VOX Compact SPANISH and ENGLISH Dictionary

Third Edition

McGraw Hill

New York Chicago San Francisco Lisbon London Madrid Mexico City
Milan New Delhi San Juan Seoul Singapore Sydney Toronto

The McGraw-Hill Companies

Library of Congress Cataloging-in-Publication Data

Vox compact Spanish and English dictionary (hardcover and vinyl) : English-Spanish, Spanish-English. — 3rd ed.
p. cm.
ISBN 0-07-149952-0 (hardcover)
ISBN 0-07-149951-2 (vinyl)
1. Spanish language—Dictionaries—English. 2. English language—Dictionaries—Spanish.

PC4640.V67 2007
463'.21—dc22 2007032043 (hardcover); 2007032465 (vinyl)

1 2 3 4 5 6 7 8 9 10 11 12 13 14 15 16 17 CTP/CTP 0 9 8 7 (0-007-149951-2)
1 2 3 4 5 6 7 8 9 10 11 12 13 14 15 16 17 CTP/CTP 0 9 8 7 (0-007-149952-0)

ISBN 978-0-07-149951-4 (vinyl)
MHID 0-07-149951-2 (vinyl)

ISBN 978-0-07-149952-1 (hardcover)
MHID 0-07-149952-0 (hardcover)

Dirección editorial: Eladio Pascual Foronda
Coordinación editorial: Maria José Simón Aragón
Realización: dos més dos edicions, s. l.
Con la colaboración de: Pauline Shaw, Carmen Soler Rodriguez, Victoria Alonso Blanco, Suzanne McCloskey, Mark Waudby, Rafael Davies, Marga Fortuny, Fernando Nápoles Tapia

McGraw-Hill books are available at special quantity discounts to use as premiums and sales promotions, or for use in corporate training programs. For more information, please write to the Director of Special Sales, Professional Publishing, McGraw-Hill, Two Penn Plaza, New York, NY 10121-2298. Or contact your local bookstore.

This book is printed on acid-free paper.

Foreword

This new thoroughly revised and updated *Compact Spanish and English Dictionary*, the most recent addition to the extensive range of VOX dictionaries, has been compiled by a team of experienced lexicographers, translators and language teachers.

It presents a large amount of up-to-date information and pays special attention to current English and Spanish usage, both European and American varieties, formal and informal registers. It contains over 150,000 translations differentiated by bracketed context indicators and field labels to guide users to the correct sense and help them to choose the right translation for a given context or express themselves correctly in the foreign language.

The basic translations are complemented by abundant examples of usage that clarify and illustrate those senses which present particular problems. There are also numerous idiomatic expressions and set phrases, ample coverage of English phrasal verbs, abbreviations and acronyms, a summary of the grammar of both languages, a table of English irregular verbs, complete conjugation tables for Spanish verbs, some examples of letters, a list of phrasal verbs, tables of numbers and weights and measures, a list of idioms and expressions, and three detailed maps.

The *VOX Compact Spanish and English Dictionary* has been designed specifically to be convenient and easy to use. The clear typography and simple, logical organization of the entries facilitate looking up and make it ideal for any student or professional who uses either language in his or her studies or at work.

We are sure that the dictionary contains all the information the user needs, whether he or she be a beginning, intermediate or advanced learner, and is up-to-date, practical, and easy to consult: an indispensable tool not only in the classroom and the workplace, but also in the home, or indeed in any situation where there is interaction between these two important world languages.

Presentación

Este *Compact Spanish and English Dictionary*, la más reciente adición a la extensa gama de diccionarios VOX, redactado por un equipo compuesto por experimentados lexicógrafos, traductores y profesores de idiomas, ha sido completamente revisado y actualizado.

Contiene gran cantidad de información totalmente puesta al día y presta especial atención a los usos actuales del inglés y del español en sus variedades europea y americana, en los niveles tanto formal como coloquial. Ofrece más de 150 000 traducciones rigurosamente acotadas por el uso de indicadores de contexto y etiquetas de tecnicismo que guían al usuario a la acepción adecuada y le ayudan a escoger la traducción idónea para cada contexto o a expresarse correctamente en el idioma extranjero.

Como complemento de las traducciones básicas de cada palabra, se incluyen muchos ejemplos de uso que aclaran e ilustran las acepciones con problemas especiales. Hay también numerosos modismos, frases hechas y expresiones idiomáticas, una amplia cobertura de los llamados *phrasal verbs* o verbos preposicionales ingleses, siglas y abreviaturas, un resumen de gramática para cada uno de los dos idiomas, la tabla de verbos irregulares ingleses, el cuadro completo de conjugación de los verbos españoles, una lista de falsos amigos, ejemplos de correspondencia, tablas de numerales y de pesos y medidas, una lista de modismos y expresiones, y tres mapas detallados.

El *VOX Compact Spanish and English Dictionary* ha sido diseñado específicamente para que resulte de cómodo y fácil empleo. La tipografía clara y la organización sencilla y lógica de los distintos elementos agilizan las consultas y lo convierten en una obra ideal para cualquier estudiante o profesional que maneje una u otra lengua en el curso de sus estudios o de su trabajo diario.

Estamos seguros de que este diccionario contiene toda la información que necesita el usuario, sea principiante, intermedio, o avanzado y que es actual, eficaz y fácil de consultar: una herramienta indispensable, no solo en el aula y en el lugar de trabajo, sino también en el hogar o en cualquier situación donde haya interacción entre estas dos grandes lenguas de importancia mundial.

Table of contents
Índice

How to consult this dictionary

headword
entrada

baby ['beɪbɪ] *n* **1** bebé *m*. **2** *(of animal)* cría. **3** *fig (infantile person)* niño,-a: **don't be such a baby!** *¡no seas niño!* ■ **to have a baby** dar a luz, tener un niño. ● **baby carriage** US cochecito de niño. ‖ **baby tooth** diente *m* de leche.
▲ *pl* **babies**.

compound nouns
compuestos

irregularities or spelling difficulties
irregularidades o dificultades ortográficas

baby-faced ['beɪbɪfeɪst] *adj* con cara de niño.
baby-sit ['beɪbɪsɪt] *vi* hacer de canguro, cuidar niños.
▲ *pt & pp* **baby-sat** ['beɪbɪsæt], *ger* **baby-sitting**.
baby-sitter ['beɪbɪsɪtəʳ] *n* canguro *mf*.

phonetic transcription
transcripción fonética

back [bæk] *n* **1** *(of person)* espalda. **2** *(of animal, book)* lomo. **3** *(of chair)* respaldo. **4** *(of hand)* dorso. **5** *(of stage, room, cupboard)* fondo. **6** *(sport - player)* defensa *mf*; *(- position)* defensa.
▷ *adj* trasero,-a, de atrás.
▷ *adv (at the rear)* atrás; *(towards the rear)* hacia atrás.
▷ *vt* **1** *(support)* apoyar, respaldar. **2** *(finance)* financiar.
■ **back to front** al revés. ‖ **to answer back** replicar. ‖ **to be back** estar de vuelta. ‖ **to come back / go back** volver. ‖ **to give back** devolver. ‖ **to put back** volver a guardar en su sitio. ‖ **to phone back** volver a llamar. ‖ **to stand back** apartarse.
⊙ **to back away** *vi* retirarse.
⊙ **to back off** *vi* apartarse.
⊙ **to back out** *vi* volverse atrás.
⊙ **to back up** *vt sep (vehicle)* dar marcha atrás a; *(support)* apoyar.

gender of translation
género de la traducción

parts of speech
categorías gramaticales

idioms
fraseología

phrasal verbs
verbos preposicionales

blanket ['blæŋkɪt] *n* **1** manta, AM frazada. **2** *(layer)* capa, manto: **a blanket of snow** *una capa de nieve*.
blond [blɒnd] *adj* rubio,-a.
Suele escribirse **blonde** cuando se refiere a una mujer.

American Spanish
español de América

grammatical explanations
explicaciones gramaticales

feet [fiːt] *n pl* → **foot**.
feign [feɪn] *vt* fingir, aparentar: **she feigned illness to get off school** *fingió estar enferma para no ir a la escuela*.
feint [feɪnt] *n fml (fencing)* finta; *(boxing)* treta.
▷ *adj (paper)* rayado,-a.
feisty ['fiːstɪ] *adj (forceful)* batallador,-ra; *(irritable)* irritable.
▲ *comp* **feistier**, *superl* **feistiest**.
feldspar ['feldspɑːʳ] *n* feldespato.
feline ['fiːlaɪn] *adj* felino,-a.
▷ *n* felino,-a.
fell[1] [fel] *adj* feroz, cruel. ■ **at one fell swoop** de un solo golpe.
fell[2] [fel] *vt* **1** *(tree)* talar. **2** *(enemy)* derribar.
fell[3] [fel] *n* GEOG *(moorland)* páramo alto; *(hilly land)* monte *m*, colina.
fell[4] [fel] *pt* → **fall**.

irregular plural cross-referenced to singular
envíos de plural irregular a singular

examples of use
ejemplos de uso

context indicators
indicadores de contexto

homonymous headwords
entradas homónimas

field label
tecnicismo

irregular past tense and past participle cross-referenced to main entry
envíos de pasado y participio irregulares a la entrada principal

gotten ['gɒtᵊn] *pp* US → **get**.
gray [greɪ] *adj* US → **grey**.

American spelling referenced to British entry
envío de grafía americana a grafía británica

jam[1] [dʒæm] *n* **1** mermelada, confitura. **2** *fam (luck)* churra. ● **jam jar** bote *m* de mermelada.

register label
etiqueta de registro lingüístico

Guía para consultar este diccionario

aquí *adv* **1** *(lugar)* here: **por aquí por favor** *this way please.* **2** *(tiempo)* now: **de aquí en adelante** *from now on.*
ara *nf (altar)* altar; *(piedra)* altar stone. ■ **en aras de** *fml* for the sake of: **en aras de la paz** *so as to keep the peace.*
árabe *adj (gen)* Arab; *(de Arabia)* Arabian.
▷ *nm & nf* Arab. ● **alfabeto árabe** Arabic alphabet.
Arabia *nf* Arabia. ● **Arabia Saudita** Saudi Arabia.
arácnido *nm* arachnid.
arado *nm* plough (US plow).

categoría gramatical / part of speech

nombres en construcciones fijas / noun compounds

arca [Takes **el** in singular.] *nf* **1** chest. **2** *(caja de caudales)* strongbox, safe. ● **arca de Noé** Noah's ark. ‖ **arcas públicas** Treasury *sing.*

explicaciones gramaticales / grammatical explanations

grammatical number of translation / número gramatical de la traducción

ascensor *nm* lift, US elevator.
asco *nm* disgust, repugnance. ■ **coger asco a algo** to get sick of sth. ‖ **dar asco** to be disgusting. ‖ **estar hecho,-a un asco 1** *(cosa)* to be filthy, look a real mess. **2** *(persona)* to be filthy, be in a right state. ‖ **hacer ascos a algo** to turn up one's nose at sth. ‖ **¡qué asco!** how disgusting!, how revolting!

traducción del inglés americano / American English translation

fraseología / idiomatic expressions

asociar [12] *vt* **1** to associate (**a/con**, with), connect, link. **2** COM to take into partnership.
▷ *vpr* **asociarse 1** *(relacionarse)* to be associated (**a/con**, with): **2** COM to collaborate, form a partnership, become partners.

elementos intercambiables / interchangeable elements

subentrada / subentry

cabalgar [7] *vi* **1** *(sobre un animal)* to ride (**en/sobre**, -). **2** *(sobre otra cosa)* to straddle (**sobre**, -), sit astride (**sobre**, -): **el niño cabalgaba sobre la silla** *the boy sat astride the chair.*

modelo de conjugación de verbo irregular / conjugation model for irregular verb

régimen preposicional del verbo / prepositional complementation of verb

dado¹ *nm* **1** *(para jugar)* die. **2** TÉC block. **3** ARQUIT dado. ■ **echar los dados** to throw the dice.
dado,-a² *adj* **1** given: **dada la base y la altura, hallar la superficie** *given the base and the height, find the area.* **2** *(en vista de)* in view of: **dada su experiencia** *in view of his experience.* ■ **dado que** since, as, given that: **dado que llueve no saldremos** *as it's raining we won't go out.* ‖ **ser dado,-a a** to be keen on, be fond of: **mi tío es muy dado a las hierbas medicinales** *my uncle is very fond of medicinal herbs.*
dama *nf* **1** *(señora)* lady. **2** *(en el juego de damas)* king; *(en ajedrez)* queen.
▷ *nf pl* **damas** draughts, (US checkers). ● **tablero de damas** draughtboard, (US checkerboard).
deceso *nm fml* decease.
decimotercero,-a *adj* thirteenth.
▷ *nm & nf* thirteenth.
See also **sexto,-a.**

ejemplos de uso / examples of use

etiqueta de nivel de uso / usage label

ortografía del inglés americano / American English spelling

envíos a otras entradas / cross-references to other entries

Abbreviations used in this dictionary

Abreviaturas empleadas en este diccionario

abr	abreviatura, abbreviation
adj	adjective, adjetivo
abbr	abbreviation, abreviatura
adv	adverb, adverbio
AER	aeronautics, aeronáutica
AGR	agriculture, agricultura
AM	American Spanish, español americano
ANAT	anatomy, anatomía
ARCH	architecture, arquitectura
arg	argot, slang
ARQ	arquitectura, architecture
ART	art, arte
art	article, artículo
art def	artículo definido, definite article
art indef	artículo indefinido, indefinite article
AUTO	automobiles, automóvil
AV	aviation, aviación
BIOL	biology, biología
BOT	botany, botánica
CHEM	chemistry, química
CINEM	cinema, cinematografía
COM	comercio, commerce
COMM	commerce, comercio
comp	comparative, comparativo
COMPUT	computing, informática
conj	conjunction, conjunción
contr	contraction, contracción
COST	costura, sewing
CULIN	cookery, cocina
def art	definite article, artículo definido
DEP	deporte, sport
EDUC	education, educación
ELEC	electricity, electricidad
etc	etcetera, etcétera
euf	uso eufemístico, euphemistic use
euph	euphemistic use, uso eufemístico
fam	familiar use, uso familiar
fig	figurative use, uso figurado
FIN	finance, finanzas
FÍS	física, physics
fml	formal use, uso formal
fut	future, futuro
GB	British English, inglés británico
gen	in general, en general
GEOG	geography, geografía
GEOL	geology, geología
ger	gerund, gerundio
GRAM	grammar, gramática
HIST	history, historia
imperat	imperative, imperativo
imperf	imperfect, imperfecto
indef art	indefinite article, artículo indefinido
indic	indicative, indicativo
inf	infinitive, infinitivo
INFORM	informática, computing
interj	interjection, interjección
iron	ironic, irónico
irón	irónico, ironic
JUR	law, derecho
LING	linguistics, lingüística
LIT	literature, literatura
loc	locución, phrase

MAR	maritime, marítimo
MAT	matemáticas, mathematics
MATH	mathematics, matemáticas
MED	medicine, medicina
METEOR	meteorology, meteorología
MIL	military, militar
MUS	music, música
MÚS	música, music
n	noun, nombre
neut	neuter, neutro
nf	feminine noun, nombre femenino
nf pl	plural feminine noun, nombre femenino plural
nm	masculine noun, nombre masculino
nm o nf	masculine or feminine noun, nombre de género ambiguo
nm & nf	masculine and feminine noun, nombre de género común
nm pl	masculine plural noun, nombre masculino plural
npl	plural noun, nombre plural
pej	pejorative, peyorativo
pers	person, persona
pey	peyorativo, pejorative
phr	phrase, locución
PHYS	physics, física
POL	politics, política
pp	past participle, participio pasado
pref	prefix, prefijo
prep	preposition, preposición
pres	present, presente
pron	pronoun, pronombre
pt	past, pasado
QUÍM	química, chemistry
RAD	radio
REL	religion, religión
SEW	sewing, costura
sím	símbolo, symbol
sing	singular
sl	slang, argot
SP	sport, deporte
subj	subjunctive, subjuntivo
superl	superlative, superlativo
symb	symbol, símbolo
TEAT	teatro, theatre
TÉC	técnica, technical
TECH	technical, técnica
THEAT	theatre, teatro
TV	television, televisión
US	American English, inglés norteamericano
v aux	auxiliary verb, verbo auxiliar
vi	intransitive verb, verbo intransitivo
vpr	pronominal verb, verbo pronominal
vt	transitive verb, verbo transitivo
vt insep	inseparable transitive phrasal verb, verbo preposicional transitivo inseparable
vt sep	separable transitive phrasal verb, verbo preposicional transitivo separable
ZOOL	zoology, zoología
→	see, véase
≈	approximately equiva lent to, aproximadamente equivalente a

English
Spanish

Gramática inglesa

Fonética

Todas las entradas inglesas en este diccionario llevan transcripción fonética basada en el sistema de la Asociación Fonética Internacional (AFI). He aquí una relación de los símbolos empleados.

El símbolo ['] delante de una sílaba indica que es ésta la acentuada.

Las consonantes

[p] pan [pæn], happy ['hæpɪ], slip [slɪp].
[b] big [bɪg], habit ['hæbɪt], stab [stæb].
[t] top [tɒp], sitting ['sɪtɪŋ], bit [bɪt].
[d] drip [drɪp], middle [mɪdᵊl], rid [rɪd].
[k] card [kɑ:d], maker ['meɪkəʳ], sock [sɒk].
[g] god [gɒd], mugger ['mʌgəʳ], dog [dɒg].
[tʃ] chap [tʃæp], hatchet ['hætʃɪt], beach [bi:tʃ].
[dʒ] jack [dʒæk], digest [daɪ'dʒest], wage [weɪdʒ].
[f] wish [wɪʃ], coffee ['kɒfɪ], wife [waɪf].
[v] very ['verɪ], never ['nevəʳ], give [gɪv].
[θ] thing [θɪŋ], cathode ['kæθəʊd], filth [fɪlθ].
[ð] they [ðeɪ], father ['fa:ðəʳ], loathe [ləʊð].
[s] spit [spɪt], stencil ['stensᵊl], niece [ni:s].
[z] zoo ['zu:], weasel ['wi:zᵊl], buzz [bɪz].
[ʃ] show [ʃəʊ], fascist [fæ'ʃɪst], gush [gʌʃ].
[ʒ] gigolo ['ʒigələʊ], pleasure ['pleʒəʳ], massage ['mæsɑ:ʒ].
[h] help [help], ahead [ə'hed].
[m] moon [mu:n], common ['kɒmən], came [keɪm].
[n] nail [neɪl], counter ['kaʊntəʳ], shone [ʃɒn].
[ŋ] linger ['fɪŋgəʳ], sank [sæŋk], thing [θɪŋ].
[l] light [laɪt], illness ['ɪlnəs], bull [bʊl].
[r] rug [rʌg], merry ['merɪ].
[j] young [jʌŋ], university [ju:nɪ'vɜ:sɪtɪ], Europe ['jʊərəp].
[w] want [wɒnt], rewind [ri:'waɪnd].
[x] loch [lɒx].
[ʳ] se llama *"linking r"* y se encuentra únicamente a final de palabra. Se pronuncia sólo cuando la palabra siguiente empieza por una vocal: mother and father came ['mʌðər ən 'fa:ðə keɪm].

Las vocales y los diptongos

[i:] sheep [ʃi:p], sea [si:], scene [si:n], field [fi:ld].
[ɪ] ship [ʃɪp], pity ['pɪtɪ], roses ['rəʊzɪz], babies ['beɪbɪz], college ['kɒlɪdʒ].
[e] shed [ʃed], instead [ɪn'sted], any ['enɪ], bury ['berɪ], friend [frend].
[æ] fat [fæt], thank [θæŋk], plait [plæt].
[ɑ:] rather ['rɑ:ðəʳ], car [kɑ:ʳ], heart [hɑ:t], clerk [klɑ:k], palm [pɑ:m], aunt [ɑ:nt].
[ɒ] lock [lɒk], wash [wɒʃ], trough [trɒf], because [bɪ'kɒz].
[ɔ:] horse [hɔ:s], straw [strɔ:], fought [fɔ:t], cause [kɔ:z], fall [fɔ:l], boar [bɔ:ʳ], door [dɔ:ʳ].
[ʊ] look [lʊk], pull [pʊl], woman ['wʊmən], should [ʃʊd].
[u:] loop [lu:p], do [du:], soup [su:p], elude [i'lu:d], true [tru:], shoe [ʃu:], few [fju:].
[ʌ] cub [kʌb], ton [tʌn], young [jʌŋ], flood [flʌd], does [dʌz].
[ɜ:] third [θɜ:d], herd [hɜ:d], heard [hɜ:d], curl [kɜ:l], word [wɜ:d], journey ['dʒɜ:nɪ].
[ə] actor ['æktəʳ], honour ['ɒnəʳ], about [ə'baʊt].
[ᵊ] opcional. En algunos casos se pronuncia y en otros se omite: trifle ['traɪfᵊl].
[eɪ] cable ['keɪbᵊl], way [weɪ], plain [pleɪn], freight [freɪt], prey [preɪ], great [greɪt].
[əʊ] go [gəʊ], toad [təʊd], toe [təʊ], though [ðəʊ], snow [snəʊ].
[aɪ] lime [laɪm], thigh [θaɪ], height [haɪt], lie [laɪ], try [traɪ], either ['aɪðəʳ].
[aʊ] house [haʊs], cow [kaʊ].
[ɔɪ] toy [tɔɪ], soil [sɔɪl].
[ɪə] near [nɪər], here [hɪər], sheer [ʃɪər], idea [aɪ'dɪə], museum [mju:'zɪəm], weird [wɪəd], pierce [pɪəs].
[eə] hare [heər], hair [heər], wear [weər].
[ʊə] pure [pjʊər], during ['djʊərɪŋ], tourist ['tʊərɪst].

Ortografía

1. El sufijo *-s/-es* según la forma de la raíz.

a) Para formar la tercera persona del singular del presente de indicativo se añade **s** al infinitivo, pero si el infinitivo acaba en **-sh, -ch, -s, -x, -z** y, a veces, **-o**, se añade **es**. Lo mismo pasa cuando se añade **s** para formar el plural de los sustantivos. (Véase también el apartado sobre los sustantivos.)

wish	→	wishes	fix	→	fixes
teach	→	teaches	buzz	→	buzzes
kiss	→	kisses	go	→	goes

b) Si la raíz acaba en cualquier consonante + **y**, ésta se convierte en **i** y se añade **-es**. Pero si la **y** va precedida de una vocal no experimenta ningún cambio.

	fry	→	fries	worry	→	worries
pero	play	→	plays			

2. Cambios ortográficos en la raíz al añadir ciertos sufijos.

a) Para formar el gerundio o participio presente se añade **-ing** al infinitivo, pero si el infinitivo acaba en cualquier consonante + **e**, ésta desaparece. Si acaba en **-ie** esta combinación se convierte en **y**.

give	→	giving	die	→	dying
move	→	moving	lie	→	lying

b) Si se trata de una raíz monosílaba que acaba en una sola consonante precedida de una sola vocal, la consonante se duplica en los siguientes casos: al añadir

- **-ing** al verbo para formar el gerundio o participio presente
- **-ed** al verbo para formar el pasado simple
- **-er** al verbo para formar el agente,
- **-er** o **-est** al adjetivo para formar el comparativo y superlativo

	stab	→	stabbing	trek	→	trekked
	swim	→	swimming	clap	→	clapped
	run	→	runner	grin	→	grinned
pero	sleep	→	sleeping	look	→	looked
	pant	→	panting	grasp	→	grasped
	sad	→	sadder, saddest	hot	→	hotter, hottest
	wet	→	wetter, wettest	big	→	bigger, biggest
pero	cold	→	colder, coldest	cool	→	cooler, coolest
	dear	→	dearer, dearest	fast	→	faster, fastest

NB Las consonantes **y, w** y **x** no se duplican.

c) También se duplica la consonante final de los verbos de más de una sílaba si el acento tónico recae en la última sílaba.

	begin	→	beginning	admit	→	admitted
	refer		referring			
pero	offer	→	offering	open	→	opened

Sin embargo, si la consonante final es **l**, ésta se duplica independientemente de donde recaiga el acento tónico. (Véase también el apartado **3f**.)

travel	→	travelling	model	→	modelled

d) Si la raíz acaba en cualquier consonante + **y**, al añadir **-ed** a la raíz del verbo o **-er** o **-est** a la del adjetivo, la **y** se convierte en **i**.

spy	→	spied	carry	→	carried
pretty	→	prettier, prettiest			

e) Si un adjetivo acaba en **-y**, al formar el adverbio añadiendo **-ly** la **y** se convierte en **i**.

happy	→	happily	gay	→	gaily

3. Las contracciones

En inglés familiar el uso de las formas contractas de ciertos verbos en las que un apóstrofo ocupa el lugar de una letra suprimida es muy frecuente. He aquí una lista de las más usuales:

's	is, has	're	are
've	have	'd	would, had
'm	am	'll	will, shall
-n't	not	can't	cannot
won't	will not		

4. Diferencias ortográficas entre el inglés británico y el americano.

Hay varias diferencias entre la ortografía británica y la americana. Aquí se resumen las diferencias regulares, pero todas las formas diferentes constan en el cuerpo del diccionario. El punto de referencia es siempre el inglés británico.

a) Algunas palabras que acaban en **-tre** se escriben con **-ter** en el inglés americano.

centre → center   mitre → miter
theatre → theater

b) Algunas palabras que acaban en **-our** se escriben con **-or** en el inglés americano.

harbour → harbor   vapour → vapor
colour → color

c) Algunas palabras que contienen el dígrafo **ae** en el ingles americano se escriben con **e**.

mediaeval → medieval   gynaecology → gynecology

d) Algunas palabras que contienen el dígrafo **oe** en el ingles americano se escriben con **e**.

manoeuvre → maneuver   oestrogen → estrogen

e) Algunas palabras que acaban en **-ogue** acaban en **-og** en el inglés americano.

catalogue → catalog   dialogue → dialog

f) A pesar de lo expresado en el apartado **2c)**, mientras que en el inglés británico una **l** final suele duplicarse independientemente de donde recaiga el acento tónico, en el inglés americano esta **l** sólo se duplica si el acento recae en la última sílaba:

travel → traveled, traveling
rebel → rebelled, rebelling.

El artículo

El artículo indefinido

El artículo indefinido es **a** y es invariable: **a man, a young woman, a boy a girl, a big dog, a tree, a planet.**

Delante de las palabras que empiecen por vocal, **a** se convierte en **an**: **an apple, an eagle, an easy test, an Indian, an untidy room.**

Sin embargo una palabra puede empezar por una vocal escrita y no empezar por sonido vocálico: esto ocurre con las palabras que empiezan por **eu-** y algunas de las que empiezan por **u-** (véanse las transcripciones fonéticas en el diccionario). En estos casos se usa **a** en vez de **an**: **a European, a euphemistic expression; a union, a university professor.**

Asimismo, si una **h** inicial se pronuncia se empleará **a** y, si es muda, **an**: **a house, a helpful person,** pero **an hour, an honest man.**

El artículo indefinido solo se pone delante de los sustantivos en singular.

a dog	*un perro*	dogs	*unos perros*
an eel	*una angula*	eels	*unas angulas*
an old house	*una casa antigua*	old houses	*casas antiguas*

El artículo definido

El artículo definido es **the** y es invariable. Sirve tanto para el singular como para el plural: **the man , the men, the woman, the women, the children, the earth, the sea.**

Su pronunciación es [ðə], pero delante de las palabras que empiecen por un sonido vocálico se pronuncia [ðɪ].

El sustantivo

Género

En inglés, a diferencia del español, los sustantivos carecen de género gramatical y los artículos y adjetivos son invariables. Sólo algunos nombres referentes a las personas tienen forma femenina y en algunos casos existen palabras diferentes para designar el varón y la hembra:

actor	→	actress	prince	→	princess	host	→	hostess
king	→	queen	boy	→	girl	son	→	daughter
cock	→	hen	bull	→	cow	ram	→	ewe

El genitivo sajón

Para indicar la relación de poseedor/posesión en inglés se usa el llamado *genitivo sajón*, que consiste en añadir **'s** al poseedor y colocarlo delante de lo poseído. Funciona para las personas y también para los animales:

Lawrence's mother	*la madre de Lawrence*
the boy's bicycle	*la bicicleta del chico*
my teacher's glasses	*las gafas de mi profesor*
the government's policies	*la política del gobierno*
our dog's tail	*la cola de nuestro perro*

Si el poseedor está en plural y acaba en **-s**, en vez de añadir **'s** se añade únicamente el apóstrofo, pero si se trata de un plural irregular que no acaba en **-s**, se añade **'s**:

the boys' bicycles	*las bicicletas de los chicos*
my parents' car	*el coche de mis padres*
your children's toys	*los juguetes de tus niños*
men's trousers	*pantalones de caballero*

Si el poseedor acaba en **-s** en el singular se suele añadir **'s**, aunque a algunos nombres extranjeros, antiguos o clásicos, se añade solo el apóstrofo:

Charles's wife	*la mujer de Charles*
Mrs Jones's house	*la casa de la Sra. Jones*
Cervantes' novels	*las novelas de Cervantes*
Aristophanes' plays	*las obras de Aristófanes*

Sustantivos contables e incontables

En inglés los sustantivos son contables o incontables. Los primeros pueden ser contados y, por tanto, pueden tener singular y plural: **boy, boys; knife, knives; pencil, pencils** (es evidente que *chicos*, *cuchillos* y *lápices* se pueden contar. Sin embargo, **electricity** es incontable, la *electricidad* no se puede contar.

Mientras que los contables pueden tener singular y plural, los incontables sólo tienen forma singular: **furniture, advice, news, information, health, chaos, honesty, peace**. No obstante, algunos de estos sustantivos incontables pueden contarse mediante el uso de **a piece of**:

furniture	los muebles	a piece of furniture	un mueble
advice	los consejos	two pieces of advice	dos consejos
news	las noticias	three pieces of news	tres noticias

Plurales irregulares

La mayoría de sustantivos en inglés son regulares y el plural se forma añadiendo **-s** (o **-es**, véase el apartado 1 de la sección de ortografía) a la forma del singular. Existen plurales irregulares y formas invariables, que aparecen en el diccionario.

Los sustantivos que acaban en **-o** pueden formar el plural añadiendo **-s**, **-es**, o bien cualquiera de las dos. Para comprobar la forma correcta, consulte la entrada en el diccionario.

Los sustantivos que acaban en **-f** pueden formar el plural añadiendo **-s**, cambiando la **f** en **v** y añadiendo **-es**, o bien de cualquiera de las dos maneras. Los que acaban en **-ff** siempre (salvo el caso de **staff** que también tiene un plural irregular) forman el plural añadiendo una sola **s**. Para comprobar la forma correcta, consulte la entrada en el diccionario.

Los sustantivos acabados en **-fe** suelen formar el plural en **-ves**, mientras que **safe** y los acabados en **-ffe** solo añaden una **-s**.

El pronombre

Cuadro de pronombres y adjetivos posesivos

pronombre sujeto	pronombre complemento directo/indirecto	adjetivo posesivo	pronombre posesivo	pronombre reflexivo
I	me	my	mine	myself
You	you	your	yours	yourself
he	him	his	his	himself
she	her	her	hers	herself
it	it	its	—	itself
we	us	our	ours	ourselves
you	you	your	yours	yourselves
they	them	their	theirs	theirselves

Los pronombres sujeto

En inglés, al contrario que es español, no se puede elidir el pronombre sujeto, que siempre debe aparecer en la frase:

I was very pleased to see him there,

aunque en una misma frase no es preciso repetir el pronombre si el sujeto no varía:

She locked the door and then put the key in her pocket.

Los pronombres de complemento directo/indirecto

El pronombre de complemento directo se coloca detrás del verbo que complementa:

She shot him; I washed and dried it.

El pronombre de complemento indirecto, si acompaña un complemento directo que es un sustantivo, se coloca también detrás del verbo que complementa:

She made me a cake; I gave him the keys,

pero cuando acompaña un complemento directo que es pronombre es más corriente usar las preposiciones to o for (nótese también el cambio de orden):

She made it for me; I gave them to him.

El pronombre con función de complemento también se usa:

1 – detrás de una preposición:	She goes out with him; Look at them.
2 – detrás de than y as ... as ... en los comparativos:	He's taller than her; She's as quick as him.
3 – en inglés informal detrás del verbo to be:	It's me, John; It wasn't me, it was him.
4 – para respuestas cortas como:	Who's got my pencil? —Me!

Los adjetivos posesivos

Los adjetivos posesivos no varían según lo poseído sino según el poseedor:

my sister, my sisters; their friend, their friends.

Los pronombres posesivos

Los pronombres posesivos se usan para sustituir la estructura adjetivo posesivo + nombre:

This is my car. Where's yours? *(= your car);* His family is bigger than mine. *(= my family).*

Los pronombres reflexivos

Los pronombres reflexivos se usan:

1 – cuando el sujeto y el complemento del verbo son el mismo: **I've hurt myself; Please help yourselves!**

2 – cuando se quiere remarcar que es una persona y no otra quien realiza la acción: **If nobody will do it for me, I'll have to do it myself.**

El pronombre impersonal

Como pronombre impersonal en inglés coloquial se usa **you**, mientras que en inglés formal se usa **one**:

You push this button if you want tea; You can't drive a car if you're under 17.
One must be sure before one makes such serious accusations.

El adjetivo

General

Los adjetivos en inglés son invariables y casi siempre van delante de los sustantivos: **an old man, an old woman; old men, old women.**

Pueden ir después de los siguientes verbos: **be, look, seem, appear, feel, taste, smell, sound.**

Si un sustantivo en una expresión numérica se usa como adjetivo, siempre va en singular: **a two-mile walk; an eight-hour day.**

El comparativo y el superlativo

Los comparativos se usan para comparar una o dos personas, cosas, etc. con otra u otras. Los superlativos se usan para comparar una persona o cosa de un grupo con dos o más personas o cosas del mismo grupo.

Añaden a la raíz **-er** para el comparativo y **-est** para el superlativo:

— los adjetivos de una sola sílaba:

big	bigger	biggest
cold	colder	coldest.

— los de dos sílabas que acaban en **-y**:

pretty	prettier	prettiest.

Forman el comparativo con **more** y el superlativo con **most**:

— la mayoría de los demás adjetivos de dos sílabas:

boring	more boring	the most boring.

— los de tres sílabas y más:

beautiful	more beautiful	the most beautiful.

Pueden formar el comparativo y superlativo de cualquiera de las dos maneras los adjetivos de dos sílabas acabados en **-er, -ure, -le** y **-ow** así como (entre otros) **common, quiet, tired, pleasant, handsome, stupid, cruel, wicked** y **polite**, aunque es más corriente la forma con **more** y **most**.

Son irregulares los siguientes:

good	better	best
bad	worse	worst
far	farther/further	farther/furthest.

El adverbio

General

Los adverbios muy a menudo pueden formarse a partir de los adjetivos añadiendo **-ly**: **sad** ⟶ **sadly, quick** ⟶ **quickly, happy** ⟶ **happily, beautiful** ⟶ **beautifully**.

Si el adjetivo acaba en **-ly** esto no es posible: los adjetivos **lovely, friendly, ugly, lonely** y **silly**, entre otros, no tienen adverbio correspondiente.

En algunos casos esta formación de un adverbio conlleva cambios ortográficos (véase el apartado de ortografía).

Algunos adverbios tienen la misma forma que el adjetivo correspondiente: **hard, late, early, fast, far, much, little, high, low, near**.

Algunos adverbios cambian de sentido respecto al adjetivo al que corresponden:

hard = duro; duramente	**hardly** = apenas
late = tarde	**lately** = últimamente
near = cercano	**nearly** = casi
high = alto	**highly** = muy; muy favorablemente

Posición

Aunque los adverbios pueden ir al principio de la frase, la posición más frecuente es después del verbo y el complemento. Sin embargo hay ciertos adverbios que suelen ir delante del verbo (después del primer auxiliar si es un tiempo compuesto) y después del verbo **be**. Los más frecuentes de este grupo son **always, usually, generally, normally, often, sometimes, occasionally, seldom, rarely, never, almost, just, still, already** y **only**.

El comparativo y el superlativo

La regla general es como la de los adjetivos; los adverbios de dos o más sílabas anteponen siempre **more** para la comparación y **most** para el superlativo, y los de una sola sílaba añaden los sufijos **-er** para el comparativo y **-est** para el superlativo:

quickly	more quickly	most quickly
beautifully	more beautifully	most beautifully
fast	faster	fastest
hard	harder	hardest
near	nearer	nearest

pero

early	earlier	earliest

Son irregulares:

well	better	best
badly	worse	worst
little	less	least
much	more	most
far	farther/further	farthest/furthest
late	later	last

El verbo

Conjugación

La conjugación del verbo inglés es sencilla. La mayoría de los verbos ingleses son regulares y el pasado simple y participio pasado se forman añadiendo **-ed** a la raíz; solo **-d** si la raíz ya tiene **-e** final. El participio presente se forma añadiendo **-ing** a la raíz. Véase también la sección de ortografía.

Infinitivo	Pasado simple	Participio pasado	Participio presente
sail	sailed	sailed	sailing
grab	grabbed	grabbed	grabbing
kiss	kissed	kissed	kissing
waste	wasted	wasted	wasting

Pronunciación del pasado y participio pasado regulares

El sufijo **-ed** siempre se escribe igual, pero se pronuncia de tres maneras distintas según la pronunciación (fíjese en la transcripción fonética) de la raíz a la que se añade.

Se pronuncia [d] si la raíz acaba en una consonante sonora [b], [g], [dʒ], [v], [ð], [z], [ʒ], [m], [n] y [l] o cualquier vocal:

— **stabbed** [stæbd], **begged** [begd], **opened** ['əʊpənd], **filled** [fɪld], **vetoed** ['viːtəʊd].

Se pronuncia [t] si la raíz acaba en una consonante sorda [p], [k], [tʃ], [f], [θ], [s], [ʃ]:

— **clapped** [klæpt], **licked** [lɪkt], **kissed** [kɪst], **wished** [wɪʃt].

Se pronuncia [ɪd] si la raíz acaba en [t] o [d];

— **tasted** ['teɪstɪd], **defended** [dɪ'fendɪd].

Para los verbos irregulares véase la tabla al final de esta sección y las respectivas entradas.

Phrasal verbs

Los *phrasal verbs* o verbos preposicionales son muy numerosos en inglés. Al añadir una partícula adverbial o preposición a un verbo, se modifica o cambia totalmente el significado del verbo original.

put *(poner)*	**put out** *(apagar)*
turn *(girar)*	**turn on** *(encender)*

En este diccionario los *phrasal verbs* aparecen en una sección al final de la entrada, introducida por el símbolo ⊙. Distinguimos tres categorías de *phrasal verbs*:

— los transitivos separables (*vt sep*),

— los transitivos inseparables (*vt insep*) y

— los intransitivos (*vi*).

Claro está, los intransitivos nunca llevan complemento directo, pero los transitivos sí lo llevan. La diferencia entre los transitivos inseparables y los separables es que en aquéllos el complemento no puede colocarse entre el verbo y la partícula:

The bigger boys were always picking on him – *Los chicos mayores siempre se metían con él*

mientras que en éstos el complemento si es sustantivo puede ir detrás de la partícula o entre el verbo y la partícula, y si es promombre debe ir forzosamente entre el verbo y la partícula:

She picked up her umbrella o **She picked her umbrella up** – *Cogió su paraguas*
She picked it up – *Lo cogió*

La formación de los tiempos verbales

Presente simple

Tiene la misma forma que el infinitivo del verbo en todas las personas excepto en la tercera persona del singular, en la que se añade la terminación **-s** o **-es** (véase el apartado de ortografía):

I sail	we sail
you sail	you sail
he/she/it sails	they sail

Los verbos **to be** y **to have** son irregulares:

I am	we are	I have	we have
you are	you are	you have	you have
he/she/it is	they are	he/she/it has	they have

Presente continuo

Se forma del presente del verbo **to be** + el participio presente: **I am resting, you are painting** etc.

Pretérito perfecto

Se forma del presente del verbo **to have** + el participio pasado:

He has arrived, they have just left etc.

Pretérito perfecto continuo

Se forma del presente del verbo **to have** + **been** + el participio presente:

I have been dreaming, we have been riding etc.

Pasado simple

Véase el principio de esta sección y la tabla de verbos irregulares. El verbo **to be** es irregular:

I was	we were
you were	you were
he/she/it was	they were

Pasado continuo

Se forma del pasado simple de **to be** + el participio presente:

It was raining, they were laughing, etc.

Pluscuamperfecto

Se forma del pasado simple de **to have** + el participio pasado:

I had lost my slippers, the dog had taken them etc.

Pluscuamperfecto continuo

Se forma del pasado simple de **to have** + **been** + el participio pasado:

He had been repairing his motorbike etc.

Futuro

Se forma de **will/shall** + el infinitivo. (Como norma general, **will** se usa para todas las personas aunque, en el lenguaje formal, **shall** lo sustituye en la primera persona tanto del singular como del plural):

It will be here next week etc.

Futuro continuo

Se forma de **will/shall** + **be** + el participio presente:

They will be lying on the beach etc.

Futuro perfecto

Se forma de **will/shall** + **have** + participio pasado:

I will have finished in ten minutes etc.

Futuro perfecto continuo

Se forma de **will/shall** + **have** + **been** + participio presente:

We will have been living here for forty years etc.

Las oraciones condicionales

Aquí damos cuenta de los tres tipos básicos de oraciones condicionales del inglés, las llamadas reales, irreales e imposibles. Las construcciones 1) y 2) hacen referencia al presente y futuro mientras que 3) describe situaciones en el pasado.

1) Condicional real (first conditional)

If + presente simple	**will/shall** + infinitivo
If it snows this week,	**we will go skiing on Saturday**

2) Condicional irreal (second conditional)

If + pasado simple	**would** + infinitivo
If we had a corkscrew,	**we would be able to open the bottle**

3) Condicional imposible (third conditional)

If + pluscuamperfecto	**would have** + participio pasado
If you had run a little faster,	**you would have caught the train.**

La voz pasiva

La voz pasiva es frecuente en inglés. Se forma de la siguente manera: se invierten el sujeto y el complemento directo, se pone el verbo **be** en el mismo tiempo que el verbo en la frase activa seguido del participio pasado del verbo, y se coloca la partícula **by** delante del sujeto:

John broke the window	→	**The window was broken by John**
Leeds United have beaten Stoke City	→	**Stoke City have been beaten by Leeds United.**

A menudo se emplea para dar más énfasis al complemento directo o cuando el sujeto no se conoce o no tiene mucha importancia:

The police will tow away your car	→	Your car will be towed away (by the police)
Someone has stolen my pen	→	My pen has been stolen.

El imperativo

Tanto en singular como en plural, el imperativo se forma con el infinitivo sin *to*:

Shut up!; Open this door!; Give me my umbrella!

Las oraciones negativas se forman con **do not** (**don't**) + infinitivo:

Do not feed the animals!; Don't put your feet on the chair!

Se usa **let's** (**let us**) + infinitivo (sin **to**) como imperativo para la primera persona del plural o para hacer sugerencias:

Let's watch the other channel; Let's not quarrel *o* Don't let's quarrel.

La construcción de las frases negativas e interrogativas

Negativas

Los tiempos compuestos forman las frases negativas intercalando *not* después del verbo auxiliar:

He has finished	→	He has not finished
It is raining	→	It is not raining
She will see you later	→	She will not see you later

En el presente simple la negación se forma empleando el infinitivo del verbo (que es invariable) junto con el verbo auxiliar **do** (**does** para la tercera persona singular) seguido de **not**:

He works on Saturdays	→	He does not work on Saturdays
You make a lot of mistakes	→	You do not make a lot of mistakes

Para el pasado simple el auxiliar **do/does** toma la forma del pasado **did** mientras que el verbo principal se mantiene en infinitivo:

He worked last Saturday	→	He did not work last Saturday
You made a lot of mistakes	→	You did not make a lot of mistakes

Interrogativas

En los tiempos compuestos se forman las frases interrogativas anteponiendo el verbo auxiliar al sujeto:

She is having a shower	→	Is she having a shower?
We shall come to help you	→	Shall we come to help you?

En el presente simple se forma empleando el infinitivo del verbo (que es invariable) junto con el verbo auxiliar **do** (**does** para la tercera persona singular) que se coloca antes del sujeto:

He works on Saturdays	→	Does he work on Saturdays?
They eat fish	→	Do they eat fish?

Para el pasado simple el auxiliar **do/does** toma la forma del pasado **did**:

He worked last Saturday	→	Did he work last Saturday?
They ate all of it	→	Did they eat all of it?

Verbos irregulares ingleses

Infinitivo	Pasado simple	Participio pasado
abide	abided/abode[1]	abided
arise	arose	arisen
awake	awoke	awaked/awoken
be	was/were	been
bear	bore	borne/born
beat	beat	beaten
become	became	become
befall	befell	befallen
beget	begot	begotten
begin	began	begun
behold	beheld	beheld
bend	bent	bent
bereave	bereft	bereft
beseech	besought/beseeched	besought/beseeched
beset	beset	beset
bet	bet/betted	bet/betted
bid	bid/bade	bid/bidden
bide	bode/bided	bided
bind	bound	bound
bite	bit	bitten
bleed	bled	bled
blow	blew	blown
break	broke	broken
breed	bred	bred
bring	brought	brought
broadcast	broadcast	broadcast
build	built	built
burn	burnt/burned	burnt/burned
burst	burst	burst
buy	bought	bought
cast	cast	cast
catch	caught	caught
chide	chided/chid	chid/chidden
choose	chose	chosen
cleave	cleft/cleaved/clove	cleft/cleaved/cloven
cling	clung	clung
clothe	clothed/clad	clothed/clad
come	came	come
cost	cost	cost
creep	crept	crept
crow	crowed/crew	crowed
cut	cut	cut
deal	dealt	dealt
dig	dug	dug
dive	dived, us dove	dived
do	did	done
draw	drew	drawn
dream	dreamed/dreamt	dreamed/dreamt
drink	drank	drunk
drive	drove	driven
dwell	dwelt/dwelled	dwelt/dwelled
eat	ate	eaten
fall	fell	fallen
feed	fed	fed
feel	felt	felt
fight	fought	fought
find	found	found

flee	fled	fled
fling	flung	flung
fly	flew	flown
forbear	forbore	forborne
forbid	forbade/forbad	forbidden
forecast	forecast/forecasted	forecast/forecasted
forego	forewent	foregone
foresee	foresaw	foreseen
foretell	foretold	foretold
forget	forgot	forgotten
forgive	forgave	forgiven
forgo	forwent	forgone
forsake	forsook	forsaken
forswear	forswore	forsworn
freeze	froze	frozen
gainsay	gainsaid	gainsaid
get	got	got, us gotten
gird	girded/girt[1]	girded/girt[1]
give	gave	given
go	went	gone
grind	ground	ground
grow	grew	grown
hamstring	hamstrung	hamstrung
hang	hung/hanged[1]	hung/hanged[1]
have	had	had
hear	heard	heard
heave	heaved/hove	heaved/hove
hew	hewed	hewed/hewn
hide	hid	hidden/hid
hit	hit	hit
hold	held	held
hurt	hurt	hurt
input	input	input
keep	kept	kept
kneel	knelt, us kneeled	knelt, us kneeled
knit	knit/knitted	knit/knitted
know	knew	known
lay	laid	laid
lead	led	led
lean	leant/leaned	leant/leaned
leap	leapt/leaped	leapt/leaped
learn	learnt/learned	learnt/learned
leave	left	left
lend	lent	lent
let	let	let
light	lighted/lit	lighted/lit
lose	lost	lost
make	made	made
mean	meant	meant
meet	met	met
mislay	mislaid	mislaid
mislead	misled	misled
misread	misread	misread
misspell	misspelled/misspelt	misspelled/misspelt
misspend	misspent	misspent
mistake	mistook	mistaken
misunderstand	misunderstood	misunderstood
mow	mowed	mowed/mown
offset	offset	offset
outbid	outbid	outbid
outdo	outdid	outdone
outgrow	outgrew	outgrown
outrun	outran	outrun

outshine	outshone	outshone
overbear	overbore	overborne
overcome	overcame	overcome
overdo	overdid	overdone
overhang	overhung	overhung
overhear	overheard	overheard
override	overrode	overridden
overrun	overran	overrun
oversee	oversaw	overseen
oversleep	overslept	overslept
overtake	overtook	overtaken
overthrow	overthrew	overthrown
pay	paid	paid
prove	proved	proved/proven
put	put	put
read	read	read
rebuild	rebuilt	rebuilt
recast	recast	recast
redo	redid	redone
re-lay	re-laid	re-laid
remake	remade	remade
rend	rent	rent
repay	repaid	repaid
rerun	reran	rerun
reset	reset	reset
retell	retold	retold
rewind	rewound	rewound
rewrite	rewrote	rewritten
rid	rid/ridded	rid/ridded
ride	rode	ridden
ring	rang	rung
rise	rose	risen
run	ran	run
saw	sawed	sawed/sawn
say	said	said
see	saw	seen
seek	sought	sought
sell	sold	sold
send	sent	sent
set	set	set
sew	sewed	sewed/sewn
shake	shook	shaken
shear	sheared	sheared/shorn
shed	shed	shed
shine	shone	shone
shoe	shod	shod
shoot	shot	shot
show	showed	shown/showed
shrink	shrank	shrunk
shut	shut	shut
sing	sang	sung
sink	sank	sunk
sit	sat	sat
slay	slew	slain
sleep	slept	slept
slide	slid	slid
sling	slung	slung
slink	slunk	slunk
slit	slit	slit
smell	smelled/smelt	smelled/smelt
smite	smote	smitten
sneak	sneaked, us snuck	sneaked, us snuck
sow	sowed	sowed/sown

speak	spoke	spoken
speed	speeded/sped	speeded/sped
spell	spelled/spelt	spelled/spelt
spend	spent	spent
spill	spilled/spilt	spilled/spilt
spin	spun/span	spun
spit	spat	spat
split	split	split
spoil	spoiled/spoilt	spoiled/spoilt
spread	spread	spread
spring	sprang	sprung
stand	stood	stood
steal	stole	stolen
stick	stuck	stuck
sting	stung	stung
stink	stank/stunk	stunk
strew	strewed	strewed/strewn
stride	strode	stridden
strike	struck	struck
string	strung	strung
strive	strove	striven
sublet	sublet	sublet
swear	swore	sworn
sweep	swept	swept
swell	swelled	swollen
swim	swam	swum
swing	swung	swung
take	took	taken
teach	taught	taught
tear	tore	torn
tell	told	told
think	thought	thought
thrive	throve/thrived	thrived/thriven
throw	threw	thrown
thrust	thrust	thrust
tread	trod	trodden/trod
undercut	undercut	undercut
undergo	underwent	undergone
understand	understood	understood
undertake	undertook	undertaken
underwrite	underwrote	underwritten
undo	undid	undone
unwind	unwound	unwound
uphold	upheld	upheld
upset	upset	upset
wake	woke	woken
waylay	waylaid	waylaid
wear	wore	worn
weave	wove	woven
wed	wedded/wed	wedded/wed
weep	wept	wept
wet	wetted/wet	wetted/wet
win	won	won
wind	wound	wound
withdraw	withdrew	withdrawn
withhold	withheld	withheld
withstand	withstood	withstood
wring	wrung	wrung
write	wrote	written

[1] Para la diferencia véase la entrada.

A

A, a [eɪ] *n* **1** *(the letter)* A, a. **2** MUS la. ● **A road** carretera principal.

a [eɪ, *unstressed* ə] *indef art* **1** un, una: **a man and a woman** *un hombre y una mujer;* **I think it's a Van Gogh** *creo que es un Van Gogh.* **2** *(not translated)*: **I'm a history teacher** *soy profesor de historia;* **two and a half litres** *dos litros y medio.* **3** *(per)* por: **three times a week** *tres veces por semana;* **£3 a kilo** *tres libras el kilo.* **4** *(a certain)* un tal, una tal: **a Mr Fletcher would like to see you** *un tal Sr. Fletcher quiere verle.*

Se usa delante de las palabras que empiezan con sonido no vocálico. Consulta también **an**.

AB ['eɪ'bi:] *abbr* US ⟶ **BA**.

aback [ə'bæk] *adv* hacia atrás. ■ **to be taken aback** asombrarse, quedarse asombrado,-a.

abacus ['æbəkəs] *n* ábaco.

abandon [ə'bændən] *vt* abandonar: **the car was abandoned at the side of the road** *el coche fue abandonado al lado de la carretera.*
▷ *n* desenfreno, abandono.

abase [ə'beɪs] *phr* **to abase** OS humillarse.

abashed [ə'bæʃt] *adj (embarrassed)* incómodo,-a; *(ashamed)* avergonzado,-a.

abate [ə'beɪt] *vi (gen)* reducirse; *(storm, anger)* amainar; *(wind)* cesar; *(pain)* ceder; *(flood waters)* descender.
▷ *vt (reduce)* reducir; *(stop)* acabar con.

abattoir ['æbətwɑ:ʳ] *n* matadero.

abbey ['æbɪ] *n* abadía.

abbot ['æbət] *n* abad *m*.

abbreviate [ə'bri:vɪeɪt] *vt* abreviar.

abbreviation [əbri:vɪ'eɪʃᵊn] *n* **1** *(shortening)* abreviación *f*. **2** *(shortened form)* abreviatura.

abdicate ['æbdɪkeɪt] *vi* abdicar.

abdomen ['æbdəmən] *n* abdomen *m*.

abdominal [æb'dɒmɪnᵊl] *adj* abdominal. ● **abdominal muscles** músculos abdominales.

abduct [æb'dʌkt] *vt* raptar, secuestrar.

abductor [æb'dʌktəʳ] *n* raptor,-ra, secuestrador,-ra.

aberrant [ə'berənt] *adj* aberrante, anormal.

aberration [æbə'reɪʃᵊn] *n* aberración *f*.

abet [ə'bet] *vt* incitar y ayudar: **the murderer was aided and abetted by his sister** *el asesino contó con la complicidad de su hermana.*
▲ *pt & pp* **abetted**, *ger* **abetting**.

abeyance [ə'beɪəns] *phr* **in abeyance** en desuso.

abhor [əb'hɔ:ʳ] *vt* aborrecer, detestar.
▲ *pt & pp* **abhorred**, *ger* **abhorring**.

abide [ə'baɪd] *vt (bear, stand)* soportar, aguantar: **I can't abide that woman** *no aguanto a esa mujer.*
⊙ **to abide by** *vt insep (promise)* cumplir con; *(rules, decision)* acatar.

ability [ə'bɪlɪtɪ] *n* **1** *(capability)* capacidad *f*, aptitud *f*. **2** *(talent)* talento.
▲ *pl* **abilities**.

abject ['æbdʒekt] *adj (conditions)* abyecto,-a.

ablation [ə'bleɪʃᵊn] *n* ablación *f*.

ablative ['æblətɪv] *n* ablativo.

ablaze [ə'bleɪz] *adj* ardiendo, en llamas.

able ['eɪbᵊl] *adj* **1** que puede: **those able to escape did so** *aquellos que podían se escaparon.* **2** *(capable)* hábil, capaz, competente: **he's a very able administrator** *es un gestor muy competente.* ■ **to be able to** poder: **we weren't able to go** *no pudimos ir.*

able-bodied [eɪbᵊl'bɒdɪd] *adj* sano,-a, robusto,-a.

abnormal [æb'nɔ:mᵊl] *adj* **1** *(not normal)* anormal. **2** *(unusual)* inusual.

abnormality [æbnɔ:'mælɪtɪ] *n* anormalidad *f*, anomalía.
▲ *pl* **abnormalities**.

aboard [ə'bɔ:d] *adv (ship, plane)* a bordo; *(train)* en el tren; *(bus)* en el autobús. ■ **to go aboard 1** *(ship, plane)* embarcar, subir a bordo. **2** *(train, bus)* subir.
▷ *prep (ship, plane)* a bordo de; *(train, bus)* en.

abode [ə'bəʊd] *n fml* morada, domicilio. ■ **of no fixed abode** sin domicilio fijo.

abolish [ə'bɒlɪʃ] *vt* **1** abolir, suprimir. **2** JUR derogar.

abolition [æbə'lɪʃᵊn] *n* **1** abolición *f*, supresión *f*. **2** JUR derogación *f*.

abominable [ə'bɒmɪnəbᵊl] *adj* abominable; *(terrible)* terrible, horrible. ● **the Abominable Snowman** el Yeti.

aboriginal [æbə'rɪdʒɪnᵊl] *adj* aborigen.
▷ *n* aborigen *mf*.

aborigine [æbə'rɪdʒɪnɪ] *n* aborigen *mf*.

abort [ə'bɔ:t] *vi* abortar.
▷ *vt* **1** *(pregnant woman)* hacer abortar. **2** *(mission, program, etc)* abortar.

abortion [ə'bɔ:ʃᵊn] *n* **1** *(of pregnancy)* aborto. **2** *(of mission, etc)* interrupción *f*. ■ **to have an abortion** abortar.

abortive [ə'bɔ:tɪv] *adj* fallido,-a.

abound [ə'baʊnd] *vi* abundar. ■ **to abound in/with** abundar en.

about [ə'baʊt] *prep* **1** *(concerning)* sobre, acerca de: **to speak about ...** *hablar de ...;* **what is the book about?** *¿de qué trata el libro?* **2** *(showing where)* por, en; *(around)* alrededor de: **he's somewhere about the house** *está por algún rincón de la casa.*
▷ *adv* **1** *(approximately)* alrededor de: **at about three o'clock** *a eso de las tres;* **it cost about $500** *costó unos quinientos dólares.* **2** *fam (almost)* casi: **she's about finished** *está a punto de acabar.* **3** *(near)* por aquí, por ahí: **there was nobody about** *no había nadie.* **4** *(around)* por ahí, en existencia: **there are lots of forged notes about** *circulan muchos billetes falsos.* ■ **to be about to ...** estar

a punto de... ‖ **how/what about +** *noun* ¿qué te parece + *sustantivo*?: **how about a pizza?** *¿qué te parece una pizza?* ‖ **how/what about +** *-ing* ¿y si + *subj*?: **how about going to Paris** *¿y si fuéramos a París?*

about-face [əbaut'feɪs] *n* US → **about-turn.**

about-turn [əbaut'tɜːn] *n* **1** MIL media vuelta. **2** *fig* cambio radical, cambio total *(de idea, opinión, postura, política, etc).*

above [ə'bʌv] *prep* **1** *(higher than)* por encima de: **above our heads** *por encima de nuestras cabezas.* **2** *(more than)* más de, más que: **above 5,000 people** *más de 5.000 personas.*

▷ *adv* **1** arriba, en lo alto: **the palace, seen from above** *el palacio, visto desde arriba.* **2** *(in writing)* arriba: **see above** *véase arriba.* ■ **above all** sobre todo.

above-board [əbʌv'bɔːd] *adj* legítimo,-a, legal.

abrasion [ə'breɪʒᵊn] *n* abrasión *f.*

abreast [ə'brest] *adv* a la misma altura: **to walk four abreast** *caminar cuatro uno al lado del otro.* ■ **to keep abreast of** mantenerse al corriente de.

abridge [ə'brɪdʒ] *vt* resumir, abreviar.

abridgement [ə'brɪdʒmənt] *n* → **abridgment.**

abridgment [ə'brɪdʒmənt] *n* resumen *m*, abreviación *f.*

abroad [ə'brɔːd] *adv (position)* en el extranjero; *(movement)* al extranjero.

abrupt [ə'brʌpt] *adj* **1** *(sudden)* repentino,-a. **2** *(rude)* brusco,-a, arisco,-a. **3** *(slope)* empinado,-a.

ABS ['eɪ'biː'es] *abbr* **(anti-lock braking system)** sistema *m* de antibloqueo; *(abbreviation)* ABS.

abscess ['æbses] *n (gen)* absceso; *(on gum)* flemón *m.*

abscissa [əb'sɪsə] *n* abscisa.

abscond [əb'skɒnd] *vi* fugarse.

abseil ['æbseɪl] *vi* hacer rappel.

absence ['æbsᵊns] *n* **1** *(of person)* ausencia. **2** *(of thing)* falta, carencia.

absent [*(adj)* 'æbsᵊnt; *(vb)* æb'sent] *adj* **1** ausente. **2** *(expression)* distraído,-a.

▷ *vt* **to absent** OS ausentarse.

absentee [æbsᵊn'tiː] *n* ausente *mf.*

absenteeism [æbsᵊn'tiːɪzᵊm] *n* absentismo.

absent-minded [æbsᵊnt'maɪndɪd] *adj* distraído,-a, despistado,-a.

absinth ['æbsɪnθ] *n* → **absinthe.**

absinthe ['æbsɪnθ] *n* absenta, ajenjo.

absolute ['æbsəluːt] *adj* **1** *(gen)* absoluto,-a. **2** *(total)* total: **there was absolute silence** *hubo silencio total.* ● **absolute zero** cero absoluto.

absolutely [æbsə'luːtlɪ] *adv* completamente, totalmente.

▷ *interj (agreement)* ¡por supuesto!, ¡desde luego!: **I think we should sell. What about you John? –Oh, absolutely!** *creo que deberíamos vender. ¿Y tú John? –Oh, ¡por supuesto!*

absolution [æbsə'luːʃᵊn] *n* absolución *f.*

absolutism ['æbsəluːtɪzᵊm] *n* absolutismo.

absolutist [æbsə'luːtɪst] *adj* absolutista.

▷ *n* absolutista *mf.*

absolve [əb'zɒlv] *vt* absolver (**of/from**, de).

absorb [əb'zɔːb] *vt* **1** *(liquids, etc)* absorber; *(shock)* amortiguar. **2** *(time)* ocupar. **3** *fig (ideas, etc)* asimilar.

absorbent [əb'zɔːbᵊnt] *adj* absorbente.

absorbing [əb'zɔːbɪŋ] *adj* absorbente, muy interesante.

absorption [əb'zɔːpʃᵊn] *n* absorción *f.*

abstain [əb'steɪn] *vi* abstenerse (**from**, de).

abstemious [æb'stiːmɪəs] *adj* abstemio,-a, sobrio,-a.

abstention [æb'stenʃᵊn] *n* abstención *f.*

abstinence ['æbstɪnəns] *n* abstinencia.

abstract [*(adj-n)* 'æbstrækt; *(vb)* æb'strækt] *adj (not concrete)* abstracto,-a.

▷ *n (summary)* resumen *m.*

absurd [əb'sɜːd] *adj* absurdo,-a.

abundance [ə'bʌndəns] *n* abundancia.

abundant [ə'bʌndənt] *adj* abundante.

abuse [*(n)* ə'bjuːs; *(vb)* ə'bjuːz] *n* **1** *(verbal)* insultos *mpl*; *(physical)* malos tratos *mpl.* **2** *(misuse)* abuso.

▷ *vt* **1** *(verbally)* insultar; *(physically)* maltratar. **2** *(misuse)* abusar de.

abusive [ə'bjuːsɪv] *adj (insulting)* injurioso,-a, insultante.

abysmal [ə'bɪzmᵊl] *adj fam* malísimo,-a, fatal.

abyss [ə'bɪs] *n* abismo.

abyssal [ə'bɪsᵊl] *adj* abisal.

AC ['eɪ'siː] *abbr* ELEC **(alternating current)** corriente *f* alterna; *(abbreviation)* CA *f.*

academic [ækə'demɪk] *adj* **1** *(gen)* académico,-a. **2** *(theoretical)* teórico: **it's a purely academic question** *es una cuestión puramente teórica.* ● **academic year** año académico.

▷ *n (lecturer)* profesor,-ra universitario,-a; *(scholar)* académico,-a.

academician [əkædə'mɪʃᵊn] *n* académico,-a.

academy [ə'kædəmɪ] *n* **1** academia. **2** *(in Scotland)* instituto de enseñanza media.

▲ *pl* **academies.**

accede [æk'siːd] *vi fml* acceder (**to**, a).

accelerate [æk'seləreɪt] *vt* acelerar.

▷ *vi* acelerarse.

acceleration [ækselə'reɪʃᵊn] *n* aceleración *f.*

accelerator [ək'seləreɪtəʳ] *n* acelerador *m.*

accent [*(n)* 'æksənt; *(vb)* æk'sent] *n* acento.

▷ *vt* acentuar.

accentuate [æk'sentʃueɪt] *vt* acentuar.

accentuation [æksentʃu'eɪʃᵊn] *n* acentuación *f.*

accept [ək'sept] *vt* **1** *(gift, offer, etc)* aceptar. **2** *(admit to be true)* admitir, aceptar: **I accept that this is true** *admito que esto es verdad.*

acceptable [ək'septəbᵊl] *adj* **1** *(satisfactory)* aceptable, admisible. **2** *(welcome)* grato,-a.

acceptance [ək'septəns] *n* **1** *(act of accepting)* aceptación *f.* **2** *(approval)* acogida.

access ['ækses] *n* acceso.

▷ *vt* COMPUT acceder a, entrar en. ● **access code** código de acceso. ‖ **access road** carretera de acceso.

accessibility [æksesɪ'bɪlɪtɪ] *n* accesibilidad *f.*

accessible [æk'sesɪbᵊl] *adj* **1** accesible. **2** *(person)* asequible, tratable.

accession [æk'seʃᵊn] *n (to throne)* advenimiento.

accessory [æk'sesərɪ] *n* **1** *(gadget)* accesorio. **2** JUR *(accomplice)* cómplice *mf.*

▷ *n pl* **accessories** *(bag, gloves, etc)* complementos *mpl.*

▲ *pl* **accessories.**

accident ['æksɪdənt] *n* 1 accidente *m*. 2 *(coincidence)* casualidad *f*: it happened quite by accident *fue una pura casualidad*. ■ **by accident** por casualidad. ● **car accident** accidente *m* de coche.

accidental [æksɪ'dentᵊl] *adj* fortuito,-a. ● **accidental death** muerte *f* por accidente.

accidentally [æksɪ'dentᵊlɪ] *adv* 1 *(by chance)* por casualidad. 2 *(unintentionally)* sin querer.

accident-prone ['æksɪdəntprəʊn] *adj* propenso,-a a los accidentes.

acclaim [ə'kleɪm] *n* 1 *(welcome)* aclamación *f*. 2 *(praise)* elogios *mpl*, alabanza.
▷ *vt* 1 *(welcome)* aclamar. 2 *(praise)* elogiar, alabar.

acclamation [æklə'meɪʃᵊn] *n* aclamación *f*.

acclimatization [əklaɪmətaɪ'zeɪʃᵊn] *n* aclimatación *f*.

acclimatize [ə'klaɪmətaɪz] *vt* aclimatar.
▷ *vi* aclimatarse.

accolade ['ækəleɪd] *n* 1 *(award)* galardón *m*, premio. 2 *(praise)* elogio.

accommodate [ə'kɒmədeɪt] *vt* 1 *(put up)* alojar. 2 *(satisfy)* complacer.

accommodation [əkɒmə'deɪʃᵊn] *n* 1 *(lodging)* alojamiento. 2 *(agreement)* acuerdo; *(compromise)* compromiso.
▷ *n pl* **accommodations** US *(lodging)* alojamiento *m sing*; *(lodging and board)* alojamiento y pensión.

accompany [ə'kʌmpənɪ] *vt* acompañar.
▲ *pt & pp* **accompanied**, *ger* **accompanying**.

accomplice [ə'kɒmplɪs] *n* cómplice *mf*.

accomplish [ə'kɒmplɪʃ] *vt* 1 *(achieve)* lograr, conseguir: I don't think your protests will accomplish anything *no creo que consigas nada con tus protestas*. 2 *(carry out)* hacer, llevar a cabo: they accomplished a great deal in a short time *hicieron mucho en poco tiempo*.

accomplished [ə'kɒmplɪʃt] *adj* cumplido,-a, consumado,-a. ● **accomplished fact** hecho consumado.

accomplishment [ə'kɒmplɪʃmənt] *n* 1 *(act of achieving)* realización *f*. 2 *(achievement)* logro.
▷ *n pl* **accomplishments** *(skills)* aptitudes *fpl*, dotes *fpl*, habilidades *fpl*.

accord [ə'kɔ:d] *n* *(agreement)* acuerdo. ■ **in accord with** de acuerdo con. ‖ **of one's own accord** espontáneamente, por propia voluntad.
▷ *vt (award)* conceder, otorgar.

accordance [ə'kɔ:dᵊns] *prep*. ■ **in accordance with** de acuerdo con.

according [ə'kɔ:dɪŋ] *prep* **according to** 1 según: according to Philip/the paper/my watch *según Philip/el periódico/mi reloj*. 2 *(consistent with)* de acuerdo con: it went according to plan *salió tal como se había previsto*.

accordion [ə'kɔ:dɪən] *n* acordeón *m*.

account [ə'kaʊnt] *n* 1 *(in bank)* cuenta. 2 *(report)* relación *f*, relato, informe *m*: he gave us an account of his experiences *nos contó sus experiencias*. 3 *(importance)* importancia: it is of no account *no tiene importancia*. ■ **on account of** por, a causa de: don't leave on my account *no te vayas por mí*. ‖ **on no account** bajo ningún concepto. ‖ **to keep the accounts** llevar las cuentas. ‖ **to take into account** tener en cuenta. ● **accounts department** sección *f* de contabilidad.
⊙ **to account for** *vi* explicar.

accountable [ə'kaʊntəbᵊl] *adj* responsable (**to**, ante).

accountancy [ə'kaʊntənsɪ] *n* contabilidad *f*.

accountant [ə'kaʊntənt] *n* contable *mf*.

accredit [ə'kredɪt] *vt (gen)* autorizar, reconocer; *(diplomat)* acreditar: an accredited representative of the company *un representante autorizado de la empresa*.

accrue [ə'kru:] *vi* FIN acumularse.

accumulate [ə'kju:mjʊleɪt] *vt* acumular.
▷ *vi* acumularse.

accumulation [əkju:mjʊ'leɪʃᵊn] *n* acumulación *f*.

accumulator [ə'kju:mjʊleɪtəʳ] *n* acumulador *m*.

accuracy ['ækjʊrəsɪ] *n* 1 *(of numbers, instrument, information)* exactitud *f*, precisión *f*. 2 *(of shot)* certeza. 3 *(of interpretation, translation)* fidelidad *f*.

accurate ['ækjʊrət] *adj* 1 *(numbers, etc)* exacto,-a, preciso,-a. 2 *(instrument)* de precisión. 3 *(shot)* certero,-a. 4 *(information, etc)* exacto,-a. 5 *(interpretation, translation)* fiel.

accusation [ækjʊ:'zeɪʃᵊn] *n* acusación *f*.

accusative [ə'kju:zətɪv] *adj* acusativo,-a.
▷ *n* acusativo.

accuse [ə'kju:z] *vt* acusar (**of**, de): she was accused of lying *la acusaron de mentir*.

accused [ə'kju:zd] *n* **the accused** *(man)* el acusado; *(woman)* la acusada.

accuser [ə'kju:zəʳ] *n* acusador,-ra.

accustom [ə'kʌstəm] *vt* acostumbrar (**to**, a).

accustomed [ə'kʌstəmd] *adj* ■ **to be accustomed to** estar acostumbrado a.

ace [eɪs] *n* 1 *(cards)* as *m*. 2 *(tennis)* ace *m*. 3 *fam (expert)* as *m*.

acephalous [ə'sefələs] *adj* acéfalo,-a.

acetate ['æsɪteɪt] *n* acetato.

acetic [ə'si:tɪk] *adj* acético,-a. ● **acetic acid** ácido acético.

acetone ['æsɪtəʊn] *n* acetona.

acetylene [ə'setɪli:n] *n* acetileno.

ache [eɪk] *n* dolor *m*.
▷ *vi* doler: my head aches *me duele la cabeza, tengo dolor de cabeza*.

achieve [ə'tʃi:v] *vt* 1 *(finish)* realizar, llevar a cabo. 2 *(attain)* lograr, conseguir.

achievement [ə'tʃi:vmənt] *n* 1 *(completion)* realización *f*. 2 *(attainment)* logro. 3 *(feat)* hazaña, proeza.

Achilles [ə'kɪli:z] *n* Aquiles. ● **Achilles' heel** *fig* talón *m* de Aquiles. ‖ **Achilles' tendon** ANAT tendón *m* de Aquiles.

acid ['æsɪd] *adj* 1 CHEM ácido,-a. 2 *(taste)* agrio,-a. 3 *fig (comment)* mordaz. ● **acid rain** lluvia ácida.
▷ *n* CHEM ácido,-a.

acidity [ə'sɪdɪtɪ] *n* acidez *f*.

acknowledge [ək'nɒlɪdʒ] *vt* 1 *(admit)* admitir: to acknowledge defeat *admitir la derrota*. 2 *(recognize)* reconocer: she's acknowledged to be the greatest living pianist *se le considera la mejor pianista contemporánea*. 3 *(an acquaintance)* saludar: he walked straight past without even acknowledging me *pasó a mi lado y ni siquiera me saludó*. 4 *(be thankful)* agradecer, expresar agradecimiento por. ■ **to acknowledge receipt of** acusar recibo de.

acknowledgement [ək'nɒlɪdʒmənt] *n* 1 *(recognition)* reconocimiento. 2 *(thanks)* muestra de agradecimiento. 3 *(reply)* contestación *f*: I received no acknowledgement of my CV *no recibí respuesta a mi currículum*.

acknowledgment [æk'nɒlɪdʒmənt] *n* → **acknowledgement**.

acne ['æknɪ] *n* acné *f*.

acorn ['eɪkɔ:n] *n* bellota.

acoustic [ə'ku:stɪk] *adj* acústico,-a.
acoustics [ə'ku:stɪks] *n (science)* acústica.
▷ *n pl (sound conditions)* acústica *f sing.*
acquaint [ə'kweɪnt] *vt* informar (with, de). ■ **to acquaint OS with STH** familiarizarse con ALGO. ‖ **to be acquainted with SB** conocer a ALGN, tener trato con ALGN. ‖ **to be acquainted with STH** conocer ALGO, tener conocimientos de ALGO.
acquaintance [ə'kweɪntəns] *n* **1** *(knowledge)* conocimiento, conocimientos *mpl*: I have a slight acquaintance with physics *tengo unos conocimientos rudimentarios de física.* **2** *(person)* conocido,-a. ■ **to make SB's acquaintance** conocer a ALGN.
acquiesce [ækwɪ'es] *vi* consentir (in, en), conformarse (in, con).
acquiescent [ækwɪ'esᵊnt] *adj* condescendiente, aquiescente.
acquire [ə'kwaɪəʳ] *vt* adquirir.
acquisition [ækwɪ'zɪʃᵊn] *n* adquisición *f.*
acquisitive [ə'kwɪzɪtɪv] *adj* codicioso,-a, acaparador,-ra.
acquit [ə'kwɪt] *vt* absolver, declarar inocente. ■ **to acquit OS well** quedar en buen lugar, quedar bien, salir airoso,-a.
▲ *pt & pp* acquitted, *ger* acquitting.
acquittal [ə'kwɪtᵊl] *n* absolución *f.*
acre ['eɪkəʳ] *n* acre *m.*
Un acre equivale a 40,47 hectáreas.
acrid ['ækrɪd] *adj* acre.
acrimonious [ækrɪ'məʊnɪəs] *adj (remark)* cáustico,-a; *(dispute)* enconado,-a, amargo,-a.
acrobat ['ækrəbæt] *n* acróbata *mf.*
acrobatic [ækrə'bætɪk] *adj* acrobático,-a.
acronym ['ækrənɪm] *n* sigla.
acropolis [ə'krɒpəlɪs] *n* acrópolis *f.*
across [ə'krɒs] *prep* **1** *(movement)* a través de, de un lado a otro de: to swim across a river *cruzar un río nadando/a nado.* **2** *(position)* al otro lado de: they live across the road *viven enfrente.*
▷ *adv* de un lado a otro: it's 4 metres across *mide 4 metros de lado a lado.*
acrylic [ə'krɪlɪk] *adj* acrílico,-a.
act [ækt] *n* **1** acto, acción *f.* **2** THEAT acto. **3** *(of parliament)* ley *f.* ● **act of God** fuerza mayor.
▷ *vi* **1** *(do something)* actuar. **2** *(behave)* portarse, comportarse: she acts like a little girl *se comporta como una niña.* **3** *(in theatre)* actuar, hacer teatro; *(in cinema)* actuar, hacer cine.
▷ *vt* hacer el papel de: she's acting (the part of) Portia *ella hace el papel de Portia.*
⊙ **to act as** *vt insep* hacer de: I had to act as interpreter *tuve que hacer de intérprete.*
⊙ **to act out** *vt sep* llevar a cabo: to act out one's fantasies *llevar a cabo su fantasías.*
⊙ **to act up** *vi (gen)* causar problemas; *(machine)* funcionar mal; *(child)* dar guerra; *(wound, injury)* doler.
acting ['æktɪŋ] *adj* en funciones, accidental.
▷ *n* **1** THEAT *(profession)* teatro: I've never done any acting *no he hecho nunca teatro.* **2** *(performance)* interpretación *f*, actuación *f*: the acting was awful *la interpretación era malísima.*
actinium [æk'tɪnɪəm] *n* actinio.
action ['ækʃᵊn] *n* **1** *(gen)* acción *f.* **2** JUR demanda. ■ **killed in action** muerto,-a en combate. ‖ **out of action** fuera de servicio. ‖ **to bring an action against SB** entablar una demanda contra ALGN. ● **action replay** repetición *f* de la jugada. ‖ **action stations** zafarrancho de combate.
activate ['æktɪveɪt] *vt* activar.
activation [æktɪ'veɪʃᵊn] *n* activación *f.*
active ['æktɪv] *adj* activo,-a. ● **the active voice** la voz activa.
activism ['æktɪvɪzᵊm] *n* activismo.
activist ['æktɪvɪst] *n* activista *mf.*
activity [æk'tɪvɪtɪ] *n* actividad *f.*
▲ *pl* activities.
actor ['æktəʳ] *n* actor *m.*
actress ['æktrəs] *n* actriz *f.*
actual ['æktʃʊəl] *adj* real, verdadero,-a.
actually ['æktjʊəlɪ] *adv* **1** en realidad, realmente, de hecho: I haven't actually decided what to do yet *en realidad, todavía no he decidido qué hacer.* **2** *(indicating surprise)* incluso, hasta: she actually accused me of stealing her bag *hasta me acusó de robarle el bolso.*
actuate ['æktjʊeɪt] *vt* **1** *(make work)* accionar. **2** *(motivate)* mover, impulsar: he was actuated by a desire for revenge *le impulsaba un deseo de venganza.*
acuity [ə'kjʊ:ɪtɪ] *n* agudeza.
acumen ['ækjʊmən] *n* perspicacia.
acupuncture ['ækjʊpʌŋktʃə] *n* acupuntura.
acupuncturist ['ækjʊpʌŋktʃərɪst] *n* acupunturista *mf.*
acute [ə'kju:t] *adj* **1** *(gen)* agudo,-a. **2** *(angle)* agudo,-a. **3** *(hearing, etc)* muy fino,-a, muy desarrollado,-a. ● **acute accent** acento agudo. ‖ **acute triangle** triángulo acutángulo.
AD ['eɪ'di:] *abbr* (Anno Domini) después de Cristo; *(abbreviation)* d.J.C.
ad [æd] *n fam* anuncio.
Adam ['ædəm] *n* Adán *m.* ● **Adam's apple** nuez *f* (de la garganta).
adamant ['ædəmənt] *adj* firme, inflexible: she was adamant about paying the bill *se empeñó en pagar la cuenta;* they were adamant *insistían.*
adapt [ə'dæpt] *vt* adaptar.
▷ *vi* adaptarse.
adaptable [ə'dæptəbᵊl] *adj (person)* capaz de adaptarse.
adaptation [ædəp'teɪʃᵊn] *n* adaptación *f.*
adapter [ə'dæptəʳ] *n* ELEC → **adaptor.**
adaptor [ə'dæptəʳ] *n* ELEC ladrón *m.*
add [æd] *vt* **1** *(gen)* añadir, agregar. **2** *(numbers)* sumar.
⊙ **to add to** *vt insep* aumentar.
⊙ **to add up** *vt sep (numbers)* sumar.
▷ *vi fig* cuadrar: there's something funny going on; it doesn't add up *pasa algo raro; es que no cuadra.*
⊙ **to add up to** *vt insep* **1** sumar: what do these numbers add up to? *¿cuánto suman estas cifras?* **2** *fig* significar, querer decir: what does it all add up to? *¿qué quiere decir todo esto?*
added ['ædɪd] *adj* añadido,-a, adicional.
addend ['ædənd] *n* MAT sumando.
adder ['ædəʳ] *n* ZOOL víbora.
addict ['ædɪkt] *n* **1** adicto,-a. **2** *fam (fanatic)* fanático,-a.
addicted [ə'dɪktɪd] *adj* adicto,-a.
addiction [ə'dɪkʃᵊn] *n* adicción *f.*
addictive [ə'dɪktɪv] *adj* que crea adicción: nicotine is addictive *la nicotina crea adicción.*

addition [ə'dɪʃᵊn] *n* 1 adición *f*, añadidura. 2 MATH adición *f*, suma. ■ **in addition to** además de.
additional [ə'dɪʃənᵊl] *adj* adicional.
additive ['ædɪtɪv] *n* aditivo.
additive-free ['ædɪtɪv'fri:] *adj* sin aditivos.
address [ə'dres] *n* 1 *(on letter)* dirección *f*, señas *fpl*. 2 *(speech)* discurso, alocución *f*. ● **address book** libro de direcciones. ‖ **form of address** tratamiento.
▷ *vt* 1 *(tackle)* abordar. 2 *(speak to)* dirigirse a.
addressee [ædre'si:] *n* destinatario,-a.
adductor [ə'dʌktəʳ] *n* ANAT aductor,-ra.
adenoids ['ædənɔɪdz] *n pl* adenoides *mpl*, vegetaciones *fpl*.
adept [ə'dept] *adj* experto,-a, diestro,-a, ducho,-a.
▷ *n* experto,-a, perito,-a.
adequate ['ædɪkwət] *adj* 1 *(enough)* suficiente. 2 *(satisfactory)* satisfactorio,-a.
adhere [əd'hɪəʳ] *vi (stick)* adherirse, pegarse.
⊙ **to adhere to** *vt insep* 1 *(cause)* adherirse a. 2 *(promise)* cumplir con. 3 *(belief)* aferrarse a, mantenerse fiel a. 4 *(rules)* observar, acatar.
adherent [əd'hɪərənt] *adj* adherente.
▷ *n (supporter)* adherido,-a, partidario,-a.
adhesive [əd'hi:sɪv] *adj* adhesivo,-a.
▷ *n* adhesivo.
ad hoc [æd'hɒk] *adj* ad hoc.
adipose ['ædɪpəʊz] *adj* adiposo,-a.
adjacent [ə'dʒeɪsənt] *adj* adyacente. ● **adjacent angles** ángulos adyacentes.
adjectival [ædʒɪk'taɪvᵊl] *adj* adjetival.
adjective ['ædʒɪktɪv] *n* adjetivo.
adjoin [ə'dʒɔɪn] *vt* lindar con.
▷ *vi* colindar.
adjoining [ə'dʒɔɪnɪŋ] *adj* 1 *(building)* contiguo,-a. 2 *(land)* colindante.
adjourn [ə'dʒɜ:n] *vt* aplazar, suspender.
▷ *vi* suspenderse.
adjournment [ə'dʒɜ:nmənt] *n* aplazamiento, suspensión *f*.
adjudicate [ə'dʒu:dɪkeɪt] *vt* juzgar.
adjudication [ə'dʒu:dɪkeɪʃᵊn] *n* 1 *(decision)* fallo. 2 *(awarding)* adjudicación *f*.
adjudicator [ə'dʒu:dɪkeɪtəʳ] *n* juez,-za, árbitro,-a.
adjust [ə'dʒʌst] *vt* ajustar, arreglar.
▷ *vi (person)* adaptarse.
adjustable [ə'dʒʌstəbᵊl] *adj* regulable. ● **adjustable spanner** llave *f* inglesa.
adjustment [ə'dʒʌstmənt] *n* 1 ajuste *m*, arreglo. 2 *(person)* adaptación *f*. 3 *(change)* cambio.
ad lib [æd'lɪb] *adj (without preparation)* improvisado,-a, espontáneo,-a.
▷ *adv* 1 *(without preparation)* improvisadamente, espontáneamente. 2 *(freely)* a voluntad.
▷ *vi (gen)* improvisar; *(actor)* meter morcillas.
adman ['ædmæn] *n* publicista *m*.
▲ *pl* admen ['ædmen].
administer [əd'mɪnɪstəʳ] *vt* 1 *(control)* administrar. 2 *(give)* administrar, dar; *(laws, punishment)* aplicar.
administration [ədmɪnɪs'treɪʃᵊn] *n* 1 administración *f*. 2 *(of law, etc)* aplicación *f*.
administrative [əd'mɪnɪstrətɪv] *adj* administrativo,-a.
administrator [əd'mɪnɪstreɪtəʳ] *n* administrador,-ra.
admirable ['ædmɪrəbᵊl] *adj* admirable.
admiral ['ædmərəl] *n* almirante *m*.
admiralty ['ædmɪtəltɪ] *n* almirantazgo.
▲ *pl* admiralties.
admiration [ædmɪ'reɪʃᵊn] *n* admiración *f*.
admire [əd'maɪəʳ] *vt* admirar.
admirer [əd'maɪərəʳ] *n (gen)* admirador,-ra; *(suitor)* pretendiente *mf*.
admissible [əd'mɪsɪbᵊl] *adj* admisible.
admission [əd'mɪʃᵊn] *n* 1 *(gen)* admisión *f*; *(to hospital)* ingreso. 2 *(price)* entrada. 3 *(acknowledgement)* reconocimiento; *(confession)* confesión *f*.
admit [əd'mɪt] *vt* 1 *(allow in)* admitir; *(to hospital)* ingresar: she was admitted to St James' yesterday *la ingresaron en el hospital de St James ayer.* 2 *(acknowledge)* reconocer; *(confess)* confesar.
▲ *pt & pp* admitted, *ger* admitting.
admittance [əd'mɪtᵊns] *n* entrada. ■ **"No admittance"** "Prohibida la entrada".
admittedly [əd'mɪtɪdlɪ] *adv* es verdad que.
admonish [əd'mɒnɪʃ] *vt* amonestar.
ado [ə'du:] *n* ajetreo, alboroto. ■ **without further ado** sin más preámbulos, sin más dilación. ‖ **much ado about nothing** mucho ruido y pocas nueces.
adobe [ə'dəʊbɪ] *n* adobe *m*.
adolescence [ædə'lesᵊns] *n* adolescencia.
adolescent [ædə'lesᵊnt] *adj* adolescente.
▷ *n* adolescente *mf*.
adopt [ə'dɒpt] *vt* 1 *(gen)* adoptar. 2 *(accept)* aceptar.
adoption [ə'dɒpʃᵊn] *n* adopción *f*.
adoptive [ə'dɒptɪv] *adj* adoptivo,-a.
adoration [ædə'reɪʃᵊn] *n* adoración *f*.
adore [ə'dɔ:ʳ] *vt* adorar.
adorn [ə'dɔ:n] *vt* adornar.
adornment [ə'dɔ:nmənt] *n* adorno.
adrenalin [ə'drenəlɪn] *n* adrenalina.
Adriatic [eɪdrɪ'ætɪk] *adj* adriático,-a. ● **the Adriatic (Sea)** el (mar) Adriático.
adrift [ə'drɪft] *adj* a la deriva. ■ **to come adrift** *fam* soltarse. ‖ **to go adrift** *(plans)* irse a pique.
adsorption [æd'zɔ:bʃᵊn] *n* adsorción *f*.
adulate ['ædjuleɪt] *vt* adular.
adult ['ædʌlt] *adj* 1 *(gen)* adulto,-a. 2 *(film, etc)* para adultos.
▷ *n* adulto,-a.
adulterate [ə'dʌltəreɪt] *vt* adulterar.
adulteration [ə'dʌltəreɪʃᵊn] *n* adulteración *f*.
adulterer [ə'dʌltərəʳ] *n* adúltero.
adulteress [ə'dʌltᵊrəs] *n* adúltera.
adultery [ə'dʌltərɪ] *n* adulterio.
advance [əd'vɑ:ns] *n* 1 *(gen)* avance *m*. 2 *(payment)* anticipo. ■ **in advance** 1 *(gen)* antes. 2 *(rent, etc)* por adelantado. ● **advance booking** reserva anticipada. ‖ **advance payment** pago anticipado.
▷ *vt* 1 *(gen)* avanzar. 2 *(money)* anticipar, adelantar. 3 *(date)* adelantar.
▷ *vi* 1 *(move forward)* avanzar. 2 *(rise)* subir: house prices continue to advance *el precio de la vivienda sigue en alza.*
advanced [əd'vɑ:nst] *adj* avanzado,-a.
advancement [əd'vɑ:nsmənt] *n* 1 *(promotion)* ascenso, promoción *f*. 2 *(encouragement)* difusión *f*, promoción *f*.

advantage [əd'vɑ:ntɪdʒ] *n* 1 ventaja. 2 *(benefit)* provecho. ■ **to take advantage of** 1 *(thing)* aprovechar. 2 *(person)* aprovecharse de.
advantageous [ædvən'teɪdʒəs] *adj* ventajoso,-a, provechoso,-a.
advent ['ædvənt] *n* advenimiento, llegada.
▷ *n* **Advent** Adviento.
adventure [əd'ventʃəʳ] *n* aventura. ● **adventure playground** parque *m* infantil.
adverb ['ædvɜ:b] *n* adverbio.
adverbial [æd'vɜ:bɪəl] *adj* adverbial.
adversary ['ædvəsərɪ] *n* adversario,-a.
▲ *pl* **adversaries.**
adversative [æd'vɜ:sətɪv] *adj* adversativo,-a.
adverse ['ædvɜ:s] *adj* desfavorable: **adverse weather conditions** *condiciones meteorológicas adversas.*
adversity [əd'vɜ:sɪtɪ] *n* adversidad *f.*
▲ *pl* **adversities.**
advert ['ædvɜ:t] *n fam* anuncio.
advertise ['ædvətaɪz] *vt* anunciar.
▷ *vi* hacer publicidad.
advertisement [əd'vɜ:tɪsmənt] *n* anuncio.
▷ *n pl* **advertisements** *(on television)* publicidad *f,* anuncios *mpl.*
advertiser ['ædvətaɪzəʳ] *n* anunciante *mf.*
advertising ['ædvətaɪzɪŋ] *n* publicidad *f.* ● **advertising agency** agencia de publicidad. ‖ **advertising campaign** campaña publicitaria.
advice [əd'vaɪs] *n* consejos *mpl.* ● **a piece of advice** un consejo.
advisable [əd'vaɪzəbᵊl] *adj* aconsejable.
advise [əd'vaɪz] *vt* aconsejar.
adviser [əd'vaɪzəʳ] *n* consejero,-a.
advisor [əd'vaɪzəʳ] *n* consejero,-a.
advocate [*(n)* 'ædvəkət; *(vb)* 'ædvəkeɪt] *n* 1 *(supporter)* partidario,-a. 2 *(lawyer)* abogado,-a defensor,-ra.
▷ *vt* abogar por, propugnar.
Aegean [ɪ'dʒi:ən] *adj* egeo,-a. ● **the Aegean (Sea)** el (mar) Egeo.
aeon ['i:ən] *n* eón *m.*
aerial ['eərɪəl] *adj* aéreo,-a.
▷ *n* antena.
aerobatics [eərə'bætɪks] *n pl (feats)* acrobacia *f sing* aérea, acrobacias *fpl* aéreas.
aerobe ['eərəub] *n* aerobio.
aerobic [eə'rəubɪk] *adj* aeróbico,-a.
aerobics [eə'rəubɪks] *n* aerobic *m,* aeróbic *m.*
aerodrome ['eərədrəum] *n* aeródromo.
aerodynamics [eərəudaɪ'næmɪks] *n* aerodinámica.
aeronautics [eərə'nɔ:tɪks] *n* aeronáutica.
aerophagia [əerə'feɪdʒɪə] *n* aerofagia.
aeroplane ['eərəpleɪn] *n* aeroplano, avión *m.*
aerosol ['eərəsɒl] *n* aerosol *m.*
aerospace ['eərəuspeɪs] *adj* aeroespacial.
aerostatic [eərə'stætɪk] *adj* aerostático,-a.
aesthetic [i:s'θetɪk] *adj* estético,-a.
aesthetics [i:s'θetɪks] *n* estética.
aetiology [i:tɪ'ɒledʒɪ] *n* etiología.
▲ *pl* **aetiologies.**
afar [ə'fɑ:ʳ] *adv* lejos. ■ **from afar** desde lejos.
affair [ə'feəʳ] *n* 1 *(matter)* asunto: **that's your affair** *eso es asunto tuyo.* 2 *(case)* caso: **the Watergate affair** *el caso Watergate.* 3 *fam (event)* acontecimiento: **the wedding was a high class affair** *la boda era un acontecimiento de mucha clase.* ● **current affairs** actualidad *f sing.*
affect [ə'fekt] *vt* 1 *(gen)* afectar. 2 *(feign)* fingir, afectar: **he affected indifference** *fingió indiferencia.*
affected [ə'fektɪd] *adj* afectado,-a, falso,-a.
affection [ə'fekʃᵊn] *n* afecto, cariño.
affectionate [ə'fekʃᵊnət] *adj* afectuoso,-a, cariñoso,-a.
affective [ə'fektɪv] *adj* afectivo,-a.
afferent ['æfərənt] *adj* aferente.
affidavit [æfɪ'deɪvɪt] *n* declaración *f* jurada, afidávit *m.*
affiliate [ə'fɪlɪət] *n* afiliado,-a.
▷ *vt* afiliar.
▷ *vi* afiliar.
affiliated [ə'fɪlɪeɪtɪd] *adj* afiliado,-a.
affinity [ə'fɪnɪtɪ] *n* afinidad *f.*
▲ *pl* **affinities.**
affirm [ə'fɜ:m] *vt* afirmar, asegurar.
affirmation [æfə'meɪʃᵊn] *n* afirmación *f.*
affirmative [ə'fɜ:mətɪv] *adj* afirmativo,-a.
affix [*(n)* 'æfɪks; *(vb)* ə'fɪks] *n* afijo.
▷ *vt* pegar, añadir, fijar.
afflict [ə'flɪkt] *vt* afligir.
affluence ['æfluəns] *n* riqueza, prosperidad *f.*
affluent ['æfluənt] *adj* rico,-a, próspero,-a.
afford [ə'fɔ:d] *vt* permitirse, costear: **I can't afford to pay £750 for a coat** *no puedo (permitirme) pagar 750 libras por un abrigo.*
afforestation [əfɒrɪ'steɪʃᵊn] *n* repoblación *f* forestal.
affricate ['æfrɪkət] *n* africada.
affricative [ə'frɪkətɪv] *adj* africado,-a.
affront [ə'frʌnt] *n* afrenta, insulto.
▷ *vt* afrentar, insultar.
Afghan ['æfgæn] *adj* afgano,-a.
▷ *n* 1 *(person)* afgano,-a. 2 *(language)* afgano.
Afghanistan [æfgænɪ'stæn] *n* Afganistán *m.*
afield [ə'fi:ld] *adv* lejos. ■ **far afield** lejos.
afloat [ə'fləut] *adj* a flote.
afoot [ə'fut] *adv* en marcha, en proceso: **there's a scheme afoot to build a prison** *hay un proyecto para construir una cárcel.*
aforementioned [əfɔ:'menʃᵊnd] *adj* arriba mencionado,-a.
aforesaid [ə'fɔ:sed] *adj* → **aforementioned.**
afraid [ə'freɪd] *adj* temeroso,-a. ■ **to be afraid** 1 *(frightened)* tener miedo. 2 *(sorry)* temer, sentir, lamentar: **I'm afraid so/not** *me temo que sí/no.*
afresh [ə'freʃ] *adv* de nuevo.
África ['æfrɪkə] *n* África. ● **South Africa** Sudáfrica.
African ['æfrɪkən] *adj* africano,-a.
▷ *n* africano,-a. ● **South African** sudafricano,-a.
Afro ['æfrəu] *adj (hairstyle)* afro.
Afro-American [æfrəuə'merɪkᵊn] *adj* afroamericano,-a.
▷ *n* afroamericano,-a.
after ['ɑ:ftəʳ] *prep* 1 *(time)* después de: **after class** *después de la clase.* 2 *(following)* detrás de: **the police are after us** *la policía nos está persiguiendo.* 3 US *(past)* y: **it's a quarter after four** *son las cuatro y cuarto.*
▷ *adv* después: **the day after** *el día después.*
▷ *conj* después que, después de que: **after he left, I went to bed** *después de que se marchara, me acosté.*
▷ *n pl* **afters** GB *fam* postre *m.*

afterbirth ['ɑ:ftəbɜ:θ] *n* placenta.
after-effect ['ɑ:ftərɪfekt] *n* efecto secundario, secuela.
afterlife ['ɑ:ftəlaɪf] *n* más allá *m*.
afternoon [ɑ:ftə'nu:n] *n* tarde *f*: in the afternoon *por la tarde*.
▷ *adv* afternoons por la tarde.
after-sales service [ɑ:ftə'seɪlzsɜ:vɪs] *n* servicio posventa.
aftershave ['ɑ:ftəʃeɪv] *n* loción *f* para después del afeitado.
aftertaste ['ɑ:ftəteɪst] *n* regusto.
afterwards ['ɑ:ftəwədz] *adv* después, luego.
again [ə'gen, ə'geɪn] *adv* 1 *(once more)* otra vez, de nuevo: play me that song again *tócame esa canción otra vez*. 2 *(in questions)*: where do you live again? *¿dónde has dicho que vives?* 3 *(also)* también: the next point is again rather a tricky one *el próximo tema es también bastante peliagudo*. ■ again and again repetidamente. ‖ now and again de vez en cuando. ‖ then again por otra parte.
against [ə'genst, ə'geɪnst] *prep* 1 *(gen)* contra: against the wall *contra la pared;* Leeds played against Liverpool *Leeds jugó contra Liverpool*. 2 *(opposed to)* en contra de: I voted against the proposal *voté en contra de la propuesta*.
agate ['ægət] *n* ágata.
age [eɪdʒ] *n* edad *f*. ■ of age mayor de edad. ‖ to come of age llegar a la mayoría de edad. ‖ under age menor de edad.
▷ *vt & vi* envejecer.
▷ *n pl* ages *fam* años *mpl*, siglos *mpl*: I haven't seen you for ages *hace años que no te veo*.
aged[1] [eɪdʒd] *adj* de (tantos años de) edad: a boy aged ten *un muchacho de diez años*.
aged[2] ['eɪdʒɪd] *adj* viejo,-a, anciano,-a. ● the aged los ancianos *mpl*.
agency ['eɪdʒənsɪ] *n* 1 *(commercial)* agencia: a travel/advertising/employment agency *una agencia de viajes/publicidad/empleo*. 2 *(governmental, etc)* organismo.
▲ *pl* agencies.
agenda [ə'dʒendə] *n* orden *m* del día.
agent ['eɪdʒənt] *n* 1 *(gen)* agente *mf*; *(representative)* representante *mf*. 2 *(active ingredient)* agente *m*.
agglomeration [əglɒmə'reɪʃən] *n* aglomeración *f*.
aggravate ['ægrəveɪt] *vt* 1 *(make worse)* agravar. 2 *fam (annoy)* irritar, molestar.
aggravation [ægrə'veɪʃən] *n* 1 *(worsening)* agravamiento. 2 *(annoyance)* exasperación *f*. 3 *fam (hassle)* follones *mpl*.
aggregate [*(n)* 'ægrɪgət; *(vb)* 'ægrɪgeɪt] *n* 1 *(total)* total *m*, totalidad *f*, conjunto. 2 *(for concrete)* conglomerado.
▷ *vt* agregar, reunir.
▷ *vi* ascender a.
aggression [ə'greʃən] *n* 1 *(act)* agresión *f*. 2 *(feeling)* agresividad *f*.
aggressive [ə'gresɪv] *adj* 1 *(gen)* agresivo,-a. 2 *(dynamic)* dinámico,-a, emprendedor,-ra.
aggressor [ə'gresəʳ] *n* agresor,-ra.
aghast [ə'gɑ:st] *adj* horrorizado,-a.
agile ['ædʒaɪl] *adj* ágil.
agility [ə'dʒɪlɪtɪ] *n* agilidad *f*.
agitate ['ædʒɪteɪt] *vt* 1 *(shake)* agitar. 2 *(worry)* inquietar, perturbar.
agitator ['ædʒɪteɪtəʳ] *n* 1 *(person)* agitador,-ra. 2 *(machine)* agitador *m*.
agnostic [æg'nɒstɪk] *adj* agnóstico,-a.
▷ *n* agnóstico,-a.
ago [ə'gəʊ] *adv* hace: ten days ago *hace diez días;* it happened a long time ago *ocurrió hace mucho tiempo*.
agog [ə'gɒg] *adj* anhelante, deseoso,-a.
agonise ['ægənaɪz] *vi* → agonize.
agonize ['ægənaɪz] *vi* agonizar.
agonizing ['ægənaɪzɪŋ] *adj* agónico,-a, angustioso,-a.
agony ['ægənɪ] *n* 1 *(pain)* dolor *m* muy agudo. 2 *(anguish)* angustia. ● agony column consultorio sentimental.
▲ *pl* agonies.
agora ['ægərə] *n* ágora.
▲ *pl* agoras o agorae ['ægəraɪ, 'ægəri:].
agoraphobia [ægərə'fəʊbɪə] *n* agorafobia.
agouti [ə'gu:tɪ] *n* agutí.
▲ *pl* agoutis o agouties.
agree [ə'gri:] *vi* 1 *(be in agreement)* estar de acuerdo (with, con): do you agree with me? *¿estás de acuerdo conmigo?* 2 *(reach an agreement)* ponerse de acuerdo (on, en): they can't agree on a name for the baby *no se ponen de acuerdo en el nombre del bebé*. 3 *(square)* concordar, encajar: the two men's stories don't agree *las historias de los dos hombres no encajan*. 4 *(food, climate, etc)* sentar bien (with, -): the prawns didn't agree with me *las gambas no me sentaron bien*.
▷ *vt (grammatically)* concordar (with, con).
agreeable [ə'gri:əbəl] *adj* 1 *(pleasant)* agradable. 2 *(in agreement)* conforme.
agreement [ə'gri:mənt] *n* 1 acuerdo. 2 *(grammatical)* concordancia.
agricultural [ægrɪ'kʌltʃərəl] *adj* agrícola.
agriculture ['ægrɪkʌltʃəʳ] *n* agricultura.
agronomist [ə'grɒnəmɪst] *n* agrónomo,-a.
agronomy [ə'grɒnəmɪ] *n* agronomía.
aground [ə'graʊnd] *adj* encallado,-a. ■ to run aground encallar.
ahead [ə'hed] *adv (in front)* delante: there's a police checkpoint ahead *hay un control de policía aquí delante;* we finished ahead of schedule *acabamos antes de lo previsto*. ■ go ahead! ¡adelante!
ahoy [ə'hɔɪ] *interj* MAR: ahoy there! *¡ah del barco!;* land ahoy! *¡tierra a la vista!*
aid [eɪd] *n (help)* ayuda; *(rescue)* auxilio. ● economic aid ayuda económica. ‖ humanitarian aid ayuda humanitaria.
▷ *vt* ayudar, auxiliar.
aide [eɪd] *n (assistant)* ayudante *mf*.
AIDS [eɪdz] *n* (Acquired Immune Deficiency Syndrome) sida *m*.
aileron ['eɪlərɒn] *n* alerón *m*.
ailing ['eɪlɪŋ] *adj* enfermo,-a.
ailment ['eɪlmənt] *n* dolencia, achaque *m*.
aim [eɪm] *n* 1 *(marksmanship)* puntería: his aim is good *tiene buena puntería*. 2 *(objective)* meta, objetivo: what's your aim in life? *¿qué objetivo tienes en la vida?*
▷ *vt* 1 *(gun)* apuntar (at, a). 2 *(attack)* dirigir (at, a).
aimless ['eɪmləs] *adj* sin objetivo, sin propósito.
ain't [eɪnt] *contr fam* → am not, is not, are not, has not, have not.
air [eəʳ] *n* aire *m*. ■ by air 1 *(send letter)* por avión. 2 *(travel)* en avión. ● air hostess azafata. ‖ air lane ruta aérea. ‖ air

pocket bache *m.* ‖ **air pressure** presión *f* atmosférica. ‖ **air raid** ataque *m* aéreo. ‖ **air rifle** escopeta de aire comprimido. ‖ **air terminal** terminal *f* aérea. ‖ **air traffic controller** controlador,-ra aéreo,-a. ‖ **fresh air** aire *m* fresco.
▷ *vt* 1 *(clothes)* airear, orear. 2 *(room)* ventilar. 3 *(opinions)* airear. 4 *(knowledge)* hacer alarde de.
airbag ['eəbæg] *n* airbag *m.*
airbase ['eəbeɪs] *n* base *f* aérea.
air-bed ['eəbed] *n* GB colchón *m* de aire.
airborne ['eəbɔːn] *adj* 1 *(troops)* aerotransportado,-a. 2 *(aircraft)* en el aire.
airbrush ['eəbrʌʃ] *n* aerógrafo.
air-conditioned [eəkən'dɪʃᵊnd] *adj* con aire acondicionado, refrigerado,-a.
air-conditioner [eəkən'dɪʃᵊnəʳ] *n* acondicionador *m* de aire.
air-conditioning [eəkən'dɪʃᵊnɪŋ] *n* aire *m* acondicionado.
aircraft ['eəkrɑːft] *n (gen)* aeronave *f*; *(plane)* avión *m.*
▲ *pl* aircraft.
aircraft-carrier ['eəkrɑːftkærɪəʳ] *n* portaaeronaves *m inv*, portaaviones *m inv.*
airdrome ['eədrəʊm] *n* US aeródromo.
airfield ['eəfiːld] *n* campo de aviación.
airforce ['eəfɔːs] *n* fuerza aérea, fuerzas *fpl* aéreas.
airlift ['eəlɪft] *n* puente *m* aéreo.
▷ *vt* transportar por avión.
airline ['eəlaɪn] *n* línea aérea.
airliner ['eəlaɪnəʳ] *n* avión *m* de pasajeros *(grande).*
airmail ['eəmeɪl] *n* correo aéreo.
airplane ['eəpleɪn] *n* US aeroplano, avión *m.*
airport ['eəpɔːt] *n* aeropuerto.
airship ['eəʃɪp] *n* dirigible *m.*
airsick ['eəsɪk] *adj* mareado,-a. ■ **to be airsick** marearse.
airspace ['eəspeɪs] *n* espacio aéreo.
airstrip ['eəstrɪp] *n* pista de aterrizaje.
airtight ['eətaɪt] *adj* hermético,-a.
airway ['eəweɪ] *n* 1 *(route)* ruta aérea, vía aérea. 2 *(airline)* línea aérea.
airy ['eərɪ] *adj* 1 *(ventilated)* bien ventilado,-a. 2 *(light)* ligero,-a.
▲ *comp* airier, *superl* airiest.
aisle [aɪl] *n* 1 *(between seats, shelves, etc)* pasillo. 2 *(section of church)* nave *f* lateral.
aitch [eɪtʃ] *n* hache *f.*
ajar [ə'dʒɑːʳ] *adj* entreabierto,-a.
akimbo [ə'kɪmbəʊ] *adv* en jarras.
akin [ə'kɪn] *adj* parecido,-a (**to**, a), semejante (**to**, a).
alabaster ['æləbɑːstəʳ] *n* alabastro.
alarm [ə'lɑːm] *n* 1 *(device)* alarma. 2 *(fear)* temor *m*, alarma. ● **alarm clock** despertador *m.*
▷ *vt* alarmar, asustar.
alarming [ə'lɑːmɪŋ] *adj* alarmante.
alarmism [ə'lɑːmɪzᵊm] *n* alarmismo.
alarmist [ə'lɑːmɪst] *adj* alarmista.
Albania [æl'beɪnɪə] *n* Albania.
Albanian [æl'beɪnɪən] *adj* albanés,-esa.
▷ *n* 1 *(person)* albanés,-esa. 2 *(language)* albanés *m.*
albatross ['ælbətrɒs] *n* albatros *m.*
albeit [ɔːl'biːɪt] *conj fml* aunque.
albinism ['ælbɪnɪzᵊm] *n* albinismo.
albino [æl'biːnəʊ] *adj* albino,-a.
▷ *n* albino,-a.
▲ *pl* albinos.
album ['ælbəm] *n* álbum *m.*
albumen ['ælbjʊmɪn, US æl'bjuːmən] *n* 1 *(white of egg)* clara de huevo. 2 *(in plants)* albumen *m.*
albumin ['ælbjʊmɪn, US æl'bjuːmən] *n* albúmina.
alcohol ['ælkəhɒl] *n* alcohol *m.*
alcohol-free ['ælkəhɒlfriː] *adj* sin alcohol.
alcoholism ['ælkəhɒlɪzᵊm] *n* alcoholismo.
alcove ['ælkəʊv] *n* hueco, hornacina, cavidad *f.*
aldehyde ['ældɪhaɪd] *n* aldehído.
alder ['ɔːldəʳ] *n* aliso.
ale [eɪl] *n* cerveza.
alert [ə'lɜːt] *adj* 1 *(quick to act)* alerta, vigilante. 2 *(lively)* vivo,-a.
▷ *n* alarma.
▷ *vt* alertar, avisar.
A-level ['eɪlevᵊl] *abbr* GB (**Advanced level**) ≈ segundo curso de bachillerato.
alfalfa [æl'fælfə] *n* alfalfa.
algae ['ældʒiː] *n pl* algas *fpl.*
▲ *sing* alga ['ælgə].
algebra ['ældʒɪbrə] *n* álgebra.
algebraic [ældʒɪ'breɪɪk] *adj* algebraico,-a.
Algeria [æl'dʒɪərɪə] *n* Argelia.
Algerian [æl'dʒɪərɪən] *adj* argelino,-a.
▷ *n* argelino,-a.
algorithm ['ælgərɪðᵊm] *n* algoritmo.
alias ['eɪlɪəs] *adv* alias.
▷ *n* alias *m.*
alibi ['ælɪbaɪ] *n* coartada.
alien ['eɪlɪən] *adj* 1 *(foreign)* extranjero,-a. 2 *(extraterrestrial)* extraterrestre. 3 *(strange)* extraño,-a, ajeno,-a: **his ideas are alien to me** *sus ideas me son ajenas.*
▷ *n* 1 *(foreigner)* extranjero,-a. 2 *(extraterrestrial)* extraterrestre *mf.*
alight [ə'laɪt] *adj* encendido,-a, ardiendo.
align [ə'laɪn] *vt* alinear (**with**, con).
alike [ə'laɪk] *adj (the same)* iguales; *(similar)* parecidos,-as: **they are alike in all respects** *son iguales en todo.*
▷ *adv* igual: **they dress alike** *visten igual.*
alimentary [ælɪ'mentᵊrɪ] *adj* alimenticio,-a. ● **alimentary canal** tubo digestivo.
alimony ['ælɪmənɪ] *n* pensión *f* alimenticia.
alive [ə'laɪv] *adj* vivo,-a. ■ **alive and kicking** vivo,-a y coleando. ‖ **alive with** lleno,-a de, infestado,-a de. ‖ **to come alive** 1 *(meeting, etc)* animarse. 2 *(narrative)* cobrar vida.
alkali ['ælkəlaɪ] *n* álcali *m.*
alkaline ['ælkəlaɪn] *adj* alcalino,-a.
all [ɔːl] *adj (singular)* todo,-a; *(plural)* todos,-as: **all the chairs** *todas las sillas*; **all day/month/year** *todo el día/mes/año.*
▷ *pron* 1 *(everything)* todo, la totalidad *f*: **all was lost in the fire** *se perdió todo en el incendio.* 2 *(everybody)* todos *mpl*, todo el mundo: **all of them helped/they all helped** *ayudaron todos.*
▷ *adv* completamente, totalmente: **she was dressed all in leather** *iba vestida toda de cuero.* ■ **after all** 1 *(despite everything)* después de todo. 2 *(it must be remembered)* no hay que olvidarlo. ‖ **all over** en todas partes. ‖ **to be all over** acabar: **in ten minutes it was all over** *en diez minutos todo había acabado.* ‖ **all right** 1 *(acceptable)*

bien, bueno,-a, satisfactorio,-a: **the film's all right, but I've seen better ones** *la película no está mal, pero las he visto mejores.* 2 *(well, safe)* bien: **are you all right?** *¿estás bien?* 3 *(accepting suggestion)* vale, bueno: **are you coming? –all right** *¿te vienes? –vale.* ‖ **all that** tan: **he's not all that fast** *no es tan rápido.* ‖ **all the** + *comp* tanto + *adj/adv*, aún + *adj/adv*: **all the better** *tanto mejor.* ‖ **all the time** todo el rato, siempre. ‖ **at all** en absoluto. ‖ **in all** en total. ‖ **not at all** no hay de qué.

Allah ['ælə] *n* Alá *m*.

allay [ə'leɪ] *vt* calmar, apaciguar.

alleged [ə'ledʒd] *adj* presunto,-a.

allegoric [ælɪ'gɒrɪk] *adj* alegórico,-a.

allegorical [ælɪ'gɒrɪkᵊl] *adj* alegórico,-a.

allegory ['ælɪgərɪ] *n* alegoría.
▲ *pl* **allegories.**

allergen ['ælədʒən] *n* alérgeno.

allergic [ə'lɜːdʒɪk] *adj* alérgico,-a (**to**, a).

allergy ['ælədʒɪ] *n* alergia.
▲ *pl* **allergies.**

alleviate [ə'liːvɪeɪt] *vt* aliviar, mitigar.

alley ['ælɪ] *n* callejuela, callejón *m*.

alliance [ə'laɪəns] *n* alianza.

allied ['ælaɪd] *adj* 1 POL aliado,-a. 2 *(related)* relacionado,-a, afín.
▷ *vt* aliar (**with**, con).
▷ *vi* aliarse (**with**, con).
▲ *pt & pp* **allied**, *ger* **allying.**

alligator ['ælɪgeɪtəʳ] *n* caimán *m*.

all-in [ɔːl'ɪn] *adj (price)* con todo incluido. ● **all-in wrestling** lucha libre.

all-inclusive [ɔːlɪn'kluːsɪv] *adj* todo comprendido, con todo incluido.

alliteration [əlɪtə'reɪʃᵊn] *n* aliteración *f*.

all-night ['ɔːlnaɪt] *adj (lasting all night)* que dura toda la noche; *(open all night)* que no cierra en toda la noche.

allocate ['æləkeɪt] *vt (money)* destinar; *(time, space, job, etc)* asignar.

allocation [ælə'keɪʃᵊn] *n* 1 *(distribution)* asignación *f*; *(of money)* distribución *f*. 2 *(gen)* lo asignado; *(money given)* cuota.

allot [ə'lɒt] *vt* asignar.
▲ *pt & pp* **allotted**, *ger* **allotting.**

all-out [ɔːl'aʊt] *adj* total.

allow [ə'laʊ] *vt* 1 *(permit)* permitir, dejar. 2 *(set aside)* conceder, dar, dejar. 3 *(admit)* admitir, reconocer.
⊙ **to allow for** *vt insep* tener en cuenta.

allowance [ə'laʊəns] *n* 1 *(from government)* subsidio, prestación *f*. 2 *(from employer)* dietas *fpl*, asignación *f*. 3 US *(pocket money)* paga semanal. ■ **to make allowances for** 1 *(take into account)* tener en cuenta. 2 *(be permissive)* tener paciencia con.

alloy ['ælɔɪ] *n* aleación *f*.

all-purpose [ɔːl'pɜːpəs] *adj* multiuso.

all-star ['ɔːlstɑːʳ] *adj* estelar: **an all-star cast** *un reparto estelar.*

all-terrain [ɔːltə'reɪn] *adj* todo terreno.

allude [ə'luːd] *vi* aludir (**to**, a).

allure [ə'ljʊəʳ] *n* atractivo, encanto.
▷ *vt* atraer, seducir.

alluring [ə'ljʊərɪŋ] *adj* seductor,-ra.

allusion [ə'luːʒᵊn] *n* alusión *f*.

alluvial [ə'luːvɪəl] *adj* aluvial.

ally ['ælaɪ] *n* aliado,-a.
▲ *pl* **allies.**

almighty [ɔːl'maɪtɪ] *adj* todopoderoso,-a.
▷ *n* **the Almighty** el Todopoderoso.

almond ['ɑːmənd] *n* almendra. ● **almond paste** mazapán *m*. ‖ **almond tree** almendro.

almost ['ɔːlməʊst] *adv* casi.

alms [ɑːmz] *n pl* limosna *f sing*, caridad *f sing*.

aloft [ə'lɒft] *adv* arriba, en lo alto.

alone [ə'ləʊn] *adj (unaccompanied)* solo,-a.
▷ *adv (only)* solo, solamente. ■ **let alone** y mucho menos: **he can't boil an egg, let alone make an omelette** *no sabe cocer un huevo, y mucho menos hacer una tortilla.* ‖ **to leave** STH **alone** no tocar ALGO. ‖ **to leave** SB **alone** dejar a ALGN en paz.

along [ə'lɒŋ] *prep* 1 por, a lo largo de: **we walked along the riverbank** *caminamos por la orilla del río.* 2 *(in)* en: **his office is along this corridor** *su despacho está en este pasillo.*
▷ *adv* adelante, hacia adelante: **move along, please** *circulen, por favor.* ■ **along with** junto con. ‖ **come along** 1 *(sing)* ven. 2 *(plural)* venid. 3 *(including speaker)* vamos.

alongside [əlɒŋ'saɪd] *prep* al lado de.
▷ *adv* al costado, al lado. ■ **to come alongside** ponerse a la misma altura.

aloof [ə'luːf] *adj* distante.
▷ *adv* a distancia.

alopecia [ælə'piːʃə] *n* alopecia.

aloud [ə'laʊd] *adv* en voz alta.

alpha ['ælfə] *n* alfa. ● **alpha ray** rayo alfa.

alphabet ['ælfəbet] *n* alfabeto, abecedario.

alphabetic [ælfə'betɪk] *adj* alfabético,-a.

alphabetical [ælfə'betɪkᵊl] *adj* alfabético,-a. ■ **in alphabetical order** por orden alfabético.

alphanumeric [ælfənjʊ'merɪk] *adj* alfanumérico,-a.

alpine ['ælpaɪn] *adj* alpino,-a.

Alps [ælps] *n pl* **the Alps** los Alpes *mpl*.

already [ɔːl'redɪ] *adv* ya: **they've already left** *ya se han ido.*

alright [ɔː'raɪt] *adv fam* → **all right.**

also ['ɔːlsəʊ] *adv* también. ■ **not only ..., but also ...** no solo ..., sino también ...

altar ['ɔːltəʳ] *n* altar *m*.

altarpiece ['ɔːltəpiːs] *n* retablo.

alter ['ɔːltəʳ] *vt (gen)* cambiar; *(clothes)* arreglar.
▷ *vi* cambiar, cambiarse.

alteration [ɔːltə'reɪʃᵊn] *n* modificación *f*.
▷ *n pl* **alterations** reformas *fpl*.

alternate [*(adj)* ɔːl'tɜːnət; *(vb)* 'ɔːltɜːneɪt] *adj* alterno,-a.
▷ *vt* alternar.
▷ *vi* alternarse.

alternating ['ɔːltɜːneɪtɪŋ] ● **alternating current** corriente *f* alterna.

alternation [ɔːltə'neɪʃᵊn] *n* alternancia.

alternative [ɔːl'tɜːnətɪv] *adj* alternativo,-a.
▷ *n (option)* opción *f*, alternativa. ● **alternative medicine** medicina alternativa.

alternatively [ɔːl'tɜːnətɪvlɪ] *adv* o bien, por otra parte.

alternator ['ɔːltəneɪtəʳ] *n* alternador *m*.

although [ɔːl'ðəʊ] *conj* aunque.

altimeter ['æltɪmiːtəʳ] *n* altímetro.

altitude ['æltɪtjuːd] *n* altitud *f*, altura.

alto ['æltəʊ] *n (male)* contralto *m*; *(female)* contralto *f*.
▲ *pl* altos.
altogether [ɔ:ltə'geðəʳ] *adv* **1** *(completely)* del todo. **2** *(on the whole)* en conjunto. **3** *(in total)* en total.
altruism ['æltrʊɪzᵊm] *n* altruismo.
aluminium [æljʊ'mɪnɪəm] *n* aluminio. ● **aluminium foil** papel *m* de aluminio, papel *m* de plata.
aluminosis [əlu:mɪ'nəʊsɪs] *n* aluminosis *fpl*.
aluminum [ə'lu:mɪnəm] *n* US aluminio.
alumna [ə'lʌmnə] *n* US ex alumna.
▲ *pl* alumnae [ə'lʌmni:].
alumnus [ə'lʌmnəs] *n* US ex alumno.
▲ *pl* alumni [ə'lʌmni:].
alveolar [ælvɪ'əʊləʳ] *adj* alveolar. ● **alveolar sacs** ANAT sacos alveolares.
alveolus [æl'vɪələs] *n* alveolo, alvéolo.
▲ *pl* alveoli [æl'vɪəlaɪ].
always ['ɔ:lweɪz] *adv* siempre.
Alzheimer's disease ['æltshaɪməsdɪzi:z] *n* enfermedad *f* de Alzheimer.
am [æm] *pres* ⟶ **be.**
AM ['eɪ'em] *abbr* RAD **(amplitude modulation)** modulación *f* de amplitud; *(abbreviation)* AM *f*.
a.m. ['eɪ'em] *abbr* **(ante meridiem)** de la mañana.
amass [ə'mæs] *vt* acumular.
amateur ['æmətəʳ] *adj* aficionado,-a.
▷ *n* aficionado,-a.
amateurish ['æmətərɪʃ] *adj* poco profesional, poco serio,-a, chapucero,-a.
amateurism ['æmətʃərɪzᵊm] *n* amateurismo.
amaze [ə'meɪz] *vt* asombrar, pasmar.
amazement [ə'meɪzmənt] *n* asombro, pasmo.
amazing [ə'meɪzɪŋ] *adj* asombroso,-a, pasmoso,-a.
amazon ['æməzᵊn] *n (warrior)* amazona.
▷ *n* **the Amazon 1** *(river)* el Amazonas *m*. **2** *(basin)* Amazonia.
Amazonian [æmə'zəʊnɪən] *adj* amazónico,-a.
ambassador [æm'bæsədəʳ] *n* embajador,-ra.
ambassadress [æm'bæsədrəs] *n* embajadora.
amber ['æmbəʳ] *n* ámbar *m*.
▷ *adj* ámbar.
ambiance ['æmbɪəns] *n* ambiente *m*.
ambidextrous [æmbɪ'dekstrəs] *adj* ambidextro,-a.
ambience ['æmbɪəns] *n* ambiente *m*.
ambient ['æmbɪənt] *adj* ambiental.
ambiguity [æmbɪ'gjʊ:ɪtɪ] *n* ambigüedad *f*.
▲ *pl* ambiguities.
ambiguous [æm'bɪgjʊəs] *adj* ambiguo,-a.
ambition [æm'bɪʃᵊn] *n* ambición *f*.
ambitious [æm'bɪʃəs] *adj* ambicioso,-a.
ambivalent [æm'bɪvələnt] *adj* ambivalente.
ambulance ['æmbjʊləns] *n* ambulancia.
ambush ['æmbʊʃ] *n* emboscada.
▷ *vt* poner una emboscada a.
ameba [ə'mi:bə] *n* US ⟶ **amoeba.**
ameliorate [ə'mi:lɪəreɪt] *vt* mejorarse.
▷ *vi* mejorar.
amelioration [əmi:lɪə'reɪʃᵊn] *n* mejora.
amen [ɑ:'men] *interj* amén.
amenable [ə'mi:nəbᵊl] *adj* tratable, bien dispuesto,-a: **he's amenable to reason** *es una persona razonable.*
amend [ə'mend] *vt (law)* enmendar; *(error)* corregir.
▷ *vi (law)* enmendarse; *(error)* corregirse.
amendment [ə'mendmənt] *n* enmienda.
amenities [ə'mi:nɪtɪz] *n pl* servicios *mpl*, prestaciones *fpl*.
America [ə'merɪkə] *n* América. ● **Central America** América Central, Centroamérica. ‖ **Latin America** América Latina, Latinoamérica. ‖ **North America** América del Norte, Norteamérica. ‖ **South America** América del Sur, Sudamérica.
American [ə'merɪkən] *adj* **1** *(gen)* americano,-a. **2** *(from USA)* estadounidense. ● **American football** fútbol *m* americano.
▷ *n* **1** *(gen)* americano,-a. **2** *(from USA)* estadounidense *mf*.
Americanism [ə'merɪkənɪzᵊm] *n* americanismo.
americium [æmə'rɪsɪəm] *n* americio.
amethyst ['æməθɪst] *n* amatista, ametista.
amiable ['eɪmɪəbᵊl] *adj* afable, amable.
amicable ['æmɪkəbᵊl] *adj* amistoso,-a, amigable.
amid [ə'mɪd] *prep* en medio de, entre.
amidst [ə'mɪdst] *prep* ⟶ **amid.**
amine [ə'mi:n] *n* amina.
amino acid [æmi:nəʊ'æsɪd] *n* aminoácido.
amiss [ə'mɪs] *adv* mal.
▷ *adj* mal. ■ **to take amiss** tomar a mal.
ammeter ['æmi:təʳ] *n* amperímetro.
ammonia [ə'məʊnɪ] *n* amoníaco, amoniaco.
ammonite ['æmənaɪt] *n* amonites.
ammunition [æmjʊ'nɪʃᵊn] *n* **1** municiones *fpl*. **2** *fig (arguments)* argumentos *mpl*.
amnesia [əm'ni:zɪə] *n* amnesia.
amnesty ['æmnəstɪ] *n* amnistía.
▲ *pl* amnesties.
amniotic [æmnɪ'ɒtɪk] *adj* amniótico,-a.
amoeba [æ'mi:bə] *n* ameba.
▲ *pl* amoebae [ə'mi:bi:].
amok [ə'mɒk] ■ **to run amok** volverse loco,-a y causar destrozos.
among [ə'mʌŋ] *prep* entre.
amongst [ə'mʌŋst] *prep* ⟶ **among.**
amorphous [ə'mɔ:fəs] *adj* amorfo,-a.
amortization [əmɔ:taɪ'zeɪʃᵊn] *n* amortización *f*.
amount [ə'maʊnt] *n (gen)* cantidad *f*; *(bill)* importe *m*.
⊙ **to amount to** *vt insep* **1** ascender a. **2** *fig* equivaler a.
amp [æmp] *n* (*abbr of* **ampere**) amperio, ampere *m*.
ampere ['æmpeəʳ] *n* amperio, ampere *m*.
ampersand ['æmpəsænd] *n el signo &.*
amphetamine [æm'fetəmi:n] *n* anfetamina.
amphibian [æm'fɪbɪən] *n* anfibio.
amphibious [æm'fɪbɪəs] *adj* anfibio,-a.
amphitheater ['æmfɪθɪətəʳ] *n* US anfiteatro.
amphitheatre ['æmfɪθɪətəʳ] *n* anfiteatro.
amphora ['æmfərə] *n* ánfora.
▲ *pl* **amphoras** o **amphorae** ['æmfəri:].
ample ['æmpᵊl] *adj* **1** *(enough)* bastante. **2** *(plenty)* más que suficiente. **3** *(large, generous)* amplio,-a.
amplification [æmplɪfɪ'keɪʃᵊn] *n* **1** *(of sound)* amplificación *f*. **2** *(of statement)* ampliación *f*.
amplifier ['æmplɪfaɪəʳ] *n* amplificador *m*.
amplify ['æmplɪfaɪ] *vt* **1** *(sound)* amplificar. **2** *(statement)* ampliar.
▲ *pt & pp* **amplified**, *ger* **amplifying**.
amplitude ['æmplɪtjʊ:d] *n* amplitud *f*.

amply ['æmplɪ] *adv* 1 *(enough)* suficientemente. 2 *(more than enough)* sobradamente. 3 *(generously)* ampliamente.
ampoule ['æmpu:l] *n* ampolla.
ampule ['æmpu:l] *n* US ampolla.
amputate ['æmpjʊteɪt] *vt* amputar.
amputation [æmpjʊ'teɪʃᵊn] *n* amputación *f.*
amuck [ə'mʌk] *adv* → **amok.**
amulet ['æmjʊlət] *n* amuleto.
amuse [ə'mju:z] *vt* entretener, divertir.
amusement [ə'mju:zmənt] *n* 1 *(enjoyment)* diversión *f,* entretenimiento. 2 *(pastime)* pasatiempo. ● **amusement arcade** salón *m* de juegos. ‖ **amusement park** parque *m* de atracciones.
amusing [ə'mju:zɪŋ] *adj* 1 *(fun)* entretenido,-a, divertido,-a. 2 *(funny)* gracioso,-a.
an [ən, æn] *indef art* 1 un, una. 2 *(per)* por.
Se usa delante de las palabras que empiezan por un sonido vocálico. Consulta también **a.**
anabolism [ə'næbəlɪzᵊm] *n* anabolismo.
anachronic [ænə'krɒnɪk] *adj* anacrónico,-a.
anaconda [ænə'kɒndə] *n* anaconda.
anaemia [ə'ni:mɪə] *n* anemia.
anaemic [ə'ni:mɪk] *adj* anémico,-a.
anaerobic [æneə'rəʊbɪk] *adj* anaerobio,-a.
anaesthesia [ænəs'θi:zɪə] *n* anestesia.
anaesthetic [ænəs'θetɪk] *adj* anestésico,-a.
▷ *n* anestésico.
anaesthetist [ə'ni:sθətɪst] *n* anestesista *mf.*
anaesthetise [ə'ni:sθətaɪz] *vt* → **anaesthetize.**
anaesthetize [ə'ni:sθətaɪz] *vt* anestesiar.
anagram ['ænəgræm] *n* anagrama *m.*
anal ['eɪnᵊl] *adj* anal.
analgesic [ænəl'dʒi:zɪk] *adj* analgésico,-a.
▷ *n* analgésico.
analog ['ænəlɒg] *adj-n* US → **analogue.**
analogical [ænə'lɒdʒɪkᵊl] *adj* analógico,-a.
analogue ['ænəlɒg] *adj* analógico,-a.
▷ *n* análogo.
analogy [ə'nælədʒɪ] *n* analogía, semejanza.
▲ *pl* **analogies.**
analyse ['ænəlaɪz] *vt* analizar.
analysis [ə'nælɪsɪs] *n* análisis *m.*
▲ *pl* **analyses** [ə'nælɪsi:z].
analyst ['ænəlɪst] *n* analista *mf.*
analytic [ænə'lɪtɪk] *adj* analítico,-a.
analytical [ænə'lɪtɪkᵊl] *adj* analítico,-a.
analytics [ænə'lɪtɪks] *n* analítica.
anaphora [ə'næfərə] *n* anáfora.
anarchic [æ'nɑ:kɪk] *adj* anárquico,-a.
anarchical [æ'nɑ:kɪkᵊl] *adj* anárquico,-a.
anarchism ['ænəkɪzᵊm] *n* anarquismo.
anarchist ['ænəkɪst] *n* anarquista *mf.*
anarchy ['ænəkɪ] *n* anarquía.
▲ *pl* **anarchies.**
anatomical [ænə'tɒmɪkᵊl] *adj* anatómico,-a.
anatomy [ə'nætəmɪ] *n* anatomía.
▲ *pl* **anatomies.**
ancestor ['ænsəstəʳ] *n* antepasado.
ancestral [æn'sestrəl] *adj* ancestral.
anchor ['æŋkəʳ] *n* 1 *(of ship)* ancla, áncora. 2 *fig* sostén *m.*
▷ *vt* 1 *(ship)* anclar. 2 *(make secure)* sujetar.
anchovy ['æntʃəvɪ] *n (salted)* anchoa; *(fresh)* boquerón *m.*
▲ *pl* **anchovies.**
ancient ['eɪnʃᵊnt] *adj* 1 antiguo,-a; *(monument)* histórico,-a. 2 *fam* viejísimo,-a. ● **ancient history** historia antigua.
ancillary [æn'sɪlərɪ] *adj* auxiliar.
and [ænd, *unstressed* ənd] *conj* 1 y; *(before* **i-** *and* **hi-**) e: **black and white** *blanco y negro;* **opinions and ideas** *opiniones e ideas.* 2 *(with infinitives)*: **go and look for it** *ve a buscarlo;* **wait and see what happens** *espera a ver lo que pasa.* 3 *(expressing repetition, increase)*: **it rained and rained** *no paró de llover.* 4 *(with numbers)*: **a hundred and twenty** *ciento veinte;* **two thousand and eighty four** *dos mil ochenta y cuatro.* 5 *(in sums)* más: **four and six are ten** *cuatro más seis son diez.*
Andes ['ændi:z] *n pl* **the Andes** los Andes *mpl.*
Andorra [æn'dɔ:rə] *n* Andorra.
Andorran [æn'dɔ:rən] *adj* andorrano,-a.
▷ *n* andorrano,-a.
androecium [æn'dri:sɪəm] *n* androceo.
▲ *pl* **androecia** [æn'dri:sɪə].
android ['ændrɔɪd] *n* androide *m.*
anecdote ['ænɪkdəʊt] *n* anécdota.
anemia [ə'ni:mɪə] *n* US → **anaemia.**
anemic [ə'ni:mɪk] *adj* US → **anaemic.**
anemometer [ænɪ'mɒmɪtəʳ] *n* anemómetro.
anemone [ə'nemənɪ] *n* BOT anémona.
anesthesia [ænəs'θi:zɪə] *n* → **anaesthesia.**
anesthesiologist [ænəsθi:zɪ'ɒlədʒɪst] *n* US anestesista *mf.*
anesthetic [ænəs'θetɪk] *adj-n* → **anaesthetic.**
anesthetist [ə'ni:sθətɪst] *n* → **anaesthetist.**
anesthetize [ə'ni:sθətaɪz] *vt* → **anaesthetize.**
aneurysm ['ænjərɪzᵊm] *n* aneurisma.
angel ['eɪndʒᵊl] *n* ángel *m.*
anger ['æŋgəʳ] *n* cólera, ira, furia.
▷ *vt* encolerizar, enojar, enfurecer.
angina [æn'dʒaɪnə] [Also **angina pectoris.**] *n* angina de pecho.
angioma [ændʒɪ'əʊmə] *n* angioma.
angiosperm ['ændʒɪəspɜ:m] *n* angiosperma.
angiospermous [ændʒɪə'spɜ:məs] *adj* angiospermo,-a.
angle¹ ['æŋgᵊl] *n* ángulo.
angle² ['æŋgᵊl] *vi* pescar, pescar con caña.
anglepoise lamp ['æŋgᵊlpɔɪzlæmp] *n* flexo.
angler [ændlᵊr] *n* pescador,-a.
Anglican ['æŋglɪkən] *adj* anglicano,-a.
▷ *n* anglicano,-a.
Anglicanism ['æŋglɪkᵊnɪzᵊm] *n* anglicanismo.
Anglicism ['æŋglɪsɪzᵊm] *n* anglicismo.
angling ['æŋglɪŋ] *n* pesca, pesca con caña.
Anglo-Saxon [æŋgləʊ'sæksᵊn] *adj* anglosajón,-ona.
▷ *n* 1 *(person)* anglosajón,-ona. 2 *(language)* anglosajón *m.*
Angola [æŋ'gəʊlə] *n* Angola.
Angolan [æŋ'gəʊlən] *adj* angoleño,-a.
▷ *n* angoleño,-a.
angry ['æŋgrɪ] *adj* 1 *(person)* enojado,-a, enfadado,-a. 2 *(wound)* inflamado,-a. 3 *(sky)* tormentoso,-a.
▲ *comp* **angrier,** *superl* **angriest.**
angstrom ['æŋstrəm] *n* ángstrom *m.*
anguish ['æŋgwɪʃ] *n* angustia.

angular ['æŋgjʊləʳ] *adj* **1** *(with angles, of angles)* angular. **2** *(person)* anguloso,-a.
anhydride [æn'haɪdraɪd] *n* anhídrido.
aniline ['ænɪlaɪn] *n* anilina.
animal ['ænɪmᵊl] *adj* animal.
▷ *n* animal *m*.
animate [*(n)* 'ænɪmət; *(vb)* 'ænɪmeɪt] *adj* animado,-a, vivo,-a.
▷ *vt* **1** animar. **2** *fig* estimular.
animated ['ænɪmeɪtɪd] *adj* animado,-a.
animation [ænɪ'meɪʃᵊn] *n* **1** animación *f*. **2** *(life)* vida, marcha.
animator ['ænɪmeɪtəʳ] *n* animador,-ra.
animism ['ænɪmɪzᵊm] *n* animismo.
anion ['ænaɪən] *n* anión *m*.
anise ['ænɪs] *n* *(plant)* anís *m*.
aniseed ['ænɪsi:d] *n* *(seed)* anís *m*.
ankle ['æŋkᵊl] *n* tobillo.
annelid ['ænəlɪd] *n* anélido.
annexe ['ænəks] *n* anexo, anejo.
annihilate [ə'naɪəleɪt] *vt* aniquilar.
anniversary [ænɪ'vɜ:sərɪ] *n* aniversario.
▲ *pl* **anniversaries**.
announce [ə'naʊns] *vt* anunciar.
announcement [ə'naʊnsmənt] *n* anuncio.
announcer [ə'naʊnsəʳ] *n* *(on TV, radio)* presentador,-ra, locutor,-ra.
annoy [ə'nɔɪ] *vt* molestar, fastidiar.
annoying [ə'nɔɪɪŋ] *adj* molesto,-a, enojoso,-a.
annual ['ænjʊəl] *adj* anual.
▷ *n* **1** *(plant)* planta anual. **2** *(book)* anuario.
annul [ə'nʌl] *vt* anular.
▲ *pt & pp* **annulled**, *ger* **annulling**.
annular ['ænjʊləʳ] *adj* anular.
anode ['ænəʊd] *n* ánodo.
anomalous [ə'nɒmələs] *adj* anómalo,-a.
anomaly [ə'nɒməlɪ] *n* anomalía.
▲ *pl* **anomalies**.
anonymous [ə'nɒnɪməs] *adj* anónimo,-a.
anopheles [ə'nɒfəli:z] *n* anofeles *m*.
anorak ['ænəræk] *n* anorak *m*.
anorexia [ænə'reksɪə] *n* anorexia.
another [ə'nʌðəʳ] *adj* otro,-a.
▷ *pron* otro,-a.
answer ['ɑ:nsəʳ] *n* respuesta, contestación *f*.
▷ *vt* **1** *(question)* responder a, contestar a. **2** *(door)* abrir; *(telephone)* contestar a, coger.
▷ *vi* *(question)* responder, contestar.
⊙ **to answer back** *vt sep* replicar.
▷ *vi* replicar.
⊙ **to answer for** *vt insep* **1** *(guarantee)* responder por, garantizar. **2** *(accept responsibility)* responder de. **3** *(speak for)* responder por, contestar por.
answering machine ['ɑ:nsərɪŋməʃi:n] *n* contestador *m* automático.
answerphone ['ɑ:nsəfəʊn] *n* contestador *m* automático.
ant [ænt] *n* hormiga. ● **ant hill** hormiguero.
Antarctic [ænt'ɑ:ktɪk] *adj* antártico,-a.
▷ *n* **the Antarctic** Antártida. ● **Antarctic Circle** Círculo polar antártico.
Antarctica [ænt'ɑ:ktɪkə] *n* Antártida.
anteater ['ænti:təʳ] *n* oso hormiguero.
antecedent [æntɪ'si:dᵊnt] *adj* antecedente.
▷ *n* antecedente *m*.
antediluvian [æntɪdɪ'lu:vɪən] *adj* antediluviano,-a.
antenatal [æntɪ'neɪtᵊl] *adj* prenatal. ● **antenatal clinic** *centro de preparación al parto*.
antenna [æn'tenə] *n* **1** [*pl* **antennae** [æn'teni:]] *(of insect)* antena. **2** [*pl* **antennas**] *(aerial)* antena.
anterior [æn'tɪərɪəʳ] *adj* anterior.
anthem ['ænθəm] *n* motete *m*.
anther ['ænθəʳ] *n* antera.
anthology [æn'θɒlədʒɪ] *n* antología.
▲ *pl* **anthologies**.
anthracite ['ænθrəsaɪt] *n* antracita.
anthrax ['ænθræks] *n* ántrax *m*.
anthropoid ['ænθrəpɔɪd] *adj* antropoide.
▷ *n* antropoide *m*.
anthropologist [ænθrə'pɒlədʒɪst] *n* antropólogo,-a.
anthropology [ænθrə'pɒlədʒɪ] *n* antropología.
antibiotic [æntɪbaɪ'ɒtɪk] *adj* antibiótico,-a.
▷ *n* antibiótico.
antibody ['æntɪbɒdɪ] *n* anticuerpo.
▲ *pl* **antibodies**.
anticipate [æn'tɪsɪpeɪt] *vt* **1** *(expect)* esperar. **2** *(get ahead of)* adelantarse a. **3** *(forsee)* anticiparse a, prever.
anticipation [æntɪsɪ'peɪʃᵊn] *n* **1** *(expectation)* expectación *f*. **2** *(foresight)* previsión *f*.
anticlimax [æntɪ'klaɪmæks] *n* anticlímax *m*.
anticline ['æntɪklaɪn] *n* anticlinal *m*.
anticlockwise [æntɪ'klɒkwaɪz] *adj* en el sentido contrario al de las agujas del reloj
anticoagulant [æntɪkəʊ'ægjələnt] *adj* anticoagulante.
▷ *n* anticoagulante *m*.
anticyclone [æntɪ'saɪkləʊn] *n* anticiclón *m*.
antidepressant [æntɪdɪ'presᵊnt] *adj* antidepresivo,-a.
▷ *n* antidepresivo.
antidote ['æntɪdəʊt] *n* antídoto.
antifreeze ['æntɪfri:z] *n* anticongelante *m*.
antigen ['æntɪdʒen] *n* antígeno.
antigenic [æntɪ'dʒenɪk] *adj* antígeno,-a.
Antigua [æn'ti:gə] *n* Antigua.
Antiguan [æn'ti:gən] *adj* antigüeño,-a.
▷ *n* antigüeño,-a.
Antilles [æn'tɪli:z] *n pl* Antillas *fpl*. ● **Greater Antilles** Grandes Antillas *fpl*. | **Lesser Antilles** Pequeñas Antillas *fpl*.
antimatter ['æntɪmætəʳ] *n* antimateria.
antimony ['æntɪmənɪ] *n* antimonio.
antioxidant [æntɪ'ɒksɪdənt] *n* antioxidante *m*.
antipathy [æn'tɪpəθɪ] *n* antipatía.
▲ *pl* **antipathies**.
antiperspirant [æntɪ'pɜ:spɪrənt] *n* antitranspirante *m*.
antipodes [æn'tɪpədi:z] *n pl* antípodas *fpl*. ● **the Antipodes** Australia y Nueva Zelanda.
antipyretic [æntɪpaɪ'retɪk] *adj* antipirético,-a.
▷ *n* antipirético.
antiquarian [æntɪ'kweərɪən] *adj* de viejo: **an antiquarian bookshop** *una librería de viejo*.
▷ *n* anticuario,-a.
antique [æn'ti:k] *adj* antiguo,-a.
▷ *n* antigüedad *f*.
antiquity [æn'tɪkwɪtɪ] *n* antigüedad *f*.
▲ *pl* **antiquities**.

anti-Semitism [æntɪ'semɪtɪzᵊm] *n* antisemitismo.
antiseptic [æntɪ'septɪk] *adj* antiséptico,-a.
▷ *n* antiséptico.
anti-terrorist [æntɪ'terərɪst] *adj* antiterrorista.
antiviral [æntɪ'vaɪrᵊl] *adj* MED antivirus.
antivirus [æntɪ'vaɪrəs] *adj* INFORM antivirus.
antlers ['æntləʳ] *n pl* cornamenta *f sing*.
antonym ['æntənɪm] *n* antónimo.
anus ['eɪnəs] *n* ano.
anvil ['ænvɪl] *n* yunque *m*.
anxiety [æŋ'zaɪətɪ] *n* **1** *(concern)* preocupación *f*, ansiedad *f*. **2** MED ansiedad *f*.
▲ *pl* anxieties.
anxious ['æŋkʃəs] *adj* **1** *(worried)* preocupado,-a (about, por). **2** *(desirous)* ansioso,-a.
any ['enɪ] *adj* **1** *(in questions)* algún,-una: are there any biscuits (US cookies) left? *¿queda alguna galleta?* **2** *(negative)* ningún,-una: he hasn't bought any milk/biscuits (US cookies) *no ha comprado leche/galletas;* without any difficulty *sin ninguna dificultad.* **3** *(no matter which)* cualquier,-ra: any old rag will do *cualquier trapo sirve.*
▷ *pron* **1** *(in questions)* alguno,-a: there are foxes round here, have you seen any? *hay zorros por aquí, ¿has visto alguno?* **2** *(negative)* ninguno,-a: they're very cheap, but I haven't sold any *son muy baratos, pero no he vendido ninguno.* **3** *(no matter which)* cualquiera: any of these books will do *cualquiera de estos libros sirve.*
▷ *adv no suele traducirse:* I don't work there any more *ya no trabajo allí;* do you want any more? *¿quieres más?.*

En preguntas y frases negativas no se usa any sino a con los sustantivos contables en singular.

anybody ['enɪbɒdɪ] *pron* **1** *(in questions)* alguien: has anybody seen my car? *¿ha visto alguien mi coche?* **2** *(negative)* nadie: there isn't anybody in the room *no hay nadie en la sala.* **3** *(no matter who)* cualquiera: anybody would tell you the same *cualquiera te diría lo mismo.*
anyhow ['enɪhaʊ] *adv* **1** ⟶ anyway. **2** *(carelessly)* de cualquier forma, de cualquier manera.
anyone ['enɪwʌn] *pron* ⟶ anybody.
anyplace ['enɪpleɪs] *adv* US ⟶ anywhere.
anything ['enɪθɪŋ] *pron* **1** *(in questions)* algo, alguna cosa: is there anything left? *¿queda algo?* **2** *(negative)* nada: there isn't anything left *no queda nada.* **3** *(no matter what)* cualquier cosa: anything will do *cualquier cosa sirve;* they can cost anything from £5 to £5000 *el precio va desde cinco libras a cinco mil.*
anyway ['enɪweɪ] *adv* **1** *(in any case)* de todas formas, de todos modos: they didn't invite me, but I didn't want to go anyway *no me invitaron, pero de todas formas no quería ir.* **2** *(all the same)* igual, de todos modos: it was dear, but I bought it anyway *era caro, pero lo compré igual.* **3** *(in conversation)* bueno, bueno pues, total, en cualquier caso: anyway, as I was saying, ... *bueno pues, como te decía, ...*
anywhere ['enɪweəʳ] *adv* **1** *(in questions - situation)* en algún sitio, en alguna parte; *(- direction)* a algún sitio, a alguna parte: have you seen my keys anywhere? *¿has visto mis llaves en alguna parte?;* are you going anywhere this weekend? *¿vas a algún sitio el fin de semana?* **2** *(negative - situation)* en ningún sitio, en ninguna parte; *(- direction)* a ningún sitio, a ninguna parte: I can't find him anywhere *no lo encuentro en ninguna parte;* we're not going anywhere *no vamos a ningún sitio.* **3** *(no matter where - situation)* donde sea, en cualquier sitio; *(- direction)* a donde sea, a cualquier sitio: I'd live anywhere as long as it's with you *viviría en cualquier sitio mientras sea contigo;* she'd travel anywhere to see Bruce *viajaría a cualquier sitio para ver a Bruce.*
aorta [eɪ'ɔːtə] *n* aorta.
apart [ə'pɑːt] *adv* **1** *(not together)* separado,-a; *(distant)* alejado,-a: these nails are too far apart *estos clavos están demasiado separados;* the villages are a long way apart *los pueblos están alejados entre sí.* **2** *(in pieces)* en piezas. ■ **apart from** aparte de. ‖ **to fall apart** deshacerse. ‖ **to tell apart** distinguir.
apartheid [ə'pɑːthaɪt] *n* apartheid *m*.
apartment [ə'pɑːtmənt] *n* piso, apartamento. ● **apartment block / apartment building** bloque *m* de pisos.
apathetic [æpə'θetɪk] *adj* apático,-a.
apathy ['æpəθɪ] *n* apatía.
ape [eɪp] *n* simio.
▷ *vt* imitar.
Apennines ['æpənaɪnz] *n* **the Apennines** los (montes) Apeninos *mpl*.
aperitif [əperɪ'tiːf] *n* aperitivo.
aperture ['æpətjəʳ] *n* abertura.
apex ['eɪpeks] *n* ápice *m*; *(of triangle)* vértice *m*.
▲ *pl* apexes o apices.
aphid ['eɪfɪd] *n* pulgón *m*.
aphorism ['æfərɪzᵊm] *n* aforismo.
aphrodisiac [æfrə'dɪzɪæk] *adj* afrodisíaco,-a.
▷ *n* afrodisíaco.
apices ['eɪpɪsiːz] *n pl* ⟶ apex.
apiculture ['eɪpɪkʌltʃəʳ] *n* apicultura.
apiece [ə'piːs] *adv* cada uno,-a: she gave us three apiece *nos dio tres a cada uno.*
apocalypse [ə'pɒkəlɪps] *n* apocalipsis *m*.
apogee ['æpədʒiː] *n* apogeo.
apolitical [eɪpə'lɪtɪkᵊl] *adj* apolítico,-a.
apologetic [əpɒlə'dʒetɪk] *adj* compungido,-a, arrepentido,-a: they were very apologetic about it *se disculparon profusamente por lo ocurrido.*
apologise [ə'pɒlədʒaɪz] *vi* ⟶ apologize.
apologize [ə'pɒlədʒaɪz] *vi* disculparse, pedir perdón.
apology [ə'pɒlədʒɪ] *n* **1** *(for mistake)* disculpa: I think I owe you an apology *creo que debo pedirte disculpas.* **2** *fml (of beliefs)* apología.
▲ *pl* apologies.
apoplexy ['æpəpleksɪ] *n* apoplejía.
▲ *pl* apoplexies.
apophthegm ['æpəθem] *n* apotema.
apostle [ə'pɒsl] *n* apóstol *m*.
apostrophe [ə'pɒstrəfɪ] *n* **1** *(punctuation)* apóstrofo. **2** *(in rhetoric)* apóstrofe *m*.
apotheosis [əpɒθɪ'əʊsɪs] *n* apoteosis *f*.
apothegm ['æpəθem] *vt* ⟶ apophthegm.
appal [ə'pɔːl] *vt* horrorizar.
▲ *pt & pp* appalled, *ger* appalling.
Appalachians [æpə'leɪʃᵊns] *n* **the Appalachians** los (montes) Apalaches *mpl*.
appall [ə'pɔːl] *vt* US ⟶ appal.
appalling [ə'pɔːlɪŋ] *adj* **1** *(horrific)* horroroso,-a. **2** *(bad)* malísimo,-a.

apparatus [æpəˈreɪtəs] *n* 1 *(equipment)* aparatos *mpl*; *(piece of equipment)* aparato. 2 *(structure)* aparato.
apparent [əˈpærənt] *adj* 1 *(obvious)* evidente. 2 *(seeming)* aparente.
apparently [əˈpærəntlɪ] *adv* 1 *(obviously)* evidentemente. 2 *(seemingly)* aparentemente.
apparition [æpəˈrɪʃən] *n* aparición *f*.
appeal [əˈpiːl] *n* 1 *(request)* ruego, llamamiento; *(plea)* súplica. 2 *(for money)* campaña de recaudación de fondos. 3 *(attraction)* atractivo. 4 JUR apelación *f*.
▷ *vi* 1 *(request)* pedir, solicitar; *(plead)* suplicar. 2 *(attract)* atraer: **it doesn't appeal to me** *no me atrae*. 3 JUR apelar (**against**, -), recurrir (**against**, -).
appealing [əˈpiːlɪŋ] *adj* 1 *(moving)* suplicante. 2 *(attractive)* atrayente, atractivo,-a.
appear [əˈpɪəʳ] *vi* 1 *(become visible)* aparecer. 2 *(before a court, etc)* comparecer (**before**, ante). 3 *(on stage, etc)* actuar. 4 *(seem)* parecer. 5 *(on TV, in film, in newspaper)* salir.
appearance [əˈpɪərəns] *n* 1 *(becoming visible)* aparición *f*. 2 *(before a court, etc)* comparecencia. 3 *(on stage)* actuación *f*. 4 *(look)* apariencia, aspecto. ■ **to all appearances** por lo que parece *(parecía, etc)*. ‖ **to keep up appearances** guardar las apariencias.
appease [əˈpiːz] *vt* aplacar, calmar.
appeasement [əˈpiːzmənt] *n* pacificación *f*.
appendices [əˈpendɪsiːz] *n pl* → **appendix**.
appendicitis [əpendɪˈsaɪtɪs] *n* apendicitis *f*.
appendix [əˈpendɪks] *n* 1 [*pl* **appendices**] *(in book)* apéndice *m*. 2 [*pl* **appendixes**] MED apéndice *m*.
appetite [ˈæpɪtaɪt] *n* apetito.
appetizer [ˈæpɪtaɪzəʳ] *n* aperitivo.
appetizing [ˈæpɪtaɪzɪŋ] *adj* apetitoso,-a.
applaud [əˈplɔːd] *vi (clap)* aplaudir.
▷ *vt* 1 *(clap)* aplaudir. 2 *(praise)* alabar.
applause [əˈplɔːz] *n* aplauso.
apple [ˈæpəl] *n* manzana. ● **apple pie** tarta de manzana. ‖ **apple tree** manzano. ‖ **the Big Apple** Nueva York.
applet [ˈæplət] *n* COMPUT applet *m*.
appliance [əˈplaɪəns] *n* 1 *(device)* aparato. 2 *(fire engine)* coche *m* de bomberos.
applicable [ˈæplɪkəbəl] *adj* aplicable.
applicant [ˈæplɪkənt] *n (for job)* candidato,-a, aspirante *mf*, solicitante *mf*.
application [æplɪˈkeɪʃən] *n* 1 *(for job)* solicitud *f*. 2 *(of ointment, theory, etc)* aplicación *f*. 3 *(effort)* diligencia.
applicator [ˈæplɪkəɪtəʳ] *n* aplicador *m*.
apply [əˈplaɪ] *vt (ointment, theory, etc)* aplicar.
▷ *vi* 1 *(be true)* aplicarse, ser aplicable. 2 *(for job)* solicitar.
▲ *pt & pp* **applied**, *ger* **applying**.
appoint [əˈpɔɪnt] *vt* 1 *(person for job)* nombrar. 2 *(day, date, etc)* fijar, señalar.
appointment [əˈpɔɪntmənt] *n* 1 *(meeting - with lawyer, etc)* cita; *(- with hairdresser, dentist, doctor)* hora: **he didn't keep the appointment** *no acudió a la cita*. 2 *(person for job)* nombramiento.
apportion [əˈpɔːʃən] *vt* repartir, distribuir.
apposition [æpəˈzɪʃən] *n* aposición *f*.
appraisal [əˈpreɪzəl] *n* valoración *f*, evaluación *f*.
appraise [əˈpreɪz] *vt* valorar, evaluar.
appreciable [əˈpriːʃəbəl] *adj* apreciable.
appreciate [əˈpriːʃɪeɪt] *vt* 1 *(be thankful for)* agradecer. 2 *(understand)* entender, comprender. 3 *(value)* valorar, apreciar.
▷ *vi* revalorizarse, valorizarse.
appreciation [əpriːʃɪˈeɪʃən] *n* 1 *(thanks)* agradecimiento, gratitud *f*. 2 *(understanding)* comprensión *f*. 3 *(appraisal)* evaluación *f*. 4 *(increase in value)* apreciación *f*, aumento en valor.
apprehend [æprɪˈhend] *vt* 1 *(arrest)* detener, capturar. 2 *(understand)* comprender.
apprehension [æprɪˈhenʃən] *n* 1 *(arrest)* detención *f*, captura. 2 *(fear)* aprensión *f*, temor *m*, recelo.
apprehensive [æprɪˈhensɪv] *adj (fearful)* aprensivo,-a.
apprentice [əˈprentɪs] *n* aprendiz,-za.
apprenticeship [əˈprentɪsʃɪp] *n* aprendizaje *m*.
approach [əˈprəʊtʃ] *n* 1 *(coming near)* aproximación *f*, acercamiento; *(arrival)* llegada. 2 *(way in)* acceso, entrada. 3 *(to problem)* enfoque *m*.
▷ *vi (come near)* acercarse, aproximarse.
▷ *vt* 1 *(come near)* acercarse a, aproximarse a. 2 *(tackle - problem)* enfocar, abordar; *(- person)* dirigirse a. ■ **to make approaches to** SB hacer propuestas a ALGN. ● **approach road** vía de acceso.
approachable [əˈprəʊtʃəbəl] *adj* 1 *(person)* tratable, accesible. 2 *(place)* accesible.
appropriate [*(adj)* əˈprəʊprɪət; *(vb)* əˈprəʊprɪeɪt] *adj* apropiado,-a, adecuado,-a, indicado,-a.
▷ *vt* 1 *(allocate)* asignar, destinar. 2 *(steal)* apropiarse de.
approval [əˈpruːvəl] *n* aprobación *f*. ■ **on approval** a prueba.
approve [əˈpruːv] *vt* aprobar, dar el visto bueno a.
⊙ **to approve of** *vt insep* aprobar, estar de acuerdo con, ver con buenos ojos.
approximate [*(adj)* əˈprɒksɪmət; *(vb)* əˈprɒksɪmeɪt] *adj* aproximado,-a.
▷ *vi* aproximarse (**to**, a).
approximation [əprɒksɪˈmeɪʃən] *n* aproximación *f*.
APR [ˈeɪˈpiːˈɑːʳ] *abbr* (**annualized percentage rate**) tasa anual equivalente; *(abbreviation)* TAE.
après-ski [æpreɪˈskiː] *n* après-ski *m*.
▷ *adj* de après-ski.
apricot [ˈeɪprɪkɒt] *n (fruit)* albaricoque *m*. ● **apricot tree** albaricoquero.
April [ˈeɪprɪl] *n* abril *m*. ● **April Fool's Day** *el día 1 de abril (≈ día de los Santos Inocentes)*.
Para ejemplos de uso, consulta **May**.
apron [ˈeɪprən] *n* 1 *(garment - domestic)* delantal *m*; *(- workman's)* mandil *m*. 2 *(at airport)* pista de estacionamiento. 3 *(in theatre)* proscenio.
apse [æps] *n* ábside *m*.
apt [æpt] *adj* 1 *(suitable)* apropiado,-a; *(remark)* acertado,-a. 2 *(liable to)* propenso,-a.
APT [ˈeɪˈpiːˈtiː] *abbr* GB (**Advanced Passenger Train**) ≈ AVE *m*.
aptitude [ˈæptɪtjuːd] *n* aptitud *f*. ● **aptitude test** prueba de aptitud.
aquamarine [ækwəməˈriːn] *n* 1 *(stone)* aguamarina. 2 *(colour)* color *m* aguamarina.
aquarium [əˈkweərɪəm] *n* acuario.
▲ *pl* **aquaria** o **aquariums**.
Aquarius [əˈkweərɪəs] *n* Acuario.
aquatic [əˈkwætɪk] *adj* acuático,-a.

aquatint ['ækwətɪnt] *n* aguatinta.
aqueduct ['ækwɪdʌkt] *n* acueducto.
aquifer ['ækwɪfəʳ] *n* acuífero.
Arab ['ærəb] *adj* árabe.
▷ *n (person)* árabe *mf.*
arabesque [ærə'besk] *n* arabesco.
Arabia [ə'reɪbɪə] *n* Arabia.
Arabian [ə'reɪbɪən] *adj* árabe, arábigo,-a.
▷ *n* árabe *mf.* ● **Arabian Peninsula** Península Arábiga. ‖ **Arabian Sea** Mar *m* Arábigo.
Arabic ['ærəbɪk] *adj* árabe.
▷ *n (language)* árabe *m.* ● **arabic numerals** números *mpl* arábigos.
arable ['ærəbᵊl] *adj* cultivable.
arachnid [ə'ræknɪd] *n* arácnido.
aragonite [ə'rægənaɪt] *n* aragonito.
arbitrary ['ɑːbɪtrərɪ] *adj* arbitrario,-a.
arbitrate ['ɑːbɪtreɪt] *vt & vi* arbitrar.
arbitration [ɑːbɪ'treɪʃᵊn] *n* arbitraje *m.*
arbor ['ɑːbəʳ] *n* US ⟶ **arbour.**
arbour ['ɑːbəʳ] *n* cenador *m.*
arc [ɑːk] *n* 1 arco. 2 ELEC arco voltaico.
arcade [ɑː'keɪd] *n* pasaje *m.* ● **shopping arcade** galerías *fpl* comerciales.
arch [ɑːtʃ] *n* 1 *(gen)* arco; *(vault)* bóveda. 2 *(of foot)* empeine *m.*
▷ *vt* 1 *(back, eyebrows)* arquear, enarcar. 2 *(vault)* abovedar.
▷ *vi* 1 *(back, eyebrows)* arquearse. 2 *(vault)* formar bóveda.
archaeological [ɑːkɪə'lɒdʒɪkᵊl] *adj* arqueológico,-a.
archaeologist [ɑːkɪ'ɒlədʒɪst] *n* arqueólogo,-a.
archaeology [ɑːkɪ'ɒlədʒɪ] *n* arqueología.
archaic [ɑː'keɪɪk] *adj* arcaico,-a.
archaism ['ɑːkeɪɪzᵊm] *n* arcaísmo.
archangel [ɑː'keɪndʒᵊl] *n* arcángel *m.*
archbishop [ɑːtʃ'bɪʃəp] *n* arzobispo.
archeological [ɑːkɪə'lɒdʒɪkᵊl] *adj* US ⟶ **archaeological.**
archeologist [ɑːkɪ'ɒlədʒɪst] *n* US ⟶ **archaeologist.**
archeology [ɑːkɪ'ɒlədʒɪ] *n* US ⟶ **archaeology.**
archer ['ɑːtʃəʳ] *n* arquero.
archery ['ɑːtʃərɪ] *n* tiro con arco.
archetype ['ɑːkɪtaɪp] *n* arquetipo.
archipelago [ɑːkɪ'pelɪgəʊ] *n* archipiélago.
▲ *pl* **archipelagos** o **archipelagoes.**
architect ['ɑːkɪtekt] *n* arquitecto,-a.
architectural [ɑːkɪ'tektʃərəl] *adj* arquitectónico,-a.
architecture ['ɑːkɪtektʃəʳ] *n* arquitectura.
archives ['ɑːkaɪvz] *n pl* archivo *m sing.*
archivist ['ɑːkaɪvɪst] *n* archivero,-a.
archway ['ɑːtʃweɪ] *n* arco.
Arctic ['ɑːktɪk] *adj* ártico,-a.
▷ *n* **the Arctic** el Ártico. ● **the Arctic Circle** el Círculo Polar Ártico. ‖ **the Arctic Ocean** el océano Ártico.
ardor ['ɑːdəʳ] *n* US ⟶ **ardour.**
ardour ['ɑːdəʳ] *n* ardor *m.*
arduous ['ɑːdjʊəs] *adj* arduo,-a.
are [ɑːʳ, əʳ] *pres* ⟶ **be.**
area ['eərɪə] *n* 1 *(extent)* área, superficie *f.* 2 *(region)* región *f*; *(of town)* zona. 3 *(field)* campo.
arena [ə'riːnə] *n* 1 *(stadium)* estadio. 2 *(in amphitheatre)* arena. 3 *fig* ámbito.
aren't [ɑːnt] *contr* ⟶ **are not.**
Argentina [ɑːdʒən'tiːnə] *n* Argentina.
Argentine ['ɑːdʒəntaɪn] *adj* argentino,-a.
▷ *n* **the Argentine** Argentina.
Argentinian [ɑːdʒən'tɪnɪən] *adj* argentino,-a.
▷ *n* argentino,-a.
argon ['ɑːgɒn] *n* argón *m.*
argot ['ɑːgəʊ] *n* jerga.
arguable ['ɑːgjʊəbᵊl] *adj* discutible.
argue ['ɑːgjuː] *vi* 1 *(quarrel)* discutir (**with**, con). 2 *(reason)* argüir, argumentar, sostener.
▷ *vt (present)* presentar, exponer.
⊙ **to argue for** *vt insep* abogar por, argumentar a favor de.
argument ['ɑːgjʊmənt] *n* 1 *(quarrel)* discusión *f*, disputa. 2 *(reasoning)* argumento. ■ **to have an argument with** SB discutir con ALGN, tener una discusión con ALGN.
aria ['ɑːrɪə] *n* aria.
arid ['ærɪd] *adj* árido,-a.
aridity [ə'rɪdɪtɪ] *n* aridez *f.*
Aries ['eəriːz] *n* 1 *(sign)* Aries *m.* 2 *(person)* Aries *mf.*
arise [ə'raɪz] *vi* surgir (**from**, de).
▲ *pt* **arose** [ə'rəʊz], *pp* **arisen** [ə'rɪzᵊn].
aristocracy [ærɪs'tɒkrəsɪ] *n* aristocracia.
▲ *pl* **aristocracies.**
aristocrat ['ærɪstəkræt, US ə'rɪstəkræt] *n* aristócrata *mf.*
aristocratic [ærɪstə'krætɪk] *adj* aristocrático,-a.
arithmetic [*(n)* ə'rɪθmətɪk; *(adj)* ærɪθ'metɪk] *n* aritmética.
▷ *adj* aritmético,-a.
arithmetical [ærɪθ'metɪkᵊl] *adj* aritmético,-a. ● **arithmetical progression** progresión *f* aritmética.
ark [ɑːk] *n* arca.
arm [ɑːm] *n* 1 ANAT brazo. 2 *(of coat, etc)* manga. 3 *(of chair)* brazo. 4 *(of organization)* rama.
▷ *vt* armar.
▷ *vi* armarse.
▷ *n pl* **arms** *(weapons)* armas *fpl.*
armada [ɑː'mædə] *n* armada, flota.
armadillo [ɑːmə'dɪləʊ] *n* armadillo.
▲ *pl* **armadillos.**
armchair [ɑːm'tʃeəʳ] *n* sillón *m.*
armed [ɑːmd] *adj* armado,-a. ● **armed forces** fuerzas *fpl* armadas. ‖ **armed robbery** robo a mano armada.
Armenia [ɑː'miːnɪə] *n* Armenia.
Armenian [ɑː'miːnɪən] *adj* armenio,-a.
▷ *n* 1 *(person)* armenio,-a. 2 *(language)* armenio.
armistice ['ɑːmɪstɪs] *n* armisticio.
armor ['ɑːməʳ] *n* US ⟶ **armour.**
armored ['ɑːməd] *adj* US ⟶ **armoured.**
armor-plated ['ɑːmə'pleɪtɪd] *adj* ⟶ **armour-plated.**
armory ['ɑːmərɪ] *n* US ⟶ **armoury.**
▲ *pl* **armories.**
armour ['ɑːməʳ] *n* 1 armadura. 2 *(on vehicle)* blindaje *m.*
armoured ['ɑːməd] *adj* 1 *(column, etc)* acorazado,-a. 2 *(vehicle)* blindado,-a. ● **armoured car** carro blindado.
armour-plated ['ɑːmə'pleɪtɪd] *adj* blindado,-a, acorazado,-a.
armoury ['ɑːmərɪ] *n* armería.
▲ *pl* **armouries.**
armpit ['ɑːmpɪt] *n* sobaco, axila.
armrest ['ɑːmrest] *n* brazo.
army ['ɑːmɪ] *n* ejército.
▲ *pl* **armies.**
aroma [ə'rəʊmə] *n* aroma *m.*

aromatic [ærəˈmætɪk] *adj* aromático,-a.
arose [əˈrəʊz] *pt* → arise.
around [əˈraʊnd] *adv* **1** *(near, in the area)* alrededor: is there anybody around? *¿hay alguien cerca?* **2** *(from place to place)*: they cycle around together *van juntos en bicicleta;* he's been around, he knows what's what *ha visto mundo, sabe de qué va la cosa.* **3** *(to face the opposite way)*: turn around please *dése la vuelta por favor.* **4** *(approximately)* alrededor de: it costs around £5,000 *cuesta unas cinco mil libras.*
▷ *prep* **1** *(near)*: there aren't many shops around here *hay pocas tiendas por aquí.* **2** *(all over)*: there were clothes around the room *había ropa por toda la habitación.* **3** *(in a circle or curve)* alrededor de: he put his arms around her *la rodeó con los brazos.* **4** *(at)* sobre, cerca de: they came around seven *vinieron sobre las siete.*
arouse [əˈraʊz] *vt* **1** *(awake)* despertar. **2** *(sexually)* excitar.
arrange [əˈreɪndʒ] *vt* **1** *(hair, flowers)* arreglar; *(furniture, etc)* colocar, ordenar. **2** *(plan)* planear, organizar. **3** *(music)* arreglar. **4** *(marriage)* concertar. **5** *(agree on)* acordar: we arranged a time for the meeting *acordamos una hora para la reunión.*
arrangement [əˈreɪndʒmənt] *n* **1** *(of flowers)* arreglo, arreglo floral. **2** *(agreement)* acuerdo, arreglo. **3** MUS arreglo.
▷ *n pl* **arrangements** *(plans)* planes *mpl*; *(preparations)* preparativos *mpl*.
array [eˈreɪ] *n* **1** *(selection)* surtido. **2** *(series)* serie *f.* **3** COMPUT matriz *f.* ■ **in battle array** en orden de batalla.
arrears [əˈrɪəz] *n pl* atrasos *mpl.*
arrest [əˈrest] *n* arresto, detención *f.*
arrival [əˈraɪvᵊl] *n* llegada.
arrive [əˈraɪv] *vi* **1** llegar. **2** *(be born)* nacer.
arrogance [ˈærəgəns] *n* arrogancia.
arrogant [ˈærəgənt] *adj* arrogante.
arrow [ˈærəʊ] *n* flecha.
arse [ɑːs] *n taboo (part of body)* culo.
arsenal [ˈɑːsənᵊl] *n* arsenal *m.*
arsenic [ˈɑːsᵊnɪk] *n* arsénico.
arson [ˈɑːsᵊn] *n* incendio provocado.
arsonist [ˈɑːsənɪst] *n* incendiario,-a, pirómano,-a.
art [ɑːt] *n (painting, etc)* arte *m.*
▷ *n pl* **arts** *(branch of knowledge)* letras *fpl.* ● **art deco** art deco *m.* ‖ **art gallery 1** *(museum)* pinacoteca. **2** *(commercial)* galería de arte. ‖ **art nouveau** art nouveau *m,* modernismo.
artefact [ˈɑːtɪfækt] *n* artefacto.
arterial [ɑːˈtɪərɪəl] *adj* **1** ANAT arterial. **2** *(road)* principal, importante.
arteriosclerosis [ɑːtɪərɪəʊskləˈrəʊsɪs] *n* arteriosclerosis *f.*
artery [ˈɑːterɪ] *n* ANAT arteria.
▲ *pl* arteries.
artesian well [ɑːtiːzɪənˈwel] *n* pozo artesiano.
arthritis [ɑːθˈraɪtəs] *n* artritis *f.*
arthropod [ɑːθˈrəpɒd] *n* artrópodo.
artichoke [ˈɑːtɪtʃəʊk] *n* alcachofa.
article [ˈɑːtɪkᵊl] *n* artículo.
▷ *n pl* **articles** contrato de aprendizaje. ● **article of clothing** prenda de vestir. ‖ **definite article** artículo determinado. ‖ **indefinite article** artículo indeterminado. ‖ **leading article** editorial *m.*
articulate [*(adj)* ɑːˈtɪkjʊlət; *(vb)* ɑːˈtɪkjʊleɪt] *adj (person)* que se expresa con facilidad; *(speech)* claro,-a.
▷ *vt* **1** articular. **2** *(pronounce)* pronunciar.
articulated [ɑːˈtɪkjʊleɪtɪd] *adj* articulado,-a. ● **articulated lorry** camión *m* articulado.
articulation [ɑːtɪkjʊˈleɪʃᵊn] *n* articulación *f.*
artifact [ˈɑːtɪfækt] *n* US → **artefact.**
artificial [ɑːtɪˈfɪʃᵊl] *adj* **1** *(flowers, light, etc)* artificial. **2** *(limb)* ortopédico,-a; *(hair)* postizo,-a. **3** *(smile, etc)* afectado,-a, fingido,-a. ● **artificial insemination** inseminación *f* artificial. ‖ **artificial intelligence** inteligencia artificial. ‖ **artificial respiration** respiración *f* artificial.
artillery [ɑːˈtɪlərɪ] *n* artillería.
artisan [ˈɑːtɪzæn] *n* artesano,-a.
artist [ˈɑːtɪst] *n* **1** artista *mf.* **2** *(painter)* pintor,-ra.
artistic [ɑːˈtɪstɪk] *adj* artístico,-a.
artistry [ˈɑːtɪstrɪ] *n* maestría.
artwork [ˈɑːtwɜːk] *n* ilustraciones *fpl.*
as [æz, *unstressed* əz] *prep* como: he works as a clerk *trabaja de oficinista;* she was dressed as a monkey *iba disfrazada de mono.*
▷ *adv (in comparatives)*: eat as much as you like *come tanto como quieras;* this is twice as expensive as the other *éste es dos veces más caro que el otro.*
▷ *conj* **1** *(while)* mientras; *(when)* cuando: as he painted, he whistled *mientras pintaba, silbaba;* as he grew older he became more tolerant *a medida que iba envejeciendo se volvía más tolerante.* **2** *(because)* ya que, como: as there were no seats we had to stand *como no había asientos tuvimos que estar de pie.* **3** *(although)* aunque: tall as he was, he still couldn't reach the shelf *aunque era alto no podía alcanzar el estante.* **4** *(showing manner)* como: everything is just as she left it *todo está tal como ella lo dejó;* as you all know, ... *como ya sabéis todos, ...* **5** *(and so too)* como, igual que: she's colour-blind, as is her mother *es daltónica, igual que su madre.* ■ **as far as** hasta. ‖ **as far as I know** que yo sepa. ‖ **as for** en cuanto a. ‖ **as if** como si. ‖ **as it is** tal como están las cosas. ‖ **as it were** por así decirlo. ‖ **as long as** mientras. ‖ **as of** desde. ‖ **as often as not** las más de las veces. ‖ **as soon as** tan pronto como. ‖ **as though** como si. ‖ **as well as** además de. ‖ **as yet** hasta ahora, de momento.
asbestos [æsˈbestəs] *n* amianto, asbesto.
ascend [əˈsend] *vt* ascender, subir a.
▷ *vi* ascender, subir.
ascendancy [əˈsendənsɪ] *n* predominio, supremacía.
▲ *pl* ascendancies.
ascendant [əˈsendᵊnt] *n* ascendiente *m.* ■ **to be in the ascendant** estar en auge.
ascendency [əˈsendənsɪ] *n* → **ascendancy.**
▲ *pl* ascendencies.
ascendent [əˈsendᵊnt] *n* → **ascendant.**
ascension [əˈsenʃᵊn] *n* ascensión *f.*
ascent [əˈsent] *n* **1** *(slope)* subida. **2** *(climb)* ascensión *f.*
ascertain [æsəˈteɪn] *vt* averiguar.
asceticism [əˈsetɪsɪzᵊm] *n* ascetismo.
ASCII [ˈæskiː] *abbr* (American standard code for information interchange) ASCII.
ascribe [əsˈkraɪb] *vt* atribuir (to, a).
asepsis [əˈsepsɪs] *n* asepsia.

aseptic [ə'septɪk] *adj* aséptico,-a.
asexual [eɪ'sekʃʊəl] *adj* asexual.
ash[1] [æʃ] *n* ceniza. ● **Ash Wednesday** miércoles *m* de ceniza.
▲ *pl* **ashes**.
ash[2] [æʃ] *n* *(tree)* fresno.
▲ *pl* **ashes**.
ashamed [ə'ʃeɪmd] *adj* avergonzado,-a.
ashbin ['æʃbɪn] *n* US cubo de la basura.
ashcan ['æʃkæn] *n* US → **ashbin**.
ashore [ə'ʃɔːʳ] *adv* *(position)* en tierra; *(movement)* a tierra. ■ **to go ashore** desembarcar.
ashtray ['æʃtreɪ] *n* cenicero.
Asia ['eɪʃə, 'eɪʒə] *n* Asia. ● **Asia Minor** Asia Menor.
Asian ['eɪʃᵊn, 'eɪʒᵊn] *adj* asiático,-a.
▷ *n* asiático,-a.
Asiatic [eɪʃɪ'ætɪk, eɪʒɪ'ætɪk] *adj* asiático,-a.
aside [ə'saɪd] *adv* al lado, a un lado. ■ **aside from** aparte de.
ask [ɑːsk] *vt* **1** *(inquire)* preguntar: **she asked me my name** *preguntó mi nombre*. **2** *(request)* pedir: **we have to ask permission** *debemos pedir permiso*. **3** *(invite)* invitar, convidar: **he asked her to go out with him** *la invitó a salir con él*.
▷ *vi* **1** *(inquire)* preguntar. **2** *(request)* pedir: **she asked to speak to the boss** *pidió hablar con el jefe*.
⊙ **to ask after** *vt insep* preguntar por.
⊙ **to ask for** *vt insep* *(thing)* pedir; *(person)* preguntar por.
⊙ **to ask out** *vt sep* invitar a salir.
askance [əs'kæns] ■ **to look askance at** mirar con recelo.
askew [əs'kjuː] *adv* de lado.
▷ *adj* ladeado,-a.
asleep [ə'sliːp] *adj* *(person)* dormido,-a; *(leg, etc)* adormecido,-a: **she fell asleep** *se durmió*.
asparagus [æs'pærəgəs] *n* *(plant)* espárrago; *(shoots)* espárragos *mpl*.
aspect ['æspekt] *n* **1** *(gen)* aspecto. **2** *(of building)* orientación *f*: **it has a west-facing aspect** *está orientada al oeste*.
aspen ['æspən] *n* álamo temblón.
aspersions [əs'pɜːʃᵊnz] ■ **to cast aspersions on** poner en duda, poner en tela de juicio.
asphalt ['æsfælt] *n* asfalto.
▷ *vt* asfaltar.
asphyxia [əs'fɪksɪə] *n* asfixia.
asphyxiate [əs'fɪksɪeɪt] *vt* asfixiar.
aspic ['æspɪk] *n* CULIN gelatina.
aspirant [əs'paɪərənt] *n* aspirante *mf*.
aspirate [*(vb)* 'æspəreɪt; *(n)* 'æspɪrət] *vt* aspirar.
▷ *n* consonante *f* aspirada.
aspiration [æspə'reɪʃᵊn] *n* **1** LING aspiración *f*. **2** *(ambition)* aspiración *f*, ambición *f*.
aspire [əs'paɪəʳ] *vi* aspirar (**to**, a).
aspirin® ['æspɪrɪn] *n* aspirina®.
ass[1] [æs] *n* *(animal)* burro,-a, asno,-a; *(person)* burro,-a, imbécil *mf*.
ass[2] [æs] *n* US *taboo* culo.
assail [ə'seɪl] *vt* **1** *(physically)* atacar. **2** *(doubts, problems, etc)* asaltar.
assailant [ə'seɪlənt] *n* atacante *mf*.
assassin [ə'sæsɪn] *n* asesino,-a.
assassinate [ə'sæsɪneɪt] *vt* asesinar.
assassination [əsæsɪ'neɪʃᵊn] *n* asesinato.
assault [ə'sɔːlt] *n* **1** MIL asalto, ataque *m*. **2** JUR agresión *f*.
▷ *vt* JUR *(gen)* agredir; *(sexually)* abusar de.
assay [ə'seɪ] *vt* ensayar.
▷ *n* ensayo.
assemble [ə'sembᵊl] *vt* **1** *(bring together)* reunir. **2** *(put together)* montar. **3** COMPUT ensamblar.
▷ *vi* reunirse.
assembler [ə'sembləʳ] *n* ensamblador *m*.
assembly [ə'semblɪ] *n* **1** *(meeting)* reunión *f*. **2** *(group, body)* asamblea. **3** TECH *(putting together)* montaje *m*; *(unit)* unidad *f*. ● **assembly hall** sala de actos. | **assembly line** cadena de montaje. | **assembly language** lenguaje *m* ensamblador. | **assembly plant** planta de montaje.
▲ *pl* **assemblies**.
assent [ə'sent] *n* asentimiento.
▷ *vi* asentir (**to**, a).
assert [ə'sɜːt] *vt* *(declare)* aseverar, afirmar.
assertion [ə'sɜːʃᵊn] *n* **1** *(statement)* aseveración *f*. **2** *(of authority, etc)* reafirmación *f*.
assess [ə'ses] *vt* **1** *(value)* tasar, valorar. **2** *(calculate)* calcular. **3** *fig* evaluar.
assessment [ə'sesmənt] *n* **1** *(valuation)* tasación *f*, valoración *f*. **2** *(calculation)* cálculo. **3** *fig* evaluación *f*. ● **continuous assessment** evaluación *f* continua.
assessor [ə'sesəʳ] *n* *(advisor)* asesor,-ra.
asset ['æset] *n* **1** *(quality)* calidad *f* positiva, ventaja. **2** *(person)* elemento valioso.
▷ *n pl* **assets** COMM activo *m sing*.
assiduity [æsɪ'djuːɪtɪ] *n* diligencia, dedicación *f*.
assiduous [ə'sɪdjʊəs] *adj* diligente, dedicado,-a.
assign [ə'saɪn] *vt* **1** *(gen)* asignar, atribuir. **2** *(person - to place)* atribuir, transferir; *(- to group)* ceder: **three new warders were assigned to the prison** *transfirieron tres nuevos celadores a la prisión*; **Spanish soldiers assigned to the peace-keeping force** *soldados españoles cedidos a la fuerza de paz*.
assignment [ə'saɪnmənt] *n* **1** *(act of assigning)* asignación *f*. **2** *(mission)* misión *f*. **3** *(task)* tarea.
assimilable [ə'sɪmɪləbᵊl] *adj* asimilable.
assimilate [ə'sɪmɪleɪt] *vt* asimilar.
▷ *vi* asimilarse.
assimilation [əsɪmɪ'leɪʃᵊn] *n* asimilación *f*.
assist [ə'sɪst] *vt & vi* ayudar.
assistance [ə'sɪstəns] *n* ayuda.
assistant [ə'sɪstənt] *n* **1** *(helper)* ayudante *mf*. **2** *(in shop)* dependiente *mf*. ● **assistant manager** subdirector,-ra, director,-ra adjunto,-a.
associate [*(adj-n)* ə'səʊʃɪət; *(vb)* ə'səʊʃɪeɪt] *adj* **1** *(company)* asociado,-a. **2** *(member)* correspondiente.
▷ *n* *(partner)* socio,-a.
▷ *vt* asociar.
▷ *vi* relacionarse (**with**, con).
association [əsəʊsɪ'eɪʃᵊn] *n* asociación *f*.
associative [ə'səʊʃɪətɪv] *adj* asociativo,-a.
associativity [əsəʊʃɪə'tɪvɪtɪ] *n* propiedad *f* asociativa.
assonance ['æsənəns] *n* asonancia.
assorted [ə'sɔːtɪd] *adj* surtido,-a, variado,-a.
assortment [ə'sɔːtmənt] *n* surtido, variedad *f*.
assume [ə'sjuːm] *vt* **1** *(suppose)* suponer. **2** *(power, responsibility)* tomar, asumir. **3** *(attitude, expression)* adoptar.

assumption [ə'sʌmpʃᵊn] *n* **1** *(supposition)* suposición *f.* **2** *(of power)* asunción *f.* ● **the Assumption** la Asunción *f.*

assurance [ə'ʃʊərəns] *n* **1** *(guarantee)* garantía. **2** *(confidence)* seguridad *f,* confianza. **3** *(insurance)* seguro. ● **life assurance** seguro de vida.

assure [ə'ʃʊəʳ] *vt* asegurar.

asterisk ['æstərɪsk] *n* asterisco.

astern [ə'stɜːn] *adv* **1** *(towards stern)* a popa; *(at stern)* en popa. **2** *(sailing backwards)* atrás.

asteroid ['æstərɔɪd] *n* asteroide *m.*

asthma ['æsmə] *n* asma.

asthmatic [æs'mætɪk] *adj* asmático,-a.
▷ *n* asmático,-a.

astigmatism [ə'stɪgmətɪzᵊm] *n* astigmatismo.

astonish [əs'tɒnɪʃ] *vt* asombrar, sorprender.

astonished [ə'stɒnɪʃt] *adj* asombrado,-a.

astonishing [əs'tɒnɪʃɪŋ] *adj* asombroso,-a, sorprendente.

astonishment [əs'tɒnɪʃmənt] *n* asombro.

astound [əs'taʊnd] *vt* pasmar, asombrar.

astral ['æstrəl] *adj* astral.

astray [ə'streɪ] *adv* extraviado,-a. ■ **to go astray 1** *(err)* descarriarse. **2** *(be lost)* extraviarse.

astringent [əs'trɪndʒənt] *adj* astringente.
▷ *n* astringente *m.*

astrolabe ['æstrəleɪb] *n* astrolabio.

astrologer [əs'trɒlədʒəʳ] *n* astrólogo,-a.

astrological [æstrə'lɒdʒɪkᵊl] *adj* astrológico,-a.

astrology [əs'trɒlədʒɪ] *n* astrología.

astronaut ['æstrənɔːt] *n* astronauta *mf.*

astronautics [æstrə'nɔːtɪks] *n* astronáutica.

astronomer [əs'trɒnəməʳ] *n* astrónomo,-a.

astronomical [æstrə'nɒmɪkᵊl] *n* astronómico,-a.

astronomy [əs'trɒnəmɪ] *n* astronomía.

astrophysics [æstrəʊ'fɪzɪks] *n* astrofísica.

astute [əs'tjuːt] *adj* astuto,-a, sagaz.

asylum [ə'saɪləm] *n* **1** *(political)* asilo, refugio. **2** *(for mentally ill)* manicomio. ● **mental asylum** manicomio.

asymmetric [æsɪ'metrɪk] *adj* asimétrico,-a. ● **asymmetric bars** barras *fpl* asimétricas.

asymmetrical [æsɪ'metrɪkəl] *adj* asimétrico,-a.

asynchronous [eɪ'sɪŋkrənəs] *adj* asíncrono,-a.

at[1] [æt, *unstressed* ət] *prep* **1** *(position)* en, a: **at home/school/work/church** *en casa/el colegio/el trabajo/la iglesia;* **they're at Alyson's** *están en casa de Alyson;* **she's at the dentist's** *ha ido al dentista;* **at the top of the mountain** *en la cumbre de la montaña.* **2** *(time)* a: **at two o'clock** *a las dos;* **at night** *por la noche;* **at midnight/noon** *a medianoche/mediodía;* **at Christmas** *en Navidad;* **at the age of 13** *a los trece años.* **3** *(direction, violence)* a, contra: **she's always shouting at them** *no para de gritarles;* **they're shooting at the minister** *disparan contra el ministro.* **4** *(with numbers)* a: **at 50 miles an hour** *a 50 millas la hora.* **5** *(state)*: **he's at breakfast/lunch/dinner** *está desayunando/comiendo/cenando;* **men at work** *hombres trabajando;* **those kids are at it again** *esos críos han vuelto a empezar.* **6** *(ability)*: **he's good at French** *va bien en francés.* ■ **at first** al principio. ‖ **at last!** ¡por fin! ‖ **at least** por lo menos. ‖ **at most** como máximo. ‖ **at the earliest** lo más pronto. ‖ **at the latest** como tarde, a lo más tardar. ‖ **at the moment** ahora. ‖ **at worst** en el peor de los casos.

at[2] [æt] *n (Internet)* arroba

ate [et, eɪt] *pt* → **eat.**

atheism ['eɪθɪɪzᵊm] *n* ateísmo.

atheist ['eɪθɪɪst] *n* ateo,-a.

Athens ['æθᵊnz] *n* Atenas.

athlete ['æθliːt] *n* atleta *mf.* ● **athlete's foot** pie *m* de atleta.

athletic [æθ'letɪk] *adj* **1** atlético,-a. **2** *(sporty)* deportista.

athletics [æθ'letɪks] *n* atletismo.

Atlantic [ət'læntɪk] *adj* atlántico,-a. ● **the Atlantic (Ocean)** el (océano) Atlántico.

atlas ['ætləs] *n* atlas *m inv.*

atmosphere ['ætməsfɪəʳ] *n* **1** atmósfera. **2** *(ambience)* ambiente *m,* atmósfera.

atmospheric [ætməs'ferɪk] *adj* atmosférico,-a. ● **atmospheric pressure** presión *f* atmosférica.

atoll ['ætɒl] *n* atolón *m.*

atom ['ætəm] *n* **1** átomo. **2** *fig* ápice *m,* pizca. ● **atom bomb** bomba atómica.

atomic [ə'tɒmɪk] *adj* atómico,-a. ● **atomic bomb** bomba atómica. ‖ **atomic energy** energía atómica. ‖ **atomic number** número atómico. ‖ **atomic pile** pila atómica. ‖ **atomic warfare** guerra atómica. ‖ **atomic weight** peso atómico.

atomiser ['ætəmaɪzəʳ] *n* → **atomizer.**

atomizer ['ætəmaɪzəʳ] *n* atomizador *m.*

atrium ['eɪtriːəm] *n* atrio.
▲ *pl* **atriums** o **atria** ['eɪtrɪə].

atrocious [ə'trəʊʃəs] *adj* **1** *(cruel)* atroz. **2** *fam* fatal, malísimo,-a.

atrocity [ə'trɒsɪtɪ] *n* atrocidad *f.*
▲ *pl* **atrocities.**

atrophy ['ætrəfɪ] *n* atrofia.
▲ *pl* **atrophies.**

attach [ə'tætʃ] *vt* **1** *(fasten)* sujetar. **2** *(tie)* atar. **3** *(stick)* pegar. **4** *(document)* adjuntar.

attachment [ə'tætʃmənt] *n* **1** TECH accesorio. **2** *(to an e-mail)* anexo. **3** *(fondness)* cariño, apego.

attack [ə'tæk] *n (gen)* ataque *m; (terrorist)* atentado.
▷ *vt* **1** *(gen)* atacar; *(terrorist)* atentar contra. **2** *(task, problem)* acometer; *(person)* agredir, atacar.

attacker [ə'tækəʳ] *n* atacante *mf,* agresor,-ra.

attain [ə'teɪn] *vt* **1** *(goal)* lograr. **2** *(rank, age)* llegar a.

attempt [ə'tempt] *n (try)* intento, tentativa.
▷ *vt* intentar.

attend [ə'tend] *vt* **1** *(be present at)* asistir a: **all her friends attended the funeral** *todos sus amigos asistieron al funeral.* **2** *(care for)* atender, cuidar: **she is attended by a nurse** *la atiende una enfermera.* **3** *(accompany)* acompañar.
▷ *vi* **1** *(be present)* asistir. **2** *(pay attention)* prestar atención.
⊙ **to attend to** *vt insep* **1** ocuparse de. **2** *(in shop)* despachar.

attendance [ə'tendəns] *n* **1** *(being present)* asistencia. **2** *(people present)* asistentes *mpl.*

attendant [ə'tendᵊnt] *n (in car park, museum)* vigilante *mf; (in cinema)* acomodador,-ra.

attention [ə'tenʃᵊn] *n* atención *f.*
▷ *interj* **attention!** MIL ¡firmes! ■ **to attract** SB**'s attention** llamar la atención a ALGN. ‖ **to pay attention** prestar atención.

attentive [ə'tentɪv] *adj* **1** *(paying attention)* atento,-a. **2** *(helpful)* solícito,-a.
attenuate [ə'tenjʊeɪt] *vt* atenuar.
attenuating [ə'tenjʊeɪtɪŋ] *adj* atenuante.
attic ['ætɪk] *n* desván *m*.
attire [ə'taɪəʳ] *n* atuendo, atavío, vestido.
▷ *vt* ataviar, vestir.
attitude ['ætɪtjuːd] *n* **1** *(way of thinking)* actitud *f*. **2** *(pose)* postura, pose *f*. ● **attitude of mind** estado de ánimo.
attorney [ə'tɜːnɪ] *n* US abogado,-a. ● **Attorney General** GB ≈ Ministro,-a de Justicia.
attract [ə'trækt] *vt* atraer.
attraction [ə'trækʃᵊn] *n* **1** *(power)* atracción *f*. **2** *(thing)* atractivo. **3** *(incentive)* aliciente *m*. ● **tourist attraction** atracción *f* turística.
attractive [ə'træktɪv] *adj* **1** *(person)* atractivo,-a. **2** *(offer)* interesante, tentador,-ra.
attribute [*(n)* æ 'trɪbjuːt, *(vb)* ə'trɪbjuːt] *n* atributo.
▷ *vt* atribuir.
attribution [ætrɪ'bjuːʃᵊn] *n* atribución *f*.
attributive [ə'trɪbjʊtɪv] *adj* atributivo,-a.
attrition [ə'trɪʃᵊn] *n* desgaste *m*. ● **war of attrition** guerra de desgaste.
atypical [eɪ'tɪpɪkᵊl] *adj* atípico,-a.
aubergine ['əʊbəʒiːn] *n* berenjena.
auburn ['ɔːbən] *adj* castaño,-a.
auction ['ɔːkʃᵊn] *n* subasta.
▷ *vt* subastar. ● **auction room** sala de subastas. ‖ **auction sale** subasta.
⊙ **to auction off** *vt sep* subastar.
auctioneer [ɔːkʃə'nɪəʳ] *n* subastador,-ra.
audacious [ɔː'deɪʃəs] *adj* **1** *(daring)* audaz, intrépido,-a. **2** *(rude)* descarado,-a, osado,-a.
audible ['ɔːdɪbᵊl] *adj* audible.
audience ['ɔːdɪəns] *n* **1** *(spectators)* público; *(to radio)* audiencia; *(to television)* telespectadores *mpl*. **2** *(interview)* audiencia.
audiotape ['ɔːdɪəʊteɪp] *n* cinta de audio.
audio-visual [ɔːdɪəʊ'vɪzjʊəl] *adj* audiovisual.
audit ['ɔːdɪt] *n* auditoría.
▷ *vt* auditar.
audition [ɔː'dɪʃᵊn] *n* prueba.
▷ *vt & vi* hacer una prueba: **she auditioned for the part of Goneril** *hizo una prueba para el papel de Goneril.*
auditor ['ɔːdɪtəʳ] *n* auditor,-ra.
auditorium [ɔːdɪ'tɔːrɪəm] *n* auditorio, sala.
▲ *pl* **auditoriums** o **auditoria** [ɔːdɪ'tɔːrɪə].
augment [ɔːg'ment] *vt fml* aumentar.
▷ *vi fml* aumentarse.
augmentative [ɔːg'mentətɪv] *adj* aumentativo,-a.
augur ['ɔːgəʳ] *vt* presagiar.
august [ɔː'gʌst] *adj* augusto,-a.
August ['ɔːgəst] *n* agosto.
Para ejemplos de uso, consulta **May**.
aunt [ɑːnt] *n* tía.
auntie ['ɑːntɪ] *n fam* tía, tita.
aunty ['ɑːntɪ] *n fam* tía, tita.
▲ *pl* **aunties**.
au pair [əʊ'peəʳ] *n* au pair *f*. ● **au pair girl** au pair *f*.
aura ['ɔːrə] *n (of person)* aura; *(of place)* sensación *f*
aural ['ɔːrᵊl] *adj* auditivo,-a.
aureola [ɔːrɪ'ələ] *n* ⟶ **aureole**.
aureole [ɔːrɪ'əʊl] *n* aureola.
auricle ['ɒrɪkᵊl] *n* **1** *(of heart)* aurícula. **2** *(of ear)* aurícula, pabellón *m* de la oreja.
auricular [ɒ'rɪkjʊləʳ] *adj* auricular.
aurora [ɔː'rɔːrə] *n* aurora. ● **aurora australis** aurora austral. ‖ **aurora borealis** aurora boreal.
auscultate ['ɔːskʌlteɪt] *vt* auscultar.
auscultation [ɔːskʌl'teɪʃᵊn] *n* auscultación *f*.
auspices ['ɔːspɪsɪz] *n pl* auspicios *mpl*.
auspicious [ɔːs'pɪʃəs] *adj (start, etc)* prometedor,-ra; *(occasion)* feliz.
Aussie ['ɒzɪ] *adj fam* australiano,-a.
▷ *n fam* australiano,-a.
austere [ɒs'tɪəʳ] *adj* austero,-a.
austerity [ɒs'terɪtɪ] *n* austeridad *f*.
Australia [ɒ'streɪlɪə] *n* Australia.
Australian [ɒ'streɪlɪən] *adj* australiano,-a.
▷ *n* **1** *(person)* australiano,-a. **2** *(language)* australiano.
Austria ['ɒstrɪə] *n* Austria.
Austrian ['ɒstrɪən] *adj* austríaco,-a, austriaco,-a.
▷ *n* austríaco,-a, austriaco,-a.
authentic [ɔː'θentɪk] *adj* auténtico,-a.
authenticate [ɔː'θentɪkeɪt] *vt* autenticar, autentificar.
authentication [ɔːθentɪ'keɪʃᵊn] *n* autenticación *f*.
author ['ɔːθəʳ] *n* autor,-ra, escritor,-ra.
authoress ['ɔːθərəs] *n* autora, escritora.
authoritarian [ɔːθɒrɪ'teərɪən] *adj* autoritario,-a.
authority [ɔː'θɒrɪtɪ] *n* **1** *(gen)* autoridad *f*. **2** *(permission)* autorización *f*, permiso.
▲ *pl* **authorities**.
authorisation [ɔːθəraɪ'zeɪʃᵊn] *n* ⟶ **authorization**.
authorise ['ɔːθəraɪz] *vt* ⟶ **authorize**.
authorization [ɔːθəraɪ'zeɪʃᵊn] *n* autorización *f*.
authorize ['ɔːθəraɪz] *vt* autorizar.
autism ['ɔːtɪzᵊm] *n* autismo.
autistic [ɔː'tɪstɪk] *adj* autista.
auto ['ɔːtəʊ] *n* US *fam* coche *m*.
▲ *pl* **autos**.
autobiography [ɔːtəbaɪ'ɒgrəfɪ] *n* autobiografía.
▲ *pl* **autobiographies**.
Autocue® ['ɔːtəʊkjuː] *n* teleapuntador *m*, teleprompter *m*.
autograph ['ɔːtəgrɑːf] *n* autógrafo.
▷ *vt* autografiar.
automat ['ɔːtəʊmæt] *n* US *restaurante autoservicio.*
automate ['ɔːtəmeɪt] *vt* automatizar.
automatic [ɔːtə'mætɪk] *adj* automático,-a.
▷ *n* **1** *(car)* coche *m* automático. **2** *(gun)* automática. **3** *(washing machine)* lavadora automática. ● **automatic pilot** piloto automático.
automation [ɔːtə'meɪʃᵊn] *n* automatización *f*.
automobile ['ɔːtəməbiːl] *n* automóvil *m*, coche *m*.
autonomous [ɔː'tɒnəməs] *adj* autónomo,-a.
autonomy [ɔː'tɒnəmɪ] *n* autonomía.
▲ *pl* **autonomies**.
autopsy ['ɔːtɒpsɪ] *n* autopsia.
▲ *pl* **autopsies**.
autosuggestion [ɔːtəʊsə'dʒestʃᵊn] *n* autosugestión *f*.
autumn ['ɔːtəm] *n* otoño.
autumnal [ɔː'tʌmnᵊl] *adj* otoñal.

auxiliary [ɔːgˈzɪljərɪ] *adj* auxiliar. ● **auxiliary verb** verbo auxiliar.
▷ *n* auxiliar *m*, ayudante *mf*.
▲ *pl* auxiliaries.
availability [əveɪləˈbɪlɪtɪ] *n* disponibilidad *f*.
available [əˈveɪləbᵊl] *adj* **1** *(thing)* disponible: **it's available in four colours** *lo hay en cuatro colores*. **2** *(person)* libre, disponible.
avalanche [ˈævəlɑːnʃ] *n* **1** alud *m*. **2** *fig* avalancha.
avant-garde [ævɒŋˈgɑːd] *n* vanguardia.
▷ *adj* vanguardista.
avarice [ˈævərɪs] *n* avaricia.
avaricious [ævəˈrɪʃəs] *adj* avaro,-a.
avenge [əˈvendʒ] *vt* vengar.
avenue [ˈævənjuː] *n* **1** *(street)* avenida. **2** *(means)* vía.
average [ˈævərɪdʒ] *n* promedio, media. ■ **above average** por encima de la media. ‖ **below average** por debajo de la media. ‖ **on average** por término medio.
▷ *adj* **1** medio,-a. **2** *(not special)* corriente, regular.
▷ *vt* **1** hacer un promedio de: **I average 10 cigarettes a day** *fumo un promedio de 10 cigarrillos al día*. **2** *(calculate)* determinar el promedio de.
⊙ **to average out at** *vt insep* salir a una media de.
averse [əˈvɜːs] *adj* reacio,-a (**to**, a).
aversion [əˈvɜːʒᵊn] *n* aversión *f*.
avert [əˈvɜːt] *vt* *(avoid)* evitar. ■ **to avert one's eyes** apartar la vista.
aviary [ˈeɪvjərɪ] *n* pajarera.
▲ *pl* aviaries.
aviation [eɪvɪˈeɪʃᵊn] *n* aviación *f*.
aviator [ˈeɪvɪeɪtəʳ] *n* aviador,-ra.
avid [ˈævɪd] *adj* ávido,-a.
avocado [ævəˈkɑːdəʊ] [Also **avocado pear**.] *n* aguacate *m*.
▲ *pl* avocados.
avoid [əˈvɔɪd] *vt* **1** evitar. **2** *(question)* eludir. **3** *(person)* esquivar.
avoirdupois [ævədəˈpɔɪs] *n sistema de pesos basado en la libra de 16 onzas usado en los países anglosajones*
avow [əˈvaʊ] *vt* confesar, declarar.
await [əˈweɪt] *vt fml* aguardar, esperar.
awake [əˈweɪk] *adj* despierto,-a.
▷ *vi* **1** despertar. **2** despertarse.
▲ *pt* **awoke** [əˈwəʊk], *pp* **awaked** o **awoken** [əˈwəʊkᵊn].
awaken [əˈweɪkᵊn] *vt-vi* ⟶ **awake**.
▲ *pt* **awakened**, *pp* **awoken** [əˈwəʊkᵊn].
award [əˈwɔːd] *n* **1** *(prize)* premio; *(medal)* condecoración *f*; *(trophy)* trofeo. **2** *(grant)* beca. **3** *(damages)* indemnización *f*.
▷ *vt* **1** *(prize, grant)* otorgar, conceder. **2** *(damages)* adjudicar.
aware [əˈweəʳ] *adj* **1** consciente. **2** *(informed)* informado,-a, enterado,-a. ■ **to be aware of** ser consciente de. ‖ **to become aware of** darse cuenta de.
awareness [əˈweənəs] *n* conciencia.
away [əˈweɪ] *adv* **1** lejos, fuera, alejándose: **he lives 4 km away** *vive a 4 km (de aquí)*; **the wedding is 6 weeks away** *faltan 6 semanas para la boda*. **2** *(indicating continuity)*: **they worked away all day** *trabajaron todo el día*. **3** *(till nothing is left)*: **she left the gas on and the milk boiled away** *dejó el gas encendido y la leche hirvió hasta evaporarse*. **4** *(in sport)* en campo contrario: **we're playing Barnsley away next week** *la semana que viene jugamos contra Barnsley en su campo*. ■ **to go away** irse, marcharse. ‖ **to put away** guardar. ‖ **to run away** irse corriendo.
awe [ɔː] *n* sobrecogimiento.
awful [ˈɔːfʊl] *adj* **1** *(shocking)* atroz, horrible. **2** *fam (very bad)* fatal, horrible, espantoso,-a.
awfully [ˈɔːfʊlɪ] *adv fam* terriblemente.
awhile [əˈwaɪl] *adv* un rato.
awkward [ˈɔːkwəd] *adj* **1** *(clumsy - person)* torpe; *(- expression)* poco elegante. **2** *(difficult)* difícil; *(uncooperative)* poco cooperativo,-a: **it's an awkward place to get to** *es difícil llegar hasta allí*. **3** *(embarrassing)* embarazoso,-a, delicado,-a. **5** *(uncomfortable)* incómodo,-a.
awl [ɔːl] *n* lezna.
awning [ˈɔːnɪŋ] *n* toldo.
awoke [əˈwəʊk] *pt* ⟶ **awake**.
awoken [əˈwəʊkᵊn] *pp* ⟶ **awake**.
ax [æks] *n* ⟶ **axe**.
axe [æks] *n* hacha.
axiom [ˈæksɪəm] *n* axioma *m*.
axis [ˈæksɪs] *n* eje *m*.
axle [ˈæksᵊl] *n* eje *m*.
axon [ˈæksəm] *n* axón *m*.
ayatollah [aɪəˈtɒlə] *n* ayatollah *m*.
azalea [əˈzeɪlɪə] *n* azalea.
Azerbaijan [æzəbaɪˈdʒɑːn] *n* Azerbaiyán *m*.
Azerbaijani [æzəbaɪˈdʒɑːnɪ] *adj* azerbaiyano,-a, azerí.
▷ *n* **1** *(person)* azerbaiyano,-a, azerí *mf*. **2** *(language)* azerí *m*, azerbaiyano.
azimuth [ˈæzɪməθ] *n* acimut *m*.
Aztec [ˈæztek] *adj* azteca.
▷ *n* **1** *(person)* azteca *mf*. **2** *(language)* azteca *m*.
azure [ˈeɪʒəʳ] *adj* azul celeste.
▷ *n* azul *m* celeste.

B

B, b [biː] *n* 1 *(the letter)* B, b *f*. 2 *(musical note)* si *m*. ● **B movie** película de la serie B. ‖ **B road** carretera secundaria.

BA [ˈbiːˈeɪ] *abbr* (**Bachelor of Arts**) licenciado,-a en letras.

babble [ˈbæbəl] *vi (meaninglessly)* balbucear.
▷ *vt (say incoherently)* farfullar.
▷ *n (confused voices)* murmullo, rumor *m*.

babe [beɪb] *n* 1 *(baby)* nene,-a, criatura. 2 US *(girl)* nena, chica.

baboon [bəˈbuːn] *n* mandril *m*, babuino.

baby [ˈbeɪbɪ] *n* 1 bebé *m*. 2 *(of animal)* cría. 3 *fig (infantile person)* niño,-a. **don't be such a baby!** *¡no seas niño!* ■ **to have a baby** dar a luz, tener un niño. ● **baby carriage** US cochecito de niño. ‖ **baby tooth** diente *m* de leche.
▲ *pl* **babies**.

baby-faced [ˈbeɪbɪfeɪst] *adj* con cara de niño.

baby-sit [ˈbeɪbɪsɪt] *vi* hacer de canguro, cuidar niños.
▲ *pt & pp* **baby-sat** [ˈbeɪbɪsɪt], *ger* **baby-sitting**.

baby-sitter [ˈbeɪbɪsɪtəʳ] *n* canguro *mf*.

baby-walker [ˈbeɪbɪwɔːkəʳ] *n* andador *m*, tacataca *m*, tacatá *m*.

bachelor [ˈbætʃələʳ] *n* soltero. ● **bachelor flat** piso de soltero. ‖ **Bachelor of Arts** licenciado,-a en letras. ‖ **Bachelor of Science** licenciado,-a en ciencias. ‖

bacillus [bəˈsɪləs] *n* bacilo.
▲ *pl* **bacilli** [bəˈsɪlaɪ].

back [bæk] *n* 1 *(of person)* espalda. 2 *(of animal, book)* lomo. 3 *(of chair)* respaldo. 4 *(of hand)* dorso. 5 *(of stage, room, cupboard)* fondo. 6 *(sport - player)* defensa *mf*; *(- position)* defensa.
▷ *adj* trasero,-a, de atrás.
▷ *adv (at the rear)* atrás; *(towards the rear)* hacia atrás.
▷ *vt* 1 *(support)* apoyar, respaldar. 2 *(finance)* financiar. ■ **back to front** al revés. ‖ **to answer back** replicar. ‖ **to be back** estar de vuelta. ‖ **to come back / go back** volver. ‖ **to give back** devolver. ‖ **to put back** volver a guardar en su sitio. ‖ **to phone back** volver a llamar. ‖ **to stand back** apartarse.
⊙ **to back away** *vi* retirarse.
⊙ **to back off** *vi* apartarse.
⊙ **to back out** *vi* volverse atrás.
⊙ **to back up** *vt sep (vehicle)* dar marcha atrás a; *(support)* apoyar.

backache [ˈbækeɪk] *n* dolor *m* de espalda.

backbencher [bækˈbenʃə] *n* diputado,-a *(que no forma parte del consejo de ministros)*.

backbite [ˈbækbaɪt] *vi* quejarse, criticar. ■ **to backbite about** SB poner a ALGN de vuelta y media.

backbone [ˈbækbəʊn] *n* columna vertebral.

backbreaking [ˈbækbreɪkɪŋ] *adj (work)* agotador,-ra: **a backbreaking job** *un trabajo agotador.*

backcloth [ˈbækklɒθ] *n* telón *m* de fondo.

backdated [bækˈdeɪtɪd] *adj (document, agreement)* con efecto retroactivo a.

backdrop [ˈbækdrɒp] *n* telón *m* de fondo.

backer [ˈbækəʳ] *n* 1 FIN promotor,-ra. 2 *(guarantor)* fiador,-ra. 3 *(supporter)* partidario,-a.

backfire [bækˈfaɪəʳ] *vi* fallar: **our plan backfired** *nos salió el tiro por la culata.*

background [ˈbækgraʊnd] *n* 1 fondo. 2 *fig (origins)* orígenes *mpl*, antecedentes *mpl*: ● **background knowledge** conocimientos *mpl* previos. ‖ **background music** música de fondo.

backhand [ˈbækhænd] *n* revés *m*. ● **backhand shot** revés *m*.

backhanded [bækˈhændɪd] *adj (compliment)* equívoco,-a.

backhander [bækˈhændəʳ] *n fam* soborno.

backing [ˈbækɪŋ] *n* 1 *(support)* apoyo, respaldo. 2 MUS acompañamiento.

backlash [ˈbæklæʃ] *n* reacción *f* violenta y repentina.
▲ *pl* **backlashes**.

backlog [ˈbæklɒg] *n* acumulación *f* de trabajo, trabajos *mpl* pendientes.

backpack [ˈbækpæk] *n* US mochila.
▷ *vi* viajar por un país o continente: **my sister's backpacking around Europe** *mi hermana está de viaje por Europa.*

backpacker [ˈbækpækəʳ] *n* mochilero,-a, trotamundos *mf*.

back-seat [ˈbæksiːt] *n* asiento trasero. ■ **to take a back-seat** desempeñar un papel secundario.

backside [bækˈsaɪd] *n fam* trasero.

backslash [ˈbækslæʃ] *n* barra inversa.

backslide [ˈbækslaɪd] *vi* reincidir.

backstage [bækˈsteɪdʒ] *n* 1 *(area)* bastidores *mpl*. 2 *(dressing-rooms)* camerinos *mpl*.

backstairs [bækˈsteəz] *adj* clandestino,-a, secreto,-a.

backstroke [ˈbækstrəʊk] *n (swimming)* espalda.

backtrack [ˈbæktræk] *vi* 1 *(retrace one's steps)* desandar lo andado. 2 *(reverse opinion)* desdecirse.

backup [ˈbækʌp] *n* 1 *(moral support)* apoyo. 2 COMPUT copia de seguridad. ● **backup file** archivo de seguridad.

backward [ˈbækwəd] *adj* 1 hacia atrás. 2 *(child)* atrasado,-a. 3 *(shy)* tímido,-a.
▷ *adv* ⟶ **backwards**.

backwardness [ˈbækwədnəs] *n* 1 *(of child)* atraso. 2 *(shyness)* timidez *f*.

backwards [ˈbækwədz] *adv* 1 hacia atrás: 2 *(the wrong way)* al revés: **he always does things backwards** *siempre hace las cosas al revés.*

backwash [ˈbækwɒʃ] *n* 1 *(wind, water)* remolino. 2 *fig* repercusión *f*, eco.

backyard [bæk'jɑːd] *n* patio de atrás.
bacon ['beɪkən] *n* tocino, bacón *m*.
bacteria ['bæktɪərɪə] *n pl* bacterias *fpl*.
▲ *sing* **bacterium**.
bacterial [bæk'tɪərɪəl] *adj* bacteriano,-a.
bacterium [bæk'tɪərɪəm] *n* bacteria.
▲ *pl* **bacteria**.
bad [bæd] *adj* **1** malo,-a; *(before masc noun)* mal: **he made a bad decision** *tomó una mala decisión*. **2** *(rotten)* podrido,-a. **3** *(serious)* grave: **they had a bad accident** *tuvieron un accidente grave*. **4** *(harmful)* nocivo,-a, perjudicial. **5** *(polluted)* viciado,-a, contaminado,-a. **6** *(naughty)* malo,-a, travieso,-a. **7** *(aches, illnesses)* fuerte, intenso,-a: **he's got a bad headache** *tiene un fuerte dolor de cabeza*. ■ **to be bad at** *(skill, subject)* ser malo,-a en: **he's bad at English** *es malo en inglés*. ▮ **to come to a bad end** acabar mal. ▮ **to have a bad leg** tener la pierna lisiada. ● **bad cheque** cheque *m* sin fondos.
▷ *adv* mal. ■ **to feel bad** encontrarse mal. ▮ **to go from bad to worse** ir de mal en peor. ▮ **to look bad 1** *(person)* tener mala cara. **2** *(situation)* pintar mal.
▷ *n* lo malo. ■ **too bad!** ¡mala pata!, ¡qué lástima!
▲ *comp* **worse**, *superl* **worst**.
baddy ['bædɪ] *n fam* malo,-a de la película.
▲ *pl* **baddies**.
bade [beɪd] *pt* → **bid**.
badge [bædʒ] *n* **1** insignia, distintivo. **2** *(metallic)* chapa. ● **lapel badge** pin *m*.
badger ['bædʒəʳ] *n* tejón *m*.
▷ *vt* acosar, importunar.
badly ['bædlɪ] *adv* **1** mal: **he behaved badly at the party** *se portó mal en la fiesta*. **2** *(seriously)* gravemente: **he was badly hurt in the bombing** *fue gravemente herido en el atentado*. **3** *(very much)* mucho,-a: **he badly needs your help** *tiene mucha necesidad de tu ayuda*.
bad-mannered [bæd'mænəd] *adj* maleducado,-a.
bad-tempered [bæd'tempəd] *adj (permanently)* de mal genio; *(temporarily)* malhumorado,-a, de mal humor.
baffle ['bæfəl] *vt* **1** *(perplex)* dejar perplejo,-a, desconcertar. **2** *(frustrate)* frustrar.
bag [bæg] *n* **1** *(paper, plastic)* bolsa; *(large)* saco. **2** *(handbag)* bolso. **3** *(for school)* cartera.
▷ *n pl* **bags 1** *(under eyes)* ojeras *fpl*. ■ **bags of** montones de. ● **bag lady** vagabunda.
baggage ['bægɪdʒ] *n* **1** equipaje *m*, bagaje *m*. **2** MIL bagaje *m*.
baggy ['bægɪ] *adj* holgado,-a, ancho,-a.
▲ *comp* **baggier**, *superl* **baggiest**.
bagpipes ['bægpaɪps] *n pl* gaita *f sing*.
bail¹ [beɪl] *n* fianza: ■ **to be on bail** estar en libertad bajo fianza.
⊙ **to bail out** *vt sep* **1** pagar la fianza a. **2** *fig* sacar de un apuro.
bail² [beɪl] *vt (water)* achicar.
bailiff ['beɪlɪf] *n* **1** *(court officer)* alguacil *m*. **2** *(steward)* administrador,-ra.
bait [beɪt] *n* **1** *(fishing)* cebo. **2** *fml fig (decoy)* señuelo, carnaza. ■ **to take the bait** picar. ▮ **to rise to the bait** *fig* caer en la trampa.
▷ *vt* **1** cebar. **2** *(torment)* atosigar.
baize [beɪz] *n* **1** *(fabric)* bayeta. **2** *(card table)* tapete *m* verde.
bake [beɪk] *vt* **1** *(bread, cakes)* cocer (en el horno). **2** *(land, earth)* endurecer.
▷ *vi* **1** cocerse. **2** *fig* achicharrarse de calor.
baked [beɪkt] *adj (cake, bread)* cocido al horno. ● **baked apple** manzana al horno. ▮ **baked beans** alubias *fpl* guisadas en salsa de tomate. ▮ **baked potato** patata asada.
baker ['beɪkəʳ] *n (of bread)* panadero,-a; *(of cakes)* pastelero,-a.
bakery ['beɪkərɪ] *n (for bread)* panadería; *(for cakes)* pastelería.
▲ *pl* **bakeries**.
baking ['beɪkɪŋ] *n (of bread, cakes)* cocción *f*; *(of ceramics)* cocedura. ■ **to do some baking** hacer unos pasteles. ● **baking powder** levadura en polvo. ▮ **baking soda** bicarbonato sódico. ▮ **baking tin** molde *m* para pasteles.
balaclava [bælə'klɑːvə] *n* pasamontañas *m*.
balance ['bæləns] *n* **1** equilibrio. **2** *(scales)* balanza. **3** *(of account, etc)* saldo. **4** *(remainder)* resto. **5** *(harmony)* equilibrio, armonía.
▷ *vi* **1** mantenerse en equilibrio. **2** FIN cuadrar. ■ **on balance** todo considerado. ▮ **to balance the books** hacer el balance.
balanced ['bælənst] *adj* equilibrado,-a.
balancing act ['bælənsɪŋækt] ■ **to perform a balancing act 1** *(in circus)* hacer equilibrismo; *(on tightrope)* andar en la cuerda floja. **2** *(with money)* hacer malabarismos.
balcony ['bælkənɪ] *n* **1** balcón *m*. **2** *(in theatre)* anfiteatro; *(gallery)* gallinero.
▲ *pl* **balconies**.
bald [bɔːld] *adj* **1** calvo,-a. **2** *(tyre)* desgastado,-a. **3** *(style)* escueto,-a. **4** *(statement)* directo,-a, franco,-a.
bale¹ [beɪl] *n* bala, fardo: **a bale of cotton** *una bala de algodón*.
▷ *vt* embalar.
bale out² ['beɪl'aʊt] *vt (water)* achicar.
▷ *vi (by parachute)* saltar en paracaídas, lanzarse en paracaídas.
Balearic [bælɪ'ærɪk] *adj* balear, baleárico,-a. ● **the Balearic Islands** las (islas) Baleares.
baleful ['beɪlfʊl] *adj (menacing)* hosco,-a, ceñudo,-a: **a baleful look** *una mirada ceñuda*.
ball [bɔːl] *n* **1** *(gen)* pelota; *(football, etc)* balón *m*; *(golf, billiards)* bola. **2** *(of paper)* bola; *(of wool)* ovillo. **3** *(of eye)* globo ocular. **4** *(dance)* baile *m*, fiesta. **5** *taboo* cojón *m*, huevo. ■ **to start the ball rolling** poner las cosas en marcha. ▮ **to play ball 1** US *(sport)* jugar a la pelota. **2** *(cooperate)* cooperar, colaborar. ▮ **the ball is in your court** ahora te toca a ti hacer algo. ▮ **that's a whole new ball game** US eso ya es otra cosa. ● **gala ball** baile *m* de etiqueta.
ballad ['bæləd] *n* balada.
ball-and-socket ['bɔːlən'sɒkɪt] ● **ball-and-socket joint** articulación *f* de rótula.
ballast ['bæləst] *n (boat, balloon)* lastre *m*.
ballerina [bælə'riːnə] *n* bailarina.
ballet ['bæleɪ] *n* ballet *m*.
ballistic [bə'lɪstɪk] *adj* balístico,-a.

ballistics [bə'lɪstɪks] *n* balística.
balloon [bə'lu:n] *n* **1** globo. **2** *(in cartoon)* bocadillo. **3** *(glass)* copa grande.
▷ *vi* **1** *(go up in a balloon)* ir en globo. **2** *(swell)* hincharse. **3** *(increase)* aumentar rápidamente.
ballooning [bə'lu:nɪŋ] *n* ascensión *f* en globo.
ballot ['bælət] *n* **1** *(vote)* votación *f*. **2** *(votes recorded)* número de votos escrutados. ■ **to take a ballot on** STH someter ALGO a votación. ● **ballot box** urna. ‖ **ballot paper** papeleta.
ballpoint ['bɔ:lpɔɪnt] [also **ballpoint pen**] *n* bolígrafo.
ballroom ['bɔ:lru:m] *n* sala de baile. ● **ballroom dancing** baile *m* de salón.
ballyhoo ['bælɪhu:] *n* **1** *(commotion)* jaleo. **2** *(publicity)* bombo: **they publicized the opening with a lot of ballyhoo** *anunciaron la inauguración a bombo y platillo.*
balm [bɑ:m] *n* bálsamo.
balmy ['bɑ:mɪ] *adj* **1** *(weather)* suave. **2** *(soothing)* balsámico,-a.
▲ *comp* **balmier**, *superl* **balmiest**.
balsam ['bɔ:lsəm] *n* ⟶ **balm**.
balsamic [bɔ:l'sæmɪk] *adj* balsámico,-a.
Baltic ['bɔ:ltɪk] *adj* báltico,-a. ● **the Baltic (Sea)** el (mar) Báltico.
baluster ['bæləstəʳ] *n* balaústre m.
balustrade [bælə'streɪd] *n* balaustrada, barandilla.
bamboo [bæm'bu:] *n* bambú *m*.
bamboozle [bæm'bu:zəl] *vt* **1** *fam (cajole)* engatusar. **2** *(cheat)* engañar.
ban [bæn] *n* prohibición *f*, interdicción *f*.
▷ *vt* prohibir.
▲ *pt & pp* **banned**, *ger* **banning**.
banal [bə'nɑ:l] *adj* **1** *(commonplace)* banal, trivial. **2** *(trite)* trillado,-a.
banality [bə'nælɪtɪ] *n* banalidad *f*.
▲ *pl* **banalities**.
banana [bə'nɑ:nə] *n* **1** *(fruit)* plátano, banana. **2** *(tree)* bananero, AM banano.
band [bænd] *n* **1** *(brass, etc)* banda; *(pop)* conjunto; *(jazz)* orquesta. **2** *(strip)* tira. **3** *(around arm)* brazalete *m*. **4** *(wrapper)* faja. **5** *(stripe)* raya. **6** PHYS banda, frecuencia. **7** TECH correa. **8** *(youths)* pandilla; *(thieves)* banda. ■ **to band together** acuadrillarse, apiñarse.
bandage ['bændɪdʒ] *n* venda, vendaje *m*.
▷ *vt* vendar.
⊙ **to bandage up** *vt sep* vendar.
Band-Aid® ['bændeɪd] *n* tirita.
B and B ['bi:ən'bi:] *abbr* (**bed and breakfast**) *casa de huéspedes que ofrece habitación con desayuno incluido.*
bandit ['bændɪt] *n* bandido,-a.
bandmaster ['bændmɑ:stəʳ] *n* director *m* de una banda.
bandstand ['bændstænd] *n* quiosco de música.
bandwagon ['bændwægən] ■ **to jump on the bandwagon** subirse al tren.
bandwidth ['bændwɪdθ] *n* ancho de banda.
bandy[1] ['bændɪ] *adj (legs)* arqueado,-a.
bandy[2] ['bændɪ] *vt* SP *(ball)* pasarse. ■ **to bandy** SB**'s name about** difamar ALGN, hablar mal de ALGN.
⊙ **to bandy about** *vt sep (story, information)* difundir.
▲ *pt & pp* **bandied**, *ger* **bandying**.
bane [beɪn] *n* **1** *(cause of trouble)* perdición *f*, ruina **2** *(poison)* veneno.
bang [bæŋ] *n* **1** *(blow)* golpe *m*. **2** *(noise)* ruido; *(of gun)* estampido; *(explosion)* estallido; *(of door)* portazo. **3** US flequillo.
▷ *vt* golpear, dar golpes en. ■ **to bang the door** dar un portazo.
▷ *adv fam* justo: **bang in the middle** *justo en medio.*
banger ['bæŋəʳ] *n* **1** *(firework)* petardo. **2** GB *fam (sausage)* salchicha. **3** *fam (car)* tartana, trasto.
bangle ['bæŋgəl] *n* brazalete *m*.
banish ['bænɪʃ] *vt (expel)* desterrar.
banishment ['bænɪʃmənt] *n* destierro, exilio.
banister ['bænɪstəʳ] *n* pasamanos *m*, barandilla.
bank[1] [bæŋk] *n* banco. ● **bank holiday** GB festivo, día festivo.
▷ *vt (deposit money)* ingresar, depositar.
⊙ **to bank on** *vt insep* contar con.
bank[2] [bæŋk] *n* **1** *(of river)* ribera; *(edge)* orilla: **on the banks of the Manzanares** *a orillas del Manzanares.* **2** *(mound)* loma; *(embankment)* terraplén *m*.
▷ *vt* **1** *(soil, earth)* amontonar. **2** *(river)* encauzar.
bank[3] [bæŋk] *n (row, line)* batería: **a bank of lights** *una batería de luces.*
bankbook ['bæŋkbʊk] *n* cartilla de ahorro.
banker ['bæŋkəʳ] *n* banquero,-a.
banking ['bæŋkɪŋ] *n* banca.
banknote ['bæŋknəʊt] *n* billete *m* de banco.
bankroll ['bæŋkrəʊl] *n* **1** US fajo de billetes. **2** *(funds)* fondos *mpl*, recursos *mpl*.
▷ *vt sl* dar apoyo financiero.
bankrupt ['bæŋkrʌpt] *adj* quebrado,-a, insolvente.
▷ *n* quebrado,-a.
▷ *vt* hacer quebrar, arruinar.
bankruptcy ['bæŋkrʌptsɪ] *n* quiebra, bancarrota.
▲ *pl* **bankruptcies**.
banner ['bænəʳ] *n* **1** *(flag)* bandera. **2** *(placard)* pancarta. **3** *(on web page)* banner *m*, anuncio.
▷ *adj* US excelente, de primera. ● **banner headlines** grandes titulares *mpl*.
banns [bænz] *n pl* amonestaciones *fpl*.
banquet ['bæŋkwɪt] *n* banquete *m*.
banter ['bæntəʳ] *n* bromas *fpl*, guasa.
▷ *vi* bromear, estar de guasa.
baptise [bæp'taɪz] *vt* ⟶ **baptize**.
baptism ['bæptɪzəm] *n* bautismo.
baptistery ['bæptɪstrɪ] *n* baptisterio.
▲ *pl* **baptisteries**.
baptistry ['bæptɪstrɪ] *n* ⟶ **baptistery**.
▲ *pl* **baptistries**.
baptize [bæp'taɪz] *vt* bautizar.
bar [bɑ:ʳ] *n* **1** *(iron, gold)* barra. **2** *(prison)* barrote *m*. **3** *(soap)* pastilla. **4** *(obstacle)* obstáculo, traba. **5** *(counter)* barra, mostrador *m*. **6** *(room)* bar *m*. **7** *(in court)* tribunal *m*: **the prisoner at the bar** *el acusado, la acusada.* ● **bar chart** gráfica estadística.
▷ *vt* **1** *(door)* atrancar; *(road, access)* cortar. **2** *(ban)* prohibir; *(from a place)* prohibir la entrada. **3** *(prevent)* impedir.
▲ *pt & pp* **barred**, *ger* **barring**.
▷ *prep* excepto, salvo: **they all came, bar his parents** *acudieron todos, excepto sus padres.* ■ **bar none** sin excepción.
▷ *n* **the Bar** JUR el colegio de abogados.
barbarian [bɑ:'beərɪən] *adj* bárbaro,-a.
▷ *n* bárbaro,-a.

barbecue ['bɑ:bəkju:] *n* barbacoa. ● **barbecue sauce** salsa barbacoa.
▷ *vt* asar a la parrilla.
▲ *ger* **barbecuing**.
barbed [bɑ:bd] *adj* **1** con púas, punzante. **2** *fig* mordaz, incisivo,-a.
barber ['bɑ:bəʳ] *n* barbero. ● **barber's shop** barbería.
barbiturate [bɑ:'bɪtʃərət] *n* barbitúrico.
bare [beəʳ] *adj* **1** *(naked)* desnudo,-a; *(head)* descubierto,-a. **2** *(land)* raso,-a; *(tree, plant)* sin hojas. **3** *(empty)* vacío,-a; *(unfurnished)* sin muebles. **4** *(scant)* escaso,-a. **5** *(worn)* gastado,-a, raído,-a.
▷ *vt* desnudar; *(uncover)* descubrir.
barefaced ['beəfeɪst] *adj* descarado,-a. ● **barefaced cheek** morro, descaro.
barefoot ['beəfʊt] *adj* descalzo,-a.
▷ *adv* descalzo,-a.
barely ['beəlɪ] *adv* apenas.
bargain ['bɑ:gən] *n* **1** *(agreement)* trato, acuerdo. **2** *(good buy)* ganga.
▷ *vi* **1** *(negotiate)* negociar. **2** *(haggle)* regatear. ● **bargain offer** oferta especial. ▮ **bargain price** precio de oferta, precio de saldo.
barge [bɑ:dʒ] *n* gabarra, barcaza.
▷ *vt* transportar en barcaza.
⊙ **to barge around** *vi* dar vueltas sin ton ni son.
⊙ **to barge into** *vt insep* irrumpir en: **he barged into the bedroom** *irrumpió en el dormitorio.*
baritone ['bærɪtəʊn] *n* barítono.
▷ *adj* barítono.
barium ['beərɪʌm] *n* bario. ● **barium meal** sulfato de bario.
bark[1] [bɑ:k] *n* **1** *(of dog)* ladrido. **2** *(cough)* tos *f* fuerte.
▷ *vi* ladrar.
▷ *vt (shout)* gritar.
▷ *vi (cough)* tener una tos fuerte.
bark[2] [bɑ:k] *n (of tree)* corteza.
barley ['bɑ:lɪ] *n* cebada.
barmaid ['bɑ:meɪd] *n* camarera.
barman ['bɑ:mən] *n* camarero, barman *m*.
▲ *pl* **barmen** ['bɑ:men].
barn [bɑ:n] *n (for grain)* granero. ● **barn dance** baile *m* popular *(que tiene lugar en un granero)*.
barnacle ['bɑ:nəkəl] *n* percebe *m*. ● **barnacle goose** barnacla *m*.
barnyard ['bɑ:njɑ:d] *n* corral *m*.
barometer [bə'rɒmɪtəʳ] *n* barómetro.
barometric [bærə'metrɪk] *adj* barométrico,-a.
baron ['bærən] *n* barón *m*.
baroness ['bærənəs] *n* baronesa.
baroque [bə'rɒk] *adj* barroco,-a.
▷ *n* barroco.
barrack[1] ['bærək] *vt (soldiers)* acuartelar.
barrack[2] ['bærək] *vt (jeer)* abuchear.
barrack-room ['bærəkru:m] *n* dormitorio de tropa.
barracks ['bærəks] *n pl* cuartel *m*.

Puede considerarse tanto singular como plural: where is/are the barracks? *¿dónde está el cuartel?*

barrage ['bærɑ:ʒ] *n* **1** *(dam)* presa, embalse *m*. **2** MIL barrera de fuego. **3** *fig (of questions)* aluvión *m*.
barrel ['bærəl] *n* **1** *(of beer)* barril *m*; *(of wine)* tonel *m*, cuba. **2** *(of gun)* cañón *m*. **3** *(of pen)* depósito. **4** TECH tambor *m*.
▷ *vt* embarrilar, poner en barriles.
▲ *pt & pp* **barrelled** (US **barreled**), *ger* **barrelling** (US **barreling**).
barren ['bærən] *adj* **1** *(land, woman)* estéril. **2** *(meagre)* escaso,-a.
barrenness ['bærənnəs] *n* esterilidad *f*.
barricade [bærɪ'keɪd] *n* barricada.
▷ *vt* poner barricadas en.
barrier ['bærɪəʳ] *n* **1** barrera. **2** *fig* obstáculo. ● **barrier reef** banco de coral, arrecife *m*.
barrister ['bærɪstəʳ] *n* abogado,-a *(capacitado,-a para actuar en tribunales superiores)*.
barrow ['bærəʊ] *n (wheelbarrow)* carretilla; *(for carrying goods)* carro.
barstool ['bɑ:stu:l] *n* taburete *m* de bar.
bartender ['bɑ:tendəʳ] *n* US camarero, barman *m*.
barter ['bɑ:təʳ] *n* trueque *m*.
▷ *vt* trocar.
barysphere ['bærɪsfɪəʳ] *n* barisfera.
basalt ['bæsɔ:lt] *n* basalto.
base[1] [beɪs] *n* **1** *(gen)* base *f*. **2** ARCH *(of column)* basa, base *f*. **3** *(of word)* raíz *f*.
▷ *vt* **1** basar. **2** MIL *(troops)* estacionar.
base[2] [beɪs] *adj* **1** bajo,-a, vil. **2** *(metal)* común, de baja ley.
baseball ['beɪsbɔ:l] *n* béisbol *m*.
baseline ['beɪslaɪn] *n* **1** SP *(tennis)* línea de saque. **2** *(diagram)* línea cero. **3** ART punto de fuga.
basely ['beɪslɪ] *adv* vilmente, rastreramente.
basement ['beɪsmənt] *n* sótano.
bash [bæʃ] *vt fam* golpear, aporrear.
▷ *n* **1** *fam (blow)* golpe *m*. **2** *fam (try)* intento.
⊙ **to bash about** *vt sep* dar una paliza.
⊙ **to bash down** *vt sep* derribar, echar abajo.
⊙ **to bash into** *vt insep* estrellarse contra.
bashful ['bæʃfʊl] *adj* vergonzoso,-a, tímido,-a, modesto,-a.
basic ['beɪsɪk] *adj* **1** básico,-a. **2** *(elementary)* elemental, para principiantes.
▷ *n pl* **the basics** lo esencial.
basically ['beɪsɪklɪ] *adv* básicamente.
basil ['bæzəl] *n* BOT albahaca.
basilica [bə'zɪlɪkə] *n* basílica.
basin ['beɪsən] *n* **1** *(bowl)* cuenco; *(washbowl)* palangana. **2** *(washbasin)* lavabo. **3** GEOG cuenca.
basis ['beɪsɪs] *n* base *f*, fundamento.
▲ *pl* **bases** ['beɪsi:z]. ■ **on the basis of ... 1** *(according to)* según. **2** *(in accordance with)* de acuerdo con. **3** *(starting from)* a partir de. **4** *(because of)* por, a causa de.
bask [bɑ:sk] *vi* tumbarse al sol.
basket ['bɑ:skɪt] *n* **1** cesta, cesto. **2** *(basketball)* canasta, cesta. **3** *(of balloon)* barquilla. **4** *sl* imbécil *mf*, capullo.
basketball ['bɑ:skɪtbɔ:l] *n* baloncesto.
Basque [bɑ:sk] *adj* vasco,-a.
▷ *n* **1** *(person)* vasco,-a. **2** *(language)* vasco, eusquera *m*, euskera *m*, vascuence *m*.
bas-relief [bæsrɪ'li:f] *n* bajorrelieve *m*.

bass[1] [beɪs] *n* 1 MUS *(singer)* bajo. 2 MUS *(notes)* graves *mpl.* 3 MUS *(guitar)* bajo.
▷ *adj* MUS bajo,-a.
bass[2] [bæs] *n (fish)* róbalo, lubina; *(freshwater)* perca.
basset ['bæsɪt] *n* ZOOL perro basset.
bassoon [bə'suːn] *n* fagot *m.*
bastard ['bɑːstəd] *n* 1 bastardo,-a. 2 *taboo* cabrón *m*: poor bastard! *¡pobre desgraciado!*
▷ *adj* ilegítimo,-a, bastardo,-a.
baste [beɪst] *vt* CULIN rociar, bañar.
bastion ['bæstɪən] *n* baluarte *m.*
bat[1] [bæt] *n* ZOOL murciélago.
bat[2] [bæt] *n* SP bate *m; (table tennis)* pala.
▷ *vi* batear.
▲ *pt & pp* batted, *ger* batting.
bat[3] [bæt] *vt* pestañear.
▲ *pt & pp* batted, *ger* batting.
batch [bætʃ] *n (gen)* lote *m*, remesa; *(of bread, etc)* hornada.
bated ['beɪtɪd] ■ **with bated breath** con ansiedad.
bath [bɑːθ] *n* 1 baño. 2 *(tub)* bañera. ■ **to run a bath** preparar un baño.
▷ *vi* bañarse. ■ **to have a bath / take a bath** bañarse.
▷ *n pl* **baths** piscina *f sing* municipal.
bathe [beɪð] *vt* 1 MED *(cut, wound)* lavar. 2 *(eyes)* bañarse. 3 *fig (with light)* bañar.
▷ *vi (in sea)* bañarse.
bather ['beɪðəʳ] *n* bañista *mf.*
bathing ['beɪðɪŋ] *n* baño. ■ **"No bathing"** "Prohibido bañarse". ● **bathing costume** traje *m* de baño. ‖ **bathing suit** traje *m* de baño.
bathrobe ['bɑːθrəʊb] *n* albornoz *m.*
bathroom ['bɑːθruːm] *n* cuarto de baño.
bathtub ['bɑːθtʌb] *n* US bañera.
bathyscaph ['bæθɪskæf] *n* batiscafo.
baton ['bætən, 'bætɒn] *n* 1 *(truncheon)* porra. 2 MUS batuta. 3 SP testigo.
batracian [bə'treɪʃən] *adj* batracio,-a.
▷ *n* batracio.
battalion [bə'tæljən] *n* batallón *m.*
batter[1] ['bætəʳ] *n* CULIN rebozado.
batter[2] ['bætəʳ] *vt (person)* golpear, apalear; *(bruise)* magullar; *(object)* maltratar, estropear.
batter[3] ['bætəʳ] *n* SP *(baseball, cricket)* bateador,-ra.
battered ['bætəd] *adj* 1 *(shabby, in bad repair)* estropeado,-a; *(carpet, coat)* raído,-a. 2 *(dented)* abollado,-a. 3 *(bruised)* lleno,-a de magulladuras.
battering ['bætərɪŋ] *n (beating)* apaleamiento.
battery ['bætərɪ] *n* 1 ELEC *(wet)* batería; *(dry)* pila. 2 MIL *(of artillery)* batería. 3 THEAT *(row of lights)* batería. 4 *(series)* batería.
▲ *pl* batteries.
battle ['bætəl] *n* 1 batalla, combate *m.* 2 *fig* lucha.
▷ *vi* pelearse, batirse.
battlefield ['bætəlfiːld] *n* campo de batalla.
battleship ['bætəlʃɪp] *n* acorazado.
bauble ['bɔːbəl] *n* 1 *(trinket)* baratija. 2 *(Christmas decoration)* bola de Navidad.
bawl [bɔːl] *vi* 1 *(shout)* chillar, gritar. 2 *(weep loudly)* llorar a lágrima viva.
bay[1] [beɪ] *n* GEOG bahía; *(large)* golfo. ● **Bay of Biscay** golfo de Vizcaya.
bay[2] [beɪ] *n (tree)* laurel *m.*
bay[3] [beɪ] *vi (howl)* aullar.
bay[4] [beɪ] *n* 1 ARCH *(recess)* hueco. 2 *(in factory)* nave *f.*
bayonet ['beɪənət] *n* MIL bayoneta.
▷ *vt* MIL pasar a la bayoneta.
bazaar [bə'zɑːʳ] *n* 1 *(eastern)* bazar *m.* 2 *(at church, etc)* venta benéfica.
BBC ['biː'biː'siː] *abbr* (British Broadcasting Corporation) compañía británica de radiodifusión; *(abbreviation)* BBC *f.*
BC ['biː'siː] *abbr* (before Christ) antes de Cristo.
be [biː] *vi* 1 *(permanent characteristic)* ser: she's clever *es inteligente.* 2 *(essential quality)* ser: diamonds are hard *los diamantes son duros.* 3 *(nationality)* ser: John's English *John es inglés.* 4 *(occupation)* ser: we are both teachers *los dos somos profesores.* 5 *(origin)* ser: they are from York *son de York.* 6 *(ownership)* ser: it's my pencil *es mi lápiz.* 7 *(authorship)* ser: this painting is by Botero *este cuadro es de Botero.* 8 *(composition)* ser: this cupboard is oak *este armario es de roble.* 9 *(use)* ser: this product is for tiles *este producto es para baldosas.* 10 *(location)* estar: San Diego is on the coast *San Diego está en la costa.* 11 *(temporary state)* estar: your supper's cold *tu cena está fría;* how are you? *¿cómo estás?* 12 *(age)* tener: Philip is 22 *Philip tiene 22 años.* 13 *(price)* costar, valer: a single ticket is £9.50 *un billete de ida cuesta 9.50 libras.* 14 tener: he's hot/cold *tiene calor/frío;* we're hungry/thirsty *tenemos hambre/sed;* she's in a hurry *tiene prisa;* he's right *tiene razón.* ■ **to be about to + inf** estar para + *inf*, estar a punto de + *inf*: the train is about to arrive *el tren está a punto de llegar.*
▷ *aux* be + *pres part (action in progress or near future)* estar: it is raining *está lloviendo;* the train is coming *viene el tren;* I am going on Thursday *iré el jueves.*
▷ *aux* to be + *pp (passive)* ser: she was arrested at the border *fue detenida en la frontera, la detuvieron en la frontera.*
▷ *aux* be + *to* + *inf (obligation)* deber, tener que; *(future)* : the King is to visit Egypt *el Rey visitará Egipto.*
▷ *phr* there is / there are hay.
▲ *pres* 1^{a} *pers* am, 2^{a} *pers sing y todas del pl* are, 3^{a} *pers sing* is; *pt* 1^{a} *y* 3^{a} *pers sing* was, 2^{a} *pers sing y todas del pl* were; *pp* been.
⊙ **to be after** *vi* querer, estar buscando: what are you after? *¿que estás buscando?*
⊙ **to be off** *vi (leave)* salir, marcharse; *(be stale, bad)* estar pasado,-a.
⊙ **to be in** *vi* 1 *(at home)* estar en casa. 2 *(in fashion)* estar de moda.
⊙ **to be out** *vi* 1 *(away)* no estar, estar fuera: John's out at the moment *John no está en estos momentos.* 2 *(published)* haber salido: the record was out last week *el disco salió la semana pasada.* 3 *(extinguished)* estar apagado,-a, haberse apagado: the fire was out *el fuego se había apagado.*
⊙ **to be away** *vi* estar fuera.
⊙ **to be back** *vi* estar de vuelta, haber vuelto.
⊙ **to be over** *vi* haber acabado, haber terminado.
beach [biːtʃ] *n* playa.
▲ *pl* beaches.
▷ *vt* varar. ■ **on the beach** en la playa.

beacon ['bi:kən] *n* 1 *(fire)* almenara. 2 *(light)* baliza. 3 *(lighthouse)* faro. 4 *(hill)* hacho.

bead [bi:d] *n* 1 *(on rosary, necklace)* cuenta; *(glass)* abalorio. 2 *(of liquid)* gota.

beady ['bi:dɪ] *adj (eye)* pequeño,-a y brillante.
▲ *comp* **beadier**, *superl* **beadiest**.

beagle ['bi:gəl] *n* beagle *m*.

beak [bi:k] *n* 1 pico. 2 *fam (nose)* nariz *f* ganchuda.

beaker ['bi:kəʳ] *n* 1 taza alta. 2 *(for measuring, playing dice)* cubilete *m*. 3 CHEM vaso de precipitación.

beam [bi:m] *n* 1 *(wooden)* viga. 2 *(of light)* rayo. 3 *(width of ship)* manga. 4 *(smile)* sonrisa radiante. 5 PHYS haz *m*.
▷ *vi* 1 *(shine)* brillar. 2 *(smile)* sonreír.
▷ *vt* irradiar, emitir. ● **electron beam** haz *m* de electrones.

beaming ['bi:mɪŋ] *adj* radiante, sonriente.

bean [bi:n] *n* 1 *(vegetable)* alubia, judía, haba. 2 *(of coffee)* grano.

beanfeast ['bi:nfi:st] *n fam* comilona.

beansprout ['bi:nspraut] *n* brote *m* de soja.

bear[1] [beəʳ] *n* 1 ZOOL oso. 2 FIN bajista *mf*, especulador,-ra a la baja. 3 *(rough person)* bruto. ● **bear cub** ZOOL osezno. | **grizzly bear** oso pardo. | **the Great Bear** la Osa Mayor. | **the Little Bear** la Osa Menor.

bear[2] [beəʳ] *vt* 1 *(carry)* llevar: **the officer bore the flag** *el oficial llevaba la bandera*. 2 *(name, date)* llevar: **the document bore the date of the meeting** *el documento llevaba la fecha de la reunión*. 3 *(show signs of)* mostrar, revelar: **the body bore no signs of violence** *el cadáver no mostraba señales de violencia*. 4 *(weight)* soportar, aguantar; *(responsibility, cost)* asumir. 5 *(tolerate)* soportar, aguantar: **I can't bear him** *no lo soporto*. 6 *(fruit)* producir. 7 FIN *(interest)* devengar. 8 *(give birth)* tener, dar a luz: **she has borne a son** *ha tenido un niño;* **her daughter was born deaf** *su hija nació sorda*.
▷ *vi (turn)* torcer a: **bear left at the next set of traffic lights** *tuerza hacia la izquierda al próximo semáforo*.
⊙ **to bear down** *vt sep lit* vencer, derrotar.
⊙ **to bear out** *vt sep* confirmar, corroborar: **his wife bore out the facts** *su mujer confirmó los hechos*.
⊙ **to bear up** *vi* ir tirando: **John's bearing up in spite of his problems** *John va tirando a pesar de sus problemas*.
⊙ **to bear with** *vt insep* tener paciencia con.
▲ *pt* **bore** [bɔ:ʳ], *pp* **borne** [bɔ:ʳn].

bearable ['beərəbəl] *adj* soportable, llevadero,-a.

beard [bɪəd] *n* 1 *(on face)* barba. 2 *(of corn)* arista, raspa.
▷ *vt* 1 *(oppose)* oponerse a. 2 *(challenge)* desafiar.

bearded ['bɪədɪd] *adj* barbudo,-a, con barba.

bearing ['beərɪŋ] *n* 1 *(posture)* porte *m*. 2 *(relevance)* relación *f*. 3 *(importance)* trascendencia. 4 TECH cojinete *m*. 5 ARCH soporte *m*, columna. 6 MAR orientación *f*.

beast [bi:st] *n* 1 bestia, animal *m*. 2 *(unpleasant person)* sinvergüenza *mf*.

beastly ['bi:stlɪ] *adj* 1 bestial. 2 *(unpleasant)* antipático,-a. 3 *sl (damn)* dichoso, -a, maldito,-a.
▲ *comp* **beastlier**, *superl* **beastliest**.

beat [bi:t] *n* 1 *(of heart)* latido. 2 *(noise)* golpe *m*, ruido; *(of rain)* tamborileo; *(of wings)* aleteo. 3 MUS ritmo. 4 *(of policeman)* ronda.
▷ *adj fam* agotado,-a, rendido,-a: **he was beat after the match** *estaba rendido después del partido*.
▷ *vt* 1 *(hit)* golpear; *(metals)* martillear; *(person)* azotar; *(drum)* tocar. 2 CULIN batir. 3 *(defeat)* vencer, derrotar; *(in competition)* ganar. 4 *fam (puzzle)* extrañar, dejar perplejo,-a.
▷ *vi* 1 *(heart)* latir. 2 *(wings)* batir.
▲ *pt* **beat**, *pp* **beaten** ['bi:tən].
⊙ **to beat back** *vt sep* hacer retroceder.
⊙ **to beat down** *vt sep* 1 *(door)* derribar, echar abajo. 2 *(price)* conseguir un precio más bajo.
⊙ **to beat up** *vt sep* dar una paliza a, vapulear.

beaten ['bi:tən] *adj* 1 *(defeated)* vencido,-a, derrotado,-a. 2 *(metal)* martillado,-a. 3 *(exhausted)* rendido,-a, agotado,-a.

beater ['bi:təʳ] *n* 1 CULIN batidora. 2 *(in hunting)* ojeador,-ra.

beating ['bi:tɪŋ] *n* 1 *(thrashing)* paliza. 2 *(defeat)* derrota. 3 *(of heart)* latidos *mpl*.

beau [bəu] *n* 1 galán *m*. 2 *(suitor)* pretendiente *m*.
▲ *pl* **beaux** [bəuz] o **beau** [bəu].

beautician [bju:'tɪʃən] *n* esteticista *mf*.

beautiful ['bju:tɪful] *adj* 1 *(person, object, place)* hermoso,-a, bonito,-a, precioso,-a; *(person)* guapo,-a. 2 *(wonderful)* maravilloso,-a, magnífico,-a. 3 *(delicious)* delicioso,-a.

beautifully ['bju:tɪfulɪ] *adv* maravillosamente, perfectamente, muy bien.

beauty ['bju:tɪ] *n* 1 belleza, hermosura. 2 *(person)* belleza. ● **beauty spot** 1 *(on face)* lunar *m*. 2 *(place)* lugar *m* pintoresco.
▲ *pl* **beauties**.

beaver ['bi:vəʳ] *n* castor *m*.

became [bɪ'keɪm] *pt* → **become**.

because [bɪ'kɒz] *conj* porque.
▷ *prep* **because of** a causa de: **they were late because of the snow** *llegaron tarde a causa de la nieve*.

become [bɪ'kʌm] *vi* 1 *(with noun)* convertirse en, hacerse, llegar a ser: **to become a doctor/teacher** *hacerse médico,-a/maestro,-a;* **to become friends** *hacerse amigos;* **to become president** *llegar a la presidencia*. 2 *(change into)* convertirse en, transformarse en: **chrysalises become butterflies** *las crisálidas se transforman en mariposas*. 3 *(irrevocable state)* volverse; *(temporary state)* ponerse; *(involuntary state)* quedarse: **to become mad** *volverse loco,-a;* **to become fat** *engordar;* **to become sad** *ponerse triste;* **to become deaf** *quedarse sordo*. ■ **what has become of ...?** ¿qué ha sido de ...?: **what has become of your sister?** *¿qué ha sido de tu hermana?*
▲ *pt* **became** [bɪ'keɪm], *pp* **become** [bɪ'kʌm].

becoming [bɪ'kʌmɪŋ] *adj* 1 *(dress, etc)* que sienta bien, favorecedor,-ra. 2 *(behaviour, language)* apropiado,-a.

bed [bed] *n* 1 cama. 2 *(for animals)* lecho. 3 *(of flowers)* arriate *m*, macizo. 4 *(of river)* lecho, cauce *m*; *(of sea)* fondo. 5 GEOL capa, yacimiento. ■ **to go to bed** acostarse. | **to put** SB **to bed** acostar a algn. | **to make the bed** hacer la cama. ● **bunk bed** litera. | **double bed** cama de matrimonio. | **single bed** cama individual. | **twin beds** camas *fpl* separadas. | **bed and board** pensión *f* completa. | **bed and breakfast** alojamiento con desayuno incluido.

bedazzle [bɪ'dæzəl] *vt* deslumbrar, encandilar.

bedbug ['bedbʌg] *n* chinche *f.*
bedclothes ['bedkləʊðz] *n pl* ropa de cama.
bedding ['bedɪŋ] *n* 1 ropa de cama. 2 *(for animals)* lecho.
bedlam ['bedləm] *n* 1 *(confusion)* alboroto, jaleo. 2 *dated* manicomio.
bedpan ['bedpæn] *n* cuña, orinal *m* de cama.
bedraggled [bɪ'drægəld] *adj* desaliñado,-a.
bedridden ['bedrɪdən] *adj* postrado,-a en cama.
bedrock ['bedrɒk] *n* 1 GEOL roca de fondo. 2 *fig* fondo de la cuestión.
bedroom ['bedru:m] *n* dormitorio, habitación *f.*
bedside ['bedsaɪd] *n* cabecera.
bedsitter [bed'sɪtəʳ] *n* estudio.
bedsore ['bedsɔ:] *n* MED llaga, úlcera.
bedspread ['bedspred] *n* cubrecama.
bedstead ['bedsted] *n* armazón *m* de la cama.
bedtime ['bedtaɪm] *n* la hora de acostarse.
bee [bi:] *n* 1 abeja. 2 US círculo de amigos. ● **carpenter bee** abeja carpintera.
beech [bi:tʃ] *n (wood)* haya. ● **beech grove** hayal *m*, hayedo. | **beech tree** haya.
beechnut ['bi:tʃnʌt] *n* hayuco.
bee-eater ['bi:i:təʳ] *n* abejaruco.
beef [bi:f] *n* 1 *(meat)* carne *f* de buey, carne *f* de vaca. 2 *(animal)* buey *m*, vaca; *(cattle)* ganado vacuno. 3 US *(complaint)* queja. ● **corned beef** carne *f* de vaca en conserva.
▷ *vi fam* quejarse.
⊙ **to beef up** *vt sep* reforzar, impulsar.
beefburger ['bi:fbɜ:gəʳ] *n* hamburguesa.
beefeater ['bi:fi:təʳ] *n* alabardero de la Torre de Londres.
beefsteak ['bi:fsteɪk] *n* bistec *m.*
beefy ['bi:fɪ] *adj* cachas, fornido,-a.
▲ *comp* beefier, *superl* beefiest.
beehive ['bi:haɪv] *n* colmena.
beekeeper ['bi:ki:pəʳ] *n* colmenero,-a, apicultor,-ra.
beekeeping ['bi:ki:pɪŋ] *n* apicultura.
beeline ['bi:laɪn] *n* línea recta.
been [bi:n, bɪn] *pp* ⟶ **be.**
beep [bi:p] *n* pitido.
▷ *vi* pitar, tocar el pito. ■ **to beep the horn** tocar el claxon.
beer [bɪəʳ] *n* cerveza.
beeswax ['bi:zwæks] *n* cera de abejas.
beet [bi:t] *n* remolacha.
beetle ['bi:təl] *n* escarabajo.
⊙ **to beetle about** *vi* ir a toda prisa.
beetroot ['bi:tru:t] *n* remolacha azucarera.
befall [bɪ'fɔ:l] *vt lit* acontecer a, suceder a: **he never knew what had befallen her** *nunca supo lo que le había sucedido.*
▲ *pt* befell [bɪ'fel], *pp* befallen [bi'fɔ:lᵊn].
befallen [bɪ'fɔ:lən] *pp* ⟶ **befall.**
befell [bɪ'fel] *pt* ⟶ **befall.**
befit [bɪ'fɪt] [Se usa únicamente en tercera persona.] *vt lit* convenir a, ser digno,-a de.
▲ *pt & pp* befitted, *ger* befitting.
befitting [bɪ'fɪtɪŋ] *adj* propio,-a, digno,-a, conveniente.
before [bɪ'fɔ:ʳ] *prep* 1 *(earlier)* antes de. 2 *(in front of)* delante de; *(in the presence of)* ante; *(for the attention of)* ante: **he's before me in the queue** *va delante de mí en la cola;* **he appeared before the judge** *compareció ante el juez.* 3 *(rather than)* antes que: **death before dishonour** *la muerte antes que la deshonra.* 4 *(ahead)* por delante. 5 *(first)* primero: **ladies before gentlemen** *las señoras primero.*
▷ *conj* 1 *(earlier than)* antes de + *inf*, antes de que + *subj*: **don't forget to say goodbye before you go** *no te olvides de despedirte antes de irte.* 2 *(rather than)* antes de + *inf*: **he would starve before he asked them for money** *preferiría morir de hambre antes de pedirles dinero.*
▷ *adv* 1 *(earlier)* antes. 2 *(previous)* anterior. 3 *(already)* ya: **we've seen it before** *ya lo hemos visto.*
beforehand [bɪ'fɔ:hænd] *adv* 1 *(earlier)* antes. 2 *(in advance)* de antemano, con antelación: **payment must be made a month beforehand** *los pagos deben efectuarse con un mes de antelación.* 3 *(before)* antes: **they arrived two hours beforehand** *llegaron dos horas antes.*
befriend [bɪ'frend] *vt* ofrecer su amistad a.
beg [beg] *vt* 1 mendigar. 2 *(ask for)* pedir. 3 *lit (beseech)* suplicar, rogar.
▷ *vi* 1 mendigar. 2 *(dog)* sentarse *(con las patas delanteras levantadas).* ■ **I beg to differ** no estoy de acuerdo.
▲ *pt & pp* begged, *ger* begging.
⊙ **to beg off** *vi* US escabullirse.
began [bɪ'gæn] *pt* ⟶ **begin.**
beget [bɪ'get] *vt* engendrar.
▲ *pt* begot [bɪ'gɒt], *pp* begotten [bɪ'gɒtᵊn], *ger* begetting.
beggar ['begəʳ] *n* 1 mendigo,-a, pordiosero,-a. 2 *fam* tipo, individuo,-a: **he's a funny beggar** *es un tipo raro.*
▷ *vt* 1 empobrecer, arruinar. 2 *fig* hacer imposible.
beggarly ['begəlɪ] *adj* pobre, miserable.
begin [bɪ'gɪn] *vt* empezar, comenzar. ■ **beginning from** a partir de: **beginning from next week** *a partir de la semana que viene.*
▲ *pt* began [bɪ'gæn], *pp* begun [bɪ'gʌn], *ger* beginning.
beginner [bɪ'gɪnəʳ] *n* principiante *mf.*
beginning [bɪ'gɪnɪŋ] *n* 1 principio, comienzo: **the beginning of the film** *el principio de la película.* 2 *(cause)* origen *m*, causa.
▷ *n pl* **beginnings** *(origins)* orígenes *mpl*: **he never discussed his humble beginnings** *nunca habló de sus orígenes humildes.*
begone [bɪ'gɒn] *interj arch* ¡retiraos!
begrudge [bɪ'grʌdʒ] *vt* 1 *(envy)* envidiar. 2 *(dis approve)* desaprobar, no ver con buenos ojos. ■ **to begrudge doing** STH hacer ALGO a regañadientes, hacer ALGO de mala gana.
begrudgingly [bɪ'grʌdʒɪŋlɪ] *adv* a regañadientes, de mala gana.
beguile [bɪ'gaɪl] *vt* 1 *(seduce)* seducir, atraer; *(bewitch)* embrujar. 2 *(cheat)* engañar.
begun [bɪ'gʌn] *pp* ⟶ **begin.**
behalf [bɪ'hɑ:f] *phr* **on behalf of** *(acting for)* en nombre de, de parte de; *(in favour of)* por, en favor de; *(for the benefit of)* para, en beneficio de.
behave [bɪ'heɪv] *vi* 1 *(people)* comportarse, portarse. 2 *(equipment, machinery)* funcionar bien: **this computer won't behave** *este ordenador no funciona bien.*

behavior [bɪ'heɪvjəʳ] *n* US → **behaviour.**
behaviour [bɪ'heɪvjəʳ] *n* **1** *(of person)* conducta, comportamiento. **2** *(of equipment, machine)* funcionamiento. **3** *(treatment)* trato.
behead [bɪ'hed] *vt* decapitar, descabezar.
beheld [bɪ'held] *pt & pp* → **behold.**
behest [bɪ'hest] *n lit* orden *m*, petición *f*.
behind [bɪ'haɪnd] *prep* detrás de.
▷ *adv* **1** detrás, atrás. **2** *(late)* atrasado,-a.
▷ *n fam (buttocks)* trasero.
behindhand [bɪ'haɪndhænd] *adv* en retraso, retrasado,-a: **he's behindhand with the payments** *está retrasado en los pagos.*
behold [bɪ'həʊld] *vt lit* contemplar, observar.
▲ *pt & pp* **beheld** [bɪ'held].
beholden [bɪ'həʊldən] *phr* **to be beholden to** SB estar en deuda con algn.
beholder [bɪ'həʊldəʳ] *n lit* observador,-ra.
beige [beɪʒ] *n* beige *m*.
▷ *adj* (de color) beige.
being ['biːɪŋ] *n* **1** *(living thing)* ser *m*. **2** *(existence)* existencia. ■ **being as** ya que, puesto que: **being as they arrived late ...** *puesto que llegaron tarde ...* ‖ **for the time being** por ahora, de momento. ‖ **to bring into being** llevar a cabo, crear. ‖ **to come into being** nacer. ● **human being** ser *m* humano.
Belarus ['belərʌs] *n* → **Byelorussia.**
belated [bɪ'leɪtɪd] *adj fam* tardío,-a, atrasado,-a.
belay [bɪ'leɪ] *vt (boat)* amarrar; *(rope in mountaineering)* asegurar, fijar.
belch [beltʃ] *n* eructo.
▷ *vi* eructar. ■ **to belch (out)** vomitar, arrojar: **the burning building belched out smoke** *el edificio en llamas arrojaba humo.*
beleaguer [bɪ'liːgəʳ] *vt* **1** *(beseige)* sitiar, cercar. **2** *(harass)* perseguir, hostigar.
belfry ['belfrɪ] *n* campanario.
▲ *pl* **belfries.**
Belgian ['beldʒən] *adj* belga.
▷ *n* belga *mf*.
Belgium ['beldʒəm] *n* Bélgica.
Belgrade [bel'greɪd] *n* Belgrado.
belie [bɪ'laɪ] *vt* **1** *(contradict)* mostrar como falso. **2** *(misrepresent)* no reflejar, ocultar. **3** *(fail to justify)* defraudar.
belief [bɪ'liːf] *n* **1** *(gen)* creencia. **2** *(opinion)* opinión *f*. **3** *(confidence)* confianza: **he has no belief in the legal system** *no tiene confianza en el sistema jurídico.* ■ **to the best of my belief** que yo sepa. ‖ **it is my firm belief that** creo firmemente que. ‖ **it is beyond belief** parece mentira.
believable [bɪ'liːvəbəl] *adj* creíble, verosímil.
believe [bɪ'liːv] *vt* **1** *(accept as true, think)* creer. **2** *(suppose)* suponer.
▷ *vi* **1** creer (**in**, en). **2** *(trust)* confiar (**in**, en). **3** *(support, be in favour of)* ser partidario,-a (**in**, de). **4** REL tener fe. ■ **it is believed that** se cree que.
believer [bɪ'liːvəʳ] *n* **1** creyente *mf*. **2** *(supporter)* partidario,-a.
belittle [bɪ'lɪtəl] *vt* menospreciar, despreciar. ■ **to belittle oneself** rebajarse.
bell[1] [bel] *n* **1** *(church, etc)* campana. **2** *(handbell)* campanilla. **3** *(on bicycle, door, etc)* timbre *m*. **4** *(on toy, hat)* cascabel *m*. **5** *(cowbell)* cencerro. **6** *(flower)* campanilla. ■ **to ring the bell** tocar el timbre.
bell[2] [bel] *n (of stag)* bramido.
▷ *vi* bramar.
bell-bottoms [bel'bɒtəmz] *n pl* pantalones *mpl* acampanados.
bellboy ['belbɔɪ] *n* botones *m*.
belle [bel] *n (beautiful woman)* belleza, beldad *f*.
bellhop ['belhɒp] *n* US botones *m*.
bellicose ['belɪkəʊs] *adj* belicoso,-a, pendenciero,-a.
belligerent [bɪ'lɪdʒərənt] *adj* beligerante.
bellow ['beləʊ] *n* bramido.
▷ *vi* **1** bramar. **2** *fig* vociferar.
▷ *n pl* **bellows** fuelle *m sing*.
belly ['belɪ] *n* **1** *(person)* vientre *m*, barriga. **2** *(animal)* panza. ● **belly button** ombligo. ‖ **belly laugh** carcajada.
▲ *pl* **bellies.**
bellyache ['belɪeɪk] *n fam* dolor *m* de barriga.
▷ *vi fam* quejarse.
bellybutton ['belɪbʌtən] *n fam* ombligo.
bellyful ['belɪfʊl] *n* panzada, hartazgo.
belong [bɪ'lɒŋ] *vi* **1** pertenecer (**to**, a), ser (**to**, de). **2** *(be a member of a club)* ser socio,-a (**to**, de); *(be a member of political party)* ser miembro (**to**, de). **3** *(have suitable qualities)* ser apto,-a (**in**, para). **4** *(fit specific environment)* estar en su ambiente natural. **5** *(be correctly placed)* estar en su sitio, deber colocarse en.
belongings [bɪ'lɒŋɪŋz] *n pl* pertenencias *fpl*, bártulos *mpl*.
beloved [*(adj)* bɪ'lʌvd, *(n)* bɪ'lʌvɪd] *adj* querido,-a, amado,-a.
▷ *n* amado,-a.
below [bɪ'ləʊ] *prep* **1** debajo de, bajo. **2** por debajo (de). **3** *(lower than)* bajo. ■ **below sea-level** por debajo del nivel del mar. ‖ **see below** véase abajo.
▷ *adv* **1** abajo. **2** de abajo.
belt [belt] *n* **1** cinturón *m*. **2** TECH correa. **3** *(area)* zona.
▷ *vt fam (hit)* arrear un tortazo.
⊙ **to belt along** *vi fam* ir a todo gas.
⊙ **to belt up** *vi fam* cerrar el pico.
bemoan [bɪ'məʊn] *vt* lamentar.
bemused [bɪ'mjuːzd] *adj* perplejo,-a.
bench [bentʃ] *n* **1** banco. **2** JUR tribunal *m*. **3** SP banquillo. ■ **to be on the bench** ser juez,-za. ● **front benches** GB *escaños ocupados por los miembros del consejo de ministros.* ‖ **back benches** GB *escaños de los diputados que no forman parte del consejo de ministros.*
bend [bend] *n* **1** *(in road, etc)* curva. **2** *(in pipe)* ángulo.
▷ *vt* **1** doblar, curvar. **2** *(head)* inclinar; *(back)* doblar, encorvar; *(knee)* doblar, flexionar.
▷ *vi* **1** doblarse, combarse: **the legs of the chair bent when he sat down** *las patas de la silla se combaron cuando se sentó.* **2** *(head)* inclinarse; *(back)* encorvarse. **3** *(road)* torcer.
▲ *pt & pp* **bent** [bent].
⊙ **to bend down** *vi* agacharse.
⊙ **to bend over** *vi* inclinarse.
beneath [bɪ'niːθ] *prep* **1** bajo, debajo de. **2** por debajo de: **the underground (**US **subway) line runs beneath our house** *la línea de metro va por debajo de nuestra casa.* **3** *fig*

indigno,-a de, no digno,-a de: it's beneath you to behave like this *es indigno de ti comportarte de esta manera.*
▷ *adv* de abajo: she lives in the flat (US apartment) beneath *vive en el piso de abajo.*
benefactor ['benɪfæktəʳ] *n* benefactor *m.*
benefice ['benɪfɪs] *n* REL beneficio.
beneficence [bɪ'nefɪsəns] *n* beneficencia.
beneficent [bɪ'nefɪsənt] *adj* benefactor,-ra.
beneficial [benɪ'fɪʃəl] *adj* beneficioso,-a, provechoso,-a.
beneficiary [benɪ'fɪʃərɪ] *n* beneficiario,-a.
▲ *pl* beneficiaries.
benefit ['benɪfɪt] *n* 1 *(advantage)* beneficio, provecho. 2 *(good)* bien *m.* 3 *(allowance)* subsidio. 4 *(charity performance)* función *f* benéfica; *(charity game)* partido benéfico.
▷ *vt* beneficiar.
▲ *pt & pp* benefited (US benefitted), *ger* benefiting (US benefitting).
▷ *vi* beneficiarse (from, de): he benefited from their help *se benefició de su ayuda.* ■ **to do STH for SB's benefit** hacer ALGO por el bien de algn. ‖ **to gain benefit from STH** sacar provecho de algo.
benevolence [bɪ'nevələns] *n* benevolencia.
benevolent [bɪ'nevələnt] *adj* benévolo,-a. ● **benevolent society** sociedad *f* benéfica.
Bengal [ben'gɔːl] *n* Bengala. ● **Bay of Bengal** golfo de Bengala.
benign [bɪ'naɪn] *adj* benigno,-a.
bent [bent] *pt & pp* → **bend.**
▷ *adj* 1 torcido,-a, doblado,-a. 2 *sl (corrupt)* corrupto,-a. 3 *sl (homosexual)* de la acera de enfrente.
▷ *n (innate ability)* facilidad *f*, don *m*: she's got a bent for maths *tiene facilidad para las matemáticas.*
benzene ['benziːn] *n* CHEM benceno.
benzine ['benziːn] *n* CHEM bencina.
bequest [bɪ'kwest] *n* legado.
bereaved [bɪ'riːvd] *adj* desconsolado,-a, afligido,-a: his bereaved wife *su desconsolada esposa.*
▷ *n pl* **the bereaved** los afligidos *mpl*, la desconsolada familia.
bereavement [bɪ'riːvmənt] *n* 1 *(loss)* pérdida. 2 *(mourning)* duelo.
bereft [bɪ'reft] *pt & pp* → **bereave.** ■ **to be bereft of STH/SB** ser privado,-a de algo/algn.
beret ['bereɪ] *n* boina.
Berlin [bɜː'lɪn] *n* Berlín.
Bermuda [bə'mjuːdə] *n* las Bermudas. ● **Bermuda shorts** bermudas *mpl.*
Berne [bɜːn] *n* Berna.
berry ['berɪ] *n* baya.
▲ *pl* berries.
berserk [bə'zɜːk] *adj* enloquecido,-a.
berth [bɜːθ] *n* 1 *(in harbour)* amarradero. 2 *(on ship)* camarote *m*, litera.
▷ *vt* poner en dique.
▷ *vi* atracar.
beryl ['berəl] *n* GEOL berilo.
beryllium [bə'rɪlɪəm] *n* CHEM berilio.
beseech [bɪ'siːtʃ] *vt lit* implorar, suplicar.
▲ *pt & pp* besought [bɪ'sɔːt] o beseeched.
beset [bɪ'set] *vt* 1 *(attack, harass)* acosar, asaltar. 2 *(hem in, surround)* acorralar, cercar.
▲ *pt & pp* beset, *ger* besetting.
beside [bɪ'saɪd] *prep* 1 al lado de. 2 *(compared to)* frente a, comparado,-a con. ■ **to be beside OS** estar fuera de sí. ‖ **to be beside OS with joy** estar loco,-a de alegría. ‖ **that's beside the point** esto no viene al caso.
besides [bɪ'saɪdz] *prep (as well as)* además de.
▷ *adv* además.
besiege [bɪ'siːdʒ] *vt* 1 MIL sitiar. 2 *fig* asediar, inundar.
besmirch [bɪ'smɜːtʃ] *vt* ensuciar.
besought [bɪ'sɔːt] *pt & pp* → **beseech.**
bespatter [bɪ'spætəʳ] *vt* salpicar (with, de).
bespoke [bɪs'pəʊk] *adj* hecho,-a a medida.
best [best] *adj (superl of* good) mejor.
▷ *adv* 1 *(superl of* well) mejor. 2 *(to a greater extent)* más: of all the girls she is the one he likes best *de todas las chicas ella es la que le gusta más.* ■ **all the best!** 1 ¡que te vaya bien! 2 *(in letter)* un saludo. ‖ **best before ...** consumir preferentemente antes de ... ‖ **it's for the best** más vale que sea así. ● **best man** padrino de boda. ‖ **the best one** el mejor, la mejor. ‖ **the best part of** casi: it cost me the best part of £5,000 *me costó casi 5.000 libras.*
▷ *n* 1 lo mejor: the best is yet to come *lo mejor aún está por venir.* 2 *(person)* el mejor, la mejor: she's the best in the class at maths *es la mejor de la clase en mates.* 3 *(in sport)* plusmarca.
▷ *vt fam* ganar, vencer.
bestial ['bestɪəl] *adj* bestial, brutal.
bestiary ['bestɪərɪ] *n* bestiario.
▲ *pl* bestiaries.
bestow [bɪ'stəʊ] *vt (honour, award)* otorgar (on, a); *(favour)* hacer (on, a); *(title)* conferir (on, a).
best-seller [best'seləʳ] *n* best-séller *m*, superventas *m.*
best-selling [best'selɪŋ] *adj* más vendido,-a: this is the best-selling novel of the year *ésta es la novela más vendida del año.*
bet [bet] *n* apuesta. ■ **to make a bet** hacer una apuesta.
▷ *vt* apostar.
▷ *vi* apostar.
▲ *pt & pp* bet o betted, *ger* betting
beta ['biːtə] *n* beta. ● **beta rays** rayos *mpl* beta.
Bethlehem ['beθlɪhem] *n* Belén.
betide [bɪ'taɪd] [Se usa únicamente en tercera persona del singular.] *vt lit* acontecer, acaecer.
betray [bɪ'treɪ] *vt* 1 traicionar. 2 *(secret)* revelar. 3 *(show signs of)* dejar ver, acusar. 4 *(deceive)* engañar. 5 *(trust)* defraudar.
betrayal [bɪ'treɪəl] *n* 1 traición *f.* 2 *(deceit)* engaño.
better[1] ['betəʳ] *adj* 1 *(comp of* good) mejor: his new novel is better than his last one *su última novela es mejor que la anterior.* 2 *(more healthy)* mejor: he's feeling better today *hoy se encuentra mejor.*
▷ *adv* 1 *(comp of* well) mejor. 2 *(to a greater extent)* más: I like this one better *me gusta más éste.*
▷ *vt* 1 *(improve)* mejorar: he has bettered their working conditions *ha mejorado sus condiciones de trabajo.* 2 *(surpass)* superar: he bettered his own record *superó su propio récord.*
▷ *n pl* **betters** superiores *mpl*: you must listen to your betters *debes escuchar a tus superiores.* ■ **to get better** recu-

perarse, mejorarse. ▮ **to like** STH/SB **better** preferir algo/a algn. ▮ **better and better** cada vez mejor. ● **better feelings** conciencia.

betterment ['betəmənt] *n* mejoría, mejora.

betting ['betɪŋ] *n* apuestas *fpl*. ■ **what's the betting that he (she, it, etc)...?** ¿qué te apuestas a que ...?: **what's the betting that he arrives late?** *¿qué te apuestas a que llega tarde?* ● **betting shop** GB administración *f* de apuestas hípicas.

between [bɪ'twi:n] *prep* entre: **choose a number between one and ten** *escoge un número entre uno y diez;* **is there a difference between a crocodile and an alligator?** *¿hay alguna diferencia entre un cocodrilo y un caimán?*

▷ *adv* [Also **in between**.] de en medio: **we could see the sea if it wasn't for the houses (in) between** *podríamos ver el mar si no fuera por las casas de en medio.* ■ **in between** en medio de, entre.

bevel ['bevəl] *n* bebida.

beverage ['bevərɪdʒ] *n* bebida.

bevy ['bevɪ] *n* 1 *(of birds)* bandada. 2 *(of women)* grupo: **a bevy of beauties** *un grupo de chicas guapas.*

▲ *pl* **bevies**.

bewail [bɪ'weɪl] *vt fml* lamentar.

beware [bɪ'weəʳ] *vi* tener cuidado (**of**, con): **beware of the dog!** *¡cuidado con el perro!*

▷ *interj* ¡ojo!, ¡cuidado!

bewilder [bɪ'wɪldəʳ] *vt* desconcertar, dejar perplejo,-a.

bewilderment [bɪ'wɪldəmənt] *n* desconcierto, perplejidad *f*, confusión *f*.

bewitch [bɪ'wɪtʃ] *vt* 1 hechizar, embrujar. 2 *fig* hechizar, fascinar.

bewitching [bɪ'wɪtʃɪŋ] *adj* hechicero,-a, fascinante.

beyond [bɪ'jɒnd] *prep* 1 más allá de: **they live beyond the mountains** *viven más allá de las montañas.* 2 *(outside)* fuera de: **it's beyond my jurisdiction** *está fuera de mi jurisdicción.*

▷ *adv* más allá, más lejos.

▷ *n* **the beyond** el más allá. ■ **it's beyond doubt** es indudable, es seguro, no cabe duda.

bezel ['bezəl] *n* bisel *m*.

biannual [baɪ'ænjuəl] *adj* bianual.

bias ['baɪəs] *n* 1 *(prejudice)* parcialidad *f*, prejuicio. 2 *(inclination)* tendencia, predisposición *f*. 3 *(in statistics)* margen *f* de error. ■ **to be biased in favour of** STH/SB ser partidario,-a de algo/algn.

▷ *vt* predisponer, influenciar.

▲ *pt & pp* **biased** o **biassed**, *ger* **biasing** o **biassing**.

biased ['baɪəst] *adj* parcial.

bib [bɪb] *n* 1 *(for baby)* babero. 2 *(top of apron, overall)* peto.

Bible ['baɪbəl] *n* Biblia.

bibliography [bɪblɪ'ɒgrəfɪ] *n* bibliografía.

▲ *pl* **bibliographies**.

bicarbonate [baɪ'kɑ:bənət] *n* CHEM bicarbonato. ● **bicarbonate of soda** bicarbonato sódico.

bicentenary [baɪsen'ti:nərɪ] *n* bicentenario.

▲ *pl* **bicentenaries**.

bicephalous [baɪ'sefələs] *adj* bicéfalo,-a.

biceps ['baɪsəps] *n* bíceps *m*.

bicker ['bɪkəʳ] *vi* discutir, porfiar.

bickering ['bɪkərɪŋ] *n* discusión *f*, altercado.

bicycle ['baɪsɪkəl] *n* bicicleta. ■ **to ride a bicycle** montar en bicicleta. ● **bicycle pump** bomba de bicicleta.

bid [bɪd] *n* 1 *(at auction)* puja: **he made a bid for the Chinese vase** *hizo una puja por el jarrón chino.* 2 *(attempt)* intento: **a failed bid for freedom** *un intento fracasado por conseguir la libertad.* 3 *(offer)* oferta: **his bid for the company was unsuccessful** *la oferta que hizo por la empresa fracasó.* 4 *(in card game)* declaración *f*.

▷ *vi* 1 *(at auction)* pujar (**for**, por). 2 *(in card game)* declarar.

▷ *vt* 1 *(at auction)* pujar, hacer una oferta de. 2 *lit (ask)* rogar. 3 [*pt* también **bade** [beɪd]; *pp* también **bidden** ['bɪdᵊn].] *lit (order)* ordenar, mandar: **she bade him come** *le ordenó que viniera.*

▲ *pt & pp* **bid**, *ger* **bidding**.

bidder ['bɪdəʳ] *n* postor,-ra, pujador,-ra, licitador,-ra.

bidding ['bɪdɪŋ] *n* 1 *(at auction)* puja, oferta. 2 *(order)* orden *f*. 3 *(card game)* declaración *f*.

bide [baɪd] *vt* **to bide one's time** esperar el momento oportuno.

▲ *pt* **bided** o **bode** [bəud], *pp* **bided**, *ger* **biding**.

bidet ['bi:deɪ] *n* bidé *m*.

bifocal [baɪ'fəukəl] *adj* bifocal.

▷ *n pl* **bifocals** lentes *fpl* bifocales.

bifurcate ['baɪfəkeɪt] *vi* bifurcarse.

▷ *adj* bifurcado,-a.

big [bɪg] *adj* 1 *(size, importance)* grande; *(before sing noun)* gran. 2 *(older)* mayor.

▲ *comp* **bigger**, *superl* **biggest**.

bigamy ['bɪgəmɪ] *n* bigamia.

big-head ['bɪghed] *n* sabihondo,-a, creído,-a.

big-hearted [bɪg'hɑ:tɪd] *adj* de buen corazón, generoso,-a.

bight [baɪt] *n* GEOG ensenada, bahía. ● **Great Australian Bight** Gran Bahía Australiana.

bigmouth ['bɪgmauθ] *n* bocazas *mf*.

bigot ['bɪgət] *n* intolerante, fanático,-a.

bigotry ['bɪgətrɪ] *n* intolerancia, fanatismo.

bigwig ['bɪgwɪg] *n fam* pez *m* gordo.

bike [baɪk] *n* 1 *fam (bicycle)* bici *f*. 2 *(motorcycle)* moto *f*.

bikeway ['baɪkweɪ] *n* carril-bici *m*.

bikini [bɪ'ki:nɪ] *n* biquini *m*, bikini *m*.

bilateral [baɪ'lætərəl] *adj* bilateral.

bile [baɪl] *n* bilis *f*, hiel *f*. ● **bile duct** conducto biliar.

biliary ['bɪlɪərɪ] *adj* biliar, biliario,-a.

bilingual [baɪ'lɪŋgwəl] *adj* bilingüe.

bilious ['bɪlɪəs] *adj* 1 MED bilioso,-a. 2 *fig (bad-tempered)* malhumorado,-a.

bilirubin [bɪlɪ'ru:bɪn] *n* bilirrubina.

bill¹ [bɪl] *n* 1 factura; *(in restaurant)* cuenta. 2 *(law)* proyecto de ley. 3 US *(banknote)* billete *m*. 4 *(poster)* cartel *m*.

▷ *vt* 1 facturar, pasar la factura. 2 THEAT programar. ● **Bill of Rights** declaración *f* de derechos.

bill² [bɪl] *n* 1 *(of bird)* pico. 2 *(headland)* cabo, promontorio.

Bill [bɪl] *n (William)* Guillermo. ● **the Old Bill** GB *sl* la bofia, la pasma.

billabong ['bɪləbɒŋ] *n (in Australia)* remanso.

billboard ['bɪlbɔ:d] *n* US valla publicitaria.

billfold ['bɪlfəuld] *n* US billetero, cartera.

billing ['bɪlɪŋ] *n* 1 *(invoicing)* facturación *f*. 2 THEAT *orden de aparición en cartel.*

billion ['bɪlɪən] *n* 1 mil millones *mpl*. 2 GB *(formerly)* billón *m*. ■ **billions of** *fig* un mogollón de, la tira de: **there were billions of people** *había la tira de gente*.

En el uso actual, tanto en EEUU como en Gran Bretaña,un **billion** equivale a mil millones.

billionaire [bɪlɪə'neəʳ] *n* multimillonario,-a.
billow ['bɪləʊ] *n* 1 *(of water)* ola. 2 *(of smoke)* nube *f*.
▷ *vt* 1 *(sea)* ondear. 2 *(sail)* hincharse.
billycan ['bɪlɪkæn] *n* cazo.
billy goat ['bɪlɪgəʊt] *n* macho cabrío.
billy-ho ['bɪlɪhəʊ] *phr* **like billy-ho** *fam* a toda pastilla: **he ran like billy-ho** *se fue corriendo a toda pastilla;* **it's raining like billy-ho** *llueven chuzos de punta*.
bimonthly [baɪ'mʌnθlɪ] *adj* 1 *(twice monthly)* bimensual. 2 *(every two months)* bimestral.
▷ *adv* 1 *(twice monthly)* dos veces al mes. 2 *(every two months)* cada dos meses.
bin [bɪn] *n* 1 *(for rubbish)* cubo de la basura; *(for paper)* papelera. 2 *(large container)* recipiente *m*.
binary ['baɪnərɪ] *adj* binario,-a. ● **binary fission** bipartición
bind [baɪnd] *n fam* fastidio, molestia.
▷ *vt* 1 *(tie up)* atar; *(cereals, corn)* agavillar. 2 CULIN *(sauce)* ligar. 3 *(book, etc)* encuadernar. 4 *(bandage)* vendar. 5 *(require)* obligar.
▲ *pt & pp* **bound** [baʊnd].
⊙ **to bind up** *vt sep (with bandage)* vendar.
⊙ **to bind over** *vt sep* JUR obligar por ley a hacer algo.
binder ['baɪndəʳ] *n* 1 *(file)* carpeta. 2 *(of books)* encuadernador,-ra.
binding ['baɪndɪŋ] *n* 1 *(of book)* encuadernación *f*. 2 SEW ribete *m*. 3 *(of skis)* fijación *f*.
▷ *adj* 1 obligatorio,-a (**on**, para). 2 que se tiene que cumplir: **a binding agreement** *un compromiso que se tiene que cumplir*.
binge [bɪndʒ] *n (drinking)* borrachera; *(eating)* atracón *m*.
▷ *vi* atiborrarse, hartarse de comida.
bingo ['bɪŋgəʊ] *n* bingo.
▲ *pl* **bingos**.
binnacle ['bɪnəkəl] *n* bitácora.
binocular [bɪ'nɒkjʊləʳ] *adj* binocular.
▷ *n pl* **binoculars** prismáticos *mpl*, gemelos *mpl*.
biochemist [baɪəʊ'kemɪst] *n* bioquímico,-a.
biochemistry [baɪəʊ'kemɪstrɪ] *n* bioquímica.
biodegradable [baɪəʊdɪ'greɪdəbəl] *adj* biodegradable.
biofeedback [baɪəʊ'fi:dbæk] *n* biorretroacción *f*.
biography [baɪ'ɒgrəfɪ] *n* biografía.
▲ *pl* **biographies**.
biological [baɪə'lɒdʒɪkəl] *adj* biológico,-a.
biologically [baɪə'lɒdʒɪkəlɪ] *adv* biológicamente.
biologist [baɪ'ɒlədʒɪst] *n* biólogo,-a.
biology [baɪ'ɒlədʒɪ] *n* biología.
biomass ['baɪəʊmæs] *n* biomasa.
biomechanics [baɪəʊmɪ'kænɪks] *n* biomecánica.
biometry [baɪ'ɒmətrɪ] *n* biometría.
bionic [baɪ'ɒnɪk] *adj* biónico,-a.
bionics [baɪ'ɒnɪks] *n* biónica.
biophysicist [baɪəʊ'fɪzɪsɪst] *n* biofísico,-a.
biophysics [baɪəʊ'fɪzɪks] *n* biofísica.
biopsy ['baɪɒpsɪ] *n* biopsia.
▲ *pl* **biopsies**.
biorhythm ['baɪərɪðəm] *n* biorritmo.
biosphere ['baɪəsfɪəʳ] *n* biosfera.
biotope ['baɪətəp] *n* biotopo.
biped ['baɪped] *adj* bípedo,-a.
▷ *n* bípedo.
biplane ['baɪpleɪn] *n* biplano.
bipolar [baɪ'pəʊləʳ] *adj* bipolar.
birch [bɜ:tʃ] *n* 1 *(tree)* abedul *m*. 2 *(rod)* vara de abedul.
▷ *vt* azotar.
bird [bɜ:d] *n* 1 *(large)* ave *f*; *(small)* pájaro. 2 GB *sl (girl)* chica. 3 *sl (person)* tipo. ● **bird of prey** ave *f* de rapiña, ave *f* de presa. ‖ **the birds and the bees** *euph* la sexualidad.
birdbrain ['bɜ:dbreɪn] *n* cabeza de chorlito.
birdcage ['bɜ:dkeɪdʒ] *n* jaula de pájaro.
birdie ['bɜ:dɪ] *n* 1 *(little bird)* pajarito. 2 *(in golf)* birdie *m*. ■ **to score a birdie** hacer menos uno: **Olazábal scored a birdie at the sixth hole** *Olazábal hizo menos uno en el hoyo seis*.
birdseed ['bɜ:dsi:d] *n* BOT alpiste *m*.
bird's-eye view [bɜ:dzaɪ'vju:] *n* vista panorámica. ■ **to get a bird's-eye view of** STH ver ALGO a vista de pájaro.
bird-watcher ['bɜ:dwɒtʃəʳ] *n* ornitólogo,-a *(cuya afición es observar las aves)*.
birefringence [baɪrɪ'frɪndʒəns] *n* refracción *f* doble.
Biro® ['baɪrəʊ] [Also written **biro**.] *n fam* boli *m*.
▲ *pl* **Biros**.
birth [bɜ:θ] *n* 1 nacimiento. 2 MED parto. 3 *(descent)* linaje *m*. ■ **to give birth to** 1 *(child)* dar a luz a. 2 *fig* dar lugar a. ● **birth certificate** partida de nacimiento. ‖ **birth control** control *m* de la natalidad.
birthday ['bɜ:θdeɪ] *n* cumpleaños *m*.
birthmark ['bɜ:θmɑ:k] *n* mancha de nacimiento, antojo.
birthplace ['bɜ:θpleɪs] *n* lugar *m* de nacimiento.
birthright ['bɜ:θraɪt] *n* derechos *mpl* de nacimiento.
Biscay ['bɪskeɪ] *n* **Bay of Biscay** golfo de Vizcaya.
biscuit ['bɪskɪt] *n* 1 galleta. 2 *(ceramics)* porcelana mate. 3 *(colour)* beige *m*.
bisect [baɪ'sekt] *vt* bisecar.
bisection [baɪ'sekʃən] *n* bisección *f*.
bisectrix [baɪ'sektrɪks] *n* bisectriz *f*.
▲ *pl* **bisectrices** [baɪ'sektrɪsi:z].
bisexual [baɪ'seksjʊəl] *adj* bisexual.
▷ *n* bisexual *mf*.
bishop ['bɪʃəp] *n* 1 obispo. 2 *(chess)* alfil *m*.
bison ['baɪsən] *n* bisonte *m*.
bissextile [baɪ'sekstaɪl] *adj* bisiesto,-a.
bisulphate [baɪ'sʌlfeɪt] *n* CHEM bisulfato.
bit¹ [bɪt] *n* 1 *(small piece)* trozo, pedacito. 2 *(small amount)* poco. 3 *fam (time)* un poco, un ratito. 4 *(part of film, play, book)* parte *f*. 5 *(coin)* moneda.
▷ *adv* **a bit** *fam (rather)* algo, un poco. ■ **a bit of** ALGO de. ‖ **quite a bit / a good bit** *fam* bastante. **that's a bit much** esto ya es pasarse. ‖ **to come to bits** hacerse pedazos.
bit² [bɪt] *n* 1 *(of bridle)* bocado. 2 *(of drill)* broca.
bit³ [bɪt] *n* COMPUT bit *m*.
bit⁴ [bɪt] *pt* → **bite**.
bitch [bɪtʃ] *n* 1 *(gen)* hembra; *(of dog)* perra. 2 *pej (woman)* bruja, lagarta.
▷ *vi fam* quejarse. ● **son of a bitch** *taboo* hijo de perra, hijo de puta.
bitchy ['bɪtʃɪ] *adj fam* malicioso,-a, rencoroso,-a.
▲ *comp* **bitchier**, *superl* **bitchiest**.

bite [baɪt] *n* 1 *(act)* mordisco. 2 *(of insect)* picadura. 3 *(of dog, etc)* mordedura. 4 *(of food)* bocado. 5 *(incisiveness)* mordacidad *f*.
▷ *vt* 1 morder. 2 *(insect, snake)* picar. 3 *(grip)* agarrar.
▷ *vi* 1 morder. 2 *(insect, snake)* picar. 3 *(fish)* picar. 4 *(grip)* agarrarse. 5 *(recession, etc)* apretar, hacerse sentir, hacerse notar.
▲ *pt* bit, *pp* bitten ['bɪtən].
⊙ **to bite off** *vt sep* arrancar con los dientes: he bit the top off *arrancó la tapa con los dientes.*
⊙ **to bite through** *vt insep* cortar de un mordisco: he bit through the rope *cortó la cuerda de un mordisco.*
biting ['baɪtɪŋ] *adj* 1 *(wind)* cortante, penetrante. 2 *(comment)* mordaz.
bitten ['bɪtən] *pp* → bite.
bitter ['bɪtəʳ] *adj* 1 *(gen)* amargo,-a; *(fruit)* ácido,-a, agrio,-a. 2 *(weather)* glacial. 3 *(person)* amargado,-a. 4 *(fight)* enconado,-a. ■ **to feel bitter about** STH guardar rencor por algo.
▷ *n* cerveza amarga.
bitterly ['bɪtəlɪ] *adv* 1 con amargura, amargamente: she complained bitterly *se quejó amargamente.* 2 *(very)* muy: it's bitterly cold *hace un frío glacial;* she was bitterly disappointed *estaba terriblemente decepcionada.*
bitterness ['bɪtənəs] *n* 1 *(gen)* amargura; *(of fruit)* acidez *f*. 2 *(of person)* amargura, rencor *m*. 3 *(of weather)* crudeza. 4 *(resentment)* rencor *m*, resentimiento.
bittersweet ['bɪtəswi:t] *adj* agridulce.
bitty ['bɪtɪ] *adj* fragmentario,-a, incompleto,-a.
▲ *comp* bittier, *superl* bittiest.
bitumen ['bɪtjʊmɪn] *n* betún *m*.
bivalent [baɪ'veɪlənt] *adj* bivalente.
bivalve ['baɪvælv] *adj* bivalvo,-a.
▷ *n* bivalvo.
biweekly [baɪ'wi:klɪ] *adj* 1 *(twice weekly)* bisemanal. 2 *(fortnightly)* quincenal.
▷ *adv* 1 *(twice weekly)* dos veces por semana. 2 *(fortnightly)* cada quincena.
bizarre [bɪ'zɑ:ʳ] *adj* 1 raro,-a, extraño,-a. 2 *(eccentric)* estrafalario,-a, extravagante.
blab [blæb] *vi* 1 *fam (gossip)* cotillear, chismear. 2 *fam (talk constantly)* rajar, parlotear.
▲ *pt & pp* blabbed, *ger* blabbing.
black [blæk] *adj* 1 negro,-a. 2 *(gloomy)* aciago,-a, negro,-a. 3 *(dirty)* sucio,-a. 4 *(threatening)* amenazador,-ra.
▷ *n* 1 *(colour)* negro. 2 *(person)* negro,-a.
▷ *vt* 1 *(make black)* ennegrecer. 2 *(boycott)* boicotear. ■ **black and white** blanco y negro. ■ **to put** STH **down in black and white** *fam* poner ALGO por escrito. ● **Black Death** HIST peste *f* negra. ■ **black economy** economía sumergida. ■ **Black Forest** GEOG Selva Negra. ■ **black widow** ZOOL *(spider)* viuda negra.
⊙ **to black out** *vt sep* 1 *(windows of house)* tapar; *(electrical supply)* apagar el alumbrado. 2 *(cause power cut)* dejar sin luz, causar un apagón.
▷ *vi (faint)* desmayarse, sufrir un desmayo.
blackberry ['blækbərɪ] *n* zarzamora, mora. ● **blackberry bush** zarza.
▲ *pl* blackberries.
blackbird ['blækbɜ:d] *n* mirlo.
blackboard ['blækbɔ:d] *n* pizarra.
blackcurrant [blæk'kʌrənt] *n* grosella negra. ● **blackcurrant bush** grosellero negro, casis *m*.
blacken ['blækən] *vt* 1 ennegrecer. 2 *fig (defame)* manchar.
blackhead ['blækhed] *n* espinilla.
blackjack ['blækdʒæk] *n (card game)* veintiuna.
blackleg ['blækleg] *n* esquirol *m*.
▷ *vi* ser un esquirol.
▲ *pt & pp* blacklegged, *ger* blacklegging.
blacklist ['blæklɪst] *n* lista negra.
▷ *vt* poner en la lista negra.
blackmail ['blækmeɪl] *n* chantaje *m*.
▷ *vt* hacer chantaje a, chantajear.
blackmailer ['blækmeɪləʳ] *n* chantajista *mf*.
blackout ['blækaʊt] *n* 1 *(through electrical fault)* apagón *m; (in wartime) oscurecimiento general de una ciudad.* 2 *(fainting)* pérdida de conocimiento, desmayo.
blacksmith ['blæksmɪθ] *n* herrero. ● **blacksmith's forge** herrería.
blackthorn ['blækθɔ:n] *n* BOT endrino.
bladder ['blædəʳ] *n* 1 vejiga. 2 *(in tyre, football)* cámara de aire.
blade [bleɪd] *n* 1 *(of sword, knife, etc)* hoja. 2 *(of ice skate)* cuchilla. 3 *(of propeller, fan, etc)* pala. 4 *(of grass)* brizna.
blame [bleɪm] *n* culpa.
▷ *vt* culpar, echar la culpa a.
blameless ['bleɪmləs] *adj* 1 *(not guilty)* libre de culpa, inocente. 2 *(virtuous)* intachable.
blameworthy ['bleɪmwɜ:ðɪ] *adj* censurable, reprobable.
blanch [blɑ:ntʃ] *vt* CULIN escaldar.
▷ *vi* palidecer.
bland [blænd] *adj* soso,-a.
blandishments ['blændɪʃments] *n lit* halago, lisonja.
blank [blæŋk] *adj* 1 *(page, etc)* en blanco. 2 *(look, etc)* vacío,-a. 3 *(cassette, tape)* virgen. ■ **my mind went blank** me quedé en blanco. ● **blank cheque** (US **check**) cheque *m* en blanco.
▷ *n* 1 *(on paper)* espacio en blanco. 2 *(bullet)* bala de fogueo. 3 *(coin, disc)* cospel *m*.
blanket ['blæŋkɪt] *n* 1 manta, AM frazada. 2 *(layer)* capa, manto: a blanket of snow *una capa de nieve.*
blare [bleəʳ] *n* 1 *(loud noise)* estruendo, fragor *m*. 2 *(of trumpet)* trompetazo.
▷ *vi* resonar, sonar.
⊙ **to blare out** *vi* sonar muy fuerte.
blasé ['blɑ:zeɪ] *adj* 1 indiferente, poco impresionado,-a. 2 *(satiated)* hastiado,-a.
blaspheme [blæs'fi:m] *vi* blasfemar (**against**, contra).
blasphemy ['blæsfəmɪ] *n* blasfemia.
▲ *pl* blasphemies.
blast [blɑ:st] *n* 1 *(of wind)* ráfaga. 2 *(of water, air, etc)* chorro. 3 *(of horn)* toque *m*. 4 *(of trumpet)* trompetazo. 5 *(explosion)* explosión *f*, voladura. 6 *(shock wave)* onda expansiva. 7 *(reprimand)* bronca.
▷ *vt* 1 *(explode)* volar, hacer volar. 2 *(criticize)* criticar. 3 *(reprimand)* echar una bronca. 4 *(ruin, spoil)* echar a perder, dar al traste con. 5 *(shoot)* pegar un tiro a. 6 *(shrivel, wither)* marchitar.
blasted ['blɑ:stɪd] *adj* maldito,-a, dichoso,-a.
blast-off ['blɑ:stɒf] *n (of rocket, missile)* despegue *m*.

blatant ['bleɪtənt] *adj* 1 descarado,-a, flagrante. 2 *(obtrusive)* llamativo,-a, intruso,-a.
blaze [bleɪz] *n* 1 *(fire)* incendio. 2 *(flame)* llamarada. 3 *(of light)* resplandor *m*. 4 *(outburst)* arranque *m*, acceso.
▷ *vi* 1 *(fire)* arder. 2 *(sun)* brillar con fuerza. 3 *(light)* resplandecer.
blazer ['bleɪzəʳ] *n* americana de sport, blazer *m*.
bleach [bliːtʃ] *n* lejía.
▷ *vt* 1 *(whiten)* blanquear. 2 *(remove colour)* desteñir, decolorar. 3 *(hair)* decolorar.
bleachers ['bliːtʃəz] *n pl* US gradas *fpl*.
bleak [bliːk] *adj* 1 *(countryside)* desolado,-a. 2 *(weather)* desapacible. 3 *(future)* poco prometedor,-ra. 4 *(welcome, reception)* frío,-a.
bleary ['blɪərɪ] *adj* 1 *(from tears)* nubloso,-a. 2 *(from tiredness)* legañoso,-a.
▲ *comp* **blearier**, *superl* **bleariest**.
bleary-eyed ['blɪərɪ'aɪd] *adj* con los ojos llenos de legañas.
bleat [bliːt] *n* balido.
▷ *vi* 1 balar. 2 *fig* gimotear.
bled [bled] *pt & pp* → **bleed**.
bleed [bliːd] *vi* MED sangrar.
▷ *vt* MED sacar sangre, sangrar. ■ **to bleed** SB **dry** sacarle a ALGN hasta el último céntimo.
▲ *pt & pp* **bled** [bled].
bleeding ['bliːdɪŋ] *adj* 1 sangriento,-a.
▷ *n* MED sangría.
bleep [bliːp] *n* pitido.
▷ *vi* pitar.
▷ *vt* localizar con un busca.
bleeper ['bliːpəʳ] *n* busca *m*, buscapersonas *m*.
blemish ['blemɪʃ] *n* 1 desperfecto, imperfección *f*.
▷ *vt* 1 *(spoil)* estropear, desmejorar. 2 *fig (reputation)* manchar, tiznar. ■ **without a blemish** *fig* intachable.
blench [blenʃ] *vi* 1 *(recoil)* retroceder. 2 *(flinch)* pestañear, inmutarse.
blend [blend] *n* mezcla, combinación *f*.
▷ *vt* 1 *(mix)* mezclar, combinar. 2 *(match)* matizar, armonizar.
blender ['blendəʳ] *n* CULIN batidora, minipímer® *m*.
bless [bles] *vt* bendecir. ■ **bless you!** *(on sneezing)* ¡Jesús!
blessed ['blesɪd] *adj* 1 *(holy)* bendito,-a, santo,-a. 2 *(content, happy)* bienaventurado,-a.
blessing ['blesɪŋ] *n* 1 bendición *f*. 2 *(advantage)* beneficio, ventaja.
blew [bluː] *pt* → **blow**.
blight [blaɪt] *n* 1 *(mildew)* tizón *m*. 2 *(calamity)* plaga.
▷ *vt fig (ruin, spoil)* echar a perder, estropear.
blimey ['blaɪmɪ] *interj* ¡jolines!, ¡caray!
blind [blaɪnd] *adj* ciego,-a.
▷ *n (on window)* persiana.
▷ *vt* 1 cegar, dejar ciego,-a. 2 *(dazzle)* deslumbrar.
blindfold ['blaɪndfəʊld] *n* venda.
▷ *vt* vendar los ojos a.
▷ *adv* con los ojos vendados.
blinding ['blaɪndɪŋ] *adj* cegador,-ra, deslumbrante.
▷ *n* deslumbramiento.
blindly ['blaɪndlɪ] *adv* ciegamente, a ciegas.
blink [blɪŋk] *n* 1 parpadeo. 2 *(gleam, glimmer)* destello. ■ **on the blink** *fam* averiado,-a.
blinkered ['blɪnkəd] *adj fig* estrecho,-a de miras.
blinkers ['blɪŋkəz] *n pl* anteojeras *fpl*.
bliss [blɪs] *n* felicidad *f*, dicha.
blister ['blɪstəʳ] *n* 1 *(on skin)* ampolla. 2 *(on paint, surface)* burbuja.
▷ *vi* ampollarse, formarse ampollas.
blithe [blaɪð] *adj* 1 *lit* alegre.
blitz [blɪts] *n* bombardeo masivo.
▷ *vt* bombardear.
blizzard ['blɪzəd] *n* tempestad *f* de nieve, ventisca.
bloated ['bləʊtɪd] *adj* hinchado,-a.
blob [blɒb] *n* 1 *(drop)* gota. 2 *(smudge)* borrón *m*. 3 *(of colour)* mancha.
bloc [blɒk] *n* POL bloque *m*.
block [blɒk] *n* 1 bloque *m*. 2 *(of wood, stone)* taco. 3 *(building)* edificio, bloque *m*. 4 *(group of buildings)* manzana. 5 *(obstruction)* obstrucción *f*. ● **block letters** mayúsculas *fpl*. ‖ **block of flats** bloque *m* de pisos. ‖ **note block** taco, bloc *m* de notas.
▷ *vt* 1 *(pipe, etc)* obstruir, atascar. 2 *(streets, etc)* bloquear.
⊙ **to block up** *vt sep (hole, window, door)* tapar.
blockade [blɒ'keɪd] *n* MIL bloqueo.
▷ *vt* bloquear.
blockage ['blɒkɪdʒ] *n* obstrucción *f*, atasco.
blockbuster ['blɒkbʌstəʳ] *n* 1 *fig (novel)* best-séller *m*, éxito de ventas. 2 *fig (film)* película de acción.
bloke [bləʊk] *n* GB *fam* tipo, tío.
blond [blɒnd] *adj* rubio,-a.
Suele escribirse **blonde** cuando se refiere a una mujer.
▷ *n* rubio,-a.
blonde [blɒnd] *adj-n* → **blond**.
blood [blʌd] *n* 1 sangre *f*. 2 *(ancestry)* parentesco, alcurnia. ● **blood cell** glóbulo. ‖ **blood pressure** tensión *f* arterial. ‖ **blood vessel** vaso sanguíneo.
bloodbath ['blʌdbɑːθ] *n* matanza, masacre *f*.
bloodhound ['blʌdhaʊnd] *n* sabueso.
bloodshed ['blʌdʃed] *n* derramamiento de sangre.
bloodshot ['blʌdʃɒt] *adj* inyectado,-a de sangre.
bloodstream ['blʌdstriːm] *n* corriente *f* sanguínea.
bloodthirsty ['blʌdθɜːstɪ] *adj* sanguinario,-a, ávido,-a de sangre.
▲ *comp* **bloodthirstier**, *superl* **bloodthirstiest**.
bloody ['blʌdɪ] *adj* 1 *(battle)* sangriento,-a. 2 *sl (damned)* puñetero,-a, mierda de. ■ **bloody hell!** ¡hostia! ● **Bloody Mary** 1 HIST María Tudor. 2 *(drink)* bloody mary *m (vodka con zumo de tomate)*.
▲ *comp* **bloodier**, *superl* **bloodiest**.
bloody-minded [blʌdɪ'maɪndɪd] *adj* 1 *(stubborn)* tozudo,-a, terco,-a. 2 *(bad-tempered)* de malas pulgas.
bloody-mindedness [blʌdɪ'maɪndɪdnəs] *n* 1 *(bad temper)* mal genio. 2 *(stubbornness)* terquedad *f*.
bloom [bluːm] *n* 1 *(flower)* flor *f*. 2 *(on fruit)* pelusa. 3 *(freshness)* frescura, lozanía.
▷ *vi* florecer.
bloomer ['bluːməʳ] *n* GB *fam* metedura de pata, pifia.
blooming ['bluːmɪŋ] *adj* 1 *(flower)* floreciente. 2 *(radiant)* radiante. 3 *fam* puñetero,-a.
blossom ['blɒsəm] *n* flor *f*.
▷ *vi* florecer. ■ **to be in blossom** florecer. ‖ **to blossom into** *fig* convertirse en.
⊙ **to blossom out** *vi* alcanzar su plenitud.

blot [blɒt] *n (of ink)* borrón *m*; *(on reputation)* mancha.
▷ *vt* 1 *(stain)* manchar. 2 *(dry)* secar.
▲ *pt & pp* **blotted**, *ger* **blotting**.
⊙ **to blot out** *vt sep* 1 *(hide)* ocultar. 2 *(memory)* borrar.
blotch [blɒtʃ] *n* mancha.
▷ *vi* 1 *(become stained)* mancharse. 2 *(skin)* salir manchas.
blotting-paper ['blɒtɪŋpeɪpəʳ] *n* papel *m* secante.
blouse [blaʊz] *n* blusa.
blow[1] [bləʊ] *n* golpe *m*.
blow[2] [bləʊ] *vi* 1 *(wind)* soplar. 2 *(instrument)* tocar, sonar; *(whistle)* pitar. 3 *(fuse)* fundirse. 4 *(tyre)* reventarse. 5 *(puff, pant)* jadear.
▷ *vt fam (money)* despilfarrar, malgastar.
▲ *pt* **blew [blu:]**, *pp* **blown [bləʊn]**.
⊙ **to blow away** *vt sep* 1 arrastrar. 2 *fam fig* mandar al otro barrio.
⊙ **to blow in** *vt sep* derribar.
⊙ **to blow off** *vi (lid, hat)* salir volando.
⊙ **to blow out** *vt sep* 1 *(flame)* apagar; *(candle)* soplar. 2 *(cheeks)* hinchar.
⊙ **to blow over** *vt sep* derribar.
▷ *vi* 1 derrumbarse. 2 *(storm)* amainar.
⊙ **to blow up** *vt sep* 1 *(explode)* (hacer) volar: **they blew up the building** *hicieron volar el edificio*. 2 *(inflate)* hinchar. 3 *(photograph)* ampliar.
▷ *vi* 1 *(explode)* explotar. 2 *(lose one's temper)* salirse de sus casillas.
blowhole ['bləʊhəʊl] *n* 1 *(of whale)* orificio nasal. 2 *(hole, air vent)* respiradero.
blowlamp ['bləʊlæmp] *n* soplete *m*.
blown [bləʊn] *pp* ⟶ **blow**.
blowout ['bləʊaʊt] *n* 1 AUTO reventón *m*, pinchazo. 2 *sl* comilona, atracón *m*.
blowtorch ['bləʊtɔ:tʃ] *n* soplete *m*.
blow-up ['bləʊʌp] *n (photograph)* ampliación *f*.
blubber ['blʌbəʳ] *n* grasa de ballena.
▷ *vi* lloriquear.
bludgeon ['blʌdʒən] *n* cachiporra.
▷ *vt* aporrear.
blue [blu:] *adj* 1 azul. 2 *(sad)* triste. 3 *(depressed)* deprimido,-a. 4 *(obscene)* verde: **a blue joke** *un chiste verde*.
▷ *n* azul *m*: **light/dark blue** *azul claro/oscuro*.
▷ *n pl* **blues** MUS blues *m*.
▷ *n pl* **the blues** la depresión *f*.
bluebell ['blu:bel] *n* BOT campanilla.
blueberry ['blu:bərɪ] *n* BOT arándano.
▲ *pl* **blueberries**.
bluebottle ['blu:bɒtəl] *n* ZOOL moscarda.
blue-collar ['blu:kɒləʳ] *adj* obrero,-a.
blueprint ['blu:prɪnt] *n fig* anteproyecto.
▷ *vt* US *(project, plan)* elaborar, desarrollar.
blues [blu:z] *n pl* ⟶ **blue**.
bluff [blʌf] *adj* 1 *(blunt)* brusco,-a, que no tiene pelos en la lengua. 2 *(hearty)* campechano,-a.
▷ *n (cliff)* acantilado.
blunder ['blʌndəʳ] *n* plancha, metedura de pata.
▷ *vi* meter la pata.
blunt [blʌnt] *adj* 1 *(knife)* desafilado,-a; *(pencil)* despuntado,-a. 2 *fig (person)* directo,-a, que no tiene pelos en la lengua.
▷ *vt* desafilar, embotar; *(pencil)* despuntar. ● **blunt angle** MATH ángulo obtuso.
bluntness ['blʌntnəs] *n* 1 *(of knife, weapon)* embotadura; *(of pencil)* despunte *m*, despuntadura. 2 *fig* brusquedad *f*, franqueza.
blur [blɜ:ʳ] *n* borrón *m*, mancha.
▷ *vt (make indistinct)* difuminar.
▷ *vi* 1 *(mark, stain)* emborronar, manchar. 2 *(become indistinct)* difuminarse.
▲ *pt & pp* **blurred**, *ger* **blurring**.
blurb [blɜ:b] *n fam pej* información *f* publicitaria.
blurred [blɜ:d] *adj* 1 borroso,-a. 2 *fig (memories)* vago,-a, confuso,-a.
blurt [blɜ:t] ■ **to blurt** STH **out** soltar ALGO bruscamente, espetar algo.
blush [blʌʃ] *n* rubor *m*, sonrojo.
▷ *vi* ruborizarse, sonrojarse.
blusher ['blʌʃəʳ] *n* colorete *m*.
blustery ['blʌstərɪ] *adj (windy)* ventoso,-a.
boa ['bəʊə] *n* ZOOL boa.
boar [bɔ:ʳ] *n* ZOOL verraco.
board [bɔ:d] *n* 1 *(piece of wood)* tabla, tablero. 2 *(food)* comida, pensión *f*. 3 *(committee)* junta, consejo. 4 *(company)* compañía: **the gas board** *la compañía del gas*. ● **board of directors** junta directiva. ‖ **board of trade** US cámara de comercio.
▷ *vt (ship, etc)* subirse a, embarcar en. ■ **on board** MAR a bordo. ‖ **to take on board** 1 *(responsibility)* asumir. 2 *(concept, idea)* abarcar. ‖ **to go back to the drawing board** volver a empezar de cero.
▷ *vi (lodge)* alojarse; *(at school)* ser interno,-a. ● **board and lodging** pensión completa.
⊙ **to board up** *vt sep (door, window)* entablar.
boarder ['bɔ:dəʳ] *n* 1 *(gen)* huésped *mf*. 2 *(at school)* interno,-a.
boarding ['bɔ:dɪŋ] *n* 1 *(ship, plane, etc)* embarque *m*. 2 *(lodging)* pensión *f*, alojamiento. ● **boarding card** tarjeta de embarque. ‖ **boarding house** casa de huéspedes. ‖ **boarding school** internado.
boardsailing ['bɔ:dseɪlɪŋ] *n* SP windsurf *m*.
boardwalk ['bɔ:dwɔ:k] *n* US paseo entablado, muelle *m* hecho de tablas de madera.
boast [bəʊst] *n* jactancia.
▷ *vi* jactarse (**about**, de), presumir (**about**, de).
▷ *vt fig* presumir de.
boat [bəʊt] *n* barco, nave *f*; *(small)* bote *m*, barca; *(large)* buque *m*, navío; *(launch)* lancha.
boater ['bəʊtəʳ] *n* canotié *m*.
boatswain ['bəʊsən] *n* contramaestre *m*.
boatyard ['bəʊtjɑ:d] *n* astillero.
bob [bɒb] *n* 1 *(jerking movement)* sacudida; *(bouncing movement)* rebote *m*. 2 *(curtsy)* reverencia.
▷ *vi* 1 *(jerk)* moverse a sacudidas; *(bounce)* rebotar. 2 *(curtsy)* hacer una reverencia.
bobbin ['bɒbɪn] *n (for textiles, wire, etc)* carrete *m*, bobina; *(for lace)* bolillo, palillo.
bobbin-lace ['bɒbɪnleɪs] *n* encaje *m* de bolillos.
bobby ['bɒbɪ] *n* GB *fam* poli *m*.
▲ *pl* **bobbies**.
bobsleigh ['bɒbsleɪ] *n* bobsleigh *m*.
▷ *vi* practicar el bobsleigh.
bode [bəʊd] *pt* ⟶ **bide**.

▷ *vt (foretell)* presagiar, augurar: **her predictions bode no good** *sus predicciones no presagiaban nada bueno.* ■ **to bode ill/well** ser de buen/mal agüero.

bodice ['bɒdɪs] *n* corpiño.

bodily ['bɒdɪlɪ] *adj* físico,-a, corporal.

▷ *adv* **1** *(in person)* físicamente. **2** *(en masse)* como un solo hombre, en pleno.

body ['bɒdɪ] *n* **1** cuerpo. **2** *(corpse)* cadáver *m.* **3** *(organization)* organismo, entidad *f,* ente *m; (association)* agrupación *f.* **4** *(of wine)* cuerpo. **5** *(of people)* grupo, conjunto. **6** AUTO *(of car)* carrocería. **7** AV fuselaje *m.* **8** *(main part)* parte *f* principal, grueso.

▲ *pl* **bodies.**

body-blow ['bɒdɪbləʊ] *n* revés *m.* ■ **to suffer a body-blow** sufrir un revés.

body-building ['bɒdɪbɪldɪŋ] *n* SP culturismo.

bodyguard ['bɒdɪgɑːd] *n* guardaespaldas *m.*

bodywork ['bɒdɪwɜːk] *n* AUTO carrocería.

Boer ['bəʊə] *adj* bóer.

▷ *n* bóer *m.*

bog [bɒg] *n* **1** pantano, cenagal *m.* **2** *sl (toilet)* meódromo.

⊙ **to bog down** *vt sep* atascar.

bogey ['bəʊgɪ] *n* **1** *(spirit)* espíritu *m* maligno; *(goblin)* duende *m.* **2** *sl* moco.

boggle ['bɒgəl] *vi* sobresaltarse, quedarse boquiabierto,-a. ■ **the mind boggles!** ¡alucina!

bogus ['bəʊgəs] *adj* **1** *(fake)* falso,-a, apócrifo,-a. **2** *(fictitious)* ficticio,-a. **3** *(sham)* simulado,-a, fingido,-a.

boil¹ [bɔɪl] *n* MED furúnculo, forúnculo.

boil² [bɔɪl] *vt (liquid)* hervir; *(food)* hervir, cocer; *(egg)* pasar por agua, cocer.

▷ *vi* **1** *(liquid)* hervir; *(food)* hervir, cocerse. **2** *fig (undulate, seethe)* bullir.

⊙ **to boil away** *vi* evaporarse, reducirse.

⊙ **to boil down to** *vt insep fig* reducirse a.

⊙ **to boil over** *vi (liquid)* salirse, rebosar; *(become over-excited)* exaltarse.

boiler ['bɔɪləʳ] *n* **1** caldera. **2** *(fowl)* gallina *(que solo sirve para el caldo).*

boiling ['bɔɪlɪŋ] *adj* hirviendo, hirviente. ● **boiling point** punto de ebullición.

boisterous ['bɔɪstərəs] *adj* **1** *(noisy, rowdy)* bullicioso,-a, alborotador,-ra. **2** *(unruly)* revoltoso,-a. **3** *(exuberant)* exuberante. **4** *(weather)* borrascoso,-a; *(sea)* agitado,-a.

bold [bəʊld] *adj* **1** *(brave)* valiente. **2** *(daring)* audaz, atrevido,-a. **3** *(cheeky)* descarado,-a, fresco,-a. **4** *(vivid)* vivo,-a. **5** *(print)* en negrita.

Bolivia [bə'lɪvɪə] *n* Bolivia.

Bolivian [bə'lɪvɪən] *adj* boliviano,-a.

▷ *n* boliviano,-a.

bollard ['bɒlɑːd] *n* **1** MAR noray *m.* **2** AUTO *(on traffic island, roadside)* poste *m.*

bollocks ['bɒləks] *n pl* **1** *taboo (testicles)* cojones *mpl.* **2** *taboo (nonsense)* gilipolleces *fpl,* chuminadas *fpl.*

Bolshevik ['bɒlʃəvɪk] *adj* POL bolchevique.

▷ *n* POL bolchevique *mf.*

Bolshevist ['bɒlʃəvɪst] *adj-n* → **Bolshevik.**

bolster ['bəʊlstəʳ] *n* **1** *(pillow)* cabezal *m,* travesaño. **2** TECH soporte *m.*

▷ *vt* **1** *(strengthen)* reforzar. **2** *(support)* apoyar.

⊙ **to bolster up** *vt sep (support)* apoyar; *(encourage)* animar, alentar.

bolt [bəʊlt] *n* **1** *(on door, etc)* cerrojo; *(small)* pestillo. **2** *(screw)* perno, tornillo. **3** *(lightning)* rayo.

▷ *vt* **1** *(lock)* cerrar con cerrojo, cerrar con pestillo. **2** *(screw)* sujetar con pernos, sujetar con tornillos. **3** *fam (food)* engullir.

▷ *vi (person)* escaparse; *(horse)* desBocarse.

⊙ **to bolt in** *vt sep (lock in)* encerrar echando el cerrojo.

▷ *vi (rush in)* entrar de golpe.

bolus ['bəʊləs] *n* bolo alimenticio.

bomb [bɒm] *n* **1** bomba. **2** US *(failure)* fracaso.

▷ *vt* MIL bombardear; *(terrorist)* colocar una bomba en.

▷ *vi* US *fam (fail)* fracasar.

⊙ **to bomb along** *vi* ir a toda leche.

⊙ **to bomb out** *vt sep* (hacer) volar la casa.

bombard [bɒm'bɑːd] *vt* **1** bombardear. **2** *fam fig* acosar (**with,** con), asediar (**with,** con).

bombardment [bɒm'bɑːdmənt] *n* bombardeo.

bombastic [bɒm'bæstɪk] *adj* rimbombante, ampuloso,-a.

bomber ['bɒməʳ] *n* **1** MIL bombardero. **2** *(terrorist)* terrorista *mf* que coloca bombas.

bombing ['bɒmɪŋ] *n* **1** MIL bombardeo. **2** *(terrorist act)* atentado con bomba. ● **bombing raid** ataque *m* aéreo.

bombproof ['bɒmpruːf] *adj* a prueba de bombas.

bombshell ['bɒmʃel] *n* **1** *fig* bomba. **2** MIL *(artillery bomb)* obús *m.* **3** *fam (attractive woman)* mujer *f* explosiva.

bona fide [bəʊnə'faɪdɪ] *adj* genuino,-a, auténtico,-a.

bonanza [bə'nænzə] *n* **1** *(prosperity)* prosperidad *f.* **2** *(source of wealth)* mina. **3** *(run of good luck)* buena racha. **4** *(mineral deposit)* bonanza.

▷ *adj* **1** *(prosperous)* próspero,-a. **2** *(productive)* productivo,-a.

bonbon ['bɒnbɒn] *n* caramelo.

bond [bɒnd] *n* **1** *(link)* lazo, vínculo: **bonds of friendship** *vínculos de amistad.* **2** FIN bono, obligación *f.* **3** JUR fianza. **4** *(agreement)* pacto, compromiso. **5** *(adhesion)* unión *f.*

▷ *vt* **1** *(stick, join)* pegar, unir. **2** *(deposit in customs)* depositar.

▷ *vi (stick, join)* pegarse, unirse.

bondage ['bɒndɪdʒ] *n* esclavitud *f,* servidumbre *f.*

bonded ['bɒndɪd] *adj* **1** *(goods)* en depósito. **2** *(debt)* avalado,-a, garantizado,-a. **3** *(material)* reforzado,-a.

bone [bəʊn] *n* **1** hueso. **2** *(of fish)* espina, raspa; *(of whale)* barba. **3** *(of corset)* ballena. ● **bone marrow** médula ósea.

▷ *vt (meat)* deshuesar; *(fish)* quitar la espina.

▷ *n pl* **bones** *(remains)* huesos *mpl,* restos *mpl* mortales.

⊙ **to bone up on** *vt insep* empollar.

bone-dry [bəʊn'draɪ] *adj* totalmente seco,-a.

bonfire ['bɒnfaɪəʳ] *n* hoguera. ● **bonfire night** GB *la noche del cinco de noviembre; se celebra con hogueras y fuegos artificiales.*

bonkers ['bɒŋkəz] *adj* GB *sl* chalado,-a.

bonnet ['bɒnɪt] *n* **1** *(child's, woman's)* gorro, gorra. **2** *(maid's)* cofia. **3** AUTO capó *m.*

bonus ['bəʊnəs] *n* 1 *(gratuity)* plus *m*, sobresueldo, prima. 2 *(benefit)* beneficio. 3 FIN *(extra dividend)* dividendo extraordinario.
▷ *adj* extra, adicional.
bony ['bəʊnɪ] *adj* 1 *(thin)* esquelético,-a. 2 *(with a lot of bone)* huesudo,-a. 3 *(like bone)* óseo,-a. 4 *(meat)* lleno,-a de huesos; *(fish)* lleno,-a de espinas.
▲ *comp* **bonier**, *superl* **boniest**.
bonze [bɒnz] *n* bonzo.
boo [buː] *n* abucheo.
▷ *vi* abuchear.
▷ *interj* ¡bu!
boob[1] [buːb] *n (mistake)* metedura de pata, plancha.
▷ *vi* meter la pata, hacer una plancha.
boob[2] [buːb] *n fam (breast)* teta.
booby ['buːbɪ] *n* 1 *(person)* bobo,-a. 2 *(bird)* alcatraz *m*.
▲ *pl* **boobies**.
booby-trap ['buːbɪtræp] *vt* colocar una trampa en.
▲ *pt & pp* **booby-trapped**, *ger* **booby-trapping**.
boogie ['buːgɪ] *n fam* bugui *m*.
▷ *vt fam* menear el esqueleto.
book [bʊk] *n* 1 libro. 2 *(of tickets)* taco; *(of matches)* cajetilla. ● **savings book** libreta de ahorro.
▷ *vt* 1 *(table, room, holiday)* reservar; *(entertainer, speaker)* contratar. 2 *(police)* multar; *(football)* advertir, amonestar. ■ **to be booked up** 1 *(hotel, restaurant)* estar completo. ▮ **to go by the book** *fig* proceder según las reglas. ▮ **in my book** *fig* a mi parecer.
▷ *n pl* **books** COMM libros *mpl*, cuentas *fpl*.
⊙ **to book in** *vt sep (in hotel)* hacer la reserva.
▷ *vi* registrarse.
bookcase ['bʊkkeɪs] *n* librería, estantería.
booking ['bʊkɪŋ] *n (table, room, holiday)* reserva, reservación *f*; *(entertainer, speaker)* contratación *f*. ● **booking office** taquilla.
bookkeeping ['bʊkkiːpɪŋ] *n* contabilidad *f*, teneduría de libros.
bookmaker ['bʊkmeɪkə[r]] *n* GB corredor,-ra de apuestas.
bookmark ['bʊkmɑːk] *n (for book)* punto de libro; *(electronic)* marcador.
▷ *vt (electronically)* poner un marcador, agregar un marcador.
bookseller ['bʊkselə[r]] *n* librero,-a.
bookshelf ['bʊkʃelf] *n* estante *m* para libros.
▲ *pl* **bookshelves**.
▷ *n pl* **bookshelves** estantería.
bookshop ['bʊkʃɒp] *n* librería.
bookstall ['bʊkstɔːl] *n* 1 *(stand selling books)* puesto de libros. 2 *(newsagent's)* quiosco, puesto de periódicos.
bookstand ['bʊkstænd] *n* 1 *(stall)* quiosco, puesto de periódicos. 2 *(bookrest)* atril *m*.
bookstore ['bʊkstɔː[r]] *n* US librería.
bookworm ['bʊkwɜːm] *n fig* ratón *m* de biblioteca.
boom[1] [buːm] *n (noise)* estampido, retumbo.
▷ *vi* tronar, retumbar.
▷ *interj* ¡bum!
▷ *vi* **to boom / boom out** *(voice)* resonar.
boom[2] [buːm] *n* 1 MAR botalón *m*. 2 *(of microphone)* jirafa. 3 *(of crane)* brazo. 4 *(barrier)* barrera.
boom[3] [buːm] *n fig (prosperity, increase)* boom *m*, auge *m*.
▷ *vi (prosper)* estar en auge.
boomerang ['buːməræŋ] *n* 1 bumerán *m*. 2 *fig* resultado contraproducente.
booming ['buːmɪŋ] *adj* 1 *(noisy)* que truena, que retumba. 2 *(voice)* resonante. 3 *(prosperous)* próspero,-a, en auge.
boost [buːst] *n* 1 *(incentive)* incentivo, estímulo. 2 *(promotion)* promoción *f*, fomento. 3 *(increase)* aumento. 4 *(push up)* empujón *m* hacia arriba, empuje *m* hacia arriba.
▷ *vt* 1 *(create an incentive)* incentivar, estimular. 2 *(promote)* promocionar, fomentar. 3 *(increase)* aumentar. 4 *(push up)* empujar hacia arriba. 5 ELEC aumentar el voltaje. 6 *(morale)* levantar.
booster ['buːstə[r]] *n* 1 ELEC elevador *m* de voltaje. 2 RAD repetidor *m*. 3 TECH motor *m* auxiliar de propulsión. ● **booster injection** MED revacunación *f*.
boot [buːt] *n* 1 *(footwear)* bota. 2 GB *(of car)* maletero, portaequipajes *m*. 3 *(kick)* patada.
▷ *vt* 1 *(kick)* dar una patada a. 2 COMPUT cargar el sistema operativo.
⊙ **to boot out** *vt sep* echar, echar a patadas.
bootblack ['buːtblæk] *n* US limpiabotas *m*, AM lustrabotas *m*.
booth [buːð] *n* 1 cabina. 2 *(at fair)* puesto. ● **telephone booth** locutorio.
bootleg ['buːtleg] *n (illegal recording)* grabación *f* pirata.
▷ *adj (alcohol)* de contrabando; *(recording)* pirata, ilegal.
bootlegger ['buːtlegə[r]] *n* contrabandista *mf* de licores.
booty ['buːtɪ] *n* botín *m*.
▲ *pl* **booties**.
booze [buːz] *n fam* trinque *m*, alcohol *m*.
▷ *vi fam* mamar.
bop [bɒp] *n* 1 *fam (dance)* baile *m*. 2 *fam (thump)* cachete *m*.
▷ *vi fam (dance)* bailar.
▲ *pt & pp* **bopped**, *ger* **bopping**.
boracic ['bəræsɪk] *adj* CHEM bórico,-a. ● **boracic acid** ácido bórico.
Bordeaux [bɔː'dəʊ] *n* 1 Burdeos. 2 *(wine)* vino de Burdeos.
border ['bɔːdə[r]] *n* 1 *(of country)* frontera. 2 *(edge)* borde *m*. 3 *(in sewing)* ribete *m*, orla. 4 *(of flowers, plants)* arriate *m*.
▷ *adj* fronterizo,-a: **border town** *pueblo fronterizo*.
▷ *vt (sew)* ribetear, orlar.
⊙ **to border on** *vt insep* 1 lindar con. 2 *fig* rayar en.
borderline ['bɔːdəlaɪn] *n* línea de demarcación.
▷ *adj* 1 fronterizo,-a. 2 *fig* incierto,-a, dudoso,-a: **a borderline case** *un caso dudoso*.
bore[1] [bɔː[r]] *pt* → **bear**.
bore[2] [bɔː[r]] *n* 1 *(of gun)* ánima, alma; *(calibre)* calibre *m*. 2 *(hole)* taladro.
▷ *vt (perforate)* perforar, taladrar, horadar.
▷ *vi* perforar, taladrar, horadar.
bore[3] [bɔː[r]] *n (person)* pelmazo,-a, pesado,-a, plasta *mf*; *(thing)* lata, rollo, tostón *m*.
▷ *vt* aburrir, fastidiar.
bored [bɔːd] *adj* aburrido,-a. ■ **to get bored** aburrirse.
boredom ['bɔːdəm] *n* aburrimiento.
borer ['bɔːrə[r]] *n* 1 *(tool)* taladro, barrena. 2 *(machine)* taladradora. 3 ZOOL barrenillo.

boric ['bɔːrɪk] *adj* CHEM bórico,-a. ● **boric acid** ácido bórico.
boring ['bɔːrɪŋ] *adj* aburrido,-a.
born [bɔːn] *adj* nato,-a: **she's a born leader** *es una líder nata.* ■ **to be born** nacer.
born-again ['bɔːnəgen] *adj* renacido,-a.
borne [bɔːn] *pp* ⟶ **bear** ².
borough ['bʌrə] *n* **1** *(district)* barrio, distrito. **2** *(town, city)* ciudad *f*. **3** *(municipality)* municipio.
borrow ['bɒrəʊ] *vt* **1** pedir prestado,-a, tomar prestado,-a: **can I borrow your pen?** *¿me dejas tu boli?;* **you can borrow it if you like** *te lo presto si quieres.* **2** *(appropriate, plagiarize)* apropiarse de, plagiar.
borstal ['bɔːstəl] *n* reformatorio, correccional *m* de menores.
Bosnia ['bɒznɪə] *n* Bosnia.
Bosnian ['bɒznɪən] *adj* bosnio,-a.
▷ *n* bosnio,-a.
bosom ['bʊzəm] *n* **1** pecho. **2** *(centre)* seno: **in the bosom of the family** *en el seno de la familia.* ● **bosom friend** amigo,-a del alma.
Bosphorus ['bɒsfərəs] *n* Bósforo.
boss [bɒs] *n* **1** jefe,-a. **2** *(of criminal organization)* capo.
⊙ **to boss around** *vt sep* mangonear.
bossy ['bɒsɪ] *adj* mandón,-ona.
▲ *comp* **bossier**, *superl* **bossiest**.
bosun ['bəʊsən] *n* MAR contramaestre *m*.
botanic [bə'tænɪk] *adj* botánico,-a.
botanical [bə'tænɪkəl] *adj* botánico,-a. ● **botanical gardens** jardín *m* botánico.
botany ['bɒtənɪ] *n* botánica.
botch [bɒtʃ] *n* chapuza.
▷ *vt* [Also **to botch up**.] *(bungle)* pifiarla, fastidiarla.
both [bəʊθ] *adj* ambos,-as, los dos, las dos.
▷ *pron* ambos,-as, los dos, las dos: **both of us** *nosotros,-as dos;* **both of you** *vosotros,-as dos;* **both of them** *los dos, las dos, ambos,-as.*
▷ *adv* a la vez: **it's both cheap and good** *es bueno y barato a la vez.* ■ **both ... and** tanto ... como: **both she and her sister are teachers** *tanto ella como su hermana son profesoras.*
bother ['bɒðəʳ] *n* **1** *(nuisance)* molestia, fastidio. **2** *(problems)* problemas *mpl*.
▷ *vt* **1** *(be a nuisance)* molestar, fastidiar. **2** *(worry)* preocupar.
▷ *vi* **1** *(take trouble)* molestarse, tomar la molestia. **2** *(worry)* preocuparse.
⊙ **to bother about** *vt insep (worry)* preocuparse por: **don't bother about me, I'm all right** *no te preocupes por mí, estoy bien.*
bothersome ['bɒðəsəm] *adj* fastidioso,-a, latoso,-a.
Botswana [bɒt'swɑːnə] *n* Botsuana.
Botswanan [bɒt'swɑːnən] *adj* botsuanés,-esa, botsuano,-a.
▷ *n* botsuanés,-esa, bostuano,-a.
bottle ['bɒtəl] *n* **1** botella; *(small)* frasco; *(for baby)* biberón *m*; *(for gas)* bombona. **2** *sl (nerve)* agallas *fpl*.
▷ *vt (wine, etc)* embotellar; *(fruit)* envasar.
⊙ **to bottle out** *vi* dar marcha atrás, acobardarse.
⊙ **to bottle up** *vt sep* reprimir.
bottle-bank ['bɒtəlbæŋk] *n* contenedor *m* para la recogida de vidrio usado.
bottled ['bɒtəld] *adj (wine, etc)* embotellado,-a; *(fruit)* envasado,-a. ● **bottled gas** gas *m* butano.
bottom ['bɒtəm] *n* **1** *(of sea, box, garden, street, etc)* fondo; *(of bottle)* culo; *(of hill, steps, page)* pie *m*; *(of ship)* quilla. **2** *(of dress)* bajo; *(of trousers)* bajos *mpl*. **3** *(buttocks)* trasero, culo. **4** *(last)* último,-a. **5** *(underneath)* parte *f* inferior, parte *f* de abajo.
▷ *adj* **1** *(position)* de abajo. **2** *(number, result)* más bajo,-a.
▷ *vt* **1** *(chair)* poner fondo a. **2** *(ship)* hacer tocar fondo.
▷ *vi (ship)* tocar fondo.
⊙ **to bottom on** *vt insep (theory, argument)* basarse en.
⊙ **to bottom out** *vi (economy)* tocar fondo.
bottomless ['bɒtəmləs] *adj* sin fondo, insondable.
boudoir ['buːdwɑːʳ] *n* tocador *m*.
bough [baʊ] *n* rama.
bought [bɔːt] *pt & pp* ⟶ **buy**.
bouillon ['buːjɒn] *n* CULIN caldo.
boulder ['bəʊldəʳ] *n* canto rodado.
boulevard ['buːləvɑːd] *n* bulevar *m*.
bounce [baʊns] *n* **1** *(of ball)* bote *m*. **2** *fig (energy)* vitalidad *f*.
▷ *vi (ball)* rebotar, botar.
▷ *vt* **1** *(cheque)* ser rechazado por el banco. **2** *(ball)* hacer botar.
⊙ **to bounce back** *vi fig* recuperarse.
bouncer ['baʊnsəʳ] *n sl* gorila *m*.
bouncing ['baʊnsɪŋ] *adj* **1** *(strong)* fuerte, robusto,-a. **2** *(healthy)* sano,-a. **3** *(boisterous)* bullicioso,-a. ■ **to be bouncing with health** rebosar de salud.
bound[1] [baʊnd] *pt & pp* ⟶ **bind**.
▷ *adj* **1** *(tied)* atado,-a. **2** *(forced)* obligado,-a. **3** *(book)* encuadernado,-a. ■ **to be bound to** ser seguro que. ‖ **to be bound by contract** estar obligado,-a por contrato.
bound[2] [baʊnd] *adj (destined)* destinado,-a: **he knew he was bound to succeed** *sabía que estaba destinado a tener éxito.* ■ **to be bound for** ir con destino, navegar con rumbo a. ‖ **-bound** con rumbo a: **Paris-bound** *con rumbo a París.*
bound[3] [baʊnd] *n (jump)* salto, brinco.
▷ *vi* saltar.
⊙ **to bound about** *vi* dar saltos, brincar.
bound[4] [baʊnd] *vt (mark the boundary)* delimitar: **the Roman wall bounds the old quarter** *la muralla romana delimita el casco antiguo.*
boundary ['baʊndərɪ] *n* límite *m*, frontera. ● **boundary stone** hito, mojón *m*.
▲ *pl* **boundaries**.
boundless ['baʊndləs] *adj* sin límites, ilimitado,-a.
bounds [baʊndz] *n pl (border)* frontera; *(boundary)* límites *mpl*. ■ **out of bounds** fuera de los límites, en zona prohibida. ‖ **beyond the bounds of possibility** más allá de los límites de la posibilidad.
bounty ['baʊntɪ] *n* **1** *(generosity)* generosidad *f*. **2** *(reward)* prima. **3** *(gift)* regalo.
▲ *pl* **bounties**.
bouquet [buː'keɪ] *n* **1** *(flowers)* ramo. **2** *(wine)* aroma *m*, buqué *m*. **3** *(compliment)* cumplido.
bourbon ['bɜːbən] *n* bourbon *m*.
Bourbon ['bʊəbən] *n* Borbón *m*.
▷ *adj* Borbónico,-a.
bourgeois ['bʊəʒwɑːʳ] *adj* burgués,-esa.
▷ *n* burgués,-esa.

bourgeoisie [bʊəʒwɑːˈziː] *n* burguesía.
bout [baʊt] *n* **1** *(period)* rato. **2** MED *(of flu, measles, etc)* ataque *m*. **3** *(boxing)* encuentro, combate.
boutique [buːˈtiːk] *n* boutique *f*, tienda.
bovine [ˈbəʊvaɪn] *adj* **1** bovino,-a, vacuno,-a. **2** *fig (dim, stupid)* torpe, lerdo,-a.
▷ *n* bovino.
bow¹ [bəʊ] *n* **1** *(for arrows)* arco. **2** *(of violin)* arco. **3** *(knot)* lazo. ● **bow saw** sierra de arco.
▷ *vt (cause to bend)* arquear, doblar.
▷ *vi* **1** *(violin)* pasar el arco (por las cuerdas). **2** *(wall)* arquearse, combarse.
bow² [baʊ] *n* MAR proa. ■ **a shot across the bows** un aviso.
bow³ [baʊ] *n (with body)* reverencia.
▷ *vt* inclinar: **he bowed his head** *inclinó la cabeza.*
▷ *vi* **to bow to** *fig (submit)* someterse a.
⊙ **to bow out** *vi (withdraw)* retirarse: **he bowed out of the championship** *se retiró del campeonato.*
bowed [baʊd] *adj* encorvado,-a.
bowel [ˈbaʊəl] *n* intestino. ● **bowel movement** evacuación *f* intestinal.
▷ *n pl* **bowels** *(entrails)* entrañas *fpl*. ■ **the bowels of the earth** las entrañas de la tierra.
bowl¹ [bəʊl] *n* **1** *(for food, etc)* cuenco, fuente *f*, bol *m*; *(large drinking bowl)* tazón *m*. **2** *(for washing)* palangana, barreño. **3** *(of toilet)* taza. **4** *(of pipe)* cazoleta. **5** *(of spoon)* cuenco. **6** US *(amphitheatre)* anfiteatro.
bowl² [bəʊl] *n (ball)* bocha.
▷ *vi (cricket)* lanzar la pelota.
⊙ **to bowl along** *vt insep* circular.
⊙ **to bowl over** *vt sep* dejar pasmado,-a.
bow-legged [bəʊˈlegd, bəʊˈlegɪd] *adj* patizambo,-a.
bowler¹ [ˈbəʊləʳ] *n (hat)* bombín *m*.
bowler² [ˈbəʊləʳ] *n* **1** *(cricket)* lanzador,-ra. **2** *(bowls player)* jugador,-ra de bochas.
bowling [ˈbəʊlɪŋ] *n (ten-pin)* bolos *mpl*; *(bowls)* las bochas. ■ **to go bowling** *(tenpin)* jugar a los bolos. ● **bowling alley** bolera.
bowls [bəʊlz] *n pl (game)* los bolos. ■ **to play bowls** jugar a los bolos.
bow-tie [bəʊˈtaɪ] *n* pajarita.
box¹ [bɒks] *n* **1** caja; *(large)* cajón *m*. **2** *(of matches)* cajetilla. **3** THEAT palco. **4** *(for sentry)* garita. **5** *(of coach)* pescante *m*. **6** GB *fam (telly)* tele *f*. **7** *(in baseball - pitcher's)* puesto del lanzador; *(- batter's)* puesto del bateador,-a; *(in football)* área de penalti. ● **box number** número de apartado de correos. | **box office** taquilla. | **post-office box** apartado de correos.
▷ *vt* meter en cajas, encajonar.
⊙ **to box in** *vt sep fig (vehicle)* bloquear la salida, impedir la salida.
box² [bɒks] *vi* boxear.
boxcar [ˈbɒkskɑːʳ] *n* US furgón *m*.
boxer [ˈbɒksəʳ] *n* **1** boxeador,-ra. **2** *(dog)* bóxer *m*.
boxing [ˈbɒksɪŋ] *n* boxeo. ● **Boxing Day** GB *el día 26 de diciembre.* | **boxing gloves** guantes *mpl* de boxeo. | **boxing ring** ring *m*.
box-office [ˈbɒksɒfɪs] *adj* taquillero,-a, de taquilla: **his last film was a box-office success** *su última película fue un éxito de taquilla.*
boxroom [ˈbɒksruːm] *n* GB trastero.
boy [bɔɪ] *n (baby)* niño; *(child)* chico, muchacho; *(youth)* joven *m*.
boyar [ˈbəʊjə] *n* boyardo.
boycott [ˈbɔɪkɒt] *n* boicoteo, boicot *m*.
▷ *vt* boicotear.
boyfriend [ˈbɔɪfrend] *n* **1** *(fiancé)* novio. **2** *(male friend)* amigo.
boyhood [ˈbɔɪhʊd] *n* infancia, niñez *f*.
▷ *adj* de la infancia.
bra [brɑː] *n* sostén *m*, sujetador *m*.
brace [breɪs] *n* **1** *(clamp)* abrazadera. **2** ARCH *(support)* riostra. **3** *(drill)* berbiquí *m*. **4** *(on teeth)* aparato. **5** [*pl* brace] *(pair of game)* par *m*: **a brace of pheasants** *un par de faisanes.* **6** MAR braza. **7** MUS corchete *m*.
▲ *pl* **braces**.
▷ *vt* **1** *(fasten tightly)* tensar. **2** *(make steady)* estabilizar. **3** ARCH reforzar. **4** MAR *(rope, sail)* bracear. **5** *(invigorate)* dar vigor, tonificar.
▷ *n pl* **braces** tirantes *mpl*.
bracelet [ˈbreɪslət] *n* **1** pulsera, brazalete *m*. **2** *(armband)* brazalete *m*.
▷ *n pl* **bracelets** *sl (handcuffs)* esposas *fpl*.
bracing [ˈbreɪsɪŋ] *adj (wind, weather)* tonificante, vigorizador,-ra.
bracken [ˈbrækən] *n* BOT helechos *mpl*.
bracket [ˈbrækɪt] *n* **1** *(round)* paréntesis *m*. **2** *(for shelf)* escuadra, soporte *m*. **3** *(group, category)* grupo, categoría *m*. ● **square bracket** corchete *m*.
▷ *vt* **1** *(put in brackets)* poner entre paréntesis. **2** *(classify)* clasificar. **3** *(group together)* agrupar.
brackishness [ˈbrækɪʃnəs] *n* salobridad *f*.
brag [bræg] *n* jactancia, fanfarria.
▷ *vi* jactarse (**about**, de).
▲ *pt & pp* **bragged**, *ger* **bragging**.
braggart [ˈbrægət] *n* fanfarrón,-ona.
braid [breɪd] *n* **1** *(on clothing)* galón *m*. **2** *(plait)* trenza.
▷ *vt* **1** *(clothing)* galonear. **2** *(plait hair)* trenzar.
Braille [breɪl] *n* braille *m*.
brain [breɪn] *n (organ)* cerebro, seso.
▷ *n pl* **brains** **1** *(intellect)* cerebro, seso, inteligencia. **2** *(as food)* sesos *mpl*. ■ **to have brains** ser un cerebro, ser inteligente. | **to have** STH **on the brain** estar obsesionado,-a con algo. ● **brain cell** célula cerebral. | **brain death** muerte *f* cerebral. | **brain drain** fuga de cerebros. | **brain scan** electroencefalograma *m*. | **brain scanner** escáner *m* cerebral. | **brain tumour** tumor *m* cerebral.
brainchild [ˈbreɪntʃaɪld] *n (idea, invention, plan)* (propia) idea, (propio) invento, (propio) proyecto: **the new road network was his brainchild** *la nueva red de carreteras fue su (propia) idea.*
▲ *pl* **brainchildren** [ˈbreɪntʃɪldrən].
brain-dead [ˈbreɪnded] *adj* clínicamente muerto,-a.
brainpower [ˈbreɪnpaʊəʳ] *n* capacidad *f* intelectual.
brainstorm [ˈbreɪnstɔːm] *n* **1** *(violent outburst)* telele *m*, ataque *m*, patatús *m*. **2** *(mental confusion)* cacao mental, empanada mental. **3** US *(brainwave)* idea genial. **4** *(brainstorming)* reunión *f* creativa.
brainstorming [ˈbreɪnstɔːmɪŋ] *n* reunión *f* creativa, lluvia de ideas.
brainwash [ˈbreɪnwɒʃ] *vt* lavar el cerebro a, comer el coco a.
brainwork [ˈbreɪnwɜːk] *n* trabajo intelectual.

brainy ['breɪnɪ] *adj fam* inteligente, sesudo,-a.
▲ *comp* **brainier**, *superl* **brainiest**.
braise [breɪz] *vt* CULIN freír y luego cocer a fuego lento.
brake¹ [breɪk] *n* freno. ● **brake arm** palanca del freno. ▮ **brake block** pastilla de freno. ▮ **brake fluid** líquido de freno.
▷ *vt* frenar, hacer frenar.
brake² [breɪk] *n (estate car)* furgoneta.
bramble ['bræmbəl] *n* BOT zarzamora, mora. ● **bramble bush** zarza.
bran [bræn] *n* salvado.
branch [brɑːntʃ] *n* **1** *(tree)* rama. **2** *(of family)* ramo. **3** *(road, railway)* ramal *m*; *(stream, river)* brazo. **4** *(of shop)* sucursal *f*; *(of bank)* oficina, sucursal *f*. **5** *(field of science, etc)* ramo. **6** *(of candelabra)* brazo.
▷ *vi (road)* bifurcarse.
⊙ **to branch off** *vi* salir de la carretera.
⊙ **to branch out** *vi* extender su campo de interés.
branchial ['bræŋkɪəl] *adj* branquial.
brand [brænd] *n* **1** marca. **2** *(type)* clase *f*, tipo. **3** *(for livestock)* hierro de marcar. **4** *(piece of burning wood)* tea.
▷ *vt (livestock)* marcar con un hierro candente. ■ **to brand** STH **as** STH calificar ALGO de ALGO.
brandish ['brændɪʃ] *vt* blandir.
brand-new [bræn'njuː] *adj* flamante, de estreno.
brandy ['brændɪ] *n* coñac *m*, brandy *m*.
▲ *pl* **brandies**.
brash [bræʃ] *adj* **1** *pej (ostentatious, showy)* ostentoso,-a. **2** *(hasty, thoughtless)* irreflexivo,-a. **3** *(imprudent)* imprudente.
brass [brɑːs] *n* **1** latón *m*. **2** *sl (money)* pasta. **3** MUS metales *mpl*.
▷ *adj* de cobre.
brassiere ['bræzɪəʳ] *n* sujetador *m*, sostén *m*.
brat [bræt] *n fam pej* mocoso,-a.
bravado [brəv'ɑːdəʊ] *n* baladronada, fanfarronada.
brave [breɪv] *adj* valiente.
▷ *n* guerrero indio.
▷ *vt* **1** *(defy)* desafiar. **2** *(confront)* afrontar, hacer frente a.
bravery ['breɪvərɪ] *n* valentía.
bravo [brɑː'vəʊ] *interj* ¡bravo!
brawl [brɔːl] *n* reyerta, pelea.
▷ *vi* pelearse.
brawn [brɔːn] *n* **1** *(muscular strength)* fuerza muscular. **2** *(muscle)* músculo. **3** CULIN carne *f* de cabeza de cerdo en gelatina.
bray [breɪ] *vi* **1** *(donkey, ass)* rebuznar. **2** *(laugh)* carcajearse.
braying ['breɪɪŋ] *n* **1** rebuzno. **2** *(harsh laugh)* carcajada.
brazen ['breɪzən] *adj* desvergonzado,-a, descarado,-a.
Brazil [brə'zɪl] *n* Brasil. ● **Brazil nut** BOT nuez *f* del Brasil.
Brazilian [brə'zɪlɪən] *adj* brasileño,-a.
▷ *n* brasileño,-a.
breach [briːtʃ] *n* **1** *(opening)* brecha, abertura. **2** *(in promise, undertaking)* incumplimiento; *(in law)* violación *f*, infracción *f*. **3** *(in relationship)* ruptura. ● **breach of faith / breach of trust** abuso de confianza. ▮ **breach of promise** incumplimiento de una promesa.
▷ *vt* **1** *(break a hole)* romper. **2** JUR violar, infringir.
bread [bred] *n* **1** pan *m*. ■ **to be on bread and water** estar a pan y agua. ▮ **to earn one's bread and butter** ganarse el pan. ● **wholemeal bread** pan *m* integral.
bread-and-butter ['bredənbʌtəʳ] *adj (commonplace)* rutinario,-a, corriente y moliente. ● **a bread-and-butter letter** carta de agradecimiento.
breadline ['bredlaɪn] *n* US *cola para recibir alimentos gratuitos*. ■ **to live on the breadline** vivir en la miseria.
breadth [bredθ] *n* **1** *(broadness)* ancho, anchura. **2** *(space)* extensión *f*, amplitud *f*. ● **breadth of mind** generosidad *f* de espíritu.
breadthwise ['bredθwaɪz] *adv* a lo ancho.
break [breɪk] *n* **1** *(in leg, etc)* rotura. **2** *(in relationship)* ruptura. **3** *(in meeting)* descanso, pausa; *(at school)* recreo.
▷ *vt* **1** romper. **2** *(record)* batir. **3** *(promise, word)* faltar a.
▷ *vi* **1** romperse. **2** *(storm)* estallar. ■ **to give** SB **a break** dar una oportunidad a algn. ▮ **to take a break** tomarse una pausa, tomarse un descanso. ▮ **without a break** sin descansar, sin parar. ▮ **at break of day** al amanecer.
▲ *pt* **broke** [brəʊk], *pp* **broken** ['brəʊkən].
⊙ **to break away** *vi (escape)* escaparse, darse a la fuga; *(leave family, job)* irse.
⊙ **to break down** *vt sep* **1** *(door)* derribar, echar abajo. **2** *(resistance)* vencer.
▷ *vi* **1** *(car)* averiarse; *(driver)* tener una avería. **2** *(burst into tears)* romper a llorar. **3** *(talks, negotiations)* fracasar.
⊙ **to break in** *vi (force entry)* entrar por la fuerza.
⊙ **to break off** *vt sep* **1** *(relationship)* romper. **2** *(discussions, negotiations)* interrumpir.
⊙ **to break out** *vi* **1** *(prisoners)* escaparse. **2** *(war, fire, etc)* estallar.
⊙ **to break through** *vt insep (obstacle, fence)* atravesar, abrirse paso por.
⊙ **to break up** *vt sep (chair, table, etc)* romper; *(ship, boat)* desguazar.
▷ *vi* **1** *(couple)* separarse. **2** *(gathering, meeting)* disolverse. **3** *(school)* empezar las vacaciones.
breakable ['breɪkəbəl] *adj* frágil, rompible.
breakage ['breɪkɪdʒ] *n* rotura.
breakdown ['breɪkdaʊn] *n* **1** *(of car, machine)* avería. **2** MED crisis *f* nerviosa. **3** *(in negotiations)* ruptura. **4** *(chemical analysis)* análisis *m*. **5** *(in negotiations)* fracaso. ● **breakdown service** (servicio de) asistencia en carretera. ▮ **breakdown van / breakdown truck** grúa.
breaker ['breɪkəʳ] *n* **1** MAR *(heavy wave)* cachón *m*. **2** *(of horse)* domador,-ra. **3** *(of cars, materials) persona que trabaja en un desguace*. ● **breaker's yard** desguace *m*.
breakfast ['brekfəst] *n* desayuno.
▷ *vi* desayunar. ● **to have breakfast** desayunar.
break-in ['breɪkɪn] *n* entrada forzada.
breaking ['breɪkɪŋ] *n* **1** *(of leg, object)* rotura. **2** *(of relationship)* ruptura. ● **breaking point** punto de ruptura. ▮ **breaking and entering** JUR allanamiento de domicilio.
break-out ['breɪkaʊt] *n (from prison)* fuga.
breakthrough ['breɪkθruː] *n* avance *m* importante.
break-up ['breɪkʌp] *n (of relationship, negotiations)* ruptura; *(of couple)* separación *f*.
breakwater ['breɪkwɔːtəʳ] *n* rompeolas *m*.
bream [briːm] *n (river fish)* brema. ● **Couch's sea bream** pagro, pargo. ▮ **gilt-head bream** dorada. ▮ **red bream** besugo. ▮ **two-banded bream** mojarra.
breast [brest] *n* **1** *(chest)* pecho; *(of woman)* pecho, seno. **2** *(of chicken, etc)* pechuga.
breastbone ['brestbəʊn] *n* ANAT esternón *m*.

breast-fed ['brestfed] *adj* amamantado,-a, criado,-a a pecho.
breast-feed ['brestfi:d] *vt* amamantar, dar el pecho a.
▲ *pt & pp* breast-fed ['brestfed].
breaststroke ['breststrəʊk] *n (swimming)* braza.
breath [breθ] *n* **1** *(of person)* aliento. **2** *(of air)* soplo. **3** *(breathing)* resuello, respiración *f*. ■ **out of breath** sin aliento. ‖ **to take a deep breath** respirar hondo. ‖ **to take one's breath away** dejar pasmado,-a a uno. ● **breath test** GB prueba del alcohol.
breathalyser® [breθəlaɪzəʳ] *n* alcoholímetro.
breathe [bri:ð] *vt (air, etc)* respirar.
▷ *vi* **1** *(air, etc)* respirar. **2** *(be alive)* respirar, vivir: **is he still breathing?** *¿respira aún?* ■ **to breathe in** aspirar. ‖ **to breathe out** espirar.
breathing ['bri:ðɪŋ] *n* respiración *f*.
breathtaking ['breθteɪkɪŋ] *adj* **1** *(amazing)* impresionante. **2** *(exciting)* emocionante.
bred [bred] *pt & pp* → **breed**.
breeches ['brɪtʃɪz] *n pl* **1** *(knee-length trousers)* calzones *mpl*. **2** *fam (trousers)* pantalones *mpl*. ● **riding breeches** pantalones *mpl* de montar.
breed [bri:d] *n (of animal)* raza; *(of plant)* variedad *f*.
▷ *vt* **1** *(animals)* criar. **2** *fig (cause)* engendrar, resultar en.
▷ *vi* **1** *(animals)* reproducirse. **2** *(disease)* propagarse, difundirse.
▲ *pt & pp* bred [bred].
breeder ['bri:dəʳ] *n* **1** *(of animals)* criador,-ra; *(of cattle)* ganadero,-a. **2** *(animal)* animal *m* criadero.
breeding ['bri:dɪŋ] *n* **1** *(of animals)* cría; *(of plants)* propagación *f*. **2** *(social background)* clase *f*; *(manners)* modales *mpl*.
breeze [bri:z] *n* METEOR brisa.
breezy ['bri:zɪ] *adj* METEOR ventoso,-a.
▲ *comp* breezier, *superl* breeziest.
brevity ['brevɪtɪ] *n fml* brevedad *f*.
brew [bru:] *n* **1** *(tea, etc)* infusión *f*. **2** *(potion)* brebaje *m*.
▷ *vt* **1** *(beer)* elaborar. **2** *(tea, etc)* preparar.
▷ *vi* **1** *(tea, etc)* reposar. **2** *(storm)* prepararse, acercarse.
brewer ['brʊəʳ] *n* fabricante *mf* de cerveza, cervecero,-a. ● **brewer's yeast** levadura de cerveza.
brewery ['brʊərɪ] *n* fábrica de cerveza, cervecería.
▲ *pl* breweries.
brewing ['brʊɪŋ] *n* elaboración *f* de cerveza.
briar ['braɪəʳ] *n* BOT *(heather)* brezo.
bribe [braɪb] *n* soborno.
▷ *vt* sobornar.
bribery ['braɪbərɪ] *n* soborno.
bric-a-brac ['brɪkəbræk] *n* baratijas *fpl*.
brick [brɪk] *n* **1** ladrillo. **2** *(toy)* cubo (de madera). **3** *fam fig (person)* buena persona.
▷ *vt* enladrillar.
bricklayer ['brɪkleɪəʳ] *n* albañil *m*.
brickwork ['brɪkwɜ:k] *n* enladrillado.
bridal ['braɪdəl] *adj* nupcial. ● **bridal gown** vestido de novia.
bride [braɪd] *n* novia, desposada. ■ **the bride and groom** los novios.
bridegroom ['braɪdgru:m] *n* novio, desposado.
bridesmaid ['braɪdzmeɪd] *n* dama de honor.
bridge [brɪdʒ] *n* **1** puente *m*. **2** *(of nose)* caballete *m*. **3** *(on ship)* puente *m* de mando.
▷ *vt (river)* tender un puente sobre.
bridle ['braɪdəl] *n* brida.
▷ *vt (horse)* embridar.
▷ *vi* mostrar desagrado (**at**, por).
brief [bri:f] *adj (short)* breve; *(concise)* conciso,-a; *(scanty)* diminuto,-a.
▷ *n* **1** *(report)* informe *m*. **2** JUR expediente *m*. **3** MIL instrucciones *fpl*.
▷ *vt* **1** *(inform)* informar (**about**, sobre). **2** *(instruct)* dar instrucciones a.
briefcase ['bri:fkeɪs] *n* maletín *m*, cartera.
briefing ['bri:fɪŋ] *n* reunión *f* informativa, briefing *m*.
briefly ['bri:flɪ] *adv* brevemente.
brigade [brɪ'geɪd] *n* MIL brigada.
▷ *vt* MIL formar una brigada con.
brigadier [brɪgə'dɪəʳ] *n* GB general *m* de brigada.
bright [braɪt] *adj* **1** *(light, eyes, etc)* brillante. **2** METEOR *(sky, day)* claro,-a, despejado,-a; *(sunny)* soleado,-a, de sol. **3** *(colour)* vivo,-a. **4** *(future)* prometedor,-ra. **5** *(clever)* inteligente, listo,-a. **6** *(cheerful)* alegre, animado,-a.
brighten ['braɪtən] *vt (colour)* avivar.
⊙ **to brighten up** *vt sep* **1** METEOR despejar. **2** *(room, house)* dar un aspecto más alegre a. **3** *(enliven)* alegrar, animar.
brightness ['braɪtnəs] *n* **1** *(light)* luminosidad *f*. **2** *(of sun)* resplandor *m*. **3** *(of day)* claridad *f*. **4** *(of colour)* viveza. **5** *(cleverness)* inteligencia.
brilliance ['brɪljəns] *n* brillo, brillantez *f*.
brilliant ['brɪljənt] *adj* **1** *(light)* brillante, reluciente. **2** *(colour)* vivo,-a. **3** *(person)* brillante, genial. **4** *fam* estupendo,-a, fantástico,-a.
brim [brɪm] *n* **1** *(of cup, glass, etc)* borde *m*. **2** *(of hat)* ala.
▷ *vi* rebosar (**with**, de): **he was brimming with pride** *rebosaba de orgullo*.
brimful [brɪm'fʊl] *adj* lleno,-a hasta el borde.
brimstone ['brɪmstəʊn] *n arch (sulphur)* azufre *m*.
brine [braɪn] *n* salmuera.
bring [brɪŋ] *vt* **1** traer. **2** *(lead)* llevar, conducir.
▲ *pt & pp* brought [brɔ:t].
⊙ **to bring about** *vt sep (accident, change, etc)* provocar, causar.
⊙ **to bring along** *vt sep (friend, colleague)* traer.
⊙ **to bring back** *vt sep* **1** *(book, record, etc)* devolver. **2** *(law, legislation)* volver a introducir. **3** *(past experience, childhood, etc)* recordar, hacer recordar.
⊙ **to bring down** *vt sep* **1** *(chair, book, etc)* bajar. **2** *(door, house, government)* derribar. **3** *(prices, temperature)* hacer bajar.
⊙ **to bring forward** *vt sep* **1** *(meeting, appointment)* adelantar. **2** *(theme, question)* presentar, plantear.
⊙ **to bring in** *vt sep* **1** *(person)* hacer pasar. **2** *(coal, food, etc into house)* traer. **3** *(law, legislation)* introducir. **4** *(yield)* rendir, producir. **5** JUR *(verdict)* emitir, pronunciar. **6** *(crowds)* atraer.
⊙ **to bring off** *vt sep (victory, result)* conseguir, lograr.
⊙ **to bring on** *vt sep (illness)* provocar.
⊙ **to bring out** *vt sep* **1** *(record)* sacar al mercado, sacar; *(book)* publicar. **2** *(talents, qualities)* sacar a relucir.
⊙ **to bring round** *vt sep* **1** *(persuade)* persuadir, convencer. **2** *(revive)* hacer volver en sí.

⊙ **to bring through** *vt sep (help survive)* ayudar a sobrevivir.
⊙ **to bring to** *vt sep* hacer volver en sí.
⊙ **to bring up** *vt sep* 1 *(chair, book, etc)* subir. 2 *(child)* criar, educar. 3 *(subject, topic)* plantear. 4 *(vomit)* devolver.
brink [brɪŋk] *n* borde *m*.
brisk [brɪsk] *adj* 1 *(energetic)* enérgico,-a, vigoroso,-a. 2 *(invigorating)* vigorizador,-ra. 3 *(business, trade)* activo,-a.
briskness ['brɪsknəs] *n* 1 *(energy)* energía, vigor *m*. 2 *(of business, trade)* actividad *f*. 3 *(of walk)* ligereza.
bristle ['brɪsəl] *n* cerda.
▷ *vi* 1 *(hair)* erizarse, ponerse de punta. 2 *(show annoyance)* mosquearse.
Britain ['brɪtən] *n* Gran Bretaña. ● **Great Britain** Gran Bretaña.
British ['brɪtɪʃ] *adj* británico,-a.
▷ *n pl* **the British** los británicos *mpl*.
Briton ['brɪtən] *n* británico,-a.
Brittany ['brɪtənɪ] *n* Bretaña.
brittle ['brɪtəl] *adj* quebradizo,-a, frágil.
broach [brəʊtʃ] *n* 1 *(drill bit)* broca. 2 *(roasting-spit)* espetón *m*.
▷ *vt (subject, theme for discussion)* abordar.
broad [brɔːd] *adj* 1 *(street, avenue)* ancho,-a; *(surface, water, plateau)* extenso,-a. 2 *fig (field of study, debate)* amplio,-a. 3 *(measurement)* de ancho. 4 *(general)* general. 5 *(main)* principal. 6 *(explicit)* claro,-a. 7 *(accent)* marcado,-a, cerrado,-a. 8 *(smile)* abierto,-a. 9 *(vowel)* abierto,-a. ● **a broad outline** un esquema general.
broadcast ['brɔːdkɑːst] *n (by TV, radio)* emisión *f*.
▷ *vt* 1 *(by TV, radio)* emitir, transmitir. 2 *(make known)* difundir.
▲ *pt & pp* **broadcast**.
broadcaster ['brɔːdkɑːstəʳ] *n* locutor,-ra, presentador,-ra.
broadcasting ['brɔːdkɑːstɪŋ] *n* 1 RAD radiodifusión *f*. 2 TV transmisión *f*.
broaden ['brɔːdən] *vt* 1 ensanchar. 2 *fig* ampliar. ■ **to broaden one's horizons** ampliar sus perspectivas.
⊙ **to broaden out** *vi* ensancharse.
broadly ['brɔːdlɪ] *adv* en términos generales.
broadly-based ['brɔːdlɪbeɪst] *adj* de base amplia.
broad-minded [brɔːd'maɪndɪd] *adj* liberal, tolerante.
broadness ['brɔːdnəs] *n* 1 anchura. 2 *fig (of accent)* lo marcado, lo cerrado.
broadsheet ['brɔːdʃiːt] *n* periódico de gran formato.
broadsword ['brɔːdsɔːd] *n* sable *m*.
broccoli ['brɒkəlɪ] *n* brécol *m*, brócoli *m*.
brochette [brə'ʃet] *n* pincho, brocheta.
brochure ['brəʊʃəʳ] *n* folleto.
broil [brɔɪl] *vt* US asar a la parrilla.
broiler ['brɔɪləʳ] *n* 1 CULIN pollo. 2 *(gridiron)* parrilla.
broke [brəʊk] *pt* → **break**.
▷ *adj fam* sin un duro, sin blanca.
broken ['brəʊkən] *pp* → **break**.
▷ *adj* 1 *(plate, window, etc)* roto,-a. 2 *(machine)* estropeado,-a. 3 *(bone)* fracturado,-a. 4 *(person)* destrozado,-a. 5 *(health)* quebrantado,-a. 6 *(language)* chapurreado,-a: **he speaks broken Spanish** *chapurrea el español*. 7 *(sleep, pattern)* interrumpido, -a.
broken-down ['brəʊkəndaʊn] *adj* 1 *(vehicle)* estropeado,-a. 2 *(building)* desmoronado,-a. 3 *(person)* destrozado,-a.
broker ['brəʊkəʳ] *n* COMM *(on Stock Exchange)* corredor,-ra, agente *mf* de Bolsa; *(middleman)* intermediario,-a sin riesgo.
brolly ['brɒlɪ] *n* GB *fam* paraguas *m*.
▲ *pl* **brollies**.
bromide ['brəʊmaɪd] *n* CHEM bromuro.
bromine ['brəʊmaɪn] *n* CHEM bromo.
bronchial ['brɒŋkɪəl] *adj* ANAT bronquial. ● **bronchial tubes** ANAT bronquios *mpl*.
bronchitis [brɒŋ'kaɪtəs] *n* MED bronquitis *f*.
bronchus ['brɒŋkəs] *n* bronquio.
▲ *pl* **bronchi** ['brɒŋkaɪ].
brontosaurus [brɒntə'sɔːrəs] *n* brontosaurio.
bronze [brɒnz] *n* 1 *(metal)* bronce *m*. 2 *(statue, sculpture)* talla de bronce. 3 *(colour)* color *m* de bronce. ● **the Bronze Age** HIST la Edad del Bronce.
▷ *vi (get a suntan)* broncearse.
bronzed [brɒnzd] *adj (suntanned)* bronceado,-a.
brooch [brəʊtʃ] *n* broche *m*.
brood [bruːd] *n* 1 *(birds)* nidada. 2 *fam fig (children)* prole *f*.
▷ *vi* 1 *(hen)* empollar. 2 *fig (worry)* apurarse, preocuparse.
⊙ **to brood about** *vt insep* dar vueltas a: **stop brooding about it!** *¡no le des más vueltas!*
⊙ **to brood over** *vt insep* rumiar, reflexionar sobre.
broody ['bruːdɪ] *adj* 1 *(hen)* clueco,-a. 2 *(thoughtful)* pensativo,-a. 3 *(melancholy)* melancólico,-a. 4 *(depressed)* deprimido, a. 5 *fam (woman)* ansiosa de tener un hijo. ● **broody hen** gallina clueca.
▲ *comp* **broodier**, *superl* **broodiest**.
brook [brʊk] *n* arroyo, riachuelo.
broom [bruːm] *n* 1 *(for sweeping)* escoba. 2 BOT hiniesta.
broomstick ['bruːmstɪk] *n* 1 *(handle)* palo de escoba. 2 *(of witch)* escoba.
Bros [brɒs] *abbr* **(Brothers)** Hermanos *mpl*; *(abbreviation)* Hnos: **Jones Bros** *Hnos Jones*.
broth [brɒθ] *n* CULIN caldo.
brothel ['brɒθəl] *n* burdel *m*.
brother ['brʌðəʳ] *n* 1 *(sibling)* hermano. 2 *(member of society, religious order, etc)* hermano. 3 US *fam (friend)* colega *m*, hermano, tío: **what's happening brother?** *¿qué pasa tío?*
brotherhood ['brʌðəhʊd] *n* hermandad *f*, cofradía.
brother-in-law ['brʌðərɪnlɔː] *n* cuñado.
▲ *pl* **brothers-in-law** ['brʌðəzɪnlɔː].
brotherly ['brʌdəlɪ] *adj* fraternal.
brought [brɔːt] *pt & pp* → **bring**.
brow [braʊ] *n* 1 *(eyebrow)* ceja. 2 *(forehead)* frente *f*. 3 *(of hill)* cresta.
browbeat ['braʊbiːt] *vt* intimidar.
▲ *pt* **browbeat**, *pp* **browbeaten** ['braʊbiːtən].
brown [braʊn] *adj* 1 marrón. 2 *(hair, etc)* castaño,-a. 3 *(skin)* moreno,-a.
▷ *n* 1 marrón *m*. 2 *(hair)* castaño. 3 *(skin)* color *m* moreno.
▷ *vi* 1 CULIN quedarse dorado,-a, dorarse. 2 *(tan)* ponerse moreno,-a, broncearse.
⊙ **to brown off** *vt sep fam* fastidiar, molestar.
brownie ['braʊnɪ] *n* US *pastelito de chocolate y nueces*.
Brownie ['braʊnɪ] *n* niña exploradora.

browse [braʊz] *vi* **1** *(grass)* pacer. **2** *(person in shop)* mirar. ■ **to have a browse** *(in shop)* ir a echar un vistazo, entrar para mirar.
⊙ **to browse through** *vt insep (book, magazine)* hojear.
browser ['braʊzəʳ] *n (Internet)* navegador *m*, explorador *m*.
bruise [bruːz] *n* **1** morado, magulladura, contusión *f*. **2** *(on fruit)* magulladura.
▷ *vt* **1** *(body)* magullar, contusionar. **2** *(fruit)* magullar.
▷ *vi* **1** *(body)* magullarse, salirle cardenales. **2** *(fruit)* magullarse.
bruiser ['bruːzəʳ] *n fam* gorila *m*, matón *m*.
brunch [brʌnʃ] *n* brunch *m*, *(desayuno que se toma sobre las doce y sustituye el almuerzo)*.
brunette [bruː'net] *n* morena.
▷ *adj* moreno,-a.
brunt [brʌnt] *n* lo más duro, lo peor.
brush [brʌʃ] *n* **1** *(for teeth, clothes, etc)* cepillo. **2** *(artist's)* pincel *m*; *(house painter's)* brocha. **3** *(unpleasant encounter)* roce *m*: **he had a brush with the police** *tuvo un roce con la policía*.
▷ *vt* **1** *(gen)* cepillar; *(teeth)* cepillar, limpiar, lavar. **2** *(touch lightly)* rozar.
⊙ **to brush aside** *vt sep (person, problem)* dejar de lado.
⊙ **to brush away** *vt sep (dirt, dust)* quitar, limpiar.
⊙ **to brush off** *vt sep* **1** *(dust, dirt)* quitar, limpiar. **2** *(rebuff, snub a person)* desairar.
⊙ **to brush up** *vt sep (knowledge)* refrescar, repasar.
brush-off ['brʌʃɒf] *n (rebuff, snub)* desaire *m*.
brushwood ['brʌʃwʊd] *n* **1** *(twigs)* broza. **2** *(undergrowth)* maleza.
brusque [brʌsk] *adj* brusco,-a, áspero,-a.
brusquely ['brʌsklɪ] *adv* bruscamente.
Brussels ['brʌsəlz] *n* Bruselas. ● **Brussels sprouts** coles *fpl* de Bruselas.
brutal ['bruːtəl] *adj* brutal, cruel.
brutalize ['bruːtəlaɪz] *vt* brutalizar.
brute [bruːt] *n* bruto,-a, bestia *mf*.
▷ *adj* brutal, bruto,-a.
BSc ['biː'es'siː] *abbr* **(Bachelor of Science)** licenciado,-a en ciencias.
bubble ['bʌbəl] *n (in liquid)* burbuja; *(of soap)* pompa.
▷ *vi* **1** burbujear. **2** *(boil)* borbotear.
bubbly ['bʌblɪ] *adj* **1** burbujeante, espumoso,-a. **2** *(person)* vivaz.
▲ *comp* **bubblier**, *superl* **bubbliest**.
bubonic [bjuː'bɒnɪk] *adj* MED bubónico,-a. ● **bubonic plague** peste *f* bubónica.
Bucharest [buːkə'rest] *n* Bucarest.
buck[1] [bʌk] *n (rabbit, hare)* macho; *(deer)* ciervo; *(goat)* macho cabrío.
▷ *adj (animal)* macho.
▷ *vt* **1** *(rider)* desarzonar. **2** US *fig (system, authority)* oponerse a, resistir a. ● **buck soldier** US soldado raso.
⊙ **to buck up** *vt sep fam* dar ánimos a: **he tried to buck her up** *intentó darle ánimos*.
▷ *vi* animarse: **buck up!** *¡anímate!*
buck[2] [bʌk] *n* US *fam* dólar *m*.
bucket ['bʌkɪt] *n* **1** cubo. **2** *(on dredger, waterwheel)* canguilón *m*.
buckle ['bʌkəl] *n (on shoe, belt)* hebilla.
▷ *vt (belt)* abrochar.
▷ *vi* **1** *(metal, object)* torcerse, combarse. **2** *(knees)* doblarse.
buckshee [bʌk'ʃiː] *adj* GB *fam* gratuito,-a.
▷ *adv* gratis, de balde.
bucolic [bjuː'kɒlɪk] *adj* bucólico,-a.
bud[1] [bʌd] *n (on tree, plant)* brote *m*, yema; *(of flower)* botón *m*, capullo.
▷ *vi (trees, plants)* echar brotes, brotar; *(flower)* empezar a echar flor.
▲ *pt & pp* **budded**, *ger* **budding**.
bud[2] [bʌd] *n* US *fam* colega *mf*: **hi bud!** *¡hola colega!*
Buddha ['bʊdə] *n* REL Buda *m*.
Buddhism ['bʊdɪzəm] *n* REL budismo.
budding ['bʌdɪŋ] *adj* en ciernes: **he's a budding politician** *es un político en ciernes*.
buddy ['bʌdɪ] *n* US *fam* amigote *m*, colega *mf*.
▲ *pl* **buddies**.
budge [bʌdʒ] *vt* **1** *(move)* mover. **2** *(make change opinion)* hacer cambiar de opinión.
budgerigar ['bʌdʒərɪgɑːʳ] *n* ZOOL periquito.
budget ['bʌdʒɪt] *n* presupuesto.
▷ *adj (good-value)* bien de precio.
▷ *vt* **to budget for** presupuestar, hacer el presupuesto para.
budgie ['bʌdʒɪ] *n* ZOOL *fam* periquito.
buff [bʌf] *n* **1** *(leather)* piel *f* de ante. **2** *(colour)* color *m* de ante. **3** *(enthusiast)* aficionado,-a.
▷ *vt* **1** *(metal, floor, etc)* dar brillo a. **2** *(leather)* aterciopelar.
buffalo ['bʌfələʊ] *n* ZOOL búfalo.
▲ *pl* **buffalo** o **buffaloes**.
buffer ['bʌfəʳ] *n* **1** *(for train)* tope *m*. **2** COMPUT memoria intermedia. **3** CHEM regulador *m*.
buffet[1] ['bʌfeɪ] *n* **1** *(bar)* bar *m*; *(at station)* bar *m*, cantina. **2** *(meal)* bufé *m* libre, bufé *m*. **3** *(sideboard)* aparador *m*.
buffet[2] ['bʌfɪt] *n (slap)* bofetada.
▷ *vt* **1** *(slap)* abofetear. **2** *(strike)* azotar, zarandear.
buffoon [bə'fuːn] *n* **1** *(idiot)* payaso. **2** *(jester)* bufón *m*.
bug [bʌg] *n* **1** *(insect)* bicho. **2** *fam (microbe)* microbio. **3** *(microphone)* micrófono oculto. **4** *fam (interest)* afición *f*. **5** *(in computer program)* error *m*.
▷ *vt* **1** *fam* ocultar micrófonos en. **2** US *(annoy)* molestar, fastidiar: **what's bugging her?** *¿qué mosca le ha picado?*
▲ *pt & pp* **bugged**, *ger* **bugging**.
bugbear ['bʌgbeəʳ] *n* bestia negra.
buggy ['bʌgɪ] *n* **1** *(horse-drawn)* calesa. **2** *(open-top vehicle)* ≈ jeep *m*. **3** US *(pram)* cochecito (de bebé).
▲ *pl* **buggies**.
bugle ['bjuːgəl] *n* MUS corneta, clarín *m*.
▷ *vi* MUS tocar la corneta.
build [bɪld] *n (physique)* constitución *f*, complexión *f*: **a strong build** *una complexión fuerte*.
▷ *vt (car, ship, etc)* construir; *(house, block of flats, etc)* construir, edificar.
▲ *pt & pp* **built** [bɪlt].
⊙ **to build in** *vt sep (as part of structure)* incorporar.
⊙ **to build on** *vt sep* **1** *(extension, part of house)* añadir. **2** *fig (base on, found)* basarse en, fundarse en.
▷ *vt insep (use profitably)* saber aprovechar.

⊙ **to build up** *vt sep (business)* desarrollar; *(reputation)* establecer; *(sales)* aumentar; *(collection, objects)* reunir, acumular; *(speed)* coger.
▷ *vi (business)* desarrollarse; *(reputation)* establecerse; *(sales, profits)* aumentarse; *(collection, objects)* acumularse.
builder ['bɪldəʳ] *n* **1** *(owner of company)* constructor,-ra. **2** *(bricklayer)* albañil *m.* **3** *(foreman)* maestro de obras. **4** *(contractor)* contratista *mf.* **5** *fig (of company, state)* fundador,-ra. ● **builder's** empresa constructora.
building ['bɪldɪŋ] *n* **1** edificio. **2** *(action)* construcción *f,* edificación *f.* ● **building society** sociedad *f* hipotecaria. ■ **the building industry / the building trade** la construcción.
build-up ['bɪldʌp] *n* **1** *(increase)* aumento: **a build-up in pollution** *un aumento de la contaminación.* **2** *(of gas)* acumulación *f.* **3** *(of troops)* concentración *f.* **4** *(of plot in film, play)* desarrollo. **5** *(favourable publicity)* bombo, publicidad *f.*
built [bɪlt] *pt & pp* ⟶ **build.** ■ **-built** de construcción ..., de fabricación .... **a Spanish-built rocket** *un cohete de construcción española.*
built-in [bɪlt'ɪn] *adj* **1** *(as component)* incorporado,-a. **2** *(recessed)* empotrado,-a.
built-up [bɪlt'ʌp] *adj* urbanizado,-a.
Bujumbura ['bʊdzəmbʊərə] *n* Buyumbura.
bulb [bʌlb] *n* **1** BOT bulbo. **2** ELEC bombilla.
Bulgaria [bʌl'geərɪə] *n* Bulgaria.
Bulgarian [bʌl'geərɪə] *adj* búlgaro,-a.
▷ *n* búlgaro,-a.
bulbous ['bʌlbəs] *adj* bulboso,-a.
bulge [bʌldʒ] *n* **1** *(lump)* bulto; *(protruberance)* protuberancia. **2** *(in surface)* pandeo.
▷ *vi* **1** *(protrude)* sobresalir; *(eyes)* saltar. **2** *(swell)* hincharse. **3** *(warp)* pandearse. **4** estar abultado,-a.
bulging ['bʌldʒɪŋ] *adj* **1** *(lumpy, bulky)* abultado,-a. **2** *(eyes, features)* saltón, ona. **3** *(swollen)* hinchado,-a. **4** *(surface)* pandeado,-a.
▷ *n* **1** *(with bulk)* abultamiento. **2** *(swelling)* hinchazón *m.* **3** *(of wall, surface)* pandeo.
bulimia [bjʊː'liːmɪə] *n* bulimia.
bulk [bʌlk] *n* **1** *(mass)* masa, bulto; *(amount, quantity)* volumen *m,* cantidad *f.* **2** *(object)* mole *f.* **3** *(weight of person)* peso. **4** *(greater part)* mayor parte *f.* **5** MAR carga.
bulk-buying ['bʌlkbaɪɪŋ] *n* compra en grandes cantidades.
bulky ['bʌlkɪ] *adj* abultado,-a, voluminoso,-a.
▲ *comp* **bulkier**, *superl* **bulkiest**.
bull[1] [bʊl] *n* **1** toro. **2** *(elephant, whale, etc)* macho. **3** FIN alcista *mf.* **4** GB *fam (target)* blanco, diana.
▷ *adj* **1** *(elephant, whale, etc)* macho. **2** FIN alcista, en alza.
▷ *vt* FIN provocar un alza en el precio de los valores, jugar al alza.
▷ *vi* FIN especular en el mercado para provocar un alza.
bull[2] [bʊl] *n* REL *(papal)* bula.
bull[3] [bʊl] *n sl (nonsense)* chorradas *fpl.* ■ **to shoot the bull** *sl* rajar, charlar.
bulldog ['bʊldɒg] *n* **1** buldog *m.* **2** *fig (person)* persona tenaz, persona porfiada.
bulldozer ['bʊldəʊzəʳ] *n* bulldozer *m,* excavadora.
bullet ['bʊlɪt] *n* bala.
bulletin ['bʊlɪtɪn] *n* **1** *(publication)* boletín *m.* **2** *(medical, etc)* parte *m.* **3** *(communiqué)* comunicado.
bulletin-board ['bʊlətɪnbɔːd] *n* US tablón *m* de anuncios.
bulletproof ['bʊlɪtpruːf] *adj* antibalas. ● **bulletproof vest** chaleco antibalas.
bullfight ['bʊlfaɪt] *n* corrida de toros, lidia. ■ **to go to a bullfight** ir a los toros.
bullfighter ['bʊlfaɪtəʳ] *n* torero,-a.
bullfighting ['bʊlfaɪtɪŋ] *n* los toros *mpl; (art)* tauromaquia.
bullion ['bʊljən] *n (gold)* oro en lingotes; *(silver)* plata en lingotes.
bullish ['bʌlɪʃ] *adj* **1** COMM alcista, en alza. **2** *(optimistic)* optimista. **3** *(impetuous)* impetuoso,-a.
bullock ['bʊlək] *n* toro castrado, buey *m.*
bullring ['bʊlrɪŋ] *n* plaza de toros.
bull's-eye ['bʊlzaɪ] *n* **1** *(target)* diana. **2** *(score)* acierto. **3** MAR *(porthole)* portilla. ■ **to score a bull's-eye** dar en el blanco.
bullshit ['bʊlʃɪt] *n taboo (nonsense)* chorradas *fpl.*
bully[1] ['bʊlɪ] *n* matón,-ona.
▲ *pl* **bullies**.
▷ *vt* **1** *(intimidate)* intimidar, atemorizar. **2** *(force, coerce)* coaccionar.
▲ *pt & pp* **bullied**, *ger* **bullying**.
bully[2] ['bʊlɪ] *n* SP *(hockey)* saque *m* inicial.
▲ *pl* **bullies**.
▷ *vi* SP *(hockey)* hacer el saque inicial.
▲ *pt & pp* **bullied**, *ger* **bullying**.
bully[3] ['bʊlɪ] *adj* US estupendo,-a.
bully-beef ['bʊlɪbiːf] *n* carne *f* de vacuno en conserva.
bully-boy ['bʊlɪbɔɪ] *n* matón *m,* gorila *m.*
bullying ['bʊlɪɪŋ] *n* **1** *(intimidation)* amenazas *fpl,* intimidación *f.* **2** *(coertion)* coacción *f.* **3** *(in school)* acoso escolar.
bulwark ['bʊlwɔːk] *n* **1** *(rampart)* baluarte *m.* **2** *(breakwater)* rompeolas *m.*
bum[1] [bʌm] *n* GB *fam (bottom)* culo, trasero.
bum[2] [bʌm] *n* **1** US *fam (tramp)* vagabundo,-a. **2** US *fam (idler)* vago,-a, holgazán,-ana. **3** US *fam (wretch)* (pobre) desgraciado,-a.
▷ *adj* **1** US *fam (faulty)* defectuoso,-a. **2** US *fam (shoddy)* de pacotilla, de mala calidad. **3** US *fam (useless object, information)* que no vale, inútil.
▷ *vt fam (scrounge)* gorrear, sablear.
bumbag ['bʌmbæg] *n* riñonera.
bumblebee ['bʌmbəlbiː] *n* ZOOL abejorro.
bumbler ['bʌmbələʳ] *n* torpe *mf,* manazas *mf.*
bumbling ['bʌmblɪŋ] *adj* torpe, manazas.
bumf [bʌmf] *n* GB *fam* propaganda, papeleo.
bummer ['bʌməʳ] *n fam* lata, latazo.
bump [bʌmp] *n* **1** *(blow)* golpe *m,* batacazo. **2** *(collision)* choque *m,* colisión *f.* **3** *(on head)* chichón *m; (swelling)* hinchazón *m; (lump)* bulto. **4** *(dent)* abolladura. **5** *(on road)* bache *m.*
▷ *vt* **1** darse un golpe en: **he bumped his head** *se dio un golpe en la cabeza.* **2** dar un golpe a.
▷ *vi* **1** chocar (**into**, con), topar (**into**, contra). **2** *(collide)* chocar, colisionar.
⊙ **to bump into** *vt insep fam* encontrar por casualidad, tropezar con.
⊙ **to bump off** *vt sep sl* cargar, liquidar.
⊙ **to bump up** *vt sep (prices)* aumentar.

bumper ['bʌmpəʳ] *n* parachoques *m*.
▷ *adj* abundante: **a bumper crop** *una cosecha abundante.*
bumper-to-bumper ['bʌmpətə'bʌmpəʳ] *adv (vehicles)* en caravana.
bumptious ['bʌmtʃəs] *adj* presumido,-a, engreído,-a.
bumpy ['bʌmpɪ] *adj* **1** *(surface)* desigual, accidentado,-a. **2** *(road)* lleno,-a de baches. **3** *(journey)* con muchos baches; *(flight)* con turbulencias.
▲ *comp* **bumpier**, *superl* **bumpiest**.
bun [bʌn] *n* **1** *(bread)* panecillo; *(sweet)* bollo. **2** *(cake)* ma(g)dalena. **3** *(hair)* moño.
bunch [bʌntʃ] *n* **1** manojo. **2** *(flowers)* ramo. **3** *(fruit)* racimo. **4** *fam (group of people)* grupo; *(gang)* pandilla.
▷ *vt* atar en un manojo.
▷ *n pl* **bunches** *(hair)* coletas *fpl*.
⊙ **to bunch together** *vt sep* agrupar.
▷ *vi* apretujarse.
bundle ['bʌndəl] *n* **1** *(clothes)* fardo, bulto. **2** *(wood)* haz *m*. **3** *(papers, banknotes)* fajo. **4** *(keys)* manojo.
▷ *vt* atar en un fardo, atar en un bulto.
⊙ **to bundle into** *vt sep (push forcibly)* introducir a empujones, meter a empujones.
bung [bʌŋ] *n* **1** *(stopper)* tapón *m*; *(of barrel)* bitoque *m*. **2** GB *(bribe)* soborno.
▷ *vt* **1** taponar. **2** GB *fam (put)* poner, meter. **3** GB *fam (serve)* poner. **4** GB *fam (throw)* tirar.
⊙ **to bung up** *vt sep fam* atascar.
bungalow ['bʌŋgələʊ] *n* bungalow *m*.
bungee ['bʌndʒɪ] *n* correa elástica, goma. ● **bungee jumping** salto elástico.
bungle ['bʌngəl] *vt* **1** *(botch)* chapucear. **2** *(mess up)* pifiar.
bungler ['bʌŋgələʳ] *n* chapucero,-a.
bungling ['bʌŋgəlɪŋ] *n (clumsiness)* torpeza.
▷ *adj* **1** *(clumsy)* torpe. **2** *(worker)* chapucero,-a.
bunion ['bʌnjən] *n* MED juanete *m*.
bunk[1] [bʌŋk] *n (bed)* litera.
bunk[2] [bʌŋk] *n (nonsense)* tonterías *fpl*.
bunk[3] [bʌŋk] *phr* **to do a bunk** irse a la francesa, poner pies en polvorosa.
bunk-bed ['bʌŋkbed] *n* litera.
▲ *pl* **bunk-beds**.
bunker ['bʌŋkəʳ] *n* **1** MIL búnker *m*. **2** *(golf)* búnker *m*. **3** *(for coal)* carbonera; *(on ship)* pañol *m* del carbón.
▷ *vt (ship)* abastecer de carbón.
bunny ['bʌnɪ] *n fam* conejito.
▲ *pl* **bunnies**.
bunting[1] ['bʌntɪŋ] *n (flags)* banderines *mpl*.
bunting[2] ['bʌntɪŋ] *n (bird)* escribano.
buoy [bɔɪ; US 'bu:ɪ] *n* **1** *(navegation mark)* boya, baliza. **2** *(lifebuoy)* boya salvavidas.
▷ *vt* señalar con balizas, señalar con boyas, abalizar.
⊙ **to buoy up** *vt sep* **1** mantener a flote. **2** *fig* dar aliento a, dar ánimos a.
buoyancy ['bɔɪənsɪ] *n* **1** flotabilidad *f*. **2** *(cheerfulness)* buen humor *m*. **3** *(optimism)* optimismo.
buoyant ['bɔɪənt] *adj* **1** flotante. **2** *(cheerful)* animado,-a. **3** *(optimistic)* optimista.
burble ['bɜ:bəl] *n (incoherent speech)* murmullo.
▷ *vi (speak incoherently)* murmullar, farfullar.
burden ['bɜ:dən] *n* carga.
▷ *vt* cargar.
bureau ['bjʊərəʊ] *n* **1** *(desk)* escritorio. **2** US *(office)* oficina. **3** US *(agency)* agencia. **4** US *(chest of drawers)* cómoda. **5** US departamento del estado. ● **bureau de change** oficina de cambio.
▲ *pl* **bureaus** o **bureaux** ['bjʊərəʊ].
bureaucracy [bjʊə'rɒkrəsɪ] *n* **1** [*pl* **bureaucracies**] *(body, administration)* burocracia. **2** [No plural.] *(paperwork)* burocracia, papeleo.
burgeon ['bɜ:dʒən] *vi* **1** *lit (flower)* florecer; *(plant, tree)* retoñar. **2** *fig (talent, potential)* desarrollarse.
burgeoning ['bɜ:dʒənɪŋ] *adj* **1** *lit (flower)* en flor; *(plant, tree)* en brote. **2** *fig* en ciernes.
burger ['bɜ:gəʳ] *n* hamburguesa.
burglar ['bɜ:gləʳ] *n* ladrón,-ona.
burglarize ['bɜ:gləraɪz] *vt* US → **burgle**.
burglar-proof ['bɜ:gləpru:f] *adj* antirrobo.
burglary ['bɜ:glərɪ] *n (gen)* robo.
▲ *pl* **burglaries**.
burgle ['bɜ:gəl] *vt* robar.
burial ['berɪəl] *n* entierro. ● **burial ground** cementerio.
burlesque [bɜ:'lesk] *n* **1** parodia burlesca. **2** *(genre)* género burlesco, vodevil *m*. **3** US *(show)* revista.
▷ *vt* parodiar.
burly ['bɜ:lɪ] *adj* fornido,-a, corpulento,-a.
▲ *comp* **burlier**, *superl* **burliest**.
burn[1] [bɜ:n] *n* quemadura.
▷ *vt* **1** quemar. **2** quemarse. **3** *(fuel)* gastar, consumir. **4** *(land, plants)* abrasar. **5** *(body)* incinerar. **6** *(harden bricks)* cocer.
▷ *vi* **1** *(blaze, glow)* arder: **we saw the building burning from the rooftop** *vimos como ardía el edificio desde el terrado.* **2** *(candle, light)* estar encendido,-a. **3** *(food)* quemarse: **the steak has burnt** *el bistec se ha quemado.* **4** *fig (passion, rage, desire)* arder (**with**, de).
▲ *pt & pp* **burnt** [bɜ:nt] o **burned**.
⊙ **to burn down** *vt sep* incendiar, quemar totalmente: **they burnt the house down** *incendiaron la casa.*
▷ *vi* quemarse, quedarse totalmente destruido,-a por las llamas.
⊙ **to burn out** *vi* **1** *(fire)* extinguirse. **2** *(fuse, bulb)* fundirse. **3** *fig (person)* quemarse; *(machine)* gastarse.
⊙ **to burn up** *vi* **1** *(building, etc)* abrasarse, quedarse totalmente destruido,-a por las llamas. **2** *fig (with heat)* abrasarse de calor, achicharrarse.
▷ *vt sep (fuel)* consumir.
burn[2] [bɜ:n] *n (stream)* arroyo.
burner ['bɜ:nəʳ] *n (on cooker, lamp)* quemador *m*.
burning ['bɜ:nɪŋ] *n* **1** *(of waste, body)* incineración *f*. **2** *(of building)* incendio. **3** *(of skin)* quemadura. **4** *(sensation)* escozor *m*.
▷ *adj* **1** *(on fire)* en llamas, ardiendo. **2** *(sun)* abrasador,-ra de justicia; *(heat)* achicharrante. **3** *(desire, need)* ardiente. ● **burning issue / burning question** cuestión *f* candente.
burnt [bɜ:nt] *pt & pp* → **burn**.
burnt-out ['bɜ:ntaʊt] *adj* **1** *(building, car)* carbonizado,-a. **2** *fig (person)* quemado,-a, caduco,-a.
burp [bɜ:p] *n fam* eructo.
▷ *vt fam (baby)* hacer eructar.
▷ *vi fam* eructar.
burr [bɜ:ʳ] *n* **1** *(whirring)* zumbido, runrún *m*. **2** TECH *(rough edge)* rebaba. **3** TECH *(dental drill)* fresa.

▷ *vi* 1 *(whirr)* zumbar, runrunear. 2 *(accent) pronunciar la "r" de forma gutural.*

burrow ['bʌrəʊ] *n* madriguera.
▷ *vt* excavar, cavar.
▷ *vi* excavar una madriguera. ■ **to burrow into** STH *fig* investigar.

bursar ['bɜːsəʳ] *n* 1 *(at college, university)* tesorero,-a. 2 *(holder of scholarship)* bursario,-a.

bursary ['bɜːsərɪ] *n (scholarship)* beca.
▲ *pl* **bursaries**.

burst [bɜːst] *n* 1 *(of balloon, pipe)* reventón *m*; *(of tyre)* pinchazo, reventón *m*. 2 *(explosion)* estallido, explosión *f*. 3 *(of activity, anger)* arranque *m*. 4 *(of speed)* arrancada. 5 *(of applause)* salva. 6 *(of gunfire)* ráfaga.
▷ *vi (balloon, pipe)* reventarse; *(tyre)* pincharse, reventarse.
▲ *pt & pp* **burst**.
⊙ **to burst in** *vi* entrar precipitadamente.
⊙ **to burst into** *vt insep* irrumpir en.
⊙ **to burst open** *vi* 1 *(bud, flower)* abrirse. 2 *fig* abrirse de golpe.
⊙ **to burst through** *vt insep* 1 *(cordon, barrier)* atravesar a empujones, romper. 2 *fig (sun)* brillar a través de.
▷ *vi (sun)* brillar repentinamente.

bursting ['bɜːstɪŋ] *adj* muy lleno,-a, lleno,-a a rebosar.

bury ['berɪ] *vt* 1 enterrar. 2 *(body)* sepultar, enterrar. 3 *fig (outlive)* enterrar.
▲ *pt & pp* **buried**, *ger* **burying**.

bus [bʌs] *n* 1 autobús *m*, bus *m*. 2 COMPUT bus *m*. ● **bus conductor** cobrador. ‖ **bus conductress** cobradora. ‖ **bus lane** carril *m* de autobuses. ‖ **bus route** línea de autobús. ‖ **bus shelter** parada de autobús cubierta. ‖ **bus station** estación *f* de autobuses. ‖ **bus stop** parada de autobús.
▲ *pl* **buses** (US **busses**).

bush¹ [bʊʃ] *n* 1 *(plant)* arbusto. 2 *(land)* breña.
▷ *n pl* **bushes** *(thicket)* matorral *m*, maleza. ● **the bush** *(in Australia)* el monte.

bush² [bʊʃ] *n* TECH *(lining)* forro.
▷ *vt* TECH forrar.

bush-baby ['bʊʃbeɪbɪ] *n* ZOOL lemúrido.
▲ *pl* **bush-babies**.

bushed [bʊʃt] *phr* **to be bushed** *fam* estar hecho,-a polvo.

bushel ['bʊʃəl] *n medida de capacidad para áridos.*

En Gran Bretaña equivale a 36,37 litros y en Estados Unidos a 35,24 litros.

Bushman ['bʊʃmən] *n* 1 *(person)* bosquimano,-a. 2 *(language)* bosquimano.
▷ *adj* bosquimano,-a.
▲ *pl* **Bushmen** ['bʊʃmen].

bushy ['bʊʃɪ] *adj* espeso,-a, tupido,-a. ■ **to have bushy eyebrows** ser cejudo,-a.
▲ *comp* **bushier**, *superl* **bushiest**.

busily ['bɪzɪlɪ] *adv* con afán.

business ['bɪznəs] *n* 1 *(commerce)* negocios *mpl*: **the business world** *el mundo de los negocios*. 2 *(firm)* negocio, empresa: **he's got a small business on the coast** *tiene un pequeño negocio en la costa.* 3 *(affair)* asunto, tema *m*: **I've got business to discuss with the manager** *tengo asuntos que tratar con el director;* **it's none of your business** *no es asunto tuyo;* **does he know about the business with the money?** *¿se ha enterado del asunto del dinero?* ■ **it's my (your, etc) business to ...** me *(te, etc)* incumbe ...: **it's my business to investigate the case** *me incumbe investigar el caso.* ‖ **to be big business** ser un buen negocio. ‖ **to be in business** dedicarse al mundo de los negocios. ‖ **to get down to business** entrar en materia. ‖ **to go out of business** quebrar. ‖ **to put** SB **out of business** hacer que ALGN quiebre. ‖ **to run a business** llevar un negocio. ‖ **to set up a business** montar un negocio. ‖ **mind your own business!** ¡no te metas donde no te llaman! ‖ **business before pleasure** primero es la obligación que la devoción. ‖ **business is business** el negocio es el negocio. ● **business administration** administración *f* de negocios. ‖ **business card** tarjeta de presentación, tarjeta comercial. ‖ **business centre** (US **center**) centro de negocios. ‖ **business consultant** asesor,-ra de empresas. ‖ **business deal** trato comercial. ‖ **business district** área de negocios, zona comercial. ‖ **business of the day** orden *m* del día. ‖ **business manager** director,-ra de empresas. ‖ **business studies** estudios *mpl* empresariales, empresariales *mpl*. ‖ **business trip** viaje *m* de negocios.

businesslike ['bɪznəslaɪk] *adj* 1 *(responsible)* formal, serio,-a. 2 *(systematic)* metódico,-a, sistemático,-a. 3 *(efficient)* eficaz. 4 *(practical)* práctico,-a.

businessman ['bɪznəsmən] *n* hombre *m* de negocios, empresario.
▲ *pl* **businessmen** ['bɪznəsmən].

business-minded [bɪznəs'maɪndɪd] *adj* comerciante.

businesswoman ['bɪznəswʊmən] *n* mujer *m* de negocios, empresaria.
▲ *pl* **businesswomen** ['bɪznəswɪmɪn].

busk [bʌsk] *vi* tocar música por la calle.

busker ['bʌskəʳ] *n* GB músico callejero,-a.

busman ['bʌsmən] *n* conductor *m* de autobús. ● **busman's holiday** tiempo libre dedicado a una actividad similar a la del trabajo habitual.

bust¹ [bʌst] *n* 1 *(bosom)* busto, pecho. 2 *(sculpture)* busto.

bust² [bʌst] *n* 1 *fam (bankruptcy)* quiebra, bancarrota. 2 *fam (police raid)* redada.
▷ *adj* 1 *fam (broken)* roto,-a. 2 *(burst)* reventado,-a. 3 *fam (bankrupt)* en quiebra, arruinado,-a.
▷ *vt* 1 *fam (break)* romper. 2 *(burst)* reventar. 3 *fam (make bankrupt)* llevar a la quiebra. 4 *fam (raid)* organizar una redada en, registrar: **the police busted the club** *la policía organizó una redada en el club.* 5 *fam (arrest)* pillar, pescar.
▷ *vi* 1 *(break)* romperse. 2 *(burst)* reventarse. ■ **to go bust** *fam* quebrar.
▲ *pt & pp* **bust** [bʌst] o **busted**.
⊙ **to bust up** *vt sep fam (marriage, relationship)* romper.
▷ *vi fam (marriage, relationship)* irse al traste.

bustard ['bʌstəd] *n* avutarda.

busted ['bʌstɪd] *adj* → **bust 2**.

bustle¹ ['bʌsəl] *n* bullicio, ajetreo: **the bustle of the city** *el bullicio de la gran ciudad.*
▷ *vi* ir y venir, no parar: **she's always bustling about** *es que no para.*
▲ *pt & pp* **busied**, *ger* **busying**.
⊙ **to bustle about** *vt insep* andar ajetreado,-a en: **she bustled about the kitchen** *andaba ajetreada en la cocina.*

⊙ **to bustle into** *vt sep* introducir sin miramientos: **they bustled her into the court** *la introdujeron en el juzgado sin miramientos.*

bustle[2] ['bʌsəl] *n (of skirt)* polizón *m.*

bustling ['bʌsəlɪŋ] *adj* **1** *(place)* bullicioso,-a. **2** *(person)* ajetreado,-a, activo,-a.

bust-up ['bʌstʌp] *n fam* riña, camorra. ■ **to have a bust-up** *fam* reñir.

busty ['bʌstɪ] *adj* tetón,-ona, pechugón,-ona.
▲ *comp* **bustier**, *superl* **bustiest**.

busy ['bɪzɪ] *adj* **1** *(person)* ocupado,-a, atareado,-a. **2** *(street, place)* concurrido,-a. **3** *(day)* ajetreado,-a. **4** US *(telephone)* comunicando: **the line was busy** *estaba comunicando.* ■ **to busy** OS **doing** STH ocuparse en hacer algo: **he busied himself washing the dishes** *se ocupó en fregar los platos.* ‖ **to be busy doing** STH estar ocupado,-a en hacer algo: **she was busy revising her notes** *estaba ocupada en repasar los apuntes.* ‖ **to be as busy as a bee** estar que no para, estar muy ocupado,-a. ‖ **to get busy 1** *fam (work)* ponerse a trabajar. **2** *(hurry)* darse prisa. ‖ **to keep** OS **busy** mantenerse ocupado,-a. ‖ **to keep** SB **busy** mantener ocupado,-a algn.
▷ *n fam (police officer)* poli *mf.* ● **the busies** *fam (police)* la poli, la pasma.
▲ *comp* **busier**, *superl* **busiest**.

busybody ['bɪzɪbɒdɪ] *n* entremetido,-a, fisgón,-ona.
▲ *pl* **busybodies**.

but [bʌt] *conj* **1** pero: **it's cold, but dry** *hace frío, pero no llueve;* **I'd like to, but I can't** *me gustaría, pero no puedo.* **2** *(after negative)* sino: **not two, but three** *no dos, sino tres.* **3** *(after negative with verb)* sino que: **she told him not to wait, but to go home** *le dijo que no se esperara, sino que se fuera para casa.* ■ **but for** de no ser por, si no fuera por: **but for him, we would have failed** *de no ser por él, habríamos fracasado;* **but for his help we would be bankrupt** *si no fuera por su ayuda estaríamos en la ruina.* ‖ **there is nothing for it but to + inf** no hay más remedio que + *inf*: **there's nothing for it but to report him** *no hay más remedio que denunciarlo.* ‖ **the last but one** el/la penúltimo,-a.
▷ *adv* (nada) más que, no ... sino, solamente, solo: **he spoke nothing but the truth** *no dijo nada más que la verdad;* **she is but three days old** *solo tiene tres días.*
▷ *prep* excepto, salvo, menos: **everyone but me** *todos menos yo;* **I can meet you any day but Friday** *te puedo ver cualquier día excepto el viernes.*
▷ *n* pero: **there are no buts about it** *no hay pero que valga.*

butane ['bjuːteɪn] *n* CHEM butano. ● **butane bottle** bombona (de butano). ‖ **butane gas** gas *m* butano.

butch [bʊtʃ] *adj fam (man)* machote; *(woman)* hombruna.

butcher ['bʊtʃəʳ] *n* carnicero,-a.
▷ *vt* **1** *(meat)* matar. **2** *(massacre)* masacrar, hacer una carnicería con. **3** *fig (book, play)* destrozar.

butcher's ['bʊtʃəz] *n* carnicería. ■ **to have a butcher's** GB *fam* echar un vistazo. ‖ **give me a butcher's** GB *fam* déjame ver. ● **butcher's block** tajo.

butchery ['bʊtʃərɪ] *n* carnicería.

butler ['bʌtləʳ] *n* mayordomo.

butt[1] [bʌt] *n (with head)* cabezazo, topetazo.
▷ *vt (goat, ram)* topetar, dar un topetazo; *(person)* dar un cabezazo.
▷ *vi (goat, ram)* dar topetazos; *(person)* dar un cabezazo.
⊙ **to butt into** *vt insep* meterse en: **he butted into our conversation** *se metió en nuestra conversación.*
⊙ **to butt in** *vi* meter baza.

butt[2] [bʌt] *n* **1** *(of rifle)* culata. **2** *(of cigarette)* colilla. **3** US *fam (bottom)* culo. ■ **to work one's butt off** US *fam* herniarse, romperse los cuernos.

butt[3] [bʌt] *n (target)* blanco.
▷ *n pl* **butts** *(shooting range)* campo de tiro. ■ **to be the butt of** SB**'s jokes** ser el blanco de las bromas de algn.

butt[4] [bʌt] *n* **1** *(barrel)* tonel *m.* **2** *(for water)* aljibe *m.*

butter ['bʌtəʳ] *n* mantequilla. ● **butter dish** mantequera. ‖ **butter knife** cuchillo para la mantequilla. ‖ **salted butter** mantequilla con sal. ‖ **unsalted butter** mantequilla sin sal. ■ **to look as if butter wouldn't melt in one's mouth** parecer no haber roto nunca un plato, parecer una mosquita muerta.
▷ *vt* untar con mantequilla.
⊙ **to butter up** *vt sep fam* dar coba a.

butter-bean ['bʌtəbiːn] *n* judión *m.*

buttercup ['bʌtəkʌp] *n* BOT botón *m* de oro, ranúnculo.

butterfingered ['bʌtəfɪŋgəd] *adj* manazas, torpe.

butterfingers ['bʌtəfɪŋgəz] *n* manazas *mf*, torpe *mf.*

butterfly ['bʌtəflaɪ] *n* **1** mariposa. **2** SP *(swimming)* braza mariposa, mariposa.
▲ *pl* **butterflies**. ■ **to have butterflies in one's stomach** *fig* sentir un cosquilleo en el estómago, estar nervioso,-a.

buttermilk ['bʌtəmɪlk] *n* suero de la leche.

buttery ['bʌtərɪ] *adj* mantecoso,-a.

buttock ['bʌtək] *n* **1** *(of person)* nalga. **2** *(of animal)* anca.
▷ *n pl* **buttocks** *(bottom)* trasero, nalgas *fpl.*

button ['bʌtən] *n* **1** *(on clothing, machine)* botón *m*; *(on doorbell)* pulsador *m*, botón *m*: **press the button** *pulse el botón.* **2** BOT *(bud)* botón *m*, yema. ■ **button your lip!** ¡punto en boca! ● **button nose** nariz *f* chata. ‖ **button mushroom** champiñón *m* pequeño.
▷ *vi* abrocharse: **how does it button?** *¿cómo se abrocha?*
▷ *vt* **to button / button up** abrochar, abrocharse: **button (up) your coat** *abróchate el abrigo.*

buttonhole ['bʌtənhəʊl] *n* **1** ojal *m.* **2** *(flower)* flor *f* que se lleva en el ojal.
▷ *vt fig* abordar y detener, enganchar: **I was buttonholed by two pollsters** *me engancharon dos encuestadores.*

buttress ['bʌtrəs] *n* ARCH contrafuerte *m.*
▷ *vt* ARCH apuntalar.

butty ['bʌtɪ] *n fam* bocata *m.*
▲ *pl* **butties**.

buxom ['bʌksəm] *adj (plump)* metida en carnes.
▷ *n (busty)* pechugona.

buy [baɪ] *n* compra.
▷ *vt* **1** comprar: **they've just bought a new flat** (US **apartment**) *acaban de comprar un piso nuevo.* **2** *(bribe)* sobornar. **3** *fam (accept, believe)* tragárselo: **he's so gullible he bought it** *es tan ingenuo que se lo tragó.* ■ **to buy it** *fam (die)* palmarla. ● **a good buy** una ganga.
▲ *pt & pp* **bought** [bɔːt].
⊙ **to buy back** *vt sep* volver a comprar.

⊙ **to buy off** *vt sep* quitar a ALGN de en medio pagándole, deshacerse de ALGN pagándole: **he bought off the blackmailers** *se deshizo de los chantajistas pagándoles.*

⊙ **to buy into** *vt insep* FIN comprar acciones de: **they bought into the business** *compraron acciones de la empresa.*

⊙ **to buy out** *vt sep* comprar la parte de: **he bought out his brother** *compró la parte de su hermano.*

⊙ **to buy up** *vt sep* comprar todas las existencias de: **he bought up the shop** *compró todas las existencias de la tienda.*

buyer ['baɪəʳ] *n* comprador,-ra. ● **buyer's market** mercado favorable al comprador.

buying power ['baɪɪŋpaʊəʳ] *n* poder *m* adquisitivo.

buzz [bʌz] *n* 1 zumbido. 2 *(of voices)* murmullo. 3 *fam fam (thrill)* emoción *f*, sensación *f*.

▷ *vi* zumbar. ■ **to get a buzz out of** STH *fam* estar entusiasmado,-a por algo: **he really gets a buzz out of hang-gliding** *está entusiasmado por el ala delta.* ‖ **buzz off!** *fam* ¡lárgate!

⊙ **to buzz around** *vi (bee)* ir zumbando de un sitio a otro; *(person)* ir y venir, no parar.

buzzard ['bʌzəd] *n* ratonero.

buzzer ['bʌzəʳ] *n* zumbador *m*, timbre *m*.

buzzing ['bʌzɪŋ] *n* zumbido.

buzz-saw ['bʌzsɔː] *n* sierra circular.

buzz-word ['bʌzwɜːd] *n* palabra pegadiza, palabra que está de moda.

by [baɪ] *prep* 1 *(agent)* por: **painted by Constable** *pintado por Constable;* **bought by a tycoon** *comprado por un magnate.* 2 *(means)* por: **by air/sea** *por avión/mar;* **by car/train** *en coche/tren;* **by hand** *a mano;* **by heart** *de memoria.* 3 *(showing difference)* por: **I won by 3 points** *gané por tres puntos;* **better by far** *muchísimo mejor.* 4 *(not later than)* para: **I need it by ten** *lo necesito para las diez.* 5 *(during)* de: **by day/night** *de día/noche.* 6 *(near)* junto a, al lado de: **sit by me** *siéntate a mi lado.* 7 *(according to)* según: **by the rules** *según las reglas.* 8 *(measurements)* por. **6 metres by 4** *6 metros por 4.* 9 *(rate)* por: **paid by the hour** *pagado por horas.* 10 MATH por: **12 divided by 3** *12 dividido por 3.* 11 *(progression)* a: **day by day** *día a día;* **little by little** *poco a poco.* 12 *(in sets)* en: **two by two** *de dos en dos.* 13 *(introducing gerund)*: **you can find out by reading the papers** *te enterarás leyendo los periódicos.* ■ **by and by** con el tiempo. ‖ **by the by** a propósito. ‖ **by** os solo,-a.

▷ *adv* al lado, delante. ■ **to go by** pasar delante.

bye [baɪ] *interj fam* ¡adiós!, ¡hasta luego!

bye-bye ['baɪbaɪ] *interj fam* ¡adiós!, ¡hasta luego! ■ **to say bye-bye** *fam* decir adiós. ‖ **to go to bye-byes** ir a dormir, ir a la cama.

by-election ['baɪɪlekʃən] *n* POL elección *f* parcial.

Byelorussia [bjeləʊ'rʌʃə] *n* Bielorrusia.

bygone ['baɪgɒn] *adj* pasado,-a: **a bygone age** *tiempos pasados.* ■ **in bygone times** antiguamente. ‖ **let bygones be bygones** lo pasado, pasado está.

▷ *n (object)* antigualla.

bylaw ['baɪlɔː] *n* ley *f* municipal.

bypass ['baɪpɑːs] *n* 1 AUTO variante *f*. 2 TECH tubo de desviación. 3 MED by-pass *m*.

▷ *vt* 1 *(traffic, road)* desviar. 2 *(avoid)* esquivar, evitar.

by-product ['baɪprɒdʌkt] *n* 1 subproducto, derivado. 2 *fig* consecuencia.

byre ['baɪəʳ] *n* establo.

by-road ['baɪrəʊd] *n* carretera secundaria.

bystander ['baɪstændəʳ] *n* espectador,-ra, curioso,-a.

byte [baɪt] *n* COMPUT byte *m*.

by-way ['baɪweɪ] *n* 1 *(road)* carretera secundaria. 2 *(remote path)* camino poco frecuentado.

byword ['baɪwɜːd] *n* 1 arquetipo, mayor *mf* exponente. 2 *(proverb)* refrán *m*, proverbio. ■ **to be a byword in** ser sinónimo de: **their products are a byword in luxury** *sus productos son sinónimo de lujo.*

Byzantine [bɪ'zæntaɪn] *n* bizantino,-a.

▷ *adj* bizantino,-a.

Byzantium [bɪ'zæntɪəm] *n* Bizancio.

C

C, c [siː] *n* 1 *(the letter)* C, c *f*. 2 MUS do.

c. ['sentʃərɪ] *abbr* **(century)** siglo; *(abbreviation)* s.: **c. 18 literature** *la literatura del s. XVIII*.

c/a [kərəntə'kaʊnt] *abbr* **(current account)** cuenta corriente; *(abbreviation)* c/c.

cab [kæb] *n* 1 *(taxi)* taxi *m*. 2 *(in vehicle)* cabina. 3 HIST cabriolé *m*. ■ **to go by cab** ir en taxi. ● **cab driver** taxista *mf*. | **cab rank** parada de taxis.

cabala [kə'bɑːlə] *n* cábala.

cabaret ['kæbəreɪ] *n* cabaret *m*.

cabbage ['kæbɪdʒ] *n* col *f*, repollo, berza.

cabbala [kə'bɑːlə] *n* cábala.

caber ['keɪbə^{r}] *n (in Scotland)* tronco.

cabin ['kæbɪn] *n* 1 *(wooden house)* cabaña. 2 *(on ship)* camarote *m*. 3 *(on plane)* cabina. ● **cabin crew** personal *m* de cabina.

cabinet ['kæbɪnət] *n* 1 *(furniture - gen)* armario; *(glass fronted)* vitrina. 2 POL gabinete *m* (ministerial), consejo de ministros. ● **cabinet meeting** consejo de ministros. | **cabinet minister** ministro,-a.

cabinet-maker ['kæbɪnətmeɪkə^{r}] *n* ebanista *mf*.

cable ['keɪb^{ə}l] *n* 1 *(rope, wire)* cable *m*. 2 *(telegram)* cable *m*, telegrama *m*.

▷ *vt (message)* cablegrafiar, telegrafiar.

cacao [kə'kɑːəʊ] *n* BOT cacao.

cache [kæʃ] *n* 1 *(store)* alijo. 2 *(computer memory)* caché *m*. ● **cache memory** memoria caché.

cackle ['kæk^{ə}l] *n* 1 *(of hen)* cacareo. 2 *(of person)* risotada, carcajada.

▷ *vi* 1 *(of hen)* cacarear. 2 *(of person)* reírse a carcajadas, carcajearse.

cacophony [kə'kɒfənɪ] *n* LING cacofonía.

cactus ['kæktəs] *n* cactus *m*.

▲ *pl* **cacti** o **cactuses.**

cad [kæd] *n* GB *fam dated* canalla *m*.

caddie ['kædɪ] *n (in golf)* cadi *m*. ● **caddie car / caddie cart** carrito de golf.

cadence ['keɪd^{ə}ns] *n* cadencia.

cadet [kə'det] *n* cadete *m*. ● **cadet school** escuela militar.

cadge [kædʒ] *vt fam* gorronear.

▷ *vi fam* gorronear (**from/off,** a).

cadger ['kædʒə^{r}] *n fam* gorrón,-ona.

cadi ['kɑːdɪ, 'keɪdɪ] *n* cadí *m*.

cadmium ['kædmɪəm] *n* cadmio.

cadre ['kɑːdə^{r}] *n* cuadro, plantel *m*.

caduceus [kə'djʊːsɪəs] *n* caduceo.

caecum ['siːkəm] *n* ciego, intestino ciego.

Caesarean [sɪ'zeərɪən] [Also **Caesarean section.**] *n* cesárea. ■ **to have a Caesarean** hacerle a una la cesárea: **I had a Caesarean** *me hicieron la cesárea*.

caesium ['siːzɪəm] *n* cesio.

café ['kæfeɪ] *n* cafetería, café *m*.

cafeteria [kæfə'tɪərɪə] *n (in factory, college, etc)* cafetería, cantina; *(restaurant)* autoservicio, self-service *m*.

caffeine ['kæfiːn] *n* cafeína.

cage [keɪdʒ] *n (gen)* jaula.

▷ *vt* enjaular.

cagey ['keɪdʒɪ] *adj fam* reservado,-a, cauteloso,-a, precavido,-a.

▲ *comp* **cagier,** *superl* **cagiest.**

cagoule [kə'guːl] *n* chubasquero.

cajole [kə'dʒəʊl] *vt* engatusar.

cake [keɪk] *n* 1 CULIN pastel *m*, tarta, torta. 2 *(of soap)* pastilla.

▷ *vi* endurecerse.

calamity [kə'læmɪtɪ] *n* calamidad *f*.

▲ *pl* **calamities.**

calcite ['kælsaɪt] *n* calcita.

calcium ['kælsɪəm] *n* calcio.

calculable ['kælkjələb^{ə}l] *adj* calculable.

calculate ['kælkjəleɪt] *vt* calcular.

▷ *vi* calcular.

⊙ **to calculate on** *vt insep* contar con.

calculated ['kælkjəleɪtɪd] *adj (risk)* calculado,-a; *(insult)* intencionado,-a; *(act)* premeditado,-a, deliberado,-a.

calculation [kælkjə'leɪʃ^{ə}n] *n* cálculo.

calculator ['kælkjəleɪtə^{r}] *n* calculador *m*, calculadora.

calculus ['kælkjələs] *n* 1 MATH cálculo matemático. 2 [*pl* **calculi** ['kælkjəlaɪ]] MED cálculo.

Calcutta [kæl'kʌtə] *n* Calcuta.

calendar ['kælɪndə^{r}] *n (gen)* calendario. ● **calendar year** año civil.

calendula [kə'lendjʊlə] *n* caléndula.

calf[1] [kɑːf] *n* ZOOL *(of cattle)* ternero,-a, becerro,-a; *(of whale)* ballenato; *(of other animals)* cría. ■ **to be in calf / be with calf** estar preñada.

▲ *pl* **calves.**

calf[2] [kɑːf] *n* ANAT pantorrilla.

▲ *pl* **calves.**

calfskin ['kɑːfskɪn] *n* piel *f* de becerro.

caliber ['kælɪbə^{r}] *n* US ⟶ **calibre.**

calibrate ['kælɪbreɪt] *vt (gun)* calibrar; *(thermometer)* graduar.

calibrator ['kælɪbreɪtə^{r}] *n* vitola.

calibre ['kælɪbə^{r}] *n (gen)* calibre *m*.

caliph ['keɪlɪf, 'kælɪf] *n* califa *f*.

caliphate ['keɪlɪfeɪt, 'kælɪfeɪt] *n* califato.

call [kɔːl] *n* 1 *(shout, cry)* grito, llamada: **a call for help** *un grito de socorro*. 2 *(by telephone)* llamada (telefónica). 3 *(of bird)* reclamo. 4 *(demand)* demanda; *(need)* motivo. 5 *(summons, vocation)* llamada; *(lure)* llamada, atracción *f*. 6 *(request, demand)* llamamiento. 7 *(short visit)* visita.

▷ *vt* **1** *(shout)* llamar. **2** *(by telephone)* llamar. **3** *(summon - meeting, strike, election)* convocar; *(announce - flight)* anunciar. **4** *(send for - police, etc)* llamar. **5** *(name, describe as)* llamar: **what's Peter's girlfriend called?** *¿cómo se llama la novia de Peter?;* **what's this called in Spanish?** *¿cómo se llama esto en español?*
▷ *vi* **1** *(shout)* llamar. **2** *(by phone)* llamar: **I just called to say I love you** *solo he llamado para decirte que te quiero.* **3** *(visit)* pasar, hacer una visita: **I called round at Martin's this afternoon** *he pasado por casa de Martin esta tarde.* **4** *(train)* parar (**at**, en). ■ **to be on call** estar de guardia. ‖ **to call for** STH/SB pasar a recoger ALGO/a ALGN. ‖ **to call in on** SB ir a ver a ALGN. ‖ **to give** SB **a call** llamar a ALGN. ‖ **to have first call on** STH tener prioridad sobre ALGO. ‖ **to have too many calls on one's time** tener muchas obligaciones, estar muy ocupado,-a. ● **call box** GB cabina telefónica.
⊙ **to call back** *vt sep (by phone)* llamar, devolver la llamada.
▷ *vi (by phone)* volver a llamar; *(visit)* volver a pasar.
⊙ **to call in** *vt sep* **1** *(summon, send for)* llamar. **2** *(recall - books, banknotes)* retirar; *(loan)* exigir el pago de.
⊙ **to call on** *vt insep* **1** *(visit)* visitar, ir a ver a. **2** *fml (invite)* invitar; *(request)* pedir; *(appeal to, urge)* apelar a.
⊙ **to call out** *vt sep* **1** *(summon - fire brigade)* llamar; *(army, troops)* hacer intervenir; *(doctor)* hacer venir; *(workers)* llamar a la huelga. **2** *(shout)* gritar, llamar.
caller ['kɔːləʳ] *n* **1** *(visitor)* visita, visitante *mf.* **2** *(by telephone)* persona que llama.
calligraphy [kə'lɪgrəfɪ] *n* caligrafía.
calling ['kɔːlɪŋ] *n (vocation)* vocación *f,* llamada; *(profession)* profesión *f.* ● **calling card** US tarjeta de visita.
callous ['kæləs] *adj* duro,-a, insensible.
call-up ['kɔːlʌp] *n* MIL llamamiento a filas.
callus ['kæləs] *n* callo.
▲ *pl* **calluses.**
calm [kɑːm] *adj* **1** *(sea)* en calma, tranquilo,-a, apacible; *(weather)* en calma, apacible. **2** *(person)* tranquilo,-a, sosegado,-a, calmado,-a: **keep calm!** *¡tranquilo!, ¡calma!*
▷ *n* **1** *(of sea, weather)* calma: **the calm before the storm** *la calma que precede a la tormenta.* **2** *(peace and quiet)* tranquilidad *f,* sosiego, serenidad *f.*
▷ *vt* calmar, tranquilizar, sosegar. ■ **to calm** OS tranquilizarse, calmarse.
⊙ **to calm down** *vt* tranquilizar, calmar.
▷ *vi* tranquilizarse, calmarse.
Calor Gas® ['kæləgæs] *n* (gas *m*) butano.
caloric [kə'lɒrɪk] *adj* calórico,-a.
calorie ['kælərɪ] *n* caloría.
calumniate [kə'lʌmnɪeɪt] *vt* calumniar.
calumny ['kæləmnɪ] *n (false statement)* calumnia; *(slander)* difamación *f.*
▲ *pl* **calumnies.**
calvary ['kælvərɪ] *n* calvario.
calve [kɑːv] *vi* parir (un becerro).
Calvinism ['kælvɪnɪzᵊm] *n* calvinismo.
Calvinist ['kælvɪnɪst] *adj* calvinista.
▷ *n* calvinista *mf.*
calyx ['keɪlɪks, 'kælɪks] *n* cáliz *m.*
camber ['kæmbəʳ] *n* **1** *(curvature - of road)* peralte *m.* **2** ARCH combadura.
Cambodia [kæm'bəʊdɪə] *n* Camboya.
Cambodian [kæm'bəʊdɪən] *adj* camboyano.
▷ *n* **1** *(person)* camboyano,-a. **2** *(language)* camboyano.
camcorder ['kæmkɔːdəʳ] *n* videocámara.
came [keɪm] *pt* → **come.**
camel ['kæmᵊl] *n* **1** ZOOL camello,-a. **2** *(colour)* (color *m*) leonado.
▷ *adj* leonado,-a.
camellia [kə'miːlɪə] *n* BOT camelia.
cameo ['kæmɪəʊ] *n* camafeo.
▲ *pl* **cameos.**
camera ['kæmᵊrə] *n* **1** *(gen)* cámara (fotográfica), máquina fotográfica. **2** *(cine, television)* cámara. ■ **in camera** a puerta cerrada.
cameraman ['kæmᵊrəmən] *n* cámara *mf.*
Cameroon [kæmə'ruːn] *n* Camerún *m.*
Cameroonien [kæmə'ruːnɪən] *adj & n* camerunés, -esa.
camomile ['kæməmaɪl] *n* BOT manzanilla, camomila. ● **camomile tea** (infusión *f* de) manzanilla.
camouflage ['kæməflɑːʒ] *n* camuflaje *m.*
▷ *vt* camuflar.
camp¹ [kæmp] *n* **1** *(gen)* campamento. **2** *(group)* bando.
▷ *vi* acampar.
camp² [kæmp] *adj (affected, effeminate)* amanerado,-a, afeminado,-a; *(affectedly theatrical)* afectado,-a.
▷ *n* amaneramiento, afectación *f.*
campaign [kæm'peɪn] *n (gen)* campaña.
▷ *vi* hacer una campaña (**for**, en favor de).
campaigner [kæm'peɪnəʳ] *n (supporter)* defensor,-ra. ● **old campaigner** veterano,-a.
camper ['kæmpəʳ] *n (person)* **1** campista *mf.* **2** [Also **camper van.**] *(vehicle)* caravana.
campfire ['kæmpfaɪəʳ] *n* fogata, hoguera.
camping ['kæmpɪŋ] *n* camping *m.* ■ **"No camping"** "Prohibido acampar". ‖ **to go camping** ir de camping. ● **camping site** camping *m,* campamento.
campus ['kæmpəs] *n* campus *m,* ciudad *f* universitaria.
▲ *pl* **campuses.**
can¹ [kæn] *n* **1** *(tin - for food, drinks)* lata, bote *m.* **2** *(container - for oil, petrol, etc)* bidón *m.* **3** US *sl (prison)* chirona, trullo. **4** US *sl (toilet)* trono.
▷ *vt (put in cans)* enlatar.
▲ *pt & pp* **canned,** *ger* **canning.**
can² [kæn] *aux* **1** *(be able to)* poder: **can you come tomorrow?** *¿puedes venir mañana?* **2** *(know how to)* saber: **he can speak Chinese** *sabe hablar chino;* **can you swim?** *¿sabes nadar?* **3** *(be allowed to)* poder, estar permitido,-a: **you can't smoke here** *no se puede fumar aquí;* **you can go now** *ya te puedes ir.* **4** *(in requests)* **can you get that box down for me?** *¿me puedes bajar esa caja?* **5** *(with verbs of perception or mental activity)*: **she couldn't see anything** *no veía nada;* **I can smell burning** *huele a quemado;* **can you hear me?** *¿me oyes?;* **I can't remember** *no me acuerdo.* **6** *(possibility)* poder: **who can it be?** *¿quién será?;* **smoking can cause cancer** *fumar puede causar cáncer.* **7** *(expressing bewilderment, incredulity)* poder: **he can't be here already!** *¡no puede ser que ya haya llegado!;* **you cannot be serious!** *¡no hablarás en serio!* **8** *(indicating typical behaviour)* poder: **he can be very annoying sometimes** *a veces es muy pesado;* **it can be very cold in Madrid** *puede llegar a hacer mucho frío en Madrid.*
▲ *pt & cond* **could** [kʊd].

Canada ['kænədɪə] *n* Canadá.

Canadian ['kænədɪən] *adj* canadiense.
▷ *n* 1 *(person)* canadiense. 2 *(language)* canadiense.

canal [kə'næl] *n* canal *m*.

canapé ['kænəpeɪ] *n* canapé *m*.

canary [kə'neərɪ] *n* canario.
▲ *pl* **canaries.**

Canary Islands [kə'neərɪaɪləndz] *n pl* Islas *fpl* Canarias.

cancel ['kænsəl] *vt* 1 *(gen)* cancelar. 2 COMM anular. 3 *(revoke - permission)* retirar; *(order, decree)* revocar. 4 *(stamp)* matasellar. 5 *(delete)* tachar. 6 MATH eliminar.
▲ *pt & pp* **cancelled** (US **canceled**), *ger* **cancelling** (US **canceling**).
⊙ **to cancel out** *vt sep* anular, compensar, contrarrestar.

cancellation [kænsə'leɪʃən] *n* 1 *(gen)* cancelación *f*. 2 COMM anulación *f*. 3 *(of stamp)* matasellos *m*. 4 *(returned ticket)* devolución *f*.

cancer ['kænsər] *n* MED cáncer *m*. ● **breast cancer** cáncer *m* de mama. ‖ **cancer research** cancerología.
▷ *n* **Cancer** *(constellation, sign)* Cáncer *m*.

cancerous ['kænsərəs] *adj* canceroso,-a.

candelabra [kændə'lɑːbrə] *n* candelabro.

candid ['kændɪd] *adj* franco,-a, sincero,-a.

candidacy ['kændɪdəsɪ] *n* candidatura.
▲ *pl* **candidacies.**

candidate ['kændɪdət] *n* 1 *(job, election)* candidato,-a. 2 *(in exam)* opositor,-ra.

candidature ['kændɪdətʃər] *n* candidatura.

candidly ['kændɪdlɪ] *adv* con franqueza.

candle ['kændəl] *n (gen)* vela; *(in church)* cirio.

candlelight ['kændəllaɪt] *n* luz *f* de vela.

candlestick ['kændəlstɪk] *n (gen)* candelero, palmatoria; *(in church)* cirial *m*.

candor ['kændər] *n* US → **candour.**

candour ['kændər] *n* franqueza, sinceridad *f*.

candy ['kændɪ] *n* US *(sweets)* caramelos *mpl*, golosinas *fpl*, dulces *mpl*; *(a sweet)* caramelo, dulce *m*.
▲ *pl* **candies.**

candyfloss ['kændɪflɒs] *n* GB algodón *m* de azúcar.

cane [keɪn] *n* 1 BOT *(of bamboo)* caña; *(of raspberry, blackberry, etc)* tallo leñoso. 2 *(stick)* bastón *m*; *(for punishment)* vara. 3 *(furniture)* mimbre *m*. 4 *(for plants)* rodrigón *m*.
▷ *vt* castigar con la palmeta.

canine ['keɪnaɪn] *adj* ZOOL canino,-a. ● **canine tooth** (diente *m*) canino, colmillo.

canister ['kænɪstər] *n (for tea, coffee, etc)* bote *m*, lata.

canned [kænd] *adj* 1 enlatado,-a, envasado,-a, en lata. 2 *(music)* grabado,-a; *(laughter)* grabado,-a. 3 *sl (drunk)* mamado,-a. ● **canned food** conservas *fpl*.

cannelloni [kænə'ləʊnɪ] *n pl* canelones *mpl*, canalones *mpl*.

cannery ['kænərɪ] *n* fábrica de conservas.
▲ *pl* **canneries.**

cannibal ['kænɪbəl] *n* caníbal *mf*.

cannibalize ['kænɪbəlaɪz] *vt* reutilizar piezas sueltas.

canning ['kænɪŋ] *n* enlatado. ● **canning factory** fábrica de conservas. ‖ **canning industry** industria conservera.

cannon ['kænən] *n* 1 MIL cañón *m*. 2 *(in billiards)* carambola.
▷ *vi* chocar (**against**, contra).
▲ *pl* **cannon** o **cannons.**

cannonball ['kænənbɔːl] *n* bala de cañón.

cannot ['kænɒt] *aux* → **can not.**

canny ['kænɪ] *adj* astuto,-a.
▲ *comp* **cannier**, *superl* **canniest.**

canoe [kə'nuː] *n* canoa, piragua.
▷ *vi* ir en canoa, ir en piragua.

canon[1] ['kænən] *n* 1 *(rule, standard)* canon *m*. 2 REL *(decree)* canon *m*. ● **cannon law** derecho canónico.

canon[2] ['kænən] *n (priest)* canónigo.

canonization [kænənaɪ'zeɪʃən] *n* canonización.

can-opener ['kænəʊpənər] *n* abrelatas *m*.

canopy ['kænəpɪ] *n* 1 *(over throne, bed, altar)* dosel *m*, baldaquín *m*; *(ceremonial)* palio; *(of terrace, balcony)* toldo. 2 AV *(of cockpit)* cubierta transparente. 3 *fig (of sky)* bóveda.
▲ *pl* **canopies.**

can't [kɑːnt] *aux* → **can.**

Cantabria [kæn'tæbrɪə] *n* Cantabria.

cantankerous [kən'tæŋkərəs] *adj* de mal genio, irascible, cascarrabias.

canteen [kæn'tiːn] *n* 1 *(restaurant)* cantina, comedor *m*. 2 *(set of cutlery)* juego de cubiertos. 3 *(flask)* cantimplora.

canter ['kæntər] *n* medio galope.
▷ *vi* ir a medio galope.

canticle ['kæntɪkəl] *n* cántico.

cantilever ['kæntɪliːvər] *n* ARCH voladizo. ● **cantilever bridge** puente *m* voladizo.

canton ['kæntɒn] *n* cantón *m*.

canvas ['kænvəs] *n* 1 *(cloth)* lona. 2 ART lienzo.

canvass ['kænvəs] *vi* POL hacer propaganda electoral (**for**, a favor de), hacer campaña (**for**, a favor de).
▷ *vt* 1 POL *(try to obtain - support, vote)* solicitar, tratar de conseguir, tratar de obtener. 2 POL *(ask - opinion)* sondear, hacer un sondeo de. 3 *(idea, plan)* proponer, presentar.

canyon ['kænjən] *n* GEOG cañón *m*. ● **the Grand Canyon** el Gran Cañón.

canyoning ['kænjənɪŋ] *n* barranquismo.

cap [kæp] *n* 1 *(type of hat - gen)* gorra; *(- soldier's, policeman's)* gorra de plato; *(- nurse's)* cofia; *(- academic, judge's)* birrete *m*; *(- cardinal's)* capelo, birrete *m*. 2 *(cover - of pen)* capuchón *m*; *(- of bottle)* tapón *m*, chapa; *(- of lens)* tapa. 3 GEOG casquete *m*. 4 *(for toy gun)* fulminante *m*. 5 *(upper limit)* tope *m*. 6 MED diafragma *m*.
▷ *vt* 1 *(mountains, etc)* cubrir, coronar. 2 *(tooth)* poner una corona en. 3 *(joke, story)* superar. 4 GB *(in sport)* seleccionar para el equipo nacional. 5 *(limit)* poner un tope a, limitar.
▲ *pt & pp* **capped**, *ger* **capping.**

capability [keɪpə'bɪlɪtɪ] *n* 1 *(ability)* capacidad *f* (**to**, para/de). 2 MIL capacidad *f*.
▲ *pl* **capabilities.**
▷ *n pl* **capabilities** *(potential)* aptitudes *fpl*, posibilidades *fpl*.

capable ['keɪpəbəl] *adj* 1 *(able)* capaz (**of**, de): **he's capable of breaking the world record** *es capaz de batir el récord mundial.* 2 *(competent)* competente, capaz: **a very capable person** *una persona muy competente.*

capacious [kə'peɪʃəs] *adj fml* espacioso,-a.

capacity [kə'pæsɪtɪ] *n* 1 *(maximum content - of container)* capacidad *f*, cabida; *(- of theatre)* aforo, capaci-

dad *f*, cabida: **the cinema has a seating capacity of 300** *el cine tiene un aforo de 300 localidades.* 2 *(ability)* capacidad *f* (**for**, de): **he has a great capacity for hard work** *tiene una gran capacidad de trabajo.* 3 *(position, role)* calidad *f*: **speaking in my capacity as club secretary** *hablando en calidad de secretario del club.*
▲ *pl* **capacities.**

cape[1] [keɪp] *n (garment)* capa.

cape[2] [keɪp] *n* cabo. ● **Cape Canaveral** Cabo Cañaveral. ‖ **Cape of Good Hope** Cabo de Buena Esperanza. ‖ **Cape Town** Ciudad *f* del Cabo. ‖ **Cape Verde** Cabo Verde.

caper[1] ['keɪpəʳ] *n* 1 *(for cooking)* alcaparra. 2 *(plant)* alcaparro. ● **caper berry** alcaparrón *m*.

caper[2] ['keɪpəʳ] *n* 1 *(jump)* brinco. 2 *fam (prank)* travesura, broma; *(scheme)* ardid *m*, estratagema, truco.
▷ *vi* brincar, dar brincos.

capillary [kə'pɪlərɪ] *n* vaso capilar, capilar *m*.
▲ *pl* **capillaries.**

capital[1] ['kæpɪtᵊl] *n* 1 *(of country, etc)* capital *f*: **what's the capital of Greece?** *¿cuál es la capital de Grecia?* 2 FIN capital *m*: **starting capital** *capital inicial.* 3 *(letter)* mayúscula: **write it in capitals** *escríbelo con mayúsculas.* ■ **to make capital out of** STH sacar provecho de ALGO, sacar partido de ALGO. ● **capital city** capital *f*.
▷ *adj* 1 JUR *(offence)* capital. 2 *(letter)* mayúscula: **capital A** *A mayúscula.* 3 *(very serious)* grave. 4 *(primary, chief, principal)* primordial, capital.

capitalism ['kæpɪtᵊlɪzᵊm] *n* capitalismo.

capitol ['kæpɪtᵊl] *n* capitolio.

capitulation [kəpɪtjə'leɪʃᵊn] *n* capitulación *f*.

caprice [kə'priːs] *n* capricho, antojo.

capricious [kə'prɪʃəs] *adj* caprichoso,-a, antojadizo,-a.

Capricorn ['kæprɪkɔːn] *n (constellation, sign)* Capricornio.

capsicum ['kæpsɪkəm] *n* pimiento.

capsize [kæp'saɪz] *vi* zozobrar.
▷ *vt* hacer zozobrar.

capsule ['kæpsjuːl] *n* cápsula.

captain ['kæptɪn] *n (rank)* capitán *m*; *(leader)* capitán, -ana.
▷ *vt* capitanear.

captaincy ['kæptɪnsɪ] *n* capitanía.

caption ['kæpʃᵊn] *n* 1 *(under picture)* leyenda, pie *m* de foto; *(short title, headline)* título. 2 CINEM subtítulo.

captivate ['kæptɪveɪt] *vt* cautivar, fascinar.

captivating ['kæptɪveɪtɪŋ] *adj* encantador,-ra, cautivador,-ra.

captive ['kæptɪv] *adj* cautivo,-a.
▷ *n* cautivo,-a.

captivity [kæp'tɪvɪtɪ] *n* cautiverio, cautividad *f*.

captor ['kæptəʳ] *n* captor,-ra.

capture ['kæptʃəʳ] *n (seizure - of person)* captura, apresamiento; *(of town)* toma, conquista.
▷ *vt* 1 *(seize - person)* capturar, apresar; *(- town)* tomar. 2 *(gain - share of market)* hacerse con; *(- votes)* conseguir, captar. 3 *fig (attract - attention, etc)* captar, atraer, acaparar; *(preserve - mood, etc)* captar, reproducir; *(on film, in painting, in words)* captar, plasmar.

car [kɑːʳ] *n* 1 AUTO coche *m*, automóvil *m*. 2 US *(railway carriage)* vagón *m*, coche *m*. ■ **to go by car** ir en coche.

carafe [kə'ræf] *n* garrafa.

caramel ['kærəmel] *n* 1 CULIN *(burnt sugar)* azúcar *m* quemado. 2 *(toffee)* caramelo.

caramelize ['kærəməlaɪz] *vt* caramelizar.

carapace ['kærəpeɪs] *n* carapacho, caparazón *m*.

carat ['kærət] *n* quilate *m*.

caravan [kærə'væn] *n* 1 GB *(trailer)* caravana, roulotte *f*. 2 GB *(covered cart)* carromato. 3 *(in desert)* caravana. ● **caravan site** camping *m* para caravanas.

caravel ['kærəvel] *n* carabela.

carbide ['kɑːbaɪd] *n* carburo.

carbine ['kɑːbaɪn] *n* carabina.

carbohydrate [kɑːbəʊ'haɪdreɪt] *n* hidrato de carbono, carbohidrato.

carbolic acid [kɑː'bɒlɪk'æsɪd] *n* fenol *m*.

carbon ['kɑːbᵊn] *n* CHEM carbono. ● **carbon dioxide** dióxido de carbono. ‖ **carbon monoxide** monóxido de carbono. ‖ **carbon paper** papel *m* carbón.

carbonate ['kɑːbəneɪt] *n* carbonato.
▷ *vt* carbonatar.

carbonated ['kɑːbᵊneɪtɪd] *adj (fizzy)* gaseoso,-a, con gas.

Carboniferous [kɑːbə'nɪfərəs] *adj* GEOL carbonífero,-a. ● **the Carboniferous** el carbonífero.

carbonize ['kɑːbᵊnaɪz] *vt* carbonizar.

carburettor [kɑːbə'retəʳ] *n* carburador *m*.

carcass ['kɑːkəs] *n* 1 *(dead animal)* res *f* muerta; *(at butcher's)* res *f* abierta en canal; *(of cooked bird)* huesos *mpl*. 2 *(frame, shell)* armazón *f*.

carcinogenic [kɑːsɪnə'dʒenɪk] *adj* MED cancerígeno,-a, carcinógeno,-a.

card[1] [kɑːd] *n* 1 *(gen)* tarjeta: **my telephone number is on the card** *mi número de teléfono está en la tarjeta.* 2 *(greetings card)* tarjeta de felicitación, felicitación *f*. 3 *(postcard)* tarjeta postal. 4 *(index card)* ficha. 5 *(of membership, identity)* carnet *m*, carné *m*. 6 *(stiff paper)* cartulina. 7 [Also **playing card.**] carta, naipe *m*: **shuffle the cards and deal them out** *baraja los naipes y repártelos.*
▷ *n pl* **cards** *(card-playing)* cartas *fpl*: **shall we play cards?** *¿jugamos a cartas?*

card[2] [kɑːd] *n (for wool)* carda.
▷ *vt* cardar.

cardamom ['kɑːdəmən] *n* cardamomo.

cardboard ['kɑːdbɔːd] *n* cartón *m*. ● **cardboard box** caja de cartón.

cardiac ['kɑːdɪæk] *adj* cardíaco,-a. ● **cardiac arrest** paro cardíaco. ‖ **cardiac sphincter** cardias.

cardigan ['kɑːdɪgən] *n* rebeca, chaqueta de punto.

cardinal ['kɑːdɪnᵊl] *adj (most important)* capital, fundamental, principal.
▷ *n* REL cardenal *m*. ● **cardinal number** número cardinal. ‖ **cardinal point** punto cardinal. ‖ **cardinal sin** pecado capital.

cardiogram ['kɑːdɪəgræm] *n* cardiograma *m*.

cardiography [kɑːdɪ'ɒgrəfɪ] *n* cardiografía.

cardiologist [kɑːdɪ'ɒlədʒɪst] *n* cardiólogo,-a.

cardiology [kɑːdɪ'ɒlədʒɪ] *n* cardiología.

care [keəʳ] *n* **1** *(attention, carefulness)* cuidado, atención *f*: **take care when driving at night** *(ten) cuidado al conducir de noche.* **2** *(sympathetic concern, protection)* cuidado, atención *f*. **3** *(charge, protection, responsibility)* cuidado: **I left the baby in the care of my mother** *dejé al bebé al cuidado de mi madre.* **4** *(worry, grief)* preocupación *f*, inquietud *f*. ■ **"Handle with care"** "Frágil". ‖ **take care! 1** *(be careful)* ¡ten cuidado! **2** *(look after yourself)* ¡cuídate! ● **medical care** asistencia médica.
▷ *vi (be worried, be concerned)* preocuparse (**about**, por), importar: **I don't care** *no me importa, me da igual;* **who cares!** *¡y a mí qué!*
▷ *vt (feel concern, mind)* importar: **no-one cares if you're late** *a nadie le importa si llegas tarde.*
⊙ **to care for** *vt insep* **1** *(look after)* cuidar, atender. **2** *(like)* gustar; *(feel affection for)* querer, sentir cariño por.
career [kə'rɪəʳ] *n* **1** *(profession)* carrera: **a career in politics** *una carrera en (la) política.* **2** *(working life)* vida profesional.
careerist [kə'rɪərɪst] *n* ambicioso,-a, trepa *mf*.
carefree ['keəfriː] *adj* despreocupado,-a, libre de preocupaciones.
careful ['keəfʊl] *adj* **1** *(cautious)* prudente, cuidadoso,-a: **a careful driver** *un conductor prudente.* **2** *(painstaking)* cuidadoso,-a. ■ **to be careful** tener cuidado.
carefully ['keəfʊlɪ] *adv* **1** *(cautiously)* con cuidado, con precaución: **drive carefully** *conduce con cuidado.* **2** *(with great attention)* cuidadosamente.
careless ['keələs] *adj (inattentive, thoughtless - person)* descuidado,-a, poco cuidadoso,-a; *(driving)* negligente; *(work)* dejado,-a, poco cuidado,-a: **he's careless with his money** *es muy descuidado con el dinero.* ● **careless mistake** descuido.
carer ['keərəʳ] *n* persona encargada de cuidar a alguien.
caress [kə'res] *n* caricia.
▷ *vt* acariciar.
caretaker ['keəteɪkəʳ] *n* conserje *m*, portero,-a. ● **caretaker government** gobierno provisional.
cargo ['kɑːgəʊ] *n (goods)* carga; *(load)* cargamento. ● **cargo ship** buque *m* de carga, carguero.
▲ *pl* **cargoes** o **cargos**.
Caribbean [kærɪ'bɪən, US kə'rɪbɪən] *adj* caribeño,-a. ● **the Caribbean (Sea)** el (mar) Caribe.
caribou ['kærɪbuː] *n* caribú *m*.
caricature ['kærɪkətjʊəʳ] *n* caricatura.
▷ *vt* caricaturizar.
caries ['keərɪz] *n* caries *f*.
caring ['keərɪŋ] *adj (kind)* bondadoso,-a, comprensivo,-a, atento,-a; *(loving)* cariñoso,-a, afectuoso,-a. ● **caring professions** profesiones *fpl* de vocación social.
carnage ['kɑːnɪdʒ] *n* carnicería, matanza.
carnal ['kɑːnᵊl] *adj* carnal.
carnation [kɑː'neɪʃᵊn] *n* clavel *m*.
carnival ['kɑːnɪvᵊl] *n* carnaval *m*.
carnivore ['kɑːnɪvɔːʳ] *n* carnívoro,-a.
carnivorous [kɑː'nɪvərəs] *adj* carnívoro,-a.
carol ['kærᵊl] *n* villancico.
Carolina [kærə'laɪnə] *n* Carolina. ● **North Carolina** Carolina del Norte. ‖ **South Carolina** Carolina del Sur.
carom ['kærəm] *n* US carambola.
carotene ['kærətiːn] *n* caroteno, carotina.
carousel [kærə'sel] *n* **1** US *(roundabout)* tiovivo, caballitos *mpl*, carrusel *m*. **2** *(for baggage)* cinta transportadora. **3** *(for slides)* carrete *m* de diapositivas.
carp¹ [kɑːp] *n (fish)* carpa.
carp² [kɑːp] *vi (complain)* quejarse (**about/at**, de).
Carpathians [kɑː'peɪðɪənz] *n* **the Carpathians** los (montes *mpl*) Cárpatos.
carpenter ['kɑːpɪntəʳ] *n* carpintero,-a.
carpentry ['kɑːpɪntrɪ] *n* carpintería.
carpet ['kɑːpɪt] *n* **1** *(gen)* alfombra; *(fitted)* moqueta. **2** *fig* alfombra.
▷ *vt* **1** alfombrar, enmoquetar. **2** *fig* cubrir, alfombrar. **3** *fam (reprimand)* echarle una bronca a.
carpeting ['kɑːpɪtɪŋ] *n* alfombrado.
carriage ['kærɪdʒ] *n* **1** HIST *(horse-drawn)* carruaje *m*. **2** GB *(railway vehicle)* vagón *m*, coche *m*. **3** *(of typewriter)* carro; *(of gun)* cureña. **4** *(cost of transport)* porte *m*, transporte *m*. **5** *dated (bearing, deportment)* porte *m*.
carriageway ['kærɪdʒweɪ] *n* GB calzada.
carrier ['kærɪəʳ] *n* **1** *(company, person)* transportista *mf*. **2** AV compañía aérea, línea aérea. **3** MED *(of disease)* portador,-ra. **4** *(on bicycle)* cesta, canasta. ● **aircraft carrier** MAR portaaviones *m*. ‖ **carrier bag** bolsa de papel, bolsa de plástico. ‖ **carrier pigeon** paloma mensajera.
carrion ['kærɪən] *n* carroña.
carrot ['kærət] *n* **1** *(vegetable)* zanahoria. **2** *fig* incentivo, aliciente *m*, estímulo.
carrousel [kærə'sel] *n* **1** *(roundabout)* tiovivo, carrusel. **2** *(for baggage reclaim)* cinta.
carry ['kærɪ] *vt* **1** *(take, bear - gen)* llevar; *(- money, passport, gun, etc)* llevar (encima). **2** *(transport - goods, load, passengers)* transportar, acarrear. **3** *(conduct, convey - water, oil, blood)* llevar; *(- electricity)* conducir. **4** *(disease)* ser portador,-ra de. **5** ARCH *(support - weight)* soportar, sostener. **6** *(take - blame, responsibility)* cargar con. **7** *(entail, involve - responsibility)* conllevar; *(- penalty, consequences)* implicar, conllevar. **8** MATH llevar(se).
▷ *vi (sound, voice)* oírse, tener alcance.
▲ *pt & pp* **carried**, *ger* **carrying**.
⊙ **to carry forward / carry over** *vt sep* llevar a la columna siguiente, llevar a la página siguiente: **carry this figure forward to the next page** *lleva esta cifra a la página siguiente.*
⊙ **to carry off** *vt sep* **1** *(part, action, duty)* realizar con éxito, salir airoso,-a de: **she carried the speech off well** *salió airosa del discurso.* **2** *(prize)* llevarse, hacerse con.
⊙ **to carry on** *vt insep (continue)* continuar con, seguir con; *(conversation)* mantener.
▷ *vi* **1** continuar, seguir. **2** *fam (make a fuss)* hacer una escena, montar un número.
⊙ **to carry out** *vt sep (plan, work)* llevar a cabo, realizar; *(test)* verificar; *(fulfil - order, threat, promise)* cumplir; *(- duty)* cumplir con.
⊙ **to carry through** *vt sep (plan, etc)* llevar a cabo.
carrycot ['kærɪkɒt] *n* capazo (de bebé).
carry-on [kærɪ'ɒn] *n* GB *fam* lío, jaleo, follón *m*.

carry-out ['kærɪaʊt] *n* **1** US *(food)* comida para llevar. **2** *(drink)* bebida para llevar.
carsick ['kɑːsɪk] *adj* mareado,-a (al ir en coche). ■ **to get carsick** marearse en coche.
cart [kɑːt] *n* **1** *(horse-drawn)* carro, carreta; *(handcart)* carretilla. **2** US *(for shopping)* carrito, carro.
▷ *vt* **1** *(carry in cart)* carretear, transportar. **2** *fam (carry in hands)* llevar: **I've been carting this umbrella around all day** *he llevado el paraguas arriba y abajo todo el día.* ■ **to put the cart before the horse** empezar la casa por el tejado.
carte blanche [kɑːt'blɑːntʃ] *n* carta blanca.
cartel [kɑː'tel] *n* cártel *m*.
Cartesian [kɑː'tiːʒᵊn] *adj* cartesiano,-a.
Carthage ['kɑːθɪdʒ] *n* Cartago.
Carthaginian [kɑːθə'dʒɪnɪən] *adj* cartaginense.
▷ *n* cartaginense *mf*.
cartilage ['kɑːtɪlɪdʒ] *n* cartílago.
cartographer [kɑː'tɒgrəfəʳ] *n* cartógrafo,-a.
cartography [kɑː'tɒgrəfɪ] *n* cartografía.
carton ['kɑːtᵊn] *n (of cream, yoghurt)* bote *m*; *(of milk, juice, cigarettes)* cartón *m*; *(of cereals, etc)* caja.
cartoon [kɑː'tuːn] *n* **1** *(drawing)* viñeta, chiste *m*; *(strip)* tira cómica, historieta. **2** *(animated)* dibujos *mpl* animados. **3** ART cartón *m*.
cartoonist [kɑː'tuːnɪst] *n* **1** *(of drawings)* dibujante *mf*, humorista *mf* gráfico,-a. **2** *(of animations)* dibujante *mf* de dibujos animados.
cartridge ['kɑːtrɪdʒ] *n* **1** MIL cartucho. **2** *(for record-player)* portaagujas *m*; *(for pen)* recambio; *(for magnetic tape)* cartucho; *(for camera)* carrete *m*.
cartwright ['kɑːtraɪt] *n* carretero.
carve [kɑːv] *vt* **1** *(wood, stone)* tallar; *(statue, etc)* esculpir; *(initials)* grabar. **2** *(meat)* cortar, trinchar.
▷ *vi* trinchar la carne, cortar la carne.
cascade [kæs'keɪd] *n* cascada.
▷ *vi* caer en cascada.
case¹ [keɪs] *n* **1** *(instance, situation, circumstances)* caso: **2** *(problem)* caso. **3** JUR *(lawsuit)* causa, litigio, pleito; *(set of arguments)* argumentos *mpl*, razones *fpl*. **4** LING caso. **5** *fam (person)* caso. ■ **in case ...** por si ..., en caso de que ... | **in no case** bajo ninguna circunstancia.
case² [keɪs] *n* **1** *(suitcase)* maleta. **2** *(box)* caja, cajón *m*; *(small, hard container)* estuche *m*; *(soft container)* funda. **3** *(in printing)* caja.
caseworker ['keɪswɜːkəʳ] *n* asistente,-a social.
cash [kæʃ] *n* **1** *(notes and coins)* dinero (en) efectivo, metálico. **2** *fam (money)* dinero.
▷ *vt (cheque)* cobrar, hacer efectivo.
⊙ **to cash up** *vi* hacer caja.
cashier [kæ'ʃɪəʳ] *n* cajero,-a.
cashmere [kæʃ'mɪəʳ] *n* cachemir *m*, cachemira.
▷ *adj* de cachemir, de cachemira.
casino [kə'siːnəʊ] *n* casino.
▲ *pl* **casinos.**
cask [kɑːsk] *n* tonel *m*, barril *m*.
casket ['kɑːskɪt] *n* **1** *(box)* cofre *m*. **2** *(coffin)* ataúd *m*.
casserole ['kæsərəʊl] *n* **1** *(dish)* cazuela. **2** *(food)* guiso, guisado.
▷ *vt* guisar.
cassette [kə'set] *n* casete *f*.
cast [kɑːst] *n* **1** *(throw)* lanzamiento. **2** THEAT reparto. **3** TECH *(mould)* molde *m*; *(product)* pieza. **4** ART *(product)* vaciado.
▷ *vt* **1** *(throw - gen)* lanzar,; *(- fishing line)* lanzar; *(- net)* echar; *(- dice)* tirar, echar. **2** *(shadow, light)* proyectar. **3** *(vote)* emitir. **4** THEAT *(part, role)* asignar el papel a. **5** *(shed - snake's skin)* mudar, mudar de.
▲ *pt & pp* **cast.** ■ **to be cast away** naufragar. | **to cast a spell on** STH/SB hechizar ALGO/a ALGN.
⊙ **to cast about for / cast around for** *vt insep* buscar, andar buscando.
⊙ **to cast out** *vt sep fml* expulsar.
castaway ['kɑːstəweɪ] *n* náufrago,-a.
caste [kɑːst] *n* casta.
caster ['kɑːstəʳ] *n (wheel)* ruedecilla. ● **caster sugar** azúcar *m* extrafino.
castigate ['kæstɪgeɪt] *vt fml* castigar.
Castile [kæ'stiːl] *n* Castilla. ● **New Castile** Castilla la Nueva. | **Old Castile** Castilla la Vieja.
Castilian [kæ'stɪlɪən] *adj* castellano,-a.
▷ *n* **1** *(person)* castellano,-a. **2** *(language)* castellano.
casting ['kɑːstɪŋ] *n* **1** TECH *(process)* fundición *f*; *(object)* pieza fundida. **2** ART vaciado. **3** THEAT *(selection)* selección *f*, casting *m*, reparto de papeles.
cast-iron ['kɑːstaɪən] *adj* **1** de hierro fundido, de hierro colado. **2** *fig (constitution, stomach)* de hierro; *(will)* férreo,-a; *(alibi)* a toda prueba; *(evidence)* irrefutable; *(guarantee, promise)* sólido,-a.
castle ['kɑːsᵊl] *n* **1** *(gen)* castillo. **2** *(chess)* torre *f*.
▷ *vi (chess)* enrocar.
castor¹ ['kɑːstəʳ] *n* → **caster.**
castor² ['kɑːstəʳ] *n* ZOOL castor *m*. ● **castor oil** aceite *m* de ricino.
castrate [kæ'streɪt] *vt* castrar, capar.
casual ['kæʒjʊəl] *adj* **1** *(chance - visit, visitor)* ocasional; *(- meeting)* fortuito,-a, casual. **2** *(unconcerned)* despreocupado,-a; *(irresponsible)* descuidado,-a . **3** *(superficial)* superficial; *(reader)* ocasional. **4** *(informal)* informal. **5** *(labour)* eventual, ocasional; *(worker)* eventual.
casually ['kæʒjʊəlɪ] *adv* **1** *(dress)* de manera informal, informalmente. **2** *(unconcernedly)* despreocupadamente; *(indifferently)* con indiferencia. **3** *(employed)* de forma eventual.
casualty ['kæʒjʊəltɪ] *n (of accident)* herido; MIL baja.
cat [kæt] *n (domestic)* gato,-a; *(lion, tiger)* felino,-a.
Catalan ['kætəlæn] *adj* catalán,-ana.
▷ *n* **1** *(person)* catalán,-ana. **2** *(language)* catalán *m*.
catalogue ['kætəlɒg] *n* catálogo.
▷ *vt* catalogar.
Catalonia [kætə'ləʊnɪə] *n* Cataluña.
catalyst ['kætəlɪst] *n* catalizador *m*.
catapult ['kætəpʌlt] *n* **1** *(for aircraft)* catapulta (de lanzamiento). **2** *(toy)* tirador *m*, tirachinas *m*.
▷ *vt* catapultar.
cataract ['kætərækt] *n* **1** *(waterfall)* catarata; *(in river)* rápido. **2** MED catarata.
catarrh [kə'tɑːʳ] *n* catarro.
catastrophe [kə'tæstrəfɪ] *n* catástrofe *f*.
catch [kætʃ] *n* **1** *(of ball)* parada. **2** *(of fish)* presa. **3** *fam (difficulty)* pega, trampa. **4** *(fastener on door)* pestillo.

▷ *vt* 1 *(grasp, take hold of)* coger, agarrar; *(capture, trap)* atrapar; *(fish)* pescar. 2 *(surprise)* pillar, sorprender; *(catch up with)* alcanzar, pillar. 3 *(train, plane - take)* coger, tomar; *(- be in time for)* alcanzar: **I just caught the last train** *cogí el último tren con el tiempo justo.* 4 *(hear, understand)* oír, entender, captar. 5 *(become infected with)* contagiarse de, contraer. 6 *(mood, likeness, etc)* captar, reflejar.
▷ *vi* 1 *(take hold of)* coger. 2 *(sleeve, etc)* engancharse (**on**, en). 3 *(burn)* prender. ■ **to catch a cold** resfriarse, coger un resfriado. ❙ **to catch** SB **red-handed** coger a ALGN con las manos en la masa, coger a ALGN in fraganti. ❙ **to catch** SB**'s attention/eye** atraer la atención de ALGN, captar la atención de ALGN.
▲ *pt & pp* **caught** [kɔ:t].
⊙ **to catch on** *vi* 1 *(understand)* entender, darse cuenta (**to**, de). 2 *(become popular)* ponerse de moda, imponerse.
⊙ **to catch out** *vt sep (doing something wrong)* pillar, sorprender; *(trick)* hacer que uno caiga.
⊙ **to catch up** *vt sep (person)* alcanzar.
▷ *vi (with news, studies, work)* ponerse al día; *(with person, country)* alcanzar.
catching ['kætʃɪŋ] *adj (contagious)* contagioso,-a.
catchment area ['kætʃmənteərɪə] *n* 1 *(of school, hospital, etc)* zona de captación. 2 GEOG cuenca.
catchword ['kætʃwɜ:d] *n* eslogan *m.*
catechism ['kætəkɪzᵊm] *n* catecismo.
categoric [kætə'gɒrɪk] *adj* categórico,-a.
categorize ['kætəgəraɪz] *vt* clasificar.
category ['kætəgᵊrɪ] *n* categoría.
▲ *pl* **categories.**
cater ['keɪtəʳ] *vi (food)* proveer comida (**for**, para).
⊙ **to cater for** *vt insep (needs, interests, tastes)* atender a, satisfacer.
caterer ['keɪtərəʳ] *n* proveedor,-ra.
catering ['keɪtərɪŋ] *n (business, course)* hostelería; *(service)* catering *m.*
caterpillar ['kætəpɪləʳ] *n* oruga.
cathedral [kə'θi:drəl] *n* catedral *f*: **cathedral city** *ciudad catedralicia*
catheter ['kæθətəʳ] *n* catéter *m.*
cathode ['kæθəʊd] *n* cátodo. ● **cathode ray** rayo catódico.
Catholic ['kæθᵊlɪk] *adj* REL católico,-a.
▷ *n* REL católico,-a.
Catholicism [kə'θɒlɪsɪzᵊm] *n* REL catolicismo.
Catholicize [kə'θɒlɪsaɪz] *vt* catolizar.
cattle ['kætᵊl] *n pl* ganado (vacuno). ● **cattle breeding** ganadería. ❙ **cattle market** feria de ganado.
catty ['kætɪ] *adj (remark)* malicioso,-a, malintencionado,-a; *(person)* malicioso,-a, rencoroso,-a, malo,-a.
▲ *comp* **cattier**, *superl* **cattiest.**
catwalk ['kætwɔ:k] *n* pasarela.
Caucasian [kɔ:'keɪʒᵊn] *adj* 1 *(race)* caucásico,-a. 2 GEOG caucáseo,-a, caucasiano,-a.
▷ *n (race)* caucásico,-a.
Caucasus ['kɔ:kəsəs] *n* **the Caucasus** 1 *(region)* el Cáucaso. 2 *(mountains)* las montañas del Cáucaso.
caucus ['kɔ:kəs] *n* 1 GB comité *m.* 2 US reunión *f* del comité central.
caught [kɔ:t] *pt & pp* ⟶ **catch.**
cauldron ['kɔ:ldrən] *n* caldero.
cauliflower ['kɒlɪflaʊəʳ] *n* coliflor *f.*
causal ['kɔ:zᵊl] *adj* causal.
causality [kɔ:'zælɪtɪ] *n* causalidad *f.*
cause [kɔ:z] *n* 1 *(origin)* causa 2 *(reason, grounds)* razón *f*, motivo. 3 *(principle, movement)* causa. 4 JUR causa, pleito.
▷ *vt* causar.
causeway ['kɔ:zweɪ] *n (road)* carretera elevada.
caustic ['kɔ:stɪk] *adj* 1 CHEM cáustico,-a. 2 *fig* cáustico,-a, mordaz. ● **caustic soda** sosa cáustica.
cauterize ['kɔ:təraɪz] *vt* cauterizar.
caution ['kɔ:ʃᵊn] *n* 1 *(care, prudence)* cautela, precaución *f*, prudencia. 2 *(warning)* aviso, advertencia. 3 GB *(from judge, etc)* advertencia.
▷ *vt* 1 *(warn)* advertir. 2 GB *(judge, etc)* amonestar.
cautionary ['kɔ:ʃᵊnᵊrɪ] *adj* aleccionador,-ra: **a cautionary tale** *un cuento con moraleja.*
cautious ['kɔ:ʃəs] *adj* cauteloso,-a, prudente, cauto,-a.
cavalcade [kævᵊl'keɪd] *n (procession - gen)* desfile *m*; *(- on horseback)* cabalgata.
cavalier [kævə'lɪəʳ] *n* caballero.
▷ *adj* arrogante, indiferente.
cavalry ['kævᵊlrɪ] *n* caballería.
▲ *pl* **cavalries.**
cavalryman ['kævᵊlrɪmən] *n* soldado de caballería.
cave [keɪv] *n* cueva. ● **cave dweller** cavernícola *mf*, troglodita *mf.* ❙ **cave painting** pintura rupestre.
⊙ **to cave in** *vi (roof, etc)* hundirse, derrumbarse; *(opposition, etc)* ceder.
caveat ['kævɪæt] *n (warning)* advertencia, salvedad *f.*
caveman ['keɪvmæn] *n* cavernícola *m*, troglodita *m*, hombre *m* de las cavernas.
cavern ['kævᵊn] *n* caverna.
cavernous ['kævᵊnəs] *adj* cavernoso,-a.
caviar ['kævɪɑ:ʳ] *n* caviar *m.*
cavil ['kævɪl] *vi* poner reparos (**about/at**, a).
▲ *pt & pp* **cavilled** (US **caviled**), *ger* **cavilling** (US **caviling**).
caving ['keɪvɪŋ] *n* espeleología. ■ **to go caving** hacer espeleología.
cavity ['kævɪtɪ] *n* 1 *(hole)* cavidad *f.* 2 *(in tooth)* caries *f.*
▲ *pl* **cavities.**
cavort [kə'vɔ:t] *vi* retozar.
caw [kɔ:] *n* graznido.
▷ *vi* graznar.
cayenne [keɪ'en] [Also **cayenne pepper.**] *n* pimienta de cayena.
cayman ['keɪmən] *n* caimán *m.* ● **Cayman Islands** Islas *fpl* Cayman.
CBI ['si:'bi:'aɪ] *abbr* GB (**Confederation of British Industry**) confederación británica de organizaciones empresariales.
CBS ['si:'bi:'es] *abbr* US (**Columbia Broadcasting System**) sociedad norteamericana de radiodifusión; *(abbreviation)* CBS.
cc ['si:'si:] *abbr* (**cubic centimetre**) centímetro cúbico; *(abbreviation)* cc.
CD ['si:'di:] *abbr* (**compact disc**) disco compacto; *(abbreviation)* CD *m.*
CD-ROM ['si:'di:'rɒm] *abbr* (**compact disc read-only memory**) CD-ROM *m.*

CE ['si:əv'i:] *abbr* **(Church of England)** Iglesia Anglicana.
cease [si:s] *vt (production, etc)* suspender.
▷ *vi* cesar. ■ **to cease fire** MIL cesar el fuego.
cease-fire [si:s'faɪəʳ] *n* alto el fuego.
ceaseless ['si:sləs] *adj* incesante.
cecum ['si:kəm] *n* US ciego, intestino ciego.
cedar ['si:dəʳ] *n* BOT cedro.
cede [si:d] *vt* ceder.
ceiling ['si:lɪŋ] *n* **1** *(of room)* techo. **2** *(upper limit)* tope *m*, límite *m*.
celebrate ['selɪbreɪt] *vt* **1** celebrar, festejar. **2** REL celebrar.
▷ *vi* divertirse.
celebrated ['selɪbreɪtɪd] *adj* célebre, famoso,-a.
celebration [selɪ'breɪʃən] *n (event)* fiesta, festejo; *(activity)* celebración *f*.
▷ *n pl* **celebrations** festividades *fpl*, festejos *mpl*.
celebrity [sə'lebrɪtɪ] *n* celebridad *f*, personaje *m* famoso.
▲ *pl* **celebrities.**
celery ['selərɪ] *n* apio.
celestial [sɪ'lestɪəl] *adj* **1** *(heavenly)* celestial. **2** *(of the skies)* celeste.
celibacy ['selɪbəsɪ] *n* celibato.
celibate ['selɪbət] *adj* célibe.
▷ *n* célibe *mf*.
cell [sel] *n* **1** *(in prison, monastery)* celda. **2** *(of honeycomb)* celdilla. **3** *(of organism)* célula. **4** ELEC *(in battery)* pila.
cellar ['seləʳ] *n* **1** *(basement)* sótano. **2** *(for wine)* bodega.
cellist ['tʃelɪst] *n* violoncelista *mf*.
cello ['tʃeləʊ] *n* violoncelo.
▲ *pl* **cellos.**
Cellophane® ['seləfeɪn] *n* celofán® *m*.
cellphone ['selfəʊn] *n* US teléfono móvil.
cellular ['seljələʳ] *adj* celular. ● **cellular telephone** teléfono móvil.
cellulite ['seljʊlaɪt] *n (fat)* celulitis *f*.
celluloid® ['seljəlɔɪd] *n* celuloide® *m*.
cellulose ['seljələʊs] *n* celulosa.
Celsius ['selsɪəs] *adj* Celsius: **30 degrees Celsius** *30 grados Celsius*.
Celt [kelt] *n* celta *mf*.
Celtiberian [keltɪ'bɪərɪən] *n* **1** *(person)* celtibérico,-a, celtíbero,-a, celtibero,-a. **2** *(language)* celtíbero, celtibero.
Celtic ['keltɪk] *adj* celta.
▷ *n (language)* celta *m*.
cement [sɪ'ment] *n* **1** *(in building)* cemento. **2** *(glue)* adhesivo; *(for filling teeth)* empaste *m*. ● **cement mixer** hormigonera.
▷ *vt* **1** *(bind)* unir con cemento; *(cover)* revestir de cemento. **2** *fig* cimentar.
cemetery ['semətrɪ] *n* cementerio.
▲ *pl* **cemeteries.**
cenotaph ['senətɑ:f] *n* cenotafio.
censor ['sensəʳ] *n* censor,-ra.
▷ *vt* censurar.
censorship ['sensəʃɪp] *n* censura.
censure ['senʃəʳ] *n fml* censura.
▷ *vt fml* censurar.
census ['sensəs] *n* censo, padrón *m*. ■ **to take a census** realizar el censo.
cent [sent] *n* centavo, céntimo.
centaur ['sentɔ:ʳ] *n* centauro.
centenary [sen'ti:nərɪ] *n* centenario.
▲ *pl* **centenaries.**
centennial [sen'tenɪəl] *n* US centenario.
▷ *adj* del centenario.
center ['sentəʳ] *n & vb* US → **centre.**
centigrade ['sentɪgreɪd] *adj* centígrado,-a.
centigram ['sentɪgræm] *n* centigramo.
centiliter ['sentɪli:təʳ] *n* US → **centilitre.**
centilitre ['sentɪli:təʳ] *n* centilitro.
centimeter ['sentɪmi:təʳ] *n* US → **centimetre.**
centimetre ['sentɪmi:təʳ] *n* centímetro.
centipede ['sentɪpi:d] *n* ciempiés *m*.
central ['sentrəl] *adj* **1** *(government, bank, committee)* central. **2** *(of, at or near centre)* céntrico,-a. **3** *(main, principal)* principal, fundamental. ● **central nervous system** sistema *m* nervioso central.
centralism ['sentrəlɪzəm] *n* centralismo.
centralization [sentrəlaɪ'zeɪʃən] *n* centralización *f*.
centralize ['sentrəlaɪz] *vt* centralizar.
centrally ['sentrəlɪ] *adv*: **it's very centrally located** *es muy céntrico*.
centre ['sentəʳ] *n* GB *(gen)* centro.
▷ *vt (put in centre)* centrar.
▷ *vi (focus on)* centrarse (**on/upon,** en); *(revolve round)* girar (**around,** alrededor de/en torno a).
centrefold ['sentəfəʊld] *n* página central.
centrepiece ['sentəpi:s] *n* **1** *(decoration)* centro de mesa. **2** *(most important, noticeable, attractive part)* plato fuerte.
centrifugal [sentrɪ'fjʊ:gəl] *adj* centrífugo,-a.
centripetal [sen'trɪpɪtəl] *adj* centrípeto,-a.
century ['sentʃərɪ] *n* siglo: **the twentieth century** *el siglo veinte*.
▲ *pl* **centuries.**
ceramic [sə'ræmɪk] *adj* de cerámica.
▷ *n* cerámica.
ceramics [sə'ræmɪks] *n (art)* cerámica; *(objects)* objetos *mpl* de cerámica.
cereal ['sɪərɪəl] *n (plant, grain)* cereal *m*; *(breakfast food)* cereales *mpl*.
cerebellum [serɪ'beləm] *adj* cerebelo.
cerebral ['serɪbrəl] *adj* cerebral. ● **cerebral palsy** parálisis *f* cerebral. ‖ **cerebral haemorrhage** (US **hemorrhage**) hemorragia cerebral.
cerebrum ['serəbrəm] *adj* cerebro.
ceremonial [serɪ'məʊnɪəl] *adj (gen)* ceremonioso,-a; *(dress)* de gala; *(occasion)* solemne.
▷ *n* ceremonial *m*.
ceremony ['serɪmənɪ] *n* ceremonia.
▲ *pl* **ceremonies.**
cert [sɜ:t] *phr* **to be a cert** *fam* no caber duda.
certain ['sɜ:tən] *adj* **1** *(sure to happen, definite)* seguro,-a: **she's certain to pass** *seguro que aprobará*. **2** *(completely sure, convinced, true)* seguro,-a: **I'm certain** *estoy seguro,-a*. **3** *(specific, particular)* cierto,-a. **4** *(named)* tal: **a certain Pedro Díaz** *un tal Pedro Díaz*. **5** *(limited, some, slight)* cierto,-a.
certainly ['sɜ:tənlɪ] *adv* **1** *(definitely, surely)* seguro. **2** *(when answering questions)* desde luego, por supuesto.

certainty ['sɜːtᵊntɪ] *n* **1** *(state of being certain)* certeza, seguridad *f*. **2** *(certain thing)* cosa segura.
▲ *pl* **certainties.**
certificate [sə'tɪfɪkət] *n (gen)* certificado: **birth certificate** *partida de nacimiento.*
certified ['sɜːtɪfaɪd] *adj* **1** *(cheque)* certificado,-a; *(document)* legalizado,-a. **2** MED declarado,-a demente.
certify ['sɜːtɪfaɪ] *vt* certificar.
▲ *pt & pp* **certified**, *ger* **certifying.**
certitude ['sɜːtɪtjuːd] *n* certeza.
cervical ['sɜːvɪkᵊl] *adj* **1** *(of neck)* cervical. **2** *(of uterus)* del (cuello del) útero. ● **cervical cancer** cáncer *m* de útero.
cervix ['sɜːvɪks] *n* **1** *fml (neck)* cerviz *f*, cuello. **2** *(uterus)* cuello del útero.
▲ *pl* **cervixes** o **cervices.**
cesium ['siːzɪəm] *n* US cesio.
cessation [se'seɪʃᵊn] *n fml* cese *m*.
cesspit ['sespɪt] *n* pozo negro.
cetacean [sɪ'teɪʃᵊn] *adj* cetáceo,-a.
▷ *n* cetáceo.
cf. ['siː'ef] *abbr* (**confer**) compárese; *(abbreviation)* cfr.
chafe [tʃeɪf] *vt* **1** *(make sore)* rozar, excoriar. **2** *(make warm)* frotar, friccionar.
▷ *vi* **1** *(become sore)* irritarse. **2** *(become irritated)* irritarse (**at**, por/con), enfadarse (**at**, por).
chaffinch ['tʃæfɪntʃ] *n* pinzón *m* vulgar.
chagrin ['ʃægrɪn] *n* disgusto, desilusión *f*.
chain [tʃeɪn] *n* **1** *(metal rings)* cadena. **2** *(of shops, hotels, etc)* cadena; *(of events)* cadena, serie *f*. ● **mountain chain** cordillera, cadena montañosa.
▷ *vt* encadenar, atar.
chair [tʃeəʳ] *n (gen)* silla; *(with arms)* sillón *m*, butaca.
▷ *vt (meeting)* presidir.
▷ *n* **the chair** *(in meeting)* presidencia; *(at university)* cátedra. ■ **to address the chair** dirigirse al presidente, dirigirse a la presidencia.
chairman ['tʃeəmən] *n* presidente *m*.
▲ *pl* **chairmen** ['tʃeəmen].
chairmanship ['tʃeəmənʃɪp] *n* presidencia.
chairperson ['tʃeəpɜːsᵊn] *n* presidente,-a.
chairwoman ['tʃeəwʊmən] *n* presidenta.
▲ *pl* **chairwomen** ['tʃeəwɪmɪn].
chaise longue [ʃeɪz'lɒŋ] *n* diván *m*.
chalet ['ʃæleɪ] *n (in mountains)* chalet *m*, chalé *m*; *(in holiday camp)* bungaló *m*, bungalow *m*.
chalice ['tʃælɪs] *n* cáliz *m*.
chalk [tʃɔːk] *n* **1** *(mineral)* creta, roca caliza. **2** *(for writing)* tiza.
▷ *vt* escribir con tiza.
⊙ **to chalk up** *vt insep fam (victory, success)* apuntarse.
challenge ['tʃælɪndʒ] *n (gen)* reto, desafío.
▷ *vt* **1** *(invite to compete)* retar, desafiar. **2** *(question, dispute - person, authority)* poner a prueba, cuestionar; *(- statement)* poner en duda, cuestionar. **3** *(stimulate)* suponer un reto para.
challenger ['tʃælɪndʒəʳ] *n (for title, leadership)* aspirante *mf*; *(opponent, rival)* contrincante *mf*, rival *mf*.
challenging ['tʃælɪndʒɪŋ] *adj (task, job, problem)* que supone un reto, que supone un desafío; *(idea)* estimulante; *(look, tone)* desafiante.
chamber ['tʃeɪmbəʳ] *n* **1** *arch (room)* cámara. **2** *(hall)* sala; *(body)* cámara. **3** ANAT cámara. **4** *(of gun)* recámara.
▷ *n pl* **chambers** JUR *(barrister's office)* gabinete *m*, bufete *m*; *(judge's room)* despacho del juez.
chambermaid ['tʃeɪmbəmeɪd] *n* camarera (de hotel).
chameleon [kə'miːlɪən] *n* camaleón *m*.
champagne [ʃæm'peɪn] *n (French)* champán *m*, champaña; *(Catalan)* cava *m*.
champion ['tʃæmpɪən] *n* **1** campeón,-ona. **2** *fig (defender)* defensor,-ra, paladín,-ina.
▷ *adj* premiado,-a.
▷ *vt fig* defender, abogar por.
championship ['tʃæmpɪənʃɪp] *n* **1** SP campeonato. **2** *fig* defensa.
chance [tʃɑːns] *n* **1** *(fate, fortune)* azar *m*, casualidad *f*. **2** *(opportunity)* oportunidad *f*, ocasión *f*: **you won't get another chance like this** *no se te presentará otra oportunidad como ésta.* **3** *(possibility, likelihood)* posibilidad *f*. **4** *(risk, gamble)* riesgo. ■ **by chance** por casualidad.
▷ *adj (meeting, discovery, occurrence)* fortuito,-a, casual.
▷ *vt (risk)* arriesgar.
chancel ['tʃɑːnsᵊl] *n* presbiterio.
chancellor ['tʃɑːnsᵊləʳ] *n* **1** POL canciller *m*. **2** GB *(of university)* rector,-ra. ● **Chancellor of the Exchequer** GB ministro,-a de Hacienda.
chancy ['tsɑːnsɪ] *adj fam* arriesgado,-a.
▲ *comp* **chancier**, *superl* **chanciest.**
chandelier [ʃændə'lɪəʳ] *n* araña (de luces).
change [tʃeɪndʒ] *n* **1** *(gen)* cambio. **2** *(of clothes)* muda. **3** *(coins)* cambio, monedas *fpl*; *(money returned)* cambio, vuelta.
▷ *vi* cambiar, cambiarse.
changeable ['tʃeɪndʒəbᵊl] *adj (weather)* variable; *(person)* inconstante, voluble.
changeless ['tʃeɪndʒləs] *adj* inmutable.
changeover ['tʃeɪndʒəʊvəʳ] *n* **1** *(gen)* cambio, conversión *f*. **2** SP *(in relay)* relevo.
changing ['tʃeɪndʒɪŋ] *adj* cambiante.
▷ *n* MIL cambio, relevo. ● **changing room** vestuario.
channel ['tʃænᵊl] *n* **1** GEOG *(sea passage)* canal *m*; *(passage for water, liquid)* canal *m*, acequia; *(bed of river, etc)* cauce *m*, lecho. **2** *fig (course, way)* vía, conducto. **3** *(on television)* canal *m*, cadena.
▷ *vt* canalizar, encauzar, dirigir.
▲ *pt & pp* **channelled** (US **channeled**), *ger* **channelling** (US **channeling**).
chant [tʃɑːnt] *n* **1** REL canto litúrgico, cántico. **2** *(of crowd)* eslogan *m*, consigna.
chaos ['keɪɒs] *n* caos *m*.
chaotic [keɪ'ɒtɪk] *adj* caótico,-a.
chap [tʃæp] *n fam* tío, tipo.
chapel ['tʃæpᵊl] *n* **1** REL *(building, room)* capilla. **2** GB *(branch of trade union)* sección *f* sindical.
chaplain ['tʃæplɪn] *n* capellán *m*.
chapter ['tʃæptəʳ] *n* **1** *(of book, of history)* capítulo. **2** REL cabildo.
char[1] [tʃɑːʳ] *vt* chamuscar, carbonizar.
▲ *pt & pp* **charred**, *ger* **charring.**
char[2] [tʃɑːʳ] *vi* trabajar de asistenta.
▲ *pt & pp* **charred**, *ger* **charring.**

character ['kærəktə^r] *n* **1** *(nature)* carácter *m*. **2** *(reputation)* reputación *f*; *(integrity, moral strength)* carácter *m*, personalidad *f*. **3** *(in film, book, play)* personaje *m*.
characteristic [kærəktə'rɪstɪk] *adj* característico,-a.
▷ *n* característica.
characterize ['kærəktəraɪz] *vt (be typical of)* caracterizar; *(describe character of)* calificar (**as**, de); *(in fiction)* caracterizar, describir.
chard [tʃɑːd] *n* acelga.
charge [tʃɑːdʒ] *n* **1** *(price)* precio; *(fee(s))* honorarios *mpl*. **2** *(responsibility)* cargo. **3** JUR cargo, acusación *f*. **4** MIL *(attack)* carga. **5** *(explosive)* carga explosiva. **6** ELEC carga.
▷ *vt* **1** *(ask as a price - customer, amount)* cobrar; *(record as debit)* cargar: **2** JUR acusar (**with**, de). **3** ELEC cargar. **4** MIL cargar contra, atacar.
charged [tʃɑːdʒd] *adj* **1** ELEC cargado,-a. **2** *fig (voice, atmosphere)* cargado,-a (**with**, de). **3** *fig (issue)* emotivo,-a.
charger ['tʃɑːdʒə^r] *n* **1** ELEC cargador *m*. **2** *(horse)* corcel *m*.
chariot ['tʃærɪət] *n* cuadriga, carro (de guerra).
charisma [kə'rɪzmə] *n* carisma *m*.
charitable ['tʃærɪtəbᵊl] *adj* **1** *(person)* caritativo,-a; *(attitude)* benévolo,-a, comprensivo,-a. **2** *(organization)* benéfico,-a.
charity ['tʃærɪtɪ] *n* **1** *(generosity, kindness)* caridad *f*. **2** *(help given, alms)* limosna, caridad *f*. **3** *(organization)* institución *f* benéfica, institución *f* de beneficencia; *(relief projects)* obras *fpl* de beneficencia.
▲ *pl* **charities.**
charlatan ['ʃɑːlətᵊn] *n (quack)* curandero,-a.
charm [tʃɑːm] *n* **1** *(quality)* encanto. **2** *(object)* amuleto. **3** *(spell)* hechizo.
▷ *vt* **1** *(delight)* encantar, cautivar, embelesar. **2** *(influence or protect by magic)* encantar, hechizar.
charmer ['tʃɑːmə^r] *n* **1** *(charming person)* persona encantadora. **2** *(of snakes)* encantador,-ra.
charming ['tʃɑːmɪŋ] *adj (delightful)* encantador,-ra.
chart [tʃɑːt] *n* **1** *(table)* tabla; *(graph)* gráfico; *(map)* carta, mapa *m*. **2** *(navigational)* carta de navegación.
▷ *vt* **1** *(make a map of)* trazar un mapa de; *(plan, plot on map)* trazar. **2** *(record)* registrar gráficamente; *(follow)* seguir; *(show)* mostrar, reflejar.
▷ *n pl* **the charts** MUS la lista de éxitos, el hit parade *m*.
charter ['tʃɑːtə^r] *n* **1** *(of town)* fuero; *(of company)* escritura de constitución, estatutos *mpl*; *(of university)* estatutos *mpl*: **by royal charter** *por cédula real*. **2** *(constitution)* carta. **3** *(hiring of plane, etc)* fletamiento.
▷ *vt* **1** *(grant rights, privileges to)* aprobar los estatutos de. **2** *(hire plane, boat, etc)* fletar, alquilar.
chartered ['tʃɑːtəd] *adj (qualified)* colegiado,-a. ● **chartered accountant** contable *mf* diplomado,-a.
chase¹ [tʃeɪs] *n (gen)* persecución *f*; *(hunt)* caza.
▷ *vt* **1** *(gen)* perseguir, dar caza a; *(hunt)* cazar. **2** *fam (job, client, etc)* ir a la caza de; *(success)* ir en busca de, perseguir.
chase² [tʃeɪs] *vt (engrave, emboss)* cincelar, grabar.
chasm ['kæzᵊm] *n* **1** GEOG sima. **2** *fig* abismo.
chassis ['ʃæsɪ] *n* chasis *m*.
▲ *pl* **chassis.**
chaste [tʃeɪst] *adj* **1** *(pure)* casto,-a, puro,-a. **2** *(not ornate)* sobrio,-a, sencillo,-a.
chasten ['tʃeɪsᵊn] *vt (discipline)* castigar, escarmentar.
chastise [tʃæs'taɪz] *vt fml* castigar.
chastity ['tʃæstɪtɪ] *n* castidad *f*.
chat [tʃæt] *n* **1** *(in general)* charla. **2** *(on Internet)* charla, chat *m*.
chatter ['tʃætə^r] *n* **1** *(rapid talk)* cháchara, parloteo. **2** *(noise - of teeth)* castañeteo; *(- of machine gun)* tableteo; *(- of birds)* gorjeo; *(- of monkeys)* chillidos *mpl*.
▷ *vi* **1** *(talk rapidly)* chacharear, parlotear, cotorrear. **2** *(teeth)* castañetear; *(birds)* piar, gorjear; *(monkeys)* chillar.
chatterbox ['tʃætəbɒks] *n fam* parlanchín,-ina, charlatán,-ana, tarabilla *mf*, cotorra *mf*.
chatty ['tʃætɪ] *adj (person)* hablador,-ra, parlanchín, -ina, conversador,-ra; *(style)* informal.
▲ *comp* **chattier**, *superl* **chattiest.**
chauffeur ['ʃəʊfə^r] *n* chófer *mf*, chofer *mf*.
chauvinism ['ʃəʊvɪnɪzᵊm] *n* chovinismo.
cheap [tʃiːp] *adj* **1** *(gen)* barato,-a; *(fare, ticket)* económico,-a. **2** *(of poor quality, shoddy)* ordinario,-a, de baratillo. **3** *(contemptible - trick, gibe, crook)* vil, bajo, -a; *(vulgar - joke, remark)* de mal gusto. **4** *(worthless, insincere)* fácil.
▷ *adv* barato.
cheapen ['tʃiːpᵊn] *vt* **1** *(in price)* abaratar, rebajar el precio de. **2** *(degrade)* degradar, rebajar.
cheaply ['tʃiːplɪ] *adv (for a low price)* barato, a bajo precio; *(in a cheap manner)* económicamente, en plan barato.
cheat [tʃiːt] *n* **1** *(person - at cards)* tramposo,-a, fullero,-a; *(in exam, etc)* tramposo,-a; *(swindler)* estafador,-ra, timador,-ra. **2** *(trick)* trampa; *(swindle)* estafa, timo.
▷ *vt (trick, deceive)* engañar; *(swindle)* estafar, timar.
▷ *vi (gen)* hacer trampa(s); *(in exam)* hacer trampa, copiar.
check [tʃek] *n* **1** *(examination - of documents, goods, people)* revisión *f*, control *m*; *(of work)* examen *m*, revisión *f*; *(of machine)* verificación *f*, inspección *f*; *(of results, facts, information)* comprobación *f*, verificación *f*. **2** *(stop, restraint)* control *m*, freno. **3** US → **cheque.** **4** US *(bill)* cuenta, nota. **5** US *(receipt, ticket)* ticket *m*, resguardo. **6** *(chess)* jaque *m*.
▷ *vi (make sure)* comprobar, verificar.
⊙ **to check in** *vi (at airport)* facturar el equipaje; *(at hotel)* registrarse.
▷ *vt sep* facturar.
⊙ **to check out** *vi* pagar la cuenta e irse, dejar el hotel.
▷ *vt sep (facts, information)* verificar, comprobar; *(place)* ir a ver; *(person)* hacer averiguaciones sobre.
checkbook ['tʃekbʊk] *n* US → **chequebook.**
checked [tʃekt] *adj* a cuadros.
checkerboard ['tʃekᵊbɔːd] *n* US → **chequerboard.**
checkered ['tʃekᵊd] *adj* US → **chequered.**
checkers ['tʃekəz] *n pl* US damas *fpl*.
checklist ['tʃeklɪst] *n* lista de control.
checkmate ['tʃekmeɪt] *n* (jaque *m*) mate *m*.
▷ *vt* dar (jaque) mate a.
checkout ['tʃekaʊt] *n (in supermarket)* caja. ● **checkout boy/girl** cajero,-a.
checkpoint ['tʃekpɔɪnt] *n* control *m*.
checkroom ['tʃekruːm] *n* US guardarropa.

checkup ['tʃekʌp] *n (by doctor)* chequeo, revisión *f* médica, reconocimiento médico; *(by dentist)* chequeo, revisión *f*.
cheek [tʃi:k] *n* **1** ANAT *(on face)* mejilla; *(buttock)* nalga. **2** *fam (nerve, impudence)* descaro, frescura, cara.
▷ *vt* insolentarse con, replicar.
cheekbone ['tʃi:kbəʊn] *n* pómulo.
cheeky ['tʃi:kɪ] *adj (person)* descarado,-a, fresco,-a; *(smile)* pícaro,-a; *(remark)* impertinente. ● **cheeky devil** caradura *mf*.
▲ *comp* **cheekier**, *superl* **cheekiest**.
cheep [tʃi:p] *n* pío, piada, gorjeo.
▷ *vi* piar, gorjear.
cheer [tʃɪəʳ] *n* **1** *(shout of joy)* viva *m*, vítor *m*, hurra *m*. **2** *(happiness)* alegría.
▷ *vt* **1** *(applaud with shouts)* vitorear, aclamar. **2** *(gladden)* animar, alegrar.
⊙ **to cheer up** *vt sep* animar, alegrar.
▷ *vi* animarse, alegrarse: **cheer up!** *¡ánimo!*
cheerful ['tʃɪəfʊl] *adj (happy - person)* alegre, animado,-a, risueño,-a.
cheerio [tʃɪərɪ'əʊ] *interj* GB *fam* ¡adiós!, ¡hasta luego!
cheerleader ['tʃɪəli:dəʳ] *n* animador,-ra (de un equipo deportivo).
cheers [tʃɪəz] *interj* **1** *fam (as toast)* ¡salud! **2** *fam (thanks)* ¡gracias! **3** *fam (goodbye)* ¡adiós!, ¡hasta luego!
cheese [tʃi:z] *n* queso.
cheetah ['tʃi:tə] *n* guepardo.
chef [ʃef] *n* chef *m*, jefe,-a de cocina.
chemical ['kemɪkəl] *adj* químico,-a.
▷ *n* producto químico, sustancia química.
chemist ['kemɪst] *n* **1** CHEM químico,-a. **2** GB *(pharmacist)* farmacéutico,-a. ● **chemist's (shop)** GB farmacia.
chemistry ['kemɪstrɪ] *n* química.
chemotherapy [ki:məʊ'θerəpɪ] *n* quimioterapia.
cheque [tʃek] *n* cheque *m*, talón *m*.
chequerboard ['tʃekəbɔ:d] *n* tablero de damas.
chequebook ['tʃekbuk] *n* talonario de cheques.
chequered ['tʃekəd] *adj* **1** *(cloth, pattern)* a cuadros. **2** *fig (past, history, career)* con altibajos, accidentado,-a.
chequers ['tʃekəz] *n pl* damas *fpl*.
cherish ['tʃerɪʃ] *vt* **1** *(person)* apreciar, querer, tenerle mucho cariño a. **2** *(hope, memory, illusion)* abrigar, albergar, acariciar.
cherry ['tʃerɪ] *n (fruit)* cereza, guinda; *(wood)* cerezo.
▲ *pl* **cherries**. ● **cherry tree** cerezo.
chess [tʃes] *n* ajedrez *m*: **a game of chess** *una partida de ajedrez*.
chessboard ['tʃesbɔ:d] *n* tablero de ajedrez.
chessmen ['tʃesmən] *n pl* piezas *fpl* de ajedrez.
chesspiece ['tʃespi:s] *n* pieza de ajedrez.
chest [tʃest] *n* **1** *(large)* arca, arcón *m*; *(small)* cofre *m*; *(tea chest, packing case)* cajón *m*; *(trunk)* baúl *m*. **2** ANAT pecho: **chest pains** *dolores de pecho*.
chestnut ['tʃesnʌt] *n* **1** BOT *(tree, wood)* castaño; *(nut)* castaña. **2** *(colour)* castaño. **3** *(horse)* alazán,-ana. **4** *(story)* historia vieja; *(joke)* chiste *m* viejo.
▷ *adj (colour)* castaño,-a; *(horse)* castaño,-a, zaino,-a, alazán,-ana.
chew [tʃʊ:] *vt (food)* mascar, masticar; *(nails, pencil)* morder; *(gum, tobacco)* mascar.
▷ *n (of tobacco)* mascada; *(sweet)* caramelo.
chewing gum ['tʃʊ:ɪŋgʌm] *n* chicle *m*, goma de mascar.
chic [ʃi:k] *adj* chic, elegante.
▷ *n* elegancia.
chick [tʃɪk] *n (young chicken)* pollito, polluelo; *(young bird)* polluelo.
chicken ['tʃɪkɪn] *n* **1** *(hen)* gallina; *(food)* pollo. **2** *fam (coward)* gallina *mf*.
▷ *adj fam* gallina. ● **chicken feed** una miseria. ‖ **chicken stock** caldo de gallina. ‖ **chicken wire** alambrera.
chickenpox ['tʃɪkɪnpɒks] *n* varicela.
chickpea ['tʃɪkpi:] *n* garbanzo.
chicory ['tʃɪkərɪ] *n* achicoria, chicoria.
chief [tʃi:f] *n (gen)* jefe,-a; *(of party)* líder *mf*; *(of tribe)* cacique *m*.
▷ *adj* principal.
chiefly ['tʃi:flɪ] *adv (mainly)* principalmente; *(especially)* sobre todo.
chieftain ['tʃi:ftən] *n* cacique *m*, jefe,-a.
chiffon ['ʃɪfɒn] *n* gasa.
chilblain ['tʃɪlbleɪn] *n* sabañón *m*.
child [tʃaɪld] *n* **1** *(boy)* niño; *(girl)* niña. **2** *(son)* hijo; *(daughter)* hija.
▲ *pl* **children**.
childbearing ['tʃaɪldbeərɪŋ] *n* maternidad *f*. ■ **of childbearing age** en edad fértil, en edad de tener hijos.
childbirth ['tʃaɪldbɜ:θ] *n* parto, alumbramiento.
childhood ['tʃaɪldhʊd] *n* infancia, niñez *f*.
childish ['tʃaɪldɪʃ] *adj (of a child)* infantil; *(immature)* pueril, infantil.
childlike ['tʃaɪldlaɪk] *adj* infantil, ingenuo,-a.
childproof ['tʃaɪldpru:f] *adj* a prueba de niños.
children ['tʃɪldrən] *n pl* → **child**.
chili ['tʃɪlɪ] *n* US → **chilli**.
chill [tʃɪl] *n* **1** MED *(cold)* resfriado; *(shiver)* escalofrío. **2** *(coldness)* fresco, frío.
▷ *adj (wind, etc)* frío,-a.
▷ *vt* **1** *(make cold)* enfriar. **2** *(wine, beer)* enfriar, poner a enfriar; *(meat)* refrigerar: **3** *fig* hacer sentir escalofríos.
chilli ['tʃɪlɪ] *n* chile *m*.
chilling ['tʃɪlɪŋ] *adj* **1** glacial. **2** *fig* espeluznante, escalofriante.
chilly ['tʃɪlɪ] *adj (gen)* frío,-a.
▲ *comp* **chillier**, *superl* **chilliest**.
chime [tʃaɪm] *n (bells)* carillón *m*; *(sound of bells)* repique *m*; *(of clock)* campanada; *(of doorbell)* campanilla.
▷ *vi (bells)* sonar, repicar; *(clock)* dar la hora, sonar.
⊙ **to chime in** *vi (interrupt)* intervenir, interrumpir.
chimney ['tʃɪmnɪ] *n* chimenea.
chimpanzee [tʃɪmpæn'zi:] *n* chimpancé *m*.
chin [tʃɪn] *n* barbilla, mentón *m*.
china ['tʃaɪnə] *n* **1** *(white clay)* loza; *(fine)* porcelana. **2** *(crockery)* vajilla, objetos *mpl* de porcelana, loza.
China ['tʃaɪnə] *n* China.
Chinese [tʃaɪ'ni:z] *adj* chino,-a.
▷ *n* **1** *(person)* chino,-a. **2** *(language)* chino.
▷ *n pl* **the Chinese** los chinos *mpl*.
chink[1] [tʃɪŋk] *n (crack - in wall, fence)* grieta, abertura; *(- in door)* rendija, resquicio.
chink[2] [tʃɪŋk] *n (noise)* tintineo.
▷ *vt* hacer tintinear, hacer sonar.

chip [tʃɪp] *n* 1 GB *(fried potato)* patata frita. 2 US patata frita (de bolsa). 3 COMPUT chip *m*: 4 *(of wood)* astilla; *(of stone)* lasca; *(of china)* pedacito, trocito. 5 *(flaw - in plate, glass)* desportilladura; *(- in furniture)* astilladura. 6 *(in gambling)* ficha.
▷ *vt* 1 GB *(potatoes)* cortar. 2 *(china, glass)* desportillar, resquebrar; *(paint)* desconchar; *(tooth)* romper un trocito de.
▲ *pt & pp* **chipped**, *ger* **chipping**.
chipboard ['tʃɪpbɔːd] *n* madera aglomerada.
chiropodist [kɪ'rɒpədɪst] *n* podólogo,-a, pedicuro,-a, callista *mf*.
chirp [tʃɜːp] *vi (insect)* chirriar; *(bird)* gorjear.
▷ *n (of grasshopper)* chirrido; *(of bird)* gorjeo.
chisel ['tʃɪzᵊl] *n (for stone)* cincel *m*.
▷ *vt (stone)* cincelar; *(wood, metal)* labrar, tallar; *(hole, etc)* grabar, cincelar.
▲ *pt & pp* **chiselled** (US **chiseled**), *ger* **chiselling** (US **chiseling**).
chit [tʃɪt] *n fam (note)* nota; *(memo)* memorándum *m*; *(receipt)* recibo, resguardo.
chitchat ['tʃɪttʃæt] *n fam* palique *m*, cháchara.
chivalrous ['ʃɪvᵊlrəs] *adj* caballeroso,-a.
chivalry ['ʃɪvᵊlrɪ] *n* caballerosidad *f*.
chives [tʃaɪvz] *n pl* BOT cebollino, cebolleta.
chloric ['klɔːrɪk] *adj* clórico,-a cloram.
chloride ['klɔːraɪd] *n* cloruro.
chlorinate ['klɔːrɪneɪt] *vt* tratar con cloro.
chlorine ['klɔːriːn] *n* cloro.
chloroform ['klɒrəfɔːm] *n* cloroformo.
chlorophyll ['klɒrəfɪl] *n* clorofila.
chock [tʃɒk] *n* calzo, cuña.
chock-a-block [tʃɒkə'blɒk] *adj fam* hasta los topes, de bote en bote.
chock-full [tʃɒk'fʊl] *adj fam* hasta los topes.
chocolate ['tʃɒkᵊlət] *n* 1 *(substance)* chocolate *m*: **a bar of chocolate** *una chocolatina, una tableta de chocolate*. 2 *(individual sweet)* bombón *m*.
choice [tʃɔɪs] *n* 1 *(act)* elección *f*, opción *f*; *(option)* opción *f*, alternativa. 2 *(person, thing chosen)* elección *f*. 3 *(variety, range)* surtido, selección *f*.
▷ *adj* 1 *(top quality)* selecto,-a, de primera calidad. 2 *iron (rude)* exquisito,-a.
choir ['kwaɪəʳ] *n (gen)* coro.
choirboy ['kwaɪəbɔɪ] *n* niño de coro.
choirmaster ['kweɪəmɑːstəʳ] *n (gen)* director *m* de coro; *(in church)* maestro de coro.
choke [tʃəʊk] *vt* 1 *(person)* ahogar, asfixiar, estrangular. 2 *(block - pipe, drain, etc)* atascar, obstruir.
▷ *n* estárter *m*.
choked [tʃəʊkt] *adj (upset)* disgustado,-a; *(disappointed)* decepcionado,-a; *(angry)* furioso,-a.
cholera ['kɒlərə] *n* cólera *m*.
cholesterol [kə'lestᵊrɒl] *n* colesterol *m*.
chomp [tʃɒmp] *vt* masticar, mascar.
▷ *vi* masticar, mascar.
choose [tʃuːz] *vt* 1 *(select)* escoger, elegir; *(elect)* elegir. 2 *(decide)* decidir, optar por.
▲ *pt* **chose** [tʃəʊz], *pp* **chosen** ['tʃəʊzᵊn], *ger* **choosing**.
choosy ['tʃuːzɪ] *adj fam* exigente, difícil de contentar.
▲ *comp* **choosier**, *superl* **choosiest**.

chop [tʃɒp] *n* 1 *(blow)* tajo, golpe *m*; *(with axe)* hachazo. 2 CULIN chuleta.
▷ *vt* 1 cortar (**up**, -). 2 CULIN *(meat)* cortar en trozos (**up**, -); *(onions)* picar (**up**, -). 3 GB *fam (reduce)* recortar, reducir.
▲ *pt & pp* **chopped**, *ger* **chopping**.
⊙ **to chop down** *vt sep (tree, etc)* cortar, talar.
⊙ **to chop off** *vt sep* cortar.
chopper ['tʃɒpəʳ] *n* 1 *(short axe)* hacha pequeña; *(butcher's)* cuchilla de carnicero. 2 *fam (helicopter)* helicóptero.
chopping board ['tʃɒpɪŋbɔːd] *n* tabla de picar.
choppy ['tʃɒpɪ] *adj (sea)* picado,-a.
▲ *comp* **choppier**, *superl* **choppiest**.
chopsticks ['tʃɒpstɪks] *n pl* palillos *mpl*.
choral ['kɔːrᵊl] *adj* coral. ● **choral society** coral *f*, orfeón *m*.
chorale [kə'rɑːl] *n* coral *f*.
chord¹ [kɔːd] *n* 1 MATH cuerda. 2 ANAT ⟶ **cord**.
chord² [kɔːd] *n* MUS acorde *m*.
chore [tʃɔːʳ] *n (job)* quehacer *m*, tarea; *(boring job)* lata.
choreography [kɒrɪ'ɒgrəfɪ] *n* coreografía.
chorister ['kɒrɪstəʳ] *n* corista *mf*.
chortle ['tʃɔːtᵊl] *vi* reírse, reírse con ganas.
chorus ['kɔːrəs] *n* 1 *(choir)* coro. 2 *(of song)* estribillo. 3 *(outburst)* coro.
chose [tʃəʊz] *pt* ⟶ **choose**.
chosen ['tʃəʊzᵊn] *pp* ⟶ **choose**.
▷ *adj* elegido,-a, escogido,-a.
Christ [kraɪst] *n* Cristo, Jesucristo.
christening ['krɪsᵊnɪŋ] *n (ritual)* bautismo; *(celebration)* bautizo.
Christian ['krɪstɪən] *adj* cristiano,-a.
▷ *n* cristiano,-a.
Christianity [krɪstɪ'ænɪtɪ] *n* cristianismo.
Christmas ['krɪsməs] *n* Navidad *f*, Navidades *fpl*. ● **Christmas Eve** Nochebuena. ‖ **Christmas Day** día *m* de Navidad.
chrome [krəʊm] *n* cromo.
chromosome ['krəʊməsəʊm] *n* cromosoma *m*.
chronic ['krɒnɪk] *adj* 1 *(disease, person, problem)* crónico,-a. 2 GB *fam (terrible)* malísimo,-a, terrible.
chronicle ['krɒnɪkᵊl] *n* crónica.
chronological [krɒnə'lɒdʒɪkᵊl] *adj* cronológico,-a.
chronology [krə'nɒlədʒɪ] *n* cronología.
chronometer [krə'nɒmɪtəʳ] *n* cronómetro.
chrysalis ['krɪsəlɪs] *n* crisálida.
▲ *pl* **chrysalises**.
chrysanthemum [krɪ'sænθəməm] *n* crisantemo.
chubby ['tʃʌbɪ] *adj (person)* regordete,-a, gordinflón,-ona, llenito,-a; *(part of body)* regordete,-a, llenito,-a.
▲ *comp* **chubbier**, *superl* **chubbiest**.
chuck [tʃʌk] *vt* 1 *fam (throw)* tirar. 2 *fam (give up)* dejar, plantar.
⊙ **to chuck away** *vt sep (rubbish)* tirar; *(money)* derrochar.
chuckle ['tʃʌkᵊl] *vi* reírse (entre dientes).
▷ *n* risita.
chuffed [tʃʌft] *adj* GB *fam* contento,-a, satisfecho,-a.
chug [tʃʌg] *n* resoplido.
▷ *vi (engine)* resoplar, dar resoplidos.
▲ *pt & pp* **chugged**, *ger* **chugging**.

chum [tʃʌm] *n fam* compinche *mf*, compañero,-a, amigote *m*.
⊙ **to chum up with** *vi* hacerse amigo,-a de.
▲ *pt & pp* **chummed**, *ger* **chumming**.
chummy ['tʃʌmɪ] *adj* amigo,-a.
▲ *comp* **chummier**, *superl* **chummiest**.
chunk [tʃʌŋk] *n fam (thick piece)* cacho, pedazo; *(large amount)* buena parte *f*.
church [tʃɜ:tʃ] *n* iglesia. ● **Church of England** Iglesia Anglicana.
churchyard ['tʃɜ:tʃjɑ:d] *n* cementerio, camposanto.
churlish ['tʃɜ:lɪʃ] *adj* grosero,-a, maleducado,-a.
churn [tʃɜ:n] *n* **1** GB *(for milk)* lechera. **2** *(for butter)* mantequera.
▷ *vt* **1** *(butter)* hacer; *(milk, cream)* batir. **2** *(water, earth)* agitar (**up**, -), revolver (**up**, -).
▷ *vi* **1** *(liquid)* arremolinarse. **2** *(stomach)* revolverse.
⊙ **to churn out** *vt sep* producir en serie, hacer como churros.
chute [ʃu:t] *n* **1** *(slide)* tobogán *m*. **2** *(for waste, rubbish)* conducto. **3** *fam* paracaídas *m*.
chutney ['tʃʌtnɪ] *n* conserva agridulce *hecha a base de frutas, especias, vinagre y azúcar*.
CIA ['si:'ai:'eɪ] *abbr* (**Central Intelligence Agency**) agencia central de información; *(abbreviation)* CIA *f*.
cicada [sɪ'kɑ:də] *n* cigarra.
cider ['saɪdəʳ] *n* sidra.
cigar [sɪ'gɑ:ʳ] *n* puro, cigarro.
cigarette [sɪgə'ret] *n* cigarrillo.
cinder ['sɪndəʳ] *n* ceniza, pavesa.
▷ *n pl* **cinders** ceniza *f sing*, carbonilla *f sing*.
Cinderella [sɪndə'relə] *n* (la) Cenicienta.
cine camera ['sɪnɪkæmᵊrə] *n* cámara cinematográfica, tomavistas *m*.
cinema ['sɪnəmə] *n* cine *m*.
cinematographic [sɪnəmætə'græfɪk] *adj* cinematográfico,-a.
cinnamon ['sɪnəmən] *n* canela.
cipher ['saɪfəʳ] *n* **1** *(code)* código, cifra, clave *f*. **2** *(zero)* cero; *(numeral)* cifra.
circa ['sɜ:kə] *prep* hacia, alrededor de.
circle ['sɜ:kᵊl] *n* **1** *(shape)* círculo; *(in geometry)* circunferencia. **2** *(ring)* círculo; *(of people)* corro. **3** *(group)* círculo.
▷ *vt* **1** *(encircle)* rodear, cercar; *(move in a circle)* dar vueltas alrededor de. **2** *(ring with pen, pencil)* trazar un círculo alrededor de, marcar con un círculo.
circuit ['sɜ:kɪt] *n* **1** *(route, journey round)* recorrido; *(of running track)* vuelta. **2** ELEC circuito. **3** JUR *(regular journey made by judge)* recorrido; *(area covered)* distrito. **4** SP *(series of tournaments)* circuito. **5** *(motor racing track)* circuito.
circuitous [sə'kju:ɪtəs] *adj fml* tortuoso,-a, indirecto,-a.
circular ['sɜ:kjələʳ] *adj* **1** *(gen)* circular; *(bus, train route)* de circunvalación. **2** *fig (argument)* que no lleva a ninguna parte, que no conduce a nada.
circulate ['sɜ:kjəleɪt] *vi (gen)* circular; *(rumour, story)* circular, correr.
▷ *vt* **1** *(pass round)* hacer circular. **2** *(send circular to)* enviar una circular a.
circulation [sɜ:kjə'leɪʃᵊn] *n* **1** *(gen)* circulación *f*. **2** *(of newspaper, magazine)* tirada.
circulatory [sɜ:kjə'leɪtərɪ] *adj* circulatorio,-a.
circumcision [sɜ:kəm'sɪʒᵊn] *n* circuncisión *f*.
circumference [sə'kʌmfᵊrəns] *n* circunferencia.
circumflex ['sɜ:kəmfleks] *n* circunflejo.
circumlocution [sɜ:kəmlə'kju:ʃᵊn] *n* circunloquio.
circumnavigate [sɜ:kəm'nævɪgeɪt] *vt* circunnavegar.
circumscribe ['sɜ:kəmskraɪb] *vt* **1** MATH circunscribir. **2** *fml (restrict)* restringir, limitar.
circumspect ['sɜ:kəmspekt] *adj* circunspecto,-a, prudente, cauto,-a, cauteloso,-a.
circumspection [sɜ:kəm'spekʃᵊn] *n* circunspección *f*.
circumstance ['sɜ:kəmstəns] *n (condition, fact)* circunstancia.
▷ *n pl* **circumstances** *(financial position)* situación *f* económica.
circumvent [sɜ:kəm'vent] *vt fml (law, rule, regulation)* burlar.
circus ['sɜ:kəs] *n* **1** *(entertainment)* circo. **2** GB *(in town)* glorieta, plaza redonda.
cirque [sɜ:k] *n* circo.
cistern ['sɪstən] *n* cisterna.
citadel ['sɪtədᵊl] *n* ciudadela.
cite [saɪt] *vt* **1** *(quote)* citar. **2** US *(military)* mencionar. **3** JUR citar.
citizen ['sɪtɪzᵊn] *n (of country)* ciudadano,-a, súbdito,-a; *(of town, city)* habitante *mf*, vecino,-a.
citizenship ['sɪtɪzᵊnʃɪp] *n* ciudadanía.
citric ['sɪtrɪk] *adj* cítrico,-a.
citrus fruit ['sɪtrəsfru:t] *n* agrio, cítrico.
city ['sɪtɪ] *n* ciudad *f*. ● **city council** GB ayuntamiento, municipio. ▮ **the City** GB el centro financiero de Londres.
▲ *pl* **cities**.
civic ['sɪvɪk] *adj (duty, pride)* cívico,-a; *(leader, event)* municipal.
civics ['sɪvɪks] *n* educación *f* cívica.
civil ['sɪvᵊl] *adj* **1** *(of citizens)* civil. **2** *(polite)* cortés, educado,-a. ● **civil servant** funcionario,-a.
civilian [sɪ'vɪljən] *adj (government, life)* civil.
▷ *n* civil *mf*. ■ **in civilian dress** de paisano.
▷ *n pl* **civilians** población *f sing* civil.
civility [sɪ'vɪlɪtɪ] *n* cortesía.
civilization [sɪvɪlaɪ'zeɪʃᵊn] *n* civilización *f*.
civilize ['sɪvɪlaɪz] *vt* civilizar.
civvies ['sɪvɪz] *n pl* GB *fam* ropa *f sing* de paisano, traje *m sing* de paisano.
cl ['si:'el] *symb* (**centilitre**) centilitro; *(symbol)* cl.
clad [klæd] *pt & pp* → **clothe**.
▷ *adj* vestido,-a.
claim [kleɪm] *n* **1** *(demand - for insurance)* reclamación *f*; *(for wages)* demanda, reivindicación *f*; *(for benefit, allowance)* solicitud *f*. **2** *(right - to title, right, property)* derecho. **3** *(assertion)* afirmación *f*. **4** *(thing claimed - land)* concesión *f*.
▷ *vt* **1** *(right, property, title)* reclamar; *(land)* reclamar, reivindicar; *(compensation)* exigir, reclamar; *(immunity)* alegar. **2** *(apply for - benefit, allowance)* solicitar; *(- expenses)* pedir, solicitar; *(receive)* cobrar. **3** *(of disaster, accident, etc)* cobrar. **4** *(assert)* afirmar, sostener, decir. **5** *(attention)* reclamar; *(time)* exigir.
▷ *vi* presentar un reclamación, reclamar.

claimant ['kleɪmənt] *n* 1 *(of benefit, allowance)* solicitante *mf*; *(of insurance)* reclamante *mf*. 2 *(to throne)* pretendiente *mf*. 3 JUR demandante *mf*.
clairvoyance [kleə'vɔɪəns] *n* clarividencia.
clam [klæm] *n* almeja.
⊙ **to clam up** *vi fam* callarse, quedarse mudo,-a.
▲ *pt & pp* clammed, *ger* clamming.
clamber ['klæmbəʳ] *vi* trepar gateando (over, a).
clammy ['klæmɪ] *adj (weather)* bochornoso,-a; *(hands)* pegajoso,-a.
▲ *comp* clammier, *superl* clammiest.
clamor ['klæməʳ] *n* US ⟶ clamour.
clamorous ['klæmərəs] *adj (demand)* clamoroso,-a; *(crowd)* vociferante, ruidoso,-a.
clamour ['klæməʳ] *n (shouting)* clamor *m*, griterío; *(loud protest)* clamor *m*.
▷ *vi* clamar, gritar, dar voces, vociferar.
clamp [klæmp] *n (gen)* abrazadera; *(in carpentry)* tornillo de banco.
▷ *vt (gen)* sujetar con abrazaderas; *(wheel)* poner un cepo a.
⊙ **to clamp down on** *vt insep* poner freno a, tomar medidas drásticas contra.
clampdown ['klæmpdaʊn] *n* medidas *fpl* drásticas.
clan [klæn] *n* clan *m*.
clandestine [klæn'destɪn] *adj* clandestino,-a.
clang [klæŋ] *n* sonido metálico (fuerte).
▷ *vi* sonar.
clank [klæŋk] *n* sonido seco y metálico.
▷ *vi* hacer ruido, sonar.
clannish ['klænɪʃ] *adj* cerrado,-a, exclusivista.
clansman ['klænzmən] *n* miembro de un clan.
▲ *pl* clansmen ['klænzmɪn].
clap [klæp] *n* 1 *(noise)* ruido seco. 2 *(applause)* aplauso. 3 *(slap)* palmada, golpecito con la mano.
▷ *vt* 1 *(applaud)* aplaudir. 2 *(slap)* dar una palmada a.
⊙ **to clap on** *vt sep (add)* agregar.
clapped-out [klæpt'aʊt] *adj* GB *fam (car, machine)* destartalado,-a; *(person)* rendido,-a, reventado,-a, hecho,-a polvo.
clapperboard ['klæpəbɔːd] *n* claqueta.
clapping ['klæpɪŋ] *n* aplausos *mpl*.
claret ['klærət] *n (wine)* clarete *m*; *(colour)* granate *m*, color *m* burdeos.
clarification [klærɪfɪ'keɪʃᵊn] *n* aclaración *f*.
clarify ['klærɪfaɪ] *vt* aclarar.
▷ *vi* aclararse.
▲ *pt & pp* clarified, *ger* clarifying.
clarinet [klærɪ'net] *n* 1 *(instrument)* clarinete *m*. 2 *(musician)* clarinete *mf*, clarinetista *mf*.
clarity ['klærɪtɪ] *n* claridad *f*.
clash [klæʃ] *n* 1 *(fight)* enfrentamiento, choque *m*; *(disagreement, argument)* desacuerdo. 2 *(conflict - of interests)* conflicto; *(- of personalities, cultures)* choque *m*; *(- of opinions)* disparidad *f*, choque *m*; *(coinciding - of times, dates, classes)* coincidencia; *(bad match - of colours)* falta de armonía. 3 *(loud noise)* sonido.
▷ *vi* 1 *(opposing forces - fight)* chocar; *(- disagree)* discutir, enfrentarse (with, a). 2 *(interests)* estar en conflicto. 3 *(dates, events)* coincidir. 4 *(colours)* desentonar (with, con). 5 *(cymbals)* sonar.
clasp [klɑːsp] *n* 1 *(on necklace)* broche *m*; *(on belt)* cierre *m*, hebilla. 2 *(grasp)* apretón *m*; *(embrace)* abrazo.
▷ *vt* 1 *(object)* agarrar, sujetar; *(person)* abrazar. 2 *(necklace, etc)* abrochar.
class [klɑːs] *n* 1 *(in society)* clase *f*. 2 EDUC clase *f*. 3 *(kind)* clase *f*, tipo. 4 *(of plant, animal)* clase *f*. 5 *(style)* clase *f*, estilo.
▷ *vt* clasificar, catalogar.
class-conscious [klɑːs'kɒnʃəs] *adj* con conciencia de clase, clasista.
classic ['klæsɪk] *adj* 1 *(high quality)* clásico,-a. 2 *(typical)* clásico,-a, típico,-a.
▷ *n (novel, film, play)* clásico.
▷ *n pl* classics *(literature)* clásicos *mpl*, obras *fpl* clásicas; *(languages)* clásicas *fpl*; *(clothes)* prendas *fpl* clásicas.
classical ['klæsɪkᵊl] *adj (gen)* clásico,-a.
classification [klæsɪfɪ'keɪʃᵊn] *n* clasificación *f*.
classified ['klæsɪfaɪd] *adj* 1 *(categorized)* clasificado,-a. 2 *(secret)* secreto,-a, confidencial.
classify ['klæsɪfaɪ] *vt* 1 *(categorize)* clasificar, catalogar. 2 *(declare secret)* clasificar como secreto,-a.
▲ *pt & pp* classified, *ger* classifying.
classmate ['klɑːsmeɪt] *n* compañero,-a de clase.
classroom ['klɑːsruːm] *n* aula, clase *f*.
classy ['klɑːsɪ] *adj sl* con clase, con estilo.
▲ *comp* classier, *superl* classiest.
clatter ['klætəʳ] *n (of pans, dishes, etc)* ruido; *(of something falling)* estrépito; *(of trains)* traqueteo; *(of typewriter)* repiqueteo.
▷ *vi (pans, dishes, etc)* hacer ruido; *(things falling)* hacer estrépito; *(trains)* traquetear; *(typewriter)* repiquetear.
▷ *vt* hacer ruido con.
clause [klɔːz] *n* 1 *(in document)* cláusula. 2 LING oración *f*, cláusula.
claustrophobia [klɔːstrə'fəʊbɪə] *n* claustrofobia.
claustrophobic [klɔːstrə'fəʊbɪk] *adj* claustrofóbico,-a.
clavichord ['klævɪkɔːd] *n* clavicordio.
clavicle ['klævɪkᵊl] *n* clavícula.
claw [klɔː] *n* 1 *(of lion, tiger, etc)* garra, zarpa; *(of cat)* uña; *(of bird)* garra; *(of crab, lobster)* pinza. 2 TECH garfio.
▷ *vi (scratch)* arañar (at, -); *(grab)* intentar agarrarse (at, a).
⊙ **to claw back** *vt sep* (lograr) recuperar.
clay [kleɪ] *n* arcilla.
clean [kliːn] *adj* 1 *(not dirty - gen)* limpio,-a; *(air)* limpio,-a, puro,-a; *(sheet of paper)* nuevo,-a, en blanco. 2 *(not rude - gen)* decente; *(joke)* inocente; *(life)* sano,-a; *(match, fight)* limpio,-a. 3 *(well-formed)* bien definido,-a, nítido,-a; *(regular, even)* limpio,-a.
▷ *adv* 1 *(fight, play)* limpio, limpiamente. 2 *fam (completely)* por completo.
▷ *n* limpieza.
▷ *vt (gen)* limpiar; *(teeth, car)* lavar.
▷ *vi* limpiarse.
⊙ **to clean out** *vt sep* 1 *(room, etc)* limpiar a fondo. 2 *fam (take all money)* dejar limpio,-a, dejar sin blanca; *(steal everything)* desplumar.
⊙ **to clean up** *vt sep* 1 *(room, mess, etc)* limpiar. 2 *fam (money, fortune)* hacer, sacar.
▷ *vi* 1 *(room, etc)* limpiar. 2 *fam (make money)* forrarse, barrer con todo.
clean-cut [kliːn'kʌt] *adj (outline, feature)* bien definido,-a, nítido,-a; *(person, appearance)* limpio,-a.

cleaner ['kli:nəʳ] *n* 1 *(person)* encargado,-a de la limpieza. 2 *(product)* limpiador *m*.
▷ *n* cleaner's *(place, shop)* tintorería, tinte *m*.
cleaning ['kli:nɪŋ] *n* limpieza.
cleanly [*(adj)* 'klenlɪ, *(adv)* 'kli:nlɪ] *adj* limpio,-a.
▷ *adv* 1 *(gen)* limpiamente. 2 SP con limpieza.
cleanse [klenz] *vt* limpiar (of, de).
cleanser ['klenzəʳ] *n (detergent)* producto de limpieza; *(lotion for skin)* leche *f* limpiadora, crema limpiadora.
cleansing ['klenzɪŋ] *n* limpieza.
clear [klɪəʳ] *adj* 1 *(glass, plastic, liquid)* transparente; *(sky, day, etc)* despejado,-a; *(skin, complexion)* bueno,-a. 2 *(not blocked - road, desk)* despejado,-a; *(free - time)* libre. 3 *(picture, outline)* nítido,-a. 4 *(voice, sound, speaker)* claro,-a. 5 *(understandable - explanation, instruction, ideas)* claro,-a.
▷ *adv* 1 *(clearly - speak)* claramente; *(hear)* perfectamente, bien. 2 *(not touching)* a distancia.
▷ *vt* 1 *(table)* quitar; *(floor, road)* despejar; *(pipe, drain)* desatascar; *(building, room - of people)* desalojar, despejar, desocupar; *(house, room - of furniture)* vaciar. 2 *(accused person)* absolver, descargar, exculpar; *(one's name)* limpiar. 3 *(approve - plans)* aprobar; *(authorize)* autorizar, dar el visto bueno a; *(plane)* dar autorización. 4 *(debt)* liquidar, saldar; *(earn - money)* sacar; *(- cheque)* conformar, dar por bueno. 5 *(obstacle)* salvar. 6 SP *(ball)* despejar.
⊙ **to clear away** *vt sep (dishes, etc)* recoger, quitar.
⊙ **to clear off** *vi fam* largarse.
▷ *vt sep (debt)* liquidar.
⊙ **to clear out** *vi fam* largarse.
▷ *vt sep (cupboard, drawers, room)* vaciar; *(old things)* tirar.
⊙ **to clear up** *vt sep* 1 *(mystery, crime)* resolver, esclarecer; *(issue, misunderstanding)* aclarar; *(loose ends)* atar. 2 *(tidy)* recoger.
▷ *vi* 1 *(tidy)* ordenar. 2 *(weather)* despejar, mejorar; *(cold, illness)* mejorarse, irse.
clearance ['klɪərəns] *n* 1 SP despeje *m*. 2 *(of land, area)* despeje *m*. 3 *(space, distance)* espacio (libre). 4 *(permission)* autorización *f*. 5 *(of cheque)* compensación *f*.
clear-cut [klɪə'kʌt] *adj* claro,-a, bien definido,-a.
clear-headed ['klɪə'hedɪd] *adj* lúcido,-a, despejado,-a.
clearing ['klɪərɪŋ] *n* 1 *(in wood)* claro. 2 *(of cheque)* compensación *f*.
clearly ['klɪəlɪ] *adv* 1 *(speak, write, think)* claramente, con claridad; *(see)* claramente. 2 *(obviously)* evidentemente: it was clearly very risky *estaba claro que era muy arriesgado.*
clearness ['klɪənəs] *n* claridad *f*.
clear-sighted [klɪə'saɪtɪd] *adj* perspicaz, lúcido,-a.
clearway ['klɪəweɪ] *n* GB *tramo de carretera donde está prohibido detenerse.*
cleave [kli:v] *vt (split)* hender, partir.
▲ *pt* cleft [kleft], cleaved o clove [klʊv], *pp* cleft [kleft], cleaved o cloven ['kləʊvᵊn], *ger* cleaving.
cleaver ['kli:vəʳ] *n* cuchillo de carnicero.
clef [klef] *n* MUS clave *f*: bass/treble clef *clave de fa/de sol.*
cleft [kleft] *pt & pp* → cleave.
▷ *adj (chin, lip)* partido,-a.
▷ *n* hendidura, grieta.
clemency ['klemənsɪ] *n* 1 *(mercy)* clemencia. 2 *(of weather)* benignidad *f*.
clementine ['klem əntaɪn] *n* clementina.
clench [klentʃ] *vt* 1 *(teeth, fist)* apretar. 2 *(grip)* apretar, agarrar.
clergy ['klɜ:dʒɪ] *n* clero.
clergyman ['klɜ:dʒɪmən] *n* clérigo.
▲ *pl* clergymen ['klɜ:dʒɪmən].
clerical ['klerɪkᵊl] *adj* 1 REL clerical, eclesiástico,-a. 2 *(of a clerk)* de oficina, administrativo,-a.
clerk [klɑ:k, US klɜ:rk] *n (office worker)* oficinista *mf*, administrativo,-a.
clever ['klevəʳ] *adj* 1 *(person - intelligent)* listo,-a, inteligente, espabilado,-a; *(skilful)* hábil. 2 *(idea, plan, gadget)* ingenioso,-a; *(move)* hábil.
cleverly ['klevəlɪ] *adv (intelligently)* con inteligencia; *(skilfully)* hábilmente, ingeniosamente.
cliché ['kli:ʃeɪ] *n* cliché *m*, tópico.
click [klɪk] *n (sound - gen)* clic *m*; *(of tongue, fingers)* chasquido.
▷ *vt (tongue, fingers)* chasquear.
▷ *vi* 1 *(make noise)* hacer clic. 2 *(understand, realize)* caer en la cuenta, darse cuenta de. 3 *(become friendly)* congeniar; *(become popular)* tener éxito.
client ['klaɪənt] *n* cliente,-a.
clientele [kli:ən'tel] *n* clientela.
cliff [klɪf] *n* acantilado, precipicio.
cliffhanger ['klɪfhæŋəʳ] *n* situación *f* de suspense.
climate ['klaɪmət] *n* 1 GEOG clima *m*. 2 *fig* clima *m*, situación *f*.
climatic [klaɪ'mætɪk] *adj* climático,-a.
climatological [klaɪmətə'lɒdʒɪkᵊl] *adj* climatológico,-a.
climatology [klaɪmə'tɒlədʒɪ] *n* climatología.
climax ['klaɪmæks] *n* 1 *(peak)* clímax *m*, punto culminante. 2 *(orgasm)* orgasmo.
climb [klaɪm] *n* 1 *(gen)* subida. 2 SP escalada.
▷ *vt (ladder, stairs)* subir; *(tree)* trepar a, subirse a; *(mountain)* escalar, subir a.
▷ *vi* 1 *(move)* trepar. 2 *(socially)* escalar, ascender. 3 *(of things)* subir, ascender; *(of plants)* trepar.
⊙ **to climb down** *vi* 1 *(descend)* bajar. 2 *fig (admit mistake, withdraw)* ceder, volverse atrás.
▷ *vt insep* bajarse de.
climb-down ['klaɪmdaʊn] *n fig* marcha atrás, vuelta atrás.
climber ['klaɪməʳ] *n* 1 SP alpinista *mf*, escalador,-ra. 2 BOT enredadera, trepadora.
climbing ['klaɪmɪŋ] *n* SP alpinismo, montañismo.
clinch [klɪntʃ] *n* 1 *fam (embrace)* abrazo apasionado. 2 SP *(in boxing)* cuerpo a cuerpo.
▷ *vt fam (deal)* cerrar; *(argument)* resolver; *(title)* hacerse con.
▷ *vi* SP *(in boxing)* abrazarse.
clincher ['klɪntʃəʳ] *n fam* factor *m* decisivo.
cling [klɪŋ] *vi* 1 *(hold tightly)* agarrarse (to, a). 2 *(stick - clothes)* pegarse, ceñirse; *(- smell)* pegarse. 3 *pej (stay too close to)* pegarse a. 4 *fig (retain - hope, belief)* aferrarse (to, a).
▲ *pt & pp* clung [klʌŋ].
clingfilm ['klɪŋfɪlm] *n* film *m* transparente.
clinging ['klɪŋɪŋ] *adj* 1 *(clothes)* ceñido,-a, ajustado,-a. 2 *(child)* enmadrado,-a; *(person)* pegajoso,-a.

clinic ['klınık] *n* 1 *(private, specialized)* clínica. 2 *(in state hospital)* ambulatorio, dispensario. 3 MED *(of students)* clase *f* práctica.
clinically ['klınıkəlı] *adv* 1 MED clínicamente. 2 *(coldly)* fríamente.
clink [klıŋk] *n (noise)* tintineo.
▷ *vt* hacer tintinear.
▷ *vi* tintinear.
clip[1] [klıp] *n* 1 *(with scissors)* tijeretada. 2 *(of film)* fragmento. 3 *fam (blow)* cachete *m*.
▷ *vt* 1 *(cut - gen)* cortar; *(ticket)* picar; *(animals)* esquilar. 2 *(cut out)* recortar. 3 *fam (hit)* dar un cachete a.
▲ *pt & pp* clipped, *ger* clipping.
clip[2] [klıp] *n* 1 *(for papers, etc)* clip *m*, sujetapapeles *m*; *(for hair)* pasador *m*, clip *m*. 2 *(brooch)* broche *m*, alfiler *m* de pecho, prendedor *m*. 3 [Also cartridge clip.] *(in rifle)* cargador *m*.
clipboard ['klıpbɔːd] *n* tablilla con sujetapapeles.
clippers ['klıpəz] *n pl (for nails)* cortaúñas *m sing*; *(for hair)* maquinilla *f sing*; *(for hedge)* tijeras de podar.
clipping ['klıpıŋ] *n (cutting)* recorte *m* de periódico, recorte *m* de prensa.
▷ *n pl* clippings *(of nails, sheep's wool)* recortes *mpl*; *(of grass)* hierba cortada.
clique [kliːk] *n pej* camarilla.
clitoridectomy [klıtərı'dektəmı] *n* ablación *f* del clítoris.
clitoris ['klıtərıs] *n* clítoris *m*.
cloak [kləʊk] *n* 1 *(garment)* capa. 2 *fig (cover)* capa, manto.
▷ *vt* encubrir.
cloakroom ['kləʊkruːm] *n* 1 *(gen)* guardarropa. 2 GB *euph (toilet)* lavabo, servicios *mpl*.
clock [klɒk] *n* 1 *(gen)* reloj *m* (de pared). 2 AUTO *fam (mileometer)* cuentakilómetros *m*; *(speedometer)* velocímetro; *(taximeter)* taxímetro.
▷ *vt* 1 *(time - athlete, race)* cronometrar. 2 *(register - speed, time)* registrar, hacer.
⊙ **to clock in/on** *vi* fichar (al llegar al trabajo).
⊙ **to clock out/off** *vi* fichar (al salir del trabajo).
⊙ **to clock up** *vt insep (miles, hours)* hacer.
clockmaker ['klɒkmeıkəʳ] *n* relojero,-a.
clockwise ['klɒkwaız] *adv* en el sentido de las agujas del reloj.
clockwork ['klɒkwɜːk] *n* mecanismo de relojería.
clog [klɒg] *n (shoe)* zueco.
▷ *vt* [Also clog up.] obstruir, atascar.
▷ *vi* [Also clog up.] obstruirse, atascarse.
▲ *pt & pp* clogged, *ger* clogging.
cloister ['klɔıstəʳ] *n* claustro.
clone [kləʊn] *n* clon *m*.
▷ *vt* clonar.
close[1] [kləʊz] *n* 1 *(end)* fin *m*, final *m*. 2 *(precincts)* recinto.
▷ *vt* 1 *(shut - gen)* cerrar. 2 *(end - deal)* cerrar; *(meeting)* cerrar, poner fin a; *(course, conference)* clausurar.
▷ *vi* 1 *(gen)* cerrar, cerrarse. 2 *(end)* concluir, terminar. 3 FIN cerrar (at, a).
⊙ **to close down** *vt sep* cerrar (definitivamente).
▷ *vi* 1 *(shop, factory, etc)* cerrar (definitivamente). 2 *(stop broadcasting)* cerrar la emisión.
⊙ **to close in** *vi* 1 *(days)* acortarse. 2 *(get nearer)* acercarse, aproximarse.
⊙ **to close up** *vi* 1 *(of wound)* cicatrizar, cerrarse. 2 *(shop, etc)* cerrar.
close[2] [kləʊs] *adj* 1 *(near)* cercano,-a (to, a), próximo,-a (to, a). 2 *(friend)* íntimo,-a, allegado,-a; *(relation, family)* cercano,-a.
▷ *adv* 1 *(in position)* cerca. 2 *(in time)* cerca.
closed [kləʊzd] *adj (gen)* cerrado,-a.
close-knit [kləʊs'nıt] *adj* unido,-a.
closely ['kləʊslı] *adv* 1 *(connect)* estrechamente, muy. 2 *(resemble)* mucho. 3 *(carefully - watch, listen)* atentamente; *(follow)* de cerca; *(question)* a fondo.
closet ['klɒzıt] *n* US armario.
▷ *adj fam (secret)* encubierto,-a.
close-up ['kləʊsʌp] *n* primer plano.
closing ['kləʊzıŋ] *n* cierre *m*.
closure ['kləʊʒəʳ] *n (gen)* cierre *m*; *(debate)* clausura.
clot [klɒt] *n* 1 *(of blood)* coágulo. 2 GB *fam* tonto,-a.
▷ *vt* coagular.
▷ *vi (blood)* coagularse; *(cream)* cuajar.
▲ *pt & pp* clotted, *ger* clotting.
cloth [klɒθ] *n* 1 *(fabric)* tela; *(thick)* paño. 2 *(rag)* trapo; *(for dishes)* trapo de cocina, bayeta; *(tablecloth)* mantel *m*.
▷ *n* the cloth el clero.

Consulta también clothes.

clothe [kləʊð] *vt* 1 *(dress, provide clothes for)* vestir (in/with, de). 2 *(cover)* revestir (in, de), cubrir (in, de).
▲ *pt & pp* clothed o clad [klæd], *ger* clothing.
clothes [kləʊðz] *n pl* ropa *f sing*.
clothing ['kləʊðıŋ] *n* ropa.
cloud [klaʊd] *n* 1 METEOR *(single)* nube *f*; *(mass)* nubes *fpl*, nubosidad *f*. 2 *(of insects, smoke, dust, etc)* nube *f*.
▷ *vt* 1 *(view, vision, eyes)* nublar; *(mirror)* empañar. 2 *fig (confuse, make difficult)* complicar; *(spoil, threaten)* obscurecer.
▷ *vi* enturbiarse.
⊙ **to cloud over** *vi (sky)* nublarse; *(face, eyes)* empañarse.
cloudy ['klaʊdı] *adj* 1 *(sky, weather, day)* nublado,-a. 2 *(liquid)* turbio,-a.
▲ *comp* cloudier, *superl* cloudiest.
clout [klaʊt] *n* 1 *fam* tortazo. 2 *fam (influence)* influencia, peso.
▷ *vt fam* dar un tortazo a.
clove[1] [kləʊv] *n (spice)* clavo.
clove[2] [kləʊv] *n (of garlic)* diente *f*.
clove[3] [kləʊv] *pt* ⟶ cleave.
cloven ['kləʊvən] *pp* ⟶ cleave.
clover ['kləʊvəʳ] *n* trébol *m*.
cloverleaf ['kləʊvəliːf] *n* 1 BOT hoja de trébol. 2 *(on motorway)* trébol *m*.
clown [klaʊn] *n* payaso, clown *m*.
cloy [klɔı] *vi* empalagar.
club [klʌb] *n* 1 *(group, society)* club *m*. 2 *(nightclub)* club *m* nocturno. 3 *(stick)* porra, garrote *m*. 4 SP *(in golf)* palo. 5 *(in cards - English pack)* trébol *m*; *(- Spanish pack)* basto.
▷ *vt* aporrear, dar garrotazos a, pegar garrotazos a.
▲ *pt & pp* clubbed, *ger* clubbing.
⊙ **to club together** *vi* pagar entre varios.

clubhouse ['klʌbhaʊs] *n* SP sede *f* de un club.
cluck [klʌk] *n* cloqueo.
▷ *vi* cloquear.
clue [klu:] *n (gen)* pista; *(in crossword)* clave *f*.
clump [klʌmp] *n* **1** *(of trees)* grupo; *(of plants)* mata, macizo. **2** *(of earth)* terrón *m*. **3** *(noise)* ruido de pisadas fuertes.
▷ *vi* andar pesada y ruidosamente, caminar pisando fuerte.
clumsy ['klʌmzɪ] *adj* **1** *(person, movement)* torpe, patoso,-a. **2** *(tool, shape)* pesado,-a y difícil de manejar; *(furniture)* mal diseñado,-a. **3** *(apology, attempt, speech)* torpe, sin tacto; *(forgery, translation)* burdo,-a.
▲ *comp* **clumsier**, *superl* **clumsiest**.
clung [klʌŋ] *pt & pp* ⟶ **cling**.
cluster ['klʌstəʳ] *n (of trees, stars, buildings, people)* grupo; *(of berries, grapes)* racimo; *(of plants)* macizo.
▷ *vi* agruparse, apiñarse (**round**, alrededor de/en torno a).
clutch [klʌtʃ] *n* **1** AUTO embrague *m*. **2** *(grasp, grip)* agarrón *m*.
▷ *vt (seize)* agarrar; *(hold tightly)* estrechar, apretar.
⊙ **to clutch at** *vt insep* tratar de agarrar.
clutter ['klʌtəʳ] *n (things)* cosas *fpl*, trastos *mpl*; *(untidy state)* desorden *m*, revoltijo.
▷ *vt* [Also **to clutter up**.] llenar, atestar, abarrotar.
cluttered ['klʌtəd] *adj* atestado,-a (**with**, de), abarrotado,-a (**with**, de).
cm ['si:'em] *symb* (**centimetre**) centímetro; *(symbol)* cm.
CND ['si:'en'di:] *abbr* GB (**Campaign for Nuclear Disarmament**) campaña para el desarme nuclear.
Co[1] [kəʊ] *abbr* (**Company**) Compañía; *(abbreviation)* Cía.
Co[2] ['kaʊntɪ] *abbr* (**County**) condado.
c/o ['keərɒv] *abbr* (**care of**) en casa de; *(abbreviation)* c/d.
coach [kəʊtʃ] *n* **1** GB *(bus)* autocar *m*. **2** *(carriage)* carruaje *m*, coche *m* de caballos. **3** *(on train)* coche *m*, vagón *m*. **4** EDUC *(tutor)* profesor,-ra particular. **5** SP *(trainer)* entrenador,-ra.
▷ *vt* **1** EDUC dar clases particulares a, preparar. **2** SP entrenar.
coaching ['kəʊtʃɪŋ] *n* **1** *(tutoring)* preparación *f*, clases *fpl* particulares. **2** *(training)* entrenamiento.
coagulate [kəʊ'ægjəleɪt] *vt* coagular.
▷ *vi* coagularse.
coagulation [kəʊægjə'leɪʃᵊn] *n* coagulación *f*.
coal [kəʊl] *n* carbón *m*, hulla.
coalesce [kəʊə'les] *vi* **1** *fml (groups)* coaligarse, unirse. **2** CHEM fundirse.
coalescence [kəʊə'lesəns] *n* **1** *(of groups)* unión *f*. **2** CHEM fusión *f*.
coalfield ['kəʊlfi:ld] *n* yacimiento de carbón.
coalition [kəʊə'lɪʃᵊn] *n* coalición *f*.
coarse [kɔ:s] *adj* **1** *(fabric)* basto,-a, burdo,-a; *(skin)* áspero,-a; *(sand, salt)* grueso,-a. **2** *(language, joke)* grosero,-a, vulgar, ordinario,-a, basto,-a; *(manners, tastes)* ordinario,-a, basto,-a.
coarsely ['kɔ:slɪ] *adv* **1** *(chop)* en trozos grandes. **2** *(speak)* de manera ordinaria.
coast [kəʊst] *n* costa, litoral *m*.
▷ *vi* **1** *(in car)* ir en punto muerto; *(on bicycle)* deslizarse sin pedalear. **2** *fig* avanzar sin ningún esfuerzo. **3** MAR costear, bordear la costa.
coastal ['kəʊstᵊl] *adj* costero,-a.
coaster ['kəʊstəʳ] *n* **1** MAR barco de cabotaje. **2** *(small mat)* posavasos *m*.
coastguard ['kəʊstgɑ:d] *n* guardacostas *mf*.
▷ *n* **the coastguard** *(organization)* los guardacostas *mpl*.
coastline ['kəʊstlaɪn] *n* costa, litoral *m*.
coat [kəʊt] *n* **1** *(overcoat)* abrigo; *(short)* chaquetón *m*. **2** *(of paint)* capa, mano *f*; *(of dust)* capa. **3** *(of animal)* pelo, pelaje *m*.
▷ *vt* **1** *(cover - gen)* cubrir (**in/with**, de). **2** CULIN *(with liquid)* cubrir (**in/with**, de), bañar (**in/with**, en); *(in breadcrumbs or batter)* rebozar.
coating ['kəʊtɪŋ] *n* **1** CULIN capa, baño. **2** *(of paint, dust, wax)* capa; *(of metal)* revestimiento.
coax [kəʊks] *vt (person)* engatusar.
coaxial [kəʊ'ækʃᵊl] *adj* coaxial.
coaxing ['kəʊksɪŋ] *n* persuasión *f*, mano *f* izquierda.
▷ *adj* persuasivo,-a.
cob [kɒb] *n* **1** *(of corn)* mazorca (de maíz). **2** *(cobnut)* avellana. **3** *(horse)* jaca. **4** *(male swan)* cisne *m* macho.
cobble ['kɒbᵊl] *n* adoquín *m*.
▷ *vt (street)* adoquinar.
cobbler ['kɒbləʳ] *n dated (shoe repairer)* zapatero (remendón).
cobblestone ['kɒbᵊlstəʊn] *n* adoquín *m*.
cobweb ['kɒbweb] *n* telaraña.
cocaine [kə'keɪn] *n* cocaína.
coccyx ['kɒksɪks] *n* coxis *m*, cóccix *m*.
▲ *pl* **coccyxes** o **coccyges**.
cochineal [kɒtʃɪ'ni:l] *n* cochinilla.
cochlea ['kɒklɪə] *n* caracol *m* del oído.
cock [kɒk] *n* **1** *(rooster)* gallo; *(any male bird)* macho. **2** *(on firearm)* percutor *m*, percusor *m*. **3** GB *fam (mate)* macho. **4** *sl (penis)* polla.
▷ *vt* **1** *(of firearm)* amartillar, montar. **2** *(head, hat)* ladear; *(ears, leg)* levantar.
cockcrow ['kɒkkrəʊ] *n* amanecer *m*.
cockeyed ['kɒkaɪd] *adj* **1** *fam (crooked)* torcido,-a; *(impractical, ridiculous)* disparatado,-a. **2** *fam (squinting, cross-eyed)* bizco,-a. **3** *fam (drunk)* borracho,-a, trompa.
cockle ['kɒkᵊl] *n* berberecho.
Cockney ['kɒknɪ] *adj del barrio obrero del este de Londres.*
▷ *n* **1** *(person) persona del barrio obrero del este de Londres.* **2** *(dialect) dialecto que se habla en el barrio obrero del este de Londres.*
cockpit ['kɒkpɪt] *n (in plane)* cabina del piloto, carlinga; *(in racing car)* cabina.
cockroach ['kɒkrəʊtʃ] *n* cucaracha.
cocktail ['kɒkteɪl] *n* cóctel *m*.
cocoa ['kəʊkəʊ] *n (powder)* cacao; *(drink)* chocolate *m*.
coconut ['kəʊkənʌt] *n* coco.
cocoon [kə'ku:n] *n* capullo.
▷ *vt fig* envolver, arropar.
COD ['si:'əʊ'di:] *abbr* GB (**cash on delivery**, US **collect on delivery**) contra reembolso.
cod [kɒd] *n* bacalao.
▲ *pl* **cod**.

code [kəʊd] *n* 1 *(set of laws, rules)* código. 2 *(system of words, letters, signs, numbers)* clave *f*, código. 3 *(telephone)* prefijo; *(postal)* código (postal).
▷ *vt* 1 *(message, etc)* poner en clave, cifrar. 2 *(mark)* codificar.
codification [kəʊdɪfɪ'keɪʃᵊn] *n* codificación *f*.
codify ['kəʊdɪfaɪ] *vt* codificar.
▲ *pt & pp* **codified**, *ger* **codifying**.
coeducation [kəʊedjə'keɪʃᵊn] *n* enseñanza mixta.
coefficient [kəʊɪ'fɪʃᵊnt] *n* coeficiente *m*.
coerce [kəʊ'ɜːs] *vt* coaccionar.
coercion [kəʊ'ɜːʃᵊn] *n* coacción *f*.
coexist [kəʊɪg'zɪst] *vi* coexistir.
C of E ['siːəv'iː] *abbr* **(Church of England)** Iglesia Anglicana.
coffee ['kɒfɪ] *n* café *m*.
coffeepot ['kɒfɪpɒt] *n* cafetera.
coffer ['kɒfəʳ] *n* arca, cofre *m*.
▷ *n pl* **coffers** fondos *mpl*, arcas *fpl*.
coffin ['kɒfɪn] *n* ataúd *m*, féretro.
cog [kɒg] *n* 1 *(teeth)* diente *m*. 2 *fig* pieza.
cogent ['kəʊdʒənt] *adj* convincente, contundente.
cognac ['kɒnjæk] *n* coñac *m*.
cognitive ['kɒgnɪtɪv] *adj* cognitivo,-a.
cohabit [kəʊ'hæbɪt] *vi* cohabitar.
cohabitation [kəʊhæbɪ'teɪʃən] *n* cohabitación *f*.
coherent [kəʊ'hɪərənt] *adj* coherente, congruente.
coil [kɔɪl] *n* 1 *(of rope, wire)* rollo; *(of cable)* carrete *m*; *(of hair)* rizo, moño; *(of smoke)* espiral *m*, voluta. 2 *(single loop)* vuelta, lazada. 3 TECH bobina. 4 **the coil** MED *(contraceptive)* espiral *f*, dispositivo intrauterino, DIU *m*.
▷ *vt* [Also **to coil up**.] enrollar.
coin [kɔɪn] *n* moneda.
▷ *vt* 1 *(money)* acuñar. 2 *(invent)* crear, acuñar.
coinage ['kɔɪnɪdʒ] *n* 1 *(coins)* monedas *fpl*; *(making coins)* acuñación *f*. 2 *(system of coins)* sistema monetario. 3 *(inventing of new word)* acuñación *f*; *(new word)* palabra de nuevo cuño; *(new phrase)* frase *f* de nuevo cuño.
coincide [kəʊɪn'saɪd] *vi* coincidir (**with**, con).
coincidence [kəʊ'ɪnsɪdəns] *n* 1 *(chance)* coincidencia, casualidad *f*. 2 *(coinciding)* coincidencia.
coincidental [kəʊɪnsɪ'dentᵊl] *adj* casual, fortuito,-a.
coincidentally [kəʊɪnsɪ'dentᵊlɪ] *adv* por casualidad, casualmente.
Coke® [kəʊk] *n* Coca Cola®.
coke [kəʊk] *n (coal)* coque *m*.
cola ['kəʊlə] *n* cola.
colander ['kʌləndəʳ] *n* colador *m*.
cold [kəʊld] *adj* 1 *(gen)* frío,-a. 2 *(unenthusiastic, unfriendly)* frío,-a.
▷ *n* 1 *(weather)* frío. 2 MED resfriado, catarro, constipado. ● **cold cuts** US embutidos *mpl*, fiambres *mpl*.
cold-blooded [kəʊld'blʌdɪd] *adj* 1 ZOOL de sangre fría. 2 *fig (person)* frío,-a, insensible; *(murderer)* despiadado,-a, cruel; *(crime)* a sangre fría.
coleslaw ['kəʊlslɔː] *n* ensaladilla de col y zanahoria.
colic ['kɒlɪk] *n* cólico.
coliseum [kɒlɪ'siːəm] *n* coliseo.
collaborate [kə'læbəreɪt] *vi* colaborar (**with**, con).
collaborator [kə'læbəreɪtəʳ] *n* 1 colaborador,-ra. 2 *(with enemy)* colaboracionista *mf*.
collage ['kɒlɑːdʒ] *n* ART collage *m*.
collapse [kə'læps] *n* 1 *(falling down)* derrumbamiento; *(falling in)* hundimiento. 2 *(failure, breakdown)* fracaso. 3 *(prices, currency)* caída en picado; *(business, company)* quiebra. 4 MED colapso.
▷ *vi* 1 *(building, bridge, etc)* derrumbarse, desplomarse; *(roof)* hundirse, venirse abajo; *(tired person)* desplomarse. 2 MED *(person)* sufrir un colapso. 3 *(fail - project, talks, etc)* fracasar, venirse abajo; *(- hopes)* desvanecerse. 4 *(prices, currency)* caer en picado; *(business, company)* quebrar, ir a la bancarrota. 5 *(chair, table)* plegarse.
▷ *vt (table)* plegar.
collapsible [kə'læpsəbᵊl] *adj* plegable.
collar ['kɒləʳ] *n* 1 *(of shirt, etc)* cuello. 2 *(for dog)* collar *m*. 3 TECH collar *m*, abrazadera.
▷ *vt fam* pescar, echar el guante a, pillar.
collarbone ['kɒləbəʊn] *n* clavícula.
collateral [kə'lætᵊrəl] *n* FIN garantía subsidiaria.
▷ *adj* 1 *(relative)* colateral. 2 *(additional)* circunstancial, colateral. ● **collateral damage** daños *mpl* colaterales.
collation [kɒ'leɪʃᵊn] *n* 1 *(comparison)* cotejo, comparación *f*. 2 *(collecting together)* reunión *f*, recopilación *f*; *(putting in order)* compaginación *f*.
colleague ['kɒliːg] *n* colega *mf*, compañero,-a.
collect [kə'lekt] *vt* 1 *(glasses, plates, belongings, etc)* recoger; *(information, data)* reunir, recopilar. 2 *(stamps, records, etc)* coleccionar. 3 *(taxes)* recaudar; *(rent)* cobrar. 4 *(for charity - money)* recaudar, hacer una colecta de; *(- old clothes, jumble)* juntar. 5 *(pick up, fetch)* ir a buscar, recoger.
▷ *vi* 1 *(dust, water)* acumularse; *(people)* reunirse, congregarse. 2 *(for charity)* recaudar dinero.
collection [kə'lekʃᵊn] *n* 1 *(of stamps, paintings, etc)* colección *f*; *(of poems, short stories)* recopilación *f*; *(of people)* grupo. 2 *(range of new clothes)* colección *f*. 3 *(for charity)* colecta. 4 *(of mail, of refuse)* recogida. 5 *(of taxes)* recaudación *f*; *(of rent)* cobro.
collective [kə'lektɪv] *adj* colectivo,-a.
▷ *n (enterprise)* cooperativa; *(people)* colectivo.
collector [kə'lektəʳ] *n* 1 *(of stamps, etc)* coleccionista *mf*. 2 *(of rent, debts, tickets)* cobrador,-ra.
college ['kɒlɪdʒ] *n* 1 *(for children education)* escuela, instituto *mf*. 2 US *(university)* universidad.
collide [kə'laɪd] *vi* 1 *(crash)* colisionar, chocar. 2 *(of people, aims, opinions, etc)* estar en conflicto, chocar.
collier ['kɒlɪəʳ] *n* 1 GB *(miner)* minero (de carbón). 2 *(ship)* barco carbonero.
colliery ['kɒljərɪ] *n* GB mina de carbón.
▲ *pl* **collieries**.
collision [kə'lɪʒᵊn] *n (between cars, trains, etc)* colisión *f*, choque *m*; *(between ships)* abordaje *m*.
collocation [kɒlə'keɪʃᵊn] *n* colocación *f*, combinación *f*.
colloquial [kə'ləʊkwɪəl] *adj* familiar, coloquial.
collusion [kə'luːʒᵊn] *n* colusión *f*, connivencia.
Cologne [kə'ləʊn] *n* Colonia.
Colombia [kə'lʌmbɪə] *n* Colombia.
Colombian [kə'lʌmbɪən] *adj & n* colombiano,-a.
colon¹ ['kəʊlən] *n* ANAT colon *m*.
colon² ['kəʊlən] *n* LING dos puntos *mpl*.

colonel ['kɜːnᵊl] *n* coronel *m*.
colonial [kə'ləʊnɪəl] *adj* colonial.
▷ *n* colono,-a.
colonialism [kə'ləʊnɪəlɪzᵊm] *n* colonialismo.
colonist ['kɒlənɪst] *n (inhabitant)* colono; *(colonizer)* colono,-a, colonizador,-ra.
colonize ['kɒlənaɪz] *vt* colonizar.
colony ['kɒlənɪ] *n (gen)* colonia.
▲ *pl* colonies.
color ['kʌlə'] *n* US → **colour.**
color-blind ['kʌləblaɪnd] *adj* US → **colour-blind.**
colored ['kʌləd] *adj & n* US → **coloured.**
colorful ['kʌləfʊl] *adj* US → **colourful.**
coloring ['kʌlərɪŋ] *n* US → **colouring.**
colorless ['kʌlələs] *adj* US → **colourless.**
colossal [kə'lɒsᵊl] *adj* colosal, descomunal.
colossus [kə'lɒsəs] *n* coloso.
colour ['kʌlə'] *n* **1** color *m*. **2** *(skin - racial characteristic, complexion)* color *m*.
▷ *adj (television, film, etc)* en color.
▷ *vt* **1** *(with pen, paint, crayon)* pintar, colorear; *(dye)* teñir. **2** *fig (affect negatively, influence)* influir en.
▷ *vi* **1** *(blush)* enrojecer, ruborizarse, sonrojarse, ponerse rojo,-a, ponerse colorado,-a. **2** *(of leaves)* ponerse amarillo,-a; *(fruit)* coger color.
▷ *n pl* **colours** GB *(worn by team, school)* colores *mpl*; MIL *(flag)* bandera, enseña.
⊙ **to colour in** *vt sep* pintar, colorear.
colour-blind ['kʌləblaɪnd] *adj* daltónico,-a.
coloured ['kʌləd] *adj* **1** *(pencils, crayons)* de color, de colores. **2** *dated (person)* de color. **3** *(biased)* parcial; *(exaggerated)* exagerado,-a.
▷ *n dated* persona de color.
▷ *adj* **Coloured** POL *(in South Africa)* mestizo,-a.
▷ *n* **Coloured** POL *(in South Africa)* mestizo,-a.
colourful ['kʌləfʊl] *adj* **1** *(full of colour, bright)* lleno,-a de color, vistoso,-a; *(brightly coloured)* de colores vivos. **2** *(interesting, exciting)* lleno,-a de color, lleno,-a de colorido; *(person)* pintoresco,-a.
colouring ['kʌlərɪŋ] *n* **1** *(substance, dye)* colorante *m*. **2** *(person's skin, hair and eye colour)* color *m*. **3** *(of animal's skin, fur, plumage)* colorido, color *m*. **4** ART *(act)* coloración *f*; *(use of colour)* colorido.
colourless ['kʌlələs] *adj* **1** *(without colour)* incoloro,-a, sin color; *(pale)* pálido,-a. **2** *fig (dull, uninteresting)* soso,-a, anodino,-a, gris.
colt [kəʊlt] *n* potro.
column ['kɒləm] *n (gen)* columna.
columnist ['kɒləmnɪst] *n* columnista *mf*.
coma ['kəʊmə] *n* MED coma *m*. ■ **to go into a coma** caer en coma, entrar en coma.
comb [kəʊm] *n* **1** *(for hair)* peine *m*; *(ornamental)* peineta. **2** *(for wool, cotton)* carda. **3** *(of bird)* cresta. **4** *(of honeycomb)* panal *m*.
▷ *vt* **1** *(hair)* peinar. **2** *(wool, cotton)* cardar, peinar. **3** *(search - area)* rastrear, peinar; *(- files)* rebuscar.
combat ['kɒmbæt] *n* combate *m*.
▷ *vt* combatir, luchar contra.
combination [kɒmbɪ'neɪʃᵊn] *n (gen)* combinación *f*.
combine [*(vb)* kəm'baɪn, *(n)* 'kɒmbaɪn] *vt* **1** *(gen)* combinar; *(efforts)* combinar, aunar; *(ingredients)* mezclar. **2** *(qualities, features)* reunir; *(activities)* combinar.
▷ *vi (gen)* combinarse; *(teams, forces)* unirse; *(companies)* fusionarse.
▷ *n* COMM grupo industrial, asociación *f*.
combined [kəm'baɪnd] *adj* combinado,-a.
combustible [kəm'bʌstɪbᵊl] *adj* combustible, inflamable.
combustion [kəm'bʌstʃᵊn] *n* combustión *f*.
come [kʌm] *vi* **1** *(gen)* venir. **2** *(arrive, reach)* llegar. **3** *(happen)* suceder. **4** *(be available)* venir, suministrarse. **5** *sl (have orgasm)* correrse.
▷ *vt (behave, play the part)* hacerse: **don't come the innocent with me** *no te hagas el inocente conmigo.*
▲ *pt* came [keɪm], *pp* come [kʌm], *ger* coming.
⊙ **to come about** *vi (happen)* ocurrir, suceder.
⊙ **to come across** *vt insep (thing)* encontrar, tropezar con; *(person)* encontrar, encontrarse con, tropezarse con.
▷ *vi* **1** *(be understood)* ser comprendido,-a. **2** *(make an impression)* causar una impresión.
⊙ **to come after** *vt insep* seguir.
⊙ **to come along** *vi* **1** *(progress)* ir, marchar. **2** *(hurry up)* darse prisa; *(give encouragement)* ir, venir. **3** *(arrive)* venir, llegar; *(appear)* aparecer.
⊙ **to come away** *vi* **1** *(become detached)* despegarse, desprenderse, soltarse, separarse. **2** *(leave, depart)* salir (**from**, de), irse (**from**, de); *(move away)* apartarse (**from**, de).
⊙ **to come back** *vi* **1** *(return)* volver (**from**, de). **2** *(remember)* volver a la memoria. **3** *(return to topic, question, idea)* volver (**to**, a); *(reply, retort)* replicar, contestar.
⊙ **to come before** *vt insep* **1** JUR comparecer ante. **2** *(be more important than)* ser más importante que.
⊙ **to come down** *vi* **1** *(gen)* bajar; *(collapse)* caerse, hundirse, venirse abajo; *(fall - rain, snow)* caer. **2** *(plane - land)* aterrizar; *(- fall)* caer. **3** *(price, temperature, etc)* bajar. **4** *(be passed down, inherited)* llegar (**to**, a).
⊙ **to come down with** *vt insep (illness)* caer enfermo,-a de, contraer, coger.
⊙ **to come in** *vi (enter)* entrar.
⊙ **to come on** *vi* **1** *(make progress)* avanzar. **2** *(hurry up)* darse prisa; *(give encouragement)* ir, venir. **3** *(follow on)* ir, venir.
⊙ **to come out** *vi* **1** *(leave)* salir (**of**, de); *(tooth, hair)* caerse; *(stain)* salir, quitarse; *(colour, dye)* desteñirse. **2** *(sun, moon, stars)* salir. **3** *(new book, record, magazine, figures)* salir, publicarse; *(film)* estrenarse. **4** *(news, truth, secret)* revelarse, salir a la luz. **5** *(declare openly that one is gay)* declararse homosexual.
⊙ **to come over** *vi* **1** *(visit)* hacer una visita. **2** *(change sides, opinions)* pasarse (**to**, a).
⊙ **to come through** *vt insep (operation, accident)* sobrevivir, salir con vida de; *(illness)* recuperarse de; *(difficult period)* pasar por, atravesar.
⊙ **to come up to** *vt insep* **1** *(equal)* alcanzar, llegar a, estar a la altura de. **2** *(approach - in space)* acercarse a; *(- in time)* ser casi.
⊙ **to come up with** *vt insep (idea)* tener, ocurrirse; *(solution)* encontrar; *(plan)* idear; *(proposal)* presentar plantear.
⊙ **to come upon** *vt insep* encontrarse con, encontrar.
comeback ['kʌmbæk] *n* **1** *fam (of person)* reaparición *f*, vuelta, retorno. **2** *(way of obtaining compensation)* reclamación *f*. **3** *(reply)* réplica, respuesta.

comedian [kə'miːdɪən] *n* cómico, humorista *m*.
comedienne [kəmiːdɪ'en] *n* cómica, humorista.
comedown ['kʌmdaʊn] *n* degradación *f*, humillación *f*.
comedy ['kɑmədɪ] *n* comedia.
▲ *pl* comedies.
comer ['kʌmə'] *n* participante *mf*, asistente *mf*.
comet ['kɒmɪt] *n* cometa *m*.
comeuppance [kʌm'ʌpəns] *n* justo castigo.
comfort ['kʌmfət] *n* 1 *(well-being)* comodidad *f*, confort *m*, bienestar *m*. 2 *(thing, luxury)* comodidad *f*. 3 *(consolation)* consuelo.
▷ *vt* consolar.
comfortable ['kʌmfətəbəl] *adj* 1 *(furniture, clothes, etc)* cómodo,-a. 2 *(patient)* tranquilo,-a. 3 *(job, income)* bueno,-a; *(life)* desahogado,-a, acomodado,-a: 4 *(lead, majority)* amplio,-a.
comfortably ['kʌmfətəblɪ] *adv* 1 *(sit, lie)* cómodamente. 2 *(live)* holgadamente. 3 *(win)* fácilmente.
comforter ['kʌmfətə'] *n* 1 *(person)* consolador,-ra. 2 *(scarf)* bufanda. 3 *(dummy)* chupete *m*.
comforting ['kʌmfətɪŋ] *adj* reconfortante.
comic ['kɒmɪk] *adj* cómico,-a.
▷ *n* 1 *(comedian)* cómico,-a, humorista *mf*. 2 *(magazine)* tebeo, cómic *m*.
coming ['kʌmɪŋ] *adj (gen)* próximo,-a; *(generation)* venidero,-a, futuro,-a:
▷ *n* 1 *(arrival)* llegada. 2 REL advenimiento.
coming-of-age ['kʌmɪŋəv'eɪdʒ] *n* mayoría de edad.
comma ['kɒmə] *n* coma. ● **inverted comma** comilla.
command [kə'mɑːnd] *n* 1 *(order)* orden *f*. 2 *(control, authority)* mando. 3 *(knowledge, mastery)* dominio.
▷ *vt* 1 *(order)* mandar, ordenar. 2 MIL *(have authority over)* estar al mando de, tener el mando de, comandar. 3 *(have at one's disposal)* disponer de, contar con, tener. 4 *(deserve - respect, admiration)* infundir, imponer, inspirar; *(- confidence)* inspirar; *(- sympathy)* merecer. 5 *(of place, fort)* dominar.
commandant ['kɒməndænt] *n* MIL comandante *m*.
commander [kə'mɑːndə'] *n* 1 MIL comandante *m*. 2 MAR capitán *m* de fragata.
commanding [kə'mɑːndɪŋ] *adj* 1 *(voice, manner, appearance)* autoritario,-a, imperioso,-a. 2 *(position)* dominante, de superioridad.
commandment [kə'mɑːndmənt] *n* REL mandamiento.
commando [kə'mɑːndəʊ] *n* comando.
▲ *pl* commandos o commandoes.
commemorate [kə'meməreɪt] *vt* conmemorar.
commencement [kə'mensmənt] *n* 1 *fml (beginning)* comienzo, inicio. 2 US *(graduation)* (ceremonia de) graduación *f*.
commend [kə'mend] *vt* 1 *(praise)* alabar (for, por), elogiar (for, por); *(recommend)* recomendar. 2 *(entrust)* encomendar (to, a).
commendable [kə'mendəbəl] *adj* encomiable, loable.
commensurate [kə'menʃərət] *adj fml* acorde.
comment ['kɒment] *n* comentario, observación *f*.
▷ *vt* comentar, observar.
commentary ['kɒməntərɪ] *n* 1 *(spoken description)* comentario, comentarios *mpl*. 2 *(set of written remarks)* comentario, crítica.
▲ *pl* commentaries.
commentate ['kɒmənteɪt] *vi* comentar un partido, retransmitir un partido (on, de).
commentator ['kɒmənteɪtə'] *n* comentarista *mf*.
commerce ['kɒmɜːs] *n* comercio.
commercial [kə'mɜːʃəl] *adj* 1 COMM comercial, mercantil. 2 *(intended to make money)* comercial.
▷ *n (advertisement)* anuncio, spot *m* publicitario.
commercialization [kə'mɜːʃəlaɪzeɪʃən] *n* comercialización *f*.
commercialize [kə'mɜːʃəlaɪz] *vt* comercializar.
commercially [kə'mɜːʃəlɪ] *adv* comercialmente.
commiserate [kə'mɪzəreɪt] *vi* compadecerse (with, de).
commiseration [kəmɪzə'reɪʃən] *n (sympathy)* conmiseración *f*.
▷ *interj* commiserations ¡mala suerte!
commissar ['kɒmɪsɑː'] *n* comisario político.
commissariat [kɒmɪ'seərɪət] *n* comisariado.
commission [kə'mɪʃən] *n* 1 COMM comisión *f*. 2 *(piece of work)* encargo. 3 *(group of people)* comisión *f*. 4 MIL *(rank)* grado de oficial; *(document)* nombramiento.
▷ *vt* 1 *(order)* encargar. 2 MIL nombrar. 3 MAR *(ship)* poner en servicio.
commissionaire [kəmɪʃə'neə'] *n* GB portero, conserje *m*.
commissioner [kə'mɪʃənə'] *n* 1 *(public official)* comisario. 2 *(member of a commission)* comisionado,-a, miembro de la comisión. ● **Commissioner for Oaths** GB ≈ notario,-a.
commit [kə'mɪt] *vt* 1 *(crime, error, sin)* cometer. 2 *(send to prison, etc)* internar. 3 *(bind)* comprometer, obligar; *(pledge)* asignar, consignar, destinar.
▲ *pt & pp* committed, *ger* committing.
commitment [kə'mɪtmənt] *n* 1 *(undertaking, obligation)* compromiso, obligación *f*; *(responsibility)* responsabilidad *f*. 2 *(dedication)* dedicación *f*, entrega.
committal [kə'mɪtəl] *n (to mental hospital)* reclusión *f*; *(to prison)* encarcelamiento.
committed [kə'mɪtɪd] *adj (to a cause)* comprometido,-a; *(dedicated)* dedicado,-a, entregado,-a.
committee [kə'mɪtɪ] *n* comité *m*, comisión *f*.
commode [kə'məʊd] *n* 1 *(chest of drawers)* cómoda. 2 *(chair)* silla con orinal.
commodity [kə'mɒdɪtɪ] *n* 1 COMM producto, artículo, mercancía. 2 FIN materia prima.
▲ *pl* commodities.
common ['kɒmən] *adj* 1 *(ordinary, average)* corriente. 2 *(usual, not scarce)* común, corriente. 3 *(shared, joint)* común. 4 *pej (vulgar)* ordinario,-a.
▷ *n (land)* campo comunal, terreno comunal, tierras *fpl* comunales.
commoner ['kɒmənə'] *n* plebeyo,-a.
common-law ['kɒmənlɔː] *adj (couple)* de hecho.
commonplace ['kɒmənpleɪs] *adj* común, corriente.
▷ *n (platitude)* lugar *m* común, tópico.
Commons ['kɒmənz] *n pl* **the Commons** GB los Comunes. ● **the House of Commons** la Cámara de los Comunes.
Commonwealth ['kɒmənwelθ] *n* GB Commonwealth *f*. ● **the Commonwealth of Nations** la Mancomunidad *f* Británica de Naciones.

commotion [kəˈməʊʃᵊn] *n (scandal)* escándalo; *(noise, excitement)* alboroto, jaleo; *(confusion)* confusión *f.*
communal [ˈkɒmjənᵊl] *adj (shared)* comunal, común; *(of a community)* comunitario,-a.
commune¹ [ˈkɒmjuːn] *n* comuna.
commune² [kəˈmjuːn] *vi lit* estar en comunión (**with**, con).
communicable [kəˈmjuːnɪkəbᵊl] *adj* **1** MED transmisible. **2** *(ideas, etc)* comunicable.
communicate [kəˈmjuːnɪkeɪt] *vt* **1** *(make known, convey)* comunicar. **2** MED transmitir, contagiar.
▷ *vi* **1** *(person)* comunicarse (**with**, con). **2** *(of rooms)* comunicarse.
communication [kəmjuːnɪˈkeɪʃᵊn] *n* **1** *(gen)* comunicación *f.* **2** *(message)* comunicación *f*, comunicado.
▷ *n pl* **communications** comunicaciones *fpl.*
communicative [kəˈmjuːnɪkətɪv] *adj* comunicativo,-a.
communion [kəˈmjuːnjən] *n fml* comunión *f.*
▷ *n* **Communion** REL Comunión *f.*
communiqué [kəˈmjuːnɪkeɪ] *n* comunicado.
communism [ˈkɒmjənɪzᵊm] *n* comunismo.
communist [ˈkɒmjənɪst] *adj* comunista.
▷ *n* comunista *mf.*
community [kəˈmjuːnɪtɪ] *n* **1** *(people living in one place)* comunidad *f.* **2** *(group of people)* comunidad *f*, colectividad *f.*
▲ *pl* **communities.**
commute [kəˈmjuːt] *vi* desplazarse diariamente al lugar de trabajo.
▷ *vt* **1** *(sentence, punishment)* conmutar. **2** *fml (money payment, pension)* conmutar (**for/into**, por).
commuter [kəˈmjuːtəʳ] *n* persona que se desplaza diariamente a su lugar de trabajo. ● **the commuter belt** los barrios *mpl* periféricos.
compact¹ [*(adj-vb)* kəmˈpækt, *(n)* ˈkɒmpækt] *adj (gen)* compacto,-a; *(style)* conciso,-a.
▷ *n* **1** *(for powder)* polvera de bolsillo. **2** US coche *m* utilitario.
▷ *vt* compactar, comprimir.
compact² [ˈkɒmpækt] *n (agreement)* pacto, acuerdo, convenio.
companion [kəmˈpænjən] *n* **1** *(partner, friend)* compañero,-a. **2** *(person employed)* persona de compañía. **3** *(either of pair or set)* compañero,-a, pareja. **4** *(guide)* guía, manual *m.*
companionship [kəmˈpænjənʃɪp] *n (relationship)* compañerismo, camaradería; *(company)* compañía.
company [ˈkʌmpᵊnɪ] *n* **1** *(companionship)* compañía. **2** *(visitors)* visita. **3** *(business)* empresa, compañía, sociedad *f.* **4** THEAT compañía. **5** MIL compañía.
▲ *pl* **companies.**
comparable [ˈkɒmpᵊrəbᵊl] *adj* comparable (**to**, a) (**with**, con), equiparable (**to**, a) (**with**, con).
comparative [kəmˈpærətɪv] *adj* **1** *(relative)* relativo, -a. **2** *(making a comparison)* comparado,-a. **3** LING comparativo,-a.
▷ *n* LING comparativo.
compare [kəmˈpeəʳ] *vt* comparar (**to/with**, con).
comparison [kəmˈpærɪsᵊn] *n* comparación *f.*
compartment [kəmˈpɑːtmənt] *n (in wallet, fridge, desk)* compartimento; *(in train)* departamento, compartimento.
compartmentalize [kɒmpɑːtˈmentᵊlaɪz] *vt* compartimentar.
compass [ˈkʌmpəs] *n* **1** *(magnetic)* brújula, compás *m*: **the points of the compass** *los puntos cardinales.* **2** [Functions as *sing* or *pl.*] *(for drawing)* compás *m*: **a pair of compasses, a compass** *un compás.* **3** *fig (range, scope)* alcance *m.* ● **compass rose** rosa de los vientos.
compassion [kəmˈpæʃᵊn] *n* compasión *f.*
compassionate [kəmˈpæʃᵊnət] *adj* compasivo,-a.
compatibility [kəmpætəˈbɪlɪtɪ] *n* compatibilidad *f.*
compatible [kəmˈpætɪbᵊl] *adj* compatible (**with**, con).
compatriot [kəmˈpætrɪət] *n* compatriota *mf.*
compel [kəmˈpel] *vt* **1** *(force)* obligar, forzar, compeler. **2** *fig (inspire - respect)* imponer, infundir, inspirar; *(- admiration)* despertar, inspirar, infundir.
▲ *pt & pp* **compelled,** *ger* **compelling.**
compelling [kəmˈpelɪŋ] *adj (novel, account, story)* irresistible; *(reason, argument)* convincente, persuasivo,-a, de peso.
compensate [ˈkɒmpənseɪt] *vt* **1** *(recompense, indemnify)* indemnizar (**for**, por), compensar (**for**, por). **2** *(counterbalance)* compensar.
▷ *vi* compensar (**for**, -).
compensation [kɒmpənˈseɪʃᵊn] *n* **1** *(money, damages)* indemnización *f* (**for**, por). **2** *(way of compensating)* compensación *f* (**for**, por).
compensatory [kɒmpenˈseɪtᵊrɪ] *adj* compensador,-ra.
compere [ˈkɒmpeəʳ] *n* GB presentador,-ra.
▷ *vt* GB presentar.
compete [kəmˈpiːt] *vi (try to win)* disputarse; *(take part in)* competir, participar.
competence [ˈkɒmpɪtəns] *n* **1** *(ability)* competencia, capacidad *f*, aptitud *f*: **a fair level of competence in German** *un buen nivel de alemán.* **2** JUR *(legal authority)* competencia.
competent [ˈkɒmpɪtənt] *adj* **1** *(person)* competente; *(work, novel, etc)* aceptable, bastante bien. **2** JUR competente.
competition [kɒmpəˈtɪʃᵊn] *n* **1** *(gen)* concurso; *(race, sporting event)* competición *f*; *(literary)* certamen *m.* **2** *(rivalry)* competencia.
competitive [kəmˈpetɪtɪv] *adj* **1** *(gen)* competitivo, -a; *(person)* competitivo,-a, que tiene espíritu competitivo. **2** COMM *(price, goods, etc)* competitivo,-a.
competitor [kəmˈpetɪtəʳ] *n* **1** COMM *(rival)* competidor,-ra, rival *mf.* **2** SP *(in race, etc)* participante *mf*; *(opponent)* contrincante *mf.* **3** *(in quiz, etc)* concursante *mf*, participante *mf*; *(in competitive examination)* opositor,-ra.
compilation [kɒmpɪˈleɪʃᵊn] *n* **1** *(act)* compilación *f*, recopilación *f.* **2** *(record, etc)* recopilación *f.*
compile [kəmˈpaɪl] *vt* **1** *(produce book, list, etc)* compilar; *(collect information)* recopilar. **2** COMPUT compilar.
complacency [kəmˈpleɪsᵊnsɪ] *n* autocomplacencia, suficiencia.
complacent [kəmˈpleɪsᵊnt] *adj (person)* satisfecho,-a de sí mismo,-a, suficiente; *(manner, attitude)* de complacencia.
complacently [kəmˈpleɪsᵊntlɪ] *adv* con suficiencia.

complain [kəm'pleɪn] *vi* quejarse (**about/of**, de).
> *vt* quejarse, protestar.

complaint [kəm'pleɪnt] *n* **1** *(gen)* queja (**about**, de); *(formal)* reclamación *f*. **2** MED enfermedad *f* (leve), achaque *m*, dolencia.

complaisant [kəm'pleɪzᵊnt] *adj fml* sumiso,-a.

complement ['kɒmplɪmənt] *n (gen)* complemento (**to**, de).
> *vt* complementar.

complementary [kɒmplɪ'mentᵊrɪ] *adj (gen)* complementario,-a.

complete [kəm'pli:t] *adj* **1** *(entire)* completo,-a. **2** *(finished)* acabado,-a, terminado,-a. **3** *(thorough, absolute, total)* total, completo,-a.
> *vt* **1** *(make whole)* completar. **2** *(finish)* acabar, terminar. **3** *(fill in - form)* rellenar.

completely [kəm'pli:tlɪ] *adv* completamente, totalmente, por completo.

completion [kəm'pli:ʃᵊn] *n (act, state)* finalización *f*, terminación *f*. ■ **on completion** en cuanto se termine.

complex ['kɒmpleks] *adj (gen)* complejo,-a.
> *n* **1** *(group, system)* complejo. **2** *(in psychology)* complejo.

complexion [kəm'plekʃᵊn] *n* **1** *(quality of skin)* cutis *m*; *(colour or tone of skin)* tez *f*. **2** *(aspect, character)* aspecto, cariz *m*, naturaleza, carácter *m*.

complexity [kəm'pleksɪtɪ] *n* complejidad *f*.
▲ *pl* **complexities**.

compliance [kəm'plaɪəns] *n* **1** *(obedience)* conformidad *f*. **2** *(tendency to agree, willingness)* buena voluntad, buena disposición *f*.

compliant [kəm'plaɪənt] *adj* sumiso,-a, dócil.

complicate ['kɒmplɪkeɪt] *vt* complicar.

complicated ['kɒmplɪkeɪtɪd] *adj* complicado,-a.

complication [kɒmplɪ'keɪʃᵊn] *n (gen)* complicación *f*.
> *n pl* **complications** MED complicaciones *fpl*.

complicity [kəm'plɪsɪtɪ] *n* complicidad *f* (**in**, en).

compliment ['kɒmplɪmənt] *vt* felicitar (**on**, por).
> *n (praise)* cumplido, halago.
> *n pl* **compliments** saludos *mpl*, felicitaciones *fpl*.

complimentary [kɒmplɪ'mentᵊrɪ] *adj* **1** *(expressing praise)* elogioso,-a, halagüeño,-a. **2** *(free)* gratuito,-a, de regalo.

comply [kəm'plaɪ] *vi (order)* obedecer (**with**, -), cumplir (**with**, con), acatar (**with**, -); *(request)* acceder (**with**, a); *(law)* acatar (**with**, -); *(standards)* cumplir (**with**, con).
▲ *pt & pp* **complied**, *ger* **complying**.

component [kəm'pəʊnənt] *adj* componente.
> *n* **1** *(gen)* componente *m*. **2** AUTO pieza.

compose [kəm'pəʊz] *vt* **1** *(music, poem)* componer; *(letter)* redactar. **2** *(constitute)* componer. **3** *(one's thoughts)* poner en orden.
> *vi* MUS componer.

composed [kəm'pəʊzd] *adj (calm)* sereno,-a, sosegado,-a, tranquilo,-a.

composer [kəm'pəʊzəʳ] *n* compositor,-ra.

composite ['kɒmpəzɪt] *adj* compuesto,-a.
> *n* combinación *f*, conjunto.

composition [kɒmpə'zɪʃᵊn] *n* **1** *(gen)* composición *f*. **2** *(essay)* redacción *f*. **3** *(substance)* mezcla.
> *adj* sintético,-a.

compost ['kɒmpɒst] *n* abono orgánico, abono vegetal, compost.

composure [kəm'pəʊʒəʳ] *n* calma, serenidad *f*, compostura.

compound¹ [*(adj-n)* 'kɒmpaʊnd, *(vb)* kəm'paʊnd] *adj* compuesto,-a.
▷ *n* **1** CHEM compuesto. **2** *(substance)* mezcla. **3** LING palabra compuesta.
▷ *vt* **1** *(mix)* componer, combinar, mezclar. **2** *(worsen, exacerbate - problem)* agravar, exacerbar; *(- difficulty)* acrecentar, aumentar.
▷ *vi* COMM *(reach agreement)* transigir (**for**, en).

compound² ['kɒmpaʊnd] *n (enclosed area)* recinto.

comprehend [kɒmprɪ'hend] *vt* **1** *(understand)* comprender. **2** *fml (include)* comprender, abarcar.

comprehensible [kɒmprɪ'hensəbᵊl] *adj* comprensible.

comprehension [kɒmprɪ'henʃᵊn] *n* comprensión *f*.

comprehensive [kɒmprɪ'hensɪv] *adj (thorough)* detallado,-a, global, completo,-a; *(broad)* amplio,-a, extenso,-a.

comprehensively [kɒmprɪ'hensɪvlɪ] *adv* exhaustivamente.

compress ['kɒmpres] *n* compresa.
▷ *vt* **1** *(air, straw)* comprimir. **2** *(text, argument, speech)* condensar.

compression [kəm'preʃᵊn] *n* compresión *f*.

compressor [kəm'presəʳ] *n* compresor *m*.

comprise [kəm'praɪz] *vt (consist of, be made up of)* comprender, constar de; *(constitute, form)* componer, constituir.

compromise ['kɒmprəmaɪz] *n* acuerdo mutuo, término medio, compromiso, solución *f* de compromiso.
▷ *vi* llegar a un acuerdo, transigir.
▷ *vt (endanger, weaken)* comprometer.

compromising ['kɒmprəmaɪzɪŋ] *adj (situation)* comprometido,-a, comprometedor,-ra; *(evidence, details, document)* comprometedor,-ra.

compulsion [kəm'pʌlʃᵊn] *n* **1** *(force)* obligación *f*, coacción *f*. **2** *(urge)* compulsión *f*.

compulsive [kəm'pʌlsɪv] *adj* **1** *(compelling, fascinating)* fascinante, irresistible, absorbente. **2** *(obsessive)* obsesivo,-a.

compulsory [kəm'pʌlsərɪ] *adj (subject, military service)* obligatorio,-a; *(retirement, redundancy)* forzoso,-a.

compunction [kəm'pʌŋkʃᵊn] *n fml* remordimiento.

computation [kɒmpjʊ'teɪʃᵊn] *n* cálculo, cómputo.

compute [kəm'pjʊ:t] *vt* computar, calcular.

computer [kəm'pjʊ:təʳ] *n* ordenador *m*, computadora. ● **computer game** juego de ordenador.

computerization [kəmpjʊ:təraɪ'zeɪʃᵊn] *n (of data)* computerización *f*, computadorización *f*; *(of system, business)* informatización *f*.

computerize [kəm'pjʊ:təraɪz] *vt (data)* computarizar, computerizar; *(system, business)* informatizar.

computing [kəm'pjʊ:tɪŋ] *n* informática.

comrade ['kɒmreɪd] *n* **1** POL camarada *mf*, compañero,-a. **2** *dated* compañero,-a.

comradeship ['kɒmreɪdʃɪp] *n* camaradería.

con¹ [kɒn] *n fam* estafa, timo.

▷ *vt fam (money)* estafar, timar; *(person)* embaucar, engañar.
▲ *pt & pp* conned, *ger* conning.
con² [kɒn] *n (disadvantage)* contra *m*.
Consulta también pro.
concave ['kɒnkeɪv] *adj* cóncavo,-a.
concavity [kɒn'kævɪtɪ] *n* concavidad *f*.
conceal [kən'siːl] *vt (gen)* ocultar; *(facts)* encubrir; *(feelings)* disimular.
concealed [kən'siːld] *adj (gen)* oculto,-a; *(lighting)* indirecto,-a.
concede [kən'siːd] *vt* 1 *(admit)* reconocer, admitir. 2 *(allow, give away)* conceder.
▷ *vi* ceder, rendirse.
conceit [kən'siːt] *n (pride)* vanidad *f*, presunción *f*, engreimiento.
conceivable [kən'siːvəbᵊl] *adj* concebible, imaginable.
conceive [kən'siːv] *vt* 1 *(child)* concebir. 2 *(devise, think up)* concebir. 3 *(understand)* entender.
concentrate ['kɒnsᵊntreɪt] *n* concentrado.
▷ *vt (gen)* concentrar (on, en).
▷ *vi* 1 *(person)* concentrarse (on, en); *(talks, book, government)* centrarse (on, en). 2 *(gather together)* concentrarse.
concentrated ['kɒnsᵊntreɪtɪd] *adj (solution, etc)* concentrado,-a; *(study, effort, fire)* intenso,-a.
concentration [kɒnsᵊn'treɪʃᵊn] *n (gen)* concentración *f* (on, en).
concentric [kən'sentrɪk] *adj* concéntrico,-a.
concept ['kɒnsept] *n* concepto.
conception [kən'sepʃᵊn] *n* 1 *(of child, idea, plan)* concepción *f*. 2 *(idea)* concepto, idea, noción *f*.
concern [kən'sɜːn] *n* 1 *(worry)* preocupación *f*, inquietud *f*. 2 *(interest)* interés *m*; *(affair)* asunto. 3 COMM *(company, business)* negocio.
▷ *vt* 1 *(affect, involve)* afectar, concernir, importar; *(interest)* interesar. 2 *(worry)* preocupar. 3 *(book, film, article, etc)* tratar de.
concerned [kən'sɜːnd] *adj* 1 *(affected)* afectado,-a; *(involved)* involucrado,-a. 2 *(worried)* preocupado,-a (about/for, por).
concerning [kən'sɜːnɪŋ] *prep* referente a, con respecto a, en cuanto a, respecto a.
concert ['kɒnsət] *n* concierto.
concerted [kən'sɜːtɪd] *adj* concertado,-a, coordinado,-a.
concerto [kən'tʃeətəʊ] *n* concierto.
▲ *pl* concertos o concerti [kən'tʃeətɪ].
concession [kən'seʃᵊn] *n* 1 *(act or thing granted)* concesión *f* (to, a). 2 COMM concesión *f*.
concessionaire [kənseʃə'neəʳ] *n* concesionario,-a.
concessionary [kən'seʃᵊnərɪ] *adj (rates, etc)* reducido,-a.
conciliate [kən'sɪlɪeɪt] *vt* conciliar.
▷ *vi* conciliar.
conciliation [kənsɪlɪ'eɪʃᵊn] *n* conciliación *f*.
conciliatory [kən'sɪlɪətᵊrɪ] *adj* conciliatorio,-a, conciliador,-ra.
concise [kən'saɪs] *adj* conciso,-a.
concisely [kən'saɪslɪ] *adv* con concisión.
concision [kən'sɪʒᵊn] *n* concisión *f*.
conclude [kən'kluːd] *vt* 1 *(end)* concluir, finalizar. 2 *(settle - deal)* cerrar; *(- agreement)* llegar a; *(- treaty)* firmar. 3 *(deduce)* concluir, llegar a la conclusión de.
▷ *vi* concluir, terminar.
concluding [kən'kluːdɪŋ] *adj* final.
conclusion [kən'kluːʒᵊn] *n* 1 *(decision)* conclusión *f*. 2 *(end)* final *m*, conclusión *f*. 3 *(settling - of deal)* cierre *m*; *(- of treaty)* firma.
conclusive [kən'kluːsɪv] *adj (evidence, proof)* concluyente, definitivo,-a; *(argument)* concluyente, decisivo,-a.
conclusively [kən'kluːsɪvlɪ] *adv* definitivamente.
concoct [kən'kɒkt] *vt* 1 *(dish, sauce, drink)* confeccionar, preparar. 2 *(story, excuse, explanation)* inventar, inventarse.
concoction [kən'kɒkʃᵊn] *n pej (food)* mejunje *m*, mezcolanza; *(drink)* brebaje *m*.
concord ['kɒŋkɔːd] *n* 1 *fml (harmony)* concordia. 2 LING concordancia.
concordance [kəŋ'kɔːdəns] *n* 1 *(similarity, concord)* concordancia. 2 *(index)* concordancias *fpl*.
concordant [kən'kɔːdənt] *adj fml* concordante.
concourse ['kɒŋkɔːs] *n* 1 *(hall)* vestíbulo; *(in station)* explanada. 2 *fml (gathering)* concurrencia, concurso.
concrete ['kɒŋkriːt] *adj* 1 *(definite, not abstract)* concreto,-a. 2 *(made of concrete)* de hormigón.
▷ *n* hormigón *m*.
▷ *vt (wall)* revestir de hormigón; *(ground)* pavimentar con hormigón.
concretely [kɒn'kriːtlɪ] *adv* concretamente.
concubine ['kɒŋkjəbaɪn] *n* concubina.
concur [kən'kɜːʳ] *vi* 1 *(agree)* estar de acuerdo, coincidir. 2 *(coincide)* coincidir, concurrir.
▲ *pt & pp* concurred, *ger* concurring.
concurrence [kən'kʌrəns] *n* 1 *(agreement)* acuerdo, coincidencia. 2 *(of events, etc)* concurrencia, coincidencia.
concurrent [kən'kʌrənt] *adj (in time)* simultáneo,-a, concurrente.
concurrently [kən'kʌrəntlɪ] *adv* simultáneamente.
concussion [kən'kʌʃᵊn] *n* MED conmoción *f* cerebral.
condemn [kən'dem] *vt* 1 *(criticize, denounce)* condenar, censurar. 2 *(sentence)* condenar. 3 *(building)* declarar en ruina.
condemnation [kɒndem'neɪʃᵊn] *n* 1 *(strong disapproval)* condena, repulsa; *(criticism)* crítica. 2 JUR condena.
condemned [kən'demd] *adj* 1 *(person)* condenado,-a. 2 *(building)* que ha sido declarado,-a en ruina.
condensation [kɒnden'seɪʃᵊn] *n* 1 CHEM *(process)* condensación *f*; *(on glass)* vaho. 2 *(of report, history, etc)* condensación *f*.
condense [kən'dens] *vt* 1 CHEM condensar. 2 *(shorten)* condensar, abreviar, resumir.
condenser [kən'densəʳ] *n* condensador *m*.
condescend [kɒndɪ'send] *vi* 1 *(deign)* condescender, dignarse. 2 *(patronize)* tratar con condescendencia.
condescending [kɒndɪ'sendɪŋ] *adj (attitude, answer)* condescendiente.
condescension [kɒndɪ'senʃᵊn] *n* condescendencia.
condiment ['kɒndɪmənt] *n* condimento.

ondition [kən'dɪʃᵊn] *n* 1 *(state)* condición *f*, estado. 2 *(requirement, provision)* condición *f*. 3 MED afección *f*, enfermedad *f*.
▷ *vt* 1 *(determine, accustom)* condicionar. 2 *(treat - hair)* acondicionar, suavizar.
▷ *n pl* **conditions** *(circumstances)* condiciones *fpl*.
onditional [kən'dɪʃənᵊl] *adj* condicional.
▷ *n* **the conditional** LING el condicional *m*.
onditioner [kən'dɪʃᵊnəʳ] *n* *(for hair)* acondicionador *m*, suavizante *m*.
ondolence [kən'dəʊləns] *n* condolencia, pésame *m*.
▷ *n pl* **condolences** pésame *m sing*.
ondom ['kɒndəm] *n* condón *m*, preservativo.
ondominium [kɒndə'mɪnɪəm] *n* 1 POL condominio. 2 US *(apartment block)* bloque *m* de pisos; *(apartment)* apartamento, piso.
ondone [kən'dəʊn] *vt* *(person)* aprobar, consentir; *(action, behaviour)* consentir.
ondor ['kɒndɔːʳ] *n* cóndor *m*.
onducive [kən'djuːsɪv] *adj* propicio,-a (**to**, para).
onduct [*(n)* 'kɒndʌkt, *(vb)* kɒn'dʌkt] *n* 1 *(behaviour)* conducta, comportamiento. 2 *(management)* dirección *f*, gestión *f*, administración *f*.
▷ *vt* 1 *(direct - survey, campaign)* llevar a cabo, realizar; *(- business)* administrar. 2 *(lead, guide)* conducir, guiar. 3 *(transmit - heat, etc)* conducir. 4 MUS dirigir.
▷ *vi* MUS dirigir.
onduction [kən'dʌkʃᵊn] *n* PHYS conducción *f*.
onductivity [kən'dʌktɪvɪtɪ] *adj* conductividad *f*.
onductor [kən'dʌktəʳ] *n* 1 *(of heat, electricity)* conductor *m*. 2 *(of orchestra)* director,-ra de orquesta. 3 *(on bus)* cobrador,-ra. 4 US *(on train)* jefe,-a de tren.
onductress [kən'dʌktrəs] *n* *(on bus)* cobradora.
onduit ['kɒndjʊɪt] *n* conducto.
one [kəʊn] *n* 1 *(shape, for traffic)* cono. 2 *(for ice cream)* cucurucho. 3 BOT *(fruit of pine, etc)* piña.
onfectioner [kən'fekʃᵊnəʳ] *n* confitero,-a, pastelero,-a.
onfectionery [kən'fekʃənᵊrɪ] *n* dulces *mpl*.
onfederacy [kən'fedᵊrəsɪ] *n* confederación *f*.
▲ *pl* **confederacies**.
onfederate [kən'fedᵊrət] *adj* confederado,-a.
▷ *n* 1 confederado,-a. 2 JUR *(accomplice)* cómplice *mf*.
▷ *vi* confederarse.
onfederation [kənfedə'reɪʃᵊn] *n* confederación *f*.
onfer [kən'fɜːʳ] *vt* *(award, grant, bestow)* conferir, conceder.
▷ *vi* *(consult, discuss)* consultar (**with**, con) (**about/on**, sobre).
▲ *pt & pp* **conferred**, *ger* **conferring**.
onference ['kɒnfᵊrəns] *n* 1 *(large event, convention)* congreso, conferencia. 2 *(meeting)* reunión *f*, conferencia, junta.
onfess [kən'fes] *vt* confesar.
▷ *vi* 1 *(admit)* confesar. 2 REL confesarse.
onfessed [kən'fest] *adj* declarado,-a.
onfession [kən'feʃᵊn] *n* confesión *f*.
onfessional [kən'feʃənᵊl] *n* confesionario.
onfessor [kən'fesəʳ] *n* REL confesor *m*.
onfetti [kən'fetɪ] *n* confeti *m*.
onfidant ['kɒnfɪdænt] *n* confidente *m*.
onfidante ['kɒnfɪdænt] *n* confidenta.

confide [kən'faɪd] *vt* 1 *(tell)* confiar. 2 *fml (entrust)* confiar (**to**, a).
⊙ **to confide in** *vi* confiar en.
confidence ['kɒnfɪdəns] *n* 1 *(trust, faith)* confianza (**in**, en), fe *f* (**in**, en). 2 *(self-confidence)* confianza, seguridad *f*. 3 *(secrecy)* confianza. 4 *(secret)* confidencia.
confident ['kɒnfɪdᵊnt] *adj* 1 *(certain)* seguro,-a. 2 *(self-confident)* seguro,-a de sí mismo,-a.
confidential [kɒnfɪ'denʃᵊl] *adj* confidencial.
confidentiality [kɒnfɪdenʃɪ'ælətɪ] *n* confidencialidad *f*, reserva.
confidentially [kɒnfɪ'denʃᵊlɪ] *adv* confidencialmente, en confianza.
confidently ['kɒnfɪdᵊntlɪ] *adv* con seguridad.
confiding [kən'faɪdɪŋ] *adj* confiado,-a.
confine [kən'faɪn] *vt* 1 *(person)* confinar, recluir; *(animal)* encerrar. 2 *(limit, restrict)* limitar.
confined [kən'faɪnd] *adj* *(space)* reducido,-a, limitado,-a.
confinement [kən'faɪnmənt] *n* 1 *(imprisonment)* reclusión *f*. 2 MED *(in childbirth)* parto.
confines ['kɒnfaɪnz] *n pl* límites *mpl*, confines *mpl*.
confirm [kən'fɜːm] *vt* 1 *(prove true, verify)* confirmar. 2 *(ratify)* ratificar. 3 REL confirmar.
confirmation [kɒnfə'meɪʃᵊn] *n* 1 *(proof, verification)* confirmación *f*. 2 *(ratification)* ratificación *f*. 3 REL confirmación *f*.
confirmed [kən'fɜːmd] *adj* *(inveterate)* empedernido,-a.
confiscate ['kɒnfɪskeɪt] *vt* confiscar.
confiscation [kɒnfɪs'keɪʃᵊn] *n* confiscación *f*.
conflict [*(n)* 'kɒnflɪkt, *(vb)* kən'flɪkt] *n* conflicto.
▷ *vi* chocar (**with**, con), estar en conflicto (**with**, con), entrar en desacuerdo (**with**, con).
conflicting [kən'flɪktɪŋ] *adj* *(evidence, accounts)* contradictorio,-a; *(opinions, interests)* contrario,-a, opuesto,-a.
confluence ['kɒnflʊəns] *n* confluencia.
conform [kən'fɔːm] *vi* 1 *(comply with rules, standards, regulations)* ajustarse (**to/with**, a), someterse (**to/with**, a), cumplir (**to/with**, con). 2 *(agree, be consistent with)* avenirse (**to**, a), conformarse (**to/with**, con), concordar (**with**, con). 3 *(fit in, behave like other people)* ser conformista.
conformist [kən'fɔːmɪst] *adj* conformista, convencional.
▷ *n* conformista *mf*.
conformity [kən'fɔːmɪtɪ] *n* conformidad *f*.
confound [kən'faʊnd] *vt* 1 *(puzzle, perplex)* confundir, desconcertar. 2 *dated (defeat)* frustrar.
confront [kən'frʌnt] *vt* 1 *(enemy, opponent)* hacer frente a, plantar cara a, enfrentarse a. 2 *(task, difficulty, reality)* enfrentar, enfrentarse a, afrontar, hacer frente a.
confrontation [kɒnfrʌn'teɪʃᵊn] *n* 1 *(dispute, conflict, opposition)* confrontación *f*, enfrentamiento. 2 JUR *(of witnesses)* careo.
confuse [kən'fjuːz] *vt* 1 *(make unclear, muddle)* confundir, complicar, enredar. 2 *(bewilder)* desconcertar, confundir, desorientar. 3 *(mix up, mistake)* confundir.
confused [kən'fjuːzd] *adj* 1 *(person)* confundido,-a, desconcertado,-a, turbado,-a. 2 *(mind, ideas, account)* confuso,-a.
confusing [kən'fjuːzɪŋ] *adj* confuso,-a.

confusion [kən'fjuːʒᵊn] *n* confusión *f.*
congeal [kən'dʒiːl] *vi (blood)* coagularse; *(fat)* solidificarse.
congenial [kən'dʒiːnɪəl] *adj (person)* simpático,-a, agradable; *(climate, environment, hobby)* agradable.
congenital [kən'dʒenɪtᵊl] *adj* 1 MED congénito,-a. 2 *fig* instintivo,-a, natural.
congested [kən'dʒestɪd] *adj* 1 *(with traffic)* colapsado,-a, congestionado,-a; *(with people)* abarrotado,-a de gente, repleto,-a de gente. 2 MED congestionado,-a.
congestion [kən'dʒestʃᵊn] *n* 1 *(with traffic)* congestión *f*; *(with people)* aglomeración *f.* 2 MED congestión *f.*
conglomerate [*(n)* kən'glɒmərət, *(vb)* kən'glɒməreɪt] *n* 1 COMM conglomerado (de empresas). 2 GEOL conglomerado.
▷ *vi* conglomerarse.
conglomeration [kəŋglɒmə'reɪʃᵊn] *n* conglomerado.
congratulate [kən'grætjəleɪt] *vt* felicitar (**on**, por), dar la enhorabuena a (**on**, por).
congratulation [kən'grætjəleɪʃᵊnz] *n* felicitación *f.*
▷ *interj* **congratulations!** ¡felicidades! *fpl*, ¡enhorabuena!
congregate ['kɒŋgrɪgeɪt] *vi* congregarse.
congregation [kɒŋgrɪ'geɪʃᵊn] *n* REL *(people gathered)* fieles *mpl*; *(parishioners)* feligreses *mpl.*
congress ['kɒŋgres] *n* congreso.
▷ *n* **Congress** US el Congreso.
congressional [kəŋ'greʃənᵊl] *adj* US del Congreso.
● **Congressional district** distrito electoral.
Congressman ['kɒŋgresmən] *n* miembro del Congreso, congresista *m.*
Congresswoman ['kɒŋgreswʊmən] *n* miembro *f* del Congreso, congresista.
▲ *pl* **Congresswomen** ['kɒŋgreswʊmɪn].
congruent ['kɒŋgrʊənt] *adj* MATH congruente.
congruous ['kɒŋrʊəs] *adj fml* congruente (**with**, con).
conic ['kɒnɪk] *adj* cónico,-a.
conifer ['kɒnɪfəʳ] *n* conífera.
conjectural [kən'dʒektʃərᵊl] *adj* conjetural, basado,-a en conjeturas.
conjecture [kən'dʒektʃəʳ] *n* conjetura, suposición *f.*
▷ *vi* hacer conjeturas.
conjugal ['kɒndʒəgᵊl] *adj* conyugal.
conjugate ['kɒndʒəgeɪt] *vt* conjugar.
▷ *vi* conjugarse.
conjugation [kɒndʒə'geɪʃᵊn] *n* conjugación *f.*
conjunction [kən'dʒʌŋkʃᵊn] *n* conjunción *f.* ■ **in conjunction with** conjuntamente con.
conjure ['kʌndʒəʳ] *vi* hacer magia, hacer juegos de manos.
⊙ **to conjure up** *vt sep (evoke - memories)* evocar, traer a la memoria; *(summon - spirits)* invocar.
conjurer ['kʌndʒərəʳ] *n* mago,-a, prestidigitador,-ra.
conk [kɒŋk] *vt* 1 GB *fam (nose)* napias *fpl.* 2 *fam* pegarle una piña a.
⊙ **to conk out** *vi* 1 *fam (machine, car)* averiarse. 2 *fam (person)* quedarse como un tronco, quedarse roque.
conker ['kɒŋkəʳ] *n fam* castaña (de Indias).
connect [kə'nekt] *vt* 1 *(join, attach - gen)* unir, enlazar, conectar; *(- wires, cables, pipes)* empalmar, conectar; *(- rooms, buildings)* comunicar, unir; *(- cities)* unir, conectar. 2 *(join to power supply)* conectar, enchufar. 3 *(associate)* relacionar, asociar. 4 *(on telephone)* pone (**with**, con).
connected [kə'nektɪd] *adj* 1 *(related, joined)* relacionado,-a, conectado,-a. 2 *(to power supply)* conectado,-a, enchufado,-a. 3 *(related by birth)* emparentado,-a.
connection [kə'nekʃᵊn] *n* 1 *(link)* unión *f*, enlace *m.* 2 *(electrical)* conexión *f*, empalme *m.* 3 *(relation)* relación *f*, conexión *f.* 4 *(train, plane)* conexión *f*, enlace *m.*
▷ *n pl* **connections** *(professional)* contactos *mpl*; *(relatives)* familia, parientes *mpl.*
connective [kə'nektɪv] *n* conector *m.*
connector [kə'nektər] *n* conector *m.*
connivance [kə'naɪvᵊns] *n* complicidad *f*, connivencia.
connive [kə'naɪv] *vi (conspire)* conspirar, confabularse.
connoisseur [kɒnə'sɜːʳ] *n* entendido,-a, conocedor,-ra.
connotation [kɒnə'teɪʃᵊn] *n* connotación *f.*
conquer ['kɒŋkəʳ] *vt (country, mountain, heart)* conquistar; *(enemy, disease, fear)* vencer.
conqueror ['kɒŋkərəʳ] *n* conquistador,-ra, vencedor,-ra.
conquest ['kɒŋkwest] *n* conquista.
consanguinity [kɒnsæŋ'gwɪnɪtɪ] *n* consanguinidad *f.*
conscience ['kɒnʃᵊns] *n* conciencia.
conscience-stricken ['kɒnʃᵊnsstrɪkᵊn] *adj* lleno,-a de remordimientos.
conscientious [kɒnʃɪ'enʃəs] *adj (work)* concienzudo,-a; *(person)* aplicado,-a, serio,-a.
conscientiously [kɒnʃɪ'enʃəslɪ] *adv* a conciencia, concienzudamente.
conscientiousness [kɒnʃɪ'enʃəsnəs] *n* escrupulosidad *f.*
conscious ['kɒnʃəs] *adj* 1 MED consciente. 2 *(aware)* consciente. 3 *(intentional, deliberate)* deliberado,-a.
conscript [*(n)* 'kɒnskrɪpt, *(vb)* kən'skrɪpt] *n* recluta.
▷ *vt* reclutar.
conscription [kən'skrɪpʃᵊn] *n* servicio militar obligatorio.
consecrate ['kɒnsɪkreɪt] *vt* consagrar.
consecutive [kən'sekjətɪv] *adj* consecutivo,-a.
consecutively [kən'sekjətɪvlɪ] *adv* consecutivamente.
consensus [kən'sensəs] *n* consenso.
consent [kən'sent] *n* consentimiento.
▷ *vi* consentir (**to**, en), acceder (**to**, en).
consequence ['kɒnsɪkwəns] *n* 1 *(result)* consecuencia. 2 *(importance)* importancia, trascendencia.
consequent ['kɒnsɪkwənt] *adj* consiguiente.
consequential [kɒnsɪ'kwenʃᵊl] *adj* 1 *(resultant)* consiguiente, resultante. 2 *fml (important)* importante, trascendente.
consequently ['kɒnsɪkwəntlɪ] *adv* por consiguiente.
conservation [kɒnsə'veɪʃᵊn] *n* conservación *f.*
conservationist [kɒnsə'veɪʃᵊnɪst] *n* ecologista *mf.*
conservatism [kən'sɜːvətɪzᵊm] *n* POL conservadurismo.
conservative [kən'sɜːvətɪv] *adj* 1 *(traditional)* conservador,-ra. 2 *(cautious)* cauteloso,-a, prudente.
▷ *n (traditionalist)* conservador,-ra.
▷ *adj* **Conservative** POL conservador,-ra.
▷ *n* **Conservative** POL conservador,-ra.
conservatoire [kən'sɜːvətwɑːʳ] *n* conservatorio.

onservatory [kən'sɜ:vətrɪ] *n* 1 MUS conservatorio. 2 *(greenhouse)* invernadero.
▲ *pl* conservatories.

onserve [kən'sɜ:v] *vt (nature, wildlife, etc)* conservar, proteger; *(save)* conservar, ahorrar; *(resources)* conservar, preservar.
▷ *n* CULIN *(jam)* confitura.

onsider [kən'sɪdər] *vt* 1 *(think about, examine, contemplate)* considerar. 2 *(regard as)* considerar. 3 *(take into account)* tener en cuenta, considerar.

onsiderable [kən'sɪdərəbəl] *adj* considerable.

onsiderably [kən'sɪdərəblɪ] *adv* bastante, considerablemente.

onsiderate [kən'sɪdərət] *adj* considerado,-a, atento,-a.

onsideration [kənsɪdə'reɪʃən] *n* 1 *(thoughtfulness)* consideración *f*. 2 *(factor to consider)* factor *m* a tener en cuenta, factor *m* que se tiene en cuenta. 3 *(attention, thought)* consideración *f*, atención *f*.

onsidering [kən'sɪdərɪŋ] *prep* teniendo en cuenta.
▷ *conj* teniendo en cuenta que, dado que.
▷ *adv* después de todo.

onsign [kən'saɪn] *vt* 1 COMM *(send - goods)* consignar. 2 *fml (entrust, hand over, give up)* confiar, encomendar.

onsignment [kən'saɪnmənt] *n* COMM remesa, envío.

onsist [kən'sɪst] *vi* 1 *fml (have as chief element)* consistir (in, en). 2 *(comprise, be composed of)* constar (of, de), estar compuesto,-a (of, de).

onsistency [kən'sɪstənsɪ] *n* 1 *(of actions, behaviour, policy)* consecuencia, coherencia, lógica. 2 *(of mixture)* consistencia.

onsistent [kən'sɪstənt] *adj (of person, behaviour, beliefs)* coherente (with, con), consecuente (with, con); *(denial, improvement)* constante.

onsistently [kən'sɪstəntlɪ] *adv (unchangingly)* consecuentemente, coherentemente; *(constantly)* constantemente.

onsolation [kɒnsə'leɪʃən] *n* consuelo.

onsole[1] ['kɒnsəʊl] *n (electrical)* consola; *(video games)* consola.

onsole[2] [kən'səʊl] *vt* consolar.

onsolidate [kən'sɒlɪdeɪt] *vt* 1 *(gen)* consolidar. 2 COMM *(merge)* fusionar.
▷ *vi* 1 *(gen)* consolidarse. 2 COMM *(merge)* fusionarse.

onsolidation [kənsɒlɪ'deɪʃən] *n* 1 *(gen)* consolidación *f*. 2 COMM fusión *f*.

onsoling [kən'səʊlɪŋ] *adj* de consuelo, consolador,-ra.

onsommé ['kɒnsɒmeɪ] *n* consomé *m*.

onsonant ['kɒnsənənt] *n* consonante *f*.

onsort [*(n)* 'kɒnsɔ:t], *(vb)* kən'sɔ:t] *n* consorte *mf*.
▷ *vi* asociarse (with, con).

onsortium [kən'sɔ:tɪəm] *n* consorcio.
▲ *pl* consortia.

onspicuous [kəns'pɪkjʊəs] *adj (clothes)* llamativo,-a; *(mistake, difference, lack)* evidente, obvio,-a.

onspicuously [kən'spɪkjʊəslɪ] *adv (loudly)* de forma llamativa; *(markedly)* notoriamente.

onspiracy [kən'spɪrəsɪ] *n* conspiración *f*: a conspiracy to murder *una conspiración de asesinato.*
▲ *pl* conspiracies.

conspirator [kən'spɪrətər] *n* conspirador,-ra.

conspiratorial [kənspɪrə'tɔ:rɪəl] *adj* conspirador,-ra.

conspire [kən'spaɪər] *vi (people)* conspirar (against, contra); *(events)* conspirar, confabularse.

constable ['kʌnstəbəl] *n* policía *mf*, guardia *mf*, agente *mf* (de policía).

constabulary [kən'stæbjələrɪ] *n* GB policía.
▲ *pl* constabularies.

constancy ['kɒnstənsɪ] *n* 1 *(freedom from change)* constancia. 2 *(faithfulness, loyalty)* fidelidad *f*, lealtad *f*.

constant ['kɒnstənt] *adj* 1 *(continual)* continuo,-a, constante. 2 *(unchanging)* constante. 3 *(loyal)* leal, fiel.
▷ *n* constante *f*.

constantly ['kɒnstəntlɪ] *adv* constantemente, continuamente.

constellation [kɒnstə'leɪʃən] *n* constelación *f*.

consternation [kɒnstə'neɪʃən] *n* consternación *f*.

constipated ['kɒnstɪpeɪtɪd] *adj* estreñido,-a.

constipation [kɒnstɪ'peɪʃən] *n* estreñimiento.

constituency [kən'stɪtjʊənsɪ] *n* circunscripción *f*, distrito electoral.
▲ *pl* constituencies.

constituent [kəns'tɪtjʊənt] *adj* 1 *(part, etc)* constitutivo,-a, constituyente. 2 POL constituyente.
▷ *n* 1 *(component)* componente *m*. 2 POL elector,-ra.

constitute ['kɒnstɪtju:t] *vt* constituir.

constitution [kɒnstɪ'tju:ʃən] *n* 1 *(gen)* constitución *f*. 2 *(of person)* constitución *f*, complexión *f*.

constitutional [kɒnstɪ'tju:ʃənəl] *adj* constitucional.
▷ *n dated* paseo.

constrain [kəns'treɪn] *vt* 1 *(oblige, force)* constreñir, obligar, forzar. 2 *(restrict, hold back)* contener.

constraint [kən'streɪnt] *n* 1 *(compulsion, coercion)* constreñimiento, coacción *f*, obligación *f*. 2 *(restriction)* restricción *f*, limitación *f*. 3 *fml (uneasiness)* inquietud *f*, confusión *f*.

constrict [kən'strɪkt] *vt* 1 *(blood vessels)* estrangular; *(breathing, movement)* dificultar; *(neck)* apretar, oprimir. 2 *fig (action, behaviour)* limitar, coartar.

constriction [kən'strɪkʃən] *n* 1 MED *(narrow part)* estrangulamiento; *(tightness)* opresión *f*. 2 *fig (limitation)* restricción *f*, limitación *f*, constricción *f*.

construct [kəns'trʌkt] *vt (gen)* construir; *(model)* armar, montar.

construction [kən'strʌkʃən] *n* 1 *(gen)* construcción *f*. 2 *fig (meaning)* interpretación *f*.

constructive [kən'strʌktɪv] *adj* constructivo,-a.

constructively [kən'strʌktɪvlɪ] *adv* constructivamente, de manera constructiva.

constructor [kən'strʌktər] *n* constructor,-ra.

construe [kən'stru:] *vt* interpretar.

consul ['kɒnsəl] *n* cónsul *mf*.

consulate ['kɒnsjələt] *n* consulado.

consult [kən'sʌlt] *vt* consultar.
▷ *vi* consultar.

consultant [kən'sʌltənt] *n* 1 *(expert, advisor)* asesor,-ra, consultor,-ra. 2 GB *(doctor)* especialista *mf*.

consultation [kɒnsəl'teɪʃən] *n* 1 *(act, process)* consulta. 2 MED consulta. 3 *(discussion)* discusión *f*, conversación *f*; *(meeting)* reunión *f*.

consultative [kən'sʌltətɪv] *adj* consultivo,-a.

consulting [kənˈsʌltɪŋ] *adj (architect, engineer)* asesor,-ra, consultor,-ra. ● **consulting room** MED consulta.
consume [kənˈsjuːm] *vt (gen)* consumir; *(fire)* consumir, reducir a cenizas.
consumer [kənˈsjuːməʳ] *n* consumidor,-ra.
consuming [kənˈsjuːmɪŋ] *adj (interest)* arrollador,-ra; *(passion)* devorador,-ra.
consummate [*(adj)* ˈkɒnsəmət, *(vb)* ˈkɒnsəmeɪt] *adj fml* consumado,-a.
▷ *vt fml* consumar.
consummation [kɒnsəˈmeɪʃᵊn] *n* consumación *f.*
consumption [kənˈsʌmpʃᵊn] *n* **1** *(of food, energy, resources)* consumo. **2** MED *dated* tisis *f.*
cont[1] [ˈkɒntents] *abbr* **(contents)** contenido.
cont[2] [kɒnˈtɪnjuːd] *abbr* **(continued)** sigue.
contact [ˈkɒntækt] *n (gen)* contacto. ● **contact lenses** lentes *fpl* de contacto.
▷ *vt* ponerse en contacto con, contactar con.
contagion [kənˈteɪdʒᵊn] *n* contagio.
contagious [kənˈteɪdʒəs] *adj* contagioso,-a.
contain [kənˈteɪn] *vt* contener.
container [kənˈteɪnəʳ] *n* **1** *(receptacle)* recipiente *m*; *(packaging)* envase *m*. **2** *(for transporting goods)* contenedor *m*, contáiner *m*.
containment [kənˈteɪnmənt] *n* contención *f.*
contaminate [kənˈtæmɪneɪt] *vt* contaminar.
contamination [kəntæmɪˈneɪʃᵊn] *n* contaminación *f.*
contemplate [ˈkɒntempleɪt] *vt* **1** *(look at)* contemplar; *(consider thoughtfully)* considerar, contemplar. **2** *(consider possibility of)* considerar, pensar (en); *(expect)* prever. **3** *(meditate)* meditar sobre.
▷ *vi* **1** pensar. **2** *(meditate)* meditar.
contemplation [kɒntemˈpleɪʃᵊn] *n* **1** *(act of looking at)* contemplación *f*; *(deep thought, meditation)* reflexión *f*, meditación *f.* **2** *(consideration, intention)* intención *f.*
contemplative [ˈkɒntempleɪtɪv] *adj (thoughtful)* pensativo,-a, meditabundo,-a.
contemporaneous [kɒntempəˈreɪnɪəs] *adj fml* contemporáneo,-a, coetáneo,-a.
contemporary [kənˈtempᵊrərɪ] *adj* **1** *(of the same period)* contemporáneo,-a, coetáneo,-a. **2** *(modern)* contemporáneo,-a, actual.
▷ *n* contemporáneo,-a.
▲ *pl* **contemporaries.**
contempt [kənˈtempt] *n* desdén *m*, menosprecio.
contemptible [kənˈtemptəbᵊl] *adj* despreciable.
contemptuous [kənˈtemptjʊəs] *adj (attitude)* despreciativo,-a, despectivo,-a; *(person)* desdeñoso,-a.
contend [kənˈtend] *vi* **1** *(compete)* contender, competir. **2** *(deal with, struggle against)* enfrentarse a, lidiar con.
▷ *vt (claim, state)* sostener, afirmar.
contender [kənˈtendəʳ] *n* contendiente *mf* (**for**, por).
content[1] [ˈkɒntent] *n* contenido.
▷ *n pl* **contents** contenido *m sing.*
content[2] [kənˈtent] *adj* contento,-a, satisfecho,-a: **he's content to watch the match at home** *se conforma con ver el partido en casa.*
▷ *n* contento.
▷ *vt* contentar, satisfacer.
contented [kənˈtentɪd] *adj* contento,-a, satisfecho,-a.
contention [kənˈtenʃᵊn] *n* **1** *(opinion, assertion)* opinión *f.* **2** *(dispute, disagreement)* discusión *f*, controversia. **3** *(competition)* competición *f.*
contentious [kənˈtenʃəs] *adj (issue, decision, view)* contencioso,-a, polémico,-a, muy discutido,-a; *(person)* discutidor,-ra.
contentment [kənˈtentmənt] *n* contento, satisfacción *f.*
contest [*(n)* ˈkɒntest, *(vb)* kənˈtest] *n* **1** *(competition gen)* concurso; *(- sports)* competición *f*; *(- boxing)* combate *m*. **2** *(struggle, attempt)* contienda, lucha.
▷ *vt* **1** *(championship, seat)* competir por, luchar por, disputarse; *(election)* presentarse como candidato,-a a. **2** *(dispute)* refutar, rebatir. **3** JUR *(appeal against)* impugnar.
contestant [kənˈtestənt] *n (in competition, quiz, game)* concursante *mf*; *(for post, position)* candidato,-a, aspirante *mf.*
context [ˈkɒntekst] *n* contexto.
contiguous [kənˈtɪgjʊəs] *adj* contiguo,-a.
continent [ˈkɒntɪnənt] *n* continente *m*.
▷ *n* **the Continent** GB Europa (continental).
continental [kɒntɪˈnentᵊl] *adj* continental.
▷ *adj* **Continental** GB europeo,-a.
contingency [kənˈtɪndʒənsɪ] *n* contingencia, eventualidad *f.* ● **contingency plan** plan *m* de emergencia.
contingent [kənˈtɪndʒᵊnt] *adj* contingente.
▷ *n* contingente *m*.
continual [kənˈtɪnjʊəl] *adj* continuo,-a, constante.
continuance [kənˈtɪnjʊəns] *n fml* continuación *f.*
continuation [kəntɪnjʊˈeɪʃᵊn] *n* **1** *(resumption)* continuación *f*; *(prolongation)* prolongación *f.* **2** *(extension)* prolongación *f*, continuación *f.* **3** US *(adjournment)* aplazamiento.
continue [kənˈtɪnjuː] *vt* continuar, seguir con.
▷ *vi* continuar, seguir.
continuous [kənˈtɪnjʊəs] *adj* continuo,-a.
continuously [kənˈtɪnjʊəslɪ] *adv* continuamente, sin interrupción.
contort [kənˈtɔːt] *vt (face)* contraer.
▷ *vi* contraerse.
contortion [kənˈtɔːʃᵊn] *n* contorsión *f.*
contour [ˈkɒntʊəʳ] *n* contorno.
contraband [ˈkɒntrəbænd] *n* contrabando.
contraception [kɒntrəˈsepʃᵊn] *n* anticoncepción *f.*
contraceptive [kɒntrəˈseptɪv] *adj* anticonceptivo,-a.
▷ *n* anticonceptivo.
contract [*(n)* ˈkɒntrækt, *(vb)* kənˈtrækt] *n (gen)* contrato; *(for public work, services)* contrata.
▷ *vt* **1** *(place under contract)* contratar. **2** *(make smaller)* contraer. **3** *fml (debt, habit, illness)* contraer.
▷ *vi* **1** *(enter into agreement)* hacer un contrato, firmar un contrato. **2** *(become smaller)* contraerse.
contraction [kənˈtrækʃᵊn] *n* contracción *f.*
contractor [kənˈtræktəʳ] *n* contratista *mf.*
contradict [kɒntrəˈdɪkt] *vt (gen)* contradecir.
▷ *vi* contradecir.
contradiction [kɒntrəˈdɪkʃᵊn] *n* contradicción *f.*
contradictory [kɒntrəˈdɪktərɪ] *adj* contradictorio,-a.
contraption [kənˈtræpʃᵊn] *n fam* cacharro, artefacto, aparato, artilugio.

ontrariness [kɒnˈtreərɪnəs] *n* terquedad *f*, obstinación *f*.

ontrary [*(adj)* ˈkɒntrərɪ, *(n)* kɒnˈtreərɪ] *adj* **1** *(opposite)* contrario,-a. **2** *(stubborn)* terco,-a, obstinado,-a, tozudo,-a.
n **the contrary** lo contrario.

ontrast [*(n)* ˈkɒntrɑːst, *(vb)* kɒnˈtrɑːst] *n* contraste *m*.
vt contrastar, comparar.
vi contrastar.

ontrasting [kənˈtrɑːstɪŋ] *adj* opuesto,-a.

ontravention [kɒntrəˈvenʃən] *n* JUR contravención *f*, infracción *f*.

ontribute [kənˈtrɪbjuːt] *vt* **1** *(money)* contribuir (**to**, a), (**towards**, para); *(ideas, information)* aportar. **2** *(article, poem, etc)* escribir.
vi **1** *(gen)* contribuir (**to**, a), (**towards**, para); *(in discussion)* participar (**to**, en). **2** *(to newspaper, magazine, etc)* colaborar (**to**, en), escribir (**to**, para).

ontributor [kənˈtrɪbjətər] *n* **1** *(to charity, appeal, etc)* donante *mf*. **2** *(to newspaper, magazine, etc)* colaborador,-ra.

ontrition [kənˈtrɪʃən] *n* contrición *f*.

ontrivance [kənˈtraɪvəns] *n* **1** *(device, tool)* artefacto, invento, cacharro, artilugio, aparato. **2** *(plan)* estratagema, artimaña, treta.

ontrive [kənˈtraɪv] *vt* **1** *(way, device)* idear, inventar; *(meeting)* arreglar; *(meal, dress, etc)* improvisar. **2** *(manage)* conseguir, lograr.

ntrived [kənˈtraɪvd] *adj* artificial, forzado,-a, afectado,-a.

ntrol [kənˈtrəʊl] *vt* **1** *(govern, rule)* controlar. **2** *(regulate - temperature, volume)* controlar, regular; *(- traffic)* dirigir.
n **1** *(power, command)* poder *m*, dominio, mando; *(authority)* autoridad *f*. **2** *(restriction, means of regulating)* control *m*. **3** *(place, people in control)* control *m*. **4** TECH *(standard of comparison)* patrón *m* de comparación. **5** *(switch, button)* botón *m*, mando.
n pl **controls** *(of vehicle)* mandos *mpl*.

ontroller [kənˈtrəʊlər] *n* **1** *(financial)* interventor,-ra. **2** *(in broadcasting)* director,-ra de programación.

ontroversial [kɒntrəˈvɜːʃəl] *adj* controvertido,-a, polémico,-a.

ntroversy [kənˈtrɒvəsɪ] *n* controversia, polémica.
▲ *pl* **controversies**.

ntusion [kənˈtjuːʒən] *n* contusión *f*.

onvalesce [kɒnvəˈles] *vi* convalecer, recuperarse.

nvalescence [kɒnvəˈlesəns] *n* convalecencia.

nvalescent [kɒnvəˈlesənt] *adj* convaleciente.

nvene [kənˈviːn] *vt* convocar.
vi reunirse.

nvenience [kənˈviːnɪəns] *n* conveniencia, comodidad *f*.

onvenient [kənˈviːnɪənt] *adj* *(time, arrangement)* conveniente, oportuno,-a; *(thing)* práctico,-a, cómodo,-a.

nvent [ˈkɒnvənt] *n* convento.

nvention [kənˈvenʃən] *n* convención *f*, congreso.

nverge [kənˈvɜːdʒ] *vi* *(lines, roads)* convergir (**on**, en), converger (**on**, en); *(people)* reunirse.

nversant [kənˈvɜːsənt] *adj* familiarizado,-a (**with**, con), versado,-a (**with**, en).

conversation [kɒnvəˈseɪʃən] *n* conversación *f*.

conversational [kɒnvəˈseɪʃənəl] *adj* coloquial, familiar.

converse[1] [ˈkɒnvɜːs] *adj* opuesto,-a, contrario,-a.

converse[2] [kənˈvɜːs] *vi* conversar, hablar.

conversely [kənˈvɜːslɪ] *adv* a la inversa.

conversion [kənˈvɜːʃən] *n* **1** *(gen)* conversión *f* (**to**, a), (**into**, en); *(of buildings)* transformación *f*. **2** REL conversión *f*. **3** SP *(in rugby)* transformación *f*, conversión *f*.

convert [*(vb)* kənˈvɜːt, *(n)* ˈkɒnvɜːt] *vt* *(gen)* convertir (**into**, en), (**to**, a).
▷ *n* REL converso,-a.

converter [kənˈvɜːtər] *n* convertidor *m*.

convertible [kənˈvɜːtəbəl] *adj* *(gen)* convertible; *(car)* descapotable.
▷ *n* AUTO descapotable *m*.

convex [ˈkɒnveks] *adj* convexo,-a.

convey [kənˈveɪ] *vt* **1** *(goods, people, electricity)* transportar, conducir; *(sound)* transmitir, llevar. **2** *(opinion, feeling, idea)* comunicar, expresar, transmitir; *(thanks)* hacer llegar, transmitir.

conveyance [kənˈveɪəns] *n* **1** *(transport)* transporte *m*. **2** *fml* *(vehicle)* vehículo. **3** JUR traspaso, transferencia.

conveyor [kənˈveɪər] *n* transportista *mf*.

convict [*(n)* ˈkɒnvɪkt, *(vb)* kənˈvɪkt] *n* presidiario,-a, recluso,-a.
▷ *vt* JUR declarar culpable, condenar.

conviction [kənˈvɪkʃən] *n* **1** *(belief)* convicción *f*, creencia. **2** JUR condena (**for**, por).

convince [kənˈvɪns] *vt* convencer.

convincing [kənˈvɪnsɪŋ] *adj* convincente.

convivial [kənˈvɪvɪəl] *adj* *(party, atmosphere)* alegre, jovial, festivo,-a, cordial; *(person)* sociable.

convocation [kɒnvəˈkeɪʃən] *n* **1** *(summoning)* convocatoria. **2** *(of academics)* asamblea.

convoke [kənˈvəʊk] *vt* convocar.

convoluted [ˈkɒnvəluːtɪd] *adj* **1** *(complicated)* complicado,-a, enredado,-a, intrincado,-a, enrevesado,-a. **2** BIOL *(twisted, coiled)* enrollado,-a.

convoy [ˈkɒnvɔɪ] *n* convoy *m*.
▷ *vt* escoltar, convoyar.

convulse [kənˈvʌls] *vt* **1** MED convulsionar. **2** *fig* convulsionar, sacudir.
▷ *vi* MED tener convulsiones.

coo [kuː] *vi* *(dove, pigeon)* arrullar; *(baby)* hacer gorgoritos.
▷ *vt* susurrar.

cook [kʊk] *n* cocinero,-a.
▷ *vt* *(food)* guisar, cocinar; *(meals)* preparar, hacer.
▷ *vi* **1** *(person)* cocinar, guisar, cocer; *(food)* hacerse, cocerse. **2** *fam* *(be planned)* cocerse, tramarse.

cooker [ˈkʊkər] *n* *(stove)* cocina.

cookie [ˈkʊkɪ] *n* **1** US *(biscuit)* galleta. **2** *(in computing)* cookie *m & f*, galleta.

cooking [ˈkʊkɪŋ] *n* cocina: **home cooking** *cocina casera*.

cool [kuːl] *adj* **1** *(weather, breeze, clothes)* fresco,-a; *(drink)* fresco,-a, frío,-a. **2** *(unfriendly, reserved)* frío,-a. **3** *(calm)* tranquilo,-a, sereno,-a. **4** *fam* *(great)* guay. **5** *(self-confident)* impasible.

coop[1] [ku:p] *n* gallinero.
coop[2] ['kəʊɒp] [Also written **co-op**.] *n* cooperativa.
cooperate [kəʊ'ɒpəreɪt] [Also written **co-operate**.] *vi* cooperar, colaborar.
coordinate [*(vb)* kəʊ'ɔ:dɪneɪt, *(n)* kəʊ'ɔ:dɪnət] [Also written **co-ordinate**.] *vt* coordinar.
▷ *n* MATH coordenada.
coordination [kəʊɔ:dɪ'neɪʃᵊn] [Also written **co-ordination**.] *n* coordinación *f*.
cop [kɒp] *n sl (policeman)* poli *mf*.
cope [kəʊp] *vi* arreglárselas, poder.
Copenhagen [kəʊpᵊn'heɪgᵊn] *n* Copenhague.
copious ['kəʊpɪəs] *adj* copioso,-a, abundante.
copper ['kɒpəʳ] *n* **1** *(metal)* cobre *m*. **2** GB *fam (coin)* penique *m*, pela, perra. **3** *sl (policeman)* poli *mf*.
copse [kɒps] *n* arboleda, bosquecillo.
copulate ['kɒpjəleɪt] *vi* copular.
copy ['kɒpɪ] *n* **1** *(reproduction)* copia. **2** *(of book, magazine, etc)* ejemplar *m*. **3** TECH *(written text to be printed)* manuscrito, texto; *(text)* artículo, texto.
▲ *pl* **copies**.
▷ *vi* copiar.
copycat ['kɒpɪkæt] *n fam* copión,-ona.
▷ *adj (crime)* inspirado,-a en otro.
copyright ['kɒpɪraɪt] *n* copyright *m*, derechos *mpl* de autor.
▷ *adj* protegido,-a por el copyright.
coral ['kɒrᵊl] *n* coral *m*.
cord [kɔ:d] *n* **1** *(string, rope)* cuerda. **2** ELEC cable *m*. **3** *(corduroy)* pana.
cordial ['kɔ:dɪəl] *adj* cordial.
▷ *n (soft drink)* refresco; *(liqueur)* licor *m*.
cordon ['kɔ:dᵊn] *n* cordón *m*.
corduroy ['kɔ:dərɔɪ] *n* pana.
core [kɔ:ʳ] *n* **1** *(of earth)* núcleo, centro; *(of magnet, nuclear reactor)* núcleo; *(of computer)* núcleo magnético. **2** *(of apple, pear, etc)* corazón *m*. **3** *(most important part)* núcleo, meollo.
▷ *vt* quitarle el corazón a.
coriander [kɒrɪ'ændəʳ] *n* cilantro.
cork [kɔ:k] *n (material)* corcho.
corkscrew ['kɔ:kskru:] *n* sacacorchos *m*, tirabuzón *m*.
corm [kɔ:m] *n* bulbo.
corn[1] [kɔ:n] *n (gen)* cereales *mpl*; *(wheat)* trigo; *(oats)* avena; *(maize)* maíz *m*.
corn[2] [kɔ:n] *n* MED callo.
corncob ['kɔ:nkɒb] *n* mazorca de maíz.
corncrake ['kɔ:nkreɪk] *n* guion *m* de codornices.
cornea ['kɔ:nɪə] *n* córnea.
corned beef [kɔ:nd'bi:f] *n* carne *f* en conserva.
corner ['kɔ:nəʳ] *n* **1** *(of street)* esquina; *(bend in road)* curva, recodo; *(of table, etc)* esquina, punta. **2** *(of room, cupboard, etc)* rincón *m*; *(of mouth)* comisura; *(of eye)* rabillo; *(of page, envelope)* ángulo. **3** SP *(kick - in football)* córner *m*, saque *m* de esquina. **4** SP *(in boxing)* esquina. **5** COMM monopolio.
▷ *vt* **1** *(enemy, animal)* arrinconar, acorralar; *(person)* arrinconar. **2** COMM acaparar, monopolizar.
cornerstone ['kɔ:nəstəʊn] *n* **1** ARCH piedra angular. **2** *fig* base *f*, pilar *m*.
cornet ['kɔ:nɪt] *n* **1** MUS corneta. **2** GB *(for ice-cream)* cucurucho.
cornflakes ['kɔ:nfleɪks] *npl* copos de maíz.
cornice ['kɔ:nɪs] *n* cornisa.
Cornwall ['kɔ:nwəl] *n* Cornualles.
corny ['kɔ:nɪ] *adj fam (joke, story)* gastado,-a, sob do,-a, malo,-a; *(film)* cursi, hortera.
▲ *comp* **cornier**, *superl* **corniest**.
corolla [kə'rɒlə] *n* corola.
coronation [kɒrə'neɪʃᵊn] *n* coronación *f*.
coroner ['kɒrənəʳ] *n* juez *mf* de instrucción.
corporal ['kɔ:pᵊrəl] *adj* corporal.
corporate ['kɔ:pᵊrət] *adj* **1** *(collective)* colectivo,-a. **2** *(a corporation)* de la empresa, de la compañía.
corporation [kɔ:pə'reɪʃᵊn] *n* **1** COMM corporación sociedad *f* anónima. **2** GB *(council)* ayuntamient corporación *f* municipal.
▷ *adj* GB municipal.
corporeal [kɔ:'pɔ:rɪəl] *adj fml* corpóreo,-a.
corps [kɔ:ʳ] *n* cuerpo.
▲ *pl* **corps** [kɔ:zʳ].
corpse [kɔ:ps] *n* cadáver *m*.
corpulence ['kɔ:pjələns] *n* corpulencia.
corpuscle ['kɔ:pəsᵊl] *n* corpúsculo, glóbulo.
corral [kə'rɑ:l] *n* US corral *m*.
correct [kə'rekt] *adj* **1** *(true, right, accurate)* correct -a, exacto,-a. **2** *(of behaviour, manners, dress)* formal
▷ *vt (person, mistake, defect)* corregir, rectificar; *(exam etc)* corregir.
correlate ['kɒrəleɪt] *vt* correlacionar.
▷ *vi* guardar correlación (**with**, con).
▷ *n* correlato.
correspond [kɒrɪs'pɒnd] *vi* **1** *(match, be consistent)* c rresponderse (**with**, con), concordar (**with**, con); *(equivalent, be similar)* corresponder (**to**, a), equival (**to**, a). **2** *(write)* escribirse (**with**, con), mantener c rrespondencia (**with**, con).
correspondence [kɒrɪs'pɒndᵊns] *n* **1** *(agreeme similarity)* correspondencia. **2** *(letters)* correo, corre pondencia.
correspondent [kɒrɪs'pɒndᵊnt] *n* corresponsal *mf*
correspondingly [kɒrɪ'spɒndɪŋlɪ] *adv (proportio ately)* proporcionalmente, en proporción; *(as a r sult)* por consiguiente, en consecuencia; *(used linker)* de la misma manera.
corridor ['kɒrɪdɔ:ʳ] *n* pasillo, corredor *m*.
corroborate [kə'rɒbəreɪt] *vt* corroborar.
corrode [kə'rəʊd] *vt* corroer.
▷ *vi* corroerse.
corrosion [kə'rəʊʒᵊn] *n* **1** *(process)* corrosión *f*. *(substance)* herrumbre *f*, orín *m*. **3** *fig* ruina, destru ción *f*.
corrugated ['kɒrəgeɪtɪd] *adj (iron, paper)* ondul do,-a.
corrupt [kə'rʌpt] *adj* **1** *(person, government, system, e* corrompido,-a, corrupto,-a; *(morals, behaviour)* de honesto,-a. **2** *(language, text)* viciado,-a.
▷ *vt* **1** *(gen)* corromper; *(bribe)* sobornar. **2** *(language,* viciar.
corruption [kə'rʌpʃᵊn] *n* **1** *(gen)* corrupción *f*. **2** *(of la guage)* deformación *f*.
corset ['kɔ:sɪt] *n* corsé *m*.
Corsica ['kɔ:sɪkə] *n* Córcega.
cortege [kɔ:'teɪʒ] [Also written **cortège**.] *n* cortejo.

cortex ['kɔ:teks] *n* corteza.
cos¹ [kɒs] [Also **cos lettuce**.] *n* lechuga romana.
cos² ['kəʊsaɪn] *abbr* (**cosine**) coseno; *(abbreviation)* cos.
cosh [kɒʃ] *n* GB porra.
▷ *vt* GB dar un porrazo a, aporrear.
cosine ['kəʊsaɪn] *n* MATH coseno.
cosmetic [kɒz'metɪk] *adj* **1** *(for skin, hair, etc)* cosmético,-a. **2** *(superficial)* superficial.
cosmic ['kɒzmɪk] *adj* cósmico,-a.
cosmonaut ['kɒzmənɔ:t] *n* cosmonauta *mf*.
cosmopolitan [kɒzmə'pɒlɪtᵊn] *adj* cosmopolita.
cosmos ['kɒzmɒs] *n* cosmos *m*.
Cossack ['kɒsæk] *adj* cosaco,-a.
▷ *n* cosaco,-a.
cosset ['kɒsɪt] *vt* mimar.
cost [kɒst] *vt* costar, valer.
▷ *n (price)* coste *m*, costo, precio; *(expense)* gasto.
▲ *pt & pp* **cost** [kost].
Costa Rica [kɑztə'ri:ke] *n* Costa Rica.
Costa Rican [kɑztə'ri:ken] *adj & n* costarricense.
cost-effective [kɒstɪ'fektɪv] *adj* rentable.
costing ['kɒstɪŋ] *n* cálculo de costes.
costly ['kɒstlɪ] *adj* costoso,-a.
▲ *comp* **costlier**, *superl* **costliest**.
costume ['kɒstju:m] *n* traje *m*.
▷ *n pl* **costumes** THEAT vestuario.
cosy ['kəʊzɪ] *adj* **1** *(room, house, atmosphere)* acogedor,-ra. **2** *(chat)* íntimo,-a y agradable.
▲ *comp* **cosier**, *superl* **cosiest**.
cot [kɒt] *n* **1** *(for baby)* cuna. **2** US *(camp bed)* cama de campaña.
cotton ['kɒtᵊn] *n* **1** *(cloth, plant)* algodón *m*. **2** *(thread)* hilo (de coser).
▷ *adj (shirt, etc)* de algodón.
couch [kaʊtʃ] *n (sofa)* canapé *m*, sofá *m*.
▷ *vt* expresar, formular.
couchette [ku:'ʃet] *n* litera.
cougar ['ku:gəʳ] *n* puma *m*.
cough [kɒf] *n* tos *f*.
▷ *vi* toser.
could [kʊd] *pt* → **can**.
▷ *aux* **1** poder. **2** *(conditional use)*: **you could have told me!** *¡podrías habérmelo dicho!*
council ['kaʊnsᵊl] *n* **1** *(elected group)* consejo. **2** GB *(of town, city)* ayuntamiento. **3** REL concilio.
councillor ['kaʊnsᵊləʳ] *n* concejal,-la.
counsel ['kaʊnsᵊl] *n* **1** *(advice)* consejo. **2** JUR abogado,-a.
▷ *vt* **1** *(advise)* aconsejar. **2** *(give professional advice)* orientar, aconsejar.
counsellor ['kaʊnsᵊləʳ] *n* **1** *(adviser)* consejero,-a, asesor,-ra. **2** US *(lawyer)* abogado,-a.
count¹ [kaʊnt] *n* **1** *(act of counting)* recuento, cómputo; *(of votes)* escrutinio; *(total)* total *m*, suma. **2** JUR *(crime)* cargo. **3** *(point in discussion, argument)* punto; *(way, reason)* motivo, razón *f*.
▷ *vt* **1** *(gen)* contar. **2** *(consider)* considerar.
count² [kaʊnt] *n (nobleman)* conde *m*.
countable ['kaʊntəbᵊl] *adj* contable.
countdown ['kaʊntdaʊn] *n* cuenta atrás.
countenance ['kaʊntənəns] *n* **1** *fml (face)* rostro, semblante *m*. **2** *fml (support, approval)* aprobación *f*.
▷ *vt fml* aprobar, dar aprobación a.
counter¹ ['kaʊntəʳ] *n* **1** *(in shop)* mostrador *m*; *(individual)* ventanilla. **2** *(in board games)* ficha.
counter² ['kaʊntəʳ] *n (apparatus)* contador *m*.
counter³ ['kaʊntəʳ] *n* SP contraataque *m*, contragolpe *m*.
▷ *adv* en contra (**to**, de).
▷ *vt (claim, accusation)* rebatir, refutar; *(tendency, threat)* contrarrestar.
▷ *vi* contestar, replicar.
counteract [kaʊntə'rækt] *vt* contrarrestar.
counterattack ['kaʊntᵊrətæk] *n* contraataque *m*.
▷ *vt* contraatacar.
counterclockwise [kaʊntə'klɒkwaɪz] *adj* US en sentido contrario a las agujas del reloj.
counterfeit ['kaʊntəfɪt] *adj* falso,-a, falsificado,-a.
▷ *n* falsificación *f*.
▷ *vt* falsificar.
counterfoil ['kaʊntəfɔɪl] *n* matriz *f*.
countermand [kaʊntə'mɑ:nd] *vt* contramandar.
▷ *n* contraorden *f*.
counterpart ['kaʊntəpɑ:t] *n* homólogo,-a.
counterproductive [kaʊntəprə'dʌktɪv] *adj* contraproducente.
countersign ['kaʊntəsaɪn] *vt* refrendar.
▷ *n* contraseña.
countess ['kaʊntəs] *n* condesa.
countless ['kaʊntləs] *adj* incontable, innumerable.
country ['kʌntrɪ] *n* **1** [*pl* **countries**.] *(state, nation)* país *m*; *(people)* pueblo; *(native land)* país *m*, patria, tierra. **2** [No *pl*.] *(rural area)* campo. **3** [No *pl*.] *(region, area of land)* región *f*, zona, territorio. **4** [Also **country music**.] MUS música country, country *m*.
▷ *adj (rural - life, lane)* rural; *(- house)* de campo.
countryman ['kʌntrɪmən] *n* **1** *(man from country)* campesino. **2** *(compatriot)* compatriota *m*.
▲ *pl* **countrymen** ['kʌntrɪmən].
countryside ['kʌntrɪsaɪd] *n (area)* campo, campiña; *(scenery)* paisaje *m*.
countrywoman ['kʌntrɪwʊmən] *n* **1** *(woman from country)* campesina. **2** *(compatriot)* compatriota.
▲ *pl* **countrywomen** ['kʌntrɪwɪmɪn].
county ['kaʊntɪ] *n* condado.
▲ *pl* **counties**.
coup [ku:] *n* golpe *m*. ● **coup d'état** golpe *m* de estado.
couple ['kʌpᵊl] *n* **1** *(two things)* par *m*; *(a few)* unos, -as. **2** *(two people)* pareja.
▷ *vt (gen)* conectar, acoplar; *(railway carriage)* enganchar, acoplar; *(people, events)* asociar.
coupling ['kʌplɪŋ] *n (for railway carriages)* enganche *m*, acoplamiento.
coupon ['ku:pɒn] *n* **1** COMM *(for discount, free gift, etc)* cupón *m*, vale *m*. **2** GB *(for competition, football pools)* boleto.
courage ['kʌrɪdʒ] *n* coraje *m*, valor *m*, valentía.
courageous [kə'reɪdʒəs] *adj (person)* valiente.
courgette [kʊə'ʒet] *n* calabacín *m*.
courier ['kʊərɪəʳ] *n* **1** *(messenger)* mensajero,-a. **2** *(guide)* guía *mf* turístico,-a.

course [kɔ:s] *n* 1 *(direction - gen)* curso, dirección *f*; *(of ship)* rumbo. 2 *(plan of action)* plan *m* de acción, línea de acción. 3 *(development, progress)* curso, marcha. 4 EDUC *(year-long)* curso; *(short)* cursillo; *(series)* ciclo; *(at university)* carrera; *(individual subject)* asignatura. 5 MED serie *f*, tanda. **a course of injections** *una tanda de inyecciones*. 6 *(of meal)* plato. 7 SP *(for golf)* campo; *(racecourse)* hipódromo; *(stretch, distance)* curso, recorrido. 8 *(of bricks)* hilada.
▷ *vi* correr, fluir.

court [kɔ:t] *n* 1 JUR *(place, people)* tribunal *m*; *(building)* juzgado. 2 *(royal)* corte *f*. 3 SP *(tennis, squash, etc)* pista, cancha. 4 *(courtyard)* patio.
▷ *vt* 1 *(woman)* cortejar, hacer la corte a; *(influential person)* tratar de ganarse el favor de. 2 *(support, approval)* tratar de ganarse, buscar; *(favour, publicity)* buscar. 3 *(failure, disaster, death, danger)* exponerse a, buscarse.
▷ *vi* tener novio, tener novia.

courteous ['kɜ:tɪəs] *adj (person, behaviour)* cortés, fino,-a, educado,-a.

courtesy ['kɜ:təsɪ] *n* 1 *(good manners)* cortesía, educación *f*. 2 *(polite act or remark)* favor *m*, atención *f*.
▲ *pl* **courtesies**.

courthouse ['kɔ:thaʊs] *n* juzgado.

courtier ['kɔ:tɪəʳ] *n* cortesano,-a.

courtly ['kɔ:tlɪ] *adj* fino,-a, distinguido,-a.

court-martial [kɔ:t'mɑ:ʃəl] *vt* someter a consejo de guerra.

courtroom ['kɔ:tru:m] *n* sala de justicia, tribunal *m*.

courtyard ['kɔ:tjɑ:d] *n* patio.

cousin ['kʌzən] *n* primo,-a.

cove [kəʊv] *n* cala, caleta, ensenada.

coven ['kʌvn] *n* aquelarre *m*.

covenant ['kʌvənənt] *n* JUR *(formal agreement)* convenio, pacto; *(clause)* cláusula, provisión *f*.

cover ['kʌvəʳ] *n* 1 *(lid)* tapa, cubierta. 2 *(thing that covers - gen)* funda; *(- book)* forro, cubierta. 3 *(outside pages - of book)* cubierta, tapa; *(- of magazine)* portada. 4 *(insurance)* cobertura. 5 *(shelter, protection)* abrigo, protección *f*.
▷ *vt* 1 *(place over - gen)* cubrir (**with**, de); *(- floor, wall)* revestir (**with**, de); *(- sofa)* tapizar; *(- book)* forrar. 2 *(with lid, hands)* tapar. 3 *(hide)* tapar; *(mask)* disimular, ocultar. 4 *(extend over surface)* cubrir. 5 *(travel - distance)* recorrer.
▷ *vi* 1 *(substitute for)* sustituir (**for**, a), suplir (**for**, a). 2 *(conceal truth)* encubrir (**for**, a).
▷ *n pl* **the covers** *(bedclothes)* las mantas *fpl*.

coverage ['kʌvərɪdʒ] *n* 1 *(in press)* cobertura. 2 *(insurance)* cobertura.

coveralls ['kʌvərɔ:lz] *n pl* US ⟶ **overalls**.

covering ['kʌvərɪŋ] *n (protective)* cubierta, envoltura; *(layer)* capa. ● **covering letter** carta adjunta.

covert ['kʌvət] *adj* secreto,-a, disimulado,-a, encubierto,-a.

cover-up ['kʌvərʌp] *n* encubrimiento.

covet ['kʌvət] *vt* codiciar.

cow[1] [kaʊ] *n* vaca. 2 GB *fam pej* arpía, bruja.

cow[2] [kaʊ] *vt* intimidar, acobardar.

coward ['kaʊəd] *n* cobarde *mf*.

cowardly ['kaʊədlɪ] *adj* cobarde.

cowboy ['kaʊbɔɪ] *n* 1 *(gen)* vaquero. 2 GB *fam pej (dishonest person)* estafador,-ra, timador,-ra.

cower ['kaʊəʳ] *vi (cringe)* agacharse; *(in fear)* encogerse de miedo.

cowgirl ['kaʊgɜ:l] *n* vaquera.

cox [kɒks] *n* timonel *mf*.

coy [kɔɪ] *adj* tímido,-a, recatado,-a.

coyote [kaɪ'əʊtɪ] *n* coyote *m*.

cozy ['kəʊzɪ] *adj* US ⟶ **cosy**.
▲ *comp* **cozier**, *superl* **coziest**.

CP ['si:'pi:] *abbr* **(Communist Party)** Partido Comunista; *(abbreviation)* PC *m*.

crab [kræb] *n (shellfish)* cangrejo.

crack [kræk] *vt* 1 *(break - cup, glass, etc)* rajar; *(- bone)* fracturar, romper. 2 *(break open - safe)* forzar; *(- egg)* cascar, romper; *(- nut)* cascar, partir; *(- bottle)* destapar, abrir, descorchar. 3 *(hit)* pegar, golpear. 4 *(whip)* hacer restallar, hacer chasquear; *(knuckles)* hacer crujir. 5 *fig (solve - problem)* solucionar, resolver, dar con la solución de; *(- code)* descifrar, dar con.
▷ *vi* 1 *(break - cup, glass)* rajarse, resquebrarse; *(- rock, plaster, paint, skin)* agrietarse; *(- lips)* partirse, agrietarse. 2 *(whip)* restallar, chasquear; *(bone)* crujir. 3 *(voice)* cascarse, quebrarse. 4 *(relationship, system)* venirse abajo; *(person)* sufrir una crisis nerviosa.
▷ *n* 1 *(in cup, glass)* raja; *(in ice, wall, ground, pavement, etc)* grieta. 2 *(slit, narrow opening)* rendija. 3 *(of whip)* restallido, chasquido; *(of shot)* estallido; *(of thunder)* estruendo; *(of bone)* crujido. 4 *(blow)* golpetazo. 5 *(wisecrack)* réplica aguda, comentario socarrón. 6 *(attempt)* intento. 7 *fig (defect)* defecto. 8 *(drug)* crack *m*.
▷ *adj (troops, regiment, shot)* de primera.

cracked [krækt] *adj fam (mad, crazy)* chiflado,-a, chalado,-a, loco,-a.

cracker ['krækəʳ] *n* 1 *(biscuit)* galleta seca. 2 *(firework)* petardo *m*.

cracking ['krækɪŋ] *adj fam (shot, goal)* de primera, sensacional; *(pace)* muy rápido,-a.

crackle ['krækəl] *n (of twigs, etc)* crujido, chasquido.
▷ *vi (twigs, etc)* chasquear; *(fire)* chisporrotear, crepitar; *(radio, telephone)* hacer ruido.

cradle ['kreɪdəl] *n* cuna *f*.
▷ *vt (baby)* acunar (en los brazos), mecer.

craft [krɑ:ft] *n* 1 *(occupation)* oficio. 2 *(art)* arte *m*; *(skill)* habilidad *f*, destreza. 3 *(boat)* embarcación *f*. 4 nave *f*.
▷ *vt* trabajar.

craftsman ['krɑ:ftsmən] *n* artesano.
▲ *pl* **craftsmen** ['krɑ:ftsmən].

craftswoman ['krɑ:ftswʊmən] *n* artesana.
▲ *pl* **craftswomen** ['krɑ'ftswɪmɪn].

crafty ['krɑ:ftɪ] *adj (person)* astuto,-a, taimado,-a, mañoso,-a; *(child)* pícaro,-a, pillo,-a; *(method, idea, etc)* hábil, artero,-a.
▲ *comp* **craftier**, *superl* **craftiest**.

crag [kræg] *n* peña, risco, peñasco.

cram [kræm] *vt (stuff, fill)* henchir (**with**, de), atestar (**with**, de), atiborrar (**with**, de):
▷ *vi fam (learn for exam)* empollar.
▲ *pt & pp* **crammed**, *ger* **cramming**.

cramp[1] [kræmp] *n* MED calambre *m*, rampa.

▷ *n pl* **cramps** *(gen)* retortijones *mpl; (period pains)* molestias *fpl* menstruales.
cramp[2] [kræmp] *vt* obstaculizar.
cramp[3] [kræmp] [Also **cramp iron**.] *n* grapa.
cramped [kræmpt] *adj* **1** *(closed in, restricted)* apretujado,-a, apretado,-a, estrecho,-a; *(schedule)* apretado,-a. **2** *(writing)* apretado,-a.
cranberry ['krænbərɪ] *n* arándano.
▲ *pl* **cranberries**.
crane [kreɪn] *n* **1** ZOOL grulla común. **2** *(machine)* grúa.
▷ *vt (neck)* estirar.
cranium ['kreɪnɪəm] *n* cráneo.
▲ *pl* **craniums** o **crania** ['kreɪnɪə].
crank [kræŋk] *n* **1** *(crankshaft)* cigüeñal *m*. **2** *(starting handle)* manivela. **3** *fam (person)* maniático,-a, bicho raro. **4** US *(grouch)* gruñón,-ona, cascarrabias *mf*.
▷ *vt* [Also **crank up**.] *(car)* arrancar con la manivela.
cranny ['krænɪ] *n* grieta, ranura.
▲ *pl* **crannies**.
crap [kræp] *n* **1** *fam (excrement)* mierda; *(act)* cagada. **2** *fam (nonsense)* estupideces *fpl*, gilipolleces *fpl*.
▷ *adj fam* malísimo,-a, de mierda.
crash [kræʃ] *n* **1** *(noise)* estrépito; *(of thunder)* trueno, estallido. **2** *(collision)* choque *m*, colisión *f*, accidente *m*. **3** COMM *(collapse)* quiebra.
crash-land [kræʃ'lænd] *vi* hacer un aterrizaje forzoso.
crass [kræs] *adj (remark, person)* grosero,-a; *(error)* craso,-a, garrafal.
crate [kreɪt] *n* caja, cajón *m* (para embalar).
▷ *vt* embalar.
crater ['kreɪtər] *n* cráter *m*.
cravat [krə'væt] *n* pañuelo *de hombre para el cuello*.
crave [kreɪv] *vt (admiration, attention)* ansiar, tener ansias de.
craving ['kreɪvɪŋ] *n (gen)* ansia (**for**, de), ansias *fpl* (**for**, de); *(in pregnancy)* antojo (**for**, de).
crawfish ['krɔːfɪʃ] *n* → **crayfish**.
crawl [krɔːl] *vi* **1** *(move slowly - person, snake)* arrastrarse; *(- baby)* gatear, andar a gatas; *(- insect)* andar. **2** *(car, traffic)* avanzar lentamente, ir a paso de tortuga. **3** *(be covered with, be full of)* estar lleno,-a de, estar plagado,-a de. **4** *fam pej (try to gain favour)* arrastrarse (**to**, ante), rebajarse (**to**, ante), humillarse (**to**, ante).
▷ *n* SP *(in swimming)* crol *m*.
crayfish ['kreɪfɪʃ] *n* cangrejo de río.
▲ *pl* **crayfish**.
crayon ['kreɪɒn] *n (charcoal)* carboncillo; *(chalk)* pastel *m*, lápiz *m* pastel; *(wax)* lápiz *m* de cera.
craze [kreɪz] *n (fashion)* moda; *(game, sport, hobby, etc)* manía.
crazed [kreɪzd] *adj (look, expression)* de loco,-a; *(person)* enloquecido,-a.
crazy ['kreɪzɪ] *adj fam* loco,-a.
▲ *comp* **crazier**, *superl* **craziest**.
creak [kriːk] *vi (floorboard, stairs, joints)* crujir, hacer un crujido; *(door, hinge)* chirriar.
cream [kriːm] *n* **1** *(of milk)* nata, crema (de leche). **2** *(cosmetic)* crema; *(medical)* pomada, crema.
▷ *n* **the cream** *fig* la crema, la flor y nata.
crease [kriːs] *n* **1** *(wrinkle)* arruga; *(fold)* pliegue *m*; *(ironed)* raya. **2** SP *(in cricket)* línea.
create [kriː'eɪt] *vt* **1** *(make - gen)* crear. **2** *(cause - sensation, impression)* producir, causar; *(- difficulty, problem)* crear, causar; *(- fuss, scandal)* armar. **3** *(invest)* nombrar.
creation [kriː'eɪʃən] *n* creación *f*.
creature ['kriːtʃər] *n* **1** *(animal)* criatura. **2** *(human being)* ser *m*.
credence ['kriːdəns] *n* crédito.
credentials [krɪ'denʃəlz] *n pl* **1** *(qualifications)* credenciales *fpl*. **2** *(documents)* cartas *fpl* credenciales.
credible ['kredɪbəl] *adj* creíble.
credit ['kredɪt] *n* **1** *(praise, approval)* mérito, reconocimiento. **2** *(cause of honour)* honor *m*. **3** *(belief, trust, confidence)* crédito. **4** FIN *(gen)* crédito; *(in accountancy)* haber *m*; *(on statement)* saldo acreedor. **5** EDUC crédito.
▷ *n pl* **credits** *(of film, programme)* ficha técnica.
creditable ['kredɪtəbəl] *adj* loable, digno,-a de crédito, encomiable, meritorio,-a.
creditor ['kredɪtər] *n* acreedor,-ra.
credulity [krɪ'djuːlətɪ] *n* credulidad *f*.
creed [kriːd] *n* credo.
creek [kriːk] *n* **1** GB cala. **2** US riachuelo, arroyo.
creep [kriːp] *vi* **1** *(move quietly)* moverse sigilosamente, deslizarse. **2** *(move with the body close to the ground)* arrastrarse, reptar. **3** *(move slowly)* ir muy despacio.
▷ *n fam pej (crawler)* pelota *mf*, pelotillero,-a; *(unpleasant person)* ser *m* repulsivo.
▲ *pt & pp* **crept** [krept].
creeper ['kriːpər] *n* (planta) trepadora.
creepy ['kriːpɪ] *adj* escalofriante, espeluznante.
▲ *comp* **creepier**, *superl* **creepiest**.
cremate [krɪ'meɪt] *vt* incinerar.
crematorium [kremə'tɔːrɪəm] *n* (horno) crematorio.
▲ *pl* **crematoriums** o **crematoria**.
crepe [kreɪp] *n* **1** *(fabric)* crepé *m*, crespón *m*. **2** *(rubber)* crepé *m*. **3** *(pancake)* crepe *m*. ● **crepe rubber** crepé *m*. ❙ **crepe paper** papel *m* crespón.
crept [krept] *pt & pp* → **creep**.
crescent ['kresənt] *n* **1** *(shape)* medialuna. **2** *(street)* calle *f* en forma de medialuna.
▷ *adj* creciente. ● **crescent moon** luna creciente.
cress [kres] *n* berro.
crest [krest] *n* **1** *(of cock)* cresta; *(of helmet)* penacho, cimera. **2** *(of hill)* cima, cumbre *f*; *(of wave)* cresta. **3** *(insignia)* blasón *m*.
crestfallen ['krestfɔːlən] *adj* abatido,-a.
cretin ['kretɪn] *n* **1** *(stupid person)* cretino,-a, imbécil *mf*. **2** MED cretino,-a.
crevasse [krə'væs] *n* grieta, fisura.
crevice ['krevɪs] *n* grieta, raja, hendedura.
crew[1] [kruː] *n* **1** *(of ship, etc)* tripulación *f*. **2** *(working team)* equipo. **3** SP *(rowing team)* equipo de remo. **4** *fam (gang)* banda, pandilla.
crew[2] [kruː] *pt* → **crow**.
crib [krɪb] *n* **1** *(manger)* pesebre *m*; *(Nativity scene)* belén *m*, pesebre *m*. **2** *(for baby)* cuna. **3** *(for cheating)* chuleta; *(copied answer)* copia.
▷ *vt* plagiar, copiar.
▲ *pt & pp* **cribbed**, *ger* **cribbing**.

crick [krɪk] *n (in neck)* tortícolis *f*.
▷ *vt* hacer un mal gesto con.
cricket[1] ['krɪkɪt] *n (insect)* grillo.
cricket[2] ['krɪkɪt] *n* SP cricket *m*.
cried [kraɪd] *pp* ⟶ **cry**.
crikey ['kraɪkɪ] *interj* ¡caramba!, ¡ostras!
crime [kraɪm] *n* **1** *(act, offence)* delito, crimen *m*; *(law-breaking, criminal activity)* delincuencia: **a life of crime** *una vida de delincuencia*. **2** *fam (sin)* crimen *m*, pecado.
criminal ['krɪmɪnəl] *adj* **1** *(case, organization)* criminal; *(act, behaviour)* delictivo,-a. **2** *(law)* penal. **3** *(disgraceful)* vergonzoso,-a, criminal.
▷ *n* delincuente *mf*, criminal *mf*.
criminology [krɪmɪ'nɒlədʒɪ] *n* criminología.
cringe [krɪndʒ] *vi* **1** *(cower)* encogerse, agacharse; *(in fear)* encogerse de miedo. **2** *pej (without self-respect)* rebajarse (**before/to**, ante), arrastrarse (**before/to**, ante). **3** *(with embarrassment)* morirse de vergüenza.
crinkle ['krɪŋkəl] *n* arruga.
▷ *vt* arrugar.
cripple ['krɪpəl] *n* lisiado,-a, tullido,-a.
▷ *vt* **1** *(person)* dejar cojo,-a, lisiar. **2** *fig (industry, country)* paralizar.
crisis ['kraɪsɪs] *n* crisis *f*.
▲ *pl* **crises ['kraɪsi:z]**.
crisp [krɪsp] *adj* **1** *(pastry, biscuits, etc)* crujiente; *(lettuce)* fresco,-a; *(paper, banknote)* nuevo,-a; *(clothes, etc)* recién planchado,-a. **2** *(weather, air)* frío,-a y seco,-a; *(snow)* crujiente. **3** *(of curls)* apretado,-a; *(of hair)* muy rizado,-a. **4** *(style, speech)* directo,-a, escueto,-a, resuelto,-a; *(picture)* nítido,-a.
▷ *n* GB patata frita *(de bolsa o churrería)*.
crisscross ['krɪskrɒs] *vt* entrecruzar.
critic ['krɪtɪk] *n* **1** *(reviewer)* crítico,-a. **2** *(negative person)* criticón,-ona.
critical ['krɪtɪkəl] *adj* **1** *(analysis, essay, work, etc)* crítico,-a. **2** *(negative, finding fault)* criticón,-ona, quisquilloso,-a. **3** *(decisive, crucial, very serious)* crítico,-a.
critically ['krɪtɪklɪ] *adv* **1** *(look)* con ojo crítico; *(speak)* en tono de crítica; *(analyse)* desde un punto de vista crítico. **2** *(ill)* gravemente; *(important)* fundamentalmente.
criticism ['krɪtɪsɪzəm] *n* crítica.
criticize ['krɪtɪsaɪz] *vt* **1** *(express disapproval)* criticar. **2** *(film, play, etc)* criticar, hacer la crítica de.
croak [krəʊk] *n* **1** *(of raven)* graznido; *(of frog)* canto. **2** *(of person)* voz *f* ronca.
Croatia [krəʊ'eɪʃə] *n* Croacia.
Croatian [krəʊ'eɪʃən] *adj & n* croata.
crochet ['krəʊʃeɪ] *n* ganchillo.
crockery ['krɒkərɪ] *n* loza, vajilla.
crocodile ['krɒkədaɪl] *n* cocodrilo.
crocus ['krəʊkəs] *n* azafrán *m*.
crony ['krəʊnɪ] *n fam* compinche *mf*, amigote *mf*.
▲ *pl* **cronies**.
crook [krʊk] *n* **1** cayado, gancho. **2** *fam (criminal)* sinvergüenza *mf*, caco, delincuente *mf*. **3** *(bend, curve - in river, path)* curva; *(- in arm)* parte *f* interior del codo.
▷ *vt (finger, arm)* doblar.
crooked ['krʊkɪd] *adj* **1** *(not straight - stick, picture)* torcido,-a; *(- path, road)* tortuoso,-a, sinuoso,-a. **2** *fam (person, deal, etc)* deshonesto,-a, corrupto,-a.
crop [krɒp] *n* **1** *(plant)* cultivo; *(harvest)* cosecha. **2** *(group, batch)* tanda. **3** *(hairstyle)* corte *m* al rape.
cross [krɒs] *n* **1** *(gen)* cruz *f*. **2** BIOL *(hybrid)* cruce *m*. **3** *fig (mixture)* mezcla.
▷ *vt* **1** *(street, river, bridge)* atravesar; *(arms, legs)* cruzar. **2** *(thwart - person)* contrariar; *(- plans, wishes)* frustrar.
▷ *vi (walk across)* cruzar (**over**, -); *(intersect, pass each another)* cruzarse.
▷ *adj* **1** *(angry)* enojado,-a, enfadado,-a, furioso,-a. **2** *(transverse)* cruzado,-a, transversal; *(winds)* lateral.
crossbar ['krɒsbɑ:ʳ] *n (of goal)* travesaño, larguero; *(of bicycle)* barra.
cross-examination [krɒsɪgzæmɪ'neɪsən] *n* interrogatorio.
crossing ['krɒsɪŋ] *n* **1** MAR travesía. **2** *(intersection, crossroads)* cruce *m*. ● **border crossing** paso fronterizo.
cross-reference [krɒs'refərəns] *n* remisión *f*.
▷ *vt* remitir.
crossroads ['krɒsrəʊdz] *n* encrucijada, cruce *m*.
cross-section ['krɒssekʃən] *n* **1** *(drawing)* sección *f*, corte *m* transversal. **2** *(representative part, group)* muestra representativa.
crossword ['krɒswɜ:d] [Also **crossword puzzle**.] *n* crucigrama *m*.
crotch [krɒtʃ] *n* entrepierna.
crotchet ['krɒtʃɪt] *n* MUS negra.
crouch [kraʊtʃ] [Also **crouch down**.] *vi (person)* agacharse, ponerse en cuclillas; *(cat)* agazaparse.
crow[1] [krəʊ] *n (bird)* cuervo.
crow[2] [krəʊ] *vi (cock)* cantar, cacarear; *(baby)* gorjear; *(person)* alardear, pavonearse.
▲ *pt* **crowed** o **crew [kru:]**, *pp* **crowed**.
crowbar ['krəʊbɑ:ʳ] *n* palanca.
crowd [kraʊd] *n* **1** *(large number of people)* muchedumbre *f*, gentío; *(at match, concert, etc)* público. **2** *(particular group)* gente *f*; *(clique)* pandilla, grupo.
crowded ['kraʊdɪd] *adj* atestado,-a de gente, abarrotado,-a de gente, concurrido,-a.
crown [kraʊn] *n* **1** *(of king, queen)* corona. **2** ANAT *(of head)* coronilla; *(of tooth)* corona. **3** *(top - of hat, tree)* copa; *(- of hill)* cima; *(- of road)* parte *f* central.
crowning ['kraʊnɪŋ] *adj (achievement, success)* supremo,-a, final, mayor; *(moment)* culminante; *(touch)* último,-a.
crucial ['kru:ʃəl] *adj* **1** *(critical)* crucial, decisivo,-a, crítico,-a. **2** GB *sl (excellent)* guay.
crucible ['kru:sɪbəl] *n* crisol *m*.
crucifix ['kru:sɪfɪks] *n* crucifijo.
crucify ['kru:sɪfaɪ] *vt (kill)* crucificar.
▲ *pt & pp* **crucified**, *ger* **crucifying**.
crude [kru:d] *n* **1** *(manners, style)* tosco,-a, grosero,-a; *(joke)* grosero,-a, ordinario,-a. **2** *(oil)* crudo,-a.
cruel ['kru:əl] *adj (gen)* cruel; *(winter)* crudo,-a; *(blow)* duro,-a; *(luck)* malo,-a.
▲ *comp* **crueller**, *superl* **cruellest**.
cruelty ['kru:əltɪ] *n* crueldad *f* (**to**, hacia).
▲ *pl* **cruelties**.
cruise [kru:z] *vi* **1** MAR *(for pleasure)* hacer un crucero; *(in wartime)* navegar, patrullar. **2** *(travel at steady*

speed - car) ir, circular *(a una velocidad constante y sin forzar el motor)*; *(- plane)* volar, desplazarse.
cruiser ['kru:zəʳ] *n* 1 *(warship)* crucero. 2 *(pleasure boat)* yate *m*.
▷ *n* crucero.
cruising speed ['kru:zɪŋspi:d] *adj* velocidad *f* de crucero.
crumb [krʌm] *n* 1 *(of bread, etc)* miga, migaja. 2 *(of information, comfort, hope)* pizca.
crumble ['krʌmbᵊl] *vt (gen)* desmenuzar, deshacer; *(bread)* desmigajar.
crumple ['krʌmpᵊl] *vt (clothes)* arrugar; *(paper)* estrujar.
crunch [krʌntʃ] *vt* 1 *(food)* mascar, ronzar. 2 *(with feet, tyres)* hacer crujir.
crunchy ['krʌntʃɪ] *adj* crujiente.
▲ *comp* crunchier, *superl* crunchiest.
crusade [kru:'seɪd] *n* cruzada.
crush [krʌʃ] *vt* 1 *(squash - gen)* aplastar; *(squeeze)* estrujar; *(- grapes)* prensar; *(- clothes)* arrugar. 2 *(smash, pound - gen)* triturar; *(- ice)* picar. 3 *(defeat)* aplastar; *(shock badly)* abatir.
▷ *n* 1 *(of people)* aglomeración *f*. 2 GB *(soft drink)* refresco.
crust [krʌst] *n* corteza.
crustacean [krʌ'steɪʃᵊn] *n* crustáceo.
crutch [krʌtʃ] *n* 1 *(for walking)* muleta. 2 *fig* apoyo. 3 GB ⟶ **crotch**.
crux [krʌks] *n* quid *m*, meollo.
cry [kraɪ] *vt* 1 *(shout, call)* gritar. 2 *(weep)* llorar.
▲ *pt & pp* cried, *ger* crying.
crying ['kraɪɪŋ] *n (weeping)* llanto, llorera.
▷ *adj fig (need)* urgente, apremiante; *(injustice)* que clama al cielo.
crypt [krɪpt] *n* cripta.
cryptic ['krɪptɪk] *adj* enigmático,-a, críptico,-a.
crystal ['krɪstᵊl] *n* cristal *m*.
▷ *adj (vase, ball)* de cristal; *(water)* cristalino,-a.
crystal-clear [krɪstᵊl'klɪəʳ] *adj (water)* cristalino,-a; *(meaning, evidence)* claro,-a, transparente, obvio,-a.
crystallize ['krɪstᵊlaɪz] *vt* cristalizar.
cu ['kju:bɪk] *abbr* (cubic) cúbico,-a.
cub [kʌb] *n* ZOOL cachorro,-a. [Also **Cub Scout**.] (niño) explorador *m*.
cube [kju:b] *n* 1 *(shape)* cubo; *(of sugar)* terrón *m*; *(of ice)* cubito; *(of cheese, meat, etc)* dado. 2 MATH cubo.
▷ *vt* MATH elevar al cubo. ● **cube root** raíz *f* cúbica.
cubic ['kju:bɪk] *adj* cúbico,-a.
cubicle ['kju:bɪkᵊl] *n (compartment)* cubículo; *(changing-room in shop)* probador *m*.
cubism ['kju:bɪzᵊm] *n* cubismo.
cuckoo ['kʊku:] *n* cuco.
▲ *pl* cuckoos.
cucumber ['kju:kʌmbəʳ] *n* pepino.
cuddle ['kʌdᵊl] *vt* abrazar, acariciar.
cudgel ['kʌdʒᵊl] *n* porra, garrote *m*.
▷ *vt* aporrear.
▲ *pt & pp* cudgelled (US cudgeled), *ger* cudgelling (US cudgeling).
cue¹ [kju:] *n* 1 *(for actor)* pie *m*; *(for musician)* entrada. 2 *(signal)* señal *f*. 3 *(example)* ejemplo.
cue² [kju:] *n (in billiards, etc)* taco. ● **cue ball** bola blanca.
cuff¹ [kʌf] *n* 1 *(of sleeve)* puño. 2 US *(of trousers)* dobladillo.
▷ *n pl* cuffs *sl* esposas *fpl*.
cuff² [kʌf] *vt* abofetear, dar un bofetada a.
▷ *n* bofetada, cachete *m*, bofetón *m*.
cufflinks ['kʌflɪŋks] *n pl* gemelos *mpl*.
cuisine [kwɪ'zi:n] *n* cocina.
cul-de-sac ['kʌldəsæk] *n* calle *f* sin salida.
culinary ['kʌlɪnᵊrɪ] *adj* culinario,-a.
cull [kʌl] *vt* 1 *(kill)* eliminar. 2 *(select)* seleccionar, escoger.
culminate ['kʌlmɪneɪt] *vi* culminar (in, en).
culottes [kju:'lɒts] *n pl* falda pantalón *f sing*.
culpability [kʌlpə'bɪlətɪ] *n* culpabilidad *f*.
culprit ['kʌlprɪt] *n* culpable *mf*.
cult [kʌlt] *n (gen)* culto; *(sect)* secta.
cultivate ['kʌltɪveɪt] *vt* cultivar.
▲ *pt & pp* cupped, *ger* cupping.
cultivated ['kʌltɪveɪtɪd] *adj* 1 *(person)* culto,-a, cultivado,-a. 2 *(land, etc)* cultivado,-a.
cultivator ['kʌltɪveɪtəʳ] *n* 1 *(person)* cultivador,-ra. 2 *(machine)* cultivadora.
culture ['kʌltʃəʳ] *n* 1 *(gen)* cultura. 2 *(growth)* cultivo.
cumbersome ['kʌmbəsəm] *adj* 1 *(thing)* incómodo,-a, voluminoso,-a, pesado,-a. 2 *(procedure)* torpe, engorroso,-a.
cumin ['kʌmɪn] *n* comino.
cumulative ['kju:mjələtɪv] *adj* acumulativo,-a.
cumulus ['kju:mjələs] *n* cúmulo.
cunning ['kʌnɪŋ] *adj (person)* astuto,-a; *(thing)* ingenioso,-a.
▷ *n* astucia.
cup [kʌp] *n* 1 *(for drinking)* taza. 2 SP *(trophy)* copa. 3 *(chalice)* cáliz *m*. 4 *(drink)* ponche *m*. 5 *(of bra)* copa.
cupboard ['kʌbəd] *n (for clothes, etc)* armario; *(for food)* alacena; *(for crockery)* aparador *m*.
cupidity [kju:'pɪdɪtɪ] *n* codicia.
cupola ['kju:pələ] *n* cúpula.
curate ['kjʊərət] *n* coadjutor *m*.
curative ['kjʊərətɪv] *adj* curativo,-a.
curator [kjʊ'reɪtəʳ] *n (of museum)* conservador,-ra.
curb [kɜ:b] *n* 1 *(for horse)* barbada. 2 *(control)* freno. 3 US bordillo.
curd [kɜ:d] *n (from milk)* cuajada. ● **curd cheese** requesón.
curdle ['kɜ:dᵊl] *vi (form curds)* cuajarse; *(go bad)* cortarse.
cure [kjʊəʳ] *vt (illness)* curar (of, de).
▷ *n (for disease, illness)* cura; *(for problem)* remedio; *(return to health)* curación *f*, restablecimiento.
cure-all ['kjʊərɑ:l] *n* panacea.
curfew ['kɜ:fju:] *n* toque *m* de queda.
curiosity [kjʊərɪ'ɒsətɪ] *n* curiosidad *f*.
▲ *pl* curiosities.
curious ['kjʊərɪəs] *adj* 1 *(inquisitive)* curioso,-a. 2 *(strange, odd)* curioso,-a, extraño,-a; *(interesting)* interesante.
curl [kɜ:l] *vt (hair)* rizar; *(leaves, paper)* enrollar.
▷ *vi (hair)* rizarse; *(smoke)* formar volutas, hacer volutas; *(leaves, paper)* enrollarse, ondularse, rizarse; *(plants, tendrils)* enrollarse; *(river, path)* serpentear.
▷ *n (of hair)* rizo; *(ringlet)* bucle *m*, tirabuzón *m*; *(of smoke)* espiral *f*, voluta.

curly ['kɜːlɪ] *adj (hair)* rizado,-a; *(tail, leaves)* enroscado,-a; *(pattern)* con volutas.
▲ *comp* curlier, *superl* curliest.

currant ['kʌrənt] *n* 1 *(dried grape)* pasa (de Corinto). 2 *(fruit)* grosella.

currency ['kʌrənsɪ] *n* 1 FIN moneda. 2 *(acceptance)* aceptación *f*. ● **foreign courrency** divisa.
▲ *pl* currencies.

current ['kʌrənt] *adj* 1 *(present, existing - gen)* actual; *(- month, year)* en curso; *(most recent - issue)* último,-a; *(- legislation, licence)* vigente. 2 *(generally accepted)* corriente, común, habitual, general. ● **current account** cuenta corriente.
▷ *n (gen)* corriente *f*.

currently ['kʌrəntlɪ] *adv* 1 *(at present)* actualmente, en la actualidad. 2 *(commonly)* comúnmente.

curriculum [kə'rɪkjələm] *n* EDUC plan *m* de estudios. ● **curriculum vitae** currículum *m*, historial *m*.

curry ['kʌrɪ] *n* CULIN curry *m*.
▲ *pl* curries.

curse [kɜːs] *n* 1 *(evil spell)* maldición *f*. 2 *(oath)* palabrota.
▷ *n* **the curse** *(period)* la regla.

cursive ['kɜːsɪv] *adj* cursivo,-a.

cursor ['kɜːsəʳ] *n* cursor *m*.

cursorily ['kɜːsərəlɪ] *adv* someramente, por encima, superficialmente.

cursory ['kɜːsərɪ] *adj (glance, look)* rápido,-a; *(study, reading)* superficial, por encima.

curt [kɜːt] *adj* seco,-a, brusco,-a, cortante.

curtail [kɜː'teɪl] *vt (spending)* reducir; *(rights, freedom)* restringir; *(speech, holiday, text)* abreviar, acortar.

curtain ['kɜːtᵊn] *n* 1 *(gen)* cortina. 2 THEAT telón *m*. 3 *fig (of rain, mist, smoke)* cortina, velo; *(of fog)* manto; *(of secrecy)* halo, velo.

curtly ['ketlɪ] *adv* secamente, bruscamente.

curtsey ['kɜːtsɪ] *n* reverencia.
▷ *vi* hacer una reverencia.

curvaceous [kɜː'veɪʃəs] *adj* curvilíneo,-a.

curvature ['kɜːvətʃəʳ] *n* 1 *(of surface)* curvatura. 2 MED encorvamiento.

curve [kɜːv] *n (gen)* curva.
▷ *vt* encorvar.
▷ *vi (of road, river, ball)* describir una curva, torcer; *(surface)* estar curvado,-a, combarse, encorvarse.

curvy ['kɜːvɪ] *adj (line)* curvo,-a; *(road)* con muchas curvas; *(figure)* curvilíneo,-a.
▲ *comp* curvier, *superl* curviest.

cushion ['kʊʃᵊn] *n* 1 *(gen)* cojín *m*; *(large)* almohadón *m*. 2 *(on billiard table)* banda. 3 *fig (protection)* amortiguador *m*.
▷ *vt fig (blow, fall)* suavizar, amortiguar; *(person)* proteger.

cusp [kʌsp] *n* 1 *(in astrology)* cúspide *f*. 2 *(of curves)* vértice *m*; *(of moon)* cuerno.

cussed ['kʌsɪd] *adj fam* terco,-a, tozudo,-a, difícil.

custard ['kʌstəd] *n (cold, set)* natillas *fpl*; *(hot, liquid)* crema. ● **custard apple** chirimoya.

custodian [kʌs'təʊdɪən] *n (of museum)* conservador,-ra; *(of morals)* guardián,-ana.

custody ['kʌstədɪ] *n* 1 *(care)* custodia, guarda. 2 *(imprisonment)* encarcelamiento.

custom ['kʌstəm] *n* 1 *(tradition, habit)* costumbre *f*: **it is his custom retire to bed early** *tiene por costumbre acostarse pronto*. 2 COMM *(patronage)* clientela.

customary ['kʌstəmərɪ] *adj (habitual)* acostumbrado,-a, habitual, de costumbre; *(traditional)* tradicional.

custom-built [kʌstəm'bɪlt] *adj* hecho,-a por encargo.

customer ['kʌstəməʳ] *n* 1 *(client)* cliente *mf*. 2 *fam (person)* tipo,-a.

customize ['kʌstəmaɪz] *vt* hacer por encargo, hacer a la medida.

custom-made [kʌstəm'meɪd] *adj (clothes, etc)* hecho,-a a medida; *(furniture)* hecho,-a de encargo, hecho,-a a medida.

customs ['kʌstəmz] *n* aduana.

Puede ser tanto singular como plural.

cut [kʌt] *vt* 1 *(gen)* cortar; *(stone, glass)* tallar; *(record)* grabar; *(key, hole)* hacer. 2 *(divide)* cortar, partir, dividir. 3 *(reduce - level, number)* reducir; *(- budget, spending)* recortar; *(- price)* rebajar, reducir. 4 *(shorten)* acortar; *(remove)* cortar; *(edit)* editar; *(censor)* hacer cortes en, censurar. 5 *(hurt feelings of, cause pain)* herir. 6 *(adulterate)* mezclar, cortar.
▲ *pt & pp* cut, *ger* cutting.
▷ *n* 1 *(wound, incision)* corte *m*; *(deep cut)* tajo; *(knife wound)* cuchillada. 2 *(of meat - joint)* corte *m*; *(- piece cut off)* trozo. 3 *(share)* parte *f*, tajada. 4 *(reduction - in budget, services, wages)* recorte *m*; *(- in level, number, price)* reducción *f*. 5 *(deletion, removal)* corte *m*; *(part deleted)* trozo omitido. 6 ELEC corte *m*, apagón *m*.
⊙ **to cut down** *vt sep (tree)* talar, cortar; *(kill)* matar.
⊙ **to cut off** *vt sep* 1 *(sever)* cortar; *(limb)* amputar, cortar. 2 *(disconnect, discontinue)* cortar: **our phone's been cut off** *nos han cortado el teléfono*; **we were cut off** *se cortó la comunicación*. 3 *(isolate, separate)* aislar: **she felt cut off** *se sentía aislada*. 4 *fig (disinherit)* desheredar.
⊙ **to cut out** *vt sep* 1 *(from newspaper)* recortar; *(in sewing)* cortar. 2 *(exclude)* suprimir, eliminar: **cut it out!** *¡basta ya!, ¡corta el rollo!*
▷ *vi (of machine, engine)* pararse.

cutaneous [kjuː'teɪnɪəs] *adj* cutáneo,-a.

cutback ['kʌtbæk] *n* reducción *f*, recorte *m*.

cute [kjuːt] *adj* 1 *(sweet)* mono,-a, rico,-a; *(good-looking)* guapo,-a, lindo,-a. 2 US *(clever)* listo,-a.

cuticle ['kjuːtɪkᵊl] *n* cutícula.

cutlass ['kʌtləs] *n* alfanje *m*.

cutlery ['kʌtlərɪ] *n* cubiertos *mpl*, cubertería.

cutlet ['kʌtlət] *n* 1 CULIN *(meat chop)* chuleta. 2 *(croquette)* croqueta *(de forma aplastada)*.

cutoff ['kʌtɒf] *n* 1 *(level, point)* límite *m*, tope *m*. 2 *(stopping)* corte *m*, cese *m*. ● **cutoff date** fecha límite, fecha tope.
▷ *n pl* **cutoffs** *(shorts)* bermudas *fpl* vaqueras.

cutout ['kʌtaʊt] *n* 1 *(shape)* recortable *m*, figura para recortar. 2 *(device, switch)* cortacircuitos *m*.

cut-price [kʌt'praɪs] *adj (goods)* a precio rebajado; *(shop)* de ocasión.

cutter ['kʌtəʳ] *n* 1 *(person)* cortador,-ra. 2 *(tool)* cúter *m*; *(machine, knife)* cortadora. 3 MAR *(ship's boat)* bote *m*; *(sailing boat)* cúter *m*; *(government ship)* patrullero guardacostas *m*.
▷ *n pl* **cutters** *(for wire)* cizalla, cortaalambres *m*.

cutthroat ['kʌtθrəʊt] *adj* feroz, salvaje.
cutting ['kʌtɪŋ] *n* 1 *(from newspaper)* recorte *m*. 2 BOT esqueje *m*. 3 *(for road, railway)* tajo.
▷ *adj (tool, blade)* cortante; *(wind)* penetrante, cortante; *(remark)* mordaz, hiriente: **the cutting edge** *el filo*. ● **cutting room** sala de montaje.
cuttlefish ['kʌtəlfɪʃ] *n* jibia, sepia.
cv ['siː'viː] *abbr* **(curriculum vitae)** currículum *m* vitae.
cwt ['hʌndrədweɪt] *abbr* **(hundredweight)** quintal *m*.
cyanide ['saɪənaɪd] *n* cianuro.
cybernetics [saɪbə'netɪks] *n* cibernética.
cyclamen ['sɪkləmən] *n* ciclamen *m*.
cycle ['saɪkəl] *n* 1 *(series of events, of songs, etc)* ciclo; *(of washing machine)* programa *m*. 2 *(bicycle)* bicicleta; *(motorcycle)* moto *f*. ● **cycle lane/path/way** carril *m* para bicicletas. ‖ **cycle track** velódromo.
▷ *vi* ir en bicicleta.
cyclic ['sɪklɪk, 'saɪklɪk] *adj* cíclico,-a.
cyclical ['sɪklɪkəl, 'saɪklɪkəl] *adj* cíclico,-a.
cycling ['saɪklɪŋ] *n* ciclismo.
cyclist ['saɪklɪst] *n* ciclista *mf*.
cyclone ['saɪkləʊn] *n (windstorm)* ciclón *m*; *(low pressure area)* ciclón *m*, borrasca.
cygnet ['sɪgnət] *n* pollo de cisne.
cylinder ['sɪlɪndəʳ] *n* 1 *(shape)* cilindro. 2 *(in engine)* cilindro. 3 *(for gas)* bombona. 4 *(of gun)* tambor *m*.
cylindrical [sɪ'lɪndrɪkəl] *adj* cilíndrico,-a.
cymbal ['sɪmbəl] *n* címbalo, platillo.
cynic ['sɪnɪk] *n* cínico,-a.
cynical ['sɪnɪkəl] *adj* cínico,-a.
cynicism ['sɪnɪsɪzəm] *n* cinismo.
cypress ['saɪprəs] *n* ciprés *m*.
Cypriot ['sɪprɪət] *adj* chipriota.
▷ *n* 1 *(person)* chipriota *mf*. 2 *(language)* chipriota *m*.
Cyprus ['saɪprəs] *n* Chipre *m*.
cyst [sɪst] *n* quiste *m*.
cystic fibrosis [sɪstɪkfaɪ'brəʊsɪs] *n* fibrosis *f* quística.
cystitis [sɪ'staɪtɪs] *n* cistitis *f*.
czar [zɑːʳ] *n* zar *m*.
Czech [tʃek] *adj* checo,-a.
▷ *n* 1 *(person)* checo,-a. 2 *(language)* checo. ● **Czech Republic** República Checa.
Czechia ['tʃekɪə] *n* Chequia.
Czechoslovak [tʃekə'sləʊvæk] *adj* checoslovaco,-a.
▷ *n* checoslovaco,-a.
Czechoslovakia [tʃekəslə'vækɪə] *n* Checoslovaquia.
Czechoslovakian [tʃekəslə'vækɪən] *adj* checoslovaco,-a.
▷ *n* checoslovaco,-a.

D

D, d [diː] *n* **1** *(the letter)* D, d *f*. **2** MUS re *m*.
'd [əd] *aux* **1** ⟶ **would.** **I'd go** *iría.* **2** ⟶ **had. he'd seen** *había visto.* **3** *fam* ⟶ **did. what'd you do?** *¿qué hiciste?*
D.A. ['diː'eɪ] *abbr* US **(District Attorney)** fiscal *mf*.
dab¹ [dæb] *n (of paint)* toque *m*; *(of perfume)* gota; *(of butter)* poquito.
▷ *vi* dar ligeros toques (**at**, en).
▷ *n pl* **dabs** GB *sl (fingerprints)* huellas *fpl* dactilares.
dab² [dæb] *n (fish)* ≈ acedía.
dabble ['dæbəl] *vi (in activity)* aficionarse (**in**, a).
▷ *vt (in water)* chapotear.
dachshund ['dækshʊnd] *n* perro salchicha.
dad [dæd] *n fam* papá *m*.
Dadaism ['dɑːdɑːɪzəm] *n* dadaísmo.
daddy ['dædɪ] *n fam* papá *m*, papi *m*.
▲ *pl* **daddies.**
daddy-longlegs [dædɪ'lɒŋlegz] *n* GB *fam* típula.
▲ *pl* **daddy-longlegs.**
daffodil ['dæfədɪl] *n* narciso.
dagger ['dægəʳ] *n* **1** *(weapon)* daga, puñal *m*. **2** *(obelisk)* cruz *f*.
daguerrotype [də'gerəʊtaɪp] *n* daguerrotipo.
dahlia ['deɪljə] *n* dalia.
daily ['deɪlɪ] *adj (newspaper, prayers)* diario,-a; *(routine)* diario,-a, cotidiano,-a.
▷ *adv* diariamente, a diario.
▷ *n (newspaper)* diario.
▷ *n* [Also **daily help.**] GB *fam (cleaning woman)* asistenta, mujer *f* de la limpieza.
▲ *pl* **dailies.**
daintily ['deɪntɪlɪ] *adv* delicadamente, finamente.
dainty ['deɪntɪ] *adj* **1** *(delicate - thing)* delicado,-a, fino,-a; *(- person)* precioso,-a, delicado,-a, refinado,-a.
▲ *comp* **daintier**, *superl* **daintiest.**
▷ *n pl* **dainties** *(small cakes)* pastelitos *mpl*.
dairy ['deərɪ] *n* **1** *(on farm)* vaquería. **2** *(shop)* lechería; *(company)* central *f* lechera. ● **dairy products** productos lácteos.
▲ *pl* **dairies.**
dairymaid ['deərɪmeɪd] *n* lechera.
dairyman ['deərɪmən] *n* lechero.
▲ *pl* **dairymen** ['deərɪmən].
dais ['deɪɪs] *n (raised platform)* tarima; *(stage)* estrado, tribuna.
▲ *pl* **daises.**
daisy ['deɪzɪ] *n* margarita.
▲ *pl* **daisies.**
dale [deɪl] *n* valle *m*.
dally ['dælɪ] *vi (waste time)* perder el tiempo; *(linger)* entretenerse (**about**, -).
▲ *pt & pp* **dallied**, *ger* **dallying.**
Dalmatian [dæl'meɪʃən] *n* dálmata *m*.
daltonic [dɔːl'tɒnɪk] *adj* daltónico,-a, daltoniano.
daltonism ['dɔːltənɪzəm] *n* daltonismo.
dam¹ [dæm] *n* **1** *(barrier)* dique *m*. **2** *(reservoir)* embalse *m*, presa.
▲ *pt & pp* **dammed**, *ger* **damming.**
⊙ **to dam up** *vt sep* **1** *(river)* represar, embalsar. **2** *(emotions)* reprimir, contener.
dam² [dæm] *n* ZOOL madre *f*.
damage ['dæmɪdʒ] *n (gen)* daño; *(to reputation, cause, health)* perjuicio, daños *mpl*; *(destruction)* destrozos *mpl*, daños *mpl*, estragos *mpl*.
damask ['dæməsk] *n* damasco.
dame [deɪm] *n* **1** US *fam* mujer *f*, tía. **2** *(in pantomime)* vieja *(representada por un hombre)*.
▷ *n* **Dame** GB *(title) título honorífico concedido a una mujer.*
damn [dæm] *interj fam* ¡mecachis!, ¡caray!
▷ *adj fam* maldito,-a, condenado,-a, puñetero,-a.
▷ *adv fam* muy, sumamente: **you were damn lucky** *tuviste mucha suerte.*
▷ *vt* **1** REL condenar. **2** *(curse)* maldecir: **damn it!** *¡maldita sea!* **3** *(criticize, condemn)* condenar.
damned [dæmd] *adj* **1** *fam* maldito,-a, condenado,-a. **2** REL condenado,-a.
▷ *n* **the damned** los condenados *mpl*.
damning ['dæmɪŋ] *adj (evidence, facts)* irrefutable, condenatorio,-a; *(criticism, indictment)* adverso,-a, mordaz, feroz, duro,-a; *(remark)* crítico,-a, mordaz.
damp [dæmp] *adj (gen)* húmedo,-a; *(wet)* mojado,-a.
▷ *n* humedad *f*.
dampcourse ['dæmpkɔːs] *n* aislante *m* hidrófugo.
dampen ['dæmpən] *vt* **1** *(make damp)* humedecer. **2** *fig (enthusiasm, ardour, etc)* hacer perder, apagar, enfriar; *(person's spirits)* desanimar.
damper ['dæmpəʳ] *n* **1** *(of chimney)* regulador *m* de tiro. **2** MUS sordina.
damsel ['dæmzəl] *n* doncella.
dance [dɑːns] *n (gen)* baile *m*; *(classical, tribal)* danza.
▷ *vi* **1** *(gen)* bailar. **2** *fig (trees, leaves, flowers, etc)* agitarse, mecerse, moverse; *(waves)* agitarse, moverse.
dancer ['dɑːnsəʳ] *n* bailarín,-ina; *(flamenco)* bailaor,-ra.
dandelion ['dændɪlaɪən] *n* diente *m* de león.
dandruff ['dændrəf] *n* caspa.
dandy ['dændɪ] *n* dandy *m*, petimetre *m*.
▷ *adj* US *fam* estupendo,-a.
▲ *pl* **dandies.**
Dane [deɪn] *n* danés,-esa.
danger ['deɪndʒəʳ] *n (peril, hazard)* peligro; *(risk)* riesgo.
dangerous ['deɪndʒərəs] *adj (gen)* peligroso,-a; *(risky)* arriesgado,-a; *(illness)* grave.
dangle ['dæŋgəl] *vt (hang)* colgar; *(swing)* balancear.
▷ *vi* colgar, pender.

Danish ['deɪnɪʃ] *adj* danés,-esa.
▷ *n (language)* danés *m*.
▷ *n pl* **the Danish** los daneses *mpl*.
dank [dæŋk] *adj* húmedo,-a y frío,-a.
Dantesque [dæn'tesk] *adj* dantesco.
Danube ['dænjuːb] *n* el Danubio.
dapper ['dæpəʳ] *adj (smart)* atildado,-a, pulcro,-a.
dappled ['dæpəld] *adj (mottled - colour, shade, sunlight)* moteado,-a; *(horse)* rodado,-a.
dapple-grey [dæpəl'greɪ] *adj* tordo,-a.
▷ *n* caballo tordo.
dare [deəʳ] *vi* atreverse (**to**, a), osar (**to**, -).
▷ *vt (challenge)* desafiar.
▷ *n* desafío, reto.
daredevil ['deədevəl] *n* atrevido,-a, temerario,-a.
daring ['deərɪŋ] *adj (bold, brave)* audaz, osado,-a, atrevido,-a.
▷ *n* osadía, atrevimiento, audacia.
dark [dɑːk] *adj* **1** *(without light)* oscuro,-a. **2** *(hair, skin)* moreno,-a; *(eyes)* negro,-a. **3** *(gloomy)* triste, sombrío,-a. **4** *(sinister)* siniestro,-a, tenebroso,-a. **5** *(secret)* misterioso,-a.
▷ *n* **1** *(darkness)* oscuridad *f*. **2** *(nightfall)* anochecer *m*.
darken ['dɑːkən] *vt* **1** oscurecer, hacer más oscuro,-a. **2** *fig* entristecer, ensombrecer.
dark-haired ['dɑːk'heəd] *adj* moreno,-a.
darkness ['dɑːknəs] *n* oscuridad *f*.
darling ['dɑːlɪŋ] *n (lover)* querido,-a, amor *m*, cariño; *(popular person)* niño,-a mimado,-a.
▷ *adj* **1** *(loved)* querido,-a. **2** *fam (charming)* precioso,-a, encantador,-ra, mono,-a.
darn [dɑːn] *n* zurcido.
▷ *vt (sock, etc)* zurcir.
darnel ['dɑːnəl] *n* cizaña.
dart [dɑːt] *n* **1** *(object)* dardo, flechilla, rehilete *m*. **2** *(rush)* movimiento rápido. **3** SEW *(fold)* pinza.
▷ *vt (look, glance)* lanzar; *(tongue)* disparar.
▷ *vi (move quickly - person)* lanzarse, precipitarse; *(- butterfly, etc)* revolotear.
dartboard ['dɑːtbɔːd] *n* diana, blanco de tiro.
Darwinism ['dɑːwɪnɪzəm] *n* darvinismo.
dash [dæʃ] *n* **1** *(sudden run)* carrera. **2** *(small amount)* poco; *(of salt, spice)* pizca; *(of liquid)* chorrito, gota. **3** *(horizontal mark)* raya; *(hyphen)* guion *m*; *(in Morse code)* raya. **4** *(style, panache)* elegancia; *(energy, vitality)* brío, dinamismo. **5** US *(dashboard)* salpicadero.
▷ *vt* **1** *(hit)* lanzar, arrojar; *(smash)* romper, estrellar. **2** *(hopes)* truncar.
dashboard ['dæʃbɔːd] *n* salpicadero.
data ['deɪtə] *n pl* datos *mpl*, información *f*.
▲ *sing* **datum.**
database ['deɪtəbeɪs] *n* COMPUT base *f* de datos.
date[1] [deɪt] *n* **1** *(in time)* fecha. **2** *(appointment)* cita, compromiso: **I've got a date with David tonight** *tengo una cita con David esta noche.* **3** US *(person)* ligue *m*, amigo,-a, pareja. **4** *(performance, booking)* actuación *f*.
▷ *vt* **1** *(write a date on)* fechar. **2** *(determine the date of)* datar. **3** *(show the age of)* demostrar la edad de. **4** US *fam (go out with)* salir con.
▷ *vi* **1** *(have existed since)* datar (**from**, de), remontarse (**back to**, a). **2** *(go out of fashion)* pasar de moda. **3** US *(go out together)* salir juntos, ser novios.
date[2] [deɪt] *n (fruit)* dátil *m*.
dated ['deɪtɪd] *adj* anticuado,-a.
dative ['deɪtɪv] *n* LING dativo.
datum ['deɪtəm] *n* dato.
▲ *pl* **data.**
daub [dɔːb] *n* **1** *(small bit, smear)* mancha. **2** *(bad painting)* pintarrajo.
▷ *vt* embadurnar.
daughter ['dɔːtəʳ] *n* hija.
daughter-in-law ['dɔːtərɪnlɔː] *n* nuera.
daunt [dɔːnt] *vt (frighten)* intimidar; *(dishearten)* desanimar, desalentar.
dauntless ['dɔːntləs] *adj* impávido,-a, intrépido,-a.
dauphin ['dɔːfɪn] *n* delfín *m*.
dawdle ['dɔːdəl] *vi (walk slowly)* andar despacio; *(waste time)* perder el tiempo, entretenerse.
dawn [dɔːn] *n* **1** alba, aurora, amanecer *m*. **2** *fig (beginning)* amanecer *m*, albores *mpl*, aurora.
▷ *vi* **1** *(day)* amanecer, clarear. **2** *(new age, year)* alborear, nacer. **3** *(become known, obvious)* brillar.
day [deɪ] *n* **1** *(24 hours)* día *m*. **2** *(time between sunrise and sunset)* día *m*. **3** *(period of work)* jornada, día *m*. **4** *(period of success)* día *m*. **5** *(period of time)* época, tiempo.
▷ *n pl* **days** *(period)* época, tiempos *mpl*.
daybreak ['deɪbreɪk] *n* amanecer *m*, alba.
daydream ['deɪdriːm] *n* ensueño, ensoñación *f*.
▷ *vi* soñar despierto,-a, fantasear.
daytime ['deɪtaɪm] *n* día *m*.
▷ *adj (flight)* diurno,-a.
daze [deɪz] *n* aturdimiento.
▷ *vt* aturdir.
dazed [deɪzd] *adj* aturdido,-a.
dazzle ['dæzəl] *n (brilliance)* resplandor *m*, brillo.
▷ *vt* deslumbrar.
dB ['diː'biː] *abbr* **(decibel)** decibelio; *(abbreviation)* dB.
D-day ['diːdeɪ] *n* **1** *(in war)* día *m* D. **2** *(important date)* el día *m* señalado.
DEA ['diː'iː'eɪ] *abbr* US **(Drug Enforcement Administration)** agencia norteamericana contra el narcotráfico; *(abbreviation)* DEA.
deacon ['diːkən] *n* diácono.
deactivate [diː'æktɪveɪt] *vt* desactivar.
dead [ded] *adj* **1** *(not alive)* muerto,-a. **2** *(obsolete - language)* muerto,-a; *(- custom)* desusado,-a, en desuso; *(finished with - topic, issue, debate)* agotado,-a, pasado,-a; *(- glass, bottle)* terminado,-a, acabado,-a. **3** *(numb)* entumecido,-a, dormido,-a. **4** *(not functioning - telephone)* desconectado,-a, cortado,-a; *(- machine)* averiado,-a; *(- battery)* descargado,-a, gastado,-a; *(- match)* gastado,-a. **5** *fam (very tired)* muerto,-a. **6** *(dull, quiet, not busy)* muerto,-a. **7** *(sounds)* sordo,-a; *(colours)* apagado,-a. **8** SP *(ball)* muerto,-a. **9** *(total)* total, completo,-a, absoluto,-a.
▷ *adv* **1** *(completely, absolutely)* completamente, sumamente; *(as intensifier)* muy: **I'm dead sure** *estoy segurísimo.* **2** *(exactly)* justo: **we arrived dead on time** *llegamos puntualísimos.*
▷ *n* **the dead** los,-las muertos,-as.

deadbeat ['dedbiːt] *n* US *fam (idler)* vago,-a, flojo,-a; *(dropout)* marginado,-a.
deaden ['dedən] *vt (pain)* calmar, aliviar; *(noise, blow)* amortiguar.
dead-end job [dedend'dʒɒb] *n* trabajo sin porvenir, trabajo sin futuro.
deadline ['dedlaɪn] *n (date)* fecha límite, fecha tope, plazo de entrega; *(time)* hora límite, hora tope.
deadlock ['dedlɒk] *n* punto muerto, impasse *m.*
deadpan ['dedpæn] *adv* de manera inexpresiva.
deaf [def] *adj* sordo,-a.
▷ *n* **the deaf** los sordos *mpl.*
deaf-aid ['defeɪd] *n* audífono.
deafen ['defᵊn] *vt* ensordecer.
deaf-mute ['defmjuːt] *n* sordomudo,-a.
deafness ['defnəs] *n* sordera.
deal [diːl] *n* **1** *(agreement)* trato, acuerdo, pacto; *(financial)* acuerdo. **2** *(treatment)* trato. **3** *(amount)* cantidad *f.* **4** *(in card games)* reparto.
▷ *vt* **1** *(cards)* repartir, dar. **2** *(drugs)* traficar.
▲ *pt & pp* **dealt** [delt].
⊙ **to deal with** *vt insep* **1** COMM *(trade with)* tratar con, tener relaciones comerciales con. **2** *(tackle - problem, etc)* abordar, ocuparse de, atacar; *(- task)* encargarse de; *(- person)* tratar (con), lidiar con.
dealer ['diːləʳ] *n* **1** COMM comerciante *mf*, negociante *mf.* **2** *(illegal - in drugs)* traficante *mf*; *(- in stolen goods)* perista *mf.* **3** FIN corredor,-ra de bolsa, corredor,-ra de valores.
dealt [delt] *pt & pp* → **deal.**
dean [diːn] *n* **1** REL deán *m.* **2** EDUC decano,-a.
deanery ['diːnərɪ] *n* decanato.
dear [dɪəʳ] *adj* **1** *(loved - person)* querido,-a; *(- thing)* preciado,-a. **2** *(as form of address)* querido,-a. **3** *fam (in letter)* querido,-a; *(more formally)* apreciado,-a, estimado,-a. **4** *(expensive)* caro,-a.
▷ *interj* ¡Dios mío!
▷ *adv* caro.
dearly ['dɪəlɪ] *adv* **1** *(very much)* mucho. **2** *(at a cost)* caro.
dearth [dɜːθ] *n* escasez *f.*
death [deθ] *n* **1** *(gen)* muerte *f*; *(decease, demise)* fallecimiento, defunción *f.* **2** *(end - of custom, institution)* fin *m.* ● **death penalty** pena de muerte.
deathly ['deθlɪ] *adj (silence)* sepulcral, de muerte, mortal; *(pallor)* cadavérico,-a, de muerte.
▲ *comp* **deathlier**, *superl* **deathliest.**
deathtrap ['deθtræp] *n fam* lugar peligroso.
debacle [deɪ'bɑːkəl] *n* debacle *m*, desastre *m*, fiasco.
debar [dɪ'bɑːʳ] *vt (from place)* excluir (**from**, de); *(of right)* privar; *(from profession)* incapacitar, inhabilitar.
▲ *pt & pp* **debarred**, *ger* **debarring.**
debase [dɪ'beɪs] *vt* **1** *(degrade, devalue - idea, principle)* desvalorizar, envilecer; *(- language)* corromper, viciar; *(word, phrase)* quitar el sentido de. **2** *(coinage)* alterar. **3** *(demean, humiliate - person)* degradar.
debasement [dɪ'beɪsmənt] *n* degradación *f.*
debate [dɪ'beɪt] *n (public meeting, in Parliament)* debate *m*; *(discussion)* debate *m*, discusión *f.*
▷ *vt* **1** *(discuss)* debatir, discutir. **2** *(consider, think over)* considerar, dar vueltas a.
debauch [dɪ'bɔːtʃ] *vt* corromper, pervertir.
debauchee [debɔː'tʃiː] *n* disoluto.
debenture [dɪ'bentʃəʳ] *n* FIN *(bond)* obligación *f*, bono
debilitate [dɪ'bɪlɪteɪt] *vt (weaken)* debilitar; *(exhaus* extenuar.
debility [dɪ'bɪlɪtɪ] *n* debilidad *f*, decaimiento.
▲ *pl* **debilities.**
debit ['debɪt] *n* FIN débito.
▷ *vt* cargar en cuenta.
debrief [diː'briːf] *vt* interrogar, pedir un informe a.
debris ['deɪbriː] *n (ruins)* escombros *mpl*; *(wreckage* restos *mpl.*
debt [det] *n (something owed)* deuda; *(indebtednes* endeudamiento.
debtor ['detəʳ] *n* deudor,-ra.
debug [diː'bʌg] *vt* **1** *(computer programme, system)* de purar. **2** *(room, building, etc)* quitar los micrófonc ocultos de.
▲ *pt & pp* **debugged**, *ger* **debugging.**
debunk [diː'bʌŋk] *vt fam (person)* desmitificar, deser mascarar; *(idea, belief)* desacreditar, desprestigiar.
debut ['deɪbjuː] *n* debut *m.*
Dec [dɪ'sembəʳ] *abbr* (**December**) diciembre.
decade ['dekeɪd] *n* década, decenio.
decadence ['dekədəns] *n* decadencia.
decaffeinated [diː'kæfɪneɪtd] *vt* descafeinado,-a.
decagon ['dekəgɒn] *n* decágono.
decagonal [dɪ'kægənᵊl] *adj* decagonal.
decagramme ['dekəgræm] *n* decagramo.
decahedron [dekə'hiːdrən] *n* decaedro.
decalcification [diːkælsɪfɪ'keɪʃᵊn] *n* descalcificación
decalcify [diː'kælsɪfaɪ] *vt* descalcificar.
decalitre ['dekəliːtəʳ] *n* decalitro.
Decalogue ['dekəlɒg] *n* decálogo.
decametre ['dekəmiːtəʳ] *n* decámetro.
decamp [dɪ'kæmp] *vi* **1** *fam (leave suddenly)* esfumars largarse. **2** MIL *(leave camp)* levantar campamento.
decant [dɪ'kænt] *vt (wine)* decantar.
▷ *vi* CHEM transvasar.
decanter [dɪ'kæntəʳ] *n* decantador *m.*
decapitation [dɪkæpɪ'teɪʃᵊn] *n* decapitación *f.*
decapod ['dekəpɒd] *n* decápodo.
decarbonate [diː'kɑːbəneɪt] *vt* descarbonatar.
decarbonize [diː'kɑːbənaɪz] *vt* descarburar.
decarburize [diː'kæbjʊraɪz] *vt* descarburar.
decasyllable [dekə'sɪləbᵊl] *n* decasílabo.
decathlete [dɪ'kæθliːt] *n* decatleta *m.*
decathlon [dɪ'kæθlɒn] *n* decatlón *m.*
decay [dɪ'keɪ] *n* **1** *(of organic matter)* descomposició *f*; *(of teeth)* caries *f.* **2** *(of building)* deterioro, desmc ronamiento. **3** *fig (of culture, values)* decadencia.
decease [dɪ'siːs] *n* fallecimiento, defunción *f.*
deceit [dɪ'siːt] *n (trick)* engaño; *(deceiving)* falsedad *f*
deceive [dɪ'siːv] *vt* engañar.
decelerate [diː'seləreɪt] *vi* reducir la velocidac desacelerar.
December [dɪ'sembəʳ] *n* diciembre *m.*

Para ejemplos de uso, consulta **May.**

decency ['diːsᵊnsɪ] *n* **1** *(seemliness)* decencia, decorc **2** *(politeness)* buena educación *f*, cortesía *f.*
▲ *pl* **decencies.**
▷ *n pl* **decencies** convenciones *fpl* sociales.
decennial [dɪ'senɪəl] *n* decenal.

decent ['di:sᵊnt] *adj* 1 *(socially acceptable- dress, behaviour, language)* decente, decoroso,-a; *(person)* decente, honrado,-a. 2 *(adequate - meal, wage, housing)* decente, adecuado,-a. 3 *fam (nice, kind)* bueno,-a, amable.

decentralize [di:'sentrəlaɪz] *vt* descentralizar.

deception [dɪ'sepʃᵊn] *n (trick)* engaño; *(deceiving)* falsedad *f.*

deceptive [dɪ'septɪv] *adj* engañoso,-a: **appearances can be deceptive** *las apariencias engañan.*

decibel ['desɪbel] *n* decibelio, decibel *m.*

decide [dɪ'saɪd] *vt* 1 *(person)* decidir. 2 *(cause to reach a decision)* decidir. 3 *(settle, determine - of event, action)* decidir, determinar.

deciduous [dɪ'sɪdjʊəs] *adj* de hoja caduca.

decigram ['desɪgræm] *n* US → **decigramme.**

decigramme ['desɪgræm] *n* decigramo.

deciliter ['desɪli:təʳ] *n* US → **decilitre.**

decilitre ['desɪli:təʳ] *n* decilitro.

decimal ['desɪmᵊl] *n* decimal *m.* ● **decimal point** coma decimal.

decimalize ['desɪməlaɪz] *vt* convertir al sistema decimal.

decimate ['desɪmeɪt] *vt* diezmar.

decimation [desɪ'meɪʃᵊn] *n* reducción *f* catastrófica, acción de diezmar.

decimeter ['desɪmi:təʳ] *n* US → **decimetre.**

decimetre ['desɪmi:təʳ] *n* decímetro.

decipher [dɪ'saɪfəʳ] *vt* descifrar.

decision [dɪ'sɪʒᵊn] *n* 1 *(choice, verdict)* decisión *f.* 2 *(resolution)* resolución *f,* decisión *f,* determinación *f.*

decisive [dɪ'saɪsɪv] *adj* 1 *(conclusive - gen)* decisivo,-a; *(- victory)* contundente. 2 *(firm, resolute - person)* decidido,-a, resuelto,-a; *(- reply, action)* firme.

deck [dek] *n* 1 *(of ship)* cubierta. 2 *(of bus, coach)* piso. 3 US *(of cards)* baraja. 4 *(of record player)* plato. 5 US *(raised roofless area)* terraza.

deckchair [dektʃeəʳ] *n* tumbona.

deckhand ['dekhænd] *n* marinero.

declaim [dɪ'kleɪm] *vt* declamar.
▷ *vi* declamar.

declamation [deklə'meɪʃᵊn] *n* declamación *f.*

declamatory [dɪ'klæmətərɪ] *adj* declamatorio,-a.

declarant [dɪ'kleərənt] *n* declarante *mf.*

declaration [deklə'reɪʃᵊn] *n* declaración *f.*

declarative [dɪ'klærətɪv] *adj* declarativo,-a.

declaratory [dɪ'klærətᵊrɪ] *adj* 1 → **declarative.** 2 *(in law)* declaratorio,-a.

declare [dɪ'kleəʳ] *vt* 1 *(gen)* declarar; *(opinion)* manifestar. 2 *(at customs)* declarar.

declared [dɪ'kleəd] *adj* declarado,-a.

declarer [dɪ'leərəʳ] *n* declarante *mf.*

declassify [dɪ'klæsɪfaɪ] *vt* levantar el secreto oficial de.
▲ *pt & pp* **declassified**, *ger* **declassifying.**

declension [dɪ'klenʃᵊn] *n* LING declinación *f.*

declinable [dɪ'klaɪnəbᵊl] *adj* declinable.

declination [deklɪ'neɪʃᵊn] *n* declinación *f,* variación *f.* ● **magnetic declination** variación *f* magnética.

decline [dɪ'klaɪn] *n* 1 *(decrease)* disminución *f,* descenso. 2 *(deterioration - gen)* deterioro, declive *m,* decadencia; *(in health)* deterioro, empeoramiento.

decode [di:'kəʊd] *vt* decodificar, descodificar, descifrar.

decompose [di:kəm'pəʊz] *vt* descomponer.
▷ *vi* 1 descomponerse, pudrirse. 2 CHEM descomponerse.

decompress [dɪkəm'pres] *vt* someter a descompresión.

decompression [dɪkəm'preʃᵊn] *n* descompresión *f.*

decongestion [di:kən'dʒetʃᵊn] *n* descongestión *f.*

decontaminate [di:kən'tæmɪneɪt] *vt* descontaminar.

decontamination [di:kəntæmɪ'neɪʃᵊn] *n* descontaminación *f.*

decor ['deɪkɔ:ʳ] *n* 1 *(furnishings)* decoración *f.* 2 THEAT decorado.

decorate ['dekəreɪt] *vt* 1 *(adorn, make beautiful)* decorar (**with**, con), adornar (**with**, con). 2 *(paint)* pintar; *(wallpaper)* empapelar. 3 *(honour)* condecorar (**for**, por).

decoration [dekə'reɪʃᵊn] *n* 1 *(act, art)* decoración *f.* 2 *(ornament)* adorno. 3 *(medal)* condecoración *f.*

decorator ['dekəreɪtəʳ] *n (designer)* decorador,-ra, interiorista *mf; (painter)* pintor,-ra; *(wallpaperer)* empapelador,-ra.

decorous ['dekərəs] *adj fml* decoroso,-a.

decorum [dɪ'kɔ:rəm] *n fml* decoro.

decoy ['di:kɔɪ] *n* 1 *(bird)* cimbel *m; (in hunting)* señuelo, reclamo. 2 *fig (lure)* señuelo, carnada, gancho.

decrease [dɪ'kri:s] *n* disminución *f,* descenso.
▷ *vt* disminuir, reducir.

decreasing [dɪ'kri:sɪŋ] *adj* decreciente.

decreasingly [dɪ'kri:sɪŋlɪ] *adv* cada vez menos.

decree [dɪ'kri:] *n* 1 *(command)* decreto. 2 US *(judgement)* sentencia.
▷ *vt* decretar.

decrepit [dɪ'krepɪt] *adj (person)* decrépito,-a; *(furniture)* destartalado,-a; *(house)* deteriorado,-a, desvencijado,-a.

decriminalize [di:'krɪmɪnᵊlaɪz] *vt* despenalizar.

decry [dɪ'kraɪ] *vt (condemn, criticize)* censurar, criticar, condenar; *(disparage)* menospreciar, despreciar.
▲ *pt & pp* **decried**, *ger* **decrying.**

decurrent [dɪ'kʌrənt] *adj* decurrente.

dedicate ['dedɪkeɪt] *vt* 1 *(devote - oneself, time, effort)* dedicar, consagrar. 2 *(book, poem, performance, etc)* dedicar. 3 REL *(consecrate)* dedicar.

dedicatory ['dedɪkətᵊrɪ] *adj* dedicatorio,-a.

deduce [dɪ'dju:s] *vt* deducir (**from**, de), inferir (**from**, de).

deduct [dɪ'dʌkt] *vt (gen)* descontar, deducir; *(from taxes)* desgravar.

deduction [dɪ'dʌkʃᵊn] *n* 1 *(subtraction)* deducción *f,* descuento; *(from taxes)* desgravación *f.* 2 *(reasoning)* deducción *f.*

deed [di:d] *n* 1 *lit (act)* acto, acción *f,* obra; *(feat)* hazaña, proeza. 2 JUR escritura.

deejay ['di:dʒeɪ] *n* pinchadiscos *mf,* discjockey *mf.*

deem [di:m] *vt fml* juzgar, considerar.

deep [di:p] *adj* 1 *(river, hole, well, etc)* hondo,-a, profundo,-a. 2 *(shelf, wardrobe)* de fondo; *(hem, border)* ancho,-a. 3 *(sound, voice)* grave, bajo,-a; *(note)* grave; *(breath)* hondo,-a.

▷ *adv* 1 *(to a great depth)* profundamente. 2 *(far from the outside)* lejos. 3 *(far in time, late)* tarde.
▷ *n* **the deep** las profundidades *fpl*, el piélago.
deepen ['di:pən] *vt* 1 *(well, channel, river)* profundizar, hacer más profundo,-a, hacer más hondo,-a. 2 *(knowledge)* profundizar, ahondar; *(sympathy)* aumentar; *(colour, emotion)* intensificar; *(sound, voice)* hacer más grave.
deep-freeze ['di:p'fri:z] *n* congelador *m*.
▷ *vt (at home)* congelar; *(commercially)* ultracongelar.
▲ *pt* **deep-froze** [di:p'frəʊz], *pp* **deep-frozen** [di:p'frəʊzən].
deep-fry [di:p'fraɪ] *vt* freír en abundante aceite.
▲ *pt & pp* **deep-fried**, *ger* **deep-frying**.
deeply ['di:plɪ] *adv* 1 *(cut, bite)* profundamente. 2 *(sigh)* profundamente, hondo; *(breathe)* hondo; *(look)* fijamente.
deep-rooted [di:p'ru:tɪd] *adj* profundamente arraigado,-a.
deep-sea ['di:psi:] *n (fishing, diving)* de altura.
deer [dɪəʳ] *n* ciervo, venado.
▲ *pl* **deer**.
deface [dɪ'feɪs] *vt (damage, spoil)* desfigurar; *(scrawl on)* pintarrajear.
de facto [deɪ'fæktəʊ] *adj* de hecho.
▷ *adv* de hecho.
defame [dɪ'feɪm] *vt fml* difamar.
default [dɪ'fɔ:lt] *n* 1 *(failure to act)* omisión *f*, negligencia. 2 *(failure to pay)* incumplimiento de pago, mora, demora.
▷ *vi* 1 *(fail to act)* faltar a sus compromisos, incumplir un acuerdo. 2 *(fail to pay)* no pagar (**on**, -), demorarse (**on**, en).
defaulter [dɪ'fɔ:ltəʳ] *n* 1 *(on loan, rent)* moroso,-a. 2 JUR rebelde *mf*.
defeat [dɪ'fi:t] *n* 1 *(of army, team)* derrota; *(of motion, bill)* rechazo. 2 *fig (of hopes, plans)* fracaso.
▷ *vt* 1 *(opponent)* derrotar, vencer; *(opposition, government)* derrotar; *(bill, motion)* rechazar. 2 *fig (hopes, plans)* frustrar.
defecate ['defəkeɪt] *vi fml* defecar.
defect [*(n)* 'di:fekt, *(vb)* dɪ'fekt] *n (gen)* defecto; *(flaw)* desperfecto, tara.
▷ *vi (party, team)* desertar, pasarse al bando contrario; *(country)* huir.
defection [dɪ'fekʃən] *n (from party, team)* deserción *f*, defección *f*; *(from country)* fuga, huida.
defective [dɪ'fektɪv] *adj* 1 *(faulty)* defectuoso,-a; *(flawed)* con desperfectos; *(incomplete, lacking)* deficiente. 2 LING defectivo,-a.
defector [dɪ'fektəʳ] *n* POL tránsfuga *mf*, trásfuga *mf*.
defence [dɪ'fens] *n* 1 *(gen)* defensa; *(protection)* defensa, protección *f*. 2 JUR defensa. 3 SP defensa.
defend [dɪ'fend] *vt (gen)* defender; *(protect)* defender, proteger.
▷ *vi* SP jugar de defensa.
defendant [dɪ'fendənt] *n* JUR *(in civil case)* demandado,-a; *(in criminal case)* acusado,-a.
defender [dɪ'fendəʳ] *n* 1 *(gen)* defensor,-ra. 2 SP defensa *mf*.
defenestration [di:fenɪ'streɪʃən] *n* defenestración *f*.
defensible [dɪ'fensəbəl] *adj (town, position)* defendible; *(idea, opinion, system)* defendible, justificable.
defensive [dɪ'fensɪv] *adj* defensivo,-a.
defer[1] [dɪ'fɜ:ʳ] *vt (postpone)* aplazar, posponer, retrasar.
▲ *pt & pp* **deferred**, *ger* **deferring**.
defer[2] [dɪ'fɜ:ʳ] *vi (submit to)* deferir (**to**, a).
▲ *pt & pp* **deferred**, *ger* **deferring**.
deference ['defərəns] *n* deferencia.
deferment [dɪ'fɜ:mənt] *n* aplazamiento.
deferral [dɪ'fɜ:rəl] *n* aplazamiento.
deferred [dɪ'fɜ:d] *adj* 1 FIN diferido,-a. 2 JUR aplazado,-a.
defiance [dɪ'faɪəns] *n* desafío.
defiant [dɪ'faɪənt] *adj (attitude, behaviour)* desafiante de desafío; *(person)* rebelde.
deficiency [dɪ'fɪʃənsɪ] *n* 1 *(lack)* deficiencia; *(shortage)* escasez *f*, falta, déficit *m*. 2 *(fault, shortcoming)* defecto, deficiencia.
▲ *pl* **deficiencies**.
deficient [dɪ'fɪʃənt] *adj* deficiente, insuficiente.
deficit ['defɪsɪt] *n* déficit *m*.
defile[1] [dɪ'faɪl] *vt* 1 *(make dirty, pollute - countryside)* dañar; *(- water, river)* contaminar; *(corrupt - mind)* corromper, envilecer; *(spoil - reputation, honour)* mancillar, manchar; *(- memory)* profanar. 2 REL *(desecrate)* profanar.
defile[2] [dɪ'faɪl] *n* desfiladero.
define [dɪ'faɪn] *vt* 1 *(word, expression, concept)* definir. 2 *(duties, role, rights, etc)* delimitar. 3 *(outline)* definir, perfilar.
definite ['defɪnət] *adj* 1 *(final, fixed - gen)* definitivo,-a; *(- opinions)* fijo,-a. 2 *(clear, distinct)* claro,-a; *(clear, appreciable)* notable, sensible; *(exact, specific)* específico,-a, preciso,-a.
definitely ['defɪnətlɪ] *adv* 1 *(without doubt)* sin duda, indudablemente, seguramente. 2 *(definitively)* definitivamente.
▷ *interj* ¡desde luego!, ¡claro que sí!
definition [defɪ'nɪʃən] *n* 1 *(explanation)* definición *f*.
definitive [dɪ'fɪnɪtɪv] *adj* 1 *(final, conclusive)* definitivo,-a. 2 *(ultimate - study, etc)* de mayor autoridad; *(- performance)* inmejorable, insuperable.
deflagrate ['defləgreɪt] *vi* deflagrar.
deflate [dɪ'fleɪt] *vt* 1 *(balloon, tyre)* desinflar, deshinchar. 2 *fig (humble)* rebajar, humillar, bajar los humos a; *(discourage)* desanimar, desalentar.
deflation [dɪ'fleɪʃən] *n* 1 *(of balloon, tyre)* desinflamiento. 2 *(economic)* deflación *f*.
deflect [dɪ'flekt] *vt* desviar.
▷ *vi* desviarse.
deflection [dɪ'flekʃən] *n* desviación *f*.
deforest [di:'fɒrɪst] *vt* deforestar.
deform [dɪ'fɔ:m] *vt* deformar.
deformation [di:fɔ:'meɪʃən] *n* deformación *f*.
deformed [dɪ'fɔ:md] *adj* deforme.
deformity [dɪ'fɔ:mɪtɪ] *n* deformidad *f*.
▲ *pl* **deformities**.
defraud [dɪ'frɔ:d] *vt* estafar.
defray [dɪ'freɪ] *vt* sufragar, costear.
defrock [di:'frɒk] *vt* expulsar del sacerdocio.
defrost [di:'frɒst] *vt* 1 *(freezer, food)* descongelar. US *(windscreen)* desempañar.
deft [deft] *adj* diestro,-a, hábil.

defunct [dɪˈfʌŋkt] *adj (person)* difunto,-a; *(practice, law)* (que ha caído,-a) en desuso, caduco,-a; *(organization, scheme)* desaparecido,-a, extinto,-a.
defuse [dɪˈfjuːz] *vt* 1 *(bomb)* desactivar. 2 *(situation)* distender, reducir la tensión de; *(anger, crisis)* calmar.
defy [dɪˈfaɪ] *vt* 1 *(ignore, refuse to give in to)* desafiar; *(disobey - law, order, authority)* desobedecer, desacatar. 2 *(make impossible)* ser imposible. 3 *(challenge)* retar, desafiar.
▲ *pt & pp* defied, *ger* defying.
degeneracy [dɪˈdʒenərəsɪ] *n* degeneración *f*.
degenerate [*(adj-n)* dɪˈdʒenərət, *(vb)* dɪˈdʒenəreɪt] *adj* degenerado,-a.
▷ *n* degenerado,-a.
▷ *vi (gen)* degenerar (into, en); *(health)* deteriorarse.
degenerative [dɪˈdʒenərətɪv] *adj* degenerativo,-a.
degradation [degrəˈdeɪʃᵊn] *n* degradación *f*.
degrade [dɪˈgreɪd] *vt* 1 *(debase)* degradar, envilecer. 2 *(break down)* degradar.
degree [dɪˈgriː] *n* 1 *(unit of measurement)* grado. 2 *(extent, level, point)* grado, nivel *m*, punto; *(amount)* algo. 3 *(stage, grade, step)* grado, etapa. 4 EDUC título.
dehiscent [dɪˈhɪsᵊnt] *adj* dehiscente.
dehumanize [diːˈhjuːmənaɪz] *vt* deshumanizar.
dehydrate [diːhaɪˈdreɪt] *vt* deshidratar.
▷ *vi* deshidratarse.
dehydrogenize [diːhaɪˈdrɒdʒənaɪz] *vt* deshidrogenar.
de-ice [diːˈaɪs] *vt* quitar el hielo a, deshelar.
de-icing [diːˈaɪsɪŋ] *n* deshielo.
deification [diːɪfɪˈkeɪʃᵊn] *n* deificación *f*, divinización *f*.
deify [ˈdeɪɪfaɪ] *vt* deificar, divinizar.
▲ *pt & pp* deified, *ger* deifying.
deign [deɪn] *vi* dignarse (to, a).
deistic [diːˈɪstɪk, deˈɪstɪk] *adj* deísta.
deity [ˈdeɪɪtɪ] *n* deidad *f*.
▷ *n* the Deity Dios *m*.
▲ *pl* deities.
dejection [dɪˈdʒekʃᵊn] *n* abatimiento, desaliento, desánimo.
delay [dɪˈleɪ] *n* retraso.
▷ *vt* 1 *(defer, postpone - gen)* aplazar, retrasar; *(payment)* aplazar, diferir. 2 *(make late - flight, train)* retrasar, demorar; *(person)* entretener.
delayed [dɪˈleɪd] *adj* retardado,-a, con retraso.
delectable [dɪˈlektəbəl] *adj* delicioso,-a.
delegate [*(adj-n)* ˈdelɪgət, *(vb)* ˈdelɪgeɪt] *n* delegado,-a.
▷ *vt (duties, responsibility, etc)* delegar (to, en).
delegation [delɪˈgeɪʃᵊn] *n* delegación *f*.
delete [dɪˈliːt] *vt (remove)* eliminar, suprimir; *(cross out)* tachar.
deleterious [delɪˈtɪərɪəs] *adj fml* nocivo,-a, perjudicial.
deliberate [*(adj)* dɪˈlɪbᵊrət, *(vb)* dɪˈlɪbəreɪt] *adj* 1 *(intentional)* deliberado,-a, intencionado,-a; *(studied)* premeditado,-a. 2 *(slow, unhurried)* pausado,-a, lento,-a; *(careful)* reflexivo,-a.
▷ *vi* deliberar (on, sobre).
deliberately [dɪˈlɪbərətlɪ] *adv* 1 *(intentionally)* a propósito, adrede, aposta, deliberadamente. 2 *(slowly)* pausadamente.
deliberation [dɪlɪbəˈreɪʃᵊn] *n* 1 *(consideration)* deliberación *f*. 2 *(slowness, carefulness)* calma, parsimonia.
delicacy [ˈdelɪkəsɪ] *n* 1 *(softness, tenderness)* delicadeza. 2 *(fragility)* fragilidad *f*. 3 *(food)* manjar *m* (exquisito), exquisitez *f*.
▲ *pl* delicacies.
delicate [ˈdelɪkət] *adj* 1 *(fine - gen)* delicado,-a; *(- embroidery, handiwork)* fino,-a, esmerado,-a. 2 *(easily damaged)* frágil. 3 *(sensitive - instrument)* sensible; *(- sense of smell, taste)* fino,-a.
delicatessen [delɪkəˈtesᵊn] *n* charcutería selecta.
delicious [dɪˈlɪʃəs] *adj* 1 *(food)* delicioso,-a, riquísimo,-a; *(taste, smell)* exquisito,-a. 2 *(delightful, attractive, pleasant)* delicioso,-a, agradable.
delight [dɪˈlaɪt] *n* 1 *(great pleasure, joy)* placer *m*, gusto, alegría, deleite *m*. 2 *(source of pleasure)* encanto, delicia, placer *m*.
▷ *vi* deleitarse (in, en/con).
delighted [dɪˈlaɪtɪd] *adj (person)* encantado,-a, contentísimo,-a; *(smile, shout, look)* de alegría.
delimit [dɪˈlɪmɪt] *vt* delimitar.
delineate [dɪˈlɪnɪeɪt] *vt* 1 *(by drawing)* delinear, esbozar, perfilar. 2 *(by describing)* trazar, describir.
delinquency [dɪˈlɪŋkwənsɪ] *n* 1 *(behaviour)* delincuencia. 2 *(act)* delito.
delinquent [dɪˈlɪŋkwənt] *adj* 1 *(youth)* delincuente; *(activity)* delictivo,-a. 2 FIN *(person)* moroso,-a.
▷ *n* delincuente *mf*.
delirious [dɪˈlɪrɪəs] *adj* 1 MED delirante. 2 *fig (happy)* loco,-a de alegría.
delirium [dɪˈlɪrɪəm] *n* 1 MED delirio, desvarío. 2 *(excited happiness)* delirio.
deliver [dɪˈlɪvəʳ] *vt* 1 *(take, give, hand over - goods, etc)* entregar; *(- message)* dar, entregar; *(distribute)* repartir (a domicilio). 2 *(hit, kick, push)* dar; *(blow, punch)* propinar, atestar; *(shot, fast ball)* lanzar. 3 *(say - speech, sermon, verdict)* pronunciar; *(lecture, sermon, ultimatum)* dar; *(warning)* hacer; *(judgement)* dictar, pronunciar, emitir. 4 *(produce, provide, fulfil)* cumplir. 5 MED *(baby)* asistir en el parto de, atender en el parto de. 6 *fml (free, save)* liberar.
▷ *vi* 1 *(goods, groceries, etc)* hacer repartos a domicilio. 2 *(fulfil promise, etc)* cumplir.
deliverance [dɪˈlɪvᵊrəns] *n fml* liberación *f*.
delivery [dɪˈlɪvᵊrɪ] *n* 1 *(act - gen)* entrega, reparto; *(- of mail)* reparto. 2 *(consignment)* partida, remesa. 3 *(manner of speaking)* modo de hablar. 4 *(of baby)* parto, alumbramiento. 5 *(throwing, launching - of ball, missile)* lanzamiento.
▲ *pl* deliveries.
dell [del] *n lit* valle *m* pequeño, hondonada.
delouse [diːˈlaʊs] *vt* espulgar, despiojar.
delta [ˈdeltə] *n* 1 GEOG delta *m*. 2 *(Greek letter)* delta.
deltoid [ˈdeltɔɪd] *adj* deltoides.
▷ *n* deltoides *m*.
delude [dɪˈluːd] *vt* engañar.
deluge [ˈdeljuːdʒ] *n* 1 *(rain)* diluvio; *(flood)* inundación *f*. 2 *fig* avalancha, alud *m*, aluvión *m*.
delusion [dɪˈluːʒᵊn] *n* 1 *(false belief)* falsa ilusión *f*; *(mistaken idea)* error *m*. 2 *(act, state)* engaño.

delusive [dɪ'lu:sɪv] *adj* 1 *(misleading)* engañoso,-a. 2 *(illusory)* ilusorio,-a.
de luxe [də'lʌks] *adj* de lujo.
delve [delv] *vi* 1 *(rummage, search)* hurgar (**into**, en). 2 *(study - gen)* ahondar (**into**, en); *(the past)* hurgar (**into**, en), escarbar (**into**, en).
demagnetize [di:'mægnətaɪz] *vt* desimanar, desimantar, desmagnetizar.
demagogue ['deməgɒg] *n* demagogo,-a.
demagogy ['deməgɒgɪ] *n* demagogia.
demand [dɪ'mɑ:nd] *n* 1 *(request)* solicitud *f*, petición *f*; *(claim)* exigencia; *(for pay rise, rights, etc)* reclamación *f*. 2 COMM demanda. 3 *(note, warning)* aviso.
▷ *vt* 1 *(call for, insist on)* exigir; *(rights, conditions, etc)* reclamar. 2 *(need, require)* exigir, requerir.
demanding [dɪ'mɑ:ndɪŋ] *adj* 1 *(person - gen)* exigente; *(awkward)* difícil. 2 *(tiring - job, etc)* agotador,-ra.
demarcate ['di:mɑ:keɪt] *vt* demarcar, acotar.
demean [dɪ'mi:n] *vi fml* degradar, rebajar.
demeanor [dɪ'mi:nər] *n* US ⟶ **demeanour**.
demeanour [dɪ'mi:nər] *n* 1 *fml (behaviour)* comportamiento, conducta. 2 *(bearing)* porte *m*.
dementia [dɪ'menʃɪə] *n* demencia.
demerit [dɪ'merɪt] *n* demérito.
demineralize [di:'mɪnərəlaɪz] *vt* desmineralizar.
demise [dɪ'maɪz] *n* 1 *(death)* fallecimiento, defunción *f*. 2 *fig (end)* desaparición *f*; *(failure)* fracaso.
demist [di:'mɪst] *vt* desempañar.
demo ['deməʊ] *n* 1 *(recording, tape)* maqueta. 2 *fam (demonstration)* manifestación *f*. 3 INFORM demo.
▲ *pl* **demos**.
demob [dɪ'mɒb] *vt* desmovilizar.
▲ *pt & pp* **demobbed**, *ger* **demobbing**.
demobilize [di:'məʊbɪlaɪz] *vt* desmovilizar.
democracy [dɪ'mɒkrəsɪ] *n* democracia.
▲ *pl* **democracies**.
democrat ['deməkræt] *n* demócrata *mf*. ● **Christian Democrat** democratacristiano,-a.
demography [dɪ'mɒgrəfɪ] *n* demografía.
demolish [dɪ'mɒlɪʃ] *vt* 1 *(building)* derribar, demoler, echar abajo. 2 *fig (theory, proposal)* destruir, echar por tierra.
demolition [demə'lɪʃən] *n* 1 *(of building)* demolición *f*, derribo. 2 *fig (of argument, idea, belief)* demolición *f*, destrucción *f*.
demon ['di:mən] *n* 1 *(evil spirit)* demonio, diablo. 2 *fam (naughty child)* diablillo. 3 *(energetic person)* fiera, bestia; *(talented person)* fiera, hacha.
demonic [dɪ'mɒnɪk] *adj* demoniaco,-a.
demonstrate ['demənstreɪt] *vt* 1 *(show, prove)* demostrar. 2 *(express, display)* demostrar, dar prueba de. 3 *(in shop, etc)* hacer una demostración de.
▷ *vi (protest)* manifestarse.
demonstration [demən'streɪʃən] *n* 1 *(act of showing)* demostración *f*, muestra. 2 *(march)* manifestación *f*.
demonstrative [dɪ'mɒnstrətɪv] *adj* 1 *(person - showing feelings)* abierto,-a, franco,-a, efusivo,-a, expresivo,-a. 2 *fml (proving something)* concluyente. 3 LING demostrativo,-a.
demonstrator ['demənstreɪtər] *n* POL manifestante *mf*.
demoralize [dɪ'mɒrəlaɪz] *vt* desmoralizar.
demote [dɪ'məʊt] *vt* 1 *(gen)* bajar de categoría. 2 MIL degradar.
demur [dɪ'mɜ:r] *vi fml (object)* oponerse, objetar.
▲ *pt & pp* **demurred**, *ger* **demurring**.
demure [dɪ'mjʊər] *adj (person)* recatado,-a; *(behaviour)* tímido,-a, discreto,-a.
demurrage [dɪ'mʌrɪdʒ] *n* estadía.
demystify [dɪ'mɪstɪfaɪ] *vt* desmitificar.
▲ *pt & pp* **demystified**, *ger* **demystifying**.
den [den] *n* 1 *(of animals)* guarida. 2 *(secret meeting-place)* antro. 3 *fam (room)* cuarto; *(for study)* estudio.
denarius [dɪ'neərɪəs] *n* denario.
denaturize [di:'neɪtʃəraɪz] *vt* desnaturalizar.
dendrite ['dendraɪt] *n* dendrita.
denial [dɪ'naɪəl] *n* 1 *(of accusation)* mentís *m*, desmentido, refutación *f*. 2 *(of principle)* negación *f*. 3 *(of rights, justice)* denegación *f*. 4 *(of request)* negativa, rechazo.
denigrate ['denɪgreɪt] *vt (person, character)* denigrar; *(achievements, efforts)* menospreciar.
denim ['denɪm] *n* tela vaquera, tela tejana.
▷ *n pl* **denims** vaqueros *mpl*, tejanos *mpl*.
denizen ['denɪzən] *n lit* habitante *mf*, morador,-ra.
Denmark ['denmɑ:k] *n* Dinamarca.
denominate [dɪ'nɒmɪneɪt] *vt* denominar.
denomination [dɪnɒmɪ'neɪʃən] *n* 1 REL confesión *f*. 2 *(standard of value)* valor *m*. 3 *(classification)* denominación *f*.
denominator [dɪ'nɒmɪneɪtər] *n* MATH denominador *m*.
denote [dɪ'nəʊt] *vt* 1 *fml (indicate, represent)* denotar, indicar. 2 LING *(mean)* denotar, significar.
denounce [dɪ'naʊns] *vt* denunciar.
dense [dens] *adj* 1 *(closely packed - population, traffic)* denso,-a; *(- forest, jungle, vegetation)* denso,-a, espeso,-a; *(- crowd)* compacto,-a, apretado,-a.
density ['densɪtɪ] *n (gen)* densidad *f*.
▲ *pl* **densities**.
dent [dent] *n (in car, metal)* abolladura.
▷ *vt* 1 *(car, metal)* abollar. 2 *(pride, reputation)* hacer mella en; *(confidence)* hacer perder.
dentist ['dentɪst] *n* dentista *mf*, odontólogo,-a.
dentistry ['dentɪstrɪ] *n* odontología.
denture ['dentʃər] *n (plate)* prótesis *f* dental.
▷ *n pl* **dentures** dentadura *f sing* postiza.
denude [dɪ'nju:d] *vt* 1 GEOG desnudar, denudar. 2 *(strip)* despojar (of, de).
denunciation [dɪnʌnsɪ'eɪʃən] *n* denuncia.
deny [dɪ'naɪ] *vt* 1 *(repudiate - accusation, fact)* negar; *(rumour, report)* desmentir; *(charge)* rechazar. 2 *(refuse - request)* denegar; *(- rights, equality)* privar de; *(- access)* negar. 3 *fml (disown - person)* desconocer, negar a; *(- faith, country)* renegar de; *(not admit, disclaim)* negar.
▲ *pt & pp* **denied**, *ger* **denying**.
deodorant [di:'əʊdərənt] *n* desodorante *m*.
deoxyribonucleic [di:ɒksɪraɪbəʊnjʊ:'kleɪɪk] *n* desoxirribonucleico,-a.
depart [dɪ'pɑ:t] *vi fml (leave)* partir, salir.
departed [dɪ'pɑ:tɪd] *adj* 1 *euph* difunto,-a. 2 *fml (youth)* perdido,-a; *(glories)* pasado,-a.
department [dɪ'pɑ:tmənt] *n* 1 *(in shop)* sección *f*; *(in company, organization)* departamento, sección *f*; *(in gov-*

ernment) ministerio. **2** *fam (responsibility)* campo, esfera, terreno.

departure [dɪ'pɑːtʃəʳ] *n* **1** *(of person)* partida, marcha; *(of plane, train, etc)* salida. **2** *fig (divergence)* desviación *f*; *(venture, type of activity)* innovación *f*.

depend [dɪ'pend] *vi* depender.

⊙ **to depend on** *vt* confiar en.

dependability [dɪpendə'bɪlətɪ] *n* *(of people)* formalidad *f*, seriedad *f*; *(of things)* fiabilidad *f*.

depict [dɪ'pɪkt] *vt* **1** *(portray visually, in music)* pintar, representar, retratar. **2** *(describe in writing)* describir.

deplete [dɪ'pliːt] *vt fml* reducir, agotar.

deplore [dɪ'plɔːʳ] *vt (condemn, criticize)* deplorar, condenar; *(regret)* lamentar, deplorar.

deploy [dɪ'plɔɪ] *vt* **1** MIL desplegar. **2** *(use effectively)* utilizar, hacer uso de.

deport [dɪ'pɔːt] *vt* deportar.

deportee [diːpɔː'tiː] *n* deportado,-a.

depose [dɪ'pəʊz] *vt* **1** *(remove from power - leader, president)* deponer, destituir; *(- king)* destronar. **2** JUR declarar, deponer.

deposit [dɪ'pɒzɪt] *n* **1** *(sediment)* sedimento, depósito; *(layer)* capa. **2** *(mining - of gold,etc)* yacimiento. **3** FIN *(payment into account)* depósito, ingreso.

depot ['depəʊ] *n (storehouse)* almacén *m*.

deprave [dɪ'preɪv] *vt* depravar.

deprecate ['deprɪkeɪt] *vt* **1** *fml (deplore)* censurar, condenar, criticar, reprobar. **2** *fml (belittle)* menospreciar, despreciar.

depreciate [dɪ'priːʃɪeɪt] *vi* FIN depreciarse.

▷ *vt* **1** FIN depreciar, amortizar. **2** *fml (denigrate)* menospreciar.

depress [dɪ'pres] *vt* **1** *(make sad)* deprimir, desanimar, abatir. **2** *(reduce - prices, sales, wages)* reducir, hacer bajar, disminuir. **3** *fml (press down)* pulsar, apretar.

depression [dɪ'preʃᵊn] *n* **1** *(sadness)* depresión *f*, abatimiento. **2** *(economic)* depresión *f*, crisis *f*. **3** *(hollow place)* depresión *f*. **4** METEOR depresión *f* (atmosférica).

depressive [dɪ'presɪv] *adj* depresivo,-a.

▷ *n (person)* depresivo,-a.

deprive [dɪ'praɪv] *vt (take away)* privar (**of**, de); *(prevent from having or using)* despojar de, privar de.

depth [depθ] *n (of hole, mine, etc)* profundidad *f*; *(of cupboard, shelf)* fondo; *(of hem, border)* ancho.

deputation [depjʊ'teɪʃᵊn] *n* delegación *f*.

depute [dɪ'pjuːt] *vt fml (work, authority)* delegar (**to**, en), encomendar (**to**, a); *(person)* diputar (**to**, para), comisionar (**to**, para).

deputize ['depjətaɪz] *vi* reemplazar (**for**, a), sustituir (**for**, a).

deputy ['depjətɪ] *n* **1** *(substitute)* sustituto,-a, suplente *mf*. **2** POL diputado,-a. **3** US ayudante *mf* del shérif. ● **deputy head** EDUC subdirector,-ra.

▲ *pl* **deputies**.

derail [dɪ'reɪl] *vt (train)* hacer descarrilar.

derange [dɪ'reɪndʒ] *vt* **1** *(drive mad)* alienar, volver loco,-a. **2** *(disturb order)* trastornar.

derby ['dɑːbɪ] *n* **1** SP *(between two local teams)* derby *m*. **2** US *(horse race)* carrera (de caballos). **3** US *(bowler hat)* bombín *m*, sombrero (de) hongo.

▲ *pl* **derbies**.

deregulate [diː'regjəleɪt] *vt* desregular, liberalizar.

derelict ['derɪlɪkt] *adj (building)* abandonado,-a, en ruinas.

deride [dɪ'raɪd] *vt* burlarse de, ridiculizar, reírse de, mofarse de.

derive [dɪ'raɪv] *vt (get, obtain)* sacar, recibir.

▷ *vi* **1** LING *(word)* derivar, derivarse (**from**, de). **2** *(stem from - problem, attitude)* provenir (**from**, de); *(- idea)* tener su origen (**from**, en).

dermatitis [dɜːmə'taɪtɪs] *n* dermatitis *f*.

dermis ['dɜːmɪs] *n* dermis *f*.

derogatory [dɪ'rɒgətᵊrɪ] *adj (remark, attitude, article)* despectivo,-a; *(meaning, sense)* peyorativo,-a.

derrick ['derɪk] *n* **1** *(crane)* grúa. **2** *(tower over oil well)* torre *f* de perforación.

descend [dɪ'send] *vt* descender, bajar.

descent [dɪ'sent] *n (by plane, climbers, etc)* descenso, bajada; *(slope)* pendiente *f*, declive *m*.

describe [dɪ'skraɪb] *vt* **1** *(depict in words)* describir. **2** *(call, characterize)* calificar, definir. **3** *(move in shape)* describir; *(draw)* trazar.

desensitize [diː'sensɪtaɪz] *vt* insensibilizar.

desert¹ ['dezət] *n* desierto.

desert² [dɪ'zɜːt] *vt (family, person, place)* abandonar; *(political party, idea)* desertar (**from**, de).

deserts [dɪ'zɜːts] *n pl* merecido.

deserve [dɪ'zɜːv] *vt (gen)* merecer, merecerse; *(attention)* merecer, ser digno,-a de.

desiccation [desɪ'keɪʃᵊn] *n* desecación *f*.

design [dɪ'zaɪn] *n* **1** ART *(gen)* diseño, dibujo; *(of fashion)* diseño de modas, creación *f*. **2** *(plan, drawing)* plano, proyecto; *(sketch)* boceto; *(of dress)* patrón *m*; *(of product, model)* modelo. **3** *fig (purpose, intention)* plan *m*, intención, proyecto.

▷ *vt* **1** *(make drawing, plan, model)* diseñar, proyectar; *(fashion, set, product)* diseñar; *(course, programme)* planear, estructurar. **2** *(develop for a purpose)* diseñar, concebir, idear; *(intend, mean)* pensar, destinar.

designate [*(vb)* 'dezɪgneɪt, *(adj)* 'dezɪgnət] *vt* **1** *fml (indicate, mark, show)* indicar, señalar. **2** *(appoint)* designar, nombrar.

desire [dɪ'zaɪəʳ] *n (wish, urge, longing)* deseo, anhelo, ansia; *(sexual)* deseo.

▷ *vt fml (gen)* desear, anhelar, ansiar.

desist [dɪ'zɪst] *vi fml* desistir (**from**, de).

desk [desk] *n* **1** *(in school)* pupitre *m*; *(in office)* escritorio. **2** *(service area)* mostrador *m*. **3** *(newspaper office)* sección *f*.

desktop [deskɒp] *n* escritorio.

desolate ['desələt] *adj* **1** *(place)* deshabitado,-a, desierto,-a, despoblado,-a, solitario,-a. **2** *(person - sad)* triste, desconsolado,-a; *(lonely)* solitario,-a.

▷ *vt* desolar.

desoxyribonucleic [dezɒksɪraɪbəʊnjuː'kleɪɪk] *n* desoxirribonucleico,-a.

despair [dɪs'peəʳ] *n* desesperación *f*, desesperanza.

▷ *vi* desesperar (**of**, de), desesperarse (**of**, por), perder la esperanza (**of**, de).

desperado [despə'rɑːdəʊ] *n* forajido,-a.

desperate ['despᵊrət] *adj (reckless, risky)* desesperado,-a.

despicable [dɪ'spɪkəbᵊl] *adj (person, act)* despreciable, vil, infame, bajo,-a; *(behaviour)* indigno,-a.

despise [dɪ'spaɪz] *vt* despreciar, menospreciar.

despite [dɪ'spaɪt] *prep* a pesar de: she went to work despite having a bad cold *se fue a trabajar a pesar de estar muy resfriada.*

despondent [dɪ'spɒndənt] *adj* desalentado,-a, desanimado,-a, abatido,-a.

despot ['despɒt] *n* déspota *mf.*

dessert [dɪ'zɜ:t] *n* postre *m.*

destabilize [di:'steɪbəlaɪz] *vt* desestabilizar.

destination [destɪ'neɪʃᵊn] *n* destino.

destined ['destɪnd] *adj* 1 *(intended, meant)* destinado,-a. 2 *(fated)* condenado,-a, destinado,-a. 3 *(bound)* con destino (for, a).

destiny ['destɪnɪ] *n* destino, sino.
▲ *pl* destinies.

destitute ['destɪtju:t] *adj* indigente, mísero,-a.

destroy [dɪ'strɔɪ] *vt* 1 *(gen)* destruir; *(vehicle, old furniture)* destrozar. 2 *(life)* arruinar. 3 *(animal)* matar, abatir.

destruction [dɪ'strʌkʃᵊn] *n* 1 *(of city, books, documents, forest)* destrucción *f*; *(of reputation, civilization)* destrucción *f*, ruina. 2 *(cause of downfall)* ruina, perdición *f*. 3 *(damage)* daños *mpl*, estragos *mpl*, destrozos *mpl*.

desultory ['desəltərɪ] *adj* 1 *fml (without clear plan, purpose)* poco sistemático,-a, poco metódico,-a, irregular. 2 *fml (showing little interest)* desganado,-a, poco entusiasta.

detach [dɪ'tætʃ] *vt* 1 *(separate, remove)* separar, quitar; *(unstick)* despegar: you can detach the collar from the coat *se puede quitar el cuello del abrigo.* 2 MIL destacar.

detached [dɪ'tætʃt] *adj* 1 *(separated - gen)* separado,-a, suelto,-a. 2 *(house)* independiente. 3 *(person, manner - impartial)* objetivo,-a, imparcial; *(- aloof)* distante, indiferente. ● detached house vivienda unifamiliar.

detail ['di:teɪl] *n* 1 *(point, fact, item)* detalle *m*, pormenor *m*. 2 ART *(of picture, pattern)* detalle *m*. 3 MIL destacamento, cuadrilla.
▷ *vt* 1 *(describe)* detallar, exponer en detalle. 2 MIL destacar.
▷ *n pl* details *(information)* información *f*; *(particulars)* datos *mpl*.

detain [dɪ'teɪn] *vt* 1 *(hold - in custody)* detener. 2 *(delay)* entretener, demorar, retener.

detainee [di:teɪ'ni:] *n* detenido,-a.

detect [dɪ'tekt] *vt* 1 *(notice, sense - gen)* detectar, advertir; *(- sarcasm, difference)* notar; *(- sound, small)* percibir. 2 *(find - object, substance)* detectar, encontrar. 3 *(discover - crime, criminal, fraud)* descubrir.

detection [dɪ'tekʃᵊn] *n* 1 *(of error)* descubrimiento; *(of substance)* detección *f*; *(of small, sound)* percepción *f*. 2 *(discovery of crime, criminal, fraud)* descubrimiento.

detective [dɪ'tektɪv] *n (private)* detective *mf*; *(in police force)* agente *mf*, oficial *mf*.

detector [dɪ'tektəʳ] *n* detector *m*.

detente ['deɪtɒnt] *n* distensión *f*.

detention [dɪ'tenʃᵊn] *n* 1 JUR *(of suspect)* detención *f*, arresto. 2 EDUC *(of pupil)* castigo.

deter [dɪ'tɜ:ʳ] *vt* 1 *(person - dissuade)* disuadir (from, de). 2 *(prevent, stop)* impedir.
▲ *pt & pp* deterred, *ger* deterring.

deterge [dɪ'tɜ:dʒ] *vt* deterger.

detergent [dɪ'tɜ:dʒənt] *n* detergente *m*.

deteriorate [dɪ'tɪərɪəreɪt] *vi (economy, health, situation, relations, material)* deteriorarse; *(weather, work)* empeorar.

deterioration [dɪtɪərɪə'reɪʃᵊn] *n (gen)* empeoramiento; *(of material)* deterioro.

determination [dɪtɜ:mɪ'neɪʃᵊn] *n* 1 *(resolution)* determinación *f*, resolución *f*, decisión *f*. 2 *fml (setting, deciding)* determinación *f*.

determine [dɪ'tɜ:mɪn] *vt* 1 *(find out, ascertain - cause, position, meaning)* determinar, establecer, averiguar. 2 *(influence)* determinar, condicionar. 3 *(settle, fix - date, price)* decidir, fijar; *(mark - boundary, limit)* determinar, definir, demarcar. 4 *fml (resolve, decide)* decidir, resolver, tomar la determinación de.

determined [dɪ'tɜ:mɪnd] *adj (person)* decidido,-a, resuelto,-a; *(attempt, effort)* enérgico,-a, persistente.

determiner [dɪ'tɜ:mɪnəʳ] *n* LING determinante *m*.

deterrent [dɪ'terənt] *adj* disuasivo,-a, disuasorio,-a.
▷ *n* fuerza disuasoria, fuerza disuasiva.

detest [dɪ'test] *vt* detestar, odiar, aborrecer: I detest cooking *odio cocinar.*

dethronement [dɪ'θrəʊnmənt] *n* destronamiento.

detonate ['detəneɪt] *vi* estallar, detonar, explotar.
▷ *vt* hacer estallar, hacer explotar.

detonation [detə'neɪʃᵊn] *n* detonación *f*.

detour ['di:tʊəʳ] *n (in traffic)* desvío.

detract [dɪ'trækt] *vt* **to detract from** *(achievement)* quitar mérito(s) a, restar valor a; *(beauty)* deslucir.

detractor [dɪ'træktəʳ] *n* detractor,-ra.

detriment ['detrɪmənt] *n fml* detrimento (to, para), perjuicio (to, para).

detrimental [detrɪ'mentᵊl] *adj fml* perjudicial (to, para).

detritus [dɪ'traɪtəs] *n* 1 GEOL detrito, detritus *m*. 2 *(debris)* desechos *mpl*.

deuce [djʊ:s] *n* 1 *(in tennis)* cuarenta *mpl* iguales. 2 *(in games)* dos *m*.

devaluation [di:væljʊ:'eɪʃᵊn] *n* FIN devaluación *f*, desvaloración *f*.

devalue [di:'vælju:] *vt* 1 FIN *(currency)* devaluar, desvalorizar. 2 *(person, achievement)* subvalorar.

devastate ['devəsteɪt] *vt* 1 *(city, area, country)* devastar. 2 *fam fig (person)* anonadar, apabullar.

devastating ['devəsteɪtɪŋ] *adj* 1 *(destructive)* devastador,-ra, asolador,-ra, desastroso,-a; *(causing severe shock)* espeluznante. 2 *(criticism, argument)* demoledor,-ra, apabullante, aplastante; *(wit)* tremendo,-a. 3 *fam (beauty, charm)* irresistible; *(insight)* brillante.

devastatingly ['devəsteɪtɪŋlɪ] *adv (witty)* tremendamente; *(beautiful)* irresistiblemente.

devastation [devə'steɪʃᵊn] *n* devastación *f*, asolación *f*, asolamiento.

develop [dɪ'veləp] *vt* 1 *(cultivate, gen)* desarrollar; *(foster - trade, arts)* fomentar, promover; *(expand - industry)* ampliar; *(build up, improve - skill, ability, talent)* perfeccionar. 2 *(elaborate, expand - idea, argu-*

ment, story) desarrollar; *(- theory, plan)* desarrollar, elaborar. **3** *(acquire - habit, quality, feature)* contraer, adquirir; *(- talent, interest)* mostrar; *(- tendency)* revelar, manifestar; *(get - illness, disease)* contraer; *(- immunity, resistance)* desarrollar. **4** *(exploit - resources)* explotar; *(- site, land)* urbanizar. 5 *(film, photograph)* revelar.

▷ *vi* **1** *(grow - person, body, nation, region, etc)* desarrollarse; *(- system)* perfeccionarse; *(feeling, interest)* aumentar, crecer. **2** *(evolve - emotion)* convertirse (**into**, en), transformarse (**into**, en), evolucionar; *(plot, novel)* desarrollarse. **3** *(appear - problem, complication, symptom)* aparecer, surgir; *(situation, crisis)* producirse. **4** *(of film, photograph)* salir.

developer [dɪ'veləpəʳ] *n* **1** *(of land, property - company)* promotora inmobiliaria, empresa constructora; *(- person)* constructor,-ra. **2** *(for photographs)* revelador *m*.

developing [dɪ'veləpɪŋ] *adj (country)* en vías de desarrollo.

development [dɪ'veləpmənt] *n* **1** *(growth, formation - gen)* desarrollo; *(- of skill, system)* perfección *f*; *(fostering)* fomento, promoción *f*; *(growth, expansion - of firm, industry, country)* desarrollo; *(evolution)* evolución *f*. **2** *(elaboration - of idea, argument, play)* desarrollo, elaboración *f*; *(evolution - of situation, events)* desarrollo, evolución *f*. **3** *(invention - of product)* creación *f*. **4** *(event, incident)* acontecimiento, suceso; *(advance)* avance *m*, conquista. **5** *(of resources)* explotación *f*; *(of site, land, etc)* urbanización *f*.

developmental [dɪveləp'mentəl] *adj* del desarrollo.

deviance ['di:vɪəns] *n* desviación *f*.

deviant ['di:vɪənt] *adj* anormal.

▷ *n* pervertido,-a.

deviate ['di:vɪeɪt] *vi (from course)* desviarse (**from**, de); *(from norm)* apartarse (from de).

device [dɪ'vaɪs] *n* **1** *(object, equipment)* aparato, artefacto; *(mechanism)* mecanismo, dispositivo. **2** *(scheme, trick)* ardid *m*, estratagema. **3** *lit (method)* recurso. **4** *(on shield)* emblema *m*.

devil ['devᵊl] *n (Satan, evil spirit)* diablo, demonio.

devilry ['devᵊlrɪ] *n* diablura.

devious ['di:vɪəs] *adj* **1** *(of route, path, etc)* tortuoso,-a, sinuoso,-a. **2** *pej (cunning, dishonest - person)* taimado,-a, artero,-a, zorro,-a; *(- plan, method, scheme)* astuto,-a.

devise [dɪ'vaɪz] *vt (plan, scheme, system)* idear, concebir, crear; *(object, tool, machine)* inventar.

devoid [dɪ'vɔɪd] *adj* carente (**of**, de), desprovisto,-a (**of**, de).

devolution [di:və'lu:ʃᵊn] *n* **1** GB *traspaso de competencias del gobierno central a un gobierno regional.* **2** *(delegation)* delegación *f*, transferencia.

devolve [dɪ'vɒlv] *vi* **1** *(work, duties)* recaer (**on/upon**, sobre); *(power, responsibility)* pasar (**to**, a). **2** *(land, goods, property)* pasar (**to**, a).

▷ *vt (power, responsibility)* delegar, transferir (**to**, a).

devote [dɪ'vəʊt] *vt (time, effort)* dedicar, consagrar.

devoted [dɪ'vəʊtɪd] *adj (loyal - friend)* fiel (**to**, a), leal (**to**, a); *(- couple)* unido,-a; *(- follower, supporter)* ferviente; *(selfless)* abnegado,-a: **your devoted daughter** *tu hija que te quiere.*

devotion [dɪ'vəʊʃᵊn] *n* **1** *(loyalty)* lealtad *f*, fidelidad *f*; *(love)* cariño, afecto, amor *m*. **2** *(to work, research, cause)* dedicación *f*, entrega. **3** REL *(devoutness)* devoción *f*; *(prayer)* oración *f*, rezo.

devour [dɪ'vaʊəʳ] *vt* **1** *(food)* devorar, zampar. **2** *(book, etc)* devorar. **3** *(destroy - of fire)* devorar, destruir.

dew [dju:] *n* rocío.

dexterity [dek'sterɪtɪ] *n (manual)* destreza, habilidad *f*, maña; *(intellectual)* habilidad *f*.

diabetes [daɪə'bi:ti:z] *n* diabetes *f*.

▲ *pl* **diabetes**.

diabolical [daɪə'bɒlɪkᵊl] *adj* **1** *(evil)* diabólico,-a, satánico,-a. **2** GB *fam (extremely bad)* espantoso,-a.

diabolo [dɪ'æbələʊ] *n* diábolo, diávolo.

diacritic [daɪə'krɪtɪk] *adj* diacrítico,-a.

▷ *n* signo diacrítico.

diadem ['daɪədem] *n* diadema.

diaeresis [daɪ'erəsɪs] *n* diéresis *fpl*.

diagnose ['daɪəgnəʊz] *vt* **1** MED diagnosticar. **2** *(fault)* descubrir.

diagnosis [daɪəg'nəʊsɪs] *n* MED diagnóstico.

▲ *pl* **diagnoses** [daɪəg'nəʊsi:s].

diagonal [daɪ'ægənᵊl] *adj (line)* diagonal; *(path)* en diagonal.

▷ *n* diagonal *f*.

diagram ['daɪəgræm] *n (gen)* diagrama *m*; *(graph)* gráfico, gráfica; *(of process, system)* esquema *m*.

diagrammatic [daɪəgrə'mætɪk] *adj* esquemático,-a.

dialect ['daɪəlekt] *n* dialecto.

dial ['daɪəl] *n* dial.

▷ *vt* marcar.

dialling ['daɪəlɪŋ] ● **dialling code** prefijo.

dialogue ['daɪəlɒg] *n* **1** *(conversation)* diálogo. **2** *(communication, talks)* diálogo, negociaciones *fpl*. **3** *(discussion)* discusión *f*, debate *m*.

diameter [daɪ'æmɪtəʳ] *n* diámetro.

diametrically [daɪə'metrɪkəlɪ] *adv* diametralmente.

diamond ['daɪəmənd] *n* **1** *(stone)* diamante *m*, brillante *m*. **2** *(shape)* rombo. **3** *(in cards)* diamante *m*.

diaper ['daɪəpəʳ] *n* US pañal *m*.

diaphragm ['daɪəfræm] *n (gen)* diafragma *m*.

diarrhoea [daɪə'rɪə] *n* diarrea.

diary ['daɪərɪ] *n* **1** *(of thoughts, events, etc)* diario. **2** *(for appointments)* agenda.

▲ *pl* **diaries**.

diastole [daɪəs'təlr] *n* diástole.

diatribe ['daɪətraɪb] *n* diatriba, invectiva.

dice [daɪs] *n* dado.

▲ *pl* **dice**.

dichotomy [daɪ'kɒtəmɪ] *n* dicotomía.

▲ *pl* **dichotomies**.

dick[1] [dɪk] *n* **1** *sl (penis)* polla. **2** *sl (stupid man)* imbécil *m*, gilipollas *m*.

dick[2] [dɪk] *n* US *sl (detective)* sabueso.

dictate [*(vb)* dɪk'teɪt, *(n)* 'dɪkteɪt] *vt* **1** *(letter, etc)* dictar. **2** *(state, lay down - law, demands, trends)* ordenar; *(terms, conditions)* imponer. **3** *(determine, influence)* determinar, condicionar.

▷ *vi (read out)* dictar.

▷ *n* mandato.

dictation [dɪk'teɪʃᵊn] *n* **1** *(of letter, passage, etc)* dictado. **2** *(giving orders)* mandato.
dictator [dɪk'teɪtəʳ] *n* dictador,-ra.
dictatorship [dɪk'teɪtəʃɪp] *n* dictadura.
diction ['dɪkʃᵊn] *n* dicción *f*.
dictionary ['dɪkʃənᵊrɪ] *n* diccionario.
▲ *pl* **dictionaries.**
did [dɪd] *pt* ⟶ **do.**
didactic [dɪ'dæktɪk] *adj* didáctico,-a.
didn't [dɪdənt] *pt* ⟶ **do.**
die [daɪ] *vi* **1** *(person, animal, plant)* morir, morirse. **2** *fam fig (be overcome)* morirse. **3** *fig (love, tradition, custom)* morir; *(flame)* extinguirse, apagarse; *(engine)* apagarse, dejar de funcionar.
⊙ **to die away** *vi (noise)* desvanecerse, irse apagando; *(breeze)* amainar.
die-hard ['daɪhɑːd] *n* intransigente *mf*.
dieresis [daɪ'erəsɪs] *n* diéresis *fpl*.
diesel ['diːzᵊl] *n* **1** *(fuel)* gasóleo, gasoil *m*. **2** *(car)* coche *m* diesel.
diet ['daɪət] *n (food)* dieta (alimenticia), alimentación *f*. **2** *(restricted food)* régimen *m*, dieta.
▷ *adj (food)* de régimen, bajo,-a en calorías.
▷ *vi* estar a régimen, estar a dieta, hacer régimen.
dietary ['daɪətərɪ] *adj* alimenticio,-a.
differ ['dɪfəʳ] *vi* **1** *(be unlike)* ser distinto,-a (**from**, de), ser diferente (**from**, de), diferir (**from**, de). **2** *(disagree)* discrepar (**about/on**, en).
difference ['dɪfᵊrəns] *n* **1** *(dissimilarity)* diferencia. **2** *(disagreement)* desacuerdo, diferencia.
different ['dɪfᵊrənt] *adj* **1** *(unlike, not the same)* diferente (**from**, de), distinto,-a (**from**, de). **2** *(various, several)* distinto,-a, vario,-a. **3** *fam (unusual, original)* diferente, original.
differential [dɪfə'renʃᵊl] *adj* diferencial.
▷ *n* **1** FIN diferencial *m*. **2** [Also **differential gear.**] AUTO diferencial *m*.
differentiate [dɪfə'renʃɪeɪt] *vt* diferenciar (**from**, de), distinguir (**from**, de).
▷ *vi* distinguir (**between**, entre).
difficult ['dɪfɪkᵊlt] *adj (gen)* difícil.
difficulty ['dɪfɪkᵊltɪ] *n* **1** *(trouble)* dificultad *f*. **2** *(problem)* dificultad *f*, problema *m*.
▲ *pl* **difficulties.**
diffidence ['dɪfɪdəns] *n* falta de seguridad en sí mismo,-a, confianza en sí mismo,-a.
diffuse [*(adj)* dɪ'fjuːs, *(vb)* dɪ'fjuːz] *adj* **1** *(light, gas)* difuso,-a. **2** *pej (speech, style, writer)* prolijo,-a.
▷ *vt (light, heat, news)* difundir.
diffusion [dɪ'fjuːʒᵊn] *n* difusión *f*.
dig [dɪg] *n* **1** *(poke, prod)* codazo. **2** *fam (gibe)* pulla; *(hint)* indirecta. **3** *(by archaeologists)* excavación *f*.
▷ *vt (ground, garden)* cavar (en); *(by machine - tunnel, trench)* excavar; *(by hand - hole)* hacer, cavar; *(potatoes, etc)* sacar; *(site)* excavar.
▲ *pt & pp* **dug**, *ger* **digging.**
⊙ **to dig into** *vt insep* **1** *(investigate, examine)* investigar. **2** *(resources, savings, reserves)* echar mano de.
⊙ **to dig out** *vt sep (trapped person, car)* sacar, desenterrar.
digest [*(n)* 'daɪdʒest, *(vb)* dɪ'dʒest] *n (summary)* resumen *m*, compendio.
▷ *vt (food)* digerir; *(facts, information)* asimilar, digerir.
digestion [dɪ'dʒestʃᵊn] *n* digestión *f*.
digestive [daɪ'dʒestɪv] *adj* digestivo,-a.
digger ['dɪgəʳ] *n* **1** *(machine)* excavadora. **2** *(person)* excavador,-ra.
digit ['dɪdʒɪt] *n* **1** MATH dígito. **2** ANAT *(finger)* dedo; *(thumb)* pulgar *m*.
digital ['dɪdʒɪtəl] *adj* **1** *(watch, display, recording)* digital. **2** ANAT dactilar, digital.
dignify ['dɪgnɪfaɪ] *vt* **1** *(ennoble)* dignificar, ennoblecer; *(make respectable)* dar categoría a. **2** *(give important name to)* dar un nombre importante a.
▲ *pt & pp* **dignified**, *ger* **dignifying.**
dignitary ['dɪgnɪtərɪ] *n* dignatario,-a.
▲ *pl* **dignitaries.**
dignity ['dɪgnɪtɪ] *n* **1** *(seriousness, calmness - of person)* dignidad *f*; *(of occasion)* solemnidad *f*. **2** *(self-respect)* dignidad *f*, amor *m* propio. **3** *fml (high rank, title)* dignidad *f*.
digress [daɪ'gres] *vi* divagar.
dilapidated [dɪ'læpɪdeɪtɪd] *adj (furniture)* desvencijado,-a, en mal estado; *(building)* ruinoso,-a; *(car)* desvencijado,-a, destartalado,-a.
dilate [daɪ'leɪt] *vt* dilatar.
dilation [daɪ'leɪʃᵊn] *n* dilatación *f*.
dilatory ['dɪlətərɪ] *adj (causing delay)* dilatorio,-a; *(slow in acting)* tardío,-a.
dilemma [dɪ'lemə] *n* dilema *m*.
diligence ['dɪlɪdʒəns] *n* diligencia.
dill [dɪl] *n* eneldo.
dilute [daɪ'luːt] *vt* **1** *(liquid, concentrate)* diluir. **2** *fig (criticism, effect, influence)* atenuar, suavizar.
▷ *adj* diluido,-a.
dilution [daɪ'luːʃᵊn] *n* **1** dilución *f*. **2** *fig* atenuación *f*.
dim [dɪm] *adj* **1** *(light)* débil, tenue; *(room, corridor, corner)* oscuro,-a, poco iluminado,-a. **2** *fam (person)* tonto,-a, corto,-a (de luces). **3** *(prospects, prospectives)* nada halagüeño,-a, nada prometedor,-ra, sombrío,-a.
▲ *comp* **dimmer**, *superl* **dimmest.**
▷ *vt (light)* atenuar, bajar; *(eyes)* nublar, empañar; *(memory)* borrar, ir borrando, difuminar.
▲ *pt & pp* **dimmed**, *ger* **dimming.**
dime [daɪm] *n* US moneda de diez centavos.
dimension [dɪ'menʃᵊn] *n* dimensión *f*.
▷ *n pl* **dimensions** dimensiones *fpl*.
diminish [dɪ'mɪnɪʃ] *vt* **1** *(reduce - size, cost)* disminuir, reducir; *(- enthusiasm)* disminuir, apagar; *(- resolve)* disminuir; *(- horror)* hacer perder. **2** *(belittle - person)* denigrar, rebajar; *(- achievements, work)* menospreciar.
diminution [dɪmɪ'njuːʃᵊn] *n* disminución *f*, reducción *f*.
diminutive [dɪ'mɪnjətɪv] *adj* **1** diminuto,-a. **2** LING diminutivo,-a.
▷ *n* LING diminutivo.
dimmer ['dɪməʳ] [Also **dimmer switch.**] *n* regulador *m* de intensidad (de la luz).
dimple ['dɪmpᵊl] *n* hoyuelo.
din [dɪn] *n (of voices)* barullo, bulla, alboroto; *(of traffic)* estruendo, ruido.
dine [daɪn] *vi fml (gen)* comer (**on**, -); *(in evening)* cenar (**on**, -).
⊙ **to dine out** *vi* cenar fuera.

diner ['daɪnəʳ] *n* 1 *(person)* comensal *mf*. 2 US restaurante *m* barato.

dinghy ['dɪŋgɪ] *n* bote *m*.

▲ *pl* dinghies.

dingy ['dɪndʒɪ] *adj (dark, depressing - room, house, street)* lúgubre, sombrío,-a, deprimente, oscuro,-a, sórdido,-a; *(drab - colour, wall, curtains)* deslucido,-a; *(dirty)* sucio,-a.

▲ *comp* dingier, *superl* dingiest.

dining car ['daɪnɪŋkɑːʳ] *n* vagón *m* restaurante.

dining room ['daɪnɪŋruːm] *n* comedor *m*.

dinner ['dɪnəʳ] *n (at midday)* comida; *(in evening)* cena. ■ **to have dinner** cenar. ■ **dinner jacket** esmoquin *m*.

dinosaur ['daɪnəsɔːʳ] *n* dinosaurio.

diocese ['daɪəsɪs] *n* diócesis *f*.

dioxide [daɪ'ɒksaɪd] *n* dióxido, bióxido.

dip [dɪp] *n* 1 *(downward slope)* declive *m*, pendiente *f*; *(in ground)* hondonada; *(drop - in prices, temperature, sales, production, profits)* caída, descenso. 2 *fam (quick swim)* chapuzón *m*. 3 *(for sheep)* baño desinfectante; *(for cleaning silver)* baño. 3 CULIN *(sauce)* salsa.

▷ *vt* 1 *(put into liquid - pen, brush, bread)* mojar; *(- hand, spoon)* meter. 2 *(sheep)* desinfectar. 3 *(lower - head)* agachar, bajar.

▷ *vi (slope down)* descender, bajar; *(move down - bird, plane)* bajar en picado; *(- sun)* desaparecer; *(drop - sales, prices, etc)* bajar.

▲ *pt & pp* dipped, *ger* dipping.

diphthong ['dɪfθɒŋ] *n* LING diptongo.

diploma [dɪ'pləʊmə] *n* diploma *m*.

diplomacy [dɪ'pləʊməsɪ] *n* diplomacia.

diplomat ['dɪpləmæt] *n* 1 *(ambassador, etc)* diplomático,-a. 2 *(tactful person)* persona diplomática.

diplomatic [dɪplə'mætɪk] *adj* diplomático,-a.

dipstick ['dɪpstɪk] *n* AUTO varilla del aceite.

dire ['daɪəʳ] *adj* 1 *(desperate, extreme)* extremo,-a, urgente. 2 *(serious, ominous)* serio,-a, grave. 3 *(terrible, dreadful)* terrible, espantoso,-a, atroz.

direct [dɪ'rekt, daɪ'rekt] *adj* 1 *(gen)* directo,-a. 2 *(exact, complete)* exacto,-a. 3 *(straightforward - person, manner)* sincero,-a; *(- answer)* claro,-a.

▷ *adv (go, write, phone)* directamente; *(broadcast)* en directo.

▷ *vt* 1 *(show the way)* indicar el camino a. 2 *(letter, parcel)* mandar, dirigir. 3 *(attention, remark)* dirigir. 4 *(traffic, organization, inquiry)* dirigir. 5 *(play, actors)* dirigir. 6 *fml (order, command)* ordenar.

direction [dɪ'rekʃᵊn, daɪ'rekʃᵊn] *n* 1 *(way, course)* dirección *f*. 2 *(control, management)* dirección *f*.

▷ *n pl* **directions** instrucciones *f pl* de uso.

directive [dɪ'rektɪv] *adj* directiva, directriz *f*.

directly [dɪ'rektlɪ, daɪ'rektlɪ] *adv* 1 *(go, fly, drive)* directamente, directo. 2 *(exactly - opposite, above)* justo. 3 *(descend)* directamente, por línea directa. 4 *(speak)* francamente. 5 *(very soon, shortly)* en seguida, dentro de poco; *(immediately, at once)* inmediatamente.

director [dɪ'rektəʳ, daɪ'rektəʳ] *n (gen)* director,-ra; *(of company)* director,-ra, directivo,-a.

directory [dɪ'rektᵊrɪ, daɪ'rektᵊrɪ] *n (telephone)* guía telefónica, listín *m* (de teléfonos); *(book, lost, index)* directorio, guía.

▷ *n* [Also **street directory**.] callejero.

▲ *pl* directories.

dirt [dɜːt] *n* 1 *(dirtiness)* suciedad *f*; *(filth, grime)* mugre *f*. 2 *(earth)* tierra. 4 *fam (scandal, gossip)* chismes *mpl*, trapos *mpl* sucios. 5 *fam (obscene thought, talk)* porquerías *fpl*, guarradas *fpl*.

dirty ['dɜːtɪ] *adj* 1 *(not clean, soiled)* sucio,-a; *(stained)* manchado,-a. 2 *(obscene - magazine, film)* porno; *(story, book)* indecente, cochino,-a, guarro,-a; *(- joke)* verde; *(- mind, sense of humour)* pervertido,-a. ● **dirty word** palabrota.

▲ *comp* dirtier, *superl* dirtiest.

▷ *vt* ensuciar.

disability [dɪsə'bɪlɪtɪ] *n (state)* invalidez *f*, discapacidad *f*, incapacidad *f*, minusvalía; *(handicap)* desventaja, hándicap *m*.

▲ *pl* disabilities.

disabled [dɪs'eɪbᵊld] *adj* minusválido,-a: **mentally disabled people** *los disminuidos psíquicos*.

▷ *n pl* **the disabled** los minusválidos. ● **disabled access** acceso para minusválidos.

disadvantage [dɪsəd'vɑːntɪdʒ] *n (drawback)* desventaja; *(obstacle)* inconveniente *m*.

disadvantaged [dɪsəd'vɑːntɪdʒd] *adj* desfavorecido,-a, desheredado,-a, discriminado,-a.

▷ *n pl* **the disadvantaged** los desfavorecidos *mpl*.

disagree [dɪsə'griː] *vi* 1 *(not agree)* no estar de acuerdo (**on**, en), (**with**, con), disentir (**with**, de), discrepar (**with**, de), (**on**, en). 2 *(food)* sentar mal (**with**, a); *(weather)* no convenir (**with**, a).

disagreeable [dɪsə'grɪəbᵊl] *adj* desagradable.

disagreement [dɪsə'griːmənt] *n* 1 *(difference of opinion)* desacuerdo, disconformidad *f*; *(argument)* discusión *f*, riña, altercado. 2 *(lack of similarity)* discrepancia.

disallow [dɪsə'laʊ] *vt (objection, claim, evidence)* denegar, rechazar, desestimar; *(goal)* anular.

disappear [dɪsə'pɪəʳ] *vi (gen)* desaparecer; *(worries, fears)* desvanecerse.

disappearance [dɪsə'pɪərəns] *n* desaparición *f*.

disappoint [dɪsə'pɔɪnt] *vt* decepcionar, desilusionar.

disappointment [dɪsə'pɔɪntmənt] *n* desilusión *f*, decepción *f*.

disapprove [dɪsə'pruːv] *vt* 1 desaprobar (**of**, -). 2 US *(legislation, plan, etc)* rechazar, no aprobar.

disarm [dɪs'ɑːm] *vt* 1 *(gen)* desarmar; *(bomb)* desactivar.

disarmament [dɪs'ɑːməmənt] *n* desarme *m*.

disarray[dɪsə'reɪ] *n* desorganización, desorden, caos *m*.

disaster [dɪ'zɑːstəʳ] *n* desastre *m*, catástrofe *f*.

disband [dɪs'bænd] *vt (group, organization)* disolver, deshacer; *(army)* licenciar.

disbelief [dɪsbɪ'liːf] *n* incredulidad *f*.

disc [dɪsk] *n (gen)* disco. ● **disc jockey** pinchadiscos *m sing*.

discard [dɪs'kɑːd] *vt* desechar, deshacerse de.

discern [dɪ'sɜːn] *vt* percibir, distinguir.

discernment [dɪ'sɜːnmənt] *n* (buen) criterio, discernimiento.

discharge [*(n)* 'dɪstʃɑ:dʒ, *(vb)* dɪs'tʃɑ:dʒ] *n* **1** descarga. **2** *(of prisoner)* liberación *f*, puesta en libertad; *(of patient)* alta. **3** *(of worker)* despido.
▷ *vt* **1** *(give, send out - sewage, waste, oil)* verter; *(smoke, fumes)* despedir; *(- electric current)* descargar. **2** *(prisoner)* liberar, soltar, poner en libertad; *(patient)* dar de alta. **3** *(dismiss)* despedir.
disciple [dɪ'saɪpəl] *n* **1** REL discípulo,-a. **2** *(follower)* seguidor,-ra, discípulo,-a.
disciplinary ['dɪsɪplɪnərɪ] *adj* disciplinario,-a.
discipline ['dɪsɪplɪn] *n* **1** *(behaviour)* disciplina. **2** *(punishment)* castigo.
disclaim [dɪs'kleɪm] *vt (knowledge, responsibility)* negar.
disclose [dɪs'kləʊz] *vt* **1** *(make known)* revelar, dar a conocer. **2** *(show)* mostrar, dejar ver.
disco ['dɪskəʊ] *n fam* disco *f*, discoteca.
▲ *pl* discos.
discoloration [dɪskʌlə'reɪʃən] *n (process, fading)* decoloración *f*; *(stain)* mancha.
discomfiture [dɪs'kʌmfɪtʃər] *n fml* desconcierto, turbación *f*.
discomfort [dɪs'kʌmfət] *n* **1** incomodidad *f*. **2** inquietud *f*, desasosiego.
disconcert [dɪskən'sɜ:t] *vt* desconcertar.
disconnect [dɪskə'nekt] *vt (from mains)* desconectar; *(gas, electricity, etc)* cortar.
disconnection [dɪskə'nekʃən] *n* desconexión *f*.
disconsolate [dɪs'kɒnsələt] *adj* desconsolado,-a.
discontent [dɪskən'tent] *n* descontento.
discontinue [dɪskən'tɪnju:] *vt (service)* suspender, interrumpir; *(model)* dejar de fabricar.
discord ['dɪskɔ:d] *n (disagreement)* discordia.
discotheque ['dɪskətek] *n fml* discoteca.
discount [*(n)* 'dɪskaʊnt, *(vb)* dɪs'kaʊnt] *n* descuento.
▷ *vt (goods)* rebajar; *(price)* reducir; *(amount, bill of exchange)* descontar.
discourage [dɪs'kʌrɪdʒ] *vt* **1** *(dishearten)* desanimar, desalentar. **2** *(dissuade)* disuadir (from, de), hacer desistir (from, de).
discouragement [dɪs'kʌrɪdʒmənt] *n (dejection)* desaliento, desánimo.
discourse ['dɪskɔ:s] *n* **1** *fml (spoken - speech)* discurso; *(- discussion)* discusión *f*, debate *m*; *(written)* disertación *f*. **2** LING discurso.
▷ *vt* disertar (on/upon, sobre).
discover [dɪ'skʌvər] *vt (find - gen)* descubrir; *(mistake, loss, fact)* descubrir, darse cuenta de; *(missing object, person)* encontrar, hallar.
discoverer [dɪ'skʌvərər] *n* descubridor,-ra.
discovery [dɪ'skʌvərɪ] *n* descubrimiento.
▲ *pl* discoveries.
discredit [dɪs'kredɪt] *n (dishonour, disgrace)* descrédito.
discreet [dɪ'skri:t] *adj (gen)* discreto,-a; *(distance)* prudencial.
discrepancy [dɪ'skrepənsɪ] *n* discrepancia.
▲ *pl* discrepancies.
discrete [dɪs'kri:t] *adj* diferenciado,-a, distinto,-a.
discretion [dɪ'skreʃən] *n* **1** *(quality of being discreet)* discreción *f*; *(prudence)* prudencia. **2** *(judgement)* criterio, juicio.
discriminate [dɪ'skrɪmɪneɪt] *vi (treat differently)* discriminar (against, a), (between, entre).
▷ *vt (see a difference)* distinguir (from, de), discriminar.
discriminating [dɪ'skrɪmɪneɪtɪŋ] *adj (person)* entendido,-a, exigente; *(judgement)* sagaz.
discrimination [dɪskrɪmɪ'neɪʃən] *n* **1** *(bias)* discriminación *f*. **2** *(distinction)* diferenciación *f*, distinción *f*. **3** *(judgement)* discernimiento, criterio.
discus ['dɪskəs] *n (object)* disco.
▷ *n* the discus *(event, sport)* el lanzamiento de disco.
▲ *pl* discuses o disci ['dɪskaɪ].
discuss [dɪ'skʌs] *vt (talk about - person)* hablar de; *(- subject, topic)* hablar de, tratar; *(- plan, problem)* discutir.
discussion [dɪ'skʌʃən] *n (gen)* discusión *f*, debate *m*.
disdain [dɪs'deɪn] *n* desdén *m*, desprecio, menosprecio.
▷ *vt* desdeñar, despreciar, menospreciar.
disease [dɪ'zi:z] *n (illness)* enfermedad *f*.
diseased [dɪ'zi:zd] *adj* **1** MED *(part of body)* afectado,-a; *(plant, animal)* enfermo,-a. **2** *fig (imagination, mind)* enfermizo,-a, morboso,-a; *(society)* enfermo,-a.
disembark [dɪsɪm'bɑ:k] *vt* desembarcar.
disembarkation [dɪsɪmbɑ:'keɪʃən] *n (of people)* desembarco; *(of goods)* desembarque *m*.
disembodied [dɪsɪm'bɒdɪd] *adj* incorpóreo,-a.
disenchanted [dɪsɪn'tʃɑ:ntɪd] *adj* desencantado,-a, desilusionado,-a.
disenchantment [dɪsɪn'tʃɑ:ntmənt] *n* desencanto, desilusión *f*.
disenfranchise [dɪsɪn'fræntʃaɪz] *vt* privar del derecho al voto.
disengage [dɪsɪn'geɪdʒ] *vt* **1** *(free - gen)* soltar (from, de); *(gears, mechanism)* desconectar. **2** MIL *(troops)* retirar (from, de).
disentail [dɪsen'teɪl] *vt* desamortizar.
disentangle [dɪsɪn'tæŋgəl] *vt (unravel)* desenredar, desenmarañar.
disfavor [dɪs'feɪvər] *n* US → **disfavour**.
disfavour [dɪs'feɪvər] *n* desaprobación *f*.
disfigure [dɪs'fɪgər] *vt (face, person)* desfigurar; *(building, town, landscape)* afear, estropear.
disgorge [dɪs'gɔ:dʒ] *vt* **1** *(liquid, waste)* verter; *(smoke, fumes)* emitir; *(people)* echar. **2** *(vomit)* devolver. **3** *fam (give up)* entregar.
▷ *vi* **1** *(of river)* desembocar. **2** *fig (crowds)* salir.
disgrace [dɪs'greɪs] *n* **1** *(loss of favour)* desgracia; *(loss of honour)* deshonra, deshonor *m*. **2** *(shame)* escándalo, vergüenza.
▷ *vt* **1** *(bring shame on)* deshonrar. **2** *(discredit)* desacreditar.
disgraceful [dɪs'greɪsfʊl] *adj* vergonzoso,-a: **it's disgraceful** *es vergonzoso, es una vergüenza.*
disgruntled [dɪs'grʌntəld] *adj* contrariado,-a disgustado,-a.
disguise [dɪs'gaɪz] *n* disfraz *m*. ● **in disguise** disfrazado,-a
▷ *vt (person)* disfrazar (as, de); *(voice, handwriting)* cambiar, disimular.
disgust [dɪs'gʌst] *n (revulsion)* asco, repugnancia *(strong disapproval)* indignación *f*.
▷ *vt (revolt)* repugnar, dar asco a; *(disapprove)* indignar.

disgusting [dɪs'gʌstɪŋ] *adj* asqueroso,-a, repugnante.
dish [dɪʃ] *n* **1** *(plate)* plato; *(for serving)* fuente *f*. **2** CULIN *(food)* plato. **3** TV antena parabólica. ● **to do the dishes** lavar los platos.
▷ *n pl* **dishes** *(crockery)* platos *mpl*, vajilla *f sing*.
dishcloth ['dɪʃklɒθ] *n* trapo, bayeta, paño.
dishearten [dɪs'hɑ:tᵊn] *vt* descorazonar, desanimar, desalentar.
dishevel [dɪ'ʃevᵊl] *vt* despeinar.
▲ *pt & pp* **dishevelled** (US **disheveled**), *ger* **dishevelling** (US **disheveling**).
dishonest [dɪs'ɒnɪst] *adj (person, answer)* deshonesto,-a, poco honrado,-a; *(means, etc)* fraudulento,-a.
dishonour [dɪs'ɒnəʳ] *n* deshonra, deshonor *m*.
▷ *vt* **1** *(family, country, team, etc)* deshonrar. **2** *(renege on - agreement)* no respetar; *(- promise)* no cumplir, faltar a; *(- cheque, debt)* no pagar.
dishonorable [dɪs'ɒnərəbᵊl] *adj* US → **dishonourable**.
dishonourable [dɪs'ɒnərəbᵊl] *adj* deshonroso,-a.
dishtowel ['dɪʃtaʊəl] *n* US paño de cocina.
dishwasher ['dɪʃwɒʃəʳ] *n (machine)* lavaplatos *m*, lavavajillas *m*; *(person)* lavaplatos *mf*.
dishwater ['dɪʃwɔ:təʳ] *n* aguachirle *m*.
dishy ['dɪʃɪ] *adj* GB *fam* guapo,-a.
▲ *comp* **dishier**, *superl* **dishiest**.
disillusion [dɪsɪ'lu:ʒᵊn] *vt* desilusionar.
disincentive [dɪsɪn'sentɪv] *n* freno.
disinclination [dɪsɪnklɪ'neɪʃᵊn] *n* aversión *f*, desgana.
disinfect [dɪsɪn'fekt] *vt* desinfectar.
disinfection [dɪsɪn'fekʃᵊn] *n* desinfección *f*.
disinformation [dɪsɪnfə'meɪʃᵊn] *n* desinformación *f*.
disinherit [dɪsɪn'herɪt] *vt* desheredar.
disintegration [dɪsɪntɪ'greɪʃᵊn] *n* desintegración *f*.
disinter [dɪsɪn'tɜ:ʳ] *vt fml* desenterrar.
▲ *pt & pp* **disinterred**, *ger* **disinterring**.
disk [dɪsk] *n (gen)* disco. ● **disk drive** COMPUT disquetera.
diskette [dɪs'ket] *n* COMPUT disquete *m*.
dislike [dɪs'laɪk] *n* aversión *f*, antipatía.
dislocation [dɪslə'keɪʃᵊn] *n* **1** MED dislocación *f*. **2** *fig* trastorno.
dislodge [dɪs'lɒdʒ] *vt* **1** *(object)* sacar. **2** *(person)* desalojar (**from**, de), desplazar (**from**, de).
disloyal [dɪs'lɔɪəl] *adj* desleal (**to**, a/con).
dismal ['dɪzməl] *adj* sombrío,-a, deprimente, lúgubre.
dismantle [dɪs'mæntᵊl] *vt (take apart - machinery)* desmontar; *(- furniture)* desarmar.
dismay [dɪs'meɪ] *n* consternación *f*.
▷ *vt* consternar.
dismember [dɪs'membəʳ] *vt* desmembrar.
dismiss [dɪs'mɪs] *vt* **1** descartar, desechar. **2** *(sack)* despedir.
dismissal [dɪs'mɪsᵊl] *n* **1** descarte *m*, abandono. **2** *(sacking - of employee)* despido; *(- of official, minister)* destitución *f*.
dismissive [dɪs'mɪsɪv] *adj* desdeñoso,-a.
dismount [dɪs'maʊnt] *vi* desmontarse (**from**, de), apearse (**from**, de), bajarse (**from**, de).
disobedience [dɪsə'bi:dɪəns] *n* desobediencia.
disobedient [dɪsə'bi:dɪənt] *adj* desobediente.
disobey [dɪsə'beɪ] *vt* desobedecer.
disobliging [dɪsə'blaɪdʒɪŋ] *adj fml* poco servicial.
disorder [dɪs'ɔ:dəʳ] *n* desorden *m*.
disordered [dɪs'ɔ:dəd] *adj* desordenado,-a.
disorganisation [dɪsɔ:gənaɪ'zeɪʃᵊn] *n* → **disorganization**.
disorganise [dɪs'ɔ:gənaɪz] *vt* → **disorganize**.
disorganised [dɪs'ɔ:gənaɪzd] *adj* → **disorganized**.
disorganization [dɪsɔ:gənaɪ'zeɪʃᵊn] *n* desorganización *f*.
disorganize [dɪs'ɔ:gənaɪz] *vt* desorganizar.
disorganized [dɪs'ɔ:gənaɪzd] *adj* desorganizado,-a.
disorient [dɪs'ɔ:rɪənt] *vt* desorientar.
disorientate [dɪs'ɔ:rɪənteɪt] *vt* desorientar.
disorientation [dɪsɔ:rɪən'teɪʃᵊn] *n* desorientación *f*.
disown [dɪs'əʊn] *vt* renegar de, repudiar.
disparage [dɪ'spærɪdʒ] *vt* menospreciar, despreciar.
disparagement [dɪs'pærədʒmənt] *n* denigración *f*.
disparaging [dɪ'spærɪdʒɪŋ] *adj* despectivo,-a.
disparagingly [dɪs'pærədʒɪŋlɪ] *adv* en tono despectivo, despectivamente.
disparate ['dɪspərɪt] *adj fml* dispar.
disparity [dɪ'spærɪtɪ] *n fml (inequality)* disparidad *f*; *(difference)* discrepancia.
▲ *pl* **disparities**.
dispassionate [dɪs'pæʃᵊnət] *adj* imparcial.
dispassionately [dɪs'pæʃᵊnətlɪ] *adv* desapasionadamente.
dispatch [dɪ'spætʃ] *n* **1** mensaje, despacho. **2** *(journalist's report)* noticia, reportaje *m*.
▷ *vt* **1** *(send)* enviar, despachar, expedir. **2** *(finish quickly)* despachar.
dispel [dɪ'spel] *vt* disipar.
▲ *pt & pp* **dispelled**, *ger* **dispelling**.
dispensable [dɪ'spensəbəl] *adj* prescindible.
dispensary [dɪ'spensərɪ] *n (in hospital)* dispensario; *(in school)* enfermeria.
▲ *pl* **dispensaries**.
dispensation [dɪspen'seɪʃᵊn] *n* **1** *fml (act of handing out)* administración *f*. **2** *(exemption, permission)* exención *f*, dispensa.
dispense [dɪ'spens] *vt* **1** *(distribute)* distribuir, repartir. **2** JUR *(justice)* administrar. **3** *fml (public service)* suministrar, administrar.
⊙ **to dispense with** *vt insep* prescindir de, pasar sin.
dispenser [dɪ'spensəʳ] *n* **1** máquina expendedora. **2** farmacéutico,-a.
dispensing chemist [dɪspensɪŋ'kemɪst] *adj* GB farmacéutico,-a.
dispersal [dɪ'spɜ:sᵊl] *n* dispersión *f*.
disperse [dɪ'spɜ:s] *vt* dispersar.
dispersed [dɪs'pɜ:st] *adj* disperso,-a.
dispirited [dɪ'spɪrɪtɪd] *adj* abatido,-a, desanimado,-a.
displace [dɪs'pleɪs] *vt* **1** *(gen)* desplazar; *(bone)* dislocar. **2** *(replace)* sustituir, reemplazar.
displacement [dɪs'pleɪsmənt] *n* **1** desplazamiento. **2** sustitución *f*, reemplazo.
display [dɪ'spleɪ] *n* **1** exposición *f*, muestra. **2** COMPUT visualización *f*.
▷ *vt* **1** exhibir, exponer. **2** COMPUT visualizar.

displease [dɪs'pliːz] *vt fml* disgustar.
displeasure [dɪs'pleʒəʳ] *n* disgusto.
disport [dɪ'spɔːθ] *vt* **to disport os** entretenerse, divertirse.
disposable [dɪ'spəʊzəbᵊl] *adj* **1** desechable, de usar y tirar. **2** disponible.
disposal [dɪ'spəʊzᵊl] *n* **1** eliminación *f*. **4** disponibilidad *f*.
dispose [dɪ'spəʊz] *vt* **1** disponer, colocar. **2** *fml* predisponer (**to/towards**, hacia).
⊙ **to dispose of** *vt insep* **1** tirar, deshacerse de, liquidar.
disposed [dɪ'spəʊzd] *adj* **1** dispuesto,-a (**to**, a). **2** propenso,-a (**to**, a).
disposition [dɪspə'zɪʃᵊn] *n* **1** *fml* carácter *m*. **2** disposición *f*.
dispossess [dɪspə'zes] *vt* desposeer, despojar.
dispossession [dɪspə'zeʃᵊn] *n* desposeimiento.
disproportion [dɪsprə'pɔːsən] *n* desproporción *f*, desmesura.
disproportionate [dɪsprə'pɔːʃᵊnət] *adj* desproporcionado,-a (**to**, a).
disproportionately [dɪsprə'pɔːʃᵊnətlɪ] *adv* desproporcionadamente.
disprove [dɪs'pruːv] *vt (theory)* refutar, rebatir.
disputable [dɪ'spjuːtəbəl] *adj* discutible.
dispute [*(n)* 'dɪspjuːt, *(vb)* dɪ'spjuːt] *n* **1** discusión *f*.
▷ *vi* discutir.
disqualification [dɪskwɒlɪfɪ'keɪʃᵊn] *n* descalificación *f*; inhabilitación *f*.
disqualify [dɪs'kwɒlɪfaɪ] *vt* descalificar; inhabilitar, incapacitar.
▲ *pt & pp* **disqualified**, *ger* **disqualifying**.
disquiet [dɪs'kwaɪət] *n* inquietud *f*.
▷ *vt fml* inquietar.
disquieting [dɪs'kwaɪətɪŋ] *adj* preocupante.
disquisition [dɪskwɪ'zɪʃᵊn] *n fml* disquisición *f* (**on**, sobre/acerca de).
disregard [dɪsrɪ'gɑːd] *n* indiferencia (**for**, hacia); despreocupación *f*.
▷ *vt (danger, difficulty)* ignorar, despreciar.
disrepair [dɪsrɪ'peəʳ] *n* mal estado.
disreputable [dɪs'repjətəbᵊl] *adj (person, place)* de mala fama.
disrepute [dɪsrɪ'pjuːt] *n* mala reputación *f*.
disrespect [dɪsrɪ'spekt] *n* falta de respeto.
disrespectful [dɪsrɪ'spektfʊl] *adj* irrespetuoso,-a; irreverente.
disrobe [dɪs'rəʊb] *vi* desnudarse.
disrupt [dɪs'rʌpt] *vt* interrumpir, perturbar el desarrollo de.
disruption [dɪs'rʌpʃᵊn] *n (of meeting)* interrupción *f*; *(of traffic)* problemas *mpl*.
disruptive [dɪs'rʌptɪv] *adj* perjudicial, nocivo,-a; perturbador,-ra.
dissatisfaction [dɪssætɪs'fækʃᵊn] *n* insatisfacción *f*, descontento.
dissatisfied [dɪs'sætɪsfaɪd] *adj* insatisfecho,-a, descontento,-a.
dissect [dɪ'sekt, daɪ'sekt] *vt* disecar, diseccionar.
dissemble [dɪ'sembəl] *vt fml* disimular.
▷ *vi fml* fingir.
disseminate [dɪ'semɪneɪt] *vt fml* divulgar, difundir, diseminar.
dissemination [dɪsemɪ'neɪʃᵊn] *n fml* diseminación *f*, difusión *f*.
dissension [dɪ'senʃᵊn] *n* disensión *f*, desacuerdo.
dissent [dɪ'sent] *n* desacuerdo, disconformidad *f*.
▷ *vi* disentir, discrepar.
dissenter [dɪ'sentəʳ] *n* disidente *mf*.
dissenting [dɪ'sentɪŋ] *adj* discrepante.
dissertation [dɪsə'teɪʃᵊn] *n* **1** *(formal discourse)* disertación *f*. **2** EDUC *(for lower degree, master's)* tesina; *(for PhD)* tesis *f* (doctoral).
disservice [dɪs'sɜːvɪs] *n* perjuicio.
dissidence ['dɪsɪdᵊns] *n* disidencia.
dissident ['dɪsɪdənt] *adj* disidente.
▷ *n* disidente *mf*.
dissimilar [dɪ'sɪmɪləʳ] *adj* diferente (**to**, de), distinto,-a (**to**, de/a).
dissimilarity [dɪsɪmɪ'lærɪtɪ] *n* diferencia.
dissimulate [dɪ'sɪmjəleɪt] *vt fml* disimular, ocultar, encubrir.
▷ *vi fml* disimular.
dissimulation [dɪsɪmjə'leɪʃᵊn] *n fml* disimulo, disimulación *f*.
dissipate ['dɪsɪpeɪt] *vt* dispersar, difundir.
▷ *vi* disiparse, desvanecerse.
dissipated ['dɪsɪpeɪtɪd] *adj* disoluto,-a, disipado,-a.
dissociate [dɪ'səʊʃɪeɪt] *vt (separate)* disociar (**from** de), separar (**from**, de).
dissociation [dɪsəʊʃɪ'eɪʃᵊn] *n* disociación *f*.
dissoluble [dɪ'sɒljəbəl] *adj* disoluble.
dissolute ['dɪsəluːt] *adj* disoluto,-a.
dissolution [dɪsə'luːʃᵊn] *n (gen)* disolución *f*.
dissolve [dɪ'zɒlv] *vt* disolver.
dissuade [dɪ'sweɪd] *vt* disuadir (**from**, de).
dissuasion [dɪ'sweɪʒᵊn] *n* disuasión *f*.
dissuasive [dɪ'sweɪsɪv] *adj* disuasorio,-a.
distance ['dɪstəns] *n (gen)* distancia.
▷ *vt* distanciar.
distant ['dɪstənt] *adj* lejano,-a, distante.
distaste [dɪs'teɪst] *n* aversión *f*, desagrado.
distasteful [dɪs'teɪstfʊl] *adj (idea, task)* desagradable; *(joke, remark)* de mal gusto.
distemper[1] [dɪs'tempəʳ] *n* ART *(paint)* temple *m* *(method)* pintura al temple.
▷ *vt* pintar al temple.
distemper[2] [dɪs'tempəʳ] *n (disease)* moquillo.
distend [dɪ'stend] *vt* dilatar, hinchar.
▷ *vi* dilatarse, hincharse.
distil [dɪs'tɪl] *vt* destilar.
▲ *pt & pp* **distilled**, *ger* **distilling**.
distill [dɪs'tɪl] *vt* US ⟶ **distil**.
distillation [dɪstɪ'leɪʃᵊn] *n* destilación *f*.
distiller [dɪs'tɪləʳ] *n* destilador,-ra.
distillery [dɪ'stɪlərɪ] *n* destilería.
▲ *pl* **distilleries**.
distinct [dɪ'stɪŋkt] *adj* distinto,-a (**from**, a), diferente (**from**, de).
distinction [dɪ'stɪŋkʃᵊn] *n* **1** diferencia, distinción *f* **2** GB ≈ matrícula de honor.
distinctive [dɪ'stɪŋktɪv] *adj* distintivo,-a, característico,-a; personal, inconfundible.

distinctly [dɪ'stɪŋktlɪ] *adv* con claridad.
distinguish [dɪ'stɪŋgwɪʃ] *vt* distinguir.
▷ *vi* distinguir (**between**, entre).
distinguishable [dɪ'stɪŋgwɪʃəbəl] *adj* distinguible.
distinguished [dɪ'stɪŋgwɪʃt] *adj* distinguido,-a.
distinguishing [dɪ'stɪŋgwɪʃɪŋ] *adj* distintivo,-a, característico,-a.
distort [dɪ'stɔ:t] *vt* deformar.
distortion [dɪ'stɔ:ʃᵊn] *n* deformación *f*.
distract [dɪ'strækt] *vt* distraer (**from**, de).
distracted [dɪ'stræktɪd] *adj* distraído,-a.
distracting [dɪ'stræktɪŋ] *adj (noise)* molesto,-a; *(presence)* que distrae.
distraction [dɪ'strækʃᵊn] *n* distracción *f*. **2** desconsuelo, aflicción *f*.
distraught [dɪ'strɔ:t] *adj* afligido,-a.
distress [dɪ'stres] *n* **1** *(mental)* aflicción *f*, angustia; *(physical)* dolor *m*; *(exhaustion)* agotamiento. **2** penuria. **3** peligro. ● **distress call** señal de socorro.
▷ *vt (upset)* afligir; *(grieve)* consternar.
distressed [dɪ'strest] *adj* consternado,-a.
distressing [dɪ'stresɪŋ] *adj* penoso,-a, angustioso,-a.
distribute [dɪ'strɪbju:t] *vt* distribuir, repartir.
distribution [dɪstrɪ'bju:ʃᵊn] *n* distribución *f*, reparto.
distributor [dɪ'strɪbjətəʳ] *n* distribuidor,-ra.
district ['dɪstrɪkt] *n (of town, city)* distrito, barrio; *(of country)* región *f*, zona.
distrust [dɪs'trʌst] *n* desconfianza, recelo.
▷ *vt* desconfiar de, no fiarse de.
distrustful [dɪ'stʌstfʊl] *adj* desconfiado,-a.
disturb [dɪ'stɜ:b] *vt* molestar.
disturbed [dɪ'stɜ:bd] *adj* perturbado,-a.
disturbing [dɪ'stɜ:bɪŋ] *adj* inquietante.
disunite [dɪsju:'naɪt] *vt* desunir.
disunity [dɪs'ju:nɪtɪ] *n* desunión *f*.
disuse [dɪs'ju:s] *n* desuso.
ditch [dɪtʃ] *n (gen)* zanja; *(at roadside)* cuneta; *(for irrigation)* acequia.
▷ *vt fam* deshacerse de.
▷ *vi* AV hacer un amerizaje forzoso.
dither ['dɪðəʳ] *vi* vacilar, titubear.
ditto ['dɪtəʊ] *n (in list)* ídem *m*.
ditty ['dɪtɪ] *n* cantinela, cancioncilla.
▲ *pl* **ditties**.
diuretic [daɪjə'retɪk] *adj* diurético,-a.
diurnal [daɪ'ɜ:nəl] *adj* diurno,-a.
divan [dɪ'væn] *n (couch)* diván *m*, canapé *m*.
dive [daɪv] *n* **1** *(into water)* zambullida, salto (de cabeza); *(in competition)* salto (de trampolín); *(underwater)* buceo; *(whale)* inmersión *f*. **2** *(of plane)* picado; *(of bird)* descenso (en picado).
▷ *vi* [US *pt* **dove** [dəʊv].] **1** *(into water)* zambullirse, tirarse (de cabeza); *(in competition)* saltar; *(underwater)* bucear; *(whale)* sumergirse. **2** *(birds, planes)* bajar en picado. **3** *(move suddenly)* precipitarse hacia.
⊙ **to dive in** *vi* zambullirse, tirarse de cabeza.
diver ['daɪvəʳ] *n* buzo, submarinista *mf*.
diverge [daɪ'vɜ:dʒ] *vi* **1** *(lines)* divergir; *(roads)* bifurcarse. **2** *(opinion, views)* divergir.
divergence [daɪ'vɜ:dʒəns] *n* divergencia.
divergent [daɪ'vɜ:dʒənt] *adj* divergente.
diverse [daɪ'vɜ:s] *adj* diverso,-a, variado,-a.
diversification [daɪvɜ:sɪfɪ'keɪʃᵊn] *n* **1** *(variety)* variedad *f*. **2** COMM diversificación *f*.
diversify [daɪ'vɜ:sɪfaɪ] *vt* diversificar.
▲ *pt & pp* **diversified**, *ger* **diversifying**.
diversion [daɪ'vɜ:ʃᵊn] *n* **1** desvío, desviación *f*. **2** diversión *f*, entretenimiento.
diversity [daɪ'vɜ:sɪtɪ] *n* diversidad *f*.
divert [daɪ'vɜ:t] *vt* **1** desviar. **2** divertir.
divest [daɪ'vest] *vt* despojar, privar (**of**, de).
divide [dɪ'vaɪd] *vt* dividir, separar.
▷ *vi* dividirse, bifurcarse.
▷ *n fml* división *f*, diferencia.
divided [dɪ'vaɪdɪd] *adj (opinion)* dividido,-a.
dividend ['dɪvɪdend] *n* dividendo.
divider [dɪ'vaɪdəʳ] *n (in file)* separador *m*; *(in room)* mampara.
dividers [dɪ'vaɪdəz] *n pl* compás *m* de punta (fija).
dividing line [dɪ'vaɪdɪŋ laɪn] *n* línea divisoria.
divination [dɪvɪ'neɪʃᵊn] *n* adivinación *f*.
divine [dɪ'vaɪn] *adj* divino,-a.
divinely [dɪ'vaɪnlɪ] *adv* **1** REL por Dios. **2** *fam* divinamente.
diviner [dɪ'vaɪnəʳ] *n* zahorí *m*.
diving ['daɪvɪŋ] *n* **1** buceo, submarinismo. **2** *(n competition)* saltos *mpl* (de trampolín).
divinity [dɪ'vɪnɪtɪ] *n* **1** *(quality, state)* divinidad *f*. **2** *(subject)* teología.
▲ *pl* **divinities**.
divisible [dɪ'vɪzəbəl] *adj* divisible.
division [dɪ'vɪʒᵊn] *n* división *f*, reparto.
divisive [dɪ'vaɪsɪv] *adj* divisivo,-a.
divisor [dɪ'vaɪzəʳ] *n* divisor *m*.
divorce [dɪ'vɔ:s] *n* divorcio.
▷ *vi* divorciarse.
divorcé [dɪ'vɔ:seɪ] *n* divorciado.
divorced [dɪ'vɔ:st] *adj* divorciado,-a.
divorcée [dɪvɔ:'si:] *n* divorciada.
divulge [daɪ'vʌldʒ] *vt* divulgar, revelar.
DIY ['di:'aɪ'waɪ] *abbr* GB (**do-it-yourself**) bricolaje *m*.
dizziness ['dɪzɪnəs] *n* mareo, vértigo.
dizzy ['dɪzɪ] *adj* **1** *(person)* mareado,-a. **2** *(speed, pace)* vertiginoso,-a; *(height)* de vértigo.
▲ *comp* **dizzier**, *superl* **dizziest**.
DJ[1] ['di:'dʒeɪ] *abbr* GB *fam* (**dinner jacket**) esmoquin *m*, smoking *m*.
DJ[2] ['di:'dʒeɪ] *abbr* (**disc jockey**) pinchadiscos *m*, discjockey *m*.
DNA ['di:'en'eɪ] *abbr* (**deoxyribonucleic acid**) ácido desoxirribonucleico; *(abbreviation)* ADN *m*.
do [du:] *vt* **1** *(gen)* hacer. **2** *(as job)* dedicarse. **3** *(be sufficient for)* ser suficiente; *(be satisfactory for, acceptable to)* ir bien a. **4** *fam (cheat, swindle)* estafar, timar.
⊙ **to do away with** *vt insep* abolir, suprimir.
⊙ **to do down** *vt sep* hablar mal de.
⊙ **to do for** *vt insep (manage)* arreglárselas para conseguir.

⊙ **to do in** *vt sep fam* matar, agotar.
⊙ **to do out** *vt sep* GB *(clean)* hacer una limpieza a fondo de; *(decorate)* decorar.
⊙ **to do out of** *vt sep fam* quitar, birlar.
⊙ **to do over** *vt sep fam* dar una paliza a.
⊙ **to do up** *vt sep* **1** *fam (fasten, belt)* abrochar(se). **2** *(wrap)* envolver. **3** *(dress up)* arreglar.
⊙ **to do with** *vt insep (need)* venir bien a.
⊙ **to do without** *vi* arreglárselas sin.
Doberman ['dəʊbəmən] *n* doberman *m.*
doc [dɒk] *n fam* doctor,-ra.
docile ['dəʊsaɪl] *adj* dócil, sumiso,-a.
dock[1] [dɒk] *n* **1** MAR *(gen)* muelle *m*; *(for cargo)* dársena. **2** JUR banquillo (de los acusados).
▷ *vt (ship)* atracar (**at**, a); *(spaceship)* acoplar.
▷ *n pl* **docks** puerto.
dock[2] [dɒk] *vt* **1** *(animal's tail)* cortar. **2** *(wages)* descontar dinero de.
dock[3] [dɒk] *n* BOT acedera.
docker ['dɒkəʳ] *n* estibador,-ra, cargador,-ra.
docket ['dɒkɪt] *n* GB *(label)* rótulo, etiqueta.
dockland ['dɒklænd] *n* zona del puerto, zona portuaria.

En Londres **Docklands** es la antigua zona portuaria cerca del río Támesis donde se han establecido muchas grandes empresas, sobre todo del sector financiero.

dockside ['dɒksaɪd] *n* dársena.
dockyard ['dɒkjɑːd] *n* astillero.
doctor ['dɒktəʳ] *n* médico,-a, doctor,-ra.
▷ *vt pej* falsificar, amañar.
doctoral ['dɒktərəl] *adj* doctoral.
doctorate ['dɒktᵊrət] *n* doctorado.
doctrinaire [dɒktrɪ'neəʳ] *adj* doctrinario,-a.
doctrinal [dɒk'traɪnəl] *adj* doctrinal.
doctrine ['dɒktrɪn] *n* doctrina.
document ['dɒkjəmənt] *n* **1** documento.
▷ *vt* documentar.
documentary [dɒkjə'mentᵊrɪ] *adj* documental.
▷ *n* documental *m.*
▲ *pl* **documentaries.**
documentation [dɒkjəmən'teɪʃᵊn] *n* documentación *f.*
dodder ['dɒdəʳ] *vi fam* andar tambaleándose.
dodderer ['dɒdərəʳ] *n fam* vejestorio,-a.
doddering ['dɒdərɪŋ] *adj fam* chocho,-a.
doddery ['dɒdərɪ] *adj fam* chocho,-a.
doddle ['dɒdᵊl] ■ **it's a doddle** *fam* es pan comido, está chupado,-a, está tirado,-a.
dodecagon [dəʊ'dekəgɒn] *n* dodecágono.
dodecagonal [dəʊde'kægənᵊl] *adj* dodecágono,-a.
dodecahedron [dəʊdekə'hiːdrən] *n* dodecaedro.
dodecaphonic [dəʊdekə'fɒnɪk] *adj* dodecafónico,-a.
dodecasyllable [dəʊdekə'sɪləbᵊl] *n* dodecasílabo.
dodecasyllablic [dəʊdekəsɪ'læbɪk] *n* dodecasílabo,-a.
dodge [dɒdʒ] *n* **1** *(quick movement)* regate *m.* **2** *fam (trick)* truco, astucia, treta, artimaña.
▷ *vt* esquivar.
dodgems ['dɒdʒəmz] *n pl* coches *mpl* de choque, autos *mpl* de choque.
dodger ['dɒdʒəʳ] *n* persona que intenta eludir algo tax dodger *evasor,-ra de impuestos.*
dodgy ['dɒdʒɪ] *adj* **1** *fam (risky)* arriesgado,-a. **2** *fam (person)* que no es de fiar.
▲ *comp* **dodgier**, *superl* **dodgiest.**
doe [dəʊ] *n (of deer)* gama; *(of rabbit)* coneja.
doer ['duːəʳ] *n* persona emprendedora, persona dinámica.
does [dʌz] *pres* ⟶ **do.**
doesn't ['dʌzᵊnt] *contr* ⟶ **does not.**
doff [dɒf] *vt* quitar.
dog [dɒg] *n* **1** *(gen)* perro,-a. **2** *fam (person)* tipo,-a.
▷ *n pl* **the dogs** las carreras *fpl* de galgos.
▷ *vt (pursue)* perseguir.
▲ *pt & pp* **dogged**, *ger* **dogging.**
dogcart ['dɒgkɑːt] *n* carro de dos ruedas tirado po un caballo.
dog-catcher ['dɒgkætʃəʳ] *n* lacero,-a.
doge [dəʊdʒ] *n* dux *m.*
dog-eared ['dɒgɪəd] *adj (book)* sobado,-a y con las esquinas dobladas.
dog-end ['dɒgend] *n* colilla.
dogfight ['dɒgfaɪt] *n* **1** *(between dogs)* pelea de perros; *(between people)* refriega, reyerta. **2** AV combate *m* aéreo.
dogfish ['dɒgfɪʃ] *n (fish)* cazón *m*, perro marino.
dogged ['dɒgɪd] *adj* terco,-a, obstinado,-a.
doggerel ['dɒgᵊrəl] *n* malos versos *mpl.*
doggie ['dɒgɪ] *n* ⟶ **doggy.**
doggy ['dɒgɪ] *n* perrito,-a.
▲ *pl* **doggies.**
doghouse ['dɒghaʊs] *n* US perrera, casita del perro
dogma ['dɒgmə] *n* dogma *m.*
dogmatic [dɒg'mætɪk] *adj* dogmático,-a.
dogmatism ['dɒgmətɪzᵊm] *n* dogmatismo.
do-gooder [duː'gʊdəʳ] *n* bienhechor,-ra, person bien intencionada.
dogsbody ['dɒgzbɒdɪ] *n* GB *fam* burro de carga.
▲ *pl* **dogsbodies.**
dog-tired ['dɒgtaɪəd] *adj* rendido,-a, hecho,-a polvo, muerto,-a de cansancio.
doh [dəʊ] *n* MUS do.
doily ['dɔɪlɪ] *n* tapete *m* (decorativo).
▲ *pl* **doilies.**
doing ['duːɪŋ] *n* obra, trabajo.
▷ *n pl* **doings** *(activities)* actividades *fpl.*
do-it-yourself [duːɪtjɔː'self] *n* bricolaje *m.*
dole [dəʊl] *n* **the dole** GB *fam* el subsidio de desempleo, el paro.
⊙ **to dole out** *vt sep* repartir, dar.
doleful ['dəʊlfʊl] *adj* triste, compungido,-a, afligido,-a.
doll [dɒl] *n* muñeca.
⊙ **to doll up** *vt sep fam* poner guapo,-a.
dollar ['dɒləʳ] *n* dólar *m.*
dollarisation [dɒləraɪ'zeɪʃən] *n* dolarización *f.*
dollop ['dɒləp] *n fam (spoonful)* cucharada; *(serving measure)* ración *f.*
dolly ['dɒlɪ] *n* **1** *(doll)* muñeca, muñequita. **2** CINE dolly *m*, plataforma móvil.
▲ *pl* **dollies.**
dolmen ['dɒlmən] *n* dolmen *m.*

Dolomites [dɒlə'maɪts] *n* **the Dolomites** los Dolomitas *mpl.*
dolphin ['dɒlfɪn] *n* delfín *m.*
domain [də'meɪn] *n* **1** *(lands)* dominios *mpl.* **2** *(in computing)* dominio. **3** *(sphere of knowledge)* campo, esfera; *(area of activity)* ámbito.
dome [dəʊm] *n* ARCH *(roof)* cúpula; *(ceiling)* bóveda.
domestic [də'mestɪk] *adj* **1** doméstico,-a: **domestic animal** *animal doméstico.* **2** hogareño,-a, casero,-a. **3** *(news, flight)* nacional; *(trade, policy)* interior; *(affairs, policy, market)* interno,-a.
▷ *n* empleado,-a doméstico,-a.
domesticate [də'mestɪkeɪt] *vt* **1** *(animal)* domesticar. **2** *(person)* volver hogareño,-a, volver casero,-a.
domesticity [dəʊme'stɪsɪtɪ] *n (of person)* vida de hogar, vida casera; *(of animal)* domesticidad *f.*
domicile ['dɒmɪsaɪl] *n* JUR domicilio.
dominance ['dɒmɪnəns] *n* dominio, control.
dominant ['dɒmɪnənt] *adj (gen)* dominante.
dominate ['dɒmɪneɪt] *vt* dominar.
▷ *vi (predominate)* predominar.
dominating ['dɒmɪneɪtɪŋ] *adj* dominante.
domination [dɒmɪ'neɪʃən] *n* dominación *f.*
domineer [dɒmɪ'nɪəʳ] *vi* avasallar.
domineering [dɒmɪ'nɪərɪŋ] *adj* dominante.
Dominica [dɒmɪ'niːkə] *n* Dominica.
Dominican [də'mɪnɪkən] *adj* dominicano,-a.
▷ *n* dominicano,-a. ● **Dominican Republic** República Dominicana.
dominion [də'mɪnjən] *n* dominio.
domino ['dɒmɪnəʊ] *n* ficha de dominó.
▲ *pl* **dominoes.**
▷ *n pl* **dominoes** *(game)* dominó *m.*
don[1] [dɒn] *n* profesor,-ra universitario,-a.
don[2] [dɒn] *vt* **1** *(put on)* ponerse. **2** *fig* asumir.
▲ *pt & pp* **donned**, *ger* **donning.**
donate [dəʊ'neɪt] *vt* donar.
donation [dəʊ'neɪʃən] *n* **1** *(act)* donación *f.* **2** *(gift)* donativo.
done [dʌn] *pp* → **do.**
▷ *adj* **1** *(finished)* terminado,-a, hecho,-a. **2** bien visto,-a.
donkey ['dɒŋkɪ] *n* burro,-a, asno.
donor ['dəʊnəʳ] *n* donante *m.*
don't [dəʊnt] *aux (do + not)* → **do.**
donut ['dəʊnʌt] *n* → **doughnut.**
doodle ['duːdəl] *vi* garabatear.
▷ *n* garabato.
doom [duːm] *n (fate)* destino; *(ruin)* fatalidad *f*; *(death)* muerte *f.*
▷ *vt (destine)* destinar; *(condemn)* condenar.
doomed [duːmd] *adj* condenado,-a.
doomsday ['duːmzdeɪ] *n* día *m* del juicio final.
door [dɔːʳ] *n* **1** *(gen)* puerta. **2** *(entrance)* puerta, entrada.
doorbell ['dɔːbel] *n* timbre *m.*
doorknob ['dɔːnɒb] *n* pomo.
doorman ['dɔːmən] *n* portero.
doormat ['dɔːmæt] *phr* felpudo, esterilla.
doorstep ['dɔːstep] *n* **1** peldaño, umbral *m.* **2** GB *fam (thick slice of bread)* rebanada gruesa de pan.
doorstop ['dɔːstɒp] *n* cuña, tope.
door-to-door [dɔːtə'dɔː] *adj* de puerta en puerta, a domicilio.
doorway ['dɔːweɪ] *n* entrada, portal *m.*
dope [dəʊp] *vt* **1** *fam (food, drink)* adulterar con drogas, poner droga en. **2** SP *(athlete, horse)* dopar, drogar.
dopey ['dəʊpɪ] *adj* **1** *sl (with drugs, sleep)* grogui, atontado,-a. **2** lelo,-a, bobo,-a.
▲ *comp* **dopier**, *superl* **dopiest.**
doping ['dəʊpɪŋ] *n* dopaje *m*, doping *m.*
dormant ['dɔːmənt] *adj* **1** *(volcano)* inactivo,-a; *(animal, plant)* aletargado,-a. **2** *fig (idea, emotion, rivalry)* latente.
dormer ['dɔːməʳ] [Also **dormer window.**] *n* buhardilla.
dormitory ['dɔːmɪtərɪ] *n* **1** *(in boarding school, hostel)* dormitorio. **2** US residencia de estudiantes, colegio mayor.
▲ *pl* **dormitories.**
dormouse ['dɔːmaʊs] *n* lirón *m.*
▲ *pl* **dormice** ['dɔːmaɪs].
dorsal ['dɔːsəl] *adj* dorsal.
dosage ['dəʊsɪdʒ] *n (amount)* dosis *f*; *(on medicine bottle)* posología.
dose [dəʊs] *n* dosis *f.*
▷ *vt* medicar.
dosh [dɒʃ] *n sl (money)* pasta.
doss [dɒs] *n fam (short sleep)* cabezada.
⊙ **to doss down** *vi* GB *fam* echarse a dormir, dormir.
dosser ['dɒsəʳ] *n* **1** *fam (tramp)* vagabundo,-a, indigente *mf.* **2** *fam (lazy person)* vago,-a.
dosshouse ['dɒshaʊs] *n* pensión *f* barata.
dossier ['dɒsɪeɪ] *n* expediente *m*, dossier *m.*
dot [dɒt] *n (spot)* punto.
▷ *vt* **1** *(letter)* poner el punto a. **2** *(scatter)* esparcir, salpicar.
▲ *pt & pp* **dotted**, *ger* **dotting.**
dotage ['dəʊtɪdʒ] *n* chochez *f.*
dote [dəʊt] *vi* **to dote on** adorar.
dotted ['dɒtɪd] *adj (line)* de puntos.
dotty ['dɒtɪ] *adj* GB *fam* chiflado,-a.
▲ *comp* **dottier**, *superl* **dottiest.**
double ['dʌbəl] *adj & n (gen)* doble.
▷ *vt* **1** *(increase twofold)* doblar, duplicar. **2** *(fold in half)* doblar por la mitad.
▷ *n pl* **doubles** *(tennis)* partido de dobles.
⊙ **to double back** *vi* volver sobre sus pasos.
⊙ **to double up** *vt sep* doblar.
▷ *vi* **1** *(with pain, laughter)* doblarse; *(with laughter)* partirse, mondarse. **2** *(share)* compartir la habitación.
double-barreled ['dʌbəlbærəld] *n* US → **double-barrelled.**
double-barrelled ['dʌbəlbærəld] *adj* **1** *(gun)* de dos cañones. **2** *(surname)* compuesto,-a.
double-breasted ['dʌbəlbrestɪd] *adj* cruzado,-a.
double-check [dʌbəl'tʃek] *vt* volver a revisar.
double-click [dʌbəl'klɪk] *vi* hacer doble clic.
double-cross [dʌbəl'krɒs] *vt fam* engañar, traicionar.
double-dealing [dʌbəl'diːlɪŋ] *n* doble juego.
double-decker [dʌbəl'dekəʳ] *n* [Also **double-decker bus.**] GB autobús *m* de dos pisos.
double-edged [dʌbəl'edʒd] *adj* de doble filo.
double-jointed [dʌbəl'dʒɔɪntɪd] *adj* con articulaciones dobles.

double-park [dʌbəl'pɑ:k] *vt* aparcar en doble fila.
double-quick ['dʌbəlkwɪk] *adj* muy rápido,-a.
▷ *adv* volando.
doubloon [də'blu:n] *n* doblón *m*.
doubly ['dʌblɪ] *adv* doblemente.
doubt [daʊt] *n (gen)* duda; incertidumbre *f*.
▷ *vi* dudar.
doubter ['daʊtəʳ] *n* escéptico,-a.
doubtful ['daʊtfʊl] *adj* dudoso,-a, incierto,-a.
doubtfully ['daʊtfʊlɪ] *adv* dudosamente.
doubtless ['daʊtləs] *adv* sin duda, indudablemente.
doubtlessly ['daʊtləslɪ] *adv* sin duda, indudablemente.
dough [dəʊ] *n* **1** CULIN masa. **2** *sl (money)* pasta.
doughiness ['dəʊɪnəs] *n* pastosidad *f*.
doughnut ['dəʊnʌt] *n* rosquilla, donut *m*.
doughy ['dəʊɪ] *adj* pastoso,-a.
dour [daʊəʳ] *adj* hosco,-a, adusto,-a.
Douro ['dʊərəʊ] *n* el Duero.
douse [daʊs] *vt* **1** *(extinguish - light, candle)* apagar. **2** *(soak)* mojar, empapar.
dove¹ [dʌv] *n (bird)* paloma (blanca).
dove² [dəʊv] *pp* US ⟶ **dive**.
dovecote ['dʌvkeʊt] *n* palomar *m*.
dovetail ['dʌvteɪl] *vt fig* sincronizar, encajar.
▷ *vi* encajar (into, en), (with, con).
▷ *n* [Also dovetail joint.] cola de milano.
dowager ['daʊədʒəʳ] *n* **1** *(widow)* viuda (de un noble). **2** *(rich old lady)* vieja dama.
dowdy ['daʊdɪ] *adj pej* sin gracia, sin estilo
▲ *comp* dowdier, *superl* dowdiest.
dowel ['daʊəl] *n* clavija.
down¹ [daʊn] *prep* **1** *(to a lower level)* (hacia) abajo. **2** *(at a lower level)* abajo. **3** *(along)* por: cut it down the middle *córtalo por la mitad*.
▷ *adv* **1** *(to lower level)* (hacia) abajo. **2** *(on paper, in writing)*: she wrote his phone number down *apuntó su teléfono*.
▷ *vt* **1** *(knock over, force to ground)* derribar, tumbar. **2** *fam (drink)* tragarse rápidamente, beberse rápidamente: he downed the glass in one *se bebió el vaso de un trago*.
▷ *interj (to dog)* ¡quieto!
down² [daʊn] *n (on bird)* plumón *m*; *(on peach)* pelusa; *(on body)* vello.
down-and-out ['daʊnənaʊt] *n* vagabundo,-a, indigente *mf*.
down-at-heel [daʊnət'hi:l] *adj (person)* desastrado,-a, desaliñado,-a.
downbeat ['daʊnbi:t] *adj fam (depressed)* deprimente; *(low-key, relaxed,)* relajado,-a.
▷ *n* MUS compás *m* acentuado.
downcast ['daʊnkɑ:st] *adj* abatido,-a.
downer ['daʊnəʳ] *n* **1** *fam (drug)* calmante *m*, sedante *m*. **2** *(blow, depressing experience)* palo.
downfall ['daʊnfɔ:l] *n* **1** *fig (of person)* perdición *f*, ruina. **2** *(of regime, dictator, etc)* caída.
downgrade [daʊn'greɪd] *vt* **1** *(demote)* bajar de categoría. **2** *(make seem unimportant)* restar importancia a.
downhearted [daʊn'hɑ:tɪd] *adj* desanimado,-a, desmoralizado,-a.
downhill [daʊn'hɪl] *adv* cuesta abajo.
▷ *n (in skiing)* descenso contrarreloj.
download ['daʊn'ləʊd] *vt* bajar; *(internet)* descargar.
downmarket [daʊn'mɑ:kɪt] *adj (newspaper, book)* popular; *(products, services)* barato,-a.
downpour ['daʊnpɔ:ʳ] *n* chaparrón *m*, aguacero.
downright ['daʊnraɪt] *adj fam* descarado,-a.
▷ *adv fam* muy, absolutamente.
downs [daʊnz] *n pl* GB colinas *fpl*.
Down's syndrome ['daʊnz sɪndrəʊm] *n* MED síndrome *m* de Down.
downstairs [daʊn'steəz] *adv (down the stairs)* abajo.
▷ *adj (room)* (del piso) de abajo.
▷ *n* planta baja.
downstream [daʊn'stri:m] *adv* río abajo.
down-to-earth [daʊntʊ'ɜ:θ] *adj* práctico,-a, realista.
downtown [daʊn'taʊn] *adj* US céntrico,-a.
▷ *n* US centro de la ciudad.
downtrodden ['daʊntrɒdən] *adj* oprimido,-a.
downturn ['daʊntɜ:n] *n (in economy)* bajón *m*, bache *m* económico.
downward ['daʊnwəd] *adj (movement)* descendente; *(direction, pressure)* hacia abajo.
downwards ['daʊnwədz] *adv* hacia abajo.
downy ['daʊnɪ] *adj* aterciopelado,-a.
▲ *comp* downier, *superl* downiest.
dowry ['daʊərɪ] *n* dote *f*.
▲ *pl* dowries.
doz ['dʌzᵊn] *abbr* (dozen) docena; *(abbreviation)* doc.
doze [dəʊz] *n* cabezada.
▷ *vi* dormitar, echar una cabezada.
⊙ **to doze off** *vi* quedarse dormido,-a.
dozen ['dʌzᵊn] *n (set of twelve)* docena.
dozy ['dəʊzɪ] *adj* **1** *(sleepy)* adormilado,-a. **2** GB *fam (stupid)* tonto,-a.
▲ *comp* dozier, *superl* dozier.
D Ph ['di:'pi:'eɪtʃ] *abbr* (Doctor of Philosophy) Doctor,-ra en Filosofía.
D Phil ['di:'fɪl] *abbr* (Doctor of Philosophy) Doctor,-ra en Filosofía.
DPP ['di:'pi:'pi:] *abbr* GB (Director of Public Prosecutions) ≈ Fiscal General del Estado.
Dr ['dɒktəʳ] *abbr* (Doctor) Doctor,-ra; *(abbreviation)* Dr., Dra.
drab [dræb] *adj* **1** *(colour)* apagado,-a; *(appearance)* soso,-a, sin gracia. **2** *(dreary - life)* monótono,-a, gris.
drachma ['drækmə] *n* dracma.
▲ *pl* drachmas o drachmae ['drɟkmi:].
Draconian [dræ'kəʊnɪən] *adj* draconiano,-a.
draft [drɑ:ft] *n* **1** *(rough copy - of letter, speech, etc)* borrador *m*; *(of plot)* esbozo; *(of plan, project)* anteproyecto. **2** FIN *(bill of exchange)* letra de cambio, giro. **3** US *(conscription)* (reclutamiento para el) servicio militar obligatorio. **4** US ⟶ **draught**.
▷ *adj (version, copy)* preliminar.
draftsman ['drɑ:ftsmən] *n* US ⟶ **draughtsman**.
drafty ['drɑ:ftɪ] *adj* US ⟶ **draughty**.
drag [dræg] *n (hindrance)* estorbo (on, para), carga (on, para).
▷ *vt (pull, cause to trail)* arrastrar, llevar a rastras.
▲ *pt & pp* dragged, *ger* dragging.

⊙ **to drag down** *vt sep* arrastrar.

⊙ **to drag in** *vt sep (subject)* traer por los pelos; *(person)* meter.

⊙ **to drag on** *vi* alargarse, prolongarse, hacerse interminable.

⊙ **to drag out** *vt sep* alargar, prolongar.

⊙ **to drag up** *vt sep* **1** *(revive, recall)* sacar a relucir. **2** GB *(raise)* criar (a la buena de Dios).

dragnet ['drægnet] *n* **1** *(net)* red barredera. **2** *(system)* operación *f* policial de captura.

dragon ['dræg°n] *n* **1** *(mythology)* dragón *m*. **2** *fam (woman)* bruja.

dragonfly ['drægənflaɪ] *n* libélula.
▲ *pl* **dragonflies.**

dragoon [drə'gu:n] *n* MIL dragón *m*.
▷ *vt* presionar, obligar.

dragster ['drægstə'] *n* coche *m* de carreras trucado.

drain [dreɪn] *n* desagüe *m*, alcantarilla.
▷ *vt* **1** *(empty)* vaciar; *(- wound, blood)* drenar. **2** *(rice, pasta, vegetables, etc)* escurrir.
▷ *vi* **1** *(discharge - pipes, rivers)* desaguar. **2** *(dry out)* escurrir (**off**, -), escurrirse (**off**, -). **3** *fig (strength, energy, etc)* irse agotando.
▷ *n pl* **the drains** *(of town)* el alcantarillado *m sing*; *(of building)* las tuberías *fpl* del desagüe.

⊙ **to drain away** *vi (liquid - empty)* vaciarse.

drainage ['dreɪnɪdʒ] *n* **1** drenaje, desagüe *m*; **2** *(drains - of town)* alcantarillado; *(of building)* desagüe *m*. ● **drainage basin** cuenca hidrográfica.

drained [dreɪnd] *adj* agotado,-a.

draining board ['dreɪnɪŋ bɔ:d] *n* escurridero.

drainpipe ['dreɪnpaɪp] *n (pipe)* tubo de desagüe.

drake [dreɪk] *n* pato (macho).

dram [dræm] *n fam* trago, chupito.

drama ['drɑ:mə] *n* **1** THEAT *(play)* obra de teatro; *(plays, literature)* teatro, drama *m*. **2** *(as school subject)* expresión *f* corporal; *(at drama school)* arte *m* dramático.

dramatic [drə'mætɪk] *adj* dramático,-a, teatral, emocionante.

dramatics [drə'mætɪks] *n* THEAT teatro.

dramatisation [dræmətaɪ'zeɪʃ°n] *n* ⟶ **dramatization.**

dramatise ['dræmətaɪz] *vt* ⟶ **dramatize.**

dramatist ['dræmətɪst] *n* dramaturgo,-a.

dramatization [dræmətaɪ'zeɪʃ°n] *n* adaptación *f* teatral, dramatización *f*.

dramatize ['dræmətaɪz] *vt* **1** THEAT hacer una adaptación teatral de. **2** *(exaggerate)* dramatizar, exagerar.

drank [dræŋk] *pt* ⟶ **drink.**

drape [dreɪp] *vt* **1** *(decorate)* drapear; *(cover)* cubrir (**in/with**, con). **2** *(part of body)* descansar, acomodar.
▷ *n pl* **drapes** US *(curtains)* cortinas *fpl*.

draper ['dreɪpə'] *n* GB pañero,-a.

drapery ['dreɪpərɪ] *n* **1** GB *(trade, goods)* pañería. **2** *(cloth)* tela; *(hanging)* colgadura.
▲ *pl* **draperies.**
▷ *n pl* **draperies** US cortinas *fpl*.

drastic ['dræstɪk] *adj* drástico,-a, severo,-a, radical.

drastically ['dræstɪklɪ] *adv* drásticamente.

draught [drɑ:ft] *n* **1** *(of cold air)* corriente *f* (de aire). **2** *(swallow of beer, etc)* trago. **3** *(medicine)* pócima. **4** MAR *(depth)* calado. **5** *(haulage)* tiro. **6** *(piece in game)* dama, pieza.
▷ *adj (animal)* de tiro.
▷ *n pl* **draughts** GB damas *fpl*.

draughtboard ['drɑ:ftbɔ:d] *n* tablero de damas.

draughtsman ['drɑ:ftsmən] *n* **1** *(artist)* delineante *mf*. **2** GB *(in game)* ficha de damas.
▲ *pl* **draughtsmen** ['drɑ:ftsmən].

draughtsmanship ['drɑ:ftsmənʃɪp] *n (drawing)* dibujo lineal; *(skill)* ejecución *f* gráfica.

draughtswoman ['drɑ:ftswumən] *n* ARCH delineante.
▲ *pl* **draughtswomen** ['drɑ:ftswɪmɪn].

draughty ['drɑ:ftɪ] *adj* con corrientes de aire.
▲ *comp* **draughtier**, *superl* **draughtiest.**

draw [drɔ:] *n* **1** *(raffle, lottery)* sorteo. **2** SP *(tie - gen)* empate *m*. **3** *(attraction)* atracción *f*.
▷ *vt* **1** *(sketch - picture)* dibujar; *(- plans)* trazar; *(describe)* pintar. **2** *(move)* llevar. **3** *(pull out, take out - gen)* sacar, extraer; *(bow)* tensar. **4** SP *(tie)* empatar. **5** *(attract)* atraer; *(- attention)* atraer la atención sobre. **6** *(produce, elicit)* provocar, obtener; *(- praise)* conseguir. **7** MAR *(of ship)* tener un calado de.
▲ *pt* **drew** [dru:], *pp* **drawn** [drɔ:n].

⊙ **to draw back** *vi* **1** *(move away)* retirarse, retroceder. **2** *(pull out)* echarse atrás, volverse atrás.

⊙ **to draw in** *vi* **1** *(of days)* acortarse. **2** *(train)* llegar.

⊙ **to draw off** *vt sep (liquid)* sacar, extraer.

⊙ **to draw on** *vt insep (make use of - experience, etc)* recurrir a, hacer uso de, inspirarse en, aprovecharse de; *(- money, savings)* utilizar, recurrir a, hacer uso de.
▷ *vi (approach - winter, night, etc)* acercarse.

⊙ **to draw out** *vt sep* **1** *(prolong)* alargar, estirar. **2** *(make talk, bring out)* hacer hablar, desatar la lengua.
▷ *vt insep (withdraw - money)* sacar; *(information)* sacar, sonsacar; *(confession)* arrancar.
▷ *vi* **1** *(of days)* hacerse más largo,-a. **2** *(train)* salir.

⊙ **to draw up** *vt sep (draft - contract, treaty, etc)* preparar, redactar; *(- list)* hacer; *(- plan)* esbozar.
▷ *vi (of vehicle)* detenerse, pararse.

drawback ['drɔ:bæk] *n* inconveniente *m*, desventaja.

drawbridge ['drɔ:brɪdʒ] *n* puente *m* levadizo.

drawee [drɔ:'i:] *n* librado,-a, girado,-a.

drawer ['drɔ:ə'] *n* **1** *(in furniture)* cajón *m*. **2** *(draughtsperson)* dibujante *mf*.

drawers [drɔ:z] *n pl dated (pants - men's)* calzoncillos *mpl*; *(- women's)* bragas *fpl*.

drawing ['drɔ:ɪŋ] *n* dibujo: **she's good at drawing** *dibuja muy bien*. ■ **to go back to the drawing board** volver a empezar, empezar de nuevo. ● **drawing board** tablero de dibujo. ‖ **drawing pin** GB chincheta. ‖ **drawing room** sala de estar, salón *m*.

drawl [drɔ:l] *n manera de hablar lenta en que se arrastran las palabras*: **a southern/Texan drawl** *un acento sureño/tejano*.
▷ *vi* hablar arrastrando las palabras.
▷ *vt* decir arrastrando las palabras.

drawn [drɔ:n] *pp* ⟶ **draw.**
▷ *adj* **1** *(face - tired, haggard)* ojeroso,-a, cansado,-a, demacrado,-a; *(- worried)* preocupado,-a: **a face**

drawn with grief *una cara transida de dolor.* **2** SP *(match, etc)* empatado,-a.

drawstring ['drɔ:strɪŋ] *n* cordón *m.* ● **drawstring waist** talle *m* fruncido con un cordón.

dread [dred] *n* terror *m*, pavor *m*: **her dread of growing old** *su terror a hacerse vieja.*

▷ *vt* temer, tener pavor a, tener terror a: **he's dreading the exam** *el examen le da terror;* **she's dreading his parents' visit** *espera la visita de sus padres con aprensión;* **I dread to think what would happen** *no quiero ni pensar en lo que pasaría.*

dreadful ['dredful] *adj* **1** *(shocking)* terrible, espantoso,-a, atroz. **2** *fam (awful)* fatal, horrible, malísimo,-a: **how dreadful!** *¡qué horror!*

dreadfully ['dredfulɪ] *adv fam (horribly)* terriblemente, fatal; *(very)* muy, sumamente: **I'm dreadfully sorry** *lo siento muchísimo.*

dream [dri:m] *n* **1** *(while asleep)* sueño: **I had a bad dream** *tuve una pesadilla;* **sweet dreams!** *¡felices sueños!* **2** *(daydream)* ensueño, sueño: **he lives in a dream** *vive en las nubes.* **3** *(hope, fantasy)* sueño (dorado), deseo, ilusión *f*: **the house of your dreams** *la casa de tus sueños.* **4** *fam (wonderful thing, person)* sueño, encanto, maravilla: **it all went like a dream** *todo salió a las mil maravillas.*

▷ *adj (imaginary)* imaginario,-a; *(ideal)* ideal, de ensueño: **your dream holiday (US vacation)** *las vacaciones de tus sueños.*

▷ *vt* **1** *(while asleep)* soñar: **I dreamt that I was flying** *soñé que volaba.* **2** *(imagine)* imaginarse: **I never dreamt you'd actually do it** *nunca me imaginé que lo harías de verdad.*

▷ *vi* **1** *(while asleep)* soñar (**about/of**, con); *(daydream)* soñar (despierto,-a): **I dreamt about you last night** *soñé contigo anoche;* **dream on** *sigue soñando.* **2** *(imagine)* soñar (**of**, con); *(contemplate)* soñar despierto: **I dream of having my own business** *sueño con tener mi propia empresa.*

▲ *pt & pp* **dreamed** o **dreamt.**

⊙ **to dream away** *vt sep* pasarse soñando.

⊙ **to dream up** *vt sep fam pej (excuse)* inventarse; *(plan)* idear.

dreamer ['dri:məʳ] *n* soñador,-ra.

dreamlike ['dri:mlaɪk] *adj* de ensueño, irreal.

dreamt [dremt] *pt & pp* → **dream.**

dreamy ['dri:mɪ] *adj* **1** *(person)* soñador,-ra, fantasioso,-a. **2** *(dreamlike - gen)* de ensueño, irreal; *(music)* etéreo,-a, sutil. **3** *fam (wonderful, desirable)* maravilloso,-a.

▲ *comp* **dreamier**, *superl* **dreamiest.**

dreariness ['drɪərɪnəs] *n* lo deprimente, lo aburrido.

dreary ['drɪərɪ] *adj* **1** *(gloomy - weather, day)* triste, deprimente; *(- room, landscape)* deprimente, lóbrego,-a, sombrío,-a. **2** *fam (dull, uninteresting)* pesado,-a, monótono,-a, aburrido,-a.

▲ *comp* **drearier**, *superl* **dreariest.**

dredge[1] [dredʒ] *vt (river, lake, etc)* dragar, rastrear.

▷ *vi (in river, lake, etc)* dragar, rastrear.

⊙ **to dredge up** *vt sep* **1** *(body)* sacar del agua. **2** *fig (scandal, etc)* desenterrar, sacar a la luz.

dredge[2] [dredʒ] *vt* CULIN *(with sugar)* espolvorear; *(with flour)* enharinar, rebozar.

dredger ['dredʒəʳ] *n* **1** *(machine)* draga; *(ship)* draga, dragador *m.* **2** CULIN espolvoreador *m.*

dregs [dregz] *n pl* **1** *(in liquid)* heces *fpl*, sedimento, poso. **2** *fig (scum)* escoria, hez *f.*

drench [drentʃ] *vt* empapar. ■ **to be/get drenched** empaparse. ‖ **to be drenched to the skin** esta[r] calado,-a hasta los huesos.

Dresden ['drezdən] *n* Dresde.

dress [dres] *n* **1** *(for women)* vestido. **2** *(clothing)* ropa vestimenta.

▷ *adj (shirt, suit)* de etiqueta.

▷ *vt* **1** *(person)* vestir. **2** MED *(wound)* vendar. **3** CULIN *(poultry, crab)* aderezar, preparar; *(salad)* aliñar. **4** *(shop window)* arreglar, decorar; *(Christmas tree,* decorar, adornar; *(hair)* arreglar.

▷ *vi (gen)* vestirse; *(formally)* vestirse de etiqueta. ■ **to be dressed** estar vestido,-a. ‖ **to be dressed in red black, etc** ir vestido,-a de rojo, negro, etc. ‖ **to be dressed to kill** ir de punta en blanco, ir de tiros largos. ‖ **to be well/badly dressed** ir bien/mal vestido,-a ‖ **to get dressed** vestirse. ‖ **to have good dress sense** tener buen gusto para vestirse. ● **dress circle** THEA[T] primer piso, piso principal. ‖ **dress rehearsal** THEA[T] ensayo general. ‖ **period dress** traje *m* de época. ‖ **su[n] dress** vestido sin mangas.

⊙ **to dress down** *vt sep (scold)* regañar; *(rebuke)* echa[r] una bronca, echar una regañina a.

▷ *vi (dress informally)* vestirse informalmente.

⊙ **to dress up** *vi (in fancy dress)* disfrazarse (**as**, de); *(dress formally)* ponerse de tiros largos, ir de tiros largos, ponerse elegante.

▷ *vt sep fig (truth, facts, etc)* disfrazar.

dresser ['dresəʳ] *n* **1** GB *(in kitchen)* aparador *m.* **2** U[S] *(chest of drawers)* tocador *m.* **3** THEAT ayudante *mf* d[e] camerino. ■ **to be a snappy/fashionable dresse[r]** vestir(se) con estilo/a la moda.

dressing ['dresɪŋ] *n* **1** *(gen)* apósito; *(bandage)* vendaje *m.* **2** *(act of getting dressed)* el vestir(se) *m.* **3** CULI[N] *(for salad)* aliño. **4** US *(stuffing)* relleno. ● **dressing gown** bata. ‖ **dressing room** THEAT camerino. ‖ **dressing table** tocador *m.*

dressing-down ['dresɪŋdaʊn] *n* reprimenda, rapapolvo, bronca. ■ **to give sb a dressing-down** echarle un rapapolvo a algn.

dressmaker ['dresmeɪkəʳ] *n (woman)* modista [f], modisto; *(man)* modista *m*, modisto.

dressmaking ['dresmeɪkɪŋ] *n* costura.

dressy ['dresɪ] *adj (clothes)* elegante, de vestir; *(person)* arreglado,-a, elegante.

▲ *comp* **dressier**, *superl* **dressiest.**

drew [dru:] *pt* → **draw.**

dribble ['drɪbᵊl] *n* **1** *(saliva)* saliva, baba. **2** *(of water, blood)* gotas *fpl*, hilo, chorrito. **3** SP dribling *m.*

▷ *vi* **1** *(baby)* babear. **2** *(liquid)* gotear.

▷ *vt* **1** *(liquid)* chorrear, dejar caer: **he's dribbling saliv[a]** *babea.* ■ **in dribs and drabs** poco a poco.

dried [draɪd] *pp* → **dry.**

▷ *adj (fruit)* seco,-a; *(milk)* en polvo.

drier ['draɪəʳ] *n* → **dryer.**

drift [drɪft] *n* **1** *(of snow)* ventisquero; *(of sand)* montón *m.* **2** MAR *(flow of water)* deriva; *(deviation - of ship)* desviación *f.* **3** *(movement)* movimiento, desplaza miento; *(tendency)* tendencia; *(shift)* cambio: **the drift of people from the country to cities** *el desplazamiento de la gente del campo a las ciudades.* **4** *(meaning, gist)* significado, sentido, idea: **do you get my drift?** *¿entiendes lo que quiero decir?* **5** GEOL *(deposits of earth, gravel, rock, etc)* terreno de acarreo.

▷ *vi* **1** *(float on water)* dejarse llevar por la corriente; *(be or go adrift)* ir a la deriva, derivar; *(float in air)* moverse empujado,-a por el viento: **we drifted out to sea** *íbamos a la deriva hacia alta mar.* **2** *(pile up - of snow, sand, leaves, etc)* amontonarse. **3** *fig (person)* ir sin rumbo, vivir sin rumbo, vagar; *(government)* ir a la deriva: **he drifts in and out of jobs** *cambia de trabajo continuamente.* ■ **to drift apart** distanciarse. ‖ **to drift off to sleep** quedarse dormido,-a.

▷ *vt (snow, sand, etc)* amontonar.

drifter ['drɪftəʳ] *n* **1** *(person - wanderer)* trotamundos *mf*, vagabundo,-a; *(- without fixed job)* persona sin ocupación fija. **2** MAR trainera, (barco) pesquero.

driftwood ['drɪftwʊd] *n* madera flotante.

drill¹ [drɪl] *n* **1** *(handtool)* taladro; *(large machine)* barreno, perforadora; *(dentist's)* fresa; *(drill head, bit)* broca: **pneumatic drill** *taladradora.* **2** MIL instrucción *f.* **3** EDUC *(exercise)* ejercicio. **4** *(rehearsal, practice)* simulacro; *(procedures to be followed)* procedimiento: **fire drill** *simulacro de incendio;* **safety drill** *instrucciones de seguridad.* **5** GB *fam (procedure)* procedimiento, trámite *m*: **what's the drill for getting paid?** *¿qué hay que hacer para cobrar?*

▷ *vt* **1** *(wood, metal, etc)* taladrar, perforar, barrenar; *(hole)* hacer, perforar. **2** MIL instruir. **3** *(teach)* hacer ejercicios (**in**, de), hacer practicar.

▷ *vi* **1** *(for oil, coal)* perforar, hacer perforaciones, sondar: **drilling for** *perforar en busca de.* **2** MIL entrenarse. ■ **to drill** STH **into** SB inculcarle ALGO a ALGN.

drill² [drɪl] *n (material)* dril *m.*

drill³ [drɪl] *n* AGR *(machine)* sembradora; *(furrow)* hilera, surco.

drily ['draɪlɪ] *adj* ⟶ **dryly.**

drink [drɪŋk] *n (gen, alcohol)* bebida; *(alcoholic drink)* copa, trago; *(soft drink)* refresco: **let's go for a drink!** *¡vamos a tomar algo!, ¡vamos a tomar una copa!*

▷ *vt (gen)* beber, tomar: **you haven't drunk your tea** *no te has bebido el té;* **what do you want to drink?** *¿qué quieres beber?* ■ **to drink a toast to** SB brindar por ALGN. ‖ **to drink to** STH/SB brindar por ALGO/ALGN. ‖ **to have** STH **to drink** tomar(se) ALGO.

▷ *vi* beber: **she doesn't drink (alcohol)** *no bebe (alcohol);* **don't drink and drive** *si bebes, no conduzcas.*

▷ *n* **the drink** *fam (the sea)* el mar, la mar.

▲ *pt* **drank** [dræŋk], *pp* **drunk** [drʌŋk].

◉ **to drink in** *vt sep (scene, sights, sounds, etc)* apreciar, empaparse de; *(success)* saborear.

◉ **to drink up** *vi* bebérselo todo,-a, terminar la copa.

▷ *vt sep* beberse.

drinkable ['drɪŋkəbəl] *adj (water)* potable; *(wine, beer, etc)* aceptable.

drink-driving [drɪŋk'draɪvɪŋ] *n* JUR conducción *f* bajo la influencia del alcohol, conducción *f* en estado de embriaguez.

drinker ['drɪŋkəʳ] *n* bebedor,-ra.

drinking ['drɪŋkɪŋ] *n (alcohol)* bebida; *(action)* beber *m.* ● **drinking fountain** fuente *f* de agua potable. ‖ **drinking water** agua potable.

drip [drɪp] *n* **1** *(drop of liquid)* goteo; *(sound)* gotear *m.* **2** MED gota a gota *m*: **they put him on a drip** *le pusieron el gota a gota.* **3** *fam (person)* soso,-a. ■ **to drip with flattery** rezumar halagos. ‖ **to drip with jewels** ir cargado,-a de joyas.

▷ *vi (fall in drops)* gotear, caer; *(fall heavily)* chorrear: **water is dripping from the ceiling** *caen gotas del techo, el techo gotea;* **the tap drips** *el grifo gotea.*

▷ *vt* dejar caer gota a gota.

▲ *pt & pp* **dripped**, *ger* **dripping.**

drip-dry ['drɪpdraɪ] *adj* de lavar y poner, que se seca rápidamente y no necesita plancha.

dripping ['drɪpɪŋ] *n* GB *(fat)* pringue *mf*, grasa de carne asada.

▷ *adj* empapado,-a.

▷ *adv* chorreando. ■ **to be dripping wet** estar chorreando.

drive [draɪv] *n* **1** *(trip)* paseo en coche, vuelta en coche; *(journey)* viaje *m*: **we went for a drive** *dimos una vuelta en coche;* **it's a two-hour drive** *es un viaje de dos horas.* **2** *(road)* calle *f*; *(driveway)* camino de entrada. **3** SP *(golf)* golpe *m* inicial, tiro de salida; *(tennis)* golpe *m* fuerte, drive *m.* **4** *(campaign)* campaña: **sales drive** *promoción;* **membership drive** *campaña para atraer socios;* **a no-smoking drive** *una campaña antitabaco.* **5** MIL ofensiva, avanzada. **6** *(energy, initiative)* energía, ímpetu *m*, empuje *m*, dinamismo. **7** *(need, compulsion)* necesidad *f*, impulso, instinto. **8** *(propulsion system)* transmisión *f*, propulsión *f*; *(of wheeled vehicle)* tracción *f*: **front-wheel drive** *tracción delantera;* **four-wheel drive** *tracción en las cuatro ruedas;* **right/left-hand drive** *con el volante a la derecha/izquierda.* **9** GB *(competition, tournament)* torneo: **whist drive** *torneo de whist.*

▷ *vt* **1** *(operate - vehicle)* conducir: **he drives a bus** *es conductor de autobús.* **2** *(take - person)* llevar (en coche): **I'll drive you home** *te llevaré a casa;* **could you drive me to the airport?** *¿podrías llevarme al aeropuerto?* **3** *(cause to move - person)* hacer, obligar a; *(- animal)* arrear: **he was driven back by the flames** *las llamas le hicieron retroceder;* **the war is driving prices up** *la guerra está haciendo subir los precios.* **4** *(of wind - blow)* llevar; *(of water)* llevarse: **the wind drove the boat off course** *el viento alejó al barco de su rumbo.* **5** *(provide power for, keep going)* hacer funcionar, mover: **the river drives the waterwheel** *el río mueve el molino.* **6** *(strike in - stake)* hincar; *(- nail)* clavar; *(hit - ball)* mandar. **7** *(construct - tunnel)* perforar, abrir; *(- motorway)* construir. **8** *(force, compel to act)* forzar, obligar; *(cause to be in state)* llevar, empujar: **you're driving me crazy** *me estás volviendo loco;* **the pain was driving her mad** *el dolor la enloquecía;* **he is driven by greed** *lo impulsa la codicia.* **9** *(make work hard, overwork)* hacer trabajar: **you've been driving yourself to hard** *te has estado exigiendo demasiado.*

▷ *vi* **1** *(vehicle)* conducir: **can you drive?** *¿sabes conducir?;* **he's learning to drive** *está aprendiendo a conducir;* **I drove here** *vine en coche;* **don't drive so fast** *no vayas tan rápido, no corras;* **in England, people drive on the** left *en Inglaterra, la gente conduce por la izquierda.* **2** *(of rain, hail, snow)* azotar, barrer. ■ **to drive a coach and horses through** STH saltarse ALGO a la torera. ‖ **to drive a hard bargain** saber cómo conseguir lo que uno,-a quiere, ser buen,-na negociador,-ra. ‖ **to drive** STH **home** hacer entender ALGO.

▲ *pt* **drove** [drəʊv], *pp* **driven** ['drɪvən].

⊙ **to drive at** *vt insep* insinuar, querer decir.

⊙ **to drive away** *vt sep (fend off - attacker, animal)* ahuyentar; *(throw out)* alejar.

⊙ **to drive off** *vt sep* ahuyentar.

▷ *vi (car, driver)* irse.

⊙ **to drive on** *vi* seguir (adelante).

▷ *vt sep* empujar, llevar a.

⊙ **to drive out** *vt sep* expulsar.

drive-in ['draɪvɪn] *n* US *(cinema)* autocine *m*; *(restaurant)* restaurante *m* donde se atiende a los clientes desde el coche. ● **drive-in bank** autobanco.

drivel ['drɪvəl] *n* tonterías *fpl*, bobadas *fpl*, memeces *fpl*.

▷ *vi* [Also **to drivel on**.] decir tonterías, decir bobadas, decir memeces.

▲ *pt & pp* **drivelled** (US **driveled**), *ger* **drivelling** (US **driveling**).

driven ['drɪvən] *pp* → **drive**.

driver ['draɪvər] *n* **1** *(of bus, car)* conductor,-ra; *(of taxi)* taxista *mf*; *(of lorry)* camionero,-a; *(of racing car)* piloto *mf*; *(of train)* maquinista *mf*: **he's a very good driver** *conduce muy bien.* **2** SP *(golf club)* madera número 1. ■ **to be in the driver's seat** estar al frente, llevar las riendas. ● **driver's licence** US carnet *m* de conducir, permiso de conducir.

driveway ['draɪvweɪ] *n* camino de entrada.

driving ['draɪvɪŋ] *n* AUTO conducción *f*: **what do you think of Mum's** (US **Mom's**) **driving?** *¿te gusta como conduce mamá?, ¿qué te parece la manera de conducir de mamá?;* **we shared the driving** *nos turnamos para conducir;* **he was found guilty of dangerous driving** *lo declararon culpable de conducción temeraria.*

▷ *adj* **1** *(dynamic - personality)* dinámico,-a; *(force)* motriz: **she was the driving force behind the company** *ella era la impulsora de la empresa.* **2** *(rain)* torrencial; *(snow, wind)* que azota. ● **driving licence** carnet *m* de conducir, permiso de conducir. ‖ **driving range** *(in golf)* campo de prácticas. ‖ **driving school** autoescuela. ‖ **driving test** examen *m* de conducir.

drizzle ['drɪzəl] *n* llovizna, chirimiri *m*.

▷ *vi* lloviznar.

droll [drəʊl] *adj (amusing)* gracioso,-a, chistoso,-a; *(odd, quaint)* curioso,-a.

dromedary ['drɒmədərɪ] *n* dromedario.

▲ *pl* **dromedaries.**

drone[1] [drəʊn] *n* **1** *(bee)* zángano. **2** GB *pej (parasite)* zángano,-a, parásito,-a.

drone[2] [drəʊn] *n* **1** *(noise - of bee, engine)* zumbido; *(- of traffic, plane)* ruido, zumbido. **2** *(monotonous talk)* cantinela, sonsonete *m*.

▷ *vi (bee, plane, engine)* zumbar.

⊙ **to drone on** *vi* hablar con monotonía, hablar en tono monótono.

drool [dru:l] *n* **1** *(of baby)* baba, babas *fpl*. **2** *(drivel)* tonterías *fpl*, bobadas *fpl*, memeces *fpl*.

▷ *vi* **1** *(of baby, dog)* babear. **2** *(of person)* babear (**over**, por), caérsele la baba a (**over**, por): **the boys were drooling over the pin-up** *a los chicos se les caía la baba mirando la foto.*

droop [dru:p] *n (of shoulders)* caída, inclinación *f*, encorvamiento.

▷ *vi* **1** *(head)* inclinarse, caerse; *(shoulders)* encorvarse; *(eyelids)* cerrar. **2** *(flower)* marchitarse, ponerse mustio,-a; *(branches)* inclinarse. **3** *(spirits)* flaquear, decaer.

droopy ['dru:pɪ] *adj* caído,-a.

▲ *comp* **droopier**, *superl* **droopiest.**

drop [drɒp] *n* **1** *(of liquid)* gota: **she carried the cup without spilling a drop** *llevó la taza sin derramar ni una gota;* **we could do with a drop of rain** *nos iría bien un poco de lluvia;* **I never touch a drop** *no pruebo ni gota (de alcohol);* **a tear drop** *una lágrima.* **2** *(sweet)* pastilla, caramelo. **3** *(descent, distance down)* desnivel *m*, caída: **a sheer drop** *una caída a plomo.* **4** *(fall - gen)* caída; *(in price)* bajada, caída; *(in sales)* disminución *f*, descenso; *(in temperature)* descenso. **5** US *(collection point)* lugar *m* de recogida: **mail drop** *dirección postal.* **6** US *(delivery - from plane)* lanzamiento; *(- from van)* entrega, reparto. ■ **a drop in the ocean** una gota de agua en el mar, un grano de arena en el desierto. ● **drop curtain** THEAT telón *m*. ‖ **drop kick** *(in rugby)* botepronto. ‖ **drop shot** dejada.

▷ *vt* **1** *(let fall - accidentally)* caérsele a uno: **he dropped the glass** *se le cayó el vaso;* **don't drop it!** *¡que no se te caiga!;* **I must have dropped it** *se me debe haber caído;* **the goalkeeper dropped the ball** *al portero se le escapó el balón.* **2** *(let fall - deliberately)* dejar caer, tirar; *(let go of)* soltar; *(launch - bomb, supplies)* lanzar: **she dropped her handkerchief by his chair** *dejó caer su pañuelo al lado de su silla;* **drop it!** *¡suéltalo!* **3** *(lower voice)* bajar; *(- speed)* reducir; *(- prices)* bajar, reducir. **4** *fam (set down - passenger)* dejar (**off**, -); *(- delivery)* dejar, pasar a dejar (**off**, -): **where shall I drop you** *¿dónde quieres que te deje?* **5** *(give up, abandon - school subject, course, etc)* dejar, abandonar; *(- idea, plan)* abandonar, renunciar a; *(- case)* abandonar; *(- charge)* retirar; *(- boyfriend, girlfriend)* plantar: **let's drop the subject** *cambiemos de tema;* **drop everything** *dejarlo todo plantado;* **drop it!** *¡déjalo ya!, ¡basta ya!, ¡ya está bien!* **6** *(omit, leave out - in speaking)* no pronunciar, comerse; *(in writing)* omitir: **don't drop your "h's"** *no te comas las "haches";* **the gerund drops the final "e"** *el gerundio pierde la "e" final.* **7** SP *(player from team)* echar, sacar, no seleccionar; *(lose)* perder. **8** *(in knitting)* soltar, dejar escapar. **9** *sl (take drug)* tomarse. ■ **to do** STH **at the drop of a hat** hacer ALGO en cualquier momento, hacer ALGO sin más ni más. **to drop a brick / drop a clanger** hacer una plancha, meter la pata. ‖ **to drop a hint** soltar una indirecta. **to drop dead** caerse muerto,-a: **drop dead!** *¡vete a la porra!, ¡vete al demonio!* ‖ **to drop names** mencionar gente importante. ‖ **to drop** SB **a line / drop** SB **a note** escribir cuatro/unas líneas a ALGN. ‖ **to have a drop too much** beber más de la cuenta. ‖ **to let drop that ...** dejar caer/escapar que ...

▷ *vi* **1** *(fall - object)* caer, caerse; *(- person)* dejarse caer, tirarse: **an orange dropped out of her bag** *se le cayó una naranja de la bolsa;* **he dropped to his knees** *cayó de rodillas.* **2** *(collapse)* desplomarse, caer rendido,-a: **dance till you drop** *baila hasta que no puedas más;* **she dropped into an armchair** *se desplomó en un sillón.* **3** *(prices)* bajar, caer, descender; *(wind)* amainar; *(temperature)* bajar, descender; *(speed)* reducirse, disminuir; *(voice)* bajar. **4** *(land, ground)* caer. **5** *(lapse)* dejar: **let it drop!** *¡déjalo ya!, ¡basta ya!*

▲ *pt & pp* **dropped**, *ger* **dropping.**

▷ *n pl* **drops** MED gotas *fpl*: **I'll give you some eye drops** *te daré un colirio.*

⊙ **to drop away** *vi* **1** *(support, interest)* disminuir. **2** *(ground)* caer.

⊙ **to drop back / drop behind** *vi* rezagarse, quedarse atrás.

⊙ **to drop by** *vi* pasar.

▷ *vt insep* pasar por.

⊙ **to drop in** *vi (visit)* pasar.

▷ *vt sep (deliver)* dejar en casa (de ALGN), pasar a dejar.

⊙ **to drop in on** *vt insep* pasar a ver a, dejarse caer por casa de.

⊙ **to drop off** *vi* **1** *fam (fall asleep)* quedarse dormido,-a, dormirse. **2** *(sales, interest, etc)* disminuir.

⊙ **to drop out** *vi (of school, etc)* dejar los estudios, abandonar los estudios, colgar los libros; *(of group)* dejar el grupo; *(of race, competition)* abandonar; *(of society)* marginarse.

⊙ **to drop round** *vi* pasar.

▷ *vt sep* pasar a dejar.

droplet ['drɒplət] *n* gotita.

dropout ['drɒpaʊt] *n (from school)* alumno,-a que no termina el curso, alumno,-a que no completa los estudios; *(from university)* estudiante *mf* que deja los estudios; *(from society)* marginado,-a.

dropper ['drɒpəʳ] *n* cuentagotas *m.*

droppings ['drɒpɪŋz] *n pl (of birds)* excremento, caca, cagadas *fpl*; *(of sheep, goats, rabbits)* cagarrutas *fpl*, caca, cacas *fpl.*

dropsy ['drɒpsɪ] *n* hidropesía.

dross [drɒs] *n* **1** *(of metal)* escoria. **2** *(rubbish)* basura.

drought [draʊt] *n* sequía.

drove [drəʊv] *pt* ⟶ **drive.**

▷ *n* **1** *(of cattle)* manada. **2** *(of people)* multitud *f*: **they came in droves** *vinieron a montones.*

drown [draʊn] *vt* **1** *(person, animal)* ahogar. **2** *(submerge - place)* inundar, anegar. **3** *(smother - food)* ahogar; *(drink)* aguar. **4** *(sound, noise, voice, etc)* ahogar (**out**, -).

▷ *vi* ahogarse, morir ahogado,-a. ■ **to be drowned** ahogarse, morir ahogado,-a. ‖ **to drown one's sorrows** ahogar las penas.

drowning ['draʊnɪŋ] *adj* que se ahoga.

drowse [draʊz] *vi* dormitar.

drowsiness ['draʊzɪnəs] *n* somnolencia, sopor *m*, modorra.

drowsy ['draʊzɪ] *adj* **1** *(person, look)* somnoliento,-a, soñoliento,-a, adormilado,-a: **these tablets make me drowsy** *estas pastillas me dan sueño.* **2** *(atmosphere, day)* somnoliento,-a, soñoliento,-a; *(village, scene)* aletargado,-a, amodorrado,-a, somnoliento,-a, soñoliento,-a. ■ **to feel drowsy** tener ganas de dormir, tener sueño.

▲ *comp* **drowsier**, *superl* **drowsiest.**

drudge [drʌdʒ] *n (person)* esclavo,-a, machaca *mf*, burro de carga.

▷ *vi* trabajar como un,-a esclavo,-a.

drudgery ['drʌdʒərɪ] *n* trabajo duro y pesado.

drug [drʌg] *n* **1** *(medicine)* medicamento, medicina, fármaco. **2** *(narcotic)* droga, estupefaciente *m*, narcótico: **hard/soft drugs** *drogas duras/blandas.* ■ **to be on/do/take drugs** drogarse. ● **drug abuse** consumo de drogas. ‖ **drug addict** drogadicto,-a, toxicómano,-a. ‖ **drug addiction** drogadicción *f*, toxicomanía. ‖ **drug dealer** traficante *mf* de drogas. ‖ **drug pusher** camello *mf*. ‖ **drug squad** brigada de estupefacientes.

▷ *vt* **1** *(person, animal)* drogar. **2** *(food, drink)* adulterar con drogas.

▲ *pt & pp* **drugged**, *ger* **drugging.**

druggist ['drʌgɪst] *n* US farmacéutico,-a.

drugstore ['drʌgstɔːʳ] *n* US *establecimiento donde se puede comprar medicamentos, cosméticos, periódicos y otras cosas.*

druid ['druːɪd] *n* druida *m.*

drum [drʌm] *n* **1** *(instrument)* tambor *m.* **2** *(container)* bidón *m.* **3** TECH tambor.

▷ *vi* **1** *(play a drum)* tocar el tambor, tamborilear. **2** *(rain, hooves)* repiquetear; *(person)* tamborilear, tabalear.

▲ *pt & pp* **drummed**, *ger* **drumming.**

▷ *n pl* **drums** *(set)* batería. ■ **to drum one's fingers** tamborilear con los dedos. ‖ **to drum** STH **into** SB hacerle aprender ALGO a ALGN a fuerza de repetírselo, hacerle aprender algo a ALGN a fuerza de machacárselo. ‖ **to play the drums** tocar la batería. ● **drum major** tambor *m* mayor. ‖ **drum majorette** bastonera.

⊙ **to drum out** *vt sep* expulsar (**of**, de).

⊙ **to drum up** *vt insep (support, votes)* conseguir, obtener; *(enthusiasm)* despertar; *(business)* fomentar, atraer.

drumbeat ['drʌmbiːt] *n* son *m* del tambor.

drummer ['drʌməʳ] *n (in marching band)* tambor *mf*; *(in pop group, jazz band)* batería *mf.*

drumstick ['drʌmstɪk] *n* **1** MUS baqueta, palillo (de tambor). **2** CULIN muslo (de ave).

drunk [drʌŋk] *pp* ⟶ **drink.**

▷ *adj* **1** *(gen)* borracho,-a. **2** *fig (elated)* ebrio,-a, borracho,-a (**with**, de).

▷ *n (person)* borracho,-a. ■ **to be blind drunk / dead drunk** estar borracho,-a perdido,-a, estar como una cuba. ‖ **to be drunk and disorderly** JUR estar en estado de embriaguez y alterando el orden público. ‖ **to get drunk** emborracharse.

drunkard ['drʌŋkəd] *n* borracho,-a.

drunken ['drʌŋkᵊn] *adj (person)* borracho,-a; *(party)* de borrachos: **drunken driver** *conductor,-ra en estado de embriaguez.* ■ **in a drunken stupor** atontado,-a por la bebida.

drunkenness ['drʌŋkənnəs] *n* embriaguez *f.*

dry [draɪ] *adj* **1** *(gen)* seco,-a; *(bread - stale)* duro,-a; *(- without butter)* sin mantequilla: **tomorrow will be**

hot and dry *mañana hará un tiempo cálido y seco;* dry white wine *vino blanco seco.* **2** *(cow)* sin leche, que no da leche. **3** *(dull, uninteresting)* aburrido,-a, árido,-a. **4** *(amusing, ironic)* agudo,-a, mordaz, cáustico,-a.

▲ *comp* drier, *superl* driest.

▷ *vt (gen)* secar: dry your hands on this towel *sécate las manos en esta toalla.*

▷ *vi (become dry)* secarse (off, -): just leave the glasses to dry *deja que los vasos se sequen.* [Also to dry up.] *(dry the dishes)* secar (los platos). ■ **there wasn't a dry eye in the house** no hubo quien no llorara. ‖ **as dry as a bone** completamente seco,-a. ‖ **as dry as dust** muy árido,-a. ‖ **to be dry / feel dry** *(thirsty)* tener la garganta seca, tener sed. ‖ **to dry one's eyes** enjugarse las lágrimas. ‖ **to dry** os **(off)** secarse. ‖ **to run dry** *(river, well)* secarse. ‖ **to wipe** STH **dry** secar ALGO. ● **dry dock** dique *m* seco. ‖ **dry goods 1** GB comestibles *mpl* no perecederos. **2** US artículos *mpl* de mercería. ‖ **dry ice** hielo seco. ‖ **dry land** tierra firme. ‖ **dry law** US ley *f* seca. ‖ **dry rot** putrefacción *f* de la madera. ‖ **dry run** simulacro.

▲ *pt & pp* dried, *ger* drying.

⊙ **to dry out** *vi* **1** *(gen)* secarse. **2** *(alcoholic)* curarse.

⊙ **to dry up** *vi* **1** *(reservoir, river, etc)* secarse; *(funds, supply, resources, etc)* agotarse. **2** *(actor, etc)* quedarse en blanco: dry up! *¡cállate!, ¡cierra el pico!*

dry-clean [draɪ'kli:n] *vt* limpiar en seco.

dry-cleaner's [draɪ'kli:nəz] *n* tintorería, tinte *m.*

dryer ['draɪəʳ] *n (for clothes)* secadora; *(for hair)* secador *m.*

dry-eyed [draɪ'aɪd] *adj* sin una lágrima.

dryly ['draɪlɪ] *adv (coldly)* secamente, con sequedad; *(ironically)* con guasa, irónicamente.

dryness ['draɪnəs] *n* **1** *(gen)* sequedad *f.* **2** *(coldness)* sequedad *f; (irony)* ironía, guasa. **3** *(dullness)* aridez *f.*

D Sc ['di:'es'si:] *abbr* (Doctor of Science) doctor,-ra en ciencias.

DTI ['di:'ti:'aɪ] *abbr* GB *(Department of Trade and Industry)* departamento de comercio e industria.

DTP ['di:'ti:'pi:] *abbr* (desktop publishing) autoedición *f* antibalístico.

DTs ['di:'ti:z] *abbr* (delirium tremens) delírium *m* trémens.

dual ['djʊ:əl] *adj (gen)* doble. ● **dual carriageway** GB carretera de doble calzada.

dual-control [djʊ:əlkən'trəʊl] *adj* de doble mando, de doble control.

dual-purpose [djʊ:əl'pɜ:pəs] *adj (utensil)* de doble uso; *(furniture)* de doble función.

dub[1] [dʌb] *vt (soundtrack)* doblar (into, a).

▲ *pt & pp* dubbed, *ger* dubbing.

dub[2] [dʌb] *vt* **1** *(give nickname)* apodar. **2** *(knight)* armar.

▲ *pt & pp* dubbed, *ger* dubbing.

dub[3] [dʌb] *n* MUS dub *m.*

dubbing ['dʌbɪŋ] *n (of soundtrack)* doblaje *m.*

dubious ['djʊ:bɪəs] *adj* **1** *(questionable, suspect - morals, activities, origin)* dudoso,-a, sospechoso,-a; *(past, record)* turbio,-a; *(compliment)* ambiguo,-a, equívoco,-a; *(character)* sospechoso,-a. **2** *(unsure)* dudoso,-a, indeciso,-a. ■ **to be dubious about sth** tener dudas sobre algo, tener reservas sobre algo.

Dublin ['dʌblɪn] *n* Dublín.

Dubliner ['dʌblɪnəʳ] *n (person)* dublinés,-esa.

ducal ['djʊ:kəl] *adj* ducal.

ducat ['dʌkət] *n* ducado.

duchess ['dʌtʃəs] *n* duquesa.

duchy ['dʌtʃɪ] *n* ducado.

▲ *pl* duchies.

duck[1] [dʌk] *n* **1** *(bird)* pato,-a. **2** CULIN pato. **3** GB *fam (as term of address)* majo,-a, guapo,-a. **4** SP *(in cricket)* cero. ■ **to be like water off a duck's back** serle indiferente a uno. ‖ **to take to sth like a duck to water** adaptarse bien a algo.

duck[2] [dʌk] *vi (bend down)* agacharse; *(hide)* esconderse: she ducked behind the sofa *se escondió detrás del sofá.*

▷ *vt* **1** *(head)* agachar, bajar. **2** *(in water)* hundir, sumergir, zambullir. **3** *(dodge - duty, responsibility)* evadir eludir; *(- question)* eludir, esquivar. ■ **to duck out of** STH escabullirse de ALGO.

duckie ['dʌkɪ] *n fam* chato, chati.

ducking ['dʌkɪŋ] *n* chapuzón *m.*

duckling ['dʌklɪŋ] *n* patito.

duct [dʌkt] *n (gen)* conducto.

ductile ['dʌktaɪl] *adj* **1** *(metal)* dúctil. **2** *fig (person)* dúctil, dócil.

dud [dʌd] *n* **1** *fam (object)* trasto inútil, engañifa; *(person)* desastre *m,* inútil *mf.* **2** *(grenade, bomb, firework etc)* granada, bomba, fuego artificial, etc que no estalla.

▷ *adj (defective)* defectuoso,-a; *(worthless, useless)* inútil que no sirve; *(valueless - note, coin)* falso,-a; *(grenade bomb, firework)* que no estalla. ● **dud cheque** cheque *m* sin fondos.

dude [djʊ:d] *n* **1** US *(city man)* ciudadano. **2** *(guy, man)* tío, tipo. ● **dude ranch** rancho para turistas.

due [djʊ:] *adj* **1** *(expected, supposed to happen)* esperado,-a: her new book is due out in December *su nuevo libro saldrá en diciembre;* the train is due (in) at five o'clock *el tren debe llegar a las cinco;* he's due back any minute *volverá en cualquier momento;* when is the baby due? *¿para cuándo espera el bebé?;* we were due there at nine o'clock *teníamos que estar allí a las nueve.* **2** *fml (proper, correct)* debido,-a: he was driving without due care and attention *conducía de forma imprudente y sin prestar la debida atención;* after due consideration *con las debidas consideraciones.* **3** *(payable, requiring immediate payment)* pagadero,-a, que vence: a bill due today *una factura que vence hoy;* the rent isn't due till next week *no hay que pagar el alquiler hasta la semana que viene.* **4** *(owed as right)* merecido,-a; *(owed as debt)* debido,-a: thanks are due to all the staff at London Hospital *gracias a todo el personal del Hospital de Londres;* credit where credit's due *hay que reconocer su mérito;* I'm due for a rise *me corresponde un aumento de sueldo;* how much are you due? *¿cuánto te deben?;* I'm still due 5 days' holiday (US vacation) *aún me deben cinco días de vacaciones.* ■ **due to** debido a. ‖ **to become due** FIN vencer, hacerse efectivo,-a. ‖ **to be due to** deberse a, ser causado,-a por. ‖ **to giv**

SB **his/her due** dar a ALGN su merecido, ser justo,-a con ALGN, hacer justicia a ALGN. ‖ **with all due respect** con el debido respeto, con todo el respeto que se merece, sin ganas de ofender. ● **due date** (fecha de) vencimiento.
▷ *n* merecido.
▷ *adv* derecho hacia: **due north** *derecho hacia el norte.*
▷ *n pl* **dues** *(charges, payments, fees)* cuota: **have you paid your dues?** *¿has pagado la cuota?*
duel ['djuːəl] *n* duelo.
▷ *vi* batirse en duelo (**with**, con).
▲ *pt & pp* **duelled** (US **dueled**), *ger* **duelling** (US **dueling**).
duet [djuː'et] *n* dúo. ■ **to play/sing a duet** tocar/cantar a dúo.
duff [dʌf] *adj* GB *fam (useless)* inútil, que no sirve; *(defective)* defectuoso,-a.
⊃ **to duff up** *vt sep* dar una paliza a.
duffel ['dʌfəl] *n* tela gruesa de lana, muletón *m.* ● **duffel bag** talego, petate *m.* ‖ **duffel coat** trenca.
duffle ['dʌfəl] *n* ⟶ **duffel.**
dug [dʌg] *pt & pp* ⟶ **dig.**
dugout ['dʌgaut] *n* **1** MIL *(shelter)* refugio subterráneo. **2** SP *(in sportsground)* banquillo *(a un nivel inferior al del campo).* **3** [Also **dugout canoe.**] *(boat)* piragua.
duke [djuːk] *n* duque *m.*
dukedom ['djuːkdəm] *n* ducado.
dull [dʌl] *adj* **1** *(boring - job)* monótono,-a, pesado,-a; *(- person, life, film)* pesado,-a, aburrido,-a, soso,-a; *(- place, town)* aburrido,-a, sin interés. **2** *(not bright - colours)* apagado,-a; *(light)* pálido,-a; *(overcast - weather, day)* gris, triste, feo,-a; *(- sky)* cubierto,-a, nublado,-a; *(not shiny - hair, complexion, eyes)* sin brillo. **3** *(muffled - sound)* sordo,-a, amortiguado,-a; *(- pain, ache)* sordo,-a; *(blunt- edge, blade)* romo,-a, embotado,-a. **4** *(slow-witted)* torpe, lerdo,-a. **5** COMM *(sluggish - trade)* flojo,-a.
▷ *vt (pain)* aliviar, calmar; *(sound)* amortiguar; *(hearing)* embotar.
dullness ['dʌlnəs] *n* **1** *(boredom)* lo soso, lo aburrido. **2** *(lack of shine)* falta de brillo.
duly ['djuːlɪ] *adv* **1** *fml (properly)* debidamente. **2** *(as expected)* como era de esperar.
dumb [dʌm] *adj* **1** *(unable to speak)* mudo,-a. **2** *(silent)* callado,-a. **3** US *fam (stupid)* tonto,-a, estúpido,-a, bobo,-a.
▷ *n pl* **the dumb** los mudos *mpl.* ■ **to act dumb** hacerse el tonto. ‖ **to be struck dumb** quedarse mudo,-a, enmudecer.
dumbbell ['dʌmbel] *n* **1** SP pesa. **2** US *(stupid person)* tonto,-a, imbécil *mf,* estúpido,-a.
dumbfound [dʌm'faund] *vt* pasmar, dejar sin habla.
dumbfounded [dʌm'faundɪd] *adj* pasmado,-a, atónito,-a.
dumbly ['dʌmlɪ] *adv* sin decir nada.
dumbstruck ['dʌmstrʌk] *adj* estupefacto,-a.
dumdum ['dʌmdʌm] [Also **dumdum bullet.**] *n* dumdum *m.*
dummy ['dʌmɪ] *n* **1** *(in shop window, dressmaker's)* maniquí *m*; *(ventriloquist's, for tests)* muñeco. **2** *(fake)* imitación *f.* **3** *(in printing)* maqueta. **4** GB *(for baby)* chupete *m.* **5** *fam* imbécil *mf.* **6** SP *(in football, rugby)* regateo, finta. **7** *(in bridge - cards)* mano *f* de muerto; *(player)* muerto.
▲ *pl* **dummies.**
▷ *adj* falso,-a, de imitación. ● **dummy run** ensayo, prueba, simulacro.
dump [dʌmp] *n* **1** *(tip - for rubbish)* vertedero, basurero; *(- for cars)* cementerio (de coches). **2** MIL depósito. **3** *fam pej (place)* lugar *m* de mala muerte; *(town)* poblacho; *(dwelling)* tugurio. **4** COMPUT volcado de memoria.
▷ *vt* **1** *(drop, unload - rubbish)* verter, descargar; *(leave)* dejar, poner: **he dumped his dirty washing on the floor** *dejó su ropa sucia en el suelo.* **2** *(get rid of, abandon - gen)* deshacerse de, tirar, abandonar; *(- boyfriend, girlfriend)* plantar, dejar. **3** COMM *pej* inundar el mercado con algo barato: **they dump these medicines in the Third World** *inundan el mercado del Tercer Mundo con estos medicamentos baratos.* **4** COMPUT volcar. ■ **to dump** OS **on** SB plantarse en casa de ALGN.
dumper-truck ['dʌmpətrʌk] [Also **dumper.**] *n* volquete *m.*
dumping ['dʌmpɪŋ] *n* vertido. ■ **"No dumping"** "Prohibido arrojar basuras". ● **dumping ground** vertedero, basurero.
dumpling ['dʌmplɪŋ] *n* CULIN *(in stew)* bola de masa hervida para acompañar carnes, etc; *(as dessert)* (tipo de) budín *m* relleno.
dumps [dʌmps] ■ **to be down in the dumps** estar depre.
dumpy ['dʌmpɪ] *adj fam* rechoncho,-a, regordete.
▲ *comp* **dumpier,** *superl* **dumpiest.**
dunce [dʌns] *n* tonto,-a, burro,-a.
dune [djuːn] [Also **sand dune.**] *n* duna.
dung [dʌŋ] *n (manure)* estiércol *m*; *(excrement)* excremento, boñiga.
dungarees [dʌŋgə'riːz] *n (garment)* pantalones *mpl* de peto, peto; *(overalls)* mono.
dungeon ['dʌndʒən] *n* calabozo, mazmorra.
dunk [dʌŋk] *vt (bread, biscuit, etc)* mojar.
dunlin ['dʌnlɪn] *n* correlimos *m.*
dunnock ['dʌnək] *n* acentor *m.*
duo ['djuːəu] *n* dúo.
▲ *pl* **duos.**
duodena [djuːə'diːnə] *n pl* ⟶ **duodenum.**
duodenal [djuːə'diːnəl] *adj* duodenal.
duodenum [djuːə'diːnəm] *n* duodeno.
▲ *pl* **duodenums** o **duodena.**
dupe [djuːp] *n* ingenuo,-a, inocentón,-ona, primo,-a.
▷ *vt* engañar, embaucar. ■ **to dupe** SB **into doing** STH embaucar a ALGN para que haga ALGO.
duplex ['djuːpleks] *n* US *(house)* casa adosada; *(flat, apartment)* dúplex *m.*
duplicate [*(adj)* 'djuːplɪkət, *(n)* 'djuːplɪkeɪt] *adj* duplicado,-a: **a duplicate key** *una copia de una llave.*
▷ *n* copia, duplicado.
▷ *vt* **1** *(copy)* duplicar, hacer copias de. **2** *(repeat)* repetir. ■ **in duplicate** por duplicado.
duplication [djuːplɪ'keɪʃᵊn] *n* **1** *(of document)* copia, duplicación *f.* **2** *(repetition)* repetición *f.*
duplicator ['djuːplɪkeɪtəʳ] *n* multicopista.
duplicity [djuː'plɪsɪtɪ] *n fml* duplicidad *f.*

durability [djʊərəˈbɪlɪtɪ] *n* durabilidad *f.*

durable [ˈdjʊərəbəl] *adj* duradero,-a.

▷ *n pl* **durables** bienes *mpl* (de consumo) duraderos.

duration [djʊəˈreɪʃən] *n* duración *f.* ■ **for the duration** MIL mientras dure la guerra.

duress [djʊˈres] *phr* **under duress** *fml* bajo coacción.

during [ˈdjʊərɪŋ] *prep* durante: **I lived in France during the war** *viví en Francia durante la guerra;* **she's out at work during the day** *trabaja fuera de casa durante el día.*

dusk [dʌsk] *n* anochecer *m.* ■ **at dusk** al anochecer.

dust [dʌst] *n (gen)* polvo: **a cloud of dust** *una polvareda.*

▷ *vt* **1** *(room, furniture, ornaments, etc)* quitar el polvo a, limpiar el polvo a. **2** *(cake, plant)* espolvorear.

▷ *vi (clean)* quitar el polvo. ■ **to bite the dust 1** *(person)* morder el polvo. **2** *(plan, etc)* irse a pique. ‖ **to dust** OS **down** sacudirse el polvo. ‖ **to gather dust** llenarse de polvo. ‖ **to give** STH **a dust** quitar el polvo a ALGO, limpiar el polvo a ALGO. ‖ **not to see** SB **for dust** poner los pies en polvorosa. ‖ **when the dust has settled** cuando se calme la borrasca, cuando haya pasado la tormenta. ● **dust bowl** GEOG región *f* de sequía, zona semi-árida, zona semidesértica. ‖ **dust cover 1** *(for furniture)* funda. **2** *(for book)* sobrecubierta. ‖ **dust jacket** sobrecubierta. ‖ **dust storm** tormenta de polvo.

dustbin [ˈdʌstbɪn] *n* GB cubo de la basura. ● **dustbin man** basurero.

dustcart [ˈdʌstkɑːt] *n* camión *m* de la basura.

duster [ˈdʌstəʳ] *n (for dusting)* paño, trapo (del polvo); *(for blackboard)* borrador *m.*

dustman [ˈdʌstmən] *n* GB basurero.

dustpan [ˈdʌstpæn] *n* recogedor *m,* pala.

dust-up [ˈdʌstʌp] *n* GB *fam (fight)* pelea.

dusty [ˈdʌstɪ] *adj* **1** *(track, town)* polvoriento,-a; *(room)* lleno,-a de polvo; *(furniture)* cubierto,-a de polvo. **2** *(of colour)* grisáceo,-a, ceniciento,-a. ■ **to get a dusty answer** recibir una evasiva.

▲ *comp* **dustier**, *superl* **dustiest**.

Dutch [dʌtʃ] *adj* holandés,-esa, neerlandés,-esa.

▷ *n (language)* holandés *m.*

▷ *n pl* **the Dutch** los holandeses *mpl.* ■ **to go Dutch (with** SB**)** pagar cada uno lo suyo, pagar a escote, pagar a la catalana. ● **Dutch courage** valor *m* que da la bebida. ‖ **Dutch elm** olmo. ‖ **Dutch elm disease** grafiosis *f* del olmo.

Dutchman [ˈdʌtʃmən] *n* holandés *m,* neerlandés *m.* ■ **I'm a Dutchman** yo soy el Papa de Roma.

▲ *pl* **Dutchmen** [ˈdʌtʃmən].

Dutchwoman [ˈdʌtʃwʊmən] *n* holandesa.

▲ *pl* **Dutchwomen** [ˈdʌtʃwɪmɪn].

dutiable [ˈdjuːtɪəbəl] *adj* sujeto,-a a derechos arancelarios.

dutiful [ˈdjuːtɪfʊl] *adj* consciente de sus deberes, obediente y respetuoso,-a.

duty [ˈdjuːtɪ] *n* **1** *(obligation)* deber *m,* obligación *f:* **I feel it's my duty to go** *creo que es mi obligación ir;* **he went to the funeral out of a sense of duty** *asistió al funeral porque le parecía que era su deber.* **2** *(task)* función *f,* cometido: **her duties include dealing with the public** *sus funciones incluyen atender al público.* **3** *(service)* guardia, servicio. **4** *(tax)* impuesto: **there's duty to pay on that** *hay que pagar un impuesto por eso.* ■ **to be off duty 1** *(doctor, nurse, etc)* no estar de guardia. **2** *(police, firefighter, etc)* no estar de servicio. ‖ **to be on duty 1** *(doctor, nurse, etc)* estar de guardia. **2** *(police, firefighter)* estar de servicio: **she's on night duty** *tiene guardia nocturna.* ‖ **to do duty as** STH servir de ALGO, hacer las veces de ALGO. ‖ **to do one's duty** cumplir con su deber. ‖ **to make it one's duty to do** STH encargarse de hacer ALGO. ‖ **to neglect one's duties** descuidar sus responsabilidades. ‖ **to take up one's duties** entrar en funciones. ● **customs duties** derechos *mpl* de aduana, aranceles *mpl.* **duty roster** lista de guardias.

▲ *pl* **duties**.

duty-bound [ˈdjuːtɪbaʊnd] *adj* moralmente obligado,-a.

duty-free [ˈdjuːtɪfriː] *adj* libre de impuestos.

▷ *adv* libre de impuestos, sin pagar impuestos.

▷ *n (object)* artículo libre de impuestos. ● **duty-free shop** duty-free *m,* tienda libre de impuestos.

duvet [ˈduːveɪ] *n* GB edredón *m.* ● **duvet cover** funda de edredón.

DV [ˈdiːˈviː] *abbr* **(Deo volente)** Dios mediante; *(abbreviation)* Dm.

DVD [ˈdiːˈviːˈdiː] *n* **(Digital Video Disc)** DVD *m.* ● **DVD player** lector *m* de DVD.

dwarf [dwɔːf] *n (gen)* enano,-a.

▲ *pl* **dwarfs** o **dwarves** [dwɔːvz].

▷ *adj* enano,-a.

▷ *vt* hacer parecer pequeño,-a.

dwell [dwel] *vi fml* morar, habitar, vivir.

▲ *pt & pp* **dwelt** [dwelt].

⊙ **to dwell on** *vt insep (think about)* pensar demasiado en; *(talk about)* hablar extensamente de, detenerse demasiado en: **let's not dwell on it** *olvidémoslo.*

dweller [ˈdweləʳ] *n* morador,-ra, habitante *mf:* **cave dweller** *cavernícola;* **city dweller** *persona que vive en la ciudad.*

dwelling [ˈdwelɪŋ] *n fml* morada, vivienda.

dwelt [dwelt] *pt & pp* ⟶ **dwell**.

dwindle [ˈdwɪndəl] *vi* menguar, disminuir, reducirse. ■ **to dwindle away to nothing** quedar reducido,-a a nada.

dwindling [ˈdwɪndlɪŋ] *adj (numbers, population)* cada vez más reducido,-a; *(resources)* cada vez más limitado,-a.

DWP [ˈdiːˈdʌbəljuːˈpiː] *abbr* GB **(Department for Work and Pensions)** departamento de servicios sociales; *(abbreviation)* ABM *m.*

dye [daɪ] *n* tinte *m,* tintura, colorante *m.*

▷ *vt* teñir: **she dyed her hair green** *se tiñó el pelo de verde.*

▷ *vi* teñirse.

dyed-in-the-wool [daɪdɪnðəˈwʊl] *adj pej* acérrimo,-a, inflexible, intransigente.

dying [ˈdaɪɪŋ] *adj (person, animal)* moribundo,-a, agonizante; *(race, breed, art, industry)* en vías de extinción; *(custom)* en vías de desaparición; *(flame, embers)* mortecino,-a; *(words, breath)* último,-a, postrero,-a.

▷ *n* muerte *f.*

▷ *n pl* **the dying** los moribundos *mpl*. ■ **to be SB's dying wish** ser el último deseo de ALGN. ■ **to one's dying day** hasta el fin de sus días, hasta que se muera.

dyke [daɪk] *n* **1** *(bank)* dique *m*, barrera; *(causeway)* terraplén *m*. **2** *sl pej (lesbian)* tortillera.

dynamic [daɪ'næmɪk] *adj (gen)* dinámico,-a.
▷ *n* TECH dinámica.

dynamics [daɪ'næmɪks] *n (science)* dinámica.

dynamism ['daɪnəmɪzəm] *n* dinamismo.

dynamite ['daɪnəmaɪt] *n* **1** *(explosive)* dinamita. **2** *fam (shocking thing)* una bomba; *(wonderful thing, person)* sensación *f*: **if the press got hold of this, it could be dynamite** *si se enterara la prensa de esto, podría ser una bomba;* **their new singer is dynamite!** *¡su nuevo cantante es sensacional!*
▷ *vt* dinamitar, volar con dinamita.

dynamo ['daɪnəməʊ] *n* dinamo *f*, dínamo *f*.
▲ *pl* dynamos.

dynastic [dɪ'næstɪk] *adj* dinástico,-a.

dynasty ['dɪnəstɪ] *n* dinastía.
▲ *pl* dynasties.

dyne [daɪn] *n* dina.

dysentery ['dɪsᵊntrɪ] *n* disentería.

dysfunction [dɪs'fʌnkʃᵊn] *n* disfunción *f*.

dyslexia [dɪs'leksɪə] *n* dislexia.

dyslexic [dɪs'leksɪk] *adj* disléxico,-a.

dysphasia [dɪs'feɪzɪə] *n* disfasia.

dysplasia [dɪs'pleɪzɪə] *n* displasia.

dystrophy ['dɪstrəfɪ] *n* distrofia.

E

E, e [i:] *n* **1** *(the letter)* E, e *f.* **2** MUS mi *m.*
E [i:st] *abbr* (east) este *m*; *(abbreviation)* E.
each [i:tʃ] *adj* cada: each day *cada día, todos los días.*
▷ *pron* cada uno,-a: they each have their own car *cada uno tiene su coche.*
▷ *adv* cada uno,-a: apples cost 15p each *las manzanas cuestan 15 peniques la pieza.*
eager ['i:gəʳ] *adj* **1** *(anxious)* ávido,-a (to, de), ansioso,-a (to, de); *(desirous)* deseoso,-a (to, de); *(impatient)* impaciente (to, por). **2** *(excited, full of interest)* ilusionado,-a, entusiasta: it was nice to see their eager faces *daba gusto ver sus caras ilusionadas.*
eagerly ['i:gəlɪ] *adv* *(enthusiastically)* con afán, con entusiasmo; *(anxiously)* con impaciencia.
eagle ['i:gᵊl] *n* **1** *(bird)* águila. **2** *(in golf)* eagle *m.* ● **golden eagle** águila real.
eaglet ['i:glət] *n* aguilucho.
ear[1] [ɪəʳ] *n* **1** ANAT oreja. **2** *(sense)* oído. ● **ear lobe** lóbulo. ‖ **ear, nose and throat specialist** otorrinolaringólogo,-a. ‖ **ear shell** oreja de mar. ‖ **ear trumpet** trompetilla. ‖ **thick ear** bofetada.
ear[2] [ɪəʳ] *n* *(of cereal)* espiga.
earache ['ɪəᵊeɪk] *n* dolor *m* de oídos.
eardrum ['ɪədᵊʌm] *n* tímpano.
earflap ['ɪəflæp] *n* orejera.
earl [ɜ:l] *n* conde *m.*
earldom ['ɜ:ldəm] *n* condado.
early ['ɜ:lɪ] *adj* **1** *(before expected)* temprano,-a, pronto,-a: we were early *llegamos temprano.* **2** *(initial)* primero,-a: take the early train *coge el primer tren de la mañana.* **3** *(near beginning)*: in the early 1960's *a principios de los sesenta.*
▲ *comp* earlier, *superl* earliest.
▷ *adv* **1** *(before expected)* temprano, pronto; *(soon)* pronto: she got up early *se levantó temprano.* **2** *(in good time)* con tiempo, con anticipación: we got there early to get a good seat *llegamos con tiempo para coger buen sitio.*
earmark ['ɪəmɑ:k] *vt* destinar (for, a), reservar (for, para).
earmuff ['ɪəmʌf] *n* orejera.
earn [ɜ:n] *vt* ganar, ganarse: how much do you earn a month? *¿cuánto ganas al mes?.*
earner ['ɜ:nəʳ] *n* **1** *(person)* persona que gana dinero: I'm the only earner in the family *soy el único de la familia que gana un sueldo.* **2** *(thing)* cosa rentable.
earnest ['ɜ:nɪst] *adj* serio,-a, formal.
earnestly ['ɜ:nɪstlɪ] *adv* seriamente.
earnings ['ɜ:nɪŋz] *n pl* **1** *(personal)* ingresos *mpl.* **2** *(of company)* ganancias *fpl.*
earphones ['ɪəfəʊnz] *n pl* auriculares *mpl.*
earpiece ['ɪəpi:s] *n* *(of telephone)* auricular *m.*
earplug ['ɪəplʌg] *n* tapón *m para los oídos.*
earring ['ɪəᵊrɪŋ] *n* pendiente *m.*
earshot ['ɪəʃɒt] ■ **out of earshot** fuera del alcance del oído. ‖ **within earshot** al alcance del oído.
earth [ɜ:θ] *n* **1** *(gen)* tierra: the highest mountain on earth *la montaña más alta de la tierra.* **2** GB toma de tierra, tierra. **3** GB *(of fox, badger)* madriguera.
▷ *vt* GB conectar a tierra.
A menudo se escribe Earth cuando se refiere al planeta.
earthbound ['ɜ:θbaʊnd] *adj* **1** *(confined to Earth)* que no puede despegar; *(heading for Earth)* que se dirige hacia la Tierra. **2** *fig (dull)* corriente, poco imaginativo,-a, prosaico,-a.
earthen ['ɜ:ðᵊn] *adj* **1** *(of earth)* de tierra. **2** *(of baked clay)* de barro, de arcilla.
earthenware ['ɜ:ðᵊnweəʳ] *n* loza.
▷ *adj* de arcilla, de barro.
earthiness ['ɜ:θɪnəs] *n* desinhibición *f.*
earthling ['ɜ:θlɪŋ] *n* terrícola *mf.*
earthly ['ɜ:θlɪ] *adj* **1** *(on earth)* terrenal. **2** *fam* posible.
earthquake ['ɜ:θkweɪk] *n* terremoto.
earthshattering ['ɜ:θʃætᵊrɪŋ] *adj* trascendental.
earthward ['ɜ:θwəd] *adj* hacia la tierra.
earthworm ['ɜ:θwɜ:m] *n* lombriz *f.*
earthy ['ɜ:θɪ] *adj* **1** *(colour)* terroso,-a; *(smell)* a tierra. **2** *(frank, straightforward)* desinhibido,-a.
▲ *comp* earthier, *superl* earthiest.
earwax ['ɪəwæks] *n* cerumen *m*, cera, cerilla.
earwig ['ɪəwɪg] *n* tijereta.
ease [i:z] *n* **1** *(lack of difficulty)* facilidad *f.* **2** *(natural manner)* soltura, naturalidad *f*, desenvoltura. **3** *(freedom from pain)* alivio. **4** *(leisure, affluence)* comodidad *f*, desahogo.
▷ *vt* **1** *(relieve, alleviate)* aliviar (of, de), calmar. **2** *(improve)* mejorar, facilitar; *(make easier)* facilitar. **3** *(move gently)* mover con cuidado. **4** *(loosen)* aflojar.
▷ *vi* **1** *(pain)* aliviarse, calmarse, disminuir; *(tension etc)* disminuir. **2** *(become easier)* mejorar.
⊙ **to ease off / ease up** *vi* **1** *(pain)* aliviarse, calmarse, disminuir; *(tension, etc)* disminuir; *(rain)* amainar. **2** *(slow down)* ir más despacio.
⊙ **to ease up on** *vt insep fam (go easy, be more moderate)* aflojar, no pasarse con.
easel ['i:zᵊl] *n* caballete *m.*
easily ['i:zɪlɪ] *adv* **1** *(without difficulty)* fácilmente, con facilidad. **2** *(by far)* con mucho; *(without doubt)* sin duda. **3** *(possibly)* fácilmente, perfectamente.
east [i:st] *adj (gen)* este, oriental; *(wind)* del este.
▷ *adv* hacia el este, en dirección este.
▷ *n (gen)* este *m.*
▷ *n* **the East** *(Asia)* Oriente *m*; *(Eastern Europe)* el Este *m.*

eastbound ['i:stbaʊnd] *adj (train)* que va en dirección este; *(carriageway)* en dirección este.
Easter ['i:stəʳ] *n* **1** REL Pascua, Pascua de Resurrección. **2** *(holiday)* Semana Santa.
easterly ['i:stəlɪ] *adj* **1** *(to the east)* al este, hacia el este. **2** *(from the east)* del este.
▷ *n* viento del este.
▲ *pl* easterlies.
eastern ['i:stᵊn] *adj* oriental, del este.
Easterner ['i:stənəʳ] *n* US *nativo,-a del Este de los Estados Unidos.*
eastward ['i:stwəd] *adj* hacia el este.
eastwards ['i:stwədz] *adv* hacia el este.
easy ['i:zɪ] *adj* **1** *(not difficult)* fácil, sencillo. **2** *(comfortable)* cómodo,-a. **3** *(unworried, relaxed)* tranquilo,-a.
▲ *comp* easier, *superl* easiest.
▷ *adv* con cuidado, con calma.
easy-going [i:zɪ'gəʊɪŋ] *adj (relaxed)* tranquilo,-a; *(easy to please)* fácil de complacer, poco exigente.
eat [i:t] *vt* comer.
▲ *pt* ate [et, eɪt], *pp* eaten ['i:tən].
▷ *vi* comer: we always eat at 7.00 *siempre cenamos a las 7.00.*
⊙ **to eat away** *vt sep (mice)* roer; *(termites)* carcomer; *(acid)* corroer; *(sea)* desgastar.
⊙ **to eat into** *vt insep* **1** *(acid, rust)* corroer. **2** *fig (cost)* comerse.
⊙ **to eat out** *vi (lunch)* comer fuera; *(dinner)* cenar fuera.
⊙ **to eat up** *vt sep* **1** *(finish food)* comerse: eat it all up! *¡cómetelo todo!* **2** *(consume)* consumir, tragar, devorar.
eatable ['i:təbᵊl] *adj* comestible.
eaten ['i:tᵊn] *pp* → eat.
eau de Cologne [əʊdəkə'ləʊn] *n* colonia.
eaves [i:vz] *n pl* alero *m sing.*
eavesdrop ['i:vzdrɒp] *vi* escuchar a escondidas (on, -).
▲ *pt & pp* eavesdropped, *ger* eavesdropping.
ebb [eb] *n* reflujo.
▷ *vi* **1** *(water)* bajar. **2** *fig* disminuir, decaer.
to ebb away *vi fig* ir disminuyendo.
ebonite ['ebənaɪt] *n* ebonita.
ebony ['ebənɪ] *n* ébano.
▷ *adj* de ébano.
ebullience [ɪ'bʌljəns] *n* exaltación *f*, euforia.
ebullient [ɪ'bʌljənt] *adj* exaltado,-a, eufórico,-a.
eccentric [ɪk'sentrɪk] *adj* **1** *(unusual)* excéntrico,-a, estrafalario,-a. **2** *(of circles)* excéntrico,-a.
▷ *n (person)* excéntrico,-a.
eccentricity [eksen'trɪsɪtɪ] *n* excentricidad *f.*
▲ *pl* eccentricities.
ecclesiastic [ɪkli:zɪ'æstɪk] *adj* eclesiástico,-a.
▷ *n* eclesiástico, clérigo.
echelon ['eʃəlɒn] *n* MIL escalón *m.* ■ **in echelon** MIL en escalafón.
▷ *n pl* echelons *(levels)* niveles *mpl*, estratos *mpl*, capas *fpl.*
echinoderm ['ɪkainəʊdɜ:m] *n* equinodermo.
echo ['ekəʊ] *n* **1** eco. **2** *fig* resonancia.
▲ *pl* echoes.
▷ *vt* **1** repetir (back, -). **2** *fig (words)* repetir, imitar; *(opinions)* hacerse eco de.
▷ *vi* hacer eco, resonar.
eclectic [ɪ'klektɪk] *adj fml* ecléctico,-a.
▷ *n* ecléctico,-a.
eclipse [ɪ'klɪps] *n* **1** eclipse *m.* **2** *fig* eclipse *m.*
▷ *vt* **1** eclipsar. **2** *fig* eclipsar, brillar más que, hacer sombra a.
ecliptic [ɪ'klɪptɪk] *n* eclíptica.
ecofriendly [ekəʊ'frendlɪ] *adj* no perjudicial para el medio ambiente, que no perjudica el medio ambiente.
ecological [i:kə'lɒdʒɪkᵊl] *adj* ecológico,-a.
ecologist [ɪ'kɒlədʒɪst] *n* ecologista *mf.*
ecology [ɪ'kɒlədʒɪ] *n* ecología.
economic [ekə'nɒmɪk, i:kə'nɒmɪk] *adj* **1** *(gen)* económico,-a. **2** *(profitable)* rentable.
economically [ekə'nɒmɪklɪ, i:kə'nɒmɪklɪ] *adv* económicamente: economically speaking *en términos económicos.*
economics [ekə'nɒmɪks, i:kə'nɒmɪks] *n* **1** *(science)* economía. **2** EDUC económicas *fpl*, ciencias *fpl* económicas.
▷ *n pl (financial aspect)* aspecto económico.
economist [ɪ'kɒnəmɪst] *n* economista *mf.*
economize [ɪ'kɒnəmaɪz] *vi* economizar (on, en), ahorrar (on, en).
economy [ɪ'kɒnəmɪ] *n* **1** *(saving)* economía, ahorro. **2** *(science)* economía; *(system)* sistema *m* económico, economía.
▲ *pl* economies.
ecosystem ['i:kəʊsɪstəm] *n* ecosistema *m.*
ecstasy ['ekstəsɪ] *n* éxtasis *m.*
▲ *pl* ecstasies.
ecstatic [ek'stætɪk] *adj* extasiado,-a.
ECU ['eɪkju:] *abbr* (European Currency Unit) unidad de cuenta europea, ECU.
Ecuador ['ekwədɔ:ʳ] *n* Ecuador *m.*
Ecuadorian [ekwə'dɔ:ʳɪən] *adj* ecuatoriano,-a.
▷ *n* ecuatoriano,-a.
ecumenic [i:kjʊ'menɪk] *adj* ecuménico,-a.
eczema ['eksɪmə] *n* eccema *m.*
eddy ['edɪ] *n* remolino.
▲ *pl* eddies.
▷ *vi* arremolinarse.
▲ *pt & pp* eddied, *ger* eddying.
edema [ɪ'di:mə] *n* US edema *m.*
Eden ['i:dᵊn] [Also the garden of Eden.] *n* el Edén *m.*
edge [edʒ] *n* **1** *(of cliff, wood, etc)* borde *m.* **2** *(of coin, step, etc)* canto. **3** *(of knife)* filo. **4** *(of water)* orilla. **5** *(of town)* afueras *fpl.* **6** *(of paper)* margen *m.* **7** *(brink)* borde *m.* **8** *(to voice)* tono.
▷ *vt* **1** *(supply with border)* bordear. **2** SEW ribetear.
▷ *vi (move in small stages)* moverse con cautela, moverse poco a poco.
⊙ **to edge away** *vi* alejarse poco a poco.
⊙ **to edge forward** *vi* avanzar lentamente, avanzar poco a poco.
⊙ **to edge out** *vt sep (displace)* eliminar, apartar, quitar.
edgeways ['edʒweɪz] *adv* de lado.
edging ['edʒɪŋ] *n* ribete *m*, orla.
edgy ['edʒɪ] *adj* nervioso,-a.
▲ *comp* edgier, *superl* edgiest.
edible ['edɪbᵊl] *adj* comestible.
edict ['i:dɪkt] *n* **1** edicto. **2** JUR decreto.
edification [edɪfɪ'keɪʃᵊn] *n fml (improvement of mind)* edificación *f.*

edifice ['edɪfɪs] *n* **1** *fml (building)* edificio, gran edificio. **2** *fig* estructura.
edify ['edɪfaɪ] *vt fml* edificar.
▲ *pt & pp* **edified**, *ger* **edifying.**
Edinburgh ['edɪnbᵊrə] *n* Edimburgo.
edit ['edɪt] *vt* **1** *(prepare for printing)* preparar para la imprenta. **2** *(correct)* corregir; *(put together)* editar. **3** *(run newspaper, etc)* dirigir. **4** *(film, programme)* montar, editar.
⊙ **to edit out** *vt sep* cortar.
edition [ɪ'dɪʃᵊn] *n* edición *f*.
editor ['edɪtəʳ] *n* **1** *(of book)* editor,-ra; *(writer)* redactor,-ra; *(proofreader)* corrector,-ra. **2** *(of newspaper, etc)* director,-ra. **3** *(of film, programme)* montador,-ra.
editorial [edɪ'tɔːᵊrɪəl] *adj* editorial.
▷ *n* editorial *m*. ● **editorial staff** redacción *f*.
educate ['edjʊkeɪt] *vt* educar, formar.
educated ['edjʊkeɪtɪd] *adj* culto,-a, cultivado,-a.
education [edjʊ'keɪʃᵊn] *n* **1** *(system of teaching)* educación *f*, enseñanza. **2** *(training)* formación *f*, preparación *f*, instrucción *f*. **3** *(acquisition of knowledge)* estudios *mpl*, formación *f* académica. **4** *(theory of teaching)* pedagogía. **5** *(knowledge, culture)* cultura.
educational [edjʊ'keɪʃᵊnəl] *adj* educativo,-a.
educationalist [edʒʊ'keɪʃᵊnəlɪst] *n* pedagogo,-a.
educationist [edʒʊ'keɪʃᵊnɪst] *n* pedagogo,-a.
educator ['edʒʊkeɪtəʳ] *n* educador,-ra.
eel [iːl] *n* anguila.
eerie ['ɪrɪ] *adj* misterioso,-a, siniestro,-a.
efface [ɪ'feɪs] *vt fml* borrar.
effect [ɪ'fekt] *n* **1** *(gen)* efecto. **2** *(impression)* impresión *f*, efecto.
▷ *vt fml* efectuar, provocar.
▷ *n pl* **effects** *(property)* efectos *mpl*.
effective [ɪ'fektɪv] *adj* **1** *(successful)* eficaz. **2** *(real, actual)* efectivo,-a. **3** *(operative)* vigente. **4** *(impressive)* impresionante; *(striking)* llamativo,-a.
effectively [ɪ'fektɪvlɪ] *adv* **1** *(efficiently)* eficazmente. **2** *(in effect)* de hecho, en efecto.
effectual [ɪ'fektʊəl] *adj fml* eficaz.
effectuate [ɪ'fektjʊeɪt] *vt* efectuar, realizar.
effeminate [ɪ'femɪnət] *adj* afeminado,-a.
effervesce [efə'ves] *vi* **1** *(of liquids)* entrar en efervescencia. **2** *fig (of people)* ser efervescente, ser muy vivo,-a.
effervescent [efə'vesᵊnt] *adj* efervescente.
effete [e'fiːt] *adj (weak)* débil, impotente; *(feeble)* agotado,-a.
efficacious [efɪ'keɪʃəs] *adj* eficaz.
efficacy ['efɪkəsɪ] *n* eficacia.
efficiency [ɪ'fɪʃᵊnsɪ] *n* **1** *(of person)* eficiencia, competencia. **2** *(of system, product)* eficacia. **3** *(of machine)* rendimiento.
efficient [ɪ'fɪʃᵊnt] *adj* **1** *(person)* eficiente, competente. **2** *(system, product)* eficaz. **3** *(machine)* de buen rendimiento.
effigy ['efɪdʒɪ] *n* efigie *f*.
▲ *pl* **effigies.**
efflorescence [eflɔː'resᵊns] *n lit* florecimiento.
effluent ['eflʊənt] *n* **1** *(waste matter)* aguas *fpl* residuales, residuos *mpl*. **2** *(stream)* corriente *f*.

effort ['efət] *n* **1** *(exertion)* esfuerzo. **2** *(attempt, struggle)* intento, tentativa. **3** *(achievement)* obra.
effrontery [ɪ'frʌntərɪ] *n* descaro, desfachatez *f*, frescura.
effusive [ɪ'fjʊːsɪv] *adj* efusivo,-a.
effusively [ɪ'fjʊːsɪvlɪ] *adv* efusivamente, con efusividad.
EFL ['iː'ef'el] *abbr* (**English as a foreign language**) inglés como idioma extranjero.
egalitarian [ɪgælɪ'teərɪən] *adj* igualitario,-a.
egg¹ [eg] *n* **1** *(laid by birds, etc)* huevo. **2** BIOL *(ovum)* óvulo.
egg² [eg] *vt* **to egg on** animar, incitar.
egghead ['eghed] *n pej* intelectual *mf*.
eggnog [eg'nɒg] *n* ponche *m* de huevo.
eggplant ['egplɑːnt] *n* berenjena.
eggshell ['egʃel] *n* cáscara de huevo.
egg-slicer ['egslaɪsəʳ] *n* cortahuevos *m*.
ego ['iːgəʊ] *n* **1** *(in psychology)* ego. **2** *fam* amor *m* propio.
▲ *pl* **egos.**
egocentric [iːgəʊ'sentrɪk] *adj* egocéntrico,-a.
egoism ['iːgəʊɪzᵊm] *n* egoísmo.
egoist ['iːgəʊɪst] *n* egoísta *mf*.
egomaniac [iːgəʊ'meɪnɪæk] *n* ególatra *mf*.
Egypt ['iːdʒɪpt] *n* Egipto.
Egyptian [ɪ'dʒɪpʃᵊn] *adj* egipcio,-a.
▷ *n* **1** *(person)* egipcio,-a. **2** *(language)* egipcio.
Egyptology [iːdʒɪp'tɒlədʒɪ] *n* egiptología.
eider ['aɪdəʳ] [Also **eider duck.**] *n* eider *m*.
eiderdown ['aɪdədaʊn] *n* edredón *m*.
eight [eɪt] *adj* ocho.
▷ *n* **1** ocho. **2** SP *(oarsmen)* ocho.
Consulta también **six.**
eighteen [eɪ'tiːn] *adj* dieciocho.
▷ *n* dieciocho.
Consulta también **six.**
eighteenth [eɪ'tiːnθ] *adj* decimoctavo,-a.
▷ *adv* en decimoctavo lugar.
▷ *n* **1** *(in series)* decimoctavo,-a. **2** *(fraction)* decimoctavo; *(one part)* decimoctava parte *f*.
Consulta también **sixth.**
eighth [eɪtθ] *adj* octavo,-a.
▷ *adv* octavo, en octavo lugar.
▷ *n* **1** *(in series)* octavo,-a. **2** *(fraction)* octavo; *(one part)* octava parte *f*.
Consulta también **sixth.**
eighties ['eɪtɪz] *n pl* **the eighties** los años *mpl* ochenta, los ochenta *mpl*.
Consulta también **sixties.**
eightieth ['eɪtɪɪθ] *adj* octogésimo,-a.
▷ *adv* en octogésimo lugar.
▷ *n* **1** *(in series)* octogésimo,-a. **2** *(fraction)* octogésimo; *(one part)* octogésima parte *f*.
Consulta también **sixtieth.**
eighty ['eɪtɪ] *adj* ochenta.
▷ *n* ochenta.
Consulta también **sixty.**
einsteinium [aɪn'staɪnɪəm] *n* einstenio.
Eire ['eərə] *n* Eire *m*.

either ['aɪðəʳ, 'i:ðəʳ] *pron* 1 *(affirmative)* cualquiera: **either of them** *cualquiera de los dos.* 2 *(negative)* ni el uno ni el otro, ni la una ni la otra, ninguno de los dos, ninguna de las dos: **I can't stand either** *no aguanto ni el uno ni el otro.*
▷ *adj* 1 cualquier. 2 *(both)* cada, los dos, las dos, ambos,-as. 3 *(neither)* ninguno de los dos, ninguna de las dos.
▷ *conj* 1 *(affirmative)* o: **he'll arrive either today or tomorrow** *llegará u hoy o mañana.* 2 *(negative)* ni: **I didn't go to either the wedding or the party** *no fui ni a la boda ni a la fiesta.*
▷ *adv (after negative)* tampoco: **Ann didn't come either** *tampoco vino Ann.*
ejaculate [ɪ'dʒækjʊleɪt] *vi* 1 *(eject fluid)* eyacular. 2 *(exclaim)* exclamar.
ejaculation [ɪdʒækʊ'leɪʃᵊn] *n* 1 *(ejection)* eyaculación *f.* 2 *(exclamation)* exclamación *f.*
eject [ɪ'dʒekt] *vt* expulsar, echar.
▷ *vi* AV eyectar(se).
ejection [ɪ'dʒekʃᵊn] *n* 1 *(gen)* expulsión *f.* 2 *(from plane)* eyección *f.*
ejector [ɪ'dʒektəʳ] *n* eyector *m.*
eke [i:k] *vt* **to eke out** *(make last)* hacer alcanzar, estirar, racionar.
elaborate [*(adj)* ɪ'læəbərt; *(vb)* ɪ'læbəreɪt] *adj* 1 *(detailed, extensive)* detallado,-a. 2 *(ornate, intricate)* muy trabajado,-a, esmerado,-a. 3 *(complex, intricate)* complicado,-a.
▷ *vt (work out in detail, refine)* elaborar, desarrollar.
▷ *vi (discuss in detail)* explicar detalladamente; *(expand)* ampliar, dar más detalles.
elaborately [ɪ'læbrrətlɪ] *adv* 1 *(in detail, extensively)* detalladamente, con todo detalle. 2 *(ornately, richly)* esmeradamente. 3 *(complexly, intricately)* de manera complicada.
elaboration [ɪlæbə'reɪʃᵊn] *n* 1 *(working out in detail)* elaboración *f*, desarrollo. 2 *(additional detail)* complicación *f*, detalle *m.*
elapse [ɪ'læps] *vi* transcurrir.
elastic [ɪ'læstɪk] *adj* 1 elástico,-a. 2 *fig* flexible.
▷ *n* elástico. ● **elastic band** goma elástica.
elasticity [ɪlæ'stɪsətɪ] *n* 1 elasticidad *f.* 2 *fig* flexibilidad *f.*
Elastoplast [ɪ'læstəplɑ:st] *n* tirita.
elated [ɪ'leɪtɪd] *adj* eufórico,-a, jubiloso,-a.
elbow ['elbəʊ] *n* 1 ANAT codo. 2 *(bend)* recodo.
⊙ **to elbow aside** *vt sep* apartar a codazos.
elder[1] ['eldəʳ] *adj* mayor.
▷ *n* 1 mayor *m.* 2 REL anciano,-a.
elder[2] ['eldəʳ] *n* BOT saúco.
elderly ['eldəlɪ] *adj* mayor, anciano,-a.
▷ *n* **the elderly** los ancianos *mpl.*
eldest ['eldɪst] *adj* mayor.
▷ *n* el mayor, la mayor.
elect [ɪ'lekt] *adj* electo,-a.
▷ *vt* 1 *(vote for)* elegir. 2 *(choose, decide)* decidir.
election [ɪ'lekʃᵊn] *n* elección *f.*
▷ *adj* electoral.
electioneering [ɪlekʃə'nɪərɪŋ] *n* electoralismo, maniobras *fpl* electorales.
▷ *adj* electoralista.
elector [ɪ'lektəʳ] *n* elector,-ra.
electoral [ɪ'lektᵊrəl] *adj* electoral. ● **electoral college** colegio electoral. ‖ **electoral roll / electoral register** censo electoral.
electorate [ɪ'lektᵊrət] *n* electorado.
electric [ɪ'lektrɪk] *adj* 1 eléctrico,-a. 2 *fig* electrizante.
electrical [ɪ'lektrɪkᵊl] *adj* eléctrico,-a.
electrician [ɪlek'trɪʃᵊn] *n* electricista *mf.*
electricity [ɪlek'trɪsɪtɪ] *n* electricidad *f.*
electrification [ɪlektrɪfɪ'keɪʃᵊn] *n* electrificación *f.*
electrify [ɪ'lektrɪfaɪ] *vt* 1 electrificar. 2 *fig* electrizar.
▲ *pt & pp* **electrified**, *ger* **electrifying.**
electrocute [ɪ'lektrəkjʊ:t] *vt* electrocutar.
electrode [ɪ'lektrəʊd] *n* electrodo.
electrolysis [ɪlek'trɒləsɪs] *n* electrólisis *f.*
electrolyte [ɪ'lektrəlaɪt] *n* electrolito, electrólito.
electromagnet [ɪlektrəʊ'mægnɪt] *n* electroimán *m.*
electromagnetism [ɪlektrəʊ'mægnɪtɪzᵊm] *n* electromagnetismo.
electromagnetic [ɪlektrəʊmæg'netɪk] *adj* electromagnético,-a.
electron [ɪ'lektrɒn] *n* electrón *m.* ● **electron gun** cañón *m* de electrones. ‖ **electron microscope** microscopio electrónico.
electronic [ɪlek'trɒnɪk] *adj* electrónico,-a.
electronics [ɪlek'trɒnɪks] *n (science, technology)* electrónica.
▷ *n pl (circuits and devices)* componentes *mpl* electrónicos.
elegance ['elɪgəns] *n* elegancia.
elegant ['elɪgənt] *adj* elegante.
elegy ['elədʒɪ] *n* elegía.
▲ *pl* **elegies.**
element ['elɪmənt] *n* 1 CHEM elemento. 2 *(necessary part of a whole)* parte *f*, componente *m.* 3 *(important feature or quality)* factor *m.* 4 *(small amount, hint)* parte *f*, algo. 5 ELEC resistencia. 6 *(group, section)* fracción *f.* 7 *(earth, air, fire, water)* elemento.
▷ *n pl* **elements** 1 *(weather)* los elementos *mpl.* 2 *(basics)* rudimentos *mpl.*
elemental [elɪ'mentᵊl] *adj* elemental, básico,-a.
elementary [elɪ'mentᵊrɪ] *adj* 1 *(basic)* elemental, básico,-a. 2 *(easy)* fácil, sencillo,-a. ● **elementary education** enseñanza primaria. ‖ **elementary particle** partícula elemental.
elephant ['elɪfənt] *n* elefante *m.* ● **elephant seal** elefante *m* marino.
elephantine [elɪ'fæntaɪn] *adj* 1 *(huge)* mastodóntico,-a, descomunal. 2 *(clumsy)* torpe, patoso,-a.
elevate ['elɪveɪt] *vt* 1 *fml (raise)* elevar; *(promote)* ascender, promover. 2 *fig (improve in quality)* elevar.
elevated ['elɪvaɪtɪd] *adj fml (fine, noble)* elevado,-a, noble.
elevation [elɪ'velʃᵊn] *n* 1 *fml (nobility)* elevación *f.* 2 *(angle)* elevación *f.* 3 *fml (in rank)* ascenso. 4 *(height)* altitud *f*, altura. 5 *fml (hill, high place)* elevación *f.* 6 ARCH alzado.
elevator ['elɪveɪtəʳ] *n* 1 US ascensor *m.* 2 *(machine)* montacargas *m.* 3 AV timón *m* de profundidad.
eleven [ɪ'levᵊn] *adj* once.
▷ *n* 1 once *m.* 2 SP equipo, once *m.*

Consulta también **six.**

elevenses [ɪ'levᵊnzɪz] *n pl* GB *fam* desayuno, almuerzo.
eleventh [ɪ'levᵊnθ] *adj* undécimo,-a.
▷ *adv* en undécimo lugar.
▷ *n* **1** *(in series)* undécimo,-a, onceno,-a. **2** *(fraction)* onceavo, undécimo; *(one part)* onceava parte *f*, undécima parte *f*.
Consulta también sixth.
elf [elf] *n* duende *m*, elfo.
▲ *pl* elves [elvz].
elfin ['elfɪn] *adj fig* delicado,-a.
elfish ['elfɪʃ] *adj* travieso,-a.
elicit [ɪ'lɪsɪt] *vt* **1** *fml (facts, information)* sonsacar, obtener. **2** *(reaction, response)* provocar.
elide [ɪ'laɪd] *vt* elidir.
▷ *vi* elidirse.
eligible ['elɪdʒəbᵊl] *adj* **1** *(qualified, suitable)* idóneo,-a, apto,-a. **2** *(desirable)* deseable.
eliminate [ɪ'lɪmɪneɪt] *vt* **1** *(remove, get rid of)* eliminar, erradicar; *(expel)* expulsar. **2** *(rule out)* descartar, excluir, eliminar. **3** *fam (kill)* eliminar, suprimir. **4** *(knock out)* eliminar, derrotar.
elimination [ɪlɪmɪ'neɪʃᵊn] *n* eliminación *f*.
eliminatory [ɪ'lɪmɪnətrɪ] *adj* eliminatorio,-a.
elision [ɪ'lɪʒᵊn] *n* elisión *f*.
elite [eɪ'li:t] *n* elite *f*.
▷ *adj* exclusivo,-a, selecto,-a.
elitist [eɪ'li:tɪst] *adj* elitista.
elixir [ɪ'lɪksəʳ] *n* elixir *m*.
Elizabethan [ɪlɪzə'bi:θᵊn] *adj* isabelino,-a.
▷ *n* isabelino,-a.
elk [elk] *n* GB alce *m*.
ellipse [ɪ'lɪps] *n* elipse *f*.
ellipsis [ɪ'lɪpsɪs] *n* elipsis *f*.
▲ *pl* ellipses [ɪ'lɪpsi'z].
elliptic [ɪ'lɪptɪk] *adj* elíptico,-a.
elm [elm] *n* olmo.
elocution [elə'kju:ʃᵊn] *n* elocución *f*.
elongate ['i:lɒŋgeɪt] *vt* alargar, extender.
elongated ['i:lɒŋgeɪtɪd] *adj* alargado,-a.
elope [ɪ'ləʊp] *vi* fugarse (para casarse).
eloquence ['eləkwəns] *n* elocuencia.
eloquent ['eləkwənt] *adj* elocuente.
else [els] *adv* más, otro,-a: anything else? *¿algo más?*; where else have you been? *¿en qué otro(s) sitio(s) has estado?*
elsewhere [els'weəʳ] *adv* en otro sitio, en otra parte.
elucidate [ɪ'lu:sɪdeɪt] *vt fml* aclarar, dilucidar, poner en claro.
elucidation [ɪlu:sɪ'deɪʃᵊn] *n* aclaración *f*, dilucidación *f*.
elude [ɪ'lu:d] *vt* **1** *(escape from)* escaparse de. **2** *(avoid)* eludir. **3** *(not remember)* no recordar, no acordarse; *(not understand)* no entenderse.
elusive [ɪ'lu:sɪv] *adj* **1** *(difficult to capture)* huidizo,-a, esquivo,-a, escurridizo,-a. **2** *(difficult to remember)* difícil de recordar; *(difficult to understand)* difícil de entender.
elver ['elvəʳ] *n* angula.
emaciated [ɪ'meɪsɪeɪtɪd] *adj (body)* enflaquecido,-a; *(face)* demacrado,-a.
e-mail ['i:meɪl] *n* correo electrónico.
emanate ['eməneɪt] *vi fml* emanar (from, de), provenir (from, de), proceder (from, de).
emanation [emə'neɪʃᵊn] *n* emanación *f*.
emancipate [ɪ'mænsɪpeɪt] *vt* emancipar.
emancipation [ɪmænsɪ'peɪʃᵊn] *n* emancipación *f*.
emasculate [ɪ'mæskjʊleɪt] *vt* **1** *fml (weaken)* debilitar. **2** *(castrate)* capar, castrar, emascular.
embalm [ɪm'bɑ:m] *vt* embalsamar.
embankment [ɪm'bæŋkmənt] *n* **1** *(wall, earth, etc)* terraplén *m*. **2** *(river bank)* dique *m*.
embargo [em'bɑ:gəʊ] *n* embargo, prohibición *f*.
▲ *pl* embargoes.
▷ *vt* **1** *(prohibit)* prohibir, imponer un embargo sobre. **2** *(seize)* embargar.
▲ *pt & pp* embargoed, *ger* embargoing.
embark [ɪm'bɑ:k] *vt (take on board)* embarcar.
⊙ **to embark on** *vt insep* emprender.
embarkation [ɪmbɑ:'keɪʃᵊn] *n* embarque *m*, embarco.
embarrass [ɪm'bærəs] *vt (make ashamed)* avergonzar, azorar, abochornar, hacer pasar vergüenza a; *(make awkward)* desconcertar.
embarrassed [ɪm'bærəst] *adj (behaviour, action)* embarazoso,-a; *(person)* avergonzado,-a, violento,-a, molesto,-a.
embarrassing [ɪm'bærəsɪŋ] *adj* embarazoso,-a, violento,-a, desconcertante.
embarrassment [ɪm'bærəsmənt] *n* **1** *(state)* turbación *f*, vergüenza, desconcierto. **2** *(person, object)* vergüenza, estorbo. **3** *(event, situation)* disgusto, vergüenza.
embassy ['embəsɪ] *n* embajada.
▲ *pl* embassies.
embed [ɪm'bed] *vt* **1** *(jewels, stones)* incrustar; *(weapon, nails)* clavar (in, en). **2** *fig* fijar, grabar.
▲ *pt & pp* embedded, *ger* embedding.
embellish [ɪm'belɪʃ] *vt* **1** *(adorn)* adornar, embellecer. **2** *fig (add details)* adornar.
embellishment [ɪm'belɪʃmənt] *n* adorno.
ember ['embəʳ] *n* **1** brasa, ascua, rescoldo. **2** *fig* vestigio.
embezzle [ɪm'bezᵊl] *vt* desfalcar, malversar.
embitter [ɪm'bɪtəʳ] *vt* amargar, acibarar.
emblem ['embləm] *n* emblema *m*.
emblematic [emblə'mætɪk] *adj* emblemático,-a, simbólico,-a.
embody [ɪm'bɒdɪ] *vt* **1** *(give visible form to)* encarnar, personificar. **2** *(express)* expresar, manifestar. **3** *(include)* incorporar, incluir, abarcar, comprender.
▲ *pt & pp* embodied, *ger* embodying.
embolden [ɪm'bəʊldᵊn] *vt fml* envalentonar, dar confianza a, encorajar.
emboss [ɪm'bɒs] *vt (leather, metal)* repujar; *(initials)* grabar en relieve.
embrace [ɪm'breɪs] *n* abrazo.
▷ *vt* **1** *(hug)* abrazar, dar un abrazo a. **2** *(include)* abarcar, incluir. **3** *fml (accept - opportunity, etc)* aprovechar; *(- offer)* aceptar. **4** *fml (adopt - religion, etc)* convertirse a; *(- political doctrine)* adherirse a; *(- new idea)* abrazar.
embrasure [ɪm'breɪʒəʳ] *n* aspillera, barbacana, saetera, tronera.

embroider [ɪm'brɔɪdəʳ] *vt* 1 SEW bordar. 2 *fig* adornar.
embroiderer [ɪm'brɔɪdəʳəʳ] *n* bordador,-ra.
embroidery [ɪm'brɔɪdᵊʳɪ] *n* 1 SEW bordado. 2 *fig* adorno.
embroil [ɪm'brɔɪl] *vt* enredar, liar.
embryo ['embrɪəʊ] *n* 1 embrión *m*. 2 *fig* germen *m*.
▲ *pl* embryos.
▷ *adj* embrionario,-a.
emend [ɪ'mend] *vt* corregir, enmendar.
emerald ['emᵊrəld] *n* 1 *(stone)* esmeralda *f*. 2 *(colour)* esmeralda *m*.
▷ *adj* (de color) esmeralda.
emerge [ɪ'mɜːdʒ] *vi* 1 *(come out)* emerger, aparecer, salir, surgir. 2 *(become known)* resultar.
emergence [ɪ'mɜːdʒəns] *n* aparición *f*, surgimiento.
emergency [ɪ'mɜːdʒənsɪ] *n* 1 emergencia, crisis *f*. 2 MED caso de urgencia, caso urgente, urgencia.
▲ *pl* emergencies.
▷ *adj* de emergencia, de urgencia.
emergent [ɪ'mɜːdʒənt] *adj* 1 *(emerging)* emergente. 2 *(of countries, nations)* en vías de desarrollo.
emeritus [ɪ'merɪtəs] *adj* emérito,-a.
emery ['emərɪ] *n* esmeril *m*.
emigrant ['emɪgrənt] *n* emigrante *mf*.
emigrate ['emɪgreɪt] *vi* emigrar.
emigration [emɪ'greɪʃᵊn] *n* emigración *f*.
émigré ['emɪgreɪ] *n* emigrado,-a.
eminence ['emɪnəns] *n* eminencia.
eminent ['emɪnənt] *adj* 1 *(of person)* eminente. 2 *(of qualities)* destacado,-a.
emir [e'mɪəʳ] *n* emir *m*.
emirate ['emɪrət] *n* emirato. ● United Arab Emirates Emiratos *mpl* Árabes Unidos.
emissary ['emɪsᵊrɪ] *n* emisario,-a.
▲ *pl* emissaries.
emission [ɪ'mɪʃᵊn] *n* emisión *f*.
emit [ɪ'mɪt] *vt (signal, heat, light, smoke)* emitir, producir; *(sound, noise)* producir; *(smell)* despedir; *(cry)* dar.
▲ *pt & pp* emitted, *ger* emitting.
emoluments [ɪ'mɒljəmənts] *n pl* emolumentos, honorarios.
emoticon [ɪ'mɒtɪkɒn] *n* COMPUT emoticón *m*, emoticono.
emotion [ɪ'məʊʃᵊn] *n* 1 *(feeling)* sentimiento. 2 *(strong feeling)* emoción *f*.
emotional [ɪ'məʊʃᵊnəl] *adj* 1 *(connected with feelings)* emocional, afectivo,-a. 2 *(moving)* conmovedor,-ra, emotivo,-a. 3 *(sensitive)* emotivo,-a, sentimental, muy sensible. 4 *(upset)* emocionado,-a, exaltado,-a.
emotionless [ɪ'məʊʃᵊnləs] *adj* impasible.
emotive [ɪ'məʊtɪv] *adj* emotivo,-a.
empathy ['empəθɪ] *n* empatía.
emperor ['empᵊrəʳ] *n* emperador *m*.
emphasis ['emfəsɪs] *n* 1 *(importance)* énfasis *m*, importancia. 2 LING acento, énfasis *m*.
▲ *pl* emphases ['emfəsiːz].
emphasize ['emfəsaɪz] *vt* 1 *(of words)* enfatizar, poner énfasis en. 2 *(stress importance)* hacer hincapié en, enfatizar, subrayar, destacar, recalcar, insistir en.
emphatic [em'fætɪk] *adj* 1 *(forceful - tone, gesture)* enfático,-a, enérgico,-a. 2 *(insistent - refusal, rejection, assertion)* categórico,-a, rotundo,-a. 3 *(definite, clear)* rotundo,-a.
empire ['empaɪəʳ] *n* imperio: the British Empire *el Imperio Británico.*
empirical [em'pɪrɪkᵊl] *adj* empírico,-a.
empiricist [em'pɪrɪsɪst] *n* empírico,-a.
emplacement [ɪm'pleɪsmənt] *n* emplazamiento.
employ [ɪm'plɔɪ] *n fml* empleo.
▷ *vt* 1 *(give work to)* emplear; *(appoint)* contratar. 2 *fml (make use of, use)* emplear, usar. 3 *(occupy)* ocupar.
employed [em'plɔɪd] *adj* 1 *(in work)* empleado,-a. 2 *(busy)* ocupado,-a.
employee [em'plɔiiː, emplɔɪ'iː] *n* empleado,-a.
employer [em'plɔɪəʳ] *n* 1 *(manager, boss)* empresario,-a; *(of domestic worker)* patrón,-ona. 2 *(company, organization)* empresa, organismo.
employment [em'plɔɪmənt] *n* 1 *(work)* trabajo; *(availability of work)* empleo. 2 *(use)* empleo, uso.
emporium [ɪm'pɔːrɪəm] *n fml* emporio (comercial), gran almacén *m*.
empower [ɪm'paʊəʳ] *vt fml* autorizar, facultar, habilitar.
empress ['emprəs] *n* emperatriz *f*.
emptiness ['emptɪnəs] *n* 1 *(nothingness)* vacío. 2 *(meaninglessness)* vacuidad *f*.
empty ['emptɪ] *adj* 1 *(gen)* vacío,-a; *(place)* desierto,-a; *(house)* desocupado,-a, deshabitado,-a; *(seat, table, place)* libre, desocupado. 2 *fam (hungry)* hambriento,-a. 3 *(purposeless)* vano,-a, inútil; *(meaningless)* carente de sentido; *(words, threats, promises)* vano,-a.
▲ *comp* emptier, *superl* emptiest.
▷ *vt* vaciar.
▷ *n pl* empties envases *mpl*, cascos *mpl*.
empty-handed ['emptɪ'hændɪd] *adj* con las manos vacías.
EMU ['iː'em'juː] *abbr* (European Monetary Union) unión monetaria europea; *(abbreviation)* UME *f*.
emulate ['emjəleɪt] *vt fml* emular.
emulation [emjə'leɪsᵊn] *n* emulación *f*.
emulsifier [ɪ'mʌlsɪfaɪəʳ] *n* emulsionante *m*, emulsivo.
emulsify [ɪ'mʌlsɪfaɪ] *vt* emulsionar.
▲ *pt & pp* emulsified, *ger* emulsifying.
emulsion [ɪ'mʌlʃᵊn] *n (gen)* emulsión *f*.
enable [ɪ'neɪbᵊl] *vt* permitir.
enabling [ɪ'neɪblɪŋ] *adj* que posibilita, que permite.
enact [ɪ'nækt] *vt* 1 *(law)* promulgar. 2 *(play)* representar.
enamel [ɪ'næmᵊl] *n* esmalte *m*.
▷ *vt* esmaltar.
enamored [ɪ'næməd] *adj* US → **enamoured.**
enamoured [ɪ'næməd] *adj* enamorado,-a.
encamp [ɪn'kæmp] *vi* acampar.
encapsulate [ɪn'kæpsjʊleɪt] *vt* encapsular.
encephalic [ensɪ'fælɪk] *adj* encefálico,-a.
enchant [ɪn'tʃɑːnt] *vt* 1 *(delight)* encantar, cautivar. 2 *(cast spell on)* hechizar.
enchanted [ɪn'tʃɑːntɪd] *adj* encantado,-a.
enchanter [ɪn'tʃɑːntəʳ] *n* hechicero, mago.
enchanting [ɪn'tʃɑːntɪŋ] *adj* encantador,-ra.
enchantment [ɪn'tʃɑːntmənt] *n* 1 *(delight)* encanto. 2 *(spell)* hechizo.
enchantress [ɪn'tʃɑːntᵊəs] *n* hechicera.

encircle [ɪn'sɜːkᵊl] *vt* rodear, cercar.
enclave ['enkleɪv] *n* enclave *m*.
enclitic [en'klɪtɪk] *adj* enclítico,-a.
enclose [ɪn'kləʊz] *vt* **1** *(surround)* encerrar; *(with wall or fence)* cercar, rodear. **2** *(include in letter)* adjuntar.
enclosure [ɪn'kləʊʒəʳ] *n* **1** *(land)* cercado; *(area)* recinto. **2** *(act)* cercamiento, encierro. **3** *(with letter)* anexo, documento adjunto.
encode [ɪŋ'kəʊd] *vt* codificar.
encompass [ɪn'kʌmpəs] *vt (include)* abarcar.
encore ['ɒŋkɔːʳ] *interj* ¡otra!
▷ *n* repetición *f*, bis *m*.
encounter [ɪn'kaʊntəʳ] *n* encuentro.
▷ *vt (meet)* encontrar, encontrarse con; *(be faced with)* tropezar con.
encourage [ɪn'kʌrɪdʒ] *vt* **1** *(cheer, inspire)* animar, alentar. **2** *(develop, stimulate)* fomentar, favorecer, estimular.
encouragement [ɪn'kʌᵊrɪdʒmənt] *n* **1** *(act)* aliento, ánimo. **2** *(development)* fomento, estímulo.
encroach [ɪn'krəʊtʃ] *vi* **to encroach on** *(territory, property)* pasar los límites de, invadir; *(rights)* cercenar, usurpar, abusar; *(time, freedom)* quitar, robar.
encrust [ɪn'krʌst] *vt* incrustar.
encrypt [en'krɪpt] *vt* cifrar.
encryption [en'krɪpʃᵊn] *n* cifrado.
encumber [ɪn'kʌmbəʳ] *vt* **1** *(physically)* estorbar. **2** *(financially)* gravar.
encumbrance [ɪn'kʌmbrəns] *n* **1** estorbo. **2** gravamen *m*.
encyclopaedia [ensaɪklə'piːdɪə] *n* enciclopedia.
encyclopedia [ensaɪklə'piːdɪə] *n* enciclopedia.
end [end] *n* **1** *(extremity - of rope)* cabo; *(- of street)* final *m*; *(- of table, sofa)* extremo; *(- of stick, tail)* punta; *(- of box)* lado. **2** *(final part, finish)* fin *m*, final *m*, conclusión *f*. **3** *(aim)* objeto, objetivo, fin *m*. **4** *(remnant)* resto, cabo; *(of cigarette)* colilla. **5** *euph* muerte *f*. **6** *(on telephone)* lado (de la línea).
▷ *adj* final, último,-a.
▷ *vt* **1** *(conclude)* acabar, terminar. **2** *(stop)* terminar, poner fin a, acabar con.
⊙ **to end in** *vi* acabar en, terminar con.
⊙ **to end off** *vt sep* acabar.
▷ *vi* acabar.
⊙ **to end up** *vi* acabar, terminar, ir a parar.
endanger [ɪn'deɪndʒəʳ] *vt* poner en peligro.
endangered [ɪn'deɪndʒəd] *adj* en peligro. ● **endangered species** especie *f* en peligro (de extinción).
endearing [ɪn'dɪərɪŋ] *adj* simpático,-a, atractivo,-a.
endeavor [ɪn'devəʳ] *n* US ⟶ **endeavour.**
endeavour [ɪn'devəʳ] *n* GB *fml* esfuerzo, empeño.
▷ *vi* esforzarse, intentar, procurar.
endemic [en'demɪk] *adj* endémico,-a.
ending ['endɪŋ] *n* **1** final *m*, conclusión *f*, desenlace *m*. **2** LING terminación *f*.
endive ['endaɪv] *n* **1** GB escarola. **2** US endibia.
endless ['endləs] *adj* interminable, eterno,-a.
endocarp ['endəʊkɑːp] *n* endocarpo, endocarpio.
endocrine ['endəʊkᵊɪn] *adj* endocrino,-a. ● **endocrine gland** glándula endocrina.
endorse [ɪn'dɔːs] *vt* **1** *(of cheque, etc)* endosar. **2** *(approve)* aprobar, apoyar, respaldar. **3** GB *(driving license)* escribir la sanción en.
endorsement [ɪn'dɔːsmənt] *n* **1** *(of cheque, etc)* endoso. **2** *(approval)* aprobación *f*, apoyo, respaldo. **3** AUTO nota de sanción.
endow [ɪn'daʊ] *vt* **1** *(bless)* dotar. **2** *(give money)* dotar (de fondos).
endowment [ɪn'daʊmənt] *n (attribute)* atributo, dote *m & f*.
▷ *n pl* **endowments** *(money)* donaciones *fpl*.
endurance [ɪn'djʊərəns] *n* resistencia, aguante *m*.
▷ *adj* de resistencia.
endure [ɪn'djʊəʳ] *vt* **1** *(suffer patiently)* soportar, resistir. **2** *(bear, tolerate)* soportar, aguantar.
▷ *vi (continue to exist, survive)* durar, perdurar.
enemy ['enəmɪ] *n* enemigo,-a.
▲ *pl* **enemies.**
▷ *adj* enemigo,-a.
energetic [enə'dʒetɪk] *adj* enérgico,-a, activo,-a.
energize ['enədʒaɪz] *vt* activar, dar energía a.
energy ['enədʒɪ] *n (gen)* energía.
▲ *pl* **energies.**
▷ *n pl* **energies** *(efforts)* energías *fpl*, fuerzas *fpl*.
enervate ['enəveɪt] *vt* enervar, debilitar.
enfeeble [ɪn'fiːbᵊl] *vt* debilitar.
enfold [ɪn'fəʊld] *vt* **1** *(embrace)* estrechar. **2** *(enclose)* envolver.
enforce [ɪn'fɔːs] *vt* **1** *(force to obey)* hacer cumplir, hacer respetar. **2** *(impose)* imponer.
enforcement [ɪn'fɔːsmənt] *n* imposición *f*.
engage [ɪn'geɪdʒ] *vt* **1** *(hire)* contratar. **2** *(take up, occupy)* ocupar, entretener. **3** *(attract)* llamar, atraer, captar. **4** *fml (attack)* entablar combate con. **5** AUTO *(gear)* engranar, meter; *(clutch)* apretar. **6** TECH engranar con.
▷ *vi* **1** TECH engranar. **2** *fml (attack)* entablar combate.
⊙ **to engage in** *vi (participate)* ocuparse en, dedicarse a.
engaged [ɪn'geɪdʒd] *adj* **1** *(to be married)* prometido,-a. **2** *(busy)* ocupado,-a.
engagement [ɪn'geɪdʒmənt] *n* **1** *(to be married)* petición *f* de mano; *(period)* noviazgo. **2** *(appointment)* compromiso, cita. **3** MIL combate *m*. **4** *(employment)* contrato, empleo.
engaging [ɪn'geɪdʒɪŋ] *adj* atractivo,-a, simpático,-a, encantador,-ra.
engender [ɪn'dʒendəʳ] *vt fml* engendrar.
engine ['endʒɪn] *n* **1** motor *m*. **2** *(of train)* máquina, locomotora. ● **engine driver** maquinista *mf*.
engineer [endʒɪ'nɪəʳ] *n* **1** *(graduate)* ingeniero,-a; *(technician)* técnico,-a. **2** US maquinista *mf*.
▷ *vt* **1** *(contrive)* maquinar, tramar, urdir. **2** *(plan as engineer)* crear por ingeniería.
engineering [endʒɪ'nɪəᵊrɪŋ] *n* ingeniería.
England ['ɪŋglənd] *n* Inglaterra.
English ['ɪŋglɪʃ] *adj* inglés,-esa.
▷ *n (language)* inglés *m*.
Englishman ['ɪŋglɪʃmən] *n* inglés *m*.
▲ *pl* **Englishmen.**
English-speaking ['ɪŋglɪʃspiːkɪŋ] *adj* de habla inglesa.
Englishwoman ['ɪŋglɪʃwʊmən] *n* inglesa.
▲ *pl* **Englishwomen** ['ɪŋglɪʃwɪmɪn].
engrave [ɪn'greɪv] *vt (gen)* grabar.

engraving [ɪn'greɪvɪŋ] *n* 1 *(picture)* grabado. 2 *(art)* grabación *f*.
engrossed [ɪn'gᵊəʊst] *adj* absorto,-a (in, en).
engulf [ɪn'gʌlf] *vt* envolver.
enhance [ɪn'hɑːns] *vt* 1 *(beauty, taste)* realzar; *(quality, chances)* mejorar; *(power, value)* aumentar. 2 COMPUT procesar.
enigma [ɪ'nɪgmə] *n* enigma *m*.
enigmatic [enɪg'mætɪk] *adj* enigmático,-a.
enjoy [ɪn'dʒɔɪ] *vt* 1 *(get pleasure from)* disfrutar de; *(like)* gustarle a uno. 2 *(benefit from)* gozar de.
enjoyment [ɪn'dʒɔɪmənt] *n* placer *m*, goce *m*, disfrute *m*, gusto.
enlarge [ɪn'lɑːdʒ] *vt (gen)* extender, aumentar, ampliar; *(photograph)* ampliar.
enlargement [ɪn'lɑːdʒmənt] *n* 1 *(photograph)* ampliación *f*. 2 extensión *f*, aumento, ampliación *f*.
enlighten [ɪn'laɪtᵊn] *vt* 1 *(free from ignorance)* iluminar, ilustrar. 2 *(inform)* informar, instruir.
enlightenment [ɪn'laɪtᵊnmənt] *n* 1 *fml (act)* aclaración *f*, explicación *f*. 2 *(liberalism)* tolerancia.
▷ *n* **the Enlightenment** la Ilustración *f*. ● **the Age of Enlightenment** el Siglo de las Luces, el Siglo de la Ilustración.
enliven [ɪn'laɪvᵊn] *vt* avivar, animar.
enmity ['enmɪtɪ] *n* enemistad *f*, hostilidad *f*.
▲ *pl* enmities.
ennoble [ɪ'nəʊbᵊl] *vt* ennoblecer.
enormity [ɪ'nɔːmɪtɪ] *n* 1 *fam (enormousness)* enormidad *f*, inmensidad *f*, magnitud *f*. 2 *(extreme wickedness)* atrocidad *f*. 3 *fml (crime)* atrocidad *f*, barbaridad *f*.
▲ *pl* enormities.
enormous [ɪ'nɔːməs] *adj* enorme, inmenso,-a, descomunal.
enough [ɪ'nʌf] *adj* bastante, suficiente.
▷ *adv* bastante, suficientemente.
enquire [ɪŋ'kwaɪəʳ] *vt* preguntar.
▷ *vi* 1 preguntar, informarse. 2 JUR investigar (into, -).
enquiry [ɪŋ'kwaɪərɪ] *n* 1 pregunta. 2 JUR investigación *f*.
▲ *pl* enquiries.
enrage [ɪn'reɪdʒ] *vt* enfurecer.
enrich [ɪn'rɪtʃ] *vt* enriquecer.
enrol [ɪn'rəʊl] *vt* matricular, inscribir.
▲ *pt & pp* enrolled, *ger* enrolling.
▷ *vi* matricularse, inscribirse, apuntarse.
enrolment [ɪn'rəʊlmənt] *n* matrícula, inscripción *f*.
ensemble [ɒn'sɒmbᵊl] *n* conjunto.
ensign ['ensaɪn] *n* 1 *(flag)* bandera, pabellón *m*. 2 US *(naval officer)* alférez *m*.
enslave [ɪn'sleɪv] *vt* esclavizar.
ensue [ɪn'sjuː] *vi* 1 *(follow)* seguir. 2 *(result)* resultar (from, de).
ensure [ɪn'ʃʊəʳ] *vt* 1 *(make sure)* asegurarse. 2 *(assure)* asegurar.
entail [ɪn'teɪl] *vt* 1 *(involve, mean)* suponer, implicar; *(make necessary, bring about)* ocasionar, acarrear. 2 JUR vincular.
entangle [ɪn'tæŋgᵊl] *vt* 1 enredar, enmarañar. 2 *fig* enredar, involucrar.
enter ['entəʳ] *vt* 1 *(gen)* entrar en. 2 *(participate)* participar en, tomar parte en; *(register)* inscribirse en. 3 *(write down, record)* anotar, apuntar. 4 *fml (present for consideration, submit)* formular, presentar.
▷ *vi* 1 *(gen)* entrar. 2 *(theatre)* entrar en escena.
⊙ **to enter for** *vt sep* inscribir en.
▷ *vi (race)* inscribirse en; *(exam)* presentarse a.
⊙ **to enter into** *vt insep* 1 *(negotiations)* iniciar; *(contract)* firmar; *(agreement)* llegar a, concertar; *(relations)* establecer (with, con); *(conversation)* entablar (with, con). 2 *(figure in)* entrar en; *(matter)* importar, contar.
⊙ **to enter on / enter upon** *vt insep fml (career)* emprender; *(term of office)* empezar.
enterprise ['entəpraɪz] *n* 1 *(venture)* empresa, proyecto. 2 *(initiative)* energía, iniciativa, espíritu *m* emprendedor. 3 *(firm)* empresa.
enterprising ['entəpraɪzɪŋ] *adj* emprendedor,-a.
entertain [entə'teɪn] *vt* 1 *(amuse)* entretener, divertir. 2 *fml (suggestion, etc)* considerar, tener en cuenta; *(doubts, etc)* abrigar. 3 *(invite)* recibir, invitar.
▷ *vi (act as host)* tener invitados.
entertaining [entə'teɪnɪŋ] *adj* divertido,-a, entretenido,-a.
entertainment [entə'teɪnmənt] *n* 1 *(amusement)* entretenimiento, diversión *f*. 2 THEAT espectáculo, función *f*.
enthral [ɪn'θᵊɔːl] *vt* cautivar.
▲ *pt & pp* enthralled, *ger* enthralling.
enthrone [ɪn'θᵊəʊn] *vt* entronizar.
enthuse [ɪn'θjuːz] *vi fam (be enthusiastic)* entusiasmarse (over, por), (about, con).
enthusiasm [ɪn'θjuːzɪæzᵊm] *n* entusiasmo (about/for, por).
enthusiast [ɪn'θjuːzɪæst] *n* entusiasta *mf*.
enthusiastic [ɪnθjuːzɪ'æstɪk] *adj* 1 *(reaction)* entusiástico,-a, caluroso,-a. 2 *(person)* entusiasta.
entice [ɪn'taɪs] *vt* persuadir, tentar, engatusar.
entire [ɪn'taɪəʳ] *adj* entero,-a, completo,-a, íntegro,-a, todo,-a.
entirely [ɪn'taɪəlɪ] *adv (totally)* enteramente, totalmente, completamente.
entirety [ɪn'taɪrətɪ] *n* totalidad *f*: **in its entirety** *en su totalidad*.
entitle [ɪn'taɪtᵊl] *vt* 1 *(give right to)* dar derecho (to, a). 2 *(book, etc)* titular.
entitlement [ɪn'taɪtᵊlmənt] *n* derecho (to, a).
entity ['entɪtɪ] *n* entidad *f*.
▲ *pl* entities.
entourage [ɒntʊ'rɑːʒ] *n* séquito.
entrails ['entreɪlz] *n pl* entrañas *fpl*, tripas *fpl*, vísceras *fpl*.
entrance¹ ['entrəns] *n* 1 *(way in)* entrada; *(door, gate)* puerta, entrada; *(hall)* vestíbulo, hall *m*, entrada. 2 *(act of entering)* entrada; *(on stage)* entrada en escena, aparición *f*. 3 *(admission)* entrada, admisión *f*; *(to school, university)* ingreso.
entrance² [ɪn'trɑːns] *vt* arrebatar, extasiar, encantar.
entrant ['entrənt] *n (competitor)* participante *mf*; *(applicant)* aspirante *mf*.
entreat [ɪn'triːt] *vt fml* suplicar, rogar.
entrée ['ɒntreɪ] *n* entrante *m*, entrada.

entrench [ɪn'trentʃ] *vt* 1 *(with trench)* atrincherar. 2 *fig (establish firmly)* reafirmar, consolidar.
entrepreneur [ɒntrəprə'nɜːʳ] *n (business person)* empresario,-a.
entrust [ɪn'trʌst] *vt* confiar, encargar, encomendar.
entry ['entᵊɪ] *n* 1 *(entrance)* entrada; *(joining)* ingreso. 2 *(right to enter)* admisión *f*, acceso. 3 US *(door, gate)* puerta, entrada. 4 *(item in accounts)* entrada, asiento; *(in diary)* anotación *f*, entrada; *(in dictionary)* entrada. 5 *(in competition - participant)* participante *mf*; *(- total number of participants)* participación *f*, número de participantes; *(- thing entered)* ejemplar *m*.
▲ *pl* entries.
entryphone ['entrɪfəʊn] *n* portero automático.
entwine [en'twaɪn] *vt* entrelazar.
enumerate [ɪ'njuːməreɪt] *vt* enumerar.
enunciate [ɪ'nʌnsɪeɪt] *vt* 1 *(pronounce)* pronunciar, articular. 2 *(express)* expresar, enunciar.
envelop [ɪn'veləp] *vt* envolver.
envelope ['envələʊp] *n (of letter)* sobre *m*; *(covering)* envoltura.
enviable ['envɪəbᵊl] *adj* envidiable.
envious ['envɪəs] *adj (person)* envidioso,-a; *(look, etc)* de envidia.
environment [ɪn'vaɪrənmənt] *n* 1 *(ecology)* medio ambiente *m*: we need to protect the environment *hemos de proteger el medio ambiente.* 2 *(surroundings)* ambiente *m*, entorno; *(habitat)* hábitat *m*.
environmental [ɪnvaɪəᵊən'mentᵊl] *adj* 1 *(ecological)* del medio ambiente, ambiental: environmental pollution *contaminación del medio ambiente.* 2 *(of surroundings)* ambiental.
environs [ɪn'vaɪrənz] *n pl* alrededores *mpl*.
envisage [ɪn'vɪzɪdʒ] *vt* 1 *(foresee)* prever. 2 *(imagine)* imaginarse.
envoy ['envɔɪ] *n* enviado,-a.
envy ['envɪ] *n* envidia (at/of, de).
▲ *pl* envies.
▷ *vt* envidiar, tener envidia de.
▲ *pt & pp* envied, *ger* envying.
enzyme ['enzaɪm] *n* enzima *m & f*.
eon [ɪən] *n* eón *m*.
épée ['epeɪ] *n* florete *m*.
ephemeral [ɪ'femᵊrəl] *adj* efímero,-a.
epic ['epɪk] *adj (poem, film, novel)* épico,-a; *(achievement)* colosal.
▷ *n (poem)* epopeya, poema *m* épico; *(film)* película épica; *(novel)* epopeya.
epicenter ['epɪsentəʳ] *n* US ⟶ epicentre.
epicentre ['epɪsentəʳ] *n* epicentro.
epicure ['epɪkjʊəʳ] *n* sibarita *mf*.
epidemic [epɪ'demɪk] *n* epidemia.
▷ *adj* epidémico,-a.
epidermis [epɪ'dɜːmɪs] *n* epidermis *f*.
epiglottis [epɪ'glɒtɪs] *n* epiglotis *f*.
epigram ['epɪgræm] *n* epigrama *m*.
epigraph ['epɪgrɑːf] *n* epígrafe *m*.
epilepsy ['epɪlepsɪ] *n* epilepsia.
epileptic [epɪ'leptɪk] *adj* epiléptico,-a.
▷ *n* epiléptico,-a.
epilogue ['epɪlɒg] *n* epílogo.
Epiphany [ɪ'pɪfənɪ] *n* epifanía.
episode ['epɪsəʊd] *n* 1 episodio. 2 *(of series)* capítulo.
epistle [ɪ'pɪsᵊl] *n* epístola.
epitaph ['epɪtɑːf] *n* epitafio.
epithelial ['epɪθelɪəl] *adj* epitelial.
epithet ['epɪθet] *n* epíteto.
epitome [ɪ'pɪtəmɪ] *n (model, perfect example)* personificación *f*.
epitomize [ɪ'pɪtəmaɪz] *vt* personificar, ejemplificar, ser la personificación de.
epoch ['iːpɒk] *n* época.
epoch-making ['iːpɒkmeɪkɪŋ] *adj* histórico,-a, transcendental, que hace historia.
eponymous [ɪ'pɒnɪməs] *adj* epónimo,-a.
equable ['ekwebᵊl] *adj* 1 *(climate)* uniforme, regular. 2 *(person)* ecuánime.
equal ['iːkwəl] *adj* 1 *(identical)* igual; *(same)* mismo,-a. 2 *(capable)* capaz.
▷ *n* igual *mf*.
▷ *vt* 1 MATH ser igual a, equivaler a. 2 *(match)* igualar.
equality [ɪ'kwɒlɪtɪ] *n* igualdad *f*.
▲ *pl* equalities.
equalize ['iːkwəlaɪz] *vi* SP empatar, lograr el empate.
▷ *vt* igualar.
equally ['iːkwəlɪ] *adv* 1 igualmente, igual de. 2 en partes iguales, equitativamente. 3 *(similarly)* del mismo modo, asimismo.
equanimity [ekwə'nɪmɪtɪ] *n* ecuanimidad *f*.
equate [ɪ'kweɪt] *vt* equiparar (with, con), comparar (with, con).
equation [ɪ'kweɪʒᵊn] *n* 1 MATH ecuación *f*. 2 *fml (relationship)* relación *f*. ● simple equation ecuación *f* de primer grado.
equator [ɪ'kweɪtəʳ] *n* ecuador *m*.
equestrian [ɪ'kwestrɪən] *adj* ecuestre.
▷ *n (man)* jinete *m*; *(woman)* amazona.
equidistant [iːkwɪ'dɪstᵊnt] *adj* equidistante.
equilateral [iːkwɪ'lætᵊrəl] *adj* equilátero,-a. ● equilateral triangle triángulo equilátero.
equilibrium [iːkwɪ'lɪbrɪəm] *n* equilibrio.
equine ['ekwaɪn] *adj* equino,-a.
equinox ['iːkwɪnɒks] *n* equinoccio.
equip [ɪ'kwɪp] *vt* 1 *(fit out, supply)* equipar (with, con), proveer (with, de). 2 *(prepare)* preparar (for/to, para).
▲ *pt & pp* equipped, *ger* equipping.
equipment [ɪ'kwɪpmənt] *n* 1 *(materials)* equipo, material *m*. 2 *(act of equipping)* equipamiento.
equipped [ɪ'kwɪpt] *adj* 1 *(supplied)* equipado,-a, provisto,-a. 2 *(prepared)* preparado,-a (for, para).
equitable ['ekwɪtəbᵊl] *adj fml* equitativo,-a.
equity ['ekwətɪ] *n* equidad *f*.
▷ *n* Equity GB sindicato de actores.
▲ *pl* equities.
equivalence [ɪ'kwɪvələns] *n* equivalencia.
equivalent [ɪ'kwɪvələnt] *adj* equivalente.
▷ *n* equivalente *m*.
equivocal [ɪ'kwɪvəkᵊl] *adj* 1 *(ambiguous)* equívoco,-a. 2 *(questionable, dubious)* dudoso,-a.
era ['ɪərə] *n* era, época.
eradicate [ɪ'rædɪkeɪt] *vt (eliminate)* erradicar, extirpar; *(uproot)* desarraigar.
eradication [ɪrædɪ'keɪʃᵊn] *n* erradicación *f*, extirpación *f*.
erase [ɪ'ᵊeɪz] *vt* borrar.

eraser [ɪ'reɪzəʳ] *n* goma de borrar.
erect [ɪ'rekt] *adj* **1** *(upright)* derecho,-a, erguido,-a. **2** ANAT erecto,-a.
> *vt (build)* erigir, levantar; *(put up - tent)* armar; *(- flagstaff)* izar.
erectile [ɪ'rektaɪl] *adj* erectil.
erection [ɪ'rekʃᵊn] *n* **1** ANAT erección *f*. **2** *(building)* construcción *f*.
ergonomic [ɜːgə'nɒmɪk] *adj* ergonómico,-a.
ermine ['ɜːmɪn] *n* armiño.
> *adj* de armiño.
erode [ɪ'rəʊd] *vt* **1** *(rock, soil)* erosionar. **2** *(metal)* corroer, desgastar. **3** *fig (power, confidence, rights, etc)* minar.
⊙ **to erode away** *vi* **1** *(rock, soil)* erosionarse. **2** *(metal)* corroerse, desgastarse. **3** *fig* irse minando.
erogenous ['ɪrɒdʒənəs] *adj* erógeno,-a.
erosion [ɪ'rəʊʒᵊn] *n* **1** *(of rock, soil)* erosión *f*. **2** *(of metal)* corrosión *f*, desgaste *m*. **3** *fig* desgaste *m*.
erosive [ɪ'rəʊsɪv] *adj* erosivo,-a, corrosivo,-a.
erotic [ɪ'rɒtɪk] *adj* erótico,-a.
err [ɜːʳ] *vi fml* errar, equivocarse.
errand ['erənd] *n* encargo, recado.
errant ['erənt] *adj* **1** *fig* errante. **2** *(of knight)* andante.
errata [ɪ'ᵊrɑːtə] *n pl* fe *f sing* de erratas.
erratic [ɪ'rætɪk] *adj (behaviour, performance)* irregular, inconstante; *(weather)* muy variable.
erratum [ɪ'rɑːtəm] *n* errata.
▲ *pl* errata [e'rɑːtə].
erroneous [ɪ'rəʊnɪəs] *adj* erróneo,-a, equivocado,-a.
error ['erəʳ] *n* error *m*, equivocación *f*.
error-free ['erərfriː] *adj* sin errores.
erudite ['erʊdaɪt] *adj* erudito,-a.
erupt [ɪ'rʌpt] *vi* **1** *(volcano)* entrar en erupción. **2** *fig (war, violence, fire)* estallar; *(sudden movement)* irrumpir. **3** *fam (people - in anger)* estallar en cólera; *(- in laughter)* estallar de risa; *(- in enthusiasm)* volverse loco,-a, exaltarse. **4** MED *(rash, spots, etc)* brotar, salir; *(tooth)* salir.
eruption [ɪ'rʌpʃᵊn] *n* **1** *(volcano)* erupción *f*. **2** *fig (war)* estallido, comienzo; *(violence)* estallido, brote *m*; *(anger)* estallido, explosión *f*; *(new force, etc)* irrupción *f*. **3** *(disease)* brote *m*, epidemia; *(rash, spots, etc)* erupción *f*.
escalate ['eskəleɪt] *vt (war)* intensificar, agravar.
> *vi* **1** *(war, violence, etc)* intensificarse, agravarse. **2** *(prices, etc)* aumentar, subir.
escalation [eskə'leɪʃᵊn] *n* **1** *(war)* intensificación *f*, agravamiento, escalada. **2** *(prices)* subida, aumento.
escalator ['eskəleɪtəʳ] *n* escalera mecánica.
escalope ['eskəlɒp] *n* escalope.
escapade ['eskəpeɪd, eskə'peɪd] *n* aventura.
escape [ɪ'skeɪp] *n* **1** *(flight)* fuga, huida (**from**, de). **2** *(of gas)* fuga, escape *m*. **3** *(escapism)* evasión *f*.
> *vi* **1** *(get free, get away)* escaparse, fugarse, huir. **2** *(gas, etc)* escapar.
> *vt* **1** *(avoid)* escapar a, salvarse de, librarse de. **2** *(be forgotten or unnoticed)* escaparse, no recordar.
escapee [ɪ'skeɪpiː] *n* fugitivo,-a.
escapism [ɪ'skeɪpɪzᵊm] *n* evasión *f*.
escapist [ɪ'skeɪpɪst] *adj* de evasión.
escarpment [ɪ'skɑːpmənt] *n* escarpa.
eschatological [eskætə'lɒdʒɪkᵊl] *adj* escatalógico,-a.
eschatology [eskə'tɒlədʒɪ] *n* escatología.
eschew [ɪs'tʃuː] *vt fml* evitar, abstenerse de.
escort [*(n)* e'skɔːt; *(vb)* ɪ'skɔːt] *n* **1** acompañante *mf*. **2** MIL escolta.
▷ *vt* **1** acompañar: **I'll escort you home** *te acompañaré a casa*. **2** MIL escoltar.
escudo [e'skuːdəʊ] *n* escudo.
Eskimo ['eskɪməʊ] *n* **1** *(person)* esquimal *mf*. **2** *(language)* esquimal *m*.
▲ *pl* **Eskimos** o **Eskimo**.
▷ *adj* esquimal.
ESL ['iː'es'el] *abbr* (**English as a second language**) inglés como segundo idioma.
esophagus [ɪ'sɒfəgəs] *n* US esófago.
esoteric [esəʊ'terɪk] *adj* esotérico,-a.
ESP[1] ['iː'es'piː] *abbr* (**extrasensory perception**) percepción *f* extrasensorial.
ESP[2] ['iː'es'piː] *abbr* (**English for Specific Purposes**) cursos de inglés especializados.
espadrille [espə'drɪl] *n* alpargata.
espagnolette [espænjə'let] *n* falleba.
especial [ɪ'speʃᵊl] *adj* especial, particular.
especially [ɪ'speʃᵊlɪ] *adv* especialmente, sobre todo.
Esperanto [espə'ræntəʊ] *n* esperanto.
espionage ['espɪənɑːʒ] *n* espionaje *m*.
esplanade [esplə'neɪd] *n* paseo marítimo.
espousal [ɪ'spaʊzᵊl] *n fml (taking up)* adhesión *f* (**of**, a), adopción *f* (**of**, de); *(support)* apoyo (**of**, de).
espouse [ɪ'spaʊz] *vt fml (take up)* abrazar, adoptar, adherirse a; *(support)* apoyar, propugnar.
espresso [es'presəʊ] *n* café *m* exprés, exprés *m*.
▲ *pl* **espressos**.
esquire [ɪ'skwaɪəʳ] *n* GB *fml* señor *m* don: **Mr David Gómez Esquire** *Sr. Don David Gómez*.
essay ['eseɪ] *n* **1** *(school)* redacción *f*, composición *f*; *(university)* trabajo. **2** *(literary)* ensayo. **3** *fml (attempt)* intento.
▷ *vt fml* intentar.
essence ['esᵊns] *n* **1** *(central quality)* esencia; *(perfect model)* personificación *f*. **2** *(extract)* esencia, perfume *m*.
essential [ɪ'senʃᵊl] *adj* **1** *(necessary)* esencial, imprescindible. **2** *(most important, basic)* fundamental, central, básico,-a.
▷ *n (necessary thing)* necesidad *f* básica.
▷ *n pl* **essentials** lo esencial *m sing*, lo fundamental *m sing*.
essentially [ɪ'senʃᵊlɪ] *adv* esencialmente, fundamentalmente.
EST ['iː'es'tiː] *abbr* US (**Eastern Standard Time**) hora del meridiano 75 al oeste de Greenwich.
establish [ɪ'stæblɪʃ] *vt* **1** *(set up)* establecer, fundar, crear. **2** *(find out, determine)* determinar, averiguar; *(prove correct, show to be true)* probar, demostrar, verificar. **3** *(cause to be accepted - precedent, theory)* sentar; *(- fame, reputation)* consolidar, consagrar; *(- habit, belief, custom)* establecer. **4** *(set up - contact, communication, etc)* establecer, entablar.
established [ɪ'stæblɪʃt] *adj* **1** *(practice, custom)* consolidado,-a, arraigado,-a. **2** *(person - set up)* establecido,-a; *(- well known)* reconocido,-a. **3** *(busi-*

ness) establecido,-a, sólido,-a; *(clientele)* fijo,-a. **4** *(order, authority)* establecido,-a; *(theory)* sentado,-a. **5** *(fact)* comprobado,-a.

establishment [ɪ'stæblɪʃmənt] *n* **1** *(setting up)* establecimiento, fundación *f*. **2** *(premises)* establecimiento; *(business)* negocio. **3** *(staff)* plantilla, personal *m*.
▷ *n* **the Establishment** GB el sistema, el poder.

estate [ɪ'steɪt] *n* **1** *(land)* finca. **2** GB *(with houses)* urbanización *f*. **3** *(money and property)* propiedad *f*, bienes *mpl*; *(inheritance)* herencia.

esteem [ɪ'sti:m] *vt* **1** *(respect)* apreciar, estimar. **2** *(regard)* considerar, estimar.
▷ *n* aprecio, estima, estimación *f*.

esthetic [i:s'θetɪk] *adj* US estético,-a.

estimate [*(n)* 'estɪmət; *(vb)* 'estɪmeɪt] *n* **1** *(calculation - of amount, size)* cálculo, estimación *f*; *(- of value, cost)* valoración *f*, estimación *f*; *(- for work)* presupuesto. **2** *(judgement)* evaluación *f*, juicio, opinión *f*.
▷ *vt* **1** *(calculate)* calcular. **2** *(judge, form opinion about)* pensar, creer, estimar.
▷ *vi (for work)* hacer un presupuesto (**for**, de).

estimated [estɪ'meɪtɪd] *adj* aproximado,-a.

estimation [estɪ'meɪʃən] *n* **1** opinión *f*, juicio. **2** *(esteem)* estima, estimación *f*, aprecio.

Estonia [e'stəunɪə] *n* Estonia.

Estonian [e'stəunɪən] *adj* estonio,-a.
▷ *n* **1** *(person)* estonio,-a. **2** *(language)* estonio.

estrange [ɪ'streɪndʒ] *vt* alejar (**from**, de).

estrangement [ɪ'streɪndʒmənt] *n* alejamiento, separación *f*.

Estremadura [estrəmə'duəʳə] *n* Extremadura.

Estremaduran [estrəmə'duəʳən] *adj* extremeño,-a.
▷ *n* extremeño,-a.

estrogen ['i:strədʒən] *n* US estrógeno.

estrus ['estrəs] *n* estro.

estuary ['estjuərɪ] *n* estuario.
▲ *pl* **estuaries.**

etcetera [et'setrə] *adv* etcétera.

etch [etʃ] *vt* **1** grabar al agua fuerte. **2** *fig* grabar.

etching ['etʃɪŋ] *n* aguafuerte *m & f*.

eternal [ɪ'tɜ:nəl] *adj* **1** *(everlasting)* eterno,-a. **2** *fam (unceasing)* incesante. **3** *(immutable)* inmutable.
▷ *n* **the Eternal** Dios.

eternally [ɪ'tɜ:nəlɪ] *adv* **1** eternamente. **2** *fam (always)* siempre.

eternity [ɪ'tɜ:nətɪ] *n* eternidad *f*.

ether ['i:θəʳ] *n* éter *m*.

ethereal [ɪ'θɪərɪəl] *adj* etéreo,-a.

ethic ['eθɪk] *n* ética.

ethical ['eθɪkəl] *adj* ético,-a, moral.

ethically ['eθɪkəlɪ] *adv* éticamente, moralmente.

ethics ['eθɪks] *n (science)* ética.
▷ *n pl (moral correctness)* moralidad *f*.

Ethiopia [i:θɪ'əupɪə] *n* Etiopía.

Ethiopian [i:θɪ'əupɪən] *adj* etíope.
▷ *n* **1** *(person)* etíope *mf*, etiope *mf*. **2** *(language)* etíope *m*.

ethnic ['eθnɪk] *adj* étnico,-a. ● **ethnic minority** minoría étnica.

ethnographer [eθ'nɒgəfəʳ] *n* etnógrafo,-a.

ethnographic [eθnə'gəæfɪk] *adj* etnográfico,-a.

ethnography [eθ'nɒgəfɪ] *n* etnografía.

ethnologic [eθnə'lɒdʒɪk] *adj* etnológico,-a.

ethnologist [eθ'nɒlədʒɪst] *n* etnólogo,-a.

ethnology [eθ'nɒlədʒɪ] *n* etnología.

ethos ['i:θɒs] *n* carácter *m* distintivo, espíritu *m*.

ethyl ['i:θaɪl, 'eθɪl] *n* CHEM etilo. ● **ethyl alcohol** alcohol *m* etílico.

etiquette ['etɪket] *n* protocolo, etiqueta. ● **professional etiquette** ética profesional.

Etruscan [ɪ'trʌskən] *adj* etrusco,-a.
▷ *n* **1** *(person)* etrusco,-a. **2** *(language)* etrusco.

etymological [etɪmə'lɒdʒɪkəl] *adj* etimológico,-a.

etymologist [etɪ'mɒlədʒɪst] *n* etimólogo,-a.

etymology [etɪ'mɒlədʒɪ] *n* etimología.
▲ *pl* **etymologies.**

eucalyptus [ju:kə'lɪptəs] *n* eucalipto. ● **eucalyptus oil** aceite *m* de eucalipto. ‖ **eucalyptus tree** eucalipto.

EU ['i:'ju:] *abbr* **(European Union)** Unión *f* Europea; *(abbreviation)* UE *f*.

Eucharist ['ju:kəʳɪst] *n* Eucaristía.

eulogize ['ju:lədʒaɪz] *vt* elogiar.

eulogy ['ju:lədʒɪ] *n* elogio.
▲ *pl* **eulogies.**

eunuch ['ju:nək] *n* eunuco.

euphemism ['ju:fəmɪzəm] *n* eufemismo.

euphemistic [ju:fɪ'mɪstɪk] *adj* eufemístico,-a.

euphonium [ju:'fəunɪəm] *n* bombardino.

euphony ['ju:fənɪ] *n* eufonía.

euphoria [ju:'fɔ:rɪə] *n* euforia.

euphoric [ju:'fɒrɪk] *adj* eufórico,-a.

Eurasian [juə'reɪʒən] *n* euroasiático,-a.
▷ *adj* euroasiático,-a.

eureka [juə'ri:kə] *interj* ¡eureka!

eurhythmics [juə'rɪðmɪks] *n* gimnasia rítmica.

euro ['juərəu] *n* euro.

Eurocheque ['juərəutʃek] *n* eurocheque *m*.

Eurocrat ['juərəkræt] *n* eurócrata *mf*.

Eurocurrency ['juərəukʌrənsɪ] *n* FIN eurodivisa.

Eurodollar ['juərəudɒləʳ] *n* FIN eurodólar *m*.

Europe ['juərəp] *n* Europa.

European [juərə'pɪən] *adj* europeo,-a.
▷ *n (person)* europeo,-a. ● **European Economic Community** Comunidad *f* Económica Europea. ‖ **European Parliament** Parlamento Europeo. ‖ **European Union** Unión *f* Europea.

Europeanization [juərəpɪənaɪ'zeɪʃən] *n* europeización *f*.

Europeanize [juərə'pɪənaɪz] *vt* europeizar.

Eurosceptic [juərəu'skeptɪk] *n* euroescéptico,-a.

Eurovision ['juərəvɪʒən] *n* eurovisión *f*.

euthanasia [ju:θə'neɪzɪə] *n* eutanasia.

evacuate [ɪ'vækjueɪt] *vt* **1** *(people)* evacuar. **2** *(place)* desalojar; *(mil)* desocupar.

evacuation [ɪvækju'eɪʃən] *n* **1** *(of people)* evacuación *f*. **2** *(of place)* desalojamiento, desalojo.

evacuee [ɪvækju'i:] *n* evacuado,-a.

evade [ɪ'veɪd] *vt* **1** *(gen)* evadir, eludir, esquivar. **2** *(question)* eludir. **3** *(tax)* evadir.

evaluate [ɪ'væljueɪt] *vt* **1** *(assess)* evaluar, juzgar; *(estimate value)* valorar, calcular (el valor de), tasar. **2** MATH hallar el valor numérico de.

evaluation [ɪvælju'eɪʃən] *n* evaluación *f*.

evanescent [i:və'nesənt] *adj* evanescente.

evangelical [iːvæn'dʒelɪkᵊl] *adj* evangélico,-a.
evangelist [ɪ'vændʒᵊlɪst] *n* evangelista *mf*.
evangelization [ɪvændʒəlaɪ'zeɪsᵊn] *n* evangelización *f*.
evangelize [ɪ'vændʒᵊlaɪz] *vt* evangelizar.
evaporate [ɪ'væpəreɪt] *vt* evaporar.
▷ *vi* **1** evaporarse. **2** *fig* desvanecerse, esfumarse.
evaporated milk [ɪ'væpəraɪtɪd'mɪlk] *n* leche *f* evaporada.
evaporation [ɪvæpə'reɪʃᵊn] *n* evaporación *f*.
evasion [ɪ'veɪʒᵊn] *n* **1** *(gen)* evasión *f*. **2** *(excuse, etc)* evasiva.
evasive [ɪ'veɪsɪv] *adj* evasivo,-a.
evasively [ɪ'veɪsɪvlɪ] *adv* de manera evasiva.
eve [iːv] *n* víspera, vigilia. ■ **on the eve of** STH en vísperas de ALGO.
even ['iːvᵊn] *adj* **1** *(level, flat)* llano,-a, plano,-a; *(smooth)* liso,-a: **this surface isn't even** *esta superficie no es plana*. **2** *(regular, steady)* uniforme, regular, constante. **3** *(evenly balanced)* igual, igualado,-a. **4** *(equal in measure, quantity, number)* igual. **5** *(number)* par. **6** *(placid - character)* apacible, tranquilo,-a; *(- voice)* imperturbable. **7** *(on the same level as)* a nivel (**with**, de).
▷ *adv* **1** hasta, incluso, aun: **it's always sunny, even in winter** *siempre hace sol, incluso en invierno*. **2** *(with negative)* siquiera, ni siquiera: **she never even said hello** *ni siquiera me saludó*. **3** *(before comparative)* aun, todavía: **she's even more beautiful than I remembered** *es aun más guapa de lo que recordaba*. ■ **even if** aun si, aunque. ‖ **even though** aunque, aun cuando.
▷ *vt* **1** *(level)* nivelar, allanar. **2** *(score)* igualar; *(situation)* equilibrar.
⊙ **to even out** *vt sep (make level)* nivelar; *(make equal)* igualar; *(spread equally)* repartir equitativamente.
⊙ **to even up** *vt sep (balance)* equilibrar; *(make equal)* igualar.
even-handed ['iːvᵊnhændɪd] *adj* imparcial.
evening ['iːvᵊnɪŋ] *n (early)* tarde *f*; *(late)* noche *f*. ● **good evening!** ¡buenas tardes! ¡buenas noches!
evenly ['iːvᵊnlɪ] *adv* **1** *(uniformly)* uniformemente, de modo uniforme, regularmente. **2** *(fairly, equally)* equitativamente, igualmente.
▷ *adj (of voice)* en el mismo tono, con calma.
evensong ['iːvᵊnɒŋ] *n* vísperas *fpl*.
event [ɪ'vent] *n* **1** *(happening)* suceso, acontecimiento. **2** SP prueba.
eventful [ɪ'ventfʊl] *adj (memorable)* lleno,-a (de acontecimientos), memorable; *(busy)* ajetreado,-a, agitado,-a; *(troubled)* accidentado,-a.
eventual [ɪ'ventʃʊəl] *adj* **1** *(final, ultimate)* final. **2** *(resulting)* consiguiente. **3** *(possible)* posible.
eventuality [ɪventʃʊ'ælɪtɪ] *n* eventualidad *f*. ▲ *pl* **eventualities**.
eventually [ɪ'ventʃʊəlɪ] *adv* finalmente, con el tiempo.
ever ['evəʳ] *adv* **1** *(in negative sentences)* nunca, jamás. **2** *(in questions)* alguna vez. **3** *(always)* siempre. **4** *(after comparative and superlative)* nunca. **5** *(emphatic use)*: **how ever did you lose your coat?** *¿cómo has podido perder el abrigo?* ● **for ever** para siempre.
evergreen ['evəgriːn] *adj* BOT de hoja perenne.
▷ *n (tree)* árbol *m* de hoja perenne; *(bush)* arbusto de hoja perenne.
everlasting [evə'lɑːstɪŋ] *adj* **1** *(eternal, lasting for ever)* eterno,-a, perpetuo,-a. **2** *(lasting for long time)* duradero,-a, perdurable. **3** *pej (incessant)* continuo,-a, incesante.
evermore [evə'mɔːʳ] *adv* eternamente. ■ **for evermore** para siempre.
every ['evrɪ] *adj* **1** *(each)* cada; *(all)* todos,-as: **every day** *cada día, todos los días*. **2** *(all possible)*: **we encourage people to help in every way** *animamos a la gente a que ayude de cualquier manera*. ■ **every other day** un día sí un día no, cada dos días.

Consulta también **each**.

everybody ['evrɪbɒdɪ] *pron* todos,-as, todo el mundo.
everyday ['evrɪdeɪ] *adj (day-to-day)* diario,-a, de todos los días; *(ordinary)* corriente, cotidiano,-a: **for everyday use** *para uso diario*.
everyone ['evrɪwʌn] *pron* → **everybody**.
everyplace ['evrɪpleɪs] *adv* US→ **everywhere**.
everything ['evrɪθɪŋ] *pron* todo.
everywhere ['evrɪweəʳ] *adv* **1** *(place)* en todas partes, por todas partes: **he's been everywhere** *ha estado en todas partes*. **2** *(movement)* a todas partes.
evict [ɪ'vɪkt] *vt* desahuciar, desalojar.
evidence ['evɪdəns] *n* **1** *(proof)* prueba, pruebas *fpl*. **2** *(sign, indication)* indicio, indicios *mpl*, señal *f*. **3** JUR *(testimony)* testimonio, declaración *f*.
▷ *vt* **1** *(prove)* demostrar, probar. **2** *(give proof of)* justificar.
evident ['evɪdənt] *adj* evidente, patente, manifiesto,-a.
evil ['iːvᵊl] *adj* **1** *(wicked)* malo,-a, malvado,-a. **2** *(harmful)* malo,-a, pernicioso,-a, nocivo,-a. **3** *(foul - smell)* horrible, fétido,-a, repugnante; *(- temper)* geniudo,-a, terrible, de perros; *(- weather)* malo,-a, de perros. **4** *(unlucky)* aciago,-a, de mal agüero.
▷ *n (wickedness)* mal *m*, maldad *f*.
evocative [ɪ'vɒkətɪv] *adj* evocador,-ra.
evoke [ɪ'vəuk] *vt* **1** *(bring to mind)* evocar. **2** *fml (produce, cause)* provocar.
evolution [iːvə'luːʃᵊn] *n* **1** *(biol)* evolución *f*. **2** *(gradual development)* desarrollo.
evolve [ɪ'vɒlv] *vt* **1** *(develop)* desarrollar. **2** *(give off)* desprender.
▷ *vi* **1** *(develop)* desarrollarse. **2** *(biol)* evolucionar.
ewe [juː] *n* oveja.
ex[1] [eks] *n fam (husband)* ex marido; *(wife)* ex mujer *f*.
ex[2] [eks] *prep* FIN sin: **ex dividend** *sin dividendo, sin cupón*; **ex interest** *sin interés*.
exacerbate [ɪg'zæsɜːbeɪt] *vt* exacerbar, agravar.
exact [ɪg'zækt] *adj* **1** *(precise)* exacto,-a. **2** *(meticulous)* meticuloso,-a. **3** *(accurate)* preciso,-a. **4** *(specific, particular)* justo.
▷ *vt* **1** *(demand, insist on)* exigir (**from**, a). **2** *(require)* exigir, requerir: **this job exacts great patience** *este trabajo requiere mucha paciencia*.
exacting [ɪg'zæktɪŋ] *adj* exigente.
exactitude [ɪg'zæktɪtjuːd] *n* exactitud *f*.

exactly [ɪg'zæktlɪ] *adv* **1** *(in precise detail, correctly, accurately)* exactamente, precisamente. **2** *(precisely)* justo, exactamente.
▷ *interj* ¡exacto!, ¡exactamente!
exaggerate [ɪg'zædʒəreɪt] *vt* exagerar.
exaggerated [ɪg'zædʒəreɪtɪd] *adj* exagerado,-a.
exalt [ɪg'zɔ:lt] *vt* **1** *fml (elevate)* exaltar, elevar. **2** *(praise, extol)* ensalzar.
exaltation [egzɔ:l'teɪʃən] *n* exaltación *f.*
exam [ɪg'zæm] *n fam* examen *m.*
examination [ɪgzæmɪ'neɪʃən] *n* **1** EDUC examen *m.* **2** *(inspection)* inspección *f*, examen *m*; *(of house, room)* registro. **3** MED reconocimiento. **4** JUR interrogatorio.
examine [ɪg'zæmɪn] *vt* **1** *(inspect)* inspeccionar, examinar; *(check)* comprobar; *(consider)* examinar, estudiar. **2** *(customs)* registrar. **3** EDUC examinar (**in/on**, de). **4** MED hacer un reconocimiento a. **5** JUR interrogar.
examinee [ɪgzæmɪ'ni:] *n* examinado,-a.
examiner [ɪg'zæmɪnər] *n* examinador,-ra.
example [ɪg'zɑ:mpəl] *n* **1** *(gen)* ejemplo. **2** *(specimen)* ejemplo. ● **for example** por ejemplo.
exasperate [ɪg'zɑ:spəreɪt] *vt* exasperar, irritar.
excavate ['ekskəveɪt] *vt* excavar.
excavation [ekskə'veɪʃən] *n* excavación *f.*
excavator ['ekskəveɪtər] *n* **1** *(person)* excavador,-ra. **2** *(machine)* excavadora.
exceed [ɪk'si:d] *vt (be greater than)* exceder, sobrepasar; *(go beyond)* exceder, sobrepasar.
excel [ɪk'sel] *vt (surpass)* aventajar, superar.
▷ *vi (be very good at)* destacar (**at/in**, en), sobresalir (**at/in**, en), descollar (**at/in**, en).
▲ *pt & pp* **excelled**, *ger* **excelling**.
excellence ['eksələns] *n* excelencia.
excellent ['eksələnt] *adj* excelente, sobresaliente.
▷ *interj fam* ¡estupendo!, ¡fantástico!
except [ɪk'sept] *prep* excepto, salvo, a excepción de, menos.
▷ *vt fml* excluir, exceptuar.
exception [ɪk'sepʃən] *n* excepción *f.*
exceptionable [ɪk'sepʃənəbəl] *adj* censurable.
exceptional [ɪk'sepʃənəl] *adj* excepcional, extraordinario,-a.
excerpt ['eksɜ:pt] *n* extracto.
excess [ɪk'ses] *n* **1** exceso. **2** COMM excedente *m.*
▷ *adj* excedente, sobrante.
▷ *n pl* **excesses** excesos *mpl.*
excessive [ɪk'sesɪv] *adj* excesivo,-a.
exchange [ɪks'tʃeɪndʒ] *n* **1** *(gen)* cambio. **2** *(of ideas, information, etc)* intercambio. **3** *(of prisoners)* canje *m.* **4** FIN cambio. **5** *(dialogue)* intercambio de palabras; *(argument)* enfrentamiento. **6** *(building)* lonja. **7** *(telephone)* central *f* telefónica. **8** EDUC *(reciprocal visit)* intercambio. **9** *(of gunfire)* tiroteo.
▷ *vt* **1** *(gen)* cambiar. **2** *(ideas, information, etc)* intercambiar. **3** *(prisoners)* canjear.
exchequer [ɪks'tʃekər] *n (treasury)* tesoro público.
▷ *n* **the Exchequer** Hacienda.
excise[1] [ɪk'saɪz] *vt fml* extirpar.
excise[2] ['eksaɪz] *n* impuesto sobre el consumo.
excision [ɪk'sɪʒən] *n fml* extirpación *f*, excisión *f.*
excite [ɪk'saɪt] *vt* **1** *(enthuse, thrill)* emocionar, entusiasmar, apasionar. **2** *fml (bring about)* provocar: **3** *(cause, arouse)* provocar, despertar. **4** *(arouse sexually)* excitar. **5** MED *(stimulate)* excitar.
excited [ɪk'saɪtɪd] *adj* **1** emocionado,-a, entusiasmado,-a, ilusionado,-a. **2** *(sexually)* excitado,-a, caliente.
excitement [ɪk'saɪtmənt] *n* **1** *(strong feeling)* emoción *f*, entusiasmo, ilusión *f.* **2** *(commotion)* agitación *f*, conmoción *f*, revuelo.
exciting [ɪk'saɪtɪŋ] *adj* emocionante, apasionante.
exclaim [ɪk'skleɪm] *vt* exclamar, gritar.
▷ *vi* exclamar.
exclamation [ekskləˈmeɪʃən] *n* exclamación *f.* ● **exclamation mark** signo de admiración. ‖ **exclamation point** US signo de admiración.
exclude [ɪk'sklu:d] *vt* **1** *(leave out, not include)* excluir, no incluir. **2** *(debar, prevent from entering)* no admitir. **3** *(reject)* excluir, descartar.
excluding [ɪk'sklu:dɪŋ] *prep (excepting)* excepto, con excepción de.
exclusive [ɪk'sklu:sɪv] *adj* **1** *(not shared, sole)* exclusivo,-a. **2** *(select)* selecto,-a, exclusivo,-a. **3** *(press)* en exclusiva.
▷ *n (press)* exclusiva.
excoriation [ɪkskɔ:rɪ'eɪʃən] *n* excoriación *f.*
excrescence [ɪk'skresəns] *n* excrecencia.
excrement ['ekskrɪmənt] *n* excremento.
excrete [ɪk'skri:t] *vt* excretar.
excretion [ɪk'skri:ʃən] *n* excreción *f.*
excretory [ɪk'skri:tərɪ] *adj* excretorio,-a, excretor,-ra
excruciating [ɪk'skru:ʃɪeɪtɪŋ] *adj* **1** insoportable atroz, agudísimo,-a. **2** *euph* fatal, horrible.
excursion [ɪk'skɜ:ʒən] *n (outing)* excursión *f*, viaje *m.*
excuse [*(n)* ɪk'skju:s; *(vb)* ɪk'skju:z] *n* **1** *(apology)* disculpa. **2** *(pretext)* excusa.
▷ *vt* **1** perdonar, disculpar. **2** *(justify)* justificar. **3** *(exempt)* dispensar, eximir.
execrable ['eksɪkrəbəl] *adj* execrable.
execrate ['eksɪkreɪt] *vt* execrar.
execute ['eksɪkju:t] *vt* **1** *(put to death)* ejecutar, ajusticiar. **2** *(carry out)* ejecutar; *(orders)* cumplir; *(tasks)* realizar, llevar a cabo. **3** *(music, etc)* interpretar. **4** JUR *(will)* cumplir.
execution [eksɪ'kju:ʃən] *n* **1** *(carrying out)* ejecución *f*; *(of order)* cumplimiento; *(of task)* realización *f.* **2** *(putting to death)* ejecución *f.* **3** JUR *(of will)* cumplimiento. **4** *(of music, etc)* interpretación *f.*
executioner [eksɪ'kju:ʃənər] *n* verdugo.
executive [ɪg'zekjətɪv] *adj* ejecutivo,-a.
▷ *n (person)* ejecutivo,-a; *(committee)* ejecutiva.
▷ *n* **the executive** *(government)* el poder ejecutivo, el ejecutivo.
executor [ɪg'zekjətər] *n* JUR albacea.
exemplary [ɪg'zemplərɪ] *adj* ejemplar.
exemplification [ɪgzemplɪfɪ'keɪʃən] *n* ejemplificación *f*, ejemplo.
exemplify [ɪg'zemplɪfaɪ] *vt* ejemplificar, servir de ejemplo para.
▲ *pt & pp* **exemplified**, *ger* **exemplifying**.
exempt [ɪg'zempt] *adj* exento,-a, libre (**from**, de).
▷ *vt* eximir, dispensar (**from**, de).

exemption [ɪg'zempʃᵊn] *n* exención *f* (from, de).
exercise ['eksəsaɪz] *n* 1 *(gen)* ejercicio. 2 *(use, application)* ejercicio, uso. ● **exercise book** cuaderno.
▷ *vt* 1 *(employ, make use of)* ejercer, emplear. 2 *(give exercise to - dog)* sacar de paseo; *(- horse)* entrenar.
▷ *vi* hacer ejercicio, entrenarse.
▷ *vt fml (trouble)* inquietar.
▷ *n pl* **exercises** US *(ceremonies)* ceremonia.
exert [ɪg'zɜːt] *vt* ejercer.
exertion [ɪg'zɜːʃᵊn] *n* 1 *(great effort)* esfuerzo. 2 *(use, application)* ejercicio, uso.
exhalation [ekshə'leɪʃᵊn] *n* exhalación *f*.
exhale [eks'heɪl] *vt (breathe out)* exhalar.
▷ *vi (give off)* despedir.
exhaust [ɪg'zɔːst] *n* 1 *(pipe)* (tubo de) escape *m*. 2 *(fumes)* gases *mpl* de combustión.
▷ *vt* 1 *(gen)* agotar. 2 *(empty)* vaciar.
exhausted [ɪg'zɔːstɪd] *adj* agotado,-a.
exhausting [ɪg'zɔːstɪŋ] *adj* agotador,-ra.
exhaustive [ɪg'zɔːstɪv] *adj* exhaustivo,-a, completo,-a.
exhaustively [ɪg'zɔːstɪvlɪ] *adv* exhaustivamente.
exhibit [ɪg'zɪbɪt] *n* 1 ART objeto expuesto. 2 JUR prueba instrumental.
▷ *vt* 1 *(display, show)* exponer, presentar. 2 *fml (manifest)* manifestar, mostrar, presentar, dar muestras de.
▷ *vi (of artist)* exponer.
exhibition [eksɪ'bɪʃᵊn] *n* 1 *(art, etc)* exposición *f*. 2 *(display)* demostración *f*, muestra.
exhibitionist [eksɪ'bɪʃᵊnɪst] *n* exhibicionista *mf*.
exhilarating [ɪg'zɪləreɪtɪŋ] *adj (invigorating)* estimulante; *(exciting)* emocionante.
exhilaration [ɪgzɪlə'reɪʃᵊn] *n (state)* alegría, regocijo; *(act)* estímulo.
exhort [ɪg'zɔːt] *vt fml* exhortar.
exhume [eks'hjuːm] *vt* exhumar, desenterrar.
exigency ['eksɪdʒənsɪ, ɪg'zɪdʒənsɪ] *n* 1 *fml (need)* exigencia. 2 *fml (emergency)* caso de emergencia.
▲ *pl* **exigencies.**
exigent ['eksɪdʒənt] *adj* 1 *fml (demanding)* exigente. 2 *fml (urgent)* urgente.
exiguous [ek'sɪgjʊəs] *adj fml* exiguo,-a.
exile ['eksaɪl] *n* 1 *(action)* destierro, exilio. 2 *(person)* desterrado,-a, exiliado,-a.
▷ *vt* desterrar, exiliar.
exist [ɪg'zɪst] *vi* 1 *(gen)* existir. 2 *(subsist)* subsistir (**on**, a base de).
existence [ɪg'zɪstᵊns] *n* existencia.
existent [ɪg'zɪstᵊnt] *adj* existente.
exit ['eksɪt] *n* 1 *(gen)* salida. 2 THEAT mutis *m*.
▷ *vi* THEAT hacer mutis, salir de escena.
exodus ['eksədəs] *n* éxodo.
exonerate [ɪg'zɒnəᵊeɪt] *vt* exonerar, exculpar.
exorbitant [ɪg'zɔːbɪtᵊnt] *adj* exorbitante, desorbitado,-a, excesivo,-a.
exorcise ['eksɔːsaɪz] *vt* 1 exorcizar. 2 *fig (memory)* borrar; *(feeling)* quitar, librar.
exorcism ['eksɔːsɪzᵊm] *n* exorcismo.
exorcist ['eksɔːsɪst] *n* exorcista *mf*.
exotic [eg'zɒtɪk] *adj* exótico,-a.
expand [ɪk'spænd] *vt* 1 *(enlarge - business)* ampliar; *(- number)* aumentar, incrementar. 2 *(gas, metal)* dilatar, expandir.
▷ *vi* 1 *(grow larger)* crecer, aumentar. 2 *(metal)* dilatarse; *(gas)* expandirse, expansionarse. 3 *(spread out)* extenderse. 4 *(become friendlier)* abrirse, volverse expansivo,-a.
⊙ **to expand on** *vt insep* ampliar, desarrollar.
expanse [ɪk'spæns] *n* extensión *f*.
expansion [ɪk'spænʃᵊn] *n* 1 crecimiento, aumento. 2 *(gas, metal)* dilatación *f*, expansión *f*. 3 *(trade)* desarrollo.
expansive [ɪk'spænsɪv] *adj* 1 *(friendly, talkative)* expansivo,-a, hablador,-ra, comunicativo,-a. 2 *(able to expand)* expansivo,-a.
expatiate [ɪk'speɪʃɪeɪt] *vi fml* extenderse.
expatriate [*(adj-n)* ek'spætrɪət; *(vb)* eks'pætrɪeɪt] *adj* expatriado,-a.
▷ *n* expatriado,-a.
▷ *vt* desterrar, expatriar.
expect [ɪk'spekt] *vt* 1 *(anticipate)* esperar: **I never expected to win** *no esperaba ganar.* 2 *(demand)* esperar, contar con. 3 GB *fam (suppose)* suponer, imaginar.
expectancy [ɪk'spektᵊnsɪ] *n (anticipation)* expectación *f*, expectativa; *(hope)* ilusión *f*.
expectant [ɪk'spektᵊnt] *adj (expecting)* expectante; *(hopeful)* ilusionado,-a.
expectation [ekspek'teɪʃᵊn] *n (hope, firm belief)* esperanza.
▷ *n pl* **expectations** *(confident feelings)* expectativas *fpl*.
expediency [ɪk'spiːdɪənsɪ] *n* conveniencia, oportunidad *f*.
expedient [ɪk'spiːdɪənt] *adj* conveniente, oportuno,-a.
▷ *n* expediente *m*, recurso.
expediently [ɪk'spiːdɪəntlɪ] *adv* oportunamente, convenientemente.
expedite ['ekspədaɪt] *vt fml (hasten, speed up)* acelerar.
expedition [ekspɪ'dɪʃᵊn] *n* 1 *(gen)* expedición *f*. 2 *fml (speed)* aceleración *f*, prontitud *f*.
expel [ɪk'spel] *vt* expulsar.
▲ *pt & pp* **expelled**, *ger* **expelling.**
expend [ɪk'spend] *vt* 1 *fml (spend, use)* gastar, emplear. 2 *fml (use up, exhaust)* agotar.
expendable [ɪk'spendəbᵊl] *adj fml* prescindible.
expenditure [ɪk'spendɪtʃəʳ] *n* gasto, desembolso.
expense [ɪk'spens] *n* gasto, desembolso.
▷ *n pl* **expenses** gastos *mpl*.
expensive [ɪk'spensɪv] *adj* caro,-a, costoso,-a.
experience [ɪk'spɪərɪəns] *n* experiencia.
▷ *vt (sensation, situation, etc)* experimentar; *(difficulty)* tener; *(loss)* sufrir.
experienced [ɪk'spɪərɪənst] *adj* experimentado,-a, con experiencia.
experiment [ɪk'sperɪmənt] *n* experimento.
▷ *vi* experimentar, hacer experimentos.
experimental [ɪksperɪ'mentᵊl] *adj* experimental.
expert ['ekspɜːt] *n* experto,-a (**at/in/on**, en).
▷ *adj* experto,-a:
expertise [ekspɜː'tiːz] *n (skill)* pericia, habilidad *f*, *(knowledge)* conocimiento (práctico).

expire [ɪk'spaɪəʳ] *vi* **1** *(come to end)* terminar, acabarse; *(die)* expirar, morir. **2** *(run out - contract)* vencer; *(- passport, ticket)* caducar. **3** MED *(breathe out)* espirar.
expiry [ɪk'spaɪəʳɪ] *n* **1** *(ending)* expiración *f*, terminación *f*. **2** *(of contract, bill of exchange)* vencimiento; *(of passport, driving licence, etc)* caducidad *f*.
explanation [ekspla'neɪʃᵊn] *n* **1** *(gen)* explicación *f*. **2** *(clarification)* aclaración *f*.
explicate ['eksplɪkeɪt] *vt fml* aclarar, explicar.
explicit [ɪk'splɪsɪt] *adj* explícito,-a.
explode [ɪk'spləʊd] *vt* **1** *(blow up - bomb, etc)* hacer estallar, hacer explotar; *(- mine)* hacer volar. **2** *(refute - theory)* refutar; *(- rumour)* desmentir.
▷ *vi* **1** *(blow up)* estallar, explotar, hacer explosión. **2** *(react violently)* reventar, explotar, estallar. **3** *(increase rapidly)* aumentar rápidamente, crecer rápidamente.
exploit [*(n)* 'eksplɔɪt; *(vb)* ɪk'splɔɪt] *n* hazaña, proeza.
▷ *vt* **1** *(work, develop fully)* explotar. **2** *(use unfairly)* aprovecharse de, explotar.
exploitation [eksplɔɪ'teɪʃᵊn] *n* explotación *f*.
exploration [ekspla'reɪʃᵊn] *n* exploración *f*.
explore [ɪk'splɔːʳ] *vt* **1** *(gen)* explorar. **2** *(examine)* examinar.
▷ *vi* explorar.
explorer [ɪk'splɔːrəʳ] *n* explorador,-ra.
explosion [ɪk'spləʊʒᵊn] *n* **1** *(gen)* explosión *f*, estallido. **2** *(violent outburst)* ataque *m*, arrebato. **3** *(increase)* aumento rápido, crecimiento rápido.
explosive [ɪk'spləʊsɪv] *adj (gen)* explosivo,-a.
exponent [ɪk'spəʊnənt] *n* **1** *(gen)* exponente *m*; *(supporter)* defensor,-ra (**of**, de), partidario,-a (**of**, de). **2** *(performer)* intérprete *mf*; *(expert)* experto,-a. **3** MATH exponente *m*.
exponential [ekspə'nenʃᵊl] *adj* MATH exponencial.
export [*(n)* 'ekspɔːt; *(vb)* ɪk'spɔːt] *n* **1** *(trade)* exportación *f*. **2** *(article)* artículo de exportación.
▷ *vt* exportar.
exporter [ek'spɔːtəʳ] *n* exportador,-ra.
expose [ɪk'spəʊz] *vt* **1** *(uncover, make visible)* exponer. **2** *(make known - secret, etc)* revelar, descubrir, desvelar, destapar; *(- person)* desenmascarar. **3** *fig (lay open)* exponerse. **4** *(introduce, acquaint with)* exponer (**to**, a), verse expuesto,-a. **5** *(photo)* exponer.
exposed [ɪk'spəʊzd] *adj (not sheltered)* desabrigado,-a, al descubierto; *(not protected)* expuesto,-a (**to**, a).
exposition [ekspə'zɪʃᵊn] *n* **1** *(exhibition)* exposición *f*. **2** *(account)* explicación *f*.
exposure [ɪk'spəʊʒəʳ] *n* **1** *(being exposed)* exposición *f*. **2** *(revelation, disclosure)* revelación *f*, descubrimiento; *(exposé)* desenmascaramiento. **3** *(in photography - picture)* fotografía; *(- time)* exposición *f*. **4** *(position of house, etc)* situación *f*, orientación *f*. **5** *(publicity)* publicidad *f*; *(coverage)* cobertura.
expound [ɪk'spaʊnd] *vt fml* exponer.
express [ɪk'spres] *adj* **1** *(explicit)* expreso,-a, claro,-a. **2** *(fast - mail)* urgente; *(- train, coach)* expreso.
▷ *adv* urgente.
▷ *n (rail)* (tren *m*) expreso.
▷ *vt* **1** expresar. **2** *fml (juice)* exprimir.
expression [ɪk'spreʃᵊn] *n* **1** *(gen)* expresión *f*; *(manifestation)* manifestación *f*. **2** MATH expresión *f*.
expressionism [ɪk'spreʃᵊnɪzᵊm] *n* expresionismo.
expressionist [ɪk'spreʃᵊnɪst] *n* expresionista *mf*.
expressive [ɪk'spresɪv] *adj* expresivo,-a.
expressway [ɪk'spresweɪ] *n* US autopista.
expropriate [ɪk'sprəʊpᵊrɪeɪt] *vt* expropiar.
expropriation [ɪksprəʊpᵊrɪ'eɪʃᵊn] *n* expropiación *f*.
expulsion [ɪk'spʌlʃᵊn] *n* expulsión *f*.
exquisite [ek'skwɪzɪt, 'ekskwɪzɪt] *adj* **1** *(delicate, etc)* exquisito,-a, perfecto,-a. **2** *fml (of emotion)* intenso,-a; *(of power to feel)* delicado,-a.
extend [ɪk'stend] *vt* **1** *(enlarge)* ampliar; *(lengthen - line, road)* prolongar, alargar. **2** *(over time)* prolongar, alargar; *(deadline)* prorrogar. **3** *(stretch out - arm, hand)* alargar, tender; *(- leg)* estirar; *(- wing)* desplegar, extender; *(- rope, ladder, etc)* extender. **4** *(offer, give)* dar, ofrecer, rendir. **5** *(enlarge - scope, range, influence)* ampliar, extender.
▷ *vi* **1** *(in space)* continuar, extenderse, llegar hasta. **2** *(in time)* prolongarse, alargarse, durar. **3** *(become extended - ladder, etc)* extenderse. **4** *(include, affect)* incluir, abarcar, extenderse a.
extended [ɪk'stendɪd] *adj (time)* prolongado,-a; *(wide, broad)* amplio,-a, extenso,-a; *(stretched out)* extendido,-a.
extension [ɪk'stenʃᵊn] *n* **1** *(widening)* ampliación *f*, extensión *f*. **2** *(of line, road, etc)* prolongación *f*. **3** *(of time)* prórroga, prolongación *f*. **4** *(of school, hospital, etc)* anexo; *(of house)* ampliación *f*. **5** *(telephone line)* extensión *f*; *(telephone)* supletorio.
extensive [ɪk'stensɪv] *adj* **1** *(area)* extenso,-a, amplio,-a. **2** *(wide-ranging)* vasto,-a, amplio,-a, extenso,-a; *(thorough)* exhaustivo, minucioso,-a. **3** *(very great in effect, widespread)* importante, múltiple.
extent [ɪk'stent] *n* **1** *(expanse)* extensión *f*. **2** *(range, scale, scope)* amplitud *f*, vastedad *f*, alcance *m*. **3** *(point)* punto.
extenuate [ɪk'stenjʊeɪt] *vt fml* atenuar.
exterior [ɪk'stɪəᵊrɪəʳ] *adj* exterior, externo,-a: **exterior walls** *paredes exteriores.*
▷ *n* **1** exterior *m*. **2** *(of person)* aspecto externo, apariencia.
exterminate [ɪk'stɜːmɪneɪt] *vt* exterminar.
extermination [ɪkstɜːmɪ'neɪʃᵊn] *n* exterminación *f*, exterminio.
external [ek'stɜːnᵊl] *adj* externo,-a, exterior.
▷ *n pl* **externals** *fml* aspecto *m sing* externo.
extinct [ɪk'stɪŋkt] *adj* **1** *(of animal)* extinguido,-a. **2** *(of volcano)* extinguido,-a, apagado,-a.
extinction [ɪk'stɪŋkʃᵊn] *n* extinción *f*.
extinguish [ɪk'stɪŋgwɪʃ] *vt* extinguir, apagar.
extinguisher [ɪk'stɪŋgwɪʃəʳ] *n* extintor *m*.
extirpate ['ekstəpeɪt] *vt fml* extirpar.
extol [ɪks'təʊl] *vt fml* ensalzar, alabar.
▲ *pt & pp* **extolled**, *ger* **extolling**.
extort [ɪk'stɔːt] *vt (money)* sacar, conseguir a la fuerza, conseguir con amenazas; *(promise, confession)* arrancar, obtener.
extortion [ɪk'stɔːʃᵊn] *n* extorsión *f*.
extra ['ekstᵊə] *adj (additional)* extra, más, otro,-a; *(spare)* de sobra; *(on top)* aparte.
▷ *adv (more than usually)* extra, muy; *(additional)* aparte.
▷ *n* **1** *(additional thing)* extra *m*, complemento; *(additional charge)* suplemento; *(luxury)* lujo. **2** CINEM extra *mf*. **3** *(press)* edición *f* especial.

extract [*(n)* 'ekstrækt; *(vb)* ɪk'strækt] *n* **1** *(product)* extracto. **2** *(excerpt)* extracto, fragmento, trozo.
▷ *vt* **1** *(pull out)* extraer, sacar. **2** *(obtain - confession, promise, etc)* arrancar, obtener; *(- information, passage, quotation)* extraer, sacar. **3** *(produce)* extraer, sacar.
extraction [ɪk'strækʃᵊn] *n* **1** *(gen)* extracción *f*. **2** *(of tooth)* extracción *f*. **3** *(descent)* origen *m*.
extractor [ɪk'stræktəʳ] *n* extractor *m*. ● **extractor fan** extractor *m* de humos.
extracurricular [ekstrəkə'ᵊɪkjʊləʳ] *adj* extracurricular, extraescolar.
extradite ['ekstrədaɪt] *vt* extraditar, extradir.
extradition [ekstrə'dɪʃᵊn] *n* extradición *f*.
extramarital [ekstrə'mæᵊrtᵊl] *adj* extramatrimonial.
extraordinary [ɪk'strɔːdənᵊɪ] *adj* **1** *(exceptional)* extraordinario,-a, fuera de lo común; *(very strange, unusual)* raro,-a. **2** *fml (special, additional)* extraordinario,-a, especial.
extrapolate [ɪk'stræpəleɪt] *vt* **1** *fml (maths)* extrapolar. **2** *fml (estimate)* extrapolar.
extrasensory [ekstrə'sensᵊᵊɪ] *adj* extrasensorial.
extraterrestrial [ekstᵊətə'ᵊestᵊrɪəl] *adj* extraterrestre.
▷ *n* extraterrestre *mf*.
extraterritorial [ekstrəteᵊɪ'tɔːᵊrɪəl] *adj* extraterritorial.
extravagance [ɪk'strævəgᵊns] *n (spending)* derroche *m*, despilfarro, lujo; *(behaviour)* extravagancia.
extravagant [ɪk'strævəgᵊnt] *adj* **1** *(wasteful - person)* derrochador,-ra, despilfarrador,-ra; *(- thing)* ineficaz, ineficiente. **2** *(extreme)* extravagante, exagerado,-a, estrafalario,-a. **3** *(luxurious)* lujoso,-a, suntuoso,-a.
extravaganza [ɪkstᵊævə'gænzə] *n* espectáculo fantástico, fantasía.
extreme [ɪk'striːm] *adj* **1** *(furthest, very great)* extremo,-a. **2** *(not moderate)* extremo,-a, radical. **3** *(severe, unusual)* excepcional.
▷ *n* extremo.
extremely [ɪk'striːmlɪ] *adv* extremadamente, sumamente.
extremism [ɪk'striːmɪzᵊm] *n* extremismo, radicalismo.
extremist [ɪk'striːmɪst] *n* extremista *mf*.
extremity [ɪk'stremɪtɪ] *n* **1** *fml (furthest point)* extremo. **2** *fml (extreme degree, situation)* extremo, situación *f* extrema, situación *f* límite.
▲ *pl* **extremities**.
▷ *n pl* **extremities** ANAT extremidades *fpl*.
extricate ['ekstrɪkeɪt] *vt fml* librar, sacar. ■ **to extricate** OS lograr salir (**from**, de).
extrinsic [ɪk'strɪnzɪk] *adj* extrínseco,-a.
extrovert ['ekstrəvɜːt] *adj* extrovertido,-a.
▷ *n* extrovertido,-a.

extrude [ɪk'struːd] *vt* extrudir.
extrusion [ɪk'struːzᵊn] *n* extrusión *f*.
exuberance [ɪg'zjuːbərəns] *n (vigour)* exuberancia; *(high spirits)* euforia.
exuberant [ɪg'zjuːbərənt] *adj* **1** *(of person)* eufórico,-a. **2** *(of plants)* exuberante. **3** *fig* vivo,-a.
exude [ɪg'zjuːd] *vt* **1** *fml (of sweat, etc)* exudar, rezumar. **2** *fig (of feeling)* rebosar: **she exudes confidence** *rebosa de confianza*.
▷ *vi (of sweat, etc)* exudar, rezumar.
exult [ɪg'zʌlt] *vi fml* regocijarse (**in**, con).
exultant [ɪg'zʌltənt] *adj* exultante, jubiloso,-a, regocijado,-a, triunfante.
exultation [ɪgzʌl'teɪʃᵊn] *n* exultación *f*, júbilo.
eye [aɪ] *n* **1** ANAT ojo: **open your eyes** *abre los ojos*. **2** *(sense)* vista. **3** *(of needle, potato, storm)* ojo.
▷ *vt (observe)* mirar, observar; *(look at longingly)* echar el ojo a.
eyeball ['aɪbɔːl] *n* globo ocular.
eyebath ['aɪbæθ] *n* lavaojos *m*.
eyebolt ['aɪbəʊlt] *n* armella, hembrilla.
eyebrow ['aɪbraʊ] *n* ceja.
eye-catching ['aɪkætʃɪŋ] *adj* llamativo,-a.
eyeful ['aɪfʊl] *n* **1** *(of dust, sand, etc)*: **I fell on the beach and got an eyeful of sand** *me caí en la playa y se me llenó el ojo de arena*. **2** *(attractive sight)* cosa atractiva: **the new secretary's an eyeful** *la nueva secretaria está como un tren*. ■ **to get an eyeful of** STH echar un vistazo a ALGO.
eyeglass ['aɪglɑːs] *n* monóculo.
eyelash ['aɪlæʃ] *n* pestaña.
eyelet ['aɪlət] *n* ojete *m*.
eyelid ['aɪlɪd] *n* párpado.
eyeliner ['aɪlaɪnəʳ] *n* lápiz *m* de ojos.
eye-opener ['aɪəʊpᵊnəʳ] *n* revelación *f*, gran sorpresa.
eyepiece ['aɪpiːs] *n* ocular *m*.
eyeshade ['aɪʃeɪd] *n* visera.
eyesight ['aɪsaɪt] *n* vista.
eyesore ['aɪsɔːʳ] *n* monstruosidad *f*.
eyestrain ['aɪstreɪn] *n* vista cansada.
eyetooth [aɪ'tuːθ] *n* colmillo.
eyewash ['aɪwɒʃ] *n* **1** MED colirio. **2** *fam (nonsense)* tonterías *fpl*: **it's all eyewash!** *¡eso son disparates!*
eyewitness ['aɪwɪtnəs] *n* testigo presencial, testigo ocular.
eyrie ['ɪərɪ] *n* aguilera.

F

F, f [ef] *n* **1** *(the letter)* F, f *f*. **2** MUS fa *m*.
F ['færənhaıt] *abbr* **(Fahrenheit)** Fahrenheit; *(abbreviation)* F.
fable ['feıbᵊl] *n* fábula.
fabled ['feıbᵊld] *adj* legendario,-a.
fabric ['fæbrık] *n* **1** *(material)* tela, tejido. **2** *(structure)* fábrica, estructura. **3** *fig* estructura.
fabricate ['fæbrıkeıt] *vt* **1** *(story)* inventar; *(document)* falsificar. **2** *(build)* fabricar.
fabrication [fæbrı'keıʃᵊn] *n* invención *f*.
fabulous ['fæbjələs] *adj* fabuloso,-a.
façade [fə'sɑːd] *n* fachada.
face [feıs] *n* **1** *(of person)* cara, rostro. **2** *(surface)* superficie *f*. **3** *(side)* cara. **4** *(of dial)* cuadrante *m*. **5** *(of watch)* esfera. **6** *fig (of earth)* faz *f*. ● **face up** boca arriba.
▷ *vt* **1** *(look towards)* mirar hacia. **2** *(look onto)* mirar hacia, estar orientado,-a hacia, dar a. **3** *(be opposite to)* estar enfrente de. **4** *(confront)* presentarse, plantearse; *(deal with)* enfrentarse a. **5** *(tolerate)* soportar. **6** *(cover - building)* revestir (**with**, de), recubrir (**with**, de); *(- material)* forrar (**with**, de).
⊙ **to face up to** *vt insep* afrontar, enfrentar, enfrentarse a.
faceless ['feısləs] *adj* anónimo,-a.
facelift ['feıslıft] *n* **1** lifting *m*, estiramiento facial. **2** *fig (building)* lavado de cara.
face-saving ['feıssaıvıŋ] *adj* para salvar las apariencias.
facet ['fæsıt] *n* faceta.
facetious [fə'siːʃəs] *adj* burlón,-ona.
facial ['feıʃᵊl] *adj* facial.
▷ *n* masaje *m* facial, tratamiento facial.
facile ['fæsaıl] *adj* **1** *pej (meaningless)* superficial. **2** *(easy)* fácil.
facilitate [fə'sılıteıt] *vt* facilitar.
facility [fə'sılıtı] *n* facilidad *f*.
▲ *pl* **facilities.**
▷ *n pl* **facilities** **1** *(equipment)* instalaciones *fpl*, servicios *mpl*. **2** *(means)* facilidades *fpl*.
facing ['feısıŋ] *n* **1** *(of garment)* forro, entretela. **2** *(of building)* revestimiento.
▷ *n pl* **facings** *(of garment)* vueltas *fpl*.
facsimile [fæk'sımılı] *n* facsímil *m*, facsímile *m*.
fact [fækt] *n* **1** *(event, happening)* hecho. **2** *(the truth)* realidad *f*. ● **in fact** de hecho.
fact-finding ['fæktfaındıŋ] *adj* investigador,-ra.
faction ['fækʃᵊn] *n (group)* facción *f*.
factor ['fæktəʳ] *n* factor *m*.
factorize ['fæktəraız] *vt* descomponer en factores.
factory ['fæktᵊrı] *n* fábrica.
▲ *pl* **factories.**
factual ['fækʃʊəl] *adj* factual.
faculty ['fækᵊltı] *n* **1** *(power, ability)* facultad *f*. **2** *(univ,* facultad *f*. **3** US *(at university)* profesorado.
▲ *pl* **faculties.**
fad [fæd] *n* **1** *(fashion)* moda pasajera. **2** *(personal,* manía.
faddy ['fædı] *adj* maniático,-a.
▲ *comp* **faddier**, *superl* **faddiest.**
fade [feıd] *vt (colour)* descolorar, descolorir, desteñir.
⊙ **to fade away** *vi* **1** *(become less intense, strong, etc,* desvanecerse, esfumarse. **2** *(die)* morirse.
⊙ **to fade in** *vt sep (camera image)* fundir.
⊙ **to fade out** *vt sep (camera image)* fundir.
▷ *vi (sound)* desvanecerse.
faded ['feıdıd] *adj* **1** *(colour)* desteñido,-a. **2** *(flower,* marchito,-a.
faecal ['fiːkᵊl] *adj* fecal.
faeces ['fiːsiːz] *n pl* heces *fpl*.
fag [fæg] *n* **1** GB *fam (cigarette)* pitillo. **2** *sl (drag)* lata rollo. **3** US *fam (gay)* marica *m*. **4** GB *(public school* fámulo.
▷ *vi* **1** *fam (work hard)* trabajar mucho. **2** GB *(work as a fag)* hacer de fámulo.
▲ *pt & pp* **fagged**, *ger* **fagging.**
faggot¹ ['fægət] *n* **1** *(sticks)* haz *m* de leña. **2** *(meat* *especie de* albóndiga.
faggot² ['fægət] *n* US *pej (homosexual)* marica *m*, ma ricón *m*.
Fahrenheit ['færənhaıt] *adj* Fahrenheit.
fail [feıl] *n* EDUC suspenso.
▷ *vt* **1** *(let down)* fallar, decepcionar; *(desert)* fallar, fal tar. **2** EDUC suspender.
▷ *vi* **1** *(neglect)* dejar de. **2** *(not succeed)* fracasar, no ha cer algo. **3** *(crops)* fallar, echarse a perder. **4** *(stop working)* fallar. **5** *(light)* acabarse, irse apagando. **6** *(become weak)* debilitarse, fallar. **7** COMM *(become bankrupt)* quebrar, fracasar.
failing ['feılıŋ] *n (fault)* defecto, fallo; *(weakness* punto débil.
▷ *prep* a falta de.
fail-safe ['feılsaıf] *adj (device, mechanism)* de seguri dad; *(plan)* infalible.
failure ['feıljəʳ] *n* **1** *(lack of success)* fracaso. **2** COM quiebra. **3** EDUC suspenso. **4** *(person)* fracasado,-a **5** *(breakdown)* fallo, avería. **6** *(of crops)* pérdida. *(inability)* incapacidad *f*; *(neglect)* falta.
faint [feınt] *adj* **1** *(sound, voice)* débil, tenue. **2** *(colour* pálido,-a; *(outline)* borroso,-a. **3** *(slight - memory, etc* vago,-a; *(- hope)* poco,-a; *(- resemblance)* ligero,-a. **4** *(giddy)* mareado,-a.
▷ *n* mareo.
▷ *vi* desmayarse (**from**, de).

faint-hearted ['feɪnt'hɑːtɪd] *adj (person)* temeroso,-a; *(attempt)* tímido,-a.

fair[1] [feəʳ] *adj* **1** *(just)* justo,-a, equitativo,-a; *(impartial)* imparcial; *(reasonable)* razonable. **2** *(considerable)* considerable. **3** *(idea, guess, etc)* bastante bueno,-a, más o menos acertado,-a. **4** *(average)* regular. **5** *(weather)* bueno,-a. **6** *(hair)* rubio,-a; *(skin)* blanco,-a. **7** *fml* bello,-a.

fair[2] [feəʳ] *n* **1** *(market)* mercado, feria. **2** *(show)* feria; *(funfair)* parque *m* de atracciones.

fairground ['feəgraʊnd] *n (site)* recinto ferial; *(show)* feria; *(funfair)* parque *m* de atracciones.

fair-haired ['feəheəd] *adj* rubio,-a.

fairly ['feəlɪ] *adv* **1** *(justly)* justamente. **2** *(moderately)* bastante. **3** *(completely)* completamente.

fair-minded [feə'maɪndɪd] *adj* justo,-a.

fairness ['feənəs] *n* **1** justicia, imparcialidad *f*. **2** *(of hair)* color *m* rubio; *(of skin)* palidez *f*, blancura.

fairway ['feəweɪ] *n* **1** *(golf)* calle *f*. **2** *(sea)* canal *m* navegable.

fairy ['feərɪ] *n* hada. ● **fairy story/tale** cuento de hadas.
▲ *pl* **fairies**.

fait accompli [feɪtə'kɒmpliː] *n* hecho consumado.

faith [feɪθ] *n* **1** fe *f*. **2** *(trust, confidence)* confianza (**in**, en), fe *f* (**in**, en). **3** REL fe *f*.

faithful ['feɪθfʊl] *adj* **1** *(loyal)* fiel (**to**, a), leal (**to**, a/con. **2** *(accurate)* fiel, exacto,-a.

faithfully ['feɪθfʊlɪ] *adv* fielmente. ● **yours faithfully** *(in letter)* atentamente.

fake [feɪk] *n* **1** falsificación *f*. **2** *(person)* impostor,-ra, farsante *mf*.
▷ *adj* falso,-a, falsificado,-a.
▷ *vt* **1** *(falsify)* falsificar. **2** *(pretend)* fingir: **she faked illness** *fingió estar enferma*.

falcon ['fɔːlkᵊn] *n* halcón *m*.

falconry ['fɔːlkᵊnrɪ] *n* halconería.

Falkland Islands ['fɔːlkləndaɪləndz] *n pl* Islas *fpl* Malvinas.

fall [fɔːl] *n* **1** *(act of falling)* caída. **2** *(of rock)* desprendimiento; *(of snow)* nevada. **3** *(decrease)* baja, descenso, disminución *f*. **4** *(defeat)* caída. **5** US *(autumn)* otoño.
▷ *vi* **1** *(gen)* caer, caerse. **2** *(decrease)* bajar, descender. **3** *(be defeated)* caer; *(be killed)* perecer. ● **to fall in love** enamorarse.
▲ *pt* **fell** [fel], *pp* **fallen** ['fɔːlən].
▷ *n pl* **falls** *(waterfall)* cascada *f sing*, cataratas *fpl*.
⊙ **to fall apart** *vi* romperse, deshacerse, caerse a pedazos.
⊙ **to fall away** *vi* **1** *(desert, leave)* disminuir. **2** *(disappear)* desaparecer. **3** *(break off)* desprenderse.
⊙ **to fall back** *vi (retreat)* retroceder, retirarse.
⊙ **to fall back on** *vt insep (resort to)* recurrir a, echar mano de, apoyarse en.
⊙ **to fall behind** *vi (be overtaken)* retrasarse, quedarse atrás, rezagarse.
⊙ **to fall down** *vi* **1** *(person)* caer, caerse; *(building)* hundirse, derrumbarse, venirse abajo. **2** *(fail)* fallar.
⊙ **to fall for** *vt insep* **1** *(be tricked)* dejarse engañar por, picar. **2** *fam (fall in love)* enamorarse de.
⊙ **to fall in** *vi* **1** *(collapse)* desplomarse, venirse abajo. **2** MIL alinearse, formar filas, ponerse en filas.
⊙ **to fall in with** *vt insep* **1** *(meet, become involved with)* encontrarse con, juntarse con. **2** *(agree with, support)* convenir en, aprobar, aceptar.
⊙ **to fall off** *vi* **1** *(decrease in quantity)* bajar, disminuir; *(in quality)* empeorar. **2** *(become detached)* desprenderse, caerse.
⊙ **to fall on** *vt insep* **1** *(be borne by)* incidir en, recaer en, tocar a. **2** *(attack)* atacar, caer sobre.
⊙ **to fall out** *vi (quarrel)* reñir (**with**, con), pelearse (**with**, con).
▷ *vi (drop)* caerse.
⊙ **to fall over** *vt insep* caer, tropezar con.
⊙ **to fall through** *vi (come to nothing)* fracasar, quedar en nada.

fallacy ['fæləsɪ] *n* falacia.
▲ *pl* **fallacies**.

fallen ['fɔːlən] *pp* → **fall**.
▷ *adj (not virtuous)* perdido,-a.

falling-off ['fɔːlɪŋɒf] *n (in quantity)* disminución *f*; *(in price, quality)* descenso.

Fallopian tube [fələʊpɪən'tjuːb] *n* trompa de Falopio.

fallout ['fɔːlaʊt] *n* lluvia radiactiva.

fallow ['fæləʊ] *adj* en barbecho.

false [fɔːls] *adj* **1** *(untrue)* falso,-a. **2** *(artificial)* postizo,-a. ● **false alarm** falsa alarma. | **false teeth** dentadura postiza.

falsification [fɔːlsɪfɪ'keɪʃᵊn] *n* falsificación *f*.

falsify ['fɔːlsɪfaɪ] *vt* **1** *(alter falsely)* falsificar. **2** *(misrepresent)* falsear.
▲ *pt & pp* **falsified**, *ger* **falsifying**.

falter ['fɔːltəʳ] *vi (person)* vacilar, titubear; *(voice)* fallar.

fame [feɪm] *n* fama.

familiar [fə'mɪlɪəʳ] *adj* **1** *(well-known)* familiar, conocido,-a (**to**, a). **2** *(aware)* al corriente (**with**, de), familiarizado,-a (**with**, con). **3** *(intimate)* íntimo,-a; *(too informal)* fresco,-a.

familiarity [fəmɪlɪ'ærɪtɪ] *n* **1** familiaridad *f*. **2** *(knowledge)* conocimiento (**with**, de).

familiarize [fə'mɪlɪəraɪz] *vt* **1** *(become acquainted)* familiarizarse (**with**, con). **2** *(divulge)* popularizar.

family ['fæmɪlɪ] *n* familia.
▷ *adj* familiar. ● **family name** apellido.
▲ *pl* **families**.

famine ['fæmɪn] *n* hambruna, hambre *f*.

famished ['fæmɪʃt] *adj fam* muerto,-a de hambre.

famous ['feɪməs] *adj* famoso,-a (**for**, por), célebre (**for**, por).

famously ['feɪməslɪ] *adv fam* estupendamente.

fan [fæn] *n* **1** *(object)* abanico. **2** ELEC ventilador *m*. **3** *(follower)* aficionado,-a; *(of pop star, etc)* admirador,-ra, fan *mf*. **4** *(of football)* hincha *mf*.
▷ *vt* **1** *(face)* abanicar; *(elec)* ventilar; *(fire)* avivar. **2** *fig* avivar, atizar.
▲ *pt & pp* **fanned**, *ger* **fanning**.
⊙ **to fan out** *vi* desplegarse en abanico.

fanatic [fə'nætɪk] *n* fanático,-a.
▷ *adj* fanático,-a (**about**, de).

fancier ['fænsɪəʳ] *n* aficionado,-a.

fanciful ['fænsɪfʊl] *adj* **1** *(idea)* imaginario,-a, fantástico,-a. **2** *(extravagant)* caprichoso,-a, rebuscado,-a, estrafalario,-a.

fancy ['fænsɪ] *n* 1 *(imagination)* fantasía, imaginación *f*. 2 *(whim)* capricho, antojo.
▷ *adj* 1 *(jewels, goods, etc)* de fantasía. 2 *(unusual)* estrafalario,-a. 3 *(high-class, posh)* elegante, de lujo. 4 *(prices)* exagerado,-a, excesivo,-a, exorbitante.
▲ *pl* fancies.
▷ *vt* 1 *(want)* apetecer, querer. 2 *(find attractive)* encontrar atractivo,-a. 3 *(think)* creer, suponer. 4 *(think likely to do well)* creer, parecer.
▲ *pt & pp* fancied, *ger* fancying.
fanfare ['fænfeəʳ] *n* fanfarria.
fang [fæŋ] *n* colmillo.
fanlight ['fænlaɪt] *n* montante *m*.
fantasize ['fæntəsaɪz] *vi* fantasear (about, sobre).
fantastic [fæn'tæstɪk] *adj* fantástico,-a.
fantasy ['fæntəsɪ] *n* fantasía.
▲ *pl* fantasies.
FAO ['ef'eɪ'əʊ] *abbr* (Food and Agriculture Organization) Organización para la Agricultura y la Alimentación; *(abbreviation)* FAO *f*.
FAQ ['ef'eɪ'kjuː] *n* (frequently asked questions) preguntas frecuentes.
far [fɑːʳ] *adj* 1 *(distant)* lejano,-a, remoto,-a. 2 *(more distant)* opuesto,-a, extremo,-a.
▲ *comp* farther o further, *superl* farthest o furthest.
▷ *adv* 1 *(a long way)* lejos. 2 *(a long time)* lejos. 3 *(much)* mucho. ■ as far as I am concerned *por lo que a mí se refiere*. ■ far away lejos. ■ so far hasta ahora.
faraway ['fɑːrəweɪ] *adj* lejano,-a, remoto,-a; *(look)* distraído,-a, en las nubes.
farce [fɑːs] *n* farsa.
farcical ['fɑːsɪkᵊl] *adj* absurdo,-a, ridículo,-a.
fare [feəʳ] *n* 1 *(price)* tarifa, precio del billete, precio del viaje; *(boat)* pasaje *m*. 2 *(passenger)* viajero,-a, pasajero,-a. 3 *(food)* comida.
▷ *vi (progress, get on)* desenvolverse.
farewell [feə'wel] *interj* ¡adiós!
▷ *n* despedida.
far-fetched [fɑː'fetʃt] *adj* 1 *(strained)* rebuscado,-a, forzado,-a. 2 *(incredible)* inverosímil.
farm [fɑːm] *n* granja.
▷ *adj* agrícola, de granja.
▷ *vt* 1 *(use land)* cultivar, labrar. 2 *(breed animals)* criar.
▷ *vi (grow crops)* cultivar la tierra.
⊙ **to farm out** *vt sep (work)* encargar a terceros, encargar fuera; *(children)* dejar con alguien.
farmer ['fɑːməʳ] *n* granjero,-a, agricultor,-ra.
farm-hand ['fɑːmhænd] *n* peón *m* agrícola.
farmhouse ['fɑːmhaʊs] *n* granja.
farming ['fɑːmɪŋ] *n* agricultura. ■ farming industry industria agropecuaria.
farmstead ['fɑːmsted] *n* alquería.
farmyard ['fɑːmjɑːd] *n* corral *m*.
far-reaching [fɑː'riːtʃɪŋ] *adj* de gran alcance.
farrier ['færɪəʳ] *n* herrero.
farrow ['færəʊ] *vi* parir.
▷ *vt* parir.
far-sighted [fɑː'saɪtɪd] *adj* previsor,-ra.
fart [fɑːt] *n* 1 *fam* pedo. 2 *(fool)* carcamal *m*, carroza *m*.
▷ *vi* tirarse un pedo.
farther ['fɑːðəʳ] *adj comp* → far: Santander is farther than Murcia *Santander está más lejos que Murcia*.
farthest ['fɑːðɪst] *adj* → far: Neptune is the farthest planet from the Sun *Neptuno es el planeta más alejado del Sol*.
▷ *adv* → far: who lives farthest from the school? *¿quién vive más lejos de la escuela?*
fascicle ['fæsɪkᵊl] *n* fascículo.
fascicule ['fæsɪkjuːl] *n* fascículo.
fascinate ['fæsɪneɪt] *vt* fascinar.
fascinating ['fæsɪneɪtɪŋ] *adj* fascinante.
fascination [fæsɪ'neɪʃᵊn] *n* fascinación *f*.
fascism ['fæʃɪzᵊm] *n* fascismo.
fascist ['fæʃɪst] *n* fascista *mf*.
▷ *adj* fascista.
fashion ['fæʃᵊn] *n* 1 *(style)* moda. 2 *(way)* modo.
▷ *vt (clay)* formar; *(metal)* labrar.
fashionable ['fæʃᵊnəbᵊl] *adj* de moda.
fast[1] [fɑːst] *adj* 1 *(gen)* rápido,-a. 2 *(tight, secure)* firme, seguro,-a. 3 *(clock)* adelantado,-a. 4 *(colours)* sólido,-a. 5 *(active)* muy activo,-a, ajetreado,-a.
▷ *adv* 1 rápidamente, deprisa. 2 *(securely)* firmemente; *(thoroughly)* profundamente.
fast[2] [fɑːst] *n* ayuno.
▷ *vi* ayunar.
fasten ['fɑːsᵊn] *vt* 1 *(attach)* fijar, sujetar. 2 *(tie)* atar. 3 *(box, door, window)* cerrar; *(belt, dress)* abrochar.
▷ *vi (box, door, etc)* cerrarse; *(dress, etc)* abrocharse.
⊙ **to fasten on/onto** *vt insep* agarrarse a, aferrarse a.
fastener ['fɑːsᵊnəʳ] *n* cierre *m*.
fastidious [fæ'stɪdɪəs] *adj* quisquilloso,-a, melindroso,-a.
fat [fæt] *adj* 1 *(person)* gordo,-a. 2 *(thick)* grueso,-a, gordo,-a. 3 *(meat)* que tiene mucha grasa. 4 *(profit, cheque, etc)* sustancioso,-a. 5 *(rich, fertile)* fértil. 6 *fam iron (very little)* poco,-a.
▲ *comp* fatter, *superl* fattest.
▷ *n* 1 *(of meat)* grasa; *(of person)* carnes *fpl*. 2 *(for cooking)* manteca; *(lard)* lardo.
fatal ['feɪtᵊl] *adj* 1 *(causing disaster)* fatal, funesto,-a; *(serious)* grave. 2 *(causing death)* mortal. 3 *(fateful)* fatídico,-a.
fatalism ['feɪtᵊlɪzᵊm] *n* fatalismo.
fatality [fə'tælɪtɪ] *n* víctima mortal.
▲ *pl* fatalities.
fatally ['feɪtᵊlɪ] *adv* mortalmente.
fate [feɪt] *n* 1 *(destiny)* destino. 2 *(person's lot)* suerte *f*.
▷ *n pl* The Fates las Parcas *fpl*.
fated ['feɪtɪd] *adj* predestinado,-a, condenado,-a.
fateful ['feɪtfʊl] *adj* fatídico,-a, aciago,-a.
fatefully ['feɪθfʊlɪ] *adv* fatídicamente.
father ['fɑːðəʳ] *n* 1 *(male parent)* padre *m*. 2 *(priest)* padre *m*.
▷ *vt* 1 *(beget)* engendrar. 2 *fig (create, originate)* inventar, crear.
▷ *n pl* fathers *(ancestors)* antepasados *mpl*.
fatherhood ['fɑːðəhʊd] *n* paternidad *f*.
father-in-law ['fɑːðərɪnlɔː] *n* suegro.
fatherland ['fɑːðəlænd] *n* patria.
fatherless ['fɑːðələs] *adj* huérfano,-a de padre.

fatherly ['fɑːðəlɪ] *adj* paternal.

fathom ['fæðəm] *n (measurement)* brazo.
▷ *vt* 1 *(measure)* sondear. 2 *fig* penetrar en, comprender.
⊙ **to fathom out** *vt sep* comprender, entender.

fatigue [fə'tiːg] *n* 1 fatiga, cansancio. 2 TECH fatiga. 3 MIL faena.
▷ *vt fml* fatigar, cansar.
▷ *n pl* **fatigues** US *(uniform)* traje *m* de faena.

fat-soluble [fæt'sɒljəbᵊl] *adj* liposoluble.

fatten ['fætᵊn] *vt* 1 *(animal)* cebar (**up**, -). 2 *(person)* engordar (**up**, -).

fattening ['fætᵊnɪŋ] *adj* que engorda: **biscuits are fattening** *las galletas engordan.*

fatty ['fætɪ] *adj (greasy)* graso,-a.
▲ *comp* **fattier**, *superl* **fattiest**.
▷ *n fam pej* gordinflón,-ona.
▲ *pl* **fatties**.

fatuous ['fætjʊəs] *adj* fatuo,-a, necio,-a.

faucet ['fɔːsɪt] *n* US grifo.

fault [fɔːlt] *n* 1 *(in character, system, etc)* defecto. 2 *(in merchandise)* defecto, desperfecto, tara. 3 *(blame)* culpa. 4 *(mistake)* error *m*, falta. 5 *(in earth)* falla. 6 *(in tennis, etc)* falta.
▷ *vt* criticar, encontrar defectos a.

faultless ['fɔːltləs] *adj* perfecto,-a, intachable, impecable.

faulty ['fɔːltɪ] *adj* defectuoso,-a.
▲ *comp* **faultier**, *superl* **faultiest**.

faun [fɔːn] *n* fauno.

fauna ['fɔːnə] *n* fauna.

faux pas [fəʊ'pɑː] *n* metedura de pata.
▲ *pl* **faux pas** [fʊ'pɑː].

favor ['feɪvəʳ] *n-vt* US ⟶ **favour**.

favorable ['feɪvᵊrəbᵊl] *adj* US ⟶ **favourable**.

favorably ['feɪvᵊrəblɪ] *adv* US ⟶ **favourably**.

favorite ['feɪvᵊrɪt] *adj* US ⟶ **favourite**.

favoritism ['feɪvᵊrɪtɪzᵊm] *n* US ⟶ **favouritism**.

favour ['feɪvəʳ] *n* 1 *(kindness)* favor *m*. 2 *(approval)* aprobación *f*, favor *m*. 3 *(favouritism)* parcialidad *f*, favoritismo.
▷ *vt* 1 *(prefer)* preferir, inclinarse por. 2 *(benefit, aid)* favorecer; *(treat with partiality)* dar un trato de favor.
▷ *n pl* **favours** *(sexual pleasure)* favores *mpl*.

favourable ['feɪvᵊrəbᵊl] *adj* 1 favorable (**to/towards**, a). 2 *(suitable)* propicio,-a (**for**, para).

favourably ['feɪvᵊrəblɪ] *adv* favorablemente.

favourite ['feɪvᵊrɪt] *n* preferido,-a, favorito,-a.
▷ *adj* preferido,-a, predilecto,-a, favorito,-a.

favouritism ['feɪvᵊrɪtɪzᵊm] *n* favoritismo.

fawn [fɔːn] *n* 1 ZOOL cervato. 2 *(colour)* beige *m*, color *m* café claro.
▷ *adj* beige, de color café claro.
⊙ **to fawn on** *vt insep* adular, lisonjear.

fax [fæks] *n* fax *m*.
▷ *vt* enviar por fax. ● **fax machine** fax *m*.

faze [feɪz] *vt fam* desconcertar, perturbar.

FBI ['ef'biː'aɪ] *abbr* **(Federal Bureau of Investigation)** oficina federal de investigación; *(abbreviation)* FBI *f*.

FC ['ef'siː] *abbr* GB **(Football Club)** Club *m* de Fútbol; *(abbreviation)* CF.

fealty ['fiəltɪ] *n* lealtad *f*.

fear [fɪəʳ] *n* miedo, temor *m*.
▷ *vt* temer, tener miedo a.
▷ *vi* temer, tener miedo.
⊙ **to fear for** *vt insep* temer por: **I fear for the children's safety** *temo por la seguridad de los niños.*

fearful ['fɪəfʊl] *adj* 1 *(frightened)* temeroso,-a (**of**, de). 2 *(terrible)* terrible, espantoso,-a, tremendo,-a.

fearfully ['fɪəfʊlɪ] *adv* temerosamente.

fearless ['fɪələs] *adj* intrépido,-a, audaz.

fearsome ['fɪəsəm] *adj* temible.

feasibility ['fiːzəbɪlɪtɪ] *n* viabilidad *f*.

feasible ['fiːzəbᵊl] *adj* 1 *(viable)* factible, viable. 2 *(plausible)* verosímil.

feast [fiːst] *n* 1 festín *m*, banquete *m*. 2 *fam* comilona. 3 REL fiesta de guardar, día *m* de fiesta.
▷ *vi* banquetear, festejar.

feat [fiːt] *n* proeza, hazaña.

feather ['feðəʳ] *n* pluma.
▷ *vt* 1 emplumar. 2 *(oar)* alzar.

featherweight ['feðəweɪt] *n (boxing)* peso pluma.

feature ['fiːtʃəʳ] *n* 1 *(of face)* rasgo, facción *f*. 2 *(characteristic)* rasgo, característica, aspecto. 3 *(press)* artículo especial, especial *m*.
▷ *vt (have)* tener; *(film)* tener como protagonista: **this car features the latest safety devices** *este coche incorpora los últimos dispositivos de seguridad.*
▷ *vi (appear)* figurar (**in**, en): **his name featured in the police report** *su nombre figuró en el informe policial.* ● **feature (film)** largometraje *m*.

featureless ['fiːtʃələs] *adj* monótono,-a.

February ['februərɪ] *n* febrero.

Para ejemplos de uso, consulta **May**.

feckless ['fekləs] *adj* incompetente, inútil.

fecund ['fiːkənd] *adj* fecundo,-a, fértil.

fecundity [fe'kʌndɪtɪ] *n* fecundidad *f*.

fed [fed] *pt & pp* ⟶ **feed**. ■ **to be fed up with** *fam* estar harto,-a de.

federal ['fedᵊrəl] *adj* federal.

federalist ['fedᵊrəlɪst] *n* federalista *mf*.

federate [*(vb)* 'fedəreɪt, *(adj)* 'fedᵊrət] *vt* federar.
▷ *adj* federado,-a.

federation [fedə'reɪʃᵊn] *n* federación *f*.

fee [fiː] *n* 1 *(doctor's, etc)* honorarios *mpl*; *(for tuition)* derechos *mpl* (de matrícula). 2 *(membership)* cuota, cuota de socio. ● **registration fee** matrícula.

feeble ['fiːbᵊl] *adj* 1 *(person)* débil. 2 *(light, sound)* tenue, débil. 3 *(argument, excuse)* de poco peso.

feebleness ['fiːbᵊlnəs] *n* debilidad *f*.

feed [fiːd] *n* 1 comida. 2 *fam* comilona. 3 *(for cattle)* pienso. 4 TECH alimentación *f*.
▷ *vt* 1 alimentar, dar de comer a: **could you feed our cat while we're away?** *¿podrías dar de comer a nuestro gato mientras estamos fuera?* 2 *(breastfeed)* amamantar a, dar de mamar a; *(bottle-feed)* dar el biberón a. 3 *fig (fire, passion)* alimentar. 4 TECH alimentar, suministrar. 5 *(insert)* introducir; *(coins)* meter.
▷ *vi (people)* comer, alimentarse (**on**, de); *(animals)* pacer.
▲ *pt & pp* **fed** [fed].
⊙ **to feed up** *vt sep (animal)* cebar; *(person)* engordar.

feedback ['fiːdbæk] *n* 1 TECH retroalimentación *f*, retroacción *f*. 2 *fig* reacción *f*, respuesta, impresión *f*.

feeder ['fiːdəʳ] *n* 1 TECH alimentador *m*. 2 *(road)* ramal *m*, carretera.
feeding ['fiːdɪŋ] ● **feeding bottle** biberón *m*. ‖ **feeding time** hora de la comida, hora de dar de comer.
feel [fiːl] *n* 1 *(sense, texture)* tacto. 2 *(atmosphere)* aire *m*, ambiente *m*.
▷ *vt* 1 *(touch)* tocar, palpar. 2 *(search with fingers)* buscar. 3 *(sense, experience)* sentir, experimentar, tener la impresión. 4 *(notice)* notar, apreciar. 5 *(suffer)* sentir, afectar. 6 *(believe)* creer.
▷ *vi* 1 *(be)* sentir(se), encontrarse, experimentar. 2 *(seem)* parecer: **it feels like leather** *parece piel.* 3 *(perceive, sense)* sentir: **she could feel all eyes upon her** *sentía que todos la miraban.* 4 *(opinion)* opinar, pensar: **how do you feel about exams?** *¿qué opinas de los exámenes?*
▲ *pt & pp* **felt** [felt].
⊙ **to feel for** *vt insep (have sympathy for)* compadecer a, compadecerse de.
⊙ **to feel up to** *vt insep* sentirse con ánimos para, sentirse con fuerzas para: **are you sure you feel up to it?** *¿seguro que te sientes con fuerzas?*
feeler ['fiːləʳ] *n* antena.
feeling ['fiːlɪŋ] *n* 1 *(emotion)* sentimiento, emoción *f*. 2 *(sensation)* sensación *f*. 3 *(sense)* sensibilidad. 4 *(concern)* compasión *f*, ternura. 5 *(impression)* impresión *f*, sensación *f*, presentimiento: **I have the feeling that...** *tengo la impresión de que...* 6 *(artistic)* sensibilidad *f*, talento. 7 *(opinion)* sentir *m*, opinión *f*, actitud *f*, parecer *m*. 8 *(atmosphere)* ambiente *m*.
▷ *adj* sensible, compasivo,-a.
▷ *n pl* **feelings** sentimientos *mpl*.
fee-paying ['fiːpeɪɪŋ] *adj* 1 *(pupil)* que paga. 2 *(school)* de pago.
feet [fiːt] *n pl* ⟶ **foot.**
feign [feɪn] *vt* fingir, aparentar: **she feigned illness to get off school** *fingió estar enferma para no ir a la escuela.*
feint [feɪnt] *n fml (fencing)* finta; *(boxing)* treta.
▷ *adj (paper)* rayado,-a.
feisty ['fiːstɪ] *adj (forceful)* batallador,-ra; *(irritable)* irritable.
▲ *comp* **feistier**, *superl* **feistiest**.
feldspar ['feldspɑːʳ] *n* feldespato.
feline ['fiːlaɪn] *adj* felino,-a.
▷ *n* felino,-a.
fell[1] [fel] *adj* feroz, cruel. ■ **at one fell swoop** de un solo golpe.
fell[2] [fel] *vt* 1 *(tree)* talar. 2 *(enemy)* derribar.
fell[3] [fel] *n* GEOG *(moorland)* páramo alto; *(hilly land)* monte *m*, colina.
fell[4] [fel] *pt* ⟶ **fall.**
fellatio [fə'leɪʃɪəʊ] *n* felación *f*.
felling ['felɪŋ] *n* tala.
fellow ['feləʊ] *n* 1 *fam (chap)* tipo, tío: **old fellow** *viejo amigo;* **poor fellow!** *¡pobrecito!* 2 *(companion, comrade)* compañero,-a, camarada *mf*. 3 *(member)* socio,-a. 4 *(univ)* miembro (del claustro de profesores). 5 US *(graduate)* graduado,-a. 6 *fml (one of a pair)* pareja. ● **fellow citizen** conciudadano,-a. ‖ **fellow countryman / fellow countrywoman** compatriota *mf*. ‖ **fellow student** compañero,-a de estudios.
fellowship ['feləʊʃɪp] *n* 1 *(group)* asociación *f*, sociedad *f*. 2 *(companionship)* compañerismo, camaradería. 3 EDUC *(scholarship)* beca.
felon ['felən] *n* criminal *mf*.
felony ['felənɪ] *n* crimen *m*, delito mayor.
▲ *pl* **felonies**.
felspar ['felspɑːʳ] *n* feldespato.
felt[1] [felt] *pt & pp* ⟶ **feel.**
felt[2] [felt] *n* fieltro.
▷ *adj* de fieltro.
felt-tip ['feltɪp] [Also **felt-tip pen.**] *n* rotulador *m*.
female ['fiːmeɪl] *n* 1 hembra. 2 *(woman)* mujer *f*; *(girl)* chica.
▷ *adj* 1 femenino,-a. 2 ZOOL hembra.
feminine ['femɪnɪn] *adj* femenino,-a.
▷ *n* femenino,-a.
femininity [femə'nɪnətɪ] *n* feminidad *f*.
feminism ['femɪnɪzᵊm] *n* feminismo.
feminist ['femɪnɪst] *n* feminista *mf*.
femoral ['fɪːmərəl] *adj* femoral.
femur ['fiːməʳ] *n* fémur *m*.
fen [fen] *n* GEOG terreno pantanoso.
▷ *n pl* **the Fens** *zona llana y pantanosa del este de Inglaterra*
fence [fens] *n* 1 *(structure)* valla, cerca. 2 *sl (buyer and seller of stolen goods)* perista *mf*. ■ **to sit on the fence** ver los toros desde la barrera.
▷ *vi* 1 SP practicar la esgrima. 2 *(land)* cercar.
⊙ **to fence in** *vt sep (animals)* encerrar en un cercado, meter en un cercado; *(land)* cercar.
⊙ **to fence off** *vt sep* separar mediante cercas.
fencing ['fensɪŋ] *n* 1 SP esgrima. 2 *(structure)* cercado. 3 *(material)* material *m* para cercas.
fend [fend] *vi* **to fend for os** valerse por sí mismo,-a, apañárselas por su cuenta.
⊙ **to fend off** *vt sep (blow)* parar, desviar; *(question)* esquivar; *(attack)* rechazar, defenderse de.
fender ['fendəʳ] *n* 1 *(for fire)* pantalla. 2 US *(on automobile)* parachoques *m*. 3 *(on boat)* defensa.
fennel ['fenᵊl] *n* hinojo.
ferment [*(n)* 'fɜːmənt; *(vb)* fə'ment] *n* 1 *(substance)* fermento. 2 *(unrest)* agitación *f*.
▷ *vt* fermentar.
▷ *vi* fermentar.
fermentation [fɜːmen'teɪʃᵊn] *n* fermentación *f*.
fern [fɜːn] *n* helecho.
ferocious [fə'rəʊʃəs] *adj* feroz.
ferocity [fə'rɒsɪtɪ] *n* ferocidad *f*.
ferret ['ferɪt] *n* hurón *m*.
▷ *vi* huronear.
⊙ **to ferret about** *vi* buscar (**for**, -), husmear (**for**, -).
⊙ **to ferret out** *vt sep* descubrir.
ferric ['ferɪk] *adj* férrico,-a.
ferrite ['feraɪt] *n* ferrita.
ferroconcrete [ferəʊ'kɒŋkriːt] *n* ferrohormigón *m*
ferrous ['ferəs] *adj* ferroso,-a.
ferrule ['feruːl] *n* casquillo.
ferry ['ferɪ] *n (small)* barca de pasaje; *(large)* transbordador *m*, ferry *m*.
▲ *pl* **ferries**.
▷ *vt* transportar.
▲ *pt & pp* **ferried**, *ger* **ferrying**.
ferryboat ['ferɪbəʊt] *n* ⟶ **ferry.**

'erryman ['ferɪmæn] *n* barquero.
▲ *pl* ferrymen ['ferɪmən].
'ertile ['fɜːtaɪl] *adj* fértil, fecundo,-a.
'ertility [fə'tɪlɪtɪ] *n* fertilidad *f*.
'ertilisation [fɜːtəlaɪ'zeɪʃᵊn] *n* → **fertilization.**
'ertilization [fɜːtəlaɪ'zeɪʃᵊn] *n* **1** *(soil)* fertilización *f*. **2** *(egg)* fecundación *f*.
'ertilize ['fɜːtɪlaɪz] *vt* **1** *(soil)* abonar. **2** *(egg)* fecundar.
'ertilizer ['fɜːtɪlaɪzəʳ] *n* fertilizante *m*, abono.
'erule¹ ['feruːl] *n* férula.
'erule² ['feruːl] *n* → **ferrule.**
'ervent ['fɜːvᵊnt] *adj* fervoroso,-a.
'ervor ['fɜːvəʳ] *n* US → **fervour.**
'ervour ['fɜːvəʳ] *n* fervor *m*.
'ester ['festəʳ] *vi* **1** MED supurar, enconarse. **2** *fig* amargarse.
'estival ['festɪvᵊl] *n* **1** *(event)* festival *m*. **2** *(celebration)* fiesta.
'estive ['festɪv] *adj* festivo,-a. ● **the festive season** las Navidades *fpl*, las fiestas *pl* de Navidad.
'estivity [fe'stɪvətɪ] *n (celebration)* fiesta, festividad *f*.
▲ *pl* festivities.
▷ *n pl* **festivities** fiestas *fpl*, festejos *mpl*.
'estoon [fe'stuːn] *n* **1** *(decoration)* adorno, guirnalda. **2** *(in sewing)* festón *m*.
▷ *vt* **1** *(decorate)* adornar, decorar (**with**, de). **2** *(in sewing)* festonear.
'etal ['fiːtᵊl] *adj* US → **foetal.**
'etch [fetʃ] *vt* **1** *(go and get)* ir por, ir a buscar, buscar; *(bring)* traer. **2** *fam (sell for)* venderse por, alcanzar.
⊙ **to fetch up** *vi* ir a parar.
'etching ['fetʃɪŋ] *adj* atractivo,-a.
'ête [feɪt] *n (party)* fiesta; *(fair)* feria.
▷ *vt* festejar.
'etid ['fetɪd] *adj* fétido,-a.
'etish ['fetɪʃ] *n* fetiche *m*.
'etishist ['fetɪʃɪst] *n* fetichista *mf*.
'etlock ['fetlɒk] *n* espolón *m*.
'etter ['fetəʳ] *vt* **1** encadenar. **2** *fig* estorbar, poner trabas a.
▷ *n pl* **fetters 1** grillo *m sing*, grilletes *mpl*, cadenas *fpl*: **they were in fetters** *estaban encadenados.* **2** *fig* trabas *fpl*.
'ettle ['fetᵊl] *n* estado, condiciones *fpl*.
'etus ['fiːtəs] *n* US → **foetus.**
'eud [fjuːd] *n* enemistad *f* (duradera): **there's been a feud between the two families for years** *hace años que existe una enemistad entre ambas familias.*
▷ *vi* disentir, reñir, pelear.
'eudal ['fjuːdᵊl] *adj* feudal.
'eudalism ['fjuːdᵊlɪzᵊm] *n* feudalismo.
'ever ['fiːvəʳ] *n* **1** *(temperature)* fiebre *f*. **2** *(nervous excitement)* fiebre *f*, excitación *f*.
'everish ['fiːvərɪʃ] *adj* **1** *(having a fever)* febril. **2** *(excited)* nervioso,-a, excitado,-a, febril.
'ew [fjuː] *adj* **1** *(not many)* poco,-a, pocos,-as: **very few cars** *muy pocos coches.* **2** *(some)* uno,-as cuantos,-as, algunos,-as: **in the next few days** *en unos días.*
▷ *pron* **1** *(not many)* pocos,-as: **many try but few succeed** *muchos lo intentan pero pocos lo consiguen.* **2** *(some)* unos,-as cuantos,-as, algunos,-as: **there are a few left** *quedan unos cuantos.*

fey [feɪ] *adj (whimsical)* fantasioso,-a; *(clairvoyant)* clarividente.
fez [fez] *n* fez *m*.
▲ *pl* fezzes.
fiancé [fɪ'ænseɪ] *n* prometido, novio.
fiancée [fɪ'ænseɪ] *n* prometida, novia.
fiasco [fɪ'æskəʊ] *n* fiasco, fracaso.
▲ *pl* fiascos, US fiascoes.
fib [fɪb] *n fam* bola, trola.
▷ *vi fam* contar bolas, contar trolas.
▲ *pt & pp* fibbed, *ger* fibbing.
fiber ['faɪbəʳ] *n* US → **fibre.**
fiberglass ['faɪbəglɑːs] *adj* US → **fibreglass.**
fibre ['faɪbəʳ] *n* **1** fibra. **2** *fig (moral)* nervio, carácter *m*. ● **fibre optics** fibra óptica. | **man-made fibre** fibra artificial.
fibreglass ['faɪbəglɑːs] *n* fibra de vidrio.
fibrosis [faɪ'brəʊsɪs] *n* fibrosis *f*.
fibrous ['faɪbrəs] *adj* fibroso,-a.
fibula ['fɪbjələ] *adj* fibroso,-a.
fickle ['fɪkᵊl] *adj* inconstante, voluble.
fiction ['fɪkʃᵊn] *n* **1** *(novels)* novela, narrativa. **2** *(invention)* ficción *f*.
fictitious [fɪk'tɪʃəs] *adj* ficticio,-a.
fiddle ['fɪdᵊl] *n* **1** *fam* violín *m*. **2** *fam (fraud)* estafa, trampa.
▷ *vi* **1** tocar el violín. **2** *fam (play)* juguetear (**with**, con).
▷ *vt fam (cheat)* amañar, falsificar.
⊙ **to fiddle about / fiddle around** *vi fam* perder el tiempo.
fiddler ['fɪdləʳ] *n* **1** *fam (violinist)* violinista *mf*. **2** *fam (cheat)* tramposo,-a.
fiddly ['fɪdlɪ] *adj fam* difícil, complicado,-a.
▲ *comp* fiddlier, *superl* fiddliest.
fidelity [fɪ'delɪtɪ] *n* fidelidad *f*.
fidget ['fɪdʒɪt] *n* persona inquieta.
▷ *vi (move about)* moverse, no poder estar(se) quieto,-a; *(play about)* jugar (**with**, con).
fidgety ['fɪdʒɪtɪ] *adj* inquieto,-a.
fiduciary [fɪ'duːʃɪərɪ] *adj* fiduciario,-a.
fief [fiːf] *n* feudo.
field [fiːld] *n* **1** *(gen)* campo. **2** *(for mining)* yacimiento. **3** *(subject, area)* campo, terreno. **4** SP *(competitors)* competidores *mpl*; *(horses)* participantes *mpl*.
▷ *vt* SP parar y devolver.
▷ *vt* SP *(select to play)* presentar.
fieldfare ['fiːldfeəʳ] *n* zorzal *m* real.
fieldmouse ['fiːldmaʊs] *n* ratón *m* de campo.
▲ *pl* fieldmice.
field-test ['fiːldtest] *n* prueba sobre el terreno.
▷ *vt* testar sobre el terreno.
fiend [fiːnd] *n* **1** demonio, diablo. **2** *fam* fanático,-a.
fiendish ['fiːndɪʃ] *adj* diabólico,-a.
fierce [fɪəs] *adj* **1** *(gen)* feroz. **2** *fig (heat, competition, etc)* fuerte, intenso,-a; *(argument)* acalorado,-a.
fiery ['faɪərɪ] *adj* **1** *(colour)* encendido,-a, rojo,-a. **2** *(burning)* ardiente. **3** *(food)* muy picante; *(drink)* muy fuerte. **4** *fig (person)* acalorado,-a, fogoso,-a; *(words)* vehemente, apasionado,-a.
▲ *comp* fierier, *superl* fieriest.
fifteen [fɪf'tiːn] *adj* quince.
▷ *n* quince *m*.
Consulta también **six.**

fifteenth [fɪf'tiːnθ] *adj* decimoquinto,-a.
▷ *adv* en decimoquinto lugar.
▷ *n* **1** *(in series)* decimoquinto,-a. **2** *(fraction)* decimoquinto; *(one part)* decimoquinta parte *f*.
Consulta también **sixth**.

fifth [fɪfθ] *adj* quinto,-a.
▷ *adv* quinto, en quinto lugar.
▷ *n* **1** *(in series)* quinto,-a. **2** *(fraction)* quinto; *(one part)* quinta parte *f*.
Consulta también **sixth**.

fifth-former ['fɪfθfɔːməʳ] *n* GB alumno,-a de quinto curso.

fifties ['fɪftɪz] *n pl* **the fifties** los años *mpl* cincuenta, los cincuenta *mpl*.
Consulta también **sixties**.

fiftieth ['fɪftɪəθ] *adj* quincuagésimo,-a.
▷ *adv* en quincuagésimo lugar.
▷ *n* **1** *(in series)* quincuagésimo,-a. **2** *(fraction)* quincuagésimo; *(one part)* quincuagésima parte *f*.
Consulta también **sixtieth**.

fifty ['fɪftɪ] *adj* cincuenta.
▷ *n* cincuenta *m*.
Consulta también **sixty**.

fifty-fifty ['fɪftɪ'fɪftɪ] *adv fam* mitad y mitad, a medias.

fig [fɪg] *n* **1** higo. **2** *(tree)* higuera.

fight [faɪt] *n* **1** *(struggle)* lucha. **2** *(physical violence)* pelea; *(quarrel)* riña; *(argument)* disputa. **3** *(boxing)* combate *m*. **4** *(resistance)* combatividad *f*, ánimo.
▷ *vi* **1** *(quarrel)* pelear(se) (**about/over**, por), discutir (**about/over**, por). **2** *(in boxing)* pelear (**against**, contra). **3** *(with physical violence)* pelearse (**with**, con) (**against**, contra), luchar (**with**, con) (**against**, contra). **4** *fig* luchar (**for**, por) (**against**, contra), combatir.
▷ *vt* **1** *(bull)* lidiar. **2** *(engage in - battle)* librar; *(- war)* hacer; *(- election)* presentarse a. **3** *(with physical violence)* pelearse, luchar. **4** *fig (strive to overcome, prevent)* luchar, combatir. **5** JUR recurrir contra. **6** *(fire)* apagar, combatir.
▲ *pt & pp* **fought** [fɔːt].
⊙ **to fight back** *vi* defenderse, resistir.
▷ *vt sep (tears)* contener.
⊙ **to fight off** *vt sep* **1** vencer, rechazar. **2** *fig (illness)* librarse de, combatir; *(sleep)* sacudirse.

fighter ['faɪtəʳ] *n* **1** *(war)* combatiente *mf*. **2** *(boxing)* boxeador,-ra. **3** *fig* luchador,-ra.

fighting ['faɪtɪŋ] *n* peleas *fpl*.
▷ *adj* de combate, militar.

fig-leaf ['fɪgliːf] *n* hoja de parra.

figment ['fɪgmənt] *n cosa imaginada*.

figurative ['fɪgərətɪv] *adj* figurado,-a.

figure ['fɪgəʳ, US 'fɪgjr] *n* **1** *(number, sign)* cifra, número. **2** *(money, price)* cantidad *f*, precio, suma. **3** *(in art)* figura. **4** *(human form)* figura, tipo, línea. **5** *(personality)* figura, personaje *m*. **6** *(diagram)* diagrama *m*, dibujo, grabado, ilustración *f*. **7** *(shape)* forma, figura.
▷ *vi (appear)* figurar, constar.
▷ *vt* US *(think)* suponer, imaginarse.
▷ *n pl* **figures** *(arithmetic)* matemáticas *fpl*.
⊙ **to figure out** *vt sep fam (gen)* comprender, enterarse; *(problem)* resolver, calcular.

filament ['fɪləmənt] *n* filamento.

filch [fɪltʃ] *vt fam (steal)* birlar, afanar, chorizar.

file [faɪl] *n* **1** *(tool)* lima. **2** *(folder)* carpeta. **3** *(archive)* archivo, expediente *m*. **4** COMPUT archivo. **5** *(line)* fila.
▷ *vt* **1** *(smooth)* limar. **2** *(put away)* archivar; *(in card index)* fichar. **3** JUR presentar.
▷ *vi (walk in line)* desfilar.

filial ['fɪlɪəl] *adj* filial.

filibuster ['fɪlɪbʌstəʳ] *n* **1** POL *(person)* obstruccionista *mf*. **2** *(speech) intervención parlamentaria hecha para impedir que una moción se vote*.
▷ *vt* obstaculizar.
▷ *vi* practicar una política obstruccionista.

filigree ['fɪlɪgriː] *n* filigrana.

filing ['faɪlɪŋ] *n* clasificación *f*.
▷ *n pl* **filings** limaduras *fpl*.

fill [fɪl] *vt* **1** *(make full)* llenar (**with**, de). **2** *(time)* ocupar. **3** *(cover)* cubrir. **4** CULIN rellenar. **5** *(tooth)* empastar. **6** *(hold a position)* ocupar; *(appoint)* cubrir. **7** *(fulfill)* satisfacer.
▷ *vi* llenarse (**with**, de).
⊙ **to fill in** *vt sep* **1** *(space, form)* rellenar. **2** *(inform)* poner al corriente (**on**, de).
⊙ **to fill in for** *vt insep* sustituir a.
⊙ **to fill up** *vt sep* llenar.
▷ *vi* llenarse.

fillet ['fɪlɪt] *n* filete *m*.
▷ *vt* cortar en filetes, filetear.

filling ['fɪlɪŋ] *n* **1** *(in tooth)* empaste *m*. **2** CULIN relleno. ● **filling station** gasolinera.

film [fɪlm] *n* **1** CINEM película, filme *m*, film *m*. **2** *(coating of dust, etc)* capa, película. **3** *(of photos)* carrete *m*, rollo.
▷ *vt* **1** *(cinem)* rodar, filmar; *(tv program)* grabar. **2** *(event)* filmar.
▷ *vi* CINEM rodar.

filmography [fɪl'mɒgrəfɪ] *n* filmografía.

filter ['fɪltəʳ] *n* filtro.
▷ *vt* filtrar.
▷ *vi* **1** filtrarse. **2** *(move gradually)* moverse poco a poco. **3** GB girar a la derecha o a la izquierda *(mientras el semáforo principal está cerrado)*.
⊙ **to filter out** *vt sep (remove)* eliminar.
▷ *vi fig (news, etc)* llegar a saberse, trascender.
⊙ **to filter through** *vi* **1** *fig (news, etc)* llegar. **2** *(sunlight, etc)* filtrarse.

filth [fɪlθ] *n* **1** *(dirt)* suciedad *f*, porquería. **2** *fig (obscenity)* obscenidades *fpl*, porquerías *fpl*. **3** *sl (police)* pasma, bofia.

filthy ['fɪlθɪ] *adj* **1** *(dirty)* sucio,-a, asqueroso,-a. **2** *(obscene)* obsceno,-a, grosero,-a, asqueroso,-a. **3** *fam (very bad)* malo,-a.
▲ *comp* **filthier**, *superl* **filthiest**.

filtration [fɪl'treɪʃən] *n* filtración *f*.

fin [fɪn] *n* aleta.

final ['faɪnəl] *adj* **1** *(last)* final, último,-a. **2** *(definitive)* definitivo,-a.
▷ *n* SP final *f*.
▷ *n pl* **finals** *(at university)* exámenes *mpl* finales.

finale [fɪ'nɑːlɪ] *n* final *m*.

finalist ['faɪnəlɪst] *n* finalista *mf*.

finality [faɪ'nælətɪ] *n* carácter *m* definitivo.

inalize ['faɪnəlaɪz] *vt (plans, arrangements)* ultimar; *(date)* fijar.
inally ['faɪnəlɪ] *adv* **1** *(at last)* por fin, al final. **2** *(lastly)* por último, finalmente. **3** *(definitively)* definitivamente, de forma definitiva.
inance ['faɪnæns] *n (management of money)* finanzas *fpl*.
vt financiar.
n pl **finances** *(money available)* fondos *mpl*.
inancier [faɪ'nænsɪər] *n* financiero,-a.
inch [fɪntʃ] *n* pinzón *m*.
ind [faɪnd] *n (act, thing found)* hallazgo.
vt **1** *(locate)* encontrar, hallar. **2** *(discover)* descubrir, encontrar. **3** *(exist)* hallarse, encontrarse, existir. **4** *(obtain, get)* encontrar. **5** *(think, consider)* encontrar, parecer. **6** *(become aware, realize)* encontrar, darse cuenta. **7** *(end up, arrive at, reach)* ir a parar a, llegar a. **8** JUR declarar.
to find out *vt sep* **1** *(enquire)* preguntar, averiguar; *(discover)* descubrir, enterarse de. **2** *(rumble)* calar, pillar, descubrir el juego.
vi **1** *(enquire)* informarse (**about**, sobre), averiguar. **2** *(discover)* enterarse (**about**, de), (llegar a) saber.
▲ *pt & pp* **found** [faʊnd].
inder ['faɪndər] *n* descubridor,-ra.
inding ['faɪndɪŋ] *n* **1** *(of inquiry)* conclusión *f*, resultado. **2** JUR fallo, veredicto.
e usa en plural con el mismo significado.
ine[1] [faɪn] *adj* **1** *(thin - hair, thread, sand, rain)* fino,-a. **2** *(delicate)* fino,-a, delicado,-a. **3** *(subtle)* sutil. **4** *(high-quality)* excelente. **5** *(metals)* puro,-a, refinado,-a. **6** *(weather)* bueno,-a. **7** *(healthy)* bien. **8** *fam (all right)* bien. **9** *iron (terrible)* menudo,-a.
adv **1** *(in small bits)* fino, finamente. **2** *fam (very well)* muy bien, a la perfección.
ine[2] [faɪn] *n (punishment)* multa.
vt multar, poner una multa.
inely ['faɪnlɪ] *adv* **1** *(very thin, in small bits)* fino, finamente. **2** *(well, splendidly)* elegantemente. **3** *(with precision, subtly)* delicadamente, minuciosamente.
inery ['faɪnərɪ] *n* galas *fpl*.
inesse [fɪ'nes] *n* delicadeza, diplomacia, sutileza.
inger ['fɪŋgər] *n* dedo.
vt **1** *(touch)* tocar. **2** *pej* manosear.
ingernail ['fɪŋgəneɪl] *n* uña.
ingerprint ['fɪŋgəprɪnt] *n* huella digital, huella dactilar.
ingerstall ['fɪŋgəstɔːl] *n* dedil *m*.
ingertip ['fɪŋgətɪp] *n* punta del dedo, yema del dedo.
inicky ['fɪnɪkɪ] *adj* **1** *(person)* remilgado,-a. **2** *(job)* engorroso,-a.
inish ['fɪnɪʃ] *n* **1** fin *m*, final *m*, conclusión *f*. **2** SP llegada, meta. **3** *(for surface)* acabado.
vt **1** *(end)* acabar, terminar. **2** *(complete)* acabar (**off**, -), terminar (**off**, -). **3** *fam (exhaust)* agotar (**off**, -), acabar con.
to finish up *vi (end up)* ir a parar a/en.
inite ['faɪnaɪt] *adj* finito,-a.
inland ['fɪnlənd] *n* Finlandia.
inn [fɪn] *n (person)* finlandés,-esa.
innish ['fɪnɪʃ] *adj* finlandés,-esa.
n (language) finlandés *m*.
ord [fɪ'ɔːd] *n* fiordo.

fir [fɜːr] *n* abeto.
fire ['faɪər] *n* **1** *(gen)* fuego. **2** *(blaze)* incendio, fuego. **3** *(heater)* estufa. **4** MIL fuego. **5** *(strong emotion)* ardor *m*, pasión *f*, entusiasmo.
▷ *vt* **1** *(weapon)* disparar; *(rocket)* lanzar. **2** *(questions, etc)* disparar, bombardear. **3** *(pottery)* cocer. **4** *fig (stimulate)* inflamar, enardecer, excitar, exaltar. **5** *fam (dismiss)* despedir.
▷ *vi* **1** *(shoot)* disparar (**at**, sobre), hacer fuego. **2** AUTO encenderse.
▷ *interj* ¡fuego!
firearm ['faɪərɑːm] *n* arma de fuego.
firebreak ['faɪəbreɪk] *n* cortafuego.
firecracker ['faɪəkrækər] *n* petardo.
firefighter ['faɪəfaɪtər] *n* bombero *mf*.
firefly ['faɪəflaɪ] *n* luciérnaga.
▲ *pl* **fireflies**.
fireguard ['faɪəgɑːd] *n* pantalla.
fireman ['faɪəmən] *n* bombero.
▲ *pl* **firemen** ['faɪəmən].
fireplace ['faɪəpleɪs] *n* **1** *(structure)* chimenea. **2** *(hearth)* hogar *m*.
fireproof ['faɪəpruːf] *adj* incombustible.
fireside ['faɪəsaɪd] *n* hogar *m*.
firewall ['faɪəwɔːl] *n* cortafuego.
firewoman ['faɪəwʊmən] *n* mujer bombero.
▲ *pl* **firewomen** ['faɪəwɪmɪn].
firewood ['faɪəwʊd] *n* leña.
fireworks ['faɪəwɜːks] *n pl* **1** fuegos *mpl* artificiales, fuegos *mpl* de artificio. **2** *fig* escándalo *m sing*.
firing ['faɪərɪŋ] *n* tiroteo.
firm[1] [fɜːm] *n (business)* empresa.
firm[2] [fɜːm] *adj* **1** *(strong, solid, steady)* firme, sólido,-a **2** *(strict, strong)* duro,-a. **3** FIN *(steady)* firme, estable.
⊙ **to firm up** *vt sep (deal, etc)* concretar, confirmar.
firmament ['fɜːməmənt] *n* firmamento.
firmly ['fɜːmlɪ] *adv* firmemente, con firmeza.
firmness ['fɜːmnəs] *n* firmeza.
first [fɜːst] *adj* primero,-a.
▷ *adv* **1** *(before anything else)* primero. **2** *(for the first time)* por primera vez. **3** *(in first place)* primero, en primer lugar. **4** *(in preference to)* antes. ● **at first** al principio.
▷ *n* la primera vez.
▷ *n* **1** *(first-class degree)* ≈ sobresaliente *m (título universitario que corresponde a la nota más alta)*. **2** *(gear)* primera: **I can't put it into first** *no puedo meter primera.*
first-aid [fɜːst'eɪd] *adj* de primeros auxilios. ● **first-aid kit** botiquín *m*.
first-born ['fɜːstbɔːn] *adj* primogénito,-a.
▷ *n* primogénito,-a.
first-class ['fɜːstklɑːs] *adj* **1** de primera clase. **2** *fig* de primera, excelente.
▷ *adv* en primera.
first-former ['fɜːstfɔːmər] *n* GB alumno,-a del primer curso.
first-hand [fɜːst'hænd] *adj* de primera mano.
▷ *adv* de primera mano, directamente.
firstly ['fɜːstlɪ] *adv* en primer lugar, ante todo.
first-rate ['fɜːstreɪt] *adj* de primera, excelente.
▷ *adv* de primera.
fiscal ['fɪskəl] *adj* fiscal.

fish [fɪʃ] *n* 1 pez *m*. 2 CULIN pescado. ● **fish farm** piscifactoría. ‖ **fish shop** pescadería.
▲ *pl* fish o fishes.
▷ *vi* pescar (for, -).
fishbowl ['fɪʃbəʊl] *n* pecera.
fish-eating ['fɪʃiːtɪŋ] *adj* ictiófago,-a.
fisherman ['fɪʃəmən] *n* pescador *m*.
▲ *pl* fishermen ['fɪʃəmən].
fishery ['fɪʃərɪ] *n* 1 *(industry)* industria pesquera. 2 *(place)* pesquería.
▲ *pl* fisheries.
fishfinger [fɪʃ'fɪŋgəʳ] *n* palito de pescado rebozado.
fish-hook ['fɪʃhʊk] *n* anzuelo.
fishing ['fɪʃɪŋ] *n* pesca. ■ **to go fishing** ir de pesca. ● **fishing line** sedal *m*. ‖ **fishing net** red *f* de pesca. ‖ **fishing rod** caña de pescar. ‖ **fishing tackle** aparejo de pescar.
fishmonger ['fɪʃmʌŋgəʳ] *n* GB pescadero,-a.
fishnet ['fɪʃnet] *n* 1 US red *f* de pesca. 2 *(mesh fabric)* red *f*.
fishwife ['fɪʃwaɪf] *n* 1 pescadera. 2 *pej* verdulera.
▲ *pl* fishwives.
fishy ['fɪʃɪ] *adj* 1 *(taste, smell)* a pescado. 2 *(suspicious)* sospechoso,-a.
▲ *comp* fishier, *superl* fishiest.
fission ['fɪʃᵊn] *n* fisión *f*.
fissure ['fɪʃəʳ] *n* fisura, grieta.
fist [fɪst] *n* puño.
fistful ['fɪstfʊl] *n* puñado.
fisticuffs ['fɪstɪkʌfs] *n pl dated* puñetazos *mpl*.
fit¹ [fɪt] *n* 1 MED ataque *m*, acceso. 2 *(of laughter)* arrebato, ataque *m*; *(of rage, panic)* arranque *m*, arrebato.
fit² [fɪt] *adj* 1 *(suitable, appropriate)* adecuado,-a, apto,-a, apropiado,-a; *(qualified for)* capacitado,-a hábil, capaz; *(worthy, deserving)* digno,-a. 2 *(in good health)* sano,-a, bien de salud, en (plena) forma; *(physically)* en forma. 3 *fam (ready)* a punto de.
▲ *comp* fitter, *superl* fittest.
▷ *n* 1 *(of clothes)*: **it's a perfect fit** *me va perfectamente*. 2 *(in space)*: **it'll be a tight fit** *vamos a estar muy apretados*.
▷ *vt* 1 *(be right size for)* sentar bien, quedar bien, ir bien a. 2 *(try (clothing) on SB)* probar. 3 *(key)* abrir. 4 *(install)* instalar, poner, colocar. 5 *fig (be appropriate)* cuadrar con, corresponder a, responder a. 6 *(adapt)* ajustar, adaptar, adecuar; *(make suitable)* capacitar.
⊙ **to fit in** *vi* 1 *(get on)* llevarse bien, integrarse. 2 *(suit)* encajar; *(harmonize)* pegar, quedar bien; *(tally)* cuadrar.
▷ *vt sep* 1 *(physically)* hacer sitio para, meter. 2 *(in timetable)* hacer un hueco para, tener tiempo para. 3 *(harmonize)* encajar, cuadrar.
▲ *pt & pp* fitted, *ger* fitting.
⊙ **to fit out** *vt sep (ship)* equipar, pertrechar; *(person)* equipar.
⊙ **to fit up** *vt sep* 1 *(building)* acondicionar. 2 GB *sl (frame)* incriminar.
fitful ['fɪtfʊl] *adj* irregular, discontinuo,-a, intermitente.
fitment ['fɪtmənt] *n* mueble *m*.
fitness ['fɪtnəs] *n* 1 *(health)* buena forma física, buen estado físico. 2 *(suitability)* capacidad *f* (for, para).

fitted ['fɪtɪd] *adj (cupboard)* empotrado,-a; *(room)* amueblado,-a; *(clothes)* entallado,-a.
fitter ['fɪtəʳ] *n* 1 TECH montador,-ra. 2 SEW probador,-ra.
fitting ['fɪtɪŋ] *adj (appropriate, proper)* apropiado,-a, adecuado,-a.
▷ *n* SEW prueba.
▷ *n pl* **fittings** 1 *(accessories)* accesorios *mpl*. 2 *(furnishings) muebles, cortinas y alfombras*.
five [faɪv] *n* cinco.
▷ *adj* cinco.
Consulta también six.
five-a-side ['faɪvə'saɪd] [Also **five-a-side football**.] fútbol sala *m*, futbito.
fiver ['faɪvəʳ] *n* GB *fam* billete *m* de cinco libras.
fix [fɪks] *n* 1 *fam (difficult situation)* apuro, aprieto. 2 *(position of ship, aircraft)* posición *f*. 3 *(dishonest arrangement)* tongo.
▷ *vt* 1 *(fasten)* fijar, sujetar. 2 *fig (stick)* fijar, grabar. 3 *(direct - eyes, attention)* fijar, clavar, poner. 4 *(decide)* decidir; *(date, meeting, etc)* fijar. 5 *(organize)* arreglar, organizar. 6 *(dishonestly)* amañar. 7 *(repair)* arreglar. 8 US *(prepare)* preparar. 9 *(photo)* fijar.
⊙ **to fix on** *vt insep (decide, select - person)* decidir, optar por, escoger; *(- date)* fijar.
⊙ **to fix up** *vt sep* 1 *(accommodate, provide with)* proveer (with, de), conseguir. 2 *(organize)* arreglar, organizar. 3 *(repair, redecorate)* arreglar; *(install)* poner.
fixation [fɪk'seɪʃᵊn] *n* obsesión *f*, idea fija.
fixed [fɪkst] *adj* 1 *(set)* fijo,-a. 2 *(dishonestly)* amañado,-a.
fixture ['fɪkstʃəʳ] *n* SP encuentro.
▷ *n pl* **fixtures** *(furniture)* muebles *mpl* empotrados.
fizz [fɪz] *n* burbujeo, efervescencia.
▷ *vi* burbujear.
fizzle ['fɪzᵊl] *vi* burbujear.
⊙ **to fizzle out** *vi* esfumarse, perder fuerza, quedar en nada.
fizzy ['fɪzɪ] *adj (gen)* gaseoso,-a, con gas; *(wine)* espumoso,-a.
▲ *comp* fizzier, *superl* fizziest.
fjord [fɪ'ɔːd] *n* fiordo.
flab [flæb] *n fam pej* michelines *mpl*.
flabbergasted ['flæbəgɑːstɪd] *adj* pasmado,-a, atónito,-a.
flabby ['flæbɪ] *adj* 1 *(part of body)* fofo,-a. 2 *fig (weak)* débil, soso,-a.
▲ *comp* flabbier, *superl* flabbiest.
flaccid ['flæksɪd] *adj* fláccido,-a.
flag¹ [flæg] *n (rock)* ⟶ **flagstone**.
flag² [flæg] *n* 1 *(gen)* bandera. 2 MAR pabellón *m*. 3 *(for charity)* banderita.
▷ *vt* 1 *(put up flags)* decorar con banderas. 2 *(mark)* señalar.
▲ *pt & pp* flagged, *ger* flagging.
⊙ **to flag down** *vt sep* hacer señales para que un coche se detenga.
flag³ [flæg] *n* BOT lirio.
flag⁴ [flæg] *vi* 1 *(lose strength)* decaer, flaquear, languidecer. 2 *(plants)* marchitarse.
▲ *pt & pp* flagged, *ger* flagging.
flagellate ['flædʒəleɪt] *vt* flagelar.

lagellum [flə'dʒeləm] *vt* flagelo.
lagon ['flægən] *n* jarro, jarra.
lagpole ['flægpəʊl] *n* asta de bandera.
lagrant ['fleɪgrənt] *adj* flagrante, escandaloso,-a, descarado,-a.
lagship ['flægʃɪp] *n* buque *m* insignia.
lagstone ['flægstəʊn] *n (large)* losa; *(small)* loseta.
lail [fleɪl] *n* mayal *m*.
▷ *vt* golpear, azotar.
▷ *vi* **to flail about** agitarse, debatirse.
lair [fleər] *n* talento, don *m*, facilidad *f*.
lak [flæk] *n* **1** MIL fuego antiaéreo. **2** *(criticism)* críticas *fpl* (negativas).
lake [fleɪk] *n* **1** *(of snow, oats)* copo. **2** *(of skin, soap)* escama. **3** *(of paint)* desconchón *m*, trozo desprendido.
▷ *vi* **to flake away/off** *(gen)* descamarse; *(paint)* desconcharse.
⊙ **to flake out** *vi (collapse)* caer rendido,-a.
lambé ['flɒmbeɪ] *adj* CULIN flameado,-a.
lamboyant [flæm'bɔɪənt] *adj* llamativo,-a, extravagante.
lame [fleɪm] *n* **1** llama. **2** *fig (intense feeling)* llama.
▷ *vi* **1** *(burn)* arder. **2** *(glow, shine)* brillar, encenderse. **3** *(become angry)* montar en cólera.
lameproof ['fleɪmpru:f] *adj* ignífugo,-a.
lame-thrower ['fleɪmθrəʊər] *n* lanzallamas *m*.
laming ['fleɪmɪŋ] *adj* **1** *(burning)* en llamas; *(glowing)* ardiente. **2** *(colour)* encendido,-a. **3** *(passionate, violent)* apasionado,-a, violento,-a, ardiente. **4** *fam (damn)* maldito,-a, condenado,-a.
lamingo [flə'mɪŋgəʊ] *n* flamenco.
▲ *pl* **flamingos** o **flamingoes.**
lammable ['flæməbəl] *adj* inflamable.
lan [flæn] *n* CULIN tarta rellena.
landers ['flɑ:ndəz] *n* Flandes *m*.
lange [flændʒ] *n (on wheel)* pestaña; *(on pipe)* reborde *m*.
lank [flæŋk] *n* **1** *(of animal)* ijada, ijar *m*. **2** MIL flanco. **3** *(of building, mountain, etc)* lado, falda.
▷ *vt* flanquear, bordear.
lannel ['flænəl] *n* **1** *(material)* franela. **2** *(for face)* toallita. **3** *fam (words)* palabrería.
lap [flæp] *n* **1** *(of envelope, pocket)* solapa. **2** *(of tent)* faldón *m*. **3** *(of plane)* alerón *m*. **4** *(of table)* hoja (abatible). **5** *(action, sound)* aleteo. **6** *fam* pánico.
▷ *vt (wings)* batir; *(arms)* agitar.
▷ *vi* **1** *(wings)* aletear. **2** *(flag, sails)* ondear. **3** *fam* inquietarse.
▲ *pt & pp* **flapped**, *ger* **flapping.**
lare [fleər] *n* **1** *(flame)* llamarada. **2** *(signal)* bengala.
▷ *vi* **1** llamear. **2** *fig* estallar, encenderse.
⊙ **to flare up** *vi (blow up, erupt)* estallar, encenderse; *(get angry)* enfadarse, montar en cólera.
lared [fleəd] *adj* acampanado,-a.
lare-up ['fleərʌp] *n* **1** *(of flame)* llamarada. **2** *(of violence)* estallido.
lash [flæʃ] *n* **1** *(of light)* destello, centelleo; *(of lightning)* relámpago. **2** *(from firearm)* fogonazo. **3** *fig* destello, rayo. **4** *(photography)* flash *m*. **5** MIL *(patch)* distintivo.
▷ *adj fam pej (showy)* ostentoso,-a, chulo,-a.
▷ *vi* **1** relampaguear, destellar. **2** *fig (eyes)* brillar. **3** *(dash)* pasar como un rayo. **4** *(expose OS)* exhibirse.
▷ *vt* **1** *(shine - light)* dirigir, lanzar; *(- torch)* encender, dirigir. **2** *(communicate with light)* hacer señales con. **3** *(transmit message)* transmitir. **4** *fig (look, smile)* lanzar. **5** *(show quickly)* enseñar rápidamente.
⊙ **to flash about / flash around** *vt sep* hacer ostentación de.
⊙ **to flash back** *vi* CINEM retroceder.
flashback ['flæʃbæk] *n* escena retrospectiva, flashback *m*.
flasher ['flæʃər] *n* exhibicionista *m*.
flashlight ['flæʃlaɪt] *n* **1** *(torch)* linterna. **2** *(photo)* flash *m*.
flashy ['flæʃɪ] *adj* llamativo,-a, ostentoso,-a.
▲ *comp* **flashier**, *superl* **flashiest.**
flask [flæsk] *n* **1** frasco. **2** CHEM matraz *m*.
flat[1] [flæt] *n (apartment)* piso.
flat[2] [flæt] *adj* **1** *(level, even)* llano,-a, plano,-a; *(smooth)* liso,-a. **2** *(shallow)* llano,-a. **3** *(shoes)* sin tacón. **4** *(tyre, ball, etc)* desinflado,-a. **5** *(battery)* descargado,-a. **6** *(drink)* sin gas. **7** *fig (dull)* monótono,-a, soso,-a. **8** *(having single price)* fijo,-a. **9** *(firm, absolute, categorical)* rotundo,-a. **10** *(exact)* justo,-a. **11** MUS *(key)* bemol; *(voice, instrument)* desafinado,-a.
▲ *comp* **flatter**, *superl* **flattest.**
▷ *n* **1** *(plain)* llano, llanura. **2** *(of hand)* palma. **3** MUS bemol *m*. **4** US *(tyre)* pinchazo.
▷ *adv* **1** *(completely)* categóricamente. **2** MUS desafinadamente. **3** *(exactly)* exactamente.
▷ *n pl* **flats** *(low level plain)* llano *sing*.
flatly ['flætlɪ] *adv* **1** *(categorically)* categóricamente, rotundamente. **2** *(voice)* con voz monótona.
flatmate ['flætmaɪt] *n* compañero,-a de piso.
flatten ['flætən] *vt* **1** *(make flat)* allanar, aplanar (**out**, -); *(smooth)* alisar. **2** *(crush)* aplastar; *(knock down)* derribar, tumbar; *(knock over)* atropellar. **3** *fig (defeat)* desconcertar.
▷ *vi* allanarse, aplanarse (**out**, -).
flatter ['flætər] *vt* **1** *(praise)* halagar, adular. **2** *(suit)* favorecer. **3** *(believe)* felicitarse, preciarse de; *(delude OS)* hacerse ilusiones.
flattering ['flætərɪŋ] *adj* **1** *(words)* lisonjero,-a, halagüeño,-a. **2** *(clothes, etc)* favorecedor,-ra.
flattery ['flætərɪ] *n* adulación *f*, halagos *mpl*.
flatulence ['flætjələns] *n fml* flatulencia.
flaunt [flɔ:nt] *vt* hacer alarde de, hacer ostentación de.
flautist ['flɔ:tɪst] *n* flautista *mf*.
flavor ['fleɪvər] *n* US → **flavour.**
flavoring ['fleɪvərɪŋ] *n* US → **flavouring.**
flavour ['fleɪvər] *n* **1** sabor *m*, gusto. **2** *fig* atmósfera.
▷ *vt* sazonar, condimentar (**with**, con).
flavouring ['fleɪvərɪŋ] *n* condimento.
flaw [flɔ:] *n* **1** *(fault - in material, product, etc)* defecto, desperfecto, tara, fallo. **2** *(failing - in character)* defecto; *(- in argument)* error *m*.
flawless ['flɔ:ləs] *adj* sin defecto, impecable, perfecto,-a.
flax [flæks] *n* lino.
flaxen ['flæksən] *adj* muy rubio,-a.

flay [fleɪ] *vt* **1** *(remove skin)* desollar, despellejar; *(whip)* azotar. **2** *fig (criticize)* despellejar.
flea [fliː] *n* pulga.
fleck [flek] *n* mota, punto.
▷ *vt* salpicar (**with**, de), motear (**with**, de).
fledgeling ['fledʒlɪŋ] *n* **1** *(bird)* pajarito. **2** *(inexperienced person)* novato,-a, pipiolo.
flee [fliː] *vt (run away)* huir de.
▷ *vi* **1** *(run away, escape)* huir. **2** *(vanish)* desaparecer.
▲ *pt & pp* **fled** [fled].
fleece [fliːs] *n* **1** *(sheep's coat, fabric)* lana. **2** *(sheared)* vellón *m*.
▷ *vt* **1** *(shear)* esquilar. **2** *fam (swindle)* desplumar, robar, timar.
fleet [fliːt] *n* **1** *(of ships)* flota. **2** *(of vehicles)* flota, parque *m* móvil.
fleeting ['fliːtɪŋ] *adj* fugaz, breve, efímero,-a.
Fleming ['flemɪŋ] *n (person)* flamenco,-a.
Flemish ['flemɪʃ] *adj* flamenco,-a.
▷ *n (language)* flamenco.
flesh [fleʃ] *n* **1** *(of animals, humans)* carne *f*. **2** *(of fruit)* carne *f*, pulpa.
▷ *n* **the flesh** *fig* la carne *f*.
⊙ **to flesh out** *vt sep (add more details)* desarrollar.
flew [fluː] *pt* → **fly**.
flex [fleks] *n* GB cable *m*.
▷ *vt (body, joints)* doblar; *(muscles)* flexionar.
flexibility [fleksɪ'bɪlɪtɪ] *n* flexibilidad *f*.
flexible ['fleksəbᵊl] *adj* flexible.
flexitime ['fleksɪtaɪm] *n* horario flexible.
flick [flɪk] *n* **1** *(jerk)* movimiento rápido, movimiento brusco. **2** *(of fingers)* capirotazo; *(of whip)* latigazo, chasquido; *(of tail)* coletazo. **3** *(of pages)* hojeada.
▷ *vt* **1** *(with finger)* dar un capirotazo a. **2** *(switch)* dar al interruptor. **3** *(whip)* chasquear, dar con el látigo; *(tail)* dar un coletazo. **4** *(remove)* sacudirse.
▷ *n pl* **the flicks** *dated* el cine *m sing*.
⊙ **to flick away** *vt sep* quitar, sacudirse.
⊙ **to flick through** *vt insep* hojear.
flicker ['flɪkəʳ] *n* **1** *(of flame, eyelids)* parpadeo; *(of light)* titileo, parpadeo. **2** *fig (slight sign)* señal *f*, muestra; *(faint emotion)* chispa, pizca.
▷ *vi* **1** *(flame)* vacilar, parpadear; *(light)* titilar, parpadear; *(shadow)* bailar. **2** *(eyelids)* parpadear. **3** *(smile)* esbozarse.
flier ['flaɪəʳ] *n* **1** *(pilot)* aviador,-ra. **2** *(bird, insect, etc)* volador,-ra. **3** *(leaflet)* folleto.
flight [flaɪt] *n* **1** *(journey by air)* vuelo: **our flight has been delayed** *nuestro vuelo se ha retrasado*. **2** *(path)* trayectoria. **3** *(flock of birds)* bandada. **4** *(of stairs)* tramo. **5** *(escape)* huida, fuga. ● **flight attendant** auxiliar *mf* de vuelo.
flimsy ['flɪmzɪ] *adj* **1** *(thin)* fino,-a, ligero,-a. **2** *(structure)* poco sólido,-a. **3** *fig (unconvincing)* flojo,-a, pobre, poco convincente.
▲ *comp* **flimsier**, *superl* **flimsiest**.
▷ *n* papel *m* cebolla.
flinch [flɪntʃ] *vi* **1** *(wince)* estremecerse. **2** *(shun)* retroceder (**from**, ante).
fling [flɪŋ] *n* **1** *(throw)* lanzamiento. **2** *(wild time)* juerga. **3** *(affair)* aventura (amorosa), romance *m*.
▷ *vt* **1** *(throw)* arrojar, tirar, lanzar. **2** *(move)* echar, lanzar. **3** *(say)* lanzar.
▲ *pt & pp* **flung** [flʌŋ].
⊙ **to fling off** *vt sep (clothes)* quitarse de prisa.
⊙ **to fling on** *vt sep (clothes)* ponerse de prisa.
⊙ **to fling out** *vt sep (thing)* tirar; *(person)* echar, expulsar.
flint [flɪnt] *n* **1** *(stone)* sílex *m*; *(piece)* pedernal *m*. **2** *(tool)* sílex *m*. **3** *(of lighter)* piedra, piedra de mechero.
flip [flɪp] *n* **1** *(light blow)* golpecito. **2** *(somersault)* voltereta (en el aire).
▷ *adj fam (flippant)* frívolo,-a, poco serio,-a.
▷ *interj fam* ¡ostras!
▷ *vt* **1** *(toss - gen)* echar, tirar al aire; *(- coin)* echar a cara o cruz. **2** *(switch)* dar a. **3** *(turn over)* dar la vuelta a.
▷ *vi fam (get angry)* perder los estribos; *(go mad)* volverse loco,-a.
▲ *pt & pp* **flipped**, *ger* **flipping**.
⊙ **to flip through** *vt insep* echar un vistazo a.
flip-flop ['flɪpflɒp] *n* chancla.
flipper ['flɪpəʳ] *n* aleta.
flirt [flɜːt] *n* coqueto,-a, ligón,-ona.
▷ *vi (coquette)* flirtear (**with**, con), coquetear (**with**, con).
flit [flɪt] *n (escape)* escapada.
▷ *vi (birds, insects)* revolotear, volar; *(people)* mover.
▲ *pt & pp* **flitted**, *ger* **flitting**.
float [fləʊt] *n* **1** *(for fishing)* boya, flotador *m*. **2** *(for swimming)* flotador *m*. **3** *(of aircraft)* pontón *m*, flotador *m*. **4** *(vehicle - in procession)* carroza; *(- for delivery)* furgoneta. **5** *(money)* cambio. **6** *(plasterer's tool)* llana.
▷ *vi (gen)* flotar.
▷ *vt* **1** poner a flote, hacer flotar. **2** FIN *(company)* lanzar a bolsa; *(shares)* emitir; *(currency)* dejar flotar. *(suggest, present)* sugerir.
flock [flɒk] *n* **1** *(of sheep, goats)* rebaño; *(of birds)* bandada. **2** *fam (crowd)* multitud *f*, tropel *m*. **3** REL grey *f*, rebaño.
floe [fləʊ] *n* témpano.
flog [flɒg] *vt* **1** *(beat)* azotar. **2** GB *fam (sell)* vender.
▲ *pt & pp* **flogged**, *ger* **flogging**.
flood [flʌd] *n* **1** *(overflow of water)* inundación *f*. *(of river)* riada. **3** *fig (great quantity)* torrente *m*, avalancha, diluvio.
▷ *vt* **1** *(gen)* inundar, anegar; *(engine)* ahogar. **2** *fig (with calls, applications, etc)* llover, inundar (**with**, de).
▷ *vi* **1** *(river)* desbordarse. **2** *fig (cover, fill)* invadir, inundar.
floodgate ['flʌdgaɪt] *n* compuerta.
flooding ['flʌdɪŋ] *n* inundación *f*.
floodlight ['flʌdlaɪt] *n* foco.
▷ *vt* iluminar con focos.
floor [flɔːʳ] *n* **1** *(surface)* suelo. **2** GEOG fondo. **3** *(storey)* piso, planta. **4** *(dance)* pista.
▷ *vt* **1** *(provide with floor)* solar, entarimar (**with**, de). *(knock down)* derribar, tumbar. **3** *fig (confuse, defeat)* apabullar, desconcertar, dejar perplejo,-a.
▷ *n* **the floor** POL la sala, el hemiciclo.
floorboard ['flɔːbɔːd] *n* tabla (del suelo).
flooring ['flɔːrɪŋ] *n* suelo, pavimento.
flop [flɒp] *n fam* fracaso.

vi **1** *(fall clumsily)* abalanzarse, arrojarse (**into**, en); *(sit or lie clumsily)* tumbarse, dejarse caer. **2** *fam (fail)* fracasar.
▲ *pt & pp* **flopped**, *ger* **flopping**.
loppy ['flɒpɪ] *adj* blando,-a, flexible. ● **floppy disk** COMPUT disco flexible, disquete *m*.
▲ *comp* **floppier**, *superl* **floppiest**.
lora ['flɔːrə] *n* flora.
lorence ['flɒrəns] *n* Florencia.
lorid ['flɒrɪd] *adj* **1** *(style)* florido,-a, recargado,-a. **2** *(ruddy)* rojizo,-a, colorado,-a.
lorist ['flɒrɪst] *n* florista *mf*. ● **florist's (shop)** floristería.
loss [flɒs] *n* seda floja.
lotsam ['flɒtsəm] *n* MAR desechos *mpl* en el mar.
lounce [flaʊns] *n* **1** SEW volante *m*. **2** *(jerk)* gesto exagerado, gesto de enfado.
vi moverse exageradamente.
to flounce in / flounce out *vi* entrar airadamente / salir airadamente.
lounder ['flaʊndəʳ] *n* *(fish)* platija.
vi **1** *(struggle, move with difficulty)* forcejear. **2** *fig (hesitate, dither)* vacilar.
lour [flaʊəʳ] *n* harina.
vt enharinar.
lourish ['flʌrɪʃ] *n* **1** *(gesture)* ademán *m*, gesto teatral, gesto exagerado. **2** *(signature)* rúbrica; *(of pen)* plumada. **3** MUS *(guitar)* floreo; *(fanfare)* toque *m* de trompeta; *(singing)* floritura.
vt (wave about) agitar, blandir.
vi **1** *(be successful)* florecer, prosperar. **2** *(plant)* crecer bien.
lout [flaʊt] *vt (rule)* mofarse de, burlarse de; *(convention, tradition)* ignorar, no hacer caso de; *(law)* desacatar.
low [fləʊ] *n* **1** *(gen)* flujo. **2** *(of river)* corriente *f*. **3** *(of traffic)* circulación *f*. **4** *(of words)* torrente *m*. **5** *(of people, goods)* afluencia. **6** *(of capital)* movimiento. **7** *(of tide)* flujo.
vi **1** *(move freely - liquid, river, blood)* fluir, discurrir, correr. **2** *(pour out - blood)* manar; *(- tears)* correr. **3** *(tide)* subir. **4** *(traffic)* circular; *(electricity)* fluir. **5** *(speech, writing, thoughts)* fluir. **6** *(hair, clothes)* ondear. **7** *(be available, abound)* abundar (**with**, -).
to flow into *vi (river)* desembocar en: **the Ebro flows into the sea at Amposta** *el Ebro desemboca en el mar en Amposta*.
lower [flaʊəʳ] *n* flor *f*.
vi florecer.
lowerbed ['flaʊəbed] *n* parterre *m*, macizo.
lowerpot ['flaʊəpɒt] *n* maceta, tiesto.
lown [fləʊn] *pp* → **fly**.
u [fluː] *n* gripe *f*: **he's got (the) flu** *tiene la gripe*.
uctuate ['flʌktjʊeɪt] *vi* fluctuar, variar.
ue [fluː] *n* **1** *(of chimney)* cañón *m*. **2** *(of stove, boiler)* conducto de humos.
uency ['fluːənsɪ] *n* **1** fluidez *f*. **2** *(of language)* dominio (**in**, de).
uent ['fluːənt] *adj* **1** *(gen)* fluido,-a. **2** *(language)* fluido,-a: **he speaks fluent English** *habla inglés con soltura*.
uff [flʌf] *n* **1** *(down, material)* pelusa, lanilla. **2** *fam (mistake, blunder)* pifia, fallo.
vt fam (do badly, fail) hacer mal.

fluffy ['flʌfɪ] *adj* **1** *(feathery)* mullido,-a. **2** *(toys)* de peluche. **3** *(light, airy)* esponjoso,-a.
▲ *comp* **fluffier**, *superl* **fluffiest**.
fluid ['fluːɪd] *adj* **1** *(not solid)* fluido,-a, líquido,-a. **2** *(smooth, graceful)* con soltura. **3** *(not fixed)* flexible.
▷ *n* fluido, líquido.
fluke [fluːk] *n fam* chiripa.
flummox ['flʌməks] *vt* desconcertar, confundir.
flung [flʌŋ] *pt & pp* → **fling**.
flunk [flʌnk] *vt* suspender, catear.
fluorescent [flʊə'resᵊnt] *adj* fluorescente. ● **fluorescent light/lamp** fluorescente *m*.
flurry ['flʌrɪ] *n* **1** *(of wind)* ráfaga; *(of snow)* nevisca. **2** *fig (burst)* nerviosismo, agitación *f*, frenesí *m*.
▲ *pl* **flurries**.
flush[1] [flʌʃ] *n (in cards)* color *m*.
flush[2] [flʌʃ] *adj* **flush with** *(level)* al mismo nivel que, alineado,-a con.
flush[3] [flʌʃ] *n* **1** *(blush)* rubor *m*. **2** *(of emotion)* acceso, arrebato. **3** *(of toilet)* cisterna.
▷ *vt* **1** *(cause to blush)* ruborizar, sonrojar. **2** *(clean)* limpiar con agua. **3** *(toilet)* tirar (de) la cadena.
▷ *vi* **1** *(blush)* ruborizarse. **2** *(toilet)* funcionar.
fluster ['flʌstəʳ] *vt* poner nervioso,-a.
▷ *n* confusión *f*, agitación *f*.
flute [fluːt] *n* flauta.
flutter ['flʌtəʳ] *n* **1** *(excitement)* agitación *f*, emoción *f*. **2** *(of wings)* aleteo. **3** *(of eyelashes)* pestañeo. **4** *fam (bet)* apuesta. **5** *(of aircraft)* vibración *f*.
▷ *vt* **1** *(eyelashes)* parpadear. **2** *(wings)* aletear.
▷ *vi* **1** *(flag)* ondear. **2** *(wings)* aletear. **3** *(flit)* revolotear. **4** *(heart)* palpitar.
fluvial ['fluːvɪəl] *adj* fluvial.
flux [flʌks] *n* **1** *(flow)* flujo. **2** *(instability)* inestabilidad *f*.
fly[1] [flaɪ] *vi* **1** volar. **2** *(go by plane)* ir en avión. **3** *(flag, hair)* ondear. **4** *(sparks)* saltar. **5** *(rush, move quickly)* irse volando, irse a toda prisa. **6** *(time)* volar, pasar volando. **7** *(flee)* largarse.
▷ *vt* **1** *(plane)* pilotar. **2** *(send by plane)* transportar. **3** *(travel over)* sobrevolar. **4** *(kite)* hacer volar. **5** *(flag)* enarbolar. **6** *(flee)* huir (**from**, de), salir de, abandonar.
▲ *pt* **flew** [fluː], *pp* **flown** [fləʊn], *ger* **flying**.
▷ *n (of tent)* doble techo.
▷ *n pl* **flies** **1** *(on trousers)* bragueta *f sing*. **2** *(theatre)* telar *m sing*.
⊙ **to fly away** *vi* irse volando.
fly[2] [flaɪ] *adj* GB *fam (smart)* astuto,-a.
▲ *comp* **flier**, *superl* **fliest**.
fly[3] [flaɪ] *n* mosca.
▲ *pl* **flies**.
flying ['flaɪɪŋ] *n* **1** AV aviación *f*. **2** *(action)* vuelo.
▷ *adj* **1** *(soaring)* volante; *(animal, machine)* volador,-ra, que vuela. **2** *(quick)* rápido,-a.
flyleaf ['flaɪliːf] *n* guarda.
flyover ['flaɪəʊvəʳ] *n* GB paso elevado.
fly-past ['flaɪpɑːst] *n* desfile *m* aéreo.
flytrap ['flaɪtræp] *n* BOT atrapamoscas *f*.
flyweight ['flaɪweɪt] *n* SP peso mosca.
foal [fəʊl] *n* potro,-a.
▷ *vi* parir.
foam [fəʊm] *n* espuma.

▷ *vi* **1** *(liquid)* hacer espuma. **2** *(person)* echar espumarajos, espumajear.
foamy [ˈfəʊmɪ] *adj* espumoso,-a.
▲ *comp* foamier, *superl* foamiest.
fob¹ [fɒb] *n* cadenilla de reloj.
fob² [fɒb] *vt* engañar, engatusar.
▲ *pt & pp* fobbed, *ger* fobbing.
focal [ˈfəʊkᵊl] *adj* focal.
focus [ˈfəʊkəs] *n* **1** foco. **2** *(centre)* centro:
▲ *pl* focuses o foci [ˈfəʊsaɪ].
▷ *vt* **1** *(camera, etc)* enfocar (on, -). **2** *fig (concentrate)* fijar (on, en), centrar (on, en).
▲ *pt & pp* focused o focussed, *ger* focussing o focusing.
fodder [ˈfɒdəʳ] *n* pienso, forraje *m*.
foe [fəʊ] *n* enemigo.
foetal [ˈfiːtᵊl] *adj* fetal.
foetus [ˈfiːtəs] *n* feto.
fog [fɒg] *n* niebla.
▷ *vt* **1** *(mirror, etc)* empañar. **2** *(photo)* velar. **3** *fig* complicar.
▷ *vi* empañarse (up/over, -).
▲ *pt & pp* fogged, *ger* fogging.
fogbound [ˈfɒgbaʊnd] *adj* inmovilizado,-a a causa de la niebla, paralizado,-a a causa de la niebla.
fogey [ˈfəʊgɪ] *n* carca *mf*, persona chapada a la antigua. ● **old fogey** carroza *mf*.
foggy [ˈfɒgɪ] *adj* **1** de niebla: **it's foggy** *hay niebla*. **2** *(confused)* confuso,-a.
▲ *comp* foggier, *superl* foggiest.
foghorn [ˈfɒghɔːn] *n* sirena de niebla.
foglamp [ˈfɒglæmp] *n* faro antiniebla.
foil¹ [fɔɪl] *n (fencing)* florete *m*.
foil² [fɔɪl] *vt (prevent, frustrate)* frustrar.
foil³ [fɔɪl] *n* **1** *(metal paper)* hoja de metal, papel *m* de plata. **2** *(contrast)* contraste *m*.
fold¹ [fəʊld] *n (for sheep)* redil *m*, aprisco.
fold² [fəʊld] *n* **1** *(crease)* pliegue *m*, doblez *m*. **2** GEOG pliegue *m*.
▷ *vt* **1** doblar, plegar (up, -). **2** *(wrap)* envolver.
▷ *vi* **1** doblarse, plegarse. **2** *(go bankrupt)* quebrar.
⊙ **to fold away** *vi* plegarse.
⊙ **to fold up** *vi (collapse - person)* doblarse; *(- business)* fracasar, quebrar.
folder [ˈfəʊldəʳ] *n* carpeta.
folding [ˈfəʊldɪŋ] *adj* plegable.
foliage [ˈfəʊlɪɪdʒ] *n fml* follaje *m*.
folio [ˈfəʊlɪəʊ] *n* **1** *(sheet)* folio. **2** *(book)* libro en folio.
▲ *pl* folios.
folk [fəʊk] *n pl* gente *f sing*.
▷ *adj* popular.
▷ *n pl* **folks** *fam (family)* familia *f sing*; *(friends)* amigos *mpl*.
folklore [ˈfəʊklɔːʳ] *n* folklor(e) *m*.
follicle [ˈfɒlɪkᵊl] *n* folículo.
follow [ˈfɒləʊ] *vt* **1** *(gen)* seguir. **2** *(pursue)* perseguir. **3** *(take interest in)* seguir, estar al corriente de.
▷ *vi* **1** *(gen)* seguir. **2** *(understand)* entender. **3** *(be logical)* resultar, derivarse.
⊙ **to follow up** *vt sep* **1** *(develop)* profundizar en. **2** *(investigate)* investigar.
following [ˈfɒləʊɪŋ] *adj* **1** siguiente. **2** *(winds, currents)* de cola.
▷ *prep* después de.
▷ *n (supporters)* seguidores *mpl*.
folly [ˈfɒlɪ] *n fml* locura, desatino.
▲ *pl* follies.
foment [fəʊˈment] *vt* instigar, provocar.
fond [fɒnd] *adj* **1** *(loving)* cariñoso,-a. **2** *(indulgent)* indulgente. **3** *(hope, belief)* vano,-a.
fondle [ˈfɒndᵊl] *vt* acariciar.
fondness [ˈfɒndnəs] *n* **1** cariño (for, a). **2** *(liking)* afición *f* (for, a/por).
font [fɒnt] *n* pila (bautismal).
food [fuːd] *n* comida, alimento.
foodstuffs [ˈfuːdstʌfs] *n pl* alimentos *mpl*, productos *mpl* alimenticios.
fool [fuːl] *n* **1** tonto,-a, loco,-a. **2** *(jester)* bufón,-ona
▷ *vt* engañar.
▷ *vi* bromear.
⊙ **to fool about / fool around** *vi* **1** *(be stupid)* hacer el tonto, hacer el payaso. **2** *(waste time)* perder el tiempo neciamente.
foolhardy [ˈfuːlhɑːdɪ] *adj* **1** *(risky)* temerario,-a. *(person)* intrépido,-a.
foolish [ˈfuːlɪʃ] *adj* **1** *(silly)* tonto,-a. **2** *(stupid)* estúpido,-a; *(unwise)* imprudente. **3** *(ridiculous)* ridículo,-a.
foolproof [ˈfuːlpruːf] *adj* **1** *(plan, method, idea)* infalible. **2** *(machine)* seguro,-a.
foot [fʊt] *n* **1** ANAT pie *m*. **2** *(measurement)* pie *m*. **3** *(bottom)* pie *m*. **4** *(of animal)* pata. ● **on foot** a pie.
▲ *pl* feet.
footage [ˈfʊtɪdʒ] *n* metraje *m*.
foot-and-mouth disease [fʊtᵊnˈmaʊθdɪziːz] fiebre *f* aftosa.
football [ˈfʊtbɔːl] *n* **1** *(game)* fútbol *m*, fútbol *m* americano **2** *(ball)* balón *m*. ● **football player** futbolista.
footbridge [ˈfʊtbrɪdʒ] *n* puente *m* para peatones
foothill [ˈfʊthɪl] *n* estribaciones *fpl*.
foothold [ˈfʊthəʊld] *n* **1** hueco para apoyar el pie **2** *(in job)* posición *f* segura.
footing [ˈfʊtɪŋ] *n* **1** equilibrio. **2** *(basis)* base *f*, nivel *m*. **3** *(relationship)* relación *f*.
footle [ˈfuːtl] *vi* perder el tiempo, hacer el tonto.
footlights [ˈfʊtlaɪts] *n pl* candilejas *fpl*.
footling [ˈfuːlɪŋ] *adj* trivial.
footloose [ˈfʊtluːs] *adj* libre.
footman [ˈfʊtmən] *n* lacayo, criado.
▲ *pl* footmen [ˈfʊtmɪn].
footmark [ˈfʊtmɑːk] *n* huella, pisada.
footnote [ˈfʊtnəʊt] *n* nota a pie de página.
footpath [ˈfʊtpɑːθ] *n* sendero, camino.
footplate [ˈfʊtpleɪt] *n* plataforma.
footprint [ˈfʊtprɪnt] *n* huella, pisada.
footslog [ˈfʊtslɒg] *vi* andar.
▲ *pt & pp* footslogged, *ger* footslogging.
footsore [ˈfʊtsɔːʳ] *adj* con los pies doloridos.
footstep [ˈfʊtstep] *n* paso, pisada.
footwear [ˈfʊtweəʳ] *n* calzado.
for [fɔːʳ] *prep* **1** *(intended)* para. **2** *(purpose)* para: **what's this for?** *¿para qué sirve esto?* **3** *(destination)* para. **4** *(in order to help, on behalf of)* por: **do it for me**

hazlo por mí. **5** *(because of, on account of)* por, a causa de. **6** *(past time)* durante; *(future time)* por; *(specific point in time)* para. **7** *(distance)*: **I walked for five miles** *caminé cinco millas.* **8** *(in exchange, as replacement of)* por. **9** *(in favour of, in support of)* por, a favor de. **10** *(despite)* a pesar de, para; *(considering, contrast)* para: **she's very tall for her age** *es muy alta para su edad.* **11** *(as)* de, como, por. **12** *(in order to obtain)* para: **for further details...** *para más información...*

▷ *conj fml lit* ya que, puesto que.

orage ['fɒrɪdʒ] *n (food)* forraje *m.*

▷ *vi (search, hunt)* buscar (**for**, -).

▷ *vt (rummage)* hurgar, revolver.

oray ['fɒreɪ] *n (attack, raid)* incursión *f*, correría.

▷ *vi* asaltar.

orbade [fɔː'beɪd] *pt* ⟶ **forbid.**

orbear [fɔː'beəʳ] *vi fml* abstenerse (**from**, de).

▲ *pt* **forbore** [fɔː'bɔːʳ], *pp* **forborne** [fɔː'bɔːn].

orbearance [fɔː'beərəns] *n* paciencia, tolerancia.

orbid [fə'bɪd] *vt* **1** *(prohibit)* prohibir. **2** *(make impossible)* impedir.

▲ *pt* **forbade** [fɔː'beɪd], *pp* **forbidden** [fə'bɪdən], *ger* **forbidding.**

orbidding [fə'bɪdɪŋ] *adj (stern)* severo,-a; *(unfriendly)* formidable; *(dangerous)* peligroso,-a.

orbore [fɔː'bɔːʳ] *pt* ⟶ **forbear.**

orborne [fɔː'bɔːn] *pp* ⟶ **forbear.**

orce [fɔːs] *n* **1** *(strength, power, violence)* fuerza. **2** PHYS fuerza. **3** MIL cuerpo.

▷ *vt (oblige)* forzar, obligar.

orced [fɔːst] *adj* **1** *(smile, laugh)* forzado,-a. **2** *(landing)* forzoso,-a.

orceful ['fɔːsfʊl] *adj (person, manner)* enérgico,-a; *(speech)* contundente; *(argument)* convincente.

orceps ['fɔːseps] *n pl* fórceps *m inv.*

orcible ['fɔːsəbᵊl] *adj* **1** *(violent)* forzoso,-a. **2** *(convincing)* convincente.

ord [fɔːd] *n* vado.

▷ *vt* vadear.

ore [fɔːʳ] *adj (on plane)* anterior, delantero,-a; *(on ship)* de proa.

orearm ['fɔːrɑːm] *n* antebrazo.

orebear [fɔː'beəʳ] *n* antepasado,-a.

orebode [fɔː'bəʊd] *vt* presagiar, anunciar.

oreboding [fɔː'bəʊdɪŋ] *n* presentimiento.

orecast ['fɔːkɑːst] *n* pronóstico, previsión *f.*

▷ *vt* pronosticar.

▲ *pt & pp* **forecast** o **forecasted.**

orecourt ['fɔːkɔːt] *n (of garage)* área de servicio.

orefathers ['fɔːfɑːðəz] *n pl* antepasados *mpl.*

orefinger ['fɔːfɪŋgəʳ] *n* (dedo) índice *m.*

orefront ['fɔːfrʌnt] *n* vanguardia.

orego¹ [fɔː'gəʊ] *vt (precede)* preceder.

▲ *pt* **forewent** [fɔː'went], *pp* **foregone** ['fɔːgɒn], *ger* **foregoing.**

orego² [fɔː'gəʊ] *vt* ⟶ **forgo.**

▲ *pt* **forewent** [fɔː'went], *pp* **foregone** ['fɔːgɒn], *ger* **foregoing.**

oregoing [fɔː'gəʊɪŋ] *adj* precedente.

oregone ['fɔːgɒn] *pp* ⟶ **forego.**

▷ *adj* inevitable.

foreground ['fɔːgraʊnd] *n* primer plano, primer término.

forehand ['fɔːhænd] *n* SP golpe *m* de derecho.

forehead ['fɒrɪd, 'fɔːhed] *n* frente *f.*

foreign ['fɒrɪn] *adj* **1** *(from abroad)* extranjero,-a. **2** *(dealing with other countries)* exterior. **3** *(strange)* ajeno,-a, extraño,-a.

foreigner ['fɒrɪnəʳ] *n* extranjero,-a.

foreman ['fɔːmən] *n* **1** *(of workers)* capataz *m.* **2** *(of jury)* presidente *m* del jurado.

▲ *pl* **foremen** ['fɔːmən].

foremost ['fɔːməʊst] *adj* principal.

forename ['fɔːneɪm] *n* nombre *m* (de pila).

forensic [fə'rensɪk] *adj* forense.

forerunner ['fɔːrʌnəʳ] *n* precursor,-ra.

foresaw [fɔː'sɔː] *pt* ⟶ **foresee.**

foresee [fɔː'siː] *vt* prever.

▲ *pt* **foresaw** [fɔː'sɔː], *pp* **foreseen** [fɔː'siːn], *ger* **foreseeing.**

foreseeable [fɔː'siːəbᵊl] *adj* previsible.

foreseen [fɔː'siːn] *pp* ⟶ **foresee.**

foresight ['fɔːsaɪt] *n* previsión *f.*

foreskin ['fɔːskɪn] *n* prepucio.

forest ['fɒrɪst] *n* **1** *(gen)* bosque *m.* **2** *(jungle)* selva.

▷ *adj* forestal.

forestall [fɔː'stɔːl] *vt* **1** *(preempt)* anticiparse a. **2** *(prevent)* prevenir.

forestry ['fɒrɪstrɪ] *n* silvicultura, selvicultura.

foretaste ['fɔːteɪst] *n* anticipo, muestra.

foretell [fɔː'tel] *vt* predecir, pronosticar.

▲ *pt & pp* **foretold** [fɔː'təʊld].

forethought ['fɔːθɔːt] *n* **1** previsión *f.* **2** JUR premeditación *f.*

foretold [fɔː'təʊld] *pt & pp* ⟶ **foretell.**

forever [fə'revəʳ] *adv* **1** *(all the time)* siempre. **2** *(for good)* para siempre.

forewarn [fɔː'wɔːn] *vt* prevenir.

forewent [fɔː'went] *pp* ⟶ **forego.**

foreword ['fɔːwɜːd] *n* prólogo.

forfeit ['fɔːfɪt] *n* **1** *(penalty)* pena, multa. **2** *(in games)* prenda.

▷ *vt* perder, perder (el derecho de).

forgave [fə'geɪv] *pt* ⟶ **forgive.**

forge¹ [fɔːdʒ] *vi* avanzar, adelantar(se).

forge² [fɔːdʒ] *n* **1** *(apparatus)* fragua. **2** *(smithy)* forja.

▷ *vt* **1** *(counterfeit)* falsificar. **2** *(metal)* forjar, fraguar. **3** *fig (links, etc)* forjar, formar.

forgery ['fɔːdʒərɪ] *n* falsificación *f.*

▲ *pl* **forgeries.**

forget [fə'get] *vt* **1** *(gen)* olvidar, olvidarse de. **2** *(leave behind)* dejar.

▷ *vi* olvidarse de, no recordar, descuidar.

▲ *pt* **forgot** [fə'gɒt], *pp* **forgotten** [fə'gɒtᵊn], *ger* **forgetting.**

forget-me-not [fə'getmɪnɒt] *n* BOT nomeolvides *f.*

forgive [fə'gɪv] *vt* **1** *(pardon)* perdonar. **2** *(let off debt)* perdonar.

▲ *pt* **forgave** [fə'geɪv], *pp* **forgiven** [fə'gɪvən].

forgiveness [fə'gɪvnəs] *n* perdón *m.*

forgo [fɔː'gəʊ] *vt* renunciar a, sacrificar.

▲ *pt* **forwent** [fɔː'went], *pp* **forgone** [fɔː'gɒn], *ger* **forgoing.**

forgone [*(pp)* fɔː'gɒn; *(adj)* fɔː'gɒn] *pp* ⟶ **forgo.**

▷ *adj* que era de prever, que estaba cantado,-a.

forgot [fə'gɒt] *pt* ⟶ **forget**.
forgotten [fə'gɒtən] *pp* ⟶ **forget**.
fork [fɔ:k] *n* **1** *(for eating)* tenedor *m*. **2** AGR horca, horquilla. **3** *(in road, river, etc)* bifurcación *f*.
▷ *vi* **1** *(road, river, etc)* bifurcarse. **2** *(person, car)* torcer, girar.
▷ *n pl* **forks** *(on bike)* horquilla.
⊙ **to fork out** *vt sep fam (money)* soltar, aflojar.
▷ *vi fam* desembolsar, soltar dinero.
fork-lift truck [fɔ:klɪft'trʌk] *n* carretilla elevadora.
forlorn [fə'lɔ:n] *adj* **1** *(forsaken)* abandonado,-a. **2** *(desolate)* triste. **3** *(hopeless)* desesperado,-a.
form [fɔ:m] *n* **1** *(shape, mode, etc)* forma. **2** *(kind)* clase *f*, tipo. **3** *(formality)* formas *fpl*; *(behaviour)* educación *f*. **4** *(physical condition)* forma. **5** *(mood, spirit)* humor *m*. **6** *(document)* formulario, impreso, hoja. **7** EDUC *(age group)* curso; *(class)* clase *f*. **8** *(bench)* banco. **9** GB *sl (criminal record)* antecedentes *mpl* penales.
▷ *vt* **1** *(mould)* moldear, modelar; *(make)* hacer, formar; *(character)* formar. **2** *(be, constitute)* formar, constituir. **3** *fig (idea)* hacerse; *(impression, opinion)* formarse; *(relationship)* hacer; *(habit)* adquirir; *(plan)* concebir.
formal ['fɔ:məl] *adj* **1** *(official)* formal, oficial. **2** *(correct)* formal; *(traditional)* tradicional. **3** *(dress, dinner)* de etiqueta. **4** *(visit)* de cumplido. **5** *(person, language)* ceremonioso,-a, formalista. **6** *(ordered)* formal, ordenado,-a.
formality [fɔ:'mælɪtɪ] *n (correctness)* formalidad *f*; *(convention)* ceremonia.
▲ *pl* **formalities**.
formalize ['fɔ:məlaɪz] *vt* **1** *(make official)* formalizar. **2** *(make formal)* dar carácter formal a. **3** *(give form to)* dar forma a.
format ['fɔ:mæt] *n* formato.
▷ *vt* COMPUT formatear.
▲ *pt & pp* **formatted**, *ger* **formatting**.
formation [fɔ:'meɪʃən] *n* **1** *(gen)* formación *f*. **2** *(establishment)* creación *f*.
former ['fɔ:mər] *adj* **1** *(earlier)* antiguo,-a; *(person)* ex. **2** *(of two)* primero,-a.
▷ *pron* **the former** aquél, aquélla.
formerly ['fɔ:məlɪ] *adv (previously)* antiguamente, antes.
formidable ['fɔ:mɪdəbəl] *adj* **1** *(impressive)* formidable. **2** *(daunting)* temible, imponente. **3** *(difficult to overcome)* enorme.
formula ['fɔ:mjələ] *n* fórmula.
▲ *pl* **formulas** o **formulae** ['fɔ:mjʊli:].
formulate ['fɔ:mjəleɪt] *vt* formular.
formulation [fɔ:mjə'leɪʃən] *n* formulación *f*.
forsake [fə'seɪk] *vt* **1** *fml (abandon)* abandonar. **2** *(give up)* renunciar a.
▲ *pt* **forsook** [fə'sʊk], *pp* **forsaken** [fə'seɪkən].
forswear [fɔ:'sweər] *vt fml* renunciar a, abjurar de.
▲ *pt* **forswore** [fɔ:'swɔ:r], *pp* **forsworn** [fɔ:'swɔ:rn].
fort [fɔ:t] *n* fuerte *m*.
forte[1] ['fɔ:teɪ] *n* fuerte *m*.
forte[2] ['fɔ:teɪ] *adj* MUS forte.
▷ *adv* forte.
forth [fɔ:θ] *adv (onwards)* en adelante.

forthcoming [fɔ:θ'kʌmɪŋ] *adj* **1** *fml (happening i near future)* próximo,-a. **2** *(available)* disponible. *(communicative)* comunicativo,-a, dispuesto,-a hablar.
forthright ['fɔ:θraɪt] *adj* **1** *(person)* franco,-a. *(speech, action, etc)* directo,-a.
forthwith [fɔ:θ'wɪθ] *adv fml* inmediatamente.
forties ['fɔ:tɪz] *n pl* **the forties** los años *mpl* cuarenta, los cuarenta *mpl*.
Consulta también **sixties**.
fortieth ['fɔ:tɪəθ] *adj* cuadragésimo,-a.
▷ *adv* en cuadragésimo lugar.
▷ *n (fraction)* cuadragésimo; *(one part)* cuadragésim parte *f*.
Consulta también **sixtieth**.
fortification [fɔ:tɪfɪ'keɪʃən] *n* fortificación *f*.
fortify ['fɔ:tɪfaɪ] *vt* **1** MIL fortificar. **2** *(strengthen)* fortalecer. **3** *(wine)* fortificar, encabezar; *(food)* enriquecer.
▲ *pt & pp* **fortified**, *ger* **fortifying**.
fortitude ['fɔ:tɪtju:d] *n* fortaleza, fuerza.
fortnight ['fɔ:tnaɪt] *n* GB quincena, quince días *mpl*
fortress ['fɔ:trəs] *n* fortaleza.
fortuitous [fɔ:'tju:ɪtəs] *adj* **1** *(lucky)* fortuito,-a, casual. **2** *(accidental)* accidental.
fortunate ['fɔ:tʃənət] *adj* afortunado,-a.
fortunately ['fɔ:tʃənətlɪ] *adv* afortunadamente, pc suerte.
fortune ['fɔ:tʃən] *n* **1** *(fate)* fortuna; *(luck)* suerte *f*. *(money)* fortuna.
▷ *n pl* **fortunes** *(luck)* suerte *f*; *(ups and downs)* vicisitudes *fpl*.
fortune-teller ['fɔ:tʃəntelər] *n* adivino,-a.
forty ['fɔ:tɪ] *adj* cuarenta.
▷ *n* cuarenta *m*.
Consulta también **sixty**.
forum ['fɔ:rəm] *n* foro.
forward ['fɔ:wəd] *adv* [Como adverbio tambié **forwards**.] **1** *(gen)* hacia adelante. **2** *(time)* en adelante.
▷ *adj* **1** *(position)* delantero,-a, frontal; *(movement)* hacia delante. **2** *(future)* a largo plazo. **3** *(advance* adelantado,-a, precoz. **4** *(too bold, too eage* atrevido,-a, descarado,-a, fresco,-a.
▷ *vt* **1** *(send on to new address)* remitir; *(send goods)* enviar, expedir. **2** *fml (further, advance)* adelantar, fomentar.
forwent [fɔ:'went] *pt* ⟶ **forgo**.
fossil ['fɒsəl] *n* fósil *m*.
▷ *adj* fósil.
fossilization [fɒsəlaɪ'zeɪʃən] *n* fosilización *f*.
fossilize ['fɒsəlaɪz] *vt* fosilizar.
▷ *vi* fosilizarse.
foster ['fɒstər] *vt* **1** *(child)* acoger temporalmente. *(encourage)* fomentar, promover.
▷ *adj* adoptivo,-a.
fought [fɔ:t] *pt & pp* ⟶ **fight**.
foul [faʊl] *adj* **1** *(dirty, disgusting)* asqueroso,-a; *(smel* fétido,-a. **2** *(language)* grosero,-a, obsceno,-a. **3** *fr (evil)* vil, atroz. **4** *(chimney, pipe, etc)* atascado,-a.
▷ *n* SP falta (**on**, contra).

▷ *vt* **1** *(dirty)* ensuciar; *(pollute)* contaminar. **2** *(snag)* enredar. **3** SP cometer una falta contra.

found[1] [faʊnd] *vt (metals)* fundir.

found[2] [faʊnd] *vt* **1** *(establish)* fundar. **2** *(base)* basar (on, en).

found[3] [faʊnd] *pt & pp* ⟶ **find.**

foundation [faʊn'deɪʃᵊn] *n* **1** *(act, organization)* fundación *f*. **2** *(basis)* fundamento, base *f*. **3** *(make-up)* base *f*.

▷ *n pl* **foundations** cimientos *mpl*.

founder[1] ['faʊndəʳ] *vi* **1** *(plan, etc)* irse a pique, fracasar, malograrse. **2** *(ship)* hundirse. **3** *(horse)* dar un traspié.

founder[2] ['faʊndəʳ] *n (person)* fundador,-ra.

foundry ['faʊndrɪ] *n* fundición *f*.

▲ *pl* **foundries.**

fountain ['faʊntᵊn] *n* **1** fuente *f*. **2** *(jet)* surtidor *m*, chorro. **3** *(source, origin)* fuente *f*.

four [fɔːʳ] *adj* cuatro.

▷ *n* cuatro.

Consulta también **six.**

fourfold ['fɔːfəʊld] *adj* cuádruple.

▷ *adv* cuatro veces.

foursome ['fɔːsəm] *n grupo de cuatro personas.*

fourteen [fɔː'tiːn] *adj* catorce.

▷ *n* catorce *m*.

Consulta también **six.**

fourteenth [fɔː'tiːnθ] *adj* decimocuarto,-a.

▷ *adv* en decimocuarto lugar.

▷ *n* **1** *(in series)* decimocuarto,-a. **2** *(fraction)* decimocuarto; *(one part)* decimocuarta parte *f*.

Consulta también **sixth.**

fourth [fɔːθ] *adj* cuarto,-a.

▷ *adv* cuarto, en cuarto lugar.

▷ *n* **1** *(in series)* cuarto,-a. **2** *(fraction)* cuarto; *(one part)* cuarta parte *f*.

Consulta también **sixth.**

fourth-former ['fɔːθfɔːməʳ] *n* GB alumno,-a del cuarto curso.

fowl [faʊl] *n* ave *f* de corral.

▲ *pl* **fowl.**

fox [fɒks] *n* **1** *(animal)* zorro,-a. **2** *(person)* zorro,-a.

▷ *vt* **1** *fam (trick)* engañar. **2** *(confuse)* dejar perplejo,-a, confundir, despistar.

foxy ['fɒksɪ] *adj* **1** *fam* astuto,-a. **2** US *sl (sexy)* sexy.

▲ *comp* **foxier,** *superl* **foxiest.**

foyer ['fɔɪeɪ, 'fɔɪəʳ] *n* vestíbulo.

Fr[1] ['fɑːðəʳ] *abbr* REL **(Father)** Padre *m*; *(abbreviation)* P., Pe.

Fr[2] [frentʃ] *abbr* **(French)** francés,-esa; *(abbreviation)* fr.

fracas ['frækɑː] *n* reyerta.

fraction ['frækʃᵊn] *n* **1** *(division)* fracción *f*. **2** *(small part, bit)* poquito.

fractional ['frækʃənᵊl] *adj* **1** *(in fractions)* fraccionario,-a. **2** *(very small)* muy pequeño,-a, ínfimo,-a.

fractious ['frækʃəs] *adj* irritable, malhumorado,-a.

fracture ['fræktʃəʳ] *n* fractura.

▷ *vt* fracturar.

▷ *vi* fracturarse.

fragile ['frædʒaɪl] *adj* **1** frágil. **2** *fig (health)* delicado,-a.

fragility [frə'dʒɪlɪtɪ] *n* fragilidad *f*.

fragment [*(n)* 'frægmənt; *(vb)* fræg'ment] *n* fragmento.

▷ *vi* fragmentarse.

fragmentation [frægmən'teɪʃᵊn] *n* fragmentación *f*.

fragrance ['freɪgrəns] *n* fragancia.

fragrant ['freɪgrənt] *adj* fragante.

frail [freɪl] *adj* **1** frágil, delicado,-a. **2** *(morally weak)* débil.

frame [freɪm] *n* **1** *(of building, machine, tent)* armazón *f*. **2** *(of bed)* armadura. **3** *(of bicycle)* cuadro. **4** *(of spectacles)* montura. **5** *(of human, animal - body)* cuerpo; *(- build)* constitución *f*. **6** *(of window, door, picture, etc)* marco. **7** *(order, system)* estructura, sistema *m*. **8** CINEM fotograma *m*. **9** *(of comic)* viñeta. **10** *(in billiards - triangle)* triángulo; *(- round)* jugada.

▷ *vt* **1** *(picture)* enmarcar. **2** *(door)* encuadrar. **3** *fam (set up)* tender una trampa a ALGN para incriminarlo. **4** *fml (question, proposal)* formular; *(plan)* elaborar.

frame-up ['freɪmʌp] *n fam* trampa.

framework ['freɪmwɜːk] *n* **1** armazón *f*. **2** *fig* estructura, sistema *m*, marco.

franc [fræŋk] *n* franco.

France [frɑːns] *n* Francia.

franchise ['fræntʃaɪz] *n* **1** COMM concesión *f*, franquicia. **2** *(vote)* derecho de voto.

frank [fræŋk] *adj* franco,-a.

▷ *vt* franquear.

frankincense ['fræŋkɪnsens] *n* incienso.

frantic ['fræntɪk] *adj* **1** *(hectic)* frenético,-a. **2** *(anxious)* desesperado,-a.

fraternal [frə'tɜːnᵊl] *adj* fraternal.

fraternity [frə'tɜːnɪtɪ] *n* **1** *(brotherhood)* fraternidad *f*. **2** *(society)* asociación *f*. **3** REL hermandad *f*, cofradía. **4** US *(university)* club *m* de estudiantes.

▲ *pl* **fraternities.**

fraternization [frætənaɪ'zeɪʃᵊn] *n* fraternización *f*.

fraternize ['frætənaɪz] *vi* fraternizar.

fraud [frɔːd] *n* **1** *(act)* fraude *m*. **2** *(person)* impostor,-ra, farsante *mf*.

fraudulent ['frɔːdjələnt] *adj* fraudulento,-a.

fraught [frɔːt] *adj* **1** *(filled, charged)* lleno,-a (**with**, de), cargado,-a (**with**, de). **2** *fam (worried)* nervioso,-a, alterado,-a, tenso,-a.

fray[1] [freɪ] *vi* **1** *(cloth)* deshilacharse, raerse. **2** *(tempers, nerves, etc)* crisparse.

fray[2] [freɪ] *n* contienda, lucha.

frazzle ['fræzᵊl] *n* agotamiento.

freak [friːk] *n* **1** *(monster)* monstruo; *(strange person)* bicho raro. **2** *(strange event)* anomalía. **3** *fam (fan)* fanático,-a. **4** *(eccentric)* estrafalario,-a.

▷ *adj (unusual)* insólito,-a, extraño,-a, anormal; *(unexpected)* inesperado,-a, imprevisto,-a.

⊙ **to freak out** *vt sep* flipar, alucinar.

freckle ['frekᵊl] *n* peca.

free [friː] *adj* **1** *(gen)* libre. **2** *(without cost)* gratuito,-a, gratis; *(exempt)* libre (**from**, de).

▷ *adv* **1** *(gratis)* gratis. **2** *(loose)* suelto,-a. **3** *(in free manner)* libremente, con toda libertad.

▷ *vt* **1** *(liberate, release - person)* poner en libertad, liberar; *(- animal)* soltar. **2** *(rid)* deshacerse (**of/from**, de),

librarse (**of/from**, de). 3 *(loosen, untie)* soltar, desatar. 4 *(exempt)* eximir (**from**, de).
freedom ['fri:dəm] *n* libertad *f*.
freehand ['fri:hænd] *adj* a mano alzada.
free-handed ['fri:hændɪd] *adj (generous)* generoso,-a, liberal.
freehold ['fri:həʊld] *n* JUR derecho de dominio absoluto.
freelance ['fri:lɑ:ns] *adj* independiente, autónomo,-a.
▷ *n* persona que trabaja por cuenta propia.
▷ *vi* trabajar por cuenta propia.
Freemason ['fri:meɪsᵊn] *n* masón,-ona, francmasón,-ona.
free-range ['fri:'reɪndʒ] *adj* de granja.
freestanding [fri:'stændɪŋ] *adj* independiente.
freestyle ['fri:staɪl] *n (swimming)* estilo libre.
freethinker [fri:'θɪŋkəʳ] *n* librepensador,-ra.
freeway ['fri:weɪ] *n* US autopista.
freewheel [fri:'wi:l] *vi (cycle)* ir a rueda libre; *(car)* ir en punto muerto.
freeze [fri:z] *n* 1 METEOR helada. 2 COMM congelación *f*.
▷ *vt (gen)* congelar.
▷ *vi* 1 *(liquid)* helarse; *(food)* congelarse. 2 METEOR helar. 3 *fig (stop suddenly)* quedarse inmóvil, quedarse paralizado,-a.
▲ *pt* **froze** ['frəʊz], *pp* **frozen** ['frəʊzən], *ger* **freezing**.
freezer ['fri:zəʳ] *n* congelador *m*.
freeze-up ['fri:zʌp] *n* helada.
freight [freɪt] *n* 1 *(transport)* transporte *m*. 2 *(goods)* carga, flete *m*. 3 *(price)* flete *m*.
▷ *vt* transportar.
freightage ['freɪtɪðz] *n* flete.
freighter ['freɪtəʳ] *n (ship)* buque *m* de carga; *(aircraft)* avión *m* de carga.
French [frentʃ] *adj* francés,-esa.
▷ *n (language)* francés *m*.
▷ *n pl* **the French** los franceses *mpl*.
Frenchman ['frentʃmən] *n* francés *m*.
▲ *pl* **Frenchmen** ['frentʃmən].
Frenchwoman ['frentʃwʊmən] *n* francesa.
▲ *pl* **Frenchwomen** ['frentʃwɪmɪn].
frenetic [frə'netɪk] *adj* frenético,-a.
frenzy ['frenzɪ] *n* frenesí *m*.
▲ *pl* **frenzies**.
frequency ['fri:kwənsɪ] *n* frecuencia.
▲ *pl* **frequencies**.
frequent [*(adj)* 'fri:kwənt; *(vb)* frɪ'kwent] *adj* frecuente.
▷ *vt* frecuentar.
frequently ['fri:kwəntlɪ] *adv* frecuentemente, con frecuencia.
fresco ['freskəʊ] *n* fresco.
▲ *pl* **frescos** o **frescoes**.
fresh [freʃ] *adj* 1 *(food)* fresco,-a. 2 *(water)* dulce. 3 *(air)* puro,-a. 4 *(weather)* fresco,-a; *(wind)* recio,-a. 5 *(complexion)* sano,-a. 6 *(clothes)* limpio,-a. 7 *fig (new)* nuevo,-a. 8 *(made recently)* reciente, fresco, -a. 9 *(original)* nuevo,-a. 10 *(refreshed, alert)* fresco,-a, lleno,-a de vigor. 11 *(bold, forward, cheeky)* fresco, -a, descarado,-a.
freshen ['freʃᵊn] *vt* refrescar.
▷ *vi* refrescarse.
freshener ['freʃᵊnəʳ] *n* ambientador *m*.
freshly ['freʃlɪ] *adv* recién.
freshman ['freʃmən] *n* US estudiante *mf* de prime[r] curso (de universidad), novato,-a.
▲ *pl* **freshmen** ['freʃmən].
freshness ['freʃnəs] *n* 1 *(brightness)* frescura. 2 *(coo[l])* frescor *m*. 3 *(newness)* novedad *f*. 4 *fam (cheek)* descaro.
freshwater ['freʃwæɔ:təʳ] *adj* de agua dulce: **fresh[]water fish** *pez de agua dulce*.
fret[1] [fret] *vi* preocuparse (**about/at/over**, por).
▷ *vt (wear away)* raer, desgastar.
▲ *pt & pp* **fretted**, *ger* **fretting**.
▷ *n (worry)* preocupación *f*.
fret[2] [fret] *n (on guitar)* traste *m*.
fret[3] [fret] *n (fretwork)* calado.
fretwork ['fretwɜ:k] *n* calado.
friar [fraɪəʳ] *n* fraile *m*.
friary ['fraɪərɪ] *n* monasterio.
▲ *pl* **friaries**.
fricassee ['frɪkəsi:] *n* estofado.
fricative ['frɪkətɪv] *adj* fricativo,-a.
▷ *n* fricativa.
friction ['frɪkʃᵊn] *n* 1 *(conflict)* fricción *f*, roces *mpl*. [2] *(rubbing)* rozamiento, roce *m*.
Friday ['fraɪdɪ] *n* viernes *m*.
Para ejemplos de uso, consulta **Saturday**.
fridge [frɪdʒ] *n* nevera, frigorífico.
fried [fraɪd] *adj* frito,-a.
friend [frend] *n* 1 amigo,-a, compañero,-a. 2 *(help[er], supporter)* amigo,-a (**of/to**, de). 3 *(Quaker)* cuáquero,-a.
friendly ['frendlɪ] *adj* 1 *(person)* simpático,-a, amable. 2 *(atmosphere)* acogedor,-ra. 3 *(smile, manne[r], etc)* amable.
▲ *comp* **friendlier**, *superl* **friendliest**.
friendship ['frendʃɪp] *n* amistad *f*.
frieze [fri:z] *n* 1 *(painted)* friso. 2 *(wallpaper)* cenefa
frigate ['frɪgət] *n* fragata.
fright [fraɪt] *n* 1 *(shock)* susto. 2 *(fear)* miedo.
frighten ['fraɪtᵊn] *vt* asustar, espantar.
frightfully ['fraɪtfʊlɪ] *adv fam* muchísimo.
frigid ['frɪdʒɪd] *adj* 1 *(sexually)* frígido,-a. 2 *(icy)* glacial, muy frío,-a. 3 *(unfriendly)* glacial.
frill [frɪl] *n (on dress)* volante *m*.
▷ *n pl* **frills** *(decorations)* adornos *mpl*.
fringe [frɪndʒ] *n* 1 *(decorative)* fleco. 2 *(of hair)* flequillo. 3 *(edge)* borde *m*.
▷ *vt* poner un fleco.
frisk [frɪsk] *vt (search)* registrar, cachear.
▷ *vi (frolic)* brincar, retozar.
frisky ['frɪskɪ] *adj (child, animal)* retozón,-ona, juguetón,-ona; *(adult)* vivo,-a, vital.
▲ *comp* **friskier**, *superl* **friskiest**.
fritter ['frɪtəʳ] *n* CULIN buñuelo.
⊙ **to fritter away** *vi pej (money)* malgastar; *(time)* desperdiciar.
frivolity [frɪ'vɒlətɪ] *n* frivolidad *f*.
▲ *pl* **frivolities**.
frizzle ['frɪzᵊl] *vi* achicharrarse.

rizzy ['frɪzɪ] *adj* crespo,-a, rizado,-a.
▲ *comp* **frizzier**, *superl* **frizziest**.

rock [frɒk] *n* vestido.

rock-coat ['frɒkkəʊt] *n* levita.

rog [frɒg] *n* rana.

rolic ['frɒlɪk] *vi* juguetear, retozar.
▷ *n* aventura.

rolicsome ['frɒlɪksəm] *adj* juguetón,-ona.

rom [frɒm] *prep* **1** *(starting at)* de; *(train, plane)* procedente de: **the train from Madrid** *el tren procedente de Madrid*. **2** *(origin, source)* de, desde. **3** *(because of)* por, a causa de. **4** *(considering, according to)* según, por. **5** *(indicating difference)* de; *(when distinguishing)* entre. **6** *(indicating position)* desde.

rond [frɒnd] *n* fronda.

ront [frʌnt] *n* **1** *(forward part)* parte *f* delantera, frente *m*. **2** *(of shirt, etc)* pechera. **3** METEOR frente *m*. **4** *(facade)* fachada. **5** MIL frente *m*. **6** *(promenade)* paseo marítimo. **7** *fig (illegal business, etc)* tapadera. **8** *fig (outward appearance)* apariencia; *(pretence)* fachada. **9** *(specific field of activity)* asunto, terreno.
▷ *adj* delantero,-a, de delante.
▷ *vi (face)* dar (**on/onto**, a).
▷ *vt* **1** *(lead, head)* encabezar. **2** *(present)* presentar.

ront-bench ['frʌntbentʃ] *adj* GB *de las dos primeras filas de escaños.*

rontier ['frʌntɪəʳ] *n* frontera.
▷ *adj* fronterizo,-a.
▷ *n pl* **the frontiers** fronteras *fpl*, límites *mpl*.

ront-page ['frʌntpeɪdʒ] *adj* de portada, de primera plana.

rost [frɒst] *n* **1** *(covering)* escarcha. **2** *(freezing)* helada.
▷ *vt* **1** helar, cubrir de escarcha. **2** *(plants)* quemar. **3** *(glass)* esmerilar. **4** *(cake, etc)* recubrir con azúcar glas, escarchar.

rostbite ['frɒstbaɪt] *n* congelación *f*.

rostbitten ['frɒstbɪtᵊn] *adj* congelado,-a.

rosted ['frɒstɪd] *adj* **1** *(glass)* esmerilado,-a. **2** CULIN recubierto,-a de azúcar glas, escarchado,-a.

rosty ['frɒstɪ] *adj* **1** METEOR *(cold with frost)* de helada; *(very cold)* helado,-a, muy frío,-a. **2** METEOR *(covered with frost)* escarchado,-a, cubierto,-a de escarcha. **3** *fig (unfriendly)* glacial.
▲ *comp* **frostier**, *superl* **frostiest**.
▷ *vi* **1** *(liquid)* hacer espuma. **2** *(from mouth)* espumajear, echar espumarajos por la boca.

rown [fraʊn] *n* ceño.
▷ *vi* fruncir el ceño.

roze [frəʊz] *pt* → **freeze**.

rozen ['frəʊzᵊn] *pp* → **freeze**.
▷ *adj* **1** *(water, ground)* helado,-a. **2** *(food)* congelado,-a.

ructify ['frʌktɪfaɪ] *vi* fructificar, dar fruto.
▲ *pt & pp* **fructified**, *ger* **fructifying**.

ructose ['frʌktəʊz] *n* fructosa.

rugal ['fruːgᵊl] *adj* frugal.

ruit [fruːt] *n* **1** *(food)* fruta. **2** BOT fruto. **3** *(result, reward)* fruto.
▷ *adj* de fruta. ● **fruit juice** zumo de fruta.
▷ *vi* dar fruto.

fruitcake ['fruːtkeɪk] *n* **1** *(cake)* plumcake *m*, pastel *m* de frutas pasas. **2** *fam (eccentric person)* excéntrico,-a.

fruitful ['fruːtful] *adj* fructífero,-a, provechoso,-a.

fruition [fruː'ɪʃᵊn] *n* realización *f*.

frustrate [frʌ'streɪt] *vt* **1** *(thwart)* frustrar. **2** *(upset)* frustrar.

frustrated [frʌ'streɪtɪd] *adj (dissatisfied)* frustrado,-a, insatisfecho,-a, descontento,-a; *(unfulfilled)* frustrado,-a.

frustration [frʌ'streɪʃᵊn] *n* frustración *f*.

fry[1] [fraɪ] *vt* freír.
▷ *vi* **1** freírse. **2** *fig (in sun)* asarse, achicharrarse.
▲ *pt & pp* **fried**, *ger* **frying**.

fry[2] [fraɪ] *n pl (fish)* alevines *mpl*.

fryer [fraɪəʳ] *n* **1** *(frying pan)* sartén *f*. **2** US pollo tomatero.

frying pan ['fraɪɪŋpæn] *n* sartén *f*.

ft ['fʊt, 'fiːt] *abbr* (**foot**, **feet**) pie *m*, pies *mpl*.

fuck [fʌk] *vt taboo* joder, follar.
▷ *phr* **the fuck** *taboo (used as intensifier)* coño, hostias.

fuddle ['fʌdᵊl] *vt (confuse)* confundir; *(intoxicate)* emborrachar.
▷ *n* confusión *f*.

fuddled ['fʊdᵊld] *adj* confuso,-a.

fuddy-duddy ['fʌdɪdʌdɪ] *n fam* persona chapada a la antigua.
▲ *pl* **fuddy-duddies**.

fudge[1] [fʌdʒ] *n dulce hecho con azúcar, leche y mantequilla.*

fudge[2] [fʌdʒ] *vt* **1** *(do clumsily)* pifiar, fallar. **2** *(falsify)* amañar. **3** *(evade)* eludir.

fuel [fjʊəl] *n* **1** *(gen)* combustible *m*. **2** *(for motors)* carburante *m*. **3** *fig* pábulo.
▷ *vt* **1** *(plane)* abastecer de combustible; *(car)* echar gasolina. **2** *fig (make worse)* empeorar; *(encourage)* alimentar.

fug [fʌg] *n fam* aire *m* cargado, aire *m* viciado.

fugitive ['fjuːdʒɪtɪv] *n (from danger, war, etc)* fugitivo,-a; *(from justice)* prófugo,-a.
▷ *adj* **1** fugitivo,-a. **2** *lit (fleeting)* fugaz, efímero,-a.

fugue [fjuːg] *n* fuga.

fulcrum ['fʊlkrəm] *n* fulcro.

fulfil [fʊl'fɪl] *vt* **1** *(promise, duty)* cumplir. **2** *(task, plan, ambition)* realizar. **3** *(role, function, order)* efectuar, desempeñar. **4** *(need, desire, wish)* satisfacer.
▲ *pt & pp* **fulfilled**, *ger* **fulfilling**.

fulfill [fʊl'fɪl] *vt* US→ **fulfil**.

fulfilled [fʊl'fɪld] *pt & pp* → **fulfill**.
▷ *adj* realizado,-a, satisfecho,-a.

full [fʊl] *adj* **1** *(gen)* lleno,-a. **2** *(week, day)* cargado,-a, movido,-a. **3** *(entire, complete)* completo,-a. **4** *(highest or greatest possible)* máximo,-a. **5** *(plump - figure)* llenito,-a, relleno,-a; *(- face)* redondo,-a, lleno,-a; *(- lips)* grueso,-a. **6** *(clothing - loose fitting)* holgado,-a, amplio,-a; *(skirt)* de mucho vuelo; *(sleeve)* ancho,-a.
▷ *adv (directly)* justo, de lleno.

full-blown ['fʊlbləʊn] *adj* **1** *(having all characteristics)* auténtico,-a, verdadero,-a. **2** *(in full bloom)* en flor.

full-length [fʊl'leŋθ] *adj* **1** *(mirror, portrait)* de cuerpo entero. **2** *(garment)* largo,-a. **3** *(film)* de largo metraje.

fullness ['fʊlnəs] *n* **1** *(being full)* plenitud *f*, abundancia. **2** *(width)* amplitud *f*.
full-scale [fʊl'skeɪl] *adj* **1** *(actual size)* de tamaño natural. **2** *(complete, total - gen)* completo,-a, total; *(- investigation, search)* a fondo.
full-time [fʊl'taɪm] *adj* a tiempo completo, de jornada completa.
▷ *adv* a tiempo completo.
fully ['fʊlɪ] *adv* **1** *(completely)* completamente, enteramente, plenamente. **2** *(at least, quite)* por lo menos.
fully-fledged ['fʊlɪfledʒd] *adj* hecho,-a y derecho,-a, con todas las de la ley.
fulminate ['fʌlmɪneɪt] *vi* tronar (**against**, contra).
fulsome ['fʊlsəm] *adj* exagerado,-a, excesivo,-a.
fumble ['fʌmb^əl] *vt* dejar caer.
▷ *vi* **to fumble for** buscar a tientas.
▷ *vi* **to fumble with** hacer torpemente.
⊙ **to fumble about / fumble around** *vi* andar a tientas.
fume [fjʊ:m] *vi* **1** *(produce smoke, etc)* echar humo. **2** *fig (show anger)* echar humo, subirse por las paredes: **when I got home my father was fuming** *cuando llegué a casa mi padre estaba que se subía por las paredes.*
▷ *n pl* **fumes** humos *mpl.*
fumigate ['fjʊ:mɪgeɪt] *vt* fumigar.
fun [fʌn] *n* **1** *(enjoyment, pleasure)* diversión *f*: **it'll be good fun when we go camping** *lo pasaremos muy bien cuando nos vayamos de camping;* **skiing is great fun!** *¡esquiar es divertidísimo!* **2** *(amusement)* gracia: **it's no fun staying in alone on Saturday night** *no tiene gracia quedarse solo en casa el sábado por la noche;* **well it's not much fun for me** *pues yo no le veo la gracia.*
▷ *adj (humorous, amusing)* divertido,-a.
function ['fʌŋkʃ^ən] *n* **1** *(purpose, use, duty)* función *f*: **that is not the function of a mere assistant** *eso no corresponde a un simple ayudante;* **in my function as chairperson** *en mi calidad de presidente.* **2** *(ceremony)* acto, ceremonia; *(reception)* recepción *f*. **3** MATH función *f*. ■ **to fulfil** (US **fullfil**) **a function** desempeñar una función. ● **function key** tecla de función.
▷ *vi* **1** *(work)* funcionar: **do you know how this machine functions?** *¿sabes cómo funciona esta máquina?* **2** *(act)* funcionar: **the human brain functions as a computer** *el cerebro humano funciona como un ordenador.*
functional ['fʌŋkʃən^əl] *adj* **1** *(operational)* funcional. **2** *(practical, useful)* práctico,-a.
functionary ['fʌŋkʃ^ənərɪ] *n* funcionario,-a.
▲ *pl* **functionaries.**
fund [fʌnd] *n* **1** *(sum of money)* fondo. **2** *(supply)* fuente *f*.
▷ *vt* **1** *(finance)* patrocinar. **2** *(debt)* consolidar.
▷ *n pl* **funds** *(financial resources)* fondos *mpl.* ■ **to be short of funds** andar corto,-a de dinero.
fundamental [fʌndə'ment^əl] *adj* **1** *(central, basic)* fundamental, básico,-a. **2** *(necessary, essential)* esencial (**to**, para).
▷ *n pl* **fundamentals** *(essential part, basic rule)* fundamentos *mpl*, reglas *fpl* básicas.
fundamentalist [fʌndə'ment^əlɪst] *adj* REL fundamentalista, integrista.
▷ *n* REL fundamentalista *mf*, integrista *mf*.
fundamentally [fʌndə'ment^əlɪ] *adv* **1** *(basically)* básicamente. **2** *(radically)* fundamentalmente.
funeral ['fjʊ:n^ərəl] *n* entierro, funeral *m*.
▷ *adj* fúnebre.
funereal [fjʊ:'nɪərɪəl] *adj* fúnebre.
funfair ['fʌnfeə^r] *n* GB feria, parque *m* de atracciones.
fungicidal [fʌndʒ'saɪd^əl] *adj* fungicida.
fungicide ['fʌndʒɪsaɪd] *n* fungicida *m*.
fungus ['fʌŋgəs] *n* hongo.
▲ *pl* **funguses** o **fungi** ['fʌŋdʒaɪ].
funicular [fjʊ:'nɪkjələ^r] *n* funicular *m*.
funk[1] [fʌnk] *n* **1** *fam (fear, anxiety)* canguelo, acojon*m*. **2** *(coward)* cagado,-a, gallina.
▷ *vt (avoid through fear)* rajarse ante, cagarse.
funk[2] [fʌnk] *n* MUS funky *m*.
funky ['fʌnkɪ] *adj* **1** MUS funky. **2** *fam (fashionable)* guay, chulo,-a.
▲ *comp* **funkier**, *superl* **funkiest.**
funnel ['fʌn^əl] *n* **1** *(for liquid)* embudo. **2** *(chimney)* chimenea.
▷ *vt* verter por un embudo.
▷ *vi* verterse.
▷ *vt fig (channel)* encauzar.
▲ *pt & pp* **funnelled** (US **funneled**), *ger* **funnelling** (US **funneling**).
funnily ['fʌnɪlɪ] *adv (strangely)* de manera extraña, de modo raro.
funny ['fʌnɪ] *adj* **1** *(amusing)* gracioso,-a, divertido,-a: **my little niece is so funny** *mi sobrinita es tan graciosa;* **I don't find your remarks at all funny** *tus comentarios no son nada graciosos.* **2** *(strange)* raro,-a, extraño,-a, curioso,-a: **the funny thing is that...** *lo curioso es que...* **3** *fam (slightly ill)* rarillo,-a, malito,-a; *(slightly mad)* chiflado,-a: **I feel funny** *no me encuentro bien.*
▲ *comp* **funnier**, *superl* **funniest.**
fur [fɜ:^r] *n* **1** *(of living animal)* pelo, pelaje *m*. **2** *(of dead animal)* piel *f*. **3** *(garment)* abrigo de piel. **4** *(on appliance)* sarro; *(on tongue)* sarro, saburra.
▷ *adj* de piel. ● **fur coat** abrigo de pieles.
▷ *vi* calcificarse.
furbish ['fɜ:bɪʃ] *vt* pulir.
⊙ **to furbish up** *vt sep* renovar, restaurar.
furious ['fjʊərɪəs] *adj* **1** *(very angry)* furioso,-a: **she'll be furious if we break anything** *se pondrá furiosa si rompemos algo;* **he's got a furious temper** *tiene muy mal genio.* **2** *(violent, wild, uncontrolled)* furioso,-a, violento,-a; *(vigorous)* vertiginoso,-a, frenético,-a.
furiously ['fjʊərɪəslɪ] *adv* **1** *(angrily)* con furia, furiosamente. **2** *(vigorously)* frenéticamente.
furl [fɜ:l] *vt* arrollar, enrollar.
▷ *vi* arrollarse, enrollarse.
furlong ['fɜ:lɒŋ] *n* ≈ *201 metros.*
furnace ['fɜ:nəs] *n* horno.
furnish ['fɜ:nɪʃ] *vt* **1** *(house, etc)* amueblar (**with**, de): **I'd like to rent a furnished flat** (US **apartment**) *quisiera alquilar un piso amueblado.* **2** *fml (supply - materials)* suministrar, proveer; *(- information, etc)* facilitar, proporcionar.

urnishings ['fɜ:nɪʃɪŋz] *n pl muebles, cortinas y alfombras.*

urniture ['fɜ:nɪtʃəʳ] *n* mobiliario, muebles *mpl*: I need some new furniture *necesito unos muebles nuevos.*

uror ['fjʊ:rɔ:ʳ] *n* US→ **furore.**

urore [fjʊ'rɔ:rɪ] *n (uproar - anger)* ola de protestas; *(- enthusiasm)* ola de entusiasmo.

urrier ['fʌrɪəʳ] *n* peletero,-a.

urrow ['fʌrəʊ] *n* **1** AGR surco. **2** *(wrinkle)* arruga.
▷ *vt* **1** AGR surcar. **2** *(forehead)* arrugar.

urry ['fɜ:rɪ] *adj* **1** *(hairy)* peludo,-a. **2** *(scaly)* sarroso,-a.
▲ *comp* furrier, *superl* furriest.

urther ['fɜ:ðəʳ] *adj* **1** *(farther)* más lejos: she lives further down the road *vive más abajo de la calle.* **2** *(more, additional)* más, adicional; *(new)* nuevo,-a: I have just one further question *tengo una pregunta más;* this office will remain closed until further notice *esta oficina permanecerá cerrada hasta nuevo aviso;* for further information, please contact... *para más información, póngase en contacto con...;* he had nothing further to say on the matter *no tuvo nada más que decir sobre el asunto;* we had to wait a further 3 hours *tuvimos que esperar otras tres horas más.* ■ **this must not go any further** esto tiene que quedar entre nosotros, esto no tiene que salir de aquí. ‖ **further to** con referencia a, referente a: further to your letter of the 6th inst *con referencia a su carta del día 6 del corriente.* ● **further education** estudios *mpl* superiores.
▷ *adv* **1** *(farther)* más lejos: is it much further? *¿queda mucho más?;* don't go any further *no vayas más lejos;* it's further to the East *está más al este;* nothing could be further from my mind *nada más lejos de mi intención;* looking further ahead *mirando más adelante.* **2** *(more, to a greater degree)* más: the police want to take the matter further *la policía quiere investigar más el asunto;* I'd like to go further into this subject *me gustaría estudiar el tema más a fondo;* and she hasn't heard anything further *y no ha vuelto a saber nada más;* the situation is still further complicated than we thought *la situación es aún más complicada de lo que pensábamos;* I don't want to detain you any further *no quiero entretenerte más.* **3** *fml (besides)* además: further, I'd like to complain about the lack of parking spaces *además, quisiera quejarme de la falta de aparcamientos.*
▷ *vt (advance, promote)* fomentar, promover: he would have gone to any lengths to further his career *hubiera hecho cualquier cosa para promover su propia carrera.*

Consulta también far.

urtherance ['fɜ:ðərəns] *n* promoción *f*, fomento, avance *m*.

urthermore [fɜ:ðə'mɔ:ʳ] *adv fml* además.

urthermost ['fɜ:ðərməʊst] *adj* → **far, further.**

urthest ['fɜ:ðɪst] *adj* → **far, farthest, further.**
▷ *adv* → **far, further.**

urtive ['fɜ:tɪv] *adj* furtivo,-a.

urtively ['fɜ:tɪvlɪ] *adv* furtivamente.

urtiveness ['fɜ:tɪvnəs] *n* sigilo.

fury ['fjʊərɪ] *n* **1** *(rage)* furia, rabia, ira: there was fury in her eyes *tenía los ojos llenos de furia;* he was speechless with fury *estaba mudo de ira.* **2** *(wild force)* furor *m*, violencia, frenesí *m*: the fury of the storm *el furor de la tormenta.* ■ **to do** STH **like fury** hacer ALGO con furia, hacer ALGO como un,-a loco,-a. ‖ **to be in a fury** estar furioso,-a. ‖ **to fly into a fury** ponerse hecho,-a una furia.
▲ *pl* furies.
▷ *n pl* **The Furies** las Furias *fpl*.

furze [fɜ:z] *n* aulaga, tojo.

fuse [fjʊ:z] *n* **1** ELEC fusible *m*, plomo: I've blown a fuse *he hecho saltar el fusible;* the fuses blew *saltaron los fusibles, se fundieron los plomos.* **2** *(wick)* mecha; *(detonator)* espoleta.
▷ *vt* **1** *(cause to stop working, melt)* fundir: you could fuse the light *podrías fundir los plomos;* the heat has fused all the metal *el calor ha fundido todo el metal.* **2** *fig (merge)* fusionar.
▷ *vi* **1** *(stop working, melt)* fundirse: the lights have fused *se han fundido los plomos.* **2** *fig (merge)* fusionarse: the two companies fused *las dos empresas se fusionaron.* ■ **to blow a fuse 1** *(appliance)* saltar el fusible de, fundirse el plomo de. **2** *(person)* estallar, explotar. ● **fuse box** caja de fusibles. ‖ **fuse wire** alambre *m* de fusible.

fuselage ['fjʊ:zəlɑ:ʒ] *n* fuselaje *m*.

fusilier [fjʊ:zə'lɪəʳ] *n* fusilero.

fusillade [fjʊ:zə'leɪd] *n* **1** tiroteo, descarga cerrada, cortina de fuego. **2** *fig* lluvia, torrente *m*.

fusion ['fjʊ:ʒən] *n* **1** fusión *f*, fundición *f*. **2** *fig* fusión *f*.

fuss [fʌs] *n* **1** *(commotion, nervous excitement)* alboroto, jaleo, bulla, ruido: what's all the fuss about? *¿por qué tanto jaleo?;* don't get in(to) such a fuss *no te pongas así, no hay para tanto;* a lot of fuss about nothing *mucho ruido y pocas nueces.* **2** *(angry scene, dispute)* escándalo, problemas *mpl*; *(complaints)* quejas *fpl*: there'll be a right fuss if Dad finds out *habrá un escándalo si se entera papá;* there was a fuss about the bill (US check) *hubo quejas por la cuenta.*
▷ *vt (pester, annoy, bother)* molestar: stop fussing me *no me molestes.*
▷ *vi* **1** *(worry, fret)* preocuparse, inquietarse: don't fuss, we'll get there on time *no te preocupes, llegaremos a tiempo;* she's always fussing about her hair *siempre se preocupa por su pelo.* **2** *(pay excessive attention to)* mimar (con exceso), preocuparse excesivamente (over, de): she loves to fuss over her grand-daughter *le encanta mimar a su nieta;* I think they fuss over him too much *creo que le miman demasiado.* ■ **to make a fuss / kick up a fuss** *(complain strongly)* armar un escándalo, armar un lío, montar una escena: he kicked up a fuss about his hotel room *armó un escándalo por su habitación;* please don't make a fuss *no montes una escena por favor.* ‖ **to make a fuss of** SB hacer mimos a ALGN, deshacerse por ALGN: everyone made a fuss of the new baby *todos hicieron mimos al nuevo bebé.* ‖ **not to be fussed** darle igual a uno: what do you want to do? –I'm not fussed *¿qué quieres hacer? –me da igual.*

fusspot ['fʌspɒt] *n* quisquilloso,-a, tiquismiquis *mf*.

fussy ['fʌsɪ] *adj* 1 *(concerned with details)* quisquilloso,-a, exigente, especial, particular: **he's very fussy about his food** *es muy exigente con la comida;* **she's very fussy about punctuality** *es muy quisquillosa con la puntualidad.* 2 *(nervous about small things)* nervioso,-a. 3 *(too elaborate)* recargado,-a.
▲ *comp* **fussier**, *superl* **fussiest.**

fusty ['fʌstɪ] *adj* 1 *(musty)* mohoso,-a, rancio,-a; *(stale)* que huele a cerrado. 2 *(old-fashioned)* chapado,-a a la antigua.
▲ *comp* **fustier**, *superl* **fustiest.**

futile ['fjuːtaɪl] *adj* 1 *(pointless)* vano,-a, inútil: **a futile attempt to save him** *un intento inútil de salvarlo.* 2 *(inane)* necio,-a, fatuo,-a, inútil.

futility [fjuː'tɪlətɪ] *n* inutilidad *f*, lo inútil.

futon [fuː'tɒn] *n* futón *m.*

future ['fjuːtʃəʳ] *adj* futuro,-a: **my future husband** *mi futuro marido;* **we arranged to meet at some future time** *quedamos para vernos en un futuro.* ■ **future tense** futuro.
▷ *n* 1 futuro, porvenir *m*: **the future is promising** *el futuro es prometedor;* **who knows what the future holds?** *¿quién sabe lo que tiene reservado el futuro?;* **it's a good idea to save for the future** *es buena idea ahorrar para el futuro;* **my job has no future** *mi trabajo no tiene porvenir.* 2 *(verb tense)* futuro. ■ **in future** en el futuro, de aquí en adelante. ‖ **in the future** en el futuro. ‖ **in the distant future** en un futuro lejano. ‖ **in the near future** en un futuro próximo. ‖ **in the not too distant future** en un futuro no muy lejano.

futurism ['fjuːtʃərɪzᵊm] *n* futurismo.

futurist ['fjuːtʃərɪst] *adj* futurista.

futuristic [fjuːtʃə'rɪstɪk] *adj* futurista.

futurologist [fjuːtʃe'rɒlədʒɪst] *n* futurólogo,-a.

futurology [fjuːtʃe'rɒlədʒɪ] *n* futurología.

fuzz [fʌz] *n (fluff)* pelusa; *(fine hair)* vello. ● **the fuzz** *sl* la bofia.

fuzzy ['fʌzɪ] *adj* 1 *(frizzy)* rizado,-a, crespo,-a; *(fluffy)* con pelusilla. 2 *(blurred)* borroso,-a, movido,-a.
▲ *comp* **fuzzier**, *superl* **fuzziest.**

fwd ['fɔːwəd] *abbr* **(forward)** adelante.

FYI ['ef'waɪ'aɪ] *abbr* **(for your information)** para su información, para que lo sepa.

G

G, g [gi:] *n* **1** *(the letter)* G, g *f*. **2** MUS sol *m*.
g [græm] *symb*(gram, gramme) gramo; *(abbreviation)* g.
gab [gæb] *n* labia, palique *m*.
▷ *vi* charlar, parlotear.
▲ *pt & pp* gabbed, *ger* gabbing.
gabardine ['gæbədi:n] *n* gabardina, impermeable *m*.
gabble ['gæbᵊl] *n* chapurreo, charloteo, farfulla.
▷ *vt* farfullar, charlotear, hablar atropelladamente.
gadabout ['gædəbaʊt] *n fam* callejero,-a.
gadfly ['gædflaɪ] *n* ZOOL tábano.
▲ *pl* gadflies.
gadget ['gædʒɪt] *n fam* aparato, artilugio, dispositivo, chisme *m*.
Gaelic ['geɪlɪk] *adj* gaélico,-a.
▷ *n (language)* gaélico.
gaff [gæf] *n (fishing)* garfio, arpón *m*.
gaffe [gæf] *n* metedura de pata, plancha.
gaffer ['gæfəʳ] *n* **1** *(in film-making)* jefe *m* de eléctricos. **2** GB *fam (foreman)* jefe *m*, encargado. **3** GB *fam (old man)* vejete *m*.
gag [gæg] *n* **1** *(cover for the mouth)* mordaza. **2** *(joke)* chiste *m*, gag *m*, broma.
▷ *vt* amordazar.
▷ *vi* tener náuseas.
▲ *pt & pp* gagged, *ger* gagging.
gaga ['gɑ:gɑ:] *adj fam* chocho,-a.
gaggle ['gægᵊl] *n (geese)* manada.
gaiety ['geɪətɪ] *n* alegría, diversión *f*, regocijo.
▲ *pl* gaieties.
gaily ['geɪlɪ] *adv* alegremente.
gain [geɪn] *n* **1** *(achievement)* logro. **2** *(profit)* ganancia, beneficio. **3** *(increase)* aumento.
▷ *vt* **1** *(achieve)* lograr, conseguir. **2** *(obtain)* ganar. **3** *(increase)* aumentar. **4** *(clock)* adelantar.
▷ *vi* **1** *(clock)* adelantar. **2** *(shares)* subir.
gait [geɪt] *n* andares *mpl*, forma de andar.
gaiter ['geɪtəʳ] *n* polaina.
gal[1] [gæl] *n fam dated* chica, muchacha, tía.
gal[2] [gæl] *abbr* (gallon) galón *m*.
gala ['gɑ:lə] *n* **1** gala, fiesta. **2** SP competición *f*, festival *m*, certamen *m*.
galactic [gə'læktɪk] *adj* galáctico,-a.
galaxy ['gæləksɪ] *n* galaxia.
▲ *pl* galaxies.
gale [geɪl] *n (wind)* vendaval *m*; *(storm)* tempestad *f*.
Galicia [gə'lɪsɪə] *n* Galicia.
Galician [gə'lɪsɪən] *adj* gallego,-a.
▷ *n* **1** *(person)* gallego,-a. **2** *(language)* gallego.
gall[1] [gæl, 'gælən] *abbr* (gallon) galón *m*.
gall[2] [gɔ:l] *n fig* descaro, caradura. ● **gall bladder** vesícula biliar.
gall[3] [gɔ:l] *vt* irritar, molestar.
gallant ['gælənt] *adj* **1** *(brave)* valiente. **2** *(chivalrous)* galante.
galleon ['gælɪən] *n* galeón *m*.
gallery ['gælərɪ] *n* **1** *(gen)* galería. **2** *(in theatre)* gallinero. **3** *(for spectators)* tribuna.
▲ *pl* galleries.
galley ['gælɪ] *n* **1** *(ship)* galera. **2** *(kitchen on ships)* cocina.
Gallic ['gælɪk] *adj* gálico,-a, galo,-a.
Gallicism ['gælɪsɪzᵊm] *n* galicismo.
gallon ['gælən] *n* galón *m*.

Equivale en GB a 4,55 litros y en US 3,78 litros.

gallop ['gæləp] *n* galope *m*.
▷ *vi* galopar.
gallows ['gæləʊz] *n pl* horca *sing*, patíbulo *sing*, cadalso *sing*.
galore [gə'lɔ:ʳ] *adj* en abundancia, en gran cantidad.
galvanize ['gælvənaɪz] *vt* galvanizar.
gamble ['gæmbᵊl] *n* **1** *(risky undertaking)* empresa arriesgada. **2** *(risk)* riesgo. **3** *(bet)* jugada, apuesta.
▷ *vt* jugar(se).
▷ *vi* **1** *(bet)* apostar. **2** *(take a risk)* arriesgarse, confiar.
gambler ['gæmbləʳ] *n* jugador,-ra.
gambling ['gæmblɪŋ] *n* juego.
gambol ['gæmbᵊl] *vi* brincar, saltar.
▲ *pt & pp* gambolled (US gamboled), *ger* gambolling (US gamboling).
game [geɪm] *n* **1** juego. **2** *(match)* partido. **3** *(of cards, chess, etc)* partida. **4** *(hunting)* caza. **5** *fig* presa.
▷ *adj* dispuesto,-a, listo,-a.
▷ *n pl* **games** GB educación *f sing* física.
gamekeeper ['geɪmki:pəʳ] *n* guardabosque *mf*.
gammon ['gæmən] *n* GB jamón *m (ahumado o curado a la sal)*.
gammy ['gæmɪ] *adj* GB *fam* lisiado,-a, tullido,-a.
▲ *comp* gammier, *superl* gammiest.
gamut ['gæmət] *n* gama, serie *f*.
gander ['gændəʳ] *n* ganso.
gang [gæŋ] *n* **1** *(criminals)* banda. **2** *(youths)* pandilla.
gangplank ['gæŋplæŋk] *n (on ship)* plancha.
gangrene ['gæŋgri:n] *n* gangrena.
gangster ['gæŋstəʳ] *n* gángster *m*.
gangway ['gæŋweɪ] *n* **1** GB *(aisle, passage)* pasillo. **2** *(on ship)* pasarela.
gantry ['gæntrɪ] *n (for barrels)* caballete *m*; *(for rocket)* torre *f* de lanzamiento; *(for railway signals)* puente *m* de señales.
▲ *pl* gantries.
gaol [dʒeɪl] *n* GB cárcel *f*.

Consulta también **jail**.

gap [gæp] *n* 1 *(hole)* abertura, hueco. 2 *(crack)* brecha. 3 *(empty space)* espacio. 4 *(blank)* blanco. 5 *(time)* intervalo.
gape [geɪp] *vi* 1 abrirse. 2 *(stare)* mirar boquiabierto,-a.
gaping ['geɪpɪŋ] *adj* 1 *(mouth)* abierto,-a; *(hole)* enorme. 2 *(person)* boquiabierto,-a. 3 *fig* profundo,-a, hondo,-a.
garage ['gærɑːʒ, 'gærɪdʒ] *n* 1 garaje *m*. 2 *(for repairs)* taller *m* mecánico. 3 *(for petrol, etc)* gasolinera.
garb [gɑːb] *n fml* atavío, atuendo, traje *m*, vestido.
▷ *vt fml* ataviar, vestir.
garbage ['gɑːbɪdʒ] *n* 1 US basura. 2 GB desperdicios *mpl*. 3 *fig* tonterías *fpl*, majaderías *fpl*, sandeces *fpl*.
garbled ['gɑːbəld] *adj* confuso,-a, incomprensible.
garden ['gɑːdən] *n* jardín *m*.
▷ *vi* cuidar el jardín.
▷ *n pl* **gardens** *(public park)* jardines *mpl*.
gardener ['gɑːdənəʳ] *n* *(gen)* jardinero,-a; *(of vegetables)* hortelano,-a.
garfish ['gɑːfɪʃ] *n* *(fish)* aguja.
gargle ['gɑːgəl] *vi* hacer gárgaras.
▷ *n (act)* gárgaras *fpl*.
gargoyle ['gɑːgɔɪl] *n* gárgola.
garish ['geərɪʃ] *adj (colour)* chillón,-ona, llamativo, -a; *(light)* cegador,-ra, deslumbrante.
garland ['gɑːlənd] *n* guirnalda.
▷ *vt* adornar con guirnaldas.
garlic ['gɑːlɪk] *n* ajo.
garment ['gɑːmənt] *n (clothes)* prenda.
garnet ['gɑːnɪt] *n* granate *m*.
garnish ['gɑːnɪʃ] *n* guarnición *f*.
▷ *vt* guarnecer.
garret ['gærət] *n (room)* buhardilla; *(attic, loft)* desván *m*.
garrison ['gærɪsən] *n* guarnición *f*.
▷ *vt* guarnecer.
garrote [gə'rɒt] *n* ⟶ **garrotte.**
garrotte [gə'rɒt] *n* garrote *m*.
▷ *vt* dar garrote a, agarrotar.
garter ['gɑːtəʳ] *n* liga.
gas [gæs] *n* 1 *(substance)* gas *m*. 2 US gasolina. 3 *(anaesthetic)* anestesia. 4 US *fig* algo divertido. ● **gas pump** surtidor *m* de gasolina. ▮ **gas station** gasolinera. ▮ **gas chamber** cámara de gas.
▲ *pl* **gases o gasses.**
▷ *vt* asfixiar con gas.
▷ *vi fam* charlotear.
gaseous ['gæsɪəs] *adj* gaseoso,-a.
gash [gæʃ] *n* cuchillada, herida profunda, raja.
▷ *vt* acuchillar, rajar.
gasket ['gæskɪt] *n* junta.
gasoline ['gæsəliːn] *n* US gasolina.
gasp [gɑːsp] *vi* 1 *(in astonishment)* quedar boquiabierto,-a. 2 *(to pant)* jadear.
▷ *n (cry of surprise, etc)* grito.
gassy ['gæsɪ] *adj* gaseoso,-a.
▲ *comp* **gassier**, *superl* **gassiest.**
gastric ['gæstrɪk] *adj* gástrico,-a.
gastronomy [gæs'trɒnəmɪ] *n* gastronmía.
gate [geɪt] *n* 1 *(door)* puerta, verja. 2 *(at airport)* puerta; *(at stadium)* entrada. 3 GB *(attendance)* asistencia.
gateau ['gætəʊ] *n* pastel *m*, tarta.
▲ *pl* **gateaux** ['gɟtəʊz].
gatecrash ['geɪtkræʃ] *vt fam* colarse en.
▷ *vi fam* colarse.
gateway ['geɪtweɪ] *n* 1 entrada, puerta. 2 *fig* camino, pasaporte *m*, puerta.
gather ['gæðəʳ] *vt* 1 *(collect)* juntar. 2 *(call together)* reunir. 3 *(pick up)* recoger. 4 *(taxes)* recaudar. 5 *(gain)* ganar, cobrar.
▷ *vi* 1 *(come together)* reunirse, juntarse. 2 *(build up)* acumularse. 3 *(form)* formarse.
⊙ **to gather round** *vi* acercarse, agruparse.
gathering ['gæðərɪŋ] *n* reunión *f*, asamblea.
▷ *adj* creciente.
gauche [gəʊʃ] *adj (awkward)* torpe, desmañado,-a. *(tactless)* sin tacto.
gaudy ['gɔːdɪ] *adj* chillón,-ona, llamativo,-a.
▲ *comp* **gaudier**, *superl* **gaudiest.**
gauge [geɪdʒ] *n* 1 *(device)* indicador *m*, calibrador *m*. 2 *(measure)* medida estándar. 3 *(railways)* ancho de vía.
▷ *vt* 1 *(measure)* medir, calibrar. 2 *fig* apreciar, calcular, determinar, estimar, juzgar.
gaunt [gɔːnt] *adj* 1 *(lean)* demacrado,-a. 2 *fig (desolate)* lúgubre; *(grim)* siniestro,-a.
gauntlet ['gɔːntlət] *n (armour)* guantelete *m*; *(glove)* guante *m*.
gauze [gɔːz] *n* gasa.
gave [geɪv] *pt* ⟶ **give.**
gawky ['gɔːkɪ] *adj* desgarbado,-a.
▲ *comp* **gawkier**, *superl* **gawkiest.**
gay [geɪ] *adj* 1 *fam (homosexual)* gay, homosexual. 2 *(happy, lively)* alegre. 3 *(bright)* vistoso,-a.
gaze [geɪz] *n* mirada fija.
▷ *vi* mirar fijamente.
gazebo [gə'ziːbəʊ] *n* belvedere *m*.
▲ *pl* **gazebos o gazeboes.**
gazelle [gə'zel] *n* gacela.
gazette [gə'zet] *n* 1 gaceta. 2 US periódico.
gazump [gə'zʌmp] *vt* GB *fam romper un compromiso de venta para vender a otro comprador a un precio más alto.*
GB ['dʒiː'biː] *abbr* GB **(Great Britain)** Gran Bretaña.
GCE ['dʒiː'siː'iː] *abbr* GB **(General Certificate of Education)** ≈ Curso de Orientación Universitaria; *(abbreviation)* COU *m*.
GCSE ['dʒiː'siː'es'iː] *abbr* GB **(General Certificate of Secondary Education)** ≈ Enseñanza Secundaria Obligatoria; *(abbreviation)* ESO *f*.
GDP ['dʒiː'diːpiː] *abbr* **(gross domestic product)** producto interior bruto; *(abbreviation)* PIB *m*.
gear [gɪəʳ] *n* 1 TECH engranaje *m*. 2 AUTO marcha, velocidad *f*. 3 *(equipment)* equipo. 4 *fam (belongings)* efectos *mpl* personales, pertenencias *fpl*; *(clothes)* ropa.
⊙ **to gear to** *vt insep* adaptar, ajustar.
gearbox ['gɪəbɒks] *n* caja de cambios.
gearstick ['gɪəstɪk] *n* AUTO palanca de cambio.
gee[1] [dʒiː] *interj* US *fam* ¡caramba!
gee[2] [dʒiː] *vt* **to gee up** arrear. ■ **gee up!** ¡arre!
gee-gee ['dziːdziː] *n* GB *fam* caballo.
geese [giːs] *n pl* ⟶ **goose.**
gel [dzel] *n* 1 gel *m*. 2 *(for hair)* gomina, fijador *m*.
▷ *vi* 1 CHEM gelificarse. 2 *fig (ideas, etc)* cuajar.
▲ *pt & pp* **gelled**, *ger* **gelling.**
gelatine ['dʒeləti:n] *n* gelatina.
gelignite ['dʒelɪgnaɪt] *n* gelignita.
gem [dʒem] *n* 1 *(jewel)* gema, piedra preciosa. 2 *fig* *(person, thing)* joya, alhaja.

Gemini [ˈdʒemɪnaɪ] *n* Géminis *m*.
gen [dʒen] *n* GB *fam dated* información *f*, datos *mpl*.
gender [ˈdʒendəʳ] *n* **1** LING género. **2** *(sex)* sexo.
gene [dʒiːn] *n* gene *m*, gen *m*.
genera [ˈdʒenərə] *n pl* ⟶ **genus**.
general [ˈdʒenᵊrəl] *adj* general. ● **general election** elecciones generales.
▷ *n* MIL general *m*.
generalize [ˈdʒenᵊrəlaɪz] *vt* generalizar.
▷ *vi* generalizar.
generally [ˈdʒenᵊrəlɪ] *adv* generalmente, por lo general, en general.
generate [ˈdʒenəreɪt] *vt* **1** *(gen)* generar. **2** *fig* producir.
generation [dʒenəˈreɪʃᵊn] *n* generación *f*.
generator [ˈdʒenəreɪtəʳ] *n* generador *m*.
generic [dʒəˈnerɪk] *adj* genérico,-a.
generosity [dʒenəˈrɒsətɪ] *n* generosidad *f*.
generous [ˈdʒenᵊrəs] *adj* **1** generoso,-a. **2** *(abundant)* abundante, copioso,-a.
genesis [ˈdʒenəsɪs] *n* génesis *f*, origen *m*.
▲ *pl* geneses [ˈdʒenɪsiˈz].
genetic [dʒəˈnetɪk] *adj* genético,-a. ● **genetic code** código genético.
genetically [dʒəˈnetɪklɪ] *adv* genéticamente. ■ **genetically modified** transgénico,-a.
genetics [dʒəˈnetɪks] *n* genética.
Geneva [ˈdʒəviːvə] *n* Ginebra.
genial [ˈdʒiːnɪəl] *adj* afable, amable, simpático,-a.
genie [ˈdʒiːnɪ] *n* genio, duende *m*.
genital [ˈdʒenɪtᵊl] *adj* genital.
▷ *n pl* **genitals** órganos *mpl* genitales, genitales *mpl*.
genitive [ˈdʒenɪtɪv] *adj* genitivo,-a.
▷ *n* genitivo.
genius [ˈdʒiːnɪəs] *n* **1** *(person)* genio. **2** *(gift)* don *m*.
▲ *pl* geniuses.
genocide [ˈdʒenəsaɪd] *n* genocidio.
genome [ˈdʒiːnəʊm] *n* genoma *m*.
genotype [ˈdʒenətaɪp] *n* genotipo.
genre [ˈʒɑːnrə] *n* género.
gent [dʒent] *n fam* caballero, señor *m*.
▷ *n pl* **gents** servicio de caballeros.
genteel [dʒenˈtiːl] *adj* **1** *dated (refined)* fino,-a, distinguido,-a. **2** *pej* afectado,-a, cursi.
gentle [ˈdʒentᵊl] *adj* **1** *(person)* bondadoso,-a, dulce, tierno,-a. **2** *(breeze, movement, touch, etc)* suave. **3** *(hint)* discreto,-a. **4** *(noble)* noble.
▲ *comp* gentler, *superl* gentlest.
gentleman [ˈdʒentᵊlmən] *n* caballero, señor *m*.
▲ *pl* gentlemen [ˈdʒentᵊlmən].
gently [ˈdʒentlɪ] *adv* **1** *(smoothly)* suavemente. **2** *(slowly)* despacio, poco a poco. **3** *(kindly)* amablemente.
gentry [ˈdʒentrɪ] *n (of high birth)* pequeña nobleza; *(of high standing)* alta sociedad *f*.
genuine [ˈdʒenjʊɪn] *adj* **1** *(authentic, true)* genuino,-a, auténtico,-a, verdadero,-a. **2** *(sincere)* sincero,-a.
genus [ˈdʒiːnᵊs] *n* género.
▲ *pl* genera [ˈdʒenərᵊ].
geocentric [dʒiːəʊˈsentrɪk] *adj* geocéntrico,-a.
geographic [dʒɪəˈgræfɪk] *adj* geográfico,-a.
geography [dʒɪˈɒgrəfɪ] *n* geografía.
geologic [dʒɪəˈlɒdʒɪk] *adj* geológico,-a.
geology [dʒɪˈɒlədʒɪ] *n* geología.
geometric [dʒɪəˈmetrɪk] *adj* geométrico,-a.
geometry [dʒɪˈɒmətrɪ] *n* geometría.
geranium [dʒəˈreɪnɪəm] *n* geranio.
geriatric [dʒerɪˈætrɪk] *adj* **1** geriátrico,-a. **2** *pej* caduco,-a, viejo,-a.
germ [dʒɜːm] *n* **1** *(gen)* germen *m*. **2** *(of a disease)* bacilo, microbio; *(bacteria)* bacteria. **3** *fig* germen *m*.
German [ˈdʒɜːmən] *adj* alemán,-ana.
▷ *n* **1** *(person)* alemán,-ana. **2** *(language)* alemán *m*.
Germanic [dʒɜːˈmænɪk] *adj* germánico,-a, germano,-a.
Germany [ˈdʒɜːmənɪ] *n* Alemania.
germ-free [ˈdʒɜːmfriː] *adj* esterilizado,-a.
germicide [ˈdʒɜːmɪsaɪd] *n* germicida *m*.
germinate [ˈdʒɜːmɪneɪt] *vi* germinar.
▷ *vt* hacer germinar.
germination [dʒɜːmɪˈneɪʃᵊn] *n* germinación *f*.
gerund [ˈdʒerənd] *n* gerundio.
gestate [ˈdʒesteɪt] *vt* **1** BIOL gestar. **2** *fig (idea, etc)* idear.
gestation [dʒesˈteɪʃᵊn] *n* **1** BIOL gestación *f*. **2** *fig (of idea, etc)* gestación *f*.
gesticulate [dʒesˈtɪkjəleɪt] *vi* gesticular.
gesture [ˈdʒestʃəʳ] *n* **1** ademán *m*, gesto. **2** *fig (token)* detalle *m*, gesto, muestra.
▷ *vi* hacer gestos, hacer ademanes.
get [get] *vt* **1** *(obtain)* obtener, conseguir: **I want to get a job** *quiero conseguir un trabajo;* **he got a bank loan** *le concedieron un crédito bancario;* **what did you get in maths?** *¿qué sacaste en mates?* **2** *(receive)* recibir: **I got your letter yesterday** *recibí tu carta ayer.* **3** *(buy)* comprar: **where did you get your jeans?** *¿dónde compraste tus vaqueros?* **4** *(fetch)* traer: **get the car** *traiga el coche.* **5** *(catch illnesses, means of transport)* coger: **she got the flu** *cogió la gripe.* **6** *(receive signal)* captar, recibir, coger. **7** *(ask)* pedir, decir; *(persuade)* persuadir, convencer: **get your brother to help you** *pídele a tu hermano que te ayude.* **8** *fam (jokes, etc)* entender, captar, coger. **9** *fam (annoy)* poner nervioso,-a, fastidiar. **10** *(earn)* ganar, cobrar. **11** *(have* STH *done)* hacer algo a uno: **she loves getting her hair done** *le encanta que le arreglen el pelo.* **12** *(wound, injure)* dar, alcanzar: **she got hit by a stray bullet** *le alcanzó una bala perdida.*
▷ *vi* **1** *(become)* ponerse, volverse: **she gets very angry if we're late** *se pone furiosa si llegamos tarde.* **2** *(go)* ir: **how do you get there?** *¿cómo se va hasta allí?*
▷ *vt fig* ir, llevar.
▷ *vi* **1** *(arrive)* llegar: **how did you get home?** *¿cómo llegaste a casa?* **2** *(come to)* llegar a. **3** *(start)* empezar a.
⊙ **to get across** *vt insep (cross - street, road)* cruzar; *(- bridge)* atravesar.
▷ *vi* hacerse entender.
⊙ **to get ahead** *vi* adelantar, progresar.
⊙ **to get along** *vi* **1** *(manage)* arreglárselas, apañárselas. **2** *(leave)* marcharse, irse.
⊙ **to get along with** *vt insep* **1** *(person)* llevarse (bien) con. **2** *(progress)* marchar, ir con.
⊙ **to get around** *vi* **1** *(person)* moverse, desplazarse; *(travel)* viajar. **2** *(news)* difundirse.
▷ *vt insep (avoid)* evitar, sortear.
⊙ **to get around to** *vi* encontrar tiempo para.
⊙ **to get away** *vi* escaparse, irse.
▷ *vt sep* alejar, quitar, sacar.
⊙ **to get away with** *vt insep* salir impune de.

⊙ **to get back** *vi* 1 *(return)* volver, regresar. 2 *(move backwards)* moverse hacia atrás, retroceder.
▷ *vt sep (recover)* recuperar: **did you get your money back?** *¿te devolvieron el dinero?*.
⊙ **to get behind** *vi* atrasarse.
⊙ **to get by** *vi* 1 *(manage)* arreglárselas. 2 *(pass)* pasar.
⊙ **to get down** *vt sep* 1 *(depress)* deprimir, desanimar. 2 *(gen)* bajar. 3 *(write down)* apuntar, anotar. 4 *(swallow)* tragar.
▷ *vi (descend)* bajarse.
⊙ **to get down to** *vi* ponerse a.
⊙ **to get in** *vi* 1 *(arrive)* llegar. 2 *(enter)* entrar; *(car)* subir; *(be elected)* ser elegido,-a.
▷ *vt sep* 1 *(insert)* meter. 2 *(harvest)* cosechar; *(washing)* recoger; *(supplies)* comprar. 3 *(summon)* llamar.
⊙ **to get into** *vt insep* 1 *(arrive)* llegar a. 2 *(enter)* entrar en; *(car)* subir a.
⊙ **to get off** *vt sep (remove)* quitarse.
▷ *vt insep (vehicle, horse, etc)* bajarse de.
▷ *vi* 1 bajarse. 2 *(leave)* salir. 3 *(begin)* comenzar. 4 *(escape)* escaparse.
⊙ **to get off with** *vt insep fam* ligar con.
⊙ **to get on** *vt insep (vehicle)* subir a, subirse a; *(bicycle, horse, etc)* montar a.
▷ *vi* 1 *(make progress)* progresar, avanzar, ir. 2 *(succeed)* tener éxito. 3 *(be friendly)* llevarse bien, avenirse, entenderse. 4 *(continue)* seguir, continuar. 5 *(grow old)* hacerse mayor, envejecerse.
⊙ **to get out** *vt sep (thing)* sacar; *(stain)* quitar.
▷ *vi* 1 *(leave)* salir. 2 *(of car, etc)* bajar de, bajarse de. 3 *(escape)* escapar(se). 4 *(news, rumours, etc)* llegar a saberse, hacerse público,-a.
⊙ **to get out of** *vt insep (avoid)* librarse de.
▷ *vi (stop)* dejar, perder la costumbre.
⊙ **to get over** *vt insep* 1 *(illness)* recuperarse de. 2 *(recover from)* sobreponerse a; *(forget)* olvidar. 3 *(obstacle)* salvar; *(difficulty)* vencer.
▷ *vt sep (idea, etc)* comunicar, hacer comprender.
⊙ **to get over with** *vt sep* acabar con.
⊙ **to get round** *vt insep* 1 *(obstacle)* salvar. 2 *(law, regulation)* evitar, soslayar. 3 *(person)* convencer, persuadir.
▷ *vi (news)* difundirse, hacerse público,-a, llegar a saber.
⊙ **to get through** *vi* 1 *(gen)* llegar. 2 *(on phone)* conseguir hablar (**to**, con). 3 *(communicate)* hacerse comprender (**to**, a).
▷ *vt insep* 1 *(finish)* acabar, terminar. 2 *(consume)* consumir; *(money)* gastar; *(drink)* beber. 3 *(exam)* aprobar.
⊙ **to get together** *vi (people)* reunirse, juntarse.
▷ *vt sep* 1 *(people)* juntar, reunir. 2 *(assemble)* montar; *(money)* recoger, reunir.
▲ *pt* got [gɒt], *pp* got [gɒt] (US gotten ['gɒtn]), *ger* getting.
⊙ **to get up** *vi* 1 *(rise)* levantarse; *(climb up)* subir. 2 *(become stronger - wind, storm)* levantarse.
⊙ **to get up to** *vt insep* 1 hacer: **what have you been getting up to?** *¿qué has estado haciendo?* 2 *(reach)* llegar a.
getaway ['getəweɪ] *n fam* fuga, huida.
get-together ['gettəgeðəʳ] *n fam (meeting)* reunión *f*; *(party)* fiesta.
getup ['getʌp] *n fam* atavío, atuendo.
geyser ['gi:zəʳ, US 'gaɪzəʳ] *n* 1 *(natural spring)* géiser *m*. 2 *(water heater)* calentador *m* de agua.
ghastly ['gɑ:stlɪ] *adj* 1 espantoso,-a, horrible, horroroso,-a. 2 *(pale)* pálido,-a, mortecino,-a.
▲ *comp* ghastlier, *superl* ghastliest.
gherkin ['gɜ:kɪn] *n* pepinillo.
ghetto ['getəʊ] *n* gueto.
▲ *pl* ghettos o ghettoes.
ghost [gəʊst] *n* fantasma *m*, espectro.
▷ *vt (literature)* escribir.
ghostwrite ['gəʊstraɪt] *vt (literature)* hacer de negro, escribir para otro.
ghoulish ['gu:lɪʃ] *adj* macabro,-a.
giant ['dʒaɪənt] *n* gigante,-a.
▷ *adj* gigante, gigantesco,-a.
gibber ['dʒɪbəʳ] *vi* farfullar, mascullar, hablar atropelladamente.
gibberish ['dʒɪbərɪʃ] *n* galimatías *m*.
gibe [dʒaɪb] *n* mofa, sarcasmo, pulla.
▷ *vi* mofarse (**about/at**, de).
giblets ['dʒɪbləts] *n pl* menudillos *mpl*.
Gibraltar [dʒɪ'brɔ:ltəʳ] *n* Gibraltar *m*.
Gibraltarian [dʒɪbrɔ:l'teərɪən] *adj* gibraltareño,-a.
giddiness ['gɪdɪnəs] *n* mareo, vértigo.
giddy ['gɪdɪ] *adj (dizzy)* mareado,-a.
▲ *comp* giddier, *superl* giddiest.
gift [gɪft] *n* 1 *(present)* regalo, obsequio. 2 *(talent)* don *m*. 3 REL ofrenda. 4 JUR donación *f*.
gifted ['gɪftɪd] *adj* dotado,-a, talentoso,-a.
gig [gɪg] *n fam (booking)* bolo; *(performance)* actuación *f*.
gigabyte ['gɪgəbaɪt] *n* gigabyte *m*, giga *m*.
gigantic [dʒaɪ'gæntɪk] *adj* gigantesco,-a.
giggle ['gɪgᵊl] *n* 1 risita, risa tonta. 2 GB *fam* broma diversión *f*.
gild [gɪld] *vt* dorar.
gill[1] [gɪl] *n (of fish)* agalla, branquia.
gill[2] [dʒɪl] *n (measurement)* cuarto de pinta *(equivale a 0,142 litros)*.
gilt [gɪlt] *adj* dorado,-a.
▷ *n* dorado.
gilt-edged ['gɪltedʒd] *adj* FIN de máxima garantía.
gilthead bream ['gɪlthed 'bri:m] *n* dorada.
gimmick ['gɪmɪk] *n fam (device)* reclamo, truco *(gadget)* artilugio.
gin [dʒɪn] *n* ginebra.
ginger ['dʒɪndʒəʳ] *n (spice)* jengibre *m*.
▷ *adj (hair)* rojo,-a; *(person)* pelirrojo,-a.
⊙ **to ginger up** *vt sep* animar, estimular.
gingerbread ['dʒɪndʒəbred] *n* pan *m* de jengibre.
gingerly ['dʒɪndʒəlɪ] *adv* cautelosamente.
▷ *adj* cauteloso,-a.
gipsy ['dʒɪpsɪ] *n* gitano,-a.
▲ *pl* gipsies.
giraffe [dʒɪ'rɑ:f] *n* jirafa.
gird [gɜ:d] *vt* 1 *lit (fasten)* ceñir. 2 *(surround)* rodea (**de**, with).
▲ *pt & pp* girt [gɜ:t] o girded.
girder ['gɜ:dəʳ] *n (construction)* viga.
girdle ['gɜ:dᵊl] *n* 1 *(clothes)* faja. 2 *fig* cinturón *m*.
▷ *vt fig* rodear.
girl [gɜ:l] *n* 1 chica, muchacha, joven *f*; *(small)* niña 2 *(daughter)* hija.
girlfriend ['gɜ:lfrend] *n* 1 *(partner)* novia. 2 *(friend)* amiga, compañera.

girlhood ['gɜ:lhʊd] *n (childhood)* niñez *f*; *(youth)* juventud *f*.

girlish ['gɜ:lɪʃ] *adj (of girl)* de niña; *(effeminate)* afeminado,-a.

giro ['dʒaɪrəʊ] *n* GB giro.
▲ *pl* giros.

girth [gɜ:θ] *n* 1 TECH *(measure)* contorno, circunferencia, perímetro. 2 *fig* gordura, obesidad *f*. 3 *(of saddle)* cincha.

gismo ['gɪzməʊ] *n fam* chisme *m*.
▲ *pl* gismos.

gist [dʒɪst] *n (general idea)* idea general, sentido general; *(fundamental idea)* lo esencial.

give [gɪv] *n (flexibility)* elasticidad *f*, flexibilidad *f*.
▷ *vt* 1 *(gen)* dar, entregar. 2 *(as a gift)* dar, regalar: **he gave her a dress** *le regaló un vestido*. 3 *(perform a concert, etc)* dar; *(speech)* pronunciar. 4 *(dedicate)* dedicar, consagrar. ● **to give way** ceder el paso.
▷ *vi (yield)* ceder; *(cloth, elastic)* dar de sí.
⊙ **to give away** *vt sep* 1 *(gen)* distribuir, repartir; *(present)* regalar; *(prize)* entregar. 2 *(betray)* delatar, traicionar; *(disclose)* revelar, descubrir.
⊙ **to give back** *vt sep (return)* devolver.
⊙ **to give in** *vi (admit defeat)* darse por vencido,-a, rendirse; *(yield)* ceder.
▷ *vt sep (hand in)* entregar.
⊙ **to give in to** *vi* ceder ante.
⊙ **to give off** *vt sep (smell, heat, etc)* despedir, desprender, emitir.
⊙ **to give onto** *vi* dar a.
⊙ **to give out** *vt sep* 1 *(distribute)* distribuir, repartir. 2 *(announce)* anunciar.
▷ *vi (supplies)* acabarse, agotarse; *(break down)* averiarse, sufrir una avería.
⊙ **to give over** *vt sep (hand over)* entregar; *(allocate)* dedicar, asignar.
▷ *vi fam (stop)* dejar de.
⊙ **to give up** *vt sep* 1 *(renounce)* dejar; *(idea)* abandonar, renunciar a. 2 *(devote)* dedicar. 3 *(surrender)* entregarse.
▷ *vi (admit defeat)* darse por vencido,-a, rendirse.
▲ *pt* gave [geɪv], *pp* given ['gɪvᵊn], *ger* giving.
⊙ **to give up on** *vt insep* abandonar, desistir.

giveaway ['gɪvəweɪ] *n* 1 *fam (unintentional disclosure)* revelación *f* involuntaria. 2 *(gift)* regalo.

given ['gɪvᵊn] *pp* → **give**.
▷ *adj* 1 *(fixed)* dado,-a, determinado,-a, previsto,-a. 2 *(prone)* dado,-a, propenso,-a.
▷ *prep* 1 *(considering)* dado,-a, teniendo en cuenta. 2 *(if)* si.

glacial ['gleɪʃᵊl] *adj* 1 GEOL glaciar. 2 *(icy)* glacial.

glacier ['glæsɪəʳ, 'gleɪʃəʳ] *n* GEOL glaciar *m*.

glad [glæd] *adj (pleased)* contento,-a; *(happy)* feliz.
▲ *comp* gladder, *superl* gladdest.

gladden ['glædᵊn] *vt* alegrar.

glade [gleɪd] *n (clearing)* claro.

gladiator ['glædɪeɪtəʳ] *n* HIST gladiador *m*.

gladiolus [glædɪ'əʊləs] *n* BOT gladiolo.
▲ *pl* gladioli [glad'əʊlaɪ].

gladly ['glædlɪ] *adv* de buena gana, con mucho gusto.

glamorous ['glæmərəs] *adj* 1 atractivo,-a. 2 *(charming)* encantador,-ra.

glamour ['glæməʳ] *n* 1 atractivo. 2 *(charm)* encanto.

glance [glɑ:ns] *n* mirada, vistazo, ojeada.
▷ *vi* dar una mirada, echar un vistazo (**at**, a).
⊙ **to glance off** *vt insep (ball, bullet, etc)* rebotar en.

glancing ['glɑ:nsɪŋ] *adj (blow)* oblicuo,-a.

gland [glænd] *n* ANAT glándula.

glare [gleəʳ] *n* 1 *(light)* luz *f* deslumbrante. 2 AUTO deslumbramiento. 3 *(look)* mirada furiosa, mirada hostil.
▷ *vi* 1 *(dazzle)* deslumbrar. 2 *(look)* lanzar una mirada furiosa.

glaring ['gleərɪŋ] *adj* 1 *(dazzling)* deslumbrador,-ra, deslumbrante; *(colour)* chillón,-ona; *(bright)* brillante, resplandeciente. 2 *(blatant)* patente, evidente.

glass [glɑ:s] *n* 1 *(material)* vidrio, cristal *m*. 2 *(for drinking)* vaso; *(with stem)* copa. 3 GB barómetro.
▷ *n pl* **glasses** gafas *fpl*.

glassblowing ['glɑ:sbləʊɪŋ] *n* soplado del vidrio.

glasshouse ['glɑ:shaʊs] *n (gardening)* invernadero.

glassware ['glɑ:sweəʳ] *n* cristalería.

glassy ['glɑ:sɪ] *adj* 1 *fig (eyes)* vidrioso,-a. 2 *(like glass)* vítreo,-a; *(smooth)* liso,-a; *(water)* cristalino,-a, transparente.
▲ *comp* glassier, *superl* glassiest.

glaze [gleɪz] *n (for pottery)* vidriado; *(lustre)* brillo, lustre *m*; *(varnish)* barniz *m*, esmalte *m*.
▷ *vt* 1 *(pottery)* vidriar, esmaltar. 2 *(windows)* poner cristales a. 3 CULIN glasear.

glazed [gleɪzd] *adj (of eyes, look, etc)* vidrioso,-a, ausente; *(of surface)* vidriado,-a.

gleam [gli:m] *n* 1 destello, rayo. 2 *fig* rayo, resquicio, vislumbre *m*.
▷ *vi* brillar, destellar, relucir.

glean [gli:n] *vt* 1 AGR espigar. 2 *fig* recoger, cosechar.

glee [gli:] *n* alegría, júbilo, regocijo.

glen [glen] *n* cañada.

glib [glɪb] *adj (person)* de mucha labia, charlatán,-ana; *(reply, etc)* superficial, fácil.
▲ *comp* glibber, *superl* glibbest.

glide [glaɪd] *n* 1 deslizamiento. 2 AV planeo, vuelo sin motor. 3 LING semivocal *f*.
▷ *vi* 1 deslizarse. 2 AV planear.

glider ['glaɪdəʳ] *n* AV planeador *m*.

gliding ['glaɪdɪŋ] *n* 1 AV planeo. 2 SP vuelo sin motor.

glimmer ['glɪməʳ] *n (light)* luz *f* tenue.
▷ *vi* brillar con luz tenue.

glimpse [glɪmps] *n* vislumbre *f*, visión *f* fugaz.
▷ *vt* vislumbrar, entrever.

glint [glɪnt] *n* destello, centelleo.
▷ *vi* destellar, centellear.

glisten ['glɪsᵊn] *vi* brillar, relucir.

glitter ['glɪtəʳ] *n* brillo.
▷ *vi* brillar, relucir.

gloat [gləʊt] *vi* regodearse (**over**, con), regocijarse (**over**, con), recrearse (**over**, con) .

global ['gləʊbᵊl] *adj* 1 mundial. 2 *(total)* global.

globalization [gləʊbəlaɪ'zeɪʃᵊn] *n* globalización *f*.

globe [gləʊb] *n* 1 globo, esfera. 2 *(map)* globo terrestre.

globe-trotter ['gləʊbtrɒtəʳ] *n fam* trotamundos *mf*.

globule ['glɒbju:l] *n* glóbulo.

gloom [glu:m] *n* 1 *(darkness)* penumbra, tenebrosidad *f*. 2 *(sadness)* tristeza, melancolía. 3 *(hopelessness)* desolación *f*, pesimismo.

gloomy ['glu:mɪ] *adj* **1** *(dark)* lóbrego,-a, oscuro,-a, tenebroso,-a. **2** *(sad)* melancólico,-a, triste; *(depressing)* deprimente, desalentador,-ra. **3** *(pessimistic)* pesimista. **4** *(weather)* gris, encapotado,-a.
▲ *comp* gloomier, *superl* gloomiest.
Gloria ['glɔ:rɪə] *n* gloria.
glorified ['glɔ:rɪfaɪd] *adj pej* pretencioso,-a.
glorify ['glɔ:rɪfaɪ] *vt (God)* glorificar; *(praise)* alabar.
▲ *pt & pp* glorified, *ger* glorifying.
glorious ['glɔ:rɪəs] *adj* **1** glorioso,-a. **2** *(wonderful)* espléndido,-a, magnífico,-a.
glory ['glɔ:rɪ] *n* **1** *(gen)* gloria. **2** *fig* esplendor *m*.
▲ *pl* glories.
▷ *vi* gloriarse (in, de).
▲ *pt & pp* gloried, *ger* glorying.
gloss [glɒs] *n* **1** lustre *m*, brillo. **2** *(explanation)* glosa. **3** *fig* oropel *m*.
▷ *vt (text)* glosar, comentar.
⊙ **to gloss over** *vt insep (play down)* paliar, suavizar; *(hide)* encubrir; *(ignore)* pasar por alto.
glossary ['glɒsərɪ] *n* glosario.
▲ *pl* glossaries.
glove [glʌv] *n* guante *m*.
glow [gləʊ] *n* **1** *(of lamp)* luz *f*; *(of jewel)* brillo. **2** *(of fire)* calor *m* vivo; *(of sky)* arrebol *m*; *(of fire, metal, etc)* incandescencia. **3** *(of face)* rubor *m*. **4** *fig* sensación *f* de bienestar, satisfacción *f*.
▷ *vi* **1** *(jewel, sun, etc)* brillar; *(of metal)* estar al rojo vivo; *(fire)* arder. **2** *fig* rebosar de.
glower ['glaʊəʳ] *vi* mirar con el ceño fruncido.
glowing ['gləʊɪŋ] *adj* **1** *fig (report, etc)* entusiasta; *(style)* cálido,-a. **2** *(fire)* incandescente; *(metal)* al rojo vivo. **3** *(fire, colour)* vivo,-a; *(light)* brillante. **4** *(complexion)* rojo,-a; *(cheeks)* encendido,-a.
glucose ['glu:kəʊz] *n* CHEM glucosa.
glue [glu:] *n* cola, pegamento.
▷ *vt* encolar, pegar.
glum [glʌm] *adj (mood)* abatido,-a, desanimado,-a, triste; *(by nature)* taciturno,-a, melancólico,-a.
▲ *comp* glummer, *superl* glummest.
glut [glʌt] *n (of the market)* superabundancia, exceso; *(of food)* saciedad *f*, hartazgo.
▷ *vt (market)* inundar, saturar.
▲ *pt & pp* glutted, *ger* glutting.
gluten ['glu:tən] *n* gluten *m*.
gluteus ['glu:tɪəs] *n* glúteo.
glutton ['glʌtᵊn] *n* glotón,-ona.
glycerine [glɪsə'rɪn] *n* glicerina.
GM ['dʒi:'em] *abbr* (genetically modifed) genéticamente modificado.
GMT ['dʒi:'em'di:] *abbr* (Greenwich Mean Time) hora media de Greenwich; *(abbreviation)* GMT.
gnarled [nɑ:ld] *adj* nudoso,-a, retorcido,-a.
gnash [næʃ] *vt (teeth)* hacer rechinar.
gnat [næt] *n* ZOOL mosquito.
gnaw [nɔ:] *vt* **1** *(bite)* roer. **2** *fig (worry)* corroer.
gnawing ['nɔ:ɪŋ] *adj (anxiety, fear)* constante, permanente; *(pain)* insistente.
gnome [nəʊm] *n* gnomo.
Gnostic ['nɒstɪk] *n* gnóstico,-a.
▷ *adj* gnóstico,-a.
Gnosticism ['nɒstɪszᵊm] *n* gnosticismo.
GNP ['dʒi:'en'pi:] *abbr* (gross national product) producto nacional bruto; *(abbreviation)* PNB *m*.
gnu [nu:] *n* ñu *m*.
go [gəʊ] *n* **1** *(energy)* energía, empuje *m*. **2** *(turn)* turno: it's my go *me toca a mí*. **3** *(try)* intento: I'd like to have a go at hang gliding *me gustaría intentar vuelo con ala delta*. **4** *(start)* principio.
▷ *vi* **1** *(gen)* ir: to go on holiday (US vacation) *irse de vacaciones*. **2** *(leave)* marcharse, irse; *(bus, train, etc)* salir: let's go! *¡vámonos!* **3** *(vanish)* desaparecer. **4** *(function)* funcionar, marchar: his business is going very well *su negocio marcha muy bien*. **5** *(become)* volverse, ponerse, quedarse: to go deaf *quedarse sordo,-a*. **6** *(fit)* entrar, caber: the bed won't go into the room *la cama no cabrá en la habitación*. **7** *(break)* romperse, estropearse; *(yield)* ceder; *(blow)* fundirse. **8** *(progress)* ir, marchar, andar: things aren't going too well for him *no le van muy bien las cosas*. **9** *(be available)* quedar, haber: is there any more meat going? *¿queda algo de carne?* **10** *(make a noise, gesture, etc)* hacer: go like this with your head *haz así con la cabeza*. **11** *(time - pass)* pasar; *(- be remaining)* faltar: the years went by slowly *los años pasaron lentamente;* only two weeks to go *solo faltan dos semanas*. **12** *(say)* decir: as the saying goes *según el dicho*.
▷ *vt* **1** *(make a noise)* hacer: it goes tick-tock *hace tic-tac*. **2** *(travel)* hacer, recorrer.
▷ *interj* go! *(starting races)* ¡ya!: ready, steady, go! *¡preparados, listos, ya!*
⊙ **to go about** *vt insep* **1** *(task)* emprender, hacer. **2** *(everyday activities)* continuar.
⊙ **to go after** *vt insep (pursue)* perseguir, andar tras.
⊙ **to go against** *vt insep (oppose)* ir en contra de; *(sentence)* ser desfavorable a.
⊙ **to go ahead** *vi (proceed)* proceder: go ahead! *¡adelante!*.
⊙ **to go ahead with** *vi (proceed)* proceder, continuar con.
⊙ **to go along** *vt insep (street, etc)* pasar por; *(progress)* progresar, ir.
▷ *vi (accompany)* ir.
⊙ **to go along with** *vt insep* estar de acuerdo con.
⊙ **to go around** *vi* **1** *(be enough)* bastar, ser suficiente, haber. **2** *(rumour, illness)* correr, circular. **3** *(travel round)* ir, andar. **4** *(spend time)* salir (with, con), andar (with, con). **5** *(revolve)* girar, dar vueltas.
▷ *vt insep* recorrer.
⊙ **to go away** *vi* marcharse.
⊙ **to go back** *vi (return)* volver, regresar; *(date from)* datar de, remontarse a.
⊙ **to go back on** *vt insep (break)* romper, no cumplir.
⊙ **to go by** *vi (time)* pasar.
▷ *vt insep (rules)* atenerse a, seguir; *(instinct)* dejarse llevar por; *(appearances)* juzgar por.
⊙ **to go down** *vi* **1** *(gen)* bajar; *(tyre)* deshincharse; *(sun)* ponerse; *(ship)* hundirse. **2** *(be received)* ser acogido,-a.
⊙ **to go down with** *vi (catch)* coger, pillar.
⊙ **to go for** *vt insep* **1** *(attack)* atacar. **2** *(fetch)* ir a buscar. **3** *fam (like)* gustar. **4** *fam (be valid)* valer para.
⊙ **to go in** *vi* entrar.

⊙ **to go in for** *vt insep (enter - race, competition)* participar en, tomar parte en; *(- exam)* presentarse a; *(- career)* dedicarse a; *(like, agree with)* ser partidario,-a de.
⊙ **to go into** *vt insep* 1 *(gen)* entrar en. 2 *(investigate)* investigar. 3 *(crash)* chocar contra.
⊙ **to go off** *vi* 1 *(leave)* marcharse. 2 *(bomb)* estallar; *(alarm)* sonar; *(gun)* dispararse. 3 *(food)* estropearse, pasarse; *(milk)* cortarse. 4 *(stop operating)* apagarse.
▷ *vt insep (stop liking)* perder el gusto por, perder el interés por.
⊙ **to go off with** *vi fam (elope)* escaparse con.
⊙ **to go on** *vi* 1 *(continue)* seguir, continuar. 2 *(happen)* pasar, ocurrir: **what's going on?** *¿qué pasa?* 3 *(complain)* quejarse (**about**, de); *(talk at length)* hablar sin parar. 4 *(light, etc)* encenderse. 5 *(age)* estar a punto de cumplir: **she's ten going on eleven** *está a punto de cumplir los once años.*
⊙ **to go out** *vi* 1 *(leave)* salir: **he goes out a lot** *sale mucho.* 2 *(fire, light)* apagarse.
⊙ **to go over** *vt insep (check, revise)* revisar, repasar.
⊙ **to go over to** *vt insep* 1 *(betray)* pasarse a. 2 *(change to)* cambiar a, pasar a.
⊙ **to go round** *vi* 1 *(gyrate)* dar vueltas, girar. 2 *(visit)* pasar por casa de, visitar.
⊙ **to go through** *vt insep* 1 *(undergo)* pasar por, sufrir, padecer. 2 *(examine)* examinar; *(search)* registrar; *(spend)* gastar; *(explain)* explicar.
▷ *vi (act, law)* ser aprobado,-a.
▲ *pt* went [went], *pp* gone [gɒn], *ger* going.
⊙ **to go through with** *vt insep* llevar a cabo.
⊙ **to go towards** *vi (reserve for)* destinar a, reservar para.
⊙ **to go under** *vi* 1 *(ship)* hundirse. 2 *fig* fracasar.
⊙ **to go up** *vi* 1 *(gen)* subir; *(approach)* acercarse. 2 *(curtain in theatre)* levantarse. 3 *(explode)* estallar; *(burst into flames)* prenderse fuego.
goad [gəʊd] *n (stick)* aguijada.
▷ *vt* aguijonear.
go-ahead ['geʊəhed] *n* visto bueno.
▷ *adj* emprendedor,-ra.
goal [gəʊl] *n* 1 SP *(area)* meta, portería. 2 SP *(point)* gol *m*, tanto. 3 *(aim)* fin *m*, objetivo, meta.
goalkeeper ['gəʊlkiːpəʳ] *n* portero,-a, guardameta *mf.*
goat [gəʊt] *n (female)* cabra; *(male)* macho cabrío.
goatee ['gəʊtiː] *n (beard)* perilla.
goatskin ['gəʊtskɪn] *n* piel *f* de cabra.
gobble ['gɒbᵊl] *vt* engullir, zamparse.
go-between ['gəʊbɪtwiːn] *n* 1 intermediario,-a. 2 *(between lovers)* alcahuete,-ta.
goblet ['gɒblət] *n* copa.
goblin ['gɒblɪn] *n* duende *m*, trasgo.
go-by ['gəʊkɑːt] *phr* **to give** STH/SB **the go-by** prescindir de ALGO/ALGN.
go-cart ['gəʊkɑːt] *n* SP kart *m.*
god [gɒd] *n (deity, idol)* dios *m.*
▷ *n* **God** Dios *m.*
god-awful ['gɒdɔːfᵊl] *adj* US *sl (film, book, etc)* espantoso,-a, horroroso,-a; *(place, town)* de mala muerte.
godchild ['gɒdtʃaɪld] *n* ahijado,-a.
▲ *pl* godchildren ['gɒdtʃɪldrən].
goddamn ['gɒdæm] *interj* US *sl* ¡maldito sea!
goddamned ['gɒdæm] *adj* US *sl* maldito,-a.
goddaughter ['gɒddɔːtəʳ] *n* ahijada.
goddess ['gɒdəs] *n* diosa.
godfather ['gɒdfɑːðəʳ] *n* padrino.
godforsaken ['gɒdfəseɪkᵊn] *adj* de mala muerte, dejado,-a de la mano de Dios.
godhead ['gɒdhed] *n* divinidad *f.*
godless ['gɒdlᵊs] *n* ateo,-a.
godmother ['gɒdmʌðəʳ] *n* madrina.
godparents ['gɒdpeərənts] *n pl* padrinos *mpl.*
godsend ['gɒdsend] *n* regalo llovido del cielo.
godson ['gɒdsʌn] *n* ahijado.
godwit ['gɒdwɪt] *n* aguja.
go-getter ['gəʊgetəʳ] *n* buscavidas *mf*, trepa *mf.*
goggle ['gɒgᵊl] *vi* quedarse atónito,-a.
goggle-eyed ['gɒgᵊlaɪd] *adj* asombrado,-a.
goggles ['gɒgᵊlz] *n pl* gafas *fpl* protectoras.
going ['gəʊɪŋ] *n* 1 *(departure)* ida, salida. 2 *(pace)* paso, ritmo. 3 *(path, road)* estado del camino.
▷ *adj* 1 *(price, rate)* actual, corriente. 2 *(business)* que marcha bien.
going-over [gəʊɪŋ'əʊvəʳ] *n* 1 *fam (inspection)* repaso, inspección *f.* 2 *(thrashing)* paliza.
goings-on [gəʊɪŋz'ɒn] *n pl fam* tejemanejes *mpl*, chanchullos *mpl.*
gold [gəʊld] *n (metal)* oro.
▷ *adj* 1 *(colour)* dorado,-a. 2 *(made of gold)* de oro.
gold-digger ['gəʊlddɪgəʳ] *n* 1 *(miner)* buscador,-ra de oro. 2 *fig (woman)* aventurera.
golden ['gəʊldᵊn] *adj* 1 de oro. 2 *(colour)* dorado,-a. 3 *(hair)* rubio,-a.
goldfinch ['gəʊldfɪntʃ] *n* jilguero.
goldfish ['gəʊldfɪʃ] *n* pez *m* de colores.
▲ *pl* goldfish ['gəʊldfɪʃ].
goldsmith ['gəʊldsmɪθ] *n* orfebre *mf.*
golf [gɒlf] *n* golf *m.* ● **golf course** campo de golf.
▷ *vi* jugar al golf.
golfer ['gɒlfəʳ] *n* jugador,-ra de golf.
golly ['gɒlɪ] *interj* GB ¡caramba!
gone [gɒn] *pp* → **go.**
▷ *adj* 1 *(time)* pasado,-a. 2 *(dead)* muerto,-a.
gong [gɒŋ] *n* 1 gong *m.* 2 *fam fig (award, prize)* galardón *m.*
good [gʊd] *adj* 1 bueno,-a; *(before m sing noun)* buen. 2 *(healthy)* sano,-a. 3 *(kind)* amable. 4 *(useful)* servible.
▲ *comp* better, *superl* best.
▷ *n* bien *m*: **its for your own good** *es por tu propio bien.*
▷ *n pl* **goods** *(property)* bienes *mpl.*; COMM *(in shop)* género *m sing*, artículos *mpl*; COMM *(merchandise)* mercancías *fpl.*
goodbye [gʊd'baɪ] [Also written **good-bye.**] *n* adiós *m.*
▷ *interj* ¡adiós!
good-hearted [gʊd'hɑːtɪd] *adj* de buen corazón.
good-for-nothing ['gʊdfənʌθɪŋ] *n* golfo.
good-humoured [gʊd'hjuːməd] *adj* de buen humor, campechano,-a.
good-looking [gʊd'lʊkɪŋ] *adj* guapo,-a.
good-natured [gʊd'neɪtʃəd] *adj* bondadoso,-a.
goodness ['gʊdnəs] *n* 1 *(virtue)* bondad *f.* 2 *(in food)* lo nutritivo.
goods [gʊdz] *n pl* → **good.**
good-tempered [gʊd'tempəd] *adj* de buen carácter.
goodwill [gʊd'wɪl] *n* buena voluntad *f.*
goody ['gʊdɪ] *n fam (in film, story)* el bueno.
▲ *pl* goodies.
▷ *n pl* **goodies** *fam (sweets)* golosinas *fpl*, chucherías *fpl.*

goof [gu:f] *n* **1** US *fam (mistake)* pifia, plancha. **2** *(person)* zoquete *m*.
▷ *vt* US *fam (botch)* chapucear, chafallar.
goofy ['gu:fɪ] *adj* **1** *fam (stupid)* necio,-a, bobo,-a. **2** *(teeth)* salido,-a; *(person)* dentón,-ona.
▲ *comp* goofier, *superl* goofiest.
google [gu:gᵊl] *vt* googlear, buscar en la web utilizando el motor de búsqueda Google.
goose [gu:s] *n* ganso, oca.
▲ *pl* geese.
gooseberry ['gʊzbrɪ, 'gu:sbᵊrɪ] *n* **1** BOT grosella espinosa. **2** GB *fam fig (person)* carabina.
▲ *pl* gooseberries.
gooseflesh ['gu:sfleʃ] *n* piel *f* de gallina.
goose-step ['gu:sstep] *n* paso de la oca.
gopher ['gəʊfəʳ] *n* ZOOL ardilla terrera.
gore[1] [gɔ:ʳ] *n* sangre *f* derramada.
gore[2] [gɔ:ʳ] *vt* cornear, dar una cornada a.
gorge [gɔ:dʒ] *n (mountain pass)* desfiladero; *(ravine)* barranco.
gorgeous ['gɔ:dʒəs] *adj* **1** magnífico,-a, espléndido,-a. **2** *(person)* guapísimo,-a.
▷ *n fam* guapo,-a.
gorilla [gə'rɪlə] *n* ZOOL gorila *m*.
gorse [gɔ:s] *n* BOT tojo, aulaga.
gosh [gɒʃ] *interj fam* ¡cielos!
goshawk ['gɒshɔ:k] *n* azor *m*.
go-slow [gəʊ'sləʊ] *n* huelga de celo.
gospel ['gɒspᵊl] *n* **1** REL evangelio. **2** MUS música gospel.
gossamer ['gɒsəməʳ] *n* **1** *(spiders' webs)* hilos *mpl* de telaraña. **2** *(cloth)* gasa fina.
▷ *adj* muy fino,-a.
gossip ['gɒsɪp] *n* **1** *(talk)* cotilleo, chismorreo. **2** *(person)* cotilla *mf*, chismoso,-a.
▷ *vi* cotillear, chismorrear.
gossipmonger ['gɒsɪpmʌŋgəʳ] *n (in general)* chismoso,-a; *(woman)* comadre *f*.
got [gɒt] *pt & pp* ⟶ **get**.
Goth [gɒθ] *n* **1** *(person)* godo,-a. **2** *(music)* música siniestra; *(person)* siniestro,-a.
Gothic ['gɒθɪk] *adj* **1** godo,-a. **2** *(language, architecture, type)* gótico,-a.
gotten ['gɒtᵊn] *pp* US ⟶ **get**.
gourd [gʊəd] *n* calabaza.
gourmand ['gʊəmənd] *n* goloso,-a.
gourmet ['gʊəmeɪ] *n* gastrónomo,-a, gurmet *mf*.
gout [gaʊt] *n* MED gota.
govern ['gʌvᵊn] *vt* **1** gobernar, dirigir. **2** LING regir. **3** *(determine)* dictar.
▷ *vi* **1** gobernar. **2** *(predominate)* predominar, prevalecer.
governess ['gʌvᵊnəs] *n* institutriz *f*.
government ['gʌvᵊnmənt] *n* gobierno.
▷ *adj* **1** *(of government)* del gobierno, gubernamental. **2** *(of a governor)* del gobernador.
governmental [gʌvᵊn'mentᵊl] *adj* gubernamental.
governor ['gʌvᵊnəʳ] *n* **1** *(town, state, bank)* gobernador,-ra. **2** *(prison)* director,-ra. **3** *(school)* administrador,-ra. **4** GB *fam (employer)* jefe *m*.
gown [gaʊn] *n* **1** vestido largo. **2** *(judge's, academic's)* toga. **3** *(surgeon's)* bata.
GP ['dʒi:'pi:] *abbr* (general practitioner) médico,-a de cabecera.
▲ *pl* GPs.
GPO ['dʒi:'pi:'əʊ] *abbr* GB (General Post Office) Oficina Central de Correos.
GPS ['dʒi:'pi:'es] *abbr* (global positioning system) sistema *m* de posicionamiento global.
grab [græb] *vt* **1** *(seize, snatch)* coger, agarrar, asir. **2** *(capture, arrest)* pillar, coger. **3** *fam* entusiasmar.
▲ *pt & pp* grabbed, *ger* grabbing.
▷ *n* **1** asimiento, agarrón *m*. **2** TECH cuchara.
⊙ **to grab at** *vt insep* intentar coger.
grace [greɪs] *n* **1** gracia, elegancia. **2** *(deportment)* garbo. **3** *(courtesy)* delicadeza, cortesía. **4** *(blessing)* bendición *f*. **5** REL gracia. **6** *(delay)* plazo.
▷ *vt* **1** *(adorn)* adornar. **2** *(honour)* honrar.
gracious ['greɪʃəs] *adj* **1** gracioso,-a. **2** *(polite)* cortés. **3** *(kind)* amable. **4** *(benevolent)* benévolo,-a.
▷ *interj* ¡Dios mío!
gradation [grə'deɪʃᵊn] *n* gradación *f*.
grade [greɪd] *n* **1** *(degree, level)* grado. **2** *(quality)* calidad *f*. **3** *(class, category)* clase *f*, categoría. **4** *(rank)* rango, grado. **5** *(mark)* nota. **6** US *(gradient)* pendiente *f*. **7** US *(form)* clase *f*.
▷ *vt* **1** *(sort, classify)* clasificar. **2** *(road)* nivelar. **3** *(student)* calificar, poner una nota. **4** *(colours)* degradar.
⊙ **to grade down** *vt sep* bajar de categoría.
⊙ **to grade up** *vt sep* subir de categoría.
gradual ['grædjʊəl] *adj* gradual, paulatino,-a.
gradually ['grædjʊəlɪ] *adv* poco a poco, gradualmente.
graduate [*(n)* 'grædjʊət, *(vb)* 'grædjʊeɪt] *n* EDUC *(after 3 year course)* diplomado,-a; *(after 5 year course)* licenciado,-a.
▷ *vt (grade, classify)* graduar.
▷ *vi (after 3 year course)* diplomarse (in, en); *(after 5 year course)* licenciarse (in, en).
graduation [grædjʊ'eɪʃᵊn] *n* **1** EDUC graduación *f*. **2** TECH graduación *f*.
graft[1] [grɑ:ft] *n (of plant, tissue)* injerto.
▷ *vt* injertar (onto, en).
graft[2] [grɑ:ft] *n* **1** US *(bribery)* soborno. **2** US *(corruption)* corrupción *f*. **3** GB *fam* trabajo.
▷ *vt* **1** US *(bribe)* sobornar. **2** US *(swindle)* timar, estafar. **3** GB *fam* trabajar duro, currar, pringar.
grafter ['grɑ:ftəʳ] *n* **1** US *(swindler)* timador,-ra, estafador,-ra. **2** *(worker)* persona trabajadora.
Grail [greɪl] *n* REL grial *m*.
grain [greɪn] *n* **1** *(gen)* grano. **2** *(cereals)* cereales *mpl*. **3** *(in wood)* veta, fibra; *(in stone)* filón *m*, veta; *(of leather)* flor *f*.
▷ *vt (give granular texture)* granular.
grammar ['græməʳ] *n* gramática. ● **grammar school** instituto de enseñanza media.
gramme [græm] *n* gramo.
gramophone ['græməfəʊn] *n* **1** gramófono. **2** *dated (record-player)* tocadiscos *m*.
gran [græn] *n fam* abuela.
granary ['grænərɪ] *n* granero.
▲ *pl* granaries.
grand [grænd] *adj* **1** *(splendid)* grandioso,-a, espléndido,-a, magnífico,-a. **2** *(impressive)* impresionante. **3** *(important - person)* distinguido,-a, importante. **4** *fam (great)* fenomenal.
grandchild ['græntʃaɪld] *n* nieto,-a.
▲ *pl* grandchildren [grən'tʃɪldrən].
granddad ['grændæd] *n fam* abuelo.

granddaughter ['grændɔːtəʳ] *n* nieta.
grandee [græn'diː] *n (nobleman)* grande *m.*
grandfather ['grændfɑːðəʳ] *n* abuelo.
grandiloquent [græn'dɪləkwənt] *adj* grandilocuente.
grandiose ['grændɪəʊs] *adj* grandioso,-a.
grandma ['grænmɑː] *n fam* abuela.
grandmaster [grænd'mɑːstəʳ] *n (chess)* gran maestro.
grandmother ['grænmʌðəʳ] *n* abuela.
grandpa ['græmpɑː] *n fam* abuelo.
grandparents ['grændpeərənts] *n pl* abuelos *mpl.*
grandson ['grændsʌn] *n* nieto.
grandstand ['grændstænd] *n* tribuna.
grange [greɪndʒ] *n* cortijo.
granite ['grænɪt] *n* granito.
▷ *adj* de granito.
granny ['grænɪ] *n fam* abuela.
▲ *pl* grannies.
grant [grɑːnt] *n* 1 EDUC beca. 2 *(subsidy)* subvención *f.* 3 JUR *(rights, property)* cesión *f.*
▷ *vt* 1 conceder, otorgar. 2 JUR ceder, transferir.
grant-aided [grɑːnt'eɪdɪd] *adj* subvencionado,-a.
granting ['grɑːntɪŋ] *n* 1 *(awarding - grant, money)* concesión *f,* otorgamiento. 2 JUR *(rights, property)* concesión *f.*
granulated ['grænjʊleɪtɪd] *adj* granulado,-a.
granule ['grænjuːl] *n* gránulo.
grape [greɪp] *n* uva.
grapefruit ['greɪpfruːt] *n* pomelo.
▲ *pl* grapefruits o grapefruit.
grapevine ['greɪpvaɪn] *n (gen)* parra; *(vine)* vid *f.*
graph [grɑːf] *n* gráfica, gráfico.
graphic ['græfɪk] *adj* 1 *(gen)* gráfico,-a. 2 *(vivid)* muy gráfico,-a, vívido,-a.
graphite ['græfaɪt] *n* grafito.
graphology [grə'fɒlədʒɪ] *n* grafología.
grapple ['græpᵊl] *vi* 1 *(person)* luchar (**with**, con), forcejear (**with**, con). 2 *(problem, etc)* lidiar (**with**, con).
grappling iron ['græplɪnaɪən] *n* garfio.
grasp [grɑːsp] *n* 1 *(grip, hold)* asimiento, apretón *m.* 2 *fig (control, power)* control *m,* dominio. 3 *(reach)* alcance *m.* 4 *(understanding)* comprensión *f; (knowledge)* conocimientos *mpl.*
▷ *vt* 1 *(seize - with hands)* agarrar, asir; *(opportunity, offer)* aprovechar. 2 *(understand)* comprender, captar.
⊙ **to grasp at** *vt insep* 1 tratar de agarrar. 2 *fig (opportunity)* aprovechar.
grasping ['grɑːspɪŋ] *adj* avaricioso,-a, avaro,-a, codicioso,-a.
grass [grɑːs] *n (plant)* hierba, yerba; *(lawn)* césped *m; (pasture)* pasto; *(dried)* paja.
▷ *vt (turf)* plantar césped en (**over**, -).
grasshopper ['grɑːshɒpəʳ] *n* saltamontes *m.*
grassy ['grɑːsɪ] *adj* cubierto,-a de hierba.
▲ *comp* grassier, *superl* grassies.
grate[1] [greɪt] *vt* 1 CULIN rallar. 2 *(scrape - gen)* rascar; *(- teeth)* hacer rechinar.
grate[2] [greɪt] *n (metal frame)* rejilla; *(fireplace)* chimenea.
grateful ['greɪtfʊl] *adj (person)* agradecido,-a; *(letter, smile)* de agradecimiento.
grater ['greɪtəʳ] *n* rallador *m.*
gratification [grætɪfɪ'keɪʃᵊn] *n* gratificación *f,* satisfacción *f,* placer *m.*
gratified ['grætɪfaɪd] *adj* satisfecho,-a, complacido,-a.
gratify ['grætɪfaɪ] *vt* 1 *(satisfy - desire, etc)* satisfacer. 2 *(give pleasure to)* complacer, gratificar.
▲ *pt & pp* gratified, *ger* gratifying.
gratis ['grætɪs, 'grɑːtɪs] *adv* gratis.
gratitude ['grætɪtjuːd] *n* gratitud *f,* agradecimiento.
gratuitous [grə'tjuːɪtəs] *adj* gratuito,-a.
gratuitously [grə'tjuːɪtəslɪ] *adv* gratuitamente.
gratuitousness [grə'truːɪtəsnəs] *n* gratuidad *f.*
gratuity [grə'tjuːɪtɪ] *n* 1 *(tip)* propina. 2 GB *(gift of money)* gratificación *f.*
▲ *pl* gratuities.
grave[1] [greɪv] *n* 1 *(tomb)* tumba, sepultura. 2 *lit (death)* tumba.
grave[2] [greɪv] *adj* 1 *(solemn - voice, look, etc)* grave. 2 *(serious - situation, consequences, error, etc)* grave, serio,-a. 3 [[grɑ'v] .] *(accent)* grave.
gravel ['grævᵊl] *n* grava, gravilla, guijo.
gravestone ['greɪvstəʊn] *n* lápida.
graveyard ['greɪvjɑːd] *n* cementerio.
gravitate ['grævɪteɪt] *vi* PHYS gravitar (**towards**, hacia).
⊙ **to gravitate to / gravitate towards** *vt insep (be drawn to)* sentirse atraído,-a por; *(move towards)* desplazarse hacia.
gravitation [grævɪ'teɪʃᵊn] *n* PHYS gravitación *f.*
gravity ['grævɪtɪ] *n* 1 PHYS gravedad *f.* 2 *(seriousness)* gravedad *f; (of person, manner)* gravedad *f,* circunspección *f.*
gray [greɪ] *adj* US ⟶ **grey.**
graying ['greɪɪŋ] *adj* US ⟶ **greying.**
graze[1] [greɪz] *n* rasguño, roce *m.*
graze[2] [greɪz] *vt (sheep, cattle)* pastar, pastorear, apacentar.
grazing ['greɪzɪŋ] *n* pastoreo.
grease [griːs] *n (gen)* grasa.
▷ *vt (part of car, machine, device)* engrasar.
greaseproof paper ['griːspruːf'peɪpəʳ] *n* papel *m* de cera.
greasy ['griːsɪ] *adj* 1 *(oily - hands)* grasiento,-a. 2 *fam pej (smarmy)* adulador,-ra, pelota.
▲ *comp* greasier, *superl* greasiest.
great [greɪt] *adj* 1 *(gen)* grande; *(before sing noun)* gran. 2 *(famous, important, outstanding)* grande, importante; *(before sing noun)* gran, importante. 3 *fam (excellent, wonderful)* estupendo,-a, fantástico,-a, sensacional, fabuloso,-a.
▷ *adv fam* muy bien, estupendamente, fenomenal.
great-aunt [greɪt'ɑːnt] *n* tía abuela.
greatcoat ['greɪtkəʊt] *n* abrigo, gabán *m.*
great-grandchild [greɪt'græntʃaɪld] *n* bisnieto,-a, biznieto,-a.
▲ *pl* great-grandchildren [greɪtgrən'tʃɪl-drən].
great-grandfather [greɪt'grændfɑːðəʳ] *n* bisabuelo.
great-grandmother [greɪt'grænmʌðəʳ] *n* bisabuela.
great-uncle [greɪt'ʌŋkəl] *n* tío abuelo.
greave [griːv] *n* greba.
Greece [griːs] *n* Grecia.
greed [griːd] *n* 1 *(for money, power)* codicia, avaricia. 2 *(for food)* gula, glotonería.

greedy ['gri:dɪ] *adj* 1 *(for money, power)* codicioso,-a. 2 *(for food)* glotón,-ona.
▲ *comp* greedier, *superl* greediest
Greek [gri:k] *adj* griego,-a.
▷ *n* 1 *(person)* griego,-a. 2 *(language)* griego.
green [gri:n] *adj* 1 *(colour)* verde. 2 *(environment friendly)* ecológico,-a. 3 *(pale)* pálido,-a. 4 *(inexperienced)* novato,-a, verde; *(gullible)* ingenuo,-a, crédulo,-a. 5 *(jealous)* envidioso,-a.
▷ *n* 1 *(colour)* verde *m*. 2 *(stretch of grass)* césped *m*; *(in golf)* green *m*; *(in village) césped público.*
▷ *n pl* greens *(vegetables)* verduras *fpl.*
▷ *n pl* the Greens POL los verdes *mpl.*
greenback ['gri:nbæk] *n* US *fam* dólar *m*, verde *m*, lechuga.
greenery ['gri:nərɪ] *n* follaje *m*, vegetación *f.*
greenfinch ['gri:nfɪntʃ] *n* verderón *m* común.
greenfly ['gri:nflaɪ] *n* pulgón *m*.
▲ *pl* greenflies.
greengage ['gri:ngeɪdʒ] *n* ciruela claudia.
greengrocer ['gri:ngrəʊsəʳ] *n* verdulero,-a. ● **greengrocer's (shop)** verdulería.
greenhorn ['gri:nhɔ:n] *n fam* novato,-a.
greenhouse ['gri:nhaʊs] *n* invernadero. ● **greenhouse effect** efecto invernadero.
greenish ['gri:nɪʃ] *adj* verdoso,-a.
Greenland ['gri:nlənd] *n* Groenlandia.
Greenlander ['gri:nləndəʳ] *n* groenlandés,-esa.
greenstuff ['gri:nstʌf] *n* verdura.
greet [gri:t] *vt* 1 *(wave at, say hello to)* saludar; *(welcome)* dar la bienvenida a; *(receive)* recibir. 2 *(react)* acoger, recibir. 3 *fig (meet)* llegar, presentarse.
greeting ['gri:tɪŋ] *n* saludo.
▷ *n pl* greetings saludos *mpl*, recuerdos *mpl.*
gregarious [gre'geərɪəs] *adj* gregario,-a, sociable.
gremlin ['gremlɪn] *n* duende *m*, duendecillo.
Grenada [grə'neɪdə] *n* Granada.
grenade [grə'neɪd] *n* granada.
grew [grʊ:] *pt* → grow.
grey [greɪ] *adj* 1 *(colour)* gris; *(hair)* cano,-a; *(sky)* nublado,-a, gris. 2 *(gloomy)* triste, gris.
▷ *n* 1 *(colour)* gris *m*. 2 *(horse)* caballo tordo.
greyhound ['greɪhaʊnd] *n* galgo.
greying ['greɪɪŋ] *adj* canoso,-a.
grid [grɪd] *n* 1 *(grating)* reja, parrilla, rejilla. 2 ELEC *(network)* red *f* nacional de tendido eléctrico. 3 *(on map)* cuadrícula.
griddle ['grɪdᵊl] *n* CULIN plancha.
gridiron ['grɪdaɪən] *n* 1 *(for cooking)* plancha. 2 US *(football)* campo.
grief [gri:f] *n* dolor *m*, pena.
grief-stricken ['gri:fstrɪkᵊn] *adj (person)* desconsolado,-a, consternado,-a.
grievance ['gri:vᵊns] *n (ground for complaint)* motivo de queja; *(complaint)* queja.
grieve [gri:v] *vt* afligir, apenar, dar pena a, entristecer.
▷ *vi* apenarse, afligirse.
griffin ['grɪfɪn] *n* grifo.
grill [grɪl] *n* CULIN *(over cooker)* gratinador *m*, grill *m*; *(on charcoal)* parrilla. → grille.
grille [grɪl] *n (partition)* reja, verja, enrejado; *(protective covering)* rejilla. [Also radiator grille.] AUTO calandra, parrilla.

grilling ['grɪlɪŋ] *n* interrogatorio.
grillroom ['grɪlrʊ:m] *n* asador *m*, grill *m*.
grim [grɪm] *adj* 1 *(serious)* austero,-a, severo,-a; *(look)* ceñudo,-a. 2 *(unpleasant)* horroroso,-a, pesimista; *(- prospect, outlook)* nefasto,-a, desalentador,-ra; *(- reality)* crudo,-a, duro,-a. 3 *(gloomy - landscape, place)* lúgubre, sombrío,-a. 4 *(resolute, unyielding)* inflexible, inexorable. 5 *(sinister - joke)* macabro,-a. 6 *fam (very bad)* malísimo,-a, penoso,-a, desastroso,-a; *(ill)* fatal.
▲ *comp* grimmer, *superl* grimmest.
grimace ['grɪməs] *n* mueca.
grime [graɪm] *n* mugre *f*, suciedad *f.*
grimly ['grɪmlɪ] *adv (severely - speak)* con gravedad, en tono grave.
▷ *adj (resolutely)* inexorablemente.
grimy ['graɪmɪ] *adj* mugriento,-a, sucio,-a.
▲ *comp* grimier, *superl* grimiest.
grin [grɪn] *n (genuine)* sonrisa (abierta); *(mocking)* sonrisa burlona.
▷ *vi* sonreír (abiertamente).
▲ *pt & pp* grinned, *ger* grinning.
grind [graɪnd] *vt* 1 *(mill)* moler; *(crush)* machacar, triturar; *(crystals, ore)* pulverizar; *(lens, mirror)* pulir; *(knife, blade)* afilar. 2 US *(mince - beef)* picar. 3 *(teeth)* rechinar. 4 *(press down hard on)* incrustar, aplastar, *(press in)* meter.
▷ *vi* 1 *(crush)* triturarse. 2 *(make harsh noise)* rechinar, chirriar. 3 US *(swot)* empollar.
▷ *n* 1 *fam (work)* trabajo pesado; *(effort)* paliza. 2 US *fam (swot)* empollón,-ona.
▲ *pt & pp* ground [graʊnd].
⊙ **to grind down** *vt sep (oppress)* oprimir.
⊙ **to grind out** *vt sep (music)* tocar.
grinder ['graɪndəʳ] *n (machine - for coffee)* molinillo, *(person - for knives, etc)* afilador,-ra.
grindstone ['graɪnstəʊn] *n* muela, piedra de afilar.
gringo ['grɪŋgəʊ] *n pej* gringo,-a.
▲ *pl* gringos.
grip [grɪp] *n* 1 *(tight hold)* asimiento. 2 *(of tyre)* adherencia, agarre *m*. 3 *fig (control, force)* control *m*, dominio. 4 SP *(way of holding)* la forma en que uno coge la raqueta, etc; *(part of handle)* asidero, empuñadura. 5 *(hairgrip)* horquilla. 6 US *(large bag)* bolsa de viaje. 7 *(in filming)* ayudante *mf* de cámara.
▷ *vt* 1 *(hold tightly - gen)* agarrar, asir, sujetar. 2 *(adhere to)* tener agarre, agarrarse, adherirse. 3 *fig (film, story, play)* captar el interés de, captar la atención de.
▷ *vi* adherirse.
▲ *pt & pp* gripped, *ger* gripping.
gripe [graɪp] *vi fam (complain)* quejarse, refunfuñar.
▷ *n fam (complaint)* queja.
▷ *n pl* the gripes *(stomach pains)* retortijones *mpl.*
gripping ['grɪpɪŋ] *adj (film, story, etc)* apasionante.
grisly ['grɪzlɪ] *adj* espeluznante, horripilante, truculento,-a.
▲ *comp* grislier, *superl* grisliest.
gristle ['grɪsᵊl] *n* cartílago, ternilla.
grit [grɪt] *n* 1 *(fine)* arena; *(coarse)* gravilla; *(dirt)* polvo. 2 *fam (determination)* valor *m*, agallas *fpl.*
gritty ['grɪtɪ] *adj* 1 *(flour)* arenoso,-a; *(mussels, cockles)* lleno,-a de arena. 2 *(determination, etc)* enérgico,-a.
▲ *comp* grittier, *superl* grittiest.

grizzle ['grɪzəl] *vi* GB *fam (whine)* lloriquear; *(complain)* refunfuñar.
grizzly ['grɪzlɪ] [Also **grizzly bear**.] *n* oso pardo.
groan [grəʊn] *n* 1 *(of pain)* gemido, quejido. 2 *fam (of disapproval)* gruñido. 3 *(creak)* crujido.
▷ *vi* 1 *(in pain)* gemir, quejarse; *(with disapproval)* gruñir. 2 *(creak)* crujir. 3 *fam (complain)* quejarse (**about**, de), refunfuñar (**about**, por), rezongar (**about**, de).
grocer ['grəʊsəʳ] *n* tendero,-a. ● **grocer's (shop)** tienda de comestibles.
groceries ['grəʊsərɪz] *n pl* comestibles *mpl*.
grocery ['grəʊsərɪ] *n* US tienda de ultramarinos, tienda de comestibles, colmado.
▲ *pl* **groceries.**
grog [grɒg] *n* grog.
groggy ['grɒgɪ] *adj fam* grogui.
▲ *comp* **groggier**, *superl* **groggiest.**
groin [grɔɪn] *n* 1 ANAT ingle *f*. 2 US ⟶ **groyne.**
groom [gruːm] *n* 1 *(bridegroom)* novio. 2 *(for horses)* mozo de cuadra.
▷ *vt* 1 *(horse)* almohazar; *(dog)* cepillar. 2 *(person)* arreglar.
groomed [gruːmd] *adj* arreglado,-a.
groove [gruːv] *n* 1 *(gen)* ranura; *(for door)* guía; *(in column)* acanaladura. 2 *(on record)* surco.
groovy ['gruːvɪ] *adj fam* guay, genial.
▲ *comp* **groovier**, *superl* **grooviest.**
grope [grəʊp] *vi (fumble)* andar a tientas.
gross [grəʊs] *adj* 1 *(flagrant - injustice)* flagrante; *(- ignorance)* craso,-a; *(- error)* grave. 2 *(fat)* muy gordo,-a, obeso,-a. 3 *(behaviour, manners)* grosero,-a, tosco,-a; *(- language)* soez; *(disgusting)* asqueroso,-a. 4 FIN *(total)* bruto,-a.
▷ *n (144 units)* gruesa, doce docenas *fpl*.
▲ *pl* **gross.**
▷ *vt (person)* obtener unos ingresos brutos de; *(film, etc)* recaudar.
⊙ **to gross out** *vt sep* US *fam* asquear, dar asco a.
grotesque [grəʊ'tesk] *adj* grotesco,-a.
grotto ['grɒtəʊ] *n* gruta.
▲ *pl* **grottoes** o **grottos.**
grotty ['grɒtɪ] *adj* GB *fam* asqueroso,-a, de mala muerte.
▲ *comp* **grottier**, *superl* **grottiest.**
grouch [graʊtʃ] *n* 1 *fam (person)* gruñón,-ona, cascarrabias *mf*. 2 *fam (complaint)* queja, protesta.
▷ *vi fam* refunfuñar, quejarse, rezongar.
ground¹ [graʊnd] *n* 1 *(surface of earth)* suelo; *(soil, earth)* tierra; *(terrain, land)* campo, terreno. 2 US *(electrical)* tierra. 3 ART *(background)* fondo. 4 *(matter, subject)* aspecto, punto. ● **ground floor** planta baja.
▷ *vt* 1 *(plane)* obligar a quedarse en tierra; *(boat)* varar, hacer encallar. 2 US *fam (child, teenager)* castigar, no dejar salir. 3 *(base)* fundar.
▷ *vi (instruct)* dar buenos conocimientos (**in**, de), enseñar los conocimientos básicos.
▷ *vt* US *(electrical apparatus)* conectar a tierra.
▷ *vi (ship)* encallar.
▷ *n pl* **grounds** *(reason, justification)* razón *f*, motivo: *(of coffee)* poso, posos *mpl*; *(gardens)* jardines *mpl*; *(area of land)* terreno.
ground² [graʊnd] *pp* ⟶ **grind.**
▷ *adj* 1 *(coffee)* molido,-a. 2 US *(beef)* picado,-a.
groundhog ['graʊndhɒg] *n* marmota.
grounding ['graʊndɪŋ] *n* base *f*, conocimientos *mpl*.
groundless ['graʊndləs] *adj* infundado,-a.
groundnut ['graʊndnʌt] *n* GB cacahuete *m*, maní *m*.
groundsheet ['graʊndʃiːt] *n* GB tela impermeable.
groundwork ['graʊndwɜːk] *n* trabajo preliminar, trabajo preparatorio.
group [gruːp] *n* 1 *(gen)* grupo. 2 MUS grupo, conjunto. 3 POL agrupación *f*, asociación *f*, colectivo, grupo.
▷ *vt* agrupar.
grouper ['gruːpəʳ] *n* mero.
groupie ['gruːpɪ] *n fam* grupi *mf*.
grouse¹ [graʊs] *n* lagópodo.
grouse² [graʊs] *n fam (complaint)* queja.
▷ *vi fam* quejarse (**about**, de), refunfuñar (**about**, por).
grove [grəʊv] *n* arboleda.
grovel ['grɒvəl] *vi (behave humbly)* humillarse, rebajarse, arrastrarse.
▲ *pt & pp* **grovelled** (US **groveled**), *ger* **grovelling** (US **groveling**).
groveller ['grɒvələʳ] *n* adulador,-ra, pelota *mf*.
grovelling ['grɒvəlɪŋ] *adj* servil, rastrero,-a.
grow [grəʊ] *vi* 1 *(gen)* crecer. 2 *(increase)* aumentar. 3 *(become)* hacerse, volverse. 4 *(begin gradually)* llegar a.
▷ *vt* 1 *(crop, plant, flower)* cultivar. 2 *(beard, etc)* dejarse (crecer); *(hair, nails)* dejarse crecer.
▲ *pt* **grew** ['gruː], *pp* **grown** [grəʊn].
⊙ **to grow apart** *vi* distanciarse.
⊙ **to grow away from** *vt insep* distanciarse de.
⊙ **to grow into** *vt insep (become)* convertirse en, hacerse.
⊙ **to grow on** *vt insep* llegar a gustar.
⊙ **to grow out of** *vt insep (habit)* perder, quitarse; *(clothes)* quedarle pequeño,-a a.
⊙ **to grow up** *vi* 1 *(become adult)* hacerse mayor; *(spend childhood)* criarse, crecer. 2 *(spring up)* surgir, nacer, desarrollarse.
grower ['grəʊəʳ] *n (farmer)* cultivador,-ra.
growl [graʊl] *n* gruñido.
▷ *vi* gruñir.
grown [grəʊn] *pp* ⟶ **grow.**
▷ *adj* adulto,-a.
grown-up ['grəʊnʌp] *adj* mayor, adulto,-a.
growth [grəʊθ] *n* 1 *(gen)* crecimiento; *(increase)* aumento; *(development)* desarrollo. 2 MED *(tumour)* bulto, tumor *m*. 3 *(of beard)* barba.
groyne [grɔɪn] *n* espigón *m*.
grub [grʌb] *n (larva)* larva, gusano.
▷ *vi* 1 *(by digging)* escarbar, hurgar. 2 *fig* rebuscar.
▲ *pt & pp* **grubbed**, *ger* **grubbing.**
⊙ **to grub out** *vt sep* arrancar.
⊙ **to grub up** *vt sep* sacar (de la tierra), desenterrar.
grubby ['grʌbɪ] *adj* 1 *(rather dirty)* mugriento,-a, sucio,-a. 2 *fig (seamy, sordid)* asqueroso,-a.
▲ *comp* **grubbier**, *superl* **grubbiest.**
grudge [grʌdʒ] *n* resentimiento, rencor *m*.
▷ *vt* 1 *(begrudge, resent)* dar a regañadientes, dar de mala gana. 2 *(envy)* envidiar.
grudging ['grʌdʒɪŋ] *adj* hecho,-a a regañadientes, hecho,-a de mala gana.
gruel ['gruːəl] *n* gachas *fpl*.
gruelling ['gruːəlɪŋ] *adj (race, journey)* agotador,-ra; *(ordeal, experience)* duro,-a, penoso,-a.

gruesome ['gruːsəm] *adj* espantoso,-a, horrible, horripilante.
gruff [grʌf] *adj (manner)* brusco,-a; *(voice)* áspero,-a, bronco,-a.
grumble ['grʌmbəl] *n* **1** *(complaint)* queja, rezongo. **2** *(of thunder)* estruendo.
▷ *vi* **1** *(moan, complain)* refunfuñar, rezongar, quejarse (**about**, de). **2** *(rumble - thunder)* retumbar; *(- stomach)* hacer ruido.
grumpy ['grʌmpɪ] *adj* gruñón,-ona, malhumorado,-a, de mal humor.
▲ *comp* **grumpier**, *superl* **grumpiest**.
grunge [grʌndʒ] *n* MUS grunge *m*.
grunt [grʌnt] *n* gruñido.
▷ *vi* gruñir.
guarantee [gærən'tiː] *n (gen)* garantía; *(certificate)* certificado de garantía.
▷ *vt* **1** *(gen)* garantizar; *(assure, promise)* asegurar. **2** *(debt)* avalar, garantizar.
guard [gɑːd] *n* **1** *(sentry, soldier)* guardia *mf*; *(security guard)* guarda *mf*, guarda jurado,-a, guarda de seguridad; *(prison officer)* carcelero,-a. **2** *(duty)* guardia. **3** GB *(on train)* jefe,-a de tren. **4** *(on machine)* dispositivo de seguridad; *(on gun)* seguro.
▷ *vt* **1** *(watch over)* vigilar, custodiar; *(protect - person, reputation)* proteger; *(keep - secret)* guardar. **2** *(control - tongue)* cuidar, controlar.
⊙ **to guard against** *vt insep (injury)* evitar; *(risks)* protegerse contra; *(infection, disease)* prevenir.
guarded ['gɑːdɪd] *adj (person, remark)* cauteloso,-a.
guardhouse ['gɑːdhaʊs] *n* MIL *(quarters)* cuartel *m*; *(prison)* prisión *f* militar, cárcel *f* militar.
guardian ['gɑːdɪən] *n* **1** *(defender)* guardián,-ana, defensor,-ra. **2** JUR *(of child)* tutor,-ra.
guardianship ['gɑːdɪənʃɪp] *n* tutela, tutoría.
guardrail ['gɑːdreɪl] *n* barandilla.
guardsman ['gɑːdzmən] *n* guardia *m*.
guava ['gwɑːvə] *n (fruit)* guayaba.
guess [ges] *n (conjecture)* conjetura; *(estimate)* cálculo.
▷ *vt* **1** *(gen)* adivinar. **2** US *fam (suppose)* suponer, pensar, creer. ● **to have a guess** adivinar.
▷ *vi* adivinar.
guesstimate ['gestɪmət] *n fam* cálculo aproximado.
guesswork ['geswɜːk] *n* conjeturas *fpl*, suposiciones *fpl*.
guest [gest] *n* **1** *(at home, to restaurant, etc)* invitado, -a; *(in hotel)* cliente,-a, huésped,-da. **2** *(on TV programme)* invitado,-a.
guesthouse ['gesthaʊs] *n* casa de huéspedes, pensión *f*.
guestroom ['gestruːm] *n* cuarto de (los) invitados.
guffaw [gʌ'fɔː] *n* carcajada, risotada.
▷ *vi* reírse a carcajadas.
Guiana [gaɪ'ænə, gɪ'ɑːnə] *n* Guayana.
guidance ['gaɪdəns] *n (help, advice)* orientación *f*, consejos *mpl*.
guide [gaɪd] *n* **1** *(person)* guía *mf*. **2** *(book)* guía. **3** *(indicator)* guía, modelo. ● **guide dog** perro lazarillo.
▷ *vt* **1** *(show the way)* guiar; *(lead)* conducir. **2** *(advise, influence)* guiar, orientar, aconsejar.
guidebook ['gaɪdbʊk] *n* guía.
guided ['gaɪdɪd] *adj* dirigido,-a.
guideline ['gaɪdlaɪn] *n* pauta, directriz *f*.
guiding ['gaɪdɪŋ] *adj* que guía, que sirve de guía. ● **guiding principle** principio rector. ‖ **guiding light** norte *m*.
guild [gɪld] *n (of workers)* gremio; *(association)* asociación *f*, agrupación *f*.
guile [gaɪl] *n (craftiness)* astucia; *(trickery)* mañas *fpl*, engaño.
guileless ['gaɪlləs] *adj* ingenuo,-a, cándido,-a.
guillotine ['gɪlətiːn] *n* guillotina.
▷ *vt (person, paper)* guillotinar.
guilt [gɪlt] *n* **1** JUR culpabilidad *f*. **2** *(blame)* culpa; *(remorse)* remordimiento.
guilty ['gɪltɪ] *adj* culpable (**of**, de). ● **to find** SB **guilty** declarar culpable a ALGN.
▲ *comp* **guiltier**, *superl* **guiltiest**.
Guinea ['gɪnɪ] *n* Guinea. ● **Equatorial Guinea** Guinea Ecuatorial. ‖ **Gulf of Guinea** golfo de Guinea. ‖ **New Guinea** Nueva Guinea.
guinea ['gɪnɪ] *n (coin)* guinea. ● **guinea fowl** gallina de Guinea, pintada. ‖ **guinea pig** conejillo de Indias, cobayo,-a.
Guinea-Bissau [gɪnɪbɪ'saʊ] *n* Guinea Bissau.
Guinean ['gɪnɪən] *adj* guineano,-a.
▷ *n* guineano,-a.
guise [gaɪz] *n* apariencia, forma, aspecto: **in various guises** *de varias formas.*
guitar [gɪ'tɑːr] *n* guitarra.
guitarist [gɪ'tɑːrɪst] *n* guitarrista *mf*.
gulf [gʌlf] *n* **1** GEOG golfo. **2** *fig* abismo. ● **Gulf of Mexico** Golfo de Méjico. ‖ **Persian Gulf** Golfo Pérsico. ‖ **the Gulf States 1** *(in Middle East)* los países del Golfo Pérsico. **2** *(in United States) los estados que lindan con el golfo de Méjico.* ‖ **Gulf Stream** Corriente *f* del Golfo. ‖ **the Gulf War** la guerra del Golfo.
gull [gʌl] *n* gaviota.
gullet ['gʌlɪt] *n* garganta, gaznate *m*.
gulley ['gʌlɪ] *n* → **gully**.
gullible ['gʌlɪbəl] *adj* crédulo,-a.
gully ['gʌlɪ] *n* **1** GEOG *(small valley, ravine)* barranco, torrentera. **2** *(deep ditch, waterway, channel)* surco cauce *m*.
▲ *pl* **gullies**.
gulp [gʌlp] *n (of drink)* trago; *(of air)* bocanada: **he drank his glass in one gulp** *se bebió todo el vaso de un trago.*
▷ *vt (drink)* beberse de un trago (**down**, -), tomarse de un trago (**down**, -); *(food)* engullir (**down**, -).
▷ *vi (swallow air)* tragar aire; *(with fear)* tragar saliva.
⊙ **to gulp back** *vt insep* tragarse.
gum[1] [gʌm] *n* ANAT encía.
gum[2] [gʌm] *n* **1** *(natural substance)* goma, resina. **2** *(chewing gum)* goma de mascar, chicle *m*. **3** *(glue)* goma (de pegar), pegamento. **4** *(gumdrop)* pastilla de goma. **5** *(gumtree)* gomero, árbol *m* del caucho.
▷ *vt* pegar (con goma).
▲ *pt & pp* **gummed**, *ger* **gumming**.
⊙ **to gum up** *vt sep* pegar.
gumboil ['gʌmbɔɪl] *n* flemón *m*.
gumboot ['gʌmbuːt] *n* bota de agua.
gummed [gʌmd] *adj* engomado,-a.

gummy ['gʌmɪ] *adj* **1** *(sticky)* pegajoso,-a. **2** *(smile)* muy amplio,-a.
▲ *comp* **gummier**, *superl* **gummiest**.
gumption ['gʌmpʃᵊn] *n fam (good sense)* sentido común, juicio, seso; *(courage)* agallas *fpl*.
gumshield ['gʌmʃi:ld] *n* protector.
gumtree ['gʌmtri:] *n* gomero, árbol *m* del caucho.
gun [gʌn] *n* **1** *(gen)* arma de fuego; *(handgun)* pistola, revólver *m*; *(rifle)* rifle *m*, fusil *m*; *(shotgun)* escopeta; *(cannon)* cañón *m*. **2** SP pistola.
⊙ **to gun for** *vt insep* andar a la caza de.
gunboat ['gʌnbəʊt] *n* (lancha) cañonera.
gunfight ['gʌnfaɪt] *n* tiroteo.
gunfire ['gʌnfaɪəʳ] *n (gen)* fuego, disparos *mpl*; *(shooting)* tiroteo; *(shellfire)* cañoneo, cañonazos *mpl*.
gunge [gʌndʒ] *n* GB *fam* porquería.
gunk [gʌŋk] *n* US *fam* porquería.
gunman ['gʌnmən] *n* pistolero.
▲ *pl* **gunmen** ['gʌnmən].
gunner ['gʌnəʳ] *n* artillero.
gunnery ['gʌnərɪ] *n* artillería.
gunpoint ['gʌnpɔɪnt] *phr* **at gunpoint** a punta de pistola.
gunpowder ['gʌnpaʊdəʳ] *n* pólvora.
gunrunner ['gʌnrʌnəʳ] *n* traficante *mf* de armas.
gunrunning ['gʌnrʌnɪŋ] *n* tráfico de armas, contrabando de armas.
gunshot ['gʌnʃɒt] *n* disparo, tiro.
gunsmith ['gʌnsmɪθ] *n* armero,-ra.
gunwale ['gʌnᵊl] *n* MAR borda.
gurgle ['gɜ:gᵊl] *n (of water)* gorgoteo, borboteo; *(of baby)* gorjeo.
▷ *vi (water, brook)* gorgotear, borbotar; *(baby)* gorjear.
gurnard ['gɜ:nəd] *n* rubio, arete.
guru ['gʊru:] *n* gurú *m*.
gush [gʌʃ] *n (of liquid)* chorro, borbotón *m*; *(of words)* torrente *m*; *(of emotion)* efusión *f*.
▷ *vi* **1** *(liquid)* salir a borbotones, brotar a chorros, salir a chorros. **2** *(person)* ser efusivo,-a: **everyone was gushing over her new baby** *todos se deshacían en elogios con su nuevo bebé*.
▷ *vt* chorrear, derramar.
gushing ['gʌʃɪŋ] *adj (person)* efusivo,-a.
gusset ['gʌsɪt] *n (gen)* escudete *m*; *(in briefs)* cuadradillo.
gust [gʌst] *n* **1** *(of wind)* ráfaga, racha; *(of rain)* chaparrón *m*. **2** *fig (of anger)* arrebato: **gust of laughter** *carcajada*.
▷ *vi* soplar.
gusto ['gʌstəʊ] *n* entusiasmo.
gusty ['gʌstɪ] *adj (wind)* racheado,-a; *(day)* ventoso,-a.
▲ *comp* **gustier**, *superl* **gustiest**.
gut [gʌt] *n* **1** ANAT intestino, tripa. **2** *fam (belly)* panza, barriga, tripa. **3** *(catgut)* cuerda de tripa.
▷ *vt* **1** *(fish)* destripar, limpiar; *(rabbit)* destripar. **2** *(building)* destruir el interior de.
▲ *pt & pp* **gutted**, *ger* **gutting**.
▷ *adj* visceral: **gut reaction** *reacción visceral*.
▷ *n pl* **guts** *(entrails)* entrañas *fpl*, tripas *fpl*, vísceras *fpl*; *fam (courage)* agallas *fpl*: **it takes guts to do what you did** *hay que tener agallas para hacer lo que hiciste*.
gutsy ['gʌtsɪ] *adj fam (person)* con agallas.
▲ *comp* **gutsier**, *superl* **gutsiest**.
gutter ['gʌtəʳ] *n (in street)* arroyo, cuneta; *(on roof)* canal *m*, canalón *m*.
▷ *n* **the gutter** *(in society)* los bajos fondos *mpl*, el arroyo, la cloaca. ● **gutter press** prensa amarilla, prensa sensacionalista.
guttural ['gʌtᵊrəl] *adj* gutural.
guy[1] [gaɪ] *n* **1** *fam (man)* tipo, tío: **he's a great guy** *es un tío estupendo*; **a tough guy** *un tipo duro*. **2** US *fam (person)* tío,-a: **come on you guys** *venga tíos*. **3** GB *(effigy)* efigie *m* de Guy Fawkes.
guy[2] [gaɪ] [Also **guy rope**.] *n* viento, cuerda (tensora).
Guyana [gaɪ'ænə] *n* Guyana, Guayana.
Guyanan [gaɪ'ænən] *adj-n* ⟶ **Guyanese**.
guzzle ['gʌzᵊl] *vt fam (eat)* zamparse, engullirse; *(drink)* chupar, tragar.
▷ *vi fam (eat)* engullir; *(drink)* chupar, tragar.
guzzler ['gʌzᵊləʳ] *n fam (person - big eater)* comilón,-ona, glotón,-ona; *(- drinker)* tragón,-ona; *(car)* que traga mucho.
gym [dʒɪm] *n* **1** *fam (gymnasium)* gimnasio. **2** *(gymnastics)* gimnasia. ● **gym shoes** zapatillas *fpl* de deporte.
gymkhana [dʒɪm'kɑ:nə] *n* gymkhana.
gymnasium [dʒɪm'neɪzɪəm] *n* gimnasio.
▲ *pl* **gymnasiums** o **gymnasia** [dʒɪm'neɪ-zɪə].
gymnast ['dʒɪmnæst] *n* gimnasta *mf*.
gymnastics [dʒɪm'næstɪks] *n* gimnasia.
gymnosperm ['dʒɪmnəʊspɜ:m] *n* gimnospermo.
gynaecological [gaɪnəkə'lɒdʒɪkᵊl] *adj* ginecológico,-a.
gynaecologist [gaɪnɪ'kɒlədʒɪst] *n* ginecólogo,-a.
gynaecology [gaɪnɪ'kɒlədʒɪ] *n* ginecología.
gynecological [gaɪnəkə'lɒdʒɪkᵊl] *adj* US ⟶ **gynaecological**.
gynecologist [gaɪnɪ'kɒlədʒɪst] *n* US ⟶ **gynaecologist**.
gynecology [gaɪnɪ'kɒlədʒɪ] *n* US ⟶ **gynaecology**.
gyp[1] [dʒɪp] *n* GB *fam (pain, trouble)* dolor *m*; *(punishment)* bronca: **my leg's been giving me gyp** *la pierna me ha estado fastidiando*.
gyp[2] [dʒɪp] *n fam (swindle)* estafa, timo.
▷ *vt* estafar, timar.
gypsum ['dʒɪpsəm] *n* yeso.
gypsy ['dʒɪpsɪ] *n* gitano,-a.
▷ *adj* gitano,-a.
▲ *pl* **gypsies**.
gyrate [dʒaɪ'reɪt] *vi* girar.
gyration [dʒaɪ'reɪsᵊn] *n* giro, rotación *f*.
gyratory ['dʒaɪrətərɪ] *adj* giratorio,-a.
gyrocompass ['dʒaɪrəʊkʌmpəs] *n* girocompás *m*, brújula giroscópica.
gyroscope ['dʒaɪrəskəʊp] *n* giroscopio, giróscopo.
gyroscopic [dʒaɪrə'skɒpɪk] *adj* giroscópico,-a.

H

H, h [eɪtʃ] *n (the letter)* H, h *f.*
ha ['hektɑːʳ] *abbr* **(hectare)** hectárea; *(abbreviation)* ha.
haberdasher ['hæbədæʃəʳ] *n* **1** GB *(shopkeeper)* mercero,-a. **2** US *(person)* camisero.
haberdashery [hæbə'dæʃərɪ] *n* **1** GB *(shop)* mercería; *(materials)* artículos *mpl* de mercería. **2** US *(shop)* tienda de ropa para caballero; *(clothes)* ropa para caballero.
habit ['hæbɪt] *n* **1** *(custom)* hábito, costumbre *f.* **2** REL *(garment)* hábito.
habitable ['hæbɪtəbᵊl] *adj fml* habitable.
habitat ['hæbɪtæt] *n* hábitat *m.*
habitation [hæbɪ'teɪʃᵊn] *n fml (the act of living in a place)* habitación *f*; *(dwelling)* morada.
habitual [hə'bɪtʃʊəl] *adj* **1** *(usual)* habitual, acostumbrado,-a. **2** *(liar, etc)* empedernido,-a, inveterado,-a.
habituate [hə'bɪtʃʊeɪt] *vt fml* acostumbrarse (**to**, a), habituarse (**to**, a).
habitué [hə'bɪtʃʊeɪ] *n* asiduo,-a, cliente,-a habitual.
hack¹ [hæk] *n (cut)* corte *m*, tajo; *(with axe)* hachazo; *(with machete)* machetazo.
⊙ **to hack about** *vt sep (in writing)* cortar, mutilar.
hack² [hæk] *n* **1** *(horse - worn-out)* jamelgo *m*; *(- hired)* caballo de alquiler. **2** *fam (writer)* escritorzuelo,-a; *(journalist)* periodista de pacotilla; *(politician)* politicastro,-a.
▷ *vi* GB *fam* montar a caballo.
hacker ['hækəʳ] *n fam (in computers)* pirata *mf.*
hacking¹ ['hækɪŋ] *adj (horseriding)* de montar.
hacking² ['hækɪŋ] *adj (cough)* áspero,-a, seco,-a.
hackles ['hækᵊlz] *n* ZOOL *(feathers)* collar *m*, plumas *fpl* del cuello; *(fur)* pelo del cuello.
hackneyed ['hæknɪd] *adj* gastado,-a, trillado,-a.
hacksaw ['hæksɔː] *n* sierra de arco para metales.
had [hæd] *pt & pp* ⟶ **have.**
hadn't [hædnt] *pt* ⟶ **have.**
haddock ['hædək] *n (fish)* eglefino.
haematoma [hiːmə'təʊmə] *n* hematoma *mf.*
haemorrhage ['hemərɪdʒ] *n* hemorragia.
haft [hɑːft, hæft] *n* TECH *(of knife)* mango; *(of sword)* puño, empuñadura.
hag [hæg] *n pej (ugly and evil old woman)* bruja, arpía.
haggard ['hægəd] *adj (look exhausted)* ojeroso,-a, trasnochado,-a; *(look drawn and pale)* macilento,-a.
haggis ['hægɪs] *n* CULIN *plato típico escocés hecho con las asaduras del cordero.*
haggish ['hægɪʃ] *adj* de bruja.
haggle ['hægᵊl] *vi* regatear (**over**, -).
haggling ['hægᵊlɪŋ] *n* regateo.
Hague [heɪg] *n* **The Hague** La Haya.
hah [hɑː] *interj* ¡ja!
ha-ha [hɑː'hɑː] *interj* ¡ja ja!
hail¹ [heɪl] *n (greeting)* saludo; *(shout)* grito.
▷ *vi* **1** *(call a taxi)* llamar. **2** *(acclaim)* aclamar.
hail² [heɪl] *n* **1** METEOR granizo, pedrisco. **2** *fig* lluvia.
▷ *vi* METEOR granizar.
hailstone ['heɪlstəʊn] *n* granizo, piedra.
hailstorm ['heɪlstɔːm] *n* granizada.
hair [heəʳ] *n* **1** *(on head)* cabello, pelo, cabellera. **2** *(on body)* vello. **3** *(horse's mane)* crin *f.*
hairband ['heəbænd] *n (for hair)* cinta.
hairbrush ['heəbrʌʃ] *n* cepillo para el pelo.
hairclip ['heəklɪp] *n* horquilla.
haircut ['heəkʌt] *n* corte *m* de pelo. ■ **to have a haircut** cortarse el pelo.
hairdo ['heəduː] *n fam* peinado.
▲ *pl* **hairdos.**
hairdresser ['heədresəʳ] *n* peluquero,-a. ● **hairdresser's** peluquería.
hairdressing ['heədresɪŋ] *n (profession)* peluquería.
hairdryer ['heədraɪəʳ] *n* secador *m* (de pelo).
hairgrip ['heəgrɪp] *n* horquilla.
hairless ['heələs] *adj* sin pelo, calvo,-a.
hairline ['heəlaɪn] *n* **1** nacimiento del pelo. **2** TECH grieta fina.
▷ *adj* fino,-a, preciso,-a, exacto,-a.
hairnet ['heənet] *n* redecilla.
hairpiece ['heəpiːs] *n* peluquín *m*, postizo.
hairpin ['heəpɪn] *n* horquilla.
hair-raising ['heəreɪzɪŋ] *adj* espeluznante, que pone los pelos de punta.
hair-remover ['heərɪmuːvəʳ] *n* depilatorio.
hairslide ['heəslaɪd] *n* pasador *m.*
hair-splitting ['heəsplɪtɪŋ] *n* sutilezas *fpl.*
▷ *adj pej* sutil, nimio,-a.
hairspray ['heəspreɪ] *n* laca para el pelo.
hairstyle ['heəstaɪl] *n* peinado.
hairy ['heərɪ] *adj* **1** peludo,-a. **2** *fig (scary)* espeluznante, espantoso,-a.
▲ *comp* **hairier**, *superl* **hairiest.**
Haiti ['heɪtɪ] *n* Haití *m.*
Haitian ['heɪʃᵊn] *adj* haitiano,-a.
▷ *n* haitiano,-a.
hake [heɪk] *n (fish)* merluza; *(young)* pescadilla.
halberd ['hælbəd] *n* alabarda.
halberdier [hælbə'dɪəʳ] *n* alabardero,-a.
halcyon ['hælsɪən] *n (in mythology)* alción *m.*
▷ *adj* **1** *lit (weather)* sereno,-a, tranquilo,-a; *(times)* próspero,-a, rico,-a. **2** *lit (days)* feliz, despreocupado,-a.
hale [heɪl] *adj* sano,-a, fuerte, robusto,-a.
half [hɑːf] *n* **1** mitad *f*: **a kilo and a half** *un kilo y medio.* **2** SP *(period)* parte *f*, mitad *f*, tiempo. **3** *(beer)* media pinta.
▲ *pl* **halves.**

▷ *adj* medio,-a: **he's been gone for half an hour** *lleva fuera media hora.* ● **half board** media pensión *f.* ‖ **half term** *vacaciones que se hacen a mitad de trimestre.*
▷ *adv* medio, a medias: **she's half Spanish** *es medio española.* ■ **half past** y media: **it's half past two** *son las dos y media.*

half-brother ['hɑ:fbrʌðə^r] *n* hermanastro.
half-caste ['hɑ:fkɑ:st] *n* mestizo,-a.
▷ *adj* mestizo,-a.
half-day [hɑ:f'deɪ] *n* media jornada.
half-hearted [hɑ:f'hɑ:tɪd] *adj* poco entusiasta.
half-hour [hɑ:f'aʊə^r] *n* media hora.
half-life ['hɑ:flaɪf] *n* CHEM media vida, período.
half-light ['hɑ:flaɪt] *n* media luz *f*, luz *f* crepuscular, penumbra.
half-mast [hɑ:f'mɑ:st] *phr* **at half-mast** a media asta.
half-note ['hɑ:fnəʊt] *n* US blanca.
halfpenny ['heɪpnɪ] *n (coin)* medio penique *m.*
▲ *pl* **halfpennies.**
half-price [hɑ:f'praɪs] *adv* a mitad de precio.
half-sister ['hɑ:fsɪstə^r] *n* hermanastra.
half-time [hɑ:f'taɪm] *n* SP descanso, media parte *f.*
half-tone ['hɑ:ftəʊn] *n* **1** *(in printing)* medio tono, media tinta. **2** MUS semitono.
halfway ['hɑ:f'weɪ] *adj* medio,-a, intermedio,-a.
▷ *adv* a medio camino, a mitad de camino.
half-yearly [hɑ:f'jɪəlɪ] *adj* semestral.
▷ *adv* semestralmente.
halibut ['hælɪbət] *n (fish)* halibut *m.*
halitosis [hælɪ'təʊsɪs] *n* halitosis *f.*
hall [hɔ:l] *n* **1** *(entrance)* vestíbulo, entrada. **2** *(for concerts, etc)* sala. **3** *(mansion)* casa solariega, mansión *f.* **4** US *(corridor)* pasillo, corredor *m.*
hallmark ['hɔ:lmɑ:k] *n* **1** *(on gold, etc)* contraste *m.* **2** *fig* sello.
hallo [hə'ləʊ] *interj* ⟶ **hello.**
hallowed ['hæləʊd] *adj fml dated* santo,-a, santificado,-a, bendito,-a.
Halloween [hæləʊ'i:n] *n* víspera de Todos los Santos.
hallstand ['hɔ:lstænd] *n* perchero.
hallucinate [hə'lu:sɪneɪt] *vi* alucinar.
hallucination [həlu:sɪ'neɪʃ^{ə}n] *n* alucinación *f.*
hallway ['hɔ:lweɪ] *n* US vestíbulo.
halo ['heɪləʊ] *n* **1** *(round moon, etc)* halo. **2** REL aureola.
▲ *pl* **haloes** o **halos.**
halogen ['hælədʒen] *n* halógeno.
halt [hɔ:lt] *n* **1** alto, parada. **2** *(railway)* apeadero.
▷ *vt* parar, detener, interrumpir.
halter ['hɔ:ltə^r] *n* cabestro, ronzal *m.*
halting ['hɔ:ltɪŋ] *adj* vacilante, titubeante.
halve [hɑ:v] *vt* **1** *(cut in two)* partir en dos. **2** *(reduce)* reducir a la mitad. **3** *(share)* compartir. **4** *(golf)* empatar.
halves [hɑ:vz] *n pl* ⟶ **half.**
halyard ['hæljəd] *n* driza.
ham[1] [hæm] *n (food)* jamón *m.*
ham[2] [hæm] *n* **1** RAD radioaficionado,-a. **2** *(actor)* comicastro,-a, histrión *m.*
▷ *vi* sobreactuar.
▲ *pt & pp* **hammed,** *ger* **hamming.**
Hamburg ['hæmbɜ:g] *n* Hamburgo.
hamburger ['hæmbɜ:gə^r] *n (food)* hamburguesa.
ham-fisted [hæm'fɪstɪd] *adj* **1** *fam* torpe, desmañado,-a. **2** *fig* torpe, manazas.
ham-handed [hæm'hændɪd] *adj* ⟶ **ham-fisted.**
hamlet ['hæmlət] *n* aldea, pueblecito.
hammer ['hæmə^r] *n* **1** *(tool)* martillo; *(piano)* macillo. **2** *(gun)* percusor *m.*
▷ *vt* **1** *(gen)* martillar, martillear; *(nail)* clavar. **2** *fam (beat)* dar una paliza, machacar.
⊙ **to hammer away** *vi* trabajar con ahínco.
⊙ **to hammer out** *vt sep (metal, dent)* trabajar con el martillo; *(deal, plan, etc)* lograr, alcanzar, llegar a.
hammerhead ['hæməhed] *n* ZOOL pez *m* martillo.
hammering ['hæmərɪŋ] *n* **1** *(knocking noise)* martilleo, golpeteo. **2** *fig* paliza.
hammock ['hæmək] *n* **1** hamaca. **2** MAR coy *m.*
hamper[1] ['hæmpə^r] *n* cesta, canasta.
hamper[2] ['hæmpə^r] *vt* estorbar, obstaculizar.
hamster ['hæmstə^r] *n* ZOOL hámster *m.*
hamstring ['hæmstrɪŋ] *n* ANAT tendón *m* de la corva.
▷ *vt* **1** desjarretar. **2** *fig* paralizar, limitar, incapacitar.
▲ *pt & pp* **hamstrung ['hamstrʊŋ].**
hand [hænd] *n* **1** mano *f.* **2** *(worker)* trabajador,-ra, operario,-a; *(sailor)* tripulante *mf*, marinero,-a. **3** *(of clock)* manecilla, aguja. **4** *(handwriting)* letra. **5** *(of cards)* mano *f*, cartas *fpl.* **6** *(applause)* aplauso. ● **at hand** a mano. ‖ **hands up!** ¡manos arriba! ‖ **on the one hand** por un lado. ‖ **by hand** a mano. ‖ **on the other hand** por otro lado. ‖ **to lend a hand** echar una mano.
▷ *vt* dar, entregar.
⊙ **to hand around** *vt sep* repartir, ofrecer, pasar.
⊙ **to hand back** *vt sep* devolver.
⊙ **to hand down** *vt sep (songs, etc)* transmitir; *(clothes)* pasar; *(possessions)* dejar en herencia.
⊙ **to hand in** *vt sep (work, etc)* entregar; *(resignation, etc)* presentar, notificar.
⊙ **to hand on** *vt sep (traditions, etc)* transmitir, heredar; *(give)* pasar, dar.
⊙ **to hand out** *vt sep (distribute)* repartir, distribuir; *(give - gen)* dar; *(- punishment)* aplicar.
⊙ **to hand over** *vt sep (give)* entregar; *(one's possessions, etc)* ceder.
handbag ['hændbæg] *n* bolso.
handball ['hændbɔ:l] *n* SP balonmano.
handbook ['hændbʊk] *n (guidebook)* guía; *(reference book)* manual *m.*
handbrake ['hændbreɪk] *n* freno de mano.
handclap ['hændklæp] *n* aplauso.
handcuff ['hændkʌf] *vt* esposar.
▷ *n pl* **handcuffs** esposas *fpl.*
handful ['hændfʊl] *n* puñado.
hand-grenade ['hændgrəneɪd] *n* granada de mano.
handgun ['hændgʌn] *n* pistola.
handicap ['hændɪkæp] *n* **1** *(physical)* discapacidad *f*; *(mental)* deficiencia, disminución *f* psíquica. **2** *(in sport)* hándicap *m.* **3** *fig* obstáculo.
▷ *vt* **1** obstaculizar, impedir, perjudicar. **2** *(in sport)* handicapar, conceder un hándicap a.
▲ *pt & pp* **handicapped,** *ger* **handicapping.**
handicapped ['hændɪkæpt] *adj* **1** *(physically)* minusválido,-a, discapacitado,-a, disminuido,-a físico,-a, *(mentally)* disminuido, a psíquico,-a. **2** *fig* desfavorecido,-a.

handicraft ['hændɪkrɑːft] *n* **1** *(job, art)* artesanía; *(objects)* objetos *mpl* de artesanía. **2** *(manual skill)* habilidad *f* manual, destreza manual.
handiwork ['hændɪwɜːrk] *n (work)* trabajo, obra; *(craft)* artesanía.
handkerchief ['hæŋkətʃiːf] *n* pañuelo.
handle ['hændl] *n* **1** *(of door)* pomo, manilla. **2** *(of drawer)* tirador *m*. **3** *(of cup)* asa. **4** *(of knife)* mango. **5** *(lever)* palanca. **6** *(crank)* manivela. **7** *fig* pretexto.
▷ *vt* **1** *(gen)* manejar, manipular. **2** *(people)* tratar. **3** *(tolerate)* aguantar. **4** *(control)* controlar, dominar. **5** *(deal with)* ocuparse de. **6** *(manage)* poder con, tener la capacidad para. **7** *(responsibility)* encargarse de.
handlebar ['hændᵊlbɑːʳ] *n* manillar *m*.
handlebar ['hændᵊlbɑːʳ] *n* manillar *m*.
handler ['hændləʳ] *n* cuidador,-ra.
handmade [hænd'meɪd] *adj* hecho,-a a mano.
handmaiden ['hændmeɪdᵊn] *n dated* criada.
handout ['hændaʊt] *n* **1** *(leaflet)* folleto, prospecto; *(political)* octavilla. **2** EDUC material *m*. **3** *(press)* comunicado de prensa, nota de prensa. **4** *(charity)* limosna, dádiva, caridad *f*.
handover ['hændəʊvəʳ] *n (power, responsibility, etc)* traspaso, transferencia.
handrail ['hændreɪl] *n* pasamano, barandilla.
handsaw ['hændsɔː] *n* serrucho.
handset ['hændset] *n* microteléfono.
handshake ['hændʃeɪk] *n* apretón *m* de manos.
handsome ['hænsəm] *adj* **1** *(man)* apuesto, guapo, de buen ver; *(woman)* bella, hermosa, guapa. **2** *(elegant)* elegante. **3** *(generous)* considerable, generoso,-a.
hands-on ['hændzɒn] *adj (for computers)* práctico,-a.
handstand ['hændstænd] *phr* **to do a handstand** hacer el pino.
hand-wash ['hænd'wɒʃ] *vt* lavar a mano.
handwriting ['hændraɪtɪŋ] *n* letra, escritura.
handy ['hændɪ] *adj* **1** *(person)* hábil. **2** *(close at hand)* a mano, cercano,-a. **3** *(useful)* práctico,-a, cómodo,-a, útil.
▲ *comp* **handier**, *superl* **handiest**.
handyman ['hændɪmæn] *n* manitas *mf*.
▲ *pl* **handymen** ['hændɪmen].
hang [hæŋ] *vt* **1** [*pt & pp* **hung** [hʌŋ]] *(gen)* colgar. **2** [*pt & pp* **hung** [hʌŋ]] *(wallpaper)* colocar. **3** [*pt & pp* **hanged**.] JUR ahorcar.
▷ *n (of dress, etc)* caída.
⊙ **to hang about / hang around** *vi* **1** esperar. **2** *(waste time)* perder el tiempo.
▷ *vt insep* frecuentar.
⊙ **to hang back** *vi* **1** quedarse atrás. **2** *fig* vacilar.
⊙ **to hang down** *vi* colgar, caer.
⊙ **to hang on** *vi* **1** *(hold tight)* agarrarse. **2** *(wait)* esperar.
⊙ **to hang out** *vt sep (washing)* tender.
▷ *vi fam* soler estar.
⊙ **to hang up** *vt sep* colgar.
hangar ['hæŋəʳ] *n* hangar *m*.
hanger ['hæŋəʳ] *n* percha.
hanger-on [hæŋər'ɒn] *n fam pej (person)* lapa, parásito.
▲ *pl* **hangers-on**.
hang-glider ['hæŋglaɪdəʳ] *n* ala delta.
hanging ['hæŋɪŋ] *adj* colgante.
▷ *n* ejecución *f* en la horca, ahorcamiento.

hangman ['hæŋmən] *n* **1** verdugo. **2** *(game)* el ahorcado.
▲ *pl* **hangmen** ['hæŋmən].
hangnail ['hæŋneɪl] *n* padrastro.
hangout ['hæŋaʊt] *n fam* guarida, lugar *m* de reunión habitual.
hangover ['hæŋəʊvəʳ] *n* **1** *(after too much drinking)* resaca. **2** *(remains)* resto, vestigio.
hang-up ['hæŋʌp] *n* **1** *fam (problem)* problema *m*. **2** *(complex)* complejo.
hank [hæŋk] *n* madeja.
hanker ['hæŋkəʳ] *vi* **to hanker after / hanker for** ansiar, anhelar.
haphazard [hæp'hæzəd] *adj* **1** desordenado,-a. **2** *(plans, etc)* improvisado,-a.
happen ['hæpᵊn] *vi* **1** *(occur)* ocurrir, pasar, suceder. **2** *(by chance)* dar la casualidad de.
happening ['hæpᵊnɪŋ] *n* acontecimiento.
happily ['hæpɪlɪ] *adv* **1** *(in a happy way)* felizmente, con alegría. **2** *(luckily)* afortunadamente.
happiness ['hæpɪnəs] *n* felicidad *f*, alegría.
happy ['hæpɪ] *adj* **1** *(cheerful)* feliz, alegre, dichoso,-a, afortunado,-a. **2** *(glad)* contento,-a, satisfecho,-a.
■ **happy birthday!** !feliz cumpleaños!
▲ *comp* **happier**, *superl* **happiest**.
harangue [hə'ræŋ] *vt* arengar.
▷ *n* arenga.
harass ['hærəs] *vt* **1** acosar, hostigar. **2** *(military)* hostilizar, hostigar. **3** *(worries, problems)* atormentar, agobiar.
harassment ['hærəsmənt] *n* acoso, hostigamiento.
harbor ['hɑːbəʳ] *n* US **harbour**.
harbour ['hɑːbəʳ] *n* puerto.
▷ *vt* **1** *(criminal)* encubrir. **2** *(doubts)* abrigar. **3** *(suspicions)* tener; *(contain, hide)* contener, esconder.
hard [hɑːd] *adj* **1** *(gen)* duro,-a; *(solid)* sólido,-a. **2** *(difficult)* difícil. **3** *(harsh)* severo,-a. **4** *(work)* arduo,-a, penoso,-a, agotador,-ra. **5** *fig* cruel, rudo,-a. **6** *(fight, match)* reñido,-a, disputado,-a; *(decision)* injusto,-a. **7** *(fact)* innegable; *(luck)* malo,-a. **8** *(final decision)* definitivo,-a, irrevocable; *(person)* severo,-a, inflexible. **9** LING fuerte. ■ **hard of hearing** duro,-a de oído. ‖ **to work hard** trabajar mucho. ● **hard court** pista dura. ‖ **hard disk** disco duro. ‖ **hard labour** (US **labor**) trabajos forzados.
▷ *adv (forcibly)* fuerte; *(diligently)* mucho, de firme, concienzudamente, con ahínco.
hardback ['hɑːdbæk] *n (in printing)* edición *f* en tela, edición *f* de tapas duras.
hard-boiled ['hɑːdbɔɪld] *adj (egg)* duro,-a; *(person)* duro,-a, insensible.
hard-core ['hɑːdkɔːʳ] *adj* irreductible, incondicional.
harden ['hɑːdᵊn] *vt* **1** endurecer. **2** *fig* insensibilizar.
hard-headed ['hɑːd'hedɪd] *adj* frío,-a, cerebral, práctico,-a.
hardhearted ['hɑːd'hɑːtɪd] *adj* cruel, duro,-a, insensible.
hardliner [hɑːd'laɪnəʳ] *n (ideas, especially in politics)* duro,-a, partidario,-a de la línea dura.
hardly ['hɑːdlɪ] *adv (scarcely)* apenas, casi; *(not easily)* difícilmente, duramente, con dificultad.

hardship ['hɑːdʃɪp] *n (usually economic)* privación *f*, apuro, dificultad *f*.

hardware ['hɑːdweəʳ] *n* **1** *(goods)* ferretería, quincallería. **2** COMPUT hardware *m*, soporte *m* físico. **3** MIL armamento. **4** TECH equipos *mpl*, maquinaria.

hardwearing [hɑːd'weərɪŋ] *adj (especially articles of clothing)* duradero,-a, resistente.

hard-working ['hɑːd'wɜːkɪŋ] *adj* trabajador,-ra.

hardy ['hɑːdɪ] *adj* **1** fuerte, robusto,-a. **2** *(plant)* resistente.

▲ *comp* **hardier**, *superl* **hardiest**.

hare [heəʳ] *n* ZOOL liebre *f*.

▷ *vi* correr muy deprisa, ir muy deprisa.

haricot bean [hærɪkəʊ'biːn] *n* alubia, judía.

harm [hɑːm] *n* mal *m*, daño, perjuicio. ■ **to do** SB **harm** hacerle daño a ALGN. ‖ **there's no harm in...** no se pierda nada...

▷ *vt* dañar, perjudicar.

harmful ['hɑːmfʊl] *adj* dañino,-a, nocivo,-a, perjudicial.

harmless ['hɑːmləs] *adj* inocuo,-a, inofensivo,-a.

harmonic [hɑː'mɒnɪk] *adj* armónico,-a.

harmonica [hɑː'mɒnɪkə] *n* MUS armónica.

harmonics [hɑː'mɒnɪks] *n* MUS armonía.

harmonize ['hɑːmənaɪz] *vt* armonizar.

harmony ['hɑːmənɪ] *n* armonía.

▲ *pl* **harmonies**.

harness ['hɑːnəs] *n* **1** *(for animals)* arreos *mpl*, guarniciones *fpl*, arneses *mpl*. **2** *(for children)* andadores *mpl*.

▷ *vt* **1** *(horse)* poner los arreos a. **2** *(hitch)* enganchar. **3** *fig (resources)* aprovechar, utilizar.

harp [hɑːp] *n* MUS arpa.

harpist ['hɑːpɪst] *n* MUS arpista *mf*.

harpoon [hɑː'puːn] *n* arpón *m*.

▷ *vt* arponear.

harpsichord ['hɑːpsɪkɔːd] *n* MUS clavicordio, clavicémbalo.

harpy ['hɑːpɪ] *n* **1** *lit* arpía. **2** *fig* arpía.

▲ *pl* **harpies**.

harrier[1] ['hærɪəʳ] *n (bird)* aguilucho.

harrier[2] ['hærɪəʳ] *n* **1** *(dog)* perro de caza. **2** *(runner)* corredor,-ra de cros.

harrow ['hærəʊ] *n* AGR grada, rastrillo.

▷ *vt* rastrillar.

harrowing ['hærəʊɪŋ] *adj* angustioso,-a, desgarrador,-ra, terrible.

harsh [hɑːʃ] *adj* **1** *(cruel)* cruel, duro,-a, severo,-a. **2** *(sound)* discordante. **3** *(rough)* áspero,-a.

hart [hɑːt] *n* ZOOL ciervo.

harvest ['hɑːvɪst] *n* **1** *(gen)* cosecha, siega; *(vegetables)* recolección *f*, cosecha. **2** *(grapes)* vendimia. **3** *fig* cosecha.

▷ *vt* **1** cosechar, recoger. **2** *(grapes)* vendimiar.

harvester ['hɑːvɪstəʳ] *n* **1** *(person)* segador,-ra. **2** *(machine)* segadora, cosechadora.

has [hæz] *pres* ⟶ **have**.

has-been ['hæzbiːn] *n fam* vieja gloria.

hash[1] [hæʃ] *n* **1** CULIN *sofrito de carne picada*. **2** *fam (mess)* embrollo, lío.

⊙ **to hash up** *vt sep fam* hacer mal, estropear, pifiar.

hash[2] [hæʃ] *n fam (drug)* hachis *m*.

hashish ['hæʃiːʃ] *n* hachís *m*.

hasp [hɑːsp] *n* **1** *(of window)* falleba; *(of door)* picaporte *m*, cierre *m*. **2** *(of padlock)* cerrojo, pestillo; *(of album, etc)* broche *m*, cierre *m*.

hassle ['hæsəl] *n* **1** *fam (nuisance)* rollo, follón *m*, jaleo; *(problem)* problema *m*, lío. **2** *(argument)* bronca, discusión *f*, pelea, riña.

▷ *vt* molestar, fastidiar.

haste [heɪst] *n* prisa, precipitación *f*.

hasten ['heɪsən] *vt fml* apresurar, acelerar el paso de, dar prisa a.

▷ *vi* darse prisa, apresurarse.

hastily ['heɪstɪlɪ] *adv (quickly)* de prisa.

hat [hæt] *n* sombrero.

hatch [hætʃ] *n* **1** *(on ship)* escotilla. **2** *(of chickens, brood)* pollada.

▷ *vt* **1** *(eggs)* empollar, incubar. **2** *fig (plot, plan)* idear, tramar.

▷ *vi* salir del cascarón, salir del huevo.

hatchet ['hætʃɪt] *n* hacha.

hate [heɪt] *n* odio.

▷ *vt* **1** *fam (detest)* odiar, detestar, aborrecer. **2** *fam (regret)* lamentar, sentir.

hatred ['heɪtrəd] *n* odio.

haughty ['hɔːtɪ] *adj* altanero,-a, arrogante, altivo,-a, engreído,-a.

▲ *comp* **haughtier**, *superl* **haughtiest**.

haul [hɔːl] *n* **1** *(pull)* tirón *m*, estirón *m*. **2** *(distance)* recorrido, camino. **3** *(fish)* redada. **4** *(loot)* botín *m*.

▷ *vt* **1** *(drag)* tirar de, arrastrar. **2** *(boat)* halar; *(car, caravan, etc)* remolcar.

haulage ['hɔːlɪdʒ] *n* **1** *(activity)* transporte *m*, acarreo. **2** *(cost)* (gastos *mpl* de) transporte *m*.

haunch [hɔːntʃ] *n* **1** ANAT cadera y muslo, anca. **2** CULIN pierna, pernil *m*.

haunt [hɔːnt] *n (of people)* sitio preferido; *(of criminals, animals)* guarida.

▷ *vt* **1** *(frequent - gen)* frecuentar; *(- ghost)* aparecer en, rondar por. **2** *(memory, thought)* obsesionar, perseguir.

haunted ['hɔːntɪd] *adj* encantado,-a, embrujado,-a.

Havana [hə'vænə] *n* La Habana.

have [hæv] *vt* **1** *(gen)* tener, poseer. **2** *(food)* comer, tomar; *(drink)* beber, tomar. **3** *(treatment)* recibir: **she's having physiotherapy** *acude a fisioterapia*. **4** *(invite)* recibir, invitar. **5** *(borrow)* pedir prestado, dejar. **6** *(party, meeting)* celebrar, tener, dar. **7** *(cause to happen)* hacer, mandar: **he had the house painted** *hizo pintar la casa*. **8** *fam (cheat)* timar. ■ **have got** tener: **he's got two sisters** *tiene dos hermanas*; **we haven't got any sugar** *no tenemos azúcar*. ‖ **to have breakfast** desayunar. ‖ **to have dinner** cenar. ‖ **to have just** acabar de: **I have just seen him** *acabo de verlo*. ‖ **to have lunch** comer, almorzar. ‖ **to have a bath** bañarse. ‖ **to have a shower** ducharse. ‖ **to have a swim** darse un baño.

▷ *aux* haber: **I have seen her** *la he visto*.

⊙ **to have on** *vt sep* **1** *(wear)* llevar puesto,-a. **2** *(tease)* tomar el pelo a.

⊙ **to have out** *vt sep (tooth)* sacarse; *(appendix)* operarse de.

▲ *3rd pers pres sing* **has** [hæz], *pt & pp* **had** [hæd], *ger* **having**.

haven ['heɪvᵊn] *n* **1** *fig* refugio, asilo. **2** *(harbour)* puerto.
haversack ['hævəsæk] *n* mochila.
havoc ['hævək] *n* estragos *mpl*.
hawk[1] [hɔ:k] *n* halcón *m*.
hawk[2] [hɔ:k] *vt* **1** *(in the street)* vender en la calle; *(door to door)* vender de puerta en puerta. **2** *(gossip, news)* divulgar, pregonar, difundir.
▷ *vi* carraspear.
hawker ['hɔ:kəʳ] *n* vendedor,-ra ambulante.
hawthorn ['hɔ:θɔ:n] *n* BOT espino.
hay [heɪ] *n* BOT heno. ● **hay fever** fiebre *f* del heno.
hayloft ['heɪlɒft] *n* pajar *m*, henar *m*.
haystack ['heɪstæk] *n* almiar *m*.
haywire ['heɪwaɪəʳ] *adj fam (confused)* en desorden, confuso,-a; *(mad)* chalado,-a, loco,-a.
hazard ['hæzəd] *n* **1** *(risk)* riesgo, peligro. **2** *(in sports in general)* obstáculo.
▷ *vt* **1** *fml* arriesgar, poner en peligro. **2** *fml (guess, remark)* aventurar, atreverse a hacer.
hazardous ['hæzədəs] *adj* arriesgado,-a, peligroso,-a, aventurado,-a.
haze [heɪz] *n* **1** neblina. **2** *fig* confusión *f*, vaguedad *f*.
▷ *vt* US hacer una novatada a.
hazel ['heɪzᵊl] *n* BOT avellano.
▷ *adj* (de color de) avellana.
hazelnut ['heɪzᵊlnʌt] *n* BOT avellana.
hazily ['heɪzɪlɪ] *adv fig* vagamente.
haziness ['heɪzɪnəs] *n* **1** nebulosidad *f*, calina. **2** *fig* nebulosidad *f*, vaguedad *f*.
he [hi:] *pron* **1** él: **he's my brother** *(él) es mi hermano.* **2** *(gen)* el que, quien.
▷ *n* **1** *(male animals)* macho. **2** *(man)* hombre *m*, varón *m*.
head [hed] *n* **1** *(gen)* cabeza; *(mind)* mente *f*. **2** *(on tape recorder, video)* cabezal *m*. **3** *(of bed, table)* cabecera. **4** *(of page)* principio. **5** *(on beer)* espuma. **6** *(cape)* cabo, punta. **7** *(of school, company)* director, -ra. **8** *(cattle)* res *f*. **9** *(coin)* cara. **10** *(of cabbage, lettuce)* cogollo; *(of cauliflower)* pella.
▷ *adj* principal, jefe.
▷ *vt* **1** *(company, list, etc)* encabezar. **2** *(ball)* rematar de cabeza, dar un cabezazo a, cabecear.
⊙ **to head for** *vt insep* dirigirse hacia.
⊙ **to head off** *vi* marcharse, irse.
▷ *vt sep (divert)* interceptar; *(avoid)* evitar.
headache ['hedeɪk] *n* **1** dolor *m* de cabeza. **2** *fig* quebradero de cabeza.
headed ['hedɪd] *adj (paper)* con membrete.
header ['hedəʳ] *n (football)* cabezazo; *(dive)* salto de cabeza.
head-first [hed'fɜ:st] *adv* de cabeza.
head-hunter [hed'hʌntəʳ] *n* **1** cazador,-ra de cabezas, jíbaro,-a. **2** *fam fig* cazatalentos *mf*.
heading ['hedɪŋ] *n* **1** *(of chapter)* encabezamiento, título. **2** *(letterhead)* membrete *m*.
headlamp ['hedlæmp] *n* AUTO faro.
headland ['hedlənd] *n* cabo, punta, promontorio.
headlight ['hedlaɪt] *n* AUTO faro.
headline ['hedlaɪn] *n* titular *m*.
▷ *vt* **1** *(newspaper)* poner en los titulares. **2** *(emphasize)* remarcar, subrayar. **3** US encabezar la lista de artistas de.
headlong ['hedlɒŋ] *adj (headfirst)* de cabeza; *(hasty)* precipitado,-a, impetuoso,-a.
▷ *adv* **1** *(hastily)* precipitadamente, impetuosamente. **2** *(headfirst)* de cabeza.
headmaster [hed'mɑ:stəʳ] *n* director *m*.
headmistress [hed'mɪstrəs] *n* directora.
head-on [hed'ɒn] *adj* frontal.
headphones ['hedfəʊnz] *n pl* auriculares *mpl*, cascos *mpl*.
headquarters ['hedkwɔ:təz] *n* **1** *(of an organization)* sede *f*; *(main office)* oficina central. **2** *(of a firm)* domicilio social. **3** MIL cuartel *m* general.

Puede usararse con verbo tanto en singular como en plural.

headrest ['hedrest] *n* cabecero, cabezal *m*.
headroom ['hedru:m] *n* **1** altura libre sobre la cabeza, espacio libre sobre la cabeza. **2** *(bridges, etc)* altura libre de paso, luz *f*.
headscarf ['hedskɑ:f] *n* pañuelo.
▲ *pl* **headscarves** ['hedskɑ:vz].
headset ['hedset] *n* auriculares *mpl*.
headship ['hedʃɪp] *n (gen)* dirección *f*.
headstand ['hedstænd] *n* posición *f* de cabeza.
headstone ['hedstəʊn] *n* **1** *(tombstone)* lápida mortuoria. **2** ARCH piedra angular.
headstrong ['hedstrɒŋ] *adj* cabezota, obstinado,-a
headteacher ['hed'ti:ʳ] *adj* director,-a.
headway ['hedweɪ] *n (progress - gen)* progreso; *(of ship)* salida.
headword ['hedwɜ:d] *n* entrada, lema.
heady ['hedɪ] *adj (intoxicating)* embriagador,-ra, fuerte
▲ *comp* **headier**, *superl* **headiest.**
heal [hi:l] *vt* **1** *(disease, patient)* curar; *(wound)* cicatrizar, curar. **2** *fig* curar, remediar.
▷ *vi* **1** *(wounds)* cicatrizar, cicatrizarse; *(people)* curarse, sanar. **2** *fig* remediarse.
⊙ **to heal up** *vi* curarse, cicatrizarse.
healer ['hi:ləʳ] *n* curador,-ra, sanador,-ra.
healing ['hi:lɪŋ] *n (of disease)* curación *f*, cura; *(of wound)* cicatrización *f*.
▷ *adj (ointment)* cicatrizante; *(remedy)* curativo,-a; *(soothing)* apaciguador,-ra, conciliador,-ra.
health [helθ] *n* **1** salud *f*. **2** *(service)* sanidad *f*. **3** *fig* prosperidad *f*. ● **health care** sanidad *f*. ‖ **health centre** (US **center**) centro de salud. ‖ **health food** alimentos *mpl* naturales.
healthy ['helθɪ] *adj* **1** *(gen)* sano,-a. **2** *(good for health)* saludable. **3** *(appetite)* bueno,-a. **4** *(prosperous)* próspero,-a; *(disposition)* sensato,-a.
▲ *comp* **healthier**, *superl* **healthiest.**
heap [hi:p] *n* montón *m*.
hear [hɪəʳ] *vt* **1** *(gen)* oír. **2** *(lecture)* asistir a; *(a news item)* saber. **3** JUR *(case)* ver; *(witness, defendant)* oír.
▲ *pt & pp* **heard** [hɛ:d].
⊙ **to hear out** *vt sep* escuchar hasta el final.
hearer ['hɪərəʳ] *n* oyente *mf*.
hearing ['hɪərɪŋ] *n* **1** *(sense)* oído. **2** *(act of hearing)* audición *f*. **3** JUR audiencia, vista.
hearsay ['hɪəseɪ] *n* rumores *mpl*.
hearse [hɜ:s] *n* coche *m* fúnebre.
heart [hɑ:t] *n* **1** ANAT corazón *m*. **2** *(centre of feeling)* corazón *m*. **3** *(courage)* valor *m*, corazón *m*. **4** *(of le*

tuce, etc) cogollo; *(of place)* corazón *m*, centro; *(of question)* fondo, quid *m*, meollo. ■ **to learn by heart** aprender de memoria. ‖ **to take heart** animarse. ‖ **to learn by heart** aprender de memoria. ■ **heart attack** ataque *m* de corazón.
▷ *n pl* **hearts** *(cards)* corazones *mpl*; *(Spanish cards)* copas *fpl*.
heartache ['hɑːteɪk] *n* **1** angustia, pena, pesar *m*. **2** *(deep feeling of sorrow)* congoja.
heartbeat ['hɑːtbiːt] *n* latido del corazón.
heartbreak ['hɑːtbreɪk] *n* angustia, congoja.
heartburn ['hɑːtbɜːn] *n* ardor *m* de estómago, acedía, ardores *mpl*.
hearten ['hɑːtᵊn] *vt* animar, alentar.
heartfelt ['hɑːtfelt] *adj* sincero,-a, cordial.
hearth [hɑːθ] *n* **1** *(of fireplace)* hogar *m*, chimenea. **2** *fig* hogar *m*.
heartless ['hɑːtləs] *adj* cruel, insensible, despiadado,-a, inhumano,-a.
heart-rending ['hɑːtrendɪŋ] *adj* angustioso,-a, desgarrador,-ra, conmovedor,-ra.
heart-throb ['hɑːtθrɒb] *n fam* ídolo, rompecorazones *mf*.
hearty ['hɑːtɪ] *adj* **1** *(person)* campechano,-a. **2** *(welcome)* cordial. **3** *(meal)* abundante.
▲ *comp* **heartier**, *superl* **heartiest**.
heat [hiːt] *n* **1** *(warmth)* calor *m*. **2** *fig* calor *m*, pasión *f*, ardor *m*, vehemencia. **3** *(heating)* calefacción *f*. **4** SP eliminatoria, serie *f*. **5** ZOOL celo.
▷ *vt* **1** calentar. **2** *fig* acalorar.
⊙ **to heat up** *vi (warm up)* calentarse; *(to raise excitement, etc)* acalorarse.
heated ['hiːtɪd] *adj* **1** *fig (argument)* acalorado,-a. **2** *(room)* con calefacción *f*.
heater ['hiːtəʳ] *n* calentador *m*.
heath [hiːθ] *n* **1** *(land)* brezal *m*. **2** *(plant)* brezo.
heathen ['hiːðᵊn] *n* **1** *(non Christian)* pagano,-a. **2** *fig* bárbaro, salvaje *m*.
heather ['heðəʳ] *n* BOT brezo.
heating ['hiːtɪŋ] *n* calefacción *f*.
heatstroke ['hiːtstrəʊk] *n* MED insolación *f*.
heatwave ['hiːtweɪv] *n* ola de calor.
heave [hiːv] *n (pull)* tirón *m*; *(push)* empujón *m*.
▷ *vt* **1** *(pull)* tirar; *(lift)* levantar. **2** *(push)* empujar. **3** *fam (throw)* lanzar, arrojar.
▷ *vi* **1** *(rise and fall)* subir y bajar; *(pant)* jadear. **2** *(retch)* tener náuseas; *(chest)* jadear. **3** [*pt & pp* **hove** [həʊv]] MAR cabecear.
⊙ **to heave to** *vi* MAR ponerse al pairo.
▲ *pt & pp* **hove** [həʊv].
heaven ['hevᵊn] *n* **1** cielo. **2** *fam* gloria, paraíso.
▷ *n pl* **heavens** cielo.
heavily ['hevɪlɪ] *adv* **1** *(fall, move, step, etc)* pesadamente; *(rain)* fuertemente, mucho. **2** *(sleep, etc)* profundamente; *(drink)* con exceso, mucho; *(breathe)* con dificultad *f*.
heavy ['hevɪ] *adj* **1** *(gen)* pesado,-a. **2** *(rain, blow)* fuerte, pesado,-a. **3** *(traffic)* denso,-a. **4** *(sleep)* profundo,-a. **5** *(crop)* abundante. **6** *(atmosphere)* cargado,-a. **7** *(loss, expenditure)* grande, considerable. ● **heavy metal** rock *m* duro, heavy metal *m*.
▲ *comp* **heavier**, *superl* **heaviest**.
heavy-duty ['hevɪ'djuːtɪ] *adj (clothes, shoes, etc)* de faena, resistente; *(equipment, machinery, etc)* reforzado,-a, robusto,-a, para grandes cargas.
heavyweight ['hevɪweɪt] *n* **1** SP peso pesado. **2** *fig* peso pesado.
Hebrew ['hiːbruː] *adj* hebreo,-a.
▷ *n* **1** *(person)* hebreo,-a. **2** *(language)* hebreo.
heckle ['hekᵊl] *vt* interrumpir, provocar.
heckling ['heklɪŋ] *n* altercado, interrupción *f* con gritos e insultos.
hectare ['hektɑːʳ] *n* hectárea.
hectic ['hektɪk] *adj* agitado,-a, ajetreado,-a, movido,-a.
hectogram ['hektəgræm] *n* hectogramo.
hector ['hektəʳ] *vt* intimidar, tiranizar.
he'd [hiːz] *contr* **1** he had. **2** he would.
hedge [hedʒ] *n* **1** seto vivo. **2** *fig* protección *f*, barrera.
▷ *vi* contestar con evasivas.
▷ *vt* **1** cercar, separar con un seto. **2** *fig (protect)* proteger, guardar; *(protect* OS *against)* protegerse.
⊙ **to hedge in** *vt sep* cercar, rodear.
hedgehog ['hedʒhɒg] *n* ZOOL erizo.
hedonist ['hiːdᵊnɪst] *n* hedonista *mf*.
heed [hiːd] *n* atención *f*.
▷ *vt* prestar atención a, hacer caso de.
heedless ['hiːdləs] *adj* desatento,-a, descuidado,-a, despreocupado,-a.
heel [hiːl] *n* **1** ANAT talón *m*. **2** *(on shoe)* tacón *m*; *(of sock)* talón *m*.
▷ *vt* **1** poner tacón a. **2** *(in rugby)* talonear. **3** MAR inclinar.
▷ *vi* MAR escorar.
hefty ['heftɪ] *adj (person)* fuerte, fornido,-a, robusto,-a; *(object)* pesado,-a; *(large quantity)* grande, importante, considerable.
▲ *comp* **heftier**, *superl* **heftiest**.
hegemony [hɪ'gemənɪ] *n* hegemonía.
height [haɪt] *n* **1** *(gen)* altura. **2** *(altitude)* altitud *f*. **3** *(of person)* estatura. **4** GEOG cumbre *f*, cima.
heighten ['haɪtᵊn] *vt* **1** *fig (enhance)* intensificar, realzar. **2** *fig (enjoyment)* aumentar. **3** elevar, levantar, hacer más alto.
▷ *vi (to increase)* aumentar; *(intensify)* intensificarse.
heinous ['heɪnəs] *adj fml lit* atroz.
heir [eəʳ] *n* heredero.
heiress ['eəres] *n* heredera.
heirloom ['eəluːm] *n* **1** reliquia, joya de familia. **2** *fig* herencia.
held [held] *pt & pp* → **hold**.
helicopter ['helɪkɒptəʳ] *n* helicóptero.
heliport ['helɪpɔːt] *n* helipuerto.
helium ['hiːlɪəm] *n* CHEM helio.
helix ['hiːlɪks] *n* hélice *f*.
hell [hel] *n* infierno.
he'll [hiːl] *contr* he will, he shall.
hellish ['helɪʃ] *adj fam* infernal.
hello [he'ləʊ] *interj* **1** ¡hola! **2** *(on telephone - answering)* ¡diga!; *(- calling)* ¡oiga! **3** *(to get* SB*'s attention)* ¡oiga!, ¡oye!
helm [helm] *n* MAR timón *m*.
helmet ['helmɪt] *n* casco.
helmsman ['helmzmən] *n* timonel *m*.
▲ *pl* **helmsmen** ['helmzmən].

help [help] *n* 1 *(gen)* ayuda. 2 *(servant)* asistenta, criada.
▷ *interj* ¡socorro!
▷ *vt* 1 *(gen)* ayudar. 2 *(be of use)* ayudar, servir. 3 *(to relieve)* aliviar. 4 *(avoid)* evitar.
⊙ **to help out** *vt sep* ayudar, echar una mano a.
helper ['helpəʳ] *n* 1 ayudante,-a *mf*, auxiliar *mf*. 2 *(collaborator)* colaborador,-ra.
helpful ['helpfʊl] *adj* 1 *(thing)* útil, práctico,-a. 2 *(person)* amable.
helpfully ['helpfʊlɪ] *adv* amablemente.
helping ['helpɪŋ] *n* ración *f*, porción *f*.
▷ *adj* ayuda.
helpless ['helpləs] *adj* 1 *(unprotected)* desamparado,-a, indefenso,-a, desvalido,-a. 2 *(powerless)* impotente, incapaz, inútil.
helpline ['helplaɪn] *n* teléfono de asistencia.
helter-skelter [heltə'skeltəʳ] *adv* atropelladamente, en desbandada.
▷ *adj* ajetreado,-a.
▷ *n* *(at fair)* tobogán *m*; *(confusion)* desbandada.
hem [hem] *n* SEW dobladillo.
▷ *vt* hacer un dobladillo en.
▲ *pt & pp* hemmed, *ger* hemming.
⊙ **to hem in** *vt sep fig* cercar, rodear.
he-man ['hi:mæn] *n* machote *m*.
▲ *pl* he-men ['hi:mən].
hematoma [hi:mə'təʊmə] *n* US ⟶ **haematoma.**
hemisphere ['hemɪsfɪəʳ] *n* hemisferio.
hemispherical [hemɪs'ferɪkᵊl] *adj* hemisférico,-a.
hemlock ['hemlɒk] *n* BOT *(plant)* cicuta; *(tree)* tsuga.
hemorrhage ['hemərɪdʒ] *n* US ⟶ **haemorrhage.**
hemp [hemp] *n* 1 BOT cáñamo. 2 *(drug)* hachís *m*, marihuana.
hen [hen] *n* *(chicken)* gallina; *(female bird)* hembra.
● **hen party** *fam* reunión *f* de mujeres, despedida de soltera.
hence [hens] *adv* 1 *fml (so)* por eso, por lo tanto, de ahí. 2 *(from now)* de aquí a, dentro de.
henceforth [hens'fɔ:θ] *adv* de ahora en adelante.
henchman ['hentʃmən] *n* 1 *pej* secuaz *m*, partidario. 2 *(bodyguard)* guardaespaldas *m*.
▲ *pl* henchmen.
henhouse ['henhaʊs] *n* gallinero.
henna ['henə] *n* BOT alheña.
hennin ['henɪn] *n* capirote *m*.
henpecked ['henpekt] *adj* dominado por la mujer: a henpecked husband *un calzonazos.*
heptagon ['heptəgən] *n* heptágono.
heptagonal [hep'tægənᵊl] *adj* heptagonal.
her [hɜ:ʳ] *pron* 1 *(direct object)* la: I love her *la quiero.* 2 *(indirect object)* le; *(with other third person pronouns)* se: give it to her *dáselo.* 3 *(after preposition)* ella: go with her *vete con ella.* 4 *fam (as subject)* ella: listen, that's her! *¡escucha, es ella!*
▷ *adj* su, sus; *(emphatic)* de ella.
herald ['herəld] *n* 1 heraldo. 2 *fig* precursor *m*, anunciador *m*.
▷ *vt fml lit* anunciar, proclamar.
heraldic [he'rældɪk] *adj* heráldico,-a.
herb [hɜ:b; US ɜ:b] *n* hierba.
herbaceous [hɜ:'beɪʃəs] *adj* herbáceo,-a.
herbal ['hɜ:bᵊl] *adj* herbario,-a, de hierbas.
herbalist ['hɜ:bᵊlɪst] *n* herbolario,-a.
herbicide ['hɜ:bɪsaɪd] *n* herbicida *m*.
herbivore ['hɜ:bɪvɔ:ʳ] *n* ZOOL herbívoro,-a.
herbivorous [hɜ:'bɪvərəs] *adj* ZOOL herbívoro,-a.
herd [hɜ:d] *n* 1 *(cattle)* manada; *(goats)* rebaño; *(pigs)* piara. 2 *fam (people)* montón *m*, multitud *f*.
▷ *vt* *(animals - group)* juntar en manada; *(- drive)* conducir en manada; *(people)* llevar.
▷ *vi* juntarse en manada, juntarse en rebaño.
herdsman ['hɜ:dzmən] *n* *(of cattle)* vaquero; *(of sheep)* pastor *m*; *(of goats)* cabrero.
▲ *pl* herdsmen ['hɜ:dzmən].
here [hɪəʳ] *adv* aquí. ■ **here you are** aquí tienes.
hereafter [hɪər'ɑ:ftəʳ] *adv* de ahora en adelante.
hereby [hɪə'baɪ] *adv fml* por la presente.
hereditary [hɪ'rədɪtᵊrɪ] *adj* hereditario,-a.
heredity [hɪ'redɪtɪ] *n* herencia.
herein [hɪə'rɪn] *adv (inside)* aquí; *(in letter, etc)* aquí mencionado,-a.
heresy ['herəsɪ] *n* herejía.
▲ *pl* heresies.
heretic ['herətɪk] *n* hereje *mf*.
heretical [he'retɪkᵊl] *adj* herético,-a.
herewith [hɪə'wɪð] *adv* adjunto,-a.
heritage ['herɪtɪdʒ] *n* herencia, patrimonio.
hermaphrodite [hɜ:'mæfrədaɪt] *adj* hermafrodita.
hermeneutic [hɜ:mɪ'nju:tɪk] *adj* hermenéutico,-a.
hermetic [hɜ:'metɪk] *adj* hermético,-a.
hermit ['hɜ:mɪt] *n* ermitaño,-a, eremita *mf*.
hermitage ['hɜ:mɪtɪdʒ] *n* ermita.
hernia ['hɜ:nɪə] *n* hernia.
hero ['hɪərəʊ] *n* 1 *(gen)* héroe *m*. 2 *(in novel)* protagonista *m*, personaje *m* principal.
▲ *pl* heroes.
heroic [hɪ'rəʊɪk] *adj* heroico,-a.
heroics [hɪ'rəʊɪks] *n pl (words)* grandilocuencia *f sing*; *(deeds)* actos heroicos *mpl*.
heroin ['herəʊɪn] *n (drug)* heroína.
heroine ['herəʊɪn] *n* 1 heroína. 2 *(in novel)* protagonista, personaje *m* principal.
heroism ['herəʊɪzᵊm] *n* heroísmo.
heron ['herən] *n* garza.
hero-worship ['hɪərəʊwɜ:ʃɪp] *n* mitificación *f*, idolatría.
▷ *vt* mitificar, idolatrar.
herpes ['hɜ:pi:z] *n* herpe *m*, herpes *m*.
herring ['herɪŋ] *n* arenque *m*.
▲ *pl* herring o herrings.
hers [hɜ:z] *pron (sing)* (el) suyo, (la) suya; *(pl)* (los) suyos, (las) suyas; *(emphatic)* de ella: this pencil is hers *este lápiz es suyo.*
herself [hɜ:'self] *pron* 1 *(reflexive use)* se: she washed herself *se lavó.* 2 *(emphatic)* ella misma: she made it all herself *lo hizo todo ella misma.*
hertz [hɜ:ts] *n* hertz *m*, hercio.
he's [hi:z] *contr* 1 he is. 2 he has.
hesitant ['hezɪtᵊnt] *adj* indeciso,-a.
hesitate ['hezɪteɪt] *vi* vacilar, dudar.
hesitation [hezɪ'teɪʃᵊn] *n* duda, indecisión.
heterodox ['hetᵊrədɒks] *adj* heterodoxo,-a.

heterogeneous [hetərəʊ'dʒiːnɪəs] *adj* heterogéneo,-a.
heterosexual [hetərəʊ'seksjʊəl] *adj* heterosexual.
hexagon ['heksəgən] *n* hexágono.
hexagonal [hek'sægənᵊl] *adj* hexagonal.
hexameter [hek'sæmɪtəʳ] *n* hexámetro.
hey [heɪ] *interj* ¡eh!, ¡oye!, ¡oiga!
heyday ['heɪdeɪ] *n* **1** auge *m*, apogeo. **2** *fig* flor *f*, los mejores años.
HGV ['eɪtʃ'dʒiː'viː] *abbr* GB (heavy goods vehicle) vehículo de carga pesada.
hi [haɪ] *interj fam* ¡hola!
hiatus [haɪ'eɪtəs] *n* **1** LING hiato. **2** *fml fig (gap)* laguna, interrupción *f*, vacío.
▲ *pl* hiatuses o hiatus.
hibernate ['haɪbəneɪt] *vi* hibernar.
hibernation [haɪbə'neɪʃᵊn] *n* hibernación *f*.
hibiscus [haɪ'bɪskəs] *n* BOT hibisco.
hiccough ['hɪkʌp] *n-vi* ⟶ **hiccup.**
hiccup ['hɪkʌp] *n* hipo: to have hiccups *tener hipo.*
hick [hɪk] *n* US *fam (yokel)* cateto,-a, paleto,-a, palurdo,-a.
hickory ['hɪkərɪ] *n* BOT nogal *m* americano.
▲ *pl* hickories.
hid [hɪd] *pt & pp* ⟶ **hide.**
hidden ['hɪdᵊn] *pp* ⟶ **hide.**
▷ *adj* **1** escondido,-a. **2** *fig* oculto,-a.
hide¹ [haɪd] *n (concealed place)* puesto de observación, escondrijo, escondite *m*.
▷ *vt (conceal)* esconder; *(obscure)* ocultar, tapar.
▲ *pt* hid [hɪd], *pp* hid [hɪð] o hidden ['hɪdᵊn].
hide² [haɪd] *n* **1** piel *f*, cuero. **2** *fig (of a person)* pellejo.
hide-and-seek [haɪdᵊn'siːk] *n* escondite *m*.
hidebound ['haɪdbaʊnd] *adj* chapado,-a a la antigua, conservador,-ra, rígido,-a.
hideous ['hɪdɪəs] *adj* **1** *(terrible)* horroroso,-a, atroz. **2** *(ugly)* horrendo,-a, espantoso.
hide-out ['haɪdaʊt] *n* escondrijo, escondite *m*, guarida.
hiding¹ ['haɪdɪŋ] *n (beating)* paliza.
hiding² ['haɪdɪŋ] *n* ocultación *f*.
hierarchic [haɪə'rɑːkɪk] *adj* jerárquico,-a.
hierarchy ['haɪərɑːkɪ] *n* jerarquía.
▲ *pl* hierarchies.
hieroglyphics [haɪərə'glɪfɪks] *n pl* jeroglíficos *mpl*.
hi-fi ['haɪfaɪ] *n* hifi *m*, alta fidelidad *f*.
high [haɪ] *adj* **1** alto,-a, elevado. **2** *(important)* alto,-a, importante; *(strong)* fuerte. **3** *(very good)* bueno,-a. **4** *(going rotten - food)* pasado,-a; *(- game)* manido,-a. **5** *(of time)* pleno,-a. **6** *sl (on drugs)* flipado,-a, colocado,-a. ● **high jump** salto de altura. ‖ **high school** instituto (de bachillerato). ‖ **high street** calle mayor. ‖ **high tide** marea alta.
▷ *n* **1** punto máximo, récord *m*. **2** METEOR zona de alta presión, anticiclón *m*.
highborn ['haɪbɔːn] *adj* de alta alcurnia.
highbrow ['haɪbraʊ] *adj* intelectual.
high-class [haɪ'klɑːs] *adj (classy)* de categoría; *(superior)* de calidad *f*.
higher ['haɪəʳ] *adj* **1** ⟶ **high.** **2** superior. **3** *(bigger)* más alto,-a; *(number, velocity, etc)* mayor. ● **higher education** enseñanza superior.
high-flown ['haɪ'fləʊn] *adj* altisonante, rimbombante.
high-flyer [haɪ'flaɪəʳ] *n fig* persona muy ambiciosa.
high-frequency [haɪ'friːkwensɪ] *adj* RAD de alta frecuencia.
high-heeled ['haɪ'hiːld] *adj* de tacón alto.
highland ['haɪlənd] *adj* montañoso,-a.
highlander ['haɪləndəʳ] *n* montañés,-esa.
highlands ['haɪləndz] *n pl* GEOG tierras *fpl* altas.
highlight ['haɪlaɪt] *vt* **1** destacar, hacer resaltar. **2** *(with pen)* marcar *(con un rotulador fosforescente).*
▷ *n* **1** ART toque *m* de luz. **2** *(hairdressing)* reflejo. **3** *fig (especially in show business)* atracción *f* principal; *(most outstanding)* punto culminante, momento culminante; *(aspect or feature)* característica notable, aspecto notable.
highly ['haɪlɪ] *adv (very)* muy; *(favourably)* muy bien.
highly-strung [haɪlɪ'strʌŋ] *adj* tenso,-a, hipertenso,-a, muy nervioso,-a.
high-minded [haɪ'maɪndɪd] *adj* noble, magnánimo,-a.
Highness ['haɪnəs] *n* Alteza *mf*.
high-pitched ['haɪ'pɪtʃt] *adj (sound, voice)* agudo,-a, estridente; *(roof)* empinado,-a.
high-powered ['haɪ'paʊəd] *adj* **1** *(engine)* de gran potencia. **2** *(person)* dinámico,-a.
high-ranking [haɪ'ræŋkɪŋ] *adj* de alta graduación, superior, de categoría.
high-rise ['haɪraɪz] *adj (buildings)* alto,-a.
▷ *n* rascacielos *m*, bloque *m* de pisos.
high-speed ['haɪspiːd] *adj* rápido,-a, de gran velocidad.
high-spirited [haɪ'spɪrɪtɪd] *adj (person)* muy animado,-a, alegre; *(horse)* fogoso,-a.
highway ['haɪweɪ] *n* **1** US autovía. **2** JUR vía pública.
hijack ['haɪdʒæk] *n* secuestro.
▷ *vt* secuestrar.
hijacking ['haɪdʒækɪŋ] *n* secuestro.
hike [haɪk] *n* **1** *(walk)* excursión *f* a pie. **2** US *fam* aumento de precio.
▷ *vi* ir de excursión, hacer una excursión.
▷ *vt fam* aumentar los precios.
hiker ['haɪkəʳ] *n* excursionista.
hiking ['haɪkɪŋ] *n* excursionismo a pie.
hilarious [hɪ'leərɪəs] *adj* graciosísimo,-a, hilarante, divertidísimo,-a.
hill [hɪl] *n* **1** colina, cerro. **2** *(slope)* cuesta.
hillside ['hɪlsaɪd] *n* ladera.
hilltop ['hɪltɒp] *n* cumbre *f*, cima.
hilt [hɪlt] *n* puño, empuñadura.
him [hɪm] *pron* **1** *(direct object)* lo: I love him *lo quiero.* **2** *(indirect object)* le; *(with other pronouns)* se: give him the money *dale el dinero;* give it to him *dáselo.* **3** *(after preposition)* él: we went with him *fuimos con él.* **4** *fam (as subject)* él: it's him! *¡es él!*
Himalayas [hɪmə'leɪəz] *n pl* **the Himalayas** el Himalaya *m sing*.
himself [hɪm'self] *pron* **1** *(reflexive)* se; *(alone)* solo, por sí mismo: he cut himself *se cortó;* he did it by himself *lo hizo solo.* **2** *(emphatic)* él mismo, sí mismo, en persona.
hind¹ [haɪnd] *adj* trasero,-a.
hind² [haɪnd] *n (deer)* cierva.

hinder ['hɪndəʳ] *vt* dificultar, entorpecer, estorbar, impedir.
hindrance ['hɪndrəns] *n* estorbo, obstáculo.
hindsight ['haɪndsaɪt] *n* retrospectiva.
Hindu [hɪn'duː, 'hɪnduː] *n* hindú *mf*.
▷ *adj* hindú.
Hinduism ['hɪnduɪzəm] *n* hinduismo.
hinge [hɪndʒ] *n* **1** TECH gozne *m*, bisagra. **2** *(for stamps)* fijasello. **3** *fig* eje *m*.
▷ *vi* girar sobre goznes.
hint [hɪnt] *n* **1** insinuación *f*, indirecta. **2** *(advice)* consejo, sugerencia. **3** *(clue)* pista. **4** *(trace)* pizca. **5** *(sign)* sombra.
▷ *vt (imply)* insinuar, aludir a.
hinterland ['hɪntəlænd] *n* GEOG interior *m*.
hip[1] [hɪp] *n* ANAT cadera.
hip[2] [hɪp] *n* BOT escaramujo.
hip[3] [hɪp] ■ **hip hip hooray!** ¡hurra!
hip[4] [hɪp] *adj sl* marchoso,-a, en la onda.
hipbone ['hɪpbəʊn] *n* ANAT hueso de la cadera.
hippie ['hɪpɪ] *n fam* hippie *mf*.
hippopotamus [hɪpə'pɒtəməs] *n* ZOOL hipopótamo.
hippy ['hɪpɪ] *n fam* hippie *(mf)*.
▲ *pl* **hippies.**
hire ['haɪəʳ] *n* alquiler *m*.
▷ *vt* **1** *(rent)* alquilar. **2** *(employ)* contratar.
⊙ **to hire out** *vt sep (equipment, vehicles, etc)* alquilar; *(people)* contratar.
his [hɪz] *adj* **1** su, sus: **his dog** *su perro*. **2** *(emphatic)* de él.
▷ *pron* (el) suyo, (la) suya, (los) suyos, (las) suyas.
Hispanic [hɪs'pænɪk] *adj* hispánico,-a.
▷ *n* US hispano,-a, latino,-a.
hiss [hɪs] *n* **1** *(gen)* siseo. **2** *(air, snake, steam, etc)* silbido. **3** *(protest)* silbido.
▷ *vt* **1** sisear, silbar. **2** *(in protest)* pitar, abuchear.
historian [hɪ'stɔːrɪən] *n* historiador,-ra.
historic [hɪ'stɒrɪk] *adj* histórico,-a.
historical [hɪ'stɒrɪkəl] *adj* histórico,-a.
history ['hɪstᵊrɪ] *n* **1** *(in general)* historia. **2** COMPUT historial *m*.
▲ *pl* **histories.**
hit [hɪt] *n* **1** *(blow)* golpe *m*. **2** *(success)* éxito, acierto. **3** *(shot)* impacto. **4** *(visit to web page)* acceso. **5** *fig (damaging remark)* pulla. **6** US *sl* asesinato.
▷ *vt* **1** *(strike)* golpear, pegar. **2** *(crash into)* chocar contra. **3** *(affect)* afectar, perjudicar. **4** *(reach)* alcanzar.
▲ *pt & pp* **hit**, *ger* **hitting.**
⊙ **to hit back** *vi (strike in return)* devolver golpe por golpe; *(reply to criticism)* defenderse.
⊙ **to hit out at / hit out against** *vt insep (condemn verbally)* condenar a, atacar a; *(try to attack)* atacar a.
hitch [hɪtʃ] *n* obstáculo, tropiezo, dificultad *f*.
▷ *vt (tie)* enganchar, atar.
▷ *vi fam* hacer autoestop, ir a dedo, hacer dedo.
hitched [hɪtʃt] *phr* **to get hitched** *fam* casarse.
hitchhike ['hɪtʃhaɪk] *vi* hacer autoestop.
hitchhiking ['hɪtʃhaɪkɪŋ] *vi* autoestop *m*, dedo.
hitherto [hɪðə'tuː] *adv fml* hasta ahora, hasta la fecha.
HIV ['eɪtʃ'aɪ'viː] *abbr* **(human immunodeficiency virus)** virus *m* de inmunodeficiencia humana; *(abbreviation)* VIH *m*.

hive [haɪv] *n* **1** colmena. **2** *fig* lugar *m* muy activo.
⊙ **to hive off** *vt sep* separar.
hives [haɪvz] *n pl* MED urticaria *f sing*.
HM ['eɪtʃ'em] *abbr* **(His Majesty, Her Majesty)** Su Majestad; *(abbreviation)* SM.
hoard [hɔːd] *n* **1** *(provisions)* reserva. **2** *(money)* tesoro escondido.
▷ *vt* **1** *(objects)* acumular. **2** *(money)* atesorar.
hoarding ['hɔːdɪŋ] *n (billboard)* valla publicitaria; *(construction)* valla.
hoarfrost ['hɔːfrɒst] *n* escarcha.
hoarse [hɔːs] *adj* ronco,-a, áspero,-a.
hoary ['hɔːrɪ] *adj lit* cano,-a, canoso,-a; *(very old person)* viejo,-a.
▲ *comp* **hoarier**, *superl* **hoariest.**
hoax [həʊks] *n (trick)* trampa, engaño; *(joke)* broma pesada.
▷ *vt* engañar a, gastar una broma a.
hob [hɒb] *n (of cooker)* encimera; *(next to fireplace)* repisa.
hobble ['hɒbᵊl] *vi (limp)* cojear, andar con dificultad *f*.
▷ *vt* **1** *(tie)* trabar, manear. **2** *fig* poner trabas a, obstaculizar.
hobby ['hɒbɪ] *n* afición *f*, hobby *m*, pasatiempo favorito.
▲ *pl* **hobbies.**
hobbyhorse ['hɒbɪhɔːs] *n* **1** *(toy)* caballito de juguete. **2** *fig (fixed idea)* caballo de batalla.
hobgoblin [hɒb'gɒblɪn] *n* duende *m*.
hobo ['həʊbəʊ] *n* US vagabundo,-a.
▲ *pl* **hoboes o hobos.**
hockey ['hɒkɪ] *n* SP hockey *m*.
hod [hɒd] *n (trough)* artesa; *(for bricks)* capacho de albañil.
hoe [həʊ] *n* azada, azadón *m*.
▷ *vt (earth)* azadonar, cavar; *(weeds)* sachar.
hog [hɒg] *n* **1** cerdo, puerco, marrano. **2** *fam pej (not a nice person)* indeseable *mf*.
▷ *vt* acaparar.
▲ *pt & pp* **hogged**, *ger* **hogging.**
hoist [hɔɪst] *n* **1** *(crane)* grúa. **2** *(lift)* montacargas *m*.
▷ *vt* **1** levantar, subir. **2** *(flag)* izar.
hold [həʊld] *n* **1** *(place to grip)* asidero. **2** *(in ship, plane)* bodega. ■ **to get hold of 1** *(grab)* agarrar, coger. **2** *(obtain)* hacerse con, encontrar.
● *vt* **1** *(keep in one's hand)* aguantar, sostener: **hold my bag** *aguántame el bolso*. **2** *(opinion)* sostener. **3** *(contain)* dar cabida a, tener capacidad para: **the stadium holds a lot of people** *el estadio tiene capacidad para mucha gente*. **4** *(meeting)* celebrar; *(conversation)* mantener: **political parties often hold meetings in parks** *los partidos políticos celebran a menudo sus mítines en los parques*. ■ **to hold** SB abrazar a ALGN.
⊙ **to hold back** *vt sep* **1** *(suspect)* retener. **2** *(information)* ocultar; *(restrain)* contener; *(feelings)* reprimir; *(keep)* guardar.
▷ *vi (hesitate)* vacilar, no atreverse; *(abstain)* abstenerse.
⊙ **to hold down** *vt sep (control)* dominar; *(job)* desempeñar.
⊙ **to hold forth** *vi* hablar largo y tendido.
⊙ **to hold off** *vt sep* mantener alejado,-a.
▷ *vi (refrain)* refrenarse.

⊙ **to hold on** *vi* 1 *(grip tightly)* agarrarse fuerte, agarrarse bien. 2 *(wait)* esperar; *(on 'phone)* no colgar.
⊙ **to hold over** *vt sep (meeting, etc)* aplazar.
⊙ **to hold up** *vt sep* 1 *(rob)* atracar, asaltar. 2 *(delay)* retrasar. 3 *(raise)* levantar. 4 *(support)* aguantar, sostener.
▷ *vi* aguantar, resistir.
⊙ **to hold with** *vt insep* estar de acuerdo con.
older ['həʊldəʳ] *n* 1 *(owner)* poseedor,-ra; *(of passport)* titular *mf*. 2 *(container)* recipiente *m*, receptáculo. 3 *(bearer - gen)* portador,-ra; *(- of bonds)* tenedor,-ra. 4 *(handle)* asidero. 5 *(tenant - on land)* arrendatario,-a; *(- of a flat)* inquilino,-a.
olding ['həʊldɪŋ] *n* 1 *(possession)* posesión *f*; *(piece of land)* propiedad *f*, terreno. 2 *(of an event)* celebración *f*. 3 *(stocks, shares, bonds)* valor *m* en cartera.
old-up ['həʊldʌp] *n* 1 *(robbery)* atraco; *(of train, etc)* asalto. 2 *(delay)* retraso. 3 AUTO atasco.
ole [həʊl] *n* 1 *(gen)* agujero; *(in ground, golf)* hoyo. 2 *(in road)* bache *m*. 3 *(of rabbits)* madriguera; *(cavity)* cavidad *f*. 4 *fam (town)* pueblucho de mala muerte. 5 *fam (place to live)* cuchitril *m*; *(unsavoury place)* antro. 6 *(a tight spot)* aprieto, apuro.
▷ *vt* 1 *(make holes - small)* agujerear; *(large)* hacer un boquete en. 2 *(at golf)* meter en el hoyo.
oliday ['hɒlɪdeɪ] *n* 1 *(one day)* fiesta, día *m* de fiesta, día *m* festivo. 2 *(period)* vacaciones *fpl*.
▷ *vi* GB *(gen)* pasar las vacaciones; *(in summer)* veranear.
olistic [həʊ'lɪstɪk] *adj* holístico,-a.
Holland ['hɒlənd] *n* Holanda.
ollow ['hɒləʊ] *adj* 1 *(sound, thing)* hueco,-a. 2 *(cheeks, etc)* hundido,-a. 3 *fig (laugh)* falso,-a; *(promise)* vacío,-a.
▷ *n* 1 hueco. 2 GEOG hondonada.
▲ *comp* **hollower**, *superl* **hollowest**.
▷ *vt* **to hollow out** vaciar.
olly ['hɒlɪ] *n* acebo.
▲ *pl* **hollies**.
ollyhock ['hɒlɪhɒk] *n* malvarrosa.
olocaust ['hɒləkɔːst] *n* holocausto.
ologram ['hɒləgræm] *n* holograma *m*.
olster ['həʊlstəʳ] *n* pistolera.
oly ['həʊlɪ] *adj* 1 REL *(sacred)* santo,-a, sagrado,-a. 2 *(blessed)* bendito,-a.
▲ *comp* **holier**, *superl* **holiest**.
omage ['hɒmɪdʒ] *n* homenaje *m*.
ome [həʊm] *n* 1 *(house)* hogar *m*, casa. 2 *fml* domicilio. 3 *(institution)* asilo. 4 *(country, village, etc)* patria, tierra. 5 ZOOL hábitat *m*. ■ **at home** en casa.
▷ *adj* 1 casero,-a. 2 POL (del) interior. 3 *(native)* natal.
omeland ['həʊmlænd] *n (gen)* patria; *(birthplace)* tierra natal.
omeless ['həʊmləs] *adj* sin hogar, sin techo.
omely ['həʊmlɪ] *adj* 1 GB *(attractive, cosy, domesticated)* sencillo,-a, casero,-a, familiar. 2 US *(unattractive)* feo,-a, sin atractivo.
ome-made ['həʊm'meɪd] *adj* casero,-a, de fabricación casera, hecho,-a en casa.
omeopath ['həʊmɪəpæθ] *n* MED homeópata *mf*.
omesick ['həʊmsɪk] *adj* nostálgico,-a.
omesickness ['həʊmsɪknəs] *n* añoranza, morriña, nostalgia.

homestead ['həʊmsted] *n* US granja.
homeward ['həʊmwəd] *adv* hacia casa.
homework ['həʊmwɜːk] *n* deberes *mpl*.
homicide ['hɒmɪsaɪd] *n* 1 *(crime)* homicidio. 2 *(criminal)* homicida *mf*.
homily ['hɒmɪlɪ] *n* homilía.
▲ *pl* **homilies**.
homing ['həʊmɪŋ] *adj* TECH buscador,-ra.
homogeneous [hɒmə'dʒiːnɪəs] *adj* homogéneo,-a.
homogenization [hɒmɒdzənaɪ'zeɪʃᵊn] *n* homogeneización *f*.
homograph ['hɒməgræf] *n* homógrafo.
homologate [hɒ'mɒləgeɪt] *vt* homologar.
homological [həʊmə'lɒdʒɪkᵊl] *adj* homólogo,-a.
homonym ['hɒmənɪm] *n* homónimo.
homonymous [hə'mɒnɪməs] *adj* homónimo,-a.
homophone ['hɒməfəʊn] *n* homófono.
homophonous [hə'mɒfənəs] *adj* homófono,-a.
homosexual [həʊməʊ'seksjʊəl] *adj & n* homosexual.
homosexuality [həʊməʊseksjʊ'ælɪtɪ] *n* homosexualidad *f*.
honest ['ɒnɪst] *adj* 1 *(trustworthy)* honrado,-a, honesto,-a. 2 *(frank)* sincero,-a, franco,-a. 3 *(fair)* justo,-a, equitativo,-a, decente.
▷ *adv fam* de verdad.
honesty ['ɒnɪstɪ] *n* honradez *f*, rectitud *f*.
honey ['hʌnɪ] *n* 1 miel *f*. 2 US *fam (dear)* cariño, cielo.
honeycomb ['hʌnɪkəʊm] *n* panal *m*.
honeymoon ['hʌnɪmuːn] *n* luna de miel, viaje *m* de novios.
honeysuckle ['hʌnɪsʌkᵊl] *n* BOT madreselva.
honk [hɒŋk] *n* 1 *(goose)* graznido. 2 *(car horn)* bocinazo.
▷ *vi* 1 *(goose)* graznar. 2 *(car)* tocar la bocina.
honor ['ɒnəʳ] *n* US → **honour**.
honorable ['ɒnᵊrəbᵊl] *adj* US → **honourable**.
honorary ['ɒnərərɪ] *adj (member)* honorario,-a; *(duties)* honorífico,-a.
honour ['ɒnəʳ] *n* 1 *(virtue)* honor *m*, honra. 2 *(title)* Su Señoría.
▷ *vt* 1 *(respect)* honrar. 2 *(cheque)* pagar, aceptar; *(promise, word, agreement)* cumplir.
honourable ['ɒnᵊrəbᵊl] *adj* 1 *(person)* honrado,-a; *(title)* honorable. 2 *(actions)* honorífico,-a, honroso,-a.
hood [hʊd] *n* 1 *(of clothes)* capucha. 2 *(on pram, etc)* capota. 3 US *(car bonnet)* capó *m*. 4 *(of hawk)* capirote *m*.
hoodlum ['huːdləm] *n sl* matón *m*, gorila *m*.
hoodwink ['hʊdwɪŋk] *vt* engañar.
hoof [huːf] *n (of sheep, cow, etc)* pezuña; *(of horse)* casco.
▲ *pl* **hoofs** o **hooves**.
hook [hʊk] *n* 1 *(gen)* gancho. 2 *(for fishing)* anzuelo.
▷ *vt* 1 *(catch)* enganchar. 2 *(fishing)* pescar, coger. 3 *(in boxing)* pegar un gancho. 4 *(in rugby)* talonear.
⊙ **to hook up** *vt sep (connect)* conectar.
hooked [hʊkt] *adj* 1 *(nose)* aquilino,-a; *(hook-shaped)* ganchudo,-a. 2 *(on drug, etc)* enganchado,-a; *(attracted)* prendado,-a.
hooker ['hʊkəʳ] *n* 1 *(in rugby)* taloneador,-ra. 2 *sl (us)* puta.
hookey ['hʊkɪ] *phr* **to play hookey** US *fam* hacer novillos.

hook-up ['hʊkʌp] *n* 1 *(in electronics, computers, etc)* conexión *f*. 2 *(by TV, radio)* emisión *f* transmitida a distintos países.
hooligan ['huːlɪgən] *n* gamberro,-a.
hoop [huːp] *n (gen)* aro; *(of barrel)* fleje *m*; *(of wheel)* llanta.
hooray [hʊ'reɪ] *interj* ¡hurra!
hoot [huːt] *n* 1 *(of owl)* ululato, grito. 2 *(of car)* bocinazo. 3 *fam (funny thing)* cosa divertida; *(funny person)* persona divertida.
hooter ['huːtəʳ] *n* 1 *(siren)* sirena. 2 *(on car)* bocina, claxon *m*. 3 GB *(nose)* narizota, napias *fpl*.
Hoover ['huːvəʳ] [Registered trademark.] *n* GB aspiradora.
hop[1] [hɒp] *n* 1 salto, brinco. 2 *fam (dance)* baile *m*. 3 AV *fam* vuelo corto.
▷ *vi* saltar, dar brincos, dar saltos.
▷ *vt* 1 US *fam (train, etc)* coger. 2 AV cruzar.
▲ *pt & pp* **hopped**, *ger* **hopping**.
hop[2] [hɒp] *n (plant)* lúpulo.
hope [həʊp] *n (gen)* esperanza; *(false)* ilusión *f*.
▷ *vt* esperar.
hopeful ['həʊpfʊl] *adj* 1 *(promising)* esperanzador, -ra, prometedor,-ra, alentador,-ra. 2 *(confident)* optimista.
hopefully ['həʊpfʊlɪ] *adv* 1 *(confidently)* con esperanza, con ilusión, con optimismo. 2 *fam (all being well)* ojalá.
hopeless ['həʊpləs] *adj* 1 desesperado,-a. 2 *fam (useless)* inútil.
horde [hɔːd] *n* 1 horda. 2 *fig* multitud *f*.
horizon [hə'raɪzᵊn] *n* horizonte *m*.
horizontal [hɒrɪ'zɒntᵊl] *adj* horizontal.
hormonal [hɔː'məʊnᵊl] *adj* hormonal.
hormone ['hɔːməʊn] *n* hormona.
horn [hɔːn] *n* 1 ZOOL asta, cuerno. 2 AUTO bocina, claxon *m*. 3 MUS cuerno, trompa.
hornet ['hɔːnɪt] *n* ZOOL avispón *m*.
horny ['hɔːnɪ] *adj* 1 *(skin, hands)* calloso,-a. 2 *fam (sexually)* cachondo,-a, caliente.
▲ *comp* **hornier**, *superl* **horniest**.
horology [hɒ'rɒlədʒɪ] *n* relojería.
horoscope ['hɒrəskəʊp] *n* horóscopo.
horrendous [hə'rendəs] *adj* horrendo,-a.
horrible ['hɒrɪbᵊl] *adj (gen)* horrible, horroroso,-a; *(person)* antipático,-a.
horrid ['hɒrɪd] *adj (horrible)* horroroso,-a, horrible; *(unkind)* antipático,-a, odioso,-a; *(child)* inaguantable, insoportable.
horrific [hə'rɪfɪk] *adj* horrendo,-a, horroroso,-a.
horrify ['hɒrɪfaɪ] *vt* horrorizar, espantar.
▲ *pt & pp* **horrified**, *ger* **horrifying**.
horror ['hɒrəʳ] *n* horror *m*, terror *m*. ● **horror film** película de terror.
hors d'oeuvre [ɔː'dɜːvʳ] *n* CULIN entremés *m*.
▲ *pl* **hors d'oeuvre o hors d'oeuvres**.
horse [hɔːs] *n* 1 ZOOL caballo. 2 *(in gym)* potro. 3 TECH caballete *m*. 4 *sl (heroin)* caballo. ● **horse riding** equitación *f*.
horseback ['hɔːsbæk] *n* a caballo.
horseman ['hɔːsmən] *n* jinete *m*.
▲ *pl* **horsemen** ['hɔːsmən].
horsepower ['hɔːspaʊəʳ] *n* 1 AUTO caballo de vapor, caballo. 2 potencia.
horseradish ['hɔːsrædɪʃ] *n* BOT rábano picante.
horseshoe ['hɔːsʃuː] *n* herradura.
horsewoman ['hɔːswʊmən] *n* amazona.
▲ *pl* **horsewomen** ['hɔːswɪmɪn].
horticulture ['hɔːtɪkʌltʃəʳ] *n* horticultura.
hose[1] [həʊz] *n (pipe)* manguera.
▲ *pl* **hose**.
▷ *vt* regar, lavar.
hose[2] [həʊz] *n pl (socks)* calcetines *mpl*; *(stockings)* medias *fpl*.
hosepipe ['həʊzpaɪp] *n* manguera.
hosiery ['həʊzɪərɪ] *n (socks)* calcetines *mpl*; *(stockings)* medias *fpl*.
hospice ['hɒspɪs] *n* 1 *(hostel)* hospicio. 2 *(hospital)* residencia para enfermos terminales.
hospitable [hɒ'spɪtəbᵊl] *adj* hospitalario,-a, acogedor,-ra.
hospital ['hɒspɪtᵊl] *n* hospital *m*.
hospitality [hɒspɪ'tælɪtɪ] *n* hospitalidad *f*.
host[1] [həʊst] *n* 1 *(person)* anfitrión,-ona; *(place)* sede *f*. 2 *(TV presenter)* presentador,-ra. 3 *(animal, plant)* huésped *m*.
▷ *vt* 1 TV presentar. 2 celebrar, albergar.
host[2] [həʊst] *n (large number)* multitud *f*.
Host [həʊst] *n* REL hostia.
hostage ['hɒstɪdʒ] *n* rehén *mf*.
hostel ['hɒstᵊl] *n* residencia, hostal *m*.
hostelry ['hɒstᵊlrɪ] *n* hospedería.
▲ *pl* **hostelries**.
hostess ['həʊstəs] *n* 1 *(at home)* anfitriona. 2 *(on plane, etc)* azafata. 3 *(in club)* camarera. 4 TV presentadora.
hostile ['hɒstaɪl] *adj* hostil, enemigo,-a.
hostility [hɒ'stɪlɪtɪ] *n* hostilidad *f*.
▲ *pl* **hostilities**.
hot [hɒt] *adj* 1 *(gen)* caliente. 2 METEOR caluroso,-a, cálido,-a. 3 *(food - spicy)* picante. 4 *(news)* de última hora. 5 *(temper)* fuerte; *(anger)* rabioso,-a, colérico,-a. 6 *(good)* bueno,-a, enterado,-a. 7 *(dangerous)* peligroso,-a. 8 *sl (stolen)* robado,-a.
▲ *comp* **hotter**, *superl* **hottest**.
hotel [həʊ'tel] *n* hotel *m*.
hotelier [həʊ'telɪeɪ] *n* hotelero,-a.
hot-headed ['hɒthedɪd] *adj* impetuoso,-a, impulsivo,-a.
hothouse ['hɒthaʊs] *n* invernadero.
hotline ['hɒtlaɪn] *n* línea directa.
hound [haʊnd] *n* perro de caza.
▷ *vt (harass)* acosar, perseguir.
hour [aʊəʳ] *n* hora.
hourly ['aʊəlɪ] *adj* cada hora.
▷ *adv* a cada hora, por horas.
house [*(n)* haʊs; *(vb)* haʊz] *n* 1 *(gen)* casa; *(official use)* domicilio. 2 POL cámara. 3 THEAT sala. 4 *(company)* empresa, casa. ● **House of Commons** Cámara de los Comunes. ‖ **House of Lords** Cámara de los Lores. **House of Representatives** Cámara de Representantes. ‖ **Houses of Parliament** Parlamento.

▷ *vt* 1 *(gen)* alojar, albergar; *(supply housing)* proveer de vivienda. 2 *(store)* guardar, almacenar; *(fit)* dar cabida a.

ousebreaking ['hausbreıkıŋ] *n* JUR allanamiento de morada.

ousehold ['haushəuld] *n* casa, familia, hogar *m*.

▷ *adj* de la casa, doméstico,-a.

ouseholder ['haushəuldəʳ] *n* dueño,-a de la casa.

ousekeeper ['hauski:pəʳ] *n* ama de llaves.

ousekeeping ['hauski:pıŋ] *n* 1 administración *f* de la casa. 2 [Also **housekeeping money**.] dinero para los gastos de la casa.

ouse-trained ['haustreınd] *adj (pet)* adiestrado,-a, limpio,-a.

ouse-warming ['hauswɔ:mıŋ] *n* inauguración *f* de una casa.

ousewife ['hauswaıf] *n* ama de casa.

▲ *pl* **housewives** ['hauswaıvz].

ousework ['hauswɜ:k] *n* quehaceres *mpl* domésticos.

ousing ['hauzıŋ] *n* 1 vivienda. 2 TECH bastidor *m*, caja.

ovel ['hɒvᵊl] *n* casucha, cuchitril *m*.

over ['hɒvəʳ] *vi* 1 *(aircraft)* permanecer inmóvil *(en el aire)*. 2 *(bird)* cernerse, revolotear. 3 *(move around)* rondar. 4 *(hesitate)* dudar, vacilar.

overcraft ['hɒvəkrɑ:ft] *n* aerodeslizador *m*.

▲ *pl* **hovercraft**.

ow [hau] *adv* 1 *(in questions - direct)* ¿cómo?; *(- indirect)* cómo: **tell me how to do it** *dime cómo se hace*. 2 *(in exclamations)* qué: **how odd!** *¡qué extraño!, ¡qué raro!* ■ **how about...?** ¿qué te parece si...? ‖ **how are you?** ¿cómo estás? ‖ **how many** cuántos,-as ‖ **how much** cuánto

owever [hau'evəʳ] *adv* 1 *(nevertheless)* sin embargo, no obstante. 2 *(with adj)* por: **however hard it may be** *por difícil que sea;* **however much** *por más que, por mucho que*.

owl [haul] *n (cry)* aullido.

▷ *vi* aullar.

◆ **to howl down** *vt sep* abuchear.

owler ['hauləʳ] *n fam* despiste *m*, pifia, plancha.

HRH ['eıtʃ'ɑ:r'eıts] *abbr* **(His/Her Royal Highness)** Su Alteza Real; *(abbreviation)* S.A.R.

HTML ['eıtʃ'ti:'em'el] *abbr* **(hypertext markup language)** HTML.

ub [hʌb] *n* 1 AUTO cubo. 2 *fig* centro, eje *m*.

ubbub ['hʌbʌb] *n (tumult)* alboroto, bullicio, jaleo; *(voices)* vocerío, griterío.

ubcap ['hʌbkæp] *n* AUTO tapacubos *m*.

uckleberry ['hʌkᵊlberı] *n* BOT arándano.

▲ *pl* **huckleberries**.

uddle ['hʌdᵊl] *n* grupo.

▷ *vi* 1 *(crouch)* acurrucarse, apiñarse, amontonarse. 2 *(cluster)* apiñarse.

Hudson ['hʌdsᵊn] *n* el río Hudson.

ue [hju:] *n (colour)* tinte *m*; *(shade)* matiz *m*.

uff [hʌf] *n* enfado, enojo.

ug [hʌg] *n* abrazo.

▷ *vt* 1 abrazar. 2 *fig (kerb, coast)* pegarse a, ceñirse a.

▲ *pt & pp* **hugged**, *ger* **hugging**.

uge [hju:dʒ] *adj* enorme, inmenso,-a.

hulk [hʌlk] *n* 1 *(ship)* buque *m* viejo, casco. 2 *(thing, person)* armatoste *m*, mole *f*, masa.

hull [hʌl] *n* 1 *(of ship)* casco. 2 BOT *(shell)* cáscara; *(pod)* vaina.

▲ *pl* **hullos**.

▷ *vt (peas, beans, etc)* desvainar.

hullabaloo [hʌləbə'lu:] *adj* griterío, follón *m*, escándalo, lío.

hullo [hʌ'ləu] *interj* ⟶ **hello**.

hum [hʌm] *n (of bees, engine)* zumbido.

▷ *vi* 1 *(bees, engine, etc)* zumbar. 2 *(sing)* tararear, canturrear. 3 *(bustling with activity)* hervir.

▷ *vt (tune)* tararear, canturrear.

▷ *vi fam (smell)* apestar.

▲ *pt & pp* **hummed**, *ger* **humming**.

human ['hju:mən] *adj* humano,-a. ● **human being** ser *m* humano.

▷ *n* ser *m* humano, humano.

humane [hju:'meın] *adj* humano,-a.

humanist ['hju:mənıst] *n* humanista *mf*.

humanitarian [hju:mænı'teərıən] *adj* humanitario,-a, filantrópico,-a.

▷ *n* filántropo,-a.

humanity [hju:'mænıtı] *n* 1 *(virtue)* humanidad *f*. 2 *(mankind)* género humano, raza humana.

▲ *pl* **humanities**.

humanization [hju:mənaı'zeıʃᵊn] *n* humanización *f*.

humanize ['hju:mənaız] *vt* humanizar.

humanly ['hju:məlı] *adv* humanamente.

humanoid ['hju:mənɔıd] *n* humanoide *mf*.

humble ['hʌmbᵊl] *adj* humilde.

▷ *vt* humillar.

▲ *comp* **humbler**, *superl* **humbliest**.

humbug ['hʌmbʌg] *n* 1 *fam (lie)* bola, embuste *m*. 2 *(person)* farsante *mf*, embaucador,-ra. 3 *(nonsense)* tonterías *fpl*, disparates *mpl*. 4 GB *(sweet)* caramelo de menta.

humdrum ['hʌmdrʌm] *adj* monótono,-a, aburrido,-a.

humerus ['hju:mərəs] *n* ANAT *(bone)* húmero.

▲ *pl* **humeri** ['hju:məraı].

humid ['hju:mıd] *adj* húmedo,-a.

humidifier ['hju:mıdıfaıəʳ] *n* humidificador *m*.

humidify [hju:'mıdıfaı] *vt* humidificar.

▲ *pt & pp* **humidified**, *ger* **humidifying**.

humidity [hju:'mıdıtı] *n* humedad *f*.

humiliate [hju:'mılıeıt] *vt* humillar.

humiliation [hju:mılı'eıʃᵊn] *n* humillación *f*.

hummingbird ['hʌmıŋbɜ:d] *n* colibrí *m*.

humor ['hju:məʳ] *n* US ⟶ **humour**.

humorous ['hju:mərəs] *adj* US ⟶ **humourous**.

humorist ['hju:mərıst] *n* 1 *(writer or teller of funny stories)* humorista *mf*. 2 *(joker)* bromista *mf*.

humorous ['hju:mərəs] *adj* 1 *(funny)* gracioso,-a, divertido,-a. 2 *(writer)* humorístico,-a, humorista.

humorously ['hju:mərəslı] *adv* jocosamente.

humour ['hju:məʳ] *n* 1 humor *m*. 2 *(of a joke)* gracia. 3 *(whim)* capricho.

▷ *vt* complacer, seguir el humor a.

hump [hʌmp] *n* 1 *(on back)* giba, joroba. 2 *(hillock)* montículo.

▷ *vt* 1 GB *fam (carry)* cargar.

humpback ['hʌmpbæk] *n* jorobado,-a.

humus ['hju:məs] *n* AGR mantillo, humus *m*.

hunch [hʌntʃ] *n* presentimiento, intuición *f*.
▷ *vt* encorvar.
hunchback ['hʌntʃbæk] *n (person)* jorobado,-a.
hundred ['hʌndrəd] *n* cien.
▷ *n pl* **hundreds** *(many)* centenares *mpl*, cientos *mpl*.
hundredth ['hʌndrədθ] *adj* centésimo,-a.
▷ *adv* en centésimo lugar.
hundredweight ['hʌndrədweɪt] *n* quintal *m*.
▲ *pl* **hundredweight** o **hundredweights**.

En Gran Bretaña equivale a 50,8 kg; en Estados Unidos equivale a 45,4 kg.

hung [hʌŋ] *pt & pp* → **hang**.
Hungarian [hʌŋ'geərɪən] *adj* húngaro,-a.
▷ *n* **1** *(person)* húngaro,-a. **2** *(language)* húngaro.
Hungary ['hʌŋgərɪ] *n* Hungría.
hunger ['hʌŋgə'] *n* **1** hambre *f*. **2** *fig* sed *f*. ● **hunger strike** huelga de hambre.
⊙ **to hunger after / hunger for** *vt insep* ansiar, anhelar, tener hambre de.
hungry ['hʌŋgrɪ] *adj* **1** hambriento,-a. **2** *fig* ávido,-a, sediento,-a. ■ **to be hungry** tener hambre.
▲ *comp* **hungrier**, *superl* **hungriest**.
hunk [hʌŋk] *n* **1** *fam (piece)* pedazo (grande), buen trozo. **2** *fam (man)* cachas *m*, machote *m*.
Hunnish ['hʌnɪʃ] *adj* huno,-a.
hunt [hʌnt] *n* **1** *(gen)* caza, cacería. **2** *(search)* búsqueda.
▷ *vt* cazar.
⊙ **to hunt down** *vt sep (corner)* acorralar, perseguir; *(to find)* dar con, encontrar.
⊙ **to hunt out / hunt up** *vt sep (to find)* encontrar; *(to look for)* buscar.
hunter ['hʌntə'] *n* **1** cazador,-ra *mf*. **2** ZOOL caballo de caza. **3** *(watch)* saboneta.
hunting ['hʌntɪŋ] *n (gen)* caza; *(expedition)* cacería, montería.
huntress ['hʌntrəs] *n* cazadora.
huntsman ['hʌntsmən] *n (gen)* cazador *m*; *(of big game)* montero.
▲ *pl* **huntsmen** ['hʌntsmən].
hurdle ['hɜːdəl] *n* **1** SP valla. **2** *fig* obstáculo.
▷ *vt* SP *(barrier)* saltar.
hurdling ['hɜːdlɪŋ] *n* SP carrera de vallas.
hurdy-gurdy ['hɜːdɪgɜːdɪ] *n* MUS organillo.
▲ *pl* **hurdy-gurdies**.
hurl [hɜːl] *vt* **1** lanzar, arrojar, tirar. **2** *(insults)* soltar.
hurling ['hɜːlɪŋ] *n* SP *juego irlandés parecido al rugby con quince jugadores en cada equipo.*
hurly-burly ['hɜːlɪbɜːlɪ] *n* alboroto, ajetreo, bullicio.
hurrah [hʊ'rɑː] *interj* ¡hurra!: **hurrah for Peter!** *¡viva Peter!*
▷ *vt* vitorear, aclamar.
hurray [hʊ'reɪ] *interj* ¡hurra!
hurricane ['hʌrɪkən, 'hʌrɪkeɪn] *n* huracán *m*.
hurried ['hʌrɪd] *adj* apresurado,-a, hecho,-a de prisa.
hurriedly ['hʌrɪdlɪ] *adv* apresuradamente, deprisa.
hurry ['hʌrɪ] *n* prisa: **are you in a hurry for the report?** *¿le corre prisa el informe?* ■ **to be in a hurry** tener prisa.
▷ *vi* apresurarse, darse prisa.
▲ *pt & pp* **hurried**, *ger* **hurrying**.
⊙ **to hurry up** *vi* darse prisa.
hurt [hɜːt] *n* **1** *(harm)* daño, dolor *m*, mal *m*. **2** *(wound)* herida. **3** *fig* daño, perjuicio.
▷ *adj* **1** *(physically)* herido,-a. **2** *(offended)* dolido,-a.
▷ *vt* **1** *(cause injury)* lastimar, hacer daño; *(to wound)* herir: **he has hurt his arm** *se ha hecho daño en el brazo*. **2** SP lesionar. **3** *(offend)* herir, ofender: **you hurt her feelings** *la has ofendido, le has herido los sentimientos*.
▷ *vi* **1** doler: **my eyes hurt** *me duelen los ojos*. **2** *fam* venir mal, ir mal.
▲ *pt & pp* **hurt**.
hurtful ['hɜːtfʊl] *adj (remark)* hiriente; *(experience)* doloroso,-a.
hurtle ['hɜːtəl] *vi* lanzarse, precipitarse.
▷ *vt* lanzar.
husband ['hʌzbənd] *n* marido, esposo.
husbandry ['hʌzbəndrɪ] *n* AGR *fml* agricultura. ● **animal husbandry** cría de ganado.
hush [hʌʃ] *n* quietud *f*, silencio.
▷ *vt* callar, silenciar.
▷ *interj* ¡silencio! ¡cállate! ¡cállese! ¡chito! ● **hush money** *fam* soborno *(que se paga para que alguien no hable)*.
⊙ **to hush up** *vt sep (affair)* echar tierra a; *(person)* hacer callar.
hush-hush ['hʌʃ'hʌʃ] *adj fam* confidencial, secreto,-a.
husk [hʌsk] *n (of cereals, etc)* cáscara; *(of beans, etc)* vaina.
▷ *vt (nuts, cereals)* descascarar, descascarillar; *(beans, peas)* pelar, desvainar.
huskiness ['hʌskɪnəs] *n* ronquera.
husky[1] ['hʌskɪ] *adj* ronco,-a: **he has a husky voice** *tiene la voz ronca*.
▲ *comp* **huskier**, *superl* **huskiest**.
husky[2] ['hʌskɪ] *n (dog)* perro esquimal.
▲ *pl* **huskies**.
hussar [hʊ'zɑː'] *n* MIL húsar *m*.
hussy ['hʌzɪ] *n dated (woman)* fresca, descarada.
▲ *pl* **hussies**.
hustings ['hʌstɪŋz] *n pl* GB *(platform)* tribuna *f sing* electoral; *(election)* elecciones *fpl*: **there have been heated debates at the hustings this year** *ha habido debates acalorados durante la campaña electoral este año*.
hustle ['hʌsəl] *n* bullicio. ● **hustle and bustle** ajetreo.
▷ *vt* **1** *(hurry)* dar prisa a. **2** *(jostle)* empujar, dar empujones a. **3** US *fam* hacerse con.
▷ *vi* apresurarse.
hustler ['hʌslə'] *n* **1** *(cheat)* estafador,-ra, buscavida *mf*. **2** US *sl (prostitute - man)* puto, chapero; *(- woman)* puta.
hut [hʌt] *n* **1** cabaña. **2** *(in garden)* cobertizo. **3** MIL barraca.
hutch [hʌtʃ] *n* jaula.
hyacinth ['haɪəsɪnθ] *n* BOT jacinto.
hyaena [haɪ'iːnə] *n* hiena.
hybrid ['haɪbrɪd] *adj* híbrido,-a.
▷ *n* vehículo híbrido.
hydra ['haɪdrə] *n* hidra.
hydrangea [haɪ'dreɪndʒə] *n* BOT hortensia.
hydrant ['haɪdrənt] *n* boca de riego.
hydrate [haɪ'dreɪt] *vt* hidratar.
hydration [haɪ'dreɪʃən] *n* hidratación *f*.

hydraulic [haɪˈdrɔːlɪk] *adj* hidráulico,-a. ● **hydraulic brake** freno hidráulico.
hydraulics [haɪˈdrɔːlɪks] *n (science)* hidráulica.
hydric [ˈhaɪdrɪk] *adj* hídrico,-a.
hydro [ˈhaɪdrəʊ] *n* GB *(spa)* balneario, estación *f* termal.
▲ *pl* **hydros.**
hydrocarbon [haɪdrəʊˈkɑːbᵊn] *n* CHEM hidrocarburo.
hydrochloric [haɪdrəˈklɒrɪk] *adj* clorhídrico,-a. ● **hydrochloric acid** ácido clorhídrico.
hydroelectric [haɪdrəʊɪˈlektrɪk] *adj* hidroeléctrico,-a. ● **hydroelectric power station** central *f* hidroeléctrica.
hydroelectricity [haɪdrəʊɪlekˈtrɪsɪtɪ] *n* hidroelectricidad *f*.
hydrofoil [ˈhaɪdrəfɔɪl] *n* hidroala *m*.
hydrogen [ˈhaɪdrədʒᵊn] *n* CHEM hidrógeno. ● **hydrogen bomb** bomba de hidrógeno.
hydrogenate [haɪˈdrɒdʒəneɪt] *vt* hidrogenar.
hydrographer [haɪˈdrɒgrəfəʳ] *n* hidrógrafo,-a.
hydrographic [haɪdrəˈgræfɪk] *adj* hidrográfico,-a.
hydrography [haɪˈdrɒgrəfɪ] *n* hidrografía.
hydrology [haɪˈdrɒlədʒɪ] *n* hidrología.
hydrolyse [ˈhaɪdrəlaɪz] *vt* hidrolizar.
hydrolysis [haɪˈdrɒlɪsɪs] *n* CHEM hidrólisis *f*.
hydrometer [haɪˈdrɒmɪtəʳ] *n* hidrómetro.
hydrometry [haɪˈdrɒmɪtrɪ] *n* hidrometría.
hydrophobia [haɪdrəˈfəʊbɪə] *n* MED hidrofobia.
hydrophobic [haɪdrəˈfəʊbɪk] *adj* hidrófobo,-a.
hydroplane [ˈhaɪdrəpleɪn] *n* hidroavión *m*, hidroplano.
hydroponics [haɪdrəˈpɒnɪks] *n* hidroponía.
hydrosphere [ˈhaɪdrəsfəʳ] *n* hidrosfera.
hydrotherapy [haɪdrəʊˈθerəpɪ] *n* MED hidroterapia.
hydroxide [haɪˈdrɒksaɪd] *n* hidróxido.
hyena [haɪˈiːnə] *n* ZOOL hiena.
hygiene [ˈhaɪdʒiːn] *n* higiene *f*.
hygienic [haɪˈdʒiːnɪk] *adj* higiénico,-a.
hygienist [haɪˈdʒiːnɪst] *n* higienista *mf*.
hygrometer [haɪˈgrɒmɪtəʳ] *n* higrómetro.
hygrometry [haɪˈgrɒmɪtrɪ] *n* higrometría.
hymen [ˈhaɪmən] *n* ANAT himen *m*.
hymenopteran [haɪməˈnɒptərən] *n* himenóptero.
hymenopterous [haɪməˈnɒptərəs] *adj* himenóptero,-a.
hymn [hɪm] *n* himno. ● **hymn book** cantoral *m*.
hymnal [ˈhɪmnᵊl] *n* cantoral *m*.
hype [haɪp] *vt fam* exagerar, dar mucho bombo a. ▷ *n fam* campaña publicitaria, bombo.
hyperactive [haɪpəˈæktɪv] *adj* hiperactivo,-a.
hyperbola [haɪˈpɜːbələ] *n* hipérbola.
▲ *pl* **hyperbole** [haɪˈpɜːbəlɪ] o **hyperbolas.**
hyperbole [haɪˈpɜːbəlɪ] *n* hipérbole *f*.
hypercorrection [haɪpəkəˈrekʃᵊn] *n* ultracorrección *f*.
hypercritical [haɪpəˈkrɪtɪkᵊl] *adj* hipercrítico,-a.
hyperglycaemia [haɪpəglaɪˈsiːmɪə] *n* hiperglucemia.
hyperglycemia [haɪpəglaɪˈsiːmɪə] *n* US hiperglucemia.
hyperlink [ˈhaɪpəlɪŋk] *n* hiperenlace.
hypermarket [ˈhaɪpəmɑːkɪt] *n* GB hipermercado.
hypermedia [ˈhaɪpəmiːdɪə] *n* hipermedia.
hypersensitive [haɪpəˈsensɪtɪv] *adj* hipersensible.
hypersonic [haɪpəˈsɒnɪk] *adj* hipersónico,-a.
hyperspace [ˈhaɪpəspeɪs] *n* hiperespacio.
hypertension [haɪpəˈtenʃᵊn] *n* MED hipertensión *f*.
hypertensive [haɪpəˈtensɪv] *adj* hipertenso,-a.
hypertext [ˈhaɪpətekst] *n* hipertexto.
hyphen [ˈhaɪfᵊn] *n* guion *m*.
hyphenate [ˈhaɪfᵊneɪt] *vt* escribir con guion, unir con guion.
hypnosis [hɪpˈnəʊsɪs] *n* MED hipnosis *f*.
hypnotic [hɪpˈnɒtɪk] *adj* hipnótico,-a.
hypnotise [ˈhɪpnətaɪz] *vt* → **hypnotize.**
hypnotism [ˈhɪpnətɪzᵊm] *n* hipnotismo.
hypnotist [ˈhɪpnətɪst] *n* hipnotizador,-ra.
hypnotize [ˈhɪpnətaɪz] *vt* hipnotizar.
hypo[1] [ˈhaɪpəʊ] *n (photography)* fijador *m*.
hypo[2] [ˈhaɪpəʊ] *n fam (syringe)* jeringa.
▲ *pl* **hypos.**
hypoallergenic [haɪpəæləˈdzenɪk] *adj (cosmetics, etc)* hipoalergénico,-a.
hypochondria [haɪpəˈkɒndrɪə] *n* hipocondría.
hypochondriac [haɪpəˈkɒndrɪæk] *n* hipocondríaco,-a. ▷ *adj* hipocondríaco,-a.
hypocrisy [hɪˈpɒkrɪsɪ] *n* hipocresía.
hypocrite [ˈhɪpəkrɪt] *n* hipócrita *mf*.
hypocritical [hɪpəˈkrɪtɪkᵊl] *adj* hipócrita.
hypodermic [haɪpəˈdɜːmɪk] *adj* hipodérmico,-a.
hypodermis [haɪpəʊˈdɜːmɪs] *n* hipodermis *f*.
hyponym [ˈhaɪpənɪm] *n* hipónimo.
hypotension [haɪpəʊˈtenʃᵊn] *n* MED hipotensión *f*.
hypotensive [haɪpəʊˈtensɪv] *adj* hipotenso,-a.
hypotenuse [haɪˈpɒtənjuːz] *n (geometry)* hipotenusa.
hypothalamus [haɪpəʊˈθæləməs] *n* hipotálamo.
hypothermia [haɪpəʊˈθɜːmɪə] *n* MED hipotermia.
hypothesis [haɪˈpɒθəsɪs] *n* hipótesis *f*.
▲ *pl* **hypotheses** [haɪˈpɒθəsiːz].
hypothetic [haɪpəˈθetɪk] *adj* hipotético,-a.
hypothetical [haɪpəˈθetɪkᵊl] *adj* hipotético,-a.
hyssop [ˈhɪsəp] *n* hisopo.
hysterectomy [hɪstəˈrektəmɪ] *n* histerectomía.
▲ *pl* **hysterectomies.**
hysteria [hɪˈstɪərɪə] *n* histeria.
hysterical [hɪˈsterɪkᵊl] *adj* histérico,-a. ● **hysterical laughter** risa incontrolable.
hysterically [hɪˈsterɪkᵊlɪ] *adv* histéricamente.
hysterics [hɪˈsterɪks] *n* **1** *(attack)* ataque *m* de histeria. **2** *fam* ataque *m* de risa. ■ **to have hysterics** mondarse de risa.
Hz [ˈeɪtʃˈzed] *abbr* (**hertz**) hercio, hercios; *(abbreviation)* Hz.

I

I, i [aɪ] *n (the letter)* I, i *f*.

I [aɪ] *pron* yo.

Iberia [aɪ'bɪərɪə] *n* Iberia.

Iberian [aɪ'bɪərɪən] *adj (modern)* ibérico,-a; *(historically)* ibero,-a, íbero,-a, ibérico,-a.
▷ *n* **1** *(person - now)* ibérico,-a; *(- historically)* ibero,-a, íbero,-a. **2** *(language)* ibero, íbero. ● **Iberian Peninsula** Península Ibérica.

ibex ['aɪbeks] *n* íbice *m*.
▲ *pl* **ibex** ['aɪbeks] o **ibexes** ['aɪbeksɪz].

ibis ['aɪbɪs] *n* ibis *f*.
▲ *pl* **ibis** ['aɪbɪs] o **ibises** ['aɪbɪsɪz].

Ibiza [ɪ'bi:θə] *n* Ibiza.

Ibizan [ɪ'bi:θᵊn] *adj* ibicenco,-a.

ice [aɪs] *n* **1** *(frozen water)* hielo. **2** *(ice-cream)* helado. ■ **ice cube** cubito de hielo. ‖ **ice hockey** hockey *m* sobre hielo. ‖ **ice lolly** polo. ‖ **ice ring** pista de hielo.
▷ *vt (cake)* glasear.
⊙ **to ice over** *vi (lake, etc)* helarse; *(windscreen, etc)* cubrirse de hielo.
⊙ **to ice up** *vi* → **ice over.**

iceberg ['aɪsbɜ:g] *n* **1** iceberg *m*. **2** *fig* persona fría.

icebound ['aɪsbaʊnd] *adj (harbour, etc)* bloqueado,-a por el hielo; *(ship)* atrapado,-a por el hielo.

icebox ['aɪsbɒks] *n* **1** US nevera. **2** *(freezing compartment)* congelador *m*.

icebreaker ['aɪsbreɪkəʳ] *n* rompehielos *m inv*.

icecap ['aɪskæp] *n* casquete *m* polar.

ice-cold ['aɪskəʊld] *adj* helado,-a.

ice-cream ['aɪskri:m] *n* helado.

iced [aɪst] *n (drink)* con hielo; *(cake)* glaseado,-a.

Iceland ['aɪslənd] *n* Islandia.

Icelander ['aɪsləndəʳ] *n (person)* islandés,-esa.

Icelandic [aɪs'lændɪk] *adj* islandés,-esa.
▷ *n (language)* islandés *m*.

ice-skate ['aɪsskeɪt] *vi* patinar sobre hielo.

ice-skating ['aɪskeɪtɪŋ] *n* patinaje *m* sobre hielo.

icicle ['aɪsɪkᵊl] *n* carámbano.

icing ['aɪsɪŋ] *n* cobertura.

icon ['aɪkən] *n* icono.

iconoclast [aɪ'kɒnəklæst] *n* iconoclasta *mf*.

iconography [aɪkə'nɒgrəfɪ] *n* iconografía.

icy ['aɪsɪ] *adj* **1** *(very cold - hand, etc)* helado,-a; *(- wind)* glacial. **2** *(covered with ice)* cubierto,-a de hielo. **3** *fig* glacial.
▲ *comp* **icier**, *superl* **iciest**.

ID ['aɪ'di:] *abbr* (**identification**) identificación *f*. ● **ID card** documento nacional de identidad, DNI *m*.

I'd [aɪd] *contr* I would, I had.

idea [aɪ'dɪə] *n* **1** *(gen)* idea; *(opinion)* opinión *f*. **2** *(intuition)* impresión *f*, sensación *f*. **3** *(concept)* concepto.
▷ *n* **the idea** *(aim, purpose)* idea, intención *f*, objetivo.

ideal [aɪ'di:l] *adj* ideal, perfecto,-a.
▷ *n* **1** *(perfect example)* ideal *m*. **2** *(principle)* principio ideal *m*.

idealist [aɪ'dɪəlɪst] *n* idealista *mf*.

idealistic [aɪdɪə'lɪstɪk] *adj* idealista.

idealization [aɪdɪəlaɪ'zeɪʃᵊn] *n* idealización *f*.

idealize [aɪ'dɪəlaɪz] *vt* idealizar: **we tend to idealize the past** *tendemos a idealizar el pasado.*

ideally [aɪ'dɪəlɪ] *adv* **1** *(perfectly)* idealmente, perfectamente. **2** *(preferably)* a ser posible.

identical [aɪ'dentɪkᵊl] *adj* **1** *(exactly alike)* idéntico,-a (**to/with**, a). **2** *(the same)* mismísimo,-a.

identifiable [aɪ'dentɪfaɪəbᵊl] *adj* identificable.

identification [aɪdentɪfɪ'keɪʃᵊn] *n* **1** *(gen)* identificación *f*. **2** *(papers)* documentación *f*.

identify [aɪ'dentɪfaɪ] *vt* **1** *(prove or show identity of, recognize)* identificar. **2** *(discover)* descubrir, averiguar, identificar. **3** *(associate)* asociar (**with**, con), relacionar (**with**, con).
⊙ **to identify with** *vt sep (associate)* relacionar con, asociar con.
▷ *vi (sympathize)* identificarse con.
▲ *pt & pp* **identified**, *ger* **identifying**.

Identikit® [aɪ'dentɪkɪt] ● **Identikit picture** retrato robot.

identity [aɪ'dentɪtɪ] *n* identidad *f*. ● **identity card** carnet *m* de identidad.
▲ *pl* **identities**.

ideogram ['ɪdɪəʊgræm] *n* ideograma *m*.

ideolect ['ɪdɪəʊlekt] *n* ideolecto.

ideological [aɪdɪə'lɒdʒɪkᵊl] *adj* ideológico,-a.

ideology [aɪdɪ'ɒlədʒɪ] *n* ideología.
▲ *pl* **ideologies**.

idiocy ['ɪdɪəsɪ] *n* **1** *(stupidity)* idiotez *f*. **2** *(stupid act, etc)* estupidez *f*.
▲ *pl* **idiocies**.

idiom ['ɪdɪəm] *n* **1** *(phrase)* locución *f*, modismo, frase *f* hecha. **2** *(language)* lenguaje *m*, idioma *m*; *(style)* estilo.

idiomatic [ɪdɪə'mætɪk] *adj* idiomático,-a.

idiosyncrasy [ɪdɪə'sɪŋkrəsɪ] *n* idiosincrasia, rareza, manía.
▲ *pl* **idiosyncrasies**.

idiosyncratic [ɪdɪəsɪŋ'krætɪk] *adj* idiosincrásico,-a.

idiot ['ɪdɪət] *n* **1** *fam* idiota *mf*, tonto,-a. **2** MED idiota *mf*.

idle ['aɪdᵊl] *adj* **1** *(lazy)* perezoso,-a, holgazán,-ana, vago,-a. **2** *(not working - person)* parado,-a, desempleado,-a, sin trabajo, inactivo,-a; *(- machinery)* parado,-a; *(- money)* improductivo,-a. **3** *(groundless - threat, hope, promise)* vano,-a, inútil; *(- fear, suspicion)* infundado,-a. **4** *(frivolous, trivial)* frívolo,-a, trivial, sin importancia, insignificante.
▲ *comp* **idler**, *superl* **idlest**.

▷ *vi* **1** *(waste time)* gandulear, holgazanear, perder el tiempo. **2** *(engine)* funcionar en vacío.
◆ **to idle away** *vt sep* desperdiciar, perder.
dler ['aɪdᵊləʳ] *n* holgazán,-ana, vago,-a, gandul,-la.
dol ['aɪdᵊl] *n* ídolo.
dolatrous [aɪ'dɒlətrəs] *adj* idólatra.
dolatry [aɪ'dɒlətrɪ] *n* idolatría.
▲ *pl* idolatries.
dolize ['aɪdəlaɪz] *vt* idolatrar.
dyll ['ɪdɪl] *n* idilio.
dyllic [ɪ'dɪlk] *adj* idílico,-a.
e ['aɪ'iː] *abbr* (id est) esto es, a saber; *(abbreviation)* i.e.
f [ɪf] *conj* **1** *(supposing)* si: if it rains, we'll stay at home *si llueve, nos quedaremos en casa;* you can come if you want *puedes venir si quieres.* **2** *(whether)* si: do you know if she got the job? *¿sabes si consiguió el trabajo?* **3** *(used after verbs expressing feelings)* que: do you mind if I open the window? *¿te importa que abra la ventana?* **4** *(but)* aunque, pero: it's good, if a little slow at times *es bueno pero algo lento a veces.* **5** *(in exclamations)*: well, if it isn't Jimmy Jazz! *vaya, ¡pero si es Jimmy Jazz!*
■ **if I were you** yo que tú, yo en tu lugar. ‖ **if only** *(present or future time)* ¡ojalá!, ¡si al menos...!
ffy ['ɪfɪ] *adj fam* dudoso,-a.
▲ *comp* iffier, *superl* iffiest.
gloo ['ɪgluː] *n* iglú *m.*
▲ *pl* igloos.
gneous ['ɪgnɪəs] *adj* ígneo,-a.
gnite [ɪg'naɪt] *vt* encender, prender fuego.
gnition [ɪg'nɪʃᵊn] *n* **1** ignición *f.* **2** AUTO encendido, arranque *m.*
gnoble [ɪg'nəubᵊl] *adj* innoble, vil, infame.
gnominious [ɪgnə'mɪnɪəs] *n* ignominioso,-a, vergonzoso,-a.
gnominy ['ɪgnəmɪnɪ] *n* ignominia, oprobio.
▲ *pl* ignominies.
gnorance ['ɪgnərəns] *n* ignorancia.
gnorant ['ɪgnərənt] *adj* **1** *(unaware)* ignorante (of, de). **2** *fam (rude)* descortés, maleducado,-a.
gnore [ɪg'nɔːʳ] *vt* **1** *(order, warning)* no hacer caso de, hacer caso omiso de; *(behaviour, fact)* pasar por alto. **2** *(person)* hacer como si no existiese.
guana [ɪ'gwɑːnə] *n* iguana.
lex ['aɪleks] *n* **1** *(holm oak)* encina. **2** *(holly)* acebo.
lk [ɪlk] *phr* of that ilk de esa clase.
ll [ɪl] *adj* **1** *(sick)* enfermo,-a. **2** *(harmful, unpropitious)* malo,-a.
▷ *n fml (harm, evil)* mal *m.*
▷ *adv* **1** *(badly)* mal. **2** *(unfavourably)* mal. **3** *(with difficulty, hardly)* mal, a duras penas.
▷ *n pl* ills *(problems, misfortunes)* desgracias *fpl.*
'll [aɪl] *contr* I will, I shall.
ll-advised [ɪləd'vaɪzd] *adj* desaconsejable, poco aconsejable, desacertado,-a.
ll-behaved [ɪlbɪ'heɪvd] *adj* maleducado,-a.
ll-bred [ɪl'bred] *adj* maleducado,-a, malcriado,-a.
ll-considered [ɪlkən'sɪdəd] *adj* poco meditado,-a, poco pensado,-a, imprudente.
ll-disposed [ɪldɪ'spəuzd] *adj fml (unfriendly)* mal dispuesto,-a, poco dispuesto,-a; *(unsympathetic)* indiferente, impasible.
llegal [ɪ'liːgᵊl] *adj* ilegal.
illegality [ɪlɪ'gælɪtɪ] *n* ilegalidad *f.*
▲ *pl* illegalities.
illegible [ɪ'ledʒɪbᵊl] *adj* ilegible.
illegitimacy [ɪlɪ'dʒɪtɪməsɪ] *n* ilegitimidad *f.*
illegitimate [ɪlɪ'dʒɪtɪmət] *adj* ilegítimo,-a.
ill-equipped [ɪlɪ'kwɪpt] *adj (equipment)* mal equipado,-a; *(ability)* mal preparado,-a.
ill-founded [ɪl'faundɪd] *adj (fear, suspicion, accusation, rumour, etc)* infundado,-a; *(confidence, hope)* vano,-a.
illicit [ɪ'lɪsɪt] *adj* ilícito,-a.
illiteracy [ɪ'lɪtᵊrəsɪ] *n* analfabetismo.
illiterate [ɪ'lɪtᵊrət] *adj* **1** *(unlettered)* analfabeto,-a. **2** *(uneducated)* ignorante, inculto,-a. **3** *(poor style)* inculto,-a, pobre.
▷ *n (unlettered person)* analfabeto,-a.
ill-mannered [ɪl'mænəd] *adj* maleducado,-a, descortés.
illness ['ɪlnəs] *n* enfermedad *f.*
▲ *pl* illnesses.
illogical [ɪ'lɒdʒɪkᵊl] *adj* ilógico,-a.
ill-treat [ɪl'triːt] *vt* maltratar.
ill-treatment [ɪl'triːtmənt] *n* malos tratos *mpl.*
illuminate [ɪ'luːmɪneɪt] *vt* iluminar.
illuminating [ɪ'luːmɪneɪtɪŋ] *adj (revealing)* revelador,-ra; *(instructive)* instructivo,-a.
illumination [ɪluːmɪ'neɪʃᵊn] *n* **1** *(light)* iluminación *f.* **2** *(clarification)* aclaración.
illusion [ɪ'luːʒᵊn] *n* ilusión *f*, falsa impresión *f.*
illusionist [ɪ'luːʒᵊnɪst] *n* ilusionista *mf.*
illusive [ɪ'luːsɪv] *adj* ilusorio,-a.
illustrate ['ɪləstreɪt] *vt* ilustrar.
illustrated ['ɪləstreɪt] *adj* ilustrado,-a.
illustration [ɪləs'treɪʃᵊn] *n* **1** *(gen)* ilustración *f.* **2** *(example)* ejemplo.
illustrative ['ɪləstrətɪv] *adj* **1** *(gen)* ilustrativo,-a, ilustrador,-ra. **2** *(example)* aclaratorio,-a.
illustrator ['ɪləstreɪtəʳ] *n* ilustrador,-ra.
illustrious [ɪ'lʌstrɪəs] *adj* ilustre.
ILO ['aɪ'el'əu] *abbr* (International Labour Organization) Organización *f* Internacional del Trabajo; *(abbreviation)* OIT *f.*
I'm [aɪm] *contr* I am.
IM ['aɪ'em] *abb* (instant messaging) mensajería instantánea.
image ['ɪmɪdʒ] *n* **1** *(gen)* imagen *f.* **2** *(reputation)* imagen *f*, fama, reputación *f.*
imagery ['ɪmɪðzᵊrɪ] *n lit* imágenes *fpl.*
imaginable [ɪ'mædʒɪnəbᵊl] *adj* imaginable, concebible.
imaginary [ɪ'mædʒɪnərɪ] *adj* imaginario,-a.
imagination [ɪmædʒɪ'neɪʃᵊn] *n (gen)* imaginación *f*; *(inventiveness)* inventiva.
imaginative [ɪ'mædʒɪnətɪv] *adj (person)* imaginativo,-a, de gran inventiva; *(creation)* lleno,-a de imaginación, lleno,-a de fantasía.
imagine [ɪ'mædʒɪn] *vt* **1** *(visualize)* imaginar. **2** *(suppose)* suponer, imaginar(se), figurarse.
imam [ɪ'mɑːm] *n* imán *m.*
imbalance [ɪm'bæləns] *n* desequilibrio, falta de equilibrio.
imbecile ['ɪmbəsiːl] *n* imbécil *mf.*
imbibe [ɪm'baɪb] *vt* **1** *fml (liquids)* beber. **2** *(knowledge)* asimilar, absorber, imbuirse de.

imbue [ɪm'bjuː] *vt fml* imbuir (**with**, de), infundir.
IMF ['aɪ'em'ef] *abbr* (**International Monetary Fund**) Fondo Monetario Internacional; *(abbreviation)* FMI *m*.
imitate ['ɪmɪteɪt] *vt (gen)* imitar, copiar; *(for fun)* imitar.
imitation [ɪmɪ'teɪʃən] *n* **1** *(gen)* imitación *f*, copia; *(for fun)* imitación *f*. **2** *(reproduction)* reproducción *f*.
▷ *adj* de imitación.
immaculate [ɪ'mækjʊlət] *adj* **1** *(perfectly clean, spotless)* inmaculado,-a; *(perfectly tidy)* perfectamente ordenado,-a; *(clothes, appearance)* impecable. **2** *(perfect, flawless)* perfecto,-a.
immaterial [ɪmə'tɪərɪəl] *adj* **1** *(unimportant)* irrelevante. **2** *(incorporeal)* inmaterial, incorpóreo,-a.
immature [ɪmə'tjʊəʳ] *adj* **1** *(gen)* inmaduro,-a; *(- plant)* joven. **2** *(childish)* inmaduro,-a, pueril.
immaturity [ɪmə'tjʊərətɪ] *n* inmadurez *f*, falta de madurez.
immeasurable [ɪ'meʒərəbəl] *adj* inconmensurable, incalculable.
immediacy [ɪ'miːdɪəsɪ] *n* **1** *(urgency)* urgencia, carácter *m* urgente. **2** *(nearness)* proximidad *f*, inmediación *f*.
immediate [ɪ'miːdɪət] *adj* **1** *(instant)* inmediato,-a; *(urgent)* urgente. **2** *(nearest)* inmediato,-a, más próximo,-a. **3** *(direct)* primero,-a, principal.
immediately [ɪ'miːdɪətlɪ] *adv (instantly, at once)* inmediatamente, de inmediato, en seguida, en el acto.
immemorial [ɪmə'mɔːrɪəl] *adj fml* inmemorial.
immense [ɪ'mens] *adj* inmenso,-a, enorme.
immensely [ɪ'menslɪ] *adv* enormemente, sumamente.
immensity [ɪ'mensɪtɪ] *n* inmensidad *f*.
immerse [ɪ'mɜːs] *vt* sumergir (**in**, en), hundir (**in**, en).
immersion [ɪ'mɜːʃən] *n* **1** inmersión *f*, sumersión *f*. **2** *fig* absorción *f*.
immigrant ['ɪmɪgrənt] *adj* inmigrante.
▷ *n* inmigrante *mf*.
immigrate ['ɪmɪgreɪt] *vi* inmigrar.
immigration [ɪmɪ'greɪʃən] *n* inmigración *f*.
imminence ['ɪmɪnəns] *n* inminencia.
imminent ['ɪmɪnənt] *adj* inminente.
immobile [ɪ'məʊbaɪl] *adj* inmóvil.
immobility [ɪmə'bɪlɪtɪ] *n* inmovilidad *f*.
immobilize [ɪ'məʊbɪlaɪz] *vt* inmovilizar.
immoderate [ɪ'mɒdərət] *adj (gen)* excesivo,-a, desmesurado,-a, descomedido,-a; *(language)* soez.
immodesty [ɪ'mɒdɪstɪ] *n* **1** *(conceitedness)* presunción *f*, engreimiento. **2** *(indecency)* indecencia, falta de pudor.
immoral [ɪ'mɒrəl] *adj* inmoral.
immortal [ɪ'mɔːtəl] *adj* **1** *(god, soul, etc)* inmortal. **2** *fig (fame, memory, etc)* imperecedero,-a, perdurable.
▷ *n* inmortal *mf*.
immortality [ɪmɔː'tælɪtɪ] *n* inmortalidad *f*.
immortalize [ɪ'mɔːtəlaɪz] *vt* inmortalizar.
immovable [ɪ'muːvəbəl] *adj (object)* inamovible.
immune [ɪ'mjuːn] *adj* **1** *(gen)* inmune (**to**, a). **2** *(exempt)* exento,-a.
immunity [ɪ'mjuːnɪtɪ] *n* **1** *(gen)* inmunidad *f*. **2** *(exemption)* exención *f*.

immunize ['ɪmjənaɪz] *vt* inmunizar (**against**, contra
immunodeficiency [ɪmjʊnəʊdɪ'fɪʃənsɪ] *n* inmunc deficiencia.
immunodeficient [ɪmjʊnəʊdɪ'fɪʃənt] *adj* inmunc deficiente.
immunology [ɪmjʊ'nɒlədʒɪ] *n* inmunología.
immutable [ɪ'mjuːtəbəl] *adj fml* inmutable, inalter ble.
imp [ɪmp] *n* **1** *(small devil)* diablillo, duendecillo. **2** *f (naughty child)* pillo,-a, diablillo.
impact [*(n)* 'ɪmpækt; *(vb)* ɪm'pakt] *n* **1** *(gen)* impacto *(crash)* choque *m*. **2** *(impression, effect)* efecto, im presión *f*, impacto.
▷ *vt* US *(have impact on)* impresionar.
impair [ɪm'peəʳ] *vt* **1** *(damage - gen)* afectar; *(- healt* afectar, perjudicar. **2** *(weaken)* debilitar.
impairment [ɪm'peəmənt] *n (dysfunction)* disfur ción; *(damage)* daños *mpl*.
impale [ɪm'peɪl] *vt (gen)* empalar; *(with sword, et* atravesar.
impalpable [ɪm'pælpəbəl] *adj* **1** *fml* impalpable, ir tangible. **2** *(difficult to understand)* abstruso,-a.
impart [ɪm'pɑːt] *vt* **1** *fml (inform)* comunicar, hac saber; *(teach)* impartir, transmitir. **2** *fml (give - fl vour)* dar; *(- quality)* otorgar, conferir.
impartial [ɪm'pɑːʃəl] *adj* imparcial.
impassable [ɪm'pɑːsəbəl] *adj (road, etc)* intransit ble, impracticable; *(barrier)* infranqueable.
impasse [æm'pɑːs] *n* punto muerto, impasse *m*.
impassive [ɪm'pæsɪv] *adj (expressionless)* impasibl imperturbable; *(indifferent)* indiferente.
impatience [ɪm'peɪʃəns] *n* **1** *(eagerness)* impacienci ansiedad *f*. **2** *(irritation)* impaciencia, irritación *f*.
impatient [ɪm'peɪʃənt] *adj* **1** *(eager)* impaciente, ar sioso,-a. **2** *(irritable)* irritable. **3** *fml (intolerant)* int lerante.
impeach [ɪm'piːtʃ] *vt* **1** JUR *(accuse)* acusar; *(try)* pr cesar. **2** *fml (question)* poner en tela de juicio.
impeachment [ɪm'piːtʃmənt] *n* JUR *(accusation)* ac sación *f*, denuncia; *(trial)* proceso.
impeccable [ɪm'pekəbəl] *adj (gen)* impecable, pe fecto,-a.
impecunious [ɪmpɪ'kjuːnɪəs] *adj fml* indigente, n cesitado,-a.
impede [ɪm'piːd] *vt (hinder)* estorbar, dificultar, in pedir; *(obstruct)* poner obstáculos a, poner trabas obstaculizar.
impediment [ɪm'pedɪmənt] *n* **1** *(gen)* impedimer to, estorbo, obstáculo (**to**, para). **2** MED defecto.
impel [ɪm'pel] *vt* impeler, impulsar.
▲ *pt & pp* **impelled**, *ger* **impelling**.
impending [ɪm'pendɪŋ] *adj* inminente.
impenetrable [ɪm'penɪtrəbəl] *adj* **1** *(gen)* impen trable. **2** *(mystery, problem, etc)* insondable, inescr table.
impenitent [ɪm'penɪtənt] *adj fml* impenitente.
imperative [ɪm'perətɪv] *adj* **1** *(indispensable)* in prescindible. **2** *(authoritative)* imperativo,-a, imp rioso,-a. **3** LING imperativo,-a.
imperceptible [ɪmpə'septəbəl] *adj* imperceptibl insensible.

mperfect [ɪm'pɜːfekt] *adj* 1 *(gen)* imperfecto,-a; *(goods, sight)* defectuoso,-a. 2 LING imperfecto,-a.
▹ *n* **the imperfect** LING el imperfecto.

mperfection [ɪmpə'fekʃᵊn] *n (gen)* imperfección *f*; *(defect)* defecto, tara, tacha; *(blemish)* mancha.

mperial [ɪm'pɪərɪəl] *adj* 1 *(gen)* imperial. 2 *(weight, measure) del sistema métrico británico.*

mperialism [ɪm'pɪərɪəlɪzᵊm] *n* imperialismo.

mperialist [ɪm'pɪərɪəlɪst] *n* imperialista *mf*.

mperil [ɪm'perəl] *vt fml* poner en peligro, arriesgar.

mperious [ɪm'pɪərɪəs] *adj* imperioso,-a, autoritario,-a.

mperishable [ɪm'perɪʃəbᵊl] *adj* imperecedero,-a.

mpermanent [ɪm'pɜːmənənt] *adj* efímero,-a.

mpermeability [ɪmpɜːmɪə'bɪlɪtɪ] *n* impermeabilidad *f*.

mpermeable [ɪm'pɜːmɪəbᵊl] *adj* impermeable.

mpermissible [ɪmpə'mɪsəbᵊl] *adj fml* prohibido,-a.

mpersonal [ɪm'pɜːsᵊnəl] *adj* impersonal.

mpersonate [ɪm'pɜːsᵊneɪt] *vt* 1 *(imitate to deceive)* hacerse pasar por. 2 *(imitate to entertain)* imitar.

mpertinence [ɪm'pɜːtɪnəns] *n* impertinencia, descaro.

mpertinent [ɪm'pɜːtɪnənt] *adj* impertinente, descarado,-a.

mperturbable [ɪmpə'tɜːbəbᵊl] *adj* imperturbable.

mpervious [ɪm'pɜːvɪəs] *adj* 1 *(rock, etc)* impermeable. 2 *(person)* insensible (**to**, a).

mpetuosity [ɪmpetjʊ'ɒsətɪ] *n* impetuosidad *f*, irreflexión *f*.

mpetuous [ɪm'petjʊəs] *adj* impetuoso,-a, irreflexivo,-a, impulsivo,-a.

mpetus ['ɪmpətəs] *n* ímpetu *m*, impulso, estímulo.

mpiety [ɪm'paɪətɪ] *n fml* impiedad *f*.

mpinge [ɪm'pɪndʒ] *vi* 1 *(affect)* afectar (**on**, a), repercutir (**on**, en), incidir (**on**, en). 2 *(encroach on)* vulnerar (**on**, -).

mplacable [ɪm'plækəbᵊl] *adj* implacable.

mplant [*(vb)* ɪm'plɑːnt; *(n)* 'ɪmplɑːnt] *vt* 1 MED implantar, injertar. 2 *(ideas, etc)* inculcar (**in**, en).
▹ *n* MED implantación *f*, injerto.

mplausible [ɪm'plɔːzəbᵊl] *adj* inverosímil, poco probable, poco convincente.

mplement [*(n)* 'ɪmpləmənt; *(vb)* 'ɪmplɪment] *n (instrument)* instrumento, utensilio; *(tool)* herramienta.
▹ *vt (plan, suggestion, etc)* llevar a cabo, poner en práctica; *(law, policy)* aplicar.

mplementation [ɪmpləmen'teɪʃᵊn] *n (of plan, etc)* puesta en práctica, desarrollo; *(of law, etc)* aplicación *f*.

mplicate ['ɪmplɪkeɪt] *vt* implicar, (**in**, en).

mplication [ɪmplɪ'keɪʃᵊn] *n* implicación *f*.

mplicit [ɪm'plɪsɪt] *adj* 1 *(implied)* implícito,-a, tácito,-a. 2 *(absolute)* absoluto,-a, incondicional.

mplied [ɪm'plaɪd] *adj* implícito,-a, tácito,-a.

mplode [ɪm'pləʊd] *vi* implosionar.

mplore [ɪm'plɔːʳ] *vt* implorar, suplicar.

mplosion [ɪm'pləʊʒᵊn] *n* implosión *f*.

mplosive [ɪm'pləʊsɪv] *adj* implosivo,-a.

mply [ɪm'plaɪ] *vt* 1 *(involve, entail)* implicar, suponer, presuponer. 2 *(mean)* significar, querer decir; *(hint)* insinuar, dar a entender.
▲ *pt & pp* implied.

impolite [ɪmpə'laɪt] *adj* maleducado,-a, descortés.

imponderable [ɪm'pɒndᵊrəbᵊl] *adj* imponderable.

import¹ ['ɪmpɔːt] *n* 1 *(article)* artículo de importación. 2 *(activity)* importación *f*.
▷ *vt* importar.

import² [ɪm'pɔːt] *n* 1 *fml (meaning)* significado. 2 *fml (importance)* importancia.
▷ *vt fml (mean)* significar.

importance [ɪm'pɔːtᵊns] *n (gen)* importancia.

important [ɪm'pɔːtᵊnt] *adj* 1 *(gen)* importante. 2 *(influential)* de categoría.

importation [ɪmpɔː'teɪʃᵊn] *n* importación *f*.

importer [ɪm'pɔːtəʳ] *n* importador,-ra.

importune [ɪm'pɔːtjuːn] *vt* importunar.

impose [ɪm'pəʊz] *vt (gen)* imponer (**on**, a).
⊙ **to impose on** *vt insep (take advantage of)* abusar de, aprovecharse de.

imposition [ɪmpə'zɪʃᵊn] *n (gen)* imposición *f*.

impossible [ɪm'pɒsɪbᵊl] *adj (gen)* imposible.

impossibly [ɪm'pɒsɪblɪ] *adv (intolerably)* insoportablemente; *(inconceivably)* increíblemente; *(hopelessly)* desesperadamente.

impostor [ɪm'pɒstəʳ] *n* impostor,-ra.

imposture [ɪm'pɒstʃəʳ] *n fml* impostura.

impotence ['ɪmpətᵊns] *n* impotencia.

impotent ['ɪmpətənt] *adj* impotente.

impound [ɪm'paʊnd] *vt* JUR confiscar, incautarse de, embargar.

impoverish [ɪm'pɒvᵊrɪʃ] *vt* 1 *(person)* empobrecer. 2 *(land)* agotar.

impoverishment [ɪm'pɒvᵊrɪsmənt] *n* empobrecimiento.

impracticable [ɪm'præktɪkəbᵊl] *adj* irrealizable, inviable, no factible.

impractical [ɪm'præktɪkᵊl] *adj* 1 *(person)* poco práctico,-a, nada práctico,-a. 2 *(project, etc)* inviable, poco viable, poco factible.

imprecation [ɪmprɪ'keɪʃᵊn] *n* imprecación *f*.

imprecise [ɪmprə'saɪs] *adj* impreciso,-a, inexacto,-a.

imprecision [ɪmprə'sɪʒᵊn] *n* imprecisión *f*, falta de precisión.

impregnable [ɪm'pregnəbᵊl] *adj* 1 *(structure)* inexpugnable. 2 *fig* inexpugnable, invulnerable.

impregnate ['ɪmpregneɪt] *vt* 1 *(saturate)* impregnar (**with**, de), empapar (**with**, de); *(pervade)* penetrar en. 2 *fig (influence)* extenderse por. 3 *fml (fertilize)* fecundar.

impregnation [ɪmpreg'neɪʃᵊn] *n* impregnación *f*.

impresario [ɪmprə'sɑːrɪəʊ] *n* empresario,-a.
▲ *pl* impresarios.

impress [ɪm'pres] *vt* 1 *(cause respect)* impresionar. 2 *(emphasize, stress)* subrayar, convencer, recalcar. 3 *fig* grabar.

impression [ɪm'preʃᵊn] *n* 1 *(gen)* impresión *f*. 2 *(imitation)* imitación *f*. 3 *(imprint, mark)* marca, señal *f*, impresión *f*; *(in wax, plaster)* molde *m*; *(of foot, etc)* huella. 4 *(reprint)* impresión *f*, edición *f*.

impressionable [ɪm'preʃᵊnəbᵊl] *adj* impresionable, influenciable.

impressionism [ɪm'preʃᵊnɪzᵊm] *n* ART impresionismo.

impressionist [ɪm'preʃᵊnɪst] *adj* ART impresionista.
▷ *n* 1 ART impresionista. 2 *(mimic)* imitador,-ra.

impressionistic [ɪmpreʃᵊn'ɪstɪk] *adj* impresionista.
impressive [ɪm'presɪv] *adj* impresionante.
imprint [*(vb)* ɪm'prɪnt; *(n)* 'ɪmprɪnt] *vt* **1** *(mark)* dejar huella (**on**, en), marcar (**on**, en); *(stamp)* imprimir (**on**, en), estampar (**on**, en). **2** *fig* grabar.
▷ *n* **1** *(physical mark)* marca, huella, señal *f*, sello, impresión *f*; *(stamp)* marca, sello; *(of hand, etc)* huella. **2** *fig* huella, marca. **3** pie *m* de imprenta.
imprison [ɪm'prɪzᵊn] *vt* encarcelar, meter en la cárcel.
imprisonment [ɪm'prɪzᵊnmənt] *n* encarcelamiento.
improbability [ɪmprɒbə'bɪlɪtɪ] *n* **1** *(of event)* improbabilidad *f*. **2** *(of story, explanation)* inverosimilitud *f*.
▲ *pl* **improbabilities.**
improbable [ɪm'prɒbəbᵊl] *adj* **1** *(event)* improbable. **2** *(story, explanation)* inverosímil.
impromptu [ɪm'prɒmptjuː] *adj (improvised)* improvisado,-a, no preparado,-a; *(unexpected)* imprevisto,-a.
▷ *adv (spontaneously)* improvisadamente; *(unexpectedly)* de improviso.
▷ *n* MUS impromptu *m*, improvisación *f*.
improper [ɪm'prɒpəʳ] *adj* **1** *(behaviour)* impropio,-a; *(method, conditions)* inadecuado,-a; *(remark)* inoportuno,-a; *(dress)* incorrecto,-a. **2** *(use)* incorrecto,-a, indebido,-a. **3** *(language)* indecente. **4** *(proposal)* deshonesto,-a.
impropriety [ɪmprə'praɪətɪ] *n fml (indecent behaviour)* impropiedad *f*, falta de decoro; *(dishonest practice)* deshonestidad *f*, indecencia.
▲ *pl* **improprieties.**
improve [ɪm'pruːv] *vt* **1** *(quality, etc)* mejorar. **2** *(skill, knowledge)* perfeccionar. **3** *(mind)* cultivar. **4** *(property)* hacer mejoras en. **5** *(increase)* aumentar.
▷ *vi (get better)* mejorar, mejorarse.
⊙ **to improve on** *vt insep (better)* superar.
improvement [ɪm'pruːvmənt] *n* **1** *(gen)* mejora, mejoramiento; *(in health)* mejoría. **2** *(in knowledge)* perfeccionamiento. **3** *(increase)* aumento.
improvidence [ɪm'prɒvɪdəns] *n* imprevisión *f*.
improvident [ɪm'prɒvɪdᵊnt] *adj fml (wasteful)* despilfarrador,-ra; *(shortsighted)* imprevisor,-ra, incauto,-a.
improvisation [ɪmprəvaɪ'zeɪʃᵊn] *n* improvisación *f*.
improvise ['ɪmprəvaɪz] *vt* improvisar.
imprudence [ɪm'pruːdᵊns] *n (unwise behaviour)* imprudencia; *(rashness)* precipitación *f*.
imprudent [ɪm'pruːdᵊnt] *adj fml (unwise)* imprudente; *(rash)* precipitado,-a.
impudence ['ɪmpjʊdᵊns] *n* insolencia, frescura, descaro.
impudent ['ɪmpjʊdᵊnt] *adj* insolente, fresco,-a, descarado,-a.
impugn [ɪm'pjuːn] *vt fml* impugnar.
impulse ['ɪmpʌls] *n* **1** *(sudden urge)* impulso, capricho; *(stimulus, drive)* impulso, estímulo, ímpetu *m*. **2** TECH impulso.
impulsive [ɪm'pʌlsɪv] *adj* impulsivo,-a, irreflexivo,-a.
impunity [ɪm'pjuːnɪtɪ] *n* impunidad *f*.
impure [ɪm'pjʊəʳ] *adj* **1** *(contaminated)* contaminado,-a; *(adulterated)* adulterado,-a. **2** *(morally - act)* impuro,-a; *(- thought)* impúdico,-a, deshonesto,-a.
impute [ɪm'pjuːt] *vt fml* imputar, atribuir.
in[1] [ɪn] *prep* **1** *(place)* en, dentro de: **it's in the box** *está en la caja.* **2** *(motion)* en, a: **we arrived in Bonn** *llegamos a Bonn.* **3** *(time - during)* en, durante: **in 1980** *e 1980.* **4** *(time - within)* en, dentro de. **5** *(wearing)* er vestido,-a de: **the woman in black** *la mujer vestida d negro.* **6** *(state, condition)* en. **7** *(ratio, measuremen number) varias traducciones*: **in twos** *de dos en do* **she's in her thirties** *tiene treinta y tantos años.* **8** *(pro fession)* en: **she's in television** *trabaja en la televisión* **9** *(weather, light) varias traducciones*: **walking in th rain** *caminando bajo la lluvia.* **10** *(after superlative)* de **the tallest in the class** *el más alto de la clase.*
▷ *adv* **1** *(motion)* dentro. **2** *(tide)* alto,-a. **3** *(fashionable)* de moda: **hats are in** *los sombreros están de moda.* *(on sale, obtainable)* disponible.
▷ *n pl* **ins and outs** *(details)* detalles *mpl*, pormenore *mpl*.
▷ *phr* **to be in** *(at home)* estar en casa; *(at work)* estar.
inability [ɪnə'bɪlɪtɪ] *n* incapacidad *f*.
inaccessible [ɪnæk'sesəbᵊl] *adj* inaccesible.
inaccuracy [ɪn'ækjərəsɪ] *n* **1** *(gen)* inexactitud *f*. *(error)* error *m*, incorrección *f*.
▲ *pl* **inaccuracies.**
inaccurate [ɪn'ækjərət] *adj (gen)* inexacto,-a; *(incor rect)* incorrecto,-a, erróneo,-a.
inaction [ɪn'ækʃᵊn] *n* inacción *f*.
inactive [ɪn'æktɪv] *adj* inactivo,-a.
inactivity [ɪnæk'tɪvətɪ] *n* inactividad *f*.
inadequacy [ɪn'ædɪkwəsɪ] *n* **1** *(lack)* insuficiencia **2** *(of person)* incapacidad *f*, incompetencia. **3** *(de fect)* defecto, imperfección *f*.
▲ *pl* **inadequacies.**
inadequate [ɪn'ædɪkwət] *adj* **1** *(not sufficient)* insuficiente; *(not appropriate)* inadecuado,-a. **2** *(person)* incapaz, incompetente. **3** *(defective)* defectuoso,-a imperfecto,-a.
inadmissible [ɪnəd'mɪsəbᵊl] *adj* **1** inadmisible, intolerable. **2** JUR improcedente.
inadvertence [ɪnəd'vɜːtᵊns] *n (oversight)* descuido error *m*, distracción *f*; *(lack of attention)* falta de atención.
inadvisable [ɪnəd'vaɪzəbᵊl] *adj* poco aconsejable imprudente, inconveniente.
inalienable [ɪn'eɪlɪənəbᵊl] *adj* inalienable.
inane [ɪ'neɪn] *adj* fatuo,-a, necio,-a, tonto,-a, estúpido,-a.
inanimate [ɪn'ænɪmət] *adj* inanimado,-a.
inapplicable [ɪn'æplɪkəbᵊl] *adj* inaplicable (**to**, a).
inappropriate [ɪnə'prəʊprɪət] *adj (unsuitable clothes, behaviour)* poco apropiado,-a, no apropiado,-a; *(- time, remark)* inoportuno,-a, inconveniente
inapt [ɪn'æpt] *adj* poco apto,-a.
inarticulate [ɪnɑː'tɪkjʊlət] *adj* **1** *(person)* incapaz d expresarse. **2** *(speech, words, writing)* mal expresado,-a, incoherente. **3** *(cry, sound)* inarticulado,-a. *(joints)* inarticulado,-a.
inattention [ɪnə'tenʃᵊn] *n* falta de atención.
inattentive [ɪnə'tentɪv] *adj (not paying attention)* poco atento,-a, distraído,-a; *(not attentive)* poco atento,-a
inaudible [ɪn'ɔːdəbᵊl] *adj* inaudible, imperceptible
inaugural [ɪ'nɔːgjʊrəl] *adj* inaugural, de inauguración, de apertura.
inaugurate [ɪ'nɔːgjʊreɪt] *vt* **1** *(building, exhibition, et* inaugurar. **2** *(president, etc)* investir.

nauguration [ɪnɔːgjʊ'reɪʃən] *n* **1** *(of building, etc)* inauguración *f.* **2** *(of president, etc)* investidura, toma de posesión.
nauspicious [ɪnɔː'spɪʃəs] *adj (start, moment)* poco propicio,-a; *(circumstance)* desfavorable, adverso,-a.
nauspiciously [ɪnɔː'spɪʃəslɪ] *adv* de modo poco propicio.
nborn ['ɪnbɔːn] *adj* innato,-a.
nbox ['ɪnbɒks] *n* bandeja de entrada.
nbred ['ɪnbred] *adj* **1** *(innate)* innato,-a. **2** *(produced by inbreeding)* endogámico,-a.
nc [ɪn'kɔːpəreɪtɪd] *abbr* US **(Incorporated)** ≈ sociedad *f* anónima; *(abbreviation)* S.A.
ncalculable [ɪn'kælkjʊləbəl] *adj* **1** *(beyond calculation)* incalculable. **2** *(uncertain, unpredictable)* imprevisible.
ncandescence [ɪnkæn'desəns] *n* incandescencia.
ncandescent [ɪnkæn'desənt] *adj* incandescente.
ncantation [ɪnkæn'teɪʃən] *n* conjuro, ensalmo.
ncapability [ɪnkeɪpə'bɪlətɪ] *n* incapacidad *f.*
ncapable [ɪn'keɪpəbəl] *adj* **1** *(unable)* incapaz. **2** *(incompetent)* incompetente. **3** *(helpless)* impotente, imposibilitado,-a.
ncapacitate [ɪnkə'pæsɪteɪt] *vt* **1** *(gen)* incapacitar, inhabilitar, imposibilitar; *(disable)* imposibilitar. **2** *(disqualify)* inhabilitar.
ncapacity [ɪnkə'pæsɪtɪ] *n* incapacidad *f.*
ncarcerate [ɪn'kɑːsəreɪt] *vt fml* encarcelar.
ncarceration [ɪnkɑːsə'reɪʃən] *n fml* encarcelamiento, encarcelación *f.*
ncarnate [ɪn'kɑːnət] *adj* **1** *(embodied)* encarnado,-a. **2** *(personified)* personificado,-a.
▷ *vt* **1** *fml (give bodily form to)* encarnar. **2** *(personify)* personificar.
ncarnation [ɪnkɑː'neɪʃən] *n* **1** *(embodiment)* encarnación *f.* **2** *(personification)* personificación *f.*
ncautious [ɪn'kɔːʃəs] *adj* incauto,-a, imprudente.
ncendiary [ɪn'sendɪərɪ] *adj* incendiario,-a.
▷ *n* **1** *(bomb)* bomba incendiaria. **2** *(person - arsonist)* pirómano,-a; *(- agitator)* agitador,-ra.
ncense¹ ['ɪnsens] *n* incienso.
ncense² [ɪn'sens] *vt (make angry)* enfurecer, poner furioso,-a, sacar de quicio.
ncentive [ɪn'sentɪv] *n* incentivo, estímulo, aliciente *m.*
nception [ɪn'sepʃən] *n fml* principio, comienzo.
ncessant [ɪn'sesənt] *adj (continuous)* incesante, ininterrumpido,-a; *(continual)* constante, continuo,-a.
ncest ['ɪnsest] *n* incesto.
ncestuous [ɪn'sestjʊəs] *adj* **1** *(gen)* incestuoso,-a. **2** *pej (group)* endogámico,-a, cerrado,-a.
nch [ɪntʃ] *n* **1** *(measurement)* pulgada. **2** *(small amount)* poco, pelo, ápice *m.*
▲ *pl* **inches.**

Equivale a 2,54 cm.

● **to inch along / inch forward** *vi* avanzar poco a poco.
ncidence ['ɪnsɪdəns] *n* **1** *(occurrence)* frecuencia, extensión *f.* **2** PHYS incidencia.
ncident ['ɪnsɪdənt] *n (event)* incidente *m*; *(violent episode)* altercado.
ncidental [ɪnsɪ'dentəl] *adj* **1** *(unimportant)* secundario,-a, incidental, de poca importancia. **2** *(inherent)* inherente. **3** *(fortuitous)* fortuito,-a, casual.
▷ *n pl* **incidentals** imprevistos *mpl.*

incidentally [ɪnsɪ'dentəlɪ] *adv* **1** *(by the way)* a propósito, por cierto, dicho sea de paso. **2** *(by chance)* por casualidad.
incinerate [ɪn'sɪnəreɪt] *vt* incinerar, quemar.
incineration [ɪnsɪnə'reɪʃən] *n* incineración *f*, quema.
incipient [ɪn'sɪpɪənt] *adj fml* incipiente.
incise [ɪn'saɪz] *vt (cut)* cortar; *(carve, engrave)* grabar, tallar.
incision [ɪn'sɪʒən] *n* incisión *f.*
incisive [ɪn'saɪsɪv] *adj* **1** *(comment, wit)* incisivo,-a, mordaz. **2** *(mind)* penetrante.
incisor [ɪn'saɪzəʳ] *n* (diente *m*) incisivo.
incite [ɪn'saɪt] *vt* **1** *(urge, encourage)* incitar, provocar. **2** *(cause, lead to)* instigar (**to**, a).
incivility [ɪnsɪ'vɪlətɪ] *n fml* descortesía, falta de cortesía.
▲ *pl* **incivilities.**
inclemency [ɪn'klemənsɪ] *n* inclemencia.
inclement [ɪn'klemənt] *adj fml* inclemente.
inclination [ɪnklɪ'neɪʃən] *n* **1** *(tendency)* inclinación *f*, tendencia; *(disposition)* disposición *f*, propensión *f.* **2** *(slope)* inclinación *f*, pendiente *f.* **3** *(bow)* inclinación *f.*
incline [*(n)* 'ɪnklaɪn; *(vb)* ɪn'klaɪn] *n* pendiente *f*, inclinación *f*, cuesta.
▷ *vt* **1** *(bend forward)* inclinar. **2** *fml (persuade, influence)* inclinar, predisponer.
▷ *vi* **1** *(slope)* inclinarse, estar inclinado,-a. **2** *(tend)* tender a, tener tendencia a.
inclined [ɪn'klaɪnd] *adj* **1** *(disposed, encouraged)* dispuesto,-a (**to**, a). **2** *(tending to)* propenso,-a. **3** *(having natural ability)* dotado,-a. **4** *(sloping)* inclinado,-a.
include [ɪn'kluːd] *vt* incluir.
including [ɪn'kluːdɪŋ] *prep* incluso, incluyendo.
inclusion [ɪn'kluːʒən] *n* inclusión *f.*
inclusive [ɪn'kluːsɪv] *adj* inclusive.
incognito [ɪnkɒg'niːtəʊ] *adv* de incógnito.
incoherence [ɪnkəʊ'hɪərəns] *n* **1** *(lack of cohesion)* incoherencia. **2** *(inarticulateness)* ininteligibilidad *f.*
incoherent [ɪnkəʊ'hɪərənt] *adj* **1** *(unclear)* incoherente, inconexo,-a. **2** *(unintelligible)* ininteligible, incoherente.
incombustible [ɪnkəm'bʌstəbəl] *adj fml* incombustible.
income ['ɪnkʌm] *n (from work)* ingresos *mpl*, renta; *(from investment)* réditos *mpl.* ● **income tax** impuesto sobre la renta.
incoming ['ɪnkʌmɪŋ] *adj* **1** *(tide)* ascendente; *(plane)* de llegada; *(passenger)* que llega; *(missile, fire)* enemigo,-a; *(message, mail, etc)* recibido,-a. **2** *(to post, job)* entrante.
incommensurable [ɪnkə'menʃərəbəl] *adj fml* inconmensurable.
incommensurate [ɪnkə'menʃərət] *adj fml* desproporcionado,-a.
incommode [ɪnkə'məʊd] *vt fml* incomodar, molestar.
incommunicable [ɪnkə'mjuːnɪkəbəl] *adj* incomunicable.
incomparable [ɪn'kɒmpərəbəl] *adj* incomparable, inigualable, sin par.
incompatibility [ɪnkəmpætə'bɪlɪtɪ] *n* incompatibilidad *f.*
▲ *pl* **incompatibilities.**

incompatible [ınkəm'pætəbᵊl] *adj* incompatible (with, con).

incompetence [ın'kɒmpətᵊns] *n* incompetencia, ineptitud *f*, incapacidad *f*.

incompetent [ın'kɒmpətᵊnt] *adj* incompetente, inepto,-a, incapaz.
▷ *n* incompetente *mf*, inepto,-a.

incomplete [ınkəm'pli:t] *adj* **1** *(not whole)* incompleto,-a; *(not finished)* inacabado,-a, sin terminar. **2** *(partial)* parcial.

incomprehensible [ınkɒmprı'hensəbᵊl] *adj* incomprensible.

incomprehension [ınkɒmprı'henʃᵊn] *n* incomprensión *f*.

inconceivable [ınkən'si:vəbᵊl] *adj* **1** inconcebible. **2** *fam* imposible, increíble.

inconceivably [ınkən'si:vəblı] *adv* increíblemente.

inconclusive [ınkən'klu:sıv] *adj* **1** *(debate, vote, etc)* no decisivo,-a. **2** *(evidence, result, etc)* no concluyente.

incongruity [ınkɒn'gru:ətı] *n* incongruencia.
▲ *pl* incongruities.

incongruous [ın'kɒŋgruəs] *adj* incongruente, incongruo,-a, fuera de lugar.

inconsequent [ın'kɒnsıkwənt] *adj* **1** *(not following logically)* inconsecuente. **2** *(inconsequential)* de poca importancia, sin trascendencia.

inconsequential [ınkɒnsı'kwenʃᵊl] *adj* de poca importancia, sin trascendencia.

inconsiderable [ınkən'sıdᵊrəbᵊl] *adj* insignificante.

inconsiderate [ınkən'sıdᵊrət] *adj* desconsiderado,-a, inconsiderado,-a, poco atento,-a.

inconsiderately [ınkən'sıdᵊrətlı] *adv* con poca consideración.

inconsistency [ınkən'sıstənsı] *n* **1** *(gen)* inconsecuencia. **2** *(contradiction)* contradicción *f*, discrepancia.
▲ *pl* inconsistencies.

inconsistent [ınkən'sıstᵊnt] *adj* **1** *(not agreeing with, at variance with)* inconsecuente; *(contradictory)* contradictorio,-a. **2** *(changeable - weather)* variable; *(- person)* inconstante, voluble, irregular; *(- behaviour)* imprevisible, irregular.

inconsolable [ınkən'səuləbᵊl] *adj* inconsolable, desconsolado,-a.

inconspicuous [ınkən'spıkjuəs] *adj* *(not noticeable)* que pasa desapercibido,-a, que no llama la atención; *(unobtrusive)* discreto,-a.

inconstant [ın'kɒnstᵊnt] *adj* **1** *(person)* inconstante, veleidoso,-a, mudable. **2** *(not fixed)* variable.

incontinence [ın'kɒntınᵊns] *n* incontinencia.

incontinent [ın'kɒntınənt] *adj* incontinente.

incontrovertible [ınkɒntrə'vɜ:təbᵊl] *adj* incontrovertible.

inconvenience [ınkən'vi:nıəns] *n* *(gen)* inconveniente *m*; *(trouble, difficulty)* molestia, dificultad *f*; *(hindrance)* estorbo, obstáculo; *(discomfort)* incomodidad *f*: I'm sorry to cause you so much inconvenience *siento causarle tanta molestia.*
▷ *vt* *(annoy)* causar molestia a, molestar; *(cause difficulty)* incomodar.

inconvenient [ınkən'vi:nıənt] *adj* **1** *(gen)* inconveniente, molesto,-a, incómodo,-a; *(place)* mal situado,-a; *(time)* mal, inoportuno,-a; *(arrangement)* poco práctico,-a. **2** *(fact)* incómodo,-a.

incorporate [ın'kɔ:pəreıt] *vt* **1** *(make part of, include in)* incorporar (in/into, a), incluir (in/into, en); *(include, contain)* incluir, contener. **2** US *(company)* constituir, constituir en sociedad.
▷ *adj* US *(company)* constituido,-a, constituido,-a en sociedad.

incorrect [ınkə'rekt] *adj* **1** *(wrong, untrue)* incorrecto,-a, erróneo,-a, equivocado,-a. **2** *(- dress)* impropio,-a, inadecuado,-a.

incorrigible [ın'kɒrıdʒəbᵊl] *adj* incorregible.

incorruptible [ınkə'rʌptəbᵊl] *adj* incorruptible.

increase [*(n)* 'ınkri:s; *(vb)* ın'kri:s] *n* *(gen)* aumento, incremento; *(in price, temperature)* subida, alza.
▷ *vt* *(gen)* aumentar, incrementar; *(temperature)* subir.

increasing [ın'kri:sıŋ] *adj* creciente.

increasingly [ın'kri:sıŋlı] *adv* cada vez más.

incredible [ın'kredıbᵊl] *adj* *(unbelievable)* increíble, inverosímil; *(amazing)* fantástico,-a.

incredulity [ınkrı'dju:lətı] *n* incredulidad *f*.

incredulous [ın'kredjələs] *adj* incrédulo,-a.

increment ['ınkrımənt] *n* aumento, incremento.

incriminate [ın'krımıneıt] *vt* incriminar.

incriminatory [ın'krımınətᵊrı] *adj* JUR incriminatorio,-a.

incrust [ın'krʌst] *vt* incrustar.

incrustation [ınkrʌ'steıʃᵊn] *n* incrustación *f*.

incubate ['ınkjubeıt] *vt* incubar.
▷ *vi* *(of eggs)* incubar; *(of bird)* empollar.

incubation [ınkju'beıʃᵊn] *n* incubación *f*.

incubator ['ınkjubeıtəʳ] *n* incubadora.

incubus ['ınkjubəs] *n* íncubo.
▲ *pl* incubuses o incubai ['ınkjubaı].

inculcate ['ınkʌlkeıt] *vt fml* inculcar (in/into, a) (with, en).

incumbency [ın'kʌmbənsı] *n* **1** *(office, duty, tenure)* titularidad *f*, mandato. **2** REL beneficio.

incumbent [ın'kʌmbənt] *n* *(holder of office)* titular *mf*; *(clergyman)* beneficiado.
▷ *adj* *(holding office)* actual, titular, en ejercicio: the incumbent president *el presidente actual.*

incur [ın'kɜ:ʳ] *vt* **1** *(blame, anger)* incurrir en, provocar. **2** *(debt, expense)* contraer, incurrir en. **3** *(injury, loss)* sufrir. **4** *(risk)* correr.
▲ *pt & pp* incurred, *ger* incurring.

incurable [ın'kjuərəbᵊl] *adj* **1** *(disease)* incurable. **2** *fig (loss)* irremediable; *(habit, optimist)* incorregible.
▷ *n* enfermo,-a incurable.

incurably [ın'kjurəblı] *adv* *(ill)* incurablemente.
▷ *adj fig* irremediablemente.

incursion [ın'kɜ:ʃᵊn] *n fml* incursión *f*, invasión *f* (into, en).

incurved [ın'kɜ:vd] *adj* curvado,-a.

indebted [ın'detıd] *adj* **1** *(in debt)* endeudado,-a. **2** *fig (grateful)* agradecido,-a.

indecency [ın'di:sᵊnsı] *n* indecencia, obscenidad *f*.

indecent [ın'di:sᵊnt] *adj* **1** *(obscene)* indecente, indecoroso,-a, obsceno,-a. **2** *(improper)* impropio,-a, indebido,-a, injustificado,-a; *(undue)* excesivo,-a.

indecipherable [ındı'saıfᵊrəbᵊl] *adj* indescifrable.

indecision [ɪndɪ'sɪʒᵊn] *n* indecisión *f*, irresolución *f*.

indecisive [ɪndɪ'saɪsɪv] *adj* **1** *(hesitant)* indeciso,-a, irresoluto,-a. **2** *(inconclusive)* poco concluyente, no concluyente, no decisivo,-a.

indecorous [ɪn'dekərəs] *adj fml* indecoroso,-a.

indecorum [ɪndɪ'kɔːrəm] *n fml* indecoro, falta de decoro.

indeed [ɪn'diːd] *adv* **1** *(yes, certainly)* efectivamente, en efecto: **are you Mr Fox? yes, indeed** *¿es el Sr Fox? sí, efectivamente.* **2** *(intensifier)* realmente, de veras, de verdad: **thank you very much indeed** *muchísimas gracias.* **3** *fml (in fact)* realmente, en realidad, de hecho; *(what is more)* es más.

indefatigable [ɪndɪ'fætɪgəbᵊl] *adj fml* incansable, infatigable.

indefensible [ɪndɪ'fensəbᵊl] *adj* **1** *(idea, statement, view, etc)* insostenible; *(behaviour)* injustificable, inexcusable. **2** *(place, building, position)* indefendible, indefensible, indefensable.

indefensibly [ɪndɪ'fensəblɪ] *adv (behaviour)* injustificablemente, inexcusablemente.

indefinable [ɪndɪ'faɪnəbᵊl] *adj* indefinible.

indefinite [ɪn'defɪnət] *adj* **1** *(vague, not precise)* indefinido,-a, vago,-a, impreciso,-a. **2** *(not fixed - period of time, amount, number)* indefinido,-a, indeterminado,-a.

indefinitely [ɪn'defɪnətlɪ] *adv* indefinidamente.

indelible [ɪn'delɪbᵊl] *adj* **1** *(ink, etc)* indeleble, imborrable. **2** *fig (memory, etc)* inolvidable, imborrable.

indelibly [ɪn'deləblɪ] *adv* indeleblemente, imborrablemente.

indelicate [ɪn'delɪkət] *adj* **1** *(rude, embarrassing)* poco delicado,-a, indelicado,-a. **2** *(tactless)* indiscreto,-a.

indemnification [ɪndemnɪfɪ'keɪʃᵊn] *n* **1** *(act)* indemnización *f*. **2** *(compensation, repayment)* indemnización *f*, reparación *f*, compensación *f*.

indemnify [ɪn'demnɪfaɪ] *vt* **1** *fml (insure)* asegurar (**against**, contra). **2** *fml (compensate)* indemnizar (**for**, por/de).
▲ *pt & pp* **indemnified**, *ger* **indemnifying**.

indemnity [ɪn'demnɪtɪ] *n* **1** *(insurance, guarantee)* indemnidad *f* (**against**, contra). **2** *(compensation)* indemnización *f* (**for**, por), reparación *f*, compensación *f*.
▲ *pl* **indemnities**.

indent [*(vb)* ɪn'dent; *(n)* 'ɪndent] *vt (text)* sangrar.
▷ *vi* GB *(order)* hacer un pedido (**for**, de), encargar (**for**, -).
▷ *n* GB *(order)* pedido.

indentation [ɪnden'teɪʃᵊn] *n* **1** *(in text)* sangría. **2** *(notch in edge, mark)* mella, muesca.

indenture [ɪn'dentʃə] *vt* contratar como aprendiz,-za.
▷ *n pl* **indentures** contrato *m sing* de aprendizaje.

independence [ɪndɪ'pendəns] *n* independencia (**from**, de).

independent [ɪndɪ'pendᵊnt] *adj (gen)* independiente.
▷ *n* POL (candidato,-a) independiente *mf*.

in-depth [ɪn'depθ] *adj* minucioso,-a, exhaustivo,-a, a fondo.

indescribable [ɪndɪ'skraɪbəbᵊl] *adj* **1** *(gen)* indescriptible. **2** *(too good)* inefable. **3** *pej (too bad)* indecible, incalificable.

indestructible [ɪndɪ'strʌktəbᵊl] *adj* indestructible.

indeterminable [ɪndɪ'tɜːmɪnəbᵊl] *adj fml* indeterminable.

indeterminate [ɪndɪ'tɜːmɪnət] *adj* indeterminado,-a.

index ['ɪndeks] *n* índice. ● **index finger** dedo índice.
▲ *pl* **indixes** o **indices** ['ɪndɪsiːz].

India ['ɪndɪə] *n* (la) India. ● **India rubber** caucho.

Indian ['ɪndɪən] *adj* indio,-a, hindú *mf*.
▷ *n* indio,-a, hindú. ● **the Indian Ocean** el océano Índico.

indicate ['ɪndɪkeɪt] *vt* indicar, señalar, marcar.
▷ *vi* AUTO poner el intermitente.

indication [ɪndɪ'keɪʃᵊn] *n (gen)* indicio, señal *f*, indicación *f*.

indicative [ɪn'dɪkətɪv] *adj* **1** *fml* indicativo,-a (**of**, de). **2** LING indicativo,-a.
▷ *n* LING indicativo.

indicator ['ɪndɪkeɪtəʳ] *n* **1** *(gen)* indicador *m*. **2** AUTO intermitente *m*.

indices ['ɪndɪsiːz] *n pl* → **index**.

indict [ɪn'daɪt] *vt* JUR acusar (**for**, de).

indictable [ɪn'daɪtəbᵊl] *adj* JUR *(offense)* que constituye delito; *(person)* procesable.

indictment [ɪn'daɪtmənt] *n* **1** JUR acusación *f*, sumario. **2** *fig (criticism)* crítica.

indifference [ɪn'dɪfᵊrəns] *n* indiferencia (**to**, ante).

indifferent [ɪn'dɪfᵊrənt] *adj* **1** *(gen)* indiferente (**to**, a). **2** *(mediocre, average)* mediocre, regular, pobre.

indigenous [ɪn'dɪdʒənəs] *adj fml* indígena, autóctono,-a (**to**, de).

indigent ['ɪndɪdʒənt] *adj fml* indigente.

indigestion [ɪndɪ'dʒestʃᵊn] *n* indigestión *f*, empacho.

indignation [ɪndɪg'neɪʃᵊn] *n* indignación *f* (**about/over**, por) (**at**, ante/por).

indigo ['ɪndɪgəʊ] *n* añil *m*.

indirect [ɪndɪ'rekt] *adj* indirecto,-a.

indirectly [ɪndɪ'rektlɪ] *adv* indirectamente.

indiscernible [ɪndɪ'sɜːnəbᵊl] *adj* imperceptible, indiscernible.

indiscipline [ɪn'dɪsəplɪn] *n* indisciplina.

indiscreet [ɪndɪ'skriːt] *adj (person)* indiscreto,-a, poco discreto,-a, poco diplomático,-a, falto de tacto.

indiscretion [ɪndɪ'skreʃᵊn] *n* indiscreción *f*.

indiscriminate [ɪndɪ'skrɪmɪnət] *adj (violence, attack, etc)* indiscriminado,-a; *(praise, reading, viewing, etc)* sin criterio, sin discernimiento.

indispensable [ɪndɪ'spensəbᵊl] *adj* indispensable, imprescindible (**to**, para).

indisposed [ɪndɪ'spəʊzd] *adj* **1** *(ill)* indispuesto,-a. **2** *fml (not willing)* poco dispuesto,-a (**to**, a).

indisposition [ɪndɪspə'zɪʃᵊn] *n (illness)* indisposición *f*.

indisputable [ɪndɪ'spjuːtəbᵊl] *adj (gen)* indiscutible, indisputable, incuestionable; *(winner, leader, etc)* indiscutible; *(fact)* irrefutable.

indissolubility [ɪndɪsɒljə'bɪlətɪ] *n* indisolubilidad *f*.

indissoluble [ɪndɪ'sɒljəbᵊl] *adj fml (cannot be dissolved)* indisoluble; *(cannot be broken)* inseparable.

indistinct [ɪndɪ'stɪŋkt] *adj (gen)* indistinto,-a, impreciso,-a; *(memory)* confuso,-a, vago,-a; *(shape, area, etc)* borroso,-a.

indistinctly [ɪndɪ'stɪŋktlɪ] *adv (gen)* indistintamente, imprecisamente; *(remember)* vagamente; *(see)* con poca claridad; *(speak)* confusamente.
indistinguishable [ɪndɪ'stɪŋgwɪʃəbᵊl] *adj* indistinguible (**from**, de).
individual [ɪndɪ'vɪdjʊəl] *adj* **1** *(single, separate)* por separado. **2** *(for one person)* individual. **3** *(particular, personal)* personal, propio,-a. **4** *(different, unique)* personal, original.
▷ *n* **1** *(person)* individuo, persona. **2** *fam* individuo, tipo, tío,-a.
individualism [ɪndɪ'vɪdʒʊəlɪzᵊm] *n* individualismo.
individualist [ɪndɪ'vɪdʒʊəlɪst] *n* individualista *mf*.
individuality [ɪndɪvɪdʒʊ'ælətɪ] *n* individualidad *f*, personalidad *f*.
individualize [ɪndɪ'vɪdʒʊəlaɪz] *vt* individualizar, personalizar.
individually [ɪndɪ'vɪdʒʊəlɪ] *adv (separately)* individualmente, por separado; *(one by one)* uno por uno.
indivisible [ɪndɪ'vɪzəbᵊl] *adj* indivisible.
indoctrinate [ɪn'dɒktrɪneɪt] *vt* adoctrinar.
indoctrination [ɪndɒktrɪ'neɪʃᵊn] *n* adoctrinamiento.
Indo-European [ɪndəʊjʊərə'pɪən] *adj* indoeuropeo,-a.
indolence ['ɪndələns] *n fml* indolencia, pereza.
indolent ['ɪndələnt] *adj fml* indolente, perezoso,-a.
indomitable [ɪn'dɒmɪtəbᵊl] *adj fml* indomable, indómito,-a.
indoor ['ɪndɔːʳ] *adj* **1** *(aerial, plant, photography, etc)* interior; *(clothes, etc)* de estar por casa. **2** SP *(swimming pool, running track)* cubierto,-a.
indoors [ɪn'dɔːz] *adv (inside house)* dentro (de casa); *(at home)* en casa; *(inside building)* a cubierto, dentro.
indubitable [ɪn'djuːbɪtəbᵊl] *adj fml* indudable.
induce [ɪn'djuːs] *vt* **1** *(persuade)* inducir, persuadir, llevar. **2** *(cause)* causar, producir, provocar.
inducement [ɪn'djuːsmənt] *n* **1** incentivo, estímulo, aliciente *m*. **2** MED inducción *f*. **3** *euph* soborno.
induct [ɪn'dʌkt] *vt* **1** *(introduce to organization)* admitir, instalar. **2** US *(recruit)* reclutar.
induction [ɪn'dvkʃᵊn] *n* **1** *(initiation - gen)* admisión *f*, ingreso; *(- of priest)* instalación *f*. **2** US *(recruitment)* reclutamiento. **3** *(logic)* inducción *f*.
inductive [ɪn'dʌktɪv] *adj* inductivo,-a.
indulge [ɪn'dʌldʒ] *vt* **1** *(satisfy - desire, whim)* satisfacer, ceder a, consentir; *(- passion)* dar rienda suelta a. **2** *(pamper - person)* complacer; *(- child)* mimar, consentir.
▷ *vi (gen)* permitirse; *(eat)* comer (lo que uno quiera); *(drink)* beber (lo que uno quiera).
indulgence [ɪn'dʌldʒᵊns] *n* **1** *(luxury)* (pequeño) lujo; *(bad habit)* vicio. **2** *(of desire, whim)* satisfacción *f*, complacencia; *(partaking - of food, drink)* abuso; *(of person)* consentimiento; *(of child)* mimo. **3** REL indulgencia.
indulgent [ɪn'dʌldʒᵊnt] *adj* indulgente (**towards**, con).
Indus ['ɪndʌs] *n* el Indo.
industrial [ɪn'dʌstrɪəl] *adj* industrial.
industrialism [ɪn'dʌstrɪəlɪzᵊm] *n* industrialismo.
industrialist [ɪn'dʌstrɪəlɪst] *n* industrial *mf*, empresario,-a.
industrialization [ɪndʌstrɪəlaɪ'zeɪʃᵊn] *n* industrialización *f*.
industrialize [ɪn'dʌstrɪəlaɪz] *vt* industrializar.
▷ *vi* industrializarse.
industrious [ɪn'dʌstrɪəs] *adj (hard-working)* trabajador,-ra, laborioso,-a; *(diligent)* diligente, aplicado,-a.
industry ['ɪndəstrɪ] *n* **1** *(gen)* industria. **2** *fml (hard work)* diligencia.
▲ *pl* industries.
inebriate [ɪ'niːbrɪət] *adj fml* ebrio,-a.
▷ *vt fml* embriagar.
inedible [ɪn'edəbᵊl] *adj* incomible, incomestible.
ineffable [ɪn'efəbᵊl] *adj fml* inefable.
inefficiency [ɪnɪ'fɪʃᵊnsɪ] *n* **1** *(gen)* ineficacia. **2** *(of person)* incompetencia, ineficiencia, ineptitud *f*.
inefficient [ɪnɪ'fɪʃᵊnt] *adj* **1** *(gen)* ineficaz. **2** *(person)* incompetente, ineficiente, poco eficiente.
inelastic [ɪnɪ'læstɪk] *adj* **1** PHYS no elástico,-a. **2** *fig (rigid)* rígido,-a, poco flexible.
ineligible [ɪn'elɪdʒəbᵊl] *adj* que no tiene derecho inelegible.
inept [ɪ'nept] *adj (person)* inepto,-a, incapaz; *(remark)* torpe.
ineptitude [ɪ'neptɪtjuːd] *n (incompetence)* ineptitud *f* incapacidad *f*; *(of remark)* torpeza.
inequality [ɪnɪ'kwɒlətɪ] *n* desigualdad *f*.
▲ *pl* inequalities.
inequitable [ɪn'ekwɪtəbᵊl] *adj fml* injusto,-a.
inequity [ɪn'ekwətɪ] *n* injusticia.
▲ *pl* inequities.
ineradicable [ɪnɪ'rædɪkəbᵊl] *adj* inextirpable.
inert [ɪ'nɜːt] *adj* **1** *(gas, matter, etc)* inerte. **2** *(immobile)* inerte, inmóvil. **3** *pej (sluggish, without vigour)* poco enérgico,-a, sin vigor.
inertia [ɪ'nɜːʃə] *n* **1** PHYS inercia. **2** *(lethargy)* inercia letargo, apatía.
inescapable [ɪnɪ'skeɪpəbᵊl] *adj* ineludible, inevitable.
inessential [ɪnɪ'senʃᵊl] *adj* no esencial, innecesario,-a.
▷ *n pl* **inessentials** cosas *fpl* sin importancia.
inestimable [ɪn'estɪməbᵊl] *adj fml (gen)* inestimable inapreciable; *(damage)* incalculable.
inevitable [ɪn'evɪtəbᵊl] *adj* **1** *(unavoidable)* inevitable. **2** *fam (usual)* sempiterno,-a, consabido,-a, de siempre.
inexact [ɪnɪg'zækt] *adj* inexacto,-a.
inexcusable [ɪnɪk'skjuːzəbᵊl] *adj* inexcusable, imperdonable, injustificable.
inexhaustible [ɪnɪg'zɔːstəbᵊl] *adj* inagotable.
inexorable [ɪn'eksᵊrəbᵊl] *adj fml* inexorable, implacable.
inexpensive [ɪnɪk'spensɪv] *adj* barato,-a, económico,-a
inexperience [ɪnɪk'spɪərɪəns] *n* inexperiencia, falta de experiencia.
inexpert [ɪn'ekspɜːt] *adj (person)* inexperto,-a, inhábil (**at**, en); *(advice, etc)* inexperto,-a.
inexplicable [ɪnɪk'splɪkəbᵊl] *adj* inexplicable.
inexpressible [ɪnɪk'spresəbᵊl] *adj* inexpresable, inefable.
inexpressive [ɪnɪk'spresɪv] *adj* inexpresivo,-a.
inextinguishable [ɪnɪk'stɪŋgwɪʃəbᵊl] *adj fml* inextinguible, inapagable.
inextricable [ɪn'ekstrɪkəbᵊl] *adj* inextricable.
infallible [ɪn'fæləbᵊl] *adj* infalible, indefectible.

infamous ['ɪnfəməs] *adj* **1** *(notorious)* infame. **2** *fml (wicked)* infame, ruin.
infamy ['ɪnfəmɪ] *n* **1** *fml (wickedness)* infamia, maldad *f*. **2** *fml (disgrace)* infamia, desgracia.
▲ *pl* infamies.
infancy ['ɪnfənsɪ] *n* **1** *(childhood)* infancia, niñez *f*. **2** GB minoría de edad.
infant ['ɪnfənt] *n* **1** *(baby)* bebé *m*, niño,-a; *(at infant school)* niño,-a, párvulo,-a. **2** GB menor *mf* de edad.
● **infant school** escuela primaria.
infanticide [ɪn'fæntɪsaɪd] *n* **1** *(crime)* infanticidio. **2** *(person)* infanticida *mf*.
infantile ['ɪnfəntaɪl] *adj* **1** infantil. **2** *pej* infantil, pueril.
infantry ['ɪnfəntrɪ] *n* infantería.
infarction [ɪn'fɑːkʃᵊn] *n* infarto.
infatuation [ɪnfætʃʊ'eɪʃᵊn] *n* encaprichamiento (**with/by**, con), enamoramiento (**with/by**, de).
infect [ɪn'fekt] *vt* **1** *(wound, cut, etc)* infectar; *(food, water, etc)* contaminar; *(person)* contagiar. **2** *fig (emotions)* contagiar. **3** *(poison)* envenenar.
infection [ɪn'fekʃᵊn] *n* **1** *(of wound, cut, etc)* infección *f*; *(of food, water, etc)* contaminación *f*; *(with illness)* infección *f*, contagio. **2** *(disease)* infección *f*.
infectious [ɪn'fekʃəs] *adj* **1** *(disease)* infeccioso,-a, contagioso,-a. **2** *fig* contagioso,-a.
infer [ɪn'fɜːʳ] *vt* inferir (**from**, de), deducir (**from**, de).
▲ *pt & pp* inferred, *ger* inferring.
inferior [ɪn'fɪərɪəʳ] *adj* inferior (**to**, a).
▷ *n* inferior *mf*.
inferiority [ɪnfɪərɪ'ɒrətɪ] *n* inferioridad *f*.
infernal [ɪn'fɜːnᵊl] *adj* **1** infernal. **2** *fam (tiresome)* maldito,-a.
inferno [ɪn'fɜːnəʊ] *n* **1** *(like hell)* infierno. **2** *(fire)* llamas *fpl*.
▲ *pl* infernos.
infertile [ɪn'fɜːtaɪl] *adj* estéril.
infertility [ɪnfə'tɪlətɪ] *n* esterilidad *f*.
infest [ɪn'fest] *vt* infestar (**with**, de), plagar (**with**, de).
infidel ['ɪnfɪdᵊl] *n* infiel *mf*.
infidelity [ɪnfɪ'delətɪ] *n* infidelidad *f*.
▲ *pl* infidelities.
infighting ['ɪnfaɪtɪŋ] *n* **1** *fam fig* luchas *fpl* internas. **2** SP *(boxing)* lucha cerrada.
infill ['ɪnfɪl] *n* relleno.
infiltrate ['ɪnfɪltreɪt] *vt* infiltrarse (**into**, en).
infiltration [ɪnfɪl'treɪʃᵊn] *n* infiltración *f*.
infiltrator [ɪnfɪl'treɪtəʳ] *n* infiltrado,-a.
infinite ['ɪnfɪnət] *adj (endless)* infinito,-a; *(very great)* sin límites.
▷ *n* **the Infinite** Dios *m*.
infinitesimal [ɪnfɪnɪ'tesɪmᵊl] *adj* infinitesimal, infinitésimo,-a.
infinitive [ɪn'fɪnɪtɪv] *n* LING infinitivo.
infinitude [ɪn'fɪnɪtjuːd] *n fml* infinidad *f*.
infinity [ɪn'fɪnɪtɪ] *n* **1** *(gen)* infinidad *f*. **2** MATH infinito.
infirm [ɪn'fɜːm] *adj* débil, endeble, enfermizo,-a, achacoso,-a.
infirmary [ɪn'fɜːmərɪ] *n* **1** *(hospital)* hospital *m*. **2** *(in school, etc)* enfermería.
▲ *pl* infirmaries.
infirmity [ɪn'fɜːmɪtɪ] *n (weakness)* debilidad *f*; *(illness)* enfermedad *f*.
▲ *pl* infirmities.
infix ['ɪnfɪks] *n* infijo.
inflame [ɪn'fleɪm] *vt (anger)* encender; *(passion)* inflamar.
inflammable [ɪn'flæməbᵊl] *adj* **1** inflamable. **2** *fam fig* explosivo,-a.
inflammation [ɪnflə'meɪʃᵊn] *n* inflamación *f*.
inflate [ɪn'fleɪt] *vt* **1** inflar, hinchar. **2** *fig* inflar, hinchar, exagerar. **3** *(economy)* inflar.
inflation [ɪn'fleɪʃᵊn] *n* inflación *f*.
inflect [ɪn'flekt] *vt* **1** LING *(verb)* conjugar; *(noun)* declinar. **2** *(voice)* modular.
inflection [ɪn'flekʃᵊn] *n* **1** LING inflexión *f*, flexión *f*. **2** *(of voice)* inflexión *f*.
inflexible [ɪn'fleksɪbᵊl] *adj* inflexible.
inflict [ɪn'flɪkt] *vt* **1** *(grief, suffering, pain)* causar (**on**, a); *(blow)* dar a, asestar a, propinar a; *(defeat, punishment)* infligir (**on**, a), imponer (**on**, a); *(grief, suffering, pain)* causar (**on**, a). **2** *fig (view, etc)* imponer (**on**, a).
infliction [ɪn'flɪkʃᵊn] *n* **1** *(act)* imposición *f*. **2** *(thing inflicted)* castigo.
inflow ['ɪnfləʊ] *n* afluencia.
influence ['ɪnflʊəns] *n (gen)* influencia.
▷ *vt (decision, etc)* influir en/sobre; *(person)* influenciar.
influential [ɪnflʊ'enʃᵊl] *adj* influyente.
influenza [ɪnflʊ'enzə] *n* gripe *f*.
influx ['ɪnflʌks] *n* afluencia, oleada.
info ['ɪnfəʊ] *n fam* información *f*.
inform [ɪn'fɔːm] *vt* informar, notificar, avisar.
informal [ɪn'fɔːmᵊl] *adj (speech)* informal, familiar; *(discussion)* informal.
informant [ɪn'fɔːmənt] *n* informante *mf*.
information [ɪnfə'meɪʃᵊn] *n (gen)* información *f*; *(facts)* datos *mpl*.
informative [ɪn'fɔːmətɪv] *adj* informativo,-a.
informer [ɪn'fɔːməʳ] *n* **1** *(gen)* delator,-ra. **2** *(to police)* informador,-ra, chivato,-a, soplón,-ona.
infraction [ɪn'frækʃᵊn] *n fml* infracción *f*.
infra dig [ɪnfrə'dɪg] *adj* degradante.
infrared [ɪnfrə'red] *adj* infrarrojo,-a.
infrastructure ['ɪnfrəstrʌktʃəʳ] *n* infraestructura.
infrequent [ɪn'friːkwənt] *adj* infrecuente, poco frecuente, raro,-a.
infringe [ɪn'frɪndʒ] *vt (law, rule, etc)* infringir, transgredir, violar; *(copyright, agreement, etc)* no respetar; *(liberty, rights)* violar, usurpar.
infuriate [ɪn'fjʊərɪeɪt] *vt* enfurecer, poner furioso,-a, sacar de quicio.
infuse [ɪn'fjuːz] *vt* **1** *(life, energy, etc)* infundir (**into**, a). **2** *(tea, herbs)* hacer una infusión.
▷ *vi (tea, herbs)* reposar.
infusion [ɪn'fjuːʒᵊn] *n* **1** *(of tea, herbs)* infusión *f*, tisana. **2** *(of capital, resources, etc)* inversión *f*; *(of life, energy, etc)* inyección *f*.
ingenious [ɪn'dʒiːnɪəs] *adj (person, thing)* ingenioso,-a; *(idea)* genial.
ingenuity [ɪndʒɪ'njuːɪtɪ] *n* ingenio, ingeniosidad *f*, inventiva.
ingenuous [ɪn'dʒenjʊəs] *adj fml* ingenuo,-a.
ingest [ɪn'dʒest] *vt fml* ingerir.

inglorious [ɪn'glɔːrɪəs] *adj* vergonzoso,-a, ignominioso,-a.
ingot ['ɪŋgət] *n* lingote *m*.
ingrained [ɪn'greɪnd] *adj* **1** *(dirt, stains, etc)* incrustado,-a. **2** *(habit, tendency, etc)* arraigado,-a.
ingratitude [ɪn'grætɪtjuːd] *n* ingratitud *f*.
ingredient [ɪn'griːdɪənt] *n* **1** CULIN ingrediente *m*. **2** *fig* componente *m*, elemento.
inhabit [ɪn'hæbɪt] *vt* habitar, vivir en, ocupar, poblar.
inhabitable [ɪn'hæbɪtəbəl] *adj* habitable.
inhabitant [ɪn'hæbɪtənt] *n* habitante *mf*.
inhalation [ɪnhə'leɪʃən] *n* inhalación *f*.
inhale [ɪn'heɪl] *vt (air)* aspirar, respirar; *(gas, vapour)* inhalar.
inherent [ɪn'hɪərənt] *adj* inherente (in, a), intrínseco,-a (in, as), propio,-a (in, de).
inherit [ɪn'herɪt] *vt* heredar (from, de).
inheritance [ɪn'herɪtəns] *n (money, property, etc)* herencia (from, de); *(succession)* sucesión *f*.
inheritor [ɪn'herɪtər] *n* heredero,-a.
inhibit [ɪn'hɪbɪt] *vt* **1** *(person)* inhibir, cohibir. **2** *(hold back - attempt)* inhibir. **3** *(prevent)* impedir, restringir.
inhibition [ɪnhɪ'bɪʃən] *n* inhibición *f*, cohibición *f*.
inhospitable [ɪn'hɒspɪtəbəl] *adj* **1** *(people)* inhospitalario,-a. **2** *(place)* inhóspito,-a.
inhuman [ɪn'hjuːmən] *adj* inhumano,-a.
inimical [ɪ'nɪmɪkəl] *adj* **1** *fml (hostile)* hostil (to, a). **2** *(harmful, unfavourable)* desfavorable (to, a), perjudicial (to, para), contrario,-a (to, a).
inimitable [ɪ'nɪmɪtəbəl] *adj* inimitable.
iniquitous [ɪ'nɪkwɪtəs] *adj fml (wicked)* inicuo,-a; *(unjust)* injusto,-a.
iniquity [ɪ'nɪkwətɪ] *n (wickedness)* iniquidad *f*; *(unjustness)* injusticia.
▲ *pl* **iniquities**.
initial [ɪ'nɪʃəl] *adj* inicial, primero,-a.
▷ *n* inicial *f*, letra inicial.
▷ *n pl* **initials** *(of name)* iniciales *fpl*; *(of abbreviation)* siglas *fpl*.
initially [ɪ'nɪʃəlɪ] *adv* al principio, en primer lugar.
initiate [*(vb)* 'ɪnɪʃɪeɪt; *(n)* ɪ'nɪʃɪət] *vt* **1** *(gen)* iniciar; *(reform, plan, etc)* promover. **2** JUR entablar. **3** *(admit, introduce)* admitir (into, en).
▷ *n* iniciado,-a.
initiation [ɪnɪʃɪ'eɪʃən] *n* **1** *(start)* iniciación *f* (of, de), principio (of, de). **2** *(admission)* admisión *f* (into, en), iniciación *f* (into, en).
initiative [ɪ'nɪʃɪətɪv] *n* iniciativa.
inject [ɪn'dʒekt] *vt* **1** *(drug, etc)* inyectar; *(person)* poner una inyección a, pinchar. **2** *fig (new ideas, enthusiasm, etc)* infundir, inyectar; *(money, resources, etc)* invertir.
injection [ɪn'dʒekʃən] *n* **1** inyección *f*.
injudicious [ɪndʒʊ:'dɪʃəs] *adj fml (gen)* poco discreto,-a, imprudente; *(time, moment)* inoportuno,-a.
injure ['ɪndʒər] *vt* **1** herir, lesionar, lastimar. **2** *fig (feelings)* herir; *(health, reputation, etc)* perjudicar.
injured ['ɪndʒəd] *adj* **1** *(hurt)* herido,-a, lesionado,-a, lastimado,-a. **2** *fig (offended - feeling)* herido,-a; *(- look, tone, etc)* ofendido,-a.
▷ *n pl* **the injured** los heridos.
injurious [ɪn'dʒʊərɪəs] *adj* **1** *fml (harmful)* perjudicial. **2** *fml (insulting)* injurioso,-a, ofensivo,-a.
injury ['ɪndʒərɪ] *n* **1** herida, lesión *f*. **2** *fig (to feelings, etc)* daño; *(to reputation)* agravio.
▲ *pl* **injuries**.
injustice [ɪn'dʒʌstɪs] *n* injusticia.
ink [ɪŋk] *n* tinta.
▷ *vt* entintar.
⊙ **to ink in** *vt sep* repasar con tinta.
inkblot ['ɪŋkblɒt] *n* borrón *m*.
inkjet printer ['ɪŋkdʒet 'prɪntər] *n* impresora de chorro de tinta.
inkling ['ɪŋklɪŋ] *n (vague idea)* noción *f*, idea; *(suspicion)* sospecha; *(hint)* señal *m*, indicio, atisbo.
inkpad ['ɪŋkpæd] *n* tampón *m* de entintar, almohadilla.
inkstand ['ɪŋkstænd] *n* escribanía.
inkwell ['ɪŋkwel] *n* tintero.
inky ['ɪŋkɪ] *adj* **1** *(dirty)* manchado,-a de tinta. **2** *(black)* negro,-a.
▲ *comp* **inkier**, *superl* **inkiest**.
inland [*(adj)* 'ɪnlənd; *(adv)* ɪn'lænd] *adj* (del) interior.
▷ *adv (travel)* tierra adentro, hacia el interior; *(live)* en el interior. ● **Inland Revenue** GB Hacienda.
inlay [*(n)* 'ɪnleɪ; *(vb)* ɪn'leɪ] *n* **1** *(in wood)* taracea; *(of gems)* incrustación *f*; *(in metal)* damasquinado; *(of marquetry)* marquetería. **2** *(in tooth)* empaste *m*.
inlet ['ɪnlet] *n* **1** *(from sea or lake)* cala, ensenada; *(between islands)* brazo de mar. **2** TECH entrada, admisión *f*.
inmate ['ɪnmeɪt] *n* **1** *(gen)* residente *mf*. **2** *(of prison)* preso,-a, interno,-a. **3** *(of hospital)* enfermo,-a. **4** *(of asylum, camp)* internado,-a.
inn [ɪn] *n (with lodgings)* posada, fonda, mesón *m*; *(in country)* venta; *(pub)* taberna.
innards ['ɪnədz] *n pl* entrañas *fpl*, tripas *fpl*.
innate [ɪ'neɪt] *adj* innato,-a.
inner ['ɪnər] *adj* **1** *(room, region, etc)* interior; *(organization)* interno,-a. **2** *(feelings, etc)* interior, íntimo,-a.
innermost ['ɪnəməʊst] *adj* **1** *(most inward)* más interior. **2** *fig (most private)* más íntimo,-a, más secreto,-a.
innocence ['ɪnəsəns] *n* inocencia.
innocent ['ɪnəsənt] *adj (gen)* inocente; *(harmless)* inocuo,-a, inofensivo,-a; *(naive)* ingenuo,-a.
innovate ['ɪnəveɪt] *vi* innovar.
innovative ['ɪnəvətɪv] *adj* innovador,-ra.
innumerable [ɪ'njuːmərəbəl] *adj* innumerable.
inoculate [ɪ'nɒkjuleɪt] *vt* inocular, vacunar.
inoffensive [ɪnə'fensɪv] *adj* inofensivo,-a.
inoperable [ɪn'ɒpərəbəl] *adj* inoperable.
inoperative [ɪn'ɒpərətɪv] *adj* inoperante.
inopportune [ɪn'ɒpətjuːn] *adj* inoportuno,-a.
inordinate [ɪn'ɔːdɪnət] *adj fml (beyond normal limits)* desmesurado,-a; *(excessive)* excesivo,-a.
inorganic [ɪnɔː'gænɪk] *adj* inorgánico,-a.
input ['ɪnpʊt] *n (of power)* entrada; *(of money, resources)* inversión *f*; *(of data)* input *m*.
▷ *vt* COMPUT entrar, introducir.
▲ *pt & pp* **input** o **inputted**.
inquest ['ɪnkwest] *n* **1** investigación *f* judicial, encuesta judicial. **2** *fam* investigación *f*.
inquire [ɪn'kwaɪər] *vi fml* preguntar, informarse.
⊙ **to inquire into** *vt insep* investigar.

inquiry [ɪn'kwaɪᵊrɪ] *n* **1** *fml (question)* pregunta. **2** *(investigation)* investigación *f*.
▲ *pl* **inquiries.**
inquisition [ɪnkwɪ'zɪʃᵊn] *n* investigación *f*, inquisición *f*. ● **the Inquisition** HIST la Inquisición *f*.
inquisitive ɪnkwɪ'zɪtɪv] *adj (person)* curioso,-a.
inroads ['ɪnrəʊds] *n pl (raid)* incursión *f sing*.
▷ *n fig (encroachment)* intrusión *f*.
insalubrious [ɪnsə'luːbrɪəs] *adj fml* insalubre.
insane [ɪn'seɪn] *adj* **1** *(person)* loco,-a, demente; *(act)* insensato,-a. **2** *fam (idea, etc)* loco,-a. ■ **to go insane** volverse loco,-a.
insanitary [ɪn'sænɪtᵊrɪ] *adj* insalubre, antihigiénico,-a.
insanity [ɪn'sænɪtɪ] *n (of person)* locura, demencia; *(of act)* insensatez *f*.
insatiable [ɪn'seɪʃəbᵊl] *adj* insaciable (**for**, de).
inscribe [ɪn'skraɪb] *vt (tombstone, ring, etc)* inscribir, grabar; *(book)* dedicar.
inscription [ɪn'skrɪpʃᵊn] *n (gen)* inscripción *f*; *(in book)* dedicatoria.
inscrutable [ɪn'skruːtəbᵊl] *adj* inescrutable, insondable, impenetrable.
insect ['ɪnsekt] *n* insecto.
insecticide [ɪn'sektɪsaɪd] *n* insecticida *m*.
insecure [ɪnsɪ'kjʊəʳ] *adj* inseguro,-a.
insecurity [ɪnsɪ'kjʊərɪtɪ] *n* inseguridad *f*.
inseminate [ɪn'semɪneɪt] *vt* inseminar.
insensibility [ɪnsensə'bɪlətɪ] *n* **1** *fml (unconsciousness)* inconsciencia, pérdida de conciencia. **2** *fml (lack of feeling)* insensibilidad *f* (**to**, hacia); *(indifference)* indiferencia (**to**, ante).
insensible [ɪn'sensəbᵊl] *adj* **1** *fml (unconscious)* inconsciente, sin conocimiento. **2** *fml (unaware)* inconsciente; *(not able to feel)* insensible.
insensitive [ɪn'sensətɪv] *adj* insensible.
inseparable [ɪn'sepᵊrəbᵊl] *adj* inseparable (**from**, de).
insert [*(vb)* ɪn'sɜːt; *(n)* 'ɪnsɜːt] *vt (gen)* introducir en, meter en; *(comment, clause, paragraph, etc)* incluir (**in**, en), insertar (**in**, en); *(advertisement)* poner (**in**, en).
▷ *n (in book, newspaper)* encarte *m*; *(in clothing)* añadido.
insertion [ɪn'sɜːʃᵊn] *n* **1** *(gen)* introducción *f*; *(of comment, clause, paragraph, etc)* inclusión *f*, inserción *f*. **2** *(advertisement)* anuncio.
inset [*(n)* 'ɪnset; *(vb)* ɪn'set] *n (diagram, etc)* recuadro.
▷ *vt* insertar (**into**, en).
▲ *pt & pp* **inset**, *ger* **insetting.**
inside [ɪn'saɪd] *n* **1** interior *m*, parte *f* interior. **2** *(driving on left)* la izquierda; *(driving on right)* la derecha.
▷ *adv (position)* dentro; *(movement)* adentro. ■ **inside out** del revés.
▷ *prep* dentro de.
▷ *n pl* **insides** *fam* entrañas *fpl*, tripas *fpl*.
insider [ɪn'saɪdəʳ] *n* persona enterada.
insight ['ɪnsaɪt] *n* **1** *(deep understanding, perception)* perspicacia, penetración *f*. **2** *(sudden understanding)* idea.
insignia [ɪn'sɪgnɪə] *n* insignia, insignias *fpl*.
▲ *pl* **insignia** [ɪn'sɪgnɪə].
insignificance [ɪnsɪg'nɪfɪkəns] *n* insignificancia.
insignificant [ɪnsɪg'nɪfɪkənt] *adj* insignificante.
insincere [ɪnsɪn'sɪəʳ] *adj* poco sincero,-a, insincero,-a, falso,-a.
insinuate [ɪn'sɪnjʊeɪt] *vt* **1** *(hint, suggest)* insinuar, dar a entender. **2** *(worm, install)* insinuarse (**into**, en).
insinuation [ɪnsɪnjʊ'eɪʃᵊn] *n* insinuación *f*, indirecta.
insipid [ɪn'sɪpɪd] *adj (food, drink)* insípido,-a, soso,-a; *(person, activity)* insulso,-a, soso,-a.
insist [ɪn'sɪst] *vt* **1** *(declare firmly)* insistir en. **2** *(demand forcefully)* exigir.
insistence [ɪn'sɪstᵊns] *n* insistencia (**on**, en), empeño (**on**, en).
insistent [ɪn'sɪstᵊnt] *adj* **1** *(person)* insistente. **2** *(urgent, compelling)* apremiante, urgente; *(repeated)* persistente.
insofar as [ɪnsəʊ'fɑːrəz] *adv* en la medida en que, en tanto que.
insole ['ɪnsəʊl] *n* plantilla.
insolence ['ɪnsələns] *n* insolencia, descaro, frescura.
insolent ['ɪnsələnt] *adj* insolente, descarado,-a, fresco,-a.
insoluble [ɪn'sɒljəbᵊl] *adj* **1** *(of substances)* insoluble, indisoluble. **2** *fig* sin solución, insoluble.
insolvent [ɪn'sɒlvənt] *adj* insolvente.
insomnia [ɪn'sɒmnɪə] *n* insomnio.
insomuch [ɪnsəʊ'mʌtʃ] *phr* **insomuch as** puesto que, visto que, ya que.
▷ *phr* **insomuch that** hasta tal punto que.
insouciance [ɪn'suːsɪəns] *n fml* despreocupación *f*, indiferencia.
inspect [ɪn'spekt] *vt (gen)* inspeccionar, examinar, revisar.
inspection [ɪn'spekʃᵊn] *n* **1** *(gen)* inspección *f*, examen, revisión *f* **2** *(of luggage)* registro.
inspector [ɪn'spektəʳ] *n (gen)* inspector,-ra; *(on train)* revisor,-ra; *(in police)* inspector,-ra de policía.
inspiration [ɪnspɪ'reɪʃᵊn] *n* **1** *(gen)* inspiración *f*. **2** *fam (good idea)* genialidad *f*.
inspire [ɪn'spaɪəʳ] *vt* **1** *(gen)* inspirar. **2** *(encourage)* estimular, animar, mover. **3** *(fill with - fear)* infundir; *(- confidence, respect)* inspirar.
instability [ɪnstə'bɪlɪtɪ] *n* inestabilidad *f*.
install [ɪn'stɔːl] [Also written **instal**.] *vt* **1** *(equipment, etc)* instalar. **2** *(person)* instalar, colocar.
installation [ɪnstə'leɪʃᵊn] *n* instalación *f*.
installment [ɪn'stɔːlmənt] *n* US → **instalment**
instalment [ɪn'stɔːlmənt] *n* **1** *(of payment)* plazo. **2** *(of book, story, etc)* entrega; *(of collection)* fascículo.
instance ['ɪnstᵊns] *n* ejemplo, caso. ■ **for instance** por ejemplo.
▷ *vt* poner por caso, citar como ejemplo.
instant ['ɪnstᵊnt] *n* instante *m*, momento.
▷ *adj* **1** *(at once)* inmediato,-a. **2** *(coffee, etc)* instantáneo,-a. **3** *fml (urgent)* urgente. **4** COMM *(of the present month)* del corriente.
instantaneous [ɪnstən'teɪnɪəs] *adj* instantáneo,-a.
instantly ['ɪnstəntlɪ] *adv* al instante, inmediatamente.
instead [ɪn'sted] *adv* en cambio, en su lugar: **Mrs Jones couldn't do the class so I did it instead** *la Señora Jones no pudo dar la clase así que yo la di en su lugar.*
▷ *prep* **instead of** en vez de, en lugar de: **we should eat more fish instead of meat** *deberíamos comer más pescado en lugar de carne.*
instep ['ɪnstep] *n* empeine *m*.

instigate ['ɪnstɪgeɪt] *vt* instigar.
instil [ɪn'stɪl] *vt (idea)* inculcar (**in**, a/en); *(respect, etc)* infundir (**in**, a).
▲ *pt & pp* **instilled**, *ger* **instilling**.
instinct ['ɪnstɪŋkt] *n* instinto.
instinctive [ɪn'stɪŋktɪv] *adj* instintivo,-a, intuitivo,-a.
institute ['ɪnstɪtjuːt] *n* **1** *(gen)* instituto, centro. **2** *(professional body)* colegio, asociación *f*; *(educational)* escuela.
▷ *vt fml (organize, establish)* instituir, establecer, fundar; *(initiate - enquiry)* iniciar, empezar; *(- proceedings)* entablar.
institution [ɪnstɪ'tjuːʃᵊn] *n* **1** *(act - gen)* institución *f*, establecimiento, introducción *f*; *(- of inquiry, proceedings)* iniciación *f*. **2** *(organization)* institución *f*, organismo, asociación *f*. **3** *(home)* asilo; *(asylum)* hospital *m* psiquiátrico, manicomio; *(orphanage)* orfanato. **4** *(custom, practice)* institución *f*, tradición *f*, costumbre *f*.
institutionalize [ɪnstɪ'tjuːsᵊnəlaɪz] *vt* institucionalizar.
instruct [ɪn'strʌkt] *vt* **1** *(teach)* instruir, enseñar; *(inform)* informar. **2** *(order)* ordenar, mandar, dar instrucciones. **3** JUR *(solicitor, barrister)* dar instrucciones a; *(jury)* instruir.
instruction [ɪn'strʌkʃᵊn] *n* **1** *(teaching)* instrucción *f*, enseñanza. **2** *(order)* orden *f*, mandato.
instructive [ɪn'strʌktɪv] *adj* instructivo,-a, formativo,-a.
instructor [ɪn'strʌktəʳ] *n (gen)* instructor,-ra; *(of driving)* profesor,-ra; *(of sport)* monitor,-ra.
instrument ['ɪnstrəmənt] *n* instrumento.
instrumental [ɪnstrə'mentᵊl] *adj* **1** MUS instrumental. **2** *(helpful, significant)* decisivo,-a.
insubordinate [ɪnsə'bɔːdɪnət] *adj* insubordinado,-a, indisciplinado,-a, desobediente, rebelde.
insubordination [ɪnsəbɔːdɪ'neɪʃᵊn] *n* insubordinación *f*, indisciplina, desobediencia, rebeldía.
insubstantial [ɪnsəb'stænʃᵊl] *adj* **1** *(gen)* insustancial; *(meal)* poco nutritivo,-a; *(structure)* poco sólido,-a, poco seguro,-a, frágil. **2** *fig (tenuous)* poco convincente, flojo,-a. **3** *(imaginary, unreal)* imaginario,-a.
insufferable [ɪn'sʌfᵊrəbᵊl] *adj* insoportable, inaguantable, insufrible.
insufficient [ɪnsə'fɪʃᵊnt] *adj* insuficiente.
insular ['ɪnsjʊləʳ] *adj* **1** *(of island)* insular. **2** *pej (narrow-minded)* estrecho,-a de miras.
insulate ['ɪnsjəleɪt] *vt* **1** TECH aislar (**against/from**, de). **2** *fig (protect)* proteger (**against**, contra), (**from**, de).
insulation [ɪnsjə'leɪʃᵊn] *n* TECH aislamiento.
insulator ['ɪnsjəleɪtəʳ] *n* TECH aislante *m*, aislador *m*.
insulin ['ɪnsjəlɪn] *n* insulina.
insult [*(n)* 'ɪnsʌlt; *(vb)* ɪn'sʌlt] *n* insulto.
▷ *vt* insultar, ofender, injuriar.
insuperable [ɪn'suːpᵊrəbᵊl] *adj fml (problems, etc)* insuperable; *(barrier, etc)* infranqueable.
insupportable [ɪnsə'pɔːtəbᵊl] *adj fml* insoportable.
insurance [ɪn'ʃʊərəns] *n* **1** seguro. **2** *fig (safeguard)* salvaguarda, protección *f*, garantía.
insure [ɪn'ʃʊəʳ] *vt* **1** asegurar (**against**, contra). **2** US *(ensure)* asegurar.
insurgent [ɪn'sɜːdʒənt] *adj* insurgente, insurrecto,-a.
insurmountable [ɪnsə'maʊntəbᵊl] *adj fml* insuperable.
insurrection [ɪnsə'rekʃᵊn] *n* insurrección *f*.
intact [ɪn'tækt] *adj* intacto,-a.
intake ['ɪnteɪk] *n* **1** *(of food, etc)* consumo; *(of breath)* inhalación *f*. **2** TECH *(of air, water)* entrada; *(of electricity, gas, water)* toma. **3** *(number of people)* número de personas inscritas.
intangible [ɪn'tændʒɪbᵊl] *adj* intangible.
integer ['ɪntɪdʒəʳ] *n* MATH entero, número entero.
integral ['ɪntɪgrəl] *adj* **1** *(intrinsic, essential)* integral, esencial, fundamental. **2** *(built-in)* incorporado,-a. **3** MATH integral.
integrate ['ɪntɪgreɪt] *vt* **1** integrar (**into/with**, en), incorporar (**into/with**, a). **2** MATH integrar.
▷ *vi* integrarse (**into/with**, en), incorporarse (**into/with**, a).
integration [ɪntɪ'greɪʃᵊn] *n* integración *f* (**into**, en).
integrity [ɪn'tegrətɪ] *n* **1** *(honesty)* integridad *f*, honradez *f*. **2** *(completeness)* totalidad *f*.
intellect ['ɪntəlekt] *n* **1** *(intelligence)* intelecto, inteligencia. **2** *(person)* intelectual *mf*.
intellectual [ɪntə'lektjʊəl] *adj* intelectual.
▷ *n* intelectual *mf*.
intelligence [ɪn'telɪdʒᵊns] *n* **1** *(gen)* inteligencia. **2** *(information)* información *f*, espionaje *m*.
intelligent [ɪn'telɪʒᵊnt] *adj* inteligente.
intelligible [ɪn'telɪdʒəbᵊl] *adj* inteligible, comprensible.
intemperate [ɪn'tempᵊrət] *adj* **1** *fml (behaviour, emotion)* inmoderado,-a, desaforado,-a, excesivo,-a; *(speech)* violento,-a, ultrajante; *(drinker)* dado,-a a la bebida. **2** *(climate)* riguroso,-a.
intend [ɪn'tend] *vt* **1** *(plan, mean, have in mind)* tener la intención de, tener el propósito de, proponerse, pensar, querer. **2** *(destine for)* ir dirigido,-a a.
intense [ɪn'tens] *adj* **1** *(gen)* intenso,-a, fuerte; *(stare)* penetrante. **2** *(emotions)* profundo,-a, grande, vivo,-a. **3** *(person)* muy serio,-a.
intensifier [ɪn'tensɪfaɪəʳ] *n* LING partícula enfática.
intensify [ɪn'tensɪfaɪ] *vt (search, campaign)* intensificar; *(effort)* redoblar; *(production, pollution, pain)* aumentar.
▲ *pt & pp* **intensified**, *ger* **intensifying**.
intensity [ɪn'tensɪtɪ] *n* **1** intensidad *f*. **2** *(of person)* seriedad *f*.
▲ *pl* **intensities**.
intensive [ɪn'tensɪv] *adj* **1** *(course, training, etc)* intensivo,-a. **2** *(search)* minucioso,-a; *(study)* profundo,-a.
● **intensive care** cuidados *mpl* intensivos.
intent [ɪn'tent] *adj* **1** *(look, etc)* atento,-a. **2** *(determined)* decidido,-a, resuelto,-a, empeñado,-a. **3** *(absorbed)* absorto,-a, concentrado,-a.
▷ *n* intención *f*, propósito.
intention [ɪn'tenʃᵊn] *n (purpose, aim, plan, determination)* intención *f*, propósito.
intently [ɪn'tentlɪ] *adv* atentamente.
inter [ɪn'tɜːʳ] *vt fml* enterrar, sepultar.
▲ *pt & pp* **interred**, *ger* **interring**.
interact [ɪntər'ækt] *vi* **1** *(people)* relacionarse, interaccionar. **2** CHEM reaccionar.
interaction [ɪntər'ækʃᵊn] *n* interacción *f*.
interactive [ɪntər'æktɪv] *adj* interactivo,-a.

intercede [ɪntə'siːd] *vi fml* interceder.
intercept [ɪntə'sept] *vt* interceptar.
interception [ɪntə'sepʃᵊn] *n* interceptación *f*.
interceptor [ɪntə'septəʳ] *n* AV avión *m* interceptor.
interchange ['ɪntətʃeɪndʒ] *n* 1 *(exchange)* intercambio. 2 *(on motorway)* enlace *m*.
▷ *vt* intercambiar (**with**, con).
inter-city [ɪntə'sɪtɪ] *adj* interurbano,-a, de largo recorrido.
intercom ['ɪntəkɒm] *n* interfono.
interconnect [ɪntəkə'nekt] *vi* interconectar.
interconnection [ɪntəkə'nekʃᵊn] *n* interconexión *f*.
intercontinental [ɪntəkɒntɪ'nentᵊl] *adj* intercontinental.
intercostal [ɪntə'kɒstᵊl] *adj* intercostal.
intercourse ['ɪntəkɔːs] *n* 1 *(dealings)* trato. 2 *(sexual)* coito, relaciones *fpl* sexuales.
interdental [ɪntə'dentᵊl] *adj* interdental.
interdict [ɪntə'dɪkt] *n (judicial)* interdicto; *(religious)* interdicto, entredicho.
▷ *vt* prohibir.
interdisciplinary [ɪntədɪsɪ'plɪnərɪ] *adj* interdisciplinario,-a.
interest ['ɪntrəst] *n* 1 *(gen)* interés *m*. 2 *(hobby)* afición *f*, interés *m*. 3 *(advantage, benefit)* provecho, beneficio. 4 COMM *(share, stake)* participación *f*, interés *m*. 5 FIN *(money)* interés *m*, rédito.
▷ *vt* interesar.
interested ['ɪntrəstɪd] *adj* interesado,-a (**in**, en).
interesting ['ɪntrəstɪŋ] *adj* interesante.
interface ['ɪntəfeɪs] *n* 1 COMPUT interface *f*, interfaz *f*. 2 *fig* terreno común.
interfacing ['ɪntəfeɪsɪŋ] *n* entretela.
interfere [ɪntə'fɪəʳ] *vi (meddle)* entrometerse (**in**, en), inmiscuirse (**in**, en).
▷ *vi (prevent advancement)* afectar (**with**, -), dificultar (**with**, -), estorbar (**with**, -), impedir (**with**, -), interferir (**with**, en); *(fiddle with, mess about with)* tocar (**with**, -), manosear (**with**, -); *(broadcasts)* interferir (**with**, -).
interference [ɪntə'fɪərəns] *n* 1 *(meddling)* intromisión *f*, entrometimiento, injerencia. 2 *(with broadcast)* interferencia.
intergovernmental [ɪntəgʌvᵊn'mentᵊl] *adj* intergubernamental.
interim ['ɪntərɪm] *adj* interino,-a, provisional.
interior [ɪn'tɪərɪəʳ] *adj* interior.
▷ *n* interior *m*, parte *f* interior.
interject [ɪntə'dʒekt] *vt* interponer.
interjection [ɪntə'dʒekʃᵊn] *n* 1 *(part of speech)* interjección *f*. 2 *(comment)* interposición *f*.
interlace [ɪntə'leɪs] *vt* entrelazar.
interlink [ɪntə'lɪŋk] *vt* entrelazar, unir.
interlock [ɪntə'lɒk] *vt (fingers)* entrelazar; *(cogs)* engranar, endentar; *(parts, pieces, units)* enganchar, trabar.
interlocutor [ɪntə'lɒkjutəʳ] *n fml* interlocutor,-ra.
interloper ['ɪntələupəʳ] *n* intruso,-a.
interlude ['ɪntəluːd] *n* 1 *(break)* intervalo, pausa; *(respite)* respiro, tregua. 2 *(music)* interludio; *(play, etc)* intermedio, descanso.
intermediary [ɪntə'miːdɪərɪ] *n* intermediario,-a.
▷ *adj* intermediario,-a.
▲ *pl* **intermediaries**.
intermediate [ɪntə'miːdɪət] *adj* intermedio,-a.
interment [ɪn'tɜːmənt] *n fml* entierro.
interminable [ɪn'tɜːmɪnəbᵊl] *adj* interminable, inacabable, sin fin.
intermission [ɪntə'mɪʃᵊn] *n* US *(interval)* intermedio, descanso.
intermittent [ɪntə'mɪtᵊnt] *adj* intermitente.
intern [*(n)* 'ɪntɜːn; *(vb)* ɪn'tɜːn] *n* US interno,-a.
▷ *vt* internar, recluir.
internal [ɪn'tɜːnᵊl] *adj* interno,-a.
internalize [ɪn'tɜːnᵊlaɪz] *vt (feelings)* interiorizar.
international [ɪntə'næʃᵊnəl] *adj* internacional.
internationalize [ɪntə'næʃnəlaɪz] *vt* internacionalizar.
internaut ['ɪntənɔːt] *n* internauta *mf*.
internecine [ɪntə'niːsaɪn] *adj* de destrucción recíproca.
internee [ɪntɜː'niː] *n* interno,-a, preso,-a.
Internet ['ɪntənet] *n* Internet *f*.
internment [ɪn'tɜːnmənt] *n* internamiento.
interpellate [ɪn'tɜːpəleɪt] *vt* interpelar.
interpersonal [ɪntə'pɜːsᵊnəl] *adj* interpersonal.
interplanetary [ɪntə'plænɪtrɪ] *adj* interplanetario,-a.
interplay ['ɪntəpleɪ] *n* interacción *f*.
Interpol ['ɪntəpɒl] *abbr* (**International Criminal Police Organization**) Interpol *f*.
interpolate [ɪn'tɜːpəleɪt] *vt fml* interpolar, intercalar.
interpose [ɪntə'pəuz] *vt* 1 *(place between)* interponer. 2 *(interrupt)* interrumpir.
interposition [ɪntəpə'zɪʃᵊn] *n fml* interposición *f*.
interpret [ɪn'tɜːprət] *vt (gen)* interpretar; *(understand)* interpretar, entender.
interpretation [ɪntɜːprə'teɪʃᵊn] *n* interpretación *f*.
interpreter [ɪn'tɜːprətəʳ] *n* intérprete *mf*.
interracial [ɪntə'reɪʃᵊl] *adj* interracial.
interrelate [ɪntərɪ'leɪt] *vt* interrelacionar.
interrogate [ɪn'terəgeɪt] *vt* interrogar.
interrogation [ɪnterə'geɪʃᵊn] *n* interrogatorio.
interrogative [ɪntə'rɒgəætɪv] *adj fml* interrogativo,-a.
▷ *n* LING *(word)* palabra interrogativa; *(phrase)* oración *f* interrogativa.
interrupt [ɪntə'rʌpt] *vt* interrumpir.
▷ *vi* interrumpir.
interruption [ɪntə'rʌpʃᵊn] *n* interrupción *f*.
intersect [ɪntə'sekt] *vt* 1 *(road, etc)* cruzar, atravesar. 2 *(in geometry)* cruzar, intersecar.
intersection [ɪntə'sekʃᵊn] *n* 1 *(of roads)* cruce *m*. 2 *(in geometry)* intersección *f*.
intersperse [ɪntə'spɜːs] *vt* 1 *(scatter)* esparcir, entremezclar. 2 *(diversify)* salpicar.
interstate ['ɪntəsteɪt] *adj (esp us)* interestatal, entre estados.
interval ['ɪntəvᵊl] *n* 1 *(in time, space)* intervalo (**between**, entre). 2 *(in play, film, etc)* intermedio, descanso; *(in play)* entreacto. 3 *(pause, break)* pausa; *(silence)* silencio; *(rest)* descanso. 4 MUS intervalo.
intervene [ɪntə'viːn] *vi* 1 *(person)* intervenir (**in**, en). 2 *(event, etc)* sobrevenir, ocurrir. 3 *fml (time)* transcurrir, mediar.
interview ['ɪntəvjuː] *n (gen)* entrevista; *(press)* entrevista.
▷ *vt* entrevistar, hacer una entrevista a, entrevistarse con.
interviewee [ɪntəvjuː'iː] *n* entrevistado,-a.
interviewer ['ɪntəvjuːəʳ] *n* entrevistador,-ra.

intervocalic [ɪntəvə'kælɪk] *adj* intervocálico,-a.
interweave [ɪntə'wiːv] *vt* 1 entretejer. 2 *fig* entrelazar, cruzar.
▲ *pt* interwove [ɪntə'wəʊv], *pp* interwoven [ɪntə'wəʊvᵊn].
intestinal [ɪn'testɪnᵊl] *adj* intestinal.
intestine [ɪn'testɪn] *n* intestino. ● large intestine intestino grueso. ‖ small intestine intestino delgado.
intimacy ['ɪntɪməsɪ] *n* 1 *(closeness)* intimidad *f*. 2 *euph (sexual activity)* relaciones *fpl* íntimas.
intimate¹ ['ɪntɪmət] *adj* 1 *(gen)* íntimo,-a; *(link, etc)* estrecho,-a. 2 *(knowledge)* profundo,-a.
▷ *n (friend)* amigo,-a íntimo,-a, íntimo,-a.
intimate² ['ɪntɪmeɪt] *vi fml* insinuar, dar a entender.
intimation [ɪntɪ'meɪʃᵊn] *n* 1 *fml (sign)* indicio; *(hint)* sugerencia, indirecta. 2 *fml (feeling)* presentimiento.
intimidate [ɪn'tɪmɪdeɪt] *vt* intimidar.
into ['ɪntʊ] *prep* 1 *(indicating movement)* en, dentro de, a; *(in direction of)* a, hacia; *(against)* contra, con. 2 *(time, age)* hasta. 3 *(indicating change)* en, a: he turned water into wine *transformó el agua en vino.* 4 MATH entre: what's four into twenty? *¿cuánto son veinte entre cuatro?*
intolerable [ɪn'tɒlᵊrəbᵊl] *adj* intolerable, insoportable, inaceptable, inadmisible.
intolerance [ɪn'tɒlərəns] *n* intolerancia, intransigencia.
intolerant [ɪn'tɒlərənt] *adj* intolerante, intransigente.
intonation [ɪntə'neɪʃᵊn] *n* entonación *f*.
intone [ɪn'təʊn] *vt* entonar.
intoxicate [ɪn'tɒksɪkeɪt] *vt* 1 *fml* embriagar, emborrachar. 2 *fig* embriagar.
intoxication [ɪntɒksɪ'keɪʃᵊn] *n* embriaguez *f*.
intractable [ɪn'træktəbᵊl] *adj fml* intratable.
intranet ['ɪntrənet] *n* red *f* local.
intransigence [ɪn'trænsɪdʒəns] *n* intransigencia, intolerancia.
intransigent [ɪn'trænsɪdʒent] *adj* intransigente, intolerante.
intransitive [ɪn'trænsɪtɪv] *adj* LING intransitivo,-a.
intrauterine [ɪntrə'juːtəraɪn] *adj* MED intrauterino,-a.
intrepid [ɪn'trepɪd] *adj* intrépido,-a, audaz.
intricacy ['ɪntrɪkəsɪ] *n* complejidad *f*.
▲ *pl* intricacies.
intricate ['ɪntrɪkət] *adj (plot, etc)* complejo,-a, complicado,-a; *(pattern)* intrincado,-a.
intrigue [ɪn'triːg] *n* 1 *(gen)* intriga; *(conspiracy)* conspiración *f*. 2 *(love affair)* amorío, aventura.
▷ *vt (fascinate)* intrigar, fascinar, interesar.
intrinsic [ɪn'trɪnsɪk] *adj* intrínseco,-a, inherente.
intro ['ɪntrəʊ] *n* 1 *fam (of person)* presentación *f*. 2 MUS introducción *f*.
▲ *pl* intros.
introduce [ɪntrə'djʊːs] *vt* 1 *(person, programme)* presentar. 2 *(bring in - gen)* introducir; *(- new product, etc)* presentar, lanzar; *(law, procedure, etc)* instituir. 3 *(to hobby, habit)* iniciar (to, en). 4 *(bring up)* proponer, sugerir, plantear. 5 *fml (insert)* introducir, meter, insertar.
introduction [ɪntrə'dʌkʃᵊn] *n* 1 *(of person, programme)* presentación *f*. 2 *(to book, speech, etc)* introducción *f*. 3 *(- of new product, etc)* presentación *f*, lanzamiento; *(- of law, procedure, etc)* introducción *f*, institución *f*. 4 *(first experience)* iniciación *f*. 5 MUS introducción *f*.
introspect [ɪntrə'spekt] *vi* practicar la introspección.
introspection [ɪntrə'spekʃᵊn] *n* introspección *f*.
introspective [ɪntə'spektɪv] *adj* introspectivo,-a.
introvert ['ɪntrəvɜːt] *n* introvertido,-a.
intrude [ɪn'truːd] *vi* 1 *(disturb)* importunar, molestar. 2 *(interfere)* entrometerse, inmiscuirse, meterse.
intruder [ɪn'truːdəʳ] *n* intruso,-a.
intrusive [ɪn'truːsɪv] *adj (intruding)* intruso,-a; *(nosy)* entrometido,-a; *(annoying, unwelcome)* que moleste, que estorba, molesto,-a.
intuit [ɪn'tjʊːɪt] *vt fml* intuir.
intuition [ɪntjʊː'ɪʃᵊn] *n* intuición *f*.
intuitive [ɪn'tjʊːɪtɪv] *adj* intuitivo,-a.
inundate ['ɪnʌndeɪt] *vt* 1 inundar (with, de). 2 *fig* inundar (with, de).
inure [ɪ'njʊəʳ] *vt fml* acostumbrar (to, a), habituar (to, a).
invade [ɪn'veɪd] *vt (gen)* invadir.
invader [ɪn'veɪdəʳ] *n* invasor,-ra.
invalid¹ ['ɪnvəlɪd] *n (disabled person)* inválido,-a, minusválido,-a; *(sick person)* enfermo,-a.
invalid² [ɪn'vælɪd] *adj (gen)* inválido,-a, no válido,-a, nulo,-a; *(out of date)* caducado,-a.
invalidate [ɪn'vælɪdeɪt] *vt (result, rule, etc)* invalidar, anular; *(argument)* refutar, demostrar el error de.
invalidity [ɪnvə'lɪdətɪ] *n (of invalid)* invalidez *f*.
invaluable [ɪn'væljʊəbᵊl] *adj* inestimable, inapreciable.
invariable [ɪn'veərɪəbᵊl] *adj* invariable, constante.
invasion [ɪn'veɪʒᵊn] *n (gen)* invasión *f*.
invasive [ɪn'veɪsɪv] *adj* invasivo,-va.
invective [ɪn'vektɪv] *n fml* invectiva, improperio.
inveigle [ɪn'veɪgᵊl] *vt* engatusar, embaucar.
invent [ɪn'vent] *vt* inventar, inventarse.
invention [ɪn'venʃᵊn] *n* 1 *(gen)* invento, invención *f*; *(lying)* invención *f*, mentira. 2 *(capacity for inventing)* inventiva.
inventive [ɪn'ventɪv] *adj* inventivo,-a.
inventor [ɪn'ventəʳ] *n* inventor,-ra.
inventory ['ɪnvəntrɪ] *n* inventario.
▲ *pl* inventories.
▷ *vt* inventariar.
▲ *pt & pp* inventoried, *ger* inventorying.
inverse [ɪn'vɜːs] *adj* inverso,-a.
inversion [ɪn'vɜːʒᵊn] *n* inversión *f*.
invert [ɪn'vɜːt] *vt* invertir. ● inverted commas comillas.
invertebrate [ɪn'vɜːtɪbrət] *adj* invertebrado,-a.
invest [ɪn'vest] *vt* 1 *(money)* invertir (in, en). 2 *(time, effort, etc)* emplear (in, en), invertir (in, en). 3 *fml (right, rank, power, etc)* investir (with, con), conferir (with, -), otorgar (with, -). 4 *fml (quality, characteristic, etc)* revestir (with, con), envolver (with, de). 5 MIL *dated* sitiar, cercar.
investigate [ɪn'vestɪgeɪt] *vt (crime)* investigar; *(cause, possibility)* examinar, estudiar.
▷ *vi fam (check)* mirar.
investigation [ɪnvestɪ'geɪʃᵊn] *n (of crime)* investigación *f* (into, sobre); *(of cause, possibility)* examen *m* (into, de), estudio (into, de).
investigator [ɪn'vestɪgeɪtəʳ] *n* investigador,-ra.

investiture [ɪn'vestɪtʃəʳ] *n* investidura.
investment [ɪn'vestmənt] *n* **1** *(of money)* inversión *f*. **2** *(investiture)* investidura.
investor [ɪn'vestəʳ] *n* inversor,-ra, inversionista *mf*.
inveterate [ɪn'vetᵊrət] *adj (person)* empedernido,-a; *(habit, feeling, etc)* arraigado,-a, consolidado,-a.
invidious [ɪn'vɪdɪəs] *adj* **1** *(task, job, etc)* odioso,-a, ingrato,-a. **2** *(comparison, choice, etc)* injusto,-a.
invigilate [ɪn'vɪdʒɪleɪt] *vt* GB vigilar.
invigorate [ɪn'vɪgəreɪt] *vt* tonificar, vigorizar.
invincible [ɪn'vɪnsəbᵊl] *adj* invencible.
inviolable [ɪn'vaɪələbᵊl] *adj* inviolable.
invisible [ɪn'vɪzəbᵊl] *adj* invisible.
invitation [ɪnvɪ'teɪʃᵊn] *n* invitación *f*.
invite [*(vb)* ɪn'vaɪt; *(n)* 'ɪnvaɪt] *vt* **1** *(guest, etc)* invitar, convidar; *(candidate, participant)* pedir, invitar. **2** *(comment, suggestion, etc)* solicitar. **3** *(criticism, disaster, etc)* provocar, incitar.
invoice ['ɪnvɔɪs] *n* COMM factura.
invoke [ɪn'vəʊk] *vt* invocar.
involuntary [ɪn'vɒləntərɪ] *adj* involuntario,-a.
involve [ɪn'vɒlv] *vt* **1** *(entail)* suponer, implicar, conllevar; *(give rise to)* acarrear, ocasionar. **2** *(include, affect, concern)* tener que ver con, afectar a. **3** *(implicate)* implicar, involucrar, meter.
involved [ɪn'vɒlvd] *adj* **1** *(complicated)* complicado,-a, enrevesado,-a. **2** *(implicated, associated)* implicado,-a, involucrado,-a; *(mixed up in)* metido,-a, envuelto,-a, mezclado,-a. **3** *(engrossed)* absorto,-a, enfrascado,-a; *(busy)* ocupado,-a. **4** *(emotionally)* enredado,-a, liado,-a, enrollado,-a.
involvement [ɪn'vɒlvmənt] *n* **1** *(participation)* participación *f*. **2** *(in crime)* complicidad *f*, implicación *f*. **3** *(affair)* enredo, lío, relación *f*.
invulnerable [ɪn'vʌlnərəbᵊl] *adj* invulnerable.
inward ['ɪnwəd] *adj* interior.
▷ *adv* hacia dentro.
inwards ['ɪnwədz] *adv* hacia dentro.
iodide ['aɪədaɪd] *n* yoduro.
iodine ['aɪədiːn] *n* yodo.
iodize ['aɪədaɪz] *vt* yodar.
ion [aɪən] *n* ion *m*.
ionize ['aɪənaɪz] *vt* ionizar.
ionosphere [aɪ'ɒnəsfɪəʳ] *n* ionosfera.
iota [aɪ'əʊtə] *n* pizca, ápice *m*.
iPod® ['aɪpɒd] *n* iPod® *m*.
IQ ['aɪ'kjuː] *abbr* **(intelligence quotient)** coeficiente *m* de inteligencia; *(abbreviation)* CI *m*.
IRA ['aɪ'ɑːr'eɪ] *abbr* **(Irish Republican Army)** Ejército Republicano irlandés; *(abbreviation)* IRA *m*.
Iran [ɪ'rɑːn] *n* Irán.
Iraq [ɪ'rɑːk] *n* Irak.
irascible [ɪ'ræsɪbᵊl] *adj fml* irascible, colérico,-a, iracundo,-a.
irate [aɪ'reɪt] *adj fml* airado,-a, iracundo,-a, furioso,-a.
ire ['aɪəʳ] *n fml* ira, cólera, enojo, enfado.
Ireland ['aɪələnd] *n* Irlanda. ● **Northern Ireland** Irlanda del norte.
iridescence [ɪrɪ'desᵊns] *n fml* iridiscencia.
iris ['aɪᵊrɪs] *n* **1** *(of eye)* iris *m inv*. **2** BOT lirio.
Irish ['aɪrɪʃ] *adj* irlandés,-esa.
Irishman ['aɪrɪʃmən] *n* irlandés *m*.
▲ *pl* **Irishmen** ['aɪrɪʃmən].
Irishwoman ['aɪrɪʃwʊmən] *n* irlandesa.
▲ *pl* **Irishwomen** ['aɪrɪʃwɪmɪn].
irk [ɜːk] *vt* fastidiar, molestar.
iron ['aɪən] *n* **1** *(metal)* hierro. **2** *(appliance)* plancha. **3** *(for golf)* hierro, palo de hierro.
▷ *adj* de hierro.
▷ *vt (clothes)* planchar.
▷ *n pl* **irons** *(fetters)* grillos *mpl*, grilletes *mpl*.
⊙ **to iron out** *vt sep* **1** *(clothes)* planchar. **2** *fig (problem, difficulty, etc)* resolver, solucionar.
ironic [aɪ'rɒnɪk] *adj* irónico,-a.
ironing [aɪ'rɒnɪŋ] *n* planchado. ■ **to do the ironing** planchar. ● **ironing board** tabla de planchar.
ironmonger ['aɪənmʌŋgəʳ] *n* GB ferretero,-a. ● **ironmonger's (shop)** ferretería.
ironmongery ['aɪənmʌŋgərɪ] *n* GB ferretería.
ironstone ['aɪənstəʊn] *n* mineral *m* de hierro.
ironware ['aɪənweəʳ] *n* objetos *mpl* de hierro, ferretería.
ironwork ['aɪənwɜːk] *n* herraje *m*.
ironworks ['aɪənwɜːks] *n pl* GB fundición *f* (de hierro).
irony ['aɪrənɪ] *n* ironía.
▲ *pl* **ironies**.
irradiate [ɪ'reɪdɪeɪt] *vt fml* irradiar.
irrational [ɪ'ræʃᵊnəl] *adj* irracional.
irreconcilable [ɪ'rekənsaɪləbᵊl] *adj fml* irreconciliable, inconciliable.
irrecoverable [ɪrɪ'kʌvᵊrəbᵊl] *adj fml (gen)* irrecuperable; *(debt)* incobrable.
irredeemable [ɪrɪ'diːməbᵊl] *adj* **1** *fml* irremediable. **2** FIN irredimible, no amortizable.
irreducible [ɪrɪ'djuːsəbᵊl] *adj fml* irreducible, irreductible.
irrefutable [ɪrɪ'fjuːtəbᵊl] *adj fml* irrefutable.
irregular [ɪ'regjələʳ] *adj* **1** *(gen)* irregular; *(uneven)* desigual. **2** *(unusual, abnormal)* raro,-a, anormal; *(against the rules)* inadmisible. **3** *(troops)* irregular.
irregularity [ɪregjə'lærɪtɪ] *n* **1** *(gen)* irregularidad *f*; *(unevenness)* desigualdad *f*. **2** *(abnormality)* anormalidad *f*, anomalía.
▲ *pl* **irregularities**.
irregularly [ɪ'regjələlɪ] *adv* irregularmente, con irregularidad, sin regularidad.
irrelevance [ɪ'reləvəns] *n* falta de pertinencia.
irrelevancy [ɪ'reləvənsɪ] *n* **1** *(state)* falta de pertinencia. **2** *(remark)* observación *f* que no viene al caso. **3** *(matter)* cosa que no viene al caso.
irrelevant [ɪ'relɪvənt] *adj* **1** *(unimportant - fact, detail, etc)* irrelevante. **2** *(out of place)* que no viene al caso: **that's irrelevant** *eso no tiene nada que ver, eso no viene al caso*.
irreligious [ɪrɪ'lɪdʒəs] *adj* irreligioso,-a.
irremediable [ɪrɪ'miːdɪəbᵊl] *adj* irremediable.
irremediably [ɪrɪ'miːdɪəblɪ] *adv* irremediablemente.
irremovable [ɪrɪ'muːvəbᵊl] *adj* inamovible.
irreparable [ɪ'repᵊrəbᵊl] *adj* irreparable.
irreplaceable [ɪrɪ'pleɪsəbᵊl] *adj* irremplazable, insustituible.
irrepressible [ɪrɪ'presəbᵊl] *adj* incontenible, incontrolable.
irreproachable [ɪrɪ'prəʊtʃəbᵊl] *adj* irreprochable, intachable.

irresistible [ɪrɪ'zɪstəbᵊl] *adj* 1 *(temptation, impulse, etc)* irresistible: **an irresistible urge** *un impulso irrefrenable.* 2 *(person, thing)* irresistible.
irresistibly [ɪrɪ'zɪstəblɪ] *adv* irresistiblemente.
irresolute [ɪ'rezəlu:t] *adj fml* indeciso,-a, vacilante, irresoluto,-a.
irresolution [ɪrezə'lu:ʃᵊn] *n* vacilación *f*, indeterminación *f*.
irrespective [ɪrɪ'spektɪv] *prep* **irrespective of** sin tener en cuenta, sin tomar en consideración, independientemente de.
irresponsibility [ɪrɪspɒnsə'bɪlətɪ] *n* irresponsabilidad *f*, falta de seriedad.
irresponsible [ɪrɪ'spɒnsəbᵊl] *adj* irresponsable, poco serio,-a.
irresponsibly [ɪrɪ'spɒnsəblɪ] *adv* irresponsablemente.
irretrievable [ɪrɪ'tri:vəbᵊl] *adj fml (object)* irrecuperable; *(mistake, damage, harm, etc)* irreparable; *(loss, situation, breakdown, etc)* irremediable.
irreverence [ɪ'revᵊrəns] *n* irreverencia, falta de respeto.
irreverent [ɪ'revᵊrənt] *adj* irreverente.
irreverently [ɪ'revᵊrəntlɪ] *adv* irreverentemente.
irreversible [ɪrɪ'vɜ:səbᵊl] *adj (process, damage)* irreversible; *(judgement, decision)* irrevocable.
irrevocable [ɪ'revəkəbᵊl] *adj fml* irrevocable, inalterable.
irrigable ['ɪrɪgəbᵊl] *adj* irrigable, regadío,-a.
irrigate ['ɪrɪgeɪt] *vt* 1 AGR regar, irrigar. 2 MED irrigar.
irrigation [ɪrɪ'geɪʃᵊn] *n* AGR riego, irrigación *f*. ● **irrigation channel** acequia, canal *m* de riego. ‖ **irrigation farming** cultivo de regadío. ‖ **irrigation system** sistema *m* de regadío.
irritability [ɪrɪtə'bɪlətɪ] *n* irritabilidad *f*, mal humor *m*.
irritable ['ɪrɪtəbᵊl] *adj* irritable, de mal humor.
irritably ['ɪrɪtəblɪ] *adv* con tono malhumorado, de mal humor.
irritant ['ɪrɪtənt] *adj* irritante.
▷ *n* 1 agente *m* irritante. 2 *fig* molestia, motivo de irritación.
irritate ['ɪrɪteɪt] *vt* 1 *(annoy)* irritar, molestar, fastidiar. 2 MED *(cause discomfort)* irritar; *(make inflamed)* inflamar.
irritating ['ɪrɪteɪtɪŋ] *adj* 1 *(annoying)* irritante, molesto,-a, fastidioso,-a, pesado,-a. 2 MED irritante.
irritation [ɪrɪ'teɪʃᵊn] *n* 1 MED irritación *f*. 2 *(cause of annoyance)* molestia, fastidio. 3 *(anger)* mal humor *m*, enfado, irritación *f*.
irruption [ɪ'rʌpʃᵊn] *n fml* irrupción *f*.
is [ɪz] *pres* → **be**.
Islam ['ɪzlɑ:m] *n* islam *m*.
Islamic [ɪz'læmɪk] *adj* islámico,-a.
island ['aɪlənd] *n* isla.
▷ *adj* isleño,-a. ● **safety island** US isla de peatones, isleta, refugio. ‖ **traffic island** isla de peatones, isleta, refugio.
islander ['aɪləndəʳ] *n* isleño,-a.
isle [aɪl] *n* isla.
islet ['aɪlət] *n* islote *m*.
isobar ['aɪsəbɑ:ʳ] *n* isobara.
isolate ['aɪsəleɪt] *vt* aislar (**from**, de): **scientists have isolated the germ** *los científicos han aislado el microbio.*
isolated ['aɪsəleɪtɪd] *adj* 1 *(solitary)* aislado,-a, apartado,-a: **an isolated house** *una casa aislada;* **I live a very isolated life** *llevo una vida muy solitaria.* 2 *(single)* aislado,-a, único,-a, excepcional: **an isolated case** *un caso aislado.*
isolation [aɪsə'leɪʃᵊn] *n* aislamiento (**from**, de).
isolationism [aɪsə'leɪʃᵊnɪzᵊm] *n* aislacionismo.
isolationist [aɪsə'leɪʃᵊnɪst] *adj* aislacionista.
▷ *n* aislacionista *mf*.
isometric [aɪsə'metrɪk] *adj* isométrico,-a.
isosceles [aɪ'sɒsəli:z] *adj* isósceles. ● **isosceles triangle** triángulo isósceles.
isotherm ['aɪsəθɜ:m] *n* isotermo.
isothermal [aɪsə'θɜ:mᵊl] *adj* isotérmico,-a.
isotope ['aɪsətəʊp] *n* isótopo.
Israel ['ɪzrɪəl] *n* Israel.
Israeli [ɪz'reɪlɪ] *adj* israelí.
▷ *n* israelí *mf*.
Israelite ['ɪzrɪəlaɪt] *adj* israelita.
▷ *n* israelita *mf*.
issue ['ɪʃu:] *n* 1 *(subject, topic)* tema *m*, cuestión *f*, asunto. 2 *(of newspaper, magazine, etc)* número. 3 *(of stamps, shares, back notes, etc)* emisión *f*; *(of book)* publicación *f*. 4 *(of passport, licence)* expedición *f*. 5 *(of equipment, supplies, etc)* distribución *f*, reparto, suministro. 6 *fml (emergence - of water, blood)* flujo. 7 *fml (children)* descendencia. 8 *fml (result, outcome)* resultado, consecuencia, desenlace *m*.
▷ *vt* 1 *(book, article)* publicar. 2 *(stamps, shares, banknotes, etc)* emitir. 3 *(passport, visa)* expedir. 4 *(equipment, supplies, etc)* distribuir, repartir, suministrar, proporcionar. 5 *(order, instruction)* dar; *(statement, warning)* dar, hacer público; *(writ, summons)* dictar, expedir; *(decree)* promulgar; *(warrant)* expedir.
▷ *vi* 1 *fml (liquid, blood)* fluir, manar; *(smell, etc)* salir. 2 *fml (result)* resultar (**from**, de), provenir (**from**, de), derivar(se) (**from**, de).
Istanbul [ɪstæn'bʊl] *n* Estambul.
isthmus ['ɪsməs] *n* istmo.
it [ɪt] *pron* 1 *(subject)* él, ella, ello: **where's my supper? it's in the oven!** *¿dónde está mi cena? ¡está en el horno!;* **whose is this coat? it's mine!** *¿de quién es este abrigo? ¡es mío!;* **is it a boy or a girl?** *¿es niño o niña?;* **who's that? who is it? it's me!** *¿quién eres? ¿quién es? ¡soy yo!* 2 *(object - direct)* lo, la; *(- indirect)* le: **I doubt it** *lo dudo;* **I've just got this letter. Can you read it for me?** *acabo de recibir esta carta. ¿Me la puedes leer?;* **do you like skiing? yes, I love it** *¿te gusta esquiar? sí, me encanta;* **she went up to the horse and patted it** *se acercó al caballo y lo acarició;* **can you manage that bag? Give it to me** *¿puedes con esa bolsa? Dámela.* 3 *(after prep)* él, ella, ello: **a vase with flowers in it** *un florero con flores dentro;* **the train was still there so I ran for it** *el tren aún estaba allí así que corrí para cogerlo;* **you're not frightened of it, are you?** *no le tienes miedo, ¿verdad?;* **tell me about it** *explícamelo, cuéntamelo.* 4 *(abstract)* ello: **let's get on with it** *vamos a por ello.* 5 *(impersonal) no se traduce*: **it's cold** *hace frío;* **it's too early** *es demasiado temprano;* **it's six o'clock** *son las seis;* **it's Wednesday** *es miércoles;* **it's cloudy** *está nublado;* **it's not far** *no está lejos;* **it's impossible** *es imposible;* **it's important** *es importante*

it's worth it *vale la pena;* it doesn't matter *no importa;* what's it like? *¿cómo es?;* it cost a fiver *costó cinco libras;* it's true *es verdad;* it seems (that) she failed *parece que suspendió.*

IT ['aɪ'tiː] *abbr* (information technology) informática.

Italian [ɪ'tælɪən] *adj* italiano,-a.
▷ *n* **1** *(person)* italiano,-a. **2** *(language)* italiano.

italic [ɪ'tælɪks] *adj* (letra) cursiva. ■ **in italics** en cursiva. ■ **my italics** la cursiva es mía.

Italy ['ɪtəlɪ] *n* Italia.

ITC ['aɪ'tiː'siː] *abbr* GB (Independent Television Commission) *ente que regula las televisiones privadas.*

Consulta también IBA.

itch [ɪtʃ] *n* **1** MED picazón *f*, picor *m*. **2** *fam fig (strong desire)* deseo, anhelo, ansia: an itch to travel *un deseo de viajar.*
▷ *vi* picar: my feet itch *me pican los pies;* I'm itching all over *me pica todo;* this blanket itches *esta manta pica.*

itchiness ['ɪtʃɪnəs] *n* picor *m*, picazón *m*.

itchy ['ɪtʃɪ] *adj* que pica: this jumper's itchy *este jersey me pica.* ■ **to feel itchy** picar, tener picor. ■ **to get/have itchy feet** tener ganas de viajar.
▲ *comp* itchier, *superl* itchiest.

it'd ['ɪtəd] *contr* **1** it had. **2** it would.

item ['aɪtəm] *n* **1** *(on list)* artículo, cosa; *(in collection)* pieza. **2** *(on agenda)* asunto, punto. **3** *(on bill)* partida, asiento. **4** *(in show)* número. ● **item of clothing** prenda de vestir.
▷ *adv* también.

itemize ['aɪtəmaɪz] *vt* **1** *(contents)* hacer una lista de. **2** *(bill)* detallar.

iterate ['ɪtəreɪt] *vt fml* iterar.

itinerant [ɪ'tɪnərənt] *adj* itinerante, ambulante.

itinerary [aɪ'tɪnᵊrərɪ] *n* itinerario, ruta.
▲ *pl* itineraries.

it'll ['ɪtᵊl] *contr* it will.

its [ɪts] *adj (one thing)* su; *(more than one thing)* sus: the cat washed its paws *el gato se lavó las patas;* the baby's in its pram *el bebé está en su cochecito;* the film has its good points *la película tiene sus puntos buenos.*

it's [ɪts] *contr* **1** → it is. **2** → it has.

itself [ɪt'self] *pron* **1** *(reflexive)* se: the bird preened itself *el pájaro se arregló las plumas;* Barcelona has opened itself up to the sea *Barcelona se ha abierto al mar.* **2** *(emphatic)* en sí: the house itself is quite old *la casa en sí es bastante vieja;* the job itself isn't that difficult *el trabajo en sí no es muy difícil;* she is politeness itself *es la cortesía personificada.* **3** *(after prep)* sí: the committee wants to keep all the profits for itself *el comité quiere guardar todos los beneficios para sí;* each dog has a kennel to itself *cada perro tiene su propia casita;* the idea in itself isn't bad *la idea en sí no está mal;* the first course was a meal in itself *el primer plato ya era una comida de por sí.* ■ **by itself** solo,-a: it switches off by itself *se apaga solo, se apaga automáticamente;* the baby did it all by itself *el niño lo hizo él solo.*

ITV ['aɪ'tiː'viː] *abbr* GB (Independent Television) *conjunto de televisiones privadas.*

I've [aɪv] *contr* I have.

ivory ['aɪvərɪ] *n (substance)* marfil *m*; *(colour)* color *m* marfil.
▷ *adj* de marfil.
▷ *n pl* **ivories** *(objects)* objetos *mpl* de marfil; *(teeth)* dientes *mpl*; *(piano keys)* teclas *fpl*. ■ **an ivory tower** una torre de marfil. ● **Ivory Coast** Costa de Marfil.

ivy ['aɪvɪ] *n* hiedra, yedra. ● **Ivy League** *ocho prestigiosas universidades privadas del nordeste de los Estados Unidos.*

J

J, J [dʒeɪ] *n (the letter)* J, j *f*.

jab [dʒæb] *n* **1** pinchazo; *(with elbow)* codazo. **2** *fam* inyección *f*: **a flu jab** *una inyección contra la gripe.* **3** *(in boxing)* gancho.

▷ *vt* pinchar; *(with elbow)* dar un codazo a.

▲ *pt & pp* **jabbed**, *ger* **jabbing**.

jabber [ˈdʒæbəʳ] *n* parloteo.

▷ *vt* farfullar, decir atropellada e ininteligiblemente: **she jabbered out a confused explanation** *farfulló una explicación confusa e ininteligible.*

▷ *vi* hablar atropellada e ininteligiblemente: **loads of people jabbering away in foreign languages** *un montón de gente parloteando en lenguas extranjeras.*

jack [dʒæk] *n* **1** AUTO gato. **2** *(in cards)* jota; *(Spanish pack)* sota. **3** *(in bowls)* boliche *m*. **4** ELEC enchufe *m*. ● **jack plug** ELEC jack *m*, clavija.

⊙ **to jack in** *vt sep* GB *sl* dejar, colgar.

⊙ **to jack up** *vt sep* **1** *(car)* levantar con gato. **2** *(prices)* subir.

jackal [ˈdʒækɔːl] *n* chacal *m*.

jackdaw [ˈdʒækdɔː] *n* grajilla.

jacket [ˈdʒækɪt] *n* **1** *(in general)* chaqueta; *(of suit)* americana; *(leather, etc)* cazadora. **2** *(of book)* sobrecubierta. **3** US *(of record)* funda. ● **jacket potato** patata asada *(con su piel)*.

jack-knife [ˈdʒæknaɪf] *n* navaja.

▷ *vi (lorry)* dar un coletazo.

jack-of-all-trades [ˈdʒækəvɔːltreɪdz] *n* **1** *(handyman)* manitas *m*. **2** *pej* persona de muchos oficios.

jackpot [ˈdʒækpɒt] *n* (premio) gordo. ■ **to hit the jackpot** tocarle a ALGN el gordo.

Jacuzzi® [dʒˈkuːzɪ] *n* jacuzzi *m*, bañera de hidromasaje.

jade [dʒeɪd] *n* jade *m*.

jaded [ˈdʒeɪdɪd] *adj* agotado,-a, cansado,-a.

jag [dʒæg] *n* GB *fam* juerga, borrachera.

jagged [ˈdʒægɪd] *adj* irregular, dentado,-a.

jaguar [ˈdʒægjʊəʳ] *n* jaguar *m*.

jail [dʒeɪl] *n* cárcel *f*, prisión *f*.

▷ *vt* encarcelar: **he was jailed for life** *lo condenaron a cadena perpetua.*

jailbird [ˈdʒeɪlbɜːd] *n* preso,-a reincidente.

jailbreak [ˈdʒeɪlbreɪk] *n* fuga de la cárcel.

jailer [ˈdʒeɪləʳ] *n* carcelero,-a.

jailhouse [ˈdʒeɪlhaʊs] *n* US cárcel *f*.

Jakarta [ˈdʒəkɑːtə] *n* Yakarta.

jalopy [dʒəˈlɒpɪ] *n fam (car)* cacharro.

▲ *pl* **jalopies**.

jam¹ [dʒæm] *n* **1** mermelada, confitura. **2** *fam (luck)* churra. ● **jam jar** bote *m* de mermelada.

jam² [dʒæm] *n (tight spot)* aprieto, apuro. ■ **to get into a jam** meterse en un apuro.

▷ *vt* **1** *(fill)* abarrotar, atestar: **thousands of people jammed the streets** *miles de personas abarrotaban las calles.* **2** *(cram)* embutir, meter a la fuerza: **she jammed all her things into the bag** *embutió todas sus cosas en la bolsa.* **3** RAD interferir. **4** *(block)* bloquear: **the switchboard was jammed with calls of complaint** *las llamadas de protesta bloquearon la centralita.*

▷ *vi* **1** *(stick)* atrancarse: **the door is jammed, I can't open it** *la puerta se ha atrancado, no puedo abrirla.* **2** *(machine parts)* atascarse, agarrotarse: **the lock has jammed, it won't open** *se ha atascado la cerradura, no abre.* **3** MUS *tocar en una sesión improvisada de jazz o rock.* ■ **to jam the brakes on** pegar un frenazo, frenar de golpe.

Jamaica [dʒəˈmeɪkə] *n* Jamaica.

Jamaican [dʒəˈmeɪkᵊn] *adj* jamaicano,-a.

▷ *n* jamaicano,-a.

jamb [dʒæm] *n* jamba.

jamboree [dʒæmbəˈriː] *n* **1** juerga. **2** *(scout meeting)* reunión *f* de boy scouts.

jam-packed [dʒæmˈpækt] *adj fam* de bote en bote, abarrotado,-a (**with**, de).

jangle [ˈdʒæŋgᵊl] *vi* sonar de un modo discordante.

▷ *vt* hacer sonar de un modo discordante.

▷ *n* sonido discordante.

janitor [ˈdʒænɪtəʳ] *n* conserje *m*, portero.

January [ˈdʒænjʊərɪ] *n* enero.

Para ejemplos de uso, consulta **May**.

Japan [dʒəˈpæn] *n* (el) Japón *m*.

Japanese [dʒæpəˈniːz] *adj* japonés,-esa.

▷ *n* **1** *(person)* japonés,-esa. **2** *(language)* japonés *m*.

jar [dʒɑːʳ] *n* **1** *(glass)* tarro, bote *m*: **a jar of strawberry jam** *un tarro de mermelada de fresa.* **2** *(earthenware)* vasija, tinaja. **3** *(shake, shock)* sacudida: **it gave me a bit of a jar** *me chocó bastante.* **4** *fam (drink)* copa: **let's go and have a few jars!** *¡vamos a tomar unas copas!*

▷ *vt (shake)* golpear, dar un golpe a.

▷ *vi* **1** *(sounds)* chirriar, discordar: **this kind of music jars on my nerves** *este tipo de música me pone los nervios a punta.* **2** *(colours)* no pegar, desentonar.

▲ *pt & pp* **jarred**, *ger* **jarring**.

jargon [ˈdʒɑːgᵊn] *n* jerga, jerigonza.

jasmine [ˈdʒæzmɪn] *n* jazmín *m*.

jasper [ˈdʒæspəʳ] *n* jaspe *m*.

jaundice [ˈdʒɔːndɪs] *n* ictericia.

jaundiced [ˈdʒɔːndɪst] *adj fig* cínico,-a.

jaunt [dʒɔːnt] *n* excursión *f*.

▷ *vi* ir de excursión.

jaunty [ˈdʒɔːntɪ] *adj* garboso,-a.

▲ *comp* **jauntier**, *superl* **jauntiest**.

Java [ˈdʒɑːvə] *n* Java.

Javan [ˈdʒɑːvᵊn] *adj* javanés,-esa.

▷ *n* javanés,-esa.

Javanese [dʒɑːvəˈniːz] *adj* javanés,-esa.
▷ *n* **1** *(person)* javanés,-esa. **2** *(language)* javanés *m*.
avelin [ˈdʒævəlɪn] *n* jabalina. ● **javelin competition** lanzamiento de jabalina.
aw [dʒɔː] *n* **1** ANAT mandíbula. ● **lower jaw** maxilar *m* inferior. ‖ **upper jaw** maxilar *m* superior. **2** ZOOL mandíbula, quijada, carrillera. **3** *fam (talk)* charla: we had a really good jaw *tuvimos una buena charla.*
▷ *vi fam (talk)* charlar, darle a la sinhueso.
awbone [ˈdʒɔːbəʊn] *n* **1** *(of person)* mandíbula, maxilar *m*. **2** *(of animal)* quijada.
awbreaker [ˈdʒɔːbreɪkəʳ] *n sl* trabalenguas *m*.
ay [dʒeɪ] *n* arrendajo común.
aywalker [ˈdʒeɪwɔːlkəʳ] *n* peatón *m* imprudente.
azz [dʒæz] *n* jazz *m*.
▷ *adj* de jazz, jazzístico,-a. ■ **and all that jazz** y demás, y toda la pesca, y todo el rollo. ‖ **don't give me that jazz!** ¡no me vengas con cuentos! ● **jazz band** conjunto de jazz.
◊ **to jazz up** *vt sep (in general)* hacer más alegre, dar vida a; *(party)* animar.
azzy [ˈdʒæzɪ] *adj* **1** *fam fig* llamativo,-a. **2** MUS jazzístico,-a.
▲ *comp* jazzier, *superl* jazziest.
ealous [ˈdʒeləs] *adj* **1** celoso,-a. **2** *(envious)* envidioso,-a. ■ **to be jealous of** SB tener celos de ALGN, estar celoso,-a de ALGN. ‖ **to make** SB **jealous** poner celoso,-a a ALGN.
ealousy [ˈdʒeləsɪ] *n* **1** celos *mpl*. **2** *(envy)* envidia.
▲ *pl* jealousies.
eans [dʒiːnz] *n pl* vaqueros *mpl*, tejanos *mpl*.
eep® [dʒiːp] *n* jeep *m*, todoterreno.
eer [dʒɪəʳ] *vi (mock)* burlarse (at, de), mofarse (at, de).
▷ *vt (boo)* abuchear.
▷ *vi (boo)* abuchear.
▷ *n pl* **jeers** *(booing)* abucheos *mpl*; *(mocking)* burlas *fpl*, mofas *fpl*, befas *fpl*.
eering [ˈdʒɪərɪŋ] *adj* burlón,-ona.
ehovah [dʒɪˈhəʊvə] *n* REL Jehová *m*. ● **Jehovah's Witness** testigo *mf* de Jehová.
ell [dʒel] *vi* cuajar.
ello [ˈdʒeləʊ] *n* US gelatina, jalea.
elly [ˈdʒelɪ] *n* **1** *(in general)* jalea. **2** *(fruit)* gelatina.
▲ *pl* jellies.
ellyfish [ˈdʒelɪfɪʃ] *n* medusa.
▲ *pl* jellyfishes.
eopardize [ˈdʒepədaɪz] *vt* poner en peligro, hacer peligrar.
eopardy [ˈdʒepədɪ] *n* peligro. ■ **to be in jeopardy** estar en peligro, peligrar. ‖ **to put in jeopardy** poner en peligro, hacer peligrar.
erk [dʒɜːk] *n* **1** *(pull)* tirón *m*; *(jolt)* sacudida. **2** *fam* imbécil *mf*, subnormal *mf*. ■ **with a jerk** bruscamente.
vt dar una sacudida a, tirar de.
vi dar una sacudida.
erkin [ˈdʒɜːkɪn] *n* **1** chaleco. **2** *(historically)* jubón *m*.
erky [ˈdʒɜːkɪ] *adj* espasmódico,-a.
▲ *comp* jerkier, *superl* jerkiest.
erry-build [ˈdʒerɪbɪld] *vt* construir mal.
▲ *pt & pp* jerry-built [ˈdʒerɪbɪlt].
errycan [ˈdʒerɪkæn] *n* bidón *m*.
jersey [ˈdʒɜːzɪ] *n* jersey *m*, suéter *m*.
jest [dʒest] *n* broma. ■ **in jest** en broma.
▷ *vi* bromear.
jester [ˈdʒestəʳ] *n* HIST bufón *m*.
Jesuit [ˈdʒezjʊɪt] *n* jesuita *m*.
Jesus [ˈdʒiːzəs] *n* Jesús *m*, Jesucristo.
▷ *interj* **Jesus!** *fam* ¡joder! ● **Jesus Christ** Jesucristo.
jet[1] [dʒet] *n* **1** *(aircraft)* reactor *m*. **2** *(stream)* chorro. **3** *(outlet)* boquilla, mechero. ● **jet engine** reactor *m*, propulsor *m* a chorro. ‖ **jet foil** deslizador *m*. ‖ **jet lag** jet lag *m*, desarreglo horario. ‖ **jet propulsion** propulsión *f* a chorro. ‖ **jet set** la jet set *f*, la jet *f*.
▷ *vi* **1** salir a chorro. **2** *fam* viajar en avión.
jet[2] [dʒet] *n (mineral)* azabache *m*.
jet-black [ˈdʒetˈblæk] *adj* negro,-a como el azabache.
jettison [ˈdʒetɪsənn] *vt* **1** MAR echar por la borda. **2** *fig* deshacerse de. **3** *(idea)* olvidarse de.
jetty [ˈdʒetɪ] *n (stone)* malecón *m*; *(wooden)* embarcadero.
▲ *pl* jetties.
Jew [dʒuː] *n* REL judío,-a.
jewel [ˈdʒuːəl] *n* **1** joya, alhaja. **2** *(stone)* piedra preciosa. **3** *(in watch)* rubí *m*.
jewelled [ˈdʒuəld] *adj* adornado,-a con piedras preciosas.
jeweller [ˈdʒuːələʳ] *n* joyero,-a.
jewellery [ˈdʒuːəlrɪ] *n* joyas *fpl*.
jewelry [ˈdʒuːəlrɪ] *n* US → jewellery.
Jewess [ˈdʒues] *n* judía.
Jewish [ˈdʒuɪʃ] *adj* judío,-a.
Jewry [ˈdʒuərɪ] *n* los judíos *mpl*, el pueblo judío.
jib [dʒɪb] *vi (animal)* plantarse; *(person)* resistirse, negarse: she jibbed at wearing the new uniform *se resistió a llevar el nuevo uniforme.*
Jibouti [dʒɪˈbuːtɪ] *n* Djibuti.
jiffy [ˈdʒɪfɪ] *n fam* instante *m*. ■ **in a jiffy** en un santiamén.
▲ *pl* jiffies.
jig [dʒɪg] *n* **1** giga. **2** TECH plantilla.
▷ *vi* bailar la giga.
▲ *pt & pp* jigged, *ger* jigging.
jigsaw [ˈdʒɪgsɔː] *n* **1** *(saw)* sierra de vaivén. **2** *(puzzle)* rompecabezas *m*, puzzle *m*.
jilt [dʒɪlt] *vi* abandonar, dejar plantado,-a a.
jingle [ˈdʒɪŋgəl] *n* **1** tintineo. **2** TV tonadilla publicitaria.
▷ *vi* tintinear.
▷ *vt* hacer sonar.
jingoistic [dʒɪŋgəʊˈɪstɪk] *adj* patriotero,-a, jingoísta *mf*.
jinks [dʒɪŋks] *n pl* **high jinks** jolgorio, juerga. ■ **to get up to high jinks** organizar una juerga.
jinx [dʒɪŋks] *n* **1** *(person)* gafe *mf*. **2** *(bad luck)* mala suerte *f*.
▷ *vt* gafar.
jitters [ˈdʒɪtəz] *n pl fam* nervios *mpl*. ■ **to get the jitters** ponerse nervioso,-a.
jittery [ˈdʒɪtərɪ] *adj* nervioso,-a.
jive [dʒaɪv] *n* **1** *(dance)* swing *m*. **2** *(back talk)* rollo. **3** US *sl (lies)* embustes *mpl*. ● **jive talk** US *sl* argot *m*, jerga.
▷ *vi* bailar el swing.
job [dʒɒb] *n* **1** *(employment)* empleo, (puesto de) trabajo: what's your job? *¿en qué trabajas?* **2** *(piece of work)* trabajo; *(task)* tarea: he did a good job (of work) *hizo*

un buen trabajo. **3** *(difficult thing)* trabajo: **it snowed so much that we had a job to get home** *nevó tanto que nos costó trabajo llegar a casa.* **4** *(duty)* deber *m*, responsabilidad *f*, misión *f*: **it's your job to lock all the doors** *es responsabilidad tuya cerrar todas las puertas.* **5** *fam (robbery)* robo; *(holdup)* atraco: **he did four bank jobs before he got caught** *atracó cuatro bancos antes de que lo cogieran.* ■ **it's a good job that ...** menos mal que... ‖ **just the job!** ¡perfecto!, ¡estupendo! ‖ **on the job** trabajando. ‖ **out of a job** parado,-a. ● **job centre** oficina de empleo. ‖ **job hunting** búsqueda de trabajo.

jobber ['dʒɒbəʳ] *n* GB corredor,-ra de bolsa.

jobbing ['dʒɒbɪŋ] *adj* GB que trabaja a destajo: **a jobbing plumber** *un fontanero que trabaja a destajo.*

jobless ['dʒɒbləs] *adj* parado,-a.

jockey ['dʒɒkɪ] *n* jockey *m*.

▷ *vt* persuadir: **we finally managed to jockey them into signing the contract** *por fin pudimos convencerles para que firmaran el contrato.* ■ **to jockey for position** maniobrar para colocarse en buena posición.

jocose [dʒə'kəʊs] *adj* jocoso,-a.

jocular ['dʒɒkjələʳ] *adj (person)* gracioso,-a; *(comment)* humorístico,-a.

jog [dʒɒg] *n* **1** *(push)* empujoncito, sacudida. **2** *(pace)* trote *m*.

▷ *vt* empujar, sacudir.

▷ *vi* hacer footing. ■ **to go for a jog** (ir a) hacer footing. ‖ **to jog** SB**'s memory** refrescarle la memoria a ALGN.

⊙ **to jog along** *vi* **1** andar a trote corto. **2** *fig* ir tirando.

jogging ['dʒɒgɪŋ] *n* footing *m*. ■ **to go jogging** hacer footing.

joggle ['dʒɒgᵊl] *vt* menear.

john [dʒɒn] *n* US váter *m*.

join [dʒɔɪn] *vt* **1** *(bring together)* juntar, unir. **2** *(connect)* unir, conectar: **the two cities are joined by a bridge** *las dos ciudades están unidas por un puente.* **3** *(company, etc)* incorporarse a: **Mr Osuna joined the company last year** *el Sr Osuna se incorporó a la empresa el año pasado.* **4** *(armed forces)* alistarse en; *(police)* ingresar en. **5** *(club)* hacerse socio,-a de. **6** *(party)* afiliarse a, ingresar en. **7** *(be with* SB*)* reunirse con, unirse a: **would you like to join us for the evening?** *¿les gustaría pasar la tarde con nosotros?*

▷ *vi* **1** juntarse, unirse. **2** *(rivers)* confluir; *(roads)* juntarse, empalmar.

▷ *n* juntura: **you can't see the join** *no se ve la juntura.*

⊙ **to join in** *vi* participar.

▷ *vt insep (debate)* intervenir en.

⊙ **to join up** *vi* alistarse.

joiner ['dʒɔɪnəʳ] *n* carpintero *que se dedica a puertas, ventanas, etc.*

joinery ['dʒɔɪnərɪ] *n* carpintería.

joint [dʒɔɪnt] *n* **1** junta, juntura, unión *f*; *(wood)* ensambladura. **2** ANAT articulación *f*. **3** CULIN *(raw)* corte *m* de carne *para asar*; *(when cooked)* asado. **4** *sl (drugs)* porro. **5** *sl (place)* antro, tugurio.

▷ *adj* colectivo,-a, mutuo,-a. ● **joint account** cuenta conjunta, cuenta indistinta. ‖ **joint owner** copropietario,-a.

▷ *vt* CULIN descuartizar.

jointed ['dʒɔɪntɪd] *adj* **1** articulado,-a. **2** *(chicken, etc)* cortado,-a a piezas.

jointly ['dʒɔɪntlɪ] *adv* conjuntamente.

joke [dʒəʊk] *n* **1** chiste *m*: **shall I tell you a joke?** *¿te cuento un chiste?* **2** *(practical)* broma: **John can't take a joke** *John no aguanta una broma.* **3** *(person)* payaso. ■ **to make a joke of** STH reírse de ALGO. ‖ **to play a joke on** SB gastar una broma a ALGN. ‖ **to tell a joke** contar un chiste.

▷ *vi* bromear. ■ **you must be joking!** ¡venga ya!

joker ['dʒəʊkəʳ] *n* **1** bromista *mf*: **some joker put salt in the sugar** *algún gracioso ha puesto sal en el azúcar.* **2** *(card)* comodín *m*. **3** *fam* idiota *mf*.

jolly ['dʒɒlɪ] *adj* **1** *(cheerful)* alegre, animado,-a: **she was a very jolly person** *era una persona muy animada.* **2** *dated (amusing)* divertido,-a: **we had a terribly jolly time** *nos divertimos muchísimo.*

▲ *comp* **jollier**, *superl* **jolliest**.

▷ *adv* GB *fam* muy: **it's jolly difficult** *es la mar de difícil*; **they played jolly well** *jugaron fenomenal.*

⊙ **to jolly along** *vt sep* dar ánimos a, animar.

⊙ **to jolly up** *vt sep* alegrar, animar.

▲ *pt & pp* **jollied**, *ger* **jollying**.

jolt [dʒəʊlt] *n* **1** sacudida. **2** *(fright)* susto.

▷ *vt* sacudir.

▷ *vi* dar tumbos.

▷ *vt fig* dar un choque a: **I was jolted out of my daydreams by a loud noise** *un fuerte ruido me sacó de mis ensoñaciones.*

Jordan ['dʒɔːdᵊn] *n* **1** *(country)* Jordania.

Jordanian [dʒɔː'deɪnɪən] *adj* jordano,-a.

▷ *n* jordano,-a.

joss stick ['dʒɒsstɪk] *n* varita de incienso.

jostle ['dʒɒsᵊl] *vt* empujar.

▷ *vi* **1** dar empujones: **the crowds jostled to get into the stadium** *el gentío daba empujones para entrar en el estadio.* **2** *fig* competir.

jot [dʒɒt] *n* pizca: **I don't care a jot** *me importa un bledo.*

▷ *vt* apuntar, anotar.

▲ *pt & pp* **jotted**, *ger* **jotting**.

⊙ **to jot down** *vt sep* apuntar.

jotter ['dʒɒtəʳ] *n* GB bloc *m*.

joule [dʒʊːl] *n* julio.

journal ['dʒɜːnᵊl] *n* **1** *(magazine)* revista. **2** *(diary)* diario.

journalism ['dʒɜːnᵊlɪzᵊm] *n* periodismo.

journalist ['dʒɜːnᵊlɪst] *n* periodista *mf*.

journey ['dʒɜːnɪ] *n* viaje *m*: **it's a 100 mile journey** *un viaje de 100 millas.*

▷ *vi* viajar.

jovial ['dʒəʊvɪəl] *adj* jovial, alegre.

jowl [dʒaʊl] *n (cheek)* carrillo.

joy [dʒɔɪ] *n* **1** alegría, júbilo: **her face was a picture of joy** *estaba radiante de alegría.* **2** *fam (satisfaction)* satisfacción *f*; *(luck)* suerte *f*; *(success)* éxito: **you can complain all you like, but you'll get no joy** *quéjate todo lo que quieras, pero no te servirá de nada.*

joyful ['dʒɔɪfʊl] *adj* jubiloso,-a, alegre.

joyous ['dʒɔɪəs] *adj lit* alegre.

joyride ['dʒɔɪraɪd] *n fam paseo en un coche robado.*

joystick ['dʒɔɪstɪk] *n* **1** AV palanca de mando. COMPUT joystick *m*.

jubilant ['dʒʊːbɪlənt] *adj* radiante de alegría.

jubilation [dʒʊːbɪ'leɪʃᵊn] *n* júbilo.

jubilee ['dʒʊːbɪliː] *n* **1** festejos *mpl*. **2** *(anniversary)* aniversario.

udder ['dʒʌdəʳ] *vi* vibrar *(violentamente)*.
▷ *n* vibración *f (violenta)*.
udge [dʒʌdʒ] *n* 1 *(man)* juez *m*; *(woman)* juez *f*, jueza. 2 *(in competition)* jurado, miembro del jurado.
▷ *vt* 1 *(court case)* juzgar. 2 *(calculate)* calcular: **it's hard to judge how much we need** *es difícil calcular cuánto necesitamos*. 3 *(consider)* considerar: **the meat was judged unfit for human consumption** *la carne se consideró no apta para el consumo humano*. 4 *(competition)* hacer de jurado en: **the competition was judged by my mother** *mi madre hizo de jurado en el concurso*.
udgement ['dʒʌdʒmənt] [Also written **judgment**.] *n* 1 *(ability)* (buen) juicio, (buen) criterio. 2 *(opinion)* juicio, opinión *f*: **in my judgement ...** *a mi juicio...* 3 *(decision)* fallo. 4 *(criticism)* crítica. ■ **to reserve judgement** reservarse la opinión.
udicial [dʒuː'dɪʃəl] *adj* judicial.
udiciary [dʒuː'dɪʃərɪ] *n* judicatura.
udicious [dʒuː'dɪʃəs] *adj* sensato,-a, prudente.
udo ['dʒuːdəu] *n* yudo, judo.
ug [dʒʌg] *n* 1 jarra, jarro. 2 *sl (prison)* chirona.
uggernaut ['dʒʌgənɔːt] *n* GB camión *m* pesado.
uggle ['dʒʌgəl] *vi* 1 hacer juegos malabares (**with**, con). 2 *fig (figures, etc)* jugar (**with**, con).
uggler ['dʒʌgələʳ] *n* malabarista *mf*.
ugular ['dʒʌgjələʳ] *adj* yugular.
▷ *n* yugular *f*. ● **jugular vein** vena yugular.
uice [dʒuːs] *n* 1 *(gen)* jugo. 2 *(of fruit)* zumo, AM jugo. 3 *fam (petrol)* gasolina; *(electricity)* fuerza, luz *f*. ● **juice extractor** licuadora.
uicy ['dʒuːsɪ] *adj* 1 jugoso,-a. 2 *fam (gossip, etc)* picante, escabroso,-a.
▲ *comp* **juicier**, *superl* **juiciest**.
ukebox ['dʒuːkbɒks] *n* máquina de discos.
uly [dʒuː'laɪ] *n* julio.
Para ejemplos de uso, consulta **May**.
umble ['dʒʌmbəl] *n* revoltijo, mezcolanza. ● **jumble sale** rastrillo benéfico.
▷ *vt* desordenar.
umbo ['dʒʌmbəu] *adj* gigante.
▷ *n* [Also **jumbo jet**.] *(plane)* jumbo.
ump [dʒʌmp] *n* 1 salto: **a parachute jump** *un salto en paracaídas*. 2 *(in prices, etc)* salto, aumento importante, disparo: **there's been a tremendous jump in profits** *ha habido un aumento importante de los beneficios*. 3 *(fence)* valla, obstáculo: **the horse refused at the first jump** *el caballo se plantó en el primer obstáculo*. ● **jump seat** asiento plegable. ‖ **jump suit** mono.
▷ *vi* 1 saltar. 2 *(rise sharply)* dar un salto: **inflation jumped 2% last month** *la inflación dio un salto de un 2% el mes pasado*.
▷ *vt* saltar: **he tried to jump the wall, but it was too high** *intentó saltar el muro, pero era demasiado alto*. ■ **to jump rope** US saltar a la comba. ‖ **to jump the lights** saltarse el semáforo en rojo. ‖ **to jump the queue** colarse.
to jump at *vt insep* aceptar sin pensarlo: **when they offered him the job, he jumped at it** *cuando le ofrecieron el trabajo lo aceptó sin pensar*.
umper[1] ['dʒʌmpəʳ] *n* 1 GB jersey *m*. 2 US *(skirt)* pichi *m*.
umper[2] ['dʒʌmpəʳ] *n* SP saltador,-ra.
umpy ['dʒʌmpɪ] *adj* nervioso,-a.
▲ *comp* **jumpier**, *superl* **jumpiest**.

junction ['dʒʌŋkʃən] *n* 1 *(railways)* empalme *m*. 2 *(roads)* cruce *m*. 3 *(motorway - entry)* acceso; *(- exit)* salida.
juncture ['dʒʌŋktʃəʳ] *n* coyuntura.
June [dʒuːn] *n* junio.
Para ejemplos de uso, consulta **May**.
jungle ['dʒʌŋgəl] *n* selva, jungla.
junior ['dʒuːnɪəʳ] *adj* 1 *(in rank)* subalterno,-a. 2 *(in age)* menor, más joven. 3 US *(after name)* hijo.
▷ *n* 1 *(in rank)* subalterno,-a. 2 *(in age)* menor *mf*: **she is three years my junior** *tiene tres años menos que yo*. 3 GB alumno,-a de EGB. 4 estudiante *mf* de penúltimo curso. 5 US hijo: **where's your mom, Junior?** *¿dónde está tu mamá, hijo?* ● **junior college** US *colegio universitario para los dos primeros cursos*. ‖ **junior high school** US instituto de enseñanza secundaria. ‖ **junior school** GB escuela primaria.
junk [dʒʌŋk] *n* trastos *mpl*. ● **junk food** comida basura. ‖ **junk mail** correo basura. ‖ **junk shop** chamarilería.
junkie ['dʒʌŋkɪ] *n sl* yonqui *mf*.
junta ['dʒʌntə] *n* POL junta (militar).
Jupiter ['dʒuːpɪtəʳ] *n* Júpiter *m*.
Jurassic [dʒu'ræsɪk] *adj* jurásico,-a.
juridical [dʒuː'rɪdɪkəl] *adj* jurídico,-a.
jurisdiction [dʒuərɪs'dɪkʃən] *n* jurisdicción *f*.
jurist ['dʒuərɪst] *n* jurista *mf*.
juror ['dʒuərəʳ] *n* jurado.
jury ['dʒuərɪ] *n* jurado.
▲ *pl* **juries**.
just[1] [dʒʌst] *adj* 1 *(fair)* justo,-a. 2 *(justifiable)* fundado,-a, justificado,-a. 3 *(deserved)* merecido,-a. ■ **to get one's just desserts** llevar su merecido.
just[2] [dʒʌst] *adv* 1 *(exactly)* exactamente, precisamente, justo: **this is just what I needed** *esto es justo lo que necesitaba*. 2 *(only)* solamente, solo: **no sugar for me, please, just milk** *no quiero azúcar, gracias, solo leche*. 3 *(barely)* apenas, por poco: **I ran all the way and (only) just caught the bus** *fui corriendo y cogí el autobús por poco*. 4 *(right now)* en este momento: **I'm just finishing it** *lo acabo ahora mismo*. 5 *(simply)* sencillamente: **we could just stay here and wait for her** *pues, sencillamente podríamos quedarnos aquí y esperarla*. 6 *(for emphasis)*: **he's just as clever as you are** *él es tan inteligente como tú*. 7 *(used to interrupt)*: **just shut up, will you?** *¡cállese, por favor!* 8 *fam (really)* realmente, verdaderamente: **the weather's just marvellous** *hace un tiempo realmente maravilloso*. ■ **just about** prácticamente. ‖ **just in case** por si acaso. ‖ **just like that!** ¡sin más! ‖ **just so** 1 *(tidy)* ordenado,-a, arreglado,-a. 2 *(as a reply)* sí, exactamente. ‖ **just then** en ese momento.
▷ *phr* **to have just** + *pres part* acabar de + *infin*: **he has just telephoned** *acaba de telefonear*.
justice ['dʒʌstɪs] *n* 1 justicia. 2 *(judge - man)* juez *m*; *(- woman)* juez *f*, jueza.
justifiable [dʒʌstɪ'faɪəbəl] *adj* justificable.
justification [dʒʌstɪfɪ'keɪʃən] *n* justificación *f*.
justified ['dʒʌstɪfaɪd] *adj* justificado,-a.
justify ['dʒʌstɪfaɪ] *vt* justificar.
▲ *pt & pp* **justified**, *ger* **justifying**.
jut [dʒʌt] *vi* sobresalir, proyectarse.
▲ *pt & pp* **jutted**, *ger* **jutting**.
juvenile ['dʒuːvənaɪl] *adj* 1 juvenil. 2 *(childish)* infantil.
▷ *n* menor *mf*.
juxtapose ['dʒʌkstəpəuz] *vt* yuxtaponer.

K

K, k [keɪ] *n (the letter)* K, k *f.*
Kaiser ['kaɪzəʳ] *n* káiser *m.*
kale [keɪl] *n* col *f* rizada.
kaleidoscope [kə'laɪdəskəʊp] *n* calidoscopio.
kamikaze [kæmɪ'kɑːzɪ] *n* kamikaze *m.*
▷ *adj* kamikaze.
Kampuchea [kæmpʊ'tʃɪə] *n* Kampuchea.
Kampuchean [kæmpʊ'tʃɪən] *adj* kampucheo,-a.
▷ *n* kampucheo,-a.
kangaroo [kæŋgə'ruː] *n* canguro.
▲ *pl* kangaroos.
kaolin ['keɪəlɪn] *n* caolín *m.*
kaput [kə'pʊt] *adj fam* roto,-a, estropeado,-a.
karaoke [kærɪ'əʊkɪ] *n* karaoke *m.*
karate [kə'rɑːtɪ] *n* kárate *m.*
karma ['kɑːmə] *n* karma *m.*
karstic ['kɑːstɪk] *adj* kárstico,-a.
kasbah ['kæzbɑː] *n* casba, casbah *f.*
Kazakh [kæ'zæk] *adj* kazajio,-a.
▷ *n* **1** *(person)* kazajio,-a. **2** *(language)* kazajio.
Kazakhstan [kæzæk'stæn] *n* Kazajstán.
kazoo [kə'zuː] *n* mirlitón *m.*
▲ *pl* kazoos.
kebab [kɪ'bæb] *n* pincho moruno, broqueta.
kedgeree ['kedʒəriː] *n plato de pescado, arroz y huevo duro.*
keel [kiːl] *n* quilla.
⊙ **to keel over** *vi (ship)* zozobrar; *(person)* desplomarse.
keen [kiːn] *adj* **1** *(eager)* entusiasta, aficionado,-a: **he's a very keen pupil** (US **student**) *es un alumno muy entusiasta.* **2** *(sharp - mind, senses, etc)* agudo,-a, vivo,-a; *(- look)* penetrante; *(- wind)* cortante; *(- edge, point)* afilado,-a. **3** *(feeling)* profundo,-a, intenso,-a. **4** *(competition)* fuerte, reñido,-a. **5** *(price)* competitivo,-a. ■ **to be as keen as mustard** ser muy entusiasta. ‖ **to be keen on** STH ser aficionado,-a a ALGO, gustarle ALGO a ALGN. ‖ **to be keen on** SB gustarle alguien a ALGN. ‖ **to take a keen interest in** mostrar un gran interés por.
keenly ['kiːnlɪ] *adv (feel)* profundamente, intensamente; *(look)* atentamente; *(work)* con entusiasmo, con interés.
keep [kiːp] *n* **1** *(board)* sustento, mantenimiento: **to earn one's keep** *ganarse el pan.* **2** *(of castle)* torreón *m,* torre *f* del homenaje.
▷ *vt* **1** *(not throw away)* guardar. **2** *(not give back)* quedarse con: **keep the change** *quédese con el cambio.* **3** *(have)* tener; *(carry)* llevar. **4** *(look after, save)* guardar: **can you keep me a loaf of bread for Friday?** *¿me guarda una barra de pan para el viernes?* **5** *(put away, store)* guardar: **where do you keep the glasses?** *¿dónde guardas los vasos?* **6** *(reserve)* reservar: **I keep the chocolates for special occasions** *reservo los bombone para las ocasiones especiales.* **7** *(detain)* retener, hace esperar; *(hold up)* entretener: **she kept me talking fo hours** *me entretuvo hablando durante horas.* **8** *(shop hotel, etc)* tener, llevar: **they keep a small hotel on th coast** *tienen un pequeño hotel en la costa.* **9** *(have i stock)* tener, vender. **10** *(support)* mantener. **11** *(ani mals)* tener: **children love keeping pets** *a los niños le encanta tener animales de compañía.* **12** *(promise* cumplir. **13** *(secret)* guardar: **can you keep a secret** *¿sabes guardar un secreto?* **14** *(appointment)* acudir a no faltar a: **please phone if you are unable to kee your appointment** *por favor, llame si no puede acud a la visita.* **15** *(order)* mantener. **16** *(tradition)* obse var. **17** *(with adj, verb, etc)* mantener: **these doo must be kept locked** *estas puertas deben manteners cerradas.*
▷ *vi* **1** *(do repeatedly)* no dejar de; *(do continuously)* s guir, continuar: **she was exhausted but kept swim ming** *estaba agotada pero siguió nadando.* **2** *(sta fresh)* conservarse. **3** *(continue in direction)* continua seguir: **keep left/right** *circula por la izquierda/derech* **4** *(with adj, verb, etc)* quedarse, permanecer: **we mu keep calm** *debemos mantener la calma.* ■ **how are yo keeping?** ¿cómo estás? ‖ **keep it up!** ¡ánimo! ‖ **to kee going** seguir (adelante). ‖ **to keep one's head** no pe der la cabeza. ‖ **to keep quiet** callarse, no hacer ru do. ‖ **to keep** SB **from doing** STH impedir que ALGN hag ALGO. ‖ **to keep** STH **from** SB ocultar ALGO a ALGN.
⊙ **to keep at** *vt insep (work, study, etc)* perseverar e algo; *(person)* no dejar en paz, machacar.
⊙ **to keep away** *vt sep* mantener a distancia (**fro** de), no dejar a uno acercarse (**from**, a): **keep plast bags away from children** *mantenga las bolsas de plá tico fuera del alcance de los niños.*
▷ *vi* mantenerse a distancia, evitar contacto con: **kee away from the fire** *manténganse alejados del fuego.*
⊙ **to keep back** *vt sep* **1** *(money, etc)* retener, guarda *(information)* ocultar, no revelar; *(emotions)* contene **2** *(enemy)* tener a raya; *(work, progress, etc)* estorba impedir. **3** mantener atrás, contener.
▷ *vi* mantenerse atrás, alejarse: **children! keep back fro the edge!** *¡niños! ¡alejaos del borde!*
⊙ **to keep down** *vt sep (oppress)* oprimir, sujeta *(price, voice)* mantener bajo; *(growth, spending)* lim tar, controlar; *(food)* mantener en el estómago.
▷ *vi (lie low)* agacharse, no levantar la cabeza.
⊙ **to keep from** *vt insep (refrain from)* abstenerse d guardarse de.
⊙ **to keep in** *vt sep* **1** *(gen)* no dejar salir; *(in schoo* hacer quedar. **2** *(feelings)* contener. **3** *(pay for)* cc

tear, pagar: **he doesn't earn enough to keep his wife in hats** *no gana para pagar los sombreros de su mujer.*
to keep in with *vi* mantener buenas relaciones con.
to keep off *vi (stay away)* mantenerse a distancia; *(of rain)* no llover: **if the rain keeps off, we'll be able to play tennis** *si no llueve, podremos jugar a tenis.*
vt sep (make stay away) no dejar entrar, no dejar acercarse; *(avoid)* no tocar, no hablar de: **"Keep off the grass"** *"No pisar la hierba".*
to keep on *vi* seguir, continuar.
vt sep (clothes) no quitarse.
to keep on about *vi* insistir en, no parar de hablar de.
to keep on at *vt insep* no dejar en paz, machacar.
to keep out *vt sep* no dejar entrar, no dejar pasar.
vi no entrar.
to keep out of *vi (place)* no entrar en; *(affair)* no meterse en.
to keep to *vt insep (rules)* atenerse a, cumplir; *(path)* no dejar, no salir de.
to keep together *vi* mantenerse juntos,-as, no separarse.
to keep under *vt sep* tener subyugado.
to keep up *vt sep* **1** *(gen)* mantener, seguir. **2** *(from sleeping)* mantener despierto,-a, tener en vela.
vi **1** *(not fall behind)* aguantar el ritmo. **2** *(stay in touch)* mantenerse al día.
▲ *pt & pp* **kept** [kept].
to keep up with *vt insep* **1** *(not fall behind)* seguir. **2** *(be aware of)* mantenerse al corriente de. **3** *(stay in touch)* mantener el contacto con.
eeper ['ki:pə[r]] *n* **1** *(in zoo)* guardián,-ana. **2** *(in park)* guarda *mf.* **3** *(in museum)* conservador,-ra; *(in archives)* archivador,-ra.
eeping ['ki:pɪŋ] *n* cuidado, custodia: **he left his keys in his mother's keeping** *le dejó las llaves a su madre.* ■ **in keeping with** conforme a, en armonía con. ■ **out of keeping with** en desacuerdo con.
eepsake ['ki:pseɪk] *n* recuerdo.
g [keg] *n* barrilete *m*, cuñete *m.*
n [ken] *n* conocimiento.
vt (Scot) saber, conocer. ■ **beyond one's ken** incomprensible para uno.
nnel ['kenəl] *n* caseta del perros.
n pl **kennels** *(boarding)* residencia *f sing* canina.
nya ['kenjə] *n* Kenia.
nyan ['kenjən] *adj* keniano,-a.
n keniano,-a.
pi ['keɪpi:] *n* quepis *m.*
pt [kept]*pt & pp* → **keep.**
rb [kɜ:b] *n* bordillo.
rchief ['kɜ:tʃɪf] *n* pañuelo.
rmes ['kɜ:mɪz] *n* quermes *m.*
rmis ['kɜ:mɪs] *n* quermés *f.*
rnel ['kɜ:nəl] *n* **1** *(of nut, fruit)* semilla. **2** *fig* núcleo, grano.
rosene ['kerəsi:n] *n* US queroseno.
tchup ['ketʃəp] *n* ketchup *m*, catsup *m.*
ttle ['ketəl] *n* tetera *(para hervir agua)*, hervidor *m*: **will you put the kettle on to make some tea?** *¿quieres poner el agua a hervir para hacer té?* ■ **that's a different kettle of fish** eso es harina de otro costal.
ttledrum ['ketəldrʌm] *n* timbal *m.*

key[1] [ki:] *n* **1** *(of door, car, etc)* llave *f.* **2** *(of clock, mechanical)* llave *f.* **3** *fig (to problem, map, code)* clave *f*; *(to exercises)* respuestas *fpl.* **4** *(on computer, piano, etc)* tecla. **5** MUS *(on wind instrument)* llave *f*, pistón *m*; *(set of notes)* clave *f*; *(tone, style)* tono. ● **key ring** llavero.
▷ *adj* clave, principal: **tourism is the country's key industry** *el turismo es la industria principal del país.*
▷ *vt* introducir, teclear: **she keyed in the data** *introdujo los datos.*
⊙ **to key to** *vt sep* adaptar.
key[2] [ki:] *n* GEOG cayo, isleta.
keyboard ['ki:bɔ:d] *n* teclado. ● **keyboard player** teclista *mf.*
▷ *n pl* **keyboards** teclados *mpl.*
keyed up [ki:d'ʌp] *adj* nervioso,-a, excitado,-a.
keyhole ['ki:həʊl] *n* ojo de la cerradura.
keynote ['ki:nəʊt] *n* **1** tónica, clave *f.* **2** *(mus)* tónica.
keystone ['ki:stəʊn] *n* **1** ARCH clave *f.* **2** *fig* piedra angular.
kg ['kɪləgræm] *abbr* **(kilogram, kilogramme)** kilo, kilogramo; *(abbreviation)* kg.
khaki ['kɑ:kɪ] *n* caqui *m.*
▷ *adj* caqui.
kHz ['kɪləhɜ:ts] *abbr* **(kilohertz)** kilohercio, kilohercios; *(abbreviation)* kHz.
kibbutz [kɪ'bʊts] *n* kibutz *m.*
kick [kɪk] *n* **1** *(by person)* puntapié *m*, patada: **2** *(sp)* golpe *m*, tiro. **3** *(by animal)* coz *f.* **4** *fam (pleasure)* diversión *f*, emoción *f*: **he gets a kick out of playing basketball** *se divierte jugando al baloncesto.* **5** *(of drink)* fuerza: **this cocktail's got a real kick to it** *este cóctel es muy fuerte.* **6** *(of gun)* culatazo.
▷ *vt* **1** *(hit ball)* dar un puntapié a, golpear, golpear con el pie; *(score)* marcar. **2** *(hit person)* dar una patada a; *(move legs)* patalear. **3** *(by animal)* dar coces a, cocear.
▷ *vi (gun)* dar un culatazo.
⊙ **to kick against** STH *vt insep* protestar contra, reaccionar contra.
⊙ **to kick around** *vi (exist, be there)* andar por ahí.
▷ *vt sep (discuss ideas, etc)* dar vueltas a.
⊙ **to kick in** *vt sep* romper a patadas.
⊙ **to kick off** *vi (sp)* sacar, hacer el saque inicial; *(begin)* empezar, comenzar.
▷ *vt sep* **1** *(begin)* empezar, comenzar, iniciar. **2** *(remove - shoes)* quitarse.
⊙ **to kick out** *vt sep* echar.
kick-off ['kɪkɒf] *n* SP saque *m* inicial.
kick-start ['kɪkstɑ:t] *n* arranque *m.*
▷ *vt (start engine)* arrancar, poner en marcha; *(begin, launch)* dar un impulso a.
kid[1] [kɪd] *n* **1** *fam* crío,-a, niño,-a, chico,-a, chaval,-la. **2** *(animal)* cabrito. **3** *(leather)* cabritilla. ■ **to treat** SB **with kid gloves** tratar a ALGN con guantes de seda.
▷ *adj (brother, sister)* menor.
kid[2] [kɪd] *vt* **1** *(deceive, tease)* tomar el pelo a, engañar. **2** *(fool OS)* engañarse a sí mismo, hacerse ilusiones.
▷ *vi* estar de broma: **you're kidding!** *¡estás de broma!, ¡no me digas!*; **no kidding!** *¡en serio!*
kidnap ['kɪdnæp] *vt* secuestrar, raptar.
▲ *pt & pp* **kidnapped**, *ger* **kidnapping.**
kidnapper ['kɪdnæpə[r]] *n* secuestrador,-ra.

kidnapping ['kɪdnæpɪŋ] *n* secuestro.
kidney ['kɪdnɪ] *n* riñón *m*. ● **kidney disease** enfermedad *f* renal. ‖ **kidney machine** riñón *m* artificial.
kill [kɪl] *n (act)* matanza; *(animal)* pieza.
▷ *vt* **1** matar, asesinar. **2** *fig (hope, conversation, etc)* destruir, acabar con; *(pain)* aliviar. **3** *(hurt)* doler mucho: **my back's killing me** *me duele mucho la espalda.* ■ **to kill** OS matarse, suicidarse. ‖ **to kill** OS **laughing** morirse de risa. ‖ **to kill time** pasar el rato, matar el tiempo. ‖ **to kill two birds with one stone** matar dos pájaros de un tiro. ‖
⊙ **to kill off** *vt sep* exterminar, rematar.
killer ['kɪlə^r] *n (person)* asesino,-a; *(thing)* mortal, que mata. ● **killer whale** orca.
killing ['kɪlɪŋ] *n* matanza; *(of person)* asesinato. ■ **to make a killing** ganar una fortuna, hacer el negocio del siglo.
▷ *adj fig* agotador,-ra, duro,-a.
killjoy ['kɪldʒɔɪ] *n* aguafiestas *mf*.
kiln [kɪln] *n* horno.
kilo ['ki:ləʊ] *n* kilo.
▲ *pl* **kilos.**
kilobyte ['kɪləbaɪt] *n* kilobyte.
kilocalorie ['kɪləkælərɪ] *n* kilocaloría.
kilogram ['kɪləgræm] *n* kilogramo.
kilogramme ['kɪləgræm] *n* US ⟶ **kilogram.**
kilohertz ['kɪləhɜ:ts] *n* kilohercio.
kiloliter ['kɪləli:tə^r] *n* US ⟶ **kilolitre.**
kilolitre ['kɪləli:tə^r] *n* kilolitro.
kilometer [kɪ'lɒmɪtə^r] *n* US ⟶ **kilometre.**
kilometre [kɪ'lɒmɪtə^r] *n* kilómetro.
kilowatt ['kɪləwɒt] *n* kilowatt *m*, kilovatio.
kilt [kɪlt] *n* falda escocesa.
kimono [kɪ'məʊnəʊ] *n* quimono.
▲ *pl* **kimonos.**
kin [kɪn] *n* parientes *mpl*, familia. ● **next of kin** pariente *m* más próximo.
kind [kaɪnd] *adj (person)* amable: **she is the sweetest, kindest person I know** *es la persona más dulce y amable que conozco;* **that's very kind of you** *eres muy amable.*
▷ *n (sort)* tipo, género, clase *f*: **what kind of ...?** *¿qué clase de ...?* ■ **to be two of a kind** ser tal para cual. ‖ **to pay in kind 1** pagar en especie. **2** *(treatment)* pagar con la misma moneda.
▷ *adv* **kind of** bastante, algo, un poco: **it's kind of difficult** *es un poco difícil;* **have you finished? – Kind of ...** *¿has acabado? –Más o menos;* **... and that kind of thing ...** *y cosas por el estilo.*
kindergarten ['kɪndəgɑ:tᵊn] *n* parvulario, guardería.
kind-hearted [kaɪnd'hɑ:tɪd] *adj* bondadoso,-a.
kindle ['kɪndᵊl] *vt* encender.
kindly ['kaɪndlɪ] *adj* bondadoso,-a, amable.
▲ *comp* **kindlier,** *superl* **kindliest.**
▷ *adv* **1** con amabilidad: **she very kindly lent me £5** *tuvo la amabilidad de prestarme cinco libras.* **2** *(please)* por favor: **kindly shut up!** *¡haz el favor de callarte!* ■ **not to take kindly to** SB/STH no gustar de ALGO/ALGN: **she doesn't take kindly to being told what to do** *no le gusta nada que le digan lo que tiene que hacer.* ‖ **to look kindly on** mirar con buenos ojos.
kindness ['kaɪndnəs] *n* **1** bondad *f*, amabilidad *f*. *(favour)* favor *m*.
kindred ['kɪndrəd] *n* familiares *mpl*.
▷ *adj (related)* emparentado,-a; *(similar)* semejante, afín ■ **kindred spirits** almas gemelas.
kinematics [kɪnə'mætɪks] *n* cinemática.
kinetic [kɪ'netɪk] *adj* cinético,-a.
kinetics [kɪ'netɪks] *n* cinética.
king [kɪŋ] *n* rey *m*. ● **the king and queen** los reye *mpl*. ‖ **the Three Kings** los Reyes *mpl* Magos.
kingdom ['kɪŋdəm] *n* reino.
kingfisher ['kɪŋfɪʃə^r] *n* martín pescador *m*.
king-size ['kɪŋsaɪz] *adj* extragrande, extralargo,-a.
kink [kɪŋk] *n* **1** *(in rope, wire, etc)* coca, enroscadur *(in hair)* rizo.
kinky ['kɪŋkɪ] *adj fam* peculiar; *(sexual)* pervertido, -a
▲ *comp* **kinkier,** *superl* **kinkiest.**
kiosk ['ki:ɒsk] *n* **1** quiosco. **2** *(telephone)* cabina tel fónica.
kip [kɪp] *vi fam* dormir.
▲ *pt & pp* **kipped,** *ger* **kipping.**
▷ *n* cabezada. ■ **to have a kip** dormir, echar una cab zada.
kipper [kɪpə^r] *n* arenque *m*.
Kiribati [kɪrɪ'bætɪ] *n* Kiribati.
kiss [kɪs] *n* beso.
▲ *pl* **kisses.**
▷ *vt* besar, dar un beso a: **he kissed her on the cheek** *dio un beso en la mejilla.*
▷ *vi* besarse, darse un beso.
kit [kɪt] *n* **1** *(equipment, gear)* equipo, equipaje *m*. *(clothes)* ropa. **3** *(model)* maqueta, kit *m*.
⊙ **to kit out** *vt sep* equipar.
kitbag ['kɪtbæg] *n* mochila.
kitchen ['kɪtʃɪn] *n* cocina. ● **kitchen garden** huerto
kite [kaɪt] *n* **1** *(bird)* milano. **2** *(toy)* cometa: **to fly kite** *hacer volar una cometa.* ■ **go fly a kite!** ¡vete p ahí! ‖ **to be as high as a kite** *(excited)* estar entusia mado,-a. ‖ **to fly a kite** *lanzar una idea para sondear opinión.*
kith [kɪθ] ● **kith and kin** parientes *mpl* y amigos.
kitten ['kɪtᵊn] *n* gatito,-a. ■ **to have kittens** tener un a que: **I nearly had kittens!** *¡por poco me da un ataque!*
kitty ['kɪtɪ] *n* **1** *fam (cat)* minino,-a. **2** *(in card gam* bote *m*; *(for bills, drinks)* fondo común.
▲ *pl* **kitties.**
kiwi ['ki:wi:] *n* **1** *(bird)* kiwi *m*. **2** *(fruit)* kiwi *m*.
klaxon ['klæksᵊn] *n* claxon *m*.
kleptomania [kleptə'meɪnɪə] *n* cleptomanía.
km [kɪ'lɒmɪtə^r, 'kɪləmi:tə^r] *abbr* **(kilometre)** kilómet *(abbreviation)* km.
knack [næk] *n (skillful method)* maña, truco, tir tranquillo; *(talent)* don *m*: **it's easy to do once you got the knack of it** *es fácil hacerlo cuando le coges tranquillo.*
knackered ['nækəd] *adj fam* reventado,-a, agota -a, hecho,-a polvo.
knapsack ['næpsæk] *n* mochila.
knead [ni:d] *vt* amasar.
knee [ni:] *n* **1** ANAT rodilla: **on one's knees** *de rodil* **2** *(of trousers)* rodillera.
▷ *vt* dar un rodillazo a.

neecap ['ni:kæp] *n* rótula.

neel [ni:l] *vi* arrodillarse.

▲ *pt & pp* **knelt** [nelt].

nee-length ['ni:leŋθ] *adj* hasta las rodillas.

neepad ['ni:pæd] *n* rodillera.

nell [nel] *n* toque *m* de difuntos.

nelt [nelt] *pt & pp* ⟶ **kneel.**

new [nju:] *pt* ⟶ **know.**

nickerbocker ['nɪkəbɒkə] *n pl* **knickerbockers** *arch* pantalones *mpl* cortos.

nickers ['nɪkəz] *n pl* bragas *fpl*: **she bought three pairs of knickers** *compró tres bragas.*

nick-knack ['nɪknæk] *n* chuchería.

nife [naɪf] *n (gen)* cuchillo; *(folding)* navaja. ■ **you could cut the atmosphere with a knife** el ambiente se podía cortar con un cuchillo. ● **knife and fork** cubierto.

▲ *pl* **knives.**

vt apuñalar, acuchillar.

night [naɪt] *n* **1** *arch* caballero. **2** *(chess)* caballo. **3** caballero, *(hombre que lleva el título de* **Sir***)*. ● **knight in shining armour** (US **armor**) príncipe *m* azul.

vt **1** *arch* armar caballero. **2** nombrar caballero a.

nighthood ['naɪthʊd] *n* título de caballero.

nit [nɪt] *vt* tejer.

vi **1** hacer punto, hacer media. **2** MED soldarse. **3** *fig* unirse. ■ **to knit one's brow** fruncir.

▲ *pt & pp* **knit** o **knitted**, *ger* **knitting.**

nitting ['nɪtɪŋ] *n (material)* punto; *(activity)* labor *f* de punto. ● **knitting machine** tricotosa. | **knitting needle** aguja de tejer.

nitwear ['nɪtweəʳ] *n* género de punto.

nives [naɪvz]*pl* ⟶ **knife.**

nob [nɒb] *n* **1** *(on door - large)* pomo; *(- small)* tirador *m*. **2** *(on stick)* puño. **3** *(natural)* bulto, protuberancia. **4** *(on radio, etc)* botón *m*.

nobbly ['nɒblɪ] *adj* nudoso,-a.

nock [nɒk] *n* **1** *(blow)* golpe *m*. **2** *(on door)* llamada: **was that a knock at the door?** *¿han llamado a la puerta?* **3** *fig (bad luck)* revés *m*.

vt **1** *(to hit)* golpear, darse un golpe en. **2** *fam (criticize)* criticar, hablar mal de: **the newspapers are forever knocking the England manager** *los periódicos siempre critican al entrenador de la selección inglesa.*

vi **1** *(at door)* llamar: **please knock before entering** *por favor, llamen antes de entrar.* **2** *(of car engine)* golpear, martillear.

to knock about *vi (travel)* rodar, recorrer; *(spend time)* andar con.

vt sep (beat up) pegar, maltratar.

to knock around *vt-vi* ⟶ **knock about.**

to knock back *vt sep* **1** *(drink)* beberse *de un trago, rápidamente o en grandes cantidades.* **2** *(cost)* soplar, costar: **how much did that car knock you back?** *¿cuánto te soplaron por aquel coche?*

to knock down *vt sep* **1** *(building)* derribar. **2** *(person - with a car)* atropellar; *(- with a blow)* derribar. **3** *(price)* rebajar.

to knock off *vt sep (make fall)* tirar.

vt insep fam (steal) birlar, mangar.

vt sep **1** *sl (kill)* cargarse, liquidar. **2** *(deduct - money)* descontar; *(reduce - time)* quitar.

▷ *vi (stop work)* acabar, salir del trabajo: **what time do you knock off work?** *¿a qué hora sales del trabajo?*

⊙ **to knock out** *vt sep* **1** *(make unconscious)* dejar sin conocimiento; *(put to sleep)* dejar dormido,-a; *(boxing)* poner fuera de combate, dejar K.O. **2** *(from competition)* eliminar. **3** *(make or do quickly)* hacer o producir rápidamente. **4** *(astonish)* dejar pasmado,-a, dejar boquiabierto,-a.

⊙ **to knock over** *vt sep* **1** *(overturn)* volcar, tirar. **2** *(run over)* atropellar.

⊙ **to knock together** *vt sep (do quickly)* hacer de prisa, hacer rápidamente.

▷ *vi (knees)* entrechocarse.

⊙ **to knock up** *vt sep* **1** GB *fam* despertar, llamar. **2** *(prepare quickly)* hacer deprisa, preparar. **3** US *sl* dejar embarazada.

▷ *vi (tennis, etc)* pelotear.

knockabout ['nɒkəbaʊt] *adj* bullicioso,-a.

▷ *n* SP peloteo.

knock-back ['nɒkbæk] *n* rechazo.

knockdown ['nɒkdaʊn] *adj* rebajado. ● **knockdown price** precio de saldo.

knocker ['nɒkəʳ] *n* **1** aldaba. **2** *(critic)* detractor,-ra.

knock-kneed [nɒk'ni:d] *adj* patizambo,-a.

knockout ['nɒkaʊt] *n* **1** SP knock-out *m*, fuera de combate *m*. **2** *fam* maravilla: **it's a knockout!** *¡es alucinante!*

knock-up ['nɒkʌp] *n* peloteo.

knot [nɒt] *n* **1** *(gen)* nudo. **2** *(people)* corrillo, grupo.

▷ *vt* anudar.

▲ *pt & pp* **knotted**, *ger* **knotting.**

know [nəʊ] *vt* **1** *(be acquainted with)* conocer: **do you know Colin?** *¿conoces a Colin?* **2** *(recognize)* reconocer: **I'd know him if I saw him again** *lo reconocería si lo volviera a ver.* **3** *(have knowledge of)* saber: **I don't know the answer** *no sé la respuesta.* ■ **as far as I know** que yo sepa. | **don't I know it!** ¿y me lo dices a mí?, ¡ni que lo digas! | **for all I know** ¡vete a saber! | **how should I know?** ¿yo qué sé? | **if only I'd known!** ¡haberlo sabido! | **I know what!** ¡ya lo tengo! | **not that I know of** que yo sepa, no. | **to be in the know** estar enterado,-a. | **to know apart** saber distinguir. | **to know better** tener más juicio. | **to know by sight** conocer de vista. | **you know best** tú sabes mejor que yo, sabes lo que más te conviene. | **you never know** nunca se sabe.

▲ *pt* **knew** [nju:], *pp* **known** [nəʊn].

⊙ **to know about** *vt insep* saber de, entender de.

⊙ **to know of** *vt insep* saber de, haber oído hablar de.

know-all ['nəʊɔ:l] *n* sabelotodo *mf*.

know-how ['nəʊhaʊ] *n* saber hacer *m*, conocimiento práctico.

knowing ['nəʊɪŋ] *adj (smile, look)* de complicidad; *(person)* sagaz, astuto,-a.

▷ *n* manera de saber.

knowingly ['nəʊɪŋlɪ] *adv (intentionally)* a sabiendas, adrede; *(look, etc)* con complicidad.

knowledge ['nɒlɪdʒ] *n* **1** *(learning, information)* conocimientos *mpl*: **his knowledge of football is amazing** *sus conocimientos de fútbol son increíbles.* **2** *(awareness)* conocimiento: **at that time I had no knowledge of what was happening** *entonces no tenía conocimiento* *de lo que estaba pasando.* ■ **to be common knowledge that ...** ser notorio que ..., todo el mundo sabe que ... ‖ **to my knowledge** que yo sepa. ‖ **it has come to my knowledge that ...** he llegado a saber que ... ‖ **to have a good knowledge of** STH conocer ALGO bien.

knowledgeable ['nɒlɪdʒəbᵊl] *adj* entendido,-a: **he's very knowledgeable about music** *es muy entendido en música.*

knowledgeably ['nɒlɪdʒəblɪ] *adv* de forma entendida, entendidamente.

known [nəʊn] *pp* → **know.**

knuckle ['nʌkᵊl] *n* nudillo.

⊙ **to knuckle down** *vi fam* ponerse a trabajar en serio.

⊙ **to knuckle under** *vi* pasar por el aro.

knuckleduster ['nʊkldʌstəʳ] *n* puño de hierro.

koala [kəʊ'ɑːlə] *n* koala *m.*

kook [kʊːk] *n* US *sl* chiflado,-a, majara *mf*, majareta *mf.*

kopeck ['kəʊpek] *n* copec *m*, copeck *m.*

kopek ['kəʊpek] *n* copec *m*, copeck *m.*

Koran [kɔː'rɑːn] *n* Alcorán *m*, Corán *m.*

Korea [kə'rɪə] *n* Corea. ● **North Korea** Corea del Norte. ‖ **South Korea** Corea del Sur.

Korean [kə'rɪən] *adj* coreano,-a.

▷ *n* **1** *(person)* coreano,-a. **2** *(language)* coreano. ● **North Korean** norcoreano,-a. ‖ **South Korean** surcoreano,-a.

kosher ['kəʊʃəʳ] *adj* **1** *(meat)* cosher *(permitido por la ley dietética judía)*. **2** *fam (genuine)* legal, auténtico,-a.

kowtow [kaʊ'taʊ] *vi* humillarse (**to**, ante), rebajarse (**to**, ante).

kph ['keɪ'piː'eɪtʃ] *abbr* (**kilometres per hour**) kilómetros *mpl* por hora; *(abbreviation)* km/h.

kraut [kraʊt] *n pej* alemán,-ana.

▷ *adj pej* alemán,-ana.

krypton ['krɪptɒn] *n* criptón *m.*

kudos ['kjuːdɒs] *n* prestigio, gloria.

kung fu [kʊŋ'fʊː] *n* kung-fu *m.*

Kurd [kɜːd] *adj* kurdo,-a.

▷ *n (person)* kurdo,-a.

Kurdish ['kɜːdɪʃ] *adj* kurdo,-a.

▷ *n (language)* kurdo.

Kuwait [kʊ'weɪt] *n* Kuwait.

Kuwaiti [kʊ'weɪtɪ] *adj* kuwaití.

▷ *n* kuwaití *mf.*

kW ['kɪləwɒt] *abbr* (**kilowatt**) kilovatio, kilowatt; *(abbreviation)* kW.

kWh [kɪləwɒt'aʊəʳ] *abbr* (**kilowatt-hour**) kilovatio, kilowatt-hora *m*; *(abbreviation)* kW/h.

L

L, l [el] *n (the letter)* L, l *f*.
l ['liːtəʳ] *symb* (**litre**, US **liter**) litro; *(symbol)* l.
lab^{1} [læb] *n fam (abbr of* **laboratory**) laboratorio.
lab^{2} ['leɪbəʳ] *abbr* (**Labour**) laborista.
label ['leɪbᵊl] *n* **1** etiqueta. **2** *(record company)* casa discográfica.
▷ *vt* **1** etiquetar, poner etiqueta a. **2** *fig* calificar (**as**, de).
▲ *pt & pp* **labelled** *(*US **labeled***), ger* **labelling** *(*US **labeling***)*.
labor ['leɪbəʳ] *n* US ⟶ **labour**.
laboratory [ləbɒrətərɪ, US 'læbrətɒrɪ] *n* laboratorio.
▲ *pl* **laboratories**.
labored ['leɪbəd] *adj* US ⟶ **laboured**.
laborer ['leɪbərəʳ] *n n* US ⟶ **labourer**.
labor-intensive [leɪbərɪntensɪv] *adj* US ⟶ **labour-intensive**.
laborious [ləbɔːrɪəs] *adj* laborioso,-a, penoso,-a.
labor-saving ['leɪbəseɪvɪŋ] *adj*US ⟶ **labour-saving**.
labour ['leɪbəʳ] *n* **1** *(work)* trabajo. **2** *(task)* labor *f*, tarea, faena; *(involving manual work)* mano *f* de obra. **3** *(workforce)* mano *f* de obra. **4** *(childbirth)* parto. **5** *(effort)* esfuerzo. ● **labour camp** campo de trabajos forzados. ‖ **Labour Day** día del trabajo. ‖ **labour force** mano *f* de obra.
▷ *vi* **1** *(work hard)* trabajar duro. **2** *(move slowly)* avanzar penosamente; *(engine)* funcionar con dificultad.
▷ *vt* machacar.
▷ *n* **Labour** GB los laboristas *mpl*, el Partido Laborista.
⊙ **to labour under** *vt insep* dejarse llevar por.
laboured ['leɪbəd] *adj* **1** *(breathing)* fatigoso,-a. **2** *(style)* forzado,-a.
labourer ['leɪbərəʳ] *n* peón *m*, jornalero,-a, bracero. ● **farm labourer** peón *m* agrícola.
labour-intensive [leɪbərɪntensɪv] *adj* con mucha mano de obra.
labour-saving ['leɪbəseɪvɪŋ] *adj* que ahorra trabajo. ● **labour-saving device** electrodoméstico.
labyrinth ['læbərɪnθ] *n* laberinto.
lace [leɪs] *n* **1** *(material)* encaje *m*. **2** *(shoestring)* cordón *m*.
▷ *vt (pull string through)* poner los cordones a.
⊙ **to lace into** *vt insep fam* meterse con, atacar.
⊙ **to lace up** *vt sep* atar los cordones de.
lacerate ['læsəreɪt] *vt* lacerar.
laceration [læsəreɪʃᵊn] *n* laceración *f*.
lachrymal ['lækrɪmᵊl] *adj* lagrimal, lacrimal.
lachrymose ['lækrɪməʊs] *adj* **1** *(tearful)* llorón,-ona, lacrimoso,-a. **2** *pej* lacrimógeno,-a.
lack [læk] *n* falta, carencia, escasez *f*: **she has no lack of self-confidence** *no le falta confianza en sí misma.* ■ **for lack of** por falta de.
▷ *vt* carecer de. ■ **for lack of** por falta de.
lackadaisical [lækədeɪzɪkᵊl] *adj pej* indiferente, apático,-a.
lacking ['lækɪŋ] *adj* carente de: **there was something lacking in the room** *en la habitación faltaba algo.*
lackluster ['læklʌstəʳ] *adj* US ⟶ **lacklustre**.
lacklustre ['læklʌstəʳ] *adj* sin interés, insulso,-a.
laconic [ləkɒnɪk] *adj* lacónico,-a.
lacquer ['lækəʳ] *n* laca.
▷ *vt (metal, wood)* lacar; *(hair)* poner laca a.
lacrimal ['lækrɪmᵊl] *adj* lacrimal.
lactation [lækteɪʃᵊn] *n* lactancia.
lactic ['læktɪk] *adj* láctico,-a.
lactose ['læktəʊs] *n* lactosa.
lacuna [lə'kjuːnə] *n* laguna, hueco.
▲ *pl* **lacunas** o **lacunae** [lə'kjuːniː].
lacy ['leɪsɪ] *adj (of lace)* de encaje.
▲ *comp* **lacier**, *superl* **laciest**.
lad [læd] *n* **1** GB *fam* muchacho, chaval *m*, chico. **2** GB *fam* diablillo, pillo: **John's a bit of a lad** *John es un poco pillo.* **3** *(stable boy)* mozo de cuadra.
ladder ['lædəʳ] *n* **1** escalera (de mano). **2** GB *(in stocking)* carrera. **3** *fig* escala. ● **rope ladder** escalera de cuerda.
▷ *vi* GB hacerse una carrera.
▷ *vt* GB hacerse una carrera en.
laden ['leɪdᵊn] *adj* cargado,-a (**with**, de). ■ **to be fully laden** estar lleno,-a hasta el tope.
ladies ['leɪdɪz] *n* GB *(toilet)* lavabo (de señoras). ● **ladies room** US lavabo (de señoras).
lading ['leɪdɪŋ] *n* embarque *m*.
ladle ['leɪdᵊl] *n* cucharón *m*.
▷ *vt* servir con cucharón.
⊙ **to ladle out** *vt sep* repartir.
lady ['leɪdɪ] *n* señora; *(of high social position)* dama.
Lady ['leɪdɪ] *n (title)* lady *f*.
▲ *pl* **ladies**.
ladybird ['leɪdɪbɜːd] *n* mariquita.
ladybug ['leɪdɪbʌg] *n* US mariquita.
lady-in-waiting [leɪdɪɪnweɪtɪŋ] *n* dama de honor.
▲ *pl* **ladies-in-waiting**.
lady-killer ['leɪdɪkɪləʳ] *n* donjuán *m*.
ladylike ['leɪdɪlaɪk] *adj* delicado,-a, elegante.
lag [læg] *n* **1** retraso. **2** GB *sl* preso. ● **time lag** retraso.
lager ['lɑːgəʳ] *n* cerveza rubia.
lagoon [ləguːn] *n* laguna.
laid [leɪd] *pt & pp* ⟶ **lay^{2}**.
lain [leɪn] *pp* ⟶ **lie^{2}**.
lair [leəʳ] *n* guarida.
laird [leəd] *n* terrateniente *m (escocés)*.
lake [leɪk] *n* lago.
lam [læm] *vt* **to lam into** *sl (physically)* apalear; *(verbally)* machacar, fustigar.
▲ *pt & pp* **lammed**, *ger* **lamming**.

lama ['lɑːmə] *n* lama *m*.
lamb [læm] *n* **1** *(animal)* cordero,-a. **2** *(meat)* carne *f* de cordero. **3** *fam (person)* cordero,-a: **poor lamb!** *¡pobrecito,-a!*
lambaste ['læmbeɪst] *vt fam* fustigar.
lambskin ['læmskɪn] *n* piel *f* de cordero.
lame [leɪm] *adj* **1** cojo,-a: **lame in one leg** *cojo,-a de una pierna*. **2** *fig* débil; *(excuse)* poco convincente; *(business)* fallido,-a. ● **lame duck** inútil *mf*.
lament [ləment] *n* lamento.
▷ *vt* lamentar, llorar.
▷ *vi* lamentarse (**over**, de).
lamentable ['læməntəbᵊl] *adj* lamentable.
laminate [*(n)* 'læmɪnət; *(vb)* 'læmɪneɪt] *vt* laminar.
▷ *n* laminado.
laminated ['læmɪneɪtɪd] *adj* **1** *(metal)* laminado,-a; *(glass)* inastillable. **2** *(paper)* plastificado,-a.
lamp [læmp] *n* **1** lámpara. **2** *(on car, train)* faro.
lampoon [læmpuːn] *n* pasquín *m*, sátira.
▷ *vt* satirizar.
lamp-post ['læmppəust] *n* (poste *m* de) farol *m*.
lamprey ['læmprɪ] *n (fish)* lamprea.
lampshade ['læmpʃeɪd] *n* pantalla (de lámpara).
lance [lɑːns] *n* **1** *(spear)* lanza. **2** MED lanceta.
▷ *vt* MED abrir con lanceta.
lancer ['lɑːnsəʳ] *n* lancero,-a.
lancet ['lɑːnsɪt] *n* lanceta.
land [lænd] *n* **1** *(gen)* tierra: **by land and sea** *por tierra y por mar*. **2** *(soil)* suelo, tierra. **3** *(country, region)* tierra, país: **in foreign lands** *en tierras extranjeras*. **4** *(property)* terreno, tierras *fpl*. ■ **land ahoy!** ¡tierra a la vista! ● **farm land** tierras *fpl* de cultivo. ‖ **land agent** GB encargado,-a de una granja.
▷ *vi* **1** *(plane, etc)* aterrizar, tomar tierra; *(bird)* posarse. **2** *(disembark)* desembarcar. **3** *(fall)* caer.
▷ *vt* **1** *(plane, etc)* hacer aterrizar. **2** *(disembark)* desembarcar; *(unload)* descargar. **3** *(fish)* sacar del agua. **4** *fam (get)* conseguir.
⊙ **to land in** *vt sep* causar, traer: **he's bound to land you in trouble** *seguro que te traerá problemas*.
⊙ **to land up** *vi* acabar.
landed ['lændɪd] *adj* hacendado,-a. ● **the landed gentry** los terratenientes *mpl*.
landing ['lændɪŋ] *n* **1** *(plane)* aterrizaje *m*. **2** *(on stairs)* descansillo, rellano. **3** *(of people)* desembarco. ● **crash landing** aterrizaje *m* de emergencia. ‖ **landing field** pista de aterrizaje. ‖ **landing gear** tren *m* de aterrizaje.
landlady ['lændleɪdɪ] *n (of flat)* propietaria, dueña; *(of house)* casera.
▲ *pl* **landladies**.
landlocked ['lændlɒkt] *adj* sin salida al mar.
landlord ['lændlɔːd] *n* **1** *(of flat)* propietario, dueño; *(of house)* casero.
landmark ['lændmɑːk] *n* **1** *fig (building, place) monumento o edificio muy conocido*. **2** *(reference point)* punto de referencia.
landmine ['lændmaɪn] *n* mina (de tierra).
landowner ['lændəunəʳ] *n* propietario,-a, terrateniente *mf*, hacendado,-a.
landscape ['lændskeɪp] *n* paisaje *m*. ● **landscape gardener** jardinista *mf*, arquitecto,-a paisajista. ‖ **landscape painter** paisajista *mf*.
▷ *vt* ajardinar.
landslide ['lændslaɪd] *n* desprendimiento de tierras.
lane [leɪn] *n* **1** *(in country)* camino, sendero, vereda *(in town)* callejuela, callejón *m*. **2** *(on road)* carril *m*. 3 *(in athletics, swimming)* calle *f*.
language ['læŋgwɪdʒ] *n* **1** *(faculty, way of speaking)* lenguaje *m*. **2** *(tongue)* idioma *m*, lengua. **3** *(school subject)* lengua. ■ **to use bad language** ser mal hablado,-a. ● **language laboratory** laboratorio de idiomas. ‖ **language school** escuela de idiomas.
languid ['læŋgwɪd] *adj* lánguido,-a.
languish ['læŋgwɪʃ] *vi* languidecer; *(in prison)* pudrirse.
languor ['læŋgəʳ] *n* languidez *f*.
lank [læŋk] *adj* lacio,-a.
lanky ['læŋkɪ] *adj* larguirucho,-a.
▲ *comp* **lankier**, *superl* **lankiest**.
lanolin ['lænəlɪn] *n* lanolina.
lantern ['læntən] *n* linterna, farol *m*.
Lao [lau] *n (language)* laosiano.
Laos [lauz, laus] *n* Laos.
Laotian ['lauʃɪən] *adj* laosiano,-a.
▷ *n* laosiano,-a.
lap[1] [læp] *n* regazo; *(knees)* rodillas *fpl*; *(skirt)* falda.
lap[2] [læp] *n* **1** SP vuelta. **2** *fig (stage)* etapa.
▷ *vt* SP *(overtake)* doblar.
▷ *vi (go round)* dar la vuelta.
▲ *pt & pp* **lapped**, *ger* **lapping**.
lap[3] [læp] *vt* **1** *(animal)* beber a lengüetadas. **2** *(waves)* lamer, besar.
▲ *pt & pp* **lapped**, *ger* **lapping**.
⊙ **to lap up** *vt sep* **1** beber a lengüetadas. **2** *fig (believe)* tragar, tragarse.
laparoscopy [læpərɒskəpɪ] *n* laparoscopia.
▲ *pl* **laparoscopies**.
lapdog ['læpdɒg] *n* perrito faldero.
lapel [ləpel] *n* solapa.
Lapland ['læplænd] *n* Laponia.
lapse [læps] *n* **1** *(in time)* intervalo, lapso. **2** *(slip)* desliz *m*. **3** *(when speaking)* lapsus *m*; *(of memory)* fallo.
▷ *vi* **1** *(time)* transcurrir. **2** *(err)* cometer un desliz. **3** *(contract, etc)* caducar.
lapsed [læpst] *adj* REL no practicante.
laptop ['læptɒp] [Also **laptop computer**.] *n* ordenador *m* portátil.
larceny ['lɑːsᵊnɪ] *n* latrocinio.
▲ *pl* **larcenies**.
larch [lɑːtʃ] *n* alerce *m*.
lard [lɑːd] *n* manteca de cerdo.
larder ['lɑːdəʳ] *n* despensa.
large [lɑːdʒ] *adj* **1** grande; *(before sing noun)* gran *(sum, amount)* importante; *(meal)* abundante. **2** *(family)* numeroso,-a. **3** *(extensive)* amplio,-a, extenso,-a. ■ **at large** *(as a whole)* en general. ‖ **by and large** por lo general.
largely ['lɑːdʒlɪ] *adv (mainly)* en gran parte, en gran medida; *(chiefly)* principalmente.
largeness ['lɑːdʒnəs] *n* **1** *(size)* magnitud *f*, amplitud *f*. **2** *(importance)* importancia.
large-scale ['lɑːdʒskeɪl] *adj* **1** de gran escala. **2** *(map)* a gran escala.
largesse [lɑːdʒes] *n fml* generosidad *f*.

ark¹ [lɑ:k] *n (bird)* alondra.
ark² [lɑ:k] *n fam (bit of fun)* broma.
⊙ **to lark about / lark around** *vi fam* hacer el indio.
arva ['lɑ:və] *n* larva.
▲ *pl* larvae ['lɑ:vi:].
aryngitis [lærɪndʒaɪtəs] *n* laringitis *f.*
arynx ['lærɪŋks] *n* laringe *f.*
▲ *pl* larynxes o larynges [lə'rɪndʒi:z].
asagna [ləzɑ:njə] *n* lasaña.
ascivious [ləsɪvɪəs] *adj* lascivo,-a.
aser ['leɪzəʳ] *n* láser *m.*
ash [læʃ] *n* **1** *(blow with whip)* latigazo, azote *m*; *(with tail)* coletazo. **2** *(whip)* látigo; *(thong)* tralla. **3** *(eyelash)* pestaña.
▲ *pl* lashes.
▷ *vt* **1** *(in general)* azotar. **2** *(fasten)* sujetar.
▷ *vi (fall hard)* caer con fuerza (**against**, contra).
⊙ **to lash out** *vi* **1** arremeter (**against/at**, contra). **2** *(splurge)* gastarse un montón (de dinero) (**on**, en).
ash-up ['læʃʌp] *n fam* chapuza.
ass [læs] *n fam* chica, chavala.
▲ *pl* lasses.
assitude ['læsɪtju:d] *n* lasitud *f.*
asso [læsu:] *n* lazo.
▲ *pl* lassos o lassoes.
▷ *vt* lazar, coger con el lazo.
▲ *pt & pp* lassoed, *ger* lassoing.
ast¹ [lɑ:st] *adj* **1** *(final)* último,-a. **2** *(most recent)* último,-a: **the last time** *la última vez.* **3** *(past)* pasado,-a; *(previous)* anterior: **last Monday** *el lunes pasado;* **the night before last** *anteanoche.*
▷ *adv* **1** por última vez: **when he last came to see me** *cuando vino a verme por última vez.* **2** *(at the end)* en último lugar; *(in race)* en última posición. ■ **at last** al fin, por fin. ‖ **at long last** por fin.
▷ *n (person)* el/la último,-a; *(thing)* lo último: **are you the last?** *¿eres tú el último?* ■ **last but one** penúltimo,-a.
▷ *vi (continue)* durar; *(hold out)* aguantar, resistir.
▷ *vt* durar.
⊙ **to last out** *vi* resistir, aguantar.
ast² [lɑ:st] *n (shoemaker's)* horma.
ast-ditch [lɑ:stdɪtʃ] *adj* último,-a, desesperado,-a.
asting ['lɑ:stɪŋ] *adj* duradero,-a.
astly ['lɑ:stlɪ] *adv* por último, finalmente.
ast-minute [lɑ:stmɪnɪt] *adj* de última hora.
atch [lætʃ] *n* pestillo: **come in, the door's on the latch** *entra, el pestillo no está echado.*
⊙ **to latch on** *vi fam* caer en la cuenta.
⊙ **to latch onto** *vt insep* **1** *fam (understand)* captar. **2** *fam (cling to)* pegarse a. **3** *(take an interest in)* poner interés en, interesarse por.
atchkey ['lætʃki:] *n* llavín *m.*
ate [leɪt] *adj* **1** *(not on time)* tardío,-a: **you're ten minutes late** *llegas diez minutos tarde.* **2** *(far on in time)* tarde: **in late May** *a finales de mayo.* **3** *euph (dead)* difunto,-a, fallecido,-a. **4** *(former)* anterior. **5** *(last-minute)* de última hora.
▷ *adv* **1** tarde: **I stayed up late last night** *anoche me acosté muy tarde.* **2** *(recently)* recientemente: **as late as yesterday** *ayer mismo.* ■ **of late** últimamente.
atecomer ['leɪtkʌməʳ] *n* persona que llega tarde.
lately ['leɪtlɪ] *adv* últimamente, recientemente.
lateness ['leɪtnəs] *n* retraso.
late-night ['leɪtnaɪt] *adj* de noche, de madrugada.
latent ['leɪtᵊnt] *adj* latente, oculto.
later ['leɪtəʳ] *adj* **1** más tardío,-a: **we'll discuss that at a later date** *hablaremos de eso más adelante.* **2** *(more recent)* más reciente.
▷ *adv* **1** más tarde: **five minutes later** *cinco minutos más tarde;* **see you later!** *¡hasta luego!* **2** *(afterwards)* después, luego. ■ **later on** más adelante, más tarde.
lateral ['lætᵊrəl] *adj* lateral.
latest ['leɪtɪst] *adj* último,-a, más reciente.
▷ *n* lo último. ■ **at the latest** como máximo.
latex ['leɪteks] *n* látex *m.*
lath [læθ, lɑ:θ] *n* listón *m.*
lathe [leɪð] *n* torno.
lather ['lɑ:ðəʳ] *n* **1** *(of soap)* espuma. **2** *(sweat)* sudor *m.*
▷ *vt* enjabonar.
Latin ['lætɪn] *adj* latino,-a.
▷ *n* **1** *(person)* latino,-a. **2** *(language)* latín *m.* ● **Latin American** latinoamericano,-a.
latitude ['lætɪtju:d] *n* latitud *f.*
latrine [lətri:n] *n* retrete *m.*
latter ['lætəʳ] *adj* **1** *(last)* último,-a: **the latter days of his life were very happy** *los últimos días de su vida fueron muy felices.* **2** *(second)* segundo,-a.
▷ *pron* **the latter** éste,-a, este,-a último,-a.
latter-day ['lætədeɪ] *adj* actual, de hoy.
lattice ['lætɪs] *n* celosía, enrejado.
Latvia ['lætvɪə] *n* Letonia.
Latvian ['lætvɪən] *adj* letón,-ona.
▷ *n* **1** *(person)* letón,-ona. **2** *(language)* letón *m.*
laud [lɔ:d] *vt arch* alabar, elogiar.
laudable ['lɔ:dəbᵊl] *adj* laudable, loable.
laugh [lɑ:f] *vi* reír, reírse: **it makes me laugh** *me da risa.* ■ **he who laughs last laughs longest** quien ríe último ríe mejor. ‖ **to laugh one's head off** *fam* partirse de risa, troncharse de risa, desternillarse de risa.
▷ *n* risa: **we had a really good laugh** *nos reímos muchísimo.*
⊙ **to laugh at** *vt insep* reírse de.
⊙ **to laugh off** *vt sep* tomar a risa.
laughable ['lɑ:fəbᵊl] *adj* ridículo,-a, irrisible; *(sum)* irrisorio,-a.
laughing ['lɑ:fɪŋ] *adj* risueño,-a.
▷ *n* risas *fpl*; *(loud)* carcajadas *fpl.* ■ **not to be a laughing matter** no ser (cosa) de risa.
laughing-stock ['lɑ:fɪŋstɒk] *n* hazmerreír *m.*
laughter ['lɑ:ftəʳ] *n* risas *fpl*: **a fit of laughter** *un ataque de risa.*
launch [lɔ:ntʃ] *vt* **1** lanzar: **it will be launched on the market next year** *se lanzará al mercado el año que viene.* **2** *(ship)* botar; *(lifeboat)* echar al mar. **3** *(film, etc)* estrenar; *(book)* presentar. **4** *(company)* fundar. **5** *(scheme, attack)* iniciar. ■ **launch pad** plataforma de lanzamiento.
▷ *n (boat)* lancha.
▲ *pl* launches.
launching ['lɔ:ntʃɪŋ] *n* **1** lanzamiento. **2** *(of ship)* botadura. **3** *(of film)* estreno; *(of book)* presentación *f.* ■ **launching pad** plataforma de lanzamiento.
launchpad ['lɔ:ntʃpæd] *n* plataforma de lanzamiento.

launder ['lɔːndəʳ] *vt* 1 *(clothes)* lavar (y planchar). 2 *fig (money)* blanquear.
launderette [lɔːndəˈret] *n* lavandería automática.
laundry ['lɔːndrɪ] *n* 1 *(place)* lavandería. 2 *(dirty)* ropa sucia, colada; *(clean)* ropa limpia, ropa lavada.
▲ *pl* **laundries.** ■ **to do the laundry** lavar la ropa.
laurel ['lɒrəl] *n* laurel *m.*
lava ['lɑːvə] *n* lava.
lavatory ['lævətərɪ] *n* 1 váter *m.* 2 *(room)* lavabo, baño.
▲ *pl* **lavatories.**
lavender ['lævɪndəʳ] *n* espliego, lavanda.
▷ *adj (colour)* de color lavanda.
lavish ['lævɪʃ] *adj* 1 *(generous)* pródigo,-a, generoso,-a. 2 *(abundant)* abundante. 3 *(luxurious)* lujoso,-a.
▷ *vt* prodigar (**on**, a).
lavishly ['lævɪʃlɪ] *adv* espléndidamente, magníficamente.
law [lɔː] *n* 1 ley *f.* 2 EDUC derecho. ■ **against the law** contra la ley. ‖ **by law** por ley. ‖ **to keep within the law** obrar según la ley. ‖ ● **law and order** orden *m* público. ‖ **law court** tribunal *m* de justicia.
law-abiding ['lɔːəbaɪdɪŋ] *adj* respetuoso,-a de la ley.
law-breaker ['lɔːbreɪkəʳ] *n* infractor,-ra de la ley.
lawful ['lɔːfʊl] *adj* legal.
lawless ['lɔːləs] *adj* 1 sin ley; *(ungovernable)* ingobernable. 2 *(person)* anárquico,-a.
lawmaker ['lɔːmeɪkəʳ] *n* legislador,-ra.
lawn [lɔːn] *n* césped *m.*
lawnmower ['lɔːnməʊəʳ] *n* cortacésped *m & f.*
lawsuit ['lɔːsjuːt] *n* pleito, juicio.
lawyer ['lɔːjəʳ] *n* abogado,-a.
lax [læks] *adj* 1 *(unstrict)* poco disciplinario,-a, flojo,-a; *(relaxed)* relajado,-a. 2 *(negligent)* negligente.
laxative ['læksətɪv] *adj* laxante.
▷ *n* laxante *m.*
laxity ['læksɪtɪ] *n* 1 *(lacking strictness)* poca disciplina, flojedad *f*; *(relaxation)* relajamiento, relajación *f.* 2 *(negligence)* negligencia.
laxness ['læksnəs] *n* laxitud *f.*
lay[1] [leɪ] *adj* 1 REL laico,-a, seglar. 2 *(non-professional)* lego,-a, no profesional.
lay[2] [leɪ] *vt* 1 *(gen)* poner, colocar; *(spread out)* extender. 2 *(bricks, carpet)* poner; *(cable, pipe)* tender; *(foundations, basis)* echar; *(bomb)* colocar. 3 *(prepare)* preparar; *(curse)* lanzar. 4 *(eggs)* poner. 5 *(bet)* apostar. 6 *(charge)* formular. ■ **to lay the table** poner la mesa.
▷ *vi (hen)* poner huevos.
⊙ **to lay about** *vt insep* agredir.
⊙ **to lay aside** *vt sep* 1 dejar a un lado. 2 *fig* dejar de lado.
⊙ **to lay before** *vt insep* presentar.
⊙ **to lay by** *vt sep* guardar; *(money)* ahorrar.
⊙ **to lay down** *vt sep* 1 *(let go)* dejar, soltar. 2 *(give up)* entregar. 3 *(establish)* imponer, fijar.
⊙ **to lay in** *vt insep* proveerse de.
⊙ **to lay into** *vt insep* atacar.
⊙ **to lay off** *vt sep (worker)* despedir.
▷ *vt insep fam (stop)* dejar en paz.
▷ *vi fam* parar: **lay off!** *¡ya está bien!, ¡para ya!*
⊙ **to lay on** *vt sep (provide)* suministrar.
▷ *vt insep (burden)* cargar.
▲ *pt & pp* **laid** [leɪd].
⊙ **to lay out** *vt sep* 1 *(spread out)* tender, extender. 2 *(arrange)* disponer, colocar. 3 *(present)* presentar, exponer. 4 *(town, etc)* hacer el trazado de; *(garden)* diseñar.
⊙ **to lay over** *vi* US *(gen)* hacer una parada (**at/in**, en); *(plane)* hacer escala (**at/in**, en).
⊙ **to lay up** *vt sep (store)* almacenar.
lay[3] [leɪ] *pp* → **lie**[2].
layabout ['leɪəbaʊt] *n* GB *fam* gandul,-la, holgazán,-ana.
lay-by ['leɪbaɪ] *n* área de descanso.
▲ *pl* **lay-bys.**
layer ['leɪəʳ] *n* 1 capa. 2 *(of rock)* estrato. 3 *(hen)* gallina ponedora.
layette [leɪet] *n* canastilla.
lay-off ['leɪɒf] *n* despido.
layout ['leɪaʊt] *n* 1 *(arrangement)* disposición *f*; *(presentation)* presentación *f.* 2 *(printing)* composición, formato. 3 *(plan)* trazado.
laziness ['leɪzɪnəs] *n* pereza.
lazy ['leɪzɪ] *adj* 1 gandul,-la, vago,-a, perezoso,-a. 2 *(river)* perezoso,-a.
▲ *comp* **lazier**, *superl* **laziest.**
lazybones ['leɪzɪbəʊnz] *n* perezoso,-a, gandul,-la.
▲ *pl* **lazybones.**
lb [paʊnd] *abbr* (**pound**) libra.
▲ *pl* **lb** o **lbs.**
L-driver ['eldraɪvəʳ] *n* GB conductor,-ra novato,-a.
lead[1] [led] *n* 1 *(metal)* plomo. 2 *(in pencil)* mina. ■ **to swing the lead** *fam* hacer el vago.
lead[2] [liːd] *vt* 1 *(guide)* llevar, conducir: **our tour guide led the way to the cathedral** *la guía nos llevó a la catedral.* 2 *(be leader of)* liderar, dirigir. 3 *(be first in)* ocupar el primer puesto en. 4 *(influence)* llevar: **he is easily led** *se deja llevar fácilmente.*
▷ *vi* 1 *(road)* conducir, llevar (**to**, a). 2 *(command)* tener el mando. 3 *(go first)* ir primero,-a.
▷ *n* 1 *(front position)* delantera. 2 SP liderato; *(difference)* ventaja. 3 THEAT primer papel *m.*
⊙ **to lead off** *vi (begin)* empezar.
▷ *vt insep (room, door)* dar a.
⊙ **to lead on** *vt sep* 1 *(deceive)* engañar, tomar el pelo a. 2 *(coerce)* coaccionar.
▷ *vi* ir adelante: **lead on!** *¡adelante!*
▲ *pt & pp* **led** [**led**].
⊙ **to lead up to** *vt insep* llevar a, conducir a.
leader ['liːdəʳ] *n* 1 POL líder *mf*, dirigente *mf.* 2 *(in race)* líder *mf* (**of/in**, de).
leadership ['liːdəʃɪp] *n* 1 *(position)* liderato, liderazgo. 2 *(qualities)* dotes *mpl* de mando. 3 *(leaders)* dirección *f.*
lead-free ['ledfriː] *adj* sin plomo.
leading ['liːdɪŋ] *adj* destacado,-a, principal.
leaf [liːf] *n* 1 *(of plant)* hoja. 2 *(of book)* hoja, página.
▲ *pl* **leaves** ['liːvz].
⊙ **to leaf through** *vt insep* hojear.
leaflet ['liːflət] *n (folded)* folleto; *(single sheet)* octavilla, hoja suelta.
▷ *vi* GB repartir folletos, repartir octavillas.
leafy ['liːfɪ] *adj* frondoso,-a.
▲ *comp* **leafier**, *superl* **leafiest.**

league [li:g] *n* liga. ■ **to be in league with** SB estar conchabado,-a con ALGN.
leak [li:k] *vi* **1** *(container)* tener un agujero; *(pipe)* tener un escape. **2** *(roof)* gotear. **3** *(gas, fluid)* escaparse.
▷ *vt* **1** *(let out)* dejar salir, dejar escapar; *(spill out)* derramar. **2** *fig (information, etc)* pasar (**to**, a).
▷ *n* **1** *(hole)* agujero. **2** *(in roof)* gotera. **3** *(of gas)* fuga, escape *m*; *(of liquid)* escape *m*. **4** *fig (of information, etc)* filtración *f*.
⊙ **to leak out** *vi* **1** *(gas, fluid)* escaparse. **2** *fig* filtrarse.
leakage ['li:kɪdʒ] *n* fuga, escape *m*.
leaky ['li:kɪ] *adj* **1** *(container)* agujereado,-a; *(pipe)* con un escape. **2** *(roof)* que tiene goteras. **3** *(pipe)* que tiene escapes.
▲ *comp* **leakier**, *superl* **leakiest**.
lean[1] [li:n] *adj* **1** *(person)* delgado,-a, flaco,-a. **2** *(meat)* magro,-a. **3** *(harvest)* malo,-a, escaso,-a; *(year)* malo,-a, pobre: **it was a lean year for car sales** *fue un mal año para la venta de coches*.
▷ *n (meat)* carne *f* magra.
lean[2] [li:n] *vi* **1** inclinarse. **2** *(for support)* apoyarse (**on**, en) (**against**, contra).
▷ *vt* apoyar.
▲ *pt & pp* **leaned** o **leant** [lent].
▷ *n* inclinación *f*.
⊙ **to lean on** *vt insep* **1** *(depend on)* depender de. **2** *(pressure)* presionar a.
⊙ **to lean towards** *vt insep* estar a favor de, tirar hacia.
leaning ['li:nɪŋ] *adj* inclinado,-a.
▷ *n* inclinación *f*, tendencia.
leant [lent] *pt & pp* ⟶ **lean**[2].
lean-to ['li:ntu] *n* cobertizo.
▲ *pl* **lean-tos**.
leap [li:p] *vi* saltar, brincar.
▲ *pt & pp* **leaped** o **leapt** [lept].
▷ *n* **1** salto, brinco. ● **leap year** año bisiesto.
⊙ **to leap at** *vt insep* no dejar escapar, aprovechar.
leapfrog ['li:pfrɒg] *n* pídola.
▷ *vt fig (skip)* saltarse.
▲ *pt & pp* **leapfrogged**, *ger* **leapfrogging**.
leapt [lept] *pt & pp* ⟶ **leap**.
learn [lɜ:n] *vt* **1** aprender: **I'd love to learn (how) to ice-skate** *me encantaría aprender a patinar sobre hielo*. **2** *(find out about)* enterarse de, saber.
▷ *vi* **1** aprender. **2** *(find out)* enterarse (**about/of**, de).
▲ *pt & pp* **learned** o **learnt** [lɜ:nt].
learned ['lɜ:nəd] *adj* erudito,-a.
learner ['lɜ:nə'] *n* estudiante *mf*. ● **learner driver** conductor,-a en prácticas.
learnt [lɜ:nt] *pt & pp* ⟶ **learn**.
lease [li:s] *n* contrato de arrendamiento *que transfiere la propiedad al arrendatario por un cierto período de tiempo*.
▷ *vt* arrendar.
leash [li:ʃ] *n* correa.
leasing ['li:sɪŋ] *n* **1** arrendamiento, arriendo. **2** FIN leasing *m*.
least [li:st] *adj* menor, menos: **he makes the least money** *es el que gana menos dinero*.
▷ *adv* menos: **when you least expect it** *cuando menos lo esperas*.
▷ *n* lo menos: **it's the least I can do** *es lo menos que puedo hacer*. ■ **at (the) least** por lo menos.
leather ['leðə'] *n* piel *f*, cuero.
▷ *adj* de piel, de cuero.
leave[1] [li:v] *vt* **1** *(go away from)* dejar, abandonar; *(go out of)* salir de: **she left home when she was 16** *se marchó de casa a los 16 años*. **2** *(stop being with)* irse de, marcharse de. **3** *(forget)* dejarse, olvidar, olvidarse. **4** *(allow to remain)* dejar: **please leave the door open** *por favor, deja la puerta abierta*. **5** *(cause to remain)* dejar: **the glass left a ring on the table** *el vaso dejó un cerco en la mesa*. **6** *(bequeath)* dejar, legar. **7** MATH dar: **two from six leaves four** *seis menos dos dan cuatro*.
▷ *vi* marcharse, irse, partir: **he left for Rome this morning** *esta mañana salió hacia Roma*.
⊙ **to leave off** *vt insep* dejar de: **there was so much noise that I had to leave off studying** *había tanto ruido que tuve que dejar de estudiar*.
▷ *vi* acabar, terminar.
▲ *pt & pp* **left**, *ger* **leaving**.
⊙ **to leave out** *vt sep* omitir, excluir.
leave[2] [li:v] *n* **1** *(time off)* permiso. **2** *(permission)* permiso. ■ **to be on leave** MIL estar de permiso.
leaven ['levᵊn] *n* levadura.
leaves [li:vz] *pl* ⟶ **leaf**.
Lebanese [lebəni:z] *adj* libanés,-esa.
▷ *n* libanés,-esa.
▷ *n pl* **the Lebanese** los libaneses *mpl*.
Lebanon ['lebənən] *n* Líbano.
lecherous ['letʃərəs] *adj* lujurioso,-a, lascivo,-a.
lechery ['letʃərɪ] *n* lujuria, lascivia.
lectern ['lektən] *n* atril *m*; *(in church)* facistol *m*.
lecture ['lektʃə'] *n* **1** conferencia. **2** *(in university)* clase *f*. **3** *(telling-off)* reprimenda, sermón *m*.
▷ *vi* **1** dar una conferencia (**on**, sobre). **2** *(in university)* dar clase.
▷ *vt (scold)* sermonear, echar una reprimenda a.
lecturer ['lektʃərə'] *n* **1** conferenciante *mf*. **2** *(in university)* profesor,-ra.
led [li:vz] *pp & pt* ⟶ **lead**[2].
ledge [ledʒ] *n* **1** *(shelf)* repisa; *(of window)* antepecho, alféizar *m*. **2** *(of rock)* saliente *m*.
lee [li:] *n* **1** MAR sotavento, socaire *m*. **2** *(shelter)* abrigo. ■ **in the lee of** al abrigo de.
leech [li:tʃ] *n* sanguijuela. ■ **to cling to** SB **like a leech** pegarse a ALGN como una lapa.
leek [li:k] *n* puerro.
leer [lɪə'] *vi* mirar con lascivia (**at**, -).
▷ *n* mirada lasciva.
leeway ['li:weɪ] *n* **1** *(freedom)* libertad *f*: **from now on I'll have a certain amount of leeway** *a partir de ahora tendré cierto margen de libertad*. **2** GB *(backlog)* tiempo perdido.
left[1] [left] *adj* **1** izquierdo,-a. **2** POL de izquierdas: **the left wing of the party** *el ala izquierda del partido*.
▷ *adv* a la izquierda, hacia la izquierda.
▷ *n* **1** izquierda: **keep to the left** *manténgase a la izquierda*. **2** *(punch)* golpe *m* de la izquierda. ■ **on the left** a mano izquierda.
left[2] [left] *pt & pp* ⟶ **leave**[1]. ■ **to be left** quedar: **is there any milk left?** *¿queda leche?* ■ **to be left over** sobrar, quedar. ● **left luggage office** consigna.

left-hand ['lefthænd] *adj* izquierdo,-a: **the shop is on the left-hand side** *la tienda está a mano izquierda.*
left-handed [lefthændɪd] *adj* **1** *(person)* zurdo,-a. **2** *(object)* para zurdos. **3** *(action)* con la mano izquierda.
left-hander [lefthændəʳ] *n (person)* zurdo,-a.
leftist ['leftɪst] *adj* izquierdista.
▷ *n* izquierdista *mf.*
leftover ['leftəʊvəʳ] *adj* sobrante, restante.
▷ *n pl* **leftovers** sobras *fpl*, restos *mpl.*
left-wing ['leftwɪŋ] *adj* de izquierdas.
left-winger [leftwɪŋəʳ] *n* izquierdoso,-a.
lefty ['leftɪ] *n* **1** GB *fam* izquierdista *mf*, izquierdoso,-a. **2** US *fam* zurdo,-a.
▲ *pl* **lefties.**
leg [leg] *n* **1** ANAT pierna; *(of animal)* pata. **2** CULIN *(lamb, etc)* pierna; *(chicken, etc)* muslo. **3** *(of furniture)* pata, pie *m.* **4** *(of trousers)* pernera. **5** *(stage)* etapa. ■ **not to have a leg to stand on** no tener en qué basarse. ‖ **to be on one's last legs** estar en las últimas. ‖ **to leg it 1** *fam (run away)* irse corriendo, poner pies en polvorosa. **2** *(walk)* ir andando. ‖ **to pull** SB**'s leg** *fam* tomarle el pelo a ALGN.
legacy ['legəsɪ] *n* legado, herencia.
▲ *pl* **legacies.**
legal ['li:gᵊl] *adj* **1** legal, lícito,-a. **2** *(relating to the law)* jurídico,-a, legal: **the legal profession** *la abogacía.* ■ **to take legal action** entablar un pleito (**against**, contra).
legality [lɪgælɪtɪ] *n* legalidad *f.*
▲ *pl* **legalities.**
legalize ['li:gᵊlaɪz] *vt* legalizar.
legate ['legət] *n* legado.
legend ['ledʒᵊnd] *n* leyenda. ■ **a legend in one's own lifetime** una leyenda viva.
legendary ['ledʒᵊndᵊrɪ] *adj* legendario,-a.
leggings ['legɪŋz] *n pl (whole leg)* mallas *fpl*; *(below knee)* polainas *fpl.*
leggy ['legɪ] *adj* zanquilargo,-a, patilargo,-a; *(woman)* de piernas esculturales.
▲ *comp* **leggier**, *superl* **leggiest.**
legible ['ledʒəbᵊl] *adj* legible.
legibly ['ledʒəblɪ] *adv* con letra clara.
legion ['li:dʒᵊn] *n* legión *f.*
legionella [li:dʒə'nelə] *n* legionella.
legionnaire [li:dʒə'neəʳ] *n* legionario. ● **legionnaire's disease** enfermedad *f* del legionario.
legislate ['ledʒɪsleɪt] *vi* legislar.
legislation [ledʒɪsleɪʃᵊn] *n* legislación *f.*
legislative ['ledʒɪslətɪv] *adj* legislativo,-a.
legislator ['ledʒɪsleɪtəʳ] *n* legislador,-ra.
legislature ['ledʒɪsleɪtʃəʳ] *n* cuerpo legislativo.
legitimate [lɪ'dʒɪtɪmət] *adj* legítimo,-a.
legitimize [lɪ'dʒɪtɪmaɪz] *vt* legitimar.
legless ['legləs] *adj fam* ciego,-a, trompa.
legroom ['legru:m] *n* sitio para las piernas.
legume ['legju:m] *n* legumbre *f.*
legwork ['legwɜ:k] *phr* **to do the legwork** *fam* hacer el trabajo duro.
leisure ['leʒəʳ, US 'li:ʒəʳ] *n* ocio, tiempo libre. ■ **at leisure 1** *(with free time)* en su tiempo libre. **2** *(calmly)* tranquilamente.
leisurely ['leʒəlɪ, US 'li:ʒərlɪ] *adj* sin prisa.
lemon ['lemən] *n* limón *m.*
▷ *adj (colour)* de color limón. ● **lemon squeezer** exprimidor *m.* ‖ **lemon tree** limonero.
lemonade [lemə'neɪd] *n* **1** *(fizzy - plain)* gaseosa; *(- lemony)* limonada. **2** *(still)* limonada.
lend [lend] *vt* **1** dejar, prestar: **could you lend me some money?** *¿me dejas un poco de dinero?* **2** *fig (add)* dotar de, prestar. ■ **to lend** OS **to** STH prestarse a ALGO, prestarse para ALGO. ‖ **to lend (**SB**) a hand** echar una mano (a ALGN).
▲ *pt & pp* **lent** [lent].
lending ['lendɪŋ] ● **lending library** biblioteca pública.
length [leŋθ] *n* **1** longitud *f.* **2** *(of time)* duración *f.* **3** *(piece)* trozo; *(of cloth)* largo. **4** *(of road)* tramo; *(of swimming pool)* largo.
lengthen ['leŋθᵊn] *vt* **1** *(skirt, etc)* alargar. **2** *(lifetime)* prolongar.
▷ *vi* **1** *(skirt, etc)* alargarse. **2** *(lifetime)* prolongarse; *(days)* crecer.
lengthways ['leŋθweɪz] *adv* a lo largo.
lengthy ['leŋθɪ] *adj (in general)* largo,-a.
▲ *comp* **lengthier**, *superl* **lengthiest.**
lenience ['li:nɪəns] *n* indulgencia, lenidad *f.*
lenient ['li:nɪənt] *adj (person)* indulgente; *(punishment)* poco severo,-a.
Leninist ['lenɪnɪst] *adj* leninista.
▷ *n* leninista *mf.*
lens [lenz] *n* **1** *(of glasses)* lente *m & f.* **2** *(of camera)* objetivo. **3** ANAT cristalino.
lent [lent] *pt & pp* → **lend.**
lentil ['lentᵊl] *n* lenteja.
Leo ['li:əʊ] *n* Leo.
leopard ['lepəd] *n* leopardo.
leotard ['li:ətɑ:d] *n* malla.
leper ['lepəʳ] *n* leproso,-a.
leprosy ['leprəsɪ] *n* lepra.
lesbian ['lezbɪən] *adj* lesbiano,-a.
▷ *n* lesbiana.
Lesotho [lɪ'su:tu:] *n* Lesotho.
less [les] *adj* menos.
▷ *pron* menos: **the less you eat, the less you'll spend** *cuanto menos comas, menos gastarás.* ■ **no less** nada menos.
▷ *adv* menos: **less and less** *cada vez menos;* **he was being less than sincere** *no fue nada sincero.* ■ **much less** menos aún.
▷ *prep* menos.
lessee [lesi:] *n* arrendatario,-a.
lessen ['lesᵊn] *vt* disminuir, reducir.
▷ *vi* disminuir, reducirse.
lesser ['lesəʳ] *adj* menor.
lesson ['lesᵊn] *n* **1** *(class)* clase *f.* **2** *(warning)* lección *f.*
lessor [lesɔ:ʳ] *n* arrendador,-ra.
lest [lest] *conj (for fear that)* por miedo a que.
let [let] *vt (allow)* dejar: **he lets the children watch cartoon videos** *a los niños les deja mirar vídeos de dibujos animados.* ■ **to let** SB **alone** dejar a ALGN en paz, no molestar a ALGN. ‖ **to let** SB **know** hacer saber a ALGN, avisar a ALGN.
▷ *aux* que + *subjuntivo*: **let him come** *que venga;* **let's go!** *¡vamos!, ¡vámonos!*
▷ *vt* GB *(rent)* alquilar: **«House to let»** *«Se alquila casa».*
▲ *pt & pp* **let**, *ger* **letting.**

▷ *n* GB *(renting)* alquiler *m*.
⊙ **to let down** *vt sep* 1 *(lower)* bajar. 2 *(lengthen)* alargar. 3 *(deflate)* desinflar. 4 *(disappoint)* fallar, defraudar.
⊙ **to let in** *vt sep* dejar entrar: **her father let me in** *me abrió su padre*.
⊙ **to let into** *vt sep* 1 dejar entrar a: **this key will let you into the garage** *con esta llave podrás entrar en el garaje*. 2 *(inlay into)* incrustar en. 3 *(reveal)* revelar.
⊙ **to let off** *vt sep* 1 *(leave off)* dejar. 2 *(bomb)* hacer explotar; *(fireworks)* hacer estallar. 3 *(person - forgive)* perdonar; *(- let leave)* dejar marcharse; *(- free)* dejar en libertad.
⊙ **to let on** *vi fam (tell)* decir, descubrir.
▷ *vt insep fam (pretend)* hacer ver.
⊙ **to let out** *vt sep* 1 *(in general)* dejar salir; *(release)* soltar (**from**, de). 2 *(utter)* soltar.
⊙ **to let through** *vt sep* dejar pasar.
⊙ **to let up** *vi* parar.
⊙ **to let up on** *vt insep fam* dejar en paz.
letdown ['letdaʊn] *n fam* disgusto, chasco, desilusión *f*.
lethal ['li:θəl] *adj* letal, mortal.
lethargic [ləθɑ:dʒɪk] *adj* aletargado,-a.
lethargy ['leθədʒɪ] *n* letargo.
letter ['letəʳ] *n* 1 *(of alphabet)* letra. 2 *(message)* carta. ■ **to the letter** al pie de la letra.● **capital letter** mayúscula. ‖ **letter box** buzón *m*. ‖ **small letter** minúscula.
letterhead ['letəhed] *n* membrete *m*.
lettering ['letərɪŋ] *n* rotulación *f*.
letter-opener ['letərəʊpənəʳ] *n* US abrecartas *m*.
letting ['letɪŋ] *n* GB piso de alquiler, casa de alquiler.
lettuce ['letɪs] *n* lechuga.
let-up ['letʌp] *n fam* respiro, tregua.
leukaemia [lu:ki:mɪə] *n* GB leucemia.
leukemia [lu:'ki:mɪə] *n* US ⟶ **leukaemia.**
leukocyte ['lu:kəsaɪt] *n* leucocito.
level ['levəl] *adj* 1 *(horizontal)* llano,-a, plano,-a. 2 *(even)* a nivel, nivelado,-a; *(spoonful, etc)* raso,-a: **the table's not level** *la mesa no está nivelada*. 3 *(equal)* igual, igualado,-a. 4 *(steady)* estable; *(voice)* llano,-a. ● **level crossing** paso a nivel.
▷ *n* 1 nivel *m*: **above sea level** *sobre el nivel del mar*. 2 *(flat ground)* llano, llanura. ■ **to be on a level with** estar al mismo nivel que.
▷ *vt* 1 *(make level, survey)* nivelar. 2 *(raze)* arrasar, rasar. 3 *(aim)* apuntar.

▷ *adv* a ras (**with**, de).
⊙ **to level off** *vi* 1 *(plane)* enderezarse; *(prices, etc)* estabilizarse. 2 *(ground)* nivelarse.
▷ *vt sep* nivelar.
▲ *pt & pp* **levelled** (US **leveled**), *ger* **levelling** (US **leveling**).
⊙ **to level out** *vi* ⟶ **to level off.**
level-headed [levəlhedɪd] *adj* sensato,-a.
lever ['li:vəʳ] *n* 1 palanca. 2 *(in lock)* guarda.
leverage ['li:vərɪdʒ] *n* 1 acción *f* de palanca. 2 *fig (influence)* influencias *fpl*, enchufe *m*.
leviathan [lɪvaɪəθən] *n* leviatán *m*.
levitate ['levɪteɪt] *vi* levitar.
▷ *vt* hacer levitar.
levy ['levɪ] *vt* recaudar; *(fine)* imponer.
▲ *pt & pp* **levied**, *ger* **levying.**
▷ *n* recaudación *f*; *(of fine)* imposición *f*.
▲ *pl* **levies.**
lewd [lu:d] *adj* 1 lascivo,-a. 2 *(obscene)* obsceno,-a.
lexical ['leksɪkəl] *adj* léxico,-a.
liability [laɪəbɪlətɪ] *n fam* desastre *m*.
▲ *pl* **liabilities.**
liable ['laɪəbəl] *adj* 1 *(likely, susceptible)* propenso,-a (**to**, a): **the car is liable to stall** *el coche tiende a calarse*. 2 *(susceptible)* susceptible (**to**, a).
liaise [lɪeɪz] *vi* comunicarse, tener contacto (**with**, con).
liaison [lɪeɪzən] *n* 1 enlace *m*. 2 *(sexual)* amorío.
liana [lɪɑ:nə] *n* liana, bejuco.
liar ['laɪəʳ] *n* mentiroso,-a, embustero,-a: **he's such a liar!** *¡menudo embustero está hecho!*
libel ['laɪbəl] *n* calumnia, difamación *f*.
▷ *vt* difamar.
▲ *pt & pp* **libelled** (US **libeled**), *ger* **libelling** (US **libeling**).
liberal ['lɪbərəl] *adj* 1 *(in general)* liberal. 2 *(abundant)* abundante.
Liberal ['lɪbərəl] *adj* POL liberal.
▷ *n* POL liberal *mf*.
liberalism ['lɪbərəlɪzəm] *n* liberalismo.
liberalization [lɪbərəlaɪzeɪʃən] *n* liberalización *f*.
liberalize ['lɪbərəlaɪz] *vt* liberalizar.
liberate ['lɪbəreɪt] *vt (in general)* liberar; *(prisoner, etc)* poner en libertad, libertar, emancipar: **a liberated woman** *una mujer liberada*. ■ **to become liberated** liberarse, emanciparse.
liberation [lɪbə'reɪʃən] *n* liberación *f*.
liberator ['lɪbəreɪtəʳ] *n* libertador,-ra.
Liberia [laɪ'bɪərɪə] *n* Liberia.
Liberian [laɪ'bɪərɪən] *adj* liberiano,-a.
▷ *n* liberiano,-a.
libertine ['lɪbəti:n] *n* libertino,-a.
▷ *adj* libertino,-a.
liberty ['lɪbətɪ] *n* libertad *f*.■ **at liberty** en libertad, libre (**to**, de). ‖ **to take liberties with** SB/STH tomarse libertades con ALGN/ALGO.
▲ *pl* **liberties.**
libido [lɪbi:dəʊ] *n* libido *f*.
▲ *pl* **libidos.**
Libra ['li:brə] *n* Libra *m*.
librarian [laɪ'breərɪən] *n* bibliotecario,-a.
library ['laɪbrərɪ] *n* 1 biblioteca. 2 *(collection)* colección *f*. ● **newspaper library** hemeroteca.
▲ *pl* **libraries.**
libretto [lɪ'bretəʊ] *n* libreto.
▲ *pl* **librettos** o **libretti** [lɪ'breti:].
Libya ['lɪbɪə] *n* Libia.
Libyan ['lɪbɪən] *adj* libio,-a.
▷ *n* libio,-a.
lice [laɪs] *pl* ⟶ **louse.**
licence ['laɪsəns] *n* 1 *(permit)* licencia, permiso. 2 *(freedom)* libertad *f*; *(excessive freedom)* licencia. ● **licence number** matrícula.
license ['laɪsəns] *n* US ⟶ **licence.**
▷ *vt* autorizar, dar licencia a.
licensed ['laɪsənst] *adj* autorizado,-a.
licensee [laɪsənsi:] *n (in general)* concesionario,-a.

licentious [laɪsenʃəs] *adj* licencioso,-a.
lichen ['laɪkᵊn, 'lɪtʃᵊn] *n* liquen *m*.
lick [lɪk] *vt* **1** lamer. **2** *fam (defeat - team)* vencer a, derrotar; *(- problem)* superar, solucionar. ■ **to lick one's lips** relamerse.
▷ *n* **1** lamedura, lengüetada. **2** *fam (of paint)* mano *f*.
licorice ['lɪkᵊrɪs, 'lɪkᵊrɪʃ] *n* regaliz *m*.
lid [lɪd] *n* **1** *(cover)* tapa. **2** *(of eye)* párpado. ■ **to take the lid off** STH *fig* destapar ALGO.
lie¹ [laɪ] *vi* mentir.
▲ *pt & pp* **lied**, *ger* **lying**.
▷ *n* mentira. ■ **to tell lies** mentir.
lie² [laɪ] *vi* **1** *(adopt a flat position)* acostarse, tumbarse. **2** *(be situated)* estar (situado,-a), encontrarse. **3** *(be buried)* yacer. **4** *(remain)* quedarse, permanecer.
▲ *pt* **lay** [leɪ], *pp* **lain** [leɪn], *ger* **lying**.
▷ *n (position)* posición *f*; *(direction)* orientación *f*.
⊙ **to lie about / lie around** *vi (person)* estar tumbado,-a; *(things)* estar tirado,-a.
⊙ **to lie back** *vi* recostarse.
⊙ **to lie down** *vi* acostarse, tumbarse, echarse.
⊙ **to lie in** *vi* GB levantarse tarde.
⊙ **to lie up** *vi* guardar cama.
Liechtenstein ['lɪktᵊnstaɪn] *n* Liechtenstein.
lie-down ['laɪdaʊn] *n* siesta.
lie-in ['laɪɪn] *phr* **to have a lie-in** *fam* levantarse tarde.
lieutenant [lef'tenənt, US luː'tenənt] *n* **1** MIL teniente *m*. **2** *(non-military)* lugarteniente *m*.
life [laɪf] *n* **1** vida. **2** *(of battery)* duración *f*. ■ **it's a matter of life and death** es cuestión de vida o muerte. ‖ **not on your life!** *fam* ¡ni hablar! ‖ **run for your life «(lives)»!** ¡sálvese quien pueda! ‖ **to bring** SB **back to life** resucitar a ALGN. ‖ **to come to life** cobrar vida. ‖ **to lose one's life** perder la vida. ‖ **to take one's own life** suicidarse. ‖ **to take** SB**'s life** matar a ALGN. ● **life belt / life buoy** salvavidas *m*. ‖ **life jacket** chaleco salvavidas. ‖ **life style** estilo de vida.
▲ *pl* **lives** [laɪvz].
life-and-death ['laɪfᵊndeθ] *adj* a vida o muerte.
lifeblood ['laɪfblʌd] *n fig* alma, impulso vital.
lifeboat ['laɪfbəʊt] *n* **1** *(on shore)* lancha de socorro. **2** *(on ship)* bote *m* salvavidas.
lifeguard ['laɪfgɑːd] *n* socorrista *mf*.
lifeless ['laɪfləs] *adj* **1** exánime, inánime. **2** *fig* sin vida, soso,-a.
lifelike ['laɪflaɪk] *adj* fiel.
lifeline ['laɪflaɪn] *n* **1** *(rope)* cuerda de salvamento. **2** *fig* cordón *m* umbilical.
lifelong ['laɪflɒŋ] *adj* de toda la vida.
life-saver ['laɪfseɪvəʳ] *n* socorrista *mf*.
life-sized ['laɪfsaɪzd] *adj* (de) tamaño natural.
lifespan ['laɪfspæn] *n* vida: **men are said to have a shorter lifespan than women** *se dice que los hombres viven menos que las mujeres*.
lifetime ['laɪftaɪm] *n* **1** vida: **in her lifetime** *en su vida*. **2** *fam* eternidad *f*.
lift [lɪft] *vt* **1** *(in general)* levantar, coger. **2** *(by plane)* transportar.
▷ *vi (of movable parts)* levantarse:.
▷ *n* GB ascensor *m*. ■ **to give** SB **a lift 1** *(in car)* llevar a ALGN en coche. **2** *(cheer up)* animar.
liftoff ['lɪftɒf] *n* despegue *m*.
ligament ['lɪgəmənt] *n* ligamento.
light¹ [laɪt] *n* **1** *(gen)* luz *f*. **2** *(lamp)* luz *f*, lámpara; *(traffic light)* semáforo. **3** *(for cigarette, fire)* fuego. ■ **in (the) light of** GB en vista de, teniendo en cuenta. ‖ **to come to light** salir a luz. ‖ **to throw light on** STH aclarar ALGO. ● **light bulb** bombilla. ‖ **light switch** interruptor *m* de la luz. ‖ **light year** año luz.
▷ *vt* **1** *(ignite)* encender. **2** *(illuminate)* iluminar, alumbrar.
▷ *vi* encenderse.
▷ *adj* **1** *(colour)* claro,-a; *(complexion)* blanco,-a. **2** *(bright)* con mucha claridad.
⊙ **to light up** *vt sep* **1** iluminar. **2** *fam (cigarette, etc)* encender.
▷ *vi* **1** iluminarse. **2** *fam* encender un cigarrillo.
▲ *pt & pp* **lighted** o **lit** [lɪt].
light² [laɪt] *adj* **1** *(not heavy)* ligero,-a; *(rain)* fino,-a; *(breeze)* suave. **2** *(sentence, wound)* leve. ● **light aircraft** avioneta.
lighten¹ ['laɪtᵊn] *vt* **1** *(colour)* aclarar. **2** *(room)* iluminar.
▷ *vi (colour)* aclararse.
lighten² ['laɪtᵊn] *vt (make less heavy)* aligerar.
▷ *vi (mood, etc)* alegrarse.
lighter ['laɪtəʳ] [Also **cigarette lighter**.] *n* encendedor *m*, mechero.
light-fingered ['laɪtfɪŋgəd] *adj* largo,-a de dedos.
light-headed [laɪthedɪd] *adj (dizzy)* mareado,-a.
lighthouse ['laɪthaʊs] *n* faro.
lighting ['laɪtɪŋ] *n* **1** *(in general)* iluminación *f*. **2** *(system)* alumbrado.
lightly ['laɪtlɪ] *adv* **1** *(not heavily)* ligeramente. **2** *(not seriously)* a la ligera.
lightning ['laɪtᵊnɪŋ] *n* rayo; *(flash only)* relámpago.
lightweight ['laɪtweɪt] *n* **1** *(boxing)* peso ligero. **2** *pej* don nadie *m*, peso ligero.
▷ *adj* **1** *(clothing)* ligero,-a. **2** *(boxing)* de peso ligero. **3** *pej* flojo,-a, poco convincente.
lignite ['lɪgnaɪt] *n* lignita.
like¹ [laɪk] *prep* **1** *(the same as)* como: **the flat (**US **apartment) looks like new** *el piso está como nuevo*. **2** *(typical of)* propio,-a de: **it isn't like her to make a scene** *no es propio de ella armar un escándalo*. ■ **to look like** SB parecerse a ALGN.
▷ *adj* **1** *(such as)* como. **2** *fml* parecido,-a.
▷ *conj fam* como.
▷ *n* algo parecido: **I've never seen the like of it** *nunca he visto cosa igual*.
like² [laɪk] *vt* **1** *(enjoy)* gustar. **2** *(want)* querer, gustar: **I'd like a cup of coffee** *me gustaría tomar un café*. ■ **to like** STH **better** preferir ALGO.
▷ *vi* querer: **if you like** *si quieres*.
▷ *n pl* **likes** gustos *mpl*.
likeable ['laɪkəbᵊl] *adj* simpático,-a.
likelihood ['laɪklɪhʊd] *n* probabilidad *f*.
likely ['laɪklɪ] *adj* probable: **he's likely to leave late** *es probable que salga tarde*.
▷ *adv* probablemente. ■ **as likely as not** *fam* lo más seguro.
like-minded [laɪkmaɪndɪd] *adj* del mismo parecer.
liken ['laɪkᵊn] *vt* comparar (**to**, con).
likeness ['laɪknəs] *n* **1** *(similarity)* semejanza, parecido. **2** *(portrait)* retrato.
likewise ['laɪkwaɪz] *adv* **1** *(the same)* lo mismo, igualmente: **to do likewise** *hacer lo mismo*.

liking ['laɪkɪŋ] *n (for thing)* gusto, afición *f*; *(for person)* simpatía; *(for friend)* cariño.
lilac ['laɪlək] *n* **1** BOT lila. **2** *(colour)* lila *m*.
▷ *adj* (de color) lila.
lilt [lɪlt] *n (in voice)* melodía; *(in song)* ritmo alegre.
lilting ['lɪltɪŋ] *adj (voice)* melodioso,-a.
lily ['lɪlɪ] *n* lirio, azucena.
▲ *pl* lilies.
lima bean ['laɪməbi:n] *n* frijol *m*.
limb [lɪmb] *n* **1** ANAT miembro. **2** *(branch)* rama.
limber ['lɪmbəʳ] *adj (person)* ágil; *(thing)* flexible.
⊙ **to limber up** *vi* SP entrar en calor.
▷ *vt sep* calentar.
lime [laɪm] *n* **1** *(citrus fruit)* lima. **2** *(citrus tree)* limero. **3** *(linden)* tilo.
lime-green ['laɪmgri:n] *adj* (de color) verde lima.
limelight ['laɪmlaɪt] *n* luz *f* de calcio. ■ **to be in the limelight** estar en el candelero.
limerick ['lɪmərɪk] *n* quintilla humorística.
limestone ['laɪmstəʊn] *n* piedra caliza.
limit ['lɪmɪt] *n* límite *m*. ■ **that's the limit!** *fam* ¡eso es el colmo! ■ **to be off limits** estar en zona prohibida (**to**, para). ■ **within limits** dentro de ciertos límites.
▷ *vt* limitar, restringir (**to**, a)
limitation [lɪmɪ'teɪʃᵊn] *n* limitación *f*.
limited ['lɪmɪtɪd] *adj* limitado,-a, restringido,-a.
limitless ['lɪmɪtləs] *adj* ilimitado,-a.
limousine [lɪmə'zi:n] *n* limusina.
limp[1] [lɪmp] *vi* cojear.
▷ *n* cojera.
limp[2] [lɪmp] *adj* **1** *(floppy)* flojo,-a, fláccido,-a; *(lettuce)* mustio,-a. **2** *(weak)* débil.
limpet ['lɪmpɪt] *n* lapa.
limpid ['lɪmpɪd] *adj lit* límpido,-a.
limy ['laɪmɪ] *adj* calizo,-a.
▲ *comp* limier, *superl* limiest.
linden ['lɪndᵊn] *n* tilo.
line [laɪn] *n* **1** *(in general)* línea: **in a straight line** *en línea recta.* **2** *(drawn on paper)* raya. **3** *(of text)* línea, renglón *m*; *(of poetry)* verso: **new line** *punto y aparte.* **4** *(row)* fila, hilera. **5** US *(queue)* cola. **6** *(cord)* cuerda, cordel *m*; *(fishing)* sedal *m*; *(wire)* cable *m*. **7** *(route)* vía. ■ **all along the line 1** *(from the beginning)* desde el principio. **2** *(in detail)* con todo detalle. ■ **in line with** *fig* conforme a. ■ **to stand in line** US hacer cola. ● **dotted line** línea de puntos. ■ **line drawing** dibujo lineal.
▷ *vt* **1** *(draw lines on)* dibujar rayas en. **2** *(mark with wrinkles)* arrugar. **3** *(form rows along)* bordear.
⊙ **to line up** *vi* ponerse en fila; *(in queue)* hacer cola.
linen ['lɪnɪn] *n* **1** *(material)* lino, hilo. **2** *(sheets, etc)* ropa blanca, lencería. ● **bed linen** ropa de cama.
liner ['laɪnəʳ] *n (mar)* transatlántico.
linesman ['laɪnzmən] *n* juez *mf* de línea, linier *m*.
▲ *pl* linesmen ['laɪnzmən].
line-up ['laɪnʌp] *n (of people)* alineación *f*, formación *f*.
linger ['lɪŋgəʳ] *vi* **1** *(stay)* quedarse. **2** *(persist)* persistir, perdurar.
lingerie ['lɑ:nʒəri:] *n fml* lencería.
lingering ['lɪŋgərɪŋ] *adj* **1** *(slow)* lento,-a. **2** *(persistent)* persistente.
lingo ['lɪŋgəʊ] *n sl* idioma *m*.
▲ *pl* lingoes.

linguist ['lɪŋgwɪst] *n* **1** lingüista *mf*. **2** *(fam)* políglota *mf*.
linguistic [lɪŋ'gwɪstɪk] *adj* lingüístico,-a.
linguistics [lɪŋ'gwɪstɪks] *n* lingüística.
liniment ['lɪnɪmənt] *n* linimento.
lining ['laɪnɪŋ] *n* forro.
link [lɪŋk] *n* **1** *(in chain)* eslabón *m*. **2** *(connection)* enlace *m*. **3** *fig* vínculo, lazo.
▷ *vt* **1** unir, conectar. **2** *fig* vincular, relacionar.
⊙ **to link up** *vi* **1** *(be related)* estar relacionado,-a (**with**, con). **2** *(meet)* encontrarse (**with**, con).
linkage ['lɪŋkɪdʒ] *n* conexión *f*.
link-up ['lɪŋkʌp] *n* **1** *(in general)* conexión *f*. **2** *(meeting)* encuentro.
linnet ['lɪnɪt] *n* pardillo.
lino ['laɪnəʊ] *n* GB *(abbr of* **linoleum***)* linóleo.
linocut ['laɪnəʊkʌt] *n* linóleo, huecorrelieve *m*.
linoleum [lɪnəʊlɪəm] *n* (suelo de) linóleo.
linseed ['lɪnsi:d] *n* linaza.
lint [lɪnt] *n* **1** hilas *fpl*. **2** US *(fluff)* pelusa.
lintel ['lɪntᵊl] *n* dintel *m*.
lion ['laɪən] *n* león *m*.
lioness ['laɪənəs] *n* leona.
▲ *pl* lionesses.
lion-hearted [laɪənhɑ:tɪd] *adj lit* valentísimo,-a.
lionize ['laɪənaɪz] *vt* venerar.
lion-like ['laɪənlaɪk] *adj* leonino,-a.
lip [lɪp] *n* **1** labio. **2** *(of cup, etc)* borde *m*.
lipid ['lɪpɪd] *n* lípido.
lip-read ['lɪpri:d] *vt* leer en los labios.
▷ *vi* leer en los labios.
▲ *pt & pp* lip-read ['lɪpred].
lip-service ['lɪpsɜ:vɪs] *n* jarabe *m* de pico, palabrería.
lipstick ['lɪpstɪk] *n (stick)* barra de labios, lápiz *m* de labios; *(substance)* pintura de labios.
liquefy ['lɪkwɪfaɪ] *vt* licuar.
▷ *vi* licuarse.
▲ *pt & pp* liquefied, *ger* liquefying.
liqueur [lɪ'kjʊəʳ, US lɪ'kɜ:ʳ] *n* licor *m*.
liquid ['lɪkwɪd] *n* líquido.
▷ *adj* líquido,-a.
liquidate ['lɪkwɪdeɪt] *vt* liquidar.
liquidation [lɪkwɪdeɪʃᵊn] *n* liquidación *f*.
liquidity [lɪkwɪdɪtɪ] *n* liquidez *f*.
liquidize ['lɪkwɪdaɪz] *vt* licuar.
liquidizer ['lɪkwɪdaɪzəʳ] *n* licuadora.
liquor ['lɪkəʳ] *n* US licor *m*.
liquorice ['lɪkərɪs, 'lɪkərɪʃ] *n* regaliz *m*.
lira ['lɪərə] *n* lira.
▲ *pl* liras o lire ['lɪərə].
lisp [lɪsp] *vi* cecear.
list[1] [lɪst] *n* lista.
▷ *vt* hacer una lista de: **your name is not listed** *su nombre no aparece en la lista.*
list[2] [lɪst] *n* MAR escora.
▷ *vi* MAR escorar.
listen ['lɪsᵊn] *vi* escuchar (**to**, -): **listen to me!** *¡escúchame!*
⊙ **to listen in** *vi (radio)* escuchar (**to**, -).
⊙ **to listen out** *vi fam* estar a la escucha, estar en escucha (**for**, de).
listener ['lɪsᵊnəʳ] *n* **1** *(in general)* oyente *mf*. **2** RAD radioyente *mf*.
listing ['lɪstɪŋ] *n* listado.

listless ['lɪstləs] *adj* lánguido,-a, apático,-a.
lit [lɪt] *pt & pp* ⟶ **light.**
litany ['lɪtᵊnɪ] *n* letanía.
▲ *pl* **litanies.**
liter ['li:təʳ] *n* US ⟶ **litre.**
literacy ['lɪtᵊrəsɪ] *n* **1** *(ability to read)* alfabetización *f.* **2** *(knowledge)* conocimientos *mpl,* nociones *fpl.*
literal ['lɪtᵊrəl] *adj* literal.
literally ['lɪtᵊrəlɪ] *adv* literalmente.
literary ['lɪtᵊrərɪ] *adj* literario,-a.
literate ['lɪtᵊrət] *adj* **1** *(able to read)* alfabetizado,-a. **2** *(with knowledge)* con conocimientos de.
literature ['lɪtᵊrətʃəʳ] *n* **1** literatura. **2** *(bibliography)* bibliografía.
lithe [laɪð] *adj* ágil.
lithium ['lɪθɪəm] *n* litio.
lithograph ['lɪθəgrɑ:f] *n* litografía.
lithosphere ['lɪθəsfɪəʳ] *n* litosfera.
Lithuania [lɪθjʊ'eɪnɪə] *n* Lituania.
Lithuanian [lɪθjʊ'eɪnɪən] *adj* lituano,-a.
▷ *n* **1** *(person)* lituano,-a. **2** *(language)* lituano.
litigation [lɪtɪgeɪʃᵊn] *n* litigio.
litigious ['lɪtɪdʒəs] *adj* pleiteador,-ra.
litre ['li:təʳ] *n* GB litro.
litter ['lɪtəʳ] *n* **1** *(rubbish)* basura, desperdicios *mpl; (paper)* papeles *mpl.* **2** *(of kittens, etc)* camada. ● **litter bin** GB papelera.
little ['lɪtᵊl] *adj* **1** *(small)* pequeño,-a: **a little cup** *una tacita.* **2** *(not much)* poco,-a: **a little milk** *un poco de leche.* ● **little finger** dedo meñique.
▲ *comp* **less,** *superl* **least.**
▷ *pron* poco: **more tea? –just a little, please** *¿quieres más té? –un poco, por favor.*
▷ *adv* poco: **I'm a little (bit) tired** *estoy un poco cansada.* ■ **little by little** poco a poco.
littoral ['lɪtərəl] *n* litoral *m.*
▷ *adj* litoral.
liturgy ['lɪtədʒɪ] *n* liturgia.
▲ *pl* **liturgies.**
livable ['lɪvəbᵊl] *adj* **1** *(habitable)* habitable: **the flat (US apartment) isn't livable (in) yet** *el piso aún no es habitable.* **2** *(bearable)* soportable.
live[1] [lɪv] *vi* vivir: **he lives in the country** *vive en el campo.*
▷ *vt* vivir. ■ **to live it up** *fam* pasárselo bomba.
⊙ **to live down** *vt sep* lograr que se olvide.
⊙ **to live for** *vt insep* vivir por.
⊙ **to live in** *vi (student)* estar internado,-a; *(servant)* vivir con la familia.
⊙ **to live off** *vt insep* vivir de.
⊙ **to live on** *vi* sobrevivir; *(memory)* seguir vivo,-a.
⊙ **to live out** *vt sep* **1** *(finish)* acabar. **2** *(fulfil)* realizar.
▷ *vi (student)* ser externo,-a; *(servant)* no vivir con la familia.
⊙ **to live through** *vt insep* sobrevivir.
⊙ **to live together** *vi* vivir juntos,-as.
⊙ **to live up to** *vt insep* cumplir con.
⊙ **to live with** *vt insep* **1** vivir con. **2** *(tolerate)* soportar.
live[2] [laɪv] *adj* **1** *(not dead)* vivo,-a: **it's a real live snake** *es una serpiente de verdad.* **2** *(still burning)* vivo,-a, candente; *(issue)* candente. **3** *(broadcast)* en directo.
▷ *adv* en directo, en vivo.
livelihood ['laɪvlɪhʊd] *n* sustento.
lively ['laɪvlɪ] *adj* **1** vivo,-a, animado,-a; *(interest)* entusiasmado,-a. **2** *(colour)* vivo,-a.
▲ *comp* **livelier,** *superl* **liveliest.**
liven ['laɪvᵊn] *vt* **to liven up** animar.
▷ *vi* **liven up** animarse.
liver ['lɪvəʳ] *n* ANAT hígado.
livery ['lɪvᵊrɪ] *n* librea.
▲ *pl* **liveries.**
lives [laɪvz] *pl* ⟶ **life.**
livestock ['laɪvstɒk] *n* ganado. ■ **livestock farming** ganadería.
livid ['lɪvɪd] *adj* **1** *fam* furioso,-a. **2** *(bluish)* lívido,-a.
living ['lɪvɪŋ] *adj* vivo,-a: **every living creature** *todo bicho viviente.*
▷ *n* vida: **what do you do for a living?** *¿cómo te ganas la vida?* ● **living room** salón *m,* sala de estar.
lizard ['lɪzəd] *n* lagarto; *(small)* lagartija.
llama ['lɑ:mə] *n* ZOOL llama.
load [ləʊd] *n* **1** *(in general)* carga. **2** *(weight)* peso. ■ **a load of ... / loads of ...** *fam* un montón de ...
▷ *vt* cargar (**with,** de).
▷ *vi* cargar.
⊙ **to load down** *vt sep* cargar (**with,** de); *(with worries etc)* agobiar (**with,** de/por).
loaded ['ləʊdɪd] *adj* **1** *(dice)* trucado,-a; *(question)* tendencioso,-a. **2** *sl (rich)* forrado,-a.
loading ['ləʊdɪŋ] *n (act)* carga.
loaf [ləʊf] *n* pan *m; (French)* barra; *(sliced)* pan *m* de molde.
▲ *pl* **loaves** [ləvz].
loafer ['ləʊfəʳ] *n* **1** *fam (person)* holgazán,-ana, vago,-a. **2** US mocasín *m.*
loan [ləʊn] *n (of money)* préstamo. ■ **on loan** prestado,-a.
loath [ləʊθ] *adj* reacio,-a.
loathe [ləʊð] *vt* odiar, aborrecer.
loathing ['ləʊðɪŋ] *n* odio, aborrecimiento.
loathsome ['ləʊðsəm] *adj* odioso,-a, repelente.
loaves [ləʊvz] *pl* ⟶ **loaf.**
lobby ['lɒbɪ] *n* **1** *(hall)* vestíbulo. **2** POL grupo de presión.
▲ *pl* **lobbies.**
▷ *vi* presionar (**for,** para) (**against,** en contra de).
▷ *vt* POL presionar, ejercer presión sobre.
lobbyist ['lɒbɪɪst] *n* POL activista *mf* de un grupo de presión.
lobe [ləʊb] *n* lóbulo.
lobster ['lɒbstəʳ] *n* bogavante *m.*
local ['ləʊkᵊl] *adj* **1** *(in general)* local. **2** *(person)* de barrio, de la zona.
▷ *n* **1** *fam (person)* vecino,-a. **2** GB *fam* bar *m,* pub *m (de barrio).* **3** US *(train)* tren *m* de cercanías; *(bus)* autobús *m*
locale [ləʊkɑ:l] *n fml (place)* lugar *m; (scene)* escenario.
locality [ləʊkælɪtɪ] *n fml* localidad *f.*
▲ *pl* **localities.**
localize ['ləʊkᵊlaɪz] *vt fml* localizar.
locally ['ləʊkᵊlɪ] *adv* **1** *(in the area)* en la localidad, en el lugar. **2** *(in particular areas)* localmente.
locate [ləʊ'keɪt] *vt* **1** *fml (find)* localizar. **2** *fml (situate)* situar, ubicar.
location [ləʊ'keɪʃᵊn] *n* **1**lugar, ubicación *m.* **2** CINEM exteriores *mpl.*
loch [lɒk] *n (in Scotland)* lago.

lock[1] [lɒk] *n* **1** *(gen)* cerradura; *(padlock)* candado. **2** *(in canal)* esclusa. **3** *(in wrestling)* llave *f*.
▷ *vt (with key)* cerrar con llave.
▷ *vi (door, etc)* cerrarse (con llave).
⊙ **to lock away** *vt sep* **1** *(valuables)* guardar bajo llave. **2** *fam (person)* encerrar.
⊙ **to lock in** *vt sep* encerrar.
⊙ **to lock onto** *vt insep (missile)* seguir el rastro de.
⊙ **to lock out** *vt sep* **1** cerrar la puerta a; *(leave outside)* dejar fuera a. **2** *(from work)* cerrar el paso a.
⊙ **to lock up** *vt sep* **1**→ **to lock away**. **2** *(building)* cerrar con llave.
lock[2] [lɒk] *n (of hair)* mecha, mechón *m*.
locker ['lɒkəʳ] *n* armario, taquilla. ● **locker room** vestuarios *mpl*.
locket ['lɒkɪt] *n (with picture)* medallón *m*.
lockout ['lɒkaʊt] *n* locáut *m*, cierre *m* patronal.
locksmith ['lɒksmɪθ] *n* cerrajero.
lockup ['lɒkʌp] *n (local prison)* cárcel *f (pequeña)*.
locomotion [ləʊkə'məʊʃᵊn] *n* locomoción *f*.
locomotive [ləʊkə'məʊtɪv] *n* locomotora.
▷ *adj* locomotor,-ra.
locust ['ləʊkəst] *n* langosta.
locution [ləkjuːʃᵊn] *n* locución *f*.
lodge [lɒdʒ] *n* **1** *(in general)* casita; *(hunter's)* refugio. **2** *(porter's)* portería. **3** *(masonic)* logia.
▷ *vi* **1** *(as guest)* alojarse, hospedarse. **2** *(become fixed)* quedarse atrapado,-a.
▷ *vt (complaint)* presentar.
lodger ['lɒdʒəʳ] *n* huésped,-da.
lodging ['lɒdʒɪŋ] *n* alojamiento. ● **lodging house** casa de huéspedes.
loft [lɒft] *n* desván *m*, buhardilla.
▷ *vt* SP lanzar al aire.
lofty ['lɒftɪ] *adj* **1** *(high)* alto,-a. **2** *pej (haughty)* altivo,-a.
▲ *comp* **loftier**, *superl* **loftiest**.
log [lɒg] *n* **1** tronco; *(for fire)* leño. **2** *(on ship)* cuaderno de bitácora; *(on plane)* diario de vuelo. **3** MATH *fam (abbr of* **logarithm**) logaritmo.
▷ *vt* **1** registrar, anotar. **2** *(cover)* recorrer.
▲ *pt & pp* **logged**, *ger* **logging**.
⊙ **to log in** *vi* COMPUT entrar (en el sistema).
⊙ **to log out** *vi* COMPUT salir (del sistema).
ogarithm ['lɒgərɪðᵊm] *n* logaritmo.
ogger ['lɒgəʳ] *n* leñador,-ra.
oggerheads ['lɒgəhedz] ■ **to be at loggerheads** estar enfrentados,-as.
oggia ['lɒdʒə] *n* logia.
ogic ['lɒdʒɪk] *n* lógica.
ogical ['lɒdʒɪkᵊl] *adj* lógico,-a.
ogically ['lɒdʒɪklɪ] *adv* lógicamente.
ogician [lədʒɪʃᵊn] *n* lógico,-a.
ogistics [lə'dʒɪstɪks] *n* logística.
ogo ['ləʊgəʊ] *n* logotipo.
▲ *pl* **logos**.
ogy ['lɒgɪ] *adj* US *fam* pesado,-a, lento,-a.
▲ *comp* **logier**, *superl* **logiest**.
oin [lɔɪn] *n* CULIN *(of pork)* lomo; *(of beef)* solomillo.
oiter ['lɔɪtəʳ] *vi* **1** *(be slow)* entretenerse; *(waste time)* perder el tiempo. **2** *(loaf about)* holgazanear.
oiterer ['lɔɪtərəʳ] *n (gen)* holgazán,-ana.
oll [lɒl] *vi* **1** *(sit)* repantigarse. **2** *(droop)* colgar.

lollipop ['lɒlɪpɒp] *n* **1** pirulí *m*, piruleta. **2** GB *(iced)* polo.
lolly ['lɒlɪ] *n* **1** GB *fam* pirulí *m*, piruleta *m*. **2** GB *fam (iced)* polo.
▲ *pl* **lollies**.
lone [ləʊn] *adj* **1** *lit (single)* solo,-a. **2** *lit (solitary)* solitario,-a. ● **lone wolf** *fig* persona solitaria.
loneliness ['ləʊnlɪnəs] *n* soledad *f*.
lonely ['ləʊnlɪ] *adj* **1** *(person)* solo,-a. **2** *(place)* solitario,-a.
▲ *comp* **lonelier**, *superl* **loneliest**.
lonesome ['ləʊnsᵊm] *adj* US→ **lonely**.
long[1] [lɒŋ] *adj* largo,-a: **a long journey** *un largo viaje*.
● **long jump** salto de longitud.
▷ *adv* mucho tiempo: **it takes a long time to climb the mountain** *se tarda mucho en escalar la montaña*. ■ **as long as** *(while)* mientras. ❙ **long ago** hace mucho tiempo.
long[2] [lɒŋ] *phr* **to long to do** STH tener muchos deseos de hacer algo.
⊙ **to long for** *vt insep (yearn)* anhelar; *(nostalgically)* añorar.
long-distance [lɒŋ'dɪstᵊns] *adj* de larga distancia.
long-drawn-out [lɒŋdrɔːnaʊt] *adj* largo,-a, interminable.
longevity [lɒndʒevɪtɪ] *n* longevidad *f*.
long-haired ['lɒŋheəd] *adj* de pelo largo.
longhand ['lɒŋhænd] *n* escritura a mano.
longing ['lɒŋɪŋ] *n (yearning)* ansia, anhelo; *(nostalgia)* nostalgia.
longitude ['lɒndʒɪtjuːd] *n* longitud *f*.
longitudinal [lɒndʒɪtjuːdɪnᵊl] *adj* longitudinal.
long-life ['lɒŋlaɪf] *adj (battery)* de larga duración; *(milk)* UHT, uperizado,-a.
long-playing [lɒŋpleɪɪŋ] *adj* de larga duración.
● **long-playing record** elepé *m*.
long-range ['lɒŋreɪndʒ] *adj* **1** *(distance)* de largo alcance. **2** *(plans, forecast)* a largo plazo.
long-standing [lɒŋstændɪŋ] *adj* antiguo,-a.
long-term [lɒŋtɜːm] *adj* a largo plazo, de largo plazo.
longways ['lɒŋweɪz] *adv* GB a lo largo.
loo [luː] *n* GB *fam* váter *m*.
▲ *pl* **loos**.
look [lʊk] *vi* **1** mirar (at, -). **2** *(seem)* parecer: **he looks tired** *parece cansado*. ■ **look out!** ¡cuidado!
▷ *vt* **1** mirar: **I can't look him in the face** *no puedo mirarle a la cara*. **2** *(seem)* parecer: **he doesn't look his age** *no aparenta la edad que tiene*.
▷ *n* **1** *(glance)* mirada: **have a look at this** *mira esto*. **2** *(appearance)* aspecto, apariencia. **3** *(fashion)* moda: **I'm not into the punk look** *no me va la moda punk*.
▷ *interj* ¡mira!
⊙ **to look after** *vt insep (deal with)* ocuparse de, atender a; *(take care of)* cuidar (de).
⊙ **to look at** *vt insep* **1** *(consider)* mirar, considerar. **2** *(examine)* mirar.
⊙ **to look back** *vi* mirar atrás.
⊙ **to look down on** *vt insep* despreciar.
⊙ **to look for** *vt insep* buscar: **what are you looking for?** *¿qué buscas?*
⊙ **to look forward to** *vt insep* esperar (con ansia).
⊙ **to look into** *vt insep* investigar.
⊙ **to look on** *vt insep* considerar.
⊙ **to look like** *vt insep* parecerse a: **he looks like his father** *se parece a su padre*.
⊙ **to look out** *vi (be careful)* ir con cuidado.

⊙ **to look out for** *vt insep* esperar.
⊙ **to look over** *vt sep (study quickly)* mirar por encima.
⊙ **to look round** *vi* **1** *(turn one's head)* volver la cabeza. **2** *(in shop, etc)* mirar.
⊙ **to look through** *vt insep (check)* revisar (bien); *(quickly)* ojear.
⊙ **to look to** *vt insep* **1** *(depend on)* contar con. **2** *(concentrate on)* centrarse en.
⊙ **to look up** *vi fam (improve)* mejorar.
▷ *vt sep* **1** *(in dictionary, etc)* consultar, buscar.
⊙ **to look up to** *vt insep* respetar.
lookalike ['lʊkəlaɪk] *n fam* doble *mf*, sosia *m*.
look-in ['lʊkɪn] *n fam* oportunidad *f*, ocasión *f*.
lookout ['lʊkaʊt] *n* **1** *(person)* vigía *mf*. **2** *(place)* atalaya.
loom[1] [lu:m] *n* telar *m*.
loom[2] [lu:m] *vi* vislumbrarse; *(causing fear)* amenazar.
⊙ **to loom up** *vi* surgir.
loony ['lu:nɪ] *adj fam* chiflado,-a, chalado,-a.
▲ *comp* **loonier**, *superl* **looniest**.
loop [lu:p] *n (in string, etc)* lazo.
▷ *vi* formar un lazo. ■ **to loop the loop** rizar el rizo.
loophole ['lu:phəʊl] *n fig* escapatoria.
loose [lu:s] *adj* **1** *(in general)* suelto,-a. **2** *(not tight)* flojo,-a; *(clothes)* holgado,-a.
▷ *vt lit* soltar.
loose-fitting [lu:s'fɪtɪŋ] *adj* holgado,-a, amplio,-a.
loosen ['lu:sᵊn] *vt (gen)* soltar, aflojar; *(belt)* desabrochar.
▷ *vi* **1** soltarse, aflojarse.
⊙ **to loosen up** *vi (relax)* relajarse.
loot [lu:t] *n* botín *m*.
looter ['lu:təʳ] *n* saqueador,-ra.
lop [lɒp] *vt* **1** podar. **2** *fig* recortar.
▲ *pt & pp* **lopped**, *ger* **lopping**.
lope [ləʊp] *vi* andar a zancadas
lopsided [lɒpsaɪdɪd] *adj* **1** *(walk, table)* cojo,-a; *(unbalanced)* desigual. **2** *fig* injusto,-a.
loquacious [lə'kweɪʃəs] *adj fml* locuaz.
lord [lɔ:d] *n* **1** señor *m*. **2** GB *(title)* lord *m*. **3** *(judge)* señoría *mf*. ■ **good Lord!** ¡ay Dios!, ¡Dios mío!
lordship ['lɔ:dʃɪp] *n (title)* señoría.
lore [lɔ:ʳ] *n* saber *m* popular.
lorry ['lɒrɪ] *n* GB camión *m*.
▲ *pl* **lorries**.
lose [lu:z] *vt* **1** *(in general)* perder: **don't lose it** *no lo pierdas*. **2** *(clock)* atrasar.
▷ *vi* **1** *(in general)* perder: **Liverpool lost to United** *el Liverpool perdió ante el United*. **2** *(clock)* atrasarse. ■ **to lose one's way** perderse. ‖ **to lose sight of** STH perder ALGO de vista.
▲ *pt & pp* **lost** [lɒst], *ger* **losing**.
⊙ **to lose out** *vi* salir perdiendo (**to**, ante).
loser ['lu:zəʳ] *n* perdedor,-ra.
loss [lɒs] *n* **1** *(in general)* pérdida. **2** MIL *(death)* baja.
▲ *pl* **losses**.
lost [lɒst] *adj* perdido,-a. ■ **to get lost** perderse.
lost-and-found [lɒstᵊn'faʊnd] [Also **lost-and-found department**.] *n* US oficina de objetos perdidos.
lot [lɒt] *n* **1** *(large number)* cantidad *f*: **he talks a lot** *habla mucho*. **2** *(group)* grupo: **the next lot of passengers** *el próximo grupo de pasajeros*. **3** *(fate)* suerte *f*. ■ **thanks a lot!** ¡muchísimas gracias!
▷ *n* **the lot** todo,-a, todos,-as.
▷ *phr* **lots of** mucho,-a, muchos,-as, cantidad de: **there were lots of people** *había mucha gente*.
lotion ['ləʊʃᵊn] *n* loción *f*.
lottery ['lɒtᵊrɪ] *n* lotería.
▲ *pl* **lotteries**.
loud [laʊd] *adj* **1** *(sound)* fuerte. **2** *(voice)* alto,-a. **3** *(colour)* chillón,-ona.
▷ *adv* fuerte, alto. ■ **out loud** en voz alta.
loudly ['laʊdlɪ] *adv (speak)* alto; *(shout)* fuerte; *(complain)* a voz en grito.
loudness ['laʊdnəs] *n (of sound)* fuerza, intensidad *f*; *(noisiness)* bullicio.
loudspeaker [laʊd'spi:kəʳ] *n* altavoz *m*.
lounge [laʊndʒ] *n* salón *m*. ● **lounge suit** *fam* traje *m*.
▷ *vi* **1** *(on sofa, etc)* repantigarse. **2** *(idle)* holgazanear.
lounger ['laʊndʒəʳ] *n (chair)* tumbona.
louse [laʊs] *n* **1** piojo. **2** *fam* canalla *mf*.
▲ *pl* **lice**.
⊙ **to louse up** *vt sep* US *sl* fastidiar.
lousy ['laʊzɪ] *adj* **1** *fam* fatal, malísimo,-a: **he felt lousy** *se encontraba fatal*.
▲ *comp* **lousier**, *superl* **lousiest**.
lout [laʊt] *n pej* patán *m*, animal *m*.
louvre ['lu:vəʳ] *n* persiana.
lovable ['lʌvəbᵊl] *adj* adorable.
love [lʌv] *n* **1** *(in general)* amor *m*; *(affection)* cariño *(liking)* afición *f* (**for**, a). **2** GB *fam (person)* guapo,-a, chato,-a. **3** *(regards)* recuerdos *mpl*: **(give my) love to your parents** *muchos recuerdos a tus padres*. ■ **to be in love with** estar enamorado,-a de. ‖ **to fall in love** enamorarse. ‖ **to make love** hacer el amor (**to**, a).
▷ *vt* **1** amar, querer: **do you love him?** *¿lo quieres?* **2** *(like a lot)* encantarle a uno, gustarle a uno mucho: **I love playing tennis** *me encanta jugar a tenis*.
lovebirds ['lʌvbɜ:zd] *n pl* tortolitos.
lovely ['lʌvlɪ] *adj* **1** *(wonderful)* estupendo,-a, maravilloso,-a. **2** *(beautiful)* hermoso,-a, precioso,-a *(charming)* encantador,-ra.
▲ *comp* **lovelier**, *superl* **loveliest**.
love-making ['lʌvmeɪkɪŋ] *n (courtship)* galanteo *(sexual)* relaciones *fpl* sexuales.
lover ['lʌvəʳ] *n* amante *mf*.
lovesick ['lʌvsɪk] *adj* enfermo,-a de amor.
loving ['lʌvɪŋ] *adj* cariñoso,-a: **your loving son, Paul** *tu hijo que te quiere, Paul*.
low [ləʊ] *adj* **1** *(in general)* bajo,-a; *(neckline)* escotado,-a: **low clouds** *nubes bajas*. **2** *(battery)* gastado,-a. **3** *(depressed)* deprimido,-a, abatido,-a. **4** MUS grave ■ **to keep a low profile** ser discreto,-a. ● **low tide** marea baja. ‖ **the Low Countries** los Países Bajos.
▷ *adv* bajo: **we're running low on petrol** (US **gas**) *se nos acaba la gasolina*.
▷ *n (low level)* punto bajo.
lowbrow ['ləʊbraʊ] *n pej* inculto,-a.
low-calorie [ləʊ'kælərɪ] *adj* bajo,-a en calorías, hipocalórico,-a.
low-cut ['ləʊkʌt] *adj* escotado,-a.
lowdown ['ləʊdaʊn] *n fam* detalles *mpl*, información *f*
▷ *adj fam* despreciable.
lower ['ləʊəʳ] *adj* inferior.
▷ *vt* **1** *(in general)* bajar; *(price)* rebajar. **2** *(flag)* arriar.
lower-class [ləʊə'klɑ:s] *adj* de clase baja.

lowest ['ləʊɪst] *adj* más bajo,-a; *(price, speed)* mínimo,-a.
▷ *n* mínimo: **at the lowest** *como mínimo.*
low-fat ['ləʊfæt] *adj* de bajo contenido graso.
low-key [ləʊki:] *adj (controlled)* discreto,-a.
lowlands ['ləʊləndz] *n pl* tierras *fpl* bajas.
lowly ['ləʊlɪ] *adj* humilde, modesto,-a.
▲ *comp* **lowlier**, *superl* **lowliest.**
low-lying [ləʊlaɪɪŋ] *adj* bajo,-a.
loyal ['lɔɪəl] *adj* leal, fiel.
loyalist ['lɔɪəlɪst] *adj* patriótico,-a.
▷ *n* patriota *mf.*
loyalty ['lɔɪəltɪ] *n* lealtad *f*, fidelidad *f.*
▲ *pl* **loyalties.**
lozenge ['lɒzɪndʒ] *n* **1** pastilla. **2** *(geometry)* rombo.
LSD ['elesdi:] *abbr* **(lysergic acid diethylamide)** dietilamida del ácido lisérgico; *(abbreviation)* LSD.
lubricant ['lu:brɪkənt] *n* lubricante *m.*
lubricate ['lu:brɪkeɪt] *vt* lubricar, engrasar.
lubrication [lu:brɪ'keɪʃᵊn] *n* lubricación *f*, engrase *m.*
lucerne ['lu:sɜ:n] *n* GB alfalfa.
lucid ['lu:sɪd] *adj* lúcido,-a.
lucidity [lu:sɪdɪtɪ] *n* lucidez *f.*
luck [lʌk] *n* suerte *f.* ■ **bad luck!** ¡mala suerte! ‖ **good luck!** ¡suerte! ‖ **to be in luck** estar de suerte.
luckily ['lʌkɪlɪ] *adv* afortunadamente.
luckless ['lʌkləs] *adj fml* desafortunado,-a.
lucky ['lʌkɪ] *adj (in general)* afortunado,-a; *(timely)* oportuno,-a: **how lucky you were!** *¡qué suerte tuviste!*
▲ *comp* **luckier**, *superl* **luckiest.**
lucrative ['lu:krətɪv] *adj* lucrativo,-a.
ludicrous ['lu:dɪkrəs] *adj* ridículo,-a.
ludo ['lu:dəʊ] *n* GB parchís *m.*
luff [lʌf] *n* orza.
lug[1] [lʌg] *vt fam* arrastrar.
▲ *pt & pp* **lugged**, *ger* **lugging.**
lug[2] [lʌg] *n fam (ear)* oreja.
luggage ['lʌgɪdʒ] *n* GB equipaje *m.* ● **luggage rack** portaequipajes *m.*
lugubrious [ləgu:brɪəs] *adj* lúgubre.
lukewarm ['lu:kwɔ:m] *adj* tibio,-a, templado,-a.
lull [lʌl] *n (in storm)* momento de calma, recalmón *m*; *(in activity)* respiro.
▷ *vt* adormecer.
lullaby ['lʌləbaɪ] *n* canción *f* de cuna, nana.
▲ *pl* **lullabies.**
lumbago [lʌmbeɪgəʊ] *n* lumbago.
lumbar ['lʌmbəʳ] *adj* lumbar.
lumber ['lʌmbəʳ] *n* **1** US *(timber)* leña. **2** GB *(junk)* trastos *mpl* viejos.
lumberjack ['lʌmbədʒæk] *n* leñador *m.*
lumberyard ['lʌmbəja:d] *n* almacén *m* de madera, almacén *m* de leña.
luminosity [lu:mɪnɒsɪtɪ] *n* luminosidad *f.*
luminous ['lu:mɪnəs] *adj* luminoso,-a.
lump [lʌmp] *n* **1** *(chunk)* pedazo, trozo; *(in sauce)* grumo. **2** *(swelling)* bulto, protuberancia; *(in throat)* nudo. **3** *(of sugar)* terrón *m.* **4** *fam (idiot)* burro,-a.
⊙ **to lump together** *vt sep* juntar.
lumpy ['lʌmpɪ] *adj* lleno,-a de bultos; *(sauce)* grumoso,-a.
▲ *comp* **lumpier**, *superl* **lumpiest.**
lunacy ['lu:nəsɪ] *n* locura.
lunar ['lu:nəʳ] *adj* lunar. ● **lunar landing** alunizaje *m.* ‖ **lunar month** mes *m* lunar.
lunatic ['lu:nətɪk] *adj* loco,-a.
▷ *n* loco,-a, lunático,-a. ● **lunatic asylum** manicomio. ‖ **the lunatic fringe** los fanáticos *mpl.*
lunch [lʌntʃ] *n* comida, almuerzo: **we'll have lunch at one** *comeremos a la una.* ● **business lunch** almuerzo de trabajo. ‖ **lunch hour** hora de comer.
▷ *vi fml* comer, almorzar.
luncheon ['lʌntʃᵊn] *n fml* almuerzo.
luncheonette [lʌntʃənet] *n* US cafetería, restaurante *m* pequeño.
lunchtime ['lʌntʃtaɪm] *n* hora de comer, hora de almorzar.
lung [lʌŋ] *n* pulmón *m*: **her little girl has a good pair of lungs!** *¡su hijita tiene buenos pulmones!* ● **lung cancer** cáncer *m* de pulmón.
lunge [lʌndʒ] *vi* arremeter, embestir (**at/towards**, contra).
▷ *n* arremetida, embestida.
lupin ['lu:pɪn] *n* altramuz *m.*
lurch [lɜ:tʃ] *vi (vehicle)* dar tumbos, dar bandazos; *(person)* tambalearse.
▷ *n (vehicle)* tumbo, bandazo; *(of person)* tambaleo.
lure [lʊəʳ] *n* **1** *(decoy)* señuelo. **2** *fig* aliciente *m.*
▷ *vt* seducir, atraer.
lurid ['lʊərɪd] *adj* **1** *(colour, etc)* chillón,-ona. **2** *(details)* horripilante, espeluznante.
lurk [lɜ:k] *vi* **1** *(wait)* estar al acecho. **2** *(hide)* esconderse.
luscious ['lʌʃəs] *adj* **1** delicioso,-a, exquisito,-a. **2** *fam (sexy)* apetitoso,-a.
lush [lʌʃ] *adj* **1** *(vegetation)* exuberante. **2** *(plush)* lujoso,-a.
lust [lʌst] *n* **1** *(sexual)* lujuria. **2** *(greed)* codicia.
⊙ **to lust after** *vt insep* codiciar; *(sexually)* desear.
lustful ['lʌstful] *adj* **1** lujurioso,-a. **2** *(greedy)* codicioso,-a.
lustre ['lʌstəʳ] *n* lustre *m*, brillo.
lusty ['lʌstɪ] *adj* fuerte, robusto,-a.
▲ *comp* **lustier**, *superl* **lustiest.**
lutanist ['lu:tᵊnɪst] *n* tañedor,-ra de laúd.
lute [lu:t] *n* laúd *m.*
luv [lʌv] *n* GB *fam* guapo,-a, chato,-a.
Luxembourg ['lʌksᵊmbɜ:g] *n* Luxemburgo.
Luxembourger ['lʌksᵊmbɜ:gəʳ] *n* luxemburgués,-esa.
luxuriant [lʌg'zjʊərɪənt] *adj* **1** *(vegetation)* exuberante; *(hair)* abundante.
luxurious [lʌg'zjʊərɪəs] *adj* lujoso,-a.
luxury ['lʌkʃərɪ] *n* lujo.
▲ *pl* **luxuries.**
lycanthrope ['laɪkənθrəʊp] *n* licántropo,-a.
lychee ['laɪtʃi:] *n* lichi *m.*
lying ['laɪɪŋ] *adj (deceitful)* mentiroso,-a.
▷ *n (lies)* mentiras *fpl.*
lymph [lɪmf] *n* linfa.
lymphatic [lɪmfætɪk] *adj* linfático,-a.
lynch [lɪntʃ] *vt* linchar.
lynching ['lɪntʃɪŋ] *n* linchamiento.
lynx [lɪŋks] *n* lince *m.*
lyre [laɪəʳ] *n* lira.
lyric ['lɪrɪk] *adj* lírico,-a.
▷ *n* poema *m* lírico.
▷ *n pl* **lyrics** *(of song)* letra *f sing.*

M

M, m [em] *n (the letter)* M, m *f.*
M ['mɪlɪən] *abbr* **(million)** millón: **£24M** *veinticuatro millones de libras.*
mac [mæk] *n* GB *fam (mackintosh)* impermeable *m.*
macabre [mə'kɑːbrə] *adj* macabro,-a.
macaroni [mækə'rəʊnɪ] *n* macarrones *mpl.*
macaroon [mækə'ruːn] *n* mostachón *m.*
macaw [mə'kɔː] *n* guacamayo, ara *m.*
mace [meɪs] *n (club, staff)* maza.
macebearer ['meɪsbeərəʳ] *n* macero,-a.
macerate ['mæsəreɪt] *vt* macerar.
▷ *vi* macerarse.
maceration [mæsə'reɪʃᵊn] *n* maceración *f.*
machete [mə'ʃetɪ] *n* machete *m.*
machinations [mækɪ'neɪʃᵊnz] *n pl* intrigas *fpl,* maquinaciones *fpl.*
machine [mə'ʃiːn] *n* **1** *(gen)* máquina, aparato. **2** *(organization, system)* organización *f,* sistema *m,* aparato. ● **machine gun** ametralladora. ‖ **machine operator** operario,-a.
▷ *vt* **1** TECH trabajar a máquina. **2** SEW coser a máquina.
▷ *n pl* **machines** *(machinery)* maquinaria *f sing.*
machine-gun [mə'ʃiːngʌn] *vt* ametrallar.
▲ *pt & pp* **machine-gunned**, *ger* **machine-gunning.**
machinery [mə'ʃiːnərɪ] *n* **1** *(machines)* maquinaria. **2** *(workings)* mecanismo. **3** *(organization)* organización *f,* sistema *m.*
machinist [mə'ʃiːnɪst] *n (gen)* operario,-a.
machismo [mə'tʃɪzməʊ] *n* machismo.
mackerel ['mækᵊrəl] *n* caballa.
mackintosh ['mækɪntɒʃ] *n* impermeable *m.*
macramé [mə'krɑːmɪ] *n* macramé *m.*
macro ['mækrəʊ] *n* COMPUT macro *f.* ● **macro lens** objetivo macro.
macrocosm ['mækrəʊkɒzᵊm] *n* macrocosmo.
macroeconomics [mækrəʊiːkə'nɒmɪks] *n* macroeconomía.
macroscopic [mækrə'skɒpɪk] *adj* macroscópico,-a.
mad [mæd] *adj* **1** *(insane)* loco,-a, demente: **she's quite mad** *está completamente loca.* **2** *fam (person)* loco,-a; *(crazy - idea, plan)* disparatado,-a, descabellado,-a. **3** *fam (enthusiastic)* loco,-a (**about**, por), chiflado,-a: **he's mad about her** *está loco por ella.* **4** *fam (angry)* enfadado,-a, furioso,-a (**at/with**, con). ■ **to drive sb mad / send sb mad** volver a algn loco,-a, traer loco,-a a algn. ‖ **to get mad** enfadarse. ‖ **to go mad** volverse loco,-a, enloquecer.
▲ *comp* **madder**, *superl* **maddest.**
Madagascan [mædə'gæskᵊn] *adj* malgache.
▷ *n (person)* malgache *mf.*
Madagascar [mædə'gæskəʳ] *n* Madagascar.
madam ['mædəm] *n fml* señora.
madcap ['mædkæp] *adj* disparatado,-a, descabellado,-a.
madden ['mædᵊn] *vt (annoy)* enfurecer, enloquecer.
made [meɪd] *pt & pp* → **make.**
▷ *adj (produced)* hecho,-a, fabricado,-a: **made in England** *hecho,-a en Inglaterra.* ■ **to be made from** STH estar hecho,-a de ALGO. ‖ **to be made of** STH ser de ALGO, estar hecho,-a de ALGO, estar compuesto,-a de ALGO.
made-to-measure [meɪdtə'meʒəʳ] *adj* hecho,-a a medida.
madhouse ['mædhaʊs] *n fam dated (mental hospital)* manicomio.
madman ['mædmæn] *n* loco.
▲ *pl* **madmen** ['mædmæn].
madness ['mædnəs] *n* **1** *(insanity)* locura, demencia. **2** *(foolishness)* locura: **it is madness to drive in this weather** *es una locura conducir con el tiempo que hace.*
madonna [mə'dɒnə] *n (in art)* madona.
▷ *n* **the Madonna** la Virgen *f.*
madwoman ['mædwʊmən] *n* loca.
▲ *pl* **madwomen** ['mædwɪmɪn].
maelstrom ['meɪlstrəʊm] *n* remolino, torbellino.
maestro ['maɪstrəʊ] *n* maestro.
▲ *pl* **maestros.**
magazine [mægə'ziːn] *n* **1** *(periodical)* revista. **2** *(on TV, radio)* magacín *m,* magazine *m.* ● **magazine rack** revistero.
magenta [mə'dʒentə] *n* magenta.
▷ *adj* (de color) magenta.
maggot ['mægət] *n* larva, cresa, gusano.
Magi ['meɪdʒaɪ] *n pl* Reyes *mpl* Magos.
magic ['mædʒɪk] *n* magia.
▷ *adj* mágico,-a. ● **magic wand** varita mágica.
magical ['mædʒɪkᵊl] *adj* mágico,-a.
magician [mə'dʒɪʃᵊn] *n* **1** *(conjurer)* prestidigitador,-ra ilusionista *mf.* **2** *(wizard)* mago,-a.
magisterial [mædʒɪ'stɪərɪəl] *adj fml (showing authority)* magistral.
magistrate ['mædʒɪstreɪt] *n* JUR magistrado,-a, juez *mf*
magma ['mægmə] *n* magma.
magnanimity [mægnə'nɪmɪtɪ] *n* magnanimidad *f.*
magnanimous [mæg'nænɪməs] *adj* magnánimo,-a
magnate ['mægneɪt] *n* magnate *m.*
magnesium [mæg'niːzɪəm] *n* magnesio.
magnet ['mægnət] *n* imán *m.*
magnetic [mæg'netɪk] *adj* **1** *(force, etc)* magnético,-a **2** *fig (personality, charm)* carismático,-a.
magnetism ['mægnɪtɪzᵊm] *n* **1** *(force)* magnetismo. **2** *fig (personal charm)* carisma *m.*
magnetize ['mægnɪtaɪz] *vt* **1** *(object)* magnetizar imantar. **2** *fig (person)* magnetizar, cautivar.
magnification [mægnɪfɪ'keɪʃᵊn] *n* **1** *(increase)* aumento, ampliación *f.* **2** *(power of lens, etc)* aumento

magnificence [mæg'nɪfɪsəns] *n* esplendor *m*.
magnificent [mæg'nɪfɪsənt] *adj (splendid)* magnífico,-a, espléndido,-a.
magnify ['mægnɪfaɪ] *vt* **1** *(enlarge)* aumentar, ampliar. **2** *fig (exaggerate)* exagerar, agrandar.
▲ *pt & pp* magnified, *ger* magnifying.
magnifying glass ['mægnɪfaɪɪŋglɑːs] *n* lupa.
▲ *pl* magnifying glasses.
magnitude ['mægnɪtjuːd] *n (size)* magnitud *f*; *(importance)* magnitud *f*, envergadura.
magnolia [mæg'nəʊlɪə] *n* **1** *(tree)* magnolio, magnolia. **2** *(flower)* magnolia.
magpie ['mægpaɪ] *n* urraca.
maharajah [mɑːhə'rɑːdʒə] *n* marajá *m*.
mahogany [mə'hɒgənɪ] *n (wood, tree)* caoba; *(colour)* color *m* caoba.
maid [meɪd] *n (servant)* sirvienta; *(in hotel)* camarera.
maiden ['meɪdən] *n (unmarried woman, girl)* doncella.
▷ *adj (first of its kind - speech, voyage)* inaugural.
mail [meɪl] *n* **1** *(system)* correo: send it by mail *envíalo por correo*. **2** *(letters, etc)* correo, correspondencia.
▷ *vt (send)* mandar por correo.
mailbag ['meɪlbæg] *n* valija, saca de correo.
mailbox ['meɪlbɒks] *n* buzón *m*.
mailing list ['meɪlɪŋlɪst] *n* lista de correo.
mailman ['meɪlmæn] *n* US cartero.
▲ *pl* mailmen ['meɪlmæn].
mailshot ['meɪlʃɒt] *n* mailing *m*, envío postal.
maim [meɪm] *vt* mutilar, lisiar.
main [meɪn] *adj (most important)* principal: be careful when you cross the main road *ten cuidado al cruzar la carretera principal*. ● main course plato principal, segundo plato. ‖ main street calle *f* mayor.
mainframe ['meɪnfreɪm] [Also mainframe computer.] *n* unidad *f* central, ordenador *m* central.
mainland ['meɪnlənd] *n continente o isla grande en contraposición a una isla cercana más pequeña*.
mainline ['meɪnlaɪn] *adj (train, etc)* interurbano,-a.
mainly ['meɪnlɪ] *adv (chiefly)* principalmente, sobre todo; *(mostly)* en su mayoría.
mainsail ['meɪnseɪl] *n* vela mayor.
mainstay ['meɪnsteɪ] *n fig (support)* pilar *m*, puntal *m*.
mainstream ['meɪnstriːm] *n* corriente *f* principal, corriente *f* dominante.
▷ *adj* convencional, dominante.
maintain [meɪn'teɪn] *vt* **1** *(preserve, keep up - gen)* mantener; *(- silence, appearances)* guardar. **2** *(support financially)* mantener, sostener.
maintenance ['meɪntənəns] *n* **1** *(preservation)* mantenimiento, conservación *f*. **2** *(running, upkeep)* mantenimiento. **3** *(upkeep of family)* manutención *f*.
maize [meɪz] *n* maíz *m*.
majestic [mə'dʒestɪk] *adj* majestuoso,-a.
majesty ['mædʒəstɪ] *n* majestad *f*.
▲ *pl* majesties.
major ['meɪdʒəʳ] *adj* **1** *(more important, greater)* mayor, principal: tourism is the major industry *el turismo es la industria principal*. **2** *(important - gen)* importante; *(- illness)* grave. **3** MUS *(key, scale)* mayor.
▷ *n* **1** MIL comandante *m*.
⊙ **to major in** *vt insep* US especializarse en
majorette [meɪdʒər'et] *n* majorette *f*.
majority [mə'dʒɒrɪtɪ] *n* mayoría. ■ to be in a/the majority ser mayoría.
▲ *pl* majorities.
▷ *adj* mayoritario,-a.
make [meɪk] *n (brand)* marca: what make is your watch? *¿de qué marca es tu reloj?*
▷ *vt* **1** *(produce - gen)* hacer; *(construct)* construir; *(manufacture)* fabricar; *(create)* crear; *(prepare)* preparar: she made some sandwiches *hizo unos bocadillos, preparó unos bocadillos*; stop making all that noise! *¡dejad de hacer tanto ruido!* **2** *(carry out, perform)* hacer: I must make a phone call *tengo que hacer una llamada*. **3** *(cause to be)* hacer, poner, volver: the gift made him happy *el regalo lo hizo feliz*. **4** *(force, compel)* hacer, obligar; *(cause to do)* hacer: they make me go to bed early *me obligan a acostarme temprano*. **5** *(be, become)* ser, hacer; *(cause to be)* hacer, convertir en: she'll make a good singer *será buena cantante, tiene madera de cantante*. **6** *(earn)* ganar, hacer. **7** *(achieve)* conseguir, alcanzar. **8** *(total, equal)* ser, equivaler a: three and four make seven *tres más cuatro son siete*.
▷ *vi (to be about to)* hacer como, hacer ademán de, simular: he made as if to kiss her *hizo como si la besara*. ■ to make like hacer ver, fingir. ‖ to make sense tener sentido. ‖ to make sure (of STH) asegurarse (de ALGO).
⊙ **to make for** *vt insep* **1** *(move towards)* dirigirse hacia. **2** *(result in, make possible)* contribuir a, crear, conducir a.
⊙ **to make of** *vt insep (think of)* pensar, opinar, parecer; *(understand)* entender.
⊙ **to make off** *vi (escape)* escaparse, largarse, huir.
⊙ **to make off with / make away with** *vt insep (steal)* llevarse, escaparse con.
⊙ **to make out** *vt sep* **1** *(write - list, receipt)* hacer; *(- cheque)* extender, hacer; *(- report)* redactar. **2** *(see)* distinguir, divisar; *(writing)* descifrar. **3** *(understand)* entender, comprender.
▷ *vt insep fam (pretend, claim)* pretender, hacerse pasar por.
⊙ **to make up** *vt sep* **1** *(invent)* inventar. **2** *(put together)* hacer; *(assemble)* montar; *(bed, prescription)* preparar; *(page)* componer; *(clothes, curtains)* confeccionar, hacer. **3** *(complete)* completar. **4** *(constitute)* componer, integrar; *(represent)* representar. **5** *(cosmetics)* maquillar.
▷ *vi* **1** maquillarse, pintarse. **2** *(become friends again)* hacer las paces, reconciliarse.
▲ *pt & pp* made, *ger* making.
⊙ **to make up for** *vt insep (compensate for)* compensar.
⊙ **to make up to** *vt sep (pay back)* recompensar, pagar.
make-believe ['meɪkbɪliːv] *n (fantasy)* fantasía, imaginación *f*; *(pretence)* simulación *f*: it's only make-believe *es pura fantasía*.
maker ['meɪkəʳ] *n (of product)* fabricante *mf*; *(of film, etc)* creador,-ra.
makeshift ['meɪkʃɪft] *adj (temporary)* provisional, temporal; *(improvised)* improvisado,-a.
make-up ['meɪkʌp] *n* **1** *(cosmetics)* maquillaje *m*: she never wears make-up *nunca se maquilla*. **2** *(composition, combination)* composición *f*. **3** *(of person)* carácter *m*.
making ['meɪkɪŋ] *n (manufacture)* fabricación *f*; *(construction)* construcción *f*; *(creation)* creación *f*; *(preparation)* preparación *f*, elaboración *f*. ■ in the making *(person)* en potencia, futuro,-a. ‖ to be of SB's own making ser culpa de uno,-a mismo,-a.

maladjusted [mælə'dʒʌstɪd] *adj* inadaptado,-a.
malaise [mæ'leɪz] *n fml* malestar *m.*
malaria [mə'leərɪə] *n* malaria, paludismo.
Malawi [mə'lɑːwɪ] *n* Malawi.
Malawian [mə'lɑːwɪən] *adj* malawiano,-a.
▷ *n* malawiano,-a.
Malaysia [mə'leɪzɪə] *n* Malaysia, Malasia.
Malaysian [mə'leɪzɪən] *adj* malasio,-a.
▷ *n* malasio,-a.
Maldives ['mɔːldaɪvz] *n* Maldivas.
Maldivian [mɔː'dɪvɪən] *adj* maldivo,-a.
▷ *n* maldivo,-a.
male [meɪl] *adj* **1** *(animal, plant)* macho; *(person, child)* varón; *(sex, hormone, character, organ)* masculino,-a. **2** *(manly)* varonil, viril.
▷ *n (man, boy)* varón *m*; *(animal, plant)* macho.
malevolent [mə'levələnt] *adj* malévolo,-a.
malformed [mæ'fɔːmd] *adj* deformado,-a.
malfunction [mæ'fʌnkʃᵊn] *n* mal funcionamiento.
▷ *vi* funcionar mal.
Mali ['mɑːlɪ] *n* Malí.
Malian ['mɑːlɪən] *adj* maliense.
▷ *n* maliense *mf.*
malice ['mælɪs] *n* malicia.
malicious [mə'lɪʃəs] *adj* **1** *(comment, person)* malicioso,-a, malintencionado,-a: **malicious gossip** *malas lenguas.* **2** *(damage)* intencional.
malignant [mə'lɪgnənt] *adj* **1** *(person)* malévolo,-a, malvado,-a, malo,-a; *(action, behaviour, influence, etc)* maligno,-a, perjudicial. **2** MED maligno,-a.
malinger [mə'lɪŋgəʳ] *vi pej* fingirse enfermo,-a.
mall [mæl, mɔːl] *n* US *(covered)* centro comercial; *(street)* zona comercial.
mallard ['mælɑːd] *n* ánade *m* real.
malleable ['mælɪəbᵊl] *adj* **1** *(metal)* maleable. **2** *fig (person)* dócil.
mallet ['mælət] *n* mazo.
mallow ['mæləʊ] *n* malva.
malnourished [mæ'nʌrɪʃt] *adj* desnutrido,-a.
malnutrition [mælnjʊː'trɪʃᵊn] *n* desnutrición *f.*
malpractice [mæ'præktɪs] *n* **1** MED negligencia. **2** JUR procedimiento ilegal.
malt [mɔːlt] *n (grain)* malta.
Malta ['mɔːltə] *n* Malta.
Maltese [mɔː'tiːz] *adj* maltés,-esa.
▷ *n* **1** *(person)* maltés,-esa. **2** *(language)* maltés *m.*
▷ *n pl* **the Maltese** los malteses *mpl.*
maltreat [mæ'triːt] *vt fml* maltratar, tratar mal.
maltreatment [mæ'trɪtmənt] *n* malos tratos *mpl.*
mambo ['mæmbəʊ] *n* mambo.
mammal ['mæmᵊl] *n* mamífero.
mammary ['mæmərɪ] *adj* mamario,-a. ● **mammary gland** mama.
mammography [mæ'mɒgrəfɪ] *n* mamografía.
▲ *pl* **mammographies.**
mammoth ['mæməθ] *n* ZOOL mamut *m.*
▷ *adj (huge)* gigantesco,-a, descomunal, inmenso,-a.
mammy ['mæmɪ] *n fam* mamá.
▲ *pl* **mammies.**
man [mæn] *n* **1** *(adult male)* hombre *m*, señor *m*: **an old man** *un hombre mayor, un señor mayor, un viejo.* **2** *(human being, person)* ser *m* humano, el hombre *m*: **all men are born equal** *todos los hombres nacen iguales.* **3** *(husband)* marido, hombre *m*; *(boyfriend)* novio; *(partner)* pareja: **man and wife** *marido y mujer.*
■ **as one man** como un solo hombre, todos a la vez.
● **man of the world** hombre *m* de mundo. ‖ **the man in the street** el hombre de la calle.
▲ *pl* **men.**
▷ *interj fam* hombre, tío, macho.
▷ *vt (operate - post, phones)* servir, atender; *(boat, plane)* tripular; *(barricades)* defender: **can you man the desk while I'm at lunch** *¿puedes atender la recepción mientras voy a comer?*
manacle ['mænəkᵊl] *vt* esposar.
▷ *n pl* **manacles** esposas *fpl*, grillos *mpl.*
manage ['mænɪdʒ] *vt* **1** *(run - business, company)* dirigir, llevar, administrar; *(- property)* administrar; *(- household)* llevar; *(handle - money, affairs)* manejar, administrar: **she manages a shop** *es la encargada de una tienda, lleva una tienda.* **2** *(handle, cope with - child, person)* llevar, manejar; *(- animal)* domar; *(- work, luggage, etc)* poder con. **3** *(succeed)* conseguir, lograr: **we managed it!** *¡lo conseguimos!* **4** *(have room for, have time for)* poder.
▷ *vi* **1** poder: **can you manage?** *¿puedes?* **2** *(financially)* arreglárselas, apañarse.
manageable ['mænɪdʒəbᵊl] *adj* manejable.
management ['mænɪdʒmənt] *n* **1** *(running of business, etc)* dirección *f*, administración *f*, gestión *f.* **2** *(people in charge)* dirección *f*, gerencia, patronal *f.*
manager ['mænɪdʒəʳ] *n* **1** *(of company, bank)* director,-ra, gerente *mf.* **2** *(of shop, restaurant)* encargado,-a; *(of department)* jefe,-a. **3** *(of actor, group, etc)* representante *mf*, manager *mf.* **4** SP *(of football team)* entrenador *m*, míster *m.*
manageress [mænɪdʒə'res] *n* **1** *(of company, bank)* directora, gerente *f.* **2** *(of shop, restaurant, etc)* encargada, jefa; *(of department)* jefa. **3** *(of actor, group)* representante *f*, manager *f.*
managing ['mænɪdʒɪŋ] *adj* directivo,-a.
manatee [mænə'tiː] *n* manatí *m.*
mandarin ['mændərɪn] *n* **1** mandarina. **2** GB *pej (government official)* mandarín *m.*
▷ *n* **Mandarin** *(language)* mandarín *m.*
mandate ['mændeɪt] *n* mandato.
▷ *vt (authorize)* autorizar.
mandatory ['mændətᵊrɪ] *adj (compulsory)* obligatorio,-a.
mandible ['mændɪbᵊl] *n* mandíbula.
mandolin ['mændəlɪn] *n* mandolina.
mandrake ['mændreɪk] *n* mandrágora.
mane [meɪn] *n (of horse)* crin *f*; *(of lion)* melena.
maneuver [mə'nuːvəʳ] *n & v* US ⟶ **manoeuvre.**
maneuvrable [mə'nuːvᵊrəbᵊl] *adj* US ⟶ **manoeuvrable.**
manganese ['mæŋgəniːz] *n* manganeso.
manger ['meɪndʒəʳ] *n* pesebre *m.*
mangle ['mæŋgᵊl] *vt (cut to pieces)* destrozar, despedazar; *(crush)* aplastar.
mango ['mæŋgəʊ] *n* mango.
▲ *pl* **mangoes** o **mangos.**
mangrove ['mæŋgrəʊv] *n* manglar *m.*
mangy ['meɪndʒɪ] *adj* **1** *(animal)* sarnoso,-a, tiñoso,-a. **2** *fig (carpet, etc)* raído,-a.
▲ *comp* **mangier**, *superl* **mangiest.**
manhandle ['mænhændᵊl] *vt* **1** *(person)* maltratar. **2** *(object)* manipular.

manhole ['mænhəʊl] *n* boca de acceso.
manhood ['mænhʊd] *n* **1** *(state)* madurez *f*. **2** *(qualities)* virilidad *f*, hombría.
manhunt ['mænhʌnt] *n* persecución *f*, búsqueda *(a gran escala)*.
mania ['meɪnɪə] *n* manía.
maniac ['meɪnɪæk] *n* **1** *fam (wild person)* loco,-a. **2** *fam (fan)* entusiasta *mf*, fanático,-a.
manic ['mænɪk] *adj* maníaco,-a, maniaco,-a.
manicure ['mænɪkjʊə(r)] *n* manicura.
▷ *vt* hacer la manicura.
manicurist ['mænɪkjʊərɪst] *n* manicuro,-a.
manifest ['mænɪfest] *adj fml* manifiesto,-a, patente.
▷ *vt fml* manifestar.
manifestation [mænɪfe'steɪʃ(ə)n] *n fml* manifestación *f*.
manifesto [mænɪ'festəʊ] *n* manifiesto.
▲ *pl* manifestos o manifestoes.
manifold ['mænɪfəʊld] *adj fml (many)* múltiples; *(varied)* varios,-as, diversos,-as.
manila [mə'nɪlə] *n* papel *m* de estraza.
manioc ['mænɪɒk] *n* mandioca, yuca.
manipulate [mə'nɪpjəleɪt] *vt* **1** *(work - machine)* manipular, manejar; *(- knob, lever)* accionar. **2** *(control, influence)* manipular.
manipulation [mənɪpjə'leɪʃ(ə)n] *n* **1** *(handling)* manipulación *f*, manejo. **2** *(control, influence)* manipulación *f*.
manipulative [mə'nɪpjələtɪv] *adj* manipulador,-ra.
manipulator [mə'nɪpjəleɪtə(r)] *n* manipulador,-ra.
mankind [mæn'kaɪnd] *n* la humanidad *f*, el género humano, los hombres *mpl*.
manly ['mænlɪ] *adj* varonil, viril, macho.
▲ *comp* manlier, *superl* manliest.
man-made [mæn'meɪd] *adj* **1** *(lake, etc)* artificial. **2** *(fabric, etc)* sintético,-a.
manna ['mænə] *n* maná *m*.
mannequin ['mænɪkɪn] *n* **1** *(dummy)* maniquí *m*. **2** *dated (model)* modelo *f*.
manner ['mænə(r)] *n* **1** *(way, method)* manera, modo: in this manner *de esta manera*. **2** *(way of behaving)* forma de ser, comportamiento, aire *m*: she has a pleasant manner *tiene una forma de ser agradable*. ■ **in a manner of speaking** hasta cierto punto.
▷ *n pl* **manners** *(social behaviour)* maneras *fpl*, modales *mpl*; *(customs)* costumbres *fpl*. ● **bad manners** falta de educación. ‖ **good manners** buenos modales *mpl*.
mannered ['mænəd] *adj (affected)* amanerado,-a, afectado,-a.
mannerism ['mænərɪz(ə)m] *n (quirk)* manía, rareza, gesto, peculiaridad *f*; *(way of speaking)* deje *m*.
mannish ['mænɪʃ] *adj* hombruno,-a.
manoeuvrable [mə'nuːv(ə)rəb(ə)l] *adj* manejable.
manoeuvre [mə'nuːvə(r)] *n (gen)* maniobra.
▷ *vt* **1** *(gen)* maniobrar. **2** *(person)* manipular, manejar.
▷ *vi* maniobrar.
manometer [mə'nɒmɪtə(r)] *n* manómetro.
manor ['mænə(r)] *n* **1** *(estate)* señorío. **2** *sl (area)* territorio.
manpower ['mænpaʊə(r)] *n* mano *f* de obra.
manservant ['mænsɜːv(ə)nt] *n* criado, sirviente *m*.
mansion ['mænʃ(ə)n] *n (gen)* casa grande; *(country)* casa solariega.
man-size ['mænsaɪz] *adj fam* extragrande, muy grande.
mantelpiece ['mænt(ə)lpiːs] *n* repisa de chimenea.
mantis ['mæntɪs] *n* mantis *f*.
▲ *pl* mantis.
mantle ['mænt(ə)l] *n* **1** *(cloak)* capa, manto. **2** *fig (layer)* manto, capa.
man-to-man [mæntə'mæn] *adj* de hombre a hombre.
manual ['mænjʊəl] *adj* manual.
▷ *n* manual *m*.
manually ['mænjʊəlɪ] *adv* a mano, manualmente.
manufacture [mænjə'fæktʃə(r)] *n (gen)* fabricación *f*; *(of clothing)* confección *f*; *(of foodstuffs)* elaboración *f*.
▷ *vt* **1** *(gen)* fabricar; *(clothing)* confeccionar; *(foodstuffs)* elaborar. **2** *fig (excuse, etc)* inventar.
manufacturer [mænjə'fæktʃərə(r)] *n* fabricante *mf*.
manufacturing [mænjə'fæktʃərɪŋ] *n* fabricación *f*.
manure [mə'njʊə(r)] *n* abono, estiércol *m*.
manuscript ['mænjəskrɪpt] *n* **1** *(historic handwritten book)* manuscrito. **2** *(original copy of text)* original *m*, texto original.
many ['menɪ] *adj* mucho,-a, muchos,-as: many people never go abroad *mucha gente nunca va al extranjero*.
▲ *comp* more, *superl* most.
▷ *pron* muchos,-as: I don't want many *no quiero muchos*. ■ **a good/great many** muchísimos,-as. ‖ **as many … as** tantos,-as … como. ‖ **how many?** ¿cuántos,-as? ‖ **not many** pocos,-as. ‖ **too many** demasiados,-as.
map [mæp] *n (of country, region)* mapa *m*; *(of town, bus, tube)* plano. ● **map of the world** mapamundi *m*.
▷ *vt (area)* trazar un mapa de.
▲ *pt & pp* mapped, *ger* mapping.
⊙ **to map out** *vt sep (future, career, etc)* proyectar, organizar; *(route)* trazar en un mapa.
maple ['meɪp(ə)l] *n (tree, wood)* arce *m*.
mapmaking ['mæpmeɪkɪŋ] *n* cartografía.
mar [mɑː(r)] *vt* estropear, echar a perder.
▲ *pt & pp* marred, *ger* marring.
marathon ['mærəθ(ə)n] *n* maratón *m*.
▷ *adj fig* maratoniano,-a, larguísimo,-a.
maraud [mə'rɔːd] *vi* merodear.
marble ['mɑːb(ə)l] *n* **1** *(stone, statue)* mármol *m*. **2** *(glass ball)* canica.
▷ *adj* **1** *(floor, statue)* de mármol, marmóreo,-a; *(industry)* del mármol. **2** *fig (like marble)* marmóreo,-a.
▷ *n pl* **marbles** **1** *(game)* canicas *fpl*. **2** ART mármoles *mpl*.
March [mɑːtʃ] *n* marzo.

Para ejemplos de uso, consulta May.

march [mɑːtʃ] *n* **1** MIL marcha. **2** *(walk)* caminata. **3** *(demonstration)* manifestación *f*. **4** MUS marcha.
▷ *vi* **1** MIL marchar, hacer una marcha. **2** *(walk)* caminar, marchar. **3** *(walk purposefully and determinedly)* ir resueltamente, ir decididamente. **4** *(demonstrate)* manifestarse.
▷ *vt* hacer marchar.
⊙ **to march past** *vi* MIL desfilar.
marcher ['mɑːtʃə(r)] *n (demonstrator)* manifestante *mf*.
marchioness ['mɑːʃənəs] *n* marquesa.
mare [meə(r)] *n* yegua.
margarine [mɑːdʒə'riːn] *n* margarina.
marge [mɑːdʒ] *n* GB *fam* margarina.
margin ['mɑːdʒɪn] *n* **1** *(gen)* margen *m*. **2** *(difference, leeway)* margen *m*: there is no margin for error *no hay margen de error*.

marginal ['mɑːdʒɪnᵊl] *adj* 1 *(small, minor)* menor, pequeño,-a, mínimo,-a. 2 *(artist)* marginal.

marginalization [mɑːdʒɪnᵊlaɪ'zeɪʃᵊn] *n* marginación *f*.

marginalize ['mɑːdʒɪnᵊlaɪz] *vt* marginar.

marginally ['mɑːdʒɪnəlɪ] *adv* ligeramente, un poco.

marigold ['mærɪgəʊld] *n* BOT maravilla, caléndula.

marihuana [mærɪ'hwɑːnə] *n* → **marijuana**.

marijuana [mærɪ'hwɑːnə] *n* marihuana, marijuana.

marina [mə'riːnə] *n* puerto deportivo.

marinade [mærɪ'neɪd] *n* adobo.
▷ *vt* adobar.

marinate ['mærɪneɪt] *vt* adobar.

marine [mə'riːn] *n (life, flora, etc)* marino,-a, marítimo,-a.
▷ *adj (law, stores, etc)* marítimo,-a.
▷ *n* soldado de infantería de marina.
▷ *n pl* **the Marines** GB la infantería de marina.

mariner ['mærɪnəʳ] *n* marinero.

marionette [mærɪə'net] *n* marioneta, títere *m*.

marital ['mærɪtᵊl] *adj (relations, problems)* matrimonial, marital; *(bliss)* conyugal. ● **marital status** estado civil.

maritime ['mærɪtaɪm] *adj* marítimo,-a.

marjoram ['mɑːdʒərəm] *n* mejorana.

mark¹ [mɑːk] *n* FIN *(currency)* marco.

mark² [mɑːk] *n* 1 *(imprint, trace)* huella; *(from blow)* señal *f*; *(stain)* mancha: **there's a mark on this blouse** *esta blusa tiene una mancha*. 2 *(sign, symbol)* marca, señal *f*: **I've put a mark by the things I'm interested in** *he señalado las cosas que me interesan*. 3 *(characteristic feature)* impronta, señal *f*, sello. 4 EDUC nota, calificación *f*, puntuación *f*: **he got a good mark in maths** *sacó una buena nota en mates*. ■ **on your marks, get set, go!** ¡preparados, listos, ya!
▷ *vt* 1 *(make mark on)* marcar, señalar, poner una señal en: **mark all the words that you don't know** *señala todas las palabras que no conoces*. 2 *(scar)* señalar, desfigurar, marcar; *(stain)* manchar. 3 *(denote, show position of)* señalar, indicar; *(show)* mostrar: **the route is marked** *la ruta está señalizada*. 4 EDUC *(correct)* corregir; *(grade - student)* poner nota a; *(- exam, essay, etc)* puntuar, calificar. 5 *(be typical of, characterize)* caracterizar.
▷ *vi (stain)* mancharse.
⊙ **to mark down** *vt sep* 1 *(reduce price of)* rebajar el precio de. 2 *(reduce marks of)* bajar la nota de. 3 *(note in writing)* apuntar.
⊙ **to mark off** *vt sep* 1 *(separate)* separar, dividir, distinguir; *(area)* delimitar; *(boundary)* trazar. 2 *(put line through)* tachar.
⊙ **to mark out** *vt sep* 1 *(area)* marcar, delimitar; *(boundary)* marcar, trazar. 2 *(choose)* señalar, seleccionar.
⊙ **to mark up** *vt sep* 1 *(increase price of)* subir (el precio de), aumentar (el precio de). 2 *(increase marks of)* subir la nota de.

marked [mɑːkt] *adj (noticeable - gen)* marcado,-a, notable; *(- improvement)* sensible, apreciable.

marker ['mɑːkəʳ] *n* 1 *(stake, pole)* jalón *m*. 2 *(bookmark)* punto de libro. ● **marker buoy** boya, baliza. ‖ **marker pen** rotulador *m*.

market ['mɑːkɪt] *n* 1 *(selling fruit, vegetables, etc)* mercado; *(selling clothes, etc)* mercadillo; *(marketplace)* plaza: **I always go to the market on Saturdays** *siempre voy al mercado los sábados*. 2 *(trade)* mercado: **the propert market** *el mercado inmobiliario*. 3 *(demand, desire to buy* demanda, salida, mercado. ■ **to be on the market** estar en venta. ‖ ● **market day** día *m* de mercado. ‖ **market forces** tendencias del mercado. ‖ **market garden** G huerta. ‖ **market price** precio de mercado.
▷ *vt (sell)* vender, poner en venta.

marketing ['mɑːkɪtɪŋ] *n* marketing *m*, mercadotecnia

marketplace ['mɑːkɪtpleɪs] *n (gen)* mercado; *(square* plaza.

marking ['mɑːkɪŋ] *n* 1 *(on bird, animal)* mancha. *(drawn, written)* marca. 3 EDUC correcciones *fpl*.

marksman ['mɑːksmən] *n* tirador *m*.
▲ *pl* **marksmen** ['mɑːksmən].

marksmanship ['mɑːksmənʃɪp] *n* puntería.

mark-up ['mɑːkʌp] *n (increase in price)* subida, au mento.

marmalade ['mɑːməleɪd] *n* mermelada (de cítricos)

maroon¹ [me'ruːn] *vt (abandon)* aislar, abandonar.

maroon² [mə'ruːn] *adj* granate.
▷ *n* (color *m*) granate *m*.

marooned [mə'ruːnd] *adj (abandoned)* abandona do,-a, aislado,-a.

marquee [mɑː'kiː] *n (large tent)* carpa, entoldado.

marquess ['mɑːkwɪs] *n* marqués *m*.

marquetry ['mɑːkɪtrɪ] *n* marquetería, taracea.

marquis ['mɑːkwɪs] *n* marqués *m*.

marriage ['mærɪdʒ] *n* 1 *(state, institution)* matrimo nio. 2 *(act, wedding)* boda, casamiento, enlace matrimonial. ■ **to be related by marriage** ser parien tes políticos. ‖ **to take** SB **in marriage** casarse co ALGN. ● **marriage bureau** agencia matrimonial. ‖ **ma riage certificate** certificado de matrimonio.

married ['mærɪd] *adj* 1 *(person, status)* casado,-a (to con): **a married couple** *un matrimonio*. 2 *(life, bliss* matrimonial, conyugal.

marrow ['mærəʊ] *n* [Also **bone marrow**.] 1 ANAT *(c bone)* tuétano, médula. 2 *fig (inner meaning)* meollo 3 [Also **vegetable marrow**.] GB calabacín *m* grande.

marry ['mærɪ] *vt* 1 *(take in marriage)* casarse con. *(unite in marriage)* casar. 3 *fig* unir.
▷ *vi* 1 casarse. 2 *fig* unirse. ■ **to get married** casarse (to con).
▲ *pt & pp* **married**, *ger* **marrying**.
⊙ **to marry into** *vt insep* emparentar con.
⊙ **to marry off** *vt sep* casar a.
⊙ **to marry up** *vi* corresponder, cuadrar.

Mars [mɑːz] *n* Marte *m*.

marsh [mɑːʃ] *n* 1 *(bog)* pantano. 2 *(area)* zona co pantanos, pantanal *m*.

marshal ['mɑːʃᵊl] *n* 1 MIL mariscal *m*. 2 *(at sports even demonstration)* oficial *mf*, organizador,-ra.
▷ *vt* 1 *(crowds, troops, etc)* reunir. 2 *fig (facts, thoughts, et* ordenar, poner en orden.
▲ *pt & pp* **marshalled** *(US* **marshaled***)*, *ger* **marshalling** *(U* **marshaling***)*.

marshland ['mɑːʃlænd] *n* tierra pantanosa.

marshmallow [mɑːʃ'mæləʊ] *n* 1 *(sweet)* golosina d merengue blando. 2 BOT malvavisco.

marshy ['mɑːʃɪ] *adj* pantanoso,-a.
▲ *comp* **marshier**, *superl* **marshiest**.

marsupial [mɑː'suːpɪəl] *n* marsupial *m*.

marten ['mɑːtᵊn] *n* marta.
martial ['mɑːʃᵊl] *adj* marcial.
Martian ['mɑːʃᵊn] *n* marciano,-a.
▷ *adj* marciano,-a.
martin ['mɑːtɪn] *n* avión *m*.
martyr ['mɑːtəʳ] *n* **1** mártir *mf*. **2** *fam* víctima (to, de).
martyrdom ['mɑːtədəm] *n* martirio.
marvel ['mɑːvᵊl] *n* **1** *(wonder)* maravilla: **it's a marvel no-one was hurt** *es un milagro que no hubiera heridos*. **2** *(person)* maravilla. ■ **to do marvels / work marvels** hacer maravillas.
▷ *vi fml* maravillarse (at, con), asombrarse (at, de).
▲ *pt & pp* **marvelled** *(*US **marveled***)*, *ger* **marvelling** *(*US **marveling***)*.
marvellous ['mɑːvᵊləs] *adj* maravilloso,-a, magnífico,-a, estupendo,-a.
marvellously ['mɑːvᵊləslɪ] *adv* maravillosamente, estupendamente.
marvelous ['mɑːvᵊləs] *adj* US ⟶ **marvellous.**
marvelously ['mɑːvᵊləslɪ] *adv* US ⟶ **marvellously.**
Marxism ['mɑːksɪzᵊm] *n* marxismo.
marzipan ['mɑːzɪpæn] *n* mazapán *m*.
mascara [mæ'skɑːrə] *n* rímel *m*.
mascot ['mæskɒt] *n* mascota.
masculine ['mɑːskjəlɪn] *adj* masculino,-a.
▷ *n* LING masculino.
masculinity [mæskjə'lɪnətɪ] *n* masculinidad *f*.
mash [mæʃ] *n* CULIN *fam (potatoes)* puré *m* de patatas.
▷ *vt* **1** *(beat, crush)* triturar (up,), machacar (up,). **2** CULIN *(potatoes)* hacer un puré de. ● **mashed potatoes** puré *m* de patatas.
mask [mɑːsk] *n (gen)* máscara; *(disguise)* careta, carátula; *(around eyes)* antifaz *m*. ● **diving mask** gafas *fpl* de bucear.
▷ *vt (gen)* enmascarar.
masked [mɑːskt] *adj* enmascarado,-a. ● **masked ball** baile *m* de disfraces, baile *m* de máscaras.
masking tape ['mɑːskɪŋteɪp] *n* cinta adhesiva.
masochism ['mæsəkɪzᵊm] *n* masoquismo.
masochist ['mæsəkɪst] *n* masoquista.
▷ *adj* masoquista.
mason ['meɪsᵊn] *n (builder)* albañil *m*.
masonic [mə'sɒnɪk] *adj* masónico,-a.
masonry ['meɪsᵊnrɪ] *n (stonework)* albañilería; *(building)* construcción *f*.
masquerade [mæskə'reɪd] *n* **1** *(pretence)* farsa, mascarada. **2** *(dance)* mascarada.
▷ *vi* disfrazarse (as, de), hacerse pasar (as, por).
mass¹ [mæs] *n* **1** *(large quantity)* montón *m*, masa; *(of people)* masa, multitud *f*, muchedumbre *f*: **a mass of books** *un montón de libros*. **2** *(majority)* mayoría.
▷ *vi (crowd)* congregarse, reunirse en gran número; *(troops)* concentrarse; *(clouds)* amontonarse.
▷ *vt* reunir.
▷ *adj* masivo,-a, multitudinario,-a, de masas: **there was a mass meeting** *se celebró un mitin multitudinario*. ● **mass media** medios *mpl* de comunicación (de masas).
▷ *n pl* **masses** *fam (lots)* cantidad *f*, montones *mpl*, mogollón *m*.
mass² [mæs] *n* REL misa.
massacre ['mæsəkəʳ] *n* masacre *f*, carnicería, matanza.
▷ *vt* masacrar, asesinar en masa.

massage ['mæsɑːʒ] *n* masaje *m*.
▷ *vt* **1** *(person, body)* dar un masaje a; *(part of body)* dar un masaje en.
masseur [mæ'sɜːʳ] *n* masajista *m*.
masseuse [mæ'sɜːz] *n* masajista.
massif [mæ'siːf] *n* macizo.
massive ['mæsɪv] *adj* **1** *(huge)* enorme, gigantesco. **2** *(solid, weighty)* sólido,-a, macizo,-a.
massively ['mæsɪvlɪ] *adv* enormemente.
mass-produce [mæsprə'djuːs] *n* fabricar en serie.
mast [mɑːst] *n* **1** MAR mástil *m*, palo. **2** *(transmitter)* torre *f*, poste *m*.
master ['mɑːstəʳ] *n* **1** *(of slave, servant, dog)* amo; *(of household)* señor *m*; *(owner)* dueño. **2** MAR *(of ship)* capitán *m*; *(of fishing boat)* patrón *m*. **3** GB *(teacher - infant school)* maestro, profesor *m*; *(- secondary)* profesor *m*. ● **master bedroom** dormitorio principal. ■ **master copy** original *m*.
▷ *n* **Master's (degree)** EDUC *(second level degree)* máster *m*.
▷ *adj (expert, skilled)* maestro,-a, experto,-a.
▷ *vt (learn - subject, skill)* llegar a dominar; *(- craft)* llegar a ser experto,-a en.
masterful ['mɑːstəful] *adj (dominating, authoritative)* autoritario,-a, dominante.
masterly ['mɑːstəlɪ] *adj* magistral, genial.
mastermind ['mɑːstəmaɪnd] *n (person)* cerebro, genio.
masterpiece ['mɑːstəpiːs] *n* obra maestra.
mastery ['mɑːstərɪ] *n (skill, expertise)* maestría, dominio (of, de).
mastodon ['mæstədɒn] *n* mastodonte *m*.
masturbate ['mæstəbeɪt] *vt* masturbar.
▷ *vi* masturbarse.
masturbation [mæstə'beɪʃᵊn] *n* masturbación *f*.
mat [mæt] *n* **1** *(rug)* alfombrilla; *(doormat)* felpudo. **2** *(rush mat)* estera; *(beach mat)* esterilla. **3** SP colchoneta.
match¹ [mætʃ] *n (light)* cerilla, fósforo.
▲ *pl* **matches.**
match² [mætʃ] *n* **1** SP *(football, hockey, etc)* partido, encuentro. **2** *(equal)* igual *mf*: **when it comes to chess, she's no match for you** *ella no puede competir contigo al ajedrez*. **3** *(marriage)* casamiento, matrimonio. **4** *(clothes, colour, etc)* juego, combinación *f*.
▲ *pl* **matches.**
▷ *vt* **1** *(equal)* igualar: **nobody can match him** *nadie lo iguala*. **2** *(go well with)* hacer juego (con), combinar (con): **her shoes match her dress** *los zapatos hacen juego con el vestido*. **3** *(be like, correspond to)* corresponder a.
▷ *vi* **1** *(go together)* hacer juego, combinar. **2** *(tally)* coincidir, concordar. **3** *(people)* llevarse bien, avenirse.
⊙ **to match up** *vi (tally)* coincidir.
▷ *vt sep (connect together)* emparejar, aparejar.
⊙ **to match up to** *vt insep (be as good as)* estar a la altura de.
matchbox ['mætʃbɒks] *n* caja de cerillas.
▲ *pl* **matchboxes.**
matching ['mætʃɪŋ] *adj* que hace juego, a juego.
mate [meɪt] *n* **1** *(school friend, fellow worker, etc)* compañero,-a, colega *mf*; *(friend)* amigo,-a, colega *mf*, compinche *mf*. **2** *(assistant)* ayudante *mf*, aprendiz,-za. **3** ZOOL pareja; *(male)* macho; *(female)* hembra.
▷ *vt* ZOOL aparear, acoplar.
▷ *vi* ZOOL aparearse, acoplarse.

material [mə'tɪərɪəl] *n* 1 *(physical substance)* materia, material *m*: raw material *materia prima;* building materials *materiales de construcción.* 2 *(cloth)* tela, tejido. 3 *(information, ideas, etc)* datos *mpl*, documentación *f*.
▷ *adj* 1 *(physical)* material. 2 *(important)* importante, substancial; *(relevant)* pertinente.
materialism [mə'tɪərɪəlɪzᵊm] *n* materialismo.
materialistic [mətɪərɪə'lɪstɪk] *adj* materialista.
materially [mə'tɪərɪəlɪ] *adv* 1 *(physically)* materialmente. 2 *(essentially)* esencialmente, en esencia.
maternal [mə'tɜːnᵊl] *adj* 1 *(motherly)* maternal. 2 *(related to mother)* materno,-a.
maternity [mə'tɜːnɪtɪ] *n* maternidad *f*.
math [mæθ] *n* US ⟶ maths.
mathematical [mæθə'mætɪkᵊl] *adj* matemático,-a. ■ to have a mathematical mind estar dotado,-a para las matemáticas.
mathematician [mæθᵊmə'tɪʃᵊn] *n* matemático,-a.
mathematics [mæθᵊ'mætɪks] *n* matemáticas *fpl*.
maths [mæθs] *n fam* mates *fpl*.
mating ['meɪtɪŋ] *n* ZOOL acoplamiento, apareamiento. ● mating call reclamo. ‖ mating season época de celo.
matriarch ['meɪtrɪɑːk] *n* matriarca.
matriculate [mə'trɪkjəleɪt] *vt* matricular.
▷ *vi* matricularse.
matriculation [mətrɪkjə'leɪʃᵊn] *n* matrícula, matriculación *f*.
matrix ['meɪtrɪks] *n* matriz *f*.
▲ *pl* matrixes o matrices ['meɪtrɪsiːz].
matron ['meɪtrən] *n* 1 GB *dated (in hospital)* enfermera jefe. 2 GB *(in school)* ama de llaves. 3 *(middle-aged married woman)* matrona.
matronly ['meɪtrənlɪ] *adj* madura y recia.
matt [mæt] *adj* mate.
matted ['mætɪd] *adj* enmarañado,-a.
matter ['mætəʳ] *n* 1 *(affair, subject)* asunto, cuestión *f*: it's a personal matter *es un asunto personal.* 2 *(trouble, problem)* problema *m*: what's the matter? *¿qué pasa?* 3 PHYS *(physical substance)* materia, sustancia. 4 *(type of substance, things of particular kind)* materia. ■ as a matter of fact en realidad, de hecho. ‖ to be another matter ser otra cosa.
▷ *vi (be important)* importar (to, a): it doesn't matter *no importa, es igual, da igual.* ■ no matter no importa: no matter what *pase lo que pase;* no matter what I say *diga lo que diga.*
matter-of-fact [mætərəv'fækt] *adj* práctico,-a, realista.
matting ['mæθɪŋ] *n* estera.
mattress ['mætrəs] *n* colchón *m*.
▲ *pl* mattresses.
mature [mə'tʃʊəʳ] *adj (gen)* maduro,-a.
▷ *vt* madurar.
▷ *vi* madurar.
maturity [mə'tʃʊərətɪ] *n* madurez *f*.
maul [mɔːl] *vt* 1 *(wound)* herir, agredir. 2 *(handle roughly)* maltratar. 3 *fig (criticize)* vapulear.
Mauritania [mɒrɪ'teɪnɪə] *n* Mauritania.
Mauritanian [mɒrɪ'teɪnɪən] *adj* mauritano,-a.
▷ *n* mauritano,-a.
Mauritian [mə'rɪʃᵊn] *adj* de Mauricio.
▷ *n* nativo o habitante *mf* de Mauricio.

mausoleum [mɔːsə'lɪəm] *n* mausoleo.
mauve [məʊv] *adj* malva.
▷ *n* malva *m*.
maverick ['mævᵊrɪk] *n* inconformista *mf*, independiente *mf*.
▷ *adj* inconformista, independiente.
mawkish ['mɔːkɪʃ] *adj* sensiblero,-a, empalagoso,-a
maxim ['mæksɪm] *n* máxima.
maximize ['mæksɪmaɪz] *vt* 1 *(increase as much as possible)* maximizar, llevar al máximo, aumentar al máximo. 2 *(make the best use of)* aprovechar al máximo.
maximum ['mæksɪməm] *adj* máximo,-a.
▷ *n* máximo, máximum *m*. ■ as a maximum como máximo. ‖ to the maximum al máximo.
May [meɪ] *n* mayo: his birthday is on the twentieth of May *su cumpleaños es el veinte de mayo;* at the beginning/end of May *a principios/finales de mayo;* in the middle of May *a mediados de mayo;* last May *en mayo del año pasado;* next May *en mayo del año que viene.*
may [meɪ] *aux* 1 *(possibility, probability)* poder, ser posible: he may come *es posible que venga, puede que venga;* you may laugh, but I think it's serious *tú bien puedes reír, pero yo creo que es grave.* 2 *(permission)* poder: may I help you? *¿en qué puedo servirle?;* may I go? *¿puedo irme?* 3 *(wish)* ojalá: may it be so *ojalá sea así.* ■ be that as it may sea como sea. ‖ SB may well ... bien puede ser que ALGN ...: he may well be angry *bien puede ser que esté enfadado.*

Consulta también might.

Maya ['maɪə] *n* 1 *(person)* maya *mf*. 2 *(language)* maya *m*
maybe ['meɪbiː] *adv* quizá, quizás, tal vez: maybe it'll rain *tal vez llueva;* maybe you're right *quizás tengas razón, a lo mejor tienes razón.*
mayday ['meɪdeɪ] *n* señal *f* de socorro, S.O.S. *m*.
mayonnaise [meɪə'neɪz] *n* mayonesa, mahonesa.
mayor [meəʳ] *n (man)* alcalde *m*; *(woman)* alcaldesa.
mayoress ['meəres] *n* alcaldesa.
maypole ['meɪpəʊl] *n* mayo.
maze [meɪz] *n* laberinto.
me¹ [miː] *n* MUS mi *m*.
me² [miː] *pron* 1 *(as object of verb)* me: follow me *sígueme;* give it to me *dámelo;* he looked at me *me miró.* *(after prep)* mí: it's for me *es para mí;* are you talking to me? *¿me lo dices a mí?* 3 *(emphatic)* yo: it's me! *¡soy yo!;* it's me, David *soy David.*
meadow ['medəʊ] *n* prado, pradera.
meagre ['miːgəʳ] *adj* 1 *(very small quantity)* escaso,-a exiguo,-a. 2 *(thin)* magro,-a.
meal¹ [miːl] *n (flour)* harina.
meal² [miːl] *n (gen)* comida: three meals a day *tres comidas al día;* ■ to have a meal 1 *(lunch)* comer. 2 *(supper)* cenar.
mealtime ['miːltaɪm] *n* hora de comer.
mealy-mouthed [miːlɪ'maʊðd] *adj pej* evasivo,-a, embustero,-a.
mean¹ [miːn] *adj* 1 *(miserly, selfish - person)* mezquino,-a, tacaño,-a, agarrado,-a; *(portion, etc)* mezquino,-a, miserable. 2 *(unkind)* malo,-a, antipático,-a; *(petty)* mezquino,-a; *(ashamed)* avergonzado,-a. 3 *fam (skilful, great)* excelente, de primera, genial. ■ to be no mean ser todo,-a un,-a: she's no mean singer *es una cantante genial.*

nean[2] [mi:n] *vt* **1** *(signify, represent)* significar, querer decir; *(to be a sign of, indicate)* ser señal de, significar: **what does «mug» mean?** *¿qué significa «mug»?, ¿qué quiere decir «mug»?* **2** *(have in mind)* pensar, tener pensado,-a, tener la intención de; *(intend, wish)* querer, pretender: **she didn't mean to do it** *lo hizo sin querer.* **3** *(involve, entail)* suponer, implicar; *(have as result)* significar: **that means we can't go on holiday** (US **vacation**) *eso significa que no podemos irnos de vacaciones.* **4** *(refer to, intend to say)* referirse a, querer decir; *(be serious about)* decir en serio: **what do you mean by that?** *¿qué quieres decir con eso?* ■ **to be meant for 1** *(be intended for)* ser para. **2** *(be destined for)* estar dirigido,-a a, ir dirigido,-a a: **these shoes are meant for light walking** *estos zapatos son para pasear.* ‖ **to be meant to 1** *(to be supposed to)* suponerse, deber, tener que. **2** *(to be fated)* estar destinado,-a: **they were meant to arrive yesterday** *tenían que llegar ayer.* ‖ **to mean well** tener buenas intenciones.

▲ *pt & pp* **meant** [ment].

nean[3] [mi:n] *adj (average)* medio,-a: **mean temperature** *temperatura media.*

n **1** *(average)* promedio. **2** MATH media. **3** *(middle term)* término medio.

neander [mɪ'ændəʳ] *vi* **1** *(river, etc)* serpentear. **2** *(person)* vagar, deambular, andar sin rumbo fijo. **3** *fig (conversation)* divagar.

n (of river, etc) meandro.

neaning ['mi:nɪŋ] *n* **1** *(sense - of word)* sentido, significado; *(- in dictionary)* acepción *f*; *(- of symbol, act)* significado: **what's the meaning of «draft»?** *¿qué significa «draft»?, ¿qué quiere decir «draft»?* **2** *(significance, importance)* sentido; *(purpose, intention)* intención *f*: **a glance full of meaning** *una mirada llena de intención.*

adj (significant) significativo,-a.

neaningful ['mi:nɪŋful] *adj (significant)* significativo,-a, importante; *(worthwhile)* útil, que vale la pena.

neaningfully ['mi:nɪŋfulɪ] *adv* significativamente.

neaningless ['mi:nɪŋləs] *adj* **1** *(word, phrase, etc)* sin sentido. **2** *(futile)* sin sentido, inútil, vano,-a.

neanness ['mi:nnəs] *n* **1** *(miserliness)* tacañería, mezquindad *f*, avaricia. **2** *(nastiness)* maldad *f*.

neans [mi:nz] *n (way, method)* medio, manera: **there's no means of escape** *no hay escapatoria, no hay manera de escapar;* **a means of transport** *un medio de transporte.*

▲ *pl* **means.**

n pl (resources) medios *mpl* de vida, recursos *mpl* económicos, ingresos *mpl*; *(income)* renta *f sing.* ■ **a means to an end** un medio de conseguir un objetivo, un medio para lograr un fin. ‖ **by all means** naturalmente, por supuesto. ‖ **by means of** por medio de, mediante. ‖ **by no means / not by any means** de ninguna manera, de ningún modo. ‖ **to live beyond one's means** vivir por encima de sus posibilidades.

neantime ['mi:ntaɪm] *adv* mientras tanto, entretanto. ■ **in the meantime** mientras tanto.

neanwhile ['mi:nwaɪl] *adv* mientras tanto, entretanto.

neasles ['mi:zᵊlz] *n* MED sarampión *m*.

neasly ['mi:zlɪ] *adj fam pej* miserable, mezquino,-a.

▲ *comp* **measlier**, *superl* **measliest.**

measurable ['meʒᵊrəbᵊl] *adj* mensurable.

measure ['meʒəʳ] *n* **1** *(system)* medida: **liquid measure** *medida para líquidos.* **2** *(indicator)* indicador *m*: **it's a measure of her popularity** *es un indicador de su popularidad.* **3** *(ruler)* regla. **4** *(measured amount, unit)* medida. **5** *(amount, degree, extent)* grado, cantidad *f*: **some measure of happiness** *cierta felicidad.* **6** *(method, step, remedy)* medida, disposición *f*: **safety measures** *medidas de seguridad.* ■ **in large measure** en gran parte, en gran medida. ‖ **in some measure** hasta cierto punto, en cierta medida. ‖ **to take measures** tomar medidas, adoptar medidas.

▷ *vt* **1** *(area, object, etc)* medir. **2** *(person)* tomar las medidas de. **3** *fig (assess)* evaluar; *(consider carefully)* sopesar, pensar bien.

▷ *vi (be)* medir: **it measures 3 feet by 6 feet** *mide 1 metro por 2 metros.*

⊙ **to measure up** *vi (be up to)* dar la talla, estar a la altura (**to**, de).

▷ *vt sep (person)* tomar las medidas de.

measured ['meʒəd] *adj* **1** *(action)* estudiado,-a; *(tone)* mesurado,-a; *(statement)* prudente, circunspecto,-a; *(language)* moderado,-a, comedido,-a. **2** *(step, etc)* acompasado,-a, regular, rítmico,-a.

measurement ['meʒəmənt] *n* **1** *(act)* medición *f*. **2** *(length, etc)* medida.

measuring ['meʒᵊrɪŋ] *n (act)* medición *f*. ● **measuring tape** cinta métrica, metro.

meat [mi:t] *n* carne *f*: **I prefer meat to fish** *me gusta más la carne que el pescado.* ● **cold meat / cooked meat** fiambre *m*.

meatball ['mi:tbɔ:l] *n* albóndiga.

meaty ['mi:tɪ] *adj* **1** *(pie, chop, bone, etc)* con mucha carne; *(smell, taste)* a carne. **2** *fig (book, discussion, etc)* sustancioso,-a.

▲ *comp* **meatier**, *superl* **meatiest.**

mechanic [mə'kænɪk] *n (person)* mecánico,-a.

mechanical [mə'kænɪkᵊl] *adj* mecánico,-a.

mechanics [mə'kænɪks] *n (science)* mecánica. ● **the mechanics** *(working parts)* el mecanismo; *(processes)* el funcionamiento.

mechanism ['mekənɪzᵊm] *n* mecanismo.

mechanization [mekənaɪ'zeɪʃᵊn] *n* mecanización *f*.

mechanize ['mekənaɪz] *vt* mecanizar.

▷ *vi* mecanizarse.

medal ['medᵊl] *n* medalla.

medallion [mə'dælɪən] *n* medallón *m*.

medallist ['medəlɪst] *n* medalla *mf*, campeón,-ona.

meddle ['medᵊl] *vi* **1** *(interfere)* entrometerse (**in**, en). **2** *(handle)* manosear (**with**, -).

meddler ['medᵊləʳ] *n* entrometido,-a, entremetido,-a.

meddlesome ['medᵊlsəm] *adj fml* entrometido,-a, entremetido,-a.

media ['mi:dɪə] *n pl* **the media** los medios *mpl* de comunicación.

Consulta también **medium.**

mediaeval [medɪ'i:vᵊl] *adj* medieval.

median ['mi:dɪən] *adj* MATH mediano,-a.

▷ *n* MATH *(line)* mediana; *(quantity)* valor *m* mediano.

mediate ['mi:dɪeɪt] *vi (arbitrate)* mediar (**between**, entre), (**in**, en).

▷ *vt (bring about)* lograr, conseguir.

mediation [mi:dɪ'eɪʃᵊn] *n* mediación *f*.
mediator ['mi:dɪeɪtəʳ] *n* mediador,-ra.
medic ['medɪk] *n fam (doctor)* médico,-a; *(medical student)* estudiante *mf* de medicina.
medical ['medɪkᵊl] *adj (treatment, care, examination)* médico,-a; *(book, student)* de medicina.
▷ *n fam (check-up)* chequeo, reconocimiento médico, revisión *f* médica.
medicate ['medɪkeɪt] *vt* medicar.
medicated ['medɪkeɪtɪd] *adj* medicinal.
medication [medɪ'keɪʃᵊn] *n* medicación *f*.
medicinal [mə'dɪsɪnᵊl] *adj* medicinal.
medicine ['medɪsᵊn] *n* 1 *(science)* medicina. 2 *(drugs, etc)* medicina, medicamento.
medieval [medɪ'i:vᵊl] *adj* medieval.
mediocre [mi:dɪ'əʊkəʳ] *adj* mediocre.
mediocrity [mi:dɪ'ɒkrətɪ] *n* mediocridad *f*.
meditate ['medɪteɪt] *vi* meditar, reflexionar (**on/upon**, sobre).
▷ *vt* meditar.
meditation [medɪ'teɪʃᵊn] *n* meditación *f*.
Mediterranean [medɪtə'reɪnɪən] *adj* mediterráneo,-a.
▷ *n* **the Mediterranean** el Mediterráneo.
medium ['mi:dɪəm] *adj (average)* mediano,-a, regular, normal. ● **medium wave** onda media.
▷ *n* 1 [*pl* **media**.] *(means)* medio. 2 [*pl* **media**.] *(environment)* medio (ambiente). 3 [*pl* **media**.] *(middle position)* punto medio, término medio. 4 [*pl* **mediums**.] *(spiritualist)* médium *mf*.
medley ['medlɪ] *n* 1 MUS popurrí *m*. 2 *(mixture)* mezcla; *(variety, assortment)* variedad *f*.
meek [mi:k] *adj* manso,-a, dócil, sumiso,-a.
meet [mi:t] *vt* 1 *(by chance)* encontrar, encontrarse con; *(in street)* cruzar con, topar con: **she met an old friend** *se encontró con un viejo amigo.* 2 *(by arrangement)* encontrar, reunirse con, citarse, quedar con; *(formally)* entrevistarse con; *(informally)* ver: **I'm meeting Rob tomorrow** *he quedado con Rob para mañana.* 3 *(meet for first time)* conocer: **I met him at a party** *lo conocí en una fiesta.* 4 *(collect)* ir a buscar, pasar a buscar; *(await arrival of)* esperar; *(receive)* ir a recibir: **he'll meet me at the station** *me vendrá a buscar a la estación;* 5 *(face - danger, difficulty)* encontrar; *(- problem)* hacer frente a.
▷ *vi* 1 *(by chance)* encontrarse: **we'll meet again** *nos volveremos a encontrar.* 2 *(by arrangement)* reunirse, verse, quedar, encontrarse; *(formally)* entrevistarse: **we arranged to meet on Saturday** *quedamos para el sábado.* 3 *(get acquainted)* conocerse: **I think we've already met** *creo que ya nos conocemos.* 4 *(join)* unirse; *(touch)* tocarse; *(rivers)* confluir; *(roads)* empalmar; *(eyes)* cruzarse.
▲ *pt & pp* **met** [met].
▷ *n* 1 SP encuentro.
⊙ **to meet up** *vi fam (by arrangement)* quedar, reunirse (**with**, con); *(by chance)* encontrar, encontrarse con.
⊙ **to meet with** *vt insep* 1 *(difficulty, problem)* encontrar, tropezar con; *(loss, accident)* sufrir; *(success)* tener. 2 US *(person)* reunirse con, entrevistarse con.
meeting ['mi:tɪŋ] *n* 1 *(gen - prearranged)* reunión *f*; *(- formal)* entrevista; *(- date)* cita. 2 *(chance encounter)* encuentro. 3 *(of club, committee, etc)* reunión *f*; *(of assembly)* sesión *f*; *(of shareholders, creditors)* junta. 4 POL *(rally)* mitin *m*. ● **meeting place** lugar *m* de encuentro, lugar *m* de reunión.
megabyte ['megəbaɪt] *n* COMPUT megabyte *m*, megaocteto.
megahertz ['megəhɜ:ts] *n* megahercio.
megalith ['megəlɪθ] *n* megalito.
megalomaniac [megələ'meɪnɪæk] *n* megalómano,-a.
▷ *adj* megalómano,-a.
megaphone ['megəfəʊn] *n* megáfono, altavoz *m*.
megaton ['megətʌn] *n* megatón *m*.
megawatt ['megəwɒt] *n* megavatio.
melamine ['meləmi:n] *n* melamina.
melancholy ['melənkəlɪ] *n* melancolía.
▷ *adj* melancólico,-a.
mellow ['meləʊ] *adj* 1 *(fruit)* maduro,-a; *(wine)* añejo,-a. 2 *(colour, voice)* suave. 3 *(person - mature, calm)* sosegado,-a, sereno,-a; *(genial, cheerful)* relajado,-a, apacible.
▷ *vt (person)* serenar, suavizar el carácter de.
▷ *vi* 1 *(colour, voice)* suavizar(se); *(fruit)* madurar; *(wine)* añejarse. 2 *(person)* serenarse; *(views)* moderarse.
melodic [mə'lɒdɪk] *adj* melódico,-a.
melodious [mə'ləʊdɪəs] *adj* melodioso,-a.
melodrama ['melədrɑ:mə] *n* melodrama *m*.
melodramatic [melədrə'mætɪk] *adj* melodramático,-a.
melody ['melədɪ] *n* melodía.
▲ *pl* **melodies**.
melon ['melən] *n (honeydew, etc)* melón *m*; *(watermelon)* sandía.
melt [melt] *vt* 1 *(ice, snow, butter, etc)* derretir. 2 *(metal)* fundir (**down**, -). 3 *(sugar, chemical)* disolver. 4 *fig* ablandar.
▷ *vi* 1 *(ice, snow)* derretirse (**away**, -). 2 *(metal)* fundirse. 3 *(sugar, chemical)* disolverse. 4 *fig (SB's heart)* ablandarse, derretirse. 5 *(colour, sound, etc)* desvanecer.
to melt into tears deshacerse en lágrimas. ‖ **to melt into the crowd** perderse entre la multitud.
⊙ **to melt away** *vi* 1 *(money, crowd, person)* desaparecer. 2 *fig (confidence, etc)* desvanecerse, esfumarse; *(anger)* disiparse, desaparecer.
melting ['meltɪŋ] *n (of metal)* fundición *f*; *(of snow)* derretimiento. ● **melting point** punto de fusión. **melting pot** crisol *m*.
member ['membəʳ] *n* 1 *(gen)* miembro *mf*; *(of club)* socio,-a; *(of union, party)* afiliado,-a: **the youngest member of the family** *el miembro más joven de la familia.* 2 POL *(of Parliament)* diputado,-a; *(of European Parliament)* eurodiputado,-a. 3 ANAT miembro.
▷ *adj (country, state)* miembro,-a.
membership ['membəʃɪp] *n* 1 *(of club - state)* calidad *f* de socio,-a, pertenencia; *(- entry)* ingreso. 2 *(of political party, union - state)* afiliación *f*; *(- entry)* ingreso. 3 *(members - of club)* miembros *mpl*, socios *mpl*; *(- political party)* afiliados *mpl*.
membrane ['membreɪn] *n* membrana.
memo ['meməʊ] *n* 1 *(official)* memorándum *m*. 2 *(personal note)* nota, apunte *m*. ● **memo pad** bloc *m* de notas.
▲ *pl* **memos**.
memoir ['memwɑ:ʳ] *n (essay)* memoria.

n pl **memoirs** *(autobiography)* memorias *fpl*, autobiografía.

emorable ['mem³rəb³l] *adj* memorable.

emorandum [meməˈrændəm] *n* **1** *(official note)* memorándum *m*, memorando. **2** *(personal note)* nota, apunte *m*.
▲ *pl* **memorandums o memoranda** [meməˈrændə].

emorial [məˈmɔːrɪəl] *adj (plaque, etc)* conmemorativo,-a.
n (monument) monumento conmemorativo; *(ceremony)* homenaje *m*.

emorize [ˈmeməraɪz] *vt* memorizar, aprender de memoria.

emory [ˈmemərɪ] *n* **1** *(ability, computers)* memoria: **she's got a good memory for names** *tiene buena memoria para los nombres.* **2** *(recollection)* recuerdo. ■ **to lose one's memory** perder la memoria. ▮ **within living memory** que se recuerde.
▲ *pl* **memories.**

en [men] *pl* ⟶ **man.**

enace [ˈmenəs] *n* **1** *(threat)* amenaza (**to**, para); *(danger)* peligro (**to**, para). **2** *fam (nuisance - person)* pesado,-a; *(- thing)* lata, molestia.
vt amenazar (**with**, de).

enacing [ˈmenəsɪŋ] *adj* amenazador,-ra, amenazante.

end [mend] *vt* **1** *(repair - gen)* reparar, arreglar; *(sew)* coser; *(patch)* remendar; *(darn)* zurcir: **can you mend my watch?** *¿me puedes arreglar el reloj?* **2** *(improve)* mejorar.
vi (health) mejorarse, reponerse; *(part of body, injury, wound)* curarse. ■ **to be on the mend** ir mejorando.
n (patch) remiendo; *(darn)* zurcido.

ender [ˈmendəʳ] *n (of shoes)* zapatero,-a, zapatero,-a remendón,-ona; *(of watches)* relojero,-a. ● **mender's shop 1** *(shoes)* zapatero. **2** *(watches)* relojería.

ending [ˈmendɪŋ] *n* **1** *(repairing - gen)* reparación *f*, arreglo. **2** *(clothes to be mended)* ropa para remendar. ■ **to do the mending 1** *(sew)* coser. **2** *(patch)* remendar. **3** *(darn)* zurcir.

enfolk [ˈmenfəʊk] *n pl* los hombres *mpl*.

enial [ˈmiːnɪəl] *adj (task, etc)* servil, bajo,-a.

eningitis [menɪnˈdʒaɪtəs] *n* MED meningitis *f*.

eniscus [mɪˈnɪskəs] *n* menisco.
▲ *pl* **meniscusses o menisci** [mɪˈnɪskaɪ].

enopause [ˈmenəʊpɔːz] *n* menopausia.

enstrual [ˈmenstrʊəl] *adj* menstrual. ● **menstrual cycle** ciclo menstrual. ▮ **menstrual period** regla, período.

enstruate [ˈmenstrʊeɪt] *vi* menstruar.

enstruation [menstrʊˈeɪʃ³n] *n* menstruación *f*, regla.

enswear [ˈmenzweəʳ] *n* ropa de caballero, ropa de hombres.

ental [ˈment³l] *adj* **1** *(of the mind)* mental: **mental effort** *esfuerzo mental;* **mental health** *salud mental.* **2** *(in the mind)* mental: **mental arithmetic** *cálculo mental;* **mental block** *bloqueo mental.* **3** *fam pej (mad)* chalado,-a, tocado,-a. ● **mental age** edad *f* mental. ▮ **mental handicap** disminución *f* psíquica. ▮ **mental home / mental hospital** (hospital *m*) psiquiátrico.

entality [menˈtælətɪ] *n* mentalidad *f*.
▲ *pl* **mentalities.**

mentally [ˈment³lɪ] *adv* mentalmente. ■ **to be mentally deranged** ser demente. ▮ **to be mentally ill** padecer una enfermedad mental.

menthol [ˈmenθɒl] *n* mentol *m*.
▷ *adj (cigarette)* mentolado,-a.

mention [ˈmenʃ³n] *n* mención *f*: **she made no mention of your visit** *no mencionó tu visita.*
▷ *vt* mencionar, hacer mención de, aludir a: **he never mentioned the money** *no mencionó el dinero.* ■ **don't mention it!** ¡de nada!, ¡no hay de qué!

mentor [ˈmentɔːʳ] *n* mentor *m*.

menu [ˈmenjuː] *n* **1** carta, menú *m*. **2** COMPUT menú *m*.
▲ *pl* **menus.**

meow [mɪˈaʊ] *n* maullido, miau *m*.
▷ *vi* maullar.

mercantile [ˈmɜːkəntaɪl] *adj* mercantil, comercial.

mercenary [ˈmɜːs³nərɪ] *adj* mercenario,-a.
▷ *n* mercenario,-a.
▲ *pl* **mercenaries.**

merchandise [ˈmɜːtʃ³ndaɪz] *n* mercancías *fpl*, géneros *mpl*.
▷ *vt (sell)* vender, poner en venta; *(promote)* promocionar.

merchant [ˈmɜːtʃ³nt] *n (trader)* comerciante *mf*; *(dealer, businessperson)* negociante *mf*; *(retailer)* detallista *mf*, minorista; *(shopkeeper)* tendero,-a. ● **merchant bank** banco comercial. ▮ **merchant navy** marina mercante.

merciful [ˈmɜːsɪfʊl] *adj* **1** *(forgiving)* misericordioso,-a (**to/towards**, con), clemente (**to/towards**, con), compasivo,-a (**to/towards**, con). **2** *(fortunate)* bienaventurado,-a.

merciless [ˈmɜːsɪləs] *adj* despiadado,-a, sin piedad.

mercurial [mɜːˈkjʊərɪəl] *adj* **1** *(people, mood)* voluble, volátil. **2** *fml (of mercury, like mercury)* mercurial.

Mercury [ˈmɜːkjərɪ] *n (planet)* Mercurio.

mercury [ˈmɜːkjərɪ] *n (metal)* mercurio.

mercy [ˈmɜːsɪ] *n* **1** *(compassion)* misericordia, clemencia, piedad *f*: **have mercy upon me!** *¡tenga piedad de mí!* **2** *fam (good fortune)* suerte *f*, milagro; *(blessing)* bendición *f*. ■ **to be at the mercy of** SB/STH estar a la merced de ALGN/ALGO.
▲ *pl* **mercies.**
▷ *adj* de ayuda, de socorro. ● **mercy killing** eutanasia.

mere [mɪəʳ] *adj* mero,-a, simple, puro,-a.
▷ *adj* **merest** *(slightest)* el/la más mínimo,-a.

merely [ˈmɪəlɪ] *adv* solamente, simplemente.

merge [mɜːdʒ] *vt (combine - gen)* unir (**with**, a), combinar (**with**, con); *(- road)* empalmar (**into**, con); *(- river)* desembocar (**into**, en); *(- firms, businesses)* fusionar.
▷ *vi* **1** *(combine - gen)* unirse, combinarse; *(- firms, businesses)* fusionarse; *(- roads, rivers)* juntarse; *(- rivers)* confluir. **2** *(blend, fade)* ir convirtiéndose (**into**, en).

merger [ˈmɜːdʒəʳ] *n* COMM fusión *f*.

meridian [məˈrɪdɪən] *n* meridiano.

meridional [məˈrɪdɪən³l] *adj* meridional.

meringue [məˈræŋ] *n* merengue *m*.

merit [ˈmerɪt] *n* **1** *(worth)* mérito, valía. **2** *(advantage, good point)* ventaja, mérito.
▷ *vt (deserve)* merecer, ser digno,-a de.

mermaid [ˈmɜːmeɪd] *n* sirena.

merrily [ˈmerɪlɪ] *adv* alegremente.

merriment [ˈmerɪmənt] *n* alegría, regocijo.

merry ['merɪ] *adj* **1** *(cheerful)* alegre; *(amusing)* divertido,-a, gracioso,-a. **2** *fam (slightly drunk)* alegre, achispado,-a. ■ **merry Christmas!** ¡felices Navidades!
▲ *comp* **merrier**, *superl* **merriest**.
merry-go-round ['merɪgəʊraʊnd] *n* tiovivo, caballitos *mpl*.
mesh [meʃ] *n* **1** *(of thread)* malla; *(of wire)* malla metálica, tela metálica; *(net)* red *f*. **2** TECH engranaje *m*.
▷ *vi* **1** TECH engranar. **2** *(fit in, harmonize)* encajar, combinar (**with**, con).
mesmerize ['mezməraɪz] *vt* **1** *(hypnotize)* hipnotizar. **2** *(fascinate)* fascinar, cautivar.
mess [mes] *n* **1** *(untidy state)* desorden *m*, revoltijo: **your room is a complete mess!** *¡tu habitación está toda desordenada!* **2** *(confusion, mix-up)* confusión *f*, lío, follón *m*; *(person, thing)* desastre *m*: **what a mess!** *¡vaya lío!*
▷ *vt (untidy)* desordenar; *(dirty)* ensuciar.
⊙ **to mess about / mess around** *vi* **1** *(idle)* gandulear; *(kill time)* pasar el tiempo; *(potter about)* entretenerse. **2** *(act the fool)* hacer el primo, tontear.
▷ *vt sep (treat badly)* fastidiar, tomar el pelo a.
⊙ **to mess about / mess around with** *vt insep (fiddle with)* tocar, manosear; *(play with)* jugar con.
▷ *vt sep (get involved with)* meterse con.
▷ *vt insep (have affair with)* tener un lío con, estar liado,-a con.
⊙ **to mess up** *vt sep* **1** *fam (untidy)* desordenar; *(dirty)* ensuciar. **2** *(spoil)* estropear, echar a perder.
⊙ **to mess with** *vt insep* **1** *(get involved with)* meterse con. **2** *(play with)* jugar con.
message ['mesɪdʒ] *n* **1** *(communication)* recado, mensaje *m*: **could you give her a message?** *¿podrías darle un recado?* **2** *(of story, film, etc)* mensaje *m*. ■ **to get the message** *(understand)* entender, darse cuenta.
messenger ['mesɪndʒəʳ] *n* mensajero,-a. ● **messenger boy** recadero.
Messiah [mə'saɪə] *n* REL Mesías *m*.
messy ['mesɪ] *adj* **1** *(untidy)* desordenado,-a, en desorden; *(- dirty)* sucio,-a. **2** *(confused)* complicado,-a, enredado,-a; *(awkward)* difícil; *(unpleasant)* desagradable.
▲ *comp* **messier**, *superl* **messiest**.
met [met] *pp & pt* ⟶ **meet**.
metabolism [mə'tæbəlɪzᵊm] *n* metabolismo.
metal ['metᵊl] *n* metal *m*.
▷ *adj* metálico,-a, de metal.
metalanguage ['metəlæŋgwɪdʒ] *n* metalenguaje *m*.
metallic [mə'tælɪk] *adj* metálico,-a. ● **metallic paint** pintura metalizada.
metallize ['metᵊlaɪz] *vt* metalizar.
metallurgist [mə'tælədʒɪst] *n* metalúrgico,-a.
metallurgy [mə'tælədʒɪ] *n* metalurgia.
metalwork ['metəlwɜ:k] *n* **1** *(craft)* metalistería. **2** *(objects)* objetos *mpl* de metal.
metamorphose [metə'mɔ:fəʊz] *vt* metamorfosear.
▷ *vi* metamorfosearse.
metamorphosis [metə'mɔ:fəsɪs] *n* metamorfosis *f*.
▲ *pl* **metamorphoses** [metə'mɔ:fəsi:z].
metaphor ['metəfɔ:ʳ] *n* metáfora.
metaphorical [metə'fɒrɪkᵊl] *adj* metafórico,-a.
metaphysical [metə'fɪzɪkᵊl] *adj* metafísico,-a.
metaphysics [metə'fɪzɪks] *n* metafísica.
metatarsus [metə'tɑ:səs] *n* metatarso
▲ *pl* **metatarsi** [metə'tɑ:saɪ].
metathesis [me'tæθəsɪs] *n* metátesis *f*.
meteor ['mi:tɪəʳ] *n* meteorito.
meteoric [mi:tɪ'ɒrɪk] *adj (gen)* meteórico,-a.
meteorite ['mi:tɪəraɪt] *n* meteorito.
meteorological [mi:tɪərə'lɒdʒɪkᵊl] *adj* meteorológico,-a.
meteorologist [mi:tɪə'rɒlədʒɪst] *n* meteorólogo,-
meteorology [mi:tɪə'rɒlədʒɪ] *n* meteorología.
meter ['mi:təʳ] *n* **1** US ⟶ **metre**. **2** contador *m*.
▷ *vt* medir.
methacrylate [meθ'ækrɪleɪt] *n* metacrilato.
methadone ['meθədəʊn] *n* metadona.
methane ['mi:θeɪn] *n* metano.
method ['meθəd] *n* **1** *(manner, way)* método, form **2** *(system, order)* sistema *m*, orden *m*, lógica.
methodical [mə'θɒdɪkᵊl] *adj* metódico,-a, ordenado,-a.
Methodist ['meθədɪst] *n* metodista *mf*.
methodology [meθə'dɒlədʒɪ] *n* metodología.
▲ *pl* **methodologies**.
meths [meθs] *n fam* alcohol *m* de quemar.
methylated spirits [meθəleɪtɪd'spɪrɪts] *n* alcoh *m* de quemar, alcohol *m* desnaturalizado.
meticulous [mə'tɪkjələs] *adj* meticuloso,-a, min cioso,-a.
metonymy [me'tɒnɪmɪ] *n* metonimia.
metre[1] ['mi:təʳ] *n (in poetry)* metro.
metre[2] ['mi:təʳ] *n (measure)* metro. ● **cubic metre** m tro cúbico.
metric ['metrɪk] *adj* métrico,-a. ● **metric system** sis ma métrico. ‖ **metric ton** tonelada métrica.
metronome ['metrənəʊm] *n* metrónomo.
metropolis [mə'trɒpəlɪs] *n* metrópoli *f*, metrópolis
▲ *pl* **metropolises**.
metropolitan [metrə'pɒlɪtᵊn] *adj* metropolitano,-
mettle ['metᵊl] *n fml (courage, spirit)* valor *m*, entere *(character)* carácter *m*.
mew [mju:] *vi* maullar.
▷ *n* maullido.
mews [mju:z] *n* GB *callejuela con antiguas caballeriz reconvertidas en viviendas.*
Mexican ['meksɪkᵊn] *adj* mejicano,-a.
▷ *n* mejicano,-a.
Mexico ['meksɪkəʊ] *n* Méjico.
mezzo-soprano ['metsəʊsə'prɑ:nəʊ] *n* mezzos prano *f*.
mg ['em'dʒi:, 'mɪlɪgræm] *symb* (**milligram, milligram** miligramo; *(symbol)* mg.
MHz ['megəhɜ:ts] *abbr* (**megahertz**) megaherz *m*; *(a breviation)* MHz.
mi [mi:] *n* MUS mi *m*.
miaow [mi:'aʊ] *n* maullido.
▷ *vi* maullar.
mice [maɪs] *pl* ⟶ **mouse**.
mickey ['mɪkɪ] ■ **to take the mickey out of** SB *fam* marle el pelo (a ALGN).
micro ['maɪkrəʊ] *n fam* microordenador *m*.
▲ *pl* **micros**.
microbe ['maɪkrəʊb] *n* microbio.

microbiology [maɪkrəʊbaɪ'ɒlədʒɪ] *n* microbiología.
microchip ['maɪkəʊtʃɪp] *n* microchip *m.*
microclimate ['maɪkrəʊklaɪmət] *n* microclima *mf.*
microcomputer [maɪkrəʊkəm'pju:təʳ] *n* microordenador *m*, microcomputador *m.*
microcosm ['maɪkrəʊkɒzᵊm] *n* microcosmos *m inv.*
microfiche ['maɪkrəʊfi:ʃ] *n* microficha.
microfilm ['maɪkrəʊfɪlm] *n* microfilme *m.*
microlight ['maɪkrəlaɪt] *n* ultraligero, avión *m* ultraligero.
micron ['maɪkrɒn] *n* micra.
microphone ['maɪkrəfəʊn] *n* micrófono.
microprocessor [maɪkrəʊ'prəʊsesəʳ] *n* microprocesador *m.*
microscope ['maɪkrəskəʊp] *n* microscopio.
microscopic [maɪkrə'skɒpɪk] *adj* microscópico,-a.
microsurgery [maɪkrəʊ'sɜ:dʒərɪ] *n* microcirugía.
microwave ['maɪkrəweɪv] *n* microonda. ● **microwave oven** horno de microondas, microondas *m inv.*
▷ *vt* cocinar en el microondas.
mid- [mɪd] *adj* medio,-a: **in mid-afternoon** *a media tarde.*
midair [mɪd'eəʳ] *adj* en el aire.
midday [mɪd'deɪ] *n* mediodía *m.*
▷ *adj* de mediodía. ■ **at midday** al mediodía.
middle ['mɪdᵊl] *adj (central)* de en medio, central; *(medium)* mediano,-a, medio,-a: **he's the middle son** *él es el hijo mediano.*
▷ *n* **1** *(centre)* medio, centro: **there's a pond in the middle of the garden** *hay un estanque en medio del jardín.* **2** *(halfway point of period, activity)* mitad *f*: **in the middle of a storm** *en medio de una tormenta.* **3** *fam (waist)* cintura. ■ **in the middle of nowhere** en el quinto pino. ‖ **to be in one's middle twenties «(thirties, etc)»** tener unos veinticinco *(treinta y cinco, etc)* años. ‖ ● **middle age** mediana edad *f.* ‖ **middle class** clase *f* media. ‖ **middle finger** dedo corazón. ‖ **middle school** GB *colegio para niños de entre 8 y 13 años.* ‖ **the Middle Ages** la Edad Media.
middle-aged [mɪdᵊ'eɪdʒd] *adj* de mediana edad.
middle-class [mɪdᵊ'klɑ:s] *adj* de la clase media.
middleman ['mɪdᵊlmən] *n* intermediario.
▲ *pl* **middlemen** ['mɪdᵊlmen].
middle-sized ['mɪdᵊlsaɪzd] *adj* de tamaño mediano, mediano,-a.
middleweight ['mɪdᵊlweɪt] *n (boxing)* peso medio.
middling ['mɪdᵊlɪn] *adj* mediano,-a, regular.
midge [mɪdʒ] *n* mosquito.
midget ['mɪdʒɪt] *n* enano,-a.
midnight ['mɪdnaɪt] *n* medianoche *f*: **we got home at midnight** *llegamos a casa a medianoche.*
midriff ['mɪdrɪf] *n* **1** *(belly)* estómago. **2** ANAT diafragma *m.*
midst [mɪdst] ■ **in our/your/their midst** entre nosotros/vosotros/ellos. ‖ **in the midst of** en medio de.
midstream [mɪd'stri:m] ■ **in midstream** *(river)* en medio de la corriente.
midsummer [mɪd'sʌməʳ] *n* pleno verano.
midway ['mɪdweɪ] *adv* a medio camino.
▷ *adj (point, etc)* intermedio,-a.
midweek ['mɪdwi:k] *adj* de entre semana.
▷ *adv* entre semana.
midwife ['mɪdwaɪf] *n* comadrona, partera, matrona.
▲ *pl* **midwives** ['mɪdwaɪvz].
midwifery ['mɪdwɪfərɪ] *n* obstetricia.
midwinter [mɪd'wɪntəʳ] *n* pleno invierno.
miffed [mɪft] *adj fam* molesto,-a, picado,-a.
might[1] [maɪt] *n* poder *m*, fuerza.
might[2] [maɪt] *aux* **1** *(possibility)* poder: **it might rain** *podría llover.* **2** *(in suggestions or requests)* poder: **you might try the hardware shop** *podrías probar en la ferretería.* **3** *(permission)* poder: **he asked if he might come in** *pidió permiso para entrar.* ■ **I might have known!** ¡debí imaginármelo!, ¡típico! ‖ **might (just) as well** más vale que.

Consulta también **may.**

mighty ['maɪtɪ] *adj* **1** *(very strong)* muy fuerte; *(powerful)* potente. **2** *(great, imposing)* enorme.
▲ *comp* **mightier**, *superl* **mightiest.**
▷ *adv* US *fam (very)* muy.
migraine ['maɪgreɪn] *n* jaqueca, migrana.
migrant ['maɪgrənt] *adj* migratorio,-a.
▷ *n (person)* emigrante *mf*; *(bird)* ave *f* migratoria.
migrate [maɪ'greɪt] *vi* migrar.
migration [maɪ'greɪʃᵊn] *n* migración *f.*
migratory ['maɪgrətərɪ] *adj* migratorio,-a.
mike [maɪk] *n fam* micro.
mild [maɪld] *adj* **1** *(person, character)* apacible, afable, dulce. **2** *(climate, weather)* benigno,-a, templado,-a, suave, blando,-a; *(soap, detergent)* suave. **3** *(protest, attempt)* ligero,-a; *(punishment, fever)* leve; *(illness, attack)* ligero,-a, leve; *(criticism, rebuke)* suave, leve.
mildew ['mɪldju:] *n* **1** *(on fabric, wall)* moho. **2** *(on plants)* mildiu *m*, mildeu *m.*
mildly ['maɪldlɪ] *adv* **1** *(softly, gently)* suavemente. **2** *(slightly)* ligeramente.
mildness ['maɪldnəs] *n* **1** *(of person, character)* apacibilidad *f*, afabilidad. **2** *(of climate, weather)* suavidad *f*, lo templado; *(of soap, detergent)* suavidad *f.* **3** *(of punishment, illness)* levedad *f.*
mile [maɪl] *n* milla (1,6 kms).
▷ *n pl* **miles** *(much)* mucho, muchísimo: **I'm miles better** *estoy mucho mejor;* **it's miles away** *está muy lejos.*
mileage ['maɪlɪdʒ] *n* **1** AUTO *(miles travelled by a car)* ≈ kilómetros *mpl*, kilometraje *m.* **2** *fam fig (benefit, advantage, use)* jugo, partido.
mileometer [maɪ'lɒmɪtəʳ] *n* AUTO cuentakilómetros *m.*
milestone ['maɪlstəʊn] *n* **1** hito, mojón *m.* **2** *fig* hito.
milieu ['mi:ljɜ:] *n* entorno, medio ambiente.
▲ *pl* **milieux** ['mi:l'jə] o **milieus** ['mi:ljəz].
militant ['mɪlɪtənt] *adj* POL militante.
▷ *n* POL militante *mf.*
militarism ['mɪlɪtərɪzᵊm] *n* militarismo.
militarist ['mɪlɪtərɪst] *n* militarista *mf.*
militarization [mɪlɪtəraɪ'zeɪʃᵊn] *n* militarización *f.*
military ['mɪlɪtᵊrɪ] *adj* militar.
▷ *n* **the military** los militares, las fuerzas armadas.
militia [mɪ'lɪʃə] *n* milicia.
milk [mɪlk] *n (gen)* leche *f.* ● **milk shake** batido. ‖ **milk tooth** diente *m* de leche.
▷ *adj (bottle, production)* de leche; *(product)* lácteo,-a.
▷ *vt* **1** *(from cow, goat)* ordeñar. **2** *(from plant, tree)* sacar, extraer; *(from snake)* extraer el veneno de. **3** *fig (exploit)* chupar, sacar jugo a.
▷ *vi (of cow, goat)* dar leche.

milking ['mɪlkɪŋ] *n* ordeño. ■ **to do the milking** ordeñar.
milkmaid ['mɪlkmeɪd] *n* lechera.
milkman ['mɪlkmən] *n* lechero, repartidor *m* de la leche.
▲ *pl* **milkmen** ['mɪlkmen].
milky ['mɪlkɪ] *adj* **1** *(liquid, jewel)* turbio,-a. **2** *(coffee, tea)* con mucha leche; *(substance)* lechoso,-a. **3** *(colour)* pálido,-a.
▲ *comp* **milkier**, *superl* **milkiest**. ● **Milky Way** Vía Láctea.
mill [mɪl] *n* **1** *(machinery)* molino. **2** *(for coffee, pepper, etc)* molinillo. **3** *(factory)* fábrica.
▷ *vt (crush, grind)* moler.
⊙ **to mill about/around** *vi* arremolinarse, apiñarse.
millennium [mɪ'lenɪəm] *n* milenio, milenario.
▲ *pl* **millenniums** o **millennia** [mɪ'lenɪə].
miller ['mɪləʳ] *n* molinero,-a.
millet ['mɪlɪt] *n* mijo.
millibar ['mɪlɪbɑːʳ] *n* milibar *m*.
milligram ['mɪlɪgræm] *n* miligramo.
milligramme ['mɪlɪgræm] *n* miligramo.
milliliter ['mɪlɪliːtəʳ] *n* US → **millilitre.**
millilitre ['mɪlɪliːtəʳ] *n* mililitro.
millimeter ['mɪlɪmiːtəʳ] *n* US → **millimetre.**
millimetre ['mɪlɪmiːtəʳ] *n* milímetro.
millinery ['mɪlɪnᵊrɪ] *n* **1** *(hats)* sombreros *mpl* de señora. **2** *(shop)* sombrerería.
million ['mɪljən] *n* millón *m*: **one million dollars** *un millón de dólares.*
▷ *n pl* **millions** *fam (lots)* millones *mpl.*
millionaire [mɪljə'neəʳ] *n* millonario,-a.
millionairess [mɪljən'eəres] *n* millonaria.
millipede ['mɪlɪpiːd] *n* milpiés *m inv*.
millisecond ['mɪlɪsekənd] *n* milésima de segundo.
millstone ['mɪlstəʊn] *n* muela, rueda de molino.
mime [maɪm] *n* **1** *(art)* mimo. **2** *(performance)* pantomima, representación *f* de mimo.
▷ *vt (express by mime)* expresar haciendo mímica.
mimic ['mɪmɪk] *n* imitador,-ra.
▷ *vt (copy)* imitar, remedar.
▲ *pt & pp* **mimicked**, *ger* **mimicking.**
mimicry ['mɪmɪkrɪ] *n (art)* mímica; *(imitation)* imitación *f*, remedo.
mimosa [mɪ'məʊzə] *n* mimosa.
mince [mɪns] *n* GB *(meat)* carne *f* picada.
▷ *vt (chop, cut)* picar.
▷ *vi (walk)* andar de manera amanerada; *(speak)* hablar con afectación.
mincemeat ['mɪnsmiːt] *n* **1** *(sweet)* conserva de picadillo de fruta. **2** US *(meat)* carne *f* picada.
mincer ['mɪnsəʳ] *n* máquina de picar carne.
mind [maɪnd] *n* **1** *(intellect)* mente *f*. **2** *(mentality)* mentalidad *f*. **3** *(brain, thoughts)* cabeza, cerebro: **her mind was very confused** *estaba confusa.*
▷ *vt* **1** *(heed, pay attention to)* hacer caso de; *(care about)* importar, preocupar: **I mind what people say** *me importa lo que dice la gente.* **2** *(be careful with)* tener cuidado con: **mind the step!** *¡cuidado con el escalón!* **3** *(look after - child)* cuidar, cuidar de; *(- house)* vigilar; *(- shop)* atender; *(- seat, place)* guardar. **4** *(object to, be troubled by)* tener inconveniente en, importar: **I don't mind staying** *no tengo inconveniente en quedarme.* **5** *(fancy, quite like)* venir bien: **I wouldn't mind a coffee** *me vendría bien un café.*
▷ *vi* **1** *(be careful)* tener cuidado: **mind (out)!** *¡cuidado ¡ojo!* **2** *(object to)* importar, molestar, tener inconveniente: **do you mind if I open the window?** *¿le importa que abra la ventana?* ■ **never mind 1** *(it doesn't matter)* no importa, da igual. **2** *(don't worry)* no te preocupes. **3** *(let alone)* ni hablar de. ‖ **to be out of one's mind** estar loco,-a. ‖ **to change one's mind** cambiar de opinión, cambiar de parecer. ‖ **to make up one's mind** decidirse. ‖ **to** SB**'s mind** en la opinión de ALGN.
minder ['maɪndəʳ] *n fam (bodyguard)* guardaespaldas *m inv*, gorila *m*.
mindful ['maɪndful] *adj fml* consciente (**of**, de).
mindless ['maɪndləs] *adj* **1** *(tedious)* monótono,-a, mecánico,-a. **2** *pej (senseless - behaviour)* absurdo,-a, estúpido,-a.
mind-reader ['maɪndriːdəʳ] *n* adivino,-a.
mine[1] [maɪn] *n (gen)* mina.
▷ *vt* **1** *(coal, gold, etc)* extraer; *(area)* explotar. **2** MIL sembrar minas en, minar.
▷ *vi* explotar una mina.
mine[2] [maɪn] *pron* (el) mío, (la) mía, (los) míos, (las) mías, lo mío: **hey! that's mine!** *¡ey! ¡eso es mío!*; **a friend of mine** *un/una amigo,-a mío,-a.*
minefield ['maɪnfiːld] *n* campo de minas.
miner ['maɪnəʳ] *n* minero,-a.
mineral ['mɪnᵊrəl] *adj* mineral.
▷ *n* mineral *m*. ● **mineral water** agua mineral. ‖ **mineral oil** GB petróleo.
mineralogy [mɪnə'rælədʒɪ] *n* mineralogía.
minesweeper ['maɪnswiːpəʳ] *n* dragaminas *m inv*.
mineworker ['maɪnwɜːkəʳ] *n* minero,-a.
mingle ['mɪŋgᵊl] *vt* mezclar.
▷ *vi* **1** *(liquids)* mezclarse; *(sounds, smells, etc)* confundirse. **2** *(people)* circular, mezclarse con la gente.
mini ['mɪnɪ] *n (skirt)* minifalda, mini *f*.
miniature ['mɪnɪtʃəʳ] *n* miniatura.
▷ *adj* (en) miniatura.
miniaturist ['mɪnɪtʃərɪst] *n* miniaturista *mf*.
minibus ['mɪnɪbʌs] *n* microbús *m*.
▲ *pl* **minibuses.**
minicab ['mɪnɪkæb] *n* GB taxi *m*.
minicomputer [mɪnɪkəm'pjuːtəʳ] *n* microordenador *m*.
minim ['mɪnɪm] *n* GB blanca.
minimal ['mɪnɪmᵊl] *adj* mínimo,-a.
minimize ['mɪnɪmaɪz] *vt (reduce)* minimizar, reducir al mínimo.
minimum ['mɪnɪməm] *adj* mínimo,-a.
▷ *n* mínimo: **a minimum of 20 people** *un mínimo de 20 personas.*
mining ['maɪnɪŋ] *n* minería, explotación *f* de minas: **coal mining** *extracción de carbón.*
▷ *adj (area, town, industry)* minero,-a. ● **mining engineer** ingeniero,-a de minas.
miniseries [mɪnɪ'sɪəriːz] *n* TV miniserie *f*.
miniskirt ['mɪnɪskɜːt] *n* minifalda.
minister ['mɪnɪstəʳ] *n* **1** *(gen)* ministro,-a (**for**, de). **2** *(priest)* pastor,-ra.
▷ *vi* atender (**to**, a), cuidar (**to**, a).
ministerial [mɪnɪ'stɪərɪəl] *adj* ministerial.
ministry ['mɪnɪstrɪ] *n (gen)* ministerio.
▷ *n* **the ministry** GB *(priesthood)* el clero..
▲ *pl* **ministries.**

ink [mɪŋk] *n* visón *m*.

innow ['mɪnəʊ] *n* piscardo.

inor ['maɪnəʳ] *adj* **1** *(unimportant)* menor; *(secondary)* secundario,-a. **2** MUS menor.
n JUR menor *mf*.

inority [maɪ'nɒrɪtɪ] *n* **1** minoría. **2** JUR minoría de edad. ■ **to be in a minority** estar en minoría.
▲ *pl* **minorities**.
adj minoritario,-a.

inster ['mɪnstəʳ] *n* catedral *f*.

instrel ['mɪnstrəl] *n* trovador *m*, juglar *m*.

int¹ [mɪnt] *n* FIN *(place)* casa de la moneda.
vt (coins, words) acuñar.

int² [mɪnt] *n* **1** BOT menta. **2** *(sweet)* caramelo de menta.

inuet [mɪnjʊ'et] *n* minué *m*.

inus ['maɪnəs] *prep* **1** MATH menos: **four minus three equals one** *cuatro menos tres es igual a uno.* **2** METEOR bajo cero: **minus five degrees** *cinco grados bajo cero.*
adj negativo,-a.
n **1** MATH menos *m*. **2** *(disadvantage)* desventaja *m*.
● **minus sign** signo de menos *m*.

inuscule ['mɪnəskjuːl] *adj* minúsculo.

inute¹ [maɪ'njuːt] *adj (tiny)* diminuto,-a, minúsculo,-a.

inute² ['mɪnɪt] *n* **1** *(of time)* minuto: **it's a five minute walk** *es un paseo de cinco minutos.* **2** *fam (moment)* momento; *(instant)* instante *m*: **I'll be back in a minute** *ahora vuelvo, vuelvo en un momento.* ■ **(at) any minute now** en cualquier momento. | **at the last minute** en el último momento, a última hora.
n pl **minutes** *(notes)* acta *f sing*, actas *fpl*.

iracle ['mɪrək°l] *n (gen)* milagro.

iraculous [mɪ'rækjələs] *adj* milagroso,-a.

irage [mɪ'rɑːʒ] *n* espejismo.

ire ['maɪəʳ] *n (mud)* fango, lodo; *(muddy area)* lodazal *m*.

irror ['mɪrəʳ] *n (gen)* espejo: **stop looking at yourself in the mirror** *deja de mirarte en el espejo.* ● **driving mirror** espejo (retrovisor).
vt reflejar.

irth [mɜːθ] *n (happiness)* alegría, regocijo; *(laughter)* risas *fpl*.

isadventure [mɪsəd'ventʃəʳ] *n* desventura, desgracia.

isanthropist [mɪ'zænθrəpɪst] *n* misántropo,-a.

isapprehension [mɪsæprɪ'henʃ°n] *n* malentendido, equivocación *f*.

isappropriate [mɪsə'prəʊprɪeɪt] *vt* malversar.

isbehave [mɪsbɪ'heɪv] *vi* portarse mal, comportarse mal.

isbehavior [mɪsbɪ'heɪvjəʳ] *n* US ⟶ **misbehaviour**.

isbehaviour [mɪsbɪ'heɪvjəʳ] *n* mala conducta, mal comportamiento.

iscalculate [mɪs'kælkjəleɪt] *vt* calcular mal.
vi calcular mal.

iscarriage [mɪs'kærɪdʒ] *n* MED aborto (espontáneo).

iscarry [mɪs'kærɪ] *vi* **1** MED abortar (espontáneamente), tener un aborto. **2** *(plans, etc)* fracasar, frustrarse, malograrse.
▲ *pt & pp* **miscarried**, *ger* **miscarrying**.

iscellaneous [mɪsɪ'leɪnɪəs] *adj (mixed, varied)* variado,-a, vario,-a, diverso,-a, misceláneo,-a.

miscellany [mɪ'selənɪ] *n* **1** *(mixture)* miscelánea. **2** *(book)* antología.
▲ *pl* **miscellanies**.

mischance [mɪs'tʃɑːns] *n fml* desgracia, mala suerte *f*.

mischief ['mɪstʃɪf] *n* **1** *(naughtiness)* travesura, diablura: **I know you're up to some mischief** *sé que estás haciendo alguna travesura.* **2** *fml* daño, mal *m*.

mischievous ['mɪstʃɪvəs] *adj* **1** *(naughty - person)* travieso,-a; *(- look, grin, etc)* pícaro,-a. **2** *(causing harm)* malicioso,-a.

misconceived [mɪskən'siːvd] *adj (badly planned)* desacertado,-a, equivocado,-a.

misconception [mɪskən'sepʃ°n] *n* idea equivocada, idea falsa, concepto erróneo, concepto falso.

misconduct [mɪs'kɒndʌkt] *n (improper behaviour)* mala conducta.
▷ *vt* administrar mal.

miscount [mɪs'kaʊnt] *vt* contar mal.
▷ *n* cómputo erróneo.

misdeed [mɪs'diːd] *n fml* delito, fechoría.

misdemeanor [mɪsdɪ'miːnəʳ] *n* US ⟶ **misdemeanour**.

misdemeanour [mɪsdɪ'miːnəʳ] *n* **1** *fam (misdeed)* fechoría. **2** JUR delito menor.

misdirect [mɪsdaɪ'rekt] *vt* **1** *(letter)* poner mal las señas en. **2** *(person)* orientar mal a, informar mal a. **3** *(energy, talent, qualities, etc)* encaminar mal, encauzar mal.

miser ['maɪzəʳ] *n* avaro,-a.

miserable ['mɪz°rəb°l] *adj* **1** *(person - unhappy)* abatido,-a, triste, deprimido,-a, infeliz; *(- bad-tempered)* antipático,-a. **2** *(place, etc)* deprimente, triste; *(weather)* horrible, malísimo,-a. **3** *(paltry)* miserable, mezquino,-a, despreciable; *(pathetic)* lamentable.

miserably ['mɪz°rəblɪ] *adv* **1** *(unhappily)* tristemente. **2** *(poorly)* miserablemente. **3** *(pathetically)* lamentablemente, de manera lamentable; *(badly)* pésimamente.

miserly ['maɪzəlɪ] *adj* avaro,-a, tacaño,-a.

misery ['mɪzərɪ] *n* **1** *(wretchedness, unhappiness)* desgracia, desdicha, tristeza. **2** *(suffering)* sufrimiento, dolor *m*, suplicio. **3** *(poverty)* pobreza, miseria.
▲ *pl* **miseries**.

misfire [mɪs'faɪəʳ] *vi* fallar.

misfit ['mɪsfɪt] *n (person)* inadaptado,-a.

misfortune [mɪs'fɔːtʃ°n] *n* infortunio, desgracia, mala fortuna.

misgiving [mɪs'gɪvɪŋ] *n (doubt)* duda, recelo; *(fear)* temor *m*; *(worry)* preocupación *f*.

misguided [mɪs'gaɪdɪd] *adj* desacertado,-a, equivocado,-a.

mishandle [mɪs'hænd°l] *vt (deal with badly)* llevar mal, manejar mal; *(treat roughly)* maltratar.

mishap ['mɪshæp] *n* percance *m*, contratiempo.

mishear [mɪs'hɪəʳ] *vt* oír mal, entender mal.
▷ *vi* oír mal.
▲ *pt & pp* **misheard** [mɪshɜːd].

mishmash ['mɪʃmæʃ] *n fam* batiburrillo, mezcolanza.

misinform [mɪsɪn'fɔːm] *vt* informar mal.

misinterpret [mɪsɪn'tɜːprət] *vt (accidentally)* interpretar mal; *(deliberately)* tergiversar.

misjudge [mɪs'dʒʌdʒ] *vt* **1** *(person, situation)* juzgar mal. **2** *(distance, speed, etc)* calcular mal.

mislay [mɪs'leɪ] *vt* extraviar, perder.
▲ *pt & pp* **mislaid** [mɪsleɪd], *ger* **mislaying**.

mislead [mɪs'li:d] *vt (muddle)* despistar; *(deceive)* engañar.
▲ *pt & pp* misled [mɪs'led], *ger* misleading.
mismanagement [mɪs'mænɪdʒmənt] *n* mala administración *f*.
misogynist [mɪ'sɒdʒənɪst] *n* misógino,-a.
misplace [mɪs'pleɪs] *vt (mislay)* perder, extraviar.
misprint ['mɪsprɪnt] *n* errata, error *m* de imprenta.
mispronounce [mɪsprə'naʊns] *vt* pronunciar mal.
misquote [mɪs'kwəʊt] *vt (accidentally)* citar incorrectamente; *(deliberately)* distorsionar las palabras de.
misread [mɪs'ri:d] *vt* **1** *(read wrongly)* leer mal. **2** *(interpret wrongly)* interpretar mal, malinterpretar.
▲ *pt & pp* misread [mɪs'red], *ger* misreading.
misrepresent [mɪsreprɪ'zent] *vt (person)* tergiversar la palabras de; *(words)* tergiversar, distorsionar.
misrepresentation [mɪsreprɪzen'teɪʃᵊn] *n (of truth, etc)* falsificación *f*, deformación *f*; *(of words, etc)* tergiversación *f*, distorsión *f*.
miss[1] [mɪs] *n* señorita.
miss[2] [mɪs] *n (catch, hit, etc)* fallo; *(shot)* tiro errado.
▷ *vt* **1** *(not to hit, score, etc)* fallar; *(shot)* errar: he missed a penalty *falló un penalti.* **2** *(not catch)* perder: I missed the bus *perdí el autobús.* **3** *(not experience)* perderse: don't miss this concert! *¡no te pierdas este concierto!* **4** *(not see)* perderse: she doesn't miss anything *no se le escapa nada.* **5** *(not attend - meeting, etc)* no asistir a; *(- class, work)* faltar a. **6** *(omit, skip)* saltarse; *(disregard)* pasar por alto; *(overlook, fail to notice)* dejarse, dejar pasar: she missed a line *se saltó una línea.* **7** *(long for - person)* echar de menos; *(- place)* añorar: she misses her family *echa de menos a su familia.*
▷ *vi* **1** *(catch, kick, etc)* fallar; *(shot)* errar el tiro. **2** *(engine)* fallar. **3** *(fail)* fallar.
⊙ **to miss out** *vt sep (omit, fail to include)* saltarse, omitir; *(overlook, disregard)* pasar por alto, dejarse.
▷ *vi (lose opportunity)* dejar pasar, perderse.
misshapen [mɪs'ʃeɪpᵊn] *adj (badly formed)* deforme; *(out of shape)* deformado,-a.
missile ['mɪsaɪl] *n* **1** *(explosive weapon)* misil *m*. **2** *(object thrown)* proyectil *m*.
missing ['mɪsɪŋ] *adj* **1** *(object - lost)* perdido,-a, extraviado,-a. **2** *(person - disappeared)* desaparecido,-a; *(- absent)* ausente: she's been missing for a week *hace una semana que desapareció.* ■ **to be missing** faltar. ● missing person desaparecido,-a.
mission ['mɪʃᵊn] *n* misión *f*.
missionary ['mɪʃᵊnərɪ] *n* misionero,-a.
▲ *pl* missionaries.
missive ['mɪsɪv] *n* misiva.
misspell [mɪs'spel] *vt (write)* escribir mal.
▲ *pt & pp* misspelled o misspelt [mɪs'spelt], *ger* misspelling.
misspend [mɪs'spend] *vt* malgastar.
▲ *pt & pp* misspent [mɪs'spent].
mist [mɪst] *n* **1** *(gen)* neblina; *(sea)* bruma; *(haze)* calima. **2** *(on window, mirror, etc)* vaho.
⊙ **to mist over / mist up** *vi* **1** *(windows, glasses, etc)* empañarse. **2** *fig (eyes)* llenarse de lágrimas, empañarse.
mistake [mɪs'teɪk] *n (error)* equivocación *f*, error *m*; *(in test)* falta; *(oversight)* descuido: there must be some mistake *debe haber algún error.* ■ **by mistake 1** *(in e rror)* por error. **2** *(unintentionally)* sin querer. ■ **to mak a mistake** equivocarse, cometer un error.
▷ *vt* **1** *(misunderstand)* entender mal. **2** *(confuse)* co fundir (**for**, con).
▲ *pt* mistook [mɪs'tʊk], *pp* mistaken [mɪs'teɪkən].
mistaken [mɪs'teɪkᵊn] *pp* ⟶ **mistake.**
▷ *adj (wrong, incorrect)* equivocado,-a, erróneo,-a, fa so,-a. ■ **to be mistaken** equivocarse.
mistakenly [mɪs'teɪkᵊnlɪ] *adv* por error.
mister ['mɪstəʳ] *n* señor *m*.
mistime [mɪs'taɪm] *vt (do at wrong time)* calcular ma
mistletoe ['mɪsᵊltəʊ] *n* muérdago.
mistook [mɪs'tʊk] *pt* ⟶ **mistake.**
mistreat [mɪs'tri:t] *vt* maltratar, tratar mal.
mistress ['mɪstrəs] *n* **1** *(owner - gen)* dueña, ama, s ñora; *(of dog)* ama, dueña. **2** *(lover)* amante *f*. **3** maestra, profesora.
mistrust [mɪs'trʌst] *n* desconfianza, recelo.
▷ *vt* desconfiar de, dudar de, recelar de.
mistrustful [mɪs'trʌstfʊl] *adj* desconfiado,-a, rec loso,-a.
misty ['mɪstɪ] *adj* **1** METEOR neblinoso,-a: it's misty *h neblina.* **2** *(window, glasses, etc)* empañado,-a.
▲ *comp* mistier, *superl* mistiest.
misunderstand [mɪsʌndə'stænd] *vt (gen)* entend mal; *(misinterpret)* malinterpretar.
▲ *pt & pp* misunderstood [mɪsʌndə'stʊd].
misunderstanding [mɪsʌndə'stændɪŋ] *n* male tendido (**about**, sobre).
misuse [*(n)* mɪs'ju:s; *(vb)* mɪs'ju:z] *n (of tool, resourc word, etc)* mal uso, uso incorrecto; *(of funds)* malve sación *f*.
▷ *vt (tool, resources, word, etc)* utilizar mal, emplear m *(funds)* malversar.
mite[1] [maɪt] *n (insect)* ácaro, acárido.
mite[2] [maɪt] *n* **1** *(small amount)* pizca, pelín *m*. **2** *(sm child)* chiquillo,-a, criatura.
miter ['maɪtəʳ] *n* US ⟶ **mitre.**
mitigate ['mɪtɪgeɪt] *vt* mitigar.
mitigating ['mɪtɪgeɪtɪŋ] *adj* mitigador,-ra. ● **mitig ing circumstances** JUR circunstancias *fpl* atenuante
mitre ['maɪtəʳ] *n* **1** REL mitra. **2** TECH inglete *m*.
mitten ['mɪtᵊn] *n (fingers covered)* manopla; *(fing exposed)* mitón *m*.
mix [mɪks] *n* **1** *(mixture - gen)* mezcla. **2** CULIN preparac
▷ *vt* **1** *(combine)* mezclar, combinar: mix the sugar w the butter *mezclar el azúcar con la mantequilla (make, prepare - plaster, cement)* amasar; *(- cockt salad, medicine)* preparar.
▷ *vi* **1** *(substances)* mezclarse. **2** *(clothes, colours, food)* co binar bien, ir bien juntos,-as. **3** *(people - come toget* mezclarse con la gente; *(- get on)* llevarse bien (**w** con).
⊙ **to mix up** *vt sep* **1** *(ingredients)* mezclar bien. **2** *(c fuse)* confundir. **3** *(mess up, put in disorder)* desor nar, revolver, mezclar.
mixed [mɪkst] *adj* **1** *(of different kinds)* variado, mixed biscuits *galletas surtidas.* **2** *(ambivalent)* sigual. **3** *(for both sexes)* mixto,-a.

mixed-up [mɪkst'ʌp] *adj* 1 *(objects, papers, etc)* revuelto,-a. 2 *(person)* desconcertado,-a, desorientado,-a, hecho,-a un lío.

mixer ['mɪksəʳ] *n (for food)* batidora. ■ **to be a good mixer** *(person)* ser sociable.

mixing bowl ['mɪksɪŋbəʊl] *n (gen)* bol *m*, tazón *m*; *(earthenware)* cuenco.

mixture ['mɪkstʃəʳ] *n (gen)* mezcla.

mix-up ['mɪksʌp] *n fam (confusion)* lío, confusión *f*; *(misunderstanding)* malentendido.

ml[1] [maɪl] *abbr* **(mile)** milla.

ml[2] ['mɪlɪlɪtəʳ] *abbr* **(millilitre)** mililitro; *(abbreviation)* ml.

mm ['mɪlɪmiːtəʳ] *symb* (*(millimetre)* milímetro; *(abbreviation)* mm.

mnemonic [nə'mɒnɪk] *adj* nemotécnico,-a, mnemotécnico,-a.

moan [məʊn] *n* 1 *(groan)* gemido, quejido. 2 *(complaint)* queja, protesta.

vi 1 *(groan)* gemir. 2 *(complain)* quejarse (**about**, de), protestar (**about**, por).

moaner ['məʊnəʳ] *n* quejica *m & f*.

moat [məʊt] *n* foso.

mob [mɒb] *n* 1 *(large crowd)* muchedumbre *f*, turba, multitud *f*. 2 *(group of friends)* pandilla, grupo, peña.

vt (crowd round) acosar, rodear; *(attack)* asaltar, atacar.

▲ *pt & pp* **mobbed**, *ger* **mobbing**.

mobile ['məʊbaɪl] *adj (object, troops, etc)* móvil, movible. ● **mobile home** caravana, remolque *m*. ‖ **mobile phone** teléfono móvil.

n (hanging ornament) móvil *m*.

mobility [mə'bɪlɪtɪ] *n* movilidad *f*.

mobilize ['məʊbɪlaɪz] *vt* movilizar.

vi movilizarse.

moccasin ['mɒkəsɪn] *n* mocasín *m*.

mock [mɒk] *adj* 1 *(object)* de imitación. 2 *(feeling)* fingido,-a, simulado,-a; *(modesty)* falso,-a.

vt (laugh at, make fun of) burlarse de, mofarse de.

vi burlarse (**at**, de).

mockery ['mɒkərɪ] *n* 1 *(ridicule)* burla, mofa. 2 *(farce)* farsa; *(travesty)* parodia. ■ **to make a mockery of** STH poner ALGO en ridículo.

mocking ['mɒkɪŋ] *adj* burlón,-ona.

mock-up ['mɒkʌp] *n (model)* maqueta, modelo a escala.

mod [mɒd] *n* mod *mf*.

modal ['məʊdᵊl] *adj* modal. ● **modal auxiliary** auxiliar *m* modal. ‖ **modal verb** verbo modal.

mode [məʊd] *n* 1 *fml (means)* medio; *(manner, way)* modo. 2 *(fashion)* moda.

model ['mɒdᵊl] *n* 1 *(small representation)* modelo, maqueta. 2 *(design)* modelo, patrón *m*. 3 *(type of car, etc)* modelo. 4 *(perfect example)* modelo, pauta. 5 *(fashion model)* modelo *mf*, maniquí *mf*; *(artist's model)* modelo *mf*.

adj 1 *(miniature)* en miniatura, a escala; *(toy)* de juguete. 2 *(exemplary)* ejemplar; *(ideal)* modelo.

vt (clay, etc) modelar.

vi 1 *(clay, etc)* modelar. 2 *(work as fashion model)* trabajar de modelo.

pt & pp **modelled** (US **modeled**), *ger* **modelling** (US **modelling**).

to model on *vt insep (form as copy of)* inspirarse en.

modem ['məʊdem] *n* COMPUT modem *m*.

moderate ['mɒdᵊrət] *adj* 1 *(average)* mediano,-a, regular: **moderate size** *tamaño mediano*. 2 *(not extreme)* moderado,-a; *(reasonable)* razonable. 3 *(talent, ability, performance)* mediocre, regular.

▷ *vt* moderar.

▷ *vi* moderarse.

moderately ['mɒdᵊrətlɪ] *adv (not very)* medianamente, bastante.

moderation [mɒdə'reɪʃᵊn] *n* moderación *f*.

moderator ['mɒdəreɪtəʳ] *n (in debate)* moderador,-ra.

modern ['mɒdᵊn] *adj* 1 *(up-to-date)* moderno,-a. 2 *(history, literature, etc)* contemporáneo,-a. ● **modern language** lengua moderna.

modernism ['mɒdᵊnɪzᵊm] *n* modernismo.

modernity [mə'dɜːnɪtɪ] *n* modernidad *f*.

modernization [mɒdᵊnaɪ'zeɪʃᵊn] *n* modernización *f*.

modernize ['mɒdᵊnaɪz] *vt* modernizar.

▷ *vi* modernizarse.

modest ['mɒdɪst] *adj* 1 *(gen)* modesto,-a, humilde. 2 *(improvement, increase)* modesto,-a; *(- price)* módico,-a.

modestly ['mɒdɪstlɪ] *adv* modestamente.

modesty ['mɒdɪstɪ] *n* 1 *(humility)* modestia, humildad *f*. 2 *(chastity)* pudor *m*, recato.

modicum ['mɒdɪkəm] *n (small amount)* atisbo, mínimo (**of**, de).

modification [mɒdɪfɪ'keɪʃᵊn] *n* modificación *f*.

modifier ['mɒdɪfaɪəʳ] *n* modificador *m*.

modify ['mɒdɪfaɪ] *vt (change)* modificar.

▲ *pt & pp* **modified**, *ger* **modifying**.

modular ['mɒdjʊləʳ] *adj* modular.

module ['mɒdjuːl] *n* módulo.

mogul ['məʊgʌl] *n* magnate *m*.

mohair ['məʊheəʳ] *n* mohair *m*.

moist [mɔɪst] *adj (damp)* húmedo,-a; *(slightly wet)* ligeramente mojado,-a: **a moist sponge cake** *un bizcocho tierno*.

moisten ['mɔɪsᵊn] *vt* humedecer.

moisture ['mɔɪstʃəʳ] *n* humedad *f*.

moisturize ['mɔːstʃəraɪz] *vt* hidratar.

moisturizer ['mɔɪstʃəraɪzəʳ] *n* hidratante *m*.

molar ['məʊləʳ] *n* muela.

molasses [mə'læsɪz] *n* melaza.

mold [məʊld] *n* → **mould**.

molding ['məʊldɪŋ] *n* → **moulding**.

moldy ['məʊldɪ] *adj* → **mouldy**.

mole[1] [məʊl] *n (on skin)* lunar *m*.

mole[2] [məʊl] *n* 1 ZOOL topo. 2 *fam (spy)* topo *mf*, espía *mf*.

molecular [mə'lekjələʳ] *adj* molecular.

molecule ['mɒlɪkjuːl] *n* molécula.

molehill ['məʊlhɪl] *n* topera.

molest [mə'lest] *vt* 1 *(attack - person)* atacar, asaltar; *(- dog)* perseguir, atacar. 2 *(sexually)* abusar sexualmente.

mollify ['mɒlɪfaɪ] *vt* aplacar, apaciguar, calmar.

▲ *pt & pp* **mollified**, *ger* **mollifying**.

mollusc ['mɒləsk] *n* molusco.

mollycoddle ['mɒlɪkɒdᵊl] *vt fam* mimar, consentir.

molt [məʊlt] *n* US → **moult**.

molten ['məʊltᵊn] *adj* fundido,-a, derretido,-a.

mom [mɒm] *n* US *fam* mamá *f*.

moment ['məʊmənt] *n (instant)* momento, instante *m*: just a moment *un momentito;* I didn't believe that story for a moment *no me creí ese cuento ni por un momento.* ■ **at any moment** de un momento a otro, en cualquier momento. ‖ **at the last moment** a última hora. ‖ **at the moment** en este momento. ‖ **for the moment** de momento, por el momento. ‖ **in a moment** dentro de un momento.
momentary ['məʊməntərɪ] *adj* momentáneo,-a.
momentous [mə'mentəs] *adj* trascendental, de suma importancia.
momentum [mə'mentəm] *n* **1** PHYS momento. **2** *(impetus)* ímpetu *m*, impulso.
mommy ['mɒmɪ] *n* US *fam* mamá.
▲ *pl* mommies.
Monaco ['mɒnəkəʊ] *n* Mónaco.
monarch ['mɒnək] *n* monarca *m*.
monarchist ['mɒnəkɪst] *n* monárquico,-a.
monarchy ['mɒnəkɪ] *n* monarquía.
▲ *pl* monarchies.
monastery ['mɒnəstᵊrɪ] *n* monasterio.
▲ *pl* monasteries.
monastic [mə'næstɪk] *adj* monástico,-a.
Monday ['mʌndɪ] *n* lunes *m inv*.
Para ejemplos de uso, consulta Saturday.
Monegasque ['mɒnəgæsk] *n* monegasco,-a.
monetary ['mʌnɪtᵊrɪ] *adj* monetario,-a.
money ['mʌnɪ] *n* **1** *(gen)* dinero: how much money have you got? *¿cuánto dinero tienes?* **2** *(currency)* moneda. ■ **to make money 1** *(person)* ganar dinero, hacer dinero. **2** *(business)* dar dinero. ‖ **to put money on** STH apostar por ALGO.
moneybox ['mʌnɪbɒks] *n* hucha.
▲ *pl* moneyboxes.
moneychanger ['mʌnɪθseɪndʒəʳ] *n* cambiante *mf*, cambista *mf*.
moneyed ['mʌnɪd] *adj* adinerado,-a, rico,-a.
moneylending ['mʌnɪlendɪŋ] *n* préstamo.
moneymaking ['mʌnɪmeɪkɪŋ] *adj* rentable.
money-spinner ['mʌnɪspɪnəʳ] *n* GB *fam* negocio rentable.
Mongol ['mɒŋgɒl] *n* mongol,-la, mogol,-la.
Mongolia [mɒŋ'gəʊlɪə] *n* Mongolia.
Mongolian [mɒŋ'gəʊlɪən] *adj* mongol,-la, mogol,-la.
▷ *n* **1** *(person)* mongol,-la, mogol,-la. **2** *(language)* mongol *m*, mogol *m*.
mongolism ['mɒŋgəlɪzᵊm] *n taboo* mongolismo.
mongoose ['mɒŋgʊːs] *n* mangosta.
mongrel ['mʌŋgrᵊl] *n (dog)* perro cruzado, perro mestizo.
monitor ['mɒnɪtəʳ] *n* **1** *(screen)* monitor *m*. **2** *(school pupil)* responsable *mf*, encargado,-a.
▷ *vt (check)* controlar; *(follow)* seguir de cerca; *(watch)* observar.
monk [mʌŋk] *n* monje *m*.
monkey ['mʌŋkɪ] *n (gen)* mono,-a; *(long-tailed)* mico,-a. ● **monkey nut** cacahuete *m*. ‖ **monkey wrench** llave *f* inglesa.
⊙ **to monkey about / monkey around** *vi* hacer tonterías, hacer el tonto.
⊙ **to monkey about with** *vt insep* juguetear con.
mono ['mɒnəʊ] *n fam* mono, monofonía.
▷ *adj fam* mono, monofónico,-a.
monochrome ['mɒnəkrəʊm] *adj (one colour)* monocromo,-a.
monocle ['mɒnəkᵊl] *n* monóculo.
monogamous [mə'nɒgəməs] *adj* monógamo,-a.
monogamy [mə'nɒgəmɪ] *n* monogamia.
monolith ['mɒnəlɪθ] *n* monolito.
monolithic [mɒnə'lɪθɪk] *adj* monolítico,-a.
monologue ['mɒnəlɒg] *n* monólogo.
monoplane ['mɒnəpleɪn] *n* monoplano.
monopolize [mə'nɒpəlaɪz] *vt* monopolizar.
monopoly [mə'nɒpəlɪ] *n* monopolio.
▲ *pl* monopolies.
monosyllabic [mɒnəsɪ'læbɪk] *adj (word)* monosílabo,-a.
monosyllable ['mɒnəsɪləbᵊl] *n* monosílabo.
monotheism ['mɒnəʊθɪɪzᵊm] *n* monoteísmo.
monotheistic [mɒnəʊθɪ'ɪstɪk] *adj* monoteísta.
monotone ['mɒnətəʊn] *n* tono monocorde. ■ **to speak in a monotone** hablar con voz monótona.
monotonous [mə'nɒtənəs] *adj* monótono,-a.
monotony [mə'nɒtənɪ] *n* monotonía.
monoxide [mə'nɒksaɪd] *n* monóxido.
monsoon [mɒn'suːn] *n* **1** *(wind)* monzón *m*. **2** *(rainy season)* estación *f* lluviosa. ● **monsoon rains** lluvias *fpl* monzónicas.
monster ['mɒnstəʳ] *n (gen)* monstruo.
▷ *adj fam (huge)* enorme, gigantesco,-a.
monstrosity [mɒn'strɒsətɪ] *n* monstruosidad *f*.
▲ *pl* monstrosities.
monstrous ['mɒnstrəs] *adj* **1** *(huge)* enorme, gigantesco,-a. **2** *(hideous)* monstruoso,-a.
montage ['mɒntɑːʒ] *n* montaje *m*.
Montenegrin [mɒntɪ'niːgrɪn] *adj* montenegrino,-a.
▷ *n* montenegrino,-a.
Montenegro [mɒntɪ'niːgrəʊ] *n* Montenegro.
month [mʌnθ] *n* mes *m*: I'm going on holiday (US vacation) at the end of the month *me voy de vacaciones a final de mes.*
monthly ['mʌnθlɪ] *adj* mensual.
▷ *adv* mensualmente, cada mes.
▷ *n (magazine)* revista mensual.
monument ['mɒnjəmənt] *n* monumento (to, a).
monumental [mɒnjə'mentᵊl] *adj* **1** *(gen)* monumental. **2** *fam (lie, blunder, etc)* garrafal, monumental.
moo [muː] *n (of cow)* mugido.
▷ *vi* mugir.
▲ *pt & pp* mooed, *ger* mooing.
mooch [muːtʃ] *vt* US *fam (cadge)* gorrear (off/from, a).
⊙ **to mooch about / mooch around** *vi* dar vueltas, deambular.
mood[1] [muːd] *n* LING modo.
mood[2] [muːd] *n* **1** *(humour)* humor *m*: her moods change very quickly *cambia de humor de repente.* ■ **to be in a good/bad mood** estar de buen/mal humor.
moody ['muːdɪ] *adj* **1** *(bad-tempered)* malhumorado,-a, de mal humor. **2** *(changeable)* de humor cambiadizo, lunático,-a.
▲ *comp* moodier, *superl* moodiest.
moon [muːn] *n* luna: full moon *luna llena.* ■ **to be over the moon** estar en el séptimo cielo.
moonbeam ['muːnbiːm] *n* rayo de luna.
moonlight ['muːnlaɪt] *n* claro de luna, luz *f* de luna.

noonlighting ['mu:nlaɪtɪŋ] *n fam* pluriempleo.
noonlit ['mu:nlɪt] *adj (landscape, etc)* iluminado,-a por la luna; *(night)* de luna.
noonstruck ['mu:nstrʌk] *adj* tocado,-a, trastornado,-a, lunático,-a.
Moor [mʊəʳ] *n* moro,-a.
noor[1] [mʊəʳ] *n (heath)* brezal *m.*
noor[2] [mʊəʳ] *vt (with rope)* amarrar; *(with anchor)* anclar.
vi (with anchor) anclar; *(with rope)* echar amarras.
nooring ['mʊərɪŋ] *n (place)* amarradero.
n pl **moorings** *(ropes, etc)* amarras *fpl.*
Moorish ['mʊərɪʃ] *adj* moro,-a.
noorland ['mʊələnd] *n* páramo.
noose [mu:s] *n* alce *m.*
noot [mu:t] *vt fml (raise, propose, suggest)* plantear, proponer, sugerir.
nop [mɒp] *n* **1** *(for floor)* fregona. **2** *fam (of hair)* mata de pelo.
vt **1** *(floor)* fregar, limpiar. **2** *(brow, tears)* enjugarse (**with**, con), secarse.
▲ *pt & pp* **mopped**, *ger* **mopping.**
to mop up *vt sep* enjugar, limpiar.
nope [məʊp] *vi* estar abatido,-a, estar deprimido,-a.
to mope about / mope around *vi* andar abatido,-a, andar deprimido,-a.
noped ['məʊped] *n* ciclomotor *m.*
noral ['mɒrᵊl] *adj* moral.
n (of story) moraleja.
n pl **morals** moral *f sing*, moralidad *f sing.*
norale [mə'rɑ:l] *n* moral *f*, estado de ánimo.
noralistic [mɒrə'lɪstɪk] *adj* moralizador,-ra.
norality [mə'rælɪtɪ] *n* moralidad *f*, moral *f.*
noralize ['mɒrəlaɪz] *vi* moralizar.
norally ['mɒrəlɪ] *adv* moralmente.
norass [mə'ræs] *n* **1** *(marsh)* cenagal *m*, ciénaga. **2** *fig* cenagal *m*, lío, maraña.
noratorium [mɒrə'tɔ:rɪəm] *n* moratoria.
▲ *pl* **moratoria** [mɒrə'tɔ:rɪə].
norbid ['mɔ:bɪd] *adj* **1** *(mind, ideas)* morboso,-a, enfermizo,-a. **2** MED mórbido,-a.
nore [mɔ:ʳ] *adj* más: **more than half an hour** *más de media hora.*
pron más: **we need some more** *necesitamos más.* ■ **the more ..., the more ...** cuanto más ..., más ... | **what is more** además, lo que es más.
adv más: **it's more expensive** *es más caro.* ■ **more and more** cada vez más. | **more or less 1** *(approximately)* más o menos. **2** *(almost)* casi.
Consulta también **many** y **much.**
noreover [mɔ:'rəʊvəʳ] *adv fml* además, por otra parte.
norgue [mɔ:g] *n* depósito de cadáveres.
noribund ['mɒrɪbʌnd] *adj* moribundo,-a.
Mormon ['mɔ:mən] *adj* mormón,-ona.
n mormón,-ona.
morning ['mɔ:nɪŋ] *n (gen)* mañana; *(early)* madrugada: **at eight o'clock in the morning** *a las ocho de la mañana;* **the following morning** *a la mañana siguiente.* ■ **good morning!** ¡buenos días! | **in the morning** *(tomorrow before noon)* mañana por la mañana.
adv **mornings** por la mañana, por las mañanas.
Moroccan [mə'rɒkᵊn] *adj* marroquí,-ina.
n marroquí,-ina.

Morocco [mə'rɒkəʊ] *n* Marruecos.
moron ['mɔ:rɒn] *n fam pej* imbécil *mf.*
morose [mə'rᵊʊs] *adj* malhumorado,-a, hosco,-a, taciturno,-a.
morpheme ['mɔ:fi:m] *n* LING morfema *m.*
morphine ['mɔ:fi:n] *n* morfina.
morphological [mɔ:fə'lɒdʒɪkᵊl] *adj* morfológico,-a.
morphology [mɔ:'fɒlədʒɪ] *n (gen)* morfología.
Morse [mɔ:s] *n* Morse *m.* ● **Morse code** alfabeto Morse.
morsel ['mɔ:sᵊl] *n (of food)* bocado.
mortal ['mɔ:tᵊl] *adj (gen)* mortal.
▷ *n* mortal *mf.*
mortality [mɔ:'tælətɪ] *n* mortalidad *f.*
mortally ['mɔ:tᵊlɪ] *adv* mortalmente: **mortally wounded** *herido de muerte.*
mortar ['mɔ:təʳ] *n* **1** *(cement)* mortero, argamasa. **2** MIL *(gun)* mortero.
mortgage ['mɔ:gɪdʒ] *n* hipoteca.
▷ *adj* hipotecario,-a.
▷ *vt* hipotecar.
mortgagee [mɔ:gɪ'dʒi:] *n* acreedor,-ra hipotecario,-a.
mortify ['mɔ:tɪfaɪ] *vt (embarrass)* avergonzar, dar vergüenza a, humillar.
▲ *pt & pp* **mortified**, *ger* **mortifying.**
mortuary ['mɔ:tʃʊərɪ] *n* depósito de cadáveres.
▲ *pl* **mortuaries.**
mosaic [mə'zeɪɪk] *adj* mosaico.
Moslem ['mʌzləm] *adj* musulmán,-ana.
▷ *n* musulmán,-ana.
mosque [mɒsk] *n* mezquita.
mosquito [məs'ki:təʊ] *n* mosquito. ● **mosquito bite** picadura de mosquito. | **mosquito net** mosquitero, mosquitera.
▲ *pl* **mosquitoes** o **mosquitos.**
moss [mɒs] *n* BOT musgo.
mossy ['mɒsɪ] *adj* musgoso,-a.
▲ *comp* **mossier**, *superl* **mossiest.**
most [məʊst] *adj* **1** *(greatest in quantity)* más: **Simon's got the most points** *Simon tiene más puntos.* **2** *(majority)* la mayoría de, la mayor parte de: **most people live in flats** (US **apartments**) *la mayoría de la gente vive en pisos.*
▷ *adv* más: **the most difficult question** *la pregunta más difícil.*
▷ *pron* **1** *(greatest part)* la mayor parte: **it rained most of the time** *llovió durante la mayor parte del tiempo.* **2** *(greatest number or amount)* lo máximo. **3** *(the majority of people)* la mayoría.
▷ *adv* **1** *(superlative)* más: **the most beautiful girl** *la chica más guapa.* **2** *(very)* muy, de lo más: **it was most kind of you** *ha sido muy amable de su parte;* **a most delightful evening** *una tarde muy agradable.* **3** US *(almost)* casi. ■ **for the most part** por lo general. | **most of all** sobre todo.
Consulta también **many** y **much.**
mostly ['məʊstlɪ] *adv* **1** *(mainly)* principalmente, en su mayor parte. **2** *(generally)* generalmente; *(usually)* normalmente.
motel [məʊ'tel] *n* motel *m.*
moth [mɒθ] *n* mariposa nocturna. ● **clothes moth** polilla.
mothball ['mɒθbɔ:l] *n* bola de naftalina.

moth-eaten ['mɒθiːtᵊn] *adj* apolillado,-a.
mother ['mʌðəʳ] *n* madre *f*: **a single mother** *una madre soltera.*
▷ *vt* **1** *(care for)* cuidar como una madre; *(rear)* criar. **2** *(spoil)* mimar. ● **Mother Nature** la Madre *f* Naturaleza. ▮ **mother ship** buque *m* nodriza. ▮ **mother tongue** lengua materna.
motherhood ['mʌðəhʊd] *n* maternidad *f*.
mother-in-law ['mʌðərɪnlɔː] *n* suegra.
▲ *pl* **mothers-in-law.**
motherland ['mʌðəlænd] *n* patria, madre *f* patria.
motherless ['mʌðələs] *adj* huérfano,-a de madre.
motherly ['mʌðəlɪ] *adj* maternal.
mother-of-pearl [mʌðərəv'pɜːl] *n* madreperla, nácar *m*.
mother-to-be [mʌðərtə'biː] *n* futura madre *f*.
▲ *pl* **mothers-to-be.**
motif [məʊ'tiːf] *n* **1** *(pattern, design)* motivo. **2** *(in music, literature - theme)* tema *m*.
motion ['məʊʃᵊn] *n* **1** *(movement)* movimiento. **2** *(gesture)* gesto, ademán *m*. **3** POL *(proposal)* moción *f*. ■ **in motion** en movimiento. ▮ **in slow motion** CINEM a cámara lenta. ● **motion picture** película. ▮ **motion pictures** el cine *m*.
▷ *vt* hacer señas.
▷ *vi* hacer señas, hacer una señal.
motionless ['məʊʃᵊnləs] *adj* inmóvil.
motivate ['məʊtɪveɪt] *vt* motivar.
motivation [məʊtɪ'veɪʃᵊn] *n* motivación *f*.
motive ['məʊtɪv] *n* **1** *(reason)* motivo. **2** JUR móvil *m*.
▷ *adj* motor,-ra, motriz. ● **motive force / motive power** fuerza motriz.
motiveless ['məʊtɪvləs] *adj* sin motivo.
motocross ['məʊtəkrɒs] *n* SP motocross *m*.
motor ['məʊtəʳ] *n* **1** *(engine)* motor *m*. **2** GB *fam (car)* coche *m*, automóvil *m*. ● **motor racing** carreras *fpl* de coches. ▮ **motor vehicle** vehículo a motor.
▷ *adj* **1** TECH motor,-ra. **2** BIOL motor,-ra, motriz.
motorbike ['məʊtəbaɪk] *n fam* motocicleta, moto *f*.
motorboat ['məʊtəbəʊt] *n* lancha motora, motora.
motorcade ['məʊtəkeɪd] *n* desfile *m* de coches.
motorcar ['məʊtəkɑːʳ] *n* coche *m*, automóvil *m*.
motorcycle ['məʊtəsaɪkᵊl] *n* motocicleta, moto *f*.
motorcycling ['məʊtəsaɪkᵊlɪŋ] *n* motociclismo.
motorcyclist ['məʊtəsaɪkᵊlɪst] *n* motociclista *mf*, motorista *mf*.
motoring ['məʊtərɪŋ] *adj* automovilístico,-a, del automóvil: **motoring offence** *infracción de tráfico.*
▷ *n* automovilismo.
motorist ['məʊtərɪst] *n* automovilista *mf*, conductor,-ra (de coche).
motorize ['məʊtəraɪz] *vt* motorizar.
motorway ['məʊtəweɪ] *n* GB autopista.
mottled ['mɒtᵊld] *adj (skin, animal)* con manchas, moteado,-a, jaspeado,-a.
motto ['mɒtəʊ] *n* lema *m*.
▲ *pl* **mottos** o **mottoes.**
mould[1] [məʊld] *n (growth)* moho.
mould[2] [məʊld] *n* **1** *(cast)* molde *m*. **2** *fig (type)* carácter *m*, temple *m*.
▷ *vt* **1** *(figure)* moldear; *(clay)* modelar.
moulding ['məʊldɪŋ] *n* **1** *(on wall, ceiling, frame)* moldura. **2** *(object produced from mould)* molde *m*. *(shaping)* modelado.
mouldy ['məʊldɪ] *adj (food, etc)* mohoso,-a; *(smell)* humedad, a moho.
▲ *comp* **mouldier**, *superl* **moldiest.**
moult [məʊlt] *vi* ZOOL mudar.
▷ *n* ZOOL muda.
mound [maʊnd] *n* **1** *(small hill)* montículo. **2** *(pile, heap)* montón *m*.
mount[1] [maʊnt] *n (mountain)* monte *m*.
mount[2] [maʊnt] *n* **1** *(horse, etc)* montura. **2** *(for machine, gun, trophy)* soporte *m*, base *f*; *(for photo, picture)* fondo; *(for jewel)* engaste *m*, engarce *m*; *(for slide)* marquito.
▷ *vt* **1** *(horse)* montar, montarse en; *(bicycle)* montar en, subir a; *(stage, platform)* subir a; *(stairs)* subir. *(fix - photo, picture)* montar; *(- stamp)* fijar; *(- jewel)* montar, engastar, engarzar. **3** *(organize - attack)* montar, preparar; *(- campaign)* montar, organizar.
▷ *vi* **1** *(go up)* subir, ascender. **2** *(get on horse)* montar. *(increase)* subir, aumentar, crecer.
⊙ **to mount up** *vi (accumulate)* amontonarse, acumularse.
mountain ['maʊntᵊn] *n* **1** GEOG montaña. **2** *fig (large amount)* montaña, montón *m*. ● **mountain bike** bicicleta de montaña. ▮ **mountain range** cordillera, sierra.
▷ *adj* de montaña.
mountaineer [maʊntə'nɪəʳ] *n* montañero,-a, alpinista *mf*, AM andinista *mf*.
mountaineering [maʊntə'nɪərɪŋ] *n* montañismo, alpinismo, AM andinismo.
mountainous ['maʊntᵊnəs] *adj* **1** *(region)* montañoso,-a. **2** *(huge)* enorme, gigantesco,-a.
mounted ['maʊntɪd] *adj* **1** *(on horse)* montado,-a. *(photo, etc)* montado,-a.
mourn [mɔːn] *vt (person)* llorar la muerte de; *(thing)* llorar, añorar.
⊙ **to mourn for / mourn over** *vt insep (person)* llorar a, llorar la muerte de; *(thing)* llorar.
mourner ['mɔːnəʳ] *n persona que asiste a los funerales de alguien.*
mournful ['mɔːnfʊl] *adj (person)* triste, afligido,-a, apenado,-a; *(occasion, music)* fúnebre, lúgubre.
mourning ['mɔːnɪŋ] *n* luto, duelo. ■ **to be in mourning for** SB estar de luto por ALGN.
mouse [maʊs] *n (gen)* ratón *m*.
▲ *pl* **mice.**
mousetrap ['maʊstræp] *n* ratonera.
mousse [muːs] *n* **1** CULIN mousse *f*. **2** *(for hair)* espuma (moldeadora).
moustache [məs'tɑːʃ] *n* bigote *m*.
mouth [*(n)* maʊθ; *(vb)* maʊð] *n* **1** ANAT boca. **2** *(of river)* desembocadura; *(of bottle)* boca; *(of tunnel, cave)* boca, entrada. **3** *(person to feed)* boca. ■ **to keep one's mouth shut** mantener la boca cerrada, no decir nada. ● **mouth organ** armónica.
▷ *vt* **1** *pej (say - without sincerity)* decir; *(- without understanding)* recitar, repetir. **2** *(say without making sound)* decir con los labios.
▷ *vi (speak without making sound)* mover los labios.

to mouth off *vi (express opinions)* fanfarronear, fardar, jactarse (**about**, de); *(complain)* protestar (**about**, por).
mouthful ['maʊθfʊl] *n* **1** *(of food)* bocado; *(of drink)* trago; *(of air)* bocanada. **2** *fam (long word, phrase)* trabalenguas *m*, palabreja.
mouthpiece ['maʊθpi:s] *n* **1** *(of instrument, pipe)* boquilla. **2** *(of phone)* micrófono. **3** *pej (newspaper, person)* voz *f*.
mouth-to-mouth [maʊθtə'maʊθ] [Also **mouth-to-mouth resuscitation**.] *n* boca a boca *m*.
mouthwash ['maʊθwɒʃ] *n* enjuague *m* bucal.
mouthwatering ['maʊθwɔ:tᵊrɪŋ] *adj* muy apetitoso,-a, delicioso,-a.
movable ['mu:vəbᵊl] *adj* movible, móvil.
move [mu:v] *n* **1** *(act of moving, movement)* movimiento: **he watched my every move** *observó todos mis movimientos*. **2** *(to new home)* mudanza; *(to new job)* traslado. **3** *(in game)* jugada; *(turn)* turno: **whose move is it?** *¿a quién le toca jugar?* **4** *(action, step)* paso, acción *f*, medida; *(decision)* decisión *f*; *(attempt)* intento. ■ **to be on the move 1** *(travel - gen)* viajar, desplazarse. **2** *(- army, etc)* estar en marcha. **3** *(be busy)* no parar. ‖ **to get a move on** darse prisa, moverse. ‖ **to make a move 1** *(leave)* irse, marcharse. **2** *(act)* dar un paso, actuar.
vt **1** *(gen)* mover; *(furniture, etc)* cambiar de sitio, trasladar; *(transfer)* trasladar; *(out of the way)* apartar: **you've moved the furniture!** *¡habéis cambiado los muebles de sitio!* **2** *(affect emotionally)* conmover. **3** *(in games)* mover, jugar. **4** *(prompt)* inducir, mover; *(persuade)* convencer, persuadir; *(change mind)* hacer cambiar de opinión: **what moved you to leave your job?** *¿qué te convenció para dejar el trabajo?* **5** *(resolution, motion, etc)* proponer.
vi **1** *(gen)* moverse; *(change - position)* trasladarse, desplazarse; *(- house)* mudarse; *(- post, department)* trasladarse: **she was so scared she couldn't move** *tenía tanto miedo que no podía moverse*.
to move about / move around *vt sep (object)* cambiar de sitio, trasladar.
vi (fidget, be restless) moverse (mucho), ir y venir; *(travel)* viajar de un lugar a otro.
to move along *vi* circular.
to move away *vi* **1** *(move aside, etc)* alejarse, apartarse. **2** *(change house)* mudarse de casa.
to move in *vi* **1** *(into new home)* instalarse. **2** *(prepare to take control, attack, etc)* acercarse.
to move off *vi (set off - person)* marcharse, ponerse en camino; *(- train)* salir; *(- car)* arrancar.
to move on *vi* **1** *(continue journey)* seguir, seguir el viaje. **2** *(go on, change to)* pasar a. **3** *(develop, progress)* avanzar, evolucionar.
vt sep (police officer's order) hacer circular.
to move out *vi* **1** *(leave house)* mudarse. **2** *(leave)* irse, marcharse.
to move over *vt sep (step aside)* apartarse.
vi (make room) correrse, moverse.
to move up *vt sep (promote)* promover, ascender.
vi **1** *(rise in grade)* ascender. **2** *(make room)* correrse.
movement ['mu:vmənt] *n* **1** *(act, motion)* movimiento; *(gesture)* gesto, ademán *m*. **2** *(of goods)* traslado; *(of troops)* desplazamiento; *(of population)* movimiento. **3** *(political, literary)* movimiento. **4** *(trend)* tendencia, corriente *f*.
▷ *n pl* **movements** *(activities)* movimientos *mpl*, actividades *fpl*.
movie ['mu:vɪ] *n* US película.
▷ *n pl* **the movies** el cine *m sing*. ■ **to go to the movies** ir al cine. ● **movie theater** *(place)* cine *m*.
moving ['mu:vɪŋ] *adj* **1** *(that moves)* móvil; *(in motion)* en movimiento, en marcha. **2** *(causing motion)* motor,-ra, motriz. **3** *(causing action, motivating)* instigador,-ra, promotor,-ra. **4** *(emotional)* conmovedor,-ra.
mow [məʊ] *vt (lawn)* cortar, segar; *(corn, wheat)* segar.
▲ *pt* **mowed**, *pp* **mowed** o **mown** [məʊn].
⊙ **to mow down** *vt sep* acribillar.
mower ['məʊəʳ] *n (for lawn)* cortacésped *m & f*, segadora de césped; *(for fields)* segadora.
mown [məʊn] *pp* ⟶ **mow**.
Mozambique [məʊzæm'bi:k] *n* Mozambique.
Mozambiquean [məʊzæm'bi:kᵊn] *adj* mozambiqueño,-a.
▷ *n* mozambiqueño,-a.
Mozarab [məʊ'zærəb] *adj* mozárabe.
▷ *n* mozárabe *mf*.
MP ['em'pi:] *abbr* (**member of Parliament**) diputado,-a.
mpg ['em'pi:'dʒi:] *abbr* (**miles per gallon**) ≈ litros/100 km.
mph ['em'pi:'eɪtʃ] *abbr* (**miles per hour**) millas por hora.
MP3 ['em'pi:'θri:] *abbr* (**Moving Pictures Experts Group Audio Layer 3**) MP3. ● **MP3 player** reproductor *m* de MP3
Mr *abbr* (**Mister**) señor; *(abbreviation)* sr.
Mrs *abbr* señora; *(abbreviation)* sra.
Ms *abbr* (**Miss**) señorita; *(abbreviation)* srta.
much [mʌtʃ] *adj* mucho,-a: **we haven't got much bread** *no tenemos mucho pan*; **he didn't have much time** *no tenía mucho tiempo*; **we've made too much jam** *hemos hecho demasiada mermelada*; **why is there so much traffic?** *¿por qué hay tanto tráfico?*; **take as much time as you need** *tómate tanto tiempo como necesites*; **how much money have you got?** *¿cuánto dinero tienes?*
▲ *comp* **more**, *superl* **most**.
▷ *pron* mucho: **there's not much to do round here** *no hay mucho que hacer por aquí*; **how much is it?** *¿cuánto vale?* ■ **a bit much** un poco demasiado, un poco excesivo,-a. ‖ **as much 1** *(equal)* equivalente a. **2** *(the same)* lo mismo. ‖ **not to be much of a ...** no ser muy buen,-na ... ‖ **that's not saying much** eso no significa gran cosa, eso no es mucho decir. ‖ **to not be up to much** no valer gran cosa.
▷ *adv* mucho: **he felt much better** *se encontraba mucho mejor*.
muck [mʌk] *n* **1** *(dirt)* suciedad *f*, porquería; *(mud)* lodo. **2** *(manure)* estiércol *m*.
⊙ **to muck about / muck around** *vi* **1** *(idle)* gandulear, perder el tiempo; *(play the fool)* hacer el tonto.
▷ *vt sep (irritate)* fastidiar, jorobar.
⊙ **to muck in** *vi fam (help)* echar una mano.
⊙ **to muck out** *vt sep (stable)* limpiar.
⊙ **to muck up** *vt sep* **1** *(clothes)* ensuciar; *(hair)* despeinar. **2** *(spoil)* estropear, echar a perder, arruinar.
muck-up ['mʌkʌp] *n fam (bungle)* chapuza, cagada, pifia; *(mess)* follón *m*, lío.

mucky ['mʌkɪ] *adj* 1 *(dirty)* sucio,-a; *(muddy)* lodoso, -a. 2 *(obscene, dirty)* obsceno,-a, verde. 3 *(of weather)* asqueroso,-a.
▲ *comp* **muckier**, *superl* **muckiest**.
mucus ['mju:kəs] *n* mucosidad *f*.
mud [mʌd] *n (gen)* barro, lodo; *(thick)* fango.
muddle ['mʌdᵊl] *n* 1 *(mess)* desorden *m*: **everything's in a muddle** *todo está en desorden*. 2 *(confusion, mix-up)* confusión *f*, embrollo, lío.
▷ *vt* [Also **to muddle up**.] *(untidy)* revolver, desordenar; *(confuse mentally)* liar, confundir; *(confuse, mix up)* confundir.
⊙ **to muddle along** *vi* actuar a la buena de Dios, actuar al buen tuntún.
⊙ **to muddle through** *vi* arreglárselas.
muddleheaded ['mʌdᵊlhedɪd] *adj (person)* despistado,-a; *(idea, argument, etc)* confuso,-a.
muddy ['mʌdɪ] *adj* 1 *(gen)* fangoso,-a. 2 *(colour)* sucio,-a. 3 *(thinking, idea, etc)* confuso,-a, turbio,-a.
▲ *comp* **muddier**, *superl* **muddiest**.
▷ *vt* 1 *(dirty - floor, etc)* ensuciar de barro, llenar de barro. 2 *fig* enredar.
mudflap ['mʌdflæp] *n* faldón *m*.
mudguard ['mʌdgɑ:d] *n* guardabarros *m inv*.
mudpack ['mʌdpæk] *n* mascarilla facial de lodo.
muesli ['mju:zlɪ] *n* muesli *m*.
muff[1] [mʌf] *n (for hands)* manguito.
muff[2] [mʌf] *vt (catch)* fallar; *(shot)* errar; *(lines, words)* salirle mal a, equivocarse con.
▷ *n* fallo, pifia. ■ **to muff it** pifiarla.
muffin ['mʌfɪn] *n* 1 GB *panecillo redondo que se come tostado y con mantequilla*. 2 US *tipo de magdalena*.
muffle ['mʌfᵊl] *vt* 1 *(sound)* amortiguar, ensordecer. 2 *(keep warm - person)* abrigar; *(face)* embozar.
muffled ['mʌfᵊld] *adj* 1 *(sound, voice)* apagado,-a. 2 *(wrapped up - person)* abrigado,-a; *(- face)* embozado,-a.
muffler ['mʌfᵊləʳ] *n* US *(silencer)* silenciador *m*.
mug[1] [mʌg] *n (large cup)* taza alta, tazón *m*.
mug[2] [mʌg] *n* 1 GB *fam (fool)* tonto,-a, ingenuo,-a, idiota *mf*. 2 *sl (face)* jeta, careto.
▷ *vt (rob violently)* atracar, asaltar.
▲ *pt & pp* **mugged**, *ger* **mugging**.
mugger ['mʌgəʳ] *n* atracador,-ra, asaltante *mf*.
mugging ['mʌgɪŋ] *n* atraco, asalto.
muggy ['mʌgɪ] *adj (weather)* bochornoso,-a.
▲ *comp* **muggier**, *superl* **muggiest**.
mulatto [mju:'lætəʊ] *n* mulato,-a.
▲ *pl* **mulattos** o **mulattoes**.
mulberry ['mʌlbərɪ] *n* 1 *(fruit)* mora. 2 *(tree)* morera, moral *m*. 3 *(colour)* morado.
▲ *pl* **mulberries**.
mule [mju:l] *n* ZOOL mulo,-a.
mull [mʌl] *vt* **to mull over** *(ponder)* reflexionar sobre.
multicoloured [mʌltɪ'kʌləd] *adj* multicolor.
multicultural [mʌltɪ'kʌltʃərəl] *adj* multicultural.
multifarious [mʌltɪ'feərɪəs] *adj* múltiple.
multilateral [mʌltɪ'lætᵊrəl] *adj* multilateral.
multimillionaire [mʌltɪmɪljə'neəʳ] *n* multimillonario,-a.
multinational [mʌltɪ'næʃᵊnəl] *adj* multinacional.
▷ *n* multinacional *f*.
multiple ['mʌltɪpᵊl] *adj* múltiple.
▷ *n* MATH múltiplo.
multiple-choice [mʌltɪpə'tʃɔɪs] *adj* tipo test.

multiplex ['mʌltɪpleks] *adj* 1 *(cinema)* multicine *mpl*. 2 TECH múltiple.
multiplication [mʌltɪplɪ'keɪʃᵊn] *n* multiplicación
● **multiplication sign** signo de multiplicar. ■ **multiplication table** tabla de multiplicar.
multiplicity [mʌltɪ'plɪsətɪ] *n* multiplicidad *f*, diversidad
multiply ['mʌltɪplaɪ] *vt* MATH multiplicar (**by**, por).
▷ *vi* multiplicarse.
▲ *pt & pp* **multiplied**, *ger* **multiplying**.
multipurpose [mʌltɪ'pɜ:pəs] *adj* multiuso *inv*.
multiracial [mʌltɪ'reɪʃᵊl] *adj* multirracial.
multistorey [mʌltɪ'stɔ:rɪ] *adj (building)* de varios pisos, de varias plantas.
multitude ['mʌltɪtju:d] *n (crowd)* multitud *f*, muchedumbre *f*.
multitudinous [mʌltɪ'tju:dɪnəs] *adj* multitudinario,-a
mum[1] [mʌm] *n* GB *fam* mamá *f*.
mum[2] [mʌm] *adj (silent)* callado,-a. ■ **to keep mum** no decir ni pío, guardar silencio.
mumble ['mʌmbᵊl] *vt (gen)* decir entre dientes, mascullar; *(prayer)* musitar.
▷ *vi* hablar entre dientes, farfullar.
mummification [mʌmɪfɪ'keɪʃᵊn] *n* momificación
mummify ['mʌmɪfaɪ] *vt* momificar.
▲ *pt & pp* **mummified**, *ger* **mummifying**.
mummy[1] ['mʌmɪ] *n (dead body)* momia.
▲ *pl* **mummies**.
mummy[2] ['mʌmɪ] *n* GB *fam (mother)* mamá *f*.
▲ *pl* **mummies**.
mumps [mʌmps] *n* MED paperas *fpl*.
munch [mʌntʃ] *vt* masticar ruidosamente.
▷ *vi* masticar ruidosamente.
mundane [mʌn'deɪn] *adj* 1 *(wordly)* mundano,-a. *pej (banal)* rutinario,-a, banal.
municipal [mju:'nɪsɪpᵊl] *adj* municipal.
municipality [mju:nɪsɪ'pælɪtɪ] *n* municipio.
▲ *pl* **municipalities**.
munitions [mju:'nɪʃᵊnz] *n pl* municiones *fpl*.
mural ['mjʊərᵊl] *n* pintura mural, mural *m*.
murder ['mɜ:dəʳ] *n* 1 asesinato, homicidio. 2 *fam* *(difficult experience)* pesadilla. ■ **to get away with murder** hacer lo que a uno le da la gana. ● **murder story** novela negra, novela policíaca.
▷ *vt* 1 *(kill)* asesinar, matar. 2 *fam fig (be angry with)* mata
murderer ['mɜ:dərəʳ] *n* asesino, homicida *mf*.
murderess ['mɜ:dərəs] *n* asesina, homicida.
murderous ['mɜ:dərəs] *adj* asesino,-a, homicida.
murky ['mɜ:kɪ] *adj* 1 *(night)* oscuro,-a, tenebroso,- *(weather, day)* gris, nublado,-a; *(place)* lóbrego,-a, sombrío,-a. 2 *(water)* turbio,-a.
▲ *comp* **murkier**, *superl* **murkiest**.
murmur ['mɜ:məʳ] *n* 1 *(of voice)* murmullo, susurro. 2 *(of traffic)* rumor *m*; *(of insects)* zumbido; *(of win* murmullo; *(of water)* susurro. 3 MED soplo.
▷ *vt* murmurar: **they murmured their approval** *hubo* *murmullo de aprobación*.
▷ *vi* 1 susurrar. 2 *(complain)* quejarse (**against/at**, de).
muscle ['mʌsᵊl] *n* 1 ANAT músculo. 2 *(muscle pow* fuerza. 3 *fig (strength, power)* poder *m*, fuerza. ■ **not move a muscle** no inmutarse.
⊙ **to muscle in** *vi (situation)* entrometerse (**on**, en); *(pl ce)* introducirse por la fuerza.
muscular ['mʌskjələʳ] *adj* 1 *(pain, tissue)* muscular. *(person)* musculoso,-a.

nuse¹ [mjuːz] *vi* meditar (on/over, -), reflexionar (on/over, sobre).
nuse² [mjuːz] *n* musa.
▸ *n pl* the Muses las Musas *fpl*.
nuseum [mjuːˈzɪəm] *n* museo.
nush [mʌʃ] *n* 1 *(food)* papilla, pasta. 2 *fam (writing, speech, film)* sentimentalismo.
nushroom [ˈmʌʃruːm] *n* 1 BOT seta, hongo. 2 CULIN *(button mushroom)* champiñón *m*; *(wild)* seta.
▸ *vi* 1 *(gather mushrooms)* recoger setas, ir a buscar setas. 2 *(spring up)* crecer de la noche a la mañana, aparecer como hongos; *(spread)* multiplicarse. ● mushroom cloud hongo nuclear.
nushy [ˈmʌʃɪ] *adj* 1 *(food)* blando,-a, como una papilla. 2 *fam (words, film, etc)* sentimentaloide.
▲ *comp* mushier, *superl* mushiest.
nusic [ˈmjuːzɪk] *n* música. ● music box caja de música. ‖ music centre equipo de música. ‖ music hall teatro de variedades. ‖ music score partitura. ‖ music stand atril *m*.
nusical [ˈmjuːzɪkəl] *adj* 1 *(gen)* musical. 2 *(person - gifted)* dotado,-a para la música; *(- fond of music)* aficionado,-a a la música, melómano,-a.
▸ *n* musical *m*. ● musical box caja de música. ‖ musical instrument instrumento musical.
nusician [mjuːˈzɪʃən] *n* músico,-a.
nusk [mʌsk] *n (substance)* almizcle *m*.
nusket [ˈmʌskɪt] *n* mosquete *m*.
nusketeer [mʌskəˈtɪəʳ] *n* mosquetero.
nuskrat [ˈmʌskræt] *n* almizclera.
Muslim [ˈmʌzlɪm] *adj* musulmán,-ana.
▸ *n* musulmán,-ana.
nuslin [ˈmʌzlɪn] *n* muselina.
nusquash [ˈmʌzkwɒʃ] *n* 1 *(animal)* almizclera. 2 *(fur)* piel de almizclera.
nussel [ˈmʌsəl] *n* mejillón *m*.
nust¹ [mʌst] *aux* 1 *(necessity, obligation)* deber, tener que: I must leave now *tengo que marcharme ahora;* must you play your music so loud? *¿es necesario poner la música tan fuerte?* 2 *(probability)* deber de: she must be tired *debe de estar cansada;* but someone must have seen her *pero alguien debe de haberla visto.* ■ if I must si no hay más remedio. ‖ if you must know, ... si te empeñas en saberlo, ...
▸ *n (need)* necesidad *f*: it's an absolute must for all film buffs *es imprescindible para todos los cinéfilos.*
nustache [məsˈtɑːʃ] *n* US → moustache.
nustard [ˈmʌstəd] *n (gen)* mostaza. ● mustard gas gas *m* mostaza.
nuster [ˈmʌstəʳ] *vt* 1 *(supporters, troops)* reunir; *(army)* lograr formar. 2 *(courage, strength)* cobrar, armarse de (up, -).
▸ *vi (supporters)* reunirse, juntarse; *(troops, soldiers)* congregarse.
nutant [ˈmjuːtənt] *n* mutante *mf*.
▸ *adj* mutante.
nutation [mjuːˈteɪʃən] *n* mutación *f*.
nute [mjuːt] *adj (dumb, silent)* mudo,-a.
▸ *n* 1 LING mudo,-a. 2 *(dumb person)* mudo,-a. 3 MUS sordina. ● deaf mute sordomudo,-a.
nuted [ˈmjuːtɪd] *adj* 1 *(sound)* apagado,-a, sordo,-a. 2 *(colour)* suave, apagado,-a. 3 *(emotion, feeling)* contenido,-a.

mutilate [ˈmjuːtɪleɪt] *vt* mutilar.
mutilation [mjuːtɪˈleɪʃən] *n* mutilación *f*.
mutineer [mjuːtɪˈnɪəʳ] *n* amotinado,-a.
mutinous [ˈmjuːtɪnəs] *adj* 1 *(guilty of mutiny)* amotinado,-a. 2 *(rebellious)* rebelde, desobediente.
mutiny [ˈmjuːtɪnɪ] *n* motín *m*, amotinamiento, sublevación *f*, rebelión *f*.
▲ *pl* mutinies.
▷ *vi* amotinarse.
▲ *pt & pp* mutinied, *ger* mutinying.
mutt [mʌt] *n* 1 *fam (dog)* perro callejero. 2 *fam (fool)* tonto,-a, estúpido,-a.
mutter [ˈmʌtəʳ] *n* murmullo, refunfuño.
▷ *vt (mumble)* murmurar, mascullar, decir entre dientes, refunfuñar.
▷ *vi* 1 *(mumble)* murmurar, hablar entre dientes. 2 *(complain)* refunfuñar, rezongar, quejarse.
muttering [ˈmʌtərɪŋ] *n* quejas *fpl*, rezongos *mpl*, refunfuños *mpl*.
mutton [ˈmʌtən] *n (sheep meat)* carne *f* de oveja, carne *f* ovina; *(lamb)* carne *f* de cordero. ■ mutton dressed up as lamb una vieja vestida de jovencita.
mutual [ˈmjuːtʃuəl] *adj* 1 *(help, love, etc)* mutuo,-a, recíproco,-a. 2 *(friend, interest, etc)* común.
mutually [ˈmjuːtʃuəlɪ] *adv* mutuamente.
muzzle [ˈmʌzəl] *n* 1 *(snout)* hocico. 2 *(guard)* bozal *m*. 3 *(of gun)* boca.
▷ *vt* 1 *(dog)* poner un bozal a. 2 *fig (person, press, etc)* amordazar.
muzzy [ˈmʌzɪ] *adj* 1 *(blurred)* borroso,-a. 2 *(groggy)* atontado,-a, espeso,-a.
▲ *comp* muzzier, *superl* muzziest.
my [maɪ] *adj* mi, mis: my book *mi libro;* my records *mis discos;* one of my friends *un amigo mío.*
▷ *interj* ¡caramba!, ¡caray!
myopia [maɪˈəupɪə] *n* miopía.
myopic [maɪˈɒpɪk] *adj* miope.
myriad [ˈmɪrɪəd] *n* miríada.
myrrh [mɜːʳ] *n* mirra.
myrtle [ˈmɜːtəl] *n* BOT arrayán *m*, mirto.
myself [maɪˈself] *pron* 1 *(reflexive)* me: I cut myself *me corté;* I helped myself *me serví.* 2 *(after preposition)* mí (mismo,-a): I kept it for myself *lo guardé para mí;* I said to myself *me dije a mí mismo.* 3 *(emphatic)* yo mismo,-a: I did it by myself *lo hice yo mismo,-a.* ■ all by myself 1 *(alone)* solo,-a. 2 *(without help)* yo solo,-a. ‖ to myself *(private)* para mí solo,-a.
mysterious [mɪˈstɪərɪəs] *adj* misterioso,-a.
mysteriously [mɪˈstɪərɪəslɪ] *adv* misteriosamente.
mystery [ˈmɪstərɪ] *n* misterio.
▲ *pl* mysteries.
mystic [ˈmɪstɪk] *adj* místico,-a.
▷ *n* místico,-a.
mystical [ˈmɪstɪkəl] *adj* místico,-a.
mysticism [ˈmɪstɪsɪzəm] *n* 1 REL misticismo. 2 LIT mística.
mystique [mɪsˈtiːk] *n* halo de misterio.
myth [mɪθ] *n* 1 *(ancient story)* mito. 2 *(fallacy)* falacia.
mythical [ˈmɪθɪkəl] *adj* 1 *(of a myth)* mítico,-a. 2 *(not real, imagined)* imaginario,-a, fantástico,-a.
mythological [mɪθəˈlɒdʒɪkəl] *adj* mitológico,-a.
mythology [mɪˈθɒlədʒɪ] *n* mitología.

N

N, n [en] *n (the letter)* N, n *f*.
N [nɔ:θ] *abbr* **(north)** norte *m*; *(abbreviation)* N.
n [ˈnju:təʳ] *abbr* **(neuter)** neutro; *(abbreviation)* n.
nab [næb] *vt fam* pillar.
▲ *pt & pp* **nabbed**, *ger* **nabbing.**
naff [næf] *adj fam* hortera.
nag [næg] *vt* **1** *(annoy)* molestar, fastidiar. **2** *(complain)* dar la tabarra a.
▷ *vi* quejarse.
▲ *pt & pp* **nagged**, *ger* **nagging.**
▷ *n* regañón,-ona, gruñón,-ona.
nail [neɪl] *n* **1** *(on finger, toe)* uña: **to bite/cut/trim one's nails** *morderse/cortarse/arreglarse las uñas.* **2** *(metal)* clavo. ● **nail clippers** cortaúñas *m*. ‖ **nail polish** esmalte *m* para las uñas. ‖ **nail varnish** esmalte *m* para las uñas. ‖ **nail varnish remover** quitaesmaltes *m*.
▷ *vt* **1** clavar, fijar con clavos. **2** *fam* pillar, coger. ■ **to hit the nail on the head** dar en el clavo.
⊙ **to nail down** *vt sep* **1** *(thing)* clavar, sujetar con clavos. **2** *fig (person)* conseguir que ALGN se comprometa: **I couldn't nail him down to a price** *no pude conseguir que me concretara un precio.*
⊙ **to nail up** *vt sep* **1** *(to wall, etc)* clavar. **2** *(completely)* cerrar con clavos.
nailbrush [ˈneɪlbrʌʃ] *n* cepillo de uñas.
nailfile [ˈneɪlfaɪl] *n* lima de uñas.
naive [naɪˈi:v] *adj* ingenuo,-a.
naked [ˈneɪkɪd] *adj* **1** *(body)* desnudo,-a; *(flame)* sin protección; *(light)* sin pantalla. **2** *(unhidden)* abierto,-a: **naked aggression** *agresión patente.* ■ **with the naked eye** a simple vista. ● **the naked truth** la pura verdad.
name [neɪm] *n* **1** *(first name)* nombre *m*; *(surname)* apellido: **his name's Richard** *se llama Richard;* **what's your name?** *¿cómo te llamas?* **2** *(fame)* fama, reputación *f*: **she made her name in the theatre** *se hizo famosa en el teatro.*
▷ *vt* **1** llamar: **they named the child Dominic after his uncle** *al niño le pusieron Dominic por su tío.* **2** *(appoint)* nombrar: **he was named Minister of Transport** *lo nombraron Ministro de Transportes.* ■ **in the name of...** en nombre de... ‖ **to call SB names** insultar a ALGN. ‖ **to put one's name down for STH** apuntarse para ALGO. ‖ **to take SB's name in vain** faltar al respeto a ALGN. ● **big name** pez *m* gordo. ‖ **name day** santo.
nameless [ˈneɪmləs] *adj* **1** *(unnamed)* anónimo,-a. **2** *(indescribable)* indescriptible. ■ **to remain nameless** permanecer en el anonimato.
namely [ˈneɪmlɪ] *adv* a saber.
namesake [ˈneɪmseɪk] *n* tocayo,-a.
Namibia [nəˈmɪbɪə] *n* Namibia.
Namibian [nəˈmɪbɪən] *adj* namibio,-a.
▷ *n* namibio,-a.
nan [næn] *n* GB *fam* yaya, abuela.
nanna [ˈnænə] *n* GB *fam* yaya, abuela.
nanny[1] [ˈnænɪ] *n* **1** *(carer)* niñera. **2** GB *fam (grandmother)* yaya, abuela.
▲ *pl* **nannies.**
nanny[2] [ˈnænɪ] *n* **nanny goat** cabra.
▲ *pl* **nannies.**
nap[1] [næp] *n* siesta. ■ **to have a nap / take a nap** echa la siesta.
▷ *vi* dormir la siesta.
▲ *pt & pp* **napped**, *ger* **napping.**
nap[2] [næp] *n (on cloth)* lanilla.
nape [neɪp] *n* nuca, cogote *m*.
napkin [ˈnæpkɪn] *n* servilleta. ● **napkin ring** servilletero
Naples [ˈneɪpəlz] *n* Nápoles.
Napoleon [nəˈpəʊlɪən] *n* Napoleón.
nappy [ˈnæpɪ] *n* GB pañal *m*.
▲ *pl* **nappies.**
narcissus [nɑ:ˈsɪsəs] *n* narciso.
▲ *pl* **narcissi o narcissuses.**
narcotic [nɑ:ˈkɒtɪk] *adj* narcótico,-a.
▷ *n* narcótico.
narrate [nəˈreɪt] *vt* narrar.
narration [nəˈreɪʃən] *n* narración *f*.
narrative [ˈnærətɪv] *adj* narrativo,-a.
▷ *n* **1** narración *f*. **2** *(genre)* narrativa.
narrator [nəˈreɪtəʳ] *n* narrador,-ra.
narrow [ˈnærəʊ] *adj* **1** estrecho,-a: **a narrow road** *una carretera estrecha.* **2** *(restricted)* reducido,-a, restringido,-a: **narrow circle of friends** *un círculo reducido de amigos.* **3** *(by very little)* escaso,-a: **to have a narrow escape** *escapar por los pelos.* **4** *(strict)* estricto,-a, exacto,-a. **5** *(limited outlook)* estrecho,-a de miras. **6** *(careful)* minucioso,-a.
▲ *comp* **narrower**, *superl* **narrowest.**
▷ *vt* **1** *(make narrower)* estrechar. **2** *(reduce)* reducir, acortar. **3** *(eyes)* entornar.
▷ *vi* **1** *(become narrower)* estrecharse: **the road narrows after the bridge** *la carretera se estrecha después del puente.* **2** *(eyes)* entornarse.
▷ *n pl* **narrows** estrecho *m sing*. ● **narrow boat** barcaza
⊙ **to narrow down** *vt sep* reducir, limitar.
narrowly [ˈnærəʊlɪ] *adv* **1** *(by very little)* por poco, por un escaso margen. **2** *(carefully)* minuciosamente.
narrow-minded [nærəʊˈmaɪndɪd] *adj* estrecho, de miras.
narrowness [ˈnærəʊnəs] *n* estrechez *f*.
NASA [ˈnæsə] *abbr* US **(National Aeronautics and Space Administration)** Administración *f* Nacional de Aeronáutica y del Espacio; *(abbreviation)* NASA *f*.
nasal [ˈneɪzəl] *adj* **1** nasal. **2** *(way of speaking)* gangoso,-a
nastily [ˈnɑ:stɪlɪ] *adv* de manera desagradable.

nastiness ['nɑːstɪnəs] *n* lo desagradable, cosas *fpl* desagradables.
nasty ['nɑːstɪ] *adj* **1** *(unpleasant)* desagradable, repugnante, horrible: **what a nasty smell!** *¡qué olor más desagradable!* **2** *(malicious)* malintencionado,-a; *(unkind)* antipático,-a: **she was really nasty to everyone** *se mostró muy antipática con todos.* **3** *(dangerous)* peligroso,-a: **this bend is really nasty** *esta curva es muy peligrosa.* **4** *(tricky)* peliagudo,-a: **it's quite a nasty little problem** *es un problemita bastante peliagudo.* **5** *(serious)* grave: **a nasty cold** *un resfriado de cuidado.*
▲ *comp* **nastier**, *superl* **nastiest.**
nation ['neɪʃ*ə*n] *n* **1** *(country)* nación *f*, país *m*. **2** *(ethnic group)* pueblo, nación *f*.
national ['næʃ*ə*nəl] *adj* nacional.
▷ *n* súbdito,-a, ciudadano,-a.
nationalism ['næʃ*ə*nəlɪz*ə*m] *n* nacionalismo.
nationalist ['næʃ*ə*nəlɪst] *adj* nacionalista.
▷ *n* nacionalista *mf*.
nationalistic ['næʃənəlɪstɪk] *adj* nacionalista.
nationality [næʃ*ə*'nælɪtɪ] *n* nacionalidad *f*.
▲ *pl* **nationalities.**
nationwide [*(adj)* 'neɪʃənwaɪd; *(adv)* neɪʃən'waɪd] *adj* de ámbito nacional, a escala nacional: **a nationwide broadcast** *una emisión a todo el país.*
▷ *adv* por todo el país.
native ['neɪtɪv] *adj* **1** *(place)* natal; *(language)* materno,-a: **her native country** *su país natal.* **2** *(plant, animal)* originario,-a: **it's native to Australia** *es originario de Australia.* **3** *(relating to natives)* de los indígenas.
▷ *n* **1** natural *mf*, nativo,-a: **she's a native of Orense** *es natural de Orense.* **2** *(original inhabitant)* indígena *mf*.
NATO ['neɪtəʊ] [Also written **Nato.**] *abbr* **(North Atlantic Treaty Organization)** Organización *f* del Tratado del Atlántico Norte; *(abbreviation)* OTAN *f*.
natter ['nætə*ʳ*] *vi* GB *fam* charlar.
▷ *n* GB *fam* charla.
natural ['nætʃər*ə*l] *adj* **1** natural: **the natural world** *el mundo natural.* **2** *(born)* nato,-a: **he's a natural footballer** *es un futbolista nato.* **3** *(usual)* natural, normal: **it's only natural to feel afraid** *es normal tener miedo.* ● **natural gas** gas *m* natural. ‖ **natural resources** recursos *mpl* naturales. ‖ **natural science** ciencias *fpl* naturales.
▷ *n* MUS *(note)* nota natural; *(sign)* becuadro.
naturally ['nætʃ*ə*rəlɪ] *adv* **1** *(by nature)* por naturaleza. **2** *(unaffectedly)* con naturalidad. **3** *(not artificially)* de manera natural. **4** *(of course)* naturalmente, por supuesto.
nature ['neɪtʃə*ʳ*] *n* **1** *(gen)* naturaleza. **2** *(character)* carácter *m*, forma de ser: **it's in her nature to be like that** *es así por naturaleza.* **3** *(type)* índole *f*. ■ **by nature** por naturaleza. ● **nature conservation** conservación *f* de la naturaleza. ‖ **nature lover** amante *mf* de la naturaleza.
naught [nɔːt] *n* nada. ■ **to come to naught** fracasar.
naughtily ['nɔːtɪlɪ] *adv* mal.
naughty ['nɔːtɪ] *adj* **1** travieso,-a, malo,-a. **2** *(risqué)* atrevido,-a.
▲ *comp* **naughtier**, *superl* **naughtiest.**
Nauru ['naʊruː, 'nɑːuːruː] *n* Nauru.
Nauruan [naʊ'ruːən] *adj* nauruano,-a.
▷ *n* nauruano,-a.

nausea ['nɔːzɪə] *n* **1** *(physical)* náusea. **2** *(disgust)* asco, repugnancia.
nauseate ['nɔːzɪeɪt] *vt* **1** *(physically)* dar náuseas a. **2** *(disgust)* dar asco a, repugnar.
nauseating ['nɔːzɪeɪtɪŋ] *adj* **1** *(physically)* nauseabundo,-a. **2** *(disgusting)* asqueroso,-a, repugnante.
nautical ['nɔːtɪk*ə*l] *adj* náutico,-a. ● **nautical mile** milla náutica.
Navaho ['nævəhəʊ] *adj* navajo,-a.
▷ *n* **1** *(person)* navajo,-a. **2** *(language)* navajo.
▲ *pl* **Navaho, Navahos** o **Navahoes.**
Navajo ['nævəhəʊ] *adj-n* → **Navaho.**
naval ['neɪvəl] *adj* naval. ● **naval base** base *f* naval. ‖ **naval battle** batalla naval. ‖ **naval base** base *f* naval. ‖ **naval officer** oficial *mf* de marina. ‖ **naval power** potencia naval.
Navarre [nə'vɑː*ʳ*] *n* Navarra.
Navarrese [nævə'riːz] *adj* navarro,-a.
▷ *n* navarro,-a.
▷ *n pl* **the Navarrese** los navarros *mpl*.
navel ['neɪv*ə*l] *n* ombligo.
navigate ['nævɪgeɪt] *vt* **1** *(river, sea)* navegar por. **2** *(steer - ship)* gobernar; *(- plane)* pilotar.
▷ *vi (when sailing, flying)* dirigir; *(when driving)* guiar: **you drive, I'll navigate** *tu conduce, yo te guiaré.*
navigation [nævɪ'geɪʃ*ə*n] *n* navegación *f*.
navigator ['nævɪgeɪtə*ʳ*] *n* MAR navegante *mf*.
navvy ['nævɪ] *n* GB peón *m*.
▲ *pl* **navvies.**
navy ['neɪvɪ] *n* marina de guerra, armada. ● **navy blue** azul marino.
▲ *pl* **navies.** ● **navy blue** azul marino.
nay [neɪ] *adv* **1** *arch (more than that)* más aun. **2** *(in votes)* no.
▷ *n* voto negativo, no: **the nays have it** *ganan los noes.*
Nazi ['nɑːtsɪ] *adj* nazi.
▷ *n* nazi *mf*.
Nazism ['nɑːtsɪz*ə*m] *n* nazismo.
NE [nɔːθ'iːst] *abbr* **(northeast)** nordeste *m*; *(abbreviation)* NE.
Neanderthal [nɪ'ændətɑːl] *adj* de Neanderthal.
neap tide ['niːp 'taɪd] *n* marea muerta.
near [nɪə*ʳ*] *adj* **1** cercano,-a: **where is the nearest bank?** *¿dónde está el banco más cercano?* **2** *(relations)* cercano,-a: **a near relative** *un pariente cercano.* **3** *(time)* próximo,-a: **in the near future** *en un futuro próximo.* **4** *(similar)* parecido,-a.
▲ *comp* **nearer**, *comp* **nearest.**
▷ *adv* cerca: **I live quite near (by)** *vivo bastante cerca.*
▷ *prep* cerca de: **near the end of the book** *hacia el final del libro.* [Also **near to.**] a punto de: **she was near to crying** *estuvo a punto de llorar.*
▷ *vt* acercarse a: **we are nearing the day when...** *nos acercamos al día en que...* ■ **to come near** acercarse. ‖ **to come near to doing** STH estar en un tris de hacer ALGO.
nearby [*(adj)* 'nɪəbaɪ; *(adv)* nɪə'baɪ] *adj* cercano,-a: **a nearby hotel** *un hotel cercano.*
▷ *adv* cerca: **is there one nearby?** *¿hay alguno cerca?*
nearly ['nɪəlɪ] *adv* casi. ■ **not nearly** ni mucho menos, ni con mucho.
▷ *adj* AUTO *(right-hand drive)* del lado izquierdo; *(left-hand drive)* del lado derecho.
near-sighted [nɪə'saɪtɪd] *adj* miope, corto,-a de vista.

neat [ni:t] *adj* 1 *(room)* ordenado,-a; *(garden)* bien arreglado,-a. 2 *(person)* pulcro,-a; *(in habits)* ordenado,-a. 3 *(writing)* claro,-a. 4 *(clever)* ingenioso,-a. 5 *(drinks)* solo,-a. 6 US fantástico,-a, estupendo,-a.

neaten ['ni:tən] *vt* arreglar, ordenar.

neatness ['ni:tnəs] *n* esmero.

necessarily [nesə'serɪlɪ] *adv* 1 necesariamente. 2 *(inevitably)* inevitablemente, forzosamente.

necessary ['nesɪsərɪ] *adj* 1 necesario,-a. 2 *(inevitable)* inevitable, forzoso,-a.
▷ *n pl* **necessaries** lo necesario, cosas *fpl* necesarias.

necessitate [nɪ'sesɪteɪt] *vt* requerir, hacer necesario,-a.

necessity [nɪ'sesɪtɪ] *n* 1 necesidad *f*: **it's a necessity** *es indispensable.* 2 *(item)* requisito indispensable.
▲ *pl* **necessities.**

neck [nek] *n* cuello.
▷ *vi fam (kiss)* morrearse; *(caress)* pegarse el lote. ■ **to be in STH up to one's neck** estar metido,-a en ALGO hasta el cuello. ‖ **to break one's neck** desnucarse. **to stick one's neck out** arriesgarse.

necklace ['nekləs] *n* collar *m*.

necklet ['neklət] *n* gargantilla.

neckline ['neklaɪn] *n* escote *m*.

necktie ['nektaɪ] *n* corbata.

née [neɪ] *adj* de soltera: **Mrs Hastings, née Lawley** *la Sra. Hastings, de soltera Lawley.*

need [ni:d] *n* 1 necesidad *f*: **there's no need for all of you to come with me** *no hace falta que me acompañéis todos.* 2 *(poverty)* necesidad *f*, infortunio: **to help SB in time of need** *ayudar a ALGN en tiempos de necesidad.*
▷ *vt* necesitar: **you'll need a pencil** *necesitarás un lápiz.*
▷ *aux* hacer falta: **need we all go?** *¿hace falta que vayamos todos?* ■ **to be in need of** necesitar.

needle ['ni:dəl] *n* 1 *(gen)* aguja. 2 GB *fam (friction)* pique *m*. 3 US *fam (injection)* inyección *f*. 4 *(leaf)* hoja: **pine needles** *hojas de pino.* ■ **it's like looking for a needle in a haystack** es como buscar una aguja en un pajar. ‖ **to get the needle** GB *fam* picarse.
▷ *vt fam* pinchar.

needless ['ni:dləs] *adj* innecesario,-a.

needlewoman ['ni:dəlwʊmən] *n* costurera.
▲ *pl* **needlewomen** ['ni:dəlwɪmɪn].

needlework ['ni:dəlwɜ:k] *n* 1 *(sewing)* costura. 2 *(embroidery)* bordado.

needy ['ni:dɪ] *adj* necesitado,-a.
▲ *comp* **needier**, *superl* **neediest.**
▷ *n pl* **the needy** los necesitados *mpl*.

negate [nɪ'geɪt] *vt* 1 *(invalidate)* anular, invalidar. 2 *(deny)* negar.

negation [nɪ'geɪʃən] *n* 1 *(denial)* negación *f*. 2 *(invalidation)* anulación *f*, invalidación *f*.

negative ['negətɪv] *adj* negativo,-a.
▷ *n* 1 LING negación *f*. 2 *(answer)* negativa. 3 *(photograph)* negativo. ■ **to answer in the negative** dar una respuesta negativa.

neglect [nɪ'glekt] *n* 1 *(of thing)* descuido, desatención *f*, abandono. 2 *(of duty)* incumplimiento.
▷ *vt* 1 *(not take care of)* tener abandonado,-a, desatender: **I've been neglecting my friends recently** *tengo abandonados a mis amigos.* 2 *(fail to attend to)* descuidar. 3 *(forget to do)* olvidar: **she neglected to lock the safe** *olvidó cerrar la caja con llave.*

neglectful [nɪ'glektfʊl] *adj* negligente, descuidado,-a. ■ **to be neglectful of** desatender, descuidar.

negligee ['neglɪʒeɪ] *n* salto de cama, deshabillé *m*.

negligence ['neglɪdʒəns] *n* negligencia.

negligible ['neglɪdʒəbəl] *adj* insignificante.

negotiation [nɪgəʊʃɪ'eɪʃən] *n* negociación *f*.

negotiator [nɪ'gəʊʃɪeɪtər] *n* negociador,-ra.

Negro ['ni:grəʊ] *adj* negro,-a.
▷ *n* negro.
▲ *pl* **Negroes.**

neigh [neɪ] *n* relincho.
▷ *vi* relinchar.

neighbor ['neɪbər] *n* US → **neighbour.**

neighborhood ['neɪbəhʊd] *n* US → **neighbourhood.**

neighbour ['neɪbər] *n* 1 vecino,-a. 2 *(fellow man)* prójimo,-a.

neighbourhood ['neɪbəhʊd] *n* 1 vecindad *f*, barrio. 2 *(people)* vecindario.

neither ['naɪðər, 'ni:ðər] *adj* ninguno de los dos, ninguna de las dos: **neither boy knew the answer** *ninguno de los dos chicos sabía la respuesta.*
▷ *pron* ninguno de los dos, ninguna de las dos: **neither is here** *ninguno de los dos está aquí.*
▷ *adv* 1 ni: **he's neither fat nor thin** *no es ni gordo ni delgado.* 2 tampoco: **I don't like it and neither does my wife** *no me gusta a mí, y a mi mujer tampoco.* ■ **neither... nor...** ni... ni...: **she neither smokes nor drinks** *ni fuma ni bebe.*

neon ['ni:ɒn] *n* neón *m*. ● **neon light** luz *f* de neón.

Nepal [nə'pɔ:l] *n* Nepal.

Nepalese [nepə'li:z] *adj* nepalés,-esa, nepalí.
▷ *n* 1 *(person)* nepalés,-esa, nepalí *mf*. 2 *(language)* nepalés *m*, nepalí *m*.
▷ *n pl* **the Nepalese** los nepaleses *mpl*, los nepalíes *mpl*.

Nepali [nə'pɔ:lɪ] *adj* → **Nepalese.**

nephew ['nevju:] *n* sobrino.

Neptune ['neptju:n] *n* Neptuno.

nerve [nɜ:v] *n* 1 nervio. 2 *(daring)* valor *m*. 3 *(cheek)* descaro, jeta, cara: **what a nerve!** *¡qué cara!* ■ **to be a bundle of nerves** estar hecho,-a un manojo de nervios.

nerve-racking ['nɜ:vrækɪŋ] *adj* angustioso,-a.

nervous ['nɜ:vəs] *adj* 1 nervioso,-a. 2 *(afraid)* miedoso,-a; *(timid)* tímido,-a. 3 *(apprehensive)* aprensivo,-a. ● **nervous breakdown** crisis *f* nerviosa. ‖ **nervous system** sistema *m* nervioso.

nest [nest] *n* 1 nido; *(hen's)* nidal *m*. 2 *(wasp's)* avispero; *(animal's)* madriguera. 3 *fig* nido, refugio.
▷ *vi* anidar, nidificar.
▷ *vt* COMPUT anidar.

nestle ['nesəl] *vi* 1 acomodarse. 2 esconderse.
▷ *vt* recostar.

net¹ [net] *n* red *f*. ● **net curtains** visillos.
▷ *vt* coger con red.
▲ *pt & pp* **netted**, *ger* **netting.**

net² [net] *adj* FIN neto,-a. ● **net result** resultado final. ‖ **net weight** peso neto.
▷ *vt* 1 *(earn)* ganar neto,-a: **he netted £8,000** *ganó ocho mil libras netas.* 2 *(produce)* reportar un beneficio neto de.
▲ *pt & pp* **netted**, *ger* **netting.**

nether ['neðər] *adj lit* inferior, de abajo.

Netherlander ['neðəlændər] *n* neerlandés,-esa.

Netherlands ['neðələndʒ] *n* **the Netherlands** los Países *mpl* Bajos.
nethermost ['neðəməust] *adj lit* más bajo,-a.
netsurfer ['netsɜ:fəʳ] *n* internauta *mf*.
netting ['netɪŋ] *n* malla, red *f*.
nettle ['netəl] *n* ortiga. ● **nettle rash** urticaria.
▷ *vt* irritar.
network ['netwɜ:k] *n* red *f*.
▷ *vt* COMPUT conectar en red.
neuron ['njuərɒn] *n* neurona.
neuter ['nju:təʳ] *adj* neutro,-a.
▷ *n* LING neutro.
▷ *vt (castrate)* castrar.
neutral ['nju:trəl] *adj* **1** *(in general)* neutro,-a: **a neutral shampoo** *un champú neutro.* **2** POL neutral: **a neutral country** *un país neutral.* **3** *(impartial)* neutral, imparcial: **a neutral Judgment** *un juicio imparcial.*
▷ *n* AUTO punto muerto.
neutron ['njuərɒn] *n* neutrón *m*.
never ['nevəʳ] *adv* nunca, jamás: **I have never been there** *jamás he estado allí;* **we never go there any more** *ya no vamos allí nunca;* **never have I heard such rubbish** *en mi vida he oído tales tonterías;* **he never so much as thanked me** *ni siquiera me dio las gracias.* ■ **never again** nunca más. ‖ **never mind!** ¡no importa!
never-ending [nevə'rendɪŋ] *adj* interminable.
nevermore [nevə'mɔ:ʳ] *adv* LIT nunca más.
nevertheless [nevəðə'les] *adv* sin embargo.
new [nju:] *adj* **1** nuevo,-a: **a new car** *un coche nuevo;* **new bread** *pan recién hecho.* **2** *(baby)* recién nacido,-a: **she's got a new baby** *acaba de tener un hijo.* ■ **as good as new** como nuevo,-a. ● **new deal** programa *m* de reformas. ‖ **new moon** luna nueva. ‖ **New Testament** Nuevo Testamento. ‖ **New World** Nuevo Mundo. ‖ **New Year** Año Nuevo. ‖ **New Year's Day** día *m* de Año Nuevo. ‖ **New York** Nueva York. ‖ **New Zealand** Nueva Zelanda.
newborn ['nju:bɔ:n] *adj* recién nacido,-a.
newcomer ['nju:kʌməʳ] *n* recién llegado,-a.
newfangled [nju:'fæŋgləd] *adj pej* novedoso,-a.
Newfoundland ['nju:fəndlənd] *n* Terranova.
newly ['nju:lɪ] *adv* recién: **newly baked bread** *pan recién hecho.*
newlywed ['nju:lɪwed] *n* recién casado,-a.
news [nju:z] *n* noticias *fpl*. ■ **no news is good news** la falta de noticias son buenas noticias. ● **a piece of news** una noticia.
newsagent ['nju:zeɪdʒənt] *n* vendedor,-ra de periódicos. ● **newsagent's (shop)** quiosco.
newsdealer ['nju:zdi:ləʳ] *n* US vendedor,-ra de periódicos.
newsflash ['nju:zflæʃ] *n* noticia de última hora.
newsgroup ['nju:zgru:p] *n* grupo de discusión.
newsletter ['nju:zletəʳ] *n* hoja informativa, boletín *m*.
newsman ['nju:zmæn] *n* periodista *m*.
▲ *pl* **newsmen** ['nju:zmen].
newspaper ['nju:speɪpəʳ] *n* diario, periódico.
newsprint ['nju:zprɪnt] *n* papel *m* de periódico.
newssheet ['nju:zʃi:t] *n* hoja informativa.
newsstand ['nju:zstænd] *n* quiosco, puesto de periódicos.
newsworthy ['nju:zwɜ:ðɪ] *adj* de interés periodístico.
newt [nju:t] *n* tritón *m*.
newton ['nju:tᵊn] *n* newton *m*.
next [nekst] *adj* **1** *(following - in order)* próximo,-a, siguiente; *(- in time)* próximo,-a, que viene: **the next street on the left** *la próxima calle a la izquierda;* **it's on the next page** *está en la página siguiente.* **2** *(room, house, etc)* de al lado: **they live in the next house** *viven en la casa de al lado.*
▷ *adv* luego, después, a continuación: **what do you want to do next?** *¿qué quieres hacer ahora?*
▷ *prep* **next to** al lado de: **it's next to the cinema** *está al lado del cine.*
next-door ['nekstdɔ:ʳ] *adj* de al lado, de la casa de al lado: **my next-door neighbours** *los vecinos de al lado.*
NGO ['en'dʒi:'əu] *abbr* **(Non-Governmental Organization)** Organización *f* no gubernamental; *(abbreviation)* ONG *f*.
NHS ['en'eɪtʃ'es] *abbr* GB **(National Health Service)** ≈ Insalud *m*.
nib [nɪb] *n* plumilla.
nibble ['nɪbᵊl] *n* **1** *(action)* mordisco: **I felt a nibble at my bait** *sentí como mordía el cebo.* **2** *(piece)* bocadito.
▷ *vi* picar: **I've been nibbling all morning so I'm not hungry** *no tengo hambre porque he estado picando toda la mañana;* **someone's been nibbling at this cheese** *alguien ha estado picando de este queso.*
Nicaragua [nɪkə'rægjuə] *n* Nicaragua.
Nicaraguan [nɪkə'rægjuən] *adj* nicaragüense.
▷ *n* nicaragüense.
nice [naɪs] *adj* **1** *(person)* amable, simpático,-a: **he's such a nice boy!** *¡es un chico tan simpático!* **2** *(thing)* bueno,-a, agradable: **nice day today, isn't it?** *hace buen día, ¿verdad?* **3** *(food)* delicioso,-a, bueno,-a. **4** *(pretty)* bonito,-a, guapo,-a. **5** *(subtle)* sutil: **a nice distinction** *una distinción sutil.* **6** *iron* menudo,-a, bonito,-a: **a nice mess you made of that, didn't you?** *menuda la hiciste, ¿eh?*
Nice [ni:s] *n* Niza.
nicely ['naɪslɪ] *adv* **1** *(well)* bien: **she was very nicely dressed** *iba muy bien vestida.* **2** *(properly)* bien: **behave nicely, dear** *compórtate bien, cariño.* **3** *fam (very well)* perfecto, estupendo.
nicety ['naɪsətɪ] *n* detalle *m*: **there isn't time for all these niceties, let's get to the point** *no hay tiempo para tantos detalles, vayamos al grano.* ■ **to a nicety** con suma precisión, a la perfección.
▲ *pl* **niceties.**
niche [ni:ʃ] *n* nicho, hornacina.
nick [nɪk] *n* **1** mella, muesca. **2** GB *fam* condiciones *fpl*: **in good/bad nick** *en buenas/malas condiciones.* **3** GB *sl (gaol)* chirona, gayola, trena.
▷ *vt* **1** *(notch)* mellar; *(cut)* cortar: **I nicked myself when I was shaving** *me corté mientras me afeitaba.* **2** *sl (steal)* birlar, mangar, chorizar: **somebody's nicked my wallet** *me han mangado la cartera.* **3** GB *sl (arrest)* trincar, pillar: **he was nicked for speeding** *lo trincaron por exceso de velocidad.* ■ **in the nick of time** justo a tiempo.
nickel ['nɪkᵊl] *n* **1** níquel *m*. **2** US moneda de cinco centavos. ● **nickel silver** metal *m* blanco.
▷ *vt* niquelar.
nickname ['nɪkneɪm] *n* apodo.
▷ *vt* apodar: **he was nicknamed «Lanky»** *lo apodaron «Lanky».*
niece [ni:s] *n* sobrina.

nifty ['nɪftɪ] *adj* **1** *fam (smart)* chulo,-a. **2** *fam (clever)* ingenioso,-a, apañado,-a; *(deft)* hábil. **3** *fam (quick)* rápido,-a.
▲ *comp* niftier, *superl* niftiest.
Niger [ni:'ʒeəʳ] *n* Níger.
Nigeria [naɪ'dʒɪərɪə] *n* Nigeria.
Nigerian [naɪ'dʒɪərɪən] *adj* nigeriano,-a.
▷ *n* nigeriano,-a.
niggard ['nɪgəd] *n* avaro,-a, tacaño,-a.
niggle ['nɪgəl] *n* **1** *(doubt)* duda. **2** *(worry)* preocupación *f*.
▷ *vi (worry)* preocupar.
▷ *vt (annoy)* molestar.
▷ *vi (fuss)* reparar en nimiedades; *(complain)* quejarse.
niggling ['nɪgəlɪŋ] *adj* **1** *(trifling)* insignificante. **2** *(persistent)* persistente. **3** *(worrying)* preocupante.
night [naɪt] *n* noche *f*. ■ **at night** de noche. | **by night** de noche. | **last night** anoche. | **night and day** noche y día. | **to have a bad night** pasar una mala noche. | **to have a late night** acostarse tarde. | **to make a night of it** salir de juerga hasta tarde. ● **night school** escuela nocturna. | **night shift** turno de noche.
▷ *adv* **nights** *fam* de noche, por la noche: **I can't sleep nights** *no puedo dormir por la noche.*
nightdress ['naɪtdres] *n* camisón *m*.
▲ *pl* nightdresses.
nightfall ['naɪtfɔ:l] *n* anochecer *m*.
nightgown ['naɪtgaʊn] *n* camisón *m*.
nightingale ['naɪtɪŋgeɪl] *n* ruiseñor *m*.
nightly ['naɪtlɪ] *adv* cada noche: **she prayed nightly for a child** *rezaba cada noche por tener un hijo.*
▷ *adj* cada noche: **his nightly medicine** *su medicina de cada noche.*
nightmare ['naɪtmeəʳ] *n* pesadilla.
nightshade ['naɪtʃeɪd] ● **deadly nightshade** belladona. | **woody nightshade** dulcamara, dulzamara, hierba mora.
nighttime ['naɪttaɪm] *n* noche *f*.
nil [nɪl] *n* **1** cero, nada: **costs have been reduced to practically nil** *los costes se han reducido prácticamente a cero.* **2** SP cero: **Lincoln beat Grantham two goals to nil** *Lincoln ganó a Grantham por dos goles a cero.*
Nile [naɪl] *n* el Nilo.
nimble ['nɪmbəl] *adj* ágil.
nine [naɪn] *adj* nueve.
▷ *n* nueve *m*. ■ **nine times out of ten** en el noventa por ciento de los casos.
Consulta también **six**.
nineteen [naɪn'ti:n] *adj* diecinueve.
▷ *n* diecinueve *m*. ■ **to talk nineteen to the dozen** hablar por los codos.
Consulta también **six**.
nineteenth [naɪn'ti:nθ] *adj* decimonono,-a.
▷ *adv* en decimonono lugar.
▷ *n* **1** *(in series)* decimonono,-a. **2** *(fraction)* decimonono; *(one part)* decimonona parte *f*.
Consulta también **sixth**.
nineties ['naɪntɪz] *n pl* **the nineties** los años *mpl* noventa, los noventa *mpl*.
Consulta también **sixties**.
ninetieth ['naɪntɪəθ] *adj* nonagésimo,-a.
▷ *adv* en nonagésimo lugar.
▷ *n* **1** *(in series)* nonagésimo,-a. **2** *(fraction)* nonagésimo; *(one part)* nonagésima parte *f*.
Consulta también **sixtieth**.
ninety ['naɪntɪ] *adj* noventa.
▷ *n* noventa *m*.
Consulta también **sixty**.
ninth [naɪnθ] *adj* nono,-a, noveno,-a.
▷ *adv* en nono lugar, en noveno lugar.
▷ *n* **1** *(in series)* nono,-a, noveno,-a. **2** *(fraction)* noveno; *(one part)* novena parte *f*.
Consulta también **sixth**.
nip [nɪp] *n* **1** *(pinch)* pellizco. **2** *(bite)* mordisco, mordedura: **the dog gave me a nip on the ankle** *el perro me pegó un mordisco en el tobillo.* **3** *(drink)* trago: **a nip of whisky** *un trago de whisky.*
▷ *vt* **1** *(pinch)* pellizcar: **a crab nipped my finger** *un cangrejo me pellizcó el dedo.* **2** *(bite)* morder *(con poca fuerza)*: **the dog nipped me** *el perro me mordió.*
▷ *vi* **1** *(pinch)* pellizcar: **crabs nip** *los cangrejos pellizcan.* **2** *(bite)* morder: **some dogs nip** *algunos perros muerden.* **3** *(go quickly)* ir (en un momento): **she's nipped out to the shop** *ha salido un momentín a la tienda.*
▲ *pt & pp* nipped, *ger* nipping.
nipple ['nɪpəl] *n* **1** *(female)* pezón *m*. **2** *(male)* tetilla. **3** *(teat)* tetilla. **4** TECH pezón *m*.
nippy ['nɪpɪ] *adj* **1** *fam (quick)* rápido,-a. **2** *fam (cold)* fresquillo,-a: **it's a bit nippy** *hace fresquillo.*
▲ *comp* nippier, *superl* nippiest.
nit [nɪt] *n* **1** liendre *f*. **2** GB *fam* imbécil *mf*.
niter ['naɪtəʳ] *n* US salitre *m*.
nitre ['naɪtəʳ] *n* salitre *m*.
nitrogen ['naɪtrədʒən] *n* nitrógeno.
nitty-gritty [nɪtɪ'grɪtɪ] ■ **to get down to the nitty-gritty** *fam* ir al grano.
nitwit ['nɪtwɪt] *n fam* imbécil *mf*.
NNE [nɔ:θnɔ:θ'i:st] *abbr* (north-northeast) nornoreste *m*; *(abbreviation)* NNE.
NNW [nɔ:θnɔ:θ'west] *abbr* (north-northwest) nornoroeste *m*; *(abbreviation)* NNO.
no [nəʊ] *adv* no: **have you seen it? –no!** *¿lo has visto? –¡no!*
▷ *adj* ninguno,-a; *(before masc sing)* ningún: **I have no time** *no tengo tiempo.*
▷ *n* no: **there were two noes and nine yeses** *hubo dos noes y nueve síes.*
No ['nʌmbəʳ] [Also written **no**; pl **Nos**, **nos.**] *abbr* (number) número; *(abbreviation)* n°, núm.
nobility [nəʊ'bɪlɪtɪ] *n* nobleza.
noble ['nəʊbəl] *adj* noble.
▲ *comp* nobler, *superl* noblest.
▷ *n* noble *mf*.
nobleman ['nəʊbəlmən] *n* noble *m*.
▲ *pl* noblemen ['nəʊbəlmən].
noblewoman ['nəʊbəlwʊmən] *n* noble *f*.
▲ *pl* noblewomen ['nəʊbəlwɪmɪn].
nobody ['nəʊbədɪ] *pron* nadie: **nobody went to the party** *no fue nadie a la fiesta.* ■ **like nobody's business** *fam* como nadie.
▷ *n* don nadie *m*.
nocturne ['nɒktɜ:n] *n* MUS nocturno.
nod [nɒd] *n* **1** saludo *con la cabeza.* **2** *(in agreement)* señal *f* de asentimiento.

▷ *vi* **1** saludar *con la cabeza.* **2** *(agree)* asentir *(con la cabeza).* ■ **to nod one's head** asentir con la cabeza.
▲ *pt & pp* **nodded**, *ger* **nodding**.
⊙ **to nod off** *vi* dormirse, dar cabezadas.
nodding acquaintance [nɒdɪŋə'kweɪntəns] *n* conocimiento superficial: **I have a nodding acquaintance with him** *lo conozco de hola y adiós.*
no-go area [nəʊ'gəʊeərɪə] *n* GB zona prohibida.
noise [nɔɪz] *n* ruido, sonido. ■ **to make a noise** hacer ruido.
▷ *n pl* **noises** comentarios *mpl.*
noiseless ['nɔɪzləs] *adj* silencioso,-a.
noisy ['nɔɪzɪ] *adj* ruidoso,-a.
▲ *comp* **noisier**, *superl* **noisiest**.
nomad ['nəʊmæd] *n* nómada *mf.*
no-man's-land ['nəʊmænzlænd] *n* tierra de nadie.
nominal ['nɒmɪnəl] *adj* **1** nominal. **2** *(price)* simbólico,-a.
nominate ['nɒmɪneɪt] *vt* **1** nombrar: **he was nominated team captain** *lo nombraron capitán del equipo.* **2** *(propose)* proponer.
nomination [nɒmɪ'neɪʃən] *n* **1** *(appointment)* nombramiento. **2** *(proposal)* nominación *f*, propuesta.
nominative ['nɒmɪnətɪv] *adj* nominativo,-a.
▷ *n* nominativo.
nominee [nɒmɪ'niː] *n* **1** *(person chosen)* nominado,-a. **2** *(person proposed)* persona propuesta, candidato,-a.
non [nɒn] *pref* no.
nonchalance ['nɒnʃələns] *n* **1** *(lack of worry)* despreocupación *f.* **2** *(calmness)* serenidad *f*, ecuanimidad *f.* **3** *(indifference)* indiferencia.
noncommissioned officer [nɒnkəmɪʃənd'ɒfɪsə'] *n* suboficial *mf.*
noncommittal [nɒnkə'mɪtəl] *adj (person)* evasivo,-a; *(answer)* no comprometedor,-ra.
nonconformism [nɒnkəm'fɔːmɪzəm] *n* inconformismo.
nonconformist [nɒnkən'fɔːmɪst] *adj* disidente.
▷ *n* **1** disidente *mf.* **2** REL *miembro de cualquiera de las Iglesias que se escindieron de la Anglicana.*
noncustodial [nɒnkə'stəʊdɪəl] *adj* **1** *(parent) que no tiene custodia legal de sus hijos.* **2** *(sentence) que no implica ingreso en prisión.*
nondescript ['nɒndɪskrɪpt] *adj* soso,-a, insulso,-a, anodino,-a, insípido,-a.
nondrinker [nɒn'drɪŋkə'] *n* abstemio,-a: **he's a non drinker** *no bebe alcohol.*
none [nʌn] *pron* ninguno,-a: **none of the keys opens the door** *ninguna de las llaves abre la puerta.*
▷ *adv* de ningún modo: **he's none the worse for his ordeal** *no le ha afectado esa mala experiencia.* ■ **none but** únicamente, solamente, solo: **none but the strongest survived** *sobrevivieron solo los más fuertes.* ‖ **none other than** nada menos que. ‖ **to have none of** no tolerar, no permitir.
nonentity [nɒ'nentɪtɪ] *n* nulidad *f.*
▲ *pl* **nonentities**.
nonetheless [nʌnðə'les] *adv* no obstante.
nonevent [nɒnɪ'vent] *n* fracaso.
nonexistent [nɒnɪg'zɪstənt] *adj* inexistente.
noninterference [nɒnɪntə'fɪərəns] *n* no injerencia.
no-nonsense [nəʊ'nɒnsens] *adj* práctico,-a.
nonplus [nɒn'plʌs] *vt* dejar perplejo,-a.
▲ *pt & pp* **nonplussed**, *ger* **nonplussing**.

non-profit-making [nɒn'prɒfɪtmeɪkɪŋ] *adj* sin fines lucrativos.
nonsense ['nɒnsəns] *n* tonterías *fpl*: **don't talk nonsense!** *¡no digas tonterías!*
nonskid ['nɒn'skɪd] *adj* antiderrapante.
nonslip ['nɒn'slɪp] *adj* antideslizante.
nonstick ['nɒn'stɪk] *adj* antiadherente.
nonstop ['nɒn'stɒp] *adj* **1** *(continuous)* continuo,-a. **2** *(flight, etc)* directo,-a, sin escalas.
▷ *adv* sin parar.
noodle ['nuːdəl] *n* fideo.
nook [nʊk] *n* rincón *m.*
noon [nuːn] *n* mediodía *m.*
no-one ['nəʊwʌn] [Also written **no one**.] *pron* nadie: **no-one went to the party** *no fue nadie a la fiesta.*
noose [nuːs] *n* **1** lazo. **2** *(hangman's)* soga, dogal *m.*
no-place ['nəʊpleɪs] *adv* US→ **nowhere**.
nor [nɔː'] *conj* **1** ni: **neither you nor I** *ni tú ni yo.* **2** tampoco: **nor do I** *yo tampoco.*
Nordic ['nɔːdɪk] *adj* nórdico,-a.
normal ['nɔːməl] *adj* normal
normality [nɔː'mælɪtɪ] *n* normalidad *f.*
Norman ['nɔːmən] *adj* **1** normando,-a. **2** *(church, etc)* románico,-a.
▷ *n* normando,-a.
Normandy ['nɔːməndɪ] *n* Normandía.
Norse [nɔːs] *adj* nórdico,-a.
▷ *n (language)* nórdico.
Norseman ['nɔːsmən] *n* vikingo.
▲ *pl* **Norsemen** ['nɔːsmən].
north [nɔːθ] *n* norte *m*: **in the north of Scotland** *en el norte de Escocia.* ● **North Pole** Polo Norte. ‖ **the North Country** GB el norte *m.*
▷ *adj* del norte: **I live in north London** *vivo en el norte de Londres.*
▷ *adv* al norte, hacia el norte: **we're travelling north** *viajamos hacia el norte.*
northeast [nɔːθ'iːst] *n* nordeste *m*, noreste *m.*
▷ *adj* del nordeste.
▷ *adv* al nordeste, hacia el nordeste.
northern ['nɔːðən] *adj* norte, del norte.
north-northeast [nɔːθnɔːθ'iːst] *n* nornoreste *m.*
▷ *adv* al nornoreste, hacia el nornoreste.
north-northwest [nɔːθnɔːθ'west] *n* nornoroeste *m.*
▷ *adv* al nornoroeste, hacia el nornoroeste.
northwest [nɔːθ'west] *n* noroeste *m.*
▷ *adj* del noroeste.
▷ *adv* al noroeste, hacia el noroeste.
Norway ['nɔːweɪ] *n* Noruega.
Norwegian [nɔː'wiːdʒən] *adj* noruego,-a.
▷ *n* **1** *(person)* noruego,-a. **2** *(language)* noruego.
nose [nəʊz] *n* **1** nariz *f.* **2** *(of animal)* hocico. **3** *(sense)* olfato. **4** *(of car, etc)* morro. ■ **it's as plain as the nose on your face** está tan claro como el agua. ‖ **just follow your nose 1** *(go straight ahead)* sigue todo recto. **2** *(follow instinct)* guíate por el instinto. ‖ **to blow one's nose** sonarse. ‖ **to get up** SB'**s nose** GB *fam* fastidiar a ALGN. ‖ **to poke/stick one's nose into** STH meter las narices en ALGO.
⊙ **to nose around** *vi* curiosear.
⊙ **to nose forward** *vi (car)* avanzar poco a poco.
⊙ **to nose out** *vi (car)* salir poco a poco.
nosebleed ['nəʊzbliːd] *n* hemorragia nasal.

nosecone ['nəʊzkəʊn] *n* morro.
nosedive ['nəʊzdaɪv] *n* picado.
▷ *vi* descender en picado, bajar en picado.
nosh-up ['nɒʃʌp] *n* GB *sl* comilona.
nostalgia [nɒ'stældʒɪə] *n* nostalgia, añoranza.
nostril ['nɒstrəl] *n* fosa nasal.
nosy ['nəʊzɪ] *adj fam* curioso,-a, entrometido,-a.
▲ *comp* nosier, *superl* nosiest.
not [nɒt] [La forma contracta es n't: isn't, aren't, doesn't.] *adv* no: are you coming or not? *¿vienes o no?* ■ not likely! ¡ni hablar!
notary ['nəʊtərɪ] *n* notario,-a.
▲ *pl* notaries.
notch [nɒtʃ] *n* 1 muesca. 2 *fig* punto: this film is several notches above his previous ones *esta película está varios puntos por encima de sus anteriores.* 3 US desfiladero.
▷ *vt* hacer muescas en.
⊙ to notch up *vt insep* apuntarse.
note [nəʊt] *n* 1 MUS nota; *(key)* tecla. 2 *(message)* nota. 3 *(money)* billete *m*: £1000 in used five pound notes *mil libras en billetes usados de cinco libras.* ■ of note digno,-a de mención ‖ to take notes tomar apuntes.
▷ *vt* 1 *(notice)* notar, advertir: I noted a certain reluctance on John's part *noté cierta reticencia por parte de John.* 2 *(pay special attention)* fijarse en: note that the plural of «child» is «children» *fijaos en que el plural de «child» es «children».* 3 *(write down)* apuntar, anotar.
▷ *n pl* notes apuntes *mpl.*
notebook ['nəʊtbʊk] *n* 1 *(book)* libreta, cuaderno. 2 *(computer)* ordenador *m* portátil.
noted ['nəʊtɪd] *adj* conocido,-a, célebre.
notepad ['nəʊtpæd] *n* bloc *m* de notas.
notepaper ['nəʊtpeɪpəʳ] *n* papel *m* de cartas.
noteworthy ['nəʊtwɜːðɪ] *adj* digno,-a de mención.
nothing ['nʌθɪŋ] *n* nada: there's nothing left *no queda nada;* it's nothing special *no es nada del otro jueves.*
▷ *adv* de ningún modo, de ninguna manera: it's nothing like a pheasant *no se parece en nada a un faisán.* ■ for nothing *fam* gratis. ‖ nothing but... únicamente..., solo... ‖ nothing doing *fam* ni hablar. ‖ nothing else nada más. ‖ nothing much nada de interés. ‖ there's nothing to it es facilísimo.
notice ['nəʊtɪs] *n* 1 *(sign)* letrero: there's a notice which says «No parking» *hay un letrero que pone «Prohibido aparcar».* 2 *(announcement)* anuncio: there's a notice in the paper about a lost dog *hay un anuncio en el diario acerca de un perro extraviado.* 3 *(criticism)* crítica, reseña, recensión *f*: the play got very good notices *la obra fue muy bien recibida por la crítica.* 4 *(attention)* atención *f*: it totally escaped my notice *se me escapó por completo.* 5 *(warning)* aviso: they gave him a month's notice to quit the flat (US apartment) *le dieron un plazo de un mes para abandonar el piso.* ■ to hand in one's notice presentar la dimisión. ‖ to take no notice of no hacer caso de. ‖ without notice sin previo aviso.
▷ *vt* notar, fijarse en, darse cuenta de.
▷ *vi fam (show)* verse: don't worry, the stain doesn't notice *no te preocupes, la mancha no se ve.*
noticeable ['nəʊtɪsəbᵊl] *adj* que se nota, evidente.
noticeboard ['nəʊtɪsbɔːd] *n* tablón *m* de anuncios.
notify ['nəʊtɪfaɪ] *vt* notificar, avisar.
▲ *pt & pp* notified, *ger* notifying.

notion ['nəʊʃᵊn] *n* noción *f*, idea, concepto.
▷ *n pl* notions US mercería *f sing.*
notorious [nəʊ'tɔːrɪəs] *adj pej* célebre: a notoriou criminal *un conocido criminal.*
notwithstanding [nɒtwɪθ'stændɪŋ] *adv* no obstante
▷ *prep* a pesar de.
nougat ['nuːgɑː] *n* turrón *m* blando.
nought [nɔːt] *n* cero: nought point six six *cero com sesenta y seis.* ● noughts and crosses tres en raya *m.*
noun [naʊn] *n* nombre *m*, sustantivo. ● noun phras sintagma *m* nominal.
nourish ['nʌrɪʃ] *vt* nutrir, alimentar.
nourishing ['nʌrɪʃɪŋ] *adj* nutritivo,-a.
nourishment ['nʌrɪʃmənt] *n* nutrición *f*, alimentación *f.*
Nova Scotia [nəʊve'skəʊʃə] *n* Nueva Escocia.
novel[1] ['nɒvəl] *adj* original, novedoso,-a: what a nov el idea! *¡qué idea más original!*
novel[2] ['nɒvəl] *n* novela.
novelist ['nɒvəlɪst] *n* novelista *mf.*
novelty ['nɒvᵊltɪ] *n* 1 novedad *f*: the novelty soon wor off *pronto dejó de ser novedad.* 2 *(trinket)* chuchería.
▲ *pl* novelties.
November [nəʊ'vembəʳ] *n* noviembre *m.*
Para ejemplos de uso, consulta May.
novice ['nɒvɪs] *n* 1 novato,-a. 2 REL novicio,-a.
now [naʊ] *adv* 1 *(at the present)* ahora; *(used contrastively)* ya: where do you work now? 2 *(immediately)* ya, ahor mismo: do it now! *¡hazlo ya!* 3 *(in past)* ya, entonces 4 *(introductory)* bueno, vamos a ver, veamos: now, let begin *bueno, empecemos.* ■ by now ya: she'll be in Mexico by now *ya debe de estar en Méjico.* ‖ for now por e momento. ‖ from now on de ahora en adelante. ‖ jus now 1 *(at this moment)* en estos momentos, ahora mis mo. 2 *(a short while ago)* hace un momento. ‖ right nov ahora mismo.
▷ *conj* [Also now that.] ahora que, ya que: now (tha we're all here, we can begin *ya que estamos todos podemos empezar.*
nowadays ['naʊədeɪz] *adv* hoy día, hoy en día, actualmente.
nowhere ['nəʊweəʳ] *adv (position)* en ninguna parte en ningún sitio, en ningún lugar; *(direction)* a ninguna parte, a ningún sitio: where are you going? –nowhere special *¿dónde vas? –a ningún sitio en especia* there's nowhere to hide *no hay donde esconderse;* sh has nowhere else to go *no tiene otro sitio donde ir;* tha will get you nowhere *eso no te llevará a ninguna parte eso no te ayudará en nada;* my keys were nowhere t be found *no encontraba mis llaves por ninguna parte.* ■ in the middle of nowhere en el quinto pino. ‖ nowher near muy lejos de: I've nowhere near finished *esto muy lejos de acabar.*
noxious ['nɒkʃəs] *adj* nocivo,-a.
nozzle ['nɒzᵊl] *n (of hose)* boca, boquilla; *(of oilcan)* pitorro; *(large calibre)* tobera.
nuance [njuː'ɑːns] *n* matiz *m.*
nub [nʌb] *n* meollo, clave *f.* ■ the nub of the matter e quid de la cuestión.
nuclear ['njuːklɪəʳ] *adj* nuclear. ● nuclear disarmamen desarme *m* nuclear. ‖ nuclear energy energía nuclea

‖ **nuclear physics** física nuclear. ‖ **nuclear waste** residuos nucleares. ‖ **nuclear weapon** arma nuclear.

nucleus ['nju:klɪəs] *n* núcleo.
▲ *pl* nuclei [nju:'klɪaɪ].

nude [nju:d] *adj* desnudo,-a.
▷ *n* desnudo. ■ **in the nude** desnudo,-a.

nudge [nʌdʒ] *n* 1 *(with elbow)* codazo. 2 empujón *m* suave.
▷ *vt* 1 *(with elbow)* dar un codazo a: **he nudged me** *me dio un codazo.* 2 empujar suavemente: **I just nudged the bike with my car and it fell over** *tan solo le di un empujoncito a la bici con el coche y se cayó.*

nudity ['nju:dɪtɪ] *n* desnudez *f*.

nugget ['nʌgɪt] *n* pepita.

nuisance ['nju:sᵊns] *n* 1 molestia, fastidio, lata. 2 *(person)* pesado,-a. ■ **to make a nuisance of** os dar la lata.

nuke [nju:k] *n fam* bomba nuclear.
▷ *vt fam* atacar con arma nuclear.

null [nʌl] *adj* nulo,-a. ■ **null and void** nulo,-a, sin efecto.

nullify ['nʌlɪfaɪ] *vt* anular.
▲ *pt & pp* **nullified**, *ger* **nullifying.**

nullity ['nʌlɪtɪ] *n* nulidad *f*.
▲ *pl* **nullities.**

numb [nʌm] *adj* entumecido,-a, insensible.
▷ *vt* 1 entumecer. 2 *(anaesthetize)* anestesiar. 3 *fig* consternar. ■ **to be numb with cold** estar helado,-a de frío. ‖ **to be numb with fear** estar paralizado,-a de miedo.

number ['nʌmbəʳ] *n* 1 número: **if I give you my number, you can call me** *si te doy mi número, me puedes llamar;* **a large number of people** *un gran número de personas;* **I thought my number was on that one!** *¡pensé que esa bala era para mí!;* **I thought my number was up!** *¡creí que me había llegado la hora!* 2 *(on car)* número de matrícula, matrícula: **did you get his number?** *¿le cogiste la matrícula?* 3 *(of magazine, etc)* número. 4 *(song)* tema *m*: **she sang a few Gershwin numbers** *cantó algunos temas de Gershwin.* 5 *(group)* grupo: **two of their number died of malaria** *dos de ellos murieron de malaria.* 6 LING número: **adjectives agree with the noun in number and gender** *los adjetivos concuerdan con el sustantivo en número y en género.* 7 *fam (garment)* modelo: **Vicky turned up in a nice little red leather number** *Vicky se presentó con un modelito de cuero rojo.* ■ **a number of...** varios,-as... ‖ **any number of...** muchísimos,-as... ‖ **number one** principal, más importante. ‖ **to be number one** ser el número uno, ser el mejor. ‖ **to have** SB**'s number** tener calado,-a a ALGN. ‖ **to look after number one** mirar por lo suyo. ‖ **without number** un sinfín de... ● **Number Ten** *el nº 10 de Downing Street: la residencia oficial del primer ministro británico.*
▷ *vt* 1 numerar: **the tickets are not numbered** *los billetes no están numerados;* **his days are numbered** *tiene los días contados.* 2 *(count)* contar: **I number her among my friends** *la cuento entre mis amigos.*

⊙ **to number off** *vi* numerarse.

numeral ['nju:mərəl] *n* número, cifra.

numerate ['nju:mərət] *adj* que tiene conocimientos de matemáticas.

numerous ['nju:mərəs] *adj* numeroso,-a.

numismatics [nju:mɪz'mætɪks] *n* numismática.

nun [nʌn] *n* monja, religiosa.

nuptial ['nʌpʃəl] *adj fml* nupcial.
▷ *n pl* **nuptials** *fml* casamiento, nupcias *fpl*.

nurse [nɜ:s] *n* 1 enfermero,-a. 2 *(children's)* niñera.
▷ *vt* 1 *(look after)* cuidar. 2 *(suckle)* amamantar. 3 *(hold)* acunar. 4 *(feeling)* guardar. ■ **to nurse a cold** intentar curarse de un resfriado. ‖ **to nurse a grudge/grievance against** SB guardar rencor a ALGN.

nursemaid ['nɜ:smeɪd] *n* niñera.

nursery ['nɜ:sᵊrɪ] *n* 1 *(in house)* cuarto de los niños. 2 *(kindergarten)* guardería. 3 *(for plants)* vivero. ● **nursery nurse** enfermero,-a puericultor,-ora. ‖ **nursery rhyme** canción *f* infantil, poema *m* infantil. ‖ **nursery school** parvulario. ‖ **nursery slope** pista para principiantes.
▲ *pl* **nurseries.**

nursing ['nɜ:sɪŋ] *n* profesión *f* de enfermera, enfermería. ● **nursing home** clínica.

nurture ['nɜ:tʃəʳ] *vt* 1 nutrir, alimentar. 2 *(child)* criar.

nut [nʌt] *n* 1 BOT fruto seco: **a selection of nuts: hazelnuts, walnuts, almonds, peanuts and cashews** *un surtido de frutos secos: avellanas, nueces, almendras, cacahuetes y anacardos.* 2 TECH tuerca: **tighten this nut with a spanner** *aprieta esta tuerca con una llave inglesa.* 3 *fam (head)* coco. 4 fanático,-a: **he's a real soccer nut** *es un fanático del fútbol.* 5 *fam (nutcase)* chalado,-a, chiflado,-a.
▷ *adj* **nuts** loco,-a, chalado,-a, chiflado,-a: **she must be nuts to go out with him** *debe de estar loca para salir con él.* ■ **to be a tough nut to crack** ser un hueso duro de roer. ‖ **to be nuts about** STH/SB estar loco,-a por ALGO/ALGN. ‖ **to be off one's nut** estar chalado,-a. ‖ **to do one's nut** subirse por las paredes. ● **nuts and bolts** lo básico.

nutcrackers ['nʌtkrækəz] *n pl* cascanueces *m inv*.

nutmeg ['nʌtmeg] *n* nuez *f* moscada.

nutrition [nju:'trɪʃᵊn] *n* nutrición *f*.

nutritious [nju:'trɪʃəs] *adj* nutritivo,-a.

nutshell ['nʌtʃel] *n* cáscara. ■ **in a nutshell** en pocas palabras.

NW [nɔ:θ'west] *abbr* **(northwest)** noroeste *m*; *(abbreviation)* NO.

nylon ['naɪlɒn] [Registered trademark.] *n* nailon *m*.
▷ *n pl* **nylons** medias *fpl* de nailon.

nymph [nɪmf] *n* ninfa.

nympho ['nɪmfəʊ] *n fam* ninfómana.
▲ *pl* **nymphos.**

nymphomania [nɪmfə'meɪnɪə] *n* ninfomanía.

nymphomaniac [nɪmfə'meɪnɪæk] *n* ninfómana.

O

O, o [əʊ] *n (the letter)* O, o *f*.

O [əʊ] *n* **1** *(the letter)* O, o. **2** *(as number)* cero.

oaf [əʊf] *n fam* patán *m*, palurdo,-a, zoquete *mf*, zopenco,-a.

oafish ['əʊfɪʃ] *adj* torpe, bruto,-a.

oak [əʊk] *n* **1** BOT roble *m*. **2** *(wood)* roble *m*.
▷ *adj* de roble.

oar [ɔːʳ] *n* remo. ■ **to stick one's oar in** entrometerse, meter las narices.

oarsman ['ɔːzmən] *n* remero.
▲ *pl* oarsmen ['ɔːzmən].

oarswoman ['ɔːzwʊmən] *n* remera.
▲ *pl* oarswomen ['ɔːzwɪmɪn].

oasis [əʊ'eɪsɪs] *n* oasis *m*.
▲ *pl* oases [əʊ'eɪsiːz].

oat [əʊt] *n (plant)* avena.
▷ *n pl* **oats** *(cereal)* avena *f sing*.
▷ *n (porridge)* copos *mpl* de avena.

oatcake ['əʊtkeɪk] *n* torta de avena.

oath [əʊθ] *n* **1** JUR juramento. **2** *(swearword)* palabrota, juramento. ■ **on my oath** lo juro. ‖ **to be on oath / be under oath** estar bajo juramento.

oatmeal ['əʊtmiːl] *n* **1** *(flour)* harina de avena. **2** US *(porridge)* copos *mpl* de avena.

obdurate ['ɒbdjərət] *n fml (stubborn)* obstinado,-a, terco,-a; *(unyielding)* inflexible.

obedience [ə'biːdɪəns] *n* obediencia.

obedient [ə'biːdɪənt] *adj* obediente.

obelisk ['ɒbəlɪsk] *n* obelisco.

obese [əʊ'biːs] *adj* obeso,-a.

obesity [əʊ'biːsɪtɪ] *n* obesidad *f*.

obey [ə'beɪ] *vt* **1** *(gen)* obedecer; *(orders)* acatar. **2** *(law)* cumplir.
▷ *vi (gen)* obedecer.

obituary [ə'bɪtjʊərɪ] *n* necrología, obituario.
▲ *pl* obituaries.

object [*(n)* 'ɒbdʒekt; *(vb)* əb'dʒekt] *n* **1** *(thing)* objeto, cosa. **2** *(aim, purpose)* objetivo, objeto, fin *m*, propósito. **3** *(focus of feelings)* objeto: **he was an object of ridicule** *fue objeto de burlas*. **4** LING complemento: **direct/indirect object** *complemento directo/indirecto*. ● **object glass / object lens** objetivo.
▷ *vt* objetar.
▷ *vi* **1** *(oppose)* oponerse (**to**, a), poner reparos (**to**, a).

objection [əb'dʒekʃᵊn] *n* objeción *f*, reparo, inconveniente.

objectionable [əb'dʒekʃᵊnəbᵊl] *adj (unacceptable)* inaceptable; *(unpleasant)* ofensivo,-a.

objective [əb'dʒektɪv] *adj* objetivo,-a.
▷ *n* **1** *(purpose)* objetivo, fin *m*. **2** *(lens)* objetivo.

objectivity [əb'dʒektɪvɪtɪ] *n* objetividad *f*.

objector [əb'dʒektəʳ] *n* objetor,-ra.

obligate ['ɒblɪgeɪt] *vt fml* obligar.

obligation [ɒblɪ'geɪʃᵊn] *n* obligación *f*, compromiso.

obligatory [ɒ'blɪgətᵊrɪ] *adj* obligatorio,-a.

oblige [ə'blaɪdʒ] *vt* **1** *(compel)* obligar: **I felt obliged to attend** *me veía obligado a asistir*. **2** *(do a favour)* hacer un favor a, ayudar a. ■ **much obliged!** ¡muy agradecido,-a!
▷ *vi (do a favour)* hacer un favor, ayudar.

obliging [ə'blaɪdʒɪŋ] *adj* servicial, complaciente.

oblique [ə'bliːk] *adj* **1** *(line, angle)* oblicuo,-a. **2** *fig (hint, reference)* indirecto,-a.
▷ *n* barra.

obliterate [ə'blɪtəreɪt] *vt* **1** *(destroy)* destruir, arrasar; *(eliminate)* eliminar. **2** *(erase, blot out)* borrar, obliterar.

oblivion [ə'blɪvɪən] *n (obscurity)* olvido.

oblivious [ə'blɪvɪəs] *adj* inconsciente (**of**, de), ajeno,-a (**of**, a).

oblong ['ɒblɒŋ] *adj* oblongo,-a, alargado,-a.
▷ *n* rectángulo.

obnoxious [əb'nɒkʃəs] *adj* repugnante.

oboe ['əʊbəʊ] *n* oboe *m*.

obscene [ɒb'siːn] *adj* **1** *(indecent)* obsceno,-a, indecente. **2** *(scandalous)* escandaloso,-a.

obscenity [əb'senɪtɪ] *n* obscenidad *f*, indecencia.
▲ *pl* obscenities.

obscure [əbs'kjʊəʳ] *adj* **1** *(unclear)* oscuro,-a, poco claro,-a. **2** *(vague, indistinct)* vago,-a, confuso,-a; *(hidden)* recóndito,-a.
▷ *vt* **1** *(make unclear, difficult to understand)* ofuscar, oscurecer. **2** *(hide)* ocultar.

obscurity [əb'skjʊərɪtɪ] *n* **1** *(state)* oscuridad *f*, olvido. **2** *(darkness)* oscuridad *f*.

obsequious [əb'siːkwɪəs] *adj* servil.

observable [əb'zɜːvəbᵊl] *adj* visible, apreciable.

observance [əb'zɜːvᵊns] *n* observancia.

observant [əb'zɜːvᵊnt] *adj* observador,-ra.

observation [ɒbz'veɪʃᵊn] *n* **1** *(watching, study)* observación *f*; *(surveillance)* vigilancia. **2** *(remark)* observación *f*, comentario.

observatory [əb'zɜːvətᵊrɪ] *n* observatorio.
▲ *pl* observatories.

observe [əb'zɜːv] *vt* **1** *(see, watch)* observar, ver; *(in surveillance)* vigilar. **2** *(law)* cumplir, respetar. **3** *fml (say)* señalar.
▷ *vi* observar.

observer [əb'zɜːvəʳ] *n* observador,-ra.

obsess [əb'ses] *vt* obsesionar.

obsessed [əb'sest] *adj* obsesionado,-a (**by/with**, con).

obsession [əb'seʃᵊn] *n* obsesión *f* (**with/about**, con).

obsessional [əb'seʃᵊnəl] *adj* obsesivo,-a.

obsessive [əb'sesɪv] *adj* obsesivo,-a.
▷ *n* obsesivo,-a.

obsolete ['ɒbsəliːt] *adj* obsoleto,-a.

obstacle ['ɒbstəkᵊl] *n* **1** obstáculo. **2** *fig* obstáculo, impedimento. ● **obstacle race** carrera de obstáculos.

obstetrics [ɒb'stetrɪks] *n* obstetricia, tocología.

obstinate ['ɒbstɪnət] *adj (person)* obstinado,-a, tenaz, terco,-a; *(problem, thing)* tenaz, pertinaz.

obstruct [əb'strʌkt] *vt* **1** *(block - gen)* obstruir; *(- pipe, etc)* bloquear; *(- view)* tapar. **2** *(make difficult)* dificultar.

obstruction [əb'strʌkʃᵊn] *n* **1** *(gen)* obstrucción *f*. **2** *(hindrance)* estorbo, obstáculo.

obtain [əb'teɪn] *vt (get, acquire)* obtener, conseguir.

obtainable [əb'teɪnəbᵊl] *adj* obtenible: **it's no longer obtainable** *ya no se puede conseguir.*

obtrusion [əb'truːʒᵊn] *n fml* intrusión *f*.

obtrusive [əb'truːsɪv] *adj (noise)* molesto,-a; *(smell)* penetrante; *(colour)* llamativo,-a.

obtuse [əb'tjuːs] *adj fml (stupid)* obtuso,-a. ● **obtuse angle** ángulo obtuso.

obverse ['ɒbvɜːs] *n* **1** *fml (back)* anverso. **2** *fml (opposite)* contrario.

obviate ['ɒbvɪeɪt] *vt* obviar, evitar.

obvious ['ɒbvɪəs] *adj (clear)* obvio,-a, evidente, patente, claro,-a: **for obvious reasons** *por razones obvias.*

obviously ['ɒbvɪəslɪ] *adv* obviamente, evidentemente, claramente.

occasion [ə'keɪʒᵊn] *n* **1** *(time)* ocasión *f*; *(event)* acontecimiento. **2** *(opportunity)* ocasión *f*, oportunidad *f*: **if the occasion arises** *si se presenta la ocasión.* ■ **on occasion** de vez en cuando. ■ **on the occasion of** con motivo de. ■ **to rise to the occasion** estar a la altura de las circunstancias, dar la talla.
▷ *vt fml* ocasionar, causar.

occasional [ə'keɪʒᵊnəl] *adj (not frequent)* esporádico,-a, eventual.

occasionally [ə'keɪʒᵊnəlɪ] *adv* de vez en cuando, ocasionalmente.

occipital [ɒk'spɪtᵊl] *adj* occipital.

occult ['ɒkʌlt] *adj* oculto,-a. ● **the occult** las ciencias *fpl* ocultas, el ocultismo.

occultism ['ɒkʌltɪzᵊm] *n* ocultismo.

occupancy ['ɒkjəpənsɪ] *n* ocupación *f*.

occupant ['ɒkjəpənt] *n (gen)* ocupante *mf*; *(tenant)* inquilino,-a.

occupation [ɒkj'peɪʃᵊn] *n* **1** *(job)* ocupación *f*, profesión *f*. **2** *(pastime)* pasatiempo. **3** *(act, state of occupying)* ocupación *f*.

occupational [ɒkj'peɪʃᵊnəl] *adj* ocupacional, profesional.

occupied ['ɒkjəpaɪd] *adj* ocupado,-a.

occupier ['ɒkjəpaɪəʳ] *n* GB *(gen)* ocupante *mf*; *(tenant)* inquilino,-a.

occupy ['ɒkjəpaɪ] *vt* **1** *(live in)* ocupar, habitar, vivir en. **2** *(take possession of)* tomar posesión de, apoderarse de. **3** *(take up, fill - space)* ocupar; *(- time)* ocupar, llevar.
▲ *pt & pp* **occupied**, *ger* **occupying.**

occur [ə'kɜːʳ] *vi* **1** *(happen - event, incident)* ocurrir, suceder; *(- change)* producirse. **2** *fml (be found, exist)* existir, darse. **3** *(come to mind)* ocurrir, ocurrirse: **it never occurred to me to ask** *no se me ocurrió preguntar.*
▲ *pt & pp* **occurred**, *ger* **occurring.**

occurrence [ə'kʌrəns] *n* **1** *(event, incident)* suceso. **2** *fml (frequency)* incidencia, frecuencia; *(existing amount)* cantidad *f*.

ocean ['əʊʃᵊn] *n* océano.
▷ *adj* oceánico,-a: **ocean currents** *corrientes oceánicas.*

ocean-going ['əʊʃəngəʊɪŋ] *adj* de alta mar, de altura.

oceanic [əʊʃɪ'ænɪk] *adj fml* oceánico,-a.

oceanography [əʊʃən'ɒgrəfɪ] *n* oceanografía.

ocher ['əʊkəʳ] *adj* US ⟶ **ochre.**

ochre ['əʊkəʳ] *adj* (de color) ocre.
▷ *n* ochre *m.*

o'clock [ə'klɒk] *adv*: **it's one o'clock** *es la una;* **at three o'clock** *a las tres.*

octagon ['ɒktəgən] *n* octágono, octógono.

octagonal [ɒk'tægənᵊl] *adj* octagonal, octogonal.

octahedron [ɒkt'hiːdrən] *n* octaedro.

octane ['ɒkteɪn] *n* octano.

octave ['ɒktɪv] *n* octava.

octet [ɒk'tet] *n* octeto.

October [ɒk'təʊbəʳ] *n* octubre *m.*

Para ejemplos de uso, consulta **May.**

octogenarian [ɒktəʊdʒ'neərɪən] *n* octogenario,-a.

octopus ['ɒktəpəs] *n* pulpo.
▲ *pl* **octopuses.**

ocular ['ɒkjələʳ] *adj* ocular.

oculist ['ɒkjəlɪst] *n* oculista *mf.*

odd [ɒd] *adj* **1** *(strange)* extraño,-a, raro,-a: **the odd thing is that...** *lo raro es que...* **2** *(number)* impar. **3** *(approximately)* y pico: **thirty odd people** *unas treinta y pico personas.* **4** *(shoe, glove, etc)* suelto,-a, desparejado,-a. **5** *(left over, spare)* suelto,-a, de más: **have you got any odd coins?** *¿tienes algunas monedas sueltas?* **6** *(occasional)* ocasional. ■ **to be the odd man out 1** *(be over)* estar de más. **2** *(be different)* ser la excepción.
▷ *n pl* **odds 1** *(probability, chances)* probabilidades *fpl*, posibilidades *fpl*: **the odds are that...** *lo más probable es que...* **2** *(in betting)* apuestas *fpl* ■ **against (all) the odds** contra todo pronóstico.

oddball ['ɒdbɔːl] *n (person)* bicho raro, estrafalario,-a, excéntrico,-a.

oddity ['ɒdɪtɪ] *n* **1** *(thing)* cosa rara, rareza, curiosidad *f*; *(person)* bicho raro, estrafalario,-a.
▲ *pl* **oddities.**

odd-jobman [ɒd'dʒɒbmæn] *n* hombre *m* que hace trabajillos, hombre *m* para todo.
▲ *pl* **odd-jobmen** [ɒd'dʒɒbmen].

odd-looking ['ɒdlʊkɪŋ] *adj* de apariencia extraña.

oddly ['ɒdlɪ] *adv* de manera extraña, extrañamente.
■ **oddly enough** por extraño que parezca, curiosamente.

oddment ['ɒdmənt] *n* retal *m.*

odds-on ['ɒdzɒn] *adj* muy probable, casi seguro,-a.

ode [əʊd] *n* oda.

odious ['əʊdɪəs] *adj* odioso,-a, detestable.

odometer [əʊ'dɒmɪtəʳ] *n* US cuentakilómetros *m.*

odontology [ɒdɒn'tɒlədʒɪ] *n* odontología.

odor ['əʊdəʳ] *adj* US ⟶ **odour.**

odorous ['əʊdərəs] *adj fml* oloroso,-a, fragante.

odour ['əʊdəʳ] *n (smell)* olor *m*; *(fragrance)* perfume *m*, fragancia.

odourless ['əʊdələs] *adj* inodoro,-a.

odyssey ['ɒdɪsɪ] *n* odisea.

oenologist [iː'nɒlədʒɪst] *n* enólogo,-a.

oenology [iːˈnɒlədʒɪ] *n* enología.

oesophagus [iːˈsɒfəgəs] *n* esófago.
▲ *pl* oesophagi [iːˈsɒfəgaɪ].

oestrogen [ˈiːstrədʒᵊn] *n* estrógeno.

of [ɒv, *unstressed* əv] *prep* **1** *(belonging to)* de: a friend of mine *un amigo mío.* **2** *(made from)* de: shoes of Spanish leather *zapatos de piel española.* **3** *(containing)* de: a bag of crisps (US chips) *una bolsa de patatas.* **4** *(showing a part, a quantity)* de: a kilo of apples *un kilo de manzanas.* **5** *(partitive use)* de: the two of us *nosotros dos.* **6** *(dates, distance)* de: the 7th of August *el 7 de agosto.* **7** *(apposition)* de: the city of London *la ciudad de Londres.* **8** *(by)* de: the works of Shakespeare *las obras de Shakespeare.* **9** *(originating from, living in)* de: the people of Liverpool *los habitantes de Liverpool.* **10** *(depicting)* de: a map of Europe *un mapa de Europa.* **11** *(cause)* de: of one's own free will *por su propia voluntad.* **12** *(connected with)* de: the estimated time of arrival *la hora de llegada prevista.* **13** *(with, having)* de: a child of five *un niño de cinco años.* **14** *(description)* de: how kind of you to buy me flowers *qué amable de tu parte comprarme flores.* **15** *(after superlative)* de: best of all was the food *lo mejor de todo fue la comida.*

off [ɒf] *prep* **1** *(movement)* de: he got off the bus *bajó del autobús.* **2** *(indicating removal)* de: he cut a branch off the tree *cortó una rama del árbol.* **3** *(distance, situation)* *diferentes traducciones*: a narrow street off the main road *una callejuela que sale a la carretera;* the ship sank off Malpica *el barco se hundió a la altura de Malpica.* **4** *(away from)* *diferentes traducciones*: the ship went off course *el barco se desvió de su rumbo;* we're a long way off finding a cure *estamos lejos de encontrar una cura.* **5** *(not wanting)*: I'm off coffee *ya no tomo café.* **6** *(not at work)*: she comes off duty at 10.00pm *acaba el turno a las 10.00.* **7** *fam (from)* a: I bought it off Eva *se lo compré a Eva.*
▷ *adv* **1** *(departure)*: he ran off *se fue corriendo;* I'm off *me voy.* **2** *(showing distance)* a: the village is three miles off *el pueblo está a tres millas.* **3** *(in theatre)* en off: voices off *voces en off.* **4** *(removed)* fuera: leave the lid off *no pongas la tapa.* **5** *(reduced in price)* menos: 70% off! *¡70% menos!* **6** *(disconnected, not working)* *diferentes traducciones*: turn the light off *apaga la luz;* she turned the tap off *cerró el grifo.* **7** *(free, on holiday)* libre: can I have the afternoon off? *¿puedo tomarme la tarde libre?* ■ **off and on / on and off** de vez en cuando, a ratos. ‖ **right off / straight off** acto seguido.
▷ *adj* **1** *(event)* cancelado,-a, suspendido,-a: the wedding's off *la boda se ha suspendido.* **2** *(not turned on - gas, water)* cerrado,-a; *(- electricity)* apagado,-a. **3** *(impolite, unfriendly)* descortés, poco amable; *(below standard)* malo,-a. **4** *(food - bad)* malo,-a, pasado,-a; *(- unavailable)* acabado,-a: the milk's off *la leche está agria.* ● **off season** temporada baja.

offal [ˈɒfᵊl] *n* asaduras *fpl*, menudos *mpl*.

offbeat [ˈɒfbiːt] *adj* poco convencional.

off-center [ˈɒfˈsentəʳ] *adj* US → **off-centre**.

off-centre [ˈɒfˈsentəʳ] *adj* descentrado,-a.

off-color [ɒfˈkʌləʳ] *adj* US → **off-colour**.

off-colour [ɒfˈkʌləʳ] [Se escribe **off colour** cuando no se usa para calificar a un nombre.] *adj* **1** *(ill)* indispuesto,-a, pachucho,-a.

offcut [ˈɒfkʌt] *n* retal *m*.

offence [əˈfens] *n* **1** JUR delito, infracción *f*: a traffic offence *una infracción de tráfico.* **2** *(insult)* ofensa. ■ **to take offence at** STH ofenderse por ALGO, sentirse ofendido,-a por ALGO.

offend [əˈfend] *vt* **1** *(insult, hurt)* ofender: she'll be offended if we don't go *se ofenderá si no vamos.*
▷ *vi* **1** *fml (do wrong to)* atentar (**against**, a). **2** JUR *fml (commit crime)* cometer un delito.

offender [əˈfendəʳ] *n* **1** JUR *(gen)* infractor,-ra; *(criminal)* delincuente *mf*. **2** *(culprit)* culpable *mf*.

offending [əˈfendɪŋ] *adj (causing problems)* problemático,-a; *(unpleasant)* desagradable.

offense [ˈɒfens] *n* US *(in sport)* ataque *m*, ofensiva.

offensive [əˈfensɪv] *adj* **1** *(insulting)* ofensivo,-a, insultante. **2** *(disgusting - gen)* repugnante; *(- smell)* desagradable. **3** *(attacking)* ofensivo,-a.
▷ *n* MIL ofensiva.

offer [ˈɒfəʳ] *vt* **1** *(gen)* ofrecer: she offered us a coffee *nos ofreció un café.* **2** *(show willingness)* ofrecerse (**to** para): he offered me a lift to the airport *se ofreció para llevarme al aeropuerto.* **3** *(propose)* proponer, sugerir.
▷ *vi* **1** *(show willingness)* ofrecerse.
▷ *n* **1** *(gen)* oferta, ofrecimiento; *(proposal)* propuesta **2** COMM oferta. ■ **to be on offer 1** *(at reduced price)* estar de oferta. **2** *(available)* disponible.

offering [ˈɒfᵊrɪŋ] *n* **1** *(act)* ofrecimiento. **2** *(thing offered)* ofrenda; *(gift)* regalo.

offhand [ɒfˈhænd] *adj (abrupt)* brusco,-a; *(inconsiderate)* descortés, desconsiderado,-a.
▷ *adv* de improviso.

office [ˈɒfɪs] *n* **1** *(room)* despacho, oficina; *(building)* oficina; *(staff)* oficina. **2** GB ministerio: the Foreign Office *el Ministerio de Asuntos Exteriores.* **3** *(post, position)* cargo. ■ **to hold office** ocupar un cargo. ● **office block** edificio de oficinas. ‖ **office boy** recadero. ‖ **office worker** oficinista *mf*.

officer [ˈɒfɪsəʳ] *n* **1** MIL oficial *mf*. **2** *(police officer)* agente *mf*. **3** *(in government)* oficial *mf*, funcionario,-a. **4** *(of club, society)* directivo,-a.

official [əˈfɪʃᵊl] *adj (gen)* oficial.
▷ *n* funcionario,-a, oficial *mf*.

officially [əˈfɪʃᵊlɪ] *adv* oficialmente.

officiate [əˈfɪʃɪeɪt] *vi* **1** *(gen)* ejercer.

officious [əˈfɪʃəs] *adj (too eager)* oficioso,-a; *(interfering)* entrometido,-a.

off-key [ɒfˈkiː] *adj* desafinado,-a.

off-licence [ˈɒflaɪsᵊns] *n* GB tienda de bebidas alcohólicas.

off-load [ɒfˈləʊd] *vt* **1** *(unload)* descargar. **2** *(get rid of)* endilgar (**onto**, a).

off-peak [ˈɒfpiːk] *adj (times, hours)* fuera de las horas punta, de menor consumo.

off-putting [ˈɒfpʊtɪŋ] *adj* GB *fam (disconcerting)* desconcertante; *(unpleasant)* desagradable.

offset [*(vb)* ɒfˈset; *(n)* ˈɒfset] *vt* compensar.
▲ *pt & pp* offset, *ger* offsetting.
▷ *n (in printing)* offset *m*.

offshoot [ˈɒfʃuːt] *n* BOT renuevo, retoño, vástago.

offshore [ɒfˈʃɔːʳ] *adj* **1** *(at sea)* a poca distancia de la costa. **2** *(breeze)* terral, de tierra. **3** *(overseas)* en el extranjero.
▷ *adv* mar adentro.

offside [ɒf'saɪd] *adj* **1** SP fuera de juego. **2** GB *(part of vehicle)* del lado del conductor.
▷ *adv* SP en fuera de juego.
▷ *n* GB *(of vehicle)* lado del conductor.
offspring ['ɔːfsprɪŋ] *n* **1** *fml (child)* descendiente *mf*; *(children)* descendencia, prole *f*. **2** *(animal - one)* cría; *(- several)* crías *fpl*.
▲ *pl* offspring.
offstage [ɒf'steɪdʒ] *adj* entre bastidores.
▷ *adv* fuera del escenario.
off-the-cuff [ɒfðə'kʌf] *adj* improvisado,-a.
off-the-peg [ɒfðə'peg] *adj (clothes)* de confección.
off-the-record [ɒfðə'rekɔːd] *adj* extraoficial, confidencial.
off-white [ɒf'waɪt] *adj* de color hueso, blancuzco,-a.
often ['ɒfən, 'ɒftən] *adv (frequently)* a menudo, con frecuencia: we often go to the theatre *vamos al teatro a menudo.* ■ more often than not la mayoría de las veces.
ogle ['əʊgəl] *vt* comerse con los ojos.
▷ *vi* comerse con los ojos (at, a).
ogre ['əʊgəʳ] *n* ogro.
oh [əʊ] *interj* ¡oh!, ¡ay!, ¡vaya!: oh, really? *¿de veras?;* oh, look! *¡eh, mira!*
ohm [əʊm] *n* ohmio, ohm *m*.
oil [ɔɪl] *n* **1** *(gen)* aceite *m*: sunflower oil *aceite de girasol.* **2** *(petroleum)* petróleo: crude oil *crudo.* **3** ART *(painting)* óleo, pintura al óleo.
▷ *vt* engrasar, lubricar, lubrificar.
▷ *n pl* oils *(paints)* óleo: she paints in oils *pinta al óleo.* ● oil industry industria petrolera. ‖ oil painting cuadro al óleo, óleo. ‖ oil rig plataforma petrolífera. ‖ oil slick marea negra. ‖ oil tanker petrolero. ‖ oil well pozo petrolífero.
oilcan ['ɔɪlkæn] *n* aceitera.
oilcloth ['ɔɪlklɒθ] *n* hule *m*.
oilfield ['ɔɪlfiːld] *n* yacimiento petrolífero.
oilfired ['ɔɪlfaɪəd] *adj* de fuel-oil.
oiliness ['ɔɪlɪnəs] *n* untuosidad *f*.
oilskin ['ɔɪlskɪn] *n* hule *m*.
▷ *n pl* oilskins chubasquero *m sing*, traje *m sing* de hule.
oily ['ɔɪlɪ] *adj* **1** *(food)* aceitoso,-a, grasiento,-a; *(skin, hair)* graso,-a. **2** *pej (manner)* empalagoso,-a.
▲ *comp* oilier, *superl* oiliest.
ointment ['ɔɪntmənt] *n* ungüento, pomada.
okay [əʊ'keɪ] *interj* ¡vale!, ¡de acuerdo!
▷ *adj* correcto,-a, bien: are you okay? *¿estás bien?*
▷ *adv* bien, bastante bien: he's doing okay at school *va bien en el colegio.*
▷ *n* visto bueno, aprobación *f*.
▷ *vt* dar el visto bueno a: the boss okayed it *el jefe ha dado el visto bueno.*
old [əʊld] *adj* **1** *(person)* viejo,-a, mayor: an old man *un anciano, un hombre mayor, un viejo.* **2** *(thing)* viejo,-a, antiguo,-a; *(wine)* añejo,-a; *(clothes)* usado,-a: the old part of the city *el casco antiguo de la ciudad.* **3** *(long-established, familiar)* viejo,-a: he's an old friend *es un viejo amigo.* **4** *(former)* antiguo,-a: in my old job *en mi antiguo trabajo.* ■ how old are you? ¿cuántos años tienes?, ¿qué edad tienes? ‖ to be... years old tener... años. ● old age vejez *f*. ‖ old hand veterano,-a. ‖ old maid solterona. ‖ the Old World el viejo mundo.
▷ *n* the old las personas *fpl* mayores, los ancianos *mpl*.
olden ['əʊldən] *adj* antiguo,-a.
older ['əʊldəʳ] *adj* **1** *(comparative)* → old. **2** *(elder)* mayor.
old-fashioned [əʊld'fæʃənd] *adj (outdated - gen)* anticuado,-a, pasado,-a de moda; *(- person)* chapado,-a a la antigua.
old-time ['əʊldtaɪm] *adj* antiguo,-a.
old-timer [əʊld'taɪməʳ] *n* **1** *(in job, etc)* veterano,-a. **2** US *(old man)* viejo.
old-world ['əʊldwɜːld] *adj (of past)* tradicional, de los tiempos antiguos; *(quaint)* pintoresco,-a.
olfactory ['ɒlfæktərɪ] *adj* olfativo,-a, olfatorio,-a. ● olfactory nerve nervio olfativo.
oligarchy ['ɒlɪgɑːkɪ] *n* oligarquía.
▲ *pl* oligarchies.
olive ['ɒlɪv] *n* **1** *(tree, wood)* olivo. **2** *(fruit)* aceituna, oliva. **3** *(colour)* verde *m* oliva. ● olive oil aceite *m* de oliva. ‖ olive tree olivo.
▷ *adj (paint)* color aceituna; *(skin)* aceitunado,-a.
Olympiad [ə'lɪmpɪæd] *n* Olimpíada, Olimpiada.
Olympic [ə'lɪmpɪk] *adj* olímpico,-a.
▷ *n pl* the Olympics los Juegos Olímpicos, la Olimpíada *f sing*. ● Olympic Games Juegos *mpl* Olímpicos.
omega ['əʊmɪgə] *n* omega.
omelette ['ɒmlət] *n* tortilla. ● plain omelette tortilla francesa.
omen ['əʊmən] *n* agüero, presagio, augurio.
ominous ['ɒmɪnəs] *adj (foreboding evil)* de mal agüero, siniestro,-a; *(prophetic)* agorero,-a.
omission [əʊ'mɪʃən] *n* omisión *f*.
omit [əʊ'mɪt] *vt* **1** *(not include, leave out)* omitir, suprimir; *(forget to include)* olvidar incluir. **2** *(fail to do)* omitir, dejar de; *(forget)* olvidarse.
▲ *pt & pp* omitted, *ger* omitting.
omnibus ['ɒmnɪbəs] *n* **1** *dated (bus)* ómnibus *m*. **2** *(collection)* antología.
omnipotent [ɒm'nɪpətənt] *adj fml* omnipotente.
omnipresent [ɒmnɪ'prezənt] *adj fml* omnipresente.
omniscient [ɒm'nɪsɪənt] *adj fml* omnisciente.
omnivorous [ɒm'nɪvərəs] *adj* ZOOL *fml* omnívoro,-a.
on [ɒn] *prep* **1** *(covering or touching)* sobre, encima de, en: it's on the table *está encima de la mesa.* **2** *(supported by, hanging from)* en: she put the picture on the wall *colgó el cuadro en la pared.* **3** *(to, towards)* a, hacia: on the right/left *a la derecha/izquierda.* **4** *(at the edge of)* en: a village on the coast *un pueblo de la costa.* **5** *(concerning)* sobre: a tax on alcohol *un impuesto sobre el alcohol.* **6** *(travelling expressions)* de: we went on a journey *nos fuimos de viaje.* **7** *(days, dates, times) no se traduce*: on Saturday *el sábado.* **8** *(at the time of, just after)* al: on arriving *al llegar.* **9** *(as a result of) diferentes traducciones*: on your advice *siguiendo tus consejos.* **10** *(as means of transport)* a, en: on foot *a pie;* on the train *en el tren.* **11** *(regarding, about)* sobre, de: a book on art *un libro de arte.* **12** *(by means of)* por: I'm speaking on the phone *estoy hablando por teléfono.* **13** *(using)* con: cars run on petrol (US gas) *los coches funcionan con gasolina.* **14** *(state, process) diferentes traducciones*: it's on sale now *ya está a la venta;* on strike *en huelga.* **15** *(working for, belonging to) diferentes traducciones*: on the staff *en plantilla;* whose side are you on? *¿de parte de quién estás?* **16** *(in possession of)* con: have you got any money on you? *¿llevas dinero?* **17** *(paid for by)* pagado por: the drinks are on me! *¡invito yo!*

▷ *adv* **1** *(not stopping)* sin parar: **she kept on talking** *siguió hablando.* **2** *(movement forward) diferentes traducciones*: **walk on until you get to the church** *sigue hasta que llegues a la iglesia;* **it's time we were moving on** *es hora de que nos vayamos.* **3** *(clothes - being worn)* puesto,-a: **she had a cap on** *llevaba puesta una gorra.* **4** *(working) diferentes traducciones*: **who left the TV on?** *¿quién dejó la TV encendida?;* **don't leave the tap on!** *¡no dejes el grifo abierto!* **5** *(happening) diferentes traducciones*: **what time is the film on?** *¿a qué hora ponen la película?;* **have we got anything on this weekend?** *¿tenemos plan para este fin de semana?* ■ **and so on** y así sucesivamente. ‖ **from that day on** a partir de aquel día. ‖ **to go on and on about** STH seguir dale que dale con ALGO.

▷ *adj* **1** *(in use) diferentes traducciones*: **is the heating on?** *¿está puesta la calefacción?;* **all the lights were on** *todas las luces estaban encendidas.* **2** *(happening) diferentes traducciones*: **the strike's on** *la huelga sigue convocada;* **is the party still on?** *¿se hace la fiesta?;* **the match is on after all** *después de todo, el partido se celebra.* **3** *(performing) diferentes traducciones*: **you're on next!** *¡sales tú el próximo!;* **they're bringing the sub on** *hacen salir a jugar al suplente.* ■ **it's not on** no hay derecho, eso no vale. ‖ **you're on!** ¡trato hecho!

once [wʌns] *adv* **1** *(one time)* una vez: **once a week** *una vez por semana.* **2** *(formerly)* antes, en otro tiempo: **I was a cook once** *antes era cocinero.* ■ **all at once** de repente. ‖ **at once 1** *(at the same time)* a la vez, de una vez. **2** *(immediately)* en seguida, inmediatamente, ahora mismo. ‖ **once again** otra vez. ‖ **once and for all** de una vez para siempre, de una vez por todas. ‖ **once in a while** de vez en cuando. ‖ **once more** una vez más. ‖ **once upon a time** érase una vez.

▷ *conj* una vez que, en cuanto: **once everyone gets here, we can start** *una vez que lleguen todos, podemos empezar.*

▷ *n* vez *f*: **just this once** *solo esta vez.*

once-over ['wʌnsəʊvəʳ] *n fam* vistazo.

oncoming ['ɒnkʌmɪŋ] *adj* **1** *(traffic)* que viene en dirección contraria. **2** *(event, season)* venidero,-a, futuro,-a.

one [wʌn] *adj* **1** *(stating number)* un, una: **I've got one brother** *tengo un hermano.* **2** *(unspecified, a certain)* un, una, algún,-una: **one day in January** *un día de enero.* **3** *(only, single)* único,-a: **it's my one chance** *es mi única oportunidad.* **4** *(same)* mismo,-a: **in one direction** *en la misma dirección.*

▷ *pron* **1** *(thing)* uno,-a: **a red one** *uno,-a rojo,-a;* **this one** *éste,-a.* **2** *(person)* él, la: **he's the one who I was telling you about** *es él de quien te estaba hablando.* **3** *(any person, you)* uno, una: **one can't think of everything** *uno no puede pensar en todo.* ■ **at one with** en armonía con. ‖ **one after another** uno,-a detrás de otro,-a. ‖ **one another** el uno al otro. ‖ **one at a time** de uno en uno. ‖ **one by one** de uno,-a en uno,-a.

▷ *n (number)* uno: **my son is one today** *mi hijo cumple un año hoy.*

one-man ['wʌnmæn] *adj* individual.

oneness ['wʌnnəs] *n (unity)* unidad *f.*

one-night stand [wʌnnaɪt'stænd] *n (show)* representación *f* única.

one-off ['wʌnɒf] *adj* GB *fam* único,-a, irrepetible.

▷ *n* GB *fam* cosa única, fuera *mf* de serie.

one-parent family ['wʌnpeərənt'fæmᵊlɪ] *n* familia monoparental.

one-piece ['wʌnpi:s] *adj* de una sola pieza.

oneself [wʌn'self] *pron* **1** *(reflexive)* se; *(emphatic)* uno,-a mismo,-a; *(after prep)* sí mismo,-a: **to wash oneself** *lavarse.* **2** *(alone)* solo,-a: **one can't do everything oneself** *uno no puede hacerlo todo solo.* ■ **(all) by oneself** solo,-a. ‖ **to oneself** para sí, para sí solo,-a.

one-sided ['wʌn'saɪdɪd] *adj* **1** *(contest)* desigual. **2** *(view, account)* parcial.

one-time ['wʌntaɪm] *adj (former)* antiguo,-a, ex-.

one-to-one ['wʌntʊwʌn] *adj* **1** *(corresponding exactly)* con una correspondencia mutua, de uno a uno. **2** *(individual)* individualizado,-a, personal.

one-way ['wʌnweɪ] *adj* **1** *(street)* de sentido único, de dirección única. **2** *(ticket)* de ida.

ongoing ['ɒngəʊɪŋ] *adj (continuing)* continuo,-a; *(unresolved)* pendiente.

onion ['ʌnɪən] *n* cebolla.

onionskin ['ʌnɪənskɪn] *n* papel *m* cebolla.

online ['ɒnlaɪn] *adj* COMPUT en línea.

▷ *adv* COMPUT en línea.

onlooker ['ɒnlʊkəʳ] *n* espectador,-ra, curioso,-a.

only ['əʊnlɪ] *adj (sole)* único,-a: **the only problem is that...** *el único problema es que...* ● **only child** hijo,-a único,-a.

▷ *adv* **1** *(just, merely)* solo, solamente: **he's only a child** *solo es un niño.* **2** *(exclusively)* solo, solamente, únicamente: **only my mother knows** *mi madre es la única que lo sabe.* ■ **not only... but also** no solamente... sino también. ‖ **only just 1** *(a moment before)* acabar de. **2** *(almost not, scarcely)* por poco. ‖ **only too...** muy...

▷ *conj* pero: **it's like yoghurt, only better** *es como el yogur, pero mejor.*

onomatopoeia [ɒnəmæt'pi:ə] *n* onomatopeya.

onrush ['ɒnrʌʃ] *n (of people)* oleada, avalancha; *(of water)* riada, crecida.

onset ['ɒnset] *n* comienzo, aparición.

onshore [ɒn'ʃɔ:ʳ] *adj (on land)* en tierra.

▷ *adv (towards land)* tierra adentro.

onslaught ['ɒnslɔ:t] *n* ataque *m* violento.

onto ['ɒntʊ] *prep* **1** *(movement)* a, en: **it fell onto the floor** *cayó al suelo.* **2** *(new subject)* a: **let's move onto a different subject** *cambiemos de tema.*

onus ['əʊnəs] *n* responsabilidad *f.*

onward ['ɒnwəd] *adj* hacia adelante.

onwards ['ɒnwədz] *adv* GB adelante, hacia adelante: **from now onwards** *de ahora en adelante.*

onyx ['ɒnɪks] *n* ónice *m.*

oodles ['ʊ:dᵊlz] *n pl* montones *mpl.*

oops [ʊ:ps] *interj* ¡ay!, ¡uy!

ooze[1] [ʊ:z] *vi* rezumar.

▷ *vt* **1** rezumar. **2** *fig* rebosar, irradiar.

ooze[2] [ʊ:z] *n* cieno, lodo.

opacity [əʊ'pæsɪtɪ] *n* **1** *(non-transparency)* opacidad *f.* **2** *(obscurity)* oscuridad *f.*

opal ['əʊpᵊl] *n* ópalo.

opaque [əʊ'peɪk] *adj* **1** *(not transparent)* opaco,-a. **2** *(difficult to understand, obscure)* obscuro,-a, oscuro,-a, poco claro,-a.

open ['əʊpᵊn] *adj* **1** *(not closed - gen)* abierto,-a; *(- wound)* abierto,-a, sin cicatrizar: **I can't keep my eyes open** *no puedo mantener los ojos abiertos.* **2** *(not enclosed)* abier to,-a: **the open sea** *el mar abierto.* **3** *(not covered - gen)* descubierto,-a: **an open car** *un coche descapotable.* **4** *(not fastened, not folded)* abierto,-a; *(not buttoned)* desabrochado,-a, abierto,-a. **5** *(ready for customers)* abierto,-a; *(ready to start being used)* inaugurado,-a. **6** *(not settled)* sin resolver; *(not decided)* sin decidir, sin concretar: **an open question** *una cuestión sin resolver.* **7** *(available)* vacante. **8** *(not hidden, not limited)* abierto,-a, manifiesto,-a. **9** *(frank, honest)* abierto,-a, sincero,-a. **10** *(that anyone can enter)* abierto,-a, libre. ● **open day** jornada de puertas abiertas. | **open letter** carta abierta. | **open season** temporada de caza.

▷ *n* SP *(competition)* open *m.*

▷ *vt* **1** *(gen)* abrir: **open your mouth** *abre la boca.* **2** *(book, newspaper)* abrir; *(map)* abrir, desplegar: **she opened the book** *abrió el libro.* **3** *(start - gen)* abrir, iniciar. **4** *(begin, set up)* abrir, montar, poner; *(inaugurate, declare open)* abrir, inaugurar. **5** *(tunnel, road, mine, etc)* abrir. ■ **to open fire** abrir fuego (**on/at**, contra).

▷ *vi* **1** *(gen)* abrir, abrirse: **the door opened** *la puerta se abrió.* **2** *(spread out, unfold)* abrirse: **the roses are opening** *las rosas se están abriendo.* **3** *(start - conference, play, book)* comenzar, empezar; *(film)* estrenarse. **4** *(begin business)* abrir.

▷ *adj* **open to** *(susceptible)* susceptible a, expuesto,-a a; *(receptive)* abierto,-a a.

▷ *n* **the open** *(the outdoors, open air)* campo, aire *m* libre.

⊙ **to open into / open onto** *vt insep* dar a: **the back door opens onto the patio** *la puerta trasera da al patio.*

⊙ **to open out** *vi* **1** *(develop - person)* volverse más abierto,-a; *(- flower)* abrirse. **2** *(become wider)* ensancharse; *(unfold)* abrirse.

⊙ **to open up** *vt sep (make available)* abrir (**to**, a).

▷ *vi* **1** *(become available)* abrirse (**to**, a). **2** *(unlock)* abrir.

open-air ['əupᵊneəʳ] *adj* al aire libre.

open-and-shut ['əupᵊnənʃʌt] *adj* claro, a, evidente.

opencast ['əupᵊnkɑ:st] *adj* GB a cielo abierto.

open-ended [əupᵊn'endɪd] *adj (indefinite - contract)* de duración indefinida; *(- discussion)* abierto,-a.

opener ['əupᵊnəʳ] *n* abridor *m.*

open-handed [əupᵊn'hændɪd] *adj (generous)* generoso,-a, dadivoso,-a.

open-heart ['əupᵊnhɑ:t] *adj (surgery)* a corazón abierto.

open-hearted [əupᵊn'hɑ:tɪd] *adj (kind)* de gran corazón; *(candid)* sincero,-a.

opening ['əupᵊnɪŋ] *n* **1** *(ceremony - gen)* inauguración *f*, comienzo. **2** *(first night)* estreno. **3** *(process of opening, unfolding)* apertura. **4** *(hole)* abertura; *(space)* hueco; *(gap)* brecha; *(clearing)* claro. **5** *(chance)* oportunidad *f* (**for**, para). **6** *(vacancy)* vacante *f* (**for**, para). ● **opening hours** horario de apertura.

▷ *adj (initial)* inicial.

openly ['əupᵊnlɪ] *adv (not secretly)* abiertamente; *(publicly)* públicamente, en público.

open-minded [əupᵊn'maɪndɪd] *adj* abierto,-a, de actitud abierta.

open-mouthed [əupᵊn'mauðd] *adj* boquiabierto,-a.

openness ['əupᵊnnəs] *n (frankness)* franqueza; *(receptiveness)* actitud *f* abierta.

open-plan ['əupᵊnplæn] *adj* de planta abierta.

opera ['ɒpᵊrə] *n* ópera.

operate ['ɒpəreɪt] *vt* **1** *(machine, etc)* hacer funcionar, manejar, operar. **2** *(manage, run - business)* dirigir, manejar, llevar.

▷ *vi* **1** *(function - machine, etc)* funcionar. **2** *(carry on trade)* operar; *(work)* trabajar. **3** MED operar (**on**, a), intervenir (**on**, a).

operatic [ɒp'rætɪk] *adj* de ópera, operístico,-a.

operating ['ɒpəreɪtɪŋ] *adj* COMM *(losses, costs)* de explotación. ● **operating room** US quirófano. | **operating system** COMPUT sistema *m* operativo. | **operating theatre** GB quirófano.

operation [ɒp'reɪʃᵊn] *n* **1** MED operación *f*, intervención *f*. **2** *(of machine - gen)* funcionamiento; *(- by person)* manejo; *(of system)* uso. **3** *(activity)* operación *f*; *(planned campaign)* campaña. **4** MIL operación *f*. **5** MATH operación *f*.

operational [ɒp'reɪʃᵊnəl] *adj* **1** *(ready for use)* operativo,-a, listo,-a para usar; *(in use)* en funcionamiento. **2** *(ocurring in practice)* de operación, operativo,-a.

operative ['ɒpᵊrətɪv] *adj* **1** *(in force)* vigente; *(effective)* operativo,-a; *(operating, in use)* en funcionamiento.

▷ *n (worker)* operario,-a; *(spy)* agente *mf.*

operator ['ɒpəreɪtəʳ] *n* **1** *(of equipment, machine)* operario,-a. **2** *(of switchboard)* operador,-ra, telefonista *mf.*

operetta [ɒp'retə] *n* opereta.

ophthalmologist [ɒfθæl'mɒlədʒɪst] *n* oftalmólogo,-a, oculista *mf.*

opinion [ə'pɪnɪən] *n* **1** *(belief)* opinión *f*, parecer *m.* **2** *(evaluation, estimation)* opinión *f*, concepto. ■ **in my opinion** en mi opinión, a mi juicio. ● **opinion poll** encuesta.

opinionated [ə'pɪnɪəneɪtɪd] *adj* dogmático,-a.

opium ['əupɪəm] *n* opio.

opponent [ə'pəunənt] *n* adversario,-a, oponente *mf.*

opportune ['ɒpətju:n] *adj* oportuno,-a.

opportunist [ɒp'tju:nɪst] *n* oportunista *mf.*

opportunity [ɒp'tju:nɪtɪ] *n* **1** *(gen)* oportunidad *f*, ocasión *f*. **2** *(prospect)* perspectiva.

▲ *pl* **opportunities.**

oppose [ə'pəuz] *vt* oponerse a.

opposed [ə'pəuzd] *adj* opuesto,-a, contrario,-a.

opposing [ə'pəuzɪŋ] *adj* contrario,-a, opuesto,-a.

opposite ['ɒpəzɪt] *adj* **1** *(facing)* de enfrente: **she lives on the opposite side of the road** *vive al otro lado de la calle.* **2** *(contrary, different)* opuesto,-a, contrario,-a.

▷ *prep* enfrente de, frente a: **the building opposite the cinema** *el edificio enfrente del cine.*

▷ *adv* enfrente: **the family who live opposite** *la familia que vive enfrente.*

▷ *n* lo contrario, lo opuesto: **the opposite of big is small** *lo contrario a grande es pequeño.*

opposition [ɒpə'zɪʃᵊn] *n* **1** *(resistance)* oposición *f*, resistencia. **2** *(rivals - in sport)* adversarios *mpl*; *(- in business)* competencia.

▷ *n* **the Opposition** POL la oposición *f.*

oppress [ə'pres] *vt* **1** *(rule)* oprimir. **2** *(make uncomfortable)* agobiar.

oppression [ə'preʃᵊn] *n* opresión *f.*

oppressive [ə'presɪv] *adj* opresivo,-a, agobiante.

oppressor [ə'presəʳ] *n* opresor,-ra.

opt [ɒpt] *vi* optar (**for**, por).

⊙ **to opt out** *vi (person)* abandonar, dejar de participar.

optative ['ɒptətɪv] *adj* optativo,-a.
optic ['ɒptɪk] *adj* óptico,-a.
optical ['ɒptɪkᵊl] *adj* óptico,-a.
optician [ɒp'tɪʃᵊn] *n* óptico,-a, oculista *mf*. ● **optician's (shop)** óptico.
optics ['ɒptɪks] *n* óptica.
optimism ['ɒptɪmɪzᵊm] *n* optimismo.
optimist ['ɒptɪmɪst] *n* optimista *mf*.
optimistic [ɒptɪ'mɪstɪk] *adj* optimista.
optimize ['ɒptɪmaɪz] *vt* optimizar.
optimum ['ɒptɪməm] *adj* óptimo,-a.
option ['ɒpʃᵊn] *n* **1** *(choice)* opción *f*, posibilidad *f*. **2** EDUC *(optional subject)* asignatura optativa.
optional ['ɒpʃᵊnəl] *adj* opcional.
opulence ['ɒpjələns] *n* opulencia.
opulent ['ɒpjələnt] *adj* opulento,-a.
or [ɔːʳ] *conj* **1** *(alternative - gen)* o; *(- before word beginning with* o *or* ho) u: **tea or coffee** *té o café*. **2** *(with negative)* ni: **she can't sing or dance** *no sabe cantar ni bailar*. **3** *(otherwise)* o: **come on, or we'll be late!** *¡date prisa o llegaremos tarde!* ■ **or so** más o menos.
oracle ['ɒrəkᵊl] *n* oráculo.
oral ['ɔːrᵊl] *adj* **1** *(spoken - gen)* oral; *(tradition)* transmitido,-a oralmente. **2** MED *(contraceptive)* oral; *(hygiene)* bucal.
▷ *n (exam)* examen *m* oral.
orange ['ɒrɪndʒ] *n* **1** *(fruit)* naranja. **2** *(colour)* naranja *m*. ● **orange blossom** azahar *m*. ‖ **orange tree** naranjo.
▷ *adj* naranja, de color naranja.
orangey ['ɒrɪndʒɪ] *adj* **1** *(colour)* anaranjado,-a. **2** *(taste)* con sabor a naranja.
orang-utan [ɔːræŋuː'tæn] *n* orangután *m*.
oration [ɔː'reɪʃᵊn] *n* oración *f*, discurso.
orator ['ɒrətəʳ] *n* orador,-ra.
oratorio [ɒr'tɔːrɪəʊ] *n* oratorio.
oratory ['ɒrətᵊrɪ] *n (art of speaking)* oratoria.
orb [ɔːb] *n* **1** *(jewelled ball)* orbe *m*. **2** *fml lit (sphere)* esfera; *(sun)* el sol *m*; *(moon)* la luna.
orbit ['ɔːbɪt] *n* **1** *(of satellite)* órbita. **2** *(area of influence)* órbita, esfera de influencia, ámbito. ■ **to go into orbit** entrar en órbita.
▷ *vt* girar alrededor de, orbitar alrededor de.
orbital ['ɔːbɪtᵊl] *adj* orbital, orbitario,-a. ● **orbital road** carretera de circunvalación.
orchard ['ɔːtʃəd] *n* huerto.
orchestra ['ɔːkɪstrə] *n* orquesta.
orchestral [ɔː'kestrəl] *adj (music)* orquestal; *(musician)* de orquesta.
orchestrate ['ɔːkɪstreɪt] *vt* **1** MUS orquestar. **2** *(campaign, etc)* organizar, montar, orquestar.
orchid ['ɔːkɪd] *n* BOT orquídea.
ordain [ɔː'deɪn] *vt* **1** REL *(priest)* ordenar. **2** *fml (decree)* decretar, ordenar.
ordeal [ɔː'diːl] *n (bad experience)* mala experiencia, terrible experiencia.
order ['ɔːdəʳ] *n* **1** *(sequence)* orden *m*, serie *f*: **in alphabetical/chronological order** *por orden alfabético/cronológico*. **2** *(condition, organization)* orden *m*, concierto: **she put her affairs in order** *puso sus asuntos en orden*. **3** *(fitness for use)* condiciones *fpl*, estado: **the car's in good working order** *el coche funciona bien*. **4** *(obedience, authority, discipline)* orden *m*, disciplina. **5** *(rules, procedures, etc)* orden *m*, procedimiento. **6** *(command)* orden *f*. **7** COMM *(request, goods)* pedido: **the waiter took our order** *el camarero tomó nota de lo que queríamos*. **8** *(group, society)* orden *f*; *(badge, sign worn)* condecoración *f*, orden *f*: **the monastic orders** *las órdenes monásticas*. ■ **in order that** para que, a fin de que. ‖ **in order to** para, a fin de. ‖ **out of order** *(not working)* que no funciona. ● **order form** hoja de pedido.
▷ *vt* **1** *(command)* ordenar, mandar. **2** *(ask for)* pedir, encargar: **I've ordered a cake for his birthday** *he encargado un pastel para su cumpleaños*. **3** *(arrange, put in order, organize)* ordenar, poner en orden.
▷ *vi (request to bring, ask for)* pedir.
⊙ **to order about / order around** *vt sep* mangonear, dar órdenes.
⊙ **to order off** *vt sep* SP expulsar.
⊙ **to order out** *vt sep* mandar salir.
ordered ['ɔːdəd] *adj* ordenado,-a.
orderly ['ɔːdəlɪ] *adj* **1** *(tidy)* ordenado,-a, metódico,-a. **2** *(well-behaved)* disciplinado,-a.
▷ *n (in hospital)* camillero,-a.
ordinal ['ɔːdɪnᵊl] *adj* ordinal.
▷ *n* ordinal *m*.
ordinarily ['ɔːdənərɪlɪ] *adv* generalmente.
ordinary ['ɔːdɪnᵊrɪ] *adj (usual, normal)* normal, usual, habitual; *(average)* normal, común. ● **ordinary seaman** marinero.
ordinate ['ɔːdɪnət] *n* MATH ordenada.
ordination [ɔːdɪ'neɪʃᵊn] *n* ordenación *f*.
ordnance ['ɔːdnəns] *n* MIL *(artillery)* artillería; *(supplies)* pertrechos *mpl*.
ore [ɔːʳ] *n* mineral *m*, mena.
oregano [ɒrɪ'gɑːnəʊ] *n* orégano.
organ ['ɔːgᵊn] *n* órgano.
organic [ɔː'gænɪk] *adj* **1** *(living)* orgánico,-a. **2** *(without chemicals)* biológico,-a, ecológico,-a.
organism ['ɔːgənɪzᵊm] *n* organismo.
organist ['ɔːgənɪst] *n* organista *mf*.
organization [ɔːgənaɪ'zeɪʃᵊn] *n* organización *f*.
organizational [ɔːgənaɪ'zeɪʃᵊnəl] *adj* organizativo,-a, de organización.
organize ['ɔːgənaɪz] *vt* organizar, ordenar.
▷ *vi* organizar.
organized ['ɔːgənaɪzd] *adj (gen)* organizado,-a.
organizer ['ɔːgənaɪzəʳ] *n* organizador,-ra.
orgasm ['ɔːgæzᵊm] *n* orgasmo.
orgiastic [ɔːdʒɪ'æstɪk] *adj* orgiástico,-a.
orgy ['ɔːdʒɪ] *n (wild party)* orgía.
▲ *pl* **orgies**.
Orient ['ɔːrɪənt] *n* **the Orient** el oriente *m*.
oriental [ɔːrɪ'entᵊl] *adj* oriental.
▷ *n* oriental *mf*.
orientate ['ɔːrɪənteɪt] *vt* orientar.
orientation [ɔːrɪen'teɪʃᵊn] *n* orientación *f*.
orienteering [ɔːrɪən'tɪərɪŋ] *n* orientación *f*.
orifice ['ɒrɪfɪs] *n* orificio.
origin ['ɒrɪdʒɪn] *n* origen *m*.
▷ *n pl* **origins** origen *m sing*.
original [ə'rɪdʒɪnᵊl] *adj* **1** *(first, earliest)* original, originario,-a, primero,-a. **2** *(not copied)* original. **3** *(new, different)* original.
▷ *n* original *m*.

originality [ərɪdʒɪ'nælɪtɪ] *n* originalidad *f.*
originally [ə'rɪdʒɪnəlɪ] *adv* **1** *(in the beginning)* originariamente, en un principio. **2** *(in a new way)* con originalidad.
originate [ə'rɪdʒɪneɪt] *vt (create)* originar, crear, dar lugar a.
▷ *vi (arise)* tener su origen (in, en), originarse (in, en), provenir (in, de).
ornament ['ɔ:nəmənt] *n (decoration)* ornamento, adorno; *(object)* adorno.
ornamental [ɔ:n'mentᵊl] *adj* decorativo,-a.
ornate [ɔ:'neɪt] *adj* **1** *(richly decorated)* ornamentado,-a, elaborado,-a. **2** *pej (overdecorated, too complicated)* recargado,-a.
ornithologist [ɔ:nɪ'θɒlədʒɪst] *n* ornitólogo,-a.
ornithology [ɔ:nɪ'θɒlədʒɪ] *n* ornitología.
orographic [ɒr'græfɪk] *adj* orográfico,-a.
orography [ɒ'rɒgrəfɪ] *n* orografía.
orphan ['ɔ:fᵊn] *n* huérfano,-a.
▷ *vt* dejar huérfano,-a ■ **to be orphaned** quedar huérfano,-a.
orphanage ['ɔ:fᵊnɪdʒ] *n* orfanato.
orthodox ['ɔ:θədɒks] *adj* ortodoxo,-a.
orthodoxy ['ɔ:θədɒksɪ] *n* ortodoxia.
orthographic [ɔ:θ'græfɪk] *adj* ortográfico,-a.
orthography [ɔ:'θɒgrəfɪ] *n* ortografía.
orthopaedic [ɔ:θəʊ'pi:dɪk] *adj* MED ortopédico,-a.
Oscar ['ɒskəʳ] *n* Óscar *m.*
Oscar-winning ['ɒskəwɪnɪŋ] *adj* ganador,-ra del Óscar.
oscillate ['ɒsɪleɪt] *vi (vacillate)* oscilar, vacilar.
oscillation [ɒsɪ'leɪʃᵊn] *n* oscilación *f.*
oscillator ['ɒsɪleɪtəʳ] *n* oscilador *m.*
osmosis [ɒz'məʊsɪs] *n* ósmosis *f*, osmosis *f.*
ostensible [ɒ'stensɪbᵊl] *adj (apparent)* aparente; *(alleged)* pretendido,-a, fingido,-a.
ostentation [ɒsten'teɪʃᵊn] *n* ostentación *f.*
ostentatious [ɒsten'teɪʃəs] *adj* ostentoso,-a.
osteopath ['ɒstɪəpæθ] *n* MED osteópata *mf.*
osteopathy [ɒstɪ'ɒpəθɪ] *n* osteopatía.
ostracism ['ɒstrəsɪzᵊm] *n* ostracismo.
ostracize ['ɒstrəsaɪz] *vt* **1** *(from society)* condenar al ostracismo. **2** *(from group)* aislar, excluir, hacer el vacío a.
ostrich ['ɒstrɪtʃ] *n* avestruz *m.*
other ['ʌðəʳ] *adj* **1** *(additional)* otro,-a: I have one other idea *tengo otra idea.* **2** *(different)* otro,-a: people from other countries *gente de otros países.* **3** *(second, remaining)* otro,-a: it's on the other side of the street *está al otro lado de la calle.* ■ **every other day** un día sí, otro no. ‖ **the other day** el otro día.
▷ *pron* otro,-a. ■ **one after the other** uno tras otro.
▷ *prep* **other than** *(except)* aparte de, salvo: there was nobody other than the teacher *aparte del profesor, no había nadie.*
otherwise ['ʌðəwaɪz] *adv* **1** *(differently)* de otra manera, de manera distinta: she couldn't do otherwise *no podía obrar de otra manera.* **2** *(apart from that, in other respects)* aparte de eso, por lo demás.
▷ *conj (if not)* si no, de no ser así, de lo contrario.
▷ *adj* distinto,-a.
otitis [əʊ'taɪtɪs] *n* otitis *f.*
otter ['ɒtəʳ] *n* nutria.

Ottoman ['ɒtəmən] *adj* otomano,-a.
ouch [aʊtʃ] *interj* ¡ay!
ought [ɔ:t] *aux* **ought to** **1** *(moral obligation)* deber: you ought to have helped them *debiste ayudarles.* **2** *(recommendation)* deber, tener que. **3** *(expectation)* deber de: they ought to be home by now *seguramente ya estarán en casa.*
ounce [aʊns] *n* **1** *(weight)* onza. **2** *fam (small quantity)* pizca.

La onza equivale a 28,35 gramos.

our [aʊəʳ] *adj* nuestro,-a: our house *nuestra casa;* our children *nuestros hijos.*
ours [aʊəz] *pron* (el) nuestro, (la) nuestra: a friend of ours *un amigo nuestro.*
ourselves [aʊ'selvz] *pron* **1** *(reflexive)* nos: we made ourselves comfortable *nos pusimos cómodos.* **2** *(emphatic)* nosotros,-as mismos,-as: we did it ourselves *lo hicimos nosotros mismos.*
oust [aʊst] *vt* **1** *(from position, job, etc)* desbancar. **2** *(from land, property)* expulsar.
out [aʊt] *adv* **1** *(outside)* fuera, afuera: could you wait out there? *¿podrías esperar allí fuera?* **2** *(move outside)* fuera: she ran out *salió corriendo.* **3** *(not in)* fuera. **4** *(expressing distance)* en: they live out in the country *viven en el campo.* **5** *(expressing removal) diferentes traducciones*: I've had a tooth out *me han sacado una muela;* she got out a handkerchief *sacó un pañuelo.* **6** *(showing disappearance) diferentes traducciones*: rub that word out *borra esa palabra;* our money ran out *se nos acabó el dinero.* **7** *(available, existing) diferentes traducciones*: the film comes out next month *la película se estrenará el mes que viene;* it's the best sandwich out *es el mejor bocadillo que hay.* **8** *(known) diferentes traducciones*: your secret's out *tu secreto ha salido a la luz;* the news is out *se sabe la noticia.* **9** *(flowers)* en flor; *(sun, stars, etc)* que ha salido: the sun's out *ha salido el sol.* **10** *(protruding)* que se sale: a nail sticking out *un clavo que sobresale.* **11** *(clearly, loudly)* en voz alta: he called out to me *me llamó en voz alta.* **12** *(to the end)* hasta el final; *(completely)* completamente, totalmente.
▷ *adj* **1** *(extinguished)* apagado,-a: the lights are out *las luces están apagadas.* **2** *(unconscious)* inconsciente; *(asleep)* dormido,-a. **3** SP *(defeated)* eliminado,-a; *(out of play)* fuera. **4** *(not fashionable)* pasado,-a de moda. **5** *(out of order)* estropeado,-a. **6** *(on strike)* en huelga. **7** *(tide)* bajo,-a. **8** *(over, finished)* acabado,-a: school's out *han terminado las clases.*
▷ *prep fam (out of)* por: she ran out the door *salió por la puerta.*
▷ *prep* **out of** **1** *(away from, no longer in)* fuera de. **2** *(from a state of)* fuera de: out of danger *fuera de peligro.* **3** *(not involved in)* fuera de: they are out of the cup *han quedado fuera de la copa.* **4** *(from among)* de: she got five out of ten in French *sacó (un) cinco sobre diez en francés.* **5** *(without)* sin: out of money *sin dinero.* **6** *(using, made from)* de: made out of wood *hecho,-a de madera.*
out-and-out ['aʊtənaʊt] *adj* empedernido,-a.
outboard motor [aʊtbɔ:d'məʊtəʳ] *n* MAR motor *m* fueraborda, fueraborda *m.*
outbound ['aʊtbaʊnd] *adj* que parte, que sale.
outbreak ['aʊtbreɪk] *n* **1** *(of violence, fighting)* brote *m;* **2** *(of disease)* brote *m*, epidemia; *(of spots)* erupción *f.*

outbuilding ['autbɪldɪŋ] *n* dependencia.
outburst ['autbɜːst] *n* **1** *(of emotion)* explosión *f*, arrebato *m*. **2** *(of activity)* explosión *f*.
outcast ['autkɑːst] *n* marginado,-a.
outclass ['autklɑːs] *vt* superar, aventajar.
outcome ['autkʌm] *n* resultado.
outcry ['autkraɪ] *n* protesta.
▲ *pl* outcries.
outdated [aut'deɪtɪd] *adj* anticuado,-a.
outdo [aut'duː] *vt* superar, ganar, sobrepasar.
▲ *pt* outdid [aut'dɪd], *pp* outdone [aut'dʌn].
outdoor [aut'dɔːʳ] *adj (gen)* exterior.
outdoors [aut'dɔːʳz] *adv* fuera, al aire libre.
outer ['autəʳ] *adj* exterior, externo,-a.
outermost ['autərməust] *adj (outer)* exterior; *(furthest away)* más remoto,-a.
outfit ['autfɪt] *n* **1** *(clothes)* conjunto; *(uniform)* uniforme *m*. **2** *fam (group of people)* grupo, equipo; *(organization)* organización *f*.
outgoing [aut'gəuɪŋ] *adj* **1** *(departing)* saliente. **2** *(sociable)* sociable, extrovertido,-a.
▷ *n pl* **outgoings** gastos *mpl*.
outgrow [aut'grəu] *vt (clothes, etc)* hacerse demasiado grande para: **he's outgrown his shoes** *se le han quedado pequeños los zapatos*.
▲ *pt* outgrew [aut'gruː], *pp* outgrown [aut'grəun].
outing ['autɪŋ] *n (trip)* salida, excursión *f*.
outlandish [aut'lændɪʃ] *adj (strange, unusual)* extravagante, estrafalario,-a.
outlast [aut'lɑːst] *vt (gen)* durar más que
outlaw ['autlɔː] *n* forajido,-a, proscrito,-a.
▷ *vt* prohibir, declarar ilegal.
outlay [*(n)* 'autleɪ; *(vb)* aut'leɪ] *n* inversión.
outlet ['autlet] *n* **1** *(opening - gen)* salida; *(for water)* desagüe *m*. **2** *fig (for emotions)* válvula de escape. **3** COMM *(shop)* punto de venta.
outline ['autlaɪn] *n* **1** *(outer edge)* contorno; *(shape)* perfil *m*. **2** *(draft)* bosquejo, esquema *m*; *(summary)* resumen *m*.
▷ *vt* **1** *(sketch)* bosquejar. **2** *(summarize)* resumir.
outlive [aut'lɪv] *vt* sobrevivir a.
outlook ['autluk] *n* **1** *(point of view, attitude)* punto de vista (on, ante). **2** *(prospect)* perspectiva, panorama *m*.
outlying ['autlaɪɪŋ] *adj* **1** *(remote)* alejado,-a, distante. **2** *(suburban)* periférico,-a.
outmanoeuvre [autməˈnuːvəʳ] *vt (opponent)* superar estratégicamente.
outmoded [aut'məudɪd] *adj* anticuado,-a.
outnumber [aut'nʌmbəʳ] *vt* ser más que.
out-of-date [autəv'deɪt] *adj (fashion)* pasado,-a de moda; *(technology)* desfasado,-a, obsoleto,-a; *(food, ticket)* caducado,-a.
out-of-the-way [autəvðəˈweɪ] *adj* **1** *(distant)* alejado, -a, distante. **2** *(uncommon)* poco corriente, insólito,-a.
outpost ['autpəust] *n* MIL avanzada.
output ['autput] *n* **1** *(gen)* producción *f*; *(of machine)* rendimiento. **2** COMPUT salida.
outrage ['autreɪdʒ] *n* **1** *(anger, resentment)* indignación *f* (at, ante). **2** *(violent action)* atrocidad *f*. **3** *(scandal)* escándalo.
▷ *vt (make angry)* ultrajar, indignar.
outrageous [aut'reɪdʒəs] *adj* **1** *(shocking - gen)* escandaloso,-a; *(crime)* atroz; *(language)* injurioso,-a; **2** *(unconventional)* extravagante.
outrider ['autraɪdəʳ] *n* escolta *mf*.
outright [*(adj)*'autraɪt; *(adv)* aut'raɪt] *adj* **1** *(gen)* absoluto,-a, total, rotundo, indiscutible. **2** *(direct - attack)* declarado,-a, abierto,-a; *(- lie)* descarado,-a.
▷ *adv* **1** *(completely - refuse)* rotundamente, categóricamente; *(ban)* totalmente; *(win)* indiscutiblemente. **2** *(directly - ask, say)* directamente, abiertamente. **3** *(instantly)* en el acto.
outrun [aut'rʌn] *vt* **1** *(run faster than)* correr más rápido que, dejar atrás. **2** *fig* superar.
▲ *pt* outran [aut'ræn], *pp* outrun [aut'rʌn], *ger* outrunning.
outsell [aut'sel] *vt* venderse más que.
▲ *pt & pp* outsold [aut'səuld].
outset ['autset] *n* comienzo, principio. ■ **at the outset** al principio.
outshine [aut'ʃaɪn] *vt* eclipsar.
▲ *pt & pp* outshone [aut'ʃɒn].
outside [*(n)* aut'saɪd, *(prep)* 'autsaɪd] *n* **1** *(exterior part)* exterior *m*, parte *f* exterior: **from the outside** *desde fuera*. **2** GB *(when driving)* derecha.
▷ *prep* **1** *(gen)* fuera de. **2** *(beyond)* más allá de, fuera de: **outside working hours** *fuera del horario laboral*. **3** *(other than)* aparte de, fuera de.
▷ *adv (gen)* fuera, afuera.
▷ *adj* **1** *(exterior)* exterior. **2** *(external)* externo,-a. **3** *(remote)* remoto,-a. ■ **at the outside** como máximo como mucho.
outsider [aut'saɪdəʳ] *n* **1** *(person- stranger)* extraño,-a forastero,-a, desconocido,-a. **2** *(unlikely winner athlete, etc)* competidor,-ra con pocas probabilidades de ganar.
outsize ['autsaɪz] *adj* enorme.
outskirts ['autskɜːts] *n pl* afueras *fpl*, alrededore *mpl*, extrarradio *m sing*.
outsmart [aut'smɑːt] *vt* burlar, engañar.
outspoken [aut'spəukᵊn] *adj* franco,-a.
outspread [aut'spred] *adj (wing)* extendido,-a, desplegado,-a; *(arm)* abierto,-a.
outstanding [aut'stændɪŋ] *adj* **1** *(excellent)* destacado,-a, notable, sobresaliente; *(exceptional)* excepcional, singular. **2** *(gen)* sin pagar, pendiente.
outstretched [aut'stretʃt] *adj* extendido,-a.
outstrip [aut'strɪp] *vt* **1** *(run faster than)* correr más rápido que, dejar atrás. **2** *(become greater than)* sobrepasar.
▲ *pt & pp* outstripped, *ger* outstripping.
outvote [aut'vəut] *vt (person)* derrotar; *(proposal, etc)* vencer.
outward ['autwəd] *adj* **1** *(appearance)* exterior; *(sign)* externo,-a, show. **2** *(journey, flight)* de ida.
outwards ['autwəðʒ] *adv (gen)* hacia fuera, hacia afuera; *(attention, etc)* hacia el exterior.
outweigh [aut'weɪ] *vt (weigh more than)* pesar más que
outwit [aut'wɪt] *vt* ser más listo,-a que.
▲ *pt & pp* outwitted, *ger* outwitting.
oval ['əuvᵊl] *adj* oval, ovalado,-a.
▷ *n* óvalo.
ovary ['əuvərɪ] *n* ovario.
▲ *pl* ovaries.
ovation [əu'veɪʃᵊn] *n* ovación *f*.

oven ['ʌvᵊn] *n* horno.
ovenproof ['ʌvᵊnpru:f] *adj* refractario,-a.
ovenware ['ʌvᵊnweəʳ] *n* vajilla refractaria.
over ['əʊvəʳ] *adv* **1** *(down) diferentes traducciones*: the boy fell over *el niño se cayó;* I knocked the glass over *tiré la copa (de un golpe).* **2** *(from one side to another) diferentes traducciones*: turn over the page *dar la vuelta a la página;* he bent over *se inclinó.* **3** *(across) diferentes traducciones*: let's cross over *crucemos al otro lado;* over here/there *aquí/allí.* **4** *(everywhere, throughout)* en todas partes: the lake is frozen over *el lago está completamente helado.* **5** *(again)* otra vez: let's start over (again) *volvamos a empezar.* **6** *(remaining)* sobrante: are there any strawberries (left) over? *¿quedan fresas?* **7** *(too much)* de más: it's 50 grams over *pesa 50 gramos de más.* **8** *(more)* más; *(older)* mayor. ■ over here aquí. ‖ over there allí.
▷ *prep* **1** *(above, higher than)* encima de: a sign over the door *un letrero encima de la puerta.* **2** *(covering, on top of)* sobre, encima de: he wore a jacket over his sweater *llevaba una americana encima del jersey.* **3** *(across)* sobre; *(on the other side of)* al otro lado de: he lives over the border *vive al otro lado de la frontera.* **4** *(during)* durante: over the past 25 years *durante los últimos 25 años.* **5** *(throughout)* por: we travelled all over Italy *viajamos por toda Italia.* **6** *(more than)* más de: she's over thirty *tiene más de treinta años.* **7** *(about)* por: an argument over money *una discusión por dinero.* **8** *(recovered from)* recuperado,-a de: he's over the flu *se ha recuperado de la gripe.* **9** *(indicating control)* sobre; *(superior)* por encima de: she has control over the class *controla la clase.* ■ over and above además de.
▷ *adj (ended)* acabado,-a, terminado,-a: the game is over *la partida ha acabado.*
overact [əʊvər'ækt] *vi* exagerar, sobreactuar.
overall [*(adj)* 'əʊvərɔ:l *(adv)* əʊvər'ɔ:l] *adj (general)* global, total.
▷ *adv (generally, on the whole)* en conjunto, por lo general, en términos generales.
▷ *n* GB *(work coat)* guardapolvo, bata.
▷ *n pl* overalls mono *m sing.*
overawe [əʊvər'ɔ:] *vt* intimidar.
overbalance [əʊve'bæləns] *vi* perder el equilibrio.
overbearing [əʊvə'beərɪŋ] *adj pej (domineering)* dominante, autoritario,-a.
overboard ['əʊvəbɔ:d] *adv* por la borda. ■ to fall overboard caer al agua. ‖ to go overboard pasarse.
overbooking [əʊvə'bʊkɪŋ] *n* sobrecontratación *f.*
overburden [əʊvə'bɜ:dᵊn] *vt* sobrecargar (with, de), agobiar (with, de).
overcame [əʊvə'keɪm] *pt* → overcome.
overcast ['əʊvəkɑ:st] *adj* METEOR nublado,-a.
overcharge [əʊvə'tʃɑ:dʒ] *vt* **1** *(charge too much)* cobrar demasiado (for, por). **2** *(overload)* sobrecargar.
overcoat ['əʊvəkəʊt] *n* abrigo.
overcome [əʊvə'kʌm] *vt* **1** *(defeat)* vencer. **2** *(overwhelm)* agobiar, abrumar, invadir, apoderarse de, vencer: he was overcome by sleep *el sueño se apoderó de él.*
▷ *vi (triumph)* vencer: we shall overcome *venceremos.*
▲ *pt* overcame [əʊvə'keɪm], *pp* overcome [əʊv'kʌm].
overconfident [əʊvə'kɒnfɪdᵊnt] *adj* confiado,-a, demasiado confiado,-a.
overcook [əʊvə'kʊk] *vt* cocer demasiado,-a.
overcrowded [əʊvə'kraʊdɪd] *adj (room, place, etc)* abarrotado,-a, atestado,-a (de gente); *(country)* superpoblado,-a.
overcrowding [əʊvə'kraʊdɪŋ] *n (of prisons, etc)* hacinamiento, masificación *f*; *(of country)* superpoblación *f.*
overdeveloped [əʊvədɪ'veləpt] *adj* **1** *(photo)* sobrerrevelado,-a. **2** *(muscle, imagination)* excesivamente desarrollado,-a.
overdo [əʊvə'du:] *vt* **1** *(exaggerate)* exagerar, pasarse con: she overdid her makeup *se pasó con el maquillaje.* **2** CULIN *(overcook)* cocer demasiado, asar demasiado; *(use too much)* pasarse con.
▲ *pt* overdid [əʊvə'dɪd], *pp* overdone [əʊvə'dʌn].
overdose ['əʊvədəʊs] *n* sobredosis *f.*
overdraft ['əʊvədrɑ:ft] *n (amount)* descubierto.
overdressed [əʊvə'drest] *adj* demasiado arreglado,-a.
overdue [əʊvə'dju:] *adj* **1** *(late)* atrasado,-a: the train is an hour overdue *el tren lleva una hora de retraso.* **2** COMM *(left unpaid)* vencido,-a y sin pagar.
overeat [əʊvə'ri:t] *vi* comer en exceso.
▲ *pt* overate [əʊv'reɪt], *pp* overeaten [əʊvə'ri:tən].
overestimate [əʊvər'estɪmeɪt] *vt* sobreestimar.
overexpose [əʊvərɪk'spəʊʒ] *vt (photo)* sobreexponer.
overflow [*(n)* 'əʊvəfləʊ; *(vb)* əʊv'fləʊ] *n* **1** *(of river, etc)* desbordamiento. **2** *(pipe)* tubo de desagüe.
▷ *vi* **1** *(river)* desbordarse; *(bath, etc)* rebosar. **2** *(people)* rebosar. **3** *(be full of)* rebosar (with, de).
▷ *vt (liquid)* salirse de.
overfly [əʊvə'flaɪ] *vt* sobrevolar.
▲ *pt* overflew [əʊv'flu:], *pp* overflown ['əʊvəfləʊ].
overgrown [əʊvə'grəʊn] *adj (garden, etc)* cubierto,-a (with, de).
overhang [*(vb)* əʊv'hæŋ; *(n)* əʊv'hæŋg] *vt* sobresalir por encima de, colgar por encima de.
▷ *vi* sobresalir, colgar por encima.
▷ *n* saliente *m.*
overhaul [*(n)* 'əʊvəhɔ:l; *(vb)* əʊv'hɔ:l] *n* revisión *f* general, puesta a punto.
▷ *vt* revisar, poner a punto.
overhead [*(adj)* 'əʊvəhed; *(adv)* əʊv'hed] *adj (cable)* aéreo,-a; *(railway)* elevado,-a.
▷ *adv* arriba, por encima de la cabeza.
overhear [əʊvə'hɪəʳ] *vt* oír por casualidad.
▲ *pt & pp* overheard [əʊvə'hɜ:d].
overheard [əʊvə'hɜ:d] *pt & pp* → overhear.
overheat [əʊvə'hi:t] *vi* recalentarse.
overindulge [əʊvəɪn'dʌldʒ] *vi* excederse.
▷ *vt* mimar demasiado.
overjoyed [əʊvə'dʒɔɪd] *adj* rebosante de alegría.
overkill ['əʊvəkɪl] *n fig* exageración *f.*
overland [*(adj)* 'əʊvəlænd; *(adv)* əʊv'lænd] *adj* por tierra.
▷ *adv* por tierra.
overlap [əʊvə'læp] *vi* superponerse, solaparse.
▲ *pt & pp* overlapped, *ger* overlapping.
▷ *n* superposición *f*, coincidencia.
overlay [*(n)* 'əʊvəleɪ; *(vb)* [əʊvə'leɪ] *n* capa, revestimiento.
▷ *vt* revestir (with, de).
▲ *pt & pp* overlaid.
overleaf [əʊvə'li:f] *adv* al dorso.
overload [*(vb)* əʊv'ləʊd; *(n)* 'əʊvələʊd] *vt* sobrecargar (with, de).

overlook [əʊvə'lʊk] *vt* **1** *(not notice)* pasar por alto; *(disregard)* no tener en cuenta. **2** *(excuse)* disculpar. **3** *(have a view of)* tener vistas a.
overly ['əʊvəlɪ] *adv* demasiado.
overmanning [əʊve'mænɪŋ] *n* exceso de personal.
overnight [əʊvə'naɪt] *adv* **1** *(during the night)* durante la noche; *(at night)* por la noche: **it rained overnight** *llovió durante la noche.* **2** *fam (suddenly)* de la noche a la mañana.
▷ *adj* **1** *(during the night)* de la noche; *(for the night)* de una noche. **2** *fam (sudden)* repentino,-a. ● **overnight bg** bolsa de viaje.
overpass ['əʊʌəpæs] *n* US paso elevado.
overpay [əʊvə'peɪ] *vt* pagar demasiado.
▲ *pt & pp* **overpaid** əʊv'peɪd].
overpopulated [əʊvə'pɒpjəleɪtɪd] *adj* superpoblado,-a.
overpower [əʊvə'paʊəʳ] *vt* **1** *(defeat)* vencer, dominar. **2** *fig (affect strongly - heat)* agobiar, sofocar; *(- smell)* marear; *(- emotion)* abrumar.
overpowering [əʊvə'paʊərɪŋ] *adj (heat)* agobiante; *(smell)* muy fuerte; *(emotion)* abrumador,-ra.
overproduction [əʊvəpr'dʌkʃᵊn] *n* superproducción *f.*
overrate [əʊvə'reɪt] *vt* sobreestimar.
overreact [əʊvərɪ'ækt] *vi* reaccionar de forma exagerada.
override [əʊvə'raɪd] *vt* **1** *(be more important than)* contar más que, ser más importante que. **2** *(not accept - verdict)* invalidar, anular; *(- advice)* hacer caso omiso de.
▲ *pt* **overrode** [əʊvə'rəʊd], *pp* **overridden** [əʊvə'rɪdən].
overriding [əʊvə'raɪdɪŋ] *adj* primordial.
overripe [əʊvə'raɪp] *adj* demasiado maduro,-a, pachucho,-a.
overrule [əʊvə'ru:l] *vt* **1** *(verdict)* invalidar, anular; *(objection)* rechazar. **2** *(person)* imponerse a.
overrun [əʊvə'rʌn] *vt* **1** *(invade)* invadir. **2** *(time, budget)* exceder, rebasar.
▷ *vi (exceed - in time)* durar más de lo previsto.
▲ *pt* **overran** [əʊv'ræn], *pp* **overrun** [əʊv'rʌn], *ger* **overrunning.**
oversaw [əʊvə'sɔ:] *pt* ⟶ **oversee.**
overseas [əʊvə'si:z] *adj (person)* extranjero,-a; *(trade)* exterior; *(investment)* en el extranjero.
▷ *adv* en ultramar. ■ **to go overseas** ir al extranjero.
oversee [əʊvə'si:] *vt* supervisar.
▲ *pt* **oversaw** [əʊvə'sɔ:], *pp* **overseen** [əʊv'si:n].
overseen [əʊvə'si:n] *pp* ⟶ **oversee.**
overshoot [əʊvə'ʃu:t] *vt (turning)* pasarse de.
▲ *pt & pp* **overshot** [əʊvə'ʃɒt].
oversight ['əʊvəsaɪt] *n* descuido: **through oversight** *por descuido.*
oversized [əʊvə'saɪzd] *adj* demasiado grande.
oversleep [əʊvə'sli:p] *vi* quedarse dormido,-a, no despertarse a tiempo.
▲ *pt & pp* **overslept** [əʊvə'slept].
overspill ['əʊvəspɪl] *n* excedente *m* de población.
overstate [əʊvə'steɪt] *vt* exagerar.
overstatement ['əʊvəsteɪtmənt] *n* exageración *f.*
overstep [əʊvə'step] *vt* pasar de.
▲ *pt & pp* **overstepped**, *ger* **overstepping.**
overt ['əʊvɜ:t, əʊ'vɜ:t] *adj (obvious)* manifiesto,-a, patente; *(deliberate)* abierto,-a.
overtake [əʊvə'teɪk] *vt* **1** GB *(a vehicle)* adelantar, pasar AM rebasar: **we overtook a sports car** *adelantamos un coche deportivo.* **2** *(surpass)* superar, sobrepasar. **3** *(happen suddenly to)* adelantarse a; *(surprise)* sorprender.
▷ *vi* GB *(vehicle)* adelantar, AM rebasar.
▲ *pt* **overtook** [əʊvə'tʊk], *pp* **overtaken** [əʊv'teɪkən].
overtaken [əʊvə'teɪkən] *pp* ⟶ **overtake.**
overthrow [*(vb)* əʊv'θrəʊ; *(n)* 'əʊvəθrəʊ] *vt (government, regime, etc)* derribar, derrocar.
▲ *pt* **overthrew** [əʊvə'θru:], *pp* **overthrown** [əʊv'θrəʊn]
▷ *n (defeat)* derrocamiento.
overtime ['əʊvətaɪm] *n (extra hours)* horas *fpl* extras.
overtly [əʊ'vɜ:tlɪ] *adv* abiertamente.
overtook [əʊvə'tʊk] *pt* ⟶ **overtake.**
overture ['əʊvətjʊəʳ] *n* MUS obertura.
overturn [əʊvə'tɜ:n] *vt* **1** *(vehicle)* volcar; *(boat)* hacer zozobrar. **2** *(government)* derrocar. **3** *fig (ruling)* anular.
▷ *vi (vehicle)* volcar; *(boat)* zozobrar.
overview ['əʊvəvju:] *n* perspectiva general.
overweight [əʊvə'weɪt] *adj (thing)* demasiado pesado,-a; *(person)* demasiado gordo,-a.
overwhelm [əʊvə'welm] *vt* **1** *(physically - defeat)* arrollar, aplastar. **2** *fig (emotionally)* abrumar.
overwhelming [əʊvə'welmɪŋ] *adj (defeat, victory)* aplastante, arrollador,-ra; *(generosity)* abrumador,-ra.
overwork [əʊvə'wɜ:k] *vt* **1** *(person, animal)* hacer trabajar demasiado. **2** *(word, phrase, etc)* usar demasiado.
▷ *vi* trabajar demasiado.
▷ *n* trabajo excesivo.
overwrought [əʊvə'rɔ:t] *adj (tense, upset)* muy nervioso,-a.
oviparous [əʊ'vɪpərəs] *adj* ovíparo,-a.
ovulate ['ɒvjəleɪt] *vi* ovular.
ovulation [ɒvj'leɪʃᵊn] *n* ovulación *f.*
ovule ['ɒvju:l] *n* óvulo.
owe [əʊ] *vt (gen)* deber: **you owe me 10 pounds** *me debes 10 libras.*
owing ['əʊɪŋ] *adj (due)* debido,-a.
▷ *prep* **owing to** debido a, a causa de.
owl [aʊl] *n* búho, lechuza.
own [əʊn] *adj* propio,-a.
▷ *pron* propio,-a: **would you like to borrow mine or do you have your own?** *¿quieres que te deje el mío o ya tienes uno propio?*
▷ *vt (possess)* poseer, ser dueño,-a de, tener: **he owns this land** *es dueño de estas tierras.*
⊙ **to own up** *vi* confesarlo.
owner ['əʊnəʳ] *n* dueño,-a, propietario,-a.
ownership ['əʊnəʃɪp] *n* propiedad *f.*
ox [ɒks] *n* buey *m.*
▲ *pl* **oxen** ['ɒksən].
oxen ['ɑksən] *npl* ⟶ **ox.**
oxidation [ɒksɪ'deɪʃᵊn] *n* US oxidación *f.*
oxide ['ɒksaɪd] *n* óxido.
oxidization [ɒksɪdaɪ'zeɪʃᵊn] *n* oxidación *f.*
oxidize ['ɒksɪdaɪz] *vt* oxidar.
▷ *vi* oxidarse.
oxtail ['ɒksteɪl] *n* rabo de buey.
oxygen ['ɒksɪdʒᵊn] *n* oxígeno.
oyster ['ɔɪstəʳ] *n (shellfish)* ostra.
oz [aʊns] *abbr* **(ounce)** onza.
ozone ['əʊzəʊn] *n* ozono.

P

P, p [piː] *n (the letter)* P, p *f*.

pace [peɪs] *n* **1** *(rate, speed)* marcha, ritmo, velocidad *f*. **2** *(step)* paso.

▷ *vt* **1** *(room, floor)* ir de un lado a otro de. **2** *(set speed for)* marcar el ritmo a.

pacemaker [ˈpeɪsmeɪkəʳ] *n* **1** SP liebre *f*. **2** MED marcapasos *m*.

pachyderm [ˈpækɪdɜːm] *n* paquidermo.

pacification [pæsɪfɪˈkeɪʃᵊn] *n* pacificación *f*.

pacifier [ˈpæsɪfaɪəʳ] *n* **1** *(peacemaker)* apaciguador,-ra. **2** US *(dummy)* chupete *m*.

pacifism [ˈpæsɪfɪzᵊm] *n* pacifismo.

pacifist [ˈpæsɪfɪst] *n* pacifista *mf*.

pacify [ˈpæsɪfaɪ] *vt* **1** *(person)* calmar, tranquilizar, apaciguar. **2** *(country)* pacificar.

▲ *pt & pp* **pacified**, *ger* **pacifying**.

pack¹ [pæk] *n* **1** *(parcel)* paquete *m*; *(bundle)* fardo, bulto; *(rucksack)* mochila. **2** US *(packet - gen)* paquete *m*; *(of cigarettes)* paquete *m*, cajetilla. **3** GB *(of cards)* baraja. **4** *pej (of thieves)* banda, partida. **5** *(of lies)* sarta. **6** *(of wolves, dogs)* manada; *(of hounds)* jauría.

▷ *vt* **1** *(goods)* empaquetar, envasar. **2** *(suitcase)* hacer; *(clothes, etc)* poner, meter. **3** *(fill)* atestar, abarrotar, llenar: **the disco was packed with young people** *la discoteca estaba abarrotada de jóvenes*. **4** *(press down)* apretar.

▷ *vi* **1** *(suitcase, etc)* hacer las maletas, hacer el equipaje: **he hasn't packed yet** *aún no ha hecho las maletas*. **2** *(people)* apiñarse, apretarse, meterse.

⊙ **to pack in** *vt sep (attract)* atraer.

⊙ **to pack off** *vt sep (send)* enviar, mandar.

⊙ **to pack up** *vi* **1** *(stop, give up)* dejarlo. **2** *(machine)* estropearse; *(car)* averiarse.

▷ *vt sep (belongings - in case)* meter en la maleta; *(gather together)* recoger.

pack² [pæk] *vt (jury, committee)* llenar de partidarios.

package [ˈpækɪdʒ] *n* **1** *(parcel)* paquete *m*. **2** *(proposals)* paquete *m*; *(agreement)* acuerdo. ● **package holiday** (US **vacation**) viaje *m* organizado.

▷ *vt (goods)* empaquetar, envasar.

packaging [ˈpækɪdʒɪŋ] *n* embalaje *m*.

packed [pækt] *adj (with people)* lleno,-a, atestado,-a de gente, abarrotado,-a, repleto,-a; *(with facts, information, etc)* lleno,-a.

packet [ˈpækɪt] *n* **1** *(small box - gen)* paquete *m*, cajita; *(of cigarettes)* paquete *m*, cajetilla; *(envelope)* sobre *m*. **2** *fam (large amount of money)* dineral *m*.

packing [ˈpækɪŋ] *n (material)* embalaje *m*. ■ **to do one's packing** hacer la maleta.

pact [pækt] *n* pacto.

pad¹ [pæd] *n* **1** *(cushioning)* almohadilla, cojinete *m*. **2** *(inkpad)* tampón *m*. **3** *(of paper)* taco, bloc *m*. **4** *(of animal)* almohadilla. **5** *(platform)* plataforma. ● **knee pad** rodillera. | **sanitary pad** compresa.

▷ *vt (chair, etc)* acolchar, rellenar, guatear; *(garment)* poner hombreras a.

▲ *pt & pp* **padded**, *ger* **padding**.

⊙ **to pad out** *vt sep (speech, etc)* meter paja en.

pad² [pæd] *vi* andar sin hacer ruido.

▲ *pt & pp* **padded**, *ger* **padding**.

padded [ˈpædɪd] *adj (chair, etc)* acolchado,-a, guateado,-a; *(garment)* con hombreras.

padding [ˈpædɪŋ] *n* **1** *(material)* relleno, acolchado. **2** *(in speech, writing, etc)* paja.

paddle¹ [ˈpædᵊl] *n (oar)* pala, remo, canalete *m*. ● **paddle boat / paddle steamer** vapor *m* de ruedas.

▷ *vt (boat, canoe)* remar con pala, remar con canalete.

▷ *vi* remar con pala, remar con canalete.

paddle² [ˈpædᵊl] *vi (walk or play in water)* mojarse los pies, chapotear.

▷ *n* chapoteo.

paddling pool [ˈpædᵊlɪŋpuːl] *n* piscina para niños, piscina infantil.

paddock [ˈpædək] *n (field)* potrero, prado.

paddy [ˈpædɪ] *n* arrozal *m*.

▲ *pl* **paddies**.

padlock [ˈpædlɒk] *n* candado.

▷ *vt* cerrar con candado.

paediatrician [piːdɪˈætrɪʃᵊn] *n* pediatra *mf*.

paedophile [ˈpiːdəfaɪl] *n* pedófilo,-a.

pagan [ˈpeɪgᵊn] *adj* pagano,-a.

▷ *n* pagano,-a.

page¹ [peɪdʒ] *n (of book)* página; *(of newspaper)* plana, página. ■ **on the front page** en primera plana.

page² [peɪdʒ] *n* **1** *(boy servant, at wedding)* paje *m*; *(in hotel, club)* botones *m*. **2** HIST escudero.

▷ *vt (over loudspeaker)* llamar por megafonía.

pageant [ˈpædʒᵊnt] *n (show)* espectáculo; *(procession)* desfile *m*; *(on horses)* cabalgata.

pageantry [ˈpædʒᵊntrɪ] *n* pompa, boato.

pageboy [ˈpeɪdʒbɔɪ] *n* **1** *(boy servant, at wedding)* paje *m*; *(in hotel, club)* botones *m*. **2** *(hairstyle)* estilo paje.

pager [ˈpeɪdʒəʳ] *n* buscapersonas *m*.

pagination [pædʒɪˈneɪʃᵊn] *n* paginación *f*.

pagoda [pəˈgəʊdə] *n* pagoda.

paid [peɪd] *pp & pt* → **pay**.

▷ *adj (purchase, holiday)* pagado,-a; *(work)* remunerado,-a.

paid-up [ˈpeɪdʌp] *adj (member)* que está al corriente de los pagos.

pail [peɪl] *n* cubo.

pain [peɪn] *n* **1** *(physical)* dolor *m*: **I've got a pain in my stomach** *me duele el estómago*. **2** *(mental suffering)* sufri-

miento, dolor *m*. 3 *(annoying thing)* lata, fastidio; *(person)* pesado,-a, pelmazo.
▷ *vt* doler, dar pena a, apenar.
▷ *n pl* **pains** *(effort)* esfuerzos *mpl*, esmero.

pained [peɪnd] *adj (hurt)* afligido,-a, apenado,-a, dolido,-a; *(look, expression)* de pena.

painful ['peɪnfʊl] *adj (physically)* doloroso,-a; *(mentally)* angustioso,-a, doloroso,-a.

painfully ['peɪnfʊlɪ] *adv* 1 *(causing pain)* dolorosamente. 2 *(extremely)* terriblemente.

painkiller ['peɪnkɪlə^r] *n* calmante *m*.

painless ['peɪnləs] *adj* 1 *(without pain)* indoloro,-a, sin dolor. 2 *(without distress)* sencillo,-a, sin complicaciones, llevadero,-a.

painstaking ['peɪnzteɪkɪŋ] *adj (person)* meticuloso,-a; *(care, research)* concienzudo,-a.

paint [peɪnt] *n* pintura: **a tin of paint** *una lata de pintura*. ■ **«Wet paint»** «Recién pintado».
▷ *vt (gen)* pintar: **we're going to paint the walls yellow** *vamos a pintar las paredes de amarillo*.
▷ *vi (gen)* pintar: **she paints in oils** *pinta al óleo*.

paintbox ['peɪntbɒks] *n* caja de pinturas.

paintbrush ['peɪntbrʌʃ] *n* 1 *(for walls, etc)* brocha. 2 *(artist's)* pincel *m*.

painter ['peɪntə^r] *n* 1 ART pintor,-ra. 2 *(decorator)* pintor,-ra de brocha gorda.

painting ['peɪntɪŋ] *n* 1 ART *(picture)* pintura, cuadro. 2 *(activity)* pintura.

paint-stripper ['peɪntstrɪpə^r] *n* quitapinturas *m sing*.

paintwork ['peɪntwɜːk] *n* pintura.

pair [peə^r] *n* 1 *(of shoes, socks, gloves, etc)* par *m*; *(of cards)* pareja: **a pair of brown eyes** *dos ojos castaños*. 2 *(of people, animals)* pareja. ■ **in pairs** de dos en dos. ● **a pair of scissors** unas tijeras. ■ **a pair of trousers** unos pantalones.
▷ *vt (people)* emparejar; *(animals)* aparear.
▷ *vi (animals)* aparearse.
⊙ **to pair off** *vt sep* emparejar (**with**, con).
▷ *vi* formar pareja (**with**, con).
⊙ **to pair up** *vt sep* emparejar.
▷ *vi* formar pareja (**with**, con).

pajamas [pə'dʒæməz] *n pl* US ⟶ **pyjamas**.

Pakistan [pɑːkɪ'stɑːn] *n* Pakistán *m*.

Pakistani [pɑːkɪ'stɑːnɪ] *adj* pakistaní.
▷ *n* pakistaní *mf*.

pal [pæl] *n fam* amigo,-a, colega *mf*.

palace ['pæləs] *n* palacio.

Palaeolithic [pælɪəʊ'lɪθɪk] *adj* paleolítico,-a.

palatable ['pælətəbᵊl] *adj* 1 *(tasty)* sabroso,-a. 2 *(acceptable)* aceptable.

palate ['pælət] *n (gen)* paladar *m*.

palatial [pə'leɪʃəl] *adj* suntuoso,-a.

palaver [pə'lɑːvə^r] *n fam (fuss)* lío, follón *m*.

pale [peɪl] *adj (complexion, skin)* pálido,-a; *(colour)* claro,-a, pálido,-a; *(light)* débil, tenue. ■ **to turn pale** palidecer.
▷ *vi* palidecer.

paleness ['peɪlnəs] *n* palidez *f*.

Palestine ['pælɪstaɪn] *n* Palestina.

Palestinian [pælɪ'stɪnɪən] *adj* palestino,-a.
▷ *n* palestino,-a.

palette ['pælət] *n* paleta.

palfrey ['pɔːlfrɪ] *n* palafrén *m*.

paling ['peɪlɪŋ] *n pl (fence)* empalizada.

pall[1] [pɔːl] *n* 1 *(cloth on coffin)* paño mortuorio. 2 US *(coffin)* féretro. 3 *fig (of smoke)* cortina.

pall[2] [pɔːl] *vi (become boring)* dejar de gustar, hacerse pesado,-a, cansar, aburrir.

pallbearer ['pɔːlbeərə^r] *n* portador,-ra del féretro.

pallet[1] ['pælət] *n* TECH paleta.

pallet[2] ['pælɪt] *n (mattress)* jergón *m*; *(bed)* camastro.

palliative ['pælɪətɪv] *adj* paliativo,-a.

pallid ['pælɪd] *adj* pálido,-a.

pallor ['pælə^r] *n* palidez *f*.

palm[1] [pɑːm] *n* BOT *(tree)* palmera; *(leaf)* palma.

palm[2] [pɑːm] *n* ANAT palma. ● **palm tree** palmera.
▷ *vt (touch ball)* dar con la mano a.
⊙ **to palm off** *vt sep* endosar (**on/onto**, a).

palmistry ['pɑːmɪstrɪ] *n* quiromancia.

palpable ['pælpəbᵊl] *adj* palpable.

palpitate ['pælpɪteɪt] *vi (heart)* palpitar.

palpitation [pælpɪ'teɪʃᵊn] *n* palpitación *f*.

paltry ['pɔːltrɪ] *adj* insignificante.
▲ *comp* **paltrier**, *superl* **paltriest**.

pamper ['pæmpə^r] *vt* mimar, consentir.

pamphlet ['pæmflət] *n* folleto.

pan[1] [pæn] *n* 1 *(saucepan)* cacerola, cazuela, cazo; *(cooking pot)* olla. 2 *(for washing gravel)* batea.
▷ *vt* 1 *(soil, gravel)* cribar con batea.
⊙ **to pan out** *vi fam (turn out)* salir, resultar.
▲ *pt & pp* **panned**, *ger* **panning**.

pan[2] [pæn] *vt* CINEM tomar una panorámica de.
▲ *pt & pp* **panned**, *ger* **panning**.

panacea [pænə'sɪə] *n* panacea.

panache [pə'næʃ] *n* garbo, salero.

panama ['pænəmɑː] *n (hat)* panamá *m*.

Panama ['pænəmə] *n* Panamá.

Panamanian [pænə'meɪnɪən] *adj* panameño,-a.
▷ *n* panameño,-a.

pancake ['pænkeɪk] *n* tortita, crepe *f*.

pancreas ['pæŋkrɪəs] *n* páncreas *m*.

panda ['pændə] *n* oso panda *m*, panda *m*.

pandemonium [pændə'məʊnɪəm] *n* pandemónium *m*.

pander ['pændə^r] *vi (person)* complacer (**to**, a).

pane [peɪn] *n* cristal *m*, vidrio.

panel ['pænəl] *n* 1 *(of door, wall, car body, etc)* panel *m*; *(on ceiling)* artesón *m*. 2 *(of controls, instruments)* tablero. 3 *(group of people)* panel *m*; *(team)* equipo.

panelling ['pænəlɪŋ] *n (of door, wall, etc)* paneles *mpl*; *(on ceiling)* artesonado.

panellist ['pænəlɪst] *n (in discussion, etc)* participante *mf*, contertulio,-a.

pang [pæŋ] *n* punzada.

panic ['pænɪk] *n* pánico: **panic spread throughout the crowd** *el pánico cundió entre la gente*.
▷ *vt* infundir pánico a.
▷ *vi* entrarle el pánico a, aterrarse.
▲ *pt & pp* **panicked**, *ger* **panicking**.

panicky ['pænɪkɪ] *adj fam (person)* asustadizo,-a; *(reaction, feeling)* aterrador,-ra.

panic-striken ['pænɪkstrɪkᵊn] *adj* preso,-a de pánico, aterrorizado,-a.

pannier ['pænɪə^r] *n (on animal)* alforja; *(on bicycle)* bolsa.

panorama [pænə'rɑːmə] *n (view)* panorama *m*.

panoramic [pænə'ræmɪk] *adj* panorámico,-a.

pansy ['pænzɪ] *n* BOT pensamiento.
▲ *pl* **pansies**.

pant [pænt] *vi* jadear, resoplar.
pantheon ['pænθɪən] *n* ARCH panteón *m*.
panther ['pænθəʳ] *n* pantera.
panties ['pæntɪz] *n pl* bragas *fpl*.
pantomime ['pæntəmaɪm] *n* **1** *(mime)* pantomima. **2** GB *(play) representación musical navideña basada en cuentos de hadas.*
pantry ['pæntrɪ] *n* despensa.
▲ *pl* **pantries.**
pants [pænts] *n pl* **1** GB *(underpants - men's)* calzoncillos *mpl*; *(- women's)* bragas *fpl*. **2** US *(trousers)* pantalón *m*, pantalones *mpl*.
papa [pæ'pɑː] *n dated* papá *m*.
papacy ['peɪpəsɪ] *n* papado, pontificado.
papal ['peɪpᵊl] *adj* papal, pontificio.
papaya [pə'paɪə] *n* papaya.
paper ['peɪpəʳ] *n* **1** *(material)* papel *m*: **take a sheet of paper** *coge una hoja de papel.* **2** *(newspaper)* periódico, diario. **3** *(examination)* examen *m*. **4** *(essay, written work)* trabajo (escrito). ■ **on paper** por escrito. ● **paper mill** fábrica de papel. ‖ **paper shop** quiosco.
▷ *vt* empapelar.
▷ *n pl* **papers** *(documents)* documentos *mpl*.
▷ *n pl* **the papers** la prensa.
paperback ['peɪpəbæk] *n* libro en rústica.
paperboy ['peɪpəbɔɪ] *n* repartidor *m* de periódicos.
paperclip ['peɪpəklɪp] *n* clip *m*, sujetapapeles *m*.
papergirl ['peɪpəgɜːl] *n* repartidora de periódicos.
paperknife ['peɪpənaɪf] *n* cortapapeles *m*.
paperweight ['peɪpəweɪt] *n* pisapapeles *m*.
paperwork ['peɪpəwɜːk] *n* papeleo.
papier-mâché [pæpɪeɪ'mæʃeɪ] *n* cartón *m* piedra.
papist ['peɪpɪst] *adj pej* papista.
paprika ['pæprɪkə] *n* pimentón *m* dulce.
Papua ['pæpjuə] *n* Papúa. ● **Papua New Guinea** Papúa Nueva Guinea.
Papuan ['pæpjuən] *adj* papú,-úa.
▷ *n* papú,-úa.
par [pɑːʳ] *n (parity)* igualdad *f*.
parable ['pærəbᵊl] *n* parábola.
parabola [pə'ræbələ] *n* MATH parábola.
parachute ['pærəʃuːt] *n* paracaídas *m*.
▷ *vi* saltar en paracaídas.
parade [pə'reɪd] *n* **1** *(procession)* desfile *m*: **fashion parade** *desfile de modelos.* **2** MIL desfile *m*.
▷ *vt* **1** MIL hacer desfilar. **2** *(flaunt - knowledge, wealth)* alardear, hacer alarde de.
▷ *vi* **1** *(gen)* desfilar. **2** MIL pasar revista.
paradigm ['pærədaɪm] *n* paradigma *m*.
paradigmatic [pærədɪg'mætɪk] *adj* paradigmático,-a.
paradise ['pærədaɪs] *n* paraíso.
paradox ['pærədɒks] *n* paradoja.
paradoxical [pærə'dɒksɪkᵊl] *adj* paradójico,-a.
paraffin ['pærəfɪn] *n* GB queroseno. ● **paraffin wax** parafina.
paragon ['pærəgən] *n* modelo, dechado.
paragraph ['pærəgrɑːf] *n* párrafo. ■ **full stop** (US **period), new paragraph** punto y aparte.
Paraguay [pærə'gwaɪ] *n* Paraguay.
Paraguayan [pærə'gwaɪən] *adj* paraguayo,-a.
▷ *n* paraguayo,-a.
parakeet ['pærəkiːt] *n* periquito, perico.
parallel ['pærəlel] *adj* **1** paralelo,-a (**to/with**, a). **2** *fig (similar)* paralelo,-a (**to/with**, a), análogo,-a (**to/with**, a).
▷ *n* **1** MATH paralela. **2** GEOG paralelo. **3** *(similarity)* paralelo, paralelismo.
▷ *vt* ser paralelo,-a a, ser análogo,-a a.
paralyse ['pærəlaɪz] *vt (gen)* paralizar. ■ **to be paralysed with fear** quedarse paralizado,-a de miedo.
paralysis [pə'ræləsɪs] *n* **1** MED parálisis *f*. **2** *fig* paralización *f*.
paralytic [pærə'lɪtɪk] *adj* MED paralítico,-a.
▷ *n* MED paralítico,-a.
paralyze ['pærəlaɪz] *vt* US → **paralyse.**
parameter [pə'ræmɪtəʳ] *n* parámetro.
paramilitary [pærə'mɪlɪtᵊrɪ] *adj* paramilitar.
paramount ['pærəmaunt] *adj* supremo,-a, primordial.
paranoia [pærə'nɔɪə] *n* paranoia.
paranoiac [pærə'nɔɪk] *adj* paranoico,-a.
▷ *n* paranoico,-a.
paranoid ['pærənɔɪd] *adj* **1** *(mentally ill)* paranoide. **2** *(obsessed)* obsesionado,-a (**about**, por).
paranormal [pærə'nɔːmᵊl] *adj* paranormal.
parapet ['pærəpɪt] *n* parapeto.
paraphernalia [pærəfə'neɪlɪə] *n* parafernalia.
paraphrase ['pærəfreɪz] *n* paráfrasis *f*.
▷ *vt* parafrasear.
paraplegia [pærə'pliːdʒə] *n* MED paraplejía.
paraplegic [pærə'pliːdʒɪk] *adj* MED parapléjico,-a.
▷ *n* MED parapléjico,-a.
parapsychology [pærəsaɪ'kɒlədʒɪ] *n* parapsicología.
parasite ['pærəsaɪt] *n* parásito,-a.
parasitic [pærə'sɪtɪk] *adj (plant, animal, etc)* parásito,-a; *(disease)* parasitario,-a.
parasol [pærə'sɒl] *n* sombrilla.
paratrooper ['pærətruːpəʳ] *n* MIL paracaidista *mf*.
parboil ['pɑːbɔɪl] *vt* cocer a medias.
parcel ['pɑːsᵊl] *n* **1** *(package)* paquete *m*. **2** *(piece of land)* parcela.
⊙ **to parcel out** *vt sep* repartir, dividir.
⊙ **to parcel up** *vt sep* empaquetar, embalar.
parched [pɑːtʃt] *adj* **1** *(very dry)* agostado,-a, reseco,-a. **2** *(thirsty)* muerto,-a de sed.
parchment ['pɑːtʃmənt] *n* pergamino.
pardon ['pɑːdᵊn] *n* **1** *(forgiveness)* perdón *m*. **2** JUR indulto. ■ **I beg your pardon!** *fml* ¡perdone! ‖ **to ask SB's pardon** pedirle perdón a ALGN.
▷ *vt* **1** *(forgive)* perdonar: **pardon me for interrupting** *perdone que le interrumpa.* **2** JUR indultar. ■ **pardon?** *(for repetition)* ¿cómo dice?, ¿cómo? ‖ **pardon me!** *(sorry)* ¡perdón! ‖ **to pardon SB STH** perdonarle ALGO a ALGN.
pardonable ['pɑːdənəbᵊl] *adj* perdonable.
pare [peəʳ] *vt* **1** *(fruit)* pelar, mondar. **2** *(nails)* cortar.
⊙ **to pare down** *vt sep* reducir, recortar.
parent ['peərənt] *n (father)* padre *m*; *(mother)* madre *f*.
▷ *n pl* **parents** padres *mpl*.
parentage ['peərəntɪdʒ] *n* familia, origen *m*.
parental [pə'rentᵊl] *adj (of both parents)* de los padres; *(parental)* paterno,-a; *(maternal)* materno,-a.
parenthesis [pə'renθəsɪs] *n* paréntesis *m*.
▲ *pl* **parentheses.**
parenthood ['peərənthud] *n (being a parent)* ser padre, ser madre; *(fatherhood)* paternidad *f*; *(motherhood)* maternidad *f*.
pariah [pə'raɪə] *n* paria *m*.

parietal [pəˈraɪətᵊl] *adj* parietal.
parish [ˈpærɪʃ] *n* **1** REL parroquia. **2** GB *(civil)* municipio.
parishioner [pəˈrɪʃənəʳ] *n* feligrés,-esa.
parity [ˈpærɪtɪ] *n (equality)* igualdad *f*.
park [pɑːk] *n* parque *m*, jardín *m* público.
▷ *vt (car)* aparcar, estacionar: **I'm parked opposite** *he aparcado enfrente.*
▷ *vi* aparcar, estacionar.
parka [ˈpɑːkə] *n* anorak *m*, parka.
parking [ˈpɑːkɪŋ] *n (act)* estacionamiento. ■ **«No parking»** «Prohibido aparcar». ● **parking meter** parquímetro.
parkland [ˈpɑːklænd] *n* jardines *mpl*.
parkway [ˈpɑːkweɪ] *n* US avenida, alameda.
parky [ˈpɑːkɪ] *adj fam* fresco,-a: **it's a bit parky** *hace fresquito.*
▲ *comp* **parkier**, *superl* **parkiest.**
parlance [ˈpɑːləns] *n fml* lenguaje *m*, habla.
parliament [ˈpɑːləmᵊnt] *n (assembly)* parlamento.
▷ *n* **Parliament** GB *(body)* Parlamento; *(period)* legislatura.
parliamentarian [pɑːləmenˈteərɪən] *n* parlamentario,-a.
parliamentary [pɑːləˈmentərɪ] *adj* parlamentario,-a.
parlor [ˈpɑːləʳ] *n* US ⟶ **parlour.**
parlour [ˈpɑːləʳ] *n* **1** US *(shop)* salón *m*, tienda. **2** *dated (room in house)* salón *m*.
parochial [pəˈrəʊkɪəl] *adj (of parish)* parroquial.
parody [ˈpærədɪ] *n* parodia.
▲ *pl* **parodies.**
▷ *vt* parodiar.
▲ *pt & pp* **parodied**, *ger* **parodying.**
parole [pəˈrəʊl] *n* libertad *f* condicional.
▷ *vt* poner en libertad condicional.
paroxysm [ˈpærəksɪzᵊm] *n* paroxismo.
parquet [ˈpɑːkeɪ] *n* parqué *m*.
parrot [ˈpærət] *n* loro, papagayo.
parry [ˈpærɪ] *vt* **1** *(blow)* parar, desviar. **2** *(question, etc)* esquivar, eludir.
▲ *pt & pp* **parried**, *ger* **parrying.**
parsimonious [pɑːsɪˈməʊɪəs] *adj fml* mezquino,-a, tacaño,-a, parsimonioso,-a.
parsley [ˈpɑːslɪ] *n* perejil *m*.
parsnip [ˈpɑːsnɪp] *n* chirivía.
parson [ˈpɑːsᵊn] *n* REL párroco, cura *m*.
part [pɑːt] *n* **1** *(gen)* parte *f*: **we spent part of the day on the beach** *pasamos parte del día en la playa.* **2** *(component)* pieza. **3** *(of serial, programme)* capítulo. **4** *(measure)* parte *f*. **5** *(in play, film)* papel *m*: **she plays the part of Scarlett** *hace el papel de Scarlett.* **6** *(role, share, involvement)* papel *m*, parte *f*: **I want no part in your dodgy deals** *no quiero saber nada de tus negocios sucios.* ■ **for my part** por mi parte. ‖ **in part** en parte. ‖ **the best part of / the better part of** la mayor parte de.
▷ *adv* en parte.
▷ *adj* parcial.
▷ *vt (separate)* separar (**from**, de).
▷ *vi* **1** *(separate)* separarse; *(say goodbye)* despedirse: **they parted as friends** *se separaron amistosamente.* **2** *(open - lips, curtains)* abrirse.
▷ *n pl* **parts** *(area)* zona, parajes *mpl*.
⊙ **to part with** *vt insep* desprenderse de, separarse de.
partake [pɑːˈteɪk] *vi* **partake of** *fml (eat)* comer; *(drink)* beber.

partial [ˈpɑːʃᵊl] *adj* **1** *(not complete)* parcial. **2** *(biased)* parcial. ■ **to be partial to** STH ser aficionado,-a a ALGO.
partiality [pɑːʃɪˈælɪtɪ] *n* **1** *(bias)* parcialidad *f*. **2** *(liking)* afición *f* (**for**, a).
partially [ˈpɑːʃəlɪ] *adv* **1** *(partly)* parcialmente. **2** *(with bias)* con parcialidad.
participant [pɑːˈtɪsɪpənt] *n (gen)* participante *mf*; *(in competition)* concursante *mf*.
participate [pɑːˈtɪsɪpeɪt] *vi* participar (**in**, en).
participation [pɑːtɪsɪˈpeɪʃᵊn] *n* participación *f*.
participle [ˈpɑːtɪsɪpᵊl] *n* participio.
particle [ˈpɑːtɪkᵊl] *n* partícula.
particular [pəˈtɪkjʊləʳ] *adj* **1** *(special)* particular, especial: **for no particular reason** *por nada en especial.* **2** *(specific)* concreto, particular. **3** *(fussy)* exigente, especial.
▷ *n pl* **particulars** *(of event, thing)* detalles *mpl*; *(of person)* datos *mpl* personales.
particularly [pəˈtɪkjʊləlɪ] *adv* especialmente.
parting [ˈpɑːtɪŋ] *n* **1** *(leaving)* despedida; *(separation)* separación *f*. **2** *(in hair)* raya.
▷ *adj* de despedida.
partisan [pɑːtɪˈzæn] *n* **1** *(supporter)* partidario,-a. **2** MI[L] partisano,-a.
▷ *adj* partidista.
partition [pɑːˈtɪʃᵊn] *n* **1** *(act)* partición *f*, división *f*. **2** *(wall)* tabique *m*; *(screen)* mampara.
▷ *vt* partir, dividir.
partly [ˈpɑːtlɪ] *adv* parcialmente, en parte.
partner [ˈpɑːtnəʳ] *n* **1** *(in an activity)* compañero,-a; *(in dancing, tennis, cards, etc)* pareja. **2** COMM socio,-a, asociado,-a. **3** *(spouse)* cónyuge *mf*; *(husband)* marido; *(wife)* mujer *f*; *(in relationship)* pareja, compañero,-a.
▷ *vt* acompañar, ser pareja de.
partnership [ˈpɑːtnəʃɪp] *n* **1** COMM *(company)* sociedad *f*. **2** *(working relationship)* asociación *f*.
partridge [ˈpɑːtrɪdʒ] *n* perdiz *f*.
▲ *pl* **partridges** o **partridge.**
part-time [pɑːtˈtaɪm] *adj (work, job)* de media jornada, a tiempo parcial.
▷ *adv* media jornada, a tiempo parcial.
part-timer [pɑːtˈtaɪməʳ] *n* trabajador,-ra a tiempo parcial.
party [ˈpɑːtɪ] *n* **1** *(celebration)* fiesta: **birthday party** *fiesta de cumpleaños.* **2** POL partido. **3** *(group)* grupo.
▲ *pl* **parties.**
▷ *adj* **1** *(dress)* de fiesta; *(mood, atmosphere)* festivo,-a. **2** POL *(member, leader)* del partido.
▷ *vi (go to parties)* ir a fiestas; *(have fun)* divertirse.
▲ *pt & pp* **partied**, *ger* **partying.**
pass [pɑːs] *n* **1** GEOG *(in mountains - gen)* puerto, pas[o] (de montaña); *(narrow)* desfiladero. **2** *(official permi[t])* pase *m*, permiso. **3** *(in exam)* aprobado. **4** SP pase *m*. ● **bus pass** abono de autobús.
▷ *vt* **1** *(go past - gen)* pasar; *(person)* cruzarse con: **I passe[d] her in the street** *me crucé con ella en la calle.* **2** *(overtake)* adelantar. **3** *(cross - border, frontier)* pasar, cruzar. **4** *(give, hand)* pasar: **pass me that screwdriver** *pásame ese destornillador.* **5** *(move)* pasar: **he passed a comb through h[is] hair** *se pasó el cepillo por el pelo.* **6** SP *(ball)* pasar. **7** *(exam, test, examinee)* aprobar; *(bill, law, proposal, motion)* aprobar; *(censor)* pasar. **8** *(time)* pasar. **9** *(say, utter - opinion)* expresar, dar; *(- remark, comment)* hacer.

▷ *vi* **1** *(go past - gen)* pasar; *(procession)* desfilar; *(people)* cruzarse: I was just passing *pasaba por aquí.* **2** *(overtake)* adelantar. **3** *(move, go)* pasar: we passed through Zaragoza *pasamos por Zaragoza.* **4** SP hacer un pase. **5** *(be transferred to)* pasar (to, a). **6** *(change)* cambiar (from, de). **7** *(of time)* pasar, transcurrir. **8** *(come to an end - pain, feeling)* pasarse; *(storm)* pasar. **9** *(exam, test)* aprobar; *(bill, motion)* ser aprobado,-a. **10** *(be acceptable)* pasar; *(be tolerated)* consentir: let it pass *déjalo correr.* **11** *(happen)* ocurrir, acontecer, suceder: it came to pass that ... *sucedió que...*

⊙ **to pass away** *vi (die)* pasar a mejor vida.

⊙ **to pass by** *vi* pasar: she watched the people passing by *miraba pasar a la gente.*

▷ *vt sep* pasar de largo.

⊙ **to pass down** *vt sep (hand down - heirloom)* pasar; *(tradition, story)* transmitir.

⊙ **to pass for** *vt insep* pasar por.

⊙ **to pass off** *vi* **1** *(happen)* pasar, transcurrir. **2** *(stop)* parar; *(disappear)* pasarse.

▷ *vt sep (succeed in presenting)* hacer pasar (as, por).

⊙ **to pass on** *vt sep (information)* pasar, dar; *(infection)* contagiar.

▷ *vi* **1** *(die)* pasar a mejor vida. **2** *(proceed)* pasar (to, a).

⊙ **to pass out** *vi* **1** *(faint)* desmayarse, perder el conocimiento. **2** MIL graduarse.

▷ *vt sep (distribute)* repartir.

⊙ **to pass over** *vt sep (ignore, overlook)* pasar por alto, dejar de lado, olvidar.

▷ *vt insep (cross)* atravesar, cruzar.

⊙ **to pass through** *vi* estar de paso.

▷ *vt insep* pasar por, atravesar.

⊙ **to pass up** *vt sep (opportunity)* dejar pasar, dejar escapar, desperdiciar; *(offer)* rechazar.

passable ['pɑːsəbᵊl] *adj* **1** *(acceptable)* pasable, aceptable. **2** *(road, bridge)* transitable.

passably ['pɑːsəblɪ] *adv* aceptablemente.

passage ['pæsɪdʒ] *n* **1** *(in street)* pasaje *m*; *(alleyway)* callejón *m*; *(narrow)* pasadizo. **2** *(in building - corridor)* pasillo. **3** *(way, movement - gen)* paso; *(of vehicle)* tránsito, paso. **4** *(of time)* paso, transcurso. **5** MAR *(journey)* travesía, viaje *m*; *(fare)* pasaje *m*. **6** *(writing, music)* pasaje *m*.

passageway ['pæsɪdʒweɪ] *n (corridor)* pasillo.

passbook ['pɑːsbʊk] *n* cartilla de ahorros.

passenger ['pæsɪndʒəʳ] *n* pasajero,-a.

passer-by [pɑːsə'baɪ] *n* transeúnte *mf*.

▲ *pl* passers-by.

passing ['pɑːsɪŋ] *adj* **1** *(fashion, thought)* pasajero,-a; *(remark, reference)* de pasada; *(glance)* rápido,-a. **2** *(vehicle)* que pasa.

▷ *n (of time)* paso, transcurso.

passion ['pæʃᵊn] *n* pasión *f*, vehemencia. ● **passion fruit** granadilla, maracuyá *m*.

passionate ['pæʃᵊnət] *adj* apasionado,-a, vehemente.

passive ['pæsɪv] *adj (gen)* pasivo,-a.

▷ *n* LING voz *f* pasiva.

passively ['pæsɪvlɪ] *adv (gen)* pasivamente.

passivity [pæ'sɪvətɪ] *n* pasividad *f*.

passkey ['pɑːskiː] *n* llave *f* maestra.

passport ['pɑːspɔːt] *n* pasaporte *m*.

password ['pɑːswɜːd] *n* contraseña.

past [pɑːst] *adj* **1** *(gone by in time)* pasado,-a; *(former)* anterior. **2** *(gone by recently)* último,-a: the past few days *los últimos días.* **3** *(finished, over)* acabado,-a, terminado,-a: summer is past *el verano ha terminado.* **4** LING pasado,-a. ■ **past participle** participio pasado. ■ **past tense** pasado.

▷ *n* **1** *(former times)* pasado: in the past *en el pasado, antes, antiguamente.* **2** *(of person)* pasado; *(of place)* historia.

▷ *prep* **1** *(farther than, beyond)* más allá de; *(by the side of)* por (delante de): it's just past the cinema *está un poco más allá del cine.* **2** *(in time)* y: it's five past six *son las seis y cinco.* **3** *(older than)* más de: he's past forty *pasa de los cuarenta (años).* **4** *(beyond the limits of)*: it's past my comprehension *me resulta incomprensible.*

▷ *adv*: a few joggers ran past *pasaron unos haciendo footing.*

pasta ['pæstə] *n* pasta, pastas *fpl*.

paste [peɪst] *n* **1** *(mixture)* pasta; *(glue)* engrudo. **2** CULIN pasta, paté *m*.

▷ *vt (stick)* pegar; *(put paste on)* encolar.

pasteboard ['peɪstbɔːd] *n* cartón *m*.

pastel ['pæstᵊl] *n* **1** *(chalk)* pastel *m*; *(drawing)* dibujo al pastel. **2** *(colour)* color *m* pastel.

▷ *adj (drawing)* al pastel; *(colour, tone, shade, etc)* pastel.

paste-up ['peɪstʌp] *n* maqueta.

pasteurization [pæstjəraɪ'zeɪʃᵊn] *n* pasteurización *f*.

pasteurize ['pɑːstjəraɪz] *vt* pasteurizar.

pastiche [pæ'stiːʃ] *n* pastiche *m*.

pastille ['pæstɪl] *n* pastilla.

pastime ['pɑːstaɪm] *n* pasatiempo.

pasting ['peɪstɪŋ] *n fam* paliza.

pastor ['pɑːstəʳ] *n* REL pastor *m*.

pastoral ['pɑːstᵊrəl] *adj* **1** *(rustic)* pastoril, bucólico,-a. **2** REL pastoral.

pastry ['peɪstrɪ] *n* **1** *(dough)* masa. **2** *(cake)* pasta, bollo.

▲ *pl* pastries.

pasture ['pɑːstʃəʳ] *n* pasto.

pasty[1] ['pæstɪ] *n* CULIN empanadilla.

pasty[2] ['peɪstɪ] *adj* **1** *(pale)* pálido,-a. **2** *(like paste)* pastoso,-a.

▲ *comp* pastier, *superl* pastiest.

pat[1] [pæt] *n* **1** *(tap)* golpecito, palmadita; *(touch)* toque *m*; *(caress)* caricia. **2** *(of butter)* porción *f*.

▷ *vt (tap)* dar palmaditas a; *(touch)* tocar; *(caress)* acariciar.

▲ *pt & pp* patted, *ger* patting.

pat[2] [pæt] *adv* de memoria.

patch [pætʃ] *n* **1** *(to mend clothes)* remiendo, parche *m*. **2** *(over eye)* parche *m*. **3** *(area on surface - gen)* trozo, zona; *(- of colour, damp, etc)* mancha. **4** *(plot of land)* parcela.

▷ *vt (mend)* remendar; *(put patch on)* poner un parche a.

⊙ **to patch up** *vt sep* **1** *(garment)* remendar, poner un parche a. **2** *(quarrel)* resolver; *(marriage)* salvar.

patchwork ['pætʃwɜːk] *n* **1** labor *f* de retales. **2** *fig (of fields)* mosaico.

▷ *adj* de retales.

patchy ['pætʃɪ] *adj* desigual, irregular.

▲ *comp* patchier, *superl* patchiest.

pâté ['pæteɪ] *n* paté *m*.

patent ['peɪtᵊnt] *n* COMM patente *f*.

▷ *adj (obvious)* patente, evidente. ● **patent leather** charol *m*.

▷ *vt* COMM patentar.

patently ['peɪtəntlɪ] *adv* evidentemente.

paternal [pə'tɜːnᵊl] *adj (fatherly)* paternal; *(on father's side)* paterno,-a, por parte de padre.

paternity [pəˈtɜːnɪtɪ] *n* paternidad *f.*
path [pɑːθ] *n* **1** *(track)* camino, sendero, senda: **keep to the path** *seguir el camino.* **2** *(course of bullet, missile)* trayectoria; *(of flight)* rumbo; *(of moon, sun)* recorrido, trayectoria.
pathetic [pəˈθetɪk] *adj* **1** *(rousing pity)* patético,-a. **2** *(awful, hopeless)* malísimo,-a.
pathetically [pəˈθetɪklɪ] *adv* **1** *(pitiably)* patéticamente. **2** *fam (badly, hopelessly)* que da lástima, que da pena.
pathological [pæθəˈlɒdʒɪkəl] *adj* patológico,-a.
pathology [pəˈθɒlədʒɪ] *n* patología.
pathos [ˈpeɪθɒs] *n* patetismo.
pathway [ˈpɑːθweɪ] *n* camino, sendero.
patience [ˈpeɪʃəns] *n* **1** *(quality)* paciencia: **I lost my patience** *perdí la paciencia.* **2** *(card game)* solitario.
patient [ˈpeɪʃᵊnt] *adj (person - gen)* paciente; *(long-suffering)* sufrido,-a: **be patient with him** *ten paciencia con él.*
▷ *n* paciente *mf*, enfermo,-a.
patiently [ˈpeɪʃᵊntlɪ] *adv* pacientemente.
patina [ˈpætɪnə] *n* pátina.
patio [ˈpætɪəʊ] *n* patio.
▲ *pl* **patios.**
patriarch [ˈpeɪtrɪɑːk] *n* patriarca *m.*
patriarchy [ˈpeɪtrɪɑːkɪ] *n* patriarcado.
▲ *pl* **patriarchies.**
patrician [pəˈtrɪʃᵊn] *adj* patricio,-a.
▷ *n* patricio.
patrimony [ˈpætrɪmənɪ] *n* patrimonio.
patriot [ˈpeɪtrɪət] *n* patriota *mf.*
patriotic [pætrɪˈɒtɪk] *adj* patriótico,-a.
patriotism [ˈpætrɪətɪzᵊm] *n* patriotismo.
patrol [pəˈtrəʊl] *n* patrulla, ronda.
▷ *vt (area)* patrullar por, estar de patrulla en.
▲ *pt & pp* **patrolled** (US **patroled**), *ger* **patrolling** (US **patroling**).
patrolman [pəˈtrəʊlmən] *n* US policía *m*, guardia *m.*
▲ *pl* **patrolmen** [pəˈtrəʊlmən].
patron [ˈpeɪtrən] *adj* **1** *(customer)* cliente,-a habitual. **2** *(sponsor)* patrocinador,-ra, mecenas *m.*
patronage [ˈpætrənɪdʒ] *n* patrocinio.
patronize [ˈpætrənaɪz] *vt* **1** *(sponsor - gen)* patrocinar. **2** *pej (condescend to)* tratar con condescendencia.
patronizing [ˈpætrənaɪzɪŋ] *adj pej* condescendiente.
patter[1] [ˈpætəʳ] *n (of rain)* repiqueteo, golpeteo; *(of footsteps)* ruido.
▷ *vi (rain)* repiquetear, golpear; *(feet, person)* corretear.
patter[2] [ˈpætəʳ] *n fam (talk)* parloteo, labia.
pattern [ˈpætən] *n* **1** *(decorative design)* dibujo; *(on fabric)* diseño, estampado. **2** *(way something develops)* orden *m*, estructura. **3** *(example, model)* ejemplo, modelo. **4** *(for sewing, knitting)* patrón *m*; *(sample)* muestra.
patterned [ˈpætənd] *adj (gen)* con dibujos, decorado,-a; *(fabric)* estampado,-a.
paunch [pɔːntʃ] *n* panza, barriga.
paunchy [ˈpɔːntʃɪ] *adj* barrigón,-ona.
▲ *comp* **paunchier**, *superl* **paunchiest.**
pauper [ˈpɔːpəʳ] *n* pobre *mf*, indigente *mf.*
pause [pɔːz] *n* **1** *(gen)* pausa; *(silence)* silencio; *(rest)* descanso. **2** MUS pausa.
▷ *vi (gen)* hacer una pausa; *(stop moving)* detenerse.
pave [peɪv] *vt* pavimentar.
pavement [ˈpeɪvmənt] *n* **1** GB acera. **2** US calzada, pavimento.
pavilion [pəˈvɪljən] *n* **1** *(at exhibition)* pabellón *m.* **2** G *(cricket)* vestuarios *mpl.*
paving [ˈpeɪvɪŋ] *n* pavimento. ● **paving stone** baldosa.
paw [pɔː] *n* **1** ZOOL *(foot)* pata; *(claw - of big cats)* zarpa, garra. **2** *fam (person's hand)* manaza.
▷ *vt* **1** *(animal)* tocar con la pata; *(lion)* dar zarpazos. **2** *pej (person)* manosear, sobar.
pawn[1] [pɔːn] *n (in chess)* peón *m.* **2** *(unimportant person)* juguete *m*, marioneta, títere *m.*
pawn[2] [pɔːn] *n (pledge)* prenda.
▷ *vt* empeñar.
pawnbroker [ˈpɔːnbrəʊkəʳ] *n* prestamista *mf.*
pawnshop [ˈpɔːnʃɒp] *n* casa de empeños.
pay [peɪ] *n (wages)* paga, sueldo, salario.
▷ *vt* **1** *(gen)* pagar; *(bill, debt)* pagar, saldar: **I paid him 1 pounds to mend my bike** *le pagué 10 libras para que me arreglara la bici.* **2** *(make, give - attention)* prestar; *(homage, tribute)* rendir; *(respects)* presentar, ofrecer; *(compliment, visit, call)* hacer. **3** FIN *(make, give - interest, dividends)* dar. **4** *(be worthwhile)* compensar, convenir.
▷ *vi* **1** *(gen)* pagar: **you don't have to pay to go in** *no hay que pagar para entrar.* **2** *fig (suffer)* pagar (**for**, -): **he'll pay for this!** *¡me las pagará!* **3** *(be profitable business, etc)* ser rentable, ser factible. **4** *(be worthwhile)* compensar, convenir. ■ **to get paid** cobrar. ‖ **to pay in advance** pagar por adelantado. ‖ **to pay cash / pay in cash** pagar en efectivo. ● **pay phone** teléfono público.
⊙ **to pay back** *vt sep* **1** *(money)* devolver; *(loan, mortgage)* pagar. **2** *fig (take revenge on)* hacer pagar a.
⊙ **to pay in** *vt sep (money, cheque)* ingresar.
⊙ **to pay off** *vt sep* **1** *(debt)* saldar, liquidar, cancelar; *(loan)* pagar; *(mortgage)* acabar de pagar. **2** *(worker)* dar el finiquito a.
▷ *vi (be successful)* dar resultado; *(prove worthwhile)* valer la pena.
⊙ **to pay out** *vt sep* **1** *(money - spend)* desembolsar (**on** en); *(- give out)* pagar. **2** *(rope)* ir soltando.
▷ *vi* pagar.
▲ *pt & pp* **paid** [peɪd].
⊙ **to pay up** *vi* pagar.
payable [ˈpeɪəbᵊl] *adj* pagadero,-a.
payday [ˈpeɪdeɪ] *n* día *m* de paga.
payee [peɪˈiː] *n* beneficiario,-a.
payer [ˈpeɪəʳ] *n* pagador,-ra.
paying guest [ˈpeɪɪŋˈgest] *adj* huésped,-a de pago.
paymaster [ˈpeɪmɑːstəʳ] *n* (oficial *mf*) pagador,-ra.
payment [ˈpeɪmənt] *n* **1** *(paying)* pago. **2** *(instalment)* plazo.
payoff [ˈpeɪɒf] *n* **1** *(payment - gen)* pago; *(of redundancy money)* indemnización *f.* **2** *(climax, outcome)* desenlace *m*, resultado.
payroll [ˈpeɪrəʊl] *n (gen)* nómina.
PDA [ˈpiːˈdiːˈeɪ] *abbr* (**Personal Digital Assitant**) ayudante *m* personal digital *f*; *(abbreviation)* PDA.
pea [piː] *n* guisante *m.*
peace [piːs] *n* **1** *(not war)* paz *f.* **2** *(tranquillity)* paz, tranquilidad *f.* ■ **at peace / in peace** en paz. ‖ **to make one's peace with** SB hacer las paces con ALGN.
peaceable [ˈpiːsəbᵊl] *adj* pacífico,-a.

eaceful ['pi:sfʊl] *adj* 1 *(non-violent)* pacífico,-a. 2 *(calm)* tranquilo,-a, sosegado,-a.
eace-keeping ['pi:ski:pɪŋ] *adj* pacificador,-ra.
eacemaker ['pi:smeɪkəʳ] *n* conciliador,-ra.
eacetime ['pi:staɪm] *n* tiempos *mpl* de paz.
each [pi:tʃ] *n* 1 *(fruit)* melocotón *m*. 2 *(colour)* (color *m*) melocotón *m*.
▷ *adj* de color melocotón. ● **peach tree** melocotonero.
eacock ['pi:kɒk] *n* pavo real.
eahen ['pi:hen] *n* pava real.
eak [pi:k] *n* 1 GEOG *(of mountain)* pico; *(summit)* cima, cumbre *f*. 2 *fig (highest point)* cumbre *f*; *(climax)* apogeo. 3 *(of cap)* visera. ● **peak hours** horas *fpl* punta.
▷ *adj (maximum)* máximo,-a.
▷ *vi* alcanzar el punto máximo.
eaked [pi:kt] *adj (cap)* con visera.
eaky ['pi:kɪ] *adj fam* pálido,-a.
▲ *comp* **peakier**, *superl* **peakiest**.
eal [pi:l] *n (of bells)* repique *m*. ● **a peal of thunder** un trueno.
▷ *vt (bells)* repicar, tocar a vuelo.
▷ *vi (bells)* repicar, tocar a vuelo.
eanut ['pi:nʌt] *n* cacahuete *m*.
▷ *n pl* **peanuts** *(small amount)* una miseria.
ear [peəʳ] *n (fruit)* pera. ● **pear tree** peral *m*.
earl [pɜ:l] *n* perla.
early ['pɜ:lɪ] *adj* nacarado,-a, perlado,-a.
▲ *comp* **pearlier**, *superl* **pearliest**.
easant ['pezᵊnt] *adj* campesino,-a, rural.
▷ *n* 1 *(gen)* campesino,-a. 2 *pej (uncultured person)* inculto,-a, palurdo,-a.
easantry ['pezəntrɪ] *n* campesinado.
eashooter ['pi:ʃu:təʳ] *n* canuto, cerbatana.
eat [pi:t] *n* turba.
eaty ['pi:tɪ] *adj* turboso.
▲ *comp* **peatier**, *superl* **peatiest**.
ebble ['pebᵊl] *n* guija, guijarro, china.
ecan ['pi:kæn] *n (nut)* pacana; *(tree)* pacanero.
eck [pek] *n (of bird)* picotazo; *(kiss)* besito.
▷ *vt (bird)* picotear; *(kiss)* dar un besito a.
▷ *vi (bird)* picotear (**at**, -).
ecking order ['pekɪŋɔ:dəʳ] *n* jerarquía.
eckish ['pekɪʃ] *adj fam* algo hambriento,-a.
ectin ['pektɪn] *n* pectina.
ectoral ['pektərəl] *adj* pectoral.
eculiar [pɪ'kju:lɪəʳ] *adj* 1 *(strange)* extraño,-a, raro,-a; *(unwell)* indispuesto,-a. 2 *(particular)* característico,-a (**to**, de), propio,-a (**to**, de).
eculiarity [pɪkju:lɪ'ærɪtɪ] *n* 1 *(oddity)* rareza, singularidad *f*. 2 *(distinctive feature, characteristic)* característica.
▲ *pl* **peculiarities**.
eculiarly [pɪ'kju:lɪərlɪ] *adv* 1 *(strangely)* de forma rara. 2 *(especially, more than usually)* especialmente. 3 *(exclusively)* típicamente.
ecuniary [pɪ'kju:nɪərɪ] *adj fml (motives, advantage)* pecuniario,-a; *(problems)* monetario,-a.
edagogy ['pedəgɒdʒɪ] *n* pedagogía.
edal ['pedᵊl] *n (gen)* pedal *m*.
▷ *vi* pedalear.
▲ *pt & pp* **pedalled** (US **pedaled**), *ger* **pedalling** (US **pedaling**).
edalo ['pedᵊləʊ] *n* patín *m*.
▲ *pl* **pedalos o pedaloes**.

pedant ['pedənt] *n* pedante *mf*.
pedantic [pə'dæntɪk] *adj* pedante.
pedantry ['pedəntrɪ] *n* pedantería.
peddle ['pedᵊl] *vt* COMM vender de puerta en puerta.
peddler ['pedləʳ] *n (drug pusher)* traficante *mf* de drogas.
pederast ['pedəræst] *n* pederasta *m*.
pedestal ['pedɪstᵊl] *n* pedestal *m*.
pedestrian [pə'destrɪən] *n* peatón,-ona. ● **pedestrian crossing** paso de peatones. ‖ **pedestrian precinct** zona peatonal.
▷ *adj (dull)* pedestre.
pediatrician [pi:dɪ'ætrɪʃᵊn] *n* US ⟶ **paediatrician**.
pedicure ['pedɪkjʊəʳ] *n* pedicura.
pedigree ['pedɪgri:] *n (of animals)* pedigrí *m*; *(of people)* linaje *m*.
▷ *adj* de raza.
pedlar ['pedləʳ] *n* vendedor,-ra ambulante.
pedophile ['pi:dəfaɪl] *n* US ⟶ **paedophile**.
pee [pi:] *n fam* pis *m*, pipí *m*.
▷ *vi fam* hacer pis, hacer pipí.
peek [pi:k] *n* ojeada, miradita.
▷ *vi* mirar (a hurtadillas).
peel [pi:l] *n (skin - gen)* piel *f*; *(- of orange, lemon, etc)* corteza, cáscara, monda, mondadura.
▷ *vt* pelar, quitar la piel de.
▷ *vi (skin)* pelarse; *(paint)* desconcharse; *(wallpaper)* despegarse.
⊙ **to peel back** *vt sep* quitar, despegar.
⊙ **to peel off** *vt sep (fruit)* pelar, quitar la piel de; *(clothes)* quitarse.
▷ *vi (skin)* pelarse; *(paint)* desconcharse; *(wallpaper)* despegarse.
peeler ['pi:ləʳ] [Also **potato peeler**.] *n* pelapatatas *m*.
peelings ['pi:lɪŋz] *n pl* peladuras *fpl*.
peep¹ [pi:p] *n (look)* ojeada, vistazo.
▷ *vi* espiar, atisbar, mirar a hurtadillas.
peep² [pi:p] *n (noise)* pío: **I don't want to hear another peep out of you!** *¡que no te oiga decir ni pío!*
peephole ['pi:phəʊl] *n* mirilla.
peeping Tom [pi:pɪŋ'tɒm] *n pej* mirón *m*.
peepshow ['pi:pʃəʊ] *n (machine)* mundonuevo, cosmorama *m*.
peer¹ [pɪəʳ] *vi (look closely)* mirar detenidamente (**at**, -).
peer² [pɪəʳ] *n* 1 *(equal)* par *mf*, igual *mf*. 2 GB *(noble)* par *mf*, noble *mf*.
peerage ['pɪərɪdʒ] *n (rank)* título nobiliario.
▷ *n* **the peerage** *(nobility)* la nobleza.
peeress ['pɪəres] *n* paresa.
peeved [pi:vd] *adj fam* mosqueado,-a.
peevish ['pi:vɪʃ] *adj fam (irritable)* malhumorado,-a.
peg [peg] *n* 1 *(for hanging clothes on)* percha, colgador *m*. 2 TECH clavija.
▷ *vt* 1 *(clothes)* tender (**out**, -); *(tent)* fijar con estacas (**down**, -). 2 *(prices)* fijar, estabilizar.
▲ *pt & pp* **pegged**, *ger* **pegging**.
⊙ **to peg out** *vi fam (die)* estirar la pata.
pejorative [pə'dʒɒrətɪv] *adj* despectivo,-a.
pelican ['pelɪkən] *n* pelícano.
pellet ['pelɪt] *n* 1 *(small ball)* bolita. 2 *(piece of shot)* perdigón *m*.
pell-mell [pel'mel] *adv* desordenadamente.
pelmet ['pelmɪt] *n* GB galería (de cortina).

pelt[1] [pelt] *vt* tirar, lanzar, arrojar: **he was pelted with questions** *lo bombardearon a preguntas.*
▷ *vi* **1** *(rain)* llover a cántaros (**down**, -). **2** *(run)* correr a toda prisa; *(move fast)* ir a toda máquina.
pelt[2] [pelt] *n (skin)* piel *f*, pellejo.
pelvis ['pelvɪs] *n* pelvis *f*.
pen[1] [pen] *n (gen)* pluma; *(ballpoint)* bolígrafo *m*.
▷ *vt (write - gen)* escribir.
▲ *pt & pp* **penned**, *ger* **penning.**
pen[2] [pen] *n* corral *m*.
⊙ **to pen in / pen up** *vt sep* encerrar, acorralar.
pen[3] [pen] *n* US *fam (penitentiary)* chirona, talego.
penal ['pi:nᵊl] *adj* penal.
penalize ['pi:nəlaɪz] *vt* **1** *(punish)* castigar, sancionar. **2** SP penalizar. **3** *(put at a disadvantage)* perjudicar.
penalty ['penᵊltɪ] *n* **1** *(gen)* pena, castigo; *(fine)* multa. **2** SP *(gen)* castigo (máximo); *(football)* penalti *m*. **3** *(disadvantage)* desventaja, inconveniente *m*. ■ **to pay the penalty for sth** pagar las consecuencias de algo.
▲ *pl* **penalties.**
pencil ['pensᵊl] *n* lápiz *m*: **write in pencil** *escribir con lápiz.* ● **pencil sharpener** sacapuntas *m*.
▷ *vt (write)* escribir con lápiz; *(draw)* dibujar con lápiz.
▲ *pt & pp* **pencilled** *(*US **penciled***)*, *ger* **pencilling** *(*US **penciling***)*.
⊙ **to pencil in** *vt sep* anotar provisionalmente.
pendant ['pendənt] *n* colgante *m*.
pending ['pendɪŋ] *adj (waiting to be decided or settled)* pendiente; *(imminent)* próximo,-a, inminente.
▷ *prep (while awaiting)* en espera de.
pendulum ['pendjʊləm] *n* péndulo.
penetrate ['penɪtreɪt] *vt* **1** *(gen)* penetrar en; *(organization)* infiltrarse en. **2** *(understand)* entender.
▷ *vi (sink in)* causar impresión, hacer mella en.
penetrating ['penɪtreɪtɪŋ] *adj (gen)* penetrante; *(mind)* penetrante, perspicaz.
penetration [penɪ'treɪʃᵊn] *n* **1** *(gen)* penetración *f*. **2** *(insight)* perspicacia, agudeza.
penfriend ['penfrend] *n* amigo,-a por correspondencia.
penguin ['peŋgwɪn] *n* pingüino.
penicillin [penɪ'sɪlɪn] *n* penicilina.
peninsula [pə'nɪnsjʊlə] *n* península.
penis ['pi:nɪs] *n* ANAT pene *m*.
▲ *pl* **penises** o **penes** ['pi:ni:z].
penitent ['penɪtent] *adj* penitente.
penknife ['pennaɪf] *n* cortaplumas *m*, navaja.
▲ *pl* **penknives** ['pennaɪvz].
pennant ['penənt] *n* banderín *m*.
penniless ['penɪləs] *adj* pobre, sin dinero.
penny ['penɪ] *n* **1** GB penique *m*. **2** US centavo.
▲ *pl* **penises** o **pence** [pens].
penny-pinching ['penɪpɪntʃɪŋ] *adj* tacaño,-a.
pennyroyal [penɪ'rɔɪəl] *n* poleo.
pension ['penʃᵊn] *n* pensión *f*.
⊙ **to pension off** *vt sep* jubilar.
pensioner ['penʃᵊnəʳ] *n* jubilado,-a, pensionista *mf*.
pensive ['pensɪv] *adj* pensativo,-a.
pentagon ['pentəgən] *n* pentágono.
pentathlon [pen'tæθlən] *n* pentatlón *m*.
penthouse ['penthaʊs] *n* ático, sobreático.
pent-up ['pentʌp] *adj* **1** *(confined)* encerrado,-a. **2** *(repressed - emotions)* reprimido,-a.

penultimate [pɪ'nʌltɪmət] *adj* penúltimo,-a.
penury ['penjʊrɪ] *n* miseria, pobreza.
peony ['pi:ənɪ] *n* BOT peonía.
▲ *pl* **peonies.**
people ['pi:pᵊl] *n pl* **1** *(gen)* gente *f*, personas *fpl*: **a lot of people** *mucha gente;* **over a hundred people** *más de cien personas;* **people say that...** *dicen que..., se dice que...* *(citizens)* ciudadanos *mpl*; *(inhabitants)* habitantes *mpl*. **old people** los viejos *mpl*, la gente *f* mayor. ▮ **people's republic** república popular. ▮ **the common people** la gente *f* corriente. ▮ **young people** los jóvenes *mpl*, la gente *f* joven.
▷ *n (nation, race)* pueblo, nación *f*.
▷ *vt* poblar.
Consulta también person
pep [pep] *n fam* energía, vitalidad *f*.
⊙ **to pep up** *vt sep* animar.
pepper ['pepəʳ] *n* **1** *(spice)* pimienta. **2** *(vegetable)* pimiento.
▷ *vt* CULIN echar pimienta a.
⊙ **to pepper with** *vt sep* **1** *(hit, pelt)* acribillar a. **2** *fig (intersperse)* salpicar de.
peppercorn ['pepəkɔ:n] *n* grano de pimienta.
peppermint ['pepəmɪnt] *n* **1** BOT menta. **2** *(sweet)* caramelo de menta.
peppery ['pepərɪ] *adj* CULIN *(taste)* a pimienta; *(spicy)* picante.
per [pɜ:ʳ] *prep* por: **100 miles per hour** *100 millas por hora.* ■ **as per** de acuerdo con, según. ▮ **per annum** por año, al año. ▮ **per cent** por ciento.
perceive [pə'si:v] *vt (see)* percibir, ver; *(notice)* notar; *(realize)* darse cuenta de.
percentage [pə'sentɪdʒ] *n* porcentaje *m*.
perceptible [pə'septəbᵊl] *adj (visible)* perceptible, visible; *(audible)* perceptible, audible; *(noticeable)* sensible, apreciable.
perception [pə'sepʃᵊn] *n* **1** *(sense)* percepción *f*. **2** *(insight)* perspicacia, agudeza. **3** *(way of understanding)* idea.
perceptive [pə'septɪv] *adj (person)* perspicaz.
perch[1] [pɜ:tʃ] *n (fish)* perca.
▲ *pl* **perch** o **perches.**
perch[2] [pɜ:tʃ] *n* **1** *(for bird)* percha. **2** *(high position)* posición *f* elevada, posición *f* privilegiada; *(pedestal)* pedestal *m*.
▷ *vt* poner, colocar.
▷ *vi (bird)* posarse (**on**, en); *(person)* sentarse (**on**, en).
percolate ['pɜ:kəleɪt] *vt (coffee)* hacer (en una cafetera eléctrica).
▷ *vi* **1** *(gen)* filtrarse; *(coffee)* hacerse.
percolator ['pɜ:kəleɪtəʳ] *n* cafetera eléctrica.
percussion [pɜ:'kʌʃᵊn] *n* percusión *f*.
percussionist [pe'kʌʃᵊnɪst] *n* percusionista *nf*.
perennial [pə'renɪəl] *adj* **1** *(plant)* perenne. **2** *(problem)* perenne, eterno,-a; *(subject)* eterno,-a, de siempre.
perfect [*(adj)* 'pɜ:fɪkt; *(vb)* pə'fekt] *adj* **1** *(gen)* perfecto,-a. **2** *(absolute, utter - fool)* perdido,-a, redomado,-a; *(- gentleman)* consumado; *(- waste of time)* auténtico,-a: **he's a perfect stranger to me** *me es totalmente desconocido.* **3** LING perfecto,-a.
▷ *n* LING perfecto.
▷ *vt* perfeccionar.
perfection [pə'fekʃᵊn] *n* **1** *(state, quality)* perfección. **2** *(act)* perfeccionamiento. ■ **to do** STH **to perfection** hacer ALGO a la perfección.

erfectionist [pəˈfekʃənɪst] *n* perfeccionista *mf*.
erforate [ˈpɜːfəreɪt] *vt* perforar.
erforation [pɜːfəˈreɪʃən] *n* perforación *f*.
erform [pəˈfɔːm] *vt* **1** *(task)* ejecutar; *(function)* hacer, cumplir. **2** *(piece of music)* interpretar, tocar; *(song)* cantar; *(play)* representar, dar; *(role)* interpretar.
▷ *vi* **1** *(actor)* actuar; *(singer)* cantar; *(musician)* tocar, interpretar; *(dancer)* bailar. **2** *(machine)* funcionar, marchar; *(person)* trabajar.
erformance [pəˈfɔːməns] *n* **1** *(of task)* ejecución *f*, realización *f*; *(of function, duty)* desempeño. **2** *(session - at theatre)* función *f*; *(- of circus, show, etc)* número, espectáculo. **3** *(action - of song, of musician)* interpretación *f*; *(- of play)* representación *f*; *(- of actor)* interpretación *f*, actuación *f*. **4** *(of machine)* funcionamiento.
erformer [pəˈfɔːmər] *n (gen)* artista *mf*, actor *m*, actriz *f*; *(musician)* artista, intérprete *mf*.
erforming arts [pəfɔːmɪŋˈɑːts] *n pl* artes *fpl* interpretativas.
erfume [ˈpɜːfjuːm] *n* perfume *m*.
▷ *vt* perfumar.
erfunctory [pəˈfʌŋktərɪ] *adj* superficial.
ergola [ˈpɜːgələ] *n* pérgola.
erhaps [pəˈhæps] *adv* quizá, tal vez: **perhaps they've got lost** *quizá se hayan perdido*.
eril [ˈperəl] *n (danger)* peligro. ■ **at one's own peril** por su cuenta y riesgo.
erilous [ˈperɪləs] *adj* peligroso,-a.
erilously [ˈperɪləslɪ] *adv* peligrosamente.
erimeter [pəˈrɪmɪtər] *n* perímetro.
eriod [ˈpɪərɪəd] *n* **1** *(length of time)* período, periodo. **2** *(epoch)* época. **3** GEOL período. **4** EDUC *(lesson)* clase *f*. **5** *(menstruation)* regla, período. **6** US *(full stop)* punto.
▷ *adj (dress, furniture)* de época.
eriodic [pɪərɪˈɒdɪk] *adj* periódico,-a. ● **periodic table** CHEM tabla periódica.
eriodical [pɪərɪˈɒdɪkəl] *adj* periódico,-a.
▷ *n* publicación *f* periódica.
eripatetic [perɪpəˈtetɪk] *adj* itinerante.
eripheral [pəˈrɪfərəl] *adj* **1** *(zone, etc)* periférico,-a. **2** *(secondary)* secundario,-a.
eriphery [pəˈrɪfərɪ] *n* **1** *(of city)* periferia. **2** *(of society)* margen *m*.
eriscope [ˈperɪskəʊp] *n* periscopio.
erish [ˈperɪʃ] *vi* **1** *(die)* fallecer. **2** *(decay)* estropearse.
▷ *vt (rubber)* deteriorar.
erishable [ˈperɪʃəbəl] *adj* perecedero,-a.
erishing [ˈperɪʃɪŋ] *adj* **it's perishing** GB *fam* hace un frío que pela.
eritonitis [perɪtəˈnaɪtəs] *n* MED peritonitis *f*.
erk [pɜːk] *n fam (benefit)* beneficio, extra *m*; *(money, goods)* gajes *mpl*.
to perk up *vt sep* animar, reanimar.
▷ *vi (person)* animarse, reanimarse.
erky [ˈpɜːkɪ] *adj* animado,-a, alegre.
▲ *comp* **perkier**, *superl* **perkiest**.
erm [pɜːm] *n fam (in hair)* permanente *f*.
ermanence [ˈpɜːmənəns] *n* permanencia.
ermanent [ˈpɜːmənənt] *adj* **1** *(lasting - gen)* permanente; *(damage)* irreparable. **2** *(job, address)* fijo,-a.
ermeable [ˈpɜːmɪəbəl] *adj* permeable (**to**, a).
ermeate [ˈpɜːmɪeɪt] *vt* impregnar.

permissible [pɜːˈmɪsəbəl] *adj (allowed)* permisible, lícito,-a; *(acceptable)* aceptable.
permission [pəˈmɪʃən] *n (gen)* permiso; *(authorization)* autorización *f*.
permissive [pəˈmɪsɪv] *adj* permisivo,-a.
permit [*(n)* ˈpɜːmɪt; *(vb)* pɜːˈmɪt] *n (gen)* permiso; *(licence)* permiso, licencia.
▷ *vt (gen)* permitir; *(authorize)* autorizar.
▷ *vi* permitir: **weather permitting** *si el tiempo lo permite*.
▲ *pt & pp* **permitted**, *ger* **permitting**.
permutation [pɜːmjʊˈteɪʃən] *n* **1** MATH permutación *f*. **2** GB *fam (in football pools)* combinación *f*.
pernicious [pɜːˈnɪsəs] *adj fml* pernicioso,-a.
pernickety [pɜːˈnɪkətɪ] *adj fam (person)* quisquilloso, -a; *(job)* delicado,-a.
perpendicular [pɜːpənˈdɪkjʊlər] *adj* **1** MATH perpendicular (**to**, a). **2** *(upright)* vertical.
▷ *n* perpendicular *f*.
perpetrate [ˈpɜːpɪtreɪt] *vt fml* perpetrar, cometer.
perpetrator [ˈpɜːpɪtreɪtər] *n* autor,-ra.
perpetual [pəˈpetjʊəl] *adj (permanent)* perpetuo,-a.
perpetuate [pəˈpetjʊeɪt] *vt* perpetuar.
perpetuity [pɜːpɪˈtjuːɪtɪ] *n* perpetuidad *f*.
perplex [pəˈpleks] *vt* dejar perplejo,-a, desconcertar.
perplexing [pəˈpleksɪŋ] *adj* desconcertante.
perplexity [pəˈpleksɪtɪ] *n* perplejidad *f*.
persecute [ˈpɜːsɪkjuːt] *vt (for beliefs)* perseguir; *(hound, harass)* atormentar, acosar.
persecution [pɜːsɪˈkjuːʃən] *n* persecución *f*.
persecutor [ˈpɜːsɪkjuːtər] *n* perseguidor,-ra.
perseverance [pɜːsɪˈvɪərəns] *n* perseverancia.
persevere [pɜːsɪˈvɪər] *vi* perseverar (**at/in/with**, en).
persevering [pɜːsɪˈvɪərɪŋ] *adj* perseverante.
persist [pəˈsɪst] *vi* **1** *(person)* persistir (**in**, en). **2** *(pain, loyalty, belief)* persistir; *(rain)* continuar.
persistence [pəˈsɪstəns] *n* **1** *(continuation)* persistencia. **2** *(determination, insistence)* perseverancia, empeño.
persistent [pəˈsɪstənt] *adj* **1** *(person)* insistente. **2** *(cough, pain, fog)* persistente; *(rain)* continuo,-a; *(denials, rumours, warnings)* continuo,-a, constante, repetido,-a.
person [ˈpɜːsən] *n* **1** *(gen)* persona: **he's a really nice person** *es una persona muy simpática;* **2** LING persona. ■ **in person** personalmente.

El plural más usual es **people**, pero **persons** se emplea en el lenguaje jurídico.

personable [ˈpɜːsənəbəl] *adj (good looking)* bien parecido,-a; *(pleasant)* amable, afable.
personal [ˈpɜːsənəl] *adj* **1** *(private)* personal, privado, -a: **for personal reasons** *por motivos personales.* **2** *(own)* particular, personal: **she's got a personal trainer** *tiene un entrenador particular.* **3** *(individual)* personal: **it's a personal opinion** *es una opinión personal.* **4** *(physical - appearance)* personal; *(hygiene)* íntimo,-a, personal. **5** *(in person)* en persona: **I'll give it my personal attention** *me encargaré de ello personalmente.* ● **personal computer** ordenador personal.
personality [pɜːsəˈnælɪtɪ] *n* **1** *(nature)* personalidad *f*. **2** *(famous person)* personaje *m*.
▲ *pl* **personalities**.
personalize [ˈpɜːsənəlaɪz] *vt* personalizar.

personally ['pɜːsənəlɪ] *adv* **1** *(in person)* personalmente, en persona. **2** *(for my part)* personalmente. **3** *(as a person)* como persona. ■ **to take** STH **personally** ofenderse.
personify [pɜː'sɒnɪfaɪ] *vt* personificar.
▲ *pt & pp* **personified**, *ger* **personifying**.
personnel [pɜːsə'nel] *n* personal *m*.
perspective [pə'spektɪv] *n* **1** ART perspectiva. **2** *fig (view, angle)* perspectiva. ■ **to get/keep things in perspective** tratar de ver las cosas objetivamente.
perspicacious [pɜːspɪ'keɪʃəs] *adj fml* perspicaz.
perspiration [pɜːspɪ'reɪʃən] *n* transpiración *f*, sudor *m*.
perspire [pə'spaɪər] *vi* transpirar, sudar.
persuade [pə'sweɪd] *vt* persuadir, convencer.
persuasion [pə'sweɪʒən] *n* **1** *(act)* persuasión *f*. **2** *(ability)* persuasiva.
persuasive [pə'sweɪsɪəv] *adj* convincente.
pert [pɜːt] *adj (cheeky)* fresco,-a; *(girl)* pizpireta.
pertain [pɜː'teɪn] *vi fml (connected with)* estar relacionado,-a (**to**, con).
pertinence ['pɜːtɪnəns] *n fml* pertinencia.
pertinent ['pɜːtɪnənt] *adj fml* pertinente (**to**, a).
perturb [pə'tɜːb] *vt* perturbar, inquietar.
Peru [pə'ruː] *n* Perú.
peruse [pə'ruːz] *vt* **1** *(read carefully)* leer detenidamente. **2** *(browse)* leer por encima.
Peruvian [pə'ruːvɪən] *adj* peruano,-a.
▷ *n (person)* peruano,-a.
pervade [pɜː'veɪd] *vt (smell)* penetrar; *(idea, feeling, mood)* extenderse, dominar.
pervasive [pɜː'veɪsɪv] *adj (smell)* penetrante; *(influence, mood)* extendido,-a, dominante.
perverse [pə'vɜːs] *adj* **1** *(delight, desire, pleasure, etc)* perverso,-a, malsano,-a. **2** *(person - stubborn)* terco,-a; *(contrary)* puñetero,-a.
perversion [pə'vɜːʃən] *n* **1** *(sexual)* perversión *f*. **2** *(distortion)* tergiversación *f*, distorsión *f*.
perversity [pə'vɜːsɪtɪ] *n (wickedness)* perversidad *f*; *(stubbornness)* terquedad *f*.
▲ *pl* **perversities**.
pervert [*(n)* 'pɜːvɜːt; *(vb)* pə'vɜːt] *n (sexual)* pervertido,-a.
▷ *vt* **1** *(corrupt)* pervertir. **2** *(truth, justice)* tergiversar.
pessimist ['pesɪmɪst] *n* pesimista *mf*.
pessimistic [pesɪ'mɪstɪk] *adj* pesimista.
pest [pest] *n* **1** plaga: **greenfly and other pests** *pulgones y otras plagas*. **2** *fam (person)* pelma *mf*, pesado,-a; *(thing)* lata, rollo.
pester ['pestər] *vt* molestar.
pesticide ['pestɪsaɪd] *n* pesticida.
pestle ['pesəl] *n* mano *f* (de mortero), maja.
pet [pet] *n (tame animal)* animal *m* de compañía, mascota.
▷ *adj* **1** *(kind person)* sol, cielo; *(term of affection)* cariño, cielo. **2** *(tame)* domesticado,-a. **3** *(favourite - theory, subject, etc)* favorito,-a. ● **pet name** nombre *m* cariñoso. ‖ **pet shop** tienda de animales.
▷ *vt (animal)* acariciar.
▷ *vi fam* tocarse y besuquearse.
▲ *pt & pp* **petted**, *ger* **petting**.
petal ['petəl] *n* pétalo.
peter out [piːtər'aʊt] *vi (supplies)* acabarse, agotarse; *(enthusiasm, interest)* decaer; *(track, path)* perderse.
petiole ['petɪəʊl] *n* pecíolo.
petite [pə'tiːt] *adj (woman)* menuda, chiquita.

petition [pə'tɪʃən] *n* **1** petición *f*, solicitud *f*. **2** JUR de manda.
▷ *vt* presentar una solicitud a.
▷ *vi* solicitar (**for**, -).
petrify ['petrɪfaɪ] *vt fam (terrify)* petrificar, aterrorizar.
▲ *pt & pp* **petrified**, *ger* **petrifying**.
petrochemical [petrəʊ'kemɪkəl] *adj* petroquímico,-a.
petrol ['petrəl] *n* gasolina. ● **petrol pump** surtidor *m* d gasolina. ‖ **petrol station** gasolinera.
petroleum [pə'trəʊlɪəm] *n* petróleo. ● **petroleum jel** vaselina.
petticoat ['petɪkəʊt] *n (underskirt)* enaguas *fpl*; *(slip* enagua, combinación *f*.
petty ['petɪ] *adj* **1** *(trivial)* insignificante, sin importar cia. **2** *(mean)* mezquino,-a. ● **petty cash** dinero par gastos *mpl* menores.
▲ *comp* **pettier**, *superl* **pettiest**.
petulant ['petjʊlənt] *adj* malhumorado,-a.
pew [pjuː] *n* banco de iglesia.
pewter ['pjuːtər] *n* peltre *m*.
phalange ['fælændʒ] *n* falange *f*.
phallic ['fælɪk] *adj* fálico,-a.
phallus ['fæləs] *n* falo.
phantom ['fæntəm] *n (ghost)* fantasma *m*.
▷ *adj (imaginary)* ilusorio,-a, imaginario,-a.
Pharaoh ['feərəʊ] *n* faraón *m*.
pharmaceutical [fɑːmə'sjuːtɪkəl] *adj* farmacéutico,-a
pharmacist ['fɑːməsɪst] *n* farmacéutico,-a.
pharmacy ['fɑːməsɪ] *n* farmacia.
▲ *pl* **pharmacies**.
pharyngitis [færɪn'dʒaɪtɪs] *n* faringitis *f*.
pharynx ['færɪŋks] *n* faringe *f*.
phase [feɪz] *n (gen)* fase *f*; *(stage)* etapa.
▷ *vt* escalonar, realizar por etapas.
⊙ **to phase in** *vt sep* introducir paulatinamente.
⊙ **to phase out** *vt sep* retirar paulatinamente.
pheasant ['fezənt] *n* faisán *m*.
phenomenal [fɪ'nɒmɪnəl] *adj* extraordinario,-a.
phenomenon [fɪ'nɒmɪnən] *n* fenómeno.
▲ *pl* **phenomenons** o **phenomena** [fɪ'nɒmɪnə].
phew [fjuː] *interj* ¡uf!
phial [faɪəl] *n* frasco.
philanthropist [fɪ'lænθrəpɪst] *n* filántropo,-a.
philately [fɪ'lætəlɪ] *n* filatelia.
philharmonic [fɪlɑː'mɒnɪk] *adj* filarmónico,-a.
Philippine ['fɪlɪpiːn] *adj* filipino,-a.
Philippines ['fɪlɪpiːnz] *n* Filipinas.
philology [fɪ'lɒlədʒɪ] *n* filología.
philosopher [fɪ'lɒsəfər] *n* filósofo,-a.
philosophical [fɪlə'sɒfɪkəl] *adj* filosófico,-a.
philosophize [fɪ'lɒsəfaɪz] *vi* filosofar.
philosophy [fɪ'lɒsəfɪ] *n* filosofía.
phlegm [flem] *n* flema.
phlegmatic [fleg'mætɪk] *adj* flemático,-a.
phobia ['fəʊbɪə] *n* fobia.
phoenix ['fiːnɪks] *n* fénix *m*.
phone [fəʊn] *n fam* teléfono. ● **phone book** listín guía telefónica.
▷ *vt* llamar (por teléfono), telefonear.
▷ *vi* llamar (por teléfono), telefonear.
Consulta también **telephone**.
phonecard ['fəʊnkɑːd] *n* tarjeta telefónica.

phone-in ['fəʊnɪn] *n* programa *m* en el que participa el público por teléfono.
phonetics [fə'netɪks] *n* fonética.
phoney ['fəʊnɪ] *adj fam (gen)* falso,-a.
▲ *comp* phonier, *superl* phoniest.
▷ *n fam (person)* farsante *mf*; *(thing)* falsificación *f*.
phonograph ['fəʊnəgrɑːf] *n* fonógrafo.
phosphorescent [fɒsfə'resᵊnt] *adj* fosforescente.
phosphorus ['fɒsfərəs] *n* fósforo.
photo ['fəʊtəʊ] *n fam* foto *f*.
photocopier ['fəʊtəʊkɒpɪəʳ] *n* fotocopiadora.
photocopy ['fəʊtəʊkɒpɪ] *n* fotocopia.
▲ *pl* photocopies.
▷ *vt* fotocopiar.
▲ *pt & pp* photocopied, *ger* photocopying.
photoelectric [fəʊtəʊɪ'lektrɪk] *adj* fotoeléctrico,-a.
photogenic [fəʊtəʊ'dʒenɪk] *adj* fotogénico,-a.
photograph ['fəʊtəgrɑːf] *n* fotografía, foto *f*: **colour photograph** *fotografía en color.* ■ **to take a photograph of** STH/SB fotografiar ALGO/a ALGN.
▷ *vt* fotografiar.
photographer [fə'tɒgrəfəʳ] *n* fotógrafo,-a.
photographic [fəʊtə'græfɪk] *adj* fotográfico,-a.
photography [fə'tɒgrəfɪ] *n* fotografía.
photosensitive [fəʊtəʊ'sensɪtɪv] *adj* fotosensible.
photosynthesis [fəʊtəʊ'sɪnθəsɪs] *n* fotosíntesis *f*.
phrasal verb [freɪzᵊl'vɜːb] *n* verbo compuesto.
phrase [freɪz] *n* **1** LING frase *f*, locución *f*. **2** *(expression)* frase *f*, expresión *f*.
▷ *vt (express)* expresar.
physical ['fɪzɪkᵊl] *adj* **1** *(gen)* físico,-a, material. **2** *(of physics)* físico,-a. **3** *fam euph (rough)* duro,-a: **it was a very physical game** *fue un partido muy duro.* ● **physical education** educación *f* física. ‖ **physical geography** geografía física.
▷ *n (medical examination)* reconocimiento médico.
physically ['fɪzɪklɪ] *adv* físicamente.
physician [fɪ'zɪʃᵊn] *n* médico,-a.
physicist ['fɪzɪsɪst] *n* físico,-a.
physics ['fɪzɪks] *n* física.
physiognomy [fɪzɪ'ɒnəmɪ] *n* fisionomía.
physiology [fɪzɪ'ɒlədʒɪ] *n* fisiología.
physiotherapist [fɪzɪəʊ'θerəpɪst] *n* fisioterapeuta *mf*.
physiotherapy [fɪzɪəʊ'θerəpɪ] *n* fisioterapia.
physique [fɪ'ziːk] *n* físico.
pianist ['pɪənɪst] *n* pianista *mf*.
piano [pɪ'ænəʊ] *n (instrument)* piano.
▲ *pl* pianos.
piccolo ['pɪkələʊ] *n* flautín *m*.
▲ *pl* piccolos.
pick[1] [pɪk] *n (tool)* pico, piqueta.
pick[2] [pɪk] *n (choice)* elección *f*, selección *f*: **take your pick** *elige el que quieras.*
▷ *vt* **1** *(choose - gen)* elegir, escoger; *(team)* seleccionar. **2** *(flowers, fruit, cotton, etc)* coger, recoger. **3** *(remove pieces from - gen)* escarbar, hurgar; *(spots)* tocarse. **4** *(remove from - hair, etc)* quitar. **5** *(open - lock)* forzar, abrir con una ganzúa. **6** *(of birds)* picotear.
⊙ **to pick at** *vt insep (gen)* tocar; *(food)* comer sin ganas.
⊙ **to pick off** *vt sep (shoot)* matar uno a uno.
⊙ **to pick on** *vt insep (victimize)* meterse con; *(choose for task)* elegir, escoger.
⊙ **to pick out** *vt sep* **1** *(choose)* elegir, escoger. **2** *(see, discern)* distinguir; *(recognize)* reconocer.
⊙ **to pick up** *vt sep* **1** *(lift)* levantar; *(from floor)* recoger; *(take)* coger; *(stitch)* coger; *(telephone)* descolgar: **don't forget to pick up all your litter** *no os olvidéis de recoger toda la basura.* **2** *(learn - language)* aprender; *(- habit)* adquirir, coger; *(- news, gossip)* descubrir, enterarse de. **3** *(illness, cold)* pescar, pillar. **4** *(acquire, get)* conseguir, encontrar. **5** *(collect - person)* recoger, pasar a buscar; *(- hitchhiker)* coger; *(- thing)* recoger: **I'll pick you up at 9.00 pm** *te vendré a buscar a las nueve.* **6** *fam (man, woman)* ligar con, ligarse. **7** *(on radio)* captar, recibir. **8** *(resume - conversation)* reanudar.
▷ *vi* **1** *(improve - health, weather, acting)* mejorar. **2** *(resume)* seguir, continuar.
⊙ **to pick up on** *vt insep (news)* hacer reseña de; *(point)* volver a; *(mistake)* señalar.
pickaxe ['pɪkæks] *n* GB pico, piqueta.
picker ['pɪkəʳ] *n* recolector,-ra.
picket ['pɪkɪt] *n* **1** *(industry)* piquete *m*. **2** *(stick)* estaca.
▷ *vt (factory, etc)* formar un piquete frente a.
▷ *vi* formar parte de un piquete.
pickle ['pɪkᵊl] *vt* encurtir, conservar en vinagre.
▷ *n* CULIN *(food)* conserva en vinagre.
▷ *n pl* **pickles** *(vegetables)* encurtidos *mpl*.
pickled ['pɪkᵊld] *adj (food)* encurtido,-a.
pick-me-up ['pɪkmiːʌp] *n* tónico, reconstituyente *m*.
pickpocket ['pɪkpɒkɪt] *n* carterista *mf*.
pick-up ['pɪkʌp] *n (on record player)* brazo (del tocadiscos), fonocaptor *m*. ● **pick-up truck** furgoneta, camioneta.
picnic ['pɪknɪk] *n* picnic *m*.
▷ *vi (go on a picnic)* ir de picnic; *(eat)* hacer un picnic.
▲ *pt & pp* picnicked, *ger* picnicking.
picnicker ['pɪknɪkəʳ] *n* excursionista *mf*.
pictorial [pɪk'tɔːrɪəl] *adj* ilustrado,-a.
picture ['pɪktʃəʳ] *n* **1** *(painting)* pintura, cuadro; *(portrait)* retrato; *(drawing)* dibujo, grabado; *(illustration)* ilustración *f*, lámina; *(photograph)* fotografía, foto *f*: **he painted her picture** *la retrató;* **I took a picture of them** *les saqué una foto.* **2** *(account, description)* descripción *f*; *(mental picture)* imagen *f*, idea, impresión *f*. **3** TV *(quality of image)* imagen *f*. **4** GB *(film)* película. ■ **to get the picture** entender, enterarse. ● **picture book** libro ilustrado. ‖ **picture window** ventanal *m*.
▷ *vt* **1** *(imagine)* imaginarse, verse: **I can't picture them married** *no me los imagino casados.* **2** *(paint)* pintar; *(draw)* dibujar.
▷ *n pl* **the pictures** GB el cine.
picturesque [pɪktʃᵊ'resk] *adj* pintoresco,-a.
pie [paɪ] *n* CULIN *(sweet)* pastel *m*, tarta; *(savoury)* pastel *m*, empanada. ■ **pie in the sky** pura fantasía.
piece [piːs] *n* **1** *(bit - large)* trozo, pedazo; *(small)* cacho; *(of broken glass)* fragmento. **2** *(part, component)* pieza, parte *f*: **a thirty-piece dinner service** *una vajilla de treinta piezas.* **3** *(coin)* moneda. **4** *(in board games)* ficha. **5** *(in newspaper)* artículo. **6** *(item, example of)* pieza: **a piece of advice** *un consejo;* **a piece of chalk** *una tiza;* **a piece of furniture** *un mueble;* **a piece of news** *una noticia;* **a piece of paper** *un papel;* **a piece of work** *un trabajo.* ■ **in one piece** *(unharmed)* sano,-a y salvo,

-a. ▮ **to be in pieces** *(dismantled)* estar desmontado,-a. ▮ **to break** STH **in pieces** hacer ALGO pedazos.
⊙ **to piece together** *vt sep (facts, events)* reconstruir; *(torn letter, etc)* recomponer; *(jigsaw)* hacer.
piecemeal ['pi:smi:l] *adv (unsystematically)* de manera poco sistemática.
▷ *adj (gradual)* gradual; *(unsystematic)* poco sistemático,-a.
piecework ['pi:swɜ:k] *n* trabajo a destajo.
pier [pɪəʳ] *n* **1** *(landing place)* muelle *m*, embarcadero. **2** ARCH *(pillar)* pilar *m*, estribo.
pierce [pɪəs] *vt* **1** *(make hole in)* perforar, agujerear; *(go through)* atravesar, traspasar. **2** *(of light, sound)* penetrar.
piercing ['pɪəsɪŋ] *adj (sound)* agudo,-a; *(scream)* desgarrador,-ra; *(look)* penetrante; *(wind)* cortante.
piety ['paɪətɪ] *n* piedad *f*.
pig [pɪg] *n* **1** ZOOL cerdo, puerco, marrano. **2** *pej (ill-mannered person)* cerdo, puerco, cochino; *(glutton)* glotón,-ona, tragón,-ona, comilón,-ona.
⊙ **to pig out** *vi* US pegarse un atracón (**on**, de).
pigeon ['pɪdʒɪn] *n (bird)* paloma; *(for eating)* pichón *m*.
pigeonhole ['pɪdʒɪnhəʊl] *n* casilla.
▷ *vt* encasillar.
piggyback ['pɪgɪbæk] *adv* a cuestas.
pig-headed [pɪg'hedɪd] *adj* terco,-a, testarudo,-a, cabezudo,-a.
piglet ['pɪglət] *n* cerdito, cochinillo.
pigment ['pɪgmənt] *n* pigmento.
pigskin ['pɪgskɪn] *n* piel *f* de cerdo.
pigsty ['pɪgstaɪ] *n* pocilga.
▲ *pl* **pigsties**.
pigswill ['pɪgswɪl] *n* bazofia.
pigtail ['pɪgteɪl] *n* coleta.
pike[1] [paɪk] *n (weapon)* pica.
pike[2] [paɪk] *n (fish)* lucio.
pilaster [pɪ'læstəʳ] *n* pilastra.
pilchard ['pɪltʃəd] *n* sardina.
pile[1] [paɪl] *n* **1** *(heap)* montón *m*, pila. **2** *fam (a lot of)* montón *m*, pila.
▷ *vt* **1** *(form a pile)* amontonar, apilar. **2** *(fill)* llenar, colmar: **the sink was piled high with dishes** *el fregadero estaba lleno de platos.*
▷ *n pl* **piles of** montones *mpl* de.
⊙ **to pile in** *vi* **1** *(squeeze in)* meterse; *(vehicle)* subir. **2** *(crowd)* entrar en tropel.
⊙ **to pile into** *vt insep* **1** *(squeeze in)* meterse en. **2** *(attack)* arremeter contra.
⊙ **to pile on** *vt sep* poner un montón de.
▷ *vi (crowd)* subir en tropel.
⊙ **to pile out** *vi (crowd)* salir en tropel.
⊙ **to pile up** *vi* **1** *(accumulate - gen)* amontonarse, acumularse; *(- money)* acumularse. **2** *(crash)* chocar en cadena.
▷ *vt sep* **1** *(books, boxes, logs, etc)* amontonar, apilar. **2** *(riches, debts)* acumular.
pile[2] [paɪl] *n* ARCH pilote *m*, pilar *m*.
pile[3] [paɪl] *n (on carpet)* pelo.
pile-driver ['paɪldraɪvəʳ] *n* martinete *m*.
pile-up ['paɪlʌp] *n* AUTO choque *m* en cadena.
pilfer ['pɪlfəʳ] *vt* hurtar.
▷ *vi* hurtar.
pilgrim ['pɪlgrɪm] *n* peregrino,-a.
pilgrimage ['pɪlgrɪmɪdʒ] *n* peregrinación *f*.
pill [pɪl] *n (gen)* píldora, pastilla.
pillage ['pɪlɪdʒ] *n* pillaje *m*, saqueo.
▷ *vt* pillar, saquear.
pillar ['pɪləʳ] *n* pilar *m*, columna. ● **pillar box** buzón *m*
pillion ['pɪlɪən] *n* asiento trasero (de una moto).
pillory ['pɪlərɪ] *n* picota.
▲ *pl* **pillories**.
▷ *vt fig* burlarse de, ridiculizar.
▲ *pt & pp* **pilloried**, *ger* **pillorying**.
pillow ['pɪləʊ] *n* almohada.
pillowcase ['pɪləʊkeɪs] *n* funda de almohada.
pilot ['paɪlət] *n* **1** AV piloto *mf*. **2** MAR práctico *mf*. **3** *(TV or radio programme)* programa *m* piloto. ● **pilot ligh[t]** piloto.
▷ *adj* piloto, experimental.
▷ *vt* **1** *(ship, etc)* pilotar. **2** *(guide)* dirigir. **3** *(test)* poner [a] prueba.
pimento [pɪ'mentəʊ] *n* pimiento morrón.
▲ *pl* **pimentos**.
pimp [pɪmp] *n* chulo, proxeneta *mf*.
pimple ['pɪmpᵊl] *n (spot)* grano.
pimply ['pɪmpəlɪ] *adj* lleno,-a de granos.
▲ *comp* **pimplier**, *superl* **pimpliest**.
pin [pɪn] *n* **1** *(gen)* alfiler *m*. **2** *(badge, brooch)* insignia, pin *m*, alfiler *m*. **3** TECH *(peg, dowel)* clavija, espiga. [4] ELEC polo. ● **pins and needles** hormigueo.
▷ *vt* **1** *(garment, hem, seam)* prender (con alfileres); *(pa[pers, etc together)* sujetar (con un alfiler); *(notice o[n] board, etc)* clavar (**up**, -); *(hair)* recoger (**up**,-). **2** *(person)* inmovilizar; *(arms)* sujetar.
▲ *pt & pp* **pinned**, *ger* **pinning**.
▷ *n pl* **pins** *fam (legs)* patas *fpl*.
pinafore ['pɪnəfɔ:ʳ] *n (apron)* delantal *m*.
pinball ['pɪnbɔ:l] *n* flipper *m*.
pincer ['pɪnsəʳ] *n (of crab, etc)* pinza.
▷ *n pl* **pincers** *(tool)* tenaza, tenazas *fpl*.
pincers ['pɪnsəz] *n pl* **1** *(tool)* tenazas *fpl*. **2** *(on crab, etc)* pinzas *fpl*.
pinch [pɪntʃ] *n* **1** *(nip)* pellizco. **2** *(small amount)* pizca.
▷ *vt* **1** *(nip)* pellizcar; *(shoes)* apretar. **2** *fam (steal)* robar.
pinched [pɪntʃt] *adj* **1** *(face - drawn)* cansado,-a, ojeroso,-a; *(- worried)* preocupado,-a. **2** *(short of)* escaso,-a (**for**, de), apretado,-a (**for**, de).
pincushion ['pɪnkʊʃᵊn] *n* acerico.
pine[1] [paɪn] *n* BOT *(tree, wood)* pino.
▷ *adj* de pino. ● **pine cone** piña. ▮ **pine nut** piñón *m*.
pine[2] [paɪn] *vi* estar triste, sufrir.
⊙ **to pine away** *vi* consumirse, morirse de pena.
pineapple ['paɪnæpᵊl] *n* piña.
ping [pɪŋ] *n (sound)* sonido metálico; *(of bullet)* silbido.
▷ *vi (gen)* hacer un sonido metálico; *(bullet)* silbar.
ping-pong ['pɪŋpɒŋ] *n* tenis *m* de mesa, ping-pong *m*.
pinion[1] ['pɪnɪən] *n* TECH piñón *m*.
pinion[2] ['pɪnjən] *vt (person)* inmovilizar; *(arms)* maniata[r].
pink [pɪŋk] *adj* (de color) rosa, rosado,-a. ■ **to go pink** [o] **turn pink** ponerse colorado,-a.
▷ *n* **1** *(colour)* (color *m*) rosa *m*. **2** BOT clavel *m*, clavellina.
pinkie ['pɪŋkɪ] *n* US *fam* dedo meñique.
pinking shears ['pɪŋkɪŋʃɪəz] *n pl* tijeras *fpl* dentadas.
pinnacle ['pɪnəkᵊl] *n* **1** *(of building)* pináculo. **2** *(of mountain)* cima, cumbre *f*.
pinny ['pɪnɪ] *n fam* delantal *m*.
▲ *pl* **pinnies**.

inpoint ['pɪnpɔɪnt] *vt (position)* localizar; *(cause, origin, time)* establecer con exactitud.
inprick ['pɪnprɪk] *n* 1 *(sensation)* pinchazo; *(hole)* agujerito. 2 *(annoying thing)* pequeño inconveniente *m*.
instripe ['pɪnstraɪp] *n (stripe)* raya fina; *(cloth)* tela de raya diplomática.
adj (suit) de raya diplomática.
int [paɪnt] *n (measurement)* pinta.
n **a pint** *fam (of beer)* una cerveza, una jarra. ■ **to go for a pint** ir a tomar una cerveza.
En Gran Bretaña equivale a 0,57 litros; en Estados Unidos equivale a 0,47 litros.
in-up ['pɪnʌp] *n* foto *f*.
ioneer [paɪə'nɪəʳ] *n* 1 *(settler)* pionero,-a. 2 *(first person, originator)* pionero,-a, precursor,-ra, iniciador,-ra.
vt (policy, industry) promover; *(technique)* iniciar, ser el/la primero,-a en aplicar.
ioneering [paɪə'nɪərɪŋ] *adj* pionero,-a.
ious ['paɪəs] *adj* 1 *(devout - person)* piadoso,-a, devoto,-a. 2 *pej (person)* beato,-a.
ip¹ [pɪp] *n (seed)* pepita.
ip² [pɪp] *n (sound)* señal *f* (corta).
ipe [paɪp] *n* 1 *(for water, gas, etc)* tubería, conducto. 2 *(for smoking)* pipa. ● **pipe dream** quimera, sueño imposible.
vt 1 *(water, gas)* llevar por tuberías; *(oil)* conducir por oleoducto.
n pl **pipes** gaita *f sing*.
to pipe down *vi* callarse.
to pipe up *vi* decir inesperadamente, salir con.
ipeline ['paɪplaɪn] *n (for water)* tubería, cañería; *(for gas)* gasoducto; *(for oil)* oleoducto. ■ **to be in the pipeline** estar en trámite.
iper ['paɪpəʳ] *n* gaitero,-a.
iping ['paɪpɪŋ] *n (for water, gas, etc)* tubería, cañería.
iquant ['pi:kənt] *adj* 1 *(taste)* picante. 2 *fig (exciting)* estimulante, intrigante.
ique [pi:k] *n* resentimiento, despecho.
iracy ['paɪərᵊsɪ] *n* piratería.
iranha [pɪ'rɑ:nə] *n (fish)* piraña.
irate ['paɪᵊrət] *n* pirata *m*.
adj pirata.
vt piratear.
irouette [pɪru'et] *n* pirueta.
vi hacer piruetas, piruetear.
isces ['paɪsi:z] *n* piscis.
iss [pɪs] *n taboo* meada.
vi sl mear. ■ **to have a piss** *sl* mear. | **to take the piss out of** SB/STH *sl* cachondearse de ALGN/ALGO.
to piss about / piss around *vi sl (play the fool)* hacer el tonto; *(idle)* gandulear.
vt sep sl (waste SB*'s time)* hacer perder tiempo a; *(take for a ride)* tomar el pelo a.
to piss down *vi sl (rain heavily)* llover a cántaros.
to piss off *vi sl* largarse, irse a la mierda.
vt sep sl cabrear, poner de mala leche.
issed [pɪst] *adj* 1 GB *sl (drunk)* trompa, bolinga, mamado,-a. 2 US *sl (annoyed)* cabreado,-a. ● **pissed off** GB cabreado,-a.
istachio [pɪs'tɑ:ʃɪəu] *n* pistacho.
▲ *pl* **pistachios**.
istil ['pɪstɪl] *n* pistilo.
istol ['pɪstᵊl] *n* pistola.
iston ['pɪstᵊn] *n* TECH pistón *m*, émbolo.

pit¹ [pɪt] *n* 1 *(hole)* hoyo, foso; *(grave)* fosa. 2 *(mine)* mina, pozo. 3 *(mark - on metal, glass)* señal *f*, marca; *(- on skin)* picadura, cicatriz *f*. 4 THEAT *(for orchestra)* foso de la orquesta.
▷ *vt (mark)* picar, marcar.
▲ *pt & pp* **pitted**, *ger* **pitting**.
▷ *n* **the pit** *(hell)* el infierno.
▷ *n pl* **the pits** *(in motor racing)* los boxes *mpl*.
pit² [pɪt] *n* US *(seed)* pepita; *(stone)* hueso.
pitch¹ [pɪtʃ] *n* 1 MUS *(of sound)* tono; *(of instrument)* diapasón *m*. 2 SP *(field)* campo, terreno; *(throw)* lanzamiento. 3 *(degree, level)* grado, punto, extremo. 4 *(position, site)* lugar *m*, sitio; *(in market)* puesto. 5 MAR *(movement)* cabezada. 6 *(slope of roof)* pendiente *f*.
▷ *vt* 1 MUS *(note, sound)* entonar. 2 *fig (aim, address)* dirigir (at, a); *(set)* dar un tono a. 3 *(throw)* tirar, arrojar; *(in baseball)* lanzar. 4 *(tent)* plantar, montar; *(camp)* montar.
▷ *vi* 1 *(fall)* caerse. 2 *(ship, plane)* cabecear. 3 SP *(in baseball)* lanzar.
⊙ **to pitch in** *vi fam (start work)* ponerse a trabajar.
⊙ **to pitch into** *vt insep fam (attack)* atacar.
pitch² [pɪtʃ] *n (tar)* brea, pez *f*.
pitch-black [pɪtʃ'blæk] *adj* muy oscuro,-a, (oscuro,-a).
pitched [pɪtʃt] *adj (roof)* en pendiente, inclinado,-a.
● **pitched battle** batalla campal.
pitcher¹ ['pɪtʃəʳ] *n (of clay)* cántaro.
pitcher² ['pɪtʃəʳ] *n* SP pítcher *mf*, lanzador,-ra.
pitchfork ['pɪtʃfɔ:k] *n* AGR horca.
piteous ['pɪtɪəs] *adj* lastimero,-a.
pitfall ['pɪtfɔ:l] *n (difficulty)* dificultad *f*, escollo; *(danger)* peligro, riesgo.
pith [pɪθ] *n* 1 *(of bone, plant)* médula; *(of orange)* piel *f* blanca. 2 *fig* meollo.
pithead ['pɪthed] *n (of mine)* bocamina.
pithy ['pɪθɪ] *adj* 1 *(bone, plant)* meduloso,-a. 2 *(description, comment, etc)* conciso,-a y contundente.
▲ *comp* **pithier**, *superl* **pithiest**.
pitiable ['pɪtɪəbᵊl] *adj (arousing pity)* lastimoso,-a.
pitiful ['pɪtɪful] *adj* 1 *(arousing pity - sight)* lastimoso,-a; *(cry)* lastimero,-a. 2 *(arousing contempt)* lamentable.
pitiless ['pɪtɪləs] *adj* 1 *(killer, tyrant, etc)* despiadado,-a. 2 *fig (sun, wind, tec)* implacable.
pittance ['pɪtəns] *n* miseria.
pitter-patter ['pɪtəpætəʳ] *n* repiqueteo.
pituitary [pɪ'tju:ɪtᵊrɪ] *adj* pituitario,-a. ● **pituitary gland** glándula pituitaria.
pity ['pɪtɪ] *n* 1 *(compassion)* piedad *f*, compasión *f*. 2 *(regret)* lástima, pena. ■ | **what a pity!** ¡qué lástima!
▲ *pl* **pities**.
▷ *vt (feel pity for)* compadecerse de, dar lástima.
▲ *pt & pp* **pitied**, *ger* **pitying**.
pitying ['pɪtɪɪŋ] *adj* compasivo,-a, de lástima.
pivot ['pɪvət] *n* 1 pivote *m*. 2 *fig* eje *m*.
▷ *vi* pivotar, girar sobre su eje.
pixel ['pɪksəl] *n* píxel *m*.
pixie ['pɪksɪ] *n* duendecillo.
pizza ['pi:tsə] *n* pizza.
pizzeria [pi:tsə'rɪə] *n* pizzería.
placard ['plækɑ:d] *n* pancarta.
placate [plə'keɪt] *vt* apaciguar, calmar.
place [pleɪs] *n* 1 *(particular position, part)* lugar *m*, sitio. 2 *(proper position)* lugar *m*, sitio; *(suitable place)* lugar *m*

adecuado, sitio adecuado. **3** *(building)* lugar *m*, sitio; *(home)* casa, piso: **let's go to my place** *vamos a mi casa.* **4** *(in book)* página. **5** *(seat)* asiento, sitio; *(at table)* cubierto. **6** *(position, role, rank)* lugar *m*; *(duty)* obligación *f*: **if I were in your place** *yo en tu lugar.* **7** *(in race, contest)* puesto, lugar *m*, posición *f*; *(in queue)* turno. **8** *(job)* puesto; *(at university, on course)* plaza; *(on team)* puesto. ■ **all over the place** por todas partes. ‖ **in place** en su sitio. ‖ **in place of** SB / **in** SB**'s place** en el lugar de ALGN. ‖ **out of place** fuera de lugar. ‖ **to take place** tener lugar.
▷ *vt* **1** *(put - gen)* poner; *(- carefully)* colocar: **she placed the vase on the shelf** *puso el florero en el estante.* **2** *(find home, job for)* colocar. **3** *(rank, class)* poner, situar. **4** *(remember - face, person)* recordar; *(- tune, accent)* identificar.

placebo [plə'si:bəu] *n* placebo.
▲ *pl* **placebos o placeboes.**

placement ['pleɪsmənt] *n* colocación *f*.

placenta [plə'sentə] *n* placenta.
▲ *pl* **placentas o placentae** [plə'senti:].

placid ['plæsɪd] *adj* plácido,-a, tranquilo,-a.

plagiarism ['pleɪdʒərɪzᵊm] *n* plagio.

plagiarize ['pleɪdʒəraɪz] *vt* plagiar.

plague [pleɪg] *n* **1** *(of insects, etc)* plaga. **2** MED peste *f*.
▷ *vt* **1** *(pester)* acosar, asediar. **2** *(afflict)* afligir, asolar, plagar, atormentar.

plaice [pleɪs] *n (fish)* platija.
▲ *pl* **plaice.**

plaid [plæd] *n* tejido escocés.

plain [pleɪn] *adj* **1** *(clear)* claro,-a, evidente: **he made it quite plain** *lo dejó muy claro.* **2** *(straightforward)* franco,-a, directo,-a: **tell me in plain language** *dímelo en lenguaje corriente.* **3** *(simple, ordinary)* sencillo,-a; *(without pattern)* liso,-a. **4** *(unattractive)* poco agraciado,-a, feúcho,-a. **5** *(chocolate)* sin leche.
▷ *adv* **1** *(absolutely)* totalmente. **2** *(clearly)* claramente.
▷ *n* GEOG llanura.

plain-spoken [pleɪn'spəukᵊn] *adj* franco,-a.

plaintiff ['pleɪntɪf] *n* demandante *mf*, querellante *mf*.

plaintive ['pleɪntɪv] *adj* lastimero,-a, triste.

plait [plæt] *n* trenza.
▷ *vt* trenzar.

plan [plæn] *n* **1** *(scheme, arrangement)* plan *m*, proyecto. **2** *(map, drawing, diagram)* plano; *(design)* proyecto; *(for essay)* esquema *m*.
▷ *vt* **1** *(make plans)* planear, proyectar, planificar; *(intend)* pensar, tener pensado: **they plan to get married next year** *tienen planeado casarse el año que viene.* **2** *(make a plan of - house, garden, etc)* hacer los planos de, diseñar; *(- economy, strategy)* planificar.
▷ *vi (make preparations)* hacer planes; *(intend)* pensar: **I'd planned on going away this weekend** *había pensado salir fuera este fin de semana.*
▲ *pt & pp* **planned,** *ger* **planning.**

plane¹ [pleɪn] *n* **1** MATH *(surface)* plano. **2** *fig (level, standard)* nivel *m*. **3** *fam (aircraft)* avión *m*.
▷ *adj* plano,-a.

plane² [pleɪn] *n (tool)* cepillo.
▷ *vt* cepillar.

plane³ [pleɪn] *n (tree)* plátano.

planet ['plænət] *n* planeta *m*.

planetarium [plænɪ'teərɪəm] *n* planetario.
▲ *pl* **planetariums o planetaria** [plænɪ'teərɪə].

planetary ['plænətərɪ] *adj* planetario,-a.

plank [plæŋk] *n (of wood)* tablón *m*, tabla.

plankton ['plæŋktən] *n* plancton *m*.

planner ['plænəʳ] *n* planificador,-ra.

planning ['plænɪŋ] *n* planificación *f*.

plant¹ [plɑ:nt] *n* BOT planta.
▷ *vt* **1** *(flowers, trees)* plantar; *(seeds, vegetables)* sembrar; *(bed, garden, etc)* plantar (**with**, de). **2** *(bomb)* colocar; *(blow)* plantar; *(kiss)* dar. **3** *(ideas, doubt)* inculcar.

plant² [plɑ:nt] *n (factory)* planta, fábrica; *(machinery)* equipo, maquinaria.

plantation [plæn'teɪʃᵊn] *n (for crops)* plantación *f*.

planter ['plɑ:ntəʳ] *n (plantation owner)* hacendado,-a.

plaque [plæk] *n* placa.

plasma ['plæzmə] *n* plasma *m*.

plaster ['plɑ:stəʳ] *n* **1** *(powder, mixture - gen)* yeso; *(for walls)* revoque *m*, enlucido. **2** MED escayola.
▷ *vt* **1** *(wall, ceiling)* enyesar, enlucir. **2** *(cover, spread)* cubrir (**with**, de).

plastered ['plɑ:stəd] *adj fam (drunk)* borracho,-a.

plasterer ['plɑ:stərəʳ] *n* yesero,-a.

plastic ['plæstɪk] *adj* **1** *(bag, cup, spoon, etc)* de plástico,-a. **2** *(malleable)* moldeable. ■ **plastic surgery** cirugía plástica. ‖ **the plastic arts** las artes *fpl* plásticas.
▷ *n* **1** plástico. **2** *fam (credit cards)* tarjetas de crédito.

Plasticine ['plæstɪsi:n] *n* GB plastilina.

plate [pleɪt] *n* **1** *(dish, plateful)* plato. **2** *(sheet of metal, glass)* placa; *(thin layer)* lámina. **3** *(illustration)* grabado. ■ **number plate** matrícula. ‖ **plate rack** escurreplatos.
▷ *vt (gen)* chapar.

plateau ['plætəu] *n* **1** GEOG meseta. **2** *(state)* estancamiento.
▲ *pl* **plateaus o plateaux** 'plætəuz].

platform ['plætfɔ:m] *n* **1** *(gen)* plataforma; *(for speaker)* tribuna; *(for band)* estrado. **2** *(railway)* andén *m*, vía.

platinum ['plætɪnəm] *n* platino.

platitude ['plætɪtju:d] *n* tópico, lugar *m* común.

platonic [plə'tɒnɪk] *adj* platónico,-a.

platoon [plə'tu:n] *n* MIL pelotón *m*.

platter ['plætəʳ] *n (dish)* fuente *f*.

platypus ['plætɪpəs] *n* ornitorrinco.

plausible ['plɔ:zɪbᵊl] *adj* admisible, verosímil.

play [pleɪ] *n* **1** *(recreation)* juego: **children at play** *niños jugando.* **2** SP *(action)* juego; *(match)* partido; *(move)* jugada. **3** THEAT obra (de teatro), pieza (teatral).
▷ *vt* **1** *(game, sport)* jugar a: **some played cards while the others played football** *algunos jugamos a cartas mientras otros jugaron a fútbol.* **2** SP *(compete against)* jugar contra; *(in position)* jugar de; *(ball)* pasar; *(card)* jugar; *(piece)* mover: **have you played David at tennis?** *¿has jugado al tenis con David?* **3** MUS tocar: **she plays the piano** *toca el piano.* ■ **to play it cool** hacer como si nada. ‖ **to play the fool** hacer el indio, hacer el tonto. ‖ **play the game** jugar limpio.
▷ *vt (joke, trick)* gastar, hacer.
▷ *vt* **1** THEAT *(part)* hacer el papel de, hacer de; *(play)* representar, dar: **she plays the part of Juliet** *hace de Julieta.* **2** *(record, song, tape)* poner.
▷ *vi* **1** *(amuse oneself)* jugar (**at**, a), (**with**, con). **2** SP *game)* jugar. **3** THEAT *(cast)* actuar, trabajar; *(show)* ser representado,-a. **4** MUS tocar.
⊙ **to play about** *vi* juguetear.

⊙ **to play along** *vi* seguir la corriente a.
⊙ **to play around** *vi (gen)* juguetear; *(have affairs)* tener líos.
⊙ **to play back** *vt sep* (volver a) poner.
⊙ **to play down** *vt sep* quitar importancia a.
⊙ **to play off** *vt sep* oponer (**against**, a).
▷ *vi* jugar el desempate.
⊙ **to play on** *vt insep* aprovecharse de, explotar.
⊙ **to play up** *vt sep (cause trouble)* dar la lata a, fastidiar.
▷ *vi* 1 *(machine)* no funcionar bien; *(child)* portarse mal.
play-act ['pleɪækt] *vi* hacer teatro.
playbill ['pleɪbɪl] *n* cartel *m*.
playboy ['pleɪbɔɪ] *n* playboy *m*.
player ['pleɪər] *n* 1 SP jugador,-ra. 2 THEAT *(actor)* actor *m*; *(actress)* actriz *f*.
playful ['pleɪfʊl] *adj* juguetón,-ona, travieso,-a.
playground ['pleɪgraʊnd] *n* patio de recreo.
playgroup ['pleɪgruːp] *n* jardín *m* de infancia, guardería.
playhouse ['pleɪhaʊs] *n* 1 *(theatre)* teatro. 2 *(for children)* casita.
playing card ['pleɪɪŋkɑːd] *n* carta, naipe *m*.
playing field ['pleɪɪŋfiːld] *n* campo deportivo.
playmate ['pleɪmeɪt] *n* compañero,-a de juego, amiguito,-a.
play-off ['pleɪɒf] *n* SP partido de desempate.
playpen ['pleɪpen] *n* parque *m* (para niños).
playroom ['pleɪruːm] *n* cuarto de juego.
playschool ['pleɪskuːl] *n* jardín *m* de infancia, guardería.
plaything ['pleɪθɪŋ] *n* juguete *m*.
playtime ['pleɪtaɪm] *n* recreo.
playwright ['pleɪraɪt] *n* dramaturgo,-a.
plea [pliː] *n* 1 *fml (request)* petición *f*, súplica. 2 JUR alegato, declaración *f*.
plead [pliːd] *vi* suplicar (**with**, -).
▷ *vt (give as excuse)* alegar.
pleading ['pliːdɪŋ] *adj (tone, voice, look)* suplicante.
▷ *n* súplica, ruego.
pleasant ['plezənt] *adj* 1 *(gen)* agradable; *(surprise)* grato,-a. 2 *(person)* simpático,-a, amable.
pleasantry ['plezəntrɪ] *n* cumplido.
▲ *pl* **pleasantries.**
please [pliːz] *vt (make happy, be agreeable to)* agradar, gustar, complacer; *(satisfy)* contentar, complacer: **you can't please everyone** *no se puede complacer a todos.*
▷ *vi* 1 *(satisfy)* contentar, complacer, satisfacer. 2 *(choose, want, like)* querer: **you can do as you please** *puedes hacer lo que quieras.*
▷ *interj* por favor: **quiet, please** *silencio, por favor.*
pleased [pliːzd] *adj (happy)* contento,-a; *(satisfied)* satisfecho,-a. ■ **pleased to meet you!** ¡encantado,-a!, ¡mucho gusto!
pleasing ['pliːzɪŋ] *adj* agradable, grato,-a.
pleasure ['pleʒər] *n* placer *m*: **it's a pleasure to be here** *es un placer estar aquí.* ■ **my pleasure** ha sido un placer. ■ **with pleasure** con mucho gusto.
pleat [pliːt] *n* pliegue *m*.
▷ *vt* plisar.
plebeian [plɪ'biːən] *adj* 1 HIST plebeyo,-a. 2 *pej* ordinario,-a.
plebiscite ['plebɪsɪt] *n* plebiscito.
pledge [pledʒ] *n* 1 *(promise)* promesa. 2 *(token)* prenda, señal *f*. 3 *(security, guarantee)* garantía, prenda.
▷ *vt* 1 *(promise)* prometer. 2 *(pawn)* empeñar, dar en prenda.
plentiful ['plentɪfʊl] *adj* abundante.
plenty ['plentɪ] *n* abundancia.
▷ *pron* mucho,-a, muchos,-as: **we've got plenty of time** *tenemos tiempo de sobra.*
pliable ['plaɪəbəl] *adj* flexible.
pliers ['plaɪəz] *n pl* alicates *mpl*, tenazas *fpl*.
plight [plaɪt] *n* situación *f* grave.
plimsolls ['plɪmsəlz] *n pl* GB playeras *fpl*, zapatillas *fpl* de lona.
plinth [plɪnθ] *n (of column, pillar)* plinto; *(of statue)* peana.
plod [plɒd] *vi* 1 *(walk slowly)* andar con paso lento. 2 *(work steadily)* hacer laboriosamente.
⊙ **to plod away** *vi* perseverar (**at**, en).
▲ *pt & pp* **plodded**, *ger* **plodding.**
plodder ['plɒdər] *n* persona tenaz.
plonk[1] [plɒŋk] *n* ruido sordo.
▷ *vt fam* dejar caer.
plonk[2] [plɒŋk] *n* GB *fam* vinaza.
plop [plɒp] *n* plaf *m*.
▷ *vi* hacer plaf (al caer).
plot[1] [plɒt] *n* 1 *(conspiracy)* conspiración *f*, complot *m*. 2 *(of book, film, etc)* trama, argumento.
▷ *vt* 1 *(plan secretly)* tramar, urdir. 2 *(course, position)* trazar.
▷ *vi* conspirar, tramar, maquinar.
▲ *pt & pp* **plotted**, *ger* **plotting.**
plot[2] [plɒt] *n* parcela, terreno, solar.
plotter ['plɒtər] *n* conspirador,-ra.
plough [plaʊ] *n* AGR arado.
▷ *vt (land, etc)* arar.
⊙ **to plough back** *vt sep (profits)* reinvertir.
⊙ **to plough into** *vt insep (crash)* estrellarse contra.
⊙ **to plough through** *vt insep* 1 *(mud, snow, etc)* abrirse camino a través de; *(sea)* surcar. 2 *fig* hacer laboriosamente.
plow [plaʊ] *adj* US ⟶ **plough.**
ploy [plɔɪ] *n* truco, ardid *m*, treta, estratagema.
pluck [plʌk] *n* valor *m*, ánimo, coraje *m*.
▷ *vt* 1 *(gen)* arrancar; *(fruit)* coger. 2 *(bird)* desplumar.
▷ *n* MUS puntear.
plucky ['plʌkɪ] *adj* valiente.
▲ *comp* **pluckier**, *superl* **pluckiest.**
plug [plʌg] *n* 1 *(for bath, sink, etc)* tapón *m*. 2 ELEC *(on lead)* enchufe *m*, clavija; *(socket)* enchufe *m*, toma de corriente. 3 *(publicity)* publicidad *f*.
▷ *vt* 1 *(hole, etc)* tapar (**up**, -). 2 *(publicize)* dar publicidad a, promocionar.
⊙ **to plug away** *vt insep* perseverar (**at**, en).
⊙ **to plug in** *vt sep* enchufar.
▷ *vi* enchufarse.
▲ *pt & pp* **plugged**, *ger* **plugging.**
⊙ **to plug into** *vt sep* enchufar a.
plug-in ['plʌgɪn] *n* plug-in *m*, conector *m*.
plum [plʌm] *n* 1 *(fruit)* ciruela. 2 *(colour)* color *m* ciruela. ■ **plum tree** ciruelo.
▷ *adj fam* fantástico,-a.
plumage ['pluːmɪdʒ] *n* plumaje *m*.
plumb [plʌm] *n* 1 *(lead weight used in building)* plomada. 2 *(for depth-sounding)* sonda.
▷ *adv* 1 ARCH a plomo, verticalmente. 2 *(exactly)* justo, de lleno.

▷ *vt* **1** ARCH aplomar. **2** *(water)* sondar. **3** *fig (mystery)* descifrar.
⊙ **to plumb in** *vt sep* instalar, conectar.
plumber ['plʌmə^r] *n* fontanero,-a.
plumbing ['plʌmɪŋ] *n* **1** *(occupation)* fontanería. **2** *(system)* tubería, cañería.
plume [plu:m] *n* penacho.
plummet ['plʌmɪt] *vi* **1** *(bird, plane)* caer en picado. **2** *fig (prices)* desplomarse; *(morale)* caer a plomo.
plump[1] [plʌmp] *adj* regordete, rollizo,-a.
⊙ **to plump up** *vt sep (pillow, etc)* ahuecar, sacudir.
plump[2] [plʌmp] *vt* **to plump for** optar por.
plunder ['plʌndə^r] *n* **1** *(action)* pillaje *m*, saqueo. **2** *(loot)* botín *m*.
▷ *vt* saquear, pillar.
plunge [plʌndʒ] *n* **1** *(dive)* zambullida, chapuzón *m*. **2** *(fall)* caída, descenso.
▷ *vi* **1** *(dive)* lanzarse, zambullirse; *(fall)* caer, hundirse. **2** *(drop - prices, etc)* caer en picado.
▷ *vt (immerse)* sumergir, hundir; *(thrust)* clavar, meter; *(in despair, poverty, etc)* sumir.
plunger ['plʌndʒə^r] *n* **1** *(for drain, etc)* desatascador *m*. **2** TECH *(piston)* émbolo.
pluperfect [plu:'pɜ:fɪkt] *n* LING pluscuamperfecto.
plural ['plʊər^əl] *adj* plural.
▷ *n* plural *m*.
plurality [plʊə'rælɪtɪ] *n* **1** pluralidad *f*. **2** US mayoría relativa.
plus [plʌs] *prep* más: **four plus five is nine** *cuatro más cinco son nueve.*
▷ *adj* **1** *(ion, number)* positivo,-a. **2** *(and more)* más de, algo más de. **3** *(advantageous)* positivo,-a.
▷ *n* **1** MATH *(sign)* signo más. **2** *(advantage)* ventaja, factor *m* positivo, pro.
plush [plʌʃ] *adj fam* lujoso,-a.
Pluto ['plu:təʊ] *n* Plutón *m*.
plutonium [plu:'təʊnɪəm] *n* plutonio.
ply[1] [plaɪ] *vt* **1** *(of ship)* navegar por. **2** *(tool)* manejar.
▷ *vi (ship, bus, etc)* hacer el trayecto, navegar.
▲ *pt & pp* **plied**, *ger* **plying**.
⊙ **to ply with** *vt sep (drink, food)* no parar de ofrecer; *(questions)* asediar a, acosar a.
ply[2] [plaɪ] *n (of wood)* chapa; *(of paper)* capa.
▲ *pl* **plies**.
plywood ['plaɪwʊd] *n* madera contrachapada.
pm ['pi:'em] *abbr* (**post meridiem**) de la tarde: **it is 5.10 p.m.** *son las cinco y diez de la tarde.*
pneumatic [njʊ:'mætɪk] *adj* neumático,-a.
pneumonia [njʊ:'məʊnɪə] *n* pulmonía.
poach[1] [pəʊtʃ] *vi (for game)* cazar furtivamente; *(for fish)* pescar furtivamente.
▷ *vt* **1** *(game)* cazar furtivamente; *(fish)* pescar furtivamente. **2** *(take, steal)* robar.
poach[2] [pəʊtʃ] *vt* CULIN *(fish)* hervir; *(eggs)* escalfar.
poacher ['pəʊtʃə^r] *n (of game)* cazador,-ra furtivo,-a; *(of fish)* pescador,-ra furtivo,-a.
pocket ['pɒkɪt] *n* **1** *(gen)* bolsillo. **2** *(small area - of air)* bolsa; *(- of resistance)* foco. ■ **to be out of pocket** salir perdiendo. ■ **to pick SB's pocket** robarle algo a ALGN.
▷ *adj (dictionary, camera, etc)* de bolsillo. ● **pocket money** *(for children)* paga, semanada.
▷ *vt* **1** *(put in pocket)* meterse en el bolsillo. **2** *(keep, take dishonestly)* embolsar, quedarse con.
pocketbook ['pɒkɪtbʊk] *n* **1** US bolso. **2** *(notebook)* libreta (de bolsillo).
pocketful ['pɒkɪtfʊl] *n* bolsillo.
pocketknife ['pɒkɪtnaɪf] *n* navaja.
▲ *pl* **pocketknives**.
pocket-sized ['pɒkɪtsaɪzd] *adj* de bolsillo.
pod [pɒd] *n* BOT vaina.
podgy ['pɒdʒɪ] *adj* gordinflón,-ona.
▲ *comp* **podgier**, *superl* **podgiest**.
podium ['pəʊdɪəm] *n* podio.
▲ *pl* **podiums** o **podia** ['pəʊdɪə].
poem ['pəʊəm] *n* poema *m*, poesía.
poet ['pəʊət] *n* poeta *mf*.
poetic [pəʊ'etɪk] *adj* poético,-a.
poetry ['pəʊətrɪ] *n* poesía.
poignant ['pɔɪnjənt] *adj (moving)* conmovedor,-ra.
point [pɔɪnt] *n* **1** *(sharp end - of knife, nail, pencil)* punta. **2** *(place)* punto, lugar *m*: **meeting point** *punto de encuentro.* **3** *(moment)* momento, instante *m*, punto: **at this point** *en este momento.* **4** *(state, degree)* punto, extremo. **5** *(on scale, graph, compass)* punto; *(on thermometer)* grado. **6** SP *(score, mark)* punto, tanto. **7** *(item, matter, idea, detail)* punto. **8** *(central idea, meaning)* idea, significado: **you've missed the point** *no has captado la idea.* **9** *(purpose, use)* sentido, propósito: **what's the point?** *¿para qué?* **10** *(quality, ability)* cualidad *f*. **11** GEOG punta, cabo. **12** MATH *(in geometry)* punto (de intersección). **13** *(in decimals)* coma: **5 point 6** *cinco coma seis.* ■ **to come to the point** ir al grano. ● **point of view** punto de vista.
▷ *vi* **1** *(show)* señalar. **2** *fig (indicate)* indicar.
▷ *vt* **1** *(with weapon)* apuntar. **2** *(direct)* señalar, indicar.
⊙ **to point out** *vt sep* **1** *(show)* señalar. **2** *(mention)* señalar, hacer notar; *(warn)* advertir.
point-blank [pɔɪnt'blæŋk] *adj* **1** *(refusal)* categórico,-a. **2** *(shot)* a quemarropa.
▷ *adv* **1** *(refuse)* categóricamente, rotundamente. **2** *(shoot)* a quemarropa.
pointed ['pɔɪntɪd] *adj* **1** puntiagudo,-a, en punta. **2** *fig (comment)* intencionado,-a, significativo,-a; *(wit)* mordaz.
pointedly ['pɔɪntɪdlɪ] *adv (significantly)* con intención; *(cuttingly)* con mordacidad.
pointer ['pɔɪntə^r] *n* **1** *(on dial, scale, etc)* aguja; *(for blackboard, etc)* puntero. **2** *(piece of advice, suggestion)* consejo, sugerencia; *(clue)* pista.
pointless ['pɔɪntləs] *adj (meaningless)* sin sentido; *(useless)* inútil.
poise [pɔɪz] *n* **1** *(bearing)* elegancia, garbo. **2** *(self-assurance)* aplomo, desenvoltura.
poised [pɔɪzd] *adj* **1** *(ready)* listo,-a, preparado,-a. **2** *(self-controlled)* sereno,-a, dueño,-a de sí mismo,-a.
poison ['pɔɪz^ən] *n* veneno.
▷ *vt* **1** *(harm, kill - person, animal)* envenenar; *(make ill)* intoxicar; *(river)* contaminar; *(arrow, dart)* envenenar. **2** *(corrupt)* envenenar, corromper.
poisoning ['pɔɪz^ənɪŋ] *n* envenenamiento.
poisonous ['pɔɪz^ənəs] *adj* **1** *(plant, berry, snake)* venenoso,-a; *(drugs, gas)* tóxico,-a. **2** *fig* pernicioso,-a.

poke [pəʊk] *n (jab)* empujón *m*, golpe *m*; *(with elbow)* codazo; *(with sharp object)* pinchazo.
▷ *vt* **1** *(jab - with finger)* dar con la punta del dedo; *(- with elbow)* dar un codazo a; *(- with pointed object)* dar un pinchazo a. **2** *(insert)* meter. **3** *(fire)* atizar. **4** *(show)* asomar.
⊃ **to poke about / poke around** *vi* fisgonear.

poker[1] ['pəʊkəʳ] *n (for fire)* atizador *m*.

poker[2] ['pəʊkəʳ] *n (card game)* póquer *m*.

Poland ['pəʊlənd] *n* Polonia.

polar ['pəʊləʳ] *adj* polar. ● **polar bear** oso polar.

polarity [pəʊ'lærɪtɪ] *n* polaridad *f*.
▲ *pl* **polarities.**

Pole [pəʊl] *n* polaco,-a.

pole[1] [pəʊl] *n (stick, post)* poste *m*, palo, pértiga.

pole[2] [pəʊl] *n (electrical, geographical)* polo. ■ **to be poles apart** ser polos opuestos.

polemic [pə'lemɪk] *n* polémica.
▷ *n pl* **polemics** polémica *f sing*.

police [pə'liːs] *n pl (body)* policía *f sing*; *(officers)* policías *mpl*. ● **police station** comisaría.
▷ *vt (keep order in)* mantener el orden en; *(keep watch on)* vigilar; *(area)* patrullar.

policeman [pə'liːsmən] *n* policía *m*, agente *m* de policía, guardia *m*.
▲ *pl* **policemen** [pə'liːsmən].

policewoman [pə'liːswʊmən] *n* policía, agente *f* de policía, guardia.
▲ *pl* **policewomen** [pə'liːswɪmɪn]

policy ['pɒlɪsɪ] *n* **1** POL política. **2** *(course of action, plan)* política, estrategia. **3** *(insurance)* póliza (de seguros).
▲ *pl* **policies.**

polio ['pəʊlɪəʊ] *n* poliomielitis *f*, polio *f*.

polish ['pɒlɪʃ] *n* **1** *(for furniture)* cera (para muebles); *(for shoes)* betún *m*; *(for floors)* cera, abrillantador *m* (de suelos); *(for nails)* esmalte *m*. **2** *(shine)* lustre *m*, brillo. **3** *fig (refinement)* refinamiento, brillo.
▷ *vt (floor, furniture)* encerar; *(shoes)* limpiar; *(silver, cutlery)* sacar brillo a; *(nails)* pintar con esmalte; *(stone)* pulir.
⊃ **to polish off** *vt sep (work)* despachar, terminar con; *(food)* zamparse, tragarse.

Polish ['pəʊlɪʃ] *adj* polaco,-a.
▷ *n* **1** *(person)* polaco,-a. **2** *(language)* polaco.
▷ *n pl* **the Polish** los polacos *mpl*.

polished ['pɒlɪʃt] *adj* **1** *(wood)* brillante; *(metal)* lustroso,-a. **2** *(manners)* refinado,-a, elegante; *(performance, style)* pulido,-a.

polite [pə'laɪt] *adj* cortés, educado,-a, cumplido,-a, correcto,-a: **he was very polite to me** *me trató con cortesía*. ■ **in polite society** entre gente educada.
▲ *comp* **politer,** *superl* **politest.**

politely [pə'laɪtlɪ] *adv* educadamente, correctamente.

politeness [pə'laɪtnəs] *n* cortesía, educación *f*.

political [pə'lɪtɪkəl] *adj (gen)* político,-a.

politically [pə'lɪtɪkəlɪ] *adv* políticamente.

politician [pɒlɪ'tɪʃən] *n* político,-a.

politicize [pə'lɪtɪsaɪz] *vt* politizar.

politics ['pɒlɪtɪks] *n* **1** *(gen)* política: **he's active in politics** *es militante (político)*. **2** *(science)* ciencias *fpl* políticas.
▷ *n pl (view, opinions)* ideas *fpl* políticas.

polka ['pɒlkə] *n (dance)* polca. ● **polka dot** lunar *m*.

poll [pəʊl] *n* **1** *(voting)* votación *f*. **2** *(survey)* encuesta, sondeo.
▷ *vt* **1** *(votes - obtain)* obtener. **2** *(ask opinion)* sondear, encuestar.
▷ *n pl* **the polls** las elecciones *fpl*, los comicios *mpl*. ■ **to go to the polls** acudir a las urnas.

pollen ['pɒlən] *n* polen *m*.

pollination [pɒlɪ'neɪʃən] *n* polinización *f*.

polling ['pəʊlɪŋ] *n* votación *f*. ● **polling station** colegio electoral.

pollster ['pəʊlstəʳ] *n* encuestador,-ra.

pollute [pə'luːt] *vt* contaminar.

pollution [pə'luːʃən] *n* contaminación *f*.

polo ['pəʊləʊ] *n* SP polo.

polo-neck ['pəʊləʊnek] *adj (sweater)* de cuello alto.

polyester [pɒlɪ'estəʳ] *n* poliéster *m*.

polygamist [pə'lɪgəmɪst] *n* polígamo,-a.

polygamy [pɒ'lɪgəmɪ] *n* poligamia.

polygon ['pɒlɪgɒn] *n* polígono.

polyphony [pə'lɪfənɪ] *n* polifonía.

polytechnic [pɒlɪ'teknɪk] *n* escuela politécnica.

pomegranate ['pɒmɪgrænət] *n* BOT *(fruit)* granada; *(tree)* granado.

pommel ['pɒməl] *n* pomo.

pomp [pɒmp] *n* pompa.

pompom ['pɒmpɒm] *n* borla, pompón *m*.

pompous ['pɒmpəs] *adj (person)* pedante, presumido,-a; *(occasion, ceremony)* pomposo,-a; *(building)* ostentoso,-a, imponente.

poncho ['pɒntʃəʊ] *n* poncho.
▲ *pl* **ponchos.**

pond [pɒnd] *n* estanque *m*.

ponder ['pɒndəʳ] *vt* considerar.
▷ *vi* reflexionar (**on/over**, sobre), meditar (**on/over**, sobre).

pontiff ['pɒntɪf] *n* pontífice *m*.

pontificate [pɒn'tɪfɪkeɪt] *vi* pontificar.

pontoon[1] [pɒn'tuːn] *n* pontón *m*.

pontoon[2] [pɒn'tuːn] *n* GB *(card game)* veintiuna.

pony ['pəʊnɪ] *n* póney *m*, poni *m*.
▲ *pl* **ponies.**

ponytail ['pəʊnɪteɪl] *n* cola de caballo.

poodle ['puːdəl] *n* caniche *m*.

pooh-pooh [puː'puː] *vt (idea, suggestion)* descartar, desechar, desdeñar.

pool[1] [puːl] *n* **1** *(of water, oil, blood, etc)* charco; *(of light)* foco. **2** *(pond)* estanque *m*; *(in river)* pozo.

pool[2] [puːl] *n* **1** *(common fund of money)* fondo común; *(in gambling)* bote *m*. **2** *(common supply of services)* servicios *mpl* comunes. **3** US *(snooker)* billar *m* americano.
▷ *vt (funds, money)* reunir, juntar; *(ideas, resources)* poner en común.
▷ *n pl* **the pools** las quinielas *fpl*.

poor [pʊəʳ] *adj* **1** *(person, family, country)* pobre. **2** *(inadequate)* escaso,-a; *(bad quality)* malo,-a; *(inferior)* inferior: **you've got a poor memory** *tienes mala memoria*. **3** *(unfortunate)* pobre: **poor Edward** *el pobre Edward*.
▷ *n pl* **the poor** los pobres *mpl*.

poorly ['pʊəlɪ] *adj (ill)* indispuesto,-a.
▷ *adv (badly)* mal: **poorly dressed** *mal vestido,-a*.

pop[1] [pɒp] *n* **1** *(of cork)* taponazo. **2** *fam (drink)* gaseosa.
▷ *vt* **1** *(burst)* hacer reventar; *(cork)* hacer saltar. **2** *(put)* poner, meter.

▷ *vi* **1** *(burst)* estallar, reventar; *(cork)* saltar. **2** *(go quickly)* ir rápidamente.
▲ *pt & pp* **popped**, *ger* **popping**.
⊙ **to pop up** *vi (appear)* aparecer.
pop² [pɒp] *n fam (music)* música pop. ● **pop art** pop-art *m*.
popcorn ['pɒpkɔːn] *n* palomitas *fpl* de maíz.
pope [pəʊp] *n* papa *m*.
poplar ['pɒpləʳ] *n* BOT álamo.
poplin ['pɒplɪn] *n* popelín *m*.
popper ['pɒpəʳ] *n* GB *(on clothes)* corchete *m*.
poppy ['pɒpɪ] *n* amapola.
▲ *pl* **poppies**.
populace ['pɒpjʊləs] *n (people)* pueblo; *(masses)* populacho.
popular ['pɒpjʊləʳ] *adj* **1** *(well-liked - gen)* popular; *(- person)* estimado,-a; *(- resort, restaurant)* muy frecuentado,-a; *(fashionable)* de moda. **2** *(of or for general public)* popular; *(prices)* económico,-a.
popularity [pɒpjʊ'lærɪtɪ] *n* popularidad *f*.
popularize ['pɒpjʊləraɪz] *vt (make popular)* popularizar; *(make accessible)* vulgarizar.
populate ['pɒpjʊleɪt] *vt* poblar.
population [pɒpjʊ'leɪʃᵊn] *n* población *f*.
populist ['pɒpjəlɪst] *adj* populista.
porcelain ['pɔːsᵊlɪn] *n* porcelana.
▷ *adj* de porcelana.
porch [pɔːtʃ] *n* **1** *(of church)* pórtico; *(of house)* porche *m*, entrada. **2** US *(veranda)* terraza.
porcupine ['pɔːkjʊpaɪn] *n* puerco espín.
pore¹ [pɔːʳ] *n* ANAT poro.
pore² [pɔːʳ] *vt* **to pore over** leer detenidamente.
pork [pɔːk] *n* carne *f* de cerdo. ● **pork butcher** charcutero,-a.
pornography [pɔː'nɒgrəfɪ] *n* pornografía.
porous ['pɔːrəs] *adj* poroso,-a.
porpoise ['pɔːpəs] *n* marsopa.
porridge ['pɒrɪdʒ] *n* gachas *fpl* de avena.
port¹ [pɔːt] *n (harbour, town)* puerto.
▷ *adj* portuario,-a.
port² [pɔːt] *n (left side)* babor *m*.
portable ['pɔːtəbᵊl] *adj* portátil.
portal ['pɔːtᵊl] *n* portal *m*.
portcullis [pɔːt'kʌlɪs] *n* rastrillo.
portent ['pɔːtent] *n fml* augurio, presagio.
porter ['pɔːtəʳ] *n* **1** *(in hotel, block of flats)* portero,-a; *(in public building, school)* conserje *m*; *(in hospital)* camillero. **2** *(at station, airport)* mozo, maletero.
portfolio [pɔːt'fəʊlɪəʊ] *n* **1** *(flat case)* carpeta. **2** POL cartera.
▲ *pl* **portfolios**.
porthole ['pɔːthəʊl] *n* portilla.
portion ['pɔːʃᵊn] *n (gen)* parte *f*; *(of food)* ración *f*.
⊙ **to portion out** *vt sep* repartir, dividir.
portly ['pɔːtlɪ] *adj* corpulento,-a.
▲ *comp* **portlier**, *superl* **portliest**.
portrait ['pɔːtreɪt] *n* retrato.
portray [pɔː'treɪ] *vt* **1** *(painting)* representar, retratar. **2** *(describe)* describir, retratar. **3** *(act)* interpretar.
portrayal [pɔː'treɪəl] *n* **1** *(painting)* representación *f*. **2** *(description)* descripción *f*. **3** *(acting)* interpretación *f*.
Portugal ['pɔːtjʊgᵊl] *n* Portugal.
Portuguese [pɔːtjʊ'giːz] *adj* portugués,-esa.
▷ *n* **1** *(person)* portugués,-esa. **2** *(language)* portugués *m*.
▷ *n pl* **the Portuguese** los portugueses *mpl*.
pose [pəʊz] *n* **1** *(position, stance)* postura, actitud *f*. **2** *pe(affectation)* pose *f*, afectación *f*.
▷ *vt (problem, question, etc)* plantear; *(threat)* representar.
▷ *vi* **1** *(for painting, photograph)* posar. **2** *pej (behave affectedly)* presumir. ■ **to pose as** hacerse pasar por.
poser ['pəʊzəʳ] *n* **1** *(question)* pregunta difícil; *(problem)* dilema *m*. **2** *(person)* presumido,-a.
posh [pɒʃ] *adj* **1** GB *fam (place, area)* elegante, de lujo *(accent)* refinado,-a. **2** *(person)* pijo,-a.
position [pə'zɪʃᵊn] *n* **1** *(place)* posición *f*. **2** *(right place)* sitio, lugar *m*: **they manoeuvred the piano into position** *colocaron el piano en su lugar.* **3** *(posture)* postura, posición *f*. **4** *(on scale, in competition)* posición *f*, lugar *m* puesto; *(social standing)* categoría social, posición *f*. **5** *(job)* puesto. **6** *(situation, circumstances)* situación *f*, lugar *m*. **7** *(opinion, point of view)* postura. **8** SP posición *f*
▷ *vt (put in place)* colocar, poner.
positive ['pɒzɪtɪv] *adj* **1** *(gen)* positivo,-a. **2** *(definite - proof, evidence)* concluyente, definitivo,-a; *(- refusal, decision)* categórico,-a; *(- instruction, order)* preciso,-a. **3** *(effective - criticism, advice)* constructivo,-a; *(- attitude, experience)* positivo,-a. **4** *(quite certain)* seguro,-a (**about**, de): **I'm absolutely positive** *estoy segurísimo.*
▷ *n* positivo.
positively ['pɒzɪtɪvlɪ] *adv* **1** *(with certainty)* categóricamente. **2** *(optimistically)* positivamente; *(favourably)* favorablemente. **3** *fam (absolutely)* verdaderamente.
possess [pə'zes] *vt* **1** *(own)* poseer, tener. **2** *(take over - anger, fear)* apoderarse de.
possessed [pə'zest] *adj (by devil)* poseído,-a, poseso,-a, endemoniado,-a.
possession [pə'zeʃᵊn] *n* **1** *(ownership)* posesión *f*, poder *m*. **2** *(thing owned)* bien *m*, posesión *f*.
possessive [pə'zesɪv] *adj* **1** *(person)* posesivo,-a; *(selfish)* egoísta. **2** LING posesivo,-a.
▷ *n* LING posesivo.
possessor [pə'zesəʳ] *n* poseedor,-ra.
possibility [pɒsɪ'bɪlɪtɪ] *n* **1** *(likelihood)* posibilidad *f*. **2** *(something possible)* posibilidad *f*.
▲ *pl* **possibilities**.
possible ['pɒsɪbᵊl] *adj* posible. ■ **as much as possible** todo lo posible. ■ **as soon as possible** cuanto antes.
▷ *n* posible candidato,-a.
possibly ['pɒsɪblɪ] *adv* **1** *(reasonably, conceivably)* posiblemente. **2** *(in requests)*: **could you possibly give me a lift to the station?** *¿me podría llevar a la estación?* **3** *(perhaps)* posiblemente, quizás.
post¹ [pəʊst] *n (of wood)* estaca, poste *m*.
post² [pəʊst] *n* **1** *(job)* puesto, empleo; *(important position)* cargo. **2** MIL puesto.
▷ *vt* MIL destinar, apostar. **2** *(employee)* mandar.
post³ [pəʊst] *n* GB *(mail)* correo; *(collection)* recogida, *(delivery)* reparto: **it's in the post** *ya está enviado.*
▷ *vt* **1** GB *(send - letter, parcel)* mandar por correo, echar al correo; *(put in postbox)* echar al buzón. ● **post office** Correos, oficina de correos.
postage ['pəʊstɪdʒ] *n* franqueo, porte *m*.
postal ['pəʊstᵊl] *adj* postal.

postbag [ˈpəʊstbæg] *n* **1** *(sack)* saca (de correos). **2** GB *(letters)* correspondencia.
postbox [ˈpəʊstbɒks] *n* GB buzón *m*.
postcard [ˈpəʊstkɑːd] *n* tarjeta postal *f*.
postcode [ˈpəʊstkəʊd] *n* GB código postal.
poster [ˈpəʊstəʳ] *n* póster *m*, cartel *m*.
posterior [pɒˈstɪərɪəʳ] *adj* posterior.
posterity [pɒsˈterɪtɪ] *n* posteridad *f*.
post-free [pəʊstˈfriː] *adj* porte pagado.
postgraduate [pəʊstˈgrædjʊət] *n* postgraduado,-a.
▷ *adj* de postgrado.
posthumous [ˈpɒstjʊməs] *adj* póstumo,-a.
posting [ˈpəʊstɪŋ] *n* destino.
postman [ˈpəʊstmən] *n* cartero.
▲ *pl* **postmen** [ˈpəʊstmən].
postmark [ˈpəʊstmɑːk] *n* matasellos *m*.
▷ *vt* timbrar, matasellar.
postmortem [pəʊstˈmɔːtəm] *n* autopsia.
postpone [pəsˈpəʊn] *vt* aplazar, posponer.
postscript [ˈpəʊstskrɪpt] *n* posdata.
postulate [ˈpɒstjəleɪt] *vt* postular.
posture [ˈpɒstʃəʳ] *n* **1** *(position of body)* postura, pose *f*. **2** *(attitude)* postura.
▷ *vi* hacer poses, adoptar poses.
postwar [ˈpəʊstwɔːʳ] *adj* de la posguerra.
postwoman [ˈpəʊstwʊmən] *n* cartera.
▲ *pl* **postwomen** [ˈpəʊstwɪmɪn].
posy [ˈpəʊzɪ] *n* ramillete *m*.
▲ *pl* **posies**.
pot [pɒt] *n* **1** CULIN *(container)* pote *m*, tarro; *(for cooking)* olla, puchero; *(earthenware)* vasija; *(teapot)* tetera; *(coffee pot)* cafetera. **2** *(of paint)* bote *m*. **3** *(flower pot)* maceta, tiesto.
▷ *vt (plant)* plantar en una maceta.
▷ *n* **the pot** *(in card games)* el bote.
potable [ˈpəʊtəbᵊl] *adj fml* potable.
potash [ˈpɒtæʃ] *n* potasa.
potassium [pəˈtæsɪəm] *n* potasio.
potato [pəˈteɪtəʊ] *n* patata.
▲ *pl* **potatoes**.
potbellied [ˈpɒtbəlɪd] *adj (fat)* barrigón,-ona, panzudo,-a.
potbelly [ˈpɒtbelɪ] *n* barriga, panza.
▲ *pl* **potbellies**.
potency [ˈpəʊtənsɪ] *n* potencia, fuerza.
potent [ˈpəʊtənt] *adj* potente, fuerte.
potentate [ˈpəʊtənteɪt] *n* potentado.
potential [pəˈtenʃəl] *adj* potencial, posible.
▷ *n* potencial *m*.
pothole [ˈpɒthəʊl] *n* **1** GEOL cueva. **2** *(in road)* bache *m*.
potholer [ˈpɒthəʊləʳ] *n* GB espeleólogo,-a.
potholing [ˈpɒthəʊlɪŋ] *n* GB espeleología.
potion [ˈpəʊʃᵊn] *n* poción *f*, pócima.
potluck [pɒtˈlʌk] *n* **to take potluck** conformarse con lo que haya.
potpourri [pəʊˈpʊərɪ] *n (gen)* popurrí *m*.
potted [ˈpɒtɪd] *adj* **1** CULIN en conserva. **2** *(plant)* en maceta, en tiesto.
potter¹ [ˈpɒtəʳ] *n* alfarero,-a.
potter² [ˈpɒtəʳ] *vi* **to potter about / potter around** entretenerse.
pottery [ˈpɒtərɪ] *n (craft)* alfarería, cerámica; *(place)* alfarería, taller *m* de cerámica.
potty [ˈpɒtɪ] *n* orinal *m*.
▲ *pl* **potties**.
pouch [paʊtʃ] *n* **1** *(gen)* bolsa (pequeña); *(for tobacco)* petaca. **2** ZOOL bolsa abdominal.
pouffe [puːf] *n (seat)* puf *m*.
poultice [ˈpəʊltɪs] *n* cataplasma, emplasto.
poultry [ˈpəʊltrɪ] *n (birds)* aves *fpl* de corral; *(food)* carne *f* de ave, aves *fpl*, volatería.
pounce [paʊns] *n* salto.
▷ *vi* saltar (**on**, sobre), abalanzarse (**on**, sobre).
pound¹ [paʊnd] *vt* **1** *(crush)* machacar. **2** *(strike, beat)* aporrear, golpear.
▷ *vi* **1** *(strike, beat)* aporrear (**at/on**, -), golpear (**at/on**, -); *(of waves)* batir (**against**, contra). **2** *(heart)* palpitar, latir con fuerza.
pound² [paʊnd] *n* **1** FIN libra: **a five-pound note** *un billete de cinco libras*. **2** *(weight)* libra: **half a pound of tomatoes** *media libra de tomates*.

Como medida de peso, equivale a 454 gramos.

pound³ [paʊnd] *n (enclosure - for dogs)* perrera; *(- for cars)* depósito.
pour [pɔːʳ] *vt (liquid)* verter, echar; *(substance)* echar; *(drink)* servir: **she poured the orange juice into a jug** *vertió el zumo de naranja en una jarra*.
▷ *vi* **1** *(blood)* manar, salir; *(water, sweat)* chorrear. **2** *fig* moverse en tropel. ■ **to pour (down/with rain)** llover a cántaros: **it's pouring** *está lloviendo a cántaros*.
pouring [ˈpɔːrɪŋ] *adj (rain)* torrencial.
pout [paʊt] *n* puchero, mohín *m*.
▷ *vi* hacer pucheros, hacer un mohín.
poverty [ˈpɒvətɪ] *n (gen)* pobreza.
powder [ˈpaʊdəʳ] *n (dust)* polvo; *(cosmetic, medicine)* polvos *mpl*.
▷ *vt* **1** *(put powder on)* poner polvos, empolvar. **2** *(pulverize)* pulverizar, reducir a polvo.
powdered [ˈpaʊdəd] *adj (milk, eggs)* en polvo.
power [ˈpaʊəʳ] *n* **1** *(strength, force)* fuerza; *(of sun, wind)* potencia, fuerza; *(of argument)* fuerza. **2** *(ability, capacity)* poder *m*, capacidad *f*: **it's beyond his power** *no está en sus manos*. **3** *(faculty)* facultad *f*. **4** *(control, influence, authority)* poder *m*; *(of country)* poderío, poder *m*: **the power of the media** *el poder de los medios de comunicación*. **5** *(nation)* potencia; *(person, group)* fuerza. **6** PHYS *(capacity, performance)* potencia; *(energy)* energía. **7** ELEC electricidad *f*, corriente *f*. **8** MATH potencia: **six to the power of four** *seis elevado a la cuarta potencia*.
▷ *vt* propulsar, impulsar: **it's powered by electricity** *funciona con electricidad*.
powerboat [ˈpaʊəbəʊt] *n* lancha motora.
powerful [ˈpaʊəfʊl] *adj* **1** *(strong - athlete, body, current)* fuerte; *(- blow, engine, machine)* potente. **2** *(influential - enemy, nation, ruler)* poderoso,-a. **3** *(effective)* impactante.
powerless [ˈpaʊələs] *adj* impotente.
pox [pɒks] *n* viruela.
practicable [ˈpræktɪkəbəl] *adj* factible.
practical [ˈpræktɪkᵊl] *adj* **1** *(gen)* práctico,-a. **2** *(good with hands)* hábil, mañoso,-a.
▷ *n (lesson)* clase *f* práctica. ● **practical joke** broma.

practically ['præktɪkᵊlɪ] *adv* **1** *(almost)* casi, prácticamente. **2** *(in a practical way)* de manera práctica, con sentido práctico.

practice ['præktɪs] *n* **1** *(repeated exercise)* práctica; *(training)* entrenamiento: **I'm out of practice** *me falta práctica.* **2** *(action, reality)* práctica: **in practice** *en la práctica.* **3** *(custom, habit)* costumbre *f.*
▷ *vt & vi* US → **practise.**

practise ['præktɪs] *vt* **1** GB *(do repeatedly - language, serve, scales)* practicar; *(song, act)* ensayar. **2** GB *(religion, belief, economy)* practicar. **3** GB *(profession)* ejercer.
▷ *vi* **1** GB *(gen)* practicar. **2** GB *(sports team)* entrenar; *(actors)* ensayar. **3** GB *(professionally)* ejercer (**as**, de/como).

practised ['præktɪst] *adj* GB experto,-a.

practising ['præktɪsɪŋ] *adj* GB *(doctor, lawyer)* en ejercicio; *(Catholic, etc)* practicante.

practitioner [præk'tɪʃᵊnəʳ] *n (medical)* médico,-a.

pragmatic [præg'mætɪk] *adj* pragmático,-a.

pragmatism ['prægmətɪzᵊm] *n* pragmatismo.

prairie ['preərɪ] *n* pradera, llanura.

praise [preɪz] *n* **1** alabanza, elogio, loa. **2** REL alabanza. ■ **to sing the praises of** alabar, elogiar.
▷ *vt* **1** elogiar. **2** REL alabar.

praiseworthy ['preɪzwɜːðɪ] *adj* digno,-a de elogio.

praline ['prɑːliːn] *n* praliné *m.*

pram [præm] *n* GB cochecito de niño.

prance [prɑːns] *vi* **1** *(horse)* hacer cabriolas. **2** *(child)* brincar (**about**, -), ir dando brincos.

prank [præŋk] *n (trick)* broma; *(of child)* travesura. ■ **to play a prank on** SB gastar una broma a ALGN.

prawn [prɔːn] *n (large)* langostino; *(medium)* gamba; *(small)* camarón *m.*

pray [preɪ] *vi* orar, rezar.

prayer [preəʳ] *n* REL *(request)* oración *f*, rezo, plegaria; *(action)* oración *f*, rezo.

preach [priːtʃ] *vt* **1** REL *(gospel)* predicar; *(sermon)* dar, hacer. **2** *(advocate)* aconsejar.
▷ *vi* REL predicar.

preacher ['priːtʃəʳ] *n* predicador,-ra.

precarious [prɪ'keərɪəs] *adj* precario,-a.

precaution [prɪ'kɔːʃᵊn] *n* precaución *f.* ■ **to take precautions** tomar precauciones.

precede [prɪ'siːd] *vt* preceder a, anteceder a.

precedence ['presɪdᵊns] *n (order of importance)* precedencia; *(priority)* preferencia, prioridad *f.*

precedent ['presɪdᵊnt] *adj* precedente *m.*

preceding [prɪ'siːdɪŋ] *adj* anterior.

precept ['priːsept] *n* precepto.

precinct ['priːsɪŋkt] *n* **1** *(of cathedral, hospital, etc)* recinto. **2** GB *(part of town)* zona.
▷ *n pl* **precincts** recinto *m sing.*

precious ['preʃəs] *adj* **1** *(jewel, stone, metal)* precioso,-a. **2** *(moment, memory, possession)* preciado,-a.

precipice ['presɪpɪs] *n* precipicio.

precipitate [*(vb)* prɪ'sɪpɪteɪt; *(adj)* prɪ'sɪpɪtət] *vt fml (hasten)* precipitar.
▷ *adj fml* precipitado,-a.

precipitation [prɪsɪpɪ'teɪʃᵊn] *n fml (haste)* precipitación *f.*

precise [prɪ'saɪs] *adj* preciso,-a, exacto,-a.

precisely [prɪ'saɪslɪ] *adv (exactly)* exactamente; *(accurately)* con precisión. ■ **precisely!** ¡exacto!, ¡eso es!

precision [prɪ'sɪʒən] *n* precisión *f*, exactitud *f.*

preclude [prɪ'kluːd] *vt fml (prevent - gen)* impedir, evitar; *(- possibility)* excluir.

precocious [prɪ'kəʊʃəs] *adj* precoz.

preconceived [priːkən'siːvd] *adj* preconcebido,-a.

precondition [priːkən'dɪʃᵊn] *n* condición *f* previa.

precook [priː'kʊkt] *adj* precocinado,-a.

precursor [prɪ'kɜːsəʳ] *n fml* precursor,-ra.

predator ['predətəʳ] *n* ZOOL depredador *m.*

predecessor ['priːdɪsesəʳ] *n* antecesor,-ra.

predestination [priːdestɪ'neɪʃᵊn] *n* predestinación *f.*

predestine [priː'destɪn] *vt* predestinar.

predetermine [priːdɪ'tɜːmɪn] *vt* predeterminar.

predicament [prɪ'dɪkəmənt] *n* apuro, aprieto.

predict [prɪ'dɪkt] *vt* predecir, pronosticar.

predictable [prɪ'dɪktəbᵊl] *adj (results, weer)* previsible.

prediction [prɪ'dɪkʃᵊn] *n* predicción *f*, pronóstico.

predilection [priːdɪ'lekʃᵊn] *n fml* predilección *f* (**for** por), preferencia (**for**, por).

predispose [priːdɪs'pəʊz] *vt fml* predisponer (**to**, a).

predisposition [priːdɪspə'zɪʃᵊn] *n* predisposición *f* (**to** a), propensión *f* (**to**, a).

predominate [prɪ'dɒmɪneɪt] *vi* predominar.

pre-eminent [priː'emɪnənt] *adj* preeminente.

pre-empt [priː'empt] *vt* **1** *(forestall)* adelantarse a. **2** *(acquire)* apropiarse de.

preen [priːn] *vt (of bird)* arreglar con el pico. ■ **to preen os** **1** *(bird)* arreglarse con el pico. **2** *(person)* acicalarse.

preface ['prefəs] *n* prefacio, prólogo.
▷ *vt* prologar.

prefect ['priːfekt] *n* **1** *(official)* prefecto. **2** GB *(in school)* monitor,-ra.

prefer [prɪ'fɜːʳ] *vt* preferir.
▲ *pt & pp* **preferred**, *ger* **preferring.**

preferable ['prefᵊrəbᵊl] *adj* preferible (**to**, a).

preference ['prefᵊrəns] *n* preferencia (**for**, por).

preferential [prefə'renʃᵊl] *adj* preferente.

prefix ['priːfɪks] *n* LING prefijo.

pregnancy ['pregnənsɪ] *n* embarazo.
▲ *pl* **pregnancies.**

pregnant ['pregnənt] *n (woman)* embarazada; *(animal)* preñada.

preheat ['priːhiːt] *vt* precalentar.

prehistoric [priːhɪ'stɒrɪk] *adj* prehistórico,-a.

prehistory [priː'hɪst
pl **pregnancies.**rɪ] *n* prehistoria.

prejudge [priː'dʒʌdʒ] *vt* prejuzgar.

prejudice ['predʒədɪs] *n (unfavourable bias)* prejuicio *(favourable)* predisposición *f.*
▷ *vt* **1** *(influence, bias)* predisponer (**against**, contra), (**in favor of**, a favor de). **2** *(harm)* perjudicar.

prejudiced ['predʒʊdɪst] *adj* parcial.

prejudicial [predʒə'dɪʃᵊl] *adj* perjudicial (**to**, para).

preliminary [prɪ'lɪmɪnᵊrɪ] *adj* preliminar.
▷ *n pl* **preliminaries** preliminares *mpl.*

prelude ['preljuːd] *n (gen)* preludio.

premature [premə'tjʊəʳ] *adj (gen)* prematuro,-a.

premeditate [prɪ'medɪteɪt] *vt* premeditar.

premeditated [priː'medɪteɪtɪd] *adj* premeditado,-a.

premenstrual [priː'menstrʊəl] *adj* premenstrual.

premier ['premɪəʳ] *adj* primero,-a, principal.
▷ *n* POL primer,-a ministro,-a.

premiere ['premɪeəʳ] *n* estreno.
premise ['premɪs] *n* premisa.
premises ['premɪsɪz] *n pl* local *m*.
premium ['pri:mɪəm] *n* FIN *(insurance)* prima; *(extra cost)* recargo.
premonition [pri:mə'nɪʃᵊn] *n* presentimiento, premonición *f*.
prenatal [pri:'neɪtəl] *adj* prenatal.
preoccupation [pri:ɒkjʊ'peɪʃᵊn] *n (worry)* preocupación *f*; *(obsession)* obsesión *f*.
preoccupied [pri:'ɒkjʊpaɪd] *adj (worried)* preocupado,-a; *(wrapped up)* absorto,-a.
preoccupy [pri:'ɒkjʊpaɪ] *vt (worry)* preocupar; *(think about too much)* pensar demasiado en.
▲ *pt & pp* **preoccupied**, *ger* **preoccupying**.
prep [prep] *n* GB *(homework)* deberes *mpl*; *(study period)* hora de estudio.
prepaid [pri:'peɪd] *adj (envelope)* franqueado,-a; *(reply)* pagado,-a por adelantado.
preparation [prepə'reɪʃᵊn] *n* **1** *(action)* preparación *f*. **2** *(substance)* preparado.
▷ *n pl* **preparations** preparativos *mpl* (**for**, para).
preparatory [prɪ'pærətərɪ] *adj* preliminar.
prepare [prɪ'peəʳ] *vt (gen)* preparar; *(report)* redactar.
▷ *vi* prepararse (**for**, para).
prepared [prɪ'peəd] *adj* **1** *(gen)* preparado,-a. **2** *(willing)* dispuesto,-a (**to**, a).
preponderance [prɪ'pɒndərəns] *n fml* preponderancia.
preposition [prepə'zɪʃᵊn] *n* preposición *f*.
preposterous [prɪ'pɒstərəs] *adj* absurdo,-a.
prerecorded [pri:rɪ'kɔ:dɪd] *adj* pregrabado,-a.
prerequisite [pri:'rekwɪzɪt] *n* requisito previo, condición *f* previa.
prerogative [prɪ'rɒgətɪv] *n* prerrogativa.
presage ['presɪdʒ] *vt lit* presagiar.
preschool [pri:'sku:l] *adj* preescolar.
prescribe [prɪs'kraɪb] *vt* **1** *(medicine, drugs, etc)* recetar; *(holiday, rest)* recomendar. **2** *fml (order)* prescribir.
prescription [prɪs'krɪpʃᵊn] *n* receta (médica).
presence ['prezᵊns] *n* **1** *(gen)* presencia; *(attendance)* asistencia. **2** *(spirit)* espíritu *m*.
present¹ ['prezᵊnt] *adj* **1** *(in attendance)* presente. **2** *(current)* actual. **3** LING presente.
▷ *n (now)* presente *m*, actualidad *f*. ■ **at present** actualmente, en este momento.
▷ *n* **the present** LING presente *m*. ● **present continuous** presente continuo. ‖ **present perfect** presente perfecto. ‖ **present tense** presente.
present² [*(vb)* prɪ'zent; *(n)* 'prezənt] *vt* **1** *(make presentation)* entregar, hacer entrega de; *(give - as gift)* regalar. **2** *(offer - report, petition, bill, cheque)* presentar; *(- argument, ideas, case)* presentar, exponer. **3** *fml (offer - apologies, respects)* presentar; *(- compliments, greetings)* dar. **4** *(give - difficulty, problem)* plantear; *(constitute)* suponer, constituir, ser. **5** *(introduce)* presentar. **6** *(play)* representar; *(programme)* presentar.
▷ *n (gift)* regalo; *(formal)* obsequio.
presentable [prɪ'zentəbᵊl] *adj* presentable.
presentation [prezən'teɪʃᵊn] *n* **1** *(of awards, prizes, gifts)* entrega. **2** *(way of presenting)* presentación *f*. **3** *(of play)* representación *f*.
present-day ['prezəntdeɪ] *adj* actual.
presenter [prɪ'zentəʳ] *n* presentador,-ra, locutor,-ra.
presentiment [prɪ'zentɪmənt] *n* presentimiento.
preservation [prezə'veɪʃᵊn] *n (of wildlife)* conservación *f*, preservación *f*; *(of food, works of art, buildings)* conservación *f*.
preservative [prɪ'zɜ:vətɪv] *n* CULIN conservante *m*.
preserve [prɪ'zɜ:v] *n* CULIN *(fruit)* conserva; *(jam)* confitura, mermelada.
▷ *vt* conservar, proteger.
preset [pri:'set] *vt* programar.
▲ *pt & pp* **preset**, *ger* **presetting**.
preside [prɪ'zaɪd] *vi* presidir (**over**, -).
presidency ['prezɪdənsɪ] *n* presidencia.
▲ *pl* **presidencies**.
president ['prezɪdᵊnt] *n* presidente,-a.
presidential [prezɪ'denʃᵊl] *adj* presidencial.
press [pres] *n* **1** *(newspapers)* prensa. **2** *(machine)* prensa, imprenta. **3** *(act of pressing)* presión *f*; *(of hand)* apretón *m*; *(act of ironing)* planchado. ● **press conference** rueda de prensa.
▷ *vt* **1** *(push down - button, switch)* pulsar, apretar, presionar; *(- accelerator)* pisar; *(- key on keyboard)* pulsar; *(- trigger)* apretar. **2** *(squeeze - hand)* apretar. **3** *(crush - fruit)* exprimir, estrujar; *(- grapes, olives, flowers)* prensar. **4** *(clothes)* planchar, planchar a vapor. **5** *(record)* imprimir. **6** *(urge, put pressure on)* presionar, instar; *(insist on)* insistir en, exigir.
▷ *vi* **1** *(push)* apretar, presionar. **2** *(crowd)* apretujarse, apiñarse. **3** *(urge, pressurize)* presionar, insistir; *(time)* apremiar.
⊙ **to press ahead / press on** *vi* seguir adelante.
pressed [prest] *adj* CULIN *(ham, chicken)* embutido,-a. ■ **to be pressed for** STH andar escaso,-a de ALGO.
pressing ['presɪŋ] *adj* urgente, apremiante.
pressman ['presmən] *n* periodista *m*.
▲ *pl* **pressmen** ['presmən].
press-up ['presʌp] *n* flexión *f*.
pressure ['preʃəʳ] *n* **1** *(gen)* presión *f*. **2** *(stress)* tensión *f*: **he's under a lot of pressure** *está sometido a una gran presión*. ● **pressure cooker** olla a presión, olla exprés.
pressurize ['preʃəraɪz] *vt* GB *(force)* presionar.
prestige [pres'ti:ʒ] *n* prestigio.
prestigious [pres'tɪdʒəs] *adj* prestigioso,-a.
presumably [prɪ'zjʊ:məblɪ] *adv* se supone que.
presume [prɪ'zjʊ:m] *vt* suponer, imaginarse, presumir: **I presume so** *supongo que sí*.
▷ *vi* **1** suponer. **2** *(venture to)* atreverse a.
presumption [prɪ'zʌmpʃᵊn] *n* **1** *(assumption - gen)* suposición *f*, presunción *f*; *(- of innocence)* presunción *f*. **2** *(boldness)* atrevimiento, audacia, presunción *f*.
presumptuous [prɪ'zʌmptjʊəs] *adj* atrevido,-a, audaz, impertinente.
presuppose [pri:sə'pəʊz] *vt* presuponer.
pretence [prɪ'tens] *n (deception, make-believe)* fingimiento, apariencia, fachada.
pretend [prɪ'tend] *vt (feign)* fingir, aparentar: **the children pretended to be asleep** *los niños fingían estar dormidos*.
▷ *vi (feign)* fingir.
▷ *adj (make-believe)* de mentirijillas.
pretension [prɪ'tenʃᵊn] *n* pretensión *f*.
pretentious [prɪ'tenʃəs] *adj* pretencioso,-a.

preterite ['pretərıt] *n* LING pretérito.
pretext ['pri:tekst] *n* pretexto.
prettiness ['prıtınəs] *n* lindeza, lo bonito.
pretty ['prıtı] *adj (girl, baby)* bonito,-a, guapo,-a, mono,-a; *(thing)* bonito,-a mono,-a: **what a pretty little girl!** *¡qué niña más bonita!*
▲ *comp* **prettier**, *superl* **prettiest**.
▷ *adv* bastante: **I'm pretty sure** *estoy bastante seguro,-a*. ■ **pretty much** más o menos. ‖ **pretty well** casi.
prevail [prı'veıl] *vi* predominar, imperar.
prevailing [prı'veılıŋ] *adj* predominante.
prevalent ['prevələnt] *adj (frequent, common - gen)* frecuente, corriente.
prevaricate [prı'værıkeıt] *vi* andarse con rodeos, buscar evasivas.
prevent [prı'vent] *vt (gen)* impedir; *(avoid - accident)* evitar; *(- illness)* prevenir. ■ **to prevent SB from doing STH** impedir a ALGN hacer ALGO.
prevention [prı'venʃən] *n* prevención *f*.
preventive [prı'ventıv] *adj* preventivo,-a.
preview ['pri:vju:] *n* preestreno.
previous ['pri:vıəs] *adj* previo,-a, anterior: **the previous day** *el día anterior.*
prewar ['pri:wɔ:r] *adj* de antes de la guerra.
prey [preı] *n* **1** *(animal)* presa. **2** *fig* presa, víctima. ■ **to fall prey to STH** caer víctima de ALGO.
⊙ **to prey on** *vt insep (animal)* alimentarse de; *(person)* explotar a, aprovecharse de.
price [praıs] *n* **1** *(gen)* precio; *(amount, cost)* importe *m*; *(value)* valor *m*. **2** *fig (cost, sacrifice)* precio. ■ **at any price** a toda costa, cueste lo que cueste.
▷ *vt (fix price of)* tener un precio; *(value)* valorar, tasar; *(mark price on)* poner el precio a.
priceless ['praısləs] *adj* inestimable.
pricey ['praısı] *adj fam* caro,-a.
▲ *comp* **pricier**, *superl* **priciest**.
prick [prık] *n (pain)* pinchazo; *(hole)* agujero.
▷ *vt (with needle, pin, fork)* pinchar.
▷ *vi (pin, thorn)* pinchar; *(itch, sting)* escocer, picar.
prickle ['prıkəl] *n* **1** *(thorn)* espina, púa; *(spine)* púa, pincho. **2** *(sensation)* picor *m*.
▷ *vi* pinchar, picar.
prickly ['prıklı] *adj* **1** *(plant)* espinoso,-a; *(animal)* con púas; *(wool, sweater)* que pica. **2** *(irritable, touchy)* enojadizo,-a, irritable, difícil.
▲ *comp* **pricklier**, *superl* **prickliest**.
pride [praıd] *n* **1** *(gen)* orgullo; *(self-respect)* amor *m* propio. **2** *(arrogance)* soberbia, orgullo. ■ **to pride OS on STH** enorgullecerse de ALGO. ‖ **to take pride in / take a pride in** *(be proud of)* enorgullecerse de.
priest [pri:st] *n* sacerdote *m*, cura *m*.
priestess ['pri:stes] *n* sacerdotisa.
priesthood ['pri:sthʊd] *n (clergy)* clero; *(office)* sacerdocio.
prig [prıg] *n pej* mojigato,-a.
prim [prım] *adj* remilgado,-a, formal.
▲ *comp* **primmer**, *superl* **primmest**.
primacy ['praıməsı] *n* primacía.
primal ['praıməl] *adj* **1** *(first, original)* primario,-a. **2** *(most important)* primordial.
primary ['praımərı] *adj* **1** *(main)* principal. **2** *(first, basic)* primario,-a. ● **primary school** escuela primaria.

primate ['praımeıt] *n* ZOOL primate *m*.
prime [praım] *adj* **1** *(main, chief)* principal, primero,-a. **2** *(first-rate - meat)* de primera (calidad); *(example, location)* excelente. ● **Prime Minister** primer,-a ministro,-a.
▷ *n (best time of life)* flor *f* de la vida.
▷ *vt* **1** *(engine, pump, bomb)* cebar; *(surface, wood)* imprimar, preparar. **2** *fig (person)* preparar, enseñar.
primer ['praımər] *n (paint)* imprimación *f*.
primeval [praı'mi:vəl] *adj* primitivo,-a.
primitive ['prımıtıv] *adj (man, tribe, culture)* primitivo,-a; *(tool, method, shelter)* rudimentario,-a, primitivo,-a.
primrose ['prımrəʊz] *n* **1** BOT primavera, prímula. **2** *(colour)* amarillo claro.
Primus ['praıməs] *n* hornillo de camping.
prince [prıns] *n* príncipe *m*.
princess ['prınses] *n* princesa.
▲ *pl* **princesses**.
principal ['prınsıpəl] *adj* principal.
▷ *n* **1** EDUC director,-ra. **2** THEAT protagonista.
principle ['prınsıpəl] *n* **1** *(basic idea, rule, law)* principio; *(basis)* base *f*. **2** *(moral rule)* principio.
print [prınt] *n* **1** *(lettering)* letra: **in large print** *en letra grande.* **2** *(photo)* copia. **3** *(printed fabric)* estampado. **4** *(mark - of finger, foot)* huella.
▷ *vt* **1** *(book, page, poster, etc)* imprimir; *(publish)* publicar, editar. **2** *(photo - negative)* imprimir; *(- copy)* sacar una copia de. **3** *(write clearly)* escribir con letra de imprenta. **4** *(fabric)* estampar. **5** *(make impression)* marcar.
⊙ **to print out** *vt sep* imprimir.
printer ['prıntər] *n (person)* impresor,-ra; *(machine)* impresora.
printing ['prıntıŋ] *n (act, process)* impresión *f*; *(industry)* imprenta.
print-out ['prıntaʊt] *n* COMPUT impresión *f*.
prior ['praıər] *adj* anterior, previo,-a. ■ **prior to** antes de.
priority [praı'ɒrıtı] *n* prioridad *f*.
▲ *pl* **priorities**.
▷ *adj* prioritario,-a.
prise [praız] *vt* GB *(open)* abrir con palanca; *(lift up)* levantar con palanca.
prism ['prızəm] *n* prisma.
prismatic [prız'mætık] *adj* prismático,-a.
prison ['prızən] *n* prisión *f*, cárcel *f*.
prisoner ['prızənər] *n (in jail)* preso,-a, recluso,-a; *(captive)* prisionero,-a.
prissy ['prısı] *adj* remilgado,-a.
▲ *comp* **prissier**, *superl* **prissiest**.
pristine ['prısti:n] *n* prístino,-a.
privacy ['praıvəsı] *n* intimidad *f*, vida privada.
private ['praıvət] *adj* **1** *(own, for own use - property, house, class)* particular; *(- letter, income)* personal. **2** *(confidential)* privado,-a, confidencial. **3** *(not state-controlled)* privado,-a; *(school)* privado,-a, de pago. **4** *(not official)* privado,-a, personal. **5** *(person)* reservado,-a. ● **private eye** detective *mf* privado,-a.
▷ *n* MIL soldado raso.
privately ['praıvətlı] *adv* **1** *(in private)* en privado; *(undisturbed, alone)* en la intimidad. **2** *(personally)* personalmente. **3** *(not by state)* de forma privada.
privation [praı'veıʃən] *n* privación *f*.
privatization [praıvətaı'zeıʃən] *n* privatización *f*.
privatize ['praıvətaız] *vt* privatizar.

privet ['prɪvɪt] *n* BOT alheña.
privilege ['prɪvɪlɪdʒ] *n* privilegio.
privileged ['prɪvɪlɪdʒd] *adj* privilegiado,-a.
privy ['prɪvɪ] *n fam (toilet)* retrete *m*.
▲ *pl* privies.
▷ *adj arch* privado,-a.
prize[1] [praɪz] *n (gen)* premio.
▷ *adj (having won a prize)* premiado,-a; *(excellent)* de primera, selecto,-a.
prize[2] [praɪz] *vt* apreciar, valorar.
prize-giving ['praɪzgɪvɪŋ] *n* entrega de premios.
prizewinner ['praɪzwɪnəʳ] *n* ganador,-ra.
probability [prɒbə'bɪlɪtɪ] *n* probabilidad *f*.
▲ *pl* probabilities.
probable ['prɒbəbəl] *adj* probable, posible.
probably ['prɒbəblɪ] *adv* probablemente: **it'll probably rain** *es probable que llueva.*
probation [prə'beɪʃən] *n* **1** JUR libertad *f* condicional. **2** *(in employment)* período de prueba.
probe [prəʊb] *n* **1** MED sonda. **2** investigación *f*.
▷ *vt* **1** MED sondar. **2** *(investigate - gen)* investigar; *(public opinion)* sondear; *(mind)* explorar.
▷ *vi* investigar (**into**, -).
probing ['prəʊbɪŋ] *adj (question)* agudo,-a, perspicaz.
problem ['prɒbləm] *n* problema *m*: **no problem!** *¡no hay problema!, ¡ningún problema!*
problematic [prɒblə'mætɪk] *adj* problemático,-a.
procedure [prə'siːdʒəʳ] *n (set of actions)* procedimiento; *(step)* trámite *m*, gestión *f*.
proceed [prə'siːd] *vi* **1** *(continue)* seguir, continuar. **2** *(progress)* marchar. **3** *fml (go along)* avanzar, circular; *(go towards)* dirigirse a.
proceedings [prə'siːdɪŋz] *n pl* **1** *(events at meeting, ceremony, etc)* actos *mpl*. **2** JUR *(lawsuit)* proceso *sing*.
process ['prəʊses] *n* **1** *(set of actions, changes)* proceso. **2** *(method)* procedimiento, proceso.
▷ *vt* **1** *(raw material, food)* procesar, tratar; *(film)* revelar. **2** *(deal with)* ocuparse de, tramitar. **3** COMPUT procesar. ■ **to be in the process of doing** STH estar haciendo ALGO.
processing ['prəʊsesɪŋ] *n* **1** *(treatment)* procesamiento, tratamiento; *(of film)* revelado. **2** *(in business, law)* tramitación *f*. **3** COMPUT procesamiento, tratamiento.
procession [prə'seʃən] *n* **1** *(gen)* desfile *m*. **2** REL procesión *f*.
processor ['prəʊsesəʳ] *n* **1** *(for food)* robot *m* de cocina. **2** COMPUT procesador *m*.
proclaim [prə'kleɪm] *vt* proclamar, declarar.
proclamation [prɒklə'meɪʃən] *n* proclamación *f*.
proclivity [prə'klɪvɪtɪ] *n fml* propensión *f*, tendencia.
▲ *pl* proclivities.
procreate ['prəʊkrɪeɪt] *vi* procrear.
procreation [prəʊkrɪ'eɪʃən] *n* procreación *f*.
procure [prə'kjʊəʳ] *vt (obtain)* conseguir, obtener.
prod [prɒd] *n* **1** *(with finger, sharp object)* golpecito, pinchazo. **2** *fig (encouragement)* pinchazo, empujón *m*.
▷ *vt* **1** *(with object)* pinchar; *(with finger)* dar golpecitos a. **2** *fig (encourage)* pinchar, estimular; *(remind)* recordar.
▲ *pt & pp* prodded, *ger* prodding.
prodigal ['prɒdɪgəl] *adj* pródigo,-a.
prodigious [prə'dɪdʒəs] *adj (great)* prodigioso,-a; *(huge)* enorme.
prodigy ['prɒdɪdʒɪ] *n* prodigio.
▲ *pl* prodigies.
produce [*(vb)* prə'djuːs; *(n)* 'prɒdjuːs] *vt* **1** *(gen)* producir, fabricar. **2** *(give birth to)* tener. **3** *(show)* enseñar, presentar. **4** *(cause)* producir, causar. **5** *(play)* poner en escena, dirigir.
▷ *n* productos *mpl*: **produce of Spain** *productos de España.*
producer [prə'djuːsəʳ] *n* **1** *(gen)* productor,-ra, fabricante. **2** *(play)* director,-ra de escena.
product ['prɒdʌkt] *n* producto.
production [prə'dʌkʃən] *n* **1** *(gen)* producción *f*, fabricación *f*. **2** *(of film)* producción *f*; *(of play)* producción *f*, puesta en escena. ● **production line** cadena de montaje.
productive [prə'dʌktɪv] *adj* productivo,-a.
productivity [prɒdʌk'tɪvɪtɪ] *n* productividad *f*.
profane [prə'feɪn] *adj* **1** *fml (language)* blasfemo,-a. **2** *fml (secular)* profano,-a.
profanity [prə'fænɪtɪ] *n* blasfemia.
▲ *pl* profanities.
profess [prə'fes] *vt* **1** *(state)* proclamar, manifestar, declarar. **2** *(claim)* pretender.
professed [prə'fest] *adj* **1** *(supporter, monarchist)* declarado,-a. **2** *(claimed, alleged)* pretendido,-a, supuesto,-a.
profession [prə'feʃən] *n (occupation)* profesión *f*: **he's a baker by profession** *es panadero de profesión.*
professional [prə'feʃənəl] *adj (gen)* profesional.
▷ *n* profesional *mf*.
professionally [prə'feʃənəlɪ] *adv (as paid occupation)* profesionalmente.
professor [prə'fesəʳ] *n* **1** GB catedrático,-a. **2** US profesor,-ra universitario,-a.
proffer ['prɒfəʳ] *vt (gift, assistance, apology)* ofrecer; *(thanks, resignation, advice)* dar.
proficiency [prə'fɪʃənsɪ] *n* competencia.
proficient [prə'fɪʃənt] *adj* muy competente.
profile ['prəʊfaɪl] *n* **1** *(side view)* perfil *m*. **2** *(description)* perfil *m*; *(written)* reseña. ■ **to keep a low profile** intentar pasar desapercibido,-a.
profit ['prɒfɪt] *n* **1** COMM ganancia, beneficio. **2** *fml (advantage)* provecho. ■ **to make a profit** sacar beneficios.
profitability [prɒfɪtə'bɪlɪθɪ] *n* rentabilidad *f*.
profitable ['prɒfɪtəbəl] *adj* **1** COMM rentable. **2** *(beneficial)* provechoso,-a.
profiteer [prɒfɪ'tɪəʳ] *n* especulador,-ra.
▷ *vi* especular.
profit-making ['prɒfɪtmeɪkɪŋ] *adj (business)* rentable; *(charity)* con fines lucrativos.
profound [prə'faʊnd] *adj* profundo,-a.
profundity [prə'fʌndɪtɪ] *n* profundidad *f*.
▲ *pl* profundities.
profuse [prə'fjuːs] *adj (gen)* profuso,-a; *(bleeding)* intenso,-a.
profusion [prə'fjuːʒən] *n* profusión *f*, abundancia.
prognosis [prɒg'nəʊsɪs] *n* pronóstico.
program ['prəʊgræm] *n* COMPUT programa *m*.
▷ *vt* COMPUT programar.
▲ *pt & pp* programmed, *ger* programming.
programme ['prəʊgræm] *n (gen)* programa *m*; *(plan)* plan *m*.
▷ *vt (gen)* programar; *(activities)* planear.
programmer ['prəʊgræməʳ] *n* programador,-ra.
progress [*(n)* 'prəʊgres; *(vb)* prəʊ'gres] *n (advance)* progreso, avance *m*; *(development)* desarrollo.

▷ *vi* **1** *(advance)* progresar, avanzar, adelantar; *(develop)* desarrollar. **2** *(improve)* mejorar, hacer progresos. ■ **to be in progress** *(work)* estar en marcha.

progression [prəˈgreʃᵊn] *n* **1** *(development)* evolución *f*, avance *m*. **2** *(series)* serie *f*.

progressive [prəˈgresɪv] *adj* **1** *(increasing)* progresivo,-a. **2** *(favouring progress)* progresista.

progressively [prəˈgresɪvlɪ] *adv* progresivamente, cada vez más.

prohibit [prəˈhɪbɪt] *vt* prohibir.

prohibition [prəʊɪˈbɪʃᵊn] *n* prohibición *f*.

prohibitive [prəˈhɪbɪtɪv] *adj* prohibitivo,-a.

project [*(n)* ˈprɒdʒekt; *(vb)* prəˈdʒekt] *n* **1** *(gen)* proyecto. **2** EDUC trabajo, estudio.

▷ *vt* **1** *(gen)* proyectar. **2** *(extrapolate)* extrapolar.

▷ *vi* sobresalir, resaltar.

projectile [prəˈdʒektaɪl] *n* proyectil *m*.

projection [prəˈdʒekʃᵊn] *n* **1** *(gen)* proyección *f*. **2** *(protuberance)* saliente *m*, resalto.

projectionist [prəˈdʒekʃᵊnɪst] *n* operador,-ra de cine.

projector [prəˈdʒektəʳ] *n* proyector *m*.

proletarian [prəʊləˈteərɪən] *adj* proletario,-a.

proletariat [prəʊləˈteərɪət] *n* proletariado.

proliferate [prəˈlɪfəreɪt] *vi* proliferar.

prolific [prəˈlɪfɪk] *adj* prolífico,-a.

prologue [ˈprəʊlɒg] *n* prólogo.

prolong [prəˈlɒŋ] *vt* prolongar, alargar.

promenade [prɒməˈnɑːd] *n* **1** GB *(at seaside)* paseo marítimo. **2** *fml (walk)* paseo.

prominence [ˈprɒmɪnəns] *n* *(conspicuousness)* prominencia; *(importance)* importancia.

prominent [ˈprɒmɪnənt] *adj* *(important)* importante; *(projecting)* prominente, saliente.

promiscuity [prɒmɪˈskjuːɪtɪ] *n* promiscuidad *f*.

promiscuous [prəˈmɪskjuəs] *adj* promiscuo,-a.

promise [ˈprɒmɪs] *n* **1** *(pledge)* promesa. **2** *(expectation, hope)* esperanza, esperanzas *fpl*.

▷ *vt* **1** prometer: **you promised to help me** *prometiste ayudarme;* **2** *(seem likely)* prometer.

▷ *vi (gen)* prometer; *(swear)* jurar: **I promise** *te lo prometo.*

promising [ˈprɒmɪsɪŋ] *adj* prometedor,-ra.

promontory [ˈprɒməntᵊrɪ] *n* promontorio.

▲ *pl* **promontories.**

promote [prəˈməʊt] *vt* **1** *(in rank)* promover, ascender. **2** *(encourage)* promover, fomentar.

promoter [prəˈməʊtəʳ] *n* promotor,-ra.

promotion [prəˈməʊʃᵊn] *n* **1** *(in rank)* promoción *f*, ascenso. **2** COMM promoción *f*. **3** *(encouragement)* promoción *f*, fomento.

prompt [prɒmpt] *adj* *(quick)* pronto,-a, rápido,-a; *(punctual)* puntual.

▷ *adv* en punto.

▷ *vt* **1** *(cause, incite)* instar, incitar, mover. **2** THEAT apuntar.

▷ *n* THEAT *(line)* apunte *m*.

prompter [ˈprɒmptəʳ] *n* THEAT apuntador,-ra.

promptly [ˈprɒmptlɪ] *adv* rápidamente.

promulgate [ˈprɒməlgeɪt] *vt* promulgar.

prone [prəʊn] *adj (face down)* boca abajo. ■ **to be prone to** STH ser propenso,-a a ALGO.

prong [prɒŋ] *n* diente *m*, punta.

pronoun [ˈprəʊnaʊn] *n* LING pronombre *m*.

pronounce [prəˈnaʊns] *vt* **1** LING pronunciar. **2** *(declare)* declarar.

▷ *vi* pronunciarse (**on**, sobre).

pronounced [prəˈnaʊnst] *adj* pronunciado,-a, marcado,-a, acusado,-a.

pronouncement [prəˈnaʊnsmənt] *n* declaración *f*.

pronunciation [prənʌnsɪˈeɪʃᵊn] *n* pronunciación *f*.

proof [pruːf] *n* **1** *(evidence)* prueba. **2** *(trial, print)* prueba.

proofread [ˈpruːfriːd] *vt* corregir.

proofreader [ˈpruːfriːdəʳ] *n* corrector,-ra de pruebas.

prop [prɒp] *n* **1** *(support)* puntal *m*. **2** *fig* apoyo, sostén *m*. **3** SP *(in rugby)* pilar *mf*.

▷ *vt* apoyar (**against**, en/contra).

▲ *pt & pp* **propped**, *ger* **propping.**

⊙ **to prop up** *vt sep* **1** *(wall, building)* sostener, apuntalar. **2** *(regime)* apoyar.

propaganda [prɒpəˈgændə] *n* propaganda.

propagate [ˈprɒpəgeɪt] *vt* propagar.

▷ *vi* propagarse.

propagation [prɒpəˈgeɪʃᵊn] *n* propagación *f*.

propane [ˈprəʊpeɪn] *n* propano.

propel [prəˈpel] *vt* propulsar, impulsar.

▲ *pt & pp* **propelled**, *ger* **propelling.**

propeller [prəˈpeləʳ] *n* hélice *f*.

propelling pencil [prəpelɪŋˈpensᵊl] *n* portaminas *m*.

propensity [prəˈpensɪtɪ] *n* propensión *f* (**to**, a).

▲ *pl* **propensities.**

proper [ˈprɒpəʳ] *adj* **1** *(suitable)* adecuado,-a, apropiado,-a; *(correct)* correcto,-a: **the proper time** *el momento oportuno.* **2** *fam (real, genuine)* verdadero,-a, de verdad; **3** *fam (thorough)* auténtico,-a, todo,-a. **4** *(respectable)* correcto,-a, decente. ● **proper name / proper noun** nombre propio.

properly [ˈprɒpəlɪ] *adv* **1** *(properly)* bien, adecuadamente. **2** *(correctly)* bien; *(as one should)* como es debido.

property [ˈprɒpətɪ] *n* **1** *(possessions, ownership)* propiedad *f*. **2** *(buildings, land)* propiedad *f*, bienes *mpl*; *(estate)* finca. **3** *fml (building)* inmueble *m*.

▲ *pl* **properties.**

prophecy [ˈprɒfəsɪ] *n* profecía.

▲ *pl* **prophecies.**

prophesy [ˈprɒfəsaɪ] *vt* **1** predecir. **2** REL profetizar.

▲ *pt & pp* **prophesied**, *ger* **prophesying.**

prophet [ˈprɒfɪt] *n* profeta *m*.

prophetic [prəˈfetɪk] *adj* profético,-a.

propitious [prəˈpɪʃəs] *adj fml* propicio,-a.

proponent [prəˈpəʊnənt] *n* defensor,-ra.

proportion [prəˈpɔːʃᵊn] *n* **1** *(ratio)* proporción *f*. **2** *(part)* parte *f*; *(percentage)* porcentaje *m*. **3** *(correct relation)* proporción *f*.

▷ *n pl* **proportions** dimensiones *fpl*, proporciones *fpl*.

proportional [prəˈpɔːʃᵊnəl] *adj* proporcional (**to**, a).

proportionate [prəˈpɔːʃənət] *adj* proporcionado,-a (**to**, con), en proporción (**to**, a).

proposal [prəˈpəʊzəl] *n* propuesta.

propose [prəˈpəʊz] *vt* **1** *(suggest)* proponer. **2** *(intend)* pensar.

▷ *vi* declararse, proponer matrimonio a.

proposed [prəˈpəʊzd] *adj* propuesto,-a.

proposition [prɒpəˈzɪʃᵊn] *n* **1** *(suggestion)* propuesta *(offer)* oferta. **2** *(assertion)* proposición *f*.

propound [prəˈpaʊnd] *vt* exponer, proponer.

proprietary [prə'praɪətᵊrɪ] *adj* patentado,-a.
proprietor [prə'praɪətəʳ] *n* propietario,-a, dueño,-a.
propriety [prə'praɪətɪ] *n* **1** *(correctness)* corrección *f*, decoro, decencia. **2** *(suitability)* conveniencia.
▲ *pl* proprieties.
propulsion [prə'pʌlʃᵊn] *n* propulsión *f*.
pro rata [prəʊ'rɑːtə] *adj* prorrateado,-a.
▷ *adv* a prorrata, proporcionalmente.
prosaic [prəʊ'zeɪɪk] *adj* prosaico,-a.
proscribe [prəʊ'skraɪb] *vt* proscribir.
prose [prəʊz] *n* LIT prosa.
prosecute ['prɒsɪkjuːt] *vt* JUR procesar.
▷ *vi* JUR *(bring a charge)* entablar una acción judicial; *(be prosecutor)* llevar la acusación.
prosecution [prɒsɪ'kjuːʃᵊn] *n* JUR *(action)* procesamiento, acción *f* judicial.
▷ *n* **the prosecution** JUR *(person)* la acusación.
prosecutor ['prɒsɪkjuːtəʳ] *n* JUR fiscal *mf*, acusador,-ra.
prospect [*(n)* 'prɒspekt *(vb)* prə'spekt] *n* **1** *(picture in mind)* perspectiva. **2** *(possibility, hope)* posibilidad *f*, probabilidad *f*. **3** *fml (wide view)* panorama *m*, vista.
▷ *vt* prospectar, explorar.
▷ *vi* buscar (**for**, -).
▷ *n pl* **prospects** perspectivas *fpl*.
prospective [prə'spektɪv] *adj* posible.
prospector [prə'spektəʳ] *n* buscador,-ra.
prospectus [prə'spektəs] *n* prospecto.
prosper ['prɒspəʳ] *vi* prosperar.
prosperity [prɒ'sperɪtɪ] *n* prosperidad *f*.
prosperous ['prɒspᵊrəs] *adj* próspero,-a.
prostate ['prɒsteɪt] *n* próstata.
prosthesis ['prɒsθəsɪs] *n* prótesis *f*.
prostitute ['prɒstɪtjuːt] *n (gen)* prostituta.
prostitution [prɒstɪ'tjuːʃᵊn] *n* prostitución *f*.
prostrate [*(adj)* 'prɒstreɪt; *(vb)* prɒ'streɪt] *adj* postrado,-a.
▷ *vt* postrar.
protagonist [prə'tægənɪst] *n* protagonista *mf*.
protect [prə'tekt] *vt (gen)* proteger; *(interests)* proteger, salvaguardar.
protection [prə'tekʃᵊn] *n (gen)* protección *f*; *(shelter)* protección *f*, amparo.
protectionism [prə'tekʃᵊnɪzᵊm] *n* proteccionismo.
protectionist [prə'tekʃᵊnɪst] *adj* proteccionista *mf*.
protective [prə'tektɪv] *adj* protector,-ra.
protector [prə'tektəʳ] *n* protector,-ra.
protectorate [prə'tektərət] *n* protectorado.
protein ['prəʊtiːn] *n* proteína.
protest [*(n)* 'prəʊtest; *(vb)* prə'test] *n (gen)* protesta; *(demonstration)* manifestación *f* de protesta.
▷ *vt* protestar de.
▷ *vi* protestar (**about**, de), (**against**, contra), (**at**, por): **they protested about the working conditions** *protestaron por las condiciones de trabajo.*
Protestant ['prɒtɪstᵊnt] *adj* protestante.
▷ *n* protestante *mf*.
protester [prə'testəʳ] *n* manifestante *mf*.
protocol ['prəʊtəkɒl] *n* protocolo.
proton ['prəʊtɒn] *n* protón *m*.
prototype ['prəʊtətaɪp] *n* prototipo.
protracted [prə'træktɪd] *adj* prolongado,-a.
protractor [prə'træktəʳ] *n* transportador *m*.
protrude [prə'truːd] *vi fml* sobresalir, salir.
protuberance [prə'tjuːbərəns] *n fml* protuberancia.
proud [praʊd] *adj* **1** *(gen)* orgulloso,-a: **I'm proud of you** *estoy orgulloso de ti.* **2** *(arrogant)* orgulloso,-a, arrogante, altanero,-a, soberbio,-a.
proudly ['praʊdlɪ] *adv (with satisfaction)* orgullosamente, con orgullo; *(arrogantly)* con arrogancia.
prove [pruːv] *vt* **1** *(show to be true)* probar, demostrar. **2** *(turn out to be)* demostrar.
▷ *vi (turn out)* resultar: **the information proved correct** *la información resultó (ser) correcta.*
▲ *pt* **proved**, *pp* **proved** o **proven** ['pruːvən], *ger* **proving**.
proven ['pruːvᵊn] *adj* probado,-a, comprobado,-a.
proverb ['prɒvɜːb] *n* proverbio, refrán *m*.
proverbial [prə'vɜːbɪəl] *adj* proverbial.
provide [prə'vaɪd] *vt* **1** *(supply)* proveer, proporcionar: **he provided us with all the information** *nos facilitó toda la información.* **2** *fig (answer, example)* ofrecer, dar.
⊙ **to provide against** *vt insep* tomar precauciones contra.
⊙ **to provide for** *vt insep* **1** *(family)* mantener. **2** *(make arrangements for)* tomar precauciones contra; *(of bill, constitution)* prever.
provided [prə'vaɪdɪd] [Also **provided that**.] *conj* siempre que, con tal que.
providence ['prɒvɪdᵊns] *n* providencia.
provident ['prɒvɪdᵊnt] *adj* previsor,-ra.
providential [prɒvɪ'denʃᵊl] *adj fml* providencial.
provider [prə'vaɪdəʳ] *n* proveedor,-ra.
province ['prɒvɪns] *n* **1** *(region)* provincia. **2** *fig* terreno, campo, competencia.
provincial [prə'vɪnʃᵊl] *adj* **1** *(government)* provincial; *(town)* de provincia(s). **2** *pej* provinciano,-a.
provision [prə'vɪʒən] *n* **1** *(supply)* suministro, abastecimiento. **2** *(preparation)* previsiones *fpl*.
▷ *n pl* **provisions** *(food)* provisiones *fpl*, víveres *mpl*.
provisional [prə'vɪʒənᵊl] *adj* provisional.
provocation [prɒvə'keɪʃᵊn] *n* provocación *f*.
provocative [prə'vɒkətɪv] *adj (controversial)* provocador,-ra; *(sexy)* provocativo,-a.
provoke [prə'vəʊk] *vt* **1** *(make angry)* provocar, irritar. **2** *(cause)* provocar.
provoking [prə'vəʊkɪŋ] *adj* **1** provocador,-ra. **2** *(irritating)* irritante.
provost ['prɒvəst] *n* GB *(of university)* rector,-ra.
prow [praʊ] *n* proa.
prowess ['praʊəs] *n fml* habilidad *f*.
prowl [praʊl] *vi* merodear, rondar.
▷ *vt* merodear por, rondar por.
▷ *n* merodeo.
prowler ['praʊləʳ] *n* merodeador,-ra.
proximity ['prɒksɪmɪtɪ] *n fml* proximidad *f*.
proxy ['prɒksɪ] *n* **1** *(authority)* poder *m*. **2** *(person)* apoderado,-a. ■ **by proxy** por poderes.
▲ *pl* **proxies**.
prude [pruːd] *n* gazmoño,-a, mojigato,-a.
prudence ['pruːdᵊns] *n* prudencia.
prudent ['pruːdənt] *adj* prudente.
prudish ['pruːdɪʃ] *adj* remilgado,-a.
prune¹ [pruːn] *n* ciruela pasa.
prune² [pruːn] *vt (hedge, rosebush, etc)* podar.
pry [praɪ] *vi* curiosear, husmear, fisgonear.
▲ *pt & pp* **pried**, *ger* **prying**.

psalm [sɑːm] *n* salmo.
pseud [sjuːd] *n fam* farsante *mf*.
pseudonym ['suːdənɪm] *n* seudónimo.
psyche ['saɪkɪ] *n* psique *f*, psiquis *f*.
psychedelic [saɪkɪ'delɪk] *adj* psicodélico,-a.
psychiatric [saɪkɪ'ætrɪk] *adj* psiquiátrico,-a.
psychiatrist [saɪ'kaɪətrɪst] *n* psiquiatra *mf*.
psychiatry [saɪ'kaɪətrɪ] *n* psiquiatría.
psychic ['saɪkɪk] *adj (mental)* psíquico,-a.
psychoanalyst [saɪkəʊ'ænəlɪst] *n* psicoanalista *mf*.
psychological [saɪkə'lɒdʒɪkəl] *adj* psicológico,-a.
psychologist [saɪ'kɒlədʒɪst] *n* psicólogo,-a.
psychology [saɪ'kɒledʒɪ] *n* psicología.
psychopath ['saɪkəʊpæθ] *n* psicópata *mf*.
psychosis [saɪ'kəʊsɪs] *n* psicosis *f*.
▲ *pl* **psychoses** [saɪ'kəʊsiːz].
psychotherapy [saɪkəʊ'θerəpɪ] *n* psicoterapia.
psychotic [saɪ'kɒtɪk] *adj* psicótico,-a.
pub [pʌb] *n* bar *m*, pub *m*, taberna.
puberty ['pjuːbətɪ] *n* pubertad *f*.
pubic ['pjuːbɪk] *adj* púbico,-a.
pubis ['pjuːbɪs] *n* pubis *m*.
public ['pʌblɪk] *adj* público,-a. ● **public convenience** servicios *mpl*, aseos *mpl*. ‖ **public holiday** fiesta nacional. ‖ **public school 1** GB colegio privado. **2** US colegio público.
▷ *n* **the public** el público.
public-address system [pʌblɪkə'dressɪstəm] *n* (sistema *m* de) megafonía.
publican ['pʌblɪkən] *n* tabernero,-a.
publication [pʌblɪ'keɪʃᵊn] *n* publicación *f*.
publicist ['pʌblɪsɪst] *n* publicista *mf*.
publicity [pʌ'blɪsɪtɪ] *n* publicidad *f*.
publicize [pʌblɪ'saɪz] *vt* **1** *(make public)* divulgar, hacer público,-a. **2** *(advertise)* promocionar.
public-spirited [pʌblɪk'spɪrɪtɪd] *adj* de espíritu cívico.
publish ['pʌblɪʃ] *vt* **1** *(book, newspaper)* publicar, editar; **2** *(make known)* divulgar.
publisher ['pʌblɪʃəʳ] *n (person)* editor,-ra; *(company)* editorial *f*.
publishing ['pʌblɪʃɪŋ] *n (profession)* industria editorial.
puce [pjuːs] *adj* castaño,-a rojizo,-a.
pucker ['pʌkəʳ] *vt (face, lips, brow)* fruncir, arrugar.
▷ *vi (lips, brow)* fruncirse, arrugarse.
pudding ['pʊdɪŋ] *n* **1** CULIN *(sweet)* budín *m*, pudín *m*; *(savoury)* pastel *m*. **2** GB *fam (dessert)* postre *m*.
puddle ['pʌdᵊl] *n* charco.
puerile ['pjʊəraɪl] *adj* pueril.
Puerto Rican [pweətəʊ'riːkᵊn] *adj* puertorriqueño,-a, portorriqueño,-a.
▷ *n* puertorriqueño,-a, portorriqueño,-a.
Puerto Rico [pweətəʊ'riːkəʊ] *n* Puerto Rico.
puff [pʌf] *n* **1** *(of wind, air)* soplo, racha, ráfaga; *(of smoke)* bocanada. **2** *(action)* soplo, soplido; *(at cigarette, pipe)* calada, chupada.
▷ *vt (blow - gen)* soplar; *(- smoke)* echar.
▷ *vi* **1** *(pipe, cigarette)* chupar (**at/on**, -), dar caladas (**at/on**, a). **2** *(pant)* jadear, resoplar. **3** *(train)* echar humo, echar vapor.
puffed [pʌft] *adj* **1** *(sleeve)* abombado,-a; *(rice)* inflado,-a. **2** *(out of breath)* sin aliento.
▷ *adj* **puffed up** *(swollen)* hinchado,-a.
puffin ['pʌfɪn] *n* frailecillo (común).
puffy ['pʌfɪ] *adj* hinchado,-a.
▲ *comp* **puffier**, *superl* **puffiest**.
pug [pʌg] *n (dog)* doguillo.
pugnacious [pʌg'neɪʃəs] *adj* pugnaz, agresivo,-a.
puke [pjuːk] *vi fam* devolver, vomitar.
pull [pʊl] *n* **1** *(tug)* tirón *m*. **2** *(of moon, current)* fuerza. **3** *(attraction)* atracción *f*; *(influence)* influencia.
▷ *vt* **1** *(draw)* tirar de; *(drag)* arrastrar: **the horse was pulling a cart** *el caballo tiraba de una carreta.* **2** *(tug forcefully)* tirar de, dar un tirón a: **don't pull my hair!** *¡no me tires del pelo!* **3** *(remove, draw out)* sacar. **4** *(damage muscle)* sufrir un tirón. **5** *fam (attract - crowd, audience)* atraer; *(boy, girl)* ligarse, ligar con.
▷ *vi* **1** *(tug)* tirar (**at/on**, de). **2** *(on pipe, cigarette)* chupar, dar caladas a. **3** *(of vehicle - veer)* tirar.
⊙ **to pull apart** *vt sep (separate)* separar; *(pull to pieces)* destrozar, hacer pedazos.
⊙ **to pull away** *vi (car, bus)* arrancar; *(train)* salir de la estación.
▷ *vt sep* separar, apartar.
⊙ **to pull down** *vt sep* derribar, tirar (abajo).
⊙ **to pull in** *vt sep* **1** *(crowd)* atraer. **2** *(money)* sacar, ganar.
▷ *vi (train)* entrar en la estación; *(bus, car)* parar.
⊙ **to pull off** *vt sep (carry out)* llevar a cabo; *(achieve)* lograr.
▷ *vt insep (of car, etc)* salir de.
⊙ **to pull out** *vt sep (gun, tooth, plug, etc)* sacar; *(troops)* retirar.
▷ *vi* **1** *(train)* salir de la estación; *(bus, car)* salir. **2** *(withdraw)* retirarse.
⊙ **to pull over** *vi* hacerse a un lado.
⊙ **to pull through** *vi* reponerse.
⊙ **to pull together** *vi* trabajar juntos.
▷ *vt sep* **to pull** os **together** calmarse.
⊙ **to pull up** *vt sep* **1** *(draw up)* subir, levantar; *(plant, weed)* arrancar. **2** *(scold)* regañar.
▷ *vi (bus, car)* detenerse, parar.
pulley ['pʊlɪ] *n* polea.
pull-out ['pʊlaʊt] *n* suplemento, separata.
pullover ['pʊləʊvəʳ] *n* pullover *m*, jersey *m*.
pulmonary ['pʌlmənərɪ] *adj* pulmonar.
pulp [pʌlp] *n* **1** *(of fruit)* pulpa, carne *f*; *(of vegetable)* pulpa; *(of wood, paper)* pasta, pulpa. **2** *(substance)* papilla. **3** *pej (books, magazines, etc)* literatura barata, basura.
▷ *vt (wood, paper)* hacer pasta de; *(fruit)* reducir a pulpa.
pulpit ['pʊlpɪt] *n* púlpito.
pulsate [pʌl'seɪt] *vi* latir, palpitar.
pulse[1] [pʌls] *n* **1** ANAT pulso. **2** PHYS pulsación *f*.
▷ *vi* palpitar, latir.
pulse[2] [pʌls] *n* BOT legumbre *f*.
pulverize ['pʌlvəraɪz] *vt* pulverizar.
puma ['pjuːmə] *n* puma *m*.
pumice stone ['pʌmɪsstəʊn] *n* piedra pómez.
pummel ['pʌmᵊl] *vt* aporrear.
▲ *pt & pp* **pummelled** (US **pummeled**), *ger* **pummelling** (US **pummeling**).
pump[1] [pʌmp] *n (machine)* bomba: **bicycle pump** *bomba de aire, bombín m.*
▷ *vt* bombear.
▷ *vi (of heart)* latir.
⊙ **to pump up** *vt sep* inflar.

pump[2] [pʌmp] *n (plimsoll)* zapatilla de lona, playera; *(for dancing)* zapatilla de ballet.
pumpkin ['pʌmpkɪn] *n* calabaza.
pun [pʌn] *n* juego de palabras, retruécano.
Punch [pʌntʃ] *n* polichinela *m*, títere *m*. ● **Punch and Judy show** función *f* de polichinelas.
punch[1] [pʌntʃ] *n* **1** *(blow)* puñetazo, golpe *m*; *(in boxing)* pegada. **2** *fig* fuerza, empuje *m*.
▷ *vt* dar un puñetazo a, pegar a.
punch[2] [pʌntʃ] *n (for making holes)* perforadora, taladro; *(in leather)* punzón *m*; *(for tickets)* máquina de picar billetes.
▷ *vt (make a hole in)* perforar; *(leather)* punzar.
punch[3] [pʌntʃ] *n (drink)* ponche *m*.
punch-drunk ['pʌntʃdrʌŋk] *adj* grogui, aturdido,-a.
punch-up ['pʌntʃʌp] *n fam* riña, pelea.
punctilious [pʌŋk'tɪlɪəs] *adj fml* puntilloso,-a.
punctual ['pʌŋktjʊəl] *adj* puntual.
punctuate ['pʌŋktjʊeɪt] *vt* **1** LING puntuar. **2** *(interrupt)* interrumpir.
punctuation [pʌŋktjʊ'eɪʃᵊn] *n* puntuación *f*. ● **punctuation mark** signo de puntuación.
puncture ['pʌŋktʃəʳ] *n* pinchazo.
▷ *vt (tyre, ball, etc)* pinchar.
pundit ['pʌndɪt] *n* experto,-a.
pungent ['pʌndʒənt] *adj* **1** *(smell, taste)* acre. **2** *(remark)* mordaz.
punish ['pʌnɪʃ] *vt* castigar.
punishable ['pʌnɪʃəbᵊl] *adj* punible, castigable.
punishing ['pʌnɪʃɪŋ] *adj (severe)* duro,-a; *(exhausting)* agotador,-ra.
punishment ['pʌnɪʃmənt] *n (gen)* castigo.
punitive ['pjuːnɪtɪv] *adj* punitivo,-a.
punk [pʌnk] *n (person)* punk *mf*; *(music)* punk *m*.
punnet ['pʌnɪt] *n* cestita.
punt [pʌnt] *n (boat)* batea.
▷ *vi* ir en batea.
punter ['pʌntəʳ] *n* **1** *fam (in betting)* jugador,-ra. **2** *(customer)* cliente,-a.
puny ['pjuːnɪ] *adj* enclenque, canijo,-a.
▲ *comp* **punier**, *superl* **puniest**.
pup [pʌp] *n (dog)* cachorro,-a; *(seal, otter)* cría.
pupil[1] ['pjuːpəl] *n* EDUC alumno,-a.
pupil[2] ['pjuːpəl] *n* ANAT pupila.
puppet ['pʌpɪt] *n* **1** títere *m*. **2** *fig* títere *m*. ● **puppet show** teatro de títeres.
puppy ['pʌpɪ] *n* cachorro,-a.
▲ *pl* **puppies**.
purchase ['pɜːtʃəs] *n fml* compra, adquisición *f*.
▷ *vt fml* comprar, adquirir.
purchaser ['pɜːtʃəsəʳ] *n fml* comprador,-ra.
pure ['pjʊəʳ] *adj (gen)* puro,-a.
purebred [pjʊə'bred] *adj* de pura sangre, de pura raza.
▷ *n (horse)* caballo de purasangre, pura *m* sangre.
purée ['pjʊəreɪ] *n* puré *m*.
purgative ['pɜːgətɪv] *n* MED purgante *m*.
purge [pɜːdʒ] *n* purga.
▷ *vt* **1** *(cleanse)* purgar. **2** POL purgar, depurar.
purification [pjʊərɪfɪ'keɪʃᵊn] *n* purificación *f*.
purifier ['pjʊərɪfaɪəʳ] *n* depurador *m*.
purify ['pjʊərɪfaɪ] *vt (gen)* purificar; *(water)* depurar.
▲ *pt & pp* **purified**, *ger* **purifying**.
purist ['pjʊərɪst] *n* purista *mf*.
puritan ['pjʊərɪtᵊn] *adj* puritano,-a.
▷ *n* puritano,-a.
purity ['pjʊərɪtɪ] *n* pureza.
purple ['pɜːpəl] *adj* morado,-a.
▷ *n* (color *m*) púrpura, (color *m*) morado.
purport [pɜː'pɔːt] *n fml* significado, sentido.
▷ *vt fml* pretender.
purpose ['pɜːpəs] *n* **1** *(aim, intention)* propósito, intención *f*, fin *m*; *(reason)* razón *f*, motivo: **what is the purpose of your visit?** *¿cuál es el motivo de su visita?* **2** *(use)* uso, utilidad *f*. **3** *(determination)* resolución *f*. ■ **on purpose** adrede, a posta. ▮ **to no purpose** en vano.
purposeful ['pɜːpəsfʊl] *adj (resolute)* decidido,-a.
purr [pɜːʳ] *n (of cat)* ronroneo.
▷ *vi (of cat)* ronronear.
purse [pɜːs] *n* **1** GB monedero, portamonedas *m*. **2** US bolso.
▷ *vt (lips)* fruncir.
purser ['pɜːsəʳ] *n* MAR contador,-ra.
pursue [pə'sjuː] *vt* **1** *(chase)* perseguir; *(follow)* seguir. **2** *(seek)* buscar; *(strive for)* esforzarse por conseguir, luchar por. **3** *(carry out - policy)* llevar a cabo; *(- matter)* investigar. **4** *(continue with)* dedicarse a, ejercer.
pursuer [pə'sjuːəʳ] *n* perseguidor,-ra.
pursuit [pə'sjuːt] *n* **1** *(chase)* persecución *f*; *(hunt)* caza. **2** *(search)* búsqueda, busca; *(striving)* lucha. **3** *(activity)* actividad *f*.
purveyor [pɜː'veɪəʳ] *n fml* proveedor,-ra.
pus [pʌs] *n* pus *m*.
push [pʊʃ] *n (shove)* empujón *m*: **we had to give the car a push** *tuvimos que empujar el coche*. ■ **to give** SB **the push 1** *(from job)* poner a ALGN de patitas en la calle, echar a ALGN. **2** *(end relationship)* dejar a ALGN.
▷ *vt* **1** *(shove)* empujar: **they pushed her in the water** *la empujaron al agua*. **2** *(press - button, bell, etc)* pulsar, apretar. **3** *(persuade forcefully)* empujar, presionar; *(harass)* apretar, presionar, exigir. **4** *(promote, try to sell)* promocionar.
▷ *vi* **1** *(shove)* empujar: **push harder!** *¡empuja más!* **2** *(move forward)* abrirse paso. **3** *(pressurize)* presionar, exigir.
⊙ **to push about / push around** *vt sep* intimidar.
⊙ **to push ahead** *vi* seguir adelante.
⊙ **to push in** *vi (in queue)* colarse.
⊙ **to push off** *vi* **1** *fam (go away)* largarse. **2** *(in boat)* desatracar.
⊙ **to push on** *vi* seguir, continuar.
⊙ **to push over** *vt sep (person)* tirar; *(thing)* volcar.
⊙ **to push through** *vt sep (legislation, bill)* hacer aprobar; *(student)* ayudar.
pushbike ['pʊʃbaɪk] *n fam* bicicleta.
pushchair ['pʊʃtʃeəʳ] *n* GB cochecito de niño, sillita de niño.
pushover ['pʊʃəʊvəʳ] *n fam (person)* incauto,-a.
push-start ['pʊʃstɑːt] *vt* arrancar empujando.
push-up ['pʊʃʌp] *n* US flexión *f*.
pushy ['pʊʃɪ] *adj fam* agresivo,-a, insistente.
▲ *comp* **pushier**, *superl* **pushiest**.
puss [pʊs] *n fam* minino,-a, gatito,-a.
pussy ['pʊsɪ] *n fam* minino,-a, gatito,-a.
pussycat ['pʊsɪkæt] *n fam* minino,-a, gatito,-a.

put [put] *vt* **1** *(gen)* poner; *(place)* colocar; *(add)* echar, añadir; *(place inside)* meter, poner: **she put the vase on the table** *puso el florero en la mesa.* **2** *(write, mark)* poner, apuntar, escribir: **what did you put for number six?** *¿qué pusiste en el número seis?* **3** *(cause to be)* poner: **this puts me in a difficult position** *esto me pone en una situación difícil.* **4** *(rate, classify)* poner: **she puts her family before her job** *antepone su familia al trabajo.* **5** *(express)* expresar, decir: **you put that very well** *lo has expresado muy bien.* **6** *(calculate, estimate)* calcular: **I'd put the cost at 100 pounds** *yo diría que cuesta 100 libras.* ■ **to put paid to sth** estropear algo. | **to put sth right** arreglar algo. | **to put the blame on sb** echar la culpa a ALGN.

⊙**to put about** *vt sep (news, rumour)* hacer correr.

▷ *vi (ship)* virar en redondo.

⊙ **to put across** *vt sep* comunicar.

⊙ **to put aside** *vt sep* **1** *(save)* ahorrar, reservar. **2** *(disregard - differences)* dejar de lado.

⊙ **to put away** *vt sep* **1** *(clothes, toys, dishes)* guardar (en su sitio); *(save - money)* ahorrar. **2** *(lock up - criminal, mad person)* encerrar.

⊙ **to put back** *vt sep* **1** *(replace, return)* devolver a su sitio. **2** *(clock)* atrasar, retrasar; *(postpone, delay)* aplazar, posponer. **3** *(drink)* beberse.

⊙ **to put by** *vt sep* ahorrar.

⊙ **to put down** *vt sep* **1** *(set down - gen)* dejar; *(- phone)* colgar; *(- baby)* acostar. **2** *(payment)* entregar, dejar (en depósito); *(deposit)* dejar. **3** *(rebellion)* sofocar. **4** *(animal)* sacrificar. **5** *(write)* apuntar, anotar, escribir.

▷ *vi* AV aterrizar.

⊙ **to put down for** *vt sep (register - for school)* inscribir; *(for trip, dinner, etc)* apuntar.

⊙ **to put down to** *vt sep (attribute)* atribuir a.

⊙ **to put forward** *vt sep* **1** *(idea, theory, plan)* proponer, presentar. **2** *(clock, meeting, wedding)* adelantar.

⊙ **to put in** *vt sep* **1** *(install, fit)* instalar. **2** *(include, insert)* poner, incluir; *(say)* agregar. **3** *(enter, submit - claim, request, bid)* presentar. **4** *(spend time working)* trabajar.

▷ *vi (ship)* hacer escala.

⊙ **to put in for** *vt insep (apply)* solicitar.

⊙ **to put off** *vt sep* **1** *(postpone)* aplazar, posponer. **2** *(distract)* distraer. **3** *(discourage)* desanimar, disuadir.

⊙ **to put on** *vt sep* **1** *(clothes)* poner, ponerse: **put your coat on** *ponte el abrigo.* **2** *(expression, attitude)* fingir, adoptar. **3** *(gain, increase)* aumentar. **4** *(present - show)* presentar, montar; *(- exhibition)* organizar. **5** *(provide, add - train, etc)* poner. **6** *(switch on - light, television)* encender; *(- music, radio)* poner. **7** *(add - gen)* añadir; *(- tax)* gravar con un impuesto; *(- bet)* apostar por.

⊙ **to put onto** *vt sep (put in touch with)* poner en contacto con.

⊙ **to put out** *vt sep* **1** *(fire, light, cigarette)* apagar. **2** *(put outside - cat, washing, rubbish)* sacar. **3** *(extend - hand)* tender, alargar; *(- tongue)* sacar; *(dislocate)* dislocar. **4** *(inconvenience)* molestar; *(upset, offend, annoy)* molestar, ofender. **5** *(publish, issue)* publicar; *(broadcast)* difundir.

⊙ **to put over** *vt sep* ⟶ **put across.**

⊙ **to put through** *vt sep* **1** *(phone - connect)* pasar, poner (to, con): **could you put me through to accounts** *¿me puede poner con contabilidad?* **2** *(cause to undergo)* someter a, hacer pasar por.

⊙ **to put to** *vt sep* **1** *(present, submit - proposal, case)* presentar, exponer; *(ask - question)* hacer; *(ask to vote on)* someter a votación. **2** *(cause to experience)* causar.

⊙ **to put together** *vt sep* **1** *(pieces)* armar, montar; *(team)* formar; *(meal, etc)* preparar, hacer. **2** *(combine)* juntar, reunir.

⊙ **to put up** *vt sep* **1** *(provide accommodation for)* alojar, hospedar. **2** *(erect - tent)* armar; *(- building, fence)* construir. **3** *(shelves, picture, decorations)* colocar; *(curtains, notice, poster)* colgar. **4** *(raise - hand)* levantar; *(flag)* izar; *(hair)* recoger; *(umbrella)* abrir. **5** *(increase - price, etc)* subir. **6** *(present - candidate)* presentar, proponer.

▷ *vt insep* **1** *(resistence, struggle)* ofrecer, oponer: **they put up a good fight** *ofrecieron mucha resistencia.* **2** *(money)* poner, aportar.

▲ *pt & pp* **put**, *ger* **putting.**

⊙ **to put up to** *vt sep* incitar, empujar.

⊙ **to put up with** *vt insep* soportar, aguantar.

⊙ **to put upon** *vt insep* explotar.

put-down ['putdaun] *n* corte *m.*

putrefaction [pjuːtrɪ'fækʃᵊn] *n* putrefacción *f.*

putrefy ['pjuːtrɪfaɪ] *vi* pudrirse.

▲ *pt & pp* **putrefied**, *ger* **putrefying.**

putrid ['pjuːtrɪd] *adj (rotting)* putrefacto,-a, podrido,-a

putt [pʌt] *n* tiro al hoyo.

▷ *vt* tirar al hoyo.

putty ['pʌtɪ] *n* masilla.

▲ *pl* **putties.**

put-up job ['putʌp'dʒɒb] *n fam* montaje *m.*

puzzle ['pʌzᵊl] *n* **1** *(jigsaw)* puzzle *m*; *(toy)* rompecabezas *m*; *(riddle)* adivinanza, acertijo; *(crossword)* crucigrama *m.* **2** *(mystery)* misterio, enigma *m.*

▷ *vt* dejar perplejo,-a, extrañar.

⊙ **to puzzle out** *vt sep (problem)* resolver; *(mystery)* descifrar.

puzzled ['pʌzᵊld] *adj* perplejo,-a, desconcertado,-a.

puzzling ['pʌzᵊlɪŋ] *adj* extraño,-a.

pygmy ['pɪgmɪ] *adj* pigmeo,-a, enano,-a.

▷ *n (small person)* pigmeo,-a, enano,-a.

pyjamas [pə'dʒɑːməz] *n pl* pijama *m sing.*

pylon ['paɪlən] *n* **1** ELEC torre *f* (de tendido eléctrico) **2** ARCH pilón *m*, pilar *m.*

pyramid ['pɪrəmɪd] *n* pirámide *f.*

pyre ['paɪəʳ] *n* pira.

Pyrex® ['paɪreks] *n* pírex *m.*

▷ *adj* de pírex.

pyrites [paɪ'raɪtiːz] *n* pirita.

pyromania [paɪrə'meɪnɪə] *n* piromanía.

pyromaniac [paɪrəʊ'meɪnɪæk] *n* pirómano,-a.

pyrotechnics [paɪrəʊ'teknɪks] *n* pirotecnia.

▷ *n pl* fuegos *mpl* artificiales.

python ['paɪθən] *n* pitón *m.*

Q

Q, q [kjuː] *n (the letter)* Q, q *f.*
Qatar [kæ'tɑːʳ] *n* Qatar.
quagmire ['kwɒgmaɪəʳ] *n* **1** cenagal *m.* **2** *fig* atolladero.
quail [kweɪl] *n* codorniz *f.*
▷ *vi* acobardarse, encogerse.
quaint [kweɪnt] *adj* **1** pintoresco,-a, típico,-a. **2** *(odd)* singular, original. **3** *(strange)* raro,-a, extraño, -a. ● **quaint fellow** tipo raro.
quake [kweɪk] *n fam* terremoto.
▷ *vi* temblar: **he quaked with fear** *temblaba de miedo.* ■ **to quake at the knees** temblarle las piernas a ALGN.
qualification [kwɒlɪfɪ'keɪʃᵊn] *n* **1** *(for job)* requisito. **2** *(ability)* aptitud *f*, capacidad *f.* **3** *(paper)* diploma *m*, título. **4** *(reservation)* reserva, salvedad *f.* **5** *(restriction)* limitación *f.* **6** *(act of qualifying)* graduación *f*: **she soon found a job after qualification** *no tardó mucho en encontrar trabajo después de graduarse.*
qualified ['kwɒlɪfaɪd] *adj* **1** *(for job)* capacitado,-a. **2** *(with qualifications)* titulado,-a: **qualified nurse** *enfermero,-a titulado,-a.* **3** *(limited, modified)* limitado,-a, restringido,-a: **a qualified agreement** *un acuerdo limitado.*
qualify ['kwɒlɪfaɪ] *vt* **1** *(entitle, make eligible)* capacitar, dar derecho, habilitar: **her excellent grades qualified her for a grant** *sus excelentes notas le dieron derecho a una beca.* **2** *(modify)* modificar, matizar, puntualizar. **3** LING calificar.
▷ *vi* **1** reunir las condiciones necesarias: **I'm afraid you don't qualify for a pension** *me temo que usted no reúne las condiciones necesarias para percibir una pensión.* **2** *(obtain degree)* obtener el título (**as**, de). **3** SP clasificarse: **he qualified for the finals** *se clasificó para las finales.*
quality ['kwɒlɪtɪ] *n* **1** *(degree of excellence)* calidad *f*: **of good quality** *de buena calidad;* **of poor quality** *de poca calidad.* **2** *(attribute)* cualidad *f*: **she has many qualities** *tiene muchas cualidades.* ● **quality control** control *m* de calidad. ǀ **quality goods** género de calidad, productos *mpl* de calidad. ǀ **quality newspapers** prensa de calidad.
▲ *pl* **qualities.**
qualm [kwɑːm] *n* **1** *(doubt)* duda; *(worry)* inquietud *f*, ansia: **she has qualms about aborting** *tiene dudas de si abortar o no.* **2** *(scruple)* escrúpulo. ■ **to have no qualms about doing** STH no tener escrúpulos en hacer ALGO. ● **qualms of conscience** remordimientos *mpl* de conciencia.
quantity ['kwɒntɪtɪ] *n* **1** cantidad *f.* **2** MATH cantidad *f.* ● **quantity surveyor** aparejador *m.*
▲ *pl* **quantities.**

quarrel ['kwɒrᵊl] *n* **1** riña, disputa, pelea. **2** *(disagreement)* desacuerdo. **3** *(complaint)* queja: **I have no quarrel with him** *no tengo ninguna queja de él, no tengo nada contra él.* ■ **to pick a quarrel with sb** meterse con algn, buscar pelea con algn.
▷ *vi (argue)* reñir, pelearse, disputar, discutir: **she is always quarreling with her mother** *siempre está discutiendo con su madre.*
▲ *pt & pp* **quarrelled** (US **quarreled**), *ger* **quarrelling** (US **quarreling**).
quarry ['kwɒrɪ] *n* **1** cantera. **2** *(in hunting)* presa.
▲ *pl* **quarries.**
▷ *vt* extraer.
▲ *pt & pp* **quarried**, *ger* **quarrying.**
quart [kwɔːt] *n* cuarto de galón. ■ **to put a quart into a pint pot** hacer algo imposible.

En Gran Bretaña equivale a 1,14 litros; en Estados Unidos equivale a 0,95 litros.

quarter ['kwɔːtəʳ] *n* **1** cuarto. **2** *(area)* barrio: **the old quarter** *el casco antiguo;* **the Latin Quarter** *el barrio latino.* **3** *(time)* cuarto: **it's a quarter to one** *es la una menos cuarto.* **4** *(weight)* cuarto de libra: **a quarter of sugar** *un cuarto de libra de azúcar.* **5** *(of moon)* cuarto. **6** *(three months)* trimestre *m.* **7** US *(amount)* veinticinco centavos; *(coin)* moneda de veinticinco centavos. ● **first quarter** cuarto creciente. ǀ **last quarter** cuarto menguante.
▷ *vt* **1** dividir en cuatro. **2** *(reduce)* reducir a la cuarta parte. **3** HIST descuartizar. **4** *(lodge)* alojar.
▷ *n pl* **quarters** alojamiento *m sing.* ■ **at close quarters** desde muy cerca. ǀ **from all quarters** de todas partes. ● **officer's quarters** residencia *f sing* de oficiales.
quarterly ['kwɔːtəlɪ] *adj* trimestral.
▷ *adv* trimestralmente.
▷ *n* revista trimestral.
▲ *pl* **quarterlies.**
quartz [kwɔːts] *n* cuarzo. ● **quartz watch** reloj *m* de cuarzo.
quash [kwɒʃ] *vt* **1** *(uprising)* sofocar, aplastar. **2** JUR anular, invalidar.
quasi ['kwɑːzɪ, 'kweɪzaɪ] *adv* casi, cuasi. ● **quasi contract** JUR cuasi contrato.
quaver ['kweɪvəʳ] *n* **1** MUS *(note)* corchea. **2** MUS *(voice)* trémolo. **3** *(trembling)* temblor *m.*
▷ *vi* temblar: **her voice quavered** *le temblaba la voz.*
quay [kiː] *n* muelle *m.*
queasy ['kwiːzɪ] *adj* **1** mareado,-a. **2** *(conscience)* delicado,-a, escrupuloso,-a. ■ **to feel queasy** sentirse mal, tener náuseas: **she felt queasy throughout the crossing** *se sintió mal durante toda la travesía.*
▲ *comp* **queasier**, *superl* **queasiest.**

queen [kwi:n] *n* **1** reina. **2** *(cards, chess)* dama, reina; *(chess)* reina. **3** *sl* loca, maricona. ● **queen bee** abeja reina. ‖ **Queen Mother** reina madre.
▷ *vt (pawn)* coronar. ■ **to queen it** pavonearse.

queer [kwɪəʳ] *adj* **1** raro,-a, extraño,-a. **2** *(ill)* malucho,-a. **3** *fam* gay. **4** *(mad)* loco,-a, chiflado,-a.
▷ *n fam* gay *m*, marica *m*, maricón *m*.
▷ *vt fam* fastidiar, estropear. ■ **in queer street 1** *(in debt)* endeudado,-a, en deuda. **2** *(in trouble)* en apuros. ‖ **to queer** SB**'s pitch** fastidiarle los planes a ALGN.

quell [kwel] *vt* **1** *(rebellion)* sofocar. **2** *(fears)* disipar.

quench [kwentʃ] *vt* **1** *(thirst)* saciar. **2** *(fire)* apagar.

querulous ['kwerjʊləs] *adj fml* quejumbroso,-a.

query ['kwɪərɪ] *n* **1** pregunta, duda. **2** LING signo de interrogación. **3** *fig* interrogante *m*.
▲ *pl* **queries.**
▷ *vt* **1** *(doubt)* poner en duda. **2** *(ask)* preguntar.
▲ *pt & pp* **queried**, *ger* **querying.**

quest [kwest] *n* búsqueda, busca. ■ **in quest of** en busca de: **in quest of the Holy Grail** *en busca del Santo Grial.*

question ['kwestʃən] *n* **1** pregunta. **2** *(in exam)* pregunta, problema *m*. **3** *(problem, issue)* cuestión *f*, problema *m*: **the Basque question** *el problema del País Vasco.* **4** *(topic, matter)* cuestión *f*, asunto: **there is still the question of expenses** *todavía queda el asunto de los gastos.* ■ **it's a question of** se trata de, es cuestión de: **it's a question of time** *es cuestión de tiempo.* ‖ **out of the question** imposible, impensable. ‖ **that is the question** de eso se trata, he aquí la dificultad. ‖ **without question** sin rechistar: **she did it without question** *lo hizo sin rechistar.* ● **question mark 1** *(punctuation mark)* signo de interrogación, interrogación *f*, interrogante *m*. **2** *(doubt)* interrogante *m*. ‖ **question tag** coletilla.
▷ *vt* **1** hacer preguntas a, interrogar: **she questioned the girl** *le hizo preguntas a la niña;* **those detained are being questioned about the holdup** *están interrogando a los detenidos sobre el atraco.* **2** *(cast doubt on)* cuestionar, poner en duda. ■ **to call into question** poner en duda, dudar de.

questioning ['kwestʃənɪŋ] *adj* inquisitivo,-a, interrogativo,-a: **she gave him a questioning glance** *le lanzó una mirada inquisitiva.*
▷ *n* preguntas *fpl*, interrogatorio: **the Police brought him in for questioning** *la policía lo detuvo para someterlo a un interrogatorio.*

questionnaire [kwestʃə'neəʳ] *n* cuestionario.

queue [kju:] *n (GB)* cola.
▷ *vi* hacer cola: **nowadays you have to queue up for everything** *hoy en día hay que hacer cola para todo.* ■ **to jump the queue** colarse.

quibble ['kwɪbᵊl] *n* **1** *(difficulty)* pega, objeción *f*. **2** *(subtlety)* sutileza. **3** *(evasion)* evasiva, subterfugio.
▷ *vi* **1** poner pegas, sutilizar: **he's always quibbling about something** *siempre pone pegas a todo.* **2** *fam* buscarle tres pies al gato.

quick [kwɪk] *adj* **1** *(fast)* rápido,-a: **let's have a quick look** *echemos un vistazo;* **I would appreciate a quick reply** *agradecería una respuesta pronta;* **he let me have it cheap for a quick sale** *me lo dejó barato porque lo quería vender rápido;* **let's have a quick snack** *comamos algo rápido;* **be quick or you'll miss it!** *¡rápido o l… perderás!, ¡date prisa o lo perderás!* **2** *(clever)* espabilado,-a, despierto,-a, listo,-a. ■ **as quick as lightnin…** como un rayo, como una bala. ‖ **quick march!** MI… ¡de frente! ‖ **to be quick on the uptake** captar algo en seguida. ‖ **to be quick to anger** tener mal genio. ‖ **t… be quick to take offence** enfadarse por nada. ‖ **to cu…** SB **to the quick** herir a ALGN en lo vivo. ‖ **to have … quick one** *fam* echar un trago, tomar una copita. ‖ **t… have a quick temper** tener un genio vivo.

quicken ['kwɪkᵊn] *vt (speed up)* acelerar: **he quickened his pace** *aceleró el paso.*
▷ *vi (speed up)* acelerarse.

quickly ['kwɪklɪ] *adv (speed up)* rápido
▷ *vi (speed up)* acelerarse.

quicksand ['kwɪksænd] *n* arenas *fpl* movedizas.

quid[1] [kwɪd] *n* GB *fam (money)* libra esterlina: **it cos… me ten quid** *me costó diez libras.*
▲ *pl* **quid.**

quid[2] [kwɪd] *n* mascada de tabaco.

quiet ['kwaɪət] *adj* **1** *(silent)* callado,-a, silencioso,-a: **he kept quiet all night** *estuvo callado toda la noche.* … *(peaceful, calm)* tranquilo,-a, sosegado,-a: **this is … very quiet village** *éste es un pueblo muy tranquilo.* … FIN apagado,-a, poco activo,-a: **business was ver… quiet in the shop today** *las ventas han sido muy floja… en la tienda.* **4** *(unobtrusive)* callado,-a, reservado,-a. **5** *(tranquil, without fuss)* tranquilo,-a: **they spent … quiet evening at home** *pasaron una velada tranquil… en casa.*
▷ *n* **1** *(silence)* silencio. **2** *(calm)* tranquilidad *f*, calm… sosiego. ■ **on the quiet** a la chita callando, a hurtad… llas, en secreto, sigilosamente: **he did it on the quiet** … *hizo en secreto.*
▷ *vt* US calmar, silenciar: **she quieted the baby down** *ca… mó a la criatura.*
▷ *vi* US calmarse.

quieten ['kwaɪətᵊn] *vt* **1** *(silence)* callar; *(calm)* tran… quilizar, calmar. **2** *(calm down)* tranquilizar.
▷ *vi (silence)* callarse; *(calm)* calmarse, tranquilizarse

quietly ['kwaɪətlɪ] *adv* **1** *(silently)* silenciosament… sin hacer ruido; *(not loudly)* bajo: **she always speak… quietly** *siempre habla en voz baja.* **2** *(calmly)* tranqu… lamente. **3** *(discreetly)* discretamente, con discre… ción. **4** *(simply)* sencillamente, con sencillez.

quietness ['kwaɪətnəs] *n* **1** *(silence)* silencio, paz *f*. … *(calm)* tranquilidad *f*, sosiego. **3** *(discretion)* discre… ción *f*, intimidad *f*.

quill [kwɪl] *n* **1** *(feather)* pluma. **2** *(porcupine)* púa. … *(part of feather)* cañón *m* de pluma. **4** *(pen)* pluma.

quilt [kwɪlt] *n* edredón *m*.

quintet [kwɪn'tet] *n* MUS quinteto.

quip [kwɪp] *n* **1** *(remark)* agudeza, ocurrencia, pull… salida. **2** *(joke)* chiste *m*.
▷ *vi* bromear.
▲ *pt & pp* **quipped**, *ger* **quipping.**

quirk [kwɜ:k] *n* **1** *(oddity)* manía, rareza, peculiar… dad *f*. **2** *(in writing)* rasgo. **3** *(of fate)* avatar *m*, vicis… tud *f*.

quit [kwɪt] *vt* **1** dejar, abandonar: **he quit his job** *de… el trabajo.* **2** *(stop)* dejar de: **she quit smoking** *dejó … fumar.*

▷ *vi* marcharse, irse. ■ **to be quits** estar iguales, estar en paz. ‖ **to call it quits** hacer las paces, estar en paz.
▲ *pt & pp* **quit**, *ger* **quitting**.

quite [kwaɪt] *adv* **1** *(rather)* bastante: **it was quite a good game** *fue un partido bastante bueno;* **they played quite well** *jugaron bastante bien;* **they're quite difficult exercises** *son ejercicios bastante difíciles;* **there are quite a few people here** *hay bastante gente aquí.* **2** *(totally)* completamente, del todo: **I quite understand** *lo entiendo perfectamente;* **you've quite ruined it** *lo has destrozado completamente;* **it isn't quite finished** *no está terminado del todo.* **3** *(exceptional)* excepcional, increíble, original: **he's quite a comedian** *es un cómico increíble;* **our trip was quite something** *nuestro viaje fue algo excepcional.* **4** *(exactly)* exactamente: **it isn't quite what I was looking for** *no es exactamente lo que buscaba.* ■ **quite so!** ¡exactamente!

quiver[1] ['kwɪvəʳ] *n* **1** *(for arrows)* carcaj *m*, aljaba. **2** *(tremble of lips, voice)* temblor *m*; *(of eyelids)* parpadeo; *(shiver)* estremecimiento.
▷ *vi* temblar, estremecerse.

quiver[2] ['kwɪvəʳ] *n (for arrows)* carcaj *m*, aljaba.

quiz [kwɪz] *n* **1** *(competition)* concurso. **2** *(enquiry)* encuesta; *(exam)* examen *m*.
▷ *vt* preguntar, interrogar.

quizzical ['kwɪzɪkᵊl] *adj* **1** *(bemused)* burlón,-ona: **she gave me a quizzical smile** *me sonrió burlonamente.* **2** *(enquiring)* curioso,-a: **he had a quizzical look on his face** *su mirada reflejaba curiosidad.*

quotation [kwəʊ'teɪʃᵊn] *n* **1** LING cita. **2** FIN cotización *f*. **3** COMM presupuesto. ● **quotation marks** comillas *fpl*.

quote [kwəʊt] *n* **1** LING cita. **2** *(price - gen)* presupuesto; *(- for shares)* cotización *f*.
▷ *vt* **1** citar, entrecomillar. **2** *(price)* dar, ofrecer. **3** FIN cotizar. ■ **to ask for a quote** pedir un presupuesto. ‖ **to give** SB **a quote** dar un presupuesto a ALGN. ‖ **to quote** SB **a price** ofrecer un precio a ALGN.

quotient ['kwəʊʃᵊnt] *n* **1** *(in mathematics)* cociente *m*. **2** *(degree)* coeficiente *m*, grado. ● **intelligence quotient** coeficiente intelectual *m*, coeficiente *m* de inteligencia.

R

R, r [ɑː] *n (the letter)* R, r *f.*
rabbi ['ræbaɪ] *n* rabí *m*, rabino.
rabbit ['ræbɪt] *n* conejo. ● **rabbit hole** madriguera de conejos. ‖ **rabbit warren** madriguera de conejos.
rabble ['ræbᵊl] *n* populacho.
rabies ['reɪbiːz] *n* rabia.
raccoon [rə'kuːn] *n* mapache *m.*
race[1] [reɪs] *n (people)* raza. ● **race relations** relaciones *fpl* raciales. ‖ **race riot** disturbio racial.
race[2] [reɪs] *n* **1** SP carrera. **2** *(current)* corriente *f* fuerte; *(channel)* canal *m.*
▷ *vi* **1** *(compete)* competir, correr. **2** *(go fast)* correr, ir deprisa. **3** *(heart)* latir deprisa. **4** *(engine)* acelerarse.
▷ *vt* **1** *(person)* competir con, echar una carrera a. **2** *(engine)* acelerar. ■ **to run a race** participar en una carrera.
racecourse ['reɪskɔːs] *n* GB hipódromo.
racehorse ['reɪhɔːs] *n* caballo de carreras.
racer ['reɪsəʳ] *n (person)* corredor,-ra; *(bicycle)* bicicleta de carreras; *(car)* coche *m* de carreras; *(horse)* caballo de carreras.
racetrack ['reɪstræk] *n* **1** *(for cars)* circuito; *(for cycles)* velódromo. **2** *(for people)* pista, pista de atletismo. **3** *(for horses)* hipódromo; *(for greyhounds)* canódromo.
racial ['reɪʃᵊl] *adj* racial. ● **racial discrimination** discriminación *f* racial.
racialism ['reɪʃᵊlɪzᵊm] *n* racismo.
racialist ['reɪʃᵊlɪst] *adj* racista.
▷ *n* racista *mf.*
racing ['reɪsɪŋ] *n* carreras *fpl.*
▷ *adj* de carreras.
racism ['reɪsɪzᵊm] *n* racismo.
racist ['reɪsɪst] *adj* racista.
▷ *n* racista *mf.*
rack[1] [ræk] *n* **1** estante *m.* **2** AUTO baca. **3** *(on train)* rejilla. **4** *(for torture)* potro.
▷ *vt* atormentar:
rack[2] [ræk] *n (destruction)* ruina.
racket[1] ['rækɪt] *n* SP raqueta.
racket[2] ['rækɪt] *n* **1** *(din)* alboroto, ruido. **2** *fam (fraud)* timo. **3** *fam (business)* asunto, negocio.
racketeer [rækə'tɪəʳ] *n* timador,-ra.
racketeering [rækɪ'tɪərɪŋ] *n* crimen *m* organizado.
racoon [rə'kuːn] *n* mapache *m.*
racquet ['rækɪt] *n* raqueta.
racy ['reɪsɪ] *adj (lively)* animado,-a; *(risqué)* atrevido,-a.
▲ *comp* **racier**, *superl* **raciest.**
radar ['reɪdɑːʳ] *n* radar *m.* ● **radar trap** control *m* de velocidad por radar.
radiance ['reɪdɪəns] *n* resplandor *m.*
radiant ['reɪdɪənt] *adj* radiante.
radiate ['reɪdɪeɪt] *vt (emit)* irradiar, radiar.
▷ *vi* **1** *(be emitted)* irradiar. **2** *(spread out)* salir.
radiation [reɪdɪ'eɪʃᵊn] *n* radiación *f.*
radiator ['reɪdɪeɪtəʳ] *n* radiador *m.* ● **radiator grille** rejilla del radiador, calandra.
radical ['rædɪkᵊl] *adj* radical.
▷ *n* radical *mf.*
radii ['reɪdɪaɪ] *n pl* → **radius.**
radio ['reɪdɪəʊ] *n* radio *f.* ● **radio cassette** radiocasete *m*
▲ *pl* **radios.**
▷ *vt (person)* llamar por radio; *(message)* enviar por radio, comunicar por radio.
▷ *vi* llamar por radio.
radioactive [reɪdɪəʊ'æktɪv] *adj* radiactivo,-a. ● **radioactive waste** residuos *mpl* radiactivos.
radioactivity [reɪdɪəʊæk'tɪvɪtɪ] *n* radiactividad *f.*
radiocarbon [reɪdɪəʊ'kɑːbᵊn] *n* radiocarbono. ● **radiocarbon dating** datación *f* por radiocarbono.
radio-controlled [reɪdɪəʊkən'trəʊld] *adj* teledirigido,-a.
radiographer [reɪdɪ'ɒgrəfəʳ] *n* radiógrafo,-a.
radiography [reɪdɪ'ɒgrəfɪ] *n* radiografía.
▲ *pl* **radiographies.**
radiologist [reɪdɪ'ɒlədʒɪst] *n* radiólogo,-a.
radiology [reɪdɪ'ɒledʒɪ] *n* radiología.
radiometry [reɪdɪ'ɒmətrɪ] *n* radiometría.
radiophonic [reɪdɪəʊ'fɒnɪk] *adj* radiofónico,-a.
radioscopy [reɪdɪ'ɒskəpɪ] *n* radioscopia.
radiotelegraphy [reɪdɪəʊtɪ'legrəfɪ] *n* radiotelegrafía
radiotelephone [reɪdɪəʊ'telɪfəʊn] *n* radioteléfono.
radiotelephony [reɪdɪəʊtɪ'lefənɪ] *n* radiotelefonía.
radiotherapist [reɪdɪəʊ'θerəpɪst] *n* radioterapeuta *mf*
radiotherapy [reɪdɪəʊ'θerəpɪ] *n* radioterapia.
radish ['rædɪʃ] *n* rábano.
radium ['reɪdɪəm] *n* radio.
radius ['reɪdɪəs] *n* radio.
▲ *pl* **radii** ['reɪdɪaɪ].
radon ['reɪdɒn] *n* radón *m.*
raffia ['ræfɪə] *n* rafia.
raffle ['ræfᵊl] *n* rifa.
▷ *vt* rifar, sortear.
raft [rɑːft] *n* **1** balsa. **2** US *fam* montón *m.*
rafter ['rɑːftəʳ] *n* viga.
rag[1] [ræg] *n* **1** harapo, andrajo, pingajo. **2** *(for cleaning)* trapo. **3** *fam (newspaper)* periodicucho.
rag[2] [ræg] *n* broma pesada.
▷ *vt* gastar bromas a.
ragamuffin ['rægəmʌfɪn] *n* pilluelo,-a.
rag-and-bone man [rægən'bəʊnmæn] *n* trapero.
ragbag ['rægbæg] *n fam* mezcolanza, batiburrillo.
rage [reɪdʒ] *n* rabia, furor *m*, cólera.
▷ *vi* **1** *(person)* rabiar, estar hecho,-a una furia. **2** *(fire, etc)* arder sin control; *(storm, sea)* bramar, rugir; *(debate, etc)* seguir candente.

agged ['rægɪd] *adj* 1 *(person)* andrajoso,-a, harapiento,-a. 2 *(clothes)* roto,-a, deshilachado,-a. 3 *(edge)* irregular. 4 *fig* desigual.
aging ['reɪdʒɪŋ] *adj* 1 *(headache, thirst)* terrible. 2 *(sea)* embravecido,-a; *(storm)* feroz, violento,-a.
aglan ['ræglən] *adj* raglán.
agout [ræ'gu:] *n* ragú *m*.
agtime ['rægtaɪm] *n* ragtime *m*.
aid [reɪd] *n* 1 MIL incursión *f*, ataque *m*. 2 *(by police)* redada. 3 *(robbery)* atraco.
▷ *vt* 1 MIL hacer una incursión en. 2 *(police)* hacer una redada en. 3 *(rob)* atracar, asaltar.
aider ['reɪdəʳ] *n* 1 *(robber)* atracador,-ra, asaltante *mf*. 2 MIL invasor,-ra.
ail[1] [reɪl] *n* 1 barra. 2 *(handrail)* pasamano, barandilla, baranda. 3 *(for train)* raíl *m*, carril *m*, riel *m*. 4 *(the railway)* ferrocarril *m*. ■ **by rail** por ferrocarril.
ail[2] [reɪl] *vt* **to rail against** despotricar contra.
ailcar ['reɪlkɑ:ʳ] *n* automotor *m*.
ailcard ['reɪlkɑ:d] *n* tarjeta de descuento *para viajar en tren*.
ailing ['reɪlɪŋz] *n* verja.
También se usa en plural con el mismo sigificado.
ailroad ['reɪlrəʊd] *n* US → **railway.**
▷ *vt* 1 *(person)* presionar. 2 *(measure, bill)* tramitar sin debate.
ailway ['reɪlweɪ] *n* ferrocarril *m*. ● **railway carriage** vagón *m*. ‖ **railway engine** locomotora. ‖ **railway line** vía férrea, vía del tren. ‖ **railway station** estación *f* de ferrocarril. ‖ **railway track** vía férrea.
ailwayman ['reɪlweɪmən] *n* ferroviario.
▲ *pl* **railwaymen** ['reɪlweɪmən].
ain [reɪn] *n* lluvia. ● **rain forest** selva tropical. ‖ **rain gauge** pluviómetro.
▷ *vi* llover.
▷ *vt fig* cubrir.
▷ *n pl* **the rains** la estación *f sing* de las lluvias.
ainbow ['reɪnbəʊ] *n* arco iris *m*.
aincoat ['reɪnkəʊt] *n* impermeable *m*.
aindrop ['reɪndrɒp] *n* gota de lluvia.
ainfall ['reɪnfɔ:l] *n* 1 precipitación *f*. 2 *(quantity)* pluviosidad *f*.
ainforest ['reɪnfɑrɪst] *n* selva tropical.
ainproof ['reɪnpru:f] *adj* impermeable.
ainstorm ['reɪnstɔ:m] *n* temporal *m* de lluvias.
ainwater ['reɪnwɔ:təʳ] *n* agua de lluvia.
ainy ['reɪnɪ] *adj* lluvioso,-a: **another rainy day** *otro día de lluvia*.
▲ *comp* **rainier**, *superl* **rainiest**.
aise [reɪz] *vt* 1 *(lift up)* levantar: **raise your hands** *levantad la mano*. 2 *(move to a higher position)* subir. 3 *(build, erect)* erigir, levantar. 4 *(increase)* subir, aumentar. 5 *(improve)* mejorar. 6 *(laugh, smile, etc)* provocar; *(doubt, fear)* suscitar. 7 *(children)* criar, educar; *(animals)* criar. 8 *(matter, point)* plantear. 9 *(funds)* recaudar; *(enough money)* conseguir, reunir; *(team, army)* formar. 10 *(by radio)* comunicar con. 11 *(at cards)* subir la apuesta.
▷ *n* US aumento de sueldo.
aisin ['reɪzᵊn] *n* pasa.
ake[1] [reɪk] *n (tool)* rastrillo.
▷ *vt* 1 *(garden)* rastrillar; *(leaves)* recoger *con el rastrillo*. 2 *(with gun)* barrer. 3 *(search)* registrar. 4 *(fire)* hurgar.
▷ *vt sep* 1 *(leaves)* recoger *con el rastrillo*. 2 *(past)* desenterrar.
rake[2] [reɪk] *n (dissolute man)* libertino, calavera *m*.
rake[3] [reɪk] *n (slope)* inclinación *f*.
rally ['rælɪ] *n* 1 *(public gathering)* reunión *f*; *(political)* mitin *m*; *(demonstration)* manifestación *f*. 2 *(car race)* rally *m*. 3 *(in tennis)* intercambio (de golpes).
▲ *pl* **rallies.**
▷ *vi (recover)* reponerse, recuperarse.
▷ *vt (bring together)* unir.
▲ *pt & pp* **rallied**, *ger* **rallying.**
ram [ræm] *n* 1 ZOOL carnero. 2 TECH pisón *m*.
▷ *vt* 1 TECH apisonar. 2 *(cram)* apretar, embutir; *(stick in)* clavar, hincar. 3 *(crash into)* chocar contra.
▲ *pt & pp* **rammed**, *ger* **ramming.**
ramble ['ræmbᵊl] *n* excursión *f*.
▷ *vi* 1 ir de excursión. 2 *(digress)* divagar.
rambler ['ræmbləʳ] *n* 1 *(walker)* excursionista *mf*. 2 *(rose)* trepador *m*.
rambling ['ræmblɪŋ] *adj* 1 *(speech, etc)* confuso,-a, incoherente. 2 *(house, etc)* laberíntico,-a.
▷ *n (activity)* excursionismo. ■ **to go rambling** ir de excursión.
▷ *n pl* **ramblings** desvaríos *mpl*.
ramp [ræmp] *n* 1 *(slope)* rampa. 2 *(steps)* escalerilla. 3 GB *(speed bump)* badén *m*, guardia *m* tumbado. 4 US *(slip road)* vía de acceso.
rampage [ræm'peɪdʒ] *vi* comportarse como un loco.
rampant ['ræmpənt] *adj* 1 *(uncontrolled)* incontrolado,-a 2 *(in heraldry)* rampante.
rampart ['ræmpɑ:t] *n* muralla.
ram-raid ['ræmreɪd] *n fam* alunizaje *m*.
ramshackle ['ræmʃækᵊl] *adj* destartalado,-a.
ran [ræn] *pt* → **run.**
ranch [ræntʃ] *n* rancho, hacienda. ● **ranch house** 1 *(type of house)* bungalow *m*. 2 *(house on ranch)* hacienda.
rancher ['ræntʃəʳ] *n* ranchero,-a.
rancid ['rænsɪd] *adj* rancio,-a.
rancor ['ræŋkəʳ] *n* US → **rancour.**
rancour ['ræŋkəʳ] *n* rencor *m*.
random ['rændəm] *adj* aleatorio,-a. ■ **at random** al azar. ● **random access memory** memoria de acceso directo.
randy ['rændɪ] *adj fam* cachondo,-a.
▲ *comp* **randier**, *superl* **randiest.**
rang [ræŋ] *pp* → **ring.**
range [reɪndʒ] *n* 1 *(choice)* gama, surtido, variedad *f*; *(of products)* gama; *(of clothes)* línea. 2 *(reach)* alcance *m*. 3 *(of mountains)* cordillera, sierra. 4 US *(prairie)* pradera. 5 *(for shooting)* campo de tiro. 6 *(of voice)* registro. 7 *(stove)* cocina económica. 8 US *(cooker)* cocina. 9 *(of car, plane)* autonomía.
▷ *vi* 1 variar, oscilar: **they range from ... to...** *van desde ... hasta ...* 2 *(wander)* vagar (**over**, por).
▷ *vt* 1 *(arrange)* colocar, disponer. 2 *(travel)* viajar por.
rangefinder ['reɪndʒfaɪndəʳ] *n* telémetro.
ranger ['reɪndʒəʳ] *n* 1 guardabosques *mf*. 2 US *(police officer)* policía *mf* montado,-a; *(soldier)* soldado *mf* de las tropas de asalto.
Rangoon [ræŋ'gu:n] *n* Rangún.
rank[1] [ræŋk] *n* 1 *(line)* fila. 2 MIL *(in hierarchy)* graduación *f*, rango. ● **the rank and file** las bases *fpl*.

▷ *vi (be)* figurar, estar.
▷ *vt (classify)* clasificar, considerar.

rank[2] [ræŋk] *adj* **1** *(plants)* exuberante. **2** *(smelly)* fétido,-a. **3** *(complete)* total, completo,-a.

ranking ['ræŋkɪŋ] *n* clasificación *f*, ranking *m*.

rankle ['ræŋkəl] *vi* doler.

ransack ['rænsæk] *vt* **1** *(plunder)* saquear. **2** *(search)* registrar.

ransom ['rænsəm] *n* rescate *m*. ■ **to hold to ransom** **1** pedir rescate por. **2** *fig* chantajear.
▷ *vt* rescatar.

rant [rænt] *vi* vociferar, desgañitarse, gritar.

rap [ræp] *n* **1** golpe *m* seco. **2** MUS rap *m*.
▷ *vi* **1** golpear, dar golpes. **2** MUS cantar rap.
▲ *pt & pp* **rapped**, *ger* **rapping.**

rapacity [rə'pæsɪtɪ] *n fml* rapacidad *f*.

rape[1] [reɪp] *n* violación *f*.
▷ *vt* violar.

rape[2] [reɪp] *n* BOT colza.

rapeseed ['reɪpsiːd] *n* semilla de colza. ● **rapeseed oil** aceite *m* de colza.

rapid ['ræpɪd] *adj* rápido,-a.
▷ *n pl* **rapids** rápidos *mpl*.

rapidity [rə'pɪdɪtɪ] *n* rapidez *f*.

rapier ['reɪpɪəʳ] *n* estoque *m*.

rapist ['reɪpɪst] *n* violador,-ra.

rapper ['ræpəʳ] *n* cantante *mf* de rap, rapero,-a.

rapport [ræ'pɔːʳ] *n* compenetración *f*, entendimiento.

rapprochement [ræ'prɒʃəmɑːn] *n* acercamiento.

rapture ['ræptʃəʳ] *n* éxtasis *m*, arrobamiento. ■ **to go into raptures over/about sth** extasiarse por algo.

rapturous ['ræptʃərəs] *adj (welcome)* muy entusiasta; *(applause)* calurosísimo,-a; *(feeling)* extático,-a.

rare [reəʳ] *adj* **1** *(uncommon)* poco común, poco frecuente, raro,-a. **2** *(air)* enrarecido,-a. **3** CULIN poco hecho,-a.

rarefied ['reərɪfaɪd] *adj* enrarecido,-a.

rarefy ['reərɪfaɪ] *vt* enrarecer, rarificar.
▲ *pt & pp* **rarefied**, *ger* **rarefying.**

rarely ['reəlɪ] *adv* raras veces, rara vez, pocas veces.

rareness ['reənəs] *n* rareza.

rarity ['reərɪtɪ] *n* rareza.
▲ *pl* **rarities.**

rascal ['rɑːskəl] *n* bribón *m*, pillo, pillín,-ina.

rash[1] [ræʃ] *n* **1** MED sarpullido, erupción *f* cutánea. **2** *(series)* sucesión *f*, serie *f*.

rash[2] [ræʃ] *adj* imprudente, precipitado,-a.

rasher ['ræʃəʳ] *n* loncha.

rashly ['ræʃlɪ] *adj* precipitadamente, sin reflexionar.

rashness ['ræʃnəs] *n* impetuosidad *f*, precipitación *f*.

rasp [rɑːsp] *n* escofina.
▷ *vt* **1** raspar. **2** *(say)* decir con voz áspera.

raspberry ['rɑːzbərɪ] *n* **1** frambuesa. **2** *fam (noise)* pedorreta. ● **raspberry cane** frambueso.
▲ *pl* **raspberries.**

rasping ['rɑːspɪŋ] *adj (voice)* áspero,-a.

rat [ræt] *n* **1** rata. **2** *fam* canalla *m*.

ratchet ['rætʃɪt] *n* trinquete *m*.

rate [reɪt] *n* **1** tasa, índice *m*. **2** *(speed)* velocidad *f*, ritmo. **3** *(price)* tarifa, precio. ■ **at any rate 1** *(anyway)* de todos modos. **2** *(at least)* al menos. ■ **first/second rate** de primera/segunda (categoría).
▷ *vt* **1** *(consider)* considerar **2** *(deserve)* merecer: **3** *(fix va ue)* tasar.
▷ *n pl* **rates** GB contribución *f sing* urbana.

rateable value ['reɪtəbəl'væljuː] *n* GB valor *m* catastral

ratepayer ['reɪtpeɪəʳ] *n* GB contribuyente *mf*.

rather ['rɑːðəʳ] *adv* **1** *(a little)* algo; *(fairly)* bastant *(very)* muy. **2** *(showing preference)*: **I'd rather go out** *pre feriría salir.* **3** *(more precisely)* o mejor dicho; *(not)* y no

ratify ['rætɪfaɪ] *vt* ratificar.
▲ *pt & pp* **ratified**, *ger* **ratifying.**

rating ['reɪtɪŋ] *n* **1** *(evaluation)* valoración *f*, tasación **2** *(position on scale)* clasificación *f*. **3** MAR marinero.
▷ *n pl* **ratings** TV índice *m sing* de audiencia.

ratio ['reɪʃɪəʊ] *n* razón *f*, relación *f*, proporción *f*.
▲ *pl* **ratios.**

ration ['ræʃən] *n* ración *f*.
▷ *vt* racionar.
▷ *n pl* **rations** víveres *mpl*.

rational ['ræʃənəl] *adj* racional.

rationale [ræʃə'nɑːl] *n* razón *f*, lógica.

rationalise ['ræʃənəlaɪz] *vt* → **rationalize.**

rationalize ['ræʃənəlaɪz] *vt* racionalizar.

rationing ['ræʃənɪŋ] *n* racionamiento.

rattle ['rætəl] *n* **1** *(object)* carraca, matraca; *(baby's)* sc najero; *(rattlesnake's)* cascabel *m*. **2** *(noise)* ruido; *(train)* traqueteo; *(vibration)* vibración *f*.
▷ *vt* hacer sonar, hacer vibrar.
▷ *vi* sonar, vibrar.
▷ *vt fam* poner nervioso,-a.

rattlesnake ['rætəlsneɪk] *n* serpiente *f* de cascabel.

ratty ['rætɪ] *adj* **1** GB *fam* malhumorado,-a. **2** US *(pe son)* desastrado,-a; *(thing)* destartalado,-a; *(clothe* andrajoso,-a, raído,-a.
▲ *comp* **rattier**, *superl* **rattiest.**

raucous ['rɔːkəs] *adj (loud)* escandaloso,-a; *(shrill)* e tridente.

ravage ['rævɪdʒ] *vt* devastar, asolar.
▷ *n pl* **ravages** estragos *mpl*.

rave [reɪv] *vi* **1** delirar. **2** *(rage)* despotricar (**agains** contra). **3** *fam* entusiasmarse.
▷ *n* GB fiesta *con música de baile y que puede durar toda noche*.

raven ['reɪvən] *n* cuervo.

ravenous ['rævənəs] *adj (appetite)* voraz; *(person)* han briento,-a.

ravine [rə'viːn] *n* barranco.

raving ['reɪvɪŋ] *adj* de atar.
▷ *n pl* **ravings** desvaríos *mpl*.

ravish ['rævɪʃ] *vt* **1** *(rape)* violar. **2** *(delight)* extasia embelesar, encantar.

ravishing ['rævɪʃɪŋ] *adj* encantador,-ra: **a ravishi beauty** *una belleza deslumbrante.*

raw [rɔː] *adj* **1** *(uncooked)* crudo,-a. **2** *(unprocessed)* br to,-a; *(unrefined)* sin refinar; *(untreated)* sin tratar. *(inexperienced)* novato,-a. **4** *(weather)* crudo,-a. ● **ra material** materia prima.

ray[1] [reɪ] *n (of light)* rayo.

ray[2] [reɪ] *n (fish)* raya.

ray[3] [reɪ] *n (note)* re *m*.

rayon ['reɪɒn] *n* rayón *m*.

raze [reɪz] *vt* arrasar.

azor [ˈreɪzəʳ] *n* **1** *(cutthroat)* navaja de afeitar; *(safety)* maquinilla de afeitar. **2** *(electric)* máquina de afeitar.
● **razor blade** hoja de afeitar.

azor-shell [ˈreɪzəʃel] *n* navaja.

e [riː] *prep* respecto a, con referencia a.

each [riːtʃ] *n* alcance *m*. ■ **beyond the reach of** fuera del alcance de. | **within reach of 1** *(at hand)* al alcance de. **2** *(near)* cerca de.
▷ *vt* **1** *(arrive in/at, get to)* llegar a. **2** *(rise to, fall to)* alcanzar. **3** *(be able to touch)* alcanzar, llegar a. **4** *(contact)* contactar, localizar. **5** *(pass)* alcanzar.
▷ *vi* **1** *(be long enough)* llegar. **2** *(extend)* extenderse. **3** *(take)* extender la mano, tender la mano.
▷ *n pl* **reaches** *(of river)* parte *f*, tramo.

eact [rɪˈækt] *vi* reaccionar.

eaction [rɪˈækʃᵊn] *n* reacción *f*.

eactor [rɪˈæktəʳ] *n* reactor *m*.

ead [riːd] *vt* **1** *(gen)* leer. **2** *(meter)* hacer la lectura de. **3** *(interpret)* interpretar. **4** *(at university)* estudiar. **5** *(instrument)* indicar. **6** *(sign, notice)* decir, poner.
▷ *vi* **1** *(gen)* leer. **2** *(text, passage)*: **this text reads like a translation** *este texto suena como una traducción*.
▲ *pt & pp* **read** [red].
▷ *n*: **this book is an excellent read** *este libro es buenísimo*.

eadable [ˈrɪdəbᵊl] *adj* **1** *(handwriting)* legible. **2** *(style)* ameno,-a.

eaddress [rɪəˈdres] *vt* remitir a una nueva dirección.

eader [ˈriːdəʳ] *n* **1** *(person - gen)* lector,-ra; *(- of proofs)* corrector,-ra. **2** *(at university)* profesor,-ra adjunto,-a. **3** *(book)* libro de lectura. **4** *(apparatus)* lector *m*.

eadership [ˈrɪdəʃɪp] *n* **1** *(of newspaper)* lectores *mpl*. **2** *(at university)* puesto de profesor,-ra adjunto,-a.

eadies [ˈredɪz] *n pl* → **ready.**

eadily [ˈredɪlɪ] *adv* **1** *(easily)* fácilmente. **2** *(willingly)* de buena gana.

eadiness [ˈredɪnəs] *n* **1** *(willingness)* buena disposición *f*, buena voluntad *f*. **2** *(preparedness)* preparación *f*.

eading [ˈriːdɪŋ] *n* **1** lectura. **2** *(of bill, law)* presentación *f*. **3** *(of instrument)* indicación *f*, lectura. **4** *(interpretation)* interpretación *f*.

eadjust [riːəˈdʒʌst] *vt (modify)* reajustar.
▷ *vi (readapt)* readaptarse.

eadout [ˈriːdaʊt] *n* lectura.

eady [ˈredɪ] *adj* **1** *(prepared)* preparado,-a, listo,-a. **2** *(willing)* dispuesto,-a. **3** *(quick)* rápido,-a; *(easy)* fácil.
▷ *vt* preparar. ■ **to get ready** prepararse. | **to get** STH **ready** preparar ALGO. | **to make ready** preparar.
▲ *pt & pp* **readied**, *ger* **readying.**
▷ *n pl* **readies** GB *fam* dinero.

eady-cooked [redɪˈkʊkt] *adj* precocinado,-a.

eady-made [redɪˈmeɪd] *adj* hecho,-a, confeccionado,-a.

eafforestation [rɪəfɒrɪˈsteɪʃᵊn] *n* GB reforestación *f*, repoblación *f* forestal.

eagent [riːˈeɪdʒənt] *n* reactivo.

eal [rɪəl] *adj* **1** verdadero,-a: **2** *(genuine)* auténtico,-a.
● **real estate** bienes *mpl* inmuebles.
▷ *adv* US *fam* muy.

ealign [rɪəˈlaɪn] *vt (bring back into line)* realinear; *(restructure)* reestructurar; *(readjust)* reajustar.

ealignment [rɪəˈlaɪnmənt] *n (bringing back into line)* realineamiento; *(readjustment)* reajuste *m*.

realisable [ˈrɪəlaɪzəbᵊl] *adj* → **realizable.**

realise [ˈrɪəlaɪz] *vt* → **realize.**

reality [rɪˈælɪtɪ] *n* realidad *f*.

realization [rɪəlaɪˈzeɪʃᵊn] *n* **1** *(of plan)* realización *f*. **2** FIN realización *f*. **3** *(understanding)* comprensión *f*.

realize [ˈrɪəlaɪz] *vt* **1** *(understand)* darse cuenta de, comprender. **2** *(know)* saber. **3** *(carry out)* realizar. **4** *(sell)* realizar, vender; *(fetch)* reportar.

really [ˈrɪəlɪ] *adv* **1** *(in fact)* en realidad. **2** *(very)* realmente. **3** *(showing interest)* ¿ah sí?, ¿en serio? *(showing surprise)* ¡no me digas! *(showing annoyance)* ¡vaya!

realm [relm] *n* **1** *(kingdom)* reino. **2** *(field)* campo, terreno.

realtor [ˈrɪəltɔːʳ] *n* agente *mf* inmobiliario,-a.

ream [riːm] *n* resma.

reanimate [rɪˈænɪmeɪt] *vt* reanimar.

reap [riːp] *vt* cosechar.

reaper [ˈriːpəʳ] *n* **1** *(person)* segador,-ra. **2** *(machine)* segadora.

reappear [riːəˈpɪəʳ] *vi* reaparecer.

reappearance [ˈriːəpɪərəns] *n* reaparición *f*.

reappraisal [riːəˈpreɪzᵊl] *n* revaluación *f*.

reappraise [riːəˈpreɪz] *vt* revaluar.

rear[1] [rɪəʳ] *adj* trasero,-a, de atrás.
▷ *n* **1** *(back part)* parte *f* de atrás. **2** *(of room)* fondo. **3** *fam (of person)* trasero.

rear[2] [rɪə] *vt* **1** *(raise)* criar. **2** *(lift up)* levantar.
▷ *vi* [Also **rear up**.] encabritarse.

rearguard [ˈrɪəgɑːd] *n* retaguardia.

rearmament [riːˈɑːməment] *n* rearme *m*.

rearmost [ˈrɪəməʊst] *adj* último,-a.

rearrange [riːəˈreɪndʒ] *vt* **1** *(objects)* colocar de otra manera. **2** *(event)* cambiar la fecha de, cambiar la hora de.

rear-view mirror [rɪəvjuːˈmɪrə] *n* retrovisor *m*.

reason [ˈriːzᵊn] *n* **1** *(cause)* motivo. **2** *(faculty)* razón *f*.
▷ *vt* deducir, llegar a la conclusión de que.
▷ *vi* razonar. ■ **it stands to reason** es lógico, es de lógica.

reasonable [ˈriːzənəbᵊl] *adj* **1** *(gen)* razonable. **2** *(acceptable)* pasable, aceptable.

reasonably [ˈriːzᵊnəblɪ] *adv* **1** *(gen)* razonablemente. **2** *(quite)* bastante.

reasoning [ˈriːzᵊnɪŋ] *n* razonamiento.

reassurance [riːəˈʃʊərəns] *n* **1** *(feeling)* tranquilidad *f*, consuelo. **2** *(words)* palabras *fpl* tranquilizadoras.

reassure [riːəˈʃʊəʳ] *vt* **1** *(comfort)* tranquilizar. **2** *(assure again)* volver a asegurar.

reawakening [riːəˈweɪkᵊnɪŋ] *n* renacer *m*.

rebate [ˈriːbeɪt] *n* **1** *(of tax)* devolución *f*. **2** *(discount)* descuento.

rebel [*(adj-n)* ˈrebᵊl; *(vb)* rɪˈbel] *adj* rebelde.
▷ *n* rebelde *mf*.
▷ *vi* rebelarse (**against**, contra).
▲ *pt & pp* **rebelled**, *ger* **rebelling.**

rebound [*(n)* ˈriːbaʊnd; *(vb)* rɪˈbaʊnd] *n* rebote *m*.
▷ *vi* rebotar.

rebuff [rɪˈbʌf] *n* rechazo.
▷ *vt* rechazar.

rebuke [rɪˈbjuːk] *n* reprimenda.
▷ *vt* reprender.

rebus [ˈriːbəs] *n* jeroglífico.

rebut [rɪˈbʌt] *vt* refutar.
▲ *pt & pp* **rebutted**, *ger* **rebutting.**

recalcitrant [rɪ'kælsɪtrənt] *adj* recalcitrante.
recall [*(n)* riːkɔːl; *(vb)* rɪ'kɔːl] *n* 1 *(memory)* memoria. 2 *(withdrawal)* retirada. 3 *(of parliament)* convocación *f* extraordinaria.
▷ *vt* 1 *(remember)* recordar. 2 *(withdraw)* retirar. 3 *(parliament)* convocar de manera extraordinaria.
recant [rɪ'kænt] *vi* retractarse.
▷ *vt* retractarse de.
recap ['riːkæp] *n fam* resumen *m*.
▷ *vt fam* resumir.
▷ *vi fam* resumir.
▲ *pt & pp* **recapped**, *ger* **recapping.**
recapitulate [riːkə'pɪtjʊleɪt] *vt* recapitular, resumir.
▷ *vi* recapitular, resumir.
recapture [riː'kæptʃəʳ] *n (of person)* nueva detención *f*; *(of territory)* reconquista.
▷ *vt* 1 *(person)* volver a detener, volver a capturar; *(territory)* reconquistar, volver a tomar. 2 *fig* recuperar.
recast [riː'kɑːst] *vt* 1 *(do again)* rehacer. 2 *(metals)* refundir. 3 *(play, film)* cambiar el reparto de; *(actor)* dar otro papel a; *(role)* asignar a otro actor, asignar a otra actriz.
▲ *pt & pp* **recast.**
recede [rɪ'siːd] *vi* 1 *(move back)* retirarse. 2 *(be left behind)* retroceder, irse retrocediendo. 3 *(fears, danger)* alejarse; *(memories, possibilities)* desvanecerse.
receipt [rɪ'siːt] *n* 1 *(document)* recibo. 2 *(act of receiving)* recepción *f*, recibo.
▷ *n pl* **receipts** COMM ingresos *mpl*, recaudación *f sing*.
receive [rɪ'siːv] *vt* 1 *(gen)* recibir. 2 *(wound)* sufrir. 3 *(radio signal)* recibir. 4 *(stolen goods)* comerciar con
▷ *vt (welcome)* recibir, acoger.
receiver [rɪ'siːvəʳ] *n* 1 *(of telephone)* auricular *m*. 2 *(of stolen goods)* perista *mf*. 3 JUR síndico,-a, síndico,-a de quiebras. 4 *(of radio signal)* receptor *m*. 5 *(in American football)* receptor,-ra.
receivership [rɪ'siːvəʃɪp] *n* quiebra, bancarrota.
recent ['riːsᵊnt] *adj* reciente: **in recent months/years** *en los últimos meses/años*.
recently ['riːsᵊntlɪ] *adv* 1 *(lately)* recientemente, últimamente. 2 *(a short time ago)* hace poco
receptacle [rɪ'septəkᵊl] *n* receptáculo, recipiente *m*.
reception [rɪ'sepʃᵊn] *n* 1 *(gen)* recepción *f*. 2 *(welcome)* acogida. 3 *(party)* recepción *f*; *(after wedding)* banquete *m*. ● **reception desk** recepción *f*. ‖ **reception room** 1 *(in public place)* salón *m*. 2 *(in house) sala de estar, sala, comedor o cualquier estancia donde se reciba a la gente*.
receptionist [rɪ'sepʃᵊnɪst] *n* recepcionista *m & f*.
recess ['riːses] *n* 1 *(in wall)* hueco. 2 *(rest)* descanso. 3 POL período de vacaciones. 4 *(secret place)* recoveco.
recession [rɪ'seʃᵊn] *n* recesión *f*.
recharge [riː'tʃɑːdʒ] *vt* recargar.
rechargeable [riː'tʃɑːdʒəbᵊl] *adj* recargable.
recipe ['resəpɪ] *n* 1 receta. 2 *fig* fórmula. ● **recipe book** 1 *(personal collection)* recetario. 2 *(cookery book)* libro de cocina.
recipient [rɪ'sɪpɪənt] *n* 1 *(gen)* persona que recibe. 2 *(of letter, etc)* destinatario,-a. 3 *(of transplant)* receptor,-ra.
reciprocate [rɪ'sɪprəkeɪt] *vi* corresponder.
▷ *vt (invitation)* devolver, corresponder a.
recitation [resɪ'teɪʃᵊn] *n* 1 *(of poetry)* recitación *f*. 2 *(of list)* enumeración *f*.
recite [rɪ'saɪt] *vt* 1 *(poetry)* recitar. 2 *(list)* enumerar.
reckless ['rekləs] *adj* 1 *(hasty)* precipitado,-a. 2 *(careless)* imprudente, temerario,-a. ● **reckless driving** conducción *f* temeraria.
reckon ['rekᵊn] *vt* 1 *(estimate)* calcular. 2 *(calculate)* calcular. 3 *(regard)* considerar. 4 *(think)* creer, considerar
reckoning ['rekᵊnɪŋ] *n* cálculos *mpl*: **by my reckoning** *... según mis cálculos, ...*
reclaim [rɪ'kleɪm] *vt* 1 *(money, right, etc)* reclamar. 2 *(land)* ganar (al mar). 3 *(recycle)* reciclar. 4 *(baggage)* recoger.
recline [rɪ'klaɪn] *vt (lean back)* reclinar; *(rest)* apoyar.
▷ *vi* reclinarse, recostarse.
reclining [rɪ'klaɪnɪŋ] *adj* reclinable.
recluse [rɪ'kluːs] *n* ermitaño,-a.
recognisable [rekəg'naɪzəbᵊl] *adj* ⟶ **recognizable.**
recognise ['rekəgnaɪz] *vt* ⟶ **recognize.**
recognition [rekəg'nɪʃᵊn] *n* reconocimiento.
recognizable [rekəg'naɪzəbᵊl] *adj* reconocible.
recognize ['rekəgnaɪz] *vt* reconocer.
recoil [*(n)* 'riːkɔɪl; *(vb)* rɪ'kɔɪl] *n (of gun)* retroceso.
▷ *vi* 1 *(person - move back)* retroceder; *(- feel disgust)* sentir repugnancia. 2 *(gun)* retroceder, dar un culatazo.
recollect [rekə'lekt] *vt* recordar.
recollection [rekə'lekʃᵊn] *n* recuerdo.
recommend [rekə'mend] *vt* 1 recomendar. 2 *(advise)* recomendar, aconsejar, sugerir.
recommendable [rekə'mendəbᵊl] *adj* recomendable
recommendation [rekəmen'deɪʃᵊn] *n* 1 recomendación *f*. 2 *(advice)* consejo, sugerencia.
recompense ['rekəmpens] *n* 1 recompensa. 2 JUR indemnización *f*.
▷ *vt* 1 recompensar. 2 JUR indemnizar.
reconcile ['rekənsaɪl] *vt* 1 *(people)* reconciliar. 2 *(ideas)* conciliar. ■ **to reconcile os to sth** resignarse a algo.
recondition [riːkən'dɪʃᵊn] *vt* revisar totalmente.
reconnaissance [rɪ'kɒnɪsᵊns] *n* reconocimiento.
reconnoiter [rekə'nɔɪtəʳ] *vt* US⟶ **reconnoitre.**
reconnoitre [rekə'nɔɪtəʳ] *vt* reconocer.
▷ *vi* hacer un reconocimiento.
reconsider [riːkən'sɪdəʳ] *vt* reconsiderar.
reconstitute [riː'kɒnstɪtjuːt] *vt* 1 *(food)* reconstituir. 2 *(group)* reconstituir, reorganizar.
reconstruct [riːkəns'trʌkt] *vt* reconstruir.
reconstruction [riːkən'strʌkʃᵊn] *n* reconstrucción *f*.
record [*(n)* 'rekɔːd; *(vb)* rɪ'kɔːd] *n* 1 *(written evidence)* constancia. 2 *(note)* relación *f*. 3 *(facts about a person)* historial *m*. 4 MUS disco. 5 SP récord *m*, marca. ■ **to break a record** batir un récord. ● **medical record** historial *m* médico. ‖ **record holder** plusmarquista *mf*. **record player** tocadiscos *m sing*.
▷ *vt* 1 *(write down)* anotar, apuntar. 2 *(voice, music)* grabar. 3 *(instrument, gauge)* registrar.
▷ *adj* récord.
▷ *n pl* **records** *(files)* archivos *mpl*.
record-breaking ['rekɔːdbreɪkɪŋ] *adj* récord.
recorded [rɪ'kɔːdɪd] *adj (written)* anotado; *(on tape, etc)* grabado,-a. ● **recorded delivery** correo certificado.
recorder [rɪ'kɔːdəʳ] *n* MUS flauta. ● **cassette recorder** casete *m*.
recording [rɪ'kɔːdɪŋ] *n* grabación *f*. ● **recording studio** estudio de grabación.

ecount [rɪ'kaʊnt] *vt (narrate)* contar, relatar.
e-count [*(n)* 'ri:kaʊnt; *(vb)* ri:'kaʊnt] *n* recuento.
vt (count again) volver a contar, hacer el recuento de.
ecoup [rɪ'ku:p] *vt (gen)* recuperar; *(losses)* resarcirse de.
ecourse [rɪ'kɔ:s] *n* recurso.
ecover [rɪ'kʌvəʳ] *vt (gen)* recuperar; *(dead body)* rescatar.
vi recuperarse, reponerse.
ecovery [rɪ'kʌvərɪ] *n* recuperación *f*.
ecreate [ri:krɪ'eɪt] *vt* recrear.
ecreation [rekrɪ'eɪʃᵊn] *n* **1** *(free time)* esparcimiento. **2** *(hobby)* pasatiempo. **3** *(in school)* recreo.
ecreational [rekrɪ'eɪʃənᵊl] *adj* de recreo.
ecriminate [rɪ'krɪmɪneɪt] *vt* recriminar.
ecrimination [rɪkrɪmɪ'neɪʃᵊn] *n* recriminación *f*.
ecruit [rɪ'kru:t] *n (soldier)* recluta *m*; *(to group)* nuevo miembro *m*; *(to company)* nuevo,-a empleado,-a.
vt (soldier) reclutar; *(employee)* contratar; *(member)* conseguir.
vi (soldiers) alistar reclutas; *(employees)* contratar empleados; *(members)* buscar socios.
ecruitment [rɪ'kru:tmənt] *n (of soldiers)* reclutamiento; *(of employees)* contratación *f*; *(of members)* búsqueda de socios.
ecta ['rektə] *n pl* ⟶ **rectum.**
ectangle ['rektæŋgᵊl] *n* rectángulo.
ectangular [rekt'æŋgjʊləʳ] *adj* rectangular.
ectifiable [rektɪ'faɪəbᵊl] *adj* rectificable.
ectify ['rektɪfaɪ] *vt* rectificar, corregir.
ector ['rektəʳ] *n* **1** *(of church)* párroco. **2** *(of university)* rector,-ra.
ectum ['rektəm] *n* recto.
▲ *pl* **rectums o recta** ['rektə].
ecuperate [rɪk'ʊ:pəreɪt] *vt (get back)* recuperar.
vi (from illness) recuperarse, reponerse.
ecuperation [rɪku:pər'eɪʃᵊn] *n* recuperación *f*.
ecur [rɪ'kɜ:ʳ] *vi* repetirse, reproducirse.
▲ *pt & pp* **recurred,** *ger* **recurring.**
ecurrence [rɪ'kʌrəns] *n* repetición *f*.
ecurrent [rɪ'kʌrənt] *adj* **1** MATH periódico,-a. **2** MED recurrente.
ecycle [ri:'saɪkᵊl] *vt* reciclar.
ecycling [ri:'saɪkᵊlɪŋ] *n* reciclaje *m*.
ed [red] *n* **1** *(colour)* rojo. **2** *(left winger)* rojo,-a.
adj **1** rojo,-a. **2** *(hair)* pelirrojo,-a.
▲ *comp* **redder,** *superl* **reddest.**
ed-blooded ['red'blʌdɪd] *adj* viril.
edbreast ['redbrest] *n* petirrojo.
ed-brick ['redbrɪk] *adj* de ladrillo rojo.
dcurrant [red'kʌrənt] *n* grosella.
dden ['redᵊn] *vt* enrojecer.
vi (gen) enrojecerse; *(blush)* ponerse rojo,-a, sonrojarse.
ddish ['redɪʃ] *adj* rojizo,-a.
deem [rɪ'di:m] *vt* **1** rescatar. **2** *(from pawn)* desempeñar. **3** *(voucher)* canjear. **4** *(promise)* cumplir. **5** REL redimir.
deemable [rɪ'di:məbᵊl] *adj (debt)* amortizable; *(pawned item)* redimible; *(voucher)* canjeable.
deeming [rɪ'di:mɪŋ] *adj* redentor,-ra
demption [rɪ'dempʃᵊn] *n* **1** *(of debt)* pago. **2** *(of voucher)* canje *m*. **3** REL redención *f*.
d-haired ['red'heəd] *adj* pelirrojo,-a.
d-handed [red'hændɪd] *adj* con las manos en la masa.
dhead ['redhed] *n* pelirrojo,-a.

red-hot [red'hɒt] *adj* al rojo vivo, candente.
redid [ri:'dɪd] *pt* ⟶ **redo.**
redirect [ri:daɪ'rekt] *vt (traffic)* desviar; *(letter)* remitir.
redistribute [ri:dɪ'strɪbju:t] *vt* redistribuir.
red-letter day [red'letədeɪ] *n* día *m* memorable.
red-light district [red'laɪtdɪstrɪkt] *n* barrio chino.
redness ['rednəs] *n* rojez *f*.
redo [ri:'du:] *vt* rehacer, volver a hacer.
▲ *pt* **redid** [ri:'dɪd], *pp* **redone** [ri:'dʌn], *ger* **redoing.**
redone [ri:'dʌn] *pt* ⟶ **redo.**
redouble [ri:'dʌbᵊl] *vt* redoblar, reduplicar.
redoubt [rɪ'daʊt] *n* reducto.
redoubtable [rɪ'daʊtəbᵊl] *adj* temible.
redpoll ['redpɒl] *n* pardillo sizerín.
redress [rɪ'dres] *n* reparación *f*.
▷ *vt* reparar, corregir.
redskin ['redskɪn] *n* piel roja *mf*.
redstart ['redstɑ:t] *n* colirrojo.
reduce [rɪ'dju:s] *vt* **1** *(gen)* reducir. **2** *(price, etc)* rebajar.
reduction [rɪ'dʌkʃᵊn] *n (gen)* reducción *f*; *(fall)* disminución *f*; *(in price)* rebaja.
redundancy [rɪ'dʌndənsɪ] *n* **1** *(dismissal)* despido. **2** *(superfluity)* superfluidad *f*. **3** LING redundancia.
▲ *pl* **redundancies.**
redundant [rɪ'dʌndənt] *adj* **1** *(dismissed)* despedido,-a. **2** *(superfluous)* superfluo,-a. **3** LING redundante.
redwing ['redwɪŋ] *n* zorzal *m* alirrojo.
redwood ['redwʊd] *n* secuoya.
reed [ri:d] *n* **1** *(plant)* caña, junco. **2** MUS lengüeta.
reedbed ['ri:dbed] *n* cañaveral *m*, juncal *m*.
reedy ['ri:dɪ] *adj (voice)* aflautado,-a.
▲ *comp* **reedier,** *superl* **reediest.**
reef [ri:f] *n* arrecife *m*.
reel[1] [ri:l] *n* **1** *(of thread, cotton)* carrete *m*; *(of camera film)* carrete *m*, rollo; *(of cine film)* bobina; *(of wire, tape)* rollo. **2** *(for fishing)* carrete *m*.
⊙ **to reel in** *vt sep (line)* recoger, cobrar; *(fish)* cobrar, sacar del agua.
reel[2] [ri:l] *vi* **1** *(stagger)* tambalearse. **2** *(spin round)* dar vueltas.
re-elect [ri:ɪ'lekt] *vt* reelegir.
reenact [ri:ɪ'nækt] *vt (event)* volver a representar; *(crime)* reconstruir.
re-enter [ri:'entəʳ] *vt* volver a entrar en, reingresar en.
reeve [ri:v] *n (in Canada)* presidente,-ta *mf* del concejo.
ref[1] ['refᵊrəns] *abbr* (reference) referencia; *(abbreviation)* ref.
ref[2] [ref] *n fam (abbr of* referee) árbitro,-a.
refectory [rɪ'fektᵊrɪ] *n* refectorio.
▲ *pl* **refectories.**
refer [rɪ'fɜ:ʳ] *vt (send)* remitir, mandar, enviar
▷ *vi* **1** *(allude to)* referirse (to, a). **2** *(mention, name)* hacer referencia (to, a). **3** *(consult)* consultar (to, -). **4** *(describe)* calificar (to, de); *(call)* llamar (to, a).
▲ *pt & pp* **referred,** *ger* **referring.**
referee [refə'ri:] *n* **1** SP árbitro,-a. **2** *(for job)* persona que da referencias personales sobre alguien.
▷ *vt* arbitrar.
reference ['refᵊrəns] *n* **1** referencia, mención **2** *(for job)* referencias *fpl*. ● **reference book** libro de consulta.
referendum [refə'rendəm] *n* referéndum *m*.
▲ *pl* **referendums o referenda** [refə'rendə].

refill [*(n)* 'ri:fɪl; *(vb)* ri:'fɪl] *n (for pen, etc)* recambio; *(for lighter)* carga.
▷ *vt (glass, pen)* volver a llenar; *(lighter)* recargar.
refine [rɪ'faɪn] *vt* **1** *(purify)* refinar. **2** *(polish, perfect)* pulir.
refined [rɪ'faɪnd] *adj* **1** *(product)* refinado,-a. **2** *(person, behaviour)* refinado,-a, fino,-a.
refinement [rɪ'faɪnmənt] *n* **1** *(genteelness)* refinamiento. **2** *(improvement)* mejora. **3** *(process of refining)* refinado.
refinery [rɪ'faɪnərɪ] *n* refinería.
▲ *pl* **refineries.**
refining [rɪ'faɪnɪŋ] *n* refinado.
reflect [rɪ'flekt] *vt* reflejar
▷ *vi (think)* reflexionar (**on**, sobre)
⊙ **to reflect on** *vt insep* perjudicar
reflection [rɪ'flekʃən] *n* **1** *(image)* reflejo. **2** *(thought)* reflexión *f*. **3** *(aspersion)* descrédito. ■ **on reflection, …** pensándolo bien, …
reflective [rɪ'flektɪv] *adj* **1** *(surface)* brillante. **2** *(person)* contemplativo,-a.
reflector [rɪ'flektər] *n (gen)* reflector *m*; *(on car)* catafaro.
reflex ['ri:fleks] *n* reflejo.
▲ *pl* **reflexes.**
reflexive [rɪ'fleksɪv] *adj* reflexivo,-a.
refloat [ri:'fləʊt] *vt* reflotar.
reforest [ri:'fɒrɪst] *vt* reforestar.
reforestation [ri:fɒrɪ'steɪʃən] *n* repoblación *f* forestal.
reform [rɪ'fɔ:m] *n* reforma.
▷ *vt* reformar.
reformat [ri:'fɔ:mæt] *vt* reformatear.
reformation [refə'meɪʃən] *n* reforma.
reformatory [rɪ'fɔ:mətərɪ] *n* reformatorio.
reformer [rɪ'fɔ:mər] *n* reformador,-ra.
reformist [rɪ'fɔ:mɪst] *adj* reformista.
▷ *n* reformista *mf*.
refract [rɪ'frækt] *vt* refractar.
▷ *vi* refractarse.
refraction [rɪ'frækʃən] *n* refracción *f*.
refrain[1] [rɪ'freɪn] *n* MUS estribillo.
refrain[2] [rɪ'freɪn] *vi* abstenerse (**from**, de).
refresh [rɪ'freʃ] *vt* refrescar.
refreshing [rɪ'freʃɪŋ] *adj* refrescante.
refreshment [rɪ'freʃmənt] *n* refresco, refrigerio.
refrigerate [rɪ'frɪdʒəreɪt] *vt* refrigerar.
refrigerator [rɪ'frɪdʒəreɪtər] *n* frigorífico, nevera.
refuel [ri:'fjʊəl] *vt* **1** *(vehicle)* poner carburante a. **2** *(emotions)* reavivar.
▷ *vi* repostar.
refuge ['refjʊ:dʒ] *n* refugio.
refugee [refjʊ:'dʒi:] *n* refugiado,-a.
refund [*(n)* 'ri:fʌnd; *(vb)* ri:'fʌnd] *n* reembolso.
▷ *vt* reembolsar.
refurbish [ri:'fɜ:bɪʃ] *vt* remozar, renovar.
refusal [rɪ'fjʊ:zəl] *n* **1** *(negative reply)* negativa, respuesta negativa. **2** *(rejection)* rechazo.
refuse[1] ['refjʊ:s] *n* basura. ● **refuse collection** recogida de basuras.
refuse[2] [rɪ'fjʊ:z] *vt* **1** *(reject)* rehusar, rechazar, no aceptar. **2** *(withhold)* negar, denegar, no conceder
▷ *vi* negarse (**to**, a)
refute [rɪ'fjʊ:t] *vt* refutar.
regain [rɪ'geɪn] *vt* **1** *(recover)* recuperar. **2** *(get back to)* volver a. ■ **to regain consciousness** volver en sí.

regard [rɪ'gɑ:d] *n* respeto, consideración. ■ **to hold** **high regard** tener en gran estima. ǀ **without regard to** si hacer caso de.
▷ *vt* **1** *(consider)* considerar. **2** *(look at)* mirar, conter plar. **3** *(heed)* hacer caso a.
▷ *n pl* **regards** recuerdos *mpl*.
regarding [rɪ'gɑ:dɪŋ] *prep* tocante a, respecto a.
regardless [rɪ'gɑ:dləs] *adv fam* a pesar de todo.
▷ *prep* **regardless of** *fam* sin tener en cuenta.
regenerate [rɪ'dʒenəreɪt] *vt* regenerar.
▷ *vi* regenerarse.
regime [reɪ'ʒi:m] [Also written **régime**.] *n* régimen *m*
regiment ['redʒɪmənt] *n* regimiento.
▷ *vt* **1** MIL regimentar. **2** *fig* disciplinar, reglamentar.
region ['ri:dʒən] *n* región *f*.
regional ['ri:dʒənəl] *adj* regional.
register ['redʒɪstər] *n (gen)* registro; *(in school)* list
● **register office** registro civil.
▷ *vt* **1** *(car, student)* matricular; *(birth, death, marriage)* in cribir en el registro. **2** *(show)* indicar; *(- feeling)* mo trar. **3** *(make known)* hacer constar. **4** *(letter)* certifica
▷ *vi* **1** *(for classes)* matricularse; *(at congress)* inscribirse; *(hotel)* registrarse.
registered ['redʒɪstəd] *adj* **1** *(person)* inscrito,-a; *(st dent)* matriculado,-a. **2** *(letter)* certificado,-a. **3** *(ca etc)* matriculado,-a. ● **registered nurse** enfermero, diplomado,-a. ǀ **registered post** (US **mail**) correo cert ficado. ǀ **registered trademark** marca registrada.
registrar [redʒɪs'trɑ:r] *n* **1** *(in office)* registrador,-ra; *(university)* secretario,-a general. **2** *(doctor)* médico, interno,-a.
registration [redʒɪs'treɪʃən] *n* **1** *(of birth, death ma riage)* inscripción *f*; *(of patent, etc)* registro. **2** *(enro ment)* inscripción *f*; *(of student)* matrícula. ● **registr tion number** AUTO matrícula.
registry ['redʒɪstrɪ] *n* registro. ● **registry office** regist civil
regress [rɪ'gres] *vi* sufrir una regresión.
regression [rɪ'greʃən] *n* regresión *f*.
regressive [rɪ'gresɪv] *adj* regresivo,-a.
regret [rɪ'gret] *n* **1** *(remorse)* remordimiento. **2** *(sa ness)* pesar *m*.
▷ *vt* **1** *(feel sorry)* lamentar, arrepentirse de. **2** *(expr one's sadness)* lamentar. **3** *(miss)* echar de menos.
▷ *n pl* **regrets** excusas *mpl*
regretful [rɪ'gretfʊl] *adj* arrepentido,-a.
regrettable [rɪ'gretəbəl] *adj* lamentable.
regular ['regjʊlər] *adj.* **1** *(gen)* regular. **2** *(normal)* nc mal, usual. **3** *(habitual)* habitual. **4** *(normal in size)* (tamaño normal. **5** US *(pleasant)* simpático,-a. ● **reg lar army** ejército regular. ǀ **regular soldier** soldado pr fesional.
▷ *n fam* cliente *mf* habitual.
regularity [regjʊ'lærətɪ] *n* regularidad *f*.
regularise ['regjʊləraɪz] *vt* → **regularize.**
regularize ['regjʊləraɪz] *vt* regularizar.
regularly ['regjʊləlɪ] *adv* con regularidad.
regulate ['regjʊleɪt] *vt* **1** *(control)* regular, control *(adjust)* regular. **2** *(impose rules)* reglamentar, regular
regulation [regjʊ'leɪʃən] *n* **1** *(control)* regulación *f*. *(rule)* regla.
rehabilitate [ri:hə'bɪlɪteɪt] *vt* rehabilitar.

rehabilitation [ri:həbɪlɪ'teɪʃᵊn] *n* rehabilitación *f.* ● **rehabilitation centre** (US **center**) centro de rehabilitación.
rehearsal [rɪ'hɜ:sᵊl] *n* ensayo.
rehearse [rɪ'hɜ:s] *vt* ensayar.
reign [reɪn] *n* reinado.
vi reinar.
reimburse [ri:ɪm'bɜ:s] *vt* reembolsar.
rein [reɪn] *n* rienda.
n pl **reins** *(child's)* andadores *mpl.*
reincarnation [ri:ɪnkɑ:'neɪʃᵊn] *n* reencarnación *f.*
reindeer ['reɪndɪəʳ] *n* reno.
▲ *pl* **reindeer** o **reindeers.**
reinforce [ri:ɪn'fɔ:s] *vt* reforzar. ● **reinforced concrete** hormigón *m* armado.
reinforcement [ri:ɪn'fɔ:smənt] *n* refuerzo.
reinstate [ri:ɪn'steɪt] *vt (to job)* readmitir.
reissue [ri:'ɪʃu:] *n (of book)* reedición *f*; *(of stamp)* nueva emisión *f.*
vt (book) reeditar; *(stamp)* volver a emitir.
reiterate [ri:'ɪtəreɪt] *vt* reiterar.
reject [*(n)* 'ri:dʒekt; *(vb)* rɪ'dʒekt] *n (thing)* artículo defectuoso; *(person)* marginado,-a.
vt (gen) rechazar, no aceptar; *(in law)* desestimar.
rejection [rɪ'dʒekʃᵊn] *n (gen)* rechazo.
rejoice [rɪ'dʒɔɪs] *vi* alegrarse, regocijarse.
rejuvenate [rɪ'dʒu:vəneɪt] *vt* rejuvenecer.
rejuvenation [rɪdʒu:və'neɪʃᵊn] *n* rejuvenecimiento.
re-laid [ri:'leɪd] *pt & pp* ⟶ **re-lay.**
relapse [rɪ'læps] *n* **1** MED recaída. **2** *(crime)* reincidencia.
vi **1** MED recaer. **2** *(crime)* reincidir.
relate [rɪ'leɪt] *vt* **1** *(tell)* relatar, contar. **2** *(connect)* relacionar (**to**, con).
vi (connect) relacionarse, estar relacionado.
related [rɪ'leɪtɪd] *adj* **1** *(connected)* relacionado,-a. **2** *(relatives)* emparentado,-a. **3** *(plants, animals, languages, etc)* de la misma familia.
relation [rɪ'leɪʃᵊn] *n* **1** *(connection)* relación *f.* **2** *(family)* pariente *mf.*
relationship [rɪ'leɪʃᵊnʃɪp] *n* **1** *(connection)* relación *f.* **2** *(between people)* relaciones *fpl.*
relative ['relətɪv] *adj* relativo,-a.
n pariente *mf*, familiar *mf.*
relatively ['relətɪvlɪ] *adv* relativamente.
relativism ['relətɪvɪzᵊm] *n* relativismo.
relativist ['relətɪvɪst] *adj* relativista.
n relativista *mf.*
relativity [relə'tɪvɪtɪ] *n* relatividad *f.*
relaunch [*(vb)* ri:'lɔ:ntʃ; *(n)* 'ri:lɔ:ntʃ] *vt* relanzar.
n relanzamiento.
relax [rɪ'læks] *vt* **1** *(gen)* relajar. **2** *(grip, hold)* aflojar. **3** *(rules, control)* suavizar, relajar.
vi **1** *(gen)* relajarse. **2** *(grip, hold)* aflojarse.
relaxation [ri:læk'seɪʃᵊn] *n* **1** *(gen)* relajación *f.* **2** *(of grip, hold)* aflojamiento. **3** *(of rules, control)* relajación *f.* **4** *(rest)* descanso. **5** *(recreation)* esparcimiento.
relaxed [rɪ'lækst] *adj* **1** *(person)* relajado,-a. **2** *(atmosphere)* distendido,-a.
relaxing [rɪ'læksɪŋ] *adj* relajante.
relay [*(n)* 'ri:leɪ; *(vb)* rɪ'leɪ] *n* **1** relevo. **2** ELEC relé *m.*
vt **1** *(pass on)* transmitir. **2** *(broadcast)* retransmitir.
release [rɪ'li:s] *n* **1** *(setting free)* liberación *f*, puesta en libertad. **2** *(relief)* alivio. **3** *(of film)* estreno; *(of record)* lanzamiento. **4** *(of gas, etc)* emisión *f.* **5** *(new thing - film)* estreno; *(- record)* novedad *f* discográfica. **6** *(statement)* comunicado.
▷ *vt* **1** *(set free)* liberar, poner en libertad. **2** *(let go of)* soltar. **3** *(brake, etc)* soltar; *(shutter)* disparar. **4** *(bring out - film)* estrenar. **5** *(gas, etc - give out)* emitir; *(- give off)* desprender. **6** *(statement, information)* dar a conocer.
relegate ['relɪgeɪt] *vt* relegar.
relent [rɪ'lent] *vi* **1** *(person)* ceder. **2** *(storm)* amainar.
relentless [rɪ'lentləs] *adj* implacable, inexorable.
relevance ['reləvəns] *n* **1** *(connection)* relación *f.* **2** *(importance)* relevancia, importancia.
relevant ['reləvənt] *adj* **1** *(connected)* pertinente. **2** *(important)* relevante, importante.
reliability [rɪlaɪə'bɪlɪtɪ] *n* fiabilidad *f.*
reliable [rɪ'laɪəbᵊl] *adj* **1** *(person)* fiable, de fiar. **2** *(news, etc)* fidedigno,-a. **3** *(machine)* fiable.
reliably [rɪ'laɪəblɪ] *adv*: **I am reliably informed that...** *fuentes fidedignas me informan que...*
reliant [rɪ'laɪənt] *phr* **to be reliant on** depender de.
relic ['relɪk] *n* **1** REL reliquia. **2** *(custom)* vestigio.
relief [rɪ'li:f] *n* **1** *(from pain, etc)* alivio. **2** *(help)* auxilio, socorro, ayuda. **3** *(person)* relevo. **4** *(lifting of siege)* liberación *f.* **5** GEOG relieve *m.*
relieve [rɪ'li:v] *vt* **1** *(lessen)* aliviar. **2** *(take over from)* relevar. **3** *(help)* ayudar. **4** *(lift siege of)* liberar. ■ **to relieve sb of sth 1** *(take away)* llevar. **2** *(steal)* robar, quitar.
religion [rɪ'lɪdʒᵊn] *n* religión *f.*
religious [rɪ'lɪdʒəs] *adj* religioso,-a.
religiously [rɪ'lɪdʒəslɪ] *adv* religiosamente.
relinquish [rɪ'lɪŋkwɪʃ] *vt* renunciar a.
reliquary ['relɪkwərɪ] *n* relicario.
▲ *pl* **reliquaries.**
relish ['relɪʃ] *n* **1** gusto, deleite *m.* **2** CULIN condimento.
▷ *vt* disfrutar de
reload [ri:'ləʊd] *vt (program, page)* recargar.
relocate [ri:ləʊ'keɪt] *vt* trasladar.
▷ *vi* trasladarse.
relocation [ri:ləʊ'keɪʃᵊn] *n* traslado.
reluctance [rɪ'lʌktəns] *n* renuencia.
reluctant [rɪ'lʌktənt] *adj* renuente, reacio,-a.
reluctantly [rɪ'lʌktəntlɪ] *adv* muy a mi *(tu, su, etc)* pesar.
rely on [rɪ'laɪ ɒn] *vt (trust)* confiar en, contar con; *(depend on)* depender de.
▲ *pt & pp* **relied.**
remade [ri:'meɪd] *pt & pp* ⟶ **remake.**
remain [rɪ'meɪn] *vi* **1** *(stay)* permanecer. **2** *(be left)* quedar, sobrar. **3** *(continue)* seguir, continuar.
▷ *n pl* **remains** restos *mpl.*
remainder [rɪ'meɪndəʳ] *n* resto.
remaining [rɪ'meɪnɪŋ] *adj* restante.
remake [*(n)*'ri:meɪk; *(vb)* ri:'meɪk] *n* nueva versión *f.*
▷ *vt* hacer una nueva versión de.
▲ *pt & pp* **remade** [ri:'meɪd].
remand [rɪ'mɑ:nd] *n* prisión *f* preventiva.
remark [rɪ'mɑ:k] *n* observación *f*, comentario.
▷ *vt* **1** *(say)* observar, comentar. **2** *(notice)* advertir.
⊙ **to remark on** *vt insep* comentar.
remarkable [rɪ'mɑ:kəbᵊl] *adj* **1** *(exceptional)* excepcional. **2** *(odd)* extraño,-a; *(surprising)* curioso,-a.
remarkably [rɪ'mɑ:kəblɪ] *adv* extraordinariamente.
remarry [ri:'mærɪ] *vt (bride, groom)* volver a casarse con.
▷ *vi* volver a casarse.

remediable [rɪ'mi:dɪəbᵊl] *adj* remediable.
remedial [rɪ'mi:dɪəl] *adj* **1** *(classes)* de recuperación. **2** *(treatment)* de rehabilitación.
remedy ['remədɪ] *n* remedio.
▲ *pl* **remedies.**
▷ *vt* remediar.
remember [rɪ'membəʳ] *vt* recordar, acordarse de. ■ **to remember to do** STH acordarse de hacer ALGO.
▷ *vi* acordarse, recordar.
remembrance [rɪ'membrəns] *n* **1** conmemoración *f*. **2** *(keepsake)* recuerdo.
remex ['remeks] *n* rémige *f*.
remind [rɪ'maɪnd] *vt* recordar.
reminder [rɪ'maɪndəʳ] *n* **1** *(note)* recordatorio. **2** *(of payment due)* aviso. **3** *(keepsake)* recuerdo.
reminisce [remɪ'nɪs] *vi* rememorar.
reminiscences [remɪ'nɪsᵊnsɪz] *n pl* memorias *fpl*.
reminiscent [remɪ'nɪsᵊnt] *adj* nostálgico,-a. ■ **to be reminiscent of** recordar.
remiss [rɪ'mɪs] *adj* negligente.
remission [rɪ'mɪʃᵊn] *n* remisión *f*.
remit [*(vb)* rɪ'mɪt; *(n)* 'ri:mɪt] *vt* remitir.
▷ *n* competencia, atribuciones *fpl*.
remittance [rɪ'mɪtəns] *n* envío.
remnant ['remnənt] *n* **1** resto. **2** *(cloth)* retal *m*. **3** *(of past)* vestigio.
remonstrance [rɪ'mɒnstrəns] *n* protesta.
remorse [rɪ'mɔ:s] *n* remordimiento.
remorseful [rɪ'mɔ:sfʊl] *adj* arrepentido,-a.
remorseless [rɪ'mɔ:sləs] *adj* **1** *(pitiless)* despiadado,-a. **2** *(inexorable)* implacable.
remote [rɪ'məʊt] *adj* **1** *(far away)* remoto,-a. **2** *(lonely)* aislado,-a. **3** *(person)* distante, inaccesible. **4** *(possibility)* muy pequeño,-a. ● **remote control** mando a distancia.
remoteness [rɪ'məʊtnəs] *n* **1** *(distance)* lejanía, lo lejano. **2** *(loneliness)* lo aislado, lo apartado.
remould ['ri:məʊld] *n* neumático recauchutado.
remount [ri:'maʊnt] *vt* **1** *(horse, etc)* volver a subir a. **2** *(picture, photo)* volver a montar.
removable [rɪ'mu:vəbᵊl] *adj (legs, wheels)* desmontable.
removal [rɪ'mu:vᵊl] *n* **1** *(getting rid of)* eliminación *f*. **2** *(moving)* traslado. **3** *(from post)* destitución *f*.
remove [rɪ'mu:v] *vt* **1** *(get rid of - gen)* quitar, eliminar; *(- surgically)* extirpar. **2** *(take out, take off)* quitar. **3** *(move)* trasladar. **4** *(dismiss)* destituir.
▷ *vi (change houses)* trasladarse.
remover [rɪ'mu:vəʳ] *n* **1** *(product)* *producto que quita algo*: **nail varnish remover** *quitaesmaltes*. **2** *(person)* empleado, a de mudanzas.
remuneration [rɪ'mju:nəreɪʃᵊn] *n* remuneración *f*.
remunerative [rɪ'mju:nərətɪv] *adj* remunerativo,-a.
renaissance [rə'neɪsᵊns] *n* renacimiento.
▷ *adj* **Renaissance** renacentista, del Renacimiento.
rename [ri:'neɪm] *vt* renombrar.
rend [rend] *vt* desgarrar.
▲ *pt & pp* **rent** [rent].
render ['rendəʳ] *vt* **1** *(give)* prestar, dar. **2** *(make)* hacer. **3** *(translate)* traducir. **4** *(song)* cantar. **5** *(wall)* enlucir. **6** *(fat)* derretir. ■ **to render thanks to** dar gracias a.
rendezvous ['rɒndɪvu:] *n* cita.
▲ *pl* **rendezvous.**
▷ *vi* encontrarse.

rendition [ren'dɪʃᵊn] *n* interpretación *f*.
renew [rɪ'nju:] *vt* **1** *(gen)* renovar; *(contract, permit, e…* prorrogar. **2** *(start again)* reanudar. **3** *(replace)* sustitu…
renewal [rɪ'nju:əl] *n* **1** renovación *f*. **2** *(new sta…* reanudación *f*. **3** *(replacement)* sustitución *f*, cambi… ● **renewable energy** energía renovable.
renounce [rɪ'naʊns] *vt* renunciar a.
renovate ['renəveɪt] *vt (building)* reformar, renovar.
renovation [renə'veɪʃᵊn] *n* reforma, renovación *f*.
renown [rɪ'naʊn] *n* renombre *m*, fama.
renowned [rɪ'naʊnd] *adj* renombrado,-a, famoso,-…
rent [rent] *n* **1** *(for flat, etc)* alquiler *m*. **2** *(for land)* arriend…
▷ *vt* **1** *(flat)* alquilar. **2** *(land)* arrendar. ■ **«For rent»** «Se a… quila».
⊙ **to rent out** *vt sep* alquilar.
rental ['rentᵊl] *n* **1** *(for flat, etc)* alquiler *m*. **2** *(for lan…* arriendo.
rented ['rentɪd] *adj* de alquiler, alquilado,-a.
rent-free [rent'fri:] *adj* gratuito.
▷ *adv* gratuitamente, gratis.
rentier ['rɒntɪeɪ] *n* rentista *mf*.
renunciation [rɪnʌnsɪ'eɪʃᵊn] *n* renuncia.
reoffend [ri:ə'fend] *vi* reincidir.
reorganise [ri:'ɔ:gənaɪz] *vt* ⟶ **reorganize.**
reorganization [ri:ɔ:gənaɪ'zeɪʃᵊn] *n* reorganización
reorganize [ri:'ɔ:gənaɪz] *vt* reorganizar.
repaid [ri:'peɪd] *pt & pp* ⟶ **repay.**
repair [rɪ'peəʳ] *n* reparación *f*.
▷ *vt* reparar, arreglar. ■ **in good repair** en buen estado
reparation [repə'reɪʃᵊn] *n* reparación *f*.
▷ *n pl* **reparations** POL indemnización *f sing*.
repay [ri:'peɪ] *vt* devolver.
▲ *pt & pp* **repaid**, *ger* **repaying.**
repayment [ri:'peɪmənt] *n* pago.
repeal [rɪ'pi:l] *n* derogación *f*, revocación *f*.
▷ *vt* abrogar, derogar, revocar.
repeat [rɪ'pi:t] *n* **1** *(gen)* repetición *f*. **2** *(on television)* r… posición *f*.
▷ *vt* repetir.
▷ *vi* repetir.
repel [rɪ'pel] *vt* **1** *(gen)* repeler. **2** *(disgust)* repugnar.
▲ *pt & pp* **repelled**, *ger* **repelling.**
repent [rɪ'pent] *vi* arrepentirse.
▷ *vt* arrepentirse de.
repentance [rɪ'pentəns] *n* arrepentimiento.
repertoire ['repətwɑ:ʳ] *n* repertorio.
repertory ['repətᵊrɪ] *n* repertorio.
repetition [repə'tɪʃᵊn] *n* repetición *f*.
repetitive [rɪ'petɪtɪv] *adj* repetitivo,-a.
replace [rɪ'pleɪs] *vt* **1** *(put back)* devolver a su sitio. *(substitute)* reemplazar, sustituir; *(change)* cambiar.
replacement [rɪ'pleɪsmənt] *n* **1** *(act)* sustitución *f*. *(person)* sustituto,-a. **3** *(thing)* otro,-a. **4** *(spare pa…* recambio.
replay [*(n)* 'ri:pleɪ; *(vb)* ri:'pleɪ] *n* **1** *(of film sequence)* rep… tición *f* de la jugada. **2** *(match)* partido de desempat…
▷ *vt* **1** *(tape, film)* volver a poner. **2** *(match)* volver a jug…
replenish [rɪ'plenɪʃ] *vt* **1** *(stocks)* reponer. **2** *(glass, e…* rellenar, llenar de nuevo.
replete [rɪ'pli:t] *adj* repleto,-a.
replicate ['replɪkeɪt] *vt* reproducir.
▷ *vi* reproducirse.

eply [rɪ'plaɪ] *n* respuesta, contestación *f*.
▲ *pl* replies.
▷ *vi* responder (to, a), contestar (to, a).
▲ *pt & pp* replied.
epopulate [riː'pɒpjəleɪt] *vt* repoblar.
epopulation [riːpɒpjə'leɪʃᵊn] *n* repoblación *f*.
eport [rɪ'pɔːt] *n* **1** *(informative document)* informe *m*. **2** *(school report)* informe *m* escolar. **3** *(piece of news)* noticia. **4** *(news story)* reportaje *m*. **5** *(rumour)* rumor *m*.
● report card boletín *m* de notas.
▷ *vi* **1** *(give information)* informar (on, sobre). **2** *(go in person)* presentarse, personarse.
▷ *vt* **1** *(say, inform)* decir. **2** *(to authority)* informar de. **3** *(to police)* dar parte de.
eported speech [rɪpɔːtɪ'spiːtʃ] *n* estilo indirecto.
eporter [rɪ'pɔːtəʳ] *n* reportero,-a, periodista *mf*.
epose [rɪ'pəʊz] *n* reposo.
vi reposar, descansar.
eprehensible [reprɪ'hensɪbᵊl] *adj* reprensible.
epresent [reprɪ'zent] *vt* representar.
epresentation [reprɪzen'teɪʃᵊn] *n* representación *f*.
■ to make representations to presentar una queja a.
epresentative [reprɪ'zentətɪv] *adj* representativo,-a.
n **1** representante *mf*. **2** US diputado,-a.
epress [rɪ'pres] *vt* reprimir.
epressed [rɪ'prest] *adj* reprimido,-a.
eprieve [rɪ'priːv] *n* **1** indulto. **2** *fig* respiro, tregua.
vt conmutar la pena a, indultar.
eprimand ['reprɪmɑːnd] *n* reprimenda, reprensión *f*.
vt reprender.
eprint [*(n)* 'riːprɪnt; *(vb)* riː'prɪnt] *n* reimpresión *f*.
vt reimprimir.
eprisal [rɪ'praɪzᵊl] *n* represalia.
eprise [rɪ'priːz] *n* repetición *f*.
eproach [rɪ'prəʊtʃ] *n* reproche *m*.
vt reprochar (for, -).
eproachful [rɪ'prəʊtʃfʊl] *adj* de reproche.
eproduce [riːprə'djuːs] *vt* reproducir.
vi reproducirse.
eproduction [riːprə'dʌkʃᵊn] *n* reproducción *f*.
eproductive [riːprə'dʌktɪv] *adj* reproductor,-ra.
eproof [rɪ'pruːf] *n* reprobación *f*, reprensión *f*.
eprove [rɪ'pruːv] *vt* reprobar, reprender.
eptile ['reptaɪl] *n* reptil *m*.
epublic [rɪ'pʌblɪk] *n* república.
epublican [rɪ'pʌblɪkən] *adj* republicano,-a.
n republicano,-a.
epudiate [rɪ'pjuːdɪeɪt] *vt* **1** *(reject)* rechazar. **2** *(deny)* negar. **3** *(disown)* repudiar.
epugnant [rɪ'pʌgnənt] *adj* repugnante.
epulse [rɪ'pʌls] *vt* **1** *(reject)* rechazar. **2** *(drive back)* repulsar.
epulsive [rɪ'pʌlsɪv] *adj* repulsivo,-a.
eputable ['repjʊtəbᵊl] *adj* de confianza.
eputation [repjʊ'teɪʃᵊn] *n* reputación *f*, fama.
epute [rɪ'pjuːt] *n* reputación *f*, fama.
eputed [rɪ'pjuːtɪd] *adj* **1** *(supposed)* presunto,-a, supuesto,-a. **2** *(respected)* respetado,-a, acreditado,-a.
equest [rɪ'kwest] *n* **1** petición *f*. **2** *(on radio)* canción *f*.
vt **1** *(gen)* solicitar; *(officially)* rogar. **2** *(on radio)* pedir.
equire [rɪ'kwaɪəʳ] *vt* **1** requerir, exigir. **2** *(need)* necesitar, requerir.
requirement [rɪ'kwaɪəment] *n* **1** *(demand)* requisito. **2** *(need)* necesidad *f*.
requisite ['rekwɪzɪt] *adj* requerido,-a, necesario,-a.
▷ *n* requisito.
reran [riː'ræn] *pt* → rerun.
rerun [*(n)* 'riːrʌn; *(vb)* riː'rʌn] *n* *(repetition)* repetición *f*; *(TV programme)* reposición *f*; *(film)* reestreno.
▷ *vt* *(TV programme)* reponer; *(film)* reestrenar.
▲ *pt* reran [riː'ræn], *pp* rerun [riː'rʌn], *ger* rerunning.
resat ['riːsɑt] *pt & pp* → resit.
rescind [rɪ'sɪnd] *vt* rescindir.
rescue ['reskjuː] *n* rescate *m*.
▷ *vt* rescatar (from, de).
research [rɪ'sɜːtʃ] *n* investigación *f*. ● research unit centro de investigaciones.
▷ *vi* investigar (into, -).
▷ *vt* documentar.
researcher [rɪ'sɜːtʃəʳ] *n* investigador,-ra.
resemblance [rɪ'zembləns] *n* parecido, semejanza.
resemble [rɪ'zembᵊl] *vt* parecerse a.
resent [rɪ'zent] *vt* ofenderse por, tomarse a mal.
resentment [rɪ'zentmənt] *n* resentimiento, rencor *m*.
reservation [rezə'veɪʃᵊn] *n* *(gen)* reserva.
reserve [rɪ'zɜːv] *n* *(gen)* reserva.
▷ *vt* reservar.
reserved [rɪ'zɜːvd] *adj* reservado,-a.
reservist [rɪ'zɜːvɪst] *n* reservista *mf*.
reservoir ['rezəvwɑːʳ] *n* **1** *(lake)* embalse *m*. **2** *(store)* reserva.
reset [riː'set] *vt* **1** *(programmer, computer)* reinicializar; *(mechanism)* rearmar. **2** *(clock)* poner en hora. **3** *(bone)* componer. **4** *(book)* recomponer.
▲ *pt & pp* reset, *ger* resetting.
reshape [riː'ʃeɪp] *vt* dar nueva forma.
reshuffle [riː'ʃʌfᵊl] *n* *(of cabinet)* remodelación *f*.
▷ *vt* **1** *(cabinet)* remodelar. **2** *(cards)* volver a barajar.
reside [rɪ'zaɪd] *vi* residir.
residence ['rezɪdəns] *n* residencia.
resident ['rezɪdᵊnt] *adj* residente.
▷ *n* *(gen)* residente *mf*; *(in hotel)* huésped,-da.
residential [resɪ'denʃᵊl] *adj* residencial.
residual [rɪ'zɪdjʊəl] *adj* residual.
residue ['rezɪdjuː] *n* residuo.
resign [rɪ'zaɪn] *vi* dimitir (from, de), presentar la dimisión. ■ to resign OS to STH resignarse a ALGO.
▷ *vt* dimitir de.
resignation [rezɪg'neɪʃᵊn] *n* **1** *(from post)* dimisión *f*. **2** *(acceptance)* resignación *f*. ■ to hand in one's resignation presentar la dimisión.
resigned [rɪ'zaɪnd] *adj* resignado,-a.
resilience [rɪ'zɪlɪəns] *n* **1** *(flexibility)* elasticidad *f*. **2** *(strength)* fuerza, resistencia.
resilient [rɪ'zɪlɪənt] *adj* **1** *(flexible)* elástico,-a. **2** *(strong)* fuerte.
resin ['rezɪn] *n* resina.
resist [rɪ'zɪst] *vt* *(not give in to)* resistir, resistirse a.
resistance [rɪ'zɪstəns] *n* **1** *(gen)* resistencia. **2** *(opposition)* oposición *f*. ■ to put up resistance oponer resistencia.
resistant [rɪ'zɪstənt] *adj* resistente.
resistor [rɪ'zɪstəʳ] *n* resistencia.
resit [*(n)* 'riːsɪt; *(vb)* riː'sɪt] *n* examen *m* de repesca.
▷ *vt* volver a presentarse a.
▲ *pt & pp* resat [riː'sæt], *ger* resitting.

resolute [ˈrezəlu:t] *adj* firme, decidido,-a.
resolution [ˈrezəlu:ʃən] *n* resolución *f*
resort [rɪˈzɔ:t] *n* **1** *(place)* lugar *m* de vacaciones. **2** *(recourse)* recurso.
▷ *vi* recurrir (**to**, a).
resource [rɪˈzɔ:s] *n* recurso.
resourceful [rɪˈzɔ:sful] *adj* ingenioso,-a.
respect [rɪˈspekt] *n* **1** *(admiration)* respeto. **2** *(aspect)* respecto.
▷ *vt* respetar.
respectable [rɪˈspektəbəl] *adj* **1** *(gen)* respetable. **2** *(decent)* decente, presentable.
respecting [rɪˈspektɪŋ] *prep* con respecto a.
respiratory [ˈrespərətərɪ] *adj* respiratorio,-a. ● **respiratory system** sistema *m* respiratorio.
respond [rɪˈspɒnd] *vi* responder.
response [rɪˈspɒns] *n* **1** *(gen)* respuesta. **2** *(reaction)* reacción *f*.
responsibility [rɪspɒnsɪˈbɪlɪtɪ] *n* responsabilidad *f*. ■ **to accept responsibility for** responsabilizarse de.
responsible [rɪˈspɒnsəbəl] *adj* **1** *(gen)* responsable. **2** *(in control)* encargado,-a. **3** *(position)* de responsabilidad.
responsibly [rɪˈspɒnsɪblɪ] *adv* con responsabilidad.
responsive [rɪˈspɒnsɪv] *adj* que muestra interés.
rest[1] [rest] *n* **1** *(repose)* descanso. **2** *(peace)* paz *f*, tranquilidad *f*. **3** *(support)* soporte *m*; *(for head)* reposacabezas *m*; *(for arms)* apoyabrazos *m*. ● **rest room** servicios *mpl*.
▷ *vt* **1** *(relax)* descansar. **2** *(lean)* apoyar.
▷ *vi* **1** *(relax)* descansar. **2** *(be calm)* quedarse tranquilo,-a. **3** *(depend)* depender (**on**, de).
▷ *vt (lean)* apoyar.
rest[2] [rest] *vi* quedar así.
▷ *n* **the rest** el resto.
restate [ri:ˈsteɪt] *vt* volver a exponer.
restaurant [ˈrestərɒnt] *n* restaurante *m*.
restful [ˈrestful] *adj* relajante.
restitution [restɪˈtju:ʃən] *n* restitución *f*.
restless [ˈrestləs] *adj* inquieto,-a. ■ **to grow restless** impacientarse.
restoration [restəˈreɪʃən] *n* **1** *(gen)* restauración *f*. **2** *(return)* devolución *f*.
restore [rɪˈstɔ:r] *vt* **1** *(gen)* restaurar. **2** *(return)* devolver. **3** *(order)* restablecer.
restrain [rɪˈstreɪn] *vt* contener.
restrained [rɪˈstreɪnd] *adj (person)* comedido,-a.
restraint [rɪˈstreɪnt] *n* **1** *(restriction)* restricción *f*, limitación *f*. **2** *(moderation)* moderación *f*.
restrict [rɪˈstrɪkt] *vt* restringir, limitar, limitarse.
restricted [rɪˈstrɪktɪd] *adj* **1** *(limited)* restringido,-a, limitado,-a. **2** *(confidential)* confidencial.
result [rɪˈzʌlt] *n* **1** resultado. **2** consecuencia.
▷ *vi* **to result from** resultar de.
⊙ **to result in** *vt insep* producir, causar.
resume [rɪˈzju:m] *vt* **1** *(begin again)* reanudar. **2** *(take over again)* volver a asumir.
▷ *vi* continuar.
résumé [ˈrezju:meɪ] *n* **1** *(summary)* resumen *m*. **2** US *(curriculum vitae)* currículo, currículum vitae *m*.
resumption [rɪˈzʌmpʃən] *n* reanudación *f*.
resurgence [rɪˈsɜ:dʒəns] *n* resurgimiento.
resuscitate [rɪˈsʌsɪteɪt] *vt* reanimar.

retail [ˈri:teɪl] *n* venta al detalle, venta al por menor.
▷ *vt* vender al detalle, vender al por menor.
▷ *vi* venderse, venderse al por menor.
▷ *adv* al detalle, al por menor.
retailer [ˈri:teɪlər] *n* detallista *mf*, minorista *mf*.
retain [rɪˈteɪn] *vt* **1** *(keep - power, moisture)* retener; *(- hea charge)* conservar. **2** SP *(lead)* mantener; *(title)* revalida **3** *(possessions)* guardar. **4** *(remember)* retener, recorda **5** *(hold back)* contener. **6** *(employ)* contratar.
retake [*(n)*ˈri:teɪk; *(vb)* ri:ˈteɪk] *n* **1** *(of scene)* nueva to ma. **2** *(exam)* examen *m* de recuperación.
▷ *vt* **1** *(scene)* volver a filmar. **2** *(exam)* volver a preser tarse a. **3** *(territory)* retomar.
▲ *pt* **retook** [ri:ˈteɪk], *pp* **retaken** [ri:ˈteɪkən].
retaliate [rɪˈtælɪeɪt] *vi* tomar represalias (**against**, contra
retard [rɪˈtɑ:d] *vt* retardar, retrasar.
retch [retʃ] *vi* tener arcadas, tener náuseas.
retentive [rɪˈtentɪv] *adj* retentivo,-a.
reticence [ˈretɪsəns] *n* reticencia, reserva.
retina [ˈretɪnə] *n* retina.
▲ *pl* **retinas** o **retinae** [ˈretɪni:].
retinue [ˈretɪnju:] *n* séquito.
retire [rɪˈtaɪər] *vt (from work)* jubilar.
▷ *vi* **1** *(from work)* jubilarse. **2** *(withdraw)* retirarse. **3** *(go bed)* acostarse.
retiring [rɪˈtaɪərɪŋ] *adj* **1** *(shy)* retraído,-a, tímido,-a. *(from post)* saliente.
retort[1] [rɪˈtɔ:t] *n* réplica.
▷ *vt* replicar.
retort[2] [rɪˈtɔ:t] *n* CHEM retorta.
retouch [ri:ˈtʌtʃ] *vt* retocar.
retrace [rɪˈtreɪs] *vt* desandar, volver sobre. ■ **to retrac one's steps** volver sobre sus pasos.
retract [rɪˈtrækt] *vt* **1** *(statement, promise)* retractarse d **2** *(claws)* retraer. **3** *(undercarriage)* replegar.
▷ *vi* **1** *(claws)* retraerse. **2** *(undercarriage)* replegarse.
retreat [rɪˈtri:t] *n* **1** *(withdrawal)* retirada. **2** *(place)* ref gio.
▷ *vi* **1** *(withdraw)* retirarse. **2** *(back down)* dar marcha atrá
retrench [ri:ˈtrentʃ] *vi* reducir gastos, economizar.
retribution [retrɪˈbju:ʃən] *n* justo castigo.
retrieve [rɪˈtri:v] *vt* **1** *(gen)* recuperar. **2** *(situation)* sa var, remediar. **3** *(in hunting)* cobrar.
retrogress [retrəuˈgres] *vi (go back)* retroceder; *(wor en)* empeorar.
retrospect [ˈretrəuspekt] *phr* **in retrospect** retrospec vamente.
retrospective [retrəˈspektɪv] *adj* **1** *(exhibition, etc)* r trospectivo,-a. **2** *(law)* retroactivo,-a.
return [rɪˈtɜ:n] *n* **1** *(coming or going back)* vuelta, regr so. **2** *(giving back)* devolución *f*. **3** SP *(of ball)* devol ción *f*; *(of service)* resto. **4** *(reappearance)* reaparición **5** *(on keyboard)* retorno. **6** *(profit)* beneficio. **7** *(ticke* billete *m* de ida y vuelta. ● **return ticket** billete *m* d ida y vuelta.
▷ *vi* **1** *(come back, go back)* volver, regresar. **2** *(reappe* reaparecer.
▷ *vt* **1** *(give back)* devolver. **2** SP *(ball)* devolver; *(serve)* re tar. **3** POL *(elect)* elegir. **4** *(verdict)* pronunciar. **5** *(intere* producir. ■ **in return for** a cambio de.
▷ *n pl* **returns** resultados *mpl* electorales.
returnable [rɪˈtɜ:nəbəl] *adj* retornable.

eunion [riːˈjuːnɪən] *n* reencuentro.
eunite [riːjuːˈnaɪt] *vt (parts)* reunir.
euse [riːjuːz] *vt (parts)* reutilizar.
evaluation [riːvæljuˈeɪʃᵊn] *n* revalorización *f*, revaluación *f*.
eveal [rɪˈviːl] *vt* **1** *(make known)* revelar. **2** *(show)* dejar ver, mostrar.
evel [ˈrevᵊl] *phr* **to revel in** deleitarse en.
▲ *pt & pp* **revelled** *(*US **reveled***)*, *ger* **revelling** *(*US **reveling***)*.
evenge [rɪˈvendʒ] *n* venganza.
▷ *vt* vengar. ■ **to revenge** os vengarse.
evenue [ˈrevənjuː] *n* ingresos *mpl*, renta.
everberate [rɪˈvɜːbəreɪt] *vt* resonar, retumbar.
evere [rɪˈvɪəʳ] *vt* reverenciar.
everence [ˈrevᵊrəns] *n* reverencia.
everie [ˈrevərɪ] *n* ensueño.
eversal [rɪˈvɜːsᵊl] *n* **1** *(in order)* inversión *f*. **2** *(of decision)* revocación *f*. **3** *(change)* cambio completo. **4** *(setback)* revés *m*.
everse [rɪˈvɜːs] *adj* inverso,-a.
▷ *n* **1** *(back - of coin, paper)* reverso; *(- of cloth)* revés *m*. **2** AUTO marcha atrás. **3** *(setback)* revés *m*.
▷ *vt* **1** *(positions, roles)* invertir. **2** *(decision)* revocar. **3** *(vehicle)* dar marcha atrás a.
▷ *vi* AUTO poner marcha atrás, dar marcha atrás.
evert [rɪˈvɜːt] *vi* **1** volver (**to**, a). **2** JUR revertir.
eview [rɪˈvjuː] *n* **1** *(magazine, show)* revista. **2** MIL revista. **3** *(examination)* examen *m*. **4** *(of book, etc)* crítica. **5** US *(for exam)* repaso.
▷ *vt* **1** *(troops)* pasar revista a. **2** *(examine)* examinar. **3** *(film, book, etc)* hacer una crítica de. **4** US *(for exam)* repasar.
evile [rɪˈvaɪl] *vt* injuriar, vilipendiar.
evise [rɪˈvaɪz] *vt* **1** revisar. **2** *(correct)* corregir. **3** *(change)* modificar. **4** *(examination topic)* repasar.
▷ *vi (for exam)* repasar.
evision [rɪˈvɪʒᵊn] *n* **1** revisión *f*. **2** *(correction)* corrección *f*. **3** *(change)* modificación *f*. **4** *(for exam)* repaso.
evitalise [riːˈvaɪtᵊlaɪz] *vt* ⟶ **revitalize**.
evitalize [riːˈvaɪtᵊlaɪz] *vt* revitalizar.
evival [rɪˈvaɪvᵊl] *n* **1** *(rebirth)* renacimiento. **2** *(of economy)* reactivación *f*. **3** *(of play)* reestreno.
evive [rɪˈvaɪv] *vt* **1** reanimar, reavivar, despertar. **2** *(economy)* reactivar. **3** *(play)* reestrenar. **4** MED reanimar, hacer volver en sí.
▷ *vi* MED volver en sí.
evolt [rɪˈvəʊlt] *n (rising)* revuelta, rebelión *f*.
▷ *vi (rise)* sublevarse (**against**, contra), rebelarse.
▷ *vt (disgust)* repugnar.
evolting [rɪˈvəʊltɪŋ] *adj* repugnante, asqueroso,-a.
evolution [revəˈluːʃᵊn] *n* revolución *f*.
evolutionary [revəlˈuːʃᵊnərɪ] *adj* revolucionario,-a.
▷ *n* revolucionario,-a.
evolutionise [revəˈluːʃᵊnaɪz] *vt* ⟶ **revolutionize**.
evolutionize [revəˈluːʃᵊnaɪz] *vt* revolucionar.
evolve [rɪˈvɒlv] *vi* girar.
▷ *vt* hacer girar.
volver [rɪˈvɒlvəʳ] *n* revólver *m*.
volving [rɪˈvɒlvɪŋ] *adj* giratorio,-a. ● **revolving door** puerta giratoria.
vue [rɪˈvjuː] *n* revista.
ward [rɪˈwɔːd] *n* recompensa.
▷ *vt* recompensar.

rewind [riːˈwaɪnd] *vt* rebobinar.
▲ *pt & pp* **rewound** [riːˈwaʊnd].
rewound [riːˈwaʊnd] *pt & pp* ⟶ **rewind**.
rewrite [*(vb)* riːˈraɪt; *(n)* ˈriːraɪt] *vt* volver a escribir.
▲ *pt* **rewrote** [riːˈreʊt], *pp* **rewritten** [riːˈrɪtən].
▷ *n* nueva versión *f*.
rewritten [riːˈrɪtən] *pp* ⟶ **rewrite**.
rewrote [riːˈrəʊt] *pt* ⟶ **rewrite**.
Reykjavik [ˈreɪkjəvɪk] *n* Reykjavik.
rhea [rɪə] *n* ñandú *m*.
rheniun [ˈriːnɪəm] *n* renio.
rhesus [ˈriːsəs] *n* rhesus *m*. ● **rhesus monkey** macaco rhesus.
rheumatism [ˈruːmətɪzᵊm] *n* reumatismo, reuma *m*.
rheumatoid arthritis [ruːmətɔɪdɑːˈθraɪtəs] *n* reumatismo articular.
Rhine [raɪn] *n* el Rin *m*.
Rhineland [ˈraɪnlænd] *n* Renania.
rhinestone [ˈraɪnstəʊn] *n* estrás *m*.
rhinoceros [raɪˈnɒsərəs] *n* rinoceronte *m*.
▲ *pl* **rhinoceroses** o **rhinoceros**.
rhizome [ˈraɪzəʊm] *n* rizoma *m*.
Rhodes [rəʊdʒ] *n* Rodas.
Rhodesia [rəʊˈdiːʃə] *n* Rhodesia.
Rhodesian [rəʊˈdiːʃᵊn] *adj* rhodesiano,-a.
▷ *n* rhodesiano,-a.
rhodium [ˈrəʊdɪəm] *n* rodio.
rhododendron [rəʊdəˈdendrən] *n* rododendro.
rhombus [ˈrɒmbəs] *n* rombo.
▲ *pl* **rhombuses** o **rhombi** [ˈrombaɪ].
Rhône [rəʊn] *n* el Ródano.
rhubarb [ˈruːbɑːb] *n* ruibarbo.
rhyme [raɪm] *n* rima.
▷ *vi* rimar (**with**, con).
rhythm [ˈrɪðᵊm] *n* ritmo.
rhythmic [ˈrɪðmɪk] *adj* rítmico,-a. ● **rhythmic gymnastics** gimnástica rítmica.
rib[1] [rɪb] *n* costilla. ● **rib cage** caja torácica.
rib[2] [rɪb] *vt* burlarse de.
▲ *pt & pp* **ribbed**, *ger* **ribbing**.
ribbon [ˈrɪbᵊn] *n* **1** cinta. **2** *(for hair)* lazo.
ribonucleic [raɪbəʊnjuˈkleɪk] *adj* ribonucleico,-a.
rice [raɪs] *n* arroz *m*. ● **rice field** arrozal *m*. ‖ **rice pudding** arroz *m* con leche.
rich [rɪtʃ] *adj* **1** rico,-a. **2** *(luxurious)* lujoso,-a. **3** *(fertile)* fértil. **4** *(food)* fuerte, pesado,-a. **5** *(voice)* sonoro,-a.
▷ *n pl* **riches** riqueza *f sing*.
richness [ˈrɪtʃnəs] *n* **1** *(wealth)* riqueza; *(sumptuousness)* suntuosidad *f*. **2** *(fertility)* fertilidad *f*. **3** *(of voice)* sonoridad *f*. **4** *(of colour)* viveza.
rickets [ˈrɪkɪts] *n pl* raquitismo *m sing*.
rickety [ˈrɪkətɪ] *adj* **1** desvencijado,-a. **2** *(unsteady)* tambaleante.
rid [rɪd] *vt* librar. ■ **to get rid of** deshacerse de.
▲ *pt & pp* **rid** o **ridded**, *ger* **ridding**.
ridden [ˈrɪdən] *pp* ⟶ **ride**.
riddle [ˈrɪdᵊl] *n* **1** acertijo, adivinanza. **2** *(sieve)* criba.
▷ *vt* **1** cribar. **2** *(with bullets)* acribillar.
ride [raɪd] *n* **1** *(on bicycle, horse)* paseo. **2** *(in car)* paseo, vuelta; *(on bus, train)* viaje *m*, trayecto.
▷ *vi* **1** *(on horse)* montar a caballo; *(on bicycle)* ir en bicicleta. **2** *(in vehicle)* viajar.

▷ *vt* **1** *(horse)* montar. **2** *(bicycle)* montar en, andar en.
▲ *pt* **rode** [rəʊd], *pp* **ridden** ['rɪdᵊn], *ger* **riding**.

rider ['raɪdəʳ] *n* **1** *(on horse - man)* jinete *m*, *(woman)* amazona. **2** *(on bicycle)* ciclista *mf*. **3** *(on motorcycle)* motorista *mf*. **4** *(clause)* cláusula adicional.

ridge [rɪdʒ] *n* **1** GEOG cresta. **2** *(of roof)* caballete *m*.

ridgepole ['rɪdʒpəʊl] *n* hilera.

ridicule ['rɪdɪkjuːl] *n* ridículo.
▷ *vt* ridiculizar, poner en ridículo.

ridiculous [rɪ'dɪkjʊləs] *adj* ridículo,-a.

riding ['raɪdɪŋ] *n* equitación *f*.

rife [raɪf] *adj* abundante. ■ **to be rife** abundar.

rifle[1] ['raɪfᵊl] *n* rifle *m*, fusil *m*.

rifle[2] ['raɪfᵊl] *vt* hurgar (**through**, en).

rifleman ['raɪfəlmən] *n* fusilero.
▲ *pl* **riflemen** ['raɪfəlmən].

rift [rɪft] *n* **1** hendidura, grieta. **2** *fig* ruptura.

rig [rɪg] *n* plataforma petrolífera.
▷ *vt* **1** MAR aparejar. **2** *fam (fix)* amañar.
▲ *pt & pp* **rigged**, *ger* **rigging**.
⊙ **to rig up** *vt sep* improvisar.

rigging ['rɪgɪŋ] *n* MAR aparejo, jarcia.

right [raɪt] *adj* **1** *(not left)* derecho,-a. **2** *(correct)* correcto,-a. **3** *(just)* justo,-a. **4** *(suitable)* apropiado,-a, adecuado,-a. **5** *fam (total)* auténtico,-a, total. **6** *fam (okay)* bien. ■ **all right!** ¡bien! ■ **right away** en seguida. ■ **to be right** tener razón. ■ **to get it right** acertar.
▷ *adv* **1** a la derecha, hacia la derecha. **2** *(correctly)* bien. **3** *(exactly)* justo. **4** *(well)* bueno, bien. **5** *fam (very)* muy.
▷ *n* **1** *(not left)* derecha. **2** *(entitlement)* derecho. ● **right angle** ángulo recto. ■ **right wing** POL derecha.
▷ *vt* **1** corregir. **2** MAR enderezar.

righteous ['raɪtʃəs] *adj* **1** recto,-a, justo,-a. **2** *(justified)* justificado,-a.

rightful ['raɪtfʊl] *adj* legítimo,-a.

right-hand ['raɪthænd] *adj* derecho,-a. ● **right-hand man** brazo derecho.

right-handed [raɪt'hændɪd] *adj* diestro,-a.

rightly ['raɪtlɪ] *adv* correctamente.

right-minded [raɪt'maɪndɪd] *adj* recto,-a.

rightness ['raɪtnəs] *n* **1** *(honesty)* rectitud *f*, honradez *f*. **2** *(justice)* justicia.

right-wing ['raɪtwɪŋ] *adj* POL de derechas, derechista.

rigid ['rɪdʒɪd] *adj* rígido,-a.

rigidity [rɪ'dʒɪdɪtɪ] *n* rigidez *f*.

rile [raɪl] *vt fam* poner nervioso,-a, irritar.

rim [rɪm] *n* **1** *(gen)* borde *m*, canto. **2** *(of wheel)* llanta. **3** *(of spectacles)* montura.

rind [raɪnd] *n* corteza.

ring[1] [rɪŋ] *n* **1** *(for finger)* anillo. **2** *(hoop)* anilla, aro. **3** *(circle)* círculo; *(of people)* corro; *(of criminals)* red *f*. **4** *(of circus)* pista. **5** *(for boxing)* ring *m*, cuadrilátero.
▷ *vt* **1** *(put a ring on)* anillar. **2** *(draw a ring round)* marcar con un círculo. **3** *(encircle)* rodear. ● **ring road** cinturón *m* de ronda.

ring[2] [rɪŋ] *n* **1** *(of bell)* tañido, toque *m*; *(of doorbell)* llamada. **2** *(phone call)* llamada.
▷ *vi* **1** *(bell)* sonar. **2** *(ears)* zumbar.
▲ *pt* **rang** [ræŋ], *pp* **rung** [rʌŋ].
▷ *vt* **1** *(call)* llamar. **2** *(bell)* tocar.
⊙ **to ring up** *vt sep* llamar por teléfono, telefonear.

ringing ['rɪŋɪŋ] *n* **1** repique *m*. **2** *(in ears)* zumbido.

ringleader ['rɪŋliːdəʳ] *n* cabecilla *mf*.

ringlet ['rɪŋlət] *n* rizo.

ringpull ['rɪŋpʊl] *n* anilla. ● **ringpull can** lata abrefácil

ringside ['rɪŋsaɪd] *n* primera fila.
▷ *adj* (asientos) de primera fila

rink [rɪŋk] *n* pista de patinaje. ● **ice rink** pista de hiel

rinse [rɪns] *vt* **1** *(clothes, hair)* aclarar. **2** *(dishes, mout* enjuagar.
▷ *n* **1** *(of clothes)* aclarado. **2** *(of dishes)* enjuague *m*. **3** *(f hair)* tinte *m*.

riot ['raɪət] *n* **1** *(in street)* disturbio. **2** *(in prison)* motín *n*
▷ *vi* **1** *(in street)* provocar disturbios. **2** *(in prison)* amot narse. ● **riot police** policía antidisturbios.

riotous ['raɪətəs] *adj* **1** *(behaviour)* revoltoso,-a. **2** *(li ing)* desenfrenado,-a.

rip [rɪp] *n* rasgón *m*, desgarrón *m*.
▷ *vt* rasgar, desgarrar.
▷ *vi* rasgarse, desgarrarse.
▲ *pt & pp* **ripped**, *ger* **ripping**.
⊙ **to rip off** *vt sep* **1** arrancar. **2** *fam* timar.
⊙ **to rip up** *vt sep* romper, hacer pedazos.

ripcord ['rɪpkɔːd] *n* cordón *m* de apertura.

ripe [raɪp] *adj* maduro,-a.

rip-off ['rɪpɒf] *n fam* timo.

ripple ['rɪpᵊl] *n* **1** *(on water)* onda. **2** *(sound)* murmull
▷ *vt* rizar.
▷ *vi* rizarse.

rise [raɪz] *n* **1** ascenso, subida. **2** *(increase)* aumento. *(slope)* subida, cuesta.
▷ *vi* **1** subir. **2** *(increase)* aumentar. **3** *(stand up)* pone de pie. **4** *(get up)* levantarse. **5** *(sun)* salir. **6** *(river)* nac **7** *(level of river)* crecer. **8** *(mountains)* elevarse.
▲ *pt* **rose** [rəʊz], *pp* **risen** ['rɪzən].

risen ['rɪsən] *pp* → **rise**.

rising ['raɪzɪŋ] *n (rebellion)* levantamiento.
▷ *adj* **1** *(prices)* en aumento. **2** *(sun)* naciente. **3** *(land)* pendiente.

risk [rɪsk] *n* riesgo, peligro.
▷ *vt* arriesgar. ■ **to take a risk** correr un riesgo.

risky ['rɪskɪ] *adj* arriesgado,-a.
▲ *comp* **riskier**, *superl* **riskiest**.

rite [raɪt] *n* rito.

rival ['raɪvᵊl] *adj* competidor,-ra, rival.
▷ *n* competidor,-ra, rival *mf*.
▷ *vt* competir con, rivalizar con.

river ['rɪvəʳ] *n* río.

river-bank ['rɪvəbænk] *n* ribera, orilla.

river-bed ['rɪvəbed] *n* lecho.

riverside ['rɪvəsaɪd] *n* ribera, orilla.

rivet ['rɪvɪt] *n* remache *m*.
▷ *vt* **1** remachar. **2** *fig* fijar, absorber.

riveting ['rɪvɪtɪŋ] *adj fig* fascinante.

roach[1] [rəʊtʃ] *n (fish)* pardilla.

roach[2] [rəʊtʃ] *n* US *fam* cucaracha.

road [rəʊd] *n* **1** carretera. **2** *(way)* camino. ● **road si** señal *f* de tráfico.

roadblock ['rəʊdblɒk] *n* control *m* policial.

roadside ['rəʊdsaɪd] *n* borde *m* de la carretera.

roadway ['rəʊdweɪ] *n* calzada.

roadworks ['rəʊdweːks] *n pl* obras.

roam [rəʊm] *vt* vagar por.
▷ *vi* vagar.

oaming ['rəʊmɪŋ] *adj* errante.

oar [rɔːʳ] *n* 1 *(of bull, person)* bramido. 2 *(of lion, sea)* rugido. 3 *(of traffic)* estruendo. 4 *(of crowd)* griterío.
▷ *vi* 1 *(bull, person)* bramar. 2 *(lion, sea)* rugir.

oaring ['rɔːrɪŋ] *adj* 1 *(fire)* crepitante; *(wind)* rugiente. 2 *fig* tremendo,-a, enorme.

oast [rəʊst] *adj* asado,-a. ● **roast beef** rosbif *m*. ▮ **roast potato** patata al horno.
▷ *n* asado.
▷ *vt* 1 *(meat)* asar. 2 *(coffee, nuts, etc)* tostar.
▷ *vi* 1 *(meat)* asarse. 2 *(person)* achicharrarse.

ob [rɒb] *vt* 1 robar. 2 *(bank)* atracar; *(shop)* asaltar, robar.
▲ *pt & pp* **robbed**, *ger* **robbing**.

obe [rəʊb] *n* 1 *(dressing gown)* bata. 2 *(ceremonial)* vestidura, toga. 3 *(dress)* vestido. ● **bath robe** albornoz *m*.

obin ['rɒbɪn] *n* petirrojo.

obot ['rəʊbɒt] *n* robot *m*.

obust [rəʊ'bʌst] *adj* robusto,-a, fuerte.

ock [rɒk] *n* 1 *(gen)* roca. 2 US piedra. 3 MUS rock *m*, música rock.
▷ *vt* 1 *(chair)* mecer. 2 *(baby)* acunar. 3 *(upset)* sacudir.
▷ *vi (chair)* mecerse.

ock-bottom [rɒk'bɒtəm] *adj (gen)* bajísimo,-a; *(price)* de regalo, regalado,-a, imbatible.

ock-climbing ['rɒkklaɪmɪŋ] *n* escalada en roca.

ocker ['rɒkəʳ] *n* 1 *(mechanism)* balancín *m*. 2 *(chair)* mecedora.

ockery ['rɒkərɪ] *n* jardín *m* de rocalla.

ocket ['rɒkɪt] *n* 1 *(missile)* cohete *m*.
▷ *vi (rise)* dispararse. ● **rocket launcher** lanzacohetes *m*.

ocking-chair ['rɒkɪŋtʃeəʳ] *n* mecedora.

ocky ['rɒkɪ] *adj* rocoso,-a.
▲ *comp* **rockier**, *superl* **rockiest**.

od [rɒd] *n* 1 *(thin)* vara. 2 *(thick)* barra.

ode [rəʊd] *pt* → **ride**.

odent ['rəʊdᵊnt] *n* roedor *m*.

oe[1] [rəʊ] *n (eggs)* hueva.

oe[2] [rəʊ] *n (deer)* corzo,-a.

oebuck ['rəʊbʌk] *n* corzo.

ogue [rəʊg] *n* bribón,-ona, pillo,-a.

oguish ['rəʊgɪʃ] *adj* pillo,-a.

ole [rəʊl] *n* papel, interpretación *m*.

ole-play ['rəʊlpleɪ] *n* dramatización *f*.

oll [rəʊl] *n* 1 *(gen)* rollo. 2 *(of film)* carrete *m*. 3 *(list)* lista. 4 *(of bread)* bollo, panecillo. 5 *(movement)* balanceo. 6 *(of thunder)* fragor *m*. ■ **to call the roll** pasar lista.
▷ *vt* 1 *(ball, coin)* hacer rodar. 2 *(flatten)* allanar, apisonar. 3 *(into a ball)* enroscar. 4 *(paper)* enrollar.
▷ *vi* 1 *(thunder)* retumbar; *(drum)* redoblar. 2 *(ball, coin)* rodar. 3 *(into a ball)* enroscarse. 4 *(paper)* enrollarse. 5 *(wallow)* revolcarse.
⊙ **to roll by** *vi* pasar *lentamente*.
⊙ **to roll out** *vt sep (pastry)* extender, estirar.
⊙ **to roll over** *vt sep* dar la vuelta a.
▷ *vi* darse la vuelta.
⊙ **to roll up** *vt sep* 1 enrollar. 2 *(into a ball)* enroscar.
▷ *vi* 1 enrollarse. 2 *(into a ball)* enroscarse.

oller ['rəʊləʳ] *n* 1 *(for painting)* rodillo. 2 *(wave)* ola grande. 3 *(for hair)* rulo. ● **roller coaster** montaña rusa. ▮ **roller skating** patinaje *m* sobre ruedas.

olling ['rəʊlɪŋ] *adj* ondulante. ● **rolling stock** material *m* rodante. ▮ **rolling pin** rodillo.

ROM [rɒm] *abbr* **(read-only memory)** memoria solo de lectura; *(abbreviation)* ROM *f*.

Roman ['rəʊmən] *adj* romano,-a.
▷ *n* romano,-a. ● **Roman numeral** número romano.

Romance [rəʊ'mæns] *adj* románico,-a.

romance [rəʊ'mæns] *n* 1 romance *m*. 2 *(novel)* novela romántica. 3 *(quality)* lo romántico. 4 *(affair)* idilio.

Romania [ruː'meɪnɪə] *n* Rumanía.

Romanian [ruː'meɪnɪən] *adj* rumano,-a.
▷ *n* 1 *(person)* rumano,-a. 2 *(language)* rumano.

Romany ['rəʊmənɪ] *adj* gitano,-a.
▷ *n* 1 *(persona)* gitano,-a. 2 *(language)* caló *m*.
▲ *pl* **Romanies**.

romp [rɒmp] *vi* jugar, retozar.
▷ *n* jugueteo.

roof [ruːf] *n* 1 tejado; *(tiled)* techado. 2 *(of mouth)* cielo. 3 *(of car, etc)* techo. ● **flat roof** azotea. ▮ **roof rack** baca.
▷ *vt* techar.

rook [rʊk] *n* 1 *(bird)* grajo. 2 *(in chess)* torre *f*.

rookie ['rʊkɪ] *n fam* novato,-a.

room [ruːm] *n* 1 habitación *f*, pieza. 2 *(space)* lugar *m*.
▷ *vi* 1 *(lodge)* alojarse. 2 *(share a room)* compartir una habitación.

roommate ['ruːmmeɪt] *n* compañero,-a de habitación.

roomy ['ruːmɪ] *adj* espacioso,-a, amplio,-a.
▲ *comp* **roomier**, *superl* **roomiest**.

roost [ruːst] *n* percha. ■ **to rule the roost** llevar la batuta.
▷ *vi* posarse.

rooster ['ruːstəʳ] *n* gallo.

root[1] [ruːt] *n* raíz *f*. ● **root vegetable** tubérculo.
▷ *vt* arraigar.
▷ *vi* arraigar. ■ **to take root** arraigar, echar raíces.
⊙ **to root out** *vt sep* erradicar.

root[2] [ruːt] *vi* **to root about / root around** hurgar.

root[3] [ruːt] *vt* **to root for** animar, alentar.

rope [rəʊp] *n (gen)* cuerda; *(thicker)* soga.
▷ *vt* atar *(con cuerdas)*, amarrar.
⊙ **to rope off** *vt sep* acordonar.

rorqual ['rɔːkwəl] *n* yubarta.

rosary ['rəʊzərɪ] *n* rosario.
▲ *pl* **rosaries**.

rose [rəʊz] *n* 1 *(flower)* rosa. 2 *(bush)* rosal *m*. 3 *(colour)* rosa *m*. 4 *(of shower, etc)* alcachofa. ● **rose garden** rosaleda. ▮ **rose window** rosetón *m*.

rosebay ['rəʊzbeɪ] *n* adelfa.

rosebud ['rəʊzbʌd] *n* capullo de rosa.

rosemary ['rəʊzmərɪ] *n* romero.

rosewood ['rəʊzwʊd] *n* palisandro.

roster ['rɒstəʳ] *n* lista.

rostrum ['rɒstrəm] *n* tribuna.
▲ *pl* **rostrums** o **rostra** ['rɒstrə].

rosy ['rəʊzɪ] *adj* 1 *(colour)* rosado,-a, sonrosado,-a. 2 *(future)* prometedor,-ra.
▲ *comp* **rosier**, *superl* **rosiest**.

rot [rɒt] *n* 1 *(decay)* putrefacción *f*. 2 *(rubbish)* tonterías *fpl*.
▷ *vt* pudrir.
▷ *vi* pudrirse.
▲ *pt & pp* **rotted**, *ger* **rotting**.

rotate [rəʊ'teɪt] *vt* 1 *(spin)* hacer girar, dar vueltas a. 2 *(alternate)* alternar.
▷ *vi* 1 *(spin)* girar, dar vueltas. 2 *(alternate)* alternarse.

rouge [ruːʒ] *n* colorete *m*.

rough [rʌf] *adj* **1** *(not smooth)* áspero,-a, basto,-a. **2** *(road)* lleno,-a de baches. **3** *(edge)* desigual. **4** *(terrain)* escabroso,-a. **5** *(sea)* agitado,-a. **6** *(weather)* tempestuoso,-a. **7** *(wine)* áspero,-a. **8** *(rude)* rudo,-a. **9** *(violent)* violento,-a; *(dangerous)* peligroso,-a. **10** *(approximate)* aproximado,-a. **11** *fam (bad)* fatal.

roughen [ˈrʌf^{ə}n] *vt* poner áspero,-a.

roughly [ˈrʌflɪ] *adv* **1** *(about)* aproximadamente; *(more or less)* más o menos. **2** *(not gently)* bruscamente.

round [raʊnd] *adj* redondo,-a.
▷ *n* **1** *(circle)* círculo. **2** *(series)* serie *f*, tanda; *(one of a series)* ronda. **3** SP *(stage of competition)* ronda; *(boxing)* asalto; *(of golf)* partido. **4** *(of drinks)* ronda. **5** *(of policeman, etc)* ronda. **6** *(for gun)* cartucho. **7** *(of bread)* rebanada. ● **round trip** viaje *m* de ida y vuelta.
▷ *adv* **1** *(in circles)*: **it goes round and round** *da vueltas y vueltas.* **2** *(about)* por ahí. **3** *(to somebody's house)* a casa.
▷ *prep* alrededor de.
▷ *vt* doblar.
⊙ **to round down** *vt sep* redondear *(a la baja)*.
⊙ **to round off** *vt sep* completar, acabar.
⊙ **to round on** *vt insep* volverse contra.
⊙ **to round up** *vt sep* **1** *(number)* redondear *(al alza)*. **2** *(cattle)* acorralar. **3** *(people)* reunir, juntar.

roundabout [ˈraʊndəbaʊt] *adj* indirecto,-a.
▷ *n* **1** tiovivo. **2** AUTO rotonda.

rouse [raʊz] *vt* **1** *(wake)* despertar. **2** *(provoke)* provocar.
▷ *vi* despertarse.

rousing [ˈraʊzɪŋ] *adj* **1** *(stirring)* apasionante, enardecedor,-ra. **2** *(moving)* conmovedor,-ra.

rout [raʊt] *n* derrota total.
▷ *vt* derrotar *de forma aplastante*.

route [ruːt; US raʊt] *n* **1** ruta, camino, vía. **2** *(of bus)* trayecto.
▷ *vt* mandar.
▷ *n* **Route** US carretera nacional.

router [ˈruːtə^{r}] *n* COMPUT direccionador *m*, enrutador *m*.

rove [rəʊv] *vi* vagar, errar.

row[1] [raʊ] *n* **1** *(fight)* riña, pelea. **2** *(din, racket)* jaleo.
▷ *vi* pelearse.

row[2] [rəʊ] *n* *(line)* fila, hilera.

row[3] [rəʊ] *n* *(in a boat)* paseo en bote, vuelta en bote.
▷ *vi (in a boat)* remar.
▷ *vt* impeler mediante remos.

rowan [ˈraʊən, ˈrəʊən] *n* serbal *m*.

rowdy [ˈraʊdɪ] *adj* **1** *(causing trouble)* alborotador,-ra. **2** *(noisy)* ruidoso,-a.
▲ *comp* **rowdier**, *superl* **rowdiest.**
▷ *n (troublemaker)* camorrista *mf*.
▲ *pl* **rowdies.**

rowing [ˈrəʊɪŋ] *n* remo. ● **rowing boat** bote *m* de remos.

royal [ˈrɔɪəl] *adj* real.

royalist [ˈrɔɪəlɪst] *adj* monárquico,-a.
▷ *n* monárquico,-a.

royally [ˈrɔɪəlɪ] *adv* magníficamente.

royalty [ˈrɔɪəltɪ] *n* **1** realeza. **2** *(people)* miembros *mpl* de la familia real.
▲ *pl* **royalties.**
▷ *n pl* **royalties** *(gen)* royalties *mpl*; *(of writer)* derechos *mpl* de autor.

rub [rʌb] *n* friega.
▷ *vt (gen)* frotar; *(hard)* restregar.
▷ *vi* rozar. ■ **to rub it in** *fam* insistir.
⊙ **to rub off** *vt sep* quitar *frotando*.
▷ *vi* **1** quitarse. **2** *fig* pegarse.
⊙ **to rub out** *vt sep* borrar.
▷ *vi* borrarse.
▲ *pt & pp* **rubbed**, *ger* **rubbing.**

rubber [ˈrʌbə^{r}] *n* **1** caucho, goma. **2** *(eraser)* goma d borrar. **3** US *fam* goma, preservativo. ● **rubber ban** goma elástica. ‖ **rubber ring** flotador *m*.

rubbery [ˈrʌbərɪ] *adj* **1** *(rubber-like)* gomoso,-a. *(chewy)* correoso,-a.

rubbish [ˈrʌbɪʃ] *n* **1** *(refuse)* basura. **2** *fam (thing)* birria porquería. **3** *(nonsense)* tonterías *fpl*. ● **rubbish bin** cu bo de la basura. ‖ **rubbish dump** vertedero, basurero.

rubble [ˈrʌb^{ə}l] *n* escombros *mpl*.

rubella [ruːˈbelə] *n* rubéola.

ruby [ˈruːbɪ] *n* rubí *m*.
▲ *pl* **rubies.**

rucksack [ˈrʌksæk] *n* mochila.

rudder [ˈrʌdə^{r}] *n* timón *m*.

rudderless [ˈrʌdələs] *adj* sin timón.

ruddy [ˈrʌdɪ] *adj* **1** *(colour)* colorado,-a. **2** GB *fam* mald to,-a.
▲ *comp* **ruddier**, *superl* **ruddiest.**

rude [ruːd] *adj* **1** *(person)* maleducado,-a, grosero,- *(behaviour)* grosero,-a; *(word)* malsonante. **2** *(improper)* grosero,-a. **3** *(crude)* rudo,-a, tosco,-a.

rue[1] [ruː] *vt (regret)* lamentar, arrepentirse de.

rue[2] [ruː] *n (plant)* ruda.

rueful [ˈruːfʊl] *adj* **1** *(repentant)* arrepentido,-a. **2** *(sa* afligido,-a, triste, compungido,-a.

ruffle [ˈrʌf^{ə}l] *n* **1** *(on shirt front)* chorrera. **2** *(on cuffs)* vo lante *m*.
▷ *vt* **1** *(disturb - gen)* agitar; *(- feathers)* erizar; *(- hair)* des peinar, alborotar. **2** *(annoy)* irritar, alterar.

ruffled [ˈrʌf^{ə}ld] *adj* **1** *(hair)* despeinado,-a. **2** *(perso* alterado,-a. ■ **to get ruffled** alterarse.

rug [rʌg] *n* alfombra, alfombrilla.

rugby [rʌgbɪ] *n* rugby *m*.

rugged [ˈrʌgɪd] *adj* **1** *(terrain)* escabroso,-a, agrest *(mountain)* escarpado,-a. **2** *(features)* duro,-a.

ruin [ˈruːɪn] *n* ruina.
▷ *vt* **1** arruinar. **2** *(spoil)* estropear.

ruined [ˈruːɪnd] *adj* **1** arruinado,-a. **2** *(spoilt)* estropea do,-a. **3** *(building)* en ruinas.

rule [ruːl] *n* **1** *(regulation)* regla, norma. **2** *(control)* dom nio. **3** *(of monarch)* reinado; *(by government)* gobiern **4** *(measure)* regla.
▷ *vt* **1** *(govern)* gobernar; *(reign)* reinar en. **2** *(decree)* d cretar, dictaminar. **3** *(draw)* trazar.
▷ *vi* **1** *(govern)* gobernar; *(reign)* reinar. **2** *(decree)* decr tar, dictaminar.
⊙ **to rule out** *vt sep* excluir, descartar.

ruled [ruːld] *adj* rayado,-a.

ruler [ˈruːlə^{r}] *n* **1** gobernante *mf*, dirigente *mf*. **2** *(mo arch)* soberano,-a, monarca *mf*. **3** *(instrument)* regla.

ruling [ˈruːlɪŋ] *adj (in charge)* dirigente; *(governing)* en poder; *(reigning)* reinante.
▷ *n* JUR fallo.

rum [rʌm] *n* ron *m*.

Rumania [ruːˈmeɪnɪə] *n* ⟶ **Romania.**

Rumanian [ruːˈmeɪnɪən] *adj-n* ⟶ **Romanian.**

umble ['rʌmbᵊl] *n (gen)* ruido sordo; *(of thunder)* estruendo; *(of stomach)* borborigmo.
▷ *vi (gen)* hacer un ruido sordo; *(thunder)* retumbar; *(stomach)* hacer ruidos, sonar.
uminant ['ruːmɪnənt] *adj* rumiante.
▷ *n* rumiante *m*.
uminate ['ruːmɪneɪt] *vi* **1** *(animal)* rumiar. **2** *(person)* rumiar, cavilar.
ummage ['rʌmɪdʒ] *vi* revolver *(buscando)*.
ump [rʌmp] *n* **1** *(of animal)* ancas *fpl*; *(of horse)* grupa; *(of cow)* cadera. **2** *(of person)* trasero.
umple ['rʌmpᵊl] *vt* **1** arrugar. **2** *(hair)* despeinar.
un [rʌn] *n* **1** carrera. **2** *(trip)* viaje *m*; *(for pleasure)* paseo. **3** *(sequence)* racha. **4** *(ski run)* pista. **5** *(in stocking)* carrera. **6** *(demand)* gran demanda. **7** THEAT permanencia en cartel. **8** *(in cricket)* carrera. **9** *(in printing)* tirada. **10** *(at cards)* escalera. ■ **to go for a run** ir a correr.
▷ *vi* **1** *(gen)* correr. **2** *(flow)* correr. **3** *(operate)* funcionar. **4** *(trains, buses)* circular. **5** *(in election)* presentarse. **6** *(play)* estar en cartel; *(contract, etc)* seguir vigente. **7** *(colour)* correrse.
▷ *vt* **1** *(gen)* correr. **2** *(race)* correr en, participar en. **3** *(take by car)* llevar, acompañar. **4** *(manage)* llevar, dirigir, regentar. **5** *(organize)* organizar, montar. **6** *(operate)* hacer funcionar. **7** *(pass, submit to)* pasar. **8** *(publish)* publicar. **9** *(water)* dejar correr.
⊙ **to run across** *vt insep* **1** *(cross over)* cruzar corriendo. **2** *(find)* encontrar, tropezar con.
⊙ **to run after** *vt insep* perseguir.
⊙ **to run along** *vi* irse.
⊙ **to run away** *vi* **1** *(gen)* irse corriendo. **2** *(from home, etc)* fugarse, escaparse.
⊙ **to run away with** *vt insep* escaparse con.
⊙ **to run down** *vt sep* **1** *(knock down)* atropellar. **2** *(criticize)* criticar. **3** *(battery)* agotar.
▷ *vt insep* bajar corriendo.
▷ *vi* **1** bajar corriendo. **2** *(battery)* agotarse. **3** *(clock)* pararse.
⊙ **to run in** *vt sep* **1** *(car)* rodar. **2** *(criminal)* detener.
▷ *vi* entrar corriendo.
⊙ **to run into** *vt insep* **1** entrar corriendo en. **2** *(car)* chocar con. **3** *(meet)* tropezar con.
⊙ **to run off** *vt sep (print)* imprimir.
▷ *vi* irse corriendo.
⊙ **to run off with** *vt insep* escaparse con, llevarse.
⊙ **to run out** *vi* **1** salir corriendo. **2** *(be used up - gen)* acabarse; *(- stocks)* agotarse. **3** *(contract)* caducar.
⊙ **to run over** *vt sep (knock down)* atropellar.
▷ *vi* **1** *(overflow)* rebosar. **2** *(spill)* derramar.
⊙ **to run through** *vt insep* **1** *(rehearse)* ensayar; *(do again)* repasar. **2** *(read)* echar un vistazo a.
⊙ **to run up** *vt insep (ascend)* subir corriendo.
▷ *vt sep* **1** *(debts)* acumular. **2** *(flag)* izar.
▷ *vi (ascend)* subir corriendo.
▲ *pt* **ran** [ræn], *pp* **run** [rʌn], *ger* **running**.
unaway ['rʌnəweɪ] *adj* **1** *(prisoner)* fugitivo,-a; *(horse)* desbocado,-a. **2** *(out of control)* incontrolado,-a; *(inflation)* galopante. **3** *(tremendous)* aplastante; *(success)* clamoroso,-a.
▷ *n (adult)* fugitivo,-a; *(youngster)* joven fugado,-a.
undown ['rʌndaʊn] *n* resumen *m*. ■ **to give sb a rundown on sth** poner a algn al corriente de algo.
run-down [rʌn'daʊn] *adj* **1** *(person)* agotado,-a. **2** *(area)* venido,-a a menos, decaído,-a.
rung[1] [rʌŋ] *n* escalón *m*.
rung[2] [rʌŋ] *pp* → **ring**.
runner ['rʌnəʳ] *n* **1** corredor,-ra. **2** *(of sledge)* patín *m*; *(of skate)* cuchilla. **3** *(carpet)* alfombrilla. **4** *(on furniture)* tapete *m*. ● **runner bean** judía verde.
running ['rʌnɪŋ] *n* **1** *(action)* el correr; *(sport)* atletismo. **2** *(management)* dirección *f*.
▷ *adj* **1** *(water)* corriente. **2** *(continuous)* continuo,-a.
▷ *adv* seguido,-a.
runny ['rʌnɪ] *adj* **1** *(liquid)* líquido,-a; *(egg)* poco hecho. **2** *(nose)* que moquea.
▲ *comp* **runnier**, *superl* **runniest**.
run-up ['rʌnʌp] *n* **1** *(period before)* etapa preliminar. **2** *(before jumping, etc)* carrerilla.
runway ['rʌnweɪ] *n* pista de aterrizaje.
rupture ['rʌptʃəʳ] *n* **1** *(hernia)* hernia. **2** *(breakage)* rotura; *(burst)* reventón *m*. **3** *fig* ruptura.
▷ *vt (break)* romper; *(burst)* reventar.
▷ *vi (break)* romperse; *(burst)* reventarse. ■ **to rupture os** herniarse.
ruse [ruːz] *n* ardid *m*, astucia.
rush[1] [rʌʃ] *n* **1** prisa. **2** *(movement)* movimiento impetuoso, avance *m* impetuoso. ● **rush hour** hora punta. ‖ **rush job** trabajo urgente.
▷ *vt* **1** *(hurry - person)* apresurar, dar prisa a, meter prisa a; *(- job, etc)* hacer demasiado deprisa. **2** *(send quickly)* enviar urgentemente, mandar urgentemente; *(take quickly)* llevar rápidamente. **3** *(attack)* abalanzarse sobre, arremeter contra. **4** *fam* cobrar.
▷ *vi* ir deprisa, precipitarse, apresurarse.
⊙ **to rush in** *vi* entrar corriendo.
⊙ **to rush out** *vi* salir corriendo.
rush[2] [rʌʃ] *n (plant)* junco.
rusk [rʌsk] *n* galleta.
Russia ['rʌʃə] *n* Rusia.
Russian ['rʌʃᵊn] *adj* ruso,-a.
▷ *n* **1** *(person)* ruso,-a. **2** *(language)* ruso.
rust [rʌst] *n* óxido, herrumbre *m*.
▷ *vt* oxidar.
▷ *vi* oxidar.
rustle ['rʌsᵊl] *n (of leaves, etc)* crujido; *(of silk)* frufrú *m*.
▷ *vt (leaves, etc)* hacer crujir.
▷ *vi (leaves, etc)* crujir.
▷ *vt (cattle)* robar.
▷ *vi (cattle)* robar ganado.
rustler ['rʌsᵊləʳ] *n* cuatrero,-a.
rustling ['rʌsᵊlɪŋ] *n* **1** *(noise)* crujido. **2** *(theft)* robo de ganado.
rustproof ['rʌstpruːf] *adj* inoxidable.
rusty ['rʌstɪ] *adj* **1** *(metal)* oxidado,-a. **2** *fig* olvidado,-a.
▲ *comp* **rustier**, *superl* **rustiest**.
rut[1] [rʌt] *n (groove)* surco.
rut[2] [rʌt] *n (of male animal)* período de celo.
ruthenium [ru'θiːnɪᵊm] *n* rutenio.
ruthless ['ruːθləs] *adj* cruel, despiadado,-a.
Rwanda [ru'ændə] *n* Ruanda.
Rwandan [ru'ændən] *adj* ruandés,-esa.
▷ *n* ruandés,-esa.
rye [raɪ] *n* centeno. ● **rye bread** pan *m* de centeno.

S

S, s [es] *n (the letter)* S, s *f*.
saber ['seɪbəʳ] *n* US ⟶ **sabre**.
Sabbath ['sæbəθ] *n (Jewish)* sábado.
sabbatical [sə'bætɪkᵊl] *n (year)* año sabático; *(term)* trimestre *m* sabático.
▷ *adj* sabático,-a.
sabotage ['sæbətɑːʒ] *n* sabotaje *m*.
▷ *vt* sabotear.
saboteur [sæbə'tɜːʳ] *n* saboteador,-ra.
sabre ['seɪbəʳ] *n* sable *m*.
saccharin ['sækᵊrɪn] *n* sacarina.
sachet ['sæʃeɪ] *n* bolsita, sobrecito.
sack[1] [sæk] *n (bag)* saco.
▷ *vt* GB *fam* despedir a, echar a. ■ **to get the sack** ser despedido,-a. ■ **to give** SB **the sack** despedir a ALGN.
sack[2] [sæk] *vt* MIL saquear.
▷ *n* MIL saqueo.
sackful ['sækfʊl] *n* saco.
sacking ['sækɪŋ] *n (material)* arpillera.
sacrament ['sækrəmənt] *n* sacramento.
sacred ['seɪkrəd] *adj* sagrado,-a, sacro,-a.
sacrifice ['sækrɪfaɪs] *n* **1** *(gen)* sacrificio. **2** *(offering)* ofrenda.
▷ *vt* **1** *(offer as sacrifice)* sacrificar. **2** *(give up)* sacrificar, renunciar a.
sacrilege ['sækrɪlɪdʒ] *n* sacrilegio.
sacrilegious [sækrɪ'lɪdʒəs] *adj* sacrílego,-a.
sacristan ['sækrɪstᵊn] *n* sacristán,-ana.
sacristy ['sækrɪstɪ] *n* sacristía.
▲ *pl* **sacristies.**
sacrum ['sækrəm] *n* ANAT sacro.
▲ *pl* **sacra** ['sækrə].
sad [sæd] *adj* **1** *(unhappy)* triste: **you look very sad** *estás muy triste.* **2** *(deplorable)* lamentable.
▲ *comp* **sadder**, *superl* **saddest**.
sadden ['sædᵊn] *vt* entristecer.
▷ *vi* entristecerse.
saddle ['sædᵊl] *n (for horse)* silla (de montar); *(of bicycle, etc)* sillín *m*.
▷ *vt* ensillar (**up**, -).
⊙ **to saddle with** *vt sep* cargar con.
saddlebag ['sædᵊlbæg] *n* alforja.
saddler ['sædᵊləʳ] *n* guarnicionero,-a.
sadism ['seɪdɪzᵊm] *n* sadismo.
sadist ['seɪdɪst] *n* sádico,-a.
sadistic [sə'dɪstɪk] *adj* sádico,-a.
sadly ['sædlɪ] *adv* tristemente.
sadness ['sædnəs] *n* tristeza.
safari [sə'fɑːrɪ] *n* safari *m*.
safe [seɪf] *adj* **1** *(gen)* seguro,-a; *(out of danger)* a salvo, fuera de peligro: **it's not safe to play in the road** *es peligroso jugar en la calle.* **2** *(unharmed)* ileso,-a, indemne. **3** *(not risky - method, investment, choice)* seguro,-a; *(subjec*[t]) no polémico,-a. ■ **safe and sound** sano,-a y salvo,-a.
▷ *n* caja fuerte, caja de caudales.
safe-breaker ['seɪfbreɪkəʳ] *n* ladrón,-ona de caja[s] fuertes.
safe-conduct [seɪf'kɒndʌkt] *n* salvoconducto.
safe-deposit ['seɪfdɪpɒzɪt] *n (in bank)* cámara acorazada
safeguard ['seɪfgɑːd] *n* salvaguardia; *(protection)* protección *f* (**against**, contra).
▷ *vt* salvaguardar, proteger (**against**, contra).
safekeeping [seɪf'kiːpɪŋ] *n* custodia.
safely ['seɪflɪ] *adv* **1** *(for certain)* con toda seguridad: **we can safely say that...** *podemos decir con toda seguridad que...* **2** *(without mishap)* sin contratiempos, sin accidentes. **3** *(securely)* de manera segura. ■ **to arrive safely** llegar a buen puerto.
safety ['seɪftɪ] *n* seguridad *f*. ● **safety belt** cinturón *m* de seguridad. ‖ **safety catch** seguro, cierre *m* de seguridad. ‖ **safety match** cerilla, fósforo. ‖ **safety pin** imperdible *m*. ‖ **safety razor** maquinilla de afeitar.
saffron ['sæfrən] *n (plant, condiment)* azafrán *m*.
▷ *adj (colour)* de color azafrán.
sag [sæg] *vi* **1** *(shelf, branch, beam, ceiling)* combarse; *(roof, bed)* hundirse. **2** *(demand, prices, etc)* caer, bajar. **3** *fig (spirits)* flaquear, decaer.
▲ *pt & pp* **sagged**, *ger* **sagging.**
saga ['sɑːgə] *n* saga.
sage[1] [seɪdʒ] *adj* sabio,-a.
▷ *n* sabio,-a.
sage[2] [seɪdʒ] *n* BOT salvia.
Sagittarius [sædʒɪ'teərɪəs] *n* Sagitario.
said [sed] *pt & pp* ⟶ **say.**
sail [seɪl] *n* **1** *(canvas)* vela. **2** *(trip)* paseo en barco; *(journey)* viaje *m* en barco. **3** *(of windmill)* aspa.
▷ *vt* **1** *(travel)* navegar; *(cross)* cruzar en barco: **she sailed the Atlantic single-handed** *cruzó el Atlántico sola.* [2] *(control ship)* gobernar.
▷ *vi* **1** *(ship, boat)* navegar; *(person)* ir en barco, navegar. **2** *(begin journey)* zarpar, hacerse a la mar. ■ **in full sail** toda vela. ‖ **to set sail** zarpar, hacerse a la mar.
⊙ **to sail into** *vt insep* arrebatar contra.
sailboard ['seɪlbɔːd] *n* tabla de windsurf.
sailcloth ['seɪlklɒθ] *n* lona.
sailing ['seɪlɪŋ] *n* **1** *(skill)* navegación *f*. **2** *(sport)* vela, navegación *f* a vela: **we go sailing every weekend** *hacemos vela todos los fines de semana.* **3** *(departure)* salida; *(crossing)* travesía. ● **sailing boat** barco de vela.
sailor ['seɪləʳ] *n* marinero. ■ **to be a good sailor** no marearse.
saint [seɪnt] *n (person)* santo,-a.
saintly ['seɪntlɪ] *adj* santo,-a.
▲ *comp* **saintlier**, *superl* **saintliest**.

sake [seɪk] *n* bien *m*: **for your own sake** *por tu propio bien;* **for the kids' sake** *por los niños.* ■ **for God's sake!** ¡por el amor de Dios!, ¡por Dios!

salad ['sæləd] *n* ensalada. ● **salad bowl** ensaladera. ‖ **salad dressing** aliño, aderezo.

salamander ['sæləmændəʳ] *n* salamandra.

salami [sə'lɑːmɪ] *n* salami *m*.

salaried ['sælərɪd] *adj* asalariado,-a.

salary ['sælərɪ] *n* sueldo, salario.
▲ *pl* **salaries.**

sale [seɪl] *n* **1** *(act, transaction)* venta. **2** *(special offer)* rebajas *fpl*, liquidación *f*: **I bought it in a sale** *lo compré en las rebajas.*
▷ *n pl* **sales** *(amount sold)* venta, ventas *fpl*; *(reductions)* rebajas *fpl*. ■ **for sale** en venta. ‖ **«For sale»** *(sign on house, etc)* «Se vende». ‖ **on sale 1** *(available)* en venta, a la venta. **2** *(reduced)* rebajado,-a. ● **clearance sale** liquidación *f*. ‖ **sale goods** artículos *mpl* rebajados.

salesclerk ['seɪlzklɑːk] *n* US dependiente,-a.

salesgirl ['seɪlzgɜːl] *n* dependienta.

salesman ['seɪlzmən] *n* **1** *(gen)* vendedor *m*; *(in shop)* dependiente *m*. **2** *(travelling)* representante *m*.
▲ *pl* **salesmen** ['seɪlzmən].

salesroom ['seɪlzruːm] *n* US sala de subastas.

saleswoman ['seɪlzwʊmən] *n* **1** *(gen)* vendedora; *(in shop)* dependienta. **2** *(travelling)* representante *f*.
▲ *pl* **saleswomen** ['seɪlzwɪmɪn].

salient ['seɪlɪənt] *adj* sobresaliente, destacado,-a.

saline ['seɪlaɪn] *adj* salino,-a.

saliva [sə'laɪvə] *n* saliva.

salivary [sə'laɪvərɪ] *adj* salival.

salivate ['sælɪveɪt] *vi* salivar.

sallow ['sæləʊ] *adj* cetrino,-a.

sally ['sælɪ] *n (remark)* agudeza, réplica.
▲ *pl* **sallies.**

◊ **to sally forth / sally out** *vi* salir a buen paso.
▲ *pt & pp* **sallied**, *ger* **sallying.**

salmon ['sæmən] *n* **1** *(fish)* salmón *m*. **2** *(colour)* color *m* salmón.
▲ *pl* **salmon.**

salmonella [sælmə'nelə] *n* **1** *(bacteria)* salmonella. **2** *(food poisoning)* intoxicación *f*.

salmon-pink ['sæmən'pɪŋk] *adj* asalmonado,-a.

salon ['sælɒn] *n (shop)* salón *m*.

saloon [sə'luːn] *n* **1** US taberna, bar *m*. **2** *(public room)* sala; *(on ship)* salón *m*.

salt [sɔːlt] *n (gen)* sal *f*. ■ **to be the salt of the earth** ser la sal de la tierra. ‖ **to rub salt into the wounds** hurgar en la herida.
▷ *adj* salado,-a.
▷ *vt* **1** *(preserve, cure)* salar, conservar en sal, curar. **2** *(season)* echar sal a, salar.
▷ *n pl* **salts** sales *fpl*.

◊ **to salt away** *vt sep (money)* guardar.

saltcellar ['sɔːltseləʳ] *n* salero.

salted ['sɔːltɪd] *adj* salado,-a.

saltpeter [sɔːlt'piːtəʳ] *n* US → **saltpetre.**

saltpetre [sɔːlt'piːtəʳ] *n* salitre *m*.

saltwater ['sɔːltwɔːtəʳ] *adj* de agua salada.

salty ['sɔːltɪ] *adj* salado,-a.
▲ *comp* **saltier**, *superl* **saltiest.**

salubrious [sə'luːbrɪəs] *adj fml (health-giving)* salubre, sano,-a, saludable.

salutary ['sæljʊtᵊrɪ] *adj* beneficioso,-a.

salute [sə'luːt] *n* **1** MIL *(gesture)* saludo; *(firing of guns)* salva. **2** *(greeting)* saludo, salutación *f*.
▷ *vt (gen)* saludar.
▷ *vi* MIL saludar.

Salvadorian [sælvə'dɔːrɪən] *adj* salvadoreño,-a.
▷ *n* salvadoreño,-a.

salvage ['sælvɪdʒ] *n* **1** *(recovery)* salvamento, rescate *m*. **2** *(things recovered)* objetos *mpl* recuperados, material *m* recuperado.
▷ *vt* salvar, rescatar, recuperar.

salvation [sæl'veɪʃᵊn] *n* salvación *f*.

salve [sælv] *n* **1** *(ointment)* pomada, ungüento, bálsamo. **2** *(comfort)* alivio, bálsamo.
▷ *vt* **1** *(apply salve)* curar con pomada, curar. **2** *fml (soothe, appease)* aliviar.

salver ['sælvəʳ] *n* bandeja (de plata).

salvo ['sælvəʊ] *n (of guns, applause)* salva.
▲ *pl* **salvos** o **salvoes.**

samba ['sæmbə] *n (dance)* samba.

same [seɪm] *adj* **1** *(not different)* mismo,-a: **the same day** *el mismo día.* **2** *(alike)* mismo,-a, igual, idéntico,-a: **he's wearing the same tie as you** *lleva una corbata igual que la tuya.* ■ **at the same time 1** *(simultaneously)* a la vez, al mismo tiempo. **2** *(however)* sin embargo, aun así.
▷ *pron* **the same** lo mismo: **it won't be the same without you** *no será lo mismo sin ti.*
▷ *adv* **the same** igual, del mismo modo: **they talk the same** *hablan igual.* ■ **all the same** a pesar de todo. ‖ **it's all the same to me** me da igual. ‖ **the same as** igual que, como.

sameness ['seɪmnəs] *n* uniformidad *f*.

Samoa [sə'məʊə] *n* Samoa.

Samoan [sə'məʊən] *adj* samoano,-a.
▷ *n* **1** *(person)* samoano,-a. **2** *(language)* samoano.

sample ['sɑːmpᵊl] *n* **1** *(gen)* muestra. **2** *(of food, drink)* muestra, cata, degustación *f*.
▷ *vt* **1** *(place, activity)* probar. **2** *(dish)* probar, degustar; *(wine)* catar, probar, degustar.

sanatorium [sænə'tɔːrɪəm] *n* sanatorio.
▲ *pl* **sanatoriums** o **sanatoria** [sænə'tɔːrɪə].

sanctify ['sæŋktɪfaɪ] *vt* santificar, consagrar.
▲ *pt & pp* **sanctified**, *ger* **sanctifying.**

sanction ['sæŋkʃᵊn] *n* sanción *f*.
▷ *vt fml* sancionar.
▷ *n pl* **sanctions** POL *(measures)* sanciones *fpl*.

sanctity ['sæŋktətɪ] *n (sacredness)* santidad *f*.

sanctuary ['sæŋktjʊərɪ] *n* **1** REL *(sacred palce)* santuario. **2** *(gen)* refugio, protección *f*. **3** *(for animals)* reserva.
▲ *pl* **sanctuaries.**

sanctum ['sæŋktəm] *n* **1** *(holy place)* lugar *m* sagrado. **2** *fig* lugar *m* privado.

sand [sænd] *n (gen)* arena.
▷ *vt (smooth)* lijar (**down**, -).
▷ *n pl* **sands** *(beach)* playa *f sing*; *(sandbank)* banco *m sing* de arena.

sandal ['sændᵊl] *n* sandalia.

sandalwood ['sændᵊlwʊd] *n* BOT sándalo.

sandbag ['sændbæg] *n* saco terrero.

sandbank ['sændbæŋk] *n* banco de arena.

sandcastle ['sænkaːsəl] *n* castillo de arena.

sandblast ['sændblɑːst] *vt* limpiar con un chorro de arena.

sander ['sændəʳ] *n (machine)* lijadora.

sandpaper ['sændpeɪpəʳ] *n* papel *m* de lija.
▷ *vt* lijar.
sandpit ['sændpɪt] *n* GB cajón *m* de arena.
sandstone ['sændstəʊn] *n* arenisca.
sandstorm ['sændstɔːm] *n* tempestad *f* de arena.
sandwich ['sænwɪdʒ] *n (French bread)* bocadillo; *(sliced bread)* sándwich *m*. ● **sandwich board** cartel *m* anunciador. ‖ **sandwich course** GB curso teórico-práctico.
▲ *pl* **sandwiches.**
▷ *vt* encajonar (**between**, entre).
sandy ['sændɪ] *adj* **1** *(beach, etc)* arenoso,-a, de arena. **2** *(hair)* rubio,-a oscuro,-a.
▲ *comp* **sandier**, *superl* **sandiest.**
sane [seɪn] *adj* **1** *(person)* cuerdo,-a; *(mind)* sano,-a. **2** *fig (solution, decision, etc)* sensato,-a.
sang [sæŋ] *pt* → **sing.**
sanguine ['sæŋgwɪn] *adj fml* optimista.
sanitary ['sænɪtᵊrɪ] *adj* **1** *(to do with health)* sanitario,-a, de sanidad. **2** *(hygienic)* higiénico,-a. ● **sanitary napkin / sanitary pad / sanitary towel** compresa.
sanitation [sænɪ'teɪʃᵊn] *n (public health)* sanidad *f* (pública); *(hygiene)* higiene *f*.
sank [sæŋk] *pt* → **sink.**
Santa Claus [sæntə'klɔːz] *n* Papá *m* Noel.
sanity ['sænətɪ] *n* **1** *(health of mind)* cordura. **2** *(good sense)* sensatez *f*, juicio.
sap¹ [sæp] *n* **1** BOT savia. **2** US *fam (person)* inocentón,-ona.
sap² [sæp] *vt (weaken)* debilitar, agotar, minar.
▲ *pt & pp* **sapped**, *ger* **sapping.**
sapling ['sæplɪŋ] *n* BOT árbol *m* joven.
sapphire ['sæfaɪəʳ] *n* zafiro.
sarcasm ['sɑːkæzᵊm] *n* sarcasmo, sorna.
sarcastic [sɑː'kæstɪk] *adj* sarcástico,-a.
sarcophagus [sɑː'kɒfəgəs] *n* sarcófago.
▲ *pl* **sarcophaguses** o **sarcophagi** [sɑː'kɒfəgaɪ].
sardine [sɑː'diːn] *n* sardina. ■ **to be packed like sardines** estar como sardinas en lata.
sat [sæt] *pt & pp* → **sit.**
sardonic [sɑː'dɒnɪk] *adj* sardónico,-a.
sarsaparilla [sæspə'rɪlə] *n* zarzaparrilla.
sash¹ [sæʃ] *n (waistband)* faja.
sash² [sæʃ] *n (frame)* marco de ventana.
sassy ['sæsɪ] *adj* **1** US *fam (rude)* descarado,-a, fresco,-a. **2** US *fam (bold)* atrevido,-a.
▲ *comp* **sassier**, *superl* **sassiest.**
satanic [sə'tænɪk] *adj* satánico,-a.
satchel ['sætʃᵊl] *n* cartera, mochila *(de colegial)*.
satellite ['sætəlaɪt] *n* satélite *m*. ● **satellite dish** TV antena parabólica. ‖ **satellite television** televisión *f* vía satélite.
satin ['sætɪn] *n* satén *m*, raso.
▷ *adj (made of satin)* de satén, de raso.
satire ['sætaɪəʳ] *n* sátira.
satirical [sə'tɪrɪkᵊl] *adj* satírico,-a.
satirist ['sætərɪst] *n* escritor,-ra satírico,-a.
satirize ['sætəraɪz] *vt* satirizar.
satisfaction [sætɪs'fækʃᵊn] *n* satisfacción *f*.
satisfactory [sætɪs'fæktᵊrɪ] *adj* **1** satisfactorio,-a. **2** EDUC suficiente.
satisfied ['sætɪsfaɪd] *adj* **1** satisfecho,-a, complacido,-a, contento,-a. **2** *(convinced)* convencido,-a.
satisfy ['sætɪsfaɪ] *vt* **1** *(please, make happy)* satisfacer, complacer, contentar: **does nothing satisfy you?** *¿no hay nada que te satisfaga?* **2** *(fulfil)* satisfacer. **3** *(convince)* convencer.
▲ *pt & pp* **satisfied**, *ger* **satisfying.**
satisfying ['sætɪsfaɪɪŋ] *adj (gen)* satisfactorio,-a; *(meal)* bueno,-a, delicioso,-a.
satsuma [sæt'suːmə] *n* mandarina.
saturate ['sætʃəreɪt] *vt* **1** *(fill)* saturar (**with**, de). **2** *(soak)* empapar (**with**, de).
saturated ['sætʃəreɪtɪd] *adj* **1** *(full)* saturado,-a. **2** *(wet)* empapado,-a.
saturation [sætʃə'reɪʃᵊn] *n* saturación *f*.
Saturday ['sætədɪ] *n* sábado: **next Saturday** *el próximo sábado;* **on Saturday morning** *el sábado por la mañana*.
Saturn ['sætɜːn] *n* Saturno.
sauce [sɔːs] *n* **1** CULIN salsa: **fish in parsley sauce** *pescado con salsa de perejil.* **2** *fam (cheek)* frescura, descaro.
saucepan ['sɔːspən] *n* cazo, cacerola.
saucer ['sɔːsəʳ] *n* platillo.
saucy [s'ɔːsɪ] *adj fam* descarado,-a, fresco,-a.
▲ *comp* **saucier**, *superl* **sauciest.**
Saudi ['saʊdɪ] *adj* saudí, saudita.
▷ *n* saudí *mf*, saudita *mf*. ● **Saudi Arabia** Arabia Saudita.
sauna ['sɔːnə] *n* sauna.
saunter ['sɔːntəʳ] *vi* pasear, pasearse.
sausage ['sɒsɪdʒ] *n (uncooked)* salchicha; *(cred)* salchichón *m*; *(spicy)* chorizo.
sauté ['səʊteɪ] *vt* saltear.
▲ *pt & pp* **sautéed** o **sautéd**, *ger* **sautéing.**
▷ *adj* salteado,-a.
savage ['sævɪdʒ] *adj* **1** *(ferocious)* feroz; *(cruel)* cruel; *(violent)* violento,-a, salvaje: **a savage attack** *un ataque duro.* **2** *pej (primitive)* salvaje, primitivo,-a.
▷ *n pej* salvaje *mf*.
▷ *vt* **1** *(animal)* embestir (contra). **2** *fig (criticize)* atacar violentamente, arremeter contra.
savageness ['sævɪdʒnəs] *n (ferocity)* ferocidad *f*; *(cruelty)* brutalidad *f*; *(violence)* violencia.
savanna [sə'vænə] *n* sabana.
save [seɪv] *vt* **1** *(rescue)* salvar (**from**, de), rescatar (**from**, de); *(preserve)* salvar (**from**, de): **you saved my life!** *¡me has salvado la vida!* **2** *(not spend - money)* ahorrar: **I've saved $200 towards my holidays** *he ahorrado 200 dólares para las vacaciones.* **3** *(not waste - fuel, work, money)* ahorrar; *(time)* ahorrar, ahorrarse, ganar: **we must all make an effort to save water** *todos debemos esforzarnos por ahorrar agua.* **4** *(keep, put by - food, strength)* guardar, reservar; *(- stamps)* coleccionar. **5** *(avoid)* evitar, ahorrar. **6** SP *(goal)* parar. **7** COMPUT guardar, archivar.
▷ *vi (not spend)* ahorrar (**up**, -).
▷ *n* SP parada.
▷ *prep fml (except)* salvo, excepto.
⊙ **to save on** *vt insep* ahorrar.
saver ['seɪvəʳ] *n (person)* ahorrador,-ra.
saving ['seɪvɪŋ] *n (of time, money)* ahorro, economía.
▷ *n pl* **savings** ahorros *mpl*. ● **savings account** cuenta de ahorros.
savior ['seɪvjəʳ] *n* US → **saviour.**
saviour ['seɪvjəʳ] *n* salvador,-ra.
savor ['seɪvəʳ] *n* US → **savour.**
savory ['seɪvᵊrɪ] *adj* US → **savoury.**
savour ['seɪvəʳ] *n* sabor *m*, gusto.
▷ *vt* saborear.
⊙ **to savour of** *vt insep* saber a, oler a.

savoury ['seɪvərɪ] *adj* 1 *(salty)* salado,-a; *(tasty)* sabroso,-a. 2 *(respectable, wholesome)* saludable, sano,-a.
▷ *n* entrante *m* salado, canapé *m.*

saw[1] [sɔː] *n (tool)* sierra, serrucho.
▷ *vt* serrar, aserrar, cortar con una sierra: **they sawed the tree down** *talaron el árbol con una sierra.*
▷ *vi* serrar, cortar.
▲ *pt* **sawed**, *pp* **sawed** o **sawn** [sɔːn].

saw[2] [sed] *pt* ⟶ **see.**

sawdust ['sɔːdʌst] *n* serrín *m.*

sawn [sɔːn] *pp* ⟶ **saw**[1].

sawmill ['sɔːmɪl] *n* aserradero, serrería.

sax [sæks] *n fam* saxo.

saxophone ['sæksəfəʊn] *n* saxofón *m.*

saxophonist [sæk'sɒfənɪst] *n* saxofonista *mf*, saxo *mf.*

say [seɪ] *vt* 1 *(gen)* decir; *(express)* expresar; *(state)* afirmar, declarar: **what did he say?** *¿qué dijo?, ¿qué ha dicho?* 2 *(prayer)* rezar; *(poem, lines)* recitar. 3 *(newspaper, sign, etc)* decir; *(clock, meter, etc)* marcar: **what does the guidebook say?** *¿qué dice la guía?, ¿qué pone en la guía?* 4 *(think)* pensar, opinar, decir: **I say we keep looking** *creo que deberíamos seguir buscando.* 5 *(suppose)* suponer, poner, decir: **come round at, say, 8.00 pm** *pásate hacia las 8.00, ¿te parece?* ■ **it is said that...** dicen que..., se dice que.... | **not to say...** por no decir.... | **that is to say** es decir. | **to say to** os decir para sí.
▲ *pt & pp* **said** [sed].
▷ *n* opinión *f.*

saying ['seɪɪŋ] *n* dicho, decir *m.*

say-so ['seɪsəʊ] *n fam (permission)* visto bueno, aprobación *f*, permiso *f.*

scab [skæb] *n* 1 MED costra, postilla. 2 *fam pej (blackleg)* esquirol *m.*

scabby ['skæbɪ] *adj* MED lleno,-a de costras.
▲ *comp* **scabbier**, *superl* **scabbiest.**

scabies ['skeɪbiːz] *n* MED sarna.

scaffold ['skæfəʊld] *n* 1 *(framework)* andamio. 2 *(for execution)* patíbulo, cadalso.

scaffolding ['skæfəldɪŋ] *n* andamiaje *m.*

scald [skɔːld] *n* escaldadura.
▷ *vt* escaldar.

scalding ['skɔːldɪŋ] *adj (extremely hot)* hirviendo.

scale[1] [skeɪl] *n* 1 *(of fish, reptile)* escama. 2 *(on skin)* escama.
▷ *vt (fish)* escamar, quitar las escamas a.
⊙ **to scale off** *vi* desconcharse.

scale[2] [skeɪl] *n* 1 *(measure)* escala: **a metric scale** *una escala métrica.* 2 *(size, amount)* escala, magnitud *f.* 3 MUS escala. ■ **on a large scale** a gran escala. ● **scale model** maqueta.
▷ *vt (climb up)* escalar.
⊙ **to scale down** *vt sep* reducir proporcionalmente.
⊙ **to scale up** *vt sep* ampliar proporcionalmente.

scale[3] [skeɪl] *n (pan)* platillo.
▷ *vi* SP *(weigh)* pesar.
▷ *n pl* **scales** *(for weighing in shop, kitchen)* balanza; *(bathroom, large weights)* báscula.

scallop ['skɒləp] *n* 1 *(mollusc)* vieira, concha de peregrino. 2 SEW festón *m.*

scalp [skælp] *n* ANAT cuero cabelludo.

scalpel ['skælpəl] *n* 1 *(surgeon's)* bisturí *m*; *(for dissecting)* escalpelo. 2 *(tool)* escoplo, gubia.

scam [skæm] *n fam* timo, estafa, chanchullo.

scamp [skæmp] *n fam* granuja *mf.*

scamper ['skæmpər] *vi* corretear.

scampi ['skæmpɪ] *n* colas *fpl* de cigala rebozadas.

scan [skæn] *vt* 1 *(examine)* escrutar, escudriñar. 2 *(glance at)* echar un vistazo a. 3 TECH *(with radar)* explorar. 4 MED, INFORM escanear.
▲ *pt & pp* **scanned**, *ger* **scanning.**
▷ *n* 1 TECH *(with radar)* exploración *f.* 2 MED *(gen)* exploración *f* ultrasónica; *(in gynaecology, etc)* ecografía.

scandal ['skændəl] *n* 1 *(outrage)* escándalo; *(disgrace)* vergüenza. 2 *(gossip)* chismorreo.

scandalize ['skændəlaɪz] *vt* escandalizar.

scandalous ['skændələs] *adj* escandaloso,-a.

scandalously ['skændələslɪ] *adv* escandalosamente, de manera escandalosa.

scanner ['skænər] *n* 1 TECH *(radar)* antena direccional. 2 MED, INFORM escáner *m.*

scant [skænt] *adj* escaso,-a.

scanty ['skæntɪ] *adj* escaso,-a.
▲ *comp* **scantier**, *superl* **scantiest.**

scapegoat ['skeɪpgəʊt] *n fig* cabeza de turco.

scapula ['skæpjʊlə] *n* ANAT escápula.

scar [skɑːr] *n* 1 cicatriz *f.* 2 *fig* marca, señal *f.*
▷ *vt* 1 *(leave scar)* dejar una cicatriz. 2 *fig* marcar, señalar.
▲ *pt & pp* **scarred**, *ger* **scarring.**

scarce [skeəs] *adj (not plentiful)* escaso,-a. ■ **to make** os **scarce** esfumarse, largarse.
▷ *adv lit* apenas.

scarcely ['skeəslɪ] *adv* 1 *(hardly)* apenas: **I scarcely know them** *apenas los conozco.* 2 *(surely not)* ni mucho menos.

scarcity ['skeəsətɪ] *n* escasez *f*, falta.

scare [skeər] *n* 1 *(fright)* susto: **what a scare you gave me!** *¡vaya susto me has dado!* 2 *(widespread alarm)* alarma, pánico.
▷ *vt* asustar, espantar: **did I scare you?** *¿te he asustado?*
▷ *vi* asustarse, espantarse.
⊙ **to scare away / scare off** *vt sep* espantar, ahuyentar.

scarecrow ['skeəkrəʊ] *n* espantapájaros *m.*

scared ['skeəd] *adj* asustado,-a, espantado,-a. ■ **to be scared** tener miedo (**of**, a/de): **I'm scared of spiders** *tengo miedo a las arañas, las arañas me dan miedo.*

scarf [skɑːf] *n (small)* pañuelo; *(silk)* fular *m*; *(long, woollen)* bufanda.
▲ *pl* **scarfs** o **scarves** [skɑːvz].

scarlet ['skɑːlət] *adj* escarlata.
▷ *n* escarlata *m.*

scary ['skeərɪ] *adj fam (situation, etc)* espantoso,-a; *(film, story)* de miedo, de terror.
▲ *comp* **scarier**, *superl* **scariest.**

scathing ['skeɪðɪŋ] *adj* mordaz, cáustico,-a.

scatter ['skætər] *vt* 1 *(crowd, birds)* dispersar. 2 *(papers, cushions, etc)* esparcir, desparramar; *(money)* desparramar, derrochar.
▷ *vi* dispersarse.

scatterbrained ['skætəbreɪnd] *adj (person)* despistado,-a, alocado,-a.

scattered ['skætəd] *adj* esparcido,-a, disperso,-a.

scattering ['skætərɪŋ] *n (singular)* un poco; *(plural)* unos,-as pocos,-as, algunos,-as: **a scattering of snow** *un poco de nieve.*

scatty ['skætɪ] *adj (scatterbrained)* despistado,-a.
▲ *comp* **scattier**, *superl* **scattiest.**

scavenge ['skævɪndʒ] *vi* **1** *(animal, bird - search)* rebuscar (for, -); *(- feed on)* comer (on, -). **2** *(person - search)* hurgar, escarbar; *(find)* encontrar en la basura: that tramp scavenges through the dustbins (US trashcans) *aquel vagabundo hurga en la basura.*

scavenger ['skævɪndʒəʳ] *n* **1** *(animal)* carroñero. **2** *(person)* rebuscador,-ra, trapero,-a.

scenario [sɪ'nɑːrɪəʊ] *n* **1** *(of film)* guion *m*; *(in theatre)* argumento. **2** *(situation)* (posible) situación *f*, panorama *m*. ▲ *pl* scenarios.

scene [siːn] *n* **1** *(place)* lugar *m*, escenario; *(sight, picture)* escena: the scene of the crime *el lugar del crimen.* **2** *(in play, book)* escena. **3** *(stage setting)* decorado, escenario. **4** *(emotional outburst)* escena, escándalo. **5** *(sphere)* ámbito, mundo, panorama *m*. ■ to come on the scene llegar, aparecer. | to set the scene **1** *(describe)* describir la escena. **2** *(prepare, help)* preparar el terreno.

scenery ['siːnᵊrɪ] *n* **1** *(landscape)* paisaje *m*. **2** THEAT *(on stage)* decorado.

scenic ['siːnɪk] *adj* **1** *(picturesque)* pintoresco,-a. **2** THEAT escénico,-a.

scent [sent] *n* **1** *(gen)* olor *m*; *(pleasant smell)* aroma *m*. **2** *(perfume)* perfume *m*. **3** *(track, trail)* pista, rastro.
▷ *vt* **1** *(animal)* olfatear. **2** *fig (suspect)* presentir, intuir. **3** *(perfume)* perfumar (with, de).

scepter ['septəʳ] *n* US → sceptre.

sceptic ['skeptɪk] *n* escéptico,-a.

sceptical ['skeptɪkᵊl] *adj* escéptico,-a.

scepticism ['skeptɪsɪzᵊm] *n* escepticismo.

sceptre ['septəʳ] *n* cetro.

schedule ['ʃedjuːl, US 'skedjʊəl] *n* **1** *(programme)* programa *m*: a work schedule *un programa de trabajo.* **2** *(list - gen)* lista. **3** US *(timetable)* horario. ■ on schedule **1** *(flight)* a la hora (prevista). **2** *(work)* al día. | to be ahead of schedule ir adelantado,-a. | to be behind schedule ir retrasado,-a.
▷ *vt* programar, fijar.

scheduled ['ʃedjuːld, US 'skedʒʊəld] *adj* previsto,-a, programado,-a.

schematic [skiː'mætɪk] *adj* esquemático,-a.

scheme [skiːm] *n* **1** *(plan)* plan *m*; *(project)* proyecto. **2** *(system, order)* sistema *m*, orden *m*; *(arrangement)* disposición *f*, combinación *f*: a colour scheme *una combinación de colores.* **3** *(plot)* complot *m*, conspiración *f*.
▷ *vi (plot)* conspirar, intrigar, confabularse.
▷ *vt (plan deviously)* tramar, maquinar.

scheming ['skiːmɪŋ] *adj* intrigante.

schism ['skɪzᵊm] *n* cisma *m*.

schizophrenia [skɪtsəʊ'friːnɪə] *n* esquizofrenia.

schizophrenic [skɪtsəʊ'frenɪk] *adj* esquizofrénico,-a.

schlep [ʃlep] *vt* US *fam (drag)* arrastrar. ▲ *pt & pp* schlepped, *ger* schlepping.

schmaltz [ʃmælts] *n fam* sentimentalismo.

scholar ['skɒləʳ] *n* **1** *(learned person)* erudito,-a; *(specialist)* especialista *mf*: Latin scholar *latinista.* **2** *(scholarship holder)* becario,-a. **3** *(good learner)* estudiante *mf*.;

scholarship ['skɒləʃɪp] *n* **1** *(grant, award)* beca. **2** *(learning)* erudición *f*.

scholastic [skə'læstɪk] *adj* escolar.

school¹ [skuːl] *n* **1** *(gen)* escuela, colegio: what are you going to do when you leave school? *¿qué harás cuando dejes el colegio?* **2** *(lessons)* clase *f*: let's meet after school *quedemos después de clase.* **3** *(university department)* facultad *f*. **4** *(group of artists, etc)* escuela: the Dutch school of painting *la escuela pictórica holandesa.* ● school age edad *f* escolar.
▷ *vt* **1** *(teach)* enseñar; *(train)* educar, formar. **2** *(discipline)* disciplinar.

school² [skuːl] *n (of fish)* banco.

schoolbook ['skuːlbʊk] *n* libro de texto.

schoolboy ['skuːlbɔɪ] *n* alumno, escolar *m*.

schoolchild ['skuːltʃaɪld] *n* alumno,-a, escolar *mf*. ▲ *pl* schoolchildren ['skuːltʃɪldrən].

schooldays ['skuːldeɪz] *n pl* años *mpl* de colegio, tiempos *mpl* del colegio.

schoolgirl ['skuːlgɜːl] *n* alumna, escolar *f*.

schooling ['skuːlɪŋ] *n* educación *f*, estudios *mpl*, escolaridad *f*.

school-leaver ['skuːlliːvəʳ] *n alumno,-a que está a punto de dejar la escuela.*

schoolmarm ['skuːlmɑːm] *n* **1** *fam* marimandona, sargenta; **2** US *fam (schoolmistress)* profesora, maestra.

schoolmaster ['skuːlmɑːstəʳ] *n (secondary school)* profesor *m*; *(primary school)* maestro.

schoolmistress ['skuːlmɪstrəs] *n (secondary school)* profesora; *(primary school)* maestra.

schoolroom ['skuːlruːm] *n* aula, clase *f*.

schoolteacher ['skuːltiːtʃəʳ] *n (secondary school)* profesor,-ra; *(primary school)* maestro,-a.

schooner ['skuːnəʳ] *n* **1** MAR goleta. **2** *(glass - for sherry)* copa; *(- for beer)* jarra.

sciatica [saɪ'ætɪkə] *n* MED ciática.

science ['saɪəns] *n* **1** *(gen)* ciencia. **2** *(subject)* ciencias *fpl*. ● science fiction ciencia ficción.

scientific [saɪən'tɪfɪk] *adj* científico,-a.

scientist ['saɪəntɪst] *n* científico,-a.

scintillating ['sɪntɪleɪtɪŋ] *adj* brillante.

scissors ['sɪzəz] *n pl* tijeras *fpl*. ■ a pair of scissors unas tijeras.

scoff¹ [skɒf] *vi (mock)* burlarse (at, de).
▷ *n pl* scoffs mofas *fpl*, burlas *fpl*.

scoff² [skɒf] *vt fam (eat greedily)* zamparse.

scold [skəʊld] *vt* reñir, regañar.

scone [skəʊn, skɒn] *n* CULIN bollo *(que se suele comer con mantequilla, mermelada, nata, etc)*.

scoop [skuːp] *n* **1** *(for flour, rice, etc)* pala. **2** *(amount)* palada, cucharada. **3** *(news story)* primicia.
▷ *vt* **1** *(take out)* sacar con una pala. **2** *(beat rival)* vencer, pisar; *(get news first)* dar la primicia. **3** *(win)* ganar; *(make profit)* forrarse.
⊙ **to scoop out** *vt sep (take out)* sacar con pala.
⊙ **to scoop up** *vt sep* recoger, levantar.

scooter ['skuːtəʳ] *n (child's)* patinete *m*, patineta; *(motorized)* escúter *m*, Vespa.

scope [skəʊp] *n* **1** *(area, range - gen)* alcance *m*; *(- of book, undertaking)* ámbito; *(ability, field)* competencia, campo: that is beyond the scope of this report *eso queda fuera del alcance de este informe.* **2** *(opportunity)* oportunidad *f*; *(room)* posibilidades *fpl*.

scorch [skɔːtʃ] *vt* **1** *(singe)* chamuscar, socarrar. **2** *(burn)* quemar, abrasar.
▷ *vi* **1** *(singe)* chamuscarse. **2** GB *fam (travel fast)* ir a toda velocidad.

scorched [skɔːtʃt] *adj* quemado,-a, abrasado,-a.

scorcher ['skɔ:tʃəʳ] *n fam (hot day)* día *m* abrasador.

scorching ['skɔ:tʃɪŋ] *adj* abrasador,-ra.

score [skɔ:ʳ] *n* **1** SP *(gen)* tanteo; *(in golf, cards)* puntuación *f*: **what's the score?** *¿cómo van?* **2** *(in exam, test)* nota, calificación *f*. **3** MUS *(written version)* partitura; *(of film, play, etc)* música. ■ **by the score** muchísimos,-as. | **on more scores than one** en más de un sentido. | **on that score** por lo que se refiere a eso. | **to keep the score** seguir el marcador. | **to know the score** estar al tanto. | **to pay/settle an old score** saldar cuentas pendientes.

▷ *vt* **1** SP *(goal)* marcar, hacer, meter; *(point)* ganar; *(run)* hacer, realizar: **he scored the winning goal** *marcó el gol decisivo*. **2** *(in exam, test)* sacar, obtener, conseguir. **3** *(give points to)* dar, puntuar: **this question scores 10 points** *esta pregunta vale 10 puntos*. **4** *(achieve, succeed)* tener, conseguir. **5** MUS *(write)* componer; *(arrange)* hacer un arreglo de, arreglar.

▷ *vi* **1** SP *(gen)* marcar (un tanto); *(goal)* marcar (un gol); *(point)* puntuar, conseguir puntos. **2** *(record points, etc)* llevar el marcador, tantear. **3** *(have success)* tener éxito.

▷ *n pl* **scores** *(very many)* muchísimos,-as.

⊙ **to score off** *vt insep* triunfar a costa de.

⊙ **to score out/through** *vt sep* tachar, rayar.

scoreboard ['skɔ:bɔ:d] *n* marcador *m*.

scorecard ['skɔ:kɑ:d] *n* SP *(golf)* tarjeta; *(at match, race)* ficha.

scorer ['skɔ:rəʳ] *n* **1** *(scorekeeper)* encargado,-a del marcador. **2** *(goal striker)* goleador,-ra.

scorn [skɔ:n] *n* desdén *m*, desprecio.

▷ *vt* desdeñar, despreciar, menospreciar.

Scorpio ['skɔ:pɪəʊ] *n* Escorpión *mf*.

scorpion ['skɔ:pɪən] *n* escorpión *m*, alacrán *m*.

Scot [skɒt] *n* escocés,-esa.

Scotland ['skɒtlənd] *n* Escocia.

Scottish ['skɒtɪʃ] *adj* escocés,-esa.

scotch [skɒtʃ] *vt (idea, plan)* frustrar, echar por tierra; *(rumour)* acallar, poner fin a.

scour[1] [skaʊəʳ] *vt (search)* recorrer, registrar.

scour[2] [skaʊəʳ] *vt (clean)* fregar, restregar.

scourer ['skaʊrəʳ] *n* estropajo.

scourge [skɜ:dʒ] *n* **1** *(whip)* azote *m*. **2** *fig (thing)* calamidad *f*; *(person)* verdugo.

▷ *vt* **1** *(flog)* azotar. **2** *fml fig* afligir, azotar.

scout [skaʊt] *n* **1** MIL *(person)* explorador,-ra; *(plane)* avión *m* de reconocimiento. **2** *(boy)* scout *m*.

▷ *vi* **1** MIL reconocer el terreno. **2** *(look for)* buscar (**about/around**, -).

scoutmaster ['skaʊtmɑ:stəʳ] *n* jefe *m* de un grupo de scouts.

scowl [skaʊl] *vi* fruncir el ceño.

▷ *n* ceño (fruncido).

scrabble ['skræbəl] *vi (among stones, etc)* escarbar; *(in bag, etc)* hurgar; *(on floor, etc)* rebuscar.

scraggy ['skrægɪ] *adj pej* flacucho,-a.

▲ *comp* **scraggier**, *superl* **scraggiest**.

scram [skræm] *vi fam* largarse: **scram!** *¡lárgate!*

▲ *pt & pp* **scrammed**, *ger* **scramming**.

scramble ['skræmbəl] *n* **1** *(difficult climb)* subida escabrosa; *(difficult walk)* caminata difícil. **2** *(struggle)* lucha, pelea; *(confusion)* confusión *f*, barullo.

▷ *vi* **1** *(climb)* trepar (**over**, por) (**up**, a), subir gateando; *(crawl)* gatear, arrastrarse; *(clamber)* moverse rápidamente: **the children scrambled over the rocks** *los niños gatearon por las rocas*. **2** *(struggle)* pelearse (**for**, por/para), luchar (**for**, para).

▷ *vt* **1** *(mix, jumble)* revolver, mezclar. **2** *(eggs)* revolver.

scrambled eggs [skræmbəld 'egz] *n pl* huevos revueltos.

scrap[1] [skræp] *n* **1** *(of paper, cloth, etc)* trozo, trocito, pedazo; *(of news, conversation)* fragmento, migaja. **2** *(of metal)* chatarra. **3** *(in negatives)* pizca, ápice *m*.

▷ *vt* **1** *(throw away)* desechar; *(cars, etc)* desguazar. **2** *fig (idea)* descartar; *(plan)* abandonar.

▷ *n pl* **scraps** *(gen)* restos *mpl*.

▲ *pt & pp* **scrapped**, *ger* **scrapping**.

scrap[2] [skræp] *n fam (fight)* pelea.

scrapbook ['skræpbʊk] *n* álbum *m* de recortes.

scrape [skreɪp] *n* **1** *(act)* raspado; *(sound)* chirrido. **2** *fam (fix, jam)* lío, apuro, aprieto.

▷ *vt* **1** *(surface, paint, etc)* raspar (**away/off**, -), rascar (**away/off**, -): **he scraped the paint off the door** *raspó la pintura de la puerta*. **2** *(graze skin)* arañarse, hacerse un rasguño en. **3** *(rub against)* rozar, raspar, rascar.

▷ *vi* **1** *(grate)* chirriar. **2** *(rub against)* raspar, rozar. **3** *(economize)* hacer economías, ahorrar.

⊙ **to scrape along / scrape by** *vi* ir tirando, arreglárselas, apañárselas.

⊙ **to scrape in** *vi (job, university)* entrar por los pelos; *(political party)* ganar por los pelos.

⊙ **to scrape through** *vt insep (exam)* aprobar de chiripa; *(round of competition)* pasar por los pelos.

⊙ **to scrape together / scrape up** *vt sep* reunir a duras penas, ir arañando.

scraper ['skreɪpəʳ] *n (tool)* rasqueta.

scrapheap ['skræphi:p] *n* vertedero.

scraping ['skreɪpɪŋ] *n pl* raspaduras *fpl*.

scrappy ['skræpɪ] *adj (report, speech)* deshilvanado,-a; *(book, structure)* incompleto,-a, fragmentario,-a.

▲ *comp* **scrappier**, *superl* **scrappiest**.

scrapyard ['skræpjɑ:d] *n* desguace *m*.

scratch [skrætʃ] *n* **1** *(on skin)* arañazo, rasguño; *(on paintwork, furniture)* arañazo, raspadura, marca, raya *m*: **there's a scratch on this record** *este disco está rayado*. **2** *(noise)* chirrido.

▷ *adj (improvised)* improvisado,-a.

▷ *vt* **1** *(with nail, claw)* arañar, rasguñar; *(paintwork, furniture, record)* rayar. **2** *(part of body)* rascar: **she scratched her leg** *se rascó la pierna*.

▷ *vi* **1** *(animal)* arañar, rascar, rasguñar; *(pen)* raspear; *(wool, sweater, towel)* raspar, picar. **2** *(itch)* rascarse.

▲ *comp* **scratchier**, *superl* **scratchiest**.

⊙ **to scratch out** *vt sep (erase)* tachar, borrar.

scrawl [skrɔ:l] *n (writing)* garabato, garabatos *mpl*.

▷ *vt* garabatear, garrapatear.

scrawny ['skrɔ:nɪ] *adj pej* flacucho,-a.

▲ *comp* **scrawnier**, *superl* **scrawniest**.

scream [skri:m] *n* **1** *(of pain, fear)* grito, chillido, alarido; *(of laughter)* carcajada. **2** *fig (screech)* chirrido. **3** *fam (funny person)* persona divertida, persona graciosa; *(funny thing)* cosa divertida: **your cousin's a scream** *tu primo es la monda, tu primo es divertidísimo*.

▷ *vt* **1** gritar, decir a gritos, vocear: **he screamed out a warning** *dio un aviso a gritos*.

▷ *vi* **1** *(gen)* gritar, berrear, chillar, pegar un grito; *(wind, siren, etc)* aullar: **she screamed for help** *pidió socorro a*

gritos; **he was screaming with laughter** *se tronchaba de risa.* **2** *fig (need)* pedir (a gritos), clamar (a gritos).
screech [skriːtʃ] *n (of person)* grito, alarido, chillido; *(of tyres, brakes, birds, etc)* chirrido; *(of siren)* aullido. ● **screech owl** lechuza.
▷ *vt* gritar, decir a gritos, chillar.
▷ *vi (person)* chillar; *(tyres, brakes, bird, etc)* chirriar; *(siren)* aullar; *(gate)* rechinar.
screen [skriːn] *n* **1** *(partition)* biombo, mampara. **2** *(for window)* alambrera, mosquitera, mosquitero. **3** *(protection, cover)* cortina, pantalla: **a screen of trees** *una cortina de árboles.* **4** *(of TV, for projection)* pantalla. **5** *(cinema in complex)* sala.
▷ *vt* **1** *(protect, shelter)* proteger (**from**, de), abrigar; *(hide, conceal)* tapar, ocultar: **she screened her face with her hand** *se tapó la cara con la mano.* **2** *fig (protect - gen)* proteger, abrigar, amparar; *(- criminal)* encubrir. **3** *(test)* investigar. **4** *(film - gen)* proyectar; *(- on TV)* emitir.
▷ *n* **the screen** la pantalla, el cine.
⊙ **to screen off** *vt insep* aislar, separar (con un biombo/una mampara).
⊙ **to screen out** *vt sep* eliminar, rechazar.
screening ['skriːnɪŋ] *n* **1** *(of film)* proyección *f*; *(on TV)* emisión *f*. **2** MED exploración *f*. **3** *(of candidates, etc)* selección *f*, investigación *f*.
screenplay ['skriːnpleɪ] *n* guion *m*.
screensaver ['skriːnseɪvəʳ] *n* salvapantallas *m*.
screenwriter ['skriːnraɪtəʳ] *n* guionista *mf*.
screw [skruː] *n* **1** *(metal pin)* tornillo. **2** *(propeller)* hélice *f*. **3** *(turn)* vuelta.
▷ *vt* **1** *(fasten with screws)* atornillar; *(tighten)* enroscar, apretar: **screw the two pieces together** *une las dos piezas con tornillos.* **2** *(crumple)* arrugar. **3** *(cheat, swindle)* timar; *(overcharge)* clavar; *(get money out of)* sacar.
▷ *vi (turn, tighten)* atornillarse, enroscarse.
⊙ **to screw up** *vt sep* **1** *(paper)* arrugar; *(face)* torcer; *(eyes)* cerrar, entornar. **2** *sl (ruin - interview, exam)* cagarla; *(- plans)* fastidiar.
▷ *vi sl (make a mess)* meter la pata, cagarla.
screwball ['skruːbɔːl] *n* US *fam (crazy person)* excéntrico,-a, chiflado,-a, loco,-a.
screwdriver ['skruːdraɪvəʳ] *n (tool)* destornillador *m*.
screw-top ['skruːtɒp] *adj* con tapa de rosca.
screwy ['skruːɪ] *adj fam (crazy)* loco,-a, excéntrico,-a.
▲ *comp* **screwier**, *superl* **screwiest**.
scribble ['skrɪbᵊl] *n* garabato, garabatos *mpl*.
▷ *vt* garabatear, garrapatear.
scribe [skraɪb] *n* **1** *(copier)* escribiente *mf*, amanuense *mf*. **2** *(in Biblical times)* escriba *m*.
scrimp [skrɪmp] *vi* hacer economías, escatimar (**on**, en).
script [skrɪpt] *n* **1** *(of film, etc)* guion *m*. **2** *(writing)* escritura; *(text)* texto; *(handwriting)* letra.
scripture ['skrɪptʃəʳ] *n* escritura, escrito.
scriptwriter ['skrɪptraɪtəʳ] *n* guionista *mf*.
scroll [skrəʊl] *n f* **1** *(parchment)* pergamino. **2** COMPUT barra de desplazamiento.
▷ *vi* COMPUT ir, desplazarse.
⊙ **to scroll down** *vi* COMPUT desplazarse hacia abajo.
⊙ **to scroll up** *vi* COMPUT desplazarse hacia arriba.
scrooge [skruːdʒ] *n fam pej* tacaño,-a.
scrotum ['skrəʊtəm] *n* ANAT escroto.
▲ *pl* **scrotums** o **scrota** ['skrəʊtə].
scrounge [skraʊndʒ] *vi fam* gorrear (**from/off**, a), gorronear, vivir de gorra.
▷ *vt (gen)* gorrear, gorronear (**from/off**, a): **he scrounges fags off his friends** *gorronea pitillos a los amigos.*
scrounger ['skraʊndʒəʳ] *n fam* gorrón,-ona.
scrub¹ [skrʌb] *n (undergrowth)* maleza.
scrub² [skrʌb] *vt* **1** *(clean)* fregar bien, estregar, restregar. **2** *fam (cancel)* cancelar.
▲ *pt & pp* **scrubbed**, *ger* **scrubbing**.
▷ *n (cleaning)* fregado, lavado.
⊙ **to scrub off** *vt sep* quitar frotando.
⊙ **to scrub up** *vi* lavarse (las manos).
scrubbing brush ['skrʌbɪŋbrʌʃ] *n (for floors)* estregadera, cepillo de fregar.
scruff¹ [skrʌf] *n (neck)* cogote *m*, pescuezo.
scruff² [skrʌf] *n fam (untidy person)* desaliñado,-a.
scruffy ['skrʌfɪ] *adj* desaliñado,-a.
▲ *comp* **scruffier**, *superl* **scruffiest**.
scrummage ['skrʌmɪdʒ] *n* SP *(rugby)* melé *f*.
scrumptious ['skrʌmpʃəs] *adj fam* delicioso,-a.
scrunch [skrʌntʃ] *vt (crumple)* estrujar (**up**, -).
▷ *vi (make noise)* crujir, ronchar, ronzar.
scruple ['skruːpᵊl] *n* escrúpulo.
scrupulous ['skruːpjʊləs] *adj (meticulous)* escrupuloso,-a, meticuloso,-a, puntilloso,-a.
scrutinize ['skruːtɪnaɪz] *vt* escudriñar.
scrutiny ['skruːtɪnɪ] *n* **1** *(examination)* examen *m* profundo. **2** GB *(of votes)* escrutinio. ■ **to be under scrutiny** ser analizado,-a.
scuba ['skjuːbə] *n* equipo de submarinismo. ● **scuba diving** submarinismo.
scuff [skʌf] *vt* **1** *(scrape floor, furniture)* rayar; *(shoes)* raspar, rayar. **2** *(drag feet)* arrastrar.
scuffle ['skʌfᵊl] *n (fight)* refriega, escaramuza.
▷ *vi* reñir (**with**, con), pelearse (**with**, con).
scull [skʌl] *n (oar)* remo de cuple.
▷ *vi* remar.
scullery ['skʌlərɪ] *n* fregadero, trascocina.
▲ *pl* **sculleries**.
sculpt [skʌlpt] *vt* esculpir.
sculptor ['skʌlptəʳ] *n* escultor,-ra.
sculptress ['skʌlptrəs] *n* escultora.
sculptural ['skʌlptʃərəl] *adj* escultural.
sculpture ['skʌlptʃəʳ] *n* escultura.
▷ *vt* esculpir (**in**, en).
scum [skʌm] *n* **1** *(froth)* espuma; *(on pond)* verdín *m*. **2** *pej (people)* escoria.
scupper ['skʌpəʳ] *vt* **1** GB *(ship)* hundir adrede, echar a pique. **2** *fam (plan, chance)* desbaratar, frustrar, hundir, echar a pique.
scurf [skɜːf] *n* caspa.
scurrilous ['skʌrɪləs] *adj (abusive, insulting)* difamatorio,-a, calumnioso,-a.
scurry ['skʌrɪ] *vi (run)* correr; *(hurry)* apresurarse.
⊙ **to scurry away / scurry off** *vi* escabullirse.
▲ *pt & pp* **scurried**, *ger* **scurrying**.
scurvy ['skɜːvɪ] *n* MED escorbuto.
scuttle¹ ['skʌtᵊl] *vi (run)* correr, corretear.
⊙ **to scuttle away/off** *vi* escabullirse.
scuttle² ['skʌtᵊl] *n (for coal)* cubo de carbón.
scuttle³ ['skʌtᵊl] *vt (sink ship)* barrenar, hundir adrede.
scythe [saɪð] *n* guadaña.

▷ *vt* guadañar, segar (con la guadaña).

sea [si:] *n* **1** mar *m* & *f*: **we love swimming in the sea** *nos encanta nadar en el mar.* **2** *fig* mar *m*, multitud *f*: **a sea of faces** *un mar de caras.* ■ **at sea** en el mar. ‖ **by the sea** a orillas del mar. ‖ **out to sea** mar adentro. ‖ **to go by sea** ir en barco. ● **sea bird** ave *f* marina. ‖ **sea captain** capitán *m* de barco. ‖ **sea horse** caballito de mar, hipocampo. ‖ **sea legs** equilibrio. ‖ **sea mile** milla marina (6000 pies o 1000 brazas o 1828,8 metros). ‖ **sea wall** dique *m*, rompeolas *m*. ‖ **sea lion** león marino.

▷ *adj* marítimo,-a, de mar.

seabed ['si:bed] *n* fondo marino.

seaboard ['si:bɔ:d] *n* US costa, litoral *m*.

seafarer ['si:feərəʳ] *n* marinero.

seafaring ['si:feərɪŋ] *adj* marinero,-a.

seafood ['si:fu:d] *n* marisco, mariscos *mpl*.

seafront ['si:frʌnt] *n (area)* puerto; *(beach)* playa; *(promenade)* paseo marítimo.

seagoing ['si:gəʊɪŋ] *adj* de alta mar.

seagull ['si:gʌl] *n* gaviota.

seashore ['si:ʃɔ:ʳ] *n (coast)* orilla del mar.

seal[1] [si:l] *n* ZOOL foca.

seal[2] [si:l] *n* **1** *(official stamp)* sello: **wax seal** *sello de lacre.* **2** *(on letter)* sello; *(on bottle, etc)* precinto. ■ **to give one's seal of approval to** STH dar el visto bueno a ALGO.

▷ *vt* **1** *(with official stamp)* sellar; *(with wax)* lacrar, sellar con lacre: **the document is signed and sealed** *el documento está firmado y sellado.* **2** *(close)* cerrar; *(bottle, etc)* precintar. **3** *(coat with sealant)* sellar, impermeabilizar.

⊙ **to seal in** *vt sep* encerrar.

⊙ **to seal off** *vt sep (block entry to)* cerrar el acceso a.

sealant ['si:lənt] *n* sellador *m*.

sealing wax ['si:lɪŋwæks] *n* lacre *m*.

sealskin ['si:lskɪn] *n* piel *f* de foca.

seam [si:m] *n* **1** SEW costura. **2** GEOL *(of mineral)* veta, filón *m*: **coal seam** *veta de carbón.* ■ **to be bursting at the seams** estar hasta los topes.

seaman ['si:mən] *n* marinero, marino.

▲ *pl* **seamen** ['si:mən].

seamanship ['si:mənʃɪp] *n* náutica.

seamless ['si:mləs] *adj* SEW sin costura.

seamstress ['semstrəs] *n* costurera.

seamy ['si:mɪ] *adj* sórdido,-a.

▲ *comp* **seamier**, *superl* **seamiest**.

seaplane ['si:pleɪn] *n* hidroavión *m*.

seaport ['si:pɔ:t] *n* puerto marítimo.

search [sɜ:tʃ] *n (gen)* búsqueda (**for**, de); *(of building)* registro; *(of person)* cacheo. ■ **in search of** en busca de. ● **search engine** INFORM buscador *m*. ‖ **search party** equipo de rescate. ‖ **search warrant** orden *f* de registro.

▷ *vt (gen)* buscar (**for**, -); *(building, suitcase, etc)* registrar; *(person)* cachear, registrar: **they searched the house for clues** *registraron la casa buscando pistas.*

▷ *vi (gen)* buscar (**through**, entre); *(pockets)* registrar.

⊙ **to search out** *vt sep* averiguar, descubrir.

searcher ['sɜ:tʃəʳ] *n* buscador,-ra.

searching ['sɜ:tʃɪŋ] *adj (look)* penetrante; *(question)* agudo,-a.

searchlight ['sɜ:tʃlaɪt] *n* reflector *m*, proyector *m*.

searing ['si:rɪŋ] *adj* **1** *(heat)* abrasador,-ra; *(pain)* punzante. **2** *fig (strong)* virulento,-a.

seashell ['si:ʃel] *n* concha (de mar).

seashore ['si:ʃɔ:ʳ] *n (coast)* orilla del mar.

seasick ['si:sɪk] *adj* mareado,-a.

seasickness ['si:sɪknəs] *n* mareo.

seaside ['si:saɪd] *n* playa, costa. ● **seaside resort** lugar *m* de veraneo en la costa.

season ['si:zᵊn] *n (of year)* estación *f*; *(time)* época; *(for sport, theatre, social activity)* temporada: **the tourist season** *la temporada turística.* ■ **to be in season 1** *(fresh food)* estar en sazón. **2** *(game)* ser temporada de: **strawberries are in season** *es temporada de fresas.* ‖ **to go in season** ir en temporada alta. ‖ **to go off/out of season** ir en temporada baja.

▷ *vt* **1** *(food)* sazonar (**with**, con), condimentar (**with**, con).

seasonable ['si:zᵊnəbᵊl] *adj* **1** *(weather)* propio,-a de la estación. **2** *(opportune, timely)* oportuno,-a.

seasonal ['si:zᵊnəl] *adj* estacional, temporal.

seasoned ['si:zənd] *adj* **1** *(food)* sazonado,-a (**with**, con), condimentado,-a (**with**, con): **highly seasoned** *picante.* **2** *fig (person)* experimentado,-a, curtido,-a.

seasoning ['si:zᵊnɪŋ] *n* CULIN condimento.

seat [si:t] *n* **1** *(chair - gen)* asiento; *(- in cinema, theatre)* butaca. **2** *(place)* plaza; *(at theatre, etc)* localidad *f*. **3** *(of trousers)* fondillos *mpl*; *(bottom, buttocks)* trasero, pompis *m*. **4** POL *(in parliament)* escaño. ■ **to take a seat** sentarse, tomar asiento. ● **seat belt** cinturón *m* de seguridad.

▷ *vt* **1** *(sit)* sentar. **2** *(accommodate)* tener sitio para; *(theatre, hall, etc)* tener cabida para. ■ **please be seated** siéntese/siéntense por favor. ‖ **to seat** OS sentarse.

seater ['si:təʳ] *n*: **a three-seater sofa** *un sofá de tres plazas.*

seating ['si:tɪŋ] *n* asientos *mpl*: **seating capacity** *aforo.*

seawater ['si:wɔ:təʳ] *n* agua de mar.

seaweed ['si:wi:d] *n* alga (marina).

seaworthy ['si:wɜ:ðɪ] *adj (boat)* en condiciones de navegar.

sebaceous [sɪ'beɪʃəs] *adj* sebáceo,-a.

secateurs [sekə'tɜ:z] *n pl* podadera.

secede [sɪ'si:d] *vi* separarse (**from**, de).

secession [sɪ'seʃᵊn] *n* secesión *f*.

seclude [sɪ'klu:d] *vt* aislar, apartar, retirar.

secluded [sɪ'klu:dɪd] *adj* aislado,-a, apartado,-a.

seclusion [sɪ'klu:ʒᵊn] *n (act of secluding)* aislamiento, reclusión *f*; *(privacy)* intimidad *f*.

second[1] ['sekənd] *n* **1** *(time)* segundo: **Christie's time was 9.9 seconds** *Christie hizo un tiempo de 9,9 segundos.* **2** *fam* momento, momentito: **I'll be back in a second** *enseguida vuelvo.* ● **second hand** *(of watch)* segundero. ‖ **second name** apellido.

second[2] [sɪ'kɒnd] *vt* GB trasladar temporalmente.

second[3] ['sekənd] *adj (gen)* segundo,-a; *(another)* otro,-a: **it's the second largest city in England** *es la segunda ciudad más grande de Inglaterra.* ■ **to have second helpings** repetir. ‖ **to have second thoughts (about** STH**)** entrarle dudas a uno (sobre ALGO), cambiar de idea (sobre ALGO). ● **second floor 1** GB segundo piso. **2** US primer piso. ‖ **second name** apellido.

▷ *pron* segundo,-a.

▷ *n* **1** *(in series)* segundo,-a. **2** GB *(degree)* ≈ notable *m*.

▷ *adv* segundo, en segundo lugar: **he came second** *llegó segundo, quedó en segundo lugar.*

▷ *vt (motion, proposal)* apoyar, secundar.

Consulta también **sixth**.

secondary ['sekənd^ərɪ] *adj* secundario,-a. ● **secondary school** colegio de enseñanza secundaria, instituto de bachillerato .
second-best [sekənd'best] *adj* segundo,-a mejor: **my second-best dress** *mi segundo mejor vestido.*
second-class [sekənd'klɑ:s] *adj* de segunda (clase).
second-degree [sekənddɪ'gri:] *adj* MED de segundo grado. ● **second-degree burns** quemaduras *fpl* de segundo grado.
seconder ['sekəndə^r] *n persona que secunda una moción, etc.*
second-guess [sekənd'ges] *vt* US *fam (criticize, evaluate with hindsight)* cuestionar posteriormente.
second-hand [sekənd'hænd] *adj* 1 *(used, not new)* de segunda mano, usado,-a, viejo,-a: **we bought a second-hand car** *compramos un coche de segunda mano.*
▷ *adv* 1 *(buy)* de segunda mano. 2 *(learn, find out)* por terceros.
second-in-command ['sekəndɪnkə'mɑ:nd] *n (in hierarchy)* segundo,-a en jefe, número dos.
secondly ['sekəndlɪ] *adv* en segundo lugar.
secondment [sɪ'kɒndmənt] *n* GB traslado temporal.
second-rate [sekənd'reɪt] *adj* de segunda categoría, de calidad inferior.
secrecy ['si:krəsɪ] *n (gen)* secreto, sigilo: **in secrecy** *en secreto, con sigilo.*
secret ['si:krət] *adj (gen)* secreto,-a: **this is my secret hiding-place** *éste es mi escondite secreto.*
▷ *n* 1 *(gen)* secreto; *(something confided)* secreto, confidencia. 2 *(method, key)* secreto, clave *f.* ■ **in secret** en secreto. ‖ **to keep a secret** guardar un secreto.
secretarial [sekrɪ'teərɪəl] *adj* de secretario,-a.
secretariat [sekrɪ'tərɪət] *n* secretariado.
secretary ['sekrət^ərɪ] *n* 1 secretario,-a. 2 *(non-elected official)* ministro,-a; *(representative below ambassador)* ministro,-a plenipotenciario,-a.
▲ *pl* **secretaries.**
secretary-general [sekrət^ərɪ'dʒen^ərəl] *n* secretario general.
▲ *pl* **secretaries-general.**
secrete [sɪ'kri:t] *vt* 1 *(emit liquid)* secretar, segregar. 2 *fml (hide)* ocultar, esconder.
secretion [sɪ'kri:ʃ^ən] *n (of liquid)* secreción *f.*
secretive ['si:krətɪv] *adj (gen)* sigiloso,-a.
secretly ['si:krətlɪ] *adv* en secreto.
sect [sekt] *n* secta.
sectarian [sek'teərɪən] *adj* sectario,-a.
section ['sekʃ^ən] *n* 1 *(of newspaper, orchestra, department)* sección *f*; *(of road)* tramo; *(of orange)* gajo. 2 *(of population, community)* sector *m.* 3 *(of drawing)* sección *f*, corte *m*: **cross section** *sección transversal.*
▷ *vt (cut)* cortar, seccionar.
sector ['sektə] *n (gen)* sector *m.*
secular ['sekjʊlə^r] *adj (education)* laico,-a; *(art, music)* profano,-a.
secure [sɪ'kjʊə^r] *adj* 1 *(job, income, etc)* seguro,-a; *(relationship, etc)* estable. 2 *(ladder, shelf, foothold)* firme; *(stronghold)* seguro,-a; *(base, foundation)* sólido,-a.
▷ *vt* 1 *(make safe)* asegurar; *(protect)* proteger (**from**, de), (**against**, contra). 2 *(fasten)* cerrar bien. 3 *(obtain)* obtener, conseguir.
securely [sɪ'kjʊəlɪ] *adv* bien.
security [sɪ'kjʊərətɪ] *n* 1 *(safety, confidence)* seguridad *f.* 2 *(protection)* seguridad *f.* ● **security service** servicio de seguridad. ‖ **security van** furgoneta blindada.
▲ *pl* **securities.**
sedan [sɪ'dæn] *n* US *(car)* berlina.
sedate[1] [sɪ'deɪt] *adj* sosegado,-a, sereno,-a.
sedate[2] [sɪ'deɪt] *vt* MED sedar.
sedation [sɪ'deɪʃ^ən] *n* sedación *f.*
sedative ['sedətɪv] *n* sedante *m*, calmante *m.*
▷ *adj* sedante.
sedentary ['sed^ənt^ərɪ] *adj* sedentario,-a.
sediment ['sedɪmənt] *n (gen)* sedimento.
sedimentary [sedɪ'ment^ərɪ] *adj* sedimentario,-a.
sedimentation [sedɪmen'teɪʃ^ən] *n* sedimentación *f.*
sedition [sɪ'dɪʃ^ən] *n* sedición *f.*
seditious [sɪ'dɪʃəs] *adj* sedicioso,-a.
seduce [sɪ'dju:s] *vt* 1 *(sexually)* seducir. 2 *fml (tempt, entice)* tentar, seducir.
seduction [sɪ'dʌkʃ^ən] *n (sexual)* seducción *f.*
seductive [sɪ'dʌktɪv] *adj* seductor,-ra.
see [si:] *vt* 1 *(gen)* ver: **you can see the sea from here** *desde aquí se ve el mar;* **see page 123** *véase la página 123.* 2 *(meet, visit)* ver; *(receive)* ver, atender; *(go out with)* salir con: **I'm seeing Pat on Friday** *he quedado con Pat el viernes.* 3 *(understand)* comprender, entender, ver: **I can see your point** *entiendo tu punto de vista.* 4 *(visualize, imagine)* imaginarse, ver; *(envisage)* creer: **can't see him working in a factory** *no me lo imagino trabajando en una fábrica.* 5 *(find out, discover)* ver; *(learn,* oír, leer: **I'll see what I can do** *veré lo que puedo hacer.* 6 *(ensure, check)* asegurarse de, procurar: **see that you arrive on time** *procura llegar a la hora.* 7 *(accompany)* acompañar: **he saw me home** *me acompañó a casa.*
▷ *vi* 1 *(gen)* ver: **she can't see without her glasses** *no ve sin las gafas.* 2 *(find out, discover)* ver: **we'll have to see** *ya veremos.* 3 *(understand)* entender, ver: **oh, I see** *ah, ya veo.* ■ **I'll be seeing you!** ¡hasta luego! ‖ **let me see let's see** a ver, vamos a ver. ‖ **seeing is believing** ver para creer. ‖ **see you around** ya nos veremos. ‖ **see you later/soon/Monday!** ¡hasta luego/pronto/el lunes! **you see** 1 *(in explanations)* verás. 2 *(in questions)* ¿sabes? ¿ves?
⊙ **to see about** *vt insep* 1 *(deal with)* arreglar, organizar. 2 *(consider)* ver, pensar.
⊙ **to see in** *vt insep (celebrate)* celebrar.
⊙ **to see off** *vt sep* 1 *(say goodbye to)* despedir. 2 *(chase off)* ahuyentar; *(remain firm)* resistir.
⊙ **to see out** *vt sep* 1 *(last)* durar; *(survive)* sobrevivir. 2 *(go to door with)* acompañar hasta la puerta.
⊙ **to see round/over** *vt insep (house, etc)* visitar, recorrer.
⊙ **to see through** *vt insep (person)* calar a, verle el plumero a.
▷ *vt sep* 1 *(support)* ayudar a salir de un apuro, ayudar a sobrellevar; *(last)* alcanzar, llegar: **my parents saw me through a bad time** *mis padres me ayudaron a sobrellevar una mala época.* 2 *(not abandon until finished)* terminar.
▲ *pt* **saw** [si:], *pp* **seen** [sɔ:n], *ger* **seeing.**
⊙ **to see to** *vt insep (deal with)* atender a, ocuparse de, encargarse de.
seed [si:d] *n* BOT *(gen)* semilla; *(of fruit)* pepita: **sunflower seeds** *pipas.*

› *vt* **1** *(plant seeds)* sembrar (**with**, de). **2** *(remove seed)* despepitar.
seedless ['si:dləs] *adj* sin pepitas.
seedling ['si:dlɪŋ] *n* planta de semillero.
seedy ['si:dɪ] *adj (place)* cutre, sórdido,-a, de mala muerte; *(person)* desastrado,-a.
▲ *comp* **seedier**, *superl* **seediest**.
seek [si:k] *vt* **1** *(look for, try to obtain)* buscar: **the homeless seek food and shelter** *la gente sin techo busca comida y alojamiento.* **2** *(ask for)* pedir, solicitar. **3** *(attempt, try)* tratar de, intentar. ■ **to seek one's fortune** probar fortuna.
› *vi (look for, try to obtain)* buscar (**after/for**, -), ir en busca de.
▲ *pt & pp* **sought** [sɔ:t].
⊙ **to seek out** *vt sep* buscar.
seem [si:m] *vi (appear)* parecer: **she seems nice** *parece maja;* **it seems like there's going to be a storm** *parece que va a haber una tormenta.* ■ **so it seems** eso parece.
seeming ['si:mɪŋ] *adj* aparente.
seemingly ['si:mɪŋlɪ] *adv* **1** *(used with adjective)* aparentemente. **2** *(used separately)* al parecer, según parece.
seen [si:n] *pp* ⟶ **see**.
seep [si:p] *vi* filtrarse.
seesaw ['si:sɔ:] *n (for children)* balancín *m*, subibaja *m*.
seethe [si:ð] *vi* **1** *(liquid)* hervir, bullir. **2** *fig (be angry)* rabiar, estar furioso,-a. **3** *fig (be crowded)* bullir. ■ **to seethe with people** estar a rebosar.
see-through ['si:θru:] *adj* transparente.
segment ['segmənt] *n (gen)* segmento; *(of orange)* gajo.
segregate ['segrɪgeɪt] *vt* segregar.
segregation [segrɪ'geɪʃᵊn] *n* segregación *f*.
seismic ['saɪzmɪk] *adj* sísmico,-a.
seize [si:z] *vt* **1** *(grab)* asir, agarrar, coger: **he seized my arm** *me agarró del brazo.* **2** *(opportunity)* aprovechar. **3** *(take control of)* tomar, apoderarse de. **4** *(person - arrest)* detener; *(- take hostage)* secuestrar. **5** *fig (strong feelings)* apoderarse de, acometer: **panic seized the guests** *el pánico se apoderó de los invitados.* ■ **to be seized with** STH *(pain, fear, panic, etc)* apoderarse algo de uno.
⊙ **to seize on/upon** *vt insep* valerse de.
⊙ **to seize up** *vi* agarrotarse.
seizure ['si:ʒəʳ] *n* **1** *(of power, territory)* toma. **2** MED ataque *m* (de apoplejía).
seldom ['seldəm] *adv* raramente, pocas veces: **we seldom eat out** *pocas veces comemos fuera.*
select [sɪ'lekt] *vt (thing)* escoger, elegir; *(team, player, candidate)* seleccionar.
› *adj* selecto,-a, escogido,-a.
selected [sɪ'lektɪd] *adj* escogido,-a.
selection [sɪ'lekʃᵊn] *n* **1** *(people or things chosen)* selección *f*; *(choosing)* elección *f*. **2** *(range to choose from)* surtido, gama.
selective [sɪ'lektɪv] *adj* selectivo,-a.
selector [sɪ'lektəʳ] *n* seleccionador,-ra.
self [self] *n* **1** ser *m*, uno,-a mismo,-a, sí mismo,-a: **he was his usual self again** *volvió a ser él mismo.* **2** *(one's own interest)* sí mismo,-a: **he thinks only of self** *solo piensa en sí mismo.* **3** *(in psychology)* yo: **my other self** *mi otro yo.*
▲ *pl* **selves**.
self-addressed [selfə'drest] *adj* con el nombre y la dirección.
self-adhesive [selfəd'hi:sɪv] *adj* autoadhesivo,-a, autoadherente.
self-appointed [selfə'pɔɪntɪd] *adj* autoproclamado,-a.
self-assembly [selfə'semblɪ] *adj* para montar uno,-a mismo,-a.
self-assertive [selfə'sɜ:tɪv] *adj* seguro,-a de sí mismo,-a.
self-assured [selfə'ʃʊəd] *adj* seguro,-a de sí mismo,-a.
self-catering [self'keɪtərɪŋ] *adj* sin servicio de comidas.
self-centered [self'sentəd] *adj* US ⟶ **self-centred**.
self-centred [self'sentəd] *adj* egocéntrico,-a.
self-confessed [selfkən'fest] *adj* confeso,-a.
self-confident [self'kɒnfɪdənt] *adj* seguro,-a de sí mismo,-a.
self-conscious [self'kɒnʃəs] *adj* cohibido,-a, tímido,-a.
self-contained [selfkən'teɪnd] *adj (person - independent)* independiente; *(- reserved)* reservado,-a.
self-control [selfkən'trəʊl] *n* dominio de sí mismo,-a, autocontrol *m*.
self-defence [selfdɪ'fens] *n* defensa personal, autodefensa. ■ **to act in self-defence** actuar en defensa propia.
self-determination [selfdɪtɜ:mɪ'neɪʃᵊn] *n* autodeterminación *f*.
self-discipline [self'dɪsɪplɪn] *n* autodisciplina.
self-drive [self'draɪv] *adj* sin chófer.
self-educated [self'edjʊkeɪtɪd] *adj* autodidacta.
self-effacing [selfɪ'feɪsɪŋ] *adj* humilde.
self-employed [selfɪm'plɔɪd] *adj* autónomo,-a, que trabaja por cuenta propia.
self-esteem [selfɪ'sti:m] *n* amor *m* propio.
self-government [self'gʌvᵊnmənt] *n* autonomía, autogobierno.
self-help [self'help] *n* autoayuda.
self-important [selfɪm'pɔ:tᵊnt] *adj* engreído,-a, presumido,-a.
self-imposed [selfɪm'pəʊzd] *adj* autoimpuesto,-a, voluntario,-a.
self-indulgent [selfɪn'dʌldʒənt] *adj* que se permite excesos.
self-interest [self'ɪntrəst] *n* interés *m* propio.
selfish ['selfɪʃ] *adj* egoísta.
selfishness ['selfɪʃnəs] *n* egoísmo.
selfless ['selfləs] *adj* desinteresado,-a.
self-locking [self'lɒkɪŋ] *adj* de cierre automático.
self-made [self'meɪd] *adj (man, woman)* que ha llegado donde está por sus propios esfuerzos, que se ha hecho a sí mismo,-a .
self-opinionated [selfə'pɪnjəneɪtɪd] *adj* testarudo,-a, terco,-a.
self-pity [self'pɪtɪ] *n* autocompasión *f*.
self-portrait [self'pɔ:treɪt] *n* autorretrato.
self-possessed [selfpə'zest] *adj* sereno,-a, dueño,-a de sí mismo,-a.
self-reliant [selfrɪ'laɪənt] *adj* independiente.
self-respect [selfrɪ'spekt] *n* amor *m* propio, dignidad *f*.
self-restraint [selfrɪ'streɪnt] *n* dominio de sí mismo,-a, autocontrol *m*.
self-righteous [self'raɪtʃəs] *adj* petulante.
self-rule [self'ru:l] *n* autogobierno.
self-sacrifice [self'sækrɪfaɪs] *n* abnegación *f*.

selfsame ['selfseɪm] *adj* mismísimo,-a.
self-satisfied [self'sætɪsfaɪd] *adj* satisfecho,-a de sí mismo,-a, ufano,-a, engreído,-a .
self-seeking [self'si:kɪŋ] *adj* egoísta.
self-service [self'sɜ:vɪs] *adj* de autoservicio.
▷ *n* autoservicio.
self-sufficient [selfsə'fɪʃᵊnt] *adj* autosuficiente.
self-taught [self'tɔ:t] *adj* autodidacta.
sell [sel] *vt* 1 *(gen)* vender: **he sold his bike to his neighbour** *vendió la bici a su vecino.* 2 *fam (convince)* convencer de. ■ **to sell** OS venderse.
▷ *vi (product)* venderse: **these plants sell at a pound each** *estas plantas se venden a una libra cada una.* ■ **to be sold on** STH estar entusiasmado,-a por ALGO. ❘ **to be sold out** estar agotado,-a.
⊙ **to sell off** *vt sep* liquidar.
⊙ **to sell out** *vi* 1 *(be disloyal)* claudicar, venderse. 2 COMM *(sell all of)* agotarse (**of**, -), acabarse (**of**, -). 3 *(sell business)* vender el negocio.
▷ *vt sep* COMM *(sell all of)* agotar, agotar las existencias de.
▲ *pt & pp* **sold** [səʊld].
⊙ **to sell up** *vi* venderlo todo.
sell-by date ['selbaɪdeɪt] *n* fecha límite de venta, fecha de caducidad.
seller ['seləʳ] *n (person)* vendedor,-ra.
selling ['selɪŋ] *n* ventas *fpl.*
Sellotape® ['seləteɪp] *n* celo®.
sell-out ['selaʊt] *n* 1 *(performance)* éxito de taquilla. 2 *fam (betrayal)* traición *f*, engaño.
semantic [sɪ'mæntɪk] *adj* semántico,-a.
semaphore ['seməfɔ:ʳ] *n (device)* semáforo.
semblance ['sembləns] *n fml* apariencia.
semen ['si:mən] *n* semen *m.*
semester [sɪ'mestəʳ] *n* semestre *m.*
semiautomatic [semɪɔ:tə'mætɪk] *adj* semiautomático,-a.
semicircle ['semɪsɜ:kᵊl] *n* semicírculo.
semicircular [semɪ'sɜ:kjʊləʳ] *adj* semicircular.
semicolon [semɪ'kəʊlən] *n* punto y coma *m.*
semiconscious [semɪ'kɒnʃəs] *adj* semiconsciente.
semidetached [semɪdɪ'tætʃt] *adj* pareado,-a.
▷ *n (house)* casa pareada.
semifinal [semɪ'faɪnᵊl] *n* semifinal *f.*
semifinalist [semɪ'faɪnᵊlɪst] *n* semifinalista *mf.*
seminal ['semɪnəl] *adj* 1 *(producing semen)* seminal. 2 *fig (influential)* fundamental.
seminar ['semɪnɑ:ʳ] *n* EDUC seminario.
seminary ['semɪnərɪ] *n* REL seminario.
▲ *pl* **seminaries.**
semiprecious [semɪ'preʃəs] *adj* semiprecioso,-a.
semiskilled [semɪ'skɪld] *adj* semicualificado,-a.
semiskimmed [semɪ'skɪmd] *adj* semidesnatado,-a, semidescremado,-a.
semolina [semə'li:nə] *n* sémola.
senate ['senət] *n* POL senado.
senator ['senətəʳ] *n* senador,-ra.
send [send] *vt* 1 *(gen)* enviar, mandar; *(telex, telegram)* enviar, poner; *(radio signal, radio message)* transmitir, emitir: **he sent me some flowers** *me mandó flores.* 2 *(order to go)* mandar, enviar: **the doctor sent me to a specialist** *el médico me mandó a un especialista.* 3 *(drive, cause to move)* mandar; *(rocket, ball)* lanzar. 4 *(cause to become)* volver, hacer: **the noise sent her mad** *el ruido la volvió loca.*
▷ *vi (send a message)* avisar.
▲ *pt & pp* **sent** [sent].
⊙ **to send away** *vt sep* despachar.
⊙ **to send away for** *vt insep* pedir por correo.
⊙ **to send back** *vt sep* 1 *(goods, etc)* devolver. 2 *(person)* hacer volver.
⊙ **to send down** *vt sep* enchironar, entalegar.
⊙ **to send for** *vt insep* 1 *(person)* llamar a, hacer llamar a. 2 *(thing)* pedir, encargar.
⊙ **to send in** *vt sep (application, request)* mandar, enviar.
⊙ **to send off** *vt sep (letter, etc)* enviar, mandar; *(goods)* despachar, mandar.
⊙ **to send off for** *vt insep* pedir por correo.
⊙ **to send on** *vt sep (letter)* hacer seguir; *(luggage, etc)* enviar, mandar (por adelantado).
⊙ **to send out** *vt sep* 1 *(leaflets, invitations)* enviar, mandar; *(goods)* despachar, mandar. 2 *(radio signals)* emitir, transmitir, dar. 3 *(light, smoke, heat)* emitir. 4 *(person)* echar, hacer salir.
⊙ **to send out for** *vt insep (food, etc)* mandar traer, mandar por, mandar a comprar.
⊙ **to send up** *vt sep* 1 *(gen)* hacer subir; *(rocket, flare)* lanzar. 2 GB *fam (satirize)* burlarse de.
sender ['sendəʳ] *n* remitente *mf.*
sendoff ['sendɒf] *n fam* despedida.
send-up ['sendʌp] *n* sátira, parodia.
Senegal [senɪ'gɔ:l] *n* Senegal.
Senegalese [senɪgə'li:z] *adj* senegalés,-esa.
▷ *n* senegalés,-esa.
▷ *n pl* **the Senegalese** los senegaleses *mpl.*
senile ['si:naɪl] *adj* senil.
senility [sɪ'nɪlətɪ] *n* senilidad *f.*
senior ['si:nɪəʳ] *adj* 1 *(in age)* mayor. **he's five years senior to me** *es cinco años mayor que yo.* 2 *(in rank)* superior; *(with longer service)* más antiguo,-a, de mayor antigüedad. ● **senior citizen** jubilado,-a.
▷ *n* 1 *(in age)* mayor *mf*; *(in rank)* superior *fm.* 2 GB *(pupil)* mayor *mf.* 3 US estudiante *mf* del último curso.
seniority [si:nɪ'ɒrətɪ] *n (in length of service)* antigüedad *f*; *(in rank)* superioridad.
sensation [sen'seɪʃᵊn] *n* 1 *(feeling)* sensación *f*; *(ability to feel)* sensibilidad *f.* 2 *(interest, excitement, etc)* sensación *f*; *(success)* éxito.
sensational [sen'seɪʃənᵊl] *adj* 1 *fam (wonderful)* sensacional. 2 *(exaggerated)* sensacionalista.
sensationalist [sen'seɪʃᵊnəlɪst] *adj* sensacionalista.
sense [sens] *n* 1 *(faculty)* sentido: **sense of smell** *sentido del olfato.* 2 *(feeling - of well-being, loss)* sensación *f*; *(awareness, appreciation - of justice, duty)* sentido. 3 *(wisdom, judgement)* sentido común, juicio, sensatez *f*, tino. 4 *(reason, purpose)* sentido. 5 *(meaning - gen)* sentido; *(- of word)* significado, acepción *f*: **in every sense of the word** *en todos los sentidos.* ■ **in a sense** hasta cierto punto, en cierto sentido. ❘ **in no sense** de ninguna manera. ❘ **to make sense** 1 *(have clear meaning)* tener sentido. 2 *(be sensible)* ser razonable, ser sensato,-a. ❘ **to talk sense** hablar con juicio. ● **sense of humour** sentido del humor.
▷ *vt* 1 *(feel, perceive)* sentir, percibir, presentir.
senseless ['sensləs] *adj* 1 *(unconscious)* inconsciente. 2 *(foolish, pointless)* absurdo,-a, sin sentido, insensato,-a.

sensibility [sensɪ'bɪlətɪ] *n* sensibilidad *f*.
▷ *n pl* **sensibilities** susceptibilidad *f sing*.
sensible ['sensɪbᵊl] *adj* **1** *(person)* sensato,-a; *(behaviour, decision)* razonable, prudente; *(choice)* acertado, -a. **2** *(clothes)* cómodo,-a.
sensibly ['sensɪblɪ] *adv* con sensatez.
sensitive ['sensɪtɪv] *adj* **1** *(person - perceptive)* sensible (**to**, a), consciente (**to**, de). **2** *(person - touchy)* susceptible (**to**, a), preocupado,-a (**about**, por). **3** *(teeth, paper, instrument, film)* sensible (**to**,-a); *(skin)* sensible, delicado,-a. **4** *(issue)* delicado,-a.
sensitivity [sensɪ'tɪvətɪ] *n* **1** *(gen)* sensibilidad *f* (**to**, a/ frente a). **2** *(touchiness)* susceptibilidad *f* (**to**, a). **3** *(of skin, issue)* delicadeza.
sensor ['sensəʳ] *n* TECH sensor *m*, detector *m*.
sensual ['sensjʊəl] *adj* sensual.
sensuous ['sensjʊəs] *adj* sensual.
sent [sent] *pt & pp* ⟶ **send**.
sentence ['sentᵊns] *n* **1** *(gen)* frase *f*; *(in grammar)* oración *f*. **2** JUR sentencia, fallo.
▷ *vt* JUR condenar.
sententious [sen'tenʃəs] *adj* sentencioso,-a.
sentiment ['sentɪmənt] *n* **1** *(sentimentality)* sentimentalismo. **2** *fml (feeling)* sentimiento. **3** *fml (opinion)* opinión *f*, parecer *m*.
sentimental [sentɪ'mentᵊl] *adj* sentimental.
sentimentality [sentɪmen'tælətɪ] *n* sentimentalismo, sensiblería.
sentinel ['sentɪnᵊl] *n dated* centinela *m*.
sentry ['sentrɪ] *n* centinela *m*.
▲ *pl* **sentries**.
sepal ['sepᵊl] *n* BOT sépalo.
separable ['sepᵊrəbᵊl] *adj* separable.
separate [*(vb)* 'sepəreɪt, *(adj)* 'sepᵊrət] *vt* **1** *(gen)* separar (**from**, de); *(divide)* dividir: **break the egg and separate the white from the yolk** *rompe el huevo y separa la clara de la yema*. **2** *(distinguish)* distinguir, separar.
▷ *vi* **1** *(gen)* separarse.
▷ *adj* **1** *(apart)* separado,-a: **keep the sheep separate from the goats** *mantén a las ovejas separadas de las cabras*. **2** *(not shared)* separado,-a, individual: **we had separate rooms** *cada uno tenía su habitación*. **3** *(different, distinct)* distinto,-a, diferente.
separated ['sepəreɪtɪd] *adj* separado,-a.
separately ['sepᵊrətlɪ] *adv* **1** *(apart)* por separado, aparte. **2** *(individually)* por separado: **we paid separately** *pagamos por separado*.
separation [sepə'reɪʃᵊn] *n* separación *f*.
separatist ['sepᵊrətɪst] *n* separatista *mf*.
sepia ['siːpɪə] *adj* sepia.
September [səp'tembəʳ] *n* septiembre *m*, setiembre *m*.
Para ejemplos de uso, consulta **May**.
septet [sep'tet] *n* MUS septeto.
septic ['septɪk] *adj* séptico,-a.
sepulcher ['sepəlkəʳ] *n* US ⟶ **sepulchre**.
sepulchre ['sepᵊlkəʳ] *n* sepulcro.
sequel ['siːkwəl] *n* **1** *(result, consequence)* secuela. **2** *(book, film, etc)* segunda parte *f*.
sequence ['siːkwəns] *n* **1** *(order)* secuencia, orden *m*. **2** *(series)* secuencia, serie *f*, sucesión *f*. **3** *(of images)* secuencia.
sequester [sɪ'kwestəʳ] *vt* **1** *fml (seclude)* aislar. **2** JUR *(sequestrate)* embargar, secuestrar.
sequestrate ['sekwɪstreɪt] *vt* embargar.
sequin ['siːkwɪn] *n* lentejuela.
sequoia [sɪ'kwɔɪə] *n* secoya, secuoya.
Serb [sɜːb] *n (person)* serbio,-a.
▷ *adj* serbio,-a.
Serbia ['sɜːbɪə] *n* Serbia.
Serbian ['sɜːbɪən] *n* **1** *(person)* serbio,-a. **2** *(dialect)* serbio.
▷ *adj* serbio,-a.
Serbo-Croat [sɜːbəʊ'krəʊæt] *n (language)* serbocroata *m*.
serenade [serə'neɪd] *n* serenata.
▷ *vt* dar una serenata a.
serene [sə'riːn] *adj* sereno,-a, tranquilo,-a.
serenely [sə'riːnlɪ] *adv* serenamente, con serenidad.
serenity [sə'renətɪ] *n* serenidad *f*.
serf [sɜːf] *n* siervo,-a.
serge [sɜːdʒ] *n* sarga.
sergeant ['sɑːdʒᵊnt] *n* **1** MIL sargento *mf*. **2** *(of police)* cabo *mf*.
serial ['sɪərɪəl] *adj* **1** consecutivo,-a, en serie. **2** *(in parts)* seriado,-a, en capítulos.
▷ *n (gen)* serie *f*, serial *m*.
serialize ['sɪərɪəlaɪz] *vt* seriar, adaptar *(para televisión, etc)*.
series ['sɪəriːz] *n (gen)* serie *f*. ■ **in series** TECH en serie.
▲ *pl* **series**.
serigraph ['serɪgræf] *n* serigrafía.
serious ['sɪərɪəs] *adj* **1** *(solemn, earnest)* serio,-a: **you can't be serious!** *¡no lo dices en serio!* **2** *(causing concern, severe)* grave, serio,-a: **no serious damage was caused** *no hubo daños importantes*.
seriously ['sɪərɪəslɪ] *adv* **1** *(in earnest)* en serio. **2** *(severely)* seriamente, gravemente.
seriousness ['sɪərɪəsnəs] *n* **1** *(severity)* seriedad *f*. **2** *(earnestness, solemnity)* seriedad *f*. ■ **in all seriousness** hablando (muy) en serio.
sermon ['sɜːmən] *n* sermón *m*.
serpent ['sɜːpᵊnt] *n lit* serpiente *f*.
serrated [sə'reɪtɪd] *adj* dentado,-a.
serum ['sɪərəm] *n* MED suero.
▲ *pl* **serums** o **sera** ['sɪərə].
servant ['sɜːvᵊnt] *n* sirviente *mf*.
serve [sɜːv] *vt* **1** *(work for)* servir (**as**, de). **2** *(customer)* servir, atender; *(food, drink)* servir: **dinner is served at 8.00 pm** *se sirve la cena a las 8.00*. **3** *(be useful to)* servir, ser útil: **it serves many different purposes** *sirve para varias cosas*. **4** *(provide with service)* prestar servicio a: **the new hospital will serve the whole region** *el nuevo hospital prestará servicio a toda la región*. **5** *(complete period of time - apprenticeship)* hacer; *(- sentence)* cumplir.
▷ *vi* **1** *(work for)* servir: **my father served in the army** *mi padre sirvió en el ejército*. **2** *(in shop)* atender; *(food, drink)* servir. **3** *(be useful to)* servir (**as**, de): **this will serve as an example** *esto servirá de ejemplo*.
▷ *n (tennis)* saque *m*.
⊙ **to serve out** *vt sep* **1** *(food)* servir. **2** *(complete period of time)* cumplir, hacer.
⊙ **to serve up** *vt sep* **1** *(excuse, etc)* ofrecer. **2** *(meal, food)* servir.
server ['sɜːvəʳ] *n (computer)* servidor *m*.
service ['sɜːvɪs] *n* **1** *(attention to customer)* servicio. **2** *(organization, system, business)* servicio: **there's a good bus**

service *hay un buen servicio de autobuses.* **3** *(work, duty)* servicio. **4** *(use)* servicio: **this machine is not in service** *esta máquina no funciona.* **5** *(maintenance of car, machine)* revisión *f.* **6** REL oficio, oficio religioso. **7** *(of dishes)* vajilla; *(for tea, coffee)* juego. **8** *(tennis)* saque *m*, servicio.
▷ *adj (for use of workers)* de servicio: **service entrance** *entrada de servicio.* ● **service area** área de servicio. ‖ **service charge 1** *(on bill)* servicio. **2** *(in banking)* comisión *f.* ‖ **service station** estación *f* de servicio.
▷ *n pl* **services** *(work, act, help)* servicios *mpl.*
▷ *n pl* **the services** MIL las fuerzas *fpl* armadas.

serviceable ['sɜːvɪsəbᵊl] *adj* útil, práctico.

serviceman ['sɜːvɪsmən] *n* militar *m.*
▲ *pl* **servicemen** ['sɜːvɪsmən].

servicewoman ['sɜːvɪswʊmən] *n* militar *f.*
▲ *pl* **servicewomen** ['sɜːvɪswɪmɪn].

serviette [sɜːvɪ'et] *n* GB servilleta.

servile ['sɜːvaɪl] *adj* servil.

servility [sɜː'vɪlɪtɪ] *n* servilismo.

serving ['sɜːvɪŋ] *n* porción *f*, ración *f.* ● **serving dish** fuente *f.*

sesame ['sesəmɪ] *n* BOT sésamo, ajonjolí *m.*

session ['seʃᵊn] *n* **1** *(formal meeting)* sesión *f*, junta, reunión *f.* **2** *(period of time, activity)* sesión *f*: **a training session** *una sesión de entrenamiento.* **3** EDUC *(term)* trimestre *m.*

set[1] [set] *n* **1** *(of golf clubs, brushes, tools, etc)* juego; *(books, poems)* colección *f*; *(of turbines)* equipo, grupo: **chess set** *juego de ajedrez;* **set of dishes** *vajilla.* **2** ELEC *(apparatus)* aparato: **they bought a TV set** *compraron un televisor.* **3** MATH conjunto. **4** SP *(tennis)* set *m.* **5** MUS *(performance)* actuación *f.* **6** *(of people)* grupo; *(clique)* pandilla, camarilla.

set[2] [set] *n* **1** *(in hairdressing)* marcado. **2** *(scenery)* decorado; *(place of filming)* plató *m.* **3** *(position, posture)* postura, posición *f.*
▷ *adj* **1** *(placed)* situado,-a: **a village set on a hill** *un pueblo situado sobre una colina.* **2** *(fixed, arranged)* fijo,-a, determinado,-a, establecido,-a: **meals are served at set times** *se sirven las comidas a horas determinadas.* **3** *(rigid, stiff)* rígido,-a, forzado,-a; *(opinion)* inflexible; *(idea)* fijo,-a. **4** *(ready, prepared)* listo,-a (**for/to**, para); *(likely)* probable: **is everyone set to go?** *¿todos estáis listos para salir?* ■ **to be all set** estar listo,-a, estar preparado,-a. ‖ **to set fire to** STH prender fuego a ALGO. ‖ **to set free** poner en libertad, liberar. ● **set lunch** menú *m* del día. ‖ **set square** cartabón *m*, escuadra.
▷ *vt* **1** *(put, place)* poner, colocar. **2** *(prepare - trap)* tender, preparar; *(- table)* poner; *(- camera, video)* preparar, *(- clock, watch, oven, etc)* poner: **set the table for dinner** *pon la mesa para la cena.* **3** *(date, time)* fijar, señalar, acordar: **have you set a date for the wedding?** *¿has fijado una fecha para la boda?* **4** *(price)* fijar; *(value)* poner. **5** *(jewel, stone)* montar, engastar. **6** *(text for printing)* componer. **7** *(exam, test, problem)* poner; *(homework)* mandar, poner; *(task)* asignar; *(text)* prescribir; *(target, aim)* fijar, proponer. **8** *(story, action)* ambientar: **the novel is set in Madrid** *la novela está ambientada en Madrid.*
▷ *vi* **1** *(sun, moon)* ponerse. **2** *(liquid, jelly)* cuajar, cuajarse.
⊙ **to set about** *vt insep* **1** *(begin)* empezar a, ponerse a. **2** *(attack)* atacar, agredir.
⊙ **to set against** *vt sep* **1** *(cause to oppose)* enemistar con. **2** *(balance, compare)* contraponer.
⊙ **to set apart** *vt sep (distinguish)* distinguir (**from**, de), hacer diferente (**from**, de).
⊙ **to set aside** *vt sep* **1** *(save)* guardar, ahorrar. **2** *(disregard)* dejar de lado.
⊙ **to set back** *vt sep* **1** *(delay)* retrasar, atrasar. **2** *fam (cost)* costar.
⊙ **to set down** *vt sep* **1** *(write)* poner por escrito, escribir. **2** GB *(passenger)* dejar.
⊙ **to set forth** *vi* emprender marcha, partir.
⊙ **to set in** *vi (bad weather)* empezar, comenzar; *(problems, etc)* surgir.
⊙ **to set off** *vi (begin journey)* salir.
▷ *vt sep* **1** *(bomb)* hacer estallar, hacer explotar; *(alarm)* hacer sonar; *(firework)* lanzar, tirar. **2** *(cause, start)* hacer empezar, provocar.
⊙ **to set on** *vt sep (cause to attack)* echar: **I'll set the dog on you** *te echaré el perro.*
⊙ **to set out** *vi* **1** *(begin journey)* partir, salir (**for**, para). **2** *(intend)* proponerse (**to**, -), tener la intención de, querer.
▷ *vt sep* **1** *(arrange)* disponer, exponer. **2** *(explain)* exponer.
⊙ **to set to** *vi* ponerse a, empezar a.
⊙ **to set up** *vt sep* **1** *(statue)* levantar, erigir; *(roadblock)* colocar; *(tent, stall)* montar; *(machine, equipment)* montar, armar. **2** *fam (drinks)* poner, servir. **3** *(business)* montar, poner; *(school, trust fund)* fundar. **4** *(provide with)* proveer de. **5** *fam (make healthier)* ayudar a reponerse. **6** *(establish person)* establecerse (**as**, como).
▷ *vi* establecerse (**as**, como).
▲ *pt & pp* **set**.

setback ['setbæk] *n* revés *m*, contratiempo.

settee [se'tiː] *n* sofá *m.*

setter ['setəʳ] *n (dog)* setter *m.*

setting ['setɪŋ] *n* **1** *(of sun)* puesta. **2** *(background)* marco, entorno; *(of film, novel)* escenario. **3** *(of machine, device, etc)* ajuste *m*, posición *f.*

setting-up [setɪŋ'ʌp] *n* fundación *f.*

settle[1] ['setᵊl] *vt* **1** *(establish)* instalar, colocar; *(make comfortable)* poner cómodo,-a: **he settled himself on the sofa** *se puso cómodo en el sofá.* **2** *(decide on, fix)* acordar, decidir, fijar. **3** *(sort out - problem, dispute)* resolver, solucionar; *(- differences)* resolver, arreglar; *(- score)* arreglar, ajustar: **we need to settle an argument** *tenemos que resolver una discusión.* **4** *(calm - nerves)* calmar; *(- stomach)* asentar.
▷ *vi* **1** *(make one's home in)* establecerse, afincarse, instalarse. **2** *(make OS comfortable)* ponerse cómodo,-a (**into**, en). **3** *(bird, fly, etc)* posarse. **4** *(sediment, dregs)* precipitarse, depositarse. **5** *(calm down)* calmarse, tranquilizarse. **6** *(pay)* pagar, saldar la deuda.
⊙ **to settle down** *vi* **1** *(establish a home)* instalarse, afincarse, establecerse; *(lead settled way of life)* empezar a llevar una vida asentada. **2** *(calm down)* calmarse, tranquilizarse. **3** *(get comfortable)* ponerse cómodo,-a.
⊙ **to settle down to** *vt insep (get used to)* adaptarse a, acostumbrarse a.
▷ *vi (begin seriously, give attention to)* ponerse a.
⊙ **to settle for** *vt insep (accept)* aceptar.

▷ **to settle in** *vi* 1 *(get used to)* acostumbrarse, adaptarse. 2 *(move in)* instalarse.
▷ **to settle on** *vt insep (decide on)* decidirse por.
▷ **to settle up** *vi* saldar la cuenta (**with**, con).
settle² ['setᵊl] *n (wooden bench)* banco.
settled ['setᵊld] *adj (habits, life)* ordenado,-a; *(weather)* estable.
settlement ['setᵊlmənt] *n* 1 *(village)* poblado, pueblo, asentamiento; *(colony)* colonia. 2 *(agreement)* acuerdo, convenio.
settler ['setᵊləʳ] *n* poblador,-ra, colono *mf*.
set-to [set'tuː] *n* riña, pelea.
▲ *pl* **set-tos**.
setup ['setʌp] *n* 1 *(arrangement, organization)* sistema *m*, situación *f*. 2 *fam (trick)* montaje *m*.
seven ['sevᵊn] *adj* siete.
▷ *n* siete *m*.
Consulta también **six**.
seventeen [sevᵊn'tiːn] *adj* diecisiete.
▷ *n* diecisiete *m*.
Consulta también **six**.
seventeenth [sevᵊn'tiːnθ] *adj* decimoséptimo,-a.
▷ *adv* en decimoséptimo lugar.
▷ *n* 1 *(in series)* decimoséptimo,-a. 2 *(fraction)* decimoséptimo; *(one part)* decimoséptima parte *f*.
Consulta también **sixth**.
seventh ['sevᵊnθ] *adj* séptimo,-a.
▷ *adv* en séptimo lugar.
▷ *n* 1 *(in series)* séptimo,-a. 2 *(fraction)* séptimo; *(one part)* séptima parte *f*.
Consulta también **sixth**.
seventieth ['sevᵊntɪəθ] *adj* septuagésimo,-a.
▷ *adv* en septuagésimo lugar.
▷ *n* 1 *(in series)* septuagésimo,-a. 2 *(fraction)* septuagésimo; *(one part)* septuagésima parte *f*.
Consulta también **sixtieth**.
seventy ['sevᵊntɪ] *adj* setenta.
▷ *n* setenta *m*.
Consulta también **sixty**.
sever ['sevəʳ] *vt* 1 *(cut)* cortar. 2 *(relations, ties)* romper; *(communications)* cortar.
several ['sevᵊrəl] *adj (some)* varios,-as: **we've been there several times** *hemos ido varias veces*.
▷ *pron (some)* varios,-as.
severance ['sevᵊrəns] *n* ruptura.
severe [sɪ'vɪəʳ] *adj* 1 *(person, punishment* severo,-a. 2 *(pain)* agudo,-a; *(injury, illness, damage)* grave, serio,-a.
severely [sɪ'vɪəlɪ] *adv* 1 *(strictly)* severamente, con severidad. 2 *(seriously)* gravemente.
severity [sɪ'verətɪ] *n* 1 *(of person, punishment, criticism)* severidad *f*. 2 *(of pain)* agudeza, intensidad *f*; *(of illness, wound)* gravedad *f*.
sew [səʊ] *vt* coser (**onto**, a).
▷ *vi* coser.
▲ *pt* **sewed**, *pp* **sewed** o **sewn** [səʊn].
▷ **to sew up** *vt sep* 1 *(hole, tear, etc)* coser; *(mend)* remendar. 2 *fam (arrange, settle)* arreglar, acordar.
sewage ['sjuːɪdʒ] *n* aguas *fpl* residuales.
sewer [sjʊəʳ] *n* alcantarilla, cloaca.
sewerage ['sjuːərɪdʒ] *n (system)* alcantarillado.
sewing ['səʊɪŋ] *n* costura. ● **sewing machine** máquina de coser.
sewn [səʊn] *pp* → **sew**.
sex [seks] *n* sexo: **the opposite sex** *el sexo opuesto*. ■ **to have sex with** SB tener relaciones sexuales con ALGN.
sexism ['seksɪzᵊm] *n* sexismo.
sexist ['seksɪst] *adj* sexista.
▷ *n* sexista *mf*.
sextet [seks'tet] *n* MUS sexteto.
sexual ['seksjʊəl] *adj* sexual.
sexuality [seksjʊ'ælətɪ] *n* sexualidad *f*.
sexy ['seksɪ] *adj (sexually attractive)* sexy; *(erotic)* erótico,-a.
▲ *comp* **sexier**, *superl* **sexiest**.
Seychelles [seɪ'ʃelz] *n* **the Seychelles** las Seychelles *fpl*.
shabby ['ʃæbɪ] *adj* 1 *(clothes)* gastado,-a, raído,-a, desharrapado,-a; *(furniture)* de aspecto lastimoso. 2 *(person)* mal vestido,-a, desaseado,-a.
▲ *comp* **shabbier**, *superl* **shabbiest**.
shack [ʃæk] *n* choza.
shackle ['ʃækᵊl] *vt* 1 poner grilletes a. 2 *fig* poner trabas a, coartar, constreñir.
▷ *n pl* **shackles** grilletes *mpl*, grillos *mpl*.
shad [ʃæd] *n* alosa.
shade [ʃeɪd] *n* 1 *(shadow)* sombra: **a temperature of 30 degrees in the shade** *una temperatura de 30 grados a la sombra*. 2 *(for lamp)* pantalla; *(for eye)* visera; *(blind)* persiana. 3 *(of colour)* tono, matiz *m*.
▷ *vt* 1 *(shelter from light)* proteger de la luz. 2 ART *(darken)* sombrear (**in**, -).
▷ *vi (change gradually)* convertirse (**into**, en).
▷ *n pl* **shades** *fam* gafas *fpl* de sol.
shading ['ʃeɪdɪŋ] *n* sombreado.
shadoof [ʃæ'duːf] *n* cigoñal *m*.
shadow ['ʃædəʊ] *n* 1 *(dark shape)* sombra. 2 *(trace)* sombra, vestigio. 3 *(follower)* sombra.
▷ *adj* GB de la oposición, en la sombra.
▷ *vt (follow)* seguir la pista a.
▷ *n pl* **shadows** *(darkness)* oscuridad *f sing*.
shadowy ['ʃædəʊɪ] *adj* 1 *(dark)* oscuro,-a; *(dim)* vago,-a, impreciso,-a, borroso,-a. 2 *(mysterious)* misterioso,-a.
shaduf [ʃæ'duːf] *n* cigoñal *m*.
shady ['ʃeɪdɪ] *adj* 1 *(place)* a la sombra; *(tree)* que da sombra. 2 *fam (person)* sospechoso,-a; *(deal, past)* turbio,-a.
▲ *comp* **shadier**, *superl* **shadiest**.
shaft [ʃɑːft] *n* 1 *(of axe, tool, golf club)* mango; *(of arrow)* astil *m*; *(of lance, spear)* asta. 2 *(of mine)* pozo; *(of lift)* hueco. 3 *(of light)* rayo.
shaggy ['ʃægɪ] *adj* 1 *(hair, beard)* desgreñado,-a, greñudo,-a, enmarañado,-a. 2 *(dog)* lanudo,-a, peludo,-a.
▲ *comp* **shaggier**, *superl* **shaggiest**.
shah [ʃɑː] *n* sha *m*.
shake [ʃeɪk] *n* 1 sacudida. 2 US *fam (milkshake)* batido.
▷ *vt* 1 *(move - carpet, person)* sacudir; *(- bottle, dice)* agitar: **shake well before use** *agítese bien antes de usar*. 2 *(upset, shock)* afectar, impresionar, conmocionar: **the news shook her badly** *la noticia le afectó mucho*. ■ **to shake hands** estrecharse la mano. ‖ **to shake one's head** negar con la cabeza.
▷ *vi (gen)* temblar.
▲ *pt* **shook** [ʃʊk], *pp* **shaken** ['ʃeɪkᵊn].

▷ *n pl* **the shakes** *(trembling)* temblequera; *(feverish)* tiritera.
⊙ **to shake out** *vt sep* sacudir.
⊙ **to shake up** *vt sep* **1** *(liquid)* agitar. **2** *(shock, upset)* afectar, impresionar, conmocionar.
shaken ['ʃeɪkᵊn] *adj (liquid)* agitado,-a.
▲ *pp* ⟶ **shake.**
shaker ['ʃeɪkəʳ] *n (for cocktails)* coctelera; *(for salt)* salero.
shake-up ['ʃeɪkʌp] *n* COMM reorganización *f*.
shaky ['ʃeɪkɪ] *adj* **1** *(hand, voice)* tembloroso,-a; *(writing)* temblón,-ona; *(step)* inseguro,-a. **2** *fig (argument, etc)* sin fundamento; *(government, currency)* débil.
▲ *comp* **shakier**, *superl* **shakiest.**
shale [ʃeɪl] *n* esquisto, pizarra.
shall [ʃæl, *unstressed* ʃᵊl] *aux* **1** [Used with 1st person *sing* & *pl.*] *(future)*: **I shall go tomorrow** *iré mañana;* **I shan't mention any names** *no daré nombres.* **2** [Used with 1st person *sing* & *pl.*] *(questions, offers, suggestions)*: **shall I close the window?** *¿cierro la ventana?;* **I'll carry it, shall I?** *lo llevaré yo, ¿quieres?* **3** *fml (emphatic, command)*: **you shall leave immediately** *te irás enseguida.*
shallot [ʃə'lɒt] *n* chalota.
shallow ['ʃæləʊ] *adj* **1** *(water, pond, etc)* poco profundo,-a; *(dish, bowl)* llano,-a, plano,-a. **2** *fig* superficial.
▷ *n pl* **shallows** bajío *m sing*.
▲ *comp* **shallower**, *superl* **shallowest.**
shallowness ['ʃæləʊnəs] *n* **1** *(of water)* poca profundidad *f*. **2** *fig* superficialidad *f*.
sham [ʃæm] *n* farsa, simulacro.
▷ *adj* falso,-a, simulado,-a.
▷ *vt* fingir, simular.
▲ *pt & pp* **shammed**, *ger* **shamming.**
shaman ['ʃeɪmən] *n* chamán *m*.
shamble ['ʃæmbᵊl] *vi* andar arrastrando los pies.
shambles ['ʃæmbᵊlz] *n fam (mess)* desastre *m*, caos *m*: **the house is in a shambles!** *¡la casa está hecha un desastre!*
shambolic [ʃæm'bɒlɪk] *adj fam* caótico,-a.
shame [ʃeɪm] *n* **1** *(disgrace, humiliation)* vergüenza; *(dishonour)* deshonra. **2** *(pity)* pena, lástima: **what a shame you couldn't go** *qué pena que no pudieras ir.*
▷ *vt* avergonzar, deshonrar.
shamefaced [ʃeɪm'feɪst] *adj* avergonzado,-a.
shameful ['ʃeɪmfʊl] *adj* vergonzoso,-a.
shameless ['ʃeɪmləs] *adj* desvergonzado,-a.
shamelessness ['ʃeɪmləsnəs] *n* descaro.
shammy ['ʃæmɪ] *n* gamuza.
▲ *pl* **shammies.**
shampoo [ʃæm'puː] *n* **1** *(product)* champú *m*. **2** *(act)* lavado.
▲ *pl* **shampoos.**
▷ *vt (hair)* lavar, lavarse (con champú).
▲ *pt & pp* **shampooed**, *ger* **shampooing.**
shamrock ['ʃæmrɒk] *n* trébol *m*.
shandy ['ʃændɪ] *n* GB cerveza con limonada.
▲ *pl* **shandies.**
shank [ʃæŋk] *n* **1** *(of anchor, key)* tija; *(of tool, drill, golf club)* mango. **2** CULIN *(of meat)* pierna.
▷ *n pl* **shanks** ANAT espinillas *fpl*, canillas *fpl*.
shan't [ʃɑːnt] *aux* ⟶ **shall.**
shanty[1] ['ʃæntɪ] *n (song)* saloma.
shanty[2] ['ʃæntɪ] *n (shack)* chabola.
▲ *pl* **shanties.**
shantytown ['ʃæntɪtaʊn] *n* chabolas *fpl*, barrio d[e] chabolas.
shape [ʃeɪp] *n* **1** *(form, appearance)* forma: **in the shap[e] of a heart** *en forma de corazón.* **2** *(outline, shadow)* figura. **3** *(state - of thing)* estado; *(- of person)* forma, condicio[n]nes *fpl*: **the team is in good shape** *el equipo está en buen[a] forma.* **4** *(framework, character)* configuración *f*. ■ **in a[ll] shapes and sizes** de todas las formas. ▮ **in shape** *(fit)* e[n] forma. ▮ **in the shape of 1** *(physically)* bajo la forma de. [2] *(figuratively)* en forma de. ▮ **to take shape** tomar forma.
▷ *vt* **1** *(gen)* dar forma a; *(clay)* modelar: **he shaped th[e] dough into a ball** *formó una bola con la masa.* **2** *(charac[ter])* formar; *(future, destiny)* decidir, determinar.
⊙ **to shape up** *vi* desarrollarse.
shaped [ʃeɪpt] *adj* en forma de.
shapeless ['ʃeɪpləs] *adj* informe, sin forma.
shapely ['ʃeɪplɪ] *adj (body)* curvilíneo,-a; *(legs)* tor[]neado,-a.
share [ʃeəʳ] *n* **1** *(portion)* parte *f*. **2** FIN acción *m*. ■ **to d[o] one's share** hacer su parte.
▷ *vt* **1** *(have or use with others)* compartir; *(have in commo[n])* compartir, tener en común: **can you share one boo[k] between two?** *¿podéis compartir un libro entre los dos?* [2] *(tell news, feelings, etc)* compartir. **3** *(divide)* repartir.
▷ *vi* compartir: **there's only one bed so you'll have to shar[e]** *solo hay una cama, así que tendréis que compartirla.*
sharecropper ['ʃeəkrɒpəʳ] *n* aparcero,-a.
sharecropping ['ʃeəkrɒpɪŋ] *n* aparcería.
shareholder ['ʃeəhəʊldəʳ] *n* accionista *mf*.
share-out ['ʃeəraʊt] *n* reparto.
shareware ['ʃeəweəʳ] *n* programas *mpl* compartidos.
shark[1] [ʃɑːk] *n* ZOOL tiburón *m*.
shark[2] [ʃɑːk] *n fam (swindler)* estafador,-ra.
sharp [ʃɑːp] *adj* **1** *(knife, etc)* afilado,-a; *(needle, penci[l])* puntiagudo,-a. **2** *(angle)* agudo,-a; *(bend)* cerrado,-a; *(slope)* empinado,-a. **3** *(outline)* definido,-a; *(photograph, etc)* nítido,-a; *(contrast)* marcado,-a. **4** *(mind, wit)* perspi[]caz; *(eyes, ears)* agudo,-a, bueno,-a: **keep a sharp ey[e] on those two** *ten bien vigilados a esos dos.* **5** *(perso[n] - clever)* listo,-a, vivo,-a; *(- quick-witted)* avispado,-a, despabilado,-a. **6** *(pain)* agudo,-a, fuerte; *(cry, noise)* agudo,-a, estridente; *(frost)* fuerte; *(wind)* cortante, pe[]netrante. **7** *(taste)* ácido,-a; *(smell)* acre. **8** *(change, etc)* brusco,-a, repentino,-a, súbito,-a. **9** *(blow)* seco,-a. **10** *(cri[]ticism)* mordaz; *(rebuke)* severo,-a; *(retort)* cortante; *(tem[]per)* arisco,-a, violento,-a; *(tone)* seco,-a. **11** MUS *(key)* sostenido,-a; *(too high)* desafinado,-a.
▷ *adv* **1** *(exactly)* en punto: **at ten o'clock sharp** *a las die[z] en punto.* **2** *(abruptly)* bruscamente. **3** MUS *(too high)* demasiado alto,-a.
sharp-edged [ʃɑːp'edʒd] *adj* afilado,-a.
sharpen ['ʃɑːpᵊn] *vt* **1** *(knife, claws)* afilar; *(pencil)* saca[r] punta a. **2** *fig (feeling, intelligence)* agudizar; *(desire)* avi[]var; *(appetite)* abrir.
▷ *vi (voice)* agudizarse.
sharpener ['ʃɑːpᵊnəʳ] *n (for knife)* afilador *m*; *(for penci[l])* sacapuntas *m*.
sharp-eyed [ʃɑːp'aɪd] *adj* que tiene vista de lince.
sharply ['ʃɑːplɪ] *adv* **1** *(abruptly, suddenly)* repentina[]mente. **2** *(acutely)* agudamente. **3** *(clearly)* marcada[]mente, claramente.

sharpness ['ʃɑ:pnəs] *n* **1** *(of knife)* lo afilado; *(of point)* lo puntiagudo; *(of features)* lo anguloso. **2** *(of taste)* acidez *f*. **3** *(abruptness, suddenness)* brusquedad *f*. **4** *(of image, etc)* nitidez *f*. **5** *(of pain)* agudeza, intensidad *f*. **6** *(harshness)* mordacidad *f*, severidad *f*.

sharpshooter ['ʃɑ:pʃu:tə^r] *n* tirador,-ra de primera.

sharp-tongued [ʃɑ:p'tʌŋd] *adj* de lengua viperina, de lengua mordaz.

sharp-witted [ʃɑ:p'wɪtɪd] *adj* perspicaz.

shatter ['ʃætə^r] *vt* **1** *(break into small pieces)* romper, hacer añicos, hacer pedazos. **2** *fig (health)* destrozar, quebrantar, minar; *(nerves)* destrozar. **3** *fam (shock)* conmocionar, afectar, dejar destrozado,-a.

▷ *vi (break)* romperse, hacerse añicos.

shattered ['ʃætəd] *adj* **1** *(broken)* hecho,-a añicos, hecho,-a pedazos. **2** *(shocked)* destrozado,-a. **3** *(exhausted)* agotado,-a.

shattering ['ʃætərɪŋ] *adj* **1** *(experience, news, etc)* terrible, demoledor,-ra. **2** *(exhausting)* agotador,-ra.

shatterproof ['ʃætəpru:f] *adj* inastillable.

shave [ʃeɪv] *n* afeitado.

▷ *vt* **1** *(face, legs, underarms)* afeitar. **2** *(wood)* cepillar.

▷ *vi (person)* afeitarse: **he shaves every morning** *se afeita cada mañana.* ■ **to have a shave** afeitarse.

shaven ['ʃeɪvən] *adj* afeitado,-a.

shaver ['ʃeɪvə^r] *n* máquina de afeitar.

shaving ['ʃeɪvɪŋ] *n (of face)* afeitado. ● **shaving brush** brocha de afeitar. ‖ **shaving cream** crema de afeitar. ‖ **shaving foam** espuma de afeitar.

▷ *n pl* **shavings** *(wood)* virutas *fpl*.

shawl [ʃɔ:l] *n* chal *m*, mantón *m*.

she [ʃi:] *pron* ella: **she's called Nina** *se llama Nina;* **she's happy** *está contenta.*

▷ *n (animal)* hembra; *(baby)* niña.

she- [ʃi:] *pref* hembra: **she-bear** *osa.*

sheaf [ʃi:f] *n* **1** *(of corn, barley, etc)* gavilla. **2** *(of papers, banknotes, etc)* fajo. **3** *(of arrows)* haz *m*.

▲ *pl* **sheaves.**

shear [ʃɪə^r] *vt* **1** *(sheep)* esquilar.

▲ *pt* **sheared,** *pp* **sheared** o **shorn** [ʃɔ:n].

▷ *n pl* **shears** *(gen)* tijeras *fpl* (grandes); *(for hedges)* podadera *f sing*.

shearer ['ʃɪərə^r] *n* esquilador,-ra.

shearing ['ʃɪərɪŋ] *n* esquileo, esquila.

sheath [ʃi:θ] *n* **1** *(for knife, scissors)* funda. **2** BOT vaina. **3** *(condom)* preservativo, condón *m*.

▲ *pl* **sheaths** [ʃi:ðz].

sheathe ['ʃi:ð] *vt (knife)* enfundar.

sheathing ['ʃi:ðɪŋ] *n (for building)* cubierta.

shed¹ [ʃed] *n (in garden, for bicycles)* cobertizo.

shed² [ʃed] *vt* **1** *(leaves, horns, skin)* mudar; *(clothes)* quitarse, despojarse de; *(workers, jobs)* deshacerse de; *(load, weight)* perder: **the snake sheds its skin** *la serpiente muda la piel.* **2** *fig (inhibitions, etc)* liberarse de. **3** *(water)* repeler. **4** *(blood, tears, etc)* derramar.

▲ *pt & pp* **shed,** *ger* **shedding.**

she'd [ʃi:d] *contr* **1** she had. **2** she would.

sheen [ʃi:n] *n* brillo, lustre *m*.

sheep [ʃi:p] *n* oveja.

▲ *pl* **sheep.**

sheepdog ['ʃi:pdɒg] *n* perro pastor.

sheepfold ['ʃi:pfəʊld] *n* redil *m*, aprisco.

sheepish ['ʃi:pɪʃ] *adj (embarrassed)* avergonzado,-a; *(lacking initiative)* borrego,-a.

sheepishly ['ʃi:pɪʃlɪ] *adv* con vergüenza.

sheepshearer ['ʃi:pʃɪərə^r] *n* esquilador,-ra.

sheepshearing ['ʃi:pʃɪərɪŋ] *n* esquileo.

sheepskin ['ʃi:pskɪn] *n* **1** *(skin, leather)* piel *f* de borrego. **2** *(parchment)* pergamino. ● **sheepskin jacket** pelliza.

sheer [ʃɪə^r] *adj* **1** *(total, utter)* total, absoluto,-a, puro,-a: **by sheer coincidence** *por pura casualidad.* **2** *(cliff)* escarpado,-a; *(drop)* vertical.

sheet [ʃi:t] *n* **1** *(on bed)* sábana: **bottom/top sheet** *sábana bajera/encimera.* **2** *(of paper)* hoja; *(of metal)* lámina, chapa; *(of glass)* lámina, placa; *(of tin)* hoja. ● **sheet music** hojas *pl* de partitura, papel pautado.

▷ *vi (rain heavily)* diluviar, llover a cántaros.

shelduck ['ʃeldʌk] *n* tarro.

shelf [ʃelf] *n* estante. ● **(set of) shelves** estantería. ‖ **shelf life** *tiempo que puede permanecer expuesto para su venta un producto perecedero.*

▲ *pl* **shelves.**

shell [ʃel] *n* **1** *(of egg, nut)* cáscara; *(of pea)* vaina; *(of tortoise, lobster, etc)* caparazón *m*; *(of snail, oyster, etc)* concha: **the children were collecting shells on the beach** *los niños recogían conchas en la playa.* **2** *(of building)* armazón *m*, esqueleto, estructura; *(of vehicle)* armazón *m*; *(of ship)* casco. **3** MIL *(for explosives)* proyectil *m*, obús *m*.

▷ *vt* **1** *(nuts, egg)* pelar; *(peas)* desvainar; *(mussels, etc)* quitar la concha a. **2** MIL bombardear.

⊙ **to shell out** *vt sep fam (money)* soltar, aflojar.

▷ *vi fam* apoquinar.

she'll [ʃi:l] *contr* she will, she shall.

shellac [ʃə'læk] *n* laca.

shellfish ['ʃelfɪʃ] *n (individual)* marisco; *(as food)* marisco, mariscos *mpl*.

▲ *pl* **shellfish.**

shelling ['ʃelɪŋ] *n* MIL bombardeo.

shell-shocked ['ʃelʃɒkt] *adj* MED traumatizado,-a por la guerra.

shelter ['ʃeltə^r] *n* **1** *(protection)* abrigo, protección *f*, cobijo: **the climbers sought shelter from the storm** *los montañeros buscaron abrigo para protegerse de la tormenta.* **2** *(place)* refugio, cobijo.

▷ *vt (protect)* abrigar, proteger, resguardar. **these trees should shelter us from the rain** *esos árboles nos resguardarán de la lluvia.*

▷ *vi (from weather, etc)* resguardarse, guarecerse; *(from danger)* refugiarse.

sheltered ['ʃeltəd] *adj* abrigado,-a. ● **sheltered sheltered housing** viviendas *fpl* vigiladas *(para ancianos y minusválidos)*.

shelve¹ [ʃelv] *vt* **1** *(put on shelf)* poner en el estante, poner en la estantería. **2** *fig (postpone, abandon)* aparcar, archivar.

shelve² [ʃelv] *vi (slope)* bajar, descender.

shelves [ʃelvz] *pl* → **shelf.**

shelving ['ʃelvɪŋ] *n* estanterías *fpl*.

shepherd ['ʃepəd] *n* pastor *m*.

▷ *vt (guide, direct)* guiar, conducir.

shepherdess ['ʃepədes] *n* pastora.

sherbet ['ʃɜ:bət] *n* **1** GB *(sweets)* polvos *mpl* picapica, sidral *m*. **2** US *(sorbet)* sorbete *m*.

sheriff ['ʃerɪf] *n* **1** US sheriff *mf*, alguacil,-la. **2** GB gobernador,-ra civil. **3** *(in Scotland)* juez *mf* presidente.

sherry ['ʃerɪ] *n* jerez *m*.
▲ *pl* **sherries.**

she's [ʃiːz] *contr* **1** she is. **2** she has.

shield [ʃiːld] *n* **1** *(for protection)* escudo. **2** TECH pantalla protectora. **3** *(of animal)* caparazón *m*.
▷ *vt (protect)* proteger (**from**, de).

shift [ʃɪft] *n* **1** *(change)* cambio: **a shift in policy** *un cambio de política.* **2** *(of work, workers)* turno: **the day/night shift** *el turno de día/de noche.* **3** *(on keyboard)* tecla de las mayúsculas. **4** *dated (trick, scheme, expedient)* expediente *m*, recurso. ● **shift key** tecla de las mayúsculas.
▷ *vt* **1** *(change)* cambiar; *(move)* desplazar, mover: **he shifted his feet** *movió sus pies.* **2** *(transfer)* traspasar, transferir. **3** GB *fam (remove, get rid of)* quitar; *(sell)* vender. **4** US *(change gear)* cambiar.
▷ *vi* **1** *(change)* cambiar: **the wind shifted** *el viento cambió de dirección.* **2** *(move)* moverse, cambiar de sitio, desplazarse; *(cargo)* correrse. **3** US *(change gear)* cambiar de marcha. ■ **to shift for** os arreglárselas solo.

shiftily ['ʃɪftɪlɪ] *adv* de manera sospechosa.

shiftless ['ʃɪftləs] *adj* perezoso,-a, vago,-a.

shifty ['ʃɪftɪ] *adj (person)* sospechoso,-a; *(behaviour)* furtivo,-a.
▲ *comp* **shiftier**, *superl* **shiftiest.**

shilling ['ʃɪlɪŋ] *n* chelín *m*.

shimmer ['ʃɪmə^r] *n (tremulous light)* luz *f* trémula, reflejo trémulo; *(shining)* brillo.
▷ *vi (shine)* relucir, brillar; *(in water)* rielar.
▲ *pt & pp* **shinned**, *ger* **shinning.**

shimmering ['ʃɪmərɪŋ] *adj* reluciente, brillante.

shin [ʃɪn] *n* ANAT espinilla, canilla. ● **shin guard / shin pad** espinillera.
⊙ **to shin down** *vi* deslizarse por.
⊙ **to shin up** *vi* trepar.

shinbone ['ʃɪnbəʊn] *n* ANAT tibia.

shine [ʃaɪn] *n* brillo, lustre *m*: **he gave his shoes a good shine** *sacó brillo a sus zapatos.*
▷ *vi* **1** *(sun, light, eyes)* brillar; *(metal, glass, shoes)* relucir, brillar; *(face)* resplandecer, irradiar: **her eyes shone with happiness** *le brillaban los ojos de alegría.* **2** *fig (excel)* sobresalir (**at**, en), destacar (**at**, en), brillar (**at**, en): **he shines at tennis** *destaca en tenis.*
▷ *vt* **1** *(light, lamp)* dirigir. **2** [*pt & pp* **shined.**] *(polish)* sacar brillo a; *(shoes)* limpiar.
▲ *pt & pp* **shone** [ʃɒn].

shiner ['ʃaɪnə^r] *n fam (black eye)* ojo morado.

shingle[1] ['ʃɪŋgəl] *n (pebbles)* guijarros *mpl.* ● **shingle beach** playa de guijarros.

shingle[2] ['ʃɪŋgəl] *n* **1** *(roof tile)* tablilla. **2** US *(name plate)* placa.

shingles ['ʃɪŋgəlz] *n* MED herpes *m*, culebrilla.

shining ['ʃaɪnɪŋ] *adj* **1** *(metal, glass)* brillante, reluciente; *(eyes)* brillante, luminoso,-a; *(face, sun)* radiante; *(hair, furniture)* lustroso,-a. **2** *fig (outstanding)* destacado,-a, ilustre, magnífico,-a.

shiny ['ʃaɪnɪ] *adj (coin, leather, glass)* brillante, reluciente; *(hair, shoes)* lustroso,-a; *(material, trousers)* brillante; *(face, nose)* brillante.
▲ *comp* **shinier**, *superl* **shiniest.**

ship [ʃɪp] *n (gen)* barco, buque *m*, navío, embarcación *f*. ● **passenger ship** buque *m* de pasajeros. ‖ **ship's company** tripulación *f*.
▷ *vt (send - gen)* enviar, mandar; *(- by ship)* enviar po barco: **we had our luggage shipped to England** *mandamos nuestro equipaje a Inglaterra por barco.*
▲ *pt & pp* **shipped**, *ger* **shipping.**
⊙ **to ship off** *vt sep (person)* despachar.

shipboard ['ʃɪpbɔːd] *n* de a bordo. ■ **on shipboard** a bordo.

shipbuilder ['ʃɪpbɪldə^r] *n* constructor,-ra naval, empresa de construcción naval .

shipbuilding ['ʃɪpbɪldɪŋ] *n* construcción *f* naval.

shipload ['ʃɪpləʊd] *n* cargamento, carga.

shipment ['ʃɪpmənt] *n (act)* embarque *m*, envío transporte *m* (marítimo).

shipowner ['ʃɪpəʊnə^r] *n* armador,-ra.

shipper ['ʃɪpə^r] *n (gen)* consignador,-ra.

shipping ['ʃɪpɪŋ] *n* **1** *(business)* transporte *m* (en barco); *(sending)* envío, embarque *m*. **2** *(ships)* barcos *mpl*, buques *mpl.* ● **shipping agent** consignatario,-a agente *mf* marítimo,-a. ‖ **shipping company** empresa naviera. ‖ **shipping lane** ruta de navegación.

shipshape ['ʃɪpʃeɪp] *adj* limpio,-a y ordenado,-a, en perfecto orden.

shipwreck ['ʃɪprek] *n* naufragio. ■ **to be shipwrecked** naufragar.

shipyard ['ʃɪpjɑːd] *n* astillero.

shire ['ʃaɪə^r] *n* GB *arch (county)* condado.

shirk [ʃɜːk] *vt (duty, etc)* esquivar, eludir.

shirker ['ʃɜːkə^r] *n* gandul,-la, vago,-a.

shirt [ʃɜːt] *n (gen)* camisa; *(for sport)* camiseta.

shirtless ['ʃɜːtləs] *adj* sin camisa.

shirtsleeve ['ʃɜːtsliːv] *n* manga de camisa. ■ **in shirtsleeves** en mangas de camisa.

shirt-tail ['ʃɜːtteɪl] *n* faldón *m* de camisa.

shirty ['ʃɜːtɪ] *adj fam* agresivo,-a, grosero,-a.
▲ *comp* **shirtier**, *superl* **shirtiest.**

shit [ʃɪt] *n fam (faeces)* mierda.
▷ *interj fam* ¡mierda!
▷ *n* **1** *fam (nonsense)* imbecilidades *fpl*, gilipolleces *fpl*: **you talk shit** *no dices más que gilipolleces.* **2** *fam (worthless thing)* mierda; *(contemptible person)* cabrón,-ona, mierda *mf.*
▷ *vi-vt fam* cagar.
▲ *pt & pp* **shitted o shit**, *ger* **shitting.**
▷ *adj fam* de mierda.

shit-scared [ʃɪt'skeəd] *adj* acojonado,-a.

shiver ['ʃɪvə^r] *n (with cold)* escalofrío, tiritón *m*, estremecimiento; *(with fear)* escalofrío.
▷ *vi (with cold)* temblar, tiritar; *(with fear)* estremecerse
▷ *n pl* **the shivers** escalofríos *mpl.*

shivery ['ʃɪvərɪ] *adj (with cold)* estremecido,-a; *(feverish)* destemplado,-a.

shoal[1] [ʃəʊl] *n (underwater sandbank)* banco de arena.

shoal[2] [ʃəʊl] *n (of fish)* banco, cardumen *m*.
▷ *n pl* **shoals** *fam* montones *mpl.*

shock[1] [ʃɒk] *n* **1** *(jolt, blow)* choque *m*, impacto, golpe *m*; *(of explosion, etc)* sacudida; *(electric)* descarga. **2** *(upset, distress)* conmoción *f*, golpe *m*; *(fright, scare)* susto: **you gave me quite a shock** *me has dado un buen susto.* **3** MED shock *m*, choque *m*. ● **shock absorber** amort guador *m*. ▮ **shock therapy / shock treatment** electrochoque *m*.

▷ *vt* **1** *(upset)* conmocionar, conmover, afectar. **2** *(startle)* asustar, sorprender; *(scandalize)* escandalizar, horrorizar.

▷ *vi* impresionar, impactar.

hock[2] [ʃɒk] *n (of hair)* mata.

hocked [ʃɒkt] *adj* horrorizado,-a, escandalizado,-a.

hocker [ˈʃɒkəʳ] *n* **1** *(bad thing)* desastre *m*. **2** *(surprise)* bombazo.

hockheaded [ˈʃɒkhedɪd] *adj* greñudo,-a.

hocking [ˈʃɒkɪŋ] *adj* **1** *(disgraceful, offensive)* chocante, escandaloso,-a, vergonzoso,-a. **2** *fam (very bad)* espantoso,-a, pésimo,-a.

hockproof [ˈʃɒkpruːf] *adj* a prueba de golpes.

hoddy [ˈʃɒdɪ] *adj* **1** *(work)* chapucero,-a; *(thing)* de pacotilla, de mala calidad. **2** *(treatment)* mezquino,-a.

▲ *comp* **shoddier**, *superl* **shoddiest**.

hoe [ʃuː] *n* **1** zapato: **I need a new pair of shoes** *necesito unos zapatos nuevos*. **2** *(for horse)* herradura. ■ **to put** OS **in** SB **else's shoes** ponerse en el lugar de ALGN. ● **shoe polish** betún *m*. ▮ **shoe shop** zapatería.

▷ *vt (horse)* herrar.

▲ *pt & pp* **shod** [ʃod].

hoebrush [ˈʃuːbrʌʃ] *n* cepillo para los zapatos.

hoehorn [ˈʃuːhɔːn] *n* calzador *m*.

hoelace [ˈʃuːleɪs] *n* cordón *m* (de zapato).

hoemaker [ˈʃuːmeɪkəʳ] *n* zapatero,-a.

hoeshine [ˈʃuːʃaɪn] *n* limpieza de zapatos. ● **shoeshine boy** limpiabotas *m*.

hoestring [ˈʃuːstrɪŋ] *n* **1** *(shoelace)* cordón *m* (de zapatos). **2** *(small amount of money)* poquísimo dinero. ■ **to do** STH **on a shoestring** hacer algo con poquísimo dinero.

hoetree [ˈʃuːtriː] *n* horma.

hone [ʃɒn] *pt* → **shine**.

hook [ʃuk] *pt* → **shake**.

hoo [ʃuː] *interj* ¡fuera!, ¡zape!

hoot [ʃuːt] *n* **1** BOT *(gen)* brote *m*, retoño; *(of vine)* sarmiento. **2** GB *(hunting party)* cacería; *(land)* coto de caza.

▷ *vt* **1** *(person, animal)* pegar un tiro a, pegar un balazo a; *(hit, wound)* herir (de bala); *(kill)* matar de un tiro, matar a tiros; *(hunt)* cazar: **she was shot in the back** *recibió un balazo en la espalda*. **2** *(fire - missile)* lanzar; *(- arrow, bullet, weapon)* disparar; *(- glance)* lanzar: **they shot questions at her** *la bombardearon a preguntas*. **3** *(film)* rodar, filmar; *(photograph)* fotografiar.

▷ *vi* **1** *(fire weapon)* disparar (**at**, a/sobre); *(hunt with gun)* cazar. **2** SP *(aim at goal)* tirar, disparar, chutar. **3** *(move quickly)* pasar volando, salir disparado,-a: **the car shot past us** *el coche nos pasó volando*. **4** CINEM rodar, filmar. **4** BOT brotar. ■ **to shoot for the moon** pedir la luna.

▲ *pt & pp* **shot** [ʃot]. ■ **to shoot pool** jugar al billar.

⊙ **to shoot down** *vt sep* **1** *(aircraft)* derribar, abatir; *(person)* matar a tiros. **2** *fig (argument, idea, etc)* rebatir.

⊙ **to shoot up** *vi (prices, costs)* dispararse; *(plant, child)* crecer mucho.

hooter [ˈʃuːtəʳ] *n sl* pistola, pipa.

hooting [ˈʃuːtɪŋ] *n* **1** *(shots)* disparos *mpl*, tiros *mpl*; *(killing)* asesinato; **2** *(hunting)* caza. **3** CINEM rodaje *m*.

▷ *adj (pain)* punzante. ● **shooting star** estrella fugaz.

shoot-out [ˈʃuːtaut] *n* tiroteo.

shop [ʃɒp] *n* **1** *(gen)* tienda; *(business)* comercio, negocio: **I'm going to the shop** *voy a la tienda*. **2** *(workshop)* taller *m*. ■ **to keep shop** tener una tienda. ▮ **to talk shop** hablar del trabajo. ● **repair shop** taller *m* de reparaciones. ▮ **shop assistant** dependiente,-a. ▮ **shop floor 1** *(part of factory)* taller *m*. **2** *(workers)* obreros *mpl*, trabajadores *mpl*. ▮ **shop window** escaparate *m*.

▷ *vi (gen)* hacer la compra, comprar: **we usually shop on Saturday mornings** *normalmente hacemos la compra los sábados por la mañana*.

▲ *pt & pp* **shopped**, *ger* **shopping**.

⊙ **to shop around** *vi* ir de tienda en tienda y comparar precios.

shopgirl [ˈʃɒpgɜːl] *n* dependienta.

shopkeeper [ˈʃɒpkiːpəʳ] *n* tendero,-a.

shoplift [ˈʃɒplɪft] *vi* hurtar (en las tiendas).

shoplifter [ˈʃɒplɪftəʳ] *n* mechero,-a.

shoplifting [ˈʃɒplɪftɪŋ] *n* hurto (en las tiendas).

shopper [ˈʃɒpəʳ] *n* comprador,-ra.

shopping [ˈʃɒpɪŋ] *n (purchases)* compra, compras *fpl*; *(activity)* compra: **I had a bit of shopping to do** *tuve que hacer unas compras*. ■ **to do the shopping** hacer la compra. ▮ **to go shopping** ir de compras, ir de tiendas, ir a comprar. ● **shopping basket** cesta de la compra. ▮ **shopping centre** centro comercial. ▮ **shopping list** lista de la compra. ▮ **shopping mall** US centro comercial. ▮ **shopping precinct** zona comercial. ▮ **shopping trolley** carrito (de la compra).

shopsoiled [ˈʃɒpsɔɪld] *adj* deteriorado,-a.

shore[1] [ʃɔːʳ] *n (of sea, lake)* orilla; *(coast)* costa; *(beach)* playa. ■ **on shore** en tierra.

shore[2] [ʃɔːʳ] *n* puntal *m*.

▷ *vt (building, tunnel)* apuntalar (**up**, -).

shorn [ʃɔːn] *pp* → **shear**.

shoring [ˈʃɔːrɪŋ] *n* apuntalamiento.

short [ʃɔːt] *adj* **1** *(not long)* corto,-a; *(not tall)* bajo,-a: **he's got short hair** *lleva el pelo corto*; **Jo is short for Joanne** *Jo es el diminutivo de Joanne*. **2** *(brief - of time)* breve, corto,-a: **the days are shorter in winter** *los días son más cortos en invierno* **3** *(deficient)* escaso,-a: **water was short** *escaseaba el agua*. **4** *(curt)* seco,-a, brusco, -a. ■ **for short** para abreviar. ▮ **in short** en pocas palabras. ▮ **in the short term** a corto plazo. ▮ **short of** a menos que, salvo que. ▮ **to be short of** STH andar escaso,-a de ALGO, estar falto,-a de ALGO: **I'm a bit short of money** *ando algo escaso de dinero*. ▮ **to run short of** STH acabarse ALGO: **we're running short of coffee** *se nos está acabando el café*. ● **short circuit** cortocircuito. ▮ **short cut 1** *(route)* atajo. **2** *(method)* método fácil, fórmula mágica. ▮ **short order** US comida rápida. ▮ **short story** cuento.

▷ *adv (abruptly)* bruscamente: **the car stopped short** *el coche se paró bruscamente*.

▷ *n* **1** *(drink)* copa, chupito. **2** CINEM cortometraje *m*, corto. **3** ELEC cortocircuito.

shortage [ˈʃɔːtɪdʒ] *n* falta, escasez *f*.

shortbread [ˈʃɔːtbred] *n galleta hecha de mantequilla, tipo mantecado*.

shortcake [ˈʃɔːtkeɪk] *n* **1** GB *galleta hecha de mantequilla, tipo mantecado*. **2** US tarta de frutas.

short-change [ʃɔ:t'tʃeɪndʒ] *vt* **1** *(give wrong change)* dar mal el cambio a, dar de menos (en el cambio) a. **2** *fam (cheat)* estafar.

short-circuit [ʃɔ:t'sɜ:kɪt] *vt* ELEC provocar un cortocircuito en.
▷ *vi* ELEC tener un cortocircuito.

shortcomings ['ʃɔ:tkʌmɪŋz] *n pl* defectos *mpl*, deficiencias *fpl*, puntos *mpl* flacos.

shortcrust pastry ['ʃɔ:tkrʌst'peɪstrɪ] *n* pasta quebradiza, pastaflora.

shorten ['ʃɔ:tᵊn] *vt* acortar.
▷ *vi* acortarse.

shortening ['ʃɔ:tᵊnɪŋ] *n* CULIN *(butter)* mantequilla; *(lard)* manteca.

shortfall ['ʃɔ:tfɔ:l] *n* déficit *m* (of/in, en).

short-haired ['ʃɔ:theəd] [Written **short haired** [ʃɔ:t'heəd] when not used to qualify a noun.] *adj* de pelo corto.

shorthand ['ʃɔ:thænd] *n* taquigrafía.

short-handed [ʃɔ:t'hændɪd] ■ **to be short-handed** no tener personal suficiente.

short-legged ['ʃɔ:t'legd] *adj* paticorto,-a.

short-list ['ʃɔ:tlɪst] *vt* incluir en la lista de preseleccionados.

short-lived ['ʃɔ:tlɪvd] *adj* efímero,-a, fugaz.

shortly ['ʃɔ:tlɪ] *adv* **1** *(soon)* dentro de poco, en breve: **shortly after/before** *poco después/antes.* **2** *(impatiently)* bruscamente.

short-necked ['ʃɔ:t'nekt] *adj* cuellicorto,-a.

shortness ['ʃɔ:tnəs] *n* **1** *(of thing, distance)* lo corto; *(of person)* baja estatura; *(of period)* brevedad *f*. **2** *(lack)* falta.

short-range ['ʃɔ:treɪndʒ] *adj* **1** MIL de corto alcance. **2** *(forecast, plan, project, etc)* a corto plazo.

shorts [ʃɔ:ts] *n pl* **1** pantalones *mpl* cortos, shorts *mpl*: **a pair of shorts** *un pantalón corto.* **2** US *(underpants)* calzoncillos *mpl*.

short-sighted ['ʃɔ:tsaɪtɪd] *adj* **1** MED miope, corto,-a de vista. **2** *(plan, policy, etc)* corto,-a de miras, estrecho,-a de miras.

short-sleeved ['ʃɔ:tsli:vd] *adj* de manga corta.

short-staffed ['ʃɔ:tstɑ:ft] ■ **to be short-staffed** no tener personal suficiente.

short-tempered ['ʃɔ:ttempəd] *adj* de mal genio.

short-term ['ʃɔ:ttɜ:m] *adj* a corto plazo.

short-wave ['ʃɔ:tweɪv] *adj* de onda corta.

short-winded [ʃɔ:t'wɪndɪd] *adj* corto,-a de resuello.

shot¹ [ʃɒt] *n* **1** *(act, sound)* tiro, disparo, balazo: **I thought I heard a shot** *creo haber oído un disparo.* **2** *(projectile)* bala, proyectil *m*. **3** *(person)* tirador,-ra. **4** SP *(in football)* chut *m*, chute *m*; *(in tennis, golf, cricket, etc)* golpe *m*; *(in basketball)* tiro. **5** *(attempt, try)* intento. **6** *fam (injection)* inyección *f*, pinchazo. **7** *(drink)* trago, chupito. **8** *(photo)* foto *f*; *(cinema)* toma. ■ **like a shot** *(without hesitation)* sin pensarlo dos veces, sin dudar.

shot² [sed] *pt & pp* → **shoot.**

shotgun ['ʃɒtgʌn] *n* escopeta.

shot-putter ['ʃɒtpʊtəʳ] *n* lanzador,-ra de peso.

should [ʃʊd] *aux* **1** *(duty, advisability, recommendation)* deber: **you should see the dentist** *deberías ir al dentista.* **2** *(probability)* deber de: **the clothes should be dry now** *la ropa ya debe de estar seca.* **3** *(subjunctive, conditional)*: **if you should see Janet by any chance** *si por casualida vieras a Janet.* **4** *(conditional, 1st person)*: **I should like t ask a question** *quisiera hacer una pregunta.* **5** *(tentativ statement)*: **I should think so** *me imagino que sí.* **6** *(disbe lief, surprise)*: **how should I know!** *¡yo qué sé!* ■ **I shoul have thought...** hubiera pensado...

shoulder ['ʃəʊldəʳ] *n* **1** ANAT hombro: **she looked ove her shoulder** *miró por encima del hombro.* **2** *(of mea* paletilla. **3** *(of hill, mountain)* ladera; *(of road)* arcén *m* andén *m*. ■ **a shoulder to cry on** un paño de lágrimas ▮ **to rub shoulders with** SB codearse con ALGN. ● **shoulder bag** bolso (de bandolera). ▮ **shoulder blade** omóplato. ▮ **shoulder strap 1** *(of garment)* tirante *m*. **2** *(c bag)* correa.
▷ *vt* **1** *(duty, responsibility)* cargar con. **2** *(load)* poners al hombro, echarse al hombro. **3** *(push)* empuja con el hombro.
▷ *n pl* **shoulders** ANAT hombros *mpl*, espalda *f sing*.

shoulder-length ['ʃəʊldəleŋθ] *adj* (que llega) hast los hombros.

shout [ʃaʊt] *n* grito.
▷ *vt* gritar (out, -): **get out! he shouted** *¡fuera! gritó.*
▷ *vi* gritar: **I don't like it when you shout at me** *no me gust que me grites.*
⊙ **to shout down** *vt sep* abuchear.

shouting ['ʃaʊtɪŋ] *n* gritos *mpl*, vocerío.

shove [ʃʌv] *n* empujón *m*: **we had to give the car shove** *tuvimos que dar un empujón al coche.*
▷ *vt* **1** *(push)* empujar: **she shoved the plate away** *apart el plato de un empujón.* **2** *(put casually)* meter.
▷ *vi (push)* empujar, dar empujones.
⊙ **to shove off** *vi* **1** *fam* largarse. **2** MAR desatracar.
⊙ **to shove over / shove up** *vi fam* correrse.

shovel ['ʃʌvᵊl] *n* **1** *(tool)* pala. **2** *(machine)* excavadora pala mecánica. ■ **to shovel food into one's mout** zamparse la comida.
▷ *vt* mover con pala, echar con pala.
▲ *pt & pp* **shovelled**, *ger* **shovelling.**

shovelful ['ʃʌvᵊlfʊl] *n* palada.

show [ʃəʊ] *n* **1** THEAT *(entertainment)* espectáculo; *(pe formance)* función *f*: **let's go and see a show** *vayamos ver un espectáculo.* **2** *(on TV, radio)* programa *m*, show *m*. **3** *(exhibition)* exposición *f*. **4** *(display)* muestra, demostración *f*: **a show of strength** *una demostración d fuerza, una exhibición de fuerza.* **5** *(outward appearanc pretence)* apariencia. ■ **the show must go on** el espectáculo debe continuar. ▮ **time will show** el tiempo l dirá. ▮ **to be all show** ser puro teatro, ser fingido,-a ▮ **to be on show** estar expuesto,-a. ● **fashion show** desfile *m* de modelos. ▮ **quiz show** programa *m* concurso ▮ **show business** el mundo del espectáculo.
▷ *vt* **1** *(display -gen)* enseñar; *(- things for sale)* mostra enseñar: **I showed her my photos** *le enseñé mis fotos.* *(point out)* indicar, señalar. **3** *(reveal - feelings)* demostrar, expresar; *(- interest, enthusiasm, etc)* demostra mostrar: **she rarely shows his feelings** *raras veces de muestra sus sentimientos.* **4** *(allow to be seen)* dejar ve **black doesn't show the dirt** *el negro no deja ver la sucie dad.* **5** *(measurement, etc)* marcar; *(profit, loss)* indica registrar, arrojar. **6** *(teach)* enseñar; *(explain)* explica **she showed us how it works** *nos enseñó cómo funciona* **7** *(prove, demonstrate)* demostrar. **8** *(depict, present)* re

presentar, mostrar: **this photo shows him swimming in the sea** *en esta foto está nadando en el mar.* **9** *(guide)* llevar, acompañar: **I'll show you to your room** *te acompañaré a tu habitación.* **10** *(painting, etc)* exponer, exhibir; *(film)* dar, poner, pasar, proyectar; *(slides)* pasar, proyectar; *(on TV)* dar, poner.

▷ *vi* **1** *(be perceptible)* verse, notarse: **the stain doesn't show** *no se ve la mancha.* **2** CINEM poner, dar, echar, proyectar, exhibir: **what's showing at the Odeon?** *¿qué dan en el Odeon?, ¿qué echan en el Odeon?*

⊙ **to show off** *vi (gen)* fanfarronear, presumir, lucirse; *(child)* hacerse el/la gracioso,-a.

▷ *vt sep* **1** *(set off)* hacer resaltar, realzar. **2** *(flaunt, parade)* hacer alarde de, presumir de.

⊙ **to show up** *vt sep* **1** *(make visible)* hacer resaltar, hacer destacar. **2** *fam (embarrass)* dejar en ridículo, poner en evidencia.

▷ *vi* **1** *(be visible)* notarse, verse. **2** *fam (arrive)* acudir, presentarse, aparecer.

▲ *pt* **showed**, *pp* **showed** o **shown** [ʃəun].

showcase ['ʃəukeɪs] *n* **1** *(cabinet)* vitrina. **2** *(opportunity, setting)* escaparate *m.*

▷ *vt* exhibir.

showdown ['ʃəudaun] *n* enfrentamiento.

shower ['ʃauəʳ] *n* **1** METEOR chubasco, chaparrón *m.* **2** *(of stones, blows, insults, etc)* lluvia. **3** *(in bathroom)* ducha. **4** US *(party)* fiesta de obsequio. ■ **to have a shower / take a shower** ducharse. ● **shower cap** gorro de baño. ● **shower gel** gel *m* de baño, gel *m* de ducha.

▷ *vt* **1** *(sprinkle)* espolvorear; *(spray)* rociar. **2** *fig (bestow, heap)* inundar, colmar, llover.

▷ *vi* **1** *(rain)* llover; *(objects)* caer, llover. **2** *(in bath)* ducharse.

showerproof ['ʃauəpru:f] *adj* impermeable.

showery ['ʃauərɪ] *adj* lluvioso,-a.

showgirl ['ʃəugɜ:l] *n (singer)* corista; *(dancer)* bailarina.

showing ['ʃəuɪŋ] *n* **1** *(of film)* pase *m*, sesión *f*, proyección *f*; *(of paintings)* exhibición *f.* **2** *(performance)* actuación *f*; *(result)* resultado.

showjumper ['ʃəudʒʌmpəʳ] *n* jinete *mf.*

showjumping ['ʃəudʒʌmpɪŋ] *n (gen)* hípica; *(event)* concurso *f* hípico.

showman ['ʃəumən] *n* **1** *(manager)* empresario (de espectáculos). **2** *(entertainer)* artista *m*, showman *m.*

▲ *pl* **showmen** ['ʃəumən].

showmanship ['ʃəumənʃɪp] *n* teatralidad *f.*

shown [ʃəun] *pp* → **show.**

show-off ['ʃəuɒf] *n fam* fanfarrón,-ona.

showpiece ['ʃəupi:s] *n* **1** *(in exhibition)* joya, objeto de valor. **2** *(fine example)* modelo (de su género).

showplace ['ʃəupleɪs] *n (place of interest)* lugar *m* de interés turístico.

showroom ['ʃəuru:m] *n* sala de exposiciones.

showy ['ʃəuɪ] *adj (thing)* llamativo,-a, vistoso,-a; *(person)* ostentoso,-a.

▲ *comp* **showier**, *superl* **showiest.**

shrank [ʃræŋk] *pt* → **shrink.**

shrapnel ['ʃræpnəl] *n* metralla.

shred [ʃred] *n* **1** *(gen)* triza; *(of cloth)* jirón *m*; *(of paper)* tira; *(of tobacco)* brizna, hebra. **2** *fig (bit)* pizca: **not a shred of truth** *ni pizca de verdad.* ■ **to tear** STH/SB **to shreds** hacer trizas ALGO/a ALGN.

▷ *vt (paper)* hacer trizas, triturar; *(vegetables - cut in strips)* cortar en tiras; *(- grate)* rallar.

▲ *pt & pp* **shredded**, *ger* **shredding.**

shredder ['ʃredəʳ] *n (for paper)* trituradora; *(for vegetables)* rallador *m.*

shrew [ʃru:] *n* ZOOL musaraña.

shrewd [ʃru:d] *adj* **1** *(person)* astuto,-a, sagaz. **2** *(decision)* muy acertado,-a; *(move)* hábil, inteligente.

shrewdly ['ʃru:dlɪ] *adv* astutamente.

shrewdness ['ʃru:dnəs] *n (gen)* astucia, sagacidad *f.*

shriek [ʃri:k] *n* chillido, grito agudo:

▷ *vi* chillar, gritar. ■ **to shriek with laughter** reírse a carcajadas.

▷ *vt* chillar, gritar.

shrike [ʃraɪk] *n* alcaudón *m.*

shrill [ʃrɪl] *adj* **1** *(voice, words, people)* agudo,-a, estridente; *(sound, whistle)* agudo,-a, estridente, penetrante. **2** *(demand, protest, criticism)* frenético,-a, estridente.

▷ *vi (whistle)* pitar; *(phone, alarm)* sonar; *(person, voice)* chillar.

shrillness ['ʃrɪlnəs] *n* estridencia.

shrimp [ʃrɪmp] *n* camarón *m*, gamba.

shrine [ʃraɪn] *n* REL *(holy place)* santuario, lugar *m* sagrado.

shrink [ʃrɪŋk] *vt (clothes, etc)* encoger.

▷ *vi* **1** *(clothes)* encoger, encogerse; *(meat)* achicarse, reducirse. **2** *(savings, numbers, profits, etc)* disminuir, reducirse. **3** *(move back)* retroceder, echarse atrás.

▲ *pt* **shrank** [ʃræŋk], *pp* **shrunk** [ʃrʌŋk].

shrinkage ['ʃrɪŋkɪdʒ] *n* **1** *(of clothes)* encogimiento; *(of metal)* contracción *f.* **2** *(of savings, numbers, etc)* reducción *f.*

shrink-wrap ['ʃrɪŋkræp] *vt* empaquetar en plástico, envolver en plástico.

▲ *pt & pp* **shrink-wrapped**, *ger* **shrink-wrapping.**

shrivel ['ʃrɪvəl] *vt (plant)* secar, marchitar.

▷ *vi (plant)* secarse, marchitarse.

shroud [ʃraud] *n* **1** REL mortaja, sudario. **2** *fig (of mist, secrecy)* velo.

▷ *vt fig* envolver. ■ **to be shrouded in** STH estar envuelto,-a en un velo de ALGO.

▲ *pt & pp* **shrivelled** (US **shriveled**), *ger* **shrivelling** (US **shriveling**).

shrub [ʃrʌb] *n* arbusto, mata.

shrubbery ['ʃrʌbərɪ] *n* arbustos *mpl.*

▲ *pl* **shrubberies.**

shrug [ʃrʌg] *vt* encoger. ■ **to shrug one's shoulders** encogerse de hombros.

▷ *vi* encogerse de hombros.

▲ *pt & pp* **shrugged**, *ger* **shrugging.**

▷ *n* encogimiento de hombros.

⊙ **to shrug off** *vt sep* quitar importancia a.

shrunk [ʃrʌŋk] *pp* → **shrink.**

shrunken ['ʃrʌŋkən] *adj (gen)* encogido,-a.

shudder ['ʃʌdəʳ] *n* **1** *(of person)* escalofrío. **2** *(of machine, engine)* vibración *f*, sacudida.

▷ *vi* **1** *(person)* estremecerse, temblar (**with**, de): **I shudder to think of it** *me dan escalofríos solo de pensarlo.* **2** *(machinery, vehicle)* vibrar, dar sacudidas.

shuffle ['ʃʌfəl] *n* **1** *(walk)* arrastre *m.* **2** *(of cards)* baraje *m*, barajadura.

▷ *vt* **1** *(feet - drag)* arrastrar; *(- move)* mover. **2** *(cards)* barajar; *(papers)* revolver.
▷ *vi (walk)* andar arrastrando los pies; *(in seat)* revolverse.
shun [ʃʌn] *vt (person)* rechazar, rehuir.
▲ *pt & pp* **shunned**, *ger* **shunning.**
shunt [ʃʌnt] *vt* **1** *(train, railway carriage)* cambiar de vía. **2** *fam (person)* apartar, relegar, trasladar; *(object)* empujar, mover.
shunting ['ʃʌntɪŋ] *n* maniobras *fpl.*
shush [ʃʊʃ] *interj* ¡chis!, ¡chitón!
shut [ʃʌt] *vt (gen)* cerrar: **shut your eyes** *cierra los ojos.* ■ **to shut one's ears to** STH hacer oídos sordos a ALGO. ‖ **to shut one's mouth/gob/trap/face** cerrar el pico.
▲ *pt & pp* **shut**, *ger* **shutting.**
▷ *vi (gen)* cerrar, cerrarse.
▷ *adj (closed)* cerrado,-a.
⊙ **to shut away** *vt sep (isolate)* encerrar.
⊙ **to shut down** *vt sep (factory, business)* cerrar.
▷ *vi (factory, business)* cerrar.
⊙ **to shut in** *vt sep (enclose, imprison)* encerrar.
⊙ **to shut off** *vt sep (gas, electricity, water)* cortar, cerrar; *(machinery, engine)* desconectar, apagar.
▷ *vi (gas, electricity, water)* cortarse, cerrarse; *(machinery, engine)* desconectarse, apagarse.
⊙ **to shut out** *vt sep* **1** *(exclude)* excluir, no dejar participar. **2** *(stop entering)* dejar fuera. **3** *fig (thought, feeling, etc)* no pensar en.
⊙ **to shut up** *vt sep* **1** *(close)* cerrar. **2** *(confine)* encerrar. **3** *fam (quieten)* callar, hacer callar.
▷ *vi* **1** *(close)* cerrar. **2** *(keep quiet)* callarse: **shut up!** *¡cállate!*
shutdown ['ʃʌtdaʊn] *n (of factory, etc)* cierre *m.*
shut-in ['ʃʌtɪn] *adj (gen)* encerrado,-a.
shutout ['ʃʌtaʊt] *n (lockout)* cierre *m* patronal.
shutter ['ʃʌtəʳ] *n* **1** *(on window)* postigo, contraventana; *(of shop)* cierre *m.* **2** *(of camera)* obturador *m.*
▷ *vt (close shutters)* cerrar los postigos, cerrar las contraventanas.
shuttle ['ʃʌtᵊl] *n* **1** AV puente *m* aéreo. **2** *(bus, train)* servicio regular de enlace. **3** *(in weaving)* lanzadera. ● **shuttle service** servicio regular de enlace.
▷ *vi (plane)* volar regularmente; *(bus, train)* viajar, ir regularmente. ■ **to shuttle back and forth** ir y venir.
shuttlecock ['ʃʌtᵊlkɒk] *n* volante *m.*
shy¹ [ʃaɪ] *adj* **1** *(person)* tímido,-a, vergonzoso,-a: **don't be shy** *no seas tímido, no tengas vergüenza.* **2** *(animal)* asustadizo,-a. ■ **to be shy of doing** STH *(wary, cautious)* tener miedo de hacer ALGO, no atreverse a hacer ALGO.
▲ *comp* **shyer** o **shier**, *superl* **shyest** o **shiest.**
▷ *vi (horse)* espantarse (**at**, de), respingar, asustarse.
⊙ **to shy away from** *vt insep (avoid)* huir de.
shy² [ʃaɪ] *vt (throw)* tirar, lanzar.
▲ *pt & pp* **shied**, *ger* **shying.**
shyly ['ʃaɪlɪ] *adv* tímidamente, con timidez.
shyness ['ʃaɪnəs] *n* timidez *f.*
shyster ['ʃaɪstəʳ] *n* US *fam (gen)* estafador,-ra, timador, -ra; *(lawyer)* picapleitos *mf.*
Siamese [saɪə'mi:z] *adj* siamés,-esa.
▷ *n* **1** *(person)* siamés,-esa. **2** *(language)* siamés *m.*
▷ *n pl* **the Siamese** los siameses *mpl.*
sibling ['sɪblɪŋ] *n fml (brother)* hermano; *(sister)* hermana.

sick [sɪk] *adj* **1** *(ill)* enfermo,-a. **2** *(nauseated, queasy)* mareado,-a. **3** *(fed up)* harto,-a; *(worried)* preocupado,-a: **I'm sick and tired of your moaning** *estoy más que harto de tus quejas.* ■ **to feel sick** estar mareado,-a, tener náuseas. ‖ **to feel sick** estar mareado,-a.
⊙ **to sick up** *vt sep* GB vomitar, devolver.
sickbay ['sɪkbeɪ] *n* enfermería.
sickbed ['sɪkbed] *n* lecho de enfermo.
sicken ['sɪkᵊn] *vt (make ill)* poner enfermo,-a; *(revolt, disgust)* dar asco, dar rabia.
▷ *vi* caer enfermo,-a. ■ **to be sickening for** STH estar incubando ALGO.
sickening ['sɪkᵊnɪŋ] *adj* **1** *(disgusting)* repugnante, asqueroso,-a. **2** *(annoying)* irritante, exasperante: **it's sickening** *da rabia.*
sickle ['sɪkᵊl] *n* hoz *f.*
sickly ['sɪklɪ] *adj* **1** *(person)* enfermizo,-a. **2** *(smell, taste)* empalagoso,-a, dulzón,-ona; *(colour)* horrible, asqueroso,-a.
▲ *comp* **sicklier**, *superl* **sickliest.**
sickness ['sɪknəs] *n* **1** *(illness)* enfermedad *f.* **2** *(nausea)* náuseas *fpl*, ganas *fpl* de vomitar.
sickroom ['sɪkru:m] *n* enfermería.
side [saɪd] *n* **1** *(gen)* lado; *(of coin, cube, record)* cara; *(of written page)* carilla, cara, plana: **there's a garage at the side of the house** *hay un garaje al lado de la casa*; **write on one side of the paper only** *solo escribir en una cara del papel.* **2** *(of hill, mountain)* ladera, falda. **3** *(of body)* lado, costado; *(of animal)* ijada, ijar *m*: **she was lying on her side** *estaba echada de lado.* **4** *(edge - gen)* borde *m*; *(- of lake, river, etc)* orilla; *(- of page)* margen *m.* **5** *(aspect)* aspecto, faceta, lado; *(position, opinion, point of view)* lado, parte *f*, punto de vista: **one side of the story** *una versión de la historia.* **6** *(participant in war, argument, debate, etc)* lado, parte *f*, bando; *(party)* partido: **whose side are you on?** *¿de qué parte estás?* **7** equipo. **8** *(line of descent)* parte *f*, lado.
▷ *adj* lateral. ■ **on the side** *(in addition to main job)* como trabajo extra. ‖ **side by side** juntos,-as, uno,-a al lado del/de la otro,-a. ‖ **to keep on the right side of** SB tratar de llevarse bien con ALGN. ● **side dish** guarnición acompañamiento. ‖ **side drum** tambor *m.* ‖ **side view** vista de perfil. ‖ **side effect** efecto secundario. ‖ **side street** callejuela.
⊙ **to side against** *vt insep* ponerse contra.
⊙ **to side with** *vt insep* ponerse de parte de.
sideboard ['saɪdbɔ:d] *n (furniture)* aparador *m.*
sideboards ['saɪdbɔ:dz] *n pl* patillas *fpl.*
sidecar ['saɪdkɑ:ʳ] *n* sidecar *m.*
sidekick ['ʃaɪdkɪk] *n* US *fam* compinche *m.*
sidelight ['saɪdlaɪt] *n* AUTO luz *f* de posición.
sideline ['saɪdlaɪn] *n* **1** SP línea de banda. **2** *(extra business)* negocio suplementario.
sidelong ['saɪdlɒŋ] *adj (glance, etc)* de reojo.
▷ *adv* de lado.
sidereal [saɪ'dɪərɪəl] *adj* sideral, sidéreo,-a.
side-saddle ['saɪdsædᵊl] *adv* a lo amazona.
sideshow ['saɪdʃəʊ] *n (at fair)* puesto de feria, barraca.
sidestep ['saɪdstep] *vt (question, issue)* eludir.
▲ *pt & pp* **sidestepped**, *ger* **sidestepping.**
sidetrack ['saɪdtræk] *vt (distract)* distraer; *(divert)* hacer desviar del tema.

idewalk ['saɪdwɔːk] *n* US acera.
ideways ['saɪdweɪz] *adj (movement, step)* lateral; *(look, glance)* de soslayo, de reojo.
▷ *adv* de lado.
iding ['saɪdɪŋ] *n (railway)* apartadero, vía muerta.
idle ['saɪdəl] *vi* moverse sigilosamente. ■ **to sidle up to sb** acercarse sigilosamente a ALGN .
iege [siːdʒ] *n* **1** MIL sitio, cerco. **2** *(by criminals, journalists)* asedio. ■ **to be under siege** estar sitiado,-a.
ierra Leone [sɪeərəlɪ'əʊn] *n* Sierra Leona.
ierra Leonean [sɪeərəlɪ'əʊnɪən] *adj* sierraleonés, -esa.
▷ *n* sierraleonés,-esa.
ieve [sɪv] *n (fine)* tamiz *m*; *(coarse)* criba; *(for liquids)* colador *m*.
▷ *vt (fine)* tamizar; *(coarse)* cribar.
ift [sɪft] *vt* **1** *(sieve)* tamizar, cribar. **2** *(sprinkle)* espolvorear.
ifter ['sɪftəʳ] *n (sieve)* tamiz *m*; *(sprinkler)* espolvoreador *m*.
igh [saɪ] *n (of person)* suspiro.
▷ *vi (person)* suspirar (**for**, por); *(wind)* susurrar, gemir: **she sighed with relief** *suspiró aliviada.*
ight [saɪt] *n* **1** *(faculty)* vista: **his sight is failing** *le está fallando la vista.* **2** *(range of vision)* vista: **we waited until he was out of sight** *esperamos hasta que hubo desaparecido.* **3** *(act of seeing, view)* vista: **it was her first sight of the countryside** *fue la primera vez que veía el campo.* **4** *(thing seen, spectacle)* espectáculo. ■ **in/within sight** a la vista. ‖ **to come into sight** aparecer. ‖ **to know SB by sight** conocer a ALGN de vista.
▷ *vt* ver, divisar.
▷ *n* **a sight** *fam (a great deal)* mucho: **a sight better** *mucho mejor.*
▷ *n pl* **sights** *(of city)* monumentos *mpl*, lugares *mpl* de interés.
ighted ['saɪtɪd] *adj* vidente.
ighting ['saɪtɪŋ] *n* observación *f*.
ightless ['saɪtləs] *adj* ciego,-a, invidente.
ightseeing ['saɪtsiːɪŋ] *n* visita turística, turismo. ■ **to go sightseeing** visitar los monumentos y lugares de interés.
ightseer ['saɪtsɪəʳ] *n* turista *mf*, visitante *mf*.
ign [saɪn] *n* **1** *(symbol)* signo, símbolo. **2** *(gesture)* gesto, seña; *(signal)* señal *f*: **wait until I give the sign** *espera hasta que dé la señal.* **3** *(indication)* señal *f*, indicio, muestra; *(proof)* prueba; *(trace)* rastro: **that must be a good sign** *eso debe de ser (una) buena señal.* **4** *(board)* letrero. ■ **as a sign of** como muestra de. ● **sign language** lenguaje *m* por señas.
▷ *vt* **1** *(letter, document, cheque, etc)* firmar: **sign your name here, please** *firme aquí, por favor.* **2** *(player, group)* fichar (**on/up**, -). **3** *(gesture)* hacer una seña/señal.
▷ *vi* **1** *(write name)* firmar. **2** *(player, group)* fichar (**for/with**, por). **3** US *(use sign language)* comunicarse por señas, hablar por señas.
⊙ **to sign away** *vt sep* ceder.
⊙ **to sign for** *vt insep (goods, parcel, etc)* firmar el recibo de.
⊙ **to sign in** *vi* firmar el registro.
⊙ **to sign off** *vi* despedirse.
⊙ **to sign on** *vt sep (worker)* contratar.
▷ *vi (student)* matricularse; *(soldier)* alistarse.
⊙ **to sign out** *vi* firmar el registro.
⊙ **to sign over** *vt sep* ceder mediante un escrito.
⊙ **to sign up** *vt sep (soldier)* reclutar; *(worker)* contratar.
▷ *vi (soldier)* alistarse; *(student)* matricularse.
signal ['sɪgnəl] *n* **1** *(gen)* señal *f*: **traffic signal** *señal de tráfico.* **2** *(radiophonic)* señal *f*. **3** *(railway)* señal *f*.
▷ *adj (achievement, triumph, success, etc)* señalado,-a, destacado,-a, notable.
▷ *vt* **1** *(indicate)* indicar, señalar, marcar; *(forecast)* pronosticar. **2** *(gesture)* hacer señas, hacer una seña: **he signalled the waiter to bring the bill** (US **check**) *le hizo una seña al camarero para que trajera la cuenta.*
▷ *vi* **1** *(gesture)* hacer señas, hacer una seña. **2** AUTO poner el intermitente.
signalman ['sɪgnəlmən] *n (railway)* guardavía *m*.
▲ *pl* **signalmen** [['sɪgnəlmən].
signatory ['sɪgnətərɪ] *n fml* firmante *mf*.
▲ *pl* **signatories.**
signature ['sɪgnɪtʃəʳ] *n (name)* firma.
signboard ['saɪnbɔːd] *n (sign)* letrero; *(noticeboard)* tablón *m* de anuncios.
signet ['sɪgnət] *n* sello.
significance [sɪg'nɪfɪkəns] *n* **1** *(meaning)* significado. **2** *(importance)* importancia: **it's of no significance** *no tiene importancia.*
significant [sɪg'nɪfɪkənt] *adj* **1** *(meaningful - gen)* significativo,-a. **2** *(important)* importante, trascendente, considerable.
significantly [sɪg'nɪfɪkəntlɪ] *adv* **1** *(considerably, notably)* considerablemente. **2** *(meaningfully - used alone)* lo cual es significativo.
signify ['sɪgnɪfaɪ] *vt fml* significar.
▲ *pt & pp* **signified,** *ger* **signifying.**
signing ['saɪnɪŋ] *n* GB *(of player, group)* fichaje *m*.
signpost ['saɪnpəʊst] *n* poste *m* indicador.
silage ['saɪlɪdʒ] *n* ensilaje *m*.
silence ['saɪləns] *n (gen)* silencio: **we walked in silence** *caminamos en silencio.* ■ **to reduce SB to silence** dejar a ALGN sin habla.
▷ *vt (person)* acallar, hacer callar; *(protest, opposition, criticism)* apagar, silenciar.
silencer ['saɪlənsəʳ] *n* silenciador *m*.
silent ['saɪlənt] *adj* **1** *(thing, place, taciturn person)* silencioso,-a. **2** *(not speaking)* callado,-a: **he was silent for a moment** *se quedó callado un momento.* **3** *(film, consonant)* mudo,-a; *(prayer)* silencioso,-a. ■ **to be silent** callarse.
silently ['saɪləntlɪ] *adv (without making a noise)* silenciosamente; *(without talking)* en silencio.
silhouette [sɪluː'et] *n* silueta.
silicon ['sɪlɪkən] *n* silicio.
silicone ['sɪlɪkəʊn] *n* silicona.
silk [sɪlk] *n* seda.
▷ *adj* de seda.
silken ['sɪlkən] *adj (like silk)* sedoso,-a; *(of silk)* de seda.
silk-screen printing ['sɪlkskriːnprɪntɪŋ] *n* serigrafía.
silkworm ['sɪlkwɜːm] *n* gusano de seda.
silky ['sɪlkɪ] *adj (cloth, hair, fur, etc)* sedoso,-a; *(voice)* aterciopelado,-a; *(skin)* suave.
▲ *comp* **silkier,** *superl* **silkiest.**
sill [sɪl] *n (of window)* alféizar *m*, antepecho.

silliness ['sɪlɪnəs] *n* estupidez *f*, necedad *f*.

silly ['sɪlɪ] *adj* 1 *(stupid)* tonto,-a, estúpido,-a: **how silly of me!** *¡qué tonto soy!* 2 *(unimportant)* trivial, sin importancia.
▲ *comp* **sillier**, *superl* **silliest**.
▷ *n* tonto,-a, bobo,-a.

silly-billy ['sɪlɪbɪlɪ] *n fam* tonto,-a, bobo,-a.

silo ['saɪləʊ] *n* silo.
▲ *pl* **silos**.

silt [sɪlt] *n* cieno, limo, légamo.
⊙ **to silt up** *vi* encenagarse.

silver ['sɪlvəʳ] *n* 1 *(metal)* plata: **sterling silver** *plata de ley*. 2 *(coins)* monedas *fpl* (de plata). 3 *(articles, ornaments, etc)* plata.
▷ *adj* 1 *(made of silver)* de plata. 2 *(in colour)* plateado,-a; *(hair)* canoso,-a, cano,-a. ● **silver foil / silver paper** papel *m* de plata. ❙ **silver medal** medalla de plata. ❙ **silver plate** plateado. ❙ **silver screen** el cine *m*.
▷ *vt (metal)* dar un baño de plata a, platear.

silver-plated [sɪlvə'pleɪtɪd] *adj* plateado,-a.

silversmith ['sɪlvəsmɪθ] *n* platero,-a, orfebre *mf*.

silver-tongued ['sɪlvətʌngd] *adj* elocuente.

silverware ['sɪlvəweəʳ] *n* plata, vajilla de plata.

similar ['sɪmɪləʳ] *adj* parecido,-a (**to**, a), similar (**to**, a), semejante (**to**, a): **those boys are very similar** *esos chicos se parecen mucho*.

similarity [sɪmɪ'lærətɪ] *n (likeness)* semejanza, parecido, similitud *f*.
▲ *pl* **similarities**.

similarly ['sɪmɪləlɪ] *adv* 1 *(in a similar way)* de modo parecido, de modo similar. 2 *(also, likewise)* del mismo modo, asimismo.

simile ['sɪmɪlɪ] *n* símil *m*.

simmer ['sɪməʳ] *vt* CULIN hervir a fuego lento.
▷ *vi* CULIN hervir a fuego lento.
⊙ **to simmer down** *vi* calmarse.

simper ['sɪmpəʳ] *n* sonrisa afectada.
▷ *vi* sonreír con afectación.

simpering ['sɪmpərɪŋ] *adj* melindroso,-a.

simple ['sɪmpᵊl] *adj* 1 *(easy, straightforward)* sencillo,-a, fácil, simple: **a simple solution** *una solución sencilla*. 2 *(plain, not elaborate)* sencillo,-a, simple: **a simple dress** *un vestido sencillo*. 3 *(not compound)* simple, sencillo,-a: **a simple form of life** *una forma de vida sencilla*. 4 *(plain, pure, nothing more than)* sencillo,-a, puro,-a, mero,-a: **for the simple reason that...** *por la sencilla razón que...* 5 *(unsophisticated, ordinary)* simple, sencillo,-a: **simple tastes** *gustos sencillos*. 6 *(genuine, sincere)* sencillo,-a; *(foolish)* tonto,-a; *(naive, easily deceived)* ingenuo,-a, inocente, simple; *(backward, weak-minded)* simple, corto,-a de alcances.
▲ *comp* **simpler**, *comp* **simplest**.

simple-minded [sɪmpᵊl'maɪndɪd] *adj* simple, ingenuo,-a.

simpleton ['sɪmpᵊltən] *n dated* simplón,-ona.

simplicity [sɪm'plɪsətɪ] *n* 1 *(easiness, incomplexity)* sencillez *f*, simplicidad *f*. 2 *(lack of sophistication)* sencillez *f*, naturalidad *f*. 3 *(foolishness)* simpleza; *(naivety)* ingenuidad *f*.

simplification [sɪmplɪfɪ'keɪʃᵊn] *n* simplificación *f*.

simplify ['sɪmplɪfaɪ] *vt* simplificar.
▲ *pt & pp* **simplified**, *ger* **simplifying**.

simplistic [sɪm'plɪstɪk] *adj* simplista.

simply ['sɪmplɪ] *adv* 1 *(easily, plainly, modestly)* simplemente, sencillamente: **she lives very simply** *vive muy sencillamente*. 2 *(only)* simplemente, solamente, solo; *(just, merely)* meramente: **I simply don't know** *sencillamente, no lo sé*. 3 *(really, absolutely)* francamente, realmente.

simulate ['sɪmjəleɪt] *vt* simular.

simulated ['sɪmjəleɪtɪd] *adj (flight, conditions, attack)* simulado,-a; *(leather, etc)* de imitación, sintético,-a.

simulation [sɪmjə'leɪʃᵊn] *n (reproduction)* simulación *f*, simulacro.

simulator ['sɪmjəleɪtəʳ] *n* simulador *m*.

simultaneity [sɪmᵊltə'neɪətɪ] *n* simultaneidad *f*.

simultaneous [sɪmᵊl'teɪnɪəs] *adj* simultáneo,-a: **simultaneous translation** *traducción simultánea*.

simultaneously [sɪmᵊ'teɪnɪəslɪ] *adv* simultáneamente, a la vez.

sin [sɪn] *n* pecado.
▷ *vi* pecar (**against**, contra).
▲ *pt & pp* **sinned**, *ger* **sinning**.

since [sɪns] *adv* desde entonces: **she arrived in 1988 and has lived here ever since** *llegó en 1988 y vive aquí desde entonces*.
▷ *prep* desde: **I've been here since four o'clock** *llevo aquí desde las cuatro*.
▷ *conj* 1 *(time)* desde que: **it's years since I went to the theatre** *hace años que no voy al teatro*. 2 *(because, seeing that)* ya que, puesto que: **since you're going to the shop...** *ya que vas a la tienda...*

sincere [sɪn'sɪəʳ] *adj* sincero,-a.

sincerely [sɪn'sɪəlɪ] *adv* sinceramente. ■ **Yours sincerely** *(in letter)* (le saluda) atentamente.

sincerity [sɪn'serətɪ] *n* sinceridad *f*.

sinecure ['saɪnɪkjʊəʳ] *n* sinecura.

sinew ['sɪnjuː] *n* tendón *m*.

sinewy ['sɪnjuɪ] *adj* nervudo,-a.

sinful ['sɪnfʊl] *adj* 1 *(person)* pecador,-ra. 2 *(thought, act)* pecaminoso,-a.

sing [sɪŋ] *vt (gen)* cantar.
▷ *vi* 1 *(person, bird)* cantar; *(wind, kettle, bullet)* silbar; *(ear, insect)* zumbar. 2 US *sl* cantar.
▲ *pt* **sang** [sæŋ], *pp* **sung** [sʌŋ].
⊙ **to sing along** *vi* cantar.
⊙ **to sing out** *vi* cantar fuerte.
⊙ **to sing up** *vi* cantar fuerte.

singe [sɪndʒ] *vt* chamuscar.
▷ *n* quemadura (superficial).

singer ['sɪŋəʳ] *n (gen)* cantante *mf*; *(in choir)* cantor,-ra: **jazz singer** *cantante de jazz*.

singer-songwriter [sɪŋə'sɒŋraɪtəʳ] *n* cantautor,-ra.

singing ['sɪŋɪŋ] *n (act)* canto, cantar *m*; *(songs)* canciones *fpl*: **he loves singing in the shower** *le encanta cantar en la ducha*.

single ['sɪŋgᵊl] *adj* 1 *(only one)* solo,-a, único,-a: **we heard a single scream** *oímos un solo grito*. 2 *(composed of one part)* simple, sencillo,-a: **single figures** *cifras de un solo dígito*. 3 *(for one person)* individual. 4 *(separate, individual)* cada: **every single day** *todos los días*. 5 *(unmarried)* soltero,-a. ■ **in single file** en fila india. ● **single cream** nata líquida. ❙ **single parent** 1 *(mother)* madre

soltera. **2** *(father)* padre *m* soltero. ■ **single room** habitación *f* individual.
n **1** GB *(single ticket)* billete *m* de ida, billete *m* sencillo. **2** *(record)* (disco) sencillo, single *m*.
n pl **singles** SP *(in tennis, badminton)* individuales *mpl*.
to single out *vt sep (choose)* escoger.
ngle-breasted [sɪŋgəl'brestɪd] *adj (jacket, suit)* recto,-a, sin cruzar.
ngle-decker [sɪŋgəl'dekəʳ] *n* autobús *m* de un solo piso.
ingle-handed [sɪŋgəl'hændɪd] *adv* sin ayuda, solo,-a.
ngle-minded [sɪŋgəl'maɪndɪd] *adj* resuelto,-a, decidido,-a.
ingle-parent ['sɪŋgəlpeərənt] *adj (family)* monoparental.
nglet ['sɪŋglət] *n* GB *(vest)* camiseta.
ingular ['sɪŋgjuləʳ] *adj* **1** *(in grammar)* singular. **2** *fml (outstanding)* extraordinario,-a.
n LING singular *m*. ■ **in the singular** en singular.
ngularity [sɪŋjə'lærətɪ] *n fml* singularidad *f*.
▲ *pl* **singularities**.
ngularly ['sɪŋgjələlɪ] *adv fml* extraordinariamente, singularmente.
nister ['sɪnɪstəʳ] *adj* siniestro,-a.
nk [sɪŋk] *n (in kitchen)* fregadero, pila; *(in bathroom)* lavabo, lavamanos *m*.
vt **1** *(ship)* hundir. **2** *fig (hopes, plans)* acabar con. **3** *(hole, shaft, tunnel)* cavar, excavar; *(well)* abrir; *(post, pipe, cable)* enterrar; *(knife)* clavar, hundir; *(teeth)* hincar (**into**, en).
▲ *pt* **sank** [sæŋk], *pp* **sunk** [sʌŋk].
vi **1** *(ship)* hundirse, irse al pique; *(stone, wood, etc)* hundirse. **2** *(land, building)* hundirse. **3** *(sun, moon)* ponerse. **4** *(figures, prices, value)* bajar; *(water, level)* descender, bajar: **his voice sank to a whisper** *su voz se convirtió en un susurro*. **5** *fig (hopes, etc)* venirse abajo: **my heart sank** *se me cayó el alma a los pies*. **6** *(person)* dejarse caer. **7** *(decline)* hundirse (**into**, en).
to sink in *vi fig (words)* causar impresión; *(news, idea, fact)* hacer impacto.
nker ['sɪŋkəʳ] *n* plomo.
nking ['sɪŋkɪŋ] *n* MAR hundimiento.
nner ['sɪnəʳ] *n* pecador,-ra.
nuous ['sɪnjuəs] *adj* sinuoso,-a.
p [sɪp] *n* sorbo.
vt sorber, beber a sorbos.
▲ *pt & pp* **sipped**, *ger* **sipping**.
phon ['saɪfən] *n (gen)* sifón *m*.
to siphon off *vt sep (liquid)* sacar con sifón; *(funds, traffic)* desviar.
r [sɜːʳ] *n* **1** *fml (gen)* señor *m*: **yes, sir** *sí, señor*. **2** *(title)* sir *m*. ■ **Dear Sir** *(in letter)* muy señor mío, muy señores míos, estimado señor.
ren ['saɪərən] *n (gen)* sirena.
rloin ['sɜːlɔɪn] *n* solomillo.
ssy ['sɪsɪ] *n fam pej (effeminate)* afeminado,-a, mariquita *mf*; *(cowardly)* miedica *mf*.
▲ *pl* **sissies**.
ster ['sɪstəʳ] *n* **1** *(relative)* hermana. **2** *(comrade)* hermana, compañera. **3** GB enfermera jefe. **4** REL *(nun)* hermana, monja; *(before name)* Sor. **5** *(company, organization)* hermana.
sisterhood ['sɪstəhʊd] *n* hermandad *f*.
sister-in-law ['sɪstərɪnlɔː] *n* cuñada.
▲ *pl* **sisters-in-law**.
sisterly ['sɪstəlɪ] *adj* (propio,-a) de hermana.
sit [sɪt] *vt* **1** *(child, etc)* sentar (**down**, -): **she sat him down on the table** *lo sentó en la mesa*. **2** *(room, hall, etc)* tener cabida para; *(table)* ser para. **3** GB *(exam)* presentarse a.
▷ *vi* **1** *(action)* sentarse (**down**, -): **I sat next to Anna** *me senté junto a Anna*. **2** *(be seated)* estar sentado,-a: **they were sitting on the floor** *estaban sentados en el suelo*. **3** *(village, building)* ubicarse, hallarse, estar, situarse; *(object)* estar; *(clothes)* sentar, quedar: **that dress sits well on you** *aquel vestido te sienta bien*. **4** *(person)* quedarse. **5** *(be a member)* ser miembro (**on**, de), formar parte (**on**, de). **6** *(parliament, etc)* reunirse (en sesión). ■ **to sit tight** mantenerse en sus trece, quedarse en un sitio.
▷ *vi fam (baby-sit)* hacer de canguro (**for**, a).
⊙ **to sit about / sit around** *vi fam* holgazanear, hacer el vago.
⊙ **to sit back** *vi* **1** *(lean back)* recostarse; *(relax)* ponerse cómodo,-a. **2** *(take no active part)* cruzarse de brazos.
⊙ **to sit by** *vi (do nothing)* quedarse sin hacer nada, estarse quieto,-a.
⊙ **to sit in for** *vt insep (take place)* sustituir a.
⊙ **to sit for** *vt insep* GB *(exam)* presentarse a.
⊙ **to sit in on** *vi (attend)* asistir a (sin participar), estar presente en.
⊙ **to sit on** *vt insep* **1** *fam (delay)* retener; *(keep secret)* mantener oculto,-a. **2** *(silence)* hacer callar; *(discipline, control)* poner en su sitio.
⊙ **to sit out** *vt sep* **1** *(stay until end)* aguantar (hasta el final). **2** *(not dance)* no bailar.
⊙ **to sit through** *vt insep (stay until end)* aguantar (hasta el final).
⊙ **to sit up** *vi* **1** *(in bed)* incorporarse (en la cama); **2** *(stay up late)* quedarse levantado,-a.
▷ *vt sep (child, etc)* sentar.
▲ *pt & pp* **sat** [sæt], *ger* **sitting**.
sit-down ['sɪtdaʊn] *n* **1** *(protest)* sentada; *(strike)* huelga de brazos cruzados. **2** *(rest)* breve descanso.
site [saɪt] *n (location)* situación *f*, emplazamiento, colocación *f*. ● **archaeological site** yacimiento arqueológico.
▷ *vt* situar, ubicar, emplazar.
sit-in ['sɪtɪn] *n (protest)* sentada.
siting ['saɪtɪŋ] *n* emplazamiento.
sitter ['sɪtəʳ] *n* **1** ART modelo *mf*. **2** *(baby sitter)* canguro *mf*.
sitting ['sɪtɪŋ] *n (of meal)* turno; *(of committee, for portrait)* sesión *f*.
▷ *adj (position)* sentado,-a. ● **sitting room** GB sala de estar, salón *m*, living *m*.
situate ['sɪtjʊeɪt] *vt fml* situar, ubicar.
situated ['sɪtjʊeɪtɪd] *adj (building, etc)* situado,-a, ubicado,-a.
situation [sɪtjʊ'eɪʃən] *n* **1** *(circumstances)* situación *f*: **we're in a difficult situation** *estamos en una situación difícil*. **2** *dated (job, position)* empleo. **3** *(location)* situa-

ción *f*, ubicación *f*. ■ **«Situations vacant»** «Demandas de trabajo».

sit-up ['sɪtʌp] *n* SP abdominal *m*.

six [sɪks] *adj* seis: **it costs six pounds** *cuesta seis libras;* **six hundred** *seiscientos,-as;* **six thousand** *seis mil.*
▷ *n* seis *m*: **she's six years old** *tiene seis años;* **it's six o'clock** *son las seis.*

sixteen [sɪks'ti:n] *adj* dieciséis.
▷ *n* dieciséis *m*.

Consulta también **six.**

sixteenth [sɪks'ti:nθ] *adj* decimosexto,-a.
▷ *adv* en decimosexto lugar.
▷ *n* **1** *(in series)* decimosexto,-a. **2** *(fraction)* decimosexto; *(one part)* decimosexta parte *f*.

Consulta también **sixth.**

sixth [sɪksθ] *adj* sexto,-a: **the sixth floor** *la sexta planta, el sexto piso.*
▷ *adv* sexto, en sexto lugar: **he came sixth** *llegó en sexto lugar.*
▷ *n* **1** *(in series)* sexto,-a; *(day)* el seis, el día seis: **the sixth of June** *el seis de junio.* **2** *(fraction)* sexto; *(one part)* sexta parte *f*. ● **sixth form** GB ≈ segundo de bachillerato. ‖ **sixth form college** GB ≈ *instituto para estudiantes de segundo de bachillerato.*

sixtieth ['sɪkstɪəθ] *adj* sexagésimo,-a.
▷ *adv* en sexagésimo lugar.
▷ *n* **1** *(in series)* sexagésimo,-a. **2** *(fraction)* sexagésimo; *(one part)* sexagésima parte *f*.

sixty ['sɪkstɪ] *adj* sesenta: **there were about sixty people** *había unas sesenta personas.*
▷ *n* sesenta *m*.

size [saɪz] *n* **1** *(gen)* tamaño; *(magnitude)* magnitud *f*: **it's the size of an egg** *es del tamaño de un huevo.* **2** *(of clothes)* talla; *(of shoes)* número; *(of person)* talla, estatura: **she's a size 12** *gasta la talla 12.* ■ **to cut SB down to size** bajarle los humos a ALGN.
▷ *vt (sort according to size)* poner la talla a.
⊙ **to size up** *vt sep (situation, problem)* evaluar; *(person)* juzgar.

sizeable ['saɪzəb^{ə}l] *adj* considerable.

sizzle ['sɪz^{ə}l] *vi* chisporrotear, crepitar.

skate[1] [skeɪt] *n (gen)* patín *m; (ice skate)* patín *m* de hielo; *(roller skate)* patín *m* de rueda.
▷ *vi* patinar.
⊙ **to skate over** *vt insep (problem, delicate issue)* tratar muy por encima.
⊙ **to skate round** *vt insep (problem)* evitar, esquivar.

skate[2] [skeɪt] *n (fish)* raya.

skateboard ['skeɪtbɔ:d] *n* monopatín *m*.

skater ['skeɪtə^{r}] *n* patinador,-ra.

skating ['skeɪtɪŋ] *n* patinaje *m*. ● **ice skating** patinaje *m* sobre hielo. ‖ **skating rink** pista de patinaje.

skein [skeɪn] *n* madeja.

skeletal ['skelɪt^{ə}l] *adj* **1** ANAT esquelético,-a, óseo,-a. **2** *(emaciated)* esquelético,-a, escuálido,-a. **3** *(report, etc)* escueto,-a.

skeleton ['skelɪt^{ə}n] *n* **1** *(of person, animal)* esqueleto. **2** *(of building, ship)* armazón *m*, estructura.
▷ *adj (staff)* reducido,-a; *(service)* básico,-a.

sketch [sketʃ] *n* **1** *(drawing)* dibujo; *(preliminary drawing)* bosquejo, esbozo. **2** *(outline, rough idea)* esquema *m*, esbozo.
▷ *vt (draw)* dibujar; *(preliminary drawing)* bosquejar, hacer un bosquejo de.
▷ *vi* hacer bosquejos, hacer bocetos.
⊙ **to sketch in/out** *vt sep (outline)* trazar las líneas generales de, dar un resumen de.

sketch-book ['sketʃbʊk] *n* bloc *m* de dibujo.

sketch-pad ['sketʃpæd] *n* bloc *m* de dibujo.

sketchy ['sketʃɪ] *adj* incompleto,-a.
▲ *comp* **sketchier**, *superl* **sketchiest.**

skewer ['skjʊə^{r}] *n* CULIN pincho, brocheta.
▷ *vt* ensartar (en un pincho, etc).

ski [ski:] *n (equipment)* esquí *m*.
▷ *vi* esquiar. ■ **to ski down** bajar esquiando. ● **ski jum**... **1** *(slope)* pista de saltos, trampolín *m*. **2** *(competitio*... saltos *mpl* de esquí. ‖ **ski lift** telesquí *m*. ‖ **ski resort** e... tación *f* de esquí. ‖ **ski slope** pista de esquí.

skid [skɪd] *n* AUTO patinazo, derrapaje *m*. ● **skid row** ... barrios *mpl* bajos, barriadas *fpl*.
▷ *vi* patinar, derrapar.
▲ *pt & pp* **skidded**, *ger* **skidding.**

skier ['skɪə^{r}] *n* esquiador,-ra.

skies [skaɪz] *pl* ⟶ **sky.**

skiff [skɪf] *n* MAR esquife *m*.

skiing ['skiɪŋ] *n* esquí *m*.

skilful ['skɪlfʊl] *adj (gen)* diestro,-a, hábil. ■ **to be sk**... **ful at STH** ser hábil para algo.

skilfully ['skɪlfʊlɪ] *adv* hábilmente.

skill [skɪl] *n* **1** *(ability)* habilidad *f*, destreza; *(talent)* t... lento, don *m*, dotes *fpl*. **2** *(technique)* técnica, arte *m*
▷ *n pl* **skills** *(expertise)* capacidad *f sing*, aptitudes *fpl*: **person with computer skills** *una persona que sepa inf*... *mática.*

skilled [skɪld] *adj* **1** *(specialized)* cualificado,-a, esp... cializado,-a. **2** *(able)* hábil, diestro,-a; *(expert)* expe... to,-a.

skillet ['skɪlɪt] *n* sartén *f*.

skillful ['skɪlfʊl] *adj* US ⟶ **skilful.**

skillfully ['skɪlfʊlɪ] *adv* US ⟶ **skilfully.**

skim [skɪm] *vt* **1** *(milk)* desnatar, descremar (**off**, a... *(soup)* espumar (**off**, a). **2** *(move over surface)* pasar (c... si) rozando. **3** *(read quickly)* hojear, leer por encima
▷ *vi* **1** *(move over surface)* pasar (casi) rozando (**across/over**, ... **2** *(read quickly)* hojear (**through/over**, -), leer por enc... ma (**through/over**, -).
▲ *pt & pp* **skimmed**, *ger* **skimming.**

skimmed [skɪmd] *adj (milk)* desnatado,-a.

skimmer ['skɪmə^{r}] *n (spoon)* espumadera.

skimp [skɪmp] *vt* escatimar.
▷ *vi* escatimar (**on**, -).

skimpy ['skɪmpɪ] *adj (dress)* ligero,-a, cortísimo,-... *(meal)* escaso,-a, pobre.
▲ *comp* **skimpier**, *superl* **skimpiest.**

skin [skɪn] *n* **1** *(of person)* piel *f*; *(of face)* cutis *m*, piel... **she has light/dark skin** *tiene la piel clara/morena.* **2** ... *animal)* piel *f*, pellejo. **3** *(of fruit, vegetable)* piel *f*. **4** ... *paint)* telilla, capa fina; *(on milk, custard, etc)* nata. ■ ... **the skin of one's teeth** por los pelos. ‖ **to jump out** ... **one's skin** llevarse un susto. ‖ **to save one's own sk**... salvar el pellejo.
▷ *vt* **1** *(animal, fish)* desollar, despellejar. **2** *(fruit, veget*... *ble)* pelar. **3** *(elbow, knee)* arañar, rascar.
▲ *pt & pp* **skinned**, *ger* **skinning.**

skin-deep [skɪn'diːp] *adj* superficial.
skin-diver ['skɪndaɪvəʳ] *n* submarinista *mf.*
skinflint ['skɪnflɪnt] *n fam* tacaño,-a.
skinhead ['skɪnhed] *n* cabeza *mf* rapada, skin *mf.*
skinny ['skɪnɪ] *adj fam* flaco,-a.
▲ *comp* skinnier, *superl* skinniest.
skint [skɪnt] *adj* pelado,-a. ■ **to be skint** estar sin blanca, estar sin un duro.
skintight ['skɪntaɪt] *adj* muy ceñido,-a.
skip¹ [skɪp] *n* salto, brinco.
▷ *vi* **1** *(move, jump)* saltar, brincar; *(with rope)* saltar a la comba. **2** *(jump, flit)* saltar.
▷ *vt (miss, omit)* saltarse: **she skipped a few pages** *se saltó unas páginas.*
▲ *pt & pp* skipped, *ger* skipping.
skip² [skɪp] *n (container)* contenedor *m.*
skipper ['skɪpəʳ] *n* **1** MAR patrón,-ona, capitán,-ana. **2** SP capitán,-ana.
skipping ['skɪpɪŋ] *n* comba. ● **skipping rope** comba, cuerda de saltar.
skirmish ['skɜːmɪʃ] *n* **1** MIL escaramuza. **2** *(fight)* refriega, pelea, trifulca.
▷ *vi (fight)* pelear; *(argue)* reñir, discutir.
skirt [skɜːt] *n (garment)* falda.
▷ *vt* **1** *(go round)* rodear, bordear. **2** *fig (problem)* esquivar, eludir (**round**, -).
skirting ['skɜːtɪŋ] [Also **skirting board**.] *n* GB zócalo, rodapié *m.*
skit [skɪt] *n* sátira, parodia;
skittish ['skɪtɪʃ] *adj* **1** *(person)* caprichoso,-a, frívolo,-a. **2** *(animal)* asustadizo,-a.
skittle ['skɪtᵊl] *n (wooden pin)* bolo.
▷ *n pl* **skittles** bolos *mpl,* boliche *m sing.*
skive [skaɪv] *vi* GB *fam (avoid work)* escaquearse.
⊙ **to skive off** *vi (avoid work)* escaquearse.
skiver ['skaɪvəʳ] *n* vago,-a.
skivvy ['skɪvɪ] *n* GB *fam (female servant)* fregona, sirvienta.
▲ *pl* skivvies.
▷ *vi* servir, trabajar como una esclava.
skulduggery [skʌl'dʌgərɪ] *n* trapicheo.
skulk [skʌlk] *vi* esconderse.
skull [skʌl] *n* **1** ANAT cráneo. **2** *(symbol)* calavera. ■ **skull and crossbones** bandera pirata.
skullcap ['skʌlkæp] *n (garment)* casquete *m.*
skunk [skʌŋk] *n* ZOOL mofeta.
sky [skaɪ] *n (gen)* cielo; *(firmament)* firmamento.
▲ *pl* skies.
sky-blue ['skaɪbluː] *adj* azul celeste.
skydiver [skaɪ'daɪvəʳ] *n* paracaidista *mf.*
skydiving ['skaɪdaɪvɪŋ] *n* paracaidismo.
sky-high [skaɪ'haɪ] *adv* por las nubes, por los aires. ■ **to blow** STH **sky-high** hacer volar ALGO por los aires.
▷ *adj* por las nubes, astronómico,-a.
skylark ['skaɪlɑːk] *n* alondra.
skylight ['skaɪlaɪt] *n* tragaluz *m,* claraboya.
skyline ['skaɪlaɪn] *n* **1** *(horizon)* horizonte *m.* **2** *(of city)* perfil *m.*
skyscraper ['skaɪskreɪpəʳ] *n* rascacielos *m.*
slab [slæb] *n (of stone)* losa; *(of cake)* trozo; *(of chocolate)* tableta.

slack¹ [slæk] *adj* **1** *(not taut)* flojo,-a: **a slack rope** *una cuerda floja.* **2** *(careless, lax)* descuidado,-a. **3** *(not busy - trade, demand)* flojo,-a.
▷ *n (part of rope, wire, etc)* parte *f* floja.
⊙ **to slack off** *vi (activity)* aflojar (el ritmo de trabajo); *(speed)* reducir, disminuir.
slack² [slæk] *n (coal)* cisco.
slacken ['slækᵊn] *vt* **1** *(rope, grip)* aflojar; *(reins)* soltar. **2** *(speed)* reducir, disminuir.
▷ *vi (speed)* reducirse, disminuir.
▲ *pt & pp* slagged, *ger* slagging.
⊙ **to slacken off / slacken up** *vi (activity)* aflojar (el ritmo de trabajo); *(speed)* reducirse.
slacks [slæks] *n pl dated* pantalón *m.*
slag [slæg] *n (of metal, etc)* escoria.
⊙ **to slag off** *vt sep* GB *fam* poner verde a.
slalom ['slɑːləm] *n* SP slalom *m,* eslalon *m.*
slam [slæm] *n (of lid, book, etc)* golpe *m*; *(of door)* portazo.
▷ *vt* **1** *(shut forcefully)* cerrar de golpe: **she slammed the door in my face** *me dio con la puerta en las narices.* **2** *(throw noisily)* arrojar, lanzar. **3** *fig (criticize)* criticar duramente. **4** *(defeat)* dar una paliza a.
▷ *vi* cerrarse de golpe. ■ **to slam on the brakes** AUTO dar un frenazo. ■ **to slam the phone down** colgar de golpe.
▲ *pt & pp* slammed, *ger* slamming.
slander ['slɑːndəʳ] *n (smear)* difamación *f.*
▷ *vt* difamar.
slanderer ['slɑːndərəʳ] *n* difamador,-ra.
slanderous ['slɑːndᵊrəs] *adj* difamatorio,-a.
slang [slæŋ] *n* argot *m,* jerga.
▷ *adj* de jerga, de argot.
slant [slɑːnt] *n* **1** *(gen)* inclinación *f.* **2** *(point of view)* enfoque *m,* punto de vista.
▷ *vt* **1** *(slope)* inclinar. **2** *fig (news, report, etc)* presentar tendenciosamente.
▷ *vi (slope)* inclinarse.
slanting ['slɑːntɪŋ] *adj (sloping)* inclinado,-a.
slap [slæp] *n (gen)* palmada; *(smack)* cachete *m*; *(in face)* bofetada, bofetón *m.* ■ **a slap in the face** *(rebuff)* un desaire, una bofetada.
▷ *adv* **1** *(straight)* de lleno: **we drove slap into a wall** *dimos de lleno contra una pared.* **2** *(right)* justo. ■ **to slap paint on a wall** dar una mano de pintura en la pared.
▷ *vt (gen)* pegar (con la mano).
▲ *pt & pp* slapped, *ger* slapping.
⊙ **to slap around** *vt sep (hit)* pegar.
⊙ **to slap down** *vt sep (force into silence)* hacer callar.
⊙ **to slap on** *vt sep (add to price)* añadir a.
slapdash ['slæpdæʃ] *adj fam* descuidado,-a.
slaphappy ['slæphæpɪ] *adj fam* descuidado,-a.
slapstick ['slæpstɪk] *n* payasadas *fpl.*
slap-up ['slæpʌp] *adj fam* excelente. ● **slap-up meal** comilona, banquete *m.*
slash [slæʃ] *n* **1** *(with sword)* tajo; *(with knife)* cuchillada. **2** *fam (oblique)* barra oblicua.
▷ *vt* **1** *(with sword)* dar un tajo a; *(with knife)* acuchillar, rajar. **2** *fig (prices, wages)* rebajar, reducir: **prices slashed** *precios de remate.*
slat [slæt] *n* tablilla, listón *m.*
slate¹ [sleɪt] *n (gen)* pizarra. ■ **to wipe the slate clean** hacer borrón y cuenta nueva.

slate[2] [sleɪt] *vt* GB *fam (criticize)* poner por los suelos, criticar duramente.

slaughter ['slɔːtəʳ] *n* matanza.
▷ *vt (animals)* matar, sacrificar; *(people)* matar brutalmente.

slaughterhouse ['slɔːtəhaʊs] *n* matadero.

slave [sleɪv] *n* esclavo,-a. ● **slave trade** trata de esclavos.
▷ *vi* trabajar como una bestia (**at**, en).

slaver[1] ['sleɪvəʳ] *n arch (ship)* barco negrero; *(person)* negrero,-a.

slaver[2] ['slævəʳ] *vi (drool)* babear: **she slavered over the baby** *se le caía la baba con el niño.*

slavery ['sleɪvərɪ] *n* esclavitud *f*.

slavish ['sleɪvɪʃ] *adj* **1** *(servile)* esclavo,-a, servil. **2** *(obedience, devotion)* ciego,-a.

slay [sleɪ] *vt lit* matar, asesinar.
▲ *pt* **slew** [sluː], *pp* **slain** [sleɪn].

sleazy ['sliːzɪ] *adj* sórdido,-a.
▲ *comp* **sleazier**, *superl* **sleaziest**.

sledge [sledʒ] *n* GB trineo.
▷ *vi* ir en trineo.

sledgehammer ['sledʒhæməʳ] *n* almádana.

sleek [sliːk] *adj* **1** *(hair, fur)* liso,-a, lustroso,-a. **2** *(appearance)* impecable, elegante.

sleep [sliːp] *n* sueño: **I'm going to have a little sleep** *voy a dormir un poco.*
▷ *vi (gen)* dormir: **I slept well** *he dormido bien.* ■ **to go to sleep 1** *(fall asleep)* dormirse. **2** *(become numb)* dormirse, entumecerse.
▲ *pt & pp* **slept** [slept].
⊙ **to sleep in** *vi (sleep late)* quedarse en la cama, dormir hasta tarde.
⊙ **to sleep through** *vt insep (not hear)* no oír; *(be asleep)* seguir durmiendo.
⊙ **to sleep together** *vi (sleep in same bed)* dormir juntos,-as; *(have sex)* tener relaciones sexuales.
⊙ **to sleep with** *vt insep* acostarse con.

sleeper ['sliːpəʳ] *n* **1** *(person)* durmiente *mf*. **2** *(train)* tren *m* con coches cama; *(sleeping car)* coche-cama *m*; *(berth)* litera. **3** *(beam of wood on track)* traviesa. ■ **to be a light sleeper / be a heavy sleeper** tener el sueño ligero / tener el sueño pesado.

sleepily ['sliːpɪlɪ] *adv* medio dormido,-a.

sleeping ['sliːpɪŋ] *adj* durmiente, dormido,-a. ● **sleeping bag** saco de dormir. ‖ **Sleeping Beauty** la Bella Durmiente. ‖ **sleeping car** coche cama *m*.

sleepless ['sliːpləs] *adj* insomne. ■ **to have a sleepless night** pasar la noche en blanco.

sleeplessness ['sliːpləsnəs] *n* insomnio.

sleepwalker ['sliːpwɔːkəʳ] *n* sonámbulo,-a.

sleepwalking ['sliːpwɔːkɪŋ] *n* sonambulismo.

sleepy ['sliːpɪ] *adj* **1** *(drowsy)* soñoliento,-a. **2** *(quiet, not busy)* tranquilo,-a.
▲ *comp* **sleepier**, *superl* **sleepiest**.

sleet [sliːt] *n* aguanieve *f*.
▷ *vi* caer aguanieve.

sleeve [sliːv] *n* **1** *(of garment)* manga. **2** *(of record)* funda. ■ **to have** STH **up one's sleeve** guardarse una carta en la manga.

sleeveless ['sliːvləs] *adj (garment)* sin mangas.

sleigh [sleɪ] *n* trineo. ● **sleigh bell** cascabel *m*.

sleight [slaɪt] ● **sleight of hand** prestidigitación *f*, jue go de manos.

slender ['slendəʳ] *adj* **1** *(person)* delgado,-a, esbelto,-a **2** *fig (hope, chance)* ligero,-a, remoto,-a; *(income, majo ity)* escaso,-a.
▲ *comp* **slenderer**, *comp* **slenderest**.

slept [slept] *pt & pp* → **sleep**.

sleuth [sluːθ] *n* detective *mf*, sabueso *mf*.

slice [slaɪs] *n* **1** *(of bread)* rebanada; *(thin - ham, etc)* lon ja, loncha; *(- meat)* tajada; *(- of salami, lemon, etc)* roda ja. **2** *(portion - of cake, pie)* porción *f*, trozo; *(- of melon etc)* raja. **3** *fig (share)* parte *f*; *(proportion)* proporción
● **sliced bread** pan *m* de molde.
▷ *vt* **1** *(cut up)* cortar a rebanadas, cortar a lonjas, co tar a rodajas: **she sliced up the ham** *cortó el jamón e lonchas.* **2** *(cut off)* cortar: **can you slice me a piece c cake?** *¿puedes cortarme un trozo de pastel?*

slick [slɪk] *adj* **1** *(skilful)* mañoso,-a, hábil, diestro,-a *(smooth)* fluido,-a. **2** *(attractive)* ingenioso,-a, logra do,-a; *(effective)* eficaz, impresionante: **a slick adverti ing campaign** *una campaña publicitaria muy lograd* **3** *pej (glib - person)* despabilado,-a, con mucha labia
▷ *n* marea negra.
⊙ **to slick down** *vt sep (hair)* alisar.

slicker ['slɪkəʳ] *n* **1** US *fam (person)* presuntuoso,-a. **2** *(raincoat)* impermeable *m*.

slid [slɪd] *pt & pp* → **slide**.

slide [slaɪd] *n* **1** *(act of sliding)* deslizamiento, desliz *(slip)* resbalón *m*. **2** *(in playground)* tobogán *m*. **3** *(ph to)* diapositiva. **4** *(of microscope)* platina, portaobjeto *m*. ● **slide projector** proyector *m* de diapositivas.
▷ *vt (gen)* deslizar, pasar; *(furniture)* correr.
▷ *vi* **1** *(slip deliberately)* deslizar, deslizarse; *(slip ac dentally)* resbalar: **she slid on the ice** *resbaló en el hi lo.* **2** *(move quietly)* deslizarse: **the drawer slid open** *cajón se abrió con facilidad.* ■ **to let** STH **slide** tener A GO abandonado,-a.
▲ *pt & pp* **slid** [slɪd].
⊙ **to slide into** *vt insep (gradually pass into)* caer en.
⊙ **to slide over** *vt insep (avoid)* esquivar, eludir.

sliding ['slaɪdɪŋ] *adj (door, window)* corredero,-a.

slight [slaɪt] *adj* **1** *(small in degree)* pequeño,-a, ligero,- *(not serious, unimportant)* leve, insignificante: **a slig change of plan** *un pequeño cambio de planes.* **2** *(pers* menudo,-a. ■ **not in the slightest** en absoluto.
▷ *n (affront)* desaire *m*, desprecio.
▷ *vt (scorn)* despreciar, menospreciar.

slightly ['slaɪtlɪ] *adv (a little)* ligeramente, un poco, go: **I know him slightly** *apenas lo conozco.* ■ **to slightly built** ser de complexión menuda.

slim [slɪm] *adj* **1** *(person, build)* delgado,-a, esbelto,- **2** *(chance, hopes, prospect)* remoto,-a.
▲ *comp* **slimmer**, *superl* **slimmest**.
▷ *vi* adelgazar, hacer régimen: **I'm slimming** *estoy a gimen.*
▲ *pt & pp* **slimmed**, *ger* **slimming**.
⊙ **to slim down** *vt sep* reducir.

slime [slaɪm] *n* **1** *(mud)* limo, cieno. **2** *(of snail)* baba.

slimmer ['slɪməʳ] *n* persona que está a régimen.

slimming ['slɪmɪŋ] *n (process)* adelgazamiento.

slimness ['slɪmnəs] *n* esbeltez *f*, delgadez *f*.

slimy ['slaımı] *adj* **1** *(muddy)* limoso,-a; *(sticky)* viscoso,-a, pegajoso,-a; *(snail)* baboso,-a. **2** *(person)* zalamero,-a, cobista.
▲ *comp* **slimier**, *superl* **slimiest**.

sling [slıŋ] *n* **1** MED cabestrillo. **2** *(catapult)* honda; *(child's)* tirador *m*. **3** *(device for lifting, carrying)* cuerda; *(for baby)* canguro.
▷ *vt* **1** *fam (throw)* tirar, arrojar: **sling it in the bin** *tíralo a la basura*. **2** *(lift, support)* colgar.
▲ *pt & pp* **slung** [slʌŋ].
⊙ **to sling out** *vt sep* echar, tirar.

slingshot ['slıŋʃɒt] *n* tirachinas *m*.

slink [slıŋk] *vi (move secretly)* moverse sigilosamente; *(in shame)* moverse avergonzado,-a.
▲ *pt & pp* **slunk** [slʌŋk].
⊙ **to slink away / slink off** *vi* escabullirse.

slip¹ [slıp] *n (of paper)* papelito.

slip² [slıp] *n* **1** *(slide)* resbalón *m*; *(trip)* traspiés *m*, tropezón *m*. **2** *(mistake)* error *m*, equivocación *f*; *(moral)* desliz *m*. **3** *(women's underskirt)* combinación *f*, *(petticoat)* enaguas *fpl*. ■ **a slip of the pen** un lapsus. ‖ **a slip of the tongue** un lapsus linguae. ‖ **to give SB the slip** dar esquinazo a ALGN.
▷ *vi* **1** *(slide)* resbalar; *(fall, get away, escape)* caer: **my foot slipped** *se me fue el pie*. **2** AUTO *(clutch, tyre)* patinar. **3** *(move - quickly)* ir de prisa; *(- secretly)* escabullirse. **4** *(decline)* decaer, empeorar.
▷ *vt* **1** *(pass, give, put)* pasar, deslizar, dar a escondidas: **she slipped the note into her bag** *disimuladamente metió la nota en el bolso*. **2** *(overlook, forget)* escaparse.
▲ *pt & pp* **slipped**, *ger* **slipping**.
⊙ **to slip away** *vi (person)* irse.
⊙ **to slip by** *vi (time)* pasar, transcurrir.
⊙ **to slip into** *vt insep (clothes)* ponerse.
⊙ **to slip off** *vt sep (clothes)* quitarse.
⊙ **to slip on** *vt sep (clothes)* ponerse.
⊙ **to slip out** *vi (secret, comment, etc)* escaparse.
⊙ **to slip out of** *vt insep (clothes)* quitarse.
⊙ **to slip up** *vi (make a mistake)* equivocarse.

slipknot ['slıpnɒt] *n* nudo corredizo.

slip-on ['slıpɒn] *adj (shoes)* sin cordones.
▷ *n pl* **slip-ons** *(shoes)* zapatos *mpl* sin cordones.

slipper ['slıpəʳ] *n* zapatilla.

slippery ['slıpərı] *adj (surface)* resbaladizo,-a.
▲ *comp* **slipperier**, *superl* **slipperiest**.

slipshod ['slıpʃɒd] *adj* chapucero,-a.

slipstream ['slıpstriːm] *n* estela.

slip-up ['slıpʌp] *n (mistake)* error *m*, descuido.

slipway ['slıpweı] *n* MAR grada.

slit [slıt] *n (opening)* abertura, hendedura; *(cut)* corte *m*, raja: **light came through the slits in the blind** *entraba la luz por las ranuras de la persiana*.
▷ *vt (cut)* cortar, rajar, hender.
▲ *pt & pp* **slit**, *ger* **slitting**.

slither ['slıðəʳ] *vi* deslizarse.

sliver ['slıvəʳ] *n (of wood, glass)* astilla; *(of ham, etc)* loncha fina, tajada fina.

slob [slɒb] *n fam (dirty, untidy)* dejado,-a.

slobber ['slɒbəʳ] *vi (dribble)* babear.
⊙ **to slobber over** *vt insep* **1** *fam (drool over)* caerse la baba con. **2** *fam (kiss)* besuquear.

slog [slɒg] *n* GB *fam (hard work)* paliza, gran esfuerzo; *(hard walk)* caminata: **digging is a real slog** *cavar es una auténtica paliza*.
▷ *vi* **1** GB *fam* sudar tinta (**away**, -). **2** *(walk)* caminar con dificultad.
▲ *pt & pp* **slogged**, *ger* **slogging**.

slogan ['sləʊgᵊn] *n* eslogan *m*, lema *m*.

sloop [sluːp] *n* MAR balandro.

slop [slɒp] *vt (spill)* derramar, verter: **she slopped paint everywhere** *derramó pintura por todas partes*.
▷ *vi* derramarse, verterse.
▲ *pt & pp* **slopped**, *ger* **slopping**.

slope [sləʊp] *n* **1** *(incline)* cuesta, pendiente *f*; *(upward)* subida; *(downward)* bajada, declive *m*: **a steep slope** *una cuesta empinada*. **2** *(of mountain)* ladera, falda, vertiente *f*; *(of roof)* vertiente *f*.
▷ *vi* inclinarse.
⊙ **to slope off** *vi* largarse, escabullirse.

sloping ['sləʊpıŋ] *adj* inclinado,-a.

sloppy ['slɒpı] *adj* **1** *(messy, careless - gen)* descuidado,-a; *(- manual work)* chapucero,-a; *(- appearance, dress)* desaliñado,-a, dejado,-a. **2** *(sentimental)* empalagoso,-a.
▲ *comp* **sloppier**, *superl* **sloppiest**.

slosh [slɒʃ] *vt* **1** *(splash)* salpicar: **he sloshed some paint on the floor** *salpicó el suelo de pintura*. **2** GB *fam (hit)* cascar, zurrar, pegar.
▷ *vi* agitarse.

sloshed [slɒʃt] *adj fam* borracho,-a.

slot [slɒt] *n* **1** *(for coin)* ranura; *(groove)* muesca; *(opening)* rendija, abertura. **2** *(programme)* espacio; *(position, place)* puesto, hueco. ● **slot machine 1** *(vending machine)* distribuidor *m* automático. **2** *(for gambling)* máquina tragaperras.
▷ *vt (insert)* insertar, introducir: **slot the coin in the machine** *insertar la moneda en la máquina*.
⊙ **to slot in** *vt sep (fit in)* meter.
▷ *vi (fit together)* encajar.
▲ *pt & pp* **slotted**, *ger* **slotting**.
⊙ **to slot together** *vi* encajar.

sloth [sləʊθ] *n* **1** *fml (laziness, idleness)* pereza, indolencia. **2** ZOOL perezoso.

slouch [slaʊtʃ] *vi (walk)* andar con los hombros caídos, andar arrastrando los pies.
▷ *n (posture)* andar *m* desgarbado.

slough¹ [slaʊ] *n (swamp, marsh)* cenagal *m*.

slough² [slʌf] *n (of snake)* muda.
▷ *vt (snake)* mudar de (**off**, -).
⊙ **to slough off** *vt sep fig* deshacerse de.

Slovak ['sləʊvæk] *adj* eslovaco,-a.
▷ *n* **1** *(person)* eslovaco,-a. **2** *(language)* eslovaco.

Slovakia [sləʊ'vækıə] *n* Eslovaquia.

Slovene ['sləʊviːn] *adj* esloveno,-a.
▷ *n* **1** *(person)* esloveno,-a. **2** *(language)* esloveno.

Slovenia [sləʊ'viːnə] *n* Eslovenia.

slovenly ['slʌvᵊnlı] *adj (careless)* descuidado,-a; *(scruffy)* desaliñado,-a, desaseado,-a.

slow [sləʊ] *adj* **1** *(gen)* lento,-a: **a slow recovery** *una recuperación lenta*. **2** *(clock, watch)* atrasado,-a: **my watch is slow** *mi reloj va atrasado*. **3** *(dull, not active)* aburrido,-a. **4** *(not quick to learn)* lento,-a, torpe; *(thick)* corto,-a de alcances: **he's a slow learner** *le cuesta aprender.* ■ **to be slow about/in doing** STH tardar en hacer ALGO.

▷ *adv* despacio, lentamente: **drive slow!** *¡conduce despacio!*

▷ *vt (vehicle, machine)* reducir la marcha de.

▷ *vi (gen)* ir más despacio.

⊙ **to slow down** *vt sep* hacer ir más despacio.

▷ *vi (gen)* ir más despacio.

slowcoach ['sləukəutʃ] *n fam* tortuga *mf.*

slowdown ['sləudaun] *n* US *(workers)* huelga de celo.

slowly ['sləulɪ] *adv* despacio, lentamente.

sludge [slʌdʒ] *n* **1** *(mud)* fango, cieno, lodo, barro. **2** *(sewage)* aguas *fpl* residuales.

slug[1] [slʌg] *n* ZOOL babosa.

slug[2] [slʌg] *n* **1** *(bullet)* bala. **2** *(drink)* trago.

slug[3] [slʌg] *vt (hit)* pegar un porrazo a.

▲ *pt & pp* **slugged**, *ger* **slugging.**

sluggish ['slʌgɪʃ] *adj (river, engine)* lento,-a; *(person)* perezoso,-a, holgazán,-ana.

sluice [slu:s] *n (gate, valve)* compuerta, esclusa; *(waterway)* canal *m.*

▷ *vt (wash)* lavar a chorro (**down/out**, -).

slum [slʌm] *n* **1** *(place, house, etc)* casuca, casucha, tugurio. **2** *fam (tip)* pocilga.

▷ *vi fam* visitar los barrios bajos.

▲ *pt & pp* **slummed**, *ger* **slumming.**

▷ *n pl* **slums** *(area)* barrios *mpl* bajos.

slumber ['slʌmbəʳ] *n lit (sleep)* sueño.

▷ *vi* dormir.

slump [slʌmp] *n (recession)* crisis *f* económica; *(drop in demand, etc)* bajón *m*, baja repentina.

▷ *vi* **1** *(economy)* hundirse; *(sales, demand, etc)* bajar en picado, caer en picado, caer de repente; *(prices)* desplomarse. **2** *(fall, flop down)* caer; *(faint)* desmayarse.

slung [slʌŋ] *pt & pp* → **sling.**

slur [slɜ:ʳ] *n* **1** *(stigma)* mancha; *(slanderous remark)* calumnia, difamación *f*; *(insult)* afrenta. **2** *(way of speaking)* dificultad *f* al hablar.

▷ *vt* **1** *(letters, words)* comerse, pronunciar mal. **2** *(slander)* manchar, mancillar.

▲ *pt & pp* **slurred**, *ger* **slurring.**

slurp [slɜ:p] *vt* sorber ruidosamente.

slush [slʌʃ] *n (melting snow)* aguanieve *f*, nieve *f* derretida. ● **slush fund** US fondos *mpl* para sobornos.

sly [slaɪ] *adj* **1** *(cunning)* astuto,-a, ladino,-a; *(deceitful)* tramposo,-a. **2** *(secretive, knowing)* furtivo,-a: **a sly smile** *una sonrisa maliciosa.* **3** *(mischievous, playful)* travieso,-a, pícaro,-a. ■ **on the sly** a escondidas.

▲ *comp* **slyer** o **slier**, *superl* **slyest** o **sliest.**

slyness ['slaɪnəs] *n* astucia.

smack[1] [smæk] *n* **1** *(slap)* bofetada, tortazo, azote *m*; *(blow)* golpe *m.* **2** *fam (loud kiss)* besote *m*, beso sonoro.

▷ *vt* **1** *(slap)* dar una bofetada a, abofetear, pegar a. **2** *(strike)* golpear.

▷ *adv* **1** *fam (with force)* de lleno, directamente. **2** *fam (exactly)* justo.

smack[2] [smæk] *n* **1** *(flavour)* sabor *m*; *(smell)* olor *m.* **2** *(hint, suggestion)* pizca. ■ **to smack one's lips** relamerse.

⊙ **to smack of** *vt insep (gen)* oler a.

smack[3] [smæk] *n* MAR barca de pesca.

small [smɔ:l] *adj* **1** *(not large)* pequeño,-a, chico,-a: **we live in a small flat** *vivimos en un piso pequeño.* **2** *(in height)* bajo,-a, pequeño,-a: **he's a small man** *es un hombre bajito.* **3** *(young)* joven, pequeño,-a: **when I was small** *cuando era pequeño.* **4** *(reduced - sum, number)* reducido,-a, módico,-a; *(slight, scant)* escaso,-a, poco,-a: **I want you to work in small groups** *quiero que trabajéis en grupos reducidos.* **5** *(small-scale)* pequeño,-a. **6** *(unimportant, trivial)* sin importancia, insignificante. **7** *(not capital)* minúscula: **with a small t** *con minúscula.* ■ **(it's) small wonder that...** no me extraña (nada) que.... ■ **in the small hours** a altas horas de la madrugada. ● **small ads** anuncios *mpl* por palabras. **small change** cambio, monedas *fpl* sueltas.

▷ *adv* pequeño: **cut it up small** *córtalo en trocitos.*

▷ *n pl* **smalls** *dated (underwear)* paños *mpl* menores, ropa *f sing* interior.

▲ *c comp* **smaller**, *comp* **smallest.**

smallholder ['smɔ:lhəuldəʳ] *n (landowner)* minifundista *mf.*

smallholding ['smɔ:lhəuldɪŋ] *n (estate)* minifundio.

smallness ['smɔ:lnəs] *n (size)* pequeñez *f*; *(lack of importance)* insignificancia.

smallpox ['smɔ:lpɒks] *n* viruela.

small-scale ['smɔ:l'skeɪl] *adj* a pequeña escala.

small-time ['smɔ:l'taɪm] *adj* de poca monta.

smalt [smɔ:lt] *n* esmalte *m.*

smarmy ['smɑ:mɪ] *adj* zalamero,-a, cobista.

▲ *comp* **smarmier**, *superl* **smarmiest.**

smart [smɑ:t] *adj* **1** *(elegant)* elegante, fino,-a; *(chic)* fino,-a, de buen tono. **2** US *(clever)* listo,-a, inteligente; *(sharp)* agudo,-a, vivo,-a; *(impudent)* fresco,-a, descarado,-a: **he thinks he's so smart** *se cree muy listo.* **3** *(quick, brisk)* rápido,-a, ligero,-a.

▷ *vi* **1** *(sting)* escocer, picar: **the smoke made my eyes smart** *el humo me escocía los ojos.* **2** *(suffer)* sufrir, dolerse.

smart-arse ['smɑ:tɑ:s] *n sl* listillo,-a.

smarten ['smɑ:tᵊn] *vt (person, house)* arreglar (**up**, -).

smash [smæʃ] *n* **1** *(noise)* estrépito, estruendo. **2** *(collision)* choque *m* violento, colisión *f.* **3** *(blow)* golpe *m.* **4** SP *(tennis)* smash *m*, mate *m.* **5** *(success, hit)* exitazo, gran éxito. ● **smash hit** gran éxito, exitazo.

▷ *vt* **1** *(break)* romper; *(shatter)* hacer pedazos, hacer añicos; *(destroy - car, room, etc)* destrozar: **the vandals smashed the place up** *los vándalos destrozaron el local.* **2** *(hit forcefully)* romper; *(crash, throw violently)* estrellar (**into**, contra). **3** *(defeat)* vencer, aplastar; *(destroy)* destrozar. **4** SP *(in tennis)* hacer un mate.

▷ *vi* **1** *(break)* romperse; *(shatter)* hacerse añicos: **the mirror smashed into tiny pieces** *el espejo se hizo añicos.* **2** *(crash)* estrellarse (**into**, contra), chocar (**into**, contra).

smashed [smæʃt] *adj fam (drunk)* borracho,-a.

smashing ['smæʃɪŋ] *adj* GB *fam* estupendo,-a, fantástico,-a, genial, fenomenal.

smash-up ['smæʃʌp] *n (crash)* choque *m* violento, colisión *f*; *(accident)* accidente *m.*

smattering ['smætᵊrɪŋ] *n* nociones *fpl*: **he has a smattering of French** *habla un poco de francés.*

smear [smɪəʳ] *n* **1** *(smudge, stain)* mancha. **2** *fig (defamation)* calumnia.

▷ *vt* **1** *(spread - butter, ointment)* untar; *(- grease, paint)* embadurnar: **he smeared butter on the bread** *untó el pan con mantequilla.* **2** *(make dirty)* manchar. **3** *fig (defame)* calumniar, difamar.

mell [smel] *n* **1** *(sense)* olfato. **2** *(odour)* olor *m*; *(perfume)* perfume *m*, aroma *m*.
vt **1** oler. **2** *fig* olfatear.
vi **1** oler. **2** *(have particular smell)* oler (a).
▲ *pt & pp* **smelled o smelt.**
to smell out *vt sep* **1** *(discover by smelling)* husmear. **2** *(stink)* apestar.
melt¹ [smelt] *vt (melt)* fundir.
melt² [smelt] *pp* ⟶ **smell.**
mile [smaɪl] *n* sonrisa.
vi (gen) sonreír.
vt (say with a smile) decir sonriendo.
to smile on *vi* sonreír a.
miley ['smaɪlɪ] *n* COMPUT emoticón *m*.
mirk [smɜːk] *n (self-satisfied)* sonrisa satisfecha; *(foolish)* sonrisa boba.
vi (with self-satisfaction) sonreír con satisfacción; *(foolishly)* sonreír bobamente.
mith [smɪθ] *n* herrero,-a.
mithy ['smɪðɪ] *n* herrería.
▲ *pl* **smithies.**
mog [smɒg] *n* niebla tóxica, smog *m*.
moke [sməʊk] *n* **1** *(gen)* humo. **2** *fam (cigarette)* cigarrillo, cigarro, pitillo.
vt **1** *(person)* fumar. **2** *(meat, fish)* ahumar.
vi **1** *(person)* fumar. **2** *(fire, chimney, etc)* echar humo, humear.
to smoke out *vt sep (insects)* ahuyentar con humo; *(people)* desalojar con bombas fumígenas.
moker ['sməʊkəʳ] *n* **1** *(person)* fumador,-ra. **2** *(on train)* vagón *m* de fumadores.
mokestack ['sməʊkstæk] *n* chimenea.
noking ['sməʊkɪŋ] *adj* humeante.
n fumar *m*.
moky ['sməʊkɪ] *adj* lleno,-a de humo.
▲ *comp* **smokier,** *comp* **smokiest.**
nooth [smuːð] *adj* **1** *(surface, texture, tyre)* liso,-a; *(skin)* suave; *(road)* llano,-a, uniforme; *(sea)* tranquilo,-a, en calma. **2** *(liquid mixture, sauce)* sin grumos. **3** *(wine, beer, etc)* suave. **4** *(style, etc)* fluido,-a. **5** *(journey, flight)* tranquilo,-a; *(take-off, landing, stop)* suave; *(take-over, transition)* sin problemas, sin obstáculos, sin complicaciones. **6** *pej (person)* zalamero,-a, meloso,-a.
vt (gen) alisar; *(with sandpaper)* lijar; *(polish)* pulir.
to smooth away *vt sep* **1** *(problems, etc)* allanar. **2** *(wrinkles)* hacer desaparecer.
nother ['smʌðəʳ] *vt* **1** *(asphyxiate)* asfixiar, ahogar. **2** *(put out - fire)* sofocar, extinguir, apagar. **3** *(stifle - yawn, cough, laughter)* contener, reprimir; *(suppress - opposition)* acallar. **4** *(cover)* cubrir (**in/with**, de); *(heap)* colmar (**in/with**, de).
vi (asphyxiate) asfixiarse, ahogarse.
nudge [smʌdʒ] *n (stain - gen)* mancha; *(- of ink)* borrón *m*.
vt (gen) manchar; *(writing)* emborronar.
vi (ink, paint, etc) correrse.
nuggle ['smʌgᵊl] *vt* **1** *(illegally)* pasar de contrabando. **2** *(sneak)* pasar a escondidas.
nuggler ['smʌgᵊləʳ] *n* contrabandista *mf*.
nack [snæk] *n (light meal)* bocado, piscolabis *m*, tentempié *m*, refrigerio; *(in afternoon)* merienda.
vi comer, comerse.
▷ *n pl* **snacks** *(gen)* cosas *fpl* para picar; *(in bar)* tapas *fpl*.
snail [sneɪl] *n* caracol *m*.
snake [sneɪk] *n (big)* serpiente *f*; *(small)* culebra.
▷ *vi fig (river, road, etc)* serpentear.
snap [snæp] *n* **1** *(sharp noise)* ruido seco; *(of fingers, branch)* chasquido. **2** *fam (snapshot)* foto *f*, instantánea. **3** *(card game) juego de naipes infantil*. **4** *fam (eagerness, zip)* afán *m*, brío, energía. **5** US *(easy thing to do)* cosa tirada. **6** US *(press-stud)* broche *m* a presión.
▷ *adj (decision, etc)* precipitado,-a, repentino,-a. ■ **snap to it!** ¡rápido!, ¡muévete! ▮ **to snap shut** cerrarse de golpe.
▷ *interj* GB ¡toma!, ¡caramba!
▷ *vt* **1** *(break)* partir en dos, romper en dos. **2** *(close)* cerrar de golpe. **3** *(click)* chasquear. **4** *(say sharply)* decir bruscamente. **5** *fam (photograph)* sacar una foto de.
▷ *vi* **1** *(break)* romperse, partirse. **2** *fig (person)* perder los nervios, sufrir una crisis nerviosa. **3** *(speak sharply)* regañar (**at**, a), hablar con brusquedad (**at**, a). **4** *(bite)* morder (**at**, -).
▲ *pt & pp* **snapped**, *ger* **snapping.**
⊙ **to snap up** *vt sep (bargain)* llevarse; *(offer)* agarrar, no dejar escapar.
snappy ['snæpɪ] *adj* **1** *(quick)* rápido,-a; *(brisk, lively)* enérgico,-a, vivo,-a. **2** *(stylish)* elegante. **3** *(short-tempered)* irritable, irascible.
▲ *comp* **snappier**, *superl* **snappiest.**
snapshot ['snæpʃɒt] *n* foto *f*, instantánea.
snare [sneəʳ] *n (trap - for animal)* lazo, trampa, cepo; *(- for person)* trampa.
▷ *vt (catch - animal)* coger con lazo, cazar con trampa; *(- person)* atrapar, cazar; *(trick)* engañar.
snarl¹ [snɑːl] *n (growl)* gruñido.
▷ *vi (growl)* gruñir (**at**, a).
▷ *vt (say)* gruñir.
snarl² [snɑːl] *n* **1** *(in wool)* maraña, enredo. **2** *(confused state)* enredo, maraña, lío.
⊙ **to snarl up** *vt sep (wool)* enmarañar, enredar; *(traffic)* atascar; *(plans)* enredar.
▷ *vi (traffic)* atascarse.
snatch [snætʃ] *n* **1** *(grab)* arrebatamiento. **2** *fam (theft)* robo, hurto. **3** *(of song, conversation)* fragmento.
▷ *vt* **1** *(grab)* arrebatar, arrancar, coger; *(steal)* robar; *(kidnap)* secuestrar. **2** *(sleep, food, etc)* coger, pillar; *(opportunity, etc)* aprovechar.
▷ *vi* arrebatar, quitar.
⊙ **to snatch at** *vt insep (ball, branch, etc)* tratar de coger.
▷ *vt sep (opportunity, etc)* aprovechar.
sneak [sniːk] *n* GB *fam* acusica *mf*, acusón,-ona, chivato,-a, soplón,-ona.
▷ *adj (attack, visit, etc)* sorpresa; *(look)* furtivo,-a.
▷ *vt (take out)* sacar (a escondidas); *(take in)* pasar (a escondidas), colar (de extranjis).
▷ *vi* **1** *(move)* moverse sigilosamente. **2** *(tell tales)* acusar (**on**, a), chivarse (**on**, de).
⊙ **to sneak up** *vi* acercarse sigilosamente.
sneakers ['sniːkəz] *n pl* US zapatillas *fpl* de deporte, bambas *fpl*, playeras *fpl*.
sneaky ['sniːkɪ] *adj* **1** *(secretive)* sigiloso,-a, furtivo,-a. **2** *(deceitful)* solapado,-a, artero,-a.
▲ *comp* **sneakier**, *superl* **sneakiest.**
sneer [snɪəʳ] *n* **1** *(look)* cara de desprecio; *(smile)* sonrisa burlona. **2** *(remark)* comentario desdeñoso.

▷ *vi (mock)* burlarse (**at**, de), mofarse (**at**, de); *(scorn)* desdeñar, despreciar.
sneeze [sni:z] *n* estornudo.
▷ *vi* estornudar.
sniff [snɪf] *n* 1 aspiración. 2 *(inhalation)* aspiración *f* (por la nariz), inhalación *f*.
▷ *vi* 1 *(with a cold)* sorber (por las narices). 2 *(when crying)* resollar.
▷ *vt* 1 *(person - gen)* oler; *(- suspiciously)* olfatear, husmear, olisquear; *(animal)* olfatear, husmear, olisquear. 2 *(say proudly)* decir con desdén; *(complainingly)* gimotear. 3 *(drugs)* esnifar; *(glue)* esnifar, inhalar; *(vapour, snuff, smelling salts)* aspirar (por la nariz), inhalar.
⊙ **to sniff at** *vt insep* 1 *(person)* oler; *(animal)* olfatear, husmear, olisquear. 2 *(turn nose up at)* despreciar, desdeñar.
⊙ **to sniff out** *vt insep* 1 *(drugs, etc)* descubrir olfateando. 2 *(secret, plot, etc)* oler, olerse.
snip [snɪp] *n* 1 *(cut with scissors)* tijeretazo, tijeretada; *(action, noise)* tijereteo. 2 *(small piece cut off)* recorte *m*. 3 GB *fam (bargain)* ganga, chollo.
▷ *vt* tijeretear.
▲ *pt & pp* **snipped**, *ger* **snipping**.
⊙ **to snip off** *vt sep* cortar con tijeras.
snippet ['snɪpɪt] *n* 1 *(small piece cut off)* recorte *m*, trocito. 2 *(of conversation, etc)* fragmento.
snob [snɒb] *n* esnob *mf*.
snoop [snu:p] *vi* 1 *(search, investigate)* husmear, fisgar, curiosear. 2 *(pry)* entrometerse, meterse (**into**, en).
▷ *n (person)* fisgón,-ona.
snooper ['snu:pəʳ] *n* fisgón,-ona.
snooze [snu:z] *n fam* cabezada, siestecilla.
▷ *vi fam* dormitar, echar una cabezada.
snore [snɔ:ʳ] *n* ronquido.
▷ *vi* roncar.
snorkel ['snɔ:kᵊl] *n (of swimmer)* tubo de respiración; *(of submarine)* esnórkel *m*.
▷ *vi* bucear con tubo de respiración.
▲ *pt & pp* **snorkelled** (US **snorkeled**), *ger* **snorkelling** (US **snorkeling**).
snorkelling ['snɔ:kᵊlɪŋ] *n* buceo (con tubo de respiración).
snort [snɔ:t] *vi* 1 *(make noise - person)* resoplar, bufar; *(- animal)* resoplar. 2 *(say angrily, etc)* bramar, gruñir.
▷ *vt (drugs)* esnifar.
▷ *n* 1 *(person)* resoplido, bufido; *(animal)* resoplido. 2 *fam (drink)* trago. 3 *(of drugs)* esnifada.
snout [snaʊt] *n* 1 *(of animal)* morro, hocico. 2 GB *fam (of person)* napias *mf*, narizotas *mf*. 3 *(of gun, bottle, etc)* morro. 4 GB *sl (tobacco)* tabaco. 5 GB *sl (informer)* soplón,-ona, chivato,-a.
snow [snəʊ] *n* 1 METEOR *(gen)* nieve *f*; *(snowfall)* nevada. 2 TV nieve *f*.
▷ *vi* nevar. ■ **to be snowed in/up** quedar aislado,-a por la nieve. ● **snow leopard** onza.
▷ *vt* US *fam (influence)* convencer, impresionar.
snowball ['snəʊbɔ:l] *n* bola de nieve.
snowboard ['snəʊbɔ:d] *n* snowboard.
snowbound ['snəʊbaʊnd] *adj* aislado,-a por la nieve, bloqueado,-a por la nieve.
snow-capped ['snəʊkæpt] *adj* nevado,-a.
snowdrift ['snəʊdrɪft] *n* ventisquero.
snowdrop ['snəʊdrɒp] *n* BOT campanilla de inviern
snowflake ['snəʊfleɪk] *n* copo de nieve.
snowman ['snəʊmæn] *n* muñeco de nieve.
snowplough ['snəʊplaʊ] *n* quitanieves *m*.
snowplow ['snəʊplaʊ] *n* US → **snowplough**.
snowshoe ['snəʊʃu:] *n* raqueta (de nieve).
snowstorm ['snəʊstɔ:m] *n* tormenta de nieve.
snowy ['snəʊɪ] *adj* de nieve, nevado,-a.
▲ *comp* **snowier**, *superl* **snowiest**.
snub [snʌb] *n (of person)* desaire *m*; *(of offer)* rechazo.
▷ *vt (person)* desairar; *(offer)* rechazar.
▲ *pt & pp* **snubbed**, *ger* **snubbing**.
▷ *adj (nose)* respingón,-ona, chato,-a.
snuff [snʌf] *vt (extinguish candle)* apagar (**out**, -); *(cut wick)* cortar.
⊙ **to snuff out** *vt sep (rebellion)* sofocar; *(hopes)* acabar co
snug [snʌg] *adj* 1 *(cosy)* cómodo,-a; *(warm)* calentito,- 2 *(tightfitting)* ajustado,-a, ceñido,-a.
▷ *n* GB *(in pub)* saloncito.
snuggle ['snʌgᵊl] *vi* acurrucarse.
so [səʊ] *conj* 1 *(therefore)* así que, por lo tanto, de man ra que. 2 *(to express purpose)* para, para que.
▷ *adv* 1 *(introductory)* así que, pues, bueno: **so you've d cided to come** *así que has decidido venir.* 2 *(very - befo adj or adv)* tan; *(- before noun or with verb)* tanto,-a: **she so bored** *está tan aburrida.* 3 *(unspecified number amount, limit)* tanto,-a: **I can only do so much** *no pue hacer más.* 4 *(thus, in this way)* así, de esta manera, este modo: **he's about so tall** *es así de alto.* 5 *(to av repetition)* que sí: **I think/hope so** *creo/espero que sí.* 6 *express agreement, also)* también: **so am I/so do I/so c I/so have I** *yo también.* ■ **and so on (and so forth)** y a sucesivamente. ‖ **so long!** ¡hasta luego! ‖ **so much f** STH: **so much for your advice!** *¡vaya consejo que me dis* ‖ **so what?** ¿y qué?
▷ *adj (factual, true)* así: **it can't be so** *no puede ser.*
soak [səʊk] *vt (put in liquid)* poner en remojo, remoja *(saturate)* empapar.
▷ *vi* 1 *(washing, dried pulses)* estar en remojo. 2 *(bathe)* b ñarse. 3 *(penetrate)* empapar, calar.
▷ *n* 1 remojón *m*. 2 *fam (drunkard)* borracho,-a.
⊙ **to soak up** *vt sep (liquid)* absorber; *(sun, atmosphe* empaparse de; *(information)* embeber.
soap [səʊp] *n* jabón *m*: **a bar/cake/tablet of soap** *u pastilla de jabón.*
▷ *vt* enjabonar, jabonar.
soapsuds ['səʊpsʌdz] *n pl* jabonaduras *fpl*, espum *sing.*
soar [sɔ:ʳ] *vi* 1 *(bird, plane - fly)* volar; *(- rise)* remontar vuelo, remontarse; *(- glide)* planear. 2 *fig (prices, cos etc)* dispararse. 3 *(building)* elevarse, alzarse.
sob [sɒb] *n* sollozo.
▷ *vi* sollozar.
▷ *vt* decir sollozando, decir entre sollozos.
▲ *pt & pp* **sobbed**, *ger* **sobbing**.
sober ['səʊbəʳ] *adj* 1 *(not drunk)* sobrio,-a. 2 *(person)* s rio,-a, formal; *(attitude)* sobrio,-a, moderado,-a, se sato,-a. 3 *(colour)* discreto,-a, sobrio,-a.
⊙ **to sober down** *vi* serenarse, calmarse, moderarse
▷ *vt sep* serenar, calmar, atemperar, moderar.
⊙ **to sober up** *vi* pasársele la borrachera a uno.
▷ *vt sep* despejar.
sobering ['səʊbərɪŋ] *adj* tranquilizador, -ra.

sobriety [s'braɪətɪ] *n (seriousness)* seriedad *f*; *(moderation)* moderación *f*, sobriedad *f*; *(good sense)* sensatez *f*.

so-called ['səʊkɔːld] *adj* llamado,-a, supuesto,-a.

soccer ['sɒkəʳ] *n* fútbol *m*.

sociable ['səʊʃəbəl] *adj* sociable.

social ['səʊʃᵊl] *adj* **1** *(gen)* social. **2** *fam (sociable)* sociable.
▷ *n (informal meeting)* acto social, reunión *f* (social); *(party)* fiesta; *(dance)* baile *m*.

socialism ['səʊʃəlɪzəm] *n* socialismo.

socialist ['səʊʃəlist] *adj & n* socialista *mf*.

socialite ['səʊʃᵊlaɪt] *n* vividor,-ra, mundano,-a.

socialize ['səʊʃᵊlaɪz] *vi (mix socially)* relacionarse, alternar; *(at party)* circular, hacer vida social.
▷ *vt* **1** TECH *(adapt to society)* socializar. **2** US *(nationalize)* nacionalizar.

society [s'saɪətɪ] *n* **1** *(community, people)* sociedad *f*. **2** *(fashionable group, upper class)* (alta) sociedad *f*. **3** *(organization, club)* sociedad *f*, asociación *f*, club *m*, círculo. **4** *fml (company)* compañía.
▲ *pl* **societies**.

sociology [səʊsɪ'ɒlədʒɪ] *n* sociología.

sock [sɒk] *n* calcetín *m*.

socket ['sɒkɪt] *n* **1** ANAT *(of eye)* cuenca, órbita; *(of joint)* glena. **2** ELEC *(for plug)* enchufe *m*, toma de corriente; *(for light bulb)* portalámparas *m*.

soda ['səʊdə] *n* **1** CHEM sosa, soda. **2** *(soda water)* soda, sifón *m*. **3** US *(pop)* refresco. **4** *(ice-cream soda)* soda con helado y almíbar.

sodden ['sɒdᵊn] *adj (soaked)* empapado,-a.

sodium ['səʊdɪəm] *n* CHEM sodio. ● **sodium bicarbonate** bicarbonato sódico. ‖ **sodium chloride** carbonato sódico.

sofa ['səʊfə] *n* sofá *m*.

soft [sɒft] *adj* **1** *(not hard)* blando,-a; *(spongy)* esponjoso,-a; *(flabby)* fofo,-a. **2** *(skin, hair, fur, etc)* suave. **3** *(light, music, colour)* suave; *(words)* tierno,-a; *(breeze, steps, knock)* ligero,-a; *(outline)* difuminado,-a; *(voz)* baja. **4** *fam (easy)* fácil. **5** *(person - lenient)* blando,-a, indulgente; *(- weak)* débil; *(- gentle, kind)* dulce; *(- easily upset)* sensiblero,-a. **6** *(water)* blando,-a. **7** LING *(consonant)* suave. ● **soft copy** datos *mpl* contenidos en la memoria del ordenador. ‖ **soft currency** moneda débil. ‖ **soft drink** refresco. ‖ **soft palate** velo del paladar.

soft-boiled ['sɒft'bɔɪld] *adj (egg)* pasado por agua.

soften ['sɒfᵊn] *vt (leather, heart)* ablandar; *(skin)* suavizar; *(light, sound, colour)* atenuar, suavizar; *(voice)* bajar.
▷ *vi (leather, heart, butter)* ablandarse; *(skin)* suavizarse; *(light, sound, colour)* atenuarse, suavizarse; *(voice)* bajar; *(attitude)* volverse más tolerante.
⊙ **to soften up** *vt sep* **1** *(person)* ablandar. **2** MIL debilitar.

softener ['sɒfənəʳ] *n* suavizante *m*.

soft-hearted ['sɒft'hɑːtɪd] *adj* tierno,-a, compasivo,-a.

softness ['sɒftnəs] *n* **1** *(gen)* blandura, lo blando. **2** *(of hair, fabric, skin)* suavidad *f*. **3** *(weakness)* debilidad *f*.

soft-spoken [sɒft'spəʊkᵊn] *adj* de voz suave.

software ['sɒftweəʳ] *n* COMPUT software *m*.

softwood ['sɒftwʊd] *n (wood)* madera de coníferas; *(tree)* conífera.

softy ['sɒftɪ] *n* ⟶ **softie**.
▲ *pl* **softies**.

soggy ['sɒgɪ] *adj* **1** *(wet)* empapado,-a, saturado, a. **2** *(too soft)* pastoso,-a, gomoso,-a.
▲ *comp* **soggier**, *superl* **soggiest**.

soil [sɔɪl] *n* **1** *(earth)* tierra. **2** *fml (country, territory)* tierra.
▷ *vt* **1** *(dirty)* ensuciar; *(stain)* manchar. **2** *fig (reputation)* manchar.
▷ *vi* ensuciarse.

soiled [sɔɪld] *adj (dirty)* sucio,-a; *(stained)* manchado,-a.

solace ['sɒlɪs] *n (comfort)* consuelo, solaz *m*.
▷ *vt lit* consolar.

solar ['səʊləʳ] *adj* solar. ● **solar cell** célula solar. ‖ **solar corona** corona solar. ‖ **solar energy** energía solar. ‖ **solar plexus** plexo solar. ‖ **the solar system** el sistema *m* solar.

solder ['sɒldəʳ] *n* soldadura.
▷ *vt* soldar.

soldering iron ['sɒldərɪŋaɪən] *n* soldador *m*.

soldier ['səʊldʒəʳ] *n (not officer)* soldado; *(military man)* militar *m*. ■ **a soldier of fortune** un mercenario.
⊙ **to soldier on** *vi* seguir adelante (a pesar de todo), seguir al pie del cañón.

sole¹ [səʊl] *n (fish)* lenguado.

sole² [səʊl] *adj* **1** *(only, single)* único,-a. **2** *(exclusive)* exclusivo,-a.

sole³ [səʊl] *n (of foot)* planta; *(of shoe, sock)* suela.
▷ *vt* poner suela a.

sol-fa ['sɒlfɑː] *n* solfeo.

solicit [s'lɪsɪt] *vt* **1** *(request)* pedir, solicitar. **2** *(of prostitute)* abordar (buscando clientes).
▷ *vi* **1** *(request)* pedir, solicitar. **2** *(of prostitute)* ejercer la prostitución, abordar a clientes.

solicitor [s'lɪsɪtəʳ] *n* **1** GB abogado,-a. **2** US oficial *mf* de justicia.

solicitous [s'lɪsɪtəs] *adj* **1** *fml (eager, kind, helpful)* solícito,-a. **2** *fml (concerned, anxious)* preocupado,-a (**about/for**, por), inquieto,-a (**about/for**, por).

solicitude [s'lɪsɪtjuːd] *n* **1** *fml (eagerness, kindness)* solicitud *f*. **2** *fml (concern, anxiousness)* preocupación *f* (**for**, por).

solid ['sɒlɪd] *adj* **1** *(not liquid or gas)* sólido,-a. **2** *(not hollow)* macizo,-a. **3** *(dense, compact)* compacto,-a. **4** *(unmixed)* puro,-a. **5** *(strong)* sólido,-a, fuerte. **6** *(reliable)* sólido,-a, de confianza, de fiar. **7** *(unanimous)* unánime. **8** *(continuous)* seguido,-a; *(unbroken)* continuo,-a. **9** TECH *(three-dimensional)* tridimensional. ● **solid geometry** geometría del espacio.
▷ *n (substance)* sólido.
▷ *n pl* **solids** *(food)* alimentos *mpl* sólidos, sólidos *mpl*.

sold [slept] *pt & pp* ⟶ **sell**.

solidification [səlɪdɪfɪ'keɪʃᵊn] *n* solidificación *f*.

solidify [s'lɪdɪfaɪ] *vt* solidificar.
▷ *vi* solidificarse.
▲ *pt & pp* **solidified**, *ger* **solidifying**.

soliloquy [s'lɪləkwɪ] *n* soliloquio.
▲ *pl* **soliloquies**.

solitary ['sɒlɪtᵊrɪ] *adj* **1** *(alone)* solitario,-a. **2** *(secluded, remote)* apartado,-a. **3** *(only, sole)* solo,-a, único,-a.
▷ *n sl (solitary confinement)* incomunicación *f*.

solitude ['sɒlɪtjuːd] *n* soledad *f*.

solo ['səʊləʊ] *n* **1** MUS solo. **2** AV vuelo en solitario. **3** *(card game)* solitario.
▲ *pl* **solos**.
▷ *adj* **1** MUS *(performance, album)* en solitario; *(instrument)* solo; *(piece)* para solista. **2** *(attempt, flight)* en solitario.
▷ *adv* **1** MUS *(play, sing)* solo,-a. **2** *(fly)* en solitario.

soloist ['səʊləʊɪst] *n* MUS solista *mf*.
Solomon ['sɒləmən] *n* Salomón. ● **Solomon Islands** Islas Salomón.
solstice ['sɒlstɪs] *n* solsticio.
soluble ['sɒljəbəl] *adj* soluble.
solution [sə'lju:ʃən] *n* solución *m*.
solve [sɒlv] *vt* resolver, solucionar.
solvent ['sɒlvənt] *adj* **1** *(not in debt)* solvente. **2** *(that can dissolve)* soluble.
▷ *n* solvente *m*, disolvente *m*.
Somali [s'mɑ:lɪ] *adj* somalí.
▷ *n* somalí *mf*.
Somalia [s'mɑ:lɪə] *n* Somalia.
sombre ['sɒmbəʳ] *adj* **1** *(colour, place)* sombrío,-a; *(day, weather)* gris, triste; *(sky)* cubierto,-a. **2** *(person)* sombrío,-a, triste, serio,-a; *(statement, occasion, thought)* pesimista, grave.
some [sʌm] *adj* **1** *(with plural noun)* unos,-as, algunos,-as; *(a few)* unos,-as cuantos,-as, unos,-as pocos,-as: **there were some flowers on the table** *había unas flores en la mesa.* **2** *(with singular noun)* algún, alguna; *(a little)* algo de, un poco de: **would you like some coffee?** *¿quieres un poco de café?* **3** *(certain)* cierto,-a, alguno,-a: **some days are better than others** *algunos días son mejores que otros.* **4** *(unknown, unspecified)* algún, alguna: **some day** *un día de éstos.* **5** *(quite a lot of)* bastante: **she's been gone some time** *hace ya bastante tiempo que se ha ido.* **6** *fam iron (none, not at all)* valiente, menudo,-a: **some help that was!** *¡valiente ayuda!* **7** *fam (quite a, a fine)* menudo,-a: **that was some meal!** *¡menuda comida!*
▷ *pron* **1** *(unspecified number)* unos,-as, algunos,-as: **I'll have to buy some potatoes** *tendré que comprar patatas.* **2** *(unspecified amount) no se traduce*: **if you want more paper, there's some in the drawer** *si te hace falta más papel, hay en el cajón.* **3** *(certain ones)* ciertos,-as, algunos,-as; *(a certain part)* algo, un poco, parte *f*: **some of my friends** *algunos amigos míos.*
▷ *adv* **1** *(approximately, about)* unos,-as, alrededor de, aproximadamente: **there were some twenty people** *había unas veinte personas.* **2** US *fam (rather, a little)* un poco: **they waited some** *esperaron un poco.*
somebody [sʌmbədɪ] *pron* alguien.
somehow ['sʌmhaʊ] *adv* **1** *(in some way)* de algún modo, de alguna manera. **2** *(for some reason)* por alguna razón.
someone ['sʌmwʌn] *pron* → **somebody.**
someplace ['sʌmpleɪs] *adv* → **somewhere.**
somersault ['sʌməsɔ:lt] *n (by acrobat)* salto mortal; *(by child)* voltereta; *(by car)* vuelta de campana.
▷ *vi (acrobat)* dar un salto mortal; *(child)* dar volteretas; *(car)* dar una vuelta de campana.
something ['sʌmθɪŋ] *pron* **1** algo. **2** *(a thing of value)* algo. **3** *(in vague or ill-defined statements)* algo.
▷ *adv*: **it costs something like 100 pounds** *cuesta unas cien libras.*
sometime ['sʌmtaɪm] *adv* algún día.
▷ *adj fml (former)* antiguo,-a, ex-.
sometimes ['sʌmtaɪmz] *adv* de vez en cuando.
somewhat ['sʌmwɒt] *adv* algo, un tanto.
somewhere ['sʌmweəʳ] *adv* **1** *(in some place)* en alguna parte; *(to some place)* a alguna parte. **2** *(approximately)* más o menos, alrededor de.
▷ *pron* un lugar, un sitio. ■ **somewhere else 1** *(in)* en otr parte, en otro sitio. **2** *(to)* a otra parte, a otro sitio.
son [sʌn] *n* hijo.
song [sɒŋ] *n (gen)* canción *f*; *(art, of bird)* canto.
songbird ['sɒŋbɜ:d] *n* pájaro cantor, ave *f* canora.
songbook ['sɒŋbʊk] *n* cancionero.
songwriter ['sɒŋraɪtəʳ] *n* compositor,-ra (de canciones
sonic ['sɒnɪk] *adj* sónico,-a.
son-in-law ['sʌnɪnlɔ:] *n* yerno.
▲ *pl* **sons-in-law.**
soon [su:n] *adv* **1** *(within a short time)* pronto, dentro d poco. **2** *(early)* pronto, temprano. **3** *(expressing prefe ence, readiness, willingness)*: **I'd (just) as soon eat in as.** *preferiría comer en casa que...* ■ **as soon as** tan pront como. ‖ **as soon as possible** cuanto antes. ‖ **soon afte wards** poco después.
sooner ['su:nəʳ] *adv* **1** *(earlier)* más temprano. **2** *(rathe* antes.
▷ *adv* **no sooner** *(immediately after)* nada más, apenas. ■ **n sooner said than done** dicho y hecho. ‖ **sooner or late** tarde o temprano. ‖ **the sooner the better** cuanto an tes mejor.
soot [sʊt] *n* hollín *m*.
soothe [su:ð] *vt* **1** *(calm)* calmar, tranquilizar, aplaca *(quieten)* acallar. **2** *(ease pain)* aliviar, calmar.
sophistication [sɒfɪstɪ'keɪʃᵊn] *n* sofisticación *f*.
sophomore ['sɒfəmɔ:ʳ] *n* US estudiante *mf* de segur do año.
sopping ['sɒpɪŋ] *adj fam* empapado,-a.
sorcerer ['sɔ:sərəʳ] *n* hechicero, brujo.
sorcery ['sɔ:sərɪ] *n* hechicería, brujería.
sordid ['sɔ:dɪd] *adj* **1** *(dishonourable)* sórdido,-a, ver gonzoso,-a. **2** *(squalid)* sórdido,-a, miserable.
sore [sɔ:ʳ] *adj* **1** *(aching)* dolorido,-a; *(painful)* doloro so,-a; *(inflamed)* inflamado,-a. **2** US *fam (angry)* enfa dado,-a (**about**, por), picado,-a (**about**, por). **3** *lit (grea* enorme, gran; *(serious)* grave; *(urgent)* urgente.
▷ *n* MED llaga, úlcera.
sorely ['sɔ:lɪ] *adv (very much, greatly)* muy; *(deeply* profundamente; *(seriously)* gravemente; *(urgently)* ur gentemente.
sorrel¹ ['sɒrᵊl] *n* ZOOL alazán *m*.
sorrel² ['sɒrᵊl] *n* BOT acedera.
sorrow ['sɒrəʊ] *n* **1** *(grief)* pena, pesar *m*, dolor *m*. **2** *(cau se of sadness)* disgusto.
▷ *vi* llorar (**at/over/for**, por).
sorrowful ['sɒrəʊfʊl] *adj* afligido,-a, apenado,-a, triste
sorry ['sɒrɪ] *adj (pitiful, wretched)* triste, lamentable.
▲ *comp* **sorrier**, *superl* **sorriest.**
▷ *interj* **1** *(apology)* ¡perdón!, ¡disculpe! **2** GB *(for repet tion)* ¿perdón?, ¿cómo? ■ **to be sorry** *(grieved, feelin sadness)* sentir. ‖ **to feel sorry for** SB compadecer. ‖ **t say sorry** disculparse, pedir perdón.
sort [sɔ:t] *n* **1** *(type, kind)* clase *f*, tipo, género, suerte *(make, brand)* marca. **2** *fam (person)* tipo,-a, tío,-a. ■ **sort of** una especie de. ‖ **of a sort / of sorts** una especi de. ‖ **sort of** en cierto modo.
▷ *vt* **1** *(classify)* clasificar. **2** *(repair)* arreglar.
▷ *vi (check)* revisar (**through**, -). ■ **a sort of** una especie de ‖ **of a sort / of sorts** una especie de. ‖ **nothing of the so** nada semejante. ‖ **sort of** en cierto modo.

▷ **to sort out** *vt sep* 1 *(classify)* clasificar; *(put in order)* ordenar, poner en orden. 2 *(separate)* separar (**from**, de). 3 *(solve - problem)* arreglar, solucionar; *(- misunderstanding)* aclarar. 4 *(arrange)* organizar, arreglar; *(set - date)* fijar. 5 *(deal with - person)* meter en vereda.
ortie ['sɔ:tɪ] *n* MIL salida.
orting ['sɔ:tɪŋ] *n* clasificación *f*.
ort-out ['sɔ:taʊt] *phr* **to have a sort-out** ordenar.
o-so ['səʊsəʊ] *adv fam* así así, regular.
ought [sɔ:t] *pt & pp* → **seek**.
ought-after ['sɔ:tɑ:ftəʳ] *adj (person)* solicitado,-a; *(object)* codiciado,-a.
oul [səʊl] *n* 1 REL alma, espíritu *m*. 2 *(spirit)* espíritu *m*; *(feeling, character)* carácter *m*, personalidad *f*. 3 *(person)* alma, persona. 4 MUS soul *m*, música soul.
oulful ['səʊlfʊl] *adj* conmovedor,-ra.
oul-searching ['səʊlsɜ:tʃɪŋ] *n* introspección *f*, examen *m* de conciencia.
ound[1] [saʊnd] *adj* 1 *(healthy)* sano,-a. 2 *(solid)* sólido,-a, firme; *(in good condition)* en buen estado. 3 *(sensible)* sensato,-a, acertado,-a; *(valid)* sólido,-a, lógico,-a, razonable; *(responsible)* responsable, formal, de fiar; *(reliable, safe)* seguro,-a. 4 *(thorough)* completo,-a; *(severe)* severo,-a. 5 *(of sleep)* profundo,-a.
ound[2] [saʊnd] *vt* 1 MAR sondar. 2 MED *(gen)* sondar; *(chest)* auscultar.
▷ *n* MED sonda.
▷ **to sound out** *vt sep (discover opinions)* sondear, tantear.
ound[3] [saʊnd] *n* GEOG estrecho, brazo de mar.
ound[4] [saʊnd] *n* 1 *(gen)* sonido; *(musical)* sonido *m*; *(noise)* ruido. 2 TV *(volume)* volumen *m*. 3 *(impression)* idea.
▷ *vt* 1 *(bell, horn, trumpet)* tocar, hacer sonar; *(alarm)* dar (la señal de); *(retreat)* tocar. 2 LING pronunciar.
▷ *vi* 1 *(bell, horn, alarm, etc)* sonar, resonar. 2 *(seem)* parecer; *(give impression)* sonar. 3 LING pronunciarse, sonar.
▷ **to sound off** *vi (express opinions)* hablar a gritos; *(complain)* quejarse (**about**, de), protestar (**about**, por).
ounding[1] ['saʊndɪŋ] *n* MAR sondeo.
▷ *n pl* **soundings** MAR *(measurements)* sondeos *mpl*. *(testing opinions)* sondeos *mpl*.
ounding[2] ['saʊndɪŋ] *adj (resonant)* resonante.
oundly ['saʊndlɪ] *adv* 1 *(sleep)* profundamente. 2 *(thoroughly)* completamente. 3 *(solidly)* sólidamente.
oundness ['saʊndnəs] *n* 1 *(physical solidity)* solidez *f*; *(good condition)* buen estado. 2 *(validity)* solidez *f*; *(sensibleness)* sensatez *f*.
oundproof ['saʊndpru:f] *adj* insonorizado,-a, a prueba de sonidos.
▷ *vt* insonorizar.
oundtrack ['saʊndtræk] *n* banda sonora.
oup [su:p] *n* CULIN *(gen)* sopa; *(clear)* caldo, consomé *m*.
▷ **to soup up** *vt sep* 1 *(car, motorbike, engine)* trucar. 2 *fam (film, play, book)* modernizar, popularizar.
our ['saʊəʳ] *adj* 1 *(fruit)* ácido,-a, agrio,-a; *(milk)* cortado,-a, agrio,-a; *(wine)* agrio,-a. 2 *(person)* amargado,-a, avinagrado,-a; *(behaviour, expression)* agrio,-a.
▷ *vt* 1 *(milk)* agriar, cortar. 2 *(person, relationship)* amargar.
▷ *vi* 1 *(milk)* agriarse, cortarse; *(wine)* agriarse. 2 *(person, character)* amargarse, avinagrarse.
ource [sɔ:s] *n* 1 *(of river)* fuente *f*, nacimiento. 2 *(origin, cause)* fuente *f*, origen *m*. 3 *(person, thing supplying information)* fuente *f*. 4 MED *(of infection)* foco.

south [saʊθ] *n* sur *m*.
▷ *adj* sur, del sur, meridional.
▷ *adv (direction)* hacia el sur; *(location)* al sur.
▷ *n* **the South** el Sur *m*, el sur *m*. ● **South American** sudamericano,-a. ‖ **the South Pacific** el Pacífico Sur. ‖ **the South Pole** el Polo Sur. ‖ **the South Seas** los mares del Sur. ‖ **South Wales** Gales del Sur.
southeast [saʊθ'i:st] *n* sudeste *m*.
▷ *adj* sudeste, del sudeste.
▷ *adv (direction)* hacia el sudeste; *(location)* al sudeste.
southeasterly [saʊθ'i:stəlɪ] *adj* del sudeste.
southeastern [saʊθ'ɜ:stᵊn] *adj* sudeste, del sudeste.
southerly ['sʌðəlɪ] *adj (direction)* hacia el sur; *(location)* al sur; *(wind)* del sur.
southern ['sʌðᵊn] *adj* del sur, meridional, austral. ● **Southern Europe** Europa del Sur.
southerner ['sʌðᵊnəʳ] *n* sureño,-a, meridional *mf*.
southward ['saʊθwəd] *adj* en dirección sur.
▷ *adv* al sur, hacia el sur.
southwards ['saʊθwədz] *adv (direction)* hacia el sur; *(location)* al sur.
southwest [saʊθ'west] *n* suroeste *m*.
▷ *adj* suroeste, del suroeste.
▷ *adv* al suroeste, hacia el suroeste.
southwesterly [saʊθ'westəlɪ] *adj* del sudoeste.
southwestern [saʊθ'westᵊn] *adj* del sudoeste.
souvenir [su:v'nɪəʳ] *n* recuerdo (**of**, de).
sovereign ['sɒvrɪn] *n* 1 soberano,-a. 2 GB *(coin)* soberano.
▷ *adj* soberano,-a.
sow[1] [saʊ] *n* ZOOL cerda, puerca.
sow[2] [səʊ] *vt (gen)* sembrar (**with**, de).
▲ *pt* **sowed**, *pp* **sowed** o **sown** [səʊn].
sower ['səʊəʳ] *n (person)* sembrador,-ra; *(machine)* sembradora.
soy [sɔɪ] *n* US soja. ● **soy sauce** salsa de soja.
soya ['sɔɪə] *n* GB soja. ● **soya bean** soja.
spa [spɑ:] *n* 1 *(resort)* balneario; *(baths)* baños *mpl*, termas *fpl*. 2 US *(jacuzzi)* jacuzzi *m*. 3 US *(gymnasium)* gimnasio.
space [speɪs] *n* 1 PHYS espacio. 2 *(continuous expanse)* espacio. 3 *(room, unoccupied area)* espacio, sitio, lugar *m*. 4 *(gap, empty place)* espacio, hueco. 5 *(in time)* espacio, lapso. ● **space probe** sonda espacial. ‖ **space shuttle** transbordador *m* espacial.
▷ *vt* espaciar (**out**, -).
space-age ['speɪseɪdʒ] *adj* de la era espacial.
space-bar ['speɪsbɑ:ʳ] *n* espaciador *m*.
spacecraft ['speɪskrɑ:ft] *n* nave *f* espacial.
▲ *pl* **spacecraft**.
spaceman ['speɪsmən] *n* astronáuta *m*.
spaceship ['speɪsʃɪp] *n* nave *f* espacial.
spacesuit ['speɪssu:t] *n* traje *m* espacial.
spacewoman ['speɪswʊmən] *n* astronauta.
▲ *pl* **spacewomen** ['speɪswɪmɪn].
spacing ['speɪsɪŋ] *n* espacio. ● **in double space** a doble espacio.
spacious ['speɪʃəs] *adj* espacioso,-a, amplio,-a.
spade[1] [speɪd] *n (playing card - international pack)* pica; *(- Spanish pack)* espada.
spade[2] [speɪd] *n (for digging)* pala.
spaghetti [spə'getɪ] *n* espagueti *m*.
Spain [speɪn] *n* España.

span[1] [spæn] *pp* ⟶ **spin.**
span[2] [spæn] *n (of horses)* tronco; *(of oxen)* yunta.
span[3] [spæn] *n* **1** *(of wings)* envergadura; *(of arch, bridge)* luz *f*, ojo; *(of hand)* palmo. **2** *(of time)* espacio, período, lapso.
▷ *vt* **1** *(cross)* atravesar, cruzar. **2** *(extend over)* abarcar, extenderse a.
▲ *pt & pp* **spanned**, *ger* **spanning.**
Spaniard ['spænjəd] *n (person)* español,-la.
spaniel ['spænjəl] *n* perro de aguas, perro de lanas, spaniel *m*.
Spanish ['spænɪʃ] *adj* español,-la.
▷ *n* **1** *(person)* español,-la. **2** *(language)* español *m*, castellano.
▷ *n pl* **the Spanish** los españoles *mpl*. ● **Spanish America** Hispanoamérica. ▮ **Spanish fly** cantárida. ▮ **Spanish guitar** guitarra clásica.
spank [spæŋk] *vt* zurrar, pegar, dar azotes a.
spanner ['spænəʳ] *n* llave *f* de tuerca.
spar[1] [spɑːʳ] *vi* **1** *(boxing)* entrenarse. **2** *(argue)* discutir.
▲ *pt & pp* **sparred**, *ger* **sparring.**
spar[2] [spɑːʳ] *n (mineral)* espato.
spar[3] [spɑːʳ] *n* MAR palo, verga.
spare [speəʳ] *adj* **1** *(reserve)* de repuesto; *(free)* libre. **2** *(thin, lean)* enjuto,-a. ● **spare time** tiempo libre. ▮ **spare tyre 1** *(wheel)* rueda de recambio. **2** *(stomach)* michelín *m*. ▮ **spare wheel** rueda de recambio.
▷ *n (spare part)* recambio, repuesto.
▷ *vt* **1** *(do without)* prescindir de, pasar sin. **2** *(begrudge)* escatimar. **3** *(save, relieve)* ahorrar, evitar. **4** *lit (not harm, not kill, show mercy)* perdonar.
sparing ['speərɪŋ] *adj (frugal)* frugal; *(economical)* económico,-a.
spark [spɑːk] *n* **1** *(from fire, electrical)* chispa. **2** *(trace)* chispa, pizca. **3** *(cause, trigger)* chispazo.
▷ *vi* echar chispas, chispear.
⊙ **to spark off** *vt insep (conflict, riot, etc)* hacer estallar, provocar, desencadenar, desatar; *(interest)* despertar, suscitar.
sparking plug ['spɑːkɪŋplʌg] *n* AUTO bujía.
sparkle ['spɑːkᵊl] *n* **1** *(of diamond, glass)* centelleo, destello, brillo; *(of eyes)* brillo. **2** *fig (liveliness)* viveza; *(wit)* brillo.
▷ *vi* **1** *(diamond, glass)* centellear, destellar, brillar; *(eyes)* brillar, chispear; *(firework)* echar chispas, chispear. **2** *fig (person)* brillar, lucirse; *(conversation)* brillar.
sparkler ['spɑːkᵊləʳ] *n* **1** *(firework)* bengala. **2** *fam (gem)* brillante *m*.
sparkling ['spɑːkᵊlɪŋ] *adj* **1** *(diamond, glass)* centelleante, brillante; *(eyes)* brillante, chispeante: **2** *fig (person, conversation, performance)* brillante, chispeante. ● **sparkling wine** vino espumoso.
sparrow ['spærəʊ] *n* gorrión *m*.
sparse [spɑːs] *adj (vegetation)* escaso,-a, poco denso,-a; *(population)* disperso,-a, esparcido,-a; *(hair)* ralo,-a; *(information)* escaso,-a.
spasm ['spæzᵊm] *n* **1** MED espasmo. **2** *(of coughing, laughing, etc)* ataque *m*, acceso; *(of anger)* arrebato, acceso. ■ **in spasms** a rachas.
spastic ['spæstɪk] *n* **1** MED espástico,-a. **2** *pej (clumsy, incompetent person)* inútil *mf*, patoso,-a, torpe.
▷ *adj* **1** MED espástico,-a. **2** *pej (clumsy, incompetent)* inútil, patoso,-a, torpe.

spat[1] [spæt] *n (gaiter)* polaina.
spat[2] [spæt] *n fam (quarrel)* rencilla.
spat[3] [spæt] *pt & pp* ⟶ **spit.**
spate [speɪt] *n* **1** *(of letters, orders)* avalancha; *(of accident bad luck)* racha; *(of activities, protests)* serie *f*; *(of word* torrente *m*. **2** GB *(of river)* avenida, crecida. ■ **to be i (full) spate 1** *(river)* estar crecido,-a. **2** *(talker)* estar e pleno discurso.
spatter ['spætəʳ] *vt (splash)* salpicar (**with**, de); *(sprinkle* rociar (**with**, de).
▷ *vi* salpicar.
▷ *n (spattered spot)* salpicadura, manchita; *(small amoun* pizca.
spawn [spɔːn] *n* **1** ZOOL huevas *fpl*, freza. **2** BOT micelio
▷ *vt fig* generar, producir, engendrar.
▷ *vi* ZOOL frezar, desovar.
spay [speɪ] *vt* esterilizar.
speak [spiːk] *vi* **1** *(gen)* hablar. **2** *(make speech)* pronunciar un discurso. **3** *(on phone)* hablar.
▷ *vt* **1** *(utter, say)* decir. **2** *(language)* hablar. ■ **personally speaking** personalmente. ▮ **speaking of...** a propósito de...
⊙ **to speak for** *vt insep (state views, wishes of)* hablar e nombre de.
⊙ **to speak out** *vi (speak openly)* hablar claro.
⊙ **to speak up** *vi* **1** *(speak more loudly)* hablar más fuerte. **2** *(give opinion)* defender.
▲ *pt* **spoke** [spəʊk], *pp* **spoken** ['spəʊkᵊn].
speaker ['spiːkəʳ] *n* **1** *(gen)* persona que habla, el qu habla, la que habla; *(in dialogue)* interlocutor,-ra; *(i public)* orador,-ra; *(lecturer)* conferenciante *mf*. **2** *(language)* hablante *mf*. **3** *(loudspeaker)* altavoz *m*.
▷ *n* **the Speaker 1** GB el/la presidente,-a de la Cáma de los Comunes. **2** US el/la presidente,-a de la Cá mara de los Representantes.
spear [spɪəʳ] *n* **1** *(gen)* lanza; *(javelin)* jabalina; *(harpoo* arpón *m*. **2** BOT punta.
▷ *vt (with fork)* pinchar; *(with harpoon)* arponear; *(impa with spear)* atravesar con una lanza.
spearhead ['spɪəhed] *n (person, group)* punta de lan za, vanguardia.
▷ *vt* encabezar.
special ['speʃᵊl] *adj* **1** *(not usual)* especial; *(exceptiona* extraordinario,-a. **2** *(specific)* específico,-a.
▷ *n* **1** *(train)* tren *m* especial. **2** *(TV programme)* program *m* especial. **3** US *(special offer)* oferta especial.
speciality [speʃɪ'ælɪtɪ] *n* especialidad *f*.
▲ *pl* **specialities.**
specialize ['speʃəlaɪz] *vi* especiliazarse.
specialty [speʃɪ'ælɪtɪ] *n* US ⟶ **speciality.**
species ['spiːʃiːz] *n* especie *f*.
▲ *pl* **species.**
specific [sp'sɪfɪk] *adj* **1** *(particular, not general)* específ co,-a; *(definite)* concreto,-a. **2** *(exact, detailed, precis* preciso,-a; *(clear in meaning)* explícito,-a.
▷ *n* MED *(drug)* específico.
▷ *n pl* **specifics** *(particulars, details)* datos *mpl* (concr tos). ● **specific gravity** peso específico.
specify ['spesɪfaɪ] *vt* especificar, precisar, concretar.
▲ *pt & pp* **specified**, *ger* **specifying.**
specimen ['spesɪmən] *n* **1** *(sample)* espécimen *m*. *(example)* ejemplar *m*. **3** *fam pej (person)* tipo,-a.

peck [spek] *n* **1** *(of dust, soot)* mota; *(stain)* manchita; *(dot)* punto negro. **2** *(trace)* pizca.

pectacle ['spektək^əl] *n (show, display)* espectáculo.
n pl **spectacles** gafas *fpl*.

pectate [spek'teɪt] *vi* mirar.

pectator [spek'teɪtə^r] *n* espectador,-ra.
n pl **the spectators** el público *m sing*.

pecter ['spektə^r] *n* US ⟶ **spectre.**

pectre ['spektə^r] *n* espectro, fantasma *m*.

pectrum ['spektrəm] *n* **1** PHYS espectro. **2** *(range)* gama.
▲ *pl* **spectra.**

peculate ['spekjəleɪt] *vi* **1** *(conjecture)* especular, hacer conjeturas (**on/about**, sobre). **2** FIN especular (**in**, en/con).

peculation [spekj'leɪʃ^ən] *n* **1** *(conjecture)* especulación *f*, conjetura, suposición *f*. **2** FIN especulación *f*.

ped [sped] *pt & pp* ⟶ **speed.**

peech [spi:tʃ] *n* **1** *(faculty, act)* habla. **2** *(spoken language, way of speaking)* habla, manera de hablar. **3** *(formal talk)* discurso, alocución *f*; *(informal talk)* charla; *(lectura)* conferencia; *(lines in play)* diálogo. ● **direct speech** estilo directo. ‖ **indirect speech** estilo indirecto. ‖ **part of speech** parte de la oración.

peed [spi:d] *n* **1** *(rate of movement)* velocidad *f*; *(quickness)* rapidez *f*; *(haste)* prisa. **2** *(sensitivity of film)* sensibilidad *f*, velocidad *f*; *(time of shutter)* tiempo de exposición, abertura. **3** *(gear)* marcha, velocidad *f*. **4** *sl (drug)* speed *m*, anfetas *fpl*.
vi **1** *(go fast)* ir corriendo, ir a toda prisa, ir a toda velocidad. **2** *(break limit)* ir a exceso de velocidad.
vt **1** *(hurry - process, matter)* acelerar. **2** *(take quickly)* hacer llegar rápidamente.
to speed up *vt sep (process, matter, production)* acelerar; *(person)* apresurar, meter prisa a.
vi (vehicle) acelerar; *(person, process, production)* acelerarse, apresurarse, darse prisa.
▲ *pt & pp* **speeded** o **sped** [sped].

peedboat ['spi:dbəʊt] *n* lancha rápida.

peeding ['spi:dɪŋ] *n* AUTO exceso de velocidad.

peedway ['spi:dweɪ] *n* **1** *(racing)* carreras *fpl* de moto. **2** *(track)* pista de carreras, circuito.

peedy ['spi:dɪ] *adj (quick)* rápido,-a, veloz; *(prompt)* pronto,-a, rápido,-a.
▲ *comp* **speedier**, *superl* **speediest.**

peleology [spi:lɪ'ɒlədʒɪ] *n* espeleología.

pell¹ [spel] *n (magical)* hechizo, encanto.

pell² [spel] *n* **1** *(period of time)* temporada, período; *(short period)* rato. **2** METEOR período, ola, racha. **3** MED *(dizziness)* mareo; *(of coughing)* acceso. **4** *(turn)* turno.
vt US *(take* SB*'s turn)* relevar.

pell³ [spel] *vt* **1** *(orally)* deletrear; *(written)* escribir correctamente. **2** *fig (mean)* significar, representar; *(bring)* traer, acarrear; *(foretell)* anunciar, presagiar.
vi saber escribir correctamente.
▲ *pt & pp* **spelled** o **spelt** [spelt].
to spell out *vt sep* **1** *(word)* deletrear. **2** *(explain in detail)* explicar con detalle, detallar, pormenorizar.

pellbound ['spelbaʊnd] *adj* embelesado,-a.

pelling ['spelɪŋ] *n* ortografía. ● **spelling mistake** falta de ortografía.

pelt [spelt] *pt & pp* ⟶ **spell.**

pend [spend] *vt* **1** *(money)* gastar (**on**, en). **2** *(pass time)* pasar. **3** *(devote time/energy)* dedicar (**on**, a), invertir (**on**, en). **4** *(use up, exhaust)* gastar, agotar.
▷ *vi (money)* gastar.
▲ *pt & pp* **spent** [spent].

spent [spent] *pt & pp* ⟶ **spend.**
▷ *adj* **1** *(used)* usado,-a, gastado,-a. **2** *(exhausted)* agotado,-a; *(finished)* acabado,-a.

sperm [spɜ:m] *n* esperma *mf*. ● **sperm whale** cachalote *m*.

spew [spju:] *vt (flames, lava, smoke, etc)* arrojar, vomitar. [Also **spew up**.] GB *fam* vomitar, devolver.
▷ *vi* salir a borbotones.
▷ *vi* [Also **spew up**.] GB *fam* vomitar, devolver, arrojar.

sphere [sfɪə^r] *n* **1** *(shape)* esfera. **2** *(area, range, extent)* esfera, ámbito.

sphincter ['sfɪŋktə^r] *n* esfínter *m*.

sphinx [sfɪŋks] *n* esfinge *f*.

spice [spaɪs] *n* **1** especia. **2** *fig* sazón *m*, sal *f*, salsa, sabor *m*.
▷ *vt* **1** CULIN sazonar, condimentar. **2** *(story, etc)* echar salsa a (**up**, -).

spicy ['spaɪsɪ] *adj* **1** CULIN *(seasoned)* sazonado,-a, condimentado,-a; *(hot)* picante. **2** *fig (story, etc)* picante.
▲ *comp* **spicier**, *superl* **spiciest.**

spider ['spaɪdə^r] *n* araña. ● **spider plant** BOT cinta. ‖ **spider's web** telaraña.

spike¹ [spaɪk] *n* **1** *(sharp point)* punta, pincho; *(sharp-pointed object)* objeto puntiagudo. **2** *(on running shoe)* clavo.
▷ *vt* **1** *(with shoes)* clavar. **2** *(drink)* echar alcohol a.
▷ *n pl* **spikes** *(running shoes)* zapatillas *fpl* de clavos.

spike² [spaɪk] *n* BOT espiga.

spill¹ [spɪl] *n (for lighting fires, lamps, pipes - of wood)* astilla; *(of paper)* trozo de papel enrollado.

spill² [spɪl] *n* **1** *(act, amount of spilling)* derrame *m*, derramamiento. **2** *fam (fall)* caída.
▷ *vt (liquid)* derramar, verter; *(knock over)* volcar.
▷ *vi* **1** *(liquid)* derramarse, verterse. **2** *(people)* salir en tropel.
▲ *pt & pp* **spilled** o **spilt** [spɪlt].
⊙ **to spill over** *vi (liquid)* salirse, desbordarse; *(people)* rebosar; *(conflict)* extenderse.

spin [spɪn] *n* **1** *(turn)* vuelta, giro, revolución *f*. **2** *(of washing machine)* centrifugado. **3** SP *(of ball)* efecto. **4** *(of plane)* barrena; *(of car)* patinazo. **5** *(ride, trip)* vuelta, paseo (en coche o en moto). **6** *fam (panic)* pánico, miedo.
▷ *vt* **1** *(make turn)* hacer girar, dar vueltas a. **2** *(washing)* centrifugar. **3** *(ball)* darle efecto a. **4** *(cotton, wool, etc)* hilar; *(spider's web)* tejer.
▷ *vi* **1** *(turn)* girar, dar vueltas. **2** *(washing machine)* centrifugar. **3** *(cotton, wool, etc)* hilar. **4** *(plane)* caer en barrena; *(car)* patinar. **5** *(move rapidly)* girar(se), darse la vuelta.
▲ *pt* **spun** [spʌn] o **span** [spæn], *pp* **spun** [spʌn], *ger* **spinning.**
⊙ **to spin out** *vt sep (holiday, speech)* prolongar, alargar; *(time, money)* estirar.

spinach ['spɪnɪdʒ] *n* **1** BOT espinaca. **2** CULIN espinacas *fpl*.

spinal ['spaɪn^əl] *adj* espinal, vertebral. ● **spinal column** columna vertebral. ‖ **spinal cord** médula espinal.

spindle ['spɪnd^əl] *n* **1** *(rod for spinning)* huso. **2** TECH *(part of machine)* eje *m*; *(of lathe)* mandril *m*.

spindly ['spɪnd^əlɪ] *adj (leg)* largo y delgado,-a, *(person)* larguirucho,-a, zanquilargo,-a; *(plant)* alto,-a.
▲ *comp* **spindlier**, *superl* **spindliest.**

spin-dryer [spɪn'draɪəʳ] *n* secador *m* centrífugo, centrifugadora.
spine [spaɪn] *n* **1** ANAT columna vertebral, espina dorsal, espinazo. **2** *(of book)* lomo. **3** ZOOL *(of hedgehog, etc)* púa. **4** BOT espina.
spineless ['spaɪnləs] *adj* **1** *(invertebrate)* invertebrado,-a. **2** *fig (weak)* débil, sin carácter.
spinner ['spɪnəʳ] *n* **1** *(thread)* hilandero,-a. **2** *(spin-dryer)* secador centrífugo, centrifugadora. **3** *(bowler)* lanzador,-ra rápido,-a. **4** *(bait for fish)* cuchara.
spinning ['spɪnɪŋ] *n (action)* hilado; *(art)* hilandería.
● **spinning top** peonza, trompo. ▮ **spinning wheel** rueca, torno de hilar.
spinster ['spɪnstəʳ] *n* solterona.
spiny ['spaɪnɪ] *adj* espinoso,-a.
▲ *comp* **spinier**, *superl* **spiniest.**
spiral ['spaɪᵊrᵊl] *n* espiral *f*.
▷ *adj* espiral, en espiral.
▷ *vi* **1** *(move in a spiral)* moverse en espiral. **2** *(increase rapidly)* dispararse.
spire ['spaɪəʳ] *n* aguja.
spirit[1] ['spɪrɪt] *n* CHEM alcohol *m*.
▷ *n pl* **spirits** *(alcoholic drink)* bebidas *fpl* alcohólicas, licores *mpl*.
spirit[2] ['spɪrɪt] *n* **1** *(soul)* espíritu *m*, alma; *(ghost)* fantasma *m*. **2** *(person)* ser *m*, alma. **3** *(force, vigour)* vigor *m*, energía; *(personality)* carácter *m*; *(courage)* valor *m*; *(vitality, liveliness)* ánimo, vitalidad *f*. **4** *(mood, attitude)* espíritu *m*, humor *m*. **5** *(central quality, real or intended meaning)* espíritu *m*, sentido. **6** *(mood, feelings)* moral *f sing*, humor *m sing*.
⊙ **to spirit away / spirit off** *vt sep* llevarse como por arte de magia.
spirited ['spɪrɪtɪd] *adj* **1** *(attack, reply)* enérgico,-a, vigoroso,-a; *(attempt)* valiente. **2** *(person)* animado,-a; *(horse)* fogoso,-a.
spiritual ['spɪrɪtjʊəl] *adj* espiritual.
▷ *n (song)* espiritual *m* negro.
spiritualism ['spɪrɪtjʊəlɪzᵊm] *n* espiritismo.
spit[1] [spɪt] *n* **1** CULIN asador *m*, espetón *m*. **2** GEOG *(of sand)* banco; *(of land)* punta, lengua.
spit[2] [spɪt] *n (saliva)* saliva, esputo.
▷ *vt (gen)* escupir.
▷ *vi* **1** *(gen)* escupir (**at**, a), (**on**, en). **2** *(rain)* chispear. **3** *(sputter)* chisporrotear.
▲ *pt & pp* **spat** [spæt].
⊙ **to spit out** *vt sep* **1** *(gen)* escupir. **2** *fig (say sharply)* soltar.
spite [spaɪt] *n (ill will)* rencor *m*, ojeriza.
▷ *vt* fastidiar. ■ **in spite of** a pesar de, pese a.
spiteful ['spaɪtfʊl] *adj (person)* rencoroso,-a, malévolo,-a; *(comment)* malicioso,-a; *(tongue)* viperino,-a.
spittle ['spɪtᵊl] *n* saliva, baba.
splash [splæʃ] *n* **1** *(noise)* chapoteo, chapaleo. **2** *(spray)* salpicadura, rociada. **3** *(small amount)* gota, chorrito, poco. **4** *fig (of light, colour, etc)* mancha.
▷ *vt* **1** *(gen)* salpicar (**with**, de), rociar (**with**, de). **2** *fam (of news, story, etc)* sacar, salir.
▷ *vi* **1** *(of liquid)* salpicar, esparcirse. **2** *(move noisily)* chapotear (**about/around**, -).
▷ *interj* ¡plaf!
⊙ **to splash down** *vi* amarar, amerizar.
⊙ **to splash out** *vi fam* darse un lujo, gastarse un dineral.
▷ *vt sep fam (money)* derrochar, gastarse.
▲ *pt & pp* **splatted**, *ger* **splatting.**
splashdown ['splæʃdaʊn] *n* amerizaje *m*, amaraje *m*.
splatter ['splætəʳ] *vt* salpicar.
▷ *vi* salpicar.
splay [spleɪ] *vt* **1** *(fingers)* abrir, separar; *(pipe)* extender, ensanchar. **2** ARCH *(window, door)* construir u derrame en.
▷ *vi (fingers)* separarse (**out**, -); *(pipe)* extenderse, ensancharse.
▷ *adj (of feet)* plano,-a.
spleen [spli:n] *n* **1** ANAT bazo. **2** *lit (anger)* cólera, ira.
splendid ['splendɪd] *adj* **1** *(excellent)* estupendo,-a, maravilloso,-a. **2** *(magnificent)* espléndido,-a, magnífico,-a.
splice [splaɪs] *vt* **1** *(rope)* empalmar. **2** CINEM montar.
splint [splɪnt] *n* tablilla.
splinter ['splɪntəʳ] *n (of wood)* astilla; *(of metal, bone, stone)* esquirla; *(of glass)* fragmento. ● **splinter group** grupo disidente, facción *f*.
▷ *vt* astillar, hacer astillas.
▷ *vi* **1** astillarse, hacerse astillas. **2** POL escindirse (**off**, -).
split [splɪt] *n* **1** *(crack, cut, break)* grieta, hendidura, raja. **2** *(tear - in garment)* desgarrón *m*, rasgón *m*; *(- at seam)* descosido. **3** *(division - gen)* división *f*, ruptura, cisma *m*; *(- in politics)* escisión *f*, cisma *m*, ruptura. *(division, sharing out)* reparto.
▷ *adj* **1** *(cracked)* partido,-a, hendido,-a, rajado,-a; *(torn)* desgarrado,-a, rasgado,-a. **2** *(divided - gen)* dividido,-a; *(- in politics)* dividido,-a, escindido,-a.
▷ *vt* **1** *(crack, break)* agrietar, hender; *(cut)* partir. **2** *(tear garment)* rajar, desgarrar; *(- seam)* descoser. **3** PHYS *(atom)* desintegrar. **4** *(divide, separate)* dividir (**up**, -); *(political party, etc)* dividir, escindir. **5** *(share)* repartir, dividir.
▷ *vi* **1** *(crack)* agrietarse, henderse, rajarse; *(in two parts)* partirse. **2** *(tear - garment)* rajarse, desgarrarse; *(- seam)* descoserse. **3** *(divide - gen)* dividirse (**up**, -); *(- in politics)* dividirse, escindirse. **4** *fam (tell tales)* acusar, soplar, chivarse (**on**, de). **5** *sl (leave)* largarse, abrirse, pirárselas. ● **split infinitive** LING *infinitivo con un adverbio intercalado entre el «to» y el verbo.*
⊙ **to split away / split off** *vt sep (branch, rock, etc)* romper, desprender.
▷ *vi* **1** *(branch, rock, etc)* romperse, desprenderse. **2** *(group)* escindirse, separarse (**from**, de).
⊙ **to split up** *vt sep (friends, lovers)* separar.
▷ *vi (crowd, meeting)* dispersarse; *(couple)* separarse, romper.
▲ *pt & pp* **split**, *ger* **splitting.**
split-level ['splɪt'levᵊl] *adj (room, flat)* en dos niveles; *(oven)* con el grill en la parte superior.
split-screen ['splɪtskri:n] *adj* con pantalla dividida.
split-second [splɪt'sekᵊnd] *adj (very rapid)* instantáneo,-a; *(accurate)* perfecto,-a.
splitting ['splɪtɪŋ] *adj (headache)* terrible, muy fuerte.
splurge [splɜ:dʒ] *vt fam* despilfarrar (**on**, en), derrochar (**on**, en), gastarse (**on**, en).
▷ *vi* gastarse un dineral (**on**, en).
▷ *n* derroche *m*.

splutter ['splʌtər] *n (of flame)* chisporroteo; *(of engine)* ruido, resoplido; *(of person)* barboteo, farfulleo.
▷ *vt (person)* mascullar, farfullar.
▷ *vi* **1** *(person)* farfullar, barbotar. **2** *(fire, candle, fat, etc)* chisporrotear, crepitar. **3** *(engine)* resoplar, renquear.

spoil [spɔɪl] *vt* **1** *(ruin)* estropear, echar a perder, arruinar. **2** *(invalidate)* anular. **3** *(make child selfish)* mimar, consentir; *(indulge)* complacer.
▷ *vi (food)* estropearse, echarse a perder.
▲ *pt & pp* **spoiled** o **spoilt** [spɔɪlt].
▷ *n pl* **spoils** botín *m sing.*

spoilt [spɔɪlt] *pp* ⟶ **spoil.**
▷ *adj* **1** *(food, etc)* estropeado,-a. **2** *(child)* mimado,-a, consentido,-a. **3** *(ballot paper)* nulo,-a.

spoke[1] [spəʊk] *n (of wheel)* radio, rayo.

spoke[2] [spəʊk] *pt* ⟶ **speak.**

spoken ['spəʊkən] *pp* ⟶ **speak.**
▷ *adj* hablado,-a, oral.

spokesperson ['spəʊkspɜːsən] *n* portavoz *mf*, AM personero,-a.

sponge [spʌndʒ] *n* **1** *(gen)* esponja. **2** GB *(cake)* bizcocho.
▷ *vt* **1** *(clean)* limpiar con esponja. **2** *fam (scrounge)* gorronear, gorrear, sablear.
▷ *vi fam (scrounge)* vivir de gorra, gorrear, dar sablazos.
⊙ **to sponge off / sponge on** *vt insep fam (scrounge)* vivir a costa de.

sponsor ['spɒnsər] *n* **1** *(gen)* patrocinador,-ra, sponsor *mf*; *(for arts)* mecenas *mf*. **2** FIN avalador,-ra, garante *mf*. **3** REL *(godfather)* padrino; *(godmother)* madrina. **4** *(of law, bill, motion)* proponente *mf*.
▷ *vt* **1** *(gen)* patrocinar; *(studies, research)* subvencionar. **2** *(support)* apoyar, respaldar. **3** FIN avalar, garantizar. **4** REL apadrinar.

spontaneous [spɒn'teɪnɪəs] *adj* espontáneo,-a.

spooky ['spuːkɪ] *adj fam* escalofriante, espeluznante, horripilante.
▲ *comp* **spookier**, *superl* **spookiest.**

spool [spuːl] *n* carrete *m*, bobina.

spoon [spuːn] *n* **1** *(gen)* cuchara; *(small)* cucharilla, cucharita; *(large)* cucharón *m*. **2** *(spoonful - gen)* cucharada; *(- small)* cucharadita.
▷ *vt (lift and move)* sacar con cuchara; *(serve)* servir con cuchara.
▷ *vi* US *fam (kiss)* besuquearse.

spoonful ['spuːnfʊl] *n* cucharada.
▲ *pl* **spoonfuls** o **spoonsful.**

sport [spɔːt] *n* **1** *(gen)* deporte *m*. **2** *(person)* buena persona. **3** *(fun)* diversión *f*. **4** *fam (fellow)* amigo,-a.
▷ *vt (wear proudly)* lucir.
▷ *vi (frolic)* retozar, juguetear.

sports [spɔːts] *n pl* deportes *mpl*.
▷ *n (meeting)* competición *f* deportiva.
▷ *adj* deportivo,-a, de deportes. ● **sports car** (coche *m*) deportivo. ‖ **sports centre/complex** polideportivo. ‖ **sports club** *club deportivo.* ‖ **sports commentator** comentarista deportivo. ‖ **sports day** *día dedicado a competiciones deportivas escolares.* ‖ **sports event** evento deportivo. ‖ **sports ground** campo de deportes. ‖ **sports jacket** chaqueta (de) sport. ‖ **sports programme** programa deportivo. ‖ **sports scholarship** beca deportiva.

sportsman ['spɔːtsmən] *n* deportista *m*.
▲ *pl* **sportsmen** ['spɔːtsmən].

sportsmanship ['spɔːtsmənʃɪp] *n* deportividad *f*, espíritu *m* deportivo.

sportswear ['spɔːtsweər] *n (for sport)* ropa de deporte; *(casual)* ropa (de) sport.

sportswoman ['spɔːtswʊmən] *n* deportista.
▲ *pl* **sportswomen** ['spɔːtswɪmɪn].

sporty ['spɔːtɪ] *adj* aficionado,-a a los deportes.
▲ *comp* **sportier**, *superl* **sportiest.**

spot [spɒt] *n* **1** *(dot)* punto; *(on fabric)* lunar *m*, mota; *(on animal)* mancha. **2** *(mark, stain)* mancha. **3** *(blemish, pimple)* grano. **4** *(place)* sitio, lugar *m*. **5** *(area of body)* punto; *(flaw)* mancha. **6** *(fix, trouble)* lío, aprieto, apuro. **7** *(place in broadcast)* espacio. **8** *fam (small amount)* poquito, poquitín *m*; *(drop)* gota. **9** *(position)* puesto. **10** *fam (spotlight)* foco. **11** US *fam (banknote)* billete *m*. ■ **on the spot 1** *(at once, then and there)* en el acto, allí mismo. **2** *(at the place of the action)* en el lugar del los hechos. **3** *(without moving away)* en el lugar. ‖ **to put** SB **on the spot** poner a ALGN en un aprieto.
▷ *vt* **1** *(notice)* darse cuenta de, notar; *(see)* ver; *(recognize)* reconocer; *(find)* encontrar, descubrir; *(catch out)* pillar. **2** *(mark with spots)* motear; *(stain)* manchar, salpicar.
▷ *vi* GB *(rain)* chispear, lloviznar.
▷ *adj (price, cash)* contante, al contado.
▲ *pt & pp* **spotted**, *ger* **spotting.**

spotlight ['spɒtlaɪt] *n (lamp)* foco, proyector *m*, reflector *m*; *(beam)* luz *f* de foco.
▷ *vt* **1** iluminar, enfocar. **2** *(draw attention to)* poner de relieve, destacar.

spotted ['spɒtɪd] *adj (with dots)* con puntos; *(fabric)* de lunares; *(speckled)* moteado,-a; *(stained)* manchado,-a; *(animal)* con manchas.

spotty ['spɒtɪ] *adj (person, face, complexion)* con granos, lleno,-a de granos.
▲ *comp* **spottier**, *superl* **spottiest.**

spouse [spaʊz] *n* cónyuge *mf*.

spout [spaʊt] *n* **1** *(of jug)* pico; *(of fountain)* surtidor *m*, caño; *(of roof-gutter)* canalón *m*; *(of teapot)* pitorro. **2** *(jet of water)* chorro.
▷ *vt* **1** *(liquid)* echar, arrojar. **2** *fam pej (poetry)* declamar; *(nonsense)* soltar.
▷ *vi* **1** *(liquid)* salir a chorros, chorrear. **2** *(of whale)* expulsar chorros de agua. **3** *fam pej (verse, etc)* declamar.

sprain [spreɪn] *n* MED torcedura.
▷ *vt* torcer.

sprang [spræŋ] *pt* ⟶ **spring.**

sprat [spræt] *n (fish)* espadín *m*.

sprawl [sprɔːl] *vi* **1** *(person)* tumbarse, echarse, repantigarse, repanchigarse. **2** *(city, suburbs, etc)* extenderse.
▷ *n (mass)* extensión *f*.

sprawling ['sprɔːlɪŋ] *adj* **1** *(mass)* extendido,-a; *(city, suburbs)* de crecimiento descontrolado. **2** *(handwriting)* garabateado,-a.

spray[1] [spreɪ] *n (of flowers)* ramita, ramillete *m*.

spray[2] [spreɪ] *n* **1** *(of water)* rociada; *(from sea)* espuma; *(from aerosol)* pulverización *f*. **2** *(aerosol)* spray *m*; *(atomizer)* atomizador *m*, vaporizador *m*; *(for plants)* pulverizador *m*.
▷ *vt (water)* rociar; *(perfume)* atomizar; *(plants)* pulverizar; *(crops)* fumigar, *(paint)* pintar a pistola.
▷ *vi (water)* rociar. ● **spray can** aerosol *m*. ‖ **spray gun** pistola pulverizadora. ‖ **spray paint** pintura spray.

spread [spred] *n* **1** *(gen)* extensión *f*; *(of ideas, news)* difusión *f*, diseminación *f*, divulgación *f*; *(of disease, fire)* propagación *f*; *(of nuclear weapons)* proliferación *f*; *(of terrorism, crime)* aumento. **2** *(scope)* extensión *f*, envergadura; *(range)* gama, abanico. **3** *(of wings, sails)* envergadura. **4** CULIN *(paste)* pasta (para untar). **5** *fam (large meal)* comilona, banquetazo. **6** *(in press)* extensión *f*. **7** US *(ranch)* finca.
▷ *vt* **1** *(lay out)* extender, tender; *(unfold)* desplegar; *(scatter)* esparcir. **2** *(butter, etc)* untar, extender; *(paint, glue, etc)* extender, repartir. **3** *(news, ideas, etc)* difundir, divulgar; *(rumour)* hacer correr; *(disease, fire)* propagar; *(panic, terror)* sembrar. **4** *(wealth, work, cost)* distribuir, repartir.
▷ *vi* **1** *(stretch out)* extenderse; *(open out, unfold)* desplegarse; *(widen)* ensancharse. **2** *(butter, etc)* extenderse. **3** *(news, ideas, etc)* difundirse, diseminarse, divulgarse; *(rumour)* correr; *(disease, fire)* propagarse; *(panic, fear)* cundir. **4** *(in time)* extenderse.
▲ *pt & pp* **spread**.
spread-eagled [spred'i:gᵊld] *adj* despatarrado,-a.
spreadsheet ['spredʃi:t] *n* hoja de cálculo.
spree [spri:] *n* juerga, jarana, parranda.
sprig [sprɪg] *n* ramita, ramito.
sprightly ['spraɪtlɪ] *adj (lively)* animado,-a, vivaz; *(energetic)* enérgico,-a; *(nimble)* ágil.
▲ *comp* **sprightlier**, *superl* **sprightliest**.
spring [sprɪŋ] *n* **1** *(season)* primavera. **2** *(of water)* manantial *m*, fuente *f*. **3** *(of mattress, seat)* muelle *m*; *(of watch, lock, etc)* resorte *m*; *(of car)* ballesta. **4** *(elasticity)* elasticidad *f*; *(active, healthy quality)* energía, brío. **5** *(leap, jump)* salto, brinco.
▷ *vi* **1** *(jump)* saltar. **2** *(appear)* aparecer (de repente).
▷ *vt* **1** *(operate mechanism)* accionar. **2** *fig (news, surprise)* espetar (**on**, a), soltar. **3** *fam (help escape, set free)* soltar.
▲ *pt* **sprang** [spræŋ], *pp* **sprung** [sprʌŋ].
⊙ **to spring from** *vt insep (result from, originate from)* surgir de, provenir de.
⊙ **to spring up** *vi (gen)* aparecer, surgir; *(friendship)* nacer; *(wind)* levantarse; *(plants)* brotar; *(buildings, towns, etc)* elevarse, levantarse.
springboard ['sprɪŋbɔ:d] *n* trampolín *m*.
springy ['sprɪŋɪ] *adj (mattress)* elástico,-a; *(step)* ligero,-a, ágil.
▲ *comp* **springier**, *superl* **springiest**.
sprinkle ['sprɪŋkᵊl] *vt* **1** *(with water)* rociar (**with**, de/con), salpicar (**with**, de/con). **2** *(with flour, sugar, etc)* espolvorear (**with**, de/con). **3** *fig* salpicar (**with**, de/con).
sprinkler ['sprɪŋkᵊləʳ] *n* **1** *(on hose)* aspersor *m*. **2** *(for fires)* extintor *m*. **3** *(for sugar, flour, etc)* espolvoreador *m*.
sprinkling ['sprɪŋkᵊlɪŋ] *n (small amount)* poco.
sprint [sprɪnt] *(dash)* carrera corta.
▷ *vi (dash)* correr a toda velocidad.
sprocket ['sprɒkɪt] *n* TECH diente *m* de engranaje. ● **sprocket wheel** rueda dentada.
sprout [spraʊt] *n* BOT *(shoot)* brote *m*, retoño. ● **(Brussels) sprouts** coles *fpl* de Bruselas.
▷ *vi* **1** *(bud, leaf)* brotar, salir; *(branch)* echar brotes; *(plant)* echar retoños, retoñar. **2** *fig* surgir, aparecer, crecer rápidamente.
▷ *vt (leaves, shoots)* echar; *(beard, etc)* salir.

spruce¹ [spru:s] *adj (neat)* pulcro,-a, acicalado,-a; *(smart)* apuesto,-a.
⊙ **to spruce up** *vt sep* acicalar, arreglar.
spruce² [spru:s] *n* BOT picea.
▲ *pl* **spruces** o **spruce**.
sprung [sprʌŋ] *pp* ⟶ **spring**.
spun [spʌn] *pt & pp* ⟶ **spin**.
spry [spraɪ] *adj (active)* activo,-a; *(lively)* vivaz, lleno,-a de vida; *(energetic)* enérgico,-a, dinámico,-a.
▲ *comp* **sprier**, *superl* **spriest**.
spud [spʌd] *n fam* patata.
spur [spɜ:ʳ] *n* **1** *(horse rider's)* espuela. **2** ZOOL *(of cock)* espolón *m*. **3** *fig (stimulus, incentive)* aguijón *m*, espuela, acicate *m*. **4** GEOG espolón *m*, estribación *f*. **5** *(railway track, road)* ramal *m*.
▷ *vt* **1** *(horse)* espolear, picar con las espuelas. **2** *fig (stimulate)* estimular, incitar, aguijonear, alentar.
▲ *pt & pp* **spurred**, *ger* **spurring**. ■ **on the spur of the moment** sin pensarlo.
spurt [spɜ:t] *n* **1** *(of liquid)* chorro. **2** *fig (of speed, effort, activity, etc)* racha, ataque *m*, esfuerzo.
▷ *vi* **1** *(liquid)* chorrear, salir a chorro. **2** *fig (make an effort)* hacer un último esfuerzo, esforzarse; *(accelerate)* acelerar.
sputter ['spʌtəʳ] *vi* **1** *(fire, fat, candle)* chisporrotear. **2** *(engine)* resoplar, renquear.
spy [spaɪ] *n (gen)* espía *mf*.
▲ *pl* **spies**.
▷ *vi* espiar (**on**, a).
▷ *vt lit* divisar, descubrir, ver.
▲ *pt & pp* **spied**, *ger* **spying**.
⊙ **to spy out** *vt insep (activities)* investigar; *(person)* espiar.
spyglass ['spaɪglɑ:s] *n* catalejo.
spyhole ['spaɪhəʊl] *n* mirilla.
squabble ['skwɒbᵊl] *n* disputa, riña, pelea.
▷ *vi* disputar, reñir, pelearse (**over**, por) (**about**, sobre).
squad [skwɒd] *n* **1** MIL pelotón *m*. **2** *(of police)* brigada. **3** SP *(team)* equipo; *(national)* selección *f*.
squadron ['skwɒdrən] *n (of soldiers)* escuadrón *m*; *(of planes)* escuadrilla; *(of ships)* escuadra.
squalid ['skwɒlɪd] *adj* **1** *(dirty, unpleasant)* sucio,-a, mugriento,-a, asqueroso,-a; *(poor)* miserable. **2** *(sordid)* sórdido,-a.
squall¹ [skwɔ:l] *n* **1** *(wind)* ráfaga; *(storm)* borrasca, chubasco, tormenta. **2** *fig (noisy argument)* bronca.
squall² [skwɔ:l] *n (cry, scream, yell)* chillido, berrido.
▷ *vi* chillar, berrear.
squalor ['skwɒləʳ] *n* **1** *(dirtiness)* suciedad *f*, mugre *f*. **2** *(poverty)* miseria.
squander ['skwɒndəʳ] *vt (money)* derrochar, malgastar, despilfarrar, tirar; *(fortune)* dilapidar; *(opportunity, time)* desperdiciar, desaprovechar.
square [skweəʳ] *n* **1** *(shape)* cuadrado; *(on fabric)* cuadro; *(on chessboard, graph paper, crossword)* casilla. **2** *(in town)* plaza; *(in barracks)* patio; *(block of houses)* manzana. **3** MATH cuadrado. **4** *(tool)* escuadra. **5** *fam (old fashioned person)* carroza *mf*; *(conservative)* carca *mf*.
▷ *adj* **1** *(in shape)* cuadrado,-a; *(forming right angle)* en ángulo recto, a escuadra. **2** MATH cuadrado,-a. **3** *fam (fair)* justo,-a, equitativo,-a; *(honest)* honesto,-a, franco,-a. **4** *(equal in points)* igual, empatado,-a; *(not owing money)* en paz. **5** *(tidy)* ordenado,-a, en orden. **6** *(old*

fashioned) carroza; *(conservative)* carca. ● **square metre** metro cuadrado. ▮ **square root** raíz *f* cuadrada.
▷ *adv* directamente.
▷ *vt* **1** *(make square)* cuadrar (**with**, con). **2** MATH cuadrar, elevar al cuadrado. **3** *(settle - debts, accounts)* saldar, pagar; *(- matters)* arreglar. **4** *(equalize)* empatar. **5** *(agree, reconcile)* conciliar. **6** *fam (bribe)* sobornar.
▷ *vi (agree)* cuadrar (**with**, con), concordar (**with**, con).
⊙ **to square off** *vt sep (wood, corner)* cuadrar; *(paper)* cuadricular.
⊙ **to square up** *vi* **1** *fam (settle debts)* ajustar cuentas, saldar cuentas. **2** *(fighters)* ponerse en guardia.
⊙ **to square up to** *vt insep* hacer frente a.
squared ['skweəd] *adj (paper)* cuadriculado,-a.
squarely ['skweəlɪ] *adv* directamente, de lleno.
squash[1] [skwɒʃ] *n* **1** *(in crowd)* apiñamiento, agolpamiento, apretujón *m*. **2** *(drink)* bebida de frutas, concentrado de frutas. **3** SP squash *m*. ● **squash rackets** *(game)* squash *m*.
▷ *vt* **1** *(crush, flatten)* aplastar, chafar, espachurrar. **2** *(squeeze)* meter apretando, apretar, apiñar. **3** *fig (crush - person)* apabullar, aplastar, desairar; *(- rumour, dissent, rebellion)* hacer callar, acallar, aplastar; *(- argument, plan, proposal)* echar por tierra, dar al traste con.
▷ *vi* **1** *(crush, flatten)* aplastarse, chafarse, espachurrarse. **2** *(squeeze)* meterse apretando, apretujarse.
⊙ **to squash up** *vi* apretarse, apretujarse.
squash[2] [skwɒʃ] *n* BOT calabaza.
squat [skwɒt] *adj (person)* rechoncho,-a y bajo,-a, achaparrado,-a; *(building)* achaparrado,-a.
▲ *comp* **squatter**, *superl* **squattest**.
▷ *n* **1** *(crouching position)* en cuclillas. **2** *(house occupied by squatters)* vivienda ocupada ilegalmente; *(action of squatting)* ocupación *f* ilegal.
▷ *vi* **1** *(crouch)* agacharse, ponerse en cuclillas. **2** *(in building)* ocupar ilegalmente.
▲ *pt & pp* **squatted**, *ger* **squatting**.
squatter ['skwɒtəʳ] *n* ocupante *mf* ilegal, okupa *mf*.
squawk [skwɔ:k] *n* **1** *(of bird)* graznido, chillido. **2** *(complaint)* queja.
▷ *vi* **1** *(bird)* graznar, chillar. **2** *(complain loudly)* gruñir.
squeak [skwi:k] *n (of mouse)* chillido; *(of wheel, hinge, etc)* chirrido, rechinamiento; *(of shoes)* crujido.
▷ *vi (mouse)* chillar; *(wheel, hinge, etc)* chirriar, rechinar; *(shoes)* chirriar.
squeal [skwi:l] *n (of animal, person)* chillido, grito; *(of tyres, brakes)* chirrido.
▷ *vi* **1** *(animal, person)* chillar; *(tyres, brakes)* chirriar. **2** *fam (inform on)* cantar, chivarse.
▷ *vt (say)* decir chillando, chillar, gritar.
squeamish ['skwi:mɪʃ] *adj* **1** *(easily made to feel sick)* remilgado,-a, delicado,-a; *(easily upset)* muy sensible, impresionable. **2** *(easily shocked morally)* escrupuloso,-a.
squeeze [skwi:z] *n* **1** *(pressure - gen)* estrujón *m*, presión *f*; *(- of hand)* apretón *m*; *(hug)* abrazo. **2** *(small amount)* unas gotas. **3** *(of crowd)* apretujón *m*, apiñamiento. **4** *(difficult situation)* restricciones *fpl*.
▷ *vt* **1** *(gen)* apretar; *(lemon, orange)* exprimir; *(sponge)* estrujar; *(cloth)* retorcer, escurrir. **2** *(fit in)* meter. **3** *(force out)* extraer, sacar.
▷ *vi (force into, through, etc)* meterse a la fuerza.
⊙ **to squeeze up** *vi* apretujarse.
squeezer ['skwi:zəʳ] *n* exprimidor *m*.
squelch [skweltʃ] *vi (move)* chapotear.
▷ *n* chapoteo.
squid [skwɪd] *n (gen)* calamar *m*; *(small)* chipirón *m*.
▲ *pl* **squid** o **squids**.
squiggle ['skwɪgᵊl] *n (line)* garabato.
squint [skwɪnt] *n* **1** MED bizquera, estrabismo. **2** *fam (quick look)* vistazo, ojeada, miradita.
▷ *vi* **1** MED bizquear, ser bizco,-a. **2** *(in sunlight)* entrecerrar los ojos.
squire [skwaɪəʳ] *n* **1** *dated (landowner)* terrateniente *m*, hacendado, señor *m*. **2** HIST *(knight's armour-carrier)* escudero. **3** GB *fam* jefe *m*.
squirm [skwɜ:m] *vi* **1** *(twist)* retorcerse. **2** *(feel embarrassment)* sentirse incómodo,-a.
squirrel ['skwɪrᵊl] *n* ardilla.
Sri Lanka [sri:'læŋkə] *n* Sri Lanka.
stab [stæb] *n* **1** *(with knife)* puñalada, navajazo. **2** *(of pain)* punzada.
▷ *vt (with knife)* apuñalar, acuchillar.
▲ *pt & pp* **stabbed**, *ger* **stabbing**.
⊙ **to stab at** *vi (jab - with finger)* golpear, dar con el dedo; *(- with pointed object)* pinchar, clavar.
stability [st'bɪlɪtɪ] *n* estabilidad *f*.
stabilizer ['steɪbᵊlaɪzəʳ] *n* **1** *(on plane, ship, bicycle)* estabilizador *m*. **2** *(in food)* estabilizante *m*.
stable[1] ['steɪbᵊl] *adj* **1** *(unchanging)* estable, constante; *(firm)* sólido,-a, estable; *(secure)* fijo,-a, estable, seguro,-a; *(person - sane)* equilibrado,-a. **2** CHEM estable.
stable[2] ['steɪbᵊl] *n* **1** *(for horses)* cuadra, caballeriza; *(for other animals)* establo. **2** *(training establishment for horses)* cuadra; *(school, theatre, club, etc)* escuela.
▷ *vt (put in stable)* encerrar en una cuadra; *(keep in stable)* guardar en una cuadra.
stack [stæk] *n* **1** *(pile, heap)* montón *m*, pila: **2** *(of grass, grain, etc)* almiar *m*. **3** *(chimney)* cañón de chimenea.
▷ *vt* **1** *(pile up)* apilar, amontonar; *(fill)* llenar. **2** *fam (in cards)* arreglar.
▷ *n pl* **stacks** *fam* montón *m*, montones *mpl*.
▷ *n pl* **stacks** *(in library)* estanterías *fpl*.
⊙ **to stack up** *vi* US *(compare, match)* comparar, equiparar (**against**, con).
stadium ['steɪdɪəm] *n* estadio.
▲ *pl* **stadiums** o **stadia** ['steɪdɪə].
staff [stɑ:f] *n* **1** *(personnel - gen)* personal *m*, empleados *mpl*, plantilla; *(- teachers)* profesorado, personal docente. **2** MIL estado mayor. **3** *(stick)* bastón *m*; *(of shepherd)* cayado; *(of bishop)* báculo; *(flagpole)* asta. **4** MUS pentagrama *m*.
▷ *vt* proveer de personal.
stag [stæg] *n* ZOOL ciervo, venado.
stage [steɪdʒ] *n* **1** *(point, period)* etapa, fase *f*. **2** *(of journey, race)* etapa; *(day's journey)* jornada. **3** *(in theatre)* escenario, escena; *(raised platform)* plataforma, tablado, estrado. **4** *fig (scene of action)* escena. **5** *(of rocket)* fase *f*. **6** *fam (stagecoach)* diligencia. ▪ **by stages / in stages** por etapas.
▷ *vt* **1** THEAT poner en escena, montar, representar. **2** *(hold, carry out)* llevar a cabo, efectuar; *(arrange)* organizar, montar.
▷ *n* **the stage** *(the theatre)* el teatro, las tablas *fpl*.
stagecoach ['steɪdʒkəʊtʃ] *n* diligencia.

stagehand ['steɪdʒhænd] *n* tramoyista *mf.*
stagger ['stægəʳ] *vi (walk unsteadily)* tambalearse.
▷ *vt* **1** *(hours, work)* escalonar. **2** *(amaze)* asombrar, pasmar.
▷ *n (unsteady walk)* tambaleo.
staggered ['stægəd] *adj* **1** *(amazed)* asombrado,-a, pasmado,-a. **2** *(hours, holidays)* escalonado,-a.
staging ['steɪdʒɪŋ] *n* **1** THEAT montaje *m*, puesta en escena. **2** *(scaffolding)* andamiaje *m.*
stagnation [stæg'neɪʃᵊn] *n (of water)* estancamiento; *(person)* anquilosamiento.
stagy ['steɪdʒɪ] *adj* teatral, efectista, exagerado,-a.
▲ *comp* **stagier**, *superl* **stagiest.**
stain [steɪn] *n* **1** *(gen)* mancha. **2** *(dye)* tinte *m*, tintura.
▷ *vt* **1** *(gen)* manchar. **2** *(dye)* teñir.
▷ *vi* mancharse.
stained [steɪnd] *adj* manchado,-a (**with**, de). ● **stained glass** vidrio de colores.
stainless ['steɪnləs] *adj (spotless)* sin mancha. ● **stainless steel** acero inoxidable.
stair [steəʳ] *n* **1** *(single step)* escalón *m*, peldaño. **2** *lit* escalera.
▷ *n pl* **stairs** escalera *f sing.*
stairway ['steəweɪ] *n* escalera.
stake[1] [steɪk] *n (stick)* estaca, palo; *(post)* poste *m*; *(for plant, tree)* rodrigón *m*; *(in surveying)* jalón *m.*
▷ *vt (fasten, support - gen)* sujetar con estacas, apoyar con estacas (**up**, -); *(- plant, tree)* arrodrigar; *(in surveying)* jalonar.
⊙ **to stake out** *vt sep* **1** *(mark, enclose)* cercar con estacas, marcar con estacas, delimitar con estacas. **2** *fam (watch secretly)* vigilar secretamente, vigilar a escondidas.
stake[2] [steɪk] *n* **1** *(bet)* apuesta. **2** *(investment, share)* interés *m*, participación *f.*
▷ *vt* **1** *(bet)* apostar, jugar(se); *(risk)* arriesgar, jugarse. **2** *(give financial support to)* invertir en.
▷ *n pl* **stakes** *(prize money)* premio *m sing*; *(horse race)* carrera *f sing* de caballos.
stale [steɪl] *adj* **1** *(food - gen)* no fresco,-a, pasado,-a; *(- bread, cake)* duro,-a; *(tobacco)* rancio,-a; *(wine, beer)* picado,-a. **2** *(air)* viciado,-a; *(smell)* a cerrado. **3** *(news)* viejo,-a, pasado,-a; *(joke)* trillado,-a. **4** *(person)* quemado,-a, cansado,-a, harto,-a.
stalemate ['steɪlmeɪt] *n* **1** *(chess)* tablas *fpl.* **2** *fig* punto muerto, impasse *m.*
staleness ['steɪlnəs] *n* **1** *(of food)* ranciedad *f*; *(of bread)* dureza. **2** *(of air)* lo viciado. **3** *(of news, joke)* lo añejo, lo viejo. **4** *(of person)* anquilosamiento.
stalk[1] [stɔːk] *vt (hunt - animals)* acechar; *(- hunter)* cazar al acecho; *(- detective, killer, etc)* acechar, cazar, perseguir; *(menace - danger, famine, disease, etc)* asolar.
▷ *vi (walk - proudly)* andar con paso majestuoso; *(- angrily)* andar indignado,-a.
stalk[2] [stɔːk] *n* **1** BOT *(of plant)* tallo; *(of fruit)* rabo, rabillo; *(of cabbage)* troncho. **2** ZOOL pedúnculo.
stall[1] [stɔːl] *vi fam (delay)* andar con rodeos, contestar con evasivas.
▷ *vt fam (delay)* entretener; *(put off)* aplazar, dar largas a.
stall[2] [stɔːl] *n* **1** *(in market)* puesto, tenderete *m*; *(at fair)* caseta, barraca. **2** *(for animal - stable)* establo; *(- stable compartment)* compartimiento (en un establo). **3** *(row of seats)* sillería. **4** *(small room, compartment)* compartimiento.
▷ *vt* **1** AUTO hacer calar. **2** *(put animal in stall)* encerrar en establo; *(keep in stall)* guardar en establo.
▷ *vi* AUTO calarse, pararse.
▷ *n pl* **stalls** *(in theatre)* platea *f sing.*
stallion ['stælɪən] *n* semental *m*, garañón *m.*
stalwart ['stɔːlwət] *adj* **1** *dated (strong)* fuerte, fornido,-a. **2** *(staunch, loyal)* leal, fiel.
▷ *n* partidario,-a incondicional.
stamen ['steɪmən] *n* BOT estambre *m.*
stamina ['stæmɪnə] *n (endurance)* resistencia, aguante *m.*
stammer ['stæməʳ] *n* tartamudeo.
▷ *vi* tartamudear.
▷ *vt (say with a stammer)* decir tartamudeando, farfullar.
stamp [stæmp] *n* **1** *(postage)* sello; *(fiscal)* timbre *m*; *(trading stamp)* cupón *m*, vale *m.* **2** *(tool - gen)* sello; *(- rubber)* sello de goma, tampón *m*; *(- metal)* cuño, troquel *m.* **3** *(seal, mark)* sello. **4** *(with foot - act)* patada, pisotón *m*; *(- sound)* paso. **5** *fml (distinguishing mark)* impronta, huella, marca. **6** *fml (kind, sort)* clase *f*, índole *f.*
▷ *vt* **1** *(letter)* franquear. **2** *(passport, document)* sellar, marcar con sello; *(metal, coin)* acuñar, troquelar. **3** *fig (impress - event)* grabar, estampar; *(- personality, authority, influence)* imprimir, dejar. **4** *(characterize - positively)* caracterizar, marcar, demostrar; *(- negatively)* tildar. **5** *(with foot)* dar una patada en; *(in dancing)* zapatear.
▷ *vi* **1** *(with foot)* dar patadas, patear, patalear; *(in dancing)* zapatear. **2** *(walk noisily)* pisar fuerte.
⊙ **to stamp on** *vt insep* **1** *(crush with foot)* pisar, pisotear. **2** *(suppress)* sofocar, aplastar.
⊙ **to stamp out** *vt sep* **1** *(eliminate - racism, violence, etc)* acabar con, erradicar; *(- rebellion, epidemic, etc)* sofocar, aplastar. **2** *(extinguish, put out)* apagar (con los pies).
stance [stæns] *n* **1** *(way of standing)* postura. **2** *(opinion, attitude)* postura (**on**, respecto a), posición *f* (**on**, respecto a), actitud *f* (**on**, respecto a).
stand [stænd] *n* **1** *(position)* lugar *m*, sitio; *(attitude, opinion)* posición *f*, postura; *(defence, resistance)* resistencia. **2** *(of lamp, sculpture, etc)* pie *m*, pedestal *m*, base *f.* **3** *(stall - in market)* puesto, tenderete *m*; *(- at exhibition)* stand *m*; *(- at fair)* caseta, barraca. **4** *(for taxis)* parada. **5** SP *(in stadium)* tribuna. **6** US *(witness box)* estrado.
▷ *vi* **1** *(person - be on one's feet)* estar de pie, estar; *(- get up)* ponerse de pie, levantarse; *(- remain on one's feet)* quedarse de pie; *(- take up position)* ponerse. **2** *(measure - height)* medir; *(- value, level)* marcar, alcanzar. **3** *(thing - be situated)* estar, encontrarse, haber. **4** *(remain valid)* seguir en pie, seguir vigente. **5** *(be in a certain condition)* estar. **6** *(be in particular situation)* estar. **7** *(take attitude, policy)* adoptar una postura. **8** *(be likely to)* poder. **9** *(liquid)* estancar; *(mixture)* reposar. **10** POL *(run)* presentarse como candidato, -a.
▷ *vt* **1** *(place)* poner, colocar. **2** *fam (bear, tolerate)* aguantar, soportar; *(endure, withstand)* soportar, resistir. **3** *fam (invite)* invitar: **I'll stand you a drink** *te invitaré a una copa.* ■ **not to stand a chance** no tener ni la más remota posibilidad. ‖ **to stand clear (of** STH**)** apartarse (de ALGO). ‖ **to stand in the way of** impedir, obstaculizar, poner trabas a. ‖ **to stand to reason** ser lógico,-a. ‖ **to stand trial** ser procesado,-a.

⊙ **to stand aside** *vi (move to one side)* apartarse, quitarse de en medio; *(take no part)* no tomar parte, mantenerse al margen.
⊙ **to stand back** *vi (move back)* apartarse, echarse hacia atrás, alejarse; *(be objective)* distanciarse (**from**, de).
⊙ **to stand by** *vi* **1** *(do nothing)* cruzarse de brazos, quedarse sin hacer nada. **2** *(be ready for action - gen)* estar preparado,-a, estar listo,-a; *(- troops)* estar en estado de alerta.
▷ *vt insep* **1** *(not desert)* no abandonar, respaldar, apoyar, defender. **2** *(keep to - decision)* atenerse a; *(- promise)* cumplir.
⊙ **to stand down** *vi* **1** *(withdraw)* retirarse; *(resign)* dimitir. **2** JUR *(leave witness box)* retirarse, abandonar el estrado.
⊙ **to stand for** *vt insep* **1** *(mean)* significar, querer decir; *(represent)* representar. **2** *(support, be in favour of)* defender, apoyar, ser partidario,-a de. **3** *(tolerate)* tolerar, permitir, consentir.
⊙ **to stand in for** *vt insep (substitute, deputize)* sustituir, suplir.
⊙ **to stand out** *vi* **1** *(building, etc)* destacar, sobresalir. **2** *(person, qualities)* destacarse, sobresalir. **3** *(be firm in opposition)* oponerse (**against**, a).
⊙ **to stand over** *vt insep (supervise, watch closely)* vigilar a, velar a.
⊙ **to stand to** *vi* MIL estar en estado de alerta.
▷ *vt sep* MIL poner en estado de alerta.
⊙ **to stand up** *vi* **1** *(get up)* ponerse de pie, levantarse; *(be standing)* estar de pie. **2** *(withstand)* resistir (**to**, -), soportar (**to**, -).
▷ *vt sep* **1** *(place upright)* poner en posición vertical. **2** *fam (fail to keep appointment)* dejar plantado,-a a.
▲ *pt & pp* **stood** [stud].
⊙ **to stand up for** *vt insep (defend)* defender; *(support)* apoyar.
⊙ **to stand up to** *vt insep (resist, defend OS)* hacer frente a, resistir a.

standard ['stændəd] *n* **1** *(level, degree)* nivel *m*; *(quality)* cualidad *f*. **2** *(criterion, yardstick)* criterio, valor *m*. **3** *(norm, rule)* norma, regla, estándar *m*. **4** *(flag)* estandarte *m*, bandera; *(of ship)* pabellón *m*. **5** *(official measure)* patrón *m*. **6** MUS tema *m* clásico, clásico.
▷ *adj* normal, estándar.
▷ *n pl* **standards** *(moral principles)* principios *mpl*, valores *mpl*.

standard-bearer ['stændədbeərəʳ] *n* MIL abanderado.

standardize ['stændədaɪz] *vt* normalizar, estandarizar.

standby ['stændbaɪ] *n* **1** *(person)* suplente *mf*, sustituto,-a, reserva *mf*. **2** *(thing)* recurso.

stand-in ['stændɪn] *n* **1** suplente *mf*, sustituto,-a (**for**, de). **2** CINEM doble *mf*.

standing ['stændɪŋ] *adj* **1** *(not sitting)* de pie. **2** *(upright, vertical)* derecho,-a, recto,-a, vertical. **3** *(permanent - committee, body)* permanente; *(- rule)* fijo,-a; *(- invitation)* abierto,-a.
▷ *n* **1** *(status)* status *m*, posición *f*; *(prestige, reputation)* prestigio. **2** *(duration)* duración *f*; *(in job)* antigüedad *f*.

standpipe ['stændpaɪp] *n (in street)* tubo vertical.

standpoint ['stændpɔɪnt] *n* punto de vista.

standstill ['stændstɪl] ■ **at a standstill** parado,-a, paralizado,-a.

stanza ['stænzə] *n* estrofa.

staple¹ ['steɪpᵊl] *adj* **1** *(food, ingredient)* básico,-a; *(product, export)* principal. **2** *(usual)* típico,-a, de siempre.
▷ *n (main food)* alimento básico; *(main product)* producto principal; *(main thing)* elemento principal.

staple² ['steɪpᵊl] *n (fastener)* grapa.
▷ *vt* grapar.

stapler ['steɪpᵊləʳ] *n* grapadora.

star [stɑːʳ] *n (gen)* estrella; *(person)* estrella, astro.
▷ *vi* CINEM protagonizar (**in**, -).
▷ *vt* **1** CINEM tener como protagonista a, presentar como estrella. **2** *(mark with star)* marcar con un asterisco.
▲ *pt & pp* **starred**, *ger* **starring.**
▷ *n pl* **stars** *(horoscope)* horóscopo *m sing*.

starboard ['stɑːbəd] *n* MAR estribor *m*.

starch [stɑːtʃ] *n (for laundry, in rice)* almidón *m*; *(in potatoes)* fécula.
▷ *vt (laundry)* almidonar.

stardom ['stɑːdəm] *n* estrellato. ■ **to rise to stardom** convertirse en estrella.

stare [steəʳ] *n* mirada fija.
▷ *vi* mirar fijamente (**at**, -), clavar la vista (**at**, en).

starfish ['stɑːfɪʃ] *n* estrella de mar.

stark [stɑːk] *adj* **1** *(landscape)* desolado,-a, desierto,-a, inhóspito,-a; *(climate)* duro,-a, severo,-a, crudo,-a; *(décor, room)* sobrio,-a, austero,-a. **2** *fig (realism, truth, facts, etc)* crudo,-a, puro,-a y duro,-a. **3** *(complete, utter)* absoluto,-a.

starlet ['stɑːlət] *n* aspirante *f* a estrella.

starlight ['stɑːlaɪt] *n* luz *f* de las estrellas.

starling ['stɑːlɪŋ] *n* estornino.

starlit ['stɑːlɪt] *adj* iluminado,-a por las estrellas.

starry ['stɑːrɪ] *adj* estrellado,-a, sembrado,-a de estrellas.
▲ *comp* **starrier**, *superl* **starriest.**

starry-eyed [stɑːrɪ'aɪd] *adj (idealistic)* idealista, ilusionado,-a; *(in love)* enamorado,-a, arrobado,-a.

start [stɑːt] *n* **1** *(gen)* principio, comienzo, inicio. **2** SP *(of race)* salida; *(advantage)* ventaja. **3** *(fright, jump)* susto, sobresalto.
▷ *vt* **1** *(begin - gen)* empezar, comenzar, iniciar; *(- conversation)* entablar. **2** *(cause to begin - fire, epidemic)* provocar; *(- argument, fight, war, etc)* empezar, iniciar. **3** *(set up - business)* montar, poner; *(- organization)* fundar, establecer, crear. **4** *(set in motion - machine)* poner en marcha; *(- vehicle)* arrancar, poner en marcha.
▷ *vi* **1** *(begin)* empezar, comenzar. **2** *(be set up - business)* ser fundado,-a, fundarse, crearse. **3** *(begin to operate)* ponerse en marcha, empezar a funcionar; *(car)* arrancar. **4** *(begin journey)* salir, partir, ponerse en camino. **5** *(jump)* asustarse, sobresaltarse.
⊙ **to start back** *vi* emprender el viaje de vuelta.
⊙ **to start off** *vi* **1** *(begin)* empezar, comenzar. **2** *(leave)* salir, ponerse en camino.
▷ *vt sep* empezar, ayudar a empezar.
⊙ **to start on** *vt insep* **1** empezar, ponerse a. **2** *(complain)* empezar a quejarse (**about**, de); *(criticize)* meterse con.
⊙ **to start out** *vi* **1** *(leave)* salir, ponerse en camino. **2** *(begin)* empezar, comenzar.
⊙ **to start over** *vi* US volver a empezar.

⊙ **to start up** *vt sep (car)* arrancar; *(engine)* poner en marcha; *(business)* montar, poner en marcha; *(conversation)* entablar.
▷ *vi (car)* arrancar; *(engine)* ponerse en marcha; *(orchestra)* empezar a tocar; *(music)* empezar a sonar.
starter ['stɑːtəʳ] *n* **1** SP *(official)* juez *mf* de salida. **2** SP *(competitor)* competidor,-ra, participante *mf*. **3** AUTO motor *m* de arranque. **4** CULIN *fam* primer plato, entrante *m*.
startle ['stɑːtᵊl] *vt* asustar, sobresaltar: **you startled me!** *¡me has asustado!*
startling ['stɑːtᵊlɪŋ] *adj* **1** *(frightening)* alarmante, sobrecogedor,-ra. **2** *(amazing)* sorprendente, asombroso,-a.
starvation [stɑː'veɪʃᵊn] *n* hambre *f*, inanición *f*.
starve [stɑːv] *vi (feel hungry)* pasar hambre; *(die)* morirse de hambre.
▷ *vt* **1** *(deprive of food)* privar de comida a, hacer pasar hambre a. **2** *fig* privar (**of**, de).
starving ['stɑːvɪŋ] *adj* famélico,-a.
stash [stæʃ] *n* alijo.
▷ *vt* [Also **to stash away**.] guardar en un lugar seguro.
state [steɪt] *n* **1** *(condition)* estado. **2** POL *(government)* estado. **3** *(country, division of country)* estado. **4** *(ceremony, pomp)* ceremonia, pompa, solemnidad *f*.
▷ *adj* POL estatal, del estado.
▷ *vt* **1** *(say, declare, express)* exponer, declarar, afirmar: **2** *(specify)* fijar.
stated ['steɪtɪd] *adj (specified)* indicado,-a, señalado,-a.
stateless ['steɪtləs] *adj* apátrida.
stately ['steɪtlɪ] *adj* majestuoso,-a, imponente. ● **stately home** casa solariega, casa señorial.
statement ['steɪtmənt] *n* **1** *(gen)* declaración *f*, afirmación *f*; *(official)* comunicado. **2** FIN estado de cuentas, extracto de cuenta. ■ **to make a statement** JUR prestar declaración.
state-of-the-art [steɪtəfðɪ'ɑːt] *adj* ultimísimo,-a, más avanzado,-a. ● **state-of-the-art technology** tecnología punta.
statesman ['steɪtsmən] *n* estadista *m*, hombre *m* de estado.
▲ *pl* **statesmen** ['steɪtsmən].
static ['stætɪk] *adj* **1** TECH estático,-a. **2** *(not moving, not changing)* estacionario,-a. ● **static electricity** electricidad *f* estática.
▷ *n (interference)* interferencias *fpl*, parásitos *mpl*.
▷ *n* **statics** PHYS estática.
station ['steɪʃᵊn] *n* **1** *(railway)* estación *f* (de ferrocarril); *(underground)* estación *f* de metro; *(bus, coach)* estación *f*, terminal *f*. **2** *(radio)* emisora, estación *f*, radio *f*; *(TV)* canal *m*. **3** AGR granja. **4** *(social rank)* condición *f* social, posición *f* social. **5** MIL puesto.
▷ *vt* **1** *(put)* colocar, emplazar, instalar. **2** MIL estacionar, apostar.
stationary ['steɪʃᵊnᵊrɪ] *adj* **1** *(not moving, still)* estacionario,-a, parado,-a, detenido,-a. **2** *(unchanging)* estacionario,-a. **3** *(cannot be moved)* fijo,-a.
stationer ['steɪʃᵊnəʳ] *n* dueño,-a de una papelería. ● **stationer's (shop)** papelería.
stationery ['steɪʃᵊnᵊrɪ] *n (paper)* papel *m* de escribir; *(pen, ink, etc)* artículos *mpl* de escritorio.
stationmaster ['steɪʃᵊnmɑːstəʳ] *n* jefe *m* de estación.
statistics [st'tɪstɪks] *n (science)* estadística.
▷ *n pl (data)* estadísticas *fpl*.
statue ['stætjuː] *n* estatua.
statuesque [stætjʊ'esk] *adj* escultural.
statuette [stætjʊ'et] *n* estatuilla, figurilla.
stature ['stætʃəʳ] *n* **1** *(height)* estatura, talla. **2** *fig (standing)* talla.
status ['steɪtəs] *n* **1** *(official position, condition)* situación *f*, condición *f*, posición *f*. **2** *(prestige, social standing)* status *m*, prestigio (social).
statute ['stætjuːt] *n* estatuto, decreto, ley *f*.
statutory ['stætjətərɪ] *adj (referring to statute)* estatutario,-a; *(penalty)* establecido,-a por la ley, reglamentario,-a; *(right, obligation)* legal; *(holiday)* legalmente establecido,-a.
staunch¹ [stɔːntʃ] *adj (loyal)* incondicional, acérrimo,-a.
staunch² [stɔːntʃ] *vt (blood)* restañar.
stave [steɪv] *n* **1** *(of barrel)* duela. **2** MUS pentagrama *m*.
⊙ **to stave in** *vt sep* romper.
▲ *pt & pp* **staved** o **stove** [stəʊv].
▷ *vi* romperse.
⊙ **to stave off** *vt sep (disaster, defeat)* evitar.
staves [steɪvz] *n pl* **1** → **staff. 2** → **stave.**
stay¹ [steɪ] *n* MAR *(guy rope)* estay *m*, viento.
stay² [steɪ] *n* **1** *(prop, support)* sostén *m*, soporte *m*, puntal *m*. **2** *(in corset)* ballena.
stay³ [steɪ] *n (time)* estancia, permanencia.
▷ *vi (remain)* quedarse, permanecer.
▷ *vt (continue to be)* seguir.
▷ *vi (reside temporarily)* alojarse, hospedarse.
▷ *vt fml (stop)* detener; *(delay)* aplazar; *(calm)* calmar.
⊙ **to stay away** *vi* alejarse (**from**, de), mantenerse lejo (**from**, de), no acercarse (**from**, a).
⊙ **to stay behind** *vi* quedarse.
⊙ **to stay down** *vi (food)* quedarse en el estómago; *(price)* mantenerse bajo,-a.
⊙ **to stay in** *vi* quedarse en casa, no salir.
⊙ **to stay on** *vi (remain)* quedarse, permanecer; *(remai in place)* quedarse en su sitio.
⊙ **to stay out** *vi (gen)* quedarse fuera; *(strikers)* seguir e huelga.
⊙ **to stay out of** *vt insep* no meterse en.
⊙ **to stay up** *vi (not go to bed)* quedarse levantado,-a, n acostarse; *(remain in position)* sostenerse, no caerse.
stayer ['steɪəʳ] *n (person)* persona de mucha resisten cia; *(horse)* caballo de fondo.
staying power ['steɪɪŋpaʊəʳ] *n* resistencia, aguante *m*
steadfast ['stedfɑːst] *adj* **1** *fml (refusal)* firme, rotun do,-a, categórico,-a; *(friend)* leal, incondicional. 2 *(steady, not moving)* constante, inmóvil.
steadily ['stedɪlɪ] *adv* **1** *(grow, improve, rise)* constante mente, a un ritmo constante; *(rain, work)* sin parar. 2 *(gaze, stare)* fijamente; *(walk)* con paso seguro, deci didamente; *(speak)* firmemente.
steadiness ['stedɪnəs] *n* **1** *(of hand, gait)* firmeza. **2** *(c prices)* estabilidad *f*; *(of demand)* lo constante. **3** *(of cha racter)* formalidad *f*, seriedad *f*.
steady ['stedɪ] *adj* **1** *(table, ladder, etc)* firme, seguro,-a *(gaze)* fijo,-a; *(voice)* tranquilo,-a, firme. **2** *(regula constant - heartbeat, pace)* regular; *(- demand, speed, im provement, decline, increase)* constante; *(- flow, rain* continuo,-a; *(rhythm)* regular, constante; *(- prices, cur rency)* estable. **3** *(regular - job)* fijo,-a, estable; *(- income*

regular, fijo,-a. **4** *(student)* aplicado,-a; *(worker, person)* serio,-a, formal.
▲ *comp* steadier, *superl* steadiest.
▷ *interj* ¡cuidado!, ¡ojo!
▷ *n (boyfriend)* novio; *(girlfriend)* novia.
▷ *vt* **1** *(hold firm - ladder, table, etc)* sujetar, sostener; *(stabilize)* estabilizar. **2** *(person, nerves)* calmar, tranquilizar.
▷ *vi (market, prices)* estabilizarse.
▲ *pt & pp* steadied, *ger* steadying.
teak [steɪk] *n* **1** *(of beef)* bistec *m*, filete *m*; *(of meat)* filete *m*; *(of salmon)* rodaja. **2** *(meat for stewing)* carne *f* de vaca para estofar.
teal[1] [sti:l] *n* US *fam (bargain)* ganga, regalo.
teal[2] [sti:l] *vt* robar, hurtar.
▷ *vi* **1** *(rob)* robar, hurtar. **2** *(move quietly, creep)* moverse con sigilo.
▲ *pt* stole [stəʊl], *pp* stolen stəʊlən].
tealth [stelθ] *n fml* cautela, sigilo.
team [sti:m] *n (gen)* vapor *m*. ● **steam engine 1** *(locomotive)* locomotora de vapor, máquina de vapor. **2** *(engine)* motor *m* de vapor. ‖ **steam iron** plancha de vapor.
▷ *vt* CULIN *(vegetables)* cocer al vapor.
▷ *vi (boat)* echar vapor; *(soup, drink, etc)* humear.
⊙ **to steam up** *vi (window, glasses)* empañarse.
⊙ **to steam off** *vt sep* quitar con vapor, despegar con vapor.
teamboat ['sti:mbəʊt] *n* vapor *m*.
teamer ['sti:mə^r] *n* **1** MAR vapor *m*, buque *m* de vapor. **2** CULIN olla a vapor.
teamroller ['sti:mrəʊlə^r] *n (vehicle)* apisonadora.
▷ *vt fam (crush, defeat)* aplastar.
teamship ['sti:mʃɪp] *n* vapor *m*, buque *m* de vapor *m*.
teamy ['sti:mɪ] *adj* **1** *(full of steam)* lleno,-a de vapor; *(window, glass)* empañado,-a. **2** *(erotic)* erótico,-a; *(passionate)* apasionado,-a, tórrido,-a.
▲ *comp* steamier, *superl* steamiest.
teel [sti:l] *n (gen)* acero.
▷ *adj (knife, girder, etc)* de acero. ● **steel industry** industria del acero ‖ **steel mill** acerería, acería. ‖ **steel wool** estropajo de acero.
teelworker ['sti:lwɜ:kə^r] *n* trabajador,-ra de una acería.
teelworks ['sti:lwɜ:ks] *n pl* acería, acerería.
teep[1] [sti:p] *vt (soak - washing)* remojar; *(- dried food)* poner en remojo; *(- fruit)* macerar.
▷ *vi (fruit)* macerarse.
teep[2] [sti:p] *adj* **1** *(hill, slope, stairs)* empinado,-a; *(rise, drop)* abrupto,-a, brusco,-a. **2** *fam (price, fee)* excesivo,-a; *(demand)* excesivo,-a, poco razonable.
teeple ['sti:p^{ə}l] *n* aguja, chapitel *m*.
teeplechase ['sti:p^{ə}lʃeɪs] *n* carrera de obstáculos.
teeplejack ['sti:p^{ə}ldʒæk] *n* reparador,-ra de chimeneas, torres, campanarios, etc.
teer[1] [stɪə^r] *n* buey *m*.
teer[2] [stɪə^r] *vt (gen)* dirigir, guiar; *(vehicle)* conducir, dirigir; *(ship)* gobernar; *(conversation)* llevar.
▷ *vi (vehicle)* ir al volante; *(ship)* llevar el timón, estar al timón.
teering ['stɪərɪŋ] *n* dirección *f*. ● **steering column** columna de (la) dirección. ‖ **steering lock 1** *(device)* seguro antirrobo. **2** *(when turning)* radio de giro. ‖ **steering wheel** volante *m*.

stem [stem] *n* **1** BOT *(of plant, flower)* tallo; *(of leaf)* pecíolo; *(of fruit)* pedúnculo. **2** *(of glass)* pie *m*; *(of tobacco pipe)* boquilla, caña. **3** LING raíz *f*, radical *m*.
▷ *vt (stop - gen)* frenar, parar; *(- bleeding)* contener, parar.
▲ *pt & pp* stemmed, *ger* stemming.
⊙ **to stem from** *vt insep* provenir de, ser el resultado de.
stench [stentʃ] *n* hedor *m*, peste *f*, fetidez *f*.
stencil ['stens^{ə}l] *n* **1** *(template)* plantilla; *(design, pattern)* estarcido. **2** *(for typewriter)* cliché *m*, matriz *f*.
▷ *vt* **1** *(design, pattern)* dibujar utilizando una plantilla. **2** *(duplicate)* multicopiar.
▲ *pt & pp* stencilled (US stenciled), *ger* stencilling (US stenciling).
stenography [st'nɒgrəfɪ] *n* US taquigrafía.
step [step] *n* **1** *(gen)* paso; *(sound)* paso, pisada. **2** *(distance)* paso. **3** *(move, act)* paso. **4** *(measure)* medida; *(formality)* gestión *f*, trámite *m*. **5** *(degree on scale, stage in process)* peldaño, escalón *m*, paso. **6** *(stair)* escalón *m*, peldaño, grada; *(of ladder)* escalón *m*, travesaño; *(of vehicle)* estribo.
▷ *vi* **1** *(move, walk)* dar un paso, andar. **2** *(tread)* pisar.
▷ *n pl* **steps** GB *(stepladder)* escalera de tijera.; *(outdoor)* escalinata; *(indoor)* escalera; *(of plane)* escalerilla.
▲ *pt & pp* stepped, *ger* stepping.
⊙ **to step aside** *vi* hacerse a un lado.
⊙ **to step back** *vi* retroceder.
⊙ **to step down** *vi (from position, job)* renunciar (**from**, a), dimitir (**from**, de).
⊙ **to step forward** *vi (volunteer)* ofrecerse.
⊙ **to step in** *vi (intervene)* intervenir.
⊙ **to step out** *vi* **1** GB *(start walking fast)* apretar el paso. **2** US *(go outside, go somewhere)* salir.
⊙ **to step up** *vt sep (increase - gen)* aumentar; *(- campaign)* intensificar; *(- security)* reforzar.
stepbrother ['stepbrʌðə^r] *n* hermanastro.
stepchild ['steptʃaɪld] *n* hijastro,-a.
▲ *pl* stepchildren ['steptʃɪldrən].
stepdaughter ['stepdɔ:tə^r] *n* hijastra.
stepfather ['stepfɑ:ðə^r] *n* padrastro.
stepladder ['steplædə^r] *n* escalera de tijera.
stepmother ['stepmʌðə^r] *n* madrastra.
steppe [step] *n* GEOG estepa.
stepping-stone ['stepɪŋstəʊn] *n* **1** pasadera. **2** *fig* trampolín *m*.
stepsister ['stepsɪʃtə^r] *n* hermanastra.
stepson ['stepsʌn] *n* hijastro.
stereo ['sterɪəʊ] *n* estéreo.
stereophonic [sterɪ'fɒnɪk] *adj* estereofónico,-a.
stereotype ['sterɪətaɪp] *n* estereotipo.
▷ *vt* estereotipar.
sterility [st'rɪlɪtɪ] *n* esterilidad *f*.
sterilize ['sterəlaɪz] *vt* esterilizar.
sterling ['stɜ:lɪŋ] *n* FIN libra esterlina, libras *fpl* esterlinas. ● **sterling silver** plata de ley. ‖ **the pound sterling** la libra esterlina.
▷ *adj fml (excellent)* excelente.
stern[1] [stɜ:n] *n* MAR popa.
stern[2] [stɜ:n] *adj (treatment, measures)* austero,-a, severo,-a; *(person)* severo,-a; *(look, face, etc)* severo,-a, adusto,-a, ceñudo,-a; *(job, task)* duro,-a.
sternum ['stɜ:nəm] *n* ANAT esternón *m*.
▲ *pl* sternums o sterna.

steroid ['sterɔɪd] *n* esteroide *m*.
stethoscope ['steθəskəʊp] *n* estetoscopio.
stevedore ['stiːvədɔːʳ] *n* estibador *m*.
stew [stjuː] *n* CULIN estofado, guisado, guiso.
▷ *vt (meat)* estofar, guisar; *(fruit)* hacer una compota de.
▷ *vi* **1** *(meat, fruit)* cocerse lentamente. **2** *fam (swelter)* ahogarse de calor.
steward ['stjuːəd] *n* **1** *(on ship)* camarero; *(on plane)* auxiliar *m* de vuelo. **2** *(manager of estate)* administrador *m*. **3** *(of club, hotel)* mayordomo. **4** GB *(in horse racing)* comisario de carreras; *(in athletics)* juez *m*; *(at demonstration, etc)* oficial *mf*.
stewardess ['stjuːədes] *n (on ship)* camarera; *(on plane)* azafata, auxiliar *f* de vuelo.
stick[1] [stɪk] *vt* **1** *(insert pointed object)* clavar, hincar. **2** *fam* poner, meter. **3** *(fix)* colocar, fijar; *(with glue)* pegar, fijar. **4** *fam (bear)* aguantar, soportar.
▷ *vi* **1** *(penetrate)* clavarse. **2** *(fix, become attached)* pegarse. **3** *(jam - drawer, key in lock)* atascarse; *(- machine part, lock)* atrancarse, encasquillarse; *(- vehicle in mud)* atascarse, atollarse. **4** *(remain)* quedarse. **5** *(in cards)* plantarse.
⊙ **to stick about / stick around** *vi fam* quedarse.
⊙ **to stick at** *vt insep* perseverar, perseguir en, seguir con.
⊙ **to stick by** *vt insep (friend)* mantenerse fiel a; *(promise)* cumplir con.
⊙ **to stick out** *vi* **1** *(project, protrude)* salir, sobresalir; *(be noticeable)* resaltar, destacarse. **2** *fam (be obvious)* ser obvio,-a, ser evidente.
▷ *vt sep* **1** *(tongue, hand)* sacar. **2** *(endure)* aguantar.
⊙ **to stick out for** *vt insep* empeñarse en conseguir.
⊙ **to stick to** *vt insep* **1** *(principles)* atenerse a; *(promise)* cumplir con; *(plans)* seguir con; *(text, rules)* ceñirse a. **2** *(limit oneself)* limitarse.
⊙ **to stick together** *vi* mantenerse unido,-a, no separarse.
⊙ **to stick up** *vi (project, protrude)* salir, sobresalir; *(hair)* ponerse de punta, erizarse.
▷ *vt sep* **1** *(poster, etc)* fijar, poner, colocar. **2** *(hands)* levantar. **3** *(bank)* atracar.
▲ *pt & pp* **stuck** [stʌk].
⊙ **to stick up for** *vt insep* defender.
⊙ **to stick with** *vt insep* seguir con.
stick[2] [stɪk] *n* **1** *(piece of wood)* trozo de madera, palo; *(twig)* ramita; *(for punishment)* palo, vara. **2** *(for walking)* bastón *m*. **3** *(for plants)* rodrigón *m*, tutor *m*. **4** MUS *(baton)* batuta; *(drumstick)* palillo. **5** SP *(for hockey)* palo. **6** *(of celery)* rama; *(of rhubarb)* tallo; *(of licorice, rock)* barrita, tira; *(of dynamite)* cartucho; *(of wax, of soap)* barra. **7** *(of furniture)* mueble *m*. **8** GB *fam (person)* tipo,-a.
▷ *n pl* **sticks** *(for fire)* astillas *fpl*, leña *f sing*.; *(remote area)* lugar *m sing* apartado.
sticker ['stɪkəʳ] *n* **1** *(label)* etiqueta adhesiva; *(with slogan, picture)* pegatina. **2** *(person)* persona tenaz.
sticking ['stɪkɪŋ] ● **sticking plaster** *(small)* tirita.; *(on roll)* esparadrapo.
stickleback ['stɪkᵊlbæk] *n (fish)* espinoso, espinosillo.
stickler ['stɪkləʳ] *n* persona quisquillosa.
stick-on ['stɪkɒn] *adj* adhesivo,-a.
stick-up ['stɪkʌp] *n fam* atraco, asalto, robo a mano armada.

sticky ['stɪkɪ] *adj* pegajoso,-a. ● **sticky tape** cinta adhesiva.
▲ *comp* **stickier**, *comp* **stickiest**.
stiff [stɪf] *adj* **1** *(hair, fabric)* rígido,-a, tieso,-a; *(card, collar, brush, lock)* duro,-a. **2** *(joint)* entumecido,-a; *(muscle)* agarrotado,-a. **3** *(door, window)* difícil de abrir, difícil de cerrar. **4** *(not liquid)* espeso,-a, consistente. *(person, manner)* estirado,-a, tieso,-a; *(smile)* forzado,-a. **6** *fig (climb, test, etc)* difícil, duro,-a; *(breeze)* fuerte *(sentence, punishment)* severo,-a. **7** *fam (price, fee)* excesivo,-a. **8** *fam (drink)* fuerte, cargado,-a.
▷ *n sl (corpse)* fiambre *m*.
stiffen ['stɪfᵊn] *vt* **1** *(card, fabric)* reforzar; *(collar)* almidonar; *(paste)* endurecer. **2** *fig (resistance, morale)* fortalecer.
▷ *vi* **1** *(material)* ponerse tieso,-a; *(mixture)* espesarse. *(muscles, joints)* agarrotarse; *(person)* ponerse tenso,-a *(corpse)* ponerse rígido,-a. **3** *fig (resistance, morale)* fortalecerse.
stiffness ['stɪfnəs] *n* **1** *(gen)* rigidez *f*, dureza; *(of muscles)* agarrotamiento; *(of joints)* entumecimiento. *(severity)* severidad *f*, dureza. **3** *(formality)* frialdad *f*.
stifle ['staɪfᵊl] *vt* **1** *(suffocate)* sofocar. **2** *(extinguish)* sofocar. **3** *(repress - rebellion, opposition)* reprimir, sofocar, ahogar; *(- sound, noise)* amortiguar, sofocar, ahogar; *(- tears, cries)* ahogar; *(- yawn, anger)* reprimir contener; *(- growth)* frenar.
▷ *vi* ahogarse, sofocarse.
stifling ['staɪfᵊlɪŋ] *adj (gen)* sofocante, agobiante.
stigma ['stɪgmə] *n (gen)* estigma *m*.
stigmatize ['stɪgmətaɪz] *vt* estigmatizar.
stiletto [stɪ'letəʊ] *n (small dagger)* estilete *m*.
▲ *pl* **stilettos**.
▷ *n pl* **stilettos** *(shoes)* zapatos *mpl* de tacón de aguja.
still[1] [stɪl] *n* **1** *(distillation apparatus)* alambique *m*. *(place)* destilería.
still[2] [stɪl] *adj* **1** *(not moving)* quieto,-a, inmóvil; *(stationary)* parado,-a; *(water)* manso,-a; *(air)* en calma. *(tranquil, calm)* tranquilo,-a; *(peaceful)* sosegado,-a *(subdued)* callado,-a, apagado,-a; *(silent)* silencioso,-a. **3** *(not fizzy - water)* sin gas; *(soft drink)* sin burbujas ● **still life** ART naturaleza muerta *m*.
▷ *adv* **1** *(so far)* todavía, aún. **2** *(even)* aún, todavía. *(even so, nevertheless)* a pesar de todo, con todo, no obstante, sin embargo. **4** *fml (besides, yet, in addition)* aún, todavía. **5** *(quiet, without moving)* quieto,-a.
▷ *n* **1** *lit (calm, silence)* silencio, quietud *f*, tranquilidad **2** CINEM *(photograph)* fotograma *m*.
stillborn ['stɪlbɔːn] *adj* nacido, a muerto,-a.
stillness ['stɪlnəs] *n* **1** *(calm)* calma, quietud *f*, tranquilidad *f*. **2** *(silence)* silencio.
stilt [stɪlt] *n (for walking)* zanco; *(for houses)* pilote *m*.
stilted ['stɪltɪd] *adj pej (style, language)* rebuscado,-a *(manner)* afectado,-a; *(conversation)* forzado,-a.
stimulant ['stɪmjələnt] *n* **1** *(drug)* estimulante *m*. *(stimulus)* estímulo, incentivo, acicate *m*.
stimulate ['stɪmjəleɪt] *vt (activate)* estimular; *(encourage)* animar, alentar.
stimulating ['stɪmjəleɪtɪŋ] *adj (gen)* estimulante; *(inspiring)* inspirador,-ra.
stimulation [stɪmj'leɪʃᵊn] *n (stimulus)* estímulo; *(action)* estimulación *f*.

stimulus ['stɪmjələs] *n* estímulo.
▲ *pl* stimuli ['stɪmjəli:].

sting [stɪŋ] *n* **1** *(organ - of bee, wasp)* aguijón *m*; *(- of scorpion)* uña; *(- of plant)* pelo urticante. **2** *(action, wound)* picadura. **3** *(pain)* escozor *m*, picazón *f*. **4** *fig (of remorse)* punzada. **5** US *(trick)* timo, golpe *m*.
▷ *vt* **1** *(gen)* picar. **2** *fig (remark)* herir en lo más hondo; *(conscience)* remorder. **3** *(provoke)* incitar, provocar (into/to, a). **4** *(overcharge, swindle)* clavar.
▷ *vi* **1** *(insects, nettles, etc)* picar; *(substance)* escocer. **2** *(be painful)* escocer.
▲ *pt & pp* stung [stʌŋ].

stinging ['stɪŋɪŋ] *adj (words)* mordaz, hiriente.
▲ *comp* stingier, *superl* stingiest.

stingray ['stɪŋreɪ] *n (fish)* raya venosa.

stingy ['stɪndʒɪ] *n (person)* tacaño,-a, roñoso,-a, agarrado,-a, rácano,-a; *(amount)* escaso,-a, mezquino,-a.

stink [stɪŋk] *n* **1** *(smell)* peste *f*, hedor *m*, hediondez *f*, fetidez *f*. **2** *fam (fuss, trouble)* escándalo, lío, follón *m*.
▷ *vi* **1** apestar (of, a), heder (of, a). **2** *fam (seem bad or dishonest)* dar asco.
▲ *pt* stank [stæŋk] o stunk [stʌŋk], *pp* stunk [stʌŋk].
⊙ **to stink out** *vt sep* **1** *(fill with bad smell)* apestar, dejar hediondo,-a. **2** *(drive away)* hacer salir.

stinking ['stɪŋkɪŋ] *adj* **1** *(smelly)* hediondo,-a, fétido,-a, apestoso,-a. **2** *(unpleasant, very bad)* horroroso,-a, asqueroso,-a.

stint [stɪnt] *n (period of work)* período, temporada; *(shift)* turno, tanda; *(fixed amount of work)* parte *f*.
▷ *vt* **1** *(food)* escatimar. **2** *(deprive)* privar.
▷ *vi* escatimar (on, -).

stipend ['staɪpend] *n* estipendio, salario.

stipulate ['stɪpjəleɪt] *vt* estipular, especificar.

stipulation [stɪpjə'leɪʃ*n] *n* estipulación *f*, condición *f*.

stir[1] [stɜ:ʳ] *n* **1** *(act)* acción *f* de agitar. **2** *(slight movement)* movimiento. **3** *fig (public excitement, commotion)* revuelo.
▷ *vt* **1** *(liquid, mixture)* remover, revolver. **2** *(move slightly)* mover, agitar. **3** *(curiosity, interest, etc)* despertar, excitar; *(anger)* provocar; *(imagination)* avivar, estimular; *(emotions)* conmover.
▷ *vi* **1** *(move)* moverse, agitarse; *(wake up)* despertarse; *(get up)* levantarse. **2** *(feelings)* despertarse. **3** *fam (cause trouble)* armar lío, meter cizaña.
⊙ **to stir up** *vt sep* **1** *(unrest, revolt, etc)* provocar; *(hatred)* fomentar, promover; *(trouble)* provocar, crear; *(memories)* despertar; *(passions)* excitar. **2** *(mud, waters, dust)* remover.
▲ *pt & pp* stirred, *ger* stirring.

stir[2] [stɜ:ʳ] *n sl dated (prison)* cárcel *f*, chirona.

stir-fry ['stɜ:rfraɪ] *vt* CULIN *freír en poco aceite sin dejar de removerlo*.
▲ *pt & pp* stir-fried, *ger* stir-frying.

stirring ['stɜ:rɪŋ] *adj (moving)* conmovedor,-ra; *(rousing, exciting)* emocionante.

stirrup ['stɪrəp] *n* **1** *(for riding)* estribo. **2** *(on trousers)* trabilla. ● **stirrup pump** bomba de mano.

stitch [stɪtʃ] *n* **1** *(in sewing)* puntada; *(in knitting)* punto. **2** MED punto (de sutura). **3** *(sharp pain)* punzada; *(when running, etc)* flato.
▷ *vt* **1** SEW coser (on, a), (up, -). **2** MED suturar (up, -).
▷ *vi* SEW coser.
⊙ **to stitch up** *vt sep* **1** *(complete satisfactorily)* arreglar, acabar. **2** *fam (double-cross)* engañar, traicionar.

stoat [stəʊt] *n* armiño.

stock [stɒk] *n* **1** *(supply)* reserva. **2** COMM *(goods)* existencias *fpl*, stock *m*; *(variety)* surtido. **3** FIN *(company's capital)* capital *m* social. **4** AGR *(livestock)* ganado. **5** CULIN *(broth)* caldo. **6** BOT *(flower)* alhelí *m*. **7** *(trunk, main part of tree)* tronco; *(of vine)* cepa. **8** *(plant from which cuttings are grown)* planta madre; *(stem onto which another plant is grafted)* patrón *m*. **9** *(descent - of person)* linaje *m*, estirpe *m*; *(- of animal)* raza. **10** *fml (standing, status)* prestigio; *(popularity)* popularidad *f*. **11** *(of gun)* culata; *(of tool, whip, fishing rod)* mango. ● **stock exchange** bolsa. | **stock market** mercado bursátil.
▷ *adj* **1** COMM *(goods, size)* corriente, normal, de serie, estándar. **2** *pej (excuse, argument, response)* de siempre, típico,-a, de costumbre; *(greeting, speech)* consabido,-a; *(phrase, theme)* gastado,-a, muy visto,-a.
▷ *vt* **1** COMM *(keep supplies of)* tener en stock; *(sell)* vender. **2** *(provide with a supply)* abastecer de, surtir de, proveer de; *(fill - larder, etc)* llenar (with, de); *(- lake, pond)* poblar.
▷ *n pl* stocks FIN *(shares)* acciones *fpl*, valores *mpl*.
⊙ **to stock up** *vi* abastecerse (on/with, de/con), aprovisionarse (on/with, de/con).

stockade [stɒ'keɪd] *n (fence)* empalizada, estacada.

stockbroker ['stɒkbrəʊkəʳ] *n* corredor,-ra de bolsa, agente *mf* de bolsa, bolsista *mf*.

stockbroking ['stɒkbrəʊkɪŋ] *n* correduría de valores.

stockholder ['stɒkhəʊldəʳ] *n* US accionista *mf*.

stocking ['stɒkɪŋ] *n* media.

stockist ['stɒkɪst] *n* almacenista *mf*, proveedor,-ra, distribuidor,-ra.

stockpile ['stɒkpaɪl] *n* reservas *fpl*.
▷ *vt (gen)* almacenar; *(accumulate)* acumular, hacer acopio de.

stockroom ['stɒkru:m] *n* almacén *m*, depósito.

stocks [stɒks] *n pl* **1** HIST *(wooden frame)* cepo. **2** MAR *(framework)* grada de construcción, astillero.

stock-still [stɒk'stɪl] *adv* inmóvil.

stocktaking ['stɒkteɪkɪŋ] *n* **1** COMM inventario. **2** *(review)* balance *m*.

stocky ['stɒkɪ] *adj (heavily-built)* robusto,-a, fornido,-a; *(strong, solid)* cuadrado,-a; *(squat)* bajito,-a.
▲ *comp* stockier, *superl* stockiest.

stodgy ['stɒdʒɪ] *adj* **1** *(food)* indigesto,-a, pesado,-a. **2** *(book, person)* pesado,-a, aburrido,-a.
▲ *comp* stodgier, *superl* stodgiest.

stoic ['stəʊɪk] *n* estoico,-a.

stoical ['stəʊɪk*l] *adj* estoico,-a.

stoicism ['stəʊɪsɪz*m] *n* estoicismo.

stoke [stəʊk] *vt* **1** *(fire - add fuel to)* alimentar, echar carbón a, echar leña a; *(- poke)* atizar, avivar. **2** *fig (feeling)* avivar, alimentar.
⊙ **to stoke up** *vi* **1** *(add fuel to fire)* alimentar el fuego; *(poke fire)* atizar el fuego, avivar el fuego. **2** *fam (fill up)* llenarse (on, de), atiborrarse (on, de).
▷ *vt sep fig (feeling)* avivar, alimentar.

stole[1] [stəʊl] *pt* → **steal**.

stole[2] [stəʊl] *n (garment)* estola.

stolen ['stəʊlən] *pp* → **steal**.

stolid ['stɒlɪd] *adj (impassive)* impasible, imperturbable.

stoma [s'təʊmə] *n* estoma *m*.
▲ *pl* stomas o stomata [s'təʊmətə].
stomach ['stʌmək] *n* **1** ANAT estómago. **2** *fam (belly)* barriga; *(abdomen)* abdomen *m*, vientre *m*.
▷ *vt fig (bear, endure)* aguantar, soportar, tragar; *(eat, drink)* tolerar.
stomachache ['stʌməkeɪk] *n* dolor *m* de estómago.
stomp [stɒmp] *vi fam* pisar fuerte.
stone [stəʊn] *n* **1** *(gen)* piedra. **2** *(on grave)* lápida. **3** *(of fruit)* hueso. **4** MED cálculo, piedra. **5** GB *(measure of weight) unidad de peso que equivale a 6,348 kg*.
▷ *adj* de piedra, pétreo,-a. ● **Stone Age** Edad *f* de Piedra.
▷ *vt* **1** *(person)* apedrear, lapidar. **2** *(fruit)* deshuesar.
stone-cold [stəʊn'kəʊld] *adj* helado,-a.
stoned [stəʊnd] *adj* **1** *sl (on drugs)* ciego,-a, flipado,-a, colocado,-a. **2** *sl (drunk)* trompa, mamado,-a.
stonemason ['stəʊnmeɪsᵊn] *n (stone cutter)* cantero,-a; *(builder)* mampostero,-a.
stonewall ['stəʊnwɔːl] *vi* **1** *(gen)* poner obstáculos, utilizar tácticas obstruccionistas. **2** POL practicar el obstruccionismo. **3** *(in cricket)* jugar a la defensiva.
▷ *vt* obstaculizar, poner obstáculos a.
stoneware ['stəʊnweəʳ] *n* gres *m*, cerámica de gres.
stone-washed [stəʊn'wɒʃt] *adj* lavado,-a a la piedra.
stonework ['stəʊnwɜːk] *n* mampostería.
stony ['stəʊnɪ] *adj* **1** *(ground, beach)* pedregoso,-a. **2** *fig (look, silence)* frío,-a, glacial.
▲ *comp* **stonier**, *superl* **stoniest**.
stood [stʊd] *pt & pp* → **stand**.
stooge [stuːdʒ] *n* **1** THEAT comparsa *mf*. **2** *pej (person)* títere *mf*, pelele *mf*.
stool [stuːl] *n* **1** *(seat)* taburete *m*, banqueta. **2** MED *(faeces)* deposición *f*, heces *fpl*.
stoop¹ [stuːp] *n* US *(porch)* entrada.
stoop² [stuːp] *n (of person)* encorvamiento, encorvadura; *(of shoulders)* espaldas *fpl* encorvadas.
▷ *vi* **1** *(bend)* inclinarse (**down**, -), agacharse (**down**, -). **2** *(have a stoop)* andar encorvado,-a, ser cargado,-a de espaldas.
⊙ **to stoop to** *vt insep fig (lower OS)* rebajarse a.
stop [stɒp] *n* **1** *(halt)* parada, alto. **2** *(stopping place)* parada. **3** *(on journey)* parada; *(break, rest)* descanso, pausa. **4** *(punctuation mark)* punto; *(in telegram)* stop *m*. **5** MUS *(on organ)* registro; *(knob)* botón *m* de registro; *(on wind instrument)* llave *f*. **6** *(in camera)* diafragma *m*.
▷ *vt* **1** *(halt - vehicle, person)* parar, detener; *(- machine, ball)* parar. **2** *(end, interrupt - production)* parar, paralizar; *(- inflation, advance)* parar, contener; *(- conversation, play)* interrumpir; *(- pain, etc)* poner fin a, poner término a, acabar con. **3** *(pay, match, holidays)* suspender; *(cheque)* cancelar; *(money from wages)* retener. **4** *(cease)* dejar de, parar de. **5** *(prevent)* impedir, evitar. **6** *(block - hole)* tapar, taponar (**up**, -); *(- gap)* rellenar (**up**, -); *(- tooth)* empastar (**up**, -). **7** MUS *(string, key)* apretar; *(hole)* cubrir.
▷ *vi* **1** *(halt)* parar, pararse, detener, detenerse. **2** *(cease)* acabarse, terminar, cesar. **3** GB *fam (stay)* quedarse.
⊙ **to stop behind** *vi* quedarse.
⊙ **to stop by** *vi (visit)* pasar.
⊙ **to stop in** *vi* quedarse en casa, no salir.
⊙ **to stop off** *vi (interrupt journey)* parar.
⊙ **to stop out** *vi* no volver a casa.
⊙ **to stop over** *vi* **1** *(interrupt journey)* parar; *(overnight)* pasar la noche, hacer noche. **2** *(on flight)* hacer escala.
⊙ **to stop up** *vi (go to bed late)* no acostarse.
▷ *vt sep* taponar.
▲ *pt & pp* **stopped**, *ger* **stopping**.
stopcock ['stɒpkɒk] *n* llave *f* de paso.
stopgap ['stɒpgæp] *n (thing)* recurso provisional, medida provisional; *(person)* sustituto,-a.
stopover ['stɒpəʊvəʳ] *n (stop)* parada; *(on flight)* escala; *(stay)* estancia.
stoppage ['stɒpɪdʒ] *n* **1** *(of work)* paro, suspensión *f*; *(strike)* huelga. **2** *(in production, play)* interrupción *f*. **3** *(cancellation, withholding)* suspensión *f*. **4** *(blockage)* obstrucción *f*.
▷ *n pl* **stoppages** *(money from wages)* retenciones *fpl*, deducciones *fpl*.
stopper ['stɒpəʳ] *n* tapón *m*.
stopping ['stɒpɪŋ] *adj* GB *(of train)* que para en todas las estaciones.
stop-press [stɒp'pres] *adj (news)* de última hora.
stopwatch ['stɒpwɒtʃ] *n* cronómetro.
▲ *pl* **stopwatches**.
storage ['stɔːrɪdʒ] *n* **1** *(act)* almacenaje *m*, almacenamiento. **2** *(place)* almacén *m*, depósito, guardamuebles *m*. **3** *(cost)* (gastos *mpl* de) almacenaje *m*. **4** COMPUT almacenamiento.
store [stɔːʳ] *n* **1** *(supply - gen)* reserva, provisión *f*; *(- of wisdom, knowledge)* reserva; *(- of jokes, etc)* colección *f*. **2** *(warehouse)* almacén *m*, depósito. **3** US *(shop)* tienda.
▷ *vt* **1** *(put away)* almacenar (**up**, -); *(keep)* guardar; *(amass)* acumular, hacer acopio de. **2** COMPUT almacenar. **3** *(put in storage)* guardar, almacenar, mandar a un depósito. **4** *fig (trouble, etc)* ir acumulando (**up**, -), ir almacenando (**up**, -). **5** *(fill with supplies)* abastecer (**with**, de).
▷ *n pl* **stores** *(provisions)* provisiones *fpl*, víveres *mpl*; MIL *(supplies, equipment)* pertrechos *mpl*; *(place)* intendencia *f sing*.
storehouse ['stɔːhaʊs] *n* almacén *m*, depósito.
storekeeper ['stɔːkiːpəʳ] *n* US tendero,-a.
storeroom ['stɔːruːm] *n (gen)* almacén *m*, depósito; *(for food)* despensa.
storey ['stɔːrɪ] *n* piso, planta.
stork [stɔːk] *n* cigüeña.
storm [stɔːm] *n* **1** *(thunderstorm)* tormenta; *(at sea)* tempestad *f*, temporal *m*; *(with wind)* borrasca. **2** *fig (uproar)* revuelo, escándalo; *(of missiles, insults)* lluvia, torrente *m*. ● **storm cloud** nubarrón *m*. ‖ **storm petrel** petrel *m*, ave *f* de las tempestades. ‖ **storm warning** aviso de tormenta.
▷ *vt* **1** *(attack)* asaltar. **2** *(say angrily)* bramar.
▷ *vi* **1** *(go or move angrily)* andar airado,-a. **2** *(shout angrily)* echar pestes, vociferar, rabiar, despotricar.
stormy ['stɔːmɪ] *adj* **1** *(weather)* tormentoso,-a. **2** *fig (meeting, discussion)* acalorado,-a; *(relationship)* tormentoso,-a, con muchos altibajos.
▲ *comp* **stormier**, *superl* **stormiest**.
story¹ ['stɔːrɪ] *n* US → **storey**.
story² ['stɔːrɪ] *n* **1** *(gen)* historia; *(tale)* cuento, relato; *(account)* relato. **2** *(anecdote)* anécdota; *(joke)* chiste *m*. **3** *(rumour)* rumor *m*; *(lie)* mentira. **4** *(newspaper article)*

artículo; (newsworthy item) artículo de interés periodístico. 5 (story-line, narrative, plot) argumento, trama.
▲ pl stories.

storybook ['stɔːrɪbʊk] n libro de cuentos.

storyteller ['stɔːrɪteləʳ] n cuentista mf.

stout [staʊt] adj 1 euph (fat) corpulento,-a, robusto,-a. 2 (strong) sólido,-a, fuerte. 3 (determined, resolute) firme, resuelto,-a, tenaz; (brave) valiente.
▷ n (beer) cerveza negra.

stove[1] [stəʊv] n 1 (for heating) estufa. 2 (cooker) cocina; (cooking ring) hornillo; (oven) horno.

stove[2] [stəʊv] pp → stave.

stow [stəʊ] vt 1 (put away, store) guardar, poner, colocar. 2 MAR (cargo) estibar, arrumar, cargar.
⊙ **to stow away** vi (on ship, plane) viajar de polizón.

stowaway ['stəʊəweɪ] n polizón mf.

straddle ['strædᵊl] vt 1 (on horse, fence, etc) sentarse a horcajadas sobre. 2 (bridge, town) extenderse sobre.
▷ n SP (high-jumping technique) tijereta.

strafe [streɪf] vt bombardear.

straggle ['strægᵊl] vi 1 (spread untidily) extenderse, desparramarse; (grow) crecer desordenadamente. 2 (lag behind) rezagarse, ir rezagado,-a.

straggler ['strægᵊləʳ] n (person) rezagado,-a.

straggly ['strægᵊlɪ] adj (of town, houses) disperso,-a, esparcido,-a; (of plant) que crece desordenadamente; (of hair) desgreñado,-a.
▲ comp stragglier, superl straggliest.

straight [streɪt] adj 1 (not curved - gen) recto,-a; (- hair) liso,-a. 2 (level, upright) derecho,-a, recto,-a. 3 (tidy, neat) en orden, arreglado,-a. 4 (honest - person) honrado,-a, de confianza; (sincere) sincero,-a, franco,-a. 5 (direct - question) directo,-a; (- refusal, rejection) categórico,-a, rotundo,-a. 6 (correct, accurate) correcto,-a. 7 (consecutive) seguido,-a. 8 (drink) solo,-a. 9 (play, actor, etc) serio,-a, dramático,-a. 10 (person - conventional) convencional; (- heterosexual) heterosexual; (non-drug user) que no toma droga. 11 fam (not in debt) solvente.
▷ adv 1 (in a straight line) recto,-a. 2 (not in a curve) derecho,-a, recto,-a. 3 (directly) directamente. 4 (immediately) en seguida. 5 (frankly) francamente, con franqueza. 6 (clearly) claro, con claridad.
▷ n 1 SP (in race) recta. 2 (in cards) escalera. 3 fam (conventional person) carca mf; (heterosexual) heterosexual mf; (non-drug user) persona que no se droga. ■ **straight away** en seguida. | **straight off** en el acto. | **straight up** en serio. | **to go straight** (criminal) reformarse.

straightaway [streɪt'weɪ] adv en seguida, inmediatamente.

straighten ['streɪtᵊn] vt 1 (wire) enderezar; (- tie, skirt, picture) poner bien, poner recto,-a; (- hair) estirar, alisar. 2 (tidy) ordenar (**up**, -), arreglar (**up**, -).
▷ vi (road) hacerse recto,-a.
⊙ **to straighten out** vt sep 1 (problem) resolver, solucionar; (confusion, misunderstanding) aclarar; (affair) arreglar. 2 (person) resolver los problemas de.
⊙ **to straighten up** vi (person) ponerse derecho,-a.

straight-faced ['steɪt'feɪst] adj serio,-a, sin reírse.

straightforward [streɪt'fɔːwəd] adj 1 (honest) honrado,-a; (sincere, open) sincero,-a, franco,-a, abierto,-a. 2 (simple, easy) sencillo,-a, simple; (clear) claro,-a.

strain[1] [streɪn] n 1 (race, breed) raza; (descent) linaje m; (of plant, virus) cepa. 2 (streak) vena.

strain[2] [streɪn] n 1 PHYS (tension) tensión f; (pressure) presión f; (weight) peso. 2 (stress, pressure) tensión f, estrés m; (effort) esfuerzo; (exhaustion) agotamiento. 3 (tension) tirantez f, tensión f. 4 MED torcedura, esguince m.
▷ vt 1 (stretch) estirar, tensar. 2 (damage, weaken - muscle) torcer(se), hacerse un esguince en; (- back) hacerse daño en; (- voice, eyes) forzar; (ears) aguzar; (- heart) cansar. 3 (stretch - patience, nerves, credulity) poner a prueba; (- resources) estirar al máximo; (- relations) someter a demasiada tensión, crear tirantez en. 4 (filter - liquid) colar; (- vegetables, rice) escurrir.
▷ vi (make great efforts) hacer un gran esfuerzo.
▷ n pl **strains** MUS son m sing, compás m sing.
⊙ **to strain at** vt insep tirar de.

strained [streɪnd] adj 1 (tense, unfriendly) tenso,-a, tirante; (unnatural, forced, artificial) forzado,-a. 2 (stressed, anxious) tenso,-a, estresado,-a; (tires) cansado,-a; (eyes, voice) forzado,-a. ■ **strained muscle** esguince m.

strainer ['streɪnəʳ] n colador m.

strait [streɪt] n GEOG estrecho.
▷ n pl **straits** (difficulties) aprietos mpl, apuros mpl.

straitjacket ['streɪtdʒækɪt] n 1 camisa de fuerza. 2 fig control m, limitaciones fpl.

strait-laced [streɪt'leɪst] adj pej puritano,-a, remilgado,-a, mojigato,-a.

strand[1] [strænd] n lit (beach) playa.

strand[2] [strænd] n 1 (of thread) hebra, hilo; (of rope, string) ramal m; (of hair) pelo; (of pearls) sarta. 2 fig (of story, argument) hilo, línea.

strand[3] [strænd] vt 1 MAR (ship, whale, fish) varar. 2 fig (person) abandonar. ■ **to be (left) stranded** 1 (boat, etc) quedar varado. 2 (person) quedarse colgado,-a. | **to leave** SB **stranded** dejar a ALGN tirado,-a.

strange [streɪndʒ] adj 1 (odd, bizarre) extraño,-a, raro,-a. 2 (unknown) desconocido,-a; (unfamiliar) nuevo,-a. ■ **strange to say** aunque parezca mentira.

strangely ['streɪndʒlɪ] adv extrañamente.

stranger ['streɪndʒəʳ] n (unknown person) extraño,-a, desconocido,-a; (outsider) forastero,-a.

strangle ['stræŋgᵊl] vt 1 (kill) estrangular. 2 fig (stifle) sofocar, ahogar.

stranglehold ['stræŋgᵊlhəʊld] n 1 SP (wrestling) llave f al cuello. 2 pej (firm control) poder m, dominio.

strangulate ['stræŋgjəleɪt] vt MED estrangular.

strap [stræp] n (on watch, camera) correa; (on bag) asa; (on shoe) tira; (on dress, etc) tirante m.
▷ vt 1 (fasten) atar con correa. 2 (bandage) vendar.
▲ pt & pp strapped, ger strapping.

strapless ['stræpləs] adj sin tirantes.

strapping ['stræpɪŋ] adj (big, strong) fornido,-a, robusto,-a.

stratagem ['strætədʒəm] n estratagema.

strategic [str'tiːdʒɪk] adj estratégico,-a.

strategist ['strætədʒɪst] n estratega mf.

strategy ['strætədʒɪ] n estrategia.
▲ pl strategies.

stratosphere ['strætəsfɪəʳ] n estratosfera.

stratum ['strɑːtəm] n 1 GEOL estrato. 2 (level, class) estrato, nivel m.
▲ pl strata ['strɑːtə].

straw [strɔː] *n* 1 *(dried stalk(s))* paja. 2 *(for drinking)* paja, pajita.
▷ *adj* de paja.

strawberry ['strɔːbᵊrɪ] *n (gen)* fresa; *(large)* fresón *m*. ● **strawberry blonde** 1 *(colour)* rubio rojizo. 2 *(person)* pelirroja. ‖ **strawberry jam** mermelada de fresa. ‖ **strawberry tree** madroño.
▲ *pl* **strawberries**.

stray [streɪ] *adj* 1 *(lost)* perdido,-a, extraviado,-a; *(animal)* callejero,-a. 2 *(isolated, odd)* perdido,-a.
▷ *n (animal)* animal *m* extraviado.
▷ *vi* 1 *(get lost)* extraviarse, perderse; *(wander away)* desviarse, apartarse, alejarse; *(from group)* separarse, apartarse, alejarse. 2 *fig (digress, wander)* divagar, apartarse del tema, desviarse del tema.

streak [striːk] *n* 1 *(line - gen)* raya, lista; *(- in mineral)* veta, filón *m*, vena; *(- in hair)* mecha; *(- in meat)* veta, nervio. 2 *(element of genius, madness, etc)* vena. 3 *(period)* racha.
▷ *vt (mark with streaks)* rayar, surcar (**with**, de).
▷ *vi* 1 *(move fast)* pasar como un rayo. 2 *(run naked)* correr desnudo,-a por un lugar público. ● **streak of lightning** rayo, relámpago.

streaky ['striːkɪ] *adj (hair)* con mechas desiguales; *(paint)* no uniforme. ● **streaky bacon** GB tocino entreverado.
▲ *comp* **streakier**, *superl* **streakiest**.

stream [striːm] *n* 1 *(brook)* arroyo, riachuelo. 2 *(current)* corriente *f*. 3 *(flow of liquid)* flujo, chorro, río; *(of blood, air)* chorro; *(of lava, tears)* torrente *m*; *(of light)* raudal *m*. 4 *fig (of people)* oleada, torrente *m*; *(of vehicles, traffic)* desfile *m* continuo, caravana; *(of abuse, excuses, insults)* torrente *m*, sarta. 5 GB *(class, pupils)* clase *f*, grupo, nivel *m (de alumnos seleccionados según su nivel académico)*.
▷ *vi* 1 *(flow, pour out)* manar, correr, chorrear; *(gush)* salir a chorros. 2 *fig (people, vehicles, etc)* desfilar. 3 *(hair, banner, scarf)* ondear.
▷ *vt* 1 *(liquid)* derramar. 2 GB poner en grupos según su nivel académico. ● **stream of consciousness** monólogo interior.

streamer ['striːməʳ] *n (decoration)* serpentina; *(flag)* banderín *m*.

streamline ['striːmlaɪn] *n (contour)* línea aerodinámica.
▷ *vt* 1 *(car)* aerodinamizar. 2 *(system, method, organization)* racionalizar.

streamlined ['striːmlaɪnd] *adj* 1 *(car)* de líneas aerodinámicas. 2 *(organization)* racionalizado,-a.

street [striːt] *n* calle *f*. ■ **at street level** a nivel de la calle. ‖ **to walk the streets** 1 *(homeless)* estar sin techo. 2 *(prostitute)* trabajar la calle. ● **one-way street** calle de sentido único. ‖ **street corner** esquina. ‖ **street directory** callejero. ‖ **street lighting** alumbrado público. ‖ **street plan** plano de la ciudad. ‖ **street market** mercadillo. ‖ **street value** valor *m* (en el mercado).

streetcar ['ʃtriːtkɑː] *n* US tranvía.

streetlamp ['striːtlæmp] *n* farol *m*, farola.

streetlight ['striːtlaɪt] *n* farol *m*, farola.

streetwise ['striːtwaɪz] *adj fam* espabilado,-a, despabilado,-a, avispado,-a.

strength [streŋθ] *n* 1 *(of person - physical)* fuerza, fuerzas *fpl*, fortaleza; *(- stamina)* resistencia, aguante *m*. 2 *(intellectual, spiritual)* fortaleza, entereza, firmeza. 3 *(o machine, object)* resistencia; *(of wind, current)* fuerza *(of light, sound, magnet, lens)* potencia. 4 *(of solution* concentración *f*; *(of drug)* potencia; *(of alcohol)* graduación *f*. 5 *(of currency)* valor *m*, fortaleza; *(of economy)* solidez *f*, fortaleza. 6 *(of argument, evidence, story* fuerza, validez *f*, credibilidad *f*; *(of emotion, conviction colour)* intensidad *f*; *(of protest)* energía. 7 *(strong point* punto fuerte, virtud *f*; *(ability, capability)* capacidad *(advantage)* ventaja. 8 *(power, influence)* poder *m*, potencia. 9 *(force in numbers)* fuerza numérica, número

strengthen ['streŋθᵊn] *vt* 1 *(wall, glass, defence, etc)* reforzar; *(muscle)* fortalecer. 2 *(character, faith, love)* fortalecer; *(support)* aumentar; *(relationship, ties)* consolidar, fortalecer; *(resolve, determination)* redoblar intensificar.
▷ *vi* 1 *(muscle)* fortalecerse. 2 *(economy, currency)* reforzarse, fortalecerse; *(relationship)* consolidarse, reforzarse, fortalecerse; *(support, opposition, feeling* intensificarse, aumentar.

strenuous ['strenjuəs] *adj* 1 *(requiring effort)* extenuante, fatigoso,-a, agotador,-ra. 2 *(denial)* enérgico,-a vigoroso,-a; *(protest)* vehemente; *(opposition)* tenaz *(supporter)* acérrimo,-a.

stress [stres] *n* 1 MED tensión *f* (nerviosa), estrés *m*. *(pressure)* presión *f*, tensión *f*. 3 TECH tensión *f*. 4 *(emphasis)* hincapié *m* (**on**, en), énfasis *m* (**on**, en). 5 LIN *(on word)* acento (tónico). ● **stress mark** acento.
▷ *vt* 1 *(emphasize)* hacer hincapié en, poner énfasis en subrayar, enfatizar. 2 LING *(word)* acentuar.

stressed [strest] *adj* 1 MED *(person)* estresado,-a. 2 PHY *(object)* tensado,-a.

stressful ['stresfʊl] *adj* estresante, de mucho estrés.

stretch [stretʃ] *n* 1 *(of land, water)* extensión *f*; *(of road* tramo, trecho. 2 *(elasticity)* elasticidad *f*. 3 *(act c stretching)* estiramiento. 4 *(period of time)* período tiempo, intervalo; *(in prison)* condena. 5 SP *(of race track)* recta.
▷ *vt* 1 *(extend - elastic, clothes, rope)* estirar; *(- canvas)* extender; *(- shoes)* ensanchar; *(- arm, leg)* alargar, estirar extender; *(- wings)* desplegar, extender. 2 *(make demands on, made to use all abilities)* exigir a. 3 *(strain money, resources)* estirar, emplear al máximo; *(- patience)* abusar; *(- meaning)* forzar, distorsionar.
▷ *vi* 1 *(elastic)* estirarse; *(fabric)* dar de sí; *(shoes)* ensancharse, dar de sí; *(person, animal - gen)* estirarse; *(person - when tired)* desperezarse. 2 *(extend - land, sea, etc* extenderse (**out**, -); *(- in time)* alargarse, prolongarse 3 *(reach)* llegar (**to**, para), alcanzar (**to**, para).
▷ *adj (material, jeans, etc)* elástico,-a.
⊙ **to stretch out** *vi (person - gen)* estirarse; *(- lie down,* tumbarse.
▷ *vt sep* 1 *(arm, leg)* alargar, estirar, extender. 2 *(money resources)* estirar.

stretcher ['stretʃəʳ] *n* camilla.

stretchmarks ['stretʃmɑːks] *n* estrías *fpl*.

stretchy ['stretʃɪ] *adj* elástico,-a.
▲ *comp* **stretchier**, *superl* **stretchier**.

strew [struː] *vt lit (scatter)* esparcir, desparramar; *(li scattered)* sembrar, cubrir.
▲ *pt* **strewed**, *pp* **strewed** o **strewn** [struːn].

strict [strɪkt] *adj* 1 *(severe - person)* severo,-a, estricto,-a; *(- discipline)* riguroso,-a, severo,-a, estricto,-a; *(- rule, law, order, etc)* estricto,-a, riguroso,-a, rígido,-a. 2 *(exact, precise)* estricto,-a, riguroso,-a; *(complete, total)* absoluto,-a.

strictly ['strɪktlɪ] *adv* 1 *(severely)* severamente, estrictamente, de manera estricta. 2 *(rigorously, rigidly)* estrictamente; *(categorically)* terminantemente. 3 *(exactly, precisely)* estrictamente, exactamente; *(completely)* totalmente, del todo, absolutamente. 4 *(exclusively)* exclusivamente. ■ **strictly speaking** en realidad.

strictness ['strɪktnəs] *n (severity)* severidad *f*; *(rigorousness)* rigurosidad *f*, rigidez *f*.

stride [straɪd] *n* 1 *(long step)* zancada; *(gait)* paso, manera de andar. 2 *(advance, development)* progresos *mpl*.
▷ *n pl* **strides** *fam (trousers)* pantalón *m sing*, pantalones *mpl*.
▷ *vi* andar a zancadas.
▲ *pt* **strode** [strəʊd], *pp* **stridden** ['strɪdᵊn].

stridden ['strɪdən] *pp* → **stride**.

strident ['straɪdᵊnt] *adj (voice, sound)* estridente; *(protest)* fuerte.

strife [straɪf] *n* conflictos *mpl*, luchas *fpl*: **industrial strife** *conflictos laborales*.

strike [straɪk] *n* 1 *(by workers, students, etc)* huelga. 2 SP *(blow - gen)* golpe *m*; *(- in tenpin bowling)* pleno; *(- in baseball)* strike *m*. 3 *(find)* hallazgo; *(of oil, gold, etc)* descubrimiento. 4 MIL ataque *m*: **air strike** *ataque aéreo*.
▷ *vt* 1 *(hit)* pegar, golpear. 2 *(knock against, collide with)* dar contra, chocar contra; *(ball, stone)* pegar contra, dar contra; *(lightning, bullet, torpedo)* alcanzar. 3 *(disaster, earthquake)* golpear, sobrevenir; *(disease)* atacar, golpear. 4 *(gold, oil)* descubrir, encontrar, dar con; *(track, path)* dar con. 5 *(coin, medal)* acuñar. 6 *(match)* encender. 7 *(of clock)* dar, tocar. 8 MUS *(note)* dar; *(chord)* tocar. 9 *(bargain, deal)* cerrar, hacer; *(balance)* encontrar, hallar; *(agreement)* llegar a. 10 *(pose, attitude)* adoptar. 11 *(give impression)* parecer, dar la impresión de. 12 *(occur to)* ocurrírsele a; *(remember)* acordarse de. 13 *(render)* dejar. 14 *(cause fear, terror, worry)* infundir. 15 *(take down - sail, flag)* arriar; *(- tent, set)* desmontar. 16 *(cutting)* plantar.
▷ *vi* 1 *(attack - troops, animal, etc)* atacar; *(- disaster, misfortune)* sobrevenir, ocurrir; *(- disease)* atacar, golpear; *(- lightning)* alcanzar, caer. 2 *(workers, etc)* declararse en huelga, hacer huelga. 3 *(clock)* dar la hora.
⊙ **to strike back** *vi* 1 *(gen)* devolver el golpe. 2 MIL contraatacar.
⊙ **to strike down** *vt sep (by illness, disease)* abatir, fulminar.
⊙ **to strike off** *vt sep* 1 *(name from list)* tachar. 2 JUR *(doctor, lawyer, etc)* inhabilitar para ejercer.
⊙ **to strike on** *vt insep (discover)* dar con, encontrar.
⊙ **to strike out** *vt sep (remove, cross out)* tachar.
▷ *vi* 1 *(attack, hit out)* arremeter (**at**, contra). 2 *(set off)* emprender el camino.
⊙ **to strike up** *vt insep (friendship)* entablar, trabar; *(conversation)* entablar, iniciar.
▷ *vi (band)* empezar a tocar.
▲ *pt & pp* **struck** [strʌk].

strikebound ['straɪkbaʊnd] *adj* paralizado,-a por una huelga.

strikebreaker ['straɪkbreɪkəʳ] *n* esquirol *mf*, rompehuelgas *mf*.

striker ['straɪkəʳ] *n* 1 *(worker)* huelguista *mf*. 2 SP *(football)* delantero,-a; *(cricket)* bateador,-ra.

striking ['straɪkɪŋ] *adj* 1 *(eye-catching)* llamativo,-a; *(stunning)* atractivo,-a. 2 *(similarity, resemblance)* sorprendente, asombroso,-a; *(feature, etc)* impresionante, destacado,-a. 3 *(on strike)* en huelga.

string [strɪŋ] *n* 1 *(cord)* cuerda, cordel *m*; *(lace)* cordón *m*; *(of puppet)* hilo. 2 *(on instrument, racket)* cuerda. 3 *(of garlic, onions)* ristra; *(of pearls, beads)* sarta, hilo. 4 *(of vehicles)* fila, hilera; *(of hotels)* cadena; *(of events)* serie *f*, sucesión *f*; *(of lies, complaints)* sarta; *(of insults)* retahíla.
▷ *vt* 1 *(beads)* ensartar, enhebrar. 2 *(guitar, racket)* encordar. 3 *(beans)* quitar la hebra a.
▷ *n pl* **the strings** MUS los instrumentos *mpl* de cuerda. ● **string orchestra** orquesta de cuerda. ‖ **string quartet** cuarteto de cuerda.
⊙ **to string along** *vi (accompany)* pegarse, venir.
▷ *vt sep (mislead)* tomar el pelo a.
▲ *pt & pp* **strung** [strʌŋ].
⊙ **to string out** *vt sep (spread in a line)* colocar a intervalos.
⊙ **to string together** *vt sep (words, phrases)* ensartar, hilar.
⊙ **to string up** *vt sep (hang)* colgar.

stringed [strɪŋd] *adj (instrument)* de cuerda.

stringent ['strɪndʒᵊnt] *adj* 1 *(laws, rules, conditions)* severo,-a, estricto,-a, riguroso,-a. 2 FIN severo,-a, difícil.

strip¹ [strɪp] *vt* 1 *(person)* desnudar, quitarle la ropa a; *(bed)* quitar la ropa de; *(room, house)* vaciar; *(wallpaper, paint)* quitar; *(leaves, bark)* arrancar. 2 *(property, rights, titles)* despojar (**of**, de). 3 *(engine)* desarmar, desmontar (**down**, -); *(ship)* desaparejar.
▷ *vi (undress)* desnudarse (**off**, -), quitarse la ropa; *(perform striptease)* hacer un strip-tease.
▲ *pt & pp* **stripped**, *ger* **stripping**.
▷ *n (striptease)* strip-tease *m*.

strip² [strɪp] *n* 1 *(of paper, leather)* tira; *(of land)* franja; *(of metal)* tira, cinta. 2 SP *(colours, kit)* equipo. 3 *(airstrip)* pista (de aterrizaje). 4 [Also **strip (cartoon)**.] historieta, tira cómica. ● **strip lighting** alumbrado fluorescente. ‖ **strip mining** US explotación *f* a cielo abierto.

stripe [straɪp] *n* 1 *(gen)* raya, lista. 2 MIL galón *m*. 3 *(kind, type)* tipo, clase *f*.
▷ *vt* pintar a rayas, dibujar a rayas.

striped [straɪpt] *adj* rayado,-a, a rayas: **a striped shirt** *una camisa a rayas*.

stripy ['staɪpɪ] *adj* rayado,-a, a rayas.
▲ *comp* **stripier**, *superl* **stripiest**.

strive [straɪv] *vi* esforzarse, procurar.
▲ *pt* **strove** [strəʊv], *pp* **striven** ['strɪvᵊn].

striven ['strɪvən] *pt* → **strive**.

strode [strəʊd] *pt* → **stride**.

stroke [strəʊk] *n* 1 *(blow)* golpe *m*. 2 *(caress)* caricia. 3 SP *(in tennis, cricket, golf)* golpe *m*, jugada; *(in billiards)* tacada; *(in rowing)* palada; *(in swimming - movement)* brazada; *(- style)* estilo. 4 SP *(oarsman)* cabo. 5 *(of pen)* trazo; *(of brush)* pincelada. 6 *(of bell)* campanada. 7 *(of engine)* tiempo; *(of piston)* carrera. 8 MED ataque *m* de apoplejía, derrame *m* cerebral. 9 *(oblique)* barra (oblicua).
▷ *vt* 1 *(caress)* acariciar. 2 *(ball)* dar un golpe a.

stroll [strəʊl] *n* paseo, vuelta.
▷ *vi* pasear, dar un paseo, dar una vuelta.
stroller ['strəʊlər] *n* 1 *(pushchair)* cochecito, sillita de niño. 2 *(person)* paseante *mf*.
strong [strɒŋ] *adj* 1 *(physically - person)* fuerte; *(- consitution)* robusto,-a. 2 *(material, furniture, shoes, etc)* fuerte, resistente. 3 *(country, army)* poderoso,-a, fuerte. 4 *(beliefs, views, principles)* firme; *(faith)* firme, sólido,-a; *(support)* mucho, firme. 5 *(argument, evidence)* contundente, convincente; *(influence)* grande; *(protest)* enérgico,-a. 6 *(colour)* fuerte, intenso,-a, vivo,-a; *(smell, food, drink)* fuerte; *(tea, coffee)* fuerte, cargado,-a; *(light)* brillante. 7 *(resemblance, accent)* fuerte, marcado,-a. 8 *(chance, likelihood, probability)* bueno,-a. 9 *(wind, current)* fuerte. 10 *(good - team)* fuerte; *(- cast)* sólido,-a. 11 *(currency, etc)* fuerte.
▷ *adv* fuerte.
strong-arm ['strɒŋɑːm] *adj* de mano dura.
strongbox ['strɒŋbɒks] *n* caja fuerte.
stronghold ['strɒŋhəʊld] *n* 1 MIL fortaleza. 2 *fig* baluarte *m*.
strongly ['strɒŋlɪ] *adv* 1 *(solidly)* sólidamente. 2 *(firmly)* firmemente; *(completely)* totalmente, profundamente; *(fervently)* con fervor, con ardor; *(forcefully)* enérgicamente, con insistencia. 3 *(intensely)* mucho, muy.
strong-minded [strɒŋ'maɪndɪd] *adj* decidido,-a.
strongroom ['strɒŋruːm] *n* cámara acorazada.
strong-willed ['strɒŋ'wɪld] *adj* tenaz, decidido,-a, obstinado,-a.
stroppy ['strɒpɪ] *adj* GB *fam* borde, de mala uva.
▲ *comp* **stroppier**, *superl* **stroppiest**.
strove [strəʊv] *pt* ⟶ **strive**.
struck [strʌk] *pt & pp* ⟶ **strike**.
structural ['strʌktʃərəl] *adj (gen)* estructural. ● **structural engineer** ingeniero,-a de estructuras.
structure ['strʌktʃər] *n* 1 *(organization, composition)* estructura. 2 *(thing constructed)* construcción *f*; *(building)* edificio.
▷ *vt (arguemnt, essay, report, etc)* estructurar; *(event)* planificar.
struggle ['strʌgəl] *n (gen)* lucha; *(physical fight)* pelea, forcejeo.
▷ *vi* 1 *(fight)* luchar; *(physically)* forcejear. 2 *(strive)* luchar (**for**, por), esforzarse (**for**, por); *(suffer)* pasar apuros; *(have difficulty)* costar, tener problemas. 3 *(move with difficulty)* con dificultad.
struggling ['strʌglɪŋ] *adj (with problems)* en apuros, que tiene problemas.
strum [strʌm] *vt* rasguear.
▷ *vi* rasguear (**on**, -).
▲ *pt & pp* **strummed**, *ger* **strumming**.
strung [strʌŋ] *pt & pp* ⟶ **string**. ■ **to be highly strung** estar muy nervioso,-a, estar muy tenso,-a.
strut [strʌt] *n* 1 ARCH *(rod, bar)* puntal *m*, riostra. 2 *(way of walking)* contoneo, pavoneo.
▷ *vi* pavonearse, contonearse.
▲ *pt & pp* **strutted**, *ger* **strutting**.
stub [stʌb] *n (of cigarette)* colilla; *(of pencil, candle)* cabo; *(of cheque, etc)* matriz *f*.
▷ *vt* darse un golpe.
▲ *pt & pp* **stubbed**, *ger* **stubbing**.
⊙ **to stub out** *vt sep* apagar.

stubble ['stʌbəl] *n* 1 *(in field)* rastrojo. 2 *(on chin)* barb incipiente.
stubborn ['stʌbən] *adj* 1 *(person, animal)* terco,-a, tes tarudo,-a, tozudo,-a, obstinado,-a; *(refusal, resistanc* obcecado,-a. 2 *(stain, cough, etc)* rebelde.
stubbornly ['stʌbənlɪ] *adv* tercamente, cabezuda mente.
stubby ['stʌbɪ] *adj* corto,-a y rechoncho,-a.
▲ *comp* **stubbier**, *superl* **stubbiest**.
stucco ['stʌkəʊ] *n* estuco.
▲ *pl* **stuccoes** o **stuccos**.
stuck [stʌk] *pt & pp* ⟶ **stick**.
▷ *adj* 1 *(unable to move)* atascado,-a. 2 *(trapped)* atrapa do,-a; *(in routine)* estancado,-a. 3 *fam (stumped)* atas cado,-a; *(in difficulties)* en apuros.
stuck-up [stʌk'ʌp] *adj fam* creído,-a, estirado,-a.
stud[1] [stʌd] *n* 1 *(on shirt)* gemelo; *(earring)* pendiente *(en forma de bolita)*. 2 *(on football boots)* taco; *(on clothin belt)* tachuela, tachón *m*; *(on furniture)* tachuela; *(o shield)* tachón *m*; *(in road)* clavo.
▷ *vt* 1 *(decorate - with studs)* tachonar (**with**, de); *(- with jew els)* incrustar (**with**, de). 2 *fig (dot)* salpicar (**with**, de).
▲ *pt & pp* **studded**, *ger* **studding**.
stud[2] [stʌd] *n* 1 *(animal)* semental *m*. 2 *pej (man)* se mental *m*. ● **stud farm** cuadra.
studded ['stʌdɪd] *adj (sky)* tachonado,-a; *(speech, e* salpicado,-a; *(crown)* con incrustaciones.
student ['stjuːdənt] *n* 1 *(university)* estudiante *mf*, un versitario,-a; *(school)* alumno,-a. 2 *fml (scholar)* estu dioso,-a.
▷ *adj* estudiantil.
studied ['stʌdɪd] *adj (style, etc)* estudiado,-a, afect do,-a, falso,-a; *(insult, indifference, etc)* calculado,-a.
studio ['stjuːdɪəʊ] *n* 1 *(TV, radio)* estudio. 2 *(artist's)* e tudio, taller *m*.
▲ *pl* **studios**.
▷ *n pl* **studios** CINEM estudios *mpl*.
studious ['stjuːdɪəs] *adj* 1 *(fond of studying)* estudios -a, aplicado,-a. 2 *fml (careful)* esmerado,-a; *(delibera* deliberado,-a.
studiously ['stjuːdɪəslɪ] *adv* deliberadamente, cuid dosamente.
study ['stʌdɪ] *n* 1 *(act of studying)* estudio; *(investigatio research)* investigación *f*, estudio. 2 *(room)* despach estudio.
▲ *pl* **studies**.
▷ *vt* 1 *(gen)* estudiar; *(university subject)* estudiar, curs *(investigate, research)* estudiar, investigar. 2 *(scrutini* estudiar, examinar.
▷ *vi* estudiar.
▲ *pt & pp* **studied**, *ger* **studying**.
▷ *n pl* **studies** *(work)* estudios *mpl*; *(subjects)* estudi *mpl*, asignaturas *fpl*.
stuff [stʌf] *n* 1 *fam (matter, material, substance)* mater material *m*. 2 *fam (things, possesions)* cosas *fpl*, trast *mpl*. 3 *fam (content)* cuento, rollo, cosas *fpl*.
▷ *vt* 1 *(fill - container, bag, box)* llenar (**with**, de); *(- cushic toy, food)* rellenar (**with**, de); *(- hole)* tapar. 2 *(dead a mal)* disecar. 3 *(push carelessly, shove)* meter, poner. *fam (beat, thrash)* dar una paliza a. 5 *sl (sod)* meter.
stuffed [stʌft] *adj* 1 *(full)* relleno,-a; *(crammed)* atib rrado,-a. 2 *(animal)* disecado,-a.

stuffing ['stʌfɪŋ] *n* relleno.

stuffy ['stʌfɪ] *adj* **1** *(room)* mal ventilado,-a; *(atmosphere)* cargado,-a. **2** *(person)* estirado,-a, remilgado,-a; *(institution)* tradicional; *(ideas, manners)* formal, serio,-a, convencional.
▲ *comp* **stuffier**, *superl* **stuffiest**.

stumble ['stʌmbᵊl] *n* tropezón *m*, traspié *m*, trompicón *m*.
▷ *vi* **1** *(trip)* tropezar (**on/over**, con), dar un traspié. **2** *(walk unsteadily)* tambalearse. **3** *(while speaking)* atrancarse, atascarse.
⊙ **to stumble across / stumble on** *vt insep* dar con, tropezar con.

stumbling block ['stʌmbᵊlɪŋblɒk] *n* escollo.

stump [stʌmp] *n* **1** *(of tree)* tocón *m*, cepa; *(of pencil, candle)* cabo; *(of arm, leg)* muñón *m*. **2** SP *(cricket)* estaca, palo.
▷ *vt fam (baffle)* desconcertar, confundir, dejar perplejo,-a a.
▷ *vi (move heavily)* pisar fuerte.
⊙ **to stump up** *vt insep fam* soltar, aflojar, apoquinar.
▷ *vi fam* soltar la pasta, aflojar la mosca.

stun [stʌn] *vt* **1** *(make unconscious)* dejar sin sentido; *(daze)* aturdir, atontar, pasmar. **2** *(surprise)* sorprender, dejar atónito,-a, dejar pasmado,-a; *(shock)* atolondrar, aturdir, dejar anonadado,-a.
▲ *pt & pp* **stunned**, *ger* **stunning**.

stung [stʌŋ] *pt & pp* → **sting**.

stunk [stʌŋk] *pt & pp* → **stink**.

stunning ['stʌnɪŋ] *adj* **1** *(surprising)* alucinante, apabullante; *(shocking)* asombroso,-a. **2** *(beautiful, impressive)* impresionante, imponente, fenomenal.

stunt[1] [stʌnt] *vt (growth)* atrofiar.

stunt[2] [stʌnt] *n* **1** *(dangerous act)* proeza; *(in film)* escena peligrosa. **2** *(trick)* truco, maniobra.

stunted ['stʌntɪd] *adj (tree, body)* raquítico,-a; *(growth)* atrofiado,-a.

stupefy ['stjʊːpɪfaɪ] *vt* **1** *(alcohol, drugs)* atontar, aturdir, aletargar. **2** *(amaze)* dejar pasmado,-a, dejar estupefacto,-a.
▲ *pt & pp* **stupefied**, *ger* **stupefying**.

stupendous [stjʊː'pendəs] *adj* **1** *(wonderful)* estupendo,-a, fabuloso,-a, formidable. **2** *(enormous)* tremendo,-a; *(unusual)* extraordinario,-a, increíble.

stupid ['stjʊːpɪd] *adj* **1** tonto,-a, bobo,-a, imbécil, estúpido,-a. **2** *(senseless)* atontado,-a. **3** *fam (annoying)* maldito,-a.
▷ *n* tonto,-a, imbécil *mf*.
▲ *comp* **stupider**, *superl* **stupidest**.

stupidity [stjʊː'pɪdɪtɪ] *n* estupidez *f*, tontería.

stupidly ['stjʊːpɪdlɪ] *adv* estúpidamente, tontamente.

stupor ['stjʊːpəʳ] *n* estupor *m*.

sturdy ['stɜːdɪ] *adj* **1** *(strong)* robusto,-a, fuerte; *(solid)* sólido,-a. **2** *(opposition, resistence, defence)* enérgico,-a, férreo,-a, tenaz, inquebrantable.
▲ *comp* **sturdier**, *superl* **sturdiest**.

sturgeon ['stɜːdʒᵊn] *n* esturión *m*.

stutter ['stʌtəʳ] *n* tartamudeo.
▷ *vi* tartamudear.
▷ *vt* decir tartamudeando, balbucear.

sty[1] [staɪ] *n (for pigs)* pocilga.

sty[2] [staɪ] *n* → **stye**.
▲ *pl* **sties**.

stye [staɪ] *n (in eye)* orzuelo.

style [staɪl] *n* **1** *(gen)* estilo. **2** *(type, model)* modelo, diseño. **3** *(of hair)* peinado. **4** *(fashion)* moda. **5** *fml (correct title)* título. **6** BOT estilo.
▷ *vt* **1** *(gen)* diseñar; *(hair)* peinar. **2** *fml (name, title)* llamar.

styling ['staɪlɪŋ] *n* diseño.

stylish ['staɪlɪʃ] *adj* **1** *(elegant)* elegante, con mucho estilo. **2** *(fashionable)* a la moda, de última moda.

stylist ['staɪlɪst] *n* **1** *(hairdresser)* estilista *mf*, peluquero,-a. **2** *(writer)* estilista *mf*.

stylized ['staɪlaɪʒd] *adj* estilizado,-a.

stylus ['staɪləs] *n* **1** *(of record player)* aguja. **2** *(for writing)* estilo.
▲ *pl* **styluses** o **styli**.

stymie ['staɪmɪ] *vt fam* frustrar.
▷ *n fam* apuro, lío.

suave [swɑːv] *adj (charming, polite)* afable, cortés; *(slick, ingratiating)* zalamero,-a.

sub [sʌb] *n* **1** *(submarine)* submarino. **2** SP *(substitute)* sustituto,-a, suplente *mf*. **3** *(subscription)* cuota, subscripción *f*, suscripción *f*. **4** *(subeditor)* redactor,-ra. **5** GB *(advance from wages)* anticipo.
▷ *vi (act as substitute)* sustituir (**for**, a).
▷ *vt* **1** GB *(give an advance)* anticipar, dar un anticipo. **2** *(subedit)* corregir, revisar.
▲ *pt & pp* **subbed**, *ger* **subbing**.

sub- [sʌb] *pref* sub.

subcommittee ['sʌbkəmɪtɪ] *n* subcomisión *f*, subcomité *m*.

subconscious [sʌb'kɒnʃəs] *adj* subconsciente.
▷ *n* **the subconscious** el subconsciente *m*.

subconsciously [sʌb'kɒnʃəslɪ] *adv* de forma subconsciente, de manera subconsciente.

subcontinent [sʌb'kɒntɪnənt] *n* subcontinente *m*.

subcontract [*(n)* sʌb'kɒntrækt, *(vb)* sʌbkən'trækt] *n* subcontrato.
▷ *vt* subcontratar (**to**, a).

subculture ['sʌbkʌltʃəʳ] *n* subcultura.

subdivide [sʌbdɪ'vaɪd] *vt* subdividir (**into**, en).

subdue [səb'djʊː] *vt* **1** *(nation, people)* someter, dominar, sojuzgar. **2** *(feelings, passions, etc)* contener, dominar. **3** *(sound, colour, light)* atenuar, suavizar.

subdued [səb'djʊːd] *adj* **1** *(person, emotion)* callado,-a, apagado,-a. **2** *(tone, voice)* bajo,-a; *(light)* tenue; *(colour)* apagado,-a.

subeditor [sʌb'edɪtəʳ] *n* redactor,-ra.

subgroup ['sʌbgrʊːp] *n* subgrupo.

subheading [sʌb'hedɪŋ] *n* subtítulo.

subhuman [sʌb'hjʊːmən] *adj* infrahumano,-a.

subject [*(n-adj)* 'sʌbdʒekt, *(vb)* səb'dʒekt] *n* **1** *(theme, topic)* tema *m*. **2** EDUC asignatura. **3** *(citizen)* súbdito, ciudadano,-a. **4** LING sujeto. **5** *(cause)* objeto (**of/for**, de). **6** *(of experiment)* sujeto. ● **subject matter 1** *(topic)* tema *m*, materia. **2** *(contents)* contenido.
▷ *vt (bring under control)* someter, sojuzgar (**to**, a).
▷ *adj (subordinate, governed)* sometido,-a. **subject to** *(bound by)* sujeto,-a a; *(prone to - floods, subsidence)* expuesto,-a a; *(- change, delay)* susceptible de, sujeto,-a a; *(- illness)* propenso,-a a.
▷ *prep* **subject to** *(conditional on)* supeditado,-a a.
⊙ **to subject to** *vt sep* someter a.

subjection [səb'dʒekʃən] *n (act)* sujeción *f* (**of**, de); *(state)* sometimiento (**to**, a).
subjective [səb'dʒektɪv] *adj* subjetivo,-a.
subjugate ['sʌbdʒəgeɪt] *vt* sojuzgar, subyugar.
subjunctive [səb'dʒʌŋktɪv] *adj* LING subjuntivo,-a.
▷ *n* LING subjuntivo.
sublet [sʌb'let] *vt* realquilar, subarrendar.
▷ *vi* realquilar, subarrendar.
▲ *pt & pp* **sublet**, *ger* **subletting**.
sublime [s'blaɪm] *adj* **1** *(beauty, music, compliment, etc)* sublime. **2** *fam (food, performance)* maravilloso,-a, sensacional. **3** *pej (indifference, ignorance, etc)* sumo,-a, supremo,-a, absoluto,-a, total.
▷ *n* **the sublime** lo sublime.
subliminal [sʌb'lɪmɪnəl] *adj* subliminal.
sub-machine-gun [sʌbm'ʃiːngʌn] *n* ametralladora, metralleta.
submarine ['sʌbməriːn] *n* submarino.
▷ *adj* submarino,-a.
submerge [səb'mɜːdʒ] *vt* sumergir (**in**, en).
▷ *vi* sumergirse.
submerged [səb'mɜːdʒd] *adj (wreck, rock, submarine)* sumergido,-a.
submission [səb'mɪʃən] *n* **1** *(subjection)* sumisión *f* (**to**, a). **2** SP *(in wrestling)* rendición *f*. **3** *(presentation)* presentación *f*. **4** *(report)* informe *m*; *(proposal)* propuesta.
submissive [səb'mɪsɪv] *adj* sumiso,-a, dócil.
submit [səb'mɪt] *vt* **1** *(present)* presentar. **2** *(subject)* someter (**to**, a). **3** JUR *(suggest)* sostener.
▷ *vi (admit defeat, surrender)* rendirse, ceder; *(to demand, wishes)* acceder.
▲ *pt & pp* **submitted**, *ger* **submitting**.
subnormal [sʌb'nɔːməl] *adj* **1** *(person)* subnormal, retrasado,-a. **2** *(temperatures)* por debajo de lo normal.
subordinate [*(adj-n)* s'bɔːdɪnət, *(vb)* s'bɔːdɪneɪt] *adj* **1** *(lower, less important)* subordinado,-a (**to**, a), secundario,-a. **2** LING subordinado,-a. ● **subordinate clause** oración *f* subordinada.
▷ *n (person)* subordinado,-a, subalterno,-a.
▷ *vt* subordinar (**to**, a), supeditar (**to**, a).
subordination [səbɔːdɪ'neɪʃən] *n* subordinación *f*.
subscribe [səb'skraɪb] *vi* **1** *(to newspaper, etc)* suscribirse (**to**, a), abonarse (**to**, a). **2** *(to charity)* hacer donaciones, contribuir con donativos (**to**, a). **3** *(to opinion, theory)* suscribir (**to**, -), estar de acuerdo (**to**, con). **4** FIN *(shares)* suscribir (**for**, -).
▷ *vt* **1** *(contribute)* contribuir, donar. **2** *fml (sign)* suscribir.
subscriber [səb'skraɪbər] *n (to newspaper, etc)* suscriptor,-ra, abonado,-a; *(to telephone service, cable television)* abonado,-a.
subscription [səb'skɪpʃən] *n (to newspaper, etc)* suscripción *f*, abono; *(to club)* cuota; *(to charity)* donativo, donación *f*.
subsection ['sʌbsekʃən] *n* JUR *(in document)* artículo.
subsequent ['sʌbsɪkwənt] *adj* subsiguiente, posterior. ■ **subsequent to** posterior a.
subsequently ['sʌbsɪkwəntlɪ] *adv* posteriormente.
subservient [səb'sɜːvɪənt] *adj* **1** *(submissive)* servil (**to**, a). **2** *fml (subordinate)* supeditado,-a (**to**, a).
subside [səb'saɪd] *vi* **1** *(land, building, road)* hundirse. **2** *fig (person)* dejarse caer. **3** *(storm, wind)* amainar; *(floods)* decrecer, bajar; *(pain, fever)* disminuir; *(noise, applause)* irse apagando; *(anger, excitement)* calmarse.
subsidence [səb'saɪdəns] *n (of land, building)* hundimiento.
subsidiary [səb'sɪdɪərɪ] *adj* **1** *(role, interest, issue)* secundario,-a. **2** *(income)* adicional, extra; *(payment, loan)* subsidiario,-a.
▷ *n* COMM filial *f*.
▲ *pl* **subsidiaries**.
subsidize ['sʌbsɪdaɪz] *vt (gen)* subvencionar; *(exports)* primar.
subsidy ['sʌbsɪdɪ] *n* subvención *f*, subsidio.
▲ *pl* **subsidies**.
subsist [səb'sɪst] *vi* subsistir.
subsistence [səb'sɪstəns] *n* subsistencia.
subsoil ['svbʃɔɪl] *n* subsuelo.
substance ['sʌbstəns] *n* **1** *(matter)* sustancia. **2** *(real matter, solid content)* sustancia, solidez *f*. **3** *(essence, gist)* esencia, sustancia. **4** *(wealth)* riqueza.
substandard [sʌb'stændəd] *adj* de calidad inferior.
substantial [səb'stænʃəl] *adj* **1** *(solid)* sólido,-a, fuerte. **2** *(large - sum, increase, loss, damage)* importante, considerable; *(- difference, change)* sustancial, notable. **3** *(meal - large)* abundante; *(nourishing)* sustancioso,-a. **4** *(wealthly)* acaudalado,-a. **5** *fml (real, tangible)* sustancial.
substantially [səb'stænʃəlɪ] *adv* **1** *(solidly)* sólidamente. **2** *(considerably)* de manera considerable; *(noticeably)* notablemente, sustancialmente. **3** *(essentially)* esencialmente, fundamentalmente; *(largely, mainly)* en gran parte.
substantiate [səb'stænʃɪeɪt] *vt (gen)* confirmar, corroborar; *(accusation)* probar.
substantive ['sʌbstəntɪv] *adj fml (research, information, evidence)* sustantivo,-a; *(matter, issue)* fundamental.
▷ *n* LING sustantivo.
substitute ['sʌbstɪtjuːt] *n* **1** *(person)* sustituto,-a, suplente *mf*. **2** *(thing)* sucedáneo (**for**, de).
▷ *vt* sustituir, reemplazar.
▷ *vi* sustituir, suplir (**for**, a).
substitution [sʌbstɪ'tjuːʃən] *n* sustitución *f*.
subterranean [sʌbt'reɪnɪən] *adj* subterráneo,-a.
subtitle ['sʌbtaɪtəl] *n* subtítulo.
▷ *vt* subtitular, poner subtítulos a.
subtle ['sʌtəl] *adj* **1** *(person - tactful)* delicado,-a, discreto,-a. **2** *(colour, difference, hint, joke)* sutil; *(taste)* delicado,-a, ligero,-a; *(lighting)* tenue, sutil. **3** *(remark, mind)* agudo,-a, perspicaz; *(plan, argument, analysis)* ingenioso,-a; *(irony)* fino,-a.
▲ *comp* **subtler**, *superl* **subtlest**.
subtlety ['sʌtəltɪ] *n* **1** *(delicacy, fine difference)* sutileza. **2** *(tact)* delicadeza.
▲ *pl* **subtleties**.
▷ *adj (perceptiveness)*perspicacia; *(ingenuity)* sutileza.
subtly ['sʌtəlɪ] *adv* **1** *(delicately)* sutilmente. **2** *(tactfully)* con delicadeza. **3** *(perceptively)* con agudeza, perspicazmente; *(ingeniously)* ingeniosamente.
subtotal [sʌb'təʊtəl] *n* subtotal *m*.
subtract [səb'trækt] *vt* restar (**from**, de).
subtraction [səb'trækʃən] *n* resta.
subtropical [sʌb'trɒpɪkəl] *adj* subtropical.

uburb ['sʌbɜ:b] *n* barrio residencial. ● **the suburbs** las afueras *fpl*.
uburban [s'bɜ:bᵊn] *adj (area)* de los barrios residenciales; *(attitude)* convencional.
uburbia [s'bɜ:bɪə] *n* los barrios *mpl* residenciales.
ubversion [sʌb'vɜ:ʃᵊn] *n* subversión *f*.
ubversive [sʌb'vɜ:sɪv] *adj* subversivo,-a.
n (person) elemento subversivo.
ubvert [sʌb'vɜ:t] *vt* subvertir.
ubway ['sʌbweɪ] *n* **1** GB *(underpass)* paso subterráneo. **2** US *(underground)* metro.
ubzero [sʌb'zi:rəʊ] *adj* bajo cero.
ucceed [sək'si:d] *vi* **1** *(be successful - person)* tener éxito, triunfar; *(- plan, marriage)* salir bien; *(- strike)* surtir efecto, dar resultado. **2** *(manage)* lograr, conseguir. **3** *(throne)* subir (**to**, a); *(title)* heredar (**to**, -).
vt **1** *(take place of)* suceder a. **2** *fml (follow after)* suceder a.
ucceeding [sək'si:dɪŋ] *adj* subsiguiente.
uccess [sək'ses] *n* **1** *(good result, achievement)* éxito. **2** *(successful person, thing)* éxito.
uccessful [sək'sesfʊl] *adj (person, career, film)* de éxito; *(plan, performance, attempt)* acertado,-a, logrado,-a; *(business)* próspero,-a; *(marriage)* feliz; *(meeting)* satisfactorio,-a, positivo,-a.
uccessfully [sʌk'sesfʊlɪ] *adv* satisfactoriamente.
uccession [sək'seʃᵊn] *n* **1** *(act of following)* sucesión *f*. **2** *(series)* serie *f*, sucesión *f*. **3** *(to post, throne)* sucesión *f*.
uccessive [sək'sesɪv] *adj* sucesivo,-a, consecutivo,-a.
uccessor [sək'sesəʳ] *n* sucesor,-ra.
uccinct [sək'sɪŋkt] *adj* sucinto,-a, conciso,-a.
ucculence ['sʌkjələns] *n* suculencia.
ucculent ['sʌkjələnt] *adj* **1** *(juicy)* suculento,-a. **2** BOT carnoso,-a.
n BOT planta carnosa, suculenta.
uccumb [s'kʌm] *vi* sucumbir (**to**, a).
uch [sʌtʃ] *adj* **1** *(of that sort)* tal, semejante. **2** *(so much, so great)* tal, tanto,-a.
adv (so very) tan.
pron (of that specified sort) tal. ■ **as such 1** *(strictly speaking)* propiamente dicho. **2** *(that way)* como tal. ‖ **in such a way that...** de tal manera que... ‖ **such as** *(like, for example)* como. ‖ **such as?** ¿por ejemplo?
uchlike ['sʌtʃlaɪk] *adj* por el estilo.
pron (things) cosas *fpl* por el estilo; *(people)* gente *f* por el estilo.
uck [sʌk] *vt* **1** *(person - liquid)* sorber; *(- lollipop, pencil, thumb, etc)* chupar; *(insect -blood, nectar)* chupar, succionar. **2** *(vacuum cleaner)* aspirar (**in**, -); *(pump)* succionar, aspirar (**in**, -); *(plant)* absorber (**up**, -). **3** *(draw powerfully)* arrastrar.
vi (person) chupar (**at/on**, -); *(baby)* mamar (**at**, -); *(vacuum cleaner)* aspirar (**up**,-); *(pump)* succionar, aspirar.
n chupada.
ucker ['sʌkəʳ] *n* **1** ZOOL ventosa. **2** BOT chupón *m*, mamón *m*. **3** *(rubber disc)* ventosa. **4** *fam (person)* primo,-a, bobo,-a, imbécil *mf*.
uckle ['sʌkᵊl] *vt* amamantar, dar de mamar a.
vi mamar.
ucrose ['sju:krəʊz] *n* sacarosa.

suction ['sʌkʃᵊn] *n (sticking together)* succión *f*; *(of water, air)* aspiración *f*. ● **suction cup** ventosa. ‖ **suction pump** bomba de aspiración.
Sudan [sʊ:'dæn] [Also **the Sudan**.] *n* Sudán.
Sudanese [sʊ:d'ni:z] *adj* sudanés,-esa.
▷ *n* sudanés,-esa.
▷ *n pl* **the Sudanese** los sudaneses *mpl*.
sudden ['sʌdᵊn] *adj* **1** *(quick)* súbito,-a, repentino,-a. **2** *(unexpected)* inesperado,-a, imprevisto,-a. **3** *(abrupt)* brusco,-a. ■ **all of a sudden** de repente. ● **sudden death** muerte *f* súbita.
suddenly ['sʌdᵊnlɪ] *adv* **1** *(unexpectedly)* de repente, de pronto. **2** *(abruptly)* bruscamente.
suddenness ['sʌdᵊnnəs] *n* **1** *(quickness)* lo repentino, lo súbito. **2** *(unexpectedness)* lo imprevisto, lo inesperado. **3** *(abruptness)* brusquedad *f*.
suds [sʌdz] *n pl* jabonaduras *fpl*, espuma *f sing* (de jabón).
sue [sʊ:] *vt* JUR demandar.
▷ *vi* JUR entablar una demanda (**for**, por).
suede [sweɪd] *n* ante *m*, gamuza.
▷ *adj* de ante, de gamuza.
suet ['sʊ:ɪt] *n* sebo.
suffer ['sʌfəʳ] *vt* **1** *(gen)* sufrir; *(pain)* padecer, sufrir; *(hunger)* padecer, pasar; *(losses)* sufrir, registrar. **2** *(bear, tolerate)* aguantar, soportar, tolerar.
▷ *vi* **1** *(gen)* sufrir. **2** *(be affected - work, studies, etc)* verse afectado,-a; *(- health)* resentirse. ■ **to suffer from 1** *(illness)* sufrir de, padecer. **2** *(shock)* sufrir los efectos de. **3** *(effects)* resentirse de.
sufferance ['sʌfᵊrᵊns] ■ **on sufferance** a regañadientes.
sufferer ['sʌfᵊrəʳ] *n* enfermo,-a.
suffering ['sʌfᵊrɪŋ] *n (affliction)* sufrimiento, aflicción *f*; *(grief)* pena, dolor *m*; *(pain)* dolor *m*.
suffice [s'faɪs] *vt fml* ser suficiente.
▷ *vi* bastar, ser suficiente (**for**, para).
sufficient [s'fɪʃᵊnt] *adj* suficiente, bastante. ■ **to be sufficient** bastar.
suffix ['sʌfɪks] *n* sufijo.
suffocate ['sʌfəkeɪt] *vt* asfixiar, ahogar.
▷ *vi* asfixiarse, ahogarse.
suffocation [sʌf'keɪʃᵊn] *n* asfixia, ahogo.
suffrage ['sʌfrɪdʒ] *n* sufragio.
suffuse [s'fjʊ:z] *vt (colour)* teñir; *(light)* bañar.
sugar ['ʃʊgəʳ] *n* **1** azúcar *m & f*. **2** US *fam (form of address)* cariño, cielo. ● **sugar beet** remolacha azucarera.
▷ *vt* azucarar.
sugar-coated [ʃʊg'kəʊtɪd] *adj* cubierto,-a de azúcar.
sugared ['ʃʊgəd] *adj* azucarado,-a.
sugary ['ʃʊgərɪ] *adj* **1** *(of/like sugar)* azucarado,-a; *(sweet)* dulce. **2** *fig (insincere)* almibarado,-a, meloso,-a; *(sentimental)* sensiblero,-a, empalagoso,-a.
▲ *comp* **sugarier**, *superl* **sugariest**.
suggest [s'dʒest] *vt* **1** *(propose)* sugerir, proponer; *(advise)* sugerir, aconsejar. **2** *(imply)* insinuar. **3** *(indicate)* indicar. **4** *(evoke)* evocar, sugerir.
suggestion [s'dʒestʃᵊn] *n* **1** *(proposal)* sugerencia, propuesta. **2** *(insinuation)* insinuación *f*. **3** *(indication, hint)* indicio; *(slight trace)* sombra, traza, asomo, nota. **4** *(in psychology)* sugestión *f*.
suggestive [s'dʒestɪv] *adj (with sexual connotations)* provocativo,-a, insinuante.

suicidal [suːɪ'saɪdᵊl] *adj* suicida.
suicide ['suːɪsaɪd] *n* **1** *(act)* suicidio. **2** *(person)* suicida *mf.* **3** *fig* suicidio. ■ **to commit suicide** suicidarse.
suit [suːt] *n* **1** *(man's)* traje *m*; *(woman's)* traje *m* de chaqueta. **2** JUR pleito, juicio. **3** *(in cards)* palo.
▷ *vt* **1** *(be convenient, acceptable)* convenir a, venir bien a; *(please)* satisfacer, agradar, contentar. **2** *(be right for)* ir bien a, sentar bien a; *(look good on)* quedar bien a, favorecer. **3** *(adapt)* adaptar (**to**, a), ajustar (**to**, a).
suitability [suːtə'bɪlɪtɪ] *n* **1** *(appropriateness)* lo apropiado; *(for job)* idoneidad *f.* **2** *(propriety)* lo apropiado, lo apto. **3** *(convenience)* conveniencia.
suitable ['suːtəbᵊl] *adj* **1** *(appropriate)* adecuado,-a (**for**, para), apropiado,-a (**for**, para); *(for job, post)* adecuado,-a, indicado,-a, idóneo,-a. **2** *(acceptable, proper)* apropiado,-a, apto,-a. **3** *(convenient)* conveniente.
suitably ['suːtəblɪ] *adv* **1** *(qualified)* adecuadamente; *(dressed)* apropiadamente, de manera adecuada. **2** *(correctly)* como es debido, como corresponde.
suitcase ['suːtkeɪs] *n* maleta.
suite [swiːt] *n* **1** *(of furniture)* juego. **2** *(in hotel)* suite *f.* **3** MUS suite *f.* **4** *(retinue)* séquito, comitiva. **5** COMPUT juego.
suited ['suːtɪd] *adj* apropiado,-a (**for**, para), adecuado,-a (**for**, para).
sulk [sʌlk] *vi* enfurruñarse, estar de mal humor.
▷ *n* malhumor *m.*
sulky ['sʌlkɪ] *adj (look, mood)* malhumorado,-a; *(person)* con tendencia a enfurruñarse.
▲ *comp* **sulkier**, *superl* **sulkiest**.
sullen ['sʌlən] *adj* **1** *(person, mood)* hosco,-a, arisco,-a, huraño,-a; *(face)* adusto,-a. **2** *lit (sky, weather)* sombrío, triste.
sully ['sʌlɪ] *vt* **1** *(dirty)* ensuciar. **2** *fig (tarnish, spoil)* manchar, mancillar.
▲ *pt & pp* **sullied**, *ger* **sullying**.
sultan ['sʌltᵊn] *n* sultán *m.*
sultana [sʌl'tɑːnə] *n* **1** *(raisin)* pasa de Esmirna. **2** *(woman)* sultana.
sultanate ['sʌltᵊneɪt] *n* sultanato.
sultry ['sʌltrɪ] *adj* **1** *(weather)* bochornoso,-a, sofocante. **2** *(person)* sensual.
▲ *comp* **sultrier**, *superl* **sultriest**.
sum [sʌm] *n* **1** MATH *(calculation)* cuenta; *(addition)* suma, adición *f.* **2** *(amount of money)* suma (de dinero), cantidad *f* (de dinero). **3** *(total amount)* suma, total *m.*
▷ *n pl* **sums** aritmética *f sing*, cálculos *mpl.* ■ **in sum** en resumen. ● **the sum total** total *m.*
⊙ **to sum up** *vt sep* **1** *(summarize)* resumir, hacer un resumen de, sintetizar. **2** *(size up - situation)* evaluar; *(- person)* catalogar.
▷ *vi (summarize)* resumir; *(of judge)* recapitular.
summarily ['sʌmerɪlɪ] *adv* sumariamente.
summarize ['sʌməraɪz] *vt* resumir, hacer un resumen de.
summary ['sʌmərɪ] *n (gen)* resumen *m.*
▷ *adj* **1** JUR *(justice, punishment)* sumario,-a: **summary trial** *juicio sumario.* **2** *(immediate - dismissal)* inmediato,-a. **3** *(brief - account)* breve, corto,-a. ■ **in summary** en resumen.
▲ *pl* **summaries**.
summer ['sʌməʳ] *n* **1** *(gen)* verano. **2** *lit* abril *m.*
▷ *adj (gen)* de verano; *(summery)* veraniego,-a.
summerhouse ['sʌməhaʊs] *n* cenador *m.*
summertime ['sʌmətaɪm] *n* verano, estío.
summery ['sʌmərɪ] *adj* de verano, veraniego,-a.
▲ *comp* **summerier**, *superl* **summeriest**.
summit ['sʌmɪt] *n* **1** *(of mountain, career)* cumbre *f,* c ma. **2** *(meeting)* cumbre *f.*
summon ['sʌmən] *vt* **1** *(person)* llamar; *(meeting, parli ment)* convocar. **2** JUR citar, emplazar.
⊙ **to summon up** *vt insep* **1** *(courage)* armarse de; *(stre gth)* reunir, cobrar; *(support)* lograr, obtener; *(resourc help)* reunir, conseguir. **2** *(memories, thoughts)* evoca
sumptuous ['sʌmptjʊəs] *adj (gen)* suntuoso,-a; *(me* opíparo,-a.
sun [sʌn] *n (gen)* sol *m.*
sunbaked ['sʌnbeɪkt] *adj (place)* quemado,-a por el s calcinado,-a; *(brick)* secado,-a por el sol.
sunbathe ['sʌnbeɪð] *vi* tomar el sol.
sunbeam ['sʌnbiːm] *n* rayo de sol.
sunbed ['sʌnbed] *n* cama solar.
sunburn ['sʌnbɜːn] *n* quemadura de sol.
sunburnt ['sʌnbɜːnt] *adj (burnt)* quemado,-a (por sol); *(tanned)* bronceado,-a, moreno,-a.
sundae ['sʌndɪ] *n* CULIN *copa de helado con fru almendras, jarabe y nata montada.*
Sunday ['sʌndɪ] *n* domingo.

Para ejemplos de uso, consulta **Saturday**.

sundial ['sʌndaɪəl] *n* reloj *m* de sol.
sundown ['sʌndaʊn] *n* US puesta de(l) sol.
sun-dried ['sʌndraɪd] *adj* secado,-a al sol.
sundry ['sʌndrɪ] *adj* diversos,-as, varios,-as.
▷ *n pl* **sundries** COMM *(goods)* artículos *mpl* diversos; *(e penses)* gastos *mpl* diversos.
sunflower ['sʌnflaʊəʳ] *n* girasol *m.* ● **sunflower se** semilla de girasol, pipa.
sung [sʌŋ] *pp* → **sing**.
sunglasses ['sʌnglɑːsɪz] *n pl* gafas *fpl* de sol.
sunhat ['sʌnhæt] *n* pamela, sombrero de ala ancha
sunk [sʌŋk] *pp* → **sink**.
sunken ['sʌnkən] *adj* **1** *(ship, treasure)* hundido,-a, s mergido,-a; *(eyes, cheeks)* hundido,-a. **2** *(terrace, ba* a un nivel más bajo.
sunlight ['sʌnlaɪt] *n* sol *m,* luz *f* del sol.
sunlit ['sʌnlɪt] *adj* soleado,-a.
sunny ['sʌnɪ] *adj* **1** *(room, house, etc)* soleado,-a; *(day)* sol. **2** *fig (person)* alegre, risueño,-a; *(future)* risueño,-a
▲ *comp* **sunnier**, *superl* **sunniest**.
sunray ['sʌnreɪ] *n* rayo de sol.
sunrise ['sʌnraɪz] *n (sun-up)* salida del sol; *(daw* amanecer *m,* alba *m.*
sunroof ['sʌnruːf] *n* **1** AUTO capota, techo corredizo *(on building)* azotea.
sunset ['sʌnset] *n (sundown)* puesta de(l) sol, ocas *(twilight)* crepúsculo, atardecer *m.*
sunshade ['sʌnʃeɪd] *n* **1** *(parasol)* sombrilla. **2** *(aw ing)* toldo.
sunshine ['sʌnʃaɪn] *n* **1** sol *m,* luz *f* de sol. **2** *fig* a gría. **3** GB *fam (friendly form of address)* corazón, ma -a; *(sarcastic)* guapo,-a.
sunstroke ['sʌnstrəʊk] *n* insolación *f.*
suntan ['sʌntæn] *n* bronceado, moreno. ● **suntan tion** bronceador *m.*
sun-tanned ['sʌntænd] *adj* bronceado,-a, moreno,-

untrap ['sʌntræp] *n* lugar *m* muy soleado, solana.
un-up ['sʌnʌp] *n* US *(sunrise)* salida de sol; *(dawn)* amanecer *m*, alba *m*.
up [sʌp] *vt* GB *(drink)* beber a sorbos.
vi arch (have supper) cenar (**on/off**, -).
▲ *pt & pp* **supped**, *ger* **supping**.
uper ['su:pəʳ] *adj fam* genial, súper, fenomenal, de primera.
n **1** GB *(superintendent)* comisario,-a de policía. **2** US *(superintendent)* portero,-a.
uperabundance [su:pər'bʌndəns] *n fml* superabundancia.
uperb [su:'pɜ:b] *adj* estupendo,-a, magnífico,-a, espléndido,-a, soberbio,-a.
uperbly [su'pɜ:blɪ] *adv* estupendamente, magníficamente, espléndidamente, soberbiamente.
upercilious [su:p'sɪlɪəs] *adj (condescending)* altanero,-a, *(disdainful)* desdeñoso,-a.
uperficial [su:p'fɪʃ°l] *adj (gen)* superficial.
uperfluous [su:'pɜ:fluəs] *adj (gen)* superfluo,-a; *(remark, comment)* de más.
uperhuman [su:p'hju:mən] *adj* sobrehumano,-a.
uperimpose [su:pərɪm'pəuz] *vt* sobreponer, superponer.
uperintendent [su:pərɪn'tendənt] *n* **1** *(person in charge - gen)* director,-ra, inspector,-ra, supervisor,-ra. **2** GB *(in police)* comisario,-a de policía. **3** US *(in apartment building)* portero,-a, conserje *mf*. **4** *(of park)* encargado,-a.
uperior [su:'pɪərɪəʳ] *adj* **1** *(gen)* superior (**to**, a). **2** *pej (attitude, tone, smile)* de superioridad.
n (senior) superior *mf*.
uperiority [su:pɪərɪ'ɒrɪtɪ] *n* superioridad *f*.
uperlative [su:'pɜ:lətɪv] *adj* **1** *(excellent)* superlativo,-a, de primera, excelente, excepcional. **2** LING superlativo,-a.
n LING superlativo.
uperman ['su:pəmæn] *n* superhombre *m*.
▲ *pl* **supermen** ['su:pəmən].
upermarket [su:p'mɑ:kɪt] *n* supermercado, autoservicio.
upernatural [su:p'nætʃ°rəl] *adj* sobrenatural.
n **the supernatural** lo sobrenatural *m*.
uperpower ['su:pəpauəʳ] *n* superpotencia.
upersede [su:p'si:d] *vt (replace)* reemplazar, sustituir, suplantar.
upersonic [su:p'sɒnɪk] *adj* supersónico,-a.
uperstar ['su:pəstɑ:ʳ] *n* superestrella.
uperstition [su:p'stɪʃ°n] *n* superstición *f*.
uperstitious [sju:p'stɪʃəs] *adj* supersticioso,-a.
uperstore ['su:pəstɔ:ʳ] *n* hipermercado.
uperstructure ['su:pəstrʌktʃəʳ] *n* superestructura.
upertanker ['su:pətæŋkəʳ] *n* superpetrolero.
upervise ['su:pəvaɪz] *vt* **1** *(watch over)* vigilar. **2** *(keep check on)* supervisar; *(run)* dirigir.
upervision [su:p'vɪʒ°n] *n* supervisión *f*.
upervisor ['su:pəvaɪzəʳ] *n* **1** *(gen)* supervisor,-ra. **2** GB *(of thesis)* director,-ra de tesis.
uperwoman ['su:pəwumən] *n* supermujer *f*.
▲ *pl* **superwomen** ['su:pəwɪmɪn].
upper ['sʌpəʳ] *n* cena. ● **to have supper** cenar.
upper-time ['sʌpətaɪm] *n* hora de cenar.

supplant [s'plɑ:nt] *vt* suplantar, reemplazar, sustituir.
supple ['sʌp°l] *adj (body, fingers)* flexible, ágil; *(material)* flexible; *(mind)* ágil; *(movement)* natural.
supplement [*(n)* 'sʌplɪmənt, *(vb)* 'sʌplɪment] *n* **1** *(charge)* suplemento. **2** *(dietary)* complemento. **3** LIT suplemento.
▷ *vt* complementar.
supplementary [sʌplɪ'ment°rɪ] *adj* **1** *(gen)* suplementario,-a, adicional. **2** MATH suplementario,-a.
supplicate ['sʌplɪkeɪt] *vt fml* suplicar.
▷ *vi fml* suplicar (**for**, -).
supplier [s'plaɪəʳ] *n* COMM proveedor,-ra, abastecedor,-ra.
supply [s'plaɪ] *n* **1** *(provision)* suministro. **2** COMM *(provision - to markets, areas, etc)* abastecimiento; *(- to individuals, houses, shops, etc)* suministro. **3** *(amount available)* reserva.
▲ *pl* **supplies**.
▷ *vt* **1** *(goods, materials)* suministrar. **2** *(a person, company, city, etc)* abastecer (**with**, de), proveer (**with**, de). **3** *(give - information, proof, facts)* facilitar, proporcionar. **4** MIL *(with provisions)* aprovisionar. **5** *fml (need, requirement)* satisfacer.
▲ *pt & pp* **supplied**, *ger* **supplying**.
▷ *n pl* **supplies** *(food)* provisiones *fpl*, víveres *mpl*; *(stock)* existencias *fpl*, stock *m*; MIL pertrechos *mpl*.
support [s'pɔ:t] *n* **1** *(physical - gen)* apoyo, sostén *m*; *(- thing worn on body)* protector *m*. **2** *(of building)* soporte *m*, puntal *m*. **3** *(moral)* apoyo, respaldo. **4** *(financial)* ayuda económica, apoyo económico; *(sustenance)* sustento; *(person)* sostén *m*. **5** *(supporters)* afición *f*. **6** *(evidence)* pruebas *fpl*.
▷ *vt* **1** *(roof, bridge, etc)* sostener; *(weight)* aguantar, resistir; *(part of body)* sujetar. **2** *(back, encourage)* apoyar, respaldar, ayudar; *(cause, motion, proposal)* apoyar, estar de acuerdo con. **3** SP *(follow)* seguir; *(encourage)* animar. **4** *(keep, sustain)* mantener, sustentar, sostener; *(feed)* alimentar. **5** *(corroborate, substantiate)* confirmar, respaldar, apoyar. **6** *fml (endure)* soportar, tolerar.
supporter [s'pɔ:təʳ] *n* **1** POL partidario,-a. **2** SP *(gen)* seguidor,-ra; *(fan)* hincha *mf*, forofo,-a.
▷ *n pl* **supporters** SP la afición *f sing*. ● **supporters' club** peña deportiva.
supporting [s'pɔ:tɪŋ] *adj (part, role)* secundario,-a.
suppose [s'pəuz] *vt* **1** *(assume, imagine)* suponer, imaginarse. **2** *(in polite requests)*: **I don't suppose you could lend me £10, could you?** *no podrías dejarme 10 libras, ¿no?* **3** *(believe)* creer. **4** *(postulate)* suponer. **5** *fml (presuppose)* suponer. ■ **I suppose not** supongo que no. ■ **I suppose so** supongo que sí.
▷ *conj* **1** *(hypothesis)* ¿y si...?, pongamos por caso, supongamos. **2** *(making suggestions)* ¿y si...?, ¿qué tal si...?
supposed [s'pəuzd] *adj* supuesto,-a. ■ **to be supposed to 1** *(supposition, reputation)* se supone que, dicen que. **2** *(obligation, responsibility)* deber, tener que. **3** *(intention)* se supone que.
supposedly [s'pəusədlɪ] *adv* supuestamente.
supposing [s'pəuzɪŋ] *conj* **1** *(hypothesis)* ¿y si...?, suponiendo. **2** *(making suggestions)* ¿y si...?, ¿qué tal si...?
supposition [səp'zɪʃ°n] *n* suposición *f*, supuesto.

suppository [s'pɒzɪtᵊrɪ] *n* supositorio.
▲ *pl* suppositories.
suppress [s'pres] *vt (gen)* suprimir; *(feelings, laugh, yawn, etc)* contener, reprimir; *(news, truth, evidence)* callar, ocultar; *(revolt, rebellion)* sofocar, reprimir.
suppression [s'preʃᵊn] *n (gen)* supresión *f*; *(of feelings)* represión *f*, inhibición *f*; *(of truth, evidence, information)* ocultación *f*; *(of book)* prohibición *f*; *(of revolt)* represión *f*.
suppressor [s'presəʳ] *n* 1 *(person, thing)* el/la/lo que suprime. 2 *(electrical)* supresor *m*.
supremacy [sʊ:'preməsɪ] *n* supremacía.
supreme [sʊ:'pri:m] *adj (highest)* supremo,-a, sumo,-a; *(greatest)* supremo,-a.
supremo [sʊ'pri:məʊ] *n* GB *fam* gran jefe,-a.
▲ *pl* supremos.
surcharge ['sɜ:tʃɑ:dʒ] *n* recargo, sobretasa.
▷ *vt (person)* aplicar un recargo a.
sure [ʃʊəʳ] *adj* 1 *(positive, certain)* seguro,-a (about/of, de); *(convinced)* convencido,-a. 2 *(certain, inevitable)* seguro,-a. 3 *(reliable)* seguro,-a.
▷ *adv* 1 *(of course)* claro, por supuesto. 2 US *(as intensifier)* realmente, de verdad.
sure-fire ['ʃʊəfaɪəʳ] *adj fam* segurísimo,-a, infalible.
sure-footed [ʃʊ'fʊtɪd] *adj* de pie firme.
surely ['ʃʊəlɪ] *adv* 1 *(doubtless)* seguramente, sin duda. 2 *(as intensifier)*: surely you haven't forgotten! *¡no se te habrá olvidado!* 3 *(in a sure manner)* con seguridad. 4 US *(certainly)* por supuesto, desde luego, claro (que sí).
surety ['ʃʊərətɪ] *n* 1 *(person)* fiador,-ra, garante *mf*. 2 *(money)* fianza, garantía.
▲ *pl* sureties.
surf [sɜ:f] *n (waves)* olas *fpl*, oleaje *m*; *(foam)* espuma.
▷ *vi* hacer surf. ■ to surf the net navegar en Internet.
surface ['sɜ:fɪs] *n* 1 *(gen)* superficie *f*; *(of road)* firme *m*. 2 *fig (exterior)* apariencia.
▷ *adj (gen)* superficial.
▷ *vt (cover road)* pavimentar; *(with asphalt)* asfaltar.
▷ *vi* 1 *(submarine, etc)* salir a la superficie; *(problems, etc)* aflorar, aparecer, surgir. 2 *(from bed)* asomarse, dejarse ver; *(after disappearance)* reaparecer.
surfboard ['sɜ:fbɔ:d] *n* tabla de surf.
surfeit ['sɜ:fɪt] *n fml* exceso.
surfer ['sɜ:fəʳ] *n* surfista *mf*.
surfing ['sɜ:fɪŋ] *n* surf *m*.
surge [sɜ:dʒ] *n* 1 *(of sea)* oleada, oleaje *m*, marejada; *(of people)* oleada, marea. 2 *(increase - in demand, etc)* aumento; *(- of support)* oleada; *(- of anger)* arranque *m*.
▷ *vi* 1 *(sea, wave)* levantarse, hincharse; *(people, crowd)* ir en tropel. 2 *(increase)* aumentar bruscamente.
surgeon ['sɜ:dʒᵊn] *n* cirujano,-a.
surgery ['sɜ:dʒərɪ] *n* 1 *(operating)* cirugía. 2 GB *(place)* consultorio, consulta; *(time)* consulta.
▲ *pl* surgeries. ■ to undergo surgery ser operado,-a.
surgical ['sɜ:dʒɪkᵊl] *adj (instrument, treatment)* quirúrgico,-a.
Surinam [sʊərɪ'næm] *n* Surinam.
surly ['sɜ:lɪ] *adj (bad-tempered)* hosco,-a, arisco,-a, malhumorado,-a; *(bad-mannered)* maleducado,-a.
▲ *comp* surlier, *superl* surliest.
surmise [sɜ:'maɪz] *n fml* conjetura, suposición *f*.
▷ *vt fml* suponerse, figurarse.
surmount [sɜ:'maʊnt] *vt* 1 *(overcome)* superar, venc… 2 ARCH rematar, coronar.
surname ['sɜ:neɪm] *n* apellido.
surpass [sɜ:'pɑ:s] *vt (better)* superar; *(exceed)* supera… sobrepasar.
surplus ['sɜ:pləs] *n (of goods, produce)* excedente *m*, s… brante *m*; *(of budget)* superávit *m*.
▷ *adj* sobrante, excedente.
surprise [s'praɪz] *n* sorpresa.
▷ *adj (visit, result)* inesperado,-a; *(attack, party)* sorpres…
▷ *vt* 1 *(cause surprise to)* sorprender. 2 *(catch unawar…* sorprender, coger desprevenido,-a.
surprised [s'praɪzd] *adj (person)* sorprendido,-a; *(loo…* de sorpresa.
surprising [s'praɪzɪŋ] *adj* sorprendente.
surprisingly [s'praɪzɪŋlɪ] *adv* sorprendentemente.
surreal [s'rɪəl] *adj* surrealista.
surrealism [s'rɪəlɪzᵊm] *n* surrealismo.
surrealist [s'rɪəlɪst] *n* surrealista *mf*.
▷ *adj* surrealista.
surrender [s'rendəʳ] *n* 1 *(capitulation)* rendición *f*; *(su… mission)* sumisión *f*, claudicación *f*. 2 *(giving up - arms)* entrega; *(- of rights)* renuncia.
▷ *vt* 1 MIL *(weapons, town)* rendir, entregar. 2 *fml (pa… port, ticket, etc)* entregar; *(claim, right, privilege)* renu… ciar a, ceder.
▷ *vi* rendirse, entregarse.
surreptitious [sʌrəp'tɪʃəs] *adj* subrepticio,-a, fur… vo,-a.
surrogate ['sʌrəgeɪt] *n fml (gen)* sustituto,-a.
surround [s'raʊnd] *vt (encircle)* rodear (with, de).
▷ *n* marco, borde *m*.
surrounding [s'raʊndɪŋ] *adj* circundante.
▷ *n pl* surroundings *(of town, city, etc)* alrededores *mpl f…* *(environment)* entorno, ambiente *m*.
surveillance [sɜ:'veɪləns] *n* vigilancia.
survey [*(n)* 'sɜ:veɪ, *(vb)* s'veɪ] *n* 1 *(investigation - of opi… ion)* sondeo, encuesta; *(- of prices, trends, etc)* estudi… *(written report)* informe *m*. 2 *(of land)* inspección *f*, … conocimiento; *(in topography)* medición *f*. 3 *(gene… view)* visión *f* general, visión *f* de conjunto. 4 GB … *house, building)* inspección *f*, peritaje *m*.
▷ *vt* 1 *(contemplate, look at)* contemplar, mirar. 2 *(stud… gen)* examinar, analizar; *(- prices, trends, etc)* estudi… hacer una encuesta sobre; *(investigate - people)* e… cuestar, hacer un sondeo de. 3 *(- land)* hacer un r… conocimiento de; *(in topography)* medir. 4 *(hou… building)* inspeccionar, hacer un peritaje de.
surveyor [s'veɪəʳ] *n (of land)* agrimensor,-ra, topógr… fo,-a; *(of house, building)* perito,-a
survival [s'vaɪvᵊl] *n* 1 *(gen)* supervivencia. 2 *(relic)* re… quia, vestigio (from, de).
survive [s'vaɪv] *vi* 1 *(gen)* sobrevivir; *(custom, traditic…* sobrevivir, perdurar; *(book, painting)* conservarse. … *fam (cope, get by)* ir tirando, arreglárselas.
▷ *vt* 1 *(disaster)* sobrevivir a. 2 *(person)* sobrevivir a.
survivor [s'vaɪvəʳ] *n* superviviente *mf*, sobrevivie… te *mf*.
susceptible [s'septɪbᵊl] *adj* 1 *(easily influenced)* s… gestionable; *(impressionable)* susceptible, sensib… impresionable (to, a); *(prone to illness)* propenso,… (to, a). 2 JUR *fml* susceptible (of, de).

uspect [*(adj-n)* 'sʌspekt, *(vb)* s'spekt] *adj (suspicious)* sospechoso,-a; *(dubious, questionable)* dudoso,-a.
▷ *n (person)* sospechoso,-a.
▷ *vt* **1** *(believe guilty)* sospechar de; *(mistrust)* recelar de, desconfiar de, dudar de. **2** *(think true)* sospechar. **3** *(suppose, guess)* imaginarse, creer.
uspend [s'spend] *vt* **1** *(stop temporarily)* suspender; *(postpone)* posponer, aplazar. **2** *(remove)* suspender. **3** *(hang)* suspender, colgar.
uspended [s'spendɪd] *adj (gen)* suspendido,-a.
uspense [səs'spens] *n (anticipation)* incertidumbre *f*; *(intrigue)* suspense *m*, intriga.
uspension [s'spenʃᵊn] *n* **1** *(halt)* suspensión *f*; *(postponement)* aplazamiento, postergación *f*. **2** *(of employee, player)* suspensión *f*; *(of pupil)* expulsión *f*. **3** CHEM suspensión *f*. **4** TECH suspensión *f*. ● **suspension points** puntos suspensivos.
uspicion [s'spɪʃᵊn] *n* **1** *(gen)* sospecha; *(mistrust)* recelo, desconfianza; *(doubt)* duda; *(hunch)* presentimiento. **2** *(slight trace)* pizca, asomo, atisbo.
uspicious [s'spɪʃəs] *adj* **1** *(arousing suspicion)* sospechoso,-a. **2** *(distrustful, wary)* receloso,-a, desconfiado,-a, suspicaz.
ustain [s'steɪn] *vt* **1** *(keep alive - gen)* sustentar; *(- spirits, hope)* mantener. **2** *(maintain - gen)* sostener; *(- interest, conversation)* mantener; *(- work)* continuar. **3** MUS *(note)* sostener. **4** *fml (suffer - loss, injury, wound, etc)* sufrir. **5** *fml (hold up)* sostener. **6** JUR admitir.
ustainable [s'steɪnəbᵊl] *adj* sostenible.
ustenance ['sʌstɪnəns] *n* sustento, alimento.
uture ['sʌtʃeʳ] *n (thread)* hilo de sutura; *(stitch)* punto de sutura.
▷ *vt* suturar.
velte [svelt] *adj (slim)* esbelto,-a.
wab [swɒb] *n* **1** MED *(cotton wool)* algodón *m*; *(gauze)* gasa. **2** MED *(specimen)* frotis *m*, muestra. **3** *(cleaning cloth)* paño, bayeta, trapo; *(mop)* fregona.
▷ *vt* **1** MED *(wound)* limpiar. **2** MAR *(deck)* limpiar, fregar.
▲ *pt & pp* **swabbed**, *ger* **swabbing**.
waddle ['swɒdᵊl] *vt* envolver.
wallow¹ ['swɒləʊ] *n (of drink, food)* trago.
▷ *vt* **1** *(food, etc)* tragar. **2** *fig (be taken in by)* tragarse.
▷ *vi* tragar.
⊙ **to swallow up** *vt sep* **1** *(engulf)* tragarse, engullir. **2** *(use up)* consumir, tragarse, comerse, absorber.
wallow² ['swɒləʊ] *n (bird)* golondrina.
wam [swɒm] *pt* → **swim**.
wamp [swɒmp] *n* pantano, ciénaga.
▷ *vt* **1** *(land)* inundar, anegar; *(boat)* hundir. **2** *fig (inundate)* inundar (**with/by**, de); *(overwhelm)* agobiar, abrumar (**with/by**, de).
wan [swɒn] *n (bird)* cisne *m*.
▷ *vi* pavonearse.
▲ *pt & pp* **swanned**, *ger* **swanning**.
wap [swɒp] *n* canje *m*, cambalache *m*.
▷ *vt fam* cambiar, intercambiar.
▷ *vi* hacer un intercambio, cambiar.
▲ *pt & pp* **swapped**, *ger* **swapping**.
⊙ **to swap over / swap round** *vt sep* cambiar (de sitio).
warm [swɔːm] *n* **1** *(of bees)* enjambre *m*. **2** *fig (of people)* enjambre *m*, nube *f*, multitud *f*.
▷ *vi* **1** *(bees)* enjambrar. **2** *fig (people)* aglomerarse, apiñarse, arremolinarse.
⊙ **to swarm with** *vt insep* estar plagado,-a de.
swarthy ['swɔːðɪ] *adj* moreno,-a, de tez morena.
▲ *comp* **swarthier**, *superl* **swarthiest**.
swat [swɒt] *vt (try to hit)* aplastar; *(kill)* matar.
▲ *pt & pp* **swatted**, *ger* **swatting**.
▷ *n (blow)* golpe *m*; *(with hand)* manotazo.
swath [swɔːθ] *n (of grass, land)* franja.
swathe¹ [sweɪð] *n* → **swath**.
swathe² [sweɪð] *vt (wrap)* envolver, vendar.
⊙ **to swathe in** *vt sep fig* envolver.
sway [sweɪ] *n* **1** *(movement)* balanceo, vaivén *m*, movimiento. **2** *fig (influence)* dominio, influencia (**over**, sobre).
▷ *vt* **1** *(swing)* balancear, bambolear. **2** *fig (influence)* influir en, influenciar, convencer.
▷ *vi* **1** *(person, tree, ladder)* balancearse, bambolearse; *(tower)* bambolearse; *(crops)* mecerse; *(person - totter)* tambalearse. **2** *fig (waver)* vacilar (**between**, entre), oscilar (**between**, entre).
swear [sweəʳ] *vt* **1** *(declare formally)* jurar; *(vow)* juramentar. **2** *fam (state firmly)* jurar.
▷ *vi* **1** *(declare formally)* jurar, prestar juramento. **2** *(curse)* decir palabrotas, soltar tacos; *(blaspheme)* jurar, blasfemar.
▲ *pt* **swore** [swɔːʳ], *pp* **sworn** [swɔːŋ].
⊙ **to swear by** *vt insep fam* tener una fe absoluta en.
⊙ **to swear in** *vt sep (in court)* tomarle juramento a.
⊙ **to swear to** *vt insep* jurar.
sweat [swet] *n* **1** *(perspiration)* sudor *m*. **2** *fam (hard work)* paliza. **3** *fam (anxious state)* nerviosismo. ● **sweat gland** glándula sudorípara.
▷ *vi* **1** *(perspire)* sudar. **2** *(cheese)* exudar humedad. **3** *(work hard)* sudar la gota gorda. **4** *fam (worry)* estar preocupado,-a, sufrir.
▷ *vt* GB *(cook gently)* rehogar.
⊙ **to sweat out** *vt sep (illness, cold)* quitarse sudando; *(toxins)* eliminar.
sweater ['swetəʳ] *n* suéter *m*, jersey *m*.
sweatshirt ['swetʃɜːt] *n* sudadera.
sweaty ['swetɪ] *adj (person, clothes)* sudoroso,-a, sudado,-a; *(day, weather)* bochornoso,-a; *(work)* que hace sudar.
▲ *comp* **sweatier**, *superl* **sweatiest**.
swede [swiːd] *n* BOT nabo sueco.
Swede [swiːd] *n (person)* sueco,-a.
Sweden ['swiːdᵊn] *n* Suecia.
Swedish ['swiːdɪʃ] *adj* sueco,-a.
▷ *n (language)* sueco.
▷ *n pl* **the Swedish** los suecos *mpl*.
sweep [swiːp] *n* **1** *(with broom)* barrido. **2** *(of arm)* movimiento amplio, gesto amplio; *(with weapon)* golpe *m*. **3** *(curve)* curva; *(area, stretch)* extensión *f*. **4** *fig (range, extent)* abanico, alcance *m*. **5** *(by police, rescuers)* peinado, rastreo. **6** *fam (chimney cleaner)* deshollinador,-ra.
▷ *vt* **1** *(room, floor)* barrer; *(chimney)* deshollinar. **2** *(with hand)* quitar de un manotazo. **3** *(move over)* azotar, barrer. **4** *(remove by force)* arrastrar, llevarse. **5** *(pass over)* recorrer. **6** *fig (spread through)* recorrer, extenderse por. **7** *(touch lightly)* rozar, pasar por.
▷ *vi* **1** *(with broom)* barrer. **2** *(move quickly)* pasar rápidamente. **3** *(extend)* recorrer, extenderse.

⊙ **to sweep aside** *vt sep* 1 *(objection, etc)* rechazar; *(suggestion)* descartar. 2 *(object)* apartar (bruscamente).
⊙ **to sweep away** *vt sep* 1 *(privilege, etc)* erradicar. 2 *(by flood, storm)* arrastrar, llevarse.
⊙ **to sweep up** *vt sep* 1 *(room, etc)* barrer; *(dust, etc)* (barrer y) recoger. 2 *(object, person)* recoger, levantar.
▷ *vi* barrer, limpiar.
▲ *pt & pp* swept [swept].

sweeping ['swi:pɪŋ] *adj* 1 *(broad)* amplio,-a; *(very general)* muy general. 2 *(overwhelming)* arrollador,-ra, aplastante; *(far-reaching)* radical; *(huge)* enorme. ● **sweeping brush** escoba.

sweet [swi:t] *adj* 1 *(taste)* dulce; *(sugary)* azucarado,-a. 2 *(pleasant)* agradable; *(smell)* fragante, bueno,-a; *(sound, music, voice)* melodioso,-a, suave, dulce. 3 *(air)* limpio,-a; *(water)* dulce. 4 *(charming)* encantador,-ra, simpático,-a; *(cute)* rico,-a, mono,-a; *(gentle)* dulce.
▷ *n* 1 GB *(candy)* caramelo, golosina; *(chocolate)* bombón *m.* 2 GB *(dessert)* postre *m.* 3 *(form of address)* cariño, cielo, amor *m,* vida. ● **sweet corn** maíz *m* tierno. ‖ **sweet pea** guisante *m* de olor. ‖ **sweet pepper** pimiento morrón. ‖ **sweet potato** boniato, batata.

sweet-and-sour ['swi:tᵊnsauəʳ] *adj* CULIN agridulce.

sweetcorn ['swi:tkɔ:n] *n* maíz *m* tierno.

sweeten ['swi:tᵊn] *vt* 1 *(drink, etc)* endulzar, azucarar; *(air, breath)* refrescar. 2 *fig (person)* endulzar (el carácter de); *(temper)* aplacar, calmar. 3 *fam (make more attractive)* hacer más apetecible.
⊙ **to sweeten up** *vt sep* ablandar.

sweetener ['swi:tᵊnəʳ] *n* 1 *(in food, drink)* edulcorante *m,* dulcificante *m.* 2 *fam (bribe)* soborno.

sweetheart ['swi:thɑ:t] *n* 1 *(dear, love)* cariño, tesoro, amor *m.* 2 *(loved one)* novio,-a.

sweetness ['swi:tnəs] *n (taste)* dulzor *m; (smell)* fragancia; *(sound)* suavidad *f; (character)* dulzura, simpatía.

sweet-tempered ['swi:t'tempəd] *adj* amable, dulce.

sweet-toothed [swi:t'tu:θt] *adj* goloso,-a.

swell [swel] *n* 1 *(of sea)* marejada, oleaje *m.* 2 MUS *(crescendo)* crescendo.
▷ *adj* US *fam (excellent)* fenomenal, bárbaro,-a, estupendo,-a.
▷ *vi* 1 *(gen)* hincharse (up, -); *(sea)* levantarse; *(river)* crecer, subir. 2 *(grow - in number)* crecer, aumentar; *(- louder)* hacerse más fuerte.
▷ *vt* 1 *(gen)* hinchar; *(river)* hacer crecer. 2 *(increase in number)* aumentar, engrosar.
▲ *pt* swelled, *pp* swollen ['swəulən].

swelling ['swelɪŋ] *n (swollen place)* hinchazón *f,* bulto; *(condition)* tumefacción *f.*

swept [swept] *pt & pp* ⟶ **sweep.**

swerve [swɜ:v] *n* 1 AUTO viraje *m* brusco, desvío brusco. 2 SP *(by player)* regate *m; (of ball)* efecto.
▷ *vi* 1 AUTO virar bruscamente, dar un viraje brusco. 2 SP *(player)* dar un regate, regatear; *(ball)* llevar efecto. 3 *fig (veer, deviate)* desviarse (from, de).

swift [swɪft] *adj* 1 *(runner, horse)* rápido,-a, veloz. 2 *(reaction, reply)* pronto,-a, rápido,-a.
▷ *n (bird)* vencejo común.

swiftness ['swɪftnəs] *n* 1 *(speed)* velocidad *f,* rapidez *f.* 2 *(promptness)* prontitud *f,* rapidez *f.*

swim [swɪm] *n* baño.
▷ *vi* 1 *(gen)* nadar. 2 *(be covered in liquid)* nadar (in, en); flotar (in, en); *(be overflowing)* estar cubierto,-a (with, de), estar inundado,-a. 3 *(spin, whirl)* dar vueltas.
▷ *vt (cross river)* cruzar a nado, cruzar nadando; *(cover distance)* nadar, hacer; *(use particular stroke)* nadar. ■ **to go for a swim** ir a nadar. ‖ **to have a swim** bañarse, nadar.
▲ *pt* swam [swɒm], *pp* swum [swʌm], *ger* swimming.

swimmer ['swɪməʳ] *n* nadador,-ra.

swimming ['swɪmɪŋ] *n* natación *f.* ■ **to go swimming** ir a nadar. ● **swimming baths** piscina cubierta. ‖ **swimming costume** bañador *m.* ‖ **swimming pool** piscina. ‖ **swimming trunks** bañador *m* (de hombre).

swimsuit ['swɪmsu:t] *n* bañador *m.*

swimwear ['swɪmweəʳ] *n* bañadores *mpl.*

swindle ['swɪndᵊl] *n (fiddle)* estafa; *(con)* timo.
▷ *vt* estafar, timar.

swine [swaɪn] *n* 1 [*pl* swine.] *arch (pig)* cerdo, puerco, cochino. 2 [*pl* swines.] *fam (person)* cerdo,-a, canalla *mf,* marrano,-a.

swing [swɪŋ] *n* 1 *(movement)* balanceo, vaivén *m; (of pendulum)* oscilación *f,* vaivén *m; (of hips)* contoneo. 2 *(plaything)* columpio. 3 *(change, shift)* giro, viraje *m,* cambio. 4 SP *(in golf, boxing)* swing *m.* 5 MUS *(jazz style)* swing *m; (rhythm)* ritmo. ● **swing door** puerta giratoria.
▷ *vi* 1 *(hanging object)* balancearse, bambolearse; *(pendulum)* oscilar; *(arms, legs)* menearse; *(child on swing)* columpiarse; *(on a pivot)* mecerse. 2 *(drive)* girar, doblar; *(walk)* caminar con energía; *(jump)* saltar. 3 *(shift)* cambiar, oscilar, virar. 4 *(music, band)* tener ritmo; *(party)* estar muy animado,-a.
▷ *vt* 1 *(gen)* balancear, bambolear; *(arms, legs)* balancear; *(child on swing)* columpiar, balancear; *(object on rope)* hacer oscilar. 2 *(cause to move)* hacer girar. 3 *(change)* cambiar. 4 *fam (arrange, achieve)* arreglar. ● **swing door** puerta giratoria.
⊙ **to swing around / swing round** *vi (person)* girar (sobre los talones), volverse bruscamente; *(vehicle)* dar un viraje, girar, virar (en redondo).
▷ *vt sep (vehicle)* hacer girar en redondo.
▲ *pt & pp* swung [swʌŋ].
⊙ **to swing at** *vt insep* intentar pegarle a, intentar darle a.

swipe [swaɪp] *n* 1 *(blow)* golpe *m.* 2 *(verbal attack)* ataque *m.* ● **swipe card** tarjeta magnética.
▷ *vt* 1 darle a. 2 *fam (pinch)* birlar, mangar, afanar.
▷ *vi* asestar un golpe (at, a), intentar darle (at, a).

swirl [swɜ:l] *n* 1 *(gen)* remolino; *(of smoke, cream)* voluta; *(of skirt)* vuelo. 2 *(pattern)* espiral *f.*
▷ *vi (whirl)* arremolinarse; *(person)* girar, dar vueltas.
▷ *vt* arremolinar.

swish [swɪʃ] *n (of water)* susurro, rumor *m; (of whip, cane)* silbido, chasquido; *(of skirt, curtain)* frufrú *m,* crujido, ruido; *(of animal's tail)* sacudida.
▷ *adj fam (smart)* muy elegante, elegantón,-ona.
▷ *vt (whip, cane)* chasquear; *(skirt)* hacer crujir; *(tail)* menear, sacudir.
▷ *vi (water)* susurrar; *(whip, cane)* dar un chasquido, producir un silbido; *(skirt)* crujir, hacer frufrú.

Swiss [swɪs] *adj* suizo,-a.
▷ *n* suizo,-a.
▷ *n pl* **the Swiss** los suizos *mpl.*

switch [swɪtʃ] *n* 1 ELEC interruptor *m,* conmutador *m.* 2 US *(on railway)* agujas *fpl.* 3 *(change, shift)* cambio *(turnround)* viraje *m*. **4** *(exchange, swap)* intercambio, trueque *m*. **5** *(stick)* vara; *(riding whip)* fusta. **6** *(hairpiece)* trenza postiza.

▷ *vt* **1** *(change)* cambiar de; *(move)* trasladar; *(attention)* desviar. **2** *(exchange)* intercambiar. **3** *(setting)* poner; *(channel)* cambiar de. **4** *(train)* desviar, cambiar de vía.

▷ *vi (gen)* cambiar (**to**, a).

⊃ **to switch off** *vt sep (light, TV, etc)* apagar; *(current, gas, electricity)* cortar, desconectar; *(engine)* parar.

▷ *vi (light, machine, heating)* apagarse; *(engine)* parar; *(person)* distraerse, desconectar, dejar de prestar atención.

⊃ **to switch on** *vt sep (light, machine, engine)* encender; *(light, radio, TV)* poner.

▷ *vi (gen)* encenderse.

⊃ **to switch over** *vi (gen)* cambiar (**to**, a); *(channel)* cambiar de canal.

witchboard ['swɪtʃbɔːd] *n* centralita.

witzerland ['swɪtsələnd] *n* Suiza.

wivel ['swɪvᵊl] *vi* girar, girarse, volverse.

▷ *vt (head)* girar; *(chair)* hacer girar. ● **swivel chair** silla giratoria.

▲ *pt & pp* **swivelled** (US **swiveled**), *ger* **swivelling** (US **swiveling**).

wollen ['swəʊlən] *pp* ⟶ **swell**.

▷ *adj (ankle, face)* hinchado,-a; *(glands)* inflamado,-a; *(river, lake)* crecido,-a.

woon [swuːn] *n lit* desmayo, desvanecimiento.

▷ *vi* **1** *lit (faint)* desmayarse, desvanecerse. **2** *fig (be emotionally affected)* derretirse (**over**, por).

woop [swuːp] *vi* **1** *(bird)* abalanzarse (**down on**, sobre), abatirse (**down on**, sobre); *(plane)* bajar en picado. **2** *fam (police)* hacer una redada (**on**, en).

▷ *n* **1** *(of bird, plane)* descenso (en picado). **2** *fam (by police)* redada.

word [sɔːd] *n* espada.

wordfish ['sɔːdfɪʃ] *n* pez *m* espada.

wore [swɔːʳ] *pt* ⟶ **swear**.

wordsman ['sɔːdzmən] *n* espadachín *m*, espada.

worn [swɔːn] *pp* ⟶ **swear**.

wot [swɒt] *n* empollón,-ona. ● *vi* empollar.

▲ *pt & pp* **swotted**, *ger* **swotting**.

wum [swʌm] *pp* ⟶ **swim**.

wung [swʌŋ] *pt & pp* ⟶ **swing**.

ybarite ['sɪbəraɪt] *n lit* sibarita *mf*.

ycamore ['sɪkəmɔːʳ] *n* BOT plátano falso, sicómoro.

yllable ['sɪləbᵊl] *n* sílaba.

yllabus ['sɪləbəs] *n* programa *m* de estudios.

▲ *pl* **syllabuses** o **syllabi**.

ylph [sɪlf] *n* sílfide *f*.

ymbiosis [sɪmbɪ'əʊsɪs] *n* simbiosis *f*.

ymbol ['sɪmbᵊl] *n* símbolo (**of**, de).

ymbolize ['sɪmbəlaɪz] *vt* simbolizar.

ymmetry ['sɪmɪtrɪ] *n* simetría.

ympathetic [sɪmp'θetɪk] *adj* **1** *(showing pity, compassion)* compasivo,-a; *(understanding)* comprensivo,-a (**to**, con); *(kind)* amable. **2** *(showing agreement, approval)* favorable (**to**, a).

sympathize ['sɪmpəθaɪz] *vi* **1** *(show pity, commiserate)* compadecer, compadecerse (**with**, de); *(understand)* comprender (**with**, -). **2** *(support - cause)* simpatizar (**with**, con); *(- request)* mostrarse favorable (**with**, a).

sympathizer ['sɪmpəθaɪzəʳ] *n* simpatizante *mf*.

sympathy ['sɪmpəθɪ] *n* **1** *(pity, compassion)* compasión *f*, lástima; *(condolences)* condolencia, pésame *m*. **2** *(understanding)* comprensión *f*; *(affinity)* afinidad *f*. **3** *(agreement, support)* acuerdo.

▲ *pl* **sympathies**.

▷ *n pl* **sympathies** *(condolences)* condolencia *f sing*, pésame *m sing*; *(loyalties, leanings)* simpatías *fpl*, tendencias *fpl*.

symphony ['sɪmfənɪ] *n* sinfonía. ● **symphony orchestra** orquesta sinfónica.

▲ *pl* **symphonies**.

symposium [sɪm'pəʊzɪəm] *n* simposio.

▲ *pl* **symposiums** o **symposia**.

symptom ['sɪmptəm] *n* **1** MED síntoma *m*. **2** *(sign)* síntoma *m*, señal *f*, indicio.

synagogue ['sɪnəgɒg] *n* sinagoga.

synchronize ['sɪŋkrənaɪz] *vt* sincronizar.

syncopation [sɪŋk'peɪʃᵊn] *n* síncopa.

syncope ['sɪŋkəpɪ] *n* MED síncope *m*.

syndicalism ['sɪndɪkᵊlɪzᵊm] *n* sindicalismo.

syndicalist ['sɪŋdɪkᵊlɪst] *n* sindicalista *mf*.

syndicate ['sɪndɪkət] *n* **1** *(gen)* corporación *f*, agrupación *f*, empresa. **2** *(news agency)* agencia (de prensa).

▷ *vt (distribute)* distribuir; *(publish)* publicar.

syndrome ['sɪndrəʊm] *n* síndrome *m*.

synonym ['sɪnənɪm] *n* sinónimo.

synopsis [sɪ'nɒpsɪs] *n* sinopsis *f*, resumen *m*.

▲ *pl* **synopses**.

syntactic [sɪn'tæktɪk] *adj* sintáctico,-a.

syntax ['sɪntæks] *n* sintaxis *f inv*.

synthesis ['sɪnθəsɪs] *n* síntesis *f inv*.

▲ *pl* **syntheses**.

synthesize ['sɪnθəsaɪz] *vt* sintetizar.

synthesizer ['sɪnθəsaɪzəʳ] *n* sintetizador *m*.

synthetic [sɪn'θetɪk] *adj* sintético,-a.

▷ *n* fibra sintética.

syphilis ['sɪfɪlɪs] *n* sífilis *f*.

Syria ['sɪrɪə] *n* Siria.

Syrian ['sɪrɪən] *adj* sirio,-a.

▷ *n* sirio,-a.

syringe [sɪ'rɪndʒ] *n* MED jeringa, jeringuilla.

▷ *vt* MED *(ear)* hacer un lavado de.

syrup ['sɪrəp] *n* **1** MED jarabe *m*. **2** CULIN almíbar *m*.

system ['sɪstəm] *n* **1** *(gen)* sistema *m*. **2** *(body)* cuerpo, organismo.

systematic [sɪst'mætɪk] *adj* sistemático,-a, metódico,-a.

systematize ['sɪstɪmətaɪz] *vt* sistematizar.

systemize ['sɪstəmaɪz] *vt* sistematizar.

systole ['sɪstəlɪ] *n* sístole *m*.

T

T, t [ti:] *n (the letter)* T, t *f*.

tab [tæb] *n* **1** *(flap)* lengüeta; *(on can)* anilla. **2** *(label)* etiqueta. **3** US *(bill)* cuenta. **4** *(on computer)* tabulador *m*.

tabby ['tæbɪ] *adj* atigrado,-a.

table ['teɪbᵊl] *n* **1** *(gen)* mesa. **2** *(chart)* tabla, cuadro. **3** SP clasificación *f*. ● **table of contents** índice *m* de materias. ‖ **table tennis** tenis *m* de mesa, pingpong *m*.
▷ *vt* GB *(motion, report, etc)* presentar.
▷ *n pl* **tables** tablas *fpl*, tablas *fpl* de multiplicar.

tablecloth ['teɪbᵊlklɒθ] *n* mantel *m*.

tablespoon ['teɪbᵊlspu:n] *n* **1** cucharón *m*. **2** cuchara grande.

tablespoonful ['teɪbᵊlspu:nfʊl] *n* cucharada grande.

tablet ['tæblɪt] *n* **1** MED pastilla, comprimido. **2** *(of stone)* lápida. **3** *(of soap)* pastilla.

tableware ['teɪbᵊlweəʳ] *n* vajilla.

tabloid ['tæblɔɪd] *n* periódico de formato pequeño.

tabulate ['tæbjʊleɪt] *vt* tabular.

tachycardia [tækɪ'kɑ:dɪə] *n* taquicardia.

tacit ['tæsɪt] *adj* tácito,-a.

taciturn ['tæsɪtɜ:n] *adj* taciturno,-a.

tack [tæk] *n* **1** *(nail)* tachuela. **2** MAR bordada, viraje *m*. **3** *(approach)* táctica. **4** SEW hilván *m*.
▷ *vt* **1** *(secure)* clavar con tachuelas. **2** SEW hilvanar.
▷ *vi* MAR dar bordadas, virar.

tackle ['tækᵊl] *n* **1** *(equipment)* equipo, avíos *mpl*, aparejos *mpl*. **2** MAR polea, aparejo. **3** SP *(football)* entrada; *(rugby)* placaje *m*.
▷ *vt* **1** *(deal with - problem)* abordar, encarar; *(- task)* emprender; *(person)* hablar con. **2** SP *(football)* entrarle a; *(rugby)* placar.

tacky ['tækɪ] *adj* **1** *(sticky)* pegajoso,-a. **2** *(in bad taste)* de mal gusto, cutre, hortera.
▲ *comp* **tackier**, *superl* **tackiest**.

tact [tækt] *n* tacto, discreción *f*, delicadeza.

tactful ['tæktfʊl] *adj* diplomático,-a, discreto,-a.

tactic ['tæktɪk] *n* táctica.

tactical ['tæktɪkᵊl] *adj* táctico,-a.

tactics ['tæktɪks] *n pl* MIL táctica *f sing*.

tactless ['tæktləs] *adj (person)* falto,-a de tacto, poco diplomático,-a; *(remark, question)* indiscreto,-a.

tad [tæd] *n* US niño.
▷ *n* **a tad** US *(a bit)* un poco.

tadpole ['tædpəʊl] *n* renacuajo.

Tadzhik ['tædʒɪk] *adj* tadjiko,-a.
▷ *n (person)* tadjiko,-a.
▲ *pl* **Tadzhik**.

Tadzhiki [tæ'dʒi:kɪ] *n (language)* tadjiko.

Tadzhikistan [tædʒi:kɪ'stæn] *n* Tadjikistán.

tag [tæg] *n* **1** *(label)* etiqueta. **2** *(on shoelace)* herrete *m*. **3** *(phrase)* coletilla. **4** *(game)* el corre que te pillo.
▷ *vt* **1** *(gen)* etiquetar, poner una etiqueta a. **2** *(on animals)* poner una chapa identificativa a.

Tagalog ['tægəlɒg] *n* tagalo.

Tagus ['teɪgəs] *n* el Tajo.

Tahiti [tə'hi:tɪ] *n* Tahití.

Tahitian [tə'hi:ʃᵊn] *adj* tahitiano,-a.
▷ *n* **1** *(person)* tahitiano,-a. **2** *(language)* tahitiano.

tail [teɪl] *n* **1** *(gen)* cola; *(of some four-legged animals)* cola, rabo. **2** *(of plane, kite, comet)* cola; *(of shirt, coat)* faldón *m*. **3** *(pursuer)* perseguidor,-ra.
▷ *vt* seguir de cerca.
▷ *n pl* **tails** *(of coin)* cruz *f sing*; *(suit)* frac *m*.

tailback ['teɪlbæk] *n (traffic jam)* caravana, cola, retención *f*.

tailcoat ['teɪlkəʊt] *n* frac *m*.

tail-end [teɪl'end] *n* final *m*, parte *f* final.

tail-gate ['teɪlgeɪt] *n* portón *m* trasero.

tail-light ['teɪllaɪt] *n* luz *f* trasera, piloto.

tailor ['teɪləʳ] *n* sastre,-a.
▷ *vt* **1** confeccionar. **2** *fig* adaptar.

tailored ['teɪləd] *adj (shirt)* entallado,-a; *(suit)* tipo sastre.

tailor-made [teɪlə'meɪd] *adj* hecho,-a a medida.

taint [teɪnt] *vt (reputation)* mancillar, manchar, empañar; *(food)* contaminar.
▷ *n* mancha, mancilla.

Taiwan [taɪ'wæn] *n* Taiwan.

Taiwanese [taɪwæ'ni:z] *adj* taiwanés,-esa.
▷ *n* taiwanés,-esa.

take [teɪk] *n* CINEM toma.
▷ *vt* **1** *(carry, bring)* llevar. **2** *(drive, escort)* llevar. **3** *(remove)* llevarse, quitar, coger. **4** *(hold, grasp)* tomar, coger. **5** *(accept - money, etc)* aceptar, coger; *(- criticism, advice, responsibility)* aceptar, asumir; *(- patients, clients)* aceptar. **6** *(win prize, competition)* ganar; *(earn)* ganar, hacer. **7** *(medicine, drugs)* tomar. **8** *(subject)* estudiar; *(course of study)* seguir, cursar. **9** *(teach)* dar clase a. **10** *(bus, train, etc)* tomar, coger. **11** *(capture)* tomar, capturar; *(in board games)* comer. **12** *(time)* tardar, llevar. **13** *(hold, contain)* tener cabida, acoger. **14** *(size of clothes)* usar, gastar; *(size of shoes)* calzar. **15** *(measurement, temperature, etc)* tomar; *(write down)* anotar. **16** *(need, require)* requerir, necesitar. **17** *(buy)* quedarse con, llevar(se). **18** *(bear)* aguantar, soportar. **19** *(react)* tomarse; *(interpret)* interpretar. **20** *(perform, adopt)* tomar, adoptar; *(exercise)* hacer. **21** *(have)* tomar(se). **22** *(suppose)* suponer. **23** *(consider)* considerar, mirar. **24** LING regir. **25** *(rent)* alquilar.
▷ *vi* **1** *(work - dye)* coger; *(- fire)* prender; *(- cutting)* prender; *(- seed)* germinar. **2** *(fish)* picar. **3** *(in draughts, etc)* comer. ■ **not to take no for an answer** no aceptar una respuesta negativa. ‖ **take it from me** escucha lo que te digo. ‖ **take it or leave it** lo tomas o lo dejas. ‖ **tak**

my word for it créeme. ▪ **to have what it takes** tener lo que hace falta.
to take apart *vt sep* 1 *(machine, etc)* desmontar, deshacer. 2 *(argument)* echar por tierra.
to take aside *vt sep* llevar a un lado.
to take away *vt sep* 1 *(remove)* llevarse, quitar. 2 *(subtract)* restar.
vi (food) llevar.
to take back *vt sep* 1 *(accept back)* recibir otra vez, aceptar algo devuelto; *(employee)* readmitir. 2 *(return)* devolver. 3 *(retract)* retirar, retractar. 4 *(in time)* hacer recordar.
to take down *vt sep* 1 *(remove, lower)* quitar, bajar. 2 *(dismantle)* desmontar. 3 *(write down)* apuntar.
vt insep (humiliate) humillar.
to take for *vt sep* tomar por.
to take in *vt sep* 1 *(shelter)* dar cobijo a, alojar, recoger. 2 *(deceive)* engañar. 3 *(grasp)* asimilar, entender, captar. 4 *(include)* incluir, abarcar. 5 *(clothes)* meterle a, estrechar.
to take off *vt sep* 1 *(clothes)* quitarse. 2 *(remove, detach)* quitar, sacar. 3 *(force to go)* llevar. 4 *(have as holiday)* tomarse. 5 *(imitate)* imitar. 6 *(deduct, discount)* descontar, rebajar.
vi 1 *(plane)* despegar. 2 *(leave hurriedly)* irse, marcharse. 3 *(become popular)* hacerse popular, tener éxito, ponerse de moda.
to take on *vt sep* 1 *(decide to do, undertake)* hacerse cargo de, encargarse de, aceptar; *(responsibility)* asumir. 2 *(employ)* contratar, coger. 3 *(challenge)* desafiar, enfrentarse con.
vt insep (begin to have, assume) asumir, tomar, adquirir.
vi (become upset) agitarse, ponerse nervioso,-a.
to take out *vt sep* 1 *(remove, extract, withdraw)* sacar, quitar. 2 *(escort, accompany)* invitar a salir; *(child, dog)* llevar de paseo. 3 *(insurance)* hacerse, sacar; *(licence, patent)* obtener. 4 US llevar comida a casa. 5 *(kill, destroy)* eliminar.
to take out on *vt sep* tomarla con, desquitarse con, descargarse.
to take over *vt sep* 1 *(country, party, etc)* tomar (posesión de), apoderarse de; *(building)* ocupar. 2 *(company, business)* absorber, adquirir; *(job, post)* hacerse cargo de; *(duty, responsibility)* asumir.
vi (assume control) tomar el poder, hacerse con el poder; *(job)* entrar en funciones, relevar.
vt insep (lines, points, argument) repasar; *(show round)* enseñar, mostrar.
to take over from *vt insep* relevar, sustituir.
to take to *vt insep* 1 *(person)* tomar cariño a. 2 *(vice)* darse a. 3 *(start to do)* empezar a, aficionarse a.
to take up *vt sep* 1 *(fill, occupy)* ocupar. 2 *(take upstairs)* llevar, subir; *(remove, lift - carpet, etc)* quitar, levantar. 3 *(space)* ocupar; *(time)* ocupar, llevar. 4 *(continue)* continuar, reanudar.
vt insep (offer) aceptar.
vt sep 1 *(start to do)* dedicarse a. 2 *(pursue - point, etc)* volver a. 3 *(sew)* acortar.
to take upon *vt sep* encargarse de.
to take up on *vt sep* 1 *(challenge)* hacer puntualizaciones sobre. 2 *(accept)* aceptar (una oferta).
⊙ **to take up with** *vt insep (form relationship with)* empezar a salir con, entrar en relaciones con.
▷ *vt sep (raise with)* hablar de.
▲ *pt* **took** [tʊk], *pp* **taken** ['teɪkᵊn].
take-away ['teɪkəweɪ] *n* 1 *(food)* comida para llevar. 2 *(restaurant)* restaurante *m* de comida para llevar.
take-home pay ['teɪkhəʊmpeɪ] *n* sueldo neto.
taken ['teɪkᵊn] *pp* ⟶ **take.**
▷ *adj (seat)* ocupado,-a.
take-off ['teɪkɔːf] *n* 1 *(aviation)* despegue *m*. 2 SP salto. 3 *(imitation)* imitación *f*, parodia.
take-out ['teɪkaʊt] *n* US *(food)* comida para llevar.
takeover ['teɪkəʊvəʳ] *n* 1 POL toma del poder, toma de posesión. 2 *(of company)* adquisición *f*.
taking ['teɪkɪŋ] *n dated* atractivo,-a. ▪ **it's there for the taking** allí está.
takings ['teɪkɪŋz] *n pl (gen)* recaudación *f sing*, caja; *(at box office)* taquilla, entrada.
talc [tælk] *n* talco.
talcum powder ['tælkəmpaʊdəʳ] *n* polvos *mpl* de talco.
tale [teɪl] *n (story)* cuento, relato, historia; *(lie)* cuento, mentira.
talent ['tælənt] *n* 1 *(special ability)* talento, dotes *mpl*. 2 *(talented people)* gente *f* de talento, gente *f* dotada. 3 *fam (attractive people)* gente *f* guapa.
talented ['tæləntɪd] *adj* de talento, dotado,-a.
talk [tɔːk] *vi* 1 *(gen)* hablar (**to**, con/a). 2 *(negotiate)* negociar. 3 *(gossip)* hablar, chismorrear.
▷ *vt* hablar (**about/of**, de).
▷ *n* 1 *(conversation)* conversación *f*. 2 *(lecture)* charla, conferencia. 3 *(rumour)* rumor *m*, voz *f*.
▷ *n pl* **talks** negociaciones *fpl*.
⊙ **to talk back** *vi* contestar, contestar de mala manera.
⊙ **to talk down** *vt insep* 1 *(person)* hacer callar. 2 *(aircraft)* dirigir por radio.
⊙ **to talk down to** *vt insep* hablar con desprecio a, hablar con aires de suficiencia a.
⊙ **to talk over** *vt sep* discutir, hablar de.
⊙ **to talk round** *vt sep* convencer.
▷ *vt insep* dar vueltas a.
talkative ['tɔːkətɪv] *adj* hablador,-ra, parlanchín,-ina, charlatán,-ana, locuaz.
talking ['tɔːkɪŋ] *n* hablar *m*.
▷ *adj* que habla.
talking-to ['tɔːkɪŋtuː] *n fam* bronca, reprimenda, rapapolvo.
tall [tɔːl] *adj* alto,-a. ● **tall story** cuento chino.
tallow ['tæləʊ] *n* sebo.
tally ['tælɪ] *n* cuenta.
▲ *pl* **tallies.**
▷ *vi* concordar, cuadrar.
▲ *pt & pp* **tallied**, *ger* **tallying.**
talon ['tælən] *n* garra.
tambourine [tæmbəˈriːn] *n* pandereta.
tame [teɪm] *adj* 1 *(by nature)* manso,-a, dócil. 2 *(tamed)* domesticado,-a. 3 *fig* soso,-a, aburrido,-a.
▷ *vt* domar, domesticar.
tamper ['tæmpəʳ] *vi* **to tamper with** *(gen)* tocar, manipular; *(lock)* intentar forzar; *(document, figures)* alterar.
tampon ['tæmpɒn] *n* tampón *m*.

tan[1] [tæn] *n* **1** *(colour)* color *m* marrón claro. **2** *(suntan)* bronceado, moreno.
▷ *adj* marrón claro.
▷ *vt* **1** *(leather)* curtir. **2** *(skin)* broncear, poner moreno,-a.
▷ *vi* broncearse, ponerse moreno,-a.
▲ *pt & pp* **tanned**, *ger* **tanning**.
tan[2] ['tændʒənt] *abbr* (**tangent**) tangente; *(abbreviation)* tang.
tang [tæŋ] *n (taste)* sabor *m* fuerte; *(smell)* olor *m* fuerte.
tangent ['tændʒənt] *n* tangente *f*.
tangerine [tændʒə'ri:n] *n* **1** *(fruit)* clementina, mandarina. **2** *(colour)* naranja.
▷ *adj* naranja.
tangible ['tændʒəbᵊl] *adj* tangible.
Tangier [tæn'dʒɪəʳ] *n* Tánger.
tangle ['tæŋgᵊl] *n (confused mass)* enredo, maraña, embrollo; *(confusion)* enredo, lío.
▷ *vt* enredar, enmarañar.
▷ *vi* enredarse.
⊙ **to tangle up** *vt sep* enredarse.
⊙ **to tangle with** *vt insep* meterse con.
tank [tæŋk] *n* **1** *(for water)* depósito, tanque *m*; *(for fuel)* depósito. **2** MIL tanque *m*. **3** US *sl (jail)* chirona. ● **think tank** grupo de expertos.
⊙ **to tank up** *vt sep* llenar el depósito, repostar.
▷ *vi (get drunk)* emborracharse.
tanker ['tæŋkəʳ] *n* **1** *(ship)* buque *m* cisterna. **2** *(for oil)* petrolero. **3** *(lorry)* camión *m* cisterna.
tanned [tænd] *adj (person)* moreno,-a, bronceado,-a; *(leather)* curtido,-a.
tanner ['tænəʳ] *n* **1** curtidor,-ra. **2** *fam dated moneda de seis peniques*.
tannery ['tænərɪ] *n* tenería, curtiduría.
tantalise ['tæntəlaɪz] *vt* → **tantalize**.
tantalising ['tæntəlaɪzɪŋ] *adj* → **tantalizing**.
tantalize ['tæntəlaɪz] *vt* atormentar (tentando).
tantalizing ['tæntəlaɪzɪŋ] *adj* tentador,-ra.
tantamount ['tæntəmaʊnt] *adj* equivalente (**to**, a).
tantrum ['tæntrəm] *n* berrinche *m*, rabieta.
Tanzania [tænzə'nɪə] *n* Tanzania.
Tanzanian [tænzə'nɪən] *adj* tanzano,-a.
▷ *n* tanzano,-a.
tap[1] [tæp] *n* **1** grifo. **2** *(light blow)* golpecito. **3** *(on phone)* micrófono de escucha. **4** *(on barrel)* espita; *(for gas)* llave *f*. ● **tap water** agua del grifo.
▷ *vt* **1** *(strike lightly)* golpear suavemente, dar un golpecito a. **2** *(on keyboard)* teclear, pulsar. **3** *(liquid)* sacar. **4** *(resources)* explotar, utilizar. **5** *(telephone)* pinchar, intervenir.
▲ *pt & pp* **tapped**, *ger* **tapping**.
⊙ **to tap out** *vt sep* **1** teclear, escribir a máquina. **2** *(in Morse code)* enviar.
tap[2] [tæp] *n* claqué *m*. ● **tap dance** claqué *m*.
tape [teɪp] *n* **1** *(audio, visual)* cinta. **2** *(recorded material)* grabación *f*. **3** SP cinta de llegada. **4** *(sticky)* cinta adhesiva. ● **tape measure** cinta métrica. ‖ **tape recorder** magnetófono.
▷ *vt* **1** *(fasten)* pegar con cinta adhesiva. **2** *(record)* grabar.
taper ['teɪpəʳ] *n* vela *delgada*.
▷ *vt* afilar, estrechar.
▷ *vi* afilarse, estrecharse.
⊙ **to taper off** *vt insep* ir disminuyendo.

tapestry ['tæpəstrɪ] *n* **1** *(art)* tapicería. **2** *(cloth)* tapiz *n*
▲ *pl* **tapestries**.
tar [tɑːʳ] *n* **1** *(for roads, in cigarettes)* alquitrán *m*. **2** *(… soap, etc)* brea.
▷ *vt* alquitranar.
▲ *pt & pp* **tarred**, *ger* **tarring**.
target ['tɑ:gɪt] *n* **1** *(of missile, goal, aim)* objetivo. **2** *(… shooting, of criticism)* blanco. **3** *(board)* diana.
▷ *vt* **1** *(aim at target)* apuntar. **2** *(cause to have effect o…)* dirigir a, destinar a.
▷ *adj (date, figure)* fijado,-a; *(audience, market)* objetivo.
tariff ['tærɪf] *n* **1** *(list of fixed charges)* tarifa. **2** *(duty … be paid on imports)* arancel *m*.
▷ *adj* arancelario,-a.
tarmac ['tɑ:mæk] *n* **1** asfalto. **2** *(area)* pista.
▷ *vt* asfaltar.
tarnish ['tɑ:nɪʃ] *vt (metal)* deslustrar; *(reputation)* emp…ñar, manchar.
▷ *vi (metal)* deslustrarse; *(reputation)* mancharse.
▷ *n* falta de lustre, falta de brillo.
tarpaulin [tɑ:'pɔ:lɪn] *n* lona.
tarsus ['tɑ:səs] *n* ANAT tarso.
▲ *pl* **tarsi**.
tart [tɑ:t] *adj* **1** *(sour)* acre, agrio,-a. **2** *(reply)* morda… áspero,-a, acre.
▷ *n* **1** *(pie)* tarta, pastel *m*.
⊙ **to tart up** *vt sep (building)* renovar, remodelar; *(pe… son)* emperifollar.
Tartar ['tɑ:təʳ] *adj* tártaro,-a.
▷ *n* **1** tártaro,-a. **2** tártaro.
tartar ['tɑ:təʳ] *n* **1** *(on teeth)* sarro. **2** *(in wine)* tártar… ● **tartar sauce** salsa tártara.
task [tɑ:sk] *n* tarea, labor *f*.
Tasman ['tæzmən] *n* **the Tasman Sea** el Mar de Ta…mania.
Tasmania [tæz'meɪnɪə] *n* Tasmania.
Tasmanian [tæz'meɪnɪən] *adj* tasmano,-a.
▷ *n* tasmano,-a.
tassel ['tæsᵊl] *n* borla.
taste [teɪst] *n* **1** *(faculty)* gusto. **2** *(flavour)* sabor *m*. *(small sample)* muestra; *(experience)* experiencia. *(ability to make good judgements)* gusto; *(liking)* aficiór (**for**, a), gusto (**for**, por). ● **taste bud** papila gustativa
▷ *vt* **1** *(try food)* probar; *(wine)* catar, degustar. **2** *(eat, drin…)* probar. **3** *(experience)* conocer. **4** *(perceive flavour)* nota…
▷ *vi* saber (**of/like**, a).
tasteful ['teɪstful] *adj* de buen gusto, elegante.
tasteless ['teɪstləs] *adj* **1** de mal gusto. **2** *(insipid)* ins…pido,-a, soso,-a.
tasty ['teɪstɪ] *adj* sabroso,-a, rico,-a.
▲ *comp* **tastier**, *superl* **tastiest**.
tattered ['tætəd] *adj* harapiento,-a, andrajoso,-a,.
tatters ['tætəz] *n pl (clothes)* harapos *mpl*, andraj… *mpl*. ■ **in tatters** **1** *(clothes)* harapiento,-a, andrajos…-a, hecho,-a jirones. **2** *(nerves, reputation, etc)* hecho,… pedazos, destrozado,-a.
tattle ['tætᵊl] *n* chismes *mpl*, habladurías *fpl*.
▷ *vi* cotorrear.
▷ *vt* US acusar, chivarse.
tattoo [tə'tu:] *n* **1** MIL retreta. **2** *(show)* espectáculo m…litar musical. **3** *(on skin)* tatuaje *m*.
▲ *pl* **tattoos**.

▷ *vt* tatuar.
▲ *pt & pp* tattooed, *ger* tattooing.
atty ['tætɪ] *adj (gen)* muy usado,-a gastado,-a; *(clothes)* gastado,-a, raído,-a.
▲ *comp* tattier, *superl* tattiest.
aught [tɔ:t] *pt & pp* ⟶ teach.
aunt [tɔ:nt] *n* mofa, pulla, insulto.
▷ *vt (mock)* bufarse de, mofarse de; *(provoke)* hostigar, provocar.
aurus ['tɔ:rəs] *n* Tauro.
aut [tɔ:t] *adj* tirante, tenso,-a.
avern ['tævᵊn] *n* taberna, mesón *m*.
awdry ['tɔ:drɪ] *adj* hortera, charro,-a.
▲ *comp* tawdrier, *superl* tawdriest.
awny ['tɔ:nɪ] *adj* leonado,-a.
ax [tæks] *n* **1** impuesto, contribución *f*. **2** *fig (burden, strain)* carga (on, sobre), esfuerzo (on, para).
▷ *vt* **1** *(impose a tax on - goods, profits)* gravar; *(- business, person)* imponer contribuciones a. **2** *fig (strain, test)* poner a prueba.
▲ *pl* taxes.
axable ['tæksəbᵊl] *adj* imponible, gravable.
axation [tæk'seɪʃᵊn] *n (taxes)* impuestos *mpl*; *(system)* sistema *m* tributario.
ax-deductible ['tæksdɪ'dʌktəbᵊl] *adj* desgravable.
ax-free ['tæks'fri:] *adj* libre de impuestos, exento,-a de impuestos.
axi ['tæksɪ] *n* taxi *m*. ● **taxi driver** taxista *mf*.
▲ *pl* taxis.
▷ *vi (plane)* rodar por la pista.
axidermy ['tæksɪdɜ:mɪ] *n* taxidermia.
axing ['tæksɪŋ] *adj (problem)* difícil; *(journey, job)* agotador,-ra.
axonomy [tæk'sɒnəmɪ] *n* taxonomía.
▲ *pl* taxonomies.
axpayer ['tækspeɪəʳ] *n* contribuyente *mf*.
ea [ti:] *n* **1** *(gen)* té *m*. **2** *(infusion)* infusión *f*.
ea-break ['ti:breɪk] *n* descanso *para tomar el té*.
each [ti:tʃ] *vt (gen)* enseñar; *(subject)* dar clases.
▷ *vi* ser profesor,-ra, dar clases. ■ **that'll teach you** así aprenderás.
▲ *pt & pp* taught [tɔ:t].
eacher ['ti:tʃəʳ] *n* maestro,-a, profesor,-ra.
each-in ['ti:tʃɪn] *n* seminario.
eaching ['ti:tʃɪŋ] *n* enseñanza.
▷ *adj* docente. ● **teaching staff** profesorado.
▷ *n pl* **teachings** doctrina, enseñanzas *fpl*.
eacup ['ti:kʌp] *n* taza para té.
eak [ti:k] *n* teca.
eal [ti:l] *n* cerceta común.
eam [ti:m] *n* **1** *(gen)* equipo. **2** *(of horses)* tiro; *(of oxen)* yunta.
▷ *adj* de equipo.
▷ *vi* combinar (with, con).
⊙ **to team up** *vt sep* asociarse (with, con), unirse (with, con).
eamwork ['ti:mwɜ:k] *n* trabajo de equipo.
eapot ['ti:pɒt] *n* tetera.
ear[1] [teəʳ] *n (rip)* rasgón *m*, desgarrón *m*, rotura.
▷ *vt* **1** *(rip, make a hole)* rasgar, desgarrar; *(pull apart, into pieces)* romper, hacer pedazos. **2** *(remove by force)* arrancar.
▷ *vi* **1** romperse, rasgarse. **2** *(rush)* ir a toda velocidad, lanzarse, precipitarse. ■ **to be torn between...** debatirse entre... ● **wear and tear** desgaste *m*.
▲ *pt* tore [tɔ:ʳ], *pp* torn [tɔ:n].
⊙ **to tear apart** *vt sep* **1** *(rip up)* despedazar, desgarrar; *(destroy)* destrozar. **2** *fig* destrozar, desgarrar.
⊙ **to tear at** *vt sep* arañar, rasgar.
⊙ **to tear away** *vt sep (snatch)* arrancar; *(force to leave)* arrancar, sacar.
⊙ **to tear down** *vt sep (building)* derribar, tirar abajo.
⊙ **to tear off** *vt sep (pull violently)* arrancar; *(clothes)* quitarse precipitadamente.
⊙ **to tear out** *vt sep* arrancar.
⊙ **to tear up** *vt sep (paper)* romper en pedazos, hacer pedazos; *(plant)* arrancar de raíz.
tear[2] [tɪəʳ] *n* lágrima.
teardrop ['tɪədrɒp] *n* lágrima.
tearful ['tɪəfʊl] *adj* lloroso,-a.
tearing ['teərɪŋ] *adj* vertiginoso,-a.
tearoom ['ti:rʊm] *n* salón *m* de té.
tease [ti:z] *vt* **1** *(make fun of - playfully)* tomar el pelo a, burlarse de; *(- annoyingly, unkindly)* atormentar, molestar. **2** *(sexually)* provocar, incitar. **3** *(wool, etc)* cardar.
▷ *vi* tomar el pelo.
▷ *n* **1** *(joker)* bromista *mf*. **2** *fam (flirt)* coqueta.
⊙ **to tease out** *vt sep (disentangle)* desenredar; *(obtain information)* sacar, sonsacar.
teasel ['ti:zᵊl] *n* cardencha.
teaser ['ti:zəʳ] *n* **1** *(puzzle)* rompecabezas *m*. **2** *(person)* bromista *mf*.
teashop ['ti:ʃɒp] *n* salón *m* de té.
teaspoon ['ti:spu:n] *n* cucharilla.
teaspoonful ['ti:spu:nfʊl] *n* cucharadita.
teat [ti:t] *n* **1** ZOOL tetilla. **2** *(on bottle)* tetina.
teatime ['ti:taɪm] *n* hora del té, hora de la merienda.
technical ['teknɪkᵊl] *adj* técnico,-a.
technicality [teknɪ'kælɪtɪ] *n (detail)* detalle *m* técnico; *(technical term)* tecnicismo.
▲ *pl* technicalities.
technically ['teknɪkᵊlɪ] *adv* **1** técnicamente. **2** *(theoretically)* en teoría.
technician [tek'nɪʃᵊn] *n* técnico,-a.
technique [tek'ni:k] *n* técnica.
technological [teknə'lɒdʒɪkᵊl] *adj* tecnológico,-a.
technology [tek'nɒlədʒɪ] *n* tecnología.
▲ *pl* technologies.
teddy bear ['tedɪbeəʳ] [Also teddy.] *n* osito de peluche.
tedious ['ti:dɪəs] *adj* tedioso,-a, aburrido,-a.
teem[1] [ti:m] *vi (rain)* llover a cántaros, diluviar.
teem[2] [ti:m] *vi (be abundant in)* abundar (with, en), estar lleno,-a (with, de).
teenage ['ti:neɪdʒ] *adj* adolescente.
teenager ['ti:neɪdʒəʳ] *n* adolescente *mf* de 13 a 19 años, quinceañero,-a.
teens [ti:nz] *n pl* adolescencia, edad *f* de 13 a 19 años.
teeny ['ti:nɪ] *adj fam* pequeñito,-a, chiquitín,-ina.
▲ *comp* teenier, *superl* teeniest.
tee-shirt ['ti:ʃɜ:t] *n* camiseta.
teeter ['ti:təʳ] *vi* **1** *(totter)* tambalearse. **2** *(hesitate)* vacilar.
teeth [ti:θ] *n pl* ⟶ tooth.
teethe [ti:ð] *vi* endentecer, echar los dientes.

teething ['tiːðɪŋ] *n* dentición *f*.
teetotaller [tiː'təutᵊlər] *n* abstemio,-a.
Teheran [teə'rɑːn] *n* → **Tehran.**
Tehran [teə'rɑːn] *n* Teherán.
telecommunications [telɪkəmjuːnɪ'keɪʃᵊnz] *n pl* telecomunicaciones *fpl*.
telegram ['telɪgræm] *n* telegrama *m*.
telegraph ['telɪgrɑːf] *n* telégrafo.
▷ *vi* telegrafiar.
telepathy [tɪ'lepəθɪ] *n* telepatía.
telephone ['telɪfəun] *n* teléfono. ● **telephone box** cabina telefónica. ‖ **telephone call** llamada telefónica. ‖ **telephone directory** listín *m* telefónico. ‖ **telephone number** número telefónico.
▷ *vt* telefonear, llamar por teléfono.
▷ *vi* hacer una llamada telefónica.
telephonist [tə'lefənɪst] *n* telefonista *mf*.
telephoto lens [telɪfəutəu'lenz] *n* teleobjetivo.
teleprinter ['telɪprɪntər] *n* teletipo.
teleprompter ['telɪprɒmptər] *n* autocue *m*, teleprompter *m*.
telescope ['telɪskəup] *n* telescopio.
▷ *vt* plegar.
▷ *vi* plegarse.
televise ['telɪvaɪz] *vt* televisar.
television ['telɪvɪʒᵊn] *n* **1** *(gen)* televisión *f*. **2** *(set)* televisor *m*.
telex® ['teleks] *n* télex *m*.
▷ *vt* enviar por télex.
tell [tel] *vt* **1** *(gen)* decir. **2** *(story, joke)* contar; *(truth, lies, secret)* decir. **3** *(talk about)* hablar de. **4** *fml* comunicar, informar. **5** *(assure)* asegurar, garantizar. **6** *(order)* decir, mandar. **7** *(show)* indicar; *(in writing)* explicar. **8** *(distinguish)* distinguir. **9** *(know)* saber, notarse. **10** *(count - votes)* escrutar; *(- rosary beads)* pasar.
▷ *vi* **1** *(reveal secret)* hablar, soplar. **2** *(have effect)* notarse, hacerse notar. **3** *(know)* saber.
▲ *pt & pp* **told** [təuld].
⊙ **to tell against** *vt insep* obrar en contra de.
⊙ **to tell apart** *vt sep* (saber) distinguir.
⊙ **to tell off** *vt sep* **1** regañar, reñir. **2** MIL destacar.
⊙ **to tell on** *vt insep (inform on)* chivarse de.
teller ['telər] *n (in bank)* cajero,-a.
telling ['telɪŋ] *adj (blow)* contundente; *(smile, reaction)* elocuente, expresivo,-a, revelador,-ra.
telling-off [telɪŋ'ɒf] *n fam* bronca, rapapolvo.
telltale ['telteɪl] *n* chivato,-a, acusica *mf*.
▷ *adj* revelador,-ra.
telly ['telɪ] *n fam* tele *f*.
▲ *pl* **tellies.**
temper ['tempər] *n* **1** *(mood)* humor *m*; *(nature)* genio, temperamento, disposición *f*. **2** *(of metal)* temple *m*.
▷ *vt* **1** *(metal)* templar. **2** *fig* atenuar, suavizar.
tempera ['tempərə] *n* temple *m*.
temperament ['tempᵊrəmənt] *n* temperamento.
temperamental [temprə'mentl] *adj* temperamental.
temperance ['tempᵊrəns] *n (gen)* moderación *f*; *(from alcohol)* abstinencia.
temperate ['tempᵊrɪt] *adj (gen)* moderado,-a; *(climate)* templado,-a.
temperature ['tempᵊrɪtʃər] *n* temperatura. ■ **to have/run a temperature** tener fiebre.
tempered ['tempəd] *adj* templado,-a.
tempest ['tempɪst] *n* tempestad *f*.
template ['templeɪt] *n* plantilla.
temple ['tempᵊl] *n* **1** *(building)* templo. **2** ANAT sien *f*.
temporary ['tempᵊrərɪ] *adj* temporal, provisional.
tempt [tempt] *vt* tentar.
temptation [temp'teɪʃᵊn] *n* tentación *f*. ■ **to yield to temptation** caer en la tentación.
tempting ['temptɪŋ] *adj* tentador,-ra.
ten [ten] *n* diez *m*.
▷ *adj* diez.
Consulta también **six.**
tenable ['tenəbᵊl] *adj* **1** *(theory, etc)* sostenible, defendible. **2** *(post, office)*: **how long is the post tenable for** *¿durante cuántos años se puede ocupar el puesto?*
tenacious [tə'neɪʃəs] *adj* tenaz.
tenacity [tə'næsɪtɪ] *n* tenacidad *f*.
tenant ['tenənt] *n* inquilino,-a, arrendatario,-a.
tend [tend] *vt (person)* cuidar de, atender; *(other)* ocuparse de.
▷ *vi (have tendency)* tender (**to**, a), tener tendencia (**to**, a).
⊙ **to tend to** *vt insep* ocuparse de.
tendency ['tendənsɪ] *n* tendencia.
▲ *pl* **tendencies.**
tender[1] ['tendər] *adj* **1** *(meat, etc)* tierno,-a. **2** *(loving)* tierno,-a, cariñoso,-a. **3** *(sore)* dolorido,-a. **4** *(delicate)* delicado,-a, sensible.
▲ *comp* **tenderer,** *comp* **tenderest.**
tender[2] ['tendə] *n* COMM *(offer)* oferta, propuesta.
▷ *vt* presentar, ofrecer.
▷ *vi* hacer una oferta (**for**, para).
tender[3] ['tendə] *n* **1** *(dinghy)* lancha (auxiliar). **2** *(of train)* ténder *m*.
tender-hearted ['tendə'hɑːtɪd] *adj* compasivo,-a, bondadoso,-a.
tenderise ['tendəraɪz] *vt* → **tenderize.**
tenderize ['tendəraɪz] *vt* ablandar, macerar.
tenderness ['tendənəs] *n* ternura.
tendon ['tendən] *n* tendón *m*.
tendril ['tendrəl] *n* zarcillo.
tenement ['tenəmənt] *n* casa de vecindad.
tenet ['tenət] *n* principio, dogma *m*.
tennis ['tenɪs] *n* tenis *m*. ● **tennis court** pista de tenis. ‖ **tennis player** jugador,-a de tenis.
tenon ['tenən] *n* espiga.
▷ *vt* despatillar.
tenor ['tənər] *n* tenor *m*.
tense [tens] *adj* **1** *(anxious)* tenso,-a. **2** *(taut)* tirante, tenso,-a.
▷ *n (of verb)* tiempo verbal.
▷ *vt* tensar.
tension ['tenʃᵊn] *n* tensión *f*.
tent [tent] *n* tienda de campaña.
tentacle ['tentəkᵊl] *n* tentáculo.
tentative ['tentətɪv] *adj* **1** de prueba, de ensayo, provisional. **2** *(person)* indeciso,-a.
tenterhooks ['tentəhuks] ■ **on tenterhooks** sobre ascuas.
tenth [tenθ] *adj* décimo,-a.
▷ *adv* en décimo lugar.
▷ *n (fraction)* décimo; *(one part)* décima parte *f*.
Consulta también **sixth.**

ent-peg ['tentpeg] *n* estaquilla.
enuous ['tenjuəs] *adj* tenue, delicado,-a.
enure ['tenjəʳ] *n* **1** *(of property)* ocupación *f.* **2** *(of position)* ejercicio. **3** EDUC titularidad *f.*
epid ['tepɪd] *adj* tibio,-a.
erebene ['terəbi:n] *n* terebenteno.
erm [tɜ:m] *n* **1** EDUC trimestre *m.* **2** *(period of time)* período. **3** *(expression, word)* término.
▷ *vt* calificar de, llamar, denominar.
▷ *n pl* **terms** *(sense)* términos *mpl;* COMM condiciones *fpl, (relations)* relaciones *fpl.*
erminal ['tɜ:mɪnᵊl] *adj* terminal.
▷ *n* **1** ELEC borne *m.* **2** COMPUT terminal *m.* **3** *(at airport, etc)* terminal *f.*
erminate ['tɜ:mɪneɪt] *vt* **1** *(gen)* terminar, poner fin a; *(contract)* rescindir. **2** *(pregnancy)* interrumpir.
▷ *vi* terminarse:
ermini ['tɜ:mɪnaɪ] *n pl* → **terminus.**
erminology [tɜ:mɪ'nɒlədʒɪ] *n* terminología.
erminus ['tɜ:mɪnəs] *n* término.
▲ *pl* **terminuses** o **termini** ['tɜ:mɪnaɪ].
ern [tɜ:n] *n* golondrina de mar.
errace ['terəs] *n* **1** *(of house, café, bar, etc)* terraza. **2** *(on hillside)* terraza, bancal *m.* **3** *(of houses)* hilera de casas.
▷ *n pl* **terraces** SP gradas *fpl.*
erraced house [terəst'haus] *n* casa adosada.
terrain [tə'reɪn] *n* terreno.
errapin ['terəpɪn] *n* tortuga de agua dulce.
errible ['terɪbᵊl] *adj* **1** terrible, espantoso,-a, atroz. **2** *fam (as intensifier)* mucho,-a.
erribly ['terɪblɪ] *adv* **1** terriblemente. **2** *fam (very)* muy.
errier ['terɪəʳ] *n* terrier *m.*
errific [tə'rɪfɪk] *adj* **1** *(wonderful)* fabuloso,-a, estupendo,-a. **2** *(huge)* tremendo,-a.
errify ['terɪfaɪ] *vt* aterrar, aterrorizar.
▲ *pt & pp* **terrified,** *ger* **terrifying.**
errifying ['terɪfaɪɪŋ] *adj* aterrador,-ra, espantoso,-a.
erritory ['terɪtᵊrɪ] *n* **1** *(gen)* territorio. **2** *(zone)* zona, área.
▲ *pl* **territories.**
error ['terəʳ] *n* **1** *(gen)* terror *m,* espanto. **2** *fam (child)* diablillo.
errorise ['terəraɪz] *vt* → **terrorize.**
errorism ['terərɪzᵊm] *n* terrorismo.
errorist ['terərɪst] *n* terrorista *mf.*
▷ *adj* terrorista.
errorize ['terəraɪz] *vt* aterrorizar.
error-stricken ['terəstrɪkən] *adj* aterrorizado,-a.
erse [tɜ:s] *adj* seco,-a, brusco,-a.
test [test] *n* **1** *(trial)* prueba. **2** EDUC *(gen)* examen *m,* prueba; *(multiple choice)* test *m.* **3** MED análisis *m.* ● **test tube** probeta.
▷ *vt* **1** *(gen)* probar. **2** *(patience, loyalty)* poner a prueba. **3** EDUC hacerle una prueba a. **4** MED analizar.
estament ['testəmənt] *n* testamento.
esticle ['testɪkᵊl] *n* testículo.
estify ['testɪfaɪ] *vt* JUR declarar, atestiguar.
▷ *vi* **1** *(bear witness)* dar fe (**to**, de). **2** JUR prestar declaración, testificar.
▲ *pt & pp* **testified,** *ger* **testifying.**
estimony ['testɪmənɪ] *n* testimonio.
▲ *pl* **testimonies.**

test-tube baby [testtju:b'beɪbɪ] *n* niño,-a probeta.
tetanus ['tetənəs] *n* tétanos *m inv.*
tether ['teðəʳ] *n (rope)* cuerda; *(chain)* cadena.
▷ *vt* atar.
Teuton ['tju:tᵊn] *n* teutón,-ona.
Teutonic [tju:'tɒnɪk] *adj* teutónico,-a.
Texan ['teksᵊn] *adj* tejano,-a.
▷ *n* tejano,-a.
Texas ['teksəs] *n* Tejas.
text [tekst] *n* texto.
textbook ['tekstbuk] *n* libro de texto.
textile ['tekstaɪl] *adj* textil.
▷ *n* textil *m.*
texture ['tekstʃəʳ] *n* textura.
Thai [taɪ] *adj* tailandés,-esa.
▷ *n* **1** *(person)* tailandés,-esa. **2** *(language)* tailandés *m.*
Thailand ['taɪlænd] *n* Tailandia.
Thames [temz] *n* el Támesis *m.*
than [ðæn, *unstressed* ðᵊn] *conj* **1** que: **he is taller than you are** *él es más alto que tú.* **2** *(with numbers)* de: **more than fifty** *más de cincuenta.* **3** *(followed by clause)* de lo que: **this is easier than we thought** *esto es más fácil de lo que pensábamos.*
thank [θæŋk] *vt* dar las gracias a, agradecer. ■ **no, thank you** no, gracias. | **thank you** gracias.
thankful ['θæŋkful] *adj* agradecido,-a.
thankless ['θæŋkləs] *adj* ingrato,-a.
thanks [θæŋks] *interj* gracias: **thanks to** *gracias a.*
▷ *n pl (gratitude)* agradecimiento. ■ **no, thanks** no, gracias.
thanksgiving [θæŋks'gɪvɪŋ] *n* acción *f* de gracias. ● **Thanksgiving Day** Día *m* de Acción de Gracias.
that [ðæt *unstressed* ðət] *adj* ese, esa; *(remote)* aquel, aquella.
▲ *pl* **those.**
▷ *pron* **1** ése *m,* ésa; *(remote)* aquél *m,* aquélla. **2** *(indefinite)* eso; *(remote)* aquello. **3** *(relative)* que. **4** *(with preposition)* que, el/la que, el/la cual.
▲ *pl* **those.**
▷ *adv fam* tan, tanto,-a, tantos,-as. ■ **that is to say** es decir. | **that's it 1** *(that's all)* eso es todo. **2** *(that's right)* eso es. **3** *(that's enough)* se acabó. | **that's right** así es. | **that's that** se acabó. | **who's that?** *(on 'phone)* ¿quién es?
thatch [θætʃ] *n* **1** *(straw)* paja; *(roof)* tejado de paja. **2** *(hair)* mata.
▷ *vt* poner techo de paja a, cubrir con techo de paja.
thaw [θɔ:] *n* deshielo.
▷ *vt (food)* descongelar; *(snow, ice)* derretir.
▷ *vi* **1** *(food)* descongelarse; *(snow, ice)* derretirse. **2** *(person)* ablandarse; *(relations)* distenderse, mejorar.
⊙ **to thaw out** *vi* descongelarse.
▷ *vt sep* descongelar.
the [ðə] [Delante de una vocal se pronuncia [ðɪ]; con enfasis [ði:].] *def art* **1** el, la; *(plural)* los, las. **2** *(per)* por: **we are paid by the hour** *nos pagan por horas.* **3** *(emphasis)* el, la, los, las: **you're not the Paul Newman, are you?** *no serás el auténtico Paul Newman, ¿verdad?*
▷ *adv (with comparatives)*: **the more you have, the more you want** *cuanto más se tiene, más se quiere.*
theater ['θɪətəʳ] *n* US → **theatre.**
theatre ['θɪətəʳ] *n* **1** *(gen)* teatro. **2** MED quirófano. **3** US cine *m.* **4** *(scene of action)* escenario.
▷ *adj* teatral, de teatro.

theatrical [θɪ'ætrɪkᵊl] *adj* teatral.
theft [θeft] *n* robo, hurto.
their [ðeəʳ] *adj* su; *(plural)* sus: they took their children and their dog *se llevaron a sus hijos y al perro.*
theirs [ðeəz] *pron* (el) suyo, (la) suya; *(plural)* (los) suyos, (las) suyas: that house is theirs *aquella casa es suya.*
them [ðem, *unstressed* ðᵊm] *pron* **1** *(direct object)* los, las; *(indirect object)* les; *(before another pronoun)* se: the Smiths are coming, do you know them? *vienen los Smith, ¿los conoces?;* take these flowers and give them to Mary *coge estas flores y se las das a Mary.* **2** *(with preposition, stressed)* ellos, ellas: don't speak to them *no hables con ellos;* **3** *fam (used with singular meaning)* lo, la, le: if anyone arrives, tell them to wait *si llega alguien, dile que espere.*
theme [θi:m] *n* tema *m.*
themselves [ðəm'selvz] *pron* **1** *(subject)* ellos/ellas mismos(as): they made it themselves *lo hicieron ellos mismos.* **2** *(object)* se: they looked at themselves in the mirror *se miraron en el espejo.* **3** *(after preposition)* sí mismos,-as: they are old enough to look after themselves *son lo bastante mayores como para cuidar de sí mismos.* ■ **by themselves** solos,-as: don't leave the children by themselves *no dejes a los niños solos.*
then [ðen] *adv* entonces, luego: I was born in 1963, life was different then *nací en 1963, entonces la vida era distinta;* I'll have soup first and then steak *primero tomaré sopa y luego un filete.*
theology [θɪ'ɒlədʒɪ] *n* teología.
theorem ['θɪərəm] *n* teorema *m.*
theoretic [θɪə'retɪk] *adj* teórico,-a.
theoretical [θɪə'retɪkᵊl] *adj* teórico,-a.
theorise ['θɪəraɪz] *vi* ⟶ **theorize.**
theorize ['θɪəraɪz] *vi* teorizar.
theory ['θɪərɪ] *n* teoría. ■ **in theory** en teoría.
▲ *pl* theories.
therapist ['θerəpɪst] *n* terapeuta *mf.*
therapy ['θerəpɪ] *n* terapia, terapéutica: she's having therapy *está recibiendo terapia.*
▲ *pl* therapies.
there [ðeəʳ] *adv* **1** allí, allá, ahí: I often go there on holiday (US vacation) *voy de vacaciones allí a menudo.* **2** *(in discussion)* acerca de eso: I agree with you there *estoy de acuerdo contigo en eso.* ■ **there and then** en el momento. ■ **there is/are, etc** ⟶ be. ■ **there you are** aquí tiene. ■ **there you go** ya está.
thereabouts [ðeərə'baʊts] *adv (near there)* por ahí, allí cerca; *(more or less)* más o menos.
thereafter [ðeə'ræftəʳ] *adv* a partir de entonces.
thereby ['ðeəbaɪ] *adv* por eso, por ello.
therefore ['ðeəfɔ:ʳ] *adv* por tanto, por lo tanto, por consiguiente.
therein [ðeər'ɪn] *adv* allí.
thereupon [ðerə'pɒn] *adv* acto seguido.
thermal ['θɜ:məl] *adj* **1** *(stream, bath, spring)* termal; *(underwear)* térmico,-a. **2** PHYS térmico,-a.
▷ *n* corriente *f* térmica.
▷ *n pl* thermals ropa *sing* interior térmica.
thermometer [θe'mɒmɪtəʳ] *n* termómetro.
thermos® ['θɜ:mɒs] *n* termo.
thermostat ['θɜ:məstæt] *n* termostato.
thesaurus [θɪ'sɔ:rəs] *n* diccionario ideológico.
these [ði:z] *adj* estos,-as: these apples are cheaper than those *estas manzanas son más baratas que aquellas.*
▷ *pron* éstos,-as: which ones do you prefer? –these *¿cuáles prefieres? –éstos.*
they [ðeɪ] *pron* **1** *(plural)* ellos,-as: where are the children? –they're in the garden (US yard) *¿dónde están los niños? –están en el jardín;* **2** *fam (singular - substitutes he or she)* él, ella: if anyone saw the accident, they should go to the police *si alguien vio el accidente, que vaya a la policía.* ■ **they say that...** se dice que...
thick [θɪk] *adj* **1** *(solid things)* grueso,-a: it's a thick book *es un libro grueso.* **2** *(liquid, gas, vegetation, etc)* espeso,-a. **3** *(beard, eyebrows)* poblado,-a. **4** *(cloud, smoke, fog, forest)* denso,-a, espeso,-a. **5** *(fur, hedge)* tupido,-a. **6** *fam (stupid)* corto,-a, corto,-a de alcances; *(unable to think)* espeso,-a. **7** *(accent)* marcado,-a, cerrado,-a; *(of speech, voice)* poco claro,-a.
▷ *adv* espesamente, gruesamente.
thicken ['θɪkᵊn] *vt* espesar.
▷ *vi* espesarse, hacerse más denso,-a.
thickener ['θɪkᵊnəʳ] *n* espesante *m.*
thicket ['θɪkɪt] *n* espesura, matorral *m.*
thickness ['θɪknəs] *n* **1** *(in size)* espesor *m*, grosor *m.* **2** *(density - of liquid)* espesura; *(- of fog)* densidad *f.* **3** *(layer)* capa.
thick-skinned ['θɪk'skɪnd] *adj* insensible.
thief [θi:f] *n (gen)* ladrón,-ona; *(mugger)* atracador,-ra.
thieve [θi:v] *vt* robar.
▷ *vi* robar.
thieves [θi:vz] *pl* ⟶ **thief.**
thigh [θaɪ] *n* muslo.
thighbone ['θaɪbəun] *n* fémur *m.*
thimble ['θɪmbᵊl] *n* dedal *m.*
thin [θɪn] *n (person)* delgado,-a, flaco,-a.
▷ *adj* **1** *(thing)* delgado,-a, fino,-a, **2** *(liquid - soup, sauce)* poco espeso,-a, claro,-a; *(- rain)* fino,-a.
▷ *n (hair)* escaso,-a, fino,-a y poco abundante; *(vegetation)* poco tupido,-a.
▷ *adj* **1** *(audience, crowd)* poco numeroso,-a; *(response, attendance)* escaso,-a. **2** *(voice)* débil. **3** *(excuse, argument)* pobre, poco convincente.
▲ *comp* thinner, *superl* thinnest.
▷ *adv* finamente.
▷ *vt (paint)* diluir; *(sauce)* hacer menos espeso,-a.
▷ *vi* **1** *(fog, mist)* disiparse. **2** *(audience, crowd, traffic)* hacerse menos denso,-a, disminuir.
⊙ **to thin down** *vi* adelgazar.
▷ *vt sep (sauce)* hacer menos espeso,-a, aclarar; *(paint)* diluir.
⊙ **to thin out** *vt insep (crowd, traffic)* mermar, disminuir.
▷ *vt sep (crops, plants)* entresacar.
thing [θɪŋ] *n* **1** *(object)* cosa, objeto. **2** *(non-material)* cosa. **3** *(affair)* asunto. **4** *(person, creature)*: you poor little thing! *¡pobrecito!* **5** *(action)*: the best thing to do *lo mejor que puedes hacer.* **6** *fam (preference)*: it's not really my thing *la verdad es que no es lo mío.* **7** *(with negative)* nada: I can't understand a thing you're saying *no entiendo nada de lo que dices.*
▷ *n* the thing *(what)* lo que: the thing I like most in life *lo que más me gusta en la vida;* the same thing *lo mismo;* the terrible thing is that... *lo malo es que...;* the latest

thing *lo último;* **the main thing** *lo principal;* **the important thing** *lo importante.*
▷ *n pl* **things** *(belongings)* cosas *fpl*, ropa *f sing*, equipaje *m sing.*

think [θɪŋk] *vi* **1** *(use mind)* pensar. **2** *(have in mind, consider)* pensar. **3** *(intend, plan)* pensar. **4** *(come to mind)* ocurrírsele a uno. **5** *(remember)* acordarse (**of**, de), recordar. **6** *(have an opinion)* pensar (**of**, de), opinar (**of**, de). **7** *(imagine)* imaginarse, pensar.
▷ *vt* **1** *(reflect, ponder)* pensar. **2** *(imagine, suppose)* pensar, imaginarse, creer. **3** *(expect)* pensar, esperar. **4** *(believe)* creer. **5** *(remember)* recordar, acordarse de. **6** *(have an opinion)* pensar, opinar.
▲ *pt & pp* **thought** [θɔ:t].
◉ **to think ahead** *vi* prevenir.
◉ **to think back** *vi* hacer memoria.
◉ **to think back to** *vi* recordar, acodarse de.
◉ **to think out** *vt sep (consider carefully)* estudiar, pensar bien.
◉ **to think over** *vt sep (reflect upon)* reflexionar, pensar.
◉ **to think through** *vt sep (consider fully)* estudiar, considerar.
◉ **to think up** *vt sep (invent - excuse)* inventar; *(- slogan)* idear, crear.

thinkable ['θɪŋkəbəl] *adj* pensable, imaginable.

thinker ['θɪŋkər] *n* pensador,-ra.

thinking ['θɪŋkɪŋ] *n* **1** *(opinion)* opinión *f*, parecer *m*. **2** *(thought)* pensamiento, ideas *fpl.*
▷ *adj* pensante, inteligente.

thinly ['θɪnlɪ] *adv* **1** → **also thin. 2** *(sparsely)* escasamente, en poca cantidad. **3** *(scarcely)* apenas.

thinner ['θɪnər] *n (for diluting)* disolvente *m.*

thinness ['θɪnnəs] *n* delgadez *f.*

third [θɜ:d] *adj* tercero,-a.
▷ *adv (in series)* tercero, en tercer lugar.
▷ *n* **1** tercero,-a. **2** *(fraction)* tercio; *(one part)* tercera parte *f*. **3** GB ≈ bien *m (título universitario que corresponde a la cuarta nota más alta).* ● **third person** LING tercera persona.

Consulta también **sixth.**

third-class ['θɜ:rdklɑ:s] *adj* de tercera clase.
▷ *adv (travel)* en tercera.

thirdly ['θɜ:dlɪ] *adv* en tercer lugar.

third-party ['θɜ:dpɑ:tɪ] *adj (insurance)* a terceros.

third-rate ['θɜ:dreɪt] *adj* de tercera (categoría).

third-world ['θɜ:dwɜ:ld] *adj (in general)* del tercer mundo; *(pejorative use)* tercermundista.

thirst [θɜ:st] *n* **1** sed *f*. **2** *fig* ansias *fpl*, afán *m*, sed *f.*
◉ **to thirst for** *vt insep* tener sed de, tener afán de.

thirsty ['θɜ:stɪ] *adj* **1** sediento,-a: **I'm thirsty** *tengo sed.* **2** *(work, etc)* que da sed. **3** *fig (eager)* ansioso,-a (**for**, por). ■ **to be thirsty** tener sed.
▲ *comp* **thirstier**, *superl* **thirstiest.**

thirteen [θɜ:'ti:n] *n* trece *m.*
▷ *adj* trece.

Consulta también **six.**

thirteenth [θɜ:'ti:nθ] *adj* decimotercero,-a.
▷ *adv* en decimotercero lugar.
▷ *n (fraction)* decimotercero; *(one part)* decimotercera parte *f.*

Consulta también **sixth.**

thirties ['θɜ:tɪz] *n pl* **the thirties** los años *mpl* treinta. ■ **to be in one's thirties** tener treinta y tantos años.

Consulta también **sixties.**

thirtieth ['θɜ:tɪəθ] *adj* trigésimo,-a.
▷ *adv* en trigésimo lugar.
▷ *n (fraction)* trigésimo; *(one part)* trigésima parte *f.*

Consulta también **sixtieth.**

thirty ['θɜ:tɪ] *n* treinta *m.*
▷ *adj* treinta.

Consulta también **sixty.**

this [ðɪs] *adj* este, esta: **whose is this book?** *¿de quién es este libro?*
▲ *pl* **these** [ði:s].
▷ *pron* **1** éste, ésta; *(indefinite)* esto: **I prefer this one** *prefiero éste;* **2** *(on 'phone)*: **this is Laura** *soy Laura.*
▲ *pl* **these** [ði:s].
▷ *adv* tan, tanto,-a: **I didn't think it was this far** *no creía que fuera tan lejos.* ■ **this is** *(introducing)* te presento a.

thistle ['θɪsəl] *n* cardo.

thorax ['θɔ:ræks] *n* tórax *m inv.*

thorn [θɔ:n] *n* espina, pincho.

thorny ['θɔ:nɪ] *adj* espinoso,-a.
▲ *comp* **thornier**, *superl* **thorniest.**

thorough ['θʌrə] *adj* **1** *(deep)* profundo,-a, a fondo. **2** *(careful)* cuidadoso,-a, minucioso,-a. **3** *(person)* concienzudo,-a. **4** *(utter, complete)* total, verdadero,-a.

thoroughbred ['θʌrəbred] *n (horse)* pura sangre *mf*; *(other animal)* animal *m* de raza.
▷ *adj (horse)* de pura sangre; *(other animal)* de raza.

thoroughfare ['θʌrəfeər] *n* vía pública.

thoroughly ['θʌrəlɪ] *adv* **1** *(carefully)* a fondo, meticulosamente. **2** *(completely)* totalmente, absolutamente.

those [ðəuz] *adj* esos,-as; *(remote)* aquellos,-as: **could you pass me those plates?** *¿me podrías pasar esos platos?*
▷ *pron* ésos,-as; *(remote)* aquéllos,-as: **if these are my books, whose are those?** *si estos libros son míos, ¿de quién son aquellos?*

though [ðəu] *conj* aunque, si bien, a pesar de que: **though he doesn't earn very much, he loves his job** *aunque no gana mucho, le encanta su trabajo.*
▷ *adv* sin embargo, a pesar de todo: **it's expensive - it's worth it though** *es caro - sin embargo, vale lo que cuesta.* ■ **even though** aun cuando, a pesar de que.

thought [θɔ:t] *pt & pp* → **think.**
▷ *n* **1** pensamiento **2** *(consideration)* consideración *f*. **3** *(idea, opinion)* idea, opinión *f*. **4** *(intention)* intención *f.*

thoughtful ['θɔ:tful] *adj* **1** *(considerate)* atento,-a, considerado,-a. **2** *(pensive)* pensativo,-a, meditabundo,-a. **3** *(considered)* serio,-a.

thoughtless ['θɔ:tləs] *adj* **1** *(unthinking)* irreflexivo,-a, descuidado,-a. **2** *(inconsiderate)* desconsiderado,-a, poco considerado,-a.

thousand ['θauzənd] *n* mil *m*: **there were thousands of people** *había miles de personas.*
▷ *adj* mil: **it costs a thousand euros** *cuesta mil euros.*

thousandth ['θauzənθ] *adj* milésimo,-a.
▷ *adv* en milésimo lugar.
▷ *n (fraction)* milésimo; *(one part)* milésima parte *f.*

thrash [θræʃ] *vt* **1** *(beat)* azotar. **2** *(defeat)* derrotar, dar una paliza a. **3** *(arm, leg, etc)* sacudir.

⊙ **to thrash about / thrash around** *vi* retorcerse.
⊙ **to thrash out** *vt sep (problem)* discutir; *(agreement)* llegar a un acuerdo sobre.
thread [θred] *n* **1** SEW hilo, hebra. **2** *(of screw, bolt)* rosca. **3** *(of story)* hilo.
▷ *vt* **1** *(needle)* enhebrar. **2** *(beads)* ensartar.
threat [θret] *n* amenaza.
threaten ['θretᵊn] *vt* amenazar (**with/to**, con).
▷ *vi* amenazar.
threatening ['θretᵊnɪŋ] *adj* amenazador,-ra, intimidatorio,-a.
three [θri:] *n* tres *m*.
▷ *adj* tres. ● **three quarters** tres cuartos.
Consulta también **six**.
threefold ['θri:fəʊld] *adj* triple.
▷ *adv* tres veces.
three-phase ['θri:feɪz] *adj* trifásico,-a.
three-piece ['θri:pi:s] *adj* de tres piezas.
threesome ['θri:sᵊm] *n* grupo de tres.
thresh [θreʃ] *vt* trillar.
thresher ['θreʃəʳ] *n (machine)* trilladora; *(person)* trillador,-ra.
threshing ['θreʃɪŋ] *adj* trilla.
threshold ['θreʃəʊld] *n* **1** umbral *m*. **2** *fig* umbral *m*, límite *m*.
threw [θru:] *pt* ⟶ **throw**.
thrift [θrɪft] *n* economía, frugalidad *f*.
thrifty ['θrɪftɪ] *adj* económico,-a, frugal.
▲ *comp* **thriftier**, *superl* **thriftiest**.
thrill [θrɪl] *n (excitement)* emoción *f*, ilusión *f*.
▷ *vt (excite)* entusiasmar, hacer ilusión a, ilusionar.
▷ *vi (de excited)* entusiasmarse.
thriller ['θrɪləʳ] *n (novel)* novela de suspense; *(film)* película de suspense; *(play)* obra de suspense.
thrilling ['θrɪlɪŋ] *adj* emocionante, apasionante.
thrive [θraɪv] *vi (plant)* crecer mucho, crecer bien; *(person)* estar estupendamente; *(business)* prosperar.
▲ *pt* **throve** [θrəʊv] **o thrived**; *pp* **thrived o thriven** ['θrɪvᵊn], *ger* **thriving**.
thriving ['θraɪvɪŋ] *adj* próspero,-a, floreciente.
throat [θrəʊt] *n* garganta.
throb [θrɒb] *n (of heart, pulse)* latido, palpitación *f*; *(of engine, music)* vibración *f*, zumbido.
▷ *vi* **1** *(heart, pulse)* latir, palpitar; *(engine, music)* vibrar, zumbar. **2** *(with pain)* dar punzadas.
▲ *pt & pp* **throbbed**, *ger* **throbbing**.
throes [θrəʊz] ■ **in the throes of** en medio de.
thrombosis [θrɒm'bəʊsɪs] *n* trombosis *f inv*.
throne [θrəʊn] *n* trono.
throng [θrɒŋ] *n* muchedumbre *f*, multitud *f*.
▷ *vi (come together)* apiñarse, agolparse; *(enter)* entrar en tropel, entrar en masa.
▷ *vt (fill)* abarrotar, atestar.
throttle ['θrɒtᵊl] *n* **1** válvula reguladora. **2** *fam* acelerador *m*.
▷ *vt* estrangular, ahogar. ■ **at full throttle** a toda pastilla.
⊙ **to throttle back / throttle down** *vt sep* desacelerar.
▷ *vi* disminuir la velocidad.
through [θrʊ:] *prep* **1** por, a través de. **2** *(because of)* por, a causa de. **3** *(from beginning to the end)* durante todo,-a, hasta el final de. **4** *(by means of)* por, a través de, mediante.
▷ *adv* **1** de un lado a otro. **2** *(to the end)* hasta el final. GB *(on phone)* conectado,-a. **4** US acabado,-a.
▷ *adj (train)* directo,-a; *(traffic)* de paso. ■ **to be throug with** STH/SB haber acabado con ALGO/ALGN. ● **n through road** calle *f* sin salida.
throughout [θrʊ:'aʊt] *prep* **1** por todo,-a, en todo,- **2** *(time)* durante todo,-a, a lo largo de.
▷ *adv* **1** *(all over)* por/en todas partes. **2** *(completel* completamente. **3** *(time)* desde el principio hasta fin, todo el tiempo.
throve [θrəʊv] *pt* ⟶ **thrive**.
throw [θrəʊ] *n* **1** lanzamiento, tiro. **2** *(of dice)* tirad lance *m*; *(in game)* jugada, turno.
▷ *vt* **1** *(gen)* tirar, arrojar, lanzar. **2** *(to the floor - rider)* de corcovar, desmontar; *(- wrestler)* derribar. **3** *(hea* echar; *(arms)* extender, abrir. **4** *fig (kiss)* echar, tira *(glance, look)* lanzar, dirigir. **5** *fam (party)* organiza dar, hacer. **6** *fam (confuse)* desconcertar. **7** *(light, sha ow)* proyectar. **8** *(shape pottery)* formar, hacer. **9** *(e tend bridge)* tender, construir. ■ **to throw in one's l with** compartir la suerte con.
⊙ **to throw about** *vt sep (money)* derrochar.
⊙ **to throw away** *vt sep* **1** *(get rid of, discard)* tirar. **2** *(waste)* desaprovechar, perder; *(money)* malgasta derrochar. **3** *(speech)* lanzar al aire.
⊙ **to throw back** *vt sep* **1** *(ball, etc)* devolver. **2** *(bedclothes)* echar atrás.
⊙ **to throw back on** *vt insep* obligar a recurrir a.
⊙ **to throw in** *vt sep* **1** *fam (include)* incluir gratis. **2** s sacar de banda.
⊙ **to throw off** *vt sep* **1** *(get rid of)* deshacerse de, libra se de. **2** *(confuse, escape, elude)* despistar. **3** *(clothe* quitarse.
⊙ **to throw on** *vt sep (clothes)* ponerse.
⊙ **to throw out** *vt sep* **1** *(expel)* echar, expulsar. **2** *(rejec* rechazar. **3** *(discard)* tirar.
⊙ **to throw together** *vt sep* **1** *(assemble)* juntar *de pris (improvise)* improvisar. **2** *(bring into contact)* juntar.
⊙ **to throw up** *vi (vomit)* vomitar, devolver.
▷ *vt sep* **1** *(give up, resign)* abandonar, renunciar a. *(produce)* arrojar, dar, aportar; *(reveal)* revelar, po ner en evidencia. **3** *(vomit)* vomitar, devolver.
▲ *pt* **threw** [θru:], *pp* **thrown** [θrəʊn].
throwaway ['θrəʊəweɪ] *adj* de usar y tirar.
throw-away ['θrəʊəweɪ] *adj (disposable)* de usar y ti rar, desechable; *(spoken casually)* hecho,-a como d pasada.
throw-in ['θrəʊɪn] *n* SP saque *m* de banda.
thrown [θrəʊn] *pp* ⟶ **throw**.
thru [θrʊ:] *prep-adv* US ⟶ **through**. **Monday thru Frida** *de lunes a viernes*.
thrush [θrʌʃ] *n* tordo.
thrust [θrʌst] *n* **1** *(gen)* empuje *m*, empujón *m*. **2** *(attack* ataque *m*, avance *m*. **3** *(hostile remark)* crítica. **4** *(wit sword)* estocada; *(with dagger)* puñalada; *(with knife)* cu chillada. **5** *(main point)* idea central, idea clave.
▷ *vt (shove)* empujar, empujar con violencia.
▷ *vi (jostle)* dar empujones.
▷ *vt (push in)* meter.
▷ *vi (pierce - with sword)* dar estocadas; *(- with other in strument)* clavar.
▲ *pt & pp* **thrust**.
⊙ **to thrust on** *vt sep* imponer.

thud [θʌd] *n* ruido sordo.
▷ *vi* caer con un ruido sordo.
▲ *pt & pp* thudded, *ger* thudding.
thumb [θʌm] *n* pulgar *m*.
▷ *vt* hacer autostop.
⊙ **to thumb through** *vt insep* hojear.
thumb-index ['θʌmɪndeks] *n* uñero.
thumbnail ['θʌmneɪl] *n* uña del pulgar.
thumbtack ['θʌmtæk] *n* US chincheta.
thump [θʌmp] *n (blow)* golpe *m*, puñetazo; *(sound)* golpazo.
▷ *vt* golpear, pegar un puñetazo.
▷ *vi (gen)* golpear; *(heart)* latir con fuerza; *(feet)* caminar con pasos pesados.
thunder ['θʌndəʳ] *n* trueno.
▷ *vi* tronar.
▷ *vt (shout)* bramar, rugir.
thunderbolt ['θʌndəbəult] *n* rayo.
thunderclap ['θʌndəklæp] *n* trueno.
thundercloud ['θʌndəklaud] *n* nubarrón *m*.
thunderous ['θʌndᵊrəs] *adj fig* ensordecedor,-ra, atronador,-ra.
thunderstorm ['θʌndəstɔ:m] *n* tormenta.
thunderstruck ['θʌndərstrʌk] *adj* atónito,-a, pasmado,-a, estupefacto,-a.
Thursday ['θɜ:zdɪ] *n* jueves *m*.
Para ejemplos de uso, consulta **Saturday**.
thus [ðʌs] *adv* **1** *(in this way, like this)* así, de este modo. **2** *(consequently)* así que, por lo tanto, por consiguiente. **3** *(to this extent)* hasta.
thwart [θwɔ:t] *vt* desbaratar, frustrar.
thyme [taɪm] *n* tomillo.
thyroid ['θaɪrɔɪd] *n* tiroides *m*. ● **thyroid gland** glándula tiroides.
tiara [tɪ'ɑ:rə] *n* **1** *(diadem)* diadema. **2** *(of Pope)* tiara.
Tiber ['taɪbəʳ] *n* el Tíber *m*.
Tiberias [taɪ'bɪərɪəs] *n* **Lake Tiberias** lago de Tiberiades.
Tibet [tɪ'bet] *n* Tíbet.
Tibetan [tɪ'betᵊn] *adj* tibetano.
▷ *n* **1** *(person)* tibetano,-a. **2** *(language)* tibetano.
tibia ['tɪbɪə] *n* tibia.
tick¹ [tɪk] *n* ZOOL garrapata.
tick² [tɪk] *n* **1** *(noise)* tictac *m*. **2** *(mark)* marca, señal *f*. **3** *fam* momento, segundito.
▷ *vi (clock)* hacer tictac.
▷ *vt* señalar, marcar.
⊙ **to tick away** *vi* transcurrir.
⊙ **to tick off** *vt sep* **1** marcar, señalar. **2** *(scold)* regañar, reñir. **3** US fastidiar, dar rabia.
⊙ **to tick over** *vi* **1** AUTO marchar al ralentí, estar en marcha. **2** *(business, etc)* ir tirando.
tick³ [tɪk] *n* GB *fam (credit)* crédito.
ticket ['tɪkɪt] *n* **1** *(for transport)* billete *m*. **2** *(for concert, cinema, etc)* entrada. **3** *(for library, etc)* carnet *m*. **4** *(label)* etiqueta. **5** *(for item deposited)* resguardo. **6** *fam (fine)* multa. **7** POL lista de candidatos.
tickle ['tɪkᵊl] *n* cosquilleo.
▷ *vt* **1** *(touch lightly)* hacer cosquillas a; *(itch)* picar. **2** *(amuse)* hacer gracia a, divertir.
▷ *vi (touch lightly)* hacer cosquillas; *(itch)* picar.
ticklish ['tɪkᵊlɪʃ] *adj* **1** cosquilloso,-a. **2** *fig* delicado,-a.
tidal ['taɪdᵊl] *adj* de la marea. ● **tidal wave 1** *(gen)* maremoto. **2** *fig* oleada.
tide [taɪd] *n* **1** marea. **2** *fig (trend)* corriente *f*. ● **high tide** pleamar *f*. ▮ **low tide** bajamar *f*.
tidemark ['taɪdmɑ:k] *n* **1** *marca que deja la marea*. **2** *fam (on bath, neck)* marca de mugre.
tidy ['taɪdɪ] *adj* **1** *(place)* ordenado,-a, bien arreglado. **2** *(person - appearance)* arreglado,-a; *(- habits)* metódico,-a. **3** *(considerable)* considerable, bastante.
▲ *comp* tidier, *superl* tidiest.
▷ *n* organizador *m*.
▷ *vt* [Also tidy up.] ordenar, poner en orden, arreglar.
▷ *vi* [Also tidy up.] poner las cosas en orden.
▲ *pt & pp* tidied, *ger* tidying.
⊙ **to tidy away** *vt sep* recoger, guardar.
⊙ **to tidy out** *vt sep* vaciar, limpiar, ordenar.
tie [taɪ] *n* **1** *(of shirt)* corbata. **2** *(for fastening)* cierre *m*. **3** *(rod, beam)* tirante *m*. **4** *fig (bond)* lazo, vínculo: **family ties are strong** *los lazos del parentesco son fuertes*. **5** *fig (restriction)* estorbo, atadura. **6** SP *(draw)* empate *m*; *(match)* encuentro, partido. **7** MUS ligadura.
▷ *vt* **1** *(fasten)* atar; *(knot, bow)* hacer. **2** *fig* ligar, vincular, relacionar. **3** *(restrict)* atar. **4** MUS ligar.
▷ *vi* **1** *(fasten)* atarse. **2** SP empatar.
⊙ **to tie down** *vt sep* **1** atar, sujetar. **2** *(restrict)* atar; *(commit oneself)* comprometerse.
⊙ **to tie in** *vt sep* relacionar, ligar.
▷ *vi* concordar, cuadrar.
⊙ **to tie up** *vt sep* **1** *(fasten)* atar; *(boat)* amarrar. **2** *(link)* conectar, ligar, relacionar. **3** *(occupy)* liar, ocupar. **4** FIN *(capital)* inmovilizar, invertir. **5** *(finalize)* finalizar, concluir, cerrar.
tiepin ['taɪpɪn] *n* aguja de corbata.
tier [tɪəʳ] *n* **1** *(in stadium)* grada. **2** *(of cake)* piso. **3** *(in hierarchy)* nivel *m*.
tiger ['taɪgəʳ] *n* tigre *m*. ● **tiger lily** lirio tigrado. ▮ **tiger moth** mariposa tigre.
tight [taɪt] *adj* **1** *(firmly fastened)* apretado,-a, duro,-a. **2** *(taut)* tensado,-a, tirante, tenso,-a; *(chest)* oprimido. **3** *(clothes)* ajustado,-a, ceñido,-a. **4** *(not leaky)* hermético,-a, impermeable. **5** *(hold)* estrecho,-a, fuerte. **6** *(packed together)* apretado,-a. **7** *(strict - schedule)* apretado,-a; *(- security)* estricto,-a, riguroso,-a. **8** *fam (mean)* agarrado,-a, tacaño,-a. **9** *fam (drunk)* borracho,-a. **10** *(not easily obtainable)* escaso,-a. **11** *(contest)* reñido,-a. **12** *(bend)* cerrado,-a. ● **tight spot** aprieto.
▷ *adv* firmemente, fuerte.
tighten ['taɪtᵊn] *vt* **1** *(gen)* apretar, ajustar; *(rope)* tensar. **2** *(make stricter - security)* hacer más estricto, reforzar; *(- credit)* restringir.
▷ *vi (gen)* apretarse; *(rope, muscles)* tensarse.
⊙ **to tighten up** *vt sep* intensificar, hacer más estricto,-a.
▷ *vi* ponerse más estricto,-a.
tight-fisted [taɪt'fɪstɪd] *adj* tacaño,-a, agarrado,-a.
tight-fitting [taɪt'fɪtɪŋ] *adj* ceñido,-a, ajustado,-a.
tight-knit ['taɪtnɪt] *adj* muy unido,-a.
tight-lipped ['taɪt'lɪpt] *adj (silent)* callado,-a; *(angry)* con los labios apretados.
tightrope ['taɪtrəup] *n* cuerda floja. ● **tightrope walker** funambulo.
tights [taɪts] *n pl* **1** *(gen)* pantys *mpl*, medias *fpl*. **2** *(thick)* leotardos *mpl*, mallas *fpl*.

tigress ['taɪgrəs] *n* tigresa.
tile [taɪl] *n (wall)* azulejo; *(floor)* baldosa; *(roof)* teja.
▷ *vt* **1** *(wall)* alicatar, poner azulejos a. **2** *(floor)* embaldosar. **3** *(roof)* tejar.
till [tɪl] *prep* hasta.
▷ *conj* hasta que.
▷ *n (for cash)* caja.
▷ *vt (cultivate)* labrar, cultivar.
tiller ['tɪləʳ] *n* caña del timón.
tilt [tɪlt] *n* **1** inclinación *f*. **2** *(with lance)* acometida.
▷ *vt* inclinar, ladear.
▷ *vi* **1** *(slope, shift)* inclinarse. **2** *(with lance)* acometer.
⊙ **to tilt at** *vt insep* arremeter contra.
timber ['tɪmbəʳ] *n* **1** *(wood)* madera (de construcción). **2** *(beam)* viga. **3** *(trees)* árboles *mpl* maderables.
▷ *interj* ¡cuidado, que cae!, ¡allá va! ● **timber mill** aserradero.
timberyard ['tɪmbəjɑːd] *n* almacén *m* de madera.
time [taɪm] *n* **1** *(period)* tiempo. **2** *(short period)* rato. **3** *(of day)* hora. **4** *(age, period, season)* época. **5** *(occasion)* vez *f*. **6** *(suitable moment)* momento. **7** MUS compás *m*. **8** GB la hora de cerrar. **9** *fam (imprisonment)* condena.
▷ *vt* **1** *(measure time)* medir la duración de, calcular; *(races, etc)* cronometrar. **2** *(schedule)* estar previsto,-a.
▷ *n pl* **times** veces *fpl*. ■ **(and) about time** ya era hora. ‖ **all the time** todo el tiempo. ‖ **at all times** siempre. ‖ **at any time** en cualquier momento. ‖ **at no time** nunca. ‖ **at one time** en un tiempo. ‖ **at the same time** al mismo tiempo. ‖ **at the time / at that time** entonces. ‖ **at times** a veces. ‖ **behind time** tarde. ‖ **for the time being** de momento. ‖ **from time to time** de vez en cuando. ‖ **in no time (at all)** en seguida. ‖ **in time 1** *(in the long run)* con el tiempo. **2** *(not late)* a tiempo. ‖ **on time** puntual. ‖ **time after time** una y otra vez. ‖ **time's up** se acabó el tiempo. ‖ **to be ahead of one's time** adelantarse a su época. ‖ **to give** SB **a hard time** ponérselo difícil a ALGN. ‖ **to have a bad time** pasarlas negras. ‖ **to have a good time** pasarlo bien. ‖ **to keep up with the times** estar al día. ‖ **to take one's time 1** *(not hurry)* hacer algo con calma. **2** *(be slow)* tardar mucho.
time-consuming ['taɪmkənsjuːmɪŋ] *adj* que lleva mucho tiempo.
time-lag ['taɪmlæg] *n* lapso, intervalo.
timeless ['taɪmləs] *adj* eterno,-a.
timely ['taɪmlɪ] *adj* oportuno,-a.
timer ['taɪməʳ] *n (machine)* temporizador *m*.
timescale ['taɪmskeɪl] *n* escala de tiempo.
time-share ['taɪmʃeəʳ] *adj (property)* en multipropiedad.
▷ *n (property)* (sistema *mf* de) multipropiedad *f*.
timetable ['taɪmteɪbᵊl] *n* horario.
timing ['taɪmɪŋ] *n* **1** *(time chosen)* momento escogido; *(judgement)* sentido de la oportunidad. **2** SP *(measurement of time)* cronometraje *m*.
tin [tɪn] *n* **1** *(metal)* estaño. **2** *(can)* lata, bote *m*. **3** *(for baking)* molde *m*.
▷ *vt* enlatar.
▲ *pt & pp* **tinned**, *ger* **tinning.**
tinder ['tɪndəʳ] *n* yesca.
tinea ['tɪnɪə] *n* tiña.
tinfoil ['tɪnfɔɪl] *n* papel *m* de estaño.
tinge [tɪndʒ] *n* tinte *m*, matiz *f*.
▷ *vt* teñir.
tingle ['tɪŋgᵊl] *n* hormigueo.
▷ *vi* hormiguear.
tinkle ['tɪŋkᵊl] *n* tintineo.
▷ *vt* hacer tintinear.
▷ *vi* **1** *(ring)* tintinear. **2** GB *fam (urinate)* hacer pipí.
tin-opener ['tɪnəupənəʳ] *n* abrelatas *m inv*.
tinsel ['tɪnsᵊl] *n* espumillón *m*.
tinsmith ['tɪnsmɪθ] *n* hojalatero,-a.
tint [tɪnt] *n* tinte *m*, matiz *f*.
▷ *vt* teñir, matizar.
tiny ['taɪnɪ] *adj* diminuto,-a.
▲ *comp* **tinier**, *superl* **tiniest.**
tip¹ [tɪp] *n (gen)* extremo, punta, cabo; *(of cigarette)* boquilla, filtro. ■ **from tip to toe** de pies a cabeza.
tip² [tɪp] *n* **1** *(gratuity)* propina. **2** *(advice)* consejo, truco; *(confidential information)* soplo, confidencia; *(prediction)* pronóstico.
▷ *vt* **1** *(give gratuity to)* dar una propina a. **2** *(predict)* pronosticar.
⊙ **to tip off** *vt sep* avisar, dar el soplo.
tip³ [tɪp] *n (for rubbish)* vertedero, basurero; *(dirty place)* porquería, desorden *m*, revoltijo.
▷ *vt* **1** *(lean, tilt)* inclinar, ladear. **2** *(pour)* verter; *(throw)* tirar; *(empty)* vaciar. **3** *(rubbish)* verter.
▷ *vi* inclinarse, ladearse.
⊙ **to tip over** *vi (overturn)* volcarse, caerse; *(boat)* zozobrar.
▷ *vt sep* volcar.
⊙ **to tip up** *vi (tilt)* ladearse; *(seats)* levantarse.
▷ *vt sep* inclinar.
▲ *pt & pp* **tipped**, *ger* **tipping.**
tipsy ['tɪpsɪ] *adj* achispado,-a, piripi.
▲ *comp* **tipsier**, *superl* **tipsiest.**
tiptoe ['tɪptəu] *vi* caminar de puntillas. ■ **on tiptoe** de puntillas.
tiptop ['tɪptɒp] *adj fam* de primera.
tirade [taɪ'reɪd] *n* invectiva.
Tirana [tɪ'rɑːnə] *n* Tirana.
tire¹ [taɪəʳ] *vt* cansar.
▷ *vi* cansarse (**of**, de).
⊙ **to tire out** *vt sep* agotar.
tire² [taɪəʳ] *n* US → **tyre.**
tired [taɪəd] *adj* **1** *(weary)* cansado,-a. **2** *(fed up)* harto,-a (**of**, de). ■ **to get tired** cansarse.
tireless ['taɪələs] *adj* incansable.
tiresome ['taɪəsəm] *adj* molesto,-a, pesado,-a.
tiring ['taɪərɪŋ] *adj* cansado,-a, agotador,-ra.
tissue ['tɪʃuː] *n* **1** *(cloth)* tisú *m*. **2** *(handkerchief)* pañuelo de papel, kleenex. **3** BIOL tejido. ● **tissue paper** papel *m* de seda.
tit [tɪt] *n (bird)* paro, herrerillo.
titbit ['tɪtbɪt] *n* **1** *(delicacy)* manjar *m*, exquisitez *f*. **2** *(gossip)* chisme *m*.
title ['taɪtᵊl] *n* **1** *(gen)* título. **2** JUR título, derecho. **3** SP título, campeonato.● **title deed** escritura de propiedad. ‖ **title page** portada. ‖ **title role** papel *m* principal.
▷ *vt* titular.
▷ *n pl* **titles** *(film credits)* créditos *mpl*.
titled ['taɪtᵊld] *adj* con título de nobleza.
titleholder ['taɪtəlhəuldəʳ] *n* campeón,-ona.
titter ['tɪtəʳ] *n* risita.
▷ *vi* reírse disimuladamente.

tizzy ['tɪzɪ] ■ **to get in a tizzy** *fam* ponerse nervioso,-a.

to [tʊ, *unstressed* tə] *prep* **1** *(with place)* a: **we're going to a concert** *vamos a un concierto.* **2** *(towards)* hacia: **the Labour party has moved to the right** *el partido laborista se ha desplazado hacia la derecha.* **3** *(as far as, until)* a, hasta: **from beginning to end** *desde el principio hasta el final.* **4** *(of time)* menos: **it's ten to two** *son las dos menos diez.* **5** *(with indirect object)* a: **I showed the letter to my mother** *le enseñé la carta a mi madre.* **6** *(indicating comparison)* a: **I prefer tea to coffee** *prefiero el té al café.* **7** *prep (ratio)* a: **they won by fourteen points to ten** *ganaron por catorce puntos a diez.* **8** *(in order to)* para, a fin de: **I worked overtime to earn some extra money** *hice horas extras para ganar más dinero.* **9** *(substituting infinitive)*: **would you like to dance? –I'd love to** *¿te gustaría bailar? –me encantaría.*

▷ *adv (of door)* ajustada: **push the door to** *ajusta la puerta.* ■ **to and fro** ir y venir.

Cuando se usa con la raíz del verbo para formar el infinitivo no se traduce: **I want to help you** *quiero ayudarte.*

toad [təʊd] *n* sapo.

toadstool ['təʊdstuːl] *n* hongo venenoso.

toast [təʊst] *n* **1** *(food)* pan *m* tostado, tostada. **2** *(drink)* brindis *m.*

▷ *vt* **1** *(cook)* tostar. **2** *(drink)* brindar por, beber a la salud de.

toaster ['təʊstəʳ] *n* tostadora.

tobacco [tə'bækəʊ] *n* tabaco.

▲ *pl* **tobaccos** o **tobaccoes.**

tobacconist's [təbækənɪsts] *n* estanco.

Tobago [tə'beɪgəʊ] *n* Tobago.

toboggan [tə'bɒgən] *n* trineo.

today [tə'deɪ] *n* hoy *m.*

▷ *adv* **1** hoy. **2** *(nowadays)* hoy en día.

toddle ['tɒdᵊl] *vi* **1** *(child)* dar los primeros pasos. **2** *(person)* andar con paso inseguro.

⊙ **to toddle off** *vi* marcharse, irse.

toddler ['tɒdləʳ] *n* niño,-a (que empieza a andar).

toe [təʊ] *n* **1** ANAT dedo del pie. **2** *(of shoe)* puntera; *(of sock)* punta.

▷ *vt* tocar con la punta del pie. ■ **to be on one's toes** estar alerta. ‖ **to step/tread on SB's toes 1** *(literally)* pisar a ALGN. **2** *(offend)* ofender a ALGN.

toecap [təʊcæp] *n* puntera.

toenail ['təʊneɪl] *n* uña del dedo del pie.

toffee ['tɒfɪ] *n* caramelo.

tog [tɒg] *vt* vestir.

⊙ **to tog out / tog up** *vt sep* vestir.

▷ *vi* vestirse.

together [tə'geðəʳ] *adv* **1** *(gen)* juntos,-as. **2** *(simultaneously)* a la vez, al mismo tiempo. **3** *(nonstop)* seguido,-a.

▷ *adj fam (confident, organized, capable)* seguro,-a de sí mismo,-a. ■ **to bring together** reunir. ‖ **to come together** juntarse. ‖ **to go together** ir juntos,-as. ‖ **together with** junto con.

Togo ['təʊgəʊ] *n* Togo.

Togolese [təʊgə'liːz] *adj* togolés,-esa.

▷ *n* togolés,-esa.

toil [tɔɪl] *n* trabajo, esfuerzo.

▷ *vi* afanarse, esforzarse.

toilet ['tɔɪlət] *n* **1** *(appliance)* váter *m*, inodoro; *(room)* lavabo, baño. **2** *(public)* servicios *mpl*, aseos *mpl.* **3** *(washing)* aseo personal, higiene *m* personal. ● **toilet paper** papel *m* higiénico.

toiletries ['tɔɪlətrɪz] *n pl* artículos *mpl* de aseo.

token ['təʊkᵊn] *n* **1** *(sign, proof)* señal *f*, prueba. **2** *(memento, souvenir)* detalle *m*, recuerdo. **3** *(coupon)* vale *m.* **4** *(coin)* ficha.

▷ *adj* simbólico,-a. ■ **by the same token** del mismo modo. ‖ **in token of** en recuerdo de.

told [təʊld] *pt & pp* → **tell.**

tolerance ['tɒlərəns] *n* tolerancia.

tolerant ['tɒlərənt] *adj* tolerante (**of/towards**, con).

tolerate ['tɒləreɪt] *vt* tolerar, aguantar, soportar.

toll¹ [təʊl] *n* **1** *(payment)* peaje *m.* **2** *(loss)* mortalidad *f*, número de víctimas mortales. ■ **to take its toll on** afectar negativamente.

toll² [təʊl] *n (of bell)* tañido.

▷ *vt* tañer, doblar.

▷ *vi* doblar.

tollgate ['təʊlgeɪt] *n* peaje *m.*

Toltec ['tɒltek] *adj* tolteca.

▷ *n* tolteca *mf.*

toluene ['tɒljuiːn] *n* tolueno.

tom [tɒm] *n* gato (macho).

tomahawk ['tɒməhɔːk] *n* hacha de guerra.

tomato [tə'mɑːtəʊ, US tə'meɪtəʊ] *n* tomate *m.*

▲ *pl* **tomatoes.**

tomb [tuːm] *n* tumba, sepulcro.

tombstone ['tuːmstəʊn] *n* lápida (sepulcral).

tomcat ['tɒmkæt] *n* gato (macho).

tome [təʊm] *n* tomo.

tomfoolery [tɒm'fuːlərɪ] *n* tonterías *fpl.*

tommyrot ['tɒmɪrɒt] *n* tonterías *fpl.*

tomorrow [tə'mɒrəʊ] *n* mañana.

▷ *adv* mañana: **tomorrow morning/afternoon** *mañana por la mañana/tarde;* **see you tomorrow!** *¡hasta mañana!*

ton [tʌn] *n* tonelada.

▷ *n pl* **tons** *fam* montones *mpl.*

tonality [təʊ'nælɪtɪ] *n* tonalidad *f.*

tone [təʊn] *n* **1** *(sound, manner of speaking)* tono; *(on phone)* señal *f.* **2** *(colour)* tonalidad *f*, tono. **3** *(mood, character)* tono, carácter *m.* **4** *(quality, respectability)* buen tono, clase *f*, nivel *m.* **5** MUS tono. **6** *(of muscle)* tono.

⊙ **to tone down** *vt sep* atenuar, suavizar.

⊙ **to tone in with** *vi* armonizar con.

⊙ **to tone up** *vt sep* tonificar.

tone-deaf ['təʊn'def] *adj* que no tiene sentido u oído musical.

Tonga ['tɒŋgə] *n* Tonga.

Tongan ['tɒŋgən] *adj* tongano,-a.

▷ *n* **1** *(person)* tongano,-a. **2** *(language)* tongano.

tongs [tɒŋz] *n pl* tenacillas *fpl*, pinzas *fpl.*

tongue [tʌŋ] *n* **1** ANAT lengua. **2** *(language)* lengua, idioma *m.* **3** *(of shoe)* lengüeta. **4** *(of bell)* badajo. **5** *(of land, flame)* lengua. ● **tongue twister** trabalenguas *m.*

tongue-tied ['tʌŋtaɪd] *adj* cortado,-a.

tonic ['tɒnɪk] *n* **1** MED tónico. **2** MUS tónica. **3** *(drink)* tónica.

▷ *adj* tónico,-a. ● **tonic water** tónica.

tonight [tə'naɪt] *n* esta noche *f.*

▷ *adv* esta noche *f.*

tonnage ['tʌnɪdʒ] *n* tonelaje *m*.
tonne [tʌn] *n* tonelada.
tonsil ['tɒnsᵊl] *n* amígdala.
tonsillitis [tɒnsᵊ'laɪtəs] *n* amigdalitis *f*.
too [tuː] *adv* **1** *(excessively)* demasiado. **2** *(also)* también. **3** *(besides)* además. **4** *(very)* muy. ■ **too many** demasiados,-as. ‖ **too much** demasiado,-a.
took [tʊk] *pt* → **take**.
tool [tuːl] *n (gen)* herramienta; *(instrument)* instrumento.
▷ *vt (book)* estampar; *(leather)* labrar.
▷ *n pl* **tools** *(gardening, etc)* útiles *mpl*.
⊙ **to tool up** *vt sep* equipar.
toolbar ['tuːlbɑːʳ] *n* barra de herramientas.
toolbox ['tuːlbɒks] *n* caja de herramientas.
toolkit ['tuːlkɪt] *n* juego de herramientas.
tool-maker ['tuːlmeɪkəʳ] *n trabajador,-ra que fabrica herramientas.*
tooth [tuːθ] *n* **1** *(gen)* diente *m*; *(molar)* muela; *(front tooth)* incisivo. **2** *(of comb)* púa. **3** *(of saw)* diente *m*.
▲ *pl* **tooth**.
toothache ['tuːθeɪk] *n* dolor *m* de muelas.
toothbrush ['tuːθbrʌʃ] *n* cepillo de dientes.
toothed [tuːðd] *adj* dentado,-a.
toothless ['tuːθləs] *adj* desdentado,-a.
toothpaste ['tuːθpeɪst] *n* pasta de dientes.
toothpick ['tuːθpɪk] *n* mondadientes *m inv*, palillo.
toothsome ['tuːθsəm] *adj* apetitoso,-a, sabroso,-a.
toothy ['tuːθɪ] *adj* dentón,-ona.
▲ *comp* **toothier**, *superl* **toothiest**.
top¹ [tɒp] *n* **1** *(highest/upper part)* parte *f* superior. **2** *(far end - of street)* final *m*; *(- of table)* cabecera. **3** *(of mountain)* cumbre *m*. **4** *(of tree)* copa. **5** *(surface)* superficie *f*. **6** *(of bottle)* tapón *m*; *(of pen)* capuchón *m*. **7** *(highest position)*: **she was top of the class** *fue la primera de la clase*. **8** *(of list)* cabeza. **9** *(of car)* capota. **10** *(clothes)* blusa (corta), camiseta, top *m*; *(of bikini)* parte de arriba. **11** *(beginning)* principio. **12** *(gear)* directa.
▷ *adj* **1** *(highest)* de arriba, superior, más alto,-a. **2** *(best, highest, leading)* mejor, principal. **3** *(highest, maximum)* principal, máximo,-a. ● **top brass** altos mandos *mpl*. ‖ **top gear** directa.
▷ *vt* **1** *(cover)* cubrir, rematar. **2** *(remove top of plant/fruit)* quitar los rabillos. **3** *sl (kill)* cargarse. **4** *(come first, head)* encabezar. **5** *(better, surpass, exceed)* superar.
▲ *pt & pp* **topped**, *ger* **topping**.
▷ *n pl* **tops** *(of plant)* hojas *fpl*.
⊙ **to top off** *vi* rematar.
⊙ **to top up** *vt sep (fill up)* acabar de llenar; *(refill)* volver a llenar.
top² [tɒp] *n* peonza. ■ **to sleep like a top** dormir como un tronco.
topaz ['təʊpæz] *n* topacio.
topcoat [tɒp'kəʊt] *n dated* abrigo.
top-heavy ['tɒp'hevɪ] *adj* demasiado pesado,-a en la parte superior, inestable.
top-hole [tɒp'həʊl] *adj* excelente.
topic ['tɒpɪk] *n* tema *m*.
topmost ['tɒpməʊst] *adj* más alto,-a.
topnotch [tɒp'nɒtʃ] *adj* de primera.
topography [tə'pɒgrəfɪ] *n* topografía.
toponym ['tɒpənɪm] *n* topónimo.
toponymy [tə'pɒnɪmɪ] *n* toponimia.
topping ['tɒpɪŋ] *n (for pizza)* ingrediente *m*; *(for ice-cream)* cubierta, guarnición.
▷ *adj* excelente.
topple ['tɒpᵊl] *vt* **1** *(overturn)* volcar, hacer caer. **2** *fig (overthrow)* derribar, derrocar.
▷ *vi (fall)* caerse; *(lose balance)* tambalearse, perder el equilibrio.
top-ranking ['tɒprænkɪŋ] *adj* de alto nivel.
tops [tɒps] *n pl* **the tops** *fam* lo mejor *m sing*.
top-secret [tɒp'siːkrət] *adj* sumamente secreto,-a, confidencial.
topside ['tɒpsaɪd] *n* redondo.
topsoil ['tɒpsɔɪl] *n* capa superficial del suelo.
tor [tɔːʳ] *n* colina, peñasco.
Torah ['tɔːrə] *n* Torá.
torch [tɔːtʃ] *n* **1** *(with naked flame)* antorcha. **2** *(electric)* linterna.
▷ *vt* quemar, prender fuego a.
torchlight ['tɔːtʃlaɪt] luz de antorcha o linterna.
tore [tɔːʳ] *pt* → **tear**.
torment [*(n)* 'tɔːmənt; *(vb)* tɔː'ment] *n (gen)* tormento, tortura; *(suffering)* angustia.
▷ *vt* **1** *(cause to suffer)* atormentar, torturar. **2** *(annoy)* molestar, hacer rabiar, martirizar.
torn [tɔːn] *pp* → **tear**.
torque [tɔːk] *n* par *m* motor. ● **torque wrench** llave dinamométrica.
torrent ['tɒrənt] *n* torrente *m*.
torrential [tə'renʃəl] *adj* torrencial.
torrid ['tɒrɪd] *adj* **1** *(hot, dry)* tórrido,-a. **2** *(passionate)* apasionado,-a.
torso ['tɔːsəʊ] *n* torso.
▲ *pl* **torsos**.
tort [tɔːt] *n* JUR agravio.
tortoise ['tɔːtəs] *n* tortuga (de tierra).
tortoiseshell ['tɔːtəsʃel] *n* **1** carey *m*. **2** *(color)* color *m* carey.
▷ *adj* **1** de carey. **2** *(colour)* de color carey.
torture ['tɔːtəʳ] *n* tortura.
Tory ['tɔːrɪ] *n* GB conservador,-ra.
▲ *pl* **Tories**.
▷ *adj* GB conservador,-ra.
tosh [tɒʃ] *n* tonterías *fpl*, bobadas *fpl*.
toss [tɒs] *n* **1** *(shake)* sacudida, movimiento. **2** *(of coin)* sorteo a cara o cruz.
▷ *vt* **1** *(move, shake)* mover, agitar, sacudir; *(pancake)* dar la vuelta a; *(salad)* mezclar. **2** *(throw)* arrojar, lanzar, tirar. ■ **to toss a coin** echarlo a cara o cruz.
▷ *vi* moverse, agitarse, sacudirse.
▲ *pt & pp* **totted**, *ger* **totting**.
total ['təʊtᵊl] *adj (overall)* total; *(complete)* completo,-a, rotundo,-a.
▷ *n* total *m*, suma.
▷ *vt* sumar.
▷ *vi* sumar, ascender a. ■ **in total** en total.
totalitarian [təʊtælɪ'teərɪən] *adj* totalitario,-a.
totality [təʊ'tælɪtɪ] *n* totalidad *f*.
totally ['təʊtəlɪ] *adv* totalmente, completamente.
totem ['təʊtəm] *n* tótem *m*. ● **totem pole** tótem *m*.
totter ['tɒtəʳ] *vi* tambalearse.
tottering ['tɒtərɪŋ] *adj (gen)* tambaleante; *(step)* inseguro,-a.

ouch [tʌtʃ] *n* **1** *(gen)* toque *m*; *(light touch)* roce *m*. **2** *(detail)* detalle *m*, toque *m*. **3** *(sense)* tacto. **4** *(connection)* contacto, comunicación *f*. **5** *(slight quantity)* poquito, pizca; *(trace)* asomo. **6** MED amago. **7** *fam (skill, ability)* habilidad *f*. **8** *(manner, style)* sello. **9** SP toque *m*. . ■ **to be in touch with** STH estar al corriente de ALGO. ‖ **to get in touch** ponerse en contacto (**with**, con).
▷ *vt* **1** *(gen)* tocar; *(lightly)* rozar. **2** *(eat)* probar. **3** *(move)* conmover. **4** *(equal, rival)* igualar. **5** *(affect)* afectar, tocar. **6** *(deal with)* tocar, abordar.
▷ *vi* tocarse
⊙ **to touch down** *vi* *(plane)* aterrizar.
⊙ **to touch off** *vt sep* provocar, causar.
⊙ **to touch on / touch upon** *vi* mencionar.
⊙ **to touch up** *vt sep* ART retocar.
ouchdown ['tʌtʃdaʊn] *n* **1** *(on land)* aterrizaje *m*. **2** *(on sea)* amerizaje *m*.
ouched [tʌtʃt] *adj* **1** *(moved)* conmovido,-a. **2** *(crazy)* tocado,-a.
ouchiness ['tʌtʃɪnəs] *n* susceptibilidad *f*.
ouching ['tʌtʃɪŋ] *adj* conmovedor,-ra.
ouch-screen ['tʌtʃskri:n] *n* pantalla táctil.
ouchstone ['tʌtʃstəʊn] *n* piedra de toque.
ouch-type ['tʌtʃtaɪp] *vi* mecanografiar sin mirar las teclas.
ough [tʌf] *adj* **1** *(strong)* fuerte, resistente. **2** *(difficult)* duro,-a. **3** *(rough, violent)* violento,-a. **4** *(severe)* severo,-a. **5** *(meat)* duro,-a. **6** *fam* malo,-a, injusto,-a.
▷ *n* tipo duro.
oughen ['tʌfᵊn] *vt (muscles, laws)* endurecer; *(person)* hacer más fuerte.
▷ *vi (muscles, approach)* endurecerse; *(person)* hacerse más fuerte.
oulouse [tu:'lu:z] *n* Tolosa.
our [tʊəʳ] *n* **1** viaje *m*, excursión *f*. **2** *(round building)* visita. **3** *(by performers)* gira; *(cycling)* vuelta. ● **tourist class** clase *f* turista. ‖ **tourist office** oficinade turismo. ‖ **tour operator** agente *m* de viajes.
▷ *vt* **1** *(gen)* recorrer, viajar por. **2** *(building)* visitar.
▷ *vi (by performers)* hacer una gira.
our de force [tʊədə'fɔ:s] *n* hazaña.
ourism ['tʊərɪzᵊm] *n* turismo.
ourist ['tʊərɪst] *n* turista *mf*.
▷ *adj* turístico,-a. ● **tourist class** clase *f* turista.
ournament ['tʊənəmənt] *n* torneo.
out [taʊt] *n* revendedor,-ra.
▷ *vt* revender.
▷ *vi* intentar captar clientes.
ow [təʊ] *vt* remolcar.
▷ *n* remolque *m*. ■ **on tow** de remolque.
oward [tə'wɔ:d] *prep* US ⟶ **towards.**
owards [tə'wɔ:dz] *prep* **1** *(in direction of)* hacia. **2** *(attitude)* con, para con. **3** *(payment)* para. **4** *(of time)* hacia, cerca de.
owbar ['təʊbɑ:ʳ] *n* barra de remolque.
owel [taʊəl] *n* toalla.
▷ *vt* secar con toalla.
▲ *pt & pp* **towelled** (US **toweled**), *ger* **towelling** (US **toweling**).
owelling ['taʊəlɪŋ] *n* felpa.
ower [taʊəʳ] *n* **1** *(gen)* torre *f*. **2** *(of church)* campanario.
▷ *vi* elevarse. ● **tower block** bloque *m* (de pisos).
⊙ **to tower above / tower over** *vt insep* dominar.

towering ['taʊərɪŋ] *adj* **1** *(tall)* muy alto,-a, elevado,-a, dominante. **2** *(rage)* violento,-a, intenso,-a, extremo,-a. **3** *(person)* destacado,-a, dominante.
town [taʊn] *n* **1** *(large)* ciudad *f*; *(small)* población *f*, municipio, pueblo. **2** *(city centre)* centro. **3** *(people)* ciudadanos *mpl*, ciudad *f*.
▷ *adj* urbano,-a, municipal. ● **town clerk** secretario del ayuntamiento. ‖ **town council** ayuntamiento. ‖ **town hall** ayuntamiento.
township ['taʊŋʃɪp] *n* **1** *(gen)* municipio, pueblo. **2** *(in South Africa)* distrito segregado.
townspeople ['taʊnzpi:pᵊl] *n pl* ciudadanos *mpl*.
towpath ['təʊpɑ:θ] *n* camino de sirga.
towrope ['təʊrəʊp] *n* cable *m* de remolque.
toxic ['tɒksɪk] *n* tóxico,-a.
toy [tɔɪ] *n* juguete *m*.
▷ *adj* **1** de juguete. **2** *(dog)* enano,-a.
⊙ **to toy with** *vt insep (object, food)* jugar con; *(idea)* acariciar; *(affections)* divertirse con.
toyshop ['tɔɪʃɒp] *n* juguetería.
trace [treɪs] *n* **1** *(mark, sign)* indicio, rastro. **2** *(small amount - material)* pizca, vestigio; *(- non-material)* dejo, asomo, nota. ● **trace element** oligoelemento.
▷ *vt* **1** *(sketch)* trazar, esbozar. **2** *(copy)* calcar. **3** *(find)* encontrar, localizar; *(follow)* seguir la pista de. **4** *(describe development)* describir. **5** *(find origin)* encontrar el origen de. **6** *(go back to)* remontarse a.
traceable ['treɪsəbᵊl] *adj* localizable.
tracer ['treɪsəʳ] *n* **1** MIL trazadora. **2** MED trazador *m*. ● **tracer bullet** bala trazadora.
trachea [trə'kɪə] *n* ANAT tráquea.
tracing ['treɪsɪŋ] *n* calco. ● **tracing paper** papel *m* de calco, papel *m* de calcar.
track [træk] *n* **1** *(mark)* pista, huellas *fpl*, rastro; *(of wheels)* rodada. **2** *(of rocket, bullet, etc)* trayectoria. **3** *(path)* camino, senda, sendero. **4** SP pista. **5** *(for motor-racing)* circuito. **6** *(of railway)* vía; *(platform)* andén *m*. **7** *(on record, etc)* tema *m*, corte *m*, canción *f*. **8** *(belt on wheels)* oruga. ■ **to be on** SB**'s tracks** seguir la pista de ALGN. ‖ **to be on the right track** ir por buen camino. ‖ **to keep track of** seguir. ‖ **to lose track of** perder de vista. ● **track and field** atletismo.
▷ *vt* **1** *(person, animal)* seguir la pista de. **2** TECH seguir la trayectoria de.
▷ *vi* CINEM hacer una toma larga con la cámara en movimiento.
⊙ **to track down** *vt sep* localizar, encontrar.
tracker ['trækəʳ] *n* rastreador,-ra.
tracksuit ['træksu:t] *n* chándal *m*.
tract[1] [trækt] *n (treatise)* tratado; *(pamphlet)* folleto.
tract[2] [trækt] *n* **1** *(land)* extensión *f*. **2** ANAT tracto. ● **digestive tract** tubo digestivo.
tractable ['træktəbᵊl] *adj (person)* tratable, dócil; *(metal)* maleable.
traction ['trækʃᵊn] *n (gen)* tracción *f*.
tractor ['træktəʳ] *n* tractor *m*.
trade [treɪd] *n* **1** *(commerce)* comercio. **2** *(business)* negocio; *(industry)* industria. **3** *(occupation)* oficio, profesión *f*. **4** *(people who work in particular industry)* comerciantes *mpl*, gente *f* del negocio.
▷ *adj* comercial. ● **trade gap** déficit *m* comercial. ‖ **trade fair** feria de muestras. ‖ **trade name** nombre *m* comer-

cial. ‖ **trade price** precio al por mayor. ‖ **trade union** sindicato. ‖ **trade winds** vientos *mpl* alisios.
▷ *vi (do business)* comerciar.
▷ *vt (exchange)* cambiar.
⊙ **to trade in** *vt sep* dar como parte del pago.
⊙ **to trade on** *vi* explotar, aprovecharse de.
trademark ['treɪdmɑːk] *n* marca registrada, marca.
trader ['treɪdəʳ] *n* comerciante *mf*.
tradesman ['treɪdzmən] *n* **1** *(businessman)* comerciante *m*; *(shopkeeper)* tendero. **2** *(deliveryman)* repartidor *m*.
▲ *pl* **tradesmen** ['treɪdzmən].
trading ['treɪdɪŋ] *n* comercio.
traduce [trə'djuːs] *vt* US calumniar, difamar.
traffic ['træfɪk] *n* **1** AUTO tráfico, circulación *f*, tránsito. **2** *(of ships, aircraft)* tráfico. **3** *(of people, goods)* tránsito, movimiento. **4** *(trade)* tráfico.
▷ *adj* de la circulación, del tráfico. ● **traffic circle** US rotonda. ‖ **traffic jam** atasco, embotellamiento. ‖ **traffic lights** semáforo. ‖ **traffic warden** guardia *mf* de tráfico.
▷ *vi* traficar (**in**, con).
trafficker ['træfɪkəʳ] *n* traficante *mf*.
tragedy ['trædʒədɪ] *n* tragedia.
▲ *pl* **tragedies**.
tragic ['trædʒɪk] *adj* trágico,-a.
trail [treɪl] *n* **1** *(path)* camino, sendero. **2** *(track, mark, scent)* rastro, pista, huellas *fpl*. **3** *(of rocket, comet)* cola; *(of dust, vapour)* estela; *(of blood)* reguero.
▷ *vt* **1** *(follow)* seguir la pista de. **2** *(drag)* arrastrar.
▷ *vi* **1** *(lag behind)* ir rezagado,-a, quedarse atrás. **2** *(drag)* arrastrarse. **3** *(plant)* arrastrarse, trepar. **4** *(lose)* perder.
⊙ **to trail away / trail off** *vi (voice)* irse apagando.
trailblazer ['treɪlblɑːzəʳ] *n* pionero,-a.
trailer ['treɪləʳ] *n* **1** AUTO remolque *m*. **2** US caravana. **3** CINEM tráiler *m*, avance *m*.
train [treɪn] *n* **1** *(transport)* tren *m*. **2** *(of dress)* cola. **3** *(line - of animals)* recua; *(- of vehicles)* convoy *m*. **4** *(retinue)* grupo, séquito. **5** *(of ideas, thoughts)* serie *f*, hilo; *(of events)* serie *f*, sucesión *f*.
▷ *vt* **1** SP entrenar, preparar. **2** *(teach)* enseñar, formar, capacitar. **3** *(one's eye, ear, voice)* educar. **4** MIL adiestrar. **5** *(animal)* enseñar; *(to perform tricks)* amaestrar, adiestrar. **6** *(direct - gun)* apuntar (**on**, a); *(- camera)* enfocar (**on**, a), dirigir (**on**, hacia); *(- plant)* guiar.
▷ *vi* **1** SP entrenarse, prepararse. **2** *(teach)* estudiar. **3** MIL adiestrarse.
trained [treɪnd] *adj* **1** *(worker - skilled)* calificado,-a, cualificado,-a; *(- qualified)* graduado,-a, diplomado,-a. **2** *(animal)* amaestrado,-a, adiestrado,-a. **3** *(voice, ear)* educado,-a.
trainee [treɪ'niː] *n* **1** *(manual work)* aprendiz,-za. **2** *(professional work) persona que está haciendo prácticas*.
trainer ['treɪnəʳ] *n* **1** SP entrenador,-ra. **2** *(of dogs)* amaestrador,-ra; *(of circus animals)* domador,-ra; *(of race horses)* preparador,-ra. **3** *(aircraft)* entrenador *m*. **4** *(shoe)* zapatilla de deporte.
training ['treɪnɪŋ] *n* **1** formación *f* (profesional), capacitación *f*. **2** SP entrenamiento, preparación *f* física.
▷ *vi* MIL instrucción *f*.
traipse [treɪps] *vi* recorrerse a pie, patearse.
trait [treɪt] *n* rasgo, característico.
traitor ['treɪtəʳ] *n* traidor,-ra.
tram [træm] *n* tranvía *m*.
tramcar ['træmkɑːʳ] *n* tranvía *m*.
tramlines ['træmlaɪnz] *n pl* **1** *(of tram)* carriles *mpl* d[e] tranvía. **2** SP *(in tennis)* líneas *fpl* laterales.
tramp [træmp] *n* **1** *(person)* vagabundo,-a. **2** camina[-]ta, excursión *f* a pie. **3** US *sl* fulana, puta.
▷ *vt* andar por, recorrer a pie.
▷ *vi (walk)* caminar (con pasos pesados), andar penc[-]samente; *(hike)* recorrer.
trample ['træmpᵊl] *vt* pisotear.
▷ *vi* pisotear (**on/over**, -).
trampoline ['træmpəliːn] *n* cama elástica.
tranquillise ['træŋkwɪlaɪz] *vt* → **tranquillize**.
tranquillize ['træŋkwɪlaɪz] *vt* tranquilizar.
tranquilliser ['træŋkwɪlaɪzəʳ] *n* → **tranquillizer**.
tranquillizer ['træŋkwɪlaɪzəʳ] *n* tranquilizante *m*, ca[l]mante *m*.
transact [træn'zækt] *vt* negociar.
▷ *vi* negociar.
transaction [træn'zækʃᵊn] *n* **1** *(deal)* operación [,] transacción *f*. **2** *(business)* negocio.
transcend [træn'send] *vt* **1** *(go beyond)* trascender. [2] *(surpass)* superar.
transcribe [træn'skraɪb] *vt* transcribir, trascribir.
transcript ['trænskrɪpt] *n* transcripción *f*.
transcription [træn'skrɪpʃᵊn] *n* transcripción *f*.
transept ['trænsept] *n* crucero.
transfer [*(n)* 'trænsfɜːʳ; *(vb)* træns'fɜːʳ] *n* **1** FIN transfe[-]rencia. **2** JUR *(of property)* traspaso. **3** *(of employee)* tras[-]lado. **4** SP *(of player)* traspaso; *(player)* fichaje *m*. [5] *(drawing)* cromo, calcomanía. **6** *(of airline passenge[rs])* transbordo, trasbordo.
▷ *vt* **1** FIN transferir. **2** JUR *(property)* traspasar. **3** *(employ[-]ee, prisoner)* trasladar. **4** SP *(player)* traspasar. **5** *(data, information, phone call)* pasar.
▷ *vi* **1** *(employee)* trasladarse. **2** *(transport)* hacer trans[-]bordo, cambiar. **3** EDUC cambiar.
▲ *pt & pp* **transferred**, *ger* **transferring**.
transfix [træns'fɪks] *vt* **1** *(render motionless)* paralizar. *(impale)* traspasar, atravesar.
transform [træns'fɔːm] *vt* transformar.
▷ *vi* transformarse (**into**, en), convertirse (**into**, en).
transfuse [træns'fjuːz] *vt* hacer una transfusión de.
transgress [træns'gres] *vt* **1** *(break moral principle)* transgredir, violar. **2** *(go beyond)* traspasar, exceder.
transience ['trænzɪəns] *n* transitoriedad *f*.
transient ['trænzɪənt] *adj* transitorio,-a, pasajero,-a.
transistor [træn'zɪstəʳ] *n* transistor.
transit ['trænsɪt] *n* tránsito. ● **transit van** furgoneta.
transition [træn'zɪʃᵊn] *n* transición *f*.
transitive ['trænsɪtɪv] *adj* transitivo,-a.
transitory ['trænsɪtᵊrɪ] *adj* transitorio,-a.
translatable [trɑːnz'leɪtəbᵊl] *adj* traducible.
translate [træns'leɪt] *vt* **1** *(gen)* traducir (**from**, de) (**int[o]**, a). **2** *(express, explain)* expresar. **3** *(transform)* transfo[r]mar.
▷ *vi (person)* traducir; *(word, book, etc)* traducirse.
translation [træns'leɪʃᵊn] *n* traducción *f*.
translator [træns'leɪtəʳ] *n* traductor,-ra.
translucent [trænz'luːsᵊnt] *adj* translúcido,-a.
transmission [trænz'mɪʃᵊn] *n* transmisión *f*.
transmit [trænz'mɪt] *vt* transmitir (**to**, a).
▲ *pt & pp* **transmitted**, *ger* **transmitting**.

ransmitter [trænz'mɪtəʳ] *n* transmisor *m*.
ransparency [træns'peərənsɪ] *n* **1** *(quality)* transparencia. **2** *(slide)* diapositiva; *(acetate)* transparencia.
▲ *pl* transparencies.
ransparent [træns'peərənt] *adj* **1** transparente. **2** *fig* claro,-a, evidente.
ranspire [træns'paɪəʳ] *vt (plants)* transpirar.
▷ *vi* **1** *(become known)* resultar. **2** *fam (happen)* pasar, ocurrir.
ransplant [*(n)* 'trænsplɑ:nt; *(vb)* træns'plɑ:nt] *n* trasplante *m*.
▷ *vt* trasplantar.
ransport [*(n)* 'trænspɔ:t; *(vb)* træns'pɔ:t] *n* transporte *m*.
▷ *vt* **1** transportar. **2** HIST deportar.
ransportation [trænspɔ:'teɪʃᵊn] *n* transporte *m*.
ranspose [træns'pəuz] *vt* **1** *(words, letters)* transponer, trasponer. **2** MUS transportar.
ransship [træn'ʃɪp] *vt* transbordar.
▲ *pt & pp* transshipped, *ger* transshipping.
rap [træp] *n* **1** *(gen)* trampa. **2** *(vehicle)* coche *m* ligero de dos ruedas. **3** *(of drain)* sifón *m*.
▷ *vt* **1** *(catch - gen)* atrapar; *(snare - animal)* cazar; *(imprison)* entrampar; *(part of body)* pillar. **2** SP *(in football)* parar con el pie. **3** *fig (trick)* engañar, tender una trampa a. **4** *(heat, light, etc)* retener.
▲ *pt & pp* trapped, *ger* trapping.
rapdoor ['træpdɔ:ʳ] *n (gen)* trampilla; *(in theatre)* escotillón *m*.
rapeze [trə'pi:z] *n* trapecio.
rapezium [trə'pi:zɪəm] *n* GB trapecio.
▲ *pl* trapeziums o trapezia [trə'pi:zɪə].
rapezoid ['træpɪzɔɪd] *n* **1** GB trapecio *m*. **1** US trapezoide.
rapper ['træpəʳ] *n* cazador,-ra, trampero,-a.
rappings ['træpɪŋz] *n pl (paraphernalia)* parafernalia, símbolos *mpl*; *(of horse)* arreos *mpl*.
rapshooting ['træpʃu:tɪŋ] *n* tiro al plato.
rash [træʃ] *n* **1** porquería, basura, bodrio. **2** US *(rubbish)* basura. **3** US *(people)* gente *f* despreciable. ● **trash can 1** *(on computer)* papelera de reciclaje. **2** *(for waste)* US cubo de la basura.
rashy ['træʃɪ] *adj* malo,-a, que no vale para nada.
▲ *comp* trashier, *superl* trashiest.
rauma ['trɔ:mə] *n* trauma *m*.
ravel ['trævᵊl] *n* viajes *mpl*, viajar *m*.
▷ *vt* viajar por, recorrer.
▷ *vi* **1** *(make a journey)* viajar; *(go)* ir. **2** *(move, go)* ir. **3** *(go fast)* ir rápido, ir a toda velocidad. **4** *(as salesperson)* ser viajante, ser representante. **5** *(wine, food, etc)* poderse transportar.
▲ *pt & pp* travelled (US traveled), *ger* travelling (US traveling).
▷ *n pl* travels *(journeys)* viajes *mpl*.
raveled ['trævᵊld] *adj* US → travelled.
raveler ['trævᵊləʳ] *n* US → traveller.
raveling ['trævᵊlɪŋ] *adj-n* US → travelling.
ravelled ['trævᵊld] *adj* que ha viajado.
raveller ['trævᵊləʳ] *n* **1** *(gen)* viajero,-a. **2** *(representative)* viajante *mf*, representante *mf*. **3** GB *persona que lleva una vida de nómada.*
ravelling ['trævᵊlɪŋ] *adj* **1** *(exhibition, etc)* ambulante. **2** *(bag, clock, etc)* de viaje.
▷ *n* viajar *m*, viajes *mpl*.
travelogue ['trævəlɒg] *n (film)* documental *m*; *(lecture)* conferencia sobre viajar.
travel-sick ['trævᵊlsɪk] *adj* mareado,-a.
travel-sickness ['trævᵊlsɪknəs] *n* mareo.
traverse [trə'vɜ:s] *vt* cruzar, atravesar.
▷ *n* **1** ARCH travesaño. **2** *(mountaineering)* travesía.
trawl [trɔ:l] *n (net)* red *f* de arrastre.
▷ *vt* **1** *(fish)* pescar (con red de arrastre). **2** *(search)* buscar (for, -).
▷ *vi* pescar al arrastre. ● **trawl line** palangre *m*.
trawler ['trɔ:ləʳ] *n* pesquero de arrastre.
tray [treɪ] *n* **1** *(for food)* bandeja. **2** *(for papers)* caja, cesta. **3** *(in photography)* cubeta.
treacherous ['tretʃərəs] *adj* **1** *(person)* traidor,-ra, traicionero,-a. **2** *(dangerous)* muy peligroso,-a, traicionero,-a.
treachery ['tretʃərɪ] *n* traición *f*.
▲ *pl* treacheries.
treacle ['tri:kᵊl] *n* GB melaza.
tread [tred] *n* **1** *(manner or sound of walking)* paso, pasos *mpl*. **2** *(on tyre)* banda de rodadura, dibujo. **3** *(on stair)* escalón *m*.
▷ *vt* **1** *(gen)* pisar, pisotear. **2** *(walk on)* andar por; *(make)* hacer.
▷ *vi* pisar, poner el pie (on, -).
▲ *pt* trod [trɒd], *pp* trodden ['trɒdᵊn] o trod.
treadle ['tredᵊl] *n* pedal *m*.
treadmill ['tredmɪl] *n* **1** HIST *(punishment)* rueda de castigo. **2** *fig* rutina.
treason ['tri:zᵊn] *n* traición *f*.
treasure ['treʒəʳ] *n* **1** *(gen)* tesoro, tesoros *mpl*. **2** *(valued person)* tesoro, joya.
▷ *vt (value, cherish)* apreciar mucho, valorar mucho.
⊙ **to treasure up** *vt sep* atesorar.
treasurer ['trəʒərəʳ] *n* tesorero,-a.
treasury ['treʒərɪ] *n* tesorería.
▲ *pl* treasuries.
treat [tri:t] *n* **1** *(meal, drink)* convite *m*. **2** *(present)* regalo. **3** *(pleasure)* placer *m*, gusto, deleite *m*.
▷ *vt* **1** *(act, behave towards)* tratar. **2** *(subject)* tratar. **3** *(consider, regard)* tomar(se). **4** *(invite)* convidar, invitar; *(give)* regalar; *(spoil* OS*)* permitirse el lujo, darse el gusto. **5** MED *(condition)* tratar, curar; *(person)* atender. **6** TECH *(wood, worm, etc)* tratar (with, con).
treatise ['tri:tɪs] *n* tratado.
treatment ['tri:tmənt] *n* **1** MED tratamiento, cura. **2** *(manner of treating)* trato; *(behaviour)* conducta. **3** *(process)* tratamiento.
treaty ['tri:tɪ] *n* tratado.
▲ *pl* treaties.
treble ['trebᵊl] *adj* **1** *(threefold)* triple. **2** MUS de tiple.
● **treble clef** clave *f* de sol.
▷ *n* MUS tiple *mf*.
▷ *vt* triplicar.
▷ *vi* triplicarse.
tree [tri:] *n* árbol *m*.
treeless ['tri:ləs] *adj* sin árboles.
tree-lined ['tri:laɪnd] *adj* con árboles en las aceras.
tree-top ['tri:tɒp] *n* copa.
trefoil ['trefɔɪl] *n* trébol *m*.
trek [trek] *n* caminata.
▷ *vi* caminar, andar.
▲ *pt & pp* trekked, *ger* trekking.

trekking ['trekɪŋ] *n* senderismo.
trellis ['trelɪs] *n (for plants)* espaldera.
tremble ['trembəl] *n* temblor *m*.
▷ *vi* temblar.
tremendous [trɪ'mendəs] *adj* **1** *(huge)* tremendo,-a, inmenso,-a. **2** *fam (great)* fantástico,-a, estupendo,-a.
tremor ['tremər] *n* temblor *m*.
trench [trentʃ] *n* **1** *(ditch)* zanja. **2** MIL trinchera.
trenchant ['trentʃənt] *adj* cáustico,-a, mordaz.
trend [trend] *n* **1** *(tendency)* tendencia (**to/towards**, hacia), tónica. **2** *(fashion)* moda.
trendsetter ['trendsetər] *n* iniciador,-ra de moda.
trendy ['trendɪ] *adj fam* moderno,-a, de moda.
▲ *comp* **trendier**, *superl* **trendiest**.
trepan [trə'pæn] *n* trépano.
▷ *vt* trepanar.
trepanation [trəpə'neɪʃən] *n* trepanación *f*.
trephination [trefɪ'neɪʃən] *n* trepanación *f*.
trephine [trɪ'fiːn] *n* trépano.
▷ *vt* trepanar.
trepidation [trepɪ'deɪʃən] *n* turbación *f*, agitación *f*.
trespass ['trespəs] *n* **1** entrada ilegal. **2** REL pecado.
▷ *vi* **1** *(on land)* entrar sin autorización; *(on patience, etc)* abusar de; *(in affairs)* meterse, entrometerse, interferir. **2** REL pecar (**against**, contra).
trespasser ['trespəsər] *n* intruso,-a.
tress [tres] *n* mechón *m*.
▷ *n pl* **tresses** melena *f sing*, cabellera *f sing*.
trestle ['tresəl] *n* caballete *m*.
trial [traɪəl] *n* **1** JUR proceso, juicio. **2** *(test)* prueba. **3** *(suffering)* aflicción *f*, sufrimiento; *(trouble)* molestia, problema *m*.
▷ *n pl* **trials** SP pruebas *fpl*.
triangle ['traɪæŋgəl] *n* triángulo.
tribe [traɪb] *n* **1** tribu *f*. **2** *fam (family)* tribu *f*, familia.
tribesman ['traɪbzmən] *n* miembro de una tribu.
▲ *pl* **tribesmen**.
tribunal [traɪ'bjuːnəl] *n* tribunal *m*.
tribune ['trɪbjuːn] *n* **1** ARCH tribuna. **2** *(Roman magistrate)* tribuno.
tributary ['trɪbjutərɪ] *n* afluente *m*.
▲ *pl* **tributaries**.
▷ *adj* tributario,-a.
tribute ['trɪbjuːt] *n* **1** *(homage)* homenaje *m*, tributo. **2** *(payment)* tributo.
trice [traɪs] ■ **in a trice** en un santiamén.
triceps ['traɪseps] *n pl* tríceps *m inv*.
trick [trɪk] *n* **1** *(skill, knack)* truco. **2** *(for entertainment)* truco, juego de manos; *(with cards)* juego de naipes; *(by animals)* número. **3** *(deception, ruse)* ardid *m*, engaño, trampa, truco. **4** *(prank, joke)* broma. **5** *(cards won)* baza. **6** *(habit)* hábito, costumbre *f*, manía.
▷ *adj* de juguete, de mentira.
▷ *vt (deceive)* engañar, burlar. ■ **to play a trick on** SB gastarle una broma a ALGN. ‖ **trick or treat** US *frase de los niños que en Halloween van por las casas pidiendo un regalo a cambio de no hacer una jugarreta*.
⊙ **to trick out / trick up** *vi* adornar (**in/with**, con).
trickery ['trɪkərɪ] *n* superchería, engaño.
trickle ['trɪkəl] *n* **1** goteo, hilo. **2** *fig* poco.
▷ *vi* **1** *(liquid)* gotear, salir gota a gota. **2** *fig* salir *(entrar, llegar, etc)* poco a poco.

trickster ['trɪkstər] *n* estafador,-ra, embustero,-a, t mador,-ra.
tricky ['trɪkɪ] *adj* **1** *(person)* taimado,-a, astuto,-a, ma ñoso,-a. **2** *(problem, situation - difficult)* difícil; *(- deli cate)* delicado,-a.
▲ *comp* **trickier**, *superl* **trickiest**.
tricycle ['traɪsɪkəl] *n* triciclo.
trident ['traɪdənt] *n* tridente *m*.
trier [traɪər] *n* persona que se esfuerza.
trifle ['traɪfəl] *n* **1** *(unimportant thing)* fruslería, bagatel nimiedad *f*, chuchería. **2** *(little money)* poco diner insignificancia. **3** GB *postre de bizcocho*. ■ **a trifle** u poco, algo.
⊙ **to trifle with** *vt insep* jugar con.
trifling ['traɪflɪŋ] *adj* insignificante, sin importancia
trigger ['trɪgər] *n* **1** *(of gun)* gatillo. **2** *(of camera, ma chine)* disparador *m*.
▷ *vt* [Also **trigger off**.] desencadenar, provocar.
trigonometry [trɪgə'nɒmətrɪ] *n* trigonometría.
trilby ['trɪlbɪ] *n* sombrero flexible.
▲ *pl* **trilbies**.
trill [trɪl] *n* **1** *(of birds)* trino, gorjeo. **2** MUS trino. **3** LIN vibración *f*.
▷ *vi* **1** trinar. **2** LING vibrar.
trillion ['trɪlɪən] *n* **1** billón *m*. **2** GB *(formerly)* trillón *m*

En el uso actual, tanto en EEUU como en Gra Bretaña, un **trillion** equivale al **billón** español, e decir, un millón de millones.

trim [trɪm] *adj* **1** *(neat, tidy)* (bien) arreglado,-a, orde nado,-a. **2** *(person, figure)* esbelto,-a, delgado,-a.
▲ *comp* **trimmer**, *superl* **trimmest**.
▷ *n* **1** *(cut)* recorte *m*. **2** *(decoration - on clothes)* adorn *mpl*; *(- along edges)* ribete *m*; *(upholstery)* tapicería. MAR asiento, estiba.
▷ *vt* **1** *(make neat)* arreglar; *(cut - hair)* cortar, recorta *(- hedge, etc)* podar. **2** *(reduce by cutting back)* recorta reducir. **3** *(decorate)* adornar (**with**, con); *(upholster)* t pizar. **4** MAR *(sails)* orientar; *(ship)* equilibrar, asentar
▲ *pt & pp* **trimmed**, *ger* **trimming**.
⊙ **to trim off** *vt sep* recortar, quitar.
trimmings ['trɪmɪŋs] *n pl* **1** CULIN *(accompaniment* guarnición *f sing*. **2** *(decorations)* adornos *mpl*. **3** *(aft cutting)* recortes *mpl*.
Trinidad ['trɪnɪdæd] *n* Trinidad. ● **Trinidad and Tobag** Trinidad y Tobago.
Trinity ['trɪnətɪ] *n* **the Trinity**
▲ *pl* **Trinities**. REL la Trinidad *f*. ● **Trinity Sunday** fies de la Trinidad.
trinket ['trɪŋkɪt] *n* chuchería, baratija.
trip [trɪp] *n* **1** *(journey)* viaje *m*. **2** *(excursion)* excursión **3** *(stumble)* tropezón *m*. **4** *sl (on drugs)* viaje *m*.
▷ *vt* **1** hacer tropezar, hacerle una zancadilla a. **2** *(set o - switch, alarm, etc)* activar, hacer que se dispare.
▷ *vi* **1** *(stumble)* tropezar (**over**, con). **2** *(move lightly)* con paso ligero. **3** *sl (on drugs)* viajar.
⊙ **to trip up** *vt sep* **1** *(make fall)* echar la zancadilla a. *(cause to make a mistake)* hacer equivocar.
▷ *vi* **1** *(fall)* tropezar. **2** *(make a mistake)* equivocarse.
▲ *pt & pp* **tripped**, *ger* **tripping**.
tripe [traɪp] *n* **1** CULIN callos *mpl*. **2** *fam* tonterías *fp* bobadas *fpl*.
triple ['trɪpəl] *adj* triple.

triplet ['trɪplət] *n* 1 *(child)* trillizo,-a. 2 MUS tresillo.
triplicate ['trɪplɪkət] *adj* triplicado,-a.
▷ *vt* triplicar. ■ **in triplicate** por triplicado,-a.
Tripoli ['trɪpəlɪ] *n* Trípoli.
tripper ['trɪpəʳ] *n* excursionista *mf.*
trite [traɪt] *adj* 1 *(subject)* trillado,-a, manido,-a. 2 *(sentiment)* banal.
triumph [traɪəmf] *n* 1 triunfo, éxito. 2 *(joy)* júbilo, alegría.
▷ *vi* triunfar (**over**, de/sobre), vencer.
triune ['traɪjuːn] *adj* trino,-a.
trivia ['trɪvɪə] *n pl* trivialidades *fpl.*
trivial ['trɪvɪəl] *adj* trivial.
trivialise ['trɪvɪəlaɪz] *vt* → **trivialize.**
trivialize ['trɪvɪəlaɪz] *vt* trivializar.
trod [trɒd] *pt* → **tread.**
trodden ['trɒdən] *pp* → **tread.**
Trojan ['trəʊdʒən] *n* troyano *mf.*
▷ *adj* troyano, a.
troll [trəʊl] *n* duende *m.*
trolley ['trɒlɪ] *n* 1 *(in supermarket, at airport)* carro, carrito. 2 *(in hospital)* cama con ruedas. 3 *(for food)* mesita de ruedas. 4 US tranvía. ■ **trolley bus** trolebús *mf.* ■ **trolley car** tranvía *mf.*
trombone [trɒm'bəʊn] *n* trombón *m.*
troop [truːp] *n* 1 *(group)* grupo. 2 MIL tropa.
▷ *vi* ir en tropel.
▷ *n pl* **troops** soldados *mpl*, tropas *fpl.*
trooper ['truːpəʳ] *n* soldado de caballería.
trophy ['trəʊfɪ] *n* trofeo.
▲ *pl* **trophies.**
tropic ['trɒpɪk] *n* trópico.
▷ *n pl* **the tropics** los trópicos *mpl.*
tropical ['trɒpɪkᵊl] *adj* tropical.
troposphere ['trɒpəsfɪəʳ] *n* troposfera.
trot [trɒt] *n* trote *m.*
▷ *vt* hacer trotar.
▷ *vi* 1 *(gen)* trotar, ir al trote; *(on horse)* cabalgar al trote. 2 *fam (go)* ir.
▲ *pt & pp* **trotted**, *ger* **trotting.**
▷ *n pl* **the trots** *fam* diarrea *f sing.*
⊙ **to trot out** *vt sep* 1 *(excuses, arguments)* salir con, soltar. 2 *(names, list)* recitar de memoria.
troth [trəʊθ] *n* fe *f.*
trotter ['trɒtəʳ] *n (horse)* trotón,-ona.
trouble ['trʌbᵊl] *n* 1 *(problems)* problema *m*, problemas *mpl.* 2 *(inconvenience, bother)* molestia, esfuerzo. 3 MED problema *m*, enfermedad *f.* 4 *(unrest, disturbance)* conflictos *mpl*, disturbios *mpl.*
▷ *vt* 1 *(cause worry, distress)* preocupar, inquietar. 2 *(hurt)* dar problemas a, doler. 3 *(bother)* molestar.
▷ *vi* molestarse, preocuparse (**about**, por).
troubled ['trʌbəld] *adj* 1 *(person, look)* preocupado,-a, inquieto,-a. 2 *(period)* turbulento,-a, agitado,-a.
trouble-free ['trʌbᵊlfriː] *adj* sin problemas, tranquilo,-a; *(demonstration, etc)* sin incidentes.
troublemaker ['trʌbᵊlmeɪkəʳ] *n* alborotador,-ra.
troubleshooter ['trʌbᵊlʃuːtəʳ] *n (mediator)* conciliador,-ra, mediador,-ra.
troublesome ['trʌbᵊlsəm] *adj (thing)* molesto,-a, fastidioso,-a; *(person)* difícil, problemático,-a; *(situation)* problemático,-a, conflictivo,-a.

trough [trɒf] *n* 1 *(for drinking)* abrevadero; *(for eating)* comedero, pesebre *m.* 2 *(channel)* canal *m*; *(gutter)* canalón *m.* 3 METEOR depresión *f*, zona de bajas presiones. 4 *(depression - in land)* depresión *f*; *(between waves)* seno. 5 *(low point in cycle)* parte *f* baja, punto más bajo.
trounce [traʊns] *vt (thrash)* zurrar, dar una paliza a; *(defeat)* derrotar.
troupe [truːp] *n* compañía, grupo.
trouper ['truːpəʳ] *n* actor *m*, actriz *f.*
trouser ['traʊzə] *adj* del pantalón.
trousers ['traʊzəz] *n pl* pantalón *m sing*, pantalones *mpl.*
trousseau ['truːsəʊ] *n* ajuar *m* de novia.
▲ *pl* **trousseaus** o **trousseaux.**
trout [traʊt] *n* trucha.
trowel [traʊəl] *n* 1 *(bricklaying tool)* paleta. 2 *(garden tool)* desplantador *m.*
Troy [trɔɪ] *n* Troya.
truancy ['truːənsɪ] *n* absentismo escolar.
truant ['truːənt] *n (from school)* persona que hace novillos. ■ **to play truant** hacer novillos.
truce [truːs] *n* tregua.
truck [trʌk] *n* 1 *(lorry)* camión *m.* 2 GB *(railway wagon)* vagón *m.* 3 US *(fruit, vegetables)* productos *mpl* agrícolas. 4 *(dealings)* tratos *mpl.*
trucker ['trʌkəʳ] *n* US camionero,-a.
truckle ['trʌkᵊl] *vi* rendirse (**to**, a), someterse (**to**, a).
truckload ['trʌkləʊd] *n (lorry)* camión *m* lleno; *(railway wagon)* vagón *m* lleno. ■ **by the truckload** a montones.
truculence ['trʌkjʊləns] *n* agresividad *f*, hostilidad *f.*
trudge [trʌdʒ] *vi* andar con dificultad.
▷ *n* caminata (larga y difícil).
true [truː] *adj* 1 *(not false)* verdadero,-a, cierto,-a. 2 *(genuine, real)* auténtico,-a, genuino,-a, real. 3 *(faithful)* fiel, leal. 4 *(exact)* exacto,-a. 5 *(accurate - aim)* acertado,-a. 6 *(straight, level - wall)* a plomo; *(- surface, level)* a nivel, nivelado,-a; *(- wheel)* centrado,-a.■ **to come true** hacerse realidad.
▷ *adv* 1 *(truthfully)* sinceramente. 2 *(accurately)* bien.
true-blue ['truːbluː] *adj* 1 leal, fiel. 2 POL hasta la médula.
true-life ['truːlaɪf] *adj* real.
truffle ['trʌfᵊl] *n* trufa.
truism ['truːɪzᵊm] *n* perogrullada.
truly ['truːlɪ] *adv* 1 *(really)* verdaderamente, de verdad, realmente. 2 *(sincerely)* sinceramente. 3 *(faithfully)* fielmente, lealmente. ■ **yours truly** *(in letters)* atentamente.
trump [trʌmp] *n (cards)* triunfo.
▷ *vt (cards)* ganar con un triunfo.
▷ *n pl* **trumps** triunfo.
⊙ **to trump up** *vt sep* inventar, falsificar.
trumpet ['trʌmpɪt] *n* MUS trompeta.
▷ *vi* 1 fanfarronear. 2 *(elephant)* barritar.
truncate [trʌŋ'keɪt] *vt* truncar.
▷ *adj* truncado,-a.
truncheon ['trʌntʃᵊn] *n* porra (de policía).
trundle ['trʌndᵊl] *vt (move on wheels)* hacer rodar; *(move)* mover (con dificultad).
▷ *vi (vehicles)* rodar (con mucho ruido), rodar (pesadamente); *(people)* ir(se) (pesadamente).
trunk [trʌŋk] *n* 1 *(of tree, body)* tronco. 2 *(large case)* baúl *m.* 3 *(elephant's)* trompa. 4 US *(of car)* maletero.

trunks [trʌŋks] *n pl* bañador *m sing* (de hombre).
truss [trʌs] *vt* **1** *(tie)* atar (up, -). **2** ARCH apuntalar.
▷ *n* **1** MED braguero. **2** ARCH cuchillo de armadura. **3** *(of hay)* haz *m*, lío. **4** *(of tomatoes, etc)* racimo; *(of flowers)* ramo.
trust [trʌst] *n* **1** *(confidence)* confianza. **2** *(responsibility)* responsabilidad *f*. **3** FIN *(money, property)* fondo de inversión. **4** JUR *(money or property held or invested for SB)* fideicomiso. **5** *(foundation)* patronato, fundación *f*. **6** FIN *(cartel)* trust *m*, cartel *m*. ● **trust fund** patronato.
▷ *vt* **1** *(have faith in, rely on)* confiar en, fiarse de. **2** *(hope, expect)* esperar. **3** *(entrust)* confiar.
▷ *vi* confiar (in, en), tener confianza (in, en).
trusted ['trʌstɪd] *adj* **1** *(loyal)* leal, fiel, de confianza. **2** *(remedy)* probado,-a, comprobado,-a.
trustee [trʌs'ti:] *n* **1** *(of money, property)* fideicomisario,-a. **2** *(in bankruptcy)* síndico. **3** *(of institution)* miembro del consejo de administración.
trustful ['trʌstfʊl] *adj* confiado,-a.
trusting ['trʌstɪŋ] *adj* confiado,-a.
trustworthy ['trʌstwɜ:ðɪ] *adj* **1** *(person)* digno,-a de confianza, honrado,-a. **2** *(news, etc)* fidedigno,-a.
trusty ['trʌstɪ] *adj* fiel, leal.
▲ *comp* trustier, *superl* trustiest.
▷ *n (prisoner)* ordenanza *m*.
▲ *pl* trusties.
truth [tru:θ] *n* **1** *(quality)* verdad *f*. **2** *(truthfulness)* veracidad *f*.
truthful ['tru:θfʊl] *adj* **1** *(account, etc)* verídico,-a, veraz. **2** *(person)* sincero,-a, veraz.
try [traɪ] *n* **1** intento, tentativa. **2** SP *(rugby)* ensayo.
▲ *pl* tries.
▷ *vt* **1** *(attempt)* intentar. **2** *(test, use)* probar, poner a prueba, ensayar; *(food)* probar. **3** JUR juzgar. **4** *(be a strain on - eyes)* cansar; *(- patience, person)* poner a prueba.
▷ *vi (make an attempt)* intentar.
▲ *pt & pp* tried, *ger* trying.
⊙ **to try for** *vi* tratar de obtener.
⊙ **to try on** *vt sep (clothes)* probarse.
⊙ **to try out** *vt sep* probar, ensayar.
trying ['traɪɪŋ] *adj* molesto,-a, difícil, pesado,-a.
tsar [zɑ:ʳ] *n* zar *m*.
tsarina [zɑ:'ri:nə] *n* zarina.
tsetse fly ['tsetsɪflaɪ] *n* mosca tsetsé.
▲ *pl* tsps.
T-shirt ['ti:ʃɜ:t] *n* camiseta.
Tuareg ['twɑ:reg] *adj* tuareg.
▷ *n* tuareg *m*.
tub [tʌb] *n* **1** *(for washing clothes)* balde *m*. **2** *(bath)* bañera, baño. **3** *(food container)* tarrina.
tuba ['tju:bə] *n* tuba.
tubby ['tʌbɪ] *adj* rechoncho,-a.
▲ *comp* tubbier, *superl* tubbiest.
tube [tju:b] *n* **1** *(pipe, container)* tubo. **2** AUTO cámara de aire.
▷ *n* **the tube** la televisión *f*.
▷ *n* **the Tube** *(underground)* el metro.
tubeless ['tju:bləs] *adj* sin cámara.
tuber ['tju:bəʳ] *n* tubérculo.
tubing ['tju:bɪŋ] *n* tubería.
tuck [tʌk] *n* **1** *(fold)* pliegue *m*. **2** GB *(sweets, etc)* golosinas *fpl*, chucherías *fpl*. **3** *(place)* meter, poner.
⊙ **to tuck away** *vt sep* esconder, ocultar.
⊙ **to tuck in** *vi (eat)* ponerse a comer, atacar.
▷ *vt sep* **1** *(clothes)* meter. **2** *(person)* arropar.
⊙ **to tuck into** *vt insep* ponerse a comer, atacar.
⊙ **to tuck up** *vt sep* arropar.
Tuesday ['tju:zdɪ] *n* martes *m inv*.

Para ejemplos de uso, consulta **Saturday**.

tuft [tʌft] *n* **1** *(of feathers)* penacho. **2** *(of hair)* mechón *m*. **3** *(of grass)* mata.
tug [tʌg] *n* **1** *(pull)* estirón *m*. **2** *(boat)* remolcador *m*.
▷ *vt* **1** *(pull)* tirar de, dar un estirón de. **2** *(boat)* remolcar.
▷ *vi* tirar (at, de).
▲ *pt & pp* tugged, *ger* tugging.
tugboat ['tʌgbəʊt] *n* remolcador *m*.
tuition [tju:'ɪʃᵊn] *n* enseñanza, instrucción *f*. ● **private tuition** clases *fpl* particulares. ‖ **tuition fees** EDUC matrícula.
tulip ['tju:lɪp] *n* tulipán *m*.
tumble ['tʌmbᵊl] *n* caída, tumbo.
▷ *vi* **1** *(fall)* caerse. **2** *(in acrobatics)* dar volteretas. **3** *(prices, etc)* caer en picado. ● **tumble drier** secadora.
⊙ **to tumble to** *vt insep* comprender, caer en la cuenta.
tumbledown ['tʌmbᵊldaʊn] *adj* ruinoso,-a.
tumbler ['tʌmbᵊləʳ] *n* **1** *(glass)* vaso. **2** *(acrobat)* volteador,-ra. **3** *(toy)* tentetieso, dominguillo.
tummy ['tʌmɪ] *n* barriga.
▲ *pl* tummies.
tun [tʌn] *n* tonel *m*.
tuna ['tju:nə] *n* atún *m*, bonito.
▲ *pl* tuna o tunas.
tune [tju:n] *n* melodía.
▷ *vt* **1** MUS afinar. **2** *(radio, etc)* sintonizar. **3** *(engine)* poner a punto. ■ **in tune** afinado,-a.
⊙ **to tune in to** *vt insep (radio, etc)* sintonizar.
⊙ **to tune up** *vt sep* afinar.
tuneful ['tju:nfʊl] *adj* melodioso,-a.
tuneless ['tju:nləs] *adj* sin armonía.
tuner ['tju:nəʳ] *n* **1** *(of piano)* afinador,-ra. **2** *(on radio)* sintonizador *m*.
tungsten ['tʌŋstən] *n* tungsteno.
tuning ['tju:nɪŋ] *n* **1** *(of instrument)* afinación *f*. **2** *(of radio)* sintonización *f*. **3** *(of engine)* puesta a punto. ● **tuning fork** diapasón *m*.
Tunis ['tju:nɪs] *n* Túnez.
Tunisia [tju:'nɪsɪə] *n* Túnez.
Tunisian [tju:'nsɪən] *adj* tunecino,-a.
▷ *n* tunecino,-a.
tunnel ['tʌnᵊl] *n (gen)* túnel *m*; *(in mine)* galería.
▷ *vt* excavar un túnel.
▷ *vi* construir un túnel. ● **tunnel vision 1** *(blindness)* ceguera. **2** *(narrow-mindedness)* estrechez *f* de miras.
▲ *pt & pp* tunnelled (US tunneled), *ger* tunnelling (US tunneling).
tunny ['tʌnɪ] *n* atún *m*, bonito.
▲ *pl* tunnies.
tuppence ['tʌpəns] *n* GB *fam* dos peniques *mpl*.
turban ['tɜ:bᵊn] *n* turbante *m*.
turbocharger ['tɜ:bəʊtʃɑ:dʒəʳ] *n* turboalimentador *m*.
turbojet ['tɜ:bəʊdʒet] *n* turborreactor *m*.
turboprop ['tɜ:bəʊprɒp] *n* turbohélice *m*.
turbot ['tɜ:bət] *n* rodaballo.
▲ *pl* turbot o turbots.

urbulent ['tɜ:bjʊlənt] *adj* turbulento,-a.

ureen [tjʊ'ri:n] *n* sopera.

urf [tɜ:f] *n* césped *m*.

▷ *vt* cubrir con césped. ● **the turf** las carreras de caballos, el turf *m*.

⊙ **to turf out** *vt sep fam* poner de patitas en la calle.

urk [tɜ:k] *n (person)* turco,-a.

urkestan [tɜ:kɪ'stæn] *n* Turquestán.

urkey ['tɜ:kɪ] *n* Turquía.

urkey ['tɜ:kɪ] *n* pavo. ■ **to talk turkey** hablar a las claras.

urkish ['tɜ:kɪʃ] *adj* turco,-a.

▷ *n (language)* turco.

▷ *n pl* **the Turkish** los turcos *mpl*.

urkistan [tɜ:kɪ'stæn] *n* Turquestán.

urkman ['tɜ:kmən] *adj* turcomano,-a.

▷ *n* **1** *(person)* turcomano,-a. **2** *(language)* turcomano.

urkmen ['tɜ:kmən] *n (language)* turcomano.

urkmenistan [tɜ:kmenɪ'stæn] *n* Turkmenistán *m*.

urkoman ['tɜ:kəmən] *adj* turcomano,-a.

▷ *n* **1** *(person)* turcomano,-a. **2** *(language)* turcomano.

urmeric ['tɜ:mərɪk] *n* cúrcuma.

urmoil ['tɜ:mɔɪl] *n* confusión *f*, agitación *f*.

urn [tɜ:n] *n* **1** *(act of turning)* vuelta. **2** *(change of direction)* giro, vuelta; *(bend)* curva, recodo. **3** *(chance, go)* turno. **4** *(change)* cambio, giro. **5** *(short walk)* vuelta, paseo. **6** *(attack of illness)* ataque *m*; *(shock)* susto. **7** *(act of kindness, favour)* favor *m*. **8** THEAT *(act)* número.

▷ *vt* **1** *(rotate)* girar, hacer girar, dar la vuelta a. **2** *(page)* pasar, volver; *(soil)* revolver; *(ankle)* torcer. **3** *(cause to change direction)* girar, dar la vuelta a. **4** *(invert)* darle la vuelta a. **5** *(change)* convertir, transformar, volver; *(milk)* agriar; *(stomach)* revolver. **6** *(pass)* pasar. **7** *(fold)* doblar. **8** *(shape)* tornear, labrar en un torno.

▷ *vi* **1** *(revolve)* girar, dar vueltas. **2** *(change direction - person)* girarse, dar la vuelta, volverse; *(- car)* girar, torcer; *(- plane, ship)* virar; *(- tide)* repuntar. **3** *(become)* hacerse, ponerse, volverse; *(milk)* agriarse, cortarse.

⊙ **to turn against** *vt insep* **1** *(cause to dislike)* poner en contra. **2** *(become hostile towards)* ponerse en contra de.

⊙ **to turn around / turn round** *vi* darse la vuelta.

▷ *vt sep* volver, darle la vuelta a.

⊙ **to turn away** *vt sep (not let in)* no dejar entrar.

▷ *vi (look away)* volver la cabeza, la espalda.

⊙ **to turn back** *vt sep* **1** *(make return)* hacer volver. **2** *(clock)* retrasar.

▷ *vi (return)* volverse atrás.

⊙ **to turn down** *vt sep* **1** *(reject)* rechazar; *(request)* denegar. **2** *(radio, etc)* bajar. **3** *(fold)* doblar.

⊙ **to turn in** *vt sep (to police)* entregar a la policía.

▷ *vi fam (go to bed)* acostarse.

⊙ **to turn into** *vt sep* convertir.

⊙ **to turn off** *vt sep* **1** *(electricity)* desconectar; *(light, gas, appliance)* apagar; *(tap)* cerrar. **2** *(dislike)* repugnar, dar asco a.

▷ *vt insep (off road)* salir de.

▷ *vi* **1** *(switch off)* apagarse. **2** *(off road)* salir.

⊙ **to turn on** *vt sep* **1** *(electricity)* conectar; *(light, gas, appliance)* encender; *(tap)* abrir; *(engine)* poner en marcha, encender. **2** *(attack)* atacar, arremeter contra; *(aim, point at)* apuntar, dirigir. **3** *fam (excite)* excitar, entusiasmar.

▷ *vt insep (hinge on)* depender de, girar en torno a.

▷ *vi* encenderse.

⊙ **to turn out** *vt sep* **1** *(light)* apagar. **2** *(produce)* producir, fabricar. **3** *(empty)* vaciar; *(cake, jelly, etc)* desmoldar. **4** *(expel)* expulsar, echar.

▷ *vi* **1** *(prove to be, happen)* salir, resultar. **2** *(go out)* salir; *(attend)* asistir, acudir; *(crowds)* salir a la calle.

⊙ **to turn over** *vt sep* **1** *(invert)* dar la vuelta a, volver, poner al revés. **2** *(idea)* dar vueltas a. **3** *(hand over)* entregar.

▷ *vt insep* **1** *(page)* volver. **2** COMM facturar, hacer.

▷ *vi* **1** *(person)* darse la vuelta; *(car)* volcar. **2** *(engine)* marchar en vacío, funcionar.

⊙ **to turn to** *vt insep* **1** *(person)* acudir a, recurrir a. **2** *(page)* buscar, pasar a; *(subject)* pasar a. **3** *(take up)* dedicarse a, recurrir a, darse a, empezar.

⊙ **to turn up** *vi (arrive)* llegar; *(appear)* aparecer.

▷ *vt sep* **1** *(fold upwards)* doblar hacia arriba, levantar; *(shorten)* acortar. **2** *(radio, gas, heat, etc)* subir, poner más fuerte.

▷ *vt insep (find)* descubrir, encontrar.

turnabout ['tɜ:nəbaʊt] *n* giro, cambio.

turnaround ['tɜ:nəraʊnd] *n* US → **turnround.**

turncoat ['tɜ:nkəʊt] *n* renegado,-a, chaquetero,-a.

turning ['tɜ:nɪŋ] *n* bocacalle *f*, esquina. ● **turning lathe** torno.

turnip ['tɜ:nɪp] *n* nabo.

turn-off ['tɜ:nɒf] *n* **1** *(road)* salida

turnout ['tɜ:naʊt] *n* **1** *(attendance)* asistencia; *(voters)* número de votantes. **2** *(clearout)* limpieza general. **3** *(appearance)* aspecto.

turnover ['tɜ:nəʊvəʳ] *n* **1** *(sales, business)* facturación *f*. **2** *(movement of employees)* movimiento; *(of stock)* rotación *f*. **3** CULIN pastelito relleno.

turnpike ['tɜ:npaɪk] *n* US autopista de peaje.

turnround ['tɜ:nraʊnd] *n* **1** *(of passengers)* operación *f* de desembarque y embarque de pasajeros; *(of freight)* operación *f* de carga y descarga. **2** *(reversal of situation)* cambio total.

turnstile ['tɜ:nstaɪl] *n* torniquete *m*.

turnstone ['tɜ:nstəʊn] *n* vuelvepiedras *m*.

turntable ['tɜ:nteɪbᵊl] *n* **1** *(on record player)* plato giratorio. **2** *(for trains)* plataforma giratoria.

turn-up ['tɜ:nʌp] *n* **1** GB *(of trousers)* vuelta. **2** *fam (chance occurrence)* acontecimiento.

turpentine ['tɜ:pəntaɪn] *n* trementina, aguarrás *m*.

turquoise ['tɜ:kwɔɪz] *n* **1** *(gem)* turquesa. **2** *(colour)* azul *m* turquesa.

▷ *adj* azul turquesa.

turret ['tʌrət] *n* **1** torrecilla. **2** MIL torreta.

turtle ['tɜ:tᵊl] *n* tortuga marina.

turtledove ['tɜ:tᵊldʌv] *n* tórtola.

turtleneck ['tɜ:tᵊlnek] *n* cuello cisne, cuello alto.

tusk [tʌsk] *n* colmillo.

tussle ['tʌsəl] *n* pelea, lucha.

▷ *vi* pelear, luchar.

tussock ['tʌsək] *n* mata de hierba.

tutelage ['tju:təlɪdʒ] *n* tutela.

tutor ['tju:təʳ] *n* **1** *(private teacher)* profesor,-ra particular. **2** *(at university)* profesor,-ra, tutor,-ra.

▷ *vt* dar clases particulares a (**in**, de).

tutorial [tjʊ:'tɔ:rɪəl] *n* clase *f* con grupo reducido.

Tuvalu [tʊ:vəˈlʊ:] *n* Tuvalu.
tuxedo [tʌkˈsi:dəʊ] *n* US esmoquin *m*.
▲ *pl* tuxedos.
TV [ˈtɜ:bjʊləns] *abbr* (television) televisión *f*, tele *f*.
twaddle [ˈtwɒdᵊl] *n fam* tonterías *fpl*.
twang [twæŋ] *n* **1** *(of instrument)* sonido vibrante, tañido. **2** *(through nose)* gangueo.
▷ *vt (strum)* puntear.
▷ *vi* vibrar.
tweak [twi:k] *vt* pellizcar.
▷ *n* pellizco.
twee [twi:] *adj* GB *fam pej* cursi.
tweed [twi:d] *n* cheviot *m*.
tweet [twi:t] *n* pío.
▷ *vi* piar.
tweeter [ˈtwi:təʳ] *n* altavoz *f* para altas frecuencias.
tweezers [ˈtwi:zəz] *n pl* pinzas *fpl*.
twelfth [twelfθ] *adj* duodécimo,-a.
▷ *adv* en duodécimo lugar.
▷ *n (fraction)* duodécimo; *(one part)* duodécima parte *f*.
Consulta también **sixth**.
twelve [twelv] *n* doce *m*.
▷ *adj* doce.
Consulta también **six**.
twenties [ˈtwentɪz] *n pl* **the twenties** los años *mpl* veinte. ■ **to be in one's twenties** tener veintitantos años.
Consulta también **sixties**.
twentieth [ˈtwentɪəθ] *adj* vigésimo,-a.
▷ *adv* en vigésimo lugar.
▷ *n (fraction)* vigésimo; *(one part)* vigésima parte *f*.
Consulta también **sixtieth**.
twenty [ˈtwentɪ] *n* veinte *m*.
▷ *adj* veinte.
Consulta también **sixty**.
twice [twaɪs] *adv* dos veces. ■ **twice over** dos veces.
twiddle [ˈtwɪdᵊl] *vt* dar vueltas a, girar.
▷ *vi* juguetear (**with**, con).
▷ *n* vuelta.
twig[1] [twɪg] *n* ramita.
twig[2] [twɪg] *vi* caer en la cuenta, darse cuenta.
▲ *pt & pp* twigged, *ger* twigging.
twilight [ˈtwaɪlaɪt] *n* crepúsculo, anochecer.
twill [twɪl] *n (fabric)* sarga, tela cruzada.
twin [twɪn] *n* gemelo,-a, mellizo,-a.
▷ *adj* gemelo,-a, mellizo,-a. ● **twin bed** cama doble.
▷ *vt* hermanar.
▲ *pt & pp* twinned, *ger* twinning.
twine [twaɪn] *n* bramante *m*.
▷ *vt* enroscar, entrelazar.
▷ *vi* enroscarse, entrelazarse.
twinge [twɪndʒ] *n* **1** *(pain)* punzada, dolor *m* agudo. **2** *fig (remorse)* remordimiento.
twinkle [ˈtwɪŋkᵊl] *n* **1** *(of light, stars)* centelleo. **2** *(in eye)* brillo.
▷ *vi* **1** *(lights, stars)* centellear, destellar. **2** *(eyes)* brillar.
twinkling [ˈtwɪŋkᵊlɪŋ] *n* centelleo. ■ **in the twinkling of an eye** en un abrir y cerrar de ojos.
twirl [twɜ:l] *n* giro, vuelta.
▷ *vt* **1** girar rápidamente, dar vueltas a. **2** *(twist, fiddle with)* retorcer, juguetear con.
▷ *vi* girar rápidamente, dar vueltas.
twist [twɪst] *n* **1** *(in road)* recodo, vuelta. **2** *(action)* torsión *m*. **3** MED torcedura, esguince *m*. **4** *(dance)* twist *m*. **5** *(development)* giro. **6** *(of lemon)* rodajita.
▷ *vt* **1** *(sprain)* torcer. **2** *(screw, coil)* retorcer. **3** *(turn, wind)* girar, dar vueltas a. **4** *(interweave)* entrelazar, trenzar. **5** *(pervert)* tergiversar, torcer.
▷ *vi* **1** *(turn)* girarse. **2** *(wind, coil)* enroscarse. **3** *(road)* serpentear. **4** *(writhe)* retorcerse. **5** *(dance)* bailar el twist.
⊙ **to twist off** *vt sep* desenroscar.
twisted [ˈtwɪstɪd] *adj* retorcido,-a.
twitch [twɪtʃ] *n* **1** *(pull)* tirón *m*. **2** *(nervous tic)* tic *m*.
▷ *vt* mover.
▷ *vi* moverse nerviosamente, palpitar.
twitchy [ˈtwɪtʃɪ] *adj* nervioso,-a.
▲ *comp* twitchier, *superl* twitchiest.
twitter [ˈtwɪtəʳ] *n* gorjeo.
▷ *vi (bird)* gorjear; *(person)* hablar sin parar.
two [tʊ:] *n* dos *m*.
▷ *adj* dos. ■ **in two** por la mitad. ■ **in twos** de dos en dos.
two-bit [ˈtʊ:bɪt] *adj* de tres al cuatro.
two-edged [ˈtʊ:ˈedʒd] *adj* de doble filo.
two-faced [ˈtʊ:ˈfeɪst] *adj* hipócrita, falso,-a.
twopence [ˈtʌpəns] *n* dos peniques *mpl*.
two-piece [ˈtʊ:pi:s] *adj* de dos piezas.
two-ply [ˈtʊ:plaɪ] *adj (wool)* de dos hebras; *(wood)* de dos capas.
two-seater [tʊ:ˈsi:təʳ] *n* biplaza *m*.
twosome [ˈtʊ:səm] *n* pareja, grupo de dos.
two-time [ˈtʊ:taɪm] *vt* engañar, poner los cuernos a.
two-tone [ˈtʊ:təʊn] *adj* de dos tonos.
two-way [tʊ:ˈweɪ] *adj (street)* de doble sentido.
tycoon [taɪˈkʊ:n] *n* magnate *m*.
type [taɪp] *n* **1** *(kind)* tipo, clase *f*. **2** *(letter)* letra.
▷ *vt* escribir a máquina, mecanografiar.
▷ *vi* escribir a máquina.
⊙ **to type up** *vt sep* pasar a máquina.
typecast [ˈtaɪpkɑ:st] *vt* encasillar.
▲ *pt & pp* typecast.
▷ *adj* encasillado,-a.
typeface [ˈtaɪpfeɪs] *n* tipografía.
typescript [ˈtaɪpskrɪpt] *n* texto escrito a máquina, texto mecanografiado.
typesetter [ˈtaɪpsetəʳ] *n (person)* cajista *mf*; *(machine)* componedora, máquina para componer tipos.
typewriter [ˈtaɪpraɪtəʳ] *n* máquina de escribir.
typewritten [ˈtaɪprɪtᵊn] *adj* mecanografiado,-a.
typhoid [ˈtaɪfɔɪd] *n* fiebre *f* tifoidea.
typhus [ˈtaɪfəs] *n* tifus *m*.
typical [ˈtɪpʊkəl] *adj* típico,-a.
typing [ˈtaɪpɪŋ] *n* mecanografía.
typist [ˈtaɪpɪst] *n* mecanógrafo,-a.
typography [taɪˈpɒgrəfɪ] *n* tipografía.
tyranny [ˈtɪrənɪ] *n* tiranía.
▲ *pl* tyrannies.
tyrant [ˈtaɪᵊrənt] *n* tirano,-a.
tyre [taɪəʳ] *n* neumático.
Tyrol [tɪˈrɒl] *n* Tirol.
Tyrolean [tɪrəˈlɪən] *adj* tirolés,-esa.
▷ *n* **1** *(person)* tirolés,-esa. **2** *(dialect)* tirolés,-esa.
Tyrrhenian [tɪˈri:nɪən] *adj* tirreno,-a. ● **the Tyrrhenian Sea** el (mar) *m* Tirreno.
tzar [zɑ:ʳ] *n* zar *m*, czar *m*.

U

, u [juː] *n (the letter)* U, u *f*.
dder ['ʌdəʳ] *n* ubre *f*.
FO ['juː'ef'əʊ] *abbr* **(unidentified flying object)** ovni *m f*, objeto volador no identificado.
ganda [juː'gændə] *n* Uganda.
gandan [juː'gændᵊn] *adj* ugandés,-esa.
n ugandés,-esa.
gly ['ʌglɪ] *adj* **1** feo,-a. **2** *(situation, etc)* desagradable. **3** *(custom, vice)* repugnante. **4** *(wound, mood)* peligroso,-a. **5** *(rumour)* inquietante, nada grato.
▲ *comp* **uglier**, *superl* **ugliest**.
kraine [juː'kreɪn] *n* Ucrania.
krainian [juː'keɪnɪən] *adj* ucraniano,-a.
n **1** *(person)* ucraniano,-a. **2** *(language)* ucraniano.
lcer ['ʌlsəʳ] *n* **1** *(external)* llaga. **2** *(in stomach)* úlcera.
lterior [ʌl'tɪərɪəʳ] *adj* **1** *(hidden)* oculto,-a. **2** *(further)* ulterior.
ltimate ['ʌltɪmət] *adj* **1** *(final)* final. **2** *(basic)* esencial, fundamental.
n **the ultimate** *(good)* el último grito; *(bad)* el colmo.
ltrasound ['ʌltrəsaʊnd] *n* ultrasonido.
ltraviolet [ʌltrə'vaɪələt] *adj* ultravioleta.
mbilical [ʌm'bɪlɪkᵊl] *adj* umbilical. ● **umbilical cord** cordón *m* umbilical.
mbrella [ʌm'brelə] *n* **1** paraguas *m*. **2** *fig (protection)* manto *f*; *(patronage)* patrocinio.
mpire ['ʌmpaɪəʳ] *n* árbitro,-a.
vt arbitrar.
nabashed [ʌnə'bæʃt] *adj* **1** *(shameless)* descarado,-a. **2** *(unperturbed)* inmutable.
nable [ʌn'eɪbᵊl] *adj* incapaz.
nabridged [ʌnə'brɪdʒd] *adj* íntegro,-a.
nacceptable [ʌnək'septəbᵊl] *adj* inaceptable.
naccompanied [ʌnə'kʌmpənɪd] *adj* **1** *(person)* solo,-a. **2** MUS sin acompañamiento.
naccomplished [ʌnə'kʌmlɪʃt] *adj* **1** *(unfinished)* inacabado,-a. **2** *(without talent)* mediocre. **3** *(ambitions, goals, etc,)* no logrado,-a.
naccountable [ʌnə'kaʊntəbᵊl] *adj* inexplicable.
naccustomed [ʌnə'kʌstəmd] *adj* desacostumbrado,-a.
naffected [ʌnə'fektɪd] *adj* **1** *(unchanged)* no afectado,-a. **2** *(for person)* afable, campechano. **3** *(indifferent)* inmutable. **4** *(style)* llano,-a.
nafraid [ʌnə'freɪd] *adj* sin miedo.
naided [ʌn'eɪdɪd] *adv* sin ayuda, solo,-a.
nanimous [juː'nænɪməs] *adj* unánime.
nannounced [ʌnə'naʊnst] *adj* **1** *(without knocking)* sin llamar. **2** *(without announcement)* sin ser anunciado,-a.
nanswered [ʌn'ɑːnsəd] *adj* **1** *(of letter)* sin contestar. **2** *(of love)* no correspondido,-a.

unapproachable [ʌnə'prəʊtʃəbᵊl] *adj* **1** inaccesible. **2** *(of person)* intratable.
unarmed [ʌn'ɑːmd] *adj* desarmado,-a.
unashamed [ʌnə'ʃeɪmd] *adj* descarado,-a.
unasked [ʌn'ɑːskt] *adv (voluntarily)* voluntariamente.
▷ *adj (not asked)* sin preguntar, sin formular.
▷ *adj* **unasked for** *(unsolicited)* no solicitado,-a.
unassailable [ʌnə'seɪləbᵊl] *adj* **1** *(fortress)* inexpugnable. **2** *(position)* inatacable. **3** *(argument)* irrebatible.
unassuming [ʌnə'sjuːmɪŋ] *adj* modesto,-a, sin pretensiones.
unattached [ʌnə'tætʃt] *adj* **1** *(loose)* suelto,-a. **2** *(not engaged or married)* sin compromiso, soltero,-a. **3** *(independent)* libre. **4** JUR *(of property, etc)* no embargado,-a.
unattended [ʌnə'tendɪd] *adj* **1** *(children)* sin vigilar. **2** *(not looked after)* desatendido,-a. **3** *(alone)* solo,-a.
unauthorized [ʌn'ɔːθəraɪzd] *adj* **1** *(person)* no autorizado,-a. **2** *(business, etc)* ilegal.
unavailable [ʌnə'veɪləbᵊl] *adj* **1** no disponible. **2** *(busy)* ocupado,-a. **3** *(out of print)* agotado,-a. **4** *(not for sale)* que no está en venta.
unavoidable [ʌnə'vɔɪdəbᵊl] *adj* **1** *(general)* inevitable. **2** *(accident)* fortuito,-a.
unaware [ʌnə'weəʳ] *adj* ignorante, inconsciente.
unawares [ʌnə'weəz] *adv* **1** desprevenido,-a. **2** *(unintentionally)* inconscientemente.
unbalance [ʌn'bæləns] *vt* **1** desequilibrar. **2** trastornar.
unbearable [ʌn'beərəbᵊl] *adj* inaguantable, insoportable, intolerable.
unbeatable [ʌn'biːtəbᵊl] *adj* **1** *(competition)* invencible. **2** *(price, quality)* insuperable, inigualable, inmejorable.
unbecoming [ʌnbɪ'kʌmɪŋ] *adj* **1** *(unsuitable)* impropio,-a. **2** *(clothes)* que no sienta bien.
unbelievable [ʌnbɪ'liːvəbᵊl] *adj* increíble.
unbend [ʌn'bend] *vt* **1** desencorvar, enderezar. **2** *fig* hacerse más amable.
▷ *vi fig* relajarse.
▲ *pt & pp* **unbent** [ʌn'bent].
unbiased [ʌn'baɪəst] *adj* imparcial.
unbiassed [ʌn'baɪəst] *adj* ⟶ **unbiased**.
unblock [ʌn'blɒk] *vt* **1** *(pipe, drain)* desatascar. **2** *(street, road)* desobstruir. **3** *(nose)* destaponar.
unbolt [ʌn'bəʊlt] *vt* descorrer el pestillo de.
unbreakable [ʌn'breɪkəbᵊl] *adj* **1** irrompible. **2** *fig* inquebrantable. **3** *(horse)* indomable.
unbroken [ʌn'brəʊkᵊn] *adj* **1** *(whole)* entero,-a, intacto,-a. **2** *(uninterrupted)* ininterrumpido,-a, continuo,-a. **3** *(record)* imbatido,-a. **4** *(untamed)* indómito,-a, sin domar.
unburden [ʌn'bɜːdᵊn] *vt fml* descargar, aliviar.

unbutton [ʌn'bʌtən] *vt* desabrochar.
▷ *vi fam* relajarse.
uncalled-for [ʌn'kɔːldfɔːr] [Written **uncalled for** when not used to qualify a noun.] *adj (unjustified)* gratuito,-a, fuera de lugar; *(unnecessary)* innecesario,-a.
uncanny [ʌn'kænɪ] *adj* extraño,-a.
▲ *comp* **uncannier**, *superl* **uncanniest**.
uncared-for [ʌn'keədfɔːr] [Written **uncared for** when not used to qualify a noun.] *adj* **1** *(appearance)* descuidado,-a. **2** *(person)* abandonado,-a, desamparado,-a.
uncaring [ʌn'keərɪŋ] *adj* indiferente, despreocupado,-a.
unceasing [ʌn'siːsɪŋ] *adj* continuo,-a.
uncertain [ʌn'sɜːtən] *adj* **1** *(not certain)* incierto,-a, dudoso,-a. **2** *(unspecified)* indeterminado,-a. **3** *(indecisive)* indeciso,-a. **4** *(changeable)* variable.
unchanged [ʌn'tʃeɪndʒd] *adj* igual, sin alterar.
unchecked [ʌn'tʃekt] *adj* **1** no comprobado,-a. **2** *(unrestrained)* libre, libremente.
uncivilized [ʌn'sɪvəlaɪzd] *adj* **1** *(tribe)* salvaje. **2** *(not cultured)* inculto,-a. **3** *fig* poco ortodoxo,-a.
unclaimed [ʌn'kleɪmd] *adj* sin reclamar.
uncle ['ʌnkəl] *n* tío.
unclean [ʌn'kliːn] *adj* **1** sucio,-a. **2** REL impuro,-a.
unclear [ʌn'klɪər] *adj* confuso,-a.
unclog [ʌn'klɒg] *vt* desatascar.
▲ *pt & pp* **unclogged**, *ger* **unclogging**.
uncoil [ʌn'kɔɪl] *vt* desenrollar.
▷ *vi* **1** *(snake)* desenroscarse. **2** *(rope)* desenrollarse.
uncomfortable [ʌn'kʌmfətəbəl] *adj* **1** *(physical)* incómodo,-a. **2** *(worrying)* inquietante. **3** *(unpleasant)* desagradable. **4** *(awkward)* incómodo,-a, molesto,-a.
uncommon [ʌn'kɒmən] *adj* **1** *(rare)* poco común. **2** *(strange)* insólito,-a; *(unusual)* extraordinario,-a. **3** *(excessive)* desmesurado,-a.
uncompromising [ʌn'kɒmprəmaɪzɪŋ] *adj* inflexible, intransigente.
unconcerned [ʌnkən'sɜːnd] *adj* despreocupado, indiferente.
unconnected [ʌnkə'nektɪd] *adj* no relacionado,-a, inconexo,-a.
unconscious [ʌn'kɒnʃəs] *adj* **1** MED inconsciente. **2** *(unaware)* inconsciente. **3** *(not on purpose)* involuntario,-a.
▷ *n* **the unconscious** el inconsciente.
unconsidered [ʌnkən'sɪdəd] *adj (hasty)* irreflexivo,-a.
uncontested [ʌnkən'testɪd] *adj* incontestado,-a.
uncontrollable [ʌnkən'trəʊləbəl] *adj* **1** *(general)* incontrolable. **2** *(people)* ingobernable. **3** *(desire)* irresistible. **4** *(child)* indisciplinado,-a.
unconventional [ʌnkən'venʃənəl] *adj* **1** poco convencional. **2** *(original)* original.
uncountable [ʌn'kaʊntəbəl] *adj* incontable.
uncouple [ʌn'kʌpəl] *vt* **1** *(railways)* desenganchar. **2** *(wheels)* desacoplar. **3** *(disconnect)* desconectar.
uncover [ʌn'kʌvər] *vt* **1** destapar. **2** *(secret)* revelar, descubrir.
unction ['ʌŋkʃən] *n* **1** REL *(act, ointment)* unción *f*. **2** *(balm)* ungüento. **3** *fig* unción *f*, fervor *m* fingido, zalamería.

uncultivated [ʌn'kʌltɪveɪtɪd] *adj* **1** *(land)* yermo,- baldío,-a. **2** *(person)* inculto,-a.
uncurbed [ʌn'kɜːbd] *adj (uncontrolled)* desenfrenado,-
uncut [ʌn'kʌt] *adj* **1** sin cortar. **2** *(gem)* en bruto, si tallar. **3** *(film)* íntegro,-a, sin cortes *mpl*. **4** *(printin books, etc)* intonso,-a.
undamaged [ʌn'dæmɪdʒd] *adj* **1** *(goods)* sin despe fectos, intacto,-a. **2** *(person)* indemne, ileso,-a. **3** *f* intacto,-a.
undated [ʌn'deɪtɪd] *adj* sin fecha.
undecided [ʌndɪ'saɪdɪd] *adj* **1** indeciso,-a. **2** *(ques tion)* no resuelto,-a. **3** *(issue)* pendiente.
undefeated [ʌndɪ'fiːtɪd] *adj* invicto,-a.
undefined [ʌndɪ'faɪnd] *adj* indefinido,-a.
undelivered [ʌndɪ'lɪvəd] *adj* sin entregar.
undeniable [ʌndɪ'naɪəbəl] *adj* innegable.
under ['ʌndər] *prep* **1** *(below)* bajo, debajo de. **2** *(le than)* menos de. **3** *(controlled, affected, influenced b* bajo. **4** *(suffering, subject to)* bajo. **5** *(according to)* co forme a, según. **6** *(known by)* con, bajo.
▷ *adv* **1** *(below)* debajo. **2** *(less)* menos.
under- ['ʌndər] *pref (below)* infra-, sub-; *(insufficientl* insuficientemente.
undercarriage ['ʌndəkærɪdʒ] *n* tren *m* de aterrizaj
undercharge [ʌndə'tʃɑːdʒ] *vt* cobrar menos de debido.
underclothes ['ʌndəkləʊðz] *n pl* ropa *f sing* interio
undercover [ʌndə'kʌvər] *adj* clandestino,-a, secr to,-a.
▷ *adv* en la clandestinidad.
undercurrent ['ʌndəkʌrənt] *n* **1** *(in sea)* corriente submarina. **2** *fig* tendencia oculta.
underdeveloped [ʌndədɪ'veləpt] *adj* **1** subdesarr llado,-a. **2** *(of photo)* insuficientemente revelado,-a
underestimate [*(n)* ʌndər'estɪmət; *(vb)* ʌndər'estɪme *n* menosprecio.
▷ *vt* infravalorar, subestimar.
underfed [ʌndə'fed] *adj* desnutrido,-a.
undergone [ʌndə'gɒn] *pp* → **undergo**.
undergraduate [ʌndə'grædjʊət] *n* estudiante universitario,-a no licenciado,-a.
▷ *adj* no graduado,-a.
underground [*(adj-n)* 'ʌndəgraʊnd; *(ad* ʌndə'graʊnd] *adj* **1** subterráneo,-a. **2** *fig* clandest no,-a. **3** *fig (cinema, music)* underground.
▷ *n* **1** *(railway)* metro. **2** *(resistance)* resistencia.
▷ *adv* **1** bajo tierra. **2** *fig (secretly)* en la clandestinida clandestinamente.
undergrowth ['ʌndəgrəʊθ] *n* maleza, monte bajo.
underhand ['ʌndəhænd] *adj* **1** *fig (method)* ilícito,- deshonesto,-a. **2** *(trick)* malo. **3** *(attack)* solapado,-a. *(service)* sacar con la mano por debajo del hombro.
underline [ʌndə'laɪn] *vt* subrayar.
underlying [ʌndə'laɪɪŋ] *adj* **1** *(hidden)* subyacente. *fig (basic)* esencial, fundamental.
undermine [ʌndə'maɪn] *vt* minar, socavar.
underneath [ʌndə'niːθ] *prep* bajo, debajo de.
▷ *adv* abajo, debajo, por debajo.
▷ *adj* de abajo, inferior.
▷ *n* parte *f* inferior, fondo.
underpaid [ʌndə'peɪd] *adj* mal pagado,-a.

underpants ['ʌndəpænts] *n pl* calzoncillos *mpl*, eslip *m sing*.
underpass ['ʌndəpɑːs] *n* paso subterráneo.
underprivileged [ʌndə'prɪʌɪlɪdʒd] *adj* marginado,-a, desamparado,-a.
▷ *n pl* **the underprivileged** los desvalidos.
underrate [ʌndə'reɪt] *vt* **1** *(danger)* subestimar, juzgar mal. **2** *(person)* menospreciar.
undershirt ['ʌndəʃɜːt] *n (us)* camiseta.
undersized [ʌndə'saɪzd] *adj* **1** *(thing)* demasiado pequeño,-a. **2** *(person)* diminuto,-a. **3** *(baby)* sietemesino,-a.
underskirt ['ʌndəskɜːt] *n* **1** *(modern use)* combinación *f*. **2** *(petticoat)* enaguas *fpl*. **3** *(lining)* forro.
understand [ʌndə'stænd] *vt* **1** entender. **2** *(believe)* tener entendido. **3** *(to get on with* SB*)* entenderse. **4** *(take for granted)* sobreentender.
▲ *pt & pp* **understood** [ʌnd'stʊd].
understanding [ʌndə'stændɪŋ] *n* comprensión.
understatement [ʌndə'steɪtmənt] *n* eufemismo.
understood [ʌndə'stʊd] *pt & pp* ⟶ **understand.**
undertake [ʌndə'teɪk] *vt (take on - job, task)* emprender; *(- responsibility)* asumir.
▷ *vi (promise)* comprometerse (**to**, a).
▲ *pt* **undertook** [ʌnd'tʊk], *pp* **undertaken** [ʌnd'teɪkᵊn].
undertaken [ʌndə'teɪkən] *pp* ⟶ **undertake.**
undertaker ['ʌndəteɪkəʳ] *n* empresario,-a de pompas fúnebres.
▷ *n pl (undertaker's)* funeraria, pompas *fpl* fúnebres.
undertaking [ʌndə'teɪkɪŋ] *n* **1** *(task)* empresa. **2** *(responsibility)* carga. **3** *(promise)* garantía.
undertook [ʌndə'tʊk] *pt* ⟶ **undertake.**
undervalue [ʌndə'væljuː] *vt* subvalorar.
underwater [ʌndə'wɔːtəʳ] *adj* submarino,-a, subacuático,-a.
▷ *adv* bajo el agua.
underwear ['ʌndəwɜːəʳ] *n* ropa interior.
underwent [ʌndə'went] *pt* ⟶ **undergo.**
underworld ['ʌndəwɜːld] *n* **1** *(of criminals)* hampa, bajos fondos *mpl*, inframundo.
undeserved [ʌndɪ'zɜːʌd] *adj* inmerecido,-a.
undesirable [ʌndɪ'zaɪᵊrəbᵊl] *adj* indeseable.
▷ *n* indeseable *mf*.
undetected [ʌndɪ'tektɪd] *adj (error)* pasado,-a por alto, no detectado,-a.
undetermined [ʌndɪ'tɜːmaɪnd] *adj* indeterminado,-a, indefinido,-a.
undeveloped [ʌndɪ'ʌeləpt] *adj* **1** sin desarrollar. **2** *(land)* sin edificar, sin cultivar. **3** *(film)* sin revelar.
undid [ʌnd'ɪd] *pt* ⟶ **undo.**
undignified [ʌn'dɪgnɪfaɪd] *adj* **1** *(person)* poco digno,-a. **2** *(act)* poco decoroso,-a.
undischarged [ʌndɪs'tʃɑːdʒd] *adj* **1** *(bankrupt)* no rehabilitado,-a. **2** *(duty)* no cumplido,-a. **3** *(debt)* sin liquidar. **4** *(rifle, battery)* sin descargar.
undisclosed [ʌndɪs'kləʊzd] *adj* sin revelar.
undisguised [ʌndɪs'gaɪzd] *adj* **1** *(person)* sin disfraz *m*. **2** *fig* franco,-a, sincero,-a.
undisputed [ʌndɪs'pjʊːtɪd] *adj* **1** *(unquestionable)* indiscutible, incuestionable. **2** *(unchallenged)* incontestable.
undo [ʌn'duː] *vt* **1** *(knot)* deshacer, desatar. **2** *(button)* desabrochar. **3** *(arrangement)* anular. **4** *(destroy)* deshacer, destruir. **5** *(to set right)* enmendar, reparar.
▲ *pt* **undid** [ʌn'dɪd], *pp* **undone** [ʌn'dʌn].
undone [ʌn'dʌn] *adj (incomplete)* inacabado,-a.
undoubted [ʌn'daʊtɪd] *adj* indudable.
undress [ʌn'dres] *vt* desnudar.
▷ *vi* desnudarse.
undue [ʌn'djuː] *adj* **1** *(exaggerated)* excesivo,-a, no justificado,-a. **2** *(not suitable)* indebido,-a.
unduly [ʌn'djʊːlɪ] *adv* indebidamente, excesivamente.
undying [ʌn'daɪɪŋ] *adj* imperecedero,-a.
unearned [ʌn'ɜːnd] *adj* **1** *(salary)* no ganado,-a. **2** *(undeserved)* inmerecido,-a.
unearth [ʌn'ɜːθ] *vt* **1** desenterrar. **2** *fig* desenterrar, sacar a la luz, descubrir.
uneasy [ʌn'iːzɪ] *adj* **1** *(worried)* intranquilo,-a, inquieto,-a, preocupado,-a; *(disturbing)* inquietante. **2** *(annoying)* incómodo,-a.
▲ *comp* **uneasier**, *superl* **uneasiest.**
uneducated [ʌn'edjʊkeɪtɪd] *adj* inculto,-a.
unemployed [ʌnɪm'plɔɪd] *adj* parado,-a, sin trabajo, en paro.
unemployment [ʌnɪm'plɔɪmənt] *n* **1** paro, desempleo. **2** *(percentage)* número de parados.
unending [ʌn'endɪŋ] *adj* interminable.
unequal [ʌn'iːkwəl] *adj* **1** *(not the same)* desigual, distinto,-a; *(pulse)* irregular. **2** *(not adequate)* poco apto, inadecuado,-a.
unequivocal [ʌnɪ'kwɪʌəkᵊl] *adj* inequívoco,-a, claro,-a.
unerring [ʌn'ɜːrɪŋ] *adj* infalible.
unethical [ʌn'eθɪkᵊl] *adj* poco ético,-a.
uneven [ʌn'iːʌᵊn] *adj* **1** *(not level)* desigual; *(bumpy)* accidentado,-a. **2** *(varying)* irregular, variable. **3** *(road)* lleno,-a de baches. **4** *(unfairly matched)* desigual. **5** MATH impar.
uneventful [ʌnɪ'ʌentfʊl] *adj* **1** tranquilo,-a. **2** *(routine)* monótono,-a, rutinario,-a.
unexceptional [ʌnɪk'sepʃᵊnəl] *adj* corriente, ordinario,-a.
unexpected [ʌnɪk'spektɪd] *adj* **1** inesperado,-a. **2** *(event)* imprevisto,-a.
unfailing [ʌn'feɪlɪŋ] *adj* **1** *(general)* indefectible; *(incessant)* constante. **2** *(patience)* inagotable; *(humour)* inalterable. **3** *(memory)* infalible.
unfair [ʌn'feəʳ] *adj* injusto,-a.
unfaithful [ʌn'feɪθfʊl] *adj* **1** *(husband, wife)* infiel. **2** *(friend)* desleal.
unfaltering [ʌn'fɔːltərɪŋ] *adj (voice)* firme; *(steps)* decidido,-a; *(courage)* extradordinario,-a.
unfamiliar [ʌnfə'mɪlɪəʳ] *adj (unknown)* desconocido,-a.
unfashionable [ʌn'fæʃᵊnəbᵊl] *adj (fashion, trends, etc)* pasado,-a de moda; *(ideas, measures)* poco popular.
unfasten [ʌn'fɑːsᵊn] *vt* **1** *(vest, button)* desabrochar. **2** *(untie)* desatar. **3** *(open)* abrir.
unfavorable [ʌn'feɪʌᵊrəbᵊl] *adj* US ⟶ **unfavourable.**
unfavourable [ʌn'feɪʌᵊrəbᵊl] *adj* **1** *(gen)* desfavorable; *(criticism)* adverso,-a. **2** *(winds)* contrario,-a.
unfeasible [ʌn'fiːzəbᵊl] *adj* irrealizable.
unfeeling [ʌn'fiːlɪŋ] *adj* **1** *(insensitive)* insensible. **2** *(unsympathetic)* sin compasión *f*.

unfinished [ʌn'fɪnɪʃt] *adj* inacabado,-a, incompleto,-a, sin acabar.
unfit [ʌn'fɪt] *adj* **1** *(person)* no apto,-a, incapaz. **2** *(physically)* incapacitado,-a, inútil. **3** *(injured)* lesionado,-a. **4** *(incompetent)* incompetente. ■ **to be unfit** no estar en forma.
unflinching [ʌn'flɪntʃɪŋ] *adj* **1** *(determined)* resuelto, -a, decidido,-a. **2** *(unafraid)* impávido,-a.
unfold [ʌn'fəʊld] *vt* **1** *(paper)* desplegar; *(sheet)* desdoblar. **2** *(newspaper)* abrir; *(map)* extender. **3** *(outline)* exponer; *(reveal)* revelar. **4** *(secret)* descubrir.
▷ *vi* **1** *(open up)* desdoblarse; *(landscape)* extenderse. **2** *(ideas, etc)* desarrollarse. **3** *(secret)* descubrirse, revelarse.
unforeseen [ʌnfɔː'siːn] *adj* imprevisto,-a.
unforgettable [ʌnfə'getəbᵊl] *adj* inolvidable.
unforgivable [ʌnfə'gɪʌəbᵊl] *adj* imperdonable.
unfortunate [ʌn'fɔːtʃᵊnət] *adj* **1** *(person)* desgraciado,-a; *(event)* desgraciado,-a. **2** *(remark)* desafortunado,-a.
unfounded [ʌn'faʊndɪd] *adj (rumour)* infundado,-a, sin base *(complaint)* injustificado,-a.
unfreeze [ʌn'friːz] *vt* **1** *(defrost)* descongelar. **2** COMM *(prices, wages, etc)* descongelar; *(account, loan)* desbloquear.
▲ *pt* **unfroze** [ʌn'frəʊz], *pp* **unfrozen** [ʌn'frəʊzᵊn].
unfriendly [ʌn'frendlɪ] *adj* poco amistoso,-a, antipático,-a, hostil.
▲ *comp* **unfriendlier**, *superl* **unfriendliest**.
unfruitful [ʌn'fruːtfʊl] *adj* **1** estéril. **2** *fig* infructuoso,-a.
unfulfilled [ʌnfʊl'fɪld] *adj* **1** *(not carried out)* incumplido,-a, frustrado,-a. **2** *(not satisfied)* insatisfecho,-a. **3** *(ambition)* frustrado,-a; *(dream)* irrealizado,-a.
unfurl [ʌn'fɜːl] *vt* desplegar.
▷ *vi* desplegarse.
unfurnished [ʌn'fɜːnɪʃt] *adj* **1** sin amueblar. **2** *(flat to let)* vacío,-a.
ungainly [ʌn'geɪnlɪ] *adj* **1** *(awkward)* torpe. **2** *(gait)* desgarbado,-a.
▲ *comp* **ungainlier**, *superl* **ungainliest**.
ungodly [ʌn'gɒdlɪ] *adj* **1** *(behaviour, language)* impío,-a. **2** *fam fig (hour)* intempestivo,-a:
▲ *comp* **ungodlier**, *superl* **ungodliest**.
ungrateful [ʌn'greɪtfʊl] *adj* **1** *(unthankful)* desagradecido,-a. **2** *(thankless)* ingrato,-a.
ungrudging [ʌn'grʌdʒɪŋ] *adj (generous - person)* generoso,-a; *(- support)* incondicional.
unguarded [ʌn'gɑːdɪd] *adj* **1** *(unprotected)* indefenso,-a, sin protección; *(without guards)* sin vigilancia. **2** *(careless)* desprevenido,-a, descuidado,-a, imprudente. **3** *(frank)* franco,-a.
unhampered [ʌn'hæmpəd] *adj* libre, sin estorbos.
unhappy [ʌn'hæpɪ] *adj* **1** *(sad)* infeliz. **2** *(miserable)* desdichado,-a. **3** *(unsuitable)* desafortunado,-a, poco afortunado,-a.
▲ *comp* **unhappier**, *superl* **unhappiest**.
unharmed [ʌn'hɑːmd] *adj* ileso,-a.
unhealthy [ʌn'helθɪ] *adj* **1** *(place)* malsano,-a, insalubre. **2** *(ill)* enfermizo,-a, enfermo,-a. **3** *fig (unnatural)* morboso,-a, malsano,-a.
▲ *comp* **unhealthier**, *superl* **unhealthiest**.
unheard [ʌn'hɜːd] *adj* no oído,-a.
unheard-of [ʌn'hɜːdɒʌ] [Written **unheard of** when not used to qualify a noun.] *adj* **1** *(preposterous)* inaudito,-a. **2** *(without precedent)* sin precedente.
unheeded [ʌn'hiːdɪd] *adj* desatendido,-a.
unhelpful [ʌn'helpfʊl] *adj (advice)* inútil, vano,-a; *(person)* poco servicial.
unhesitating [ʌn'hezɪteɪtɪŋ] *adj* **1** *(person)* resuelto, -a, decidido,-a. **2** *(answer)* pronto,-a, inmediato, -a.
unholy [ʌn'həʊlɪ] *adj* **1** *(place, etc)* profano,-a; *(person)* impío,-a. **2** *fam* infernal, terrible.
▲ *comp* **unholier**, *superl* **unholiest**.
unhook [ʌn'hʊk] *vt* **1** desenganchar. **2** *(take down)* descolgar. **3** *(dress)* desabrochar.
unhoped-for [ʌn'həʊptfɔːʳ] [Written **unhoped for** when not used to qualify a noun.] *adj* inesperado,-a.
unhurried [ʌn'hʌrɪd] *adj* pausado,-a.
unhurt [ʌn'hɜːt] *adj* ileso,-a, indemne.
unhygienic [ʌnhaɪ'dʒiːnɪk] *adj* antihigiénico,-a.
unicorn ['juːnikɔːn] *n* unicornio.
unidentified [ʌnaɪ'dentɪfaɪd] *adj* no identificado,-a, sin identificar.
uniform ['juːnɪfɔːm] *adj* **1** uniforme. **2** *(temperature)* constante.
▷ *n* uniforme *m*.
unify ['juːnɪfaɪ] *vt* unificar.
▲ *pt & pp* **unified**, *ger* **unifying**.
unimpaired [ʌnɪm'peəd] *adj* **1** *(strength)* no disminuido,-a. **2** *(unharmed)* intacto,-a; *(health)* inalterado,-a.
unimportant [ʌnɪm'pɔːtənt] *adj* insignificante, sin importancia, poco importante.
unimpressive [ʌnɪm'presɪʌ] *adj* **1** poco impresionante, mediocre, poco convincente. **2** *(not moving)* poco conmovedor,-ra.
uninformed [ʌnɪn'fɔːmd] *adj* **1** mal informado,-a, ignorante. **2** *(opinion)* sin base.
uninhabited [ʌnɪ'hæbɪtɪd] *adj* **1** deshabitado,-a. **2** *(deserted)* despoblado,-a.
uninhibited [ʌnɪn'hɪbɪtɪd] *adj* sin inhibición.
uninitiated [ʌnɪ'nɪʃɪeɪtɪd] *adj* no iniciado,-a, lego,-a, ignorante.
uninspired [ʌnɪn'spaɪəd] *adj* **1** *(performance)* mediocre, poco inspirado,-a. **2** *(person)* sin inspiración.
unintentional [ʌnɪn'tenʃᵊnəl] *adj* involuntario,-a.
uninteresting [ʌn'ɪntrəstɪŋ] *adj* sin interés.
uninterrupted [ʌnɪntə'rʌptɪd] *adj* ininterrumpido, -a, continuo,-a.
uninvited [ʌnɪn'ʌaɪtɪd] *adj* **1** *(guest)* no invitado,-a. **2** *(remark)* gratuito,-a.
union ['juːnɪən] *n* **1** unión *f*. **2** *fig (marriage)* enlace *m*. **3** *(of workers)* sindicato. **4** TECH unión *f*.
▷ *adj* sindical, del sindicato.
unionize [juːnjə'naɪz] *vt* sindicalizar.
▷ *vi* agremiarse, sindicalizarse.
unique [juː'niːk] *adj* **1** *(singular)* único,-a. **2** *(outstanding)* extraordinario,-a.
unit ['juːnɪt] *n* **1** unidad *f*. **2** *(furniture)* módulo, elemento. **3** MIL unidad *f*. **4** MATH unidad *f*. **5** TECH grupo. **6** *(centre)* centro; *(department)* servicio. **7** *(team)* equipo.
unite [juː'naɪt] *vt (join)* unir; *(assemble)* reunir.
▷ *vi* unirse, reunirse.
United Kingdom [juː'naɪtɪd 'kɪŋdəm] *n* Reino Unido

nited Nations [juːˈnaɪtɪd ˈneɪʃəns] *n* Naciones *fpl* Unidas.

nited States [juːˈnaɪtɪd ˈsteɪts] *n* Estados *mpl* Unidos.

nity [ˈjuːnɪtɪ] *n (union)* unidad *f*; *(harmony)* armonía.

niverse [ˈjuːnɪvɜːs] *n* universo.

niversity [juːnɪˈvɜːsətɪ] *n* universidad *f*.
adj universitario,-a.
▲ *pl* universities.

njust [ʌnˈdʒʌst] *adj (unfair)* injusto,-a; *(unfounded)* sin fundamento, infundado,-a.

nkempt [ʌnˈkempt] *adj* 1 *(general)* descuidado,-a. 2 *(hair)* despeinado,-a. 3 *(appearance)* desaliñado,-a.

nkind [ʌnˈkaɪnd] *adj* 1 *(unpleasant)* desconsiderado,-a. 2 *(cruel)* cruel; *(criticism)* despiadado,-a.

nknowing [ʌnˈnəʊɪŋ] *adj (unaware)* inconsciente; *(ignorant)* ignorante.

nknown [ʌnˈnəʊn] *adj* desconocido,-a.
n lo desconocido.

nlabeled [ʌnˈleɪbəld] *adj* US ⟶ **unlabelled.**

nlabelled [ʌnˈleɪbəld] *adj* sin etiqueta.

nlawful [ʌnˈlɔːfʊl] *adj (illegal)* ilegal; *(illegitimate)* ilegítimo,-a.

nleash [ʌnˈliːʃ] *vt* 1 *(dog)* soltar. 2 *fig (free - gen)* liberar; *(- passions)* desatar. 3 *(fury)* provocar.

nless [ənˈles] *conj* a menos que, a no ser que.
prep salvo, excepto.

nlike [ʌnˈlaɪk] *adj (different)* diferente a, distinto de; *(not characteristic)* impropio,-a.
prep a diferencia de

nlikely [ʌnˈlaɪklɪ] *adj (improbable)* improbable, poco probable; *(unexpected, unusual)* inverosímil.
▲ *comp* unlikeller, *superl* unlikeliest.

nlimited [ʌnˈlɪmɪtɪd] *adj* ilimitado,-a.

nlit [ʌnˈlɪt] *adj* 1 *(place)* sin luz, oscuro,-a. 2 *(fire, etc)* sin encender, no encendido,-a.

nload [ʌnˈləʊd] *vt* 1 *(gen)* descargar. 2 *(get rid of)* deshacerse de.
vi descargar.

nlock [ʌnˈlɒk] *vt* 1 *(door)* abrir (con llave). 2 *fig (secret)* revelar; *(enigma)* resolver.

nlooked-for [ʌnˈlʊktfɔːʳ] [Written unlooked for when not used to qualify a noun.] *adj* inesperado, -a, imprevisto,-a.

nluckily [ʌnˈlʌkɪlɪ] *adv* desafortunadamente, desgraciadamente, por desgracia.

nlucky [ʌnˈlʌkɪ] *adj* 1 *(unfortunate)* desafortunado, -a, desgraciado,-a. 2 *(fateful)* aciago,-a, nefasto,-a.
▲ *comp* unluckier, *superl* unluckiest.

nmanageable [ʌnˈmænɪdʒəbəl] *adj* 1 *(people)* ingobernable; *(child, etc)* indomable. 2 *(large object)* inmanejable, poco manejable.

nmanned [ʌnˈmænd] *adj (spacecraft)* no tripulado, -a, sin tripulación *f*.

nmarried [ʌnˈmærɪd] *adj* soltero,-a.

nmask [ʌnˈmɑːsk] *vt* 1 desenmascarar. 2 *fig (conspiracy)* descubrir.

nmatched [ʌnˈmætʃt] *adj (unique)* sin par, sin igual, incomparable.

nmerciful [ʌnˈmɜːsɪfʊl] *adj* despiadado,-a.

nmistakable [ʌnmɪsˈteɪkəbəl] *adj* inconfundible, inequívoco,-a.

unmitigated [ʌnˈmɪtɪgeɪtɪd] *adj* 1 *(absolute)* absoluto,-a, total; *(liar)* rematado,-a. 2 *(grief)* profundo,-a. 3 *(hatred)* implacable.

unmolested [ʌnməˈlestɪd] *adj* tranquilo,-a.

unmoved [ʌnˈmuːʌd] *adj* 1 *(indifferent)* impasible, indiferente. 2 *(in place)* en su sitio, sin mover. 3 *(unfeeling)* insensible.

unnamed [ʌnˈneɪmd] *adj* 1 sin nombre. 2 *(anonymous)* anónimo,-a.

unnecessary [ʌnˈnesəsərɪ] *adj* innecesario,-a.

unnoticed [ʌnˈnəʊtɪst] *adj* inadvertido,-a, desapercibido,-a.

unnumbered [ʌnˈnʌmbəd] *adj* 1 sin numerar. 2 *(countless)* innumerable.

unobserved [ʌnəbˈzɜːʌd] *adj* desapercibido,-a, inadvertido,-a.

unobtainable [ʌnəbˈteɪnəbəl] *adj* inalcanzable, inasequible, que no se puede conseguir.

unoccupied [ʌnˈɒkjʊpaɪd] *adj* 1 *(house)* deshabitado, -a. 2 *(person)* desocupado,-a. 3 *(post)* vacante. 4 *(area)* despoblado,-a. 5 *(seat)* libre. 6 MIL no ocupado,-a.

unofficial [ʌnəˈfɪʃəl] *adj* extraoficial, oficioso,-a.

unopened [ʌnˈəʊpənd] *adj* sin abrir.

unorthodox [ʌnˈɔːθədɒks] *adj* 1 *(behaviour, etc)* poco ortodoxo,-a, poco convencional. 2 REL heterodoxo,-a, no ortodoxo,-a.

unpack [ʌnˈpæk] *vt* 1 *(objects)* desempaquetar, desenvolver. 2 *(suitcase)* deshacer. 3 *(boxes)* desembalar.
▷ *vi* deshacer las maletas.

unpaid [ʌnˈpeɪd] *adj* 1 *(bill, debt)* sin pagar, por pagar. 2 *(work)* no retribuido,-a.

unpalatable [ʌmˈpælətəbəl] *adj* 1 *(taste)* desagradable, de mal sabor. 2 *fig* difícil de aceptar.

unparalleled [ʌnˈpærəleld] *adj* 1 *(of quality)* incomparable, sin par. 2 *(unprecedented)* sin precedente.

unpardonable [ʌnˈpɑːdənəbəl] *adj* imperdonable.

unperturbed [ʌnpəˈtɜːbd] *adj* impertérrito,-a, impasible, impávido,-a.

unplanned [ʌnˈplænd] *adj* inesperado,-a.

unplayable [ʌnˈpleɪəbəl] *adj* 1 *(of music)* intocable, que no se puede tocar. 2 *(a ball in sport)* imposible de jugar. 3 *(sports field)* impracticable, que no está en condiciones.

unpleasant [ʌnˈplezənt] *adj* 1 *(disagreable, nasty)* desagradable, molesto,-a. 2 *(unfriendly)* antipático,-a. 3 *(words)* grosero,-a, mal educado,-a.

unplug [ʌnˈplʌg] *vt* desenchufar.
▲ *pt & pp* unplugged, *ger* unplugging.

unpolluted [ʌnpəˈluːtɪd] *adj* no contaminado,-a.

unpopular [ʌnˈpɒpjələʳ] *adj* impopular.

unprecedented [ʌnˈpresɪdentɪd] *adj* 1 *(without precedent)* sin precedente. 2 *(unheard of)* inaudito,-a.

unpredictable [ʌnprɪˈdɪktəbəl] *adj* 1 imprevisible. 2 *(of person)* de reacciones imprevisibles. 3 *(whimsical)* antojadizo,-a.

unprepared [ʌnprɪˈpeəd] *adj* 1 *(talk, etc)* improvisado,-a. 2 *(not ready)* desprevenido,-a.

unpretentious [ʌnprɪˈtenʃəs] *adj* 1 *(simple)* modesto,-a, sencillo,-a. 2 *(humble)* sin pretensiones *fpl*.

unprintable [ʌnˈprɪntəbəl] *adj (book)* impublicable; *(remark, etc)* intranscribible.

unproductive [ʌnprəˈdʌktɪʌ] *adj* 1 *(inefficient)* improductivo,-a. 2 *fig (fruitless)* infructuoso,-a.
unprofitable [ʌnˈprɒfɪtəbəl] *adj* 1 *(efficient)* poco rentable. 2 *(fruitless)* infructuoso,-a, poco provechoso,-a. 3 *(business)* improductivo, no lucrativo,-a.
unprotected [ʌnprəˈtektɪd] *adj* indefenso,-a, sin protección.
unprovable [ʌnˈpruːʌəbəl] *adj* indemostrable.
unprovoked [ʌnprəˈʌəʊkt] *adj* 1 no provocado,-a. 2 *(attack)* gratuito,-a.
unpublished [ʌnˈpʌblɪʃt] *adj* inédito,-a, no publicado,-a.
unpunished [ʌnˈpʌnɪʃt] *adj (person)* sin castigo; *(crime)* impune.
unqualified [ʌnˈkwɒlɪfaɪd] *adj* 1 *(lacking qualification)* sin título; *(incompetent)* incompetente. 2 *(absolute)* incondicional; *(denial)* rotundo,-a. 3 *(endorsement)* sin reserva; *(success)* total, sin paliativos.
unquenchable [ʌnˈkwentʃəbəl] *adj* 1 *fig* inextinguible, inapagable. 2 *(thirst)* insaciable.
unquestioned [ʌnˈkwestʃənd] *adj (right)* indiscutido,-a, incontrovertido,-a; *(undoubted)* indudable.
unquestioning [ʌnˈkwestʃənɪŋ] *adj (general)* incondicional; *(loyalty)* ciego,-a.
unquote [ʌnˈkwəʊt] *adv* fin de la cita.
unravel [ʌnˈræʌəl] *vt* 1 *(untangle)* desenmarañar, desenredar. 2 *fig (mystery, problem)* desenmarañar, desembrollar.
▷ *vi* 1 *(become untangled)* desenredarse. 2 *(mystery)* desenmarañarse, desembrollarse.
▲ *pt & pp* unravelled *(*US unraveled*), ger* unravelling *(*US unraveling*).*
unreachable [ʌnˈriːtʃəbəl] *adj* inalcanzable.
unread [ʌnˈred] *adj* 1 *(book)* sin leer, no leído,-a. 2 *(person)* poco leído,-a, inculto,-a.
unreadable [ʌnˈriːdəbəl] *adj* 1 *(handwriting)* ilegible. 2 *(book)* imposible de leer; *(understand)* incomprensible.
unready [ʌnˈredɪ] *adj* desprevenido,-a.
unreal [ʌnˈrɪəl] *adj* irreal.
unrealistic [ʌnrɪəˈlɪstɪk] *adj* poco realista.
unreasonable [ʌnˈriːzənəbəl] *adj* 1 irrazonable. 2 *(irrational)* irracional. 3 *(excessive)* desmesurado,-a; *(prices)* exorbitante. 4 *(hour)* inoportuno,-a.
unrecognizable [ʌnrekəgˈnaɪzəbəl] *adj* irreconocible.
unrecognized [ʌnˈrekəgnaɪzd] *adj (leader, talent)* no reconocido,-a.
unrecorded [ʌnrɪˈkɔːdɪd] *adj* 1 *(music, etc)* no grabado,-a, sin grabar. 2 *(remark, etc)* no mencionado,-a; *(event)* sin registrar. 3 COMM no registrado,-a, sin registrar.
unrefined [ʌnrɪˈfaɪnd] *adj* 1 *(product)* no refinado,-a, sin refinar. 2 *(person)* inculto,-a, rudo,-a, tosco,-a, basto,-a.
unrehearsed [ʌnrɪˈhɜːst] *adj* 1 *(not prepared)* improvisado,-a. 2 THEAT sin ensayar.
unrelated [ʌnrɪˈleɪtɪd] *adj* 1 *(unconnected)* no relacionado,-a, inconexo,-a. 2 *(family)* sin parentesco.
unreliable [ʌnrɪˈlaɪəbəl] *adj* 1 *(person)* de poca confianza, poco formal, que no es de fiar. 2 *(information)* que no es de fiar, poco seguro,-a. 3 *(machine)* poco fiable, poco seguro,-a. 4 *(news)* poco fidedigno,-a.
unrelieved [ʌnrɪˈliːʌd] *adj* 1 *(boredom)* absoluto,-a, total. 2 *(pain)* no aliviado,-a. 3 *(landscape)* monótono,-a.
unremitting [ʌnrɪˈmɪtɪŋ] *adj* 1 *(unceasing)* continuo,-a. 2 *(person)* incansable.
unreserved [ʌnrɪˈzɜːʌd] *adj* 1 *(not booked)* no reservado,-a, libre. 2 *(unconditional)* incondicional, sin reserva. 3 *(character)* abierto,-a.
unresolved [ʌnrɪˈzɒlʌd] *adj* 1 *(problem)* sin resolver, no resuelto,-a. 2 *(person)* irresoluto,-a.
unresponsive [ʌnrɪˈspɒnsɪʌ] *adj* insensible.
unrest [ʌnˈrest] *n* 1 *(uneasiness)* malestar *m*. 2 *(restlessness)* inquietud *f*; *(political disturbance)* agitación *f*, disturbios *mpl*.
unrewarded [ʌnrɪˈwɔːdɪd] *adj* sin recompensa.
unripe [ʌnˈraɪp] *adj* verde, inmaduro,-a.
unrivaled [ʌnˈraɪʌəld] *adj* US → **unrivalled.**
unrivalled [ʌnˈraɪʌəld] *adj* único,-a, sin par, sin rival.
unroll [ʌnˈrəʊl] *vt* desenrollar.
▷ *vi* desenrollarse.
unruffled [ʌnˈrʌfəld] *adj* 1 *(hair)* liso,-a. 2 *(water)* tranquilo,-a. 3 *(person)* imperturbable.
unruly [ʌnˈruːlɪ] *adj* 1 *(child)* revoltoso,-a, indisciplinado,-a. 2 *(hair)* rebelde, despeinado,-a.
▲ *comp* unrulier, *superl* unruliest.
unsaddle [ʌnˈsædəl] *vt* 1 *(horse)* desensillar. 2 *(horseman)* desmontar.
unsafe [ʌnˈseɪf] *adj* 1 *(risky)* inseguro,-a, arriesgado,-a. 2 *(dangerous)* peligroso,-a.
unsaid [ʌnˈsed] *adj* sin decir.
unsalaried [ʌnˈsælərɪd] *adj* sin sueldo, no remunerado,-a.
unsanitary [ʌnˈsænɪtərɪ] *adj* antihigiénico,-a.
unsatisfactory [ʌnsætɪsˈfæktərɪ] *adj* insatisfactorio,-a, poco satisfactorio,-a.
unsavory [ʌnˈseɪʌərɪ] *adj* US → **unsavoury.**
unsavoury [ʌnˈseɪʌərɪ] *adj* 1 *(taste, etc)* desagradable; *(tasteless)* insípido,-a. 2 *(morally not right)* deshonroso,-a, infame, sospechoso,-a; *(person)* indeseable.
unscented [ʌnˈsentɪd] *adj* sin perfume.
unscramble [ʌnˈskræmbəl] *vt (code)* descifrar.
unscrew [ʌnˈskruː] *vt* destornillar, desatornillar.
unscripted [ʌnˈskrɪptɪd] *adj* no preparado,-a, sin guion previo.
unseasonable [ʌnˈsiːzənəbəl] *adj (of weather)* atípico,-a, anormal, impropio,-a.
unseasoned [ʌnˈsiːzənd] *adj* 1 *(food)* sin sazonar. 2 *fig* inexperimentado,-a, inexperto,-a. 3 *(unripe)* inmaduro,-a, verde.
unseat [ʌnˈsiːt] *vt* 1 POL quitar el escaño a. 2 POL derribar, derrocar. 3 *(horseriding)* derribar.
unseemly [ʌnˈsiːmlɪ] *adj* 1 indecoroso,-a. 2 *(unsuitable)* impropio,-a.
unseen [ʌnˈsiːn] *adj (invisible)* no visto,-a, invisible; *(unnoticed)* inadvertido,-a.
unselfish [ʌnˈselfɪʃ] *adj* desinteresado,-a.
unserviceable [ʌnˈsɜːʌɪsəbəl] *adj* inservible, inútil.
unsettled [ʌnˈsetəld] *adj* 1 *(weather)* inestable. 2 *(person)* nervioso,-a, intranquilo; *(situation)* inestable. 3 *(country, etc)* agitado,-a. 4 *(question, matter)* pendiente; *(account, etc)* sin saldar. 5 *(land)* sin colonizar, sin poblar.

nshakable [ʌn'ʃeɪkəbᵊl] *adj (faith)* firme, inquebrantable; *(person)* firme.
nshakeable [ʌn'ʃeɪkəbᵊl] *adj* → **unshakable.**
nshaven [ʌn'ʃeɪʌᵊn] *adj* sin afeitar.
nsheathe [ʌn'ʃi:ð] *vt* desenvainar.
nshrinkable [ʌn'ʃrɪŋkəbᵊl] *adj* inencogible, que no encoge.
nsightly [ʌn'saɪtlɪ] *adj* feo,-a, antiestético,-a, desagradable.
▲ *comp* **unsightlier**, *superl* **unsightliest.**
nskilful [ʌn'skɪlfʊl] *adj* torpe, desmañado,-a, inexperto.
nskilled [ʌn'skɪld] *adj* **1** *(worker)* no cualificado,-a. **2** *(job)* no especializado,-a. **3** *(untalented)* inexperto,-a.
nskillful [ʌn'skɪlfʊl] *adj* → **unskilful.**
nsold [ʌn'səʊld] *adj* sin vender.
nsolved [ʌn'sɒlʌd] *adj* sin resolver.
nsound [ʌn'saʊnd] *adj* **1** *(goods)* defectuoso,-a, *(fruit)* podrido,-a. **2** *(idea)* erróneo,-a, falso,-a, equivocado,-a. **3** *(unstable)* inestable, débil; *(not solid)* poco sólido,-a. **4** *(sleep)* ligero,-a. **5** JUR *(mentally unstable)* demente. **6** COMM poco seguro,-a, especulativo.
nsparing [ʌn'speərɪŋ] *adj* generoso,-a, pródigo,-a.
nspeakable [ʌn'spi:kəbᵊl] *adj* **1** *(ineffable)* indecible, inexpresable, inenarrable. **2** *(atrocious)* atroz, terrible.
nspecified [ʌn'spesɪfaɪd] *adj* indeterminado,-a, sin especificar.
nspoiled [ʌn'spɔɪld] *adj* **1** *(undamaged)* sin estropear. **2** *(child)* no mimado,-a.
nspoken [ʌn'spəʊkᵊn] *adj* **1** *(tacit)* tácito,-a, implícito,-a. **2** *(unuttered word)* sobreentendido,-a; *(feelings)* no expresado,-a.
nstable [ʌn'steɪbᵊl] *adj* inestable.
nsteady [ʌn'stedɪ] *adj* **1** *(not firm)* inseguro,-a, inestable; *(furniture)* cojo,-a, inestable. **2** *(voice, hand)* tembloroso,-a, poco firme. **3** *(weather conditions)* variable; *(pulse)* irregular.
▲ *comp* **unsteadier**, *superl* **unsteadiest.**
nstoppable [ʌn'stɒpəbᵊl] *adj* imparable.
nstressed [ʌn'strest] *adj* LING átono,-a.
nstuck [ʌn'stʌk] *adj* despegado,-a.
nsubscribe [ʌnsʌb'skraɪb] *vi* darse de baja (**from**, de).
nsubstantiated [ʌnsʌb'stænʃɪeɪtɪd] *adj (accusation)* sin probar *(rumour)* infundado,-a.
nsuccessful [ʌnsək'sesfʊl] *adj* **1** fracasado,-a, sin éxito. **2** *(useless)* inútil, infructuoso,-a; *(examination)* suspendido,-a. **3** *(candidate in elections)* derrotado,-a, vencido,-a.
nsuited [ʌn'su:tɪd] *adj* **1** *(person)* no apto,-a; *(thing)* impropio,-a, inadecuado,-a. **2** *(people)* incompatible.
nsullied [ʌn'sʌlɪd] *adj* inmaculado,-a.
nsupported [ʌnsə'pɔ:tɪd] *adj (person)* sin apoyo; *(statement)* infundado,-a, sin fundamento.
nsure [ʌn'ʃʊəʳ] *adj* inseguro,-a, poco seguro,-a.
nsurmountable [ʌnsə'maʊntəbᵊl] *adj* insuperable.
nsurpassable [ʌnsɜ:'pɑ:səbᵊl] *adj* inmejorable.
nsurpassed [ʌnsə'pɑ:st] *adj* no superado,-a.
nsuspected [ʌnsəs'pektɪd] *adj (not suspected)* insospechado,-a; *(unknown)* desconocido,-a, ignorado,-a.
nsuspecting [ʌnsəs'pektɪŋ] *adj* confiado,-a.
nsweetened [ʌn'swi:tənd] *adj* sin azucarar, no azucarado,-a.
unswerving [ʌn'swɜ:ʌɪŋ] *adj (faith, loyalty)* firme, inquebrantable.
unsympathetic [ʌnsɪmpə'θetɪk] *adj (unfeeling)* poco compasivo, sin compasión *f*, indiferente; *(lacking understanding)* poco comprensivo,-a.
unsystematic [ʌnsɪstə'mætɪk] *adj* sin sistema, poco metódico,-a.
untainted [ʌn'teɪntɪd] *adj* **1** *(water, food)* fresco,-a, no contaminado,-a. **2** *fig (reputation)* no manchado,-a, no corrompido,-a.
untamable [ʌn'teɪməbᵊl] *adj* indomable.
untangle [ʌn'tæŋgᵊl] *vt* desenredar.
untapped [ʌn'tæpt] *adj (resources)* sin explotar.
untarnished [ʌn'tɑ:nɪʃt] *adj* **1** *(metal)* sin oxidar. **2** *fig* sin mancha, sin tacha.
untempered [ʌn'tempəd] *adj (metals)* sin templar.
untenable [ʌn'tenəbᵊl] *adj* insostenible, indefendible.
untested [ʌn'testɪd] *adj* **1** *(not tried out)* no probado,-a. **2** *(not proved)* sin comprobar.
unthinkable [ʌn'θɪŋkəbᵊl] *adj* impensable, inconcebible.
unthread [ʌn'θred] *vt* desenhebrar.
untidy [ʌn'taɪdɪ] *adj* **1** *(room, person)* desordenado,-a. **2** *(scruffy)* desaliñado,-a, desaseado,-a; *(hair)* despeinado,-a.
▲ *comp* **untidier**, *superl* **untidiest.**
untie [ʌn'taɪ] *vt* **1** *(unfasten)* desatar. **2** *(liberate)* soltar, desligar.
until [ʌn'tɪl] *prep* hasta.
▷ *conj* hasta que.
untimely [ʌn'taɪmlɪ] *adj* **1** inoportuno,-a. **2** *(premature)* prematuro,-a.
▷ *adv (early)* prematuramente; *(inopportunely)* inoportunamente.
untiring [ʌn'taɪərɪŋ] *adj* incansable, infatigable.
untold [ʌn'təʊld] *adj* **1** *(not told)* no contado,-a. **2** *fig (uncalculably great)* incalculable, fabuloso,-a, inaudito,-a; *(unspeakable)* indecible, inefable.
untouched [ʌn'tʌtʃt] *adj* **1** *(not touched)* intocado,-a, sin tocar. **2** *(not affected)* no afectado,-a; *(unmoved)* insensible. **3** *(unhurt)* ileso,-a, indemne. **4** *(photos)* sin retocar.
untoward [ʌn'təwɔ:d] *adj* **1** *fml (unfortunate)* desafortunado,-a; *(adverse)* adverso,-a, contrario,-a. **2** desgraciado,-a.
untrained [ʌn'treɪnd] *adj* **1** inexperto,-a. **2** *(unskilled)* sin formación (profesional), no cualificado,-a; *(nurse)* sin título. **3** *(animals)* no amaestrado,-a; *(sport)* carente de preparación *f*, sin preparar.
untried [ʌn'traɪd] *adj* **1** *(not tested)* no probado,-a. **2** *(inexperienced)* inexperto,-a, no experimentado,-a. **3** JUR no procesado,-a, no juzgado,-a; *(case)* no visto,-a.
untrue [ʌn'tru:] *adj* **1** falso,-a. **2** *(unfaithful)* infiel, desleal. **3** *(inexact)* inexacto,-a, erróneo,-a.
untrustworthy [ʌn'trʌstwɜ:ðɪ] *adj (person)* poco fiable, informal; *(source)* dudoso,-a, no fidedigno,-a.
untruth [ʌn'tru:θ] *n (falsehood)* mentira; *(lacking in truthfulness)* falsedad *f*.
untruthful [ʌn'tru:θfʊl] *adj (person)* mentiroso,-a; *(statement)* falso,-a.
untuned [ʌn'tju:nd] *adj* MUS desafinado,-a.

unusable [ʌn'ju:zəbᵊl] *adj* inservible.

unused *adj* 1 [ʌn'ju:zd] *(new)* nuevo,-a, sin estrenar; *(not in use)* que no se utiliza. 2 [ʌn'ju:st] *(unaccustomed)* desacostumbrado,-a.

unusual [ʌn'jʊ:ʒʊəl] *adj* 1 *(rare, strange)* insólito,-a, poco común. 2 *(different)* original; *(exceptional)* extraordinario,-a.

unusually [ʌn'jʊ:ʒʊəlɪ] *adv* excepcionalmente, extraordinariamente.

unutterable [ʌn'ʌtərəbᵊl] *adj* indecible.

unvarying [ʌn'ʌeərɪɪŋ] *adj* constante.

unveil [ʌn'ʌeɪl] *vt* 1 *(uncover)* descubrir. 2 *fig (reveal)* descubrir, desvelar; *(secret)* revelar.

unventilated [ʌn'ʌentɪleɪtɪd] *adj* sin ventilación *f*, sin aire *m*.

unverifiable [ʌnʌerɪ'faɪəbᵊl] *adj* incomprobable, que no puede verificarse.

unvoiced [ʌn'ʌɔɪst] *adj* 1 *(untold)* no expresado,-a. 2 LING *(consonant)* sordo,-a; *(vowel)* mudo,-a.

unwanted [ʌn'wɒntɪd] *adj* 1 *(child)* no deseado,-a. 2 *(advice, etc)* no solicitado,-a, no pedido,-a. 3 *(superfluous)* superfluo,-a.

unwarranted [ʌn'wɒrəntɪd] *adj* 1 *(without justification)* injustificado,-a; *(remark)* gratuito,-a. 2 *(interference)* indebido,-a. 3 *(unauthorized)* no autorizado,-a.

unwary [ʌn'weərɪ] *adj* incauto,-a, imprudente.
▲ *comp* unwarier, *superl* unwariest.

unwashed [ʌn'wɒʃt] *adj* sin lavar, sucio,-a.

unwavering [ʌn'weɪʌərɪŋ] *adj* 1 *(steady)* constante, firme; *(courage)* inquebrantable. 2 *(look)* fijo,-a.

unweaned [ʌn'wi:nd] *adj* lactante.

unwelcome [ʌn'welkəm] *adj* 1 *(guest)* inoportuno,-a, molesto,-a; *(news)* desagradable. 2 *(uncomfortable)* incómodo,-a.

unwell [ʌn'wel] *adj (sick, ill)* indispuesto,-a, malo,-a.

unwholesome [ʌn'həʊlsəm] *adj* 1 *(climate, etc)* insalubre. 2 *(morally)* malsano,-a, indeseable, depravado,-a.

unwieldly [ʌn'wi:ldlɪ] *adj* → unwieldy.

unwieldy [ʌn'wi:ldɪ] *adj* 1 *(hard to handle)* difícil de manejar; *(cumbersome)* voluminoso,-a. 2 *(heavy)* pesado,-a; *(clumsy)* torpe, patoso,-a.
▲ *comp* unwieldier, *superl* unwieldiest.

unwilling [ʌn'wɪlɪŋ] *adj* reacio,-a, poco dispuesto,-a.

unwind [ʌn'waɪnd] *vt* desenrollar.
▷ *vi* 1 desenrollarse. 2 *fam (relax)* relajarse.
▲ *pt & pp* unwound [ʌn'waʊnd].

unwise [ʌn'waɪz] *adj* 1 *(foolish)* imprudente; *(senseless)* insensato,-a. 2 *(ill-advised)* desaconsejable, poco aconsejable.

unwitting [ʌn'wɪtɪŋ] *adj* inconsciente, involuntario,-a.

unwittingly [ʌn'wɪtɪŋlɪ] *adv* sin querer, involuntariamente, inconscientemente.

unworkable [ʌn'wɜ:kəbᵊl] *adj* 1 *(not feasible)* impracticable; *(not possible)* irrealizable. 2 inexplotable.

unworldly [ʌn'wɜ:ldlɪ] *adj* 1 poco mundano,-a, poco realista. 2 *(spiritual)* espiritual; *(naïve)* ingenuo,-a.
▲ *comp* unworldlier, *superl* unworldliest.

unworthy [ʌn'wɜ:ðɪ] *adj* indigno,-a, despreciable.
▲ *comp* unworthier, *superl* unworthiest.

unwound [ʌn'waʊnd] *pt & pp* → unwind.

unwrap [ʌn'ræp] *vt (present)* desenvolver; *(parcel, package)* abrir, deshacer.
▲ *pt & pp* unwrapped, *ger* unwrapping.

unwritten [ʌn'rɪtᵊn] *adj* 1 *(not written)* no escrito,- *(agreement)* verbal. 2 *(tradition)* oral. 3 JUR *(comm law)* no escrito,-a.

unyielding [ʌn'ji:ldɪŋ] *adj* inflexible, rígido,-a.

unzip [ʌn'zɪp] *vt* 1 bajar la cremallera de. 2 COMP descomprimir.
▲ *pt & pp* unzipped, *ger* unzipping.

up [ʌp] *adv* 1 *(upwards)* hacia arriba, arriba. 2 *(out bed)* levantado,-a. 3 *(sun, moon)*: the sun is up *ha sa do el sol.* 4 *(roadworks)* levantado,-a, en obras. 5 *(wards)* hacia. 6 *(northwards)* ir hacia el norte: 7 *(tota finished)* acabado,-a. 8 *(into pieces)* a trozos, a porci nes, a raciones.
▷ *prep* 1 *(movement)*: to go up the stairs *subir la escaler* 2 *(position)* en lo alto de.
▷ *vt* subir, aumentar.
▲ *pt & pp* upped, *ger* upping.

up-and-coming [ʌpən'kʌmɪŋ] *adj* prometedor,- que promete mucho.

up-and-down [ʌpᵊn'daʊn] *adj* 1 *(motion)* vertic *(varying)* variable. 2 *(eventful)* accidentado,-a; *(peric* con altibajos.

upbringing ['ʌpbrɪŋɪŋ] *n* educación *f*.

upcoming ['ʌpkʌmɪŋ] *adj* próximo,-a.

update [*(n)* 'ʌpdeɪt; *(vb)* ʌp'deɪt] *n* actualización puesta al día.
▷ *vt* actualizar, poner al día, modernizar.

upfront [ʌp'frʌnt] *adj* sincero,-a, franco,-a.

upgrade [*(vb)* ʌp'greɪd; *(n)* 'ʌpgreɪd] *vt* 1 *(promote)* a cender, subir de categoría. 2 *(improve)* mejorar.
▷ *n* mejora.

upheaval [ʌp'hi:ʌᵊl] *n fig* trastorno, agitación *f*.

upheld [ʌp'həeld] *pt & pp* → uphold.

uphill [*(adj)* 'ʌphɪl; *(adv)* ʌp'hɪl] *adj* 1 ascendente. 2 *(task, struggle)* arduo,-a, difícil, duro,-a, penoso,-a.
▷ *adv* cuesta arriba.

uphold [ʌp'həʊld] *vt* 1 *(opinion)* sostener, manten *(to support)* apoyar. 2 *(defend)* defender. 3 *(confir* confirmar.
▲ *pt & pp* upheld [ʌp'held].

upholster [ʊp'həʊlstəʳ] *vt* tapizar.

upkeep ['ʌpki:p] *n (maintenance)* conservación *(costs)* gastos *mpl* de mantenimiento.

uplift [ʌp'lɪft] *vt (lift up)* elevar, levantar; *(soul, voi* inspirar, elevar, alzar.
▷ *n fig* edificación *f*, inspiración *f*.

uplifting [ʌp'lɪftɪŋ] *adj fig* edificante.

upload [ʌp'ləʊd] *vt (Internet)* publicar en la red, sub a la red.

up-market ['ʌpmɑ:kɪt] *adj* de calidad *f* superior, categoría.

upon [ə'pɒn] *prep fml* en, sobre.
Consulta también on.

upper ['ʌpəʳ] *adj* 1 *(position)* superior. 2 *(in geograph* alto,-a; superior.
▷ *n (of shoe)* pala.

uppermost ['ʌpəməʊst] *adj* 1 más alto,-a. 2 *fig* pri cipal, dominante.

uppish ['ʌpɪʃ] *adj* GB *fam* engreído,-a, presumido,-a

upright ['ʌpraɪt] *adj* 1 derecho,-a, vertical. 2 *(hone* recto,-a, honrado,-a.
▷ *adv* derecho, en posición *f* vertical.

▷ *n* SP poste *m*, palo.
uprising [ʌp'raɪzɪŋ] *n* alzamiento, levantamiento, sublevación *f*.
uproar ['ʌprɔːʳ] *n* alboroto, tumulto.
uproot [ʌp'ruːt] *vt* **1** *(plant, etc)* desarraigar, arrancar; *(people)* desarraigar. **2** *(eliminate)* eliminar, extirpar.
upset [*(adj-vb)* ʌp'set; *(n)* 'ʌpset] *adj* **1** *(angry)* disgustado,-a, contrariado,-a. **2** *(mentally or physically)* trastornado,-a; *(worried)* preocupado,-a. **3** *(nerves)* desquiciado,-a; *(a little unwell)* indispuesto,-a. **4** *(stomach)* trastornado,-a. **5** *(overturned)* volcado,-a; *(spoiled)* desbaratado,-a.
▷ *n* **1** *(reversal)* revés *m*, contratiempo; *(slight ailment)* malestar *m*. **2** *(emotion, stomach, etc)* trastorno; *(plans, etc)* trastorno. **3** *(trouble, difficulty)* molestia *f*. **4** *(sport)* un resultado inesperado.
▷ *vt* **1** *(overturn)* volcar; *(capsize)* hacer zozobrar. **2** *(spill)* derramar. **3** *(shock)* trastornar. **4** *(person)* contrariar; *(worry)* preocupar; *(displease)* disgustar. **5** *(stomach)* sentar mal. **6** *(plans)* desbaratar. **7** *(to cause disorder)* desordenar, revolver.
▲ *pt & pp* **upset** [ʌp'set], *ger* **upsetting.**
upsetting [ʌp'setɪŋ] *adj* desconcertante, inquietante, preocupante.
upshot ['ʌpʃɒt] *n* *(outcome)* resultado.
upside down [ʌpsaɪd'daʊn] *adv* **1** al revés. **2** *fig (disorder)* patas arriba.
upstage [ʌp'steɪdʒ] *adj* THEAT del fondo del escenario.
▷ *adv* THEAT *(movement)* hacia el fondo del escenario; *(position)* en el fondo del escenario.
upstairs [*(adv)* ʌp'steəz; *(n)* 'ʌpsteəz] *adv* *(direction)* al piso de arriba; *(position)* en el piso de arriba.
▷ *adj* de arriba.
▷ *n* piso de arriba, piso superior.
upstanding [ʌp'stændɪŋ] *adj* **1** *fml fig* honrado,-a, recto,-a. **2** *(strong)* robusto,-a, fuerte.
upstart ['ʌpstɑːt] *n* **1** *pej* arribista. **2** *(arrogant)* insolente *mf*.
upstream [ʌp'striːm] *adv* **1** aguas arriba. **2** *(against the current)* a contracorriente.
upsurge ['ʌpsɜːdʒ] *n* **1** *(increase)* aumento; *(anger)* acceso. **2** *fig (strong increase in feelings, etc)* resurgimiento; *(of violence)* ola.
uptight [ʌp'taɪt] *adj sl* nervioso,-a.
up-to-date [ʌptə'deɪt] *adj* **1** al día. **2** *(modern)* moderno,-a, a la moda; *(informed)* al tanto, al corriente, al día.
upturn ['ʌptɜːn] *n* *(improvement)* mejora; *(increase)* aumento.
upturned ['ʌptɜːnd] *adj* **1** *(nose)* respingón,-na. **2** *(car)* volcado,-a.
upward ['ʌpwəd] *adj* hacia arriba.
▷ *adv* hacia arriba.
▷ *adj* COMM *(tendency)* al alza *m*.
upwards ['ʌpwədz] *adv* **1** hacia arriba. **2** *fam* algo más de.
Urals ['jʊərəlz] *n* los Urales *m*.
uranium [jʊ'reɪnɪəm] *n* CHEM uranio.
Uranus [jʊ'reɪnəs] *n* Urano.
urban ['ɜːbᵊn] *adj* urbano,-a.
urbane [ɜː'beɪn] *adj* cortés, urbano,-a.
ureter [jʊə'riːtəʳ] *n* uréter *m*.
urethra [jʊ'rɪθrə] *n* uretra.
urge [ɜːdʒ] *n* impulso, deseo.
▷ *vt* **1** encarecer, preconizar, instar, insistir. **2** *(incite)* incitar; *(plead)* exhortar. **3** *(encourage)* animar.
urgency ['ɜːdʒənsɪ] *n* urgencia.
urinal [jʊ'raɪnᵊl] *n* *(toilet)* urinario.
urinary ['jʊərɪnərɪ] *adj* urinario,-a.
urinate ['jʊərɪneɪt] *vi* orinar.
urine ['jʊərɪn] *n* orina.
urology [jʊ'rɒlədʒɪ] *n* MED urología.
urn [ɜːn] *n* urna.
Ursa ['ɜːrsə] *(constellation)* *n* la Osa.
Uruguay ['jʊərəgwaɪ] *n* Uruguay.
Uruguayan [jʊərə'gwaɪən] *adj* uruguayo,-a.
▷ *n* uruguayo,-a.
us [ʌs, ʌz] *pron* **1** nos; *(with preposition)* nosotros,-as. **2** *fam* me.
usable ['juːzəbᵊl] *adj* utilizable, aprovechable.
usage ['juːsɪdʒ] *n* **1** uso, manejo. **2** *(custom)* uso, costumbre *f*, usanza. **3** LING uso. **4** *(way of speaking)* habla *m*, lenguaje *m*.
use [*(n)* juːs; *(vb)* juːz] *n* **1** uso, empleo, utilización *f*. **2** *(handling)* manejo. **3** *(usefulness)* utilidad *f*. **4** *(right to use, power to use)* uso.
▷ *vt* **1** utilizar. **2** *(consume)* gastar, consumir. **3** *(exploit unfairly)* aprovecharse de. **4** *fam (need)* necesitar.
▷ *aux* [In this sense, if no habit is involved, translate using the imperfect.] *(past habits)* soler, acostumbrar.
⊙ **to use up** *vt sep* gastar, acabar.
useable ['juːzəbᵊl] *adj* → **usable.**
⊙ **used** *adj* **1** [juːzd] *(second-hand)* usado,-a. **2** [juːst] *(accustomed)* acostumbrado,-a.
Consulta también **use.**
useful ['juːsfʊl] *adj* útil.
useless ['juːsləs] *adj* **1** inútil. **2** *fam (person)* inepto,-a, incompetente.
user ['juːzəʳ] *n* usuario,-a.
usual ['juːʒʊəl] *adj* habitual, corriente.
▷ *n* **1** lo habitual. **2** *fam (drink, etc)* lo de siempre.
uterus ['juːtərəs] *n* útero.
▲ *pl* **uteruses** o **uteri** ['juːtᵊraɪ].
utilitarian [juːtɪlɪ'teərɪən] *adj* **1** *(useful)* utilitario,-a. **2** *(in philosophy)* utilitarista.
▷ *n* *(in philosophy)* utilitarista *mf*.
utility [juː'tɪlɪtɪ] *n* **1** utilidad *f*. **2** *(company)* empresa de servicio público.
▲ *pl* **utilities.**
utmost ['ʌtməʊst] *adj* sumo,-a, extremo,-a.
▷ *n* máximo.
utter ['ʌtəʳ] *adj* completo,-a, total.
▷ *vt* **1** *(words)* pronunciar, articular; *(feelings)* expresar. **2** *(lies curses, etc)* soltar; *(shouts, cries, etc)* lanzar, dar. **3** *(theatre)* proferir; *(sounds)* emitir.
utterly ['ʌtəlɪ] *adv* totalmente.
uvula ['juːʌjʊlə] *n* úvula, campanilla.
▲ *pl* **uvulas** o **uvulae** ['juːvjʊliː].
Uzbek ['ʊzbek] *adj* uzbeco,-a.
▷ *n* **1** *(person)* uzbeco,-a. **2** *(language)* uzbeco.
Uzbekistan [ʊzbekɪ'stæn] *n* Uzbekistán.

V

V, v [viː] *n (the letter)* V, v *f.*
V [vəʊlt] *symb* **(volt)** voltio; *(symbol)* V.
vacancy ['veɪk^{ə}nsɪ] *n* **1** *(job)* vacante *f.* **2** *(room)* habitación *f* libre. ■ **"No vacancies"** «Completo».
▲ *pl* **vacancies.**
vacant ['veɪk^{ə}nt] *adj* **1** *(gen)* vacío. **2** *(job)* vacante. **3** *(room)* libre. **4** *(mind, expression)* vacío,-a.
vacate [və'keɪt] *vt* **1** *fml (job)* dejar (vacante). **2** *fml (flat, etc)* desocupar, desalojar.
vacation [və'keɪʃ^{ə}n] *n* vacaciones *fpl.*
▷ *vi* US pasar las vacaciones (**in/at**, en).
vacationer [veɪ'keɪʃ^{ə}nə^{r}] *n* US veraneante *mf.*
vaccinate ['væksɪneɪt] *vt* vacunar.
vaccination [væksɪ'neɪʃ^{ə}n] *n* vacunación *f.*
vaccine ['væksiːn] *n* vacuna.
vacuum ['vækjʊəm] *n* **1** vacío. **2** *fam (vacuum cleaner)* aspiradora. ● **vacuum cleaner** aspirador *m.* ‖ **vacuum flask** termo.
▷ *vt* limpiar con aspiradora, pasar la aspiradora por.
vacuum-packed ['vækjʊəmpækt] *adj* envasado,-a al vacío.
vagina [və'dʒaɪnə] *n* vagina.
▲ *pl* **vaginas** o **vaginae** [və'dʒaɪniː].
vaginae [və'dʒaɪnɪː] *n pl* ⟶ **vagina**.
vagrant ['veɪgrənt] *adj* vagabundo,-a.
▷ *n* vagabundo,-a.
vague [veɪg] *adj* **1** *(imprecise)* vago,-a, impreciso,-a. **2** *(indistinct)* borroso,-a.
vain [veɪn] *adj* **1** *(conceited)* vanidoso,-a. **2** *(hopeless)* vano,-a, inútil. ■ **in vain** en vano.
valence ['veɪləns] *n* US valencia.
Valencian [və'lensɪən] *adj* valenciano,-a.
▷ *n* **1** *(person)* valenciano,-a. **2** *(language)* valenciano.
valency ['veɪlənsɪ] *n* GB valencia.
▲ *pl* **valencies.**
valerian [və'leərɪən] *n* valeriana.
valid ['vælɪd] *adj* **1** válido,-a. **2** *(ticket)* valedero,-a.
validate ['vælɪdeɪt] *vt fml* validar.
validation [vækɪ'deɪʃ^{ə}n] *n* validación *f.*
validity [və'lɪdɪtɪ] *n* validez *f.*
valise [və'liːz] *n* maletín *m*, bolsa de viaje.
Valletta [və'letə] *n* La Valetta.
valley ['vælɪ] *n* valle *m.*
valor ['vælə^{r}] *n* US ⟶ **valor.**
valour ['vælə^{r}] *n* valor *m*, valentía.
valuation [væljʊ'eɪʃ^{ə}n] *n* **1** *(act)* valoración *f.* **2** *(price)* valor *m.*
value ['væljuː] *n* valor *m.*
▷ *vt* **1** *(estimate value of)* tasar. **2** *(appreciate)* valorar.
valve [vælv] *n* **1** *(in general)* válvula. **2** RAD lámpara. **3** ZOOL valva. **4** MUS llave *f.*
vampire ['væmpaɪə^{r}] *n* vampiro.
van[1] [væn] *n* **1** furgoneta. **2** GB *(on train)* furgón *m.*
van[2] [væn] *phr* **in the van** *fml* en la vanguardia.
vanadium [və'neɪdɪəm] *n* vanadio.
vandalism ['vændəlɪzəm] *n* vandalismo.
vane [veɪn] *n* **1** *(weather, etc)* veleta. **2** *(of fan, etc)* aspa
vanilla [və'nɪlə] *n* vainilla.
vanish ['vænɪʃ] *vi* desaparecer.
vanity ['vænɪtɪ] *n* vanidad.
vanquish ['væŋkwɪʃ] *vt lit* vencer.
Vanuatu ['vænʊːætuː] *n* Vanuatu.
vapid ['væpɪd] *adj fml* insípido,-a.
vapor ['væɪə^{r}] *n* US ⟶ **vapour.**
vaporise ['veɪpəraɪz] *vt* ⟶ **vaporize.**
vaporize ['veɪpəraɪz] *vt* vaporizar.
▷ *vi* vaporizarse.
vapour ['veɪpə^{r}] *n* **1** vapor *m.* **2** *(on windowpane)* vahc
variable ['veərɪəb^{ə}l] *adj* variable.
▷ *n* variable *f.*
variance ['veərɪəns] ■ **to be at variance** *fml (ideas, etc)* n concordar. *(person)* estar en desacuerdo (**with**, con).
variant ['veərɪənt] *n* variante *f.*
varicose ['værɪkəʊs] *adj* varicoso,-a. ● **varicose vei** varices *fpl.*
varied ['veərɪd] *adj* variado,-a, diverso,-a.
variety [və'raɪətɪ] *n* **1** *(diversity)* variedad *f.* **2** *(asso ment)* surtido.
▲ *pl* **varieties.**
various ['veərɪəs] *adj* **1** *(different)* diverso,-a, distintc a. **2** *(several)* varios,-as.
varnish ['vɑːnɪʃ] *n* **1** *(for wood, metals)* barniz *m.* **2** *(f nails)* esmalte *m.*
▷ *vt* **1** *(wood, metals)* barnizar. **2** *(nails)* pintar.
vary ['veərɪ] *vi* variar.
▷ *vt* variar de.
▲ *pt & pp* **varied**, *ger* **varying.**
vascular ['væskjələ^{r}] *adj* vascular.
vase [vɑːz, US veɪz] *n* jarrón *m*, florero.
vassal ['væs^{ə}l] *n* vasallo,-a.
vast [vɑːst] *adj (extensive)* inmenso,-a; *(huge)* enorme
vat [væt] *n* tina, cuba.
Vatican ['vætɪk^{ə}n] *adj* vaticano,-a.
▷ *n* **the Vatican** el Vaticano. ● **Vatican City** Ciudad *f* d Vaticano.
vault[1] [vɔːlt] *n* **1** *(ceiling)* bóveda. **2** *(in bank)* cáma acorazada. **3** *(for dead)* panteón *m*; *(in church)* cripta. *(cellar)* sótano; *(for wine)* bodega.
vault[2] [vɔːlt] *vt* saltar.
▷ *vi* saltar.
▷ *n (gymnastics)* salto.
veal [viːl] *n* ternera.
vector ['vektə^{r}] *n* vector *m.*

'eer [vɪər] *vi* 1 *(ship, car)* virar; *(road)* torcer. 2 *(wind)* cambiar de dirección.
'egetable ['vedʒtəbəl] *n* 1 *(as food)* verdura, hortaliza. 2 *(as plant)* vegetal *m*. 3 *fam (person)* vegetal *m*.
'egetarian [vedʒɪ'teərɪən] *adj* vegetariano,-a.
▷ *n* vegetariano,-a.
'egetation [vedʒɪ'teɪʃən] *n* vegetación *f*.
'ehicle ['vi:əkəl] *n* 1 TECH vehículo. 2 *fig* medio.
'eil [veɪl] *n* velo.
▷ *vt* velar.
'ein [veɪn] *n* 1 ANAT vena. 2 BOT vena, nervio. 3 *(of mineral)* veta, vena, filón *m*. 4 *(mood)* humor *m*, vena.
'eined [veɪnd] *adj* 1 *(marble)* veteado,-a. 2 *(hand)* venoso,-a.
'ellum ['veləm] *n* vitela.
elocity [və'lɒsɪtɪ] *n* velocidad *f*.
▲ *pl* **velocities.**
elour [və'lʊər] *n* terciopelo (por urdimbre).
'elum ['vi:ləm] *n* velo (del paladar).
▲ *pl* **vela** ['vi:lə].
elvet ['velvɪt] *n* terciopelo.
ending machine ['vendɪŋməʃi:n] *n* máquina expendedora.
endor ['vendər] *n* vendedor,-ra.
eneer [və'nɪər] *n* 1 chapa. 2 *fig* apariencia.
▷ *vt* chapear, chapar.
enereal [və'nɪərɪəl] *adj* venéreo,-a.
'enetian [və'ni:ʃən] *adj* veneciano,-a.
▷ *n* veneciano,-a.
'enezuela [venə'zweɪlə] *n* Venezuela.
'enezuelan [venə'zweɪlən] *adj* venezolano,-a.
▷ *n* venezolano,-a.
engeance ['vendʒəns] *n* venganza.
'enice ['venɪs] *n* Venecia.
enison ['venɪsən] *n* (carne *f* de) venado.
enom ['venəm] *n* 1 veneno. 2 *fig* odio.
enous ['vi:nəs] *adj* venoso,-a.
ent [vent] *n* 1 *(opening)* abertura. 2 *(hole)* orificio, respiradero. 3 *(grille)* rejilla de ventilación.
▷ *vt* descargar.
entilate ['ventɪleɪt] *vt* ventilar.
entricle ['ventrɪkəl] *n* ventrículo.
enture ['ventʃər] *vt* arriesgar, aventurar.
▷ *vi* arriesgarse.
▷ *n* aventura, empresa arriesgada. ● **business venture** empresa comercial. ‖ **joint venture** empresa conjunta. ‖ **venture capital** capital *m* riesgo.
enue ['venju:] *n* 1 *(place)* local *m*. 2 *(scene)* escenario.
enus ['vi:nəs] *n* Venus *f*. ● **Venus flytrap** dionea.
eranda [və'rændə] *n* porche *m*.
erb [vɜ:b] *n* verbo.
erbal ['vɜ:bəl] *adj* verbal. ● **verbal noun** gerundio.
erbalise ['vɜ:bəlaɪz] *vt* → **verbalize.**
erbalize ['vɜ:bəlaɪz] *vt* GB verbalizar.
erbatim [vɜ:'beɪtɪm] *adj* textual.
▷ *adv* textualmente.
erbena [vɜ:'bi:nə] *n* verbena.
erdict ['vɜ:dɪkt] *n* 1 veredicto. 2 *(opinion)* opinión *f*.
erge [vɜ:dʒ] *n* 1 borde *m*. 2 *(of road)* arcén *m*.
● **to verge on** *vt insep* 1 *(condition)* rayar en. 2 *(age)* rondar.
erify ['verɪfaɪ] *vt* verificar, comprobar.
▲ *pt & pp* **verified**, *ger* **verifying.**
veritable ['verɪtəbəl] *adj* verdadero,-a.
vermicelli [vɜ:mɪ'selɪ] *n* fideos *mpl*.
vermin ['vɜ:mɪn] *n pl* 1 *(small animals)* alimañas *fpl*. 2 *(insects)* bichos *mpl*, sabandijas *fpl*. 3 *(people)* gentuza *f sing*, chusma *f sing*.
verruca [və'ru:kə] *n* verruga.
▲ *pl* **verrucas** o **verrucae** [və'ru:ki:].
versatility [vɜ:sə'tɪlɪtɪ] *n* 1 *(of person)* carácter *m* polifacético. 2 *(of object)* múltiples aplicaciones *fpl*. 3 ZOOL versatilidad *f*.
verse [vɜ:s] *n* 1 *(poetry)* versos *mpl*, poesía. 2 *(set of lines)* estrofa. 3 *(song, set of lines)* estrofa. 4 *(in Bible)* versículo.
version ['vɜ:ʒən] *n* 1 versión *f*. 2 MUS interpretación *f*. 3 AUTO modelo. ● **stage version** THEAT adaptación *f* teatral.
versus ['vɜ:səs] *prep* 1 *(against)* contra. 2 *(as opposed to)* frente a.
vertebra ['vɜ:tɪbrə] *n* vértebra.
▲ *pl* **vertebrae** ['vɜ:tɪbri:].
vertebral ['vɜ:tɪbrəl] *adj* vertebral.
vertebrate ['vɜ:tɪbrət, 'vɜ:tɪbreɪt] *adj* vertebrado,-a.
▷ *n* vertebrado.
vertex ['vɜ:teks] *n* vértice *m*.
▲ *pl* **vertexes** o **vertices** ['vɜ:tɪsi:z].
vertical ['vɜ:tɪkəl] *adj* vertical.
verve [vɜ:v] *n* brío, vigor *m*, empuje *m*.
very ['verɪ] *adv* 1 *(extremely)* muy. 2 *(emphatic)* muy.
▷ *adj* 1 *(extreme)* de todo. 2 *(precise)* mismo,-a, exacto,-a.
vesicle ['vesɪkəl] *n* vesícula.
vespers ['vespəz] *n pl* vísperas *fpl*.
vessel ['vesəl] *n* 1 *(ship)* nave *f*, buque *m*. 2 *(container)* recipiente *m*, vasija. 3 ANAT vaso.
vest [vest] *n* 1 GB camiseta. 2 US chaleco.
vestibule ['vestɪbju:l] *n* 1 *(entrance hall)* vestíbulo, entrada. 2 ANAT vestíbulo.
vestment ['vestmənt] *n* vestidura.
vetch [vetʃ] *n* algarroba, arveja.
veteran ['vetərən] *adj* veterano,-a:
▷ *n* 1 veterano,-a. 2 *(soldier, etc)* excombatiente *mf*.
veterinarian [vetərɪ'neərɪən] *n* US veterinario,-a.
veterinary ['vetərɪnərɪ] *adj* veterinario,-a. ● **veterinary surgeon** veterinario,-a.
veto ['vi:təʊ] *n* veto.
▲ *pl* **vetoes.**
▷ *vt* vetar; *(forbid)* prohibir, vedar.
▲ *pt & pp* **vetoed**, *ger* **vetoing.**
vex [veks] *vt dated (annoy)* disgustar, vejar.
vexation [vek'seɪʃən] *n fml* vejación *f*, disgusto.
vexed [vekst] *adj* disgustado,-a.
via ['vaɪə] *prep* 1 *(through)* vía, por. 2 *(by means of)* por medio de, a través de.
viable ['vaɪəbəl] *adj* viable, factible.
vibrant ['vaɪbrənt] *adj* 1 *(sound)* vibrante. 2 *(personality)* vital, fuerte; *(city)* animado,-a.
vibrate [vaɪ'breɪt, US 'vaɪbreɪt] *vi* vibrar (**with**, con).
▷ *vt* hacer vibrar.
vibration [vaɪ'breɪʃən] *n* vibración *f*.
vicarious [vɪ'keərɪəs] *adj* experimentado,-a por otro.
vice[1] [vaɪs] *n* vicio.
vice[2] [vaɪs] *n (tool)* torno de banco, tornillo de banco.
vice[3] [vaɪs] *pref* vice-. ● **vice president** vicepresidente,-ta.
vicelike ['vaɪslaɪk] *adj* firme, férreo,-a.

vicereine [vaɪs'reɪn] *n* virreina.
viceroy ['vaɪsrɔɪ] *n* virrey *m*.
vicinity [və'sɪnətɪ] *n* 1 inmediaciones *fpl*. 2 *fml* proximidad *f*.
vicious ['vɪʃəs] *adj* 1 *(cruel)* cruel; *(malicious)* malintencionado,-a. 2 *(violent)* virulento,-a, violento,-a. 3 *(dangerous)* peligroso,-a.
viciousness ['vɪʃəsnəs] *adj* saña.
victim ['vɪktɪm] *n* víctima.
victor ['vɪktəʳ] *n fml* vencedor,-ra.
Victorian [vɪk'tɔːrɪən] *adj* victoriano,-a.
▷ *n* victoriano,-a.
victory ['vɪktᵊrɪ] *n* victoria, triunfo.
▲ *pl* **victories.**
victuals ['vɪtᵊlz] *n pl* vituallas *fpl*, víveres *mpl*.
vicuna [vɪ'kjuːnə] *n* vicuña.
video ['vɪdɪəʊ] *n* 1 *(in general)* vídeo. 2 *(pop video)* videoclip *m*. ● **video game** videojuego.
▲ *pl* **videos.**
▷ *vt* grabar en vídeo.
videoconference [vɪdɪəʊk'kɒnfərəns] *n* videoconferencia.
videodisc ['vɪdɪəʊdɪsk] *n* videodisco.
videophone ['vɪdɪəfəʊn] *n* videoteléfono, videófono.
videorecorder [vɪdɪəʊrɪ'kɔːdəʳ] *n* vídeo.
video-tape ['vɪdɪəʊteɪp] *n* cinta de video
▷ *vt* grabar en vídeo.
videotext ['vɪdɪəʊtekst] *n* videotexto.
vie [vaɪ] *vi* competir (**for**, por).
Vienna [vɪ'enə] *n* Viena.
Viennese [vɪə'niːz] *adj* vienés,-esa.
▷ *n* vienés,-esa.
▷ *n pl* **the Viennese** los vieneses *mpl*.
Vietnam [vɪet'næm] *n* Vietnam.
Vietnamese [vɪetnə'miːz] *adj* vietnamita.
▷ *n* 1 *(person)* vietnamita *mf*. 2 *(language)* vietnamita *m*.
▷ *n pl* **the Vietnamese** los vietnamitas *mpl*.
view [vjuː] *n* 1 vista, panorama *m*. 2 *(opinion)* opinión *f*.
▷ *vt* 1 *(consider)* considerar, ver. 2 *(regard, think about)* enfocar. 3 *(examine)* ver; *(visit)* visitar. 4 *(watch)* ver; *(critically)* visionar.
viewer ['vjuːəʳ] *n* 1 TV telespectador,-ra, televidente *mf*. 2 *(photography)* visionadora.
viewfinder ['vjuːfaɪndəʳ] *n* visor *m*.
viewpoint ['vjuːpɔɪnt] *n* punto de vista.
vigil ['vɪdʒɪl] *n* vela, vigilia. ■ **to keep vigil** velar.
vigilant ['vɪdʒɪlənt] *adj* atento,-a. ■ **to remain vigilant** mantener la vigilancia.
vignette [vɪn'jet] *n* 1 *(artwork)* viñeta. 2 *(description)* estampa.
vigor ['vɪgəʳ] *n* US → **vigour.**
vigour ['vɪgəʳ] *n* vigor *m*, energía.
Viking ['vaɪkɪŋ] *adj* vikingo,-a.
▷ *n* vikingo,-a.
vile [vaɪl] *adj* 1 vil, despreciable. 2 *fam (taste, smell)* asqueroso,-a. 3 *fam (temper)* espantoso.
villa ['vɪlə] *n* 1 *(for holidays)* chalet *m*; *(in country)* casa de campo. 2 *(Roman)* villa. 3 GB *(large house)* villa.
village ['vɪlɪdʒ] *n (gen)* pueblo; *(small)* pueblecito.
villager ['vɪlɪdʒəʳ] *n* habitante *m* del pueblo, aldeano,-a.
villain ['vɪlən] *n* 1 *(bad character)* malo,-a, malo,-a de la película. 2 GB *fam* malvado,-a.
vim [vɪm] *n fam* marcha.
vindicate ['vɪndɪkeɪt] *vt* 1 *(exonerate)* vindicar, exculpar. 2 *(justify)* justificar.
vindictive [vɪn'dɪktɪv] *adj* vengativo,-a, rencoroso,-a.
vine [vaɪn] *n* 1 vid *f*. 2 *(made to climb)* parra. ● **vine grower** viticultor,-ra. ‖ **vine leaf** hoja de parra.
vinegar ['vɪnɪgəʳ] *n* vinagre *m*. ● **vinegar bottle** vinagrera. ‖ **wine vinegar** vinagre *m* de vino.
vine-growing ['vaɪngrəʊɪŋ] *adj* vitícola.
vineyard ['vɪnjəd] *n* viña, viñedo.
vintage ['vɪntɪdʒ] *n* cosecha.
▷ *adj* 1 *(wine)* de añada. 2 *(classic)* clásico,-a; *(high-quality)* glorioso,-a, maravilloso,-a. 3 *fam* lo mejor de.
vintner ['vɪntnəʳ] *n dated* vinatero,-a.
viola[1] [vaɪ'əʊlə] *n* MUS viola.
viola[2] [vaɪ'əʊlə] *n* BOT violeta.
violate ['vaɪəleɪt] *vt* violar; *(law)* infringir, transgredir.
violation [vaɪə'leɪʃᵊn] *n* violación *f*; *(of law)* infracción *f*.
violator ['vaɪəleɪtəʳ] *n* infractor,-ra, transgresor,-ra.
violence ['vaɪələns] *n* violencia.
violet ['vaɪələt] *n* 1 BOT violeta *f*. 2 *(colour)* violáceo,-a.
▷ *adj* (de color) violeta, violado,-a. ● **shrinking violet** *fam* mosquita muerta.
violin [vaɪə'lɪn] *n* violín.
violinist [vaɪə'lɪnist] *n* violinista *mf*.
viper ['vaɪpəʳ] *n* víbora.
viral ['vaɪrᵊl] *adj* viral, vírico,-a.
virgin [vaɪə'lɪnist] *adj* virgen.
Virginia [və'dʒɪnɪə] *n* Virginia.
Virgo ['vɜːgəʊ] *n* Virgo.
virtual ['vɜːtʃʊəl] *adj* virtual. ● **virtual reality** realidad virtual.
virtue ['vɜːtʃuː] *n* 1 virtud *f*. 2 *(advantage)* ventaja. ■ **by virtue of** en virtud de.
virtuosity [vɜːtʃʊ'ɒsɪtɪ] *n* virtuosismo.
virus ['vaɪᵊrəs] *n* virus *m*. ● **virus infection** infección vírica.
▲ *pl* **viruses.**
visa ['viːzə] *n* visado, *am* visa. ● **entry visa** visado de entrada. ‖ **exit visa** visado de salida.
▷ *vt* estampar un visado en.
▲ *pt & pp* **visaed**, *ger* **visaing.**
visage ['vɪzɪdʒ] *n* rostro, semblante *m*.
vis-à-vis [viːzɑː'viː] *prep* respecto a, con respecto a, respecto de.
viscose ['vɪskəʊs] *n* 1 *(textile)* viscosilla. 2 CHEM viscosa.
viscosity [vɪs'kɒsɪtɪ] *n* viscosidad *f*.
visible ['vɪzɪ'bəl] *adj* visible.
visibility [vɪzɪ'bɪlətɪ] *n* visibilidad *f*.
vision ['vɪʒᵊn] *n* 1 *(gen)* visión *f*. 2 *(eyesight)* vista. ■ **man of vision** un hombre con visión de futuro.
visionary ['vɪʒᵊnərɪ] *adj* 1 *(showing vision)* con visión de futuro. 2 *(unrealistic)* visionario,-a.
▷ *n* visionario,-a.
▲ *pl* **visionaries.**
visit ['vɪzɪt] *vt* 1 *(person)* visitar, hacer una visita a. 2 *(place)* visitar, ir a.
▷ *vi* estar de visita.
▷ *n* visita. ■ **to pay SB a visit** hacer una visita a ALGN. ‖ **to visit with SB** US charlar con ALGN.

isiting ['vɪzɪtɪŋ] *adj* 1 *(for visiting)* de visita. 2 *(guest)* visitante. ● **visiting card** tarjeta de visita. ‖ **visiting hours** horas *fpl* de visita. ‖ **visiting team** equipo visitante.
isitor ['vɪzɪtər] *n* 1 *(at home)* invitado,-a, visita. 2 *(tourist)* turista *mf*, visitante *mf*.
isor ['vaɪzər] *n* visera.
ista ['vɪstə] *n* 1 vista, panorama *m*. 2 *fig* perspectiva.
isual ['vɪʒuəl] *adj* visual. ● **visual aid** medio visual. ‖ **visual arts** artes *mpl* visuales. ‖ **visual display unit** pantalla.
ital ['vaɪtəl] *adj* 1 vital. 2 *(essential)* esencial, imprescindible. ■ **of vital importance** de suma importancia. ● **vital organ** órgano vital. ‖ **vital signs** señales *fpl* de vida. ‖ **vital statistics** 1 datos *mpl* demográficos. 2 *fam* medidas *fpl*.
▷ *n pl* órganos *mpl* vitales.
itally ['vaɪtəlɪ] *adv* sumamente.
itamin ['vɪtəmɪn, 'vaɪtəmɪn] *n* vitamina. ● **vitamin C** vitamina C. ‖ **vitamin content** contenido vitamínico.
itro ['vi:trəʊ] ■ **in vitro** in vitro.
iva ['vaɪvə] *n* GB *fam (abbr of* **viva voce***)* examen *m* oral.
ivacious [vɪ'veɪʃəs] *adj* vivaz, animado,-a.
ivid ['vɪvɪd] *adj* 1 vivo,-a, intenso,-a. 2 *(description)* gráfico,-a. ■ **to have a vivid imagination** tener mucha imaginación.
iviparous [vɪ'vɪpərəs] *adj* vivíparo,-a.
ixen ['vɪksən] *n* 1 zorra. 2 *lit* arpía.
iz [vɪz] *adv (abbr of* **videlicet***)* a saber.
-neck ['vi:nek] *n* cuello de pico.
ocabulary [və'kjæbjʊlərɪ] *n* vocabulario.
▲ *pl* **vocabularies**.
ocal ['vəʊkəl] *adj* 1 vocal. 2 *fam (noisy)* escandaloso,-a. ● **vocal cords** cuerdas *fpl* vocales.
ocational [vəʊ'keɪʃənəl] *adj* profesional. ● **vocational guidance** orientación *f* profesional. ‖ **vocational guidance counsellor** tutor,-ra.
ocative ['vɒkətɪv] *n* vocativo.
▷ *adj* vocativo,-a.
ogue [vəʊg] *n* boga, moda. ■ **to be all the vogue** estar muy en boga. ● **to be in vogue** estar en boga.
oice [vɔɪs] *n* voz *f*. ■ **at the top of one's voice** a voz en grito. ‖ **in a loud voice** en voz alta. ‖ **in a low/soft voice** en voz baja, a media voz. ‖ **the voice of experience** la voz de la experiencia. ‖ **to lose one's voice** quedarse afónico,-a, quedarse sin voz. ‖ **to lower/raise one's voice** bajar/levantar la voz. ‖ **with one voice** de una voz, a una, a coro. ● **voice box** laringe *f*. ‖ **voice off-stage** THEAT voz *f* en off.
▷ *vt* 1 expresar. 2 LING sonorizar. ■ **to give voice to one's feelings** expresar sus sentimientos.
oiced [vɔɪst] *adj* LING sonoro,-a.
oiceless ['vɔɪsləs] *adj* 1 *(hoarse)* afónico,-a. 2 LING sordo,-a.
oid [vɔɪd] *adj* 1 vacío,-a (**of**, de): **void of interest** *falto,-a de interés*. 2 JUR nulo,-a, inválido,-a.
▷ *n* vacío.
▷ *vt* 1 *(empty)* vaciar. 2 JUR anular, invalidar. ■ **to make STH void** anular ALGO.
ol-au-vent ['vɒləʊvɒn] *n* volován *m*.
olcano [vɒl'keɪnəʊ] *n* volcán *m*.
▲ *pl* **volcanos** o **volcanoes**.
olcanology [vɒlkə'nɒlədʒɪ] *n* vulcanología.
ole [vəʊl] *n* campañol *m*.

volition [və'lɪʃən] *n* volición *f*, voluntad *f*. ■ **of/on one's own volition** por voluntad propia.
volley ['vɒlɪ] *n* 1 MIL descarga. 2 *fig (of stones, curses)* aluvión *m*; *(of blows)* tanda; *(of applause)* salva. 3 *(tennis)* volea.
▷ *vi* 1 MIL lanzar una descarga. 2 *(tennis)* hacer una volea.
▷ *vt (sp)* volear.
volleyball ['vɒlɪbɔ:l] *n* voleibol *m*.
volt [vəʊlt] *n* voltio.
voltage ['vəʊltɪdʒ] *n* voltaje *m*, tensión *f*.
voltmeter ['vəʊltmi:tər] *n* voltímetro.
volubility [vɒljə'bɪlətɪ] *n* locuacidad *f*.
voluble ['vɒljəbəl] *adj* locuaz, hablador,-ra.
volume ['vɒlju:m] *n* 1 volumen *m*. 2 *(book)* tomo. ■ **to speak volumes** decirlo todo. ‖ **to turn down/up the volume** bajar/subir el volumen.
voluntary ['vɒləntərɪ] *adj* voluntario,-a. ■ **to take voluntary redundancy** acogerse al despido voluntario. ● **voluntary organization** organización *f* benéfica. ‖ **voluntary society** sociedad *f* benéfica. ‖ **voluntary work** obras *fpl* benéficas. ‖ **voluntary helper/worker** voluntario,-a.
volunteer [vɒlən'tɪər] *n* voluntario,-a. ● **volunteer army** ejército de voluntarios.
▷ *vt* ofrecer.
▷ *vi* 1 ofrecerse (**for**, para). 2 MIL alistarse como voluntario,-a (**for**, en).
vomit ['vɒmɪt] *n* vómito.
▷ *vi* vomitar, devolver.
▷ *vt* vomitar, devolver.
vortex ['vɔ:teks] *n* 1 vórtice *m*. 2 *fig* vorágine *f*.
▲ *pl* **vortexes** o **vortices** ['vɔ:tɪsi:z].
Vosges [vəʊʒ] *n* los Vosgos *mpl*.
vote [vəʊt] *n* 1 voto. 2 *(voting)* voto, votación *f*. 3 *(right to vote)* sufragio, (derecho al) voto.
▷ *vi* votar.
▷ *vt* 1 votar. 2 *(elect)* elegir. 3 *fam* considerarse: **the party was voted a complete flop** *la fiesta se consideró un desastre total*. ■ **to vote on STH / take a vote on STH** someter ALGO a votación. ● **vote of confidence** voto de confianza.
⊙ **to vote down** *vt sep* rechazar.
⊙ **to vote through** *vt sep* aprobar.
voter ['vəʊtər] *n* votante *mf*.
vouch for ['vaʊtʃ fɔ:r] *vt (a person)* responder por; *(a thing)* responder de, dar fe de.
voucher ['vaʊtʃər] *n* GB vale *m*, bono; JUR comprobante *m*, justificante *m*.
vow [vaʊ] *n* 1 promesa solemne. 2 REL voto. ■ **to take a vow of poverty** hacer voto de pobreza.
▷ *vt* jurar.
vowel ['vaʊəl] *n* vocal *f*.
voyage ['vɔɪɪdʒ] *n* viaje *m*; *(by sea)* viaje *m* en barco; *(crossing)* travesía.
▷ *vi fml* viajar.
vulcanology [vʌlkə'nɒlədʒɪ] *n* vulcanología.
vulgar ['vʌlgər] *adj* 1 *(in poor taste)* de mal gusto. 2 *(coarse)* ordinario,-a. 3 LING vulgar. ● **Vulgar Latin** latín *m* vulgar.
vulgarity [vʌl'gærɪtɪ] *n* 1 *(poor taste)* mal gusto. 2 *(coarseness)* vulgaridad *f*, ordinariez *f*, grosería.
vulnerable ['vʌlnərəbəl] *adj* vulnerable.
vulture ['vʌltʃər] *n* buitre *m*.
vulva ['vʌlvə] *n* vulva.
▲ *pl* **vulvas** o **vulvae** ['vʌlvi:].

W

W, w ['dʌbəlju:] *n (the letter)* W, w *f*.
W¹ [wɒt] *symb* (Watt) watt, vatio; *(symbol)* W.
W² [west] *abbr* (west) oeste *m*; *(abbreviation)* O.
wade [weɪd] *vi* caminar por el agua.
▷ *vt* vadear.
⊙ **to wade in** *vi* **1** *(get involved)* meterse. **2** *(start work)* ponerse.
⊙ **to wade into** *vt insep (attack)* arremeter contra.
⊙ **to wade through** *vt insep* leer *(con dificultad)*.
wader ['weɪdəʳ] *n (bird)* ave *f* zancuda.
▷ *n pl* waders botas *fpl* de pescador.
wafer ['weɪfəʳ] *n (for ice cream)* barquillo; *(biscuit)* galleta de barquillo.
wage [weɪdʒ] *n* sueldo, salario.
▷ *n pl* wages sueldo *m sing*, salario *m sing*.
waggon ['wægən] *n* GB→ **wagon.**
wagon ['wægən] *n* **1** *(cart)* carro; *(covered)* carromato. **2** GB *(railway truck)* vagón *m*. **3** US *(trolley)* carrito, mesa camarera.
wagon-lit [vægɒn'li:] *n* coche-cama *m*.
▲ *pl* wagons-lits.
waif [weɪf] *n* niño,-a abandonado,-a.
wail [weɪl] *n (of pain, grief)* lamento, gemido; *(of siren)* aullido.
▷ *vi* **1** *(person - cry)* gemir, llorar; *(- complain)* quejarse (about/over, de), lamentarse (about/over, de). **2** *(siren)* aullar, ulular; *(wind)* ulular. **3** *(mourn)* plañir.
wailing ['weɪlɪn] *n* llanto, lamentaciones *fpl*, gemidos *mpl*.
waist [weɪst] *n* **1** ANAT cintura. **2** *(of garment)* talle *m*. **3** *(of guitar, etc)* parte estrecha.
waistband ['weɪstbænd] *n* cinturilla.
waistcoat ['weɪskəʊt] *n* chaleco.
waistline ['weɪstlaɪn] *n* **1** ANAT cintura. **2** SEW talle *m*.
wait [weɪt] *n (gen)* espera; *(delay)* demora.
▷ *vi* esperar (for, -), aguardar (for, -).
▷ *vt* esperar, aguardar. ■ **to wait at table** servir la mesa.
⊙ **to wait about / wait around** *vi* esperar, perder el tiempo.
⊙ **to wait on** *vt insep* servir.
⊙ **to wait up** *vi* esperar levantado,-a:
waiter ['weɪtəʳ] *n* camarero. ● **head waiter** maitre *m*.
waiting ['weɪtɪŋ] *n* espera.
waitress ['weɪtrəs] *n* camarera.
▲ *pl* waitresses.
waive [weɪv] *vt fml (claim, right, etc)* renunciar a; *(rule)* no aplicar.
⊙ **to wake up to** *vt insep (become aware)* darse cuenta de.
wake¹ [weɪk] *vt* despertar (up, -).
▷ *vi* despertarse (up, -).
▲ *pt* woke [wəʊk], *pp* woken ['wəʊkən].
⊙ **to wake up to** *vt insep (become aware)* darse cuenta de.

wake [weɪk] *n (in water)* estela.
wakeful ['weɪkfʊl] *adj (unable to sleep)* desvelado,-a; *(alert, vigilant)* alerta, vigilante.
Wales [weɪlz] *n* País *m* de Gales.
walk [wɔ:k] *n* **1** *(gen)* paseo; *(distance)* camino; *(long)* caminata, excursión *f*; *(sport)* marcha. **2** *(path, route)* paseo, ruta; *(long)* excursión *f*. **3** *(gait)* modo de andar *mpl*.
▷ *vi* andar, caminar, pasear.
▷ *vt* **1** *(cover on foot)* ir a pie, ir andando, andar. **2** *(person)* acompañar; *(animal)* pasear.
⊙ **to walk away** *vi* alejarse.
⊙ **to walk away from** *vt insep (come out unhurt)* salir ileso,-a.
⊙ **to walk away with** *vt insep* **1** *(win easily)* ganarse con facilidad. **2** *fam (steal)* birlar.
⊙ **to walk into** *vt insep* **1** *(get caught)* caer en. **2** *(bump into)* tropezar con.
⊙ **to walk off with** *vt insep* ⟶ **walk away with.**
⊙ **to walk out** *vi* **1** *(leave suddenly)* marcharse. **2** *(go on strike)* ir a la huelga.
⊙ **to walk out on** *vt insep (abandon)* abandonar a.
walkabout ['wɔ:kəbaʊt] *n (of VIP)* paseo informal.
walker ['wɔ:kəʳ] *n* **1** *(gen)* paseante *mf*; *(hiker)* excursionista *mf*. **2** *(athlete)* marchador,-ra. **3** *(for babies)* andador *m*; *(for disabled)* andador *m*.
walkie-talkie [wɔ:kɪ'tɔ:kɪ] *n* walkie-talkie *m*.
walkman® [wɔ:kmən] *n* walkman® *m*.
▲ *pl* walkmen [wɔ:kmən].
walkout ['wɔ:kaʊt] *n (strike)* huelga.
walkway ['wɔ:kweɪ] *n* US pasaje *m* peatonal.
wall [wɔ:l] *n* **1** *(exterior)* muro; *(defensive, city)* muralla; *(garden)* tapia; *(sea)* dique *m*. **2** *(interior)* pared *f*; *(partition)* tabique *m*; *(party)* pared *f* medianera; *(main)* pared *f* maestra. **3** ANAT *(of artery, blood vessel)* pared; *(of abdomen)* pared *f* abdominal. **4** *fig (barrier)* barrera, muro. **5** SP barrera.
▷ *vt (surround with wall)* amurallar.
⊙ **to wall in** *vt sep* tapiar.
⊙ **to wall off** *vt sep* tapiar.
⊙ **to wall up** *vt sep (door, window)* tapiar, tabicar.
walled [wɔ:ld] *adj (city)* amurallado,-a; *(garden)* tapiado,-a.
wallet ['wɒlɪt] *n* cartera.
wallflower ['wɔ:lflaʊəʳ] *n* BOT alhelí *m*.
Walloon [wɒ'lu:n] *adj* valón,-ona.
▷ *n* **1** *(person)* valón,-ona. **2** *(language)* valón *m*.
wallop ['wɒləp] *n fam (blow)* golpazo.
▷ *vt* **1** *fam (hit hard)* pegar fuerte. **2** *fam (defeat)* dar una paliza a.
walloping ['wɒləpɪŋ] *n fam (beating)* paliza, zurra; *(defeat)* paliza.
▷ *adj fam (very big)* enorme, colosal.

wallow ['wɒləʊ] *vi* 1 *(animal)* revolcarse (in, en); *(ship)* bambolearse. 2 *(person - in luxury, etc)* disfrutar (in, de), nadar (in, en); *(- in grief, self-pity)* sumirse (in, en).
wallpaper ['wɔːlpeɪpəʳ] *n* 1 papel *m* pintado. 2 *(for computer screen)* papel *m* tapiz.
▷ *vt* empapelar.
wally ['wɒlɪ] *n fam* idiota *mf*, inútil *mf*.
▲ *pl* wallies.
walnut ['wɔːlnʌt] *n (fruit)* nuez *f*; *(wood)* nogal *m*. ● walnut tree nogal *m*.
walrus ['wɔːlrəs] *n* morsa.
▲ *pl/* walruses.
waltz [wɔːls] *n* vals *m*.
▲ *pl* waltzes.
▷ *vi* 1 *(dance)* valsar, bailar el vals. 2 *fam (move casually, confidently)* moverse con desenvoltura, moverse despreocupadamente.
⊙ **to waltz off with** *vt insep* 1 *(win easily)* llevarse con facilidad. 2 *(steal)* robar, birlar.
wan [wɒn] *adj* 1 *(face)* pálido,-a, macilento,-a. 2 *(look, smile)* triste, apagado,-a. 3 *fig (light)* débil.
▲ *comp* wanner, *superl* wannest.
wander ['wɒndəʳ] *vi* 1 *(roam)* deambular, errar, vagar; *(stroll)* pasear, caminar. 2 *(stray)* apartarse, desviarse, alejarse; *(get lost)* extraviarse. 3 *(river, road)* serpentear. 4 *(mind, thoughts)* desviarse, divagar; *(person)* apartarse, desviarse.
▷ *vt (streets, area)* vagar por, recorrer.
▷ *n* vuelta, paseo.
wanderer ['wɒndᵊrəʳ] *n (traveller)* trotamundos *m*; *(nomad)* nómada *mf*.
wandering ['wɒndᵊrɪŋ] *adj (gen)* errante, errabundo,-a; *(itinerant)* ambulante, itinerante; *(nomadic)* nómada.
▷ *n pl* wanderings andanzas *fpl*, viajes *mpl*. ● wandering Jew BOT tradescantia.
wanderlust ['wɒndəlʌst] *n* ansia de viajar.
wane [weɪn] *vi (moon)* menguar.
▷ *vt (strength, influence)* menguar, decrecer; *(emotion, interest)* decaer, decrecer, declinar, disminuir.
want [wɒnt] *n* 1 *(lack)* falta, carencia. 2 *(desire, need)* necesidad *f*. 3 *(poverty)* miseria, indigencia.
▷ *vt* 1 *(gen)* querer. 2 *fam (need)* necesitar. 3 *fam (ought to)* deber. 4 *fml (lack)* necesitar, carecer de, faltar. 5 *(require to be present)* buscar, requerir la presencia de; *(seek, hunt)* buscar. 6 *(desire)* desear, querer.
⊙ **to want for** *vt insep* carecer de, necesitar.
⊙ **to want in** *vi* querer entrar.
⊙ **to want out** *vi* 1 querer salir. 2 *(in plan, project, etc)* querer dejarlo.
wanted ['wɒntɪd] *adj* 1 *(for work)* necesario,-a. 2 *(by police)* buscado,-a.
wanting ['wɒntɪŋ] *adj (deficient)* deficiente; *(inadequate)* insuficiente.
wanton ['wɒntᵊn] *adj* 1 *(gratuitous)* gratuito,-a. 2 *fml (unrestrained)* desenfrenado,-a; *(licentious)* disipado,-a, licencioso,-a.
war [wɔːʳ] *n* guerra.
▷ *vi arch* guerrear.
▲ *pt & pp* warred, *ger* warring.
warble ['wɔːbᵊl] *n* gorjeo.
▷ *vt* gorjear.
▷ *vi* gorjear.

ward [wɔːd] *n* 1 *(in hospital)* sala. 2 GB *(for elections)* distrito electoral. 3 JUR pupilo,-a. 4 *(in lock)* guarda.
⊙ **to ward off** *vt sep* 1 *(illness)* prevenir; *(danger)* evitar. 2 *(blow)* parar, desviar; *(attack)* rechazar.
warden ['wɔːdᵊn] *n* 1 *(of hostel, home)* encargado,-a. 2 US *(of prison)* alcaide *m*, director,-ra. 3 *(of university)* rector,-ra.
warder ['wɔːdəʳ] *n* GB carcelero.
wardrobe ['wɔːdrəʊb] *n* 1 armario (ropero), guardarropa *m*. 2 *(clothes)* vestuario. 3 *(theatre)* vestuario.
wardship ['wɔːdʃɪp] *n* JUR tutela.
warehouse ['weəhaʊs] *n* almacén *m*, depósito.
▷ *vt* almacenar, depositar.
wares [weəz] *n pl* mercancías *fpl*.
warfare ['wɔːfeəʳ] *n* 1 *(war)* guerra. 2 *(conflict, struggle)* lucha, batalla.
warhead ['wɔːhed] *n* ojiva, cabeza.
warhorse ['wɔːhɔːs] *n* 1 caballo de guerra. 2 *fig* veterano,-a.
warily ['weərɪlɪ] *adv* con cautela, cautamente. ■ to tread warily andar con pies de plomo.
wariness ['weərɪnəs] *n* cautela, precaución *f*.
warlike ['wɔːlaɪk] *adj* belicoso,-a, guerrero,-a.
warm [wɔːm] *adj* 1 *(climate, wind)* cálido,-a; *(day)* caluroso,-a, de calor. 2 *(hands, etc)* caliente; *(liquid)* tibio,-a, templado,-a. 3 *(clothing)* de abrigo, que abriga. 4 *(colour)* cálido,-a. 5 *(welcome, applause, etc)* cálido,-a, caluroso,-a. 6 *(character)* afectuoso,-a. 7 *(scent)* fresco,-a; *(in game)* caliente.
▷ *vt (gen)* calentar.
▷ *vi* calentarse.
▷ *n* the warm el calor *m*.
⊙ **to warm over** *vt sep* 1 US *(reheat)* calentar, recalentar. 2 US *(use again)* volver a utilizar.
⊙ **to warm to** *vt insep* 1 *(person)* coger simpatía a. 2 *(subject, etc)* entusiasmarse con.
⊙ **to warm up** *vt sep* 1 *(food)* calentar, recalentar; *(engine)* calentar. 2 *(audience, party)* animar.
▷ *vi* 1 *(food, engine, etc)* calentarse. 2 *(audience, party)* animarse. 3 SP hacer ejercicios de calentamiento.
warm-blooded ['wɔːm'blʌdɪd] [Written warm blooded when not used to qualify a noun.] *adj* de sangre caliente.
warm-hearted ['wɔːm'hɑːtɪd] [Written warm hearted when not used to qualify a noun.] *adj* afectuoso,-a.
warming ['wɔːmɪŋ] *adj* que calienta.
warmly ['wɔːmlɪ] *adv* 1 *(with heat)* con ardor. 2 *(thank)* con efusión; *(recommend)* con entusiasmo; *(welcome, greet)* calurosamente. 3 *(dress)* con ropa de abrigo.
warmth [wɔːmθ] *n* 1 *(heat)* calor *m*. 2 *fig* afecto, cordialidad *f*.
warm-up ['wɔːmʌp] *n* SP calentamiento, precalentamiento.
warn [wɔːn] *vt* 1 avisar (of, de), advertir (of, de), prevenir (about, sobre), (against, contra). 2 *(instead of punishing)* amonestar.
warning ['wɔːnɪŋ] *n* 1 *(of danger)* aviso, advertencia. 2 *(instead of punishment)* amonestación *f*. 3 *(advance notice)* aviso.
▷ *adj (shot, glance)* de aviso, de advertencia; *(letter)* admonitorio.

warpath ['wɔːpæθ] ■ **to be on the warpath** *(ready to fight)* estar en pie de guerra. *(angry)* estar furioso,-a.

warped [wɔːpt] *adj* **1** *(bent, twisted)* alabeado,-a, combado,-a, torcido,-a. **2** *fig* pervertido,-a, retorcido,-a.

warrant ['wɒrənt] *n* **1** JUR orden *f* judicial, mandamiento judicial. **2** *(voucher)* bono, vale *m*. **3** *fml (justification)* justificación *f*.
▷ *vt* **1** *fml (justify)* justificar; *(deserve)* merecer, ser digno,-a de. **2** *(guarantee)* garantizar. ● **warrant officer** suboficial *m*.

warranty ['wɒrəntɪ] *n* **1** COMM *(guarantee)* garantía. **2** *fml (authority)* autorización *f*.
▲ *pl* **warranties.**

warren ['wɒrən] *n* **1** conejera. **2** *fig* laberinto.

warrior ['wɒrɪəʳ] *n* guerrero,-a.

Warsaw ['wɔːsɔː] *n* Varsovia.

warship ['wɔːʃɪp] *n* buque *m* de guerra.

wart [wɔːt] *n* verruga. ● **wart hog** jabalí *m* verrugoso.

wartime ['wɔːtaɪm] *n* tiempos *mpl* de guerra.
▷ *adj* de guerra.

wary ['weərɪ] *adj (cautious)* cauto,-a, cauteloso,-a, prudente; *(suspicious)* desconfiado,-a.
▲ *comp* **warier**, *superl* **wariest.**

was [wɒz, *unstressed* wəz] *pt* ⟶ **be.**

wash [wɒʃ] *n* **1** *(act)* lavado. **2** *(laundry)* ropa sucia, colada. **3** *(of ship)* estela; *(of water)* remolinos *mpl*; *(sound)* chapoteo. **4** MED enjuague *m*. **5** *(thin layer of paint)* capa. **6** *(swill)* bazofia.
▷ *vt* **1** *(gen)* lavar; *(dishes)* fregar. **2** *(carry)* llevar, arrastrar. **3** *(flow against, flow past)* lamer. **4** *(form by erosion)* erosionar. **5** *(cover thinly)* bañar.
▷ *vi* **1** *(gen)* lavarse. **2** *(flow, lap)* batir. **3** *fam (be believed)* colar.
⊙ **to wash away** *vt sep* **1** *(destroy and carry away)* llevarse, arrastrar. **2** *(remove)* borrar.
⊙ **to wash down** *vt sep* **1** *(clean)* lavar, regar. **2** *(with wine, etc)* acompañar (**with**, de), regar (**with**, con).
⊙ **to wash off** *vt sep (remove by washing)* quitar (lavando).
▷ *vi* quitarse lavando.
⊙ **to wash out** *vt sep* **1** *(remove by washing)* quitar lavando. **2** *(rinse)* enjuagar. **3** *(prevent)* imposibilitar, impedir.
▷ *vi* quitarse lavando.
⊙ **to wash up** *vt sep* **1** fregar. **2** arrastrar a la playa.
▷ *vi* **1** fregar los platos. **2** US lavarse las manos y la cara, lavarse rápidamente.

washable ['wɒʃəbᵊl] *adj* lavable.

washbasin ['wɒʃbeɪsᵊn] *n (fixed to wall)* lavabo; *(bowl)* palangana.

washbowl ['wɒʃbəʊl] *n* US palangana.

washday ['wɒʃdeɪ] *n* día *m* de la colada.

washed-out ['wɒʃt'aʊt] [Written **washed out** when not used to qualify a noun.] *adj* **1** *(tired)* agotado,-a, sin energía; *(pale)* pálido,-a. **2** *(faded)* descolorido,-a, desteñido,-a.

washed-up ['wɒʃt'ʌp] [Written **washed up** when not used to qualify a noun.] *adj fam* acabado,-a.

washer ['wɒʃəʳ] *n* **1** TECH *(metal)* arandela; *(rubber)* junta. **2** *fam (machine)* lavadora.

washerwoman ['wɒʃəwʊmən] *n* lavadera.
▲ *pl* **washerwomen** ['wɒʃəwɪmɪn].

washing ['wɒʃɪŋ] *n* **1** *(action)* lavado, el lavar *m*. **2** *(dirty clothes)* colada, ropa sucia, ropa para lavar *(clean clothes)* colada; *(clothes hanging out)* ropa tendida. ■ **to do the washing** hacer la colada. ● **washing machine** lavadora. ‖ **washing powder** detergente *m*.

washing-up [wɒʃɪŋ'ʌp] *n* **1** *(action)* fregado, el fregar *m*. **2** *(dishes)* platos *mpl*. ■ **to do the washing-up** fregar los platos. ● **washing-up liquid** lavavajillas *m*.

washout ['wɒʃaʊt] *n fam* fracaso.

washroom ['wɒʃruːm] *n* US *euph* servicios *mpl*.

washtub ['wɒʃtʌb] *n* tina.

wasp [wɒsp] *n* avispa. ● **wasp's nest** avispero.

wastage ['weɪstɪdʒ] *n (waste, loss)* pérdida, merma, desgaste *m*; *(amount wasted)* pérdidas *fpl*.

waste [weɪst] *n* **1** *(gen)* derroche *m*, desperdicio; *(of money, energy)* derroche *m*, despilfarro; *(of time)* pérdida, desperdicio. **2** *(matter)* desechos *mpl*, desperdicios *mpl*; *(rubbish)* basura.
▷ *adj* **1** *(unwanted)* desechado,-a. **2** *(land)* yermo,-a, baldío,-a.
▷ *vt* **1** *(gen)* desperdiciar, malgastar; *(resources)* derrochar; *(money)* despilfarrar, derrochar; *(time, chance)* desperdiciar, desaprovechar, perder. **2** *(because of disease)* atrofiar, debilitar.
▷ *n pl* **wastes** extensiones *fpl* desoladas.
⊙ **to waste away** *vi* consumirse, demacrarse.

wasted ['weɪstɪd] *adj (life, youth)* desperdiciado,-a. *(body)* atrofiado,-a.

wasteful ['weɪstfʊl] *adj (person)* pródigo,-a, derrochador,-ra, despilfarrador,-ra; *(process, habit, use)* ruinoso,-a.

wastepaper basket [weɪst'peɪpəbɑːskɪt] *n* papelera.

watch [wɒtʃ] *n* **1** *(small clock)* reloj *m*. **2** *(look-out)* vigilancia, guardia; *(person)* vigilante *mf*, guardia *mf*, centinela *mf*, guarda *mf*. **3** MAR *(period, body)* guardia; *(individual)* vigía. **4** HIST ronda.
▲ *pl* **watches.**
▷ *vt* **1** *(look at, observe)* mirar, observar; *(television, sport)* ver. **2** *(keep an eye on)* vigilar, observar; *(spy on)* espiar, vigilar. **3** *(be careful about)* tener cuidado con, cuidar de.
▷ *vi (look)* mirar, observar. ■ **watch out!** ¡cuidado!
⊙ **to watch for** *vt insep (look and wait for)* esperar, aguardar.
⊙ **to watch out for** *vt insep* **1** *(look out for, be alert)* estar alerta, estarse al tanto de, estar pendiente de. **2** *(be careful of)* tener cuidado con.
⊙ **to watch over** *vt insep (guard and protect)* vigilar.

watchdog ['wɒtʃdɒg] *n* **1** perro guardián. **2** *fig* guardián,-ana.

watcher ['wɒtʃəʳ] *n* observador,-ra, espectador,-ra.

watchful ['wɒtʃfʊl] *adj* vigilante, atento,-a.

watchfulness ['wɒtʃfʊlnəs] *n* vigilancia.

watchmaker ['wɒtʃmeɪkəʳ] *n* relojero,-a.

watchman ['wɒtʃmən] *n* **1** vigilante *m*. **2** *dated (on Spanish street)* sereno.

watchstrap ['wɒtʃstræp] *n* correa (de reloj).

watchtower ['wɒtʃtaʊəʳ] *n* atalaya.

watchword ['wɒtʃwɜːd] *n* **1** *(password)* contraseña. **2** *(catchphrase, slogan)* consigna, lema *m*.

water ['wɔːtəʳ] *n* **1** *(gen)* agua. **drinking water:** agua potable; **mineral water:** agua mineral; **running water**

agua corriente; **spring water:** agua de manantial. **2** *(tide)* marea.
▷ *vt* **1** *(plant, river)* regar. **2** *(animals)* abrevar.
▷ *vi (eyes)* llorar, lagrimear; *(mouth)* hacerse la boca agua.
▷ *n pl* **waters** *(sea, etc)* aguas *fpl*; *(of a pregnant woman)* aguas *fpl*. **coastal waters** *aguas costeras;* **territorial waters** *aguas jurisdiccionales.* ● **hot water bottle** bolsa de agua caliente. ‖ **water bottle** *(flask)* cantimplora. ‖ **water closet** *dated* váter *m*, retrete *m*. ‖ **water hole** charca. ‖ **water jump** ría. ‖ **water level 1** *(in reservoir)* nivel del agua. **2** *(of ship)* línea de flotación. ‖ **water main** conductora *f* del agua. ‖ **water pipe** cañería. ‖ **water power** energía hidráulica. ‖ **water supply** abastecimiento de agua, suministro de agua. ‖ **water table** nivel *m* freático. ‖ **water tank** depósito de agua. ‖ **water vapour** (US **vapor**) vapor *m* de agua. ‖ **water wheel 1** *(for power)* rueda hidráulica. **2** *(for irrigation)* noria.
⊙ **to water down** *vt sep* **1** *(drink)* aguar, mezclar con agua. **2** *fig* descafeinar.

waterbed ['wɔːtəbed] *n* colchón *m* de agua.

watercolor ['wɔːtəkʌləʳ] *n* → **watercolour.**

watercolour ['wɔːtəkʌləʳ] *n* acuarela.
▷ *n pl* **watercolours** acuarelas *fpl.*

water-cooled ['wɔːtəkuːld] *adj* TECH refrigerado,-a por agua.

watercourse ['wɔːtəkɔːs] *n* **1** *(channel, bed)* lecho, cauce *m*, canal *m*. **2** *(stream)* arroyo; *(river)* río.

watercress ['wɔːtkres] *n* berro.

watered-down ['wɔːtəd'daun] [Written **watered down** when not used to qualify a noun.] *adj* **1** *(drink)* aguado,-a. **2** *fig* descafeinado,-a.

waterfall ['wɔːtəfɔːl] *n* cascada, salto de agua, catarata.

waterfowl ['wɔːtəfaul] *n* ave *f* acuática.
▲ *pl* **waterfowl** o **waterfowls.**

waterfront ['wɔːtəfrʌnt] *n* *(port)* puerto, zona del puerto; *(promenade)* paseo marítimo.

watering ['wɔːtᵊrɪŋ] *n* riego. ● **watering can** regadera. ‖ **watering hole 1** *(for animals)* abrevadero. **2** *(pub)* bar *m*. ‖ **watering place 1** *(for animals)* charca, abrevadero. **2** *(spa)* balneario.

waterlogged ['wɔːtəlɒgd] *adj* empapado,-a, anegado,-a.

watermark ['wɔːtəmɑːk] *n* filigrana.

watermelon ['wɔːtəmelən] *n* sandía.

watermill ['wɔːtəmɪl] *n* molino de agua.

waterpark ['wɔːtəpɑːk] *n* parque *m* acuático.

waterpipe ['wɔːtəpaɪp] *n* cañería.

waterproof ['wɔːtəpruːf] *adj* **1** *(material)* impermeable. **2** *(watch)* sumergible.
▷ *n (coat)* impermeable *m*.
▷ *vt* impermeabilizar.

watershed ['wɔːtəʃed] *n* **1** GEOG línea divisoria de aguas. **2** *fig* coyuntura crítica, punto decisivo.

waterside ['wɔːtəsaɪd] *n* ribera.
▷ *adj* ribereño,-a.

water-ski ['wɔːtəskiː] *n* esquí *m* acuático.
▷ *vi* hacer esquí acuático.

waterspout ['wɔːtəspaut] *n* tromba.

watertight ['wɔːtətaɪt] *adj* **1** estanco,-a, hermético,-a. **2** *fig* irrefutable, irrebatible.

waterway ['wɔːtəweɪ] *n* vía fluvial; canal *m* (navegable).

water-wheel ['wɔːtəwiːl] *n* **1** *(for power)* rueda hidráulica. **2** *(for irrigation)* noria.

waterworks ['wɔːtəwɜːks] *n* depuradora, planta de tratamiento de aguas.
▷ *n pl* GB *fam euph* aparato urinario.

watery ['wɔːtᵊrɪ] *adj* **1** *(like water)* acuoso,-a; *(soup, milk)* aguado,-a; *(coffee)* flojo,-a, aguado,-a. **2** *(eyes)* lacrimoso,-a; *(smile)* débil; *(colour, sun)* pálido,-a, tenue.
▲ *comp* **waterier**, *superl* **wateriest.**

watt [wɒt] *n* ELEC watt *m*, vatio.

wattage ['wɒtɪdʒ] *n* potencia en vatios.

wave [weɪv] *n* **1** *(in sea)* ola. **2** *(in hair)* onda. **3** PHYS onda. **4** *(of hand)* ademán *m*, movimiento; *(in greeting)* saludo con la mano. **5** *(steady increase)* ola, oleada. **6** *(influx)* oleada; *(sudden increase)* oleada, ola.
▷ *vi* **1** *(greet)* saludar (con la mano). **2** *(flag)* ondear; *(corn)* ondular. **3** *(hair)* ondular.
▷ *vt* **1** *(brandish)* agitar. **2** *(direct)* indicar con la mano. **3** *(hair)* marcar, ondular.
⊙ **to wave aside** *vt sep* rechazar, desechar.
⊙ **to wave down** *vt sep* hacer señales para que pare *(un coche).*
⊙ **to wave off** *vt sep* despedirse de.

waveband ['weɪvbænd] *n* RAD banda.

wavelength ['weɪvleŋθ] *n* RAD longitud *f* de onda.

waver ['weɪvəʳ] *vi* **1** *(hesitate, dither)* vacilar, titubear, dudar; *(oscillate)* oscilar (**between**, entre). **2** *(falter - gen)* vacilar, flaquear, flojear; *(- voice)* temblar, fallar. **3** *(flicker)* vacilar, parpadear.

wavy ['weɪvɪ] *adj* ondulado,-a.
▲ *comp* **wavier**, *superl* **waviest.**

wax¹ [wæks] *n* **1** *(gen)* cera. **2** *(in ear)* cerumen *m*. ● **paraffin wax** parafina. ‖ **sealing wax** lacre *m*. ‖ **wax candle** vela. ‖ **wax paper** papel *m* encerado. ‖ **wax polish** cera para abrillantar.
▷ *vt (polish)* encerar.

wax² [wæks] *vi* **1** *(moon)* crecer. **2** *dated (become)* ponerse.

waxwing ['wækswɪŋ] *n* ampelis *mpl.*

waxwork ['wækswɜːks] *n* figura de cera.
▷ *n pl* **waxworks** museo *m sing* de cera.

way [weɪ] *n* **1** *(right route, road, etc)* camino. **2** *(direction)* dirección *f*. **3** *(distance)* distancia. **4** *(manner, method)* manera, modo. **5** *(behaviour, custom)* manera, forma, modo. **6** *(area)* zona, área. ■ **all the way 1** *(distance)* todo el viaje. **2** *(completely)* totalmente. ‖ **by the way** *(incidentally)* a propósito, por cierto. ‖ **in a way** en cierto modo, en cierta manera. ‖ **in some ways** en algunos aspectos. ‖ **in this way** *(thus)* de este modo, de esta manera. ‖ **one way or the other** *(somehow)* de algún modo, de una manera u otra, como sea. ‖ **out of the way 1** *(remote)* apartado,-a, remoto,-a. **2** *(exceptional)* excepcional, particular, original. ‖ **that way 1** *(direction)* por allá. **2** *(like that)* así. ‖ **to be in the way** estorbar, estar por en medio. ‖ **to be on the way** *(coming)* estar en camino, estar al llegar, avecinarse. ‖ **to get under way 1** *(meeting, match)* empezar. **2** *(travellers, work)* ponerse en marcha. ‖ **to give way 1** *(collapse)* ceder, hundirse. **2** *(yield)* ceder (**to**, a). **3** *(when driving)*

ceder el paso. ● **way in** entrada. ‖ **way out 1** *(exit)* salida. **2** *(solution)* solución *f*, remedio.
▷ *adv fam* muy.
▷ *n pl* **ways** *(customs)* costumbres *fpl*; *(habits, behaviour)* manías *fpl*.
wayfarer ['weɪfeərəʳ] *n fml* caminante *mf*, viajero,-a.
wayside ['weɪsaɪd] *n* borde *m* del camino.
wayward ['weɪwəd] *adj* **1** *(person - wilful)* voluntarioso,-a; *(- unruly)* revoltoso,-a, indisciplinado,-a, rebelde; *(- erratic)* voluble, inconstante; *(- capricious)* caprichoso,-a. **2** *(behaviour)* irregular, imprevisible.
we [wiː, *Unstressed* wɪ] *pron* nosotros,-as.
weak [wiːk] *adj* **1** *(gen)* débil; *(person)* débil, endeble; *(light, voice)* débil, tenue; *(team, piece of work)* flojo,-a. **2** *(argument, excuse, etc)* poco convincente, pobre, de poco peso, débil. **3** *(tea, coffee, etc)* aguado,-a, flojo,-a, poco cargado,-a.
▷ *n pl* **the weak** los necesitados *mpl*, los inválidos *mpl*.
weaken ['wiːkᵊn] *vt* **1** *(gen)* debilitar. **2** *(argument)* quitar fuerza a; *(morale)* socavar.
▷ *vi* **1** *(person)* debilitarse, desfallecer. **2** *(resolve, influence)* flaquear. **3** *(currency)* aflojar, caer. **4** *(give in)* ceder.
weak-kneed ['wiːk'niːd] [Written **weak kneed** when not used to qualify a noun.] *adj fig* medroso,-a, pusilánime.
weakling ['wiːklɪŋ] *n pej (physical)* débil *mf*, debilucho, alfeñique *m*; *(moral)* cobarde *mf*.
weakly ['wiːklɪ] *adv* **1** *(gen)* débilmente. **2** *(lamely)* sin convicción.
weak-minded [wiːk'maɪndɪd] [Written **weak minded** when not used to qualify a noun.] *adj* **1** *(indecisive)* indeciso,-a; *(weak-willed)* de poca voluntad. **2** *(mentally deficient)* deficiente mental.
weakness ['wiːknəs] *n* **1** *(gen)* debilidad *f*, flaqueza. **2** *(lack of conviction)* falta de peso, pobreza. **3** *(defect, fault, flaw)* flaqueza, punto flaco.
▲ *pl* **weaknesses**.
weak-willed ['wiːk'wɪld] [Written **weak willed** when not used to qualify a noun.] *adj* de poca voluntad.
weal [wiːl] *n* cardenal *m*, equimosis *f inv*.
wealth [welθ] *n* **1** *(riches)* riqueza. **2** *fig* abundancia, profusión *f*.
wealthy ['welθɪ] *adj* rico,-a, adinerado,-a, acaudalado,-a.
▲ *comp* **wealthier**, *superl* **wealthiest**.
▷ *n pl* **the wealthy** los ricos *mpl*.
wean [wiːn] *vt (child)* destetar.
weapon ['wepᵊn] *n* arma.
wear [weəʳ] *n* **1** *(clothing)* ropa: **evening wear** *traje de noche;* **ladies' wear** *ropa para señoras;* **men's wear** *ropa para hombres.* **2** *(use)* uso: **for everyday wear** *para todos los días.* **3** *(deterioration)* desgaste *m*, deterioro. **4** *(capacity for being used)* durabilidad *f*.
▷ *vt* **1** *(clothing, jewellery, etc)* llevar, llevar puesto,-a, vestir, usar; *(shoes)* calzar. **2** *fam (accept, tolerate)* tolerar, aceptar, soportar. **3** *(damage by use)* desgastar.
▷ *vi* **1** *(become damaged by use)* desgastarse. **2** *(endure)* durar. ● **wear and tear** desgaste *m*.
⊙ **to wear away** *vt sep* **1** *(grass, rocks, stone, etc)* erosionar, desgastar. **2** *(inscription)* borrar.
▷ *vi* **1** *(stone, etc)* erosionarse, desgastarse. **2** *(inscription)* borrarse.
⊙ **to wear down** *vt sep* **1** *(tread, stone, etc)* desgastar. **2** *(person, resistance)* agotar, cansar.
▷ *vi (heels, teeth)* desgastarse.
⊙ **to wear off** *vi (pain, shock, novelty, etc)* pasar, desaparecer.
⊙ **to wear on** *vi (time)* transcurrir, pasar, avanzar.
⊙ **to wear out** *vt sep* **1** *(shoes, etc)* gastar, desgastar, romper con el uso. **2** *(person)* agotar, rendir.
▷ *vi (shoes, etc)* gastarse, desgastarse, romperse con el uso.
▲ *pt* **wore** [wɔːᵊ], *pp* **worn** [wɔːn].
wearable ['weərəbᵊl] *adj* que se puede llevar, que se puede poner.
wearily ['wɪərɪlɪ] *adv* con cansancio, cansadamente.
weariness ['wɪərɪnəs] *n* cansancio, fatiga.
wearing ['weərɪŋ] *adj (tiring)* cansado,-a, agotador,-ra; *(tiresome)* pesado,-a.
wearisome ['wɪərɪsəm] *adj* **1** *(tiring)* cansado,-a, fatigoso,-a. **2** *(boring)* pesado,-a.
weary ['wɪərɪ] *adj* **1** *(exhausted)* cansado,-a, agotado,-a, fatigado,-a, exhausto,-a. **2** *(fed up)* cansado,-a, harto,-a. **3** *(tiring)* cansado,-a, agotador,-ra, fatigoso,-a.
▲ *comp* **wearier**, *superl* **weariest**.
▷ *vt* cansar.
▷ *vi* cansarse de.
weasel ['wiːzᵊl] *n* comadreja.
weather ['weðəʳ] *n (gen)* tiempo.
▷ *vt* **1** *(withstand, survive)* aguantar, soportar, resistir. **2** *(rocks)* erosionar. **3** *(wood)* curar.
▷ *vi (rocks)* desgastarse; *(wood)* resistir la intemperie. ● **weather forecast** parte *m* meteorológico. ‖ **weather vane** veleta.
weather-beaten ['weðəbiːtᵊn] *adj* **1** *(building, etc)* deteriorado,-a por la intemperie. **2** *(person)* curtido,-a.
weathercock ['weðəkɒk] *n* veleta.
weatherman ['weðəmən] *n* hombre *m* del tiempo.
▲ *pl* **weathermen** ['weðmen].
weatherproof ['weðəpruːf] *adj (clothing)* impermeable; *(house)* impermeabilizado,-a.
weave [wiːv] *n* tejido.
▷ *vt* **1** *(cloth)* tejer. **2** *(fence, basket, nest, etc)* trenzar, entretejer, tejer. **3** *(one's way)* serpentear, zigzaguear. **4** *fig (plot, story)* tramar, urdir, tejer.
▷ *vi* **1** *(cloth)* tejer. **2** *(zigzag about)* serpentear, zigzaguear.
▲ *pt* **wove** [wəʊv], *pp* **woven** ['wəʊvᵊn], *ger* **weaving**.
weaver ['wiːvəʳ] *n* tejedor,-ra.
weaving ['wiːvɪŋ] *n (activity)* tejido.
web [web] *n* **1** *(spider's)* telaraña. **2** *fig* red *f*, sarta, embrollo. **3** *(of animals' feet)* membrana interdigital. **4** *(Internet)* web *f*.
webbed [webd] *adj* palmeado,-a.
web-footed ['web'fʊtɪd] *adj* palmípedo,-a.
webmaster ['webmɑːstəʳ] *n* administrador,-ra de web.
website ['websaɪt] *n* web *f*, sitio web.
wed [wed] *vt* casarse con.
▲ *pt & pp* **wedded** o **wed**, *ger* **wedding**.

wedded ['wedɪd] *adj* 1 casado,-a (**to**, con). 2 *(devoted)* aferrado,-a (**to**, a).

wedding ['wedɪŋ] *n* boda, casamiento.

wedge [wedʒ] *n* 1 *(gen)* cuña, calza, calce *m*; *(for splitting)* cuña. 2 *(of cake, cheese)* trozo grande. 3 *(golf)* wedge *m*.
▷ *vt* 1 *(force apart)* acuñar, calzar. 2 *(pack tightly)* apretar.

wedlock ['wedlɒk] *n* matrimonio.

Wednesday ['wenzdɪ] *n* miércoles *m inv*.

Para ejemplos de uso, consulta **Saturday**.

weed [wi:d] *n* 1 BOT *(in garden)* mala hierba; *(in water)* algas *fpl*. 2 *fam pej (person)* debilucho,-a, canijo,-a. 3 *fam (tobacco)* tabaco, el fumar *m*.
▷ *vt* escardar.
▷ *vi* escardar.
◉ **to weed out** *vt sep* desherbar, escardar.

weeding ['wi:dɪŋ] *n* escarda.

weedkiller ['wi:dkɪlə^r] *n* herbicida *m*.

weedy ['wi:dɪ] *adj pej* debilucho,-a, esmirriado,-a, canijo,-a.
▲ *comp* **weedier**, *superl* **weediest**.

week [wi:k] *n* semana.

weekday ['wi:kdeɪ] *n* día *m* laborable.

weekend ['wi:kend, wi:'kend] *n* fin *m* de semana.
▷ *vi* pasar el fin de semana. ● **long weekend** puente *m*.

weekly ['wi:klɪ] *adj* semanal.
▷ *adv* semanalmente, cada semana: **twice weekly** *dos veces por semana.*
▷ *n (press)* semanario.

weep [wi:p] *vi* 1 *fml (person)* llorar. 2 *(wound)* supurar.
▷ *vt (tears)* derramar.
▲ *pt & pp* **wept** [wept].

weeping ['wi:pɪŋ] *adj* lloroso,-a.
▷ *n* llanto. ● **weeping willow** BOT sauce *m* llorón.

weepy ['wi:pɪ] *adj (person)* llorón,-ona, lloroso,-a; *(film)* lacrimógeno,-a.
▲ *comp* **weepier**, *superl* **weepiest**.

weever ['wi:və^r] *n* araña.

weevil ['wi:vəl] *n* gorgojo.

weft [weft] *n* trama.

weigh [weɪ] *vt* 1 *(gen)* pesar. 2 *fig (consider carefully)* ponderar, sopesar (**up**, -); *(compare carefully)* contraponer (**with/against**, a).
▷ *vi* 1 *(gen)* pesar. 2 *(be important to, have influence on)* influir en, pesar.
◉ **to weigh down** *vt sep* 1 cargar. 2 *fig* agobiar, abrumar, sobrecargar.
◉ **to weigh in** *vi* 1 SP pesarse. 2 *(join in)* intervenir (**with**, con).
◉ **to weigh on** *vt insep (worry)* pesar sobre.
◉ **to weigh out** *vt sep (food, etc)* pesar.
◉ **to weigh up** *vt sep* 1 *(consider carefully)* evaluar, ponderar, sopesar. 2 *(assess)* juzgar, calar.

weighbridge ['weɪbrɪdʒ] *n* báscula de puente.

weigh-in ['weɪɪŋ] *n* SP pesaje *m*.

weight [weɪt] *n* 1 *(gen)* peso. 2 *(of scales, clock, gym)* pesa; *(heavy object)* peso, cosa pesada: 3 *fig (burden, worry)* peso, carga. 4 *fig (importance, influence)* peso, importancia, influencia. ■ **to lose weight** perder peso, adelgazar. ▮ **to put on weight** engordar, ganar peso. ● **weights and measures** pesos *mpl* y medidas.
▷ *vt* 1 *(make heavy)* cargar con peso, añadir peso a; *(fishing net)* lastrar. 2 *fig (statistics, etc)* ponderar.

weightless ['weɪtləs] *adj* ingrávido,-a.

weightlifter ['weɪtlɪftə^r] *n* SP levantador,-ra de pesas, halterófilo,-a.

weighty ['weɪtɪ] *adj* 1 *(gen)* pesado,-a. 2 *fig (argument)* de peso; *(problem, decision)* importante, grave.
▲ *comp* **weightier**, *superl* **weightiest**.

weir [wɪə^r] *n* presa.

weird [wɪəd] *adj* 1 *(bizarre)* raro,-a, extraño,-a. 2 *(eerie)* siniestro,-a.

welcome ['welkəm] *adj* 1 *(gen)* bienvenido,-a. 2 *(news, sight, etc)* grato,-a, agradable; *(change)* oportuno,-a, beneficioso,-a.
▷ *interj* bienvenido,-a (**to**, a).
▷ *n* bienvenida, acogida.
▷ *vt* 1 *(greet)* acoger, recibir; *(officially)* dar la bienvenida a. 2 *(approve of, support)* acoger con agrado. ■ **you're welcome** *(not at all)* no hay de qué, de nada.

welcoming ['welkəmɪŋ] *adj (smile)* acogedor,-ra; *(speech)* de bienvenida.

weld [weld] *n* soldadura.
▷ *vt* 1 soldar. 2 *fig* soldar, unir.
▷ *vi* soldarse.

welder ['weldə^r] *n* soldador,-ra.

welding ['weldɪŋ] *n* soldadura.

welfare ['welfeə^r] *n* 1 *(well-being)* bienestar *m*; *(health)* salud *f*. 2 *(care, help)* protección *f*. 3 US *(money)* seguridad *f* social. ● **welfare state** estado de bienestar. ▮ **welfare worker** asistente *mf* social.

well[1] [wel] *n* 1 *(for water)* pozo. 2 *(of staircase)* hueco de la escalera; *(of lift)* hueco del ascensor. 3 GB *(in court) área de los abogados*.
▷ *vi (tears, blood)* brotar (**up**, -), manar (**up**, -).

well[2] [wel] *adj* 1 *(in good health)* bien. 2 *(satisfactory, right)* bien.
▷ *adv* 1 *(gen)* bien. 2 *(with modals)* bien. 3 *(much)* bien.
▷ *interj* 1 *(gen)* bueno, bien, pues. 2 *(surprise)* ¡vaya! ■ **as well** *(also, too)* también. ▮ **as well as** además de. ▮ **to do well** 1 *(business, etc)* ir bien, tener éxito. 2 *(person - success)* irle bien las cosas. 3 *(- health)* encontrarse bien. ▮ **very well** muy bien, bueno. ▮ **well done!** ¡muy bien!, ¡así se hace! ▮ **well I never!** ¡vaya!, ¡habráse visto! ▮ **well off** *(comfortable, rich)* acomodado,-a.

well-balanced ['wel'bæləns t] [Written **well balanced** when not used to qualify a noun.] *adj* equilibrado,-a.

well-behaved ['welbɪ'heɪvd] [Written **well behaved** when not used to qualify a noun.] *adj* formal, educado,-a.

wellbeing [wel'bi:ɪŋ] *n* bienestar *m*.

well-bred ['wel'bred] [Written **well bred** when not used to qualify a noun.] *adj* bien educado,-a.

well-built ['wel'bɪlt] [Written **well built** when not used to qualify a noun.] *adj* 1 *(building)* de construcción sólida. 2 *(person)* fornido,-a.

well-chosen ['wel'tʃəuzən] [Written **well chosen** when not used to qualify a noun.] *adj* acertado,-a.

well-disposed ['weldɪs'pəuzd] [Written **well disposed** when not used to qualify a noun.] *adj* bien dispuesto,-a (**towards**, hacia).

well-done ['wel'dʌn] [Written **well done** when not used to qualify a noun.] *adj* muy hecho,-a.

well-earned ['wel'ɜːnd] [Written **well earned** when not used to qualify a noun.] *adj* merecido,-a, bien merecido,-a.
well-educated [wel'edjəkeɪtɪd] [Written **well educated** when not used to qualify a noun.] *adj* culto,-a, instruido,-a.
well-founded ['wel'faʊndɪd] [Written **well founded** when not used to qualify a noun.] *adj* bien fundado,-a.
well-informed ['welɪn'fɔːmd] [Written **well informed** when not used to qualify a noun.] *adj* bien informado,-a.
wellington ['welɪŋtən] [Also **Wellington**.] *n* botas de agua.
well-intentioned ['welɪn'tenʃənd] [Written **well intentioned** when not used to qualify a noun.] *adj* bien intencionado,-a.
well-judged ['wel'dʒʌdʒd] [Written **well judged** when not used to qualify a noun.] *adj* bien calculado,-a.
well-known [wel'nəʊn] *adj* (bien) conocido,-a.
well-liked ['wel'laɪkt] [Written **well liked** when not used to qualify a noun.] *adj* popular.
well-lit ['wel'lɪt] [Written **well lit** when not used to qualify a noun.] *adj* bien iluminado,-a.
well-mannered ['wel'mænəd] [Written **well mannered** when not used to qualify a noun.] *adj* educado,-a, cortés.
well-meaning ['wel'miːnɪŋ] [Written **well meaning** when not used to qualify a noun.] *adj* bien intencionado,-a.
well-meant ['wel'ment] [Written **well lit** when not used to qualify a noun.] *adj* bienintencionado,-a.
well-nigh ['welnaɪ] *adj* casi.
well-off ['wel'ɒf] [Written **well off** when not used to qualify a noun.] *adj* rico,-a, acomodado,-a, pudiente.
well-spoken ['wel'spəʊkən] [Written **well spoken** when not used to qualify a noun.] *adj* con acento culto.
well-timed ['wel'taɪmd] [Written **well timed** when not used to qualify a noun.] *adj* oportuno,-a.
well-to-do ['weltə'duː] *adj* acomodado,-a, pudiente.
▷ *n pl* **the well-to-do** la gente pudiente.
well-turned ['wel'tɜːnd] *adj (phrase)* rotundo,-a.
well-wisher ['welwɪʃəʳ] *n persona que llama o escribe a otra deseándole suerte, una pronta recuperación, etc.*
well-worn ['wel'wɔːn] [Written **well worn** when not used to qualify a noun.] *adj* 1 *(clothes)* gastado,-a, raído,-a; *(path)* trillado,-a. 2 *(phrase)* gastado,-a, trillado,-a.
Welsh [welʃ] *adj* galés,-esa.
▷ *n (language)* galés *m*.
▷ *n pl* **the Welsh** los galeses *mpl*.
Welshman ['welʃmən] *n* galés *m*.
▲ *pl* **Welshmen** ['welʃmən].
Welshwoman ['welʃwʊmən] *n* galesa.
▲ *pl* **Welshwomen** ['welʃwɪmɪn].
welt [welt] *n* 1 *(weal)* verdugón *m*, cardenal *m*. 2 *(of shoe)* vira.
welter ['weltəʳ] *n* mezcla confusa, mezcolanza.
wen [wen] *n* lobanillo.
wend [wend] *phr* **to wend one's way** dirigir sus pasos (towards, hacia).

went [went] *pt* ⟶ **go**.
wept [wept] *pt & pp* ⟶ **weep**.
were [wɜːʳ] *pt* ⟶ **be**.
werewolf ['wɪəwʊlf] *n* hombre *m* lobo.
▲ *pl* **werewolves** ['wɪəwʊlvz].
west [west] *n* oeste *m*, occidente *m*.
▷ *adj* occidental, del oeste.
▷ *adv* al oeste, hacia el oeste.
▷ *n* **the West** POL Occidente *m*, los países *mpl* occidentales. ● **West Indies** las Antillas. ‖ **West Indian** antillano,-a.
westbound ['westbaʊnd] *adj* en dirección al oeste.
westerly ['westəlɪ] *adj* 1 *(point, direction)* oeste: **in a westerly direction** *en dirección al oeste*. 2 *(wind)* del oeste.
western ['westən] *adj* del oeste, occidental.
▷ *n (cinema)* western *m*.
westerner ['westənəʳ] *n* occidental *mf*.
west-northwest [westnɔːθ'west] *n* oesnoroeste *m*.
▷ *adv* al oesnoroeste, hacia el oesnoroeste.
west-southwest [westsaʊθ'west] *n* oesudoeste *m*.
▷ *adv* al oesudoeste, hacia el oesudoeste.
westward ['westwəd] *adj* hacia el oeste.
westwards ['westwədz] *adv* hacia el oeste.
wet [wet] *adj* 1 *(gen)* mojado,-a; *(damp)* húmedo,-a. 2 *(weather)* lluvioso,-a. 3 *(paint, ink)* fresco,-a. 4 *fam (person)* apocado,-a, soso,-a.
▲ *comp* **wetter**, *superl* **wettest**.
▷ *n* 1 *(damp)* humedad *f*. 2 *(rain)* lluvia. 3 *fam (person)* apocado,-a; *(politician)* moderado,-a.
▷ *vt* mojar, humedecer.
▲ *pt & pp* **wet** o **wetted**, *ger* **wetting**. ● **wet suit** traje *m* isotérmico.
wetness ['wetnəs] *n* humedad *f*.
whack [wæk] *n* 1 *(blow)* golpe *m*, porrazo. 2 *fam (share)* parte *f*, porción *f*. 3 *fam (attempt)* tentativa.
▷ *vt (hit hard - gen)* pegar, zurrar; *(- ball)* golpear fuerte.
whacked [wækt] *adj fam (tired out)* agotado,-a.
whacking ['wækɪŋ] *adj fam* enorme, grandísimo,-a.
▷ *adv fam (very)* muy.
▷ *n (beating)* paliza, zurra.
whale [weɪl] *n* ballena.
whalebone ['weɪlbəʊn] *n* (barba de) ballena.
whaler ['weɪləʳ] *n (gen)* ballenero,-a.
whaling ['weɪlɪŋ] *n* caza de ballenas. ● **whaling industry** industria ballenera.
wharf [wɔːf] *n* muelle *m*, embarcadero.
▲ *pl* **wharfs** o **wharves**.
what [wɒt] *adj* 1 *(direct questions)* qué: **what time is it?** *¿qué hora es?*. 2 *(indirect questions)* qué: **I don't know what to do** *no sé qué hacer*. 3 *(exclamations)* qué: **what a man!** *¡qué hombre!*. 4 *(all the)* todo,-a: **what oil we have is here** *todo el aceite que tenemos está aquí*.
▷ *pron* 1 *(direct questions)* qué: **what is it?** *¿qué es?*. 2 *(indirect questions)* qué: **he didn't know what to say** *no sabía qué decir*. 3 lo que: **that's what he told me** *eso es lo que me dijo*. ■ **guess what?** ¿sabes qué? ‖ **what about...?** ¿qué te parece...?. ‖ **what for?** 1 *(why)* ¿por qué? 2 *(for what purpose)* ¿para qué? ‖ **what if...?** ¿y si...? ‖ **what is it?** 1 *(what's wrong?)* ¿qué pasa? 2 *(definition)* ¿qué es?
▷ *interj* ¡cómo!: **what! you've lost it!** *¡cómo! ¡lo has perdido!*

whatever [wɒt'evəʳ] *adj* 1 *(any)* cualquiera que. 2 *(at all)* en absoluto.
▷ *pron* 1 *(anything, all that)* (todo) lo que. 2 *(no matter what)*: **whatever happens** *pase lo que pase.* 3 *(surprise)* qué. 4 *fam (show indifference)* lo que sea.
whatsoever [wɒtsəʊ'evəʳ] *adj* en absoluto.
wheat [wiːt] *n* trigo.
wheatmeal ['wiːtmiːl] *n* harina integral de trigo.
wheedle ['wiːdᵊl] *vt* engatusar.
wheel [wiːl] *n* 1 rueda. 2 *(steering wheel)* volante *m*.
▷ *vt (push)* empujar.
▷ *vi* 1 girar: 2 *(birds)* revolotear.
▷ *n pl* **wheels** coche *m sing.*
⊙ **to wheel out** *vt sep* sacar.
wheelbarrow ['wiːlbærəʊ] *n* carretilla de mano.
wheelchair ['wiːltʃeəʳ] *n* silla de ruedas.
wheeze [wiːz] *n (sound)* resuello; *(act)* respiración *f* sibilante.
▷ *vi* respirar con dificultad, resollar.
▷ *vt* decir resollando.
wheezy ['wiːzɪ] *adj (person)* asmático,-a; *(breathing)* sibilante.
▲ *comp* **wheezier**, *superl* **wheeziest**.
whelp [welp] *n* cachorro,-a.
▷ *vi* parir.
when [wen] *adv* 1 *(direct questions)* cuándo: **when did it happen?** *¿cuándo pasó?* 2 *(indirect questions)* cuándo: **tell me when you're ready** *dime cuándo estés listo.* 3 *(at which, on which)* cuando, en que: **there are times when I can't cope** *hay momentos en que no puedo más.*
▷ *conj* 1 *(at the time that)* cuando: **when I arrived** *cuando llegué yo.* 2 *(whenever)* cuando, siempre que: **when I have a free moment** *cuando tenga un momento libre.* 3 *(considering)* cuando, si: **why do you want to move?** *¿por qué te quieres mudar?* 4 *(although)* cuando, aunque: **they said it was red when in fact it was blue** *dijeron que era roja cuando en realidad era azul.*
▷ *pron* cuando: **that was when it broke** *fue entonces cuando se rompió.*
whence [wens] *adv fml* de dónde.
whenever [wen'evəʳ] *conj* 1 *(at any time, when)* cuando quiera que. 2 *(every time that)* siempre que.
▷ *adv (surprise)* cuándo.
where [weəʳ] *adv* 1 *(direct question - place)* dónde; *(- direction)* adónde: **where is it?** *¿dónde está?*. 2 *(indirect question)* dónde, adónde: **tell me where it is** *dime dónde está.* 3 *(at, in or which)* donde, en que; *(to which)* adonde, a donde: **this is where it all happened** *es aquí donde pasó todo.*
▷ *conj* 1 donde: **where I come from we don't do that** *de donde soy yo eso no se hace.* 2 *(when)* cuando: **where possible** *cuando sea posible.*
whereabouts [*(n)* 'weərəbaʊts *(adv)* weərə'baʊts] *n* paradero.
▷ *adv* (por) dónde.
whereas [weər'æz] *conj* 1 mientras que. 2 JUR considerando que.
whereby [weə'baɪ] *adv fml* por el/la/lo cual.
wherein [weə'rɪn] *adv* en donde.
whereupon ['weərəpɒn] *adv* con lo cual.
wherever [weər'evəʳ] *conj* 1 *(in any place, where)* dondequiera que. 2 *(everywhere)* dondequiera.
▷ *adv* 1 *(in questions)* dónde, adónde. 2 *(unspecified place)* en cualquier parte.
whet [wet] *vt* 1 *(appetite)* despertar, abrir. 2 *fml (knife)* afilar.
▲ *pt & pp* **whetted**, *ger* **whetting**.
whether ['weðəʳ] *conj* 1 si. 2 *(no matter if)* aunque.
whey [weɪ] *n* suero.
which [wɪtʃ] *adj* 1 *(direct questions)* qué, cuál, cuáles: **which size?** *¿qué tamaño/talla?* 2 *(indirect questions)* qué: **I can't remember which department she's in** *no recuerdo en qué sección trabaja.*
▷ *pron* 1 *(questions)* cuál, cuáles: **which do you want?** *¿cuál quieres?* 2 *(indirect questions)* cuál: **ask him which is his** *pregúntale cuál es el suyo.* 3 *(defining relative)* que; *(with preposition)* que, el/la que, el/la cual, los/las que, los/las cuales: **the shoes which I bought** *los zapatos que compré.* 4 *(non-defining relative)* el/la cual, los/las cuales: **two glasses, one of which was dirty** *dos copas, una de las cuales estaba sucia.* 5 *(referring to a clause)* lo que, lo cual: **he lost, which was sad** *perdió, lo cual era triste.*
whichever [wɪtʃ'evəʳ] *adj* 1 *(any one)* cualquier, el/la que. 2 *(no matter which)* cualquiera que, no importa. 3 *(interrogative)* cuál.
▷ *pron* 1 cualquiera, el/la que. 2 *(interrogative)* cuál.
whiff [wɪf] *n* 1 *(of air, smoke)* bocanada. 2 *(faint smell)* olor *m* fugaz, olor *m* pasajero, olorcillo. 3 *fam (bad smell)* tufo. 4 *fig (of scandal, etc)* indicio, atisbo, sospecha.
while [waɪl] *n (time)* rato, tiempo: **we talked for a while** *charlamos durante un rato.*
▷ *conj* 1 *(when)* mientras: **somebody stole our car while we were on holiday** (US **vacation**) *nos robaron el coche mientras estábamos de vacaciones.* 2 *(although)* aunque: **while I sympathize with the cause, I cannot support your methods** *aunque simpatizo con la causa, no puedo apoyar tus métodos.* 3 *(whereas)* mientras que: **he prefers to go out, while I like staying in** *él prefiere salir mientras que a mí me gusta quedarme en casa.*
⊙ **to while away** *vt sep* pasar: **they whiled away the time reminiscing about the past** *pasaron el rato rememorando el pasado.*
whim [wɪm] *n* antojo, capricho.
whimper ['wɪmpəʳ] *n (of person)* gimoteo, quejido; *(of dog)* gemido.
▷ *vi (person)* lloriquear, gimotear; *(dog)* gemir.
whimsical ['wɪmsɪkᵊl] *adj (person, idea, etc)* caprichoso,-a; *(smile)* enigmático,-a; *(story, etc)* fantástico,-a.
whinchat ['wɪntʃæt] *n* tarabilla norteña.
whine [waɪn] *n* 1 *(of child)* gimoteo, quejido; *(of dog)* gemido. 2 *(of engine)* zumbido, sonido; *(of siren)* aullido.
▷ *vi* 1 *(child)* gimotear, lloriquear; *(dog)* gemir. 2 *(complain)* quejarse; *(in pain)* gimotear.
whiner ['waɪnəʳ] *n (person)* quejica *mf.*
whinge [wɪndʒ] *vi* GB *fam (complain)* quejarse (**about**, de).
whinny ['wɪnɪ] *n* relincho.
▲ *pl* **whinnies**.
▷ *vi* relinchar.
▲ *pt & pp* **whinnied**, *ger* **whinnying**.
whip [wɪp] *n* 1 *(for animals)* látigo; *(for punishment)* azote *m*; *(for riding)* fusta. 2 CULIN *(desert)* batido.

▷ *vt* 1 *(person)* azotar; *(horse)* fustigar. 2 *(wind)* azotar. 3 CULIN *(ingredients)* batir; *(cream, egg whites)* montar. 4 GB *fam (steal)* birlar, mangar. 5 *(act quickly)* hacer algo deprisa.
▷ *vi (move quickly)* ir volando.
▲ *pt & pp* whipped, *ger* whipping.
⊙ **to whip up** *vt sep* 1 *(arouse - enthusiasm, etc)* despertar, avivar, animar; *(- help, support)* conseguir; *(- hatred)* fomentar; *(- strife, tension)* provocar, crear. 2 *(prepare quickly)* preparar en un momento, improvisar.
whiplash ['wɪplæʃ] *n* latigazo, trallazo. ● **whiplash injury** MED traumatismo cervical.
whippet ['wɪpɪt] *n* galgo pequeño.
whipping ['wɪpɪŋ] *n* azotaina, paliza. ● **whipping cream** nata para montar.
whippletree ['wɪpəltri:] *n* volea.
whip-round ['wɪpraʊnd] *n* GB *fam* colecta.
whirl [wɜ:l] *n* 1 *(movement)* giro, vuelta. 2 *fig* torbellino.
▷ *vi* 1 *(move round)* girar, dar vueltas; *(of dust, leaves, etc)* arremolinarse. 2 *(move quickly)* ir como un relámpago. 3 *fig (of brain, senses)* dar vueltas.
▷ *vt* 1 *(spin)* hacer girar, dar vueltas a. 2 *(move quickly)* llevar rápidamente.
whirlpool ['wɜ:lpu:l] *n* vorágine *m*, remolino.
whirlwind ['wɜ:lwɪnd] *n* torbellino, remolino.
▷ *adj fig* vertiginoso,-a, relámpago.
whirr [wɜ:r] *n* zumbido.
▷ *vi* zumbar.
whisk [wɪsk] *n* 1 *(quick movement)* movimiento brusco, sacudida. 2 CULIN *(hand)* batidor *m*; *(electric)* batidora.
▷ *vt* 1 *(of animal's tail)* sacudir (la cola). 2 CULIN batir. 3 *(take quickly)* llevar rápidamente.
whisker ['wɪskər] *n (single hair)* pelo (de la barba).
▷ *n pl* **whiskers** *(man's)* patillas *fpl*. *(of cat, etc)* bigote *m*, bigotes *mpl*.
whiskey [wɪskɪ] *n* ⟶ **whisky**.
whisper ['wɪspər] *n* 1 *(quiet voice)* susurro. 2 *(rumour)* rumor *m*, voz *f*.
▷ *vt* 1 *(gen)* susurrar, decir en voz baja. 2 *(rumour)* correr la voz, rumorearse.
▷ *vi* 1 *(gen)* susurrar, cuchichear, hablar en voz baja. 2 *(of wind, leaves)* susurrar.
whispering ['wɪspərɪŋ] *n (gen)* cuchicheo; *(of leaves)* murmullo.
whistle ['wɪsəl] *n* 1 *(instrument)* silbato, pito. 2 *(noise)* silbido, pitido; *(of train)* pitido; *(of wind)* silbido.
▷ *vt (tune)* silbar.
▷ *vi* 1 *(person, kettle, wind)* silbar; *(referee, police, train)* pitar. 2 *(call)* llamar con un silbido, silbar; *(protest)* silbar, pitar. 3 *(move swiftly)* pasar silbando.
whistle-stop ['wɪsəlstɒp] *n* US apeadero.
whit [wɪt] *n* pizca, ápice *m*: **you haven't changed a whit** *no has cambiado un ápice*.
white [waɪt] *adj* 1 blanco,-a: 2 *(pale)* pálido,-a.
▷ *n* 1 blanco, color *m* blanco. 2 *(person)* blanco,-a. 3 *(of egg)* clara. 4 *(of eye)* blanco.
▷ *n pl* **whites** *(linen)* ropa *f sing* blanca; *(for tennis)* ropa *f sing* de jugar al tenis. ● **white (blood) cell** glóbulo blanco. ‖ **white heat** incandescencia.
white-collar [waɪt'kɒlər] *adj* oficinista *mf*.
white-hot ['waɪt'hɒt] [Written **white hot** when not used to qualify a noun.] *adj* candente, incandescente.
whiten ['waɪtən] *vt* blanquear, emblanquecer.
whitener ['waɪtənər] *n* blanqueador,-ra.
whiteness ['waɪtnəs] *n* blancura.
whitening ['waɪtənɪŋ] *n* blanco de España.
whitethroat ['waɪtθrəʊt] *n* curruca zarcera.
white-tie [waɪt'taɪ] *adj (party, etc)* de etiqueta.
whitewash ['waɪtwɒʃ] *n* 1 cal *f*, lechada, jalbegue *m*. 2 *fig* encubrimiento.
▷ *vt* 1 encalar, enjalbegar, blanquear. 2 *fig* encubrir.
whither ['wɪðər] *adv* adónde.
whiting[2] ['waɪtɪŋ] *n (whitening)* blanco de España.
whitish ['waɪtɪʃ] *adj* blanquecino,-a.
whittle ['wɪtəl] *vt (sharpen)* afilar, sacar punta a; *(shape)* tallar.
⊙ **to whittle away** *vt sep* mermar, ir reduciendo, ir disminuyendo.
⊙ **to whittle down** *vt sep* reducir.
whiz [wɪz] *n* ⟶ **whizz**.
whizz [wɪz] *n (sound)* zumbido, silbido.
▷ *vi* 1 *(make sound)* zumbar, silbar. 2 *(car, bullet)* pasar zumbando, pasar silbando; *(time)* pasar volando.
who [hu:] *pron* 1 *(direct questions)* quién, quiénes: **who is it?** *¿quién es?* 2 *(indirect questions)* quién, quiénes: **I don't know who they are** *no sé quiénes son*. 3 *(defining relative)* que: **you're the only one who can help me** *eres el único que puede ayudarme*. 4 *(non-defining relative)* que, quien, quienes, el/la cual, los/las cuales: **the workers, who were on strike,...** *los trabajadores, los cuales estaban en huelga,...*
whoever [hu:'evər] *pron* 1 *(the person who)* quien, quienquiera que, el que. 2 *(no matter who)* quienquiera que, cualquiera que. 3 *(questions, exclamations)* quién?
whole [həʊl] *adj* 1 *(entire, all (the), the full amount of)* entero,-a, íntegro,-a, todo,-a. 2 *(intact, not broken)* intacto,-a, sano,-a; *(in one piece, complete)* entero,-a.
▷ *n* conjunto, todo. ■ **as a whole** en conjunto, en su totalidad. ‖ **on the whole** en general. ● **whole number** número entero.
wholefood ['həʊlfu:d] *n* alimento integral.
wholehearted [həʊl'hɑ:tɪd] *adj (support)* absoluto,-a, incondicional; *(attention)* completo,-a; *(sympathy)* sincero,-a; *(effort)* entusiasta.
wholemeal ['həʊlmi:l] *adj* integral.
wholesale ['həʊlseɪl] *adj* 1 COMM al por mayor. 2 *(complete, indiscriminate)* total, general, masivo,-a, sistemático,-a, absoluto,-a, indiscriminado,-a.
▷ *adv* 1 COMM al por mayor. 2 *(on a large scale)* de modo general, en su totalidad, en masa, de manera sistemática.
▷ *n* COMM venta al por mayor.
wholesome ['həʊlsəm] *adj* 1 *(food)* sano,-a; *(appearance)* sano,-a, saludable. 2 *fig (good in effect)* saludable.
wholly ['həʊlɪ] *adv* enteramente, completamente.
whom [hu:m] *pron* 1 *fml (direct questions)* a quién/quiénes: **to whom should I address it?** *¿a quién debería ir dirigido?* 2 *fml (relative - defining)* que, quien, quienes; *(- after preposition)* quien, quienes, el cual, la cual, los cuales, las cuales: **pupils** (US **students**) **whom I have**

taught *alumnos a quienes he dado clase.* **3** *(relative - non-defining)* quien, quienes, el cual, la cual, los cuales, las cuales: **our guest, of whom you must all have heard,...** *nuestro invitado, de quien todos deben haber oído hablar,...*

whooping cough ['hu:pɪŋkɒf] *n* MED tos *f* ferina.

whopper ['wɒpəʳ] *n* **1** *fam (large thing)* cosa enorme, cosa descomunal. **2** *fam (lie)* trola, bola.

whose [hu:z] *pron* **1** *(direct questions)* de quién/quiénes: **whose is this?** *¿de quién es esto?* **2** *(indirect questions)* de quién/quiénes: **I don't know whose it is** *no sé de quién es.*

▷ *adj* **1** *(direct questions)* de quién/quiénes: **whose dog is this?** *de quién es este perro?* **2** *(indirect questions)* de quién/quiénes: **I wonder whose books these are** *me pregunto de quién serán estos libros.* **3** *(relative)* cuyo,-a, cuyos,-as: **the woman whose car was stolen** *la mujer cuyo coche fue robado.*

why [waɪ] *adv* **1** *(direct questions - for what reason)* por qué; *(- for what purpose)* para qué: **why didn't you go?** *¿por qué no fuiste?* **2** *(indirect questions - for what reason)* por qué; *(- for what purpose)* para qué: **I asked him why he did it** *le pregunté por qué lo hizo.* **3** *(relative)* por eso: **that is why he left** *por eso se fue.* ■ **why not?** ¿por qué no?

▷ *interj* ¡vaya!, ¡anda!, ¡toma!

▷ *n* porqué *m.*

wick [wɪk] *n* mecha.

wicked ['wɪkɪd] *adj* **1** *(evil - person)* malvado,-a, malo,-a; *(- action)* malo,-a, perverso,-a, inicuo,-a. **2** *(harmful)* peligroso,-a, dañino,-a, nocivo,-a. **3** *(mischievous)* travieso,-a, pícaro,-a. **4** *fam fig (very bad - gen)* malísimo,-a; *(- weather)* feo,-a, horrible; *(- temper, price)* terrible; *(- waste)* vergonzoso,-a; *(humour)* cruel.

▷ *n pl* **the wicked** los malos.

wicker ['wɪkəʳ] *n* mimbre *m.*

▷ *adj* de mimbre.

wickerwork ['wɪkəwɜ:k] *n (articles)* artículos *mpl* de mimbre; *(art)* cestería.

▷ *adj* de mimbre.

wicket ['wɪkɪt] *n* **1** *(in cricket - stumps)* palos *mpl*; *(- pitch)* terreno. **2** *(small door, gate)* postigo, portillo.

wide [waɪd] *adj* **1** *(broad)* ancho,-a; *(space, hole, gap)* grande. **2** *(having specified width)* de ancho. **3** *(large - area)* amplio,-a, extenso,-a; *(- knowledge, experience, repercussions)* amplio,-a; *(- coverage, range)* extenso,-a. **4** *(eyes, smile)* abierto,-a. **5** *(off target)* desviado,-a.

▷ *adv* **1** *(fully - gen)* completamente. **2** *(off target)* desviado.

wide-angle ['waɪdæŋgᵊl] *adj* amplio,-a. ● **wide-angle lens** objetivo gran angular.

wide-awake ['waɪdə'weɪk] [Written **wide awake** when not used to qualify a noun.] *adj* **1** *(fully awake)* completamente despierto,-a. **2** *(alert)* despierto,-a, despabilado,-a, espabilado,-a.

wide-eyed ['waɪd'aɪd] [Written **wide eyed** when not used to qualify a noun.] *adj* **1** *(surprised)* con los ojos muy abiertos. **2** *(innocent, naive)* inocente, ingenuo,-a.

widely ['waɪdlɪ] *adv* **1** *(over wide area or range of things)* extensamente; *(generally)* generalmente. **2** *(to a large degree)* mucho.

widen ['waɪdᵊn] *vt* **1** *(road, etc)* ensanchar. **2** *fig (knowledge, etc)* ampliar, extender.

▷ *vi* **1** *(road, etc)* ensancharse; *(eyes)* abrirse. **2** *(project, etc)* extenderse; *(difference, gap)* aumentar.

wide-ranging ['waɪd'reɪndʒɪŋ] [Written **wide ranging** when not used to qualify a noun.] *adj* **1** *(interests, products, subjects)* múltiples, muy diversos,-as, muy variados,-as; *(discussion)* amplio,-a. **2** *(effects, implications)* de gran alcance; *(survey, study, investigation)* a fondo, de gran alcance.

widescreen ['waɪdskri:n] *adj* TV pantalla panorámica.

widespread ['waɪdspred] *adj (concern, confusion, unrest, use, belief)* generalizado,-a; *(damage, disease, news)* extenso,-a, extendido,-a. ■ **to become widespread 1** *(gen)* generalizarse. **2** *(illness, news)* extenderse, difundirse.

widow ['wɪdəʊ] *n* viuda.

widower ['wɪdəʊəʳ] *n* viudo.

width [wɪdθ] *n* **1** *(gen)* anchura. **2** *(of material)* ancho. **3** *(of swimming pool)* ancho.

wield [wi:ld] *vt* **1** *(weapon, tool, etc)* empuñar, blandir, manejar. **2** *fig (power, control, etc)* ejercer.

wife [waɪf] *n* esposa, mujer *f.*

▲ *pl* **wives.**

wig [wɪg] *n* **1** *(gen)* peluca. **2** JUR peluquín *m.*

wigeon ['wɪdʒən] *n* ánade *m* silbón.

wiggly ['wɪgᵊlɪ] *adj (wavy)* ondulado,-a; *(moving)* sinuoso,-a.

▲ *comp* **wigglier**, *superl* **wiggliest.**

wild [waɪld] *adj* **1** *(animal)* salvaje, bravío,-a. **2** *(plant, flower)* silvestre; *(vegetation)* salvaje. **3** *(country, landscape)* agreste, bravo,-a, salvaje. **4** *(weather - wind)* furioso,-a, borrascoso,-a; *(- sea)* bravo,-a; *(- night)* tempestuoso,-a, de tormenta. **5** *(tribe)* salvaje. **6** *(violent, angry - person)* furioso,-a, colérico,-a, frenético,-a; *(- behaviour)* incontrolado,-a, desenfrenado,-a; *(- blow, attack)* violento,-a, salvaje, brutal. **7** *(very excited - person)* loco,-a (**with**, de), alocado,-a; *(very exciting - party, etc)* escandaloso,-a, desmadrado,-a. **8** *(showing lack of thought - thoughts, talk)* disparatado,-a; *(- guess)* al azar; *(- idea, scheme)* descabellado,-a, desorbitado,-a, loco,-a, alocado,-a; *(- decision)* precipitado,-a, impetuoso,-a; *(- exaggeration, speculation)* enorme. **9** *fam (fantastic, crazy)* bárbaro,-a, salvaje.

▷ *n* **the wild** estado salvaje, estado natural, naturaleza.

▷ *n pl* **the wilds** las regiones *fpl* salvajes. ● **wild boar** jabalí *m.*

wildcat ['waɪldkæt] *n* gato,-a montés. ● **wildcat strike** huelga espontánea.

wildebeest ['wɪldəbi:st] *n* ñu *m.*

wilderness ['wɪldənəs] *n* **1** *(desert)* yermo, desierto; *(wasteland)* páramo. **2** *pej (garden)* selva, jungla.

wildfire ['waɪldfaɪəʳ] *n* fuego incontrolable, fuego arrasador.

wildfowl ['waɪldfaʊl] *n* ave *f* de caza.

▲ *pl* **wildfowl** o **wildfowls.**

wild-goose chase [waɪld'gu:stʃeɪs] *n* búsqueda inútil.

wildlife ['waɪldlaɪf] *n* fauna. ● **wildlife park** reserva natural.

wildly ['waɪldlɪ] *adv* **1** *(run, etc)* como un loco,-a, frenéticamente; *(talk)* exageradamente, sin ton ni son, incoherentemente; *(applaud)* fervorosamente; *(hit)* violentamente, furiosamente. 2 *(guess)* al azar, sin pensar; *(shoot)* sin apuntar, a lo loco. 3 *(very)* muy, totalmente, absolutamente.

wildness ['waɪldnəs] *n* 1 *(of landscape)* lo agreste; *(of storm, sea, wind)* furia. 2 *(of behaviour)* desenfreno, locura; *(of imagination, etc)* extravagancia.

wiles [waɪlz] *n pl (tricks)* artimañas *fpl*, artificios *mpl*; *(cunning)* astucia.

wilful ['wɪlfʊl] *adj* 1 *(headstrong, obstinate)* voluntario-so,-a, terco,-a. 2 JUR *(intentional)* premeditado,-a, deliberado,-a.

will[1] [wɪl] *n* 1 *(control, volition)* voluntad *f*; *(free will)* albedrío. 2 JUR testamento, últimas *fpl* voluntades.

▷ *vt* 1 *(make or intend to happen by power of mind)* desear, querer. 2 *fml (intend, desire)* querer, ordenar, mandar. 3 JUR legar, dejar en testamento. ■ **against one's will** contra su voluntad. ● **last will and testament** última voluntad *f*.

will[2] [wɪl] *aux* 1 *(future)*: **she will be here tomorrow** *estará aquí mañana.* 2 *(be disposed to, be willing to)*: **(no), I won't** *no quiero.* 3 *(requests)* querer: **will you do me a favour?** *¿quieres hacerme un favor?* 4 *(general truths, custom)*: **accidents will happen** *siempre habrá accidentes.* 5 *(orders, commands)*: **will you be quiet!** *¡quieres callarte!* 6 *(insistence, persistence)* insistir en: **she will play her music at full volume** *insiste en poner la música a tope.* 7 *(can, possibility)* poder: **this phone will accept credit cards** *este teléfono va con tarjetas de crédito.* 8 *(supposition, must, probability)* deber de: **that'll be John** *será John, debe de ser John.*

▷ *vi fml dated (wish)* querer.

willing ['wɪlɪŋ] *adj* 1 *(without being forced)* complaciente, de gran voluntad, dispuesto,-a; *(eager)* entusiasta. 2 *(ready, prepared, disposed)* dispuesto,-a (**to**, a). 3 *(given/done gladly)* voluntario,-a. ■ **to show willing** dar pruebas de buena voluntad.

willingly ['wɪlɪŋlɪ] *adv* de buena gana, de buen grado.

willingness ['wɪlɪŋnəs] *n (good will)* buena voluntad *f*; *(readiness)* buena disposición *f*.

will-o'-the-wisp [wɪləðə'wɪsp] *n* fuego fatuo.

willow ['wɪləʊ] *n* sauce *m*.

willowy ['wɪləʊɪ] *adj* esbelto,-a.

willpower ['wɪlpaʊə'] *n* (fuerza de) voluntad *f*.

wilt [wɪlt] *vt* marchitar, secar.

▷ *vi* 1 *(plant)* marchitarse, secarse. 2 *(person - become weak or tired)* debilitarse, decaer, languidecer; *(- lose confidence)* desanimarse.

wily ['waɪlɪ] *adj* astuto,-a, zorro,-a, mañoso,-a.

▲ *comp* **wilier**, *superl* **wiliest**.

wimp [wɪmp] *n fam pej* esmirriado,-a, canijo,-a.

wimpish ['wɪmpɪʃ] *adj* ñoño,-a.

win [wɪn] *n* victoria,

▷ *vt* 1 *(gen)* ganar; *(victory)* conseguir, ganar. 2 *(prize, cup, etc)* ganar, llevarse. 3 *(gain, obtain, achieve - gen)* conseguir, obtener, ganar; *(- friendship, respect)* granjearse; *(- sympathy, affection)* ganarse, granjearse; *(- support)* atraer, captar; *(- heart, love)* conquistar.

▷ *vi* ganar.

▲ *pt & pp* **won**, *ger* **winning**.

⊙ **to win back** *vt sep (money, love, support)* recuperar; *(land)* reconquistar.

⊙ **to win over / win round** *vt sep (person)* convencer, persuadir; *(supporter)* atraerse, captar, ganarse; *(lover)* conquistar.

⊙ **to win through / win out** *vi* conseguir triunfar, triunfar al final.

wince [wɪns] *n* rictus *m*, mueca de dolor.

▷ *vi (in pain)* hacer un rictus, hacer una mueca de dolor; *(in embarrassment)* hacer una mueca.

winch [wɪntʃ] *n* torno, cabrestante *m*.

▷ *vt* levantar con un torno.

wind[1] [wɪnd] *n* 1 METEOR viento, aire *m*. 2 *(breath)* aliento. 3 *(flatulence)* gases *mpl*, flato; *(air)* gases *mpl* del estómago. 4 *pej (talk)* palabrería.

▷ *adj* MUS de viento.

▷ *vt* 1 dejar sin aliento, cortar la respiración: 2 *(baby)* hacer eructar. ● **wind instrument** instrumento de viento.

wind[2] [waɪnd] *vt* 1 *(handle)* dar vueltas a, girar. 2 *(on reel)* arrollar, devanar. 3 *(tape, film)* bobinar. 4 *(clock)* dar cuerda a (**up**, -). 5 *(bandage, scarf)* envolver; *(wool)* ovillar.

▷ *vi (road, river)* serpentear, zigzaguear; *(staircase)* formar una espiral.

▷ *n (bend)* curva, recodo, vuelta.

⊙ **to wind down** *vi* 1 *(clock)* quedarse sin cuerda. 2 *(person)* relajarse.

⊙ **to wind up** *vt sep* 1 *(business, company)* concluir, cerrar; *(meeting, speech)* clausurar, terminar, acabar. 2 *(annoy)* fastidiar; *(kid)* tomar el pelo, quedarse con.

▷ *vi fam* acabar en.

▲ *pt & pp* **wound** [waʊnd].

windbag ['wɪndbæg] *n* charlatán,-ana.

windbreak ['wɪndbreɪk] *n* protección *f* contra el viento.

windcheater ['wɪndtʃiːtə'] *n* cazadora.

windfall ['wɪndfɔːl] *n* 1 *(fruit)* fruta caída. 2 *fig* suerte *f* inesperada, ganancia inesperada o caída del cielo.

winding ['waɪndɪŋ] *adj (road, river)* sinuoso,-a, tortuoso,-a; *(staircase)* de caracol, espiral.

windlass ['wɪndləs] *n* torno.

windmill ['wɪndmɪl] *n* molino de viento.

window ['wɪndəʊ] *n* 1 *(gen)* ventana. 2 *(in vehicle, bank, theatre, etc)* ventanilla. 3 *(of shop)* escaparate *m*. 4 *(glass)* cristal *m*. 5 COMPUT ventana.

window-dressing ['wɪndəʊdresɪŋ] *n* 1 decoración *f* de escaparates, escaparatismo. 2 *fig* fachada, apariencias *fpl*.

windowpane ['wɪndəʊpeɪn] *n* cristal *m*.

windowsill ['wɪndəʊsɪl] *n* alféizar *m*.

windpipe ['wɪndpaɪp] *n* tráquea.

windscreen ['wɪndskriːn] *n* AUTO parabrisas *m inv*.

windshield ['wɪndʃiːld] *n* US→ **windscreen**.

windsurf ['wɪndsɜːf] *vi* hacer windsurfing.

windsurfing ['wɪndsɜːfɪŋ] *n* windsurf *m*.

windswept ['wɪndswept] *adj (place)* azotado,-a por el viento; *(person, hair)* despeinado,-a (por el viento).

wind-up ['waɪndʌp] *n* tomadura de pelo, burla.

windward ['wɪndwəd] *adj* de barlovento.

▷ *adv* por barlovento.

▷ *n* barlovento. ■ **to windward** a barlovento.

windy ['wɪndɪ] *adj* 1 *(day, weather)* ventoso,-a; *(place)* expuesto,-a al viento: 2 *(speech)* rimbombante.

▲ *comp* **windier**, *superl* **windiest**.

wine [waɪn] *n* 1 vino. **red/rosé/white wine** *vino tinto/rosado/blanco.* 2 *(colour)* (color *m*) morado, granate *m.* ● **wine cellar** bodega. ‖ **wine grower** vinicultor,-ra. ‖ **wine merchant** vinatero,-a. ‖ **wine taster** catavinos *mf.*

winery ['waɪnərɪ] *n* bodega.
▲ *pl* **wineries.**

wineskin ['waɪnskɪn] *n* odre *m*, bota.

wing [wɪŋ] *n* 1 *(gen)* ala. 2 AUTO aleta. 3 SP *(side)* banda; *(player)* extremo,-a.
▷ *vi* volar.
▷ *n pl* **wings** THEAT bastidores *mpl.*

winged [wɪŋd] *adj* alado,-a, con alas.

winger ['wɪŋəʳ] *n* SP extremo,-a.

wingspan ['wɪŋspæn] *n* envergadura.

wink [wɪŋk] *n* guiño.
▷ *vi* 1 *(person)* guiñar el ojo. 2 *(of light, star)* titilear, parpadear. ■ **not to get/have a wink of sleep / not to sleep a wink** no pegar ojo.
⊙ **to wink at** *vt insep* hacer la vista gorda.

winker ['wɪnkəʳ] *n* GB *(indicator)* intermitente *m.*

winkle ['wɪŋkᵊl] *n* bígaro, bigarro.

winner ['wɪnəʳ] *n* 1 ganador,-ra, vencedor,-ra. 2 *fam (idea, etc)* éxito.

winning ['wɪnɪŋ] *adj* 1 *(person, team, etc)* ganador,-ra. 2 *(ticket, number, etc)* premiado,-a. 3 *(stroke, goal)* decisivo,-a. 4 *(smile, ways)* atractivo,-a, encantador,-ra.
▷ *n pl* **winnings** ganancias *fpl.* ● **winning post** meta.

winsome ['wɪnsəm] *adj fml* atractivo,-a, encantador,-ra.

winter ['wɪntəʳ] *n* invierno.
▷ *vi fml* invernar, pasar el invierno. ● **winter solstice** solsticio de invierno.

wipe [waɪp] *vt (clean)* limpiar; *(dry)* enjugar.
▷ *vi (dishes)* enjugar.
▷ *n* 1 *(clean)* lavado, fregado. 2 *(cloth)* paño, trapo.
⊙ **to wipe out** *vt sep* 1 *(destroy - army)* aniquilar; *(- population, species)* exterminar. 2 *(clean inside)* limpiar el interior de. 3 *(cancel - debts)* saldar, liquidar, cancelar; *(- profit)* borrar, anular.

wiper ['waɪpəʳ] *n* AUTO limpiaparabrisas *m inv.*

wire ['waɪəʳ] *n* 1 *(metal)* alambre *m.* 2 ELEC cable *m*, hilo. 3 *(fence)* alambrada, valla. 4 US telegrama *m.*
▷ *vt* 1 *(fasten, join)* atar con alambre. 2 *(house)* hacer la instalación eléctrica de; *(equipment, appliance)* conectar (a la toma eléctrica). 3 US *(telegram)* enviar un telegrama a; *(money)* mandar un giro telegráfico a. ● **wire cutters** cortaalambres *m inv.*

wired ['waɪəd] *adj* conectado,-a.

wireless ['waɪələs] *n* 1 *(set)* radio *f.* 2 *(system)* radiofonía. ● **wireless operator** radiotelegrafista *mf.*

wiretapping ['waɪətæpɪŋ] *n* intervención *f* de teléfonos.

wiring ['waɪrɪŋ] *n* cableado.

wiry ['waɪərɪ] *adj (person)* nervudo,-a; *(hair)* estropajoso,-a.
▲ *comp* **wirier**, *superl* **wiriest.**

wisdom ['wɪzdəm] *n* 1 *(knowledge)* sabiduría, saber *m.* 2 *(good sense - of person)* cordura, (buen) juicio, tino; *(- of action)* prudencia, sabiduría, sensatez *f.*

wise¹ [waɪz] *adj* 1 *(learned, knowledgeable)* sabio,-a. 2 *(sensible, prudent - person)* prudente, sensato,-a; *(- action, remark)* prudente; *(- advice)* sabio,-a; *(- decision, choice, move)* atinado,-a, acertado,-a. ● **wise guy** sabelotodo.
⊙ **to wise up** *vi (realize, become aware)* darse cuenta; *(become informed)* enterarse; *(wake up)* espabilarse.

wise² [waɪz] *n arch* manera, modo, guisa.

wish [wɪʃ] *vt* 1 *(want)* querer, desear. 2 *fml (demand, want)* querer. 3 *(hope)* desear.
▷ *vi* 1 desear (**for**, -). 2 *fml (want)* querer.
▷ *n* deseo.
▷ *n pl* **wishes** *(greeting)* deseos *mpl*; *(in letter)* saludos *mpl*, recuerdos *mpl.*
⊙ **to wish on** *vt sep*: **I wouldn't wish that on anyone** *eso no se lo desearía a nadie.*

wishbone ['wɪʃbəʊn] *n* espoleta.

wishful ['wɪʃfʊl] *adj fml* de ensueño. ● **wishful thinking** ilusiones *fpl.*

wisp [wɪsp] *n* 1 *(of grass, straw, etc)* brizna; *(of hair, wool, etc)* mechón *m*; *(of smoke, cloud)* voluta. 2 *(person)* persona menuda.

wispy ['wɪspɪ] *adj* 1 *(delicate, slight)* tenue, delgado,-a. 2 *(straggly)* desordenado,-a.
▲ *comp* **wispier**, *superl* **wispiest.**

wistful ['wɪstfʊl] *adj* pensativo,-a, nostálgico,-a, melancólico,-a.

wit [wɪt] *n* 1 *(clever humour)* agudeza, ingenio, chispa, sal *f*, gracia. 2 *(intelligence)* inteligencia, presencia de ánimo. 3 *(person)* persona salada, chistoso,-a.

witch [wɪtʃ] *n* bruja. ● **witch doctor** hechicero. ‖ **witch hazel** 1 *(tree)* hamamélide *f* de Virginia. 2 *(liquid)* solución *f* de hamamélide de Virginia.
▲ *pl* **witches.**

witchcraft ['wɪtʃkrɑːft] *n* brujería.

witch-hunt ['wɪtʃhʌnt] *n* caza de brujas.

with [wɪð, wɪθ] *prep* 1 *(accompanying)* con: **come with me** *ven conmigo.* 2 *(having, possessing)* con, de; *(including, and also)* con, incluido. **the man with the beard** *el hombre de la barba.* 3 *(using, by means of)* con: **cut it with a knife** *córtalo con un cuchillo.* 4 *(cover, fill, contain)* de: **you fill it with water** *lo llenas de agua.* 5 *(agreeing, in support of)* con: **we're with you all the way!** *¡estamos contigo hasta el final!* 6 *(against)* con: **I've had a row with Daniel** *he discutido con Daniel.* 7 *(because of, on account of)* de: **trembling with fear** *temblando de miedo.* 8 *(indicating manner)* con: **with pleasure** *con mucho gusto.* 9 *(in same direction as)* con: **with the flow** *con la corriente.* 10 *(at the same time and rate as)* con: **wine improves with age** *el vino mejora con los años.* 11 *(regarding, concerning)* con: **this has nothing to do with you** *esto no tiene nada que ver contigo.* 12 *(in the case of, as regards)* con respecto a, en cuanto a: **with Mrs Smith what happened was that...** *en el caso de la Señora Smith lo que pasó fue que...* 13 *(as an employee or client of)* en: **she's with the council now** *trabaja en el ayuntamiento ahora.* 14 *(remaining)*: **with only half an hour to go** *cuando tan solo falta media hora.* 15 *(despite, in spite of)* con: **with all his faults** *con todos sus defectos.* 16 *(in comparisons)* con: **if we compare this brand with a cheaper one** *si comparamos esta marca con una más barata.* 17 *(illness)* con: **he's in bed with flu** *está en cama con la gripe.* 18 *(according to)* según, de acuerdo con: **prices vary with the seasons** *los precios varían según la temporada.*

withdraw [wɪð'drɔ:] *vt* 1 *(take out)* retirar, sacar. 2 *fml (retract, take back - statement)* retractarse de, retirar; *(- offer)* renunciar a; *(- charge, support)* retirar.
▷ *vi (retire, not take part in)* retirarse. ■ **to withdraw into oneself** retraerse.
▲ *pt* **withdrew** [wɪð'dru:], *pp* **withdrawn** [wɪð'drɔ:n].
withdrawal [wɪð'drɔ:əl] *n* 1 *(gen)* retirada. 2 *(of words)* retractación *f*. 3 *(psychology, behaviour)* retraimiento. ● **withdrawal symptoms** síndrome *m* de abstinencia.
withdrawn [wɪðdrɔ:n] *pp* ⟶ **withdraw.**
withdrew [wɪðdru:] *pt* ⟶ **withdraw.**
wither ['wɪðəʳ] *vt* 1 *(plant)* marchitar, secar. 2 *(crush)* fulminar, aplastar, intimidar.
▷ *vi* 1 *(plant)* marchitarse (**away**, -), secarse (**away**, -). 2 *fig (hopes, etc)* desvanecerse, menguar.
withering ['wɪðərɪŋ] *adj* 1 *(look)* fulminante. 2 *(remark)* mordaz.
withhold [wɪð'həuld] *vt* 1 *(money)* retener; *(information)* ocultar; *(consent)* negar. 2 *(laughter, etc)* contener.
▲ *pt & pp* **withheld** [wɪð'held].
within [wɪ'ðɪn] *prep* 1 *fml (inside)* dentro de. 2 *(inside range or limits of)* al alcance de. 3 *(less than - distance)* a menos de. 4 *(less than - time)* dentro de.
▷ *adv fml* dentro, en el interior.
without [wɪ'ðaut] *prep* 1 sin. 2 *arch* fuera de.
▷ *adv* 1 fuera. 2 sin.
withstand [wɪð'stænd] *vt (gen)* resistir; *(pain)* aguantar, soportar.
▲ *pt & pp* **withstood** [wɪð'stud].
withstood [wɪð'stud] *pt & pp* ⟶ **withstand.**
witness ['wɪtnəs] *n* 1 *(person)* testigo *mf*. 2 *fml (testimony, evidence)* testimonio.
▷ *vt* 1 *(see)* presenciar, ver. 2 *(document)* firmar como testigo. 3 *(be a sign or proof of)* testimoniar; *(look at the example of)* ver, notar, considerar.
▷ *vi* JUR *fml (give evidence, testify)* atestiguar (**to**, -), declarar (**to**, -).
witty ['wɪtɪ] *adj (person)* ingenioso,-a, agudo,-a, salado,-a; *(remark)* agudo,-a; *(speech)* gracioso,-a.
▲ *comp* **wittier**, *superl* **wittiest.**
wives [waɪvz] *n pl* ⟶ **wife.**
wizard ['wɪzəd] *n* 1 *(male witch)* brujo, hechicero. 2 *(genius)* lince *mf*, genio, experto,-a.
wizened ['wɪzᵊnd] *adj (skin, face)* arrugado,-a; *(fruit)* seco,-a.
wobble ['wɒbᵊl] *n (table, chair, ladder)* tambaleo, bamboleo; *(bicycle)* movimiento; *(voice, jelly)* temblor *m*.
▷ *vi (table, chair, ladder)* cojear; *(bicycle, tooth)* moverse; *(legs, jelly, voice)* temblar; *(wheel)* bailar; *(person)* tambalearse, bambolearse, vacilar.
▷ *vt (table, ladder)* mover.
wobbly ['wɒbᵊlɪ] *adj* 1 *(table, chair, ladder)* cojo,-a; *(bicycle, tooth)* que se mueve; *(writing)* de trazo poco firme; *(voice)* tembloroso,-a. 2 *(person)* débil.
▲ *comp* **wobblier**, *superl* **wobbliest.**
▷ *n* ataque *m*, pataleta.
▲ *pl* **wobblies.**
woe [wəu] *n fml dated (sorrow)* aflicción *f*, congoja.
▷ *n pl* **woes** males *mpl*, penas *fpl*, desgracias *fpl*.
woeful ['wəuful] *adj* 1 *fml (very sad)* afligido,-a, apenado,-a, triste. 2 *(deplorable)* lamentable, deplorable, penoso,-a, malísimo,-a.
woke [wəuk] *pt* ⟶ **wake.**
woken [weukən] *pp* ⟶ **have, wake.**
wolf [wulf] *n* lobo. ● **wolf cub** lobezno.
▲ *pl* **wolves.**
▷ *vt* [Also **wolf down.**] tragarse, zamparse, devorar.
wolfhound ['wulfhaund] *n* perro lobo.
wolfram ['wulfrəm] *n* wolframio, volframio, wolfram *m*.
wolverine ['wulvəri:n] *n* glotón *m*.
wolves [wulvz] *pl* ⟶ **wolf.**
woman ['wumən] *n* mujer *f*, señora.
▲ *pl* **women** ['wɪmɪn].
▷ *adj*: **woman doctor** *doctora.*
womanhood ['wumənhud] *n* condición *f* de mujer.
womanly ['wumənlɪ] *adj* femenino,-a.
womb [wu:m] *n* útero, matriz *f*.
women ['wɪmɪn] *n pl* ⟶ **woman.**
won [wʌn] *pt & pp* ⟶ **win.**
wonder ['wʌndəʳ] *n* 1 *(thing)* maravilla, milagro. 2 *(feeling)* admiración *f*, asombro.
▷ *adj* milagroso,-a.
▷ *vt* 1 *fml (be surprised)* sorprenderse, extrañarse. 2 *(ask oneself)* preguntarse. 3 *(polite request)*: **I wonder if you can help me** *a ver si puede ayudarme.*
▷ *vi* 1 *(reflect, ponder)* pensar (**about**, en); *(doubt)* tener dudas. 2 *fml (marvel)* asombrarse, maravillarse, admirarse. ■ **I shouldn't wonder if «+ indic»** no me extrañaría que + *subj*. ■ **it's a wonder (that) «+ indic»** es un milagro que + *subj*. ■ **no/little/small wonder (that) «+ indic»** no es de extrañar que + *subj*.
wonderful ['wʌndəful] *adj* maravilloso,-a, estupendo,-a.
wonderland ['wʌndəlænd] *n* mundo maravilloso.
wonderment ['wʌndəmənt] *n* admiración *f*, asombro.
wondrous ['wʌndrəs] *adj fml* maravilloso,-a.
wont [wəunt] *n* costumbre *f*, hábito.
won't [wəunt] *contr* (**will not**) ⟶ **will.**
wood [wud] *n* 1 *(material)* madera. 2 *(for fire)* leña. 3 *(forest)* bosque *m*. 4 SP *(golf)* palo de madera; *(bowling)* bola.
▷ *n pl* **woods** bosque *m sing*. ● **wood pigeon** paloma torcaz. ■ **wood pulp** pulpa de madera. ■ **wood shaving** virutas *fpl*.
woodcut ['wudkʌt] *n* grabado en madera.
woodcutter ['wudkʌtəʳ] *n* leñador,-ra.
wooded ['wudɪd] *adj* arbolado,-a, cubierto,-a de bosques.
wooden ['wudᵊn] *adj* 1 de madera. 2 *fig (expression, style)* rígido,-a; *(movement)* tieso,-a; *(acting)* sin expresión.
woodland ['wudlənd] *n* bosque *m*, arbolado, monte *m*.
woodpecker ['wudpekəʳ] *n* pico, pájaro carpintero.
woodwork ['wudwɜ:k] *n* 1 *(craft)* carpintería. 2 *(of building)* maderaje *m*, maderamen *m*.
woodworm ['wudwɜ:m] *n* carcoma: **it has woodworm** *está carcomido,-a.*
woody ['wudɪ] *adj* 1 *(wooded)* arbolado,-a. 2 *(like wood)* leñoso,-a.
▲ *comp* **woodier**, *superl* **woodiest.**

wool [wul] *n* lana.
▷ *adj* 1 *(made of wool)* de lana. 2 COMM lanero,-a.
woolen ['wulən] *adj-n* US→ **woollen.**
woollen ['wulən] *adj* 1 *(made of wool)* de lana. 2 COMM lanero,-a.
▷ *n pl* **woollens** géneros *mpl* de lana.
woolly ['wulı] *adj* 1 *(made of wool)* de lana, lanoso,-a, lanudo,-a. 2 *(like wool)* lanoso,-a, lanudo,-a. 3 *fig (idea, argument)* confuso,-a, vago,-a; *(outline)* borroso,-a; *(sound)* impreciso,-a; *(person, mind)* espeso,-a.
▲ *comp* **woollier**, *superl* **woolliest.**
▷ *n (clothing)* prenda de lana.
▲ *pl* **woollies.**
woolly-headed ['wulı'hedıd] [Written **woolly headed** when not used to qualify a noun.] *adj* espeso,-a.
wooly ['wulı] *adj* → **woolly.**
word [wɜ:d] *n* 1 *(gen)* palabra: **tell me what happened in your own words** *explícame con tus propias palabras lo que pasó.* 2 *(message, news)* noticia: **word came that...** *llegó noticia (de) que...* 3 *(promise)* palabra: **I give you my word** *te doy mi palabra.* 4 *(command)* orden *f*: **wait until I give the word** *espera hasta que dé la orden.* 5 LING palabra, vocablo, voz *f*. 6 **the word** *(rumour)* voz *f*, rumor *m*: **the word is that Macy is pregnant** *corre la voz de que Macy está embarazada.* ■ **in a word** en una palabra. ‖ **in other words** o sea, es decir. ‖ **not in so many words** no exactamente. ‖ **to keep one's word** cumplir su palabra. ‖ **to put** STH **into words** expresar ALGO con palabras. ‖ **word for word** palabra por palabra. ● **a word of advice** un consejo. ‖ **a word of warning** una advertencia. ‖ **word processor** procesador *m* de textos.
▷ *n pl* **words** *(lyrics)* letra *f sing*. *(discussion, talk)* palabras *fpl*.
▷ *vt* expresar, formular, redactar: **a well-worded letter** *una carta bien redactada.*
wording ['wɜ:dıŋ] *n* redacción *f*, expresión *f*, palabras *fpl*, términos *mpl*.
word-perfect [wɜ:d'pɜ:fekt] *adj (correct in every detail)* correcto,-a hasta la última palabra.
wordy ['wɜ:dı] *adj* prolijo,-a, verboso,-a.
▲ *comp* **wordier**, *superl* **wordiest.**
wore [wɔ:ʳ] *pt* → **wear.**
work [wɜ:k] *n* 1 *(gen)* trabajo. 2 *(employment)* empleo, trabajo. 3 *(building work, roadworks)* obras *fpl*. 4 *(product, results)* trabajo, obra. 5 *(literary, etc)* obra.
▷ *vt* 1 *(person)* hacer trabajar. 2 *(machine)* manejar; *(mechanism)* accionar. 3 *(mine, oil well)* explotar; *(land, fields)* trabajar, cultivar. 4 *(produce)* hacer. 5 *(wood, metal, clay)* trabajar; *(dough)* amasar. 6 *(make by work or effort)* trabajar. 7 *fam (arrange)* arreglar. 8 *(move gradually)*: **work the fat into the flour** *vaya mezclando la mantequilla con la harina.* ■ **to be in work** tener trabajo. ‖ **to be out of work** estar en el paro. ‖ **to get down/set to work** ponerse a trabajar.
▷ *vi* 1 *(gen)* trabajar. 2 *(machine, system)* funcionar. 3 *(medicine, cleaner)* surtir efecto; *(plan)* tener éxito. 4 *(move)*: **they eventually worked round to my way of thinking** *finalmente coincidieron con mi parecer.*
▷ *n pl* **works** *(factory)* fábrica *f sing*. *(parts)* mecanismo *m sing*. *fam (everything)* todo, todo el tinglado.
⊙ **to work in** *vt sep (include)* introducir, incluir, insertar, meter.
⊙ **to work off** *vt sep (anger)* desahogarse; *(debt, loan)* saldar trabajando; *(weight)* rebajar haciendo ejercicio.
⊙ **to work on** *vt insep* 1 *(gen)* trabajar en, preparar; *(case)* investigar; *(car, etc)* reparar. 2 *(principle)* atenerse a, guiarse por; *(fact, idea, assumption, etc)* basarse en, partir de.
⊙ **to work out** *vt sep* 1 *(calculation, sum)* calcular, hacer. 2 *(plan, scheme)* planear, elaborar; *(itinerary)* planear; *(details, idea)* desarrollar. 3 *(problem)* solucionar, resolver; *(solution)* encontrar. 4 *(person)* calar, entender.
▷ *vi* 1 *(calculation)* salir (**at**, por), resultar. 2 *(turn out well - things)* salir bien; *(- problem)* resolverse. 3 SP hacer ejercicio.
⊙ **to work over** *vt sep* sacudir el polvo a, dar una paliza a.
⊙ **to work to** *vt insep (budget)* no pasarse de; *(deadline)* respetar, trabajar con miras a.
⊙ **to work up** *vt sep* 1 *(excite, rouse)* exaltar, acalorar; *(make nervous)* poner nervioso,-a, emocionar. 2 *(develop)* hacer, desarrollar. 3 *(increase)* aumentar, fomentar; *(complete, improve)* desarrollar, elaborar.
⊙ **to work up to** *vt insep* preparar el terreno para.
workable ['wɜ:kəbᵊl] *adj* 1 *(plan, scheme)* factible, viable. 2 *(mine, land)* explotable.
workaday ['wɜ:kədeı] *adj (ordinary)* rutinario,-a; *(everyday)* de cada día.
workaholic [wɜ:kə'hɒlık] *n fam* adicto,-a al trabajo.
workbench ['wɜ:kbentʃ] *n* banco de trabajo.
workbook ['wɜ:kbuk] *n* cuaderno, libreta de ejercicios.
workday ['wɜ:kdeı] *n* US día *m* laborable.
worker ['wɜ:kəʳ] *n (gen)* trabajador,-ra; *(manual)* obrero,-a, operario,-a; *(office)* oficinista *mf*, administrativo,-a. ● **worker bee** abeja obrera.
workforce ['wɜ:kfɔ:s] *n (of company, factory, etc)* personal *m*, plantilla; *(of country)* población *f* activa.
workhorse ['wɜ:khɔ:s] *n* burro de carga.
work-in ['wɜ:kın] *n* encierro (en la fábrica, etc).
working ['wɜ:kıŋ] *adj* 1 *(clothes, conditions, surface)* de trabajo; *(week, day, life)* laborable. 2 *(population, partner, etc)* activo,-a; *(person, mother)* que trabaja.
▷ *n (machine, model)* que funciona; *(part)* móvil.
▷ *adj* 1 *(majority)* suficiente. 2 *(hypothesis, etc)* de trabajo.
▷ *n (of machine)* funcionamiento; *(of pit)* explotación *f*.
▷ *n pl* **workings** *(of mine, quarry)* pozos *mpl*. *(mechanics)* funcionamiento.
working-class [wɜ:kıŋ'klɑ:s] *adj (person)* de clase obrera, de clase trabajadora; *(area)* obrero,-a.
workload ['wɜ:kləud] *n* volumen *m* de trabajo.
workman ['wɜ:kmən] *n (gen)* trabajador *m*; *(manual)* obrero, operario.
▲ *pl* **workmen** ['wɛ:kmᵊn].
workmanlike ['wɜ:kmənlaık] *adj (person)* concienzudo,-a, hábil, eficiente; *(work)* bien hecho,-a.
workmanship ['wɜ:kmənʃıp] *n* habilidad *f*, arte *m*, destreza, trabajo: **a fine piece of workmanship** *un trabajo primoroso;* **shoddy workmanship** *trabajo de mala calidad.*
workmate ['wɜ:kmeıt] *n* compañero,-a de trabajo.
work-out ['wɜ:kaut] *n* SP entrenamiento.
workplace ['wɜ:kpleıs] *n* lugar *m* de trabajo.
workroom ['wɜ:kru:m] *n* taller *m*.
work-sharing ['wɜ:kʃeərıŋ] *n* repartición *f* de trabajo.

workshop ['wɜ:kʃɒp] *n* taller *m*.
workshy ['wɜ:kʃaɪ] *adj* gandul,-la, holgazán,-ana, vago,-a.
worktop ['wɜ:ktɒp] *n* encimera.
world [wɜ:ld] *n* **1** *(earth)* mundo: **I'd love to travel round the world** *me encantaría dar la vuelta al mundo.* **2** *(sphere)* mundo: **the world of show business** *el mundo del espectáculo.* **3** *(life)* mundo, vida: **in this world** *en esta vida.* **4** *(people)* mundo: **in the eyes of the world** *a los ojos del mundo.* **5** *(large amount, large number)*: **this will make a world of difference to the disabled** *esto cambiará totalmente la vida de los minusválidos.*
▷ *adj (population, peace)* mundial; *(politics, trade)* internacional: **world record** *récord mundial;* **world power** *potencia mundial.* ■ **out of this world** fenomenal. ● **World Bank** Banco Mundial. ‖ **world champion** campeón,-ona mundial. ‖ **World Cup** el Mundial, los Mundiales. ‖ **world fair** exposición *f* internacional. ‖ **world music** música étnica.
world-class ['wɜ:ld'klɑ:s] [Written **world class** when not used to qualify a noun.] *adj* de categoría mundial.
world-famous ['wɜ:ld'feɪməs] [Written **world famous** when not used to qualify a noun.] *adj* de fama mundial.
worldliness ['wɜ:ldlɪnəs] *n* mundanería.
worldly ['wɜ:ldlɪ] *adj* mundano,-a.
▲ *comp* **worldlier**, *superl* **worldliest**. ● **worldly goods** bienes *mpl* materiales.
world-weary ['wɜ:ldwi:rɪ] *adj* hastiado,-a del mundo.
▲ *comp* **world-wearier**, *superl* **world-weariest**.
worldwide ['wɜ:ldwaɪd] *adj* mundial, universal.
▷ *adv* mundialmente.
worm [wɜ:m] *n* **1** *(grub, maggot)* gusano; *(earthworm)* lombriz *f.* **2** *pej (person)* gusano, canalla. **3** TECH *(of screw)* tornillo.
▷ *vt* **1** *(make one's way)* deslizarse; *(insinuate)* insinuarse (**into**, en). **2** MED quitar las lombrices a, desparasitar.
▷ *n pl* **worms** MED lombrices *fpl*.
⊙ **to worm out** *vt sep (extract)* sacar, sonsacar.
worm-eaten ['wɜ:mi:tᵊn] *adj (wood)* carcomido,-a; *(fruit)* agusanado,-a.
wormwood ['wɜ:mwʊd] *n* ajenjo.
wormy ['wɜ:mɪ] *adj* **1** *(like a worm)* agusanado,-a. **2** *(wood)* carcomido,-a; *(fruit)* agusanado,-a.
▲ *comp* **wormier**, *superl* **wormiest**.
worn [wɔ:n] *pp* → **wear**.
worn-out ['wɔ:n'aʊt] [Written **worn out** when not used to qualify a noun.] *adj* **1** *(thing)* gastado,-a, estropeado,-a. **2** *(person)* rendido,-a, agotado,-a.
worried ['wʌrɪd] *adj (person)* inquieto,-a, preocupado,-a (**about**, por); *(look, voice)* de preocupación.
worrier ['wʌrɪəʳ] *n* sufridor,-ra.
worry ['wʌrɪ] *n (state, feeling)* preocupación *f*, inquietud *f*, intranquilidad *f*; *(problem)* preocupación *f*, problema *m*; *(responsibility)* responsabilidad *f*.
▲ *pl* **worries**.
▷ *vt* **1** inquietar, preocupar. **2** *(annoy, disturb)* molestar. **3** *(of dog)* acosar, perseguir.
▷ *vi* inquietarse, preocuparse (**about/over**, por).
▲ *pt & pp* **worried**, *ger* **worrying**.
worrying ['wʌrɪɪŋ] *adj* inquietante, preocupante, desconcertante.
worse [wɜ:s] *adj (comp of* **bad**) peor.
▷ *adv (comp of badly)* peor; *(more intensely)* más.
▷ *n* lo peor. ■ **to be worse off 1** *(financially)* andar pe de dinero. **2** *(physically)* estar peor. ‖ **to get worse** em peorar. ‖ **to get worse and worse** ir de mal en peor. ‖ **t go from bad to worse** ir de mal en peor. ‖ **to mak matters worse** por si fuera poco.
worsen ['wɜ:sᵊn] *vt* empeorar.
▷ *vi* empeorarse.
worship ['wɜ:ʃɪp] *n* **1** REL adoración *f*, veneración culto; *(service)* culto, oficio. **2** *(devotion, love)* amor *n* culto, idolatría.
▷ *vt* **1** REL adorar, venerar. **2** *(idolize)* rendir culto a, ido latrar.
▷ *vi (attend church)* ir a misa, ser feligrés,-esa.
▲ *pt & pp* **worshipped**, *ger* **worshipping**.
worst [wɜ:st] *adj (superl)* peor.
▷ *adv (superl)* peor.
▷ *n (indefinite)* lo peor; *(person)* el/la peor, los/las peore ■ **at (the) worst** en el peor de los casos. ‖ **if the wors comes to the worst** si pasa lo peor. ‖ **to come off wors** llevarse la peor parte.
worsted ['wʊstəd] *n* SEW estambre *m*.
worth [wɜ:θ] *n* **1** *(in money)* valor *m*. **2** *(of person)* valía *(of thing)* valor *m*.
▷ *adj* **1** *(having certain value)* que vale, que tiene un va lor de. **2** *(deserving of)* que vale la pena, que merec la pena, digno,-a de, merecedor,-ra de. ■ **to ge one's money's worth** sacarle jugo al dinero. ‖ **to b worth** SB**'s while** valer la pena.
worthiness ['wɜ:θɪnəs] *n* mérito.
worthless ['wɜ:θləs] *adj* **1** *(gen)* sin valor. **2** *(useless* inútil, sin ningún valor. **3** *(person)* despreciable.
worthwhile [wɜ:θ'waɪl] *adj (gen)* que vale la pena que merece la pena.
worthy ['wɜ:ðɪ] *adj* **1** *(deserving)* digno,-a (**of**, de), me recedor,-ra (**of**, de), que vale la pena; *(winner, oppo nent, successor)* digno,-a. **2** *(action, cause)* meritorio,-a bueno,-a, justo,-a; *(effort)* meritorio,-a, encomiabl **3** *(citizen)* honorable, admirable, respetable.
▲ *comp* **worthier**, *superl* **worthiest**.
▷ *n iron* prócer *m*, dignatario,-a.
▲ *pl* **worthies**.
would [wʊd] *aux* **1** *(conditional)*: **I would love to** *me en cantaría.* **2** *(polite requests)*: **would you be so kind as t close the window?** *¿me haría usted el favor de cerrar l ventana?* **3** *(offers, invitations)*: **would you like a drink** *¿quieres tomar algo?* **4** *(willingness)*: **he wouldn't hel me** *se negó a ayudarme, no quiso ayudarme.* **5** *(givin advice)*: **I wouldn't dwell on it** *yo que tú no pensaría e ello.* **6** *(conjecture)*: **that would have been in 1978** *es debe haber sido en 1978.* **7** *(past habit, custom)* sole **we would often go out together** *a menudo salíamo juntos.* **8** *(insistence, persistence)*: **you would say that!** *¡e típico de ti decir eso!*
would-be ['wʊdbi:] *adj* **1** *(hopeful)* aspirante a. **2** *p (so-called)* supuesto,-a. **3** *(failed)* frustrado,-a, fraca sado,-a.
wound[1] [wu:nd] *n* herida.
▷ *vt* herir.

wound^2 [waʊnd] *pt & pp* → **wind**^{2}.

wounded ['wu:ndɪd] *adj* herido,-a.
▷ *n pl* **the wounded** los heridos.

wounding ['wu:ndɪŋ] *adj* hiriente.

wove [wəʊv] *pt* → **weave**.

woven ['wəʊvən] *pp* → **weave**.

wrangle ['ræŋgəl] *n* disputa, riña.
▷ *vi* discutir (**about/over**, por), reñir (**about/over**, por).

wrap [ræp] *vt* 1 *(cover)* envolver. 2 *fig (surround, immerse)* envolver (**in**, de), rodear (**in**, de).
▲ *pt & pp* **wrapped**, *ger* **wrapping**.
▷ *n (scarf, shawl)* chal *m*; *(cape)* capa; *(robe)* bata.
⊙ **to wrap up** *vi* 1 *(wear warm clothes)* abrigarse. 2 *(shut up)* callarse, cerrar el pico.
▷ *vt sep (complete)* conseguir; *(conclude)* concluir, dar fin a.

wrapper ['ræpər] *n (of food)* envoltorio, envoltura; *(of book)* sobrecubierta.

wrapping ['ræpɪŋ] *n* envoltura, envoltorio. ■ **wrapping paper** 1 *(plain)* papel *m* de envolver. 2 *(fancy)* papel *m* de regalo.

wrath [rɒθ] *n* cólera, ira.

wreak [ri:k] *vt* causar, provocar, sembrar. ■ **to wreak damage/havoc on** STH hacer estragos en ALGO.

wreath [ri:θ] *n (of flowers)* corona.

wreathe [ri:ð] *vt (circle)* envolver; *(adorn)* adornar; *(crown)* coronar.

wreck [rek] *n* 1 MAR *(action)* naufragio; *(ship)* barco naufragado o hundido. 2 *(of car, plane)* restos *mpl*; *(of building)* ruinas *fpl*, escombros *mpl*. 3 *fig (person)* ruina.
▷ *vt* 1 MAR *(ship)* hacer naufragar. 2 *(car, plane)* destrozar; *(machine)* desbaratar, estropear. 3 *fig (health, career)* arruinar; *(life, marriage)* destrozar; *(hopes)* destruir, echar por tierra; *(plans)* estropear, desbaratar; *(chances)* echar a perder.

wreckage ['rekɪdʒ] *n* 1 *(of vehicle)* restos *mpl*; *(of building)* ruinas *fpl*, escombros *mpl*. 2 *fig* ruina.

wrecked [rekt] *adj* 1 MAR *(ship)* naufragado,-a; *(sailor)* náufrago,-a. 2 *(car, plane)* destrozado,-a; *(building)* destruido,-a.
▷ *n fig (life, career, hopes)* arruinado,-a, destrozado,-a; *(plans)* estropeado,-a.
▷ *adj fam fig (stoned)* ciego,-a, colocado,-a, pasado,-a.

wrecker ['rekər] *n* 1 US *(of building)* demoledor,-ra. 2 US *(breakdown van)* grúa.

wren [ren] *n* chochín *m*.

wrench [rentʃ] *n* 1 *(pull)* tirón *m*, arranque *m*. 2 MED torcedura. 3 *fig* separación *f* dolorosa. 4 GB *(tool)* llave *f* inglesa. 5 US *(tool)* llave *f*.
▲ *pl* **wrenches**.
▷ *vt* 1 *(pull)* arrancar (de un tirón), arrebatar. 2 MED torcer.

wrest [rest] *vt* 1 *(object)* arrancar, arrebatar. 2 *(confession)* sonsacar, arrancar; *(victory, control)* conseguir a duras penas.

wrestle ['resəl] *vi* 1 *(fight)* luchar (**with**, con/contra). 2 *fig (problem, conscience)* luchar (**with**, con), lidiar (**with**, con).
▷ *vt* luchar contra.
▷ *n* lucha.

wrestler ['resələr] *n* SP luchador,-ra.

wrestling ['resəlɪŋ] *n* lucha.

wretch [retʃ] *n* 1 *(unfortunate person)* desdichado,-a, infeliz, desgraciado,-a. 2 *fam (rascal)* pícaro,-a, granuja *mf*. 3 *(bad person)* canalla *mf*, malvado,-a.

wretched ['retʃɪd] *adj* 1 *(condition)* miserable, lamentable. 2 *(unhappy)* desdichado,-a, desgraciado,-a. 3 *(ill)* muy mal, fatal. 4 *fam (very bad)* horrible, malísimo,-a, espantoso,-a. 5 *fam (damned)* maldito,-a, condenado,-a.

wretchedness ['retʃɪdnəs] *n* 1 *(unhappiness, misfortune)* desdicha, desgracia. 2 *(of conditions)* miseria.

wriggle ['rɪgəl] *vi* retorcerse, menearse, moverse.
▷ *vt* menear, mover.
▷ *n* meneo. ■ **to wriggle free** escapar deslizándose, escabullirse.
⊙ **to wriggle out of** *vt insep (situation, responsibility)* librarse hábilmente de, ingeniárselas para librarse de, escaquearse de; *(physically)* escabullirse, escaparse de.

wriggly ['rɪgəlɪ] *adj* sinuoso,-a.
▲ *comp* **wrigglier**, *superl* **wriggliest**.

wring [rɪŋ] *vt* 1 *(one's hands)* torcer, retorcer; *(person's hand)* apretar; *(bird's neck)* retorcer. 2 *(clothes)* escurrir (**out**, -), retorcer (**out**, -). 3 *fig (heart)* partir. 4 *fig (confession, truth, etc)* sonsacar, arrancar, sacar.
▲ *pt & pp* **wrung** [rʌŋ].
▷ *n (of clothes)*: **give it a good wring** *escúrrelo bien*.

wringer ['rɪŋər] *n* escurridor *m*, rodillo.

wringing wet ['rɪŋɪŋwet] *adj (garment)* empapado,-a; *(person)* calado,-a hasta los huesos.

wrinkle ['rɪŋkəl] *n* arruga.
▷ *vt* arrugar.
▷ *vi* arrugarse.

wrinkled ['rɪŋkəld] *adj* arrugado,-a.

wrist [rɪst] *n* 1 ANAT muñeca. 2 *(of clothes)* puño.

wristband ['rɪstbænd] *n* 1 *(of clothes)* puño. 2 *(sweatband)* muñequera.

wristwatch ['rɪstwɒtʃ] *n* reloj *m* de pulsera.
▲ *pl* **wristwatches**.

writ [rɪt] *n* mandato judicial, orden *f* judicial, auto.

write [raɪt] *vt (gen)* escribir; *(article)* redactar; *(cheque)* extender.
▷ *vi (gen)* escribir (**about**, sobre). ■ **to be nothing to write home about** no ser nada del otro mundo. ■ **to be written all over** SB**'s face** llevar (algo) escrito en la cara.
▲ *pt* **wrote** [rəʊt], *pp* **written** ['rɪtən], *ger* **writing**.
⊙ **to write away for** *vt insep* pedir por correo.
⊙ **to write back** *vi* contestar (por carta).
⊙ **to write down** *vt sep (note)* anotar, apuntar.
⊙ **to write in** *vt sep (gen)* escribir; *(include)* incluir.
⊙ **to write in for** *vt insep* escribir pidiendo.
⊙ **to write into** *vt sep (include)* incluir.
⊙ **to write off** *vt sep* 1 *(debt)* anular, saldar. 2 GB *(car)* destrozar. 3 *fig (accept as useless or failure)* dar por acabado,-a, dar por perdido,-a.
⊙ **to write off for** *vt insep* pedir por correo.
⊙ **to write out** *vt sep* 1 *(write in full)* escribir (en su forma completa). 2 *(cheque, receipt, etc)* extender.
⊙ **to write up** *vt sep (notes, minutes, etc)* pasar a limpio; *(describe)* redactar, escribir; *(diary, etc)* poner al día.

write-off ['raɪtɒf] *n* 1 *(car)* ruina, siniestro total. 2 FIN *(debt)* cancelación *f*.

writer ['raɪtəʳ] *n* **1** *(by profession)* escritor,-ra; *(of book, letter)* autor,-ra. **2** *(of handwriting)*: **she's a neat writer** *tiene buena letra.* ● **writer's cramp** agarrotamiento de la mano por escribir.

write-up ['raɪtʌp] *n fam (review)* crítica, reseña.

writhe [raɪð] *vi (physically)* retorcerse, contorsionarse.

writing ['raɪtɪŋ] *n* **1** *(script)* escritura; *(handwriting)* letra. **2** *(written work)* composición *f*, trabajo. **3** *(occupation)* profesión *f* de escritor,-ra, trabajo literario; *(activity)* escribir *m*. ■ **in writing** por escrito. ‖ **the writing on the wall** los malos presagios. ● **writing desk** escritorio. ‖ **writing materials** objetos *mpl* de escritorio. ‖ **writing paper** papel *m* de escribir.

▷ *n pl* **writings** obra, escritos *mpl*.

written ['rɪtᵊn] *adj* escrito,-a. ■ **the written word** la palabra escrita. ● **written consent** consentimiento por escrito. ‖ **written exam** examen *m* escrito.

▲ *pp* ⟶ **write.**

wrong [rɒŋ] *adj* **1** *(erroneous)* erróneo,-a, equivocado,-a, incorrecto,-a: **a wrong answer** *una respuesta incorrecta.* **2** *(mistaken)* equivocado,-a: **we proved him wrong** *demostramos que estaba equivocado.* **3** *(evil, immoral)* malo,-a; *(unacceptable, unfair)* injusto,-a: **stealing is wrong** *robar es malo.* **4** *(amiss)* mal: **is anything wrong?** *¿pasa algo?* **5** *(unsuitable)* inadecuado,-a, impropio,-a; *(time)* inoportuno,-a: **she's the wrong person for the job** *no es la persona adecuada para el puesto;* **I think I said the wrong thing** *creo que he dicho algo que no debía;* **he was in the wrong place at the wrong time** *estaba en el sitio equivocado en el momento inoportuno.*

▷ *adv* mal, incorrectamente, equivocadamente.

▷ *n* **1** *(evil, bad action)* mal *m*. **2** *(injustice)* injusticia; *(offenc* agravio.

▷ *vt (treat unfairly)* ser injusto,-a con; *(judge unfairly)* juzgar mal; *(offend)* agraviar. ■ **to be from the wrong sid of the tracks** ser de los barrios bajos. ‖ **to be in th wrong 1** *(mistaken)* estar equivocado,-a. **2** *(at faul* tener la culpa. ‖ **to be wrong** *(person)* estar equivocado,-a, no tener razón, equivocarse. ‖ **to have/get th wrong number** *(tel)* confundirse de número, equivocarse de número. ‖ **to get** SB **wrong** malinterpretar ALGN. ‖ **to get** STH **wrong** equivocarse, no acertar. ‖ **t go down the wrong hole/way** atragantarse. ‖ **to g wrong 1** *(things in general)* salir mal. **2** *(make a mistak* equivocarse. **3** *(go wrong way)* equivocarse de camino. *(machine, device)* romperse, estropearse. *(plar* fallar, fracasar. ‖ **to right a wrong** deshacer un entueto. ‖ **two wrongs don't make a right** no se subsana u error cometiendo otro. ‖ **wrong side out** al revés. **you can't go wrong** *(giving directions)* no tiene pérdida

wrongdoer ['rɒŋduəʳ] *n* malhechor,-ra.

wrongdoing ['rɒŋduːɪŋ] *n* maldad *f*, fechoría.

wrongful ['rɒŋful] *adj (unfair)* injusto,-a; *(illegal)* ilega

wrongly ['rɒŋlɪ] *adv* **1** *(incorrectly)* mal, incorrectamente. **2** *(mistakenly)* sin razón, equivocadament erróneamente. **3** *(unjustly)* injustamente.

wrote [rəut] *pt* ⟶ **write.**

wrought [rɔːt] *adj* **1** *(iron)* forjado,-a; *(silver)* labrado,- **2** *(made and decorated)* hecho,-a, elaborado,-a, decorado,-a.

▲ *pp arch* ⟶ **work.**

wrung [rʌŋ] *pt & pp* ⟶ **wring.**

wry [raɪ] *adj* irónico,-a, sardónico,-a.

wryness ['raɪnəs] *n* socarronería.

X

, x [eks] *n (the letter)* X, x *f.*
enon ['zenɒn] *n* xenón *m.*
enophobia [zenə'fəʊbɪə] *n* xenofobia.
enophobic [zenə'fəʊbɪk] *adj* xenófobo,-a.
erography [zɪ'rɒgrəfɪ] *n* xerografía.
erox® ['zɪərɒks] *n* xerocopia, fotocopia.
vt xerocopiar, fotocopiar.
X-ray ['eksreɪ] *n* **1** rayo X. **2** *(photograph)* radiografía.
▷ *vt* radiografiar.
xylene ['zaɪliːn] *n* xileno.
xylograph ['zaɪləgrɒːf] *n* xilografía.
xylography [zaɪ'lɒgrəfɪ] *n* xilografía.
xylophone ['zaɪləfəʊn] *n* xilófono.

Y

Y, y [waɪ] *n (the letter)* Y, y *f*.
yacht [jɒt] *n* **1** yate *m*. **2** *(with sails)* velero, yate *m*. ● **yacht club** club *m* náutico. ‖ **yacht race** regata.
yachting ['jɒtɪŋ] *n* deporte *m* de la vela, vela.
yak [jæk] *n* yac *m*, yak *m*.
yam [jæm] *n* ñame *m*.
yank [jæŋk] *n fam* tirón *m*.
▷ *vt fam* tirar de.
⊙ **to yank out** *vt sep* arrancar, sacar de un tirón.
Yaoundé [jæ'uːnde] *n* Yaundé.
yap [jæp] *n (dog)* ladrido, ladrido agudo.
▷ *vi* **1** *(dog)* ladrar. **2** *fam (person)* cotorrear.
▲ *pt & pp* **yapped**, *ger* **yapping**.
yard [jɑːd] *n* **1** *(measure)* yarda. **2** GB *(of house)* patio. **3** US *(of house)* jardín *m*. **4** *(industrial)* almacén *m*. **5** *(naut)* verga. ● **Scotland Yard** *oficina central de la policía británica en Londres*.

Una **yarda** equivale a 0,914 metros.

yardstick ['jɑːdstɪk] *n fig* criterio, norma.
yarn [jɑːn] *n* **1** hilo. **2** *(story)* cuento. ■ **to spin a yarn 1** *(story)* contar un cuento. **2** *(lie)* venir con cuentos.
yawn [jɔːn] *vi* **1** bostezar. **2** *(gap, etc)* abrirse.
▷ *n* **1** bostezo. **2** *fam (boring event)* rollo.
▲ *pl* **yds.**
year [jɪəːʳ] *n* **1** año. **2** EDUC curso. ■ **all the year round** durante todo el año. ‖ **since the year dot** desde el año de la nana. ‖ **to put years on** SB envejecer. ‖ **to take years off** SB rejuvenecer a ALGN. ‖ **year in, year out** año tras año.
yearbook ['jɪəbʊk] *n* anuario.
yearling ['jɪəlɪŋ] *n* primal,-la.
▷ *adj* primal.
yearly ['jɪəlɪ] *adj* anual.
▷ *adv* anualmente.
yearn [jɜːn] *vi (desire)* anhelar (**for**, -), ansiar (**for**, -); *(nostalgically)* añorar. ■ **to yearn to do** STH suspirar por hacer ALGO.
yearning ['jɜːnɪŋ] *n (desire)* anhelo (**for**, de); *(nostalgia)* añoranza (**for**, de).
▷ *adj* anhelante.
yeast [jiːst] *n* levadura.
yell [jel] *n* grito, alarido.
▷ *vi* gritar, dar alaridos.
yellow ['jeləʊ] *adj* **1** amarillo,-a. **2** *(cowardly)* cobarde.
▷ *n* amarillo. ● **yellow card** *(sp)* tarjeta amarilla. ‖ **yellow fever** fiebre *f* amarilla. ‖ **yellow jersey** *(sp)* maillot *m* amarillo. ‖ **yellow line** raya amarilla. ‖ **Yellow Pages** páginas amarillas. ‖ **yellow press** prensa sensacionalista.
▷ *vt* ponerse amarillo.
▷ *vi* amarillear.
yellowhammer ['jeləʊhæməʳ] *n* escribano cerillo.
yelp [jelp] *n* gañido.
▷ *vi* gañir.
Yemen ['jemən] *n* Yemen.
Yemeni ['jemənɪ] *adj* yemení.
▷ *n* yemení *mf*.
yeoman ['ɪəʊmən] *n* HIST pequeño terrateniente *m* ● **yeoman of the guard** alabardero de la Torre de Londres.
yes [jes] *adv* **1** sí. **2** *(answering person)* dime; *(answering phone)* ¿dígame?
▷ *n* sí *m*. ■ **to say yes** decir que sí. ‖ **to say yes to** STH consentir ALGO, decir que sí a ALGO.
yesterday ['jestədɪ] *adv* ayer.
▷ *n* ayer *m*. ● **the day before yesterday** anteayer.
yesteryear ['jestəjɪəʳ] *adv lit* antaño.
yet [jet] *adv* **1** todavía, aún. **2** *(until now)* hasta la fecha, hasta ahora. **3** *(even)* aún, todavía. **4** *(expressing future possibility, hope, etc)* aún: **don't give up, you may win yet** *no te rindas, aún puedes ganar*.
▷ *conj* pero, aunque: **a cheap yet effective solution to the problem** *una solución barata pero efectiva para el problema*. ■ **yet again** otra vez. ‖ **yet another...** otro a... más: **yet another gold medal for Broddle** *otra medalla de oro más para Broddle*.
yew [juː] *n* tejo.
yield [jiːld] *n* **1** *(harvest)* cosecha. **2** FIN *(return)* rendimiento, rédito.
▷ *vt* **1** *(produce)* producir, dar. **2** *(give, hand over)* entregar. **3** FIN rendir.
▷ *vi* **1** *(surrender)* rendirse (**to**, ante), ceder (**to**, a). **2** *(break)* ceder. **3** US ceder el paso.
⊙ **to yield up** *vt sep (secrets)* revelar.
yielding ['jiːldɪŋ] *adj* **1** *(material)* flexible, blando,-a. **2** *(person)* dócil, complaciente.
yodel ['ɪəʊdrl] *vi* cantar a la tirolesa.
▲ *pt & pp* **yodelled** *(*‖us‖ **yodeled***)*, *ger* **yodelling** *(*‖us‖ **yodeling***)*.
yoghourt ['jɒgət] *n* → **yoghurt**.
yoghurt ['jɒgət] *n* yogur *m*.
yogurt ['jɒgət] *n* → **yoghurt**. ● **yogurt maker** yogurtera.
yoke [jəʊk] *n* **1** *(for carrying, pulling)* yugo. **2** *(pair of oxen)* yunta. **3** SEW canesú *m*. **4** *fig* yugo.
▷ *vt* **1** *(oxen)* uncir. **2** *fig* unir.
yolk [jəʊk] *n* yema.
you [juː] *pron* **1** *(subject, familiar, singular)* tú: **and what did you say?** *y tú, ¿qué dijiste?* **2** *(subject, familiar, plural - men)* vosotros; *(- women)* vosotras: **you two where are you going?** *vosotros dos, ¿adónde vais?* **3** *(subject, polite, singular)* usted, Vd., Ud.: **you must wait here until the doctor arrives** *usted debe esperar aquí hasta que llegue el médico*. **4** *(subject, polite, plu-*

ral) ustedes, Vds., Uds.: **you must both wait here** *ustedes dos deben esperar aquí.* **5** *(subject, impersonal)* se, uno: **you can go by coach or train** *se puede ir en tren o en autocar.* **6** *(object, familiar, singular)* te; *(with prep)* ti; *(if prep is* **con***)* contigo: **I'm going with you** *voy contigo.* **7** *(object, familiar, plural)* os; *(with preposition)* vosotros,-as: **I'll go with you** *iré con vosotros.* **8** *(direct object, polite, singular - man)* lo, le; *(- woman)* la; *(with preposition)* usted: **good morning, sir, can I help you?** *buenos días, señor, ¿puedo ayudarlo?* **9** *(direct object, polite, plural - men)* los; *(- women)* las; *(with preposition)* ustedes: **I wanted to talk to you two ladies** *quería hablar con ustedes dos.* **10** *(indirect object, polite, singular)* le: **I'll send you a letter** *le mandaré una carta.* **11** *(indirect object, polite, plural)* les: **I sent both of you a card** *les mandé una felicitación a los dos.* **12** *(object, impersonal)*: **cyanide kills you** *el cianuro mata.*

oung [jʌŋ] *adj (gen)* joven; *(brother, sister)* menor. ■ **to be young at heart** ser joven de espíritu. ● **young lady 1** *(woman)* señorita. **2** *(girlfriend)* novia. ‖ **young man 1** *(man)* joven *m*, muchacho. **2** *(boyfriend)* novio. ‖ **young woman** joven *f*, muchacha.
n **the young** *(humans)* los jóvenes *mpl*, la juventud *f*, la gente *f* joven; *(animals)* las crías *fpl*.

oungish ['jʌŋɪʃ] *adj* bastante joven, juvenil.

oungster ['jʌŋstəʳ] *n* joven *mf*.

our [jɔːʳ] *adj* **1** *(familiar, singular)* tu, tus; *(plural)* vuestro,-a, vuestros,-as. **2** *(polite)* su, sus. **3** *fml (address)* Su: **Your Majesty** *Su Majestad.*

yours [jɔːz] *pron* **1** *(familiar, singular)* (el) tuyo, (la) tuya, (los) tuyos, (las) tuyas; *(plural)* (el) vuestro, (la) vuestra, (los) vuestros, (las) vuestras. **2** *(polite)* (el) suyo, (la) suya, (los) suyos, (las) suyas. **3** *(letters)* le saluda...: **Yours sincerely...** *le saluda atentamente...*

yourself [jɔː'self] *pron* **1** *(familiar singular)* te; *(emphatic)* tú mismo,-a. **2** *(polite singular)* se; *(emphatic)* usted mismo,-a.

yourselves [jɔː'selvz] *pron* **1** *(familiar plural)* os; *(emphatic)* vosotros,-as mismos,-as. **2** *(polite plural)* se; *(emphatic)* ustedes mismos,-as.

youth [juːθ] *n* **1** *(period)* juventud *f*. **2** *(young person)* joven *mf*. **3** *(young people)* juventud *f*, los jóvenes *mpl*. ● **youth club** club *m* juvenil. ‖ **youth hostel** albergue *m* juvenil.

youthful ['juːθful] *adj* joven, juvenil.

youthfulness ['juːθfulnəs] *n* juventud *f*.

yowl [jaul] *n* aullido.
▷ *vi* aullar.

yucca ['jʌkə] *n* yuca.

yucky ['jʌkɪ] *adj fam* asqueroso,-a.
▲ *comp* **yuckier**, *superl* **yuckiest**.

Yugoslav ['juːgəslɑːv] *n (person)* yugoslavo,-a.

Yugoslavia [juːgə'slɑːvɪə] *n* Yugoslavia.

Yugoslavian [juːgə'slɑːvɪən] *adj* yugoslavo,-a.
▷ *n* yugoslavo,-a.

Yule [juːl] *n* Navidad *f*.

Yuletide ['juːltaɪd] *n* → **Yule**.

yuppie ['jʌpɪ] *n* yuppie *mf*.

Z

Z, z [zed] *n (the letter)* Z, z *f*.
Zaire [zɑː'ɪə] *n* Zaire.
Zairean [zɑː'ɪrɪən] *adj* zaireño,-a.
▷ *n* zaireño,-a.
Zambesi [zæm'biːzɪ] *n* el Zambesi *m*.
Zambia ['zæmbɪə] *n* Zambia.
Zambian ['zæmbɪən] *adj* zambiano,-a.
▷ *n* zambiano,-a.
zany ['zeɪnɪ] *adj* **1** *fam* estrafalario,-a. **2** *(mad)* chiflado,-a.
▲ *comp* **zanier**, *superl* **zaniest**.
zap [zæp] *vt* **1** *fam (kill)* cargarse. **2** *(attack)* atacar.
▷ *vi (hurry)* apresurarse.
▲ *pt & pp* **zapped**, *ger* **zapping**.
▷ *n* marcha.
Zapotec ['zæpətek] *adj* zapoteca.
▷ *n* **1** *(person)* zapoteca *mf*. **2** *(language)* zapoteca *m*.
zappy ['zæpɪ] *adj fam* marchoso,-a.
▲ *comp* **zappier**, *superl* **zappiest**.
zeal [ziːl] *n* celo, entusiasmo.
zealot ['zelət] *n* fanático,-a.
zealous ['zeləs] *adj (fanatical)* celoso,-a; *(enthusiastic)* entusiasta.
zebra ['ziːbrə, 'zebrə] *n* cebra. ● **zebra crossing** paso de peatones, paso de cebra.
zebu ['ziːbuː, 'ziːbjuː] *n* cebú *m*.
zed [zed] *n* GB zeta.
zee [ziː] *n* US zeta.
Zen [zen] *n* Zen *m*.
zenith ['zenɪθ] *n* **1** cenit *m*. **2** *fig* apogeo.
zephyr ['zefəʳ] *n* céfiro.
zeppelin ['zeprlɪn] *n* zepelín *m*.
zero ['zɪərəʊ] *n* cero.
▲ *pl* **zeros** o **zeroes**.
zest [zest] *n* **1** *(eagerness)* brío, entusiasmo. **2** *(spice)* emoción *f*. **3** *(of lemon, etc)* cáscara.
zestful ['zestfʊl] *adj* entusiasta.
zigzag ['zɪgzæg] *n* zigzag *m*.
▷ *vi* zigzaguear.
▲ *pt & pp* **zigzagged**, *ger* **zigzagging**.
zilch [zɪltʃ] *n* US *sl* nada, nada de nada.
zillion ['zɪljən] *n fam* cantidad *f*, mogollón *m*.
Zimbabwe [zɪm'bɑːbweɪ] *n* Zimbabwe.
Zimbabwean [zɪm'bɑːbwɪən] *adj* zimbabwense, zimbabuo,-a.
▷ *n* zimbabwense *mf*, zimbabuo,-a.
zinc [zɪŋk] *n* cinc *m*, zinc *m*.
Zion ['zaɪən] *n* Sion *m*.
Zionism ['zaɪənɪzrm] *n* sionismo.
Zionist ['zaɪənɪst] *adj* sionista.
▷ *n* sionista *mf*.
zip [zɪp] *n* **1** cremallera. **2** *fam (energy)* vigor *m*, energía. **3** *fam (hiss)* zumbido.
▷ *vt* COMPUT comprimir. ● **zip code** US código postal. **zip fastener** cremallera.
⊙ **to zip by** *vt insep* pasar como un rayo.
▷ *vi* pasar como un rayo.
⊙ **to zip past** *vt-vi* ⟶ **zip by**.
⊙ **to zip up** *vt sep* cerrar con cremallera.
zipped [zɪpt] *adj* COMPUT comprimido,-a.
zipper ['zɪpəʳ] *n* US cremallera.
zirconite ['zɜːkənaɪt] *n* circonita *f*.
zit [zɪt] *n* US *sl* grano.
zodiac ['zəʊdɪæk] *n* zodiaco, zodíaco.
zombie ['zɒmbɪ] *n* zombi *mf*, zombie *mf*.
zonal ['zəʊnrl] *adj* zonal.
zone [zəʊn] *n* zona.
▷ *vt* dividir en zonas.
zoning ['zəʊnɪŋ] *n* división *f* en zonas.
zonked [zɒnkt] *adj* **1** *fam (exhausted)* reventado,-a, molido,-a. **2** *(drunk)* ciego,-a, colocado,-a. **3** *(drugged)* colocado,-a, flipado,-a.
zoo [zuː] *n* zoo *m*, parque *m* zoológico, zoológico.
▲ *pl* **zoos**.
zoological [ʒʊə'lɒdʒɪkrl] *adj* zoológico,-a.
zoologist [zʊ'ɒlədʒɪst] *n* zoólogo,-a.
zoology [zʊ'ɒlədʒɪ] *n* zoología.
zucchini [zuː'kiːnɪ] *n* US calabacín *m*.
▲ *pl* **zucchini** o **zucchinis**.
zygote ['zaɪɪgəʊt] *n* cigoto.

Español

Inglés

Spanish grammar

lain spelling difficulties

he letters *b* and *v*

hese two letters are pronounced in exactly the same way. The letter **b** is used in all words in which this ound is followed by a consonant: **bruma, blanco, abstenerse**, but the letter **v** is used after **b, d** and **n**: **obvio, dvertir, convencer**. Apart from this there are no general rules which govern their use; in case of doubt check the dictionary.

he letters *c*, *k* and *q*

hese three letters are used to represent the sound [k]. Before the vowels **a, o, u**, before a consonant, and in ome cases at the end of a word **c** is used: **casa, color, cuna, frac**. Before the vowels **e** or **i**, **qu** is written: **querer, uitar**. The letter **k** is used in words of foreign origin in which the original spelling has been maintained: **tsch**.

he letters *c* and *z*

hese two letters are used to represent the sound [θ]. Before the vowels **e** and **i** the letter **c** is used; before the owels **a, o, u** and at the end of a word **z** is used: **cero, cima, zapato, azote, zurra, pez**. There are a few xceptions to this rule: **zigzag, zipizape, ¡zis, zas!** Some words may also be written with either **c** or **z**: **ácimo/ zimo, acimut/azimut, eccema/eczema, ceta/zeta, cinc/zinc**.

ote that a final **z** changes to **c** in the plural: **pez ⟶ peces**.

he letters *g* and *j*

he letter **j** is always pronounced [x] (as in the Scottish "loch").

he letter **g** is pronounced [x] when it is followed by the vowels **e** and **i**, but [g] (as in "golf", "get") when it followed by the vowels **a, o** or **u**.

the group **gu + e/i** the **u** is silent and the pronunciation is [g], but when **gu** is followed by **a** or **o** the **u** is ronounced giving the sound [gw].

he group **gü**, with a dieresis over the **u**, is written only before **e** or **i**, and is pronounced [gw].

o summarize:

the sound [x] is written	**j**	before **a, o** and **u**
	j or **g**	before **e** and **i**
the sound [g] is written	**g**	before **a, o, u**
	gu	before **i** and **e**
the sound [gw] is written	**gu**	before **a** and **o**
	gü	before **e** and **i**.

he letters *r* and *rr*

he letter **r** is used to represent two different sounds: the one-tap [r] sound when it appears either in the iddle of a word or in the final position: **carta, ardor**; and the multiple vibrant [rr] when it appears in initial osition or follows the consonants **l, n** or **s**: **roca, honra**.

he double **rr** always represents the multiple vibrant [rr] sound and is written only between vowels: **barro, orrar**.

tress in Spanish

he written accent

Vords stressed on the final syllable require a written accent on that syllable when they end in a vowel or the onsonants **n** or **s**:

vendrá, café, jabalí, miró, tabú, sillón, Tomás, chochín

ut **calor, carril, merced, sagaz, carcaj**.

Words stressed on the penultimate syllable require a written accent on that syllable whenever the wor does not end in a vowel or the consonants **n** or **s**:

árbol, inútil, fémur, Gómez, fútbol
but **cosa, venden, acento, examen, pisos.**

Words stressed on the antepenultimate syllable or earlier always require a written accent on the stresse syllable:

pájaro, carámbano, cómpratelo, pagándoselas.

Generally speaking, monosyllabic words do not require written accents, but in some cases one is used t distinguish two different words with the same spelling: **él** (he, him) - **el** (the); **té** (tea) - **te** (the letter T). Thes will be found in the dictionary.

Note that in the case of adverbs ending in **-mente** any written accent in the root adjective is retained:

fácil → **fácilmente; económico** → **económicamente**

Diphthongs, triphthongs and hiatus

A group of two vowels that make one syllable is called a diphthong; a group of three is called a triphthon A diphthong is formed by one weak vowel (**i** or **u**) in combination with one strong vowel (**a**, **e** or **o**). triphthong is one strong vowel be tween two weak ones. As far as stress is concerned the general rule apply, with both diphthongs and triphthongs being treated as if they were one syllable. If a stresse dipththong or triphthong requires a written accent (following the rules above), this is placed above th strong vowel:

miércoles, acariciéis.

Hiatus occurs when groups of consecutive vowels do not form diphthongs or triphthongs. In these case the group is usually made up of strong vowels; the stressed vowel will carry a written accent or not i accordance with the rules above: **neón, tebeo, traéis**. However, when the stressed vowel is a weak vowel, it the weak vowel which carries the written accent in order to distinguish the group from a diphthong c triphthong:

María, reían, frío.

The combination **ui** is always considered a diphthong: **contribuir, ruin.**

The article

	definite		indefinite	
	masculine	femenine	masculine	masculine
singular	el	la	un	una
plural	los	las	unos	unas

Observations

With reflexive verbs the definite article is equivalent to an English possessive adjective in sentences such as

me lavo la cara *(I wash my face)* **cámbiate de ropa** *(change your clothes)*

The definite article may acquire the pronominal value of the English "the one" or "the ones": **el del traje azu** *(the one in the blue suit)*.

The masculine article (**el, un**) is used with feminine nouns which begin with a stressed **a-** or **ha-**, when thes are used in the singular: **el agua, un hacha**. Note however that the plural forms are regular: **las aguas, una hachas**. Nouns which behave in this way are marked in the dictionary.

The prepositions **a** and **de** and the article **el** contract to give the forms **al** and **del**.

There is also a neuter article **lo** which may be used with an adjective to signify a general quality:

me gusta lo bello	*(I like all that is beautiful)*
lo extraño es que...	*(what is strange is that ..., the strange thing is that ...)*

he noun

ender indication in the dictionary

nlike their English counterparts, Spanish nouns have grammatical gender. In this dictionary the gender of ery Spanish headword is given, but in the translations on the English-Spanish side, unmarked nouns ding in **-o** are to be taken to be masculine and those ending in **-a** are to be taken to be feminine; gender is arked in those cases where this does not apply.

asculine and feminine forms

many cases gender is shown by the ending which is added to the root. Nouns denoting men or male imals commonly end in **-o** while their counterparts denoting women and female animals end in **-a**:

chico → chica, gato → gata.

asculine nouns ending in a consonant add **-a** to form the feminine: **señor → señora.**

ome nouns denoting persons have the same form for both sexes. In these cases the gender is indicated only the article used: **un pianista** *(a male pianist)*; **una pianista** *(a female pianist)*.

the case of some nouns denoting animals gender is not indicated by the article but by placing the word **acho** or **hembra** after the noun: **una serpiente** *(a snake)*; **una serpiente macho** *(a male snake)*; **una serpiente embra** *(a female snake)*.

some cases a change in gender signifes a change in meaning. For example, **la cólera** means "anger" and **el lera**, "cholera". Such changes of meaning will be found in the dictionary. However there are a very few ords which are either masculine or feminine with no change in meaning whatever. Two examples are **mar** d **azúcar**; one may say **el mar está agitado** or **la mar está agitada**. Words of this type are marked *nm & nf* in e dictionary.

rmation of the plural

ouns whose plural is formed by adding **-s** are:

— those ending in an unstressed vowel: **pluma, plumas.**
— those ending in a stressed **-é**: **bebé, bebés.**

ouns whose plural is formed by adding **-es** are:

— the names of vowels: **a, aes; i, íes; o, oes; u, úes.**
— nouns ending in a consonant or stressed **-i**: **color → colores; anís → anises.**

hen a compound noun is written as separate elements only the first element indicates the plural:

ojos de buey, patas de gallo.

ll irregular plurals are indicated at the appropriate entries in the dictionary.

he adjective

he adjective usually goes after the noun, and agrees with it in gender and number:

un coche rojo; las chicas guapas.

owever, indefinite, interrogative and exclamative adjectives are placed before the noun, as are adjectives xpressing cardinal numbers:

¡qué vergüenza!; ¿cuántos leones hay?; hay treinta leones.

rmation of the masculine and feminine

ost adjectives have a double ending, one for the feminine and one for the masculine. The common are ose ending in **-o/-a, -or/-ora** and those ending in or **-és/-esa** formed from place names: **guapo,-a, trabajador, ra, arcelones,-esa.**

Some, however, have a single ending: those which end in **-a, -e, -i, -í, -n, -l, -r, -s, -z** and **-ista**:

alegre, marroquí, común, fiel, familiar, cortés, capaz.

Formation of the plural

The adjective follows the same rules as are given for the noun above.

Comparative and superlative

The comparative is formed with **más ... que** or **menos ... que**:

Pedro es más alto que Alberto
los perros corren menos que los tigres.

When **que** in a comparative expression is followed by a verb, it is replaced by **de lo que**:

esto es más complicado de lo que parece.

The English comparative phrases "as ... as" and "so ... as" are rendered by **tan ... como**:

mi patio es tan grande como el tuyo.

The superlative is formed with **el más ... de** or **el menos ... de**:

el chico más listo de la clase.

The absolute superlative is formed by placing **muy** before the adjective or by adding the suffix **-ísimo/-ísima**:

muy preocupado, preocupadísimo.

Observations

A few adjectives have special forms for the comparative and superlative:

	comparative	superlative
bueno,-a	mejor	óptimo
malo,-a	peor	pésimo,-a
grande	mayor	mayor

Comparative and superlative forms ending in **-or** do not change when forming the feminine singular: la mejor solución.

Demonstrative adjectives

		near me	near you	away from both
masculine	singular	este	ese	aquel
	plural	estos	esos	aquellos
femenine	singular	esta	esa	aquella
	plural	estas	esas	aquellas

'ossessive adjectives

one possessor		yo		tú		él, ella, usted	
masculine possession	singular plural	mi mis	mío míos	tu tus	tuyo tuyos	su sus	suyo suyos
femenine possession	singular plural	mi mis	mía mías	tu tus	tuya tuyas	su sus	suya suyas

Iote that the forms on the left are those which precede the noun; those on the right follow it:

es mi pariente ⟶ es pariente mía
son sus problemas ⟶ son problemas suyos

several possessors		nosotros,-as	vosotros,-as	ellos,-as, ustedes	
masculine possession	singular plural	nuestro nuestros	vuestro vuestros	su sus	suyo suyos
femenine possession	singular plural	nuestra nuestras	vuestra vuestras	su sus	suya suyas

'he pronoun

'emonstrative pronouns

		near me	near you	away from both
masculine	singular plural	éste éstos	ése ésos	aquél aquellos
femenine	singular plural	ésta éstas	ésa ésas	aquélla aquéllas
neuter	singular	esto	eso	aquello

hese are used to convey the distance between the person or thing they represent and the speaker or peakers: **no viajaré en este coche, viajaré en aquél.**

'ossessive pronouns

one possessor		yo	tú	él, ella, usted
masculine possession	singular plural	mío míos	tuyo tuyos	suyo suyos
femenine possession	singular plural	mía mías	tuya tuyas	suya suyas

ike the adjective, the possessive pronoun agrees with the noun denoting the thing possessed: **esta camisa es ía, la tuya está en el armario.**

several possessors		nosotros,-as	vosotros,-as	ellos,-as, ustedes
masculine possession	singular plural	nuestro nuestros	vuestro vuestros	suyo suyos
femenine possession	singular plural	nuestra nuestras	vuestra vuestras	suya suyas

Personal pronouns

The following table shows recommended use, although in colloquial Spanish variations will be encountered.

subject	strong object	weak object	
		direct	indirect
yo	mí	me	me
tú	ti	te	te
él	él	lo	le
ella	ella	la	le
usted *m*	usted	lo	le
usted *f*	usted	la	le
nosotros,-as	nosotros,-as	nos	nos
vosotros,-as	vosotros,-as	os	os
ellos	ellos	los	les
ellas	ellas	las	les
ustedes *m pl*	ustedes	las	les
ustedes *f pl*	ustedes	las	les

Use

The Spanish subject pronoun is used only for emphasis or to prevent ambiguity as the person of the subjec is already conveyed by the verb. When neither of these reasons for its use exists, its presence in the sentenc renders the style heavy and is to be avoided.

The strong object pronouns are always used as complements or objects preceded by a preposition:

> **esta carta es para ti, aquélla es para mí**
> **¿son de ustedes estos papeles?**

Weak object pronouns precede a verb or are suffixed to an infinitive, imperative or gerund:

> **lo tienes que hacer; tienes que hacerlo; haciéndolo así se gana tiempo; ¡hazlo ya!**

When several weak pronouns accompany the verb, whether preceding or following it, the second and firs person pronouns come before the third: **póntelo; se lo ha dicho**. The pronoun se always precedes the others **pónselo**.

Note that while it is considered acceptable to use **le** as a weak object pronoun instead of **lo** when a man is being referred to, this is incorrect when referring to women or to objects of either gender, the same is true c **les** instead of **los**:

	direct object	indirect object
(el jarrón)	lo tiró a la basura	le quitó el asa
(Domingo)	acabo de conocerlo/le	le di mil pesetas
(María)	la vimos ayer	le dio un abrazo
(la botella)	la he descorchado	le he sacado el tapón
(los niños)	hay que escucharlos/les	les compraron muchos juguetes
(Pepe y Jaime)	los/les invitó a cenar	les concedieron un premio

(las plantas)	**estaba regándolas**	**tendría que quitarles las hojas secas**
(Ana y Bea)	**las llamé por teléfono**	**les pediré disculpas**

e may also be an impersonal subject equivalent to the English "one", "you", "they", "people" or the passive oice:

hay tantos accidentes porque se conduce demasiado rápido.

Vhen **le** and **les** precede another third person pronoun they are replaced by **se** as in **se lo mandaron**. It is ıcorrect to say **le lo mandaron**.

sted and **ustedes** are the second person pronouns used for courtesy. The accompanying verb is in the third erson.

os is used in several Latin American countries instead of **tú**.

'he preposition

ieneral

'he most usual Spanish prepositions are: **a, ante, bajo, cabe, con, contra, de, desde, en, entre, hacia, hasta, para, or, según, sin, so, sobre, tras**. Consult the dictionary for their use.

ses of *por* and *para*

'he basic difference between these prepositions is that **por** looks back to the roots, origins or causes of a ıing, while **para** looks forwards to the result, aim, goal or destination.

or is used to express:

- cause, reason, motive (usually to say why something has happened): **lo hizo por amor**.
- the period in which the action takes place: **vendrán por la mañana**.
- the place where the action takes place: **pasean por la calle**.
- the means: **lo enviaron por avión**.
- the agent of the passive voice: **el incendio fue provocado por el portero**.
- substitution, equivalence: **aquí puedes comer por mil pesetas**.
- distribution, proportion: **cinco por ciento; trescientas pesetas por persona**.
- multiplication and measurements: **cinco por dos son diez**.
- "in search of" with verbs of movement (**ir, venir** ...): **voy por pan**.
- **estar + por +** infinitive expresses:
  - an action still to be performed: **la cena está por hacer**.
  - an action on the point of being performed: **estaba por llamarte**.
- **tener/dar + por** expresses opinion: **lo dieron por perdido**.

ara is used to express:

- purpose: **esto sirve para limpiar los cristales**
- finality, destiny (often in the future): **es para tu padre, compra pescado para la cena**.
- direction of movement, i.e. "towards": **salen para Valencia**.
- deadlines: **lo quiero para mañana**.
- comparison: **es muy alta para la edad que tiene**.
- **estar + para +** infinitive expresses imminence: **está para llegar**.

'he adverb

osition of the adverb

.s a rule, when the word to be qualified is an adjective or an adverb, the adverb is placed immediately efore it: **un plato bien cocinado**.

When the word to be qualified is a verb, the adverb may be placed before or after it:

> **hoy iré al mercado; iré al mercado hoy.**

Negative adverbs are always placed before the verb:

> **no lo he visto; nunca volverás a verme.**

Very rarely, adverbs may be placed between the auxiliary verb and the principal verb:

> **ha llegado felizmente a su destino.**

The verb

Moods

Spanish verbs have three moods, the *indicative*, *subjunctive* and *imperative*.
The indicative is generally used to indicate real actions. It is mainly used in independent statements:

> **los coches circulan por la calzada.**

The subjunctive is mainly used in subordinate statements where the actions are considered to be potenti[al] or doubtful, but not real: **es posible que venga**; or else necessary or desired:

> **¡ojalá venga!**

The imperative is used to express orders:

> **¡Ven!; ¡Venid pronto!.**

In negative imperatives the subjunctive is used:

> **¡No vengas!**

Person

The endings of verbs vary according to whether the subject is the first, second or third person, singular o[r] plural (see *Personal pronouns*). While in English it is not possible to omit the subject, this is quite common i[n] Spanish since the ending of the verb indicates the subject.

Formation of tenses

For the formation of all tenses of both regular and irregular verbs see the Spanish verb conjugation tables a[t] the end of this section.

Pronominal or reflexive verbs

Pronominal or reflexive verbs are those which are conjugated with a personal pronoun functioning as complement, coinciding in person with the subject: for example the verb **cambiar** has a pronominal for[m] which is **cambiarse:**

> **cambia moneda; se cambia de ropa.**

The personal pronouns (**me, te, se, nos, os, se**) are placed before the verb in all tenses and persons of th[e] indicative and subjunctive moods, but are suffixed onto the infinitive, gerund and imperative.
In compound tenses the pronoun is placed immediately before the auxiliary verb.

The passive voice

The passive voice in Spanish is formed with the auxiliary verb **ser** and the past participle of the conjugatin[g] verb:

> **el cazador hirió al jabalí ⟶ el jabalí fue herido por el cazador.**

The use of this form of passive statement is less frequent than in English. However, another construction the reflexive (or impersonal) passive is quite common:

se vende leña; se alquilan apartamentos; se habla inglés.

Uses of *ser* and estar

The English verb "to be" may be rendered in Spanish by two verbs: ser and estar.

When followed by a noun:

— ser is used without a preposition to indicate occupation or profession:
Jaime es el director de ventas *(Jaime is the sales manager)*
Eduardo es médico *(Eduardo is a doctor)*.

— ser with the preposition de indicates origin or possession:

soy de Salamanca *(I am from Salamanca)*.
es de Alberto *(it is Alberto's)*

— ser with para indicates destination:

el disco es para Pilar *(the record is for Pilar)*.

— estar cannot be followed directly by a noun, it always takes a preposition and the meaning is dictated by the preposition. It is worth noting, however, its special use with de to indicate that someone is performing a function which thet do not usually perform:

Andrés está de secretario *(Andrés is acting as secretary)*

Where the verb is followed by an adjective:

— ser expresses a permanent or inherent quality:

Jorge es rubio; sus ojos son grandes.

— estar expresses a quality which is neither permanent nor inherent:

Mariano está resfriado; el cielo está nublado.

Sometimes both verbs may be used with the same adjective, but there is a change of meaning. For example, Lorenzo es bueno means that Lorenzo is a good man but Lorenzo está bueno means either that he is no longer ill or, colloquially, that he is good-looking.

Finally, estar is used to indicate position and geographical location:

tu cena está en el microondas; Tafalla está en Navarra.

Spanish verb conjugation tables

Models for the conjugation of regular verbs

Simple tenses

1st conjugation – **AMAR**

Present indicative	amo, amas, ama, amamos, amáis, aman.
Preterite	amé, amaste, amó, amamos, amasteis, amaron.
Imperfect indicative	amaba, amabas, amaba, amábamos, amabais, amaban.
Future indicative	amaré, amarás, amará, amaremos, amaréis, amarán.
Conditional	amaría, amarías, amaría, amaríamos, amaríais, amarían.
Present subjunctive	ame, ames, ame, amemos, améis, amen.
Imperfect subjunctive	amara, amaras, amara, amáramos, amarais, amaran; amase, amases, amase, amásemos, amaseis, amasen.
Future subjunctive	amare, amares, amare, amáremos, amareis, amaren.
Imperative	ama (tú), ame (él/Vd.), amemos (nos.) amad (vos.) amen (ellos/Vds.).
Gerund	amando.
Past participle	amado,-a.

2nd conjugation – **TEMER**

Present indicative	temo, temes, teme, tememos, teméis, temen.
Preterite	temí, temiste, temió, temimos, temisteis, temieron.
Imperfect indicative	temía, temías, temía, temíamos, temíais, temían.
Future indicative	temeré, temerás, temerá, temeremos, temeréis, temerán.
Conditional	temería, temerías, temería, temeríamos, temeríais, temerían.
Present subjunctive	tema, temas, tema, temamos, temáis, teman.
Imperfect subjunctive	temiera, temieras, temiera, temiéramos, temierais, temieran; temiese, temieses, temiese, temiésemos, temieseis, temiesen.
Future subjunctive	temiere, temieres, temiere, temiéremos, temiereis, temieren.
Imperative	teme (tú), tema (él/Vd.), temamos (nos.) temed (vos.) teman (ellos/Vds.).
Gerund	temiendo.
Past participle	temido,-a.

3rd conjugation – **PARTIR**

Present indicative	parto, partes, parte, partimos, partís, parten.
Preterite	partí, partiste, partió, partimos, partisteis, partieron.
Imperfect indicative	partía, partías, partía, partíamos, partíais, partían.
Future indicative	partiré, partirás, partirá, partiremos, partiréis, partirán.
Conditional	partiría, partirías, partiría, partiríamos, partiríais, partirían.
Present subjunctive	parta, partas, parta, partamos, partáis, partan.
Imperfect subjunctive	partiera, partieras, partiera, partiéramos, partierais, partieran; partiese, partieses, partiese, partiésemos, partieseis, partiesen.
Future subjunctive	partiere, partieres, partiere, partiéremos, partiereis, partieren.
Imperative	parte (tú), parta (él/Vd.), partamos (nos.) partid (vos.) partan (ellos/Vds.).
Gerund	partiendo.
Past participle	partido,-a.

Note that the imperative proper has forms for the second person (*tú* and *vosotros*) only; all other forms are taken from the present subjunctive.

Compound tenses

Present Perfect	he, has, ha, hemos, habeis, han	amado / temido / partido
Pluperfect	había, habías, había, habíamos, habíais, habían	amado / temido / partido
Future Perfect	habré, habrás, habrá, habremos, habreis, habrán	amado / temido / partido
Conditional Perfect	habría, habrías, habría, habríamos, habríais, habrían	amado / temido / partido
Past Anterior	hube, hubiste, hubo, hubimos, hubisteis, hubieron	amado / temido / partido
Present Perfect subjunctive	haya, hayas, haya, hayamos, hayáis, hayan	amado / temido / partido
Pluperfect subjunctive	hubiera, hubieras, hubiera, hubiéramos, hubierais, hubieranhubiese, hubieses, hubiese, hubiésemos, hubieseis, hubiesen.	amado / temido / partido

Models for the conjugation of irregular verbs

Only the tenses which present irregularities are given here; other tenses follow the regular models above. Irregularities are shown in bold type.

1. SACAR (c *changes to* qu *before* e)
Preterite **saqué**, sacaste, sacó, sacamos, sacasteis, sacaron.
Present subjunctive **saque, saques, saque, saquemos, saquéis, saquen.**
Imperative saca (tú), **saque** (él/Vd.), **saquemos** (nos.), sacad (vos.), **saquen** (ellos/Vds.).

2. MECER (c *changes to* z *before* a *and* o)
Present indicative **mezo**, meces, mece, mecemos, mecéis, mecen.
Present subjunctive **meza, mezas, meza, mezamos, mezáis, mezan.**
Imperative mece (tú), **meza** (él/Vd.), **mezamos** (nos.), meced (vos.), **mezan** (ellos/Vds.).

3. ZURCIR (c *changes to* z *before* a *and* o)
Present indicative **zurzo**, zurces, zurce, zurcimos, zurcís, zurcen.
Present subjunctive **zurza, zurzas, zurza, zurzamos, zurzáis, zurzan.**
Imperative zurce (tú), **zurza** (él/Vd.), **zurzamos** (nos.), zurcid (vos.), **zurzan** (ellos/Vds.).

4. REALIZAR (z *changes to* c *before* e)
Preterite **realicé**, realizaste, realizó, realizamos, realizasteis, realizaron.
Present subjunctive **realice, realices, realice, realicemos, realicéis, realicen.**
Imperative realiza (tú), **realice** (él/Vd.), **realicemos** (nos.), realizad (vos.), **realicen** (ellos/Vds.).

5. PROTEGER (g *changes to* j *before* a *and* o)
Present indicative **protejo**, proteges, protege, protegemos, protegéis, protegen.
Present subjunctive **proteja, protejas, proteja, protejamos, protejáis, protejan.**
Imperative protege (tú), **proteja** (él/Vd.), **protejamos** (nos.), proteged (vos.), **protejan** (ellos/Vds.).

6. DIRIGIR (g *changes to* j *before* a *and* o)
Present indicative **dirijo**, diriges, dirige, dirigimos, dirigís, dirigen.
Present subjunctive **dirija, dirijas, dirija, dirijamos, dirijáis, dirijan.**
Imperative dirige (tú), **dirija** (él/Vd.), **dirijamos** (nos.), dirigid (vos.), **dirijan** (ellos/Vds.).

7. LLEGAR (g *changes to* gu *before* e)
Preterite **llegué**, llegaste, llegó, llegamos, llegasteis, llegaron.
Present subjunctive **llegue, llegues, llegue, lleguemos, lleguéis, lleguen.**
Imperative llega (tú), **llegue** (él/Vd.), **lleguemos** (nos.), llegad (vos.), **lleguen** (ellos/Vds.).

8. DISTINGUIR (gu *changes to* g *before* a *and* o)
Present indicative **distingo**, distingues, distingue, distinguimos, distinguís, distinguen.
Present subjunctive **distinga, distingas, distinga, distingamos, distingáis, distingan.**
Imperative distingue (tú), **distinga** (él/Vd.), **distingamos** (nos.), distinguid (vos.), **distingan** (ellos/Vds.).

9. DELINQUIR (qu *changes to* c *before* a *and* o)

Present indicative **delinco**, delinques, delinque, delinquimos, delinquís, delinquen.
Present subjunctive **delinca, delincas, delinca, delincamos, delincáis, delincan.**
Imperative delinque (tú), **delinca** (él/Vd.), **delincamos** (nos.), delinquid (vos.), **delincan** (ellos/Vds.).

10. ADECUAR* (*unstressed or stressed* u)

Present indicative **adecuo** o **adecúo**, **adecuas** o **adecúas**, **adecua** o **adecúa**, **adecuamos**, **adecuáis**, **adecuan** o **adecúan**.
Present subjunctive **adecue** o **adecúe**, **adecues** o **adecúes**, **adecue** o **adecúe**, **adecuemos**, **adecuéis**, **adecuen** o **adecúen**.
Imperative **adecua** (tú) o **adecúa** (tú), **adecue** (él/Vd.) o **adecúe** (él/Vd.), **adecuemos** (nos.), **adecuad** (vos.), **adecuen** (ellos/Vds.) o **adecúen** (ellos).

11. ACTUAR (*stressed* ú *in certain persons of certain tenses*)

Present indicative **actúo, actúas, actúa**, actuamos, actuáis, **actúan**.
Present subjunctive **actúe, actúes, actúe**, actuemos, actuéis, **actúen**.
Imperative **actúa** (tú), **actúe** (él/Vd.), actuemos (nos.), actuad (vos.), **actúen** (ellos/Vds.).

12. CAMBIAR* (*unstressed* i)

Present indicative **cambio, cambias, cambia, cambiamos, cambiáis, cambian.**
Present subjunctive **cambie, cambies, cambie, cambiemos, cambiéis, cambien.**
Imperative **cambia** (tú), **cambie** (él/Vd.), **cambiemos** (nos.), **cambiad** (vos.), **cambien** (ellos/Vds.).

13. DESVIAR (*stressed* í *in certain persons of certain tenses*)

Present indicative **desvío, desvías, desvía**, desviamos, desviáis, **desvían**.
Present subjunctive **desvíe, desvíes, desvíe**, desviemos, desviéis, **desvíen**.
Imperative **desvía** (tú), **desvíe** (él/Vd.), desviemos (nos.), desviad (vos.), **desvíen** (ellos/Vds.).

14. AUXILIAR (i *may be stressed* or *unstressed*)

Present indicative **auxilío, auxilías, auxilía**, auxiliamos, auxiliáis, **auxilían**.auxilio, auxilias, auxilia, auxiliamos, auxiliáis, auxilian.
Present subjunctive **auxilíe, auxilíes, auxilíe**, auxiliemos, auxiliéis, **auxilíen**.auxilie, auxilies, auxilie, auxiliemos, auxiliéis, auxilien.
Imperative **auxilía** (tú), **auxilíe** (él/Vd.), auxiliemos (nos.), auxiliad, (vos.), **auxilíen** (ellos/Vds.), auxilia (tú), auxilie (él/Vd.), auxiliemos (nos.), auxiliad (vos.), auxilien (ellos/Vds.).

15. AISLAR (*stressed* í *in certain persons of certain tenses*)

Present indicative **aíslo, aíslas, aísla**, aislamos, aisláis, **aíslan**.
Present subjunctive **aísle, aísles, aísle**, aislemos, aisléis, **aíslen**.
Imperative **aísla** (tú), **aísle** (él/Vd.), aislemos (nos.), aislad (vos.), **aíslen** (ellos/Vds.).

16. AUNAR (*stressed* ú *in certain of persons certain tenses*)

Present indicative **aúno, aúnas, aúna**, aunamos, aunáis, **aúnan**.
Present subjunctive **aúne, aúnes, aúne**, aunemos, aunéis, **aúnen**.
Imperative **aúna** (tú), **aúne** (él/Vd.), aunemos (nos.), aunad (vos.), **aúnen** (ellos/Vds.).

17. DESCAFEINAR (*stressed* í *in certain persons of certain tenses*)

Present indicative **descafeíno, descafeínas, descafeína**, descafeinamos, descafeináis, **descafeínan**.
Present subjunctive **descafeíne, descafeínes, descafeíne**, descafeinemos, descafeinéis, **descafeínen**.
Imperative **descafeína** (tú), **descafeíne** (él/Vd.), descafeinemos (nos.), descafeinad (vos.), **descafeínen** (ellos/Vds.).

18. REHUSAR (*stressed* ú *in certain persons of certain tenses*)

Present indicative **rehúso, rehúsas, rehúsa**, rehusamos, rehusáis, **rehúsan**.
Present subjunctive **rehúse, rehúses, rehúse**, rehusemos, rehuséis, **rehúsen**.
Imperative **rehúsa** (tú), **rehúse** (él/Vd.), rehusemos (nos.), rehusad (vos.), **rehúsen** (ellos/Vds.).

19. REUNIR *(stressed* ú *in certain persons of certain tenses)*
Present indicative **reúno**, **reúnes**, **reúne**, reunimos, reunís, **reúnen**.
Present subjunctive **reúna**, **reúnas**, **reúna**, reunamos, reunáis, **reúnan**.
Imperative **reúne** (tú), **reúna** (él/Vd.), reunamos (nos.), reunid (vos.), **reúnan** (ellos/Vds.).

20. AMOHINAR *(stressed* í *in certain persons of certain tenses)*
Present indicative **amohíno**, **amohínas**, **amohína**, amohinamos, amohináis, **amohínan**.
Present subjunctive **amohíne**, **amohínes**, **amohíne**, amohinemos, amohinéis, **amohínen**.
Imperative **amohína** (tú), **amohíne** (él/Vd.), amohinemos (nos.), amohinad (vos.), **amohínen** (ellos/Vds.).

21. PROHIBIR *(stressed* í *in certain persons of certain tenses)*
Present indicative **prohíbo**, **prohíbes**, **prohíbe**, prohibimos, prohibís, **prohíben**.
Present subjunctive **prohíba**, **prohíbas**, **prohíba**, prohibamos, prohibáis, **prohíban**.
Imperative **prohíbe** (tú), **prohíba** (él/Vd.), prohibamos (nos.), prohibid (vos.), **prohíban** (ellos/Vds.).

22. AVERIGUAR *(unstressed* u*;* gu *changes to* gü *before* e*)*
Preterite **averigüé**, averiguaste, averiguó, averiguamos, averiguasteis, averiguaron.
Present subjunctive **averigüe**, **averigües**, **averigüe**, **averigüemos**, **averigüéis**, **averigüen**.
Imperative averigua (tú), **averigüe** (él/Vd.), **averigüemos** (nos.), averiguad (vos.), **averigüen** (ellos/Vds.).

23. AHINCAR *(stressed* í *in certain persons of certain tenses; the* c *changes to* qu *before* e*)*
Present indicative **ahínco**, **ahíncas**, **ahínca**, ahincamos, ahincáis, **ahíncan**.
Preterite **ahinqué**, ahincaste, ahincó, ahincamos, ahincasteis, ahincaron.
Present subjunctive **ahínque**, **ahínques**, **ahínque**, **ahinquemos**, **ahinquéis**, **ahínquen**.
Imperative **ahínca** (tú), **ahínque** (él/Vd.), **ahinquemos** (nos.), ahincad (vos.), **ahínquen** (ellos/Vds.).

24. ENRAIZAR *(stressed* í *in certain persons of certain tenses; the* z *changes to* c *before* e*)*
Present indicative **enraízo**, **enraízas**, **enraíza**, enraizamos, enraizáis, **enraízan**.
Preterite **enraicé**, enraizaste, enraizó, enraizamos, enraizasteis, enraizaron.
Present subjunctive **enraíce**, **enraíces**, **enraíce**, **enraicemos**, **enraicéis**, **enraícen**.
Imperative **enraíza** (tú), **enraíce** (él/Vd.), **enraicemos** (nos.), enraizad (vos.), **enraícen** (ellos/Vds.).

25. CABRAHIGAR *(stressed* í *in certain persons of certain tenses; the* g *changes to* gu *before* e*)*
Present indicative **cabrahígo**, **cabrahígas**, **cabrahíga**, cabrahigamos, cabrahigáis, **cabrahígan**.
Preterite **cabrahigué**, cabrahigaste, cabrahigó, cabrahigamos, cabrahigasteis, cabrahigaron.
Present subjunctive **cabrahígue**, **cabrahígues**, **cabrahígue**, **cabrahiguemos**, **cabrahiguéis**, **cabrahíguen**.
Imperative **cabrahíga** (tú), **cabrahígue** (él/Vd.), **cabrahiguemos** (nos.), cabrahigad (vos.), **cabrahíguen** (ellos/Vds.).

26. HOMOGENEIZAR *(stressed* í *in certain persons of certain tenses, the* z *changes to* c *before* e*)*
Present indicative **homogeneízo**, **homogeneízas**, **homogeneíza**, homogeneizamos, homogeneizáis, **homogeneízan**.
Preterite **homogeneicé**, homogeneizaste, homogeneizó, homogeneizamos, homogeneizasteis, homogeneizaron.
Present subjunctive **homogeneíce**, **homogeneíces**, **homogeneíce**, **homogeneicemos**, **homogeneicéis**, **homogeneícen**.
Imperative **homogeneíza** (tú), **homogeneíce** (él/Vd.), **homogeneicemos** (nos.), homogeneizad (vos.), **homogeneícen** (ellos/Vds.).

27. ACERTAR *(*e *changes to* ie *in stressed syllables)*
Present indicative **acierto**, **aciertas**, **acierta**, acertamos, acertáis, **aciertan**.
Present subjunctive **acierte**, **aciertes**, **acierte**, acertemos, acertéis, **acierten**.
Imperative **acierta** (tú), **acierte** (él/Vd.), acertemos (nos.), acertad (vos.), **acierten** (ellos/Vds.).

28. ENTENDER (e *changes to* ie *in stressed syllables)*

Present indicative	**entiendo**, **entiendes**, **entiende**, entendemos, entendéis, **entienden**.
Present subjunctive	**entienda**, **entiendas**, **entienda**, entendamos, entendáis, **entiendan**.
Imperative	**entiende** (tú), **entienda** (él/Vd.), entendamos (nos.), entended (vos.), **entiendan** (ellos/Vds.).

29. DISCERNIR (e *changes to* ie *in stressed syllables)*

Present indicative	**discierno**, **disciernes**, **discierne**, discernimos, discernís, **disciernen**.
Present subjunctive	**discierna**, **disciernas**, **discierna**, discernamos, discernáis, **disciernan**.
Imperative	**discierne** (tú), **discierna** (él/Vd.), discernamos (nos.), discernid (vos.), **disciernan** (ellos/Vds.).

30. ADQUIRIR (i *changes to* ie *in stressed syllables)*

Present indicative	**adquiero**, **adquieres**, **adquiere**, adquirimos, adquirís, **adquieren**.
Present subjunctive	**adquiera**, **adquieras**, **adquiera**, adquiramos, adquiráis, **adquieran**.
Imperative	**adquiere** (tú), **adquiera** (él/Vd.), adquiramos (nos.), adquirid (vos.), **adquieran** (ellos/Vds.).

31. CONTAR (o *changes to* ue *in stressed syllables)*

Present indicative	**cuento**, **cuentas**, **cuenta**, contamos, contáis, **cuentan**.
Present subjunctive	**cuente**, **cuentes**, **cuente**, contemos, contéis, **cuenten**.
Imperative	**cuenta** (tú), **cuente** (él/Vd.), contemos (nos.), contad (vos.), **cuenten** (ellos/Vds.).

32. MOVER (o *changes to* ue *in stressed syllables)*

Present indicative	**muevo**, **mueves**, **mueve**, movemos, movéis, **mueven**.
Present subjunctive	**mueva**, **muevas**, **mueva**, movamos, mováis, **muevan**.
Imperative	**mueve** (tú), **mueva** (él/Vd.), movamos (nos.), moved (vos.), **muevan** (ellos/Vds.).

33. DORMIR (o *changes to* ue *in stressed syllables or to* u *in certain persons of certain tenses)*

Present indicative	**duermo**, **duermes**, **duerme**, dormimos, dormís, **duermen**.
Preterite	dormí, dormiste, **durmió**, dormimos, dormisteis, **durmieron**.
Present subjunctive	**duerma**, **duermas**, **duerma**, **durmamos**, **durmáis**, **duerman**.
Imperfect subjunctive	**durmiera**, **durmieras**, **durmiera**, **durmiéramos**, **durmierais**, **durmieran**; **durmiese**, **durmieses**, **durmiese**, **durmiésemos**, **durmieseis**, **durmiesen**.
Future subjunctive	**durmiere**, **durmieres**, **durmiere**, **durmiéremos**, **durmiereis**, **durmieren**.
Imperative	**duerme** (tú), **duerma** (él/Vd.), **durmamos** (nos.), dormid (vos.), **duerman** (ellos/Vds.).

34. SERVIR (e *weakens to* i *in certain persons of certain tenses)*

Present indicative	**sirvo**, **sirves**, **sirve**, servimos, servís, **sirven**.
Preterite	serví, serviste, **sirvió**, servimos, servisteis, **sirvieron**.
Present subjunctive	**sirva**, **sirvas**, **sirva**, **sirvamos**, **sirváis**, **sirvan**.
Imperfect subjunctive	**sirviera**, **sirvieras**, **sirviera**, **sirviéramos**, **sirvierais**, **sirvieran**; **sirviese**, **sirvieses**, **sirviese**, **sirviésemos**, **sirvieseis**, **sirviesen**.
Future subjunctive	**sirviere**, **sirvieres**, **sirviere**, **sirviéremos**, **sirviereis**, **sirvieren**.
Imperative	**sirve** (tú), **sirva** (él/Vd.), **sirvamos** (nos.), servid (vos.), **sirvan** (ellos/Vds.).

35. HERVIR (e *changes to* ie *in stressed syllables or to* i *in certain persons of certain tenses)*

Present indicative	**hiervo**, **hierves**, **hierve**, hervimos, hervís, **hierven**.
Preterite	herví, herviste, **hirvió**, hervimos, hervisteis, **hirvieron**.
Present subjunctive	**hierva**, **hiervas**, **hierva**, **hirvamos**, **hirváis**, **hiervan**.
Imperfect subjunctive	**hirviera**, **hirvieras**, **hirviera**, **hirviéramos**, **hirvierais**, **hirvieran**; **hirviese**, **hirvieses**, **hirviese**, **hirviésemos**, **hirvieseis**, **hirviesen**.
Future subjunctive	**hirviere**, **hirvieres**, **hirviere**, **hirviéremos**, **hirviereis**, **hirvieren**.
Imperative	**hierve** (tú), **hierva** (él/Vd.), **hirvamos** (nos.), hervid (vos.), **hiervan** (ellos/Vds.).

36. CEÑIR *(the* i *of certain endings is absorbed by* ñ*; the* e *changes to* i *in certain persons of certain tenses)*

Present indicative ciño, ciñes, ciñe, ceñimos, ceñís, ciñen.
Preterite ceñí, ceñiste, ciñó, ceñimos, ceñisteis, ciñeron.
Present subjunctive ciña, ciñas, ciña, ciñamos, ciñáis, ciñan.
Imperfect subjunctive ciñera, ciñeras, ciñera, ciñéramos, ciñerais, ciñeran; ciñese, ciñeses, ciñese, ciñésemos, ciñeseis, ciñesen.
Future subjunctive ciñere, ciñeres, ciñere, ciñéremos, ciñereis, ciñeren.
Imperative ciñe (tú), ciña (él/Vd.), ciñamos (nos.), ceñid (vos.), ciñan (ellos/Vds.).
Gerund ciñendo

37. REÍR *(loss of the* e *in certain persons of certain tenses)*

Present indicative río, ríes, ríe, reímos, reís, ríen.
Preterite reí, reíste, rió, reímos, reísteis, rieron.
Present subjunctive ría, rías, ría, riamos, riáis, rían.
Imperfect subjunctive riera, rieras, riera, riéramos, rierais, rieran; riese, rieses, riese, riésemos, rieseis, riesen.
Future subjunctive riere, rieres, riere, riéremos, riereis, rieren.
Imperative ríe (tú), ría (él/Vd.), riamos (nos.), reíd (vos.), rían (ellos/Vds.).
Past participle reído, -a

38. TAÑER *(the* i *of endings is absorbed by* ñ *in certain persons of certain tenses)*

Preterite tañí, tañiste, tañó, tañimos, tañisteis, tañeron.
Imperfect subjunctive tañera, tañeras, tañera, tañéramos, tañerais, tañeran; tañese, tañeses, tañese, tañésemos, tañeseis, tañesen.
Future subjunctive tañere, tañeres, tañere, tañéremos, tañereis, tañeren.
Gerund tañendo

39. EMPELLER *(the* i *of endings is absorbed by* ll *in certain persons of certain tenses)*

Preterite empellí, empelliste, empelló, empellimos, empellisteis, empelleron.
Imperfect subjunctive empellera, empelleras, empellera, empelléramos, empellerais, empelleran; empellese, empelleses, empellese, empellésemos, empelleseis, empellesen.
Future subjunctive empellere, empelleres, empellere, empelléremos, empellereis, empelleren.
Gerund empellendo

40. MUÑIR *(the* i *of endings is absorbed by* ñ *in certain persons of certain tenses)*

Preterite muñí, muñiste, muñó, muñimos, muñisteis, muñeron.
Imperfect subjunctive muñera, muñeras, muñera, muñéramos, muñerais, muñeran; muñese, muñeses, muñese, muñésemos, muñeseis, muñesen.
Future subjunctive muñere, muñeres, muñere, muñéremos, muñereis, muñeren.
Gerund muñendo

41. MULLIR *(the* i *of endings is absorbed by the* ll *in certain persons of certain tenses)*

Preterite mullí, mulliste, mulló, mullimos, mullisteis, mulleron.
Imperfect subjunctive mullera, mulleras, mullera, mulléramos, mullerais, mulleran; mullese, mulleses, mullese, mullésemos, mulleseis, mullesen.
Future subjunctive mullere, mulleres, mullere, mulléremos, mullereis, mulleren.
Gerund mullendo

42. NACER *(*c *changes to* zc *before* a *and* o*)*

Present indicative nazco, naces, nace, nacemos, nacéis, nacen.
Present subjunctive nazca, nazcas, nazca, nazcamos, nazcáis, nazcan.
Imperative nace (tú), nazca (él/Vd.), nazcamos (nos.), naced (vos.), nazcan (ellos/Vds.).

43. AGRADECER *(*c *changes to* zc *before* a *and* o*)*

Present indicative agradezco, agradeces, agradece, agradecemos, agradecéis, agradecen.
Present subjunctive agradezca, agradezcas, agradezca, agradezcamos, agradezcáis, agradezcan.
Imperative agradece (tú), agradezca (él/Vd.), agradezcamos (nos.), agradeced (vos.), agradezcan (ellos/Vds.).

44. CONOCER (c *changes to* zc *before* a *and* o)

Present indicative	conozco, conoces, conoce, conemos, conocéis, conocen.
Present subjunctive	conozca, conozcas, conozca, conozcamos, conozcáis, conozcan.
Imperative	conoce (tú), conozca (él/Vd.), conozcamos (nos.), conoced (vos.), conozcan (ellos/Vds.).

45. LUCIR (c *changes to* zc *before* a *and* o)

Present indicative	luzco, luces, luce, lucimos, lucís, lucen.
Present subjunctive	luzca, luzcas, luzca, luzcamos, luzcáis, luzcan.
Imperative	luce (tú), luzca (él/Vd.), luzcamos (nos.), lucid (vos.), luzcan (ellos/Vds.).

46. CONDUCIR (c *changes to* zc *before* a *and* o; *the preterite is irregular)*

Present indicative	conduzco, conduces, conduce, conducimos, conducís, conducen.
Preterite	conduje, condujiste, condujo, condujimos, condujisteis, condujeron.
Present subjunctive	conduzca, conduzcas, conduzca, conduzcamos, conduzcáis, conduzcan.
Imperfect subjunctive	condujera, condujeras, condujera, condujéramos, condujerais, condujeran; condujese, condujeses, condujese, condujésemos, condujeseis, condujesen.
Future subjunctive	condujere, condujeres, condujere, condujéremos, condujereis, condujeren.
Imperative	conduce (tú), conduzca (él/Vd.), conduzcamos (nos.), conducid (vos.), conduzcan (ellos/Vds.).

47. EMPEZAR (e *changes to* ie *in stressed syllables and* z *changes to* c *before* e)

Present indicative	empiezo, empiezas, empieza, empezamos, empezáis, empiezan.
Past ind	empecé, empezaste, empezó, empezamos, empezasteis, empezaron.
Present subjunctive	empiece, empieces, empiece, empecemos, empecéis, empiecen.
Imperative	empieza (tú), empiece (él/Vd.), empecemos (nos.), empezad (vos.), empiecen (ellos/Vds.).

48. REGAR (e *changes to* ie *in stressed syllables;* g *changes to* gu *before* e)

Present indicative	riego, riegas, riega, regamos, regáis, riegan.
Preterite	regué, regaste, regó, regamos, regasteis, regaron.
Present subjunctive	riegue, riegues, riegue, reguemos, reguéis, rieguen.
Imperative	riega (tú), riegue (él/Vd.), reguemos (nos.), regad (vos.), rieguen (ellos/Vds.).

49. TROCAR (o *changes to* ue *in stressed syllables;* c *changes to* qu *before* e)

Present indicative	trueco, truecas, trueca, trocamos, trocáis, truecan.
Preterite	troqué, trocaste, trocó, trocamos, trocasteis, trocaron.
Present subjunctive	trueque, trueques, trueque, troquemos, troquéis, truequen.
Imperative	trueca (tú), trueque (él/Vd.), troquemos (nos.), trocad (vos.), truequen (ellos/Vds.).

50. FORZAR (o *changes to* ue *in stressed syllables;* z *changes to* c *before* e)

Present indicative	fuerzo, fuerzas, fuerza, forzamos, forzáis, fuerzan.
Preterite	forcé, forzaste, forzó, forzamos, forzasteis, forzaron.
Present subjunctive	fuerce, fuerces, fuerce, forcemos, forcéis, fuercen.
Imperative	fuerza (tú), fuerce (él/Vd.), forcemos (nos.), forzad (vos.), fuercen (ellos/Vds.).

51. AVERGONZAR (*in stressed syllables* o *changes to* ue *and* g *to* gü; z *changes to* c *before* e)

Present indicative	avergüenzo, avergüenzas, avergüenza, avergonzamos, avergonzáis, avergüenzan.
Preterite	avergoncé, avergonzaste, avergonzó, avergonzamos, avergonzasteis, avergonzaron.
Present subjunctive	avergüence, avergüences, avergüence, avergoncemos, avergoncéis, avergüencen.
Imperative	avergüenza (tú), avergüence (él/Vd.), avergoncemos (nos.), avergonzad (vos.), avergüencen (ellos/Vds.).

2. COLGAR (o *changes to* ue *in stressed syllables;* g *changes to* gu *before* e)

resent indicative **cuelgo**, **cuelgas**, **cuelga**, colgamos, colgáis, **cuelgan**.
reterite **colgué**, colgaste, colgó, colgamos, colgasteis, colgaron.
resent subjunctive **cuelgue**, **cuelgues**, **cuelgue**, **colguemos**, **colguéis**, **cuelguen**.
mperative **cuelga** (tú), **cuelgue** (él/Vd.), **colguemos** (nos.), colgad (vos.), **cuelguen** (ellos/Vds.).

3. JUGAR (u *changes to* ue *in stressed syllables and* g *changes to* gu *before* e)

resent indicative **juego**, **juegas**, **juega**, jugamos, jugáis, **juegan**.
reterite **jugué**, jugaste, jugó, jugamos, jugasteis, jugaron.
resent subjunctive **juegue**, **juegues**, **juegue**, **juguemos**, **juguéis**, **jueguen**.
mperative **juega** (tú), **juegue** (él/Vd.), **juguemos** (nos.), jugad (vos.), **jueguen** (ellos/Vds.).

4. COCER (o *changes to* ue *in stressed syllables and* c *changes to* z *before* a *and* o)

resent indicative **cuezo**, **cueces**, **cuece**, cocemos, cocéis, **cuecen**.
resent subjunctive **cueza**, **cuezas**, **cueza**, **cozamos**, **cozáis**, **cuezan**.
mperative **cuece** (tú), **cueza** (él/Vd.), **cozamos** (nos.), coced (vos.), **cuezan** (ellos/Vds.).

5. ELEGIR (e *changes to* i *in certain persons of certain tenses;* g *changes to* j *before* a *and* o)

resent indicative **elijo**, **eliges**, **elige**, elegimos, elegís, **eligen**.
reterite elegí, elegiste, **eligió**, elegimos, elegisteis, **eligieron**.
resent subjunctive **elija**, **elijas**, **elija**, **elijamos**, **elijáis**, **elijan**.
mperfect subjunctive **eligiera**, **eligieras**, **eligiera**, **eligiéramos**, **eligierais**, **eligieran**; **eligiese**, **eligieses**, **eligiese**, **eligiésemos**, **eligieseis**, **eligiesen**.
uture subjunctive **eligiere**, **eligieres**, **eligiere**, **eligiéremos**, **eligiereis**, **eligieren**.
mperative **elige** (tú), **elija** (él/Vd.), **elijamos** (nos.), elegid (vos.), **elijan** (ellos/Vds.).

6. SEGUIR (e *changes to* i *in certain persons of certain tenses;* gu *changes to* g *before* a *and* o)

resent indicative **sigo**, **sigues**, **sigue**, seguimos, seguís, **siguen**.
reterite seguí, seguiste, **siguió**, seguimos, seguisteis, **siguieron**.
resent subjunctive **siga**, **sigas**, **siga**, **sigamos**, **sigáis**, **sigan**.
mperfect subjunctive **siguiera**, **siguieras**, **siguiera**, **siguiéramos**, **siguierais**, **siguieran**; **siguiese**, **siguieses**, **siguiese**, **siguiésemos**, **siguieseis**, **siguiesen**.
uture subjunctive **siguiere**, **siguieres**, **siguiere**, **siguiéremos**, **siguiereis**, **siguieren**.
mperative **sigue** (tú), **siga** (él/Vd.), **sigamos** (nos.), seguid (vos.), **sigan** (ellos/Vds.).
erund **siguiendo**

7. ERRAR (e *changes to* ye *in stressed syllables)*

resent indicative **yerro**, **yerras**, **yerra**, erramos, erráis, **yerran**.
resent subjunctive **yerre**, **yerres**, **yerre**, erremos, erréis, **yerren**.
mperative **yerra** (tú), **yerre** (él/Vd.), erremos (nos.), errad (vos.), **yerren** (ellos/Vds.).

8. AGORAR (o *changes to* ue *in stressed syllables and* g *changes to* gü *before* e)

resent indicative **agüero**, **agüeras**, **agüera**, agoramos, agoráis, **agüeran**.
resent subjunctive **agüere**, **agüeres**, **agüere**, agoramos, agoréis, **agüeren**.
mperative **agüera** (tú), **agüere** (él/Vd.), agoremos (nos.), agorad (vos.), **agüeren** (ellos/Vds.).

9. DESOSAR (o *changes to* hue *in stressed syllables)*

resent indicative **deshueso**, **deshuesas**, **deshuesa**, desosamos, desosáis, **deshuesan**.
resent subjunctive **deshuese**, **deshueses**, **deshuese**, desosemos, desoséis, **deshuesen**.
mperative **deshuesa** (tú), **deshuese** (él/Vd.), desosemos (nos.), desosad (vos.), **deshuesen** (ellos/Vds.).

0. OLER (o *changes to* hue *in stressed syllables)*

resent indicative **huelo**, **hueles**, **huele**, olemos, oléis, **huelen**.
resent subjunctive **huela**, **huelas**, **huela**, olamos, oláis, **huelan**.
mperative **huele** (tú), **huela** (él/Vd.), olamos (nos.), oled (vos.), **huelan** (ellos/Vds.).

61. LEER *(the* i *ending changes to* y *before* o *and* e*)*

Preterite	leí, leíste, leyó, leímos, leísteis, leyeron.
Imperfect subjunctive	leyera, leyeras, leyera, leyéramos, leyerais, leyeran;
	leyese, leyeses, leyese, leyésemos, leyeseis, leyesen.
Future subjunctive	leyere, leyeres, leyere, leyéremos, leyereis, leyeren.
Gerund	leyendo
Past participle	leído,-a

62. HUIR *(*i *changes to* y *before* a*,* e*, and* o*)*

Present indicative	huyo, huyes, huye, huimos, huís, huyen.
Preterite	huí, huiste, huyó, huimos, huisteis, huyeron.
Present subjunctive	huya, huyas, huya, huyamos, huyáis, huyan.
Imperfect subjunctive	huyera, huyeras, huyera, huyéramos, huyerais, huyeran;
	huyese, huyeses, huyese, huyésemos, huyeseis, huyesen.
Future subjunctive	huyere, huyeres, huyere, huyéremos, huyereis, huyeren.
Imperative	huye (tú), huya (él/Vd.), huyamos (nos.), huid (vos.), huyan (ellos/Vds.).
Gerund	huyendo

63. ARGÜIR *(*i *changes to* y *before* a*,* e*, and* o*;* gü *becomes* gu *before* y*)*

Present indicative	arguyo, arguyes, arguye, argüimos, argüís, arguyen.
Preterite	argüí, argüiste, arguyó, argüimos, argüisteis, arguyeron.
Present subjunctive	arguya, arguyas, arguya, arguyamos, arguyáis, arguyan.
Imperfect subjunctive	arguyera, arguyeras, arguyera, arguyéramos, arguyerais, arguyeran;
	arguyese, arguyeses, arguyese, arguyésemos, arguyeseis, arguyesen.
Future subjunctive	arguyere, arguyeres, arguyere, arguyéremos, arguyereis, arguyeren.
Imperative	arguye (tú), arguya (él/Vd.), arguyamos (nos.), argüid (vos.), arguyan (ellos/Vds.).
Gerund	arguyendo

64. ANDAR

Preterite	anduve, anduviste, anduvo, anduvimos, anduvisteis, anduvieron.
Imperfect subjunctive	anduviera, anduvieras, anduviera, anduviéramos, anduvierais, anduvieran;
	anduviese, anduvieses, anduviese, anduviésemos, anduvieseis, anduviesen.
Future subjunctive	anduviere, anduvieres, anduviere, anduviéremos, anduviereis, anduvieren.

65. ASIR

Present indicative	asgo, ases, ase, asimos, asís, asen.
Present subjunctive	asga, asgas, asga, asgamos, asgáis, asgan.
Imperative	ase (tú), asga (él/Vd.), asgamos (nos.), asid (vos.), asgan (ellos/Vds.).

66. CABER

Present indicative	quepo, cabes, cabe, cabemos, cabéis, caben.
Preterite	cupe, cupiste, cupo, cupimos, cupisteis, cupieron.
Future indicative	cabré, cabrás, cabrá, cabremos, cabréis, cabrán.
Conditional	cabria, cabrias, cabria, cabriamos, cabriais, cabrian.
Present subjunctive	quepa, quepas, quepa, quepamos, quepáis, quepan.
Imperfect subjunctive	cupiera, cupieras, cupiera, cupiéramos, cupierais, cupieran;
	cupiese, cupieses, cupiese, cupiésemos, cupieseis, cupiesen.
Future subjunctive	cupiere, cupieres, cupiere, cupiéremos, cupiereis, cupieren.
Imperative	cabe (tú), quepa (él/Vd.), quepamos (nos.), cabed (vos.), quepan (ellos/Vds.).

67. CAER

Present indicative	caigo, caes, cae, caemos, caéis, caen.
Preterite	caí, caíste, cayó, caímos, caísteis, cayeron.
Present subjunctive	caiga, caigas, caiga, caigamos, caigáis, caigan.
Imperfect subjunctive	cayera, cayeras, cayera, cayéramos, cayerais, cayeran;
	cayese, cayeses, cayese, cayésemos, cayeseis, cayesen.

Future subjunctive	**cayere, cayeres, cayere, cayéremos, cayereis, cayeren.**
Imperative	cae (tú), **caiga** (él/Vd.), **caigamos** (nos.), caed (vos.), **caigan** (ellos/Vds.).
Gerund	**cayendo**
Past participle	**caído,-a**

68. DAR

Present indicative	**doy**, das, da, damos, dais, dan.
Preterite	**di, diste, dio, dimos, disteis, dieron.**
Present subjunctive	**dé**, des, **dé**, demos, deis, den.
Imperfect subjunctive	**diera, dieras, diera, diéramos, dierais, dieran;** **diese, dieses, diese, diésemos, dieseis, diesen.**
Future subjunctive	**diere, dieres, diere, diéremos, diereis, dieren.**
Imperative	da (tú), **dé** (él/Vd.), demos (nos.), dad (vos.), den (ellos/Vds.).

69. DECIR

Present indicative	**digo, dices, dice**, decimos, decís, **dicen**.
Preterite	**dije, dijiste, dijo, dijimos, dijisteis, dijeron.**
Future indicative	**diré, dirás, dirá, diremos, diréis, dirán.**
Conditional	**diría, dirías, diría, diríamos, diríais, dirían.**
Present subjunctive	**diga, digas, diga, digamos, digáis, digan.**
Imperfect subjunctive	**dijera, dijeras, dijera, dijéramos, dijerais, dijeran;** **dijese, dijeses, dijese, dijésemos, dijeseis, dijesen.**
Future subjunctive	**dijere, dijeres, dijere, dijéremos, dijereis, dijeren.**
Imperative	**di (tú), diga** (él/Vd.), **digamos** (nos.), decid (vos.), **digan** (ellos/Vds.).
Past participle	**dicho,-a.**

70. ERGUIR

Present indicative	**irgo, irgues, irgue**, erguimos, erguís, **irgen;yergo, yergues, yergue**, erguimos, erguís, **yergen.**
Preterite	erguí, erguiste, **irguió**, erguimos, erguisteis, **irguieron**.
Present subjunctive	**irga, irgas, irga, irgamos, irgáis, irgan;** **yerga, yergas, yerga, irgamos, irgáis, yergan.**
Imperfect subjunctive	**irguiera, irguieras, irguiera, irguiéramos, irguierais, irguieran;** **irguiese, irguieses, irguiese, irguiésemos, irguieseis, irguiesen.**
Future subjunctive	**irguiere, irguieres, irguiere, irguiéremos, irguiereis, irguieren.**
Imperative	**irgue, yergue** (tú), **irga, yerga** (él/Vd.), **irgamos** (nos.), erguid (vos.), **irgan, yergan** (ellos/Vds.).
Gerund	**irguiendo**

71. ESTAR

Present indicative	**estoy**, estás, está, estamos, estáis, están.
Imperfect indicative	estaba, estabas, estaba, estábamos, estabais, estaban.
Preterite	**estuve, estuviste, estuvo, estuvimos, estuvisteis, estuvieron.**
Future indicative	estaré, estarás, estará, estaremos, estaréis, estarán.
Conditional	estaría, estarías, estaría, estaríamos, estaríais, estarían.
Present subjunctive	esté, estés, esté, estemos, estéis, estén.
Imperfect subjunctive	**estuviera, estuvieras, estuviera, estuviéramos, estuvierais, estuvieran;** **estuviese, estuvieses, estuviese, estuviésemos, estuvieseis, estuviesen.**
Future subjunctive	**estuviere, estuvieres, estuviere, estuviéremos, estuviereis, estuvieren.**
Imperative	está (tú), esté (él/Vd.), estemos (nos.), estad (vos.), estén (ellos/Vds.).

72. HABER

Present indicative	**he, has, ha, hemos**, habéis, **han**.
Imperfect subjunctive	había, habías, había, habíamos, habíais, habían.
Preterite	**hube, hubiste, hubo, hubimos, hubisteis, hubieron.**
Future indicative	**habré, habrás, habrá, habremos, habréis, habrán.**

Conditional	habría, habrías, habría, habríamos, habríais, habrían.
Present subjunctive	haya, hayas, haya, hayamos, hayáis, hayan.
Imperfect subjunctive	hubiera, hubieras, hubiera, hubiéramos, hubierais, hubieran; hubiese, hubieses, hubiese, hubiésemos, hubieseis, hubiesen.
Future subjunctive	hubiere, hubieres, hubiere, hubiéremos, hubiereis, hubieren.
Imperative	he (tú), haya (él/Vd.), hayamos (nos.), habed (vos.), hayan (ellos/Vds.).

73. HACER

Present indicative	hago, haces, hace, hacemos, hacéis, hacen.
Preterite	hice, hiciste, hizo, hicimos, hicisteis, hicieron.
Future indicative	haré, harás, hará, haremos, haréis, harán.
Conditional	haría, harías, haría, haríamos, haríais, harían.
Present subjunctive	haga, hagas, haga, hagamos, hagáis, hagan.
Imperfect subjunctive	hiciera, hicieras, hiciera, hiciéramos, hicierais, hicieran; hiciese, hicieses, hiciese, hiciésemos, hicieseis, hiciesen.
Future subjunctive	hiciere, hicieres, hiciere, hiciéremos, hiciereis, hicieren.
Imperative	haz (tú), haga (él/Vd.), hagamos (nos.), haced (vos.), hagan (ellos/Vds.).
Past participle	hecho,-a.

74. IR

Present indicative	voy, vas, va, vamos, vais, van.
Imperfect subjunctive	iba, ibas, iba, íbamos, ibais, iban.
Preterite	fui, fuiste, fue, fuimos, fuisteis, fueron.
Present subjunctive	vaya, vayas, vaya, vayamos, vayáis, vayan.
Imperfect subjunctive	fuera, fueras, fuera, fuéramos, fuerais, fueran; fuese, fueses, fuese, fuésemos, fueseis, fuesen.
Future subjunctive	fuere, fueres, fuere, fuéremos, fuereis, fueren.
Imperative	ve (tú), vaya (él/Vd.), vayamos (nos.), id (vos.), vayan (ellos/Vds.).
Gerund	yendo

75. OÍR

Present indicative	oigo, oyes, oye, oímos, oís, oyen.
Preterite	oí, oíste, oyó, oímos, oísteis, oyeron.
Present subjunctive	oiga, oigas, oiga, oigamos, oigáis, oigan.
Imperfect subjunctive	oyera, oyeras, oyera, oyéramos, oyerais, oyeran; oyese, oyeses, oyese, oyésemos, oyeseis, oyesen.
Future subjunctive	oyere, oyeres, oyere, oyéremos, oyereis, oyeren.
Imperative	oye (tú), oiga (él/Vd.), oigamos (nos.), oíd (vos.), oigan (ellos/Vds.).
Gerund	oyendo
Past participle	oído,-a

76. PLACER

Present indicative	plazco, places, place, placemos, placéis, placen.
Preterite	plací, placiste, plació *or* plugo, placimos, placisteis, placieron *or* pluguieron.
Present subjunctive	plazca, plazcas, plazca, plegue, plazcamos, plazcáis, plazcan.
Imperfect subjunctive	placiera, placieras, placiera *or* pluguiera, placiéramos, placierais, placieran placiese, placieses, placiese *or* pluguiese, placiésemos, placieseis, placiesen.
Future subjunctive	placiere, placieres, placiere *or* pluguiere, placiéremos, placiereis, placieren.
Imperative	place (tú), plazca (él/Vd.), plazcamos (nos.), placed (vos.), plazcan (ellos/Vds.).

77. PODER

Present indicative	puedo, puedes, puede, podemos, podéis, pueden.
Preterite	pude, pudiste, pudo, pudimos, pudisteis, pudieron.
Future indicative	podré, podrás, podrá, podremos, podréis, podrán.
Conditional	podría, podrías, podría, podríamos, podríais, podrían.
Present subjunctive	pueda, puedas, pueda, podamos, podáis, puedan.

Imperfect subjunctive pudiera, pudieras, pudiera, pudiéramos, pudierais, pudieran;
pudiese, pudieses, pudiese, pudiésemos, pudieseis, pudiesen.
Future subjunctive pudiere, pudieres, pudiere, pudiéremos, pudiereis, pudieren.
Imperative **puede** (tú), **pueda** (él/Vd.), podamos (nos.), poded (vos.), **puedan** (ellos/Vds.).
Gerund **pudiendo**

78. PONER
Present indicative **pongo**, pones, pone, ponemos, ponéis, ponen.
Preterite **puse, pusiste, puso, pusimos, pusisteis, pusieron.**
Future indicative **pondré, pondrás, pondrá, pondremos, pondréis, pondrán.**
Conditional **pondría, pondrías, pondría, pondríamos, pondríais, pondrían.**
Present subjunctive **ponga, pongas, ponga, pongamos, pongáis, pongan.**
Imperfect subjunctive **pusiera, pusieras, pusiera, pusiéramos, pusierais, pusieran;**
pusiese, pusieses, pusiese, pusiésemos, pusieseis, pusiesen.
Future subjunctive **pusiere, pusieres, pusiere, pusiéremos, pusiereis, pusieren.**
Imperative **pon** (tú), **ponga** (él/Vd.), **pongamos** (nos.), poned (vos.), **pongan** (ellos/Vds.).
Past participle **puesto,-a.**

79. PREDECIR
Present indicative **predigo, predices, predice**, predecimos, predecís, **predicen.**
Preterite **predije, predijiste, predijo, predijimos, predijisteis, predijeron.**
Present subjunctive **prediga, predigas, prediga, predigamos, predigáis, predigan.**
Imperfect subjunctive **predijera, predijeras, predijera, predijéramos, predijerais, predijeran;**
predijese, predijeses, predijese, predijésemos, predijeseis, predijesen.
Future subjunctive **predijere, predijeres, predijere, predijéremos, predijereis, predijeren.**
Imperative **predice** (tú), **prediga** (él/Vd.), **predigamos** (nos.), predecid (vos.),
predigan (ellos/Vds.).
Gerund **prediciendo**
Past participle **predicho,-a**

80. QUERER
Present indicative **quiero, quieres, quiere**, queremos, queréis, **quieren.**
Preterite **quise, quisiste, quiso, quisimos, quisisteis, quisieron.**
Future indicative **querré, querrás, querrá, querremos, querréis, querrán.**
Conditional **querría, querrías, querría, querríamos, querríais, querrían.**
Present subjunctive **quiera, quieras, quiera**, queramos, queráis, **quieran.**
Imperfect subjunctive **quisiera, quisieras, quisiera, quisiéramos, quisierais, quisieran;**
quisiese, quisieses, quisiese, quisiésemos, quisieseis, quisiesen.
Future subjunctive **quisiere, quisieres, quisiere, quisiéremos, quisiereis, quisieren.**
Imperative **quiere** (tú), **quiera** (él/Vd.), queramos (nos.), quered (vos.), **quieran** (ellos/Vds.).

81. RAER
Present indicative **rao, raigo, rayo**, raes, rae, raemos, raéis, raen.
Preterite raí, raíste, **rayó**, raímos, raísteis, **rayeron.**
Present subjunctive **raiga, raigas, raiga, raigamos, raigáis, raigan;**
raya, rayas, raya, rayamos, rayáis, rayan.
Imperfect subjunctive **rayera, rayeras, rayera, rayéramos, rayerais, rayeran;**
rayese, rayeses, rayese, rayésemos, rayeseis, rayesen.
Future subjunctive **rayere, rayeres, rayere, rayéremos, rayereis, rayeren.**
Imperative rae (tú), **raiga, raya** (él/Vd.), **raigamos, rayamos** (nos.), raed (vos.), **raigan,**
rayan (ellos/Vds.).
Gerundio **rayendo**
Past participle **raído,-a**

82. ROER
Present indicative **roo, roigo, royo**, roes, roe, roemos, roéis, roen.
Preterite roí, roíste, **royó**, roímos, roísteis, **royeron.**

Present subjunctive	roa, roas, roa, roamos, roáis, roan; **roiga, roigas, roiga, roigamos, roigáis, roigan; roya, royas, roya, royamos, royáis, royan.**
Imperfect subjunctive	**royera, royeras, royera, royéramos, royerais, royeran; royese, royeses, royese, royésemos, royeseis, royesen.**
Future subjunctive	**royere, royeres, royere, royéremos, royereis, royeren.**
Imperative	roe (tú), roa, **roiga, roya** (él/Vd.), roamos, **roigamos, royamos** (nos.), roed (vos.), roan, **roigan, royan** (ellos/Vds.).
Gerundio	**royendo**
Past participle	**roído,-a**

83. SABER

Present indicative	**sé**, sabes, sabe, sabemos, sabéis, saben.
Preterite	**supe, supiste, supo, supimos, supisteis, supieron.**
Future indicative	**sabré, sabrás, sabrá, sabremos, sabréis, sabrán.**
Conditional	**sabría, sabrías, sabría, sabríamos, sabríais, sabrían.**
Present subjunctive	**sepa, sepas, sepa, sepamos, sepáis, sepan.**
Imperfect subjunctive	**supiera, supieras, supiera, supiéramos, supierais, supieran; supiese, supieses, supiese, supiésemos, supieseis, supiesen.**
Future subjunctive	**supiere, supieres, supiere, supiéremos, supiereis, supieren.**
Imperative	sabe (tú), **sepa** (él/Vd.), **sepamos** (nos.), sabed (vos.), **sepan** (ellos/Vds.).

84. SALIR

Present indicative	**salgo**, sales, sale, salimos, salís, salen.
Future indicative	**saldré, saldrás, saldrá, saldremos, saldréis, saldrán.**
Conditional	**saldría, saldrías, saldría, saldríamos, saldríais, saldrían.**
Present subjunctive	**salga, salgas, salga, salgamos, salgáis, salgan.**
Imperative	**sal** (tú), **salga** (él/Vd.), **salgamos** (nos.), salid (vos.), **salgan** (ellos/Vds.).

85. SATISFACER

Present indicative	**satisfago**, satisfaces, satisface, satisfacemos, satisfacéis, satisfacen.
Preterite	**satisfice, satisficiste, satisfizo, satisficimos, satisficisteis, satisficieron.**
Future indicative	**satisfaré, satisfarás, satisfará, satisfaremos, satisfaréis, satisfarán.**
Conditional	**satisfaría, satisfarías, satisfaría, satisfaríamos, satisfaríais, satisfarían.**
Present subjunctive	**satisfaga, satisfagas, satisfaga, satisfagamos, satisfagáis, satisfagan.**
Imperfect subjunctive	**satisficiera, satisficieras, satisficiera, satisficiéramos, satisficierais, satisficieran; satisficiese, satisficieses, satisficiese, satisficiésemos, satisficieseis, satisficiesen.**
Future subjunctive	**satisficiere, satisficieres, satisficiere, satisficiéremos, satisficiereis, satisficieren.**
Imperative	**satisfaz,** satisface (tú), **satisfaga** (él/Vd.), **satisfagamos** (nos.), satisfaced (vos.), **satisfagan** (ellos/Vds.).
Past participle	**satisfecho,-a.**

86. SER

Present indicative	**soy, eres, es, somos, sois, son.**
Imperfect subjunctive	**era, eras, era, éramos, erais, eran.**
Preterite	**fui, fuiste, fue, fuimos, fuisteis, fueron.**
Future indicative	seré, serás, será, seremos, seréis, serán.
Conditional	sería, serías, sería, seríamos, seríais, serían.
Present subjunctive	sea, seas, sea, seamos, seáis, sean.
Imperfect subjunctive	**fuera, fueras, fuera, fuéramos, fuerais, fueran; fuese, fueses, fuese, fuésemos, fueseis, fuesen.**
Future subjunctive	**fuere, fueres, fuere, fuéremos, fuereis, fueren.**
Imperative	**sé** (tú), sea (él/Vd.), seamos (nos.), **sed** (vos.), sean (ellos/Vds.).
Past participle	**sido,-a.**

7. TENER

resent indicative	tengo, tienes, tiene, tenemos, tenéis, tienen.
reterite	tuve, tuviste, tuvo, tuvimos, tuvisteis, tuvieron.
uture indicative	tendré, tendrás, tendrá, tendremos, tendréis, tendrán.
onditional	tendría, tendrías, tendría, tendríamos, tendríais, tendrían.
resent subjunctive	tenga, tengas, tenga, tengamos, tengáis, tengan.
nperfect subjunctive	tuviera, tuvieras, tuviera, tuviéramos, tuvierais, tuvieran; tuviese, tuvieses, tuviese, tuviésemos, tuvieseis, tuviesen.
uture subjunctive	tuviere, tuvieres, tuviere, tuviéremos, tuviereis, tuvieren.
nperative	ten (tú), tenga (él/Vd.), tengamos (nos.), tened (vos.), tengan (ellos/Vds.).

8. TRAER

resent indicative	traigo, traes, trae, traemos, traéis, traen.
reterite	traje, trajiste, trajo, trajimos, trajisteis, trajeron.
resent subjunctive	traiga, traigas, traiga, traigamos, traigáis, traigan.
nperfect subjunctive	trajera, trajeras, trajera, trajéramos, trajerais, trajeran; trajese, trajeses, trajese, trajésemos, trajeseis, trajesen.
uture subjunctive	trajere, trajeres, trajere, trajéremos, trajereis, trajeren.
nperative	trae (tú), traiga (él/Vd.), traigamos (nos.), traed (vos.), traigan (ellos/Vds.).
erund	trayendo
ast participle	traído,-a

9. VALER

resent indicative	valgo, vales, vale, valemos, valéis, valen.
uture indicative	valdré, valdrás, valdrá, valdremos, valdréis, valdrán.
onditional	valdría, valdrías, valdría, valdríamos, valdríais, valdrían.
resent subjunctive	valga, valgas, valga, valgamos, valgáis, valgan.
nperative	vale (tú), valga (él/Vd.), valgamos (nos.), valed (vos.), valgan (ellos/Vds.).

0. VENIR

resent indicative	vengo, vienes, viene, venimos, venís, vienen.
reterite	vine, viniste, vino, vinimos, vinisteis, vinieron.
uture indicative	vendré, vendrás, vendrá, vendremos, vendréis, vendrán.
onditional	vendría, vendrías, vendría, vendríamos, vendríais, vendrían.
resent subjunctive	venga, vengas, venga, vengamos, vengáis, vengan.
mperfect subjunctive	viniera, vinieras, viniera, viniéramos, vinierais, vinieran; viniese, vinieses, viniese, viniésemos, vinieseis, viniesen.
uture subjunctive	viniere, vinieres, viniere, viniéremos, viniereis, vinieren.
mperative	ven (tú), venga (él/Vd.), vengamos (nos.), venid (vos.), vengan (ellos/Vds.).
erund	viniendo.

1. VER

resent indicative	veo, ves, ve, vemos, veis, ven.
reterite	vi, viste, vio, vimos, visteis, vieron.
mperfect subjunctive	viera, vieras, viera, viéramos, vierais, vieran; viese, vieses, viese, viésemos, vieseis, viesen.
uture subjunctive	viere, vieres, viere, viéremos, viereis, vieren.
mperative	ve (tú), vea (él/Vd.), veamos (nos.), ved (vos.), vean (ellos/Vds.).
ast participle	visto,-a.

2. YACER

resent indicative	yazco, yazgo, yago, yaces, yace, yacemos, yacéis, yacen.
resent Subjunctive	yazca, yazcas, yazca,yazcamos, yazcáis, yazcan;

	yazga, yazgas, yazga, yazgamos, yazgáis, yazgan; yaga, yagas, yaga, yagamos, yagáis, yagan.
Imperative	yace, **yaz** (tú), **yazca**, **yazga**, **yaga** (él/Vd.), **yazcamos**, **yazgamos**, **yagamos** (nos.), yaced (vos.), **yazcan**, **yazgan**, **yagan** (ellos/Vds.).

A

a *nf (la letra)* A, a.
▲ *pl* as o aes.
prep **1** *(dirección)* to: **girar a la derecha** *to turn (to the) right;* **irse a casa** *to go home;* **subir al autobús** *to get on the bus;* **llegar a Barcelona** *to arrive in Barcelona, reach Barcelona.* **2** *(destino)* to, towards. **3** *(distancia)* away: **a diez kilómetros de casa** *ten kilometres (away) from home.* **4** *(lugar)* at, on: **a la entrada** *at the entrance;* **a la izquierda** *on the left.* **5** *(tiempo)* at: **a las once** *at eleven;* **a los tres días** *three days later;* **a tiempo** *in time;* **al final** *in the end;* **a la mañana siguiente** *(on) the following morning.* **6** *(modo)* by, in: **a ciegas** *blindly;* **a oscuras** *in the dark.* **7** *(instrumento)* by, in: **a mano** *by hand;* **a pie** *on foot.* **8** *(precio)* a: **a tres euros el kilo** *three euros a kilo.* **9** *(medida)* at: **a 90 kilómetros por hora** *at 90 kilometres an hour.* **10** *(finalidad)* to: **él vino a vernos** *he came to see us.* **11** *(complemento directo persona)*: **vi a Juanita** *I saw Juanita.* **12** *(complemento indirecto)* to: **dámelo** *give it to me.* **13** *(como imperativo)*: **¡a dormir!** *bedtime!* **14** *verbo* + **a** + *inf* to: **aprender a nadar** *to learn (how) to swim;* **empezaba a nevar** *it began to snow.* ■ **a que...** I bet...: **¡a que no lo haces!** *I bet you don't do it!*

ee also **al**.

sím **(amperio)** ampere, amp; *(símbolo)* A.

baco *nm* abacus.

bad *nm* abbot.

badejo *nm* pollack.

badesa *nf* abbess.

badía *nf* **1** *(edificio)* abbey. **2** *(dignidad)* abbacy.

bajo *adv* **1** *(lugar)* below, down: **ahí abajo** *down there.* **2** *(en una casa)* downstairs. **3** *(dirección)* down, downward: **calle abajo** *down the street.*
interj down with!: **¡abajo el dictador!** *down with the dictator!*

balanzarse [4] *vpr* **1** *(lanzarse)* to rush forward, spring forward. **2 abalanzarse sobre** to rush at; *(león, tigre)* to pounce on; *(águila, etc)* to swoop down on.

balorio *nm* **1** *(collar)* string of beads. **2** *(cuentecilla)* glass bead.

banderado,-a *pp* ⟶ **abanderar**.
nm & nf **1** *(portaestandarte)* standard bearer. **2** *fig* leader, champion.

banderar *vt* **1** *(un barco)* to register. **2** *(una causa)* to defend: **siempre abanderó la causa de las mujeres** *she always defended women's rights.*

bandonado,-a *pp* ⟶ **abandonar**.
adj **1** abandoned: **un barco abandonado** *an abandoned ship;* **se sintió abandonada** *she felt she had been deserted.* **2** *(descuidado)* neglected: **tiene el despacho abandonado** *his office hasn't been looked after.* **3** *(desaseado)* untidy, unkempt.

abandonar *vt* **1** *(desamparar)* to abandon, forsake: **la suerte le ha abandonado** *luck has forsaken him.* **2** *(lugar)* to leave, quit: **abandonar el barco** *to abandon ship.* **3** *(actividad)* to give up, withdraw from. **4** *(traicionar)* to desert. **5** *(renunciar)* to relinquish, renounce. **6** *(descuidar)* to neglect. **7** DEP *(retirarse)* to withdraw from.
▷ *vpr* **abandonarse 1** *(descuidarse)* to neglect OS, let OS go. **2** *(entregarse)* to give OS up (**a**, to): **se abandonó a la bebida** *he gave himself up to drink.* **3** *(ceder)* to give in.

abandono *nm* **1** *(acción)* abandoning, desertion. **2** *(idea, actividad)* giving up. **3** *(descuido)* neglect, lack of care. **4** *(dejadez)* apathy, carelessness. **5** DEP withdrawal: **ganaron por abandono** *they won by default.* **6** MAR abandonment. ■ **en estado de abandono** in an abandoned state.

abanicar [1] *vt* to fan.

abanico *nm* **1** fan. **2** *fig* range: **un abanico de posibilidades** *a range of possibilities.* ■ **en abanico** fan-shaped. | **abrirse en abanico** to fan out.

abaratar *vt* to reduce the price of, make cheaper.
▷ *vpr* **abaratarse** *(precio)* to come down, fall; *(artículo)* to become cheaper, come down in price.

abarcar [1] *vt* **1** *(englobar)* to cover, embrace: **sus conocimientos abarcan el campo de la psicología** *her knowledge covers the field of psychology.* **2** *(abrazar)* to embrace, get one's arms around. **3** *(trabajo)* to undertake, take on.

abarquillado,-a *pp* ⟶ **abarquillar**.
▷ *adj* warped.

abarquillar *vt (madera)* to warp; *(cartón)* to curl up.
▷ *vpr* **abarquillarse** *(madera)* to warp; *(cartón)* to curl up.

abarrotado,-a *pp* ⟶ **abarrotar**.
▷ *adj (cosas)* packed (**de**, with), crammed (**de**, with); *(personas)* jam-packed (**de**, with), packed (**de**, with).

abastecer [43] *vt* to supply, provide.
▷ *vpr* **abastecerse** *(uso reflexivo)* to stock up (**de/con**, with), lay in supplies (**de/con**, of): **se abastecieron de víveres** *they laid in supplies.*

abastecimiento *nm* supplying, provision: **quieren mejorar el abastecimiento de agua** *they want to improve the water supply.*

abasto *nm* **1** *(abastecimiento)* supplying, provision. **2** *(abundancia)* abundance.
▷ *nm pl* **abastos** provisions, supplies. ■ **dar abasto** *fam* to be sufficient for: **no doy abasto para corregir tantos ejercicios** *I've got so many exercises to correct that I just can't cope.*

abatible *adj* folding, collapsible: **asiento abatible** *folding seat;* **cama abatible** *folding bed.*

abatido,-a *pp* ⟶ **abatir**.

▷ *adj* 1 *(deprimido)* dejected, depressed. 2 *(despreciable)* despicable, low. 3 *(fruta)* fallen, drooping.

abatir *vt* 1 *(derribar)* to knock down, pull down. 2 *(matar)* to kill; *(herir)* to wound. 3 *(bajar)* to lower, take down. 4 *(desanimar)* to depress. 5 *(humillar)* to humiliate.

▷ *vpr* **abatirse** 1 *(ave)* to swoop (**sobre**, down on); *(avión)* to dive (**sobre**, down on). 2 *(ceder)* to give in. 3 *(desanimarse)* to lose heart, become depressed. 4 *fig (descender)* to fall upon.

abdicación *nf* abdication.

abdicar [1] *vt* 1 *(soberanía)* to abdicate, renounce. 2 *(ideales, ideas)* to give up, renounce.

▷ *vi* 1 *(soberanía)* to abdicate: **abdicó en su hija** *he abdicated in favour of his daughter.* 2 *(ideales)* to give up (**de**, -).

abdomen *nm* abdomen.

abdominal *adj* abdominal.

▷ *nm pl* **abdominales** *(ejercicios)* sit-ups.

abductor *adj* abductor.

abecedario *nm* 1 *(alfabeto)* alphabet. 2 *(libro)* spelling book. 3 *(nociones)* rudiments *pl*, basics *pl*.

abedul *nm* birch tree, birch.

abeja *nf* 1 *(animal)* bee. 2 *fig (persona)* busy bee. ● **abeja obrera** worker bee. ‖ **abeja reina** queen bee.

abejaruco *nm* bee-eater.

abejón *nm* 1 *(zángano)* drone. 2 *(abejorro)* bumblebee.

abejorro *nm* 1 *(himenóptero)* bumblebee. 2 *(coleóptero)* cockchafer. 3 *fig (persona)* bore, nuisance.

aberración *nf* aberration.

aberrante *adj* aberrant.

abertura *nf* 1 *(agujero)* opening, gap; *(grieta)* crack, slit. 2 *(valle)* pass. 3 *(ensenada)* cove, creek.

abeto *nm* fir tree, fir. ● **abeto blanco** silver fir. ‖ **abeto falso** spruce. ‖ **abeto rojo** spruce.

abiertamente *adv* openly, frankly.

abierto,-a *pp* ⟶ **abrir.**

▷ *adj* 1 open, unlocked. 2 *(grifo)* (turned) on: **dejó el grifo abierto** *she left the tap running.* 3 *fig (sincero)* open, frank. 4 *(tolerante)* open-minded. 5 LING open. ■ **abierto,-a al mar** seaward-looking. ‖ **abierto,-a de par en par** wide open.

abigarrado,-a *adj* 1 *(multicolor)* multicoloured (US multicolored), many-coloured (US many-colored). 2 *(mezclado)* jumbled, mixed.

abisal *adj* abyssal.

abismal *adj* abysmal: **hay una diferencia abismal** *there is a world of a difference.*

abismo *nm* abyss: **entre tu y yo media un abismo** *we are worlds apart.* ■ **estar al borde del abismo** *fig* to be on the brink of ruin.

abjurar *vt* to abjure, forswear.

▷ *vi* to abjure (**de**, -), renounce (**de**, -): **abjuró de su religión** *he renounced his religion.*

ablación *nf* 1 *(acción geológica)* ablation. 2 *(cirugía)* surgcal removal, ablation.

ablandar *vt* 1 to soften. 2 *fig (persona)* to soothe, soften up, appease.

▷ *vi (frío)* to get warmer, get milder; *(hielo, nieve)* to melt.

▷ *vpr* **ablandarse** 1 to soften, get softer. 2 *(persona)* to soften up. 3 *(acobardarse)* to lose one's nerve, become frightened. 4 *(frío)* to get warmer, get milder; *(nieve, hielo)* to melt.

ablativo *nm* ablative (case).

ablución *nf* [Also used in plural with the sam meaning.] ablution.

▷ *nf pl* **abluciones** water and wine *sing.*

abnegación *nf* abnegation, self-denial.

abnegado,-a *pp* ⟶ **abnegar.**

▷ *adj* selfless, self-sacrificing.

abobado,-a *pp* ⟶ **abobar.**

▷ *adj* 1 *(tonto)* stupid, silly. 2 *(distraído)* absent-minded. 3 *(pasmado)* bewildered.

abocado,-a *pp* ⟶ **abocar.**

▷ *adj* 1 *(expuesto)* exposed to: **es un proyecto aboca al fracaso** *it's a project that is doomed to failure.* 2 *(vin* medium dry, smooth.

abocar [1] *vt* 1 *(verter)* to pour out. 2 *(asir)* to catch one's mouth. 3 *(acercar)* to bring near, draw up: **l olas abocaron el barco a la orilla** *the waves washed t boat to the shore.*

▷ *vi* MAR to enter (**en**, -): **el barco abocó en el puerto** *t boat entered the harbour.*

▷ *vpr* **abocarse** *(reunirse)* to meet, gather.

abochornado,-a *pp* ⟶ **abochornar.**

▷ *adj* ashamed, embarrassed.

abochornar *vt* 1 *(avergonzar)* to shame. 2 *(acalorc* to make flushed.

▷ *vpr* **abochornarse** 1 *(avergonzarse)* to become er barrassed. 2 *(planta)* to wilt.

abocinado,-a *pp* abocinar.

▷ *adj* 1 trumpet-shaped. 2 ARQUIT splayed.

abofetear *vt* to slap.

abogacía *nf* legal profession.

abogado,-a *nm & nf* 1 lawyer, solicitor; *(tribun supremo)* barrister. 2 *fig* advocate, champion. ■ **eje cer de abogado** to practise law, be a lawyer. ● **ab gado de oficio** legal-aid lawyer. ‖ **abogado defens** counsel for the defense. ‖ **abogado del diablo** devi advocate. ‖ **abogado laborista** union lawyer.

abogar [7] *vi* 1 to plead. 2 *fig* to intercede. ■ **aboga favor de** to plead for. ‖ **abogar por** 1 *(preconizar)* advocate, propose. 2 *(defender)* to defend. 3 *(luch por)* to fight for.

abolengo *nm* ancestry, lineage.

abolición *nf* abolition.

abolicionista *adj* abolitionist.

▷ *nm o nf* abolitionist.

abolir *vt* to abolish.

Used only in forms which include the letter i i their endings: **abolía, aboliré, aboliendo,** etc.

abolladura *nf (hundimiento)* dent; *(bollo)* bump.

abollar *vt* 1 to dent. 2 ARTE to emboss.

▷ *vpr* **abollarse** to get dented.

abombado,-a *pp* ⟶ **abombar.**

▷ *adj* convex.

abombar *vt* 1 to make convex. 2 *fam (aturdir)* deafen, confuse.

▷ *vpr* **abombarse** to become convex.

abominable *adj* abominable, loathsome.

abominar *vt* to abominate, loathe.

▷ *vi* to abominate (**de**, -), loathe (**de**, -).

abonado,-a *pp* ⟶ **abonar.**

▷ *adj* 1 *(tierra)* fertilized. 2 FIN paid.

nm & nf (al teléfono, a revista) subscriber; *(a teatro, tren, etc)* season ticket holder.

bonar *vt* **1** FIN to pay. **2** *(avalar)* to guarantee, answer for: **les abonó su buena reputación** *their good reputation spoke for itself.* **3** *(tierra)* to fertilize. **4** *(subscribir)* to subscribe.
vpr **abonarse** *(a revista)* to subscribe (**a**, to); *(a teatro, tren, etc)* to buy a season ticket (**a**, for).

bono *nm* **1** *(pago)* payment. **2** *(aval)* guarantee. **3** *(fertilizante)* fertilizer; *(acción)* fertilizing. **4** *(a revista)* subscription; *(a teatro, tren, etc)* season-ticket.

bordaje *nm* **1** *(choque)* collision, fouling. **2** *(ataque)* boarding. ■ **¡al abordaje!** stand by to board!

bordar *vt* **1** MAR *(chocar)* to run foul of, collide with; *(atacar)* to board. **2** MAR *(arribar)* to reach port. **3** *fig (persona)* to approach; *(asunto, tema)* to tackle.

borigen *adj* aboriginal, native.
nm aborigine, native.
▲ *pl* **aborígenes.**

borrecer [43] *vt* **1** to abhor, hate, detest. **2** *(aves)* to abandon.

borrecible *adj* hateful, detestable, loathsome.

bortar *vi* **1** *(voluntariamente)* to abort, have an abortion; *(involuntariamente)* to miscarry, have a miscarriage. **2** *(fracasar)* to fail, fall through.
vt (interrumpir) to stop; *(frustrar)* to foil, thwart: **tuvieron que abortar la misión** *the mission had to be aborted.*

bortivo,-a *adj* abortive.
nm **abortivo** abortifacient.

borto *nm* **1** *(provocado)* abortion; *(espontáneo)* miscarriage. **2** *pey (persona)* ugly person, freak; *(cosa)* abortion.

botargado,-a *pp* ⟶ **abotargarse.**
adj swollen.

botonar *vt (ropa)* to button, button up.
vi (planta) to bud.
vpr **abotonarse** to do one's buttons up.

bovedado,-a *pp* ⟶ **abovedar.**
adj vaulted, arched.

boyar *vt* to buoy.

brasado,-a *pp* ⟶ **abrasar.**
adj burnt.

brasador,-ra *adj* **1** burning, scorching. **2** *fig* consuming: **pasión abrasadora** *consuming passion.*

brasar *vt* **1** *(quemar)* to burn, scorch. **2** *(calentar)* overheat.
vi to burn (up): **esta sopa abrasa** *this soup is scalding hot.*
vpr **abrasarse** to burn. ■ **abrasarse de calor** *fig* to be sweltering.

brasivo,-a *adj* abrasive.
nm **abrasivo** abrasive.

brazadera *nf* clamp, brace.

brazar [4] *vt* **1** to embrace, hug: **se abrazaron** *they embraced each other.* **2** *(ceñir)* to clasp. **3** *(incluir)* to include, comprise. **4** *(adoptar)* to adopt. **5** *fig (adherirse)* to embrace.

brazo *nm* hug, embrace. ■ **dar un abrazo a** ALGN to embrace sb. ‖ **un abrazo (de)** *(en carta)* with best wishes from.

brebotellas *nm inv* bottle opener.

abrecartas *nm inv* letter-opener, paperknife.

abrelatas *nm inv* tin-opener, US can-opener.

abrevadero *nm* drinking trough.

abreviado,-a *pp* ⟶ **abreviar.**
▷ *adj* concise.

abreviar [12] *vt* **1** *(acortar)* to shorten, cut short. **2** *(texto)* to abridge; *(palabra)* to abbreviate.

abreviatura *nf* abbreviation: **la abreviatura de etcétera es, etc** *the abbreviation of etcetera is, etc.*

abridor *nm* opener.

abrigado,-a *pp* ⟶ **abrigar.**
▷ *adj (lugar)* sheltered, protected; *(persona)* wrapped up.

abrigar [7] *vt* **1** *(contra el frío)* to wrap up; *(ropa)* to be warm: **abriga bien al niño, que hace mucho frío en la calle** *wrap him up well, it's very cold outside.* **2** *(proteger)* to shelter, protect. **3** *fig (sospechas)* to harbour (US harbor), have. **4** *fig (esperanzas)* to foster, cherish.
▷ *vpr* **abrigarse** *(uso reflexivo)* to wrap OS up.

abrigo *nm* **1** *(prenda)* coat, overcoat. **2** *(refugio)* shelter. ■ **al abrigo de** protected from, sheltered from. ‖ **al abrigo de la ley** under the protection of the law. ● **ropa de abrigo** warm clothing, warm clothes *pl.*

abril *nm* **1** April. **2** *fig* springtime.
▷ *nm pl* **abriles** *fig* summers: **una chica de veinte abriles** *a girl of twenty summers.*

For examples of use, see **marzo.**

abrillantador,-ra *nm & nf (persona)* polisher.
▷ *nm* **abrillantador 1** *(producto)* polish. **2** *(instrumento)* polishing tool, polisher.

abrillantar *vt* **1** to polish, make shine, burnish. **2** *fig* to enhance.

abrir *vt* **1** *(gen)* to open: **abre la ventana** *open the window;* **abrid vuestros libros en la página diez** *open your books at page ten.* **2** *(con llave)* to unlock: **sacó una llave y abrió la caja** *he took out a key and unlocked the safe.* **3** *(cremallera)* to undo: **abrió la cremallera de la maleta** *she undid the zip (US zipper) on the case, she unzipped the case.* **4** *(negocio)* to open. **5** *(túnel)* to dig; *(agujero)* to make. **6** *(luz)* to switch on, turn on; *(gas, grifo)* to turn on. **7** *(iniciar)* to start, begin. **8** *(encabezar)* to head, lead.
▷ *vpr* **abrirse 1** *(gen)* to open: **la puerta se abre hacia fuera** *the door opens outwards.* **2** *(flor)* to open, come out: **las rosas se están abriendo** *the roses are opening.* **3** *(iniciarse)* to begin, start, open. **4** *(extenderse)* to spread out, unfold. **5** *(dar)* to open (**a**, onto), look (**a**, onto): **la casa se abre al mar** *the house looks onto the sea.* **6** *(ligamentos)* to sprain. **7** *fig (sincerarse)* to open out. **8** *argot (largarse)* to clear off, be off,: **¡adiós, me abro!** *bye, I'm off!,* US *I'm out of here!* ■ **abrir fuego** MIL to open fire. ‖ **abrir la mano** *fig* to relax standards. ‖ **abrir paso** to make way. ‖ **abrir un expediente** JUR to start proceedings. ‖ **abrir una posibilidad** to open up a possibility. ‖ **abrirse paso en la vida** *fig* to make one's way in life. ‖ **en un abrir y cerrar de ojos** *fam* in the twinkling of an eye. ‖ **no abrir (la) boca** *fig* not to say a word.
▲ *pp* **abierto,-a.**

abrochar *vt* **1** *(camisa)* to button, button up; *(zapato)* to tie up, do up. **2** *(botones)* to do up; *(broche, corche-*

te) to fasten: **abróchense los cinturones** *please fasten your seat belts.*

abrumar *vt* to overwhelm, crush: **la abrumó con sus atenciones** *his attentions made her feel uncomfortable.*
▷ *vpr* **abrumarse** to become misty.

abrupto,-a *adj* 1 *(terreno)* rugged; *(pendiente)* steep, abrupt. 2 *(persona)* abrupt, sudden.

absceso *nm* abscess.

abscisa *nf* abscissa.

absentismo *nm* 1 *(laboral)* absenteeism. 2 *(del terrateniente)* absentee landlordism.

ábside *nm* apse.

absolución *nf* 1 REL absolution. 2 JUR acquittal.

absolutismo *nm* absolutism.

absoluto,-a *adj* absolute. ■ **en absoluto** not at all, by no means. | **estar prohibido,-a en absoluto** to be absolutely forbidden. | **nada en absoluto** nothing at all.

absolver [32] *vt* 1 REL to absolve. 2 JUR to acquit.
▲ *pp* **absuelto,-a.**

absorbente *adj* 1 absorbent. 2 *fig (trabajo)* absorbing, engrossing; *(exigente)* demanding. 3 *fig (persona)* overbearing, domineering.
▷ *nm* absorbent.

absorber *vt* 1 *(líquidos)* to absorb, soak up. 2 *fig (conocimientos)* to absorb. 3 *fig (consumir)* to use up. 4 *fig (cautivar)* to captivate.

absorción *nf* absorption.

absorto,-a *adj* 1 *(pasmado)* amazed, bewildered. 2 *(ensimismado)* absorbed (**en**, in), engrossed (**en**, in): **estaba absorta en sus pensamientos** *she was lost in thought.*

abstemio,-a *adj* abstemious, teetotal.
▷ *nm & nf* teetotaller.

abstención *nf* abstention.

abstenerse [87] *vpr* to abstain (**de**, from), refrain (**de**, from): **se abstuvieron de votar** *they abstained from voting.* ■ **ante la duda, abstenerse** when in doubt, don't.

abstinencia *nf* abstinence. ● **síndrome de abstinencia** withdrawal symptoms *pl.*

abstracción *nf* 1 abstraction. 2 *(concentración)* concentration.

abstracto,-a *adj* abstract: **en abstracto** *in the abstract.*

abstraer [88] *vt* to abstract.
▷ *vi (prescindir)* to leave aside (**de**, -).
▷ *vpr* **abstraerse** *(ensimismarse)* to become lost in thought; *(concentrarse)* to engross OS (**en**, in).

abstraído,-a *pp* → **abstraer.**
▷ *adj* 1 *(absorto)* absorbed, engrossed. 2 *(distraído)* absent-minded.

absuelto,-a *pp* → **absolver.**
▷ *adj* 1 REL absolved. 2 JUR acquitted.

absurdo,-a *adj* absurd: **sería absurdo que dejaras el trabajo** *it would be crazy to leave your job.*
▷ *nm* **absurdo** absurdity, nonsense.

abuchear *vt* to boo, jeer at.

abuela *nf* 1 grandmother; *(familiarmente)* grandma, granny. 2 *(vieja)* old woman. ■ **no tener abuela** *fam* not to be afraid of blowing one's own trumpet. | **¡tu abuela!** *fam* rubbish!

abuelo *nm* 1 grandfather; *(familiarmente)* granddad, grandpa. 2 *(viejo)* old man.
▷ *nm pl* **abuelos** 1 grandparents. 2 *fig* ancestors, forebears.

abulia *nf* apathy, lack of willpower.

abúlico,-a *adj* apathetic, lacking in willpower.

abultado,-a *pp* → **abultar.**
▷ *adj* bulky, big.

abultar *vt* 1 to enlarge, increase. 2 *fig* to exaggerate.
▷ *vi* to be bulky: **la caja abulta mucho** *the box takes up a lot of space.*

abundancia *nf* abundance, plenty.

abundante *adj* abundant, plentiful.

abundar *vi* 1 *(haber en cantidad)* to abound, be plentiful: **las manzanas abundan** *there are plenty of apples.* 2 **abundar en** *(tener en cantidad)* to be rich in, abound in: **esta región abunda en aceite de oliva** *this region is rich in olive oil.* 3 *fig (adherirse)* to share, support.

aburrido,-a *pp* → **aburrir.**
▷ *adj* 1 *(ser aburrido)* boring, tedious; *(monótono)* dull, dreary. 2 *(estar aburrido)* bored, weary; *(cansado)* tired of; *(harto)* fed up with.

aburrimiento *nm* boredom. ■ **¡menudo aburrimiento!** how boring!, what a bore! | **ser un aburrimiento** to be a bore.

aburrir *vt* 1 to bore. 2 *(cansar)* to tire.
▷ *vpr* **aburrirse** to get bored (**con/de/por**, with).

abusar *vi* 1 *(propasarse)* to go too far, abuse (**de**, -): **abusar de** ALGN *to take unfair advantage of sb.* 2 *(usar mal)* to misuse (**de**, -): **abusar de la bebida** *to drink too much.*

abusivo,-a *adj* excessive, exorbitant. ● **trato abusivo** ill-treatment.

abuso *nm* 1 abuse, misuse. 2 *(injusticia)* injustice.

abyecto,-a *adj* abject, wretched.

a.C. *abrev* (**antes de Cristo**) before Christ; *(abreviatura)* BC.

acá *adv* 1 *(lugar)* here, over here. 2 *(tiempo)* now, at this time. ■ **de acá para allá** to and fro, up and down. | **de un tiempo acá** lately. | **más acá** nearer.

acabado,-a *pp* → **acabar.**
▷ *adj* 1 *(terminado)* finished; *(perfecto)* perfect, complete: **acabado,-a de hacer** *freshly made.* 2 *fig (malparado)* worn-out, spent: **una persona acabada** *a has-been;* **un actor acabado** *a burnt-out actor.*
▷ *nm* **acabado** finish: **se presenta con tres acabados distintos** *it comes in three different finishes.*

acabar *vt* 1 *(gen)* to finish, finish off; *(completar)* complete: **he acabado el trabajo** *I've finished the work.* 2 *(consumir)* to use up.
▷ *vi* 1 *(gen)* to finish, end; *(pareja)* to split up: **acaba en punta** *it has a pointed end;* **Pilar y Juan han acabado** *Pilar and Juan have split up.* 2 **acabar por** + *gerund* to end up + *-ing*: **acabé por comprar el vestido** *I ended up buying the dress.*
▷ *vpr* **acabarse** to end, finish, come to an end; *(no quedar)* to run out: **el partido se acabó con empate a dos goles** *the match ended in a two-all draw;* **se acabó la fiesta** *the party's over.* ■ **acabar bien** to have a happy ending. | **acabar con** 1 *(destruir)* to destroy, put an end to. 2 *(terminar)* to finish, finish off. | **acabar de** + *inf* to have just + *pp*: **no lo toques, acabo de pintar**

ahora mismo *don't touch it, I've just painted it.* ‖ **acabar mal 1** *(cosa)* to end badly. **2** *(persona)* to come to a bad end: como sigas así acabarás mal *if you carry on like that you'll come to a bad end.* ‖ **¡se acabó!** that's it!

ademia *nf* **1** *(institución)* academy. **2** *(escuela)* school, academy. ● **La Real Academia Española** the Spanish Academy.

allar *vt* **1** to silence, hush. **2** *fig (persona)* to pacify; *(críticas)* to silence.

alorado,-a *pp* → acalorar.
adj **1** hot; *(cara)* flushed. **2** *fig (persona)* excited, worked up; *(debate)* heated, angry.

alorar *vt* **1** to warm up, heat up. **2** *fig* to excite; *(pasiones)* to inflame, arouse.
vpr **acalorarse 1** to warm up, heat up, get warm, get hot. **2** *fig (persona)* to get excited, get worked up; *(debate, etc)* to become heated.

ampada *nf* camping. ● **zona de acampada** camp site.

ampar *vi* to camp.
vt to camp.

analado,-a *pp* → acanalar.
adj **1** grooved. **2** ARQUIT fluted.

antilado,-a *adj* **1** *(costa)* steep, sheer; *(rocoso)* rocky, craggy. **2** *(fondo del mar)* shelving.
nm **acantilado** cliff.

aparar *vt* **1** *(productos)* to hoard; *(mercado)* to corner, buy up. **2** *(monopolizar)* to monopolize, keep for os.

aramelado,-a *pp* → acaramelar.
adj **1** *(sabor)* oversweet. **2** *(color)* caramel-coloured (US caramel-colored). **3** *fig (pareja)* lovey-dovey, starry-eyed; *(voz)* syrupy, sugary.

ariciar [12] *vt* **1** to caress, fondle. **2** *(pelo, animal)* to stroke. **3** *fig (esperanzas, etc)* to cherish; *(idea, plan)* to have in mind.
vpr **acariciarse** *(uso recíproco)* to caress each other.

aro *nm* mite.

arrear *vt* **1** *(transportar)* to carry, transport. **2** *fig (producir)* to cause, bring, give rise to.

aso *adv* perhaps, maybe: acaso esté enfermo *maybe he's ill;* ¿acaso no lo viste? *didn't you see him?*
nm (suerte) chance. ■ **por si acaso** just in case. ‖ **si acaso 1** *(en todo caso)* if anything. **2** *(hipótesis)* if: si acaso lo ves *if you see him.*

atar *vt* **1** *(leyes, etc)* to obey, observe, comply with. **2** *(respetar)* to respect.

atarrarse *vpr* to catch a cold.

audalado,-a *pp* → acaudalar.
adj wealthy, rich, well-off.

ceder *vi* **1** *(consentir)* to consent (a, to), agree (a, to). **2** *(tener entrada)* to enter. **3** *(alcanzar)* to accede (a, to).

cesible *adj* accessible; *(persona)* approachable.

ceso *nm* **1** *(entrada)* access, entry; *(a una ciudad)* approach. **2** *(de tos)* fit; *(de fiebre)* attack, bout. **3** *fig (ataque)* fit, outburst. **4** INFORMÁ access: acceso directo *random access.*

cidentado,-a *pp* → accidentarse.
adj **1** *(persona)* injured. **2** *(con incidentes)* eventful, agitated. **3** *(terreno)* uneven, rough, bumpy.
nm & nf casualty, accident victim.

accidental *adj* accidental: no fue más que un encuentro accidental *it was nothing but a chance meeting.*

accidente *nm* **1** accident: sufrir un accidente *to have an accident.* **2** *(terreno)* unevenness, irregularity. **3** MED faint. ■ **por accidente** by chance. ● **accidente de trabajo** industrial accident. ‖ **accidente de tráfico** road accident. ‖ **accidentes geográficos** geographical features.

acción *nf* **1** action; *(acto)* act, deed. **2** *(efecto)* effect. **3** COM share. **4** JUR action, lawsuit. **5** TEAT plot. **6** MIL action. ■ **entrar en acción** MIL to go into action. ‖ **ponerse en acción** to start doing sth. ● **acción de gracias** thanksgiving. ‖ **película de acción** adventure film.

accionar *vt (máquina)* to drive, work, activate.
▷ *vi* to gesticulate.

accionista *nm o nf* shareholder, stockholder.

acechar *vt* **1** *(vigilar)* to watch, spy on; *(esperar)* to lie in wait for. **2** *(caza)* to stalk. **3** *(amenazar)* to threaten, lurk: un gran peligro acecha *great danger lies ahead.*

acecho *nm* watching. ■ **estar al acecho de 1** *(vigilar)* to be on the lookout for. **2** *(esperar)* to lie in wait for.

aceite *nm* oil. ● **aceite de girasol** sunflower oil. ‖ **aceite de maíz** corn oil. ‖ **aceite de oliva** olive oil. ‖ **aceite de ricino** castor oil.

aceitera *nf* **1** oil bottle. **2** AUTO oil can.
▷ *nf pl* **aceiteras** oil and vinegar set *sing*, cruet *sing*.

aceitoso,-a *adj* **1** oily. **2** *(grasiento)* greasy.

aceituna *nf* olive. ● **aceituna rellena** stuffed olive.

aceleración *nf* acceleration. ● **poder de aceleración** AUTO acceleration.

acelerador,-ra *adj* accelerating.
▷ *nm* **acelerador** AUTO accelerator.

acelerar *vt* **1** to accelerate; *(paso)* to quicken. **2** *fig* to speed up.
▷ *vpr* **acelerarse 1** *fig (azorarse)* to be embarrassed. **2** *fig (apresurarse)* to hasten, hurry up.

acelga *nf* chard.

acento *nm* **1** *(tilde)* accent (mark). **2** *(tónico)* stress. **3** *(pronunciación)* accent: acento andaluz *Andalusian accent.* **4** *(énfasis)* emphasis, stress. ● **acento ortográfico** written accent, accent.

acentuación *nf* accentuation.

acentuar [11] *vt* **1** *(tilde)* to accentuate; *(tónico)* to stress. **2** *(resaltar)* to emphasize, stress.
▷ *vpr* **acentuarse** to become more pronounced, become more marked.

acepción *nf* meaning, sense.

aceptable *adj* acceptable.

aceptación *nf* **1** acceptance. **2** *(aprobación)* approval; *(éxito)* success: la película tuvo poca aceptación *the film wasn't popular, the film met with little success.*

aceptar *vt* **1** to accept, receive. **2** *(aprobar)* to approve of.

acequia *nf* irrigation channel, ditch.

acera *nf* pavement, US sidewalk. ■ **ser de la acera de enfrente** *fam* to be gay, be queer.

acerca de *adv* about, concerning, on.

acercar [1] *vt* **1** to bring near, bring nearer, draw up: acércate *come closer;* ¿me acercas el agua? *can you pass the water?* **2** *fig* to bring together.

▷ *vpr* **acercarse 1** *(aproximarse)* to be near: **se acerca el verano** *summer is near.* **2** *(ir)* to go: **acércate a la esquina** *go to the corner.* **3** *(visitar)* to drop in, drop by.

acero *nm* **1** steel. **2** *(espada)* sword, steel.
▷ *nm pl* **aceros** *(valor)* courage *sing*, bravery *sing*. ● **acero inoxidable** stainless steel.

acertado,-a *pp* → **acertar**.
▷ *adj* **1** *(opinión, etc)* right, correct; *(comentario)* fitting; *(idea, decisión)* clever; *(color)* well-chosen; *(palabra)* exact. **2** *(conveniente)* suitable. ■ **estar acertado,-a** to be wise.

acertante *adj* winning.
▷ *nm o nf (concurso, quiniela)* winner; *(problema)* solver.

acertar [27] *vt* **1** *(en un objetivo)* to hit. **2** *(dar con lo cierto)* to get right: **solo acertó cinco preguntas** *she only got five questions right.* **3** *(por azar)* to guess correctly; *(concurso, quinielas)* to win. **4** *(encontrar)* to find: **acertó la casa a la primera** *he found the house at the first attempt.*
▷ *vi* **1** *(encontrar)* to find: **acertó con el libro enseguida** *he found the book at once.* **2** *(dar con lo cierto)* to get right, be right. ■ **acertar a** + *inf* to happen to + *inf*: **yo acertaba a estar allí** *I happened to be there.*

acertijo *nm* riddle.

acético,-a *adj* acetic.

acetileno *nm* acetylene.

achacar [1] *vt* to impute, attribute.

achantar *vi fam (intimidar)* to scare, frighten.
▷ *vpr* **achantarse 1** *(acobardarse)* to get frightened, lose one's nerve. **2** *(esconderse)* to hide. **3** *fam (callarse)* to shut up.

achaque *nm* ailment, complaint. ■ **con achaque de** under the pretext of. ‖ **en achaque de** in the matter of, on the subject of.

achatado,-a *pp* → **achatar**.
▷ *adj* flattened.

achicar [1] *vt* **1** *(amenguar)* to diminish, reduce, make smaller. **2** *(amilanar)* to intimidate. **3** *(agua)* to drain; *(en barco)* to bale out.
▷ *vpr* **achicarse 1** *(amenguarse)* to get smaller. **2** *(amilanarse)* to lose heart.

achicharrar *vt* to scorch; *(comida)* to burn: **hace un sol que achicharra** *it's roasting.*
▷ *vi (molestar)* to bother, pester: **le achicharraron a/con preguntas** *he was plagued with questions.*
▷ *vpr* **achicharrarse** to roast.

achicoria *nf* chicory.

achinado,-a *adj* oriental-looking; *(ojos)* slanting.

achuchado,-a *pp* → **achuchar**.
▷ *adj fam* difficult.

achuchar *vt* **1** *(azuzar)* to nag at: **me anda achuchando para que lave el coche** *she keeps nagging at me to wash the car.* **2** *(abrazar)* to hug, squeeze: **había una pareja achuchándose en el rincón** *there was a couple having a cuddle in the corner.* **3** *(dar empujones)* to jostle. **4** *(empujar)* to shove.

achuchón *nm* **1** *fam (empujón)* push, shove: **el delantero apartó al portero de un achuchón** *the forward pushed the goalkeeper aside.* **2** *fam (indisposición)* ailment: **le dio un achuchón** *he had a funny turn.* **3** *fam (abrazo)* hug, squeeze.

acicalar *vt* to smarten up.
▷ *vpr* **acicalarse** to dress up, smarten up.

acicate *nm* **1** *(espuela)* spur. **2** *fig (incentivo)* spur, i centive, stimulus.

acidez *nf* **1** *(sabor)* sourness, sharpness. **2** QUÍM aci ity. ● **acidez de estómago** heartburn.

ácido,-a *adj* **1** *(sabor)* sharp, tart. **2** QUÍM acidic. **3** *(. no)* harsh.
▷ *nm* **ácido 1** QUÍM acid. **2** *argot (droga)* acid, LS ● **ácido sulfúrico** sulphuric acid. ‖ **ácido úrico** uric ac

acierto *nm* **1** *(adivinación)* correct guess, right a swer. **2** *(buena idea)* good choice/idea. **3** *(log* good shot. **4** *(tino)* wisdom, good judgement. *(casualidad)* chance. **6** *(éxito)* success. **7** *(habilida* skill.

aclamación *nf* acclamation, acclaim.

aclamar *vt* to acclaim.

aclaración *nf* explanation.

aclarar *vt* **1** *(cabello, color)* to lighten, make lighter. *(líquido)* to thin (down). **3** *(enjuagar)* to rinse. **4** *(e plicar)* to explain; *(poner en claro)* to make cle clarify. **5** *fig (mejorar)* to improve.
▷ *vi (mejorar el tiempo)* to clear (up).
▷ *vpr* **aclararse 1** *(entender)* to understand: **no me ac ro con esta lección** *I can't understand this lesson. (explicarse)* to explain OS. **3** *(decidirse)* to make u one's mind. **4** [Used only in the 3rd person; it do not take a subject.] *(el tiempo)* to clear (up).

aclaratorio,-a *adj* explanatory.

aclimatación *nf* acclimatization, US acclimation.

aclimatar *vt* to acclimatize (**a**, to), US acclimate (**a**, tc
▷ *vpr* **aclimatarse 1** to become acclimatized (**a**, to), b come US acclimated (**a**, to). **2** *fig* to get used to.

acné *nf* acne.

acobardar *vt* to frighten, unnerve.
▷ *vpr* **acobardarse** to become frightened, lose one's ner shrink back (**ante**, from).

acodar *vt* **1** *(plantas)* to layer. **2** *(doblar)* to bend.
▷ *vpr* **acodarse** to lean/rest on one's elbows.

acogedor,-ra *adj* **1** *(persona)* welcoming, friend **2** *(lugar)* cosy, warm.

acoger [5] *vt* **1** *(recibir)* to receive; *(a invitado)* to w come. **2** *(admitir)* to admit, accept. **3** *(proteger)* shelter, protect. **4** *(ideas, etc)* to accept, take to.
▷ *vpr* **acogerse 1** *(refugiarse)* to take refuge (**a**, in). **2** *una ley, etc)* to have recourse to; *(amnistía, prome* to avail OS of.

acogida *nf* **1** reception, welcome. **2** *fig* shelter. *(aceptación)* popularity. ■ **tener buena acogida** to welcomed.

acojonado,-a *pp argot* → **acojonar**.
▷ *adj* **1** *argot (asustado)* shit-scared. **2** *argot (asombra* gobsmacked.

acojonar *vt* **1** *argot (atemorizar)* to scare the shit o of. **2** *argot (asombrar)* to knock out:
▷ *vpr* **acojonarse** *argot* to shit OS, shit bricks.

acolchar *vt* **1** *(prenda)* to quilt. **2** *(superficie)* to pad.

acometer *vt* **1** *(embestir)* to attack. **2** *(emprender)* undertake. **3** *(empezar repentinamente)* to be seiz by: **le acometió la risa** *he burst out laughing;* **le acom tió la duda** *she was nagged by doubt;* **le acometió tos** *she had a coughing fit.*

acometida *nf* **1** *(ataque)* attack, assault. **2** *(derivaci* connection.

comodado,-a *pp* ⟶ acomodar.
adj 1 *(conveniente)* suitable. 2 *(rico)* well-to-do, well off. 3 *(precio)* reasonable, moderate. 4 *(ordenado)* arranged. 5 *(adaptado)* adapted.
comodador,-ra *nm & nf (hombre)* usher; *(mujer)* usherette.
compañamiento *nm* 1 accompaniment. 2 *(comitiva)* retinue, escort. 3 *(guarnición de plato)* accompaniment to a main dish, side dish. 4 MÚS accompaniment.
compañante *adj* accompanying.
nm o nf 1 companion, escort. 2 MÚS accompanist.
compañar *vt* 1 to accompany, go with: **te acompaño a la puerta** *I'll see you to the door;* **nos acompañó al cine** *she came with us to the cinema.* 2 *(adjuntar)* to enclose, attach. 3 MÚS to accompany.
vpr **acompañarse** MÚS to accompany OS (**a**, on). ■ **acompañar en el sentimiento** *fml* to express one's condolences to.
compasar *vt* 1 MÚS to mark the time of, mark the rhythm of. 2 *(adaptar)* to keep in time, adjust.
complejar *vi* to give a complex.
vpr **acomplejarse** to develop a complex (**por**, about).
condicionado,-a *pp* ⟶ acondicionar.
adj equipped, fitted-out: **la casa no está acondicionada para vivir** *the house is not fit to be lived in.*
condicionador *nm* conditioner. ● **acondicionador de aire** air conditioner. ● **acondicionador del cabello** hair conditioner.
condicionar *vt* 1 to fit up, set up. 2 *(mejorar)* to improve.
congojar *vt* to distress, grieve, make suffer.
vpr **acongojarse** to be distressed.
consejable *adj* advisable: **nada/poco aconsejable** *inadvisable.*
consejar *vt* to advise: **necesita que le aconsejes** *he needs your advice.*
vpr **aconsejarse** to seek advice.
contecer [43] *vi* [Used only in the 3rd person.] to happen, take place.
contecimiento *nm* event, happening.
copiar [12] *vt* to gather, collect.
copio *nm* 1 *(acción)* storing. 2 *(cosa)* store, stock. ■ **hacer acopio de** to store up.
coplamiento *nm* 1 fitting, adaptation. 2 TÉC *(acción)* coupling, connection; *(junta)* joint. 3 *(de naves espaciales)* docking. 4 INFORMÁ handshaking.
coplar *vt* 1 *(juntar)* to fit (together), join, adjust. 2 TÉC to couple, connect. 3 *(aparear)* to mate, pair.
vpr **acoplarse** 1 to fit, join. 2 *(aparearse)* to mate, pair. 3 *(naves espaciales)* to dock.
corazado,-a *pp* ⟶ acorazar.
adj armoured (US armored), armour-plated (US armor-plated).
nm **acorazado** battleship.
cordar [31] *vt* 1 to agree. 2 *(decidir)* to decide. 3 *(conciliar)* to reconcile. 4 MÚS to tune.
vpr **acordarse** to remember (**de**, -): **no se acuerda de nada** *she can't remember anything.*
corde *adj* in agreement, agreed.
nm MÚS chord: **a los acordes de la marcha nupcial** *to the strains of the wedding march.*

acordeón *nm* accordion.
acordonar *vt* 1 *(atar)* to lace, tie. 2 *(rodear)* to surround, draw a cordon around, cordon off.
acorralado,-a *pp* ⟶ acorralar.
▷ *adj* cornered; *(ganado)* penned in, rounded up.
acorralar *vt* to corner; *(ganado)* to pen in, round up.
acortar *vt* to shorten, make shorter: **acortar distancias** *to cut down the distance.*
▷ *vi* to shorten.
▷ *vpr* **acortarse** *fig* to be shy.
acosar *vt* to pursue, chase. ■ **acosar a preguntas** to bombard with questions.
acoso *nm* 1 pursuit, chase. 2 *fig* hounding. ● **acoso sexual** sexual harassment.
acostar [31] *vt* 1 *(en cama)* to put to bed. 2 *(estirar)* to lay down. 3 MAR to bring alongside.
▷ *vpr* **acostarse** 1 *(estirarse)* to lie down. 2 *(irse a dormir)* to go to bed: **es hora de acostarse** *it's bedtime.* ■ **acostarse con** *fam* to sleep with, go to bed with.
acostumbrado,-a *pp* ⟶ acostumbrar.
▷ *adj* 1 *(persona)* accustomed (**a**, to), used (**a**, to). 2 *(hecho)* usual, customary: **es lo acostumbrado** *it is the custom.*
acostumbrar *vt* 1 *(habituar)* to accustom to: **los acostumbró muy pronto** *she got them used to it very soon.* 2 *(soler)* to be in the habit of.
▷ *vpr* **acostumbrarse** *(habituarse)* to become accustomed (**a**, to), get used (**a**, to).
acotación *nf* 1 *(en escrito)* marginal note. 2 TEAT stage direction. 3 *(topográfica)* elevation mark.
acotar[1] *vt* 1 *(área)* to enclose, demarcate. 2 *fig* to delimit.
acotar[2] *vt* 1 *(poner notas)* to add notes; *(texto)* to annotate. 2 *(topografía)* to mark with elevations.
acre *nm (medida)* acre.
acrecentar [27] *vt* to increase.
▷ *vpr* **acrecentarse** to increase.
acreditado,-a *pp* ⟶ acreditar.
▷ *adj* 1 *(prestigioso)* reputable, well-known, prestigious. 2 *(representante, embajador)* accredited.
acreditar *vt* 1 *(probar)* to prove: **¿tiene algún documento que acredite su identidad?** *have you any documents which would prove your identity?* 2 FIN to credit: **hemos acreditado a su cuenta la suma de 1000 dólares** *we have credited your account with the sum of 1000 dollars.* 3 *(embajador)* to accredit.
▷ *vpr* **acreditarse** to gain a reputation, make one's name, become famous.
acreedor,-ra *adj* deserving: **ser/hacerse acreedor a** *to be worthy of.*
▷ *nm & nf* FIN creditor.
acribillar *vt* 1 to riddle, pepper. 2 *fig* to harass, pester: **acribillar a ALGN a preguntas** *to bombard sb with questions.*
acrílico,-a *adj* acrylic.
acritud *nf* 1 *(sabor)* sourness, bitterness; *(olor)* acridity. 2 *(dolor)* intensity. 3 *fig (mordacidad)* acrimony.
acrobacia *nf* 1 acrobatics. 2 [Also used in plural with the same meaning.] *fig (equilibrios)* manoeuvre (US maneuver).
acróbata *nm o nf* acrobat.

acta *nf* 1 [Also used in plural with the same meaning.] *(relación)* minutes *pl*, record (of proceedings); *(publicación)* transactions *pl*. 2 *(certificado)* certificate, official document. ■ **levantar acta** to draw up the minutes. ● **acta notarial** affidavit.
actinia *nf* sea anemone.
actitud *nf* *(disposición)* attitude; *(postura)* position.
activar *vt* 1 TÉC to activate; *(acelerar)* to expedite. 2 INFORMÁ to enable. 3 *fig (avivar)* to liven up, quicken.
▷ *vpr* **activarse** to become activated.
actividad *nf* activity.
activo,-a *adj* active: **estar en activo** *to be on active service.*
▷ *nm* **activo** FIN asset, assets *pl*.
acto *nm* 1 act, action. 2 *(ceremonia)* ceremony, meeting, public function: **acto inaugural** *opening ceremony.* 3 TEAT act. 4 REL Act. ■ **en el acto** at once.
actor *nm* actor.
actriz *nf* actress. ● **primera actriz** leading lady.
actuación *nf* 1 *(en cine, teatro)* performance. 2 *(intervención)* intervention, action. 3 JUR legal proceedings *pl*.
actual *adj* 1 present, current: **dadas las circunstancias actuales** *under the present circumstances.* 2 *(actualizado)* up-to-date: **ese es un tema muy actual** *that's a very topical subject.*
▷ *nm fml* this month: **el doce del actual** *the 12th of this month.*
actualidad *nf* 1 present (time). 2 *(hechos)* current affairs *pl*; *(estado)* the current state of things: **este programa te da toda la actualidad cinematográfica** *this programme gives you all the latest cinema news.* ■ **en la actualidad** at present.
actualizar [4] *vt* 1 *(poner al día)* to bring up to date, update. 2 *(filosofía)* to actualize.
actualmente *adv* *(hoy en día)* nowadays, these days; *(ahora)* at present, at the moment.
actuar [11] *vi* 1 *(ejercer)* to act (**como/de**, as). 2 *(comportarse)* to act: **actuaron como debían** *they did what they had to do.* 3 *(en obra, película)* to perform, act.
▷ *vt (poner en acto)* to actuate, work.
acuarela *nf* watercolour (US watercolor).
acuario *nm* aquarium.
Acuario *nm inv* Aquarius.
acuartelar *vt* 1 MIL *(alojar)* to quarter. 2 *(retener)* to confine to barracks.
acuático,-a *adj* aquatic, water: **animal acuático** *aquatic animal.*
acuchillar *vt* 1 *(seres vivos)* to knife, stab. 2 *(prendas)* to slash. 3 *(madera)* to plane (down).
acuclillarse *vpr* to squat, crouch, crouch down.
acudir *vi* 1 *(ir)* to go; *(venir)* to come, arrive. 2 *(presentarse)* to come back. 3 *(ir a socorrer)* to help, come forward. 4 *(recurrir)* to call on, turn to: **acudir al médico** *to consult one's doctor.*
acueducto *nm* aqueduct.
acuerdo *nm* agreement. ■ **¡de acuerdo!** all right!, O.K.! ‖ **de acuerdo con** in accordance with. ‖ **estar de acuerdo** to agree (**con**, with). ‖ **llegar a un acuerdo** to come to an agreement. ‖ **ponerse de acuerdo** to agree.
acumulación *nf* accumulation.
acumular *vt* to accumulate; *(datos)* to gather; *(dinero)* to amass.
▷ *vpr* **acumularse** 1 to accumulate, pile up, build u[p]. 2 *(gente)* to gather.
acunar *vt* to rock.
acuñar *vt* 1 *(monedas)* to strike, coin, mint. 2 *(u[na] frase)* to coin. 3 *(poner cuñas)* to wedge.
acuoso,-a *adj* 1 watery. 2 *(jugoso)* juicy.
acupuntura *nf* acupuncture.
acurrucarse [1] *vpr* to curl up, snuggle up.
acusación *nf* 1 accusation. 2 JUR charge.
acusado,-a *pp* → **acusar.**
▷ *adj* 1 accused: **acusada de asesinato** *charged with mu[r]der.* 2 *(marcado)* marked, noticeable.
▷ *nm & nf* accused, defendant.
acusar *vt* 1 *(echar la culpa)* to accuse (**de**, of). 2 JUR charge (**de**, with). 3 *(manifestar)* to give away.
▷ *vpr* **acusarse** 1 *(confesarse)* to confess: **se acusó d[el] crimen** *he confessed (to) the crime.* 2 *(acentuarse)* to b[e]come more pronounced.
acusativo *nm* accusative.
acuse ● **acuse de recibo** acknowledgement of receip[t].
acústica *nf* acoustics.
adaptación *nf* adaptation.
adaptado,-a *pp* → **adaptar.**
▷ *adj* adapted.
adaptar *vt* 1 *(acomodar)* to adapt. 2 *(ajustar)* to a[d]just, fit.
▷ *vpr* **adaptarse** *(persona)* to adapt OS (**a**, to); *(cosa)* fit, adjust.
adecentar *vt* to tidy (up), clean (up).
▷ *vpr* **adecentarse** *(uso reflexivo)* to tidy OS up.
adecuado,-a *pp* → **adecuar.**
▷ *adj* adequate, suitable, appropriate.
adecuar [10] *vt* to adapt, make suitable.
a. de J.C. *abrev* (**antes de Jesucristo**) before Chris[t] *(abreviatura)* BC.
adelantado,-a *pp* → **adelantado.**
▷ *adj* 1 *(precoz)* precocious. 2 *(aventajado)* advanced. [3] *(desarrollado)* developed. 4 *(reloj)* fast. 5 *(atrevid[o])* bold, forward. ■ **por adelantado** in advance.
adelantamiento *nm* overtaking. ■ **hacer un ade[lantamiento]** to overtake.
adelantar *vt* 1 to move forward. 2 *(reloj)* to put fo[r]ward. 3 *(pasar delante)* to pass. 4 AUTO to overtak[e]. 5 *(dinero)* to pay in advance.
▷ *vi* 1 *(progresar)* to make progress. 2 *(reloj)* to be fas[t].
▷ *vpr* **adelantarse** 1 *(ir delante)* to go ahead. 2 *(lleg[ar] temprano)* to be early. 3 *(anticiparse)* to get ahead ([of]). 4 *(reloj)* to gain, be fast.
adelante *adv* forward, further.
▷ *interj* 1 *(pase)* come in! 2 *(siga)* go ahead!, carry o[n]. ■ **de aquí en adelante** from here on. ‖ **en adelan[te]** henceforth. ‖ **más adelante** 1 *(tiempo)* later on. 2 *(e[s]pacio)* further on.
adelanto *nm* 1 *(avance)* advance: 2 *(tiempo)* advanc[e]: **llegó con una hora de adelanto** *she arrived an hour [in] advance.* 3 *(pago)* advance.
adelgazante *adj* slimming.
adelgazar [4] *vt (afinar)* to make slim.
▷ *vi (perder peso)* to slim, lose weight.
▷ *vpr* **adelgazarse** to slim, lose weight.

demán *nm (gesto)* gesture, movement.
nm pl **ademanes** manners. ■ **hacer ademán de** to look as if one is about to.
demás *adv* 1 *(también)* also, as well. 2 *(es más)* furthermore, what is more: **¡y además, el coche es mío!** *and what's more, the car's mine!* ■ **además de** as well as, in addition to: **además de gordo es feo** *as well as being fat, he's ugly.*
denoides *nm* adenoids.
dentrarse *vpr* 1 *(penetrar)* to penetrate (**en**, into), enter deep (**en**, into). 2 *fig (profundizar)* to go deeply (**en**, into), study thoroughly (**en**, -), delve (**en**, into).
dentro *adv* inside: **se fueron muy adentro** *they went too far in.*
nm pl **adentros** inward mind *sing*: **para sus adentros** *in his heart.* ■ **mar adentro** out to sea.
depto,-a *adj* who follows, who supports.
nm & nf follower, supporter.
derezar [4] *vt* 1 *(condimentar)* to season; *(ensalada)* to dress; *(bebida)* to prepare, mix. 2 *(preparar)* to prepare. 3 *fig (personas)* to make beautiful; *(cosas)* to embellish.
vpr **aderezarse** *(arreglarse)* to dress up, get ready.
derezo *nm* 1 *(condimento)* seasoning; *(de ensalada)* dressing. 2 *(preparación)* preparation, disposition. 3 *(joyas)* set of jewellery. 4 *(arreos)* harness, trappings *pl.*
deudar *vt* 1 *(deber)* to owe, have a debt of. 2 FIN to debit, charge.
vpr **adeudarse** *(endeudarse)* to get into debt.
dherente *adj* adherent, adhesive.
dherir [35] *vt (pegar)* to stick on.
vi (pegarse) to stick (**a**, to).
vpr **adherirse** 1 *(pegarse)* to stick (**a**, to). 2 *fig (unirse)* to adhere to, follow.
dhesión *nf* 1 adhesion, adherence. 2 *(apoyo)* support.
dhesivo,-a *adj* adhesive.
nm **adhesivo** adhesive.
dicción *nf* addiction. ■ **crear adicción** to be addictive.
dicional *adj* additional.
dictivo,-a *adj* addictive.
dicto,-a *adj* 1 *(drogas)* addicted (**a**, to). 2 *(dedicado)* fond (**a**, of), keen (**a**, on). 3 *(partidario)* supporting.
nm & nf 1 *(drogas)* addict. 2 *(partidario)* supporter, follower.
diestramiento *nm* training, instruction.
diestrar *vt* to train, instruct.
dinerado,-a *pp* → **adinerarse.**
adj rich, wealthy.
nm & nf rich person.
diós *interj* 1 *(gen)* goodbye!; *(familiarmente)* bye!, bye-bye! 2 *(al cruzarse con alguien)* hello! ■ **decir adiós a** ALGO *fig* to say goodbye to STH.
nm goodbye.
▲ *pl* **adioses.**
diposo,-a *adj* adipose.
ditivo,-a *adj* additive.
nm **aditivo** additive.
divinanza *nf* riddle, puzzle.
divinar *vt* 1 *(descubrir)* to guess: **le adivinó el pensamiento** *she read his mind.* 2 *(predecir)* to forecast, foretell. 3 *(enigma)* to solve.
adivino,-a *nm & nf* fortune-teller.
adjetivar *vt* 1 to use as an adjective. 2 *fig* to label, describe.
adjetivo,-a *adj* adjective, adjectival.
▷ *nm* **adjetivo** adjective.
adjudicación *nf* 1 award, awarding. 2 *(en subasta)* sale.
adjudicar [1] *vt* 1 *(premio)* to award. 2 *(venta)* to sell, knock down: **¡adjudicado!** *sold!* 3 *(obras)* to award a contract to.
▷ *vpr* **adjudicarse** 1 *(apropiarse)* to appropriate, take over. 2 *(obtener)* to win.
adjuntar *vt* to enclose, attach: **adjunto un folleto** *leaflet enclosed.*
adjunto,-a *adj* 1 *(en carta)* enclosed. 2 *(asistente)* assistant.
▷ *nm & nf* assistant teacher.
administración *nf* 1 *(gobierno)* administration, authorities *pl.* 2 *(empresa)* administration, management. 3 *(cargo)* post of administrator, post of manager. 4 *(despacho)* administrator's office, manager's office. 5 *(oficina)* branch. ● **administración de lotería** lottery office. | **administración pública** public administration.
administrador,-ra *adj* administrating.
▷ *nm & nf* 1 administrator: 2 *(manager)* manager. ● **administrador,-ra de fincas** estate agent. | **administrador de web** webmaster.
administrar *vt* 1 *(bienes, justicia)* to administer. 2 *(dirigir)* to manage, run. 3 *(suministrar)* to give: **le administró una aspirina** *she gave him an aspirin.*
▷ *vpr* **administrarse** *(manejarse)* to manage one's own money, manage one's own affairs.
administrativo,-a *adj* administrative.
▷ *nm & nf (funcionario)* official, civil servant; *(de empresa, banco)* office worker.
admirable *adj* admirable.
admiración *nf* 1 admiration: **sentía admiración por ella** *he admired her;* **les causó admiración** *she impressed them.* 2 *(signo)* exclamation mark.
admirador,-ra *adj* admiring.
▷ *nm & nf* admirer.
admirar *vt* 1 *(estimar)* to admire. 2 *(sorprender)* to amaze, surprise, astonish.
▷ *vpr* **admirarse** *(asombrarse)* to be astonished (**de**, at), be amazed (**de**, at).
admisible *adj* admissible, acceptable.
admisión *nf* 1 admission. 2 *(aceptación)* acceptance. 3 TÉC inlet, intake. ■ **«Reservado el derecho de admisión»** «The management reserves the right to refuse admission». ● **plazo de admisión** closing date.
admitir *vt* 1 *(dar entrada)* to admit, let in. 2 *(aceptar)* to accept, admit: **«No se admiten propinas»** *«No tipping», «Tipping not allowed».* 3 *(permitir)* to allow: **su obra admite varias interpretaciones** *his work is open to various interpretations.* 4 *(reconocer)* to admit. 5 *(tener capacidad)* to hold.
admón. *abrev* (**administración**) office: **admón. de Hacienda** *tax office.*
ADN *abrev* MED (**ácido desoxirribonucleico**) desoxyribonucleic acid; *(abreviatura)* DNA.

adobar *vt* 1 *(reparar)* to mend. 2 CULIN to marinate, marinade. 3 *(pieles)* to tan. 4 *fig (amañar)* to twist.
adobe *nm* adobe.
adobo *nm* 1 *(acción)* marinating, marinading. 2 *(salsa)* marinade.
adoctrinar *vt* to indoctrinate.
adolescencia *nf* adolescence.
adolescente *adj* adolescent.
▷ *nm o nf* adolescent.
adonde *adv* where.
adónde *adv* where.
adopción *nf* adoption.
adoptante *adj* adoptive, foster.
▷ *nm o nf* adoptive parent, foster parent.
adoptar *vt* to adopt.
adoptivo,-a *adj (hijo)* adopted, adoptive; *(padres)* adoptive: lo nombraron hijo adoptivo de la ciudad *he was given the title of honorary citizen.* ● **patria adoptiva** country of adoption.
adoquín *nm* 1 cobble, paving stone. 2 *fam (persona)* idiot, clod.
adorable *adj* adorable.
adoración *nf* 1 REL adoration, worship. 2 *fig* adoration, worshipping.
adorador,-ra *adj* 1 REL worshipping. 2 *fig* adoring.
▷ *nm & nf* 1 REL worshipper. 2 *fig* adorer, worshipper.
adorar *vt* 1 REL to worship. 2 *fig* to adore.
adormecer [43] *vt* 1 to make sleepy. 2 *(calmar)* to soothe.
▷ *vpr* **adormecerse** 1 *(dormirse)* to doze off. 2 *(entumecerse)* to go to sleep, go numb.
adormilarse *vpr* to doze, drowse.
adornar *vt* 1 to adorn, decorate. 2 *fig* to embellish.
adorno *nm* 1 decoration, adornment. 2 COST trimming. 3 CULIN garnish. ■ **de adorno** decorative.
adosado,-a *pp* → **adosar.**
▷ *adj* semidetached: casas adosadas *semidetached houses.*
adquirir [30] *vt* to acquire; *(comprar)* to buy.
adquisición *nf* acquisition; *(compra)* buy, purchase.
adrede *adv* deliberately, on purpose, purposely.
adrenalina *nf* adrenalin.
adscribir *vt* 1 *(atribuir)* to attribute. 2 *(destinar)* to appoint to.
▷ *vpr* **adscribirse** *(afiliarse)* to affiliate (**a**, to).
▲ *pp* adscrito,-a.
adscrito,-a *pp* → **adscribir.**
aduana *nf* 1 customs *pl*: el alcohol paga aduana *there's duty on spirits.* 2 *(oficinas)* customs building. ■ **pasar (por) la aduana** to go through customs.
aducir [46] *vt* to adduce, allege.
adueñarse *vpr* 1 to take possession (**de**, of). 2 *fig* to seize: la ira se adueñó de Eva *Eve was seized with anger.*
adulación *nf* adulation, flattery.
adulador,-ra *adj* adulating, flattering.
▷ *nm & nf* adulator, flatterer.
adular *vt* to adulate, flatter, soft-soap.
adulterar *vt* to adulterate.
adulterio *nm* adultery.
adúltero,-a *adj* adulterous.
▷ *nm & nf (hombre)* adulterer; *(mujer)* adulteress.
adulto,-a *adj* adult: persona adulta *adult.*
▷ *nm & nf* adult: los adultos *the grown-ups.*

advenimiento *nm* 1 advent, coming. 2 *(al tron*… accession.
adverbio *nm* adverb.
adversario,-a *adj* opposing.
▷ *nm & nf* adversary, opponent.
adversidad *nf* adversity, misfortune, setback.
adverso,-a *adj* 1 adverse, unfavourable (US unfavo… rable). 2 *(opuesto)* opposite. 3 *(adversario)* opposin… ● **condiciones adversas** adverse conditions.
advertencia *nf* 1 warning. 2 *(consejo)* piece of ad… vice. 3 *(nota)* notice. ■ **hacer una advertencia** t… warn.
advertir [35] *vt* 1 *(darse cuenta)* to notice, realize. … *(llamar la atención)* to warn: ya te lo advertí *I told yo*… 3 *(aconsejar)* to advise. 4 *(informar)* to inform.
adviento *nm* Advent.
adyacente *adj* adjacent.
aéreo,-a *adj* 1 aerial. 2 AV air. ● **tráfico aéreo** air traffic…
aerobic *nm* aerobics.
aerobio,-a *adj* aerobic.
▷ *nm* **aerobio** aerobe.
aerobús *nm* airbus.
▲ *pl* aerobuses.
aeroclub *nm* flying club.
aerodeslizador *nm* hovercraft.
aerodinámico,-a *adj* aerodynamic: línea aerodiná… mica *streamlined.*
aeródromo *nm* aerodrome, US airfield.
aeroespacial *adj* aerospace.
aerofagia *nf* aerophagia.
aerógrafo *nm* airbrush.
aerolínea *nf* airline.
aeronáutica *nf* aeronautics.
aeronáutico,-a *adj* aeronautic, aeronautical.
aeronaval *adj* air-sea.
aeronave *nf* airship. ● **aeronave espacial** spaceship…
aeroplano *nm* aeroplane, US airplane.
aeropuerto *nm* airport.
aerosol *nm* aerosol, spray.
aerostático,-a *adj* aerostatic.
aerostato *nm* hot-air balloon.
aeróstato *nm* hot-air balloon.
aerotaxi *nm* air taxi.
afabilidad *nf* affability.
afable *adj* affable, kind.
afablemente *adv* affably, kindly.
afamado,-a *pp* → **afamar.**
▷ *adj* famous, well-known.
afán *nm* 1 *(celo)* zeal; *(interés)* keenness, eagerness… con afán *keenly.* 2 *(esfuerzo)* effort.
afanador,-ra *adj* zealous, eager.
▷ *nm & nf* 1 zealous person, eager person. 2 *fam (la… drón)* thief.
afanar *vt fam (robar)* to nick, pinch.
▷ *vpr* **afanarse** to work with zeal. ■ **afanarse en** to wor… hard at. ■ **afanarse por** to strive to, do one's best to.
afanoso,-a *adj* 1 *(persona)* eager, keen, zealous. … *(tarea)* hard, laborious, tough.
afear *vt* 1 to make ugly, disfigure. 2 *fig (vituperar)* t… reproach: mi padre me afeaba la conducta *my fath… reproached me for my behaviour.*

fección *nf* 1 *(enfermedad)* complaint, disease: **afección hepática** *liver complaint.* 2 *(afición)* fondness.
fectación *nf* affectation.
fectado,-a *pp* → **afectar.**
adj 1 *(gen)* affected. 2 *(emocionado)* affected, upset. ■ **estar afectado,-a de** to be suffering from.
fectar *vt* 1 *(aparentar)* to affect: **afectar la voz** *to talk in an affected way.* 2 *(impresionar)* to move. 3 *(dañar)* to damage. 4 *(concernir)* to concern.
vpr **afectarse** *(impresionarse)* to be affected, be moved.
fectísimo,-a ■ **suyo,-a afectísimo,-a** *fml (en correspondencia)* yours faithfully.
fectivo,-a *adj* 1 *(sensible)* sensitive. 2 *(psicología)* affective.
fecto,-a *adj* 1 *(aficionado)* fond (**a**, of). 2 *(enfermo)* suffering (**de**, from).
nm **afecto** affection: **con todo mi afecto** *with all my love.* ■ **tomarle afecto a** ALGN to become fond of SB.
fectuoso,-a *adj* affectionate.
feitar *vt* 1 *(pelo)* to shave. 2 *(toro)* to blunt the horns of.
feminado,-a *pp* → **afeminar.**
adj effeminate.
nm effeminate man; *(familiarmente)* sissy.
ferrar *vt* to clutch, grasp.
vi to cling, clutch, grasp.
vpr **aferrarse a** to clutch to, cling to.
ffaire *nm (caso)* case, affair; *(amoroso)* love affair.
fgano,-a *adj* Afghan.
nm & nf (persona) Afghan.
nm **afgano** *(idioma)* Afghan.
fianzamiento *nm* strengthening, reinforcement; *(definitivo)* consolidation.
fianzar [4] *vt* 1 *(sujetar)* to strengthen, reinforce. 2 *fig* to support, back. 3 *(dar fianza)* to stand bail for.
vpr **afianzarse** 1 *(estabilizarse)* to steady OS. 2 *(convencerse)* to become surer, become more convinced:
fiche *nm* poster.
fición *nf* 1 *(inclinación)* liking, penchant: **tener afición por algo** *to be fond of sth.* 2 *(ahínco)* interest, zeal: **con mucha afición** *keenly.* 3 **la afición** the fans *pl*, the supporters *pl*.
ficionado,-a *pp* → **aficionar.**
adj 1 keen, fond: **ser aficionado a algo** *to be fond of* STH. 2 *(no profesional)* amateur.
nm & nf 1 fan, enthusiast: 2 *(no profesional)* amateur.
ficionar *vt* to make fond (**a**, of).
vpr **aficionarse** to become fond (**a**, of), take a liking (**a**, to): **se aficionó a la música** *he became a music lover.*
fijo,-a *adj* affixed.
nm **afijo** affix.
filar *vt* to sharpen.
vpr **afilarse** to grow sharp.
filiado,-a *pp* → **afiliar.**
adj affiliated, member.
nm & nf affiliate, member.
filiar [12] *vt* to affiliate.
vpr **afiliarse** *(uso reflexivo)* to join (**a**, to), become affiliated (**a**, to).
fín *adj* 1 *(semejante)* similar, kindred. 2 *(relacionado)* related. 3 *(próximo)* adjacent, next.
afinar *vt* 1 to perfect, polish. 2 MÚS to tune. 3 *(puntería)* to sharpen. 4 *(metales)* to purify, refine.
afinidad *nf* 1 affinity. 2 QUÍM similarity.
afirmación *nf* 1 *(aseveración)* statement, assertion. 2 *(afianzamiento)* strengthening.
afirmar *vt* 1 *(afianzar)* to strengthen, reinforce. 2 *(aseverar)* to state, say, declare.
▷ *vi (asentir)* to assent.
▷ *vpr* **afirmarse** *(ratificarse)* to maintain (**en**, -): **se afirmó en su negativa** *she continued to refuse.*
afirmativo,-a *adj* affirmative. ■ **en caso afirmativo** if the answer is yes.
aflicción *nf* affliction, grief, suffering.
afligido,-a *pp* → **afligir.**
▷ *adj* afflicted, grieved, troubled.
afligir [6] *vt* to afflict, grieve, trouble.
▷ *vpr* **afligirse** to grieve, be distressed.
aflojar *vt* 1 *(soltar)* to loosen. 2 *fig (esfuerzo)* to relax. 3 *fam fig (dinero)* to pay up.
▷ *vi (disminuir)* to let up: **el calor ha aflojado** *the heat has let up.*
▷ *vpr* **aflojarse** to come loose.
aflorar *vi* 1 *(mineral)* to crop out/up, outcrop. 2 *fig (aparecer)* to come up to the surface, appear.
afluencia *nf* 1 inflow, influx: **afluencia de público** *flow of people.* 2 *(abundancia)* affluence.
afluente *adj (caudaloso)* flowing, inflowing.
▷ *nm (río)* tributary.
afluir [62] *vi* to flow (**a**, into).
afonía *nf* loss of voice.
afónico,-a *adj* hoarse, voiceless. ■ **estar afónico** to have lost one's voice.
aforo *nm* 1 *(capacidad)* seating capacity. 2 TÉC gauging.
afortunadamente *adv* luckily, fortunately.
afortunado,-a *adj* 1 lucky, fortunate: **fue una pregunta poco afortunada** *it was a rather inappropriate question.* 2 *(dichoso)* happy.
afrenta *nf fml* affront, outrage. ■ **hacerle una afrenta a** ALGN to affront sb.
africano,-a *adj* African.
▷ *nm & nf* African.
afrontar *vt* 1 to face, confront: **afrontaron las consecuencias** *they faced up to the consequences.* 2 *(poner enfrente)* to face. 3 JUR to confront, bring face to face.
afterhours *nm* after-hours club.
afuera *adv* outside: **la parte de afuera** *the outside;* **salir afuera** *to come/go out.*
▷ *interj* out of the way!
▷ *nm pl* **afueras** outskirts.
agachar *vt* to lower, bow.
▷ *vpr* **agacharse** 1 *(encogerse)* to cower. 2 *(protegerse)* to duck (down). 3 *(agazaparse)* to crouch (down), squat.
agalla *nf* 1 *(de pez)* gill. 2 *(de ave)* temple. 3 BOT gal.
▷ *nf pl* **agallas** 1 *fam* courage *sing*, guts, pluck *sing*: **tener agallas** *to have guts.* 2 *(anginas)* sore throat *sing.*
agarradero *nm* 1 *(asa)* handle. 2 *(excusa)* excuse.
▷ *nm pl* **agarraderos** *(influencias)* influence *sing*, pull *sing.*
agarrado,-a *pp* → **agarrar.**
▷ *adj fam* stingy, tight. ■ **bailar agarrado** to dance cheek to cheek.
agarrar *vt* 1 *(con la mano)* to clutch, seize, grasp: **agárrala fuerte** *hold it tight.* 2 *fam (pillar)* to catch. 3 *fam*

(conseguir) to take advantage of: **hay que agarrar las oportunidades** *one has to grasp one's opportunities.* ■ **agarrar un cabreo** to fly off the handle. | **agarrar una borrachera** to get drunk/pissed.
▷ *vpr* **agarrarse 1** *(cogerse)* to hold on, cling (**a**, to). **2** *(pegarse)* to stick. **3** *fam (pelearse)* to quarrel, fight.
agarrotado,-a *pp (SEE agarrotar)* tight.
▷ *adj* **1** *(apretado)* tight. **2** *(músculo)* stiff. **3** *(motor)* seized up.
agarrotar *vt* **1** *(atar fuerte)* to tighten, tie up tightly. **2** *(oprimir)* to squeeze. **3** *(músculo)* to stiffen. **4** *(dar garrote)* to garotte.
▷ *vpr* **agarrotarse 1** *(los músculos)* to stiffen. **2** *(encasquillarse)* to seize up.
agasajar *vt* **1** *(obsequiar)* to smother with attention, treat well. **2** *(dar agasajo)* to wine and dine.
ágata [Takes **el** in singular.] *nf* agate.
agazapar *vt* to grab (hold of).
▷ *vpr* **agazaparse 1** *(esconderse)* to hide. **2** *(agacharse)* to crouch (down), squat.
agencia *nf* agency; *(sucursal)* branch. ● **agencia de turismo** tourist office. | **agencia de viajes** travel agency.
agenda *nf* **1** *(libro)* diary. **2** *(orden del día)* agenda.
agente *adj* agent. ● **agente de cambio y bolsa** stockbroker. | **agente de policía 1** *(hombre)* policeman. **2** *(mujer)* policewoman. | **agente de tráfico 1** *(hombre)* traffic policeman. **2** *(mujer)* traffic policewoman.
▷ *nm o nf* agent.
▷ *nm* agent.
ágil *adj* agile.
agilidad *nf* agility: **con agilidad** *swiftly.*
agilizar [4] *vt* **1** to make agile. **2** *fig* to speed up.
agitación *nf* **1** agitation. **2** *fig* restlessness.
agitado,-a *pp* ⟶ **agitar.**
▷ *adj* **1** *(movido)* agitated, shaken; *(mar)* rough, choppy. **2** *(ansioso)* anxious. **3** *(ajetreado)* hectic.
agitar *vt* **1** *(mover)* to agitate, shake; *(pañuelo)* to wave: **«Agítese antes de usarlo»** *«Shake before use».* **2** *(intranquilizar)* agitate, excite.
▷ *vpr* **agitarse 1** *(moverse)* to move restlessly. **2** *(inquietarse)* to become agitated/disturbed. **3** *(mar)* to become rough.
aglomeración *nf* **1** agglomeration. **2** *(de gente)* crowd.
aglomerado,-a *adj* ⟶ **aglomerar.**
▷ *nm* **aglomerado 1** *(madera)* chipboard. **2** *(combustible)* briquette.
aglomerar *vt (acumular)* to agglomerate, amass.
▷ *vpr* **aglomerarse 1** *(acumularse)* to agglomerate, amass. **2** *(gente)* to crowd.
aglutinar *vt* **1** to agglutinate, bind. **2** *fig* to bring together.
▷ *vpr* **aglutinarse 1** to agglutinate. **2** *fig* to come together.
agnosticismo *nm* agnosticism.
agnóstico,-a *adj* agnostic.
▷ *nm & nf* agnostic.
agobiado,-a *pp* ⟶ **agobiar.**
▷ *adj* **1** *(doblado)* bent over/down, weighed down. **2** *fig (cansado)* exhausted; *(abrumado)* overwhelmed: **agobiado de trabajo** *up to one's eyes in work.*
agobiar [12] *vt* **1** *(doblar)* to weigh/bend down. *(abrumar)* to overwhelm.
▷ *vpr* **agobiarse** *(angustiarse)* to worry too much, g worked up.
agobio *nm* burden, fatigue, suffocation.
agolparse *vpr* to crowd, throng: **se le agolpaban lágrimas en sus ojos** *tears welled up in her eyes.*
agonía *nf* **1** dying breath, last gasp: **murió despu de una larga agonía** *she died after a long illness;* **en agonía** *on her deathbed.* **2** *(sufrimiento)* agony, grie sorrow.
▷ *nm o nf* **agonías** *fam (quejica)* moaner; *(pesimista)* pe simist.
agonizante *adj* dying.
▷ *nm o nf* dying person.
agonizar [4] *vi* **1** to be dying: **está agonizando** *s could die any moment now.* **2** *(acabarse)* to fail, fac away. **3** *(sufrir)* to suffer.
agosto *nm* August. ■ **hacer su agosto** *fig* to make packet/pile, feather one's nest.

For examples of use, see **marzo.**

agotado,-a *pp* ⟶ **agotar.**
▷ *adj* **1** *(cansado)* exhausted, worn out. **2** *(libros)* out print; *(mercancías)* sold out.
agotador,-ra *adj* exhausting.
agotamiento *nm* exhaustion. ● **agotamiento físi** physical strain.
agotar *vt* **1** *(cansar)* to exhaust, tire/wear out. **2** *(ga tar)* to exhaust, use up.
▷ *vpr* **agotarse 1** *(cansarse)* to become exhausted, b come tired out. **2** *(gastarse)* to run out. **3** COM to l sold out.
agraciado,-a *pp* ⟶ **agraciar.**
▷ *adj* **1** *(bello)* attractive, beautiful. **2** *(ganador)* winnin
▷ *nm & nf* lucky winner. ■ **ser poco agraciado, -a** to l unattractive/plain.
agradable *adj* nice, pleasant: **poco agradable** *u pleasant.*
agradar *vi* to please: **esto me agrada** *I like this.*
agradecer [43] *vt* **1** to thank for, be grateful for. *(uso impersonal)* to be welcome: **siempre se agrade una ayuda** *help is always welcome.*
agradecido,-a *pp* ⟶ **agradecer.**
▷ *adj* grateful, thankful: **le quedaría muy agradecido si** *I should be very much obliged if…*
agradecimiento *nm* gratefulness, gratitud thankfulness.
agrado *nm* pleasure: **no es de su agrado** *it isn't to h liking.*
agrandar *vt* **1** *(hacer grande)* to enlarge, make large **2** *(exagerar)* to exaggerate.
▷ *vpr* **agrandarse 1** *(hacerse grande)* to enlarge, becon larger. **2** *(acentuarse)* to become more intense.
agrario,-a *adj* agrarian, land, agricultural. ● **políti agraria** agricultural policy.
agravante *adj* aggravating.
▷ *nm & nf* **1** added difficulty. **2** JUR aggravating circun stance.
agravar *vt* to aggravate, worsen.
▷ *vpr* **agravarse** to get worse, worsen.
agraviar [12] *vt* to offend, insult.
agravio *nm* offence, insult.

agredir *vt* to attack.
Used only in forms which include the letter i in their endings: agredía, agrediré, agrediendo.

agregado,-a *pp* → agregar.
▷ *adj* aggregate.
▷ *nm & nf* 1 *(de instituto)* senior teacher; *(de universidad)* senior lecturer. 2 POL attaché.

agregar [7] *vt* 1 *(añadir)* to add. 2 *(unir)* to gather. 3 *(destinar)* to appoint.
▷ *vpr* **agregarse** *(unirse)* to join.

agresión *nf* aggression, attack.

agresividad *nf* agressiveness.

agresivo,-a *adj* aggressive.

agresor,-ra *adj* attacking.
▷ *nm & nf* aggressor, attacker.

agreste *adj* 1 *(salvaje)* wild. 2 *(abrupto)* rugged; *(rocoso)* rocky. 3 *(sin cultivar)* uncultivated. 4 *fig (rudo)* uncouth, coarse.

agriar [12] *vt* 1 to sour. 2 *fig (persona)* to embitter.
▷ *vpr* **agriarse** to turn sour.

agrícola *adj* agricultural, farming: **las técnicas agrícolas han cambiado** *farming techniques have changed.*

agricultor,-ra *nm & nf* farmer.

agricultura *nf* agriculture, farming.

agridulce *adj* 1 bittersweet. 2 CULIN sweet and sour.

agrietar *vt* to crack; *(piel)* to chap.
▷ *vpr* **agrietarse** to crack; *(piel)* to get chapped.

agrio,-a *adj* sour.
▷ *nm pl* **agrios** citrus fruits.

agronomía *nf* agronomy.

agrónomo,-a *adj* farming.
▷ *nm & nf* agronomist.

agropecuario,-a *adj* agricultural, farming.

agrupación *nf* 1 grouping, group. 2 *(asociación)* association.

agrupamiento *nf* 1 grouping, group. 2 *(asociación)* association.

agrupar *vt* to group, put into groups.
▷ *vpr* **agruparse** 1 to group together, form a group. 2 *(asociarse)* to associate.

agrura *nf* sourness, tartness.

agua [Takes **el** in singular.] *nf* 1 water: **echarse al agua** *to dive in.* 2 *(lluvia)* rain. 3 ARQUIT slope of a roof: **tejado a dos aguas** *pitched roof.* ■ **claro como el agua** crystal clear. ‖ **como agua de mayo** a godsend. ● **agua dulce** fresh water. ‖ **agua corriente** running water. ‖ **agua de colonia** (eau de) cologne. ‖ **agua del grifo** tap water. ‖ **agua mineral con gas** sparkling mineral water. ‖ **agua oxigenada** hydrogen peroxide. ‖ **agua potable** drinking water. ‖ **aguas jurisdiccionales** territorial waters.
▷ *nf pl* **aguas** 1 *(del mar, río)* waters: **aguas arriba** *upstream.* 2 *(de brillante)* water *sing*, sparkle *sing*.

aguacate *nm (árbol)* avocado; *(fruto)* avocado (pear).

aguacero *nm* heavy shower, downpour.

aguado,-a *pp* → aguar.
▷ *adj* watered down, wishy-washy: **leche aguada** *watered-down milk.*

aguafiestas *nm o nf inv* killjoy, wet blanket.

aguafuerte [Takes **el** in singular.] *nm & nf* 1 ARTE etching: **grabar algo al aguafuerte** *to etch sth.* 2 QUÍM nitric acid.

aguamarina *nf* aquamarine.

aguanieve [Takes **el** in singular.] *nf* sleet.

aguantar *vt* 1 *(contener)* to hold (back). 2 *(sostener)* to hold, support. 3 *(soportar)* to tolerate: **no aguanto más** *I can't stand any more, I can't take any more.*
▷ *vpr* **aguantarse** 1 *(contenerse)* to keep back; *(risa, lágrimas)* to hold back. 2 *(resignarse)* to resign OS. ■ **¡que se aguante!** *fam* that's her/his tough luck!

aguante *nm* 1 *(paciencia)* patience, endurance. 2 *(fuerza)* strength. ■ **tener mucho aguante** 1 *(paciente)* to be very patient. 2 *(resistente)* to be strong, have a lot of stamina.

aguar [22] *vt* to water down, add water to.
▷ *vpr* **aguarse** to become flooded. ■ **aguar la fiesta a ALGN** to spoil SB's fun.

aguardar *vt* to wait (for), await: **no sé lo que me aguarda el futuro** *I don't know what the future holds for me.*
▷ *vi* to wait.

aguardiente *nm* eau de vie, spirit, liquor. ● **aguardiente de caña** sugar cane liquor.

aguarrás *nm* turpentine.

agudeza *nf* 1 sharpness, keenness; *(dolor)* acuteness. 2 *fig (viveza)* wit, wittiness. 3 *fig (ingenio)* witticism, witty saying.

agudizar [4] *vt* 1 *(afilar)* to sharpen. 2 *(empeorar)* to worsen, intensify, make more acute.
▷ *vpr* **agudizarse** 1 *(afilarse)* to become sharper. 2 *(empeorar)* to worsen, intensify, become more acute.

agudo,-a *adj* 1 *(afilado)* sharp. 2 *(dolor)* acute. 3 *fig (ingenioso)* witty; *(mordaz)* sharp. 4 *fig (sentido)* sharp, keen. 5 *(voz)* high-pitched. 6 *(sonido)* treble, high. 7 LING *(palabra)* oxytone; *(acento)* acute.

agüero *nm* omen, presage. ■ **ser de mal agüero** to be ill-omened. ‖ **ser pájaro de mal agüero** *fig* to be a bird of ill omen.

aguijón *nm* 1 ZOOL sting. 2 BOT thorn, prickle. 3 *fig (estímulo)* sting, spur. 4 *(espuela)* spur.

aguijonear *vt* 1 *(punzar)* to goad. 2 *fig (estimular)* to spur on.

águila [Takes **el** in singular.] *nf* eagle.

aguileño,-a *adj* aquiline: **nariz aguileña** *aquiline/hook nose.*

aguilucho *nm* 1 *(cría del águila)* eaglet. 2 *(ave)* harrier.

aguinaldo *nm* 1 *(de Navidad)* Christmas bonus/box. 2 *(paga extra)* bonus. 3 *(villancico)* Christmas carol.

aguja *nf* 1 needle; *(de tricotar)* knitting needle. 2 *(de reloj)* hand; *(de tocadiscos)* stylus. 3 *(de arma)* firing pin. 4 *(obelisco)* obelisk; *(capitel)* spire, steeple. 5 *(de tren)* point, US switch. 6 *(pez)* garfish. 7 *(ave)* godwit. 8 *(pastel dulce)* sweet pastry; *(pastel salado)* meat/fish pastry.
▷ *nf pl* **agujas** ribs: **carne de agujas** *shoulder.*

agujerear *vt* to pierce, perforate, make holes in.

agujero *nm* 1 hole. 2 *fig (falta de dinero)* shortfall: **encontraron un agujero de varios millones de euros** *they found that several million euros were missing.* ● **agujero negro** black hole.

agujetas *nf pl* stiffness *sing*: **tener agujetas** *to be stiff.*

aguzar [4] *vt* 1 *(afilar)* to sharpen. 2 *(estimular)* to spur on, prick. ■ **aguzar el oído** to prick up one's ears.

■ **aguzar la vista** to look attentively. ‖ **la necesidad aguza el ingenio** necessity is the mother of invention.
▷ *vpr* **aguzarse** to become sharper.
ah *interj* **1** *(caer en la cuenta)* ah!, oh!: **¡ah, ya te entiendo!** *ah, now I see!* **2** *(sorpresa, admiración)* oh!
ahí *adv* there, in that place. ■ **de ahí que** hence, therefore. ‖ **por ahí 1** *(lugar)* round there. **2** *(aproximadamente)* more or less.
ahijado,-a *pp* → **ahijar.**
▷ *nm & nf* **1** godchild; *(chico)* godson; *(chica)* goddaughter. **2** *(adoptivo)* adopted child.
ahínco *nm* eagerness, keenness, enthusiasm: **con ahínco** *eagerly, enthusiastically.*
ahogado,-a *pp* → **ahogar.**
▷ *adj* **1** drowned. **2** *(asfixiado)* suffocated. **3** *fig (deudas, etc)* up to one's neck. **4** *(sitio)* stuffy, close.
▷ *nm & nf* drowned person.
ahogar [7] *vt* **1** *(asfixiar)* to choke, suffocate. **2** *(en el agua)* to drown. **3** *(plantas)* to overwater. **4** *(motor)* to flood. **5** *(fuego)* to put out, extinguish. **6** *fig (reprimir)* to stifle, put down.
▷ *vpr* **ahogarse 1** to be drowned, drown: **se cayó al río y se ahogó** *he fell into the river and drowned.* **2** *(sofocarse)* to choke, suffocate. **3** *(motor)* to flood. ■ **ahogarse en un vaso de agua** *fig* to make a mountain out of a molehill.
ahogo *nm* **1** *(al respirar)* breathlessness, shortness of breath. **2** *(congoja)* anguish, sorrow, distress. **3** *(penuria)* financial difficulty.
ahondar *vt* **1** *(hacer profundo)* to deepen, make deeper. **2** *(meter en profundidad)* to go deep.
▷ *vi* **1** to go deep. **2** *(investigar)* to examine: **ahondar en un problema** *to examine a problem in depth.*
ahora *adv* **1** *(en este momento)* now: **ahora no tengo tiempo** *I haven't got time now.* **2** *(hace un momento)* just a moment ago: **lo acabo de ver ahora** *I've just seen it.* **3** *(dentro de un momento)* in a minute, shortly: **ahora te lo preparo** *I'll get it ready for you in a minute.* ■ **de ahora en adelante** from now on. ‖ **hasta ahora** until now, so far. ‖ **por ahora** for the time being.
▷ *conj (adversativa)* however: **gana poco; ahora, tampoco trabaja mucho** *he doesn't earn very much; but then, he doesn't work very hard.*
ahorcar [1] *vt* to hang. ■ **se ahorcó con el cinturón** he hanged himself with his belt.
ahorrador,-ra *adj* thrifty.
▷ *nm & nf* thrifty person.
ahorrar *vt* **1** *(dinero, energía, etc)* to save. **2** *(molestia, problema)* to save, spare:
▷ *vpr* **ahorrarse** to save OS: **te ahorrarás problemas si lo haces como yo te digo** *you'll save yourself problems if you do it the way I say.*
ahorro *nm* **1** saving. **2** *(cualidad)* thrift.
▷ *nm pl* **ahorros** savings.
ahuecar [1] *vt* **1** to hollow out. **2** *(esponjar)* to fluff up; *(tierra)* to loosen. **3** *(voz)* to deepen.
▷ *vpr* **ahuecarse** *(engreírse)* to become conceited, give OS airs.
ahumado,-a *pp* → **ahumar.**
▷ *adj* smoked; *(bacon)* smoky.
▷ *nm* **ahumado** *(proceso)* smoking.
ahumar [16] *vt* **1** *(tratar con humo)* to smoke. **2** *(llenar de humo)* to fill with smoke, smoke out.
▷ *vi (echar humo)* to give off smoke, smoke.
▷ *vpr* **ahumarse 1** *(adquirir color)* to blacken, turn black; *(adquirir olor)* to develop a smoky smell; *(adquirir sabor)* to acquire a smoky taste. **2** *fam (emborracharse)* to get drunk.
ahuyentar *vt* **1** to drive away, scare away. **2** *fig* to dismiss.
airado,-a *pp* → **airarse.**
▷ *adj* angry, furious, irate.
airar [15] *vt* to anger, make furious.
▷ *vpr* **airarse** to get angry.
airbag [Registered trademark.] *nm* airbag.
aire *nm* **1** air. **2** *(viento)* wind; *(corriente)* draught: **hace aire** *it's windy.* **3** *fig (aspecto)* air, appearance: **tiene un aire cansado** *she looks tired.* **4** *fig (parecido)* resemblance, likeness: **tienen un aire de familia** *there's a family likeness to them.* **5** *fig (estilo)* style, manner, way: **lo hizo a su aire** *he did it his way.* **6** *fig (gracia)* gracefulness, elegance. **7** *fig (ambiente)* atmosphere: **había mucha tensión en el aire** *the atmosphere was very tense.* **8** MÚS air, melody. ■ **al aire libre** in the open air, outdoors. ‖ **tomar el aire** to take the air, get some fresh air. ● **aire acondicionado** air conditioning. ‖ **aire puro** clean air.
airear *vt* **1** *(ventilar)* to air. **2** *fig (un asunto)* to publicize.
▷ *vpr* **airearse 1** *(tomar el aire)* to take/get some fresh air. **2** *(resfriarse)* to catch a cold.
airoso,-a *adj* **1** *(lugar)* windy. **2** *(persona)* graceful, elegant. ■ **salir airoso,-a** to do well, be successful: **salió airoso de la entrevista** *he did well in the interview.*
aislado,-a *pp* → **aislar.**
▷ *adj* **1** *(suelto)* isolated. **2** TÉC insulated.
aislante *adj* insulating.
▷ *nm* insulator.
aislar [15] *vt* **1** *(dejar separado)* to isolate. **2** TÉC to insulate.
▷ *vpr* **aislarse** *(uso reflexivo)* to isolate OS (**de**, from).
ajá *interj* good!
ajar *vt (deslucir)* to spoil, wear out.
▷ *vpr* **ajarse 1** *(persona)* to become worn out, wear OS out. **2** *(piel)* to become wrinkled, wrinkle.
ajardinar *vt* to landscape, lay out with gardens.
a. J.C. *abrev* → **a. de J.C.**
ajedrez *nm* **1** *(juego)* chess. **2** *(tablero y piezas)* chess set.
ajeno,-a *adj* **1** *(de otro)* another's, belonging to other people: **esta semana el equipo juega en campo ajeno** *our team plays away from home this week.* **2** *(distante)* detached. **3** *(impropio)* inappropriate, unsuitable. **4** *(extraño)* not involved: **es ajeno al escándalo de las escuchas telefónicas** *he's not involved in the phone tapping affair.*
ajetreo *nm* activity, bustle.
ají *nm* AM red pepper, chilli.
ajillo *nm.* ■ **al ajillo** fried with garlic.
ajo *nm* garlic. ■ **estar en el ajo** *fam fig* to be involved, be in the thick of it. ● **ajo tierno** young garlic.
ajustado,-a *pp* → **ajustar.**

▷ *adj* 1 *(precio)* very low, rock-bottom; *(presupuesto)* tight. 2 *(apretado)* tight-fitting, tight.

ajustar *vt* 1 *(adaptar)* to adjust, regulate. 2 *(apretar)* to tighten. 3 *(encajar)* to fit, fit tight. 4 *(acordar)* to fix, agree on, set. ■ **ajustar cuentas** 1 COM to settle up.

▷ *vi* to fit.

▷ *vpr* **ajustarse** 1 *(ceñirse)* to fit. 2 *(ponerse de acuerdo)* to come to an agreement; *(estar de acuerdo)* to agree with, fit in with: **esto no se ajusta a mi presupuesto** *this is outside my price range.*

ajuste *nm* 1 *(unión)* adjustment, fitting. 2 TÉC assembly. 3 COM settlement, fixing. 4 *(tipografía)* make-up, composition. ● **ajuste de cuentas** *fig* settling of scores.

ajusticiar [12] *vt* to execute.

al [Contraction of a + el.] *contr* ⟶ **a.** ■ **al** + *inf* on + *ger*: **me lo encontré al salir de casa** *I met him when I was leaving, I met him on leaving* ; **al quedarse sin dinero, tuvo que ponerse a trabajar** *when he ran out of money, he had to get down to work.* ‖ **está al caer** it's about to happen.

ala [Takes **el** in singular.] *nf* 1 wing: **de dos alas** *two-winged.* 2 *(de sombrero)* brim. 3 *(de hélice)* blade. 4 DEP winger. 5 *(de mesa)* leaf, flap.

▷ *nf pl* **alas** *(atrevimiento)* daring *sing.* ● **ala delta** 1 *(aparato)* hang glider. 2 *(aparato)* hang gliding.

alabanza *nf* 1 *(elogio)* praise. 2 *(jactancia)* boasting, bragging.

alabar *vt (elogiar)* to praise.

▷ *vpr* **alabarse** *(jactarse)* to boast.

alabastro *nm* alabaster.

alacena *nf* cupboard.

alacrán *nm* scorpion.

alado,-a *adj* 1 *(con alas)* winged. 2 *(veloz)* fast, quick.

alambique *nm* still.

alambrar *vt* to fence (off) with wire.

alambre *nm* wire. ● **alambre de púas** barbed wire.

alameda *nf* 1 poplar grove. 2 *(paseo)* avenue, promenade, boulevard.

álamo *nm* poplar.

alano,-a *adj* mastiff, wolfhound.

alarde *nm* display, bragging, boasting. ■ **hacer alarde de** to flaunt, show off, parade.

alardear *vi* to boast, brag, show off.

alargadera *nf* 1 TÉC extension. 2 QUÍM adapter.

alargado,-a *pp* ⟶ **alargar.**

▷ *adj* long, elongated.

alargador,-ra *adj* lengthening, extending.

▷ *nm* **alargador** extension lead.

alargar [7] *vt* 1 to lengthen. 2 *(estirar)* to stretch. 3 *(prolongar)* to prolong. 4 *(dar)* to hand, pass.

▷ *vpr* **alargarse** to lengthen.

alargo *nm* extension lead.

alarido *nm* screech, yell, shriek: **dar un alarido** *to howl.*

alarma *nf* alarm. ■ **dar la alarma** to give the alarm, raise the alarm. ● **alarma aérea** air-raid warning.

alarmante *adj* alarming.

alarmar *vt* to alarm.

▷ *vpr* **alarmarse** to be alarmed, alarm OS.

alarmista *nm o nf* alarmist.

alazán,-ana *adj* light chestnut, sorrel.

▷ *nm & nf (caballo)* sorrel horse.

alba [Takes **el** in singular.] *nf* 1 dawn, daybreak. 2 REL alb. ■ **al rayar/romper el alba** at dawn, at daybreak.

albacea *nm o nf* JUR *(hombre)* executor; *(mujer)* executrix.

albahaca *nf* basil.

albanés,-esa *adj* Albanian.

▷ *nm & nf (persona)* Albanian.

▷ *nm* **albanés** *(idioma)* Albanian.

Albania *nf* Albania.

albañil *nm (de ladrillos)* bricklayer; *(en general)* building worker.

albañilería *nf* 1 *(oficio)* bricklaying. 2 *(obra)* brickwork: **techo de albañilería** *brick ceiling.*

albarán *nm* delivery note, despatch note.

albaricoque *nm* 1 *(fruta)* apricot. 2 *(árbol)* apricot tree.

albedrío *nm* will. ● **libre albedrío** free will.

alberca *nf* reservoir.

albergar [7] *vt* 1 *(alojar)* to lodge, house, accommodate. 2 *fig (sentimientos)* to cherish, harbour (US harbor).

▷ *vpr* **albergarse** to stay.

albergue *nm* 1 *(hostal)* hostel. 2 *(refugio)* shelter, refuge. ■ **dar albergue** to take in, put up. ● **albergue juvenil** youth hostel.

albino,-a *adj* albino.

▷ *nm & nf* albino.

albis ■ **in albis** left in the dark. ‖ **quedarse in albis** not to know a thing.

albóndiga *nf* meatball.

alborada *nf* 1 *(alba)* dawn, break of day. 2 *(música)* dawn song. 3 *(toque militar)* reveille.

alborear *vi* [Used only in the 3rd person; it does not take a subject.] to dawn.

albornoz *nm* bathrobe.

▲ *pl* **albornoces.**

alborotador,-ra *adj* 1 *(rebelde)* rebellious, turbulent. 2 *(ruidoso)* noisy, rowdy. 3 *(mar)* rough, tempestuous.

▷ *nm & nf* troublemaker, agitator.

alborotar *vt* 1 *(agitar)* to agitate, excite. 2 *(desordenar)* to make untidy, turn upside down. 3 *(sublevar)* to incite to rebel.

▷ *vi* to make a racket.

▷ *vpr* **alborotarse** 1 *(excitarse)* to get excited. 2 *(el mar)* to get rough. 3 *(alarmarse)* to be alarmed.

alboroto *nm* 1 *(gritería)* din, racket, row. 2 *(desorden)* uproar, commotion, disturbance. 3 *(sobresalto)* shock, alarm.

alborozar [4] *vt* to delight, fill with joy.

▷ *vpr* **alborozarse** to be overjoyed.

alborozo *nm* joy, merriment, gaiety.

albufera *nf* lagoon.

álbum *nm* album.

▲ *pl* **álbumes.**

albúmina *nf* albumin.

alcachofa *nf* 1 *(planta)* artichoke. 2 *(pieza)* rose, sprinkler.

alcalde *nm* mayor.

alcaldesa *nf* 1 *(cargo)* lady mayor, mayoress. 2 *(mujer del alcalde)* mayoress.

alcaldía *nf* 1 *(cargo)* mayorship. 2 *(oficina)* mayor's office, mayoralty. 3 *(territorio)* land under the jurisdiction of a mayor.
alcalino,-a *adj* alkaline.
alcaloide *nm* alkaloid.
alcance *nm* 1 reach, grasp: **está al alcance de todo el mundo** *it's within everyone's reach.* 2 *(de arma)* range. 3 *(trascendencia)* scope, importance. 4 *(inteligencia)* intelligence: **persona de pocos alcances** *person of low intelligence.*
alcanfor *nm* camphor.
alcantarilla *nf* 1 *(conducto)* sewer. 2 *(boca)* drain.
alcantarillado *nm* sewer system.
alcanzar [4] *vt* 1 *(gen)* to reach: **no alcanzo el libro** *I can't reach the book.* 2 *(persona)* to catch up, catch up with: **los alcanzamos en la esquina** *we'll catch up with them at the corner.* 3 *(pasar)* to pass, hand over: **alcánzame el agua** *pass me some water.* 4 *(entender)* to understand, grasp. 5 *(conseguir)* to attain, achieve: **alcanzamos los objetivos** *we achieved the goals.* 6 *(golpear)* to hit. 7 *(afectar)* to affect.
▷ *vi* 1 *(ser suficiente)* to be sufficient (**para**, for), be enough (**para**, for), suffice (**para**, for): **eso no alcanza para todos** *that's not enough for all of us.* 2 *(ser capaz)* to manage, succeed: **no alcanzo a verlo** *I can't see it.*
alcaparra *nf* 1 *(fruto)* caper. 2 *(planta)* caper bush.
alcayata *nf* hook.
alcázar *nm* 1 *(fortaleza)* fortress, citadel. 2 *(palacio)* palace, castle.
alce *nm* elk, moose.
alcoba *nf* bedroom. ● **secretos de alcoba** *fig* intimacies.
alcohol *nm* 1 *(sustancia)* alcohol. 2 *(bebida)* alcohol, spirits *pl.* ● **alcohol desnaturalizado/metílico/de quemar** methylated spirits, methylated spirit.
alcoholemia *nf* alcohol: **tasa/nivel de alcoholemia** *blood alcohol level.*
alcohólico,-a *adj* alcoholic.
▷ *nm & nf* alcoholic. ● **Alcohólicos Anónimos** Alcoholics Anonymous.
alcoholímetro *nm* breathalyzer.
alcoholismo *nm* alcoholism.
alcohómetro *nm* breathalyzer.
alcornoque *nm* 1 BOT cork oak. 2 *fig* blockhead, idiot, dimwit.
alcorque *nm* basin, pit.
aldaba *nf* 1 *(llamador)* door knocker. 2 *(barra)* bar. 3 *(pestillo)* bolt.
aldea *nf* hamlet, small village.
aldeano,-a *adj* 1 *(de aldea)* village. 2 *fig (rústico)* rustic.
▷ *nm & nf* villager.
aldehído *nm* aldehyde.
aleación *nf* alloy.
aleatorio,-a *adj* random, chance, fortuitous.
aleccionar *vt* 1 *(instruir)* to teach, instruct. 2 *(adiestrar)* to train.
alegación *nf* allegation, plea, claim.
alegar [7] *vt* to allege, plead, claim: **alegó diferentes motivos** *he put forward several reasons.*
alegato *nm* 1 *(argumento)* claim, plea. 2 *(razonamiento)* reasoned allegation.
alegoría *nf* allegory.
alegórico,-a *adj* allegorical, allegoric.
alegrar *vt* 1 *(causar alegría)* to make happy, mak[e] glad, cheer up. 2 *fig (avivar)* to brighten (up), enli[ven]. 3 *fam (achispar)* to make tipsy.
▷ *vpr* **alegrarse** 1 to be pleased, be glad. 2 *fam (achisparse)* to get tipsy.
alegre *adj* 1 *(contento)* happy, glad. 2 *(color)* bright. 3 *(música)* lively. 4 *(espacio)* cheerful, pleasant. 5 *fam (achispado)* tipsy. 6 *euf (irreflexivo)* thoughtless, irresponsible, rash.
alegría *nf* 1 *(felicidad)* happiness, joy: **¡qué alegría!** *that's wonderful!, how marvellous!* 2 *pey (irresponsabilidad)* irresponsibility, thoughtlessness, rashness.
alejamiento *nm* 1 *(separación)* distance, separation. 2 *(enajenación)* estrangement.
alejar *vt* 1 *(llevar lejos)* to remove, move away. 2 *fig (ahuyentar)* to keep away: **aleja esa idea** *get rid of that idea.*
▷ *vpr* **alejarse** to go/move away.
aleluya *nm & nf* hallelujah, alleluia.
▷ *nf fam (pareado)* couplet.
▷ *interj* hallelujah!
alemán,-ana *adj* German.
▷ *nm & nf (persona)* German.
▷ *nm* **alemán** *(idioma)* German.
Alemania *nf* Germany. ● **Alemania Occidental** West Germany. ‖ **Alemania Oriental** East Germany.
alentador,-ra *adj* encouraging.
alentar [27] *vi* 1 *arc (respirar)* to breathe. 2 *fig (existir)* to exist, live on.
▷ *vt* 1 *(animar)* to encourage. 2 *(tener)* to harbour (US harbor), cherish.
▷ *vpr* **alentarse** *(recuperarse)* to get well.
alérgeno *nm* allergen.
alergia *nf* allergy.
alérgico,-a *adj* allergic (**a**, to).
alero *nm* 1 ARQUIT eaves *pl.* 2 *(coche)* wing.
alerta *adv (vigilante)* on the alert.
▷ *nf (atención)* alert.
▷ *nm (señal)* alert, warning.
▷ *interj* look/watch out!
alertar *vt* to alert (**de**, to).
▷ *vi* to be alert.
aleta *nf* 1 *(de pez)* fin; *(de mamífero, de nadador)* flipper. 2 *(de nariz)* wing, ala. 3 *(de avión)* aileron; *(de coche)* wing.
aletargar [7] *vt* to make drowsy/sleepy.
▷ *vpr* **aletargarse** to become drowsy/sleepy.
aletear *vi* 1 *(ave)* to flutter, flap its wings. 2 *(pez)* to move its fins. 3 *(persona)* to wave one's arms about.
alfabetizar [4] *vt* 1 *(enseñar)* to teach to read and write. 2 *(ordenar)* to alphabetize, put in alphabetical order.
alfabeto *nm* 1 *(abecedario)* alphabet. 2 *(código)* code. ● **alfabeto Morse** Morse code.
alfalfa *nf* alfalfa, lucerne.
alfarería *nf* 1 *(arte)* pottery. 2 *(taller)* potter's workshop. 3 *(tienda)* pottery shop.
alféizar *nm* sill, windowsill.
alférez *nm* second lieutenant.
▲ *pl* **alféreces.**

fil *nm* bishop.

filer *nm* 1 *(costura)* pin: **sujetó la falda con alfileres** *she pinned up her dress.* 2 *(joya)* brooch, pin. 3 *(del pelo)* clip; *(de tender ropa)* peg. 4 *(de corbata)* tiepin.

fombra *nf* 1 carpet, rug. 2 *(de baño)* bathmat. 3 *(alfombrilla)* rug, mat.

fombrar *vt* to carpet.

fombrilla *nf* rug, mat.

forja *nf* 1 *(para caballerías)* saddlebag. 2 *(para el hombro)* knapsack. 3 *fig* provisions *pl.*

ga [Takes **el** in singular.] *nf* alga; *(marina)* seaweed.

garroba *nf* 1 *(fruto)* carob bean. 2 *(planta)* vetch.

garrobo *nm* carob tree.

gebra [Takes **el** in singular.] *nf* algebra.

gido,-a *adj* 1 *(frío)* icy, very cold. 2 *fig* culminating: **el punto álgido** *the height.*

go *pron (afirmación)* something; *(negación, interrogación)* anything: **vamos a tomar algo** *let's have something to drink;* **¿quieres algo?** *do you want anything?* *adv (un poco)* a bit, a little, somewhat: **te queda algo grande** *it's a bit too big for you.* ■ **algo es algo** something is better than nothing.

godón *nm* cotton. ■ **criado,-a entre algodones** pampered. ● **algodón dulce/de azúcar** candyfloss, (US cotton candy). ‖ **algodón en rama** raw cotton. ‖ **algodón hidrófilo** cotton wool (US absorbent cotton).

goritmo *nm* algorithm.

guacil *nm* bailiff. ● **alguacil de moscas** *(araña)* zebra spider.

guien *pron (afirmativo)* somebody, someone; *(interrogativo, negativo)* anybody, anyone: **preguntemos a alguien** *let's ask someone;* **¿hay alguien?** *is anyone there?*

lgún [Used before singular masculine nouns.] *adj* → **alguno,-a.**

lguno,-a *adj (afirmativo)* some; *(interrogativo, negativo)* any: **alguna noche voy al cine** *some nights I go to the cinema;* **¿ha habido alguna llamada?** *has anyone phoned?, have there been any phone calls?;* **el ministro no facilitó dato alguno** *the minister didn't provide any information.*
▷ *pron (afirmativo)* someone, somebody; *(interrogativo, negativo)* anybody: **que venga alguno que sepa francés** *get someone who speaks French.* ■ **alguno que otro** some, a few.

lhaja *nf* 1 jewel, gem. 2 *fig (cosa, persona)* gem, treasure.

liado,-a *pp* → **aliar.**
▷ *adj* allied.
▷ *nm & nf* ally. ● **los Aliados** the Allies.

lianza *nf* 1 *(pacto)* alliance. 2 *(anillo)* wedding ring.

liar [13] *vt* to ally.
▷ *vpr* **aliarse** *(uso recíproco)* to become allies, form an alliance (**con**, with).

lias *adv* alias.
▷ *nm inv* alias.

licaído,-a *adj* 1 *fig (débil)* weak, feeble. 2 *fig (deprimido)* depressed, down.

licates *nm pl* pliers.

liciente *nm* 1 *(incentivo)* incentive, inducement. 2 *(atractivo)* attraction, lure, charm.

alienación *nf* 1 *(gen)* alienation. 2 MED derangement, madness.

alienígena *nm o nf* alien.

aliento *nm* 1 *(respiración)* breath, breathing. 2 *fig (ánimo)* spirit, courage. ■ **cobrar aliento** to get one's breath back. ‖ **dar aliento a** ALGN to encourage sb. ‖ **quedarse sin aliento** 1 *(respirando mal)* to be breathless, be out of breath. 2 *(sorprendido)* to gasp.

aligerar *vt* 1 *(descargar)* to lighten, make lighter. 2 *(aliviar)* to relieve, ease, soothe. 3 *(apresurar)* to speed up.
▷ *vi (apresurar)* to speed up. ■ **¡aligera!** *fam* hurry up! ‖ **aligerar el paso** to quicken one's pace.

alijo *nm* consignment: **un alijo de armas** *a consignment of smuggled arms, an arms cache.*

alimaña *nf* pest.
▷ *nf pl* **alimañas** vermin.

alimentación *nf* 1 *(acción)* feeding. 2 *(alimento)* food; *(dieta)* diet. 3 TÉC feed. ● **bomba de alimentación** feed pump.

alimentar *vt* 1 *(dar alimento)* to feed. 2 *(mantener)* to keep, support. 3 *fig (alentar)* to encourage, foster, nurture; *(pasiones)* to feed, fuel, nurture. 4 *(uso técnico)* to feed.
▷ *vi (servir de alimento)* to nourish, be nutritious:
▷ *vpr* **alimentarse** to live (**de/con**, on): **se alimenta de patatas** *he lives on potatoes.*

alimenticio,-a *adj* 1 *(nutritivo)* nutritious, nutritive. 2 *(de la comida)* food.

alimento *nm* 1 *(comida)* food. 2 *(valor nutritivo)* nutritional value, nourishment. 3 *fig* fuel: **los recuerdos eran el alimento de su ilusión** *he lived off his memories.*

alineación *nf* 1 *(colocación)* alignment, lining up. 2 *(equipo)* line-up. 3 POL alignment. ● **política de no alineación** non-alignment policy.

alineado,-a *pp* → **alinear.**
▷ *adj* aligned, lined-up. ● **países no alineados** non-aligned countries.

alinear *vt* 1 *(poner en línea)* to align, line up. 2 DEP to pick, select. 3 MIL to form up.
▷ *vpr* **alinearse** 1 *(unirse)* to become aligned, align OS (**con**, with). 2 MIL to fall in.

aliñar *vt (gen)* to season, flavour (US flavor); *(ensalada)* to dress.

aliño *nm (gen)* seasoning; *(para ensalada)* dressing.

alioli *nm* garlic mayonnaise.

alisar *vt* to smooth.
▷ *vpr* **alisarse** to smooth: **se alisó el pelo** *he smoothed his hair down.*

alistar *vt* to enlist, recruit.
▷ *vpr* **alistarse** to enlist, join up, enrol (US enroll).

aliviar [12] *vt* 1 *(aligerar)* to lighten, make lighter. 2 *fig (enfermedad, dolor)* to relieve, ease, alleviate, soothe. 3 *(consolar)* to comfort, console. 4 *(apresurar)* to hurry.
▷ *vpr* **aliviarse** *(dolor)* to get better, diminish.

alivio *nm* 1 *(aligeramiento)* lightening. 2 *(mejoría)* relief: **¡qué alivio!** *what a relief!* 3 *(consuelo)* comfort, consolation. ■ **ser de alivio** 1 *fam (persona)* to be a fine one 2 *(cosa)* to be awful: **un resfriado de alivio** *a stinking cold.*

aljibe *nm* cistern, tank.

allá *adv* 1 *(lugar)* there, over there: **más allá** *further (on);* **allá va tu madre** *there goes your mother.* 2 *(tiempo)* back: **allá por los años sesenta** *back in the sixties.*

allanamiento *nm* 1 *(aplanamiento)* levelling. 2 *fig* smoothing out. ● **allanamiento de morada** 1 unlawful entry. 2 *(robo)* housebreaking, breaking and entering.

allanar *vt* 1 *(aplanar)* to level, flatten. 2 *(dificultad, etc)* to smooth out, solve, resolve. 3 *(pacificar)* to pacify, subdue: 4 *(entrar a la fuerza)* to break into: **allanar un domicilio** *to break into a house.*

▷ *vpr* **allanarse** 1 *(nivelarse)* to level out. 2 *fig (avenirse)* to agree, comply (**a**, with).

allegado,-a *pp* → **allegar.**

▷ *adj* close, related.

▷ *nm & nf (familia)* relative; *(amigo)* close friend.

allí *adv* 1 *(lugar)* there, over there: **allí abajo/arriba** *down/up there;* **por allí** *over there, round there.* 2 *(tiempo)* then, at that moment.

alma [Takes **el** in singular.] *nf* soul. ■ **agradecer a ALGN con toda el alma** to thank sb from the bottom of one's heart. ‖ **caerse el alma a los pies** to become disheartened. ‖ **no había ni una alma** there wasn't a soul, there was nobody there. ‖ **no poder ALGN con su alma** to be absolutely exhausted. ‖ **parecer una alma en pena** to look like a ghost. ● **alma gemela** kindred spirit.

almacén *nm* 1 *(local)* warehouse, storehouse. 2 *(habitación)* storeroom.

▷ *nm pl* **almacenes** department store *sing.* ● **grandes almacenes** department store *sing.*

almacenar *vt* 1 to store, warehouse. 2 *(acumular)* to store up, keep.

almeja *nf* clam.

almena *nf* merlon.

▷ *nf pl* **almenas** battlements.

almendra *nf* 1 almond. 2 *(semilla)* kernel, stone.

almendro *nm* almond tree.

almíbar *nm* syrup.

almidón *nm* starch.

almidonar *vt* to starch.

almirante *nm* admiral.

almirez *nm* mortar.

▲ *pl* **almireces.**

almizcle *nm* musk.

almohada *nf* pillow. ■ **consultar algo con la almohada** *fam* to sleep on sth.

almohadilla *nf* 1 *(gen)* small cushion. 2 COST *(para coser)* sewing cushion; *(para alfileres)* pincushion. 3 *(tampón)* inkpad. 4 *(de animal)* pad. 5 ARQUIT *(de capitel)* volute cushion.

almohadón *nm* 1 *(gen)* cushion, large pillow. 2 *(funda)* pillow case. 3 ARQUIT springer.

almorrana *nf fam* pile.

almorzar [50] *vi (al mediodía)* to have lunch; *(de desayuno)* to have breakfast; *(a media mañana)* to have elevenses, have a mid-morning snack.

▷ *vt (al mediodía)* to have for lunch; *(de desayuno)* to have for breakfast; *(a media mañana)* to have for elevenses, have for a mid-morning snack.

almuerzo *nm* 1 *(a mediodía)* lunch. 2 *(a media mañ na)* mid-morning snack, elevenses *pl.* 3 *(desayun* breakfast.

alocado,-a *adj* 1 *(distraído)* scatterbrained. 2 *(loc* crazy, wild, reckless. 3 *(irreflexivo)* thoughtles rash, impetuous.

▷ *nm & nf (despistado)* scatterbrain; *(loco)* fool.

alojamiento *nm* lodging, accommodation: **dar al jamiento a ALGN** *to give accommodation to sb.*

alojar *vt* 1 *(hospedar)* to lodge, put up, accomm date; *(dar vivienda a)* to house. 2 MIL to billet, qua ter. 3 *(meter)* to put, place.

▷ *vpr* **alojarse** 1 *(persona)* to stay; *(ba la, etc)* to be lodge **nos alojamos en un hotel frente al mar** *we stayed in hotel on the seafront.* 2 MIL to be billeted, be qua tered.

alomorfo,-a *adj* allomorphic.

▷ *nm* **alomorfo** allomorph.

alondra *nf* lark. ● **alondra común** skylark.

alopatía *nf* allopathy.

alopecia *nf* alopecia.

alpaca[1] *nf (animal, tela)* alpaca.

alpaca[2] *nf (metal)* nickel silver, German silver, a paca.

alpargata *nf rope-soled* sandal, espadrille.

Alpes *nm pl* **los Alpes** the Alps.

alpinismo *nm* mountaineering, mountain climb ing.

alpinista *nm o nf* mountaineer, mountain climber.

alpiste *nm* 1 birdseed, canary grass. 2 *fam (comid* food; *(bebida)* booze.

alquilar *vt* 1 *(dar en alquiler - período largo)* to ren rent out, let; *(- período corto)* to hire out: **alquila hab taciones a estudiantes** *she rents out rooms to student she lets rooms to students.* 2 *(recibir en alquiler - perío largo)* to rent; *(- período corto)* to hire. ■ **«Se alquila** «To let».

alquiler *nm* 1 *(acción - de casa)* renting, letting; *(- d coche)* hire: **el alquiler de coches es caro** *car hire is e pensive.* 2 *(cuota - de casa)* rent; *(- de TV, etc)* renta **¿has pagado el alquiler del piso?** *have you paid th rent on the flat?* ■ **«En alquiler»** «To let», US «Fo rent».

alquimia *nf* alchemy.

alquitrán *nm* tar. ● **alquitrán de hulla** coal tar.

alrededor *adv* 1 *(lugar)* round, around: **mira alred dor** *look around.* 2 **alrededor de** *(tiempo)* around: **alr dedor de las cuatro** *around four o'clock.* 3 *(aproxima damente)* about: **alrededor de veinte** *about twenty.*

▷ *nm pl* **alrededores** surrounding area *sing:* **en los alr dedores de Sevilla** *in the vicinity of Seville, just outsid Seville.*

alta *nf* [Takes **el** in singular.] 1 *(de un enfermo)* dis charge: **dieron de/el alta al enfermo** *the patient wa discharged from hospital.* 2 *(de un empleado)* registra tion *with Social Security.* 3 *(entrada, admisión)* admis sion; *(ingreso)* membership. 4 *(en el ejército)* enro ment, enlistment.

altanero,-a *adj* arrogant, haughty, conceited.

altar *nm* altar.

altavoz *nm* loudspeaker.

▲ *pl* **altavoces.**

lteración *nf* 1 *(cambio)* alteration, change. 2 *(excitación)* agitation, uneasiness, restlessness. 3 *(alboroto)* disturbance, quarrel, row. ■ **alteración del orden público** breach of the peace, disturbance of the peace.

lterar *vt* 1 *(cambiar)* to change, modify, alter: **alteró nuestros planes** *he changed our plans.* 2 *(estropear)* to spoil, upset; *(comida)* to make go off, turn bad. 3 *(enfadar)* to annoy, upset: **todo le altera** *the slightest thing upsets him.* 4 *(inquietar)* to unnerve, make feel restless.

vpr **alterarse** 1 *(cambiar)* to change. 2 *(deteriorarse)* to go bad, go off. 3 *(enfadarse)* to lose one's temper, get upset.

ltercado *nm* argument, quarrel.

lternar *vt (gen)* to alternate.

vi 1 *(turnar)* to alternate. 2 *(relacionarse)* to meet people, socialize (**con**, with), mix (**con**, with). 3 *(en salas de fiesta, bar)* to entertain.

vpr **alternarse** *(turnarse)* to take turns: **se alternaron para conducir** *they took turns at driving.*

lternativa *nf* alternative, option, choice. ■ **tomar una alternativa** to decide, choose.

lternativamente *adv* alternatively.

lternativo,-a *adj* alternative.

lterno,-a *adj* alternate, alternating: **días alternos** *alternate days.*

lteza *nf* Highness. ● **Su Alteza Real** 1 *(hombre)* His Royal Highness. 2 *(mujer)* Her Royal Highness.

ltibajos *nm pl* ups and downs: **los altibajos de la vida** *the ups and downs of life.*

ltiplano *nm* high plateau.

ltisonante *adj* grandiloquent, pompous.

ltitud *nf* height, altitude.

ltivamente *adv* arrogantly.

ltivez *nf* haughtiness, arrogance, conceit.

ltivo,-a *adj* haughty, arrogant, conceited.

lto[1] *nm (parada)* stop: **hicieron un alto para comer** *they stopped for lunch.*

▷ *interj* halt!; *(policía)* stop!

lto,-a[2] *adj* 1 *(persona, edificio, árbol)* tall: **es una mujer muy alta** *she's a very tall woman.* 2 *(montaña, pared, techo, precio)* high. 3 *(elevado)* top, upper: **viven en los pisos altos** *they live on the upper floors.* 4 *(importancia)* high, top. 5 *(voz, sonido)* loud: **lo dijo en voz alta** *she said it aloud.*

▷ *adv* **alto** 1 high (up): **colocaron los platos muy alto** *they put the dishes very high up.* 2 *(voz)* loud, loudly: **¿podrías hablar más alto?** *could you speak a bit louder?*

▷ *nm* 1 *(altura)* height: **solo hace dos metros de alto** *it's only two metres high.* 2 *(elevación)* hill, high ground. ■ **a altas horas de la noche** late at night. ▮ **en lo alto de** on the top of. ▮ **pasar por alto** to pass over. ▮ **por todo lo alto** *fig* in a grand way. ● **alta cocina** haute cuisine. ▮ **alta sociedad** high society. ▮ **alta tecnología** high technology.

ltramuz *nm* lupin.

▲ *pl* **altramuces.**

ltruismo *nm* altruism.

ltura *nf* 1 *(gen)* height: **el edificio tiene una altura de 80 metros** *the building is 80 metres high.* 2 *(altitud)* altitude. 3 *(nivel)* level, par; *(punto)* point: **¿a qué altura de la calle vives?** *how far up the street do you live?* 4 *fig (mérito, valía, calidad)* merit, worth; *(dignidad)* dignity, excellence. ■ **estar a la altura de** to measure up to, match up to, be on a par with.

▷ *nf pl* **alturas** REL heavens. ■ **a estas alturas** by now, at this stage.

alubia *nf* bean.

alucinación *nf* hallucination.

alucinado,-a *pp* → **alucinar.**

▷ *adj argot* amazed, stunned, gobsmacked.

alucinante *adj* 1 hallucinatory. 2 *argot (extraordinario)* brilliant, fantastic, amazing, incredible, mind-blowing.

alucinar *vt* 1 *(producir sensaciones)* to hallucinate. 2 *fig (cautivar)* to fascinate, amaze, astound, flip out, stun.

▷ *vi argot* to be amazed, be gobsmacked: **¡alucinas!** *you're out of your mind!, you're crazy!*

alud *nm* avalanche.

aludido,-a *pp* → **aludir.**

▷ *adj* above-mentioned, in question. ■ **darse por aludido,-a** to take the hint.

aludir *vi* to allude (**a**, to), mention (**a**, -), refer (**a**, to).

alumbrado,-a *pp* → **alumbrar.**

▷ *adj* 1 *(iluminado)* lit, lighted. 2 *fam (achispado)* tipsy, merry.

▷ *nm* **alumbrado** TÉC lighting, lights *pl*; *(coche)* lights *pl*.

alumbramiento *nm* 1 *(eléctrico)* lighting. 2 *(nacimiento)* childbirth.

alumbrar *vt* 1 *(iluminar)* to light, give light to, illuminate. 2 *fig (enseñar)* to enlighten.

▷ *vi* 1 *(iluminar)* to give light. 2 *(parir)* to give birth to.

▷ *vpr* **alumbrarse** *fam (embriagarse)* to get tipsy.

aluminio *nm* aluminium, US aluminum.

alumnado *nm (de colegio)* pupils *pl*; *(de universidad)* student body.

alumno,-a *nm & nf (de colegio)* pupil (US student); *(de universidad)* student. ● **alumno externo** day pupil. ▮ **alumno interno** boarder. ▮ **antiguo alumno** 1 *(de colegio)* old boy, former pupil. 2 *(de universidad)* old student, former student.

alunizar [4] *vi* to land on the moon.

alusión *nf* allusion, reference.

alusivo,-a *adj* allusive (**a**, to), referring (**a**, to).

aluvión *nm* 1 alluvion: **tierra de aluvión** *alluvium, alluvial soil.* 2 *fig* flood: **un aluvión de insultos** *a barrage of insults.*

alveolar *adj* alveolar.

alveolo *nm* 1 ANAT alveolus. 2 *(de panal)* cell.

alza [Takes **el** in singular.] *nf* 1 *(aumento)* rise, increase. 2 *(impresión)* underlay. 3 *(de calzado)* raised insole. 4 *(de rifle)* rear sight, sight. ■ **al alza / en alza** rising. ▮ **estar en alza** *fig* to be up and coming, be on the rise.

alzamiento *nm* 1 *(aumento)* raising, lifting. 2 *(rebelión)* uprising, insurrection.

alzar [4] *vt* 1 *(levantar)* to raise, lift: **alzó la mano** *he raised his hand.* 2 *(construir)* to build, erect. 3 *(un plano)* to draw up, make out. 4 *(quitar)* to remove, take off, take away. 5 *(una cosecha)* to get in, gather in. 6 *(cortar la baraja)* to cut. 7 REL to elevate. 8 *(en impre-*

sión) to gather. ■ **alzar el vuelo** to take off. ■ **alzar los ojos** to look up.
▷ *vpr* **alzarse 1** *(levantarse)* to rise up, get up. **2** *(sublevarse)* to rise, rebel: **alzarse en rebelión** *to rise up in rebellion.* **3** *(sobresalir)* to stand out. **4** JUR to lodge an appeal.
a.m. *abrev* **(ante meridiem)** ante meridiem; *(abreviatura)* a.m.
ama [Takes **el** in singular.] *nf* **1** *(señora)* lady of the house. **2** *(propietaria)* landlady. ● **ama de casa** housewife.
amabilidad *nf* kindness, affability: **tenga la amabilidad de...** *would you be so kind as to...?*
amable *adj* kind, nice: **¿sería usted tan amable de...?** *would you be so kind as to...?*
amaestrado,-a *pp* ⟶ **amaestrar.**
▷ *adj (adiestrado)* trained; *(domado)* tamed: **ratón amaestrado** *performing mouse.*
amaestrar *vt (adiestrar)* to train; *(domar)* to tame.
amago *nm* **1** *(amenaza)* threatening. **2** *(señal)* sign, indication: **amago de infarto** *mild heart attack.*
amainar *vi* **1** *(viento)* to die down, drop. **2** *fig (calmarse)* to calm down.
amalgamar *vt* to amalgamate.
amamantar *vt* to breast-feed, suckle.
amanecer [43] *vi* **1** [Used only in the 3rd person; it does not take a subject.] to dawn, get light: **en verano amanece pronto** *day breaks early in summer.* **2** *(estar)* to be at dawn, be at daybreak: **amanecimos en Barcelona** *we were in Barcelona at dawn.* **3** *(despertar)* to wake up.
▷ *nm* dawn, daybreak. ■ **al amanecer** at daybreak.
amanerado,-a *pp* ⟶ **amanerar.**
▷ *adj* affected, mannered.
amansar *vt* **1** *(animal)* to tame; *(caballo)* to break in. **2** *fig (persona)* to tame, calm down; *(pasión, etc)* to soothe, appease.
▷ *vpr* **amansarse** to become tame.
amante *adj* loving, fond (**de**, of).
▷ *nm o nf* lover.
amañar *vt* **1** *(falsear)* to fiddle, fix; *(documentos)* to tamper with, doctor; *(cuentas)* to cook; *(elecciones)* to rig. **2** *(componer)* to fix, arrange.
▷ *vpr* **amañarse** *(darse maña)* to be skilful (US skillful). ■ **amañárselas** *fam* to manage.
amaño *nm (disposición)* skill.
▷ *nm pl* **amaños 1** *(instrumentos)* tools. **2** *(trucos)* tricks.
amapola *nf* poppy.
amar *vt* to love.
▷ *vpr* **amarse** *(uso recíproco)* to love each other, be in love (with each other).
amarar *vi (hidroavión)* to land at sea; *(nave espacial)* to splash down.
amargado,-a *pp* ⟶ **amargar.**
▷ *adj* embittered, resentful: **estar amargado,-a** *to feel very bitter.*
▷ *nm & nf* bitter person.
amargar [7] *vi (tener sabor amargo)* to taste bitter: **este pan amarga** *this bread tastes bitter.*
▷ *vt* **1** *(hacer amargo)* to make bitter. **2** *fig (disgustos, etc)* to embitter, make bitter. **3** *fig (estropear)* to spoil, ruin: **la lluvia nos amargó el día** *the rain put a damp on our day.*
▷ *vpr* **amargarse 1** *(volverse amargo)* to become bitte **2** *fig* to become embittered, become bitter. ■ **a n die le amarga un dulce** a gift is always welcome.
amargo,-a *adj* **1** *(sabor)* bitter. **2** *fig (carácter)* sou *(experiencia)* bitter, sour, painful.
▷ *nm* **amargo** bitterness.
amargura *nf* **1** bitterness. **2** *(dolor)* sorrow, grie sadness.
amarillo,-a *adj* yellow.
▷ *nm* **amarillo** yellow. ● **prensa amarilla** sensationali press.
amarra *nf* mooring rope.
▷ *nf pl* **amarras** *fam fig* connections. ■ **soltar las amarras 1** MAR to cast off, let go. **2** *fig* to break loose.
amarrar *vt* **1** *(atar)* to tie (up), fasten. **2** MAR to moo tie up.
amarre *nm* mooring.
amasar *vt* **1** CULIN to knead; *(cemento)* to mix. **2** *fi (reunir)* to amass. **3** *fam (urdir)* to cook up.
amasijo *nm* **1** *(masa)* dough; *(cemento, yeso)* mixture **2** *fam (mezcolanza)* hotchpotch, jumble.
amateur
▲ *pl* **amateurs.** *adj* amateur.
▷ *nm o nf* amateur.
amatista *nf* amethyst.
amazona *nf* **1** *(mitología)* Amazon. **2** *(jinete)* horsewoman.
Amazonas *nm* **el Amazonas** the Amazon.
amazónico,-a *adj* Amazonian.
ambages *nm pl* circumlocution *sing*: **dímelo sin ambages** *tell it to me straight, don't beat about the bush.* ■ **hablar sin ambages** to speak plainly.
ámbar *nm* amber.
ambición *nf* ambition, aspiration.
ambicionar *vt* to want: **siempre ambicionó ser rico** *was always his ambition to be rich.*
ambicioso,-a *adj (plan, etc)* ambitious; *(persona)* ambitious, enterprising.
▷ *nm & nf* ambitious person, go-getter.
ambidextro,-a *adj* ambidextrous.
▷ *nm & nf* ambidextrous person.
ambientación *nf* **1** *(ambiente)* atmosphere. **2** *(localización)* setting.
ambientador *nm* air freshener.
ambiental *adj* **1** *(del ambiente)* environmental. **2** *(de fondo)* background.
ambientar *vt* **1** *(dar ambiente)* to give atmosphere to. **2** *(localizar)* to set.
▷ *vpr* **ambientarse** to adapt, get used (**a**, to).
ambiente *nm* **1** *(aire)* air, atmosphere. **2** *(entorno)* environment, atmosphere: **no hay mucho ambiente de noche** *there is not much going on at night.* ■ **cambiar de ambiente** to have a change of scene.
ambigüedad *nf* ambiguity.
ambiguo,-a *adj* ambiguous.
ámbito *nm* **1** *(espacio)* sphere, space. **2** *(marco)* field **en el ámbito de la informática** *in the computer science field.*
ambivalente *adj* ambivalent.
amblar *vi* to amble.

mbos,-as *adj* both: **por ambos lados** *on both sides.* *pron* both: **me gustan ambos** *I like both of them, I like them both.*
mbulancia *nf* ambulance.
mbulante *adj* itinerant, travelling: **biblioteca ambulante** *mobile library.*
mbulatorio,-a *adj* **1** ambulatory. **2 ambulatorio** surgery, clinic.
meba *nf* amoeba (US ameba).
medrentar *vt* to frighten, scare.
vpr **amedrentarse** *(asustarse)* to be frightened, be scared; *(acobardarse)* to become intimidated.
melgar *vt* to furrow.
melonado,-a *adj* **1** melon-shaped. **2** *fam* lovesick.
mén¹ *nm* REL amen. ■ **decir amén a todo/todos** *fam* to agree with everything/everybody. ‖ **en un decir amén** *fam* in the twinkling of an eye.
▲ *pl* **amenes.**
mén² ■ **amén de** *(excepto)* except for. *(además de)* in addition to, as well as.
menaza *nf* threat, menace.
menazar [4] *vt* & *vi* to threaten.
menidad *nf* amenity, pleasantness, agreeableness.
menizar [4] *vt* to liven up, make entertaining, make enjoyable.
meno,-a *adj* lively, entertaining, enjoyable.
menorrea *nf* amenorrhoea (US amenorrhea).
mérica *nf* America. ● **América Central** Central America. ‖ **América del Norte** North America. ‖ **América del Sur** South America. ‖ **América Latina** Latin America.
mericana *nf* jacket.
mericano,-a *adj* American.
▷ *nm & nf* American.
meritar *vt* to deserve.
merizar [4] *vi* ⟶ **amarar.**
metralladora *nf* machine gun.
metrallar *vt* **1** to machine-gun. **2** *fig (acosar)* to chase, pursue, besiege.
mianto *nm* asbestos.
migable *adj* amicable, friendly.
mígdala *nf* tonsil.
migdalitis *nf inv* tonsillitis.
migo,-a *adj* **1** *(amigable)* friendly: **es muy amigo de Julio** *he's very friendly with Julio.* **2** *(aficionado)* fond (**de**, of): **no es muy amiga de discotecas** *she's not keen on discos.*
▷ *nm & nf* **1** friend: **una amiga mía** *a friend of mine;* **son amigos íntimos** *they are close friends.* **2** *(novio)* boyfriend; *(novia)* girlfriend. **3** *(amante)* lover. ■ **hacerse amigo,-a de** to make friends with.
migote *nm fam* pal, mate, chum.
miguismo *nm* contacts *pl*, string-pulling.
minoácido *nm* amino acid.
minoración *nf* reduction, decrease: **aminoración de la velocidad** *reduction in speed.*
minorar *vt* to reduce, decrease. ■ **aminorar el paso** to slow down.
mistad *nf* friendship.
▷ *nf pl* **amistades** friends. ■ **hacer amistades** to make friends.
amistoso,-a *adj* friendly: **partido amistoso** *friendly match.*
amnesia *nf* amnesia, loss of memory: **amnesia temporal** *blackout.*
amniótico,-a *adj* amniotic.
amnistía *nf* amnesty.
amo *nm* **1** *(señor)* master. **2** *(dueño)* owner. **3** *(jefe)* boss. ■ **hacerse el amo** *fig* to be the boss (**de**, of), rule the roost.
amodorrar *vt* to make drowsy, make sleepy.
▷ *vpr* **amodorrarse** *(adormecerse)* to feel drowsy, feel sleepy; *(dormirse)* to fall into a stupor.
amoldar *vt* to adapt, adjust.
▷ *vpr* **amoldarse** to adapt, adjust (**a**, to): **se amoldó a las costumbres españolas** *he adapted himself to Spanish customs.*
amonestación *nf* **1** *(reprensión)* reprimand, admonition, admonishment. **2** *(advertencia)* warning. **3** DEP caution, booking.
▷ *nf pl* **amonestaciones** banns.
amonestar *vt* **1** *(reprender)* to reprimand, admonish. **2** *(advertir)* to warn. **3** DEP to caution, book. **4** *(en una boda)* to publish the banns of.
amoníaco *nm* ammonia.
amontonar *vt* **1** to heap up, pile up. **2** *(juntar)* to collect, gather, accumulate.
▷ *vpr* **amontonarse 1** to heap up, pile up. **2** *(gente)* to crowd together. **3** *fam* to live together.
amor *nm* **1** *(gen)* love. **2** *(cuidado)* loving care; *(devoción)* devotion.
▷ *nm pl* **amores** *(asuntos)* love affairs, loves. ■ **con/de mil amores** *fam* willingly, with pleasure. ‖ **hacer el amor** to make love. ● **amor cortés** courtly love. ‖ **amor libre** free love. ‖ **amor propio** self-esteem.
amoral *adj* amoral.
amoratado,-a *pp* ⟶ **amoratarse.**
▷ *adj* **1** *(de frío)* blue with cold. **2** *(de un golpe)* bruised, black and blue.
amordazar [4] *vt (persona)* to gag; *(perro)* to muzzle.
amorfo,-a *adj* **1** amorphous. **2** *fig (persona)* characterless, insipid, weak.
amorío *nm* love affair, fling.
amoroso,-a *adj* loving, affectionate.
amortiguador,-ra *adj (de golpe)* cushioning, softening; *(de dolor)* alleviating, mitigating; *(de ruido)* muffling; *(de luz)* subduing.
▷ *nm* **amortiguador 1** AUTO shock absorber. **2** TÉC damper.
amortiguar [22] *vt (golpe)* to cushion; *(dolor)* to alleviate, ease, soothe; *(ruido)* to muffle; *(luz)* to subdue, dim.
amortizar [4] *vt* **1** *(pagar)* to repay, pay off. **2** *(recuperar - lo pagado)* to get one's money's worth out of; *(- lo invertido)* to get a return on, recoup.
amotinar *vt* **1** to incite to rebellion. **2** MIL to incite to mutiny.
▷ *vpr* **amotinarse 1** to rebel, rise up, riot. **2** MIL to mutiny.
amparar *vt* **1** *(proteger)* to protect, shelter. **2** *(ayudar)* to help; *(favorecer)* to favour (US favor).

▷ *vpr* **ampararse 1** *(protegerse)* to take shelter, protect OS. **2** *(acogerse)* to avail OS of the protection (**en**, of), seek protection (**en**, in).

amparo *nm* protection, shelter. ■ **al amparo de** under the protection of.

amperio *nm* ampere.

ampliación *nf* **1** enlargement, extension. **2** ARQUIT extension. **3** *(fotografía)* enlargement. ● **ampliación de estudios** furthering of studies.

ampliar [13] *vt* **1** to enlarge, extend. **2** ARQUIT to build an extension onto. **3** *(fotografía)* to enlarge. **4** *(capital)* to increase. **5** *(estudios)* to further. **6** *(tema, idea)* to develop, expand on.

amplificación *nf* amplification.

amplificador,-ra *adj* amplifying.

▷ *nm* **amplificador** amplifier.

amplificar [1] *vt* to amplify.

amplio,-a *adj* **1** *(extenso)* large: **amplia mayoría** *large majority.* **2** *(espacioso)* roomy, spacious. **3** *(ancho)* wide, broad. **4** *(holgado)* loose. ■ **en el sentido más amplio de la palabra** in the broadest sense of the word.

amplitud *nf* **1** *(extensión)* extent, range. **2** *(espacio)* room, space, spaciousness. **3** *(anchura)* width. **4** *(holgadura)* looseness. **5** FÍS amplitude.

ampolla *nf* **1** MED blister. **2** *(burbuja)* bubble. **3** *(vasija)* flask, bottle. **4** *(tubito)* ampoule, phial.

ampuloso,-a *adj* inflated, pompous, bombastic.

amputar *vt* **1** to amputate. **2** *fig* to cut out.

Amsterdam *nm* Amsterdam.

amueblado,-a *pp* → **amueblar.**

▷ *adj* furnished.

amueblar *vt* to furnish. ■ **sin amueblar** unfurnished.

amuleto *nm* amulet, charm. ● **amuleto de la suerte** lucky charm.

amurallar *vt* to wall.

anabaptismo *nm* Anabaptism.

anabolizante *adj* anabolic.

anaconda *nf* anaconda.

anacoreta *nm o nf* anchorite.

anacronismo *nm* anachronism.

anaerobio,-a *adj* anaerobic.

▷ *nm* **anaerobio** anaerobe, anaerobium.

anagrama *nm* anagram.

anal *adj* anal.

analfabetismo *nm* illiteracy.

analfabeto,-a *adj* **1** illiterate. **2** *fig* stupid.

▷ *nm & nf* **1** illiterate person. **2** *fig* stupid person, ignoramus.

analgésico,-a *adj* analgesic.

▷ *nm* **analgésico** analgesic, painkiller.

análisis *nm inv* analysis. ● **análisis de orina** urine test. ‖ **análisis de sangre** blood test.

analizar [4] *vt* to analyse (US analyze).

analogía *nf* analogy.

analógico,-a *adj* analogical.

análogo,-a *adj* analogous, similar.

ananá *nf* pineapple.

▲ *pl* **ananaes.**

anaquel *nm* shelf.

anarquía *nf* anarchy.

anárquico,-a *adj* anarchic, anarchical.

anarquista *adj* anarchist.

▷ *nm o nf* anarchist.

anatema *nm* anathema. ■ **lanzar anatemas contra** curse, hurl abuse at.

anatomía *nf* anatomy.

anca [Takes **el** in singular.] *nf* haunch. ● **ancas de r**na frogs' legs.

ancestral *adj* ancestral, ancient.

ancho,-a *adj* **1** *(gen)* broad, wide. **2** *(prenda - holg*da)* loose-fitting; *(- grande)* too big.

▷ *nm* **ancho 1** *(anchura)* breadth, width: **¿qué ancho ti**ne? *how wide is it?;* **tiene cuatro metros de ancho** *i four metres wide.* **2** *(en costura)* width. ■ **a sus anch** *fam* comfortable, at ease. ‖ **estar más ancho,-a q** **largo,-a** to be full of OS. ‖ **quedarse tan ancho,-a** *fam* behave as if nothing had happened, not bat an ey lid.

anchoa *nf* anchovy.

anchura *nf* breadth, width. ● **anchura de pecho/ci tura/caderas** bust/waist/hip measurement.

anciano,-a *adj* very old, elderly, aged.

▷ *nm & nf* old person, elderly person.

▷ *nm pl* **los ancianos** old people, the elderly.

ancla [Takes **el** in singular.] *nf* anchor. ■ **echar ancl** to drop anchor.

anclar *vi* MAR to anchor.

▷ *vt* TÉC to anchor.

andadas *nf pl fam* old ways. ■ **volver a las andad** to go back to one's old tricks.

andadura *nf* **1** *(viaje)* journey. **2** *(trayectoria - de pers na)* career; *(- de organización, etc)* activity, functio ing: **este libro resume la andadura de la asociaci** *this book summarizes the activities of the associatio* ■ **iniciar su andadura / comenzar su andadura 1** *(pers na)* to start out. **2** *(organización)* to start up.

Andalucía *nf* Andalusia.

andaluz,-za *adj* Andalusian.

▷ *nm & nf (persona)* Andalusian.

▷ *nm* **andaluz** *(dialecto)* Andalusian.

andamio *nm* scaffold.

andanada *nf* **1** MAR broadside. **2** *(reprensión)* repr mand, rebuke. **3** *(en plaza de toros)* covered stand.

andante *adj* **1** walking. **2** MÚS andante.

▷ *adv* MÚS andante.

▷ *nm* MÚS andante. ● **caballero andante** knight errant.

andanza *nf* event, occurrence.

▷ *nf pl* **andanzas** adventures.

andar [64] *vi* **1** *(moverse)* to walk: **está cerca, irem andando** *it's not far, we'll walk.* **2** *(trasladarse)* t move: **este coche anda despacio** *this car goes ve slowly.* **3** *(funcionar)* to work, run, go: **este reloj r anda** *this watch doesn't work.* **4** *(estar)* to be: **¿cór andas?** *how are you?, how's it going?* **5** *(juntarse)* t mix (**con**, with). ■ **andar a gatas** to crawl. ‖ **andar c puntillas** to tiptoe. ‖ **andar con cien ojos** to keep one wits about one. ‖ **andar con rodeos** to beat about th bush. ‖ **andar con cuidado / andarse con cuidado** to b careful. ‖ **andar por las nubes** to be absent-minded **andarse por las ramas** *fig* to beat about the bush.

▷ *vt* to walk: **no puede andar ni cien metros** *she can't eve walk a hundred yards.*

▷ *nm* walk, gait.

interj **¡anda!** well!, oh!: **¡anda ya!** *come off it!;* **bésame, anda** *go on, give me a kiss.*
ndén *nm* platform.
ndes *nm pl* **los Andes** the Andes.
ndino,-a *adj* Andean.
nm & nf Andean.
ndorra *nm* Andorra.
ndorrano,-a *adj* Andorran.
nm & nf Andorran.
ndrajo *nm* rag, tatter.
ndrajoso,-a *adj* ragged, in tatters.
ndrógeno *nm* androgen.
ndrógino,-a *adj* androgynous.
ndroide *nm* android.
nécdota *nf* anecdote.
necdótico,-a *adj* anecdotic, anecdotal.
negar [7] *vt* 1 *(inundar)* to flood. 2 *(ahogar)* to drown.
vpr **anegarse** 1 *(inundarse)* to be flooded, flood. 2 *(ahogarse)* to be drowned. ■ **anegarse en llanto/lágrimas** to fill with tears, dissolve into tears.
nejo,-a *adj* adjoining, attached (**a**, to).
nm **anejo** annexe (US annex).
nélido *nm* annelid.
nemia *nf* anaemia (US anemia).
nemona *nf* anemone. ● **anemona de mar** sea anemone.
nestesia *nf* anaesthesia (US anesthesia).
nestésico,-a *adj* anaesthetic (US anesthetic).
nm **anestésico** anaesthetic (US anesthetic).
nexar *vt* to annex.
nexión *nf* annexation
nexionar *vt* to annex.
nexo,-a *adj* adjoining, attached (**a**, to).
nm **anexo** annexe (US annex).
nfetamina *nf* amphetamine.
nfibio,-a *adj* amphibious.
nm **anfibio** amphibian.
nm pl **los anfibios** amphibia *pl.*
nfiteatro *nm* 1 amphitheatre (US amphitheater). 2 *(en universidad)* lecture theatre (US theater). 3 *(en teatro, cine)* circle.
nfitrión,-ona *nm & nf (hombre)* host; *(mujer)* hostess.
ngel *nm* angel. ■ **ángel caído** fallen angel. ‖ **tener ángel** to be charming. ● **ángel custodio/de la guarda** guardian angel.
ngelical *adj* angelic, angelical.
ngina *nf* angina. ■ **tener anginas** to have a sore throat. ● **angina de pecho** angina pectoris.
nglicano,-a *adj* Anglican.
nm & nf Anglican. ● **la Iglesia Anglicana** the Anglican Church, the Church of England.
nglosajón,-ona *adj* Anglo-Saxon.
nm & nf (persona) Anglo-Saxon.
nm **anglosajón** *(idioma)* Anglo-Saxon.
ngola *nf* Angola.
ngora *nf* angora.
ngosto,-a *adj* narrow.
ngostura *nf* 1 *(estrechez)* narrowness. 2 *(bebida)* angostura.
ngstrom *nm* angstrom.

anguila *nf* eel. ● **anguila de mar** conger eel.
angula *nf* elver.
angular *adj* angular. ● **(objetivo) gran angular** *(fotografía)* wide-angle lens.
ángulo *nm* 1 angle: **formar ángulo con** *to be at an angle to.* 2 *(rincón)* corner. ■ **en ángulo con** at an angle to. ● **ángulo recto** right angle.
anguloso,-a *adj* angular.
angustia *nf* 1 anguish, affliction, distress: **¡qué angustia!** *how distressing!* 2 *(física)* sickness, nausea. ● **angustia vital** anxiety state, angst.
angustiar [12] *vt* 1 *(afligir)* to distress, upset. 2 *(preocupar)* to worry, make anxious.
▷ *vpr* **angustiarse** 1 *(afligirse)* to become distressed, get upset. 2 *(preocuparse)* to worry, get anxious.
angustioso,-a *adj (situación)* distressing, worrying; *(mirada)* anguished.
anhelante *adj* longing, yearning.
anhelar *vt* to long for, yearn for: **anhela ser famosa** *she longs to be famous.*
anhelo *nm* longing, yearning.
anhídrido *nm* anhydride.
anidar *vi* 1 *(pájaro)* to nest, make one's nest. 2 *fig* to live, dwell: **el miedo anida en su corazón** *fear lingers in her heart.*
▷ *vt fig* to shelter.
anilla *nf (aro)* ring.
▷ *nf pl* **anillas** DEP rings. ● **anilla de lata** ringpull.
anillo *nm* 1 ring. 2 *(de planeta)* ring. 3 ARQUIT annulet. 4 *(de gusano)* annulus; *(de culebra)* coil. ■ **caérsele a ALGN los anillos** to be beneath sb. ‖ **venir como anillo al dedo** to be just what sb needed, suit sb fine.
ánima [Takes **el** in singular.] *nf* 1 soul. 2 *(de arma)* bore.
▷ *nf pl* **ánimas** *(toque)* evening bell *sing.* ● **ánima bendita** soul in purgatory.
animación *nf* 1 *(actividad)* activity, movement, bustle. 2 *(viveza)* liveliness: **dar animación** *to liven up.* 3 CINE animation.
animado,-a *pp* → **animar.**
▷ *adj* 1 *(movido)* animated, lively, jolly. 2 *(concurrido)* bustling, full of people. 3 *(alegre)* cheerful, in high spirits, excited.
animador,-ra *adj* cheering, encouraging.
▷ *nm & nf* 1 *(artista)* entertainer. 2 *(de un equipo)* cheerleader.
animadversión *nf* antagonism, hostility, ill will, animosity. ■ **sentir animadversión por ALGN** to feel hostile towards sb.
animal *adj* 1 animal. 2 *fig (basto)* rough; *(necio)* ignorant, stupid; *(grosero)* rude, coarse, uncouth.
▷ *nm* 1 animal. 2 *fig (basto)* rough person, brute, lout; *(necio)* dunce; *(grosero)* rude person: **¡animal!** *you brute!* ● **animal doméstico** pet. ‖ **reino animal** animal kingdom.
animar *vt* 1 *(alegrar a ALGN)* to cheer up. 2 *(alegrar algo)* to brighten up, liven up. 3 *(alentar)* to encourage.
▷ *vpr* **animarse** 1 *(persona)* to cheer up. 2 *(fiesta, etc)* to brighten up, liven up. 3 *(decidirse)* to make up one's mind: **anímate a venir** *say that you'll come.*
ánimo *nm* 1 *(espíritu)* spirit; *(mente)* mind; *(alma)* soul. 2 *(intención)* intention, purpose: **sin ánimo de ofen-**

der *no offence intended.* 3 *(valor)* courage: **no tengo ánimos de nada** *I don't feel up to anything.* 4 *(aliento)* encouragement.
▷ *interj* cheer up! ■ **dar ánimos a ALGN** to encourage SB.
animosidad *nf* animosity, ill will, hostility.
animoso,-a *adj (atrevido)* brave, courageous; *(decidido)* determined.
aniñado,-a *pp* ⟶ **aniñarse.**
▷ *adj* 1 childlike. 2 *pey* childish.
anión *nm* anion.
aniquilar *vt* to annihilate, destroy: **aniquilar al enemigo** *to wipe out the enemy.*
anís *nm* 1 *(planta)* anise; *(grano)* aniseed. 2 *(bebida)* anisette. 3 *(confite)* aniseed ball. ■ **no ser grano de anís** *fam* to be no trifle.
aniversario *nm* anniversary.
ano *nm* anus.
anoche *adv (late)* last night; *(early)* yesterday evening. ■ **antes de anoche** the night before last.
anochecer [43] *vi* 1 [Used only in the 3rd person; it does not take a subject.] to get dark: **cuando anocheció** *when it got dark.* 2 to be at nightfall, reach at nightfall.
▷ *nm* nightfall, dusk, evening. ■ **al anochecer** at nightfall, at dusk.
anodino,-a *adj* 1 MED anodyne. 2 *(ineficaz)* ineffective, inefficient. 3 *(soso)* insipid, dull.
▷ *nm* **anodino** MED anodyne.
ánodo *nm* anode.
anofeles *nm inv* anopheles.
anomalía *nf* anomaly.
anómalo,-a *adj* anomalous.
anonadado,-a *pp* ⟶ **anonadar.**
▷ *adj* dumbfounded, speechless. ■ **dejar anonadado,-a a ALGN** to dumbfound SB, amaze SB, take SB aback, leave SB speechless.
anonimato *nm* anonymity. ■ **permanecer en el anonimato** to remain anonymous, remain nameless.
anónimo,-a *adj* 1 *(desconocido)* anonymous. 2 *(sociedad)* limited, US incorporated.
▷ *nm* **anónimo** 1 *(carta)* anonymous letter; *(obra)* anonymous work. 2 *(anonimato)* anonymity.
anorak *nm* anorak.
▲ *pl* **anoraks.**
anorexia *nf* anorexia.
anormal *adj* 1 *(no normal)* abnormal. 2 *(inhabitual)* unusual: **comportamiento anormal** *abnormal behaviour.* 3 MED subnormal.
▷ *nm o nf* MED subnormal person.
anotación *nf* 1 *(acotación)* annotation. 2 *(nota)* note. 3 *(apunte)* noting.
anotar *vt* 1 *(acotar)* to annotate, add notes to. 2 *(apuntar)* to take down, jot down, make a note of.
anquilosar *vt* to ankylose, anchylose.
▷ *vpr* **anquilosarse** 1 to ankylose, anchylose. 2 *fig* to stagnate, be paralysed.
ansia [Takes **el** in singular.] *nf* 1 *(ansiedad)* anxiety; *(angustia)* anguish. 2 *(deseo)* eagerness, longing, yearning: **tener ansia de poder** *to be longing for power.* 3 MED sick feeling.
ansiar [13] *vt* to long for, yearn for: **ansiaba la paz** *she longed for peace.*
ansiedad *nf* 1 anxiety. 2 MED nervous tension. ■ **co ansiedad** anxiously.
ansioso,-a *adj* 1 *(desasosegado)* anguished, anxiou desperate. 2 *(deseoso)* eager, longing (**por/de**, to): **e taba ansioso de verla** *he couldn't wait to see her, h was dying to see her.* 3 *(avaricioso)* greedy, covetous
antagónico,-a *adj* antagonistic.
antagonismo *nm* antagonism.
antagonista *adj* antagonistic.
▷ *nm o nf* antagonist.
antaño *adv* formerly, in olden times, long ago: **la costumbres de antaño** *age-old traditions.*
antártico,-a *adj* Antarctic.
Antártida *nf* Antarctica.
ante[1] *prep* 1 before, in the presence of. 2 *(considerando)* in the face of: **ante estas circunstancias** *under th circumstances.* ■ **ante todo** 1 *(primero)* first of all. 2 *(p encima de)* above all.
ante[2] *nm* 1 ZOOL elk, moose. 2 *(piel)* suede.
anteanoche *adv* the night before last.
anteayer *adv* the day before yesterday.
antebrazo *nm* forearm.
antecedente *adj* previous, preceding.
▷ *nm* 1 precedent. 2 GRAM antecedent. 3 MED history
▷ *nm pl* **antecedentes** record *sing.* ■ **poner en antecedentes** to put in the picture. ‖ **tener malos antecedentes** to have a bad record.
anteceder *vt* to precede, come before.
antecesor,-ra *nm & nf* 1 *(en un cargo)* predecesso 2 *(antepasado)* ancestor.
antedicho,-a *adj* aforesaid, aforementioned.
▷ *nm & nf* person mentioned before, aforementioned person.
antelación *nf* precedence: **con cinco días de antelación** *five days beforehand.* ■ **con antelación** in advance.
antemano ■ **de antemano** beforehand, in advance
antena *nf* 1 RAD TV aerial, antenna. 2 ANAT antenna feeler. ■ **estar en antena** to be on the air. ● **antena parabólica** satellite dish.
anteojo *nm* telescope.
▷ *nm pl* **anteojos** 1 *(binóculos)* binoculars, field glasses 2 *(gafas)* glasses, spectacles.
antepasado,-a *adj* previous, prior.
▷ *nm* **antepasado** ancestor.
▷ *nm pl* **antepasados** forefathers, forbears.
antepenúltimo,-a *adj* antepenultimate: **el episodio antepenúltimo** *the second from last episode.*
anteponer [78] *vt* 1 *(poner delante)* to place in fron (**a**, of), put in front (**a**, of); *(poner antes)* to put before. 2 *(preferir)* to prefer (**a**, to).
▲ *pp* **antepuesto,-a.**
antera *nf* anther.
anterior *adj* 1 *(tiempo)* previous, preceding, before **el día anterior** *the day before.* 2 *(lugar)* front: **la part anterior** *the front part.*
▷ *nm o nf* the previous one.
anterioridad *nf* priority. ■ **con anterioridad** previously. ‖ **con anterioridad a** prior to, before.
anteriormente *adv* previously, before.
antes *adv* 1 *(tiempo)* before, earlier: **llámame antes d salir** *ring me before you leave;* **llegué antes que él** *I a*

rived before him; **antes del partido** *before the match;* **deberías estar allí antes de las nueve** *you should be there before nine.* **2** *(en el pasado)* before, in the past. **3** *(lugar)* in front, before.
▷ *conj* on the contrary, quite the opposite, rather: **no la aborrece, antes la ama** *he doesn't hate her, on the contrary he loves her.*
▷ *adj* before. ■ **antes de nada** first of all. ‖ **lo antes posible** as soon as possible.
antesala *nf* anteroom, antechamber. ■ **hacer antesala** to wait. ‖ **en la antesala de** *fig* on the verge of.
antiadherente *adj* nonstick.
antiaéreo,-a *adj* anti-aircraft.
antibalas *adj* bullet-proof.
antibiótico,-a *adj* antibiotic.
▷ *nm* **antibiótico** antibiotic.
anticaspa *adj* anti-dandruff: **champú anticaspa** *dandruff shampoo.*
anticatarral *adj* anticatarrhal.
anticiclón *nm* anticyclone, high pressure area.
anticiclónico,-a *adj* anticyclonic.
anticipación *nf* anticipation, advance. ■ **con anticipación** in advance.
anticipado,-a *pp* → **anticipar.**
▷ *adj* brought forward; *(temprano)* early: **gracias anticipadas** *thanks in advance;* **pago anticipado** *payment in advance.* ■ **por anticipado** in advance.
anticipar *vt* **1** to anticipate, advance, bring forward. **2** *(dinero)* to advance.
▷ *vpr* **anticiparse 1** *(llegar antes)* to come early. **2** *(adelantarse)* to beat to it: **él se me anticipó** *he beat me to it.*
anticipo *nm* **1** *(gen)* foretaste, preview. **2** *(pago)* advance, advance payment.
anticlerical *adj* anticlerical.
▷ *nm o nf* anticlerical.
anticlinal *nm* anticline.
anticonceptivo,-a *adj* contraceptive.
▷ *nm* **anticonceptivo** contraceptive.
anticongelante *adj* antifreeze.
▷ *nm* **anticongelante** antifreeze.
anticonstitucional *adj* unconstitutional.
anticorrosivo,-a *adj* anticorrosive.
▷ *nm* **anticorrosivo** anticorrosive.
anticuado,-a *adj* antiquated, old-fashioned, obsolete, out-of-date.
anticuario *nm (conocedor)* antiquary, antiquarian; *(comerciante)* antique dealer.
anticuerpo *nm* antibody.
antidemocrático,-a *adj (no democrático)* undemocratic; *(que ataca la democracia)* antidemocratic.
antidepresivo,-a *adj* antidepressant.
▷ *nm* **antidepresivo** antidepressant.
antideslizante *adj (neumático)* nonskid; *(suelo)* nonslip.
▷ *nm* nonskid device.
antidisturbios *adj* riot. ● **material antidisturbios** riot gear. ‖ **policía antidisturbios** riot police.
antidoping *adj* anti-doping, anti-drug.
antídoto *nm* antidote.
antiestético,-a *adj* ugly, unsightly, unattractive.
antifascismo *nm* anti-fascism.
antifaz *nm* mask.
▲ *pl* **antifaces.**
antígeno,-a *adj* antigenic.
▷ *nm* **antígeno** antigen.
antigripal *adj* flu.
▷ *nm* flu remedy.
antigualla *nf pey* antique, relic.
antiguamente *adv* in the old days, in the past.
antigüedad *nf* **1** *(período)* antiquity. **2** *(en empleo)* seniority. **3** *(objeto)* antique. ■ **en la antigüedad** in olden days, in former times. ● **tienda de antigüedades** antique shop.
antiguo,-a *adj* **1** *(gen)* ancient, old; *(coche)* vintage, old. **2** *(en empleo)* senior. **3** *(pasado)* old-fashioned. **4** *(anterior)* former: **el antiguo primer ministro** *the former Prime Minister.*
▷ *nm pl* **los antiguos** the ancients.
antihéroe *nm* antihero
antihigiénico,-a *adj* unhygienic, unhealthy.
antihistamínico,-a *adj* antihistamine.
▷ *nm* **antihistamínico** antihistamine.
antiimperialismo *nm* anti-imperialism.
antiinflacionista *adj* anti-inflationary.
antiinflamatorio,-a *adj* anti-inflammatory.
▷ *nm* **antiinflamatorio** anti-inflammatory.
antílope *nm* antelope.
antimilitarismo *nm* antimilitarism.
antimonio *nm* antimony.
antinatural *adj* unnatural, contrary to nature.
antiniebla *adj inv* anti-fog. ● **faros antiniebla** foglamps. ‖ **luces antiniebla** foglamps.
antinuclear *adj* antinuclear.
antioxidante *adj (para alimentos)* antioxidant; *(para metales)* antirust.
▷ *nm (para alimentos)* antioxidant; *(para metales)* antirust substance.
antipatía *nf* antipathy, dislike, aversion. ■ **coger antipatía a ALGN** to take a dislike to sb. ‖ **tener antipatía a ALGN** to dislike sb.
antipático,-a *adj* unfriendly, unpleasant, unkind: **Eva me cae antipática** *I don't like Eva.*
▷ *nm & nf* unpleasant person.
antípoda *adj* antipodean, antipodal.
▷ *nm o nf (persona)* antipodean.
▷ *nm & nf* [Also used in plural with the same meaning.] *(punto)* antipode, antipodes *pl.*
antipulgas ● **collar antipulgas** flea collar.
antiquísimo,-a *adj* very old, ancient.
antirrábico,-a *adj* anti-rabies, anti-rabic.
antirreglamentario,-a *adj* DEP against the rules.
antirreumático,-a *adj* anti-rheumatoid.
▷ *nm* **antirreumático** anti-rheumatoid drug.
antirrobo *adj inv* anti-theft. ● **alarma antirrobo 1** *(para casa)* burglar alarm. **2** *(para coche)* anti-theft device, car alarm.
antisemitismo *nm* anti-Semitism.
antiséptico,-a *adj* antiseptic.
▷ *nm* **antiséptico** antiseptic.
antiterrorista *adj* antiterrorist.
antítesis *nf inv* antithesis.
antitetánico,-a *adj* anti-tetanus.
antitético,-a *adj* antithetic, antithetical.
antitranspirante *adj* antiperspirant.
▷ *nm* antiperspirant.

antituberculoso,-a *adj* antitubercular.
antivirus *nm* 1 *(fármaco)* antivirus drug. 2 INFORMÁ antivirus.
antojarse *vpr* 1 *(encapricharse)* to feel like, fancy, take a fancy to: **se le antojó un patinete** *she fancied a scooter;* **cuando se le antoje** *when he feels like it, when it appeals to him.* 2 *(suponer)* to think, imagine, suppose, seem: **se me antoja que no vendrá** *I have the feeling that she won't come.* ■ **hacer lo que se le antoja** to do what one fancies.
antojo *nm* 1 *(capricho)* whim, fancy; *(de embarazada)* craving. 2 *(en la piel)* birthmark. ■ **a su** *(mi, tu, etc)* **antojo** arbitrarily.
antología *nf* anthology. ■ **de antología** *fig* remarkable, outstanding.
antónimo,-a *adj* antonymous.
▷ *nm* **antónimo** antonym.
antonomasia *nf* antonomasia. ■ **por antonomasia** par excellence.
antorcha *nf* 1 torch. 2 *fig* guiding light.
antracita *nf* anthracite.
ántrax *nm inv* anthrax.
antro *nm* 1 *(caverna)* cavern. 2 *(tugurio)* dump, hole, dive. ● **antro de perdición** den of vice.
antropofagia *nf* cannibalism.
antropoide *adj* anthropoid, anthropoidal.
▷ *nm o nf* anthropoid.
antropología *nf* anthropology.
anual *adj* annual, yearly: **gastos anuales** *yearly expenses.*
anualidad *nf* annual payment, annuity.
anuario *nm* yearbook.
anudar *vt* 1 *(atar)* to knot, tie, fasten. 2 *fig* to join, tie together.
▷ *vpr* **anudarse** to tie, knot. ■ **anudarse la voz/lengua** to become tongue-tied.
anulación *nf* 1 *(gen)* annulment, cancellation; *(de ley)* repeal; *(de sentencia)* quashing, overturning. 2 DEP *(de gol)* disallowing. ● **anulación de matrimonio** annulment of marriage.
anular[1] *adj* ring-shaped.
▷ *nm* ring finger.
anular[2] *vt* 1 *(matrimonio)* to annul; *(una ley)* to repeal; *(una sentencia)* to quash. 2 *(un pedido, viaje)* to cancel; *(un contrato)* to invalidate, cancel. 3 DEP *(un gol)* to disallow. 4 *fig (desautorizar)* to deprive of authority.
▷ *vpr* **anularse** to lose one's authority.
anunciación *nf* REL Annunciation.
anunciante *adj* → **anunciador,-ra.**
anunciar [12] *vt* 1 *(avisar)* to announce, make public. 2 *(hacer publicidad)* to advertise.
▷ *vpr* **anunciarse** to put an advert (**en**, in).
anuncio *nm* 1 *(aviso)* announcement; *(signo)* sign. 2 *(publicidad)* advertisement, advert, ad: **pusimos un anuncio en el diario** *we put an ad in the paper.* 3 *(valla publicitaria)* hoarding, US billboard. 4 *(cartel)* poster, notice. ● classified adverts, small ads. ‖ **anuncios por palabras** classified adverts, small ads.
anverso *nm* 1 *(de moneda)* obverse. 2 *(de página)* recto.
anzuelo *nm* 1 fish-hook. 2 *fig* lure, bait. ■ **echar el anzuelo,-a** to try to hook. ‖ **tragar/morder/picar el anzuelo** to swallow the bait.
añadido,-a *pp* → **añadir.**
▷ *adj* added.
▷ *nm* **añadido** 1 *(postizo)* switch, hairpiece. 2 *(añadidura)* addition, addendum.
añadidura *nf* addition, addendum. ■ **por añadidura** besides, in addition.
añadir *vt* to add (**a**, to): **añádele un poco de sal** *add a bit of salt (to it).*
añejo,-a *adj* 1 *(vino, queso)* mature; *(jamón)* cured. 2 *(viejo)* old.
añicos *nm pl* bits, pieces. ■ **hacer añicos** to smash to pieces. ‖ **hacerse añicos** to shatter, smash to bits.
añil *adj* indigo, blue.
▷ *nm* 1 *(arbusto)* indigo plant. 2 *(color)* indigo. 3 *(sustancia)* blue.
año *nm* year: **el año pasado** *last year;* **el año que viene** *next year;* **una vez al año** *once a year;* **los años sesenta** *the sixties;* **en estos últimos años** *in recent years.* ● **año escolar** school year. ‖ **año fiscal** tax year. ‖ **año luz** light year.
▷ *nm pl* years, age *sing*: **¿cuántos años tienes?** *how old are you?;* **tengo 20 años** *I'm 20 years old.* ■ **hace años** a long time ago, years ago. ‖ **¡por muchos años!** 1 *(cumpleaños)* many happy returns! 2 *(brindis)* here's to your health!
añoranza *nf* longing (**de**, for), yearning (**de**, for), nostalgia (**de**, for): **sentir añoranza de su país** *to be homesick.*
añorar *vt* 1 *(gen)* to long for, miss, yearn for. 2 *(país)* to be homesick for, miss. 3 *(persona fallecida)* to mourn.
▷ *vi* to pine.
aorta *nf* aorta.
aovar *vi* to lay eggs.
apabullar *vt* 1 *(dejar confuso)* to bewilder, confuse. 2 *(abrumar)* to overwhelm.
apacentar [27] *vt* 1 *(pacer)* to graze, put out to pasture. 2 *(alimentar)* to feed. 3 *fig (instruir)* to teach. 4 *fig (alimentar pasiones, etc)* to gratify.
▷ *vpr* **apacentarse** to pasture, graze.
apachurrar *vt* to squash, flatten.
apacible *adj (persona)* gentle, calm, placid; *(vida)* quiet, peaceful; *(clima, tiempo)* mild; *(mar)* calm.
apaciguar [22] *vt* to pacify, appease, placate, calm down.
▷ *vpr* **apaciguarse** *(persona)* to calm down; *(tormenta)* to abate; *(mar)* to become calm.
apadrinar *vt* 1 *(en bautizo)* to act as godfather to. 2 *(en boda)* to be the best man for. 3 *(en duelo)* to act as second to. 4 *(artista)* to sponsor.
apagado,-a *pp* → **apagar.**
▷ *adj* 1 *(luz, etc)* out, off. 2 *(persona)* spiritless, lifeless. 3 *(voz)* sad; *(mirada)* expressionless, lifeless. 4 *(color)* dull. 5 *(volcán)* extinct.
apagar [7] *vt* 1 *(fuego)* to extinguish, put out. 2 *(luz)* to turn out, turn off, put out. 3 *(televisión, etc)* to switch off, turn off: **apaga la radio** *turn the radio off.* 4 *(color)* to soften. 5 *fig (dolor)* to soothe; *(pena)* to heal. 6 *fig (sed)* to quench.
▷ *vpr* **apagarse** 1 *(luz)* to go out; *(televisión)* to go off. 2 *(emoción)* to fade, wane. 3 *fig (morirse)* to pass away. ■ **apaga y vámonos** *fig* let's call it a day.

apagón *nm* power cut, blackout.
apaisado,-a *adj* **1** oblong. **2** INFORMÁ landscape.
apalabrar *vt* **1** *(concertar)* to make a verbal agreement on: **apalabrar una venta** *to make a verbal agreement on a sale.* **2** *(contratar)* to engage verbally.
apalancar [1] *vt (levantar)* to lever up; *(abrir)* to lever open: **apalancó la puerta** *he levered the door open.*
▷ *vpr* **apalancarse 1** *argot* to settle OS, settle down: **se apalancó ante la tele** *she settled down in front of the TV.* **2** *argot* to get stuck in a rut.
apalear[1] *vt (pegar)* to beat, cane, thrash.
apalear[2] *vt (grano)* to winnow.
apaleo *nm* **1** *(acción)* winnowing. **2** *(época)* winnowing time.
apantanar *vt* to flood.
apañado,-a *pp* → **apañar.**
▷ *adj* **1** *(ordenado)* tidy; *(limpio)* clean; *(arreglado)* well-dressed, smart. **2** *(hábil)* skilful (US skilfull), clever; *(mañoso)* handy. **3** *(apropiado)* suitable. ■ **estar apañado,-a / ir apañado,-a** *fam* to be in for a shock, have had it: **estamos apañados si no nos llega el dinero** *we've had it if the money doesn't arrive.*
apañar *vt* **1** *(ordenar)* to tidy; *(limpiar)* to clean. **2** *(recoger)* to collect. **3** *fam (robar)* to steal, snatch, nick, lift, swipe. **4** *(ataviar)* to smarten up. **5** *(remendar)* to patch, mend. **6** *(componer)* to fix, arrange.
▷ *vpr* **apañarse 1** to manage, get by, make do: **ya se apañará sola** *she'll manage on her own.* **2** to cohabit. ■ **apañárselas** to manage, get by.
apaño *nm* **1** *(remiendo, compostura)* repair, mend, patch. **2** *(acuerdo)* agreement, deal. **3** *(habilidad)* skill. **4** *fam (lío amoroso)* (love) affair, fling; *(amante)* lover. ■ **tener un apaño** *fam* to have a bit on the side.
aparador *nm* **1** *(escaparate)* shop window. **2** *(mueble)* sideboard, cupboard, buffet.
aparato *nm* **1** *(mecanismo)* (piece of) apparatus, set; *(eléctrico)* appliance: **aparatos eléctricos** *equipment.* **2** *(dispositivo)* device; *(instrumento)* instrument. **3** *(teléfono)* telephone: **está al aparato** *he's on the phone.* **4** *(avión)* plane. **5** *(exageración)* exaggeration. **6** *(ostentación)* pomp, display, show: **con mucho aparato** *very pompously.* **7** *(tormenta)* flashes of lightning *pl*: **una tormenta con gran aparato (eléctrico)** *a storm with tremendous flashes of lightning.* ● **aparato auditivo** hearing aid. ‖ **aparato de radio** radio set. ‖ **aparato digestivo** ANAT digestive system. ‖ **aparato ortopédico** orthopedic aid.
aparatoso,-a *adj* **1** *(ostentoso)* pompous, showy, ostentatious. **2** *(exagerado)* exaggerated. **3** *(caída, accidente)* spectacular.
aparcamiento *nm* **1** *(acción)* parking. **2** *(en la calle)* place to park, parking place. **3** *(parking)* car park, US parking lot.
aparcar [1] *vt* **1** to park. **2** *fig (tema)* to put on one side.
▷ *vi* to park. ■ **«Prohibido aparcar»** «No parking».
aparcero,-a *nm & nf* sharecropper.
aparear *vt* **1** *(cosas)* to pair off, match up. **2** *(animales)* to mate.
▷ *vpr* **aparearse** *(uso recíproco)* to mate.
aparecer [43] *vi* **1** to appear: **no aparece en la lista de invitados** *she's not on the guest list.* **2** *(dejarse ver)* to show up, turn up: **espero que no aparezca por mi casa** *I hope he doesn't show his face near my house.* **3** *(en el mercado)* to come out (**en**, onto): **ya ha aparecido su nuevo libro** *her new book has just been published.*
▷ *vpr* **aparecerse** to appear.
aparejado,-a *pp* → **aparejar.**
▷ *adj* suitable, fit. ■ **ir aparejado,-a con** to go along with. ‖ **llevar/traer aparejado,-a** to entail.
aparejador,-ra *nm & nf (de obras)* clerk of works; *(perito)* quantity surveyor.
aparentar *vt* **1** *(simular)* to pretend, affect: **aparenta indiferencia** *she pretends not to care, she affects indifference.* **2** *(tener aspecto de)* to look: **no aparenta la edad que tiene** *he doesn't look his age.*
▷ *vi* to show off.
aparente *adj* **1** apparent. **2** *(conveniente)* suitable. **3** *(lucido)* showy, smart.
aparición *nf* **1** appearance. **2** *(visión)* apparition.
apariencia *nf* appearance, aspect. ■ **en apariencia** apparently, by all appearances. ‖ **guardar las apariencias** *fig* to keep up appearances. ‖ **tener apariencia de** to look like.
apartado,-a *pp* → **apartar.**
▷ *adj* **1** *(alejado)* remote, distant; *(aislado)* isolated, cut off. **2** *(retirado)* retired.
▷ *nm* **apartado 1** post office box. **2** *(párrafo)* section. ■ **mantenerse apartado,-a de** ALGO/ALGN to keep away from STH/SB
apartamento *nm* small flat, apartment.
apartar *vt* **1** *(alejar)* to move away: **aparta la planta del sol** *move the plant out of the sun.* **2** *(separar)* to separate; *(preservar de)* to protect from, keep away from: **lo que haga falta para apartar al menor del peligro** *whatever is necessary to protect the child from danger.* **3** *(reservar)* to put aside, set aside. **4** *(de un cargo)* to remove.
▷ *vpr* **apartarse 1** *(alejarse)* to move away. **2** *(separarse)* to withdraw, move away: **se apartó del tema** *she veered off the subject.* ■ **apartar los ojos de** to take one's eyes off.
aparte *adv* apart, aside, separately.
▷ *adj (distinto)* special: **eso es caso aparte** *that's completely different.*
▷ *nm* **1** TEAT aside. **2** LING paragraph: **punto y aparte** *full stop (US period), new paragraph.* ■ **aparte de 1** *(excepto)* apart from. **2** *(además de)* as well as, besides.
apasionado,-a *pp* → **apasionar.**
▷ *adj* passionate, enthusiastic, fervent.
▷ *nm & nf* lover, enthusiast: **es un apasionado del boxeo** *he's a boxing fanatic.* ■ **apasionado,-a por** very fond of.
apasionante *adj* exciting, fascinating.
apasionar *vt* to excite, fascinate, thrill.
▷ *vpr* **apasionarse 1** to get excited, become enthusiastic (**por/de**, about). **2** *(enamorarse)* to fall head over heels in love (**por/de**, with).
apatía *nf* apathy.
apático,-a *adj* apathetic.
▷ *nm & nf* apathetic person.
apátrida *adj* stateless.
▷ *nm o nf* stateless person.

apeadero *nm* halt.
apear *vt* **1** *(desmontar)* to take down. **2** *(terreno)* to survey. **3** ARQUIT to prop up. **4** *fam* to dissuade.
▷ *vpr* **apearse** *(del tren, autobús, etc.)* to get off; *(del coche)* to get out of; *(del caballo)* to dismount.
apechugar [7] *vi* to grin and bear it, lump it: **no pienso apechugar con todo el trabajo** *I don't intend to get lumbered with all the work.*
apedrear *vt* **1** *(tirar piedras)* to throw stones at. **2** *(matar a pedradas)* to stone (to death).
apegarse [7] *vpr* to become very fond (**a**, of), get attached (**a**, to).
apego *nm* attachment, affection, liking, fondness. ■ **tomar apego a** to become attached to.
apelación *nf* **1** JUR appeal. **2** *(llamamiento)* appeal, call. **3** *fig* help.
apelar *vi* **1** JUR to appeal: **apelar una sentencia** *to appeal against a sentence.* **2** *fig (recurrir)* to resort to: **tuvo que apelar a sus padres** *he had to go to his parents.*
apelativo,-a *adj* appellative.
▷ *nm* **apelativo** appellative, name.
apellidar *vt* to call.
▷ *vpr* **apellidarse** to be called, have as a surname.
apellido *nm* family name, surname, (US last name).
apelmazado,-a *pp* ⟶ **apelmazar.**
▷ *adj (comida)* heavy, stodgy; *(colchón)* lumpy; *(libro, estilo)* dense, stodgy; *(lana)* matted.
apelmazar [4] *vt* to compress, squeeze together.
▷ *vpr* **apelmazarse** **1** *(comida)* to go stodgy; *(colchón)* to go lumpy; *(lana)* to get matted. **2** *(gente)* to crowd, throng.
apelotonar *vt* **1** *(amontonar)* to pile up, put into a pile; *(gente)* to cluster. **2** *(hacer una pelota)* to roll into a ball.
▷ *vpr* **apelotonarse** *(gente)* to crowd together.
apenado,-a *pp* ⟶ **apenar.**
▷ *adj* troubled.
apenar *vt* to make sad, sadden, grieve.
▷ *vpr* **apenarse** to be grieved, be upset.
apenas *adv* **1** *(casi no)* scarcely, hardly: **apenas lo conozco** *I hardly know him.* **2** *(con dificultad)* only just. **3** *(tan pronto como)* as soon as, no sooner: **apenas entramos, sonó el teléfono** *no sooner had we had come in than the phone rang.* ■ **apenas si** hardly: **apenas si se oía** *it could hardly be heard.*
apéndice *nm* **1** *(órgano interno)* appendix. **2** *(de libro)* appendix. **3** *(parte unida)* appendage.
apendicitis *nf inv* appendicitis.
apercibir *vt* **1** *(preparar)* to prepare, get ready. **2** *(avisar)* to warn.
▷ *vpr* **apercibirse** *(darse cuenta)* to notice (**de**, -).
aperitivo,-a *adj* appetizing.
▷ *nm* **aperitivo** **1** *(bebida)* apéritif. **2** *(comida)* appetizer, snack.
apero *nm* implement.
▷ *nm pl* **aperos** *(aperos)* equipment *sing*, tools. ● **aperos de labranza** farming implements.
apertura *nf* **1** *(comienzo)* opening, beginning. **2** POL liberalization. ● **sesión de apertura** opening session.
aperturista *adj* progressive.
▷ *nm o nf supporter of progressive political ideas.*

apesadumbrar *vt* to sadden, distress.
apestar *vi (oler mal)* to stink.
▷ *vt (causar la peste)* to infect with the plague.
apetecer [43] *vi (agradar)* to feel like, fancy: **¿te apetece ir al teatro?** *do you fancy going to the theatre?*
▷ *vt fig (desear)* to long for, yearn for.
apetecible *adj* **1** *(empleo)* desirable; *(idea)* appealing. **2** *(comida)* tasty, appetizing.
apetito *nm* appetite. ■ **abrir el apetito** to whet one's appetite. ■ **tener apetito** to be hungry.
apetitoso,-a *adj* **1** *(aspecto de comida)* appetizing; *(comida)* tasty, delicious. **2** *(oferta)* tempting.
apiadar *vt* to inspire pity in, move to pity.
▷ *vpr* **apiadarse** to take pity (**de**, on).
ápice *nm* **1** *(punta)* apex. **2** *fig* tiny bit, speck, iota. ■ **ni un ápice** not one bit.
apicultura *nf* beekeeping, apiculture.
apilamiento *nm* piling up, heaping up.
apilar *vt* to pile up, heap up.
▷ *vpr* **apilarse** to pile up, heap up.
apiñar *vt (apretar)* to pack, press together, jam.
▷ *vpr* **apiñarse** to crowd (**en**, into).
apio *nm* celery.
apisonadora *nf* steamroller, roadroller.
aplacar [1] *vt* to placate, calm, soothe.
▷ *vpr* **aplacarse** *(persona)* to calm down; *(viento)* to abate, die down.
aplanar *vt* **1** *(igualar)* to smooth, level, make even. **2** *fig (deprimir)* to depress, dishearten.
▷ *vpr* **aplanarse** *(desanimarse)* to become depressed become disheartened.
aplastante *adj* crushing, overwhelming. ● **triunfo/victoria aplastante** *(electoral)* landslide victory.
aplastar *vt* **1** *(gen)* to flatten, squash, crush. **2** *fig (destruir)* to crush, destroy.
aplatanarse *vpr fam* to become apathetic.
aplaudir *vt* **1** to clap, applaud. **2** *fig (aprobar)* to applaud, approve.
aplauso *nm* **1** applause. **2** *fig (aprobación)* applause, praise, acclaim.
aplazamiento *nm (gen)* adjournment, postponement; *(de pago)* deferment.
aplazar [4] *vt (gen)* to adjourn, postpone, put off; *(un pago)* to defer.
aplicación *nf* **1** *(gen)* application. **2** *(adorno)* appliqué.
aplicado,-a *pp* ⟶ **aplicar.**
▷ *adj (estudioso)* studious, diligent, hard-working: **es un alumno aplicado** *he's a hard-working pupil* (US *student).* ● **ciencias aplicadas** applied sciences.
aplicar [1] *vt* **1** *(gen)* to apply: **aplicó una pomada sobre la herida** *she put some ointment on the wound.* **2** *(destinar)* to assign.
▷ *vpr* **aplicarse** *(esforzarse)* to apply OS, work hard.
aplique *nm* **1** *(adorno)* appliqué. **2** *(lámpara)* wall light, wall lamp.
aplomo *nm* composure, aplomb, self-possession.
apocado,-a *pp* ⟶ **apocar.**
▷ *adj* **1** *(intimidado)* intimidated, frightened. **2** *(tímido)* shy, timid.
apocalipsis *nm inv* apocalypse.
apocar [1] *vt* **1** *(intimidar)* to intimidate, frighten. **2** *(humillar)* to humiliate, belittle.

▷ *vpr* **apocarse** *(intimidarse)* to be intimidated.
apócope *nm* apocope, apocopation.
apodar *vt* to call, nickname.
▷ *vpr* **apodarse** to be nicknamed.
apoderado,-a *pp* ⟶ **apoderar.**
▷ *adj* 1 authorized. 2 JUR with power of attorney (**para**, to).
▷ *nm & nf* 1 agent, representative. 2 *(de torero, deportista)* manager.
apoderar *vt* 1 to authorize, empower. 2 JUR to grant power of attorney.
▷ *vpr* **apoderarse** to take possession (**de**, of), seize (**de**, -): **el miedo se apoderó de él** *he was seized by fear.*
apodo *nm* nickname.
apogeo *nm* 1 *(de órbita)* apogee. 2 *fig (punto culminante)* summit, height, climax, peak. ■ **estar en pleno apogeo** to be at its height.
apolillado,-a *pp* ⟶ **apolillar.**
▷ *adj* moth-eaten.
apolillar *vt* to eat away at, make holes in.
▷ *vpr* **apolillarse** to become moth-eaten.
apolítico,-a *adj* apolitical.
apología *nf* apology, defence (US defense).
apoltronarse *vpr* 1 *(vegetar)* to grow lazy, get lazy, become idle. 2 *(sentarse)* to sit back, lounge about.
apoplejía *nf* apoplexy, stroke.
apoquinar *vt fam* to cough up, fork out.
aporrear *vt (persona)* to beat, hit, thrash; *(puerta)* to bang on; *(piano)* to bang (away) on.
aportación *nf* contribution.
aportar *vt* 1 *(contribuir)* to contribute. 2 *(proporcionar)* to give, provide.
aporte *nm* contribution.
aposentar *vt (alojar)* to lodge.
▷ *vpr* **aposentarse** to lodge, stay.
aposento *nm* 1 *(cuarto)* room. 2 *(hospedaje)* lodgings *pl.*
apósito *nm* dressing.
aposta *adv* on purpose, deliberately, intentionally.
apostar[1] [31] *vt* to bet (**por**, on): **apostó todo su dinero por Red Rum** *he bet all his money on Red Rum.*
▷ *vi* to bet (**por**, on): **apostó por él** *she bet on him.*
▷ *vpr* **apostarse** to bet.
apostar[2] *vt (situar)* to post, station.
apostilla *nf* 1 note, comment. 2 JUR apostille.
apóstol *nm* 1 apostle. 2 *fig (defensor)* apostle, champion.
apostrofar *vt* 1 to apostrophize. 2 *(reñir)* to reprimand, tell off.
apóstrofe *nm & nf* 1 GRAM apostrophe. 2 *(reprimenda)* reprimand, rebuke.
apotema *nf* apothem.
apoteósico,-a *adj* enormous, tremendous.
apoyar *vt* 1 to lean, rest: **apoyar la cabeza** *to rest one's head.* 2 *(fundar)* to base, found: **apoya su teoría en pruebas concluyentes** *he bases his theory on hard evidence.* 3 *fig (defender algo)* to support; *(defender a alguien)* to back, support: **sus padres le apoyan en todo** *her parents support everything she does.*
▷ *vpr* **apoyarse** 1 *(descansar)* to lean (**en**, on), rest (**en**, on), stand (**en**, on): **apóyate en mí** *lean on me.* 2 *(dar el brazo)* to hold on (**en**, to). 3 *fig (basarse)* to be based (**en**, on).
apoyo *nm* 1 support. 2 *fig* support, backing, help.

apreciable *adj* 1 *(perceptible)* appreciable, noticeable. 2 *(estimable)* valuable, precious.
apreciación *nf* 1 *(valorización)* appreciation, appraisal, evaluation. 2 *(juicio)* appraisal, assessment; *(percepción)* perception. 3 *(opinión)* view, opinion. 4 *(en valor)* appreciation.
apreciar [12] *vt* 1 *(valorar)* to appraise (**en**, at). 2 *(sentir aprecio)* to regard highly, hold in high esteem: **apreciar a** ALGN *to be fond of sb.* 3 *(reconocer valor)* to appreciate. 4 *(percibir)* to notice, see, perceive.
▷ *vpr* **apreciarse** *(notarse)* to be noticed, be noticeable.
aprecio *nm* esteem, regard. ■ **sentir aprecio por** ALGN to be fond of sb.
aprehender *vt* 1 *(apresar)* to apprehend. 2 *(confiscar)* to seize. 3 *(percibir)* to understand.
aprehensión *nf* 1 *(captura)* apprehension, arrest. 2 *(de contrabando)* seizure. 3 *(percepción)* comprehension, understanding.
apremiante *adj* urgent, pressing.
aprender *vt* 1 to learn. 2 *(memorizar)* to learn by heart.
▷ *vpr* **aprenderse** to learn, learn by heart.
aprendiz,-za *nm & nf* apprentice, trainee: **aprendiza de peluquera** *trainee hairdresser.*
aprendizaje *nm* 1 *(situación)* apprenticeship. 2 *(tiempo)* training period. 3 *(en pedagogía)* learning.
aprensión *nf (miedo)* apprehension; *(asco)* squeamishness. ■ **sentir aprensión** to feel apprehensive.
aprensivo,-a *adj* apprehensive.
▷ *nm & nf* apprehensive.
apresar *vt* 1 *(tomar por fuerza)* to seize, capture. 2 *(asir)* to clutch.
aprestar *vt* 1 *(preparar)* to get ready, prepare. 2 *(tejidos)* to size.
apresto *nm* 1 *(preparación)* preparation. 2 *(tejidos)* sizing; *(material)* size.
apresurado,-a *pp* ⟶ **apresurar.**
▷ *adj* 1 *(persona)* in a hurry. 2 *(cosa)* hurried, rushed, quick.
apresurar *vt* to hurry up, speed up, accelerate.
▷ *vpr* **apresurarse** to hurry, hurry up.
apretado,-a *pp* ⟶ **apretar.**
▷ *adj* 1 *(objeto)* tight. 2 *(en un espacio)* jammed; *(personas)* crowded, cramped. 3 *(ocupado)* busy. 4 *(difícil)* tight, difficult.
apretar [27] *vt* 1 *(estrechar)* to squeeze, hug. 2 *(tornillo)* to tighten; *(cordones, nudo)* to do up tight. 3 *(comprimir)* to compress, press together, pack tight. 4 *(activar)* to press, push. 5 *fig (acosar)* to keep on at; *(presionar)* to put pressure on, pressurize.
▷ *vi* 1 *fig (aumentar)* to increase, get worse: **el calor aprieta** *it's getting hotter and hotter.* 2 *(prendas)* to fit tight, be tight on. 3 *(esforzarse)* to work hard. ■ **apretar el paso** to quicken one's pace.
▷ *vpr* **apretarse** 1 *(apiñar)* to narrow, tighten. 2 *(agolparse)* to crowd together; *(acercarse)* to squeeze up.
apretón *nm* squeeze.
▷ *nm pl* **apretones** crush *sing.* ● **apretón de manos** handshake.
apretujar *vt* to squeeze, crush.
▷ *vpr* **apretujarse** to squeeze together, cram together.
apretujón *nm fam* squeeze, crush.

aprieto *nm* tight spot, difficulty, scrape, fix. ■ **poner a** ALGN **en un aprieto** to put sb in an awkward situation. ‖ **salir del aprieto** to get out of trouble.

aprisa *adv* quickly.

aprisionar *vt* **1** *(encarcelar)* to imprison, put in prison. **2** *(sujetar)* to hold tight.

aprobación *nf (gen)* approval; *(ley)* passing.

aprobado,-a *pp* → **aprobar.**
▷ *adj* approved, passed.
▷ *nm* **aprobado** EDUC pass (mark). ■ **sacar/tener un aprobado** to get a pass.

aprobar [31] *vt* **1** *(gen)* to approve; *(ley)* to pass. **2** *(estar de acuerdo)* to approve of. **3** EDUC *(examen, asignatura)* to pass.
▷ *vi* to pass.

apropiación *nf* appropriation. ● **apropiación indebida** JUR theft.

apropiado,-a *pp* → **apropiar.**
▷ *adj* suitable, fitting, appropriate.

apropiar [12] *vt (acomodar)* to make suitable, adapt.
▷ *vpr* **apropiarse** to appropriate (**de**, -), take possession (**de**, of).

aprovechable *adj* usable.

aprovechado,-a *pp* → **aprovechar.**
▷ *adj* **1** *(tiempo)* well used, well spent. **2** *(espacio)* well-planned. **3** *(diligente)* diligent, studious, hardworking. **4** *(que saca provecho de todo)* thrifty, economical, resourceful. **5** *pey (egoísta)* selfish; *(gorrón)* sponging, scrounging. ■ **mal aprovechado,-a** wasted.
▷ *nm & nf fam (gorrón)* sponger, scrounger; *(oportunista)* opportunist.

aprovechamiento *nm* **1** *(uso)* use, exploitation: **el aprovechamiento de los recursos naturales** *the exploitation of natural resources.* **2** *(provecho)* improvement, progress.

aprovechar *vt* **1** *(emplear útilmente)* to make good use of, make the most of. **2** *(sacar provecho)* to benefit from, take advantage of.
▷ *vi* **1** to be useful, make the most of it. **2** *(avanzar)* to improve, progress.
▷ *vpr* **aprovecharse** *(de alguien)* to take advantage (**de**, of); *(de algo)* to make the most (**de**, of). ■ **¡que aproveche!** enjoy your meal!

aprovisionamiento *nm* supply, supplying, provision.

aproximación *nf* **1** *(gen)* approximation. **2** *(acercamiento)* bringing together; *(de países)* rapprochement. **3** *(lotería)* consolation prize.

aproximadamente *adv* approximately, roughly, around, about.

aproximado,-a *pp* → **aproximar.**
▷ *adj* approximate, estimated. ● **cálculo aproximado** rough estimate.

aproximar *vt* to bring near, put near.
▷ *vpr* **aproximarse** to come near, come closer: **el verano se aproxima** *summer is getting nearer.*

aptitud *nf* **1** *(habilidad)* aptitude, ability: **demuestra aptitud para la música** *he has a gift for music.* **2** *(idoneidad)* suitability, aptness.

apto,-a *adj* **1** *(apropiado)* suitable, appropriate: **no es apto para este trabajo** *he's not suitable for this job.* **2** *(capaz)* capable, able. **3** *(físicamente)* fit. ■ **no apto,** CINE for adults only.

apuesta *nf* bet, wager.

apuesto,-a *adj (gen)* good-looking; *(hombre)* hanc some.

apuntador,-ra *nm & nf* TEAT prompter.

apuntalar *vt* to prop (up), shore up, underpin.

apuntar *vt* **1** *(señalar)* to point (**a**, at). **2** *(arma)* t aim. **3** *(anotar)* to note down, make a note of. **4** *(e tar encaminado)* to be aimed (**a**, at), be designed (to). **5** *(insinuar)* to suggest, indicate. **6** *(sujetar)* t stitch, pin lightly, tack lightly. **7** TEAT to promp **8** *fam (en un examen)* to whisper the answer to.
▷ *vi* **1** to begin to appear. **2** TEAT to prompt.
▷ *vpr* **apuntarse 1** *(inscribirse)* to enrol. **2** *fam (participa* to take part (**a**, in): **¿te apuntas?** *are you game?*

apunte *nm* **1** note. **2** *(dibujo)* sketch. **3** *(apuntado* prompter; *(voz del apuntador)* prompt; *(libreto d apuntador)* prompt book.
▷ *nm pl* **apuntes** *(de clase)* notes.

apuñalar *vt* to stab.

apurado,-a *pp* → **apurar.**
▷ *adj* **1** *(avergonzado)* embarrassed. **2** *(necesitado)* in neec **apurado,-a de dinero** *hard up for money.* **3** *(dificultos* awkward, difficult. **4** *(exacto)* accurate, precise.

apurar *vt* **1** *(terminar)* to finish up. **2** *(apremiar)* t urge, put pressure on. **3** *(purificar)* to purify. **4** *(ave riguar)* to investigate. **5** AM *(dar prisa)* to hurry, rush
▷ *vpr* **apurarse 1** *(preocuparse)* to get worried, be wo ried. **2** AM *(darse prisa)* to hurry, rush.

apuro *nm* **1** fix, tight spot; *(de dinero)* hardship. **2** *(ve güenza)* embarrassment. ■ **estar/encontrarse en u apuro** to be in a tight spot. ‖ **pasar apuros 1** *(económ cos)* to be hard up. **2** *(dificultades)* to be in a tigh spot.

aquejado,-a *pp* → **aquejar.**
▷ *adj* suffering (**de**, from).

aquejar *vt* to afflict, affect: **le aqueja una enfermeda desconocida** *he is suffering from an unknown illness.*

aquel,-ella *adj* **1** that. **2 aquellos,-as** those.

aquél,-élla *pron* **1** that one; *(el anterior)* the forme **aquél es el mío** *that one is mine.* **2 aquéllos,-as** those *(los anteriores)* the former. ■ **aquél que...** he who... ‖ **todo aquél que...** anyone who..., whoever...

aquella *adj* → **aquel.**

aquélla *pron* → **aquél.**

aquello *pron* that, it.

aquellos,-as *adj* → **aquel,-ella.**

aquéllos,-as *pron* → **aquél,-éllas.**

aquí *adv* **1** *(lugar)* here: **por aquí por favor** *this way please* **2** *(tiempo)* now: **de aquí en adelante** *from now on*

ara *nf (altar)* altar; *(piedra)* altar stone. ■ **en aras de** *fm* for the sake of: **en aras de la paz** *so as to keep th peace.*

árabe *adj (gen)* Arab; *(de Arabia)* Arabian.
▷ *nm & nf* Arab. ● **alfabeto árabe** Arabic alphabet.

Arabia *nf* Arabia. ● **Arabia Saudita** Saudi Arabia.

arácnido *nm* arachnid.

arado *nm* plough (US plow).

arameo,-a *adj* Aramaean, Aramean.
▷ *nm & nf (persona)* Aramaean, Aramean.
▷ *nm* **arameo** *(idioma)* Aramaic.

rancel *nm* tariff, customs duty.
rándano *nm* bilberry, blueberry.
randela *nf* washer.
raña *nf* 1 *(arácnido)* spider. 2 *(pez)* weever. 3 *(planta)* love-in-a-mist. 4 *(lámpara)* chandelier. ● **araña de mar** spider crab. ‖ **tela de araña** spider's web.
rañar *vt* 1 *(raspar)* to scratch. 2 *fig (recoger)* to scrape together.
▷ *vpr* **arañarse** to scratch.
rañazo *nm* scratch.
rar *vt* to plough (US plow).
rbitraje *nm* 1 *(desacuerdo)* arbitration. 2 DEP *(fútbol, boxeo)* refereeing; *(cricket, tenis)* umpiring.
rbitral *adj* of the referee: **decisión arbitral** *referee's ruling.* ● **sentencia arbitral** JUR judgement by arbitration.
rbitrar *vt* 1 to arbitrate. 2 DEP *(en fútbol, boxeo)* to referee; *(en cricket, tenis)* to umpire. 3 *(obtener)* to contrive; *(reunir)* to collect: **arbitrar fondos** *to raise funds.*
rbitrariedad *nf* 1 *(acción)* arbitrary act. 2 *(condición)* arbitrariness.
rbitrario,-a *adj* arbitrary.
rbitrio *nm* 1 *(voluntad)* will; *(juicio)* judgement. 2 *(decisión)* power, choice. 3 *(medio)* mean. ■ **dejar** ALGO **al arbitrio de** ALGN to leave STH to SB's discretion.
rbitro,-a *nm & nf* 1 arbiter, arbitrator. 2 DEP *(fútbol, boxeo)* referee; *(cricket, tenis)* umpire.
rbol *nm* 1 BOT tree. 2 TÉC axle, shaft. 3 MAR mast. 4 *(gráfico)* tree (diagram).
rboleda *nf* grove, wood, copse, spinney.
rboricultura *nf* arboriculture.
rbusto *nm* shrub, bush.
rca [Takes **el** in singular.] *nf* 1 chest. 2 *(caja de caudales)* strongbox, safe. ● **arca de Noé** Noah's ark. ‖ **arcas públicas** Treasury *sing.*
rcada *nf* 1 *(conjunto de arcos)* arcade. 2 *(de puente)* arch. 3 *(vómitos)* retching.
rcaico,-a *adj* archaic.
rce *nm* maple (tree). ● **arce menor** common maple, field maple. ‖ **arce real** Norway maple. ‖ **arce rojo** red maple.
rcén *nm* side of the road, verge; *(de autopista)* hard shoulder.
rchi- *pref* really, very, extremely: **un actor archiconocido** *a really famous actor.*
rchipiélago *nm* archipelago.
rchivador,-ra *nm & nf (en archivo)* archivist; *(en oficina)* filing clerk.
▷ *nm* **archivador** *(mueble)* filing cabinet; *(carpeta)* file.
rchivar *vt* 1 *(ordenar)* to file (away). 2 INFORMÁ to save. 3 *(arrinconar)* to shelve. 4 *fam (guardar)* to put (away).
rchivo *nm* 1 *(informe, ficha)* file. 2 *(documentos)* files *pl*, archives *pl*. 3 INFORMÁ file. 4 *(lugar)* archive. 5 *(archivador)* filing cabinet. 6 *fig (modelo)* model, example.
rcilla *nf* clay.
rco *nm* 1 ARQUIT arch. 2 *(en geometría)* arc. 3 *(arma)* bow. 4 *(de violín, etc)* bow. ● **arco de medio punto** semicircular arch. ‖ **arco iris** rainbow. ‖ **arco voltaico** electric arc.
rcón *nm* large chest.
arder *vi* 1 to burn; *(completamente)* to burn down; *(sin llama)* to smoulder: **el edificio está ardiendo** *the building is in flames.* 2 *(resplandecer)* to glow. 3 *fig* to burn.
▷ *vt* to burn.
ardid *nm* scheme, trick.
ardiente *adj* 1 *(encendido)* burning, hot, scalding. 2 *fig (intenso)* passionate, ardent; *(fervoroso)* eager.
ardilla *nf* squirrel.
ardor *nm* 1 burning sensation, burn; *(calor)* heat. 2 *fig (ansia)* ardour (US ardor), fervour (US fervor). ■ **con ardor** passionately. ● **ardor de estómago** heartburn.
arduo,-a *adj* arduous, very difficult, awkward.
área [Takes **el** in sing.] *nf* 1 *(zona)* area, zone. 2 *(medida)* are. 3 *(superficie)* area.
arena *nf* 1 sand: **playa de arena** *sandy beach.* 2 *(de circo romano)* arena. 3 *(plaza de toros)* bullring. ● **arenas movedizas** quicksand *sing.*
arenal *nm* sands *pl*, sandy area.
arenga *nf* harangue. ■ **echar/dirigir/pronunciar una arenga** to harangue.
arenilla *nf* fine sand.
▷ *nf pl* **arenillas** *(cálculos)* stones.
arenisca *nf* sandstone.
arenoso,-a *adj* sandy.
arenque *nm* herring.
argamasa *nf* mortar.
Argel *nm* Algiers.
Argelia *nm* Algeria.
argelino,-a *adj* Algerian.
▷ *nm & nf* Algerian.
Argentina *nf* Argentina, the Argentine.
argentino,-a *adj* Argentinian.
▷ *nm & nf* Argentinian.
argolla *nf* 1 *(aro)* (large) ring. 2 *fig* shackles *pl.*
argón *nm* argon.
argot *nm* 1 *(popular)* slang. 2 *(técnico)* jargon.
argucia *nf* sophism, subtlety.
argüir [63] *vt* 1 *(deducir)* to deduce, conclude. 2 *(probar)* to prove. 3 *(reprochar)* to reproach.
▷ *vi (discutir)* to argue (**contra**, with).
argumentación *nf* 1 *(proceso)* arguing, argument. 2 *(argumento)* argument.
argumentar *vt (deducir)* to deduce.
▷ *vi (discutir)* to argue (**contra**, with).
argumento *nm* 1 argument. 2 *(de novela, etc)* plot.
aria *nf* aria.
aridez *nf* 1 aridity. 2 *fig* dryness.
árido,-a *adj* 1 arid. 2 *fig* dry.
▷ *nm pl* **áridos** dry goods.
Aries *nm inv* Aries.
ariete *nm* 1 *(fútbol)* centre (US center) forward. 2 *(máquina)* battering ram.
ario,-a *adj* Aryan.
arisco,-a *adj* 1 *(persona - altiva)* unsociable, unfriendly; *(- áspera)* surly, gruff; *(- huidiza)* shy. 2 *(animal)* unfriendly.
arista *nf* 1 *(línea)* edge. 2 *(filamento del trigo)* beard. 3 ARQUIT *(de viga)* arris; *(de bóveda)* groin. 4 *(de montaña)* arête.
▷ *nf pl* **aristas** *fig (dificultades)* difficulties.

aristocracia *nf* aristocracy.
aristócrata *nm o nf* aristocrat.
aristotélico,-a *adj* Aristotelian.
aritmético,-a *adj* arithmetical, arithmetic.
arma [Takes **el** in singular.] *nf* weapon, arm.
▷ *nf pl* **armas 1** *(profesión)* army *sing*; *(fuerzas armadas)* armed forces; *(empresa militar)* military combat *sing*. **2** *(heráldica)* arms, armorial bearings. ■ **alzarse en armas** to rise up in arms. ‖ **ser de armas tomar** *fig* to be formidable. ● **arma blanca** knife. ‖ **arma de doble filo** *fig* double-edged sword. ‖ **arma de fuego** firearm.
armada *nf* navy, naval forces *pl*.
armadillo *nm* armadillo.
armado,-a *pp* → **armar.**
▷ *adj* **1** armed: **ir armado,-a** *to be armed*. **2** *(en mecánica)* mounted, assembled.
armador,-ra *nm & nf* shipowner.
armadura *nf* **1** *(traje)* suit of armour (US armor). **2** *(armazón)* frame. **3** ARQUIT framework.
armamentista *adj* arms.
▷ *nm o nf* **1** *(partidario)* rearmament supporter. **2** *(fabricante)* arms manufacturer. ● **la carrera armamentista** the arms race.
armamento *nm (acción)* armament, arming.
▷ *nm pl* **armamentos** *(armas)* armaments, arms.
armar *vt* **1** *(dar armas)* to arm. **2** *(cargar)* to load; *(bayoneta)* to fix. **3** *(montar - mueble)* to assemble; *(- tienda)* to pitch, put up; *(- trampa)* to set. **4** *(preparar)* to arrange, prepare; *(organizar)* to organize. **5** *fam (causar, originar)* to cause, kick up, create: **armó un lío tremendo** *he kicked up a tremendous fuss*. **6** *(embarcación)* to fit out. **7** *(tela)* to stiffen. **8** TÉC to reinforce. ■ **armarla** *fam* to cause trouble, kick up a fuss.
▷ *vpr* **armarse 1** *(proveerse)* to provide OS (**de**, with), arm OS (**de**, with): **se armó de pintura y pincel y se puso a pintar** *he provided himself with paint and paintbrush and began to paint*. **2** *(producirse)* to be, break out: **se armó un jaleo** *there was a right row*. ■ **armarse de paciencia** to summon up patience. ‖ **armarse de valor** to pluck up courage.
armario *nm (para ropa)* wardrobe, US closet; *(de cocina)* cupboard. ● **armario empotrado** built-in wardrobe, built-in cupboard.
armatoste *nm* **1** *(cosa)* monstrosity; *(máquina)* useless contraption. **2** *(persona)* useless great oaf.
armazón *nm & nf* **1** frame, framework; *(de madera)* timberwork. **2** ARQUIT shell; *(de escultura)* armature.
armería *nf* **1** *(tienda)* gunsmith's (shop). **2** *(oficio)* gunsmith's craft. **3** *(museo)* armoury (US armory), museum of arms.
armiño *nm* ermine.
armisticio *nm* armistice.
armonía *nf* harmony.
armónica *nf* harmomica, mouth organ.
armónico,-a *adj* harmonic.
▷ *nm* **armónico** MÚS harmonic.
armonioso,-a *adj* harmonious.
armonizar [4] *vt* to harmonize.
▷ *vi* to harmonize.
arnés *nm (armadura)* armour (US armor).
▷ *nm pl* **arneses** harness *sing*, trappings.
aro *nm* **1** hoop, ring. **2** *(juego)* hoop. **3** *(servilletero)* serviette ring, US napkin ring. **4** *(sortija)* ring. **5** *(pendiente)* earring, sleeper.
aroma *nm* aroma; *(del vino)* bouquet.
aromaterapia *nf* aromatherapy.
aromático,-a *adj* aromatic, fragrant.
arpa [Takes **el** in singular.] *nf* harp.
arpía *nf* **1** harpy. **2** *fam fig* dragon, old witch, harpy.
arpillera *nf* sackcloth, burlap, hessian, sacking.
arpón *nm* harpoon.
arquear *vt (doblar)* to arch, bend, curve.
▷ *vpr* **arquearse** to arch, bend, curve.
arqueología *nf* archaeology (US archeology).
arqueólogo,-a *nm & nf* archaeologist (US archeologist).
arquero,-a *nm & nf* archer.
arquetipo *nm* archetype.
arquitecto,-a *nm & nf* architect.
arquitectura *nf* architecture.
arquitrabe *nm* architrave.
arquivolta *nf* archivolt.
arrabal *nm* poor area, working-class area *(on the edge of town)*.
▷ *nm pl* **arrabales** outskirts.
arrabalero,-a *adj* **1** *(del arrabal) of or from a poor area*. **2** *pey (grosero)* vulgar, common, ill-bred.
▷ *nm & nf pey (grosero)* vulgar person, common person, ill-bred person.
arracimarse *vpr* to cluster together, bunch together.
arraigado,-a *pp* → **arraigar.**
▷ *adj* (deeply) rooted.
arraigar [7] *vi* to take root.
▷ *vt (fijar)* to establish, strengthen.
▷ *vpr* **arraigarse** *(establecerse)* to settle down.
arraigo *nm* **1** *(acción)* act of taking root. **2** *fig (raíces)* roots: **con mucho arraigo** *deeply-rooted*.
arrancar [1] *vt* **1** *(árbol)* to uproot; *(flor)* to pull up. **2** *(plumas, cejas)* to pluck; *(cabello, diente)* to pull out; *(con violencia - página)* to tear out. **3** *(arrebatar)* to snatch, grab: **me arrancó el bolso** *he snatched my bag*. **4** *(obtener - aplausos, sonrisa)* to get; *(- confesión, información)* to extract. **5** *fig (rescatar)* to rescue, save. **6** *(coche)* to start.
▷ *vi* **1** *(partir)* to begin, start. **2** *(salir)* to go, leave. **3** *(coche)* to start; *(tren)* to pull out. **4** *fig (provenir)* to stem (**de**, from).
arranque *nm* **1** TÉC starting mechanism. **2** *(comienzo)* start. **3** *fig (arrebato)* outburst, fit. **4** ARQUIT *(de escalera)* foot; *(de arco)* base. **5** *(decisión, valentía)* courage, determination. **6** *(ocurrencia ingeniosa)* joke, witticism.
arrasar *vt* **1** *(destruir)* to raze, destroy. **2** *(allanar)* to level, smooth.
▷ *vi (disco, libro, película)* to be a smash hit, sweep the board; *(deportista)* to sweep to victory.
arrastrar *vt* **1** *(gen)* to drag, pull: **no arrastres los pies** *don't drag your feet*. **2** *(corriente, aire)* to sweep along. **3** *fig* to sway, win over, draw: **este grupo arrastra a muchas quinceañeras** *this group draws lots of teenage girls*. **4** *(traer como consecuencia)* to cause, bring, lead to. **5** *fig (tener)* to have: **arrastra ese catarro desde hace un mes** *she's had that cold for a month*.
▷ *vi* to drag, trail.

▷ *vpr* **arrastrarse 1** to drag OS, crawl. **2** *fig (humillarse)* to creep, crawl.

arrastre *nm* **1** *(acción)* dragging, pulling. **2** *(telesquí)* drag lift. **3** *(en naipes)* lead.

arre *interj* gee up!, giddy up!

arrear *vt* **1** *(animales)* to spur on, urge on. **2** *(apresurar)* to hurry up. **3** *fam (pegar)* to hit: **le arreó una bofetada** *she slapped him round the face.*

▷ *vi fam* to hurry.

arrebatado,-a *pp* → **arrebatar.**

▷ *adj* **1** *(impetuoso)* rash, impetuous. **2** *(encolerizado)* furious, enraged. **3** *(ruborizado)* blushing, flushed.

arrebatar *vt* **1** *(quitar)* to grab, snatch. **2** *fig (cautivar)* to captivate, fascinate. **3** *(agostar)* to wither.

▷ *vpr* **arrebatarse 1** *(enfurecerse)* to become furious; *(exaltarse)* to get carried away **2** *(agostarse)* to wither. **3** *(cocer muy deprisa)* to burn, overcook.

arrebato *nm (arranque)* fit, outburst.

arreciar [12] *vi* to get stronger, get worse.

arrecife *nm* reef.

arreglado,-a *pp* → **arreglar.**

▷ *adj* **1** *(solucionado)* settled, fixed, sorted out. **2** *(ordenado)* tidy, neat, arranged, orderly. **3** *(bien vestido)* well-dressed, smart. **4** *(precio)* reasonable.

arreglar *vt* **1** *(gen)* to settle, sort out, fix. **2** *(ordenar)* to tidy up, clear up. **3** *(reparar)* to mend, fix, repair. **4** MÚS to arrange. **5** *fam* to sort out: **¡ya te arreglaré!** *I'll teach you!, I'll sort you out.*

▷ *vpr* **arreglarse 1** *(componerse)* to get ready, dress up; *(cabello)* to do. **2** *(solucionarse)* to get sorted out, work out; *(pareja)* to get back together again. ■ **arreglárselas** to manage, cope: **arréglatelas como puedas** *do the best you can.*

arreglo *nm* **1** *(acuerdo)* arrangement, agreement, settlement. **2** *(reparación)* repair. **3** *(orden)* order, tidiness. **4** *(limpieza)* cleaning, tidying; *(personal)* cleanliness. **5** MÚS arrangement. ■ **llegar a un arreglo** to come to an arrangement, reach an agreement. ● **arreglo de cuentas** settling of scores, settling-up.

arremangar [7] *vt* to roll up.

▷ *vpr* **arremangarse 1** to roll up one's sleeves. **2** *fig* to get serious, get down to it: **vamos, arremángate que hay que terminar el trabajo** *come on, get down to it, we've got to finish this job.*

arremeter *vi* **1** *(gen)* to attack, charge; *(el toro)* to charge. **2** *(verbalmente)* to attack.

arremetida *nf* attack, onslaught.

arrendamiento *nm* **1** renting, leasing, letting. **2** *(precio)* rent.

arrendar [27] *vt (dar en alquiler)* to let, lease; *(tomar en alquiler)* to rent, lease.

arrendatario,-a *adj* renting, leasing.

▷ *nm & nf* **1** *(que da en arriendo)* leaseholder, lessee. **2** *(inquilino)* tenant.

arreos *nm pl* **1** *(de caballerías)* harness *sing*, trappings. **2** *(adornos)* adornment *sing.*

arrepentido,-a *pp* → **arrepentirse.**

▷ *adj* regretful, repentant.

▷ *nm & nf* penitent.

arrepentimiento *nm* regret, repentance: **después le vino el arrepentimiento** *afterwards he felt sorry.*

arrepentirse [35] *vpr* **1** *(gen)* to regret (**de**, -). **2** REL to repent (**de**, of).

arrestar *vt* **1** to arrest, detain. **2** *(poner en prisión)* to imprison, jail, put in prison.

arresto *nm* arrest.

arriar [13] *vt* **1** *(velas)* to lower. **2** *(bandera)* to strike.

arriba *adv* **1** up; *(encima)* on (the) top: **ponlo más arriba** *put it higher up.* **2** *(piso)* upstairs: **vive arriba** *he/she lives upstairs.* **3** *(en escritos)* above: **véase más arriba** *see above.*

▷ *interj* up!: **¡arriba la República!** *long live the Republic!, up the Republic!* ■ **de arriba abajo** from top to bottom. ‖ **hacia arriba** upwards.

arribista *adj* ambitious, self-seeking.

▷ *nm o nf* arriviste, social climber, parvenu.

arriendo *nm* lease; *(de un piso)* renting. ■ **dar en arriendo** to let out on lease. ‖ **tomar en arriendo** to take on lease.

arriesgado,-a *pp* → **arriesgar.**

▷ *adj* **1** *(peligroso)* risky, dangerous. **2** *(temerario)* bold, daring, fearless.

arriesgar [7] *vt* **1** to risk; *(dinero)* to stake. **2** *(aventurar)* to venture.

▷ *vpr* **arriesgarse** *(uso reflexivo)* to risk: **se arriesgó mucho y fracasó** *he took many risks and failed.* ■ **arriesgarse a hacer** ALGO to dare to do STH, risk doing STH.

arrimar *vt (acercar)* to move closer.

▷ *vpr* **arrimarse 1** to move close, get close. **2** *fam* to cohabit, live together. ■ **arrimarse a** ALGN *fig* to seek SB's protection. ‖ **arrimarse al sol que más calienta** *fig* to get on the winning side.

arrinconar *vt* **1** *(poner en un rincón)* to put in a corner. **2** *(retirar)* to lay aside, put away. **3** *(acorralar)* to corner.

arritmia *nf* arrhythmia.

arroba *nf* **1** *(medida de peso) measure of weight equal to 11.502 kg, 25.3 lbs; (medida de capacidad) variable liquid measure.* **2** *(Internet)* at, @.

arrodillarse *vpr* to kneel down, get down on one's knees.

arrogancia *nf* **1** *(orgullo)* arrogance. **2** *(gallardía)* gallantry, valour (US valor), bravery.

arrogante *adj* **1** *(orgulloso)* arrogant. **2** *(gallardo)* gallant, valiant, brave.

arrojar *vt* **1** *(tirar)* to throw, fling. **2** *(echar con violencia)* to throw out, kick out. **3** *(vomitar)* to vomit, throw up. **4** *(emitir - humo)* to send out, belch out; *(- olor)* to give off; *(- lava)* to spew out. **5** *(cuentas, etc)* to show, produce, give.

▷ *vi* to vomit.

▷ *vpr* **arrojarse** to throw OS: **se arrojó sobre él** *she jumped on him.*

arrojo *nm* boldness, dash, bravery, daring.

arrollador,-ra *adj* overwhelming, irresistible.

arrollar *vt* **1** *(envolver)* to roll (up). **2** *(el viento)* to sweep away. **3** *(al enemigo)* to crush, rout. **4** *(atropellar)* to run over.

arropar *vt* to wrap up.

arroyo *nm* **1** *(corriente de agua)* stream, brook. **2** *(en la calle)* gutter. **3** *fig (corriente)* flood, stream.

arroz *nm* rice. ● **arroz blanco 1** *(seco)* white rice. **2** *(hervido)* boiled rice. ‖ **arroz con leche** rice pudding. ‖ **arroz integral** brown rice.
▲ *pl* **arroces.**

arruga *nf (piel)* wrinkle; *(ropa)* crease.

arrugar [7] *vt (piel)* to wrinkle; *(ropa)* to crease; *(papel)* to crumple (up).
▷ *vpr* **arrugarse 1** *(piel)* to wrinkle; *(ropa)* to crease; *(papel)* to crumple (up). **2** *fam (acobardarse)* to get the wind up.

arruinar *vt* **1** to bankrupt, ruin. **2** *(estropear)* to damage: **la tormenta ha arruinado la cosecha** *the storm has ruined the crops.*
▷ *vpr* **arruinarse** to be bankrupt, be ruined.

arrullar *vt* **1** *(ave)* to coo. **2** *(adormecer)* to lull.
▷ *vpr* **arrullarse** *fig (acariciarse)* to bill and coo.

arrumar *vt* to stow.
▷ *vpr* **arrumarse** to cloud over.

arsenal *nm* **1** MAR shipyard. **2** *(de armas)* arsenal. **3** *fig (cantidad)* storehouse, mine.

arsénico *nm* arsenic.

arte *nm* **1** art. **2** *(habilidad)* craft, skill. **3** *(astucia)* cunning. **4** *(pesca)* fishing gear. ■ **con malas artes** by evil means.

artefacto *nm* **1** device, appliance; *(explosivo)* explosive device. **2** *(en arqueología)* artefact.

arteria *nf* artery. ● **arteria carótida** carotid artery. ‖ **arteria coronaria** coronary artery.

artesa *nf* trough.

artesanal *adj (objeto)* handmade; *(comida)* homemade. ● **actividades artesanales** arts and crafts. ‖ **industria artesanal** craft industry.

artesanía *nf* **1** *(calidad)* craftsmanship. **2** *(arte, obra)* crafts *pl*, handicrafts *pl*.

artesano,-a *adj* handmade.
▷ *nm & nf (hombre)* craftsman; *(mujer)* craftswoman.

artesonado,-a *adj* panelled, coffered.
▷ *nm* **artesonado** panelled ceiling, coffered ceiling.

ártico,-a *adj* Arctic.
▷ *nm* **el Ártico** the Arctic. ● **el Círculo Ártico** the Arctic Circle. ‖ **el océano Ártico** the Arctic Ocean.

articulación *nf* **1** LING articulation. **2** ANAT joint, articulation. **3** TÉC joint.

articulado,-a *pp* → **articular.**
▷ *adj* **1** *(lenguaje)* articulate. **2** *(objeto)* articulated.
▷ *nm* **articulado** articles *pl*.

articular *adj* articulated.
▷ *vt* **1** to articulate. **2** JUR to article.

artículo *nm* **1** article. **2** *(mercancía)* article, product. ● **artículo de fondo** leading article, editorial. ‖ **artículos de primera necesidad** basic commodities.

artífice *nm o nf* **1** *(artista)* craftsman, artist. **2** *(autor)* author: **Pepe ha sido el artífice de todo esto** *this is all Pepe's doing.*
▷ *nm fig* architect: **él ha sido el artífice de este éxito** *he's the man behind this success story.*

artificial *adj* artificial.

artificio *nm* **1** *(habilidad)* skill, dexterity. **2** *(mecanismo)* device. **3** *(falta de naturalidad)* affectation. **4** *(engaño)* artifice, trick. ● **artificio pirotécnico** firework.

artificioso,-a *adj* **1** *(hábil)* skilful (US skillful), dexterous. **2** *(afectado)* affected. **3** *fig (disimulado)* sly, crafty.

artillería *nf* artillery.

artillero *nm* artilleryman.

artilugio *nm* **1** *(mecanismo)* device, gadget. **2** *fig (trampa)* trick, scheme.

artimaña *nf* artifice, trick, ruse.

artista *nm o nf* artist. ● **artista de cine** film star.

artístico,-a *adj* artistic.

artritis *nf inv* arthritis.

artrópodo *nm* arthropod.

artrosis *nf inv* arthrosis.

arzobispo *nm* archbishop.

as *nm* **1** *(naipes)* ace. **2** *(dados)* one. **3** *fig* ace, star, wizard: **Fangio fue un as del volante** *Fangio was an ace driver.*

asa [Takes **el** in singular.] *nf* handle.

asado,-a *pp* → **asar.**
▷ *adj* roast, roasted.
▷ *nm* **asado** roast.

asador *nm* **1** *(utensilio)* roaster. **2** *(establecimiento)* grill room, grill house.

asaduras *nf pl* offal; *(de ave)* giblets *pl*. ■ **echar las asaduras** *fam* to make a tremendous effort.

asalariado,-a *pp* → **asalariar.**
▷ *adj* salaried.
▷ *nm & nf* wage earner, salaried worker.

asalmonado,-a *adj* salmon-pink.

asaltante *adj* assaulting, attacker.
▷ *nm o nf* attacker; *(en robo)* raider, robber.

asaltar *vt* **1** to assault, attack; *(para robar)* to raid, rob. **2** *(abordar)* to approach, come up to. **3** *fig (surgir)* to assail.

asalto *nm* **1** assault, attack; *(con robo)* raid, robbery. **2** *(boxeo)* round.

asamblea *nf* assembly, meeting.

asambleísta *nm o nf* member of an assembly, member of a meeting.

asar *vt* **1** *(cocer)* to roast. **2** *fig (importunar)* to annoy, pester.
▷ *vpr* **asarse 1** *(cocerse)* to roast. **2** *fig (pasar calor)* to be roasting, be boiling hot. ■ **asar a la parrilla** to grill. ‖ **asar al horno** to roast.

ascendencia *nf* **1** ancestry, ancestors *pl*: **era alemán, pero de ascendencia polaca** *he was German, but of Polish descent.* **2** *(influencia)* ascendancy.

ascender [28] *vt* to promote.
▷ *vi* **1** *(subir)* to climb. **2** *(de categoría)* to be promoted (**a**, to). **3** *(sumar)* to amount (**a**, to).

ascendiente *adj* ascending, ascendant.
▷ *nm o nf (antepasado)* ancestor.
▷ *nm (influencia)* ascendancy, power.

ascensión *nf (subida)* climb, climbing. ● **día de la Ascensión** REL Ascension Day.

ascenso *nm* **1** *(subida)* climb, ascent. **2** *(aumento)* rise (**de**, in). **3** *(promoción)* promotion.

ascensor *nm* lift, US elevator.

asceta *nm o nf* ascetic.

ascético,-a *adj* ascetic.

asco *nm* disgust, repugnance. ■ **coger asco a algo** to get sick of sth. ‖ **dar asco** to be disgusting. ‖ **estar**

hecho,-a un asco 1 *(cosa)* to be filthy, look a real mess. **2** *(persona)* to be filthy, be in a right state. ‖ **hacer ascos a algo** to turn up one's nose at sth. ‖ **¡qué asco!** how disgusting!, how revolting!

ascua [Takes **el** in singular.] *nf* live coal.

aseado,-a *pp* ⟶ **asear.**

▷ *adj* clean, neat, tidy.

asear *vt (adecentar)* to clean, tidy up.

▷ *vpr* **asearse** *(arreglarse)* to wash, get washed.

asediar [12] *vt* **1** to besiege, lay siege to. **2** *fig* to besiege, pester, harass.

asedio *nm* **1** siege. **2** *fig* harassment.

asegurado,-a *pp* ⟶ **asegurar.**

▷ *adj* **1** *(con seguro)* insured. **2** *(garantizado)* secure: **tiene el futuro asegurado** *his future is secure.* **3** *(seguro)* secured, tightened: **el tornillo está bien asegurado** *the screw is well tightened.*

asegurar *vt* **1** *(fijar)* to secure. **2** COM to insure. **3** *(garantizar)* to assure, guarantee: **te aseguro que lo haré** *I assure you that I'll do it.*

▷ *vpr* **asegurarse 1** *(cerciorarse)* to make sure. **2** COM to insure os.

asemejar *vt* to make alike, make similar.

▷ *vpr* **asemejarse a** to look like, be like.

asentar [27] *vt* **1** *(establecer)* to establish; *(apoyar)* to base. **2** *(colocar - gen)* to locate; *(- colonos)* to settle. **3** *(fijar)* to fix, set. **4** *(calmar)* to calm, settle. **5** *(anotar)* to enter, note down. **6** *(golpes)* to deal.

▷ *vpr* **asentarse 1** *(establecerse)* to settle. **2** *(aves)* to perch.

asentir [35] *vi* to assent, agree; *(con la cabeza)* to nod.

aseo *nm* **1** *(acción)* cleaning, tidying up. **2** *(limpieza)* cleanliness, tidiness. **3** *(habitación)* bathroom, toilet (US restroom). ● **cuarto de aseo** bathroom.

aséptico,-a *adj* **1** aseptic. **2** *fig* cold, indifferent.

asequible *adj* accessible: **a un precio asequible** *at a reasonable price, at an affordable price;* **la casa que ha comprado no es asequible para todo el mundo** *the house he bought is not within everybody's reach.*

aserradero *nm* sawmill.

aserrado,-a *adj* serrated.

▷ *nm* **aserrado** sawing.

aserrar [27] *vt* to saw (up).

aserrín *nm* sawdust.

asesinar *vt* **1** to kill, murder. **2** *(magnicidio)* to assassinate.

asesinato *nm* **1** killing, murder. **2** *(magnicidio)* assassination.

asesino,-a *adj* murderous: **no hallaron el arma asesina** *they couldn't find the murder weapon.*

▷ *nm & nf* killer; *(hombre)* murderer; *(mujer)* murderess.

asesor,-ra *adj* advisory.

▷ *nm & nf* adviser, consultant.

asesorar *vt* **1** *(dar consejo)* to advise, give advice. **2** COM to act as a consultant to.

▷ *vpr* **asesorarse** *(tomar consejo)* to take advice, consult (**de**, -).

asesoría *nf* **1** *(cargo)* consultancy. **2** *(oficina)* consultant's office.

asestar *vt* **1** *(arma)* to aim. **2** *(golpe)* to deal, give. **3** *(tiro)* to fire. ■ **asestar un puñetazo** to punch

aseveración *nf* asseveration, assertion.

asfaltado,-a *pp* ⟶ **asfaltar.**

▷ *nm* **asfaltado 1** *(acción)* asphalting. **2** *(pavimento)* asphalt, asphalted surface.

asfalto *nm* asphalt.

asfixia *nf* asphyxia, suffocation, asphyxiation.

asfixiar [12] *vt* to asphyxiate, suffocate.

▷ *vpr* **asfixiarse** to asphyxiate, suffocate.

así *adv* **1** *(de esta manera)* thus, (in) this way. **2** *(de esa manera)* (in) that way: **por decirlo así** *so to speak;* **y así sucesivamente** *and so on.* **3** *(tanto)* as: **así usted como yo** *both you and I.* **4** *(por tanto)* therefore. **5** *(tan pronto como)* as soon as: **así que lo sepa** *as soon as I know.*

▷ *adj* such: **un hombre así** *a man like that, such a man.* ■ **así así** so-so. ‖ **así que** so: **llovía, así que cogimos el paraguas** *it was raining, so we took our umbrella.*

Asia *nf* Asia.

asiático,-a *adj* Asian.

▷ *nm & nf* Asian.

asidero *nm* **1** *(asa)* handle. **2** *fig (excusa)* pretext.

asiduidad *nf* assiduity, frequency. ■ **con asiduidad** frequently, regularly.

asiduo,-a *adj* assiduous, frequent, regular.

▷ *nm & nf* regular: **es un asiduo del cine** *he's a regular cinema-goer* (US *movie-goer).*

asiento *nm* **1** *(silla, etc)* seat. **2** *(emplazamiento)* site. **3** *(sedimento)* sediment. **4** *fig (orden)* establishment. **5** COM entry, registry. **6** *(de vasija)* bottom. **7** ARQUIT settling. ■ **tomar asiento** to take a seat.

asignación *nf* **1** *(acción)* assignment, allocation. **2** *(nombramiento)* appointment, assignment. **3** *(remuneración)* allocation, allowance; *(sueldo)* wage, salary.

asignar *vt* **1** to assign, allot, allocate. **2** *(nombrar)* to appoint, assign.

asignatura *nf* subject.

asilado,-a *pp* ⟶ **asilar.**

▷ *nm & nf person who lives in a home or in care.* ● **asilado,-a político,-a** political refugee.

asilo *nm* **1** *(institución)* asylum, home, institution. **2** *fig (protección)* protection, assistance. ■ **dar asilo** to shelter. ● **asilo de ancianos** old people's home. ‖ **asilo político** political asylum.

asimetría *nf* asymmetry.

asimilar *vt* to assimilate.

asimismo *adv* **1** *(también)* also, as well. **2** *(de esta manera)* likewise. **3** *(además)* moreover.

asir [65] *vt (agarrar)* to grab, seize, grasp, take hold of.

asistencia *nf* **1** *(presencia)* attendance, presence. **2** *(público)* audience: **hubo mucha asistencia al concierto** *there was a large audience at the concert.* **3** *(ayuda)* assistance, help, aid. ● **asistencia económica** financial aid. ‖ **asistencia jurídica** legal aid. ‖ **asistencia médica** medical assistance. ‖ **asistencia técnica** technical backup. ‖ **falta de asistencia** absence.

asistenta *nf* cleaning lady.

asistente *adj* **1** *(que está)* attending. **2** *(que ayuda)* assistant.

▷ *nm o nf* **1** *(que está)* member of the audience: **los asistentes al acto se quejaron del retraso** *those present at the ceremony complained about the delay.* **2** *(que ayuda)* assistant. ● **asistente social** social worker.

asistir *vi* to attend, be present: **la niña asiste a la escuela cada día** *the little girl goes to school every day.*

▷ *vt (ayudar)* to help, assist; *(a los enfermos)* to attend, care for.
asma [Takes el in singular.] *nf* asthma.
asno *nm* 1 ass, donkey. 2 *fam (persona)* ass, idiot.
asociación *nf* association. ● **asociación de vecinos** residents' association.
asociado,-a *pp* → **asociar.**
▷ *adj* associated, associate.
▷ *nm & nf* associate, partner.
asociar [12] *vt* 1 to associate (**a/con**, with), connect, link. 2 COM to take into partnership.
▷ *vpr* **asociarse** 1 *(relacionarse)* to be associated (**a/con**, with): 2 COM to collaborate, form a partnership, become partners.
asolar [31] *vt (epidemia)* to ravage; *(ejército)* to lay waste to, raze; *(incendio, tempestad)* to devastate.
asomar *vi (empezar a aparecer)* to appear, begin to show, come out.
▷ *vt (mostrar)* to show, put out, stick out: **el chico asomó la cabeza por la ventana** *the boy stuck his head out of the window.*
▷ *vpr* **asomarse** 1 *(a ventana)* to stick one's head out (**a**, of), lean out (**a**, of); *(a balcón)* to come out (**a**, onto). 2 *(aparecer)* to appear.
asombrar *vt* to amaze, astonish, surprise.
▷ *vpr* **asombrarse** to be astonished, be amazed, be surprised: **nos asombramos de su altura** *we were amazed at her height.*
asombro *nm* amazement, astonishment, surprise.
asombroso,-a *adj* amazing, astonishing, surprising.
asomo *nm* sign, trace, hint. ■ **ni por asomo** by no means.
asonante *adj* assonant.
aspa [Takes el in singular.] *nf* 1 *(cruz)* cross. 2 *(de molino)* sail; *(de ventilador)* blade; *(armazón)* arms *pl*.
aspaviento *nm* fuss. ■ **hacer aspavientos** to make a great fuss.
aspecto *nm* 1 *(faceta)* aspect, side, angle. 2 *(apariencia)* look, appearance: **¿qué aspecto tenía?** *what did he look like?*
aspereza *nf* roughness, coarseness, asperity.
áspero,-a *adj* 1 *(cosa)* rough, coarse. 2 *fig (persona)* surly. 3 *(clima, tiempo)* harsh.
aspersión *nf* sprinkling.
aspersor *nm* sprinkler.
aspiración *nf* 1 *(al respirar)* inhalation, breathing in. 2 LING aspiration. 3 TÉC intake. 4 *fig (ambición)* aspiration, ambition.
aspirador,-ra *adj* sucking: **bomba aspiradora** *suction pump.*
▷ *nm* **aspirador** vacuum cleaner, Hoover.
aspirante *adj* suction.
▷ *nm o nf* candidate, applicant.
aspirar *vt* 1 *(al respirar)* to inhale, breathe in. 2 *(absorber)* to suck in, draw in. 3 LING to aspirate.
▷ *vi fig (desear)* to aspire (**a**, to): **aspiraba a convertirse en una estrella de cine** *he aspired to becoming a film star.*
aspirina® *nf* aspirin.
asquear *vt* to disgust, revolt, make sick.
asqueroso,-a *adj* 1 *(sucio)* dirty, filthy. 2 *(desagradable)* disgusting, foul. 3 *(que siente asco)* squeamish.
▷ *nm & nf* 1 *(sucio)* filthy person, revolting person. 2 *(que siente asco)* squeamish person.
asta [Takes el in singular.] *nf* 1 *(de bandera)* staff pole. 2 *(de lanza)* shaft; *(pica)* lance. 3 *(cuerno)* horn.
asterisco *nm* asterisk.
asteroide *adj* asteroid.
▷ *nm* asteroid.
astigmatismo *nm* astigmatism.
astilla *nf* splinter, chip.
astillero *nm* shipyard, dockyard.
astrágalo *nm* 1 ANAT astragalus. 2 ARQUIT astragal.
astringente *adj* astringent.
▷ *nm* astringent.
astro *nm* star.
astrofísica *nf* astrophysics.
astrología *nf* astrology.
astrólogo,-a *nm & nf* astrologer.
astronauta *nm o nf* astronaut.
astronomía *nf* astronomy.
astrónomo,-a *nm & nf* astronomer.
astroso,-a *adj* 1 *(desastrado)* shabby, untidy. 2 *(despreciable)* contemptible. 3 *(desdichado)* unfortunate.
astucia *nf* 1 astuteness, cunning, shrewdness. 2 *(treta)* trick, ruse.
astuto,-a *adj* astute, cunning, shrewd.
asueto *nm* time off, free time, rest: **mi tarde de asueto** *my afternoon off.*
asumir *vt* to assume, take on, take upon OS: **el coronel asumió el mando de las tropas** *the colonel assumed command of the troops.*
asunto *nm* 1 *(cuestión)* matter, issue; *(tema)* subject; *(de obra)* theme: **no quiero hablar del asunto** *I don't want to discuss the matter.* 2 *(negocio)* affair, business: **no es asunto tuyo** *it's none of your business.* 3 *(aventura)* affair, love affair. ● **asuntos exteriores** POL Foreign Affairs.
asustado,-a *adj* frightened, scared.
asustar *vt* to frighten, scare.
▷ *vpr* **asustarse** to be frightened, be scared.
atacar [1] *vt* 1 *(gen)* to attack. 2 *(criticar)* to attack, criticize. 3 *(afectar)* to attack, affect: **esas pastillas pueden atacar al estómago** *those pills can upset your stomach.*
atadura *nf* 1 *(acción)* tying, binding, fastening. 2 *(cosa)* binding, string, cord. 3 *fig (unión)* tie. 4 *fig (impedimento)* tie, hindrance.
atajar *vi* to take a short cut.
▷ *vt* 1 *(interrumpir)* to interrupt. 2 *(entorpecer el paso)* to halt.
atajo *nm* 1 *(camino)* short cut. 2 *(rebaño)* herd. 3 *fig (grupo)* bunch. ■ **echar por el atajo / tirar por el atajo** *fig* to take a shortcut, take the easiest way out.
atalaya *nf (torre)* watchtower, lookout; *(mirador)* vantage point.
▷ *nm (persona)* watcher, lookout.
atañer [38] [used only in the 3rd person.] *vi* to concern (**a**, -).
ataque *nm* 1 attack. 2 MED fit. ● **ataque de nervios** nervous breakdown.
atar *vt* 1 to tie. 2 *fig* to tie down. ■ **atar cabos** *fig* to put two and two together.

atardecer [43] *vi* [Used only in the 3rd person; it does not take a subject.] to get dark, grow dark.
▷ *nm* evening, dusk.

atareado,-a *pp* ⟶ **atarear.**
▷ *adj* busy, occupied.

atascar [1] *vt* **1** *(bloquear)* to block up, clog. **2** *fig (obstaculizar)* to hamper, hinder, obstruct.
▷ *vpr* **atascarse 1** *(bloquearse)* to get blocked, get blocked up, get clogged. **2** *(mecanismo)* to jam, get jammed, get stuck. **3** *fig (estancarse)* to get tangled up, get bogged down.

atasco *nm* **1** *(acción)* obstruction, blockage. **2** *(de tráfico)* traffic jam.

ataúd *nm* coffin.

ataviar [13] *vt* **1** *(arreglar)* to dress up. **2** *(adornar)* to adorn, deck.

atavío *nm* **1** *(adorno)* decoration, adornment, ornament. **2** *(vestido)* dress, attire.

ateísmo *nm* atheism.

atemorizar [4] *vt* to frighten, scare.
▷ *vpr* **atemorizarse** to be frightened, be scared.

Atenas *nf* Athens.

atenazar [4] *vt fig* to torture, torment.

atención *nf* **1** *(gen)* attention: **lo hace solo para que le prestes atención** *she's only doing it to get attention.* **2** *(detalle)* nice thought: **fue una atención por su parte** *it was a nice thought, it was very kind of him.*
▷ *interj* **¡atención!** *(gen)* your attention please!; *(cuidado)* watch out!, look out! ■ **a la atención de** ALGN *(en cartas)* for the attention of SB. ‖ **llamar la atención** to attract attention: **procura no llamar la atención** *try not to attract attention.* ‖ **llamar la atención a** ALGN to take SB to task. ‖ **prestar atención** to pay attention (**a**, to).

atender [28] *vt* **1** *(servir - cliente)* to serve, attend to, see to: **¿ya la atienden a usted?** *are you being served?* **2** *(cuidar)* to take care of, look after. **3** *(negocio)* to take care of; *(teléfono)* to answer. **4** *(consejo, advertencia)* to heed, pay attention to; *(ruego, deseo, protesta)* to attend to; *(instrucción)* to follow, carry out.
▷ *vi* **1** *(prestar atención)* to pay attention (**a**, to), attend (**a**, to). **2** *(cumplir con)* to meet (**a**, -), fulfil (US fulfill) (**a**, -). **3** *(tener en cuenta)* to bear in mind.

atenerse [87] *vpr* **1** *(ajustarse)* to abide (**a**, by), comply (**a**, with). **2** *(acogerse)* to rely (**a**, on).

atentado *nm* **1** *(ataque)* attack, assault: **eso puede considerarse un atentado contra su vida** *it can be considered an attempt on his life.* **2** *(afrenta)* affront. ● **atentado terrorista** terrorist attack.

atentamente *adv* **1** attentively, carefully. **2** *(amablemente)* politely; *(en carta)* sincerely, faithfully: **«Le saluda atentamente»** *«Yours sincerely», «Yours faithfully».*

atentar [27] *vi* **1** *(físicamente - a una institución)* to attack (**a/contra**, -), make an attack (**a/contra**, on); *(- a una persona)* to attempt to kill, make an attempt on sb's life. **2** *(violar)* to violate (**a/contra**, -). **3** *(amenazar)* to threaten (**a/contra**, -).

atento,-a *adj* **1** attentive. **2** *(amable)* polite, courteous. ■ **estar atento,-a a algo 1** *(prestar atención)* to pay attention to sth. **2** *(estar alerta)* to be on the alert for sth, keep an eye out for sth, be on the lookout for.

atenuante *adj* **1** attenuating. **2** JUR extenuating.
▷ *nm* JUR extenuating circumstance.

atenuar [11] *vt* **1** to attenuate. **2** JUR to extenuate.

ateo,-a *adj* atheistic.
▷ *nm & nf* atheist.

aterciopelado,-a *adj* velvety, velvet: **tenía una voz aterciopelada** *she had a velvety voice.*

aterrador,-ra *adj* terrifying, frightful.

aterrar *vt (asustar)* to terrify.
▷ *vpr* **aterrarse** to be terrified.

aterrizaje *nm* landing. ● **aterrizaje forzoso** emergency landing.

aterrizar [4] *vi* **1** to land. **2** *fig* to show up, arrive.

aterronar *vt* to cake, harden.
▷ *vpr* **aterronarse** to go lumpy, cake, harden.

aterrorizar [4] *vt* **1** *(gen)* to terrify. **2** *(terrorista)* to terrorize.
▷ *vpr* **aterrorizarse** to be terrified.

atesorar *vt* **1** *(acumular)* to hoard, accumulate, store up. **2** *fig* to possess.

atestado¹ *nm* JUR affidavit, statement.
▷ *nm pl* **atestados** testimonials.

atestado,-a² *pp* ⟶ **atestar 2.**
▷ *adj* packed (**de**, with), crammed (**de**, with).

atestar¹ *vt* JUR to testify.

atestar² [27] *vt (atiborrar)* to cram (**de**, with), pack (**de**, with).
▷ *vpr* **atestarse** *(de comida)* to stuff OS (**de**, with).

atestiguar [22] *vt* **1** JUR to testify to, bear witness to, give evidence of. **2** *(ofrecer muestras)* to attest, testify, vouch for.

atiborrar *vt (llenar)* to pack, cram, stuff (**de**, with).
▷ *vpr* **atiborrarse** *fam (de comida)* to stuff OS (**de**, with).

ático *nm* **1** *(vivienda)* penthouse, attic flat. **2** ARQUIT attic, loft.

atinar *vi* **1** *(dar con)* to hit upon, find: **si no atinas con la calle, llámame** *if you can't find the street, call me.* **2** *(acertar)* to get it right, be right, succeed: **atiné en el blanco** *I hit the target.*

atípico,-a *adj* atypical.

atisbar *vt* **1** *(observar)* to spy on, observe, watch. **2** *fig (vislumbrar)* to make out, discern.

atisbo *nm* **1** *(acción)* spying, watching. **2** *fig (indicio)* inkling, slight sign.

atizar [4] *vt* **1** *(fuego)* to poke; *(vela)* to snuff. **2** *fig (pasiones)* to rouse, excite; *(rebelión)* to stir up. **3** *(dar - golpe)* give, deal.
▷ *vpr* **atizarse** *fam (zamparse - comida)* to put away; *(- bebida)* to knock back. ■ **¡atiza!** wow!

atlántico,-a *adj* Atlantic. ● **el (océano) Atlántico** the Atlantic (Ocean).

atlas *nm inv* atlas.

atleta *nm o nf* athlete.

atlético,-a *adj* athletic.

atletismo *nm* athletics.

atmósfera *nf* atmosphere.

atolondrado,-a *pp* ⟶ **atolondrar.**
▷ *adj* **1** *(desatinado)* scatterbrained, reckless, silly. **2** *(aturdido)* stunned, bewildered.

atómico,-a *adj* atomic.

atomizador *nm* atomizer, spray, scent spray.

átomo *nm* **1** atom. **2** *fig* atom, particle, speck. ■ **ni un átomo de** not a trace of. ● **átomo de vida** spark of life.

atónito,-a *adj* astonished, amazed: **escuchó las noticias atónito** *he listened to the news in amazement.*

átono,-a *adj* atonic, unstressed.

atontado,-a *pp* → **atontar.**
▷ *adj* **1** *(aturdido)* stunned, confused, bewildered. **2** *(tonto)* stupid, silly, foolish.

atontar *vt* **1** *(volver tonto)* to make stupid, stupefy, turn into a vegetable. **2** *(aturdir)* to confuse, bewilder, stun; *(con un golpe)* to stun, daze; *(marear)* to make dopey.
▷ *vpr* **atontarse 1** *(volverse tonto)* to go stupid, turn into a vegetable. **2** *(aturdirse)* to get confused, be bewildered; to become groggy, begin to feel groggy.

atormentar *vt* **1** *(torturar)* to torture. **2** *fig (causar disgusto)* to torment, harass.
▷ *vpr* **atormentarse** *(sufrir)* to torment OS.

atornillar *vt* to screw on, screw down, screw together.

atosigar [4] *vt* to harass, pester.

atracador,-ra *nm & nf (de banco)* (bank) robber; *(en la calle)* attacker, mugger, thief.

atracar [1] *vt* **1** *(robar - banco, tienda)* to hold up, rob; *(- persona)* to mug. **2** *(de comida)* to stuff, fill.
▷ *vi* MAR *(a otra nave)* to come alongside; *(a tierra)* to tie up, dock, berth.
▷ *vpr* **atracarse** *(de comida)* to gorge OS (**de**, on), stuff OS (**de**, with); *(de bebida)* to guzzle (**de**, -).

atracción *nf (gen)* attraction: **sentía atracción por él** *she felt attracted to him.*
▷ *nf pl* **atracciones** *(de feria)* rides *pl.*

atraco *nm* hold-up, robbery.

atracón *nm fam* binge, blowout. ■ **darse/pegarse un atracón** to make a pig of OS.

atractivo,-a *adj* attractive, charming, appealing.
▷ *nm* **atractivo** attraction, charm, appeal: **el nuevo modelo tiene mucho atractivo** *the new model is very attractive.*

atraer [88] *vt* **1** *(gen)* to attract. **2** *(captivar)* to captivate, charm: **no me atrae el tema de la obra** *the subject of the play doesn't appeal to me.*

atragantarse *vpr* **1** *(no poder tragar)* to choke (**con**, on), swallow the wrong way. **2** *(atravesarse)* to get stuck in one's throat. **3** *fig (causar fastidio)* to turn off.

atrancar [1] *vt* **1** *(puerta)* to bar, bolt. **2** *(obstruir)* to obstruct, block up.
▷ *vpr* **atrancarse 1** *(atascarse)* to get stuck. **2** *(al leer)* to stumble over one's words.

atrapamoscas *nf inv (dionea)* Venus flytrap; *(drósera)* sundew.

atrapar *vt* to seize, capture, catch.

atrás *adv* **1** back: **dio un salto atrás** *she jumped back.* **2** *(tiempo)* ago: **días atrás** *several days ago.*
▷ *interj* stand back!, move back! ■ **ir hacia atrás** to go backwards.

atrasado,-a *pp* → **atrasar.**
▷ *adj* **1** *(desfasado)* outdated. **2** *(pago)* overdue. **3** *(reloj)* slow. **4** *(país)* backward, underdeveloped; *(alumno)* slow, backward.

atrasar *vt (gen)* to delay, postpone, put back; *(reloj)* to put back.
▷ *vi (reloj)* to be slow.
▷ *vpr* **atrasarse 1** *(tren, etc)* to be late. **2** *(quedarse atrás)* to fall behind.

atraso *nm* **1** delay. **2** *(de reloj)* slowness: **el tren lleva mucho atraso** *the train is very late.* **3** *(de un país)* backwardness.
▷ *nm pl* **atrasos** COM arrears.

atravesar [27] *vt* **1** *(cruzar)* to cross, go across, go over; *(pasar por)* to go through, pass through. **2** *(experimentar - gen)* to go through, experience; *(enfermedad, etc)* to suffer. **3** *(poner oblicuamente)* to put across, lay across. **4** *(con bala, etc)* to go through *(con espada)* to run through. **5** *(situación)* to go through.
▷ *vpr* **atravesarse 1** *(estar atravesado)* to be in the way, be across. **2** *(inmiscuirse)* to interfere, meddle.

atrayente *adj* attractive.

atreverse *vpr* to dare, venture: **¿te atreves?** *are you game?* ■ **atreverse a hacer algo** to dare to do sth.

atrevido,-a *pp* → **atreverse.**
▷ *adj* **1** *(osado)* daring, bold. **2** *(insolente)* insolent, impudent. **3** *(indecoroso)* daring, risqué.

atribución *nf* **1** *(acción)* attribution. **2** *(poder)* power, authority.

atribuir [62] *vt* to attribute (**a**, to), ascribe.
▷ *vpr* **atribuirse** to assume.

atributo *nm* attribute, quality.

atril *nm (para libros)* lectern, bookrest; *(para música)* music stand.

atrio *nm* **1** *(patio)* atrium. **2** *(vestíbulo)* vestibule.

atrocidad *nf* **1** *(barbaridad)* atrocity, outrage. **2** *(disparate - acción)* something stupid, foolish thing; *(- dicho)* silly remark, stupid remark.

atropellado,-a *pp* → **atropellar.**
▷ *adj* **1** *(persona)* hasty, rash. **2** *(comportamiento)* abrupt, brusque.

atropellar *vt* **1** AUTO to knock down, run over. **2** *(arrollar)* to trample over. **3** *(empujar)* to push, jostle. **4** *fig (oprimir)* to oppress; *(sentimientos)* to outrage, offend, affront; *(derechos)* to disregard, violate.
▷ *vpr* **atropellarse** to rush, hurry.

atropello *nm* **1** *(accidente)* accident, collision; *(de coche)* knocking down, running over. **2** *(apresuramiento)* haste. **3** *fig (agravio)* outrage, abuse; *(de derechos)* violation.
▷ *nm pl* **atropellos** pushing and shoving *sing.* ■ **con atropello** in a hurry, in a rush.

atroz *adj* **1** *(bárbaro)* atrocious, outrageous. **2** *fam (enorme)* enormous, huge, awful.
▲ *pl* **atroces.**

atuendo *nm* attire, dress, outfit.

atún *nm* tuna, tuna fish, tunny.

aturdido,-a *pp* → **aturdir.**
▷ *adj* **1** *(confundido)* stunned, dazed, bewildered. **2** *(atolondrado)* reckless, harebrained.

aturdir *vt* **1** *(por golpe)* to stun, daze; *(por ruido)* to deafen; *(por droga)* to stupefy. **2** *fig (atolondrar)* to stun, dumbfound; *(confundir)* to bewilder, confuse.
▷ *vpr* **aturdirse** *(atolondrarse)* to be stunned, be confused, be bewildered.

audacia *nf* audacity, boldness, daring.

audaz *adj* audacious, bold, daring.
▲ *pl* **audaces.**

audición *nf* 1 *(acción)* hearing; *(radio, televisión)* reception. 2 TEAT audition. 3 MÚS concert.
audiencia *nf* 1 *(recepción)* audience, hearing. 2 *(entrevista)* formal interview. 3 JUR high court. 4 *(público)* audience.
audífono *nm* hearing aid, deaf aid.
audiovisual *adj* audio-visual.
▷ *nm* audio-visual.
auditar *vt* to audit.
auditivo,-a *adj* auditory: **el nervio auditivo** *the auditory nerve.*
▷ *nm* **auditivo** *(auricular)* earpiece, receiver.
auditor,-ra *nm & nf* FIN auditor.
▷ *adj* auditing.
▷ *nm* **auditor** MIL legal adviser.
auditorio *nm* 1 *(público)* audience. 2 *(lugar)* auditorium, hall.
auge *nm* 1 *(del mercado)* boom. 2 *(de precios)* boost. 3 *(de fama, etc)* peak, summit. 4 *(de órbita)* apogee.
augurio *nm* augury.
aula [Takes **el** in singular.] *nf (en escuela)* classroom; *(en universidad)* lecture room.
aullar [16] *vi* to howl, yell, bay.
aullido *nm* howl, yell.
aumentar *vt* 1 to augment, increase; *(precios)* to put up; *(producción)* to step up. 2 *(óptica)* to magnify. 3 *(fotos)* to enlarge. 4 *(sonido)* to amplify.
▷ *vi* to rise, go up.
aumento *nm* 1 increase, growth. 2 *(óptica)* magnification. 3 *(fotos)* enlargement. 4 *(sonido)* amplification. 5 *(salario)* rise, US raise. ■ **ir en aumento** to be on the increase.
aun *adv* even: **aun los tontos lo saben** *even a fool knows that.*
▷ *conj (+ gerundio o participio)* although, even though: **aun llegando tarde, lo recibieron amablemente** *although he was late, he was given a warm reception.* ■ **aun así** even so, even then. ‖ **aun cuando** although, even though. ‖ **aun más** even more.
aún *adv (afirmación)* still; *(negación, interrogación)* yet: **aún no ha llamado** *he hasn't phoned yet.*
aunar [16] *vt* to unite, combine, join. ■ **aunar esfuerzos** to join forces.
aunque *conj* 1 *(valor concesivo)* although, though; *(con énfasis)* even if, even though. 2 *(valor adversativo)* but.
aúpa *interj* up!, get up!
aupar [16] *vt* 1 *(levantar)* to help up. 2 *fig (alabar)* to praise.
aureola *nf* aureole, halo.
aurícula *nf* auricle.
auricular *adj* auricular, of the ear.
▷ *nm* 1 *(teléfono)* receiver, earpiece. 2 *(dedo)* little finger.
▷ *nm pl* **auriculares** earphones, headphones.
aurora *nf* dawn, daybreak. ● **aurora boreal/borealis** aurora borealis, northern lights *pl.*
auscultar *vt* to sound (with a stethoscope).
ausencia *nf* absence. ■ **brillar por su ausencia** to be conspicuous by one's absence.
ausentarse *vpr* 1 *(faltar)* to be absent. 2 *(irse)* to leave.
ausente *adj* 1 absent. 2 *(distraído)* lost in thought.
▷ *nm o nf* 1 absentee. 2 JUR missing person.
auspicio *nm* auspice.
austeridad *nf* 1 *(sobriedad)* austerity. 2 *(severidad)* severity.
austero,-a *adj* 1 *(sobrio)* austere. 2 *(severo)* stern.
Australia *nf* Australia.
australiano,-a *adj* Australian.
▷ *nm & nf (persona)* Australian.
australopiteco *nm* australopithecine.
Austria *nf* Austria.
austriaco,-a *adj* Austrian.
▷ *nm & nf* Austrian.
autarquía[1] *nf (autosuficiencia)* autarky.
autarquía[2] *nf (autocracia)* autarchy.
auténtico,-a *adj* authentic, genuine, real: **con chocolate auténtico** *with real chocolate.*
auto[1] *nm (coche)* car. ● **autos de choque** bumper cars.
auto[2] *nm* 1 JUR decree, writ. 2 LIT mystery play, religious play.
▷ *nm pl* **autos** papers, documents.
autoadherente *adj* self-adhesive.
autoadhesivo,-a *adj* self-adhesive.
autobiografía *nf* autobiography.
autobús *nm* bus.
autocar *nm* coach.
autocontrol *nm* self-control.
autóctono,-a *adj* indigenous.
autodefensa *nf* self-defence (US self-defense).
autodeterminación *nf* self-determination.
autodidacta *nm o nf* self-taught person.
autoescuela *nf* driving school, school of motoring.
autoestop *nm* → **autostop.**
autoestopista *nm o nf* → **autostopista.**
autógrafo,-a *adj* autographic.
▷ *nm* **autógrafo** autograph.
autómata *nm* automaton.
automático,-a *adj* automatic.
automatización *nf* automation.
automóvil *nm* automobile, car.
automovilismo *nm* 1 motoring. 2 DEP motor racing.
automovilista *nm o nf* motorist, driver.
automovilístico,-a *adj* car.
autonomía *nf* 1 *(gen)* autonomy. 2 *(capacidad para funcionar sin recargar)* range.
autonómico,-a *adj* autonomous, self-governing.
autónomo,-a *adj* 1 *(región)* autonomous. 2 *(trabajador)* self-employed.
▷ *nm & nf* COM self-employed person.
autopista *nf* motorway, US highway.
autopsia *nf* 1 autopsy. 2 *fig* postmortem.
autor,-ra *nm & nf* 1 *(escritor)* writer, author; *(hombre)* author; *(mujer)* authoress. 2 *(inventor)* inventor. 3 *(responsable - gen)* person responsible; *(- de delito)* perpetrator.
autoridad *nf* authority.
autoritario,-a *adj* authoritarian.
autorización *nf* authorization.
autorizado,-a *pp* → **autorizar.**
▷ *adj* 1 *(oficial)* authorized, official. 2 *(experto)* authoritative, expert.
autorizar [4] *vt* 1 to authorize. 2 JUR to legalize. 3 *(aprobar)* to approve of, give authority to.
autorretrato *nm* self-portrait.

autoservicio *nm* 1 *(restaurante)* self-service restaurant, cafeteria. 2 *(supermercado)* supermarket.
autostop *nm* hitchhiking.
autostopista *nm o nf* hitch-hiker.
autosuficiencia *nf* self-sufficiency.
autovía *nf* dual carriageway, US highway.
auxiliar [14] *adj* auxiliary, assistant.
▷ *nm* 1 *(persona)* assistant. 2 GRAM *(verbo)* auxilliary.
▷ *vt (ayudar)* to help, assist; *(a un enfermo)* to attend; *(a un país)* to give aid to. ● **auxiliar administrativo** administrative assistant.
auxilio *nm* help, aid, assistance, relief.
▷ *interj* help! ● **primeros auxilios** first aid *sing*.
aval *nm* endorsement, guarantee.
avalancha *nf* avalanche.
avalar *vt* to guarantee, endorse.
avance *nm* 1 *(acción)* advance. 2 *(pago)* advance payment; *(balance)* balancing; *(presupuesto)* estimate. 3 *(de película)* trailer. ● **avance informativo** TV news preview, US news brief.
avanzar [4] *vi* to advance, go forward.
▷ *vt* 1 *(mover adelante)* to advance, move forward. 2 *(dinero)* to advance. 3 *(promover)* to promote. 4 *(una propuesta)* to put forward.
avaricia *nf (tacañería)* avarice, meanness, miserliness; *(codicia)* greed, avarice. ■ **con avaricia** *fam* extremely: **es feo con avaricia** *he's as ugly as sin.*
avaricioso,-a *adj* ⟶ **avariento,-a.**
avaro,-a *adj (tacaño)* avaricious, miserly, mean; *(codicioso)* greedy, avaricious.
▷ *nm & nf (tacaño)* miser; *(codicioso)* greedy person.
avasallar *vt* to subjugate, subdue.
avatar *nm* change, transformation. ● **los avatares de la vida** the ups and downs of life.
ave [Takes **el** in singular.] *nf* bird. ● **ave de rapiña** bird of prey. ‖ **aves de corral** poultry *sing.*
avecinarse *vpr* to approach (**a**, -).
avellana *nf* hazelnut.
avemaría *nf* Ave Maria, Hail Mary.
avena *nf* oats *pl.*
avenencia *nf* agreement, accord; *(comercial)* deal.
avenida *nf* 1 *(calle)* avenue. 2 *(riada)* flood, spate. 3 *(concurrencia)* gathering, meeting.
avenido,-a *pp* ⟶ **avenir.** ■ **bien avenidos,-as** in agreement, on good terms. ‖ **mal avenidos,-as** in disagreement, on bad terms.
avenir [90] *vt* to reconcile, bring together.
▷ *vpr* **avenirse** 1 *(llevarse bien)* to be on good terms, get on well. 2 *(estar de acuerdo)* to agree (**a**, to), be in agreement (**a**, with).
aventajar *vt* 1 *(exceder)* to surpass, beat: **nadie lo aventaja en amabilidad** *nobody can be kinder than him.* 2 *(ir en cabeza)* to lead, be ahead; *(llegar)* to come first, come ahead (**a**, of).
aventura *nf* 1 adventure. 2 *(riesgo)* hazard, risk. 3 *(relación amorosa)* (love) affair.
aventurado,-a *pp* ⟶ **aventurar.**
▷ *adj* 1 *(arriesgado)* dangerous, risky. 2 *(atrevido)* daring, bold.
aventurar *vt* 1 *(poner en peligro)* to hazard, risk. 2 *(idea, opinión, etc)* to venture, dare, hazard.
▷ *vpr* **aventurarse** to venture, dare.
aventurero,-a *adj* adventurous.
▷ *nm & nf (hombre)* adventurer; *(mujer)* adventuress.
aventurismo *nm* adventurism.
avergonzado,-a *pp* ⟶ **avergonzar.**
▷ *adj* embarrassed, ashamed.
avergonzar [51] *vt (causar vergüenza)* to shame, pu to shame; *(turbar)* to embarrass.
▷ *vpr* **avergonzarse** to be ashamed (**de**, of), be embar rassed (**de**, about).
avería *nf* 1 *(en productos)* damage. 2 TÉC failure. 3 AUTO breakdown.
averiado,-a *pp* ⟶ **averiar.**
▷ *adj* 1 *(en productos)* damaged. 2 TÉC faulty, not working, out of order. 3 AUTO broken down.
averiar [13] *vt* 1 *(productos)* to damage, spoil. 2 TÉC to cause to malfunction. 3 AUTO to cause a break down to.
▷ *vpr* **averiarse** 1 *(productos)* to get damaged. 2 TÉC to malfunction, go wrong. 3 AUTO to break down.
averiguación *nf* inquiry, investigation.
averiguar [22] *vt* to inquire, investigate, find ou about: **averigua quién viene** *find out who's coming.*
aversión *nf* aversion. ■ **sentir aversión por** to loathe
avestruz *nm* ostrich.
▲ *pl* **avestruces.**
aviación *nf* 1 aviation. 2 MIL air force. ● **accidente de aviación** air crash.
aviador,-ra *nm & nf* aviator, flier; *(hombre)* airman *(mujer)* airwoman.
avicultura *nf* aviculture; *(de aves de corral)* poultry keeping, poultry farming.
avidez *nf* avidity, eagerness.
ávido,-a *adj* avid, eager: **el chico estaba ávido de aventuras** *the boy was thirsty for adventure.*
avión *nm* aeroplane (US airplane), plane, aircraft.
avioneta *nf* light plane, light aircraft.
avisar *vt* 1 *(informar)* to inform, notify, announce. 2 *(advertir)* to warn. 3 *(mandar llamar)* to call for.
aviso *nm* 1 *(información)* notice. 2 *(advertencia)* warning. ■ **hasta nuevo aviso** until further notice. ‖ **sin previo aviso** without prior notice.
avispa *nf* wasp.
avispero *nm* 1 *(conjunto de avispas)* swarm of wasps 2 *(nido de avispas)* wasp's nest. 3 *fig (lío)* tight spot mess. 4 MED carbuncle.
avivar *vt* 1 *(fuego)* to stoke (up). 2 *(anhelos, deseos)* to enliven. 3 *(pasiones, dolor)* to intensify. 4 *(paso)* to quicken 5 *(colores, luz)* to brighten up.
▷ *vi* to become brighter, become livelier.
axial *adj* axial.
axila *nf* 1 *(del cuerpo)* armpit, underarm. 2 MED axilla 3 *(de planta)* axil.
axioma *nm* axiom.
ay *interj* 1 *(dolor)* ouch!, ow! 2 *(pena)* alas!: **¡ay de mí** *woe is me!, poor me!* 3 *(temor)* oh!
▷ *nm (quejido)* moan, groan; *(suspiro)* sigh. ■ **¡ay de mi** woe is me!
aya *nf* 1 *arc (ama)* wet nurse. 2 *(niñera)* nanny. 3 *(institutriz)* governess.
ayer *adv* 1 *(el día anterior)* yesterday. 2 *(en el pasado)* in the past, formerly.

nm past. ■ **ayer por la mañana/tarde** yesterday morning/afternoon. ‖ **ayer por la noche** last night.
yo *nm arc* private tutor.
yuda *nf* 1 help, aid, assistance. 2 *(lavativa)* enema. ■ **ir en ayuda de** ALGN to come to sb's assistance. ‖ **prestar ayuda** to help (**a**, -).
yudar *vt* to help, aid, assist: **¿en qué podemos ayudarte?** *how can we help you?*
vpr **ayudarse** *(apoyarse)* to make use (**de/con**, of).
yunar *vi* to fast.
yunas ■ **en ayunas** 1 on an empty stomach: **tómalo en ayunas** *take it on an empty stomach.* 2 *fig* in the dark.
yuno *nm* fast, fasting. ■ **guardar ayuno** to fast.
yuntamiento *nm* 1 *(corporación)* town council, city council. 2 *(edificio)* town hall, city hall. ● **ayuntamiento carnal** *fml* sexual intercourse.
zabache *nm* jet. ■ **negro,-a como el azabache** jet-black.
zada *nf* hoe.
zafata *nf* 1 *(de avión)* air hostess, stewardess. 2 *(de congresos)* hostess.
zafrán *nm* saffron.
zahar *nm (de naranjo)* orange blossom; *(de limonero)* lemon blossom. ● **agua de azahar** orange flower water.
zalea *nf* azalea.
zar *nm* 1 chance. 2 *(percance)* misfortune, accident. ■ **al azar** at random. ‖ **por puro azar** by pure chance.
zorar *vt* to embarrass.
▷ *vpr* **azorarse** to be embarrassed.
azotar *vt* 1 *(con látigo)* to whip, flog. 2 *(golpear)* to beat down on. 3 *(viento, olas)* to lash. 4 *fig (peste, hambre, etc)* to ravage.
azote *nm* 1 *(instrumento)* whip, scourge. 2 *(golpe)* lash, stroke (of the whip). 3 *(manotada)* smack. 4 *(del viento, del agua)* lashing. 5 *fig* scourge.
azotea *nf* flat roof. ■ **estar mal de la azotea** *fam* to have a screw loose.
azteca *adj* Aztec.
▷ *nm o nf* Aztec.
azúcar *nm & nf* sugar. ● **azúcar blanco** refined sugar. ‖ **azúcar moreno/negro** brown sugar.
azucarado,-a *pp* → **azucarar.**
▷ *adj* 1 *(con azúcar)* sugared, sweetened. 2 *(como el azúcar)* sugar-like; *(dulce)* sweet. 3 *fig* sugary.
azucarero,-a *adj* sugar.
▷ *nm* **azucarero** *(vasija)* sugar bowl.
azucarillo *nm* 1 *(terrón)* sugar lump. 2 *(pasta)* lemon candy
azucena *nf* white lily.
azufre *nm* sulphur (US sulfur).
azul *adj* blue.
▷ *nm* blue. ● **azul celeste** sky blue, light blue. ‖ **azul cielo** sky blue, light blue. ‖ **azul eléctrico** electric blue. ‖ **azul marino** navy blue. ‖ **azul turquesa** turquoise. ‖ **sangre azul** blue blood.
azulejo *nm (baldosa)* tile, glazed tile.
azuzar *vt* to egg on. ■ **azuzar los perros a** ALGN to set the dogs on sb.

B

B, b *nf (la letra)* B, b.

baba *nf* **1** *(de animal, adulto)* spittle, saliva; *(de niño)* dribble. **2** *(de caracol, babosa)* slime. ■ **caérsele a uno la baba** *fam* to drool.

babear *vi* **1** *(adulto, animal)* to slobber, slaver; *(niño)* to dribble. **2** *fig* to drool, slobber.

babero *nm* **1** bib. **2** *(babi)* child's overall.

babi *nm* child's overall.

Babia ■ **estar en Babia** to have one's head in the clouds.

babor *nm* port.

babosa *nf* slug.

baboso,-a *adj* **1** *(adulto, animal)* slobbering, slavering; *(niño)* dribbling, dribbly: **ese niño es muy baboso** *that child dribbles a lot.* **2** *fam fig* sloppy.

babucha *nf* slipper.

baca *nf* rack, roof rack, luggage rack.

bacalao *nm* cod. ■ **cortar el bacalao** to be the boss, give the orders, wear the trousers.

bacanal *adj* Bacchanalian.
▷ *nf* orgy.

bache *nm* **1** *(en carretera)* pothole. **2** *(de aire)* air pocket. **3** *fig* bad patch.

bachiller *nm o nf person who has the Spanish certificate of secondary education.*

bachillerato *nm* **1** Spanish certificate of secondary education. **2** Spanish non-compulsory secondary education.

bacilo *nm* bacillus.

bacón *nm* bacon.

bacteria *nf* bacterium.

bacteriano,-a *adj* bacterial.

badén *nm* **1** *(bache)* pothole. **2** *(vado)* ford. **3** *(canal)* channel. **4** *(obstáculo)* speed bump.

bádminton *nm* badminton.

bafle *nm* loudspeaker.

bagaje *nm* baggage. ● **bagaje cultural** experience, background.

bagatela *nf* bagatelle, trifle.

Bahamas *nf pl* **las Bahamas** the Bahamas.

bahía *nf* bay. ● **Gran Bahía Australiana** Great Australian Bight.

bailaor,-ra *nm & nf* flamenco dancer.

bailar [15] *vt* **1** to dance. **2** *(hacer girar)* to spin: **bailó una moneda en la mesa** *she spun a coin on the table.*
▷ *vi* **1** to dance: **¿bailas?** *do you want to dance?, would you like to dance?* **2** *(girar)* to spin: **mira cómo baila la peonza** *look how the top spins.* **3** *(ser grande)* to be too big: **me bailan estos zapatos** *these shoes are too big for me.* **4** *(moverse; cosa)* to wobble; *(persona)* to move about, fidget: **esta silla baila** *this chair wobbles.* **5** *(estar suelto)* to be loose: **este tornillo baila** *this screw is loose.* ■ **ir a bailar** to go dancing. ■ **q… me** *(te, le, etc)* **quiten lo bailado** they can't take t… memories away from me *(you, him, her, etc).*

bailarín,-ina *adj (que baila)* dancing; *(que gusta … bailar)* who likes dancing: **es muy bailarina** *she lov… dancing.*
▷ *nm & nf* dancer.

baile *nm* **1** dance. **2** *(de etiqueta)* ball. **3** *(sala)* dan… hall. ● **baile clásico** ballet. ■ **baile de disfraces** mask… ball, fancy dress ball, US costume ball.

baja *nf* **1** *(descenso)* fall, drop. **2** MIL casualty. **3** *(p… enfermedad)* sick leave; *(justificante)* medical certi… cate, doctor's note.

bajada *nf* **1** *(disminución)* drop, fall: **esto represen… una bajada del 10%** *this represents a drop of 10%.* … *(descenso)* descent; *(de telón, barrera)* lowering. **3** *(c… mino)* way down. **4** *(en carretera, etc)* slope, hill. ● **b… jada de bandera** minimum fare.

bajamar *nf* low tide.

bajar *vt* **1** *(coger algo de un lugar alto)* to get dow… take down. **2** *(dejar más abajo)* to lower: **ese cuad… está muy alto, bájalo un poco** *that picture's too hig… bring it down a bit;* **3** *(reducir)* to lower, reduce, bri… down: **nuestro objetivo es bajar la inflación** *our a… is to reduce inflation.* **4** *(reducir en intensidad)* to lowe… *(voz)* to lower; *(sonido, luz, gas)* to turn down. … *(alargar)* to lengthen, let down: **la modista me ba… un poco la falda** *the dressmaker let my skirt down… bit.* **6** *(recorrer de arriba abajo)* to go down, co… down: **bajamos la escalera** *we went down the stairs.* … *(en informática)* to download.
▷ *vi* **1** *(ir abajo - acercándose)* to come down; *(- alejá… dose)* to go down: **bajó corriendo/volando** *he ra… flew down.* **2** *(reducirse)* to fall, drop, come dow… **ha bajado la temperatura** *the temperature h… dropped.* **3** *(hinchazón)* to go down; *(fiebre)* to … down, come down. **4** *(marea)* to go out. **5** *(apear … - de coche)* to get out (**de**, of); *(de bicicleta, caballo)* to g… off (**de**, -); *(de avión, tren, autobús)* to get off (**de**, -).
▷ *vpr* **bajarse 1** *(ir abajo - acercándose)* to come dow… *(- alejándose)* to go down. **2** *(apearse - de coche)* … get out (**de**, -); *(bicicleta, caballo)* to get off (**de**, … *(avión, tren, autobús)* to get off (**de**, -). **3** *(agachars…* to bend down, bend over.

bajeza *nf* **1** *(acción)* base action, despicable act, vi… deed. **2** *fig* baseness: **bajeza moral** *moral baseness.*

bajo,-a *adj* **1** *(gen)* low: **precios bajos** *low prices.* … *(persona)* short, not tall. **3** *(cabeza)* bowed, he… low; *(ojos)* lowered, downcast. **4** *(marea)* out: … **marea está baja** *the tide is out.* **5** *(despreciable)* desp… cable, contemptible, base. **6** *(territorio, río)* lower. … *(época)* later: **la Baja Edad Media** *the late Middle A…*

es. 8 *(inferior)* poor, low: **es de baja calidad** *it's poor quality.*

ajo *nm* 1 *(piso)* ground floor, US first floor. 2 *(de prenda)* bottoms *pl*, US cuff. 3 MÚS *(instrumento)* bass; *(contrabajo)* double bass.
nm o nf MÚS *(músico)* bass player; *(cantante)* bass.
adv 1 *(en el aire)* low. 2 *(voz)* softly, quietly, in a low voice: **habla muy bajo** *she speaks very quietly.*
prep 1 under. 2 *(temperatura)* below: **10 grados bajo cero** *10 degrees below zero.*
nm pl **bajos** *(planta baja)* ground floor; *(sótano)* basement. ● **bajos fondos** underworld *sing.*

ajón *nm* 1 sharp fall, sharp drop, slump: **la bolsa ha dado un considerable bajón** *there has been a sharp fall in share prices.* 2 *(de ánimos)* depression. 3 *(de salud)* relapse: **tuvo un bajón** *he suffered a relapse.* 4 MÚS bassoon.

ajorrelieve *nm* bas-relief.

ajura ■ **de bajura** inshore.

ala *nf* 1 bullet. 2 *(paquete)* bale.

alada *nf* ballad.

alance *nm* 1 *(movimiento)* rocking. 2 COM *(operación)* balance; *(hoja)* balance sheet. 3 *(cálculo)* total. 4 *(resultado)* outcome, result: **el balance de la reunión ha sido positivo** *on balance, the meeting was successful.* 5 *(equilibrio)* balance. ■ **hacer un balance de** to take stock of, weigh up, evaluate.

alancear *vt (mecer)* to rock; *(columpio)* to swing.
vi (mecer) to rock; *(columpio, brazo)* to swing.
vpr **balancearse** *(mecerse)* to rock; *(columpio, brazo)* to swing.

alanceo *nm (gen)* swinging; *(suave)* rocking.

alancín *nm* 1 *(mecedora)* rocking chair. 2 *(columpio)* seesaw. 3 *(de motor)* rocker arm. 4 *(de volatinero)* balance pole.

alanza *nf* 1 *(aparato)* scales *pl.* 2 COM balance. ● **balanza comercial** trade balance, balance of trade.

alar *vi* to bleat, baa.

alaustrada *nf* balustrade; *(en escalera)* banister.

albucear *vi* to babble.
vt to babble: **balbuceó una excusa tonta** *he babbled some stupid excuse.*

albuceo *nm* babbling.

albucir *vi* → **balbucear.**

alcanes *nm pl* **los Balcanes** the Balkans.

alcón *nm* 1 *(en edificio)* balcony. 2 *(mirador)* vantage point: **desde su balcón en lo alto del peñasco...** *from his vantage point at the top of the rocky crag...*

alde *nm* bucket, pail. ■ **de balde** free, for nothing. ‖ **en balde** in vain.

aldío,-a *adj* 1 *(tierra - sin cultivar)* uncultivated; *(- estéril)* barren. 2 *(vano)* vain, useless.
nm **baldío** wasteland.

aldón *nm* 1 *(insulto)* insult, affront, slur. 2 *(deshonra)* disgrace.

aldosa *nf* floor tile.

aldosín *nm* tile, wall tile.

alear *adj* Balearic.
nm o nf Balearic islander. ● **Islas Baleares** Balearic Islands.

alido *nm* bleat, baa.

alín *nm* pellet.

balístico,-a *adj* ballistic.

baliza *nf* 1 *(de mar)* buoy. 2 *(de tierra)* beacon.

ballena *nf* 1 *(animal)* whale. 2 *(material)* whalebone; *(tira de corsé)* stay.

ballenero,-a *adj* whaling.
▷ *nm & nf (persona)* whaler.
▷ *nm* **ballenero** *(barco)* whaling ship, whaler, whaleboat.

ballesta *nf* 1 *(arma)* crossbow. 2 AUTO spring.

ballet *nm* ballet.
▲ *pl* **ballets.**

balneario,-a *adj* spa.
▷ *nm* **balneario** spa, health resort.

balompié *nm* football, soccer, US soccer.

balón *nm* 1 DEP ball; *(de fútbol)* ball, football; *(de voleibol)* ball, volleyball; *(de rugby)* ball, rugby ball; *(de baloncesto)* ball, basketball. 2 *(para gas)* cylinder.

baloncesto *nm* basketball.

balonmano *nm* handball.

balonvolea *nm* volleyball.

balsa *nf* 1 pool. 2 MAR raft. ■ **como una balsa de aceite** 1 *(mar)* like a millpond. 2 *fig* very peaceful.

bálsamo *nm* 1 balsam, balm. 2 *fig* comfort.

báltico,-a *adj* Baltic. ● **el (mar) Báltico** the Baltic (Sea).

baluarte *nm* 1 *(fortificación)* bastion. 2 *fig* bastion, stronghold.

bambalina *nf* drop cloth, drop. ■ **entre bambalinas** in the wings.

bambolear *vi* to sway.
▷ *vpr* **bambolearse** to sway.

bamboleo *nm* swaying.

bambolla *nf* pretence (US pretense).

bambú *nm* bamboo.
▲ *pl* **bambúes o bambús.**

banal *adj* trivial.

banana *nf* banana.

banca *nf* 1 COM banking; *(bancos)* (the) banks *pl.* 2 *(asiento)* bench. 3 *(en juego)* bank.

bancada *nf* 1 *(banco)* long bench. 2 *(superficie)* work surface.

bancal *nm* 1 *(en pendiente)* terrace. 2 *(en llano)* plot.

bancario,-a *adj (de un banco)* bank; *(de los bancos)* banking.

bancarrota *nf* bankruptcy. ■ **estar en bancarrota** to be bankrupt.

banco *nm* 1 bank. 2 *(asiento)* bench; *(de iglesia)* pew. 3 *(mesa)* bench, work bench. 4 *(de peces)* shoal. ● **banco de datos** data bank. ‖ **banco de niebla** fog bank.

banda[1] *nf* 1 *(faja)* sash. 2 *(lista)* band. 3 *(tira)* strip. 4 *(lado)* side. 5 *(en billar)* cushion. ● **banda magnética** magnetic strip. ‖ **banda sonora** sound track.

banda[2] *nf* 1 *(músicos)* band. 2 *(maleantes)* gang. 3 *(pájaros)* flock.

bandada *nf* 1 *(de pájaros)* flock; *(de insectos)* swarm; *(de peces)* shoal. 2 *(de personas)* horde.

bandear *vi* to move from side to side.

bandeja *nf (gen)* tray. ■ **poner** ALGO **a** ALGN **en bandeja** *fig* to hand STH to SB on a plate.

bandera *nf* flag. ■ **arriar la bandera** to strike one's colours (US colors), surrender. ● **bandera blanca** white flag. ‖ **bandera nacional** national flag.

banderilla *nf* 1 *(tauromaquia)* banderilla *(barbed dart stuck into the bull's back)*. 2 *(tapa) pickled onion, carrot, gherkin, pepper, etc on a cocktail stick*.
banderín *nm* pennant. ● **banderín de córner** corner flag.
bandido,-a *nm & nf* bandit.
bando *nm* 1 *(facción)* faction, party, camp. 2 *(de aves)* flock; *(de insectos)* swarm; *(de peces)* shoal. 3 *(edicto)* edict, proclamation.
bandolera *nf* bandolier. ■ **en bandolera** slung crossways over the shoulder.
bandolero *nm* bandit.
bandurria *nf* bandurria, *(small guitar-like instrument with six pairs of strings)*.
banjo *nm* banjo.
banquero,-a *nm & nf* banker.
banqueta *nf* 1 *(taburete)* stool; *(para los pies)* footstool. 2 *(banco) little* bench.
banquete *nm* banquet, feast. ● **banquete de bodas** wedding reception. ‖ **banquete de gala** gala reception. ‖ **banquete nupcial** wedding breakfast.
banquillo *nm* 1 *(en tribunal)* dock: **el procesado se sentó en el banquillo de los acusados** *the accused sat in the dock*. 2 *(en deporte)* bench.
bañador *nm (gen)* swimsuit; *(de mujer)* swimming costume, bathing costume; *(de hombre)* swimming trunks *pl*.
bañar *vt* 1 *(gen)* to bathe: **la cálida luz del sol bañaba toda la estancia** *warm sunlight bathed the whole room*. 2 *(lavar)* to bath: **me baño cada mañana** *I have a bath every morning*. 3 *(cubrir)* to coat; *(en oro, etc)* to plate: **bañó los pasteles en chocolate** *she coated the cakes in chocolate*.
▷ *vpr* **bañarse** to bathe; *(nadar)* to have a swim, go for a swim: **se bañaban desnudos** *they were bathing naked*.
bañera *nf* bath, bathtub.
bañista *nm o nf* bather, swimmer.
baño *nm* 1 *(gen)* bath; *(en piscina, mar)* dip, swim: **me voy a dar un baño caliente** *I'm going to have a hot bath*. 2 *(cuarto)* bathroom; *(servicio)* toilet. 3 *(bañera)* bath, bathtub. 4 *(capa)* coat, coating; *(de oro, etc)* plating. ● **baño de vapor** steam bath. ‖ **baño María** bain-marie. ‖ **baño turco** Turkish bath.
▷ *nm pl* **baños** *(balneario)* spa *sing*.
baqueta *nf* 1 *(de arma)* ramrod. 2 *(de tambor)* drumstick.
bar *nm* 1 *(cafetería)* café, snack bar; *(de bebidas alcohólicas)* bar. 2 FÍS bar.
▲ *pl* **bares**.
barahúnda *nf (ruido)* racket, din; *(caos)* chaos, pandemonium.
baraja *nf* 1 *(naipes)* pack, deck. 2 *(gama)* range.
barajar *vt* 1 *(naipes)* to shuffle. 2 *fig (considerar - posibilidades, etc)* to consider; *(- cifra)* to talk about. 3 *(problema)* to solve; *(obstáculo)* to overcome.
baranda *nf* handrail, banister.
barandilla *nf* handrail, banister.
baratija *nf* trinket, knick-knack.
baratillo *nm* 1 *(tienda)* junk shop; *(mercado)* flea market. 2 *(baratijas)* junk.
barato,-a *adj* cheap.
▷ *adv* **barato** cheaply, cheap.

barba *nf* 1 ANAT chin. 2 *(pelo)* beard. ■ **dejarse bar** to grow a beard. ‖ **por barba** per head, a head, eac
barbacoa *nf* barbecue.
barbaridad *nf* 1 *(crueldad - cualidad)* cruelty; *(- ac* atrocity, act of cruelty. 2 *(disparate)* piece of no sense. 3 **una barbaridad** *fam (mogollón)* loads tons *pl*: **pesa una barbaridad** *it weighs a ton*. ■ **¡q barbaridad!** how awful!, how terrible!
barbarismo *nm* barbarism.
bárbaro,-a *adj* 1 HIST barbarian. 2 *(cruel)* barbar savage, cruel. 3 *(temerario)* daring. 4 *fam (grana* enormous, tremendous. 5 *fam (espléndido)* fanta tic, terrific.
▷ *nm & nf* HIST barbarian.
▷ *adv* **bárbaro**: **lo pasamos bárbaro** *we had a great tim*
barbecho *nm* fallow land.
barbería *nf* barber's shop, barber's.
barbero *nm* barber.
barbilampiño,-a *adj* beardless.
barbilla *nf* chin.
barbo *nm* barbel.
barbotar *vt* to splutter.
barca *nf* boat, small boat. ■ **en la misma barca** in t same boat.
barcaza *nf* lighter.
barco *nm (gen)* boat; *(grande)* ship. ● **barco cister** tanker. ‖ **barco de guerra** warship. ‖ **barco de pasajer** passenger ship. ‖ **barco de pesca** fishing boa ‖ **barco de vapor** steamer. ‖ **barco de vela** sailing boa
bardana *nf* burdock.
bardo *nm* bard.
baremo *nm* 1 *(para calcular)* ready reckoner. 2 *(ta fas)* scale, table.
baricentro *nm* barycentre (US barycenter).
bario *nm* barium.
barítono *nm* baritone.
barlovento *nm* windward.
barman *nm* barman, US bartender.
▲ *pl* **bármanes**.
barniz *nm* 1 *(para madera)* varnish; *(para cerámic* glaze. 2 *(noción)* smattering, general idea.
▲ *pl* **barnices**.
barnizar [4] *vt (madera)* to varnish; *(cerámica)* glaze.
barómetro *nm* barometer.
barón *nm* baron.
baronesa *nf* baroness.
barquero,-a *nm & nf (hombre)* boatman; *(muje* boatwoman.
barquillo *nm (gen)* wafer; *(cucurucho)* cornet.
barra *nf* 1 *(en bar, cafetería)* bar. 2 *(vara)* bar; *(pa cortinas)* rod; *(de bicicleta)* crossbar. 3 *(de helad* block. 4 *(de pan)* loaf. 5 *(en tribunal)* bar, rail. 6 *(si no de puntuación)* slash, solidus. 7 *(de arena)* sar bar. ● **barra de labios** lipstick. ‖ **barra libre** free bar.
barrabasada *nf* dirty trick.
barraca *nf* 1 *(casita)* cottage *(typical in Valencia a Murcia)*. 2 *(puesto)* stall; *(caseta de feria)* booth. *(chabola)* shack.
barracón *nm* hut, large hut.
barranco *nm* 1 *(precipicio)* precipice. 2 *(torrenter* gully; *(más profunda)* ravine.

arranquismo *nm* canyoning.
arraquismo *nm* slums *pl.*
arrena *nf (gen)* drill; *(manual)* gimlet. ■ **entrar en barrena** to go into a spin.
arrenar *vt* 1 to drill. 2 *(desbaratar)* to foil, thwart.
arrendero,-a *nm & nf* road sweeper.
arreno *nm* 1 *(barrena)* large drill. 2 *(agujero)* drill hole, bore hole; *(para carga)* blast hole.
arreño *nm* large bowl.
arrer *vt* 1 *(suelo)* to sweep; *(hojas, migas, etc)* to sweep up. 2 *(dejar sin nada)* to clean out: **entraron ladrones y les barrieron la casa** *burglars broke in and cleaned them out.* 3 *(limpiar)* to sweep away: **el viento barrió las nubes del cielo** *the wind swept the clouds from the sky.* 4 *(derrotar)* to trounce, wipe the floor with.
▷ *vi (arrasar)* to sweep the board.
arrera *nf* 1 *(gen)* barrier. 2 *(en plaza de toros - valla)* barrier; *(asientos)* front row. 3 *fig* obstacle.
arricada *nf* barricade. ■ **levantar barricadas** to erect barricades.
arriga *nf* belly, stomach, tummy.
arril *nm* barrel, keg. ■ **de barril** draught.
arrio *nm* neighbourhood (US neighborhood); *(zona)* district, area.
arriobajero,-a *adj* common, vulgar, low.
▷ *nm & nf* common person.
arrizal *nm* quagmire.
arro *nm* 1 *(lodo)* mud. 2 *(arcilla)* clay: **objetos de barro** *earthenware sing.* 3 *(objeto)* earthenware object. ■ **de barro** earthenware.
arroco,-a *adj* 1 ARTE baroque. 2 *fig* ornate.
▷ *nm* **barroco** baroque.
arrote *nm* 1 bar. 2 *(de escalera, silla)* rung.
ártulos *nm pl* things, stuff *sing.* ■ **liar los bártulos** to pack up, pack one's bags.
arullo *nm* noise, din, racket.
asar *vt* to base (**en**, on).
▷ *vpr* **basarse** *(cosa)* to be based (**en**, on); *(persona)* to base oneself on.
asca *nf* 1 nausea. 2 *fam (pandilla)* crowd.
áscula *nf* 1 *(gen)* scales *pl*; *(de farmacia)* weighing machine. 2 *(para vehículos)* weighbridge.
ascular *vi* 1 to tilt. 2 *(oscilar)* to swing. 3 *(variar)* to swing, alternate.
ase *nf* 1 *(gen)* base. 2 *fig* basis. 3 QUÍM base, alkali. 4 MAT base. 5 *(en béisbol)* base. ■ **a base de** 1 *(por)* through, by means of, using. 2 *(de)* consisting of. ‖ **a base de bien** *fam* really well. ‖ **en base a** based on, on the basis of. ● **base de datos** database.
▷ *nf pl* **bases** 1 *(de concurso)* rules. 2 **las bases** *(de partido, etc)* grass roots, rank and file.
ásico,-a *adj* 1 *(gen)* basic. 2 *(imprescindible)* essential, indispensable.
asílica *nf* basilica.
asta¹ *nf* tacking stitch.
asta² *interj* enough!, stop it! ■ **¡basta de...!** that's enough...!, no more...!
astante *adj* 1 enough, sufficient. 2 *(abundante)* quite a lot of: **había bastante gente** *there were quite a lot of people.*
▷ *adv* 1 enough: **son lo bastante ricos como para poder permitírselo** *they're rich enough to be able to afford it.* 2 *(un poco)* fairly, quite: **es bastante alto** *it's fairly high.* 3 *(tiempo)* some time, quite a while.
bastar *vi* to be enough, be sufficient, suffice: **mi sueldo no basta para pagar el alquiler** *my salary is not enough to pay the rent.* ■ **bastar con** to be enough: **es muy concentrado, basta con una gota** *it's highly concentrated, one drop is enough.* ‖ **bastarse a sí mismo** to be self-sufficient.
bastardillo,-a *adj* italic. ■ **en bastardilla** in italics. ● **letra bastardilla** italic type.
bastardo,-a *adj* 1 illegitimate, bastard. 2 *(despreciable)* base, mean.
▷ *nm & nf* bastard.
bastidor *nm* 1 frame. 2 *(de lienzo)* stretcher. 3 *(de coche)* chassis. 4 TEAT wing. ■ **entre bastidores** 1 in the wings. 2 *fig* behind the scenes.
basto¹ *nm* ≈ club.
▷ *nm pl* **bastos** ≈ clubs: **el as de bastos** ≈ *the ace of clubs.* ■ **pintan bastos** things are getting tough.
basto,-a² *adj* 1 *(grosero)* coarse, rough. 2 *(sin pulimentar)* rough, unpolished.
bastón *nm* 1 stick, walking stick, US cane. 2 *(de esquí)* stick, ski stick. 3 *(insignia)* baton.
basura *nf* 1 *(cosa)* rubbish, US garbage. 2 *(persona despreciable)* swine. ■ **bajar la basura / sacar la basura** to put the rubbish out.
basurero *nm* 1 *(persona)* dustman, US garbage man. 2 *(lugar)* tip, rubbish dump.
bata *nf* 1 *(prenda ligera)* housecoat; *(albornoz)* dressing gown, US robe. 2 *(de trabajo)* overall; *(de médicos, etc)* white coat.
batacazo *nm (golpe)* thump, bump, bang, crash; *(caída)* heavy fall.
batalla *nf* battle. ■ **de batalla** *fam* ordinary, everyday: **zapatos de batalla** *everyday shoes.*
batallador,-ra *adj* fighting: **es muy batalladora** *she's a real fighter.*
▷ *nm & nf* fighter.
batallar *vi* to battle, fight.
batallón *nm* 1 MIL battalion. 2 *(multitud)* horde.
batata *nf* BOT sweet potato.
bate *nm* bat.
batear *vi* to bat.
▷ *vt* to hit.
batel *nm* skiff.
batería *nf* 1 *(eléctrica)* battery. 2 MIL battery. 3 TEAT footlights *pl.* 4 *(conjunto de cosas)* set; *(de preguntas)* barrage. 5 MÚS drums *pl.*
▷ *nm o nf* drummer. ■ **recargar las baterías** to recharge one's batteries. ● **batería de cocina** pots and pans *pl.*
batido,-a *pp* → **batir**.
▷ *adj* 1 *(camino)* well-worn, well-trodden, beaten. 2 *(seda)* shot.
▷ *nm* **batido** 1 CULIN beaten eggs. 2 *(bebida)* milk shake.
batidor,-ra *nm & nf (de caza)* beater.
▷ *nm* **batidor** CULIN *(manual)* whisk.
batidora *nf* blender, mixer.
batín *nm* short dressing gown.
batir *vt* 1 *(huevos)* to beat; *(nata, claras)* to whip. 2 *(palmas)* to clap. 3 *(metales)* to beat. 4 *(alas)* to flap,

beat. **5** *(derribar)* to knock down. **6** *(vencer)* to beat, defeat. **7** DEP *(marca, récord)* to break. **8** *(explorar)* to reconnoitre; *(registrar)* to comb, search. **9** *(cazador)* to beat.

▷ *vpr* **batirse** to fight.

batracio,-a *adj* batrachian.

▷ *nm* **batracio** batrachian.

batuta *nf* baton. ■ **llevar la batuta** to be the boss.

baúl *nm (cofre)* chest; *(de viaje)* trunk.

baudio *nm* baud.

bautismo *nm* **1** *(de niño)* baptism, christening. **2** *(de barco)* naming.

bautista *nm o nf* Baptist.

bautizar [4] *vt* **1** to baptize, christen. **2** *(poner nombre a)* to name. **3** *(el vino)* to water down.

bautizo *nm (de niño)* baptism, christening; *(de barco)* naming.

bauxita *nf* bauxite.

baya *nf* berry.

bayeta *nf* **1** baize. **2** *(paño)* cloth.

bayo,-a *adj* bay, whitish yellow.

▷ *nm* **bayo** *(caballo)* bay.

bayoneta *nf* bayonet. ■ **calar las bayonetas** to fix bayonets.

baza *nf* **1** *(naipes)* trick. **2** *(ventaja)* asset, advantage. **3** *(ocasión)* chance. ■ **meter baza** *fig* to butt in, stick one's oar in. ‖ **no poder meter baza** not to be able to get a word in edgeways.

bazar *nm* **1** *(oriental)* bazaar. **2** *(tienda)* electrical goods and hardware shop.

bazo *nm* spleen.

bazofia *nf* **1** *(restos de comida)* scraps *pl*, leftovers *pl*. **2** *(comida mala)* pigswill. **3** *(basura)* rubbish: **¡vaya bazofia de película!** *what a rubbishy film!*

bazuca *nm & nf* bazooka.

beatificar [1] *vt* to beatify.

beato,-a *adj* **1** *(beatificado)* blessed. **2** *(devoto)* devout. **3** *pey* sanctimonious. **4** *(feliz)* happy.

▷ *nm & nf (persona beatificada)* beatified person.

bebé *nm* baby. ● **bebé probeta** test-tube baby.

bebedero,-a *adj* drinkable: **agua bebedera** *drinking water.*

▷ *nm* **bebedero 1** *(abrevadero)* water trough. **2** *(pico de vasija)* spout. **3** *(vasija)* drinking dish.

bebedor,-ra *adj* hard-drinking.

▷ *nm & nf* hard drinker.

beber *vt* to drink.

▷ *vi* **1** to drink. **2** *(emborracharse)* to drink, drink heavily: **bebe mucho** *he's a heavy drinker.*

bebida *nf* drink, beverage.

bebido,-a *pp* → **beber.**

▷ *adj* merry, tipsy.

beca *nf (gen)* grant; *(concedida por méritos)* scholarship, award.

becar [1] *vt (gen)* to award a grant to; *(por méritos)* to award a scholarship to.

becario,-a *nm & nf* grant holder, scholarship holder.

becerro,-a *nm & nf* calf *(up to one year old)*.

▷ *nm* **becerro 1** *(en tauromaquia)* young bull *(up to four years old)*. **2** *(piel)* calfskin.

bechamel *nf* bechamel sauce, white sauce.

becuadro *nm* natural, natural sign.

bedel,-la *nm & nf* porter.

beduino,-a *adj* Bedouin.

▷ *nm & nf* Bedouin.

befa *nf* jeer, taunt.

begonia *nf* begonia.

beicon *nm* bacon.

beige *adj* beige.

▷ *nm* beige.

béisbol *nm* baseball.

belén *nm* **1** REL nativity scene, crib. **2** *fig* mess.

belfo,-a *adj* thick-lipped.

▷ *nm* **belfo** thick lip.

belga *adj* Belgian.

▷ *nm & nf* Belgian.

Bélgica *nf* Belgium.

Belgrado *nm* Belgrade.

Belice *nm* Belize.

bélico,-a *adj* military. ● **conflicto bélico** armed con- flict, war. ‖ **material bélico** military equipment.

beligerante *adj* belligerent: **las parte beligerante** *the warring parties.*

▷ *nm o nf* belligerent person.

bellaco,-a *adj* **1** *(malo)* wicked. **2** *(astuto)* cunning, sly

▷ *nm & nf* villain, rogue.

belleza *nf* beauty.

bello,-a *adj* **1** beautiful. **2** *(bueno)* fine, noble.

bellota *nf* acorn.

bemol *adj* MÚS flat.

▷ *nm* MÚS flat.

▷ *nm pl* **bemoles** *argot* guts. ■ **tener bemoles 1** *argot (se difícil)* to be tough, be tricky. **2** *(ser demasiado)* to b too much, be rich.

benceno *nm* benzene.

bencina *nf* benzine.

bendecir [79] *vt* **1** to bless. **2** *(alabar)* to praise.

bendición *nf* blessing.

▷ *nf pl* **bendiciones** wedding ceremony *sing.*

bendito,-a *adj* **1** *(bienaventurado)* blessed. **2** *iró (maldito)* damned, blessed. **3** *(feliz)* happy: **¡bendit la hora en que la conocí!** *happy the hour I met her!* *(poco inteligente)* simple.

▷ *nm & nf* simple soul.

benefactor,-ra *adj* beneficent.

▷ *nm & nf (hombre)* benefactor; *(mujer)* benefactress.

beneficencia *nf* beneficence, charity.

beneficiar [12] *vt* **1** to benefit, favour (US favor). *(mina)* to work. **3** COM to sell below par.

▷ *vpr* **beneficiarse 1** to benefit. **2** COM to profit. ■ **beneficiarse de** ALGO to do well out of STH, benefi from STH.

beneficiario,-a *nm & nf* beneficiary.

beneficio *nm* **1** *(ganancia)* profit. **2** *(bien)* benefit. ■ **e beneficio de** for the good of, for the benefit of, i the interest of: **la derecha ha perdido escaños en beneficio de la izquierda** *the right has lost seats to th left.* ‖ **a beneficio de** in aid of. ‖ **sacar beneficio de** t profit from.

beneficioso,-a *adj* beneficial.

benéfico,-a *adj* charitable. ● **causa benéfica** charitable cause. ‖ **función benéfica** charity performance.

beneplácito *nm* approval: **contamos con el beneplácito del ministro** *we have the minister's approval.*

benevolencia *nf* 1 benevolence, kindness. 2 *(comprensión)* understanding.
benevolente *adj* → **benévolo.**
benévolo,-a *adj* 1 benevolent, kind. 2 *(comprensivo)* understanding.
bengala *nf* 1 *(de aviso, etc)* flare. 2 *(para fiestas, etc)* sparkler.
benigno,-a *adj* 1 *(persona)* benign, gentle. 2 *(tumor)* benign. 3 *(clima)* mild.
benjamín,-ina *nm & nf* 1 *(en familia - gen)* youngest child; *(hijo)* youngest son; *(hija)* youngest daughter. 2 *(en grupo)* youngest person. 3 DEP *competitor of the youngest age group (9 or 10 years old).*
▷ *adj* DEP *of the youngest age group (9 or 10 years old).*
berberecho *nm* cockle, common cockle.
berenjena *nf* aubergine, US eggplant.
berilio *nm* beryllium.
berilo *nm* beryl.
Berlín *nm* Berlin.
bermejo,-a *adj* reddish.
bermellón *nm* vermilion.
bermudas *nm pl* Bermudas, Bermuda shorts.
Berna *nf* Bern, Berne.
berrear *vi* 1 *(becerro)* to bellow. 2 *(persona)* to bawl; *(niño)* to howl, bawl.
berrido *nm* 1 *(de becerro)* bellow. 2 *(de persona)* howl.
berrinche *nm* rage, tantrum, anger. ■ **coger un berrinche** to throw a tantrum.
berro *nm* watercress.
berza *nf* cabbage.
▷ *nm o nf* **berzas** idiot, moron.
besamel *adj* bechamel.
▷ *nf* bechamel, bechamel sauce, white sauce. ● **salsa besamel** white sauce, bechamel sauce.
besar *vt* to kiss.
▷ *vpr* **besarse** 1 *(uso recíproco)* to kiss. 2 *fam (chocar)* to collide.
beso *nm* 1 kiss. 2 *fam (choque)* bump.
bestia *nf (animal)* beast.
▷ *nm o nf (persona - bruto)* brute; *(- ignorante)* ignorant fool; *(- torpe)* clumsy oaf.
▷ *adj* 1 *(bruto)* brutish. 2 *(ignorante)* ignorant; *(grosero)* rude; *(torpe)* clumsy. 3 *(asombroso)* fantastic, amazing. ■ **a lo bestia** 1 *(fuerte)* hard. 2 *(a lo loco)* like a madman. 3 *(rápido)* like mad. 4 *(en cantidad)* in enormous amounts.
bestial *adj* 1 *(brutal)* beastly, bestial. 2 *fam (enorme)* enormous. 3 *fam (extraordinario)* great, fantastic.
bestialidad *nf* 1 bestiality, brutality. 2 *(tontería)* stupidity. 3 *fam (gran cantidad)* tons *pl*, loads *pl*, stacks *pl*: **una bestialidad de comida** *tons of food.*
bestiario *nm* bestiary.
best-seller *nm* best-seller.
besucón,-ona *adj* fond of kissing: **es muy besucón** *he's always kissing you.*
▷ *nm & nf* person who's always kissing.
besugo *nm* 1 *(pez)* sea bream. 2 *(persona)* idiot.
besuquear *vt* to kiss again and again.
▷ *vpr* **besuquearse** *(uso recíproco)* to smooch, neck.
betún *nm* 1 *(para zapatos)* shoe polish. 2 QUÍM bitumen.
bianual *adj* biannual.
biberón *nm* baby's bottle, feeding bottle.
Biblia *nf* Bible.
bibliografía *nf* bibliography.
biblioteca *nf* 1 library. 2 *(mueble)* bookcase, bookshelf.
bibliotecario,-a *nm & nf* librarian.
bicameralismo *nm* bicameralism.
bicarbonato *nm* bicarbonate.
bicentenario,-a *adj* two-hundred-year-old.
▷ *nm* **bicentenario** bicentenary, US bicentennial.
bíceps *nm inv* biceps.
bicho *nm* 1 *(animal)* animal, creature; *(insecto)* bug, creepy-crawly. 2 *(persona)* odd character; *(niño)* little devil, little monkey. ● **bicho raro** oddball, weirdo.
bici *nf fam* bike.
bicicleta *nf* bicycle. ● **bicicleta de carreras** racing bike. ‖ **bicicleta de montaña** mountain bike.
bicolor *adj* two-coloured (US two-colored).
bidé *nm* bidet.
bidimensional *adj* two-dimensional.
bidón *nm (normal)* drum; *(pequeño)* can.
biela *nf* AUTO connecting rod.
bien *adv* 1 *(gen)* well: **canta bien** *she sings well.* 2 *(como es debido)* properly, right: **si no pronuncias bien, no te van a entender** *if you don't pronounce the words properly, they won't understand you.* 3 *(acertadamente)* right, correctly: **contestó bien a todas las preguntas** *she answered all the questions correctly.* 4 *(con éxito)* successfully. 5 *(de acuerdo)* O.K., all right: **–ven mañana a las dos, –bien** *–come tomorrow at two, –all right.* 6 *(de buena gana)* willingly, gladly: **bien me iría contigo si no tuviera que trabajar** *I'd gladly go with you if I didn't have to work.* 7 *(mucho)* very: **es bien sencillo** *it's really simple.* 8 *(fácilmente)* easily: **bien podrías haberme avisado** *you might have warned me.* 9 *(de gusto, olor, aspecto, etc)* good, nice, lovely: **esta cerveza está muy bien** *this beer's very good.* 10 *(de salud)* well: **¿te encuentras bien?** *are you feeling all right?* 11 *(físicamente)* good-looking: **su novio está muy bien** *her boyfriend's very good-looking.*
▷ *adj (acomodado)* well-off.
▷ *nm* 1 good: **el bien siempre triunfa sobre el mal** *good always triumphs over evil.* 2 *(bienestar)* benefit: **lo hice por el bien de todos** *I did it for the good of everyone.* ● **bien de consumo** consumer item. ‖ **bien de equipo** capital asset.
▷ *nm pl* **bienes** property *sing*, possessions. ● **bienes de consumo** consumer goods. ‖ **bienes de equipo** capital goods, capital assets. ‖ **bienes inmuebles** real estate *sing*. ‖ **bienes muebles** movables, personal property *sing*. ‖ **gente bien** *fam* the upper classes *pl*.
▷ *conj* **bien... bien** either... or: **se lo enviaremos bien por correo, bien por mensajero** *we'll send it to you either by post or by messenger.* ■ **en bien de** for the sake of. ‖ **estarle bien ALGO a ALGN** to serve SB right: **lo han despedido y le está bien** *he's got the sack and it serves him right;* **le está bien lo que le ha pasado** *he deserves what happened to him.* ‖ **hacer bien** to do good. ‖ **bien que** although. ‖ **tener a bien de hacer** ALGO to be good enough to do STH. ‖ **¡ya está bien!** that's enough!
bienal *adj* biennial.
▷ *nf* biennial exhibition, biennial festival.

bienestar *nm* wellbeing, welfare: **bienestar social** *social welfare.*
bienhechor,-ra *adj* beneficent, beneficial.
▷ *nm & nf (hombre)* benefactor; *(mujer)* benefactress.
bienio *nm* **1** *(periodo)* two-year period, biennium. **2** *(aumento)* two-yearly increment.
bienvenido,-a *adj* welcome: **tus consejos serán bienvenidos** *your advice will be welcome.*
bies *nm* bias binding. ■ **al bies** on the bias.
bífido,-a *adj* forked.
bifocal *adj* bifocal. ● **gafas bifocales** bifocals.
bifurcación *nf* **1** bifurcation. **2** *(de la carretera)* fork; *(de ferrocarril)* junction.
bifurcarse [1] *vpr* to fork, branch off.
bigamia *nf* bigamy.
bígamo,-a *adj* bigamous.
▷ *nm & nf* bigamist.
bigote *nm* **1** moustache (US mustache). **2** *(de gato)* whiskers *pl.*
bigotudo,-a *adj* mustachioed.
bikini® *nm* → **biquini.**
bilabial *adj* bilabial.
▷ *nf* bilabial.
bilateral *adj* bilateral.
biliar *adj* biliary, bile.
bilingüe *adj* bilingual.
bilingüismo *nm* bilingualism.
bilis *nf inv* **1** bile. **2** *fig* spleen.
billar *nm* **1** billiards. **2** *(mesa)* billiard table. ● **billar americano** pool.
▷ *nm pl* **billares** billiard room.
billete *nm* **1** *(moneda)* note, US bill: **un billete de cincuenta euros** *a fifty-euro note.* **2** *(de transporte, sorteo, teatro, etc)* ticket. ● **billete de ida y vuelta** return ticket, US round-trip ticket.
billetera *nf* wallet, US billfold.
billetero *nm* purse, US change purse.
billón *nm* trillion.

Spanish usage coincides with former British usage: a **billón** is a million million.

binario,-a *adj* binary.
bingo *nm* **1** *(juego)* bingo. **2** *(sala)* bingo hall. ■ **¡bingo!** bingo!
binóculo *nm* pince-nez.
binomio *nm* binomial.
biodegradable *adj* biodegradable.
biografía *nf* biography.
biográfico,-a *adj* biographical.
biógrafo,-a *nm & nf* biographer.
biología *nf* biology.
biológico,-a *adj* biological.
biólogo,-a *nm & nf* biologist.
biomasa *nf* biomass.
biombo *nm* screen, folding screen.
biopsia *nf* biopsy.
bioquímica *nf* biochemistry.
biorritmo *nm* biorhythm.
biosfera *nf* biosphere.
bióxido *nm* dioxide.
bipartidismo *nm* two-party system.
bípedo,-a *adj* biped.
▷ *nm* **bípedo** biped.
biplaza *adj* two-seater.
▷ *nm* two-seater.
bipolar *adj* bipolar.
biquini [Registered trademark.] *nm* **1** *(traje de baño)* bikini. **2** CULIN *(en Cataluña)* toasted ham and cheese sandwich.
birlar *vt fam* to pinch, nick.
Birmania *nf* Burma.
birra *nf fam* beer.
birria *nf* **1** *fam (cosa fea)* monstrosity. **2** *(cosa mala)* rubbish.
bis *adv* **1** *(en dirección)*: **viven en el 23 bis** *they live a 23A.* **2** MÚS repeat, bis.
▷ *nm* [*pl* **bises**.] encore.
bisabuelo,-a *nm & nf* great-grandparent; *(hombre)* great-grandfather; *(mujer)* great-grandmother.
bisagra *nf* hinge.
biscote *nm* piece of Melba toast.
bisección *nf* bisection.
bisectriz *nf* bisector, bisectrix.
▲ *pl* **bisectrices.**
bisel *nm* bevel.
biselado,-a *pp* → **biselar.**
▷ *adj* bevelled (US beveled).
▷ *nm* **biselado** bevelling (US beveling).
biselar *vt* to bevel.
bisexual *adj* bisexual.
▷ *nm o nf* bisexual.
bisiesto *adj* leap, bissextile. ● **año bisiesto** leap year
bisilábico,-a *adj* → **bisílabo,-a.**
bismuto *nm* bismuth.
bisnieto,-a *nm & nf* great-grandchild; *(chico)* great-grandson; *(chica)* great-granddaughter.
bisonte *nm* bison.
bisoño,-a *adj* inexperienced.
▷ *nm & nf* novice.
bistec *nm* steak.
bisturí *nm* scalpel.
▲ *pl* **bisturíes o bisturís.**
bisutería *nf* costume jewellery (US jewelry).
bit *nm* bit.
▲ *pl* **bits.**
biunívoco,-a *adj* one-to-one.
bivalente *adj* bivalent, divalent.
bivalvo,-a *adj* bivalve, bivalvular.
▷ *nm* **bivalvo** bivalve.
bizco,-a *adj* cross-eyed.
▷ *nm & nf* cross-eyed person.
bizcocho *nm* sponge, sponge cake.
biznieto,-a *nm & nf* → **bisnieto,-a.**
bizquear *vi* to squint, be cross-eyed.
▷ *vt (guiñar)* to wink at.
blanco,-a *adj* **1** white. **2** *(complexión)* fair-skinned.
▷ *nm & nf (gen)* white; *(hombre)* white man; *(mujer)* white woman.
▷ *nm* **blanco** **1** *(color)* white. **2** *(objetivo)* target, mark. **3** *fig* object: **fue el blanco de todas sus críticas** *he was the target of all their criticism.* **4** *(hueco)* blank, gap; *(en escrito)* blank space. **5** *(vino)* white wine. ■ **dar en el blanco** **1** to hit the mark. **2** *fig* to hit the nail on the head. ■ **en blanco** blank: **me dio un cheque en blanco** *he gave me a blank cheque (US check).* ■ **quedarse en**

blanco **1** *(no entender)* to fail to grasp the point. **2** *(olvidarlo todo)* to forget everything: **me quedé en blanco** *my mind went blank.*

lancura *nf* whiteness.

landir *vt* to brandish, wave.

'sed only in forms which include the letter *i* in ıeir endings: **blandía, blandiré, blandiendo,** etc.

lando,-a *adj* **1** *(gen)* soft. **2** *(poco severo)* soft, lenient. **3** *fig (benigno)* gentle, mild. **4** *(cobarde)* cowardly.

landura *nf* **1** softness. **2** *fig (dulzura)* gentleness, sweetness.

lanquear *vt* **1** to whiten, make white. **2** *(con cal)* to whitewash. **3** *(con lejía)* to bleach. **4** *(dinero)* to launder. **5** *(verduras)* to blanch. **6** *(pulir)* to polish. *vi* to whiten, turn white.

lanquecino,-a *adj* whitish, off-white.

lanqueo *nm* **1** whitening. **2** *(con cal)* whitewashing. **3** *(de dinero)* laundering.

lasfemar *vi* **1** *(contra Dios)* to blaspheme (**contra,** against). **2** *(decir palabrotas)* to swear, curse.

lasfemia *nf* **1** *(contra Dios)* blasphemy. **2** *(palabrota)* curse.

lasfemo,-a *adj* blasphemous.
nm & nf blasphemer.

ledo *nm* common amaranth. ■ **me importa un bledo** *fam* I don't care less, I couldn't give a damn

lindado,-a *pp* → **blindar.**
adj armoured (US armored), armour-plated (US armor-plated). ● **puerta blindada** reinforced door.

lindaje *nm* **1** armour (US armor), armour-plating (US armor-plating). **2** *(de puerta)* reinforcing.

lindar *vt* **1** to armour-plate (US armor-plate). **2** *(puerta)* to reinforce.

loc *nm* notepad, pad.
▲ *pl* **blocs.**

loque *nm* **1** block. **2** *(papel)* pad, notepad. **3** POL bloc. ■ **en bloque** en bloc.

loquear *vt* **1** *(gen)* to block: **esto podría bloquear el proceso de paz** *this could block the peace process.* **2** MIL to blockade. **3** *(precios, cuentas)* to freeze. **4** *(mecanismo)* to jam; *(coche, etc)* to immobilize.
vpr **bloquearse** *(persona)* to have a mental block.

loqueo *nm* **1** *(gen)* blocking. **2** MIL blockade. **3** *(precios, cuenta)* freezing. ● **bloqueo económico** trade boycott, economic boycott. ‖ **bloqueo mental** mental block.

lues *nm inv* blues.

lusa *nf* blouse.

lusón *nm* loose blouse, smock.

oa *nf (serpiente)* boa.
nm (prenda) boa, feather boa.

obada *nf* silliness, foolishness. ■ **decir bobadas** to talk nonsense. ‖ **hacer bobadas** to act the fool.

obina *nf* **1** reel, bobbin. **2** ELEC coil.

obo,-a *adj* silly, foolish.
nm & nf fool.

oca *nf* **1** ANAT mouth. **2** *(de río)* mouth. **3** *(abertura)* entrance, opening: **hay una boca de metro en la esquina** *there's an entrance to the underground on the corner.* ■ **boca abajo** face downwards. ‖ **boca arriba** face upwards. ‖ **callarse la boca** to shut up, shut one's mouth. ● **boca a boca** kiss of life, mouth-to-mouth resuscitation. ‖ **boca de incendios** fire hydrant. ‖ **boca del estómago** pit of the stomach.

bocacalle *nf* **1** entrance to a street: **tuerce por la primera bocacalle a la derecha** *take the first turning on the right.* **2** *(calle secundaria)* side street.

bocadillo *nm* **1** sandwich. **2** *(en cómics)* speech balloon.

bocado *nm* **1** mouthful. **2** *(piscolabis)* snack, bite to eat. **3** *(mordedura)* bite. **4** *(de caballo)* bit.

bocajarro ■ **a bocajarro 1** *(disparar)* at point-blank range. **2** *(decir algo)* point-blank.

bocata *nm fam* sandwich, sarnie.

bocazas *nm o nf inv* bigmouth.

boceto *nm* sketch; *(proyecto)* outline.

bocha *nf (bola)* bowl.
▷ *nf pl* **bochas** *(juego)* bowls.

bochorno *nm* **1** *(calor)* sultry weather, close weather, muggy weather, stifling heat; *(viento)* hot wind. **2** *fig (rubor)* embarrassment, shame.

bochornoso,-a *adj* **1** *(sofocante)* hot, sultry, muggy. **2** *fig (vergonzoso)* disgraceful, shameful.

bocina *nf* **1** *(de coche)* horn; *(de fábrica)* siren. **2** *(instrumento músico)* horn. **3** *(para ampliar la voz)* megaphone. **4** *(de gramófono)* horn.

boda *nf* marriage, wedding.

bodega *nf* **1** *(almacén)* wine cellar. **2** *(tienda)* wine shop. **3** *(fábrica)* winery. **4** *(de barco)* hold.

bodegón *nm* still life.

bodrio *nm fam* rubbish, trash: **¡qué bodrio!** *what a load of junk!;* **¡vaya bodrio de película!** *what a useless film!*

body *nm* body.
▲ *pl* **bodies.**

bofetada *nf* slap, slap in the face.

bofetón *nm* hard slap.

bofia *nf* **la bofia** *argot* the fuzz *pl*, the cops *pl*.

boga *nf* vogue. ■ **estar en boga** to be in fashion.

bogavante *nm* lobster.

Bogotá *nm* Bogotá.

bohemio,-a *adj* **1** *(vida, etc)* bohemian. **2** *(de Bohemia)* Bohemian.
▷ *nm & nf* **1** *(artista, etc)* bohemian. **2** *(persona de Bohemia)* Bohemian.
▷ *nf* **la bohemia** bohemian life style.

boicot *nm* **1** *(no participación)* boycott. **2** *(sabotaje)* sabotage.
▲ *pl* **boicots.**

boicotear *vt* **1** *(no participar)* to boycott. **2** *(sabotear)* to sabotage.

boicoteo *nm* → **boicot.**

boina *nf* beret.

boîte *nf* nightclub.
▲ *pl* **boîtes.**

boj *nm* **1** *(árbol)* box tree. **2** *(madera)* boxwood.
▲ pl **bojes.**

bol *nm* bowl.
▲ *pl* **boles.**

bola *nf* **1** *(gen)* ball. **2** *fam* fib, lie. ● **bola de nieve** snowball. ‖ **bola de cristal** crystal ball.

bolera *nf* bowling alley.

boletería *nf* 1 AM *(de teatro)* box office. 2 *(de estación)* ticket office.
boletero,-a *nm & nf* AM ticket seller.
boletín *nm* 1 *(revista)* periodical. 2 *(de noticias)* bulletin, news bulletin. 3 *(impreso)* form. 4 *(de colegio)* report.
boleto *nm* 1 ticket. 2 *(quiniela)* coupon.
boli *nm fam* ballpen, biro.
boliche *nm* 1 *(bola pequeña)* jack. 2 *(juego de bolos)* bowling, skittles *pl*. 3 *(bolera)* bowling alley. 4 *(juguete) cup-and-ball game.*
bólido *nm* 1 *(en el espacio)* meteor, fireball. 2 *fam (coche)* racing car.
bolígrafo *nm* ballpoint pen, ballpoint, biro.
bolívar *nm* bolivar *(monetary unit of Venezuela)*.
Bolivia *nf* Bolivia.
boliviano,-a *adj* Bolivian.
▷ *nm & nf* Bolivian.
▷ *nm* **boliviano** *(moneda)* boliviano.
bollo *nm* 1 *(de pan)* bread roll, roll, breadbun; *(dulce)* pastry, bun. 2 *(abolladura)* dent. 3 *(chichón)* bump.
bolo *nm* 1 skittle, ninepin. 2 *(necio)* dunce, idiot.
▷ *nm pl* **bolos** skittles.
bolsa[1] *nf* 1 *(gen)* bag: **¿tiene una bolsa de plástico?** *have you got a plastic bag?* 2 *(bajo los ojos)* bag. 3 *(beca)* grant, scholarship. 4 *(en prenda)* bag. 5 *(de pobreza, fraude, etc)* pocket. 6 *(para dinero)* purse. 7 *(premio)* purse. 8 *(de canguro, etc)* pouch. 9 AM jacket. ● **bolsa de aseo** toilet bag. ‖ **bolsa de basura** rubbish bag, bin liner, US garbage bag. ‖ **bolsa de deportes** sports bag. ‖ **bolsa de estudios** scholarship. ‖ **bolsa de viaje** travelling bag (US traveling bag).
bolsa[2] *nf* 1 stock exchange. 2 *(valores)* share prices: **la bolsa ha subido dos puntos** *share prices are up two points.*
bolsillo *nm* pocket. ■ **de bolsillo** pocket: **una calculadora de bolsillo** *a pocket calculator.* ‖ **rascarse el bolsillo** to dip into one's pocket.
bolso *nm (gen)* bag; *(de señora)* handbag, US purse. ● **bolso de mano** bag: **se puede llevar un solo bolso de mano** *you may take only one piece of hand luggage.*
bomba *nf* 1 *(explosivo)* bomb: **pusieron una bomba en el hotel** *they planted a bomb in the hotel.* 2 *(noticia)* bombshell. 3 pump. ■ **a prueba de bomba** bombproof. ‖ **pasarlo bomba** to have a whale of a time. ● **bomba fétida** stink bomb. ‖ **bomba nuclear** nuclear bomb. ‖ **bomba de agua** water pump.
bombacho,-a *adj* loose-fitting, baggy.
▷ *nm pl* **bombachos** baggy trousers.
bombardear *vt* 1 *(con artillería)* to bombard, shell; *(desde el aire)* to bomb. 2 *fig* to bombard: **me bombardearon a preguntas** *they bombarded me with questions.*
bombardeo *nm (con artillería)* bombardment, shelling; *(desde el aire)* bombing.
bombardero *nm* bomber.
bombazo *nm* 1 *(explosión)* bomb blast, explosion. 2 *(cosa inesperada)* bombshell. 3 *(exitazo)* smash hit, smash.
bombear *vt (agua)* to pump.
bombero,-a *nm (gen)* firefighter; *(hombre)* fireman; *(mujer)* firewoman.
bombilla *nf* light bulb, bulb.
bombín *nm* 1 *(sombrero)* bowler, bowler hat. 2 *(cerradura)* cylinder.
bombo *nm* 1 *(tambor)* bass drum. 2 *(elogio)* build-u hype. 3 *(para sorteo)* drum.
bombón *nm* 1 chocolate. 2 *fam (persona)* knoc out.
bombona *nf* cylinder. ● **bombona de butano** buta cylinder.
bonachón,-ona *adj* kind, good-natured.
▷ *nm & nf* kind soul.
bonanza *nf* 1 *(mar)* calm sea. 2 *(tiempo)* fair weath 3 *fig* prosperity.
bondad *nf* 1 goodness. 2 *(afabilidad)* kindness. 3 *(am bilidad)* kindness.
bondadoso,-a *adj* kind, good, good-natured.
boniato *nm* sweet potato.
bonificar [1] *vt* 1 COM to allow, discount. 2 *(mejor* to improve.
bonito *nm (pez)* bonito, Atlantic bonito.
bonito,-a *adj* lovely, nice.
Bonn *nm* Bonn.
bono *nm* 1 FIN bond. 2 *(vale)* voucher. 3 *(billete)* tick **he comprado un bono mensual** *I've bought a month ticket.*
bonobús *nm multiple-journey* bus ticket.
bonoloto *nm Spanish state-run* lottery.
boñiga *nf* cow dung.
boquerón *nm (pez)* anchovy.
boquete *nm* hole. ■ **abrir un boquete en** to make hole in.
boquiabierto,-a *adj* 1 open-mouthed, agape. 2 *(e bobado)* dumbfounded, flabbergasted, agape. 3 *(s poder hablar)* speechless.
boquilla *nf* 1 *(de pipa, instrumento)* mouthpiece. *(de tubo)* nozzle. 3 *(sujetacigarrillos)* cigarette hold 4 *(filtro de cigarrillo)* tip. 5 *(de cigarro puro)* lit end.
borbotear *vi* to bubble.
borbotón *nm* → **borbollón.**
borda *nf* MAR gunwale. ■ **tirar por la borda 1** to thro overboard. 2 *fig* to throw away.
bordado,-a *pp* → **bordar.**
▷ *adj* embroidered.
▷ *nm* **bordado** embroidering, embroidery.
bordar *vt* 1 to embroider. 2 *fig* to perform exqu sitely.
borde[1] *adj* 1 *(tonto)* stupid. 2 *(antipático)* unpleasar *(malhumorado)* stroppy. 3 *(planta - silvestre)* wild.
▷ *nm o nf* idiot.
borde[2] *nm* 1 *(extremo)* edge. 2 *(de vaso, copa)* rim. *(de barco, carretera)* side; *(de río)* bank; *(de mar)* shor 4 *(de prenda)* hem.
bordear *vt* 1 to skirt, go round. 2 *(aproximarse)* border on, verge on: **esto bordea el ridículo** *this verging on the ridiculous.*
bordillo *nm* kerb, US curb.
bordo *nm* MAR board. ■ **a bordo** on board.
boreal *adj* boreal, northern.
bóreas *nm* north wind.
borgoña *nm (vino)* Burgundy.
bórico,-a *adj* boric.

borla *nf* 1 tassel. 2 *(de gorra)* pompom. 3 *(para polvos)* powder puff.
borra *nf* 1 *(pelusa)* fluff. 2 *(para cojines, etc)* flock. 3 *(palabras de relleno)* waffle, padding.
borrachera *nf* drunken state. ■ **coger una borrachera** to get drunk.
borracho,-a *adj* 1 *(persona)* drunk. 2 *(pastel)* soaked in alcoholic syrup.
▷ *nm & nf* drunkard, drunk.
▷ *nm* **borracho** *sponge cake soaked in alcoholic syrup.* ■ **borracho,-a como una cuba** blind drunk.
borrador *nm* 1 *(escrito)* rough version, first draft. 2 *(croquis)* rough sketch. 3 *(de pizarra)* duster. 4 *(goma)* eraser, GB rubber. 5 *(libro)* rough book.
borrar *vt* 1 *(lo escrito)* to erase, rub out; *(superficie)* to clean: **borra la pizarra** *clean the blackboard.* 2 *(cinta)* to erase. 3 INFORMÁ to delete. 4 *(tachar)* to cross out, cross off. 5 *(dar de baja)* to cancel the membership of.
▷ *vpr* **borrarse** to disappear.
borrasca *nf* 1 *(ciclón)* depression, low-presssure area. 2 *(tormenta)* storm. 3 *(en un negocio, etc)* bad spell, bad patch.
borrego,-a *nm & nf* 1 lamb. 2 *(ignorante)* moron. ■ **como borregos** like sheep.
borrón *nm* 1 *(mancha)* blot, ink blot. 2 *fig* blemish. 3 *(boceto)* rough sketch. ■ **hacer borrón y cuenta nueva** to wipe the slate clean.
borroso,-a *adj (visión)* blurred, hazy; *(foto)* blurred; *(idea, etc)* vague, hazy.
Bosnia *nf* Bosnia. ● **Bosnia-Herzegovina** Bosnia Herzegovina.
bosnio,-a *adj* Bosnian.
▷ *nm & nf* Bosnian.
bosque *nm (pequeño)* wood; *(grande)* forest.
bosquejar *vt* 1 *(trazar rasgos)* to sketch, outline. 2 *(explicar sin detalles)* to outline, give an outline of.
bosquejo *nm (dibujo)* sketch; *(plan, etc)* outline.
bosquimán *adj-nm o nf* → **bosquimano,-a**.
bosquimano,-a *adj* Bushman.
▷ *nm & nf (persona)* Bushman.
▷ *nm* **bosquimano** *(idioma)* Bushman.
bostezar [4] *vi* to yawn.
bostezo *nm* yawn.
bota[1] *nf* boot. ■ **ponerse las botas** *fam* to stuff OS. ● **botas de agua** gum boots, US rubber boots, Wellington boots, wellingtons.
bota[2] *nf (de vino)* wineskin.
botana *nf* AM snack.
botánico,-a *adj* botanical.
▷ *nm & nf* botanist.
botar *vi* 1 *(pelota)* to bounce. 2 *(persona)* to jump, jump up and down.
▷ *vt* 1 *(pelota)* to bounce. 2 *(barco)* to launch. 3 *fam (persona - del trabajo)* to fire, sack; *(- de un local)* to throw out, kick out, boot out. ■ **está que bota** he's hopping mad.
bote[1] *nm* MAR small boat. ● **bote salvavidas** lifeboat.
bote[2] *nm (salto)* bounce.
bote[3] *nm* 1 *(lata)* tin, can. 2 *(tarro)* jar. 3 *(para propinas)* jar for tips, box for tips. 4 *(fondo)* kitty. 5 *(premio)* jackpot.
bote[4] ■ **de bote en bote** jam-packed.
botella *nf* 1 bottle. 2 *(de gas)* cylinder.
botellín *nm* small bottle.
botijo *nm* earthenware jar *(with spout and handle for drinking)*.
botín[1] *nm* 1 *(zapato)* ankle boot. 2 *(cubierta)* gaiter.
botín[2] *nm* 1 *(de guerra)* spoils *pl*, booty. 2 *(de robo)* haul. ● **botín de guerra** spoils *pl* of war.
botiquín *nm* first-aid kit.
botón *nm* 1 *(gen)* button. 2 *(tirador)* knob. 3 BOT bud.
▷ *nm o nf* **botones** *(de hotel)* bellboy, US bellhop; *(recadero - chico)* errand boy; *(- chica)* errand girl.
boutique *nf* boutique.
bóveda *nf* vault.
box *nm* 1 *(de caballo)* stall. 2 *(en carrera de coches)* pit.
▲ *pl* **boxes.**
boxeador,-ra *nm & nf* boxer.
boxear *vi* to box.
boxeo *nm* boxing.
bóxer *nm (perro)* boxer.
▲ *pl* **bóxers.**
boya *nf* 1 MAR buoy. 2 *(corcho)* float.
boyante *adj* 1 MAR buoyant. 2 *fig* prosperous, successful, flourishing.
bozal *nm* muzzle.
bracear *vi* 1 to wave one's arms about. 2 *(nadar)* to swim. 3 *fig (forcejear)* to struggle.
braga *nf* 1 [Usually used in plural.] *(prenda)* panties *pl*, knickers *pl*. 2 *fam* rubbish.
bragueta *nf* fly, flies *pl*.
braille *nm* Braille.
bramar *vi* 1 *(toro, ciervo)* to bellow. 2 *(persona - de cólera)* to roar, bellow; *(- de dolor)* to howl.
brandy *nm* brandy.
▲ *pl* **brandys.**
branquia *nf* gill.
brasa *nf* ember, live coal. ■ **a la brasa** barbecued.
brasero *nm* brazier.
Brasil *nm* Brazil.
brasileño,-a *adj* Brazilian.
▷ *nm & nf* Brazilian.
bravata *nf* 1 *(amenaza)* threat. 2 *(fanfarronada)* boast: **déjate de bravatas** *stop boasting, stop showing off.*
braveza *nf* 1 *(valor)* bravery. 2 *(violencia)* violence. 3 *(fiereza)* ferocity.
bravío,-a *adj* 1 *(animal)* wild, fierce. 2 *(planta)* wild. 3 *(persona)* uncouth. 4 *(aguas)* rough, wild.
bravo,-a *adj* 1 *(valiente)* brave, courageous. 2 *(fiero)* fierce, ferocious. 3 *(bueno)* fine, excellent. 4 *(mar)* rough. 5 *(enojado)* angry, violent.
▷ *interj* **¡bravo!** well done!, bravo!
bravura *nf* 1 *(valentía)* bravery, courage. 2 *(fiereza)* fierceness, ferocity.
braza *nf* 1 *(medida)* fathom. 2 *(natación)* breaststroke.
brazada *nf* 1 *(natación)* stroke. 2 *(cantidad)* armful.
brazalete *nm* bracelet, bangle.
brazo *nm* 1 *(de persona)* arm. 2 *(de vestido)* arm, sleeve. 3 *(de silla, balanza)* arm. 4 *(de animal)* foreleg. 5 *(de río, candelabro, árbol)* branch. 6 *(de grúa)* jib.
▷ *nm pl* **brazos** hands, workers.

brea *nf* tar, pitch.
brebaje *nm* brew, potion.
brecha *nf* 1 break, opening. 2 *fig* breach.
Bretaña *nf* 1 *(británica)* Britain. 2 *(francesa)* Brittany.
● **Gran Bretaña** Great Britain.
breve *adj* short, brief.
▷ *nf* MÚS breve.
▷ *nf pl* **breves** *(en periódico)* news-in-brief section *sing.*
■ **en breve** soon, shortly.
brevedad *nf* brevity, briefness.
brezo *nm* heather, heath.
bricolaje *nm* do-it-yourself, DIY.
brida *nf* 1 *(de caballo)* bridle. 2 TÉC flange.
bridge *nm* bridge.
brigada *nf* 1 *(unidad militar)* brigade. 2 *(de policía)* squad; *(de otros efectivos)* team.
▷ *nm (soldado)* warrant officer.
brillante *adj* 1 *(extraordinario)* brilliant: **un alumno brillante** *a brilliant student.* 2 *(pelo, metal, zapatos)* shiny; *(ojos)* sparkling; *(luz, color)* bright; *(pintura)* gloss.
▷ *nm (diamante)* diamond.
brillantina *nf* brilliantine.
brillar *vi* 1 *(luz, sol, luna, pelo, zapatos)* to shine. 2 *(ojos)* to sparkle; *(estrella)* to twinkle; *(metal, dientes)* to gleam; *(cosa húmeda)* to glisten. 3 *fig* to be outstanding.
brillo *nm* 1 *(gen)* shine. 2 *(de estrella)* twinkling; *(de ojos)* sparkle; *(de pelo, zapatos)* shine; *(de cosa húmeda)* glistening. 3 *(en televisor)* brightness. 4 *fig* brilliance.
brincar [1] *vi (cabra, etc)* to skip; *(pájaro)* to hop; *(persona)* to leap, bound.
brinco *nm (de cabra)* skip, hop; *(de pájaro)* hop; *(de persona)* leap, bound.
brindar *vi* to toast (**por**, to), drink (**por**, to): **¡brindemos por el futuro!** *let's drink to the future!*
▷ *vt (ofrecer)* to offer, provide.
▷ *vpr* **brindarse** to offer (**a**, to), volunteer (**a**, to).
brindis *nm inv* toast.
brío *nm* 1 *(espíritu)* spirit, verve; *(de motor)* go. 2 *(pujanza)* strength. 3 *(resolución)* determination. 4 *(valentía)* courage.
brisa *nf* breeze. ● **brisa marina** sea breeze.
británico,-a *adj* British.
▷ *nm & nf* British person, Briton, Britisher.
brizna *nf (gen)* bit; *(hebra)* strand; *(de hierba)* blade.
broca *nf (barrena)* drill, bit.
brocha *nf* brush, paintbrush.
brochada *nf* brushstroke.
brochazo *nf* brushstroke.
broche *nm* 1 *(cierre)* fastener. 2 *(joya)* brooch.
broma *nf* joke: **no es broma** *I'm not joking, it's not a joke.*
bromear *vi* to joke.
bromista *adj* fond of joking.
▷ *nm o nf* joker.
bronca *nf* 1 *(lío)* row. 2 *(riña)* quarrel; *(discusión)* argument; *(pelea)* fight. 3 *(reprimenda)* telling-off.
bronce *nm* 1 bronze. 2 *(medalla)* bronze, bronze medal.
bronceado,-a *pp* → **broncear.**
▷ *adj* 1 bronzed. 2 *(piel)* tanned.
▷ *nm* **bronceado** tan, suntan.
bronceador,-ra *adj* tanning.
▷ *nm* **bronceador** *(crema)* suntan cream, suntan l-tion; *(aceite)* suntan oil.
broncear *vt* 1 *(metal)* to bronze. 2 *(persona)* to tar suntan.
▷ *vpr* **broncearse** to tan, get a tan.
bronco,-a *adj* 1 *(superficie)* rough; *(terreno)* rugge 2 *(voz)* rough, gruff; *(tos)* rasping; *(sonido)* harsh. 3 *(pe sona)* rude, surly.
bronquio *nm* bronchus.
bronquitis *nf inv* bronchitis.
brotar *vi* 1 *(plantas - nacer)* to sprout; *(- echar brote* to come into bud. 2 *(agua)* to spring; *(sangre)* t flow; *(lágrimas)* to well up. 3 *(estallar)* to break ou 4 *fig* to spring.
brote *nm* 1 *(renuevo)* shoot, sprout. 2 *(estallido)* out break.
broza *nf* 1 *(hojas)* dead leaves; *(ramitas)* dead twig 2 *(maleza)* scrub, brush. 3 *(suciedad)* dirt. 4 *(despe dicios)* rubbish.
bruces ■ **caerse de bruces** to fall flat on one's face.
bruja *nf* 1 *(hechicera)* witch. 2 *(mujer - fea)* old hag; *(- ma intencionada)* witch.
brujería *nf* witchcraft, sorcery.
brujo,-a *adj* enchanting.
▷ *nm* **brujo** wizard, sorcerer.
brújula *nf* compass.
bruma *nf* mist.
bruñido,-a *pp* → **bruñir.**
▷ *adj* burnished.
▷ *nm* **bruñido** burnishing.
brusco,-a *adj* 1 *(repentino)* sudden. 2 *(persona)* brus que, abrupt.
Bruselas *nf* Brussels.
brusquedad *nf* 1 *(de carácter)* abruptness. 2 *(rapi dez)* suddenness. ■ **con brusquedad** sharply.
brutal *adj* 1 *(cruel)* brutal, savage. 2 *fig (enorme)* enor mous, colossal. 3 *fig (magnífico)* terrific, fantastic.
brutalidad *nf* 1 *(crueldad)* brutality. 2 *(necedad)* stu pid thing. 3 *(cantidad)* tremendous amount.
bruto,-a *adj* 1 *(cruel)* brutal. 2 *(necio)* stupid, thick. 3 *(tos co)* rough, coarse. 4 *(torpe)* clumsy. 5 *(grosero)* rude 6 *(peso)* gross. 7 *(piedra)* rough, uncut. 8 *(petróleo)* crude.
▷ *nm & nf (persona - violenta)* brute, beast; *(necio)* ig noramus; *(grosero)* rude person.
bubónico,-a *adj* bubonic.
bucal *adj* oral, mouth.
bucanero *nm* buccaneer.
Bucarest *nm* Bucharest.
bucear *vi* 1 *(en el agua)* to dive. 2 *fig (investigar)* to delve into.
bucle *nm* 1 curl, ringlet. 2 INFORMÁ loop.
bucólico,-a *adj* bucolic.
Budapest *nm* Budapest.
budismo *nm* Buddhism.
budista *adj* Buddhist.
▷ *nm o nf* Buddhist.
buen *adj* [Used before a singular masculine noun. → **bueno,-a.**
bueno,-a *adj* 1 *(gen)* good. 2 *(persona - amable)* kind *(- agradable)* nice, polite. 3 *(tiempo)* good, nice. 4

(apropiado) right, suitable; *(correcto)* right. **5** *(de salud)* well.
› *interj* **¡bueno!** *(sorpresa)* well, very well; *(de acuerdo)* all right!
See also **buen.**
uey *nm* ox, bullock. ● **carne de buey** beef. ‖ **buey de mar** crab. ‖ **buey marino** sea cow.
úfalo *nm* buffalo.
ufanda *nf* scarf.
ufar *vi* **1** *(toro)* to snort. **2** *(persona)* to be fuming: **bufar de coraje** *to be fuming with rage.*
ufé *nm* buffet.
▲ *pl* **bufés.** ● **bufé libre** self-service buffet meal.
ufete *nm* **1** *(mesa)* writing desk. **2** *(de abogado)* lawyer's office: **abrir bufete** *to set up as a lawyer.*
ufido *nm* snort: **entró en el despacho dando bufidos** *he came raging into the office.*
ufón,-ona *adj* buffoon.
› *nm & nf* buffoon, jester.
uhardilla *nf* → **buharda.**
úho *nm* owl. ● **búho real** eagle owl.
uitre *nm (ave y persona)* vulture.
ujía *nf* **1** *(de motor)* spark plug. **2** *(vela)* candle. **3** *(candelero)* candlestick.
ulbo *nm* bulb. ● **bulbo raquídeo** medulla oblongata.
ulevar *nm* boulevard.
ulgaria *nf* Bulgaria.
úlgaro,-a *adj* Bulgarian.
› *nm & nf (persona)* Bulgarian.
› *nm* **búlgaro** *(idioma)* Bulgarian.
ulla *nf* **1** *(ruido)* din, uproar, racket, row. **2** *(multitud)* crowd.
ulldozer *nm* bulldozer.
ullicio *nm* **1** *(ruido)* noise, racket. **2** *(tumulto)* bustle, hustle and bustle, hurly-burly.
ullicioso,-a *adj* **1** *(ruidoso)* noisy. **2** *(animado)* lively; *(con ajetreo)* busy.
ullir [41] *vi* **1** *(líquido - hervir)* to boil; *(- agitarse)* to bubble up; *(mar)* to seethe; *(calle, etc)* to swarm with, seethe with. **2** *(insectos)* to swarm; *(gente)* to bustle about.
ulto *nm* **1** *(tamaño)* volume, size, bulk. **2** *(forma)* shape, form. **3** *(abultamiento - en cosa)* bulge; *(- en piel)* lump. **4** *(equipaje)* piece of luggage, item of luggage; *(fardo)* bundle; *(paquete)* package.
um *interj* boom!
umerán *nm* boomerang.
ungalow *nm* bungalow.
▲ *pl* **bungalows.**
únker *nm* bunker.
▲ *pl* **búnkers.**
uñuelo *nm* fritter: **buñuelos de bacalao** *cod fritters.*
UP *abrev* EDUC **(Bachillerato Unificado Polivalente)** former General Certificate of Secondary Education studies.
uque *nm* MAR ship, vessel.
burbuja *nf* bubble. ■ **con burbujas** *(bebida)* fizzy. ‖ **sin burbujas** *(bebida)* still.
burbujear *vi* to bubble.
burdel *nm* brothel.
burdo,-a *adj* **1** *(tejido)* coarse, rough. **2** *(persona)* coarse, crude.
burgués,-esa *nm & nf* **1** bourgeois, middle-class. **2** member of the middle-class.
burguesía *nf* bourgeoisie, middle class. ● **alta burguesía** upper middle-class.
burla *nf* **1** *(mofa)* mockery, gibe. **2** *(broma)* joke. **3** *(engaño)* deception, trick.
burlar *vt* **1** to deceive, trick. **2** *(eludir)* to dodge, evade.
▷ *vpr* **burlarse** to mock (**de**, -), make fun (**de**, of), laugh (**de**, at).
burlón,-ona *adj* mocking.
▷ *nm & nf* joker.
burocracia *nf* **1** bureaucracy. **2** *pey* red tape.
burócrata *nm o nf* bureaucrat.
burrada *nf* **1** drove of asses. **2** *fig* foolishness, blunder. **3** **una burrada** *fam (cantidad)* loads *pl*, lots *pl*, tons *pl*. **4** *fam* a lot: **me gusta una burrada** *I love it.*
burro,-a *adj* stupid.
▷ *nm & nf* **1** *(animal)* donkey, ass. **2** *(persona ignorante)* ass.
▷ *nm* **burro** *(de carpintero)* sawhorse. ■ **no ver tres en un burro** to be as blind as a bat.
bus *nm* **1** AUTO bus. **2** INFORMÁ bus.
▲ *pl* **buses.**
busca *nf* search, hunt.
▷ *nm fam* bleeper, pager. ■ **ir en busca de** to search for, hunt for.
buscador *nm* search engine.
buscapersonas *nm* bleeper, pager.
buscar [1] *vt* **1** *(gen)* to look for, search for. **2** *(en lista, índice, etc)* to look up: **búscalo en el diccionario** *look it up in the dictionary.* **3** *(ir a coger)* to go and get, fetch. **4** *(recoger)* to pick up: **iré a buscarte a la estación** *I'll pick you up at the station.* **5** *(intentar conseguir)* to try to achieve.
▷ *vi (mirar)* to look.
buscavidas *nm o nf inv* **1** go-getter. **2** *(chismoso)* snooper, busybody.
buscón,-ona *nm & nf (ladrón)* petty thief.
buscona *nf* whore.
búsqueda *nf* search.
busto *nm* **1** *(figura)* bust. **2** *(pecho - de mujer)* bust; *(- de hombre)* chest.
butaca *nf* **1** *(sillón)* armchair. **2** TEAT seat.
butacón *nm* easy chair.
butano *nm* butane.
buzo *nm* diver.
buzón *nm* letter box, US mailbox.
byte *nm* INFORMÁ byte.

C

C, c *nf (la letra)* C, c.
C¹ *sím* **(Celsius)** Celsius; *(símbolo)* C.
C² *sím* **(centígrado)** centigrade; *(símbolo)* C.
ca *interj* not at all!, not a bit of it!, never!
cabal *adj* **1** *(exacto)* exact, precise. **2** *(completo)* complete. **3** *fig (persona)* honest, upright. ■ **estar en sus cabales** to be in one's right mind.
cábala *nf* **1** *(ciencia oculta)* cabala, cabbala. **2** [In this sense, also used in plural with the same meaning.] *fig (conjetura)* guess, divination. **3** *fig (intriga)* plot.
cabalgar [7] *vi* **1** *(sobre un animal)* to ride (**en/sobre**, -). **2** *(sobre otra cosa)* to straddle (**sobre**, -), sit astride (**sobre**, -): **el niño cabalgaba sobre la silla** *the boy sat astride the chair.*
cabalgata *nf* cavalcade.
caballa *nf* mackerel.
caballería *nf* **1** *(cabalgadura)* mount. **2** MIL cavalry. **3** HIST chivalry, knighthood. ● **caballería andante** knight errantry.
caballeriza *nf* **1** *(cuadra)* stable. **2** *(personal)* stable hands *pl*, grooms *pl*. **3** *(conjunto de caballos)* stud.
caballero,-a *adj* riding, mounted: **caballero en su rocín** *riding a nag.*
▷ *nm* **caballero** **1** gentleman, sir. **2** HIST knight, cavalier. **3** *(hombre generoso, cortés)* gentleman. **4** *(noble)* gentleman.
caballete *nm* **1** *(de pintor)* easel. **2** ARQUIT ridge. **3** TÉC trestle. **4** *(de nariz)* bridge.
caballito *nm* small horse.
▷ *nm pl* **caballitos** *(tiovivo)* merry-go-round *sing*, US carrousel *sing*. ● **caballito de mar** sea horse. ‖
caballo *nm* **1** ZOOL horse. **2** TÉC horsepower. **3** *(ajedrez)* knight. **4** *(naipes)* queen. ■ **montar a caballo** to ride.
cabaña *nf* **1** *(choza)* cabin, hut, shack. **2** *(conjunto de ganados)* livestock.
cabaré *nm* cabaret, nightclub.
▲ *pl* **cabarés.**
cabecear *vi* **1** *(mover la cabeza)* to move one's head; *(para negar)* to shake one's head. **2** *(dar cabezadas)* to nod. **3** *(inclinarse)* to lean, slope. **4** MAR to pitch.
cabecera *nf* **1** *(gen)* top, head. **2** *(de cama)* headboard. **3** *(de un río)* source, headwaters *pl*. **4** *(de un periódico)* headline; *(de un libro)* headband.
cabecilla *nm o nf* leader.
cabellera *nf* **1** hair, head of hair. **2** *(de cometa)* tail.
cabello *nm* hair.
caber [66] *vi* **1** *(encajar)* to fit (**en**, into): **cabe ahí arriba** *it'll fit up there.* **2** *(pasar)* to fit, go. **3** *(ser posible)* to be possible: **cabe la posibilidad de que vengan** *they might come.* **4** MAT to go: **ocho entre dos caben a cuatro** *two into eight goes four times, eight divided by two is four.*
cabestrillo *nm* sling: **llevaba el brazo en cabestrillo** *she had her arm in a sling.*
cabeza *nf* **1** *(gen)* head: **diez mil por cabeza** *ten thousand a head.* **2** *fig (juicio)* good judgement; *(talento)* talent, intelligence. **3** *(de región)* main town. ■ **cabeza abajo** upside down. ‖ **estar mal de la cabeza** *fig* not to be right in the head. ‖ **meterse** ALGO **en la cabeza** *fam* to get STH into one's head. ● **cabeza cuadrada** *fam* bigot. ‖ **cabeza de ajo** bulb of garlic. ‖ **cabeza de turco** scapegoat. ‖ **cabeza rapada** skinhead.
cabezada *nf* **1** *(golpe recibido)* blow on the head; *(golpe dado)* butt, head butt. **2** *(saludo, al dormirse)* nod. **3** *(correaje)* cavesson. **4** MAR pitch, pitching. ■ **dar cabezadas** *fam* to nod.
cabezal *nm* TÉC head, headstock.
cabezón,-ona *adj* **1** *fam (de cabeza grande)* with a big head. **2** *fam fig (terco)* pig-headed, stubborn.
cabida *nf* capacity, room, space.
cabina *nf* **1** *(gen)* cabin, booth. **2** *(de barco, avión)* cabin. ● **cabina telefónica** telephone box, US telephone booth.
cabizbajo,-a *adj* crestfallen.
cable *nm (maroma)* cable.
cabo *nm* **1** *(extremo)* end, stub. **2** *(parte pequeña)* bit, piece. **3** *fig* end: **al cabo de un mes** *in a month's time.* **4** *(cuerda)* rope, line. **5** GEOG cape. **6** MIL corporal. ■ **al cabo** finally. ‖ **llevar a cabo** to carry out. ‖ **no dejar cabo suelto** *fig* to leave no loose ends.
cabra *nf* goat. ■ **estar como una cabra** *fam* to be off one's rocker, be nuts.
cabrear *vt fam* to annoy, make angry.
▷ *vpr* **cabrearse** *fam* to get angry, get worked up.
cabreo *nm fam* anger. ■ **agarrar un cabreo** *fam* to fly off the handle, hit the roof.
cabriola *nf* **1** *(brinco)* caper, skip. **2** *(salto de caballo)* capriole. **3** *fig (voltereta)* somersault.
cabritilla *nf* kid, kidskin.
cabrito *nm* **1** ZOOL kid. **2** *argot (cabrón)* bugger, bastard. **3** *fig (que consiente el adulterio)* cuckold.
cabrón,-ona *nm & nf tabú (hombre)* bastard; *(mujer)* bitch.
▷ *nm* **cabrón** **1** ZOOL he-goat, billy-goat. **2** *tabú (que consiente el adulterio)* cuckold.
cabuya *nf* agave, pita.
caca *nf* **1** *fam euf (excremento)* pooh. **2** *fam (en lenguaje infantil)* dirt: **3** *fig* shit, rubbish.
cacahuate *nm* → **cacahuete.**
cacahuete *nm* **1** *(planta)* groundnut. **2** *(fruto)* peanut.
cacao *nm* **1** BOT cacao. **2** *(polvo, bebida)* cocoa. **3** *fam (jaleo)* mess, cockup.
cacarear *vi (gallina)* to cluck; *(gallo)* to crow.
▷ *vt fam fig* to crow about, brag about.

acatúa *nf* **1** *(ave)* cockatoo. **2** *fam fig (mujer fea, vieja)* old hag, old bag.

acería *nf* hunting, hunt. ■ **ir de cacería** to go hunting.

acerola *nf* saucepan, casserole.

achalote *nm* cachalot, sperm whale.

acharro *nm* **1** *(de cocina)* crock, piece of crockery. **2** *fam (cosa)* thing, piece of junk. **3** *fam pey (coche)* banger.

achear *vt* to search, frisk.

achemira *nf (tejido)* cashmere.

acheo *nm* searching, frisking.

achet *nm* **1** *(elegancia)* cachet. **2** *(cotización de un artista)* fee.

achetada *nf* slap.

achete *nm* **1** *(bofetada)* slap. **2** *(golpe)* blow, punch. **3** *(carrillo)* cheek.

achivache *nm fam* thing, piece of junk, knick-knack.

acho *nm fam* bit, piece.

achondearse *vpr fam* to take the mickey (**de**, out of), make fun (**de**, of): **¿te estás cachondeando de mí?** *are you making fun of me?*

achondeo *nm* **1** *fam (jarana)* messing about. **2** *fam (burla)* joke.

achondo,-a *adj* **1** *(excitado)* hot, randy, horny. **2** *fam* funny.

achorro,-a *nm & nf (de perro)* pup, puppy; *(de gato)* kitten; *(de león, oso, zorro, tigre)* cub; *(de otros mamíferos)* young.

acique *nm* **1** *(jefe indio)* chief, cacique. **2** POL local political boss. **3** *fig (déspota)* tyrant.

aco *nm fam* thief.

acto *nm* cactus.

ada *adj* **1** *(de dos)* each; *(de varios)* every: **cada cuatro días** *every four days.* **2** *fam (intensificador)* such: **¡dice cada cosa!** *he says such strange things!* ■ **cada día** every day. ‖ **cada vez más** more and more, increasingly.

adalso *nm* **1** *(patíbulo)* scaffold. **2** *(plataforma)* platform.

adáver *nm* **1** *(de persona)* corpse, cadaver, body, dead body. **2** *(de animal)* body, carcass.

adena *nf* **1** *(gen)* chain; *(de perro)* leash, lead. **2** *(grupo de empresas)* chain. **3** *(industrial)* line. **4** *(montañosa)* range. **5** *(musical)* music centre (US center). **6** TV channel. **7** RAD chain of stations. **8** *fig (serie)* series, sequence: **una cadena de acontecimientos** *a series of events.* ● **cadena trófica** food chain. ‖ **reacción en cadena** chain reaction. ‖ **trabajo en cadena** assembly-line work.

adencia *nf* **1** cadence, rhythm. **2** MÚS cadenza.

adera *nf* hip.

adete *nm* cadet.

aducar [1] *vi* **1** *(documento, etc)* to expire: **mi pasaporte caduca este año** *my passport expires this year.* **2** *(alimento)* to pass its sell-by date; *(medicina)* to expire.

aducidad *nf* expiry.

aduco,-a *adj* **1** *(pasado)* past its sell-by date, out-of-date. **2** JUR expired, lapsed. **3** *(decrépito)* decrepit, senile. **4** BOT deciduous.

caer [67] *vi* **1** *(gen)* to fall: **caer de espalda** *to fall on one's back.* **2** *(derrumbar)* to fall down, collapse. **3** *(hallarse)* to be: **el camino cae a la derecha** *the road is on the right.* **4** *(coincidir fechas)* to fall on, be: **el día cuatro cae en jueves** *the fourth falls on a Thursday.* **5** *(premio)* to go (**en**, to). **6** *fam (entender)* to understand, get it: **ya caigo** *I see, I get it.* **7** MIL *(rendirse)* to surrender; *(morir)* to fall, die. **8** *(el sol)* to set; *(el día)* to draw in; *(el viento)* to drop.

▷ *vpr* **caerse 1** *(gen)* to fall, fall down. **2** *(desprenderse)* to fall out: **se le cae el pelo** *he's losing his hair.* ■ **caerse de sueño** *fig* to be dead on one's feet, be ready to drop. ‖ **no tener dónde caerse muerto,-a** *fam* to have nothing to one's name.

café *nm* **1** *(gen)* coffee. **2** *(cafetería)* café, coffee bar, coffee shop. ● **café con leche** white coffee. ‖ **café molido** ground coffee. ‖ **café solo** black coffee. ‖ **café soluble** instant coffee.

cafeína *nf* caffeine.

cafetera *nf* **1** *(para hacer café)* coffee-maker. **2** *(para servir café)* coffeepot. **3** *fam (coche viejo)* old banger, old crock.

cafetería *nf (gen)* snack bar, coffee bar; *(en un tren)* buffet car.

cafetero,-a *adj* **1** coffee. **2** *fam (persona)* coffee-loving.

cagar [7] *vi tabú* to shit, have a crap.

▷ *vt* **1** *tabú* to shit. **2** *tabú (echar a perder)* to ruin, spoil, mess up, muck up, cock up.

▷ *vpr* **cagarse 1** *tabú* to shit OS. **2** *tabú fig (acobardarse)* to be shit-scared. ■ **cagarse de miedo** *tabú* to be shit-scared.

caído,-a *pp* → **caer.**

▷ *adj* **1** *(gen)* fallen. **2** *(hombros)* sloping. **3** *fig (desanimado)* downhearted, crestfallen.

▷ *nm pl* **los caídos** the fallen.

caimán *nm* alligator, cayman.

caja *nf* **1** *(gen)* box. **2** *(de madera)* chest; *(grande)* crate. **3** *(de bebidas)* case. **4** *(en comercio)* cash desk, till; *(en banco)* cashier's desk; *(en supermercado)* checkout. **5** *(féretro)* coffin. **6** AUTO body. **7** *(tipografía)* case. **8** *(banco)* bank: **caja de ahorros** *savings bank.* **9** TÉC housing, casing. **10** *(de piano)* case; *(de violín)* body. ● **caja negra** AV black box. ‖ **caja registradora** cash register.

cajero,-a *nm & nf* cashier. ● **cajero automático** cash point, automatic cash dispenser, ATM.

cajetilla *nf* **1** *(de tabaco)* packet, US pack. **2** *(de cerillas)* box.

cajón *nm* **1** *(en mueble)* drawer. **2** *(caja grande)* crate. **3** *(casilla)* stall. **4** *(entre estantes)* shelf space. ● **cajón de sastre** *fig* jumble.

cal *nf* lime. ● **cal viva** quicklime.

cala *nf* **1** *(ensenada)* cove, creek. **2** *(paraje para pescar)* fishing ground. **3** *(planta)* arum lily.

calabacín *nm* **1** *(pequeño)* courgette, US zucchini. **2** *(grande)* marrow, US squash.

calabaza *nf* gourd, pumpkin.

calabozo *nm (prisión)* jail, prison. **2** *(celda)* cell.

calado,-a *pp* → **calar.**

▷ *adj fam* soaked.

▷ *nm* **calado 1** *(de un barco)* draught (US draft).

calamar *nm* squid.
calambre *nm* 1 *(contracción)* cramp. 2 *(descarga eléctrica)* electric shock.
calamidad *nf* 1 *(desgracia)* calamity, disaster. 2 *fig (persona)* dead loss, good-for-nothing.
calaña *nf pey* kind, type, sort: **esos hombres son de la misma calaña** *those men are all the same type.*
calar *vt* 1 *(mojar)* to soak through, soak, drench. 2 *(agujerear)* to go through, pierce, puncture. 3 *(el sombrero)* to jam on. 4 COST to do openwork on. 5 TÉC to do fretwork on. 6 *(las velas)* to strike; *(las redes)* to lower. 7 *fig (penetrar)* to have an effect on. 8 *fam* to rumble, find out: **¡te han calado!** *they have got your number!*
▷ *vi* MAR to draw.
▷ *vpr* **calarse** 1 *(mojarse)* to get soaked. 2 *(sombrero)* to pull down. 3 AUTO to stop, stall.
calavera *nf (cabeza del esqueleto)* skull.
▷ *nm fig (hombre)* madcap, tearaway, reckless fellow.
calcar [1] *vt* 1 to trace. 2 *fig (imitar)* to copy, imitate.
calce *nm* 1 *(llanta)* rim. 2 *(cuña)* wedge.
calceta *nf* 1 *(prenda)* stocking. 2 *(punto)* knitting. ■ **hacer calceta** to knit.
calcetín *nm* sock.
cálcico,-a *adj* calcium, calcic.
calcificar [1] *vt* to calcify.
▷ *vpr* **calcificarse** to calcify.
calcina *nf* concrete.
calcinación *nf* calcination.
calcinamiento *nm* calcination.
calcinar *vt* 1 to calcine. 2 *fig* to burn.
▷ *vpr* **calcinarse** to calcine.
calcio *nm* calcium.
calcita *nf* calcite.
calco *nm* 1 *(de dibujo)* tracing. 2 *(copia)* copy. 3 *fig (imitación)* imitation, copy.
calcomanía *nf* transfer.
calculador,-ra *adj* calculating.
▷ *nm & nf* calculator. ● **calculadora de bolsillo** pocket calculator.
calcular *vt* 1 to calculate, work out: **calcular una suma** *to calculate a figure.* 2 *(suponer)* to think, suppose, figure, guess.
cálculo *nm* 1 calculation, estimate. 2 *(conjetura)* conjecture, reckoning. 3 MAT calculus. 4 MED gallstone.
caldear *vt* 1 *(calentar)* to warm, heat. 2 *fig (excitar)* to heat up, warm up.
caldera *nf* 1 boiler. 2 *(caldero)* cauldron. ● **las calderas de Pedro Botero** *fam* hell.
calderilla *nf* small change.
caldo *nm* 1 CULIN stock, broth. 2 *(sopa)* consommé.
▷ *nm pl* **caldos** *(vinos)* wines.
calefacción *nf* heating. ● **calefacción central** central heating.
calefactor *nm* 1 *(persona)* heating engineer. 2 *(máquina)* heater.
calendario *nm* calendar. ● **calendario académico** school year.
calentador,-ra *nm* heater.
calentar [27] *vt* 1 *(comida, habitación, cuerpo)* to warm up; *(agua, horno)* to heat. 2 DEP to warm up, tone up. 3 *fig (exaltar)* to heat up, inflame: **calentar el ambien[te]** *to heat up the atmosphere.* 4 *fig (irritar)* to annoy.
▷ *vpr* **calentarse** 1 to get hot, get warm. 2 *fig (enfada[rse])* to get heated, get annoyed. 3 *fig (exaltarse)* [to] get excited. 4 *fam (excitarse sexualmente)* to g[et] horny, get randy.
calentura *nf* fever, temperature.
calibrar *vt* 1 *(graduar)* to calibrate. 2 *(medir)* to gau[ge] (US gage), bore. 3 *fig (estudiar)* to gauge (US gage), weigh up, judge.
calibre *nm* 1 *(de arma)* calibre. 2 TÉC bore, gauge (US gage). 3 *fig (importancia)* importance.
calidad *nf* 1 quality. 2 *(cualidad)* kind, types. 3 *(condición)* rank, capacity. ■ **de calidad superior** superio[r] ‖ **de primera calidad** first-class. ● **calidad de vid[a]** quality of life.
cálido,-a *adj* warm: **un clima cálido** *a warm climate.*
caliente *adj* 1 *(mayor intensidad)* hot; *(menor intensidad)* warm. 2 *fig (acalorado)* heated, spirited. 3 *fam fig (lujurioso)* hot, randy. ■ **en caliente** 1 *(ahora)* righ[t] now. 2 *(entonces)* there and then.
calificación *nf* 1 *(gen)* qualification. 2 *(nota)* mark.
calificar [1] *vt* 1 *(determinar las cualidades)* to describe, qualify. 2 EDUC to mark, grade. 3 *(llamar)* to call. [4] LING to qualify.
caligrafía *nf* 1 *(arte)* calligraphy. 2 *(escritura de una persona)* handwriting. ● **ejercicios de caligrafía** handwriting exercises.
cáliz *nm* 1 REL chalice. 2 BOT calyx. 3 *lit (copa)* cup. ▲ *pl* **cálices**.
caliza *nf* limestone.
callado,-a *pp* → **callar**.
▷ *adj* 1 *(silencioso)* silent, quiet. 2 *(reservado)* reserved, quiet.
callandito *adv* 1 *fam (en silencio)* quietly, silently. [2] *fam (con sigilo)* on the quiet, on the sly.
callando *adv* → **callandito**.
callar *vi* 1 *(no hablar)* to be quiet, keep quiet. 2 *(dejar de hablar)* to stop talking, shut up: **cuando calló todos aplaudieron** *when he stopped talking everybody clapped.* 3 *(un ruido)* to stop.
▷ *vt (esconder)* to keep to OS, not mention. ■ **¡cállate!** keep quiet!, be quiet!
calle *nf* 1 street, road. 2 DEP lane. ■ **dejar a** ALGN **en la calle** 1 *(sin trabajo)* to fire SB. 2 *(sin casa)* to leave SB homeless.
callejero,-a *adj* 1 *(que gusta de callejear)* fond of wandering about. 2 *(relativo a la calle)* street, in the street: **fiesta callejera** *street party.*
▷ *nm* **callejero** *(de calles)* street directory.
callejón *nm* back street, back alley. ■ **en un callejón sin salida** *fig* at an impasse, deadlocked. ● **callejón sin salida** cul-de-sac, dead end, blind alley.
callejuela *nf* narrow street, lane.
callo *nm* 1 MED callus, corn. 2 *fam (persona fea)* ugly sight.
▷ *nm pl* **callos** CULIN tripe *sing.*
calma *nf* 1 calmness, calm, tranquillity (US tranquility). 2 COM slack period, lull. ■ **tomárselo con calma** to take it easy.
calmante *adj* soothing, sedative, tranquillizing (US tranquilizing).

calmar *vt* 1 *(persona)* to calm (down). 2 *(dolor)* to relieve, soothe.
▷ *vpr* **calmarse** 1 *(persona)* to calm down. 2 *(dolor, etc)* to abate, ease off.
calor *nm* 1 heat, warmth: **hace calor** *it is hot.* 2 *fig (actividad)* heat. 3 *fig (afecto)* warmth. ■ **entrar en calor** 1 to get warm. 2 DEP to warm up.
caloría *nf* calorie.
calumnia *nf* 1 calumny. 2 JUR slander.
calumniar [12] *vt* 1 to calumniate. 2 JUR to slander.
calumnioso,-a *adj* calumnious, slanderous.
caluroso,-a *adj* 1 *(tiempo)* warm, hot. 2 *fig* warm, enthusiastic.
calva *nf* 1 *(de la cabeza)* bald patch. 2 *(de un bosque)* clearing.
calvario *nm fig (sufrimiento)* ordeal, calvary.
calvicie *nf* baldness.
calvo,-a *adj* 1 *(persona)* bald. 2 *(terreno)* bare, barren.
▷ *nm & nf* bald person.
calzada *nf* road, roadway, US pavement.
calzado,-a *pp* ⟶ **calzar**.
▷ *adj* 1 wearing shoes, with shoes on. 2 REL calced.
▷ *nm* **calzado** footwear, shoes *pl*.
calzar [4] *vt* 1 *(poner calzado)* to put shoes on. 2 *(llevar calzado)* to wear: **¿qué número calzas?** *what size do you take?* 3 *(poner una cuña)* to wedge, scotch.
▷ *vpr* **calzarse** *(forma reflexiva)* to put (one's shoes) on.
calzo *nm (calce)* wedge, scotch.
calzón *nm en desuso* trousers *pl*.
calzoncillos *nm pl* underpants, pants, briefs.
cama *nf* 1 *(gen)* bed. 2 *fig (de animales)* lair. ■ **estar en cama** to be confined to bed, stay in bed. ‖ **guardar cama** to be confined to bed, stay in bed. ‖ **hacer la cama** to make the bed. ‖ **irse a la cama** to go to bed. ● **cama de matrimonio** double bed. ‖ **cama individual** single bed.
camada *nf (gen)* litter; *(de pájaros)* brood.
camafeo *nm* cameo.
camaleón *nm* chameleon.
cámara *nf* 1 *(sala, pieza)* chamber, room. 2 *(institución)* chamber. 3 *(para el grano)* granary. 4 *(de parlamento)* house. 5 *(de rueda)* inner tube. 6 TÉC chamber. 7 *(fotográfica, de cine)* camera. 8 ANAT cavity.
▷ *nm o nf (hombre)* cameraman; *(mujer)* camerawoman.
▷ *nf pl* **cámaras** *(diarrea)* diarrhoea *sing* (US diarrhea). ● **cámara alta** POL upper house. ‖ **cámara baja** POL lower house. ‖ **cámara de aire** air chamber. ‖ **cámara de cine** cine camera, (US movie camera). ‖ **cámara de comercio** chamber of commerce. ‖ **cámara de gas** gas chamber.
camarada *nm o nf* 1 *(de trabajo)* colleague, fellow worker, workmate; *(de colegio)* schoolmate, schoolfellow. 2 POL comrade.
camarero,-a *nm & nf* 1 *(de bar, restaurante - hombre)* waiter; *(mujer)* waitress. 2 *(detrás de la barra - hombre)* barman; *(mujer)* barmaid. 3 *(en barco, avión - hombre)* steward; *(mujer)* stewardess.
camarilla *nf* 1 clique. 2 POL pressure group, lobby.
camarón *nm* prawn, common prawn.
camarote *nm* cabin.
cambiante *adj* 1 *(gen)* changing. 2 *(carácter)* moody.
cambiar [12] *vt* 1 *(gen)* to change: **han cambiado las sillas** *the chairs have been changed.* 2 *(intercambiar)* to exchange. 3 *(de sitio)* to shift, move. 4 *(dar cambio de moneda)* to change, give change for: 5 *(moneda extranjera)* to change, exchange. 6 *(alterar)* to change.
▷ *vi (gen)* to change: **has cambiado mucho** *you have changed a lot.*
▷ *vpr* **cambiarse** 1 *(mudarse de ropa)* to change, get changed. 2 *(mudarse de casa)* to move.
cambio *nm* 1 change, changing. 2 *(intercambio)* exchange, exchanging. 3 *(dinero suelto)* change, loose change; *(vuelta)* change. 4 *(acciones)* price, quotation; *(divisas)* exchange rate. 5 *(tren)* switch. 6 AUTO gear change. ■ **a cambio de** in exchange for. ‖ **en cambio** on the other hand, but, whereas. ● **cambio de marchas** 1 *(acción)* gear change. 2 *(caja)* gearbox. ‖ **libre cambio** free trade.
camelar *vt* 1 *fam (galantear)* to flirt with. 2 *fam (engañar)* to cajole, sweet-talk, get round.
camelia *nf* camellia.
camello *nm* 1 ZOOL camel. 2 *argot (drogas)* drug pusher, pusher, dope dealer.
camelo *nm* 1 *fam (galanteo)* courting, flirting. 2 *fam (engaño)* hoax, sham. 3 *fam (cuento)* cock-and-bull story.
camerino *nm* dressing room.
camilla *nf* 1 *(para enfermos)* stretcher. 2 *(cama)* small bed. 3 *(mesa camilla)* round table with a brazier underneath.
caminante *nm o nf* traveller (US traveler), walker.
caminar *vi* 1 *(andar)* to walk. 2 *(viajar)* to travel: **caminar a Sevilla** *to travel to Seville.* 3 *fig (seguir su curso)* to move, make its way.
▷ *vt (recorrer)* to cover, travel: **he caminado cinco kilómetros** *I have covered five kilometres.*
caminata *nf* long walk, trek.
camino *nm* 1 *(vía)* path, track. 2 *(ruta)* way, route. 3 *(viaje)* journey: **dos horas de camino** *a two-hour journey.* 4 *fig (medio)* way. ■ **a medio camino** half-way. ‖ **ir camino de** to be on one's way to. ‖ **ponerse en camino** to set off (on a journey).
camión *nm* lorry, US truck. ● **camión cisterna** tanker. ‖ **camión de mudanzas** removal van.
camionero,-a *nm & nf* lorry driver, US truck driver.
camioneta *nf* van.
camisa *nf* 1 *(prenda)* shirt. 2 *(de la culebra)* slough. 3 *(de frutos)* skin. 4 TÉC *(de horno)* lining; *(de cilindro)* sleeve. 5 *(de libro)* jacket. 6 *(carpeta)* folder. ■ **cambiar de camisa** *fig* to change sides. ‖ **meterse en camisa de once varas** *fig* to meddle in other people's business. ● **camisa de fuerza** straitjacket.
camisería *nf* 1 *(tienda)* shirt shop, outfitters. 2 *(industria)* shirt industry.
camiseta *nf* 1 *(ropa interior)* vest, US undershirt. 2 *(niqui)* T-shirt. 3 DEP shirt, jersey.
camisola *nf* 1 *arc (camisa)* camisole. 2 *(camiseta deportiva)* shirt, jersey.
camisón *nm* nightdress, nightgown, nightie.
camorra *nf fam* row, quarrel, fight. ■ **armar camorra** *fam* to kick up a row. ‖ **buscar camorra** *fam* to look for trouble.
campal ● **batalla campal** pitched battle.

campamento *nm* 1 *(acción de acampar)* camping. 2 *(lugar)* camp.
campana *nf* 1 *(gen)* bell. 2 *(de chimenea)* mantelpiece. 3 *fam (extractora)* extractor hood, (US stove extractor hood).
campanada *nf* 1 stroke of a bell, peal of a bell, ring of a bell. 2 *fig (escándalo)* scandal, sensation.
campanario *nm* belfry, bell tower.
campanilla *nf* 1 *(gen)* small bell; *(de mano)* handbell. 2 *(adorno)* tassel. 3 ANAT uvula. 4 *(flor)* morning glory.
campanilleo *nm* ringing.
campante *adj fam (despreocupado)* cool, unconcerned: **se quedó tan campante cuando vio que había suspendido** *she didn't bat an eyelid when she knew she had failed.*
campaña *nf* 1 *(conjunto de actividades)* campaign. 2 *(campo plano)* plain. 3 *(expedición militar)* expedition.
campechano,-a *adj* 1 *fam (franco, alegre)* frank, open, good-humoured (US good-humored). 2 *fam (sencillo)* unaffected, natural.
campeón,-ona *nm & nf* champion.
campeonato *nm* championship.
campero,-a *adj* 1 country, rural. 2 *(al descubierto)* open-air.
campesino,-a *adj* country, rural.
▷ *nm & nf (gen)* peasant; *(hombre)* countryman; *(mujer)* countrywoman.
campestre *adj* country, rural.
camping *nm* camp site. ■ **hacer camping / ir de camping** to go camping.
▲ *pl* **campings.**
campo *nm* 1 *(campiña)* country, countryside: **vivir en el campo** *to live in the country.* 2 *(agricultura)* field. 3 *(de deportes)* field, pitch. 4 *(espacio)* space: **en el campo de la medicina** *in the field of medicine.* 5 *fig* field, scope. ■ **dejarle a ALGN el campo libre** *fig* to leave the field open for SB. ● **campo de batalla** battlefield. ‖ **campo de fútbol** football pitch.
camuflaje *nm* camouflage.
cana *nf* grey hair, white hair.
Canadá *nm* Canada.
canadiense *adj* Canadian.
▷ *nm & nf* Canadian.
canal *nm* 1 *(artificial)* canal. 2 *(natural)* channel.
▷ *nm & nf* 1 *(de tejado)* gutter. 2 TÉC channel. 3 *(animal)* open carcass.
canalizar [4] *vt* 1 *(agua, área)* to canalize. 2 *(riego)* to channel. 3 *fig (opiniones)* to direct; *(dinero)* to channel.
canalla *nf pey (chusma)* riffraff, mob, rabble.
▷ *nm pey (hombre ruin)* rascal, scoundrel, swine, rotter.
canalón *nm (por el borde del tejado)* gutter; *(hacia el suelo)* drainpipe.
canapé *nm* 1 *(sofá)* couch, sofa. 2 CULIN canapé.
Canarias *nf pl* **Islas Canarias** Canary Islands.
canario,-a *adj* GEOG Canarian.
▷ *nm & nf* Canarian.
▷ *nm* **canario** *(pájaro)* canary.
canasta *nf* 1 *(cesto)* basket. 2 *(juego de cartas)* canasta. 3 *(en baloncesto)* basket.
canastilla *nf* 1 *(cestilla)* small basket. 2 *(de bebé)* layette.
canasto *nm (cesto)* basket, hamper.
cáncamo *nm* screweye.
cancela *nf* ironwork gate.
cancelación *nf* cancellation.
cancelar *vt* 1 *(anular)* to cancel. 2 *(saldar una deuda)* to settle, pay.
cáncer *nm* 1 [*pl* **cánceres.**] *(enfermedad)* cancer. 2 **Cáncer** *pl* **Cáncer.**] *(signo zodiacal)* Cancer.
cancerígeno,-a *adj* carcinogenic.
cancha *nf (gen)* ground; *(tenis)* court.
canciller *nm* chancellor.
canción *nf* song. ● **canción de cuna** lullaby.
cancionero *nm* 1 *(poemas)* collection of poems. 2 MÚS songbook.
candado *nm* padlock.
candela *nf* 1 *(vela)* candle. 2 *(lumbre)* fire. 3 *(flor de castaño)* blossom. 4 FÍS candle, candela.
candelabro *nm* candelabra, candelabrum.
candelero *nm* candlestick. ■ **estar en el candelero** *fig* to be at the top, be very popular.
candidato,-a *nm & nf* candidate.
candidatura *nf* 1 *(aspiración)* candidacy, candidature: **presentó su candidatura** *she put forward her candidature.* 2 *(lista de candidatos)* list of candidates.
candidez *nf* ingenuousness, innocence.
cándido,-a *adj* 1 ingenuous, innocent. 2 *lit (níveo)* white, snowy.
candil *nm* oil lamp.
candileja *nf (candil)* oil lamp.
▷ *nf pl* **candilejas** footlights.
candor *nm* 1 *lit (suma blancura)* whiteness. 2 *fig* innocence.
canela *nf* cinnamon.
canelón *nm* 1 *(canalón)* gutter (on a roof). 2 *(labor de pasamanería)* cord.
▷ *nm pl* **canelones** *(pasta)* cannelloni.
cangrejo *nm (de mar)* crab.
canguro *nm* ZOOL kangaroo.
▷ *nm o nf fam* baby-sitter.
caníbal *adj* 1 cannibal. 2 *fig (hombre cruel)* savage.
▷ *nm o nf* cannibal.
canica *nf* marble: **jugar a las canicas** *to play marbles.*
caniche *nm* poodle.
canijo,-a *adj fam* weak, puny.
canilla *nf* 1 ANAT long bone; *(de ave)* wing bone. 2 *(de barril)* tap. 3 *(carrete)* reel, bobbin.
canillera *nf (espinillera)* shin guard.
canino,-a *adj* canine.
canjear *vt* to exchange.
cano,-a *adj* white, grey (US gray).
canoa *nf* canoe; *(bote)* boat.
canódromo *nm* greyhound track, dog track.
canon *nm* 1 *(regla)* canon, norm. 2 *(composición musical)* canon. 3 *(parte de la misa)* canon. 4 *(cantidad de dinero)* tax.
canónigo *nm* canon.
canonizar [4] *vt* to canonize.
canoso,-a *adj* grey-haired (US gray-haired), white-haired: **el pelo canoso** *white hair, grey (US gray) hair.*
cansado,-a *pp* → **cansar.**
▷ *adj* 1 *(gen)* tired, weary: **estoy cansada** *I'm tired.* 2 *(que fatiga)* tiring: **es un trabajo muy cansado** *it's a very tiring job.* 3 *(pesado)* boring, tiresome. 4 *(harto)* tired (**de**, of), fed up (**de**, with).

cansancio *nm* tiredness, weariness.
cansar *vt* **1** *(causar cansancio)* to tire, tire out, make tired. **2** *(molestar)* to annoy; *(aburrir)* to tire, bore. **3** *(tierra)* to exhaust.
▷ *vi (causar cansancio)* to be tiring.
▷ *vpr* **cansarse 1** *(padecer cansancio)* to get tired, tire. **2** *fig (hartarse)* to get tired (**de**, of), get fed up (**de**, with): **me cansé de sus chistes y me fui** *I got tired of their jokes and I left.*
Cantabria *nf* Cantabria.
cantábrico,-a *adj* Cantabrian. ● **mar Cantábrico** Bay of Biscay.
cántabro,-a *adj* Cantabrian.
▷ *nm & nf* Cantabrian.
cantante *adj* singing.
▷ *nm o nf* singer.
cantaor,-ra *nm & nf* flamenco singer.
cantar *vt* **1** to sing: **cantó una canción preciosa** *she sang a beautiful song.* **2** *(en juegos de naipes)* to call. **3** *fam (confesar)* to tell, reveal, confess; *(delatar)* to give away.
▷ *vi* **1** to sing. **2** *(pájaros)* to sing, chirp; *(insectos)* to chirp. **3** *fam (confesar)* to spill the beans, talk, confess. **4** *fam (oler mal)* to stink.
▷ *nm* song.
cántaro *nm* **1** *(vasija)* pitcher. **2** *(contenido)* pitcherful. ■ **llover a cántaros** *fig* to rain cats and dogs.
cante *nm* **1** MÚS singing. **2** *fam fig* blunder. **3** *fam fig (regañina)* scolding.
cantera *nf* **1** *(de piedra)* quarry. **2** *fig* breeding ground. **3** DEP *fig* young players *pl.*
cantero *nm* stonemason.
cántico *nm* canticle.
cantidad *nf (gen)* quantity; *(de dinero)* amount, sum.
▷ *adv fam* a lot: **llovía cantidad** *it was pouring with rain.*
cantimplora *nf* water bottle.
cantina *nf* **1** *(comedor)* canteen. **2** *(de estación)* buffet.
canto *nm* **1** *(arte)* singing. **2** *(canción)* song. **3** LIT canto. **4** *(extremo)* edge: **tiene tres centímetros de canto** *it's three centimetres thick.* **5** *(de cuchillo)* blunt edge. **6** *(esquina)* corner. **7** *(piedra)* stone, pebble. ● **canto rodado 1** *(grande)* boulder. **2** *(pequeño)* pebble.
cantor,-ra *adj* singing.
▷ *nm & nf* singer. ■ **pájaro cantor** songbird.
canturrear *vi* to hum.
canuto *nm* **1** *(tubo)* tube. **2** BOT internode. **3** *argot (porro)* joint.
caña *nf* **1** *(planta)* reed. **2** *(tallo)* cane, stem. **3** ANAT bone marrow. **4** *(de pescar)* rod. **5** *(de cerveza)* small glass of draught beer. ● **caña de azúcar** sugar cane.
cañada *nf* **1** GEOG glen, dell, hollow. **2** *(sendero)* cattle track.
cáñamo *nm* **1** BOT hemp. **2** *(tela)* hempen cloth.
cañería *nf* piping.
caño *nm* **1** *(tubo)* tube. **2** *(chorro)* jet. **3** *(galería de mina)* gallery. **4** *(canal)* navigation channel.
cañón *nm* **1** *(de artillería)* gun; *(antiguamente)* cannon. **2** *(de arma)* barrel. **3** *(tubo)* tube, pipe. **4** *(de chimenea)* flue. **5** GEOG canyon. **6** *(foco)* spotlight. **7** *(de pluma)* quill.
caoba *nf* mahogany.
caolín *nm* kaolin.
caos *nm inv* chaos.
caótico,-a *adj* chaotic.
capa *nf* **1** *(prenda)* cloak, cape. **2** GEOL stratum, layer. **3** *(de pintura)* coat; *(de polvo)* layer; *(de chocolate, etc)* coating, layer. **4** *fig (estrato social)* class, stratum. **5** *(estrato social)* stratum. ■ **andar de capa caída** *fig* to be on the decline, have seen better days. ■ **defender ALGO a capa y espada** *fig* to defend STH to the last.
capacidad *nf* **1** *(gen)* capacity: **hay capacidad para cinco personas** *there's room for five people.* **2** *fig (habilidad)* capability, ability.
capacitar *vt* **1** *(instruir)* to train, qualify. **2** *(autorizar)* to qualify, entitle.
capar *vt* **1** to geld, castrate. **2** *fam fig* to curtail.
caparazón *nm* **1** shell, carapace. **2** *fig* cover, protection.
capataz,-za *nm & nf (hombre)* foreman; *(mujer)* forewoman.
capaz *adj* **1** *(competente)* capable, able: **es una persona muy capaz** *she's very capable.* **2** *(cualificado)* qualified. **3** *(capaz)* capable (**de**, of): **no es capaz de eso** *he's incapable of doing that.*
capazo *nm* **1** *(cesto)* basket. **2** *(para bebé)* carry cot.
capellán *nm* chaplain.
caperuza *nf* **1** *(prenda)* hood. **2** *(tapa)* cap, top.
capicúa *adj* reversible.
capilla *nf* **1** *(iglesia)* chapel. **2** MÚS choir. **3** *(capucho)* hood. **4** *fig (grupo de adictos)* clan. ● **capilla ardiente** funeral chapel, mortuary chapel.
capital *adj* **1** *(principal)* capital, principal, main, chief: **es de importancia capital** *it's of capital importance.* **2** *(ciudad)* capital.
▷ *nm* FIN capital.
▷ *nf* capital, chief town.
capitalismo *nm* capitalism.
capitalista *adj* capitalist, capitalistic.
▷ *nm o nf* capitalist.
capitán,-ana *nm & nf* **1** *(oficial)* captain. **2** *(jefe)* leader, chief. **3** DEP captain.
capitanear *vt* **1** *(gen)* to lead; *(tropas)* to command. **2** *(equipo)* to captain. **3** *(buque grande)* to captain; *(pesquero)* to skipper.
capitel *nm* capital, chapiter.
capitular *vi* **1** MIL *(rendirse)* to capitulate. **2** *(pactar)* to come to an agreement, reach an agreement.
capítulo *nm* **1** *(gen)* chapter. **2** *fig (tema)* subject, matter.
capó *nm* bonnet, US hood.
caporal *nm* **1** *(jefe)* head, leader. **2** *(en una granja)* farm manager.
capota *nf* **1** *(sombrero femenino)* bonnet. **2** *(cubierta plegadiza)* folding hood, folding top.
capote *nm* **1** *(capa con mangas)* cloak with sleeves, cape. **2** *(prenda militar)* greatcoat. **3** *(capa de torero)* cape.
capricho *nm* **1** *(deseo)* caprice, whim, fancy. **2** MÚS caprice, capriccio.
caprichoso,-a *adj* capricious, whimsical, fanciful.
▷ *nm & nf* whimsical person.
caprichudo,-a *adj* → **caprichoso,-a.**
Capricornio *nm* Capricorn.

cápsula *nf* 1 *(gen)* capsule. 2 *(de arma)* cap. 3 *(de botella)* cap, top.
captar *vt* 1 *(ondas)* to receive, pick up; *(agua)* to harness. 2 *(entender)* to understand, grasp. 3 *(atraer a personas)* to attract, recruit. 4 *(atención, interés)* to hold; *(confianza)* to win, gain.
captura *nf* capture.
capturar *vt* to capture, seize.
capucha *nf* hood.
capuchón *nm (de estilográfica, etc)* cap.
capullo *nm* 1 *(de insectos)* cocoon. 2 BOT bud. 3 *tabú (prepucio)* foreskin. 4 *tabú (estúpido)* silly bugger, dickhead.
caqui *adj* khaki.
cara *nf* 1 *(rostro)* face. 2 *(expresión)* face, expression: **tenía la cara muy triste** *he looked sad.*3 *(lado)* side; *(de moneda)* right side. 4 *(superficie)* face. 5 *fig (aspecto)* look. 6 *fam fig (desvergüenza)* cheek, nerve: **¡vaya cara!** *what a cheek!*
▷ *nm o nf fam (caradura)* cheeky person. ■ **a la cara** to SB's face: **se lo dijo a la cara** *he said it to her face.* ‖ **dar la cara** *fig* to face the consequences. ‖ **poner buena cara** to look pleased. ‖ **poner mala cara** to pull a long face. ‖ ● **cara de circunstancias** *fig* serious look. ‖ **cara dura** *fig* cheek, nerve.
carabina *nf* 1 *(arma)* carbine, rifle. 2 *fam fig* chaperon, chaperone.
caracol *nm* 1 *(de tierra)* snail. 2 *(de mar)* winkle. 3 *(concha)* sea shell. 4 *(del oído)* cochlea. 5 *(rizo)* kiss curl. 6 *(del reloj)* snail wheel. 7 *(de caballo)* caracole.
caracola *nf* conch.
carácter *nm* 1 *(personalidad)* character. 2 *(condición)* nature, kind. 3 *(imprenta)* letter.
▲ *pl* **caracteres.** ■ **tener buen carácter** to be good-natured. ‖ **tener mal carácter** to be bad-tempered.
característico,-a *adj* characteristic.
▷ *nm & nf (actor)* character actor; *(actriz)* character actress.
caracterización *nf* characterization.
caracterizar [4] *vt* 1 *(determinar)* to characterize, portray. 2 *(enaltecer)* to characterize. 3 *(representar)* to play well.
▷ *vpr* **caracterizarse** 1 *(distinguirse)* to be characterized: **se caracteriza por su sinceridad** *she is noted for her sincerity.* 2 *(vestirse, arreglarse)* to dress up (**de**, as).
caradura *adj fam* cheeky.
carajillo *nm fam coffee with a dash of brandy.*
caramba *interj* 1 *(extrañeza)* good heavens!, my God! 2 *(enfado)* damn it!
carambola *nf (billar)* cannon, US carom. ■ **por carambola** *fam* by a fluke, by chance.
caramelo *nm* 1 *(dulce)* sweet, US candy. 2 *(azúcar quemado)* caramel, caramel syrup. ■ **a punto de caramelo** 1 syrupy. 2 *fig* just right.
carátula *nf* 1 *(máscara)* mask. 2 *(cubierta)* cover. 3 *fig* theatre (US theater).
caravana *nf* 1 *(expedición)* caravan. 2 *(atasco)* traffic jam, tailback. 3 *(remolque)* caravan, US trailer.
caray *interj* good heavens!, God!
carbón *nm (gen)* coal.
carboncillo *nm* charcoal.
carbónico,-a *adj* carbonic. ● **anhidrido carbónico** carbon dioxide.
carbonífero,-a *adj* carboniferous.
carbonilla *nf* 1 *(residuo de carbón)* coal dust. 2 *(de locomotora)* soot.
carbonizar [4] *vt* 1 *(reducir a carbón)* to carbonize. 2 *(quemar)* to burn, char.
carbono *nm* carbon. ● **dióxido de carbono** carbon dioxide.
carburador *nm* carburettor (US carburetor).
carburante *nm* fuel.
carcajada *nf* burst of laughter, guffaw. ■ **reír(se) a carcajadas** to laugh one's head off, roar with laughter.
cárcel *nf* 1 jail, gaol, prison. 2 *(aparato para sujetar)* clamp. 3 *(ranura)* groove.
carcelero,-a *adj* prison, goal, jail.
carcoma *nf* 1 *(insecto)* woodworm. 2 *(polvo)* wood dust.
carcomer *vt* 1 *(roer)* to eat away. 2 *fig (salud)* to undermine, eat away at; *(envidia, etc)* to eat up, consume.
carcomido,-a *pp* → **carcomer.**
▷ *adj (roído)* wormeaten, riddled with woodworm.
cardamomo *nm* cardamom.
cardenal *(hematoma)* bruise. *nm* REL cardinal.
cardiaco,-a *adj* cardiac, heart.
cardinal *adj* cardinal.
cardiología *nf* cardiology.
cardiólogo,-a *nm & nf* cardiologist.
cardo *nm* BOT *(espinoso)* thistle; *(comestible)* cardoon.
carecer [43] *vi* to lack (**de**, -): **el pueblo carecía de alumbrado público** *the village lacked street lighting, the village had no street lighting* .
carencia *nf* lack (**de**, of).
carente *adj* lacking (**de**, -).
carestía *nf* 1 *(falta)* lack, shortage. 2 *(precio alto)* high cost, high price.
careta *nf (máscara)* mask. ● **careta antigás** gas mask.
carey *nm* 1 *(animal)* sea turtle. 2 *(concha)* tortoiseshell.
carga *nf* 1 *(acción)* loading. 2 *(lo cargado)* load; *(de avión, barco)* cargo, freight. 3 *(peso)* weight. 4 *(de pluma, bolígrafo)* refill. 5 *(de arma)* charge. 6 *(ataque)* charge. 7 ELEC *(de condensador)* charge; *(de circuito)* load. 8 *(tributo)* tax, charge. 9 *fig (responsabilidad)* responsibility, duty. 10 *fig (molestia)* burden. ■ **volver a la carga** *fig* to go on and on about STH.
cargado,-a *pp* → **cargar.**
▷ *adj* 1 *(atmósfera)* heavy, dense. 2 *(bebida)* strong. 3 *fam (borracho)* drunk, (US loaded). 4 *fig* burdened, weighed down: **cargado,-a de responsabilidades** *weighed down with responsibility.*
cargador,-ra *adj* loading.
▷ *nm* **cargador** 1 *(de arma)* magazine. 2 *(de batería)* battery charger. 3 *(de pluma, etc)* filler.
cargamento *nm (gen)* load; *(de avión, barco)* cargo, freight.
cargante *adj fam fig* boring, annoying.
cargar [7] *vt* 1 *(poner peso)* to load. 2 *(arma, máquina de fotos)* to load. 3 ELEC to charge: **cargar las pilas** *to charge the batteries.* 4 *(pluma, etc)* to fill. 5 *(precio)* to charge; *(en cuenta)* to debit. 6 *fig (poner muchas cosas)*

to fill (**de**, with), cram (**de**, with): **cargó su habitación de adornos** *she filled her room with ornaments.* **7** *fig (trabajo)* to burden with, lumber with; *(responsabilidad)* to burden (**de**, with); *(culpa)* to put on, lay on. **8** *fam fig (molestar)* to bother, annoy: **ese tipo me carga** *that guy annoys me.* **9** JUR to charge. **10** INFORMÁ to load. **11** MIL to charge. **12** *(naipes)* to trump; *(dados)* to load.
▷ *vi* **1** *(gen)* to load. **2** *(batería)* to charge. **3** *(toro, elefante, etc)* to charge. **4** *(atacar)* to charge (**contra/sobre**, -). **5 cargar con** *(algo que pesa)* to carry; *(una obligación)* to shoulder, take on.
▷ *vpr* **cargarse 1** *(llenarse)* to load OS (**de**, with): **cargarse de trabajo** *to burden OS with work.* **2** *(el cielo)* to get cloudy, become overcast. **3** ELEC to become charged. **4** EDUC *fam (suspender)* to fail. **5** *fam (destrozar)* to smash, ruin. **6** *fam (matar)* to knock off. ■ **cargar** ALGO **en la cuenta de** ALGN COM to debit SB's account with STH.

cargo *nm* **1** *(peso)* load, weight. **2** *(empleo)* post, position. **3** *(gobierno, custodia)* charge, responsibility. **4** FIN charge, debit. **5** JUR *(falta)* charge, accusation. ■ **correr a cargo de** ALGN to be the responsibility of SB: ‖ **hacerse cargo de 1** *(responsabilizarse de)* to take charge of. **2** *(entender)* to realize: **me hago cargo** *I realize that.*

Caribe *nm* **el Caribe** the Caribbean.

caribeño,-a *adj* Caribbean.

caricatura *nf* caricature.

caricia *nf* caress, stroke.

caridad *nf* charity.

caries *nf inv (enfermedad)* tooth decay, caries *pl*; *(lesión)* cavity.

cariño *nm* **1** *(amor)* love, affection. **2** *(esmero)* loving care. **3** *(apelativo)* darling, love, US honey. **4** *fig (expresión)* caress, hug, kiss, cuddle. ■ **coger/tomar cariño a** ALGN/ALGO to grow fond of SB/STH.

cariñoso,-a *adj* loving, affectionate.

carisma *nm* charisma.

carismático,-a *adj* charismatic.

caritativo,-a *adj* charitable.

cariz *nm* aspect, look.

carmín *adj (color)* carmine.
▷ *nm* **1** *(color)* carmine. **2** *(rosal)* wild rose. **3** *(pintalabios)* lipstick.

carnada *nf* bait.

carnal *adj* **1** carnal. **2** *(pariente)* first.

carnaval *nm* carnival.

carne *nf* **1** ANAT flesh. **2** CULIN meat. **3** *(de fruta)* pulp. **4** *fig (cuerpo)* flesh. ■ **en carne viva** red raw. ‖ **en carne y hueso** *fig* in person. ● **carne de cerdo** pork. ‖ **carne de cordero** lamb. ‖ **carne de gallina** *fig* goose pimples *pl*, goose bumps, goose flesh: ‖ **carne de ternera** veal. ‖ **carne de vaca** beef. ‖ **carne picada** mince, mincemeat, US ground meat, loose meat. ‖ **carne viva** raw flesh.

carné *nm* card. ● **carné de conducir** driving licence. ‖ **carné de identidad** identity card.
▲ *pl* **carnés.**

carnicería *nf* **1** butcher's, butcher's shop. **2** *fig* carnage, slaughter.

carnicero,-a *nm & nf* **1** *(profesión)* butcher. **2** *fig (persona)* butcher.

carnívoro,-a *adj* carnivorous.
▷ *nm & nf* carnivore.

caro,-a *adj (costoso)* expensive, dear.
▷ *adv* **caro** at a high price. ■ **costar caro,-a / salir caro,-a 1** *(ser costoso)* to cost a lot. **2** *(causar daño)* to cost dear.

carótida *nf* carotid.

carozo *nm* cob.

carpa *nf* **1** *(pez)* carp. **2** *(de circo)* big top, marquee. **3** *(tenderete)* stall.

carpeta *nf (archivador)* folder, file; *(informática)* folder.

carpintería *nf* **1** *(establecimiento)* carpenter's shop. **2** *(obra y oficio)* carpentry.

carpintero,-a *adj* carpenter.
▷ *nm & nf* carpenter.

carraca *nf (instrumento)* rattle.

carraspear *vi* to clear one's throat.

carraspera *nf fam* hoarseness.

carrera *nf* **1** *(acción)* run. **2** *(trayecto - de desfile)* route; *(- de taxi)* ride, journey. **3** *(camino)* road. **4** DEP race. **5** *(estudios)* degree course, university education. **6** *(profesión)* career. **7** *(de media)* ladder, US run. **8** *(calle)* street, avenue. ● **carrera contra reloj** race against the clock. ‖ **carrera armamentística** arms race. ‖ **carrera diplomática** diplomatic career.

carreta *nf* cart.

carrete *nm* **1** *(de hilo)* bobbin, reel. **2** ELEC coil. **3** *(de caña de pescar)* reel. **4** *(de película)* spool; *(de fotos)* film, roll of film. **5** *(de máquina de escribir)* cartridge. ■ **dar carrete** *fam (dar conversación)* to go on and on: **¡con la prisa que tenía y él, venga a darme carrete!** *I was in such a hurry and he kept going on and on!* ‖ **tener carrete** *fam (hablar mucho)* to go on and on.

carretear *vt* to cart.

carretera *nf* road. ● **carretera comarcal** B road. ‖ **carretera nacional** A road, main road. ‖ **carretera de acceso** approach road. ‖ **carretera de circunvalación** ring road.

carretilla *nf* wheelbarrow.

carril *nm* **1** *(de ferrocarril)* rail. **2** *(de carretera)* lane. **3** *(surco)* furrow. **4** *(de cortina)* rail. ● **carril bus** bus lane.

carrillo *nm* cheek.

carrito *nm (para la compra)* trolley, US cart.

carro *nm* **1** *(vehículo)* cart. **2** *(de supermercado, aeropuerto)* trolley, US cart. **3** MIL tank. **4** *(carga de un carro)* cartload. **5** *fam (coche)* car. ● **carro blindado** armoured (US armored) car. ‖ **carro de la compra** shopping trolley, US shopping cart.

carrocería *nf* body, bodywork.

carromato *nm* covered wagon.

carroña *nf* carrion.

carroñero,-a *adj* carrion-eating.
▷ *nm & nf* scavenger.

carroza *adj fam* old, old-fashioned.
▷ *nf (tirado por caballos)* coach, carriage.

carruaje *nm* carriage, coach.

carrusel *nm* **1** *(ejercicio ecuestre)* horse tattoo. **2** *(tiovivo)* merry-go-round, US carrousel.

carta *nf* 1 *(misiva)* letter. 2 *(naipe)* card. 3 *(minuta)* menu. 4 *(documento jurídico)* charter. 5 *(mapa)* chart. ■ **a la carta** à la carte. ‖ **echar una carta** to post a letter, US mail a letter. ‖ ● **carta blanca** carte blanche. ‖ **carta de presentación / carta de recomendación** letter of introduction. ‖ **carta de vinos** wine list.

cartabón *nm* set square, triangle.

cartearse *vpr* to correspond (**con**, with), exchange letters (**con**, with), write (**con**, to).

cartel *nm* poster, bill. ■ **«Prohibido fijar carteles»** «Post no bills».

cártel *nm* cartel, trust.

cartelera *nf* 1 *(para carteles)* hoarding, US billboard. 2 *(en periódicos)* entertainment section. ■ **en cartelera** running, on.

cárter *nm* 1 TÉC housing. 2 *(de bicicleta)* chain guard. 3 *(de coche)* crankcase.

cartera *nf* 1 *(monedero)* wallet. 2 *(de colegial)* satchel, school bag. 3 *(de ejecutivo)* briefcase. 4 *fig* portfolio: **ministro sin cartera** *minister without portfolio.* 5 COM portfolio.

carterista *nm o nf* pickpocket.

cartero,-a *nm & nf (hombre)* postman; *(mujer)* postwoman.

cartílago *nm* cartilage.

cartilla *nf* 1 *(para aprender)* first reader. 2 *(tratado breve)* primer. 3 *(cuaderno)* book. ● **cartilla de ahorros** savings book.

cartón *nm* 1 *(material)* cardboard. 2 *(de cigarrillos)* carton. 3 *(dibujo)* sketch. ● **cartón piedra** papier-mâché.

cartucho *nm (de explosivo)* cartridge.

cartulina *nf* thin cardboard.

casa *nf* 1 *(vivienda)* house. 2 *(piso)* flat. 3 *(edificio)* building. 4 *(hogar)* home: **vete a casa** *go home;* **nos quedamos en casa** *we stayed at home;* **fuimos a casa de Ana** *we went to Ana's.* 5 *(familia)* family. 6 *(linaje)* house: **la casa de los Austria** *the House of Hapsburg.* 7 *(empresa)* firm, company. ■ **buscar casa** to go house-hunting. ‖ **echar la casa por la ventana / tirar la casa por la ventana** *fig* to spare no expense, push the boat out. ● **casa de socorro** first aid post.

casaca *nf* fitted short coat.

casado,-a *adj* married.

casamiento *nm* 1 *(contrato)* marriage. 2 *(ceremonia)* wedding.

casar *vt* 1 *(disponer matrimonio)* to marry. 2 *(unir)* to join, fit.

▷ *vi* 1 *(casarse)* to marry (**con**, -), get married (**con**, to). 2 *(armonizar)* to match, go together, fit together.

▷ *vpr* **casarse** to get married (**con**, to) marry (**con**, -).

cascabel *nm* bell.

cascada *nf* cascade, waterfall.

cascado,-a *adj* 1 *(sonido, voz)* harsh, hoarse. 2 *(objeto)* broken-down, clapped-out. 3 *fam (persona)* worn-out.

cascanueces *nm inv* nutcrackers *pl.*

cascar [1] *vt* 1 *(romper)* to crack. 2 *fam (pegar)* to hit, beat up.

▷ *vpr* **cascarse** 1 *(romperse)* to crack.

cáscara *nf* 1 *(de huevo, nuez)* shell. 2 *(de fruta)* skin, peel.

cascarilla *nf* 1 *(de metal)* sheet. 2 *(de cacao)* cocoa.

cascarón *nm* eggshell.

cascarrabias *nm o nf inv fam* grumpy person, bad tempered person.

casco *nm* 1 *(para la cabeza)* helmet. 2 *(cráneo)* skull. 3 *(fragmento)* broken piece, fragment. 4 *(de metralla)* piece of shrapnel. 5 *(de sombrero)* crown. 6 *(envase)* empty bottle. 7 *(de barco)* hull. 8 *(de caballería)* hoof.

caserío *nm* 1 *(casa)* country house. 2 *(pueblo)* hamlet, small village.

casero,-a *adj* 1 *(persona)* home-loving. 2 *(productos)* home-made: **pan casero** *home-made bread.* 3 *(familiar)* family. 4 DEP *(árbitro, juez)* favouring (US *favoring*) *the home team.*

▷ *nm & nf* 1 *(dueño - hombre)* landlord; *(mujer)* landlady. 2 *(guarda)* keeper.

caseta *nf* 1 *(casita)* hut, booth. 2 *(de feria)* stall, stand. 3 *(de bañistas)* bathing hut, US bath house. 4 DEP changing room. 5 *(de perro)* kennel, doghouse.

casete *nm (magnetófono)* cassette player, cassette recorder.

▷ *nf (cinta)* cassette, cassette tape.

casi *adv* almost, nearly: **había casi cincuenta personas** *there were almost fifty people.* ■ **casi no** hardly. ‖ **casi nunca** hardly ever.

casilla *nf* 1 *(casita)* hut, lodge. 2 *(de casillero)* pigeonhole. 3 *(cuadrícula)* square.

casillero *nm* pigeonholes *pl.*

casino *nm* casino.

casis *nm inv* blackcurrant bush.

caso *nm* 1 *(ocasión)* case, occasion. 2 *(suceso)* event, happening. 3 *(asunto)* affair: **el caso Clinton** *the Clinton affair.* 4 *(policial, medical)* case: **es un caso clínico** *it's a clinical case.* 5 *(gramatical)* case. ■ **en caso de que** if: **en caso de que te pierdas, llámame** *if you get lost, call me.* ‖ **en cualquier caso** in any case. ‖ **en el mejor de los casos** at best. ‖ **en todo caso** anyhow, at any rate.

caspa *nf* dandruff.

casquete *nm (prenda)* skullcap.

casquillo *nm* 1 TÉC ferrule, metal tip. 2 *(de cartucho)* case.

casta *nf* 1 *(grupo social)* caste. 2 *(linaje)* lineage, descent. 3 *(de animales)* breed.

castaña *nf* BOT chestnut.

castañetear *vi (dientes)* to chatter.

castaño,-a *adj* chestnut-brown, chestnut; *(pelo)* brown.

▷ *nm* **castaño** 1 BOT *(árbol)* chestnut tree. 2 *(madera)* chestnut.

castañuela *nf* castanet.

castellano,-a *adj* Castilian.

▷ *nm & nf (persona)* Castilian.

▷ *nm* **castellano** *(idioma)* Castilian, Spanish.

castidad *nf* chastity.

castigar [7] *vt* 1 *(aplicar una pena)* to punish. 2 *(dañar)* to damage, ruin.

castigo *nm* 1 *(gen)* punishment. 2 *(en deporte)* penalty.

castillo *nm* castle.

casting *nm* casting, audition.

castizo,-a *adj* pure, authentic.

casto,-a *adj* chaste.

castor *nm* beaver.

castrar *vt (capar)* to castrate.
castrense *adj* military.
casual *adj* accidental, chance.
casualidad *nf* 1 chance, accident. 2 *(coincidencia)* coincidence. ■ **dar la casualidad** to just happen. ‖ **de casualidad / por casualidad** by chance.
casualmente *adv* by chance, by accident.
catabolismo *nm* catabolism.
cataclismo *nm* cataclysm.
catacumbas *nf pl* catacombs.
catalán,-ana *adj* Catalan, Catalonian.
▷ *nm & nf (persona)* Catalan.
▷ *nm* **catalán** *(idioma)* Catalan.
catalejo *nm* telescope.
catalizador,-ra *adj* catalytic.
▷ *nm* **catalizador** 1 catalyst. 2 AUTO catalytic converter, catalyser (US catalyzer).
catalizar [4] *vt* 1 QUÍM to catalyse (US catalyze). 2 *fig* to act as a catalyst for.
catalogar [7] *vt* 1 to catalogue (US catalog). 2 *fig* to classify, class.
catálogo *nm* catalogue (US catalog).
Cataluña *nf* Catalonia.
catamarán *nm* catamaran.
cataplasma *nf* 1 poultice, cataplasm. 2 *fam fig (pelma)* bore.
cataplines *nm pl fam* nuts, balls.
catapulta *nf* catapult.
catar *vt* 1 *(probar)* to taste. 2 *(examinar)* to examine.
catarata *nf* 1 waterfall. 2 MED cataract.
catarro *nm* cold, catarrh: **cogí un catarro** *I caught a cold.*
catastro *nm* cadastre, cadaster, official register.
catástrofe *nf* catastrophe.
catastrófico,-a *adj* catastrophic.
catear *vt* EDUC *fam* to fail, US flunk.
catecismo *nm* catechism.
cátedra *nf* 1 *(cargo de universidad)* professorship; *(de instituto)* post of head of department. 2 *(departamento)* department. 3 *(aula)* lecture room.
catedral *adj* cathedral.
▷ *nf* cathedral.
catedrático,-a *nm & nf (de universidad)* professor; *(de instituto)* head of department.
categoría *nf* category, class; *(social)* class: **un restaurante de primera categoría** *a first-class restaurant.*
categórico,-a *adj* categoric, categorical.
catequesis *nf inv* catechism.
cateto *nm (de triángulo)* side of a right-angled triangle forming the right angle. *nm & nf pey (palurdo)* dimwit, yokel.
catión *nm* cation.
cátodo *nm* cathode.
catolicismo *nm* Catholicism.
católico,-a *adj* Catholic.
catorce *adj (cardinal)* fourteen; *(ordinal)* four
catorceavo,-a *adj* fourteenth.
▷ *nm & nf* fourteenth.

See also **sexto,-a**

catre *nm* 1 *(plegable)* folding bed; *(de campaña)* camp bed.
cauce *nm* 1 *(de río)* bed. 2 *(conducto descubierto)* ditch, trench. 3 *fig (canal)* channel, way.
caucho *nm* rubber.
caudal *adj (de la cola)* caudal: **aleta caudal** *caudal fin.*
▷ *nm* 1 *(de río)* flow. 2 *(bienes)* wealth, riches *pl.* 3 *fig (abundancia)* abundance, wealth.
caudaloso,-a *adj* 1 *(río)* deep, plentiful. 2 *fig (persona)* wealthy.
caudillo *nm* leader, head.
causa *nf* 1 *(gen)* cause. 2 *(motivo)* cause, reason, motive. 3 JUR *(caso)* case, lawsuit; *(juicio)* trial. ■ **a causa de** because of, on account of.
causal *adj* causal.
causalidad *nf* causality.
causante *adj* causal, causing.
causar *vt* 1 *(provocar)* to cause, bring about. 2 *(proporcionar)* to make, give.
cáustico,-a *adj* caustic.
cautela *nf* caution, cautiousness.
cauteloso,-a *adj* cautious, wary.
cauterizar [4] *vt* 1 to cauterize, fire. 2 *fig* to apply drastic measures to.
cautivador,-ra *adj* 1 captivating. 2 *(encantador)* charming.
cautivar *vt* 1 to take prisoner, capture. 2 *fig (atraer)* to captivate, charm: **su sonrisa me cautivó** *I was captivated by his smile.*
cautivo,-a *adj* captive.
▷ *nm & nf* captive.
cauto,-a *adj* cautious, wary.
cava *nm (bebida)* cava, champagne.
▷ *nf (bodega)* wine cellar.
cavar *vt* to dig.
caverna *nf* 1 cavern, cave. 2 MED cavity.
cavernícola *nm o nf* 1 cave dweller, caveman. 2 *fam fig (reaccionario)* reactionary.
caviar *nm* caviar.
cavidad *nf* cavity.
cavilar *vi* to ponder, think about, brood over.
caza *nf* 1 *(acción)* hunting. 2 *(de animales)* game. 3 *fig (persecución)* pursuit, chase. ■ **ir de caza** to go hunting. ● **caza mayor** big game. ‖ **caza menor** small game.
cazabombardero *nm* fighter bomber.
cazador,-ra *nm & nf* hunter.
cazadora *nf (chaqueta)* jacket.
cazar [4] *vt* 1 to hunt. 2 *fam (conseguir)* to catch, land. 3 *fam (descubrir)* to find out, discover: **las mentiras siempre se cazan** *lies always catch up with you.*
cazo *nm* 1 *(cucharón)* ladle. 2 *(cacerola)* saucepan.
cazoleta *nf* 1 *(de espada)* hand guard. 2 TÉC housing. 3 *(de pipa)* bowl.
cazuela *nf* 1 *(utensilio)* casserole, saucepan. 2 *(guiso)* casserole, stew.
cazurrería *nf* sullenness, surliness.
cazurro,-a *adj* sullen, surly.
CE *abrev* **(Comunidad Europea)** European Community; *(abreviatura)* EC.
cebada *nf* barley.
cebar *vt* 1 *(animal)* to fatten, fatten up. 2 *(poner cebo)* to bait. 3 TÉC *fig* to prime.
▷ *vpr* **cebarse** 1 *fig (dedicarse)* to devote OS (en, to). 2 *fig (ensañarse)* to show no mercy (**en/con**, towards), take it out (**en/con**, on), vent one's anger (**en/con**, on).

cebo *nm* 1 *(para animales)* food. 2 *(para pescar)* bait. 3 *fig (de arma)* primer. 4 *fig (señuelo)* bait, lure.

cebolla *nf* 1 onion. 2 *(bulbo)* bulb. 3 *(de ducha)* rose, nozzle.

cebolleta *nf* 1 *(especia)* chives *pl*. 2 *(cebolla)* spring onion.

cebollino *nm* 1 *(especia)* chives *pl*. 2 *(cebolla)* spring onion. 3 *fam fig (persona)* idiot, nitwit.

cebra *nf* zebra. ● **paso cebra** zebra crossing, US crosswalk.

cecear *vi* to lisp.

ceceo *nm* lisp.

cecina *nf* cured meat.

cedazo *nm* sieve.

ceder *vt* 1 *(dar)* to cede, give: 2 DEP *(balón)* to pass.
▷ *vi* 1 *(rendirse)* to yield (**a**, to), give way (**a**, to). 2 *(caerse)* to fall, give way. 3 *(disminuir)* to diminish, slacken, go down: **la fiebre ha cedido** *his temperature has gone down*. ■ **ceder el paso** AUTO to give way, US yield.

cedro *nm* cedar.

cédula *nf* 1 document, certificate. 2 FIN bond, warrant. ● **cédula de citación** JUR summons. ‖ **cédula hipotecaria** mortgage bond.

CEE *abrev* **(Comunidad Económica Europea)** European Economic Community; *(abreviatura)* EEC.

cefalópodo,-a *adj* cephalopod.
▷ *nm* **cefalópodo** cephalopod.

cefalotórax *nm* cephalothorax.

cegar [48] *vt* 1 *(gen)* to blind: **el sol me cegó** *the sun blinded me*. 2 *(tapar)* to block up; *(puerta, ventana)* to wall up.
▷ *vpr* **cegarse** *fig* to become blind, be blinded.

cegato,-a *adj fam* short-sighted.

ceguera *nf* 1 blindness. 2 *fig* obsession, blindness.

ceja *nf* 1 eyebrow. 2 *fig (parte saliente)* projecting edge; *(de un libro)* joint. 3 MÚS bridge. ■ **tener** ALGO **entre ceja y ceja** *fig* to have STH in one's head.

cejar *vi* 1 *(retroceder)* to back up. 2 *fig (aflojar)* to give up, let up.

celda *nf* cell. ● **celda de castigo** punishment cell.

celebración *nf* 1 *(fiesta)* celebration. 2 *(de una reunión, etc)* holding. 3 *(aplauso)* praise, applause.

celebrar *vt* 1 *(festejar)* to celebrate. 2 *(organizar)* to hold: **celebraron el debate ayer** *the debate was held yesterday*. 3 *(alabar)* to praise: **celebrar virtudes** *to praise virtues*. 4 *(estar contento)* to be happy about.
▷ *vpr* **celebrarse** *(tener lugar)* to take place, be held.

célebre *adj* well-known, famous, celebrated.

celebridad *nf* celebrity, fame.

celeste *adj* 1 celestial. 2 *(color)* sky-blue.
▷ *nm (color)* sky blue.

celestial *adj* 1 celestial, heavenly. 2 *fig (delicioso)* heavenly, delightful.

celestina *nf* procuress, bawd.

celíaco,-a *adj* coeliac (US celiac).

celibato *nm* celibacy.

célibe *nm o nf* celibate.

celo[1] [Registered trademark.] *nm fam* sellotape, US Scotch tape.

celo[2] *nm* 1 *(cuidado)* zeal, fervour (US fervor). 2 BIOL *(macho)* rut; *(hembra)* heat.
▷ *nm pl* **celos** jealousy *sing*. ■ **dar celos** to make jealous

celofán [Registered trademark.] *nm* cellophane.

celosía *nf* 1 *(reja)* lattice. 2 *(ventana)* lattice window.

celoso,-a *adj* 1 *(cuidadoso)* zealous, conscientious. 2 *(envidioso)* jealous. 3 *(receloso)* suspicious.

Celsius *nm* Celsius.

celta *adj* Celtic.
▷ *nm o nf (persona)* Celt.
▷ *nm (idioma)* Celtic.

celtíbero,-a *adj* Celtiberian.
▷ *nm & nf* Celtiberian.

céltico,-a *adj* Celtic.

célula *nf* cell.

celular *adj* cell, cellular.

celulitis *nf inv* 1 *(grasa)* cellulite. 2 *(inflamación)* cellulitis.

celulosa *nf* cellulose.

cementerio *nm* cemetery, graveyard.

cemento *nm* 1 *(gen)* concrete, cement. 2 *(de los dientes)* cement. ● **cemento armado** reinforced concrete.

cena *nf (gen)* supper; *(formal)* dinner.

cenagal *nm* 1 marsh, swamp. 2 *fig* jam, tight spot.

cenar *vi* to have supper, have dinner.
▷ *vt* to have for supper, have for dinner.

cencerro *nm* cowbell. ■ **estar como un cencerro** to be nuts, be crackers.

cenefa *nf* 1 *(sobre tejido)* edging, trimming. 2 *(sobre muro, pavimento, etc)* ornamental border, frieze.

cenicero *nm* ashtray.

cenit *nm* zenith.

ceniza *nf* ash, ashes *pl*.
▷ *nf pl* **cenizas** *(restos)* ashes.

censar *vt (hacer el censo)* to take a census of.

censo *nm* 1 *(padrón)* census. 2 JUR tax. ● **censo electoral** electoral roll.

censura *nf* 1 censorship: **la película pasó por la censura** *the film went through the censors*. 2 *(crítica)* censure, criticism, condemnation.

censurar *vt* 1 to censor: **el libro fue censurado** *the book was censored*. 2 *(criticar)* to censure, criticize.

centavo,-a *adj* hundredth.
▷ *nm* **centavo** 1 *(parte)* hundredth, hundredth part. 2 *(moneda)* cent, centavo.

See also **sexto,-a**.

centella *nf* 1 *(rayo)* lightning. 2 *(chispa)* spark, flash. 3 *fig* spark.

centellear *vi* 1 *(gen)* to sparkle, flash. 2 *(estrellas)* to twinkle.

centena *nf* hundred.

centenar *nm* hundred. ■ **a centenares / por centenares** in hundreds.

centenario,-a *adj* 1 *(persona)* hundred-year-old, centenarian. 2 *(periodo, fecha)* centenary, centennial. 3 *(cifra, cantidad)* three-figure.
▷ *nm & nf (persona)* centenarian.
▷ *nm* **centenario** *(aniversario)* centenary, centennial, hundredth anniversary.

centeno *nm* rye.

centésimo,-a *adj* hundredth.
▷ *nm & nf* hundredth.
▷ *nm* **centésimo** *(moneda)* cent, centesimo.

See also **sexto,-a**.

centiárea *nf* square metre (US meter).
centígrado,-a *adj* centigrade.
centigramo *nm* centigram, centigramme.
centilitro *nm* centilitre (US centiliter).
centímetro *nm* centimetre (US centimeter).
céntimo *nm* cent, centime. ■ **estar sin un céntimo** *fam* to be penniless.
centinela *nm & nf* 1 MIL sentry. 2 *(guardián)* watch, lookout.
centollo *nm* spider crab.
centrado,-a *adj* 1 centred (US centered) (**en**, on). 2 *fig (equilibrado)* balanced. 3 *fig (atento)* devoted (**en**, to).
central *adj* central.
▷ *nf* 1 *(oficina principal)* head office, headquarters *pl*. 2 *(eléctrica)* power station. ● **central nuclear** nuclear power station. ‖ **central telefónica** telephone exchange.
centralista *adj* centralist, centralistic.
▷ *nm o nf* centralist.
centralita *nf* switchboard.
centralización *nf* centralization.
centralizar [4] *vt* to centralize.
centrar *vt* 1 *(gen)* to centre (US center). 2 *fig (atención, etc)* to centre (US center), focus. 3 *fig (basar)* to centre (US center) around, base on.
▷ *vpr* **centrarse** 1 to centre (US center) (**en**, on), focus (**en**, on): **se centró en el tema principal** *he focused on the main topic*. 2 *(concentrarse)* to concentrate (**en**, on).
céntrico,-a *adj* central, US downtown.
centrifugadora *nf* centrifuge; *(para ropa)* spin-dryer.
centrifugar [7] *vt* 1 to centrifuge. 2 *(ropa)* to spin-dry.
centrífugo,-a *adj* centrifugal.
centrípeto,-a *adj* centripetal.
centro *nm* 1 centre (US center), middle. 2 *(de ciudad)* town centre, city centre, US downtown area. 3 *(asociación)* centre (US center), association, institution. 4 DEP cross, centre (US center). 5 POL centre (US center). ● **centro comercial** shopping centre, US mall. ‖ **centro cultural** cultural centre (US center). ‖ **centro de mesa** centrepiece (US centerpiece).
centrocampista *nm o nf* midfield player.
céntuplo,-a *adj* centuple, hundredfold.
▷ *nm* **céntuplo** centuple, hundredfold.
centuria *nf* century.
ceñir [36] *vt* 1 *(estrechar)* to cling to, be tight on. 2 *(rodear)* to surround, encircle. 3 *(abrazar)* to embrace. 4 *(la espada)* to gird.
▷ *vpr* **ceñirse** 1 *(atenerse)* to keep (**a**, to), limit OS (**a**, to): **ceñirse al tema** *to keep to the subject*. 2 *(adaptarse)* to adhere (**a**, to), stick (**a**, to), abide (**a**, by): **se ciñe a la normativa** *she sticks to the rules*. 3 *(ajustarse una prenda)* to cling.
ceño *nm* frown. ■ **arrugar el ceño / fruncir el ceño** to frown.
cepa *nf* 1 *(de vid)* vine. 2 *(tronco)* stump; *(de vid)* stock, rootstock.
cepillar *vt* 1 *(gen)* to brush. 2 *(madera)* to plane. 3 *fam (adular)* to butter up.
cepillo *nm* 1 brush. 2 *(de carpintería)* plane. 3 *(para limosnas)* collection box. ● **cepillo de dientes** toothbrush. ‖ **cepillo del pelo** hairbrush.
cepo *nm* 1 *(rama)* bough, branch. 2 *(de yunque)* stock. 3 *(de reo)* pillory, stocks *pl*. 4 *(trampa)* trap. 5 *(para auto)* clamp.
cera *nf* 1 wax; *(de abeja)* beeswax. 2 *(de la oreja)* earwax, cerumen. 3 *(pulimento)* wax, polish.
cerámica *nf* 1 *(arte)* ceramics, pottery. 2 *(objeto)* piece of pottery.
ceramista *nm o nf* ceramist, potter.
cerca[1] *nf (vallado)* fence, wall.
cerca[2] *adv (lugar y tiempo)* near, close: **el museo está muy cerca** *the museum is nearby;* **vente más cerca** *come closer;* **aquí cerca** *near here*. ■ **cerca de** 1 *(cercano a)* near, close. 2 *(aproximadamente)* nearly, about, around. ‖ **de cerca** closely.
cercado *nm* 1 *(lugar)* enclosure. 2 *(cerca)* fence, wall.
cercanía *nf* proximity, nearness.
▷ *nf pl* **cercanías** outskirts, suburbs.
cercano,-a *adj* 1 *(inmediato)* near, close: **el fin está cercano** *the end is near*. 2 *(vecino)* nearby, neighbouring (US neighboring). 3 *(pariente)* close.
cercar [1] *vt* 1 *(poner una cerca)* to fence in, enclose: **cercaron la hacienda** *they fenced in the property*. 2 *(rodear)* to surround, encircle: **unos árboles cercan la plaza** *several trees encircle the square*. 3 MIL to besiege.
cerciorar *vt* to assure, affirm.
▷ *vpr* **cerciorarse** to make sure (**de**, of).
cerco *nm* 1 *(lo que rodea)* circle, ring. 2 *(aureola)* halo. 3 *(marco)* frame. 4 *(asedio)* siege.
cerdo,-a *nm & nf fam pey (persona sucia)* pig, slob; *(persona despreciable)* pig, swine, bastard.
▷ *nm* **cerdo** 1 *(animal)* pig. 2 *(carne)* pork.
cereal *adj* cereal.
▷ *nm* cereal.
cerebro *nm* 1 ANAT brain. 2 *fig* brains *pl*: **es el cerebro de la banda** *he's the brains behind the gang*.
ceremonia *nf* 1 ceremony.
ceremonial *adj* ceremonial.
ceremonioso,-a *adj* 1 *(que observa las ceremonias)* ceremonious, formal. 2 *pey (que gusta de cumplimientos)* pompous, stiff.
cereza *nf* cherry.
cerezo *nm* cherry tree.
cerilla *nf (fósforo)* match.
cerner [28] *vt* 1 *(harina)* to sift. 2 *fig* to observe.
▷ *vpr* **cernerse** 1 *(pájaro)* to hover. 2 *(amenazar)* to threaten, loom, hang.
cernícalo *nm* 1 *(ave)* kestrel. 2 *fig* blockhead, dolt, dimwit.
cero *nm* 1 MAT zero. 2 *(cifra)* nought, zero. 3 DEP nil: **ganamos tres a cero** *we won three nil*. ■ **ser un cero a la izquierda** *fig* to be useless, be a good-for-nothing.
cerrado,-a *pp* → **cerrar**.
▷ *adj* 1 shut, closed. 2 LING close, closed: **vocal cerrada** *close vowel*. 3 *(acento)* broad, thick. 4 *(curva)* tight, sharp. 5 *(ovación)* thunderous. 6 *(barba)* bushy, thick. 7 *(noche)* black, dark; *(cielo)* overcast, dark. 8 *fig (oculto)* obscure, hidden. 9 *fig (persona introvertida)* uncommunicative, reserved. 10 *fig (intransigente)* intransigent, unyielding. 11 *fam fig (torpe)* thick, dim.
cerradura *nf* lock.
cerrajería *nf* 1 *(oficio)* locksmith's trade. 2 *(negocio)* locksmith's shop.

cerrajero,-a *nm & nf* locksmith.
cerrar [27] *vt* **1** to close, shut: **cierra la puerta** *close the door;* **cerró los ojos** *she closed her eyes.* **2** *(grifo, gas)* to turn off; *(luz)* to turn off, switch off. **3** *(cuenta)* to close. **4** *(cremallera)* to zip (up). **5** *(un negocio)* to close; *(- definitivamente)* to close down. **6** *(carta)* to seal. **7** *(discusión)* to end, finish. **8** *(compra)* to close, conclude. **9** *(agujero)* to plug; *(grieta)* to fill. **10** *(paraguas)* to close, shut, put down. **11** *(los puños)* to clench, close. **12** *(frontera, puerto)* to close; *(camino)* to block. **13** *(en dominó)* to block.
▷ *vi* **1** to close, shut. **2** *(punto)* to cast off. **3** *(una herida)* to close up, heal.
▷ *vpr* **cerrarse 1** to close, shut. **2** *(una herida)* to close up, heal. **3** AUTO *(meterse)* to cut in. **4** METEOR to cloud over. **5** *fig (obstinarse)* to dig one's heel in, stand fast; *(ponerse en actitud intransigente)* to close one's mind (**a**, to): **se cerró en sus ideas** *he stuck fast to his ideas.*
cerro *nm* hill.
cerrojo *nm* **1** bolt. **2** *(en fútbol)* blanket defence (US defense). ■ **echar el cerrojo / correr el cerrojo** to bolt.
certamen *nm* competition, contest.
certero,-a *adj* **1** *(disparo)* accurate, good. **2** *(seguro)* certain, sure.
certeza *nf* certainty.
certidumbre *nf* certainty.
certificado,-a *adj (envío)* registered.
▷ *nm* **certificado 1** *(documento)* certificate. **2** *(carta)* registered letter; *(paquete)* registered package. ● **certificado médico** medical certificate.
certificar [1] *vt* **1** *(gen)* to certify. **2** *(carta, paquete)* to register.
cerumen *nm* earwax, cerumen.
cervato *nm* fawn.
cervecería *nf* **1** *(bar)* pub, bar. **2** *(destilería)* brewery.
cerveza *nf* beer, ale. ● **cerveza de barril** draught (US draft) beer. **I** **cerveza dorada** lager. **I** **cerveza ligera** lager. **I** **cerveza negra** stout.
cervical *adj* cervical, neck.
cesante *adj (gen)* dismissed; *(ministro)* removed from office; *(embajador)* recalled.
▷ *nm o nf* suspended official.
cesar *vi* **1** to cease, stop: **cesó de llover** *it stopped raining.* **2** *(en un empleo)* to leave, quit. ■ **sin cesar** incessantly.
cesárea *nf* caesarean (US Cesarean), Caesarean (US Cesarean) section .
cese *nm* **1** cessation. **2** *(despido)* dismissal.
cesión *nf* **1** cession. **2** JUR assignment, transfer.
césped *nm* lawn, grass.
cesta *nf* **1** basket. **2** DEP *(baloncesto)* basket; *(pelota)* pelota basket, jai-alai basket. ● **cesta de la compra** shopping basket.
cesto *nm* basket. ● **cesto de los papeles** wastepaper basket.
cetáceo,-a *adj* cetacean.
▷ *nm* **cetáceo** cetacean.
cetro *nm* sceptre (US scepter).
CFC *abrev* **(clorofluorocarbono)** chloro-fluorocarbon; *(abreviatura)* CFC.
cg *sím* **(centigramo)** centigram, centigramme; *(símbolo)* cg.
chabacano,-a *adj* coarse, vulgar.
chabola *nf* shack: **un barrio de chabolas** *a shanty town.*
chacal *nm* jackal.
chacha *nf* **1** *fam (niñera)* nanny, nursemaid. **2** *fam (sirvienta)* maid.
cha-cha-chá *nm* cha-cha, cha-cha-cha.
cháchara *nf fam (conversación)* small talk, chatter.
▷ *nf pl* **cháchars** *(baratijas)* trinkets, junk *sing.* ■ **estar de cháchara** to have a yap.
chachi *adj fam* → **chanchi.**
chacho,-a *nm & nf fam (muchacho)* boy, lad; *(muchacha)* girl, lass.
chacinería *nf* pork butcher's shop.
chador *nm* chuddar, chudder, chuddah.
chafar *vt* **1** *(aplastar)* to squash, crush, flatten. **2** *(arrugar)* to crumple, crease. **3** *fam (interrumpir)* to butt in on. **4** *fam (estropear)* to ruin, spoil. **5** *fam fig (abatir)* to crush; *(desengañar)* to disappoint.
▷ *vpr* **chafarse** *(aplastarse)* to be squashed, be crushed, be flattened; *(arrugarse)* to become creased, become crumpled.
chaflán *nm* **1** *(bisel)* chamfer. **2** *(esquina)* corner.
chal *nm* shawl.
chalado,-a *pp* → **chalar.**
▷ *adj (loco)* mad, crazy, nuts.
chalar *vt fam (enloquecer)* to drive crazy.
▷ *vpr* **chalarse** *fam* to go mad, go crazy, go nuts.
chaleco *nm* waistcoat, US vest; *(de punto)* sleeveless pullover, tank top. ● **chaleco salvavidas** life jacket.
chalet *nm* **1** *(casa individual)* house, detached house. **2** *(en el campo)* country house, cottage; *(en la montaña)* mountain chalet. **3** *(de lujo)* villa. **4** *(adosado)* semidetached house.
▲ *pl* **chalets.**
chalupa *nf (embarcación)* boat, launch.
▷ *adj fam fig (chalado)* nuts, crazy; *(muy enamorado)* crazy, mad.
chamán *nm* sorcerer, wizard, shaman.
chamarra *nf (zamarra)* sheepskin jacket.
chamiza *nf* **1** *(hierba)* chamiso. **2** *(leña)* brushwood.
chamizo *nm* **1** *(árbol chamuscado)* half-burnt tree. **2** *(leño quemado)* half-burnt log. **3** *(choza)* thatched hut. **4** *pey (tugurio)* hovel, shack.
champaña *nm* champagne.
champiñón *nm* mushroom.
champú *nm* shampoo.
▲ *pl* **champúes o champús.**
chamuscar [1] *vt* to singe, scorch.
▷ *vpr* **chamuscarse** to be singed, get scorched.
chamusquina *nf* **1** scorching, singeing. **2** *fam fig* quarrel, fight. ■ **esto huele a chamusquina** *fam* there's something fishy going on.
chance *nm* chance.
chancho *nm* AM *(animal)* pig; *(carne)* pork.
chanchullo *nm fam* fiddle, wangle, racket.
chancla *nf* **1** *(zapato viejo)* old shoe. **2** *(chancleta)* flip-flop.
chancleta *nf* flip-flop.
chándal *nm* track suit, jogging suit.
chanquete *nm* transparent goby.

chantaje *nm* blackmail. ■ **hacer chantaje a** ALGN to blackmail SB.
chantajear *vt* to blackmail.
chanza *nf* joke.
chao *interj fam* bye-bye!, cheerio!, so long!, ciao!
chapa *nf* **1** *(de metal)* sheet, plate. **2** *(de madera)* panel, sheet; *(enchapado)* veneer; *(contrachapado)* plywood. **3** *(tapón)* bottle top, cap. **4** *(ficha metálica)* metal tag, tally, token. **5** *(medalla)* badge, disc. **6** *fam fig (sentido común)* common sense. **7** AUTO bodywork.
▷ *nf pl* **chapas** game *sing* of tossing up coins.
chapado,-a *adj* **1** *(metal)* plated: **chapado,-a en plata** *silver-plated*. **2** *(madera)* veneered, finished. ■ **estar chapado,-a a la antigua** *fig* to be old-fashioned.
chaparrón *nm* **1** *(lluvia)* downpour, heavy shower: **cayó un buen chaparrón** *there was a downpour*. **2** *fig* shower, bombardment.
chapista *nm o nf* **1** sheet metal worker. **2** AUTO panel beater.
chapotear *vi (agitar en el agua)* to splash about.
▷ *vt (humedecer)* to moisten, dampen, sponge.
chapucear *vt* to botch, bungle.
chapucero,-a *adj (trabajo)* botched, slapdash, shoddy; *(persona)* bungling, clumsy.
▷ *nm & nf* **1** *(que trabaja mal)* bungler, botcher, shoddy worker. **2** *(embustero)* con artist, trickster; *(mentiroso)* liar.
chapurrear *vt* **1** to speak a little, have a smattering of: **chapurreo el inglés** *I have a smattering of English, I speak a little English* . **2** *fam (mezclar)* to mix.
chapuza *nf* **1** *(trabajo sin importancia)* odd job. **2** *(trabajo mal hecho)* botched job, shoddy piece of work.
chapuzón *nm* **1** *(zambullida)* duck, dive. **2** *(baño)* dip. ■ **darse un chapuzón** to have a dip.
chaqué *nm* morning coat.
▲ *pl* **chaqués**.
chaqueta *nf* jacket. ● **chaqueta de punto** cardigan. ‖ **chaqueta de smoking** dinner jacket.
chaquetero,-a *nm & nf fam* turncoat.
chaquetón *nm* winter jacket.
charanga *nf* **1** brass band. **2** *fam (bulla)* din, racket.
charca *nf* pool, pond.
charco *nm* puddle, pond.
charcutería *nf* pork butcher's shop, delicatessen.
charla *nf* **1** *(conversación)* talk, chat. **2** *(conferencia)* talk, informal lecture.
charlar *vi* to chat, talk.
charlatán,-ana *adj* **1** *(hablador)* talkative. **2** *(chismoso)* gossipy.
▷ *nm & nf* **1** *(parlanchín)* chatterbox. **2** *(chismoso)* gossip; *(bocazas)* bigmouth. **3** *(embaucador)* trickster.
charlotear *vi fam* to chatter, prattle.
charloteo *nm fam* chatter, prattle.
charnego,-a *nm & nf pey person from another region of Spain who has settled in Catalonia* .
chárter *adj inv* charter.
▷ *nm* charter.
chascarrillo *nm fam (chiste)* crack, joke; *(anécdota)* witty anecdote.
chasco *nm* **1** *(engaño)* trick; *(broma)* joke. **2** *fig (decepción)* disappointment. ■ **llevarse un chasco** to be disappointed.
chasis *nm* **1** *(del coche)* chassis. **2** *(en fotografía)* plate holder.
chasquear *vi* **1** *(lengua)* to click; *(dedos)* to snap. **2** *(látigo, madera)* to crack. **3** *(un manjar)* to crunch.
chasquido *nm* **1** *(de la lengua)* click; *(de los dedos)* snap. **2** *(de látigo, madera)* crack. **3** *(de manjar)* crunch.
chat *nm* INFORMÁ chat.
chatarra *nf* **1** *(escoria)* slag. **2** *(hierro viejo)* scrap iron, scrap. **3** *fam pey (calderilla)* small change. **4** *fam pey (joyas)* junk jewellery (US jewelry). **5** *fam fig (trasto)* piece of junk.
chatear *vi* INFORMÁ *fam* to chat (**con**, with/to).
chateo *nm* INFORMÁ *fam* chat, chatting.
chati *adj fam* duckie, love, US honey.
chato,-a *adj* **1** *(nariz)* snub; *(persona)* snub-nosed. **2** *(objeto)* flat, flattened; *(barco)* flat, shallow; *(torre)* low, squat.
▷ *nm* **chato** *fam (vaso de vino)* (small) glass of wine.
chauvinista *adj* chauvinist.
▷ *nm o nf* chauvinist.
chaval,-la *adj fam* young.
▷ *nm & nf* **1** *(joven)* kid, youngster; *(chico)* lad, boy; *(chica)* lass, girl. **2** *(apelativo)* mate.
chavo *nm fam* brass farthing.
▷ *nm pl* **chavos** *(dinero)* money *sing*, cash *sing*. ■ **estar sin un chavo** *fam* to be penniless, be broke. ‖ **no tener un chavo** *fam* to be skint, be broke.
checo,-a *adj* Czech.
▷ *nm & nf (persona)* Czech.
▷ *nm* **checo** *(idioma)* Czech. ● **República Checa** Czech Republic.
chef *nm* chef.
▲ *pl* **chefs**.
chelín *nm* shilling.
cheque *nm* cheque (US check). ■ **cobrar un cheque** to cash a cheque (US check). ‖ **extender un cheque** to write a cheque (US check). ● **cheque al portador** cheque (US check) payable to bearer. ‖ **cheque de viaje** traveller's cheque (US traveler's check).
chequear *vt* **1** *(controlar)* to check. **2** *(comprobar)* to check up on. **3** MED to give a checkup to.
chequeo *nm* MED checkup.
Chequia *nf* Czechia.
chica *nf* **1** *(muchacha)* girl. **2** *(criada)* maid.
chicana *nf* **1** *(artimaña)* chicanery, trickery. **2** *(broma)* joke.
chicarrón,-ona *nm & nf fam (chico)* strapping lad; *(chica)* strapping lass.
chícharo *nm* AM *(guisante)* pea.
chicharra *nf* **1** *(cigarra)* cicada. **2** *(timbre)* buzzer. **3** *fig (persona habladora)* chatterbox.
chicharro *nm* **1** *(chicharrón)* pork crackling, fried pork rind. **2** *(pez)* scad, horse mackerel.
chicharrón *nm* **1** *(de cerdo)* pork crackling, fried pork rind. **2** *fig (persona)* sunburnt person.
chichón *nm* bump, lump: **ayer me pegué un buen chichón en la cabeza** *I got a nasty bump on the head yesterday*.
chicle *nm* chewing gum.
chico,-a *adj (pequeño)* small, little.
▷ *nm & nf (gen)* kid, youngster.

▷ *nm* **chico 1** *(muchacho)* boy. **2** *(aprendiz)* errand boy; *(de oficina)* office boy.
chicote,-a *nm & nf fam (hombre)* fine lad; *(mujer)* fine lass.
▷ *nm* **1** *fig (cigarro puro)* cigar. **2** *(extremo de cuerda)* rope end.
chifla *nf (silbato)* whistle.
chiflado,-a *adj fam* mad, crazy, barmy, nuts, bonkers.
▷ *nm & nf fam* nut, loony, headcase. ■ **estar chiflado,-a con/por** ALGO *fam* to be crazy about STH, be mad about STH.
chiflar *vi (silbar)* to hiss, whistle.
▷ *vt* **1** *(silbar)* to hiss, boo. **2** *fam (gustar)* to fascinate, enchant.
▷ *vpr* **chiflarse** *fam (enloquecer)* to go mad, go crazy, go round the bend.
chiflido *nm* whistle, whistling.
chií *adj* Shiite.
▲ *pl* **chiíes.**
▷ *nm o nf* Shiite.
chiíta *adj-nm o nf* → **chií.**
chilaba *nf* jellabah, jellaba.
chile *nm (pimiento)* chili, chili pepper.
Chile *nm* Chile.
chileno,-a *adj* Chilean.
▷ *nm & nf* Chilean.
chillar *vi* **1** *(persona)* to scream, shriek, shout: **2** *(cerdo)* to squeal; *(ratón)* to squeak; *(pájaro)* to squawk, screech. **3** *(radio)* to blare; *(frenos)* to screech, squeal; *(puerta, ventana)* to creak, squeak. **4** *(colores)* to be loud, be gaudy, clash. **5** *fam (reñir)* to tell off. **6** *fig (protestar)* to protest, complain.
chillido *nm* **1** *(de persona)* shriek, scream, cry. **2** *(de cerdo)* squeal; *(de ratón)* squeak; *(de pájaro)* squawk, screech. **3** *(de puerta, ventana)* creak, creaking, squeaking.
chillón,-ona *adj* **1** *(que chilla mucho)* screaming, loud. **2** *(voz)* shrill, high-pitched; *(sonido)* harsh, strident. **3** *fig (color)* loud, gaudy.
▷ *nm & nf* loudmouth.
chimenea *nf* **1** chimney. **2** *(hogar)* fireplace, hearth. **3** *(de barco)* funnel, stack. **4** *fam (cabeza)* nut, block.
chimpancé *nm* chimpanzee.
▲ *pl* **chimpancés.**
China *nf* China.
chinchar *vt fam* to annoy, pester, bug.
▷ *vpr* **chincharse** *fam* to grin and bear it, put up with it, lump it. ■ **¡chínchate!** *fam* hard luck!, tough luck!
chinche *nm & nf* ZOOL bedbug, bug.
▷ *nm o nf fam fig (persona)* bore, nuisance, pest.
chincheta *nf* drawing pin, US thumbtack.
chinchilla *nf* chinchilla.
chinchón *nm* aniseed liquor.
chingar [7] *vt* **1** *tabú* to fuck, screw. **2** *tabú (robar)* to pinch.
chino[1] *nm (piedrecita)* pebble.
▷ *nm pl* **chinos** guessing game *sing.*
chino,-a[2] *adj* Chinese.
▷ *nm & nf (persona)* Chinese person.
▷ *nm* **chino 1** *(idioma)* Chinese. **2** *(colador)* sieve.
chip *nm* INFORMÁ chip.
▲ *pl* **chips.**
▷ *nm pl* **chips** *fam* crisps, US potato chips.
chipirón *nm* baby squid.
Chipre *nm* Cyprus.
chipriota *adj* Cypriot.
▷ *nm o nf* Cypriot.
chips *nm pl* → **chip.**
chiquillo,-a *nm & nf* kid, youngster.
chiquito,-a *adj* tiny, very small, weeny.
▷ *nm & nf* tiny tot, kid.
▷ *nm* **chiquito** small glass of wine.
chiribita *nf (chispa)* spark.
▷ *nf pl* **chiribitas** *fam* spots before the eyes. ■ **echa chiribitas** *fam* to be livid.
chirimoya *nf* custard apple.
chiringuito *nm fam (en playa)* refreshment stall, refreshment stand; *(en carretera)* roadside snack bar hot food stand.
chiripa *nf* **1** *(en el billar)* fluke, lucky stroke, scratch **2** *fig (suerte)* fluke. ■ **de chiripa / por chiripa** *fam* by a fluke, by sheer luck.
chirivía *nf* **1** *(planta)* parsnip. **2** *(ave)* wagtail.
chirla *nf* small clam.
chirona *nf argot* clink, nick.
chirriar [13] *vi* **1** *(al freír comida, etc)* to sizzle. **2** *(rueda, frenos)* to screech, squeal; *(puerta)* to creak. **3** *(aves,* to squawk. **4** *fig (persona)* to sing out of tune.
chirrido *nm* **1** *(de rueda, frenos)* screech; *(de puerta,* creak, creaking. **2** *(de aves)* squawk, squawking.
chis *interj* sh!, ssh!, hush!
chisme *nm* **1** *(comentario)* piece of gossip. **2** *(trasto,* knick-knack; *(de cocina, etc)* gadget; *(cosa)* thing thingamajig.
chismorrear *vi fam* to gossip.
chismoso,-a *adj* gossipy, gossiping.
▷ *nm & nf* gossip.
chispa *nf* **1** *(de lumbre, eléctrica, etc)* spark. **2** *(brillo,* sparkle, glitter. **3** *(brillante pequeño)* small diamond **4** *fam fig (un poco)* bit. **5** *(de lluvia)* drop, droplet. **6** *fig (ingenio, gracia)* wit, sparkle; *(inteligencia)* intelligence; *(viveza)* liveliness. **7** *(mentira)* lie.
chispear *vi* **1** *(echar chispas)* to spark, throw out sparks. **2** [In this sense used only in the 3rd pers; it does not take a subject.] METEOR to drizzle, spit. **3** *fig (relucir)* to sparkle, shine.
chisporrotear *vi* **1** *fam (el fuego)* to spark; *(la leña)* to crackle. **2** *fam (el aceite)* to spit.
chisporroteo *nm* **1** *fam (del fuego)* sparking; *(de la leña)* crackling. **2** *fam (del aceite)* spitting.
chist *interj* **1** *(silencio)* sh!, ssh!, hush! **2** *(para llamar,* psst!
chistar *vi* to speak. ■ **sin chistar** without saying a word.
chiste *nm* **1** *(dicho)* joke, funny story. **2** *(dibujo)* cartoon. ■ **contar un chiste** to tell a joke. ● **chiste verde** blue joke, dirty joke.
chistera *nf* **1** *(de pescador)* fish basket, angler's basket. **2** *fig (sombrero)* top hat. **3** DEP pelota basket.
chistorra *nf thin spicy pork sausage.*
chistoso,-a *adj* **1** *(persona)* witty, funny, fond of joking. **2** *(suceso)* funny, amusing.
▷ *nm & nf (persona)* joker, comic, comedian.
chitón *interj fam* sh!, ssh!, hush!, silence!

chivar *vt* 1 *fam (molestar)* to annoy, pester. 2 *fam (delatar)* to squeal on, tell on.
▷ *vpr* **chivarse** *fam* to tell, squeal, split.

chivato,-a *nm & nf fam (delator)* informer, squealer, grass; *(acusica)* telltale.
▷ *nm* **chivato** 1 *(dispositivo)* gadget. 2 ZOOL kid, young goat.

chivo,-a *nm & nf (cría macho)* kid, young goat; *(cría hembra)* kid, young she-goat. ● **chivo expiatorio** *fig* scapegoat.

choc *nm* shock.

chocante *adj* 1 *(divertido)* funny. 2 *(sorprendente)* surprising, striking, startling. 3 *(raro)* strange, odd. 4 *(escandaloso)* shocking, offensive.

chocar [1] *vi* 1 *(colisionar con algo)* to collide (**contra/con**, with), crash (**contra/con**, into), run (**contra/con**, into). 2 *(colisionar entre sí)* to collide (with each other), crash (into each other). 3 *(una pelota)* to hit (**contra**, -), strike (**contra**, -). 4 *fig (pelear)* to fight, clash. 5 *fig (en una discusión)* to clash, fall out.
▷ *vt* 1 *fig (sorprender)* to surprise; *(extrañar)* to shock. 2 *(las manos)* to shake. 3 *(copas)* to clink.

chochear *vi* 1 to dodder, be senile. 2 *fig (de cariño)* to be tender, be soft: **chochea por su nieto** *her grandson makes her soft.*

chocho,-a *adj* 1 doddering, senile. 2 *fig (de cariño)* tender, soft.

choco *nm* small cuttlefish.

chocolate *nm* 1 *(sólido)* chocolate. 2 *(líquido)* drinking chocolate, cocoa. 3 *argot (hachís)* dope, hash. ● **chocolate a la taza** drinking chocolate. ǀ **chocolate con leche** milk chocolate.

chocolatera *nf* 1 *(vasija)* chocolate pot. 2 *fam fig (coche viejo)* old banger.

chocolatería *nf* 1 *(fábrica)* chocolate factory. 2 *(tienda)* chocolate shop. 3 *(donde se toma)* café specializing in drinking chocolate.

chocolatero,-a *adj (aficionado al chocolate)* fond of chocolate, chocolate-loving.
▷ *nm & nf* 1 *(aficionado al chocolate)* chocolate lover. 2 *(fabricante)* chocolate maker. 3 *(vendedor)* chocolate seller.

chocolatina *nf* → **chocolatín.**

chófer *nm* 1 *(particular)* chauffeur. 2 *(de autocar, etc)* driver.
▲ *pl* **chóferes.**

chollo *nm* 1 *fam (ganga)* bargain, snip, gift. 2 *(trabajo)* cushy job.

chopera *nf* poplar grove.

chopo *nm (árbol)* poplar.

choque *nm* 1 *(gen)* collision, impact; *(de coche, tren, etc)* crash, smash, collision. 2 *fig (enfrentamiento)* clash. 3 MIL skirmish. 4 *(discusión)* dispute, quarrel. 5 MED shock.

chorizar *vt fam* to pinch, nick.

chorizo,-a *nm & nf fam (carterista)* thief, pickpocket; *(delincuente)* yob.
▷ *nm* **chorizo** 1 chorizo *(highly-seasoned pork sausage)*. 2 *(balancín)* balancing pole.

chorrada *nf* 1 *(de líquido)* extra drop. 2 *fam (necedad)* piece of nonsense. 3 *(regalito)* little something. 4 *fam (adorno superfluo)* frill. 5 *fam (fruslería)* trinket, knick-knack.

chorrear *vi* 1 *(caer a chorro)* to spout, gush, spurt. 2 *(gotear)* to drip. 3 *fam (ir sin interrupción)* to flow.

chorro *nm* 1 *(de líquido)* jet, spout, spurt, gush. 2 *(de gas)* jet, blast. 3 *(de poca cantidad)* trickle. 4 *(de luz)* flood. 5 *fig (de cosas)* stream, flood, torrent: **un chorro de insultos** *a torrent of abuse.* ■ **a chorros** in abundance: **tiene dinero a chorros** *he's got plenty of money, he's loaded (with money).* ǀ **beber a chorro** *to drink by directing a stream of liquid into the mouth.*

choteo *nm fam* fun, joking: **¡ya basta de choteo!** *stop joking!* ■ **tomarse** ALGO **a choteo** to take STH as a joke.

choto,-a *nm & nf* 1 *(cabrito)* kid, young goat; *(cabrita)* female kid, young she-goat. 2 *(ternero)* sucking calf.

chovinista *adj* excessively patriotic, chauvinist.
▷ *nm o nf* excessively patriotic person, chauvinist.

choza *nf* hut, shack.

christmas *nm inv* Christmas card.

chubasco *nm* 1 *(chaparrón)* heavy shower, downpour. 2 *fig (adversidad)* setback, adversity.

chubasquero *nm* raincoat.

chubesqui *nm* stove.

chuche *nm fam* sweet, US candy.

chuchería *nf* 1 *fam (golosina)* sweet, US candy. 2 *fam (fruslería)* trinket, knick-knack. 3 *fam (bocado)* titbit, delicacy.

chucho,-a *nm & nf fam (perro)* mutt, US pooch.

chucrut *nm* sauerkraut.

chufa *nf* 1 *(planta)* chufa; *(fruto)* tiger nut. 2 *fam fig (bofetada)* slap.

chulear *vi fam (presumir)* to brag, show off: **mira a Felipe cómo chulea con su coche nuevo** *look at Felipe showing off his new car.*

chuleta *nf* 1 *(costilla)* chop, cutlet. 2 *fam fig (entre estudiantes)* crib, crib note, US trot. 3 *fam fig (bofetada)* slap.

chulo,-a *adj* 1 *fam (descarado)* cocky, cheeky. 2 *fam (vistoso)* showy, flashy. 3 *fam (bonito)* nice, pretty.
▷ *nm* **chulo** *fam (proxeneta)* pimp. ■ **ponerse chulo,-a** *fam* to get cocky, get cheeky.

chungo,-a *adj* 1 *fam (malo)* bad, dud, naff. 2 *argot (estropeado)* broken down, on the blink. 3 *argot (divertido)* funny.

chupa *nf fam (chaqueta)* short jacket, bomber jacket.

chupado,-a *pp* → **chupado,-a.**
▷ *adj* 1 *fig (muy flaco)* skinny, thin; *(mejillas, cara)* hollow. 2 *fig (ajustado)* tight. 3 *argot fig (muy fácil)* dead easy.

chupar *vt* 1 to suck. 2 *(absorber)* to absorb, soak up, suck up. 3 *(hacienda)* to drain, sponge on. 4 *fam (aprovecharse)* to milk.

chupete *nm* 1 dummy, US pacifier. 2 *(tetina)* teat.

chupón,-ona *adj* 1 *(que chupa)* sucking. 2 *fam fig (gorrón)* sponging, scrounging. 3 *fam fig (en deporte, que retiene mucho tiempo el balón)* selfish.
▷ *nm & nf* 1 *fam fig (gorrón)* sponger, scrounger. 2 *fam fig (en deporte, que retiene mucho tiempo el balón)* player who hogs the ball.

churrería *nf* fritter shop.

churro *nm* **1** *(dulce)* fritter, US cruller. **2** *fam (chapuza)* botch, slapdash job. **3** *fam (malo)* rubbish, mess. **4** *fam (suerte)* fluke.
chusco,-a *adj (divertido)* funny, witty.
chusma *nf* riffraff, rabble, mob.
chut *nm* DEP shot, kick.
chutar *vi* DEP to shoot, kick.
▷ *vpr* **chutarse** *argot (droga)* to shoot up.
chute *nm argot* fix.
cianhídrico,-a *adj* hydrocyanic.
cianita *nf* cyanite.
cianuro *nm* cyanide. ● **cianuro potásico** potassium cyanide.
ciática *nf* sciatica.
cibercafé *nm* Internet café.
ciberespacio *nm* cyberspace.
cibernauta *nm o nf* Net user.
cibernética *nf* cybernetics.
cicatriz *nf* scar.
cicatrizar [4] *vi* to heal, cicatrize.
▷ *vpr* **cicatrizarse** to heal, cicatrize.
cicerone *nm o nf* guide, cicerone.
cíclico,-a *adj* cyclic, cyclical.
ciclismo *nm* cycling.
ciclista *adj* cycle, cycling.
▷ *nm o nf* cyclist.
ciclomotor *nm* moped.
ciclón *nm* cyclone.
ciego,-a *adj* **1** *(persona)* blind. **2** *(conducto)* blocked up. ■ **a ciegas 1** *(sin ver)* blindly. **2** *(sin pensar)* without thinking.
▷ *nm* **ciego** ANAT caecum (US cecum), blind gut.
cielo *nm* **1** *(gen)* sky. **2** *(clima)* weather, climate. **3** REL heaven. **4** *fig (Dios)* God. **5** *fig (techo)* ceiling; *(de cama)* canopy. **6** *fig (de boca)* roof.
▷ *interj* **cielos** good heavens! ■ **llovido,-a del cielo** *fig* heaven-sent. ‖ **ser un cielo (de persona)** *fam* to be an angel.
ciempiés *nm inv* centipede.
cien *adj* [Used only before plural nouns.] one hundred, a hundred: **cien libras** *one hundred pounds.*
▷ *nm* one hundred, a hundred. ■ **cien por cien** one hundred per cent.
See also **ciento** and **seis.**
ciénaga *nf* marsh, bog.
ciencia *nf* **1** *(disciplina)* science. **2** *(saber)* knowledge, learning. ● **ciencia ficción** science fiction. ‖ **ciencias naturales** natural sciences.
cienmilésimo,-a *adj* hundred thousandth.
▷ *nm & nf* hundred thousandth.
See also **sexto,-a.**
cienmillonésimo,-a *adj* hundred millionth.
▷ *nm & nf* hundred millionth.
See also **sexto,-a.**
cieno *nm* mud, mire.
científico,-a *adj* scientific.
▷ *nm & nf* scientist.
ciento *adj* one hundred, a hundred: **ciento ocho** *one hundred and eight.*
▷ *nm* **1** *(número)* hundred. **2 un ciento** *(centena)* about a hundred. ■ **por ciento** per cent.
See also **cien.**
cierne *nm* blossoming, blooming. ■ **en cierne / en ciernes** *fig* in embryo, potential, budding.
cierre *nm* **1** *(acción)* closing, shutting; *(de fábrica)* shutdown; *(de radio, etc)* close-down. **2** *(de prenda)* fastener; *(de bolso)* clasp; *(de cinturón)* buckle, clasp. **3** *(de tienda)* shutter, blind; *(de puerta)* catch; *(de automóvil)* choke. ● **cierre patronal** lockout.
cierto,-a *adj* **1** *(seguro)* certain, sure. **2** *(verdadero)* true: **no es cierto** *that's not true.* **3** *(algún)* certain, some.
▷ *adv* **cierto** certainly. ■ **estar en lo cierto** to be right. **lo cierto es que ...** the fact is that .... ‖ **por cierto** by the way.
ciervo,-a *nm & nf (gen)* deer; *(macho)* stag, hart; *(hembra)* doe, hind.
cifra *nf* **1** *(número)* figure, number. **2** *(cantidad)* amount, number. **3** *(código)* cipher, code.
cifrar *vt* **1** *(codificar)* to encode; *(en informática)* to encrypt. **2** *(compendiar)* to summarize. **3** *fig (poner)* to place (**en**, in), pin (**en**, on).
▷ *vpr* **cifrarse** *(valorar)* to come (**en**, to).
cigala *nf* Dublin Bay prawn.
cigarra *nf* cicada.
cigarrillo *nm* cigarette.
cigarro *nm* **1** *(puro)* cigar. **2** *(cigarrillo)* cigarette.
cigoto *nm* zygote.
cigüeña *nf* **1** *(ave)* stork. **2** TÉC crank.
cilindrada *nf* cylinder capacity.
cilíndrico,-a *adj* cylindric, cylindrical.
cilindro *nm* cylinder.
cima *nf* **1** *(de montaña)* summit, top; *(de árbol)* top. **2** *fig (cumbre)* summit, peak.
cimborrio *nm* dome.
cimentar [27] *vt* **1** ARQUIT to lay the foundations of. **2** *fig (afianzar)* to strengthen, consolidate. **3** *fig (establecer)* to found, establish.
cimiento [Also used in plural with the same meaning.] *nm* **1** ARQUIT foundation, foundations *pl*. **2** *fig* basis, origin. ■ **echar los cimientos / poner los cimientos** to lay the foundations.
cinabrio *nm* cinnabar.
cinc *nm* zinc.
cincel *nm* chisel.
cincelar *vt* to chisel, engrave.
cincha *nf* **1** *(de caballo)* girth, US cinch. **2** *(de silla, etc)* webbing.
cinco *adj (cardinal)* five; *(ordinal)* fifth.
▷ *nm (número)* five.■ **¡choca esos cinco! / ¡venga esos cinco!** *fam* put it there!, give me five!
See also **seis.**
cincuenta *adj (cardinal)* fifty; *(ordinal)* fiftieth.
▷ *nm (número)* fifty.
See also **seis.**
cincuentavo,-a *adj* fiftieth.
▷ *nm & nf* fiftieth.
See also **sexto,-a.**
cine *nm* **1** *(local)* cinema, US movie theater: **ir al cine** *to go to the cinema,* US *go to the movies.* **2** *(arte)* cinema. ■ **hacer cine** to make films, US make movies.
cineasta *nm o nf* film director, film-maker.
cineclub *nm* **1** *(organización)* film society, film club. **2** *(local)* cinema, US movie theater.
▲ *pl* **cineclubs.**

cinéfilo,-a *nm & nf* film buff, US movie buff.
cinegética *nf* hunting.
cinegético,-a *adj* of hunting, related to hunting, cynegetic.
cinemática *nf* kinematics.
cinematografía *nf* film-making, cinematography, US movie-making.
cinematográfico,-a *adj* cinematographic: **la industria cinematográfica** *the film industry,* US *the movie industry.*
cinematógrafo *nm* film projector, US movie projector.
cinética *nf* kinetics.
cinético,-a *adj* kinetic.
cínico,-a *adj* cynical.
▷ *nm & nf* cynic.
cinismo *nm* cynicism.
cinta *nf* **1** *(gen)* band, strip, *(decorativa)* ribbon. **2** COST braid, edging. **3** *(para el pelo)* headband. **4** TÉC tape. **5** *(de máquina de escribir)* ribbon. **6** CINE film. **7** *(casete)* tape. **8** *(de recogida de equipaje)* carrousel. ● **cinta adhesiva** adhesive tape. ‖ **cinta magnética** magnetic tape. ‖ **cinta métrica** tape measure. ‖ **cinta transportadora** conveyor belt.
cintura *nf* waist.
cinturilla *nf* waistband.
cinturón *nm* belt. ● **cinturón de seguridad** safety belt, seat belt.
ciprés *nm* cypress.
circo *nm* **1** *(gen)* circus. **2** GEOG cirque.
circonita *nf* zirconite.
circuito *nm* **1** *(eléctrico)* circuit. **2** *(contorno)* circumference. **3** *(recorrido)* tour, circuit. **4** *(de carreras)* track, circuit.
circulación *nf* **1** *(gen)* circulation. **2** *(de vehículos)* traffic. ● **circulación sanguínea** blood circulation. ‖ **código de (la) circulación** highway code.
circular *adj* circular.
▷ *nf (carta)* circular, circular letter.
▷ *vi* **1** *(gen)* to circulate, move, go round. **2** *(líquido, electricidad)* to circulate, flow. **3** *(coche)* to drive; *(trenes, autobuses)* to run; *(peatón)* to walk. **4** *fig (rumor, etc)* to spread, get round.
círculo *nm* **1** *(gen)* circle. **2** *(asociación)* club, circle.
▷ *nm pl* **círculos** *(ambientes)* circles. ● **círculo familiar** family circle. ‖ **círculo polar antártico** Antarctic Circle. ‖ **círculo polar ártico** Arctic Circle. ‖ **círculo vicioso** *fig* vicious circle.
circuncisión *nf* circumcision.
circundar *vt* to surround.
circunferencia *nf* circumference.
circunflejo,-a *adj* circumflex.
▷ *nm* **circunflejo** circumflex.
circunloquio *nm* circumlocution.
circunscribir *vt* to circumscribe.
▷ *vpr* **circunscribirse** *(ceñirse)* to confine OS (**a**, to), limit OS (**a**, to).
▲ *pp* **circunscrito,-a.**
circunscripción *nf* district, area. ● **circunscripción electoral** constituency.
circunscrito,-a *pp* ⟶ **circunscribir.**
circunstancia *nf* circumstance. ■ **en estas circunstancias** under the circumstances.
circunstancial *adj* circumstantial.
circunvalar *vt* to go round.
cirio *nm* long wax candle. ■ **armar un cirio** *fam* to kick up a rumpus.
cirrosis *nf inv* cirrhosis.
ciruela *nf* plum. ● **ciruela claudia** greengage. ‖ **ciruela pasa** prune.
ciruelo *nm* plum tree.
cirugía *nf* surgery. ● **cirugía estética / cirugía plástica** plastic surgery.
cirujano,-a *nm & nf* surgeon.
cisma *nm* **1** REL schism. **2** *(desacuerdo)* discord, split. **3** POL split.
cisne *nm* swan. ● **canto del cisne** swan song.
cisterciense *adj* Cistercian.
▷ *nm o nf* Cistercian.
cisterna *nf* cistern, tank.
cistitis *nf inv* cystitis.
cita *nf* **1** *(para negocios, médico, etc)* appointment: **tengo una cita con mi abogado** *I have an appointment with my lawyer.* **2** *(amorosa)* date. **3** *(mención)* quotation. ■ **darse cita 1** to meet. **2** *fig* to come together. ‖ **tener una cita** to have an appointment, have an engagement. ● **cita a ciegas** blind date.
citación *nf* **1** *(mención)* quotation. **2** JUR citation, summons.
citar *vt* **1** *(dar cita)* to make an appointment with, arrange to meet. **2** *(mencionar)* to quote. **3** JUR to summon.
▷ *vpr* **citarse** to arrange to meet (**con**, -).
citerior *adj* hithermost.
citología *nf* cytology.
citoplasma *nm* cytoplasm.
cítrico,-a *adj* citric.
▷ *nm pl* **cítricos** citrus fruits.
ciudad *nf* city, town. ● **ciudad dormitorio** dormitory suburb, dormitory town, commuter suburb. ‖ **ciudad universitaria** university campus.
ciudadanía *nf* citizenship.
ciudadano,-a *adj* civic.
▷ *nm & nf* citizen.
▷ *nm pl* **los ciudadanos** townspeople, city dwellers.
ciudadela *nf* citadel, fortress.
cívico,-a *adj* civic.
civil *adj* **1** civil. **2** *(no militar)* civilian. **3** *(no eclesiástico)* lay, secular.
civilización *nf* civilization.
civilizado,-a *pp* ⟶ **civilizar.**
▷ *adj* civilized.
civilizar [4] *vt* to civilize.
civismo *nm* **1** good citizenship, community spirit. **2** *(al servicio de los demás)* civility.
cizalla [Also used in plural with the same meaning.] *nf* **1** *(tijeras)* metal shears *pl*, wire cutters *pl*. **2** *(fragmento de metal)* metal clippings *pl*, metal cuttings *pl*.
cizaña *nf* BOT bearded darnel. ■ **meter cizaña / sembrar cizaña** *fig* to cause trouble, stir up trouble.
cl *sím* **(centilitro)** centilitre (US centiliter); *(símbolo)* cl.

clamar *vi* to clamour (US clamor) (**por**, for), cry out (**por**, for).
▷ *vt* to cry out for.
clamor *nm* 1 *(griterío)* shouting, din, noise. 2 *(voces de protesta o queja)* clamour (US clamor), outcry. 3 *(toque de campanas)* knell, toll.
clamoroso,-a *adj* 1 *(de voces)* clamorous, loud. 2 *(de quejas)* complaining. 3 *(éxito)* overwhelming.
clan *nm* clan.
clandestinidad *nf* secrecy. ■ **en la clandestinidad** in secret, underground.
clandestino,-a *adj* clandestine, underground, secret.
claqué *nm* tap dancing.
claqueta *nf* clapperboard.
claraboya *nf* skylight.
clarear *vt* 1 *(dar claridad)* to light up, illuminate. 2 *(aclarar un color)* to make lighter.
▷ *vi* [Used only in the 3rd pers; it does not take a subject.] 1 *(amanecer)* to dawn. 2 *(despejar el cielo)* to clear up.
▷ *vpr* **clarearse** 1 *(transparentarse)* to let the light through, be transparent. 2 *fig (delatarse)* to give OS away.
claridad *nf* 1 *(luminosidad)* light, brightness. 2 *(del agua, voz, etc)* clearness. 3 *(inteligibilidad)* clearness, clarity. ■ **con claridad** clearly.
clarificar [1] *vt* to clarify, clear up.
clarín *nm (instrumento)* bugle.
▷ *nm o nf (músico)* bugler.
clarinete *nm (instrumento)* clarinet.
▷ *nm o nf (músico)* clarinettist, clarinetist.
clarinetista *nm o nf* clarinettist, clarinetist.
clarividencia *nf* 1 *(percepción paranormal)* clairvoyance. 2 *(comprensión)* lucidity.
claro,-a *adj* 1 *(gen)* clear. 2 *(iluminado)* bright, well-lit. 3 *(color)* light: **azul claro** *light blue.* 4 *(salsa, etc)* thin; *(café, chocolate, etc)* weak. 5 *(evidente)* clear.
▷ *adv* clearly.
▷ *nm* **claro** 1 *(gen)* gap, space; *(de bosque)* clearing. 2 *(en el pelo)* bald patch.
▷ *interj* ¡claro! of course! ■ **dejar ALGO claro** to make STH clear. ‖ **estar claro** to be clear. ‖ **¡lo llevas claro! / ¡lo tienes claro!** *fam* you've got it coming to you! ‖ **más claro,-a que el agua** *fam* as clear as daylight. ‖ **poner en claro** to make plain, clear up. ‖ **sacar en claro** to get out.
clase *nf* 1 *(grupo, categoría)* class. 2 *(aula)* classroom; *(de universidad)* lecture hall. 3 *(tipo)* type, sort. ■ **asistir a clase** to attend class. ‖ **dar clase** to teach. ‖ **tener clase** to have class. ‖ **toda clase de** all sorts of. ● **clase alta** upper class. ‖ **clase baja** lower class. ‖ **clase de conducir** driving lesson. ‖ **clase dirigente** ruling class. ‖ **clase media** middle class. ‖ **clase obrera** working class. ‖ **clase particular** private class, private lesson. ‖ **clase preferente** business class. ‖ **primera clase** first class.
clasicismo *nm* classicism.
clásico,-a *adj* 1 *(de los clásicos)* classical: **literatura clásica** *classical literature.* 2 *(típico)* classic, typical. 3 *(tradicional)* classic.
▷ *nm* **clásico** classic: **este libro es un clásico de la ciencia ficción** *this book is a science-fiction classic.*
clasificación *nf* 1 *(gen)* classification. 2 *(distribución)* sorting, filing. 3 DEP league, table. 4 *(de discos)* top twenty, hit parade.
clasificar [1] *vt* 1 to class, classify. 2 *(distribuir)* to sort, file.
▷ *vpr* **clasificarse** 1 DEP to qualify. 2 *(llegar)* to come.
clasista *adj* class-conscious.
▷ *nm o nf* class-conscious person.
claudicar [1] *vi* to yield, give in.
claustro *nm* 1 ARQUIT cloister. 2 *(estado monástico)* monastic life. 3 *(conjunto de profesores)* staff. 4 *(junta de profesores)* staff meeting; *(de universidad)* senate.
claustrofobia *nf* claustrophobia.
claustrofóbico,-a *adj* claustrophobic.
cláusula *nf* clause.
clausura *nf* 1 *(cierre)* closure. 2 *(acto)* closing ceremony, closing session.
clausurar *vt* 1 *(poner fin)* to close, conclude. 2 *(cerrar)* to close (down).
clavado,-a *pp* → **clavar**.
▷ *adj* 1 *(con clavos)* nailed, nail-studded. 2 *fam (preciso)* exact, precise. 3 *(fijo)* firmly fixed. ■ **ser clavado,-a a ALGN** *fam* to be the spitting image of SB.
clavar *vt* 1 *(con clavos)* to nail. 2 *(un clavo)* to bang, hammer in; *(estaca)* to drive. 3 *fig (atención)* to fix; *(ojos)* to rivet. 4 *fam (cobrar caro)* to sting, fleece.
▷ *vpr* **clavarse** *(gen)* to stick.
clave *nf* 1 *(de un enigma, etc)* key, clue: **la clave del éxito** *the key to success.* 2 *(de signos)* code, key, cipher: **un mensaje en clave** *a coded message.* 3 MÚS key. 4 ARQUIT keystone.
▷ *nm (instrumento)* harpsichord.
▷ *adj (importante)* key: **el hombre clave es el ministro de Hacienda** *the key man is the Chancellor of the Exchequer.*
clavel *nm* carnation.
clavicémbalo *nm* harpsichord.
clavicordio *nm* clavichord.
clavícula *nf* clavicle, collarbone.
clavija *nf* 1 TÉC peg. 2 ELEC *(de enchufe)* pin.
clavijero *nm* MÚS pegbox.
clavillo *nm* 1 *(de abanico, tijeras)* pivot, pin. 2 *(de piano)* wrest pin.
clavo *nm* 1 nail. 2 BOT clove. 3 *(callo)* corn. 4 *tabú (polvo)* screw: **echar un clavo** *to have a screw.* ■ **dar en el clavo** *fig* to hit the nail on the head. ‖ **no dar ni clavo** *fam* not to lift a finger.
claxon® *nm* horn, hooter.
▲ *pl* **cláxones**.
clemencia *nf* clemency, mercy.
clemente *adj* forgiving, merciful.
clerical *adj* clerical.
clérigo *nm* priest.
clero *nm* clergy.
clic *nm* click. ■ **hacer clic** 1 *(hacer ruido)* to click, go click. 2 INFORMÁ to click.
clicar *vt* to click on.
▷ *vi* to click.
cliché *nm* 1 *(imprenta)* plate. 2 *(fotografía)* negative. 3 *fig (lugar común)* cliché.
clienta *nf* client, customer.
cliente *nm o nf* client, customer.
clientela *nf* customers *pl*, clients *pl*, clientele.

lima *nm* 1 climate. 2 *fig* atmosphere, climate.
imático,-a *adj* climatic, climatical.
imatización *nf* air-conditioning.
imatizado,-a *pp* → **climatizar.**
adj air-conditioned.
imatizar [4] *vt* to air-condition.
imatología *nf* climatology.
ímax *nm inv* climax.
ínica *nf* 1 *(departamento)* clinic. 2 *(hospital)* clinic, private hospital.
ínico,-a *adj* clinical: **muerte clínica** *clinical death.*
nm & nf (médico) clinician, physician.
ip *nm* 1 *(para papel)* paper clip. 2 *(para pelo)* hairgrip, US bobby pin. 3 *(pendiente)* clip-on earring.
▲ *pl* **clips.**
isé *nm* → **cliché.**
ítoris *nm inv* clitoris.
oaca *nf* sewer, drain.
on *nm* clone.
onación *nf* cloning.
onar *vt* to clone.
ónico,-a *adj* cloned.
nm **clónico** *(ordenador)* clone.
oquear *vi* to cluck.
oramfenicol *nm* chloramphenicol.
orato *nm* chlorate.
orhídrico,-a *adj* hydrochloric. ● **ácido clorhídico** hydrochloric acid.
órico,-a *adj* chloric.
oro *nm* chlorine.
orofila *nf* chlorophyll.
orofílico,-a *adj* chlorophyllous.
oroformo *nm* chloroform.
oruro *nm* chloride. ● **cloruro sódico** sodium chloride.
own *nm* clown.
▲ *pl* **clowns.**
ub *nm* club, society. ● **club de fútbol** football club. ‖ **club de tenis** tennis club. ‖ **club náutico** yacht club.
▲ *pl* **clubs o clubes.**
uniacense *adj* Cluniac.
nm Cluniac.
m *sím* **(centímetro)** centimetre (US centimeter); *(símbolo)* cm.
oacción *nf* coercion, compulsion.
oaccionar *vt* to coerce, compel.
oagulación *nf* coagulation, clotting.
oagular *vt (gen)* to coagulate, clot; *(leche)* to curdle.
vpr **coagularse** to coagulate, clot; *(leche)* to curdle.
oágulo *nm* coagulum, clot.
oala *nm* koala, koala bear.
oalición *nf* coalition.
oartada *nf* alibi.
oartar *vt* to limit, restrict.
oaxial *adj* coaxial.
oba *nf fam* soft soap. ■ **dar coba a** ALGN *fam* to soft-soap SB.
obalto *nm* cobalt.
obarde *adj* cowardly.
nm o nf coward.
obardía *nf* cowardice.
obaya *nm* guinea pig.
cobertizo *nm* shed, shack.
cobertura *nf* 1 *(gen)* cover. 2 *(de una red, servicio)* coverage. ● **cobertura de chocolate** chocolate coating. ‖ **cobertura de seguros** insurance cover.
cobijar *vt* 1 *(cubrir)* to cover. 2 *fig* to shelter. 3 *fig (a un criminal)* to harbour (US harbor).
▷ *vpr* **cobijarse** to take shelter.
cobijo *nm* 1 *(hospedaje)* lodging. 2 *(refugio)* shelter. 3 *fig* protection, refuge.
cobol *nm* INFORMÁ COBOL.
cobra *nf (serpiente)* cobra.
cobrador,-ra *nm & nf* 1 *(de luz, etc)* collector. 2 *(de transporte - hombre)* conductor; *(- mujer)* conductress.
cobrar *vt* 1 *(fijar precio por)* to charge; *(cheques)* to cash; *(salario)* to earn. 2 *(caza)* to retrieve. 3 to get: **si no te estás quieto vas a cobrar una torta** *if you don't keep still you'll get a smack.* 4 *fig (adquirir)* to gain, get.
▷ *vi* to be in for it.
▷ *vpr* **cobrarse** 1 *(dinero)* to take, collect. 2 *(víctimas)* to claim. 3 *(recuperar)* to recover (**de**, from); *(volver en sí)* to come round.
cobre *nm* 1 *(metal)* copper. 2 *(batería de cocina)* copper pans *pl.* ■ **batir el cobre** *fam* to go hard at it.
cobrizo,-a *adj* copper, copper-coloured (US copper-colored), coppery .
cobro *nm* 1 *(pago)* payment. 2 *(cobranza)* collection; *(de cheque)* cashing. 3 *(en caza)* retrieval. ■ **llamar a cobro revertido** to reverse the charges, US call collect. ● **cobro revertido** reverse-charge, US collect.
coca *nf* 1 *(arbusto)* coca. 2 *argot* coke. 3 *fam (bebida)* Coke®.
cocaína *nf* cocaine.
cocción *nf (gen)* cooking; *(en agua)* boiling; *(en horno)* baking.
cóccix *nm inv* coccyx.
cocear *vi* to kick.
cocer [54] *vt (gen)* to cook; *(hervir)* to boil; *(al horno)* to bake.
▷ *vi (hervir)* to boil.
▷ *vpr* **cocerse** 1 *(gen)* to cook; *(hervir)* to boil; *(al horno)* to bake. 2 *fam (de calor)* to be roasting, be boiling. 3 *fam (tramarse)* to be cooking, be afoot, be going on.
cochambroso,-a *adj fam* filthy, dirty.
coche *nm* 1 *(automóvil)* car, automobile, motorcar: **fuimos en coche** *we went by car.* 2 *(de tren, de caballos)* carriage, coach. 3 *(de niño)* pram, US baby carriage. ● **coche cama** sleeping car. ‖ **coche de alquiler** hired car, US rented car. ‖ **coche de bomberos** fire engine. ‖ **coche de carreras** racing car. ‖ **coches de choque** dodgems, bumper cars.
cochera *nf* depot.
cochinillo *nm* sucking pig.
cochino,-a *adj* 1 *(sucio)* filthy, disgusting. 2 *(miserable)* damn, bloody, lousy.
▷ *nm & nf* 1 ZOOL *(gen)* pig; *(macho)* swine; *(hembra)* sow. 2 *fam (persona)* dirty person, filthy person, pig.
cocido,-a *pp* → **cocer.**
▷ *adj* cooked; *(en agua)* boiled; *(al horno)* baked.
▷ *nm* **cocido** CULIN stew.
cociente *nm* quotient.

cocina *nf* 1 *(lugar)* kitchen. 2 *(gastronomía)* cooking: **cocina española** *Spanish cooking, Spanish cuisine.* 3 *(aparato)* cooker, US stove. ● **cocina casera** home cooking. ‖ **cocina de gas** gas cooker, US gas stove. ‖ **cocina de mercado** seasonal produce. ‖ **cocina eléctrica** electric cooker, US electric stove.

cocinar *vt* to cook.
▷ *vi* to cook.

cocinero,-a *nm & nf* cook. ● **primer cocinero** chef.

cocker *nm* cocker, cocker spaniel.
▲ *pl* **cockers.**

coco[1] *nm* 1 BOT *(árbol)* coconut palm. 2 *(fruta)* coconut. ● **coco rallado** desiccated coconut.

coco[2] *nm* 1 *fam (fantasma)* bogeyman. 2 *argot (cabeza)* noddle, noggin, nut. ■ **comer el coco a** ALGN *fam* to brainwash SB. ‖ **comerse el coco** *fam* to get worked up, worry about it.

cocodrilo *nm* crocodile.

cocotero *nm* coconut palm.

cóctel *nm* 1 *(bebida)* cocktail. 2 *(fiesta)* cocktail party.

coctelera *nf* cocktail shaker.

Cód. *abrev* (**código**) code.

coda *nf* MÚS coda.

codazo *nm* 1 *(golpe)* poke with one's elbow, blow with one's elbow: **le pegó un codazo** *she poked him with her elbow.* 2 *(señal)* nudge with one's elbow. ■ **abrirse paso a codazos** to elbow one's way through.

codear *vi (empujar)* to elbow.
▷ *vpr* **codearse** to rub shoulders (**con**, with), hobnob (**con**, with) .

codera *nf* elbow patch.

códice *nm* codex.

codicia *nf* greed, covetousness, coveting.

codiciado,-a *pp* → **codiciar.**
▷ *adj* coveted, much desired.

codiciar [12] *vt* to covet, desire, crave for.

codicilo *nm* codicil.

codicioso,-a *adj* covetous, greedy.
▷ *nm & nf* covetous person, greedy person.

codificación *nf* 1 *(de leyes)* codification. 2 *(de mensajes)* encoding. 3 INFORMÁ coding, code.

codificador,-ra *adj* 1 JUR codifying. 2 *(de mensajes)* encoding.
▷ *nm & nf* 1 JUR codifier. 2 *(de mensajes)* encoder.
▷ *nm* **codificador** INFORMÁ encoder.

codificar *vt* 1 *(leyes)* to codify. 2 *(mensajes)* to encode. 3 INFORMÁ to code.

código *nm* code. ● **código de barras** bar code. ‖ **código de la circulación** highway code. ‖ **código de señales** MAR flag signals. ‖ **código Morse** Morse code.

codillo *nm* 1 *(del brazo)* elbow. 2 *(en cocina)* shoulder. 3 *(de tubería)* elbow.

codo *nm* 1 ANAT elbow. 2 TÉC bend. ■ **alzar el codo / empinar el codo** *fam* to have a few drinks, knock them back. ‖ **codo a codo / codo con codo** *fig* side by side, closely. ‖ **de codos** on one's elbows. ‖ **hablar por los codos** *fam* to talk nineteen to the dozen, talk nonstop. ‖ **romperse los codos** *fig* to study a lot, swot, cram.

codorniz *nf* quail.
▲ *pl* **codornices.**

coeficiente *nm* 1 MAT coefficient. 2 *(grado)* degre rate. ● **coeficiente de inteligencia** intelligence quo tient, IQ.

coercer [2] *vt* to coerce.

coercitivo,-a *adj* coercive.

coetáneo,-a *adj* contemporary.
▷ *nm & nf* contemporary.

coexistencia *nf* coexistence. ● **coexistencia pacífi** peaceful coexistence.

coexistir *vi* to coexist.

cofia *nf* bonnet.

cofrade *nm o nf (gen)* member; *(hombre)* brothe *(mujer)* sister.

cofradía *nf* 1 *(hermandad)* brotherhood. 2 *(asocia ción)* association. 3 *(gremio)* guild.

cofre *nm (grande)* trunk, chest; *(pequeño)* box, cas ket.

coger [5] *vt* 1 *(asir)* to seize, take hold of: **coge al beb** *hold the baby.* 2 *(apresar)* to capture, catch. 3 *(toma* to take: **coge algo para beber** *take a drink.* 4 *(contra tar)* to take on. 5 *(tren, etc)* to catch. 6 *(tomar presta do)* to borrow: **te he cogido el libro** *I've borrowe your book.* 7 *(recolectar frutos, etc)* to pick; *(del suelo)* gather. 8 *(enfermedad, balón)* to catch: **cogí un resfri do** *I caught a cold.* 9 *(acento, costumbres)* to pick u 10 *(velocidad, fuerza)* to gather. 11 *(atropellar)* to ru over, knock down. 12 *(emisora, canal)* to pick u get: **coger la BBC** *to get the BBC.* 13 *(notas)* to tak take down. 14 *(oír)* to catch. 15 *(entender)* to unde stand, get: **no cogí el final** *I didn't get the end.* 16 A *tabú* to fuck. ■ **coger cariño a** ALGO/ALGN to becom fond of STH/SB, take a liking to STH/SB. ‖ **coger p sorpresa** to catch by surprise.
▷ *vi* 1 *(plantas, colores)* to take: **el limonero no ha cogid** *the lemon tree didn't take.* 2 *(ir)* to turn, take, go: **cog a la izquierda** *turn left;* 3 *fam (caber)* to fit.
▷ *vpr* **cogerse** 1 *(pillarse)* to catch. 2 *(agarrarse)* to hol on: **cógete fuerte** *hold on tight.* ■ **cogerse un cabre** *fam* to get very angry. ‖ **no hay por dónde cogerlo** h hasn't got a leg to stand on.

cogida *nf* gore, goring.

cogido,-a *pp* → **coger.**
▷ *adj* 1 *(sujeto)* fixed. 2 *(atrapado)* trapped, caught.
▷ *nm* **cogido** *(pliegue)* gather, pleat; *(de cortina)* tie.

cognición *nf* cognition.

cognoscitivo,-a *adj* cognitive.

cogollo *nm* 1 *(de lechuga, etc)* heart. 2 *(brote)* shoot. *fig* heart, centre (US center). 4 **el cogollo** *fig* th cream, the best.

cogote *nm* back of the neck, nape of the neck.

cohabitar *vi* to cohabit, live together.

cohecho *nm* JUR bribery.

coherencia *nf* coherence, coherency.

coherente *adj* coherent, connected.

cohesión *nf* cohesion.

cohete *nm* rocket.

cohibido,-a *pp* → **cohibir.**
▷ *adj* inhibited, restrained.

cohibir [21] *vt* to inhibit, restrain.
▷ *vpr* **cohibirse** to feel inhibited, feel embarrassed.

coincidente *adj* coincident, coinciding.

oincidir *vi* 1 *(estar de acuerdo)* to agree (**en**, on), coincide (**en**, in). 2 *(ajustarse)* to coincide. 3 *(ocurrir al mismo tiempo)* to be at the same time (**con**, as), coincide (**con**, with); *(en el mismo lugar)* to meet.

oito *nm* coitus, intercourse.

ojear *vi* 1 *(persona)* to limp, hobble. 2 *(muebles)* to wobble. 3 *fam fig (adolecer)* to falter. ■ **cojear del mismo pie** *fam* to have the same faults.

ojera *nf* limp, lameness.

ojín *nm* cushion.

ojo,-a *adj* 1 *(persona)* lame, crippled. 2 *(mueble)* wobbly. 3 *fig (defectuoso)* faulty, incomplete.
nm & nf lame person, cripple.

ol *nf* cabbage. ● **col de Bruselas** Brussels sprout.

ola¹ *nf* 1 *(gen)* tail. 2 *(de vestido)* train; *(de chaqueta)* tail. 3 *(fila)* queue, US line. ■ **hacer cola** to queue up, US stand in line. ● **cola de caballo** *(peinado)* ponytail.

ola² *nf (pegamento)* glue.

olaboración *nf* 1 collaboration. 2 *(prensa)* contribution.

olaborador,-ra *adj* collaborating.
nm & nf 1 collaborator. 2 *(prensa)* contributor.

olaborar *vi* 1 to collaborate (**con**, with). 2 *(prensa)* to contribute (**en**, to).

olación *nf* 1 *(comparación)* collation. 2 *(refrigerio)* light meal, snack, collation. ■ **sacar a colación / traer a colación** to mention, bring up.

olada *nf* 1 *(lavado)* washing, laundry; *(con lejía)* bleaching. 2 *(ropa)* washing, wash. 3 *(de metal)* tapping. 4 *(volcánica)* outflow. ■ **hacer la colada** to do the washing, do the laundry.

olado,-a *pp* → **colar**.
adj 1 *fam fig (enamorado)* madly in love, head over heels in love. 2 *(metal)* cast.

olador *nm* 1 *(de té, café)* strainer. 2 *(de caldo, alimentos)* colander, sieve.

olapsar *vt (ciudad, aeropuerto, etc)* to paralyse; *(tráfico)* to bring to a standstill, bring to a halt.
vi to collapse.

olapso *nm* 1 MED collapse. 2 *fig* breakdown.

olar [31] *vt* 1 *(líquido)* to strain, filter. 2 *(lavar)* to wash; *(con lejía)* to bleach. 3 *(metales)* to cast. 4 *fam (hacer pasar)* to pass, slip; *(moneda)* to pass off; *(historia)* to give.
vi fam to wash: **veremos si cuela** *we'll see if it washes.*
vpr **colarse** 1 *(escabullirse)* to slip in, gatecrash. 2 *(en una cola)* to push in, jump the queue, US jump the line. 3 *fam (equivocarse)* to slip up, make a mistake.

olcha *nf* bedspread.

olchón *nm* mattress. ● **colchón de aire** air cushion. ‖ **colchón neumático** air mattress.

olchoneta *nf* small mattress.

ole *nm fam* school.

olear *vi* 1 *(perro, etc)* to wag its tail; *(vaca, caballo, etc)* to swish its tail. 2 *fam* to drag on.

olección *nf* collection.

oleccionar *vt* to collect.

oleccionista *nm o nf* collector.

olecta *nf* collection.

olectividad *nf* community.

olectivo,-a *adj* collective, group.
▷ *nm* **colectivo** 1 *(asociación)* association, guild. 2 LING collective noun.

colector,-ra *adj* collecting.
▷ *nm* **colector** 1 *(caño)* water pipe. 2 *(cloaca)* main sewer.

colega *nm o nf* 1 colleague. 2 *argot (amigo)* chum, mate, US buddy.

colegiado,-a *pp* → **colegiarse**.
▷ *adj* collegiate.
▷ *nm & nf* collegian.
▷ *nm* **colegiado** DEP referee.

colegial,-la *nm & nf (gen)* schoolchild; *(chico)* schoolboy; *(chica)* schoolgirl.

colegio *nm* 1 *(escuela)* school: **van al colegio en autobús** *they go to school by bus.* 2 *(asociación)* college, association. 3 *(residencia)* hall of residence, US dormitory: **colegio cardenalicio** *college of cardinals.* ● **colegio de abogados** the Bar. ‖ **colegio público** state school.

coleóptero *nm* coleopteron.

cólera *nf* 1 *(bilis)* bile. 2 *fig (ira)* anger, rage. *nm* MED cholera.

colérico,-a *adj* furious, irascible.

colesterol *nm* cholesterol.

coleta *nf* pigtail, ponytail.

colgado,-a *pp* → **colgar**.
▷ *adj* hanging (**de**, from).

colgador *nm* (coat) hanger.

colgante *adj* hanging.
▷ *nm* 1 ARQUIT festoon. 2 *(joya)* pendant.

colgar [52] *vt* 1 *(gen)* to hang (up). 2 *(la colada)* to hang out. 3 *(ahorcar)* to hang. 4 *(atribuir)* to pin. 5 *(el teléfono)* to put down. 6 *fam (suspender)* to fail. 7 *(abandonar)* to give up.
▷ *vi* 1 *(estar colgado)* to hang (**de**, from): **cuelga del techo** *it hangs from the ceiling.* 2 *(una prenda)* to hang down, be crooked. 3 *(teléfono)* to hang up, ring off: **¡no cuelgue!** *please hold!, hold the line, please!*
▷ *vpr* **colgarse** *(ahorcarse)* to hang OS. ■ **colgar de un hilo** *fig* to hang by a thread.

colibrí *nm* humming bird.

cólico *nm* colic.

coliflor *nf* cauliflower.

colilla *nf* cigarette end, cigarette butt, butt.

colina *nf* hill, slope.

colirio *nm* eye drops *pl.*

colisión *nf* 1 *(de vehículos)* collision, crash. 2 *fig (conflicto)* clash, conflict.

colisionar *vi* 1 *(chocar)* to collide (**con/contra**, with), crash (**con/contra**, into). 2 *(enfrentarse)* to clash.

colitis *nf inv* colitis.

collar *nm* 1 *(adorno)* necklace. 2 *(de animal)* collar. 3 TÉC collar, ring.

collarín *nm* 1 *(alzacuello)* bands *pl.* 2 *(aparato ortopédico)* surgical collar. 3 *(de botella)* label.

colmado,-a *pp* → **colmar**.
▷ *adj* full, filled: **una cuchara colmada** *a heaped spoonful.*
▷ *nm* **colmado** grocer's (shop), grocery store.

colmar *vt* 1 *(gen)* to fill (**de**, with); *(vaso, copa)* to fill to the brim. 2 *fig* to shower (**de**, with), overwhelm (**de**, with).

colmena *nf* beehive.

colmillo *nm* **1** eye tooth, canine tooth. **2** *(de carnívoro)* fang; *(de jabalí, elefante, morsa)* tusk.
colmo *nm* height, summit. ■ **¡esto es el colmo!** this is the last straw!, this is the limit!
colocación *nf* **1** *(situación)* positioning. **2** *(de una alfombra, moqueta)* laying; *(de un cuadro)* hanging. **3** *(de dinero)* investment. **4** *(empleo)* employment, job. **5** LING collocation.
colocado,-a *pp* → **colocar.**
▷ *adj* **1** *(empleado)* employed: **está bien colocada** *she has a good job.* **2** *argot (embriagado)* sozzled; *(drogado)* stoned, high.
colocar [1] *vt* **1** *(gen)* to place, put; *(alfombra)* to lay; *(cuadro)* to hang. **2** *(dar empleo)* to get a job for.
▷ *vpr* **colocarse 1** *(situarse)* to place OS, put OS, find OS a place. **2** *(trabajar)* to find a job (**de**, as), get a job (**de**, as). **3** *argot (embriagarse)* to get sozzled; *(drogarse)* to get stoned.
colofón *nm* **1** *(apéndice)* colophon. **2** *fig (remate)* crowning, climax, culmination.
Colombia *nf* Colombia.
colombiano,-a *adj* Colombian.
▷ *nm & nf* Colombian.
colon *nm* ANAT colon.
colonia *nf* **1** *(grupo)* colony. **2** [Usually plural.] *(vacaciones infantiles)* summer camp. **3** *(perfume)* cologne.
colonial *adj* **1** POL colonial. **2** *(importado)* imported.
colonialismo *nm* colonialism.
colonización *nf* colonization.
colonizador,-ra *adj* colonizing.
▷ *nm & nf* colonizer, colonist.
colonizar [4] *vt* to colonize, settle.
colono *nm* **1** *(habitante)* colonist, settler. **2** AGR tenant farmer.
coloquial *adj* colloquial.
coloquio *nm* talk, discussion.
color *nm* **1** colour (US color): **es de color verde** *it's green.* **2** *fml fig (carácter)* character. **3** *fig (tendencia)* tendency. ■ **de color 1** *(en color)* in colour (US color), coloured (US colored). **2** *(persona)* coloured (US colored). ■ **en color / en colores** *(cine, foto)* in colour (US color).
colorado,-a *adj* **1** coloured (US colored). **2** *(rojo)* red. ■ **ponerse colorado,-a** to blush, go red.
colorante *nm* colouring (US coloring), dye.
colorear *vt* to colour (US color).
colorete *nm* rouge, blusher.
colorido *nm* colour (US color).
colosal *adj* **1** colossal, giant, huge. **2** *fig* splendid, excellent.
coloso *nm* colossus.
columna *nf* **1** *(gen)* column. **2** ANAT spine. **3** *(elemento central)* backbone. ● **columna vertebral 1** *(de un cuerpo)* vertebral column, spinal column. **2** *(de un sistema)* backbone.
columpiar [12] *vt* to swing.
▷ *vpr* **columpiarse 1** to swing (**de**, on). **2** *(al caminar)* to swing one's hips.
columpio *nm* swing.
colza *nf* rape. ● **aceite de colza** rapeseed oil, US canola oil.
coma[1] *nf* **1** *(puntuación)* comma. **2** *(en música)* comma. **3** MAT point: **cuatro coma cinco** *four point five.*

coma[2] *nm* MED coma. ■ **entrar en coma** to go into coma.
comadreja *nf* weasel.
comadrona *nm & nf* midwife.
comandante *nm* **1** *(oficial)* commander, commanding officer. **2** *(graduación)* major. **3** *(piloto)* pilot.
comandar *vt* to command.
comando *nm* **1** MIL commando. **2** INFORMÁ comman[d].
comarca *nf* area, region.
comba *nf* **1** *(de cuerda, cable)* bend, curve. **2** *(de vig[a,] pared)* sag, bulge. **3** *(de carretera)* camber. **4** *(cuerd[a])* skipping rope. **5** *(juego)* skipping. ■ **saltar a la comb[a]** to skip, US skip rope.
combar *vt* to bend.
▷ *vpr* **combarse** *(una cuerda)* to bend; *(viga, pared)* to sa[g,] bulge.
combate *nm* **1** *(gen)* combat, battle. **2** MIL battle. [3] *(boxeo)* fight, contest.
combatiente *adj* fighting.
▷ *nm o nf* fighter, combatant.
▷ *nm (ave)* ruff.
combatir *vi* to fight (**contra**, against /-), struggle (**co[n]tra**, against).
▷ *vt* **1** *(luchar contra)* to fight: **combatir el cáncer** *to fig[ht] cancer.* **2** *fig* to combat, fight. **3** *fig (batir, golpear)* t[o] beat, lash.
combativo,-a *adj* spirited, aggressive.
combinación *nf* **1** combination. **2** *(prenda)* slip. [3] *(cóctel)* cocktail. **4** *(lotería, quiniela)* permutatio[n of] numbers *pl.* **5** *fig (artimaña)* fiddle, wangle.
combinado,-a *pp* → **combinar.**
▷ *nm* **combinado 1** *(cóctel)* cocktail. **2** DEP all-star tea[m]. **3** QUÍM compound, combination.
combinar *vt* **1** *(gen)* to combine. **2** *(disponer)* to a[r]range, plan. **3** QUÍM to combine. **4** *(colores)* to matc[h] (**con**, -), go (**con**, with).
combustible *adj* combustible.
▷ *nm* fuel.
combustión *nf* combustion, burning.
comecocos *nm inv* **1** *argot (juego)* Pacman. **2** *arg[ot] (asunto, libro, etc)* brainwasher.
comedero *nm* feeding trough, manger.
comedia *nf* **1** TEAT comedy, play. **2** *fig* farce, pre[]tence (US pretense).
comediante,-a *nm & nf* **1** *(hombre)* actor; *(muje[r])* actress. **2** *fig* hypocrite, comedian.
comedido,-a *pp* → **comedirse.**
▷ *adj* **1** *(cortés)* courteous, polite. **2** *(moderado)* mode[r]ate, restrained, reserved.
comedirse [34] *vpr* to restrain OS.
comedor,-ra *nm (sala)* dining room; *(en una fábric[a])* canteen; *(en universidad)* refectory, dining hall.
comensal *nm o nf* person at the table, diner.
comentar *vt* **1** *(texto)* to comment on. **2** *(expres[ar] una opinión)* to talk about, discuss.
comentario *nm* **1** *(observación)* remark, comment. [2] *(explicación, narración)* commentary.
▷ *nm pl* **comentarios** *(murmuración)* gossip *sing.*
comentarista *nm o nf* commentator.
comenzar [47] *vt* to begin, start.
▷ *vi* to begin, start: **comenzó a reír** *he began to laug[h], he began laughing.* ■ **comenzar con** to begin with

▮ **comenzar + *ger*** to start by + *ger*: **comenzó explicando...** *he started by explaining ...*

omer *vt* **1** to eat. **2** *(tomar)* to have. **3** *(color)* to fade. **4** *(corroer)* to corrode. **5** *fig (gastar)* to eat away; *(combustible)* to use, use up. **6** *(en ajedrez)* to take, capture.
▷ *vi (gen)* to eat; *(a mediodía)* to have lunch, lunch; *(por la noche)* to have dinner, dine.
▷ *nm* eating.
▷ *vpr* **comerse 1** to eat. **2** *fig (saltarse)* to omit; *(párrafo)* to skip; *(palabra)* to swallow. **3** *(color)* to fade. **4** *(el mar, la tierra)* to swallow.

omercial *adj* **1** *(del comercio)* commercial. **2** *(de tiendas)* shopping.
▷ *nm o nf (vendedor)* seller; *(hombre)* salesman; *(mujer)* saleswoman.

omercializar [4] *vt* to commercialize, market.

omerciante *adj* business-minded.
▷ *nm o nf* **1** merchant. **2** *(interesado)* moneymaker.

omerciar [12] *vi* **1** *(comprar y vender)* to trade, deal, buy and sell. **2** *(hacer negocios)* to do business (**con**, with).

omercio *nm* **1** *(ocupación)* commerce, trade. **2** *(tienda)* shop, store. **3** *fig (trato sexual)* dealings *pl*, intercourse. ■ **comercio al por mayor** wholesale trade. ▮ **comercio al por menor** retail trade. ● **comercio exterior** foreign trade. ▮ **libre comercio** free trade.

omestible *adj* edible, eatable.
▷ *nm pl* **comestibles** groceries, food *sing*, foodstuffs *pl*.

ometa *nm (cuerpo celeste)* comet.
▷ *nf (juguete)* kite.

ometer *vt (crimen)* to commit; *(falta, error)* to make.

ometido *nm* **1** *(encargo)* task, assignment. **2** *(deber)* duty.

omezón *nf* itch, itching.

ómic *nm* comic.

omicios *nm pl* POL elections.

ómico,-a *adj* **1** *(divertido)* comic, comical, funny. **2** *(de comedia)* comedy.
▷ *nm & nf (actor)* comedian, comic.

omida *nf* **1** *(alimento)* food: **2** *(desayuno, etc)* meal. **3** *(almuerzo)* lunch.

omidilla *nf fam fig* gossip, talk.

omienzo *nm* start, beginning. ■ **a comienzos de** at the beginning of. ▮ **dar comienzo** to begin, start.

omillas *nf pl* inverted commas, quotation marks. ■ **entre comillas** in inverted commas.

omilona *nf* big meal, blowout.

omino *nm* BOT cumin, cummin. ■ **me importa un comino** *fam* I don't give a damn.

omisaría *nf* **1** commissariat. **2** *(de policía)* police station.

omisario *nm* **1** commissioner, delegate. **2** *(de policía)* police inspector.

omisión *nf* **1** *(retribución)* commission. **2** *(comité)* committee. **3** *(encargo)* assignment, commission. **4** JUR perpetration, committing. ■ **a comisión / con comisión** on a commission basis. ● **comisión bancaria** service charge, bank commission.

omisura *nf* corner, angle.

omité *nm* committee.

omitiva *nf* suite, retinue.

como *adv* **1** *(modo)* how: **lo hizo como quiso** *he did it the way he wanted to.* **2** *(comparación)* as, like: **negro como la noche** *as dark as night.* **3** *(en calidad de)* as: **como invitado** *as a guest.* **4** *(según)* as: **como dice tu amigo** *as your friend says.* **5** *fam (aproximadamente)* about: **había como unos cien** *there were about a hundred.*
▷ *conj* **1** *(así que)* as: **como llegaban se presentaban** *they introduced themselves as they arrived.* **2** *(si)* if: **como lo vuelvas a hacer...** *if you do it again....* **3** *(porque)* as, since: **como llegamos tarde no pudimos entrar** *since we arrived late we couldn't get in.* ■ **como quiera que 1** *(no importa cómo)* however. **2** *(ya que)* since, as, inasmuch as. ▮ **como sea** whatever happens, no matter what. ▮ **hacer como si** to pretend to +*inf*. **hace como si no viese nada** *he's pretending not to see anything.*

cómo *adv* **1** *(interrogativo)* how. **2** *(por qué)* why. **3** *(admiración)* how: **¡cómo corre el tiempo!** *how time flies!* ■ **¿a cómo están... ?** how much are... ? ▮ **¿cómo?** *fam* what? ▮ **¿cómo es eso?** how come? ▮ **¿cómo es que...?** how is it that...? ▮ **¡cómo no!** but of course!, certainly!

cómoda *nf* chest of drawers, commode.

comodidad *nf* **1** *(confort)* comfort. **2** *(facilidad)* convenience. ■ **con comodidad** comfortably.

comodín *nm (mono)* joker; *(otra carta)* wild card.

cómodo,-a *adj* **1** comfortable, cosy. **2** *(útil)* convenient, handy. **3** *(carácter)* easy-going.

comoquiera *adv* **comoquiera que** anyway, anyhow.

compactar *vt* to compact, compress.

compacto,-a *adj* **1** *(gen)* compact. **2** *(denso)* dense.
▷ *nm* **compacto** compact disc.

compadecer [43] *vt* to pity, feel sorry for.
▷ *vpr* **compadecerse** to take pity (**de**, on), pity (**de**, -), feel sorry (**de**, for).

compadre *nm* **1** *(padrino)* godfather. **2** *(padre)* father. **3** *fam (amigo)* mate, pal, friend.

compaginar *vt* **1** *(combinar)* to combine, make compatible. **2** *(en impresión)* to make up.
▷ *vpr* **compaginarse** to go together, be compatible.

compañerismo *nm* companionship, fellowship, comradeship.

compañero,-a *nm & nf* **1** *(sentimental, pareja)* partner. **2** *(colega)* companion, mate; *(camarada)* comrade. **3** *fig (guante, zapato, etc)* the other one, the one that goes with this one. ● **compañero,-a de colegio** schoolmate. ▮ **compañero,-a de piso** flatmate. ▮ **compañero,-a de trabajo** workmate, colleague.

compañía *nf* company. ■ **en compañía de** in the company of. ▮ **hacer compañía a** ALGN to keep SB company.

comparación *nf* comparison. ■ **en comparación con** compared to, in comparison to.

comparar *vt* to compare:

comparativo,-a *adj* comparative.

comparecer [43] *vi* **1** JUR to appear (**ante**, before). **2** *(presentarse)* to show up.

compartimento *nm* compartment: **compartimento de primera clase** *first-class compartment.*

compartir *vt* **1** *(dividir)* to divide (up), split, share (out). **2** *(poseer en común)* to share.

compás *nm* 1 *(instrumento)* compass, compasses *pl.* 2 *(brújula)* compass. 3 MÚS *(división)* time; *(intervalo)* beat; *(ritmo)* rhythm. ■ **al compás de** in time to. ‖ **llevar el compás** 1 *(con la mano)* to beat time. 2 *(al bailar)* to keep time. ‖ **perder el compás** to lose the beat.
compasión *nf* compassion, pity.
compasivo,-a *adj* compassionate, sympathetic.
compatibilidad *nf* compatibility.
compatibilizar [4] *vt* to make compatible.
compatible *adj* compatible.
compendiar [12] *vt* to summarize, abridge, sum up.
compendio *nm* summary, digest, précis, synopsis.
compenetrarse *vpr* 1 *(uso recíproco)* to understand each other. 2 FÍS to interpenetrate.
compensación *nf* compensation, indemnity. ■ **en compensación** 1 *(en pago)* in payment, as compensation. 2 *(a cambio)* in exchange.
compensar *vt* 1 *(pérdida, error)* to make up for. 2 *(indemnizar)* to compensate, indemnify. 3 TÉC to balance, compensate. 4 *fam (merecer la pena)* to be worth one's while.
competencia *nf* 1 *(rivalidad)* competition, rivalry. 2 *(competidores)* competitors *pl*, rival company. 3 *(habilidad)* competence, ability, proficiency. 4 *(incumbencia)* responsibility; *(jurisdicción)* jurisdiction.
competente *adj* 1 *(capaz)* competent, capable, proficient. 2 *(adecuado)* adequate. 3 JUR competent.
competer *vi* 1 *(corresponder)* to be incumbent (**a**, on), be the responsibility (**de**, of). 2 *(incumbir)* to come under the jurisdiction (**a**, of).
competición *nf* competition, contest.
competidor,-ra *adj* 1 *(que compite)* competing. 2 *(rival)* rival.
▷ *nm & nf* 1 *(rival)* competitor. 2 *(en competición deportiva)* competitor. 3 *(participante)* contestant, candidate.
competir [34] *vi* to compete.
competitividad *nf* competitiveness.
competitivo,-a *adj* competitive.
compilar *vt* to compile.
compinche *nm o nf* 1 *fam (amigo)* chum, pal, mate, US buddy. 2 *fam pey (cómplice)* accomplice, sidekick.
complacencia *nf* 1 *(placer)* pleasure, satisfaction. 2 *(indulgencia)* indulgence.
complacer [76] *vt* 1 *(satisfacer)* to satisfy, gratify, oblige. 2 *(agradar)* to please. 3 *fml* to please, give pleasure.
▷ *vpr* **complacerse** to take pleasure (**en**, in).
complaciente *adj* 1 obliging, helpful. 2 *(marido)* complaisant.
complejo,-a *adj* complex.
▷ *nm* **complejo** complex. ● **complejo industrial** industrial complex.
complementar *vt* to complement.
▷ *vpr* **complementarse** to complement each other, be complementary to each other .
complementario,-a *adj* complementary.
complemento *nm* 1 *(gen)* complement. 2 GRAM object, complement. 3 *(perfección)* perfection, culmination. ● **complemento circunstancial** adverbial complement. ‖ **complemento directo** direct object ‖ **complemento indirecto** indirect object.
completamente *adv* completely.
completar *vt* 1 *(gen)* to complete. 2 *(acabar)* to fi[n]ish; *(perfeccionar)* to round off.
completo,-a *adj* 1 *(terminado)* finished, complete[d]. 2 *(lleno)* full. ■ **al completo** full up, filled to capacit[y] ‖ **por completo** completely.
complexión *nf* constitution, build: **su hermano e[s] de complexión fuerte** *his brother is well-built.*
complicación *nf* complication. ■ **buscarse compl[i]caciones** to make life difficult for OS.
complicado,-a *pp* → **complicar.**
▷ *adj* 1 *(gen)* complicated, complex. 2 *(carácter)* co[m]plex. 3 *(implicado)* involved: **estaba complicado en [la] estafa** *he was involved in the fraud.*
complicar [1] *vt* 1 *(gen)* to complicate, make com[p]licated. 2 *(implicar)* to involve (**en**, in).
cómplice *nm o nf* accomplice.
complicidad *nf* complicity.
complot *nm* plot, conspiracy.
componente *adj* component, constituent.
▷ *nm* 1 *(pieza)* component, constituent; *(ingrediente)* i[n]gredient. 2 *(miembro)* member.
componer [78]
▲ *pp* **compuesto,-a.** *vt* 1 *(formar)* to compose, mak[e] up, form. 2 *(reparar)* to fix, repair, mend. 3 *(adorna[r])* to adorn, decorate. 4 *(música, versos)* to compose.
▷ *vpr* **componerse** 1 *(consistir)* to consist (**de**, of), b[e] made up (**de**, of): **las palabras se componen de sílaba[s]** *words are made up of syllables.*
comportamiento *nm* behaviour (US behavior) conduct.
comportar *vt (implica)* to involve, entail: **eso com[]porta un cambio de planes** *that involves a change [o]f plan.*
▷ *vpr* **comportarse** *(portarse)* to behave: **se comport[ó] mal** *she misbehaved.*
composición *nf* 1 *(gen)* composition. 2 *(acuerd[o])* agreement. 3 *(arreglo)* arrangement. 4 *(en impresión)* setting, composition. ■ **hacer composición de luga[r]** 1 *(decidirse)* to make a plan of action. 2 *(formarse un[a] idea)* to get a picture of a situation.
compositor,-ra *nm & nf* composer.
compostura *nf* 1 *(composición)* composition. 2 *(re[]paración)* repair, mending. 3 *(ajuste)* settlement, ad[]justment. 4 *(aseo)* neatness, tidiness.
compota *nf* compote.
compra *nf* purchase, buy. ■ **hacer la compra** to do th[e] shopping, go shopping. ‖ **ir de compras** to go shop[]ping. ● **compra a plazos** hire purchase, US instalmen[t] buying.
comprador,-ra *nm & nf* purchaser, buyer, shoppe[r]
comprar *vt* 1 to buy. 2 *fig (sobornar)* to bribe, bu[y] off.
compraventa *nf* buying and selling, dealing.
comprender *vt* 1 *(entender)* to understand: **lo com[]prendiste mal** *you misunderstood it.* 2 *(contener)* t[o] comprise, include. ■ **¿comprendes?** *(en conversació[n])* you see?
comprensión *nf* understanding.

omprensivo,-a *adj* 1 *(tolerante)* understanding. 2 *(que comprende o incluye)* comprehensive.

ompresa *nf* 1 *(higiénica)* sanitary towel. 2 *(vendaje)* compress.

omprimido,-a *pp* → **comprimir**.
adj compressed.
nm **comprimido** tablet.

omprimir *vt* 1 *(apretar)* to compress; *(gente)* to cram together. 2 *(reprimir)* to restrain.

omprobante *nm* 1 *(recibo)* receipt, voucher. 2 JUR document in proof.

omprobar [31] *vt* 1 *(verificar)* to verify, check. 2 *(demostrar)* to prove. 3 *(observar)* to see, observe: **como podrán ustedes comprobar** *as you can see for yourselves.* 4 *(confirmar)* to confirm.

omprometedor,-ra *adj* 1 *(situación, etc)* compromising. 2 *(persona)* troublemaking.

omprometer *vt* 1 *(exponer a riesgo)* to endanger, jeopardize, risk; *(a una persona)* to compromise. 2 *(implicar)* to involve, implicate. 3 *(obligar)* to commit. 4 *(poner en un aprieto)* to embarrass. 5 *(juzgar un tercero)* to submit to arbitration.
vpr **comprometerse** 1 *(contraer una obligación)* to commit OS, pledge. 2 *(involucrarse)* to get involved. 3 *(establecer relaciones formales)* to get engaged. ■ **comprometerse a hacer ALGO** to undertake to do STH.

omprometido,-a *pp* → **comprometer**.
adj 1 *(difícil, arriesgado)* difficult, in jeopardy. 2 *(escritor, artista, etc)* committed. 3 *(involucrado)* involved. 4 *(para casarse)* engaged.

ompromisario,-a *adj* representative.
nm & nf representative.

ompromiso *nm* 1 *(obligación)* commitment, obligation: **cumplió sus compromisos** *she fulfilled her obligations.* 2 *(acuerdo)* agreement. 3 *(cita)* appointment; *(amorosa)* date. 4 *(dificultad)* difficult situation, bind. 5 *(matrimonial)* engagement.

ompuerta *nf* sluice, floodgate.

ompuesto,-a *pp* → **componer**.
adj 1 *(gen)* compound. 2 *(reparado)* repaired, mended. 3 *(elegante)* dressed up; *(arreglado)* tidy. 4 *fig (comedido)* composed.

ompulsa *nf* 1 *(cotejo)* collation, comparison. 2 JUR certified true copy.

ompulsar *vt* 1 *(cotejar)* to collate. 2 JUR to make a certified true copy of.

ompulsión *nf* compulsion.

ompulsivo,-a *adj* compelling, compulsive.

ompunción *nf* 1 *(arrepentimiento)* compunction. 2 *fig (tristeza)* sorrow, sadness.

ompungido,-a *pp* → **compungir**.
adj 1 *(arrepentido)* remorseful. 2 *fig (triste)* sorrowful, sad.

ompungir [6] *vt fml (entristecer)* to sadden, make sad.
vpr **compungirse** *(entristecerse)* to be saddened, feel sad.

ompuse *pt indef* → **componer**.

omputable *adj* computable.

omputación *nf* computing.

omputador *nm* computer.

omputadora *nf* computer.

omputadorización *nf* computerization.

omputadorizar [4] *vt* to computerize.

computar *vt* 1 *(calcular)* to compute, calculate. 2 *fml (tomar en cuenta)* to take into account, count.

computarizar [4] *vt* to computerize.

computerización *nf* computerization.

computerizar *vt* to computerize.

cómputo *nm* computation, calculation.

comulgante *adj* communicant.
▷ *nm o nf* communicant.

comulgar [7] *vi* REL to receive Holy Communion.

comulgatorio *nm* communion rail, altar rail.

común *adj* 1 *(gen)* common: **eso es poco común** *that's unusual.* 2 *(compartido)* shared, communal. 3 *(amigos)* mutual.

comuna *nf* commune.

comunal *adj* communal.

comunicable *adj* 1 communicable. 2 *(persona)* sociable.

comunicación *nf* 1 *(gen)* communication. 2 *(comunicado)* communication; *(oficial)* communiqué. 3 *(telefónica)* connection. 4 *(unión)* link, connection.
▷ *nf pl* **comunicaciones** communications.

comunicado,-a *pp* → **comunicar**.
▷ *adj* served. ● **comunicado de prensa** press release.

comunicador,-ra *adj* transmitting.
▷ *nm & nf* RAD TV *(persona)* communicator.

comunicante *adj* communicating.
▷ *nm o nf* informer.

comunicar [1] *vt* 1 *(hacer partícipe)* to communicate, convey, transmit. 2 *(hacer saber)* to communicate, make known, tell. 3 *(conectar)* to connect.
▷ *vi* 1 *(ponerse en comunicación)* to communicate; *(por carta)* to correspond. 2 *(teléfono)* to be engaged, US be busy. 3 *(estar conectado)* to communicate, be connected.
▷ *vpr* **comunicarse** 1 *(tener relación)* to communicate; *(ponerse en contacto)* to get in touch, get in contact (**con**, with). 2 *(extenderse)* to spread. 3 *(estar conectado)* to be connected (**con**, to).

comunicativo,-a *adj* 1 *(actitud, sentimiento)* catching, infectious. 2 *(persona)* communicative, sociable, open.

comunidad *nf* community. ● **comunidad autónoma** autonomous region. ‖ **Comunidad Económica Europea** European Economic Community.

comunión *nf* 1 communion, fellowship. 2 REL Holy Communion.

comunismo *nm* communism.

comunista *adj* communist.
▷ *nm o nf* communist.

comunitario,-a *adj* 1 *(gen)* of the community, relating to the community.

comúnmente *adv (normalmente)* commonly, usually, generally; *(frecuentemente)* often.

con *prep* 1 *(instrumento, medio)* with. 2 *(modo, circunstancia)* in, with. 3 *(juntamente, en compañía)* with. 4 *(contenido)* with. 5 *(relación)* to. 6 *(reciprocidad)*. 7 *(comparación)* compared to. 8 *(a pesar de)* in spite of, despite. 9 **con** + *inf* by + *ger.* 10 *(aunque)* in spite of. ■ **con que / con tal de que / con tal que** provided, as long as. ‖ **con todo (y eso)** nevertheless, even so.

conato *nm* 1 *(intento)* attempt. 2 *(principio)* beginnings *pl*, start.

concadenar *vt* → **concatenar.**
concatenación *nf* concatenation.
concatenar *vt* to concatenate, link together.
concavidad *nf* concavity.
cóncavo,-a *adj* concave.
concavoconvexo,-a *adj* concavo-convex.
concebible *adj* conceivable, imaginable.
concebir [34] *vt* **1** *(engendrar)* to conceive. **2** *fig (comprender)* to understand. **3** *fig (comenzar a sentir)* to experience, have.
▷ *vi (quedarse embarazada)* to become pregnant, conceive.
conceder *vt* **1** *(otorgar)* to grant, concede; *(premio)* to award. **2** *(atribuir)* to give, attach. **3** *(oportunidad, tiempo)* to give. **4** *(admitir)* to concede, admit.
concejal,-la *nm & nf* town councillor.
concejalía *nf* councillorship.
concejo *nm* town council, council.
concelebrar *vt* to concelebrate.
concentración *nf* **1** *(gen)* concentration. **2** *(de gente)* gathering, rally.
concentrado,-a *nm* **concentrado** concentrate, extract.
concentrar *vt* to concentrate.
▷ *vpr* **concentrarse 1** *(reunirse)* to concentrate. **2** *(fijar la atención)* to concentrate (**en**, on).
concéntrico,-a *adj* concentric.
concepción *nf* conception.
conceptismo *nm* conceptism.
concepto *nm* **1** *(idea)* concept, conception, idea. **2** *(opinión)* opinion, view. **3** FIN heading, section. ■ **bajo ningún concepto** under no circumstances. ‖ **en concepto de** by way of.
conceptual *adj* conceptual.
conceptualismo *nm* conceptualism.
conceptualizar [4] *vt* to conceptualize.
conceptuar [11] *vt* to deem, think, consider.
conceptuoso,-a *adj* high-sounding, affected.
concerniente *adj* concerning, relating. ■ **en lo concerniente a** *fml* with regard to.
concernir [29] *vi* [Used only in the third persons of pres indic, imperf indic and pres subj; and nonpersonal forms.] *(afectar)* to concern, touch. ■ **en lo que a mí** *(ti, él, etc)* **concierne** as far as I am *(you are, he is, etc)* concerned. ‖ **por lo que a mí** *(ti, él, etc)* **concierne** as far as I am *(you are, he is, etc)* concerned.
concertación *nf* agreement, reconciliation.
concertadamente *adv* **1** *(de acuerdo)* of a common accord. **2** *(en orden)* systematically.
concertado,-a *pp* → **concertar.**
▷ *adj* concerted.
concertar [27] *vt* **1** *(planear)* to plan, coordinate. **2** *(entrevista)* to arrange; *(acuerdo)* to reach; *(tratado, negocio)* to conclude, settle. **3** *(precio)* to agree on. **4** MÚS to harmonize.
▷ *vi* **1** *(concordar)* to agree, match up; *(números)* to tally. **2** LING to agree. **3** MÚS to harmonize, be in tune.
concertina *nf* concertina.
concertino *nm* first violin.
concertista *nm o nf* soloist.
concesión *nf* **1** concession, granting. **2** *(de premio)* awarding.
concesionario,-a *nm & nf* concessionaire, licenc holder, licensee.
▷ *nm* **concesionario** *(de coches)* dealer.
concesivo,-a *adj* LING concessive.
concha *nf* **1** *(caparazón)* shell. **2** *(carey)* tortoiseshel **3** *(ostra)* oyster. **4** TEAT prompt box.
conchabarse *vpr fam (confabularse)* to plot, schem
conciencia *nf* **1** *(moral)* conscience. **2** *(conocimient* consciousness, awareness. ■ **a conciencia** consc entiously. ‖ **remorderle a** ALGN **la conciencia** to weig on SB's conscience. ● **conciencia de clase** class-cor sciousness.
concienciado,-a *pp* → **concienciar.**
▷ *adj* aware.
concienciar [12] *vt* to make aware (**de**, of).
▷ *vpr* **concienciarse** to become aware (**de**, of).
concienzudamente *adv* conscientiously.
concienzudo,-a *adj* conscientious.
concierto *nm* **1** MÚS *(sesión)* concert; *(composició* concerto. **2** *(acuerdo)* agreement. **3** *(armonía)* cor cert, concord.
conciliábulo *nm* secret meeting.
conciliación *nf* conciliation, reconciliation.
conciliador,-ra *adj* conciliatory, conciliating.
conciliar [12] *adj* conciliar.
▷ *vt* **1** *(gen)* to conciliate, bring together. **2** *(enemigos)* t reconcile.
conciliatorio,-a *adj* conciliatory.
concilio *nm* council.
concisión *nf* concision, conciseness.
conciso,-a *adj* concise, brief.
concitar *vt* to excite, incite, stir up, raise.
conciudadano,-a *nm & nf* fellow citizen.
conclave *nm* **1** REL conclave. **2** *fig (reunión)* privat meeting.
concluir [62] *vt* **1** *(terminar)* to finish. **2** *(trato, negoci* to close. **3** *(inferir)* to conclude, infer.
▷ *vi (finalizar)* to finish, come to an end, conclude.
conclusión *nf* **1** *(final)* conclusion, end. **2** *(deducción* conclusion. ■ **en conclusión** in conclusion. ‖ **llegar una conclusión** to come to a conclusion.
concluso,-a *adj* adjourned pending sentence.
concluyente *adj* conclusive, decisive.
concomerse *vpr* to be consumed (**de**, with), itc (**de**, with).
concomitancia *nf* concomitance.
concomitante *adj* concomitant.
concordancia *nf* **1** concordance, agreement. **2** LIN agreement.
concordante *adj* concordant.
concordar [31] *vt* **1** *(poner de acuerdo)* to bring int agreement, reconcile. **2** LING to make agree.
▷ *vi* **1** *(convenir)* to agree, coincide, match; *(números)* t tally. **2** LING to agree.
concordato *nm* concordat.
concorde *adj* in agreement.
concordia *nf* concord, harmony.
concreción *nf* **1** *(concisión)* concision, conciseness **2** *(cálculo)* stone. **3** *(de minerales)* concretion.
concretamente *adv (exactamente)* exactly.

oncretar *vt* 1 *(precisar)* to specify, state explicitly. 2 *(hora, precio)* to fix, set. 3 *(resumir)* to sum up. 4 *(limitar)* to limit, confine.
vpr **concretarse** *(tomar forma)* to take shape.
oncreto,-a *adj* 1 *(real)* concrete, real. 2 *(particular)* particular, specific. ■ **en concreto** *(en particular)* in particular, specifically.
oncubina *nf* concubine.
oncubinato *nm* concubinage.
onculcar [1] *vt* to infringe, break, violate: **conculcó la ley** *he broke the law.*
oncupiscencia *nf* concupiscence, lustfulness.
oncupiscente *adj* concupiscent, lustful.
oncurrencia *nf* 1 *(confluencia)* combination, concurrence. 2 *(público)* audience. 3 *(participación)* participation.
oncurrente *nm o nf* 1 *(persona presente)* person present. 2 *(público)* member of the audience. 3 *(competidor)* competitor, contestant.
concurrido,-a *adj* 1 *(lugar público)* busy, crowded. 2 *(espectáculo)* well-attended, popular.
concurrir *vi* 1*(juntarse en un lugar - gente)* to gather, come together, meet. 2 *(tomar parte - concurso, etc)* to compete, take part; *(- elección)* to stand, run; *(- examen)* to be a candidate.
concursante *nm o nf* 1 *(a concurso)* contestant, participant, competitor. 2 *(a empleo)* candidate.
concursar *vi* 1 *(competir)* to compete, take part. 2 *(para un empleo)* to be a candidate.
concurso *nm* 1 *(gen)* competition; *(de belleza, deportivo)* contest; *(en televisión)* quiz. 2 *(para puestos)* public examination. 3 *fml (concurrencia)* gathering; *(de factores, circunstancias)* combination. 4 *(licitación)* tender.
condado *nm* county.
conde *nm* count.
condecoración *nf* decoration, medal.
condecorar *vt* to decorate.
condena *nf* JUR sentence, conviction.
condenable *adj* condemnable, blameworthy.
condenación *nf* condemnation.
condenado,-a *adj* 1 JUR convicted. 2 REL damned. 3 *(cegado)* condemned. 4 *(sin remedio)* hopeless. 5 *fig (maldito)* damn, damned.
condenar *vt* 1 JUR *(declarar culpable)* to convict, find guilty. 2 JUR *(decretar condena)* to sentence, condemn. 3 *(desaprobar)* to condemn.
condenatorio,-a *adj* condemnatory.
condensable *adj* condensable.
condensación *nf* 1 *(acción)* condensing. 2 *(efecto)* condensation.
condensado,-a *adj* condensed.
condensador,-ra *adj* condensing.
condensar *vt* to condense.
condesa *nf* countess.
condescendencia *nf* 1 *(deferencia)* condescension. 2 *(amabilidad)* affability.
condescender [28] *vi (adaptarse)* to comply (**a**, with), consent (**a**, to).
condescendiente *adj (complaciente)* obliging.
condestable *nm* High Constable.
condición *nf* 1 *(naturaleza)* nature, condition. 2 *(carácter)* nature, character. 3 *(circunstancia)* circumstance, condition. 4 *(estado social)* status, position. 5 *(calidad)* capacity. 6 *(exigencia)* condition.
▷ *nf pl* **condiciones** 1 *(estado)* condition *sing,* state *sing.* 2 *(aptitud)* aptitude *sing,* talent *sing.* ■ **a condición de que...** provided (that).... ■ **con la condición de que...** on the condition that... ■ **estar en condiciones de hacer** ALGO 1 *(físicas)* to be fit to do STH. 2 *(posición, autoridad)* to be in a position to do STH.
condicionado,-a *adj* conditioned.
condicional *adj* conditional.
▷ *nm* conditional.
condicionamiento *nm* conditioning.
condicionar *vt* 1 *(influir en)* to condition, determine. 2 *(supeditar)* to make conditional.
cóndilo *nm* condyle.
condimentación *nf* seasoning, flavouring (US flavoring).
condimentar *vt* to season, flavour (US flavor).
condimento *nm* seasoning, flavouring (US flavoring).
condiscípulo,-a *nm & nf* fellow pupil, fellow student, schoolmate.
condolencia *nf* condolence, sympathy.
condolerse [32] *vpr* to sympathize (**de**, with), feel sorry (**de**, for), feel pity (**de**, for).
condominio *nm* 1 *(copropiedad)* joint ownership. 2 *(de un territorio)* condominium.
condón *nm* condom.
condonación *nf* condonation, remission.
condonar *vt* 1 *(perdonar)* to condone. 2 *(una deuda)* to cancel, remit.
cóndor *nm* condor.
conducción *nf* 1 FÍS conduction. 2 *(transporte)* transportation. 3 *(por tubería)* piping; *(eléctrica)* wiring. 4 AUTO driving. 5 *(cañería)* pipe, intake.
conducir [46] *vt* 1 *(guiar)* to lead, take, show. 2 *(coche, animales)* to drive. 3 *(negocio)* to manage. 4 *(transportar)* to transport.
▷ *vi* 1 *(un coche)* to drive. 2 *(llevar)* to lead (**a**, -).
conducta *nf* conduct, behaviour (US behavior).
conductancia *nf* conductance.
conductibilidad *nf* conductivity.
conductismo *nm* behaviourism.
conductista *nm o nf* behaviourist, (US behaviorist).
conductividad *nf* conductivity.
conductivo,-a *adj* conductive.
conducto *nm* 1 *(tubería)* pipe, conduit. 2 *(eléctrico)* cable, lead. 3 ANAT duct, canal. 4 *fig* channel.
conductor,-ra *adj* FÍS conductive.
▷ *nm & nf* AUTO driver.
▷ *nm* **conductor** FÍS conductor.
condumio *nm fam* grub, nosh, food.
conectar *vt* 1 *(gen)* to connect (up). 2 *(aparato eléctrico)* to switch on, plug in.
▷ *vi* 1 RAD TV *(coger)* to tune in (**con**, to); *(dar conexión)* to tune in (**con**, with). 2 *fam (llevarse bien)* to hit it off, get on well.
conector *nm* connector.
conejera *nf* 1 *(conejal)* rabbit hutch. 2 *(madriguera)* rabbit warren, rabbit burrow.
conejero,-a *nm & nf* rabbit breeder.

conejillo *nm* young rabbit. ● **conejillo de Indias** guinea pig.
conejo,-a *nm & nf* rabbit.
conexión *nf* 1 TÉC connection. 2 *fig* relationship, connection.
conexionar *vt* to connect.
conexo,-a *adj* connected, related.
confabulación *nf* conspiracy, plot.
confabulador,-ra *nm & nf* conspirator, plotter.
confabular *vi* to confabulate, discuss.
▷ *vpr* **confabularse** to conspire, plot.
confección *nf* 1 *(acción)* dressmaking, tailoring; *(ropa)* off-the-peg clothes *pl*, ready-to-wear clothes *pl*. 2 *(realización)* making, making up.
confeccionador,-ra *nm & nf* 1 COST outfitter. 2 *(realizador)* maker; *(de un escrito)* writer, author.
confeccionar *vt (vestido)* to make, make up; *(list)* to draw up; *(plato)* to prepare.
confeccionista *nm o nf* outfitter.
confederación *nf* confederation, confederacy.
confederal *adj* confederative.
confederar *vt* to confederate.
conferencia *nf* 1 *(charla)* talk, lecture. 2 POL conference, meeting. 3 *(teléfono)* long-distance call. ■ **dar una conferencia sobre** ALGO to lecture on STH, give a lecture on STH.
conferenciante *nm o nf* lecturer.
conferenciar [12] *vi* to confer.
conferir [35] *vt* 1 *(conceder)* to confer, bestow, award. 2 *(dar)* to give.
confesar [27] *vt* 1 *(reconocer)* to confess, admit. 2 *(un crimen)* to own up to.
▷ *vpr* **confesarse** to go to confession, confess.
confesión *nf* 1 *(expresión)* confession, admission. 2 *(credo)* confession, faith.
confesional *adj* denominational.
confesionario *nm* confessional.
confeso,-a *adj* 1 JUR self-confessed. 2 *(judío)* converted.
confesor *nm* confessor.
confeti *nm* confetti.
confiado,-a *adj* 1 *(crédulo)* unsuspecting, gullible. 2 *(seguro)* confident, self-confident.
confianza *nf* 1 *(seguridad)* confidence. 2 *(familiaridad)* familiarity, intimacy. 3 *(presunción)* conceit. ■ **de confianza** 1 *(fiable)* reliable. 2 *(de responsabilidad)* trustworthy. ‖ **en confianza** confidentially, in confidence. ‖ **tener confianza en uno mismo** to be self-confident.
confiar [13] *vi* 1 *(tener fe)* to trust (**en**, -), confide (**en**, in). 2 *(estar seguro)* to be confident, trust. 3 *(contar)* to count (**en**, on), rely (**en**, on).
▷ *vt* 1 *(depositar)* to entrust. 2 *(secretos, problemas, etc)* to confide.
▷ *vpr* **confiarse** 1 *(entregarse)* to entrust OS.
confidencia *nf* confidence, secret.
confidencial *adj* confidential.
confidencialidad *nf* confidentiality.
confidente,-a *nm & nf* 1 *(hombre)* confidant; *(mujer)* confidante. 2 *(de la policía)* informer.
configuración *nf* 1 configuration, shape. 2 INFORMÁ configuration.
configurar *vt* 1 to form, shape. 2 INFORMÁ to configure.
confín *adj* bordering.
▷ *nm* [Often used in plural.] limit, boundary: **los confines de la tierra** *the ends of the earth.*
confinamiento *nm* 1 *(encarcelamiento)* confinement. 2 *(exilio)* exile, banishment.
confinar *vt (recluir)* to confine.
confirmación *nf* confirmation.
confirmar *vt* to confirm.
confirmatorio,-a *adj* confirmatory.
confiscación *nf* confiscation.
confiscar [1] *vt* to confiscate.
confitado,-a *pp* → **confitar.**
▷ *adj (fruta)* candied, glacé. ● **frutas confitadas** candied fruit *sing*.
confitar *vt (frutas)* to candy; *(carne)* to preserve.
confite *nm* sweet, US candy.
confitería *nf* confectioner's, sweet shop, US candy shop.
confitero,-a *nm & nf* confectioner.
confitura *nf* preserve, jam.
conflagración *nf* 1 *(incendio)* conflagration. 2 *(de guerra)* flare-up.
conflictividad *nf* disputes *pl*.
conflictivo,-a *adj (situación)* difficult; *(tema)* controversial.
conflicto *nm* 1 *(choque)* conflict. 2 *fig (apuro)* dilemma. ● **conflicto laboral** industrial dispute.
confluencia *nf* confluence.
confluir [62] *vi (personas)* to converge, come together; *(ríos, caminos, etc)* to meet, converge.
conformación *nf* shape, structure.
conformar *vt* 1 *(dar forma)* to shape. 2 *(adaptar)* to conform, adjust.
▷ *vpr* **conformarse** *(contentarse)* to resign OS (**con**, to), be content (**con**, with), make do (**con**, with).
conforme *adj* 1 *(satisfecho)* satisfied. 2 *(de acuerdo)* in accordance with, in keeping with. 3 *(resignado)* resigned.
▷ *adv* 1 *(según, como)* as. 2 *(en cuanto)* as soon as. 3 *(a medida que)* as. ■ **conforme a** in accordance with, according to.
conformidad *nf (aprobación)* approval, consent. ■ **en conformidad con** ALGO in conformity with STH, in agreement with.
conformismo *nm* conformism.
conformista *nm o nf* conformist.
confort *nm* comfort.
▲ *pl* **conforts.**
confortable *adj* comfortable.
confortablemente *adv* comfortably.
confortante *adj* 1 *(que fortalece)* invigorating. 2 *fig (consolador)* comforting, cheering.
confortar *vt* 1 *(dar vigor)* to invigorate. 2 *fig (consolar)* to comfort. 3 *fig (animar)* to cheer.
confraternal *adj* fraternal, brotherly.
confraternar *vi* to fraternize.
confraternidad *nf* confraternity, brotherhood.
confraternizar [4] *vi* to fraternize.
confrontación *nf* 1 *(enfrentamiento)* confrontation. 2 *(comparación)* comparison, collation.

onfrontar *vt* 1 *(gen)* to confront; *(carear)* to bring face to face. 2 *(cotejar)* to compare (con, with), collate (con, with).
onfundir *vt* 1 *(mezclar)* to mix up. 2 *(equivocar)* to confuse (con, with), mistake (con, for). 3 *(turbar)* to confound, embarrass.
▷ *vpr* confundirse 1 *(mezclarse)* to mingle; *(colores, formas)* to blend. 2 *(equivocarse)* to get mixed up, make a mistake. 3 *(turbarse)* to be confused, be embarrassed.
onfusamente *adv* confusedly.
onfusión *nf* 1 *(desorden)* confusion, chaos. 2 *(equivocación)* mistake, confusion.
onfusionismo *nm* confusion.
onfuso,-a *adj* 1 *(ideas)* confused. 2 *(estilo, etc)* obscure, confused. 3 *fig (turbado)* confused, embarrassed.
onga *nf* conga.
ongelación *nf* 1 *(gen)* freezing. 2 *(precios, salarios, etc)* freeze. 3 MED *(gen)* exposure; *(extremidades)* frostbite.
ongelado,-a *adj* 1 *(gen)* frozen. 2 MED frostbitten.
▷ *nm pl* congelados frozen food *sing*.
ongelador *nm* freezer.
ongelar *vt* 1 *(gen)* to freeze. 2 MED to cause frostbite on.
▷ *vpr* congelarse 1 to freeze. 2 MED to get frostbite.
ongénere *adj* congeneric, congenerous.
▷ *nm o nf* sort, kind.
ongeniar [12] *vi* to get on.
ongénito,-a *adj* 1 congenital. 2 *fig* innate.
ongestión *nf* congestion.
ongestionar *vt* to congest.
▷ *vpr* congestionarse 1 to become congested. 2 *(la cara)* to go red, blush.
onglomeración *nf* conglomeration.
onglomerado *nm* 1 TÉC conglomerate. 2 *fig* conglomeration, collection.
onglomerar *vt* to conglomerate.
▷ *vpr* conglomerarse to conglomerate.
ongoja *nf* 1 *(angustia)* anguish, distress. 2 *(pena)* grief, sorrow.
ongraciar [12] *vt* to win over.
▷ *vpr* congraciarse to ingratiate OS (con, with).
ongratulación *nf fml* congratulation.
ongratular *vt fml* to congratulate on.
▷ *vpr* congratularse *fml* to congratulate OS (de/por, on).
congregación *nf* 1 *(reunión)* assembly. 2 REL congregation.
congregante *nm o nf* member of a congregation.
congregar [7] *vt* to congregate, assemble.
▷ *vpr* congregarse to congregate, assemble.
congresista *nm o nf* 1 *(que asiste a un congreso)* congress participant. 2 *(diputado)* member of congress; *(hombre)* congressman; *(mujer)* congresswoman.
congreso *nm* congress. ● congreso de los Diputados Parliament, US Congress.
congrio *nm* conger, conger eel.
congruencia *nf* 1 *(conveniencia)* congruity. 2 MAT congruence.
congruente *adj* 1 *(coherente)* coherent, suitable. 2 MAT congruent.
cónico,-a *adj* 1 conical. 2 *(en geometría)* conic.
conífera *nf* conifer.
conjetura *nf* conjecture. ■ hacer conjeturas to make conjectures.
conjeturar *vt* to conjecture.
conjugable *adj* conjugable.
conjugación *nf* conjugation.
conjugado,-a *adj (enlazado)* combined.
conjugar [7] *vt* 1 to conjugate. 2 *fig* to join, combine, bring together.
conjunción *nf* conjunction.
conjuntado,-a *adj* coordinated.
conjuntamente *adv* jointly, together.
conjuntar *vt* to coordinate.
conjuntiva *nf* conjunctiva.
conjuntivitis *nf inv* conjunctivitis.
conjuntivo,-a *adj* conjunctive.
conjunto,-a *adj* 1 *(compartido)* joint. 2 *(combinado)* combined.
▷ *nm* conjunto 1 *(grupo)* group, collection. 2 *(todo)* whole. 3 *(prenda)* outfit, ensemble; *(jersey y chaqueta)* twinset. 4 MÚS *(clásico)* ensemble; *(pop)* band, group. 5 MAT set. 6 DEP team. ■ en conjunto altogether, on the whole.
conjura *nf* plot, conspiracy.
conjuración *nf* plot, conspiracy.
conjurado,-a *nm & nf* conspirator, plotter.
conjurar *vt* 1 *(gen)* to exorcise; *(peligro)* to avert, stave off, ward off. 2 *lit (rogar)* to beseech.
▷ *vi (conspirar)* to conspire (contra, against).
▷ *vpr* conjurarse to conspire (contra, against).
conjuro *nm* 1 *(exorcismo)* exorcism. 2 *(encantamiento)* spell, incantation.
conllevar *vt (implicar)* to involve, entail.
conmemoración *nf* commemoration.
conmemorar *vt* to commemorate.
conmemorativo,-a *adj* commemorative.
conmigo *pron* with me, to me.
conminación *nf* threat, commination.
conminador,-ra *adj* threatening, menacing.
conminar *vt* to threaten, menace.
conminativo,-a *adj* 1 threatening, menacing. 2 *(sentencia)* coercive.
conminatorio,-a *adj* → conminativo,-a.
conmiseración *nf fml* commiseration, pity.
conmoción *nf* 1 commotion, shock: causar conmoción *to cause a commotion.* 2 MED concussion. 3 *(levantamiento)* riot. ● conmoción cerebral concussion.
conmocionar *vt* 1 to shock. 2 MED to concuss. 3 *fig* to trouble, disturb.
conmovedor,-ra *adj* moving, touching.
conmover [32] *vt* 1 *(persona)* to move, touch. 2 *(cosa)* to shake.
conmutable *adj* commutable.
conmutación *nf* commutation.
conmutador *nm* switch.
conmutar *vt* 1 *(cambiar)* to exchange. 2 JUR to commute. 3 ELEC to commutate.
conmutativo,-a *adj* commutative.
connatural *adj* connatural, inherent.
connivencia *nf* connivance, collusion.
connotación *nf* connotation.

connotar *vt* to connote.
cono *nm* cone.
conocedor,-ra *nm & nf* expert (**de**, on), connoisseur (**de**, of).
conocer [44] *vt* **1** *(gen)* to know; *(noticia)* to hear. **2** *(persona)* to meet, get to know. **3** *(reconocer)* to recognize. **4** *(país, lugar)* to have been to.
▷ *vi* **1** *(saber)* to know (**de**, about). **2** JUR to hear (**de**, -).
▷ *vpr* **conocerse** *(a sí mismo)* to know OS; *(dos o más personas)* to know each other; *(por primera vez)* to meet, get to know. ■ **dar a conocer** to make known.
conocido,-a *adj* **1** known. **2** *(famoso)* well-known.
conocimiento *nm* **1** [In **1**, also used in plural with the same meaning.] *(saber)* knowledge. **2** *(sensatez)* good sense. **3** *(conciencia)* consciousness. ■ **tener conocimiento de** ALGO to know about STH.
conque *conj* so.
conquista *nf* conquest. ■ **hacer una conquista** *(amorosa)* to make a conquest.
conquistador,-ra *adj* conquering.
conquistar *vt (con las armas)* to conquer.
consabido,-a *adj* **1** *fml (usual)* usual, familiar. **2** *(ya sabido)* well-known.
consagración *nf* **1** REL consecration. **2** *(artista, etc)* recognition. **3** *(de una costumbre)* establishment. **4** *(dedicación)* dedication.
consagrado,-a *adj* **1** REL consecrated. **2** *(reconocido)* recognized, established.
consagrar *vt* **1** REL to consecrate. **2** *(palabra, expresión)* to establish. **3** *(dedicar)* to dedicate. **4** *(artista, etc)* to confirm, establish.
consanguíneo,-a *adj* consanguineous.
▷ *nm & nf* blood relation.
consanguinidad *nf* consanguinity, blood relationship.
consciente *adj* **1** conscious, aware. **2** MED conscious. **3** *(responsable)* reliable, responsible. ■ **estar consciente** to be conscious. | **ser consciente de** ALGO to be aware of STH.
consecuencia *nf* **1** consequence, result. **2** *(coherencia)* consistency. ■ **a consecuencia de** as a consequence of, as a result of. | **como consecuencia de** as a consequence of, as a result of.
consecuente *adj* **1** *(siguiente)* consequent. **2** *(resultante)* resulting. **3** *(coherente)* consistent.
consecutivamente *adv* consecutively.
consecutivo,-a *adj* consecutive.
conseguir [56] *vt* **1** *(cosa)* to obtain, get; *(objetivo)* to attain, achieve. **2** *(lograr)* to manage, succeed in.
consejería *nf* **1** *(lugar)* Council. **2** *(cargo)* councillor.
consejero,-a *nm & nf* **1** *(asesor)* adviser, advisor, counsellor. **2** POL councillor. **3** *(de un consejo de administración)* member (of a board of directors).
consejo *nm* **1** *(recomendación)* advice. **2** *(junta)* council, board. ■ **pedir consejo a** ALGN to ask SB for advice.
● **consejo de administración** *(reunión)* board meeting. | **consejo de ministros** cabinet.
consenso *nm* **1** *(acuerdo)* consensus. **2** *(consentimiento)* consent, assent.
consensual *adj* consensual.
consensuar [11] *vt* to reach a consensus on.
consentido,-a *adj (mimado)* spoiled, spoilt.
▷ *nm & nf (persona)* spoiled person, spoilt person; *(niño)* spoiled child, spoilt child.
consentimiento *nm* consent.
consentir [35] *vt* **1** *(tolerar)* to allow, permit, tolerate. **2** *(mimar)* to spoil. **3** *(admitir)* to take, withstand.
▷ *vi* **1** *(admitir)* to consent (**en**, to), agree (**en**, to). **2** *(ceder)* to weaken.
conserje *nm* **1** *(portero)* porter; *(de hotel)* hall porter. **2** *(encargado)* caretaker.
conserjería *nf* **1** *(lugar)* porter's lodge, reception. **2** *(oficio)* job of porter.
conserva [Also used in plural with the same meaning.] *nf* **1** *(en lata)* tinned food, canned food. **2** *(dulces)* preserves *pl*.
conservación *nf (de alimentos)* preservation.
conservador,-ra *adj* POL conservative.
▷ *nm & nf* **1** POL conservative. **2** *(de museos)* curator.
conservadurismo *nm* conservatism.
conservante *nm* preservative.
conservar *vt* **1** *(alimentos)* to preserve. **2** *(guardar)* to keep, save.
▷ *vpr* **conservarse** **1** *(tradición, etc)* to survive. **2** *fig (mantenerse)* to keep well.
conservatorio *nm* conservatory, conservatoire school of music.
conservería *nf* **1** *(industria)* canning industry. **2** *(fábrica)* cannery.
conservero,-a *adj* canning: **industria conservera** *canning industry.*
considerable *adj* considerable.
considerablemente *adv* considerably.
consideración *nf* **1** *(reflexión)* consideration, attention: **este tema merece nuestra consideración** *this subject deserves our attention.* **2** *(respeto)* regard. ■ **con consideración** *(respeto)* respectfully. | **de consideración** serious. | **en consideración a** considering.
considerado,-a *adj* **1** *(atento)* considerate, thoughtful. **2** *(apreciado)* respected.
considerar *vt (reflexionar)* to consider, think over, think about.
consigna *nf* **1** *(en estación, etc)* left-luggage office, US check-room. **2** *(señal, lema)* watchword.
consignación *nf* **1** *(asignación)* allocation. **2** *(de mercancías)* consignment.
consignar *vt* **1** *(mercancías)* to consign, ship, dispatch. **2** *(destinar - dinero, etc)* to allocate; *(- cantidad)* to assign. **3** *(anotar)* to note down, take down.
consignatario,-a *nm & nf* **1** *(depositario)* trustee, mortgagee. **2** COM consignee.
consigo *pron* **1** *(3ª persona singular - hombre)* with him; *(- mujer)* with her; *(- cosa, animal)* with it. **2** *(usted)* with you. **3** *(3ª persona plural)* with them. **4** *(ustedes)* with you.
consiguiente *adj* consequent, resulting, resultant. ■ **por consiguiente** therefore, consequently.
consistencia *nf (dureza)* consistency.
consistente *adj* **1** *(firme)* firm, solid. **2** *fig* sound, solid. **3** CULIN thick. ■ **consistente en** consisting of.
consistir *vi* **1** *(estribar)* to lie (**en**, in), consist (**en**, in). **2** *(estar formado)* to consist (**en**, of).

onsistorial *adj* REL consistorial. ● **casa consistorial** town hall.
onsistorio *nm* 1 *(ayuntamiento)* town council. 2 REL consistory.
onsola *nf* 1 *(mueble)* console table. 2 *(de ordenador, etc)* console. ● **consola de videojuegos** games console.
onsolación *nf* consolation, comfort.
onsolador,-ra *adj* consoling, comforting.
onsolar [31] *vt* to console, comfort.
onsolidación *nf* consolidation.
onsolidar *vt* to consolidate.
onsomé *nm* clear soup, consommé.
onsonancia *nf* 1 LIT consonance, rhyme. 2 *fig* harmony.
onsonante *nf* consonant.
onsonántico,-a *adj* consonantal, consonant.
onsorcio *nm* consortium, partnership, association.
onsorte *nm o nf (cónyuge)* spouse.
onspiración *nf* conspiracy, plot.
onspirador,-ra *nm & nf* conspirator.
onspirar *vi* to conspire, plot.
onstancia *nf* 1 *(perseverancia)* constancy, perseverance. 2 *(evidencia)* evidence, proof. ■ **dejar constancia de ALGO** 1 *(registrar)* to put STH on record. 2 *(probar)* to prove STH.
onstante *adj* 1 *(invariable)* constant. 2 *(persona)* steadfast.
▷ *nf* MAT constant.
onstantemente *adv* constantly.
onstar *vi* 1 *(consistir en)* to consist (**de**, of), be made up (**de**, of), comprise (**de**, -). 2 *(figurar)* to figure, be included, appear. 3 *(ser cierto)* to be a fact. 4 *(quedar claro)* to be clear, be known. ■ **hacer constar** 1 *(señalar)* to point out, state. 2 *(escribir)* to put down, include.
onstatación *nf* verification.
onstatar *vt* to verify, confirm.
onstelación *nf* constellation.
onstelado,-a *adj* 1 *(estrellado)* starry. 2 *fig* strewn (**de**, with).
onsternación *nf* consternation, dismay.
onsternar *vt* to dismay, shatter.
onstipado,-a *nm* MED cold. ■ **estar constipado,-a** to have a cold.
onstiparse *vpr* to catch a cold.
onstitución *nf* constitution.
onstitucional *adj* constitutional.
▷ *nm o nf* constitutionalist.
onstituir [62] *vt* 1 *(formar)* to comprise, make up, constitute. 2 *(ser)* to be, constitute. 3 *(crear)* to create, set up, establish.
onstitutivo,-a *adj* constituent, component.
onstituyente *adj* constituent.
▷ *nm o nf (componente)* constituent.
onstreñir [36] *vt* 1 *(forzar)* to constrain, compel, force. 2 *(limitar)* to limit, restrict. 3 MED *(cerrar)* to constrict.
onstricción *nf* constriction.
onstrictor *adj* constricting, constrictive.
▷ *nm* **constrictor** constrictor.
construcción *nf* 1 construction: **la industria de la construcción** *the construction industry.* 2 *(edificio)* building. ■ **en construcción** under construction.
constructivo,-a *adj* constructive.
constructor,-ra *adj* construction, building.
▷ *nm & nf (de edificios)* builder; *(de barcos)* shipbuilder.
construir [62] *vt* to construct, build.
consubstancial *adj* consubstantial.
consuelo *nm* consolation, comfort.
consuetudinario,-a *adj* habitual, customary.
cónsul *nm o nf* consul.
consulado *nm* 1 *(oficina)* consulate. 2 *(cargo)* consulship.
consular *adj* consular.
consulta *nf* 1 *(acción)* consultation. 2 MED surgery, US doctor's office; *(consultorio)* consulting room. ■ **pasar consulta** to see patients, hold surgery.
consultar *vt* 1 *(pedir opinión)* to consult (**con**, with/-), seek advice (**con**, from): **consulté con mis padres** *I consulted with my parents.* 2 *(buscar en un libro)* to look up. ■ **consultar con un abogado** to consult a lawyer, take legal advice.
consultivo,-a *adj* consultative, advisory.
consultor,-ra *nm & nf* consultant.
consultoría *nf (servicio)* consultancy.
consultorio *nm* 1 MED *(consulta)* surgery, US doctor's office; *(habitación)* consulting room. 2 *(de información)* office. 3 *(en periódicos)* problem page, advice column; *(en radio)* phone-in.
consumación *nf* consummation, completion; *(de un crimen)* perpetration.
consumado,-a *adj* 1 *(perfecto)* consummate, accomplished. 2 *fam* complete, perfect.
consumar *vt* 1 *(terminar)* to complete, carry out. 2 *(crimen)* to commit. 3 *(matrimonio)* to consummate.
consumición *nf* 1 consumption. 2 *(bebida)* drink.
consumido,-a *adj* 1 *fig (muy flaco)* thin, emaciated. 2 *fig (afligido)* consumed.
consumidor,-ra *nm & nf* consumer.
consumir *vt* 1 *(gastar, usar)* to consume, use. 2 *(destruir)* to destroy, consume.
▷ *vpr* **consumirse** 1 *(extinguirse)* to burn out. 2 *fig (afligirse)* to waste away.
consumismo *nm* consumerism.
consumista *nm o nf* consumerist.
consumo *nm* consumption.
consunción *nf* consumption.
consustancial *adj* innate (**a**, in), inherent (**a**, in).
contabilidad *nf* 1 *(profesión)* accountancy; *(carrera)* accounting. 2 *(de empresa, etc)* accounting, bookkeeping. ■ **llevar la contabilidad** to keep the books.
contabilizar [4] *vt* to enter in the books.
contable *nm o nf* bookkeeper, accountant.
contactar *vt* to contact, get in touch (**con**, with).
contacto *nm* 1 contact. 2 AUTO ignition. ■ **ponerse en contacto con** to get in touch with, get in contact with. ■ **perder el contacto** to lose touch. ● **contacto sexual** sexual contact.
contado,-a *adj* few. ■ **en contadas ocasiones** seldom, rarely.
contador,-ra *nm & nf (contable)* accountant.
▷ *nm* **contador** meter.

contaduría *nf* 1 *(oficio)* accountancy. 2 *(oficina)* accountant's office.
contagiar [12] *vt* 1 *(enfermedad)* to transmit, pass on. 2 *fig* to infect, pass on, give.
▷ *vpr* **contagiarse** 1 *(enfermar)* to get infected. 2 *(transmitirse)* to be contagious: **esta enfermedad no se contagia** *this disease is not contagious.*
contagio *nm* MED contagion, infection.
contagioso,-a *adj* infectious, contagious: **enfermedad contagiosa** *infectious disease;* **risa contagiosa** *infectious laugh.*
contáiner *nm* container.
contaminación *nf* contamination; *(de agua, aire)* pollution.
contaminador,-ra *adj* contaminating; *(de agua, aire)* polluting.
contaminante *nm* polluting agent.
contaminar *vt* 1 to contaminate; *(agua, aire)* to pollute. 2 *fig* to contaminate, corrupt.
contante *adj (dinero)* cash.
contar [31] *vt* 1 *(calcular)* to count. 2 *(explicar)* to tell: **me contó un cuento** *she told me a story.*
▷ *vi* to count: **los niños saben contar** *the children know how to count.*
contemplación *nf (acción)* contemplation.
contemplar *vt (mirar)* to contemplate.
contemplativo,-a *adj* contemplative.
contemporáneo,-a *adj, nm & nf* contemporary.
contemporizar [4] *vi* to compromise, be compliant.
contención *nf (moderación)* control.
contencioso,-a *adj* 1 contentious. 2 JUR litigious.
contender [28] *vi* 1 *(pelear)* to contend, fight. 2 *(competir)* to contest.
contendiente *nm o nf* contender.
contenedor,-ra *adj* containing.
▷ *nm* **contenedor** container.
contener [87] *vt* 1 *(incluir)* to contain, hold. 2 *(detener)* to hold back, restrain. 3 *(reprimir)* to restrain, hold back, contain; *(respiración)* to hold.
contenido,-a *adj (moderado)* moderate, reserved.
▷ *nm* **contenido** content, contents *pl.*
contentar *vt (satisfacer)* to please, content.
▷ *vpr* **contentarse** *(conformarse)* to make do (**con**, with), be satisfied (**con**, with).
contento,-a *adj* happy, pleased: **estoy contento de conocerle** *I'm pleased to meet you.*
▷ *nm* **contento** happiness, joy, contentment.
contertulio,-a *nm & nf* fellow guest.
contestable *adj* debatable.
contestación *nf (respuesta)* answer, reply.
contestador *nm* answering machine. ● **contestador automático** answering machine.
contestar *vt (responder)* to answer.
contestatario,-a *adj* anti-establishment.
▷ *nm & nf* rebel.
contexto *nm* context.
contextualizar [4] *vt* to put into context, contextualize.
contextura *nf* 1 *(de materiales)* contexture. 2 *(de persona)* build.
contienda *nf* contest, dispute, struggle.
contigo *pron* with you.
contigüidad *nf* contiguity.
contiguo,-a *adj* contiguous (**a**, to), adjoining, adja cent (**a**, to).
continencia *nf* continence.
continental *adj* continental.
continente *nm* GEOG continent.
contingencia *nf* 1 *(probabilidad)* contingency, even tuality. 2 *(riesgo)* risk, hazard.
contingente *adj (posible)* contingent.
▷ *nm* 1 MIL contingent. 2 *(cuota)* quota, share.
continuación *nf* continuation, follow-up. ■ **a con tinuación** next.
continuador,-ra *adj* continuing.
▷ *nm & nf* continuator.
continuamente *adv* continuously.
continuar [11] *vt (proseguir)* to continue, carry on.
continuidad *nf* continuity.
continuo,-a *adj* 1 *(seguido)* continuous. 2 *(continuad* continual, constant.
contonearse *vpr (mujer)* to swing one's hips, wig gle; *(hombre)* to swagger.
contoneo *nm (de mujer)* swinging of the hips, wiggle *(de hombre)* swaggering, swagger.
contornar *vt* 1 *(dar vueltas)* to skirt. 2 *(hacer los perfi les)* to trace the outline of.
contorno *nm* 1 *(perfil)* outline; *(perímetro)* perimeter 2 *(canto)* rim, edge.
▷ *nm pl* **contornos** *(afueras)* surroundings *pl,* environ ment.
contorsión *nf* contortion.
contorsionarse *vpr* to contort OS, twist OS.
contorsionista *nm o nf* contortionist.
contra *prep* 1 against: **tres contra uno** *three agains one.* 2 for: **un producto contra las picaduras de mos quitos** *a product for mosquito bites.* ■ **en contra** against **estaba en contra** *he was against it.* ǁ **en contra de l que...** contrary to...: **en contra de lo que decían** *con trary to what they said.*
contraatacar [1] *vt* to counterattack.
contraataque *nm* counterattack.
contrabajo *nm* 1 *(instrumento)* double bass. 2 *(voz* low bass.
contrabandista *nm o nf* smuggler.
contrabando *nm* 1 smuggling, contraband; *(de ar mas)* gunrunning. 2 *(mercancías)* smuggled goods *pl,* contraband. ■ **pasar** ALGO **de contrabando** to smuggle STH in.
contracción *nf* contraction.
contracepción *nf* contraception.
contraceptivo,-a *adj* contraceptive.
▷ *nm* **contraceptivo** contraceptive.
contrachapado *nm* plywood.
contracorriente *nf* crosscurrent.
contráctil *adj* contractile.
contractilidad *nf* contractility.
contractual *adj* contractual.
contractura *nf* contracture.
contracultura *nf* counterculture.
contradanza *nf* contredanse, contradance.
contradecir *vt (decir lo contrario)* to contradict.
contradicción *nf* contradiction. ■ **estar en contradic ción con** to be inconsistent with, contradictory to.

ontradictorio,-a *adj* contradictory.
ontraer [88] *vt* 1 *(encoger)* to contract: **contraer un músculo** *to contract a muscle.* 2 *(enfermedad)* to catch. 3 *(deuda)* to contract, incur; *(hábito)* to pick up. 4 LING to contract.
▷ *vpr* **contraerse** *(encogerse)* to contract.
ontraespionaje *nm* counterespionage.
ontrafuerte *nm* ARQUIT buttress.
ontrahecho,-a *adj* deformed, hunchbacked.
▷ *nm & nf* deformed person, hunchback.
ontrahuella *nf* riser.
ontraindicación *nf* MED contraindication.
ontraindicar *vt* MED to contraindicate.
ontralmirante *nm* rear admiral.
ontralto *nm o nf* contralto.
ontraluz *nm o nf* view against the light, back light. ▲ *pl* **contraluces.** ■ **a contraluz** against the light.
ontramaestre *nm* 1 *(capataz)* foreman. 2 MAR boatswain.
ontramano ■ **a contramano** the wrong way: **circulaba a contramano** *he was driving on the wrong side of the road.*
ontraofensiva *nf* counteroffensive.
ontraorden *nf* countermand.
ontrapartida *nf* 1 COM balancing entry. 2 *fig* compensation.
ontrapelo ■ **a contrapelo** *(contra la inclinación del pelo)* the wrong way: **para empezar, se cepilla el perro a contrapelo** *to start with, brush the dog's fur the wrong way.* ‖ **a contrapelo de** contrary to, against.
ontrapesar *vt* 1 to counterbalance, counterpoise. 2 *fig* to balance, offset.
ontrapeso *nm* 1 counterweight. 2 *fig* counterbalance.
contraponer [78] *vt* 1 *(oponer)* to set in opposition (**a**, to). 2 *fig (contrastar)* to contrast (**a**, with).
▷ *vpr* **contraponerse** *(oponerse)* to be opposed.
contraportada *nf* back page.
contraposición *nf* 1 *(contraste)* contrast. 2 *(oposición)* conflict, clash: **contraposición de intereses** *conflict of interests.* ■ **estar en contraposición** to clash.
contraprestación *nf* contractual obligation.
contraproducente *adj* counterproductive.
contraproposición *nf* counterproposal.
contrapropuesta *nf* counterproposal.
contrapuesto,-a *pp* → **contraponer.**
▷ *adj* opposed.
contrapunto *nm* counterpoint.
contra-reloj *adj* against the clock.
▷ *nm (en ciclismo)* time trial; *(en esquí)* downhill event.
contrariado,-a *adj (disgustado)* upset, cross.
contrariamente *adv* contrary (**a**, to).
contrariar [13] *vi* 1 *(oponerse)* to oppose, go against. 2 *(disgustar)* to annoy, upset: **no quería contrariarte** *I didn't want to upset you.* 3 *(dificultar)* to obstruct, hinder.
contrariedad *nf* 1 *(oposición)* opposition. 2 *(disgusto)* annoyance. 3 *(dificultad)* setback, obstacle.
contrario,-a *adj* 1 *(opuesto)* contrary, opposite: **iba en sentido contrario** *he was going in the opposite direction.* 2 *(perjudicial)* harmful (**a**, to), bad (**a**, for): **el fumar es contrario a la salud** *smoking is bad for your health.*
▷ *nm & nf* opponent, adversary, rival. ■ **al contrario** on the contrary. ‖ **de lo contrario** otherwise. ‖ **llevar la contraria a** ALGN to oppose SB. ‖ **por el contrario** on the contrary. ‖ **todo lo contrario** quite the opposite.
contrarreforma *nf* Counter Reformation.
contrarreloj *adj* against the clock.
▷ *nf* race against the clock. ● **(etapa) contrarreloj** time trial.
contrarrestar *vt* 1 *(hacer frente)* to resist, oppose. 2 *(neutralizar)* counteract, neutralize. 3 *(pelota)* to return.
contrarrevolucionario,-a *adj* counter-revolutionary.
▷ *nm & nf* counter-revolutionary.
contrarrevolución *nf* counter-revolution.
contrasentido *nm* 1 *(contradicción)* contradiction. 2 *(disparate)* piece of nonsense: **eso es un contrasentido** *that's nonsense.* 3 *(mala interpretación)* misinterpretation.
contraseña *nf* 1 *(seña)* secret sign; *(palabra)* password. 2 MIL password, watchword, countersign.
contrastar *vt* 1 *(hacer frente)* to resist, repel: **contrastar al enemigo** *to resist the enemy.* 2 *(comprobar)* to check, verify. 3 *(pesos y medidas)* to check. 4 *(oro y plata)* to hallmark.
▷ *vi (oponerse)* to contrast (**con**, with).
contraste *nm* 1 *(oposición)* contrast. 2 *(pesos y medidas)* verification. 3 *(oro y plata)* hallmark.
contrata *nf* contract.
contratación *nf* 1 *(contrato - obrero)* hiring; *(- empleado)* engagement. 2 *(pedido)* total orders *pl*, volume of business.
contratar *vt* 1 *(servicio, etc)* to sign a contract for. 2 *(obrero)* to hire; *(empleado)* to engage; *(deportista)* to sign up. 3 *(un arriendo)* to take on.
contratiempo *nm (contrariedad)* setback, hitch; *(accidente)* mishap.
contratista *nm o nf* contractor. ● **contratista de obras** building contractor.
contrato *nm* contract. ● **contrato de alquiler / contrato de arrendamiento** lease, leasing agreement. ‖ **contrato de compraventa** contract of sale. ‖ **contrato de trabajo** work contract. ‖ **contrato temporal** temporary contract.
contravenir [90] *vt* to contravene, infringe, violate: **contravenir las leyes** *to infringe the law.*
contraventana *nf* shutter.
contrayente *adj* contracting.
▷ *nm o nf (en matrimonio)* contracting party.
contribución *nf* 1 contribution. 2 *(impuesto)* tax.
contribuir [62] *vt (pagar)* to pay.
▷ *vi* 1 *(aportar)* to contribute: **contribuir a los gastos** *to contribute to the expenses.* 2 *(pagar impuestos)* to pay taxes.
contributivo,-a *adj* contributory.
contribuyente *adj* taxpaying.
▷ *nm o nf* taxpayer.
contrición *nf* contrition.
contrincante *nm* opponent, rival.
contrito,-a *adj* contrite, repentant.

control *nm* 1 *(gen)* control. 2 *(comprobación)* check. 3 *(sitio)* checkpoint. ■ **estar bajo control** to be under control. ‖ **estar fuera de control** to be out of control. ‖ **llevar el control** to be in control. ‖ **perder el control** to lose control. ● **control a distancia** remote control. ‖ **control de calidad** quality control. ‖ **control de natalidad** birth control.
controlable *adj* controllable.
controlador,-ra *adj* control.
▷ *nm & nf (aéreo)* air traffic controller.
controlar *vt* 1 *(gen)* to control. 2 *(comprobar)* to check.
▷ *vpr* **controlarse** *(moderarse)* to control OS.
controversia *nf* controversy, argument.
controvertido,-a *pp* → **controvertir**.
▷ *adj* controversial.
controvertir *vt* to dispute, argue about.
▷ *vi* to argue.
contubernio *nm* 1 *(cohabitación)* cohabitation. 2 *fig (confabulación)* conspiracy, collusion.
contumacia *nf* 1 *(obstinación)* obstinacy; *(rebeldía)* insubordination. 2 JUR contumacy.
contumaz *adj* 1 *(obstinado)* obstinate, stubborn. 2 *(rebelde)* insubordinate. 3 JUR contumacious.
contundencia *nf* 1 *(de arma)* contusive properties *pl.* 2 *fig (convicción)* weight: **la contundencia de un argumento** *the weight of an argument.*
contundente *adj* 1 *(arma)* blunt. 2 *fig (categórico)* convincing, overwhelming, weighty: **un «no» contundente** *a firm «no».*
conturbado,-a *adj* anxious, dismayed, perturbed.
conturbar *vt* to trouble, dismay, perturb.
▷ *vpr* **conturbarse** to be troubled, be dismayed, become perturbed.
contusión *nf* contusion, bruise.
contusionar *vt* to contuse, bruise.
conurbación *nf* conurbation.
convalecencia *nf* convalescence.
convalecer [43] *vi* to convalesce (**de**, after), recover (**de**, from).
convaleciente *adj* convalescent.
▷ *nm o nf* convalescent.
convalidación *nf* 1 EDUC validation. 2 *(documentos)* ratification, authentication.
convalidar *vt* 1 EDUC to validate. 2 *(documentos)* to ratify, authenticate.
convección *nf* convection.
convector *nm* convector.
convencer [2] *vt* 1 *(de algo)* to convince; *(para hacer algo)* to persuade: **lo convencieron de su error** *they convinced him of his mistake.* 2 *fam (en frases negativas)* to like, be keen on: **ese color no me acaba de convencer** *I'm not sure about that colour.*
▷ *vi* to be convincing: **el equipo local no convenció con su actuación** *the local team's performance was not very convincing.*
▷ *vpr* **convencerse** to become convinced, be convinced, convince OS: **se convenció de que era guapo** *he convinced himself that he was good-looking.*
convencimiento *nm* conviction. ■ **llegar al convencimiento de que...** to be convinced that...

convención *nf* 1 *(congreso)* convention, congress. *(acuerdo)* convention, treaty. 3 *(costumbre)* convention.
convencional *adj* conventional.
convencionalismo *nm* conventionalism, conventionality.
convenido,-a *adj* agreed, set, arranged.
conveniencia *nf* 1 *(utilidad)* usefulness. 2 *(oportundad)* suitability, advisability: **la conveniencia de estas medidas** *the advisability of these measures.* 3 *(provecho)* interest, benefit: **solo se preocupa de su propi conveniencia** *he only looks out for his own interests.* *(convenio)* agreement. ● **conveniencias sociales** socia conventions. ‖ **matrimonio de conveniencia** marriag of convenience.
conveniente *adj* 1 *(útil)* useful. 2 *(oportuno)* suitabl convenient. 3 *(ventajoso)* advantageous. 4 *(aconsejable)* advisable. 5 *(precio)* good, fair. ■ **creer conveniente** to think advisable, be better. ‖ **en el moment conveniente** at the right time.
convenientemente *adv (adecuadamente)* suitably *(bien)* properly.
convenio *nm* agreement, treaty. ● **convenio colectivo / convenio laboral** collective agreement.
convenir [90] *vt (acordar)* to agree, arrange: **convenimos el precio** *we agreed the price.*
▷ *vi* 1 *(acordar)* to agree: **convinimos en la fecha** *we agree on the date.* 2 *(ser oportuno o conveniente)* to be goo for: **no te conviene hacer esfuerzos** *it's not good for yo to exert yourself.* 3 *(ser adecuado o propio)* to suit: **es chico no te conviene** *that boy is not right for you.* ■ **conviene** + *inf* it is as well to + *inf*: **conviene mencionar que...** *it's as well to mention that...* ‖ **conviene qu + *subj*** it is better that, it is advisable + *inf*: **convien que te vayas** *it is better that you go.*
convento *nm (de monjas)* convent; *(de monjes)* monastery.
conventual *adj* conventual.
convergencia *nf* convergence.
convergente *adj* convergent, converging, concurring.
converger [5] *vi* to converge, come together.
convergir [6] *vi* to converge, come together.
conversación *nf* conversation, talk. ■ **dar conversación a** ALGN to talk to SB, keep SB chatting. ‖ **entabla conversación con** ALGN to get into conversation wit SB, engage SB in conversation. ‖ **tener poca conversación** not to be very talkative. ‖ **trabar conversació con** ALGN to strike up a conversation with SB, get int conversation with SB.
conversador,-ra *adj* talkative.
▷ *nm & nf* conversationalist, talker.
conversar *vi* to converse (**con**, with), talk (**con**, to).
conversión *nf* conversion.
convertir [29] *vt* 1 *(transformar)* to change, turn transform, convert. 2 *(valores, monedas)* to change exchange. 3 REL to convert: **la convirtió al cristianismo** *he converted her to Christianity.*
▷ *vpr* **convertirse** 1 *(transformarse)* to turn (**en**, into) change (**en**, into). 2 *(volverse)* to become (**en**, -), tur (**en**, into): **su sueño se convirtió en realidad** *his drea came true.* 3 REL to be converted (**a**, to).

onvexidad *nf* convexity.
convexo,-a *adj* convex.
convicción *nf* conviction: tengo la convicción de que vendrán *I firmly believe that they'll come.*
convicto,-a *adj* guilty, convicted.
convidado,-a *adj* invited.
▷ *nm & nf* guest.
convidar *vt* 1 *(invitar)* to invite: me convidó a una fiesta *he invited me to a party.* 2 *(ofrecer)* to offer: nos convidó a pastel *he offered us some cake.* 3 *fig (incitar, mover, animar)* to prompt, inspire, move: este tiempo convida a pasear *this weather makes you want to go for a walk.*
convincente *adj* convincing.
convincentemente *adv* convincingly.
convite *nm* 1 *(invitación)* invitation. 2 *(comida)* meal; *(fiesta)* party.
convivencia *nf* 1 living together. 2 *fig* coexistence.
convivir *vi* 1 to live together. 2 *fig* to coexist. ■ **saber convivir** to give and take.
convocar [1] *vt* to convoke, summon, call together. ■ **convocar una reunión** to call a meeting.
convocatoria *nf* 1 *(citación)* convocation, summons *sing*, call to a meeting. 2 EDUC examination: convocatoria de septiembre *(September) resits pl.*
convoy *nm* 1 *(escolta)* convoy. 2 *(tren)* train.
▲ *pl* convoyes.
convulsión *nf* 1 MED convulsion. 2 *fig* upheaval.
convulsionar *vt* 1 MED to convulse. 2 *fig* to throw into confusion: los atentados han convulsionado el país *the bombings have thrown the country into confusion.*
convulso,-a *adj* convulsed (de, with): convulso de dolor *convulsed with pain.*
conyugal *adj* conjugal. ● **vida conyugal** married life.
cónyuge *nm o nf (gen)* spouse, partner; *(marido)* husband; *(mujer)* wife.
▷ *nm pl* **cónyuges** husband and wife, married couple *sing.*
coña *nf* 1 *tabú (broma)* joke. 2 *tabú (molestia)* nuisance, pain, drag, pain in the neck: es una coña tener que levantarse tan temprano *it's a pain having to get up so early.* ■ **estar de coña** 1 *tabú (estar de broma)* to be joking, be kidding. 2 *(estar muy bien)* to be terrific, be brilliant. ‖ **¡ni de coña!** no way! ‖ **tomar ALGO a coña** *tabú* to take STH as a joke, treat STH as a joke.
coñac *nm* cognac, brandy.
▲ *pl* coñacs.
coñazo *nm tabú* pain, drag. ■ **dar el coñazo** *tabú* to be a real pain, pester, hassle.
coño *nm tabú* cunt.
▷ *interj tabú (sorpresa)* bloody hell, bugger me!, fuck me!; *(disgusto)* for God's sake, for fuck's sake!
coop. *abrev* (cooperativa) cooperative; *(abreviatura)* coop, co-op.
cooperación *nf* cooperation.
cooperador,-ra *adj* cooperative, collaborating, participating.
▷ *nm & nf* collaborator, cooperator.
cooperar *vi* to cooperate.
cooperativa *nf* cooperative.
cooperativista *adj* cooperative.
▷ *nm o nf (socio)* member of a cooperative.
cooperativo,-a *adj* cooperative.
coordenada *nf* coordinate.
coordinación *nf* coordination.
coordinado,-a *adj* coordinated.
coordinador,-ra *adj* coordinating.
▷ *nm & nf* coordinator.
coordinadora *nf (comité)* coordinating committee.
coordinar *vt* to coordinate: coordinaron la compaña *they coordinated the campaign.*
copa *nf* 1 *(vaso)* glass; *(bebida)* drink: ¿te apetece una copa? *do you fancy a drink?* 2 *(de árbol)* top. 3 *(trofeo)* cup. 4 *(de sujetador)* cup.
▷ *nf pl* **copas** *(naipes)* hearts. ■ **ir de copas** to go out drinking, go on a pub crawl. ‖ **llevar una copa de más** to have had one too many. ‖ **tomar una copa** to have a drink.
copar *vt* 1 *(acaparar)* to win, take: el equipo sueco copó el primer puesto *the Swedish team took the first place.* 2 *(llenar)* to fill. 3 *(en juegos de azar)* to go banco. 4 *fig (en una elección)* to win all the seats. 5 MIL to capture, take.
Copenhague *nm* Copenhagen.
copeo *nm* pub crawl. ■ **ir de copeo** to go on a pub crawl, go out drinking.
copete *nm* 1 *(cabello)* tuft. 2 *(penacho)* crest. 3 *(de caballo)* forelock. 4 *(de mueble)* ornamental top, ornamentation; *(de montana, helado)* top. 5 *fig (atrevimiento)* arrogance.
copia *nf* 1 *(gen)* copy. 2 *(de fotografía)* print. 3 *fig (persona)* image: es la copia de su padre *he's the image of his father.* 4 *lit (abundancia)* abundance. ■ **sacar una copia** to make a copy.
copiadora *nf* photocopier.
copiar [12] *vt* 1 *(gen)* to copy: lo copió del libro *he copied it from the book.* 2 EDUC to cheat, copy. 3 *(escribir)* to take down. ■ **copiar al pie de la letra** to copy word for word.
copiloto *nm* 1 AV copilot. 2 AUTO co-driver.
copión,-ona *nm & nf* 1 EDUC *fam* cheat, copier. 2 *fam (imitador)* copycat.
copiosamente *adv (gen)* abundantly, copiously; *(llover, nevar)* heavily: copiosamente ilustrado *copiously illustrated.*
copioso,-a *adj* 1 *fml (abundante)* plentiful, abundant, copious. 2 *fml (lluvia)* heavy; *(cabello)* long.
copista *nm o nf* copyist.
copla *nf* 1 *(verso, estrofa)* verse, stanza. 2 *(canción)* popular folk song. 3 *fam (monserga)* story, tale.
copo *nm (gen)* flake; *(de nieve)* snowflake; *(de algodón)* ball (of cotton). ● **copos de avena** rolled oats.
copón *nm* REL ciborium. ■ **del copón** *tabú* a hell of a: me has dado un susto del copón *you gave me one hell of a shock.*
coprocesador *nm* coprocessor.
coproducción *nf* co-production, joint production.
coproductor,-ra *nm & nf* co-producer.
copropiedad *nf* joint ownership.
copropietario,-a *nm & nf* joint owner, co-owner, co-proprietor.
coprotagonista *nm o nf* co-star.
coprotagonizar *vt* to co-star (-, in).

cópula *nf* 1 *(nexo)* link. 2 *(coito)* copulation, intercourse. 3 LING conjunction.
copular *vi* to copulate (**con**, with).
copulativo,-a *adj* copulative.
coque *nm* coke.
coqueta *nf* 1 *(mujer)* flirt, coquette. 2 *(mueble)* dressing table.
coquetear *vi* to flirt.
coqueteo *nm* flirtation.
coquetería *nf* coquetry, flirting, flirtation.
coqueto,-a *adj* flirtatious.
coquetón,-ona *adj* 1 *(persona)* coquettish. 2 *fam (habitación, etc)* cute, charming.
coracha *nf* leather bag.
coraje *nm* 1 *(valor)* courage, toughness. 2 *(ira)* anger. ■ **dar coraje** *fam* to infuriate, make furious: **me da coraje que haya ganado él** *it makes me furious that he won.* ‖ **echarle coraje a ALGO** to put some spirit into STH.
corajudo,-a *adj* 1 *(valiente)* tough, brave. 2 *(irritable)* quick-tempered.
coral[1] *adj* MÚS choral.
▷ *nf* MÚS *(grupo)* choir, choral society.
▷ *nm* MÚS *(composición)* choral, chorale.
coral[2] *nm* ZOOL coral.
▷ *nm pl* **corales** coral beads.
coralina *nf* coralline.
coralino,-a *adj* coral.
Corán *nm* Koran.
coránico,-a *adj* Koranic.
coraza *nf* 1 *(armadura)* armour (US armor), cuirass. 2 *(caparazón)* shell, carapace. 3 *fig (protección)* armour (US armor), protection.
corazón *nm* 1 ANAT heart. 2 *fig (parte central)* heart, core: **en el corazón de la ciudad** *in the heart of the city.* 3 *(de fruta)* core. 4 *(apelativo)* darling, dear, sweetheart. ■ **abrir el corazón a ALGN** *fig* to open one's heart to SB. ‖ **de corazón / de todo corazón** *fig* sincerely, in all sincerity. ‖ **estar con el corazón en un puño** *fig* to have one's heart in one's mouth. ‖ **estar enfermo del corazón** to have heart trouble.
▷ *nm pl* **corazones** *(naipes)* hearts.
corazonada *nf* 1 *(sentimiento)* hunch, feeling, inkling: **tuve la corazonada de que él no estaba** *I had a hunch that he wasn't there.* 2 *(impulso)* impulse.
corbata *nf* 1 tie, US necktie: **iba con corbata** *he was wearing a tie.* 2 *(de bandera)* sash, tassel.
corbatín *nm* bow tie.
corbeta *nf* corvette.
Córcega *nf* Corsica.
corcel *nm lit* steed, charger.
corchea *nf* quaver.
corchero,-a *adj* cork.
corchete *nm* 1 COST hook and eye, snap fastener. 2 *(signo impreso)* square bracket.
corcho *nm* 1 cork; *(corteza)* cork bark. 2 *(tapón)* cork. 3 *(para pescar, nadar)* float. 4 *(tabla)* cork mat. 5 *(tablón para anuncios, notas)* cork board.
córcholis *interj fam* goodness me!, US gee!
corcova *nf* hunchback, hump.
corcovado,-a *pp* → **corcovar.**
▷ *adj* hunchbacked.
▷ *nm & nf* hunchback.
cordada *nf* rope.
cordaje *nm* 1 *(cuerdas)* ropes *pl*, cordage. 2 MAR rigging.
cordel *nm* rope, cord.
cordelería *nf* 1 *(oficio)* ropemaking. 2 *(cuerdas)* rope *pl*. 3 MAR rigging.
cordelero,-a *adj* ropemaking.
▷ *nm & nf* ropemaker.
cordero,-a *nm & nf* 1 lamb. 2 *fig (persona dócil)* lamb, angel.
▷ *nm* **cordero** 1 *(piel)* lambskin. 2 *(carne - joven)* lamb; *(- crecido)* mutton. ■ **ser manso como un cordero** to be as gentle as a lamb.
cordial *adj* 1 *(afectuoso)* cial, friendly, warm: **una bienvenida cordial** *a warm welcome.* 2 *(que fortalece)* cordial, stimulating.
▷ *nm (bebida)* cordial.
cordialidad *nf* cordiality, warmth, friendliness.
cordialmente *adv* 1 cordially, warmly. 2 *(despedida en carta)* sincerely.
cordillera *nf* mountain range, mountain chain.
cordón *nm* 1 *(cuerda)* string. 2 *(de zapatos)* shoelace, shoestring. 3 *(de adorno)* braid, cord. 4 ELEC flex. 5 REL cord. 6 *(cadena humana)* cordon. ● **cordón umbilical** umbilical cord.
cordoncillo *nm* 1 *(en tejido)* rib, ribbing. 2 *(bordado)* braid, piping.
cordura *nf* good sense. ■ **con cordura** sensibly, prudently, wisely.
Corea *nf* Korea. ● **Corea del Norte** North Korea. ‖ **Corea del Sur** South Korea.
coreano,-a *adj* Korean.
▷ *nm & nf (persona)* Korean.
▷ *nm* **coreano** *(idioma)* Korean.
corear *vt* 1 *(cantar)* to chorus, sing in chorus. 2 *(hablar)* to chorus, speak in chorus. 3 *fig (aclamar)* to applaud.
coreografía *nf* choreography.
coreografiar *vt* to choreograph.
coreográfico,-a *adj* choreographic.
coreógrafo,-a *nm & nf* choreographer.
corifeo *nm* 1 coryphaeus. 2 *fig* leader.
corindón *nm* corundum.
corinto,-a *adj* maroon.
▷ *nm* **corinto** *(color)* maroon.
corista *nf* chorus girl.
coriza *nf* coryza.
cormorán *nm* cormorant.
cornada *nf* goring.
cornalina *nf* cornelian, carnelian.
cornamenta *nf (gen)* horns *pl*; *(del ciervo)* antlers *pl*.
cornamusa *nf* bagpipe.
córnea *nf* cornea.
cornear *vt* to gore.
corneja *nf* crow.
cornejo *nm* dogwood.
córneo,-a *adj* hornlike, corneous.
córner *nm* DEP *(lugar)* corner; *(golpe)* corner, corner kick. ■ **lanzar un córner / sacar un córner / tirar un córner** to take a corner.
corneta *nf (instrumento)* bugle.

▷ *nm o nf* MIL *(persona)* bugler. ■ **a toque de corneta** under the bugle call.
cornete *nm* **1** *(de nariz)* turbinate, turbinate bone. **2** *(de helado)* cornet, cone.
cornetín *nm (instrumento)* cornet.
▷ *nm o nf (persona)* cornet player.
cornisa *nf* ARQUIT cornice.
cornisamiento *nm* entablature.
corno *nm* **1** BOT *(cornejo)* dogwood. **2** MÚS horn.
cornucopia *nf* **1** *(vaso)* cornucopia, horn of plenty. **2** *(espejo)* small mirror.
coro *nm* **1** MÚS choir. **2** TEAT chorus. ■ **a coro** *fig* all together. ‖ **hacer coro** *fig* to join in the chorus.
corografía *nf* chorography.
coroides *nf inv* choroid.
corola *nf* corolla.
corolario *nm* corollary.
corona *nf* **1** *(aro, cerco)* crown. **2** *(de flores, etc)* wreath, garland, crown. **3** *fig (dignidad real)* King's, Queen's: **el discurso de la corona** *the King's speech.* **4** *fig (reino)* crown, kingdom. **5** *(coronilla)* crown, crown of the head. **6** *(aureola)* halo. **7** *(de diente, moneda)* crown. **8** *(en geometría)* annulus, ring. ● **corona solar** solar corona.
coronación *nf* **1** coronation. **2** *fig (culminación)* crowning.
coronamento *nm* → **coronamiento.**
coronamiento *nm* **1** *fig (culminación)* crowning. **2** ARQUIT *fig* crown.
coronar *vt* to crown.
▷ *vi* to crown.
coronario,-a *adj* coronary. ● **insuficiencia coronaria** cardiac arrest.
coronel *nm* colonel.
coronilla *nf* **1** *(parte de la cabeza)* crown of the head. **2** *(tonsura)* tonsure. ■ **estar hasta la coronilla** *fam* to be fed up (**de**, with).
corpiño *nm* bodice.
corporación *nf* corporation. ● **corporación metropolitana** city corporation.
corporal *adj* corporal, body.
▷ *nm* REL corporal, corporale.
corporativismo *nm* corporativism.
corporativo,-a *adj* corporative, corporate. ● **imagen corporativa** corporate image.
corporeidad *nf* corporeity.
corpóreo,-a *adj* corporeal, bodily.
corpulencia *nf* corpulence, stoutness.
corpulento,-a *adj* corpulent, stocky, stout.
corpus *nm (conjunto)* corpus.
corpuscular *adj* corpuscular.
corpúsculo *nm* corpuscle.
corral *nm* **1** *(de casa)* yard, courtyard. **2** *(de granja)* farmyard, US corral. **3** *(para niños)* playpen. **4** TEAT open-air theatre.
correa *nf* **1** *(tira de piel)* strap, leather strip. **2** *(de perro)* lead, leash. **3** *(de reloj)* watchstrap. **4** *(cinturón)* belt. **5** TÉC belt. **6** *(elasticidad)* elasticity, stretch.
correaje *nm* straps *pl.*
correazo *nm* lash with a belt.
corrección *nf* **1** *(rectificación)* correction. **2** *(educación)* courtesy, correctness, politeness, good manners *pl.* **3** *(reprensión)* rebuke. **4** *(en impresión)* proofreading. ■ **tratar con corrección** to be polite. ● **corrección de pruebas** proofreading.
correccional *adj* correctional.
▷ *nm* detention centre, reformatory.
correctamente *adv* **1** *(sin errores)* correctly, accurately. **2** *(con educación)* correctly, politely, properly.
correctivo,-a *adj* corrective.
▷ *nm* corrective.
correcto,-a *adj* **1** *(sin errores)* correct, accurate. **2** *(adecuado)* suitable. **3** *(educado)* polite, courteous. **4** *(conducta)* proper.
corrector,-ra *adj* corrective.
▷ *nm & nf (de pruebas impresas)* proofreader.
corredera *nf* TÉC runner, groove, track.
corredero,-a *adj* sliding: **ventana corredera** *sliding window.*
corredizo,-a *adj* sliding.
corredor,-ra *adj* **1** running. **2** *(ave)* flightless: **ave corredora** *flightless bird.*
▷ *nm & nf* **1** DEP runner; *(de coches)* driver. **2** FIN broker.
▷ *nm* **corredor** *(pasillo)* corridor, gallery. ● **corredor,-ra de bolsa** stockbroker. ‖ **corredor,-ra de coches** racing driver. ‖ **corredor,-ra de fondo** long-distance runner.
correduría *nf* brokerage. ● **correduría de seguros** insurance brokerage.
corregible *adj* rectifiable, which can be corrected.
corregidor *nm* **1** HIST *(magistrado)* corregidor. **2** HIST *(alcalde)* mayor.
corregir [55] *vt* **1** *(amendar)* to correct, rectify. **2** *(reprender)* to reprimand, scold, tell off. **3** EDUC to mark. **4** *(en impresión)* to read, proofread.
correlación *nf* correlation.
correlacionar *vt* to correlate.
▷ *vpr* **correlacionarse** to be correlated.
correlativo,-a *adj* correlative.
▷ *nm* **correlativo** correlative.
correlato *nm* correlate.
correligionario,-a *nm & nf* co-religionist (US coreligionist).
correo *nm* **1** *(servicio, correspondencia)* post, US mail. **2** *(persona)* courier. **3** MIL dispatch rider.
▷ *nm pl* **correos** *(oficina)* post office *sing.* ■ **echar al correo** to post, US mail. ‖ **por correo** by post, US by mail. ● **apartado de correos** (post office) box. ‖ **correo aéreo** airmail. ‖ **correo certificado** registered post, US registered mail. ‖ **correo electrónico** electronic mail, e-mail. ‖ **correo urgente** special delivery.
correoso,-a *adj* **1** *(flexible)* flexible. **2** *fig (alimento)* tough, leathery.
correr *vi* **1** *(gen)* to run: **se marchó corriendo** *she ran off.* **2** *(darse prisa)* to rush, hurry: **¡corre, es tarde!** *hurry up, it's late!* **3** *(viento)* to blow. **4** *(agua)* to flow, run. **5** *(tiempo)* to pass, fly. **6** *(noticias)* to spread, circulate: **el rumor corría por la ciudad** *the rumour spread throughout the city.* **7** *(conductor)* to drive fast. **8** *(coche)* to go fast. **9** *(sueldo, interés)* to be payable. **10** *(puerta, ventana)* to slide. **11** *(moneda)* to be legal tender.
▷ *vt* **1** *(distancia)* to cover; *(país)* to travel through. **2** *(carrera)* to run; *(caballo)* to race, run. **3** *(echar)* to close; *(cortina)* to draw; *(cerrojo)* to bolt. **4** *(mover)*

to pull up, move, draw up: **corre la mesa** *move the table.* **5** *(estar expuesto)* to run: **correr un peligro** *to run a risk.* **6** *(aventura)* to have. **7** *(avergonzar)* to make ashamed.
▷ *vpr* **correrse 1** *(persona)* to move over; *(objeto)* to shift, slide. **2** *(color, tinta)* to run. **3** *(media)* to ladder. **4** *(avergonzarse)* to blush, go red. ■ **a todo correr** at full speed. ‖ **correr mundo** to be a globe-trotter. ‖ **correr un peligro** to be in danger. ‖ **correrla** *fam* to live it up. ‖ **deprisa y corriendo** in a hurry.

correría *nf* **1** MIL *(incursión)* raid, foray. **2** *(viaje)* trip, journey.
▷ *nf pl* **correrías** *fam (aventuras)* adventures; *(viajes)* travels.

correspondencia *nf* **1** *(gen)* correspondence. **2** *(cartas)* post, US mail. **3** *(de trenes, etc)* connection. ■ **mantener correspondencia con** ALGN to correspond with SB. ● **curso por correspondencia** correspondence course.

corresponder *vi* **1** *(ser adecuado)* to become, befit; *(color, aspecto)* to match, go with: **los zapatos no corresponden al vestido** *the shoes don't go with the dress.* **2** *(encajar)* to correspond (**a**, to), tally (**a**, with); *(descripción)* to fit. **3** *(pertenecer)* to belong, pertain: **esta mesa corresponde a mi habitación** *this table belongs in my bedroom.*
▷ *vt* **1** *(ser el turno)* to be one's turn: **me corresponde a mi** *it's my turn.* **2** *(en un reparto)* to get. **3** *(incumbir)* to be the job of, be the responsibility of: **eso te corresponde a ti** *that's your job.* **4** *(devolver)* to return; *(amabilidad)* to repay.
▷ *vpr* **corresponderse 1** *(ajustarse)* to correspond; *(cifras)* to tally: **la dirección que te dio no se corresponde con la que yo tengo** *the address he gave you doesn't correspond to the one I have.* **2** *(armonizar)* to be in harmony, go with. **3** *(amarse)* to love each other.

correspondiente *adj* **1** *(que corresponde)* corresponding (**a**, to). **2** *(apropiado)* suitable, appropriate. **3** *(respectivo)* own. **4** *(miembro)* correspondent.

corresponsal *nm o nf* correspondent.

corresponsalía *nf* post of correspondent.

corretear *vi* **1** *fam (correr)* to run about. **2** *fam (vagar)* to hang about.

correteo *nm* running about, hustle and bustle.

correvedile *nm o nf* **1** *fam fig (chismoso)* tell-tale, gossip. **2** *fam fig (alcahuete)* go-between.

corrida *nf* **1** *(carrera)* run, race. **2** *(de toros)* bullfight. ■ **de corrida 1** *(rápidamente)* hastily, in a flash. **2** *(de memoria)* by heart.

corrido,-a *adj* **1** *(peso)* good: **una tonelada corrida** *a good ton.* **2** *(seguido)* full, continuous: **balcón corrido** *continuous balcony.* **3** *fig (avergonzado)* abashed. **4** *fig (experimentado)* experienced. **5** *(tiempo)* running. ■ **de corrido 1** *(sin parar)* without stopping. **2** *(con fluidez)* fluently: **recitar de corrido** *to reel off.*

corriente *adj* **1** *(común)* ordinary, average: **personas corrientes** *ordinary people.* **2** *(agua)* running. **3** *(fecha)* current, present: **el cinco del corriente mes** *the fifth of this month.* **4** *(cuenta)* current.
▷ *nm (mes)* current month, this month.
▷ *nf* **1** *(masa de agua)* current, stream, flow. **2** *(de aire)* draught (US draft). **3** ELEC current. ■ **al corriente 1** *(actualizado)* up to date. **2** *(enterado)* aware. **3** *(informado)* informed, in the know: **¿estás al corriente de lo que ha pasado?** *do you know what's happened?* ‖ **ir a contra corriente** *fig* to go against the tide. ‖ **seguirle la corriente a** ALGN to humour (US humor) SB. ‖ **tener al corriente** to keep informed. ● **corriente sanguínea** bloodstream.

corrientemente *adv* usually, normally.

corrillo *nm* **1** *(corro)* small group of people talking, clique. **2** *(en la bolsa)* round enclosure.

corrimiento *nm* **1** *(acción)* slipping, sliding. **2** MED discharge. **3** *fig (vergüenza)* embarrassment. ● **corrimiento de tierras** landslide.

corro *nm* **1** *(cerco)* circle, ring. **2** *(juego)* ring-a-ring o'roses. **3** *(en la bolsa)* round enclosure. ■ **entrar en el corro** to join in the circle. ‖ **hacer corro aparte** *fig* to form a small circle.

corroboración *nf* corroboration.

corroborar *vt* to corroborate: **corroborar con pruebas** *to corroborate with proof.*

corroer [82] *vt* **1** *(desgastar)* to corrode. **2** GEOL to erode. **3** *fig (perturbar)* to corrode, eat away, eat up: **los celos lo corroen** *he's eaten up with jealousy.*
▷ *vpr* **corroerse 1** *(desgastarse)* to become corroded. **2** *fig* to be eaten up (**de**, with).

corromper *vt* **1** *(pudrir)* to turn bad. **2** *(pervertir)* to corrupt, pervert. **3** *(sobornar)* to bribe.
▷ *vpr* **corromperse 1** *(pudrirse)* to go bad, rot. **2** *(pervertirse)* to become corrupted.

corrosión *nf* **1** corrosion, rust. **2** GEOL erosion.

corrosivo,-a *adj* **1** corrosive. **2** *fig* caustic.
▷ *nm* **corrosivo** corrosive.

corrupción *nf* **1** *(putrefacción)* rot, decay. **2** *fig* corruption, degradation. **3** *fig (soborno)* bribery.

corruptela *nf* corruption, sharp practice.

corrupto,-a *adj* corrupt.

corruptor,-ra *adj* corrupting.
▷ *nm & nf* corrupter, perverter.

corrusco *nm fam* crust of stale bread.

corsario,-a *adj* privateer.
▷ *nm* **corsario** privateer.

corsé *nm* corset.

corsetería *nf* ladies' underwear shop.

corta *nf* tree felling.

cortaalambres *nm inv* wire cutters *pl.*

cortacésped *nm & nf* lawnmower.

cortacircuitos *nm inv* circuit breaker.

cortado,-a *pp* → **cortar.**
▷ *adj* **1** *(troceado)* cut; *(en lonchas)* sliced. **2** *(leche)* sour. **3** *fig (estilo)* concise, clipped. **4** *fam (aturdido)* dumbfounded.
▷ *nm* **cortado** *(café)* coffee with a dash of milk. ■ **quedarse cortado,-a 1** *fam (sin palabras)* to be speechless, be lost for words. **2** *(avergonzado)* to become embarrassed.

cortador,-ra *adj* cutting.
▷ *nm & nf (sastre, zapatero)* cutter.

cortadora *nf* cutting machine.

cortadura *nf* **1** *(corte)* cut. **2** *(paso)* gorge.

cortafrío *nm* cold chisel.

cortafuego *nm* **1** *(en el campo)* firebreak. **2** *(en un edificio)* firewall. **3** INFORMÁ firewall.

cortahuevos *nm inv* egg-slicer.
cortalápices *nm inv* pencil sharpener.
cortante *adj* **1** *(que corta)* cutting, sharp. **2** *fig (aire)* biting. **3** *fig (persona, estilo)* sharp, brusque.
cortapapeles *nm inv* **1** paper knife. **2** TÉC guillotine.
cortapisa *nf* **1** *(condición)* condition, restriction. **2** *(dificultad)* difficulty, obstacle. ■ **poner cortapisas** to impose conditions. ‖ **sin cortapisas** with no strings attached.
cortaplumas *nm inv* penknife.
cortar *vt* **1** *(gen)* to cut. **2** *(pelo)* to cut, trim. **3** *(árbol)* to cut down. **4** *(carne)* to carve. **5** *(pastel)* to cut up. **6** *(cabeza, teléfono, gas)* to cut off. **7** *(mayonesa, leche)* to curdle. **8** *(piel)* to chap, crack. **9** *(viento, frío)* to chill, bite. **10** COST to cut out. **11** *(interrumpir)* to cut off, interrupt. **12** *(bloquear)* to block: **cortaron la carretera** *the road was blocked.* **13** *(suprimir)* to cut out. **14** *fig (separar)* to divide, split, cut.
▷ *vpr* **cortarse 1** to cut: **este metal se corta fácilmente** *this metal cuts easily.* **2** *(herirse)* to cut, cut OS: **me he cortado** *I've cut myself.* **3** *(el pelo - por otro)* to have one's hair cut; *(- uno mismo)* to cut one's hair: **¿te has cortado el pelo?** *have you had your hair cut?* **4** *(piel)* to become chapped. **5** *(leche)* to go off, curdle; *(mayonesa)* to curdle. **6** *(comunicación)* to be cut off. ■ **¡corta el rollo!** *fam* knock it off! ‖ **cortar con** ALGN *fam* to split up with SB. ‖ **cortar el bacalao** *fam* to be the boss. ‖ **cortar en seco** *fig* to cut short. ‖ **cortar la digestión** to give one indigestion, upset one's stomach. ‖ **cortar la palabra** to interrupt. ‖ **cortar por lo sano** *fam* to take drastic measures.
cortaúñas *nm inv* nail clippers.
corte[1] *nf* **1** *(del rey, etc)* court. **2** *(séquito)* retinue. **3** AM *(tribunal)* court.
▷ *nf pl* **las Cortes** the Spanish Parliament *sing.*
corte[2] *nm* **1** *(gen)* cut: **me he hecho un corte en el dedo** *I've cut my finger.* **2** *(filo)* edge. **3** *(sección)* section: **corte horizontal** *horizontal section.* **4** *(de pelo)* cut, haircut. **5** *(de helado)* wafer, US ice-cream sandwich. **6** *fam fig (vergüenza)* embarrassment: **le daba corte entrar y se quedó fuera** *he was too embarrassed to go in so he stayed outside.* ■ **dar un corte a** ALGN *fam* to cut SB dead.
cortejar *vt* to court.
cortejo *nm* **1** *(acompañantes)* entourage, retinue. **2** *(galanteo)* courting.
cortés *adj* courteous, polite.
cortesana *nf (prostituta)* courtesan, courtezan.
cortesano,-a *adj* **1** *(de la corte)* court. **2** *(cortés)* courteous, courtly.
▷ *nm & nf (de la corte)* courtier.
cortesía *nf* **1** *(educación)* courtesy, politeness. **2** *(en cartas)* formal ending. **3** *(tratamiento)* title. **4** *(reverencia)* bow, curtsy. **5** *(regalo)* present: **esta bolsa es una cortesía de la empresa** *this bag is courtesy of the company.*
cortésmente *adv* courteously, politely.
corteza *nf* **1** *(de árbol)* bark. **2** *(de pan)* crust. **3** *(de fruta)* peel, skin. **4** *(de queso)* rind. **5** *fig (apariencia)* outside appearance, outward appearance. ● **corteza cerebral** cerebral cortex. ‖ **la corteza terrestre** the earth's crust.
cortical *adj* cortical.
cortina *nf* **1** curtain. **2** *fig* curtain, screen. ■ **correr las cortinas** to draw the curtains. ● **cortina de humo** *fig* smoke screen.
cortinaje *nm* drapery.
cortinilla *nf* small lace curtain.
corto,-a *adj* **1** *(extensión)* short: **distancia corta** *short distance.* **2** *(duración)* short, brief: **una película corta** *a short film.* **3** *(escaso)* scant, meagre (US meager). **4** *fig (tonto)* thick, dim. **5** *fig (tímido)* shy, timid.
▷ *nm* **corto** short film, short. ■ **corto,-a de miras** *fam* narrow-minded. ‖ **corto,-a de vista** short-sighted. ‖ **quedarse corto,-a 1** *(ropa)* to become too short: **el pantalón se me ha quedado corto** *my trousers have become too short for me.* **2** *(calcular mal)* to underestimate, miscalculate: **te quedaste corto con los bocadillos** *you didn't make enough sandwiches.* **3** *(un tiro)* to fall short. **4** *(no decir todo)* to hold something back, not say enough.
cortocircuito *nm* short circuit.
cortometraje *nm* short film, short.
corva *nf* back of the knee.
corvadura *nf* curvature, curve.
corvejón *nm* **1** *(de caballo)* hock. **2** *(de gallo)* spur. **3** *(ave)* cormorant.
corveta *nf* curvet.
córvido *nm* crow: **los córvidos** *the crow family.*
corvina *nf* corvina.
corvo,-a *adj* **1** arched, curved. **2** *(nariz)* hooked.
corzo,-a *nm & nf (macho)* roe buck; *(hembra)* roe deer.
cosa *nf* **1** *(gen)* thing: **coge tus cosas** *take your things, take your stuff.* **2** *(asunto)* matter, business: **es cosa tuya** *it's your business.* **3** *(nada)* nothing, not anything: **no hay cosa igual** *there's nothing like it.*
▷ *nf pl* **cosas** *fam (manías)* hang-ups: **son cosas de niños** *kids do that kind of thing.* ■ **como cosa tuya** as if it were your idea. ‖ **como están las cosas** as things stand. ‖ **como si tal cosa** just like that. ‖ **es cosa de... 1** *(tiempo)* it's time to... **2** *(cuestión)* it's a matter of... ‖ **no valer gran cosa** not to be worth much. ‖ **ser cosa hecha** *fam* to be no sooner said than done. ‖ **ser poquita cosa** *fam* not to be much, not to amount too much.
cosaco,-a *adj* Cossack.
▷ *nm* **cosaco** Cossack.
coscorrón *nm* blow on the head, knock on the head.
cosecante *nf* cosecant.
cosecha *nf* **1** harvest, crop. **2** *(tiempo)* harvest time. **3** *(año del vino)* vintage. ■ **de cosecha propia 1** *(hortalizas, fruta)* home-grown. **2** *fig (ideas, etc)* of one's own invention.
cosechador,-ra *nm & nf* harvester.
cosechadora *nf* combine harvester.
cosechar *vi* to harvest, reap.
▷ *vt* **1** *(recoger)* to harvest. **2** *(cultivar)* to grow. **3** *fig* to reap, harvest, win: **cosechar éxitos** *to achieve success.*
cosechero,-a *nm & nf* harvester, grower.
coseno *nm* cosine.
coser *vt* **1** *(unir)* to sew; *(un botón)* to sew on; *(pespuntes, etc)* to stitch: **le cosí los pantalones** *I sewed up her trousers.* **2** MED to stitch up. **3** *(grapar)* to staple together.

4 *fig (unir)* to join. 5 *fig (atravesar)* to pierce. ■ **eso es coser y cantar** *fam* it's plain sailing, it's a piece of cake, it's child's play .
cosido *nm* 1 sewing. 2 MED stitching.
cosificar [1] *vt* to trivialize, belittle.
cosino *nm* cosine.
cosmética *nf* cosmetics *pl*: **línea de cosmética** *range of cosmetics.*
cosmético,-a *adj* cosmetic.
▷ *nm* **cosmético** cosmetic.
cósmico,-a *adj* cosmic.
cosmogonía *nf* cosmogony.
cosmografía *nf* cosmography.
cosmográfico,-a *adj* cosmographic, cosmographical.
cosmología *nf* cosmology.
cosmológico,-a *adj* cosmologic, cosmological.
cosmonauta *nm o nf* cosmonaut.
cosmonave *nf* spaceship, spacecraft.
cosmopolita *adj* cosmopolitan.
▷ *nm o nf* cosmopolitan.
cosmopolitismo *nm* cosmopolitanism.
cosmorama *nm* cosmorama.
cosmos *nm inv* cosmos.
coso *nm* 1 *(lugar cercado)* arena, enclosure. 2 *(calle)* main street. 3 *lit (plaza de toros)* bullring.
cosquillas *nf pl* tickling *sing*. ■ **hacer cosquillas a** ALGN to tickle SB. ‖ **tener cosquillas** to be ticklish. ‖ **buscarle las cosquillas a** ALGN *fam* to needle SB, annoy SB.
cosquillear *vt* to tickle.
cosquilleo *nm* tickling.
costa[1] *nf (litoral)* coast, coastline; *(playa)* beach, seaside, US shore: **tenemos una casa en la costa** *we have a house at the seaside,* US *we have a house on the shore.*
costa[2] *nf* FIN cost, price. ■ **a costa de** 1 *(aprovechándose)* at the expense of. 2 *(a base de)* by, by dint of, by means of: **lo consiguió a costa de muchos sacrificios** *he managed it by making a lot of sacrifices.* ‖ **a toda costa** at all costs, at any price.
▷ *nf pl* **costas** JUR costs.
Costa de Marfil *nf* Ivory Coast.
costado *nm* 1 side. 2 MIL flank.
▷ *nm pl* **costados** lineage *sing*. ■ **por los cuatro costados** through and through.
costal *nm* sack.
costalada *nf* fall.
costalero *nm* 1 *(mozo)* porter. 2 *(de un paso)* bearer.
costanero,-a *adj* 1 *(inclinado)* sloping. 2 *(costero)* coastal.
costanilla *nf* steep street.
costar [31] *vi* 1 *(valer)* to cost: **¿cuánto costó?** *how much was it?* 2 *(ser difícil)* to be hard, be difficult; *(resultar difícil)* to be difficult for: **cuesta encontrar trabajo** *it's hard to find a job.* 3 *(tiempo)* to take: **me costó cuatro horas** *it took me four hours.* ■ **costar barato,-a** to be cheap. ‖ **costar caro,-a** 1 to be expensive, cost a lot. 2 to pay dearly for STH: **esa afirmación le costará cara** *he'll pay dearly for saying that.* ‖ **costar mucho / costar trabajo** to be difficult, be hard work.
Costa Rica *nf* Costa Rica.
costarricense *adj* Costa Rican.
▷ *nm o nf* Costa Rican.
costarriqueño,-a *adj-nm & nf* → **costarricense.**
coste *nm* cost, price, expense. ● **coste de la vida** cost of living.
costear *vt (pagar)* to pay for, afford: **su padre le costeó el viaje** *his father paid for his journey.*
▷ *vpr* **costearse** to pay one's way.
costera *nf* 1 *(costado)* side. 2 *(tiempo de pesca)* fishing season.
costero,-a *adj* coastal, coast.
▷ *nm* **costero** *(barco)* coasting vessel, coaster.
costilla *nf* 1 ANAT rib. 2 CULIN cutlet. 3 *fam fig (mujer)* wife, better half.
▷ *nf pl* **costillas** *fam (espalda)* back *sing.*
costillar *nm* ribs *pl.*
costo *nm* cost, price.
costoso,-a *adj* 1 *(caro)* costly, expensive. 2 *(difícil)* hard, difficult.
costra *nf* 1 crust. 2 MED scab.
costroso,-a *adj* scabby.
costumbre *nf* 1 *(hábito)* habit: **tengo la costumbre de comer temprano** *I'm in the habit of having lunch early.* 2 *(tradición)* custom: **es una costumbre rusa** *it's a Russian custom.* 3 JUR usage.
▷ *nf pl* **costumbres** *(personales)* ways, manner *sing*; *(de un pueblo)* customs. ■ **como de costumbre** as usual. ‖ **tener por costumbre** + *inf* to be in the habit of + *ger*. ● **la fuerza de la costumbre** the force of habit. ‖ **persona de buenas costumbres** respectable person.
costumbrismo *nm* folk literature.
costumbrista *adj* about local customs.
▷ *nm o nf* writer of folk literature.
costura *nf* 1 *(cosido)* sewing. 2 *(línea de puntadas)* seam: **medias sin costura** *seamless stockings.* 3 *(confección)* dressmaking. ■ **meter a** ALGN **en costura** *fig* to bring SB to reason. ● **cesto de la costura** sewing basket.
costurera *nf* seamstress.
costurero *nm* 1 *(estuche)* sewing basket, sewing kit. 2 *(mueble)* workbox.
costurón *nm* 1 *(cosido)* untidy seam. 2 *(cicatriz)* noticeable scar.
cota[1] *nf (traje)* tabard. ● **cota de malla** coat of mail.
cota[2] *nf* 1 *(altura)* height above sea level: **la cota mil** *one thousand metres above sea level.* 2 *(número en mapa)* spot height. 3 *fig (nivel)* level: **la xenofobia está llegando a cotas muy altas** *xenophobia is showing an alarming increase.*
cotangente *nf* cotangent.
cotarro *nm fam fig* noisy gathering. ■ **ser el amo del cotarro** *fam* to be the boss, run the show.
cotejable *adj* comparable.
cotejar *vt (gen)* to compare; *(textos)* to collate.
cotejo *nm (gen)* comparison; *(textos)* collation, comparison.
coterráneo,-a *adj* compatriot, from the same country, from the same region.
▷ *nm & nf (hombre)* fellow countryman; *(mujer)* fellow countrywoman.
cotidianamente *adv* daily, everyday.
cotidiano,-a *adj* daily, everyday: **la vida cotidiana** *everyday life.*
cotiledón *nm* cotyledon.
cotilla *nf (faja)* corset.
▷ *nm o nf fam* busybody, gossip.

cotillear *vi fam* to gossip, tittle-tattle.
cotilleo *nm fam* gossip, gossiping, tittle-tattle.
cotillo *nm* hammerhead.
cotillón *nm* 1 *(danza)* cotillion, cotillon. 2 *(fiesta)* party, celebration *especially on New Year's Eve.*
cotizable *adj quoted on the stock exchange.* ● **acciones cotizables en bolsa** stock market shares.
cotización *nf* 1 FIN quotation, market price. 2 *(cuota)* membership fee, subscription. ● **cotización máxima** high.
cotizar [4] *vt* FIN to quote, price.
▷ *vi (pagar cuota)* to pay a subscription.
▷ *vpr* **cotizarse** 1 *(acciones)* to sell (a, at): **las acciones del banco se cotizan a diez euros con veintitrés** *the bank's shares are selling at ten euros twenty-three.* 2 *fig (valorarse)* to be valued, be in demand: **este pintor se cotiza mucho** *this painter is in great demand.*
coto[1] *nm* 1 *(terreno)* enclosure, reserve. 2 *(poste)* boundary mark. 3 *(límite)* restriction. ■ **poner coto a** ALGO to put a stop to STH. ● **coto de caza** game preserve.
coto[2] *nm (pez)* miller's thumb.
cotorra *nf* 1 *(ave)* parrot. 2 *fam fig* chatterbox. ■ **hablar como una cotorra** to be a chatterbox.
cotorrear *vi fam fig* to chatter, prattle (on).
cotorreo *nm fam fig* chatter, prattle.
coturno *nm* cothurnus.
COU *abrev* EDUC (**Curso de Orientación Universitaria**) ≈ *former pre-university course.*
covacha *nf* small cave.
covachuela *nf* small cellar, small cave.
cowboy *nm* cowboy.
▲ *pl* **cowboys.**
coxis *nm inv* coccyx.
coyote *nm* coyote.
coyuntura *nf* 1 ANAT joint, articulation. 2 *fig (circunstancia)* moment, juncture. ● **coyuntura económica** economic situation.
coz *nf* kick. ■ **dar una coz** to kick.
▲ *pl* **coces.** ■ **tratar a** ALGN **a coces** *fig* to treat SB like dirt.
crac *nm* 1 *(quiebra)* crash, bankruptcy: **el crac de la bolsa de Nueva York** *the Wall Street crash.* 2 *(onomatopeya)* crack, snap: **el brazo me hizo crac** *my arm gave a crack.*
crack *nm* 1 *(droga)* crack. 2 *(persona)* star, ace: **es un auténtico crack del fútbol** *he's a crack football player.*
crampón *nm* crampon.
▲ *pl* **crampones.**
craneal *adj* cranial.
craneano,-a *adj* cranial.
cráneo *nm* cranium, skull. ■ **ir de cráneo** *fam* to have a lot on one's plate, have one's work cut out.
crápula *nf* 1 *(borrachera)* drunkenness. 2 *fig (disipación)* dissipation, debauchery.
▷ *nm (hombre)* reprobate, rake.
craso,-a *adj* 1 *(gordo)* fat, gross. 2 *fig (error)* gross, crass.
cráter *nm* crater.
crawl *nm* crawl.
creación *nf* 1 *(gen)* creation. 2 *(fundación)* foundation, establishment, setting up.
creador,-ra *adj* creative.
▷ *nm & nf* creator, maker.
crear *vt* 1 *(gen)* to create: **crear problemas** *to create problems.* 2 *(fundar)* to found, establish; *(partido)* to set up. 3 *(inventar)* to invent.
▷ *vpr* **crearse** 1 to make, make for OS: **crearse enemigos** *to make enemies for OS.* 2 *(imaginarse)* to imagine.
creatividad *nf* creativity.
creativo,-a *adj* creative.
crecepelo *nm* hair restorer.
crecer [43] *vi* 1 *(persona, planta)* to grow: **has crecido mucho** *you've grown a lot.* 2 *(incrementar)* to increase, grow, get bigger: **la población ha crecido un uno por ciento** *the population has grown by one per cent.* 3 *(corriente, marea)* to rise. 4 *(luna)* to wax. 5 *(días)* to get longer: **los días crecen** *the days are getting longer.* 6 *(en labor de punto)* to add, increase.
▷ *vpr* **crecerse** *(tomar mayor fuerza)* to grow in confidence: **se crece ante las dificultades** *he comes into his own when faced with problems.*
creces *nf pl* increase *sing* in volume. ■ **con creces** fully: **el dinero recaudado superó con creces lo que se necesitaba** *the money collected far exceeded what was needed.*
crecida *nf* flood, spate.
crecido,-a *adj* 1 *(persona)* grown, grown-up. 2 *(cantidad)* big, large. 3 *(río)* in flood, in spate. 4 *fig (engreído)* vain, conceited.
creciente *adj* 1 *(que crece)* growing; *(que aumenta)* increasing: **un interés creciente** *an increasing interest.* 2 *(precios)* rising. 3 *(luna)* crescent (in the first quarter).
▷ *nf (de agua)* flood, spate.
crecimiento *nm* 1 *(desarrollo)* growth, increase. 2 *(subida)* rise. 3 *(de un río)* flooding, rising.
credencial *adj* credential.
▷ *nf pl* **credenciales** credentials. ● **cartas credenciales** credentials.
credibilidad *nf* credibility.
crediticio,-a *adj* credit.
crédito *nm* 1 COM credit. 2 *(confianza)* credit, belief, credence. 3 *(fama)* reputation, standing. ■ **a crédito** on credit. ‖ **dar crédito a** *(creer)* to believe (in): **no doy crédito a mis oídos** *I can't believe what I'm hearing.* ‖ **ser digno,-a de crédito** to be reliable. ● **crédito hipotecario** debt secured by a mortgage.
credo *nm* 1 REL creed. 2 MÚS Credo. 3 *fig (creencias)* credo, creed.
credulidad *nf* credulity, gullibility.
crédulo,-a *adj* credulous, gullible.
creencia *nf* belief. ● **creencia religiosa** religious belief.
creer [61] *vt* 1 *(dar por cierto)* to believe: **si no lo veo no lo creo** *I've got to see it to believe it.* 2 *(suponer, opinar)* to think, suppose: **¿y tú que crees?** *what do you think?* 3 *(tener fe)* to believe. ■ **creer a ciencia cierta** to be convinced. ‖ **¡no creas!** do you really think so?, I'm not so sure. ‖ **¡que te crees tú eso!** that's what you think! ‖ **¡ya lo creo!** of course!
▷ *vpr* **creerse** 1 *(aceptar)* to believe: **no me lo creo** *I don't believe it, I can't believe it.* 2 *(considerarse)* to think: **¿quién te has creído que eres?** *who do you think you are?*
creíble *adj* credible, believable.

creído,-a *adj* arrogant, vain, conceited. ■ **ser un creído,-a** to be full of OS.
crema *nf* 1 *(de leche, licor, ungüento)* cream. 2 *(natillas)* custard. 3 *(betún)* shoe polish. 4 *fig (lo mejor)* cream.
▷ *adj* cream, cream coloured (US cream colored). ● **crema bronceadora** suntan cream. ‖ **crema catalana** *type of crème brûlée.* ‖ **crema de afeitar** shaving cream. ‖ **crema hidratante** moisturizing cream.
cremación *nf* cremation.
cremallera *nf* 1 *(de vestido)* zip, zip fastener (US zipper). 2 TÉC rack.
crematística *nf* 1 *(economía política)* chrematistics. 2 *fam* money matters *pl*.
crematístico,-a *adj* chrematistic.
crematorio *nm* crematorium.
cremoso,-a *adj* creamy: **queso cremoso** *full-fat cheese.*
crencha *nf* 1 *(raya)* parting. 2 *(parte)* side of the hair.
crepe *nf (torta)* pancake, crepe.
crepé *nm* 1 *(postizo)* hairpiece. 2 *(tejido, caucho)* crepe.
crepería *nf* creperie.
crepitante *adj* crackling.
crepitar *vi* to crackle.
crepuscular *adj* twilight.
crepúsculo *nm* twilight.
crespo,-a *adj* 1 *(pelo)* frizzy. 2 *(estilo)* obscure. 3 *fig (irritado)* angry.
crespón *nm* crepe.
cresta *nf* 1 *(de ave)* crest; *(de gallo)* comb. 2 *(de pelo)* toupée. 3 *(de montaña, ola)* crest. ■ **dar a ALGN en la cresta** *fam* to deflate SB, bring SB down to earth. ‖ **estar en la cresta de la ola** *fam* to be on the crest of a wave.
crestón *nm* outcrop.
Creta *nf* Crete.
cretense *adj* Cretan.
▷ *nm o nf* Cretan.
cretinismo *nm* 1 *(enfermedad)* cretinism. 2 *fam fig* cretinism, stupidity.
cretino,-a *adj* stupid, cretinous.
▷ *nm & nf* cretin, idiot.
cretona *nf* cretonne.
creyente *adj* believing.
▷ *nm o nf* believer.
crezco *pres indic* → **crecer**.
cría *nf* 1 *(acto de criar)* nursing; *(de animal)* breeding, raising. 2 *(cachorro)* young. 3 *(camada - ovíparos)* brood; *(- mamíferos)* litter.
criada *nf* maid.
criadero *nm* 1 *(de plantas)* nursery; *(de animales)* breeding farm; *(de peces)* hatchery. 2 *(mina)* seam. ● **criadero de ostras** oyster bed.
criado,-a *pp* → **criar**.
▷ *adj (animal)* reared, raised; *(persona)* bred, brought up.
▷ *nm & nf* servant. ■ **mal criado,-a** ill-bred, spoilt.
criador *nm & nf* breeder.
crianza *nf* 1 *(de animales)* breeding. 2 *(lactancia)* nursing. 3 *(educación)* upbringing. ● **vino de crianza** mature wine.
criar [13] *vt* 1 *(educar niños)* to bring up, rear, care for: **lo crió una tía** *his aunt brought him up.* 2 *(nutrir)* to feed (**con**, -); *(con pecho)* to suckle, nurse, breastfeed. 3 *(animales)* to breed, raise, rear. 4 *(producir)* to have, grow; *(vinos)* to make, mature.
▷ *vpr* **criarse** 1 *(crecer)* to grow; *(formarse)* to be brought up. 2 *(producirse)* to grow.
criatura *nf* 1 creature. 2 *(niño)* baby, child. 3 *fig* baby.
criba *nf* 1 *(tamiz)* sieve. 2 *fig (selección)* screening. ■ **hacer una criba** 1 to screen. 2 *(en examen)* to fail lots of students.
cribar *vt* 1 *(colar)* to sift, sieve. 2 *fig (seleccionar)* to screen.
cric *nm* jack.
▲ *pl* **crics**.
cricquet *nm* cricket.
▲ *pl* **cricquets**.
crimen *nm* 1 *(delito)* crime. 2 *(asesinato)* murder.
criminal *adj* 1 criminal. 2 *fam (muy malo)* awful, criminal, appalling.
▷ *nm o nf* criminal.
criminalidad *nf* criminality.
criminalista *nm o nf* 1 *(abogado)* criminal lawyer. 2 *(estudioso)* criminologist.
criminología *nf* criminology.
criminólogo,-a *nm & nf* criminologist.
crin [Also used in plural with the same meaning.] *nf* mane.
crío,-a *nm & nf fam* kid, child.
▷ *adj fam* young: **todavía eres muy crío** *you're still too young.* ■ **ser un crío,-a** *fam* to be childish.
criollo,-a *adj* Creole.
▷ *nm & nf (persona)* Creole.
▷ *nm (idioma)* Creole.
cripta *nf* crypt.
críptico,-a *adj* cryptic.
criptografía *nf* cryptography.
criptograma *nm* cryptogram.
criptón *nm* krypton.
críquet *nm* cricket.
▲ *pl* **críquets**.
crisálida *nf* chrysalis.
crisantemo *nm* chrysanthemum.
crisis *nf inv* 1 *(dificultad)* crisis. 2 *(ataque)* fit, attack: **crisis de asma** *asthma attack.* 3 *(escasez)* shortage: **crisis de alimentos** *food shortage.* ■ **estar en crisis** to be in crisis, reach crisis point. ● **crisis de gobierno** cabinet crisis. ‖ **crisis nerviosa** nervous breakdown.
crisma *nm & nf* 1 REL chrism. 2 *fam (cabeza)* head, nut.
crisol *nm* 1 crucible. 2 *fig* melting pot.
crisólito *nm* chrysolite.
crispación *nf fig* tension: **un clima de crispación** *a tense atmosphere.*
crispado,-a *adj* on edge, touchy, tense: **tengo los nervios crispados** *my nerves are shot.*
crispante *adj* annoying, irritating.
crispar *vt* 1 ANAT to contract, tense. 2 *fig (irritar)* to irritate, annoy, infuriate: **ese tipo me crispa** *that guy infuriates me.* ■ **crispar los nervios a ALGN** *fig* to get on SB's nerves.
▷ *vpr* **crisparse** 1 ANAT to contract, tense. 2 *fig (irritarse)* to get annoyed, get angry.

cristal *nm* 1 *(mineral)* crystal. 2 *(vidrio)* glass. 3 *(de ventana)* window pane, pane. 4 *(de lente)* lens. 5 *(de coche)* window.
▷ *nm pl* **cristales** 1 *(trozos)* glass *sing*: **ten cuidado, hay cristales por el suelo** *be careful, there's some broken glass on the floor.* 2 *(ventanas)* windows. ● **botella de cristal** glass bottle. | **cristal de cuarzo** quartz crystal. | **cristal de roca** rock crystal.
cristalera *nf* 1 *(mueble)* display cabinet. 2 *(escaparate)* window, shop window. 3 *(conjunto de cristales)* windows *pl*; *(puertas)* glass doors *pl*; *(techo)* glass roof.
cristalería *nf* 1 *(fábrica)* glassworks. 2 *(tienda)* glassware shop. 3 *(conjunto)* glassware; *(vasos)* glasses *pl*.
cristalero,-a *nm & nf* glazier.
cristalino,-a *adj* transparent, crystal-clear.
▷ *nm* **cristalino** crystalline lens.
cristalización *nf* 1 crystallization. 2 *fig* consolidation.
cristalizar [4] *vt* to crystallize.
▷ *vi* 1 to crystallize. 2 *fig* to crystallize (**en**, into).
▷ *vpr* **cristalizarse** to crystallize.
cristalografía *nf* crystallography.
cristaloide *nm* crystalloid.
cristiandad *nf* Christendom.
cristianismo *nm* Christianity.
cristianizar [4] *vt* to convert to Christianity.
cristiano,-a *adj* 1 REL Christian.
Cristo *nm* 1 REL Christ. 2 *(crucifijo)* crucifix. ■ **antes de Cristo** before Christ. | **armar un Cristo** *fam* to kick up a big fuss. | **después de Cristo** anno Domini.
criterio *nm* 1 *(en lógica)* criterion. 2 *(juicio)* judgement, discernment. 3 *(opinión)* opinion, point of view. ■ **cambiar de criterio** to change one's mind.
crítica *nf* 1 *(juicio, censura)* criticism. 2 *(prensa)* review, write-up. 3 *(conjunto de críticos)* critics *pl*. ■ **tener buena crítica** to get good reviews. ● **crítica teatral** theatre (US theater) column.
criticar [1] *vt* to criticize.
▷ *vi (murmurar)* to gossip.
crítico,-a *adj* critical.
▷ *nm & nf* critic.
criticón,-ona *adj fam* fault finding, nit-picking, hypercritical.
▷ *nm & nf fam* fault finder, nit-picker.
Croacia *nf* Croatia.
croar *vi* to croak.
croata *adj* Croatian, Croat.
▷ *nm o nf (persona)* Croat, Croatian.
▷ *nm (idioma)* Croat, Croatian.
crocante *nm* almond brittle.
crocanti *nm* almond brittle.
croché *nm* crochet.
croissant *nm* croissant.
▲ *pl* **croissants**.
croissantería *nf* croissant shop.
crol *nm* crawl.
cromado,-a *pp* → **cromar**.
▷ *adj* chrome.
▷ *nm* **cromado** chroming.
cromar *vt* to chrome.
cromático,-a *adj* chromatic.
cromatismo *nm* chromatism.
crómlech *nm* cromlech.
cromo *nm* 1 *(metal)* chromium, chrome. 2 *(cromolitografía)* chromolithograph, chromo. 3 *(estampa)* picture card, sticker: **un álbum de cromos** *a picture-card album.* ■ **ir hecho,-a un cromo** *fam* to look a sight.
cromolitografía *nf* colour printing.
cromosoma *nm* chromosome.
crónica *nf* 1 *(gen)* account, chronicle. 2 *(en periódico)* article, column, feature. 3 RAD TV *(programa)* programme (US program); *(reportaje)* feature, report. 4 HIST chronicle.
crónico,-a *adj* 1 chronic. 2 *fig* deeply rooted.
cronicón *nm* short chronicle.
cronista *nm o nf* 1 HIST chronicler. 2 *(de prensa)* columnist, feature writer. 3 RAD TV commentator.
crono *nm* 1 *(cronómetro)* chronometer. 2 DEP *(tiempo)* time.
cronógrafo,-a *nm & nf* chronographer.
▷ *nm* **cronógrafo** chronograph.
cronología *nf* chronology.
cronológicamente *adv* chronologically.
cronológico,-a *adj* chronological.
cronometraje *nm* timing.
cronometrar *vt* to time.
cronómetro *nm* 1 chronometer. 2 DEP stopwatch.
croquet *nm* croquet.
croqueta *nf* croquette.
croquis *nm inv* sketch, outline.
cros *nm inv (a pie)* cross-country race; *(en moto)* motocross race.
cruasán *nm* croissant.
▲ *pl* **cruasanes**.
cruce *nm* 1 cross, crossing. 2 AUTO crossroads. 3 *(de razas)* crossbreeding. 4 *(interferencia telefónica, etc)* crossed line: **hay un cruce** *there's a crossed line.* 5 ELEC short circuit.
crucería *nf* ARQUIT ogives *pl*, ribs *pl*.
crucero *nm* 1 *(buque)* cruiser. 2 *(viaje)* cruise. 3 ARQUIT transept.
crucial *adj* 1 crucial. 2 *fig* crucial, critical.
crucificado,-a *adj* crucified.
crucificar [1] *vt* 1 to crucify. 2 *fam fig* to torture.
crucifijo *nm* crucifix.
crucifixión *nf* crucifixion.
cruciforme *adj* cruciform, cross-shaped.
crucigrama *nm* crossword (puzzle).
crudeza *nf* 1 *(sin cocer)* rawness; *(sin madurar)* unripeness. 2 *(rudeza)* crudeness, rudeness, coarseness. 3 *(del clima)* harshness.
crudo,-a *adj* 1 *(sin cocer)* raw; *(poco hecho)* underdone: **la carne está cruda** *the meat is underdone, the meat isn't cooked enough.* 2 *fig (duro)* crude, coarse. 3 *(color)* natural, unbleached. 4 *(clima)* harsh. ■ **verlo muy crudo** *fam* not to hold out much hope. ● **seda cruda** raw silk.
▷ *nm* **crudo** *(petróleo)* crude oil, crude.
cruel *adj* 1 *(persona)* cruel (**con/para**, to). 2 *(clima)* harsh, severe.
crueldad *nf* 1 cruelty. 2 *(dureza)* harshness, severity.
cruelmente *adv* cruelly.
cruentamente *adv* bloodily.

cruento,-a *adj* bloody.
crujido *nm* 1 *(de puerta)* creak, creaking. 2 *(de patatas fritas)* crunching. 3 *(seda, papel)* rustle, rustling. 4 *(de dientes)* grinding.
crujiente *adj* 1 *(alimentos)* crunchy. 2 *(seda)* rustling.
crujir *vi* 1 *(puerta)* to creak. 2 *(patatas fritas)* to crunch. 3 *(seda, hojas)* to rustle. 4 *(dientes)* to grind.
crupier *nm o nf* croupier.
crustáceo *nm* crustacean.
cruz *nf* 1 *(gen)* cross. 2 *(de moneda)* tails *pl*: ¿cara o cruz? *heads or tails?* 3 *fig (carga)* burden, cross.
cruzada *nf* 1 HIST crusade. 2 *(campaña)* campaign.
cruzado,-a *adj* 1 *(gen)* crossed. 2 *(animal, planta)* crossbred. 3 *(prenda)* double-breasted. 4 *(brazos)* folded.
▷ *nm* **cruzado** HIST crusader.
cruzamiento *nm* 1 crossing. 2 *(de animales)* crossbreeding.
cruzar [4] *vt* 1 *(gen)* to cross: cruzar una calle *to cross a street.* 2 *(poner atravesado)* to lay across; *(estar atravesado)* to lie across. 3 *(en geometría)* to intersect. 4 *(animales)* to cross. 5 *(miradas, palabras)* to exchange.
▷ *vpr* **cruzarse** 1 *(encontrarse)* to cross, pass each other. 2 *(intercambiarse)* to exchange. ■ **cruzar a nado** to swim across. ‖ **cruzar los brazos** to fold one's arms.
cuaderna *nf* frame.
cuadernillo *nm* booklet.
cuaderno *nm (libreta)* notebook, journal; *(escolar)* exercise book.
cuadra *nf* 1 *(establo)* stable. 2 AM *(manzana)* block, block of houses.
cuadradillo *nm* 1 *(azúcar)* lump. 2 *(barra de hierro)* square iron bar. 3 *(regla)* square ruler.
cuadrado,-a *adj* 1 *(forma)* square. 2 *fam (persona)* broad, stocky. 3 *fig (mente)* rigid, one-track.
▷ *nm* **cuadrado** square. ■ **elevar al cuadrado** to square.
cuadrafonía *nf* quadraphonics.
cuadrafónico,-a *adj* quadraphonic.
cuadragésimo,-a *adj* fortieth.
▷ *nm & nf* fortieth.
See also sexto,-a.
cuadrangular *adj* quadrangular.
cuadrángulo *nm* quadrangle.
cuadrante *nm* 1 *(reloj)* sundial. 2 *(instrumento)* quadrant. 3 *(cojín)* square pillow.
cuadrar *vt* 1 *(dar figura cuadrada)* to square, make square. 2 *(geometría, matemáticas)* to square. 3 COM to balance.
▷ *vi* 1 *(coincidir)* to square, agree. 2 COM to tally, add up: las cuentas de este mes no cuadran *the accounts don't add up this month.* 3 *fig (ir bien)* to suit: el estilo no cuadra con el tema *the style doesn't suit the subject.*
▷ *vpr* **cuadrarse** 1 MIL to stand to attention. 2 *fig* to stand firm, stick to one's guns, dig one's heels in.
cuadrático,-a *adj* quadratic.
cuadratura *nf* quadrature.
cuádriceps *nm inv* quadriceps.
cuadrícula *nf* squares *pl*, grid.
cuadriculado,-a *adj* squared.
▷ *nm* **cuadriculado** squares *pl*, grid.
cuadricular *vt* to square, divide into squares.
▷ *adj* squared.
cuadrienio *nm* quadrennium.
cuadriga *nf* chariot.
cuadrilátero,-a *adj* quadrilateral, four-sided.
▷ *nm* **cuadrilátero** *(boxeo)* ring.
cuadrilla *nf* 1 *(grupo)* party, gang. 2 *(de bandidos, etc)* gang, band. 3 *(de obreros)* gang, team. 4 MIL squad. 5 *(de toreros)* bullfighter's team.
cuadrilongo,-a *adj* rectangular.
cuadripartito,-a *adj* quadripartite.
cuadriplicar [1] *vt* to quadruple.
▷ *vi* to quadruple.
cuadro *nm* 1 *(cuadrado)* square. 2 *(pintura)* painting, picture. 3 TEAT scene. 4 *(descripción)* description, picture. 5 MIL cadre. 6 *(dirigentes)* leaders *pl*; *(personal)* staff. 7 *(conjunto de datos)* chart, graph. 8 *(tablero de control)* panel. 9 *(de un jardín, etc)* bed, patch, plot. 10 *fig (escena)* scene, sight: desde la cima se ofrecía un cuadro maravilloso *there was a wonderful view from the summit.* 11 *(de bicicleta)* frame. 12 *(armazón)* frame. ■ **a cuadros** checked, US checkered: tela a cuadros *checked (US checkered) cloth.* ● **cuadro clínico** clinical pattern. ‖ **cuadro de mandos** control panel. ‖ **cuadro sinóptico** diagram, chart.
cuadrumano,-a *adj* quadrumanous.
▷ *nm* **cuadrumano** quadrumane.
cuadrúpedo,-a *adj* quadruped.
▷ *nm* **cuadrúpedo** quadruped.
cuádruple *adj* quadruple, fourfold.
cuadruplicado,-a *adj* quadruplicate.
cuadruplicar *vt* to quadruple.
▷ *vi* to quadruple.
cuajada *nf (leche)* curd; *(requesón)* cottage cheese.
cuajado,-a *adj* 1 *(leche)* curdled; *(sangre)* clotted; *(huevo)* set. 2 *(lleno)* full, filled. 3 *fig (asombrado)* dumbfounded, astonished.
cuajar *vt* 1 *(gen)* to coagulate; *(leche)* to curdle; *(sangre)* to clot. 2 *(huevo)* to set. 3 *fig (recargar de adornos)* to fill with, cover.
▷ *vi* 1 *(nieve)* to lie. 2 *fig (tener éxito)* to be a success, come off: la cosa no cuajó *it didn't come off.* 3 *fig (gustar)* to fit in, hit it off with: Iván ha cuajado muy bien entre sus compañeros *Iván has really hit it off with his workmates.*
▷ *vpr* **cuajarse** 1 to coagulate; *(leche)* to curdle; *(sangre)* clot. 2 *(huevo)* to set. 3 *fig (llenarse)* to fill up.
cuajo *nm* 1 *(cuajadura)* rennet. 2 *fam fig* phlegm, calmness. ■ **arrancar** ALGO **de cuajo** to tear STH out by the roots.
cuákero,-a *adj-nm & nf* → **cuáquero,-a.**
cual *pron* 1 *(precedido de artículo - persona)* who, whom: la gente a la cual preguntamos *the people whom we asked.* 2 *(precedido de artículo - cosa)* which: la ciudad en la cual nací *the city where I was born.*
▲ *pl* cuales.
▷ *adv fml* as, like: se enamoró cual si tuviese quince años *he fell in love like a teenager.* ■ **cada cual** everyone, everybody.
cuál [pl cuáles.] *pron* 1 *(interrogativo)* which, which one, what: ¿cuál es el más alto? *which one is the tallest?* 2 *(valor distributivo)* some. 3 *(exclamativo)* how, what: ¡cuál no sería mi asombro! *imagine my amazement!*

▷ *adj (interrogativo)* which. ■ **a cuál más** equally: **a cuál más listo** *each as clever as the other.*

cualidad *nf* **1** *(de persona)* quality, attribute. **2** *(de cosa)* quality, property.

cualificado,-a *adj* qualified, skilled.

cualificar [1] *vt* to qualify.

▷ *vpr* **cualificarse** to become qualified, complete one's training.

cualitativo,-a *adj* qualitative.

cualquier *adj (indefinido)* any: **cualquier otro día** *any other day;* **cualquier cosa** *anything;* **cualquier persona** *anyone.*

▲ *pl* **cualesquier.**

See also **cualquiera.**

cualquiera *adj* **1** *(indefinido)* any: **un día cualquiera** *any day.* **2** *(ordinario)* ordinary: **no es una corbata cualquiera** *it's not an ordinary tie.*

▲ *pl* **cualesquiera.**

▷ *pron* **1** *(persona indeterminada)* anybody, anyone; *(cosa indeterminada)* any, any one: **cualquiera lo compraría** *anybody would buy it.* **2** *(nadie)* nobody: **¡cualquiera lo coge!** *nobody would take it!*

▷ *nf* **1** *pey (prostituta)* hussy, floozy, tart. **2 cualquiera que** *(persona)* whoever; *(cosa)* whatever, whichever: **cualquiera que diga eso, miente** *whoever says that is lying.*

cuan *adv* [Used only before adjectives and adverbs.] *fml* as: **cayó cuan largo era** *he fell flat on the floor.*

See also **cuanto.**

cuán *adv* [Used only before adjectives and adverbs.] *(interrogativo)* how: **¡cuán idiota!** *how stupid!*

See also **cuanto.**

cuando *adv (tiempo)* when: **cuando tenía diez años** *when he was ten.*

▷ *conj* **1** *(temporal)* when, whenever: **ven a verme cuando quieras** *come and see me whenever you want.* **2** *(condicional)* if: **cuando él lo dice** *if he says so.* **3** *(causal)* since.

▷ *prep* during, at the time of: **cuando la guerra** *during the war.* ■ **de vez en cuando** now and then, from time to time. | **hasta cuando** until.

cuándo *adv (interrogativo)* when: **¿cuándo es tu cumpleaños?** *when is your birthday?*

▷ *nm* when: **no sé el cómo ni el cuándo** *I don't know how or when.*

cuantía *nf* **1** *(cantidad)* quantity; *(importe)* amount: **la cuantía de una factura** *the amount of a bill.* **2** *(dimensión)* extent: **la cuantía del desastre ecológico** *the extent of the ecological disaster.* ■ **de mayor cuantía** important.

cuantificar [1] *vt* to quantify, measure.

cuantioso,-a *adj (grande - en cantidad)* substantial, considerable; *(- en número)* numerous.

cuantitativo,-a *adj* quantitative.

cuanto[1] *nm* FÍS quantum: **la teoría de los cuantos** *the quantum theory.*

cuánto,-a[2] *adj* **1** *(pregunta - singular)* how much; *(- plural)* how many: **¿cuántos años tienes?** *how old are you?* **2** *(exclamación)* what a lot of, so many, so much: **¡cuánta gente!** *there are so many people!, what a lot of people!*

▷ *pron (singular)* how much; *(plural)* how many: **¿cuánto es?** *how much is it?*

▷ *adv* how, how much: **¡cuánto me alegro!** *I'm so glad!*

cuanto,-a[3] *adj (singular)* as much as; *(plural)* as many as: **puedes beber cuanta agua quieras** *you can drink as much water as you want.*

▷ *pron* **1** *(singular)* everything, all: **escribe cuanto quieras** *write as much as you want.* **2** *(plural)* all who, everybody who: **cuantos entraron se asustaron** *everybody who came in was frightened.* ■ **cuanto antes** as soon as possible. | **en cuanto** as soon as, when: **en cuanto llegue dile...** *as soon as he arrives tell him...*

▲ *pl* **cuantos,-as.** ■ **unos,-as cuantos,-as** some, a few.

cuáquero,-ra *adj* Quaker.

▷ *nm & nf* Quaker.

cuarcita *nf* quartzite.

cuarenta *adj (cardinal)* forty; *(ordinal)* fortieth.

▷ *nm (número)* forty. ■ **cantarle las cuarenta a ALGN** to give SB a piece of one's mind.

See also **seis.**

cuarentavo,-a *adj* fortieth.

▷ *nm & nf* fortieth.

See also **sexto,-a.**

cuarentena *nf* **1** *(exacto)* forty; *(aproximado)* about forty. **2** MED quarantine. ■ **poner a ALGN en cuarentena 1** MED to quarantine SB, put SB in quarantine. **2** *(no hablarle)* to send SB to Coventry.

cuarentón,-ona *adj* forty-year-old.

▷ *nm & nf (hombre)* forty-year-old man, man in his forties; *(mujer)* forty-year-old woman, woman in her forties.

cuaresma *nf* Lent.

cuarta *nf* **1** *(palmo)* span. **2** *(cuadrante)* quadrant.

See also **cuarto,-a.**

cuartear *vt* **1** *(dividir en cuatro)* to quarter, divide into four. **2** *(descuartizar)* to quarter. **3** *(rajar)* to crack.

▷ *vpr* **cuartearse** *(rajarse)* to crack, split.

cuartel *nm* **1** MIL barracks *pl.* **2** *(cuarta parte)* quarter. ■ **no dar cuartel** *fig* to show no mercy.

cuartelazo *nm* putsch, military uprising.

cuartelero,-a *adj* barrack, barracks.

cuartelillo *nm* post, station. ■ **dar cuartelillo a ALGN** *fam* to bail SB out.

cuarterón,-ona *nm & nf (mestizo)* quadroon.

▷ *nm* **cuarterón** *(de puerta)* panel.

cuarteta *nf* quatrain.

cuarteto *nm* quartet.

cuartilla *nf* sheet of paper.

cuartillo *nm liquid measure equivalent to 0.504 litres (lusl liters)* .

cuarto *nm* **1** *(parte)* quarter: **un cuarto de hora** *a quarter of an hour.* **2** *(de animal)* quarter. **3** *(de ropa)* quarter: **un chaquetón tres cuartos** *a three-quarter length jacket.* **4** *(habitación)* room. ■ **de tres al cuarto** *fam* worthless, third-rate. | **estar sin un cuarto** *fam* to be broke. ● **cuarto creciente** first quarter. | **cuarto de baño** bathroom. | **cuarto trastero** junk room.

▷ *nm pl* **cuartos** *fam (dinero)* money *sing,* dough *sing.* ■ **tres cuartos de lo mismo** *fam* almost exactly the same. ● **cuartos de final** DEP quarter finals. | **cuatro cuartos** *fam* very little money *sing.*

cuarto,-a *adj (ordinal)* fourth: **llegó cuarto** *he arrived in fourth place, he came fourth.*
▷ *nm & nf* fourth.
cuartofinalista *nm o nf* quarterfinalist.
cuartucho *nm fam* hovel, cramped room.
cuarzo *nm* quartz.
cuasi *adv* quasi.
cuaternario,-a *adj* quaternary.
▷ *nm* **el cuaternario** the quaternary.
cuatrero *nm* cattle thief, rustler.
cuatrienio *nm* quadrennium, four-year period.
cuatrillizo,-a *adj* quadruplet.
▷ *nm & nf* quadruplet.
cuatrillón *nm* quadrillion, US septillion.
cuatrimestral *adj (en frecuencia)* four-monthly; *(en duración)* four-month.
cuatrimestre *nm* four-month period: **en el primer cuatrimestre de 2007** *in the first four months of 2007.*
cuatrimotor *nm* four-engined plane.
cuatrisílabo,-a *adj* quadrisyllabic.
▷ *nm* **cuatrisílabo** quadrisyllable.
cuatro *adj (cardinal)* four; *(ordinal)* fourth.
▷ *nm (número)* four. ■ **caer cuatro gotas** *fam* to rain very lightly, spit. ‖ **decirle cuatro cosas a** ALGN to tell SB off. ● **cuatro gatos** *fam* just a few people, hardly anyone.

See also **seis.**

cuatrocientos,-as *adj* four hundred.
▷ *nm* **cuatrocientos** *(número)* four hundred.

See also **seis.**

cuatrojos *nm o nf inv fam* four-eyes.
cuba *nf* cask, barrel.
Cuba *nf* Cuba.
cubalibre *nm* rum and coke.
cubano,-a *adj* Cuban.
▷ *nm & nf* Cuban.
cubata *nm fam* rum and coke.
cubero,-ra *nm & nf* cooper, barrel-maker.
cubertería *nf* cutlery.
cubeta *nf* **1** *(rectangular)* tray, tank, dish. **2** *(cubo)* bucket. **3** *(de barómetro)* bulb.
cubicaje *nm (gen)* cubic capacity; *(de coche)* engine size.
cubicar *vt* **1** MAT to cube. **2** *(motor)*: **el motor del Seat cubica 2000 cc** *the Seat has a two litre engine.*
cúbico,-a *adj* cubic: **raíz cúbica** *cube root.*
cubículo *nm* cubicle.
cubierta *nf* **1** *(gen)* cover, covering. **2** *(de libro)* cover. **3** ARQUIT roof. **4** *(de neumático)* tyre (US tire). **5** *(capó)* bonnet, US hood. **6** *(de barco, avión)* deck. ■ **en cubierta** on deck.
cubierto,-a *adj* **1** *(gen)* covered. **2** *(cielo)* overcast. **3** *(plaza)* filled.
▷ *nm* **cubierto 1** *(techumbre)* cover. **2** *(en la mesa)* place setting. **3** *(menú)* meal at a fixed price: **el cubierto costó veinticinco euros** *the meal was twenty-five euros a head.* ● **precio del cubierto** cover charge.
▷ *nm pl* **cubiertos** cutlery *sing.* ■ **ponerse a cubierto** to take cover. ‖ **tener las espaldas cubiertas** *fam* to be well-heeled.
cubil *nm* den, lair.
cubilete *nm* **1** *(molde)* mould (US mold). **2** *(de dados)* dice cup, dice shaker; *(juego)* cup.
cubiletero *nm* CULIN *(molde)* pastry mould (US mold).
cubismo *nm* cubism.
cubista *adj* cubist.
▷ *nm o nf* cubist.
cubito *nm* **1** little cube. **2** *(de hielo)* ice cube.
cúbito *nm* cubitus.
cubo[1] *nm* **1** *(recipiente)* bucket. **2** *(de rueda)* hub. ● **cubo de la basura** rubbish bin, US garbage can.
cubo[2] *nm* MAT cube. ■ **elevar al cubo** to cube.
cubrecama *nm* bedspread.
cubrir *vt* **1** *(gen)* to cover. **2** CULIN to coat (**de**, with). **3** *(poner tejado)* to put a roof on. **4** *(niebla, etc)* to shroud (**de**, in), cloak. **5** *(ocultar)* to hide. **6** *(llenar)* to fill (**de**, with), cover (**de**, with): **cubrir de agua** *to fill with water.* **7** *(alcanzar)* to come up: **el agua le cubría hasta los tobillos** *the water came up to his ankles.*
▷ *vpr* **cubrirse 1** *(abrigarse)* to cover OS. **2** *(la cabeza)* to put one's hat on. **3** *fig (protegerse)* to protect OS. **4** *(cielo)* to become overcast. **5** *(llenarse)* to be filled.
cucamonas *nf pl fam* caresses.
cucaña *nf* **1** *(palo, juego)* greasy pole. **2** *fam (bicoca)* easy-pickings *pl.*
cucaracha *nf* cockroach.
cuchara *nf* spoon.
cucharada *nf* spoonful. ● **cucharada colmada** heaped spoonful. ‖ **cucharada rasa** level spoonful. ‖ **cucharada sopera** tablespoonful.
cucharadita *nf* teaspoonful.
cucharilla *nf* teaspoon. ● **cucharilla de café** coffee spoon.
cucharita *nf* teaspoon.
cucharón *nm* ladle.
cuché *adj* coated: **papel cuché** *coated paper.*
cuchichear *vi* to whisper.
cuchicheo *nm* whispering.
cuchilla *nf (hoja)* blade. ● **cuchilla de afeitar** razor blade.
cuchillada *nf (golpe)* stab, slash; *(herida)* stab wound, knife wound.
cuchillería *nf* cutler's shop.
cuchillo *nm* **1** knife. **2** ARQUIT support.
cuchipanda *nf fam (juerga)* spree; *(comilona)* feast.
cuchitril *nm* **1** *(establo)* pigsty. **2** *fam (cuartucho)* hovel.
cuchufleta *nf fam* joke.
cuclillas *loc* **en cuclillas** crouching. ■ **ponerse en cuclillas** to crouch down.
cuclillo *nm* cuckoo.
cuco[1] *nm (insecto)* caterpillar.
cuco,-a[2] *adj* **1** *fam (coquetón)* cute. **2** *(taimado)* shrewd, crafty.
▷ *nm* **cuco** *(ave)* cuckoo.
cucú *nm* **1** *(canto)* cuckoo. **2** *(reloj)* cuckoo clock.
▲ *pl* **cucúes.**
cucurucho *nm* **1** *(de papel)* paper cone. **2** *(helado)* cornet, cone. **3** *(capirote)* pointed hood.
cuelgaplatos *nm inv* plate rack.
cuellicorto,-a *adj* short-necked.
cuellilargo,-a *adj* long-necked.

:uello *nm* 1 ANAT neck. 2 *(de camisa, vestido, abrigo)* collar; *(de jersey)* neck: **un jersey de cuello alto** *a polo neck jumper,* US *a turtleneck jumper.* 3 *(de botella)* bottleneck.

:uenca *nf* 1 *(escudilla)* wooden bowl. 2 ANAT socket. 3 GEOG basin. 4 *(minera)* coalfield.

:uenco *nm (vasija)* earthenware bowl.

:uenta *nf* 1 *(bancaria)* account. 2 *(factura)* bill. 3 *(cálculo)* count, counting. 4 *(de collar, etc)* bead. ■ **caer en la cuenta** to realize: **y entonces caí en la cuenta de que...** *and then I realized that..., and then it dawned on me that... .* ‖ **cargar ALGO en cuenta de ALGN** to charge STH to SB's account. ‖ **dar a cuenta** to give on account. ‖ **en resumidas cuentas** in short. ‖ **hacer cuentas** to do sums. ‖ **más de la cuenta** too much, too many: **comió más de la cuenta** *she ate too much.* ‖ **pedir cuentas** to ask for an explanation. ‖ **por la cuenta que le trae** in one's own interest. ‖ **sacar cuentas** to work out. ‖ **tener en cuenta** to take into account. ‖ **trabajar por cuenta propia** to be self-employed. ● **cuenta atrás** countdown. ‖ **cuenta corriente** current account. ‖ **cuenta de correo electrónico** e-mail account.

:uentagotas *nm inv* dropper.

:uentakilómetros *nm inv (de velocidad)* speedometer; *(de distancia)* mileometer.

:uentarrevoluciones *nm inv* rev counter.

:uentavueltas *nm inv* rev counter.

:uentista *adj fam* overdramatic.

▷ *nm o nf* 1 *(autor)* story writer; *(narrador)* storyteller. 2 *fam (que exagera)* over-dramatic person; *(que miente)* fibber, liar.

:uentitis *nf inv pretending to be ill to get out of something.*

:uento *nm* 1 *(relato)* story, tale. 2 LIT short story. 3 *fam (chisme)* gossip. 4 *fam (embuste)* fib, story. ■ **dejarse de cuentos** 1 *fam (ir al grano)* to get to the point. 2 *(decir mentiras)* to stop telling fibs. ‖ **ir con el cuento a ALGN** to go and tell SB. ‖ **tener mucho cuento** *fam* to make a lot of fuss. ‖ **venir a cuento** to be pertinent. ● **cuento chino** tall story. ‖ **cuento de hadas** fairy tale.

:uerda *nf* 1 *(cordel)* rope, string. 2 *(instrumento)* string, cord; *(voz)* voice. 3 *(de reloj)* spring: **dar cuerda a un reloj** *to wind up a watch.* 4 *(en geometría)* chord. 5 DEP interior. ● **cuerdas vocales** vocal chords.

▷ *nf pl* **cuerdas** 1 *(boxeo)* ropes. 2 MÚS strings.

:uerdamente *adv* wisely.

:uerdo,-a *adj* 1 *(persona)* sane. 2 *(acción)* prudent, sensible.

▷ *nm & nf (persona)* sane person, person in one's right mind.

:uerna *nf* 1 *(cornamenta)* antlers *pl,* horns *pl.* 2 *(caza)* hunting horn.

:uerno *nm* 1 horn; *(de ciervo)* antlers *pl.* 2 *(de antena)* antlers *pl.* 3 MIL wing. 4 MÚS horn.

▷ *interj* golly!, gosh!

:uero *nm* 1 *(de animal)* skin, hide. 2 *(curtido)* leather: **pantalón de cuero** *leather trousers.* 3 *(odre)* wineskin. 4 *(balón)* ball. ■ **quedarse en cueros** *fam* to strip off.

:uerpo *nm* 1 ANAT body. 2 *(constitución)* build. 3 *(figura)* figure; *(tronco)* trunk. 4 *(tronco)* trunk. 5 *(grupo)* body, force, corps: **el cuerpo de bomberos** *the fire brigade* (US *the fire department).* 6 *(cadáver)* corpse, body. 7 QUÍM substance. 8 FÍS body. 9 *(vino, tela, etc)* body. 10 DEP length. ■ **cuerpo a cuerpo** hand-to-hand. ‖ **de cuerpo entero** full-length. ‖ **en cuerpo y alma** *fig* heart and soul, body and soul. ● **cuerpo diplomático** diplomatic corps. ‖ **cuerpo geométrico** regular solid. ‖ **cuerpos celestes** heavenly bodies.

cuervo *nm (córvido en general)* crow; *(específico)* raven.

cuesco *nm* 1 *(hueso)* stone. 2 *fam (pedo)* fart.

cuesta *nf (pendiente)* slope. ■ **a cuestas** on one's back, on one's shoulders. ‖ **hacérsele a uno ALGO cuesta arriba** *fig* to find STH an uphill struggle, find STH very difficult . ‖ **ir cuesta abajo** *fig* to go downhill.

cuestación *nf* charity collection. ■ **hacer una cuestación** to raise money for charity.

cuestión *nf* 1 *(pregunta)* question. 2 *(asunto)* business, matter, question. 3 *(discusión)* dispute, quarrel, argument. ■ **en cuestión** in question. ‖ **en cuestión de...** *(tiempo)* in just a few..., in a matter of... ‖ **eso es otra cuestión** that's a whole different matter.

cuestionable *adj* questionable.

cuestionar *vt* to question.

cuestionario *nm* questionnaire.

cuestor *nm* 1 *(magistrado)* quaestor. 2 *(el que pide)* collector.

cueto *nm* 1 *(sitio elevado)* protected peak. 2 *(colina peñascosa)* rocky peak.

cueva *nf* cave.

cuévano *nm* pannier.

cuezo *nm* trough.

cuidado *nm* 1 *(atención)* care, carefulness. 2 *(recelo)* worry.

▷ *interj* look out!, watch out!: **¡cuidado con la moto!** *mind the motorbike!* ■ **andarse con cuidado** to go carefully. ‖ **«Cuidado con el perro»** «Beware of the dog». ‖ **con cuidado** carefully. ‖ **tener cuidado** to be careful. ‖ **traer sin cuidado** not to care. ● **cuidados intensivos** intensive care *sing.*

cuidador,-ra *nm & nf* keeper.

cuidadosamente *adv* carefully.

cuidadoso,-a *adj* 1 *(atento)* careful. 2 *(celoso)* cautious.

cuidar *vt* to look after, take care of, care for.

▷ *vpr* **cuidarse** to take care of OS, look after OS: **¡cuídate mucho!** *take good care of yourself!*

cuita *nf* trouble, sorrow, worry.

cuitado,-a *adj* worried, troubled.

culada *nf* fall on one's backside.

culantro *nm* coriander.

culata *nf* 1 *(de arma)* butt. 2 AUTO cylinder head. 3 *(carne)* haunch, hindquarters *pl.*

culatazo *nm* kick, recoil.

culear *vi fam (mover el culo)* to wiggle one's bottom.

culebra *nf* snake.

culebrear *vi* 1 *(persona)* to zigzag. 2 *(río)* to meander, wind.

culebrilla *nf* 1 MED ringworm. 2 *(de cometa)* zigzag.

culebrina *nf* forked lightning.

culebrón *nm* television serial, soap opera.

culero,-a *adj (perezoso)* lazy

culín *nm fam (de recipiente)* tiny bit, drop.

culinario,-a *adj* culinary, cooking: **arte culinario** *cuisine.*

culito *nm fam* botty.

culminación *nf* culmination, climax.

culminante *adj (momento)* culminating, climatic; *(punto)* highest.
culminar *vi* **1** to reach a peak. **2** *fig (acabar)* to finish, end.
culo *nm* **1** *fam* bottom, bum, arse (US ass). **2** *fam (ano)* arse (US ass).
culón,-ona *adj fam* big-bottomed.
culpa *nf* **1** *(culpabilidad)* guilt, blame. **2** *(falta)* fault: **esto es culpa mía** *it's my fault.* ■ **echar la culpa a** ALGN to put the blame on SB. ‖ **tener la culpa** to be to blame (**de**, for): **yo no tengo la culpa** *I'm not to blame, it's not my fault.*
culpabilidad *nf* guilt, culpabilility.
culpable *adj* guilty.
▷ *nm o nf* offender, culprit.
culpar *vt* **1** *(gen)* to blame (**de**, for). **2** *(de un delito)* to accuse (**de**, of).
culteranismo *nm* Gongorism.
cultismo *nm* cultism.
cultivable *adj* cultivable.
cultivado,-a *pp* ⟶ **cultivar**.
▷ *adj* **1** cultivated. **2** *fig (con cultura)* cultured, refined.
cultivador,-ra *nm & nf* cultivator, grower.
cultivar *vt* **1** to cultivate, farm. **2** *(ejercitar facultades)* to work at, practise (US practice), improve: **cultivar la memoria** *to improve one's memory.* **3** *(en biología)* to produce. ■ **cultivar las amistades** *fig* to cultivate friendships.
cultivo *nm* **1** *(acción)* cultivation, farming. **2** *(cosecha)* crop. **3** BIOL culture. **4** *fig (desarrollo)* development, growth.
culto,-a *adj* **1** *(persona)* cultured, educated. **2** *(estilo)* refined.
▷ *nm* **culto** worship. ■ **rendir culto a** to pay homage to, worship.
cultura *nf* culture. ■ **de cultura** educated.
cultural *adj* cultural.
culturismo *nm* body-building.
culturista *nm o nf* body-builder.
cumbia *nf Columbian dance.*
cumbre *nf* **1** *(de montaña)* summit, top. **2** *fig (culminación)* pinnacle. **3** *(reunión)* summit conference, summit meeting.
cumpleaños *nm inv* birthday.
cumplidamente *adv* **1** *(ampliamente)* sufficiently. **2** *(totalmente)* completely.
cumplido,-a *pp* ⟶ **cumplir**.
▷ *adj* **1** *(completo)* complete, full. **2** *(abundante)* large, ample. **3** *(perfecto)* perfect. **4** *(educado)* polite, courteous.
▷ *nm* **cumplido** compliment. ■ **sin cumplidos** informally.
cumplidor,-ra *adj* **1** *(que cumple)* who delivers the goods: **es una chica muy cumplidora** *she always delivers the goods, she always fulfils her promises.* **2** *(fiable)* reliable, dependable.
cumplimentar *vt* **1** *(felicitar)* to congratulate. **2** *(ejecutar)* to carry out, execute.
cumplimiento *nm* **1** *(orden)* carrying out, execution; *(deber, deseo)* fulfilment (US fulfillment)). **2** *(cumplido)* compliment.
cumplir *vt* **1** *(orden)* to carry out; *(deseo)* to fulfil (US fulfill); *(deber)* to do. **2** *(promesa)* to keep. **3** JUR *(ley)* to observe, abide by; *(pena)* to serve. **4** *(años)* to be turn: **¡que cumplas muchos más!** *many happy returns* **5** *(satisfacer)* to do, carry out, fulfil (US fulfill). ■ **cum plir con el deber** to do one's duty. ‖ **cumplir con s palabra** to keep one's word. ‖ **para cumplir** as a for mality.
▷ *vi* **1** *(plazo)* to expire, end. **2** *(deuda, pago)* to fall due
▷ *vpr* **cumplirse 1** *(realizarse)* to be fulfilled, come true **se cumplió la profecía** *the prophecy came true.* **2** *(fe cha)* to be: **hoy se cumplen cinco años de nuestra bo da** *it's our fifth wedding anniversary today;* **se cumpl una semana del comienzo del curso** *it's a week sinc the course began.*
cúmulo *nm* **1** *(montón)* load, pile, heap; *(cantidad)* se ries, host, string: **un cúmulo de desgracias** *a series of mis fortunes.* **2** METEOR cumulus.
cumulonimbo *nm* cumulonimbus.
cuna *nf* **1** *(cama)* cradle. **2** *(linaje)* birth, lineage, stock **3** *fig (origen)* cradle, birthplace: **la cuna de la filosofí** *the cradle of philosophy.* **4** *(lugar de nacimiento)* birth place.
cundir *vi* **1** *(extenderse)* to spread: **cundió el pánic** *panic spread.* **2** *(dar de sí)* to go a long way, go far **una hora cunde muy poco** *you can't do much in a hour.* **3** *(aumentar de volumen)* to swell, expand: **lo fideos cunden al cocerse** *noodles expand whe cooked.*
cuneiforme *adj* cuneiform.
cunero,-a *adj* **1** *(expósito)* foundling. **2** *fig (toro)* un pedigreed.
▷ *nm & nf (expósito)* foundling.
cuneta *nf* **1** *(de carretera)* verge. **2** *(zanja)* ditch.
cunicultor,-ra *nm & nf* rabbit breeder.
cunicultura *nf* rabbit breeding.
cuña *nf* **1** *(pieza)* wedge. **2** *fig (influencia)* influence **3** *(anuncio)* jingle. **4** *(para el enfermo)* bedpan.
cuñado,-a *nm & nf (hombre)* brother-in-law; *(mujer* sister-in-law.
cuño *nm* **1** *(troquel)* die, stamp. **2** *(sello)* stamp, mark.
cuota *nf* **1** *(pago)* membership fee, dues *pl.* **2** *(por ción)* quota, share.
cuotidiano,-a *adj* daily.
cupe *pt indef* ⟶ **caber**.
cupé *nm* coupé.
cupido *nm* Cupid.
cuplé *nm popular lyrical song.*
cupletista *nf* music-hall singer.
cupo *nm* **1** *(cuota)* quota. **2** MIL contingent.
cupón *nm* **1** *(vale)* coupon, voucher. **2** COM tradin stamp. **3** *(de lotería)* ticket.
cúprico,-a *adj* cupric.
cúpula *nf* cupola, dome.
cuquería *nf* **1** *(astucia)* craftiness. **2** *fam (monada* pretty little thing.
cura *nm* REL priest.
▷ *nf* **1** cure, healing. **2** *(tratamiento)* treatment: **cura d adelgazamiento** *slimming treatment.* ■ **hacer las pri meras curas** to give first aid.
curable *adj* curable.
curación *nf* **1** *(gen)* cure. **2** *(de herida)* healing. **3** *(re cuperación)* recovery.

urado,-a *adj* 1 *(carne, pescado)* cured, salted; *(piel)* tanned. 2 *fig (persona)* hardened.
urador,-ra *nm & nf* healer.
uranderia *nf* quackery.
uranderismo *nm* 1 *(charlatanismo)* quackery. 2 *(de curador)* folk healing.
urandero,-a *nm & nf* 1 *(charlatán)* quack. 2 *(curador)* folk healer.
urar *vt* 1 *(sanar)* to cure. 2 *(herida)* to dress; *(enfermedad)* to treat. 3 *(carne, pescado)* to cure; *(piel)* to tan; *(madera)* to season.
▷ *vi* 1 *(cuidar)* to take care (**de**, of). 2 *(recuperarse)* to recover, get well. 3 *(herida)* to heal (up).
▷ *vpr* **curarse** 1 *(recuperarse)* to recover (**de**, from), get well. 2 *(herida)* to heal up.
urare *nm* curare.
urasao *nm* curaçao.
urativo,-a *adj* curative: **poder curativo** *healing power.*
úrcuma *nf* turmeric.
urda *nf fam* drunkenness.
urdo,-a *adj* Kurdish.
▷ *nm & nf* Kurd.
uria *nf* 1 REL curia. 2 JUR Bar.
uriana *nf* black beetle.
urio *nm* curium.
uriosamente *adv* 1 *(con curiosidad)* curiously, strangely. 2 *(limpiamente)* cleanly.
uriosear *vi* 1 *(fisgar)* to pry, nose around. 2 *(mirar)* to look around.
▷ *vt (fisgar)* to pry into.
uriosidad *nf* 1 *(gen)* curiosity. 2 *(aseo)* cleanliness, tidiness. 3 *(cuidado)* care. ■ **tener curiosidad de** ALGO to be curious about STH.
urioso,-a *adj* 1 curious. 2 *(indiscreto)* inquisitive. 3 *(aseado)* clean, tidy, neat. 4 *(extraño)* strange, odd.
▷ *nm & nf* 1 *(mirón)* onlooker. 2 *pey (indiscreto)* nosy parker, busybody.
urrante *nm o nf argot* worker.
urrar *vi argot* to grind, slave, graft.
urre *nm argot* job, meal ticket.
urrelo *nm argot* job, meal ticket.
urrículo *nm* curriculum, curriculum vitae.
urro *nm argot* job, meal ticket.
urruca *nf* warbler.
urry *nm* curry.
ursado,-a *adj* 1 *(versado)* experienced. 2 *(cartas)* dispatch.
ursante *nm o nf* student.
ursar *vt* 1 *(estudiar)* to study. 2 *(enviar)* to send, dispatch; *(orden)* to give. 3 *(tramitar)* to make an application.
ursi *adj fam (afectado)* pretentious, affected, twee.
▷ *nm o nf fam* pretentious person, affected person.
ursilada *nf* 1 *(cualidad)* affectation, pretentiousness. 2 *(hecho)* pretentious thing to do, posh thing to do. 3 *(obra, cosa)* pretentious thing: **las películas románticas me parecen una cursilada** *for me romantic films are just sentimental slush.*
cursillista *nm & nf* person on a course.
cursillo *nm* short course, training course.
cursiva *nf (escritura)* cursive; *(tipografía)* italics *pl.*
cursivo,-a *adj* cursive: **letra cursiva** *italics pl.*
curso *nm* 1 *(dirección)* course, direction: **el curso de los acontecimientos** *the course of events.* 2 EDUC *(nivel)* year, class; *(materia)* course; *(escolar)* school year: **vamos al mismo curso** *we are in the same class.* 3 *(río)* flow, current. ● **curso acelerado** crash course.
cursor *nm* 1 INFORMÁ cursor. 2 TÉC slide.
curtido,-a *pp* ⟶ **curtir.**
▷ *adj* 1 *(por el sol)* tanned, sunburnt. 2 *(cuero)* tanned. 3 *fig (endurecido)* hardened.
▷ *nm* **curtido** *(operación)* tanning.
▷ *nm pl* **curtidos** tanned leather *sing.*
curtidor,-ra *nm & nf* tanner.
curtiduría *nf* tannery.
curtir *vt* 1 *(piel)* to tan. 2 *fig (acostumbrar)* to harden, toughen.
▷ *vpr* **curtirse** 1 *(por el sol)* to get tanned. 2 *fig (acostumbrarse)* to become hardened.
curva *nf* 1 *(gen)* curve. 2 *(de carretera)* bend. 3 *(gráfico)* curve, graph. ■ **trazar una curva** to draw a curve.
▷ *nf pl* **curvas** *fam (cuerpo de mujer)* curves, curvy figure *sing.*
curvar *vt* 1 *(gen)* to curve, bend. 2 *(espalda)* to arch.
curvatura *nf* curvature.
curvilíneo,-a *adj* 1 curvilinear, curvilineal. 2 *fam (del cuerpo)* curvaceous, shapely.
curvo,-a *adj* curved, bent.
cuscús *nm* couscous.
cúspide *nf* 1 *(cumbre)* summit, peak. 2 *(en geometría)* apex. 3 *fig* peak.
custodia *nf* 1 custody, care. 2 REL monstrance. ■ **bajo custodia** in custody.
custodiar [12] *vt* 1 *(proteger)* to keep, take care of. 2 *(vigilar)* to guard, watch over.
custodio *nm* custodian, guard, keeper.
cutáneo,-a *adj* cutaneous, skin: **enfermedad cutánea** *skin disease.*
cúter *nm* 1 *(barco)* cutter. 2 *(cuchillo)* cutter.
cutí *nm* ticking.
cutícula *nf* cuticle.
cutis *nm inv* skin, complexion.
cutre *adj* 1 *(tacaño)* mean, stingy. 2 *fam (sórdido)* grotty, seedy.
cuyo,-a *pron* 1 *(personas)* whose, of whom: **esta mujer, cuya hermana trabaja en Alemania...** *this woman, whose sister works in Germany..., this woman, the sister of whom works in Germany...* 2 *(cosas)* whose, of which: **un árbol cuyas hojas presentan esta enfermedad** *a tree with leaves that show signs of this disease.* ■ **en cuyo caso** in which case.
CV[1] *sím* **(caballos de vapor)** horse power; *(símbolo)* HP.
CV[2] *abrev* **(currículum vítae)** curriculum vitae (US resumé); *(abreviatura)* CV.
czar *nm* czar, tsar.
czarina *nf* czarina, tsarina.

D

D, d *nf (la letra)* D, d.
dactilar *adj* digital. ● huellas dactilares fingerprints.
dactilografía *nf* typing, typewriting.
dactilógrafo,-a *nm & nf* typist.
dadaísmo *nm* Dadaism.
dadaísta *adj* Dadaist.
▷ *nm o nf* Dadaist.
dádiva *nf* 1 *(regalo)* gift, present. 2 *(donación)* donation.
dado[1] *nm* 1 *(para jugar)* die. 2 TÉC block. 3 ARQUIT dado. ■ echar los dados to throw the dice.
dado,-a[2] *adj* 1 given: dada la base y la altura, hallar la superficie *given the base and the height, find the area.* 2 *(en vista de)* in view of: dada su experiencia *in view of his experience.* ■ dado que since, as, given that: dado que llueve no saldremos *as it's raining we won't go out.* ‖ ser dado,-a a to be keen on, be fond of: mi tío es muy dado a las hierbas medicinales *my uncle is very fond of medicinal herbs.*
daga *nf* dagger.
daguerrotipo *nm* 1 *(arte)* daguerreotypy. 2 *(aparato, retrato)* daguerreotype.
daiquiri *nm* daiquiri.
Dakota *nf* Dakota. ● Dakota del Norte North Dakota. ‖ Dakota del Sur South Dakota.
dalai lama *nm* Dalai Lama.
dalia *nf* dahlia.
dálmata *adj* Dalmatian.
▷ *nm* Dalmatian.
daltoniano,-a *adj* colour-blind (US color-blind), daltonic.
▷ *nm & nf* person who is colour-blind (US color-blind).
daltónico,-a *adj* colour-blind (US color-blind), daltonic.
daltonismo *nm* colour (US color) blindness, daltonism.
dama *nf* 1 *(señora)* lady. 2 *(en el juego de damas)* king; *(en ajedrez)* queen.
▷ *nf pl* damas draughts, (US checkers). ● tablero de damas draughtboard, (US checkerboard).
damajuana *nf* demijohn.
damasco *nm* 1 *(tejido)* damask. 2 *(árbol, fruto)* damson.
Damasco *nm* Damascus.
damasquina *nf* French marigold.
damasquinado,-a *adj* damascene.
damasquinar *vt* to damascene, damask.
damero *nm* draughtboard, US checkerboard.
damisela *nf irón* young lady, damsel.
damnificado,-a *adj* 1 *(persona)* injured, harmed. 2 *(cosa)* damaged.
▷ *nm & nf* victim.
damnificar [1] *vt* 1 *(a una persona)* to injure, harm. 2 *(cosa)* to damage.
dandy *nm* dandy.
▲ *pl* dandys.
danés,-esa *adj* Danish.
▷ *nm & nf (persona)* Dane.
▷ *nm* danés *(idioma)* Danish.
Danubio *nm* el Danubio the Danube.
danza *nf* 1 *(baile)* dance. 2 *fig (negocio sucio)* shady business, shady deal; *(lío)* mess: no te metas en esa danza *don't get mixed up in a deal like that.* 3 *fam fig (riña)* row.
danzante *adj* dancing.
▷ *nm o nf* 1 dancer. 2 *fam fig (intrigante)* busybody, meddler. 3 *fam fig (botarate)* scatterbrain.
danzar [4] *vt (bailar)* to dance.
▷ *vi* 1 *(bailar)* to dance (con, with). 2 *(zascandilear)* to wander: se pasó la mañana danzando y no hizo los deberes *he spent the morning milling about and he didn't do his homework.*
danzarín,-ina *nm & nf* dancer.
dañado,-a *adj* damaged, spoiled.
dañar *vt* 1 *(causar dolor)* to hurt, harm. 2 *(estropear)* to damage, spoil. 3 *fig* to damage, stain: ese asunto dañará su reputación *that affair will damage his reputation.*
▷ *vpr* dañarse *(estropearse)* to get damaged, spoil; *(alimentos)* to go bad, go off.
dañino,-a *adj* harmful (para, to), damaging (para, to).
daño *nm (a persona)* harm, injury; *(a cosa)* damage; *(perjuicio)* wrong. ■ hacer daño 1 *(doler)* to hurt. 2 *(causar dolor a* ALGN*)* to hurt. 3 *(ser malo para* ALGO*)* to damage, harm. *(ser malo para* ALGN*)* to do SB harm: me hizo daño con sus palabras *her words hurt me.* ‖ hacerse daño to hurt OS: se hizo daño en la mano *she hurt her hand.* ● daños y perjuicios JUR damages.
dar [68] *vt* 1 *(gen)* to give: te daré un libro *I'll give you a book.* 2 *(poner en las manos, entregar)* to deliver, hand over; *(poner al alcance)* to pass, hand: dame la sal *pass me the salt.* 3 *(proporcionar, ofrecer, procurar algo no material a una persona - noticia)* to tell, announce, report; *(consejo)* to give; *(recuerdos, recados)* to pass on, give. 4 *(permitir tener algo, conceder)* to give. 5 *(pagar a cambio)* to give, pay: ¿cuánto me daría por esto? *how much would you give me for it?* 6 *(realizar una acción)*. 7 *(producir - cosecha)* to produce, yield; *(fruto, flores)* to bear, produce; *(beneficio, interés)* to produce, yield: la higuera da higos *the fig tree bears figs.* 8 *(celebrar, tener lugar - película)* to show, screen; *(obra de teatro)* to perform, put on; *(musical)* to play, perform; *(concierto)* to give, perform, pu

on; *(fiesta)* to give, throw: **daremos una fiesta** *we'll have a party.* **9** *(pegar)* to hit. **10** *(comunicar felicitaciones, pésames, etc)* to say. **11** *(afectar, causar)* to hit, make: **el sol me daba en los ojos** *the sun was shining in my eyes.* **12** *(expeler, desprender)* to give off: **eso da humo** *it gives off smoke.* **13** *(sonar el reloj las horas)* to strike. **14** *(untar, recubrir una superficie)* to apply, give. **15** *(abrir el paso de conductos)* to turn on: **he dado el gas** *I've turned the gas on.* **16** *(en naipes)* to deal. ■ **¡dale! 1** *fam (seguir)* go on! **2** *(venga)* come on! ‖ **dar a entender que...** to give to understand that..., imply that...: **dio a entender que no vendría** *she implied she wouldn't come.* ‖ **dar a luz** to give birth (**a**, to). ‖ **dar ALGO por** to assume, consider. ‖ **dar con** *(encontrar algo)* to find, discover. *(encontrar a alguien)* to meet, come across, bump into. *(acertar)* to find: **dio con la solución** *he found the solution.* ‖ **dar de sí 1** *(ropa)* to stretch, give. **2** *(dinero, comida)* to go a long way. ‖ **dar igual** to be all the same, not matter: **le daba igual** *it didn't matter to him, he didn't care.* ‖ **dar la mano a ALGN** to shake hands with SB. ‖ **dar lo mismo** to be all the same, not matter: **me da lo mismo** *I don't mind.* ‖ **dar gusto +** *infinitivo* to be nice + *to* + *inf*: **da gusto verla jugar** *it's nice to see her playing.* ‖ **darle a uno ALGO** *(sobrevenirle)* to have: **le dio un ataque de tos** *she had a coughing fit.* ‖ **darle a uno por hacer ALGO** to take it into one's head to do STH. ‖ **no dar una** *fam* not to get anything right. ‖ **¡y dale!** *fam* there he *(you, they, etc)* goes *(go)* again!

▷ *vi* **1** *(pegar, golpear)* to hit: **la pelota le dio en toda la cara** *the ball hit him right in the face.* **2** *(en naipes)* to deal. **3 dar a** *(botón, interruptor)* to press: **dale al botón** *press the button.* **4** *(mirar una cosa hacia una parte)* to look out onto, overlook; *(ir a parar a una parte)* to lead to, open onto. **5 dar de** *(caer)* to fall: **dio de narices en el suelo** *he fell flat on his face.* **6 dar de** *(suministrar)* to give. **7 dar en** *(acertar)* to find, hit on. **8 dar para** *(ser suficiente)* to be enough for, be sufficient for: **la sopa da para cuatro** *the soup serves four.*

▷ *vpr* **darse 1** *(entregarse)* to give in, surrender. **2** *(suceder, existir)* to happen, occur: **a veces se da este caso** *this sometimes happens.* **3** *(crecer)* to grow; *(cultivarse)* to be found, grow. **4 darse a** *(consagrarse)* to devote OS to; *(a un vicio)* to take to, abandon OS to: **se dio al estudio** *she devoted herself to study.* **5 darse con/contra** *(chocar)* to crash (**contra/con**, into).

dardo *nm* **1** *(arma)* dart, arrow. **2** *fig (dicho)* cutting remark, caustic remark.

dársena *nf* dock, basin.

darvinismo *nm* Darwinism.

darvinista *nm o nf* Darwinist.

datación *nf* dating. ● **datación por radiocarbono** radiocarbon dating.

datar *vt* **1** *(poner la data)* to date, put a date on. **2** COM to credit, enter.

▷ *vi (tener origen)* to date (**de**, from), date back (**de**, to): **esa iglesia data del siglo XI** *that church dates from the eleventh century.*

dátil *nm* **1** date. **2** *fam (dedo)* finger.

datilera *nf* date palm.

dativo,-a *adj* dative.

▷ *nm* **dativo** dative. ■ **en dativo** in the dative.

dato *nm (información)* fact, piece of information, datum. ● **datos personales** personal details.

dB *sím* **(decibelio)** decibel; *(símbolo)* dB.

d.C. *abrev* **(después de Cristo)** Anno Domini; *(abreviatura)* AD.

DDT *abrev* **(diclorodifeniltricloroetano)** dichlorodiphenyltrichloroethane; *(abreviatura)* DDT.

de *prep* **1** *(posesión, pertenencia)* of: **la mesa de mi habitación** *the table in my bedroom.* **2** *(procedencia, origen)* from: **viene de Barcelona** *she comes from Barcelona.* **3** *(descripción)* with: **el señor del abrigo azul** *the man in the blue coat.* **4** *(tema)* of, on, about: **hablaron del tiempo** *they talked about the weather.* **5** *(materia)* made of, of: **un anillo de oro** *a gold ring.* **6** *(contenido)* of: **un vaso de agua** *a glass of water.* **7** *(uso)* for: **gallo de pelea** *fighting cock.* **8** *(oficio)* by, as: **trabaja de profesor** *he works as a teacher.* **9** *(modo)* on, in, as: **de pie** *standing up.* **10** *(tiempo)* at, by, in: **de día** *by day, during the day.* **11** *(lugar) varias traducciones*: **la vecina de arriba** *our upstairs neighbour.* **12** *(precio)* at: **manzanas de dos euros el kilo** *apples at two euros a kilo.* **13** *(medida)* measuring: **una botella de dos litros** *a two litre bottle.* **14** *(causa)* with, because of, of: **llorar de alegría** *to cry with joy.* **15** *(agente)* by: **es una obra de Lope** *a play by Lope.* **16** *(con superlativo)* in, of: **el mayor de los tres** *the eldest of the three.* **17** *(suposición)* if: **de haberlo dicho** *if he had told us.* **18** *(en una aposición)* of: **la ciudad de Barcelona** *the city of Barcelona.*

See also **del**.

deambular *vi* to saunter, stroll.

deambulatorio *nm* ambulatory.

debacle *nf* disaster, downfall.

debajo *adv* below, underneath: **el libro verde está debajo** *the green book is underneath.* ■ **debajo de** under, below, underneath. ‖ **por debajo** underneath: **tuvieron que pasar por debajo** *they had to go underneath.* ‖ **por debajo de** below, under: **eso es por debajo del nivel del mar** *that's below sea level.*

debate *nm* debate, discussion.

debatir *vt* to debate, discuss.

▷ *vpr* **debatirse** *(forcejear)* to struggle.

debe *nm* debit side.

deber *vt* **1** *(estar obligado a algo)* to owe: **debemos respeto a nuestros padres** *we owe respect to our parents.* **2** *(dinero, cosa)* to owe: **te debo cincuenta euros** *I owe you fifty euros.*

▷ *aux* **1** *(obligación presente)* must, have to, have got to: **debo ir a comprar** *I must go shopping.* **2** *(obligación pasada)* should, ought to: **debía haberlo comprado ayer** *I should have bought it yesterday.* **3** *(obligación futura)* must, have to, have got to: **deberás tenerlo a las cinco** *you must have it ready by five o'clock.* **4** *(obligación moral)* should, ought to: **no deberías haberlo hecho** *you shouldn't have done it.* **5 deber de** *(probabilidad)* must; *(negativa)* can't: **deben de ser las seis** *it must be six o'clock;* **debes de haberlo oído** *you must have heard it;* **no deben de haber llegado** *they can't have arrived.*

▷ *vpr* **deberse 1** *(ser consecuencia)* to be due (**a**, to). **2** *(tener una obligación)* to have a duty (**a**, to).

▷ *nm* **deber** *(obligación)* duty, obligation.

▷ *nm pl* **deberes** *(escolares)* homework *sing.* ■ **cumplir con su deber** to do one's duty. ‖ **hacer los deberes** to do one's homework.
debidamente *adv* duly, properly.
debido,-a *adj* 1 *(merecido)* due: **con el debido respeto,...** *with all due respect,...* 2 *(conveniente)* right. 3 *(adecuado)* proper, necessary. ■ **como es debido** 1 *(correctamente)* right, properly. 2 *(como es merecido)* deservedly: **siéntate en la silla como es debido** *sit properly on the chair.* ‖ **debido,-a** due to, owing to, because of: **las carreteras están cortadas debido al mal tiempo** *the roads have been closed due to bad weather.*
débil *adj* 1 *(persona)* weak, feeble. 2 *(ruido)* faint; *(luz)* dim, feeble. 3 LING weak.
▷ *nm o nf* weak person.
▷ *nm pl* **los débiles** the weak.
debilidad *nf* 1 *(de una persona)* weakness, feebleness; *(de un sonido)* faintness. 2 *fig* weakness: **los coches de carreras son su debilidad** *he has a weakness for racing cars.* ■ **tener debilidad por** 1 *(algo)* to have a weakness for. 2 *(alguien)* to have a soft spot for.
debilitación *nf* weakening, debilitation.
debilitador,-ra *adj* weakening, debilitating.
debilitamiento *nm* weakening.
debilitar *vt* to weaken, debilitate.
▷ *vpr* **debilitarse** to weaken, get weak, become weak.
débilmente *adv* weakly.
debilucho,-a *adj pey* weak, frail, delicate.
▷ *nm & nf* weakling.
débito *nm* 1 *(deuda)* debt. 2 *(debe)* debit.
debut *nm* debut, début.
debutante *nm o nf (actor)* first-time actor; *(actriz)* first-time actress.
▷ *nf (en sociedad)* debutante.
debutar *vi* to make one's debut, make one's début.
década *nf* decade.
decadencia *nf* decadence, decline, decay.
decadente *adj* decadent.
▷ *nm o nf* decadent.
decaedro *nm* decahedron.
decaer [67] *vi* 1 *(perder fuerzas)* to weaken; *(- entusiasmo, interés)* to flag; *(- salud)* to go down, deteriorate, decay; *(- belleza, etc)* to lose: **su interés está decayendo** *his interest is flagging.* 2 *(imperio, costumbre)* to decay. 3 *(fiebre)* to go down. 4 *(negocio)* to fall off, decline. 5 *(ánimo)* to lose heart: **su ánimo no decae** *she doesn't lose heart.*
decagonal *adj* decagonal.
decágono *nm* decagon.
decagramo *nm* decagram, decagramme.
decaído,-a *adj* 1 *(débil)* weak. 2 *(triste)* sad, depressed, low.
decaimiento *nm* 1 *(debilidad)* weakness, weakening. 2 *(tristeza)* sadness.
decalitro *nm* decalitre (US decaliter).
decálogo *nm* Decalogue.
decámetro *nm* decametre (US decameter).
decano,-a *nm & nf* 1 *(cargo)* dean. 2 *(miembro más antiguo)* senior member; *(hombre)* doyen; *(mujer)* doyenne.
decantación *nf* decanting.
decantar[1] *vt (verter)* to decant, pour off.
decantar[2] *vt (alabar)* to praise, laud.
▷ *vpr* **decantarse** *(preferir)* to prefer (**hacia/por**, -): **el público se decantó por el equipo local** *the spectators were on the side of the local team.*
decapar *vt* 1 *(óxido, cal)* to descale. 2 *(pintura)* to strip (off).
decapitar *vt* to behead, decapitate.
decápodo *nm* decapod.
decasílabo,-a *adj* decasyllabic.
▷ *nm* **decasílabo** decasyllable.
decatlón *nm* decathlon.
deceleración *nf* deceleration.
decelerar *vi* to decelerate.
decena *nf* 1 *(exacto)* ten. 2 *(aproximado)* about ten: **he invitado a una decena de personas** *I have invited ten or so people.*
decenal *adj* ten-year, decennial.
decencia *nf* 1 *(decoro)* decency, propriety. 2 *(honestidad)* honesty.
decenio *nm* decade.
decentar [27] *vt* 1 *(empezar a cortar)* to start. 2 *fig (empezar a destruir)* to erode.
▷ *vpr* **decentarse** *(ulcerarse)* to ulcerate.
decente *adj* 1 *(decoroso)* decent, proper. 2 *(honesto)* honest, upright; *(respetable)* decent, respectable. 3 *(limpio)* tidy, clean. 4 *(adecuado)* suitable, right.
decentemente *adv* decently.
decepción *nf* disappointment, disenchantment.
decepcionado,-a *adj* disappointed.
decepcionante *adj* disappointing.
decepcionar *vt* to disappoint, let down: **no nos decepciones** *don't disappoint us.*
deceso *nm fml* decease.
dechado *nm* model, example.
decibel *nm* decibel.
decibelio *nm* decibel.
decididamente *adv* 1 *(con determinación)* resolutely, with determination: **solicitó el trabajo decididamente** *he applied for the job with determination.* 2 *(definitivamente)* definitely: **decididamente no compraremos esa casa** *we definitely won't buy that house.*
decidido,-a *adj* determined, resolute: **está decidido a acabar el trabajo** *he's determined to finish the job.*
decidir *vt* 1 *(gen)* to decide; *(asunto)* to settle. 2 *(convencer)* to persuade, convince: **aquellas circunstancias la decidieron a marchar** *those circumstances persuaded her to leave.* 3 *(resolver)* to resolve, decide: **decidió dejar de fumar** *he resolved to stop smoking.*
▷ *vi* to decide, choose: **tuvo que decidir entre los dos** *she had to decide between the two.*
▷ *vpr* **decidirse** to make up one's mind. ■ **decidirse por** to decide on: **se decidió por la falda roja** *she decided on the red skirt.*
decidor,-ra *adj* eloquent, silver-tongued, witty.
▷ *nm & nf* wit.
decigramo *nm* decigram, decigramme.
decilitro *nm* decilitre (US deciliter).
décima *nf* LIT stanza of ten octosyllabic lines. ■ **tener (unas) décimas** *fam* to have a slight temperature.
decimal *adj* decimal.
▷ *nm* decimal.

lecímetro *nm* decimetre (US decimeter).

lécimo,-a *adj* tenth.

▷ *nm & nf* tenth.

▷ *nm* **décimo** *tenth part of a* lottery ticket.

See also **sexto,-a**.

lecimoctavo,-a *adj* eighteenth.

▷ *nm & nf* eighteenth.

See also **sexto,-a**.

lecimocuarto,-a *adj* fourteenth.

▷ *nm & nf* fourteenth.

See also **sexto,-a**.

lecimonónico,-a *adj* nineteenth-century: **un escritor decimonónico** *a nineteenth-century writer.*

lecimonono,-a *adj* nineteenth.

▷ *nm & nf* nineteenth.

See also **sexto,-a**.

lecimonoveno,-a *adj-nm & nf* → **decimonono,-a**.

See also **sexto,-a**.

lecimoquinto,-a *adj* fifteenth.

▷ *nm & nf* fifteenth.

See also **sexto,-a**.

lecimoséptimo,-a *adj* seventeenth.

▷ *nm & nf* seventeenth.

See also **sexto,-a**.

lecimosexto,-a *adj* sixteenth.

▷ *nm & nf* sixteenth.

See also **sexto,-a**.

lecimotercero,-a *adj* thirteenth.

▷ *nm & nf* thirteenth.

See also **sexto,-a**.

lecir [69] *vt* **1** *(gen)* to say. **2** *(contar, revelar)* to tell: **dijo la verdad** *she told the truth.* **3** *(nombrar, llamar)* to call: **le dicen Cuca** *she's called Cuca.* **4** *(opinar)* to have to say. **5** *(denotar)* to tell, show. **6** *(sugerir)* to mean. **7** *(recitar)* to recite: **dijo un poema** *he recited a poem.* **8** *(un texto)* to read, say: **el texto dice lo siguiente** *the text reads as follows.* ■ **¿cómo diría yo?** how shall I put it? ‖ **digan lo que digan** whatever they say. ‖ **digo yo** in my opinion, I think. ‖ **el qué dirán** what people say. ‖ **es decir** that is (to say). ‖ **¡no me digas!** really! ‖ **querer decir** to mean: **quiero decir,...** *I mean,...* ‖ **se dice...** they say..., it is said... ‖ **¡y que lo digas!** you bet!

lecisión *nf* **1** *(resolución)* decision: **sus padres tuvieron que tomar una decisión** *his parents had to make a decision.* **2** *(determinación)* determination, resolution.

lecisivo,-a *adj* **1** *(importante)* decisive. **2** *(concluyente)* decisive, final: **un argumento decisivo** *a decisive argument.*

leclamación *nf* **1** *(acción)* recitation. **2** *(arte)* declamation.

leclamar *vi* to declaim, recite.

▷ *vt* to declaim, recite.

leclamatorio,-a *adj* declamatory.

leclaración *nf* **1** *(gen)* declaration: **declaración de renta** *income tax return.* **2** [Also used in plural with the same meaning.] *(explicación pública)* statement, comment. **3** JUR evidence. **4** *(en bridge)* bid. ■ **prestar declaración** JUR to give evidence.

declarar *vt* **1** *(gen)* to declare; *(manifestar)* to state: **lo declararon vencedor** *he was declared the winner.* **2** JUR to find. **3** *(en bridge)* to bid, declare.

▷ *vi* **1** to declare. **2** JUR to testify.

▷ *vpr* **declararse 1** *(amor)* to declare one's love (**a**, for). **2** *(fuego, guerra, etc)* to break out, start: **se declaró un incendio en el monte** *a fire broke out on the mountain.*

declinable *adj* declinable.

declinación *nf* **1** *(gramatical)* declension. **2** *(astronómica)* declination.

declinar *vi* **1** *(brújula)* to decline. **2** *(disminuir)* to decline, come down. **3** *(acercarse al fin)* to end, draw to an end.

▷ *vt* **1** *(rechazar)* to decline, refuse. **2** GRAM to decline.

declive *nm* **1** *(inclinación)* slope, incline. **2** *fig (decadencia)* decline. ■ **en declive** *fig* on the decline.

decodificar *vt* to decode.

decolorar *vt* **1** *(perder el color)* to discolour (US discolor). **2** *(blanquear)* to bleach.

▷ *vpr* **decolorarse 1** *(perder el color)* to fade, become discoloured (US discolored). **2** *(blanquearse)* to be bleached.

decomiso *nm* **1** *(acción)* confiscation, seizure. **2** *(lo confiscado)* confiscated article, confiscated goods *pl.*

decoración *nf* **1** *(gen)* decoration. **2** TEAT scenery, set.

decorado *nm* **1** *(efecto)* decoration. **2** TEAT scenery, set.

decorador,-ra *adj* decorating.

▷ *nm & nf* **1** decorator. **2** TEAT set designer.

decorar *vt (gen)* to decorate, adorn, embellish; *(una casa)* to decorate.

decorativo,-a *adj* decorative, ornamental.

decoro *nm* **1** *(honor)* decorum; *(respeto)* respect. **2** *(pudor)* modesty, decency.

decorosamente *adv* **1** *(como se debe)* with decorum. **2** *(con dignidad)* with dignity. **3** *(con decencia)* decently.

decoroso,-a *adj* **1** *(apropiado)* decorous, proper. **2** *(digno)* decent, respectable. **3** *(respetable)* respectable, honourable (US honorable): **un trabajo decoroso** *an honourable job.* **4** *(decente)* decent.

decrecer [43] *vi (gen)* to decrease, diminish; *(aguas)* to subside, go down; *(días)* to get shorter, draw in; *(interés)* to decline.

decreciente *adj* decreasing, diminishing.

decrepitud *nf* decrepitude.

decretar *vt* **1** *(con decreto)* to decree. **2** *(ordenar)* to ordain, order.

decreto *nm* decree, order.

decúbito *nm* position. ● **decúbito supino** supine position.

décuplo,-a *adj* tenfold.

▷ *nm* **décuplo** ten times.

dedal *nm* thimble.

dedicación *nf* **1** dedication, devotion. **2** REL dedication, consecration. ■ **de dedicación exclusiva** full-time.

dedicar [1] *vt* **1** *(una dedicatoria)* to dedicate, inscribe. **2** *(tiempo, dinero)* to devote (**a**, to). **3** *(palabras)* to address. **4** *(tener admiración, atenciones, etc)* to show, have: **le dedica muchas atenciones** *she devotes a lot of attention to him.*

dedicatoria *nf* dedication, inscription.

dedo *nm* 1 *(de la mano)* finger; *(del pie)* toe. 2 *(medida)* finger, digit. ■ **hacer dedo** *fam* to hitchhike. ‖ **no tener dos dedos de frente** *fig* to be as thick as two short planks. ● **dedo anular** ring finger, third finger. ‖ **dedo del corazón** middle finger. ‖ **dedo gordo** 1 *(de la mano)* thumb. 2 *(del pie)* big toe. ‖ **dedo índice** forefinger, index finger. ‖ **dedo meñique** little finger. ‖ **dedo pulgar** thumb. ‖ **yema del dedo** fingertip.

deducción *nf* deduction.

deducible *adj* 1 deducible, inferable. 2 COM deductible.

deducir [46] *vt* 1 to deduce, infer. 2 *(dinero)* to deduct, subtract.
▷ *vpr* **deducirse** to follow: **de aquí se deduce que...** *from this it follows that...*

deductivo,-a *adj* deductive.

defecar [1] *vi* to defecate.

defecto *nm* 1 *(gen)* defect, fault; *(de una joya)* imperfection, flaw. 2 *(de persona - moral)* fault, shortcoming; *(- física)* handicap. ■ **en defecto de** for lack of. ‖ **por defecto** INFORMÁ default: **la impresora por defecto** *the default printer.*

defectuoso,-a *adj* defective, faulty.

defender [28] *vt* 1 *(gen)* to defend (**contra/de**, against). 2 *(mantener una opinión, afirmación)* to defend, uphold; *(respaldar a* ALGN*)* to stand up for, support. 3 *(proteger)* to protect (**contra/de**, against/from). 4 JUR *(algo)* to argue, plead; *(a alguien)* to defend.
▷ *vpr* **defenderse** *(espabilarse)* to manage, get by, get along: **¿qué tal se defiende en inglés?** *how does she get by in English?, what's her English like?*

defendible *adj* 1 *(que se puede defender)* defensible. 2 *(que se puede justificar)* justifiable.

defenestrar *vt* to throw out the window.

defensa *nf* defence (US defense).
▷ *nm o nf* DEP *(jugador)* back, defender; *(conjunto de jugadores)* defence (US defense), defenders *pl.*

defensiva *nf* defensive. ■ **estar a la defensiva** to be on the defensive. ‖ **ponerse a la defensiva** to go on the defensive.

defensivo,-a *adj* defensive.

defensor,-ra *adj* defending.
▷ *nm & nf* 1 defender. 2 JUR counsel for the defence (US defense). ● **defensor del pueblo** ombudsman.

deferente *adj* deferential.

deficiencia *nf* 1 *(defecto)* deficiency, defect, shortcoming. 2 *(insuficiencia)* lack.

deficiente *adj* 1 *(defectuoso)* deficient, faulty. 2 *(insuficiente)* lacking, insufficient.
▷ *nm o nf* mentally retarded person. ● **deficiente mental** mentally retarded person.

déficit *nm inv* 1 COM deficit. 2 *fig* shortage.

deficitario,-a *adj* showing a deficit.

definición *nf* definition. ■ **por definición** by definition.

definido,-a *adj* defined, definite.

definir *vt* to define.
▷ *vpr* **definirse** 1 to be defined. 2 *(explicarse)* to make OS clear, define one's position.

definitivamente *adv* 1 *(para siempre)* for good, once and for all: **se marchó definitivamente** *she left for good.* 2 *(finalmente)* finally.

definitivo,-a *adj* definitive, final. ■ **en definitiva** f nally, in short, all in all.

deflación *nf* deflation.

deflagración *nf* deflagration.

defoliante *adj* defoliant.

defoliar *vt* to defoliate.

deforestación *nf* deforestation.

deforestar *vt* to deforest.

deformación *nf* deformation, distortion.

deformar *vt (gen)* to deform, put out of shape; *(ca ra)* to disfigure; *(realidad, imagen, etc)* to distort.

deforme *adj (persona)* deformed; *(cosa)* misshaper out of shape; *(imagen, cara)* distorted.

deformidad *nf* 1 deformity, malformation. 2 *fi* fault, shortcoming.

defraudado,-a *adj (decepcionado)* disappointed.

defraudar *vt* 1 *(estafar)* to defraud, cheat. 2 *(decep cionar)* to disappoint, deceive. 3 *fig (frustrar)* to be tray: **defraudar las esperanzas** *to dash one's hopes.*

defunción *nf fml* death, decease.

degenerado,-a *adj* degenerate.
▷ *nm & nf* degenerate.

degenerar *vi* to degenerate.

degenerativo,-a *adj* degenerative.

deglutir *vt* to swallow.
▷ *vi* to swallow.

degollar [58] *vt* 1 *(cortar la garganta)* to slit the throa of. 2 *(decapitar)* to behead, decapitate.

degradación *nf* 1 degradation, debasement. 2 MI demotion. 3 ARTE gradation.

degradante *adj* degrading, humiliating.

degradar *vt* 1 to degrade, debase. 2 MIL to demote
▷ *vpr* **degradarse** to demean OS, degrade OS.

degustación *nf* tasting.

degustar *vt* to taste, sample, try.

dehesa *nf* pasture, meadow.

deidad *nf* deity, divinity.

deificar [1] *vt* 1 to deify. 2 *fig* to glorify.

dejadez *nf* 1 *(negligencia de sí mismo)* neglect, sloven liness. 2 *(negligencia)* negligence, carelessness. 3 *(pereza)* laziness, apathy.

dejado,-a *adj* 1 *(descuidado)* untidy, slovenly. 2 *(ne gligente)* negligent. 3 *(perezoso)* lazy.
▷ *nm & nf* untidy person, slovenly person.

dejar *vt* 1 *(colocar)* to leave, put. 2 *(abandonar - perso na, lugar)* to leave; *(- hábito, cosa, actividad)* to giv up: **dejó el tabaco** *he gave up smoking.* 3 *(permitir)* to allow, let: **déjale jugar** *let him play.* 4 *(prestar)* to lend. 5 *(ceder)* to give. 6 *(producir dinero)* to bring in make. 7 *(producir humo, ceniza)* to produce, leave. 8 *(aplazar)* to put off: **dejémoslo hasta mañana** *let' leave it till tomorrow.* 9 *(omitir)* to leave out, omit. 10 *(causar un efecto)* to make: **le película me ha dejado triste** *the film made me sad.* 11 *(legar)* to bequeath leave. ■ **dejar** ALGO **por imposible** to give up on STH. **dejar en paz** to leave alone. ‖ **dejar preocupado,-a** to worry. ‖ **dejarse llevar por** ALGN to be influenced by SB. ‖ **dejarse oír** 1 *(gen)* to be heard. 2 *(gritar)* to make OS heard.
▷ *aux* 1 **dejar de** + *inf (cesar - voluntariamente)* to stop + ger, give up + *ger*; *(- involuntariamente)* to stop + *ger*: **ha dejado de llover** *it's stopped raining.* 2 **no dejar de**

+ *inf* not to fail *to + inf*: **no deja de sorprenderme** *she never fails to surprise me.* 3 **dejar + *pp***: **lo dejó escrito en su agenda** *he wrote it down in his diary.*

▷ *vpr* **dejarse** 1 *(abandonarse)* to neglect OS, let OS go. 2 *(olvidar)* to forget, leave behind: **me he dejado las llaves en casa** *I've left my keys at home.* 3 *(permitir)* to let OS, allow OS to. ■ **dejarse llevar por** ALGN to be influenced by SB. ‖ **dejarse oír** 1 *(gen)* to be heard. 2 *(gritar)* to make OS heard.

▷ *vpr* **dejarse de** *(cesar)* to stop: **déjate de tonterías** *don't be silly.*

del *contr (de + el)* → **de**.

delación *nf* denunciation, accusation.

delantal *nm* apron, pinafore.

delante *adv* 1 *(enfrente)* in front; *(adelantado)* in front, ahead. 2 **de delante** in front. 3 **delante de** in front of, ahead of, before: **delante de mis ojos** *before my eyes.* 4 **por delante** in front, ahead: **tenemos mucho tiempo por delante** *we've got plenty of time ahead.*

delantera *nf* 1 *(frente)* front (part). 2 DEP forward line, forwards *pl.* 3 *(ventaja)* lead, advantage. ■ **llevar la delantera** to be in the lead, be ahead.

delantero,-a *adj* 1 front, front part: **el asiento delantero** *the front seat.* 2 MAR fore.

▷ *nm* **delantero** 1 DEP forward. 2 COST front. ● **delantero centro** centre (US center) forward.

delatar *vt* 1 to inform on. 2 *(revelar)* to give away, reveal.

▷ *vpr* **delatarse** to give OS away.

delator,-ra *adj* 1 accusing, denouncing. 2 *(reveladora)* which gives away.

▷ *nm & nf* accuser, denouncer.

delegación *nf* 1 *(gen)* delegation. 2 *(cargo)* office. 3 *(oficina)* branch, local office.

delegado,-a *adj* delegated.

▷ *nm & nf* 1 delegate. 2 COM representative.

delegar [7] *vt* to delegate.

deleitar *vt* to delight, please.

▷ *vpr* **deleitarse** to delight (**con/en**, in), take delight (**con/en**, in).

deleite *nm* pleasure, delight.

deletrear *vt* 1 to spell, spell out. 2 *fig (descifrar)* to decipher.

deletreo *nm* 1 spelling (out). 2 *fig (desciframiento)* deciphering.

deleznable *adj* 1 *(que se rompe fácilmente)* fragile, crumbly. 2 *(resbaladizo)* slippery. 3 *fig (inconsistente)* weak. 4 *fig (despreciable)* despicable, contemptible.

delfín[1] *nm* HIST dauphin.

delfín[2] *nm (animal)* dolphin.

delgadez *nf* 1 *(esbeltez)* slenderness, slimness. 2 *(flacura)* thinness.

delgado,-a *adj* 1 *(poco ancho)* thin. 2 *(esbelto)* slim, slender. 3 *(flaco)* thin. 4 *fig (voz)* soft.

delgaducho,-a *adj pey* skinny, scrawny.

deliberación *nf* deliberation.

deliberadamente *adv* deliberately.

deliberado,-a *adj* deliberate, intentional.

deliberar *vt* to decide.

▷ *vi* to deliberate (**sobre**, on).

delicadeza *nf* 1 *(finura)* delicacy, daintiness. 2 *(tacto)* thoughtfulness; *(refinamiento)* refinement. 3 *(de salud)* frailty, delicacy.

delicado,-a *adj* 1 *(fino)* delicate; *(exquisito)* exquisite; *(refinado)* refined. 2 *(difícil)* delicate, difficult: **una situación delicada** *a delicate situation.* 3 *(frágil)* fragile.

delicia *nf* delight, pleasure.

delicioso,-a *adj* delightful, charming; *(una comida)* delicious.

delictivo,-a *adj* criminal, punishable.

delimitar *vt* 1 *(terreno)* to delimit, mark off. 2 *(definir)* to define, specify.

delincuencia *nf* delinquency.

delincuente *adj* delinquent.

▷ *nm o nf* delinquent.

delineante *nm o nf (hombre)* draughtsman; *(mujer)* draughtswoman.

delinear *vt* to delineate, outline, sketch.

delinquir [9] *vi* to break the law, commit an offence (US offense).

delirante *adj* delirious, frenzied.

delirar *vi* 1 to be delirious. 2 *fig (decir despropósitos)* to talk nonsense.

delirio *nm* 1 *(desvarío)* delirium. 2 *fig (disparate)* nonsense. ● **delirios de grandeza** delusions of grandeur.

delito *nm* offence (US offense), crime.

delta *nf* 1 *(letra)* delta. 2 *(ala delta)* hang-gliding.

▷ *nm* GEOG delta.

deltoides *adj inv* deltoid.

▷ *nm* deltoid.

demacración *nf* emaciation.

demacrado,-a *pp* demacrar.

▷ *adj (gen)* emaciated; *(cara)* haggard, drawn.

demagogia *nf* demagoguery, demagogy.

demagógico,-a *adj* demagogic, demagogical.

demagogo,-a *nm & nf* demagogue.

demanda *nf* 1 *(petición)* petition, request. 2 *(pregunta)* inquiry. 3 COM *(pedido de mercancías)* demand. 4 JUR lawsuit. ■ **en demanda de** asking for. ‖ **presentar una demanda contra** ALGN to take legal action against SB.

demandado,-a *nm & nf* defendant.

demandante *nm o nf* 1 JUR plaintiff. 2 *(persona que busca)* → **seeker, hunter.** *(persona que compra)* buyer. ● **demandante de empleo** job hunter.

demandar *vt* 1 *(pedir)* to request, ask for; *(desear)* to desire. 2 JUR to sue.

demarcación *nf* 1 *(separación)* demarcation. 2 *(territorio)* district, zone.

demarcar [1] *vt* to demarcate.

demás *adj* other, rest of.

▷ *pron* the other, the rest: **los demás llegaron tarde** *the others arrived late.*

▷ *adv* besides, moreover. ■ **por demás** 1 *(inútil)* in vain, useless. 2 *(muy, demasiado)* too. ‖ **por lo demás** apart from that, otherwise. ‖ **todo lo demás** everything else.

demasía *nf* 1 *(exceso)* excess, surplus. 2 *(abuso)* abuse, outrage. 3 *(descaro)* insolence, impudence.

demasiado,-a *adj (singular)* too much; *(plural)* too many.

▷ *adv (modificador de adjetivo)* too; *(modificador de verbo)* too much: **es demasiado gordo** *he's too fat;* **bebes demasiado** *you drink too much.*

demencia *nf* **1** insanity, madness, dementia. **2** *fig (disparate)* silly thing. ● **demencia senil** senile dementia.

demencial *adj* chaotic.

demente *adj* mad, insane.
▷ *nm o nf* **1** *(persona enferma)* mental patient. **2** *(loco, chalado)* lunatic.

demiurgo *nm* demiurge.

democracia *nf* democracy.

demócrata *adj* democratic.
▷ *nm o nf* democrat.

democrático,-a *adj* democratic.

democratización *nf* democratization.

democratizar [4] *vt* to democratize.
▷ *vpr* **democratizarse** to democratize.

demografía *nf* demography.

demográfico,-a *adj* demographic.

demoledor,-ra *adj* **1** demolishing. **2** *fig* devastating: **fue una crítica demoledora** *that was a devastating criticism.*

demoler [32] *vt* **1** to demolish, pull down, tear down. **2** *fig* to demolish, tear to pieces.

demolición *nf* demolition.

demoniaco,-a *adj* demoniacal, demonic, possessed by the devil.

demonio *nm* demon, devil. ■ **¿cómo/dónde/quién/qué demonios...?** *fam* how/where/who/what the hell...? ‖ **¡demonios!** *fam* hell!, damn!

demora *nf* delay.

demorar *vt (retrasar)* to delay, hold up.
▷ *vpr* **demorarse 1** *(retrasarse)* to be delayed, be held up. **2** *(detenerse en alguna parte)* to stop, linger.

demostrable *adj* demonstrable.

demostración *nf* **1** *(gen)* demonstration. **2** *(manifestación)* show, display: **una demostración deportiva** *a sports display.* **3** MAT proof.

demostrar [31] *vt* **1** *(probar)* to prove, show. **2** *(hacer una demostración)* to demonstrate, show. **3** *(manifestar)* to show: **demostró buena voluntad** *she showed goodwill.* **4** MAT to prove.

demostrativo,-a *adj* demonstrative.
▷ *nm* demonstrative.

demudar *vt (gen)* to change, alter.

dendrita *nf* dendrite.

denegación *nf (rechazo)* refusal; *(negación)* denial.

denegar [48] *vt (desestimar)* to refuse; *(negar)* to deny.

dengue *nm* **1** *(melindre)* affectation, fussiness. **2** *(enfermedad)* dengue fever.

denigración *nf* denigration, disparagement.

denigrante *adj* denigrating, disparaging.

denigrar *vt* **1** to denigrate, disparage, run down. **2** *(insultar)* to insult, revile.

denominación *nf* **1** *(acción)* denomination, naming. **2** *(nombre)* denomination, name. ● **denominación de origen** *(vinos)* guarantee of origin, ± appellation d'origine contrôlée.

denominado,-a ● **número denominado** MAT compound number.

denominador,-ra *adj* denominative.
▷ *nm* **denominador** MAT denominator. ● **mínimo co mún denominador** lowest common denominator.

denominar *vt* to denominate, name.

denotar *vt* to denote, indicate, show: **su rostro de notaba cierto disgusto** *his face showed displeasure.*

densidad *nf* **1** *(gen)* density. **2** *fig (espesura)* thick ness, denseness. **3** *fig (oscuridad)* darkness. ● **dens dad de población** population density. ‖ **doble dens dad** double density. ‖ **alta densidad** high density.

densificar [1] *vt* **1** to make dense, densify. **2** *(espe sar)* to thicken.

denso,-a *adj* **1** *(gen)* dense; *(espeso)* dense, thick. **2** *f (oscuro)* dark.

dentado,-a *adj* **1** *(con dientes)* toothed. **2** *(cuchill* serrated. **3** BOT dentate.
▷ *nm* **dentado** perforation.

dentadura *nf* teeth *pl*, set of teeth. ● **dentadur postiza** false teeth *pl*, dentures *pl.*

dental *adj* dental.
▷ *nm* LING dental. ● **cepillo dental** toothbrush. ‖ **crem dental** toothpaste.

dentellada *nf* **1** *(movimiento)* snap of the jaws. **2** *(mo disco)* bite. **3** *(señal)* tooth mark.

dentellear *vt* to nibble (at).

dentera *nf fig (envidia)* envy. ■ **dar dentera a** ALG **1** *(dar grima)* to set SB's teeth on edge. **2** *(dar envidi* to make SB green with envy.

dentición *nf* **1** *(acción de dentar)* teething, dentitior cutting of the teeth. **2** *(época en que dentan los niños* dentition. **3** *(serie de dientes)* set of teeth.

dentífrico,-a *adj* tooth. ● **pasta dentífrica** tooth paste.
▷ *nm* **dentífrico** toothpaste.

dentina *nf* dentine (US dentin).

dentista *nm o nf* dentist. ■ **ir al dentista** to go to th dentist's.

dentro *adv* inside; *(de edificio)* indoors, inside: **est ahí dentro** *it's in there.* ■ **dentro de 1** *(lugar)* in, in side. **2** *(tiempo)* in: **dentro de la casa** *in the house;* **den tro de una semana** *in a week, in a week's time.* ‖ **den tro de lo posible** as far as possible. ‖ **dentro de poc** soon, shortly. ‖ **por dentro 1** *(de una cosa)* (on the inside. **2** *(de una persona)* deep down, inside, in wardly.

denuedo *nm* bravery, courage.

denuesto *nm* insult, affront.

denuncia *nf* **1** *(acusación)* accusation, formal com plaint, report; *(delación)* denunciation. **2** JUR *(acción* reporting; *(documento)* report. ■ **presentar una de nuncia contra** ALGN to lodge a complaint against SB bring an action against SB, report SB.

denunciar [12] *vt* **1** *(poner una denuncia)* to report. **2** *(da noticia)* to denounce. **3** *(indicar)* to indicate.

deontología *nf* deontology.

deparar *vt* **1** *(presentar)* to bring, hold in store: **nadi sabe lo que el destino nos deparará** *nobody know what fate holds in store for us.* **2** *(proporcionar)* to give afford.

departamento *nm* **1** *(sección)* department, sectior **2** *(provincia)* district, province. **3** *(de tren)* compart ment. **4** *(de un objeto)* compartment, section.

departir *vi fml* to talk, converse.

dependencia *nf* 1 *(hecho de depender)* dependence. 2 *(política)* dependency. 3 *(departamento)* department, section. 4 *(habitación)* room, outbuilding. 5 *(sucursal)* branch.

depender *vi* 1 to depend (**de**, on): **depende de ti** *it's up to you.* 2 *(estar bajo el mando o autoridad)* to be under, be answerable to; *(necesitar)* to be dependent on: **aún depende de sus padres** *she's still dependent on her parents.*

dependienta *nf* shop assistant, salesgirl, saleswoman.

dependiente *adj* dependent (**de**, on).
▷ *nm o nf* shop assistant, salesman.

depilación *nf* depilation, hair removal. ■ **depilación a la cera** waxing.

depilar *vt* to depilate, remove the hair from; *(cejas)* to pluck.

depilatorio,-a *adj* depilatory. ● **crema depilatoria** hair-removing cream.
▷ *nm* **depilatorio** depilatory.

deplorable *adj* deplorable, regrettable.

deplorar *vt* to deplore, lament, regret deeply.

deponente *adj* 1 JUR testifying. 2 LING deponent.
▷ *nm o nf* JUR deponent, witness.
▷ *nm* LING deponent verb.

deponer [78] *vt* 1 *(dejar)* to lay down, set aside; *(las armas)* to lay down. 2 *(destituir)* to remove from office; *(a un rey)* to depose. 3 JUR *(exponer)* to declare, testify, give evidence about.
▷ *vi (defecar)* to defecate.
▲ *pp* **depuesto,-a**.

deportación *nf* deportation.

deportado,-a *adj* deported.
▷ *nm & nf* deportee, deported person.

deportar *vt* to deport.

deporte *nm* sport: **¿practicas algún deporte?** *do you do any sport?, do you play any sport?* ■ **hacer deporte** to do some sport.

deportista *adj* sporty, keen on sport.
▷ *nm o nf (hombre)* sportsman; *(mujer)* sportswoman.

deportividad *nf* sportsmanship.

deportivo,-a *adj* 1 *(aficionado al deporte)* sporting, sporty. 2 *(relacionado con el deporte)* sports: **club deportivo** *sports club.* 3 *(informal)* casual: **ropa deportiva** *casual clothes.* 4 *fig (correcto)* sportsmanlike, sporting.
▷ *nm* **deportivo** *(coche)* sports car.

deposición *nf* 1 *(destitución)* removal from office; *(de un rey)* deposition, deposal. 2 JUR testimony, deposition, evidence. 3 *fml (defecación)* defecation.

depositar *vt* 1 *(dinero, joyas)* to deposit. 2 *(colocar)* to place, put. 3 *fig (dar, conceder)* to place: **depositó en ella su confianza** *he placed his trust in her.* 4 *(almacenar)* to store. 5 *(sedimentar)* to deposit.
▷ *vpr* **depositarse** *(caer en el fondo)* to settle.

depositario,-a *nm & nf* 1 *(de algo material)* depositary, trustee; *(de algo inmaterial)* repository. 2 *(tesorero)* treasurer.

depósito *nm* 1 *(recipiente)* tank. 2 *(almacén)* store, warehouse, depot. 3 *(financiero)* deposit. 4 *(sedimento)* deposit, sediment. ■ **en depósito** in bond. ● **depósito de cadáveres** mortuary, morgue. ‖ **depósito de gasolina** petrol tank.

depravado,-a *adj* depraved.
▷ *nm & nf* depraved person, degenerate.

depre *nf fam* depression, downer.
▷ *adj fam* low, down, depressed.

depreciación *nf* depreciation.

depreciar [12] *vt* to depreciate.
▷ *vpr* **depreciarse** to depreciate.

depredación *nf* 1 *(saqueo)* pillaging, plundering. 2 *(malversación)* misappropriation (of funds), embezzlement.

depredador,-ra *adj* depredatory.
▷ *nm & nf* depredator, pillager.

depredar *vt* to depredate, pillage.

depresión *nf* depression: **depresión atmosférica** *atmospheric depression.* ● **depresión nerviosa** nervous breakdown.

depresivo,-a *adj* 1 *(deprimente)* depressing. 2 MED depressive.

deprimente *adj* depressing.

deprimido,-a *adj* depressed.

deprimir *vt* to depress.
▷ *vpr* **deprimirse** to get depressed.

deprisa *adv* quickly.

depuración *nf* 1 *(del agua)* purification; *(de la sangre)* cleansing. 2 *fig (purga)* purge, purging.

depurado,-a *adj (pulido)* elaborate, carefully worked: **un estilo depurado** *a carefully worked style.*

depurador,-ra *adj* purifying.
▷ *nm* **depurador** *(sustancia)* depurative; *(aparato)* purifier.

depurar *vt* 1 *(purificar agua)* to purify, depurate; *(sangre)* to cleanse. 2 POL to purge. 3 *fig (perfeccionar)* to purify, refine.

derecha *nf* 1 *(mano)* right hand. 2 *(lugar)* right: **dame el de la derecha** *give me the one on the right.* 3 **la derecha** POL the right, the right wing.

derechista *adj* right-wing, rightist.
▷ *nm & nf* right-winger, rightist.

derecho,-a *adj* 1 right: **la mano derecha** *the right hand.* 2 *(recto)* straight, upright.
▷ *adv* **derecho** straight: **se fue derecho a la cama** *he went straight to bed.*
▷ *nm* **derecho** 1 *(leyes)* law. 2 *(privilegio)* right: **los derechos de las minorías** *the rights of minority groups.* 3 *(de una tela, calcetín, etc)* right side. ■ **estar en su derecho** to be within one's rights. ‖ **no hacer nada a derechas** *fig* to do nothing right. ‖ **¡no hay derecho!** it's not fair! ‖ **tener derecho a** to be entitled to, have the right to. ● **derecho civil** civil law. ‖ **derecho de admisión** right *sing* to refuse admission. ‖ **derecho mercantil** commercial law, mercantile law. ‖ **derecho penal** criminal law. ‖ **derecho político** constitutional law. ‖ **derechos humanos** human rights.
▷ *nm pl* **derechos** *(impuestos)* duties, taxes; *(tarifa)* fees. ● **derechos de matrícula** registration fees.

deriva *nf* drift. ■ **ir a la deriva** to drift.

derivación *nf* 1 LING derivation. 2 *(en electricidad)* shunt. 3 *(de una carretera)* turn-off, diversion.

derivada *nf* MAT derivative.

derivado,-a *adj* derived, derivative.

▷ *nm* **derivado 1** LING derivative. **2** *(subproducto)* derivative, byproduct.

derivar *vi* **1** *(proceder)* to spring, arise, come, stem. **2** MAR to drift. **3** LING to be derived (**de**, from), derive (**de**, from). **4** *(conducir)* to drift: **la conversación derivó hacia otro tema** *the conversation drifted onto a different subject.*

▷ *vt* **1** *(dirigir)* to direct, divert. **2** LING to derive. **3** *(en electricidad)* to shunt. **4** MAT to derive.

▷ *vpr* **derivarse 1** *(proceder)* to result (**de**, from), stem (**de**, from). **2** LING to be derived (**de**, from).

derivativo,-a *adj* derivative.

▷ *nm* **derivativo** derivative.

dermatitis *nf inv* dermatitis.

dermatología *nf* dermatology.

dermatólogo,-a *nm & nf* dermatologist.

dermatosis *nf inv* dermatosis.

dérmico,-a *adj* dermal, dermic, skin.

dermis *nf inv* dermis.

dermoprotector,-ra *adj* which is kind to the skin.

derogación *nf* abolition, repeal.

derogar [7] *vt* **1** JUR to abolish, repeal. **2** *(contrato)* to rescind, cancel.

derramar *vt* **1** to pour out, spill. **2** *(sangre, lágrimas)* to shed. **3** *(impuestos, etc)* to share out, distribute.

derrame *nm* **1** pouring out, spilling. **2** *(de sangre, lágrimas)* shedding. **3** *(pérdida)* leak, leakage. **4** MED discharge. **5** ARQUIT splay. ● **derrame cerebral** MED brain haemorrhage.

derrapaje *nm* skid.

derrapar *vi* to skid.

derrape *nm* skid.

derredor *nm* surroundings *pl*. ■ **al/en derredor** round, around.

See also **alrededor**.

derretido,-a *adj (gen)* melted; *(metales)* molten: **nieve derretida** *melted snow.* ■ **estar derretido,-a por** ALGN *fig* to be madly in love with SB.

derretir [34] *vt* **1** *(gen)* to melt; *(hielo, nieve)* to melt, thaw; *(metal)* to melt down. **2** *(dilapidar)* to waste, squander.

▷ *vpr* **derretirse 1** *(fundirse)* to melt; *(hielo, nieve)* to melt, thaw. **2** *fig (de amor)* to burn (**de**, with).

derribar *vt* **1** *(demoler)* to pull down, demolish, knock down. **2** *(hacer caer a una persona)* to knock over; *(de un caballo)* to throw. **3** *(avión, enemigo)* to shoot down, bring down. **4** *(una puerta)* to batter down. **5** *fig (gobierno)* to overthrow; *(ministro)* to topple.

derribo *nm (demolición)* demolition, knocking down, pulling down.

derrocar [1] *vt* **1** *(demoler)* to pull down, demolish, knock down. **2** *(gobierno)* to overthrow, bring down; *(ministro)* to oust from office, topple.

derrochar *vt* **1** *(dilapidar)* to waste, squander. **2** *fig (rebosar)* to be full of.

derroche *nm* **1** *(despilfarro)* waste, squandering. **2** *(abundancia)* profusion, abundance: **un derroche de energía** *a burst of energy.*

derrota *nm* **1** *(de un ejército)* defeat. **2** *(fracaso)* failure, setback.

derrotado,-a *adj* **1** defeated. **2** *(ropa)* worn out. *(andrajoso)* in tatters, ragged. **4** *fam (cansado)* tired bushed, whacked; *(deprimido)* depressed.

derrotar *vt* to defeat, beat: **me derrotó al tenis** *h beat me at tennis.*

derrotero *nm* **1** MAR *(rumbo)* course; *(dirección)* direction. **2** MAR *(libro)* book of charts. **3** *fig (camino, medio)* path, course of action.

derrotismo *nm* defeatism.

derrotista *adj* defeatist.

▷ *nm o nf* defeatist.

derruido,-a *adj* in ruins.

derruir [62] *vt* to pull down, demolish, knock down.

derrumbar *vt (demoler)* to pull down, demolish knock down.

▷ *vpr* **derrumbarse 1** *(un edificio)* to collapse, fall down *(un techo)* to fall in, cave in. **2** *fig* to collapse.

desabastecido,-a *adj* out of.

desabotonar *vt (desabrochar)* to unbutton, undo.

▷ *vi (abrirse las flores)* to open out, bloom, blossom.

desabrido,-a *adj* **1** *(comida)* tasteless, insipid. **2** *f (persona)* surly; *(tono)* harsh, sharp. **3** *(tiempo)* unpleasant.

desabrigado,-a *adj* **1** *(lugar)* open, exposed. **2** *f (sin protección)* unprotected, defenceless.

desabrigar [7] *vt (ropa)* to take someone's coat off

▷ *vpr* **desabrigarse** *(uso reflexivo)* to take off one's coat *(en la cama)* to throw off the bedclothes.

desabrochar *vt* to undo, unfasten.

▷ *vpr* **desabrocharse** *(una prenda)* to come undone come unfastened.

desacato *nm* **1** *(falta de respeto)* lack of respect (a for), disrespect (**a**, for). **2** JUR contempt (**a**, for). ■ **desacato a la autoridad** contempt.

desaceleración *nf* deceleration.

desacelerar *vi* to decelerate.

desacertado,-a *adj* **1** *(erróneo)* wrong, mistaken. **2** *(inadecuado)* unfortunate, unwise, inappropriate; *(sin tacto)* tactless: **un comentario desacertado** *a tactless remark, an unfortunate remark.*

desacertar [27] *vi* **1** *(fallar)* to be wrong, be mistaken. **2** *(faltar de tacto)* to lack tact, be tactless.

desacierto *nm* **1** *(error)* mistake. **2** *(falta de tacto)* lack of tact.

desacomodado,-a *adj* **1** *(sin empleo)* unemployed. **2** *(falto de medios económicos)* badly off, poor.

desaconsejable *adj* ill-advised, unwise.

desaconsejar *vt* to advise against.

desacorde *nm* **1** MÚS discordant. **2** *fig* clashing, discordant, conflicting; *(colores)* clashing: **opiniones desacordes** *conflicting opinions.*

desacostumbrado,-a *adj* unusual, strange.

desacostumbrar *vt (hacer perder un uso)* to break of a habit, get out of a habit.

▷ *vpr* **desacostumbrarse 1** *(perder la costumbre)* to get out of the habit (**de**, of), lose the habit (**de**, of), give up (**de**, -). **2** *(perder la tolerancia)* to be no longer used (**a**, to): **me he desacostumbrado al calor** *I'm no longer used to the heat, I can't take the heat any more.*

desacreditar *vt* to discredit, bring discredit on bring into discredit.

esactivar *vt* to defuse.

lesacuerdo *nm* disagreement. ■ **estar en desacuerdo con** to be in disagreement with.

lesafecto,-a *adj* disaffected, opposed.

▷ *nm* **desafecto** lack of affection, coldness.

lesafiante *adj* challenging, defiant.

lesafiar [13] *vt* 1 *(gen)* to defy. 2 *(no hacer caso a)* to flout; *(no obedecer)* to defy. 3 *(plantar cara a - persona)* to defy, stand up to; *(- dificultad)* to brave. ■ **desafiar a** ALGN **a hacer** ALGO to challenge SB to do STH, dare SB to do STH.

lesafilado,-a *adj* blunt.

lesafilar *vt* to blunt.

▷ *vpr* **desafilarse** to go blunt.

lesafinado,-a *adj* out of tune.

lesafinar *vi (gen)* to be out of tune; *(cantar)* to sing out of tune; *(tocar)* to play out of tune.

▷ *vt* to put out of tune.

▷ *vpr* **desafinarse** to go out of tune.

lesafío *nm* 1 *(reto)* challenge. 2 *(duelo)* duel. 3 *(provocación)* provocation, defiance.

lesaforado,-a *adj* 1 *(exagerado)* huge, enormous, terrible: **hizo un esfuerzo desaforado** *he made a great effort.* 2 *(escandaloso)* outrageous. 3 *(fuera de la ley)* lawless.

lesafortunadamente *adv* unfortunately.

lesafortunado,-a *adj* 1 *(sin suerte)* unlucky, unfortunate. 2 *(sin tino)* unfortunate.

lesagradable *adj* disagreeable, unpleasant.

lesagradar *vi* to displease: **me desagrada su música** *I don't like her music.*

lesagradecido,-a *adj* ungrateful.

▷ *nm & nf* ungrateful person.

lesagrado *nm* displeasure, discontent. ■ **con desagrado** reluctantly.

lesagraviar [12] *vt* 1 *(reparar el agravio)* to make amends for, make up for. 2 *(compensar el agravio)* to indemnify, compensate.

lesagravio *nm* amends *pl*, compensation.

lesaguar [22] *vt (extraer el agua)* to drain.

▷ *vi* 1 *(un líquido)* to drain, drain off/away; *(un contenedor)* to drain. 2 *(desembocar)* to flow (**en**, into), drain (**en**, into).

desagüe *nm* 1 *(acción)* draining, drainage. 2 *(agujero)* drain, outlet. 3 *(cañería)* waste pipe, drainpipe.

desaguisado,-a *adj* 1 *(contra la ley)* illegal, unlawful. 2 *(contra la razón)* outrageous.

▷ *nm* **desaguisado** 1 *(delito)* offence (US offense); *(atropello)* outrage. 2 *fig (destrozo)* damage; *(fechoría)* mischief.

desahogado,-a *adj* 1 *(espacioso)* roomy, spacious. 2 *(con dinero)* well-off, well-to-do, comfortable: **una posición desahogada** *comfortable circumstances.* 3 *fig (descarado)* cheeky, shameless, insolent.

desahogar [7] *vt* 1 *(consolar)* to comfort; *(aliviar)* to relieve. 2 *fig (mostrar)* to vent, pour out: **desahogó sus penas** *he vented his grief.*

▷ *vpr* **desahogarse** 1 *(desfogarse)* to let off steam: **¡desahógate!** *don't bottle it up!* 2 *(confiarse)* to open one's heart (**con**, to). 3 *(descargar un problema)* to get off one's chest.

desahogo *nm* 1 *(alivio)* relief. 2 *(esparcimiento)* amusement, relaxation. 3 *fig (económico)* comfort, ease: **viven con desahogo** *they live comfortably.*

desahuciado,-a *adj* 1 *(enfermo)* hopeless. 2 *(inquilino)* evicted.

desahuciar [12] *vt* 1 to deprive of all hope. 2 JUR *(inquilino)* to evict.

desahucio *nm* eviction.

desairado,-a *pp* → **desairar.**

▷ *adj* 1 *(sin gracia)* ungraceful; *(sin éxito)* unsuccessful; *(desagradable)* awkward. 2 *(humillante)* humiliating.

desairar *vt* 1 *(desatender)* to slight, snub. 2 *(desestimar)* to reject.

desaire *nm* 1 *(menosprecio)* slight, rebuff. 2 *(falta de gracia)* lack of charm. ■ **hacerle un desaire a** ALGN to snub SB.

desajustar *vt* 1 *(máquina)* to put out of order. 2 *fig (planes, etc)* to upset, spoil.

▷ *vpr* **desajustarse** *(máquina)* to go wrong, break down; *(piezas)* to come apart, pull apart; *(tornillo)* to come loose.

desajuste *nm* 1 *(mal funcionamiento)* maladjustment; *(avería)* breakdown. 2 *fig (planes, etc)* upsetting.

desalado,-a *adj* CULIN desalted.

desalar *vt* to desalt, remove the salt from.

desalentador,-ra *adj* discouraging, disheartening.

desalentar [27] *vt* 1 *(dificultar el aliento)* to leave breathless, make get out of breath. 2 *fig (quitar el ánimo)* to discourage, dishearten.

▷ *vpr* **desalentarse** to lose heart, get discouraged.

desaliento *nm* discouragement.

desalinear *vt* to put out of line.

desaliñado,-a *adj* untidy, unkempt, scruffy.

desaliñar *vt* to make untidy, make scruffy.

desaliño *nm* untidiness, scruffiness.

desalmado,-a *adj* 1 *(malvado)* wicked. 2 *(cruel)* cruel, heartless.

▷ *nm & nf* 1 *(malvado)* wicked person. 2 *(cruel)* cruel person, heartless person.

desalojar *vt* 1 *(marcharse)* to evacuate, clear, move out of. 2 *(inquilino)* to evict (**de**, from). 3 MAR to displace.

▷ *vi (mudarse)* to move house, move out.

desamarrar *vt* 1 *(desatar)* to untie. 2 MAR to unmoor, cast off.

desambientado,-a *adj* 1 *(persona)* out of place. 2 *(lugar)* lacking in atmosphere.

desamor *nm* 1 *(desafecto)* lack of affection. 2 *(frialdad)* coldness, indifference. 3 *(antipatía)* dislike.

desamortización *nf* disentailment.

desamortizar [4] *vt* to disentail.

desamparado,-a *adj* 1 *(persona)* helpless, unprotected. 2 *(lugar)* abandoned, forsaken.

desamparar *vt* 1 to abandon, desert, leave helpless. 2 JUR to renounce, relinquish.

desamparo *nm* 1 *(abandono)* abandonment, desertion. 2 *(falta de ayuda)* helplessness.

desamueblado,-a *adj* unfurnished.

desamueblar *vt* to remove the furniture from, clear the furniture from.

desandar [64] *vt* to go back over, retrace. ■ **desandar lo andado** to retrace one's steps.
desangelado,-a *adj* insipid, lacking in charm.
desangrar *vt* 1 *(sangrar)* to bleed. 2 *(desaguar)* to drain. 3 *fig (empobrecer)* to bleed dry.
▷ *vpr* **desangrarse** to bleed heavily, lose blood.
desanimado,-a *adj* 1 *(decaído)* dejected, downhearted. 2 *(espectáculo, etc)* dull, lifeless.
desanimar *vt* to discourage, dishearten.
▷ *vpr* **desanimarse** to be discouraged, be disheartened, lose heart.
desánimo *nm* despondency, discouragement, dejection.
desapacible *adj (gen)* unpleasant, disagreeable; *(tiempo)* nasty, unpleasant; *(sonido, tono)* harsh, unpleasant.
desaparecer [43] *vi (dejar de estar)* to disappear.
desaparecido,-a *adj* missing.
▷ *nm & nf* missing person: **había diez desaparecidos** *there were ten missing.*
desaparición *nf* disappearance.
desapasionado,-a *adj* dispassionate, objective, impartial.
desapasionar *vt* to make lose interest.
▷ *vpr* **desapasionarse** to lose interest.
desapegar [7] *vt* to estrange.
▷ *vpr* **desapegarse** to become estranged (**de**, from), distance OS (**de**, from).
desapego *nm* 1 *(indiferencia)* indifference. 2 *(distanciamiento)* distancing. 3 *(falta de afecto)* coolness, lack of affection.
desapercibido,-a *adj* 1 *(inadvertido)* unnoticed. 2 *(desprevenido)* unprepared, unready. ■ **pasar desapercibido,-a** to go unnoticed.
desaprensión *nf* unscrupulousness.
desaprensivo,-a *adj* unscrupulous.
▷ *nm & nf* unscrupulous person.
desaprobación *nf* disapproval.
desaprobar [31] *vt* to disapprove of.
desaprovechado,-a *adj* 1 *(falto de rendimiento)* unused: 2 *(desperdiciado)* wasted.
desaprovechar *vt* 1 *(no sacar suficiente provecho)* not to take advantage of. 2 *(desperdiciar)* to waste. ■ **desaprovechar una ocasión** to miss an opportunity, waste an opportunity.
desarbolar *vt* to dismast.
desarmado,-a *adj* 1 *(sin armas)* unarmed. 2 *(desmontado)* dismantled, taken to pieces.
desarmar *vt* 1 *(quitar las armas)* to disarm. 2 *(desmontar)* to dismantle, take apart, take to pieces: **el mecánico desmontó el motor** *the mechanic stripped the engine down.*
desarme *nm* 1 disarmament. 2 *(de una máquina)* dismantling. ● **desarme nuclear** nuclear disarmament.
desarraigado,-a *adj* 1 *(árbol)* uprooted. 2 *fig (persona)* rootless, without roots, uprooted. 3 *fig (eliminado)* eradicated.
desarraigar [7] *vt* 1 *(árbol, persona)* to uproot. 2 *fig (eliminar)* to eradicate, wipe out.
▷ *vpr* **desarraigarse** 1 *(árbol)* to become uprooted. 2 *fig (persona)* to pull up one's roots.
desarraigo *nm* 1 *(de árbol, persona)* uprooting. 2 *f (de hábito, etc)* eradication.
desarreglar *vt* 1 *(desordenar)* make untidy, mes up, untidy. 2 *(estropear)* to spoil, upset.
desarreglo *nm* mess, untidiness, disorder, confu sion.
desarrollado,-a *adj* developed: **es un país desarro llado** *it's a developed country;* **este niño está muy de sarrollado para su edad** *this boy is quite grown up f his age.*
desarrollar *vt* 1 *(gen)* to develop. 2 *(deshacer un roll* to unroll, unfold. 3 *(exponer)* to expound, explai 4 *(llevar a cabo)* to carry out: **desarrollar un proyect** *to carry out a project.* 5 MAT to expand, develop.
▷ *vpr* **desarrollarse** 1 *(crecer)* to develop. 2 *(transcurri* to take place: **la novela se desarrolla en el siglo XI** *the novel is set in the 19th century.*
desarrollo *nm* 1 *(gen)* development. 2 MAT expan sion. 3 DEP run, course. ● **país en vías de desarroll** developing country.
desarticulado,-a *adj* disjointed: **un discurso desa ticulado** *a disjointed speech.*
desarticular *vt* 1 MED to disarticulate, put out o joint, dislocate. 2 *(un mecanismo)* to take to pieces 3 *fig (organización, banda, plan, etc)* to break up, dis mantle.
desaseado,-a *adj* 1 *(sucio)* untidy, dirty. 2 *(dejado* untidy, slovenly, unkempt, scruffy.
▷ *nm & nf* untidy person, scruff.
desasear *vt* 1 *(ensuciar)* to dirty. 2 *(desordenar)* t mess up.
desasir [65] *vt* to release, let go of.
▷ *vpr* **desasirse** *fig (desprenderse)* to rid OS (**de**, of), ge rid (**de**, of).
desasistido,-a *adj* neglected.
desasistir *vt* to abandon, desert, forsake.
desasnar *vt fam* to civilize, refine, teach good man ners to.
desasosegado,-a *adj* restless, anxious.
desasosegar [48] *vt* to make restless, make un easy.
▷ *vpr* **desasosegarse** to become restless, become un easy.
desasosiego *nm* uneasiness, anxiety, restlessness
desastrado,-a *adj* 1 *(desgraciado)* unfortunate. 2 *(desa seado)* untidy, slovenly, unkempt, scruffy.
▷ *nm & nf* untidy person, scruff.
desastre *nm* 1 *(catástrofe)* disaster, catastrophe. 2 *fan (calamidad)* disaster, flop: **la excursión fue un desas tre** *the trip was a washout.*
desastroso,-a *adj* disastrous.
desatar *vt* 1 *(soltar - gen)* to untie, undo, unfasten; *(- pe rro, etc)* to let loose: **desata al perro** *let the dog loose.* 2 *fig (desencadenar)* to spark off, give rise to; *(pasiones,* to unleash.
▷ *vpr* **desatarse** 1 *(soltarse)* to come untied, come un done, come unfastened. 2 *fig (desencadenarse)* tc break, explode: **se desató una gran tormenta** *a grea storm broke.*
desatascador *nm* plunger.
desatascar [1] *vt* to unblock, clear.

desatención *nf* 1 *(falta de atención)* lack of attention. 2 *(descortesía)* impoliteness, discourtesy, disrespect.

desatender [28] *vt* 1 *(no prestar atención)* to pay no attention to. 2 *(no hacer caso)* to neglect, disregard: desatendió las órdenes *he disregarded the orders.*

desatento,-a *adj* 1 *(distraído)* inattentive: está muy desatento *he doesn't pay attention.* 2 *(descortés)* discourteous, impolite.

▷ *nm & nf (descortés)* impolite person, discourteous person.

desatinado,-a *adj* 1 *(imprudente)* rash, reckless. 2 *(tonto)* foolish, silly.

desatinar *vi (hacer)* to act foolishly; *(decir)* to talk nonsense.

▷ *vt* to make act foolishly.

desatino *nm* 1 *(error)* mistake, blunder. 2 *(locura)* foolishness; *(tontería)* nonsense, silly thing: decir desatinos *to talk nonsense.* 3 *(falta de tacto)* clumsiness, heavy-handedness.

desatornillar *vt* to unscrew.

desatrancar *vt* 1 *(una puerta - con tranca)* to unbar; *(- con cerrojo)* to unbolt. 2 *(un conducto)* to unblock, clear.

desautorización *nf* 1 disapproval. 2 *(mentís)* denial. 3 *(descrédito)* discredit.

desautorizado,-a *adj* 1 unauthorized. 2 *(prohibido)* banned, forbidden. 3 *(desmentido)* denied. 4 *(desacreditado)* discredited.

desautorizar [4] *vt* 1 *(desaprobar)* to disapprove. 2 *(prohibir)* to ban, forbid: el gobierno desautorizó la manifestación *the Government banned the demonstration.* 3 *(desmentir)* to deny. 4 *(desacreditar)* to discredit.

desavenencia *nf* 1 *(desacuerdo)* disagreement, discord. 2 *(riña)* quarrel, row.

desavenir [90] *vt* to cause to quarrel.

▷ *vpr* desavenirse to quarrel.

desayunar *vi* to have breakfast, breakfast.

▷ *vt* to have for breakfast.

desayuno *nm* breakfast.

desazón *nf* 1 *(desabrimiento)* lack of flavour (US flavor), tastelessness. 2 *fig (disgusto)* grief, affliction, worry.

desazonado,-a *adj* 1 *fig (disgustado)* upset. 2 *fig (inquieto)* anxious, uneasy. 3 *(soso)* tasteless, insipid.

desazonar *vt* 1 *(quitar el sabor)* to make tasteless. 2 *fig (disgustar)* to annoy, upset. 3 *fig (inquietar)* to make uneasy, worry.

▷ *vpr* desazonarse 1 *fig (disgustarse)* to get upset. 2 *fig (inquietarse)* to worry. 3 *fig (sentirse indispuesto)* to feel unwell, feel off-colour (US off-color).

desbancar [1] *vt* 1 *(en el juego)* to clean out. 2 *fig (suplantar)* to supplant, replace, take the place of.

desbandada *nf* scattering.

desbandarse *vpr* to scatter, disperse.

desbarajuste *nm* disorder, confusion, mess: ¡qué desbarajuste! *what a mess!*

desbaratamiento *nm* 1 *(desarreglo)* wrecking, destruction. 2 *(frustración)* frustration. 3 *(derroche)* waste, squandering. 4 MIL rout.

desbaratar *vt* 1 *(desarreglar)* to spoil, ruin, wreck. 2 *(frustrar)* to spoil, ruin: nos desbarató los planes *she spoilt our plans.* 3 *(malgastar)* to waste, squander. 4 MIL to rout, throw into confusion.

desbarrar *vi* 1 *fig (hablar)* to talk nonsense. 2 *fig (actuar)* to act foolishly, do silly things.

desbastar *vt* 1 *(madera)* to rough plane; *(piedra)* to smooth down; *(metal)* to rough down. 2 *fig* to refine, polish.

desbloquear *vt* 1 TÉC to free. 2 FIN to unfreeze. 3 *(un sitio)* to lift the blockade on.

desbloqueo *nm* 1 TÉC freeing. 2 FIN unfreezing. 3 *(de un sitio)* lifting of the blockade.

desbocado,-a *adj* 1 *(arma)* wide-mouthed, bell-mouthed. 2 *(jarra)* with a chipped mouth. 3 *(caballo)* runaway. 4 *(una prenda)* loose-fitting. 5 *(río)* overflowing. 6 *fig (imaginación)* wild. 7 *fig (mal hablado)* foul-mouthed.

desbocar [1] *vt* 1 *(jarra)* to break the mouth of. 2 *(una prenda)* to tear open, rip open.

▷ *vi (desembocar)* to flow (en, into).

▷ *vpr* desbocarse 1 *(caballo)* to run away, bolt. 2 *(una prenda)* to tear open. 3 *fig (persona)* to blow up, let out a stream of abuse.

desbordar *vt* 1 *(sobrepasar)* to overflow. 2 *fig (exceder)* to surpass, exceed: eso desborda mis conocimientos *that's way over my head.*

▷ *vi (salirse)* to overflow: el río desbordó *the river overflowed.*

▷ *vpr* desbordarse 1 *(salirse)* to overflow, flood. 2 *fig* to burst.

desbrozar [4] *vt (terreno)* to clear of weeds, clear of undergrowth; *(paso)* to clear.

descabalar *vt* 1 *(dejar incompleto)* to leave incomplete. 2 *(desnivelar)* to make uneven.

descabalgar [7] *vi* to dismount.

descabellado,-a *adj fig* wild, crazy: eso es totalmente descabellado *that's absolutely crazy;* una idea descabellada *a crackpot idea.*

descacharrar *vt fam (romper)* to break; *(estropear)* to ruin, mess up, spoil.

descafeinado,-a *adj* 1 decaffeinated. 2 *fam fig* watered-down.

▷ *nm* descafeinado decaffeinated coffee.

descafeinar [17] *vt* to decaffeinate.

descalabrar *vt* 1 *(herir)* to injure; *(en la cabeza)* to injure in the head. 2 *fig (causar daño)* to ruin, damage.

▷ *vpr* descalabrarse to injure one's head.

descalabro *nm* misfortune, damage, loss: sufrir un descalabro *to suffer a misfortune.*

descalcificación *nf* decalcification.

descalcificar [1] *vt* to decalcify.

▷ *vpr* descalcificarse to become decalcified.

descalificación *nf* 1 disqualification. 2 *(descrédito)* discredit.

descalificar [1] *vt* 1 to disqualify. 2 *(desacreditar)* to discredit.

descalzar [4] *vt (zapatos)* to take off SB's shoes.

▷ *vpr* descalzarse 1 *(persona)* to take off one's shoes. 2 *(caballo)* to lose a shoe.

descalzo,-a *adj* 1 barefoot, barefooted. 2 REL barefoot. 3 *fig (pobre)* poor.

▷ *nm & nf* REL *(hombre)* barefoot monk; *(mujer)* barefoot nun.
descamación *nf* desquamation, flaking, flakiness.
descamarse *vpr* to desquamate, flake off.
descampado,-a *nm* open space, open field.
descansado,-a *adj* **1** rested, refreshed. **2** *(tranquilo)* easy, effortless.
descansar *vi* **1** *(gen)* to rest, have a rest; *(un momento)* to take a break. **2** *(dormir)* to sleep: **¡que descanses!** *sleep well!* **3** *(confiar)* to rely (**en**, on): **se puede descansar en él** *you can rely on him.* **4** *(apoyarse)* to rest (**sobre**, on), be supported (**sobre**, by).
descansillo *nm* landing.
descanso *nm* **1** rest, break. **2** *(en un espectáculo)* interval; *(en un partido)* interval, half-time. **3** *(alivio)* relief, comfort: **¡qué descanso!** *what a relief!* **4** *(rellano)* landing.
descapitalizar [4] *vt (perder el capital)* to undercapitalize.
descapotable *adj* convertible.
▷ *nm* convertible.
descarado,-a *adj* **1** *(actitud)* shameless, brazen, insolent; *(persona)* cheeky. **2** *(patente)* blatant: **es una copia descarada de mi novela** *it's a blatant copy of my novel.*
▷ *nm & nf* shameless person, cheeky person.
descarga *nf* **1** *(acción)* unloading. **2** *(eléctrica)* discharge. **3** *(de fuego)* discharge, firing. **4** INFORMÁ download. ● **descarga cerrada** volley.
descargador *nm* **1** *(gen)* unloader. **2** *(estibador)* docker, stevedore.
descargar [7] *vt* **1** *(quitar una carga)* to unload. **2** *(disparar una arma)* to fire, discharge, shoot; *(vaciar una arma)* to unload: **descargaron salvas en su honor** *they fired a salute in his honour.* **3** INFORMÁ to download.
▷ *vi* **1** ELEC to discharge. **2** *(tormenta)* to break; *(nubes)* to burst. **3** *(desembocar)* to flow.
▷ *vpr* **descargarse 1** *(pilas, baterías)* to discharge. **2** *(desahogarse)* to blow up. **3** JUR to clear OS.
descargo *nm* **1** *(descarga)* unloading. **2** COM credit. **3** *fig (excusa)* excuse; *(alivio)* relief. ■ **en/para su descargo** in his defence (US defense).
descarnado,-a *adj fig* straightforward, plain.
descaro *nm* impudence, cheek, nerve. ■ **¡qué descaro!** what a cheek!, what a nerve!, of all the cheek!
descarriado,-a *adj fig* lost. ■ **ser la oveja descarriada** *fig* to be the lost sheep.
descarriar [13] *vt* **1** *(apartar del camino)* to send the wrong way, put on the wrong road, misdirect. **2** *fig* to lead astray.
▷ *vpr* **descarriarse 1** *(perderse)* to lose one's way, get lost, go the wrong way. **2** *fig* to go astray.
descarrilar *vi* to be derailed, run off the rails, go off the rails.
descartar *vt* to discard, reject, rule out: **descartamos esa posibilidad** *we ruled out that possibility.*
descascarillar *vt* to husk.
▷ *vpr* **descascarillarse** to chip, peel, flake off.
descastado,-a *adj* **1** *(poco cariñoso)* unaffectionate, cold. **2** *(desagradecido)* ungrateful.
▷ *nm & nf* **1** *(poco cariñoso)* unaffectionate person. **2** *(desagradecido)* ungrateful person.
descendencia *nf* offspring, descendants *pl.*
descendente *adj* descending, downward.
descender [28] *vi* **1** to descend, go down, com[e] down. **2** *(temperatura, nivel, etc)* to drop, fall, g[o] down. **3** *(ser descendiente)* to descend (**de**, from), is[sue] (**de**, from). **4** *(provenir)* to come (**de**, from).
▷ *vt* **1** *(llevar más bajo)* to take down, bring dow[n,] lower. **2** *(bajar)* to go down: **descendió la escaler[a] muy rápidamente** *he went down the stairs very quickl[y]*
descendiente *nm o nf* descendant; *(hijos)* off[]spring.
descenso *nm* **1** *(acción)* descent, lowering. **2** *(de temperatura)* drop, fall. **3** *fig (declive)* decline, fall. **4** DE[P] *(de división)* relegation; *(en esquí)* downhill race.
descentrado,-a *adj* **1** off-centre (US off-center). **2** *fi[g] (desorientado)* disoriented, all-at-sea.
descentralización *nf* decentralization.
descentralizar [4] *vt* to decentralize.
descentrar *vt* **1** to put off-centre (US off-center). **2** *fig* to disorientate, throw, put off.
▷ *vpr* **descentrarse 1** to go off-centre (US off-center). **2** *fi[g]* to become disorientated.
descifrar *vt* **1** to decipher, decode. **2** *fig (llegar a comprender)* to solve, figure out.
desclavar *vt* **1** *(quitar los clavos)* to remove the nail[s] from. **2** *(desprender)* to take off.
descodificador *nm* decoder.
descodificar [1] *vt* to decode.
descolgar [52] *vt* **1** *(cuadro, etc)* to take down. **2** *(bajar)* to lower, let down. **3** *(el teléfono)* to pick up, lift[:] **dejó el teléfono descolgado** *she left the telephone of[f] the hook.*
▷ *vpr* **descolgarse** *(escurrirse)* to slip down, slide down[:] **se descolgó por la pared** *he slid down the wall.*
descollar [31] *vi* to stand out, excel.
descolocado,-a *adj* unemployed, out of a job, ou[t] of work.
descolonización *nf* decolonization.
descolonizar [4] *vt* to decolonize.
descolorar *vt* to discolour (US discolor), fade; *(pelo)* to bleach.
descolorido,-a *adj* **1** discoloured (US discolored)[,] faded. **2** *fig* dull, lifeless.
descombrar *vt* to clear.
descombro *nm* clearing.
descomedido,-a *adj* **1** *(excesivo)* excessive, immoderate. **2** *(descortés)* rude, impolite.
▷ *nm & nf* rude person, impolite person.
descomedimiento *nm* rudeness, insolence.
descompasar *vt (hacer perder el compás)* to make lose the beat.
▷ *vpr* **descompasarse** to be rude.
descompensado,-a *adj* unbalanced.
descompensar *vt* to unbalance, upset, throw out of kilter.
descomponer [78] *vt* **1** *(separar)* to break down, split up. **2** *(estropear)* to break. **3** *(desorganizar)* to mess up, upset. **4** *(desordenar)* to mess up: **me ha descompuesto toda la habitación** *he messed up my bedroom.* **5** FÍS to resolve. **6** QUÍM to decompose. **7** MAT to split up. **8** *fig (molestar)* to disturb, upset; *(irritar)* irritate. **9** *(pudrir)* to rot.

▷ *vpr* **descomponerse 1** *(pudrirse)* to decompose, rot. **2** *(estropearse)* to break down. **3** *(enfermar)* to feel ill. **4** *(enfadarse)* to lose one's temper, get angry: **me descompongo cuando dices tantas tonterías** *it makes me angry when you say such nonsense.* **5** FÍS to resolve. **6** QUÍM to decompose. **7** MAT to split.

descomposición *nf* **1** *(pudrimiento)* decomposition, decay. **2** *fig (decadencia)* decline, decadence. **3** *fam (diarrea)* diarrhoea (US diarrhea).

descompresión *nf* decompression.

descompresor *nm* decompression valve.

descomprimir *vt* to decompress, depressurize.

descompuesto,-a *adj* **1** *(podrido)* decomposed, decayed, rotten. **2** *(estropeado)* out of order, broken down. **3** *fig (alterado)* upset. **4** *fig (atrevido)* insolent, impudent. ■ **estar descompuesto,-a** to have diarrhoea (US diarrhea).

descomunal *adj* huge, enormous.

desconcertado,-a *adj* disconcerted, confused, upset.

desconcertante *adj* disconcerting, upsetting.

desconcertar [27] *vt* **1** *(perturbar)* to disconcert, upset, disturb. **2** *(desorientar)* to confuse. **3** MED to dislocate.

▷ *vpr* **desconcertarse 1** *(perturbarse)* to be disconcerted. **2** *(desorientarse)* to be bewildered, be confused. **3** MED to be dislocated.

desconchado,-a *nm* **desconchado** *(pared)* flaking, peeling; *(loza)* chipping.

desconchar *vt (pared)* to peel off, flake; *(loza)* to chip.

▷ *vpr* **desconcharse** to peel off, flake off; *(loza)* to chip.

desconchón *nm (en pared)* bare patch; *(en loza)* chip.

desconcierto *nm* disorder, confusion, chaos.

desconectado,-a *adj fig* cut off (**de**, from).

desconectar *vt* **1** ELEC to disconnect. **2** *(un aparato)* to switch off, turn off. **3** *(desenchufar)* to unplug. **4** *fam fig* to turn off, switch off.

▷ *vpr* **desconectarse** *fam fig (separarse)* to cut OS off (**de**, from): **me desconecté de mis amigos del colegio** *I lost touch with my school friends.*

desconexión *nf* disconnection.

desconfiado,-a *adj* distrustful, suspicious, wary.

▷ *nm & nf* distrustful person, suspicious person, wary person.

desconfianza *nf* distrust, mistrust, suspicion.

desconfiar [13] *vi* **1** *(faltar la confianza)* to distrust (**de**, -), mistrust (**de**, -), be suspicious (**de**, of). **2** *(dudar)* to doubt (**de**, -). **3** *(tener cuidado)* to beware (**de**, of).

descongelar *vt* **1** *(comida)* to thaw, thaw out. **2** *(nevera)* to defrost. **3** FIN to unfreeze.

descongestión *nf (nasal)* unblocking, clearing, decongestion; *(del tráfico)* easing of congestion.

descongestionar *vt* to clear.

desconocer [44] *vt* **1** not to know, be unaware of: **desconozco su nombre** *I don't know her name.* **2** *(no reconocer)* not to recognize. **3** *(rechazar)* to disown. **4** *(no prestar atención)* not to pay attention to, ignore.

desconocido,-a *adj* **1** *(no conocido)* unknown. **2** *(no reconocido)* unrecognized. **3** *(extraño)* strange.

▷ *nm & nf* stranger, unknown person.

▷ *nm* **lo desconocido** the unknown.

desconocimiento *nm* ignorance (**de**, of).

desconsideración *nf* lack of consideration, inconsiderateness, thoughtlessness.

desconsiderado,-a *adj* inconsiderate, thoughtless.

▷ *nm & nf* inconsiderate person, thoughtless person.

desconsolado,-a *adj* disconsolate, grief-stricken, inconsolable.

desconsolar [31] *vt* to distress, grieve.

▷ *vpr* **desconsolarse** to be distressed.

desconsuelo *nm* affliction, grief, sorrow.

descontaminar *vt* to decontaminate.

descontar [31] *vt* **1** *(restar)* to deduct, take off, knock off. **2** *(excluir)* to leave out, exclude. **3** *fig* to discount. **4** DEP to add on.

descontento,-a *adj* displeased, unhappy, dissatisfied, discontented.

▷ *nm & nf* malcontent.

▷ *nm* **descontento** discontent, dissatisfaction.

descontrol *nm fam* lack of control, chaos.

descontrolado,-a *adj* **1** uncontrolled, out of control. **2** *fam fig* out of control, wild.

descontrolarse *vpr (persona)* to lose control; *(avión, etc)* to go out of control.

desconvocar [1] *vt* to cancel, call off.

descorazonador,-ra *adj* disheartening, discouraging.

descorazonar *vt* to dishearten, discourage.

▷ *vpr* **descorazonarse** to lose heart, get discouraged.

descorchar *vt* to uncork.

descorrer *vt* **1** *(cortinas)* to draw; *(cerrojo)* to unbolt. **2** *(volver atrás)* to retrace, go back over.

descortés *adj* impolite, rude, discourteous.

descortesía *nf* impoliteness, rudeness, discourtesy.

descortezar [4] *vt* **1** *(árbol)* to bark, remove the bark from. **2** *(pan)* to remove the crust from; *(fruta)* to peel. **3** *fig (desbastar)* to refine, polish.

descoser *vt* to unpick.

▷ *vpr* **descoserse** to come unstitched.

descosido,-a *adj* **1** *fig (hablador)* talkative. **2** *fig (incoherente)* disconnected.

▷ *nm* **descosido** open seam. ■ **como un descosido** *fam (con exceso)* like wild, too much: **hablar como un descosido** *to talk nineteen to the dozen.*

descoyuntar *vt* **1** *(hueso)* to dislocate, disjoint. **2** *fig (cansar)* to exhaust, tire out.

▷ *vpr* **descoyuntarse** to become dislocated. ■ **descoyuntarse de risa** *fam* to split one's sides laughing.

descrédito *nm* discredit, disrepute: **el gobierno cayó en descrédito** *the government was discredited.*

descreer [61] *vt* to disbelieve.

descreído,-a *adj* disbelieving, unbelieving.

▷ *nm & nf* disbeliever, unbeliever.

descreimiento *nm* disbelief, unbelief.

descremado,-a *adj* skimmed. ● **yogur descremado** low-fat yoghurt.

descremar *vt* to skim.

describir *vt* **1** to describe. **2** *(trazar)* to trace, describe.

descripción *nf* **1** description. **2** *(acción de trazar)* tracing, describing, description.

descriptivo,-a *adj* descriptive.

descrito,-a *adj* 1 described. 2 *(trazado)* traced, described.
descruzar [4] *vt* to uncross.
descuajar *vt* 1 *(liquidar)* to liquefy. 2 *(arrancar de raíz)* to uproot. 3 *fig (desesperanzar)* to dishearten.
descuajaringar [7] *vt (desvencijar)* to pull to pieces, take to pieces.
▷ *vpr* **descuajaringarse** 1 *fam fig (cansarse)* to be exhausted, be worn out. 2 *fam fig (reírse)* to fall about laughing.
descuartizar [4] *vt* 1 *(persona)* to quarter; *(animal)* to quarter, cut up. 2 *fam fig* to pull to pieces, tear apart.
descubierto,-a *adj* 1 open, uncovered: **el cielo está descubierto** *the sky is clear.* 2 *(sin sombrero)* bareheaded.
▷ *nm* **descubierto** FIN overdraft. ■ **al descubierto** in the open.
descubridor,-ra *nm & nf* discoverer.
descubrimiento *nm* discovery.
descubrir *vt* 1 *(gen)* to discover; *(petróleo, oro, minas)* to find; *(conspiración)* to uncover; *(crimen)* to bring to light. 2 *(revelar)* to reveal. 3 *(averiguar)* to find out, discover: **descubrimos sus intenciones** *we found out his intentions.* 4 *(delatar)* to give away. 5 *(divisar)* to make out, see. 6 *(destapar)* to uncover: **el ministro descubrió la estatua** *the minister unveiled the statue.*
▷ *vpr* **descubrirse** 1 *(la cabeza)* to take off one's hat. 2 *fig (abrirse)* to open one's heart (**a/con**, to).
descuento *nm* 1 discount, reduction, deduction. 2 DEP injury time. ■ **con descuento** at a discount, on offer.
descuidado,-a *adj* 1 *(negligente)* careless, negligent. 2 *(desaseado)* slovenly, untidy, neglected. 3 *(desprevenido)* unprepared.
descuidar *vt* 1 to neglect, overlook: **ha descuidado su higiene** *he has neglected his personal hygiene.* 2 *(distraer)* to distract. 3 *(liberar)* to free, release.
▷ *vpr* **descuidarse** 1 *(no tener cuidado)* to be careless: **se descuidó y se perdió** *he was careless and got lost.* 2 *(no arreglarse)* to neglect OS, let OS go. ■ **¡descuida!** don't worry!
descuido *nm* 1 *(negligencia)* negligence, carelessness, neglect. 2 *(distracción)* oversight, slip, mistake. 3 *(desaliño)* slovenliness, untidiness. ■ **por descuido** inadvertently, by mistake.
desde *prep* 1 *(tiempo)* since: **desde 1992** *since 1992.* 2 *(lugar)* from: **desde allí** *from there.* ■ **desde ahora** from now on. ‖ **desde luego** 1 *(en realidad)* really. 2 *(como respuesta)* of course, certainly.
desdecir [79] *vi* 1 *(no ser igual)* not to be equal (**de**, to), not live up (**de**, to): **ese libro desdice mucho del anterior** *that book doesn't measure up to the previous one.* 2 *(no armonizar)* not to match (**de**, -), not to go (**de**, with). 3 *(orígenes, familia, raza)* to be unworthy (**de**, of).
▷ *vpr* **desdecirse** to go back on one's word, recant.
desdén *nm* disdain, scorn, contempt. ■ **con desdén** scornfully, disdainfully.
desdentado,-a *adj* toothless.
▷ *nm* **desdentado** ZOOL edentate.
desdeñable *adj* 1 *(despreciable)* contemptible, despicable. 2 *(insignificante)* negligible, insignificant.
desdeñar *vt* 1 *(despreciar)* to disdain, scorn. 2 *(rechazar)* to turn down.
desdeñoso,-a *adj* disdainful, contemptuous, scornful.
desdibujado,-a *adj* blurred, faint.
desdibujar *vt* to blur.
▷ *vpr* **desdibujarse** to become blurred, become faint.
desdicha *nf* misfortune, misery, adversity. ■ **para colmo de desdichas** to top it all.
desdichado,-a *adj* unfortunate, wretched, unlucky.
▷ *nm & nf* poor devil, wretch.
desdoblar *vt* 1 to unfold. 2 *fig (duplicar)* to split.
desdoro *nm* tarnishing.
desdramatizar [4] *vt* to make less traumatic, play down.
deseable *adj* desirable.
deseado,-a *adj* desired: **en el momento deseado** *at the right time.*
desear *vt* 1 *(querer)* to want: **deseo que venga** *I want him to come.* 2 *(anhelar)* to long for, wish for, desire. *(para alguien)* to wish: **¿qué desea?** *can I help you? what can I do for you?* 3 *(sexualmente)* to desire.
desecar [1] *vt* 1 *(gen)* to dry up. 2 *(pantano, laguna etc)* to drain.
▷ *vpr* **desecarse** to dry up.
desechable *adj* disposable, throw-away.
desechar *vt* 1 *(tirar)* to discard, throw out, throw away. 2 *(rechazar)* to refuse, reject; *(proyecto, idea)* to drop, discard. 3 *(apartar de sí)* to put aside, cast aside: **deberías desechar esa idea** *you should give up that idea.*
desecho *nm* 1 *(residuo)* reject. 2 *(ropa)* castoff.
▷ *nm pl* **desechos** waste *sing*, rubbish *sing*.
desembalar *vt* to unpack.
desembarazar [4] *vt* 1 *(dejar libre)* to free. 2 *(desocupar)* to empty, clear.
▷ *vpr* **desembarazarse** *(librarse)* to rid OS (**de**, of), get rid (**de**, of).
desembarcar [1] *vi* to disembark, land, go ashore.
▷ *vt (mercancías)* to unload; *(personas)* to disembark, put ashore.
▷ *vpr* **desembarcarse** to disembark, land, go ashore.
desembarco *nm (mercancías)* landing, unloading; *(personas)* disembarkation, landing; *(tropas)* landing.
desembocadura *nf* 1 *(de río)* mouth, outlet. 2 *(salida)* way out, exit.
desembocar [1] *vi* 1 *(río)* to flow (**en**, into). 2 *(calle)* to end (**en**, at), lead (**en**, into). 3 *fig* to lead (**en**, to), end (**en**, in): **todo desembocó en un final feliz** *it all ended well.*
desembolsar *vt* to pay out.
desembolso *nm* 1 *(entrega de dinero)* payment; *(plazo)* instalment (US installment). 2 *(gasto)* expense, outlay, expenditure.
desembotar *vt fig* to liven up.
desembozar [4] *vt* 1 *(quitar el embozo)* to unmask, uncover. 2 *fig* to uncover, bring out into the open.
desembragar [7] *vt* 1 TÉC to disengage. 2 AUTO to release.
▷ *vi* AUTO to release the clutch, declutch.

desembrague *nm* **1** TÉC disengaging. **2** AUTO declutching.
desembrollar *vt* to clarify, clear up.
desembrujar *vt* to remove a spell from.
desembuchar *vt* **1** *(aves)* to disgorge. **2** *fam fig* to let out, come clean about.
▷ *vi* to come clean, spill the beans: **¡desembucha de una vez!** *come out with it once and for all!*
desempadronar *vt* **1** *(dar de baja en el padrón)* to remove from the register. **2** *fig (matar)* to kill.
▷ *vpr* **desempadronarse** to remove OS from the register.
desempalmar *vt* to disconnect.
desempañar *vt* to wipe the steam from, demist.
desempapelar *vt* to strip.
desempaquetar *vt* to unpack, unwrap.
desemparejado,-a *adj* **1** *(sin pareja)* without a partner. **2** *(suelto)* odd: **un calcetín desemparejado** *an odd sock.*
desemparejar *vt* to separate.
desempatar *vt* to break a tie between.
▷ *vi* DEP *(desempatar un resultado)* to break the deadlock; *(jugar un partido de desempate)* to play a deciding match, play off.
desempate *nm* **1** tie-break, tiebreaker: **los miembros del jurado tuvieron que hacer una votación de desempate** *the members of the jury had to take a deciding vote.* **2** DEP play-off, tie-break. ● **partido de desempate** play off, deciding match.
desempeñar *vt* **1** *(sacar lo empeñado)* to redeem, take out of pawn. **2** *(liberar a una persona de deudas)* to pay the debts of. **3** *(cumplir una obligación)* to discharge, fulfil (US fulfill), carry out; *(un cargo)* to fill, hold, occupy. **4** *(papel)* to play: **desempeña un papel vital** *she plays a vital role.*
desempeño *nm* **1** *(de algo empeñado)* redeeming; *(deuda)* payment. **2** *(obligaciones, cargo)* carrying out, fulfilment (US fulfillment). **3** TEAT performance, acting.
desempleado,-a *adj* unemployed, out of work.
▷ *nm & nf* unemployed person.
▷ *nm pl* **los desempleados** the unemployed.
desempleo *nm* unemployment. ■ **cobrar el desempleo** to be on the dole, (US be on welfare).
desempolvar *vt* **1** *(quitar el polvo)* to dust. **2** *fig (volver a usar)* to unearth. ■ **desempolvar recuerdos** *fig* to revive memories.
desenamorar *vt* to make fall out of love (**de**, with).
▷ *vpr* **desenamorarse** to fall out of love.
desencadenamiento *nm* **1** *(de algo encadenado)* unchaining. **2** *fig* outbreak, outburst.
desencadenar *vt* **1** *(quitar la cadena)* to unchain. **2** *(pasiones)* to unleash. **3** *fig (producir)* to spark off, give rise to.
▷ *vpr* **desencadenarse 1** *(desatarse)* to break loose. **2** *(guerra, tormenta)* to break out: **se desencadenó una tormenta** *a storm broke.* **3** *(acontecimientos)* to start.
desencajado,-a *adj* **1** *(desunido)* out of place, out of joint. **2** *fig (rostro)* distorted; *(ojos)* wild.
desencajar *vt (desunir)* to take apart, disjoint.
▷ *vpr* **desencajarse 1** *(desunirse)* to come apart, come loose. **2** *fig (rostro)* to become distorted, become twisted; *(ojos)* to look wild.

desencallar *vt* to refloat.
desencaminado,-a *adj* on the wrong track: **no vas muy desencaminado** *you're not far wrong.*
desencantamiento *nm* disenchantment.
desencantar *vt* **1** *(deshacer el encantamiento)* to disenchant. **2** *(desilusionar)* to disillusion, disappoint.
▷ *vpr* **desencantarse** to be disappointed, be disillusioned.
desencanto *nm* **1** *(pérdida del encantamiento)* disenchantment. **2** *(desilusión)* disillusionment, disappointment.
desencapotar *vt* **1** *en desuso (quitar el capote)* to uncloak. **2** *fig (descubrir)* to uncover.
▷ *vpr* **desencapotarse** *fig (despejar el cielo)* to clear.
desencarcelar *vt* to release from prison, free.
desencargar [7] *vt* to cancel an order for.
desenchufar *vt* to unplug, disconnect.
desencofrar *vt* to remove the shuttering from.
desencoger [5] *vt (estirar)* to stretch out; *(desdoblar)* to unfold.
▷ *vpr* **desencogerse 1** *(extenderse)* to stretch, give. **2** *fig (perder el encogimiento)* to come out of one's shell, become more confident.
desencolar *vt* to unglue, unstick.
▷ *vpr* **desencolarse** to come unglued, come unstuck.
desencuadernar *vt* to unbind.
▷ *vpr* **desencuadernarse** to come unbound.
desendiosar *vt fig* to humble, bring down to earth.
desenfadadamente *adv* **1** *(con desenvoltura)* casually, with ease, confidently. **2** *(con humor)* lightheartedly.
desenfadado,-a *adj* **1** *(despreocupado)* free and easy, carefree. **2** *(cómico)* light-hearted. **3** *(ropa)* casual.
desenfadar *vt* to calm down.
▷ *vpr* **desenfadarse** to calm down.
desenfado *nm* **1** *(soltura)* self-confidence, assurance. **2** *(franqueza)* frankness, openness. **3** *(facilidad)* ease.
desenfocado,-a *adj* **1** out of focus. **2** *fig* wrongly approached.
desenfocar [1] *vt* **1** to take out of focus. **2** *fig* to approach wrong.
desenfoque *nm* **1** incorrect focusing. **2** *fig* wrong approach (**de**, to).
desenfrenado,-a *adj* **1** *(gen)* frantic, uncontrolled, wild. **2** *(pasiones, vicios)* unbridled, uncontrolled.
desenfreno *nm (vicio)* licentiousness, debauchery; *(falta de control)* lack of control, wild abandon.
desenfundar *vt* **1** *(quitar)* to draw out, pull out. **2** *(destapar)* to uncover.
desenganchar *vt* **1** *(gen)* to unhook, unfasten; *(despegar)* to unstick. **2** *(caballerías)* to uncouple, unhitch.
desengañado,-a *adj* **1** *(desilusionado)* disillusioned. **2** *(decepcionado)* disappointed, let down.
desengañar *vt* **1** *(hacer conocer la verdad)* to open the eyes of, put in the know. **2** *(decepcionar)* to disappoint. **3** *(desilusionar)* to disillusion.
▷ *vpr* **desengañarse 1** *(ver la verdad)* to have one's eyes opened (**de**, about). **2** *(tener una decepción)* to be disappointed. **3** *(tener una desilusión)* to become

disillusioned, be let down. ■ **¡desengáñate!** face facts!, don't delude yourself!, stop kidding yourself!

desengaño *nm* 1 *(conocimiento de la verdad)* eye-opener. 2 *(desilusión)* disillusion; *(decepción)* disappointment. ■ **llevarse/sufrir un desengaño** to be disappointed.

desengrasar *vt* to remove the grease from.

desenhebrar *vt* to unthread.

▷ *vpr* **desenhebrarse** to come unthreaded.

desenjaular *vt* to let out of a cage, release.

desenlace *nm* 1 *(resultado)* outcome, result. 2 *(de una obra)* ending, denouement. 3 *(final)* end.

desenlazar [4] *vt* 1 *(desatar)* to untie, undo. 2 *fig* to unravel, solve.

▷ *vpr* **desenlazarse** 1 *(desatarse)* to come undone. 2 *fig (resolverse una acción)* to unfold, turn out: **todo se desenlaza como el espectador espera** *everything turns out as the viewer expects.*

desenmarañar *vt* 1 *(desenredar)* to untangle, unravel. 2 *fig (poner en claro)* to unravel, clear up; *(un asunto)* to sort out.

desenmascarar *vt* to unmask.

desenredar *vt* to untangle, disentangle.

▷ *vpr* **desenredarse** to get out (**de**, of), extricate OS (**de**, from).

desenrollar *vt* to unroll, unwind.

desenroscar [1] *vt* to unscrew, uncoil.

▷ *vpr* **desenroscarse** to unscrew, uncoil.

desentenderse [28] *vpr* 1 *(afectar ignorancia)* to pretend not to know (**de**, -/about), ignore (**de**, -), feign ignorance (**de**, of): **se desentiende de mí** *she ignores me.* 2 *(no tomar parte en algo)* to take no part (**de**, in), have nothing to do (**de**, with) .

desenterrar [27] *vt* 1 *(un objeto)* to unearth, dig up; *(cadáver)* to disinter, exhume. 2 *fig (recuerdos)* to recall, revive.

desentonar *vi* 1 MÚS *(instrumento)* to be out of tune; *(cantante)* to sing out of tune. 2 *fig (combinar)* not to match (**con**, -). 3 *fig (estar fuera de lugar)* to be out of place, not to fit in (**con**, with).

desentrañar *vt* 1 *(sacar las entrañas)* to disembowel. 2 *fig* to find out, solve, unravel.

desentrenado,-a *adj* out of training.

desentrenarse *vpr* to be out of training, get out of training.

desentumecer [43] *vt (gen)* to loosen up; *(piernas)* to stretch.

desenvainar *vt* to unsheathe, draw.

desenvoltura *nf* 1 *fig (soltura)* confidence, assurance. 2 *fig (gracia)* grace, ease. 3 *fig (atrevimiento)* boldness, forwardness.

desenvolver [32] *vt* 1 *(quitar lo que envuelve)* to unwrap. 2 *(aclarar)* to clear up.

▷ *vpr* **desenvolverse** 1 *(desembalarse)* to come unwrapped. 2 *(transcurrir)* to develop, go. 3 *(manejarse)* to manage, cope: **se desenvuelve muy bien en los negocios** *he manages very well in business.*

desenvuelto,-a *adj* 1 *(seguro)* confident, self-assured. 2 *(natural)* easy-going, natural, relaxed. 3 *(hábil)* graceful, natural. 4 *(descarado)* bold, forward.

desenzarzar [4] *vt* 1 *(sacar de las zarzas)* to disentangle from brambles. 2 *fig (separar)* to separat (**de**, from).

deseo *nm* wish, desire. ■ **formular un deseo** to mak a wish. ● **buenos deseos** good intentions.

deseoso,-a *adj* desirous, eager, anxious. ■ **estar deseoso,-a de hacer** ALGO to be eager to do STH.

desequilibrado,-a *adj* 1 unbalanced, out of balance. 2 *(persona)* mentally unbalanced.

desequilibrar *vt* 1 to unbalance, throw off balance. 2 *fig* to unbalance.

▷ *vpr* **desequilibrarse** *fig* to become unbalanced, become mentally disturbed.

desequilibrio *nm* 1 lack of balance, imbalance. 2 *fig (mental)* unbalanced state of mind.

deserción *nf* 1 MIL desertion. 2 *fig (abandono)* abandonment, desertion.

desertar *vi* 1 MIL to desert. 2 *fig (abandonar)* to abandon, desert.

desértico,-a *adj* desert.

desertización *nf* desertification.

desertor,-ra *nm & nf* deserter.

desesperación *nf* 1 despair, desperation. 2 *(irritación)* exasperation.

desesperadamente *adv* desperately, frantically.

desesperado,-a *adj* 1 *(sin esperanza)* hopeless, desperate. 2 *(irritado)* exasperated, infuriated.

▷ *nm & nf* desperate person.

desesperante *adj* exasperating, infuriating.

desesperanza *nf* despair, desperation, hopelessness.

desesperanzar [4] *vt* to drive to despair.

▷ *vpr* **desesperanzarse** to despair, lose hope, give up hope (**de**, of).

desesperar *vt* 1 *(hacer perder la paciencia)* to drive to despair, make lose one's patience. 2 *(exasperar)* to exasperate.

▷ *vpr* **desesperarse** 1 *(desesperanzar)* to lose hope, despair. 2 *(irritarse)* to get irritated, become exasperated: **se desespera por todo** *everything exasperates her.*

desestabilización *nf* destabilization.

desestabilizador,-ra *adj* destabilizing.

desestabilizar [4] *vt* to destabilize.

desestima *nf* disrespect, lack of respect.

desestimar *vt* 1 to disregard, underestimate. 2 JUR to reject, refuse.

desfachatez *nf* cheek, nerve.

desfalcador,-ra *adj* embezzling.

▷ *nm & nf* embezzler.

desfalcar [1] *vt* FIN to embezzle.

desfalco *nm* embezzlement.

desfallecer [43] *vt (disminuir las fuerzas)* to weaken.

▷ *vi* 1 *(debilitar)* to weaken, lose strength. 2 *(decaer)* to lose heart.

desfallecido,-a *adj* weak, faint.

desfallecimiento *nm* faintness.

desfasado,-a *adj* outdated, out of date; *(persona)* old-fashioned, behind the times.

desfasar *vt* TÉC to phase out.

▷ *vpr* **desfasarse** 1 TÉC to change phase. 2 *(persona)* to be out of synch.

desfase *nm* 1 *(diferencia)* imbalance, gap. 2 TÉC phase difference. ● **desfase horario** 1 *(entre países)* time difference. 2 *(al volar en avión)* jet lag.
desfavorable *adj* unfavourable (US unfavorable).
desfavorecer [43] *vt* 1 *(perjudicar)* to disadvantage, put at a disadvantage. 2 *(afear)* not to suit, not flatter.
desfiguración *nf* disfigurement.
desfigurado,-a *adj* 1 *(persona)* disfigured. 2 *(estatua, etc)* defaced. 3 *fig (hecho)* distorted.
desfigurar *vt* 1 *(cara)* to disfigure. 2 *(estatua, etc)* to deface. 3 *fig (realidad, hechos, etc)* to distort.
▷ *vpr* **desfigurarse** *(descomponerse)* to become distorted.
desfiladero *nm* defile, gorge, narrow pass.
desfilar *vi* 1 *(gen)* to march. 2 MIL to march, march past, parade. 3 *(moda)* to parade, walk up and down.
desfile *nm* 1 *(gen)* parade, procession. 2 MIL parade. 3 *(moda)* fashion show.
desfogar [7] *vt* 1 *(descargar)* to give vent to, vent. 2 *(la cal)* to slake. 3 *(dar salida al fuego)* to vent.
▷ *vi* MAR *(tormenta)* to burst, break.
▷ *vpr* **desfogarse** to let off steam, vent one's anger.
desgajar *vt* 1 *(rama)* to tear off; *(página)* to rip out, tear out. 2 *(romper)* to break. 3 *(despedazar)* to tear to pieces.
▷ *vpr* **desgajarse** to break off, come off.
desgana *nf* 1 *(inapetencia)* lack of appetite. 2 *(tedio)* boredom, weariness. ■ **con desgana** reluctantly.
desganado,-a *adj* 1 *(sin gana)* not hungry: **está desganado** *he has no appetite.* 2 *(apático)* apathetic, half-hearted.
desganar *vt* 1 *(quitar el apetito)* to spoil the appetite of. 2 *(quitar las ganas)* to turn off.
▷ *vpr* **desganarse** 1 *(perder el apetito)* to lose one's appetite. 2 *(perder el interés)* to lose interest (**de**, in), go off (**de**, -).
desgañitarse *vpr fam* to shout OS hoarse, shout one's head off.
desgarbado,-a *adj* ungainly, ungraceful, clumsy.
desgarrador,-ra *adj* 1 heartbreaking, heart-rending. 2 *(aterrador)* bloodcurdling.
desgarramiento *nm* ripping, tearing.
desgarrar *vt* 1 *(rasgar)* to tear, rip. 2 *fig (herir los sentimientos)* to break, rend.
▷ *vpr* **desgarrarse** *(rasgarse)* to tear, rip.
desgarro *nm* 1 *(rompimiento)* tear, rip. 2 *fig (desvergüenza)* effrontery, insolence. 3 *fig (fanfarronada)* brag, boast.
desgarrón *nm* 1 tear, rip. 2 *(jirón)* tatter.
desgastar *vt* 1 *(ropa)* to wear out, wear away; *(tacones)* to wear down. 2 *(erosionar)* to erode. 3 *fig (debilitar)* to weaken.
▷ *vpr* **desgastarse** 1 *(gastarse)* to wear out, get worn. 2 *fig (debilitarse)* to weaken. 3 *fig (persona)* to wear OS out.
desgaste *nm* 1 *(gen)* wear; *(metal)* corrosion; *(cuerda)* fraying; *(piedra)* erosion. 2 *(deterioro)* damage, deterioration. 3 *fig (debilitamiento)* weakening.
desglosar *vt* 1 *(escrito)* to detach. 2 *(gastos)* to break down.
desglose *nm* breakdown, separation.
desgobierno *nm* misgovernment, mishandling, mismanagement.
desgracia *nf* 1 *(desdicha)* misfortune. 2 *(mala suerte)* bad luck, mischance. 3 *(pérdida de favor)* disfavour (US disfavor). 4 *(accidente)* mishap, accident. ■ **por desgracia** unfortunately.
desgraciadamente *adv* unfortunately.
desgraciado,-a *adj* 1 *(sin suerte)* unfortunate, unlucky. 2 *(infeliz)* unhappy.
▷ *nm & nf* wretch, unfortunate person.
desgraciar [12] *vt* 1 *(echar a perder)* to spoil. 2 *(herir)* to injure. 3 *fam (deshonrar a una mujer)* to dishonour (US dishonor), disgrace.
▷ *vpr* **desgraciarse** *(malograrse)* to fail, be spoiled; *(plan, proyecto)* to fall through.
desgranar *vt* 1 *(guisante, maíz)* to shell; *(trigo)* to thresh; *(un racimo de uvas)* to pick the grapes from. 2 *(soltar)* to reel off.
▷ *vpr* **desgranarse** *(soltarse)* to come apart, come unstrung.
desgravación *nf* deduction. ● **desgravación fiscal** tax deduction.
desgravar *vt* to deduct.
desguace *nm* 1 *(de barco)* breaking up; *(coche)* car breaking, scrapping. 2 *(lugar)* breaker's yard, scrapyard.
desguazar [4] *vt* 1 *(barco)* to break up; *(coche)* to scrap. 2 *(madera)* to rough-hew.
deshabitado,-a *adj (pueblo, lugar)* uninhabited; *(casa, piso)* unoccupied.
deshabitar *vt* to leave, abandon, vacate.
deshabituar [11] *vt (hacer perder el hábito)* to break from the habit.
▷ *vpr* **deshabituarse** to get out of the habit (**a**, of), give up (**a**, -).
deshacer [73] *vt* 1 *(destruir)* to destroy. 2 *(estropear)* to ruin, damage; *(romper)* to break; *(desordenar)* to upset. 3 *(nudo)* to untie, loosen; *(paquete)* to undo, unwrap; *(cama)* to strip; *(equipaje)* to unpack; *(puntadas)* to unpick. 4 *(romper un acuerdo)* to break off. 5 *(disolver)* to dissolve; *(derretir)* to melt. 6 *(desandar)* to retrace. 7 *(desmontar)* to take apart, take to pieces. 8 *(planes, proyectos)* to spoil, ruin.
▷ *vpr* **deshacerse** 1 *(nudo)* to come undone, come untied; *(puntada)* to come unsewn. 2 *(disolverse)* to dissolve; *(derretirse)* to melt. 3 *(desaparecer)* to disappear, fade away. 4 *(librarse)* to get rid (**de**, of).
desharrapado,-a *adj* ragged, in tatters.
▷ *nm & nf* person dressed in rags.
deshebrar *vt* 1 *(sacar las hebras)* to ravel out, undo. 2 *fig (deshacer en partes delgadas)* to tear into shreds.
deshecho,-a *adj* 1 *(destruido)* destroyed. 2 *(estropeado)* damaged, ruined. 3 *(nudo)* untied, undone; *(paquete)* unwrapped; *(cama)* unmade; *(equipaje)* unpacked. 4 *(disuelto)* dissolved; *(derretido)* melted. 5 *fig (cansado)* shattered, exhausted. 6 *fig (abatido)* devastated, shattered.
deshelar [27] *vt* 1 to thaw, melt. 2 *(congelador)* to defrost. 3 *(coche)* to de-ice.
▷ *vpr* **deshelarse** to thaw out, melt.
desherbar [27] *vt* to weed.

desheredado,-a *adj* 1 disinherited. 2 *fig* deprived, underprivileged.
▷ *nm & nf* 1 disinherited person. 2 *fig* deprived person, underprivileged person.
▷ *nm pl* **los desheredados** the deprived.

desheredar *vt* to disinherit.

deshidratación *nf* dehydration.

deshidratado,-a *adj* dehydrated.

deshidratar *vt* to dehydrate.
▷ *vpr* **deshidratarse** to become dehydrated.

deshielo *nm* 1 thaw; *(de congelador)* defrosting; *(de parabrisas)* de-icing. 2 *fig* thaw.

deshilachado,-a *adj* frayed.

deshilachar *vt* to fray.

deshilvanado,-a *adj* 1 untacked. 2 *fig* disconnected, incoherent, disjointed.

deshilvanar *vt* to untack.

deshinchado,-a *adj* 1 *(neumático, etc)* flat, deflated. 2 *(sin hinchazón)* not swollen: **la rodilla ya la tienes deshinchada** *the swelling in your knee has gone down.*

deshinchar *vt* 1 *(neumático, etc)* to deflate, let down. 2 *(reducir la hinchazón)* to reduce the swelling of.
▷ *vpr* **deshincharse** 1 to deflate, go down. 2 *(reducirse la hinchazón)* to go down.

deshojar *vt* 1 *(flor)* to strip the petals off; *(árbol)* to strip the leaves off. 2 *(libro)* to tear the pages out of.
▷ *vpr* **deshojarse** *(flor)* to lose its petals; *(árbol)* to lose its leaves.

deshollinador *nm* chimney sweep.

deshollinar *vt* to sweep.

deshonestamente *adv* dishonestly.

deshonestidad *nf* 1 *(sin honestidad)* dishonesty. 2 *(impudor)* indecency, immodesty.

deshonesto,-a *adj* 1 *(sin honestidad)* dishonest. 2 *(inmoral)* immodest, indecent.

deshonor *nm* dishonour (US dishonor), disgrace.

deshonra *nf* dishonour (US dishonor), disgrace.

deshonrar *vt* 1 *(gen)* to dishonour (US dishonor), disgrace. 2 *(injuriar)* to insult, defame. 3 *(a una mujer)* to dishonour (US dishonor).

deshonroso,-a *adj* dishonourable (US dishonorable), shameful, disgraceful.

deshora *nf* inconvenient time. ■ **a deshora** 1 *(inoportuno)* at an inconvenient time. 2 *(muy tarde)* very late.

deshumanizado,-a *adj* dehumanized.

deshumanizar [4] *vt* to dehumanize.

desiderativo,-a *adj* desiderative.

desidia *nf* negligence.

desierto,-a *adj* 1 *(sin habitantes)* uninhabited, deserted: **una isla desierta** *a desert island.* 2 *(vacío)* deserted, empty. 3 *(no adjudicado)* void.
▷ *nm* **desierto** desert.

designación *nf* 1 *(nombre)* name, designation. 2 *(nombramiento)* designation, appointment.

designar *vt* 1 *(denominar)* to designate. 2 *(nombrar para un cargo)* to appoint, name, assign. 3 *(fijar)* to set, arrange, fix.

designio *nm* intention, plan.

desigual *adj* 1 *(gen)* unequal, uneven. 2 *(diferente)* different, unequal. 3 *(irregular)* uneven, irregular. 4 *(no liso)* uneven, rough. 5 *(variable)* changeable: **tiene un carácter muy desigual** *she is very changeable*

desigualar *vt* 1 *(hacer diferente)* to make unequal, make different; *(tratar de modo distinto)* to treat unequally. 2 *(un terreno)* to make uneven, make rough.

desigualdad *nf* 1 *(gen)* inequality, difference. 2 *(irregularidad)* unevenness. 3 *(terreno)* unevenness, roughness. 4 *(inconstancia)* changeability.

desilusión *nf* disappointment, disillusion, disillusionment.

desilusionado,-a *adj* disappointed, disillusioned, disheartened.

desilusionar *vt* to disappoint, disillusion, dishearten.
▷ *vpr* **desilusionarse** to be disappointed, become disillusioned.

desimantar *vt* to demagnetize.

desincrustar *vt* to descale.

desinencia *nf* ending, desinence.

desinfección *nf* disinfection.

desinfectante *adj* disinfectant.
▷ *nm* disinfectant.

desinfectar *vt* to disinfect.

desinflamar *vt* to reduce the inflammation in, reduce the swelling in.
▷ *vpr* **desinflamarse** to go down, become less swollen.

desinflar *vt* *(gen)* to deflate; *(una rueda)* to let down.
▷ *vpr* **desinflarse** 1 to go down, deflate. 2 *fam fig (desanimarse)* to lose heart, become disheartened.

desinformación *nf* disinformation.

desinformar *vi* to misinform.

desinsectar *vt* to fumigate.

desintegración *nf* 1 disintegration. 2 *fig* disintegration, break-up.

desintegrar *vt* 1 to disintegrate. 2 *fig* to disintegrate, break up. 3 FÍS to split.
▷ *vpr* **desintegrarse** 1 to disintegrate. 2 *fig* to break up. 3 FÍS to split.

desinterés *nm* 1 *(generosidad)* unselfishness, generosity. 2 *(falta de interés)* lack of interest, indifference.

desinteresadamente *adv* unselfishly, generously.

desinteresado,-a *adj* disinterested, unselfish.

desinteresarse *vpr* 1 *(perder el interés)* to lose interest (**de**, in), go off (**de**, -). 2 *(desentenderse)* to have nothing to do (**de**, with).

desintoxicación *nf* detoxication, detoxification.

desintoxicar [1] *vt* 1 to detoxicate, detoxify. 2 *(alcohol)* to dry out.

desistir *vi* 1 *(gen)* to desist, give up. 2 *(de una querella, etc)* to abandon, relinquish.

deslavado,-a *adj (desteñido)* washed out, faded.

deslavar *vt* to half-wash.

deslavazado,-a *adj* 1 *(insulso)* insipid. 2 *(mal compuesto)* disjointed. 3 *(falto de vigor)* limp.

desleal *adj* disloyal.

deslealtad *nf* disloyalty.

desleír [37] *vt* 1 *(sólido)* to dissolve; *(líquido)* to dilute. 2 *fig* to dilute.
▷ *vpr* **desleírse** *(sólido)* to dissolve; *(líquido)* to be diluted.

deslenguado,-a *adj fig (descarado)* insolent, cheeky; *(grosero)* coarse, foul-mouthed.
desligar [7] *vt* 1 *(desatar)* to untie, unfasten. 2 *fig (separar)* to separate (**de**, from). 3 *fig (librar de una obligación)* to release (**de**, from), free (**de**, from).
▷ *vpr* **desligarse** 1 *(desatarse)* to break away (**de**, from). 2 *(librarse)* to release OS (**de**, from), free OS (**de**, from).
deslindar *vt* 1 to delimit, mark the boundaries of. 2 *fig* to clarify, define, outline.
deslinde *nm* 1 delimitation, demarcation. 2 *fig* definition.
desliz *nm* 1 *(resbalón)* slide, slip. 2 *fig (error)* slip, mistake error. ■ **cometer/tener un desliz** *fig* to slip up, make a slip.
▲ *pl* **deslices.**
deslizamiento *nm* slipping, slip. ● **deslizamiento de tierra** landslide.
deslizante *adj* sliding.
deslizar [4] *vt* 1 *(pasar)* to slide, slip. 2 *(decir o hacer por descuido)* to slip.
▷ *vi (resbalar)* to slide, slip.
▷ *vpr* **deslizarse** 1 *(gen)* to slide; *(sobre agua)* to glide. 2 *(salir)* to slip out (**de**, of); *(entrar)* to slip (**en**, into): **se deslizó en la habitación** *he slipped into the room.*
deslomar *vt* 1 *(dañar la espalda)* to break the back of. 2 *(agotar)* to wear out.
▷ *vpr* **deslomarse** *(trabajar mucho)* to wear OS out, break one's back.
deslucido,-a *adj* 1 *(sin brillantez)* faded, dull. 2 *(sin gracia)* unimpressive, unexciting, dull, lacklustre (US lackluster).
deslucir [45] *vt* 1 *(quitar la brillantez)* to tarnish, take the shine off; *(descolorar)* to fade. 2 *fig (quitar la gracia)* to mar, spoil; *(desacreditar)* to discredit.
deslumbrar *vt* to dazzle.
deslustrar *vt* 1 *(telas)* to take the shine off, dull. 2 *(vidrio)* to grind, frost. 3 *(metal)* to tarnish. 4 *fig (desacreditar)* to tarnish.
▷ *vpr* **deslustrarse** *(metal)* to become dull.
desmadejar *vt fig* to tire out, exhaust.
desmadrado,-a *adj fam fig* wild, unruly.
desmadrar *vt* to take from its mother.
▷ *vpr* **desmadrarse** *fam fig* to go wild.
desmadre *nm fam* chaos: **la fiesta fue un desmadre total** *the party was really wild.*
desmagnetizar [4] *vt* to demagnetize.
desmandar *vt (revocar)* to revoke.
▷ *vpr* **desmandarse** 1 *(descomedirse)* to rebel, misbehave, get out of hand. 2 *(animal)* to stray from the herd; *(caballo)* to bolt.
desmantelar *vt* 1 to dismantle. 2 MAR to dismast, unrig.
desmaquillador,-ra *adj* cleansing.
▷ *nm* **desmaquillador** make-up remover.
desmaquillar *vt* to remove make-up from.
▷ *vpr* **desmaquillarse** to remove one's make-up.
desmarcarse [1] *vpr* 1 DEP to get into an unmarked position. 2 *(distanciarse)* to distance OS (**de**, from), disassociate OS (**de**, from). 3 *fig (escabullirse)* to skive off, slip away.
desmayado,-a *adj* 1 *(color)* dull, washed-out. 2 *(inconsciente)* unconscious. 3 *(cansado)* exhausted, worn-out. ■ **caer desmayado,-a** to faint.
desmayar *vt (causar desmayo)* to make faint.
▷ *vi fig (acobardarse)* to lose heart.
▷ *vpr* **desmayarse** *(perder el sentido)* to faint, lose consciousness.
desmayo *nm* 1 *(desaliento)* discouragement. 2 *(pérdida del conocimiento)* faint, fainting fit. ■ **sufrir/tener un desmayo** to faint.
desmedido,-a *adj* 1 *(desproporcionado)* excessive, disproportionate, out of all proportion. 2 *(sin límite)* boundless, unbounded.
desmejorar *vt* to spoil, make worse, damage.
▷ *vi* to deteriorate, get worse, go downhill.
▷ *vpr* **desmejorarse** to deteriorate, get worse, go downhill. ■ **estar desmejorado,-a** to look unwell, look worse.
desmelenado,-a *adj* tousled, dishevelled (US disheveled), ruffled.
desmelenar *vt (desgreñar)* to tousle, dishevel.
▷ *vpr* **desmelenarse** *fam (desmadrarse)* to let one's hair down.
desmembrar [3] *vt* 1 to dismember. 2 *fig* to split up, break up, divide.
desmemoriado,-a *adj* forgetful, absent-minded.
▷ *nm & nf* forgetful person, absent minded person.
desmentir [35] *vt* 1 *(negar)* to deny. 2 *(contradecir)* to contradict, belie. 3 *(desmerecer)* not to live up to.
desmenuzar [4] *vt* 1 *(gen)* to break into little pieces; *(carne)* to chop up; *(pan)* to crumble; *(pescado)* to flake. 2 *fig (examinar)* to examine, look into, analyse (US analyze).
desmerecer [43] *vt (quitar mérito a)* to mar, detract from.
▷ *vi* 1 *(perder valor)* to lose value, deteriorate. 2 *(ser inferior)* to compare unfavourably (US unfavorably) (**de**, with), be inferior (**de**, to).
desmesurado,-a *adj* 1 *(excesivo)* excessive, disproportionate. 2 *(descortés)* insolent, discourteous, rude.
desmilitarizar [4] *vt* to demilitarize.
desmirriado,-a *adj fam* weedy, puny.
desmitificar [1] *vt* to demystify.
desmoldar *vt* to remove from a mould, turn out.
desmontable *adj* that can be taken to pieces.
desmontar *vt* 1 *(desarmar)* to take to pieces, take down, dismantle. 2 *(edificio)* to knock down. 3 *(arma)* to uncock. 4 *(cortar en un bosque)* to clear. 5 *(allanar)* to level. 6 *(quitar de la montura)* to unset, unmount. 7 *(motor)* to strip.
▷ *vi (del caballo)* to dismount (**de**, -).
desmoralizador,-ra *adj* demoralizing.
desmoralizar [4] *vt* to demoralize.
▷ *vpr* **desmoralizarse** to become demoralized.
desmoronamiento *nm* crumbling, disintegration, fall.
desmoronar *vt* to crumble, destroy.
▷ *vpr* **desmoronarse** 1 to crumble, collapse, fall to pieces. 2 *(venir a menos)* to crumble, collapse. 3 *fig (decaer el ánimo)* to lose heart, fall apart.
desnacionalizar [4] *vt* to denationalize, privatize.

desnatado,-a *adj (leche)* skimmed; *(yogur)* low-fat.
desnaturalización *nf* 1 QUÍM denaturation. 2 *(destierro)* banishment. 3 *(adulteración)* adulteration.
desnaturalizar [4] *vt* 1 *(adulterar)* to adulterate. 2 QUÍM to denature, denaturize. 3 *(desterrar)* to banish.
desnivel *nm* 1 unevenness. 2 *(cuesta)* slope, drop. 3 *fig* difference.
desnivelar *vt* 1 *(sacar de nivel)* to make uneven, put on a different level. 2 *(desequilibrar)* to throw out of balance; *(balanza)* to tip.
desnucar [1] *vt* to break the neck of.
▷ *vpr* **desnucarse** to break one's neck.
desnudar *vt* 1 to undress. 2 *fig (despojar)* to strip. 3 *fig (desenvainar)* to unsheathe.
▷ *vpr* **desnudarse** 1 *(persona)* to get undressed, take one's clothes off. 2 *fig (rechazar)* to cast aside (**de**, -).
desnudez *nf* nudity, nakedness.
desnudo,-a *adj* 1 *(persona)* naked, nude; *(parte del cuerpo)* bare. 2 *fig (falto de lo que cubre o adorna)* plain, bare.
▷ *nm* **desnudo** ARTE nude.
desnutrición *nf* malnutrition, undernourishment.
desnutrido,-a *adj* undernourished.
desobedecer [43] *vt* to disobey.
desobediente *adj* disobedient.
▷ *nm o nf* disobedient person.
desocupado,-a *adj* 1 *(libre)* free, vacant. 2 *(ocioso)* free, not busy. 3 *(desempleado)* unemployed, out of work.
desocupar *vt* to vacate, leave, empty.
desodorante *nm* deodorant.
desoír [75] *vt* to ignore, take no notice of, turn a deaf ear to.
desolación *nf* 1 desolation. 2 *(tristeza)* affliction, grief.
desolado,-a *pp* → **desolar**.
▷ *adj* 1 *(devastado)* desolated, devastated. 2 *(triste)* distressed, heartbroken.
desolador,-ra *adj* 1 *(devastador)* devastating, ravaging. 2 *(desconsolador)* heartbreaking, devastating.
desorbitado,-a *adj* exorbitant, exaggerated, disproportionate.
desorden *nm* 1 disorder, disarray, mess, untidiness. 2 *(irregularidad)* irregularity.
desordenado,-a ▷ *adj* 1 *(habitación, etc)* untidy, messy. 2 *(persona)* slovenly. 3 *(ideas)* confused. 4 *fig (vida)* licentious.
desordenar *vt* to untidy, disarrange, mess up; *(alterar)* to disturb.
desorganizar [4] *vt* to disorganize, disrupt.
desorientar *vt* 1 to disorientate. 2 *fig (confundir)* to confuse.
▷ *vpr* **desorientarse** 1 to lose one's bearings, lose one's sense of direction, get lost. 2 *fig (confundirse)* to get confused.
desovar *vi (insectos)* to lay eggs; *(peces)* to spawn.
desove *nm (insectos)* egg-laying; *(peces)* spawning.
desoxidante *adj* deoxidizing.
▷ *nm* deoxidizer.
desoxidar *vt* to deoxidize.
desoxirribonucleico,-a *adj* deoxyribonucleic.
despabilado,-a *adj* 1 *(desvelado)* wide-awake. 2 *fig (listo)* smart, sharp, quick.
despabilar *vt* 1 *(quitar el pábilo)* to snuff. 2 *fig (despertar)* to wake up.
▷ *vpr* **despabilarse** 1 *(despertarse)* to wake up. 2 *(avivarse)* to get one's act together, buck one's ideas up, wise up.
despachar *vt* 1 *(terminar)* to finish, dispatch. 2 *(resolver)* to resolve, get through; *(tratar un asunto)* to deal with, attend. 3 *(enviar)* to send, dispatch. 4 *(despedir)* to dismiss, sack, fire. 5 *(en tienda)* to serve; *(vender)* to sell.
despacho *nm* 1 *(envío)* sending, dispatch. 2 *(oficina)* office; *(estudio)* study. 3 *(venta)* sale, selling. 4 *(lugar de venta)* office. ● **despacho de billetes/localidades** ticket/box office.
despacio *adv (gen)* slowly.
desparasitar *vt (piojos)* to delouse; *(lombrices)* to worm.
desparejar *vt* to separate.
desparpajo *nm* 1 *(desenvoltura)* ease, self-assurance. 2 *(descaro)* nerve, impudence.
desparramar *vt* 1 to spread, scatter; *(un líquido)* to spill. 2 *(divulgar)* to spread.
despecho *nm* spite. ■ **por despecho** out of spite.
despectivo,-a *adj* 1 contemptuous, disparaging. 2 GRAM pejorative, derogatory.
despedida *nf* 1 farewell, goodbye. 2 *(en una carta)* closing formula. 3 MÚS last verse.
despedir [34] *vt* 1 *(lanzar)* to shoot, fire: 2 *(echar)* to throw out. 3 *(del trabajo)* to dismiss, fire, sack. 4 *(decir adiós)* to see off, say goodbye to.
▷ *vpr* **despedirse** *(decirse adiós)* to say goodbye (**de**, to).
despegar [7] *vt (desenganchar)* to unstick, take off, detach.
▷ *vi (avión)* to take off; *(nave espacial)* to lift off, blast off.
▷ *vpr* **despegarse** *(separarse)* to come unstuck.
despegue *nm (avión)* takeoff; *(nave espacial)* liftoff, blast-off.
despeinar *vt* to dishevel, ruffle.
▷ *vpr* **despeinarse** to mess up one's hair.
despejar *vt* 1 *(desalojar)* to clear. 2 MAT to find. 3 INFORMÁ to clear.
▷ *vpr* **despejarse** 1 METEOR to clear up. 2 *(espabilarse)* to wake OS up, clear one's head.
despeluznante *adj* horrible, dreadful.
despenalizar [4] *vt* to legalize, decriminalize.
despender *vt* 1 *(gastar)* to spend. 2 *(malgastar)* to waste, squander.
despensa *nf* 1 *(lugar)* pantry, larder. 2 *(víveres)* provisions *pl*, stock of food.
despeñar *vt* to throw over a cliff.
▷ *vpr* **despeñarse** 1 *(caer)* to fall over a cliff. 2 *fig (perderse)* to go off the straight and narrow.
desperdiciar [12] *vt* to waste, squander; *(oportunidad)* to throw away.
desperdicio *nm* waste.
▷ *nm pl* **desperdicios** *(basura)* rubbish *sing*; *(desechos)* scraps, leftovers.
desperdigar [7] *vt* to scatter, disperse.
▷ *vpr* **desperdigarse** to scatter, disperse.

desperezarse [4] *vpr* to stretch.
desperfecto *nm* 1 *(daño)* damage. 2 *(defecto)* flaw, defect.
despertador *nm* alarm clock.
despertar [27] *vt* 1 to wake, wake up, awaken. 2 *(apetito)* to whet.
▷ *vi* to wake up, awake.
▷ *vpr* **despertarse** to wake up, awake.
despiadado,-a *adj* ruthless, merciless.
despido *nm* dismissal, sacking.
despierto,-a *adj* 1 awake. 2 *(espabilado)* lively, smart, sharp, bright.
despilfarrar *vt* to waste, squander.
despilfarro *nm* waste.
despistado,-a *adj (distraído)* absent-minded.
despistar *vt* 1 *(hacer perder la pista)* to lose, give the slip. 2 *fig (desorientar)* to mislead, confuse.
▷ *vpr* **despistarse** 1 *(perderse)* to get lost, lose one's way. 2 *(distraerse)* to get confused, get muddled.
despiste *nm* 1 *(distracción)* absent-mindedness. 2 *(error)* mistake, slip.
desplante *nm fig* impudent remark, impudent act.
desplazado,-a *adj* out of place.
desplazamiento *nm* 1 *(traslado)* moving, removal. 2 MAR displacement.
desplazar [4] *vt* 1 *(mover)* to move, shift. 2 *fig (sustituir)* to replace, take over from.
▷ *vpr* **desplazarse** to travel.
desplegar [48] *vt* 1 *(extender)* to unfold, spread (out), open (out); *(alas)* to spread. 2 MIL to deploy. 3 *fig (aclarar)* to clarify. 4 *fig (ejercitar)* to show, display.
despliegue *nm* 1 MIL deployment. 2 *fig (exhibición)* display, show, manifestation.
desplomar *vt (hacer perder la verticalidad)* to put out of plumb.
▷ *vpr* **desplomarse** 1 *(caer una pared)* to tumble down. 2 *(caer algo de peso)* to fall down, collapse, topple over.
despoblar [31] *vt* 1 to depopulate. 2 *fig (despojar)* to clear; *(de árboles)* to deforest.
▷ *vpr* **despoblarse** to become depopulated, become deserted.
despojar *vt (quitar)* to deprive (**de**, of), strip.
▷ *vpr* **despojarse** 1 *(quitarse ropa)* to take off (**de**, -). 2 *(desposeerse voluntariamente)* to forsake (**de**, -), give up (**de**,-). 3 *fig* to free OS (**de**, of).
despojo *nm (botín)* plunder, booty.
▷ *nm pl* **despojos** 1 *(sobras)* leavings, scraps, leftovers. 2 *(de un animal)* offal *sing.*
desposar *vt fml* to marry.
▷ *vpr* **desposarse** *fml (casarse)* to get married (**con**, to).
desposeer [61] *vt* 1 *(gen)* to dispossess. 2 *(autoridad)* to remove.
déspota *nm o nf* despot, tyrant.
despreciar [12] *vt* 1 *(desdeñar)* to despise, scorn, look down on. 2 *(desestimar)* to reject; *(ignorar)* to disregard, ignore.
desprecio *nm* 1 *(desestima)* contempt, scorn, disdain. 2 *(desaire)* slight, snub.
desprender *vt* 1 *(separar)* to detach, remove. 2 *(soltar)* to release. 3 *(emanar)* to give off.
▷ *vpr* **desprenderse** 1 *(soltarse)* to come off, come away. 2 *(renunciar)* to part with, give away. 3 *fig (liberarse)* to rid OS (**de**, of), free OS (**de**, from). 4 *(deducirse)* to follow, be inferred, be implied.
desprendimiento *nm (acción de desprenderse)* detachment, loosening.
despreocupado,-a *adj* 1 *(tranquilo)* unconcerned, unworried. 2 *(negligente)* negligent, careless, sloppy. 3 *(indiferente)* indifferent.
despreocuparse *vpr* 1 *(dejar de preocuparse)* to stop worrying. 2 *(desentenderse)* to be unconcerned (**de**, about), be indifferent (**de**, to).
desprestigiar [12] *vt* to discredit, ruin the reputation of.
desprevenido,-a *adj* unprepared, unready. ■ **coger/pillar a** ALGN **desprevenido,-a** to catch SB unawares, take SB by surprise.
desproporcionado,-a *adj* disproportionate, out of proportion.
despropósito *nm* absurdity, nonsense.
desprovisto,-a *adj* lacking (**de**, -), devoid (**de**, of), without (**de**, -).
después *adv* 1 afterwards, later. 2 *(entonces)* then. 3 *(luego)* next. ■ **después de** 1 *(tiempo)* after. 2 *(desde)* since. 3 *(+ pp)* after, once: **después de la cena** *after supper;* **después de ella, nadie más lo consiguió** *no one else did it since she did.* ■ **después de todo** after all: **después de todo no está tan mal** *it's not that bad after all.*
despuntar *vt* 1 *(quitar la punta)* to blunt, make blunt. 2 MAR to round.
▷ *vi* 1 *(planta)* to sprout; *(flor)* to bud. 2 *(destacar)* to excel, stand out.
desquite *nm (venganza)* revenge, retaliation.
destacamento *nm* detachment.
destacar [1] *vi (despuntar)* to stand out.
▷ *vt* 1 MIL to detach. 2 *fig (dar énfasis)* to point out, emphasize.
▷ *vpr* **destacarse** to stand out.
destajo *nm* piecework. ■ **a destajo** by the piece.
destapar *vt* 1 *(gen)* to open: **destapé la caja y vi que estaba vacía** *I opened the box and saw it was empty.* 2 *(tapón)* to uncork; *(tapa)* to take the lid off. 3 *fig (descubrir)* to reveal, uncover.
▷ *vpr* **destaparse** *(en la cama)* to take the bedclothes off, take the covers off.
destellar *vi (gen)* to sparkle, glitter; *(estrella)* to twinkle.
destello *nm* 1 *(resplandor)* sparkle, flash; *(brillo)* gleam, shine. 2 *fig (atisbo)* glimmer, flash.
destemplado,-a *adj* 1 MÚS out of tune. 2 *(voz, gesto)* sharp, snappy. 3 *(carácter)* irritable, tetchy. 4 *(tiempo)* unpleasant.
desteñir [36] *vt* to discolour (US discolor), fade.
▷ *vi* to lose colour (US color), fade, run:
desternillarse ■ **desternillarse de risa** *fam* to split one's sides laughing, be in stitches.
desterrar [27] *vt* 1 to exile, banish. 2 *fig* to banish.
destiempo ■ **a destiempo** inopportunely, at the wrong time, at the wrong moment: **llegó a destiempo** *he arrived at the wrong moment.*

destierro *nm* **1** *(pena)* banishment, exile. **2** *(lugar)* place of exile. **3** *fig (lugar muy apartado)* back of beyond.

destilar *vt* to distil (US distill).

destilería *nf* distillery.

destinado,-a *adj* destined (**a**, to), bound (**a**, for).

destinar *vt* **1** *(asignar)* to assign, set aside, destine; *(dinero)* to allocate, set aside. **2** *(persona)* to appoint, assign, send, post. **3** MIL to post.

destinatario,-a *nm & nf* **1** *(de carta)* addressee. **2** *(de mercancías)* consignee.

destino *nm* **1** *(sino)* destiny, fate. **2** *(uso)* purpose, use. **3** *(lugar)* destination. **4** *(empleo)* post. ■ **con destino a** bound for, going to. | **salir con destino a** to leave for.

destitución *nf* dismissal, removal.

destituir [62] *vt* to dismiss, remove from office.

destornillador *nm* screwdriver.

destornillar *vt* to unscrew.

destrabar *vt* **1** *(quitar las trabas)* to unfetter. **2** *(desprender)* to remove, detach.

destreza *nf* skill, dexterity: **tiene destreza** *she's skilful.*

destronar *vt* **1** to dethrone. **2** *fig* to overthrow, unseat.

destrozar [4] *vt* **1** *(romper)* to destroy, shatter, wreck; *(despedazar)* to tear to pieces, tear to shreds. **2** *fig (gastar)* to wear out: **destroza los zapatos** *she wears her shoes out.* **3** *fig (estropear)* to ruin, spoil; *(corazón)* to break. **4** *fig (causar daño moral)* to crush, shatter, devastate.

destrozo *nm* **1** *(acción)* destruction. **2** [Often used in plural with the same meaning.] *(daño)* damage.

destrucción *nf* destruction.

destruir [62] *vt* **1** to destroy. **2** *fig* to destroy, ruin, wreck: **han destruido sus esperanzas** *they've shattered her hopes.*

desunir *vt* **1** *(separar)* to divide, separate. **2** *fig* to cause discord, disunite.

desuso *nm* disuse: **eso está en desuso** *that's obsolete, that's outdated.*

desvalido,-a *adj* needy, destitute.

desvalijar *vt* **1** *(a alguien)* to rob. **2** *(un lugar)* to burgle.

desván *nm* loft, attic.

desvanecer [43] *vt* **1** *(hacer desaparecer)* to clear, dispel, disperse. **2** *(color)* to fade; *(contorno)* to blur. **3** *fig (recuerdo, etc)* to dispel, banish.

▷ *vpr* **desvanecerse** **1** *(disiparse)* to disperse, clear. **2** *fig (desaparecer)* to vanish, disappear; *(recuerdos)* to fade. **3** *fig (desmayarse)* to faint.

desvanecimiento *nm (desmayo)* faint, fainting fit.

desvariar [13] *vi* to be delirious, rave, talk nonsense.

desvarío *nm* **1** *(delirio)* delirium, raving. **2** *(disparate)* nonsense, act of madness. **3** *(capricho)* fancy, whim.

desvelar *vt* **1** *(quitar el sueño)* to keep awake. **2** *fig (revelar)* to reveal, disclose: **nos desveló el secreto** *she revealed the secret to us.*

▷ *vpr* **desvelarse** **1** to be unable to sleep. **2** *fig (dedicarse)* to devote OS (**por**, to): **siempre se ha desvelado por su familia** *she has always devoted herself to her family.*

desvelo *nm (dedicación)* devotion, dedication.

desvencijado,-a *adj* rickety, broken-down, dilapidated.

desventaja *nf* **1** disadvantage, drawback. **2** *(problema)* problem. ■ **estar en desventaja** to be at a disadvantage.

desventura *nf* misfortune, bad luck.

desvergonzado,-a *adj (sinvergüenza)* shameless, brazen.

desvergüenza *nf (falta de decoro)* shamelessness.

desvestir [34] *vt* to undress.

▷ *vpr* **desvestirse** to undress, get undressed.

desviación *nf* **1** deviation. **2** *(de carretera)* diversion, detour.

desviar [13] *vt* **1** *(gen)* to deviate, change the course of: **desvió la mirada** *she looked away.* **2** *(golpe, balón)* to deflect. **3** *(carretera, río, barco, avión)* to divert. **4** *fig (tema)* to change.

▷ *vpr* **desviarse** **1** *(avión, barco)* to go off course; *(coche)* to make a detour. **2** *(golpe, balón)* to be deflected. **3** *(persona, camino)* to leave.

desvío *nm* diversion, detour.

desvivirse *vpr* **1** *(desvelarse)* to do one's utmost (**por**, for), be devoted (**por**, to). **2** *(desear)* to be mad (**por**, about).

detallado,-a *adj* detailed, thorough.

detallar *vt* **1** to detail, give the details of, tell in detail. **2** *(especificar)* to specify. **3** COM to retail, sell retail.

detalle *nm* **1** *(pormenor)* detail, particular. **2** *(delicadeza)* nice gesture, nice thought. **3** *(toque decorativo)* touch. ■ **al detalle** COM retail. | **tener un detalle** to be considerate, be thoughtful.

detallista *nm o nf* COM retailer, retail trader.

detectar *vt* to detect.

detective *nm o nf* detective.

detener [87] *vt* **1** *(parar)* to stop, halt; *(proceso, negociación)* to hold up. **2** *(retener)* to keep, delay, detain.

▷ *vpr* **detenerse** **1** *(pararse)* to stop, halt: **el tren se detuvo** *the train stopped.* **2** *(entretenerse)* to hang about, linger.

detenidamente *adv* carefully, thoroughly.

detenido,-a *adj* **1** *(parado)* held up. **2** *(minucioso)* detailed, thorough, careful. **3** JUR under arrest: **está detenido** *he's under arrest.*

▷ *nm & nf* JUR prisoner.

detenimiento ■ **con detenimiento** carefully, thoroughly.

detergente *nm* detergent.

deteriorar *vt (estropear)* to damage, spoil; *(gastar)* to wear out.

▷ *vpr* **deteriorarse** *(estropearse)* to get damaged; *(gastarse)* to wear out.

deterioro *nm* **1** *(daño)* damage, deterioration; *(desgaste)* wear and tear. **2** *fig (empeoramiento)* deterioration, worsening.

determinación *nf* **1** *(valor)* determination, resolution. **2** *(decisión)* decision. **3** *(firmeza)* firmness. ■ **tomar una determinación** to make a resolution, make a decision.

determinado,-a *adj* **1** *(preciso)* definite, precise, certain, given, particular. **2** *(día, hora, etc)* fixed, set,

appointed. 3 *(resuelto)* determined, decisive, resolute. 4 GRAM definite. 5 MAT determinate.
determinante *adj* decisive, determinant.
▷ *nm* MAT determinant.
determinar *vt* 1 *(decidir)* to resolve, decide, determine. 2 *(señalar)* to determine. 3 *(fijar)* to fix, set, appoint. 4 *(estipular)* to stipulate, specify. 5 *(causar)* to bring about, cause.
▷ *vpr* **determinarse** *(decidirse)* to make up one's mind, decide.
determinismo *nm* determinism.
detestar *vt* to detest, hate, abhor.
detonación *nf* detonation.
detonador *nm* detonator.
detonante *adj* detonating, explosive.
▷ *nm* 1 detonator. 2 *fig* trigger.
detractor,-ra *nm & nf* critic, detractor.
detrás *adv* 1 behind: **detrás de la puerta** *behind the door.* 2 *(en la parte posterior)* at the back, in the back. 3 *(después)* then, afterwards. ■ **ir detrás de** to go after.
detrimento *nm* 1 detriment. 2 *fig (daño moral)* harm, damage. ■ **en detrimento de** to the detriment of.
detrito *nm* detritus.
deuda *nf* 1 debt. 2 REL trespass. ● **deuda pública** national debt.
deudor,-ra *nm & nf* debtor.
devaluación *nf* devaluation.
devaluar [11] *vt* to devalue.
devanar *vt (hilo)* to wind, reel; *(alambre)* to coil.
devastar *vt* to devastate, ravage, lay waste.
devenir [90] *vi* to happen, occur.
devoción *nf* 1 devotion, devoutness. 2 *(afición)* devotion, dedication. ■ **con devoción** devoutly.
devolver [32] *vt* 1 *(volver algo a un estado anterior)* to put back, return. 2 *(por correo)* to send back, return. 3 *(restituir un dinero)* to refund, return. 4 *(una visita, un cumplido, etc)* to return, pay back. 5 *fam (vomitar)* to vomit, throw up, bring up.
▲ *pp* **devuelto,-a.**
▷ *vi fam (vomitar)* to throw up, be sick.
devorar *vt* 1 to devour.
devoto,-a *adj* 1 *(piadoso)* devout, pious. 2 *(digno de devoción)* devotional. 3 *fig (dedicado)* devoted.
devuelto,-a *nm* **devuelto** *(vómito)* vomit.
dextrina *nf* dextrin, dextrine.
Dg *sím* **(decagramo)** decagram; *(símbolo)* Dg.
dg *sím* **(decigramo)** decigram; *(símbolo)* dg.
día *nm* 1 day. 2 *(con luz)* daylight, daytime: **ya es de día** *it's daylight.* 3 *(tiempo)* day, weather. ■ **al día siguiente / al otro día** the following day. ‖ **¡buenos días!** good morning! ‖ **cada día / todos los días** each day, every day. ‖ **dar los buenos días** to say good morning. ‖ **de día** during the day. ‖ **del día** fresh. ‖ **día a día** day by day. ‖ **el día de mañana** *fig* in the future. ‖ **estar al día** *fig* to be up to date. ‖ **hacer buen/mal día** to be a nice/horrible day. ‖ **ser de día** to be daylight. ‖ **vivir al día** *fig* to live from hand to mouth, not to save a penny. ● **día de año nuevo** New Year's Day. ‖ **día de descanso** day off. ‖ **día de fiesta / día festivo** holiday, bank holiday. ‖ **día de paga** payday. ‖ **día entre semana** weekday.
▷ *nm pl* **días** *(vida)* days.

diabetes *nf inv* diabetes.
diabético,-a *adj* diabetic.
diablo *nm* devil, demon. ● **un pobre diablo** a poor devil.
diablura *nf* mischief, naughtiness.
diabólico,-a *adj* diabolic, devilish, diabolical.
diacrítico,-a *adj* diacritic, diacritical.
diacrónico,-a *adj* diachronic.
diadema *nf* 1 *(joya)* diadem. 2 *(adorno para el pelo)* hairband.
diafragma *nm* 1 ANAT diaphragm. 2 *(en fotografía)* aperture. 3 MED diaphragm, cap.
diagnóstico,-a *nm* diagnosis.
diagonal *adj* diagonal. ■ **en diagonal** diagonally.
diagrama *nm* diagram. ● **diagrama de flujo** INFORMÁ flow chart.
dial *nm* dial.
dialéctico,-a *adj* dialectical.
dialecto *nm* dialect.
diálisis *nf inv* dialysis.
dialogar [7] *vi* 1 *(conversar)* to talk, have a conversation. 2 *fig (negociar)* to negotiate, hold talks (**sobre**, on).
diálogo *nm* dialogue, conversation.
diamante *nm* diamond.
diámetro *nm* diameter.
diana *nf* 1 MIL reveille. 2 DEP *(objeto)* target; *(para dardos)* dartboard, *(blanco)* bull's eye.
diapositiva *nf* slide.
diario,-a *adj* daily, everyday.
▷ *nm* **diario** 1 *(prensa)* daily, paper, daily newspaper. 2 *(íntimo)* diary, journal. ■ **a diario** daily, every day. ● **diario de sesiones** parliamentary report.
diarrea *nf* diarrhoea (US diarrhea).
diástole *nf* diastole.
dibujante *nm o nf* 1 artist, drawer. 2 *(de dibujos animados)* cartoonist. 3 TÉC *(hombre)* draughtsman (US draftsman); *(mujer)* draughtswoman (US draftswoman).
dibujar *vt* 1 to draw, sketch. 2 TÉC to design. 3 *fig (describir)* to describe.
dibujo *nm* 1 *(arte)* drawing, sketching. 2 *(imagen)* drawing. 3 *(motivo)* pattern, design. ● **dibujo artístico** artistic drawing. ‖ **dibujo lineal** draughtsmanship (US draftsmanship). ‖ **dibujos animados** cartoons.
diccionario *nm* dictionary.
dicho,-a *adj* said, mentioned: **dicha casa...** *the said house...;* **dicho esto se marchó** *having said this he left.* ■ **dicho y hecho** no sooner said than done.
diciembre *nm* December.

See also **marzo**.

dictado,-a *nm* **dictado** dictation.
dictador,-ra *nm & nf* dictator.
dictadura *nf* dictatorship.
dictáfono® *nm* Dictaphone.
dictamen *nm* 1 *(opinión)* opinion. 2 *(informe)* report.
dictar *vt* 1 to dictate. 2 JUR *(ley)* to enact, decree, announce; *(sentencia)* to pronounce, pass. 3 *fig (sugerir)* to suggest, say.
didáctico,-a *adj* didactic.
diecinueve *adj (cardinal)* nineteen; *(ordinal)* nineteenth.
▷ *nm* 1 *(número)* nineteen. 2 *(fecha)* nineteenth.

See also **seis**.

dieciocho *adj (cardinal)* eighteen; *(ordinal)* eighteenth.
▷ *nm* **1** *(número)* eighteen. **2** *(fecha)* eighteenth.
See also **seis**.
dieciséis *adj (cardinal)* sixteen; *(ordinal)* sixteenth.
▷ *nm* **1** *(número)* sixteen. **2** *(fecha)* sixteenth.
See also **seis**.
diecisiete *adj (cardinal)* seventeen; *(ordinal)* seventeenth.
▷ *nm* **1** *(número)* seventeen. **2** *(fecha)* seventeenth.
See also **seis**.
diente *nm* **1** *(gen)* tooth. **2** *(de ajo)* clove. ■ **apretar los dientes** to grit one's teeth. ‖ **echar los dientes** to teethe. ‖ **hablar entre dientes** *fig* to mumble, mutter. ● **diente de leche** milk tooth.
diéresis *nf inv* diaeresis, dieresis.
diesel *adj* diesel.
diestro,-a *adj* **1** *lit* right. **2** *(hábil)* skilful (US skillful). ■ **a diestro y siniestro** left, right and centre (US center).
dieta *nf (régimen, alimentación)* diet.
dietético,-a *adj* dietary, dietetic.
diez *adj (cardinal)* ten; *(ordinal)* tenth.
▷ *nm* **1** *(número)* ten. **2** *(fecha)* tenth.
See also **seis**.
diezmilésimo,-a *adj* ten-thousandth.
▷ *nm & nf* ten-thousandth.
See also **sexto,-a**.
diezmo *nm* tithe.
difamar *vt* **1** to defame, slander. **2** *(por escrito)* to libel.
diferencia *nf* difference.
diferenciar [12] *vt (distinguir)* to differentiate, distinguish (**entre**, between).
▷ *vpr* **diferenciarse 1** to differ, be different (**por**, because of). **2** *(destacarse)* to distinguish OS, stand out (**por**, because of).
diferente *adj* different.
diferido,-a ■ **en diferido** recorded.
diferir [35] *vi* to differ, be different (**de/entre**, from).
difícil *adj* **1** difficult, hard. **2** *(improbable)* unlikely: **es difícil que nos encontremos allí** *it's unlikely that we'll meet there.*
dificultad *nf* **1** difficulty. **2** *(obstáculo)* obstacle; *(problema)* trouble, problem.
difuminar *vt* to blur, soften.
difundir *vt* **1** *(luz, calor)* to diffuse. **2** *fig (noticia, enfermedad)* to spread. **3** RAD TV to broadcast.
▷ *vpr* **difundirse 1** *(luz, calor)* to be diffused. **2** *fig (noticia, enfermedad)* to spread.
difunto,-a *nm & nf* deceased.
difusión *nf* **1** *(de luz, calor)* diffusion. **2** *fig (de noticia, enfermedad, etc)* spreading. **3** RAD broadcast, broadcasting.
digestión *nf* digestion.
digestivo,-a *adj* digestive.
digital *adj* digital.
digitalizar *vt* to digitize.
dígito *nm* digit.
dignarse *vpr* to deign (**a**, to), condescend (**a**, to).
dignidad *nf* **1** *(cualidad)* dignity. **2** *(cargo)* rank, office, post.
digno,-a *adj* **1** *(merecedor)* worthy, deserving. **2** *(adecuado)* fitting, appropiate. **3** *(respetable)* worthy, honourable (US honorable). **4** *(decente)* decent. ■ **digno,-a de admiración** worthy of admiration, admirable. ‖ **digno,-a de mención** worth mentioning.
digresión *nf* digression.
dilatación *nf* **1** dilation. **2** FÍS expansion.
dilatado,-a *adj* **1** dilated. **2** *(vasto)* vast, extensive, large. **3** FÍS expanded.
dilatar *vt* **1** to dilate. **2** FÍS to expand. **3** *(prolongar)* to prolong, extend. **4** *(retrasar)* to put off, delay, postpone.
dilema *nm* dilemma.
diligencia *nf* **1** *(cuidado)* diligence, care. **2** *(rapidez)* rapidity, speed. **3** *(carreta)* stagecoach.
▷ *nf pl* **diligencias** JUR *(trámites)* steps, measures; *(investigaciones)* investigations; *(resultados)* results of the investigations, findings; *(actuación)* proceedings.
diligente *adj* **1** *(cuidadoso)* diligent. **2** *(rápido)* quick.
dilucidar *vt* to elucidate, clear up, throw light on.
diluir [62] *vt* **1** *(un sólido)* to dissolve. **2** *(un líquido)* to dilute.
▷ *vpr* **diluirse 1** *(un sólido)* to dissolve. **2** *(un líquido)* to dilute.
diluviar [12] *vi* [Used only in 3rd person singular; it does not take a subject.] to pour with rain, pour down.
diluvio *nm* **1** flood. **2** *fig* torrent, deluge, flood: **un diluvio de preguntas** *a deluge of questions.*
dimensión *nf* **1** [Also used in plural with the same meaning.] dimension, size. **2** *fig (importancia)* importance.
diminutivo,-a *adj* diminutive.
▷ *nm* **diminutivo** diminutive.
diminuto,-a *adj* tiny, minute.
dimisión *nf* resignation.
dimitir *vi* to resign (**de**, from).
dimorfismo *nm* dimorphism.
Dinamarca *nf* Denmark.
dinamarqués,-esa *adj-nm & nf* → **danés,-esa**.
dinamismo *nm* dynamism.
dinamita *nf* **1** dynamite. **2** *fig* dynamite.
dinamitar *vt* to dynamite, blow up.
dinamo *nf* dynamo.
dinamómetro *nm* dynamometer.
dinastía *nf* dynasty.
dineral *nm* fortune.
dinero *nm* **1** money. **2** *(fortuna)* wealth. ■ **andar mal/escaso,-a de dinero** to be short of money. ‖ **tirar el dinero por la ventana** to throw money down the drain. ● **dinero en metálico** cash. ‖ **dinero negro/sucio** dirty money.
dinosaurio *nm* dinosaur.
dintel *nm* lintel.
diodo *nm* diode.
dioptría *nf* dioptre (US diopter).
dios *nm* god. ■ **¡Dios le bendiga!** God bless you! ‖ **¡Dios mío!** my God!, good heavens! ‖ **¡por Dios!** for goodness sake!, for God's sake!
diosa *nf* goddess.
dióxido *nm* dioxide.
diploma *nm* diploma.
diplomacia *nf* diplomacy.
diplomado,-a *adj* qualified, having a diploma.

diplomático,-a *adj* diplomatic.
▷ *nm & nf* diplomat.
díptico *nm* diptych.
diptongo *nm* diphthong.
diputación *nf* 1 *(cargo de diputado)* post of deputy, *member of the Spanish Parliament.* 2 *(conjunto de diputados)* deputies *pl.* ● **diputación provincial** county council.
diputado,-a *nm & nf (miembro del Congreso)* deputy, *member of the Spanish Parliament.*
dique *nm* 1 *(muro)* dike, breakwater. 2 *fig* barrier, obstacle, check.
dirección *nf* 1 *(acción de dirigir)* management, running. 2 *(cargo)* directorship, position of manager; *(de un partido)* leadership; *(de un colegio)* headship; *(de editorial)* position of editor. 3 *(junta)* board of directors, management. 4 *(oficina)* head office, headquarters *pl.* 5 *(sentido)* direction, way. 6 *(destino)* destination: **salió con dirección a Cádiz** *he left for Cádiz.* 7 *(domicilio)* address. 8 TÉC steering. ● **calle de dirección única** one-way street. ‖ **dirección asistida** AUTO power assisted steering, power steering.
directivo,-a *adj* directive, managing.
▷ *nm & nf* director, manager, board member.
directo,-a *adj* direct, straight.
▷ *nm* **directo** DEP straight hit. ■ **en directo** TV live.
director,-ra *nm & nf* 1 director, manager. 2 *(de colegio - hombre)* headmaster; *(mujer)* headmistress. 3 *(de universidad)* rector. 4 *(de editorial)* editor. 5 *(de cárcel)* governor. 6 *(de orquesta)* conductor. ● **director,-ra de cine** film director. ‖ **director,-ra de escena** stage manager.
directorio,-a *nm* **directorio** 1 *(gobierno)* governing body. 2 *(de direcciones)* directory, guide. 3 *(normas)* instructions *pl,* directive. 4 INFORMÁ directory.
dirigente *adj* leading, directing.
▷ *nm o nf* 1 leader. 2 *(de empresa)* manager.
dirigir [6] *vt* 1 *(empresa)* to manage; *(negocio, escuela)* to run; *(un periódico)* to edit. 2 *(orquesta)* to conduct; *(película)* to direct; *(obra de teatro)* to direct, produce. 3 *(coche)* to drive, steer; *(barco)* to steer; *(avión)* to pilot. 4 *(un partido)* to lead; *(expedición, revuelta)* to head; *(negociaciones)* to conduct. 5 *(carta, protesta)* to address; *(consejos)* to aim; *(esfuerzos, atención)* to concentrate. 6 *(apuntar - arma, telescopio)* to direct, aim, point; *(- mirada)* to turn.
▷ *vpr* **dirigirse** 1 *(ir)* to go (**a**, to), make one's way (**a**, to), make (**a**, for). 2 *(hablar)* to address (**a**, -), speak (**a**, to): **se dirigió a su padre** *she addressed her father.* 3 *(escribir)* to write.
discapacitado,-a *adj* handicapped, disabled.
disciplina *nf* 1 *(conjunto de reglas)* discipline. 2 *(doctrina)* doctrine. 3 *(asignatura)* subject. 4 *(azote)* scourge, discipline.
disciplinado,-a *adj* disciplined.
discípulo,-a *nm & nf* 1 *(seguidor)* disciple, follower. 2 *(alumno)* pupil, student.
disc-jockey *nm o nf* disc jockey, DJ.
disco *nm* 1 disc. 2 DEP discus. 3 *(de música)* record. 4 INFORMÁ disk. ● **disco duro** hard disk.
disconforme *adj* in disagreement, not in agreement.
disconformidad *nf* disagreement, disconformity.
discontinuo,-a *adj* discontinuous. ● **línea discontinua** *(en carretera)* broken white line.
discordia *nf* discord.
discoteca *nf (local)* discotheque, nightclub.
discreción *nf* 1 *(sensatez)* discretion, tact. 2 *(agudeza)* wit. ■ **a discreción** 1 *(a voluntad)* at one's discretion. 2 *(sin límite)* in great amounts.
discrecional *adj* optional.
discrepar *vi* 1 *(diferenciarse)* to differ (**de**, from). 2 *(disentir)* to disagree (**de**, with): **discrepó de su padre** *she disagreed with her father.*
discreto,-a *adj* 1 *(prudente)* discreet, prudent, tactful. 2 *(sobrio)* sober, discreet. 3 *(moderado)* moderate, average, reasonable.
discriminación *nf* discrimination. ● **discriminación racial** racial discrimination.
discriminar *vt* 1 *(diferenciar)* to discriminate, distinguish. 2 *(por raza, religión, etc)* to discriminate against.
disculpa *nf* excuse, apology. ■ **dar disculpas** to make excuses. ‖ **pedir disculpas a** ALGN to apologize to SB.
disculpar *vt* 1 *(descargar de culpa)* to excuse: **su enfermedad le disculpa** *his illness excuses him.* 2 *(perdonar)* to excuse, forgive: **¡disculpe!** *excuse me!*
▷ *vpr* **disculparse** to apologize (**por**, for), excuse OS.
discurrir *vi* 1 *(andar)* to walk, wander. 2 *(fluir)* to flow, run. 3 *(transcurrir)* to pass, go by. 4 *fig (reflexionar)* to think (**sobre**, about), ponder (**sobre**, on/over), meditate (**sobre**, on).
discurso *nm (conferencia)* speech, lecture, discourse.
discusión *nf* 1 *(charla)* discussion. 2 *(disputa)* argument.
discutir *vi* 1 *(examinar)* to discuss (**de**, -). 2 *(contender)* to argue.
disecar [1] *vt* 1 *(dividir en partes)* to dissect. 2 *(rellenar animales)* to stuff. 3 *(planta)* to dry. 4 *fig* to dissect.
diseminar *vt* to disseminate, scatter, spread.
▷ *vpr* **diseminarse** to spread.
disentir [35] *vi* to dissent, disagree (**de**, with).
diseñador,-ra *nm & nf* designer.
diseñar *vt* to design.
diseño *nm* design.
disertar *vt* to discourse (**sobre**, on/upon), lecture (**sobre**, on).
disfraz *nm* 1 *(para engañar)* disguise. 2 *(para una fiesta, etc)* fancy dress outfit, fancy dress costume.
disfrazar [4] *vt* 1 *(persona)* to disguise, dress up. 2 *(emoción)* hide, conceal; *(voz)* disguise.
▷ *vpr* **disfrazarse** 1 *(para engañar)* to disguise OS (**de**, as). 2 *(para una fiesta, etc)* to dress up (**de**, as).
disfrutar *vt* 1 *(poseer)* to own, enjoy, possess; *(pensión, renta)* to receive. 2 *(aprovechar)* to make the most of.
▷ *vi* 1 *(poseer)* to enjoy (**de**, -), have (**de**, -), possess (**de**, -): **disfruta de buena salud** *he enjoys good health.* 2 *(gozar)* to enjoy, enjoy OS: **disfruté mucho en el cine** *I enjoyed myself very much at the cinema.*

disgustar *vt* 1 *(molestar)* to displease, annoy, upset. 2 *(desagradar)* to dislike: **me disgusta ese sabor dulce** *I don't like that sweet taste.*
▷ *vpr* **disgustarse** 1 *(enfadarse)* to get angry, get upset. 2 *(pelearse)* to quarrel (**con**, with).
disgusto *nm* 1 *(enfado)* displeasure, annoyance, anger. 2 *fig (pelea)* argument, quarrel. ■ **a disgusto** against one's will, reluctantly, unwillingly. ǀ **dar un disgusto** to upset. ǀ **llevarse un disgusto** to get upset.
disidente *nm o nf* dissident.
disimular *vt (ocultar)* to hide, conceal.
▷ *vi* to pretend, dissemble: **no disimules** *stop pretending.*
disimulo *nm* pretence (US pretense), dissemblance.
disipar *vt* 1 *(derrochar)* to squander, dissipate. 2 *fig (dudas, temores)* to dispel; *(esperanzas)* to destroy; *(sospechas)* to allay.
▷ *vpr* **disiparse** 1 *(desvanecerse)* to clear, disperse, dissipate. 2 *(evaporarse)* to evaporate. 3 *fig* to vanish, be dispelled.
dislexia *nf* dyslexia.
dislocar [1] *vt* 1 *(sacar de lugar)* to dislocate. 2 *(dispersar)* to disperse. 3 *fig (desmembrar)* to dismember.
disminución *nf* decrease, reduction.
disminuido,-a *adj* disabled.
disminuir [62] *vt* 1 *(gen)* to decrease. 2 *(medidas, velocidad)* to reduce.
▷ *vi* 1 *(gen)* to diminish. 2 *(temperatura, precios)* to drop, fall.
disolución *nf* 1 *(gen)* dissolution. 2 *(anulación)* invalidation. 3 *fig (relajación)* looseness, dissoluteness. 4 QUÍM solution, dissolution.
disolvente *adj* solvent, dissolvent.
▷ *nm* solvent, dissolvent.
disolver [32]
▲ *pp* **disuelto,-a.** *vt* 1 *(gen)* to dissolve. 2 *(anular)* to annul. 3 *(destruir)* to destroy.
▷ *vpr* **disolverse** 1 *(gen)* to dissolve. 2 *fig* to be dissolved.
disonante *adj* 1 MÚS dissonant, discordant. 2 *fig* discordant.
dispar *adj* unlike, different, disparate.
disparar *vt* 1 *(arma)* to fire; *(bala, flecha)* to shoot. 2 *(lanzar)* to hurl, throw. 3 DEP to shoot.
▷ *vi fig (disparatar)* to talk nonsense.
disparatado,-a *adj* absurd, foolish, ridiculous.
disparo *nm* 1 *(acción)* firing. 2 *(efecto)* shot. 3 DEP shot.
dispensar *vt* 1 *(conceder)* to give, grant; *(elogios)* to confer. 2 *(medicamentos)* to dispense. 3 *(eximir)* to exempt, free. 4 *(disculpar)* to forgive, pardon. ■ **dispense** excuse me, pardon me.
dispersar *vt* 1 *(gen)* to disperse, scatter. 2 *(manifestantes)* to break up. 3 *fig (esfuerzos, atención, etc)* to spread, divide.
▷ *vpr* **dispersarse** 1 *(gen)* to disperse, scatter.
disperso,-a *adj (esparcido)* scattered.
disponer [78] *vt* 1 *(colocar)* to dispose, arrange, set out. 2 *(preparar)* to prepare, get ready. 3 *(ordenar)* to order, decree.
▲ *pp* **dispuesto,-a.**
▷ *vi* 1 *(tener)* to have (**de**, -). 2 *(hacer uso)* to make use (**de**, of), have the use (**de**, of).
▷ *vpr* **disponerse** *(prepararse)* to get ready (**a**, to), prepare (**a**, to).
disponibilidad *nf* availability.
disponible *adj* 1 *(gen)* available. 2 *(tiempo)* spare, free.
disposición *nf* 1 *(colocación)* arrangement, layout. 2 *(aptitud)* aptitude, talent, gift. 3 JUR order, regulation.
dispositivo *nm* device, gadget.
dispuesto,-a *adj* 1 *(decidido)* determined. 2 *(preparado)* prepared, ready, willing.
disputa *nf (discusión)* dispute, argument, quarrel.
disputar *vt* 1 *(competir)* to compete for, contend for. 2 DEP to play: **los equipos disputaron un partido amistoso** *the teams played a friendly match.*
disquete *nm* diskette, floppy disk.
disquetera *nf* disk drive.
distancia *nf* 1 distance. 2 *fig (diferencia)* difference, gap. ■ **a distancia** from a distance: **lo vimos a distancia** *we saw it from a distance.*
distanciar [12] *vt* to distance, separate.
▷ *vpr* **distanciarse** 1 to move away, become separated. 2 *fig (no tratarse)* to grow apart, drift apart. 3 *fig (desvincularse)* to distance OS, disassociate OS.
distante *adj* 1 *(en el espacio)* distant, far; *(en el tiempo)* distant, remote. 2 *fig* distant.
distendido,-a *adj* 1 *(en medicina)* distended. 2 *(ambiente, etc)* relaxed.
distensión *nf* 1 *(acción)* slackening. 2 MED strain. 3 *fig* easing. 4 POL détente.
distinción *nf* 1 *(gen)* distinction. 2 *(elegancia)* distinction, elegance, refinement. 3 *(deferencia)* deference, respect, consideration.
distinguido,-a *adj* 1 distinguished. 2 *(elegante)* elegant.
distinguir [8] *vt* 1 *(diferenciar)* to distinguish. 2 *(caracterizar)* to mark, distinguish. 3 *(ver)* to see, make out.
▷ *vpr* **distinguirse** 1 *(destacar)* to stand out, distinguish OS.
distinto,-a *adj* 1 *(diferente)* different. 2 *(claro)* distinct.
▷ *adj vpr* **distintos,-as** various, several.
distorsión *nf* distortion.
distracción *nf* 1 *(divertimiento)* amusement, pastime, recreation, entertainment. 2 *(despiste)* distraction, absent-mindedness. 3 *(error)* oversight, slip.
distraer [88] *vt* 1 *(divertir)* to amuse, entertain. 2 *(atención)* to distract; *(pena, dolor, preocupaciones)* to take one's mind off.
▷ *vpr* **distraerse** 1 *(divertirse)* to amuse OS, enjoy OS. 2 *(despistarse)* to get distracted, be inattentive, be absent-minded.
distraído,-a *adj* 1 *(desatento)* absent-minded. 2 *(entretenido)* entertaining, fun.
distribución *nf* 1 distribution. 2 *(colocación)* arrangement. 3 *(reparto)* delivery. 4 *(disposición de una casa, etc)* layout.
distribuidor,-ra *adj* distributing, distributive.
▷ *nm & nf* 1 distributor. 2 COM wholesaler.

distribuir [62] *vt* 1 *(repartir)* to distribute. 2 *(correo)* to deliver; *(trabajo)* to share, allot; *(agua, gas, etc)* to supply. 3 *(un piso)* to lay out.
distrito *nm* district.
disturbio *nm* disturbance, riot.
disuadir *vt* to dissuade (**de**, from).
disuasión *nf* dissuasion.
disuasivo,-a *adj* dissuasive, deterrent.
disuasorio,-a *adj* dissuasive, deterrent.
DIU *abrev* MED **(dispositivo intrauterino)** intrauterine device; *(abreviatura)* IUD.
diurno,-a *adj* daily, daytime.
diva *nf* MÚS prima donna, diva.
divagar [7] *vi* to digress, ramble.
diván *nm* divan, couch.
díver *adj inv fam* great fun.
divergencia *nf* divergence.
divergente *adj* divergent, diverging.
divergir [6] *vi* to diverge.
diversidad *nf* diversity, variety.
diversificar [1] *vt* to diversify, vary.
diversión *nf* fun, amusement, entertainment.
diverso,-a *adj* different.
▷ *adj vpr* **diversos;-as** several, various.
divertido,-a *adj* 1 *(gracioso)* funny, amusing. 2 *(entretenido)* fun, entertaining, enjoyable.
divertir [35] *vt* to amuse, entertain.
▷ *vpr* **divertirse** to enjoy OS, have a good time: **¡diviértete!** *enjoy yourself!*
dividendo *nm* dividend.
dividir *vt* 1 to divide. 2 *(separar)* to divide, separate: **el río divide las dos comarcas** *the river separates the two counties.* 3 *(repartir)* to divide, split.
▷ *vpr* **dividirse** *(separarse)* to divide, split up.
divino,-a *adj* 1 divine. 2 *fam (bonito)* beautiful, gorgeous; *(extraordinario)* wonderful, fantastic.
divisa *nf* 1 *(emblema)* badge, emblem. 2 *(en heráldica)* device. 3 *(moneda)* currency, foreign currency.
divisar *vt* to discern, make out, distinguish.
divisible *adj* 1 dividable. 2 MAT divisible.
división *nf* 1 división. 2 *fig* division, divergence.
divisor,-ra *nm* **divisor** 1 divider. 2 MAT divisor. ● **máximo común divisor** MAT highest common factor, (US highest common denominator). ‖ **mínimo común divisor** MAT lowest common factor, (US lowest common denominator).
divo,-a *nm & nf* star.
divorciado,-a *adj* divorced.
▷ *nm & nf (hombre)* divorcé; *(mujer)* divorcée.
divorciar [12] *vt* to divorce.
▷ *vpr* **divorciarse** to get divorced (**de**, from).
divorcio *nm* divorce.
divulgar [7] *vt* 1 *(difundir)* to divulge, spread, disclose. 2 *(por radio)* to broadcast. 3 *(propagar)* to popularize.
▷ *vpr* **divulgarse** to become known, spread.
Djibouti *nm* Djibouti, Jibouti.
dl *sím* **(decilitro)** decilitre (US deciliter); *(símbolo)* dl.
Dl *sím* **(decalitro)** decalitre (US decaliter); *(símbolo)* Dl.
dm *sím* **(decímetro)** decimetre (US decimeter); *(símbolo)* dm.
Dm *sím* **(decámetro)** decametre (US decameter); *(símbolo)* Dm.
do *nm (de solfa)* doh, do; *(de escala diatónica)* C.
dobladillo *nm* 1 *(de vestido, etc)* hem. 2 *(de pantalones)* turn-up, US cuff.
doblado,-a *adj* 1 *(mediana estatura y recio)* thickset. 2 *(curvo)* bent. 3 *(película)* dubbed. 4 *fam (agotado)* dead beat.
doblaje *nm* dubbing.
doblar *vt* 1 *(duplicar)* to double: **le doblo la edad** *I'm twice as old as she is.* 2 *(plegar)* to fold. 3 *(torcer)* to bend: **doblar un dedo** *to bend a finger.* 4 *(esquina)* to turn, go round. 5 *(película)* to dub. 6 *(a un actor)* to stand in (**a**, for), double (**a**, for).
▷ *vpr* **doblarse** 1 *(plegarse)* to fold. 2 *(torcerse)* to bend. 3 *(rendirse)* to give in.
doble *adj* 1 double. 2 *(nacionalidad)* dual. 3 *(fornido)* thickset. 4 *fig (engañoso)* two-faced.
▷ *nm* 1 double: **tiene el doble que yo** *he's got twice as much as I have.* 2 *(duplicado)* duplicate.
▷ *nm o nf* CINE stand-in, double; *(hombre)* stunt man; *(mujer)* stunt woman.
▷ *adv* double.
▷ *nm pl* **dobles** *(tenis)* doubles. ■ **ver doble** to see double.
doblez *nm (pliegue)* fold.
doce *adj (cardinal)* twelve; *(ordinal)* twelfth.
▷ *nm* 1 *(número)* twelve. 2 *(fecha)* twelfth.

See also **seis.**

docena *nf* dozen. ■ **a docenas** COM by the dozen.
docente *adj* teaching.
dócil *adj* docile, obedient.
doctor,-ra *nm & nf* doctor.
doctrina *nf* 1 doctrine. 2 *(enseñanza)* teachings *pl.*
documentación *nf* 1 documentation, documents *pl.* 2 *(para identificar)* papers *pl,* identification.
documentado,-a *adj* 1 documented, researched. 2 *fam (enterado)* informed.
documental *adj* documentary.
▷ *nm* documentary.
documentalista *nm o nf* 1 *(cineasta)* documentary maker. 2 *(investigador)* researcher.
documentar *vt* 1 to document. 2 *(a una persona)* to give information.
▷ *vpr* **documentarse** to research (**sobre**, -), get information (**sobre**, about/on).
documento *nm* document.
dodecaedro *nm* dodecahedron.
dodecasílabo,-a *nm* **dodecasílabo** dodecasyllable, Alexandrine.
dogma *nm* dogma.
dogmático,-a *adj* dogmatic.
dólar *nm* dollar.
dolencia *nf* ailment, illness.
doler [32] *vi* 1 to ache, hurt. 2 *(afligir)* to distress, sadden, upset, hurt: **me duele tal pobreza** *such poverty distresses me.* 3 *(sentir)* to be sorry, be sad: **me duele habérselo dicho** *I'm sorry I told her about it.*
▷ *vpr* **dolerse** 1 *(arrepentirse)* to repent (**de**, of), feel sorry (**de**, for). 2 *(lamentarse)* to complain (**de**, of). 3 *(notar el efecto)* to feel the effects (**de**, of).
dolido,-a *adj fig* hurt.
dolor *nm* 1 pain, ache. 2 *fig* pain, sorrow, grief. ■ **causar dolor** *fig* to sadden, hurt, upset. ● **dolor de cabeza** headache.

dolorido,-a *adj* 1 sore, aching. 2 *fig* sorrowful, sad, hurt.

doloroso,-a *adj* 1 painful. 2 *fig* painful, distressing.

domador,-ra *nm & nf* tamer; *(de caballos)* horse breaker.

domar *vt* 1 to tame; *(caballos)* to break in. 2 *fig* to tame, control.

domesticar [1] *vt* 1 to domesticate, tame. 2 *(adiestrar)* to train. 3 *fig* to subdue.

doméstico,-a *adj* domestic.
▷ *nm & nf* domestic, servant.

domiciliación *nf* payment by direct debit.

domiciliar [12] *vt* 1 *(dar domicilio)* to house, lodge. 2 FIN to pay by direct debit.

domicilio *nm* 1 residence, home, abode. 2 *(dirección)* address.

dominante *adj* 1 dominant, dominating. 2 *(que avasalla)* domineering.

dominar *vt* 1 *(tener bajo dominio)* to dominate. 2 *(avasallar)* to domineer. 3 *(controlar)* to control, restrain. 4 *(conocer a fondo)* to master: **domina el inglés** *she has a good command of English.*
▷ *vi* 1 *(ser superior)* to dominate. 2 *(destacar)* to stand out: **domina mucho el rojo** *red is the predominant colour.* 3 *(predominar)* to predominate.
▷ *vpr* **dominarse** *(controlarse)* to control OS, restrain OS.

domingo *nm* Sunday.

See also **jueves.**

dominguero,-a *nm & nf pey (conductor)* Sunday driver; *(excursionista)* day tripper.

Dominica *nf* Dominica.

dominicano,-a *adj* Dominican.
▷ *nm & nf* Dominican. ● **República Dominicana** Dominican Republic.

dominio *nm* 1 *(soberanía)* dominion. 2 *(poder)* power, control. 3 *(supremacía)* supremacy. 4 *(de conocimientos)* mastery, good knowledge; *(de un idioma)* good command. 5 *(territorio)* domain. 6 INFORMÁ domain.

dominó *nm* 1 *(juego)* dominoes *pl*. 2 *(fichas)* set of dominoes. 3 *(disfraz)* domino.

don[1] *nm* 1 *(regalo)* gift, present. 2 *(talento)* talent, natural gift.

don[2] *nm* Mr: **Señor Don Juan Pérez** *Mr Juan Pérez.*

Courtesy title placed before the first names of men.

donante *nm o nf* donor. ● **donante de sangre** blood donor.

donar *vt fml* to donate, give.

donativo *nm* donation.

donde *adv* where, in which. ■ **de donde / desde donde** from where, whence.

dónde *pron* where: **¿dónde está?** *where is it?;* **no sé dónde está** *I don't know where it is;* **¿a dónde va?** *where is he going?;* **¿hasta dónde?** *how far?*

dondequiera *adv (en cualquier parte)* anywhere; *(en todas partes)* everywhere: **dondequiera que esté lo encontraremos** *wherever he is we'll find him.*

dónut [Registered trademark.] *nm* doughnut.
▲ *pl* **dónuts.**

doña *nf* Mrs: **Doña Elena Suárez** *Mrs Elena Suárez.*

Courtesy title placed before first names of women.

dopaje *nm* doping.

dopar *vt* to dope, drug.

doping *nm* doping, drug-taking.

dorada *nf* gilthead bream.

dorado,-a *adj* golden; *(cubierto de oro)* gold-plated, gilt.
▷ *nm* **dorado** TÉC gilding.

dorar *vt* 1 *(cubrir con oro)* to gild. 2 *(dar un baño de oro)* to gold-plate. 3 CULIN to brown.

dórico,-a *nm* **dórico** Doric. ● **orden dórico** Doric order.

dormido,-a *adj* 1 asleep. 2 *(soñoliento)* sleepy: **tengo el brazo dormido** *my arm has gone numb, my arm has gone to sleep.* ■ **quedarse dormido,-a** 1 *(dormir)* to fall asleep. 2 *(dormirse más de la cuenta)* to oversleep.

dormilón,-ona *adj fam* fond of sleeping.
▷ *nm & nf fam* sleepyhead.

dormir [33] *vi* 1 to sleep: **tengo ganas de dormir** *I feel sleepy.* 2 *(pernoctar)* to spend the night.
▷ *vt* to put to sleep.
▷ *vpr* **dormirse** 1 to fall asleep, nod off. 2 *fig* to go to sleep: **se me ha dormido el pie** *my foot has gone to sleep.* 3 *fig (dejar de esforzarse)* to let things slide. ■ **¡a dormir!** to bed! ‖ **dormir a pierna suelta** *fam* to sleep like a log. ‖ **dormir como un lirón** *fam* to sleep like a log. ‖ **dormir la siesta** to have a nap.

dormitorio *nm* 1 *(en una casa)* bedroom. 2 *(colectivo)* dormitory. 3 *(muebles)* bedroom suite.

dorsal *adj* 1 dorsal, back. 2 LING dorsal.
▷ *nm* DEP number.

dorso *nm* back, reverse. ● **dorso de la mano** back of the hand.

dos *adj (cardinal)* two; *(ordinal)* second: **entre ellas dos** *between the two of them.*
▷ *nm (número)* two; *(fecha)* second. ■ **cada dos por tres** *fam* every five minutes. ● **dos veces** twice: **es dos veces mayor que su hermana** *she's twice as old as her sister.*

See also **seis.**

doscientos,-as *adj (numeral)* two hundred; *(cardinal)* two-hundredth.
▷ *nm & nf* two hundred.

See also **seis.**

dosel *nm* canopy.

dosificador *nm* dispenser.

dosificar [1] *vt* 1 *(gen)* to dose. 2 *(esfuerzos, etc)* to measure.

dosis *nf inv* dose.

dossier *nm* dossier.
▲ *pl* **dossieres.**

dotación *nf* 1 *(con lo que se dota)* endowment. 2 *(tripulación)* complement, crew. 3 *(personal)* staff, personnel.

dotado,-a *adj* 1 *(equipado)* equipped, provided: **está dotado con airbag** *it's equipped with an airbag.* 2 *(con dotes)* gifted: **está muy dotado para las matemáticas** *he has a talent for mathematics.*

dotar *vt* 1 *(dar dote)* to give a dowry. 2 *(proveer de personal)* to staff (**de**, with); *(de material)* to equip (**de**, with). 3 *(bienes, dinero)* to assign. 4 *fig (dones y cualidades)* to endow (**de**, with), provide (**de**, with):

la naturaleza la dotó de un sexto sentido *nature endowed her with a sixth sense.*

dote *nm & nf* dowry.
▷ *nf pl* **dotes** gift *sing*, talent *sing*: **tiene dotes para el violín** *he's a gifted violinist.*

dovela *nf* voussoir.

dracma *nm* drachma.

dragado *nm* dredging.

dragaminas *nm inv* minesweeper.

dragar [7] *vt* to dredge.

drago *nm* dragon tree.

dragón *nm* **1** *(reptil)* flying dragon. **2** *(animal fabuloso)* dragon. **3** *(planta)* snapdragon. **4** *(pez)* greater weever. **5** *(soldado)* dragoon.

dralón [Registered trademark.] *nm* dralon.

drama *nm* drama.

dramático,-a *adj* dramatic.
▷ *nm & nf* dramatist.

dramatismo *nm* dramatism, drama.

dramatización *nf* dramatization.

dramatizar [4] *vt* to dramatize.

dramaturgia *nf* dramatics.

dramaturgo,-a *nm & nf* playwright, dramatist.

dramón *nm fam* melodrama.

drapeado,-a *adj* draped.
▷ *nm* **drapeado** drapery.

drástico,-a *adj* drastic.

drenaje *nm* drainage.

drenar *vt* to drain.

Dresde *nf* Dresden.

dribling *nm* dribbling.

dril *nm* **1** *(tela)* drill, drilling. **2** *(mono)* drill.

drive *nm* drive.

droga *nf* **1** drug. **2** *fig (cosa desagradable)* nuisance. ● **droga blanda/dura** soft/hard drug.

drogadicción *nf* drug addiction.

drogadicto,-a *adj* addicted to drugs.
▷ *nm & nf* drug addict.

drogado,-a *adj* drugged (up).
▷ *nm & nf* drug addict.

drogar [7] *vt* to drug.
▷ *vpr* **drogarse** to take drugs.

drogata *nm o nf argot* junkie.

drogodependencia *nf* drug addiction, drug dependency.

drogodependiente *nm o nf* drug addict.

droguería *nf* hardware shop.

dromedario *nm* dromedary.

drosera *nf* sundew.

druida,-esa *nm & nf* druid.

dual *adj* dual.
▷ *nm* dual. ● **emisión en dual** bilingual broadcast.

dualidad *nf* duality.

dualismo *nm* dualism.

dualista *adj* dualistic.

dubitativo,-a *adj* doubtful.

Dublín *nm* Dublin.

dublinés,-esa *adj* of Dublin, from Dublin.
▷ *nm & nf* Dubliner.

ducado *nm* **1** dukedom, duchy. **2** *(antigua moneda)* ducat.

ducal *adj* duke's, ducal.

ducentésimo,-a *adj* two-hundredth.
▷ *nm & nf* two-hundredth.

ducha *nf* shower. ■ **darse/tomar una ducha** to take a shower, have a shower. ‖ **una ducha de agua fría** *fam* a blow, a shock.

duchar *vt* to give a shower.
▷ *vpr* **ducharse** to take a shower, have a shower.

ducho,-a *adj* knowledgeable. ■ **estar ducho,-a en la materia** to be well versed in the subject, be an expert on the subject .

dúctil *adj* ductile.

ductilidad *nf* ductility.

duda *nf* doubt. ■ **no hay duda** there is no doubt. ‖ **no te quepa duda** make no mistake about it. ‖ **sacar a** ALGN **de dudas** to dispel SB's doubts. ‖ **salir de dudas** to shed one's doubts. ‖ **sin duda** no doubt, without a doubt.

dudar *vi* **1** to doubt, have doubts. **2** *(titubear)* to hesitate: **dudo entre quedarme o marcharme** *I'm not sure whether to stay or leave.*
▷ *vt* to doubt: **lo dudo** *I doubt it.* ■ **dudar de** ALGN to doubt SB, mistrust SB.

dudoso,-a *adj* **1** *(incierto)* doubtful, uncertain. **2** *(vacilante)* hesitant, undecided. **3** *(sospechoso)* suspicious, dubious. **4** *(poco seguro)* questionable.

duelo[1] *nm (combate)* duel. ■ **batirse en duelo** to fight a duel.

duelo[2] *nm* **1** *(dolor)* grief, affliction. **2** *(luto)* mourning; *(reunión de parientes)* wake; *(cortejo)* cortege, funeral procession.

duende *nm* **1** *(espíritu travieso)* goblin, elf. **2** *(encanto)* charm, magic.

duendecillo *nm* imp, pixie.

dueño,-a *nm & nf* **1** *(propietario)* owner: **¿quién es la dueña?** *who is the owner?* **2** *(de casa, piso - hombre)* landlord; *(mujer)* landlady. ■ **hacerse dueño,-a de la situación** *fig* to get the situation under control. ‖ **ser dueño,-a de sí mismo,-a** to be self-possessed.

Duero *nm* **el Duero** the Douro.

dueto *nm* short duet.

dulce *adj* **1** *(gen)* sweet. **2** *(clima)* mild. **3** *fig* soft, gentle.
▷ *nm* CULIN *(caramelo)* sweet; *(pastel)* cake. ● **dulce de membrillo** quince jelly.

dulcería *nf* **1** confectionery. **2** *(tienda)* confectioner's, US candy store.

dulcificar [1] *vt* **1** to sweeten. **2** *fig* to soften.

dulzón,-ona *adj* sickly sweet, oversweet.

dulzor *nm* **1** sweetness. **2** *fig* gentleness, sweetness, softness.

dulzura *nf* **1** sweetness. **2** *fig* softness, gentleness, sweetness. **3** *fig (clima)* mildness.

dumping *nm* dumping.

duna *nf* dune.

dúo *nm* duet.

duodécimo,-a *adj* twelfth.
▷ *nm & nf* twelfth.

See also **sexto,-a**.

duodenal *adj* duodenal.

duodeno *nm* duodenum.

dúplex *adj inv* duplex.

▷ *nm* **1** *(casa)* duplex, duplex apartment. **2** TÉC duplex.

duplicado,-a *adj* duplicate.

▷ *nm* **duplicado** duplicate, copy. ■ **por duplicado** in duplicate.

duplicar [1] *vt (gen)* to duplicate; *(cantidad)* to double.

▷ *vpr* **duplicarse** to double.

duplicidad *nf* **1** duplicity. **2** *fig* duplicity, falseness.

duplo,-a *adj* double.

▷ *nm & nf* double.

duque *nm* duke.

duquesa *nf* duchess.

durable *adj* durable, lasting.

duración *nf* **1** duration, length: **¿cuál es la duración de la obra?** *how long is the play?* **2** *(coche, máquina, etc)* life. ■ **de larga duración 1** *(periodo de tiempo)* long, long-term. **2** *(bombilla, etc)* long-life. **3** *(enfermedad)* long-term.

duradero,-a *adj* durable, lasting.

duralex [Registered trademark.] *nm* duralex.

duramen *nm* duramen.

▲ *pl* **durámenes.**

duramente *adv* **1** *(con dificultad)* hard. **2** *(con severidad)* harshly.

durante *adv* during, in, for: **viví allí durante un año** *lived there for a year;* **durante el verano** *during the summer;* **durante todo el día** *all day long.*

durar *vi* **1** to last, go on for: **la película duró tres hora** *the film went on for three hours.* **2** *(ropa, calzado)* to wear well, last: **ese abrigo le duró mucho** *he got a lo of wear out of that coat.*

durativo,-a *adj* **1** lasting. **2** GRAM durative.

duraznero *nm* peach tree.

durazno *nm* **1** *(fruto)* peach. **2** *(árbol)* peach tree.

dureza *nf* **1** hardness, toughness. **2** *fig (de carácter)* toughness, harshness, severity. **3** *(callosidad)* corn ● **dureza de corazón** hardheartedness, callousness.

durmiente *adj* sleeping.

▷ *nm* sleeper. ● **la Bella Durmiente** Sleeping Beauty.

duro,-a *adj* **1** hard. **2** *(carne)* tough; *(pan)* stale. **3** *(difícil)* hard, difficult. **4** *(cruel)* tough, hardhearted callous. **5** *(resistente)* strong, tough. **6** *(obstinado)* obstinate, stubborn.

▷ *nm* **duro 1** *(antiguamente)* five pesetas; *(moneda)* five-peseta coin. **2** *fam* tough guy.

▷ *adv* hard: **dale duro** *hit him hard.* ■ **ser duro,-a de mollera** to be thick, be as thick as two short planks.

dux *nm inv* HIST doge.

DVD *nm* **(Disco Versátil Digital)** DVD.

E

E, e *nf (la letra)* E, e.

e *conj* and.

Used instead of **y** before words beginning with **i** or **hi compramos manzanas e higos** *we bought some apples and figs.*

EAU *abrev* **(Emiratos Árabes Unidos)** United Arab Emirates; *(abreviatura)* UAE.

ebanista *nm o nf* cabinet-maker.

ebanistería *nf* **1** *(oficio)* cabinet-making. **2** *(taller)* cabinet-maker's.

ébano *nm* ebony.

ebonita *nf* ebonite.

ebrio,-a *adj* **1** drunk, intoxicated, inebriated. **2** *fig* blind: **ebrio de ira** *blind with anger.*

ebullición *nf* **1** *(hervor)* boil, boiling. **2** *fig (agitación)* excitement, turmoil, ebullience.

eccema *nm* eczema.

echado,-a *adj (tumbado)* lying down.

echar *vt* **1** *(lanzar)* to throw. **2** *(dejar caer)* to put, drop. **3** *(líquido)* to pour; *(comida)* to give; *(sal)* to add, put in. **4** *(carta)* to post, US mail. **5** *(expulsar)* to throw out: **lo han echado del cine** *he was thrown out of the cinema.* **6** *(despedir de empleo)* to sack, dismiss, fire. **7** *(brotar, salir - plantas)* to sprout; *(- dientes)* to cut; *(- pelo)* to grow. **8** *(decir)* to tell. **9** *(emanar)* to give out, give off: **la caja de fusibles echa chispas** *sparks are coming out of the fuse box.* **10** *(suponer, calcular)* to guess: **yo le echo 40** *I think she's 40.* **11** *(poner, aplicar)* to put on, apply. **12** *(llave)* to lock, turn; *(cerrojo)* to bolt, fasten. **13** *(multas, tributos)* to give, impose. **14** *(en naipes)* to deal. **15** *fam (en el cine, teatro)* to show, put on: **echan una buena película en la tele** *there's a good film on TV.*
▷ *vi* **1 echar a** + *inf (empezar)* to begin to: **echó a correr** *she ran off.* **2 echar de** + *inf (dar)*: **echar de comer** *to feed.*
▷ *vpr* **echarse 1** *(arrojarse)* to throw OS. **2** *(tenderse)* to lie down. **3** *(ponerse)* to put on. **4** *(novio, novia)* to get OS. **5 echarse a** + *inf (empezar)* to begin to: **se echó a reír** *he burst out laughing.*

eclesiástico,-a *adj* ecclesiastic, ecclesiastical, church.

eclipsar *vt* **1** *(astro)* to eclipse. **2** *fig* outshine.

eclipse *nm* eclipse.

eclíptica *nf* ecliptic.

eclíptico,-a *adj* ecliptic.

eclosión *nf* **1** ZOOL hatching, emergence. **2** BOT blossoming. **3** *fig* upsurge, flowering, emergence.

eclosionar *vi* to break out, emerge, burst out.

eco *nm* **1** echo. **2** *fig* echo, response.

ecografía *nf* ultrasound scan.

ecógrafo *nm* ultrasound scanner.

ecología *nf* ecology.

ecológico,-a *adj* ecological.

ecologismo *nm* ecology movement.

ecologista *adj* ecological: **partido ecologista** *ecology party.*
▷ *nm o nf* ecologist.

economato *nm* company store.

economía *nf* **1** *(administración)* economy. **2** *(ciencia)* economics. **3** *(ahorro)* economy, saving. **4** *(moderación)* economy, thrift, thriftiness.

económico,-a *adj* **1** *(gen)* economic. **2** *(barato)* cheap, economical, inexpensive. **3** *(persona)* thrifty, careful with money. ● **crisis económica** economic crisis, recession.

economista *nm o nf* economist.

economizar [4] *vt* **1** *(ahorrar)* to economize, save. **2** *(usar con cuidado)* to use sparingly.
▷ *vi* to economize, save.

ecosistema *nm* ecosystem.

ectoplasma *nm* ectoplasm.

ecuación *nf* equation. ● **ecuación de primer grado** simple equation. | **ecuación de segundo grado** quadratic equation.

ecuador *nm* **1** GEOG equator. **2** EDUC half-way point. ■ **pasar el ecuador** to cross the equator.

Ecuador *nm* Ecuador.

ecualizador *nm* equalizer. ● **ecualizador gráfico** graphic equalizer.

ecuánime *adj* **1** *(temperamento)* calm, placid, equable, even-tempered. **2** *(juicio, opinión)* fair, impartial.

ecuanimidad *nf* **1** *(temperamento)* equanimity. **2** *(juicio)* impartiality, fairness.

ecuatoguineano,-a *adj* of Equatorial Guinea, from Equatorial Guinea.
▷ *nm & nf* person from Equatorial Guinea, inhabitant of Equatorial Guinea.

ecuatorial *adj* equatorial.

ecuatoriano,-a *adj* Ecuadorian.
▷ *nm & nf* Ecuadorian.

ecuestre *adj* equestrian.

ecuménico,-a *adj* ecumenical, ecumenic.

eczema *nm* eczema.

edad *nf* **1** age. **2** *(tiempo, época)* time, period.

edema *nm* oedema (US edema).

edén *nm* **1** Eden. **2** *fig* paradise, heaven.

edición *nf* **1** *(ejemplares)* edition. **2** *(publicación)* publication; *(de sellos)* issue: **Ediciones Biblograf** *Biblograf Publications.* **3** INFORMÁ editing.

edicto *nm* edict, proclamation.

edificación *nf* building, construction.

edificante *adj* edifying, uplifting.

edificar [1] *vt* **1** *(construir)* to build, construct. **2** *fig (crear)* to build, create. **3** *fig (dar ejemplo)* to edify, uplift.

edificio *nm* building.

edil,-la *nm & nf (concejal)* town councillor.
▷ *nm* **edil** *(magistrado romano)* aedile.
Edimburgo *nm* Edinburgh.
editar *vt* 1 *(libros, revistas)* to publish; *(discos)* to release. 2 INFORMÁ to edit.
editor,-ra *adj* publishing.
▷ *nm & nf (que edita)* publisher; *(que prepara)* editor.
▷ *nm* **editor** INFORMÁ editor. ● **editor de textos** text editor.
editorial *adj* publishing.
▷ *nm (artículo)* editorial, leading article, leader.
▷ *nf* publishing house, publisher.
edredón *nm* eiderdown, US comforter.
educación *nf* 1 *(preparación)* education. 2 *(crianza)* upbringing. 3 *(modales)* manners *pl*, politeness.
educado,-a *adj* polite.
educador,-ra *adj* educating.
▷ *nm & nf* educator, teacher.
educar [1] *vt* 1 *(enseñar)* to educate, teach. 2 *(criar)* to bring up. 3 *(en la cortesía, etc)* to teach manners. 4 *(sentidos)* to educate, train.
educativo,-a *adj* educational: **sistema educativo** *education system.*
edulcorante *nm* sweetener.
edulcorar *vt* 1 to sweeten. 2 *fig* to soften, alleviate.
EE UU *abrev* **(Estados Unidos)** the United States of America; *(abreviatura)* USA.
efe *nf name of the letter* **f**.
efectista *adj* showy, stagy.
efectivamente *adv* 1 *(realmente)* in fact, actually. 2 *(de verdad)* indeed.
efectividad *nf* effectiveness.
efectivo,-a *adj* 1 *(real)* real, true, actual. 2 *(que tiene efecto)* effective. 3 *(empleo)* permanent.
▷ *nm* **efectivo** 1 *(dinero)* cash. 2 *(plantilla)* staff.
▷ *nm pl* **efectivos** MIL forces.
efecto *nm* 1 *(resultado)* effect, result, end. 2 *(impresión)* impression: **la escena le hizo un gran efecto** *the scene made a great impression on her.* 3 *(fin)* aim, object. 4 DEP spin. 5 COM bill, draft.
▷ *nm pl* **efectos** *(bienes)* effects, possessions; *(mercancías)* goods; *(personales)* effects, belongings.
efectuar [1] *vt* 1 *(gen)* to carry out, perform, make, do. 2 *(pago)* to make; *(pedido)* to place. 3 *(suma, etc)* to do. 4 *(viaje, visita, etc)* to make.
▷ *vpr* **efectuarse** *(realizarse)* to be carried out; *(acto, etc)* to take place.
efervescente *adj* 1 *(gen)* effervescent. 2 *(bebida)* sparkling, fizzy. 3 *(pastilla)* soluble. 4 *fig* high-spirited.
eficacia *nf* 1 *(persona)* efficiency, effectiveness; *(cosas)* efficacy, effectiveness. 2 *(rendimiento)* efficiency.
eficaz *adj* 1 *(eficiente)* efficient. 2 *(cosa)* efficacious, effective. 3 *(que produce rendimiento)* efficient.
eficiencia *nf* efficiency.
eficiente *adj* efficient.
efigie *nf* effigy.
efímero,-a *adj* ephemeral, brief.
efluvio *nm* 1 emanation, effusion, flow. 2 *fig* surge.
efusión *nf* 1 *(derramamiento)* effusion, pouring out. 2 *fig* effusiveness, warmth.
efusivo,-a *adj* effusive, warm.
EGB *abrev* EDUC **(Enseñanza General Básica)** ≈ *former Primary School Education.*
egeo,-a *adj* Aegean.
egipcio,-a *adj* Egyptian.
▷ *nm & nf (persona)* Egyptian.
▷ *nm* **egipcio** *(idioma)* Egyptian.
Egipto *nm* Egypt.
egiptología *nf* Egyptology.
egiptólogo,-a *nm & nf* Egyptologist.
égloga *nf* eclogue.
ego *nm* ego.
egocéntrico,-a *adj* egocentric, self-centred (US self centered).
egocentrismo *nm* egocentricity.
egoísmo *nm* selfishness, egoism.
egoísta *adj* selfish, egoistic, egoistical.
▷ *nm o nf* egoist, selfish person.
ególatra *adj* egomaniacal.
▷ *nm o nf* egomaniac.
egolatría *nf* egomania, self-worship.
eh *interj* 1 *fam (para llamar)* hey!, hey you! 2 *fam (pregunta)* you what? 3 *fam (al final de frase)* OK?, right?
einstenio *nm* einsteinium.
Eire *nm* Eire.
eje *nm* 1 *(línea, recta)* axis. 2 TÉC shaft, spindle. 3 AUTO axle. 4 *fig (zona principal)* centre (US center), main area: **el eje comercial de la ciudad** *the city's main shopping area.* 5 *fig (parte esencial)* crux, main idea, core. 6 *(calle, carretera)* thoroughfare. 7 **el Eje** POL the Axis.
ejecución *nf* 1 *(de una orden, etc)* carrying out, execution. 2 MÚS performance. 3 *(ajusticiamiento)* execution. 4 JUR seizure.
ejecutar *vt* 1 *(una orden, etc)* to carry out. 2 MÚS to perform, play. 3 *(ajusticiar)* to execute. 4 JUR to seize. 5 INFORMÁ to run.
ejecutiva *nf* executive, executive committee.
ejecutivo,-a *adj* 1 executive. 2 *(rápido)* prompt.
▷ *nm & nf* executive.
▷ *nm* **el ejecutivo** *(gobierno)* the government. ● **poder ejecutivo** the executive.
ejemplar *adj* exemplary, model: **un ciudadano ejemplar** *a model citizen.*
▷ *nm* 1 *(copia)* copy, number. 2 *(prototipo)* specimen.
ejemplificar [1] *vt* to illustrate, exemplify.
ejemplo *nm* 1 example. 2 *(modelo)* model. ■ **dar ejemplo** to set an example. ■ **poner de ejemplo** to give as an example. ■ **por ejemplo** for example, for instance.
ejercer [2] *vt* 1 *(profesión, etc)* to practise (US practice), be in practice as. 2 *(usar)* to exercise; *(influencia)* to exert. ■ **ejercer el derecho de** to exercise one's right to.
▷ *vi* to practise (US practice), work: **ejerce de médico** *he works as a doctor.*
ejercicio *nm* 1 *(de profesión)* practice; *(de derecho)* use, exercise. 2 EDUC exercise; *(examen)* test; *(deberes)* homework. 3 DEP exercise. 4 FIN year.
ejercitar *vt* 1 *(profesión)* to practise (US practice). 2 *(enseñar)* to train.
▷ *vpr* **ejercitarse** *(aprender)* to train.
ejército *nm* army.
el *determinante* 1 the: **el agua** *water.* 2 **el de** the one: **el de hoy** *today's.* 3 **el que** *(persona - sujeto)* the one who; *(- objeto)* the one, the one that, the one whom: **el que vi** *the one I saw.* 4 *(cosa)* the one, the one that, the one which: **el que me diste** *the one (that) you gave me.*

él *pron* 1 *(sujeto - persona)* he; *(- cosa, animal)* it: **él vive aquí** *he lives here.* 2 *(objeto - persona)* him; *(- cosa, animal)* it: **comió con él** *she had lunch with him.* ■ **de él** *(posesivo)* his: **es de él** *it's his.* ■ **él mismo** himself.
elaboración *nf* 1 *(producto)* manufacture, production. 2 *(madera, metal, etc)* working. 3 *(idea)* working out, development. ■ **de elaboración casera** home-made.
elaborar *vt* 1 *(producto)* to make, manufacture, produce. 2 *(madera, metal, etc)* to work. 3 *(idea)* to work out, develop.
elasticidad *nf* 1 *(gen)* elasticity. 2 *(tela)* stretch. 3 *fig* flexibility.
elástico,-a *adj* 1 elastic. 2 *(telas)* elastic, stretch. 3 *fig* flexible: **un horario elástico** *a flexible timetable.*
▷ *nm* **elástico** elastic.
▷ *nm pl* **elásticos** braces, US suspenders.
ele *nf name of the letter* l.
elección *nf* 1 *(nombramiento)* election. 2 *(opción)* choice.
▷ *nf pl* **elecciones** elections.
electo,-a *adj* elect.
elector,-ra *nm & nf* voter, elector.
electorado *nm* electorate, voters *pl*.
electoral *adj* electoral.
electoralista *adj pey* electioneering.
electricidad *nf* electricity.
electricista *adj* electrical.
▷ *nm & nf* electrician.
eléctrico,-a *adj* electric, electrical.
electrificar [1] *vt* to electrify.
electrizar [4] *vt* 1 to electrify. 2 *fig* to electrify, thrill.
electrocardiograma *nm* electrocardiogram.
electrochoque *nm* electroconvulsive therapy.
electrocutar *vt* to electrocute.
▷ *vpr* **electrocutarse** to be electrocuted, electrocute OS.
electrodo *nm* electrode.
electrodoméstico *nm* electrical appliance.
electroencefalograma *nm* electroencephalogram.
electrógeno,-a *adj* generating, generating.
▷ *nm* **electrógeno** electricity generator.
electroimán *nm* electromagnet.
electrólisis *nf inv* electrolysis.
electrolito *nm* electrolyte.
electromagnetismo *nm* electromagnetism.
electromagnético,-a *adj* electromagnetic.
electromecánica *nf* electromecanics.
electrometalurgia *nf* electrometallurgy.
electromotor,-ra *adj* electromotive.
▷ *nm* **electromotor** electric motor.
electromotriz *adj* electromotive.
electrón *nm* electron.
electronegativo,-a *adj* electronegative.
electrónica *nf* electronics.
electrónico,-a *adj* electronic.
electronvoltio *nm* electron volt.
electropositivo,-a *adj* electropositive.
electroquímica *nf* electrochemistry.
electroscopio *nm* electroscope.
electrostática *nf* electrostatics.
electrotécnico,-a *adj* electrical.
electroterapia *nf* electrotherapy.
electrotermia *nf* electrothermy, electrothermics.
elefante,-a *nm & nf (macho)* elephant; *(hembra)* cow elephant, female elephant. ● **elefante marino** elephant seal.
elegancia *nf* elegance, smartness, style.
elegante *adj* elegant, smart, stylish.
elegía *nf* elegy.
elegiaco,-a *adj* 1 elegiac. 2 *fig* elegiac, plaintive.
elegido,-a *pp* → **elegir**.
▷ *adj* 1 *(escogido)* chosen. 2 *(predilecto)* preferred. 3 POL elected.
▷ *nm & nf* 1 chosen one. 2 POL elected person.
▷ *nm pl* **los elegidos** the chosen few.
elegir [55] *vt* 1 *(escoger)* to choose. 2 POL to elect.
elemental *adj* 1 *(del elemento)* elemental. 2 *(obvio)* elementary, basic.
elemento *nm* 1 *(gen)* element. 2 *(parte)* component, part. 3 *(individuo)* type, sort.
▷ *nm pl* **elementos** 1 *(atmosféricos)* elements. 2 *(fundamentos)* rudiments, basic principles.
elenco *nm* 1 *(catálogo)* index, catalogue (US catalog). 2 *(actores)* cast. 3 *(personal)* staff.
elepé *nm* LP (record).
elevación *nf* 1 *(de terreno)* elevation, rise. 2 *(precios)* rise, raising, increasing; *(voz, tono)* raising; *(peso)* raising, lifting. 3 MAT raising. 4 REL elevation.
elevado,-a *adj* 1 *(gen)* high. 2 *fig* lofty, noble. ■ **elevado,-a a** MAT raised to: **elevado al cuadrado** *squared.*
elevador,-ra *adj* elevating.
▷ *nm* **elevador** AM lift, US elevator.
elevalunas *nm inv* window winder.
elevar *vt* 1 *(peso, etc)* to elevate, raise, lift. 2 *(precios)* to raise, increase, put up; *(tono, voz)* to raise. 3 *(enaltecer)* to promote, raise. 4 MAT to raise.
▷ *vpr* **elevarse** 1 *(subir)* to rise (up): **el humo se elevaba** *the smoke was rising up.* 2 *(alcanzar)* to reach. 3 *(erguirse, levantarse)* to stand. 4 *(sumar)* to amount to, come to.
eliminación *nf* elimination.
eliminar *vt* 1 *(gen)* to eliminate. 2 *(esperanzas, miedos, etc)* to get rid of, cast aside. 3 *fam (matar)* to kill.
eliminatoria *nf* heat, qualifying round.
eliminatorio,-a *adj* eliminatory.
elipse *nf* ellipse.
elipsis *nf inv* ellipsis.
elipsoidal *adj* ellipsoidal.
elíptico,-a *adj* elliptic, elliptical.
elite *nf* elite.
elitismo *nm* elitism.
elitista *adj* elitist.
elixir *nm* elixir.
ella *pron* 1 *(sujeto - persona)* she; *(- cosa, animal)* it. 2 *(objeto - persona)* her; *(- cosa, animal)* it.
elle *nf name of the digraph ll.*
ello *pron* it: **no me digas nada de ello** *don't tell me anything about it.*
ellos,-as *pron* 1 *(sujeto)* they. 2 *(objeto)* them: **vino con ellos** *she came with them.* ■ **ellos,-as mismos,-as** themselves.
elocuencia *nf* eloquence.
elocuente *adj* eloquent.
elogiar [12] *vt* to praise, eulogize.
elogio *nm* praise, eulogy.
elucubrar *vt* to lucubrate.

eludir *vt* 1 *(responsabilidad, justicia, etc)* to evade. 2 *(pregunta)* to avoid, evade; *(persona)* to avoid.
emanación *nf* emanation.
emanar *vi* 1 *(olor, etc)* to emanate. 2 *(derivar)* to derive (**de**, from), come (**de**, from).
emancipación *nf* emancipation.
emancipado,-a *adj* emancipated, free.
emancipar *vt* to emancipate, free.
▷ *vpr* **emanciparse** to become emancipated, become free.
embadurnar *vt* to daub, smear.
embajada *nf* 1 *(cargo)* ambassadorship, post of ambassador. 2 *(edificio)* embassy.
embajador,-ra *nm & nf* ambassador.
embalaje *nm* packing, packaging.
embalar *vt (empaquetar)* to pack, wrap.
▷ *vpr* **embalarse** 1 *(acelerar)* to speed up. 2 *fig (al hablar)* to gabble.
embalsamar *vt* to embalm.
embalse *nm* 1 *(acción)* damming. 2 *(presa)* reservoir.
embarazada *adj-nf* pregnant woman.
embarazar [4] *vt* 1 *(mujer)* to make pregnant. 2 *(estorbar)* to hinder. 3 *(turbar)* to embarrass.
embarazo *nm* 1 *(preñez)* pregnancy. 2 *(obstáculo)* obstruction, obstacle. 3 *(turbación)* embarrassment.
embarazoso,-a *adj* embarrassing, troublesome.
embarcación *nf (nave)* boat, vessel, craft.
embarcadero *nm* pier, jetty, quay.
embarcar [1] *vt* 1 *(personas)* to embark, put on board; *(mercancías)* to load. 2 *fig* to involve, implicate.
▷ *vpr* **embarcarse** 1 *(en barco)* to embark, go on board; *(en avión)* to board. 2 *fig* to embark upon, engage in.
embarco *nm* embarkation.
embargar [7] *vt* 1 JUR to seize, sequestrate, impound. 2 *(emociones)* to overcome.
embargo *nm* 1 *(de bienes)* seizure of property. 2 *(prohibición)* embargo. ■ **sin embargo** nevertheless, however.
embarque *nm (de personas)* boarding; *(de mercancías)* loading.
embarrar *vt* 1 *(untar de barro)* to cover with mud. 2 *(embadurnar)* to daub, smear.
▷ *vpr* **embarrarse** to get covered in mud.
embarullar *vt* 1 *(mezclar)* to muddle. 2 *(hacer mal)* to bungle. 3 *fam (liar)* to confuse.
▷ *vpr* **embarullarse** *(liarse)* to get muddled up.
embastar *vt* to baste, tack.
embate *nm* 1 *(de olas)* dashing, breaking. 2 *(viento)* summer sea breeze. 3 *fig (acometida)* outburst.
embaucador,-ra *adj* deceitful.
▷ *nm & nf* cheat, swindler, trickster.
embaucar [1] *vt* to deceive, trick, dupe, cheat, swindle.
embeber *vt* 1 *(absorber)* to soak up. 2 *(empapar)* to soak, drench. 3 COST to take in. 4 *fig (incorporar)* to insert.
▷ *vi (encogerse)* to shrink: **la lana embebe** *wool shrinks.*
▷ *vpr* **embeberse** to become absorbed (**en**, in).
embelesado,-a *adj* fascinated, delighted.
embelesar *vt* to charm, delight, fascinate.
embellecedor,-ra *adj* beautifying.
▷ *nm* **embellecedor** AUTO hubcap.
embellecer [43] *vt* to make beautiful, beautify.
▷ *vpr* **embellecerse** to make OS beautiful, beautify OS.
embestida *nf* 1 *(gen)* onslaught. 2 *(de toro)* charge.
embestir [34] *vt* 1 *(atacar)* to assault, attack. 2 *(toro)* to charge. 3 *(coche)* to smash (into).
emblema *nm* 1 emblem, badge. 2 *(de marca)* logo.
embobado,-a *adj* fascinated, entranced.
embobar *vt* to fascinate, amaze, entrance.
▷ *vpr* **embobarse** to be fascinated, be entranced.
embocadura *nf* 1 *(de río)* mouth. 2 MÚS mouthpiece. 3 *(de vino)* taste, flavour (US flavor).
embolia *nf* embolism, clot.
émbolo *nm* TÉC piston; *(de cafetera)* plunger.
embolsar *vt* 1 to pocket. 2 *(cobrar)* to collect.
▷ *vpr* **embolsarse** *(cobrar)* to make, earn; *(ganar)* win.
emborrachar *vt* to make drunk.
▷ *vpr* **emborracharse** to get drunk.
emborronar *vt* 1 *(echar borrones)* to blot. 2 *(hacer garabatos)* to scribble on. 3 *fig (escribir mal)* to scribble.
emboscada *nf* ambush. ■ **tender una emboscada** to lay an ambush.
embotellado,-a *adj* bottled.
▷ *nm* **embotellado** bottling.
embotellamiento *nm* AUTO *fig* traffic jam.
embozar *vt* 1 *(el rostro)* to muffle. 2 *fig (ocultar)* to disguise.
▷ *vpr* **embozarse** *(el rostro)* to muffle OS up.
embrague *nm* clutch.
embriagar [7] *vt* 1 to make drunk. 2 *fig* to transport.
▷ *vpr* **embriagarse** 1 to get drunk. 2 *fig* to be enraptured.
embriaguez *nf* 1 intoxication, drunkenness. 2 *fig* intoxication, rapture.
embrión *nm* 1 embryo. 2 *fig (idea, etc)* beginnings *pl*, embryo; *(revolución)* seeds *pl.*
embrionario,-a *adj* embryonic, embryonal.
embrollar *vt* to confuse, muddle.
▷ *vpr* **embrollarse** to get confused, get muddled.
embrollo *nm* 1 *(confusión)* muddle, mess. 2 *(mentira)* lie. 3 *fig (situación embarazosa)* embarrassing situation.
embrujar *vt* 1 *(persona)* to bewitch; *(lugar)* to haunt. 2 *fig (fascinar)* to bewitch, enchant.
embrujo *nm* 1 spell, charm. 2 *fig (fascinación)* fascination, attraction.
embrutecer [43] *vt (facultades, etc)* to dull, deaden.
▷ *vpr* **embrutecerse** to become dull, become stupefied.
embuchado *nm (embutido)* processed cold meat.
embudo *nm* 1 funnel. 2 *fig* trick.
embuste *nm (mentira)* lie; *(engaño)* trick.
embustero,-a *adj* lying, deceitful.
▷ *nm & nf* liar.
embutido *nm* 1 *(alimento)* cold cut. 2 *(incrustación)* inlay.
embutir *vt (llenar)* to stuff, cram, squeeze.
eme *nf name of the letter* **m**.
emergencia *nf* 1 *(imprevisto)* emergency. 2 *(salida)* emergence. ■ **en caso de emergencia** in an emergency, in case of emergency.
emerger [5] *vi* 1 to emerge. 2 *(aparecer)* to appear, emerge, come into view. 3 *fig* to result.
emigración *nf* 1 emigration. 2 *(aves, pueblo)* migration.
emigrante *adj* emigrant.
▷ *nm o nf* emigrant.
emigrar *vi* to emigrate; *(aves, pueblo)* to migrate.
eminencia *nf* 1 *(elevación)* height, elevation, hill. 2 *fig (mérito)* prominence. 3 *fig (persona)* eminence.
eminente *adj* 1 *(elevado)* high. 2 *fig* eminent.

mirato *nm* emirate. ● **Emiratos Árabes Unidos** United Arab Emirates.

misión *nf* **1** *(gen)* emission. **2** *(sellos, monedas, etc)* issue. **3** RAD TV *(programa)* broadcast; transmission.

misor,-ra *adj* **1** *(banco, etc)* issuing. **2** RAD TV broadcasting, transmitter.
▷ *nm & nf (banco, etc)* issuer.
▷ *nm* **emisor** RAD radio transmitter.

misora *nf* broadcasting station, radio station.

mitir *vt* **1** *(sonido, luz)* to emit; *(olor)* to give off. **2** *(manifestar)* to express. **3** *(bonos, monedas, sellos)* to issue. **4** RAD TV to broadcast, transmit.
▷ *vi* RAD TV to transmit.

moción *nf* **1** *(sentimiento)* emotion, feeling. **2** *(excitación)* excitement.

mocionado,-a *adj* (deeply) moved.

mocionante *adj* **1** *(conmovedor)* moving, touching. **2** *(excitante)* exciting, thrilling.

mocionar *vt* **1** *(conmover)* to move, touch. **2** *(excitar)* to excite, thrill.
▷ *vpr* **emocionarse 1** *(conmoverse)* to be moved, be touched. **2** *(excitarse)* to get excited.

moticón *nm* INFORMÁ emoticon.

moticono *nm* INFORMÁ emoticon.

motivo,-a *adj (persona)* emotional; *(acto, etc)* moving, touching; *(palabras)* emotive, stirring, rousing.

mpachado,-a *adj* **1** *(apocado)* slow-witted. **2** *(ahíto)* bloated, full.

mpachar *vt* **1** *(comer demasiado)* to give indigestion. **2** *(impedir)* to obstruct. **3** *fig (aburrir)* to bore, make sick.
▷ *vpr* **empacharse** *(de comer)* to have indigestion, get indigestion, get an upset stomach.

mpacho *nm* **1** *(indigestión)* indigestion, upset stomach. **2** *fig (turbación)* embarrassment.

mpadronar *vt* **1** *(hacer el censo)* to take a census of. **2** *(apuntar)* to register in a census.
▷ *vpr* **empadronarse** to register.

mpalagoso,-a *adj* **1** *(dulces)* too sweet, sickly. **2** *fig (persona)* sickly sweet, cloying.

mpalmar *vt (unir)* to join, connect.
▷ *vi* **1** *(enlazar)* to join, connect. **2** *(seguir)* to follow on from.
▷ *vpr* **empalmarse** *tabú* to get a hard-on.

empalme *nm* **1** *(gen)* connection. **2** *(cinta, cuerda, película)* splice. **3** DEP volley. **4** *(ferrocarril)* junction; *(carretera)* intersection, T-junction.

empanada *nf* pasty, pie.

empanadilla *nf* pasty.

empanar *vt* **1** *(rebozar)* to coat in breadcrumbs. **2** *(poner entre masa)* to fill.

empantanar *vt (inundar)* to flood.
▷ *vpr* **empantanarse** *(inundarse)* to become flooded.

empañar *vt* **1** *(cristal)* to steam up. **2** *fig (honor, etc)* to taint, tarnish.
▷ *vpr* **empañarse 1** *(cristal)* to steam up. **2** *fig (honor, etc)* to become tainted, become tarnished.

empapar *vt* **1** *(humedecer)* to soak; *(penetrar)* to soak, drench. **2** *(absorber)* to soak up.
▷ *vpr* **empaparse 1** *(humedecerse)* to get soaked. **2** *(persona)* to get soaked, get drenched. **3** *fig (ideas, etc)* to soak up. **4** *fig (enterarse bien)* to swot up (**de**, on).

empapelar *vt* **1** *(envolver)* to wrap up in paper. **2** *(una pared)* to wallpaper, paper. **3** *fam fig (persona)* to try.

empaquetar *vt (hacer paquetes)* to pack (up).

emparedado *nm* sandwich.

emparedar *vt* **1** *(entre paredes)* wall in. **2** *(en prisión)* to imprison, confine.

emparejar *vt (cosas)* to put into pairs, match; *(personas)* to pair off.

empastar *vt (diente)* to fill, put a filling in.

empaste *nm* **1** *(de diente)* filling. **2** *(encuadernación)* binding. **3** *(pintura)* impasting.

empate *nm (en fútbol, rugby)* draw, US tie; *(en carrera, votación)* tie: **el gol del empate** *the equalizer.*

empatía *nf* empathy.

empecinarse *vpr* to be stubborn (**en**, about), be pigheaded (**en**, about).

empedernido,-a *adj* confirmed, inveterate.

empedrado,-a *adj* **1** *(calle)* cobbled. **2** *(cielo)* cloudy.
▷ *nm* **empedrado 1** *(adoquines)* cobbles *pl*, cobblestones *pl*. **2** *(acción)* cobbling, paving.

empedrar [27] *vt* to cobble, pave.

empeine *nm* **1** *(pie, zapato)* instep. **2** *(pubis)* groin.

empeñar *vt* **1** *(objetos)* to pawn, US hock. **2** *(palabra)* to pledge.
▷ *vpr* **empeñarse 1** *(endeudarse)* to get into debt. **2** *(insistir)* to insist (**en**, on). ■ **estar empeñado,-a** to be in debt.

empeño *nm* **1** *(insistencia)* determination. **2** *(deuda)* pawn.

empeorar *vi* to worsen, deteriorate.

emperador *nm* **1** emperor. **2** *(pez)* swordfish.

emperatriz *nf* empress.

emperrarse *vpr* to dig one's heels in.

empezar [47] *vt* to begin, start.

empinado,-a *adj* **1** *(alto)* very high. **2** *fig (inclinado)* steep; *(vertical)* upright.

empinar *vt (levantar)* to raise, lift.
▷ *vpr* **empinarse 1** *(persona)* to stand on tiptoe; *(animal)* to rear up. **2** *(alcanzar altura)* to tower.

empírico,-a *adj* empirical.

empirismo *nm* empiricism.

emplasto *nm* MED poultice.

emplazar[1] [4] *vt (citar)* to call together.

emplazar[2] [4] *vt (situar)* to locate, place, situate.

empleado,-a *nm & nf* employee, clerk.

emplear *vt* **1** *(dar empleo)* to employ. **2** *(usar)* to use. **3** *(dinero)* to spend. **4** *(tiempo)* to invest, spend.
▷ *vpr* **emplearse 1** *(usarse)* to be used: **este tipo de ordenador ya no se emplea** *this type of computer is no longer used.* **2** *(tener trabajo)* to be employed.

empleo *nm* **1** *(trabajo)* occupation, job. **2** POL employment. **3** *(uso)* use.

emplomar *vt* **1** *(cubrir)* to cover with lead. **2** *(soldar)* to join with lead, seal with lead. **3** *(sellar)* to seal with lead.

empobrecer [43] *vi* to impoverish.
▷ *vpr* **empobrecerse** to become poor.

empollar *vt* **1** *(huevos)* to hatch. **2** *fam (estudiar)* to swot, swot up, US bone up on.

empollón,-ona *nm & nf fam pey* swot.

emponzoñar *vt* **1** to poison. **2** *fig* to corrupt.

empotrado,-a *adj* fitted, built-in.

emprendedor,-ra *adj* enterprising, resourceful.

emprender *vt* 1 *(gen)* to start. 2 *(misión)* to tackle; *(viaje)* to set off on; *(tarea)* to undertake.
empreñar *vt* 1 *(fecundar)* to mate with. 2 *fam fig (molestar)* to bother, bug.
empresa *nf* 1 *(compañía)* firm, company. 2 *(dirección)* management. 3 *(acción)* undertaking, venture. ● **empresa multinacional** multinational company.
empresario,-a *nm & nf (gen)* employer, manager; *(hombre)* businessman, manager; *(mujer)* businesswoman, manageress.
empréstito *nm* loan.
empujar *vt* 1 to push, shove, thrust. 2 *fig* to force, urge, press: **la empujó a estudiar** *she pushed her into studying.*
empuje *nm* 1 push, thrust, drive. 2 *(presión)* pressure. 3 *fig (energía)* energy, drive.
empujón *nm* push, shove.
emular *vt* to emulate.
emulsión *nf* emulsion.
emulsionar *vt* to emulsify.
en *prep* 1 *(lugar - gen)* in, at: **en Valencia** *in Valencia;* **en casa** *at home;* **en el trabajo** *at work.* 2 *(- en el interior)* in, inside: **en el cajón** *in the drawer.* 3 *(lugar - sobre)* on: **en la mesa** *on the table.* 4 *(año, mes, estación)* in; *(día)* on; *(época, momento)* at: **en 1994** *in 1994;* **en aquel momento** *at that moment.* 5 *(dirección)* into: **entró en su casa** *he went into his house.* 6 *(transporte)* by: **ir en coche** *to go by car.* 7 *(tema, materia)* at, in: **experto en economía** *expert in economics.* 8 *(modo, manera)* in: **en inglés** *in English.* ■ **en cuanto** as soon as. ▮ **en camino** on the way.
enagua [Also used in plural with the same meaning.] *nf* petticoat, underskirt.
enajenación *nf* 1 *(distracción)* distraction, absent-mindedness. 2 *(transferencia)* transfer, alienation.
enajenar *vt* 1 *(propiedad)* to alienate. 2 *fig (sacar de sí)* to drive mad, drive to distraction.
enaltecer [43] *vt* 1 *(ennoblecer)* to do credit to, ennoble. 2 *(alabar)* to praise, extol.
enamoradizo,-a *adj* easily infatuated.
enamorado,-a *adj* in love, lovesick.
▷ *nm & nf* lover, sweetheart.
enamoramiento *nm* infatuation, falling in love.
enamorar *vt* to win the heart of.
▷ *vpr* **enamorarse** to fall in love (**de**, with).
enano,-a *adj* dwarf.
▷ *nm & nf* dwarf.
enarbolar *vt* 1 *(bandera)* to hoist. 2 *(arma)* to brandish. 3 *fig (defender)* to defend.
enardecer [43] *vt fig (excitar)* to excite, inflame, kindle.
encabezamiento *nm* 1 *(gen)* heading. 2 *(fórmula)* form of address. 3 *(preámbulo)* preamble.
encabezar [4] *vt* 1 *(carta, lista)* to head. 2 *(acaudillar)* to lead. 3 DEP *(carrera)* to lead; *(clasificación)* to head, top.
encadenar *vt* 1 *(poner cadenas)* to chain (up). 2 *fig (enlazar)* to connect, link up.
encajar *vt* 1 *(ajustar)* to fit. 2 *(hueso)* to set. 3 *(recibir)* to take, withstand. 4 *(soportar)* to bear; *(hacer aguantar)* to force to sit through. 5 *(indirecta, comentario)* to get in. 6 *(dar un golpe)* to land. 7 TÉC to gear.
encaje *nm* 1 *(acto)* fit, fitting. 2 *(hueco)* socket; *(caja)* housing. 3 COST lace.
encalar *vt* to whitewash.
encallar *vi* 1 MAR to run aground. 2 *fig* to flounder, fail.

encaminar *vt (guiar, orientar)* to direct, guide, set c the right road, put on the right road.
▷ *vpr* **encaminarse** *(dirigirse)* to head (**a**, for) (**hacia**, towards).
encandilar *vt (deslumbrar)* to dazzle.
encantado,-a *adj* 1 *(contento)* pleased, delighted: **estc encantada de conocerlo** *I'm pleased to meet you.* 2 *f (embrujado)* haunted. 3 *(distraído)* absent-minded.
encantador,-ra *adj* enchanting, charming.
encantar *vt* 1 *(hechizar)* to cast a spell on, bewitch. 2 *fa (gustar)* to delight, love.
encanto *nm* 1 *(hechizo)* spell, enchantment, charn 2 *fig (cosa)* delight, enchantment; *(persona)* charm.
encapotado,-a *adj* overcast, cloudy.
encapotar *vt (cubrir)* to put a cloak on.
▷ *vpr* **encapotarse** 1 *(persona)* to frown, look grin 2 [Used only in the 3rd pers; it does not take subject.] *(cielo)* to become overcast, become cloudy.
encapricharse *vpr* 1 *(empeñarse)* to set one's min (**con/en**, to). 2 *(encariñarse)* to take a fancy (**con**, to *(enamorarse)* to get a crush (**con**, on).
encapuchado,-a *adj* hooded.
encaramar *vt (levantar)* to raise, lift up.
▷ *vpr* **encaramarse** 1 *(subirse)* to climb up, get high up 2 *fig (encumbrarse)* to reach a high position.
encarar *vt (afrontar)* to face, face up to, confront.
▷ *vpr* **encararse** 1 *(situación, problema)* to face up (**a/con** to). 2 *(persona)* to stand up (**a/con**, to).
encarcelar *vt* to imprison, jail, incarcerate.
encarecer [43] *vt (precios)* to put up the price of.
▷ *vpr* **encarecerse** *(precio)* to become more expensive.
encargado,-a *adj* in charge.
▷ *nm & nf* 1 COM *(hombre)* manager; *(mujer)* manageress. 2 *(empleado)* person in charge.
encargar [7] *vt* 1 *(encomendar)* to entrust, put in charge of. 2 *(recomendar)* to recommend, advise. 3 COM *(pedir)* to order, place an order for.
▷ *vpr* **encargarse de** to take charge of, look after, see to
encargo *nm* 1 *(recado)* errand. 2 *(empleo)* job, assignment. 3 COM order, commission. ■ **hacer un encargo** *(recado)* to run an errand. 2 *(pedido)* to place an order.
encariñarse *vpr* to become fond (**con**, of), get attached (**con**, to).
encarnación *nf* 1 REL incarnation. 2 *fig* embodiment incarnation.
encarnado,-a *adj* 1 *(hecho carne)* incarnate. 2 *(color)* red.
encarnar *vt fig (personificar)* to embody, personify.
encarnizado,-a *adj* bloody, fierce.
encarrilar *vt* 1 *(vehículo)* to put on the road, put on the rails. 2 *fig (encaminar)* to direct, guide.
encasillar *vt* 1 *(poner en casillas)* to pigeonhole. 2 *(clasificar)* to classify, class. 3 *(actor, actriz)* to typecast.
encasquillarse *vpr* to jam.
encauzar [4] *vt* 1 to channel. 2 *fig* to direct, guide.
encéfalo *nm* encephalon.
encefalograma *nm* encephalogram.
encendedor *nm* lighter.
encender [28] *vt* 1 *(hacer arder)* to light, set fire to *(cerilla)* to strike, light; *(vela)* to light. 2 *(luz, radio, tv* to turn on, switch on, put on; *(gas)* to turn on, light
▷ *vpr* **encenderse** 1 *(incendiarse)* to catch fire, ignite: **e edificio se encendió** *the building caught fire.* 2 *(luz)* tc

go on, come on; *(llama)* to flare up. **3** *fig (excitarse)* to flare up. **4** *fig (ruborizarse)* to blush, go red.
encendido,-a *adj* **1** *(incendiado)* on fire, burning. **2** *(cigarrillo, etc)* lit. **3** *(luz, etc)* on. **4** *(color)* glowing, fiery. **5** *(rostro)* red, flushed.
▷ *nm* **encendido 1** *(gen)* lighting. **2** AUTO ignition.
encerado *nm* **1** *(lienzo)* tarpaulin. **2** *(capa de cera)* wax coating. **3** *(pizarra)* blackboard.
encerar *vt* to wax, polish.
encerrar [27] *vt* **1** *(gen)* to shut in, shut up. **2** *(con llave)* to lock in, lock up. **3** *(palabras, frases, etc)* to put: **encerrar entre paréntesis** *to put in brackets.*
▷ *vpr* **encerrarse** *(recogerse)* to go into retreat.
encerrona *nf fig (trampa)* trap.
encestar *vt* to score a basket.
enceste *nm* basket.
encharcar [1] *vt* to flood, swamp.
▷ *vpr* **encharcarse** *(terreno)* to swamp, get flooded.
enchufado,-a *adj fam* well-connected.
▷ *nm & nf fam (gen)* person with friends in the right places, US wirepuller; *(en la escuela)* teacher's pet.
enchufar *vt* **1** ELEC to connect, plug in. **2** *(unir)* to join, connect, fit. **3** *fam fig* to pull strings for: **enchufó a su hija en su empresa** *he got his daughter a job in his company.*
enchufe *nm* **1** ELEC *(hembra)* socket; *(macho)* plug. **2** *fam fig (trabajo)* easy job; *(influencias)* contacts *pl.* ■ **tener enchufe** *fam* to have contacts.
encía *nf* gum.
enciclopedia *nf* encyclopaedia, encyclopedia.
encierro *nm (protesta)* sit-in.
encima *adv* **1** *(más arriba)* above, overhead; *(sobre)* on top. **2** *(ropa, etc)* on, on top: **ponte algo encima** *put something on.* **3** *(además)* in addition, besides. **4** *fam (por si fuera poco)* besides. ■ **encima de 1** *(a más altura)* over, above. **2** *(sobre)* on. **3** *(además)* besides, as well as, on top of that. ■ **por encima de 1** *(más importante)* above. **2** *(más allá)* beyond: **está por encima de sus posibilidades** *it's beyond her capabilities.*
encina *nf* holm oak, evergreen oak, ilex.
encinta *adj* pregnant.
enclave *nm* enclave.
encoger [5] *vt* **1** *(contraer)* to contract. **2** *(tejido)* to shrink.
▷ *vi (tejido)* to shrink.
▷ *vpr* **encogerse 1** *(contraerse)* to contract. **2** *(tejido)* to shrink.
encolar *vt* **1** *(dar cola)* to glue. **2** *(en pintura)* to size, paste. **3** *(películas)* to splice. **4** *(vinos)* to clarify.
encolerizar [4] *vt* to anger, irritate, exasperate.
▷ *vpr* **encolerizarse** to get angry, lose one's temper.
encontrar [31] *vt* **1** *(gen)* to find. **2** *(una persona sin buscar)* to come across, meet, bump into. **3** *(dificultades)* to run into, come up against.
▷ *vpr* **encontrarse 1** *(estar)* to be: **se encuentra enfermo** *he's ill.* **2** *(persona)* to meet; *(por casualidad)* to bump into, run into, meet: **nos encontraremos allí** *we'll meet there.* **3** *(dificultades)* to run into. **4** *(chocar)* to collide. **5** *fig (sentirse)* to feel, be: **me encuentro mal** *I feel bad.*
encorsetado,-a *adj fig* strict, rigorous.
encorsetar *vt* **1** to corset. **2** *fig* to limit, restrict.
encorvado,-a *adj (cosa)* bent; *(persona)* stooping.
encorvar *vt* to bend, curve.
▷ *vpr* **encorvarse 1** to bend, curve. **2** *(persona)* to become round-shouldered.
encrespar *vt* **1** *(pelo)* to curl, frizz. **2** *(mar)* to make choppy, make rough. **3** *fig (enfurecer)* to infuriate.
▷ *vpr* **encresparse 1** *(pelo)* to stand on end. **2** *(mar)* to get rough. **3** *fig (enfurecerse)* to get cross, get irritated.
encrucijada *nf* **1** intersection. **2** *fig* crossroads.
encuadernación *nf* **1** *(arte)* bookbinding. **2** *(cubierta)* binding.
encuadernador,-ra *nm & nf* bookbinder.
encuadernar *vt* to bind.
encuadrar *vt* **1** *(cuadro, etc)* to frame. **2** *fig (encajar)* to fit in, insert. **3** *fig (servir de límite)* to frame. **4** *fig (en un grupo)* to incorporate.
▷ *vpr* **encuadrarse** *(incorporarse)* to join.
encuadre *nm* framing.
encubierto,-a *pp* fraud.
▷ *adj* **1** *(secreto)* secret, hidden, concealed. **2** *(fraudulento)* fraudulent, underhand.
encubridor,-ra *nm & nf* accessory, abettor.
encubrir *vt* **1** *(ocultar)* to conceal, hide. **2** JUR *(delito)* to cover up; *(criminal)* to cover up for.
encuentro *nm* **1** *(de personas)* meeting. **2** DEP meeting, clash; *(partido)* match, game. **3** *(choque)* collision.
encuesta *nf* **1** *(sondeo)* poll, survey. **2** *(pesquisa)* inquiry, investigation. ■ **hacer una encuesta** to carry out an opinion poll.
encuestador,-ra *nm & nf* pollster.
encuestar *vt* to poll.
encumbrar *vt fig* to exalt, elevate.
encurtidos *nm pl* pickles.
endeble *adj fml* feeble, weak, puny.
endecasílabo,-a *adj* hendecasyllabic.
endecha *nf* lament.
endémico,-a *adj* **1** MED endemic. **2** *fig* endemic.
endemoniado,-a *adj* **1** *(poseso)* possessed. **2** *fig (diabólico)* diabolical. **3** *fig (maldito)* evil, wretched.
enderezar [4] *vt* **1** *(poner derecho)* to straighten out. **2** *(poner vertical)* to set upright. **3** *fig (situación, etc)* to put right. **4** *fig (comportamiento)* to sort out.
▷ *vpr* **enderezarse** *(ponerse recto)* to straighten up.
endeudarse *vpr* to get into debt, fall into debt.
endiablado,-a *adj* **1** *(poseso)* possessed. **2** *fig (malo)* evil, wicked. **3** *fig (maldito)* cursed. **4** *fig (travieso)* devilish.
endibia *nf* endive.
endocardio *nm* endocardium.
endocarpio *nm* endocarp.
endocrino,-a *adj* endocrine, endocrinal.
▷ *nm & nf fam* endocrinologist. ● **glándula endocrina** endocrine gland.
endogamia *nf* endogamy, inbreeding.
endomingado,-a *adj fam* in one's Sunday best.
endosar *vt* **1** to endorse. **2** *fam fig* to lumber with.
endoscopia *nf* endoscopy.
endulzar [4] *vt* **1** to sweeten. **2** *fig (suavizar)* to soften.
endurecer [43] *vt* **1** to harden, make hard. **2** *fig* to harden, toughen.
endurecimiento *nm* hardening, toughening.
ene *nf name of the letter* **n**.
▷ *adj (indeterminado)* n: **ene veces** *n times.*
ENE *sím* **(estenordeste)** east-northeast; *(símbolo)* ENE.
eneágono *nm* nonagon.

enebro *nm* juniper.

eneldo *nm* dill.

enema *nm* enema.

enemigo,-a *adj* enemy, hostile.
▷ *nm & nf* enemy, foe.

enemistad *nf* hostility, enmity, hatred.

enemistar *vt* to make enemies of, set at odds.
▷ *vpr* **enemistarse** to become enemies.

energético,-a *adj* energy, power.

energía *nf* 1 energy, power. 2 *fig* vigour (US vigor).

enérgico,-a *adj* 1 energetic, vigorous. 2 *fig (decisión)* firm; *(palabra)* strong.

energúmeno,-a *nm & nf* 1 energumen. 2 *fam fig (hombre)* madman; *(mujer)* mad woman.

enero *nm* January.

See also **marzo**.

enervación *nf* 1 MED enervation. 2 *fam (irritación)* irritation, exasperation.

enervante *adj* 1 MED enervating. 2 *fam (irritante)* irritating, exasperating.

enervar *vt* 1 MED to enervate. 2 *fam (irritar)* to irritate, exasperate, get on one's nerves.
▷ *vpr* **enervarse** *fam* to get flustered, get worked up.

enésimo,-a *adj* 1 nth: **a la enésima potencia** *to the nth power.* 2 *fam* umpteenth.

enfadado,-a *adj* angry, cross, annoyed, US mad.

enfadar *vt* to make angry, make cross, annoy.
▷ *vpr* **enfadarse** 1 to get angry (**con**, with), get cross (**con**, with). 2 *(pelearse)* to fall out (**con**, with) (**por**, about).

enfado *nm* anger, irritation.

enfaenado,-a *adj* hard at work.

enfangar [7] *vt (ropa, persona)* to cover with mud; *(camino)* to turn to mud.

énfasis *nm & nf inv* emphasis, stress.

enfatizar [4] *vt* to emphasize, stress.

enfermar *vi* to fall ill, become ill, be taken ill.

enfermedad *nf* 1 illness, disease, sickness. 2 *fig* malaise, sickness.

enfermería *nf* infirmary, sick bay.

enfermero,-a *nm & nf (hombre)* male nurse; *(mujer)* nurse.

enfermizo,-a *adj* 1 sickly, unhealthy. 2 *fig* morbid.

enfermo,-a *adj* sick, ill.

enfilar *vt* 1 *(poner en fila)* to line up. 2 *(una calle)* to go along; *(túnel)* to go through. 3 *(dirigir)* to direct.

enfisema *nm* emphysema.

enflaquecer [43] *vt* 1 *(poner flaco)* to make thin. 2 *fig (debilitar)* to weaken.
▷ *vi (adelgazar)* to lose weight, get thin.

enfocar [1] *vt* 1 to focus, focus on, get into focus. 2 *(luz)* to shine a light on. 3 *fig (problema, etc)* to focus on.

enfoque *nm* 1 *(acción)* focus, focusing. 2 *fig* focus, approach, angle.

enfrascado,-a *adj* absorbed.

enfrascarse [1] *vpr* 1 *fig* to become absorbed (**en**, in), become engrossed (**en**, in). 2 *fig (en lectura)* to bury OS (**en**, in).

enfrentamiento *nm* confrontation.

enfrentar *vt* 1 *(poner frente a frente)* to bring face to face, confront. 2 *(encarar)* to face, confront.
▷ *vpr* **enfrentarse** 1 *(hacer frente)* to face (**a/con**, -), confront (**a/con**, -). 2 DEP to meet (**a/con**, -). 3 *(pelearse)* to have an argument (**a**, with), fall out (**a**, with); *(chocar)* to clash (**a/con**, with).

enfrente *adv* 1 opposite, in front, facing. 2 *fig* opposed to, against.

enfriamiento *nm* 1 *(acción)* cooling. 2 MED cold, chill.

enfriar [13] *vt* 1 to cool (down), chill. 2 *fig* to cool down.
▷ *vpr* **enfriarse** 1 *(lo demasiado caliente)* to cool down; *(ponerse demasiado frío)* to go cold, get cold. 2 *(tener frío)* to get cold; *(resfriarse)* to catch a cold, get a cold. 3 *fig* to cool off.

enfundar *vt (espada)* to sheathe; *(pistola)* to put into one's holster.

enfurecer [43] *vt* to infuriate, enrage.
▷ *vpr* **enfurecerse** 1 to get furious, lose one's temper. 2 *(mar)* to become rough.

enfurecimiento *nm* fury, infuriation, temper, rage.

enfurruñarse *vpr fam* to sulk, get in a huff.

engalanado,-a *adj* decked out, festooned.

engalanar *vt (cosa)* to festoon, deck out.
▷ *vpr* **engalanarse** *(persona)* to dress up, get dressed up.

enganchar *vt* 1 *(agarrar con gancho)* to hook. 2 *(colgar)* to hang. 3 *(animales)* to harness. 4 *(vagones)* to couple.
▷ *vpr* **engancharse** 1 to get caught (**en**, on). 2 MIL to enlist, join up. 3 *argot (drogas)* to get hooked (**a**, on).

enganche *nm* 1 *(gancho)* hook. 2 *(de animales)* harnessing. 3 *(de vagones)* coupling. 4 MIL recruitment.

enganchón *nm* snag.

engañabobos *nm fam (trampa)* con trick, trap.

engañar *vt* 1 *(gen)* to deceive, mislead, fool, take in. 2 *(estafar)* to cheat, trick.
▷ *vpr* **engañarse** 1 *(ilusionarse)* to deceive OS. 2 *(equivocarse)* to be mistaken, be wrong.

engaño *nm* 1 deceit, deception. 2 *(estafa)* fraud, trick, swindle. 3 *(mentira)* lie. 4 *(error)* mistake.

engañoso,-a *adj* 1 *(gen)* deceptive. 2 *(palabras)* deceitful; *(consejo)* misleading.

engarce *nm* 1 *(de perlas, etc)* threading, stringing. 2 *(de piedra)* setting, mounting.

engarzar [4] *vt* 1 *(perlas, etc)* to string. 2 *(piedras)* to mount, set. 3 *fig (palabras, frases)* to string together.

engastar *vt* to set, mount.

engaste *nm* setting, mounting.

engatusar *vt fam* to get round, coax, cajole.

engendrar *vt* 1 to engender, beget. 2 *fig* to generate.

engendro *nm* 1 *(feto)* foetus (US fetus). 2 *(ser informe)* malformed child. 3 *fam fig (persona)* freak. 4 *fig (cosa)* monstrosity.

englobar *vt* 1 *(incluir)* to include, comprise. 2 *(reunir)* to bring together, lump together.

engolado,-a *adj* 1 *(persona)* arrogant, pompous. 2 *(estilo, etc)* high-flown.

engomado,-a *adj (gomoso)* sticky.
▷ *nm* **engomado** gum, glue.

engomar *vt* to gum, glue, stick.

engominarse *vpr (brillantina)* to put hair cream on; *(fijador)* to gel one's hair, put hair gel on.

engordar *vt* to fatten, fatten up, make fat.
▷ *vi* 1 *(persona)* to put on weight, get fatter. 2 *(alimento)* to be fattening.

engorde *nm* fattening (up).

engorro *nm fam* bother, nuisance.

engorroso,-a *adj fam* bothersome, annoying.

engranaje *nm* 1 TÉC gears *pl*. 2 *(de reloj)* cogs *pl*. 3 *fig* machinery.
engranar *vi* 1 TÉC to engage, mesh. 2 *fig (enlazar)* to connect, link.
▷ *vt* 1 TÉC to engage, mesh. 2 *fig* to connect, link.
engrandecer [43] *vt* 1 *(hacer grande)* to enlarge, magnify. 2 *(exaltar)* to extol, exalt. 3 *fig (enaltecer)* to enhance. 4 *fig (mente, espíritu)* to widen, broaden.
engrasar *vt* 1 *(dar grasa)* to grease, oil, lubricate. 2 *(manchar)* to make greasy, stain with grease. 3 *fam fig (sobornar)* to grease SB's palm.
engrase *nm* 1 *(acción)* greasing, lubrication, oiling. 2 *(sustancia)* lubricant.
engreído,-a *adj* vain, conceited, stuck-up.
engreimiento *nm* vanity, conceit.
engreír [37] *vt (envanecer)* to make vain, make conceited.
▷ *vpr* **engreírse** to become vain, become conceited.
engrescar [1] *vt (incitar)* to cause trouble between; *(animar)* to get going, arouse, excite.
▷ *vpr* **engrescarse** to get embroiled.
engrosar [31] *vt* 1 *(hacer grueso)* to thicken. 2 *fig (aumentar)* to increase, swell.
▷ *vi (engordar)* to get fat.
engrudo *nm* paste, flour and water paste.
engrumecerse [43] *vpr (gen)* to go lumpy; *(sangre)* to clot; *(leche)* to curdle.
enguantado,-a *adj* gloved.
enguatar *vt* to pad.
enguijarrado *nm* cobbles *pl*.
enguirnaldar *vt* to garland.
engullir [41] *vt* to swallow.
enharinar *vt* 1 *(cubrir)* to flour; *(manchar)* to sprinkle with flour. 2 *(la cara)* to whiten.
enhebrar *vt* 1 to thread. 2 *fig* to connect, link.
enhiesto,-a *adj* erect, upright.
enhilar *vt* 1 *(enhebrar)* to thread. 2 *fig (ideas, etc)* to connect, link. 3 *fig (dirigir)* to direct, guide.
enhorabuena *nf* congratulations *pl*.
▷ *adv* thank God.
enhornar *vt* to put into the oven.
enigma *nm* enigma, puzzle, mystery.
enigmático,-a *adj* enigmatic, mysterious, puzzling.
enjabonar *vt* 1 to soap. 2 *fig* to soft-soap, butter-up.
enjaezar [4] *vt* to harness.
enjalbegar [7] *vt* 1 *(pared, etc)* to whitewash. 2 *(la cara)* to paint.
enjambrar *vt* to hive.
▷ *vi* to swarm.
enjambre *nm* 1 swarm. 2 *fig* swarm, throng, crowd.
enjarciar [12] *vt* to rig up: **enjarciaron el barco** *they rigged up the boat.*
enjaretar *vt* 1 *fam fig (discurso, etc)* to reel off. 2 *fam fig (trabajo, etc)* to palm off.
enjaular *vt* 1 to cage. 2 *fam fig* to put in jail, put inside.
enjoyar *vt* 1 to adorn with jewels. 2 *fig* to adorn, decorate. 3 *(engastar)* to set.
▷ *vpr* **enjoyarse** *fam* to put on lots of jewellery (US jewelry), be dripping with jewels.
enjuagar [7] *vt* to rinse.
▷ *vpr* **enjuagarse** to rinse one's mouth out.
enjuague *nm* 1 *(acción)* rinse. 2 *(líquido)* mouthwash. 3 *fig (intriga)* scheme, plot.
enjugar *vt* 1 *(secar)* to dry, wipe (away), mop up. 2 FIN to clear, wipe out.
enjuiciamiento *nm* 1 *(opinión)* judgement, judgment. 2 JUR *(civil)* lawsuit; *(criminal)* trial, prosecution.
enjuiciar [12] *vt* 1 *(juzgar)* to judge; *(examinar)* to examine. 2 JUR *(civil)* to sue; *(criminal)* to indict, prosecute.
enjundia *nf* 1 *(grasa)* fat. 2 *fig (sustancia)* substance; *(importancia)* importance. 3 *fig (fuerza)* force, vitality. 4 *fig (carácter)* character.
enjundioso,-a *adj* 1 *(grasoso)* fatty. 2 *fig* meaty, substantial.
enjuto,-a *adj* thin, skinny, lean.
enlace *nm* 1 *(conexión)* link, connection. 2 *(boda)* marriage. 3 *(tren, etc)* connection. 4 *(intermediario)* liaison, link. 5 QUÍM bond.
enladrillado,-a *adj* brick.
▷ *nm* **enladrillado** brick paving.
enladrillar *vt* to pave with bricks.
enlatado,-a *adj* canned, tinned.
▷ *nm* **enlatado** canning, tinning.
enlatar *vt* to can, tin.
enlazar [4] *vt* 1 *(unir)* to link, connect, tie (together). 2 *(ideas, etc)* to link, connect, relate. 3 *(carreteras, etc)* to connect.
▷ *vi (trenes, etc)* to connect (**con**, with).
▷ *vpr* **enlazarse** 1 *(unirse)* to be linked, be connected. 2 *(casarse)* to get married, marry. 3 *(familias)* to become linked by marriage.
enlodar *vt* 1 to muddy, cover with mud. 2 *fig* to stain, besmirch, sully.
▷ *vpr* **enlodarse** to get muddy.
enloquecedor,-ra *adj* maddening.
enloquecer [43] *vt* 1 *(volver loco)* to drive mad. 2 *fam (gustar)* to be mad/crazy about, be wild about.
▷ *vi (volverse loco)* to go mad/crazy, go out of one's mind.
enlosado *nm (de losas)* paving; *(de baldosas)* tiling.
enlosar *vt (losas)* to pave; *(baldosas)* to tile.
enlucir *vt* 1 *(paredes, etc)* to plaster. 2 *(metales)* to polish.
enlutado,-a *adj* mourning, in mourning.
enmadrado,-a *adj* tied to one's mother's apron strings.
enmadrarse *vpr* to be tied to one's mother's apron strings.
enmarañar *vt* 1 *(enredar)* to tangle. 2 *fig* to embroil, muddle up, confuse.
▷ *vpr* **enmarañarse** 1 *(enredarse)* to get tangled. 2 *fig* to get into a muddle, get confused.
enmarcar [1] *vt* 1 to frame. 2 *(rodear)* to surround.
enmascarado,-a *adj* masked.
▷ *nm & nf* masked person.
enmascarar *vt* 1 to mask. 2 *fig* to mask, disguise, conceal.
enmasillar *vt* to putty.
enmendar [27] *vt* 1 to correct, put right. 2 *(un daño)* to repair, put right. 3 JUR to amend.
▷ *vpr* **enmendarse** to reform, mend one's ways.

enmienda *nf* 1 correction. 2 *(de daño)* repair, indemnity, compensation. 3 JUR amendment. ■ **hacer propósito de enmienda** to turn over a new leaf.
enmohecer [43] *vt* 1 *(pan, queso, etc)* to make mouldy (US moldy); *(metal)* to rust. 2 *fig* to make rusty.
▷ *vpr* **enmohecerse** 1 *(pan, queso, etc)* to go mouldy (US moldy); *(metal)* to rust, go rusty. 2 *fig* to go rusty.
enmoquetar *vt* to carpet.
enmudecer [43] *vt (hacer callar)* to silence.
▷ *vi* 1 *(quedar mudo)* to be struck dumb; *(perder la voz)* to lose one's voice. 2 *(callar)* to fall silent, keep quiet.
ennoblecer [43] *vt* 1 to ennoble. 2 *fig (dignificar)* to do honour (US honor) to, be a credit to. 3 *fig (dar distinción)* to add distinction, add refinement.
enojado,-a *adj* angry, cross.
enojar *vt* to anger, annoy, make angry.
▷ *vpr* **enojarse** to get angry (**con**, with), get annoyed (**con**, with), lose one's temper (**con**, with).
enojo *nm* anger, annoyance, irritation.
enojoso,-a *adj* annoying, irritating.
enología *nf* oenology (US enology).
enólogo,-a *nm & nf* oenologist.
enorgullecer [43] *vt* to fill with pride.
▷ *vpr* **enorgullecerse** to be proud (**de**, of), pride OS (**de**, on).
enorme *adj* 1 *(grande)* enormous, huge, vast. 2 *(desmedido)* tremendous, great. 3 *fam (muy bueno)* very good, excellent.
enormidad *nf* 1 *(grandeza)* enormity, hugeness. 2 *(monstruosidad)* monstrous thing. 3 *fam (mucho)* a lot, loads: **comimos una enormidad** *we ate loads.*
enquistarse *vpr* to encyst.
enrabiar [12] *vt* to enrage, infuriate.
▷ *vpr* **enrabiarse** to become enraged, be furious.
enraizado,-a *adj* rooted.
enraizar [24] *vi* 1 BOT to take root. 2 *fig (persona)* to put down roots.
▷ *vpr* **enraizarse** *(planta, árbol)* to take root; *(persona)* to put down roots.
enramada *nf* 1 *(ramas)* branches *pl*. 2 *(adorno)* decoration made of branches. 3 *(cobertizo)* bower, arbour.
enrarecer [43] *vt* 1 *(aire)* to rarefy. 2 *(hacer escaso)* to make scarce. 3 *fig (situación, relación, etc)* to put a strain on.
▷ *vpr* **enrarecerse** 1 *(aire)* to rarefy. 2 *(escasear)* to become scarce. 3 *fig (situación, relación, etc)* to become strained.
enrarecido,-a *adj* 1 *(aire)* rarefied. 2 *fig (situación, ambiente)* tense, strained.
enredadera *nf* creeper, climbing plant.
enredar *vt* 1 *(engatusar)* to involve, implicate. 2 *(meter cizaña)* to sow discord, cause trouble. 3 *(enmarañar)* to tangle up, entangle. 4 *fig (asunto, etc)* to confuse, complicate; *(trabajo)* to make a mess of.
▷ *vpr* **enredarse** *(hacerse un lío)* to get tangled up, get entangled, get into a tangle.
enredo *nm* 1 *(maraña)* tangle. 2 *(confusión)* mess, muddle, confusion, mix-up. 3 *(engaño)* deceit. 4 *(travesura)* mischief. 5 *(amoroso)* love affair.
enrejado *nm* 1 *(reja)* railings *pl*, grating. 2 *(de celda, etc)* bars *pl*; *(de jardín)* trellis; *(de ventana)* lattice; *(alambrada)* wire netting.
enrejar *vt* 1 *(puerta, ventana)* to put a grating on. 2 *(vallar)* to fence, put railings round.
enrevesado,-a *adj* complicated, difficult.
enriquecer [43] *vt* 1 *(hacer rico)* to make rich. 2 *fig* to enrich.
▷ *vpr* **enriquecerse** to become rich, get rich.
enriquecimiento *nm* enrichment, enhancement.
enristrar *vt (ajos, etc)* to string together.
enrocar [1] *vi (ajedrez)* to castle.
▷ *vt (ajedrez)* to castle.
enrojecimiento *nm* 1 *(metal)* reddening, glowing. 2 *(rostro)* blushing.
enrolar *vt* 1 to enrol (US enroll), sign on, sign up. 2 MIL to enlist.
▷ *vpr* **enrolarse** 1 to enrol (US enroll), sign on. 2 MIL to enlist, join up.
enrollable *adj* that rolls up.
enrollado,-a *adj* 1 *(papel)* rolled up; *(cable)* coiled. 2 *fam (guay)* cool, great. 3 *(ocupado)* busy, wrapped up (**con**, in), engrossed (**con**, in).
enrollar *vt* 1 *(papel)* to roll up; *(hilo)* to wind up; *(cable)* to coil. 2 *(a alguien)* to involve, mix up.
▷ *vpr* **enrollarse** 1 *fam fig (hablar)* to go on and on (**con**, to), chatter (**con**, to). 2 *fam fig (tener relaciones)* to have an affair (**con**, with). 3 *fam fig (liarse)* to get involved (**con**, with).
enroque *nm* castling.
enroscado,-a *adj* curly.
enroscar [1] *vt* 1 *(gen)* to wind, coil (round); *(cable)* to twist. 2 *(tornillo)* to screw in.
▷ *vpr* **enroscarse** to wind, coil; *(cable)* to roll up; *(serpiente)* to coil itself (up).
ensaimada *nf spiral-shaped pastry made of light dough.*
ensalada *nf* 1 salad. 2 *fig* mix-up, mess.
ensaladera *nf* salad bowl.
ensaladilla *nf* vegetable salad.
ensalzar [4] *vt* 1 *(enaltecer)* to exalt. 2 *(elogiar)* to praise, extol (US extoll).
ensamblador *nm* 1 *(carpintería)* joiner. 2 INFORMÁ assembler.
ensamblaje *nm* assembly, joining.
ensamblar *vt* to join, assemble.
ensanchar *vt* 1 *(gen)* to widen, enlarge, extend. 2 COST to let out.
▷ *vpr* **ensancharse** 1 to get wider, expand, spread, stretch. 2 *fig (envanecerse)* to become conceited.
ensanche *nm* 1 *(gen)* widening, enlargement, extension. 2 *(de ciudad)* urban development.
ensangrentado,-a *adj* bloodstained, bloody.
ensangrentar [27] *vt* to stain with blood.
▷ *vpr* **ensangrentarse** to get stained with blood.
ensañamiento *nm* cruelty, brutality.
ensañar *vt* to enrage.
▷ *vpr* **ensañarse** to be cruel (**con**, to), be brutal (**con**, with).
ensartar *vt* 1 *(cuentas)* to string (together), thread; *(aguja)* to thread. 2 *fig* to reel off, rattle off.
ensayar *vt* 1 TEAT to rehearse. 2 MÚS to practise (US practice). 3 *(probar)* to try out, test.
ensayista *nm o nf* essayist.
ensayo *nm* 1 TEAT rehearsal. 2 MÚS practice. 3 *(prueba)* testt. 4 *(literario, etc)* essay. 5 *(rugby)* try.

enseguida [Also written **en seguida**.] *adv* at once, straight away, immediately.

ensenada *nf* cove, inlet.

enseña *nf* ensign, standard.

enseñado,-a *adj (educado)* educated, instructed; *(adiestrado)* trained.

enseñante *adj* teaching.
▷ *nm o nf* teacher.

enseñanza *nf* 1 *(educación)* education, teaching. 2 *(doctrina)* teaching, doctrine. ● **enseñanza general básica** general basic education. ‖ **enseñanza primaria** primary education.

enseñar *vt* 1 *(en escuela, etc)* to teach, train, instruct. 2 *(educar)* to educate. 3 *(mostrar, dejar ver)* to show: **me enseñó el libro** *he showed me the book.* 4 *(señalar)* to point out.

enseres *nm pl (bienes)* belongings, goods; *(material)* equipment *sing; (herramientas)* tools.

ensilladura *nf* 1 *(de la caballería)* back. 2 *(encorvadura)* curvature.

ensillar *vt* to saddle (up), put a saddle on.

ensimismado,-a *adj* engrossed, absorbed, lost.

ensimismamiento *nm* absorption.

ensimismarse *vpr* 1 *(absorberse)* to become engrossed. 2 *(abstraerse)* to become lost in thought.

ensombrecer [43] *vt* to cast a shadow over.
▷ *vpr* **ensombrecerse** 1 to darken. 2 *fig (entristecerse)* to become gloomy.

ensoñación *nf* daydream, pipe dream.

ensoñador,-ra *adj* dreamy.
▷ *nm & nf* dreamer.

ensoñar [31] *vt* to daydream about.

ensordecedor,-ra *adj* deafening.

ensordecer [43] *vt* to deafen.
▷ *vi* to go deaf.

ensortijado,-a *adj* curly.

ensortijar *vt (gen)* to wind; *(cabello)* to curl.

ensuciar [12] *vt* 1 to dirty, make dirty. 2 *fig (reputación, etc)* to tarnish, sully.
▷ *vpr* **ensuciarse** 1 *(mancharse)* to get dirty. 2 *fam (evacuar)* to mess OS, soil OS.

ensueño *nm* dream, fantasy. ■ **de ensueño** dream.

entablado *nm* 1 *(entarimado)* planking, planks *pl.* 2 *(suelo)* wooden floor.

entablar *vt* 1 *(poner tablas)* to plank, board. 2 *(conversación)* to begin, start, open; *(amistad)* to strike up; *(negocio)* to start; *(relaciones)* to establish. 3 *(ajedrez, etc)* to set up.

entablillar *vt* to splint, put in a splint.

entallar *vt* 1 *(esculpir)* to carve. 2 COST to take in at the waist.

entarimado *nm* parquet floor.

entarimar *vt* to cover with parquet.

ente *nm* 1 *(ser)* being. 2 *(institución)* entity, body, organization. 3 *fig* oddball.

enteco,-a *adj* weak, puny, frail.

entelequia *nf* entelechy.

entendederas *nm pl fam* brains. ■ **ser duro,-a de entendederas** *fam* to be slow on the uptake.

entender [28] *nm (opinión)* understanding, opinion.
▷ *vt* 1 *(comprender)* to understand. 2 *(darse cuenta)* to realize. 3 *(discurrir)* to think, believe: **entiendo que sería mejor ir** *I think it would be better to go.* 4 *(conocer a alguien)* to know. 5 *(interpretar)* to understand, take it.
▷ *vi* 1 *(tener conocimiento)* to know (**de**, about). 2 *(ser autoridad)* to be an expert (**en**, in); *(encargarse)* to deal (**en**, with).
▷ *vpr* **entenderse** 1 *(comprenderse)* to be understood. 2 *fam (conocerse)* to know what one is doing: **yo ya me entiendo** *I have my reasons.* 3 *fam (llevarse bien)* to get along.

entendido,-a *nm & nf* expert.

entendimiento *nm* 1 *(comprensión)* understanding, comprehension. 2 *(sentido común)* understanding, sense, judgement. 3 *(inteligencia)* intelligence.

entente *nf* agreement.

enterado,-a *adj* knowledgeable, well-informed.
▷ *nm & nf fam* expert, authority. ■ **darse por enterado,-a de** ALGO to be aware of STH. ‖ **estar enterado,-a** to be in the know.

enterar *vt* to inform (**de**, about/of); *(poner al corriente)* to acquaint (**de**, with), tell (**de**, about).
▷ *vpr* **enterarse** 1 *(averiguar)* to find out (**de**, about). 2 *(tener conocimiento)* to learn, hear. 3 *(darse cuenta)* to realize.

entereza *nf* 1 entirety, wholeness. 2 *fig (de carácter, etc)* integrity, strength.

enternecedor,-ra *adj* moving, touching.

enternecer [43] *vt* 1 *(ablandar)* to soften. 2 *(conmover)* to move, touch.
▷ *vpr* **enternecerse** to be moved, be touched.

entero,-a *adj* 1 *(completo)* entire, whole, complete. 2 *fig (recto)* honest, upright. 3 *fig (firme)* firm, resolute.
▷ *nm* **entero** 1 FIN point. 2 MAT whole number.

enterrador *nm* gravedigger.

enterramiento *nm* burial, interment.

enterrar [27] *vt* 1 to bury, inter. 2 *fig (olvidar)* to forget, give up.

entibiar [12] *vt* 1 to cool, make lukewarm. 2 *fig* to cool down, temper.
▷ *vpr* **entibiarse** 1 to become lukewarm. 2 *fig* to cool off.

entidad *nf* 1 *(esencia)* entity. 2 *(asociación, etc)* firm, company. 3 *fig (importancia)* importance, significance.

entierro *nm* 1 *(acción)* burial. 2 *(ceremonia)* funeral.

entintar *vt* 1 *(manchar)* to stain with ink. 2 *(en impresión)* to ink. 3 *fig (teñir)* to dye.

entoldado *nm* 1 *(toldos)* awnings *pl.* 2 *(para fiestas, etc)* marquee.

entomología *nf* entomology.

entomólogo,-a *nm & nf* entomologist.

entonación *nf* intonation.

entonar *vt* 1 *(nota)* to pitch; *(canción)* to sing, intone. 2 *(organismo)* to tone up. 3 *(colores)* to match.
▷ *vi* 1 MÚS to intone. 2 *(colores)* to match. 3 *fig (armonizar)* to be in harmony (**con**, with), be in tune (**con**, with).

entonces *adv* 1 *(en aquel momento)* then. 2 *(en tal caso)* so, then: **entonces no lo quieres** *so you don't want it.* ■ **desde entonces** since then. ‖ **en aquel entonces** at that time.

entornado,-a *adj (ojos, etc)* half-closed; *(puerta)* ajar.

entornar *vt* **1** *(ojos, etc)* to half-close. **2** *(puerta)* to leave ajar.

entorno *nm* **1** environment, surroundings *pl*. **2** INFORMÁ environment.

entorpecer [43] *vt* **1** to make numb, make dull. **2** *fig (dificultar)* to obstruct, impede, hinder; *(retardar)* to delay.

entorpecimiento *nm* **1** dullness, numbness. **2** *fig (obstrucción)* obstruction, hindrance; *(retraso)* delay.

entrada *nf* **1** *(gen)* entrance, entry. **2** *(vestíbulo)* hall, entrance. **3** *(billete)* ticket, admission. **4** *(público)* audience. **5** *(recaudación)* takings *pl*, receipts *pl*; *(ingresos)* receipts *pl*, earnings *pl*. **6** *(de libro, oración, etc)* opening; *(de año, mes)* beginning: **la entrada de la primavera** *the beginning of spring*. **7** *(pago inicial)* down payment, deposit. **8** *(en libro cuentas)* entry. **9** CULIN entrée, starter. **10** INFORMÁ input. **11** DEP tackle. **12** *(en diccionario)* entry. ■ **de entrada 1** *(desde el principio)* straight away, from the outset. **2** *(en comida)* for starters. ‖ **«Prohibida la entrada»** «No admittance».

entramado *nm* wooden framework.

entrampar *vt* **1** *(animal)* to trap. **2** *fig (engañar)* to trick. **3** *fig (enredar)* to mess up, muddle.

▷ *vpr* **entramparse 1** *(enredarse)* to get into a mess. **2** *(endeudarse)* to get into debt.

entrante *adj* entering, coming, incoming: **el año entrante** *the coming year;* **el mes entrante** *next month*.

▷ *nm* CULIN starter.

entrañable *adj* **1** *(amistad)* intimate, close. **2** *(amigo)* dear. **3** *(recuerdo)* fond.

entrañar *vt* **1** *(introducir)* to bury deep. **2** *(contener)* to contain; *(implicar)* to involve, entail.

entrañas *nf pl* **1** *(órgano)* entrails *pl*, bowels *pl*. **2** *fig (parte importante)* core, heart. **3** *fig (parte oculta)* bowels. **4** *fig (sentimiento, afecto)* feelings.

entrar *vi* **1** *(ir adentro)* to come in, go in. **2** *(tener entrada)* to be welcome. **3** *(en una sociedad, etc)* to join; *(en una profesión)* to take up, join. **4** *(encajar, caber)* to fit: **este tornillo no entra** *this screw doesn't fit*. **5** *(empezar - año, estación)* to begin, start; *(- período, época)* to enter; *(- libro, carta)* to begin, open: **ya ha entrado el verano** *summer has begun*. **6** *(venir)* to come over, come on: **me entraron ganas de llorar** *I felt like crying*. **7** *(alcanzar)* to reach: **ha entrado en los cuarenta** *he has reached forty*. **8** *(deberes, planes)* to come, enter. **9** *(adoptar)* to enter (into), get (into): **entrar en las modas** *to get into fashion*. **10** INFORMÁ to access. **11** AUTO to engage, change into: **no me entró la primera** *I couldn't change into first gear*. **12** MÚS to come in, enter; *(al escenario)* to enter.

▷ *vt* **1** *(meter)* to put. **2** *(de contrabando)* to smuggle. **3** COST to take in.

entre *prep* **1** *(dos términos)* between. **2** *(varios)* among, amongst: **entre los periódicos** *among the newspapers*. **3** *(sumando)* counting: **entre todos éramos veinte** *there were twenty of us all together*. **4** *(en)* in: **entre la lluvia** *in the rain*. **5** *(entremedio)* somewhere between: **entre azul y verde** *somewhere between blue and green*. ■ **de entre** from among, out of: ‖ **entre tanto** meanwhile, in the meantime.

entreabierto,-a *adj (ojos, etc)* half-open; *(puerta)* ajar.

entreabrir *vt* **1** *(ojos)* to half open. **2** *(puerta, etc)* to leave ajar.

entreacto *nm* interval.

entrecejo *nm* space between the eyebrows; *(ceño)* frown.

entrecerrar [27] *vt* to half close.

entrecomillado,-a *adj* in inverted commas, in quotation marks.

entrecomillar *vt* to put in inverted commas, put in quotation marks.

entrecortado,-a *adj* **1** *(voz)* faltering, hesitant; *(respiración)* laboured (US labored), difficult. **2** *(intermitente)* intermittent.

entrecortar *vt* **1** to cut partially. **2** *fig* to cut off, interrupt.

entrecot *nm* entrecôte.

▲ *pl* **entrecots.**

entredicho *nm* **1** *(prohibición)* prohibition, ban. **2** REL interdict. **3** *(duda)* doubt, question. ■ **poner** ALGO **en entredicho** to have one's doubts about STH, call STH into question, cast doubt on STH.

entredós *nm* **1** COST insertion, panel. **2** *(mueble)* cabinet, dresser.

entrega *nf* **1** *(gen)* handing over. **2** *(de premios)* presentation. **3** COM delivery. **4** *(de posesiones)* surrender. **5** *(fascículo)* instalment (US installment), part. **6** *fig (devoción)* selflessness, devotion. **7** DEP pass. ● **entrega a domicilio** home delivery.

entregar [7] *vt* **1** *(dar)* to hand over. **2** *(deberes, ejercicios)* to hand in, give in; *(premios)* to present, award. **3** COM to deliver. **4** MIL to surrender.

▷ *vpr* **entregarse 1** *(rendirse)* to give in (**a**, to), surrender. **2** *(dedicarse)* to devote OS (**a**, to), be devoted (**a**, to). **3** *pey (caer en)* to give OS over (**a**, to), take (**a**, to).

entreguerras ■ **de entreguerras** between the wars.

entrelazar [4] *vt* to entwine, interweave, interlace.

entremedias *adv* **1** in between. **2** *(mientras tanto)* meanwhile, in the meantime. ■ **entremedias de** between, among.

entremés *nm* **entremeses** *(entrante)* hors d'oeuvre.

entremezclar *vt* to intermingle.

▷ *vpr* **entremezclarse** to intermingle.

entrenador,-ra *nm & nf* trainer, coach.

entrenamiento *nm* training.

entrenar *vt* to train, coach.

▷ *vpr* **entrenarse** to train.

entreno *nm* training.

entrepierna *nf* crotch, crutch.

entresacar [1] *vt* **1** *(elegir)* to select, pick out. **2** *(pelo, plantas)* to thin out.

entresijo *nm fig* secret, mystery. ■ **conocer todos los entresijos** *fig* to know all the ins and outs.

entresuelo *nm* mezzanine, GB first floor, US second floor.

entretanto *adv* meanwhile, for the time being.

entretejer *vt* to interweave, intertwine.

entretela *nf* COST interfacing, interlining.

entretener [87] *vt* **1** *(detener)* to hold up, detain; *(retrasar)* to delay. **2** *(ocupar)* to keep busy. **3** *(distraer)* to occupy, keep occupied. **4** *(divertir)* to entertain, amuse, distract. **5** *(hambre)* to kill, stave off; *(tiempo)* to while away.

▷ *vpr* **entretenerse 1** *(retrasarse)* to be delayed, be held up. **2** *(distraerse)* to keep OS occupied. **3** *(divertirse)* to amuse OS.

entretenido,-a *adj* **1** *(divertido)* entertaining, amusing. **2** *(complicado)* time-consuming: **un trabajo entretenido** *a time-consuming job.*

entretenimiento *nm* **1** *(distracción)* entertainment, distraction, amusement. **2** *(mantenimiento)* maintenance, upkeep.

entretiempo *nm* period between seasons; *(primavera)* spring; *(otoño)* autumn. ■ **un traje de entretiempo** a lightweight suit.

entrever [91] *vt* **1** to glimpse, catch sight of, make out. **2** *fig (conjeturar)* to guess, suspect. ■ **dejar entrever** to hint.

entreverado,-a *adj* **1** mixed. **2** CULIN streaky.

entreverar *vt* to mix, mix up.

entrevía *nf* gauge.

entrevista *nf* **1** *(prensa)* interview. **2** *(reunión)* meeting. ■ **hacer una entrevista a ALGN** to interview SB.

entrevistador,-ra *nm & nf* interviewer.

entrevistar *vt* to interview.

▷ *vpr* **entrevistarse 1** *(prensa)* to have an interview (**con**, with). **2** *(reunirse)* to have a meeting (**con**, with).

entristecedor,-ra *adj* saddening.

entristecer [43] *vt* to sadden, make sad.

▷ *vpr* **entristecerse** to be sad (**por**, about).

entrometerse *vpr* to meddle, interfere.

entrometido,-a *adj* interfering, nosy.

▷ *nm & nf* meddler, busybody, nosy parker.

entroncar [1] *vt* to relate, link, connect.

▷ *vi (parentesco)* to be related; *(por matrimonio)* to be related by marriage.

entronización *nf* enthronement.

entronizar [4] *vt* **1** to enthrone, put on the throne. **2** *fig* to worship, put on a pedestal.

entropía *nf* entropy.

entuerto *nm (agravio)* wrong, injustice.

entumecer [43] *vt* to numb, make numb.

▷ *vpr* **entumecerse 1** to go numb, go to sleep. **2** *fig (mar, río)* to swell.

entumecido,-a *adj* numb.

entumecimiento *nm* **1** numbness. **2** *(mar, río)* swelling.

enturbiar [12] *vt* **1** to make muddy, make cloudy, cloud. **2** *fig* to cloud, muddle, obscure.

▷ *vpr* **enturbiarse 1** to get muddy, become cloudy. **2** *fig* to get confused, get muddled.

entusiasmado,-a *adj* excited.

entusiasmar *vt* **1** *(causar entusiasmo)* to fill with enthusiasm, excite. **2** *(gustar)* to like, love: **me entusiasma la ópera** *I love opera.*

▷ *vpr* **entusiasmarse 1** to get enthusiastic (**con**, about), get excited (**con**, about). **2** *(gustar)* to love (**con**, -), like (**con**, -).

entusiasmo *nm* enthusiasm. ■ **con entusiasmo** keenly, enthusiastically.

entusiasta *adj* enthusiastic.

▷ *nm & nf* lover, fan.

enumeración *nf (cómputo)* enumeration, count, reckoning; *(relación)* listing, enumeration.

enumerar *vt* to enumerate.

enunciado *nm* **1** *(teoría, etc)* enunciation. **2** LING statement. **3** *(problema, etc)* wording.

enunciar [12] *vt* **1** *(teoría)* to enunciate. **2** *(expresar)* to express, state, word.

enunciativo,-a *adj* enunciative. ● **oración enunciativa** statement.

envalentonar *vt* to make bold, make daring.

▷ *vpr* **envalentonarse 1** *(volverse valiente)* to become bold, become daring. **2** *(insolentarse)* to become arrogant, become aggressive.

envanecer [43] *vt* to make vain, make proud.

▷ *vpr* **envanecerse** to become conceited (**de/por**, about), become vain (**de/por**, about).

envarado,-a *adj* **1** *(tieso)* stiff. **2** *(orgulloso)* conceited, proud.

envaramiento *nm* stiffness.

envarar *vt (entumecer)* to numb, make numb.

▷ *vpr* **envararse 1** *(entumecerse)* to go numb. **2** *fam fig (engreírse)* to become vain, become conceited.

envasado,-a *adj (bebidas)* bottled; *(conservas)* canned, tinned; *(paquetes)* packed.

▷ *nm* **envasado** *(bebidas)* bottling; *(conservas)* canning; *(paquetes)* packing. ● **envasado al vacío** vacuum-packed.

envasar *vt (botellas)* to bottle; *(latas)* to can, tin; *(paquetes)* to pack.

envase *nm* **1** *(acción - paquetes)* packing; *(- botellas)* bottling; *(- latas)* canning. **2** *(recipiente)* container. **3** *(botella vacía)* empty. ● **envase de cartón** carton. ‖ **envase de plástico** plastic container. ‖ **envase sin retorno** nonreturnable bottle.

envejecer [43] *vt* to age, make look old.

▷ *vi* to get old, grow old.

envejecido,-a *adj* aged, old, old-looking: **Pablo está muy envejecido** *Pablo looks very old.*

envejecimiento *nm* ageing, growing old.

envenenamiento *nm* poisoning.

envenenar *vt* **1** to poison. **2** *fig (palabras, acciones)* to interpret wrongly. **3** *fig (corromper)* to corrupt, poison.

envergadura *nf* **1** *(de pájaro)* spread, span, wingspan. **2** MAR breadth (of sail). **3** *fig (de avión)* span, wingspan. **4** *fig (importancia)* importance, scope. ■ **de gran envergadura** very important, consequential, far-reaching.

envés *nm inv* **1** *(de página)* back, reverse. **2** *(de tela)* wrong side. **3** BOT reverse.

enviado,-a *nm & nf* messenger, envoy. ● **enviado,-a especial** special correspondent.

enviar [13] *vt* **1** *(gen)* to send. **2** COM to dispatch, remit; *(por barco)* to ship.

enviciar [12] *vt (pervertir)* to corrupt, pervert.

▷ *vi* **1** BOT to produce too many leaves and not enough fruit. **2** *fig (deformarse)* to become distorted.

▷ *vpr* **enviciarse** *(pervertirse)* to become corrupted, fall into bad habits; *(aficionarse demasiado)* to become addicted (**en**, to).

envidar *vi* to bid, bet.

envidia *nf* envy. ■ **dar envidia** to make envious. ‖ **tener envidia de ALGO/ALGN** to envy STH/SB.

envidiable *adj* enviable.

envidiar [12] *vt* to envy, be envious of.

envidioso,-a *adj* envious.
envilecer [43] *vt* to debase, degrade.
▷ *vi* to lose value, be debased.
▷ *vpr* **envilecerse** to debase OS, degrade OS: **bebió tanto que se envileció** *he debased himself by drinking so much.*
envilecimiento *nm* degradation, debasement.
envío *nm* 1 *(acción)* sending, dispatch. 2 COM dispatch, shipment. 3 *(remesa)* consignment; *(paquete)* parcel. 4 *(mensaje electrónico)* posting. ■ **hacer un envío** COM to dispatch an order. ● **envío contra reembolso** cash on delivery. ‖ **gastos de envío** postage and packing.
envite *nm* 1 *(apuesta)* bet. 2 *fig (ofrecimiento)* offer, bid. 3 *(empujón)* push.
enviudar *vi (hombre)* to become a widower, lose one's wife; *(mujer)* to become a widow, lose one's husband.
envoltorio *nm* 1 *(de caramelo, etc)* wrapper. 2 *(lío)* bundle.
envoltura *nf* wrapping, wrapper.
envolvente *adj* enveloping.
envolver [32] *vt* 1 *(con papel)* to wrap, wrap up. 2 *(con ropa)* to wrap, wrap up: **estaba envuelta en una manta** *she was wrapped in a blanket.* 3 *(hilo, cinta)* to wind. 4 *(pasteles, etc)* to coat, cover. 5 *fig (rodear)* to envelop, shroud: **la niebla envolvía el campanario** *the fog enveloped the bell tower.* 6 *fig (implicar)* to involve (**en**, in), implicate (**en**, in): **lo envolvieron en aquel asunto** *they involved him in that affair.* 7 *fig (confundir)* to confound. 8 MIL to surround, encircle.
enyesado *nm* 1 plastering. 2 MED plaster cast.
enyesar *vt* 1 to plaster. 2 MED to put in plaster.
enzarzar [4] *vt* 1 *(de zarzas)* to cover with brambles. 2 *fig (engrescar)* to sow discord among, set at odds.
▷ *vpr* **enzarzarse** 1 *(enredarse en zarzas)* to get entangled in brambles. 2 *fig (discusión, asunto)* to get involved (**en**, in).
enzima *nm & nf* enzyme.
eñe *nf name of the letter* **ñ**.
eoceno,-a *adj* Eocene.
▷ *nm* **eoceno** Eocene.
eólico,-a *adj* wind: **energía eólica** *wind power.*
eón *nm* aeon (US eon).
epatar *vt argot* to knock dead.
épica *nf* epic poetry.
epicarpio *nm* epicarp.
epiceno *adj* epicene.
epicentro *nm* epicentre (US epicenter).
épico,-a *adj* epic, heroic.
epicureísmo *nm* Epicureanism.
epicúreo,-a *adj* Epicurean.
epidemia *nf* epidemic.
epidémico,-a *adj* epidemic.
epidérmico,-a *adj* epidermic, skin: **enfermedad epidérmica** *skin disease.*
epidermis *nf inv* epidermis, skin.
epifanía *nf* Epiphany, Twelfth Night.
epiglotis *nf inv* epiglottis.
epígono *nm* epigone.
epígrafe *nm* 1 *(cita)* epigraph. 2 *(título)* title, heading.
epigrafía *nf* epigraphy.
epigrama *nm* epigram, satirical poem.
epilepsia *nf* epilepsy.
epiléptico,-a *adj* epileptic.
▷ *nm & nf* epileptic.
epílogo *nm* 1 *(parte final)* epilogue (US epilog). 2 *(resumen)* summary.
episcopado *nm* 1 *(obispos)* episcopacy. 2 *(lugar)* bishopric. 3 *(época)* episcopate.
episcopal *adj* episcopal.
episódico,-a *adj* episodic.
episodio *nm* 1 *(literario)* episode. 2 *(suceso)* incident, event.
epístola *nf fml* epistle, letter.
epitafio *nm* epitaph.
epitelio *nm* epithelium.
epíteto *nm* epithet.
epítome *nm* epitome, abstract, summary.
época *nf* 1 time, age. 2 HIST period, epoch: **muebles de época** *period furniture.* 3 AGR season, time: **la época de la recolección** *harvest time.* ■ **por aquella época** about that time. ‖ **ser de su época** to be with the times.
epónimo,-a *adj* eponymous.
▷ *nm* **epónimo** eponym.
epopeya *nf* 1 LIT epic poem. 2 *(hecho)* heroic deed.
equidad *nf* 1 JUR equity. 2 *(moderación)* fairness, reasonableness.
equidistancia *nf* equidistance.
equidistante *adj* equidistant.
equidistar *vi* to be equidistant (**de**, from).
equilátero,-a *adj* equilateral.
equilibrado,-a *adj* 1 balanced. 2 *(persona)* sensible, well-balanced.
equilibrar *vt* 1 to balance, poise. 2 *fig* to balance, adjust.
▷ *vpr* **equilibrarse** 1 to balance (**en**, on). 2 *fig* to recover one's balance.
equilibrio *nm* 1 *(estabilidad)* balance: **perdió el equilibrio** *he lost his balance.* 2 FÍS equilibrium. 3 *fig (armonía)* balance, harmony. 4 *fig (serenidad)* poise, composure. ■ **hacer equilibrios** *fig* to perform a balancing act. ‖ **mantener el equilibrio** to keep one's balance.
equilibrismo *nm (gen)* balancing act; *(de funámbulo)* tightrope walking.
equilibrista *nm o nf (funámbulo)* tightrope walker.
equino,-a *adj* equine, horse.
equinoccio *nm* equinox.
equinodermo *nm* echinoderm.
equipaje *nm* 1 luggage, baggage. 2 *(instrumental)* equipment, outfit. 3 *(tripulación)* crew. ● **equipaje de mano** hand luggage.
equipar *vt* 1 to equip, furnish. 2 *(barco)* to fit out.
▷ *vpr* **equiparse** *(uso reflexivo)* to kit OS out (**con/de**, with), equip OS (**con/de**, with).
equiparable *adj* comparable (**a/con**, to/with).
equiparar *vt* to compare (**a/con**, with), liken (**a/con**, to).
equipo *nm* 1 *(prestaciones)* equipment. 2 *(ropas, utensilios)* outfit, kit. 3 *(de personas)* team. ● **equipo de alta fidelidad** hi-fi system. ‖ **equipo de fútbol** football team. ‖ **equipo de música** music centre, stereo system.
equis *nf inv* 1 *name of the letter* **x**. 2 MAT x, unknown quantity.
equitación *nf* horsemanship, horse riding, US horseback riding.

equitativo,-a *adj* equitable, fair.
equivalencia *nf* 1 *(igualdad)* equivalence. 2 *(sustitución)* compensation.
equivalente *adj* 1 *(igual)* equivalent. 2 *(que sustituye)* compensatory.
▷ *nm* equivalent.
equivaler [89] *vi* 1 *(ser igual)* to be equivalent (a, to), be equal (a, to). 2 *(significar)* to be tantamount (a, to), amount (a, to), mean (a, -).
equivocación *nf* 1 *(error)* mistake, error. 2 *(malentendido)* misunderstanding. ■ **cometer una equivocación** to make a mistake.
equivocado,-a *adj* mistaken, wrong.
equivocar [1] *vt* 1 to mistake, get wrong. 2 *(cambiar)* to get mixed up: **equivoqué vuestros regalos** *I got your presents mixed up.*
▷ *vpr* **equivocarse** to make a mistake, be mistaken, be wrong; *(de dirección, camino, etc)* to go wrong, get wrong. **me equivoqué de calle** *I got the wrong street.*
equívoco,-a *adj* equivocal, misleading, ambiguous.
▷ *nm* **equívoco** 1 ambiguity, double meaning. 2 *(malentendido)* misunderstanding.
era *nf (tiempo)* era, age. ● **era cristiana** Christian era.
erario *nm* exchequer, treasury.
erasmismo *nm* Erasmianism.
erbio *nm* erbium.
ere *nf name of the letter* r.
erección *nf* 1 *(levantamiento)* erection, raising. 2 *(órgano)* erection. 3 *(institución)* foundation, establishment.
eréctil *adj* erectile.
erecto,-a *adj* erect.
eremita *nm* hermit, eremite.
eretismo *nm* erethism.
ergio *nm* erg.
ergonomía *nf* ergonomics.
ergonómico,-a *adj* ergonomic.
erguido,-a *adj* 1 erect, upright, straight. 2 *fig* proud.
erguir [70] *vt* to raise (up straight), erect, lift up.
▷ *vpr* **erguirse** 1 *(ponerse derecho)* to straighten up, stand up straight. 2 *(alzarse)* to rise. 3 *fig (engreírse)* to swell with pride.
erial *adj* uncultivated, untilled.
▷ *nm* uncultivated land.
erigir [6] *vt* 1 *(alzar)* to erect, build. 2 *(instituir)* to establish, found. 3 *(elevar de categoría)* to make: **le erigieron jefe de la pandilla** *they made him gang leader.*
Eritrea *nf* Eritrea.
eritreo,-a *adj* Eritrean.
▷ *nm & nf (persona)* Eritrean.
erizado,-a *adj* 1 bristly, prickly. 2 *fig* fraught (de, with), full (de, of).
erizar [4] *vt (pelo - animal)* to bristle; *(- persona)* make stand on end.
▷ *vpr* **erizarse** *(pelo - de animal)* to bristle; *(- de persona)* to stand on end: **el pelo se le erizó** *his hair stood on end.*
erizo *nm* 1 *(animal)* hedgehog. 2 *(planta)* burr. 3 *fig (persona)* surly person, prickly character. ● **erizo de mar** sea urchin.
ermita *nf* hermitage, shrine.
ermitaño,-a *adj* recluse.
▷ *nm & nf (persona solitaria)* hermit.
▷ *nm* **ermitaño** ZOOL hermit crab.
erógeno,-a *adj* erogenous, erogenic.
erosión *nf* 1 erosion, wearing away. 2 *fig* wear and tear.
erosionar *vt* 1 to erode. 2 *(gastar)* to wear away.
erosivo,-a *adj* erosive.
erótico,-a *adj* erotic.
erotismo *nm* eroticism.
erotizar [4] *vt* to eroticize.
errabundo,-a *adj* 1 wandering, vagrant. 2 *fig* aimless.
erradicación *nf* 1 eradication. 2 *(de enfermedad)* stamping out.
erradicar [1] *vt* 1 to eradicate. 2 *(enfermedad)* to stamp out.
errado,-a *adj* mistaken, wrong, erroneous.
errante *adj* wandering, vagrant, errant.
errar [57] *vt (objetivo)* to miss, get wrong.
▷ *vi* 1 *(vagar)* to wander, rove, roam. 2 *(equivocarse)* to be mistaken, be wrong.
errata *nf* erratum, misprint.
errático,-a *adj* erratic.
erre *nf name of the digraph* rr.
erróneo,-a *adj* erroneous, wrong, mistaken, unsound: **juicio erróneo** *unsound judgement;* **explicación errónea** *wrong explanation;* **identificación errónea** *mistaken identity.*
error *nm* error, mistake.
eructar *vi* to belch, burp.
eructo *nm* belch, burp.
erudición *nf* erudition, learning, scholarship.
erudito,-a *adj* erudite, learned, scholarly.
▷ *nm & nf* scholar, expert.
erupción *nf* 1 *(volcánica)* eruption. 2 *(cutánea)* rash. ■ **entrar en erupción** to erupt.
eruptivo,-a *adj* eruptive.
esbeltez *nf* 1 slenderness, slimness. 2 *(elegancia)* gracefulness.
esbelto,-a *adj* 1 slim, slender, willowy. 2 *(elegante)* graceful.
esbirro *nm* 1 HIST bailiff. 2 *(ayudante)* henchman.
esbozar [4] *vt* to sketch, outline. ■ **esbozar una sonrisa** *fig* to force a smile, smile weakly.
esbozo *nm* sketch, outline, rough draft.
escabechado,-a *adj* pickled, in brine; *(arenque)* pickled, soused.
escabechar *vt* 1 to pickle, preserve in brine; *(arenque)* to souse, pickle. 2 *fam fig (matar)* to do in, bump off. 3 *fam fig (suspender)* to fail.
escabeche *nm* brine, pickle.
escabechina *nf fam* massacre.
escabroso,-a *adj* 1 *(desigual)* uneven, rough: **terreno escabroso** *rough terrain.* 2 *fig (carácter)* harsh, rude. 3 *fig (difícil)* tough, difficult. 4 *fig (indecente)* indecent.
escabullirse [41] *vpr* 1 *(entre las manos)* to slip through. 2 *fig (persona)* to slip away, sneak off, disappear.
escacharrar *vt* 1 *fam (romper)* to break. 2 *fam (estropear)* to ruin, spoil. 3 *fam (coche)* to smash up.
escafandra *nf* diving suit.
escafandrista *nm o nf* diver.
escala *nf* 1 *(escalera - de mano)* ladder; *(- de tijera)* stepladder. 2 *(graduación)* scale; *(de colores)* range. 3 *(mapa, plano, etc)* scale: **lo dibujó a escala** *he drew it to scale.* 4 *(puerto)* port of call; *(aeropuerto)* stopover. 5 MÚS scale.

escalada *nf* **1** *(montaña)* climb, climbing; *(pendiente)* scaling. **2** *fig (precios, etc)* rise, increase; *(armas)* escalation.
escalador,-ra *nm & nf* climber, mountaineer.
escalafón *nm* **1** *(de personas)* roll, promotion list. **2** *(graduación)* ladder; *(de salarios)* salary scale, wage scale.
escalar *vt* **1** *(montaña)* to climb; *(pendiente)* to scale. **2** *(asaltar)* to burgle. **3** *fig (subir)* to climb; *(armas, guerra)* to escalate.
escaldado,-a *adj* **1** scalded. **2** *fig* wary, cautious.
escaleno *adj* scalene.
▷ *nm* scalene.
escalera *nf* **1** stairs *pl*, staircase. **2** *(escala)* ladder. **3** *(naipes)* run, sequence.
escalerilla *nf* **1** *(de barco)* gangway; *(de avión)* steps *pl*. **2** *(en naipes)* run of three cards.
escalfar *vt* to poach: **huevos escalfados** *poached eggs.*
escalinata *nf* outside steps *pl*.
escalofriante *adj* chilling, bloodcurdling, hair-raising.
escalofrío *nm (de frío)* shiver; *(de miedo)* shudder, shiver; *(de fiebre)* chill, shiver. ■ **tener escalofríos** to shiver.
escalón *nm* **1** *(peldaño)* step, stair; *(de escala)* rung. **2** *fig (grado)* degree, level, grade. **3** *fig (paso, medio)* stepping stone. **4** MIL echelon.
escalonado,-a *adj* **1** *(espaciado)* spaced out, at regular intervals. **2** *(graduado)* graded. **3** *(corte de pelo)* in layers, layered.
escalonar *vt* **1** *(espaciar)* to place at intervals, space out. **2** *(graduar)* to grade. **3** *(cabello)* to layer, cut in layers.
escalpelo *nm* scalpel.
escama *nf* **1** scale. **2** *fig (de piel, de jabón)* flake.
escamado,-a *adj fam fig* wary, suspicious.
escamar *vt* **1** *(quitar escamas)* to scale, remove the scales from. **2** *fam fig* to make suspicious, make wary.
▷ *vpr* **escamarse** *fam fig* to become suspicious, become wary, smell a rat.
escamotear *vt* **1** *(hacer desaparecer)* to make vanish, make disappear. **2** *fam (robar)* to pinch, lift; *(quitar)* to take, withhold, keep back. **3** *fam (problema, dificultad)* to skip, skirt round. **4** *(ocultar)* to keep secret.
escampar *vt* to clear out.
▷ *vi* [Used only in the 3rd person; it does not take a subject.] METEOR to stop raining, clear up.
escandalizar [4] *vt* to scandalize, shock.
▷ *vpr* **escandalizarse** to be shocked (**de/por**, at), be scandalized (**de/por**, by).
escándalo *nm* **1** scandal. **2** *(alboroto)* racket, fuss, din, uproar. **3** *fig (asombro)* astonishment, shock. ■ **armar un escándalo** to kick up a fuss.
escandaloso,-a *adj* **1** scandalous, shocking. **2** *(alborotado)* noisy, rowdy. **3** *(color)* loud; *(risa)* uproarious.
Escandinavia *nf* Scandinavia.
escandinavo,-a *adj* Scandinavian.
▷ *nm & nf* Scandinavian.
escanear *vt* to scan.
escáner *nm* scanner.
escaño *nm* **1** *(banco)* bench. **2** POL seat.
escapada *nf* **1** *fam (salida)* quick trip. **2** DEP breakaway. **3** *(huida)* escape.
escapar *vi* **1** *(huir)* to escape, get away. **2** *(librarse)* to escape. **3** *(quedar fuera del alcance)* to be beyond.
▷ *vpr* **escaparse 1** *(huir)* to escape, run away, get away. **2** *(librarse)* to escape, avoid. **3** *(gas, etc)* to leak. **4** *(autobús, etc)* to miss: **se me escapó el autobús** *I missed the bus.*
escaparate *nm* shop window.
escapatoria *nf* **1** *(huida)* escape, flight. **2** *(excusa)* excuse, way out. **3** *fam (escapada)* quick trip.
escape *nm* **1** *(huida)* escape, flight, getaway. **2** *(de gas, etc)* leak. **3** TÉC exhaust.
escaquearse *vpr fam* to shirk, skive off, wriggle out of: **¡no te escaquees!** *don't try and wriggle out of it!*
escarabajo *nm* **1** beetle. **2** *fam fig (persona)* little squirt. **3** *(de tejido)* flaw.
escaramujo *nm* **1** *(rosal)* wild rose, dog rose. **2** *(fruto)* rosehip. **3** *(crustáceo)* barnacle.
escaramuza *nf* **1** MIL skirmish. **2** *(riña)* run-in.
escarbar *vt* **1** *(suelo)* to scratch. **2** *(dientes, orejas)* to pick. **3** *(fuego)* to poke. **4** *(bolsillo, papeles)* to rummage in. **5** *fig (inquirir)* to inquire into, delve into.
escarcha *nf* frost, hoarfrost.
escarlata *adj* scarlet.
escarlatina *nf* scarlet fever.
escarmentar [27] *vt* to punish severely.
▷ *vi* to learn one's lesson: **a ver si escarmientas** *that'll teach you (a lesson).*
escarmiento *nm* punishment, lesson.
escarnio *nm* derision, mockery, ridicule.
escarola *nf* curly endive.
escarpado,-a *adj* **1** *(inclinado)* steep. **2** *(abrupto)* craggy.
escarpia *nf* spike, hook.
escasear *vi (faltar)* to be scarce, get scarce.
escasez *nf* **1** *(carencia)* scarcity, lack, shortage. **2** *(mezquindad)* meanness, stinginess.
escaso,-a *adj* **1** *(insuficiente)* scarce, scant, very little, small. **2** *(recursos)* slender; *(dinero)* tight; *(público)* small; *(lluvias, salario)* low; *(tiempo)* very little. **3** *(poco de algo)* few: **escasos días** *few days.* **4** *(que le falta poco)* hardly, scarcely, barely: **un kilo escaso** *barely a kilo.*
escatológico,-a *adj (de excrementos)* scatological.
escayola *nf* **1** *(yeso)* plaster of Paris; *(estuco)* stucco. **2** MED plaster.
escayolar *vt* to put in plaster, plaster.
escena *nf* **1** TEAT *(parte)* scene; *(lugar)* stage. **2** *fig* scene.
escenario *nm* **1** TEAT stage. **2** CINE scenario. **3** *fig* scene, setting.
escenificación *nf* **1** *(de novela)* to dramatize. **2** *(de obra de teatro)* to stage.
escenificar *vt* **1** *(novela)* to dramatize. **2** *(obra de teatro)* to stage.
escenografía *nm* **1** CINE set design. **2** TEAT stage design.
escenógrafo,-a *nm & nf* **1** CINE set designer. **2** TEAT stage designer.
escepticismo *nm* scepticism (US skepticism).
escéptico,-a *adj* sceptic (US skeptic).
▷ *nm & nf* sceptic (US skeptic).
escindir *vt* to split, divide.
▷ *vpr* **escindirse** to split (off) (**en**, into).
escisión *nf* **1** split, division. **2** FÍS fission. **3** MED excision.
esclarecer [43] *vt* **1** *(iluminar)* to light up, illuminate. **2** *fig (poner en claro)* to clear up, make clear, shed light on. **3** *fig (entendimiento)* to enlighten.
▷ *vi (amanecer)* to dawn.

esclavitud *nf* slavery, servitude.
esclavizar [4] *vt* to enslave.
esclavo,-a *adj (literalmente)* enslaved; *(uso figurado)* tied: **es esclavo de su familia** *he's tied to his family.*
▷ *nm & nf (gen)* slave.
esclusa *nf* lock, sluicegate, floodgate.
escoba *nf* brush, broom.
escobilla *nf* 1 small brush. 2 AUTO windscreen-wiper blade.
escobón *nm* large brush, large broom.
escocedura *nf* 1 *(herida)* sore. 2 *(dolor)* soreness.
escocer [54] *vi* 1 to smart, sting: **le escuecen sus heridas** *his cuts sting.* 2 *fig* to hurt.
escocés,-a *adj* Scottish.
▷ *nm & nf (persona)* Scot; *(hombre)* Scotsman; *(mujer)* Scotswoman.
▷ *nm* **escocés** *(idioma)* Scottish Gaelic.
Escocia *nf* Scotland. ● **Nueva Escocia** Nova Scotia.
escoger [5] *vt* to choose, pick out, select.
escogido,-a *adj* chosen, selected; *(selecto)* choice.
escolar *adj* school, scholastic.
▷ *nm o nf (chico)* schoolboy; *(chica)* schoolgirl.
escolástico,-a *adj* scholastic.
escollera *nf* breakwater, jetty.
escollo *nm* 1 MAR reef, rock. 2 *fig* difficulty, pitfall.
escolopendra *nf* centipede.
escolta *nf* escort.
escoltar *vt* 1 to escort. 2 MAR to convoy.
escombros *nm pl* rubble *sing*, debris *sing*.
esconder *vt* to hide, conceal.
▷ *vpr* **esconderse** to hide.
escondidas ■ **hacer** ALGO **a escondidas de** ALGN to do STH behind SB's back.
escondite *nm* 1 *(lugar)* hiding place. 2 *(juego)* hide-and-seek.
escopeta *nf* shotgun.
escoplo *nm* chisel.
escorar *vi* to list, heel (over): **el barco está escorado** *the ship is listing.*
escorbuto *nm* scurvy.
Escorpio *nm* Scorpio.
escorpión *nm* 1 [*pl* **escorpiones**.] scorpion. 2 **Escorpión** [*pl* **Escorpión**.] *(signo zodiacal)* Scorpio.
escorzo *nm* foreshortening.
escotado,-a *adj* COST low-necked, low-cut.
escote[1] *nm* COST low neckline.
escote[2] *nm (parte)* share. ■ **pagar a escote** to share the cost of.
escozor *nm* 1 stinging, smarting. 2 *fig* pain, grief.
escribiente *nm* (office) clerk.
escribir *vt* 1 *(gen)* to write. 2 *(deletrear)* to spell, write.
▷ *vi* to write.
▷ *vpr* **escribirse** 1 *(deletrear)* to spell, be spelt: **¿cómo se escribe?** *how do you spell it?* 2 *(uso recíproco)* to write to each other. ■ **escribir a mano** to write in longhand.
escrito,-a *pp* ⟶ **escribir.**
▷ *adj* written; *(mencionado)* stated.
▷ *nm* **escrito** 1 *(documento)* writing, document, text. 2 *(obra)* work, writing.
escritor,-ra *nm & nf* writer.
escritorio *nm* 1 *(mueble)* writing desk. 2 *(oficina)* office.
escritura *nf* 1 *(gen)* writing: **escritura fonética** *phonetic script.* 2 *(caligrafía)* handwriting, writing. 3 JUR deed, document.
escroto *nm* scrotum.
escrúpulo *nm* 1 [Often used in plural with the same meaning.] *(recelo)* scruple, doubt, qualm. 2 [Often used in plural with the same meaning.] *(aprensión)* fussiness: **eso me da escrúpulos** *I'm finicky about it, I'm fussy about it.* 3 *fig (cuidado)* extreme care: **lo hizo con escrúpulo** *he did it with extreme care.*
escrupuloso,-a *adj* 1 scrupulous. 2 *(aprensivo)* finicky, fussy. 3 *fig (exacto)* scrupulous, meticulous.
escrutar *vt* 1 *(examinar)* to scrutinize, examine carefully. 2 *(votos)* to count.
escrutinio *nm* 1 *(examen)* scrutiny, examination. 2 *(de votos)* count.
escuadra *nf* 1 *(instrumento -de dibujo)* set square; *(-de carpintería)* square; *(pieza de metal)* bracket. 2 *(de tropas)* squad; *(de buques)* squadron, fleet. 3 *(fútbol)* angle.
escuadrilla *nf* squadron.
escuadrón *nm* squadron.
escuálido,-a *adj* 1 *(delgado)* emaciated, extremely thin, skinny. 2 *(sucio)* squalid, filthy.
escucha *nf (acción)* listening.
▷ *nm* 1 MIL scout. 2 *(aparato)* monitor.
▷ *nm & nf (persona)* programme monitor. ■ **estar a la escucha de** to be listening out for. ● **escuchas telefónicas** phone tapping *sing*.
escuchar *vt* 1 to listen to; *(oír)* to hear. 2 *(atender)* to listen to, pay attention to: **no escuchaba mis consejos** *he didn't listen to my advice.*
escudería *nf* racing team.
escudo *nm* 1 *(arma)* shield. 2 *(de armas)* coat of arms. 3 *(moneda)* escudo. 4 *fig (amparo)* protection, shield.
escudriñar *vt (examinar)* to scrutinize, examine; *(inquirir)* to inquire into, investigate.
escuela *nf* 1 *(gen)* school. 2 *(experiencia)* experience.
escueto,-a *adj* 1 *(sin adornos)* bare, plain, unadorned. 2 *(conciso)* concise, brief, succinct.
esculpir *vt (gen)* to sculpt, sculpture; *(madera)* to carve; *(metal)* to engrave.
escultor,-ra *nm & nf* 1 *(hombre)* sculptor; *(mujer)* sculptress. 2 *(en madera)* carver; *(en metal)* engraver.
escultura *nf (gen)* sculpture; *(en madera)* carving; *(en metal)* engraving.
escupir *vi* to spit.
▷ *vt* 1 to spit out. 2 *fig (despedir)* to belch out: **la fábrica escupía humo** *the factory belched out smoke.* 3 *fam fig (confesar)* to come clean, confess.
escurreplatos *nm inv* plate rack.
escurridizo,-a *adj* 1 slippery. 2 *fig* slippery, elusive.
escurridor *nm* 1 *(colador)* strainer, colander. 2 *(de platos)* plate rack. 3 *(para ropa)* wringer, mangle.
escurrir *vt (platos, etc)* to drain; *(ropa)* to wring out; *(comida)* to strain.
▷ *vi* 1 *(destilar)* to drip, trickle. 2 *(deslizar)* to slip, slide.
▷ *vpr* **escurrirse** 1 *(platos, etc)* to drain. 2 *(líquido)* to drip, trickle. 3 *(deslizarse)* to slip, slide. 4 *fam (escapar)* to run away, slip away. 5 *fam (decir demasiado)* to let slip.
esdrújulo,-a *adj* proparoxytone, stressed on the antepenultimate syllable.

▷ *nm* **esdrújulo** proparoxytone, word stressed on the antepenultimate syllable.
ese *nf name of the letter* s.
▷ *nf pl* **eses** zigzags.
ese,-a *adj* that; *(plural)* those.
ése,-a *pron* **1** *(cosa)* that one. **2** *(hombre - sujeto)* he; *(mujer - sujeto)* she: **ése me lo dijo** *he told me.* **3** *(hombre - complemento)* him; *(mujer - complemento)* her: **se lo dio a ésa** *he gave it to her.* **4** *(anterior)* the former.
▲ **pl ésos,-as.**
The written accent may be omitted when no confusion with adjectives is possible.
ESE *sím* **(estesudeste)** east-southeast; *(símbolo)* ESE.
esencia *nf* **1** essence. **2** *(perfume)* essence, perfume.
esencial *adj* essential. ■ **lo esencial** the main thing.
esfera *nf* **1** sphere, globe. **2** *(de reloj)* dial, face. **3** *fig (campo)* field, sphere; *(ambiente)* sphere, circle.
esférico,-a *adj* spherical.
▷ *nm* **esférico** *(balón)* ball.
esferoide *nm* spheroid.
esfinge *nf* sphinx.
esforzar [50] *vt* **1** *(forzar)* to strain. **2** *(animar)* to encourage, spur on.
▷ *vpr* **esforzarse** *(físicamente)* to make an effort, exert OS; *(moralmente)* to try hard, strive: **se ha esforzado para llegar a la cumbre** *she has striven to get to the top.*
esfuerzo *nm* **1** effort, endeavour (US endeavor). **2** *(valor)* courage, spirit. ■ **sin esfuerzo** effortlessly.
esfumar *vt* **1** *(esfuminar)* to stump, blend. **2** *(colores)* to tone down.
▷ *vpr* **esfumarse** *fam (largarse)* to disappear, fade away.
esgrima *nf* fencing.
esgrimir *vt* **1** *(arma)* to wield, brandish. **2** *fig (argumento)* to put forward.
▷ *vi* to fence.
esguince *nm* **1** MED sprain. **2** *(gesto)* swerve, dodge. **3** *(gesto de disgusto)* frown.
eslabón *nm* link.
eslalon *nm* slalom.
eslavo,-a *adj* Slavonic.
▷ *nm & nf (persona)* Slav.
▷ *nm* **eslavo** *(idioma)* Slavonic.
eslip *nm* **1** *(ropa interior)* men's briefs *pl*, underpants *pl.* **2** *(bañador)* trunks *pl.*
▲ *pl* **eslips.**
eslogan *nm* slogan. ● **eslogan publicitario** advertising slogan.
▲ *pl* **eslóganes.**
eslora *nf* length.
eslovaco,-a *adj* Slovak.
▷ *nm & nf (persona)* Slovak.
▷ *nm* **eslovaco** *(idioma)* Slovak.
Eslovaquia *nf* Slovakia.
Eslovenia *nf* Slovenia.
esloveno,-a *adj* Slovene.
▷ *nm & nf (persona)* Slovene.
▷ *nm* **esloveno** *(idioma)* Slovene.
esmaltar *vt* **1** to enamel. **2** *(uñas)* to varnish. **3** *fig (adornar)* to decorate, adorn.
esmalte *nm* **1** *(gen)* enamel. **2** *(de uñas)* nail varnish, nail polish. **3** *(objeto esmaltado)* enamelled object. **4** *(color)* smalt.
esmerado,-a *adj* **1** *(trabajo)* careful, neat. **2** *(persona)* careful, painstaking, conscientious.
esmeralda *nf* emerald.
esmerar *vt (pulir)* to polish.
▷ *vpr* **esmerarse** to do one's best (**en/por**, to), take great pains (**en/por**, over).
esmero *nm* great care, neatness.
esmoquin *nf* dinner jacket, US tuxedo.
esnifar *vt argot* to sniff, snort.
esnob *adj (persona)* snobbish; *(lugar, etc)* posh.
▷ *nm o nf* snob.
esnobismo *nm* snobbery, snobbishness.
eso *pron* that: **eso es lo que dijo** *that's what she said.*
ESO *abrev* EDUC **(Enseñanza Secundaria Obligatoria)** *compulsory secondary education up to 16.*
esófago *nm* oesophagus (US esophagus), gullet.
esos,-as *adj* those.
See also **ese,-a.**
ésos,-as *pron* those (ones).
See also **ése,-a.**
esotérico,-a *adj* esoteric.
espacial *adj* **1** MAT spatial, spacial. **2** *(del cosmos)* space.
espaciar [12] *vt* to space out.
espacio *nm* **1** *(gen)* space. **2** *(que se ocupa)* space, room: **necesitamos más espacio** *we need more room.* **3** *(de tiempo)* period, space. **4** *(programa)* programme (US program).
espacioso,-a *adj* **1** *(ancho)* spacious **2** *(lento)* slow.
espada *nf* **1** *(arma)* sword. **2** *(naipe)* spade.
▷ *nf pl* **espadas** *(palo de baraja)* spades.
espaguetis *nm pl* spaghetti *sing.*
espalda *nf* **1** [Also used in plural with the same meaning.] *(gen)* back. **2** *(natación)* backstroke.
espantapájaros *nm inv* scarecrow.
espantar *vt* **1** *(asustar)* to frighten, scare, scare off. **2** *(ahuyentar)* to frighten away.
▷ *vpr* **espantarse 1** *(asustarse)* to be frightened, be scared. **2** *(asombrarse)* to be amazed, be astonished.
espanto *nm* **1** *(miedo)* fright, dread, terror. **2** *(asombro)* astonishment, amazement. ■ **¡qué espanto!** how awful!
espantoso,-a *adj* **1** *(terrible)* frightful, dreadful. **2** *(asombroso)* astonishing, amazing. **3** *(desmesurado)* dreadful, terrible.
España *nf* Spain.
español,-la *adj* Spanish.
▷ *nm & nf (persona)* Spaniard.
▷ *nm* **español** *(idioma)* Spanish, Castilian.
esparadrapo *nm* sticking plaster.
esparcir [3] *vt* **1** *(desparramar)* to scatter. **2** *fig (divulgar)* to spread. **3** *fig (divertir)* to amuse.
▷ *vpr* **esparcirse 1** *(desparramarse)* to scatter, be scattered. **2** *fig (divulgarse)* to spread out. **3** *fig (divertirse)* to amuse OS.
espárrago *nm* asparagus.
esparto *nm* esparto grass.
espasmo *nm* spasm.
espatarrarse *vpr* **1** *fam (abrir)* to open one's legs wide, sprawl. **2** *fam (al caer)* to go sprawling.
espato *nm* spar. ● **espato flúor** fluorspar.
espátula *nf* **1** *(gen)* spatula. **2** *(de pintor)* palette knife; *(de cristalero)* putty knife. **3** TÉC stripping knife. **4** *(ave)* spoonbill.

especia *nf* spice.
especial *adj* 1 *(gen)* special. 2 *(remilgado)* fussy (**para**, about), finicky (**para**, about): **es un poco especial para la comida** *she's a bit finicky about food.* ■ **en especial** especially.
especialidad *nf* 1 *(gen)* speciality (US specialty). 2 EDUC main subject, specialized field.
especialista *adj* specialist.
▷ *nm o nf* 1 specialist. 2 CINE stand-in; *(hombre)* stunt man; *(mujer)* stunt woman.
especialización *nf* specialization.
especializado,-a *adj* specialized.
especializar [4] *vi* to specialize.
▷ *vt* to specialize.
▷ *vpr* **especializarse** to specialize (**en**, in).
especialmente *adv* 1 *(exclusivamente)* specially. 2 *(particularmente)* especially.
especie *nf* 1 *(de animales, plantas)* species. 2 *(tipo)* kind, sort. 3 *(tema)* matter, notion, idea; *(noticia)* piece of news. ■ **en especie** in kind: **pagar en especie** *to pay in kind.*
especiería *nf* 1 *(tienda)* grocer's shop. 2 *(especias)* spices *pl*.
especiero,-a *nm & nf* grocer.
▷ *nm* **especiero** spice rack.
especificación *nf* specification.
específicamente *adv* specifically.
especificar [1] *vt* to specify.
específico,-a *adj* specific.
▷ *nm* **específico** *(medicamento)* specific; *(especialidad)* patent medicine. ● **peso específico** specific gravity.
espécimen *nm* specimen.
espectacular *adj* spectacular.
espectacularidad *nf* spectacular nature.
espectáculo *nm* 1 spectacle, sight. 2 *(diversión)* entertainment. 3 *(TV, radio, etc)* performance, show. 4 *(escándalo)* scandal.
espectador,-ra *nm & nf* 1 *(de deportes)* spectator. 2 *(de obra, película)* member of the audience; *(de televisión)* viewer. 3 *(de accidente, etc)* onlooker.
▷ *nm pl* **espectadores** *(de obra, película)* audience *sing*; *(de programa televisivo)* viewers.
espectral *adj* spectral, ghostly.
espectro *nm* 1 FÍS spectrum. 2 *(fantasma)* spectre (US specter), ghost, apparition. 3 *fig (persona)* ghost. 4 *(conjunto, serie)* range.
espectrografía *nf* spectrography.
especulación *nf* speculation.
especulador,-ra *adj* speculating.
▷ *nm & nf* speculator.
especular *vt fig (reflexionar)* to speculate about.
▷ *vi* 1 *(comerciar)* to speculate (**en**, in); *(en bolsa)* to speculate (**en**, on). 2 *(conjeturar)* to speculate (**sobre**, about).
especulativo,-a *adj* speculative, theoretical.
espejismo *nm* 1 mirage. 2 *fig* mirage, illusion.
espejo *nm* 1 mirror. 2 *fig (imagen)* mirror, reflection. 3 *fig (modelo)* model.
espeleología *nf* potholing, speleology.
espeleólogo,-a *nm & nf* potholer, speleologist.
espeluznante *adj* hair-raising, terrifying, horrifying.
espeluznar *vt* to horrify, terrify, make one's hair stand on end.
espera *nf* 1 wait, waiting. 2 *(paciencia)* patience. 3 JUR respite. ■ **en espera de...** waiting for.... ■ **estar a la espera** to be waiting, be expecting.
esperanza *nf* hope, expectance. ■ **abrigar esperanzas** to foster hopes. ■ **con la esperanza de...** in the hope of.... ■ **tener muchas esperanzas** to have high hopes. ● **esperanza de vida** life expectancy.
esperanzador,-ra *adj* encouraging.
esperanzar [4] *vt* to give hope to.
▷ *vpr* **esperanzarse** to have hope.
esperar *vt* 1 *(tener esperanza)* to hope for, expect: **esperan un milagro** *they're hoping for a miracle.* 2 *(contar, creer)* to expect: **no te esperábamos hasta mañana** *we didn't expect you till tomorrow.* 3 *(aguardar)* to wait for, await: **espera un momento** *wait a moment.* 4 *(desear)* to hope: **espero verlo** *I hope to see him.* 5 *(ser inevitable)* to await, be ahead: **mala noche nos espera** *there's a bad night ahead.* 6 *fig (bebé)* to expect.
▷ *vi* to wait: **esperaré hasta que lleguen** *I'll wait until they get here.*
▷ *vpr* **esperarse** 1 *(aguardar)* to wait: **espérense en recepción** *please wait in reception.* 2 *(creer, contar)* to expect: **se espera que seas puntual** *you're expected to be punctual.* 3 *(desear)* to hope: **se espera que lo hayan pasado bien** *we hope you've had a good time.*
esperma *nm* sperm.
espermatozoide *nm* spermatozoon, sperm.
espermicida *adj* spermicidal.
▷ *nm* spermicide.
espesante *nm* thickener.
espesar *vt (salsa, etc)* to thicken; *(tejido, etc)* to make thicker.
▷ *vpr* **espesarse** 1 *(gen)* to get thicker. 2 *(salsa, etc)* to thicken.
espeso,-a *adj* 1 *(líquido, sustancia, objeto)* thick. 2 *(bosque, niebla)* thick, dense. 3 *(pasta, masa)* stiff. 4 *fig (libro)* dense, difficult. ■ **estar espeso,-a** *fam* not to be able to think straight.
espesor *nm* thickness.
espesura *nf* 1 *(de líquido, objeto)* thickness. 2 *(de niebla, etc)* denseness. 3 *fig (en bosque)* thicket, dense wood.
espetar *vt* 1 *(carne, etc)* to skewer. 2 *(clavar)* to stab. 3 *fig (decir)* to blurt out.
espetón *nm* spit, skewer.
espía *nm o nf* spy.
espiar [13] *vt* to spy on, watch.
espiga *nf* 1 *(gen)* spike; *(de trigo)* ear. 2 *(de tejido)* herringbone. 3 *(clavija)* peg, pin. 4 *(de cuchillo)* tang; *(de tornillo)* bolt; *(de clavo)* shank. 5 *(de campana)* clapper.
espigado,-a *adj* 1 BOT ripe. 2 *(en forma de espiga)* ear-shaped. 3 *fig (persona)* tall, lanky.
espigar [7] *vt* 1 AGR to glean. 2 *fig (datos)* to glean, collect.
▷ *vpr* **espigarse** *(persona)* to shoot up.
espigón *nm* 1 MAR breakwater, jetty. 2 *(punta)* sharp point, spike. 3 *(cerro)* peak.
espina *nf* 1 *(de planta)* thorn. 2 *(de pez)* fishbone. 3 *(columna vertebral)* spine, backbone. 4 *fig (pesar)* sadness, sorrow, grief. 5 *fig (duda)* suspicion, doubt. 6 *fig (dificultad)* difficulty, problem.
espinaca *nf* spinach.
espinal *adj* spinal: **médula espinal** *spinal marrow.*
espinazo *nm* spine, backbone.

espinilla *nf* **1** *(de la pierna)* shinbone. **2** *(grano)* blackhead.
espinillera *nf* shinpad.
espino *nm* **1** *(árbol)* hawthorn. **2** *(alambre)* barbed wire. ● **espino albar** common hawthorn. ‖ **espino negro** blackthorn.
espinoso,-a *adj* **1** *(planta)* thorny. **2** *(pez)* spiny. **3** *fig* thorny, prickly, difficult, tricky.
espionaje *nm* spying, espionage: **película de espionaje** *spy film.*
espira *nf (vuelta de espiral)* spire.
espiración *nf* breathing out, exhalation, expiration.
espiral *adj* spiral: **escalera espiral** *spiral staircase.*
▷ *nf* **1** spiral. **2** *(de reloj)* hairspring.
espirar *vt* to exhale, breathe out.
▷ *vi* to breathe.
espiritismo *nm* spiritualism.
espiritista *adj* spiritualistic.
▷ *nm o nf* spiritualist.
espiritoso *adj* **1** *(animoso)* spirited. **2** *(licor, etc)* spirituous.
espíritu *nm* **1** *(gen)* spirit. **2** *(alma)* soul, spirit. **3** *(fantasma)* ghost, spirit. **4** *(licores)* spirits *pl.* **5** *fig (idea central)* spirit, essence, soul.
espiritual *adj* spiritual.
espiritualidad *nf* spirituality.
espiritualismo *nm* spiritualism.
espiritualista *adj* spiritualist.
espiritualizar [4] *vt* to spiritualize.
espiritualmente *adv* spiritually.
espita *nf* tap, US spigot.
espitoso,-a *adj* spaced out, high.
espléndidamente *adv* **1** *(con magnificencia)* splendidly, magnificently. **2** *(con generosidad)* generously, lavishly.
esplendidez *nf* **1** *(magnificencia)* magnificence, splendour (US splendor). **2** *(generosidad)* generosity.
espléndido,-a *adj* **1** *(magnífico)* splendid, magnificent. **2** *(generoso)* generous, lavish.
esplendor *nm* **1** *(resplandor)* brilliance, shining. **2** *fig (magnificencia)* magnificence, splendour (US splendor). **3** *(auge)* glory.
esplendoroso,-a *adj* **1** *(resplandeciente)* brilliant, radiant, shining. **2** *(grandioso)* magnificent, lavish.
espliego *nm* lavender.
esplín *nm* melancholy, spleen.
espolada *nf* **1** *(golpe)* prick with a spur. **2** *(trago)* swig.
espoleadura *nf* spur wound.
espolear *vt* **1** to spur on. **2** *fig* to spur on, encourage.
espoleta[1] *nf (de bomba, etc)* fuse.
espoleta[2] *nf (de ave)* wishbone.
espolón *nm* **1** *(de ave)* spur. **2** *(de caballería)* fetlock. **3** *(de nave)* ram. **4** *(malecón)* sea wall. **5** *fam (sabañón)* chilblain.
espolvoreador *nm* sifter.
espolvorear *vt* **1** *(despolvorear)* to dust. **2** *(esparcir)* to powder, sprinkle.
espondeo *nm* spondee.
espongiforme *adj* spongiform.
esponja *nf* **1** sponge. **2** *fig (gorrón)* sponger. **3** *fig (bebedor)* hard drinker. **4** *(tejido)* towelling.
esponjar *vt (ahuecar)* to fluff up; *(tierra)* to loosen.
▷ *vpr* **esponjarse 1** *fig (envanecerse)* to swell with pride **2** *fig (físicamente)* to glow with health.
esponjoso,-a *adj (gen)* spongy; *(bizcocho)* light.
esponsales *nm pl fml* betrothal *sing,* engagement *sing.*
espontáneamente *adv* spontaneously.
espontaneidad *nf* spontaneity.
espontáneo,-a *adj* **1** *(cosa)* spontaneous; *(discurso)* impromptu. **2** *(persona)* natural, unaffected.
espora *nf* spore.
esporádicamente *adv* sporadically.
esporádico,-a *adj* sporadic.
esportillo *nm* esparto basket.
esposa *nf* wife.
esposado,-a *adj* **1** *(casado)* married. **2** *(con esposas)* handcuffed.
esposar *vt* to handcuff, put handcuffs on.
esposas *nf pl* handcuffs.
esposo *nm* husband.
esprint *nm* sprint.
esprintar *vi* to sprint.
esprínter *nm o nf* sprinter.
espuela *nf* **1** spur. **2** *fig* spur, stimulus.
espuerta *nf* two-handled rush basket.
espulgar [7] *vt* **1** *(desparasitar)* to delouse. **2** *fig (examinar)* to examine, scrutinize.
espuma *nf* **1** *(gen)* foam; *(de jabón)* lather; *(de cerveza)* froth, head; *(olas)* surf. **2** *(impurezas)* scum. **3** *(tejido)* foam.
espumadera *nf* skimmer.
espumante *nm* foaming agent.
espumar *vt (quitar espuma)* to skim.
▷ *vi (hacer espuma - jabón)* to lather; *(- cerveza)* to froth; *(- vino)* to sparkle; *(- olas)* to foam.
espumarajo *nm* foam, froth.
espumillón *nm* tinsel.
espumosidad *nf* frothiness.
espumoso,-a *adj (ola)* foamy, frothy; *(jabón)* lathery; *(vino)* sparkling.
espurio,-a *adj* **1** *(bastardo)* illegitimate. **2** *fig (falso)* spurious, false.

The form **espúreo,-a** is incorrect.

espurrear *vt* to sprinkle.
esputar *vt* to spit (out).
esputo *nm* sputum, spit.
esqueje *nm* cutting.
esquela *nf* **1** *(carta)* short letter. **2** *(mortuoria)* obituary notice.
esquelético,-a *adj* **1** *(del esqueleto)* skeletal. **2** *fam (delgado)* skinny, bony.
esqueleto *nm* **1** ANAT skeleton. **2** ARQUIT framework.
esquema *nm* **1** *(gráfica)* diagram. **2** *(plan)* outline, plan.
esquemático,-a *adj* schematic, diagrammatic.
esquematizar [4] *vt* **1** *(plan, idea)* to outline. **2** *(plano, etc)* to sketch.
esquí *nm* **1** *(tabla)* ski. **2** DEP skiing. ● **esquí acuático** water-skiing. ‖ **esquí náutico** water-skiing.
▲ *pl* **esquís.**
esquiador,-ra *nm & nf* skier.
esquiar [13] *vi* to ski.
esquila[1] *nf (campanilla)* small bell, handbell, cow-bell.
esquila[2] *nf* **1** *(camarón)* squilla. **2** *(cebolla)* squill.
esquila[3] *nf (esquileo)* sheepshearing.

esquilador,-ra *nm & nf* sheepshearer.
esquiladora *nf* shears *pl*.
esquilar *vt* 1 *(pelo)* to clip. 2 *(ovejas)* to shear.
esquileo *nm* 1 *(acción)* sheep-shearing. 2 *(época)* shearing time.
esquilmar *vt* 1 *(cosecha, etc)* to harvest. 2 *fig (agotar)* to exhaust. 3 *fig (abusar)* to fleece.
esquilón *nm* large cowbell.
esquimal *adj* Eskimo.
▷ *nm o nf* Eskimo.
▷ *nm (idioma)* Eskimo.
esquina *nf* corner.
esquinado,-a *adj fig (persona)* difficult, irritable.
esquinar *vt* 1 *(hacer esquina)* to form a corner with, be on the corner of. 2 *(poner en esquina)* to put in a corner.
esquinazo *nm* corner. ■ **dar el esquinazo a** ALGN *fam* to give SB the slip.
esquirla *nf* splinter.
esquirol *nm* blackleg, scab.
esquisto *nm* shale.
esquivar *vt* 1 *(persona)* to avoid, shun. 2 *(golpe)* to dodge, elude.
esquivo,-a *adj* cold, aloof.
esquizofrenia *nf* schizophrenia.
esquizofrénico,-a *adj* schizophrenic.
▷ *nm & nf* schizophrenic.
esquizoide *adj* schizoid.
estabilidad *nf* stability.
estabilización *nf* stabilization.
estabilizador,-ra *adj* stabilizing.
estabilizante *nm* stabilizer.
estabilizar [4] *vt* to stabilize, make stable.
▷ *vpr* **estabilizarse** to become stable, become stabilized.
estable *adj* stable, steady.
establecer [43] *vt* 1 *(gen)* to establish; *(fundar)* to found, set up. 2 *(récord)* to set. 3 *(ordenar)* to state, lay down, establish.
▷ *vpr* **establecerse** *(en un lugar)* to settle; *(en un negocio)* to set up in business.
establecimiento *nm* 1 *(acto)* establishment, founding, setting-up. 2 *(de gente)* settlement. 3 *(local)* establishment, shop, store.
establo *nm* 1 stable, cowshed, stall. 2 *fig* filthy place, pigsty.
estabulación *nf* stabling.
estabular *vt* to stable.
estaca *nf* 1 *(palo con punta)* stake, post; *(para tienda de campaña)* peg. 2 *(garrote)* stick, cudgel. 3 *(rama)* cutting. 4 *(clavo)* spike.
estacada *nf* 1 *(obra)* fence, fencing. 2 MIL stockade.
estacazo *nm* blow with a stick.
estación *nf* 1 *(del año, temporada)* season. 2 *(de tren, radio)* station. 3 REL station.
estacional *adj* seasonal.
estacionalmente *adv* seasonally.
estacionamiento *nm* 1 AUTO *(acción)* parking; *(lugar)* car park, US parking lot. 2 MIL stationing. 3 *fig (estancamiento)* impasse.
estacionar *vt* 1 *(colocar)* to position. 2 AUTO to park.
▷ *vpr* **estacionarse** 1 *(estancarse)* to be stationary, remain in the same place. 2 AUTO to park.
estacionario,-a *adj* stationary, stable.
estadía *nf* 1 *(estancia)* stay. 2 *(indemnización)* demurrage. 3 *(del modelo)* sitting.
estadio *nm* 1 *(lugar)* stadium. 2 *(fase)* stage, phase. 3 *arc (medida)* stadium, furlong.
estadista *nm o nf* 1 POL *(hombre)* statesman; *(mujer)* stateswoman. 2 MAT statistician.
estadística *nf* 1 *(ciencia)* statistics. 2 *(dato)* statistic, figure.
estadísticamente *adv* statistically.
estadístico,-a *adj* statistical.
▷ *nm & nf* statistician.
estado *nm* 1 *(situación)* state, condition: **su estado es delicado** *his condition is delicate*. 2 *(en orden social)* status. 3 HIST estate. 4 POL state.
Estados Unidos *nm pl* The United States.
estadounidense *adj* American, from the United States.
▷ *nm o nf* American, person from the United States.
estafa *nf* fraud, swindle.
estafador,-ra *nm & nf* racketeer, swindler, trickster.
estafar *vt* to swindle, trick, cheat, defraud.
estafeta *nf* branch post office.
estafilococo *nm* staphylococcus.
estalactita *nf* stalactite.
estalagmita *nm* stalagmite.
estalinismo *nm* Stalinism.
estalinista *adj* Stalinist.
▷ *nm o nf* Stalinist.
estallar *vi* 1 *(reventar)* to explode, blow up. 2 *(neumático)* to burst; *(bomba)* to explode, go off; *(cristal)* to shatter. 3 *(volcán)* to erupt. 4 *(látigo)* to crack. 5 *fig (rebelión, epidemia)* to break out. 6 *fig (pasión, sentimientos)* to burst: **estallar en lágrimas** *to burst into tears*.
estallido *nm* 1 *(explosión)* explosion. 2 *(de trueno)* crash; *(de látigo)* crack. 3 *fig* outbreak.
estambre *nm* 1 COST worsted, woollen yarn (US woolen yarn). 2 BOT stamen.
Estambul *nm* Istanbul.
estamento *nm* class, stratum.
estaminífero,-a *adj* staminate.
estampa *nf* 1 *(imagen)* picture. 2 *fig (aspecto)* appearance, look, aspect.
estampación *nf* printing.
estampado,-a *adj (gen)* patterned, print; *(tela)* printed; *(metal)* stamped.
▷ *nm* **estampado** *(tela)* print.
estampar *vt* 1 *(imprimir)* to print. 2 *(metales)* to stamp. 3 *(dejar huella)* to stamp. ■ **estampar la firma** to sign.
estampida *nf* 1 *(ruido)* bang. 2 *(de animales)* stampede.
estampido *nm* bang.
estampilla *nf* stamp, rubber stamp.
estampillar *vt (gen)* to stamp; *(documento)* to rubber-stamp.
estampita *nf* religious print.
estancado,-a *adj* 1 *(agua)* stagnant. 2 *fig (asunto, negocio)* at a standstill; *(negociaciones)* deadlocked; *(persona)* stuck, bogged down.
estancamiento *nm* 1 stagnation. 2 *fig* deadlock.
estancar [1] *vt* 1 *(aguas)* to hold up, hold back, dam; *(flujo)* to check. 2 *fig (progreso)* to check, block, hold up.
▷ *vpr* **estancarse** 1 *(líquido)* to stagnate, become stagnant. 2 *fig* to stagnate, get bogged down.

estancia *nf* 1 *(permanencia)* stay. 2 *(aposento)* room. 3 *(estrofa)* stanza.
estanco,-a *adj* watertight.
▷ *nm* **estanco** 1 *(monopolio)* state monopoly. 2 *(tienda)* tobacconist's.
estándar *adj* standard, standardized: **modelo estándar** *standard model;* **reglas estándar** *set rules.*
estandarización *nf* standardization.
estandarizar [4] *vt* to standardize.
estandarte *nm* standard, banner.
estanque *nm* 1 *(de peces, etc)* pool, pond. 2 *(para proveer agua)* reservoir, tank.
estanquero,-a *nm & nf* tobacconist.
estanquidad *nf* watertightness.
estante *nm* 1 *(anaquel)* shelf; *(para libros)* bookcase. 2 *(de máquina)* stand.
estantería *nf* shelving, shelves *pl.*
estañado *nm* tin plating.
estañar *vt* 1 *(con estaño)* to tin-plate. 2 *(soldar)* to solder.
estaño *nm* tin.
estaquilla *nf* 1 *(de madera)* peg, pin; *(de tienda de campaña)* tent peg. 2 *(clavo)* tack, spike.
estar [71] *vi* 1 *(lugar, posición)* to be: **estamos en casa** *we are at home.* 2 *(permanecer)* to be, stay: **estuvimos allí diez días** *we stayed there for ten days.* 3 *(cualidades transitorias)* to be: **está cansado** *he's tired.* 4 *(una prenda)* to suit, be: **te está grande** *it's too big for you.*
▷ *aux* 1 **estar** + *gerundio* to be: **estaban cantando** *they were singing.* 2 **estar a** *(precio)* to be, sell at; *(fecha)* to be: **estamos a 15 de marzo** *it's the 15th of March.* 3 **estar con** *(tener)* to have; *(estar de acuerdo)* to agree with: **estoy con Ana** *I agree with Ana.* 4 **estar de** *(gen)* to be; *(trabajar)* to be, be working as; *(ir vestido)* to be, be dressed in: **estar de vacaciones** *to be on holiday* (US *vacation);* **está de uniforme** *he's in uniform.* 5 **estar en** *(consistir)* to be, lie; *(entender)* to understand; *(creer)* to think, believe; *(depender de uno)* to be up to. 6 **estar para** *(estar a punto)* to be about to; *(estar acabado)* to be finished, be ready; *(estar de humor)* to feel like, be in the mood for. 7 **estar por** *(no haberse ejecutado)* to remain to be; *(estar determinado)* to be for; *(ir a)* to be going to; *(a favor)* to be for. 8 **estar que** *fam* to be nearly, be really, be practically: **está que se hunde** *it's practically ruined.* 9 **estar sin** + *inf* not to have been + *pp*: **el coche está sin lavar** *the car hasn't been washed, the car still needs washing.*
▷ *vpr* **estarse** *(permanecer)* to spend, stay: **se estuvo todo el día leyendo** *she spent all day reading.*
estarcido *nm* stencil.
estarcir [3] *vt* to stencil.
estasis *nf inv* stasis.
estatal *adj* state.
estática *nf* statics.
estático,-a *adj* static.
estatificar [1] *vt* to nationalize.
estatismo *nm* 1 *(inmovilidad)* immobility. 2 *(poder del estado)* statism.
estator *nm* stator.
estatoscopio *nm* statoscope.
estatua *nf* statue.
estatuaria *nf* statuary.
estatuario,-a *adj* 1 statuary. 2 *fig* statuesque.
estatuilla *nf* statuette, figurine.
estatura *nf* height, stature.
estatutario,-a *adj* statutory.
estatuto *nm* statute. ● **estatuto de autonomía** statute of autonomy.
este[1] *adj* 1 east, eastern. 2 *(dirección)* easterly; *(viento)* east, easterly.
▷ *nm* 1 east. 2 *(viento)* east wind.
este,-a[2] *adj* this; *(plural)* these: **este libro** *this book;* **estas manzanas** *these apples.*
éste,-a *pron* 1 *(cosa)* this one: **dame éste** *give me this one.* 2 *(hombre - sujeto)* he; *(mujer - sujeto)* she: **ésta me lo dijo** *she told me.* 3 *(hombre - complemento)* him; *(mujer - complemento)* her: **se lo dio a éste** *she gave it to him.* 4 *(este último)* the latter: 5 *pey* this one.

> The written accent may be omitted when no confusion with adjectives is possible.

estearina *nf* stearin.
estela[1] *nf* 1 *(de barco)* wake, wash; *(de avión)* vapour (US vapor) trail; *(de cometa)* tail. 2 *fig* trail.
estela[2] *nf (monumento)* stela, stele.
estelar *adj* 1 *(sideral)* stellar. 2 *fig* star.
estenografía *nf* shorthand, stenography.
estenografiar [13] *vt* to take down in shorthand, stenograph.
estenográfico,-a *adj* (in) shorthand, stenographic.
estenógrafo,-a *nm & nf* shorthand writer, shorthand typist, stenographer.
estenordeste *nm* 1 east-northeast. 2 *(viento)* east-northeast wind.
estenotipia *nf* 1 *(arte)* stenotypy. 2 *(máquina)* Stenotype(r).
estenotipista *nm o nf* stenotypist.
estentóreo,-a *adj* stentorian, thundering, booming.
estepa[1] *nf (llanura)* steppe.
estepa[2] *nf (planta)* rockrose.
estepario,-a *adj* steppe, from the steppes.
éster *nm* ester.
estera *nf* rush mat.
esterar *vt* to cover with rush matting.
estercolar *vt (abonar)* to manure.
▷ *vi (excremento)* to dung.
estercolero *nm* 1 dunghill, dung heap. 2 *fig* pigsty.
estéreo *nm* stereo.
estereofonía *nf* stereo, stereophony.
estereofónico,-a *adj* stereo, stereophonic.
estereografía *nf* stereography.
estereográfico,-a *adj* stereographic.
estereógrafo,-a *nm & nf* stereographer.
estereograma *nm* stereogram.
estereometría *nf* stereometry.
estereoscopia *nf* stereoscopy.
estereoscopio *nm* stereoscope.
estereotipado,-a *adj fig* stereotyped, standard, set.
estereotipar *vt* to stereotype.
estereotipia *nf* 1 *(arte)* stereotypy. 2 *(máquina)* stereotype. 3 *fig (de un gesto)* stereotypy.
estereotipo *nm* stereotype.
estereotomía *nf* stereotomy.
estéril *adj* 1 *(tierra)* sterile, barren. 2 *(hombre)* sterile; *(mujer)* sterile. 3 *(aséptico)* sterile. 4 *fig* futile, useless.
esterilidad *nf* 1 *(de terreno)* sterility, barrenness. 2 *(de hombre)* sterility; *(de mujer)* sterility. 3 *fig* futility.

esterilización *nf* sterilization.
esterilizador,-ra *nm* sterilizer.
esterilizar [4] *vt* to sterilize.
esterilla *nf* 1 *(felpudo)* small mat. 2 *(de cañamazo)* rush matting. 3 *(trencilla)* gold braid, silver braid.
esterlina *adj* sterling.
▷ *nf* sterling.
esternocleidomastoideo *adj* sternocleidomastoid.
▷ *nm* sternocleidomastoid.
esternón *nm* sternum, breastbone.
esteroide *nm* steroid.
estertor *nm* death-rattle.
estesudeste *nm* 1 east-southeast. 2 *(viento)* east-southeast wind.
esteta *nm o nf* aesthete (US esthete).
estética *nf* aesthetics (US esthetics).
estéticamente *adv* aesthetically.
esteticismo *nm* aestheticism (US estheticism).
esteticista *nm o nf* beautician.
estético,-a *adj* aesthetic (US esthetic).
estetoscopia *nf* stethoscopy.
estetoscopio *nm* stethoscope.
estiaje *nm* low water level.
estiba *nf* MAR stowing, loading.
estibador *nm* docker, stevedore.
estibar *vt* 1 *(apretar)* to compress. 2 MAR *(distribuir los pesos)* to trim; *(colocar)* to stow.
estiércol *nm* dung, manure.
estigma *nm* 1 *(gen)* stigma. 2 *(marca)* brand, mark; *(de nacimiento)* birthmark. 3 REL stigma.
estigmatizar [4] *vt* 1 *(marcar con hierro)* to brand. 2 REL to stigmatize. 3 *fig (afrentar)* to stigmatize, brand.
estilar *vi (acostumbrar)* to be in the habit of.
▷ *vpr* **estilarse** *(ser costumbre)* to be customary; *(estar de moda)* to be fashionable, be in vogue, be in fashion.
estilete *nm* 1 *(punzón)* stylus. 2 *(puñal)* stiletto. 3 MED probe.
estilismo *nm* stylism.
estilista *nm o nf* 1 *(escritor)* stylist. 2 *(diseñador)* stylist.
estilística *nf* stylistics.
estilístico,-a *adj* stylistic.
estilización *nf* stylization.
estilizar [4] *vt* 1 to stylize. 2 *(hacer delgado)* to make thinner.
estilo *nm* 1 *(gen)* style. 2 *(modo)* manner, fashion. 3 GRAM speech. 4 *(natación)* stroke.
estilográfica *nf* fountain pen.
estima *nf* 1 esteem, respect. 2 MAR dead reckoning.
estimable *adj* 1 esteemed, reputable, worthy. 2 *(cantidad)* considerable.
estimación *nf* 1 *(afecto)* esteem, respect. 2 *(valoración)* estimation, evaluation. 3 *(cálculo)* estimate.
estimado,-a *adj* 1 *(apreciado)* esteemed, respected. 2 *(valorado)* valued, estimated: **el precio estimado** *the estimated price.*
estimar *vt* 1 *(apreciar)* to esteem, respect, hold in esteem, admire. 2 *(valorar)* to value. 3 *(juzgar, creer)* to consider, think, reckon.
estimativo,-a *adj* estimated, approximate.
estimulación *nf* stimulation.
estimulante *adj* stimulating, encouraging.
▷ *nm* stimulant.
estimular *vt* 1 *(animar)* to encourage, stimulate. 2 *(apetito, pasiones)* to whet.
estímulo *nm* 1 stimulus, stimulation. 2 *fig* encouragement. 3 COM incentive.
estío *nm* summer.
estipendiar [12] *vt* to remunerate.
estipendio *nm* stipend, fee, remuneration.
estipulación *nf* 1 JUR stipulation, condition, proviso. 2 *(acuerdo)* agreement.
estipular *vt* to stipulate.
estirada *nf* DEP dive.
estirado,-a *adj* 1 *fig (en el vestir)* stiff, formal, starchy. 2 *fig (orgulloso)* stiff, conceited, haughty.
▷ *nm* **estirado** 1 *(textil)* drawing. 2 *(del pelo)* straightening; *(de la piel)* lift.
estiramiento *nm* stretch.
estirar *vt* 1 *(gen)* to stretch. 2 *(cuello)* to crane. 3 *(medias)* to pull up; *(falda)* to pull down. 4 *fig (escrito, opinión, etc)* to spin out, stretch out. 5 *fig (dinero)* to spin out, make go further.
▷ *vi (crecer)* to shoot up.
▷ *vpr* **estirarse** 1 *(crecer)* to shoot up. 2 *(desperezarse)* to stretch.
estirón *nm* pull, jerk, tug.
estirpe *nf* stock, lineage, race.
estival *adj* summer.
esto *pron* this: **esto me gusta** *I like this.*
estocada *nf* stab, thrust.
Estocolmo *nm* Stockholm.
estofa *nf fig* class, type.
estofado *nm* CULIN stew.
estofar *vt* CULIN to stew.
estoicismo *nm* stoicism.
estoico,-a *adj* stoic, stoical.
▷ *nm & nf* stoic.
estola *nf* stole.
estolidez *nf fml* stupidity, denseness.
estólido,-a *adj fml* stupid, thick, dense.
estoma *nm* stoma.
estomacal *adj* 1 *(del estómago)* stomach, of the stomach. 2 *(digestivo)* digestive.
▷ *nm (bebida)* digestive liqueur.
estómago *nm* stomach. ● **dolor de estómago** stomachache.
estomatología *nf* stomatology.
estomatólogo,-a *nm & nf* stomatologist.
Estonia *nf* Estonia.
estonio,-a *adj* Estonian.
▷ *nm & nf (persona)* Estonian.
▷ *nm* **estonio** *(idioma)* Estonian.
estopa *nf* 1 *(fibra)* tow. 2 *(tela)* burlap.
estoque *nm* 1 *(espada)* sword. 2 BOT gladiolus.
estoquear *vt* to stab, thrust at.
estor *nm* roller blind.
estorbar *vt* 1 *(dificultar)* to hinder, get in the way; *(obstruir)* to obstruct, block, hold up. 2 *fig (molestar)* to annoy, bother, disturb.
▷ *vi (ser obstáculo)* to be in the way.
estorbo *nm* 1 *(obstáculo)* obstruction, obstacle. 2 *(molestia)* hindrance, encumbrance; *(persona)* nuisance.
estornino *nm* starling.
estornudar *vi* to sneeze.

estornudo *nm* sneeze.
estos,-as *adj* these.
See also este,-a.
éstos,-as *pron* these (ones).
See also éste,-a.
estrabismo *nm* strabismus, squint: **tengo estrabismo** *I have a squint.*
estrado *nm* stage, platform; *(tarima)* dais.
▷ *nm pl* **estrados** JUR courtrooms.
estrafalario,-a *adj* **1** *fam (desaliñado)* slovenly. **2** *fam fig (extravagante)* eccentric, weird, outlandish.
estragar *vt* **1** *(dañar)* to devastate, ruin, ravage. **2** *(viciar)* to corrupt, deprave.
estrago *nm* havoc, ruin, ravage.
estragón *nm* tarragon.
estrambote *nm* additional verses *pl.*
estrambótico,-a *adj fam* outlandish, eccentric, weird.
estramonio *nm* thorn apple.
estrangulación *nf* **1** strangling. **2** MED strangulation.
estrangulador,-ra *adj* strangling.
▷ *nm & nf* strangler.
▷ *nm* **estrangulador** AUTO choke.
estrangular *vt* **1** *(ahogar)* to strangle. **2** MED to strangulate. **3** AUTO to throttle.
estraperlear *vi* to deal in black-market goods.
estraperlista *nm o nf* black marketeer.
estraperlo *nm* black market.
estrás *nm* strass, paste, rhinestone.
Estrasburgo *nm* Strasbourg.
estratagema *nf* **1** MIL stratagem. **2** *fam fig* trick.
estratega *nm o nf* strategist.
estrategia *nf* strategy.
estratégicamente *adv* strategically.
estratégico,-a *adj* strategic.
estratificación *nf* stratification.
estratificar [1] *vt* to stratify.
▷ *vpr* **estratificarse** to be stratified.
estrato *nm* **1** GEOL stratum. **2** *(capa)* stratum. **3** *(nivel social)* stratum, class. **4** *(nube)* stratus.
estratocúmulo *nm* stratocumulus.
estratosfera *nf* stratosphere.
estraza *nf* rag, piece of cloth.
estrechamente *adv* **1** *(con estrechez)* narrowly, tightly. **2** *fig (con intimidad)* closely, intimately: **están estrechamente unidos** *they're very close.*
estrechamiento *nm* **1** *(de valle, carretera, etc)* narrowing. **2** *(de prenda)* taking in. **3** *(lugar estrecho)* narrow point. **4** *fig* coming closer together, rapprochement: **estrechamiento de relaciones diplomáticas** *rapprochement in diplomatic relations.*
estrechar *vt* **1** *(carretera)* to make narrower. **2** *(prenda)* to take in. **3** *(abrazar)* to squeeze, hug; *(mano)* to shake: **nos estrechamos las manos** *we shook hands.* **4** *fig (obligar)* to compel, constrain. **5** *fig (relaciones, lazos)* to strengthen.
▷ *vpr* **estrecharse 1** *(valle, etc)* to narrow, become narrower. **2** *(apretarse)* to squeeze together, squeeze up. **3** *fig (relaciones, etc)* to strengthen, get stronger. **4** *fig (gastos, etc)* to economize, tighten one's belt.
estrechez *nf* **1** *(poco ancho)* narrowness. **2** *(falta espacio)* lack of space. **3** *(prendas)* tightness. **4** *fig (económica)* want, need. **5** *fig (amistad)* closeness, intimacy. **6** *fig (apuro)* tight spot. ■ **pasar estrecheces** *fig* to be hard up.
estrecho,-a *adj* **1** *(poco ancho)* narrow. **2** *(ropa)* tight; *(calzado)* tight, small. **3** *(habitación)* cramped, poky, small. **4** *(sin espacio)* packed, jam-packed. **5** *fig (amistad, etc)* close, intimate.
▷ *nm* **estrecho** GEOG strait, straits *pl.*
estrechura *nf (de paso)* narrowness, narrow point.
estrella *nf* **1** *(gen)* star. **2** *fig (destino)* destiny, fate.
estrellado,-a *adj* **1** *(cielo)* starry, star-spangled, full of stars. **2** *(forma)* star-shaped. **3** *(hecho pedazos)* smashed.
estrellar *vt* **1** *(llenar de estrellas)* to cover with stars. **2** *fam (hacer pedazos)* to smash (to pieces), shatter. **3** *(freír)* to fry.
▷ *vpr* **estrellarse 1** *(llenarse de estrellas)* to be full of stars. **2** *(hacerse pedazos)* to smash, shatter. **3** *(chocar)* to crash.
estrellato *nm* stardom.
estremecedor,-ra *adj* **1** startling. **2** *(grito)* bloodcurdling.
estremecer [43] *vt* **1** *(gen)* to shake. **2** *fig (asustar)* to startle, frighten.
▷ *vpr* **estremecerse 1** *(temblar)* to shake. **2** *(de miedo)* to tremble; *(de frío)* to shiver, tremble. **3** *fig* to shudder.
estremecido,-a *adj* shaking, trembling.
estremecimiento *nm* **1** *(movimiento)* tremor, vibration. **2** *(de miedo)* trembling, shuddering; *(de frío)* shiver, trembling.
estrenar *vt* **1** *(gen)* to use for the first time; *(ropa)* to wear for the first time. **2** *(obra)* to perform for the first time, give the first performance of; *(película)* to release, put on release.
▷ *vpr* **estrenarse** to make one's debut.
estreno *nm* **1** *(de algo)* first use. **2** *(persona)* début, first appearance. **3** *(de obra)* first performance; *(de película)* premiere.
estreñido,-a *adj* **1** constipated. **2** *fig* mean, stingy.
estreñimiento *nm* constipation.
estreñir [36] *vt* to constipate, make constipated.
▷ *vpr* **estreñirse** to become constipated.
estrépito *nm* **1** din, racket, clatter. **2** *fig* ostentation, fuss.
estrepitosamente *adv* noisily.
estrepitoso,-a *adj* **1** noisy, clamorous. **2** *(ruido)* deafening. **3** *fig (éxito)* resounding; *(fracaso)* spectacular.
estreptococo *nm* streptococcus.
estreptomicina *nf* streptomycin.
estrés *nm* stress.
estresado,-a *adj* under stress.
estresante *adj* stressful.
estría *nf* **1** *(ranura)* groove. **2** ARQUIT flute. **3** *(en la piel)* stretch mark.
estriación *nf* striation.
estriar [13] *vt* **1** *(hacer ranuras)* to groove. **2** ARQUIT to flute. **3** *(piel)* to give stretch marks.
▷ *vpr* **estriarse** *(piel)* to get stretch marks.
estribación *nf* spur.
estribar *vi* **1** *(apoyarse)* to rest (**en**, on). **2** *fig (basarse)* to lie (**en**, in).
estribillo *nm* **1** *(de poesía)* refrain; *(de canción)* chorus. **2** *(muletilla)* pet phrase, pet saying.
estribo *nm* **1** *(de jinete)* stirrup. **2** *(de carruaje, tren)* step. **3** AUTO running board; *(de moto)* footrest. **4** ARQUIT

buttress; *(de puente)* pier, support. 5 *(del oído)* stirrup bone. 6 *(de alpinista)* rope ladder.
estribor *nm* starboard.
estricnina *nf* strychnine.
estricto,-a *adj* strict, rigorous.
estridencia *nf* 1 *(ruido)* stridency, shrillness. 2 *(color, etc)* loudness, garishness, gaudiness.
estridente *adj* 1 *(ruido)* strident, shrill. 2 *(color, etc)* loud, garish, gaudy.
estroboscópico,-a *adj* stroboscopic.
estroboscopio *nm* stroboscope, strobe.
estrofa *nf* stanza, verse.
estrógeno,-a *nm* **estrógeno** oestrogen (US estrogen).
estroncio *nm* strontium.
estropajo *nm* 1 *(para fregar)* scourer. 2 *(planta)* loofah. 3 *fig (desecho)* useless thing.
estropajoso,-a *adj* 1 *(lengua)* furry. 2 *(carne, etc)* gristly, tough. 3 *(pelo)* straw-like.
estropear *vt* 1 *(máquina)* to damage, break, ruin. 2 *(cosecha)* to spoil, ruin. 3 *(plan, etc)* to spoil, ruin.
▷ *vpr* **estropearse** 1 *(máquina)* to break down. 2 *(cosecha)* to be spoiled, get damaged. 3 *(plan, etc)* to fail, fall through, go wrong. 4 *(comida)* to go bad.
estropicio *nm* 1 *fam (rotura)* breakage, damage; *(ruido producido)* crash, clatter, smash. 2 *fam (desorden)* mess; *(jaleo)* fuss, rumpus.
estructura *nf* 1 *(gen)* structure. 2 *(armazón)* framework.
estructuración *nf* structure, organization.
estructurado,-a *adj* structured, organized.
estructural *adj* structural.
estructuralismo *nm* structuralism.
estructuralista *adj* structuralist.
▷ *nm o nf* structuralist.
estructurar *vt* to structure, organize.
▷ *vpr* **estructurarse** to be structured, be organized.
estruendo *nm* 1 *(ruido)* great noise, din. 2 *(confusión)* uproar, tumult.
estruendoso,-a *adj (ruido)* noisy, deafening; *(aplauso)* thunderous.
estrujar *vt* 1 *(exprimir)* to squeeze. 2 *(apretar - alguien)* to crush; *(- algo)* to screw up. 3 *(ropa)* to wring. 4 *fig (sacar partido)* to drain, bleed dry.
▷ *vpr* **estrujarse** *(apretujarse)* to crowd, throng.
estrujón *nm* tight squeeze, big hug.
estuario *nm* estuary.
estucado *nm* stucco, stucco work.
estucar [1] *vt* to stucco.
estuche *nm* 1 *(caja)* case, box. 2 *(vaina)* sheath. 3 *(conjunto)* set.
estuco *nm* stucco.
estudiado,-a *adj (afectado)* affected, studied; *(rebuscado)* elaborate, recherché.
estudiantado *nm* students *pl*, student body.
estudiante *nm o nf* student.
estudiantil *adj* student, of students.
estudiar [12] *vt* 1 *(gen)* to study, learn.
▷ *vi* to study.
▷ *vpr* **estudiarse** to consider.
estudio *nm* 1 *(gen)* study. 2 *(apartamento)* studio flat (US apartment), bedsit.
▷ *nm pl* **estudios** *(conocimientos)* studies, education *sing*.
estudioso,-a *adj* studious.
estufa *nf (calentador)* heater, stove; *(de gas, eléctrica)* fire.
estufilla *nf (brasero)* brazier, foot warmer.
estulticia *nf lit* stupidity, foolishness.
estulto,-a *adj lit* stupid, foolish.
estupa *nf argot (grupo)* drug squad.
▷ *nm o nf (oficial)* drug-squad officer.
estupefacción *nf* stupefaction, astonishment.
estupefaciente *adj* stupefying.
▷ *nm* drug, narcotic.
estupefacto,-a *adj* astounded, dumbfounded.
estupendamente *adv* marvellously (US marvelously), wonderfully.
estupendo,-a *adj* marvellous (US marvelous), wonderful, super.
estupidez *nf* stupidity, stupid thing.
estúpido,-a *adj* stupid, silly.
▷ *nm & nf* berk, idiot.
estupor *nm* stupor, amazement, astonishment. ■ **causar estupor** to astonish.
estupro *nm* rape.
estuquista *nm o nf* stucco worker.
esturión *nm* sturgeon.
esvástica *nf* swastika.
etano *nm* ethane.
etapa *nf* 1 period, stage. 2 *(parada)* stop, stage. 3 DEP leg, stage.
éter *nm* 1 QUÍM ether. 2 *(celestial)* ether, heavens *pl*, sky.
etéreo,-a *adj* ethereal.
eternamente *adv* eternally.
eternidad *nf* 1 eternity. 2 *fam* ages *pl*.
eternizar [4] *vt* 1 to eternize, eternalize. 2 *fam* to prolong endlessly.
▷ *vpr* **eternizarse** 1 *fam (ser interminable)* to be interminable, be endless; *(discusión)* to drag on. 2 *fam (tardar mucho)* to take ages.
eterno,-a *adj* eternal, everlasting, endless.
ética *nf* ethics *pl*, ethic.
éticamente *adv* ethically.
ético,-a *adj* ethical.
▷ *nm & nf* ethicist.
etileno *nm* ethylene.
etílico,-a *adj* ethylic.
etilo *nm* ethyl.
etimología *nf* etymology.
etimológico,-a *adj* etymological.
etimologizar [4] *vt* to etymologize.
etiología *nf* aetiology (US etiology).
etíope *adj* Ethiopian.
▷ *nm o nf (persona)* Ethiopian.
▷ *nm* **etíope** *(idioma)* Ethiopian, Ethiopic.
Etiopía *nf* Ethiopia.
etiópico,-a *adj* Ethiopian.
▷ *nm & nf (persona)* Ethiopian.
▷ *nm* **etiópico** *(idioma)* Ethiopian, Ethiopic.
etiqueta *nf* 1 *(rótulo)* label, tag. 2 *(formalidad)* etiquette, formality, ceremony.
etiquetar *vt* to label, put a label on.
etmoides *nm inv* ethmoid bone.
etnia *nf* ethnic group.
étnicamente *adv* ethnically.
étnico,-a *adj* ethnic.
etnografía *nf* ethnography.

etnográfico,-a *adj* ethnographic, ethnographical.
etnógrafo,-a *nm & nf* ethnographer.
etnología *nf* ethnology.
etnológico,-a *adj* ethnologic, ethnological.
etnólogo,-a *nm & nf* ethnologist.
eucalipto *nm* eucalyptus.
eucaristía *nf* Eucharist.
eucarístico,-a *adj* Eucharistic.
eufemismo *nm* euphemism.
eufemístico,-a *adj* euphemistic.
eufonía *nf* euphony.
eufónico,-a *adj* euphonic, euphonious.
euforia *nf* euphoria, elation.
eufórico,-a *adj* euphoric, elated.
Éufrates *nm* **el Éufrates** the Euphrates.
eunuco *nm* eunuch.
eureka *interj* eureka!
euritmia *nf* eurythmics.
euro *nm* euro.
euroafricano,-a *adj* Eurafrican.
▷ *nm & nf* Eurafrican.
euroasiático,-a *adj* Eurasian.
▷ *nm & nf* Eurasian.
eurocomunismo *nm* Eurocommunism.
eurocomunista *adj* Eurocommunist.
▷ *nm o nf* Eurocommunist.
eurócrata *nm o nf* Eurocrat.
eurodiputado,-a *nm & nf* Member of the European Parliament, MEP, Euro MP.
eurodivisa *nf* Eurocurrency.
eurodólar *nm* Eurodollar.
euroescéptico,-a *nm & nf* Eurosceptic.
euromisil *nf* Euromissile.
Europa *nf* Europe.
europeidad *nf* Europeanity.
europeísmo *nm* Europeanism.
europeísta *adj* pro-European.
▷ *nm o nf* pro-European.
europeización *nf* Europeanization.
europeizar [26] *vt* to Europeanize.
europeo,-a *adj* European.
▷ *nm & nf* European. ● **Comunidad Europea** European Community. ‖ **Unión Europea** European Union.
eurovisión *nf* Eurovision.
euscalduna *adj* 1 Basque. 2 *(que habla vasco)* Basque-speaking.
▷ *nm o nf* Basque speaker.
Euskadi *nm* the Basque Country.
euskera *nm (idioma)* Basque.
eutanasia *nf* euthanasia.
evacuación *nf* evacuation.
evacuado,-a *nm & nf* evacuee.
evacuar [10] *vt* 1 *(lugar)* to evacuate. 2 ANAT to empty.
evadido,-a *adj* escaped.
▷ *nm & nf* escapee, fugitive.
evadir *vt* 1 *(peligro, respuesta)* to avoid; *(responsabilidad)* to shirk. 2 *(capital, impuestos)* to evade.
▷ *vpr* **evadirse** *(escaparse)* to escape.
evaluación *nf* 1 evaluation, assessment. 2 EDUC *(acción)* assessment; *(examen)* exam.
evaluador,-ra *nm & nf* assessor.
evaluar [11] *vt* to evaluate, assess.
evanescente *adj* evanescent.
evangélico,-a *adj* evangelical.
evangelio *nm* gospel.
evangelismo *nm* evangelism.
evangelista *nm* evangelist.
evangelización *nf* evangelization, evangelizing.
evangelizador,-ra *nm & nf* evangelist.
evangelizar [4] *vt* to evangelize, preach the gospel to.
evaporación *nf* evaporation.
evaporar *vt* to evaporate.
▷ *vpr* **evaporarse** 1 to evaporate. 2 *fig* to vanish.
evasión *nf* 1 *(fuga)* escape, flight. 2 *fig* escapism.
evasiva *nf* evasive answer.
evasivo,-a *adj* evasive.
evento *nm* 1 *(acontecimiento)* event. 2 *(imprevisto)* eventuality, contingency.
eventual *adj* 1 *(casual)* chance; *(probable)* possible. 2 *(trabajo)* casual, temporary, provisional. 3 *(ingresos, gastos)* incidental.
▷ *nm o nf* casual worker, temporary worker.
eventualidad *nf* eventuality, contingency.
evidencia *nf (claridad)* obviousness, clearness; *(certeza)* certainty.
evidenciar [12] *vt* to show, make evident, prove.
evidente *adj* evident, obvious.
evidentemente *adv* evidently, obviously.
evitable *adj* avoidable, preventable.
evitar *vt* 1 *(gen)* to avoid. 2 *(impedir)* to prevent, avoid. 3 *(ahorrar)* to spare, save.
evocación *nf* evocation, recollection, recalling.
evocador,-ra *adj* evocative.
evocar [1] *vt* 1 *(recuerdo)* to evoke, call up. 2 *(recordar)* to evoke, bring to mind.
evolución *nf* 1 *(cambio)* evolution; *(desarrollo)* development. 2 *(vuelta)* turn. 3 MIL manoeuvre (US maneuver).
evolucionar *vi* 1 *(gen)* to evolve, develop. 2 *(dar vueltas)* to turn. 3 MIL to manoeuvre (US maneuver).
evolucionismo *nm* evolutionism.
evolucionista *adj* evolutionist.
▷ *nm o nf* evolutionist.
evolutivo,-a *adj* evolutionary, evolving.
ex- *pref* ex-, former: **el ex primer ministro** *the former prime minister.*
exabrupto *nm* sharp comment, sudden outburst.
exacción *nf* 1 *(impuestos)* exaction. 2 *(extorsión)* extortion.
exacerbación *nf* 1 *(agravamiento)* exacerbation, aggravation. 2 *(irritación)* exacerbation, exasperation.
exacerbante *adj* 1 *(agravante)* aggravating. 2 *(irritante)* irritating, exasperating.
exacerbar *vt* 1 *(agravar)* to exacerbate, aggravate, make worse. 2 *(irritar)* to exacerbate, exasperate.
exactamente *adv* exactly, precisely.
exactitud *nf (fidelidad)* exactness; *(precisión)* accuracy.
exacto,-a *adj* 1 *(fiel)* faithful, true; *(preciso)* accurate, exact. 2 *(verdad)* true: **eso no es exacto** *that's not true.*
exageración *nf* exaggeration.
exagerado,-a *adj (gen)* exaggerated.
exagerar *vt* to exaggerate.
▷ *vi* 1 to exaggerate. 2 *(abusar)* to overdo it, do too much.
exaltación *nf* 1 *(júbilo)* exaltation, elation. 2 *(excitación)* overexcitement.

exaltado,-a *adj* 1 *(discusión, etc)* heated, impassioned. 2 *(persona)* hot-headed, worked up.
exaltar *vt* 1 *(elevar)* to raise, promote. 2 *fig (alabar)* to exalt, praise, extol.
▷ *vpr* **exaltarse** *(excitarse)* to get overexcited, get worked up, get carried away.
examen *nm* 1 examination, exam. 2 *(estudio)* consideration, examination, study. ● **examen final** final examination. ‖ **examen oral** oral examination.
examinador,-ra *adj* examining.
▷ *nm & nf* examiner.
examinando,-a *nm & nf* candidate, examinee.
examinar *vt (gen)* to examine.
▷ *vpr* **examinarse** to take an examination, sit an examination.
exangüe *adj* 1 *(desangrado)* bloodless. 2 *fig (débil)* weak, lifeless.
exánime *adj* 1 *(muerto)* dead. 2 *fig (débil)* worn-out, exhausted; *(desmayado)* lifeless.
exasperación *nf* exasperation.
exasperante *adj* exasperating.
exasperar *vt* to exasperate.
▷ *vpr* **exasperarse** to get exasperated.
excarcelar *vt* to release (from prison).
excavación *nf* 1 excavation. 2 *(arqueológica)* dig.
excavador,-ra *nm & nf (persona)* excavator, digger.
excavadora *nf (máquina)* digger.
excavar *vt* to excavate, dig.
excedencia *nf* 1 *(de funcionario, etc)* leave. 2 *(de profesor)* sabbatical leave.
excedente *adj (sobrante)* excess, surplus.
▷ *nm* COM surplus, excess.
exceder *vt* 1 *(superar)* to excel, surpass. 2 *(sobrepasar)* to exceed, be in excess of.
▷ *vpr* **excederse** 1 *(pasarse)* to overdo it, go too far. 2 *(en atenciones, etc)* to be extremely kind.
excelencia *nf* excellence.
excelente *adj* excellent, first-rate.
excelso,-a *adj* lofty, sublime.
excentricidad *nf* eccentricity.
excéntrico,-a *adj* eccentric.
excepción *nf* exception. ■ **a excepción de** with the exception of, except for. ‖ **de excepción** exceptional.
excepcional *adj* 1 *(extraordinario)* exceptional, outstanding. 2 *(raro)* exceptional, unusual.
excepto *adv* except (for), apart from, excepting.
exceptuación *nf* exception, exclusion.
exceptuar [11] *vt* to except, leave out, exclude.
excesivo,-a *adj* excessive.
exceso *nm* 1 excess. 2 COM surplus. ● **exceso de equipaje** excess baggage.
excipiente *nm* excipient.
excisión *nf* excision.
excitabilidad *nf* excitability.
excitable *adj* excitable, easily worked up.
excitación *nf* 1 *(acción)* excitation. 2 *(sentimiento)* excitement.
excitante *adj* 1 exciting. 2 MED stimulating.
▷ *nm* stimulant.
excitar *vt* 1 to excite. 2 *(emociones)* to stimulate.
▷ *vpr* **excitarse** to get excited, get worked up.
exclamación *nf* exclamation; *(grito)* cry.
exclamar *vt* to exclaim, cry out.
▷ *vi* to exclaim, cry out.
exclamativo,-a *adj* exclamatory.
exclamatorio,-a *adj* exclamatory.
exclaustrar *vt* to secularize.
▷ *vpr* **exclaustrarse** to secularize.
excluir [62] *vt* 1 to exclude, shut out. 2 *(rechazar)* to reject; *(descartar)* to rule out; *(expulsar)* to throw out.
exclusión *nf* exclusion, shutting out.
exclusiva *nf* 1 COM sole right. 2 *(prensa)* exclusive.
exclusividad *nf* exclusiveness, exclusivity.
exclusivismo *nm* exclusivism.
exclusivista *adj* exclusivist.
exclusivo,-a *adj* exclusive.
excluyente *adj* exclusive.
excomulgar [7] *vt* to excommunicate.
excoriar [12] *vt* 1 *(rozar)* to chafe. 2 *(raspar)* to graze.
▷ *vpr* **excoriarse** 1 *(roce)* to be chafed. 2 *(raspadura)* to be grazed.
excrecencia *nf* excrescence.
excreción *nf* excretion.
excremento *nm* excrement.
excretar *vi* to excrete.
excretor,-ra *adj* excretory.
exculpar *vt* 1 to exonerate. 2 JUR to acquit.
excursión *nf* excursion, trip.
excursionismo *nm* hiking, rambling.
excursionista *nm o nf* tripper; *(a pie)* hiker, rambler.
excusa *nf* 1 *(pretexto)* excuse. 2 *(disculpa)* apology.
excusable *adj* excusable, forgivable, pardonable.
excusar *vt* 1 *(justificar)* to excuse. 2 *(disculpar)* to pardon, forgive, excuse.
▷ *vpr* **excusarse** *(justificarse)* to excuse OS; *(disculparse)* to apologize.
execrable *adj* execrable, abominable.
execración *nf* execration.
execrar *vt* to execrate, abhor, deplore.
exégesis *nf inv* exegesis.
exegeta *nm* exegete.
exención *nf* exemption.
exento,-a *adj* 1 free (**de**, from), exempt (**de**, from). 2 JUR exempt. 3 *(descubierto)* open.
exequias *nf pl* obsequies, funeral rites.
exfoliación *nf* exfoliation.
exfoliar [12] *vt* to exfoliate.
▷ *vpr* **exfoliarse** to exfoliate.
exhalación *nf* 1 exhalation. 2 *(estrella)* shooting star; *(rayo)* flash of lightning.
exhalar *vt* 1 *(gases, vapores, etc)* to give off; *(aire)* to exhale, breathe out. 2 *fig (suspiros, etc)* to heave, let out; *(quejas)* to utter.
exhaustivo,-a *adj* exhaustive, thorough.
exhausto,-a *adj* exhausted.
exhibición *nf* 1 *(exposición)* exhibition. 2 CINE showing.
exhibicionismo *nm* exhibitionism.
exhibicionista *nm o nf* exhibitionist.
exhibir *vt* 1 to exhibit, display. 2 *(ostentar)* to show off.
▷ *vpr* **exhibirse** *(ostentar)* to show off.
exhortación *nf* exhortation.
exhortar *vt* to exhort.
exhortativo,-a *adj* exhortative.
exhumación *nf* exhumation.

exhumar *vt* 1 to exhume. 2 *fig* to revive, recall.
exigencia *nf* 1 demand, exigency. 2 *(requisito)* requirement.
exigente *adj* demanding, exacting.
exigir [6] *vt* 1 *(pedir por derecho)* to demand. 2 *fig (necesitar)* to require, call for.
exiguo,-a *adj* 1 *(pequeño)* small, tiny, slight. 2 *(escaso)* scanty, meagre (US meager).
exilado,-a *nm & nf* exile.
exilar *vt* to exile, send into exile.
▷ *vpr* **exilarse** to go into exile.
exilio *nm* exile.
eximio,-a *adj* distinguished, eminent.
existencia *nf (vida)* existence, life.
▷ *nf pl* **existencias** stock *sing*, stocks.
existencial *adj* existential.
existencialismo *nm* existentialism.
existencialista *adj* existentialist.
▷ *nm o nf* existentialist.
existente *adj* 1 existing, existent. 2 COM in stock.
existir *vi* to exist, be.
éxito *nm* success.
exitoso,-a *adj* successful.
exocrino,-a *adj* exocrine.
éxodo *nm* exodus.
exogamia *nf* exogamy.
exógamo,-a *adj* exogamic.
exógeno,-a *adj* exogenous.
exonerar *vt* 1 to exonerate. 2 *(despedir)* to dismiss.
exorbitante *adj* exorbitant, excessive.
exorcismo *nm* exorcism.
exorcista *nm o nf* exorcist.
exorcizar [4] *vt* to exorcise.
exotérico,-a *adj* exoteric.
exótico,-a *adj* exotic.
exotismo *nm* exoticism.
expandir *vt* 1 *(dilatar)* to expand. 2 *fig (divulgar)* to spread.
▷ *vpr* **expandirse** 1 *(dilatarse)* to expand. 2 *fig (divulgarse)* to spread.
expansión *nf* 1 *(dilatación)* expansion. 2 *(difusión)* spreading. 3 *(aumento)* expansion, increase, growth.
expansionarse *vpr* 1 *(dilatarse)* to expand. 2 *fig (divertirse)* to amuse OS, relax.
expansionista *adj* expansionist.
expansivo,-a *adj* 1 *(gas, etc)* expansive. 2 *fig (franco)* expansive, open, frank.
expatriación *nf (exilio)* expatriation; *(emigración)* emigration.
expatriar [14] *vt* to expatriate, banish.
▷ *vpr* **expatriarse** *(emigrar)* to emigrate, become an expatriate; *(exilarse)* to go into exile.
expectativa *nf* 1 *(esperanza)* expectation, hope. 2 *(posibilidad)* prospect.
expectoración *nf* 1 *(acción)* expectoration. 2 *(flema)* sputum, phlegm.
expectorante *adj* expectorant.
▷ *nm* expectorant.
expectorar *vt* to expectorate.
▷ *vi* to expectorate.
expedición *nf* 1 *(gen)* expedition. 2 *(grupo de personas)* expedition, party. 3 *(acción de expedir)* dispatch shipping; *(remesa)* shipment.
expedientar *vt* to take disciplinary action against open a file on.
expediente *nm* 1 JUR proceedings *pl*, action: **expediente judicial** *legal proceedings*. 2 *(informe)* dossier record; *(ficha)* file. 3 *(recurso)* expedient.
expedir [34] *vt* 1 *(mercancías)* to send, dispatch, ship *(correo)* to send, dispatch. 2 *(pasaporte, título)* to issue 3 *(contrato, documento)* to draw up.
expeditivamente *adv* expeditiously.
expeditivo,-a *adj* expeditious.
expedito,-a *adj* 1 *(libre)* free, clear. 2 *(rápido)* expeditious, speedy, prompt.
expelente *adj* expelling.
expendeduría *nf* tobacconist's (shop).
expendedor,-ra *adj* selling, retailing, retail.
▷ *nm & nf* dealer, retailer, seller.
expender *vt* 1 *(gastar)* to spend. 2 *(vender)* to sell. 3 *(vender al menudeo)* to retail, sell.
expensas *nf pl* expenses, charges, costs.
experiencia *nf* 1 *(gen)* experience. 2 *(experimento)* experiment.
experimentación *nf* experimentation, testing.
experimentado,-a *adj* 1 *(persona)* experienced. 2 *(método)* tested, tried.
experimental *adj* experimental.
experimentar *vt* 1 *(hacer experimentos)* to experiment, test. 2 *(probar)* to test, try out. 3 *(sentir, notar)* to experience, feel; *(- cambio)* to undergo; *(- aumento)* to show; *(- pérdida, derrota)* to suffer.
experimento *nm* experiment, test.
experto,-a *adj* expert.
▷ *nm & nf* expert.
expiación *nf* expiation, atonement.
expiar [13] *vt* to expiate, atone for.
expiración *nf* expiration; *(mes, plazo)* expiry.
expirar *vi* to expire.
explanada *nf* esplanade.
explanar *vt* 1 *(allanar)* to level, grade. 2 *fig (explicar)* to explain, elucidate.
explayar *vt fml (extender)* to extend, spread out.
▷ *vpr* **explayarse** *(dilatarse al hablar)* to dwell (**en**, on), talk at length (**en**, about).
explicable *adj* explicable, explainable.
explicación *nf* 1 explanation. 2 *(motivo)* reason.
explicar [1] *vt* 1 *(gen)* to explain, expound, tell. 2 *(justificar)* to justify.
▷ *vpr* **explicarse** *(expresarse)* to explain OS, make OS understood, make OS clear.
explicativo,-a *adj* explanatory.
explícitamente *adv* explicitly.
explicitar *vt* to state explicitly.
explícito,-a *adj* explicit.
exploración *nf* 1 *(gen)* exploration. 2 TÉC scanning. 3 MIL reconnaissance.
explorador,-ra *nm & nf* 1 *(persona)* explorer. 2 *(niño)* boy scout; *(niña)* girl guide, US girl scout.
explorar *vt* 1 *(gen)* to explore. 2 MED to probe. 3 MIL to reconnoitre. 4 TÉC to scan. 5 *(de mina)* to drill, prospect.

exploratorio,-a *adj* 1 exploratory. 2 MED exploratory, probing.
explosión *nf* 1 explosion, blast, blowing up. 2 *fig* outburst.
explosionar *vt* to explode.
▷ *vi* to explode, blow up.
explosiva *nf* LING plosive.
explosivo,-a *adj* 1 explosive. 2 LING plosive.
▷ *nm* **explosivo** explosive.
explotable *adj* 1 *(mina)* exploitable, workable. 2 *(terreno)* which can be farmed, which can be cultivated.
explotación *nf* 1 *(gen)* exploitation. 2 *(de terreno)* cultivation, farming. 3 *(de industria)* running, operating. 4 *(de recursos)* tapping, exploitation.
explotador,-ra *nm & nf pey* exploiter.
explotar *vt (sacar provecho)* to exploit; *(mina)* to work; *(tierra)* to cultivate; *(industria)* to operate, run; *(recursos)* to tap, exploit.
▷ *vi (explosionar)* to explode, blow up.
expoliación *nf* plundering, pillaging, despoiling.
expoliar [12] *vt* to plunder, pillage, despoil.
expolio *nm* 1 *(acción)* plundering, pillaging, despoiling. 2 *(botín)* loot, booty.
exponencial *adj* exponential.
exponencialmente *adv* exponentially.
exponente *adj* exponent, expounding.
▷ *nm* 1 MAT index, exponent. 2 *(prototipo)* exponent.
exponer [78] *vt* 1 *(explicar)* to expound, explain; *(propuesta)* to put forward; *(hechos)* to state, set out. 2 *(mostrar)* to show, exhibit; *(mercancías)* to display. 3 *(arriesgar)* to expose, risk, endanger.
▷ *vpr* **exponerse** *(arriesgarse)* to expose OS (**a**, to), run the risk (**a**, of).
exportable *adj* exportable, for exportation.
exportación *nf* export, exportation.
exportador,-ra *adj* exporting.
▷ *nm & nf* exporter.
exportar *vt* to export.
exposición *nf* 1 *(de arte)* exhibition, show; *(de mercancías)* display. 2 *(explicación)* account, explanation; *(hechos, ideas)* exposé. 3 *(al sol, etc)* exposure.
expositivo,-a *adj* explanatory.
exprés *adj* 1 *(tren)* express. 2 *(café)* expresso. 3 *(olla)* pressure.
expresar *vt* 1 *(gen)* to express. 2 *(manifestar)* to state; *(comunicar)* to convey.
▷ *vpr* **expresarse** to express OS.
expresión *nf* expression.
expresionismo *nm* expressionism.
expresionista *adj* expressionist.
▷ *nm o nf* expressionist.
expresividad *nf* expressivity.
expresivo,-a *adj* 1 *(elocuente)* expressive. 2 *(mirada)* meaningful; *(silencio)* eloquent.
expreso,-a *adj (especificado)* express.
exprimidor *nm* lemon squeezer, US juicer.
exprimir *vt (fruto)* to squeeze; *(zumo)* to squeeze out.
expropiación *nf* expropriation.
expropiar [12] *vt* to expropriate.
expuesto,-a *adj (peligroso)* dangerous
expulsar *vt* 1 *(expeler)* to expel, eject, throw out; *(humo, etc)* to belch out. 2 DEP to send off.
expulsión *nf* 1 expulsion, ejection. 2 DEP sending off. 3 *(alumno)* expulsion; *(de universidad)* sending down, US expulsion.
expurgación *nf* 1 expurgation. 2 *fig* purge, purging.
expurgar [7] *vt* 1 to expurgate. 2 *fig* to purge.
exquisitamente *adv* exquisitely.
exquisitez *nf* 1 exquisiteness. 2 *(manjar)* delicacy.
exquisito,-a *adj* 1 *(gen)* exquisite. 2 *(gusto)* refined; *(sabor)* delicious, exquisite.
extasiado,-a *adj* ecstatic.
extasiar [13] *vt* to enrapture.
▷ *vpr* **extasiarse** to go into ecstasies, go into raptures.
éxtasis *nm inv* ecstasy, rapture.
extático,-a *adj* extatic.
extender [28] *vt* 1 *(mapa, papel)* to spread (out), open (out). 2 *(brazo, etc)* to stretch (out); *(alas)* to spread. 3 *(mantequilla, etc)* to spread. 4 *(documento)* to draw up; *(cheque)* to make out; *(pasaporte, certificado)* to issue.
▷ *vpr* **extenderse** 1 *(durar)* to extend, last. 2 *(terreno)* to stretch. 3 *fig (difundirse)* to spread, extend.
extendido,-a *adj* 1 *(difundido)* widespread. 2 *(mano, etc)* outstretched.
extensible *adj* extendable.
extensión *nf* 1 *(gen)* extension. 2 *(dimensión)* extent, size; *(superficie)* area, expanse. 3 *(duración)* duration.
extensivo,-a *adj* extendable, extensive.
extenso,-a *adj* 1 *(amplio)* extensive, vast; *(grande)* large. 2 *(largo)* lengthy, long.
extenuación *nf* 1 *(agotamiento)* exhaustion. 2 *(debilidad)* weakening. 3 *(enflaquecimiento)* emaciation.
extenuado,-a *adj* 1 *(agotado)* exhausted. 2 *(débil)* weak. 3 *(flaco)* emaciated.
extenuante *adj* exhausting.
extenuar [11] *vt* 1 *(agotar)* to exhaust. 2 *(debilitar)* to weaken.
▷ *vpr* **extenuarse** *(agotarse)* to exhaust OS, wear OS out.
exterior *adj* 1 *(gen)* exterior, outer. 2 *(ventana, puerta)* outside. 3 *(aspecto)* outward. 4 *(extranjero)* foreign.
▷ *nm* 1 *(superficie externa)* exterior. 2 *(extranjero)* abroad. 3 *(de una persona)* appearance. 4 DEP outside.
▷ *nm pl* **exteriores** CINE location shots.
exterioridad *nf* outward appearance, external appearance.
exteriorización *nf* manifestation, externalization.
exteriorizar [4] *vt* to show, reveal, express outwardly.
exteriormente *adv* outwardly, externally.
exterminación *nf (supresión)* extermination, wiping out; *(destrucción)* destruction.
exterminador,-ra *adj* exterminating.
▷ *nm & nf* exterminator.
exterminar *vt (suprimir)* to exterminate, wipe out; *(destruir)* to destroy.
exterminio *nm* extermination, wiping out; *(destrucción)* destruction.
externado *nm* day school.
externamente *adv* externally, outwardly.
externo,-a *adj* 1 external, outward: parte externa *outside*. 2 *(alumno)* day.
extinción *nf* extinction.
extinguir [8] *vt* 1 *(fuego, etc)* to extinguish, put out. 2 *(especie, deuda, epidemia)* to wipe out.

▷ *vpr* **extinguirse 1** *(fuego, etc)* to go out. **2** *(especie, etc)* to become extinct, die out. **3** *(plazo)* to expire, run out.
extinto,-a *adj* **1** *(fuego, etc)* extinguished, out. **2** *(raza, etc)* extinct.
extintor *nm* fire extinguisher.
extirpable *adj* **1** MED removable. **2** *fig* eradicable.
extirpación *nf* **1** MED removal, extraction. **2** *fig* eradication, wiping out, stamping out.
extirpar *vt* **1** MED to remove, extract. **2** *fig* to eradicate, wipe out, stamp out.
extorsión *nf* **1** *(usurpación)* extortion. **2** *fig (molestia)* inconvenience, trouble.
extorsionar *vt* **1** *(usurpar)* to extort, exact. **2** *fig (molestar)* to inconvenience, cause inconvenience to.
extra *adj* **1** *fam* extra. **2** *fam (superior)* top-quality, best-quality. **3** *(paga)* bonus.
▷ *nm* **1** *fam (gasto)* additional expense. **2** *fam (plus)* bonus.
extracción *nf* **1** *(gen)* extraction; *(de lotería)* draw. **2** *(origen)* descent, extraction. • **extracción de datos** INFORMÁ data retrieval.
extractar *vt* to summarize.
extracto *nm* **1** *(sustancia)* extract. **2** *(trozo)* extract, excerpt. **3** *(resumen)* summary.
extractor *nm* extractor.
extradición *nf* extradition.
extradir *vt* to extradite.
extraditar *vt* to extradite.
extradós *nm* extrados.
extraer [88] *vt* **1** *(gen)* to extract. **2** *(conclusión)* to draw.
extraescolar *adj* out of school, extracurricular. • **actividades extraescolares** extracurricular activities.
extrafino,-a *adj* superfine, best quality.
extralargo,-a *adj* king-size.
extralimitación *nf* abuse.
extralimitarse *vpr fig* to go too far, overstep.
extramatrimonial *adj* extramarital.
extramuros *adv* outside the city.
extranjería *nf* status of foreigners.
extranjerizar [4] *vt* to introduce foreign customs into, make foreign.
extranjero,-a *adj* foreign, alien.
▷ *nm & nf* foreigner.
▷ *nm* **extranjero** foreign countries *pl*, abroad.
extrañamente *adv* strangely, oddly.
extrañamiento *nm* **1** *(destierro)* banishment, exile. **2** *(sorpresa)* surprise, astonishment.
extrañar *vt* **1** *(sorprender)* to surprise. **2** *(notar extraño)* to find strange, not to be used to.
▷ *vpr* **extrañarse 1** *(desterrarse)* to go into exile. **2** *(sorprenderse)* to be surprised (**de/por**, at).
extrañeza *nf* **1** strangeness. **2** *(sorpresa)* surprise, wonder, astonishment.
extraño,-a *adj* **1** *(no conocido)* alien, foreign. **2** *(particular)* strange, peculiar, odd, funny.
▷ *nm & nf* stranger.
extraoficial *adj* **1** unofficial, informal. **2** *(declaración, etc)* off-the-record.
extraoficialmente *adv* unofficially.
extraordinaria *nf (paga)* bonus payment.
extraordinariamente *adv* extraordinarily, unusually.
extraordinario,-a *adj* **1** *(fuera de lo común)* extraordinary, unusual; *(sorprendente)* surprising; *(admirable)* outstanding, exceptional. **2** *(raro)* queer, odd. **3** *(gastos, etc)* extra; *(paga)* bonus. **4** *(revista, etc)* special.
▷ *nm* **extraordinario 1** *(correo)* special delivery. **2** *(revista, etc)* special issue.
extraplano,-a *adj* slimline.
extrapolar *vt* to extrapolate.
extrarradio *nm* outskirts *pl*, suburbs *pl*.
extrasensorial *adj* extrasensory.
extraterreno,-a *adj* extraterrestrial, extramundane.
extraterrestre *adj* extramundane, extraterrestrial.
▷ *nm o nf* alien.
extraterritorialidad *nf* extraterritoriality.
extraterritorial *adj* extraterritorial.
extrauterino,-a *adj* extra-uterine.
extravagancia *nf* extravagance, eccentricity.
extravagante *adj* extravagant outrageous.
▷ *nm o nf* flamboyant person.
extravenarse *vpr* to extravasate.
extraversión *nf* extraversion.
extraviado,-a *adj* **1** *(disoluto)* dissolute. **2** *(perdido - persona, objeto)* missing, lost; *(- perro, niño)* stray.
extraviar [13] *vt* **1** *(persona)* to mislead. **2** *(objeto)* to mislay, lose.
▷ *vpr* **extraviarse 1** *(persona)* to get lost, lose one's way. **2** *(objeto)* to get mislaid.
extravío *nm (persona)* misleading; *(cosa)* mislaying.
extremadamente *adv* extremely.
extremado,-a *adj* extreme.
extremar *vt* to carry to extremes, carry to the limit.
▷ *vpr* **extremarse** to do one's best, do one's utmost, take great pains.
extremaunción *nf* extreme unction.
extremidad *nf* **1** *(parte extrema)* extremity; *(punta)* end, tip. **2** ANAT limb, extremity.
extremismo *nm* extremism.
extremista *adj* extremist.
▷ *nm o nf* extremist.
extremo,-a *adj* **1** *(exagerado)* extreme. **2** *(distante)* further. **3** *fig (intenso)* utmost.
▷ *nm* **extremo 1** *(punta)* extreme, end. **2** *(asunto, materia)* matter, question. **3** DEP wing.
extremoso,-a *adj* **1** effusive, demonstrative. **2** *(vehemente)* extreme, excessive.
extrínseco,-a *adj* extrinsic.
extroversión *nf* extroversion.
extrovertido,-a *adj* extroverted.
▷ *nm & nf* extrovert.
extrudir *vt* to extrude.
extrusión *nf* extrusion.
exuberancia *nf* exuberance.
exuberante *adj* **1** exuberant. **2** *(vegetación)* lush.
exudar *vi* to exude, ooze (out).
▷ *vt* to exude, ooze (out).
exultación *nf* exultation.
exultar *vi* to rejoice, exult.
exvoto *nm* votive offering.
eyaculación *nf* ejaculation.
eyacular *vi* to ejaculate.
eyección *nf* ejection.
eyectable *adj* ejectable.
eyectar *vt* to eject.
eyector *nm* ejector.

F

F, f *nf (la letra)* F, f.

F *sím* (Fahrenheit) Fahrenheit; *(símbolo)* F.

fa *nm* F.

fabada *nf* bean stew *including pork sausage and bacon.*

fábrica *nf* **1** *(industria)* factory, plant. **2** *(fabricación)* manufacture. **3** ARQUIT masonry: **las paredes son de fábrica** *the walls are made of stone.*

fabricación *nf* manufacture, production, making. ■ **de fabricación casera** home-made. ● **fabricación en cadena** mass production.

fabricante *nm o nf* manufacturer, maker.

fabricar [1] *vt* **1** *(producir)* to make, manufacture, produce. **2** *fig (inventar)* to fabricate, invent. ■ **fabricar en serie** to mass-produce.

fábula *nf* **1** LIT fable. **2** *(mito)* myth, legend. **3** *(mentira)* invention.

fabular *vt* **1** *(contar fábulas)* to fable. **2** *(imaginar)* to imagine.

fabuloso,-a *adj* **1** *(fantástico)* fabulous, fantastic. **2** LIT fabulous, mythical.

facción *nf* POL faction.
▷ *nf pl* **facciones** *(rasgos)* facial features, features.

faceta *nf* facet.

facha[1] *nf* **1** *fam (aspecto)* appearance, look. **2** *(mamarracho)* mess, sight. ■ **estar hecho,-a una facha** to look a mess, look a sight.

facha[2] *adj pey* fascist.
▷ *nm o nf pey* fascist, extreme right-winger.

fachada *nf* **1** ARQUIT façade, front. **2** *fam (apariencia)* outward show.

facial *adj* facial.

fácil *adj* **1** easy. **2** *(probable)* probable, likely.

facilidad *nf* **1** *(simplicidad)* ease, facility. **2** *(aptitud)* talent, gift: **tiene facilidad para la música** *he has a gift for music.* ● **facilidad de palabra** fluency.
▷ *nf pl* **facilidades** *(medios que facilitan)* facilities.

facilitar *vt* **1** *(simplificar)* to make easy, make easier, facilitate. **2** *(proporcionar)* to provide with, supply with: **nos facilitaron información muy útil** *they provided us with some very useful information.*

facilón,-ona *adj* **1** *fam (muy fácil)* dead easy. **2** *(trivial)* hackneyed, lacking originality.

facsímil *nm* facsimile.

factible *adj* feasible, practicable, workable.

fáctico,-a *adj* **1** *(relativo a hechos)* factual, of fact. **2** *(basado en hechos)* factual, real, actual. ● **poderes fácticos** extraparlamentary political powers.

factor *nm* **1** *(gen)* factor. **2** *(empleado de ferrocarriles)* luggage clerk.

factoría *nf* **1** COM trading post. **2** *(fábrica)* factory, mill.

factura *nf* invoice, bill.

facturación *nf* **1** COM invoicing. **2** *(de equipajes)* registration, check-in.

facturar *vt* **1** COM to invoice, charge for. **2** *(equipaje)* to register, check in.

facultad *nf* **1** *(capacidad)* faculty, ability. **2** *(poder)* faculty, power. **3** *(universitaria)* faculty, school.

facultativo,-a *adj* **1** *(opcional)* optional. **2** *(profesional)* professional.
▷ *nm & nf* doctor, physician.

faena *nf* **1** *(tarea)* task, job. **2** *fam (mala pasada)* dirty trick.

fagocito *nm* phagocyte.

fagot *nm (instrumento)* bassoon.
▷ *nm o nf (músico)* bassoonist.

faisán *nm* pheasant.

faja *nf* **1** *(cinturón)* band, belt. **2** *(ropa interior)* corset, girdle. **3** *(banda)* sash. **4** *(correo)* wrapper.

fajar *vt* to bind, wrap.

fajo *nm* bundle; *(de billetes)* wad.

falacia *nf* **1** *(error)* fallacy. **2** *(engaño)* deceit, trick.

falaz *adj* **1** *(erróneo)* fallacious. **2** *(engañoso)* deceitful, false.
▲ *pl* **falaces.**

falda *nf* **1** *(prenda)* skirt. **2** *(regazo)* lap. **3** *(ladera)* slope. **4** *(corte de carne)* brisket. **5** *(de mesa camilla)* tablecloth.

faldón *nm* **1** *(de traje)* coat-tail; *(de camisa)* shirt-tail. **2** *(prenda de bebé)* wraparound skirt. **3** *(de tejado)* gable.

falible *adj* fallible.

fálico,-a *adj* phallic.

falla *nf* **1** *(defecto)* defect, fault. **2** GEOG fault.

fallar *vi* **1** JUR to pass sentence, pass judgement. **2** *(premio)* to award a prize. **3** *(fracasar, no funcionar)* to fail. **4** *(puntería)* to miss; *(plan)* to go wrong.
▷ *vt* **1** JUR to pass, pronounce. **2** *(premio)* to award.

fallecer [43] *vi fml* to pass away, die.

fallecimiento *nm* decease, demise.

fallo *nm* **1** JUR judgement, ruling. **2** *(en concurso)* decision. **3** *(error)* mistake, blunder; *(fracaso)* failure. **4** *(defecto)* fault, defect.

falo *nm* phallus.

falseamiento *nm* falsification.

falsear *vt* **1** *(deformar un informe, etc)* to falsify; *(unos hechos, la verdad)* to distort. **2** *(falsificar)* to counterfeit, forge.

falsedad *nf* **1** *(hipocresía)* falseness, hypocrisy; *(doblez)* duplicity. **2** *(mentira)* falsehood, lie.

falsete *nm* falsetto.

falsificador,-ra *adj (de firma, cuadro)* forging; *(de dinero)* counterfeiting.

▷ *nm & nf (de firma, cuadro)* forger; *(de dinero)* counterfeiter.

falsificar [1] *vt* 1 *(gen)* to falsify. 2 *(firma, cuadro)* to forge; *(dinero)* to counterfeit, forge.

falso,-a *adj* 1 *(no verdadero)* false, untrue. 2 *(moneda)* false, counterfeit; *(cuadro, sello)* forged. 3 *(persona)* insincere, false; *(sonrisa)* false.

▷ *nm & nf (persona)* insincere person.

falta *nf* 1 *(carencia)* lack: **falta de sensibilidad** *lack of sensitivity.* 2 *(escasez)* shortage: **existe una falta de agua** *there is a water shortage.* 3 *(ausencia)* absence. 4 *(error)* mistake: **has hecho una falta de ortografía** *you've made a spelling mistake.* 5 *(defecto)* fault, defect. 6 *(mala acción)* misdeed. 7 MED missed period. 8 JUR misdemeanour (US misdemeanor). 9 DEP *(fútbol)* foul; *(tenis)* fault. ■ **a falta de...** for want of..., for lack of ... ‖ **echar en falta** to miss. ‖ **sin falta** without fail.

faltar *vi* 1 *(no estar una cosa)* to be missing; *(una persona)* to be absent: **¿quién falta?** *who's missing?* 2 *(haber poco)* to be lacking, be needed: **falta (más) leche** *we need (more) milk.* 3 *(no tener)* to lack, not have (enough). 4 *(quedar)* to remain, be left: **falta poco para que...** *it won't be long till...* ■ **faltar a su palabra** to break one's word. ‖ **faltar al respeto a ALGN** to be rude to SB, insult SB. ‖ **¡lo que me** *(te, le, etc)* **faltaba!** that's all I *(you, he, etc)* needed!

falto,-a ■ **estar falto,-a de** 1 to lack, be short of, be without: **estamos faltos de dinero** *we're short of money.*

fama *nf* 1 *(renombre)* fame, renown. 2 *(reputación)* reputation.

famélico,-a *adj* starving, famished.

familia *nf* 1 family. 2 *(prole)* children *pl*, family. ■ **en familia** 1 *(con la familia)* with the family. 2 *(con muy poca gente)* in private.

familiar *adj* 1 *(de la familia)* family, of the family. 2 *(conocido)* familiar, well-known. 3 *(tamaño)* family. 4 LING colloquial.

▷ *nm o nf* relation, relative.

familiaridad *nf* familiarity, informality.

familiarizar [4] *vt* to familiarize (**con**, with), make familiar (**con**, with).

▷ *vpr* **familiarizarse** to get to know, familiarize OS: **familiarízate con el teclado** *get to know the keyboard, get used to the keyboard.*

familiarmente *adv* familiarly.

famoso,-a *adj* famous, well-known.

fan *nm o nf* fan, admirer. ■ **ser un,-a fan de ALGO** to be mad about STH.

fanático,-a *adj* fanatic, fanatical.

▷ *nm & nf* fanatic.

fanatismo *nm* fanaticism.

fanerógamo,-a *adj* phanerogamic, phanerogamous.

▷ *nm* **fanerógamo** phanerogam.

fanfarrón,-ona *adj fam* swanky, boastful.

▷ *nm & nf* show-off, swank, braggart.

fanfarronear *vi* 1 *fam (chulear)* to show off, swank. 2 *(bravear)* to brag, boast.

fango *nm* 1 *(barro)* mud, mire. 2 *fig* degradation.

fantasear *vi* 1 *(forjar en la imaginación)* to daydream, dream. 2 *(presumir)* to boast, show off.

▷ *vt (imaginar)* dream.

fantasía *nf* 1 *(imaginación)* fantasy. 2 *(irrealidad)* fancy. ■ **de fantasía** 1 *(gen)* fancy. 2 *(joya)* imitation.

fantasioso,-a *adj* imaginative.

fantasma *nm* 1 *(espectro)* phantom, ghost. 2 *fam (fanfarrón)* braggart, show-off.

fantasmal *adj* ghostly.

fantástico,-a *adj* 1 fantastic. 2 *(estupendo)* wonderful.

fantoche *nm* 1 *(títere)* puppet, marionette. 2 *pey (fanfarrón)* braggart, show-off.

faquir *nm* fakir.

faradio *nm* farad.

farallón *nm* crag, rock.

farándula *nf* 1 *(compañía de teatro)* group of strolling players. 2 *(profesión, mundo del teatro)* acting the theatre (US theater), the stage.

faraón *nm* Pharaoh.

faraónico,-a *adj* Pharaonic.

fardada *nf* 1 *argot (acción)* show, display. 2 *argot (objeto)* flash thing: **esa moto es una fardada** *that motorbike's really flash.*

fardar *vi* 1 *argot (presumir)* to show off, swank. 2 *(lucir)* to be classy, be flash.

fardo *nm (paquete)* bundle, pack.

fardón,-ona *adj argot* classy, flash.

farero,-a *nm & nf* lighthouse keeper.

farfullar *vt* to gabble, jabber.

farfullero,-a *adj* 1 *(tartamudo)* gabbling, jabbering 2 *(chapucero)* slapdash, shoddy.

faringe *nf* pharynx.

faríngeo,-a *adj* pharyngeal.

faringitis *nf inv* pharyngitis.

farmacéutico,-a *adj* pharmaceutical.

▷ *nm & nf* 1 *(licenciado)* pharmacist. 2 *(en una farmacia)* chemist, US druggist, pharmacist.

farmacia *nf* 1 *(estudios)* pharmacy. 2 *(tienda)* chemist's (shop), US drugstore, pharmacy.

fármaco *nm* medicine, medication.

farmacología *nf* pharmacology.

farmacológico,-a *adj* pharmacological.

farmacólogo,-a *nm & nf* pharmacologist, pharmacist.

faro *nm* 1 *(torre)* lighthouse, beacon. 2 *(coche)* headlight. 3 *fig (guía)* guiding light, guide.

farol *nm* 1 *(luz)* lantern; *(farola)* streetlamp, streetlight. 2 *argot (fardada)* bragging, swank; *(engaño)* bluff.

farola *nf* streetlight, streetlamp; *(de gas)* gas lamp.

farolear *vi fam* to brag, boast, swank.

farolero,-a *adj fam (que fanfarronea)* boastful.

▷ *nm & nf fam (fanfarrón)* show-off.

▷ *nm* **farolero** *(de profesión)* lamplighter.

farolillo *nm* 1 *(farol de papel)* Chinese lantern. 2 BOT Canterbury bell.

farra *nf fam* binge, spree.

farragoso,-a *adj* confused, rambling.

farruco,-a *adj fam* conceited, cocky.

farsa *nf* 1 TEAT farce. 2 *(enredo)* sham, farce.

farsante *adj* lying, deceitful.

▷ *nm o nf* fake, impostor.

fascículo *nm* instalment (US installment), fascicule.

fascinación *nf* fascination.

ascinador,-ra *adj* fascinating.
ascinante *adj* fascinating.
ascinar *vt* to fascinate, captivate.
ascismo *nm* fascism.
ascista *adj* fascist.
▷ *nm o nf* fascist.
ase *nf* 1 *(etapa)* phase, stage. 2 *(en electricidad)* phase.
astidiado,-a *adj* 1 *(hastiado)* sickened, disgusted. 2 *(molesto)* annoyed. 3 *(dañado)* damaged, in bad condition. 4 *fam (estropeado)* ruined, spoilt. 5 *fam (mal de salud)* ill, sick, in a bad way; *(órgano, miembro)* bad: **tenía el estómago fastidiado** *she had a bad stomach.*
astidiar [12] *vt* 1 *(hastiar)* to sicken, disgust. 2 *(molestar)* to annoy, bother. 3 *(partes del cuerpo)* to hurt: **le fastidia el estómago** *he's got a bad stomach.* 4 *fam (estropear)* to damage, ruin; *(planes)* to spoil, upset, mess up.
▷ *vpr* **fastidiarse** 1 *(aguantarse)* to put up with, grin and bear it. 2 *fam (estropearse)* to go wrong, break down: **se ha fastidiado la tele** *the TV has gone wrong.*
fastidio *nm* 1 *(molestia)* bother, nuisance. 2 *(aburrimiento)* boredom. 3 *(repugnancia)* repugnance, revulsion.
fastidioso,-a *adj* 1 *(molesto)* annoying, irksome. 2 *(aburrido)* boring, tedious.
fasto *nm* pomp, display.
fastos *nm pl* annals, archives.
fastuoso,-a *adj* 1 *(cosa)* splendid, lavish. 2 *(persona)* lavish, ostentatious.
fatal *adj* 1 *(inexorable)* fateful. 2 *(mortal)* deadly, fatal: **el accidente fue fatal** *the accident was fatal.*
▷ *adv fam* awfully, terribly.
fatalidad *nf* 1 *(destino)* fate. 2 *(desgracia)* misfortune.
fatalismo *nm* fatalism.
fatalista *adj* fatalistic.
▷ *nm o nf* fatalist.
fatídico,-a *adj* 1 *(desastroso)* disastrous, calamitous. 2 *fml (profético)* fateful, ominous.
fatiga *nf (cansancio)* fatigue.
▷ *nf pl* **fatigas** *(penalidades)* troubles, difficulties.
fatigar [7] *vt* 1 *(cansar)* to wear out, tire. 2 *(molestar)* to annoy.
fatigoso,-a *adj* 1 *(cansado)* tiring, exhausting. 2 *(respiración)* laboured (US labored).
fatuo,-a *adj* 1 *(necio)* fatuous. 2 *(vano)* vain.
fauces *nf pl* 1 *(en anatomía)* fauces, gullet *sing.* 2 *fig* jaws.
fauna *nf* fauna.
fauvismo *nm* fauvism.
fauvista *nm o nf* fauvist.
favor *nm* favour (US favor). ■ **a favor de** in favour (US favor) of. ‖ **en favor de** in favour (US favor) of. ‖ **hacer un favor** to do a favour (US favor). ‖ **por favor** please.
favorable *adj* favourable (US favorable); *(condiciones)* suitable. ■ **mostrarse favorable a** ALGO to be in favour (US favor) of STH.
favorecer [43] *vt* 1 *(ayudar)* to favour (US favor), help. 2 *(agraciar)* to flatter, suit: **el azul no me favorece** *blue doesn't suit me.*
favoritismo *nm* favouritism (US favoritism).
favorito,-a *adj* favourite (US favorite).
▷ *nm & nf* favourite (US favorite).
fax *nm* 1 *(sistema, documento)* fax. 2 *(aparato)* fax machine, fax.
faz *nf lit (cara)* face.
fe *nf* 1 faith. 2 JUR *(certificado)* certificate. ■ **de buena fe** in good faith, with good intentions.
fealdad *nf* ugliness.
febrero *nm* February.

See also **marzo**.

febril *adj* 1 MED feverish. 2 *(muy intenso)* hectic, restless.
fecha *nf* 1 date: **¿qué fecha es hoy?** *what's the date today?* 2 *(día)* day.
▷ *nf pl* **fechas** *(época)* time *sing*: **por esas fechas** *at that time.* ■ **fijar la fecha** to fix a date. ● **fecha de nacimiento** date of birth.
fechoría *nf* misdeed, misdemeanour (US misdemeanor); *(de niño)* mischief.
fécula *nf* starch.
fecundación *nf* fertilization.
fecundar *vt* to fertilize.
fecundidad *nf* 1 *(fertilidad)* fertility. 2 *(productividad)* productivity, fruitfulness.
fecundo,-a *adj* fertile, fecund.
federación *nf* federation.
federado,-a *adj* federated.
federal *adj* federal.
▷ *nm o nf* federal.
federalismo *nm* federalism.
federalista *adj* federalist.
▷ *nm o nf* federalist.
federar *vt* to federate.
fehaciente *adj fml (irrefutable)* incontrovertible, irrefutable; *(fiable)* reliable.
fehacientemente *adv* for certain.
feldespato *nm* feldspar, felspar.
felicidad *nf* happiness. ■ **¡(muchas) felicidades!** 1 *(éxitos)* congratulations! 2 *(cumpleaños)* happy birthday! 3 *(Navidad)* Merry Christmas!
felicitación *nf* 1 *(acción)* congratulation. 2 *(tarjeta)* greetings card.
felicitar *vt* to congratulate (**por**, on).
feligrés,-esa *nm & nf* parishioner.
felino,-a *adj* feline.
▷ *nm* **felino** feline.
feliz *adj* 1 happy. 2 *(acertado)* fortunate.
felizmente *adv* 1 *(con felicidad)* happily. 2 *(por suerte)* fortunately.
felpa *nf* plush.
felpudo,-a *adj (textil)* plushy, velvety.
▷ *nm* **felpudo** *(alfombrilla)* mat, doormat.
femenino,-a *adj* 1 feminine. 2 *(sexo)* female; *(equipo, asociación)* women's.
feminidad *nf* femininity.
feminismo *nm* feminism.
feminista *adj* feminist.
▷ *nm o nf* feminist.

femoral *adj* femoral.
fémur *nm* femur.
fenecer [43] *vi* **1** *arc (terminar)* to come to an end, expire. **2** *euf (morir)* to pass away, die.
fénix *nm inv* **1** *(mitología)* phoenix. **2** *(genio)* genius, prodigy.
fenol *nm* phenol.
fenomenal *adj* **1** *(relativo al fenómeno)* phenomenal. **2** *fam (fantástico)* great, terrific. **3** *fam (enorme)* colossal, huge.
▷ *adv* wonderfully, marvellously.
fenómeno *nm* **1** *(manifestación)* phenomenon. **2** *(prodigio)* genius. **3** *(monstruo)* freak.
▷ *adj fam (fantástico)* fantastic, terrific.
▷ *interj* terrific!, fantastic!
fenotipo *nm* phenotype.
feo,-a *adj* **1** *(persona - nada atractiva)* ugly; *(- poco atractiva)* plain. **2** *(aspecto, situación, tiempo, etc)* nasty, horrible, unpleasant, awful.
▷ *nm & nf* ugly person.
▷ *nm* **feo** *(ofensa)* slight, snub. ■ **hacerle un feo a** ALGN to slight SB, snub SB.
féretro *nm* coffin.
feria *nf* **1** COM fair. **2** *(fiesta)* fair, festival.
feriante *nm o nf* **1** *(vendedor)* stallholder, trader. **2** *(comprador)* fair-goer.
fermentación *nf* fermentation.
fermentar *vi* to ferment.
fermento *nm* ferment.
ferocidad *nf* ferocity, fierceness.
feroz *adj* fierce, ferocious.
férreo,-a *adj* **1** ferreous. **2** *fig (tenaz)* iron: **voluntad férrea** *iron will*.
ferretería *nf (tienda)* ironmonger's (shop), hardware store.
ferretero,-a *nm & nf* ironmonger, hardware dealer.
férrico,-a *adj* ferric.
ferrita *nf* ferrite.
ferrocarril *nm* railway, US railroad.
ferroso,-a *adj* ferrous.
ferroviario,-a *adj* railway, rail, US railroad.
▷ *nm & nf (trabajador)* railway worker, US railroad worker.
ferruginoso,-a *adj* ferruginous.
fértil *adj* fertile, rich.
fertilidad *nf* fertility, fecundity.
fertilización *nf* fertilization.
fertilizante *adj* fertilizing.
▷ *nm (abono)* fertilizer.
fertilizar [4] *vt* to fertilize.
ferviente *adj* fervent, passionate.
fervor *nm* fervour (US fervor).
fervoroso,-a *adj* fervent, passionate.
festejar *vt (celebrar)* to celebrate.
festejo *nm* **1** feast, entertainment. **2** *(galanteo)* courting, courtship.
▷ *nm pl* **festejos** festivities.
festín *nm* feast, banquet.
festival *nm* festival.
festividad *nf* **1** *(fiesta)* festivity, celebration. **2** *(día)* feast day, holiday.
festivo,-a *adj* **1** *(alegre)* festive, merry. **2** *(humorístico)* witty.
festón *nm* **1** COST festoon. **2** *(adorno floral)* garland.
festonear *vt* to festoon.
fetal *adj* foetal (US fetal). ● **posición fetal** foetal position.
fetichismo *nm* fetishism.
fetichista *adj* fetishist.
▷ *nm o nf* fetishist.
fétido,-a *adj* stinking, fetid.
feto *nm* **1** foetus (US fetus). **2** *fam (feo)* monster, ugly sod.
feudal *adj* feudal.
feudalismo *nm* feudalism.
feudo *nm* fief, feud.
fiabilidad *nf* reliability, trustworthiness.
fiable *adj* reliable, trustworthy.
fiado,-a *adj* **1** COM on credit. **2** *(confiado)* trusting.
fiambre *adj* **1** served cold, cold. **2** *irón (noticia, etc)* stale, old.
▷ *nm* **1** CULIN cold meat, cold cut. **2** *fam (cadáver)* stiff corpse.
fiambrera *nf* lunch box.
fianza *nf* **1** *(depósito)* deposit, security. **2** JUR bail. ■ **bajo fianza** on bail.
fiar [13] *vt* **1** *(vender)* to sell on credit. **2** *(confiar)* to confide, entrust.
▷ *vpr* **fiarse** *(confiarse)* to trust (**de**, -). ■ **de fiar 1** *(persona)* trustworthy, reliable. **2** *(cosa)* reliable.
fiasco *nm* fiasco, failure.
fibra *nf* **1** *(filamento)* fibre (US fiber); *(de madera)* grain. **2** *fig (carácter)* push, go. ● **fibra óptica** optical fibre (US fiber).
fibroma *nm* fibroma.
fibroso,-a *adj* fibrous.
fíbula *nf* fibula.
ficción *nf* fiction.
ficha *nf* **1** *(tarjeta)* index card, file card. **2** *(de teléfono)* token. **3** *(en juegos)* counter; *(naipes)* chip; *(ajedrez)* piece, man; *(dominó)* domino. **4** *(de un deportista)* signing-on fee.
fichaje *nm* signing (up).
fichar *vt* **1** *(anotar)* to put on an index card; *(registrar)* to open a file on. **2** *fam (conocer)* to size up. **3** DEP to sign up, sign on.
▷ *vi* **1** *(al entrar)* to clock in; *(al salir)* to clock out. **2** DEP to sign up (**por**, with): **finalmente fichó por el Barcelona** *he finally signed up with Barcelona F.C.*
fichero *nm* **1** *(archivo)* card index. **2** *(mueble)* filing cabinet, file. **3** INFORMÁ file.
ficticio,-a *adj* fictitious.
ficus *nm inv* rubber plant.
fidedigno,-a *adj* trustworthy, reliable.
fidelidad *nf* **1** *(lealtad)* fidelity, faithfulness. **2** *(exactitud)* accuracy. ● **alta fidelidad** high fidelity, hi-fi.
fideo *nm* noodle.
fiebre *nf* **1** *(enfermedad)* fever, temperature: **tiene la fiebre muy alta** *she has a very high temperature.* **2** *(agitación)* fever, excitement. ■ **tener fiebre** to have a temperature. ● **fiebre del heno** hay fever.
fiel *adj* **1** *(leal)* faithful, loyal. **2** *(exacto)* accurate; *(memoria)* reliable.
▷ *nm (de balanza)* needle, pointer.
▷ *nm pl* **los fieles** the faithful.

fielmente *adv* **1** *(con lealtad)* faithfully, loyally. **2** *(con exactitud)* accurately, exactly.
fieltro *nm* felt.
fiera *nf* **1** *(animal)* wild animal, wild beast. **2** *fig (persona)* beast, brute.
fiero,-a *adj* **1** *(animal salvaje)* wild; *(feroz)* fierce, ferocious. **2** *(persona)* cruel.
fiesta *nf* **1** *(día no laborable)* holiday: **el viernes es fiesta** *Friday's a holiday.* **2** *(reunión)* party.
▷ *nf pl* **fiestas** *(festividades)* festivity, fiesta.
figura *nf* **1** *(gen)* figure. **2** *(forma)* shape. **3** *(en obra, película)* character.
figuración *nf* imagination. ■ **son figuraciones mías** *(tuyas, suyas, etc)* it's just my *(your, his, etc)* imagination.
figurado,-a *adj* figurative. ■ **en sentido figurado** figuratively.
figurar *vt* **1** *(representar)* to represent: **estas líneas figuran una casa** *these lines represent a house.* **2** *(simular)* to simulate, feign.
▷ *vi* **1** *(encontrarse)* to appear, be, figure: **figura como director** *he appears as director.* **2** *(destacar)* to stand out, be important.
▷ *vpr* **figurarse** *(imaginarse)* to imagine, suppose.
figurativo,-a *adj* figurative.
figurín *nm* **1** *(dibujo)* sketch. **2** *(revista)* fashion magazine.
fijación *nf* **1** *(colocación)* setting, fixing. **2** *(sujeción)* fastening. **3** *(obsesión)* obsession.
fijador,-ra *adj* fixing.
▷ *nm* **fijador** *(para pelo)* hairspray, hair gel.
fijar *vt* **1** *(sujetar)* to fix, fasten; *(puerta)* to hang; *(ventana)* to put in. **2** *(pegar)* to stick.
▷ *vpr* **fijarse** **1** *(darse cuenta)* to notice. **2** *(poner atención)* to pay attention, watch: **fíjate cómo se hace** *watch how it's done.*
fijo,-a *adj* **1** *(sujeto)* fixed, fastened. **2** *(establecido)* set, definite, firm: **fecha fija** *set date.* **3** *(firme)* steady, stable, firm. **4** *(permanente)* permanent: **residencia fija** *fixed address.*
fila *nf* **1** *(línea)* file, line. **2** *(de local)* row.
▷ *nf pl* **filas** *(de ejército, partido)* ranks. ■ **cerrar filas** MIL to close ranks.
Filadelfia *nf* Philadelphia.
filamento *nm* filament.
filantropía *nf* philanthropy.
filantrópico,-a *adj* philanthropic.
filántropo,-a *nm & nf* philanthropist.
filarmónico,-a *adj* philharmonic.
filatelia *nf* philately, stamp collecting.
filatélico,-a *adj* philatelic.
filete *nm (de carne, pescado)* fillet (US filet); *(solomillo)* sirloin steak.
filiación *nf* **1** *(datos personales)* particulars *pl.* **2** POL affiliation.
filial *adj* **1** *(del hijo)* filial. **2** COM subsidiary.
▷ *nf* COM subsidiary, branch.
filigrana *nf (orfebrería)* filigree.
Filipinas *nf pl* **las Filipinas** the Philippines.
filipino,-a *adj* Filipino.
▷ *nm & nf (persona)* Filipino.
▷ *nm* **filipino** *(idioma)* Filipino.
film *nm* film, US movie.
filmar *vt* to film, shoot.
fílmico,-a *adj* film, cinema.
filmina *nf* slide, transparency.
filmografía *nf* filmography, films *pl.*
filmoteca *nf* **1** *(archivo)* film library. **2** *(sala de proyección)* film institute. **3** *(colección)* film collection.
filo *nm* cutting edge, edge.
filo- *pref* philo-.
filología *nf* philology.
filólogo,-a *nm & nf* philologist.
filón *nm* **1** *(mineral)* seam, vein. **2** *(buen negocio)* gold mine.
filosofar *vi* to philosophize.
filosofía *nf* philosophy.
filosófico,-a *adj* philosophical.
filósofo,-a *nm & nf* philosopher.
filoxera *nf* phylloxera.
filtración *nf* **1** filtration. **2** *(de información)* leak.
filtrar *vt* **1** *(hacer pasar)* to filter. **2** *(seleccionar)* to filter. **3** *(divulgar)* to leak.
▷ *vpr* **filtrarse** *(pasar a través)* to filter.
filtro *nm (material)* filter.
fimosis *nf inv* phimosis.
fin *nm* **1** *(final)* end. **2** *(objetivo)* purpose, aim. ■ **a fin de** in order to, so as to. | **a fin de que** so that. | **en fin** anyway. ● **fin de semana** *(tiempo)* weekend.
final *adj (último)* final, last.
▷ *nm* **1** end. **2** MÚS finale.
▷ *nf* DEP final. ■ **al final del día** at the end of the day. ● **final feliz** happy ending.
finalidad *nf* purpose, aim.
finalista *adj* in the final.
▷ *nm o nf* finalist.
finalizar [4] *vt* to end, finish.
▷ *vi* to end, finish.
financiación *nf* financing.
financiar [12] *vt* to finance.
financiero,-a *adj* financial.
▷ *nm & nf* financier.
finanzas *nf pl* finances.
finca *nf* property, estate. ● **finca rústica** country property. | **finca urbana** building.
finés,-esa *adj* Finnish.
▷ *nm & nf (persona)* Finn.
▷ *nm* **finés** *(idioma)* Finnish.
fingir [6] *vt* to feign, pretend: **fingió indiferencia** *he feigned indifference.*
▷ *vpr* **fingirse** to pretend to be: **se finge cojo** *he pretends to be lame.*
finiquito *nm* **1** *(acción)* settlement. **2** *(documento)* final discharge.
finito,-a *adj* finite.
finlandés,-esa *adj* Finnish.
▷ *nm & nf (persona)* Finn.
▷ *nm* **finlandés** *(idioma)* Finnish.
Finlandia *nf* Finland.
fino,-a *adj* **1** *(delicado)* fine, delicate. **2** *(alimentos)* choice, select. **3** *(sentidos)* sharp, acute. **4** *(delgado)* thin. **5** *(educado)* refined, polite. **6** *(sutil)* subtle.
▷ *nm* **fino** *(vino)* dry sherry.
fiordo *nm* fiord, fjord.

firma *nf* 1 *(autógrafo)* signature. 2 *(acto)* signing. 3 *(empresa)* firm.
firmamento *nm* firmament.
firmar *vt* to sign.
firme *adj* 1 *(estable)* firm, steady. 2 *(color)* fast.
firmeza *nf* firmness, steadiness.
fiscal *adj* fiscal, tax.
▷ *nm o nf* 1 JUR public prosecutor, US district attorney. 2 *fig* snooper, informer.
fisco *nm* exchequer, US treasury.
fisgar [7] *vt fam* to pry, snoop.
fisgón,-ona *adj (espía)* snooper; *(curioso)* busybody.
fisgonear *vt* to pry, snoop.
física *nf* physics.
físico,-a *adj* physical.
▷ *nm & nf (profesión)* physicist.
▷ *nm* **físico** *(aspecto)* physique.
fisicoquímica *nf* physical chemistry.
fisiología *nf* physiology.
fisiológico,-a *adj* physiological.
fisiólogo,-a *nm & nf* physiologist.
fisión *nf* fission.
fisioterapeuta *nm o nf* physiotherapist.
fisioterapia *nf* physiotherapy.
fisonomía *nf* physiognomy, appearance.
fisura *nf* fissure.
fito- *pref* phyto-.
Fiyi *nm* Fiji.
fiyiano,-a *adj* Fijian.
▷ *nm & nf (persona)* Fijian.
▷ *nm* **fiyiano** *(idioma)* Fijian.
fláccido,-a *adj* flaccid, flabby.
flaco,-a *adj* 1 *(delgado)* thin, skinny. 2 *(débil)* weak, frail.
flagelo *nm* 1 *(objeto)* whip. 2 *(calamidad)* calamity. 3 BIOL flagellum.
flagrante *adj* flagrant.
flamante *adj* 1 *(vistoso)* splendid, brilliant. 2 *(nuevo)* brand-new.
flamenco,-a *adj* 1 *(de Flandes)* Flemish. 2 *(gitano)* Andalusian gypsy. 3 *(música)* flamenco. 4 *(robusto)* sturdy; *(saludable)* healthy.
▷ *nm & nf (persona)* Fleming.
▷ *nm* **flamenco** 1 *(idioma)* Flemish. 2 *(música)* flamenco music, flamenco. 3 *(ave)* flamingo.
flan *nm* 1 *(dulce)* crème caramel. 2 *(de arena, arroz, etc)* pie. ■ **estar como un flan** to be shaking like a leaf. ‖ **estar hecho,-a un flan** SEE estar como un flan.
flanco *nm* flank, side.
flanera *nf* mould (US mold).
flaquear *vi* 1 *(ceder)* to weaken, give in. 2 *(fallar)* to fail: **su memoria ya flaquea** *his memory is already failing.*
flaqueza *nf* weakness, frailty.
flash *nm* 1 *(fotografía)* flash, flashlight. 2 *(noticia breve)* newsflash.
▲ *pl* **flashes.**
flato *nm (dolor)* stitch: **le dio flato** *he got a stitch.*
flatulencia *nf* flatulence, wind.
flatulento,-a *adj* flatulent.
flauta *nf (instrumento)* flute.
▷ *nm o nf (músico)* flautist (US flutist), flute player.
flautista *nm o nf* flute player, flautist (US flutist).
flecha *nf* 1 *(arma)* arrow; *(dardo)* dart. 2 ARQUIT spire flèche. 3 *(indicación)* arrow.
flechazo *nm* 1 *(disparo)* arrow shot. 2 *(herida)* arrow wound. 3 *fig (enamoramiento)* love at first sight.
fleco *nm* 1 *(adorno)* fringe.
flema *nf* phlegm.
flemático,-a *adj* phlegmatic.
flemón *nm (en la encía)* gumboil; *(en el cuerpo)* abscess.
flequillo *nm* fringe, US bangs *pl*.
fletar *vt* to charter, freight.
flete *nm* 1 *(alquiler)* freightage. 2 *(carga)* cargo.
flexibilidad *nf* flexibility.
flexible *adj* flexible.
flexión *nf* 1 *(doblegamiento)* flexion, bending. 2 LING inflection.
flexionar *vt (músculo)* to flex; *(cuerpo)* to bend.
flexo *nm* adjustable table lamp, anglepoise lamp.
flipante *adj argot* incredible, unbelievable, amazing
flipar *vt argot (gustar mucho)* to drive wild: **me flipa este disco** *I really love this record.*
▷ *vi* 1 *(asombrarse)* to be amazed, be stunned. 2 *(pasárselo bomba)* to freak out: **la música era una caña la gente flipaba** *the music was brilliant, everyone was freaking out.*
flirtear *vi* to flirt.
flojear *vi* 1 *(disminuir)* to fall off, go down. 2 *(debilitarse)* to weaken, grow weak.
flojera *nf fam* weakness, faintness.
flojo,-a *adj* 1 *(suelto)* loose; *(no tensado)* slack. 2 *(débil)* weak. 3 *(perezoso)* lazy, idle. 4 *(mediocre)* poor **es un estudiante flojo** *he's a poor student.* 5 *(poco activo)* slack, slow.
flor *nf* 1 BOT flower. 2 *(piropo)* compliment. ■ **a flor de piel** skin-deep. ‖ **echar flores a** ALGN to pay SB compliments.
flora *nf* flora.
floración *nf (plantas)* flowering, blooming; *(árboles)* blossoming.
floreado,-a *adj* flowered, flowery.
florecer [43] *vi* 1 *(plantas)* to flower, bloom; *(árboles)* to blossom. 2 *(prosperar)* to flourish, thrive.
floreciente *adj* flourishing, prosperous.
Florencia *nf* Florence.
florentino,-a *adj* Florentine.
▷ *nm & nf* Florentine.
florería *nf* florist's (shop).
florero *nm* vase.
floresta *nf* wood, thicket.
florido,-a *adj* 1 *(con flores)* flowery. 2 *(selecto)* choice, select. 3 *(lenguaje, estilo)* florid.
florista *nm o nf* florist.
floristería *nf* florist's (shop).
floritura *nf pey* heavy ornamentation.
flota *nf* fleet.
flotación *nf* flotation, floating.
flotador *nm* 1 float. 2 *(de niño)* rubber ring. 3 *(de cisterna)* float, ballcock.
flotar *vi* 1 to float. 2 *(ondear)* to wave, flutter.
flote ■ **a flote** afloat. ‖ **salir a flote** *(superar dificultades)* to get back on one's feet, get out of difficulty.

lotilla *nf* flotilla.
luctuación *nf* fluctuation.
luctuar [11] *vi* 1 *(variar)* to fluctuate. 2 *(vacilar)* to hesitate.
luidez *nf* 1 *(facilidad de paso)* fluidity. 2 *(facilidad de expresión)* fluency.
luido,-a *adj* 1 *(sin obstáculos)* fluid. 2 *(lenguaje, estilo)* fluent.
▷ *nm* **fluido** FÍS fluid. ● **fluido eléctrico** current, power.
luir [62] *vi* to flow.
lujo *nm* 1 *(brote)* flow. 2 *(marea)* rising tide. 3 FÍS flux. 4 MED discharge. 5 INFORMÁ discharge.
lúor *nm* fluorine.
luorescente *adj* fluorescent.
▷ *nm* fluorescent light.
luoruro *nm* fluoride.
luvial *adj* fluvial, river.
obia *nf* phobia.
oca *nf* 1 seal. 2 *fam (persona)* fat lump.
ocal *adj* focal.
oco *nm* 1 *(centro)* centre (US center), focal point. 2 *(en física)* focus. 3 *(lámpara)* spotlight, floodlight. 4 *fig (lugar)* centre (US center).
ofo,-a *adj* 1 *(material)* soft, spongy. 2 *(persona)* flabby.
ogata *nf* bonfire.
ogón *nm (de cocina)* kitchen range, stove.
ogonazo *nm* flash.
ogoso,-a *adj* fiery, spirited.
ogueo ■ **de fogueo** blank.
olclore *nm* 1 folklore. 2 *(juerga, jaleo)* binge.
olclórico,-a *adj* 1 *(popular)* folkloric, popular, traditional. 2 *fam pey* quaint.
folículo *nm* follicle.
folio *nm* folio, leaf.
foliolo *nm* leaflet.
folk *nm* folk music.
follaje *nm* 1 BOT foliage, leaves *pl*. 2 *(palabrería)* verbiage, verbosity.
folletín *nm* 1 *(relato)* newspaper serial. 2 *fig (melodrama)* melodrama, saga.
folleto *nm (prospecto)* pamphlet, leaflet, brochure; *(explicativo)* instruction leaflet; *(turístico)* brochure.
follón *nm* 1 *fam (alboroto)* rumpus, shindy. 2 *fam (enredo, confusión)* mess, trouble. ■ **armar (un) follón** *fam* to kick up a rumpus. ‖ **meterse en un follón** to get into a mess, get into trouble.
fomentar *vt* to promote, encourage, foster.
fonación *nf* phonation.
fonda *nf (mesón)* inn.
fondear *vt* 1 *(sondear)* to sound. 2 *(registrar)* to search. 3 *fig (examinar)* to get to the bottom of, delve into.
▷ *vi* to anchor.
fondista *nm o nf* DEP long-distance runner.
fondo *nm* 1 *(parte más baja)* bottom: **en el fondo del pozo** *at the bottom of the well.* 2 *(parte más lejana)* end, back: **al fondo de la sala** *at the back of the hall.* 3 *(segundo término)* background. 4 *(profundidad)* depth: **tiene poco fondo** *it's not very deep.* 5 *(aguante)* stamina. 6 FIN fund. 7 *(de libros, etc)* stock. 8 *(motivo)* reason; *(raíz)* root. ■ **a fondo** 1 *(adjetival)* thorough. 2 *(adverbial)* thoroughly. ‖ **en el fondo** *fig* deep down, at heart. ● **fondo común** kitty. ‖ **fondo del mar** sea bed.
▷ *nm pl* **fondos** *(dinero)* funds, money *sing*.
fondón,-ona *adj fam* big-bottomed, fat.
fonema *nm* phoneme.
fonendoscopio *nm* stethoscope.
fonético,-a *adj* phonetic.
fónico,-a *adj* phonic.
fono- *pref* phono-.
fonología *nf* phonology.
fonológico,-a *adj* phonological.
fonoteca *nf* record library.
fontanería *nf* plumbing.
fontanero,-a *nm & nf* plumber.
footing *nm* jogging. ■ **hacer footing** to go jogging.
forastero,-a *adj* foreign, alien.
▷ *nm & nf* stranger, outsider.
forcejear *vi* to wrestle, struggle.
forcejeo *nm* struggle, struggling.
fórceps *nm inv* forceps *pl*.
forense *adj* forensic, legal.
▷ *nm o nf* forensic surgeon. ● **médico forense** forensic surgeon.
forestal *adj* forest.
forja *nf* 1 *(fragua)* forge. 2 *(forjado)* forging.
forjado,-a *adj* forging.
▷ *nm* **forjado** ARQUIT *(entramado)* framework.
forjar *vt* 1 *(metales)* to forge. 2 *fig (crear)* to create, make. 3 *fig (imaginar)* to imagine: **forjar sueños** *to dream.*
▷ *vpr* **forjarse** *(crearse)* to forge for OS: **forjarse un buen futuro** *to forge a fine future for OS.*
forma *nf* 1 *(gen)* form, shape: **en forma de X** *X-shaped.* 2 *(manera)* way. 3 DEP form.
▷ *nf pl* **formas** 1 *(modales)* manners, social conventions. 2 *fam (de mujer)* curves. ■ **de esta forma** in this way. ‖ **de forma que** so that. ‖ **de todas formas** anyway, in any case. ‖ **estar en forma** to be in shape, be fit.
formación *nf* 1 *(gen)* formation. 2 *(educación)* upbringing. 3 *(enseñanza)* education, training. ● **formación profesional** vocational training.
formal *adj* 1 *(con los requisitos necesarios)* formal: **promesa formal** *formal promise.* 2 *(serio)* serious, serious-minded. 3 *(cumplidor)* reliable, dependable. 4 *(cortés)* polite.
formalidad *nf* 1 *(norma de comportamiento)* formality. 2 *(seriedad)* seriousness. 3 *(fiabilidad)* reliability. 4 *(trámite)* formality, requisite.
formalizar [4] *vt* 1 *(hacer formal)* to make formal: **formalizaron su noviazgo** *they made their engagement formal.* 2 *(legalizar)* to formalize.
formalmente *adv* 1 *(con formalidad)* formally. 2 *(con seriedad)* seriously. 3 *(con cortesía)* politely. 4 *(respecto a la forma)* formally.
formar *vt* 1 *(gen)* to form. 2 *(integrar, constituir)* to form, constitute: **formar parte de algo** *to be a part of* STH. 3 *(educar)* to bring up. 4 *(enseñar)* to educate.
▷ *vpr* **formarse** 1 *(desarrollarse)* to grow, develop. 2 *(educarse)* to be educated, be trained.
formatear *vt* to format.

formativo,-a *adj* 1 *(que forma)* formative. 2 *(que educa)* educational.
formato *nm* 1 *(gen)* format. 2 *(del papel)* size.
fórmico,-a *adj* formic.
formidable *adj* 1 *(tremendo)* tremendous, formidable. 2 *(maravilloso)* wonderful, terrific.
formol *nm* formol.
formón *nm* firmer chisel.
Formosa *nf* Formosa.
fórmula *nf* 1 *(gen)* formula. 2 *(receta)* recipe. 3 AUTO *(categoría)* formula: **fórmula uno** *formula one.*
formulación *nf* formulation.
formular *vt* 1 *(una teoría)* to formulate. 2 *(quejas, peticiones)* to express, make; *(deseo)* to make; *(pregunta)* to ask.
▷ *vi* QUÍM to write formulae.
formulario,-a *nm* 1 *(documento)* form: **formulario de solicitud** *application form.* 2 *(recetario)* formulary, collection of formulae.
fornido,-a *adj* strapping, hefty.
foro *nm* 1 HIST forum. 2 *(tribunal)* law court, court of justice. 3 TEAT back (of the stage). 4 *(reunión)* meeting.
forofo,-a *nm & nf fam* fan, supporter.
forraje *nm* 1 *(pienso)* fodder, forage. 2 *fam (mezcla)* hotch-potch.
forrar *vt* 1 *(por dentro)* to line. 2 *(por fuera)* to cover. 3 *(tapizar)* to upholster.
▷ *vpr* **forrarse** *fam (de dinero)* to make a fortune, make a packet.
forro *nm* 1 *(interior)* lining. 2 *(funda)* cover, case. 3 *(tapizado)* upholstery.
fortalecer [43] *vt* to fortify, strengthen.
▷ *vpr* **fortalecerse** to strengthen, become stronger.
fortaleza *nf* 1 *(vigor)* strength, vigour (US vigor). 2 *(de espíritu)* fortitude. 3 *(recinto fortificado)* fortress, stronghold.
fortificación *nf* fortification, fortifying.
fortificar [1] *vt* to fortify, strengthen.
fortín *nm* small fort, bunker.
fortuito,-a *adj* chance, fortuitous.
fortuna *nf* 1 *(destino)* fortune, fate. 2 *(suerte)* luck. 3 *(capital)* fortune. 4 *(éxito, aceptación)* success. ■ **por fortuna** fortunately. ‖ **probar fortuna** to try one's luck. ● **buena fortuna** good luck.
forúnculo *nm* boil, furuncle.
forzado,-a *adj* 1 *(obligado)* forced. 2 *(rebuscado)* forced, strained. ● **risa forzada** forced laugh.
forzar [50] *vt* 1 *(persona)* to force, compel. 2 *(cosa)* to force open, break open. 3 *(violar)* to rape.
forzoso,-a *adj* 1 *(inevitable)* inevitable, unavoidable. 2 *(obligatorio)* obligatory, compulsory.
forzudo,-a *adj* strong, brawny.
fosa *nf* 1 *(sepultura)* grave. 2 *(hoyo)* pit, hollow. 3 ANAT cavity, fossa. 4 *(en el océano)* trench, deep. ● **fosas nasales** nostrils.
fosfato *nm* phosphate. ● **fosfato de cal** calcium phosphate.
fosforescente *adj* phosphorescent.
fosfórico,-a *adj* phosphoric.
fosforito *adj* fluorescent.
▷ *nm* highlighter: **señalo los errores con un fosforito** *I highlight the mistakes.*
fósforo *nm* 1 QUÍM phosphorus. 2 *(cerilla)* match.
fósil *adj* fossil.
▷ *nm* fossil.
fosilización *nf* fossilization.
foso *nm* 1 *(hoyo)* hole, pit. 2 *(de fortaleza)* moat. 3 *(e… teatro, deportes)* pit. 4 *(en un garaje)* inspection pit.
foto *nf fam* photo, picture.
fotocélula *nf* photoelectric cell.
fotocomposición *nf* filmsetting, US photosetting.
fotocopia *nf* photocopy.
fotocopiadora *nf* photocopier, photocopying machine.
fotocopiar [12] *vt* to photocopy.
fotoeléctrico,-a *adj* photoelectric. ● **célula fotoeléctrica** photoelectric cell.
fotogénico,-a *adj* photogenic.
fotograbado *nm* photogravure, photoengraving
fotografía *nf* 1 *(proceso)* photography. 2 *(retrato)* photograph. ■ **hacer fotografías** to take photographs.
fotografiar [13] *vt* to photograph, take a photograph of.
fotógrafo,-a *nm & nf* photographer.
fotograma *nm* shot.
fotómetro *nm* light meter, exposure meter.
fotomontaje *nm* photomontage.
fotón *nm* photon.
fotonovela *nf* photo romance.
fotosíntesis *nf inv* photosynthesis.
foxterrier *nm o nf* fox terrier.
▲ *pl* **foxterriers.**
FP *abrev* EDUC **(Formación Profesional)** Professional Formation *(vocational training).*
frac *nm* dress coat, tails *pl.*
▲ *pl* **fracs o fraques.**
fracasar *vi* to fail, be unsuccessful, fall through.
fracaso *nm* failure.
fracción *nf* 1 *(gen)* fraction. 2 POL faction.
fraccionar *vt* to divide, break up, split up.
fractura *nf* fracture.
fragancia *nf* fragrance.
fragata *nf* frigate.
frágil *adj* 1 *(quebradizo)* fragile, breakable. 2 *(débil)* frail, weak.
fragilidad *nf* 1 *(cualidad)* fragility. 2 *(debilidad)* frailty, weakness.
fragmentar *vt* 1 *(partir)* to fragment. 2 *(dividir)* to divide up.
fragmentario,-a *adj* fragmentary.
fragmento *nm* 1 *(pedazo)* fragment, piece. 2 *(literario)* passage.
fragua *nf* forge.
fraguar [22] *vt* 1 *(metal)* to forge. 2 *fig (plan)* to dream up, fabricate; *(conspiración)* to hatch.
▷ *vi (endurecerse)* to set, harden.
fraile *nm* friar, monk.
frambuesa *nf* raspberry.
francamente *adv* 1 *(con franqueza)* frankly. 2 *(claramente)* clearly.
francés,-esa *adj* French.
▷ *nm & nf (persona)* French person; *(hombre)* Frenchman; *(mujer)* Frenchwoman.
▷ *nm* **francés** *(idioma)* French.

Francfort *nm* Frankfurt.
Francia *nf* France.
franciscano,-a *adj* Franciscan.
▷ *nm & nf* Franciscan.
francmasón,-ona *nm & nf* freemason.
francmasonería *nf* freemasonry.
franco,-a¹ *adj* HIST Frankish.
▷ *nm & nf* HIST *(persona)* Frank.
▷ *nm* **franco** HIST *(idioma)* Frankish.
franco,-a² *adj* 1 *(persona)* frank, open. 2 *(cosa)* clear, obvious. 3 COM free.
francófono,-a *adj* French-speaking, francophone.
▷ *nm & nf* French speaker, francophone.
francotirador,-ra *nm & nf* sniper.
franela *nf* flannel.
franja *nf* 1 *(banda)* band, strip. 2 *(de tierra)* strip. 3 COST fringe, border.
franquear *vt* 1 *(dejar libre)* to free, clear. 2 *(atravesar)* to cross; *(superar)* to overcome. 3 *(carta)* to frank.
franqueo *nm* postage.
franqueza *nf* 1 *(sinceridad)* frankness, openness. 2 *(confianza)* familiarity, intimacy.
franquicia *nf* 1 exemption. 2 COM franchise.
frasco *nm* flask.
frase *nf* 1 *(oración)* sentence. 2 *(expresión)* phrase. ● **frase hecha** set phrase, set expression, idiom.
fraternal *adj* fraternal, brotherly.
fraternidad *nf* fraternity, brotherhood.
fraternizar [4] *vi* to fraternize.
fraterno,-a *adj* fraternal, brotherly.
fratricida *adj* fratricidal.
▷ *nm o nf* fratricide.
fraude *nm* fraud. ● **fraude fiscal** tax evasion.
fraudulento,-a *adj* fraudulent.
fray *nm* Brother.
frazada *nf* AM blanket.
freático,-a *adj* phreatic. ● **nivel freático,-a** water table.
frecuencia *nf* frequency. ■ **con frecuencia** frequently, often. ● **frecuencia modulada** frequency modulation.
frecuentar *vt* to frequent, visit.
frecuente *adj* 1 *(repetido)* frequent. 2 *(usual)* common.
frecuentemente *adv* frequently, often.
fregadero *nm* kitchen sink.
fregado *nm* 1 *(lavado)* washing; *(frotado)* scrubbing. 2 *fam (riña)* fight, quarrel; *(lío)* mess, muddle.
fregar [48] *vt* 1 *(lavar)* to wash. 2 *(frotar)* to scrub. 3 *(el suelo)* to mop. ■ **fregar los platos** to wash the dishes, GB do the washing up, wash up.
fregona *nf* 1 *pey (sirvienta)* drudge, GB skivvy. 2 *(utensilio)* mop. 3 *(mujer ordinaria)* common woman.
freidora *nf* fryer, deep fryer.
freír [37] *vt* 1 *(guisar)* to fry. 2 *fig* to annoy, exasperate.
frenar *vt* 1 to brake. 2 *fig* to restrain, check.
▷ *vi* to brake: **frenó de golpe** *he jammed on the brakes.*
frenazo *nm* sudden braking. ■ **dar un frenazo** to jam on the brakes.
frenesí *nm* frenzy.
▲ *pl* **frenesíes.**
frenético,-a *adj* 1 *(exaltado)* frenzied, frantic. 2 *(colérico)* wild, mad.
freno *nm* 1 *(de auto)* brake. 2 *(de caballería)* bit. 3 *fig (contención)* curb, check. ■ **poner freno a** ALGO *fig* to curb STH.
frente *nm* 1 *(gen)* front. 2 MIL front, front line.
▷ *nf* ANAT forehead. ■ **al frente de** 1 *(delante)* at the head of. 2 *(hacia delante)* ahead. ‖ **de frente** 1 *(hacia adelante)* straight ahead. 2 *(sin rodeos)* straight. ‖ **frente a frente** face to face. ‖ **ponerse al frente de** ALGO to take command of STH.
fresa *nf* 1 *(planta)* strawberry plant. 2 *(fruto)* strawberry.
▷ *adj* strawberry.
fresco,-a *adj* 1 *(temperatura)* cool, cold: **viento fresco** *cool wind;* **agua fresca** *cold water.* 2 *(tela, vestido)* light, cool. 3 *(aspecto)* healthy, fresh. 4 *(comida)* fresh. 5 *(reciente)* fresh, new: **noticias frescas** *latest news sing.* 6 *fig (impasible)* cool, calm, unworried. 7 *(desvergonzado)* cheeky, shameless.
▷ *nm* **fresco** 1 *(frescor)* fresh air, cool air. 2 ARTE fresco. ■ **al fresco** in the cool. ‖ **quedarse tan fresco,-a** not to bat an eyelid. ‖ **tomar el fresco** to get some fresh air.
frescor *nm* coolness, freshness.
frescura *nf* 1 *(frescor)* freshness, coolness. 2 *(desvergüenza)* cheek, nerve. 3 *(calma)* coolness, calmness. ■ **¡qué frescura!** what a nerve!
fresno *nm* ash tree.
frialdad *nf* 1 *(frío)* coldness. 2 *(indiferencia)* coldness, indifference.
fricativo,-a *adj* fricative.
fricción *nf* 1 *(roce)* friction. 2 *(friega)* rub, rubbing. 3 *(desacuerdo)* friction, discord.
friega *nf* rub, rubbing.
friegaplatos *nm o nf inv* dishwasher.
frigidez *nf* frigidity.
frigorífico,-a *adj* refrigerating.
▷ *nm* **frigorífico** 1 *(electrodoméstico)* refrigerator, fridge. 2 *(cámara frigorífica)* cold store.
frijol *nm* bean, kidney bean.
frío,-a *adj* 1 *(gen)* cold. 2 *(indiferente)* cold, cool, indifferent; *(pasmado)* stunned: **la película me dejó frío** *the film left me cold.*
▷ *nm* **frío** cold. ■ **coger a** ALGN **en frío** *fig* to catch SB on the hop. ‖ **hace un frío que pela** *fam* it's freezing cold. ‖ **hacer frío** to be cold. ‖ **tener frío / pasar frío** to be cold.
friolero,-a *adj* sensitive to the cold.
friso *nm* 1 ARQUIT frieze. 2 *(zócalo)* skirting board.
frito,-a *adj* 1 CULIN fried. 2 *fam* fed up, sick: **este niño me tiene frita** *I'm sick and tired of this kid.*
▷ *nm* **frito** piece of fried food. ■ **quedarse frito,-a** 1 *fam (dormido)* to fall fast asleep. 2 *(muerto)* to snuff it.
frivolidad *nf* frivolity.
frívolo,-a *adj* frivolous.
frondoso,-a *adj* leafy, luxuriant.
frontal *adj* 1 ANAT frontal. 2 *(choque, etc)* head-on. 3 *(delantero)* front.
▷ *nm* ANAT frontal bone.
frontera *nf* 1 frontier, border. 2 *fig* limit, bounds *pl*, borderline.
frontis *nm inv* 1 *(fachada)* façade, front. 2 *(frontón)* pediment. 3 *(en artes gráficas)* frontispiece.
frontón *nm* 1 *(juego)* pelota. 2 *(edificio)* pelota court. 3 ARQUIT pediment.

frotar *vt* to rub. ■ **frotarse las manos** to rub one's hands together.
fructífero,-a *adj* 1 BOT fruit-bearing. 2 *fig* fruitful.
fructosa *nf* fructose.
frugal *adj* frugal.
frugalidad *nf* frugality, frugalness.
fruición *nf* pleasure, delight, enjoyment.
fruncir [3] *vt* 1 COST to gather. 2 *(los labios)* to purse, pucker. ■ **fruncir el ceño** to frown, knit one's brow.
fruslería *nf* 1 *(chuchería)* trinket. 2 *fam (tontería)* trifle.
frustración *nf* frustration.
frustrar *vt* 1 *(cosa)* to frustrate, thwart. 2 *(persona)* to disappoint.
▷ *vpr* **frustrarse** 1 *(proyectos, planes)* to fail, come to nothing. 2 *(persona)* to get frustrated, get disappointed.
fruta *nf* fruit.
frutería *nf* fruit shop.
frutero,-a *nm & nf* fruit seller, fruiterer.
▷ *nm* **frutero** fruit dish, fruit bowl.
fruto *nm* 1 *(fruta)* fruit. 2 *(resultado)* fruit, result, product. ■ **dar fruto** to bear fruit. ‖ **sacar fruto de** ALGO to profit from STH. ● **frutos secos** 1 *(almendras, etc)* nuts. 2 *(pasas, etc)* dried fruit *sing*.
fucsia *nf* fuchsia.
fuego *nm* 1 fire. 2 *(lumbre)* light. 3 *(cocina)* burner, ring. 4 *(ardor)* ardour (US ardor), zeal. ■ **a fuego lento** 1 on a low flame. 2 *(al horno)* in a slow oven. ‖ **poner las manos en el fuego por** ALGO/ALGN to stake one's life on STH/SB. ‖ **prender fuego a** ALGO to set fire to STH. ● **fuegos artificiales** fireworks.
fuel *nm* fuel oil.
fuelle *nm (aparato)* bellows *pl*.
fuente *nf* 1 *(manantial)* spring. 2 *(artificial)* fountain. 3 *(recipiente)* serving dish, dish. 4 *fig* source.
fuera *adv* 1 *(exterior)* out, outside: **salimos fuera** *we went out, we went outside.* 2 *(alejado)* away; *(en el extranjero)* abroad.
▷ *interj* get out!
▷ *prep* **fuera de** *(un lugar)* out of; *(más allá de)* outside, beyond; *(excepto)* except for, apart from. ■ **estar fuera de sí** to be beside OS. ‖ **fuera de lo normal** extraordinary, very unusual. ‖ **fuera de serie** extraordinary. ● **fuera de juego** offside.
fueraborda *nm (motor)* outboard engine, outboard motor.
fuero *nm* 1 *(ley)* code of laws. 2 *(privilegio)* privilege; *(exención)* exemption. 3 *(jurisdicción)* jurisdiction.
fuerte *adj* 1 *(gen)* strong: **tiene un sabor fuerte** *it has a strong taste.* 2 *(en asignatura)* strong, good: **está muy fuerte en historia** *she's very strong on history.* 3 *(viento)* strong; *(lluvia, nevada)* heavy; *(tormenta, seísmo)* severe; *(calor)* intense. 4 *(escena - violento)* violent; *(- escandaloso)* shocking; *(- inquietante)* disturbing. 5 *(dolor, enfermedad)* severe, bad. 6 *(golpe)* hard, heavy. 7 *(sonido)* loud. 8 *(subida)* steep, sharp; *(bajada)* sharp: **un fuerte descenso en el precio del petróleo** *a sharp fall in the price of oil.* 9 *(discusión)* heated, violent; *(protesta)* violent, vigorous; *(polémica)* bitter; *(aplauso)* loud, thunderous. 10 *(presión)* intense; *(influencia)* powerful, strong. 11 *(suma de dinero)* large: **pagaron una fuerte suma de dinero** *they paid a large sum of money.* 12 *(comida - pesado)* heavy; *(- cargado)* rich. 13 *(color)* intense. 14 *(contraste)* marked, sharp; *(tendencia)* strong, marked. 15 *(cosa fija)* stiff, tight. 16 *fam (terrible)* awful.
▷ *nm* 1 *(fortificación)* fort. 2 *(punto fuerte)* forte, strong point.
▷ *adv* 1 *(mucho)* a lot: **comer fuerte** *to eat a lot.* 2 *(con fuerza)* hard: **empuja fuerte** *push hard.* 3 *(volumen)* loud: **la música sonaba fuerte** *the music was loud.*
fuerza *nf* 1 *(gen)* strength. 2 *(violencia)* force, violence. 3 *(militar)* force. 4 *(en física)* force. 5 *(electricidad)* power, electric power. 6 *(poder)* power.
▷ *nf pl* **fuerzas** *(el poder)* authorities. ■ **a fuerza de** by dint of, by force of. ‖ **a la fuerza** by force. ‖ **con fuerza** 1 *(gen)* strongly. 2 *(llover)* heavily. 3 *(apretar, agarrar)* tightly. *(pegar, empujar)* hard. ‖ **por fuerza** by force. ● **fuerza de voluntad** willpower. ‖ **fuerza mayor** force majeure.
fuga *nf* 1 *(huida)* flight, escape. 2 *(escape)* leak. 3 MÚS fugue.
fugacidad *nf* fleetingness.
fugarse [7] *vpr (gen)* to flee, escape; *(de casa)* to run away from home; *(de casa y con amante)* to elope (**con**, with).
fugaz *adj* fleeting, brief.
fugitivo,-a *adj* 1 *(en fuga)* fleeing. 2 *fig (efímero)* ephemeral, fleeting.
▷ *nm & nf* fugitive, runaway.
fulano,-a *nm & nf* so-and-so; *(hombre)* what's his name; *(mujer)* what's her name.
▷ *nm* **fulano** *fam pey* guy, GB bloke.
fular *nm* foulard, scarf.
fulgor *nm* 1 *(resplandor)* brilliance, glow. 2 *fig (esplendor)* splendour (US splendor).
fulgurante *adj* 1 *(brillante)* brilliant, shining. 2 *fig (rápido)* rapid.
fulminado,-a *adj* struck by lightning.
fulminante *adj* 1 *(que arroja rayos)* fulminating. 2 *fig (instantáneo)* instantaneous; *(rápido)* swift; *(súbito)* sudden. 3 *(enfermedad)* sudden.
fulminar *vt* 1 to strike with lightning. 2 *fig* to strike dead. ■ **fulminar a** ALGN **(con la mirada)** to look daggers at SB.
fumador,-ra *adj* smoking.
▷ *nm & nf* smoker. ■ **los no fumadores** nonsmokers.
fumar *vt* to smoke.
fumigar [7] *vt* to fumigate.
funámbulo,-a *nm & nf* tightrope walker.
función *nf* 1 *(gen)* function. 2 *(cargo)* duty. 3 *(espectáculo)* performance, show. ■ **en función de** according to. ‖ **en funciones** acting. ‖ **entrar en función** *(persona)* to take up one's post. ‖ **estar en funciones** to be in office. ● **función de noche** evening performance. ‖ **función de tarde** matinée.
funcional *adj* functional.
funcionalidad *nf* functionality.
funcionalismo *nm* functionalism.
funcionalista *adj* functionalist.
▷ *nm* functionalist.
funcionamiento *nm* operation, working.
funcionar *vi (desempeñar una función)* to work, function: **funciona con gasolina/diesel** *it runs on petrol (US gas)/diesel.*

funcionariado *nm* civil service, civil servants *pl.*
funcionario,-a *nm & nf* functionary, employee. ● **funcionario,-a público,-a** civil servant.
funda *nf* 1 *(flexible)* cover. 2 *(rígida)* case. 3 *(de arma blanca)* sheath. 4 *(de disco)* sleeve. ● **funda de almohada** pillowcase.
fundación *nf* foundation.
fundado,-a *adj* firm, well-founded, justified. ■ **mal fundado,-a** ill-founded.
fundador,-ra *nm & nf* founder.
fundamental *adj* fundamental.
fundamentalismo *nm* fundamentalism.
fundamentalista *adj* fundamentalist.
▷ *nm o nf* fundamentalist.
fundamentalmente *adv* fundamentally, basically.
fundamentar *vt* 1 *fig* to base (**en**, on). 2 *(construcción)* to lay the foundations of.
fundamento *nm* 1 *(base)* basis, grounds *pl.* 2 *(seriedad)* seriousness; *(confianza)* reliability. ■ **sin fundamento** unfounded.
fundar *vt* 1 *(crear)* to found; *(erigir)* to raise: **su padre fundó la empresa** *her father founded the company.* 2 *(basar)* to base, found: **funda su teoría en falsos argumentos** *he bases his theory on false arguments.*
▷ *vpr* **fundarse** 1 *(crearse)* to be founded. 2 *(teoría, afirmación)* to be based (**en**, on); *(persona)* to base OS (**en**, on): **la teoría se funda en falsos argumentos** *the theory is based on false arguments.*
fundición *nf* 1 *(derretimiento)* melting. 2 *(de metales)* smelting. 3 *(acción de dar forma)* casting. 4 *(lugar)* foundry, smelting works.
fundido *nm (entrando)* fade-in; *(saliendo)* fade-out.
fundidor *nm* smelter, caster.
fundir *vt* 1 *(derretir)* to melt: **el sol funde la nieve** *the sun melts the snow.* 2 *(separar mena y metal)* to smelt. 3 *(dar forma)* to cast: **fundir una figura en bronce** *to cast a figure in bronze.* 4 *(bombilla, plomos)* to blow. 5 *(unir)* to unite, join. 6 *fam (despilfarrar)* to waste, blow: **fundió todo el dinero en aquel regalo** *he blew all his money on that present.*
▷ *vpr* **fundirse** 1 *(derretirse)* to melt: **la nieve se funde** *snow melts.* 2 *(bombilla, plomos)* to fuse, go, blow, burn out: **se han fundido los plomos** *the fuses have gone.* 3 *(unirse)* to merge.
fúnebre *adj* 1 *(mortuorio)* funeral. 2 *(lúgubre)* mournful, lugubrious.
funeral *adj* funeral.
▷ *nm* [Also used in plural with the same meaning.] 1 *(entierro)* funeral. 2 *(conmemoración)* memorial service.
funerala ■ **a la funerala** MIL with reversed arms. ● **ojo a la funerala** *fam* black eye.
funeraria *nf* undertaker's, US funeral parlor.
funerario,-a *adj* funerary, funeral.
funesto,-a *adj* ill-fated, fatal.
fungicida *adj* fungicidal.
▷ *nm* fungicide.
funicular *nm* funicular, funicular railway.
furgón *nm* 1 AUTO van, truck. 2 *(de tren)* (goods) wagon, US boxcar. ● **furgón de cola** guard's van.
furgoneta *nf* van.
furia *nf* fury, rage.
furibundo,-a *adj* furious, enraged.
furiosamente *adv* furiously.
furioso,-a *adj* 1 *(colérico)* furious. 2 *(tempestad, vendaval)* raging. ■ **ponerse furioso,-a** to get angry.
furor *nm* fury, rage. ■ **hacer furor** *fig* to be all the rage.
furtivamente *adv* furtively.
furtivo,-a *adj* furtive.
furúnculo *nm* boil.
fusa *nf* demisemiquaver, US thirty-second note.
fuseaux *nm* ski pants *pl.*
fuselaje *nm* fuselage.
fusible *adj* fusible.
▷ *nm* fuse.
fusil *nm* rifle, gun.
fusilamiento *nm* shooting, execution.
fusilar *vt* 1 *(ejecutar)* to shoot, execute. 2 *(plagiar)* to plagiarize.
fusilería *nf* 1 *(fusiles)* rifles *pl.* 2 *(soldados fusileros)* fusiliers *pl.* 3 *(descarga)* rifle fire, rifle shots *pl.*
fusilero *nm* fusilier, rifleman.
fusión *nf* 1 *(de metales)* fusion, melting; *(de hielo)* thawing, melting. 2 *(de intereses, partidos, ideas)* fusion. 3 *(de empresas)* merger, amalgamation.
fusionar *vt* 1 *(fundir)* to fuse. 2 *(unir)* to join, unite. 3 COM to merge: **proponen fusionar ambas empresas** *they propose to merge the two companies.*
▷ *vpr* **fusionarse** *(unir)* to join, unite; *(empresas)* to merge.
fusta *nf* riding whip.
fuste *nm* 1 *(palo)* stick. 2 *(de columna)* shaft. 3 *(importancia)* importance: **una empresa de fuste** *an important firm;* **un hombre de fuste** *a man of consequence.*
futbito *nm* five-a-side football.
fútbol *nm* football, soccer. ● **fútbol americano** American football.
futbolín [Registered trademark.] *nm* table football.
futbolista *nm o nf* footballer, football player, soccer player.
futbolístico,-a *adj* football.
futón *nm* futon.
futurista *adj* futuristic.
▷ *nm o nf* futurist.
futuro,-a *adj* future.
▷ *nm & nf (prometido)* fiancé, intended; *(prometida)* fiancée, intended.
▷ *nm* **futuro** future. ■ **en un futuro próximo** in the near future. ● **futuro imperfecto** future. ‖ **futuro perfecto** future perfect.
▷ *nm pl* **futuros** *(financieros)* futures.

G

G, g *nf (la letra)* G, g.
g *sím* **(gramo)** gram, gramme; *(símbolo)* g.
gabacho,-a *nm & nf pey* frog.
gabán *nm* overcoat.
gabardina *nf* **1** *(impermeable)* raincoat. **2** *(tela)* gabardine.
gabinete *nm* **1** *(habitación)* study. **2** POL cabinet. **3** *(despacho)* office.
Gabón *nm* Gabon.
gabonés,-esa *adj* Gabonese.
▷ *nm & nf* Gabonese.
gacela *nf* gazelle.
gaceta *nf (publicación)* gazette.
gacha *nf (masa)* paste.
▷ *nf pl* **gachas** *(papilla)* porridge *sing.*
gacho,-a *adj* drooping, bent.
gaélico,-a *adj* Gaelic.
▷ *nm* **gaélico** Gaelic.
gafa *nf pl* **gafas 1** spectacles, glasses. **2** *(de motorista, esquí, natación)* goggles. ● **gafas de bucear** diving mask *sing.* ‖ **gafas de sol** sunglasses.
gafe *adj fam* jinx.
▷ *nm o nf fam* jinx.
gag *nm* gag, sketch.
gaita *nf* **1** bagpipes *pl*, pipes *pl*. **2** *fam* bother, drag, pain.
gaitero,-a *nm & nf* MÚS piper, bagpipe player.
gajes *nm pl (dietas)* allowance *sing*, expenses. ● **gajes del oficio** *irón* occupational hazards.
gajo *nm (de fruta)* segment.
gala *nf* **1** *(espectáculo)* gala. **2** *(vestido)* best dress. ■ **hacer gala de** to make a show of. ‖ **tener ALGO a gala** to be proud of STH. ● **cena de gala** gala dinner. ‖ **noche de gala** gala night.
▷ *nf pl* **galas** *(adorno)* finery *sing.* ■ **lucir sus mejores galas** to be dressed in all one's finery.
galáctico,-a *adj* galactic.
galán *nm* **1** *(atractivo)* handsome young man; *(mujeriego)* ladies' man. **2** TEAT hero.
galante *adj* courteous, gallant, chivalrous.
galantear *vt* to court, woo.
galantería *nf* **1** *(caballerosidad)* gallantry, chivalry. **2** *(piropo)* compliment.
galápago *nm* **1** *(animal)* turtle. **2** *(lingote)* ingot. **3** *(silla de montar)* light saddle.
Galápagos *nf pl* **las (islas) Galápagos** the Galápagos Islands.
galardón *nm* prize.
galardonado,-a *adj* prizewinning.
▷ *nm & nf* prizewinner.
galardonar *vt (premio)* to award a prize to; *(medalla)* to award a medal to.
galaxia *nf* galaxy.
galena *nf* lead sulphide.
galeno *nm fam* doctor.
galeón *nm* galleon.
galeote *nm* galley slave.
galera *nf (mar)* galley.
galería *nf* **1** *(gen)* gallery. **2** *(corredor descubierto)* balcony, verandah. **3** TEAT gallery, balcony. **4** *(para cortinas)* pelmet, US cornice. ● **galerías comerciales** shopping centre *sing.*
galés,-a *adj* Welsh.
▷ *nm & nf (persona)* Welsh person; *(hombre)* Welshman; *(mujer)* Welshwoman.
▷ *nm* **galés** *(idioma)* Welsh.
Gales *nm* Wales. ● **País de Gales** Wales.
galgo,-a *nm & nf* greyhound.
gálibo *nm* loading gauge. ● **luces de gálibo** clearance lights.
gallardía *nf* **1** *(elegancia)* elegance, poise. **2** *(arresto)* gallantry, bravery.
gallardo,-a *adj* **1** *(apuesto)* elegant, handsome. **2** *(valeroso)* brave, gallant.
galleta *nf* CULIN biscuit, US cookie.
gallina *nf* hen.
▷ *nm o nf fam* chicken, coward. ■ **jugar a la gallina ciega** to play blind man's buff.
gallinero *nm* **1** henhouse. **2** *fam* bedlam, madhouse. **3 el gallinero** TEAT the gods *pl.*
gallo *nm* **1** cock, rooster. **2** *(pez)* John Dory. **3** *fig (al cantar)* false note; *(al hablar)* squeak. **4** *fam fig (mandón)* cock of the walk. ■ **en menos que canta un gallo** in a flash.
galo,-a *adj* **1** HIST Gaulish. **2** *irón* French: **el país galo** *France.*
▷ *nm & nf* HIST *(persona)* Gaul.
galón[1] *nm* **1** *(cinta)* braid. **2** MIL stripe, chevron.
galón[2] *nm (medida)* gallon.
galopar *vi* to gallop.
galope *nm* gallop. ■ **a galope / al galope 1** at a gallop. **2** *fig* in a rush. ‖ **a galope tendido** at full gallop.
galvanización *nf* galvanization.
galvanizado,-a *adj* galvanized.
▷ *nm* **galvanizado** FÍS galvanization.
galvanizar [4] *vt* to galvanize.
galvanómetro *nm* galvanometer.
gama *nf* **1** MÚS scale. **2** *(gradación, variedad)* range.
gamba[1] *nf* ZOOL prawn; *(pequeña)* shrimp.
gamba[2] *nf argot (pierna)* leg. ■ **meter la gamba** *fam* to put one's foot in it.
gamberrada *nf* act of hooliganism, act of vandalism.
gamberro,-a *adj* loutish, rowdy.
▷ *nm & nf* vandal, hooligan, lout.

Gambia *nf* Gambia.

gambiano,-a *adj* Gambian.
▷ *nm & nf* Gambian.

gambito *nm* gambit.

gameto *nm* gamete.

gamma *nf* gamma. ● **rayos gamma** gamma rays.

gammaglobulina *nf* gamma globulin.

gamo *nm* fallow deer.

gamuza *nf* 1 ZOOL chamois. 2 *(piel)* chamois leather. 3 *(paño)* duster.

gana *nf* 1 *(deseo)* wish (**de**, for), desire. 2 *(apetito)* appetite; *(hambre)* hunger. ■ **dar a** ALGN **la gana de hacer** ALGO *fam* to feel like doing STH. ‖ **de buena gana** willingly. ‖ **tener ganas de (hacer)** ALGO to feel like (doing) STH.

ganadería *nf* 1 *(crianza)* cattle raising, stockbreeding. 2 *(ganado)* cattle, livestock.

ganadero,-a *adj* cattle.
▷ *nm & nf* 1 *(propietario)* cattle breeder, stockbreeder. 2 *(cuidador de ganado)* herdsman, US herder.

ganado *nm* livestock, stock; *(vacas)* cattle. ● **ganado bovino** cattle *pl*. ‖ **ganado vacuno** cattle *pl*.

ganador,-ra *adj* winning.
▷ *nm & nf* winner.

ganancia *nf* gain, profit.

ganancial *adj* relating to profit, relating to earnings.

ganar *vt* 1 *(partido, concurso, premio)* to win. 2 *(dinero)* to earn: **¿cuánto ganas al año?** *how much do you earn a year?* 3 *(alcanzar)* to reach: **ganaron la cima** *they reached the summit.* 4 *(lograr)* to win.
▷ *vi* 1 *(mejorar)* to improve. 2 *(cambiar favorablemente)* to gain.
▷ *vpr* **ganarse** 1 to earn: **se gana bien la vida** *he makes a good living.* 2 *(ser merecedor)* to deserve: **se lo han ganado** *they deserve it.* ■ **ganar a** ALGN **en** ALGO to be better than SB at STH.

ganchillo *nm* 1 *(aguja)* crochet hook. 2 *(labor)* crochet work. ■ **hacer ganchillo** to crochet.

gancho *nm* 1 hook. 2 *(para ropa)* peg. 3 *fam (atractivo)* attractiveness, charm. 4 *fam (compinche de un estafador)* bait, decoy. 5 *(en boxeo)* hook. 6 *(en baloncesto)* hook shot. ■ **tener gancho** *fam* to be attractive, have charm.

gandul,-la *adj* lazy, idle.
▷ *nm & nf* idler, loafer, lazybones, slacker.

gandulear *vi* to idle, loaf around, laze around, slack.

gandulería *nf* idleness, laziness.

ganga[1] *nf* 1 *(algo barato)* bargain, good buy. 2 *fam (algo fácil)* gift, cinch, piece of cake. 3 *(ave)* sandgrouse. ● **precio de ganga** bargain price.

ganga[2] *nf (en minería)* gang, gangue.

Ganges *nm* **el Ganges** the Ganges.

ganglio *nm* ganglion.

gangoso,-a *adj* nasal, twanging.

gangrena *nf* gangrene.

gangrenarse *vpr* to become gangrenous.

gángster *nm* gangster.
▲ *pl* **gángsteres.**

gansada *nf fam* silly thing to say, silly thing to do.

ganso,-a *nm & nf* 1 ZOOL goose; *(macho)* gander. 2 *(torpe)* dimwit, fool. 3 *(bromista)* clown, prankster.

Gante *nm* Ghent.

ganzúa *nf* 1 *(garfio)* picklock. 2 *(ladrón)* burglar. 3 *(sonsacador)* coaxer, wheedler.

gañán *nm* 1 *(mozo de labranza)* farm hand. 2 *(hombre tosco)* big brute.

gañote *nm fam* throat, gullet.

garabatear *vt (escribir)* to scribble, scrawl; *(dibujar)* to doodle.
▷ *vi (escribir)* to scribble, scrawl; *(dibujar)* to doodle.

garabato *nm* 1 *(gancho)* hook. 2 *(dibujo)* doodle; *(escritura)* scrawl, scribble.

garaje *nm* garage.

garante *nm o nf* guarantor.

garantía *nf* 1 *(seguridad)* guarantee, security. 2 COM guarantee, warranty. 3 JUR bond, warranty, security. ● **certificado de garantía** guarantee. ‖ **garantías constitucionales** constitutional guarantees.

garantizado,-a *adj* 1 guaranteed. 2 JUR secured.

garantizar [4] *vt* 1 to guarantee. 2 COM to warrant. 3 *(responder por)* to vouch for, stand as guarantor for.

garapiñar *vt* 1 *(gen)* to coat with sugar. 2 *(fruta)* to candy. ● **almendra garapiñada** sugared almond.

garbanzo *nm* chickpea.

garbearse *vpr fam* to take a stroll.

garbeo *nm* 1 *fam* walk, stroll. 2 *(viaje)* trip.

garbo *nm* 1 *(airosidad al andar)* gracefulness, poise. 2 *(gracia)* grace, stylishness.

garboso,-a *adj (airoso)* graceful, stylish.

gardenia *nf* gardenia.

garduña *nf* marten.

garete ■ **ir(se) al garete** to collapse, fail.

garfio *nm* hook, grapple.

gargajo *nm* spit, phlegm.

garganta *nf* 1 *(cuello)* throat. 2 *(desfiladero)* gorge, narrow pass.

gargantilla *nf* short necklace, choker.

gárgaras *nm pl* gargles *pl*, gargling *sing*. ■ **hacer gárgaras** to gargle.

gargarismo *nm* 1 *(gárgaras)* gargles *pl*, gargling. 2 *(líquido)* gargling solution.

gárgola *nf* gargoyle.

garita *nf* 1 *(caseta)* box, cabin, hut; *(de centinela)* sentry box. 2 *(portería)* porter's lodge.

garito *nm* 1 *(casa de juego)* gambling den, gaming house. 2 *(antro de diversión)* dive, joint.

garlopa *nf* jack plane.

garnacha *nf* 1 *(uva)* sweet reddish-black grape. 2 *(vino)* wine made from this grape.

Garona *nm* **el Garona** the Garonne.

garra *nf (de mamífero)* paw, claw; *(de ave)* talon.
▷ *nf pl* **garras** *(poder)* clutches. ■ **caer en las garras de** ALGN *fig* to fall into SB's clutches. ‖ **tener garra** 1 *(relato, etc)* to be compelling. 2 *(persona)* to have charisma.

garrafa *nf* carafe. ■ **de garrafa** *fam* cheap, bad quality.

garrafal *adj* monumental, huge, terrible.

garrafón *nm* demijohn, large carafe.

garrapata *nf* tick.

garrapatear *vi (escribir)* to scribble, scrawl; *(dibujar)* to doodle.

garrapatoso,-a *adj* scrawled, scribbled.

garrota *nf* thick stick, cudgel.

garrotazo *nm* blow with a stick.

garrote *nm* 1 thick stick, cudgel, club. 2 *(pena capital)* garrotte.
garrulería *nf* garrulity.
garrulo,-a *adj* uncouth.
▷ *nm & nf* uncouth person.
gárrulo,-a *adj* 1 *(ave)* twittering. 2 *(persona)* garrulous.
garza *nf* heron. ● **garza real** grey heron.
gas *nm (gen)* gas. ● **gas butano** butane gas.
▷ *nm pl* **gases** *(flatulencias)* wind *sing*, flatulence *sing*, US gas *sing*.
gasa *nf* 1 gauze. 2 *(pañal)* gauze nappy, US gauze diaper.
gascón,-ona *adj* Gascon.
▷ *nm & nf* Gascon.
Gascuña *nf* Gascony.
gaseosa *nf* GB lemonade, US soda, pop.
gaseoso,-a *adj* 1 gaseous, gassy. 2 *(bebida)* carbonated, fizzy.
gasificación *nf* gasification.
gasificar [1] *vt* to gasify.
gasoducto *nm* gas pipeline.
gasógeno *nm* gazogene.
gasoil *nm* diesel oil.
gasóleo *nm* diesel oil.
gasolina *nf* petrol, US gasoline, gas. ■ **poner gasolina** to get some petrol.
gasolinera *nf* 1 petrol station, US gas station. 2 *(lancha)* motorboat.
gasómetro *nm* gasometer.
gastado,-a *adj* 1 *(desgastado)* worn-out. 2 *(acabado)* finished, empty, used up. 3 *(manido)* hackneyed, well-worn.
gastador,-ra *adj (derrochador)* spendthrift.
gastar *vt* 1 *(consumir dinero, tiempo)* to spend; *(gasolina, electricidad)* to use (up), consume: **este coche gasta mucha gasolina** *this car uses a lot of petrol* (US *gas*). 2 *(malgastar)* to waste. 3 *(usar perfume, jabón)* to use; *(ropa)* to wear: **¿qué número gastas?** *what size do you take?*
▷ *vpr* **gastarse** 1 *(desgastarse)* to wear out. 2 *(consumirse)* to run out.
gasterópodo *nm* gastropod.
gasto *nm* expenditure, expense. ● **gastos de mantenimiento** running costs, maintenance costs. ‖ **gastos diarios** daily expenses.
gástrico,-a *adj* gastric.
gastritis *nf inv* gastritis.
gastroenteritis *nf inv* gastroenteritis.
gastronomía *nf* gastronomy.
gastronómico,-a *adj* gastronomic, gastronomical.
gastrónomo,-a *nm & nf* 1 *(especialista)* gastronome. 2 *(aficionado a comer bien)* gourmet.
gata *nf* she-cat, cat.
See also **gato**.
gatas ■ **a gatas** on all fours. ‖ **andar a gatas** to crawl.
gatear *vi* 1 *(andar a gatas)* to crawl. 2 *(trepar)* to climb.
gatera *nf* cat door, cat flap.
gatillo *nm* trigger.
gatito,-a *nm & nf fam* kitty, pusy.
gato,-a *nm* **gato** 1 cat, tomcat. 2 *(de coche)* jack. ■ **buscarle tres/cinco pies al gato** *fam* to split hairs, complicate things. ‖ **dar gato por liebre** *fam* to take SB in, con SB. ‖ **hay gato encerrado** *fam* there's something fishy going on.
gatuno,-a *adj* catlike, feline.
gaveta *nf* 1 *(cajón)* drawer. 2 *(mueble)* chest of drawers.
gavia *nf* topsail.
gavilán *nm* sparrowhawk.
gavilla *nf* 1 *(de ramas, etc)* sheaf. 2 *pey (de gente)* gang, band.
gaviota *nf* seagull, gull.
gay *adj* gay, homosexual.
▷ *nm* gay, homosexual.
gazapo[1] *nm* ZOOL young rabbit.
gazapo[2] *nm* 1 *(mentira)* lie. 2 *(error)* blunder, slip.
gazmoñería *nf* prudishness, prudery.
gazmoñero,-a *adj* prudish.
gazmoño,-a *adj* prudish.
gaznate *nm* gullet.
gazpacho *nm cold soup made of tomatoes and other vegetables.*
ge *nf name of the letter* **g**.
géiser *nm* geyser.
geisha *nf* geisha.
gel *nm* gel.
gelatina *nf* 1 *(sustancia)* gelatine. 2 *(preparado alimenticio)* jelly.
gelatinoso,-a *adj* gelatinous, jelly-like.
gélido,-a *adj* icy, icy cold.
gelignita *nf* gelignite.
gema *nf* 1 BOT bud. 2 *(piedra)* gem.
gemación *nf* gemmation.
gemelo,-a *adj* twin.
▷ *nm & nf* twin.
▷ *nm* **gemelo** *(músculo)* calf muscle.
▷ *nm pl* **gemelos** 1 *(botones)* cufflinks. 2 *(anteojos)* binoculars.
gemido *nm* 1 *(quejido)* groan, moan. 2 *(gimoteo)* whimper.
geminado,-a *adj* geminate.
Géminis *nm* Gemini.
▲ *pl* **Géminis**.
gemir [34] *vi (quejarse)* to moan, groan.
gemología *nf* gemology.
gen *nm* gene.
genciana *nf* gentian.
gendarme *nm* gendarme.
gendarmería *nf* gendarmerie.
genealogía *nf* genealogy.
genealógico,-a *adj* genealogical. ● **árbol genealógico** family tree.
generación *nf* generation.
generacional *adj* generation, generational.
generador,-ra *nm* **generador** *(máquina)* generator.
general *adj* 1 general. 2 *(común)* common, usual, widespread. ■ **en general** in general, generally.
▷ *nm (oficial)* general.
generalidad *nf* 1 *(gen)* generality. 2 *(mayoría)* majority. 3 *(generalización)* general statement.
▷ *nf pl* **generalidades** *(nociones)* basic knowledge *sing*.
generalización *nf* 1 *(gen)* generalization. 2 *(extensión)* spread, spreading.
generalizado,-a *adj* widespread, common.

generalizar [4] *vt* 1 *(gen)* to generalize. 2 *(extender)* to spread, popularize.
▷ *vpr* **generalizarse** to spread, become widespread, become common.
generalmente *adv* generally, usually.
generar *vt* to generate.
generativo,-a *adj* generative.
generatriz *nf* generatrix.
genéricamente *adv* generically.
genérico,-a *adj* generic.
género *nm* 1 *(clase)* kind, sort. 2 *(tela)* cloth. 3 *(mercancía)* article, piece of merchandise. 4 GRAM gender. 5 BIOL genus. 6 *(literario)* genre.
generosamente *adv* generously.
generosidad *nf* generosity, unselfishness.
generoso,-a *adj* generous (**con/para**, to).
génesis *nf inv* genesis.
▷ *nm* **el Génesis** Genesis.
genética *nf* genetics *sing*.
genético,-a *adj* genetic.
genetista *nm o nf* geneticist.
genial *adj* 1 brilliant, inspired. 2 *fam* terrific, great, smashing.
▷ *adv fam* great.
genialidad *nf* 1 *(idea)* brilliant idea, stroke of genius. 2 *(acción)* peculiarity. 3 *(cualidad)* genius.
genio *nm* 1 *(carácter)* temper, disposition. 2 *(facultad)* genius: **Einstein fue un genio** *Einstein was a genius.* 3 *(espíritu)* spirit: **el genio del Renacimiento** *the Renaissance spirit.* 4 *(ser fantástico)* genie. ■ **estar de mal genio** to be in a bad mood. ‖ **tener mal genio** to have a bad temper.
genital *adj* genital.
▷ *nm pl* **genitales** genitals.
genitivo *nm* genitive.
genocidio *nm* genocide.
genoma *nm* genome, genom.
genotipo *nm* genotype.
Génova *nf* Genoa.
genovés,-esa *adj* Genoese.
▷ *nm & nf* Genoese.
gente *nf* 1 people *pl*. 2 *(familia)* family, folks *pl*, people *pl*: **me gusta estar con mi gente** *I like being with my family.* 3 *(personal)* staff. ● **gente menuda** *fam* nippers *pl*, kids *pl*.
gentil *adj* 1 *(amable)* kind. 2 *(apuesto)* charming.
gentileza *nf* 1 *(gracia)* grace, elegance, poise. 2 *(cortesía)* politeness, kindness.
gentilicio *adj* gentile.
▷ *nm* gentile.
gentío *nm* crowd.
gentuza *nf pey* mob, rabble, riffraff.
genuino,-a *adj* genuine, authentic.
geocéntrico,-a *adj* geocentric.
geodésico,-a *adj* geodesic.
geofísica *nf* geophysics *sing*.
geografía *nf* geography.
geógrafo,-a *nm & nf* geographer.
geología *nf* geology.
geológico,-a *adj* geologic, geological.
geólogo,-a *nm & nf* geologist.
geomagnetismo *nm* geomagnetism.
geometría *nf* geometry. ● **geometría del espacio** solid geometry. ‖ **geometría descriptiva** descriptive geometry.
geométrico,-a *adj* geometric, geometrical.
geomorfología *nf* geomorphology.
Georgia *nf* Georgia. ● **Georgia del Sur** South Georgia.
georgiano,-a *adj* Georgian.
▷ *nm & nf (persona)* Georgian.
▷ *nm* **georgiano** *(idioma)* Georgian.
geranio *nf* geranium.
gerencia *nf (actividad)* management.
gerente *nm o nf (hombre)* manager; *(mujer)* manageress.
geriatría *nf* geriatrics *sing*.
geriátrico,-a *adj* geriatric.
▷ *nm* **geriátrico** *(sanatorio)* geriatric hospital, *(residencia)* old people's home.
germano,-a *adj* Germanic.
germen *nm* germ.
germinar *vi* to germinate.
gerundio *nm* gerund.
gesta *nf arc* heroic deed, exploit.
gestación *nf* 1 gestation. 2 *(período)* gestation period.
gestante *adj* gestating.
▷ *nf* expectant mother.
gesticular *vi* to gesticulate.
gestión *nf* 1 [Also used in plural with the same meaning.] *(trámite)* step, measure, move. 2 [Also used in plural with the same meaning.] *(negociación)* negotiation. ● **gestión de datos** data management.
gestionar *vt* 1 *(negociar)* to negotiate. 2 *(administrar)* to manage, run.
gesto *nm* 1 *(movimiento)* gesture. 2 *(mueca)* grimace. ■ **hacer gestos a** *fam* to make gestures at.
gestor,-ra *nm & nf* 1 *(administrador)* manager, director. 2 *person who transacts official business on his clients' behalf*, ≈ solicitor.
Ghana *nf* Ghana.
ghanés,-a *adj* Ghanaian.
▷ *nm & nf* Ghanaian.
giba *nf* hump, hunch.
Gibraltar *nm* Gibraltar.
gibraltareño,-a *adj* Gibraltarian.
▷ *nm & nf* Gibraltarian.
giga *nf (gigabyte)* giga, gigabyte.
gigabyte *nm* gigabyte.
gigante *nm & nf (hombre)* giant; *(mujer)* giantess.
▷ *adj* giant, gigantic, huge.
gigantesco,-a *adj* giant, gigantic.
gilipollas *adj inv tabú* stupid.
▷ *nm o nf* jerk, arsehole (US asshole), GB prat.
gimnasia *nf* gymnastics *sing*.
gimnasio *nm* gymnasium, gym.
gimnosperma *nf* gymnosperm.
gincana *nf* gymkhana.
ginebra *nf* gin.
Ginebra *nf* Geneva.
ginecología *nf* gynaecology (US gynecology).
ginecólogo,-a *nm & nf* gynaecologist (US gynecologist).
gineta *nf* genet.
gingko *nm* ginkgo, gingko, maidenhair tree.

gira *nf* tour.
girar *vi* 1 *(dar vueltas)* to rotate, whirl, spin. 2 *(torcer)* to turn: **girar a la izquierda** *to turn left.* 3 *fig (versar)* to deal with: **la conversación giró en torno al teatro** *the conversation evolved around theatre.*
▷ *vt* 1 COM to issue: **girar una letra** *to issue a draft.* 2 *(cambiar de sentido)* to turn, turn around: **girar el cuerpo** *to turn one's body.*
girasol *nm* sunflower.
giratorio,-a *adj* rotating, gyratory.
giro *nm* 1 *(vuelta)* turn, turning. 2 *(dirección)* course, direction. 3 COM draft. 4 *(frase)* turn of phrase, expression. ● **giro postal** money order.
gitano,-a *nm & nf* 1 gypsy, gipsy.
glaciación *nf* glaciation.
glacial *adj* 1 glacial. 2 *fig* glacial, icy: **tuvo un recibimiento glacial** *he had an icy reception.*
glaciar *nm* glacier.
gladiador *nm* gladiator.
gladiolo *nm* gladiolus.
glándula *nf* gland.
glicerina *nf* glycerin, glycerine.
global *adj* global, comprehensive, overall.
globo *nm* 1 *(esfera)* globe, sphere. 2 *(tierra)* globe. 3 *(de aire)* balloon.
glóbulo *nm* globule. ● **glóbulo blanco** white corpuscle. ▮ **glóbulo rojo** red corpuscle.
gloria *nf* 1 *(bienaventuranza)* glory. 2 *(fama)* fame, honour (US honor). 3 *fam (placer)* bliss, delight.
glorieta *nf* 1 *(en un jardín)* arbour (US arbor). 2 *(plazoleta)* small square.
glorificar [1] *vt* to glorify.
glorioso,-a *adj* glorious.
glosa *nf* 1 *(explicación, comentario)* gloss, comment note. 2 *(poema)* gloss.
glosar *vt* 1 *(explicar)* to gloss. 2 *(interpretar)* to interpret. 3 *(comentar)* to comment on, speak about.
glosario *nm* glossary.
glotón,-ona *adj* greedy, gluttonous.
▷ *nm & nf* glutton.
glotonería *nf* gluttony, greed.
glúcido *nm* glucide.
glucosa *nf* glucose.
gluten *nm* gluten.
gneis *nm inv* gneiss.
gnomo *nm* gnome.
gnosticismo *nm* Gnosticism.
gnóstico,-a *adj* Gnostic.
▷ *nm & nf* Gnostic.
gobernador,-ra *nm & nf* governor.
gobernante *adj* ruling, governing.
▷ *nm o nf* ruler, leader.
gobernar [27] *vt* 1 *(gen)* to govern. 2 *(un país)* to rule. 3 *(un negocio)* to run, handle. 4 *(un barco)* to steer.
gobierno *nm* 1 POL government. 2 *(mando)* command, running, handling. 3 *(conducción)* direction, control; *(de un barco)* steering; *(de timón)* rudder.
goce *nm* pleasure, enjoyment.
godo,-a *adj* Gothic.
▷ *nm & nf (persona)* Goth.
▷ *nm* **godo** *(idioma)* Gothic.
gofre *nm* waffle.
gol *nm* goal.
goleador,-ra *nm & nf* scorer. ● **el máximo goleado[r]** the top scorer.
golear *vt* to hammer.
golf *nm* 1 *(deporte)* golf. 2 *(terreno)* golf course.
golfista *nm o nf* golfer.
golfo[1] *nm* gulf, large bay.
golfo,-a[2] *nm & nf (holgazán)* good-for-nothing, lay[-]about; *(niño)* rascal, little devil.
golondrina *nf (ave)* swallow.
golosina *nf* sweet, US candy.
goloso,-a *adj* sweet-toothed.
golpe *nm* 1 blow, knock; *(puñetazo)* punch: **le dio u[n] golpe** *he hit him.* 2 *(de coche)* collision; *(fuerte)* bang[;] *(ligero)* bump. 3 *fig (desgracia)* blow, misfortune. 4 *fa[m] (robo)* hold-up, robbery. 5 *(militar)* coup. ■ **de golp[e]** suddenly, all of a sudden. ▮ **no dar golpe** *fam* not t[o] lift a finger, not do a blessed thing. ● **golpe bajo** *fi[g]* punch below the belt. ▮ **golpe de Estado** coup, cou[p] d'état. ▮ **golpe de vista** quick glance.
golpear *vt (gen)* to hit, strike; *(personas)* to thump hit, punch; *(puerta)* to knock on.
golpista *nm o nf* person involved in a coup d'état.
goma *nf* 1 *(material)* gum, rubber. 2 *(de borrar)* rubber US eraser. 3 *(de pegar)* glue, gum. 4 *(banda elástica)* rubber band. ● **goma arábiga** gum arabic. ▮ **goma de mascar** chewing gum. ▮ **suela de goma** rubber sole.
gomaespuma *nf* foam rubber.
gomina *nf* hair cream.
gominola *nf* jelly bean, jelly.
gong *nm* gong.
gordo,-a *adj* 1 *(carnoso)* fat: **se puso gordo** *he got fat.* 2 *(grueso)* thick. 3 *(grave)* serious. 4 *(importante)* big. **¡qué mentira tan gorda!** *what a big lie!*
▷ *nm & nf* fat person; *(familiarmente)* fatty.
▷ *nm* **gordo** 1 *fam (grasa)* fat. 2 **el gordo** the first prize *in the lottery.*
gordura *nf* fatness.
gorila *nm* 1 *(animal)* gorilla. 2 *fam (guardaespaldas)* bodyguard; *(en club)* bouncer.
gorjear *vi* to chirp, twitter.
gorra *nf* 1 *(gen)* cap. 2 *(con visera)* peaked cap. ■ **de gorra** *fam* free, for nothing.
gorrión,-ona *nm & nf* sparrow.
gorro *nm* 1 cap. 2 *(de bebé)* bonnet. 3 *(de cocinero)* chef's hat.
gorrón,-ona *adj fam* scrounging, sponging.
▷ *nm & nf* sponger, scrounger.
gorronear *vi* to scrounge, be a parasite.
gota *nf* 1 drop. 2 *(de sudor)* bead. 3 *(de aire)* breath. 4 MED gout. ■ **caer cuatro gotas** to be spitting with rain. ▮ **gota a gota** drop by drop. ▮ **ni gota** not a bit, nothing at all. ● **gota fría** cold air pool.
gotear *vi* 1 *(grifo)* to drip; *(tejado)* to leak. 2 [Used in 3rd person only; it does not take a subject.] *(lluvia)* to drizzle.
gotera *nf* 1 *(agujero)* leak. 2 *(agua)* drip.
gótico,-a *adj* Gothic.
gourmet *nm o nf* gourmet.
gozar [4] *vi* 1 *(poseer, disfrutar)* to enjoy (**de**, -): **goza de muy buena salud** *he enjoys very good health.*

2 *(sentir placer)* to enjoy OS: **gozamos con su presencia** *we really enjoy her company.*

gozne *nm* hinge.

gozo *nm* joy, delight, pleasure.

grabación *nf* recording.

grabado,-a *nm* 1 *(arte)* engraving. 2 *(dibujo)* picture, drawing.

grabar *vt* 1 ARTE to engrave. 2 *(registrar)* to record. 3 INFORMÁ to save. ■ **grabarse en la memoria** *fig* to be engraved on one's memory.

gracia *nf* 1 *(favor)* favour (US favor). 2 *(atractivo)* grace, charm. 3 *(chiste)* joke. ■ **caer en gracia a** ALGN to make a hit with SB. ‖ **hacer gracia, tener gracia** *(diversión)* to be funny. ‖ **¡qué gracia!** how funny!

▷ *nf pl* **gracias** thank you, thanks. ■ **dar gracias a** ALGN to thank SB. ‖ **gracias a** thanks to.

gracioso,-a *adj* 1 *(atractivo)* graceful, charming. 2 *(bromista)* witty, facetious. 3 *(divertido)* funny, amusing. 4 *(tratamiento)* Gracious: **Su Graciosa Majestad** *Her Gracious Majesty.*

▷ *nm & nf* TEAT jester, clown, fool. ■ **hacerse el gracioso** to to try to be funny.

grada *nf* 1 *(peldaño)* step, stair. 2 *(gradería)* tier.

▷ *nf pl* **gradas** stands, terraces.

gradación *nf* 1 gradation. 2 MÚS scale. 3 *(retórica)* climax.

gradería *nf* stands *pl*, terraces *pl*.

grado *nm* 1 *(gen)* degree: **estábamos a 27 grados** *it was 27 degrees.* 2 *(estado)* stage. 3 EDUC *(curso)* class, year, US grade. 4 EDUC *(título)* degree. 5 *(peldaño)* step. 6 MIL rank. 7 LING degree.

graduación *nf* 1 *(gen)* graduation. 2 *(de alcohol)* strength. 3 MIL rank, degree of rank. 4 EDUC graduation.

graduado,-a *nm & nf* EDUC graduate. ● **gafas graduadas** prescription glasses. ‖ **graduado escolar** *certificate of elementary school studies.*

gradual *adj* gradual.

graduar [11] *vt* 1 *(termómetro)* to graduate, calibrate. 2 *(regular)* to adjust, regulate. 3 *(conceder un diploma)* to confer a degree on, US graduate; *(conceder un grado)* to confer a rank. 4 *(medir)* to gauge, measure; *(la vista)* to test, check.

▷ *vpr* **graduarse** to graduate, get one's degree. ■ **graduarse la vista** to have one's eyes tested.

grafía *nf* 1 *(signo)* graphic symbol. 2 *(escritura)* writing. 3 *(ortografía)* spelling.

gráficamente *adv* graphically.

grafía *nf* graph, diagram.

gráfico,-a *adj* 1 graphic. 2 *fig (vívido)* vivid, graphic.

▷ *nm* **gráfico** *(dibujo)* sketch, chart.

grafiti *nm pl* graffiti.

grafito *nm* graphite.

gragea *nf* pill, tablet.

grajo,-a *nm & nf* rook.

gramática *nf* grammar.

gramatical *adj* grammatical.

gramático,-a *adj* grammatical.

▷ *nm & nf* grammarian.

gramíneo,-a *adj* gramineous, graminaceous.

▷ *nf pl* **gramíneas** grasses, the grass family *sing.*

gramo *nm* gram, gramme.

gramófono *nm* gramophone.

gramola [Registered trademark.] *nf* gramophone.

gran *adj* [Used before singular nouns.] 1 *(fuerte, intenso)* great: **se llevaron un gran susto** *they were terribly shocked.* 2 *(excelente)* great: **aquél era un gran libro** *that was a great book.*

See also **grande**.

granada *nf* 1 BOT pomegranate. 2 MIL grenade, shell.

granate *adj* maroon, claret.

▷ *nm* 1 *(color)* maroon, claret. 2 *(mineral)* garnet.

grande *adj* 1 *(tamaño)* large, big. 2 *(fuerte, intenso)* great: **su partida les produjo una pena muy grande** *his departure caused them great sorrow.* 3 *(mayor)* grown-up, old, big.

▷ *nm (de elevada jerarquía)* great. ■ **a lo grande** on a grand scale, in a big way. ‖ **estar grande una cosa a** ALGN to be too big on SB. ‖ **pasarlo en grande** *fam* to have a great time.

See also **gran**.

grandeza *nf* 1 *(tamaño)* size. 2 *(generosidad)* generosity.

grandioso,-a *adj* grandiose, grand, magnificent.

granel ■ **a granel** 1 *(sin envase)* in bulk. 2 *(en abundancia)* tons of, lots of.

granero *nm* granary, barn.

granítico,-a *adj* granitic, granite.

granito *nm* granite.

granívoro,-a *adj* granivorous.

granizada *nf* 1 hailstorm. 2 *fig (lluvia)* hail, shower.

granizado,-a *nm* iced drink.

granizar [4] *vi* [3rd person only; it does not take a subject.] to hail.

granizo *nm* hail, hailstone.

granja *nf* farm.

granjearse *vpr* to win, obtain, earn.

granjero,-a *nm & nf* farmer.

grano *nm* 1 grain; *(de café)* bean. 2 MED pimple, spot. ■ **ir al grano** *fam* to come to the point, get to the point.

▷ *nm pl* **granos** cereals.

granuja *nf (uva)* grapes *pl*.

▷ *nm* 1 *(pilluelo)* ragamuffin, urchin. 2 *(estafador)* crook, trickster.

granujada *nf* nasty trick.

granujería *nf* gang of rogues, gang of urchins.

granulación *nf* granulation.

granulado,-a *adj* granulated.

gránulo *nm* 1 granule. 2 *(en farmacia)* small pill.

granuloso,-a *adj* 1 *(superficie)* granular. 2 *(piel)* pimply.

grapa *nf* 1 *(para papel)* staple. 2 *(en construcción)* cramp iron. 3 *(de uvas)* bunch, bunch of grapes.

grapadora *nf* stapler.

grapar *vt* to staple.

grasa *nf* grease, fat.

grasiento,-a *adj* greasy, oily.

graso,-a *adj* greasy, oily, fatty.

grasoso,-a *adj* greasy, oily.

gratamente *adv* pleasantly.

gratén *nm* gratin.

gratificación *nf* 1 *(satisfacción)* gratification. 2 *(recompensa)* reward. 3 *(extra)* bonus.

gratificador,-ra *adj* gratifying, rewarding.
gratificante *adj* gratifying, rewarding.
gratificar [1] *vt* 1 *(satisfacer)* to gratify. 2 *(recompensar)* to reward, tip.
gratinador *nm* grill.
gratinar *vt* to cook under the grill.
gratis *adv* free.
gratitud *nf* gratitude.
grato,-a *adj* pleasant, pleasing (**para**, to).
gratuidad *nf* gratuitousness.
gratuitamente *adv* 1 *(de balde)* free of charge, free. 2 *(sin fundamento)* unfoundedly.
gratuito,-a *adj* 1 *(de balde)* free. 2 *(sin fundamento)* arbitrary, gratuitous.
grava *nf* 1 *(guijas)* gravel. 2 *(piedra machacada)* crushed stone.
gravable *adj* taxable.
gravamen *nm* 1 *(carga)* burden, obligation. 2 *(impuesto)* tax, duty.
gravar *vt* to tax.
grave *adj* 1 *(pesado)* heavy. 2 *(serio)* grave, serious. 3 *(voz, nota)* deep, low. 4 LING *(acento)* grave; *(palabra)* paroxytone. ■ **estar grave** to be seriously ill.
gravedad *nf* 1 FÍS gravity. 2 *(importancia)* seriousness.
gravemente *adv* 1 *(seriamente)* seriously. 2 *(solemnemente)* solemnly, gravely.
gravidez *nf* pregnancy. ■ **en estado de gravidez** pregnant.
grávido,-a *adj* 1 *fml (lleno)* full. 2 *(embarazada)* pregnant, gravid.
gravilla *nf* fine gravel.
gravitación *nf* gravitation.
gravitacional *adj* gravitational.
gravitar *vi* 1 FÍS to gravitate. 2 *(apoyarse en)* to rest (**sobre**, on).
gravitatorio,-a *adj* gravitational.
gravoso,-a *adj (costoso)* costly, expensive.
graznar *vi* 1 *(cuervo)* to caw, croak. 2 *(oca)* to honk. 3 *(pato)* to quack.
graznido *nm* 1 *(de cuervo)* caw, croak. 2 *(de oca)* honk. 3 *(de pato)* quack.
greca *nf* fret, fretwork.
Grecia *nf* Greece.
grecolatino,-a *adj* Graeco-Latin.
grecorromano,-a *adj* Graeco-Roman.
greda *nf* fuller's earth, clay.
gregario,-a *adj* gregarious.
gregoriano,-a *adj* Gregorian. ● **canto gregoriano** Gregorian chant.
greguería *nf* 1 *(algarabía)* hubbub. 2 LIT *type of* aphorism.
gremial *adj* 1 trade union, union. 2 HIST guild.
gremio *nm* 1 HIST guild, corporation. 2 *(sindicato)* union. 3 *(profesión)* profession.
Grenada *nf* Grenada.
greña *nf* lock of entangled hair.
▷ *nf pl* **greñas** untidy mop of hair.
gres *nm* stoneware.
gresca *nf* 1 *(bulla)* racket. 2 *(riña)* row.
griego,-a *adj* Greek.
▷ *nm & nf (persona)* Greek.
▷ *nm* **griego** *(idioma)* Greek.
grieta *nf* 1 crack, crevice. 2 *(en la piel)* chap, crack.
grifería *nf* taps *pl*, US faucets *pl*.
grifo *nm* 1 *(llave)* tap, US faucet. 2 *(animal)* griffin gryphon, griffon.
grill *nm* grill.
grillete *nm* shackle.
grillo *nm* ZOOL cricket.
grima *nf* displeasure, disgust, annoyance.
gripal *adj* related to flu.
gripe *nf* flu, influenza. ■ **tener la gripe** to have (the) flu.
griposo,-a *adj* flu. ■ **estar griposo** to have (the) flu.
gris *adj* 1 grey (US gray). 2 *fig (mediocre)* mediocre, third-rate. 3 *fig (triste)* grey (US gray), gloomy.
▷ *nm (color)* grey (US gray).
grisáceo,-a *adj* greyish.
grisalla *nf* chiaroscuro, grisaille.
grisú *nm* firedamp.
gritar *vi (gen)* to shout; *(chillar)* cry out, scream: **¡no me grites!** *don't shout at me!*
griterío *nm* shouting, uproar.
grito *nm* shout; *(chillido)* cry, scream. ■ **a grito limpio** at the top of one's voice. ‖ **dar un grito** 1 to shout. 2 *(chillar)* to scream. ‖ **el último grito** *fig* the latest thing, the last word. ‖ **pedir** ALGO **a gritos** *fig* to be crying out for STH, be badly in need of STH. ‖ **pegar un grito** 1 to shout. 2 *(chillar)* to scream.
gritón,-ona *adj* noisy, loudmouthed.
▷ *nm & nf* loudmouth.
groenlandés,-esa *adj* Greenlandic.
▷ *nm & nf (persona)* Greenlander.
▷ *nm* **groenlandés** *(idioma)* Greenlandic.
Groenlandia *nf* Greenland.
grogui *adj* 1 DEP punch-drunk, groggy. 2 *fig* groggy, half-asleep.
grosella *nf* redcurrant.
grosellero *nm* redcurrant bush.
groseramente *adv* grossly, crudely, rudely.
grosería *nf* 1 *(ordinariez)* rude word, rude expression. 2 *(rusticidad)* rudeness, coarseness. ■ **decir una grosería** to say something rude.
grosero,-a *adj* 1 *(tosco)* coarse, crude. 2 *(maleducado)* rude.
▷ *nm & nf* rude person.
grosor *nm* thickness.
grotesco,-a *adj* grotesque, ridiculous.
grúa *nf* 1 *(construcción)* crane, derrick. 2 AUTO breakdown van, US tow truck.
gruesa *nf (doce docenas)* gross.
grueso,-a *adj* 1 *(objeto)* thick. 2 *(persona)* fat, stout.
▷ *nm* **grueso** 1 *(grosor)* thickness. 2 *(parte principal)* bulk.
grulla *nf* crane.
grumete *nm* cabin boy.
grumo *nm* lump; *(de sangre)* clot; *(de leche)* curd.
grumoso,-a *adj* lumpy, clotted.
gruñido *nm* grunt, growl.
gruñir [40] *vi* to grunt.
gruñón,-ona *adj* grumbling, grumpy.
grupa *nf* croup, hindquarters *pl*.
grupi *nm o nf* groupie.
grupo *nm* 1 group. 2 TÉC unit, set. ● **grupo electrógeno** power plant. ‖ **grupo sanguíneo** blood group.
gruta *nf* cavern, grotto, cave.

gruyere *nm* gruyère.
gua *nm* 1 *(juego)* marbles *pl.* 2 *(hoyo)* hole for the marbles.
guacamayo *nm* macaw.
guache *nm* gouache.
Guadalupe *nf* Guadaloupe.
guadaña *nf* scythe.
guagua *nf* worthless thing.
gualdo,-a *adj* yellow.
guanaco *nm* guanaco.
guano *nm* 1 *(abono natural)* guano. 2 *(abono artificial)* manure, fertilizer.
guantada *nf* slap.
guantazo *nm* slap.
guante *nm* glove. ■ **echar el guante a** ALGO *fam* to nick STH.
guantera *nf* glove compartment.
guaperas *adj inv fam* good-looking, US cute.
▷ *nm o nf* good looker, looker, US cutie.
guapetón,-ona *adj fam* good-looking.
guapo,-a *adj* 1 good-looking, US cute; *(hombre)* handsome; *(mujer)* beautiful, pretty. 2 *argot (bonito)* nice, smart.
guapote,-a *adj fam* good-looking.
guapura *nf fam* good looks *pl.*
guarda *nm o nf (persona)* guard, keeper.
▷ *nf* 1 *(custodia)* custody, care. 2 *(de la ley, etc)* observance. 3 *(en cerradura - pieza fija)* ward; *(- pieza móvil)* lever. 4 *(de libro)* flyleaf.
guardabarrera *nm o nf* gatekeeper.
guardabarros *nm inv* mudguard, US fender.
guardabosque *nm* forester.
guardacoches *nm o nf inv* parking attendant.
guardacostas *nm o nf inv (persona)* coastguard.
▷ *nm* coastguard vessel.
guardaespaldas *nm o nf inv* bodyguard.
guardafrenos *nm o nf inv* guard.
guardagujas *nm o nf inv (hombre)* pointsman, US switchman; *(mujer)* pointswoman, US switchwoman.
guardameta *nm o nf* goalkeeper.
guardamuebles *nm inv* furniture warehouse.
guardapolvo *nm* 1 *(cubierta)* dust cover. 2 *(mono)* overalls *pl.*
guardar *vt* 1 *(cuidar)* to keep, watch over, keep an eye on. 2 *(conservar)* to keep, hold. 3 *(la ley)* to observe, obey; *(un secreto)* to keep. 4 *(poner en un sitio)* to put away: **guárdatelo en el bolsillo** *put it in your pocket.* 5 *(reservar)* to save, keep: **le guardaron el mejor sitio** *they saved the best seat for him.* 6 INFORMÁ to save. 7 **guardarse de** *(precaverse, evitar)* to guard against, avoid, be careful not to. ■ **guardar las formas** to be polite.
guardarropa *nm* 1 *(armario)* wardrobe. 2 *(cuarto)* cloakroom.
guardarropía *nf* wardrobe for props.
guardavía *nm (hombre)* signalman.
guardería *nf* 1 crèche, nursery. 2 *(oficio de guarda)* keeping. ● **guardería infantil** nursery, nursery school.
guardia *nf* 1 *(vigilancia)* watch, lookout. 2 *(servicio)* duty, call. 3 *(tropa)* guard.
▷ *nm o nf (hombre)* policeman; *(mujer)* policewoman. ■ **estar de guardia** 1 *(doctor)* to be on duty, be on call. 2 *(soldado)* to be on guard duty. 3 *(marino)* to be on watch. ● **farmacia de guardia** duty chemist's. ‖ **médico de guardia** doctor on duty.
guardián,-ana *nm & nf* guardian, keeper, custodian.
guardilla *nf* attic, garret.
guarecer [43] *vt* to take shelter (**de**, from), shelter (**de**, from).
guarida *nf* 1 ZOOL haunt, den, lair. 2 *pey (refugio)* hide-out.
guarnecer [43] *vt* 1 *(decorar)* to adorn, decorate; *(en cocina)* to garnish. 2 *(proveer)* to provide (**de**, with).
guarnición *nf* 1 *(gen)* decoration, trimmings *pl.* 2 *(de joya)* setting. 3 CULIN *accompaniment to a main dish.* 4 MIL garrison.
guarnicionería *nf* saddlery.
guarrada *nf* 1 *fam* something dirty, disgusting thing: **¡no hagas guarradas!** *don't do such filthy things!* 2 *fam (mala pasada)* dirty trick.
guarro,-a *adj* dirty, filthy.
▷ *nm & nf* pig, dirty pig.
guasa *nf* jest, fun, mockery. ■ **estar de guasa** to be joking.
guasón,-ona *adj* funny, joking.
▷ *nm & nf* jester, joker.
guata *nf* 1 *(algodón)* raw cotton. 2 *(relleno)* padding.
guateado,-a *adj* padded, quilted.
Guatemala *nf* Guatemala.
guatemalteco,-a *adj* Guatemalan.
▷ *nm & nf* Guatemalan.
guateque *nm* party.
guau *interj* 1 *(perro)* woof!, bow-wow! 2 *(asombro)* wow!
guay *adj fam* great, cool.
guayaba *nf* guava.
guayabera *nf* summer shirt *for men.*
guayabo *nm* guava tree.
Guayana *nf* Guiana. ● **Guayana Francesa** French Guiana.
guayanés,-esa *adj* Guianese.
▷ *nm & nf* Guianese.
guayaquileño,-a *adj* of Guayaquil, from Guayaquil.
▷ *nm & nf* person from Guayaquil, inhabitant of Guayaquil.
gubernamental *adj* government, governmental.
gubernativo,-a *adj* government, governmental.
gubia *nf* gouge.
guepardo *nm* cheetah.
guerra *nf* war. ■ **dar guerra** *fam* to cause problems, cause trouble. ‖ **declarar la guerra a** to declare war on. ● **guerra civil** civil war. ‖ **guerra fría** cold war. ‖ **guerra mundial** world war. ‖ **la Primer Guerra Mundial** World War I, the First World War. ‖ **la Segunda Guerra Mundial** World War II, the Second World War.
guerrear *vi* to war.
guerrera *nf (chaqueta)* army jacket.
guerrero,-a *adj* 1 warlike. 2 *fam (niño)* difficult.
▷ *nm & nf* warrior, soldier.
guerrilla *nf* 1 *(guerra)* guerrilla warfare. 2 *(banda)* guerrilla band.
guerrillero,-a *nm & nf* guerrilla.
gueto *nm* ghetto.

guía *nm o nf (persona)* guide, leader.
▷ *nf* **1** *(norma)* guidance, guideline. **2** *(libro)* guidebook. ● **guía de teléfonos** telephone directory, phone book.
guiar [13] *vt* **1** to guide, lead. **2** *(conducir automóvil)* to drive; *(barco)* to steer; *(avión)* to pilot; *(caballo, bici)* to ride.
▷ *vpr* **guiarse** to be guided.
guijarral *nm* pebbly place.
guijarro *nm* pebble, stone.
guillarse *vpr* **1** *fam (chiflarse)* to become a real loony, go bonkers. **2** *fam (escabullirse)* to get away.
guillotina *nf* guillotine.
guillotinar *vt* to guillotine.
guinda *nf* **1** *(fruta)* sour cherry, morello cherry. **2** *(remate)* finishing touch, final touch.
guindilla *nf* **1** red pepper, chilli. **2** *fam (policía)* cop.
guindo *nm* morello cherry tree. ■ **caerse** ALGN **del guindo** *fam* to cotton on, twig.
guinea *nf* guinea.
Guinea *nf* Guinea. ● **Guinea Ecuatorial** Equatorial Guinea. ‖ **Guinea-Bissau** Guinea-Bissau. ‖ **Nueva Guinea** New Guinea.
guineano,-a *adj* Guinean.
▷ *nm & nf* Guinean.
guiñapo *nm* **1** *(andrajo)* rag, tatter. **2** *fig (persona)* wreck.
guiñar *vt* **1** to wink: **me guiñó un ojo** *he winked at me.* **2** MAR to yaw.
guiño *nm* wink.
guiñol *nm* puppet theatre.
guiñolesco,-a *adj* like a puppet show.
guion *nm* **1** *(esquema)* notes *pl*, sketch, outline. **2** GRAM hyphen, dash. **3** CINE script. **4** *(estandarte)* standard, banner.
guionista *nm o nf* scriptwriter.
guipar *vt* **1** *fam (ver)* to see, spot. **2** *fam (descubrir)* to see through.
guiri *nm o nf argot* foreigner.
guirigay *nm* **1** *(lenguaje)* gibberish. **2** *(griterío)* racket, noise, din.
guirlache *nm* almond brittle.
guirnalda *nf* garland, wreath.
guisa *nf* manner, way.
guisado,-a *adj* cooked, stewed.
▷ *nm* **guisado** stew.
guisante *nm* pea.
guisar *vt* to cook, stew.
▷ *vpr* **guisarse** to cook, stew:
guiso *nm* stew.
güisqui *nm* whisky.
guita *nf argot* dough, bread. ■ **quedarse sin guita** *argot* to be broke.
guitarra *nf* guitar.
▷ *nm o nf* guitarist.
guitarrero,-a *nm & nf* **1** *(vendedor)* guitar seller. **2** *(fabricante)* guitar maker.
guitarrillo *nm* small four-string guitar.
guitarrista *nm o nf* guitarist.
gula *nf* gluttony.
guripa *nm* **1** *fam (soldado)* soldier. **2** *fam (policía)* cop **3** *fam (granuja)* scoundrel.
gurmet *nm o nf* gourmet.
▲ *pl* **gurmets.**
gurriato *nm* **1** *(ave)* young sparrow. **2** *fam (niño)* kid, nipper.
gurú *nm* guru.
gusanillo *nm* **1** little worm. **2** *(espiral)* spiral binding. **3** *(intranquilidad)* niggling doubt. ■ **matar el gusanillo** *fam* to have a snack.
gusano *nm* **1** worm; *(oruga)* caterpillar. **2** *fig (persona)* worm. ● **gusano de seda** silkworm.
gustar *vt* **1** *(agradar)* to like. **2** *(probar)* to taste, try.
gustativo,-a *adj* gustative. ● **papila gustativa** taste bud.
gustazo *nm fam* great pleasure. ■ **darse el gustazo de** ALGO *fam* to take great pleasure in STH, take great delight in STH.
gustillo *nm* **1** *fam (regusto)* aftertaste. **2** *fam (satisfacción)* satisfaction, pleasure.
gusto *nm* **1** *(sentido, sabor)* taste. **2** *(inclinación)* liking, taste. **3** *(placer)* pleasure: **tengo el gusto de presentarle a mi hermano** *may I introduce you to my brother?* **4** *(capricho)* whim, fancy. ■ **con mucho gusto** with pleasure. ‖ **dar gusto** to please, delight: **me da gusto verla comer** *I enjoy watching her eat.* ‖ **estar a gusto** to feel comfortable, feel at ease. ‖ **hacer** ALGO **a gusto** to enjoy doing STH. ‖ **hacer** ALGO **por gusto** to do STH for fun. ‖ **¡qué gusto!** how lovely! ‖ **tanto gusto** pleased to meet you. ‖ **tener buen gusto** to have good taste.
gustosamente *adv* with pleasure, gladly, willingly.
gustoso,-a *adj* **1** *(sabroso)* tasty, savoury, palatable. **2** *(agradable)* agreeable, pleasant. **3** *(con gusto)* glad, willing, ready: **aceptó gustosa** *she accepted willingly.*
gutapercha *nf* gutta-percha.
gutural *adj* guttural.
Guyana *nf* Guyana.
guyanés,-esa *adj* Guyanese.
▷ *nm & nf* Guyanese.
gymkhana *nf* gymkhana.

H

H, h *nf (la letra)* H, h.
ha *sím* (hectárea) hectare; *(símbolo)* ha.
haba *nf (legumbre)* broad bean.
habanera *nf* music and dance from Havana.
habano ,-a *adj* of Havana, from Havana.
▷ *nm* **habano** Havana cigar.
haber [72] *vi (impersonal)* to be: **hay un coche** *there's a car.*
▷ *aux* **1** *(en tiempos compuestos)* to have: **lo has hecho** *you have done it.* **2 haber de +** *infin (obligación)* to have to, must, should: **han de venir hoy** *they must come today.* **3 haber que +** *infin (obligación)* must, have to: **habrá que hacerlo** *we'll have to do it.* ■ **¡haberlo dicho!** why didn't you say so! ‖ **había una vez...** once upon a time there was..., there was once... ‖ **¡habráse visto!** what a cheek! ‖ **¡hay que ver!** well, really!, well, I never! ‖ **no hay de qué** you're welcome, don't mention it. ‖ **no hay (nada) como...** there's nothing like... ‖ **¿qué hay?** hello!, hi!, how are you doing? ‖ **ser de lo que no hay** *fam* to be impossible.
▷ *nm* COM credit, assets *pl.*
▷ *nm pl* **haberes 1** *(posesiones)* property *sing*, assets. **2** *(sueldo)* salary *sing*, pay *sing*, wages.
habichuela *nf (gen)* bean; *(judía blanca)* haricot bean; *(judía verde)* French bean, green bean.
hábil *adj* **1** *(diestro)* skilful (US skillful). **2** *(despabilado)* clever, smart. **3** *(acto)* clever. **4** *(apto, adecuado)* good, suitable. ■ **ser hábil en** ALGO **/ ser hábil para** ALGO *(persona)* to be good at STH. ● **día hábil** working day.
habilidad *nf* **1** *(aptitud)* skill. **2** *(astucia)* cleverness, smartness. ■ **tener habilidad para** ALGO to be good at STH.
habilidoso ,-a *adj* skilful (US skillful), clever.
habilitar *vt* **1** *(espacio)* to fit out; *(tiempo)* to set aside: **habilitó una habitación para consulta** *he fitted a bedroom out as a consulting room.* **2** *(capacitar)* to entitle, qualify; *(autorizar)* to empower, authorize.
habitable *adj* habitable, livable, liveable.
habitación *nf* **1** *(gen)* room. **2** *(dormitorio)* bedroom. ● **habitación doble** double room. ‖ **habitación individual** single room.
habitáculo *nm (vivienda)* dwelling.
habitante *nm o nf* inhabitant.
habitar *vt* to live in, inhabit.
▷ *vi* to live.
hábitat *nm* habitat.
▲ *pl* **hábitats.**
hábito *nm* **1** *(costumbre)* habit, custom. **2** *(vestido)* habit. ■ **tener el hábito de...** to be in the habit of...
habitual *adj* **1** usual, habitual, customary. **2** *(asiduo)* regular.
habitualmente *adv (repetidamente)* usually; *(regularmente)* regularly.
habituar [11] *vt* to accustom (**a**, to).
▷ *vpr* **habituarse** to become accustomed (**a**, to), get used (**a**, to) .
habla [Takes **el** in singular.] *nf* **1** *(facultad)* speech. **2** *(idioma)* language; *(dialecto)* dialect. ■ **de habla española / de habla hispana** Spanish-speaking. ‖ **estar al habla con** ALGN to be in touch with SB. ‖ **perder el habla** to lose one's power of speech.
hablado ,-a *adj* spoken, oral: **francés hablado** *spoken French.*
hablador ,-ra *adj* **1** *(parlanchín)* talkative. **2** *(chismoso)* gossipy.
habladuría [Also used in plural with the same meaning .] *nf (chisme)* piece of gossip; *(rumor)* rumour (US rumor).
hablante *adj* speaking.
▷ *nm o nf* speaker.
hablar *vi* **1** *(gen)* to speak, talk: **habló conmigo** *he spoke to me.* **2** *(mencionar)* to talk, mention: **no me habló de eso** *she didn't mention that.* ■ **hablar a solas** to talk to OS. ‖ **hablar bajo** to speak softly. ‖ **hablar claro** to speak plainly. ‖ **hablar en broma** to be joking. ‖ **hablar en nombre de** ALGN to speak on SB's behalf. ‖ **¡quién fue a hablar!** look who's talking!
▷ *vt* **1** *(idioma)* to speak: **habla francés** *he speaks French.* **2** *(tratar)* to talk over, discuss: **ya lo hablaremos después** *we'll discuss it later.* ■ **«Se habla inglés»** «English spoken».
▷ *vpr* **hablarse** *(uso recíproco)* to speak, talk: **ayer nos hablamos por teléfono** *we spoke on the 'phone yesterday.* ■ **no hablarse con** ALGN not to be on speaking terms with SB.
hacendado ,-a *adj* landed.
▷ *nm & nf* landowner.
hacendoso ,-a *adj* house-proud, hard-working.
hacer [73] *vt* **1** *(producir, fabricar, crear)* to make: **hice un pastel** *I made a cake;* **¿has hecho los deberes?** *have you done your homework?* **2** *(arreglar, disponer - uñas)* to do; *(- barba)* to trim; *(- cama)* to make; *(- maleta)* to pack. **3** *(obrar, ejecutar)* to do: **haz lo que quieras** *do what you want.* **4** *(conseguir - amigos, dinero)* to make. **5** *(obligar)* to make: **nos hizo leer** *she made us read.* **6** *(recorrer)* to do: **hacer noventa kilómetros por hora** *to do ninety kilometres per hour.* **7** *(en suma)* to make: **con esta hacen ochenta** *that makes eighty.* **8** *(ocupar un lugar)* to be: **él hace el número cuatro** *he's the fourth on the list.* **9** *(hacer parecer)* to make look: **ese vestido te hace mayor** *that dress*

makes you look older. **10** *(acostumbrar)* to accustom. **11** *(practicar)* to do: **¿haces deporte?** *do you do any sport?* ■ **a medio hacer** half-done, half-finished. ‖ **¡así se hace!** that's it! ‖ **¿hace?** OK? ‖ **hace mucho** a long time ago. ‖ **hacer bien en...** to be right to...: **hice bien en ir** *I was right to go.* ‖ **hacer el ridículo** to make a fool of OS. ‖ **hacer gracia** to amuse. ‖ **hacer mal** to do the wrong thing. ‖ **hacer tiempo** to kill time.

▷ *vi* **1** *(actuar)* to play (**de**, -); *(representar)* to act: **hizo de abuela** *she played the grandmother.* **2** *(comportarse)* to pretend to be, act: **hacer el tonto** *to act the fool.* **3** *(clima)* to be: **hace buen día** *it's a fine day.* **4** *(tiempo pasado)* ago: **hace tres años** *three years ago.* ■ **hacer como que +** *ind* to pretend, act as if: **hizo como que no sabía nada** *he acted as if he knew nothing.* ‖ **hacer como si +** *subj* to pretend, act as if: **hizo como si supiera la verdad** *she acted as if she knew the truth.*

▷ *vpr* **hacerse 1** *(volverse)* to become, get: **hacerse rico** *to get rich.* **2** *(crecer)* to grow: **se ha hecho mucho** *he's grown a lot.* **3** *(resultar)* to become, go on, seem: **la película se hizo muy larga** *the film went on too long, I found the film too long.* **4** *(simular)* to pretend: **se hizo la elegante** *she pretended to be elegant.* **5** *(mandar hacer)* to have made, have done: **me hice un vestido en la modista** *I had a dress made at the dressmaker's.* ■ **hacerse el/la sordo,-a** *fig* to turn a deaf ear. ‖ **hacerse una idea de ALGO** to imagine STH.

hacha [Takes **el** in singular.] *nf (instrumento)* axe (US ax).

hache *nf (la letra)* aitch.

hachís *nm* hashish.

hacia *prep* **1** *(dirección)* towards, to. **2** *(tiempo)* at about, at around: **estaremos ahí hacia las dos** *we'll be there at about two.* ■ **hacia abajo** downward(s), down. ‖ **hacia acá** this way. ‖ **hacia adelante** forward(s): **inclínate hacia delante** *lean forward.* ‖ **hacia allá** that way. ‖ **hacia atrás** backward(s), back. ‖ **hacia casa** home, homeward, towards home.

hacienda *nf* **1** *(bienes)* property, wealth, possessions *pl.* **2** *(finca)* estate, property, US ranch. **3** FIN Treasury. ● **hacienda pública** public funds *pl,* public finances *pl.* ‖ **Ministerio de Hacienda** Finance Ministry, GB Exchequer, US Treasury.

hacinamiento *nm (de cosas)* piling, heaping; *(de personas)* overcrowding.

hacinar *vt* **1** AGR to stack. **2** *fig (amontonar)* to pile up, heap up.

▷ *vpr* **hacinarse** *fig (personas)* to be packed, be crowded.

hada [Takes **el** in singular.] *nf* fairy.

hado *nm* destiny, fate.

Haití *nm* Haiti.

haitiano ,-a *adj* Haitian.

▷ *nm & nf* Haitian.

hala *interj* **1** *(dar prisa)* go on!, get moving! **2** *(infundir ánimo)* come on! **3** *(sorpresa)* oh dear! **4** *(fuera)* clear off!, get out! **5** *(exageración)* come off it!

halagador ,-ra *adj* flattering.

halagar [7] *vt* **1** *(lisonjear)* to flatter. **2** *(satisfacer)* to please.

halago *nm* compliment, flattery.

halcón *nm* falcon.

hale *interj* **1** *(dar prisa)* get going!, get a move on! **2** *(sorpresa)* oh dear!

hálito *nm* **1** *(aliento)* breath. **2** *(vapor)* vapour (US vapor). **3** *lit* gentle breeze.

halitosis *nf inv* halitosis, bad breath.

hallar *vt* **1** *(encontrar)* to find. **2** *(averiguar)* to find out; *(descubrir)* to discover. **3** *(ver, notar)* to see, observe.

▷ *vpr* **hallarse** *(estar)* to be: **se hallaba enfermo** *he was ill.*

hallazgo *nm* **1** *(descubrimiento)* finding, discovery. **2** *(cosa descubierta)* find.

halo *nm* halo, aura.

halógeno ,-a *adj* halogenous.

halterofilia *nf* weightlifting.

hamaca *nf* **1** *(de red)* hammock. **2** *(tumbona)* deck chair.

hambre [Takes **el** in singular.] *nf* hunger, starvation, famine. ■ **matar el hambre** *fig* to stave off hunger. ‖ **pasar hambre** to be hungry, go hungry. ‖ **ser más listo, -a que el hambre** *fig* to be a cunning devil. ‖ **tener hambre** to be hungry.

hambriento ,-a *adj* **1** hungry, starving. **2** *fig* hungry, longing: **hambriento de justicia** *longing for justice.*

hambruna *nf* famine.

hamburguesa *nf* hamburger, beefburger.

hamburguesería *nf* hamburger restaurant.

hampa [Takes **el** in singular.] *nf* underworld.

hámster *nm* hamster.

▲ *pl* **hámsters.**

hándicap *nm* handicap.

▲ *pl* **hándicaps.**

haragán ,-ana *adj* lazy, idle.

▷ *nm & nf* lazybones, idler.

haraganear *vi* to idle, loaf around.

harapiento ,-a *adj* ragged, tattered, in rags.

harapo *nm* rag, tatter.

hardware *nm* hardware.

harén *nm* harem.

▲ *pl* **harenes.**

harina *nf* flour.

harpillera *nf* burlap.

hartar *vt* **1** *(atiborrar)* to satiate, fill up. **2** *fig (deseo, etc)* to satisfy. **3** *(fastidiar)* to annoy, irritate: **me harta con sus tonterías** *his silly remarks get on my nerves.* **4** *(cansar)* to tire, bore.

▷ *vpr* **hartarse 1** *(atiborrarse)* to eat one's fill, stuff OS. **2** *(cansarse)* to get fed up (**de**, with), get tired (**de**, of): **me harté de esperarla** *I got tired of waiting for her.* ■ **hasta hartarse** to repletion.

harto ,-a *adj* **1** *(repleto)* full, satiated. **2** *fam (cansado)* tired (**de**, of), fed up (**de**, with): **estoy harto de leer** *I'm tired of reading.*

▷ *adv* **harto** *en desuso (muy)* quite, very: **harto bueno** *very good.*

hasta *prep* **1** *(tiempo)* until, till, up to: **hasta el sábado** *until Saturday;* **desde las diez hasta las dos** *from ten to two.* **2** *(lugar)* as far as, up to, down to. **3** *(cantidad)* up to, as many as. **4** *(incluso)* even: **hasta sabe escribir** *she even knows how to write.* **5** *(como despedida)* → **see you. ¡hasta mañana!** *see you tomorrow!* ■ **desde... hasta...** from... to... ‖ **¿hasta cuándo?** until when?, how long? ‖ **hasta que** until.

hastiar [13] *vt* to bore.

▷ *vpr* **hastiarse** to get sick (**de**, of), get tired (**de**, of).
hastío *nm* 1 *(repugnancia)* disgust, loathing. 2 *fig (aburrimiento)* boredom, weariness.
hatajo *nm* 1 small herd, small flock. 2 *fig* heap, lot, bunch: **un hatajo de disparates** *a load of nonsense.*
hatillo *nm* small bundle.
Hawai *nm* Hawaii.
hawaiano ,-a *adj* Hawaian.
▷ *nm & nf* Hawaian.
haya *nf* 1 BOT beech. 2 *(madera)* beech, beech wood.
hayedo *nm* beech groove.
hayuco *nm* beechnut.
haz *nm* 1 *(de cosas)* bundle. 2 *(de mieses, etc)* sheaf. 3 *(de luz)* shaft, beam.
▲ *pl* **haces.**
hazaña *nf* deed, exploit, heroic feat.
hazmerreír *nm* laughing stock.
he *interj* hey!
hebilla *nf* buckle.
hebra *nf* 1 *(de hilo)* thread, piece of thread. 2 *(de carne)* sinew; *(de legumbre)* string; *(de madera)* grain; *(de planta)* strand.
hebreo ,-a *adj* Hebrew.
▷ *nm & nf (persona)* Hebrew.
▷ *nm* **hebreo** *(idioma)* Hebrew.
hecatombe *nf* 1 HIST hecatomb. 2 *(desgracia)* disaster, catastrophe.
hechicería *nf* 1 *(arte)* sorcery, witchcraft. 2 *(hechizo)* spell, charm.
hechicero ,-a *nm & nf (hombre)* sorcerer, wizard; *(mujer)* sorceress, witch.
hechizar [4] *vt* 1 *(embrujar)* to bewitch, cast a spell on. 2 *fig (cautivar)* to charm, bewitch.
hechizo *nm* 1 *(embrujo)* charm, spell. 2 *fig (embelesamiento)* fascination, charm.
hecho ,-a *adj* 1 *(carne)* done. 2 *(persona)* mature. 3 *(frase, expresión)* set. 4 *(ropa)* ready-made. ■ **¡bien hecho!** well done! ‖ **de hecho** in fact. ‖ **estar hecho,-a un,-a...** to be...: **está hecho un vago** *he's a real waster.* ‖ **hecho,-a a mano** handmade. ‖ **lo hecho hecho está** what's done is done. ‖ **muy hecho,-a** 1 *(carne)* well-cooked. 2 *(pasada)* overdone. ‖ **ser un hombre hecho y derecho** to be a real man.
▷ *nm* **hecho** 1 *(realidad)* fact. 2 *(suceso)* event, incident.
hectárea *nf* hectare.
hectogramo *nm* hectogramme (US hectogram).
hectolitro *nm* hectolitre (US hectoliter).
hectómetro *nm* hectometre (US hectometer).
hectovatio *nm* hectowatt.
hediondez *nf* stink, stench.
hediondo ,-a *adj (apestoso)* stinking, foul-smelling.
hedonismo *nm* hedonism.
hedonista *adj* hedonistic, hedonic.
▷ *nm o nf* hedonist.
hedor *nm* stink, stench.
hegemonía *nf* hegemony.
hégira *nf* Hegira, Hejira.
helada *nf* METEOR frost.
heladera *nf* 1 *(nevera)* refrigerator. 2 *(máquina de helados)* ice-cream maker.
heladería *nf* ice-cream parlour (US parlor).
heladero ,-a *nm & nf (hombre)* ice-cream man; *(mujer)* ice-cream woman.
helado ,-a *adj* 1 *(gen)* frozen: **estoy helado** *I'm frozen.* 2 *(muy frío)* icy, freezing cold. 3 *(café, té)* iced. 4 *fig (pasmado)* dumbfounded. ■ **dejar a** ALGN **helado,-a** to stun SB.
▷ *nm* **helado** ice-cream.
helador ,-ra *adj* icy, freezing.
helar [27] *vt* 1 *(congelar)* to freeze. 2 *(plantas)* to kill, freeze.
▷ *vi* [Used only in the 3rd person; it does not take a subject.] METEOR to freeze: **anoche heló** *it froze last night.*
▷ *vpr* **helarse** 1 *(congelarse)* to freeze: **el estanque se ha helado** *the pond has frozen over.* 2 *(planta)* to be killed by frost. 3 *(persona)* to freeze, freeze to death: **me estoy helando** *I'm freezing.*
helecho *nm* fern.
helenismo *nm* Hellenism.
helenístico ,-a *adj* Hellenistic, Hellenistical.
heleno ,-a *adj* Hellene, Hellenian, Greek.
▷ *nm & nf* Hellene, Greek.
heliaco ,-a *adj* heliacal.
hélice *nf* 1 *(espiral)* helix. 2 *(propulsor)* propeller.
helicoidal *adj* helicoidal.
helicóptero *nm* helicopter.
helio *nm* helium.
heliocéntrico ,-a *adj* heliocentric.
heliograbado *nm* photogravure.
heliografía *nf* heliography.
heliotropo *nm* heliotrope.
helipuerto *nm* heliport.
Helvecia *nf* Helvetia.
helvético ,-a *adj* Helvetian, Swiss.
▷ *nm & nf* Helvetian, Swiss.
hematíe *nm* red blood corpuscle.
hematites *nf inv* haematite (US hematite).
hematología *nf* haematology (US hematology).
hematoma *nm* haematoma (US hematoma), bruise.
hembra *nf* 1 *(animal)* female. 2 *(mujer)* woman. 3 TÉC female.
hemeroteca *nf* newspaper library.
hemiciclo *nm* 1 *(semicírculo)* hemicycle. 2 *(parlamento)* floor.
hemiplejia *nf* hemiplegia.
hemipléjico ,-a *adj* hemiplegic.
hemíptero *nm* hemipteran.
hemisférico ,-a *adj* hemispheric, hemispherical.
hemisferio *nm* hemisphere.
hemodiálisis *nf inv* haemodialysis (US hemodialysis).
hemofilia *nf* haemophilia (US hemophilia).
hemoglobina *nf* haemoglobin (US hemoglobin).
hemorragia *nf* haemorrhage (US hemorrhage). ● **hemorragia nasal** nosebleed.
hemorroide *nf* haemorrhoid (US hemorrhoid).
▷ *nf pl* **hemorroides** piles, haemorrhoids (US hemorrhoids).
henchir [34] *vt (llenar)* to fill (**de**, with), stuff (**de**, with), cram (**de**, with).

hender [28] *vt* 1 *(cortar)* to cleave, split, crack. 2 *fig (agua, olas)* to cut. 3 *fig (abrirse paso)* to make one's way through.
hendidura *nf* cleft, crack.
heno *nm* hay.
hepático ,-a *adj* hepatic, liver.
hepatitis *nf inv* hepatitis.
heptaedro *nm* heptahedron.
heptagonal *adj* heptagonal.
heptágono ,-a *adj* heptagonal.
▷ *nm* **heptágono** heptagon.
heptasílabo ,-a *adj* heptasyllabic.
▷ *nm* **heptasílabo** heptasyllable.
heráldica *nf* heraldry.
herbario ,-a *adj* herbal.
▷ *nm & nf (botánico)* botanist.
▷ *nm* **herbario** *(colección)* herbarium.
herbicida *nm* weedkiller, herbicide.
herbívoro ,-a *adj* herbivorous, grass-eating.
▷ *nm & nf* herbivore.
herbolario ,-a *nm & nf (persona)* herbalist.
▷ *adj fig (botarate)* crazy, foolish.
▷ *nm* **herbolario** *(tienda)* herbalist's (shop).
herboristería *nf* herbalist's (shop).
hercio *nm* hertz.
hercúleo ,-a *adj* Herculean.
heredable *adj* inheritable.
heredad *nf* 1 *(terreno)* country estate. 2 *(bienes)* private estate, property.
heredar *vt* 1 to inherit. 2 *fig* to inherit: **ha heredado los ojos de su padre** *he's got his father's eyes.*
heredero ,-a *nm & nf (hombre)* heir; *(mujer)* heiress.
hereditario ,-a *adj* hereditary.
hereje *nm o nf* 1 heretic. 2 *fig (descarado)* rascal.
herejía *nf* 1 heresy. 2 *fam fig (disparate)* nonsense.
herencia *nf* 1 inheritance, legacy. 2 *(genética)* heredity.
herético ,-a *adj* heretical.
herida *nf* 1 wound. 2 *fig* wound, outrage.
herido ,-a *adj* 1 *(físicamente)* wounded, injured, hurt: **el niño resultó herido** *the boy was injured.* 2 *fig (emocionalmente)* hurt, wounded. ■ **herido,-a de gravedad** badly injured.
▷ *nm & nf* wounded person, injured person.
herir [35] *vt* 1 *(dañar)* to wound, injure, hurt. 2 *fig (ofender)* to hurt, offend.
hermafrodita *adj* hermaphrodite.
▷ *nm o nf* hermaphrodite.
hermanado ,-a *adj* 1 *fig (semejante)* similar, alike. 2 *(a juego)* matched. 3 *(ciudad, pueblo)* twinned.
hermanar *vt* 1 *(unir)* to unite, join. 2 *(combinar)* to combine. 3 *(personas)* to unite spiritually. 4 *(ciudades)* to twin.
hermanastro ,-a *nm & nf (hombre)* stepbrother; *(mujer)* stepsister.
hermandad *nf (de hermanos)* fraternity, brotherhood; *(de hermanas)* fraternity, sisterhood.
hermano ,-a *nm & nf (hombre)* brother; *(mujer)* sister: **¿cuántos hermanos tienes?** *how many brothers and sisters have you got?*
hermenéutica *nf* hermeneutics *sing.*
herméticamente *adv* hermetically.
hermético ,-a *adj* 1 hermetic, hermetical, airtight. 2 *fig* impenetrable, secretive.
hermetismo *nm* 1 hermetism. 2 *fig* impenetrability, secrecy, secretiveness.
hermoso ,-a *adj* 1 *(gen)* beautiful, lovely: **hace un día hermoso** *it's a lovely day.* 2 *(hombre)* handsome.
hermosura *adj (cualidad - de mujer, lugar)* beauty, loveliness; *(- de hombre)* handsomeness.
▷ *nf* 1 *(mujer hermosa)* beautiful woman, beauty. 2 *(persona, cosa)* beautiful thing.
hernia *nf* hernia, rupture.
herniarse [12] *vpr* to rupture OS.
héroe *nm* hero.
heroicamente *adv* heroically.
heroico ,-a *adj* heroic.
heroína *nf* 1 *(mujer)* heroine. 2 *(droga)* heroin.
heroísmo *nm* heroism.
herpes *nm inv* herpes, shingles.
herradura *nf* horseshoe.
herraje *nm* iron fittings *pl*, ironwork.
herramienta *nf* tool.
herrar [27] *vt* 1 *(caballo)* to shoe. 2 *(ganado)* to brand.
herrería *nf* 1 *(fábrica)* ironworks *pl.* 2 *(taller)* forge, smithy, blacksmith's.
herrerillo *nm* great tit.
herrero *nm* blacksmith, smith.
herrumbre *nf* 1 *(óxido)* rust. 2 *(sabor)* rusty taste.
hervir [35] *vt* to boil.
▷ *vi* 1 to boil: **el agua ya hierve** *the water is boiling.* 2 *fig (el mar)* to surge.
hervor *nm* boiling, bubbling. ■ **dar un hervor a ALGO** to blanch STH.
heterodoxia *nf* heterodoxy.
heterodoxo ,-a *adj* heterodox, unorthodox.
heterogéneo ,-a *adj* heterogeneous.
heterónomo ,-a *adj* heteronomous.
heterosexual *adj* heterosexual.
▷ *nm o nf* heterosexual.
hexaedro *nm* hexahedron.
hexagonal *adj* hexagonal.
hexágono *nm* hexagon.
hexámetro *nm* hexameter.
Hg *sím* **(hectogramo)** hectogramme; *(símbolo)* Hg.
hiato *nm* hiatus.
hibernación *nf* hibernation.
hibernar *vi* to hibernate.
hibisco *nm* hibiscus.
híbrido ,-a *adj* hybrid.
▷ *nm & nf* hybrid.
hidalgo ,-a *nm* **hidalgo** nobleman, gentleman.
hidra *nf* 1 *(culebra)* sea snake. 2 *(pólipo)* hydra.
hidrácido *nm* hydracid.
hidratación *nf* 1 hydration. 2 *(de la piel)* moisturizing.
hidratante *adj* moisturizing.
▷ *nf* moisturizing cream.
hidratar *vt* 1 to hydrate. 2 *(piel)* to moisturize.
hidrato *nm* hydrate. ● **hidrato de carbono** carbohydrate.
hidráulica *nf* hydraulics *sing.*
hidráulico ,-a *adj* hydraulic.
hídrico ,-a *adj* hydric.

hidroavión *nm* seaplane, US hydroplane.
hidrocarburo *nm* hydrocarbon.
hidrodinámico ,-a *adj* hydrodynamic.
hidroeléctrico ,-a *adj* hydroelectric.
hidrófilo ,-a *adj* 1 *(organismo)* hydrophilous. 2 *(absorbente)* absorbent: **algodón hidrófilo** *cotton wool, US absorbent cotton.*
hidrófugo ,-a *adj* water-repellent.
hidrógeno *nm* hydrogen.
hidrográfico ,-a *adj* hydrographic.
hidrólisis *nf inv* hydrolysis.
hidrolizar [4] *vt* to hydrolyse.
hidromasaje ● **bañera de hidromasaje** Jacuzzi®, whirlpool bath.
hidroplano *nm* 1 *(hidroavión)* seaplane, US hydroplane. 2 *(embarcación)* hydroplane.
hidrosfera *nf* hydrosphere.
hidrosoluble *adj* soluble in water.
hidrostático ,-a *adj* hydrostatic.
hidroterapia *nf* hydrotherapy.
hidróxido *nm* hydroxide.
hiedra *nf* ivy.
hiel *nf* 1 bile. 2 *fig* bitterness, gall.
hielo *nm* 1 ice. 2 *fig (frialdad)* coldness. ● **cubito de hielo** ice cube.
hiena *nf* hyaena, hyena.
hierático ,-a *adj (rígido)* rigid.
hierba *nf* 1 grass. 2 CULIN herb. 3 *argot (marihuana)* grass.
▷ *nf pl* **hierbas** 1 *(veneno)* poison *sing*, potion *sing*. 2 *(pastos)* grass *sing*, pastureland *sing*. ● **finas hierbas** mixed herbs.
hierbabuena *nf* mint.
hierbajo *nm* weed.
hierro *nm* 1 *(metal)* iron. 2 *(punta)* head, point. 3 *(marca)* brand. 4 *fig (arma)* steel, weapon. ● **hierro forjado** wrought iron. ‖ **hierro fundido** cast iron.
hígado *nm* liver.
higiene *nf* hygiene.
higiénico ,-a *adj* hygienic.
higienista *nm o nf* hygienist.
higienizar [4] *vt* to make hygienic.
higo *nm* fig. ■ **de higos a brevas** *fig* once in a blue moon. ● **higo chumbo** prickly pear.
higuera *nf* fig tree.
hijastro ,-a *nm & nf (niño, niña)* stepchild; *(hijo)* stepson; *(hija)* stepdaughter.
hijo ,-a *nm & nf (niño, niña)* child; *(chico)* son; *(chica)* daughter: **tiene dos hijos y dos hijas** *he has two sons and two daughters.*
▷ *nm pl* **hijos** children: **tiene cuatro hijos** *she has four children.* ● **hijo,-a adoptivo,-a** 1 *(niño, niña)* adopted child. 2 *(chico)* adopted son. 3 *(chica)* adopted daughter. ‖ **hijo,-a único,-a** 1 *(niño, niña)* only child. 2 *(chico)* only son. 3 *(chica)* only daughter.
hilacha *nf* 1 *(hilacho)* loose thread. 2 *(resto)* rest.
hilada *nf* 1 *(hilacho)* loose thread. 2 *(de ladrillos)* course.
hilado ,-a *adj* spun.
▷ *nm* **hilado** 1 *(operación)* spinning. 2 *(hilo)* thread. ● **fábrica de hilados** spinning mill.
hilandería *nf* 1 *(arte)* spinning. 2 *(fábrica)* spinning mill; *(de algodón)* cotton mill.
hilandero ,-a *nm & nf* spinner.
hilar *vt* 1 to spin. 2 *fig* to work out.
hilarante *adj* hilarious: **gas hilarante** *laughing gas.*
hilaridad *nf fml* hilarity, mirth.
hilatura *nf* 1 *(arte)* spinning. 2 *(industria)* spinning mill.
hilera *nf (línea)* line, row.
hilo *nm* 1 thread; *(grueso)* yarn. 2 *(lino)* linen. 3 *(alambre, cable)* wire. 4 *fig (de luz)* thread, thin beam; *(de líquido)* trickle, thin stream. 5 *fig (de historia, discurso)* thread; *(de pensamiento)* train. 6 *fig (de la vida)* course. ■ **estar pendiente de un hilo** *fig* to be hanging by a thread. ‖ **mover los hilos** *fig* to pull the strings. ‖ **perder el hilo** *fig* to lose the thread. ● **hilo musical** piped music, Musak.
hilván *nm* 1 *(costura)* tacking, basting. 2 *(punto)* tack, tacking stitch, basting stitch.
hilvanar *vt* 1 to tack, baste. 2 *fig* to put together, outline.
himenóptero ,-a *nm* **himenóptero** hymenopteran.
himno *nm* hymn. ● **himno nacional** national anthem.
hincapié ■ **hacer hincapié** *(insistir)* to insist on. *(subrayar)* to emphasize (**en**, -), put emphasis (**en**, on), stress (**en**, -).
hincar [1] *vt* 1 *(clavar)* to drive (in). 2 *(apoyar)* to set firmly.
hincha *nm o nf* DEP fan, supporter.
hinchada *nf* DEP *fam* fans *pl*, supporters *pl*.
hinchado,-a *adj* 1 *(inflado)* inflated, blown up. 2 *(piel)* swollen, puffed up; *(estómago)* bloated.
hinchar *vt* 1 *(inflar)* to inflate, blow up; *(con bomba)* to pump up: **hinchar un globo** *to blow up a balloon.* 2 *fig (exagerar)* to inflate, blow up, exaggerate.
▷ *vpr* **hincharse** 1 MED to swell (up): **se me ha hinchado el pie** *my foot has swollen up.* 2 *fam (comer)* to stuff OS.
hinchazón *nf* swelling, inflation.
hindi *nm* Hindi.
hindú *adj* Hindu.
▷ *nm o nf* Hindu.
hinduismo *nm* Hinduism.
hinojo *nm* BOT fennel.
hipar *vi (tener hipo)* to hiccup, hiccough, have the hiccups, have the hiccoughs.
hiperactivo ,-a *adj* hyperactive.
hipérbaton *nm* hyperbaton.
hipérbole *nf* hyperbole.
hiperbólico ,-a *adj* hyperbolic, hyperbolical.
hipercrítico ,-a *adj* hypercritical.
hiperglucemia *nf* hyperglycaemia (US hyperglycemia).
hypermedia *nf* hypermedia.
hipermercado *nm* hypermarket, superstore.
hipermétrope *adj* long-sighted.
▷ *nm o nf* long-sighted person.
hipermetropía *nf* long-sightedness.
hipersensible *adj* hypersensitive.
hipertensión *nf* high blood pressure, hypertension.
hipertenso ,-a *adj* hypertensive.
▷ *nm & nf* hypertensive.
hipertexto *nm* hypertext.

hipertextual *adj* hypertext: **un salto hipertextual** *a hypertext link.*
hípica *nf* horse riding.
hípico ,-a *adj* horse, equestrian.
hipnosis *nf inv* hypnosis.
hipnótico ,-a *adj* hypnotic.
hipnotismo *nm* hypnotism.
hipnotizador ,-ra *adj* hypnotizing.
▷ *nm & nf* hypnotist.
hipnotizar [4] *vt* to hypnotize.
hipo *nm* hiccup, hiccough. ■ **quitar el hipo** *fig* to take one's breath away.
hipoalergénico ,-a *adj* hypoallergenic.
hipocalórico ,-a *adj* low-calorie.
hipocampo *nm* sea horse.
hipocentro *nm* hypocentre (US hypocenter).
hipocondría *nf* hypochondria.
hipocondríaco ,-a *adj* hypochondriac.
hipocondrio *nm* hypochondrium.
hipocrático ,-a *adj* Hippocratic.
hipocresía *nf* hypocrisy.
hipócrita *adj* hypocritical.
▷ *nm o nf* hypocrite.
hipodérmico ,-a *adj* hypodermic.
hipodermis *nf inv* hypodermis.
hipódromo *nm* racetrack, racecourse.
hipófisis *nf inv* hypophysis.
hipopótamo *nm* hippopotamus.
hipotálamo *nm* hypothalamus.
hipoteca *nf* 1 mortgage. 2 *fig* drawback.
hipotecar [1] *vt* 1 to mortgage. 2 *fig* to jeopardize.
hipotecario ,-a *adj* mortgage.
hipotensión *nf* low blood pressure, hypotension.
hipotenso ,-a *adj* hypotensive.
hipotenusa *nf* hypotenuse.
hipotermia *nf* hypothermia.
hipótesis *nf inv* hypothesis.
hipotético ,-a *adj* hypothetic, hypothetical.
hippie *adj* hippy.
▷ *nm o nf* hippy.
hiriente *adj* 1 wounding. 2 *fig* hurtful, cutting, wounding.
hirsuto ,-a *adj* 1 hirsute, hairy; *(cerdoso)* bristly. 2 *fig (persona)* rough, brusque, surly.
hisopo *nm* 1 BOT hyssop. 2 REL aspergillum, sprinkler.
hispánico ,-a *adj* Hispanic, Spanish. ● **filología hispánica** *(carrera)* Spanish language and literature.
hispanidad *nf* 1 *(carácter)* Spanishness. 2 *(mundo hispánico)* Spanish world, Hispanic world.
hispanismo *nm* 1 *(cultural)* Hispanism, Hispanic studies *pl.* 2 *(lingüístico)* Hispanicism.
hispanista *nm o nf* Hispanist.
hispano ,-a *adj* 1 *(de España)* Spanish, Hispanic. 2 *(de América)* Spanish-American.
▷ *nm & nf* 1 *(de España)* Spaniard. 2 *(de América)* Spanish American, US Hispanic.
hispanoamericano ,-a *adj* Spanish American, Latin American.
Hispanoamérica *nf* Spanish America, Latin America.
hispanoárabe *adj* Hispano-Arabic.
▷ *nm o nf* Spanish Arab.
hispanohablante *adj* Spanish-speaking.
▷ *nm o nf* Spanish speaker.
histamina *nf* histamine.
histeria *nf* hysteria.
histérico ,-a *adj* hysterical.
▷ *nm & nf* hysteric. ■ **poner histérico,-a a** ALGN *fam* to drive SB mad, wind SB up.
histerismo *nm* 1 hysteria. 2 *fig* hysterics *pl.*
histología *nf* histology.
histológico ,-a *adj* histological.
historia *nf* 1 *(estudio)* history. 2 *(narración)* story, tale. 3 *fig (cuento)* story, take, excuse. ■ **pasar a la historia** to go down in history. ● **historia natural** natural history. | **historia universal** world history.
historiado ,-a *adj fig* overelaborate, florid.
historiador ,-ra *nm & nf* historian.
historial *nm* 1 MED medical record, case history. 2 *(currículo)* curriculum vitae. 3 *(antecedentes)* background. 4 INFORMÁ history.
historiar [13] *vt* 1 *(contar)* to tell the story of; *(acontecimientos)* to recount. 2 *(escribir)* to write the history of; *(acontecimientos)* to chronicle. 3 *(en pintura)* to depict.
histórico ,-a *adj* 1 *(relativo a la historia)* historical. 2 *(importante)* historic, memorable. 3 *(cierto)* factual, true.
historieta *nf* 1 *(cuento)* short story, tale, anecdote. 2 *(viñetas)* comic strip, cartoon.
historiografía *nf* historiography.
histrión *nm* 1 *(actor)* player, actor. 2 *fig* clown, buffoon.
histriónico ,-a *adj* histrionic.
hito *nm* 1 *(mojón - para distancias)* milestone; *(- para límites)* boundary stone. 2 *fig (hecho importante)* milestone, landmark.
Hl *sím* **(hectolitro)** hectolitre (US hectoliter); *(símbolo)* Hl.
Hm *sím* **(hectómetro)** hectometre (US hectometer); *(símbolo)* Hm.
hobby *nm* hobby.
▲ *pl* **hobbys.**
hocico *nm* 1 *(de animal)* snout, muzzle. 2 *pey (de persona)* nose, snout.
hocicón ,-ona *adj* 1 *(animal)* big-snouted. 2 *(persona)* big-mouthed.
hockey *nm* hockey. ● **hockey sobre hielo** ice hockey.
hogar *nm* 1 *(de chimenea)* hearth, fireplace. 2 *fig (casa)* home. 3 *fig (familia)* family.
hogareño ,-a *adj* 1 *(vida)* home, family. 2 *(persona)* home-loving, stay-at-home.
hogaza *nf* large loaf (of bread).
hoguera *nf* 1 bonfire. 2 *fig* blaze.
hoja *nf* 1 *(gen)* leaf. 2 *(pétalo)* petal. 3 *(de papel)* sheet; *(impreso)* handout, printed sheet. 4 *(de libro)* leaf, page. 5 *(de cuchillo, etc)* blade. 6 *(de puerta, ventana)* leaf; *(de mesa)* leaf, flap: **una ventana de dos hojas** *a double-leaf window.* ■ **de hoja perenne** BOT evergreen. ● **hoja de afeitar** razor blade. | **hoja de cálculo** spreadsheet.
hojalata *nf* tin, tin plate.
hojalatería *nf (taller, tienda)* tinsmith's.
hojalatero *nm* tinsmith.

hojaldrado ,-a *adj* puff: **pasta hojaldrada** *puff pastry.*
hojaldre *nm & nf* [Usually considered masculine.] puff pastry.
hojarasca *nf (hojas caídas)* fallen leaves *pl,* dead leaves *pl.*
hojeada *nf* flick.
hojear *vt* to leaf through, flick through.
hola *interj fam* hello!, hullo!, US hi!
Holanda *nf* Holland.
holandés ,-esa *adj* Dutch.
▷ *nm & nf (persona)* Dutch person; *(hombre)* Dutchman; *(mujer)* Dutchwoman.
▷ *nm* **holandés** *(idioma)* Dutch.
holandesa *nf (papel)* quarto sheet.
holding *nm* holding company.
▲ *pl* **holdings.**
holgadamente *adv* 1 *(con amplio margen)* easily: **ganaron holgadamente** *they won easily.* 2 *(con comodidad)* comfortably.
holgado ,-a *adj* 1 *(ropa)* loose, baggy. 2 *(espacio)* roomy. 3 *(posición)* comfortable, well-off.
holgar [52] *vi* 1 *(descansar)* to rest. 2 *(estar ocioso)* to be idle. ■ **huelga decir que...** needless to say (that)...
holgazán ,-ana *adj* idle, lazy.
▷ *nm & nf* lazybones, layabout.
holgazanear *vi* to laze around, loaf around, idle.
holgazanería *nf* idleness, laziness.
holgura *nf* 1 *(ropa)* looseness. 2 *(espacio)* room, spaciousness. 3 *fig (bienestar)* affluence, comfort.
holístico ,-a *adj* holistic.
hollar [31] *vt (comprimir)* to tread (on), set foot on.
hollejo *nm* skin, peel.
hollín *nm* soot.
holocausto *nm* holocaust.
holografía *nf* holography.
holograma *nm* hologram.
hombre *nm* 1 *(individuo)* man. 2 *(especie)* man, mankind. 3 *fam (marido)* husband.
▷ *interj (asombro)* hey!, hey there!, well!: **¡hombre, Pedro, no te esperaba!** *hey, Pedro, I didn't expect you!* ● **hombre de letras** man of letters. ‖ **hombre orquesta** one-man band. ‖ **hombre rana** frogman.
hombrera *nf* 1 *(almohadilla)* shoulder pad. 2 MIL epaulette.
hombría *nm* manliness, virility.
hombro *nm* shoulder. ■ **a hombros** on one's shoulders. ‖ **arrimar el hombro** to help out, lend a hand.
hombruno ,-a *adj* mannish, manly.
homenaje *nm* homage, tribute. ■ **en homenaje a** in honour (US honor) of. ‖ **rendir homenaje a** ALGN to pay homage to SB, pay tribute to SB.
homenajear *vt* to pay tribute to.
homeópata *nm o nf* homeopath.
homeopatía *nf* homeopathy.
homeopático ,-a *adj* homeopathic.
homicida *adj* homicidal, murder: **el arma homicida** *the murder weapon.*
▷ *nm o nf (hombre)* murderer; *(mujer)* murderess.
homicidio *nm (voluntario)* homicide, murder; *(involuntario)* manslaughter.
homilía *nf* homily, sermon.
homínido *adj* hominoid.
▷ *nm* hominid, hominoid.
homófono ,-a *adj* homophonous, homophonic.
▷ *nm* **homófono** homophone.
homogeneidad *nf* homogeneity, uniformity.
homogeneizar [26] *vt* to homogenize, make homogeneous.
homogéneo ,-a *adj* homogeneous, uniform.
homologable *adj* equivalent.
homologación *nf* 1 *(registro)* official approval, official recognition. 2 DEP ratification. 3 *(equiparación)* parity.
homologado ,-a *adj* 1 *(centro, estudios)* officially approved, officially recognized. 2 *(productos)* authorized.
homologar [7] *vt* 1 *(comprobar)* to approve, recognize, authorize. 2 DEP to ratify.
homólogo ,-a *adj* equivalent, homologous.
▷ *nm & nf* opposite number, counterpart.
homónimo ,-a *adj* homonymous.
▷ *nm* **homónimo** homonym.
homosexual *adj* homosexual.
▷ *nm o nf* homosexual.
homosexualidad *nf* homosexuality.
honda *nf* sling.
hondear *vi* 1 *(reconocer el fondo)* to sound. 2 *(descargar)* to unload.
hondo ,-a *adj* 1 deep. 2 *fig* profound, deep.
hondonada *nf* hollow, depression.
hondura *nf* depth.
Honduras *nm* Honduras.
hondureño ,-a *adj* Honduran.
▷ *nm & nf* Honduran.
honestidad *nf* 1 *(honradez)* honesty, uprightness. 2 *(decencia)* decency. 3 *(recato)* modesty.
honesto ,-a *adj* 1 *(honrado)* honest, upright. 2 *(decente)* decent. 3 *(recatado)* modest.
hongo *nm* 1 *(gen)* fungus; *(comestible)* mushroom; *(venenoso)* toadstool. 2 *(sombrero)* bowler, bowler hat.
honor *nm* 1 *(virtud)* honour (US honor). 2 *(reputación)* reputation, honour (US honor), good name. 3 *(de la mujer)* virtue. ■ **en honor a la verdad** to be fair, in all fairness. ‖ **hacer honor a** to live up to.
▷ *nm pl* **honores** 1 *(título)* title *sing,* distinction *sing.* 2 *(agasajo)* honours (US honors).
honorable *adj* honourable (US honorable).
honorario ,-a *adj* honorary.
▷ *nm pl* **honorarios** fee *sing,* fees, emoluments.
honorífico ,-a *adj* honorary.
honra *nf* 1 *(honor)* honour (US honor). 2 *(buena reputación)* reputation, good name.
▷ *nf pl* **honras** *(fúnebres)* last honours (US honors).
honradez *nf* honesty, integrity.
honrado ,-a *adj (honesto)* honest.
honrar *vt (gen)* to honour (US honor): **nos honró con su presencia** *he honoured us with his presence.*
▷ *vpr* **honrarse** to be honoured (US honored).
honroso ,-a *adj* 1 *(que honra)* honourable (US honorable). 2 *(decoroso)* respectable, reputable.

hora *nf* 1 *(unidad de tiempo)* hour: **media hora** *half an hour.* 2 *(tiempo)* time: **¿qué hora es?** *what time is it?* 3 *(cita)* appointment: **tengo hora para las cuatro y media** *I have an appointment at half past four.* ■ **a altas horas** in the small hours. ‖ **¡a buenas horas!** and about time too! ‖ **a la hora** at the proper time, on time. ‖ **a primera hora** first thing in the morning. ‖ **dar la hora** to strike the hour. ‖ **de última hora** last-minute: **una noticia de última hora** *some last-minute news.* ‖ **pedir hora** to make an appointment. ‖ **por horas** by the hour: **cobro por horas** *I get paid by the hour.* ● **hora de comer** lunch time, dinner time. ‖ **hora punta** rush hour.

horadar *vt* 1 *(perforar)* to pierce. 2 *(taladrar)* to drill (through), bore (through).

horario ,-a *adj* time.

▷ *nm* **horario** 1 timetable, US schedule. 2 *(jornada laboral)* hours *pl*, timetable: **tengo horario de mañana** *I work mornings.* 3 *(de reloj)* hour hand. ● **horario comercial** *(tienda)* opening hours *pl*. ‖ **horario laboral** working hours *pl*.

horca *nf* 1 *(patíbulo)* gallows *pl*, gibbet. 2 AGR hayfork, pitchfork.

horcajadas ■ **a horcajadas** astride.

horchata *nf* sweet milky drink made from tiger nuts or almonds.

horchatería *nf* bar where *horchata* is sold.

horda *nf* 1 horde, mob. 2 *fig* gang.

horizontal *adj* horizontal.

horizontalidad *nf* horizontality.

horizonte *nm* horizon.

horma *nf* 1 mould (US mold), form. 2 *(de zapato)* last.

hormiga *nf* ant.

hormigón *nm* concrete. ● **hormigón armado** reinforced concrete.

hormigonera *nf* concrete mixer.

hormiguear *vi* to itch, tingle: **me hormigueaba la mano** *I had pins and needles in my hand.*

hormigueo *nm* pins and needles *pl*, tingling sensation, itching sensation.

hormiguero *nm* ant hill, ant's nest.

hormona *nf* hormone.

hormonal *adj* hormonal.

hornacina *nf* niche.

hornada *nf* 1 batch. 2 *fig* set, batch.

hornear *vi* to bake.

▷ *vt* to bake.

hornillo *nm* 1 TÉC small furnace. 2 *(para cocinar)* stove.

horno *nm* 1 *(de cocina)* oven. 2 TÉC furnace. 3 *(cerámica, ladrillos)* kiln. 4 *(panadería)* bakery. ● **horno (de) microondas** microwave oven. ‖ **horno eléctrico** electric oven.

horóscopo *nm* horoscope.

horquilla *nf (de pelo)* hairgrip, hairclip, US bobby pin.

horrendo ,-a *adj* horrible, horrifying, awful, frightful.

hórreo *nm* granary.

horrible *adj* horrible, dreadful, awful.

horripilante *adj* hair-raising, horrifying, terrifying.

horripilar *vt* to horrify, scare stiff, give the creeps.

horror *nm* 1 *(repulsión)* horror, terror. 2 *(temor)* hate. 3 *fig (atrocidad)* atrocity. ■ **¡qué horror!** how awful!

horrorizar [4] *vt* 1 *(causar horror)* to horrify, terrify. 2 *fam (disgustar)* to disgust, turn off.

▷ *vpr* **horrorizarse** to be horrified.

horroroso ,-a *adj* 1 *(que causa miedo)* horrifying, terrifying. 2 *fam (feo)* ghastly, hideous.

hortaliza *nf* vegetable.

hortelano ,-a *nm & nf* market gardener, US truck farmer.

hortense *adj* vegetable.

hortensia *nf* hydrangea.

hortera *adj fam (grosero)* common, vulgar, tasteless; *(cursi)* corny, tacky; *(ostentoso)* flashy.

horterada *nf fam (cosa)* tacky thing; *(acto)* tacky thing to do.

hortícola *adj* horticultural.

horticultor ,-ra *nm & nf* horticulturist.

horticultura *nf* horticulture.

hosco ,-a *adj* 1 *(insociable)* sullen, surly. 2 *(lugar)* gloomy, dark.

hospedaje *nm* 1 *(acción)* lodging; *(precio)* cost of lodging. 2 *(lugar)* lodgings *pl*, accommodation.

hospedar *vt* to lodge, put up.

▷ *vpr* **hospedarse** to stay (**en**, at).

hospicio *nm* 1 *(de huérfanos)* orphanage. 2 *(de peregrinos)* hospice. 3 *(de pobres)* poorhouse.

hospital *nm* hospital, infirmary.

hospitalidad *nf* hospitality.

hospitalizar [4] *vt* to send into hospital, hospitalize.

hostal *nm* hostel, hotel.

hostelería *nf* 1 *(actividad)* catering business. 2 *(estudios)* hotel management.

hostia *nf* 1 REL host, Eucharistic wafer. 2 *tabú (choque)* bump, bash; *(torta)* slap, smack, punch.

hostigamiento *nm* harassment.

hostigar [7] *vt* 1 *(azotar)* to whip. 2 *fig (perseguir)* to plague, persecute; *(al enemigo)* to harass. 3 *fig (molestar)* to pester.

hostil *adj* hostile.

hostilidad *nf* hostility.

▷ *nf pl* **hostilidades** hostilities.

hotel *nm (establecimiento)* hotel.

hotelero ,-a *adj* hotel.

▷ *nm & nf* hotel manager, hotelier.

hoy *adv* 1 *(día)* today. 2 *fig (actualmente)* now, nowadays. ■ **de hoy en adelante** from now on. ‖ **hoy (en) día** nowadays, today, these days.

hoyo *nm* 1 *(agujero)* hole, pit. 2 *(sepultura)* grave. 3 *(hoyuelo)* dimple. 4 *(golf)* hole.

hoyuelo *nm* dimple.

hoz[1] *nf* AGR sickle.

▲ *pl* **hoces.**

hoz[2] *nf* GEOG ravine, gorge.

▲ *pl* **hoces.**

hucha *nf* moneybox, piggy bank.

hueco ,-a *adj* 1 hollow: **pared hueca** *hollow wall, stud wall.* 2 *(vacío)* empty. 3 *(cóncavo)* concave. 4 *(sonido)* hollow; *(voz)* deep.

▷ *nm* **hueco 1** *(cavidad)* hollow, hole. **2** *(de tiempo)* slot, free time; *(de espacio)* empty space. **3** *fig (vacante)* vacancy.
huecograbado *nm* photogravure.
huelga *nf* strike. ■ **estar en huelga / estar de huelga** to be on strike. ● **huelga a la japonesa** work-in. ‖ **huelga de brazos caídos** go-slow. ‖ **huelga de celo** work-to-rule. ‖ **huelga general** general strike. ‖ **huelga de hambre** hunger strike.
See also **holgar.**
huelguista *nm o nf* striker.
huella *nf* **1** *(de pie)* footprint; *(de ruedas)* track. **2** *fig (vestigio)* trace, sign: **las huellas del tiempo** *the traces of time.* ■ **dejar huella** to leave one's mark (**en**, on). ● **huella dactilar** fingerprint.
huérfano ,-a *adj* orphan, orphaned.
▷ *nm & nf* orphan.
huero ,-a *adj fig* empty.
huerta *nf (terreno)* market garden, US truck garden.
huerto *nm (de verduras)* vegetable garden, kitchen garden; *(de frutas)* orchard.
hueso *nm* **1** ANAT bone. **2** *(de fruta)* stone, US pit. **3** *fam fig (cosa difícil)* struggle, problem: **las mates son un hueso para mí** *I find maths really hard.* **4** *fam fig (profesor)* strict teacher, stickler. ■ **ser un hueso duro de roer** *fig* to be a hard nut to crack.
huesoso ,-a *adj* bony.
huésped ,-da *nm & nf (invitado)* guest.
hueste *nf* [Also used in plural with the same meaning.] MIL army, host.
huesudo ,-a *adj* bony.
hueva *nf* roe, spawn.
huevera *nf* **1** *(copa)* egg cup. **2** *(cartón)* egg box.
huevería *nf* egg shop.
huevero ,-a *nm & nf (persona)* egg seller.
huevo *nm* **1** egg. **2** COST darning egg. ■ **costar un huevo** *fam* to cost an arm and a leg. ● **huevo duro** hard-boiled egg. ‖ **huevo frito** fried egg. ‖ **huevo pasado por agua** soft-boiled egg.
huevón ,-ona *adj* sluggish.
huevos *nm pl* → **huevo.**
huida *nf* **1** flight, escape. **2** *(de caballo)* shying, bolting.
huidizo ,-a *adj* **1** *(esquivo)* fleeting, elusive. **2** *(tímido)* shy.
huir [62] *vi* **1** *(escapar)* to flee, run away. **2** *(evitar)* to avoid (**de**, -), keep away (**de**, from), shun (**de**, -).
hule *nm* oilcloth, oilskin.
hulla *nf* coal.
hullero ,-a *adj* coal. ● **explotación hullera 1** *(industria)* mining. **2** *(mina)* mine.
humanamente *adv* **1** *(como humano)* humanly. **2** *(con humanidad)* humanely.
humanidad *nf* **1** *(género humano)* humanity, mankind. **2** *(cualidad)* humanity, humaneness. **3** *(benignidad)* compassion, benevolence, kindness.
▷ *nf pl* **humanidades** EDUC humanities.
humanismo *nm* humanism.
humanista *nm o nf* humanist.
humanístico ,-a *adj* humanistic.
humanitario ,-a *adj* humanitarian.
humanitarismo *nm* humanitarianism.
humanización *nf* humanization.
humanizar [4] *vt* to humanize.
▷ *vpr* **humanizarse** to become more human.
humano ,-a *adj* **1** human. **2** *(benigno)* humane.
humareda *nf* cloud of smoke.
humazo *nm* dense smoke.
humeante *adj* **1** *(de humo)* smoky, smoking. **2** *(de vaho)* steaming.
humear *vi* **1** *(humo)* to smoke, give off smoke. **2** *(vaho)* to steam, give off steam.
humectador *nm* humidifier.
humectante *adj* moistening.
humedad *nf* **1** humidity. **2** *(de vapor)* moisture.
humedecer [43] *vt* to moisten, dampen.
▷ *vpr* **humedecerse** to become damp, become moist.
húmedo ,-a *adj* **1** *(clima)* humid, damp. **2** *(impregnado)* damp, moist, wet.
húmero *nm* humerus.
humidificador *nm* humidifier.
humidificar *vt* to humidify.
humildad *nf* humility, humbleness.
humilde *adj* humble, modest.
humildemente *adv* humbly.
humillación *nf* humiliation, humbling.
humillante *adj* humiliating, humbling.
humillar *vt* to humiliate, humble.
▷ *vpr* **humillarse** to humble OS, lower OS.
humo *nm* **1** smoke. **2** *(gas)* fumes *pl.* **3** *(vapor)* steam, vapour (US vapor).
▷ *nm pl* **humos** *fig (vanidad)* conceit *sing*, airs. ■ **bajarle los humos a** ALGN *fig* to put SB in his/her place.
humor *nm* **1** *(ánimo)* mood. **2** *(carácter)* temper. **3** *(gracia)* humour (US humor). ■ **estar de buen humor** to be in a good mood. ‖ **estar de humor para** ALGO to feel like (doing) STH, feel in the mood for (doing) STH.
humorada *nf* **1** *(gracia)* joke, witticism. **2** *(extravagancia)* caprice, whim.
humorismo *nm* humour (US humor).
humorista *adj* humorous.
▷ *nm o nf (autor)* humorist; *(cómico)* comedian.
humorístico ,-a *adj* humorous, funny, amusing.
humus *nm inv* humus.
hundible *adj* sinkable.
hundido ,-a *adj* **1** *(barco, etc)* sunken. **2** *(ojos)* deep-set; *(mejillas)* hollow. **3** *fig (abrumado)* demoralized.
hundimiento *nm* **1** *(barco)* sinking. **2** *(tierra)* subsidence. **3** *(edificio)* collapse.
hundir *vt* **1** *(sumir)* to submerge, plunge: **hundió la mano en la arena** *she plunged her hand into the sand.* **2** *(barco)* to sink. **3** *(derrumbar)* to demolish, ruin: **el terremoto hundió el edificio** *the earthquake caused the building to collapse.*
▷ *vpr* **hundirse 1** *(barco)* to sink. **2** *(derrumbarse)* to collapse, fall down. **3** *(arruinarse)* to be ruined, collapse.
húngaro ,-a *adj* Hungarian.
▷ *nm & nf (persona)* Hungarian.
▷ *nm* **húngaro** *(idioma)* Hungarian.
Hungría *nf* Hungary.
huracán *nm* hurricane.
huracanado ,-a *adj* hurricane: **vientos huracanados** *hurricane winds.*
huraño ,-a *adj* sullen, unsociable.

hurgar [7] *vt* **1** *(remover)* to poke, rake. **2** *(bolsillo, bolso, etc)* to rummage in, go through. **3** *fig (fisgar)* to stir up. **4** *fig (incitar)* to poke at.
▷ *vpr* **hurgarse** to pick.
hurí *nf* houri.
hurón ,-ona *nm (animal)* ferret.
huronear *vi* **1** *(cazar con hurón)* to ferret. **2** *fig (escudriñar)* to pry, snoop, ferret.
hurra *interj* hurray!, hurrah!
hurraca *nf* magpie.
hurtadillas ■ **a hurtadillas** stealthily, on the sly.
hurtar *vt* **1** *(robar)* to steal, pilfer. **2** *(no dar el peso)* to cheat on the weight. **3** *fig (desviar)* to dodge. **4** *fig (plagiar)* to plagiarize.
hurto *nm* petty theft, pilfering.
húsar *nm* hussar.
husmeador ,-ra *adj* **1** *(con la nariz)* sniffing. **2** *fig (fisgón)* prying, snooping.
▷ *nm & nf fig (fisgón)* snooper.
husmear *vt* **1** *(con el olfato)* to sniff, scent. **2** *fig (indagar)* to pry (**en**, into), snoop (**en**, into).
▷ *vi* **1** to sniff. **2** *fig* to snoop around.
husmeo *nm* **1** sniffing. **2** *fig* prying, snooping.
huso *nm (para hilar)* spindle, bobbin. ● **huso horario** time zone.
huy *interj* **1** *(sorpresa)* well!, wow!: **¡huy qué grande!** *wow! it's huge!* **2** *(dolor)* ouch!, ow! **3** *(miedo)* argh!, aah!
huyuyuy *interj (reproche)* tut, tut, tut!
Hz *sím* **(hertzio)** hertz; *(símbolo)* Hz.

I

I, i *nf (la letra)* I, i. ● **i griega** *name of the letter* **y**. ‖ **i latina** *name of the letter* **i**.
▲ *pl* **íes**.
Iberia *nf* Iberia.
ibérico,-a *adj* Iberian. ● **Península Ibérica** Iberian Peninsula.
ibero,-a *adj-nm & nf* → **íbero,-a**.
íbero,-a *adj* Iberian.
▷ *nm & nf (persona)* Iberian.
▷ *nm* **íbero** *(idioma)* Iberian.
Iberoamérica *nf* Latin America.
iberoamericano,-a *adj* Latin American.
▷ *nm & nf* Latin American.
íbice *nm* ibex.
ibis *nm inv* ibis.
iceberg *nm* iceberg.
▲ *pl* **icebergs**.
icono *nm* icon.
iconoclasta *adj* iconoclastic.
▷ *nm o nf* iconoclast.
iconografía *nf* iconography.
ictericia *nf* jaundice.
ida *nf (acción)* going; *(salida)* departure. ■ **de ida sola** single, US one-way. ‖ **de ida y vuelta** *(billete)* return, US round-trip.
idea *nf* 1 idea. 2 *(noción)* notion. 3 *(ingenio)* imagination.
ideal *adj* 1 ideal. 2 *fam (perfecto)* marvellous.
▷ *nm* ideal.
idealismo *nm* idealism.
idealista *adj* idealistic.
▷ *nm o nf* idealist.
idealizar [4] *vt* to idealize.
idear *vt* 1 *(concebir)* to conceive. 2 *(inventar)* to design.
ideario *nm* ideology.
idéntico,-a *adj* identical.
identidad *nf* identity. ● **carnet de identidad** identity card.
identificar [1] *vt* to identify.
▷ *vpr* **identificarse** 1 *(mostrar la documentación)* to identify OS. 2 *(solidarizarse)* to identify (**con**, with).
identificativo,-a *adj* identity.
ideología *nf* ideology.
ideólogo,-a *nm & nf* ideologist.
idílico,-a *adj* idyllic.
idilio *nm* 1 *lit* idyll. 2 *fam* romance.
idiolecto *nm* idiolect.
idioma *nm* language.
idiomático,-a *adj* idiomatic.
idiosincrasia *nf* idiosyncrasy.
idiota *adj* 1 MED idiotic. 2 *fam (tonto)* stupid.
▷ *nm o nf* idiot.
idiotez *nf* 1 MED idiocy. 2 *(estupidez)* stupid thing to say, stupid thing to do.
idiotizar [4] *vt* to turn into an idiot.
ido,-a *adj* 1 *(loco)* mad. 2 *(despistado)* absent-minded.
■ **estar ido,-a** *fam (loco)* to be mad.
idolatrar *vt* 1 to worship. 2 *fig* to idolize.
idolatría *nf* idolatry.
ídolo *nm* idol.
idóneo,-a *adj* suitable.
iglesia *nf* 1 *(edificio)* church. 2 *(institución)* Church.
iglú *nm* igloo.
▲ *pl* **iglúes**.
ígneo,-a *adj* igneous.
ignición *nf* ignition.
ignífugo,-a *adj* flameproof, noninflammable.
ignominia *nf* ignominy, public shame.
ignominioso,-a *adj* ignominious.
ignorancia *nf* ignorance.
ignorante *adj* ignorant.
▷ *nm o nf* ignoramus.
ignorar *vt* 1 *(desconocer)* not to know, not be aware of, be unaware of. 2 *(no hacer caso)* to ignore.
igual *adj* 1 *(parte)* equal. 2 *(lo mismo)* the same. 3 *(muy parecido)* just like. 4 MAT equal.
▷ *nm* 1 *(persona)* equal. 2 MAT *(signo)* equals sign.
▷ *adv* 1 *(en comparativas)* the same. 2 *fam* maybe, perhaps: **igual no vienen** *they may well not come.*
igualar *vt* 1 to make equal. 2 *(allanar)* to level; *(pulir)* to smooth. 3 *(comparar)* to match: **no hay nadie que lo iguale** *nobody can match him, he has no equal.* 4 DEP *(partido)* to draw; *(tanteo)* to equalize.
▷ *vpr* **igualarse** 1 *(ser iguales)* to be equal. 2 *(compararse)* to be compared.
igualdad *nf* 1 equality. 2 *(de superficie)* levelness.
iguana *nf* iguana.
ilativo,-a *adj* inferential.
ilegal *adj* illegal.
ilegalidad *nf* illegality.
ilegalmente *adv* illegally.
ilegible *adj* unreadable, illegible.
ilegítimo,-a *adj* illegitimate.
íleon *nm* 1 *(intestino)* ileum. 2 *(hueso)* ilium.
ileso,-a *adj* unharmed, unhurt.
iletrado,-a *adj* illiterate.
ilícito,-a *adj* unlawful, illicit.
ilimitado,-a *adj* unlimited.
ilion *nm* ilium.
ilógico,-a *adj* illogical.
iluminación *nf* 1 *(de una sala)* lighting; *(de una feria)* illumination; *(de una película, un espectáculo)* lighting. 2 *(de manuscritos)* illumination.
iluminar *vt* 1 to light, light up. 2 *(manuscrito)* to illuminate. 3 *fig* to enlighten.

ilusión *nf* 1 *(no real)* illusion, illusory hope. 2 *(esperanza)* hope. 3 *(sueño)* dream. 4 *(emoción)* excitement.
ilusionado,-a *adj* excited.
ilusionar *vt* 1 *(crear ilusiones)* to raise hopes. 2 *(entusiasmar)* to excite.
▷ *vpr* **ilusionarse** 1 *(esperanzarse)* to build up one's hopes. 2 *(entusiasmarse)* to be excited (**con**, about).
ilusionismo *nm* conjuring.
ilusionista *nm o nf* conjurer, illusionist.
iluso,-a *adj* naive, gullible.
ilustración *nf* 1 *(de un texto)* illustration. 2 *(erudición)* learning, erudition. 3 **la Ilustración** HIST the Enlightenment.
ilustrado,-a *adj* 1 *(texto)* illustrated. 2 *(culto)* learned, erudite. 3 HIST of the Enlightenment.
ilustrar *vt* 1 *(texto)* to illustrate. 2 *(instruir)* to enlighten.
▷ *vpr* **ilustrarse** to learn.
ilustre *adj* 1 *(célebre)* renowned, illustrious. 2 *(distinguido)* distinguished.
imagen *nf* 1 image. 2 TV picture. ■ **ser la viva imagen de** ALGN to be the spitting image of SB.
imaginación *nf* imagination, fantasy.
imaginar *vt* 1 *(gen)* to imagine. 2 *(pensar)* to think, imagine. 3 *(idear)* to devise, think up.

The form imaginarse is also used in all senses, especially in colloquial speech.

imaginario,-a *adj* imaginary.
imaginativo,-a *adj* imaginative.
imaginería *nf* religious images *pl*.
imán[1] *nm* magnet.
imán[2] *nm* REL imam.
imantación *nf* magnetization.
imantar *vt* to magnetize.
imbatible *adj* unbeatable.
imbécil *adj* 1 MED *(retrasado)* imbecile. 2 *fam* stupid.
▷ *nm o nf* 1 MED imbecile. 2 *fam* idiot, imbecile.
imbecilidad *nf* 1 MED imbecility. 2 *fam* stupid thing to do.
imberbe *adj* beardless.
imborrable *adj* indelible.
imbricación *nf* interweaving.
imbricar *vt* to interweave.
▷ *vpr* **imbricarse** to be interwoven.
imbuir *vt* to imbue.
▷ *vpr* **imbuirse** to become imbued (**de**, with).
imitación *nf* 1 *(copia)* imitation. 2 *(parodia)* impression.
imitador,-ra *adj* imitative.
▷ *nm & nf* 1 imitator. 2 *(cómico)* impressionist.
imitar *vt* to copy, imitate; *(gestos)* to mimic; *(persona)* to mimic, do an impression of.
impaciencia *nf* impatience.
impacientar *vt* to make lose one's patience.
▷ *vpr* **impacientarse** to lose one's patience.
impaciente *adj* impatient, anxious.
impactado,-a *adj* impacted.
impactante *adj* striking, powerful.
impactar *vt* 1 *(físicamente)* to hit. 2 *(impresionar)* to make an impression on. 3 *(influir, afectar)* to affect.
impacto *nm* 1 *(choque)* impact. 2 *(marca)* mark.
impago *nm* nonpayment.
impala *nm* impala.
impar *adj* odd.
imparable *adj* unstoppable.
imparcial *adj* impartial, fair.
imparcialidad *nf* impartiality.
impartir *vt (justicia)* to administer; *(lección)* to give.
impasible *adj* impassive.
impávido,-a *adj* dauntless.
impecable *adj* impeccable, faultless.
impedido,-a *adj* disabled, handicapped.
▷ *nm & nf* disabled person, handicapped person.
impedimento *nm* 1 *(gen)* impediment; *(obstáculo)* hindrance, obstacle; *(problema)* hitch. 2 JUR *(a un matrimonio)* impediment.
impedir [34] *vt* 1 *(hacer imposible)* to prevent, stop: **¿hay algo que te lo impida?** *is there anything stopping you?* 2 *(obstaculizar)* to hinder, impede.
impeler *vt* 1 to drive forward, propel. 2 *fig (incitar)* to impel, incite.
impenetrable *adj* 1 *(bosque)* impenetrable. 2 *fig (misterio)* impenetrable. 3 *(persona, actitud)* inscrutable.
impensable *adj* unthinkable.
impepinable *adj fam* unavoidable, certain, inevitable.
imperante *adj* prevailing.
imperar *vi* to rule, prevail.
imperativo,-a *adj* imperative.
▷ *nm* **imperativo** LING imperative.
imperceptible *adj* imperceptible.
imperdible *nm* safety pin.
imperdonable *adj* unforgivable, inexcusable.
imperecedero,-a *adj* 1 *(producto)* imperishable. 2 *fig* everlasting.
imperfección *nf* 1 imperfection. 2 *(defecto)* fault.
imperfecto,-a *adj* 1 imperfect. 2 LING imperfect.
▷ *nm* **imperfecto** imperfect, imperfect tense.
imperialismo *nm* imperialism.
imperialista *adj* imperialist.
▷ *nm o nf* imperialist.
impericia *nf* inexperience.
imperio *nm* empire.
imperioso,-a *adj* 1 *(autoritario)* imperious. 2 *(necesario)* urgent, pressing.
impermeabilizar [4] *vt* to waterproof.
impermeable *adj* 1 *(gen)* impermeable, impervious; *(tejido, ropa)* waterproof. 2 *fig* impervious.
▷ *nm* raincoat.
impersonal *adj* impersonal.
impersonalidad *nf* impersonality.
impertérrito,-a *adj* imperturbable, undaunted.
impertinencia *nf* 1 impertinence. 2 *(palabras)* impertinent remark.
impertinente *adj* impertinent.
▷ *nm pl* **impertinentes** lorgnette *sing*.
imperturbable *adj* imperturbable.
ímpetu *nm* 1 *(fuerza)* vigour (US vigor); *(entusiasmo)* enthusiasm; *(energía)* energy. 2 *(impulso)* impetus.
impetuoso,-a *adj* 1 *(persona)* impetuous. 2 *(viento)* violent.
impío,-a *adj* impious.
▷ *nm & nf* infidel.
implacable *adj* implacable, relentless.
implantar *vt* 1 to introduce. 2 MED to implant.
implante *nm* implant.

implicar [1] *vt* 1 *(conllevar)* to imply. 2 *(involucrar)* to implicate, involve (**en**, in).
implícito,-a *adj* implicit.
implorar *vt* to implore, entreat, beg.
implosión *nf* implosion.
impoluto,-a *adj* immaculate, spotless.
imponderable *adj (factor)* imponderable.
imponente *adj* impressive.
imponer [78] *vt* 1 *(ley, límite, sanción)* to impose. 2 *(obediencia)* to exact. 3 *(respeto)* to inspire. 4 FIN *(cantidad)* to deposit.
▷ *vi (asustar)* to be frightening.
▷ *vpr* **imponerse** 1 to impose one's authority (**a**, on). 2 *(obligarse)* to force OS to. 3 *(prevalecer)* to prevail. 4 *(predominar)* to become fashionable.
impopular *adj* unpopular.
impopularidad *nf* unpopularity.
importación *nf* 1 *(acción)* importation, import. 2 *(productos)* imports *pl*.
importador,-ra *adj* importing.
▷ *nm & nf* importer.
importancia *nf* importance.
importante *adj* 1 *(gen)* important; *(por su gravedad)* serious; *(por su cantidad)* considerable. 2 *(influyente)* important.
importar *vt* 1 COM *(traer de fuera)* to import. 2 *(valer)* to amount to.
▷ *vi* 1 *(tener importancia)* to matter. 2 *(molestar)* to mind.
importe *nm (gen)* price; *(cantidad)* amount; *(tarifa)* fare.
importunar *vt (molestar)* to pester; *(uso formal)* to importune.
imposibilidad *nf* impossibility.
imposibilitar *vt (impedir)* to make impossible.
imposible *adj* impossible.
imposición *nf* 1 *(gen)* imposition. 2 FIN *(cantidad)* deposit; *(impuesto)* tax.
impositivo,-a *adj* tax.
impostor,-ra *nm & nf* 1 *(farsante)* impostor. 2 *(difamador)* slanderer.
impotencia *nf* impotence.
impotente *adj* impotent.
imprecar *vt* to imprecate.
impreciso,-a *adj* imprecise, vague.
impredecible *adj (persona)* unpredictable; *(circunstancia)* unforeseeable.
imprenta *nf* 1 *(arte)* printing. 2 *(taller)* printer's.
imprescindible *adj* essential, indispensable.
impresión *nf* 1 *(en imprenta)* printing. 2 *(huella)* impression, imprint. 3 *fig (efecto)* impression; *(negativo)* shock. 4 *(opinión)* impression.
impresionable *adj* impressionable.
impresionante *adj* 1 *(admirable)* impressive. 2 *(impactante)* powerful; *(inquietante)* disturbing. 3 *(sorprendente)* astonishing, amazing. 4 *fam (gen)* incredible; *(negativamente)* terrible; *(enorme)* tremendous.
impresionar *vt* 1 *(causar admiración)* to impress: **nos impresionó su facilidad de palabra** *we were impressed by her articulateness*. 2 *(afectar)* to affect; *(inquietar)* to disturb. 3 *(película)* to expose.
impresionismo *nm* impressionism.
impresionista *adj* impressionist.
▷ *nm o nf* impressionist.
impreso,-a *adj* printed.
▷ *nm* **impreso** *(formulario)* form.
impresor,-ra *nm & nf (persona)* printer.
impresora *nf (máquina)* printer.
imprevisible *adj (hecho)* unforeseeable.
imprevisto,-a *adj (circunstancia)* unforeseen.
▷ *nm pl* **imprevistos** *(gastos)* incidental expenses.
imprimir *vt* 1 *(gen)* to print. 2 *(dejar huella)* to stamp. 3 *fig (grabar)* to fix.
improbable *adj* improbable, unlikely.
improcedente *adj* 1 inappropriate. 2 JUR inadmissible.
improductivo,-a *adj* unproductive.
impronta *nf* mark.
improperio *nm* insult.
impropio,-a *adj* 1 *(inadecuado)* unsuitable, inappropriate. 2 *(incorrecto)* improper.
improvisación *nf* improvisation.
improvisado,-a *adj (gen)* improvised.
improvisar *vt* to improvise.
▷ *vi* to improvise.
improviso ■ **de improviso** *(repentinamente)* suddenly.
imprudencia *nf* 1 *(falta de prudencia)* imprudence. 2 *(acción imprudente)* rash move; *(indiscreción)* indiscretion.
imprudente *adj* imprudent, careless.
▷ *nm o nf (imprudente)* imprudent person, careless person; *(indiscreto)* indiscreet person.
impudente *adj* bold-faced, brassy.
impúdico,-a *adj* 1 *(indecente)* immodest, indecent. 2 *(desvergonzado)* shameless.
impuesto,-a *nm* **impuesto** tax, duty.
impugnación *nf* 1 *(de lo reglamentado)* contestation. 2 *(de una teoría)* refutation.
impugnar *vt* 1 *(resultado)* to contest. 2 *(teoría)* to refute.
impulsar *vt* 1 to impel. 2 TÉC to drive forward. 3 *(potenciar)* to promote. 4 *(incitar)* to drive.
impulsivo,-a *adj* impulsive.
▷ *nm & nf* impulsive person.
impulso *nm* 1 impulse. 2 *(fuerza, velocidad)* momentum.
impulsor,-ra *nm & nf* promoter, driving force.
impune *adj* unpunished.
impunidad *nf* impunity.
impureza *nf* impurity.
impuro,-a *adj* impure.
imputación *nf* imputation, accusation.
imputar *vt* to impute.
inabarcable *adj* huge, vast.
inabordable *adj* unapproachable.
inacabable *adj* interminable, endless.
inaccesible *adj* inaccessible.
inaceptable *adj* unacceptable.
inactividad *nf* inactivity.
inactivo,-a *adj* inactive.
inadaptación *nf* maladjustment.
inadaptado,-a *adj* maladjusted.
▷ *nm & nf* misfit.
inadecuado,-a *adj* 1 unsuitable. 2 *(inapropiado)* inappropriate.
inadvertido,-a *adj* 1 *(no visto)* unseen. 2 *(distraído)* inattentive.
inagotable *adj* 1 *(cantidad)* inexhaustible. 2 *(persona)* tireless.
inaguantable *adj* unbearable.

inalámbrico,-a *adj* cordless.
inalcanzable *adj* unattainable, unreachable.
inalienable *adj* inalienable.
inalterable *adj* 1 *(propiedad)* unchanging. 2 *(color)* fast. 3 *(persona, vida)* impassive, imperturbable.
inanición *nf* starvation.
inanimado,-a *adj* inanimate, lifeless.
inapelable *adj (sentencia)* unappealable.
inapetente *adj* lacking in appetite.
inaplazable *adj* which cannot be postponed.
inaplicable *adj* inapplicable.
inapreciable *adj* 1 *(insignificante)* imperceptible, insignificant. 2 *(valioso)* invaluable, priceless.
inapropiado *adj* inappropriate.
inasequible *adj* 1 *(objetivo)* unattainable. 2 *(precio)* prohibitive. 3 *(persona)* unapproachable.
inatacable *adj* 1 *(posición, fortaleza)* unassailable. 2 *(idea, postura)* irrefutable.
inaudible *adj* inaudible.
inaudito,-a *adj (nunca oído)* unheard-of.
inauguración *nf* opening, inauguration.
inaugurar *vt* to inaugurate, open.
inca *adj* Inca.
▷ *nm o nf* Inca.
incalculable *adj* incalculable.
incalificable *adj (intolerable)* unspeakable.
incandescente *adj* incandescent.
incansable *adj* tireless.
incapacidad *nf* 1 *(gen)* incapacity, inability. 2 *(insuficiencia)* disability. 3 JUR incapacity.
incapacitado,-a *adj (físicamente)* incapacitated, handicapped, disabled; *(mentalmente)* unfit.
incapacitar *vt* 1 *(impedir)* to incapacitate. 2 JUR to disqualify.
incapaz *adj* 1 incapable (**de**, of). 2 *(incompetente)* incompetent.
incautación *nf* seizure.
incautarse *vpr* **incautarse de** JUR *(confiscar)* to seize.
incauto,-a *adj (crédulo)* gullible.
▷ *nm & nf* gullible person.
incendiar [12] *vt* to set on fire, set fire to.
▷ *vpr* **incendiarse** to catch fire.
incendiario,-a *adj* 1 *(bomba)* incendiary. 2 *fig (escrito)* inflammatory.
▷ *nm & nf* arsonist.
incendio *nm* fire.
incentivo *nm* incentive.
incertidumbre *nf* uncertainty.
incesante *adj* incessant, unceasing.
incesto *nm* incest.
incestuoso,-a *adj* incestuous.
incidente *nm* incident, event.
incidir *vi* **incidir en** 1 *(repercutir en)* affect. 2 *(incurrir en)* to fall into. 3 *(tratar)* to touch upon.
incienso *nm* incense.
incierto,-a *adj* 1 *(poco seguro)* uncertain, doubtful. 2 *(desconocido)* unknown.
incineración *nf (de basuras)* incineration; *(de cadáveres)* cremation.
incinerar *vt (basura)* to incinerate; *(cadáveres)* to cremate.
incipiente *adj* incipient.
incisión *nf* incision.
inciso,-a *nm (comentario)* comment, passing remark; *(de un artículo)* subsection.
incitante *adj* 1 *(estimulante)* inciting. 2 *(provocativo)* provocative.
incitar *vt* to incite (**a**, to).
inclasificable *adj* unclassifiable.
inclemencia *nf* inclemency, harshness.
inclinación *nf* 1 *(desviación)* slant. 2 *(tendencia)* leaning. 3 *(afición, cariño)* penchant. 4 *(saludo)* bow; *(asentimiento)* nod.
inclinar *vt* 1 *(ladear)* to tilt. 2 *fig (persuadir)* to dispose.
▷ *vpr* **inclinarse** 1 *(doblarse)* to bend, lean; *(como saludo)* to bow. 2 **inclinarse a** *fig (propender a)* to incline to, incline towards. 3 **inclinarse por** *(escoger)* to choose, opt for.
incluido,-a *adj (gen)* included; *(adjunto)* enclosed.
incluir [62] *vt* 1 to include. 2 *(contener)* to contain, comprise. 3 *(adjuntar - en carta, etc)* to enclose.
incluso *adv* even.
▷ *prep* even.
incógnita *nf* 1 MAT unknown quantity. 2 *fig (misterio)* mystery.
incógnito,-a *adj* unknown.
incoherencia *nf (falta de coherencia)* incoherence.
incoherente *adj* incoherent, disconnected.
incomible *adj* uneatable, inedible.
incomodar *vt* 1 *(causar molestia)* to inconvenience. 2 *(fastidiar)* to annoy, bother. 3 *(enojar)* to anger.
▷ *vpr* **incomodarse** 1 *(tomarse la molestia)* to put OS out. 2 *(enfadarse)* to get annoyed, get angry.
incómodo,-a *adj* uncomfortable.
incomparable *adj* incomparable.
incompetencia *nf* incompetence.
incompetente *adj* incompetent.
incompleto,-a *adj* 1 incomplete. 2 *(inacabado)* unfinished.
incomprensión *nf* lack of understanding.
incomunicado,-a *adj* 1 *(aislado)* isolated. 2 *(por la nieve)* cut off. 3 *(preso)* in solitary confinement.
inconcebible *adj* inconceivable, unthinkable.
inconcluso,-a *adj* unfinished.
incondicional *adj* 1 *(rendición)* unconditional. 2 *(amistad, admiración)* unquestioning.
▷ *nm o nf* staunch supporter.
inconexo,-a *adj* disconnected.
inconfesable *adj* shameful.
inconformista *adj* nonconformist.
▷ *nm o nf* nonconformist.
inconfundible *adj* unmistakable.
incongruencia *nf* incongruity.
inconsciencia *nf* 1 MED unconsciousness. 2 *(irreflexión)* thoughtlessness.
inconsciente *adj* 1 MED unconscious. 2 *(irreflexivo)* thoughtless.
inconsecuente *adj* inconsistent.
▷ *nm o nf* inconsistent person.
inconsistente *adj* 1 *(sin firmeza)* flimsy. 2 *(sin rigor)* weak.
inconstante *adj* 1 *(indolente)* lacking in discipline. 2 *(variable)* inconstant, changeable.
inconstitucional *adj* unconstitutional.
incontable *adj* countless, uncountable.
incontestable *adj* indisputable.
incontinencia *nf* incontinence.

incontrolable *adj* uncontrollable.
inconveniencia *nf* 1 *(gen)* inconvenience. 2 *(imprudencia)* tactless remark.
inconveniente *adj (gen)* inconvenient.
▷ *nm (desventaja)* drawback; *(dificultad)* problem.
incordiar [12] *vt* to pester, bother.
incorporación *nf* 1 *(llegada)* arrival; *(inclusión)* inclusion; *(unión)* joining. 2 *(del cuerpo)* sitting-up.
incorporar *vt* 1 *(añadir)* to incorporate, include. 2 CULIN *(añadir)* to add. 3 *(enfermo)* to help to sit up.
▷ *vpr* **incorporarse** 1 *(levantarse)* to sit up. 2 *(a un trabajo)* to start; *(a una empresa, equipo, etc)* to join.
incorrección *nf* 1 *(falta de corrección)* incorrectness. 2 *(error)* mistake.
incorrecto,-a *adj* 1 *(inexacto)* incorrect. 2 *(descortés)* impolite.
incorregible *adj* incorrigible.
incrédulo,-a *adj* 1 incredulous. 2 REL unbelieving.
increíble *adj* incredible, unbelievable.
incrementar *vt* to increase.
incremento *nm* increase, rise.
increpar *vt* 1 *(reprender)* to rebuke. 2 *(insultar)* to abuse.
incriminar *vt* to incriminate.
incruento,-a *adj* bloodless.
incrustar *vt* 1 to incrust, encrust. 2 *(arte)* to inlay.
▷ *vpr* **incrustarse** to become embedded (**en**, in).
incubar *vt* to incubate.
inculcar [1] *vt* to inculcate, instil.
inculpar *vt* to accuse (**de**, of).
inculto,-a *adj* 1 *(persona)* uneducated. 2 *(terreno)* uncultivated, untilled.
▷ *nm & nf (persona)* ignorant person, ignoramus.
incumbir *vi* to be incumbent (**a**, upon).
incumplimiento *nm (de una promesa)* failure to keep; *(de una orden)* noncompliance; *(de un deber)* negligence.
incumplir *vt (promesa)* to break; *(deber)* to fail to fulfil; *(contrato)* to break; *(orden)* to disobey.
incurable *adj* incurable.
incurrir *vi* **incurrir en** 1 *(error)* to fall into; *(delito)* to commit. 2 *(ira, etc)* to incur.
indagar [7] *vt* to investigate, inquire into.
indecencia *nf* 1 indecency. 2 *(acción indecente)* scandal.
indecente *adj* 1 *(impúdico)* indecent. 2 *(indigno)* miserable. 3 *(vil)* wretched.
indecible *adj* indescribable.
indecisión *nf* indecision.
indeciso,-a *adj* 1 *(persona)* indecisive; *(- puntualmente)* undecided. 2 *(asunto - no resuelto)* undecided.
▷ *nm & nf (persona)* ditherer.
indecoroso,-a *adj* indecorous.
indefenso,-a *adj* defenceless, helpless.
indefinido,-a *adj* 1 *(periodo de tiempo)* indefinite. 2 *(impreciso)* indefinite, indefinable. 3 LING indefinite.
indemne *adj (persona)* unharmed; *(cosa)* undamaged.
indemnización *nf* 1 *(compensación)* compensation, indemnity. 2 *(acción)* indemnification.
indemnizar [4] *vt* to compensate (**de/por**, for), indemnify (**de/por**, for).
independencia *nf* independence.
independiente *adj* 1 independent. 2 *(individualista)* self-sufficient.
independizar [4] *vt* to make independent.
▷ *vpr* **independizarse** to become independent (**de**, of).
indeterminado,-a *adj* 1 *(gen)* indeterminate. 2 *(impreciso)* vague. 3 LING *(artículo)* indefinite.
indexar *vt* to index.
India *nf* India.
indicación *nf* 1 *(indicio)* indication, mention. 2 *(gesto, señal)* sign. 3 *(instrucción)* instruction; *(recomendación)* recommendation; *(sugerencia)* suggestion.
indicado,-a *adj* appropriate, suitable.
indicador,-ra *adj (gen)* which indicates, indicating.
▷ *nm (gen)* indicator.
indicar [1] *vt* 1 to indicate. 2 *(aconsejar)* to advise.
indicativo,-a *adj* indicative.
▷ *nm* **indicativo** LING indicative.
índice *nm* 1 *(gen)* index; *(indicio)* sign, indicator. 2 *(de un libro)* index. 3 *(dedo)* index finger, forefinger.
indicio *nm* 1 *(señal)* sign. 2 *(resto)* trace.
índico,-a *adj* East Indian, Indian. ● **el (océano) Indico** the Indian Ocean.
indiferencia *nf* indifference.
indiferente *adj* indifferent.
indigente *adj* indigent, poverty-stricken.
▷ *nm o nf* poor person: **los indigentes** *the needy.*
indigestión *nf* indigestion.
indigesto,-a *adj (alimento)* hard to digest, indigestible.
indignación *nf* indignation.
indignar *vt* to infuriate.
▷ *vpr* **indignarse** to become indignant (**por**, at/about).
indigno,-a *adj* 1 unworthy (**de**, of). 2 *(vil)* low, contemptible.
indio, a *adj* Indian.
▷ *nm & nf* Indian. ■ **hacer el indio** *fam* to muck about.
indirecto,-a *adj* indirect.
indisciplina *nf* indiscipline, lack of discipline.
indisciplinado,-a *adj* undisciplined.
▷ *nm & nf* undisciplined person.
indiscreción *nf* indiscretion.
indiscreto,-a *adj* indiscreet.
▷ *nm & nf* indiscreet person.
indiscutible *adj* indisputable, unquestionable.
indisoluble *adj (sustancia)* indissoluble.
indispensable *adj* indispensable, essential.
indisponer [78] *vt* 1 *(enemistar)* to set (**contra**, against). 2 MED to upset, make unwell. 3 *(plan, proyecto)* to upset.
▷ *vpr* **indisponerse** 1 *(enemistarse)* to fall out (**con**, with). 2 *(enfermarse)* to be unwell.
indispuesto,-a *adj* 1 MED indisposed, unwell. 2 *(enemistado)* on bad terms (**con**, with).
indistinto,-a *adj* 1 *(indiferente)* immaterial: **es indistinto** *it makes no difference.* 2 *(difuso, impreciso)* indistinct. 3 *(indiferenciado)* not differentiated. 4 FIN *(cuenta)* joint.
individual *adj* individual.
▷ *nm pl* **individuales** DEP singles.
individualista *adj* individualistic.
▷ *nm o nf* individualist.
individualizar [4] *vt* 1 *(hacer individual)* to individualize. 2 *(diferenciar)* to single out.
individuo,-a *nm & nf pey (gen)* character, individual.
▷ *nm* **individuo** person.
indivisible *adj* indivisible.
indocumentado,-a *adj* 1 *(sin documentación)* without means of identification. 2 *pey (ignorante)* ignorant.

índole *nf* 1 *(carácter)* disposition. 2 *(tipo)* type, kind.
indolente *adj* indolent.
indoloro,-a *adj* painless.
indómito,-a *adj* indomitable.
Indonesia *nf* Indonesia.
indonesio,-a *adj* Indonesian.
▷ *nm & nf* Indonesian.
inducir [46] *vt* 1 *(incitar)* to induce. 2 *(inferir)* to infer, deduce. 3 ELEC to induce.
inductivo,-a *adj* inductive.
inductor,-ra *adj* 1 *(instigador)* instigating. 2 FÍS inductive.
indulgencia *nf* indulgence, leniency.
indultar *vt* 1 JUR to pardon. 2 *(eximir)* to exempt.
indulto *nm* pardon, amnesty.
indumentaria *nf* clothing, clothes *pl*.
industria *nf* 1 *(gen)* industry. 2 *(fábrica)* factory.
industrial *adj* industrial.
▷ *nm o nf* industrialist, manufacturer.
industrializar [4] *vt* to industrialize.
inédito,-a *adj* 1 *(libro)* unpublished. 2 *(nuevo)* new, unheard of. 3 *(desconocido)* unknown.
inefable *adj* ineffable.
ineficaz *adj* 1 *(incompetente)* inefficient. 2 *(improductivo)* ineffective.
ineficiente *adj* inefficient.
ineludible *adj* unavoidable, inevitable.
INEM *abrev* (**Instituto Nacional de Empleo**) ≈ Unemployment Benefit Office; *(abreviatura)* UBO.
inenarrable *adj* indescribable.
ineptitud *nf* incompetence, ineptitude.
inepto,-a *adj (persona)* incompetent, inept.
▷ *nm & nf* incompetent person.
inercia *nf* 1 inertia. 2 *(pasividad)* apathy.
inerte *adj* 1 *(materia, gas)* inert. 2 *(cadáver)* lifeless.
inesperado,-a *adj* unexpected.
inestable *adj* unstable, unsteady.
inevitable *adj* inevitable, unavoidable.
inexacto,-a *adj* inexact, inaccurate.
inexcusable *adj* 1 *(imperdonable)* inexcusable. 2 *(obligatorio)* unavoidable.
inexistente *adj* nonexistent.
inexorable *adj* inexorable.
inexperiencia *nf* inexperience.
inexperto,-a *adj* inexperienced.
inexplicable *adj* inexplicable.
inexpresivo,-a *adj (cara, persona)* inexpressive.
infalible *adj* infallible.
infame *adj* 1 *(vil)* despicable, vile. 2 *(muy malo)* awful.
infamia *nf (deshonra)* disgrace.
infancia *nf* 1 *(de una persona - gen)* childhood. 2 *(de un proyecto, etc)* infancy. 3 *(los niños)* children *pl*.
infante,-a *nm* **infante** 1 *lit (niño)* infant. 2 *(soldado)* infantryman.
infantería *nf* infantry.
infantil *adj* 1 *(literatura, juego)* children's; *(equipo)* junior. 2 *(aniñado)* childlike. 3 *(inmaduro)* childish.
infarto *nm* 1 *(de miocardio)* heart attack. 2 *(de otros órganos)* infarction. ● **infarto de miocardio** heart attack.
infatigable *adj* indefatigable, tireless.
infección *nf* infection.
infectar *vt* to infect (**de**, with).
▷ *vpr* **infectarse** to become infected (**de**, with).
infecundo,-a *adj* infertile.
infeliz *adj* 1 *(desdichado)* unhappy. 2 *(ingenuo)* ingenuous.
inferior *adj* 1 *(situado debajo)* lower. 2 *(cantidad)* less, lower. 3 *(en calidad)* inferior (**a**, to).
▷ *nm o nf (en rango)* subordinate; *(en calidad)* inferior.
inferioridad *nf* inferiority.
inferir [35] *vt* 1 *(deducir)* to infer (**de**, from), conclude. 2 *(daño físico)* to inflict; *(daño moral)* to cause.
infernal *adj* 1 *(del infierno)* infernal. 2 *fam fig* hellish.
infestar *vt (invadir)* to infest.
infidelidad *nf* 1 *(sexual)* infidelity, unfaithfulness. 2 *(de un amigo)* disloyalty. 3 *(inexactitud)* inaccuracy.
infiel *adj* 1 *(esposo)* unfaithful (**a/con/para**, to); *(amigo)* disloyal (**a**, to). 2 *(inexacto)* inaccurate. 3 REL unbelieving, infidel.
▷ *nm o nf* REL unbeliever, nonbeliever, infidel.
infiernillo *nm* portable stove.
infierno *nm* hell. ■ **¡vete al infierno!** go to hell!, get lost!
infiltrar *vt* to infiltrate.
▷ *vpr* **infiltrarse** 1 to infiltrate (**en**, -). 2 *(líquido)* to seep (**en**, into); *(luz)* to filter (**en**, into).
ínfimo,-a *adj (en calidad)* lowest, poorest.
infinidad *nf* 1 *(infinito)* infinity. 2 *(gran cantidad)* great number, infinite number.
infinitesimal *adj* infinitesimal.
infinitivo,-a *nm* **infinitivo** infinitive.
infinito,-a *adj* infinite.
▷ *nm* **el infinito** the infinite, infinity.
inflación *nf* inflation.
inflamable *adj* inflammable.
inflamación *nf* 1 MED inflammation. 2 *(combustión)* combustion, ignition.
inflamar *vt* MED to inflame.
▷ *vpr* **inflamarse** MED to become inflamed.
inflamatorio,-a *adj* inflammatory.
inflar *vt* 1 *(balón)* to blow up, inflate. 2 *fig (hechos, noticias)* to exaggerate. 3 *(precios)* to inflate.
▷ *vpr* **inflarse** 1 to inflate one's opinion of OS. 2 *fam (hartarse de comer)* to stuff OS (**de**, with).
inflexible *adj* inflexible.
inflexión *nf* inflection.
infligir [6] *vt (castigo)* to inflict; *(pena)* to cause.
influencia *nf* influence.
influenciar [12] *vt* to influence.
influir [62] *vt* to influence.
▷ *vi* to have influence.
influjo *nm* influence.
influyente *adj* influential.
información *nf* 1 *(conocimiento)* information. 2 *(noticia)* piece of news; *(conjunto de noticias)* news. 3 *(oficina)* information department; *(mesa)* information desk. 4 *(en telefónica)* directory enquiries *pl*, US information.
informal *adj* 1 *(desenfadado)* informal. 2 *(persona)* unreliable.
informante *adj* providing information, informing.
▷ *nm o nf (en encuesta)* informant.
informar *vt (dar noticia)* to inform (**de**, about).
▷ *vi* to inform (**de**, about), tell (**de**, about).
▷ *vpr* **informarse** to find out (**de**, about).
informática *nf* computer science, computing.
informático,-a *adj* computer, computing.
▷ *nm & nf* computer expert.

nformativo,-a *adj* 1 *(ilustrativo)* informative: **una campaña con carácter informativo** *a public awareness campaign*. 2 *(programa)* news.
▷ *nm* **informativo** news programme, news.
nformatizar [4] *vt* to computerize.
nforme *adj (sin forma)* shapeless, formless.
▷ *nm* report.
▷ *nm pl* **informes** references.
nfracción *nf* infraction, infringement.
nfractor,-ra *adj* offending.
▷ *nm & nf* offender.
nfraestructura *nf* 1 *(de una organización)* infrastructure. 2 *(de una edificación)* foundations *pl*.
nfranqueable *adj* 1 impassable. 2 *fig* insurmountable.
nfrarrojo,-a *adj* infrared.
nfravalorar *vt* to underestimate.
nfrecuente *adj* infrequent.
nfringir [6] *vt (gen)* to infringe; *(ley)* to break.
nfructuoso,-a *adj* fruitless, unsuccessful.
nfundado,-a *adj* unfounded, groundless.
nfundir *vt (respeto)* to command; *(miedo)* to fill with; *(valor)* to instil; *(deseo)* to infuse with.
infusión *nf (acción)* infusion; *(bebida)* herbal tea, infusion.
ingeniar [12] *vt* to devise.
▷ *vpr* **ingeniárselas** to manage, find a way, contrive.
ingeniería *nf* engineering.
ingeniero,-a *nm & nf* engineer.
ingenio *nm* 1 *(talento)* talent; *(chispa)* wit. 2 *(habilidad)* ingenuity. 3 *(individuo)* genius. 4 *(aparato)* device.
ingenioso,-a *adj (inteligente)* ingenious; *(con chispa)* witty.
ingenuo,-a *adj* naive, ingenuous.
▷ *nm & nf* naive person.
ingerir [35] *vt (alimentos)* to eat; *(bebida)* to drink.
ingestión *nf* ingestion, consumption, swallowing.
Inglaterra *nf* England.
ingle *nf* groin.
inglés,-esa *adj* English.
▷ *nm & nf (persona)* English person; *(hombre)* Englishman; *(mujer)* Englishwoman.
▷ *nm* **inglés** *(idioma)* English.
ingratitud *nf* ingratitude, ungratefulness.
ingrato,-a *adj* 1 *(persona)* ungrateful. 2 *(trabajo, tarea)* thankless. 3 *(tiempo)* unpleasant.
ingrediente *nm* ingredient.
ingresar *vt (dinero)* to pay in, deposit.
▷ *vi* **ingresar en** 1 *(entrar)* to join. 2 *(hospital)* to be admitted to.
ingreso *nm* 1 *(en club, ejército)* joining; *(en hospital)* admission. 2 *(entrada)* entry. 3 FIN deposit.
▷ *nm pl* **ingresos** *(sueldo, renta)* income *sing*.
inhabilitar *vt* JUR to disqualify.
inhabitable *adj* uninhabitable.
inhalador *nm* inhaler.
inhalar *vt* to inhale, breathe in.
inherente *adj* inherent (**a**, in).
inhibir *vt* 1 *(reprimir)* to inhibit. 2 MED to inhibit.
▷ *vpr* **inhibirse** 1 *(reprimirse)* to be inhibited. 2 *(abstenerse)* to refrain (**de**, from); *(negarse)* to refuse (**de**, to).
inhóspito,-a *adj* inhospitable.
inhumano,-a *adj* 1 *(persona)* inhuman, cruel. 2 *(dolor, sufrimiento)* inhuman.
inhumar *vt* to bury.
iniciación *nf* 1 *(comienzo)* start, beginning. 2 *(de una persona)* initiation, introduction (**a**, to).
inicial *adj* initial.
▷ *nf* initial.
inicialización *nf* INFORMÁ initialization.
inicializar *vt* INFORMÁ to initialize.
iniciar [12] *vt* 1 *(empezar)* to start, begin. 2 *(introducir)* to initiate (**en**, in).
▷ *vpr* **iniciarse** *(empezar)* to start, begin.
iniciativa *nf* initiative.
inicio *nm* beginning, start.
inigualable *adj* unrivalled.
inimaginable *adj* unimaginable.
inimitable *adj* inimitable.
ininteligible *adj* unintelligible.
injerencia *nf* interference.
injertar *vt* to graft.
injerto *nm* graft.
injuria *nf* 1 insult, affront. 2 JUR slander.
injuriar [12] *vt* 1 *(insultar)* to insult. 2 JUR to slander.
injusticia *nf* injustice, unfairness.
injusto,-a *adj* unfair, unjust.
inmadurez *nf* immaturity.
inmaduro,-a *adj* immature.
inmediaciones *nf pl (de una zona)* surrounding area *sing*.
inmediato,-a *adj* 1 *(poco después)* immediate. 2 *(contiguo)* next (**a**, to), adjoining (**a**, -).
inmejorable *adj (gen)* unbeatable, unsurpassable.
inmensidad *nf* 1 immensity. 2 *(gran cantidad)* great number.
inmenso,-a *adj* immense, vast.
inmersión *nf (gen)* immersion; *(de un buceador, etc)* dive.
inmerso,-a *adj* immersed (**en**, in).
inmigración *nf* immigration.
inmigrante *adj* immigrant.
▷ *nm o nf* immigrant.
inmigrar *vi* to immigrate.
inminente *adj* imminent.
inmobiliario,-a *adj* property, US real estate.
▷ *nf* **(agencia) inmobiliaria** estate agency, US real estate company.
inmodestia *nf* arrogance, immodesty.
inmolación *nf* immolation.
inmolar *vt* to immolate, sacrifice.
inmoral *adj* immoral.
inmoralidad *nf* immorality.
inmortal *adj* immortal.
▷ *nm o nf* immortal.
inmortalidad *nf* immortality.
inmortalizar [4] *vt* to immortalize.
inmotivado,-a *adj* 1 *(sin motivo)* uncalled for. 2 *(sin motivación)* unmotivated.
inmóvil *adj* 1 still. 2 *fig (constante)* determined.
inmovilidad *nf* immobility.
inmovilismo *nm* immobilism.
inmovilista *adj* reactionary.
▷ *nm o nf* reactionary.
inmovilización *nf* immobilization.
inmovilizar [4] *vt* to immobilize.
inmueble *nm* building.
inmundicia *nf* 1 *(suciedad)* dirt. 2 *(basura)* rubbish.
inmundo,-a *adj* 1 *(sucio)* dirty, filthy. 2 *fig* dirty.

inmune *adj* 1 MED immune (a, to). 2 *(exento)* exempt (de, from).
inmunidad *nf* immunity.
inmunitario,-a *adj* immune.
inmunización *nf* immunization.
inmunizar [4] *vt* to immunize.
inmunodeficiencia *nf* immunodeficiency.
inmunodeficiente *adj* immunodeficient.
▷ *nm o nf* immnunodeficient.
inmunodepresor,-ra *adj* immunosuppressive.
▷ *nm* inmunodepresor immunosuppressant.
inmunología *nf* immunology.
inmunoterapia *nf* immunotherapy.
inmutabilidad *nf* immutability.
inmutable *adj* unchangeable, immutable.
inmutar *vt* to affect.
▷ *vpr* inmutarse to react.
innato,-a *adj* innate, inborn.
innecesario,-a *adj* unnecessary.
innegable *adj* undeniable.
innoble *adj* ignoble.
innoblemente *adv* ignobly.
innombrable *adj* unmentionable.
innominado,-a *adj* nameless.
innovación *nf* innovation.
innovador,-ra *adj* innovatory.
▷ *nm & nf* innovator.
innovar *vi* to innovate.
innumerable *adj* innumerable, countless.
inobservancia *nf* nonobservance (de, of).
inocencia *nf* 1 innocence. 2 *(ingenuidad)* naivety.
inocentada *nf* practical joke.
inocente *adj* 1 innocent. 2 *(ingenuo)* naive, innocent.
▷ *nm o nf* 1 innocent person. 2 naive person.
inocentón,-ona *adj fam* naive.
▷ *nm & nf fam* naive person, gullible person.
inocuidad *nf* harmlessness, innocuousness.
inoculación *nf* inoculation.
inocular *vt* to inoculate.
inocuo,-a *adj* innocuous, harmless.
inodoro,-a *adj* odourless.
▷ *nm* inodoro toilet.
inofensivo,-a *adj* harmless, inoffensive.
inolvidable *adj* unforgettable.
inoperable *adj* inoperable.
inoperancia *nf* ineffectiveness.
inoperante *adj* ineffective, inoperative.
inopia ■ estar en la inopia *fam (distraído)* to have one's head in the clouds.
inopinado,-a *adj* unexpected.
inoportuno,-a *adj (visita, etc)* inopportune, untimely.
inorgánico,-a *adj* inorganic.
inoxidable *adj* rustproof.
input *nm* input.
inquebrantable *adj* unbreakable.
inquietante *adj* disturbing.
inquietar *vt* to worry.
▷ *vpr* inquietarse to worry (por, about).
inquieto,-a *adj* 1 *(agitado)* restless. 2 *(preocupado)* worried, anxious. 3 *(interesado)* eager, interested.
inquietud *nf* 1 *(agitación)* restlessness. 2 *(preocupación)* worry, anxiety. 3 *(interés)* interest.
inquilino,-a *nm & nf* tenant.
inquina *nf* animosity, antipathy.
inquirir [30] *vt* to inquire, investigate.
inquisitivo,-a *adj* inquisitive.
insaciable *adj* insatiable.
insalubre *adj* insalubrious, unhealthy.
insalubridad *nf* insalubrity.
insano,-a *adj* 1 *(no sano)* unhealthy. 2 *(loco)* insane.
insatisfacción *nf* dissatisfaction.
insatisfactorio,-a *adj* unsatisfactory.
insatisfecho,-a *adj* dissatisfied, unsatisfied.
inscribir *vt* 1 *(grabar)* to inscribe. 2 *(apuntar)* to register; *(en un curso)* to enrol (US enroll).
▷ *vpr* inscribirse *(gen)* to register; *(para un curso)* to enrol (US enroll).
inscripción *nf* 1 *(grabado)* inscription. 2 *(registro)* registration; *(en un curso)* enrolment (US enrollment).
insecticida *adj* insecticidal.
▷ *nm* insecticide.
insectívoro,-a *adj* insectivorous.
▷ *nm* insectívoro insectivore.
insecto *nm* insect.
inseguridad *nf* 1 *(falta de confianza)* insecurity. 2 *(duda)* uncertainty. 3 *(peligro)* lack of safety.
inseguro,-a *adj* 1 *(sin confianza)* insecure. 2 *(que duda)* uncertain. 3 *(peligroso)* unsafe.
inseminación *nf* insemination.
inseminar *vt* to inseminate.
insensatez *nf* foolishness.
insensato,-a *adj* foolish.
▷ *nm & nf* fool.
insensibilidad *nf* insensitivity.
insensibilizar *vt* 1 MED to desensitize. 2 to make insensitive.
insensible *adj* 1 insensitive, unfeeling, thoughtless. 2 MED insensible. 3 *(imperceptible)* insensible.
inseparable *adj* inseparable.
insepulto,-a *adj* unburied.
inserción *nf* insertion.
insertar *vt* to insert (en, into).
inserto,-a *adj* inserted.
inservible *adj* useless.
insigne *adj* distinguished, eminent.
insignia *nf* 1 *(distintivo)* badge. 2 *(bandera)* flag.
insignificancia *nf* 1 *(cualidad)* insignificance. 2 *(pequeñez)* trifle.
insignificante *adj* insignificant.
insinceridad *nf* insincerity.
insincero,-a *adj* insincere.
insinuación *nf* 1 *(indicación)* insinuation, hint. 2 *fam (amorosa)* overture.
insinuante *adj* 1 *(gen)* insinuating. 2 *(provocativo)* suggestive.
insinuar [11] *vt* to insinuate, hint.
▷ *vpr* insinuarse *(amorosamente)* to a pass (a, at).
insipidez *nf* insipidity.
insípido,-a *adj* 1 *(comida)* tasteless. 2 *fig* insipid.
insistencia *nf (acción)* insistence, persistence.
insistente *adj* insistent.
insistir *vi* 1 to insist (en, on). 2 *(enfatizar)* to stress (en, -)
insobornable *adj* incorruptible.
insociable *adj* unsociable.

insolación *nf* 1 MED sunstroke. 2 *(en meteorología)* sunshine, sunlight.
insolencia *nf* 1 *(atrevimiento)* insolence. 2 *(palabra)* cheeky remark; *(acción)* cheeky thing to do.
insolente *adj* 1 *(descarado)* insolent. 2 *(soberbio)* haughty.
insolidaridad *nf* lack of solidarity.
insolidario,-a *adj* unsupportive, selfish.
insólito,-a *adj* extremely unusual.
insoluble *adj* insoluble.
insolvencia *nf* insolvency.
insolvente *adj* insolvent.
insomne *adj* sleepless.
▷ *nm o nf* insomniac.
insomnio *nm* insomnia.
insondable *adj* unfathomable.
insonorización *nf* soundproofing.
insonorizado,-a *adj* soundproof.
insonorizar [4] *vt* to soundproof.
insoportable *adj* unbearable.
insoslayable *adj* unavoidable.
insospechable *adj* 1 *(inimaginable)* unforeseeable. 2 *(sorprendente)* amazing, outlandish.
insospechado,-a *adj* 1 *(no sospechado)* unsuspected. 2 *(inesperado)* unexpected.
insostenible *adj* untenable.
inspección *nf (gen)* examination; *(policial)* search.
inspeccionar *vt (gen)* to inspect.
inspector,-ra *nm & nf* inspector.
inspiración *nf* 1 inspiration. 2 *(inhalación)* inhalation.
inspirado,-a *adj* inspired.
inspirador,-ra *adj* inspiring, stimulating.
▷ *nm & nf* inspirer.
inspirar *vt* 1 *(aspirar)* to inhale. 2 *(infundir)* to inspire.
▷ *vpr* **inspirarse** to be inspired (**en**, by).
INSS *abrev* (**Instituto Nacional de la Seguridad Social**) *national institute for social security*.
instalación *nf* 1 *(de un aparato)* installation. 2 *(de personas)* settling in; *(de empresas)* establishment, setting up.
▷ *nf pl* **instalaciones** *(de un servicio)* facilities *pl*.
instalador,-ra *nm & nf* installer, fitter.
instalar *vt* 1 *(colocar)* to install. 2 *(equipar)* to fit out. 3 *(acomodar)* to put, put up, house.
▷ *vpr* **instalarse** *(persona)* to settle; *(empresa)* to set up.
instancia *nf* 1 *(petición)* request. 2 JUR instance.
instantánea *nf (foto)* snapshot, snap.
instantáneo,-a *adj* 1 *(inmediato)* instantaneous, immediate. 2 *(momentáneo)* brief, fleeting.
instante *nm* moment, instant.
instar *vi (insistir)* to press, urge.
instauración *nf* establishment.
instaurar *vt* to establish.
instigación *nf* instigation.
instigador,-ra *adj* instigating.
instigar [7] *vt (a una persona)* to instigate.
instintivo,-a *adj* instinctive.
instinto *nm* instinct.
institución *nf* 1 *(organismo)* institution. 2 *(creación)* establishment, institution.
institucional *adj* institutional.
institucionalización *nf* institutionalization.
institucionalizar *vt* to institutionalize.
instituir [62] *vt* 1 *(crear)* to institute, establish. 2 *(nombrar)* to appoint.
instituto *nm* 1 *(asociación)* institute. 2 EDUC state secondary school, US high school. ● **instituto de bachillerato** state secondary school, US high school.
institutriz *nf* governess.
instrucción *nf* 1 *(enseñanza)* instruction; *(cultura)* education. 2 MIL military training. 3 JUR *(de un expediente)* preliminary investigation. 4 *(orden)* instruction.
▷ *nf pl* **instrucciones** *(indicaciones)* instructions.
instructivo,-a *adj* instructive.
instructor,-ra *adj* 1 *(gen)* instructing. 2 JUR *(juez)* examining, investigating.
▷ *nm & nf* instructor.
instruido,-a *adj* well-educated.
instruir [62] *vt* 1 *(enseñar)* to instruct. 2 MIL to train. 3 JUR to examine, investigate.
instrumentación *nf* instrumentation.
instrumental *adj (música)* instrumental.
▷ *nm* instruments *pl*, instrumentation.
instrumentar *vt (gen)* to arrange.
instrumentista *nm o nf* 1 *(músico)* instrumentalist. 2 *(fabricante)* instrument maker.
instrumento *nm* instrument.
insubordinación *nf* insubordination.
insubordinado,-a *adj* insubordinate.
▷ *nm & nf* insubordinate person.
insubordinar *vt* to stir up.
▷ *vpr* **insubordinarse** to rebel.
insubstancial *adj* insubstantial.
insubstancialidad *nf* insubstantiality.
insubstituible *adj* irreplaceable.
insuficiencia *nf* 1 *(escasez)* shortage. 2 MED failure.
insuficiente *adj* insufficient.
▷ *nm* EDUC fail.
insufrible *adj* insufferable.
ínsula *nf* LIT island.
insular *adj* insular.
▷ *nm o nf* islander.
insulina *nf* insulin.
insulsez *nf* insipidity.
insulso,-a *adj* 1 *(comida)* insipid. 2 *(persona)* dull.
insultante *adj* insulting.
insultar *vt* to insult.
insulto *nm* insult.
insumisión *nf* 1 *(gen)* rebelliousness. 2 MIL refusal to do military service.
insumiso,-a *adj* rebellious.
▷ *nm & nf* MIL *person who refuses to do military service or community service in lieu*.
insuperable *adj (calidad, capacidad)* unbeatable; *(obstáculo, miedo, complejo)* unsurmountable, insuperable.
insurgente *adj* insurgent.
▷ *nm o nf* insurgent.
insurrección *nf* insurrection, uprising.
insurrecto,-a *adj* insurgent.
▷ *nm & nf* insurgent.
intachable *adj* irreproachable.
intacto,-a *adj* intact.
intangible *adj* intangible.
integración *nf* integration.

integral *adj* 1 *(intrínseco)* integral; *(completo)* full. 2 *(pan, pasta)* wholemeal; *(arroz)* brown.
▷ *nf* MAT integral.
integralmente *adv* completely.
íntegramente *adv* entirely.
integrante *adj* integral.
▷ *nm o nf* member.
integrar *vt* 1 *(formar)* to make up. 2 *(ayudar a la integración)* to integrate, fit in.
▷ *vpr* **integrarse** to integrate.
integridad *nf* integrity.
integrismo *nm (gen)* reaction; *(religioso)* fundamentalism.
integrista *adj (gen)* reactionary; *(religioso)* fundamentalist.
▷ *nm o nf (gen)* reactionary; *(en religión)* fundamentalist.
íntegro,-a *adj* 1 *(completo)* whole, entire; *(versión)* unabridged. 2 *(honrado)* honest, upright.
intelecto *nm* intellect.
intelectual *adj* intellectual.
▷ *nm o nf* intellectual.
intelectualidad *nf* intellectuals *pl*, intelligentsia.
intelectualizar *vt* to intellectualize.
inteligencia *nf* intelligence. ● **inteligencia artificial** artificial intelligence.
inteligente *adj* 1 intelligent. 2 *(edificio)* smart.
inteligibilidad *nf* intelligibility.
inteligible *adj* intelligible.
intemperante *adj* intolerant.
intemperie *nf* bad weather. ■ **a la intemperie** in the open (air), outdoors.
intempestivo,-a *adj* untimely, inopportune.
intemporal *adj* timeless.
intención *nf* 1 *(propósito)* intention. 2 *(malicia)* maliciousness.
intencionado,-a *adj* deliberate, intentional.
intencional *adj* intentional.
intencionalidad *nf* intent, intention.
intendencia *nf* MIL *(cuerpo)* ± service corps, US quartermaster corps.
intendente *nm* 1 supervisor. 2 MIL quartermaster general.
intensamente *adv* intenselly.
intensidad *nf* 1 *(gen)* intensity. 2 *(del viento)* force; *(de un ruido)* loudness, high volume. 3 *(de una enfermedad)* severity; *(del dolor)* acuteness. 4 *(de la luz, del color)* brightness, intensity; *(del amor, de la fe)* strength.
intensificación *nf* intensification.
intensificar [1] *vt* to intensify.
intensivo,-a *adj* intensive.
intenso,-a *adj* 1 *(gen)* intense. 2 *(dolor)* acute. 3 *(luz, color)* bright, intense. 4 *(amor)* passionate.
intentar *vt* to try.
intento *nm* attempt, try.
intentona *nf* frustrated attempt.
interacción *nf* interaction.
interactivo,-a *adj* interactive.
interbancario,-a *adj* interbank.
intercalar *vt* to insert.
intercambiable *adj* interchangeable.
intercambiar [12] *vt* to exchange.
intercambio *nm* exchange, interchange.
interceder *vi* to intercede.
interceptación *nf* interception.
interceptar *vt* 1 *(mensaje, correspondencia)* to inte[r]cept. 2 *(obstruir)* to block; *(tráfico)* to hold up.
interceptor *adj* intercepting.
▷ *nm* interceptor.
intercesión *nf* intercession, mediation.
intercesor,-ra *adj* interceding.
▷ *nm & nf* intercessor.
intercomunicación *nf* intercommunication.
interconectar *vt* interconnect.
interconexión *nf* interconnection.
intercontinental *adj* intercontinental.
intercostal *adj* intercostal.
intercultural *adj* cross-cultural.
interdental *adj* interdental.
interdependencia *nf* interdependence.
interdependiente *adj* interdependent.
interdicción *nf* interdiction.
interdicto *nm* interdict.
interdisciplinario,-a *adj* interdisciplinary.
interés *nm* 1 *(gen)* interest; *(propio)* self-interest. 2 FI[N] interest.
interesado,-a *adj* 1 *(gen)* interested. 2 *(egoísta)* sel[f]ish, self-interested.
▷ *nm & nf* 1 *(gen)* interested party. 2 *(egoísta)* selfis[h] person.
interesante *adj* interesting.
interesar *vt* 1 to interest. 2 *(despertar interés)* to inter[]est. 3 *(afectar)* to concern. 4 *(ser útil)* to be in SB's in[]terest.
▷ *vpr* **interesarse** to take an interest (**por**, in).
interestatal *adj* interstate.
interface *nf* interface.
interfaz *nf* interface.
▲ *pl* **interfaces**.
interfecto,-a *nm & nf* 1 JUR victim. 2 *fam* person i[n] question.
interferencia *nf* 1 *(gen)* interference; *(intencionada)* jamming. 2 *fig* interference.
interferir [35] *vt* 1 *(transmisión, programa)* to jam. 2 *(obstaculizar)* to interfere in.
▷ *vi* to meddle, interfere.
interfono *nm* intercom.
intergubernamental *adj* intergovernmental.
ínterin ■ **en el ínterin** meanwhile.
interina *nf (asistenta)* cleaning lady.
interino,-a *adj* 1 temporary, provisional. 2 *(director, presidente)* acting.
▷ *nm & nf (sustituto)* stand-in.
interior *adj* 1 *(bolsillo)* inside; *(habitación)* without a view, interior; *(jardín)* interior. 2 *(del país)* domestic, internal. 3 GEOG inland.
▷ *nm* 1 *(en una vivienda)* inside: **pasemos al interior** *let's go inside.* 2 *(conciencia)* inside. 3 GEOG interior.
interiorismo *nm* interior design.
interiorista *nm o nf* interior designer.
interiorización *nf* 1 *(de una creencia)* internalization. 2 *(de sentimientos)* suppression, repression.
interiorizar [4] *vt* 1 *(creencia, principio)* to internalize. 2 *(sentimiento)* to suppress, repress.
interiormente *adv* inside.

interjección *nf* interjection.
interlineador *nm* line spacer.
interlocutor,-ra *nm & nf* speaker, interlocutor.
interludio *nm* interlude.
intermediar *vi* to mediate.
intermediario,-a *nm & nf (en negocios)* middleman; *(gen)* intermediary; *(en disputas)* mediator.
intermedio,-a *adj (gen)* intermediate; *(tamaño)* medium; *(calidad)* average, medium; *(tiempo)* transitional, intervening; *(espacio)* between.
▷ *nm* **intermedio** *(de un espectáculo)* interval, intermission.
interminable *adj* endless, interminable.
interministerial *adj* interministerial.
intermitencia *nf* intermittence.
intermitente *adj (gen)* intermittent; *(luz, destello)* flashing.
▷ *nm* AUTO indicator, US blinker.
internacional *adj* international.
internacionalismo *nm* internationalism.
internacionalidad *nf* internationality.
internacionalista *adj* internationalist.
internacionalizar *vt* to internationalize.
internacionalmente *adv* internationally.
internado,-a *nm* **internado** boarding school.
internamente *adv* internally.
internamiento *nm (en un hospital)* confinement.
internar *vt (en un colegio)* to send to boarding school; *(en un hospital)* to confine (**en**, to).
▷ *vpr* **internarse** *(penetrar)* to penetrate.
internauta *nm o nf* internaut, netsurfer.
internista *nm o nf* internist.
interno,-a *adj* 1 *(órgano)* internal. 2 *(política)* domestic, home. 3 *(alumno)* boarding.
▷ *nm & nf* 1 *(alumno)* boarder. 2 *(médico)* intern. 3 *(preso)* prisoner.
interparlamentario,-a *adj* interparliamentary.
interpelación *nf* 1 POL interpellation. 2 *(gen)* question.
interpelar *vt* POL to interpellate.
interpersonal *adj* interpersonal.
interplanetario,-a *adj* interplanetary.
Interpol *nf* Interpol.
interpolación *nf* interpolation.
interpolar *vt* to interpolate.
interponer [78] *vt* 1 to interpose. 2 JUR to lodge.
▷ *vpr* **interponerse** 1 *(físicamente)* to interpose OS. 2 *fig* to intervene.
interposición *nf* 1 interposition. 2 JUR lodging.
interpretación *nf* 1 *(gen)* interpretation. 2 *(de pieza, obra)* performance. 3 *(de idiomas)* interpreting.
interpretar *vt* 1 to interpret. 2 *(obra, pieza)* to perform; *(papel)* to play; *(canción)* to sing.
interpretativo,-a *adj* interpretative.
intérprete *nm o nf* 1 *(traductor)* interpreter. 2 *(actor, músico)* performer.
interracial *adj* interracial.
interregno *nm* interregnum.
interrelación *nf* interrelation.
interrelacionar *vt* to interrelate.
interrogación *nf* 1 *(acción)* interrogation, questioning. 2 *(signo)* question mark, interrogation mark. 3 *(pregunta)* question.
interrogador,-a *nm & nf* interrogator.
interrogante *nm (incógnita)* question mark.
interrogar [7] *vt* 1 to question. 2 *(a testigo, etc)* to interrogate.
interrogativo,-a *adj* interrogative.
interrogatorio *nm* interrogation.
interrumpir *vt* 1 *(gen)* to interrupt. 2 *(obras)* to stop, halt; *(discurso)* to break off; *(vacaciones)* to cut short; *(tráfico)* to block.
interrupción *nf* interruption.
interruptor *nm* switch.
intersección *nf* intersection.
intersticio *nm* interstice.
interurbano,-a *adj (gen)* inter-city; *(llamada)* trunk, long-distance.
intervalo *nm* 1 *(de tiempo)* interval. 2 *(de espacio)* gap.
intervención *nf* 1 *(gen)* intervention. 2 *(discurso)* speech. 3 MED operation. 4 *(de una empresa)* auditing. 5 *(de un teléfono)* tapping.
intervencionismo *nm* interventionism.
intervencionista *adj* interventionist.
▷ *nm o nf* interventionist.
intervenir [90] *vi* 1 *(tomar parte)* to take part (**en**, in); *(mediar)* to intervene. 2 *(interrumpir)* to intervene. 3 *(hablar)* to speak (**en**, at).
▷ *vt* 1 MED to operate on. 2 *(alijo, mercancía)* to seize. 3 *(teléfono)* to tap. 4 *(cuentas)* to audit.
interventor,-ra *nm & nf* 1 *(gen)* inspector, auditor; *(de ayuntamiento)* treasurer. 2 *(en elecciones)* scrutineer.
interviú *nm* interview.
intervocálico,-a *adj* intervocalic.
intestado,-a *adj* intestate.
intestinal *adj* intestinal.
intestino *nm* intestine.
intimar *vi* to become close (**con**, to).
intimidación *nf* intimidation.
intimidad *nf* 1 *(amistad)* intimacy. 2 *(vida privada)* privacy, private life.
intimidar *vt* to intimidate.
intimidatorio,-a *adj* intimidating, threatening.
intimismo *nm* intimism.
intimista *adj* intimist.
íntimo,-a *adj* 1 *(vida)* private. 2 *(amigo, relación)* close. 3 *(sentimiento, emoción)* most intimate. 4 *(higiene)* personal.
▷ *nm & nf (amigo)* close friend.
intocable *adj* untouchable.
intolerable *adj* intolerable, unbearable.
intolerancia *nf* intolerance: **intolerancia a la lactosa** *intolerance of lactose.*
intolerante *adj* intolerant.
intoxicación *nf* poisoning.
intoxicar [1] *vt* to poison.
▷ *vpr* **intoxicarse** to poison OS.
intraducible *adj* untranslatable.
intramuros *adv* within the city walls.
intramuscular *adj* intramuscular.
intranquilidad *nf* worry, uneasiness.
intranquilizar [4] *vt* to worry.
▷ *vpr* **intranquilizarse** to worry, get worried.
intranquilo,-a *adj* worried, uneasy.
intranscribible *adj* unprintable.

intransferible *adj* nontransferable.
intransigencia *nf* intransigence.
intransigente *adj* intransigent.
intransitable *adj* impassable.
intransitivo,-a *adj* intransitive.
intrascendencia *nf* unimportance, insignificance.
intrascendente *adj* unimportant, insignificant.
intratable *adj* 1 *(persona)* bad-tempered, unsociable. 2 *(asunto)* intractable.
intrauterino,-a *adj* intrauterine.
intravenoso,-a *adj* intravenous.
intrepidez *nf* fearlessness, courage.
intrépido,-a *adj* intrepid.
intriga *nf* 1 *(maquinación secreta)* intrigue. 2 *(curiosidad)* curiosity. 3 *(de una narración, película)* intrigue.
intrigado,-a *adj* intrigued.
intrigante *adj* 1 *(curioso, interesante)* intriguing. 2 *pey* scheming.
▷ *nm o nf (persona)* intriguer, schemer.
intrigar [7] *vt (interesar)* to intrigue.
▷ *vi (maquinar)* to intrigue, plot, scheme.
intrincado,-a *adj* 1 *(asunto)* intricate, complicate. 2 *(camino)* winding, roundabout.
intrínseco,-a *adj* intrinsic.
introducción *nf* introduction.
introducir [46] *vt* 1 *(gen)* to introduce; *(legislación)* to introduce, bring in; *(cambios)* to make (**en**, to). 2 *(meter)* to put, place; *(insertar)* insert. 3 *(importar)* to bring in, import; *(clandestinamente)* to smuggle in.
▷ *vpr* **introducirse** *(entrar)* to go in, get in, enter.
introductor,-ra *adj* introductory.
▷ *nm & nf* introducer.
introductorio,-a *adj* introductory.
intromisión *nf* interference, meddling.
introspección *nf* introspection.
introspectivo,-a *adj* introspective.
introversión *nf* introversion.
introvertido,-a *adj* introverted.
▷ *nm & nf* introvert.
intrusión *nf* intrusion.
intrusismo *nm* quackery.
intruso,-a *adj* intrusive.
▷ *nm & nf* intruder.
intuición *nf* intuition.
intuir [62] *vt* to sense, feel.
intuitivo,-a *adj* intuitive.
inundación *nf* flood, flooding.
inundar *vt* 1 to flood. 2 *fig* to inundate.
inusitado,-a *adj* uncommon, rare.
inusual *adj* unusual.
inútil *adj* 1 *(gen)* useless. 2 *(intento)* vain, futile.
▷ *nm o nf fam (persona)* hopeless case.
inutilidad *nf* uselessness.
inutilizable *adj* unusable.
inutilizar [4] *vt* 1 to render useless. 2 *(máquina)* to put out of action.
invadir *vt* to invade.
invalidación *nf* invalidation.
invalidar *vt* to invalidate.
invalidez *nf* 1 JUR *(nulidad)* invalidity. 2 MED *(incapacidad)* disablement, disability.
inválido,-a *adj* 1 JUR *(nulo)* invalid. 2 *(persona)* disabled, handicapped.
▷ *nm & nf* disabled person.
invariabilidad *nf* invariability.
invariable *adj* invariable.
invasión *nf* invasion.
invasivo,-va *adj* invasive.
invasor,-ra *adj* invading.
▷ *nm & nf* invader.
invectiva *nf* invective.
invencible *adj (ejército)* invincible; *(obstáculo)* unsurmountable.
invención *nf* 1 *(invento)* invention. 2 *(mentira)* fabrication.
invendible *adj* unsaleable.
inventar *vt* 1 *(crear)* to invent. 2 *(imaginar)* to imagine. 3 *(mentir)* to make up, fabricate.
inventariar *vt* to make an inventory of.
inventario *nm* inventory.
inventiva *nf* inventiveness.
inventivo,-a *adj* inventive.
invento *nm* invention.
inventor,-ra *nm & nf* inventor.
invernáculo *nm* greenhouse, hothouse.
invernadero *nm* greenhouse, hothouse.
invernal *adj* winter, wintry.
invernar [27] *vi* 1 to (spend the) winter (**en**, in). 2 *(animales)* to hibernate.
inverosímil *adj* unlikely.
inverosimilitud *nf* improbability, unlikelihood.
inversión *nf* 1 *(gen)* inversion. 2 FIN investment.
inversionista *nm o nf* investor.
inverso,-a *adj* inverse, opposite.
inversor,-ra *nm & nf* investor.
invertebrado,-a *adj* invertebrate.
▷ *nm* **invertebrado** invertebrate.
invertido,-a *adj* 1 reversed, inverted. 2 homosexual.
invertir [35] *vt* 1 *(orden)* to invert, reverse. 2 *(dirección)* to reverse. 3 *(tiempo)* to spend (**en**, on). 4 FIN to invest (**en**, in).
investidura *nf* investiture.
investigación *nf* 1 *(indagación)* investigation, enquiry. 2 *(estudio)* research.
investigador,-ra *adj* 1 *(que indaga)* investigating. 2 *(que estudia)* research.
▷ *nm & nf* 1 *(científico)* researcher. 2 *(detective)* investigator.
investigar [7] *vt* 1 *(indagar)* to investigate. 2 *(campo)* to do research on.
investir [34] *vt* to invest.
inveterado,-a *adj* deep-rooted.
inviable *adj* non-viable, unfeasible.
invicto,-a *adj* unconquered.
invidente *adj* blind.
▷ *nm o nf* blind person.
invierno *nm* winter.
inviolabilidad *nf* inviolability.
inviolable *adj* inviolable.
inviolado,-a *adj* inviolate.
invisibilidad *nf* invisibility.
invisible *adj* invisible.
invitación *nf* invitation.

invitado,-a *adj* invited.
▷ *nm & nf* guest.
invitar *vt* to invite.
▷ *vi (incitar)* to encourage; *(a la violencia)* to incite.
invocación *nf* invocation.
invocar [1] *vt* to invoke.
involución *nf* 1 BIOL involution. 2 POL regression, reaction.
involucionista *adj* POL reactionary.
▷ *nm o nf* POL reactionary.
involucrar *vt* to involve (**en**, in).
involuntario,-a *adj (reflejo, movimiento)* involuntary; *(error)* unintentional.
involutivo,-a *adj* 1 BIOL involutional. 2 POL regressive.
invulnerabilidad *nf* invulnerability.
invulnerable *adj* invulnerable.
inyección *nf* injection.
inyectable *adj* injectable.
▷ *nm* injection.
inyectar *vt* to inject (**en**, into).
inyector *nm* injector.
iodo *nm* iodine.
ion *nm* ion.
iónico,-a *adj* ionic.
ionización *nf* ionization.
ionizador *nm* ionizer.
ionizar *vt* to ionize.
ionosfera *nf* ionosphere.
ir [74] *vi* 1 *(gen)* to go; *(acudir)* to come. 2 *(camino, etc)* to lead. 3 *(funcionar)* to work, go. 4 *(sentar bien)* to suit; *(agradar)* to like. 5 *(tratar)* to be about.
▷ *aux* **ir + a +** *infin* 1 going to: **voy a venderlo** *I'm going to sell it.* 2 **ir +** *gerundio*: **fuimos andando** *we walked, we went on foot.* 3 **ir +** *pp* to be: **ir cansado,-a** *to be tired.*
▷ *vpr* **irse** 1 *(marcharse)* to go away, leave. 2 *(deslizarse)* to slip. 3 *(gastarse)* to go, disappear.
ira *nf* wrath, rage.
iracundo,-a *adj* irritable, irate.
Irak *nm* Iraq.
Irán *nm* Iran.
iraní *adj* Iranian.
▷ *nm o nf* Iranian.
▲ *pl* **iraníes.**
iranio,-a *adj* Iranian.
▷ *nm & nf (persona)* Iranian.
▷ *nm* **iranio** *(idioma)* Iranian.
iraquí *adj* Iraqi.
▷ *nm o nf (persona)* Iraqi.
▷ *nm (idioma)* Iraqi.
▲ *pl* **iraquíes.**
irascibilidad *nf* irascibility.
irascible *adj* irascible, irritable.
iridiscencia *nf* iridescence.
iridiscente *adj* iridescent.
iris *nm inv* iris.
irisación *nf* iridescence.
irisado,-a *adj* iridescent.
Irlanda *nf* Ireland. ● **Irlanda del Norte** Northern Ireland.
irlandés,-esa *adj* Irish.
▷ *nm & nf (persona - hombre)* Irishman; *(- mujer)* Irish woman.
▷ *nm* **irlandés** *(idioma)* Irish.
ironía *nf* irony.
irónico,-a *adj* 1 ironic. 2 *(burlón)* mocking.
ironizar [4] *vt* to make fun of.
IRPF *abrev* **(Impuesto sobre la Renta de las Personas Físicas)** income tax.
irracional *adj* irrational.
irracionalidad *nf* irrationality.
irradiación *nf* irradiation.
irradiar [12] *vt* to irradiate, radiate.
irrazonable *adj* unreasonable.
irreal *adj* unreal.
irrealidad *nf* unreality.
irrealizable *adj* unfeasible.
irrealizado,-a *adj* unfulfilled.
irrebatible *adj* irrefutable.
irreconciliable *adj* irreconcilable.
irreconocible *adj* unrecognizable.
irrecuperable *adj* irretrievable.
irredimible *adj* irredeemable, beyond redemption.
irreducible *adj* irreducible.
irreductible *adj* irreducible.
irreemplazable *adj* irreplaceable.
irreflexión *nf* rashness.
irreflexivo,-a *adj (acto)* rash; *(persona)* impetuous.
irrefrenable *adj* uncontrollable.
irrefutable *adj* irrefutable.
irregular *adj* irregular.
irregularidad *nf* irregularity.
irrelevante *adj* irrelevant.
irreligioso,-a *adj* irreligious.
irremediable *adj (daño)* irremediable; *(pérdida)* irreplaceable; *(vicio)* incurable.
irremisible *adj* unpardonable, unforgivable.
irremplazable *adj* irreplaceable.
irreparable *adj* irreparable.
irrepetible *adj* unrepeatable.
irreprimible *adj* irrepressible.
irreprochable *adj* irreproachable.
irresistible *adj* 1 irresistible. 2 *pey (insoportable)* unbearable.
irrespetuoso,-a *adj* disrespectful.
irrespirable *adj* 1 *(aire)* unbreathable. 2 *(ambiente)* oppressive.
irresponsabilidad *nf* irresponsibility.
irresponsable *adj* irresponsible.
▷ *nm o nf* irresponsible person.
irreverente *adj* irreverent.
irreversible *adj* irreversible.
irrevocable *adj* irrevocable.
irrigación *nf* irrigation.
irrigar *vt* to irrigate.
irrisible *adj* laughable.
irrisión *nf* derision.
irrisorio,-a *adj* 1 derisory, ridiculous. 2 *(insignificante)* insignificant.
irritabilidad *nf* irritability.
irritable *adj* irritable.
irritación *nf* irritation.

irritante *adj* irritating, aggravating, annoying.
irritar *vt* to irritate.
▷ *vpr* **irritarse** to lose one's temper, get annoyed.
irrompible *adj* unbreakable.
irrumpir *vi* to burst (**en**, into).
irrupción *nf* irruption.
isla *nf* island.
islam *nm* Islam.
islámico,-a *adj* Islamic.
islamismo *nm* Islam.
islamista *adj* 1 *(estudioso)* Islamist. 2 *(fundamentalista)* Islamic fundamentalist.
▷ *nm o nf* 1 *(estudioso)* Islamist. 2 *(fundamentalista)* Islamic fundamentalist.
islandés,-esa *adj* Icelandic.
▷ *nm & nf (persona)* Icelander.
▷ *nm* **islandés** *(idioma)* Icelandic.
Islandia *nf* Iceland.
isleño,-a *adj* island.
▷ *nm & nf* islander.
islote *nm* small unhinhabited island.
ismo *nm* ism.
isobara *nf* isobar.
isométrico,-a *adj* isometric.
isósceles *adj* isosceles.
isotérmico,-a *adj* isothermal.
isotermo *nm* isotherm.
isótopo *nm* isotope.
Israel *nm* Israel.
israelí *adj* Israeli.
▷ *nm o nf* Israeli.
israelita *adj* HIST Israelite.
▷ *nm o nf* HIST Israelite.
istmo *nm* isthmus.
Italia *nf* Italy.
italiano,-a *adj* Italian.
▷ *nm & nf (persona)* Italian.
▷ *nm* **italiano** *(idioma)* Italian.
itálica *nf (letra)* italics.
itálico,-a *adj* Italic.
itinerante *adj* itinerant.
itinerario *nm* itinerary.
IVA *abrev* (**impuesto sobre el valor añadido**) value-added tax; *(abreviatura)* VAT.
izar [4] *vt* to hoist.
izquierda *nf* 1 *(mano)* left hand; *(pierna)* left leg. 2 POL the left.
izquierdista *adj* left-wing.
▷ *nm o nf* left-winger.
izquierdo,-a *adj* left.

J

j *nf (la letra)* J, j.
a *interj* ¡**ja, ja!** *(risa)* ha, ha!
abalí *nm* wild boar.
abalina *nf* DEP javelin.
abato *nm* **1** ZOOL young wild boar. **2** *(hombre valiente)* daredevil.
abón *nm* soap. ● **jabón de tocador** toilet soap.
abonera *nf* **1** soap dish. **2** BOT soapwort.
abonoso,-a *adj* soapy.
aca *nf* cob, small horse.
acinto *nm* hyacinth.
acobeo,-a *adj* of Saint James. ● **la ruta jacobea** *the pilgrim's route to Santiago de Compostela.*
acobino,-a *adj* HIST Jacobin.
nm & nf HIST Jacobin.
actarse *vpr* to boast, brag (**de**, about).
acuzzi [Registered trademark.] *nm* jacuzzi.
ade *nm* jade.
adear *vi* to pant.
adeo *nm* panting.
aguar *nm* jaguar.
alar *vt* **1** *(tirar de)* to pull, heave. **2** *fam (comer)* to wolf down.
alea *nf* jelly. ● **jalea real** royal jelly.
alear *vt* **1** *(animar)* to cheer (on), clap and shout at. **2** *(caza)* to urge on.
aleo *nm* **1** *(alboroto)* din, racket: **no se oye nada con este jaleo** *I can't hear a thing with all this racket.* **2** *(escándalo)* fuss, commotion: **cuando se enteren se va a montar un jaleo tremendo** *there'll be a terrible fuss when they find out.*
aleoso,-a *adj (enredoso)* complicated, mixed-up.
alón *nm* **1** *(estaca)* stake, post. **2** *fig* milestone, landmark.
alonar *vt (con estacas)* to stake out.
amaica *nf* Jamaica.
amaicano,-a *adj* Jamaican.
▷ *nm & nf* Jamaican.
amás *adv (+ indic)* never; *(+ subj)* ever: **jamás volveré** *I shall never return.* ■ **jamás de los jamases** never ever. ‖ **por siempre jamás** for ever (and ever).
amba *nf* jamb.
amón *nm* **1** *(curado)* cured ham; *(pata del cerdo)* leg of ham. **2** *fam (muslo)* thigh. ● **jamón de York/jamón en dulce** boiled ham. ‖ **jamón serrano** cured ham.
apón *nm* Japan.
aponés,-esa *adj* Japanese.
▷ *nm & nf (persona)* Japanese.
▷ *nm* **japonés** *(idioma)* Japanese.
aque *nm* check. ● **jaque mate** checkmate.
aqueca *nf* migraine, headache.
ara *nf* rockrose.

jarabe *nm* **1** CULIN syrup. **2** MED syrup, mixture, medicine. ● **jarabe para la tos** cough syrup.
jardín *nm* garden. ● **jardín botánico** botanical garden. ‖ **jardín de infancia** nursery school.
jardinera *nf* **1** *(mujer)* gardener. **2** *(mueble para tiestos)* plant stand; *(en ventana)* window box.
jardinería *nf* gardening.
jardinero,-a *nm & nf* gardener.
jarra *nf* **1** *(para servir)* jug, US pitcher. **2** *(para beber)* tankard, beer mug. ■ **con los brazos en jarras** arms akimbo, hands on hips.
jarro *nm* **1** *(recipiente)* jug. **2** *(contenido)* jugful.
jarrón *nm* **1** vase. **2** ARTE urn.
jaspeado,-a *adj* mottled, speckled.
Jauja *nf (sitio)* promised land; *(situación)* the good life. ■ **esto es Jauja** this is the life!
jaula *nf* cage.
jauría *nf* **1** pack of hounds. **2** *fig* gang.
Java *nf* Java.
javanés,-esa *adj* Javanese.
▷ *nm & nf* Javanese.
jazmín *nm* jasmine.
jazz *nm* jazz.
J.C. *abrev* (**Jesucristo**) Jesus Christ; *(abreviatura)* J.C.
je *interj* ha!
jeep [Registered trademark.] *nm* jeep.
jefatura *nf* **1** *(sede)* central office; *(militar)* headquarters. **2** *(cargo, dirección)* leadership.
jefe,-a *nm & nf* **1** boss, head, chief. **2** COM *(hombre)* manager; *(mujer)* manageress. **3** POL leader. **4** MIL officer in command. **5** *(de una tribu)* chief. ● **jefe de cocina** chef. ‖ **jefe de estación** station master. ‖ **jefe de Estado** Head of State.
jengibre *nm* ginger.
jeque *nm* sheik, sheikh.
jerarca *nm* hierarch.
jerarquía *nf* **1** hierarchy. **2** *(grado)* scale. **3** *(categoría)* rank. **4** *(persona)* high-ranking person.
jerárquico,-a *adj* hierarchical, hierarchic.
jerez *nm* sherry.
jerga *nf* **1** *(lenguaje)* jargon. **2** *pey (jerigonza)* gibberish, jargon.
jergón *nm (colchón)* pallet.
jeringuilla *nf* syringe, hypodermic syringe.
jeroglífico,-a *adj* hieroglyphic.
▷ *nm* **jeroglífico 1** hieroglyph, hieroglyphic. **2** *(juego)* rebus.
jersey *nm* sweater, pullover, jumper.
Jerusalén *nm* Jerusalem.
Jesucristo *nm* Jesus Christ.
jesuita *adj* Jesuit.
▷ *nm o nf* Jesuit.

Jesús *nm* Jesus.
▷ *interj* **1 ¡Jesús!** *(al estornudar)* bless you! **2 ¡Jesús, (por Dios)!** *fam (como queja)* for God's sake!, for goodness' sake!; *(con sorpresa)* oh my God!

jet *nm* jet.
▷ *nf* **la jet** *(famosos)* the jet set.

jeta *nf fam (cara)* mug, face.
▷ *nm o nf fam* cheeky monkey, cheeky bugger. ■ **tener jeta** *fam* to be cheeky, have a nerve.

jibia *nf* cuttlefish.

jijona *nm type of soft* nougat.

jilguero *nm* goldfinch.

jineta *nf* ZOOL genet.

jinete *nm* rider, horseman.

jipi *nm o nf* hippy.

jirafa *nf* **1** giraffe. **2** *fam (persona)* beanpole. **3** *(de micrófono)* boom.

jirón *nm* shred: **una camisa hecha jirones** *a tattered shirt.*

JJ.OO. *abrev* **(Juegos Olímpicos)** Olympic Games.

jockey *nm* jockey.

jocosamente *adv* jocularly, humorously.

jocosidad *nf* **1** *(humor)* jocularity. **2** *(broma)* joke.

jocoso,-a *adj (persona)* jocular; *(tono)* humorous, jokey.

joder *vt* **1** *tabú (copular)* to fuck, screw. **2** *tabú (fastidiar)* to pester, annoy, piss off.

jofaina *nf* washbasin.

jogging *nm* jogging: **practican el jogging** *they go jogging.*

jolgorio *nm* **1** *(juerga)* binge. **2** *(algazara)* party.

jolín *interj* **1** *fam (asombro)* wow!, good grief! **2** *(enfado)* blast!, damn!

jónico,-a *adj* **1** *(mar)* Ionian; *(pueblo, dialecto)* Ionian, Ionic. **2** *(orden, capitel)* Ionic.

Jordania *nf* Jordan.

jordano,-a *adj* Jordanian.
▷ *nm & nf* Jordanian.

jornada *nf* **1** *(día de trabajo)* working day: **una jornada de ocho horas** *an eight-hour day.* **2** *(camino recorrido)* day's journey. **3** *(en periodismo)* day: **las noticias de la jornada** *today's news.*
▷ *nf pl* **jornadas** conference *sing.* ● **jornada intensiva** *eight-to-three working day without a lunch break.* ■ **media jornada** half-day.

jornal *nm* day's wage.

jornalero,-a *nm & nf* day labourer.

joroba *nf (deformidad)* hump.

jorobado,-a *adj* hunchbacked, humpbacked.
▷ *nm & nf* hunchback, humpback.

jorobar *vt* **1** *fam (fastidiar)* to bother, pester, annoy. **2** *fam (romper)* to smash up, break. **3** *fam (estropear)* to ruin, wreck.

jota *nf popular Spanish dance and music.*

joven *adj* young.
▷ *nm o nf (hombre)* youth, young man; *(mujer)* young lady, girl.

jovial *adj* jovial, cheerful, good-humoured.

jovialidad *nf* joviality, cheerfulness.

joya *nf* jewel, piece of jewellery (US jewelry).

joyería *nf* **1** *(tienda)* jewellery (US jewelry) shop, jeweller's shop, US jeweler's store. **2** *(comercio)* jewellery (US jewelry) trade.

joyero,-a *nm & nf* jeweller (US jeweler).
▷ *nm* **joyero** jewellery (US jewelry) case.

joystick *nm* joystick.

juanete *nm (en el pie)* bunion.

jubilación *nf* **1** *(acción)* retirement. **2** *(dinero)* pension.

jubilado,-a *adj* retired.
▷ *nm o nf* pensioner, retired person, US retiree.

jubilar *vt* **1** *(retirar)* to retire. **2** *(persona)* to pensio[n] off; *(objeto)* to get rid of, ditch.
▷ *vpr* **jubilarse** *(retirarse)* to retire.

jubileo *nm (perdón)* indulgence.

júbilo *nm* jubilation, joy.

jubiloso,-a *adj* jubilant, joyful.

jubón *nm arc* doublet.

judaico,-a *adj* Judaic.

judaísmo *nm* Judaism.

judas *nm inv* traitor, Judas.

judeocristiano,-a *adj* Judaeo-Christian.

judería *nf* Jewish quarter.

judía *nf (planta)* bean. ● **judía verde** French bea[n], green bean.

judicatura *nf* **1** *(profesión)* judgeship. **2** *(cuerpo)* ju[]diciary, judicature. **3** *(duración del cargo)* term of o[f]fice *as a judge.*

judicial *adj* judicial.

judío,-a *adj* **1** *(gen)* Jewish. **2** HIST *(de Judá)* Judaea[n]. **3** *fam pey* miserly.
▷ *nm & nf* **1** *(persona)* Jew. **2** HIST *(de Judá)* Judaea[n]. **3** *fam pey* miser, scrooge.

judo *nm* judo.

judoca *nm o nf* judoka.

juego *nm* **1** *(actividad recreativa)* game; *(actividad de[]portiva)* sport. **2** *(con dinero)* gambling. **3** *(acción d[e] jugar)* playing. **4** *(en tenis)* game; *(en naipes)* round, game. **5** *(conjunto de piezas)* set: **un juego de llaves** *set of keys.* ● **juego de azar** game of chance. ■ **jueg[o] de café/té** coffee/tea service.

juerga *nf fam* rave-up, bash.

juerguista *adj* fun-loving.
▷ *nm o nf* raver.

jueves *nm inv* Thursday. ● **Jueves Santo** Maund[y] Thursday.

juez,-za *nm & nf* judge. ● **juez de línea** linesman. ■ **juez de paz** justice of the peace.

jugada *nf* **1** *(en ajedrez)* move; *(en billar)* shot; *(e[n] dardos)* throw. **2** *(momento del juego)* move, piece o[f] play. **3** *fam* dirty trick.

jugador,-ra *nm & nf* **1** player. **2** *(apostador)* gam[]bler.

jugar [53] *vi* **1** to play. **2** *(burlarse)* to play: **estás ju[]gando con mis sentimientos** *you're playing with m[y] feelings.*
▷ *vt* **1** *(intervenir)* to play, go: **¿quién juega?** *whose go i[s] it?* **2** *(hacer uso - una pieza)* to move; *(- una carta)* t[o] play.
▷ *vpr* **jugarse** **1** *(arriesgar)* to risk: **se jugó la vida por m[í]** *he risked his life for me.* **2** *(apostarse)* to bet: **¿cuánt[o] te juegas a que no viene?** *what's the betting he won['t] come?*

jugarreta *nf fam* dirty trick.

juglar *nm* minstrel.

juglaresco,-a *adj* minstrel.
juglaría *nf* minstrelsy.
jugo *nm* 1 *(gen)* juice. 2 *(interés)* substance: **una novela con mucho jugo** *it's a meaty novel.*
jugoslavo,-a *adj* Yugoslav, Yugoslavian.
▷ *nm & nf* Yugoslav, Yugoslavian.
jugoso,-a *adj* 1 *(fruta, carne)* juicy.
juguete *nm* 1 toy. 2 *fig* plaything.
juguetear *vi* to play (**con**, with).
jugueteo *nm* playing.
juguetería *nf* 1 *(tienda)* toy shop. 2 *(industria)* toy business.
juguetón,-ona *adj* playful, frolicsome.
juicio *nm* 1 *(gen)* judgement: **a mi juicio** *in my opinion.* 2 *(sensatez)* reason, common sense. 3 JUR trial, lawsuit. ■ **en su sano juicio** in one's right mind. ‖ **llevar a ALGN a juicio** to take legal action against SB, sue SB. ‖ **perder el juicio** to go mad.
juicioso,-a *adj (persona)* sensible, wise; *(decisión)* judicious.
julepe *nm (juego) type of card game.*
juliana *nf* damewort.
julio[1] *nm* July.
For examples of use, see **marzo.**
julio[2] *nm* FÍS joule.
jumbo *nm* jumbo jet.
jumento *nm* ass, donkey.
juncal *adj* 1 BOT rushlike. 2 *lit* graceful.
▷ *nm* BOT reedbed.
juncia *nf* sedge.
junco[1] *nm* 1 BOT rush, reed. 2 *(bastón)* walking stick, cane.
junco[2] *nm* MAR junk.
jungla *nf* jungle.
junio *nm* June.
For examples of use, see **marzo.**
júnior *adj* DEP junior.
▲ *pl* **júniors.**
junquillo *nm* 1 BOT jonquil. 2 *(moldura)* beading.
junta *nf* 1 *(reunión)* meeting, assembly, conference. 2 *(conjunto de personas)* board, council, committee.
juntar *vt* 1 *(unir)* to join together, put together; *(piezas)* to assemble. 2 *fam (coleccionar)* to collect. 3 *(reunir - dinero)* to raise; *(- gente)* to gather together.
▷ *vpr* **juntarse** 1 *(unirse)* to join, get together; *(ríos, caminos)* to meet. 2 *(acercarse)* to squeeze up: **juntaos un poco que no quepo** *squeeze up, I can't get in.* 3 *(relacionarse)* to go out (**con**, with), mix (**con**, with). 4 *(amancebarse)* to move in (**con**, with), start living together.
junto,-a *adj* together. ■ **junto a** next to. ‖ **junto con** along with, together with.
jura *nf (acción)* oath; *(ceremonia)* swearing-in, pledge.
jurado,-a *adj* sworn.
▷ *nm* **jurado** JUR *(tribunal)* jury; *(miembro del tribunal)* juror, member of the jury.
juramentar *vt* to swear in.
▷ *vpr* **juramentarse** to take the oath.
juramento *nm* 1 JUR oath. 2 *(blasfemia)* swearword.
jurar *vt* to swear, take an oath.
▷ *vi (blasfemar)* to curse, swear.
jurásico,-a *adj* Jurassic.
jurel *nm* scad, horse mackerel.
jurídico,-a *adj* legal, juridical.
jurisdicción *nf* jurisdiction.
jurisdiccional *adj* jurisdictional.
jurispericia *nf* jurisprudence.
jurisperito,-a *nm & nf* jurist, legal expert.
jurisprudencia *nf* jurisprudence.
jurista *nm o nf* jurist, lawyer.
justicia *nf* 1 *(equidad, derecho)* justice, fairness. 2 **la justicia** *(organismo)* the law.
justiciero,-a *adj* avenging.
justificable *adj* justifiable.
justificación *nf* justification.
justificante *adj* justifying.
▷ *nm (prueba)* written proof.
justificar [1] *vt* 1 *(acción)* to justify. 2 *(persona)* to excuse.
▷ *vpr* **justificarse** *(persona)* to justify OS; *(acción)* to be justified.
justiprecio *nm* valuation.
justo,-a *adj* 1 *(persona, decisión)* just, fair; *(sentencia)* just. 2 *(ropa)* tight. 3 *(exacto)* exact: **tengo el dinero justo para el autobús** *I have the exact money for the bus.* 4 *(escaso)* just enough: **me queda lo justo para llegar a fin de mes** *I have just enough money to get by.*
▷ *adv* **justo** *(en el preciso momento)* just; *(en el preciso lugar)* right: **vivo justo en el centro de la ciudad** *I live right in the centre of town,* US *I live right downtown.*
juvenil *adj* 1 young, youthful. 2 DEP junior, youth.
juventud *nf* 1 *(período)* youth. 2 *(los jóvenes)* young people *pl*, youth *pl.*
juzgado *nm (local)* court. ● **juzgado de guardia** court, police court.
juzgar [7] *vt* 1 *(formar juicio)* to judge. 2 *(considerar)* to consider, think: **juzgo conveniente que se le traslade a otra oficina** *I think that he should be moved to a different office.*

K

K, k *nf (la letra)* K, k.
kaki *nm* **1** *(árbol)* persimmon tree. **2** *(fruta)* persimmon.
Kampuchea *nf* Kampuchea.
kampucheo,-a *adj* Kampuchean.
▷ *nm & nf* Kampuchean.
karaoke *nm* **1** *(práctica)* karaoke. **2** *(aparato)* karaoke machine.
kárate *nm* karate.
karateca *nm o nf* karateist.
karateka *nm o nf* karateist.
karma *nf* karma.
karst *nm* karst.
kárstico,-a *adj* karstic.
kart® *nm* go-kart, kart.
▲ *pl* **karts.**
karting *nm* go-kart racing, karting.
Kathmandu *nm* Katmandu, Kathmandu.
katiuska *nf* Wellington boot, rubber boot.
kayac *nm* kayak.
▲ *pl* **kayacs.**
kazajio,-a *adj* Kazakh.
▷ *nm & nf (persona)* Kazakh.
▷ *nm* **kazajio** *(idioma)* Kazakh.
Kazajstán *nm* Kazakhstan.
kéfir *nm* kefir.
kendo *nm* kendo.
Kenia *nf* Kenya.
keniano,-a *adj* Kenyan.
▷ *nm & nf* Kenyan.
keroseno *nm* kerosene.
ketchup *nm* ketchup.
kg *sím* **(kilogramo)** kilogram; *(símbolo)* kg.
Khartum *nm* Khartoum.
kibutz *nm* kibbutz.
kilo *nm* **1** kilogram. **2** *argot (antiguamente)* million pesetas.
kilobyte *nm* kilobyte.
kilocaloría *nf* kilocalorie.
kilogramo *nm* kilogram.
kilohertz *nm inv* kilohertz.
kilolitro *nm* kilolitre, US kiloliter.
kilometraje *nm* ≈ mileage.
kilometrar *vt* to measure the distance of *(in kilometres)*.
kilométrico,-a *adj* **1** kilometric: **este mapa indica la distancia kilométrica entre las ciudades** *this map shows the distance in kilometres between towns.* **2** *fam (larguísimo)* endless.
▷ *nm* **kilométrico** runabout ticket.
kilómetro *nm* kilometre, US kilometer.
kilowatt *nm* kilowatt.
kirguís *adj* Kirghiz.
▷ *nm o nf (persona)* Kirghiz.
▷ *nm (idioma)* Kirghiz.
Kirguizistán *nm* Kirghizstan, Kirghizia.
Kiribati *nm* Kiribati.
kit *nm* kit.
▲ *pl* **kits.**
kitsch *adj* kitsch.
▷ *nm (arte)* kitsch; *(objeto)* piece of kitsch.
kiwi *nm* **1** *(ave)* kiwi. **2** *(fruta)* kiwi, kiwi fruit.
Kl *sím* **(kilolitro)** kilolitre (US kiloliter); *(símbolo)* Kl.
kleenex [Registered trademark.] *nm* Kleenex, tissue.
km *sím* **(kilómetro, kilómetros)** kilometre, (US kilometer); *(símbolo)* km.
km/h *abrev* **(kilómetros hora)** kilometres (US kilometers) per hour; *(abreviatura)* kph.
knock-out *nm* knockout.
KO *abrev* **(knock-out)** knockout; *(abreviatura)* KO. ■ **dejar a** ALGN **KO** to knock SB out.
koala *nm* koala.
kung-fu *nm* kung-fu.
kurdo,-a *adj* Kurdish.
▷ *nm & nf (persona)* Kurd.
▷ *nm* **kurdo** *(idioma)* Kurdish.
Kuwait *nm* Kuwait.
kuwaití *adj* Kuwaiti.
▷ *nm & nf* Kuwaiti.
kW *sím* **(kilovatio)** kilowatt; *(símbolo)* kW.
kW/h *abrev* **(kilovatios hora)** kilowatts per hour; *(abreviatura)* kWh.

L

L, l *nf (la letra)* L, l.
l *sím* **(litro)** litre (US liter); *(símbolo)* l.
la¹ *art def* the: **la casa** *the house.*
la² *pron (persona)* her; *(cosa)* it: **la invité a cenar** *I invited her to supper;* **no la he leído** *I haven't read it.*
See also **las.**
la³ *nm* MÚS la, lah, A.
laberíntico,-a *adj* labyrinthic, labyrinthine.
laberinto *nm* labyrinth, maze.
labia *nf fam* loquacity.
labiado,-a *adj* labiate.
labial *adj (gen)* labial.
▷ *nf* LING labial.
lábil *adj* **1** *(no estable)* unstable; *(frágil)* fragile. **2** QUÍM labile.
labio *nm* lip. ● **labio leporino** harelip.
labor *nf* **1** *(gen)* work. **2** [Also used in plural with the same meaning.] *(costura)* embroidery, needlework; *(punto)* knitting.
laborable *adj (de trabajo)* working.
laboral *adj* labour (US labor).
laboralista *adj (abogado)* labour (US labor) relations.
laboratorio *nm* laboratory.
laborioso,-a *adj* **1** *(trabajador)* industrious, diligent. **2** *(trabajoso)* laborious.
laborismo *nm* Labour Movement.
laborista *adj* Labour.
▷ *nm o nf* Labour (Party) member.
labrado,-a *nm* **labrado** *(de piedra, mármol)* carving.
labrador,-ra *nm & nf* farmer.
labranza *nf* farming.
labrar *vt* **1** AGR *(campo)* to work; *(con arado)* to plough (US plow). **2** *(metal)* to work; *(madera)* to carve; *(piedra)* to cut.
labriego,-a *nm & nf* farm worker.
laca *nf* **1** *(en arte)* lacquer; *(resina)* shellac. **2** *(para pelo)* hair spray.
lacar *vt* to lacquer.
lacayo *nm* lackey, footman.
laceración *nf* laceration.
lacerante *adj lit (dolor)* searing.
lacerar *vt* **1** to lacerate, tear. **2** *fig* to harm, damage.
lacero,-a *nm & nf* **1** *(de ganado)* lassoer. **2** *(furtivo)* poacher. **3** *(de perros)* dog-catcher.
lacio,-a *adj* **1** *(cabello)* straight. **2** *(marchito)* withered. **3** *(sin vigor)* limp.
lacón *nm* ham.
lacónico,-a *adj* laconic.
laconismo *nm* laconism, laconicism.
lacra *nf* **1** *(señal)* mark, scar. **2** *(mal)* evil, scourge. **3** *(defecto)* fault.
lacrado,-a *adj (sobre)* sealed with wax.
lacrar *vt* to seal (with sealing wax).
lacre *nm* sealing wax.
lacrimal *adj* tear, lacrimal, lachrymal.
lacrimógeno,-a *adj* tearful: **una historia lacrimógena** *a tear-jerker.*
lacrimoso,-a *adj* tearful.
lactancia *nf (acción)* lactation; *(periodo)* breast-feeding.
lactante *nm o nf* unweaned baby.
lácteo,-a *adj* milk, milky. ● **productos lácteos** dairy products.
láctico,-a *adj* lactic.
lactosa *nf* lactose.
lacustre *adj* lake.
ladear *vt* to tilt.
ladeo *nm* tilt.
ladera *nf* hillside.
ladilla *nf* crab louse.
ladino,-a *adj* sly.
▷ *nm* **ladino** *(lengua)* ladino.
lado *nm (gen)* side. ■ **al lado de** ALGN next to SB: **me puse a su lado** *I sat next to her.* ‖ **al lado de** ALGO beside STH: **la casa de al lado** *next door.* ‖ **estar al lado** *(muy cerca)* to be very near. ‖ **hacerse a un lado** to get out of the way. ‖ **por un lado... por otro...** on the one hand... on the other hand...
ladrador,-ra *adj* barking.
ladrar *vi* to bark.
ladrido *nm* bark. ■ **dar ladridos** to bark.
ladrillazo *nm* blow with a brick.
ladrillo *nm* **1** *(en construcción)* brick. **2** *fam* pain, bore.
ladrón,-ona *nm & nf (persona - que roba)* thief; *(- que tima, engaña)* crook.
▷ *nm* **ladrón** *(enchufe)* adaptor.
ladronzuelo,-a *nm & nf* petty thief.
lagar *nm* press.
lagartija *nf* small lizard.
lagarto,-a *nm & nf* **1** *(animal)* lizard. **2** *fam (pícaro)* sly devil.
lago *nm* lake.
lagópodo *nm* grouse.
lágrima *nf* **1** *(ocular)* tear. **2** *(de lámpara, pendiente)* teardrop. ■ **llorar a lágrima viva** *fam* to cry one's eyes out.
lagrimal *adj* tear, lachrymal.
▷ *nm* corner of the eye.
lagrimear *vi* **1** *(ojos)* to run, water. **2** *(persona)* to cry easily.
lagrimeo *nm* **1** *(del ojo)* watering. **2** *(llanto)* weeping, shedding of tears.
lagrimón *nm* large teardrop, large tear.

laguna *nf* 1 small lake, lagoon. 2 *fig (de conocimiento)* gap; *(de la memoria)* memory lapse.
laicismo *nm* laicism, secularism.
laico,-a *adj* lay, secular.
▷ *nm & nf (hombre)* layman; *(mujer)* laywoman.
laísmo *nm incorrect use of* la *and* las *as indirect objects instead of* le *and* les.
laja *nf* slab.
lama[1] *nm* REL lama.
lama[2] *nf* 1 *(lámina)* slat. 2 *(barro)* slime.
lamé *nm* lamé.
lamentable *adj (injusticia)* regrettable, deplorable; *(estado)* sorry, pitiful.
lamentar *vt* to regret.
▷ *vpr* **lamentarse** to complain.
lamento *nm* moan, cry.
lamer *vt* to lick.
lametazo *nm* lick.
lametón *nm* lick.
lámina *nf* 1 *(gen)* sheet, plate. 2 *(ilustración)* illustration; *(grabado)* engraving.
laminado,-a *adj* laminated.
▷ *nm* **laminado** lamination.
laminar *vt* to laminate.
lámpara *nf* 1 lamp. 2 RAD valve.
lamparón *nm fam* stain.
lampista *nm o nf fam (gen)* handyman; *(fontanero)* plumber; *(electricista)* electrician.
lamprea *nf* lamprey.
lana *nf* wool. ■ **de lana** woollen (US woolen).
lanar *adj* wool-bearing.
lance *nm* 1 *(suceso)* event. 2 *(infortunio)* incident. 3 *(pelea)* quarrel. 4 DEP move.
lanceolado,-a *adj* lanceolate.
lancero *nm* lancer.
lanceta *nf* lancet, lance.
lancha *nf (bote)* launch, boat; *(a motor)* speedboat, motorboat. ● **lancha salvavidas** lifeboat.
landa *nf* moor.
lanero,-a *adj* wool.
langosta *nf* 1 *(crustáceo)* crawfish, spiny lobster. 2 *(insecto)* locust.
langostino *nm type of* prawn.
languidecer [43] *vi* to languish.
languidez *nf* 1 *(falta de vigor)* languor. 2 *(flaqueza)* listlessness.
lánguido,-a *adj* 1 *(falto de vigor)* languid, languorous. 2 *(débil)* listless.
lanilla *nf* 1 *(tejido)* flannel. 2 *(pelusilla)* fluff.
lanolina *nf* lanolin, lanoline.
lanza *nf* 1 lance, spear. 2 *(de carro)* shaft.
lanzacohetes *nm inv* rocket launcher.
lanzadera *nf* shuttle.
lanzado,-a *adj (impetuoso)* impetuous.
lanzador,-ra *nm & nf (de jabalina)* thrower; *(de béisbol)* pitcher; *(de cricket)* bowler.
lanzagranadas *nm inv* grenade launcher.
lanzallamas *nm inv* flame-thrower.
lanzamiento *nm* 1 *(acción de lanzar)* throwing. 2 *(de cohete)* launching. ● **lanzamiento de peso** shot put.
lanzaminas *nm inv* minelayer.
lanzamisiles *nm inv* missile launcher.
lanzar [4] *vt* 1 *(gen)* to throw. 2 *(cohete)* to launch. 3 *fig (grito)* to let out; *(insulto)* to fire; *(mirada)* to gave: **me lanzó una mirada furtiva** *she gave me a furtive look.* 4 *(producto)* to launch.
▷ *vpr* **lanzarse** *(actuar decididamente)* to throw OS, launch OS into: **se lanzaron a la calle en protesta por la nueva ley** *they went out onto the streets to protest against the new law.*
Laos *nm* Laos.
laosiano,-a *adj* Laotian.
▷ *nm & nf (persona)* Laotian.
▷ *nm* **laosiano** *(idioma)* Laotian.
lapa *nf* 1 *(molusco)* limpet. 2 *pey (persona)* bore.
laparoscopia *nf* laparoscopy.
lapicero *nm* pencil.
lápida *nf (sepulcral)* tombstone, slab.
lapidar *vt* to stone.
lapidario,-a *adj (frase - concisa)* terse, concise; *(- contundente)* categorical.
lapislázuli *nm* lapis lazuli.
lápiz *nm* pencil. ● **lápiz de ojos** eyeliner. ‖ **lápiz óptico** light pen.
▲ *pl* **lápices**.
lapón,-ona *adj* Lapp.
▷ *nm & nf* Laplander, Lapp.
Laponia *nf* Lapland.
lapso *nm (de tiempo)* period of time, lapse.
lapsus *nm inv (error)* slip; *(de memoria)* memory lapse, lapse of memory.
laquear *vt* to lacquer.
largar [7] *vt* 1 *fam (dar)* to give: **le largó un discurso de media hora** *he gave him a half-hour speech.* 2 *fam (contar)* to tell: **esa lo larga todo** *she can't keep anything to herself.*
▷ *vpr* **largarse** *fam (irse)* to go, leave: **me largo** *I'm off,* US *I'm out of here.*
largo,-a *adj* 1 *(en longitud)* long. 2 *(alto)* tall: **se cayó cuan larga era** *she fell flat on her face.* 3 *(en cantidad)* good: **llevo una hora larga esperándote** *I've been waiting for you for over an hour.*
▷ *nm* **largo** 1 length: **¿qué mide de largo?** *how long is it?, what length is it?* 2 *(de tela)* length: **con dos largos te basta para una falda** *two lengths will be enough for a skirt.* 3 *(de piscina)* length, US lap. 4 MÚS largo. ■ **a la larga** in the long run. ‖ **a lo largo de** along, throughout: **a lo largo del año** *throughout the year.* ‖ **dar largas a** ALGN to put SB off. ‖ **pasar de largo** to pass by.
largometraje *nm* feature film, full-length film.
larguero *nm* 1 *(en fútbol)* crossbar. 2 *(en construcción)* crossbeam.
larguirucho,-a *adj fam* lanky.
largura *nf* length.
laringe *nf* larynx.
laríngeo,-a *adj* laryngeal.
laringitis *nf inv* laryngitis.
laringología *nf* laryngology.
laringólogo,-a *nm & nf* laryngologist.
larva *nf* larva.
larvario,-a *adj* larval.
las *art def* the: **las casas** *the houses.*
▷ *pron (objeto directo)* them: **las vi** *I saw them.*

See also **la**.

asaña *nf* lasagna, lasagne.
asca *nf* chip.
ascivo,-a *adj* lascivious, lewd.
áser *nm inv* laser.
asitud *nf* lassitude, weariness.
ástima *nf* pity.
astimar *vt (herir)* to hurt, injure.
▷ *vpr* **lastimarse** to hurt OS.
astimero,-a *adj* pitiful.
astimoso,-a *adj* pitiful, sorry.
astrar *vt* 1 MAR to ballast. 2 *fig* to hinder.
astre *nm* 1 MAR ballast. 2 *fig* dead weight, burden.
ata *nf* 1 *(hojalata)* tin plate. 2 *(envase)* tin, can. 3 *(fastidio)* bore, drag: **es una lata tener que rellenar estos formularios** *it's a drag having to fill in all these forms.*
atente *adj* latent.
ateral *adj* 1 *(gen)* side. 2 *(parentesco)* lateral.
▷ *nm (de carretera)* service lane; *(de avenida)* side lane.
átex *nm inv* latex.
atido *nm* beat.
atifundio *nm (finca)* latifundium *(large estate).*
atifundismo *nm distribution of land in large estates.*
atifundista *adj* relating to **latifundismo**.
▷ *nm o nf* estate owner, large land owner.
atigazo *nm* 1 *(golpe de látigo)* lash. 2 *(sonido)* crack.
átigo *nm* whip.
atín *nm* Latin.
atinismo *nm* Latinism.
atinista *nm o nf* Latinist.
atinizar *vt* to Latinize.
atino,-a *adj* Latin.
▷ *nm & nf* Latin.
atinoamérica *nf* Latin America.
atinoamericano,-a *adj* Latin American.
▷ *nm & nf* Latin American.
atir *vi* to beat.
atitud *nf* latitude.
▷ *nf pl* **latitudes** *fig (zona, región)* area *sing.*
atitudinal *adj* latitudinal.
atón *nm* brass.
atoso,-a *adj fam* annoying, boring.
▷ *nm & nf fam* bore.
atrocinio *nm fml* theft, robbery.
aúd *nm* lute.
áudano *nm* laudanum.
audatorio,-a *adj* laudatory.
aureada *nf* MIL *(insignia)* decoration.
aureado,-a *adj* prizewinning.
aurear *vt* 1 to award a prize to. 2 *(militar)* to decorate.
aurel *nm (árbol)* bay.
ava *nf* lava.
avable *adj* washable.
avabo *nm* 1 *(pila)* washbasin. 2 *(cuarto de baño)* washroom. 3 *(público)* toilet.
avada *nf* big wash.
avadero *nm* 1 *(en casa)* laundry room. 2 *(público)* public washing place. 3 *(pila)* sink. 4 *(de una mina)* washery.
avado,-a *nm* **lavado** wash. ● **lavado de cerebro** brainwashing.
lavadora *nf* washing machine.
lavafrutas *nm inv* finger bowl.
lavamanos *nm inv* washbasin.
lavanda *nf* lavender.
lavandería *nf (automática)* launderette, US laundromat; *(con servicio completo)* laundry.
lavaplatos *nm inv* dishwasher.
lavar *vt* 1 *(ropa, cuerpo, etc)* to wash. 2 *(platos)* to wash up.
▷ *vpr* **lavarse** to wash OS, have a wash.
lavativa *nf* enema.
lavavajillas *nm inv* dishwasher.
laxante *nm* laxative.
laxitud *nf* laxity, laxness.
laxo,-a *adj* 1 *(sin tensión)* slack. 2 *(poco estricto)* lax.
lazada *nf* 1 *(nudo)* knot. 2 *(lazo)* bow.
lazar [4] *vt* to lasso.
lazarillo *nm* guide. ● **perro lazarillo** guide dog.
lazo *nm* 1 *(cinta)* ribbon; *(de adorno)* bow. 2 *fig (vínculo)* tie, bond. 3 *(trampa)* snare, trap.
lb *sím* **(libra)** pound; *(símbolo)* lb.
le *pron* 1 *(objeto directo)* him; *(usted)* you: **¿quién le sirvió?** *who served you?* 2 *(objeto indirecto - a él)* him; *(- a ella)* her; *(- a usted)* you: **le regalaron un perrito** *they gave him a puppy;* **le repito la pregunta** *I'll repeat the question for you.*

See also **les** and **leísmo**.

leal *adj* 1 loyal, faithful. 2 *(justo)* fair.
lealtad *nf* loyalty, faithfulness.
lebrel *nm* greyhound.
lebrillo *nm* bowl.
lección *nf* lesson. ■ **dar una lección a** ALGN *fig* to teach SB a lesson.
lechada *nf* whitewash.
lechal *adj* sucking.
lechazo *nm (cordero)* sucking lamb.
leche *nf* 1 milk. 2 *fam (golpe)* knock; *(accidente)* crash. 3 *tabú (fastidio)* drag, bastard, bummer. 4 *fam (suerte)* luck. ■ **a toda leche** *fam* at full belt, flat out. ‖ **estar de mala leche** *fam* to be in a foul mood. ‖ **tener mala leche** *fam (mal carácter)* to have a foul temper. ● **leche condensada** condensed milk. ‖ **leche desnatada** skimmed milk.
lechera *nf (recipiente - de mesa)* milk jug; *(- para llevar leche)* milk churn.
lechería *nf* dairy.
lechero,-a *nm* milkman, dairyman.
lecho *nm (gen)* bed; *(de un río)* river bed.
lechón *nm (animal)* piglet; *(en cocina)* sucking pig.
lechuga *nf* lettuce.
lechuza *nf* owl.
lectivo,-a *adj* school.
lector,-ra *nm & nf* 1 reader. 2 EDUC foreign language assistant.
▷ *nm* **lector** TÉC scanner. ● **lector óptico** optical scanner.
lectorado *nm* language assistantship.
leer [61] *vt* 1 *(gen)* to read. 2 *(tesis)* to defend.
▷ *vi* to read.
legado,-a *nm* **legado** 1 *(herencia)* legacy, bequest. 2 *(persona)* legate, representative.
legajo *nm* dossier.

legal *adj* 1 *(gen)* legal. 2 *argot (persona)* above-board, upfront.
legalidad *nf* 1 *(de una acción, etc)* legality, lawfulness. 2 *(sistema de leyes)* law.
legalista *adj* legalistic.
▷ *nm o nf* legalist.
legalización *nf* 1 *(de una situación, unión)* legalization. 2 *(de documento, firma)* to authenticate.
legalizar [4] *vt* 1 *(situación, unión)* to legalize. 2 *(documento, firma)* to authenticate.
▷ *vpr* **legalizarse** to become legal.
legaña *nf* sleep.
legañoso,-a *adj* bleary-eyed.
legar [7] *vt* 1 to bequeath. 2 *fig* to hand down, pass on.
legatario,-a *nm & nf* legatee.
legendario,-a *adj* legendary.
legibilidad *nf* legibility.
legible *adj* legible.
legión *nf* 1 MIL legion. 2 *fig* crowd: **una legión de seguidores** *a crowd of followers.*
legionario,-a *adj* legionary.
▷ *nm* **legionario** legionary, legionnaire.
legionella *nf* 1 *(enfermedad)* Legionnaire's disease. 2 *(bacteria)* legionella bacterium.
legislación *nf* legislation.
legislador,-ra *adj* legislative.
▷ *nm & nf* legislator.
legislar *vi* to legislate.
legislativo,-a *adj* legislative.
legislatura *nf* 1 *(período)* term of office. 2 *(cuerpo)* legislative body.
legitimación *nf* legitimization.
legitimar *vt* to legitimate.
legitimidad *nf* legitimacy.
legítimo,-a *adj* 1 JUR legitimate. 2 *(genuino)* real, authentic.
lego,-a *adj* 1 lay, secular. 2 *(ignorante)* ignorant.
legua *nf (medida)* league.
legumbre *nf* 1 *(planta)* legume. 2 *(fruto)* pulse.
leguminoso,-a *adj* leguminous.
▷ *nf pl* **leguminosas** leguminous plants.
leído,-a *adj* well-read.
leísmo *nm incorrect use of* **le** *and* **les** *as direct object instead of* **lo** *and* **los**.
leísta *adj given to* **leísmo**.
▷ *nm o nf person who is given to* **leísmo**.
leitmotiv *nm* leitmotiv.
▲ *pl* **leitmotivs**.
lejanía *nf* distance.
lejano,-a *adj (tierra, país)* distant, far-off, far-away; *(pariente, familia)* distant.
lejía *nf* bleach.
lejos *adv* far, far away, far off. ■ **a lo lejos** in the distance, far away. ‖ **de lejos** from a distance. ‖ **lejos de** far from: **lejos de reponerse, empeoró y al final murió** *far from recovering, he got worse and eventually died.*
lelo,-a *adj fam* gormless, stupid.
lema *nm (gen)* motto; *(en publicidad)* slogan.

lencería *nf* 1 *(ropa interior)* lingerie. 2 *(ropa blanc*
linen. 3 *(tienda - de ropa interior)* lingerie shop; *(-*
ropa blanca) linen shop.
lengua *nf* 1 ANAT tongue. 2 *(idioma)* language. 3 *(*
tierra) strip. ■ **irse de la lengua** *fam* to let the cat o
of the bag. ‖ **tener ALGO en la punta de la lengua** *fig*
have STH on the tip of one's tongue. ‖ **tirar de**
lengua a ALGN *fam* to pump SB for informatio
● **lengua materna** mother tongue.
lenguado *nm* sole.
lenguaje *nm* 1 *(gen)* language. 2 *(habla)* speech.
lenguaraz *adj (hablador)* garrulous; *(descarado)* i
solent.
▲ *pl* **lenguaraces**.
lengüeta *nf* 1 MÚS reed. 2 *(de zapato)* tongue.
lente *nm & nf* lens.
▷ *nm pl* **lentes** glasses, spectacles. ● **lentes de conta**
to contact lenses.
lenteja *nf* lentil.
lentejuela *nf* sequin.
lentilla *nf* contact lens.
lentitud *nf* slowness. ■ **con lentitud** slowly.
lento,-a *adj* slow.
▷ *adv* **lento** slowly.
leña *nf* 1 wood, firewood. 2 *fam fig (paliza)* hiding
(violencia) trouble.
leñador,-ra *nm & nf* woodcutter, lumberjack.
leñera *nf* woodshed.
leño *nm* 1 log. 2 *fig (tonto)* blockhead, thickhead.
leñoso,-a *adj* ligneous, woody.
Leo *nm (signo)* Leo.
▷ *nm o nf (persona)* Leo.
león,-ona *nm & nf* 1 *(animal - macho)* lion; *(- hem*
bra) lioness. 2 *(persona)* lion-hearted person. ■ **n**
es tan fiero el león como lo pintan he's not as bad a
he's made out to be. ● **león marino** sea lion.
leonera *nf* 1 lion's den. 2 *fig (habitación)* tip.
leonino,-a *adj* 1 *(de león)* lion-like, leonine. 2 *(con*
trato) unfair.
leopardo *nm* leopard.
leotardos *nm pl* thick woollen tights.
lepidóptero,-a *adj* lepidopterous.
▷ *nm* **lepidóptero** lepidopteran.
lepra *nf* leprosy.
leproso,-a *adj* leprous.
▷ *nm & nf* leper.
lerdo,-a *adj fam* slow-witted.
les *pron* 1 *(objeto directo)* them; *(ustedes)* you: **dice qu**
les vio ayer *she says she saw them yesterday;* **no le**
entiendo *I don't understand you.* 2 *(objeto indirecto*
them; *(a ustedes)* you: **entraron en casa ladrones y le**
robaron *burglars broke in and robbed them;* **les do**
una oportunidad más *I'll give you one more chance.*

See also **le**.

lesbiana *nf* lesbian.
lesbianismo *nm* lesbianism.
lésbico,-a *adj* lesbian.
lesión *nf* 1 *(daño físico)* wound. 2 *(perjuicio)* harm.
lesionado,-a *adj* injured.
▷ *nm & nf* injured person.
lesionar *vt* 1 *(herir)* to injure. 2 *(perjudicar)* to harm.
▷ *vpr* **lesionarse** to get injured.

lesivo,-a *adj* damaging, injurious.
Lesotho *nm* Lesotho.
letal *adj* lethal, deadly.
letanía *nf* **1** REL litany. **2** *fam (lista)* long list; *(sermón)* spiel.
letargo *nm* lethargy.
letón,-ona *adj* Latvian.
▷ *nm & nf (persona)* Latvian.
▷ *nm* **letón** *(idioma)* Latvian.
Letonia *nf* Latvia.
letra *nf* **1** *(del alfabeto)* letter. **2** *(de imprenta)* character. **3** *(escritura)* handwriting. **4** *(de canción)* lyrics *pl*, words *pl*. **5** *(de cambio)* bill of exchange. ● **letra de cambio** bill of exchange, draft. ‖ **letra de imprenta** block capitals *pl*. ‖ **letra mayúscula** capital letter. ‖ **letra minúscula** small letter.
▷ *nf pl* **letras** EDUC arts; *(literatura)* letters. ■ **aprender las primeras letras** to learn to read and write.
letrado,-a *adj* learned, erudite.
▷ *nm & nf* lawyer.
letrero *nm* sign, notice.
letrina *nf* latrine.
leucemia *nf* leukaemia, US leukemia.
leucocito *nm* leucocyte, white blood cell.
leva *nf* **1** MIL levy. **2** MAR weighing anchor.
levadizo,-a *adj* which can be raised.
levadura *nf* yeast.
levantamiento *nm* **1** *(de objeto, peso)* lifting. **2** *(de una sanción)* lifting, raising. **3** *(de un ejército, etc)* uprising, revolt. **4** *(de un edificio)* erection, raising.
levantar *vt* **1** *(alzar)* to raise, lift: **no lo puedo levantar, pesa mucho** *I can't lift it, it's heavy.* **2** *(construir)* to erect, build. **3** *(empresa - hacer rentable)* to get off the ground; *(- establecer)* to set up. **4** *(despegar)* to loosen, unstick: **el agua ha levantado el parqué** *the water lifted the parquet floor.* **5** *(suprimir)* to lift. ■ **levantar el campamento** to strike camp. ‖ **levantar la moral a** ALGN to cheer SB up, raise SB's spirits. ‖ **levantar la vista** to look up.
▷ *vpr* **levantarse 1** *(alzarse)* to rise. **2** *(ponerse de pie)* to stand up. **3** *(dejar la cama)* to get up, get out of bed. **4** *(sublevarse)* to rebel, rise up. **5** *(viento, oleaje)* to get up: **se levantó una tormenta violentísima** *a violent storm got up.*
levante *nm* **1** *(este)* East. **2** *(viento)* east wind.
levar *vt (ancla)* to weigh.
leve *adj* **1** *(ligero, suave)* slight; *(de poco peso)* light. **2** *(poco importante)* slight, trifling; *(poco grave)* minor.
levedad *nf* **1** *(ligereza)* lightness. **2** *(poca importancia)* insignificance.
levitar *vi* to levitate.
lexema *nm* lexeme.
léxico,-a *adj* lexical.
▷ *nm* **léxico 1** *(diccionario)* lexicon. **2** *(vocabulario)* vocabulary.
lexicografía *nf* lexicography.
lexicón *nm* lexicon.
ley *nf* **1** *(gen)* law; *(proyecto de ley)* bill, act; *(regla)* rule. **2** *(de metal)* purity. ■ **aprobar una ley** to pass a bill. ‖ **con todas las de la ley** proper. ‖ **de ley 1** *(oro)* pure. **2** *(plata)* sterling. **3** *(persona)* genuine. ‖ **por ley** by law.
leyenda *nf* **1** *(narración)* legend. **2** *(inscripción)* inscription.
lezna *nf* awl.
liado,-a *adj* **1** *(ocupado)* busy. **2** *(confuso)* mixed up.
liana *nf* liana.
liar [13] *vt* **1** *(atar)* to tie up, bind; *(envolver)* to wrap up. **2** *(cigarrillo)* to roll. **3** *(lana)* to wind. **4** *fam (complicar)* to mix up, make a mess of; *(confundir)* to confuse: **cuéntale la verdad y no lo líes más** *tell him the truth and stop messing him about.* **5** *fam (engatusar)* to involve: **me han liado para que me meta en el negocio** *they managed to get me involved in the deal.*
▷ *vpr* **liarse a** + *sustantivo* to start + *ger*: **se liaron a discutir** *they started arguing.*
libanés,-esa *adj* Lebanese.
▷ *nm & nf* Lebanese.
Líbano *nm* **el Líbano** the Lebanon.
libar *vt* **1** *(néctar)* to suck. **2** *lit (bebida)* to imbibe.
libélula *nf* dragonfly.
liberación *nf* **1** *(de una dependencia)* liberation; *(de una persona)* freeing, release: **la liberación de la mujer** *Women's Lib.* **2** *(de hipoteca)* redemption.
liberado,-a *adj* liberated.
liberador,-ra *adj* liberating.
▷ *nm & nf* liberator.
liberal *adj* liberal.
▷ *nm o nf* **1** liberal. **2** *(del partido liberal)* Liberal.
liberalismo *nm* liberalism.
liberalización *nf (en política)* liberalization; *(en economía)* relaxation of restrictions.
liberar *vt* **1** *(persona, animal)* to free; *(país, ciudad)* to liberate. **2** *(energía)* to release.
Liberia *nf* Liberia.
liberiano,-a *adj* Liberian.
▷ *nm & nf* Liberian.
libertad *nf (gen)* freedom, liberty. ■ **poner en libertad** to free, release. ‖ **tomarse la libertad de** + *inf* to take the liberty of + *ger*. ● **libertad de expresión** freedom of expression.
libertar *vt* to liberate.
libertario,-a *adj* libertarian.
▷ *nm & nf* libertarian.
libertino,-a *adj* licentious.
▷ *nm & nf* libertine.
Libia *nf* Libya.
libido *nf* libido.
libio,-a *adj* Libyan.
▷ *nm & nf* Libyan.
libra *nf* **1** *(moneda, medida)* pound. **2** *argot (antiguamente)* a hundred pesetas. **3 Libra** [*pl* **Libra.**] *(signo zodiacal)* Libra. ● **libra esterlina** pound sterling.
librar *vt* **1** to save (**de**, from): **me libraron de toda responsabilidad** *they absolved me of all responsibility.* **2** *(batalla)* to fight, wage.
▷ *vi fam (tener libre)* to be off, not to work: **libro todos los lunes** *I've got Mondays off, I'm off on Mondays.*
▷ *vpr* **librarse** to escape (**de**, from).
libre *adj* **1** *(gen)* free. **2** *(asiento)* free, vacant: **¿está libre?** *is this seat free?* **3** *(sin ocupación)* free: **mañana tenemos el día libre** *we've got the day off tomorrow.* **4** *(exento)* free. **5** *(alumno)* external. ■ **ir por libre** *fam*

to do one's own thing. ● **entrada libre** free admittance.
librecambio *nm* free trade.
librería *nf* 1 *(tienda)* bookshop, bookstore. 2 *(mueble)* bookcase; *(estantería)* bookshelf.
librero,-a *nm & nf* bookseller.
libreta *nf* 1 *(para anotar)* notebook. 2 *(de ahorros)* savings book. ● **libreta de ahorros** savings book.
libreto *nm* libretto.
libro *nm (gen)* book. ● **libro de bolsillo** paperback. ‖ **libro de consulta** reference book. ‖ **libro de familia** *book recording details of births, marriages, etc in a family.* ‖ **libro de reclamaciones** complaints book. ‖ **libro de texto** textbook.
licencia *nf* 1 *(permiso)* licence (US license), permission. 2 *(documento)* licence (US license), permit. 3 MIL discharge. ● **licencia fiscal** *tax paid by businesses and the self-employed in order to operate legally.* ‖ **licencia poética** poetic licence (US license).
licenciado,-a *nm & nf* 1 EDUC graduate. 2 *(abogado)* lawyer.
▷ *nm* **licenciado** MIL discharged soldier.
licenciar *vt* 1 EDUC to award a degree to. 2 MIL to discharge.
▷ *vpr* **licenciarse** to graduate.
licenciatura *nf (four year)* university degree.
liceo *nm* 1 *(colegio)* secondary school. 2 *(sociedad)* literary society, recreational society.
licitación *nf* bid.
licitador,-ra *nm & nf* bidder.
lícito,-a *adj* 1 *(legal)* licit, lawful. 2 *(justo)* fair.
licor *nm (dulce)* liqueur; *(bebida alcohólica)* liquor, spirits *pl*.
licuadora *nf* juice extractor.
licuar [10] *vt* to liquefy.
lid *nf* 1 contest, fight. 2 *fig (controversia)* dispute.
líder *nm o nf* leader.
liderar *vt* to lead.
liderazgo *nm* leadership.
lidia *nf* 1 *(de toros)* bullfight. 2 *(lucha)* fight, struggle.
liebre *nf* 1 *(animal)* hare. 2 DEP pacemaker.
Liechtenstein *nm* Liechtenstein.
lienzo *nm* 1 ARTE *(tela)* canvas; *(cuadro)* painting. 2 *(tejido)* linen.
lifting *nm* facelift.
▲ *pl* **liftings.**
liga *nf* 1 *(para media)* garter. 2 *(asociación)* league, alliance. 3 DEP league.
ligadura *nf* 1 *(atadura)* tie, bond. 2 MED ligature.
ligamento *nm* ligament.
ligar *vt* 1 *(atar)* to tie, bind. 2 *(unir)* to link, connect. 3 CULIN to bind.
▷ *vi fam (conquistar)* to score.
ligero,-a *adj* 1 *(liviano)* light. 2 *(sin importancia)* minor, light. 3 *(rápido)* swift. 4 *(ágil)* agile. 5 *(frívolo)* flippant. ■ **a la ligera** lightly, flippantly.
light *adj* 1 *(comida)* low-calorie; *(refresco)* diet. 2 *(cigarrillo)* light.
lignito *nm* lignite.
ligón,-ona *nm & nf fam* flirt.
ligue *nm fam* pick-up, date.
liguero,-a *adj (de la liga)* league.
▷ *nm* **liguero** *(de las medias)* suspender belt.
lija *nf (papel)* sandpaper.
lijar *vt* to sand.
lila *adj (color)* lilac.
▷ *nf (flor)* lilac.
lima *nf* 1 *(herramienta)* file; *(para uñas)* nail file. 2 *(fruta)* lime; *(árbol)* lime tree.
limar *vt* 1 *(pulir)* to file. 2 *fig (perfeccionar)* to polish up.
limeño,-a *adj* of Lima, from Lima.
▷ *nm & nf* person from Lima, inhabitant of Lima.
limitación *nf* limitation.
limitado,-a *adj* limited.
limitar *vt (gen)* to limit. ■ **limitarse a** + *inf* to restrict OS to + *ger*, do no more than + *inf*: **una persona inteligente no se limita a ver la televisión** *an intelligent person does not restrict himself to watching television.*
▷ *vi* **limitar con** to border with.
límite *nm* 1 *(extremo)* limit; *(en un terreno)* boundary. 2 *(frontera)* boundary. ■ **sin límites** boundless. ● **límite de velocidad** speed limit.
limítrofe *adj* bordering.
limo *nm* slime.
limón *nm* lemon.
limonada *nf* lemonade.
limonero,-a *adj (del limón)* lemon.
▷ *nm* **limonero** lemon tree.
limonita *nf* limonite.
limosna *nf* alms *pl*, charity. ■ **pedir limosna** to beg.
limpiabotas *nm inv* bootblack.
limpiacristales *nm inv (producto)* window cleaning fluid.
▷ *nm o nf (persona)* window cleaner.
limpiador,-ra *adj* cleaning.
▷ *nm & nf (persona)* cleaner.
▷ *nm* **limpiador** *(producto)* cleaning product.
limpiamente *adv* cleanly.
limpiaparabrisas *nm inv* windscreen wiper, US windshield wiper.
limpiapipas *nm* pipe cleaner.
limpiar [12] *vt* 1 *(gen)* to clean, cleanse. 2 *(con paño)* to wipe. 3 *fig (purificar)* to purify. 4 *fam (robar)* to pinch, nick.
limpieza *nf* 1 *(ausencia de suciedad)* cleanliness. 2 *(acción de limpiar)* cleaning. 3 *(pureza)* purity. 4 *(honradez)* honesty, fairness.
limpio,-a *adj* 1 *(sin suciedad)* clean. 2 *(claro)* neat, tidy. 3 *(puro)* pure. 4 *(honesto)* honest, fair.
▷ *adv* fairly: **no juegan limpio, hacen trampa** *they don't play fair, they cheat.*
linaje *nm (ascendencia)* lineage.
linaza *nf* linseed.
lince *nm* 1 ZOOL lynx. 2 *fig (persona)* sharp-eyed person.
linchar *vt* to lynch.
lindar *vi* to border (**con**, on), adjoin (**con**, -).
linde *nm & nf* boundary.
lindo,-a *adj* pretty, nice, lovely.
línea *nf* 1 *(gen)* line. 2 *(tipo)* figure. ■ **en líneas generales** in general. ‖ **guardar la línea** to keep one's figure. ● **línea aérea** airline. ‖ **línea continua** solid line, unbroken line.
lineal *adj* linear.

linfático,-a *adj* lymphatic.
lingote *nm* ingot.
lingüística *nf* linguistics.
lingüístico,-a *adj* linguistic.
linier *nm* linesman.
lino *nm* 1 *(tela)* linen. 2 BOT flax.
linotipista *nm o nf* typesetter.
linotipo *nm* Linotype.
linterna *nf* 1 *(de pilas)* torch. 2 *(farol)* lantern, lamp. 3 ARQUIT lantern.
lío *nm* 1 *(embrollo)* mess. 2 *(aventura amorosa)* affair. 3 *(fardo)* bundle. ■ **hacerse un lío** 1 *(uso literal)* to get tangled up. 2 *(uso figurado)* to get muddled up. ■ **meterse en un lío** to get OS into a mess.
liofilizado,-a *adj* freeze-dried.
lípido *nm* lipid.
lipotimia *nf* blackout.
liquen *nm* lichen.
liquidación *nf* 1 *(venta)* sale. 2 *(pago)* settlement. 3 *(de activos)* liquidation.
liquidar *vt* 1 *(deuda)* to settle, liquidate. 2 *(mercancías)* to sell off. 3 *fam (dinero)* to spend, blow.
líquido,-a *adj* 1 *(gen)* liquid. 2 *(neto)* net. 3 *(en metálico)* in cash.
▷ *nm* **líquido** liquid.
lira *nf* 1 MÚS lyre. 2 *(moneda)* lira.
lírica *nf* poetry, lyric poetry.
lirio *nm* lily.
lirón *nm* dormouse. ■ **dormir como un lirón** to sleep like a log.
lis *nf (planta)* lily.
liso,-a *adj* 1 *(sin desigualdades)* smooth, even. 2 *(sin desniveles)* flat. 3 *(sin arrugas)* smooth. 4 *(pelo)* straight. 5 *(color)* plain.
lista *nf* 1 *(relación)* list. 2 *(raya)* stripe. 3 *(tira)* strip, slip.
listo,-a *adj* 1 *(inteligente)* clever, smart. 2 *(preparado)* ready: **¿estás lista?** *are you ready?* 3 *(acabado)* finished. ■ **pasarse de listo,-a** *fam* to be too clever by half.
litera *nf* bunk bed; *(en barco)* bunk; *(tren)* couchette.
literal *adj* literal.
literario,-a *adj* literary.
literatura *nf* literature.
litigar [7] *vi* 1 JUR to litigate. 2 *(disputar)* to argue, dispute.
litigio *nm* 1 JUR litigation, lawsuit. 2 *(disputa)* dispute.
litio *nm* lithium.
litografía *nf* 1 *(arte)* lithography. 2 *(reproducción)* lithograph.
litoral *adj* coastal.
▷ *nm* coast.
litosfera *nf* lithosphere.
litro *nm* litre, US liter.
Lituania *nf* Lithuania.
lituano,-a *adj* Lithuanian.
▷ *nm & nf (persona)* Lithuanian.
▷ *nm* **lituano** *(idioma)* Lithuanian.
liturgia *nf* liturgy.
liviano,-a *adj* 1 *(ligero)* light. 2 *fig (inconstante)* frivolous. 3 *fig (lascivo)* lewd.
lívido,-a *adj* livid.
llaga *nf (gen)* sore; *(en la boca)* ulcer.
llagar *vt* to cover with ulcers.
llama *nf* 1 *(de fuego)* flame. 2 ZOOL llama.
llamada *nf* 1 *(gen)* call. 2 *(a la puerta)* knock, ring.
llamamiento *nm* 1 *(petición)* appeal. 2 *(convocatoria)* call.
llamar *vt* 1 *(gen)* to call. 2 *(convocar)* to summon: **habrá que llamar al médico** *we'll have to call the doctor.* 3 *(dar nombre)* to name. 4 *(atraer)* to appeal to. ■ **llamar por teléfono** to call, phone, GB ring, ring up.
▷ *vi (a la puerta)* to knock; *(al timbre)* to ring; *(al teléfono)* to ring, call, phone.
▷ *vpr* **llamarse** *(tener nombre)* to be called.
llamativo,-a *adj* showy, flashy.
llamear *vi* to blaze.
llano,-a *adj* 1 *(plano)* flat, even, level. 2 *(franco)* open, frank. 3 *(sencillo)* simple.
▷ *nm* **llano** *(llanura)* plain.
llanta *nf* wheel rim, rim.
llanto *nm* crying, weeping.
llanura *nf* 1 *(llano)* plain. 2 *(igualdad)* plainness.
llave *nf* 1 *(de puerta, etc)* key. 2 TÉC wrench. 3 *(en judo)* lock. 4 *(en texto)* bracket. 5 MÚS key.
llavero *nm* key ring.
llegada *nf* 1 *(entrada)* arrival. 2 DEP finishing line.
llegar [7] *vi* 1 to arrive (**a**, at/in), get (**a**, at), reach (**a**, -): **llegó el primero** *he arrived first.* 2 *(alcanzar)* to reach: **¿llegas a ese estante?** *can you reach that shelf?* 3 *(ser suficiente)* to be enough, suffice: **¿te llega con diez euros?** *is ten euros enough?* 4 *(conseguir)* to manage. 5 *(cantidad)* to amount (**a**, to). 6 **llegar a** + *inf (uso enfático)*: **llegó a llamarme tonto** *he even called me a silly.*
▷ *vpr* **llegarse a** *fam (ir a)* to go over to, nip over to, slip over to, hop over to.
llenar *vt* 1 *(espacio, recipiente)* to fill. 2 *(formulario)* to fill in. 3 *(tiempo)* to fill, occupy. 4 *(satisfacer)* to fulfil, please: **el trabajo que hago no me llena** *I don't find my job very fulfilling.*
▷ *vpr* **llenarse** 1 *(gen)* to fill. 2 *(de gente)* to fill up. 3 *(de comida)* to get full, overeat. 4 **llenar de** *(alegría)* to fill with.
lleno,-a *adj* 1 full (**de**, of): **está lleno de gente** *it's full of people.* 2 *(cubierto)* covered (**de**, with).
▷ *nm* **lleno** TEAT full house: **hoy hay lleno total** *it's a full house today.*
llevadero,-a *adj* bearable.
llevar *vt* 1 *(gen)* to take: **llévale esto a tu abuela** *take this to your granny.* 2 *(tener)* to have; *(tener encima)* to have, carry: **¿qué llevas ahí?** *what's that you've got there?* 3 *(prenda)* to wear, have on: **no me gusta llevar sombrero** *I don't like wearing a hat.* 4 *(aguantar)* to cope with. 5 *(dirigir)* to be in charge of: **¿quién lleva los pedidos?** *who's in charge of orders?* 6 *(conducir - coche)* to drive; *(moto)* - to ride: **Lleva un Seat azul** *he drives a blue Seat.* 7 *(pasar tiempo)* to be: **llevo un mes aquí** *I have been here for a month.* 8 *(libros, cuentas)* to keep. 9 *(años)* to be older: **te llevo tres años** *I'm three years older than you.* 10 *(vida)* to lead: **lleva una vida muy ajetreada** *she leads a hectic life.* 11 *(tiempo, esfuerzo)* to take: **este trabajo nos llevará más**

de un mes *this job will take us over a month.* **12** *(compás, paso, ritmo)* to keep.
▷ *vi* **1 llevar a** *(conducir)* to take, lead: **esta senda lleva a la cima** *this path takes you to the summit.* **2 llevar a + inf** *(inducir)* to lead to, make: **esto me lleva a pensar que ...** *this leads me to think that...*
▷ *vpr* **llevarse 1** *(obtener)* to get; *(ganar)* to win: **los rusos se llevaron todas las medallas** *the Russians won all the medals.* **2** *(recibir)* to get: **se llevó un buen susto** *he got quite a shock.* **3** *(estar de moda)* to be fashionable: **este color ya no se lleva** *this colour is not fashionable any more.* **4** *(entenderse)* to get on (**con**, with), get along (**con**, with): **se lleva bien con sus padres** *he gets on well with his parents.* **5** MAT to carry over.
llorar *vi* **1** to cry, weep. **2** *fam (quejarse)* to moan.
▷ *vt* to mourn.
llorón,-ona *nm & nf fam* crybaby.
lloroso,-a *adj* tearful, weeping.
llover [32] *vi* [Used only in the 3rd pers; it does not take a subject.] to rain: **llueve** *it's raining.*
lloviznar *vi* [Used only in the 3rd pers, it does not take a subject.] to drizzle.
lluvia *nf* **1** rain. **2** *fig* shower, barrage.
lo *art neut* the.
▷ *pron* **1** *(objeto directo - él)* him; *(- usted)* you: **no lo conozco de nada** *I don't know him from Adam;* **2** *(objeto directo - cosa, animal)* it: **¿lo has probado?** *have you tried it?* ■ **con lo cual** so. ‖ **lo cual** which. ‖ **lo que** what.
loar *vt* to praise, extol.
lobezno,-a *nm & nf* ZOOL wolf cub.
lobo,-a *nm & nf (macho)* wolf; *(hembra)* she-wolf. ● **lobo de mar** *(persona)* sea dog.
lóbulo *nm* lobe.
local *adj* local.
▷ *nm (para negocio)* premises *pl.*
localidad *nf* **1** *(ciudad)* town. **2** TEAT *(asiento)* seat; *(billete)* ticket. ■ **«Agotadas las localidades»** «Sold out».
localizar *vt* **1** *(encontrar)* to locate, find. **2** *(infección, incendio)* to localize.
locativo,-a *adj* locative.
▷ *nm* **locativo** locative.
loción *nf* lotion.
loco,-a *adj* **1** *(gen)* mad, crazy, insane. **2** *(muy ocupado)* terribly busy. **3** *fam (asombroso)* amazing.
▷ *nm & nf* lunatic, insane person. ■ **volverse loco,-a** to go mad.
locomoción *nf* locomotion.
locomotor,-ra *adj* locomotive.
locomotora *nf* locomotive.
locución *nf* phrase, locution.
locura *nf* **1** *(perturbación)* madness, insanity. **2** *(insensatez)* folly.
locutor,-ra *nm & nf (gen)* announcer; *(de noticias)* news reader.
locutorio *nm* **1** *(de teléfonos)* telephone booth. **2** *(de radio)* studio.
lodo *nm* mud.
logarítmico,-a *adj* logarithmic.
logaritmo *nm* logarithm.
lógica *nf* logic.
lógico,-a *adj* **1** *(de la lógica)* logical. **2** *(natural)* normal, to be expected.
logística *nf* logistics.
logopeda *nm o nf* speech therapist.
logotipo *nm* logo, logotype.
logrado,-a *adj (conseguido)* successful.
lograr *vt (conseguir)* to manage to get, achieve; *(sueño)* to fulfil; *(victoria, premio)* to win.
logro *nm* **1** *(éxito)* success, achievement. **2** *(beneficio)* gain, profit.
loísmo *nm incorrect use of* **lo** *and* **los** *as indirect objects instead of* **le** *and* **les**.
loma *nf* hill.
lombarda *nf* red cabbage.
lombriz *nf (de tierra)* earthworm; *(intestinal)* worm.
lomo *nm* **1** CULIN *(de cerdo)* loin; *(de ternera)* sirloin. **2** ANAT back. **3** *(de libro)* spine.
lona *nf* canvas.
loncha *nf (de jamón, queso, etc)* slice; *(de tocino, bacon)* rasher.
londinense *adj* of London, from London.
▷ *nm o nf* Londoner.
Londres *nm* London.
longaniza *nf cured pork sausage.*
longitud *nf* **1** length. **2** GEOG longitude. ● **longitud de onda** wavelength.
lonja *nf* **1** *(mercado)* exchange, market. **2** ARQUIT raised porch. **3** *(loncha)* slice, rasher.
lontananza *nf (fondo)* background.
loor *nm lit* praise.
lord *nm* lord.
loriga *nf* HIST cuirass.
loro *nm (pájaro)* parrot.
los *art def* the: **los niños** *the boys.*
▷ *pron (objeto directo)* them; *(ustedes)* you: **los vi** *I saw them;* **a ustedes dos no los quiero volver a ver** *I don't want to see you two again.*

See also **lo, el**.

losa *nf* **1** flagstone, slab. **2** *(de sepulcro)* gravestone.
loseta *nf* floor tile.
lotería *nf* lottery.
loto *nm (flor)* lotus.
loza *nf* **1** *(cerámica)* china. **2** *(de cocina)* crockery.
lozanía *nf (de persona)* healthiness, lustiness.
lozano,-a *adj* **1** *(persona)* healthy, lusty. **2** *(planta)* fresh.
lubina *nf* bass.
lubricante *adj* lubricating.
▷ *nm* lubricant.
lubricar [1] *vt* to lubricate.
lucerna *nf* skylight.
lucero *nm* bright star.
lucha *nf* **1** *(gen)* fight, struggle. **2** DEP wrestling. ● **lucha libre** free-style wrestling.
luchador,-ra *nm & nf* **1** *(gen)* fighter. **2** DEP wrestler.
luchar *vi* **1** *(gen)* to fight. **2** DEP to wrestle.
lucidez *nf* lucidity.
lucido,-a *adj* beautiful.
lúcido,-a *adj* lucid, clear-headed.
luciérnaga *nf* glow-worm.
lucífero,-a *adj lit* resplendent.

lucimiento *nm* 1 *(oportunidad de lucirse)* showing off. 2 *(brillo)* brilliance.
lucio *nm* pike.
lución *nm* slowworm.
lucir [45] *vt (mostrar)* to show, display; *(ropa)* to wear.
▷ *vpr* **lucirse** *(sobresalir)* to be brilliant.
lucrarse *vpr* to make a profit.
lucrativo,-a *adj* lucrative, profitable.
lucro *nm* gain, profit. ● **afán de lucro** profit motive: **lo hizo sin afán de lucro** *he did it with no profit motive in mind.*
luctuoso,-a *adj lit* mournful, sorrowful.
lúdico,-a *adj* recreational: **actividades lúdicas** *recreational activities, recreation.*
ludópata *nm o nf* compulsive gambler.
ludopatía *nf* compulsive gambling.
luego *adv* 1 *(después)* then, afterwards, next. 2 *(más tarde)* later.
▷ *conj* so, therefore.
lugar *nm* 1 *(sitio, ciudad)* place. 2 *(posición, situación)* place, position: **tú ponte en mi lugar y lo entenderás** *put yourself in my position and you'll understand.* 3 *(espacio)* room, space: **ya no hay lugar para más muebles** *there's no room for any more furniture.* ■ **en lugar de** instead of.
lugareño,-a *adj* local.
▷ *nm & nf* local.
lugarteniente *nm* deputy.
lúgubre *adj (triste)* bleak, lugubrious; *(fúnebre)* sombre (US somber), mournful.
lujo *nm* luxury.
lujosamente *adv* luxuriously.
lujoso,-a *adj* luxurious.
lujuria *nf* lewdness, lust, lechery.
lujurioso,-a *adj* lustful, lecherous.
▷ *nm & nf* lecher.
lumbago *nm* lumbago.
lumbar *adj* lumbar.
lumbre *nf* 1 *(fuego)* fire; *(candela)* light. 2 *(para cigarrillo)* light: **¿me das lumbre?** *could you give me a light please?* ■ **a la luz de la lumbre** by the light of the fire.
lumbrera *nf (persona)* genius, luminary; *(con ironía)* bright spark.
luminaria *nf* 1 *(en iglesia)* altar lamp. 2 *(en fiestas)* light.
lumínico,-a *adj* light.
luminiscencia *nf* luminiscence.
luminiscente *adj* luminiscent.
luminosidad *nf* brightness, luminosity.
luminoso,-a *adj* bright, luminous.
luminotecnia *nf* lighting.
luminotécnico,-a *adj* lighting.
luna *nf* 1 *(satélite)* moon. 2 *(cristal)* window pane; *(de coche)* window; *(de ventana)* glass. 3 *(espejo)* mirror. ● **luna llena** full moon. ‖ **luna de miel** honey moon.
lunación *nf* lunation.
lunar *adj* lunar, moon: **las fases lunares** *the phases of the moon.*
▷ *nm (en la piel)* beauty spot. ■ **de lunares** spotted.
lunático,-a *nm & nf* lunatic.
lunes *nm inv* Monday.

See also **jueves**.

luneta *nf car* window. ● **luneta térmica** heated rear windscreen.
lunfardo *nm Buenos Aires slang.*
lúnula *nf* half-moon, lunule.
lupa *nf* magnifying glass. ■ **con lupa** meticulously.
lúpulo *nm* hop.
lustrabotas *nm o nf* bootblack.
lustrar *vt* to polish.
lustre *nm* 1 *(brillo)* polish, shine, lustre, US luster. 2 *fig (esplendor)* glory.
lustro *nm* five years *pl.*
lustroso,-a *adj* shiny.
luteranismo *nm* Lutheranism.
luterano,-a *adj* Lutheran.
▷ *nm & nf* Lutheran.
luto *nm* 1 mourning. 2 *fig* grief.
lux *nm* lux.
luxación *nf* dislocation.
Luxemburgo *nm* Luxembourg.
luxemburgués,-esa *adj* of Luxembourg, from Luxembourg.
▷ *nm & nf* Luxembourger.
luz *nf* 1 *(gen)* light. 2 *fam (electricidad)* electricity. 3 *(iluminación)* lighting.
▷ *nf pl* **luces** *fam* intelligence *sing*: **es un hombre de pocas luces** *he's not very bright.* ■ **dar a luz** to give birth. ‖ **salir a la luz** to come out. ● **luces de cruce** dipped headlights. ‖ **luces de posición** sidelights. ‖ **luz del sol** sunlight.

M

M, m *nf (la letra)* M, m.
m¹ *sím* **(metro)** metre (US meter); *(símbolo)* m.
m² *sím* **(milla)** mile; *(símbolo)* m.
m³ *abrev* **(minuto)** minute; *(abreviatura)* min.
maca *nf* **1** *(en fruta)* bruise. **2** *(señal)* flaw, blemish.
macabro,-a *adj* macabre.
macaco,-a *nm & nf* ZOOL macaque.
macarrón *nm* **1** *(pasta italiana)* piece of macaroni. **2** *(dulce)* macaroon. **3** TÉC *(de cable)* sheath, sheathing.
▷ *nm pl* **macarrones** macaroni.
macarrónico,-a *adj fam* broken.
macedonia *nf* fruit salad. ● **macedonia de frutas** fruit salad.
Macedonia *nf* Macedonia.
macedonio,-a *adj* Macedonian.
▷ *nm & nf (persona)* Macedonian.
▷ *nm* **macedonio** *(idioma)* Macedonian.
maceración *nf* **1** *(remojo - de fruta)* maceration, soaking; *(- de carne, pescado)* marinading. **2** *(a golpes)* pounding, tenderizing.
macerar *vt (poner en remojo - fruta)* to macerate, soak; *(- carne, pescado)* to marinade.
maceta *nf* **1** flowerpot. **2** *(herramienta)* mallet.
macetero *nm* flowerpot holder.
macha *adj (almeja) type of* clam.
machaca *nm o nf argot (persona)* dogsbody.
machacar [1] *vt* **1** *(triturar)* to crush. **2** *fam (vencer)* to hammer, thrash. **3** *fam (dañar)* to kill; *(cansar, agotar)* to wear out, kill. **4** *fam (insistir en)* to harp on about, go on about.
▷ *vi* **1** *(estudiar)* to swot up, cram, US grind. **2** *(insistir en)* to go on (**con**, about), harp on (**con**, about).
machacón,-ona *adj fam* insistent, repetitive.
▷ *nm & nf fam* pain.
machaque *nm* **1** *(golpes repetidos)* beating. **2** *(trituración)* crushing, pounding. **3** *(insistencia)* dogged insistence.
machetazo *nm* blow with a machete.
machete *nm* machete.
machihembrado,-a *nm (ranura y lengüeta)* tongue and groove joint; *(caja y espiga)* mortise and tenon joint.
machismo *nm* male chauvinism.
machista *adj* male chauvinist.
▷ *nm o nf* male chauvinist.
macho *adj* **1** *(animal, planta)* male. **2** *(persona)* macho, tough.
▷ *nm* **1** *(animal, planta)* male. **2** *fam (hombre)* macho man, tough guy. **3** *fam (como apelativo)* mate, pal, man.
machote,-a *adj* **1** *(valiente)* tough. **2** *fam (hombre)* manly, tough; *(mujer)* tomboyish.
macilento,-a *adj* wan, pallid.
macizo,-a *adj* **1** *(plata)* solid. **2** *(fuerte)* solid, well-built. **3** *fam (persona)* good-looking.
▷ *nm* **macizo** **1** *(montañoso)* massif, mountain mass **2** *(de flores)* bed.
macramé *nm* macramé.
macro *nf* INFORMÁ macro.
macrobiótica *nf* macrobiotics.
macrobiótico,-a *adj* macrobiotic.
▷ *nm & nf* macrobiotic.
macrocefalia *nf* macrocephaly, macrocephalia.
macrocosmos *nm inv* macrocosm.
macroeconomía *nf* macroeconomics.
macroeconómico,-a *adj* macroeconomic.
macroscópico,-a *adj* macroscopic.
mácula *nf lit* blemish.
macuto *nm* knapsack, rucksack.
Madagascar *nm* Madagascar.
madeja *nf (de lana)* skein, hank.
madera *nf* **1** *(en el árbol)* wood; *(cortada)* timber, US lumber: **es de madera** *it's made of wood, it's wooden.* **2** *fig (aptitudes)* talent. ■ **tener madera de...** to have the makings of a...
maderero,-a *adj (industria)* timber.
madero *nm* **1** piece of timber. **2** *argot (policía)* cop.
madona *nf* Madonna.
madrastra *nf* stepmother.
madraza *nf fam* doting mother.
madre *nf* **1** mother. **2** *(monja)* sister. ● **madre política** mother-in-law. ‖ **madre soltera** single mother. ‖ **madre superiora** mother superior.
madreselva *nf* honeysuckle.
madrigal *nm* madrigal.
madriguera *nf* **1** *(de conejo)* burrow, warren; *(de zorro)* den, lair; *(de tejón)* set. **2** *(de gente)* den, lair, hideout.
madrina *nf* **1** *(de bautizo)* godmother. **2** *(de boda)* ≈ matron of honour *(usually the bridegroom's mother)*. **3** *(de un acto oficial)* lady president. **4** *(de barco) woman who launches a ship.*
madroño *nm* **1** *(árbol)* strawberry tree. **2** *(fruto) fruit of the strawberry tree.* **3** *(borla)* tassel.
madrugada *nf* **1** *(alba)* dawn, daybreak. **2** *(después de medianoche)* early morning: **a las cinco de la madrugada** *at five o'clock in the morning.*
madrugador,-ra *nm & nf* early riser.
▷ *adj* who gets up early.
madrugar [7] *vi* **1** *(levantarse pronto)* to get up early. **2** *(adelantarse)* to get there first.
madrugón ■ **darse un madrugón / pegarse un madrugón** *fam* to get up at the crack of dawn.
madurar *vi* **1** *(fruto)* to ripen. **2** *(persona)* to mature.

▷ *vt* 1 *(fruto)* to ripen. 2 *(plan, proyecto)* to think about carefully, develop fully.

madurez *nf* 1 *(de la persona)* maturity. 2 *(de la fruta)* ripeness.

maduro,-a *adj* 1 *(persona)* mature. 2 *(fruta)* ripe.

maestre *nm* HIST master.

maestría *nf* 1 *(destreza)* mastery, skill. 2 *(título)* mastership.

maestro,-a *adj (principal)* master; *(pared, viga)* main, supporting.

▷ *nm & nf* 1 *(de primaria - hombre)* schoolmaster; *(- mujer)* schoolmistress. 2 *(instructor)* teacher: **fue mi maestro en todo** *he taught me everything I know.* 3 *(experto)* master. 4 *(que alecciona)* teacher: **la vida es la mejor maestra** *life is the best teacher.*

▷ *nm* **maestro** 1 *(compositor)* composer; *(director)* conductor. 2 *(de un oficio)* master. ● **maestro de escuela** schoolteacher. ‖ **maestro de obras** foreman.

mafia *nf* mafia.

mafioso,-a *nm & nf* mafioso.

magacín *nm* 1 *(revista)* magazine. 2 *(programa)* chat show.

magdalena *nf* small sponge cake.

magenta *nf* magenta.

magia *nf* magic.

mágico,-a *adj* 1 *(pócima, palabra)* magic; *(ritual)* magical. 2 *(maravilloso)* magical, wonderful.

magisterio *nm* 1 *(estudios)* teacher training. 2 *(profesión)* teaching profession. 3 *(profesores)* teachers *pl.*

magistrado,-a *nm & nf* 1 *(juez)* judge. 2 *(miembro del Tribunal Supremo)* High Court judge, US Supreme Court judge.

magistral *adj* 1 EDUC magisterial. 2 *(interpretación)* masterly, masterful.

magistratura *nf* 1 *(cuerpo)* judges *pl.* 2 *(profesión)* judgeship.

magma *nf* magma.

magnanimidad *nf* magnanimity.

magnánimo,-a *adj* magnanimous.

magnate *nm* tycoon, magnate.

magnesio *nm* magnesium.

magnético,-a *adj* magnetic.

magnetismo *nm* magnetism.

magnetización *nf* magnetization.

magnetizar [4] *vt* 1 *(cuerpo)* to magnetize. 2 *fig (persona)* to hypnotize, captivate.

magnetofónico,-a *adj* sound recording.

magnetófono *nm* tape recorder.

magnicidio *nm* assassination.

magnificar [1] *vt* 1 *(ensalzar)* to praise, extol. 2 *(exagerar)* to exaggerate, magnify.

magnificencia *nf* 1 *(grandiosidad)* magnificence, splendour. 2 *(generosidad)* lavishness, generosity.

magnífico,-a *adj* magnificent, splendid.

magnitud *nf* 1 FÍS magnitude. 2 *fig (importancia)* magnitude, extent, size.

magno,-a *adj* great.

magnolia *nf (árbol, flor)* magnolia.

magnolio *nm* magnolia.

mago,-a *nm & nf (gen)* magician, conjurer; *(de los cuentos)* wizard.

magro,-a *adj* lean.

▷ *nm* **magro** *(de carne de cerdo)* loin of pork. ● **carne magra** lean meat.

magulladura *nf* bruise, contusion.

magullar *vt* to bruise.

▷ *vpr* **magullarse** to bruise OS, be bruised.

mahometano,-a *adj* Muslim.

▷ *nm & nf* Muslim.

maicena *nf* cornflour.

mailing *nm* mailshot.

maillot *nm* 1 *(de ciclista)* jersey. 2 *(de baile)* leotard. 3 *(de natación)* swimsuit.

maitre *nm o nf* head waiter, maître d'hôtel.

maíz *nm* 1 *(planta)* maize, US corn. 2 *(grano)* sweet corn, US corn.

maizal *nm* maize field, US corn field.

majada *nf* sheepfold.

majadería *nf* nonsense, balderdash.

majadero,-a *adj* stupid, dim-witted.

▷ *nm & nf* idiot, dimwit.

majar *vt* to crush.

majara *adj fam* loony, nuts, crazy.

▷ *nm o nf* loony, nutter.

majestad *nf* 1 *(distinción)* majesty. 2 *(tratamiento)* Majesty.

majestuoso,-a *adj* majestic.

majo,-a *adj (persona - simpático)* nice; *(- bonito)* nice, good-looking; *(cosa)* nice, lovely.

majorette *nf* majorette.

majuelo *nm (viña)* young vine.

mal *nm* 1 evil. 2 *(daño)* harm. 3 *(enfermedad)* sickness.

▷ *adj (forma apocopada de malo)* bad.

▷ *adv* 1 *(no adecuadamente)* badly: **se portó mal con nosotros** *he treated us badly.* 2 *(enfermo)* ill, sick: **me encuentro mal** *I feel ill, I don't feel well.* 3 *(incorrectamente)* wrong: **lo has hecho mal** *you've done it wrong.* 4 *(difícilmente)* hardly, scarcely: **veo muy mal desde aquí** *I can hardly see from here.* 5 *(desagradablemente)* bad: **aquí huele mal** *it smells bad in here.* 6 *(en frases negativas)* bad, badly: **la película no está mal** *the film's not bad.* ● **mal de altura** altitude sickness. ‖ **mal de ojo** evil eye.

malabarismo *nm* juggling. ■ **hacer malabarismos** to juggle.

malabarista *nm o nf* juggler.

malacostumbrado,-a *adj* spoilt.

malacostumbrar *vt* 1 *(malcriar)* to spoil. 2 *(viciar)* to get into bad habits.

malaquita *nf* malachite.

malaria *nf* malaria.

malasio,-a *adj* Malaysian.

▷ *nm & nf* Malaysian.

malaventura *nf* misfortune.

malaventurado,-a *adj* ill-fated, unfortunate.

▷ *nm & nf* unfortunate person.

Malawi *nm* Malawi.

malawiano,-a *adj* Malawian.

▷ *nm & nf* Malawian.

malayo,-a *adj* Malay.

▷ *nm & nf (persona)* Malay.

▷ *nm* **malayo** *(idioma)* Malay.

Malaysia *nf* Malaysia.

malcarado,-a *adj* 1 *(enfadado)* grim-faced, annoyed. 2 *(de poco fiar)* suspicious-looking.
malcomer *vi* not to eat enough.
malcriado,-a *adj (maleducado)* ill-mannered; *(mimado)* spoilt.
▷ *nm & nf* spoilt child.
malcriar [13] *vt* to spoil.
maldad *nf* 1 *(cualidad)* evil, wickedness. 2 *(acto)* evil thing, wicked thing.
maldecir [79] *vt* to curse, damn.
▷ *vi* to curse.
maldiciente *adj* 1 *(que difama)* slanderous, defamatory. 2 *(que blasfema)* foul-mouthed.
▷ *nm o nf* 1 *(difamador)* slanderer. 2 *(blasfemo)* foul-mouthed person.
maldición *nf* curse.
maldito,-a *adj* 1 *(no bendito)* damned. 2 *fam (que causa molestia)* damned, wretched, bloody, damn: malditas las ganas que tengo de verlo *I'm not looking forward to seeing to him one bit.*
Maldivas *nm* Maldives.
maldivo,-a *adj* Maldivian.
▷ *nm & nf* Maldivian.
maleabilidad *nf* malleability.
maleable *adj* malleable.
maleante *nm o nf* delinquent, criminal.
malear *vt* 1 *(dañar)* to spoil, damage. 2 *(pervertir)* to corrupt, lead astray.
▷ *vpr* malearse 1 *(cosecha, producto)* to go bad. 2 *(pervertirse)* to go astray.
malecón *nm (dique, rompeolas)* mole, breakwater; *(embarcadero)* jetty.
maledicencia *nf* 1 *(en la vida política)* slander. 2 *(en la vida civil)* evil talk, gossip.
maleducado,-a *adj* bad mannered, rude.
▷ *nm & nf* bad-mannered person, rude person: es una maleducada *she's really rude.*
maleducar *vt (niño)* to spoil.
maleficio *nm* curse, evil spell.
maléfico,-a *adj* evil, harmful.
malentendido *nm* misunderstanding.
malestar *nm* 1 *(incomodidad)* discomfort. 2 *fig (inquietud)* unease, unrest.
maleta *nf* suitcase, case. ■ hacer la maleta 1 *(empacar)* to pack. 2 *(irse)* to pack up.
maletero *nm* 1 AUTO boot, US trunk. 2 *(mozo)* porter; *(en aeropuerto)* baggage handler.
maletín *nm* briefcase.
malévolo,-a *adj* malevolent.
maleza *nf (malas hierbas)* weeds *pl.*
malformación *nf* malformation.
malgache *adj* Madagascan, Malagsy.
▷ *nm o nf* Madagascan.
malgastador,-ra *nm & nf* spendthrift, squanderer.
malgastar *vt* to waste, squander.
malhablado,-a *adj* foul-mouthed.
malhecho,-a *adj (cuerpo, persona)* deformed.
malhechor,-ra *adj* criminal.
▷ *nm & nf* wrongdoer, criminal.
malherir [35] *vt* to wound badly.
malhumor *nm* bad temper.
malhumorado,-a *adj* bad-tempered. ■ estar malhumorado,-a to be in a bad mood.
Malí *nm* Mali.
malicia *nf* 1 *(mala intención)* malice. 2 *(maldad)* evil, maliciousness. 3 *(astucia)* slyness, craftiness, cunning.
maliciosamente *adv* maliciously, spitefully.
malicioso,-a *adj* 1 *(malintencionado)* malicious, spiteful. 2 *(malpensado)* suspicious-minded.
maliense *adj* Malian.
▷ *nm o nf* Malian.
maligno,-a *adj* malignant.
malintencionado,-a *adj* malicious, spiteful.
▷ *nm & nf* malicious person.
malinterpretar *vt* to misinterpret.
malísimo,-a *adj* really bad, terrible, awful.
malla *nf* 1 *(red)* mesh. 2 *(prenda)* leotard.
▷ *nf pl* mallas *(medias sin pie)* leggings.
malnacido,-a *adj* despicable.
▷ *nm & nf* despicable person.
malnutrición *nf* malnutrition.
malnutrido,-a *adj* malnourished.
malo,-a *adj* 1 bad: ¡qué día tan malo hace! *what dreadful weather!* 2 *(malvado)* wicked, evil: es muy mala persona *he's a nasty piece of work.* 3 *(travieso)* naughty: ¡qué niño más malo! *what a naughty child!* 4 *(nocivo)* harmful: el tabaco es malo para la salud *smoking is bad for you.* 5 *(enfermo)* ill, sick: no ha venido a trabajar porque está malo con gripe *he's off sick with flu.* 6 *(estropeado)* off: este pescado ya está malo *this fish has gone off already.* ■ estar de malas 1 *(malhumorado)* to be in a bad mood. 2 *(desafortunado)* to be unlucky.
▷ *nm & nf (en la ficción)* baddy, villain: ¿quién es el malo? *who's the baddy?*
malogrado,-a *adj* 1 *(desaprovechado)* wasted. 2 *(frustrado)* abortive, failed.
malograr *vt (desaprovechar)* to waste.
▷ *vpr* malograrse 1 *(plan, proyecto)* to fail, fall through; *(cosecha)* to fail, be ruined. 2 *(persona)* to die before one's time.
maloliente *adj* foul-smelling, stinking.
malparado,-a ■ salir malparado,-a to come off badly.
malpensado,-a *adj* nasty-minded.
malsano,-a *adj (ambiente, vida)* unhealthy; *(curiosidad)* morbid, unhealthy; *(mente)* sick.
malsonante *adj (grosero)* offensive, rude.
malta *nf* malt.
Malta *nf* Malta.
maltear *vt* to malt.
maltés *adj* Maltese.
▷ *nm & nf (persona)* Maltese.
▷ *nm* maltés *(idioma)* Maltese.
maltratar *vt (tratar mal)* to ill-treat, mistreat; *(pegar)* to batter.
maltrato *nm* mistreatment, ill-treatment.
maltrecho,-a *adj* 1 *(persona)* battered, wrecked. 2 *(cosa)* damaged, destroyed.
maltusianismo *nm* Malthusianism.
maltusiano,-a *adj* Malthusian.
▷ *nm & nf* Malthusian.
malva *adj (color)* mauve.
▷ *nf* BOT mallow.

malvado,-a *adj* wicked, evil.
▷ *nm & nf* villain, evil person.
malvarrosa *nf* hollyhock.
malvasía *nf (uva)* malvasia; *(vino)* malmsey, malvasia.
malvavisco *nm* marshmallow.
malvender *vt* to sell at a loss.
malversación *nf* misappropriation, embezzlement. ● **malversación de fondos** embezzlement.
malversar *vt* to embezzle, misappropriate.
Malvinas *nf pl* **Islas Malvinas** Falkland Islands, Falklands.
malvinense *adj* of the Falklands, from the Falklands.
▷ *nm o nf* Falklander, Falkland islander.
malvivir *vi* to live very badly, eke out a living, get by.
mama *nf* 1 *(pecho)* breast; *(de animal)* mammary gland. 2 *fam (madre)* mum.
mamá *nf fam* mum, mummy, US mom.
mamar *vt* 1 *(succionar)* to suck. 2 *fig (aprender de pequeño)* to grow up with.
▷ *vi (bebé)* to feed; *(animal)* to suckle. ■ **dar de mamar** to breast-feed.
mamario,-a *adj* mammary.
mambo *nm* mambo.
mamífero,-a *adj* mammalian.
mamografía *nf (técnica)* mammography; *(radiografía)* mammogram, mammograph.
mamotreto *nm (armatoste)* monstrosity, massive thing.
mampara *nf* screen.
mampostería *nf* masonry, stone work.
mamut *nm* mammoth.
maná *nm* manna.
manada *nf (vacas, elefantes)* herd; *(ovejas)* flock; *(lobos, perros)* pack. ■ **en manada** en masse.
mánager *nm o nf (hombre)* manager; *(mujer)* manageress.
manantial *nm* spring.
manar *vi* 1 *(salir)* to flow (**de**, from), pour (**de**, from), well (**de**, from). 2 *fig (abundar)* to abound in, be rich in.
manatí *nm* manatee.
manazas *adj inv* clumsy.
mancha *nf* 1 stain, spot. 2 *fig* blemish.
manchado,-a *adj* stained.
manchar *vt* 1 to stain, dirty. 2 *fig* to tarnish.
▷ *vpr* **mancharse** to get dirty.
manchú *adj* Manchu.
▷ *nm o nf (persona)* Manchu.
▷ *nm* **manchú** *(idioma)* Manchu.
Manchuria *nf* Manchuria.
mancillar *vt arc* to sully.
manco,-a *adj (sin un brazo)* one-armed; *(sin brazos)* armless; *(sin una mano)* one-handed; *(sin manos)* without hands.
mancomunidad *nf* 1 *(asociación)* community, association. 2 *(de municipios)* association.
mandamiento *nm* 1 REL commandment. 2 JUR warrant, order.
mandar *vt* 1 *(ordenar)* to order, tell. 2 *(enviar)* to send.
▷ *vi (dirigir - un grupo)* to be in charge; *(- un país)* to be in power.
mandarín *nm* 1 *(persona)* mandarin. 2 *(idioma)* Mandarin, Mandarin Chinese.
mandarina *nf* mandarin, tangerine.
mandarino *nm* mandarin, mandarin orange tree.
mandatario,-a *nm & nf* 1 JUR agent. 2 POL leader.
mandato *nm* 1 *(orden)* order, command. 2 JUR mandate. 3 POL term of office. ● **mandato judicial** court order.
mandíbula *nf* jaw.
mandil *nm* apron.
mandioca *nf* manioc, cassava.
mando *nm* 1 *(autoridad)* command: **le han relevado en el mando** *he's been dismissed.* 2 *(período)* term of office. 3 *(persona)* person in charge; *(oficial)* officer. 4 *(dispositivo)* control. ● **mando a distancia** 1 *(sistema)* remote control. 2 *(aparato)* remote control unit.
mandolina *nf* mandolin.
mandón,-ona *adj fam* bossy.
▷ *nm & nf fam* bossy boots.
mandrágora *nf* mandrake.
mandril *nm* 1 ZOOL mandril. 2 TÉC mandrel.
manecilla *nf (de reloj)* hand.
manejable *adj* manageable, easy-to-handle.
manejar *vt* 1 *(manipular)* to handle, operate, use. 2 *(dirigir)* to run, manage. 3 *(manipular)* to manipulate. 4 AM to drive.
▷ *vpr* **manejarse** to manage, get by.
manejo *nm* 1 *(uso)* handling, use. 2 *(funcionamiento)* running. 3 *(de un negocio)* management. 4 *(ardid)* trick, scheme. 5 AM *(de coche)* driving.
manera *nf (gen)* way, manner. ■ **de cualquier manera** 1 *(en cualquier caso)* in any case. 2 *(sin cuidado, consideración, interés)* carelessly. | **de ninguna manera** certainly not.
▷ *nf pl* **maneras** *(educación)* manners. ■ **de todas maneras** in any case, anyhow.
manga *nf* 1 sleeve: **en mangas de camisa** *in shirt sleeves.* 2 *(manguera)* hose (pipe). 3 *(de pescar)* casting net. 4 CULIN *(de pastelero)* icing bag; *(de filtrar)* muslin strainer. 5 DEP round.
manganeso *nm* manganese.
mangar [7] *vt fam* to pinch, nick, swipe.
manglar *nm* mangrove swamp.
mango[1] *nm* handle.
mango[2] *nm* BOT mango.
mangonear *vt fam (dominar)* to boss around, boss about.
▷ *vi fam (entrometerse)* to be a busybody; *(dominar)* to be bossy.
mangoneo *nm fam (entrometimiento)* meddling.
mangosta *nf* mongoose.
manguera *nf* 1 *(de riego)* hose, hosepipe. 2 *(de bombero)* hose, fire hose.
manguito *nm* 1 *(de manos)* muff. 2 *(de manga)* oversleeve. 3 TÉC sleeve.
maní *nm* peanut.
▲ *pl* **manises.**
manía *nf* 1 MED mania. 2 *(ojeriza)* dislike, grudge. 3 *(costumbre)* habit; *(rareza)* quirk, peculiar habit; *(obsesión)* obsession, mania: **tiene la manía de morderse las uñas** *she has a habit of biting her nails.* 4 *(pasión)* craze,

fad, mania: **ahora le ha dado la manía por las antigüedades** *she's really into antiques at the moment.*
maníaco,-a *adj* MED manic.
▷ *nm & nf fam* maniac.
maniatar *vt* to tie up.
maniático,-a *adj (raro)* cranky; *(quisquilloso)* fussy, finicky.
▷ *nm & nf* 1 *(quisquilloso)* fusspot. 2 *(loco)* crackpot, crank.
manicomio *nm* mental hospital.
manicura *nf* manicure. ■ **hacerse la manicura** to have a manicure.
manido,-a *adj* 1 *(frase)* hackneyed; *(tema)* stale. 2 *(objeto)* well-worn.
manierismo *nm* mannerism.
manierista *adj* manneristic.
▷ *nm o nf* mannerist.
manifestación *nf* 1 *(de protesta, etc)* demonstration. 2 *(expresión - gen)* sign; *(- artística)* example.
manifestante *nm o nf* demonstrator.
manifestar [27] *vt* 1 *(declarar)* to state; *(expresar)* to express. 2 *(mostrar)* to show.
▷ *vpr* **manifestarse** 1 *(hacerse evidente)* to become apparent. 2 to demonstrate: **se manifestaron a favor del desarme nuclear** *they demonstrated in favour of nuclear disarmament.* 3 to declare OS, express.
manifiesto,-a *adj* obvious, evident.
▷ *nm* **manifiesto** manifesto. ■ **poner de manifiesto** to make evident.
manija *nf* handle.
manilla *nf* 1 *(grillete)* handcuff. 2 *(de reloj)* hand.
manillar *nm* handlebars *pl.*
maniobra *nf* 1 *(con un coche)* manoeuvre (US maneuver). 2 *(táctica)* manoeuvre (US maneuver), ploy.
▷ *nf pl* **maniobras** MIL manoeuvres (US maneuvers).
maniobrar *vi* to manoeuvre (US maneuver).
manipulación *nf* 1 *(ilícita)* manipulation. 2 *(de alimentos)* handling.
manipulador,-ra *adj* manipulative.
▷ *nm & nf* manipulator.
manipular *vt* 1 *(persona)* to manipulate. 2 *(mercancías, alimentos)* to handle. 3 *(aparato, máquina)* to use, operate. 4 *fig* to interfere with.
maniqueísmo *nm (doctrina)* Manichaeism.
maniquí *nm (muñeco)* dummy, mannequin.
▷ *nm o nf (modelo)* model.
▲ *pl* **maniquíes.**
manirroto,-a *adj fam* spendthrift, extravagant.
▷ *nm & nf fam* spendthrift.
manitas *nm o nf (hombre)* handyman; *(mujer)* handy woman.
manivela *nf* crank, handle.
manjar *nm* delicious dish, delicacy.
mano *nf* 1 ANAT hand. 2 ZOOL *(de caballo)* forefoot; *(de gato, perro, etc)* paw. 3 *(lado)* side: **el lavabo está a mano derecha** *the toilet is on the right.* 4 *(de pintura)* coat. 5 *(de jabón)* soaping. 6 *(habilidad)* skill: **tienes muy buena mano con los niños** *you're very good with children.* 7 *(influencia)* influence. 8 *(ayuda)* hand. ■ **a mano** 1 *(escrito)* handwritten, by hand. 2 *(hecho)* handmade, by hand. 3 *(cerca)* to hand, handy, near. ‖ **darse la mano** 1 *(dos personas)* to shake hands. 2 *(dos cosas)* to be very similar. ‖ **echar una mano** to give a hand, lend a hand. ‖ **tener mano izquierda** to have a lot of tact.
▷ *nf pl* **manos** *(poder)* hands *sing*, power *sing.* ■ **poner manos a la obra** to get down to work, get cracking. ‖ **traerse** ALGO **entre manos** to be planning STH.
manojo *nm* bunch.
manoletina *nf (calzado) open, low-heeled shoe, similar to those used by bullfighters.*
manómetro *nm* pressure gauge.
manopla *nf (guante)* mitten.
manotazo *nm* slap, smack, swipe.
mansarda *nf* attic.
mansedumbre *nf* 1 *(de una persona)* meekness, docility. 2 *(de un animal)* tameness.
mansión *nf* mansion.
manso,-a *adj* 1 *(animal)* tame. 2 *(persona)* docile, meek.
manta *nf (gen)* blanket.
▷ *nm o nf fam (perezoso)* lazybones. ■ **liarse la manta a la cabeza** to take the plunge, throw caution to the wind. ‖ **tirar de la manta** to let the cat out of the bag.
mantear *vt* to toss in a blanket.
manteca *nf (de animal)* fat; *(elaborado)* lard; *(de leche)* cream. ● **manteca de cacao** cocoa butter. ‖ **manteca de cerdo** lard.
mantecado *nm* 1 *(dulce) very crumbly shortbread (eaten particularly at Christmas).* 2 *(helado)* dairy ice cream.
mantecoso,-a *adj* greasy.
mantel *nm (de mesa)* tablecloth; *(del altar)* altar cloth.
mantelería *nf* table linen.
mantener [87] *vt* 1 *(conservar)* to keep. 2 *(tener)* to keep: **«Mantener en posición vertical»** *«Keep vertical».* 3 *(sostener)* to support, hold up, hold: **estos pilares mantienen el techo** *these pillars support the roof.* 4 *(sustentar)* to support, maintain: **ella sola mantiene a toda la familia** *she supports the whole family by herself.* 5 *(conversación, relaciones)* to have; *(reunión)* to hold, have; *(correspondencia)* to keep up; *(promesa, palabra)* to keep.
▷ *vpr* **mantenerse** 1 *(sostenerse)* to remain, stand. 2 *(continuar en un estado, una posición)* to keep: **se mantuvo a distancia** *she kept her distance.* 3 *(sostenerse)* to manage, maintain OS, support OS. ■ **mantenerse aparte** to stay out of it, not get involved.
mantenimiento *nm* 1 *(gen)* maintenance. 2 *(alimento)* sustenance.
mantequera *nf (para servir mantequilla)* butter dish; *(para hacerla)* churn.
mantequería *nf* 1 *(tienda)* delicatessen. 2 *(fábrica)* dairy.
mantequilla *nf* butter.
mantilla *nf* 1 *(de mujer)* mantilla. 2 *(de niño)* shawl.
mantillo *nm* 1 *(abono del suelo)* humus. 2 *(abono del estiércol)* manure.
mantis *nf* mantis. ● **mantis religiosa** praying mantis.
manto *nm* 1 *(capa)* cloak. 2 *(de la Tierra)* layer, stratum. 3 *fig* veil, cloak.
mantón *nm* large shawl.
manual *adj* manual.
▷ *nm* manual, handbook.
manualidad *nf* handicraft.
▷ *nf pl* **manualidades** arts and crafts.

manubrio *nm* crank, crankhandle.
manufacturar *vt* to manufacture.
manuscrito,-a *adj* handwritten, manuscript.
▷ *nm* **manuscrito** manuscript.
manutención *nf* **1** *(gen)* maintenance. **2** *(alimenticia)* food, board.
manzana *nf* **1** BOT apple. **2** *(de casas)* block.
manzanilla *nf* **1** *(planta)* camomile. **2** *(infusión)* camomile tea.
manzano *nm* apple tree.
maña *nf* **1** *(habilidad)* skill, knack. **2** *(astucia)* trick.
mañana *nf* morning: **hace una mañana preciosa** *it's a beautiful morning.*
▷ *nm* tomorrow, future: **tienes que pensar en el mañana** *you have to think of the future.*
▷ *adv* tomorrow: **mañana no tengo que ir a trabajar** *I don't have to go to work tomorrow.* ■ **¡hasta mañana!** see you tomorrow! ‖ **por la mañana** in the morning.
mañoso,-a *adj (habilidoso)* handy, skilful, US skillful.
maoísmo *nm* Maoism.
maoísta *adj* Maoist.
▷ *nm o nf* Maoist.
maorí *adj* Maori.
▷ *nm & nf (persona)* Maori.
▷ *nm (idioma)* Maori.
mapa *nm* map.
mapache *nm* racoon.
mapamundi *nm* map of the world.
maqueta *nf* **1** *(de edificio, monumento, etc)* scale model. **2** *(de libro)* dummy. **3** *(de disco)* demo.
maquetar *vt* to do the page layout of.
maquetista *nm o nf* **1** *(de maquetas)* model maker, modeller (US modeler). **2** *(de libros)* page designer.
maquiavélico,-a *adj* Machiavellian.
maquillador,-ra *nm & nf* make-up assistant.
maquillaje *nm* make-up.
maquillar *vt* to make up.
▷ *vpr* **maquillarse** *(ponerse maquillaje)* to make OS up.
máquina *nf* **1** *(gen)* machine. **2** *(de un tren)* engine. **3** *fig* machinery. **4** *(expendedora)* vending machine. ■ **a máquina 1** *(cosido)* machine-sewn. **2** *(escrito)* typewritten. ● **máquina de afeitar** shaver, electric razor. ‖ **máquina de coser** sewing machine. ‖ **máquina de escribir** typewriter. ‖ **máquina de fotos** camera. ‖ **máquina de lavar** washing machine.
maquinar *vt* to scheme, plot.
maquinaria *nf* **1** *(conjunto de máquinas)* machinery. **2** *(mecanismo)* mechanism.
maquinilla *nf* razor.
maquinista *nm o nf* **1** *(operador)* machinist. **2** *(de tren)* engine driver, US engineer. **3** CINE camera assistant.
maquis *nm inv* underground resistance movement.
▷ *nm o nf* resistance fighter.
mar *nm & nf* **1** *(gen)* sea. **2** *(marejada)* swell. ■ **en alta mar** on the high sea, on the open sea. ‖ **la mar de...** *(muy)* very, really. ‖ **llover a mares** to rain cats and dogs, bucket down.
marabunta *nf* **1** swarm of ants. **2** *fam fig* mob, crowd.
maraca *nf* maraca.
maracuyá *nf* passion fruit.
marajá *nm* maharajah.
maraña *nf* **1** *(espesura)* thicket. **2** *(enredo)* tangle. **3** *(asunto confuso)* muddle, mess.
maratón *nm* marathon.
maratoniano,-a *adj* marathon.
maravilla *nf* wonder, marvel. ■ **a las mil maravillas** wonderfully well. ‖ **de maravilla** wonderfully.
maravillar *vt* to astonish, amaze.
▷ *vpr* **maravillarse** to marvel (**de**, at).
maravilloso,-a *adj* wonderful, marvellous.
marca *nf* **1** *(señal)* mark, sign. **2** *(en comestibles, productos del hogar)* brand; *(en otros productos)* make. **3** DEP record. **4** *(acción)* marking. ■ **de marca** brand: **productos de marca** *brand products.* ● **marca registrada** registered trademark.
marcado,-a *adj* **1** *(señalado)* marked. **2** *(evidente)* distinct, definite; *(acento)* marked, pronounced.
marcador *nm* **1** DEP scoreboard. **2** INFORMÁ bookmark.
marcapasos *nm inv* pacemaker.
marcar [1] *vt* **1** *(señalar)* to mark; *(ganado)* to brand. **2** DEP *(gol, canasta)* to score. **3** DEP *(al contrario)* to mark. **4** *(pelo)* to set. **5** *(cantidad)* to indicate, show: **el termómetro marca 20 grados** *the thermometer shows 20 degrees.* **6** *(en teléfono)* to dial. **7** *(resaltar)* to show.
marcha *nf* **1** *(de protesta, soldados)* march. **2** *(progreso)* course, progress. **3** *(partida)* departure; *(abandono)* leaving: **lamentaremos su marcha** *we'll be sorry when he leaves.* **4** *(velocidad)* speed. **5** AUTO gear. **6** MÚS march. **7** DEP walk. **8** *fam (de persona)* go, energy; *(de lugar, ambiente)* life. ■ **dar marcha atrás 1** *(coche)* to reverse. **2** *(proyecto)* to fall through. ‖ **estar en marcha 1** *(máquina)* to be on, be working. **2** *(cambio, proyecto)* to be under way. ‖ **ir de marcha** *(por la noche)* to go out on the razzle, go out on the town ‖ **poner en marcha 1** *(coche)* to start. **2** *(proyecto)* to start up.
marchante *nm o nf* dealer. ● **marchante de arte** art dealer.
marchar *vi* **1** *(ir)* to go, walk. **2** *(funcionar)* to work, run. **3** MIL to march.
▷ *vpr* **marcharse** to leave.
marchitar *vt* to wither.
▷ *vpr* **marchitarse** to wither.
marchito,-a *adj (planta)* withered; *(belleza)* faded.
marchoso,-a *adj fam (persona)* fun-loving, wild; *(música, sitio)* lively.
▷ *nm & nf* raver, fun-lover.
marcial *adj* martial.
marciano,-a *adj* Martian.
▷ *nm & nf* Martian.
marco *nm* **1** *(de cuadro, ventana)* frame. **2** *fig* framework, setting. **3** *(moneda)* mark. **4** DEP goalpost.
marea *nf* **1** tide. **2** *(multitud)* sea: **una marea de gente** *a sea of people.* ● **marea alta** high tide. ‖ **marea baja** low tide. ‖ **marea negra** oil slick. ‖
mareado,-a *adj (en general)* sick; *(en el coche)* carsick; *(en el mar)* seasick; *(en avión)* airsick: **estoy mareado** *I feel sick.*
mareante *adj* **1** *(que marea)* sickening. **2** *(pesado)* tedious.
marear *vt* **1** *(producir malestar)* to make sick. **2** *(aturdir)* to make dizzy: **este ruido marea** *this noise makes your*

head spin. 3 *fam (molestar)* to annoy: **deja ya de marear, niño** *stop being a nuisance.*
▷ *vpr* **marearse** 1 *(en general)* to get sick; *(en el coche)* to get carsick; *(en el mar)* to get seasick; *(en avión)* to get airsick. 2 *(sentir vértigo)* to get dizzy; *(a punto de desmayarse)* to feel faint. 3 *(emborracharse)* to get tipsy.
marejada *nf* swell.
marejadilla *nf* slight swell.
maremoto *nm (seísmo)* seaquake; *(ola)* tidal wave.
marengo ● **gris marengo** dark grey.
mareo *nm* 1 *(en general)* sickness; *(en el mar)* seasickness; *(en el coche)* carsickness; *(en avión)* airsickness. 2 *(aturdimiento)* dizziness. 3 *(confusión)* muddle, mess.
marfil *nm* ivory.
marfileño,-a *adj* 1 *(color, piel)* ivory. 2 *(de Costa de Marfil)* of the Ivory Coast, from the Ivory Coast.
▷ *nm & nf* native of the Ivory Coast, inhabitant of the Ivory Coast.
marga *nf* marl.
margarina *nf* margarine.
margarita *nf* 1 BOT daisy. 2 *(de máquina)* daisywheel.
margen *nm & nf* 1 *(extremidad)* border, edge. 2 *(de río)* bank; *(de camino)* edge.
▷ *nm* 1 *(del papel)* margin. 2 *(oportunidad)* chance. 3 COM margin. ■ **al margen de ...** apart from..., out of... ‖ **mantenerse al margen** not to get involved.
marginación *nf* 1 *(rechazo social)* ostracism, marginalization. 2 *(exclusión)* exclusion.
marginado,-a *adj* 1 *(proyecto)* pushed aside, excluded. 2 *(persona)* marginalized, alienated.
▷ *nm & nf* social outcast, social misfit.
marginal *adj* 1 *(ilustración, nota)* marginal, in the margin. 2 *(tema, asunto)* marginal, minor. 3 *(persona)* marginalized.
marginar *vt* 1 *(persona)* to leave out, exclude; *(grupo social)* to ostracize, marginalize. 2 *(asunto)* to push aside.
marica *nm fam pey* poof, queer.
maridaje *nm* 1 *(entre parejas)* married life, marriage. 2 *(entre empresas)* close cooperation.
marido *nm* husband.
marihuana *nf* marijuana.
marimacho *nm fam (niña, joven)* tomboy; *(mujer)* butch woman.
marimandón,-ona *nm & nf fam* bossy boots.
marina *nf* 1 *(flota)* navy. 2 *(zona)* seacoast. 3 *(pintura)* seascape. 4 *(navegación)* seamanship.
marinar *vt* to marinate.
marine *nm* marine.
marinero,-a *adj* 1 *(embarcación)* seaworthy; *(nación)* seafaring: **un pueblo marinero** *a fishing village.* 2 *(blusa, cuello)* sailor.
▷ *nm* **marinero** sailor.
marino,-a *adj (corriente, animal)* marine.
▷ *nm* **marino** *(profesional)* seaman, sailor.
marioneta *nf* 1 *(muñeco)* puppet, marionette. 2 *pey (persona)* puppet. ● **(teatro de) marionetas** puppet show.
mariposa *nf* 1 *(insecto)* butterfly. 2 *(natación)* butterfly.
mariposear *vi* 1 *(ser inconstante)* to be fickle; *(en el amor)* to flirt; *(en el trabajo)* to flit. 2 *(andar alrededor)* to buzz around.
mariquita *nf* ZOOL ladybird, US ladybug.
marisabidilla *nf fam* know-all.
mariscada *nf (comida)* seafood dish; *(en menú)* seafood platter.
mariscal *nm* marshal.
mariscar *vi* to fish for shellfish.
marisco *nm* seafood, shellfish.
marisma *nf* salt marsh.
marismeño,-a *adj (cultivo)* marshy.
marisquería *nf* seafood restaurant.
marital *adj* marital.
marítimo,-a *adj (legislación)* maritime; *(ciudad)* coastal; *(ruta, transporte)* sea.
marketing *nm* marketing.
marmita *nf* casserole, cooking pot.
mármol *nm* marble.
marmolería *nf (taller)* marble cutter's workshop.
marmolista *nm o nf* marble cutter, monumental mason.
marmóreo,-a *adj* marmoreal, marble.
marmota *nf* 1 ZOOL marmot. 2 *fam (dormilón)* sleepyhead. 3 *fam* scullery maid.
maroma *nf* thick rope.
marqués,-esa *nm & nf (hombre)* marquis, marquess; *(mujer)* marchioness.
marquesina *nf (de un hotel)* canopy; *(de una parada de autobús)* bus shelter.
marquetería *nf* marquetry, inlaid work.
marrano,-a *adj* 1 *fam (sucio)* filthy, dirty. 2 *fam (sinvergüenza)* swine.
▷ *nm & nf* 1 *fam (sucio)* filthy pig, dirty pig. 2 *fam (sinvergüenza)* swine.
▷ *nm* **marrano** ZOOL pig.
marrasquino *nm* maraschino.
marrón *adj* brown.
▷ *nm* 1 *(color)* brown. 2 *argot (condena)* sentence. 3 *argot (fastidio)* pain, drag.
marroquí,-ina *adj* Moroccan.
▷ *nm & nf* Moroccan.
marroquinería *nf* 1 *(fabricación)* leather industry. 2 *(artículos)* leather goods *pl*.
Marruecos *nm* Morocco.
marrullería *nf fam (engaño)* craftiness.
marrullero,-a *adj fam (gen)* crafty, devious; *(jugador)* dirty.
marsupial *adj* marsupial.
▷ *nm* marsupial.
marsupio *nm* marsupium.
marta *nf* marten.
Marte *nm* Mars.
martes *nm* Tuesday.
See also **jueves**.
martillazo *nm* blow with a hammer.
martillear *vt* to hammer.
martilleo *nm* hammering.
martillo *nm* hammer.
martinete *nm* 1 *(ave)* heron. 2 *(penacho)* plume.
martingala *nf* 1 *fam (artimaña)* ruse, trick. 2 *fam (asunto pesado)* pain, drag.

Martinica *nf* Martinique.
martín pescador *nm* kingfisher.
mártir *nm o nf* martyr.
martirio *nm* 1 martyrdom. 2 *fig* torture, torment.
martirizar [4] *vt* 1 to martyr. 2 *fig* to torment, torture.
marxismo *nm* Marxism.
marxista *adj* Marxist.
▷ *nm o nf* Marxist.
marzo *nm* March: el día 16 de marzo *March the sixteenth, the sixteenth of March;* nací el 6 de marzo de 1993 *I was born on March 6th 1993;* durante el mes de marzo *in March;* en marzo del año pasado *last March;* en marzo del año que viene *next March;* a principios de marzo *at the beginning of March;* a mediados de marzo *in mid-March;* a finales de marzo *at the end of March.*
mas *conj* but.
más *adv* 1 *(comparativo)* more: este año ha llovido más *it has rained more this year.* 2 *(con números o cantidades)* more: más de tres *more than three.* 3 *(superlativo)* most: el más caro *the most expensive;* es la más guapa *she's the prettiest.* 4 *(después de pron interrog e indef)* else: ¿algo más? *anything else?* 5 *(exclamativo)* so: ¡qué película más buena! *what a wonderful film!*
▷ *prep* MAT plus: dos más dos igual a cuatro *two plus two is four.*
▷ *nm (signo)* plus sign. ■ **de más** spare, extra. ■ **más bien** rather. ■ **más o menos** more or less. ■ **ni más ni menos** exactly. ■ **por más (que)** however much. ■ **¿qué más da?** what difference does it make?, what does it matter?
masa *nf* 1 *(en general)* mass. 2 FÍS mass: unidad de masa *unit of mass.* 3 CULIN *(para pan)* dough; *(para tartas)* pastry; *(para pasteles)* mixture. 4 *(de gente)* mass, crowd. 5 ELEC earth, US ground.
masacre *nf* massacre.
masaje *nm* massage.
masajear *vt* to massage.
masajista *nm o nf (hombre)* masseur; *(mujer)* masseuse.
▷ *nm & nf* DEP *(en fútbol)* physiotherapist, physio.
mascar [1] *vt* to chew.
máscara *nf* 1 *(careta)* mask. 2 *fig (disfraz, pretexto)* mask, front.
mascarilla *nf* 1 mask. 2 *(cosmética - de belleza)* face mask; *(- de barro)* face pack. 3 MED face mask.
mascota *nf* 1 *(figura)* mascot. 2 *(animal doméstico)* pet.
masculinidad *nf* masculinity.
masculino,-a *adj* 1 male: la población masculina *the male population.* 2 *(propio de hombres)* masculine, manly. 3 GRAM masculine.
mascullar *vt* to mumble, mutter.
masificado,-a *adj* overcrowded.
masilla *nf* putty.
masivo,-a *adj* mass, massive, on a mass scale.
masón,-ona *adj* masonic.
▷ *nm & nf* Mason, Freemason.
masonería *nf* Masonry, Freemasonry.
masónico,-a *adj* masonic.
masoquismo *nm* masochism.
masoquista *adj* masochistic.
▷ *nm o nf* masochist.
master *nm* EDUC Master's degree.
máster *nm* 1 *(copia)* master, master copy. 2 *(estudios)* master's degree.
masticar [1] *vt* to chew, masticate.
mástil *nm* 1 *(asta)* mast, pole. 2 MAR mast.
mastodóntico,-a *adj fam* huge, enormous.
mastoides *nf inv* mastoid.
masturbar *vt* to masturbate.
▷ *vpr* **masturbarse** to masturbate.
mata *nf* 1 *(arbusto)* shrub, bush. 2 *(ramita)* sprig. 3 AM *(bosque)* forest. ● **mata de pelo** head of hair.
matadero *nm* slaughterhouse, abattoir.
matador,-ra *adj fam (agotador)* exhausting, killing.
▷ *nm* **matador** matador, bullfighter.
matalahúva *nf* 1 *(planta)* anise. 2 *(semilla)* aniseed.
matamoscas *nm* 1 *(insecticida)* fly spray. 2 *(pala)* fly swat.
matanza *nf* 1 *(gen)* slaughter. 2 *(del cerdo)* pig killing. 3 *(carne)* pork products *pl.*
matar *vt* 1 *(persona - gen)* to kill; *(- asesinar)* to murder. 2 *(animal - gen)* to kill; *(- para alimentación)* to slaughter. 3 *fam (incomodar, causar dolor)* to kill; *(volver loco)* to drive mad: estos zapatos me están matando *this shoes are killing me.* 4 *(pasar)* to kill: mientras, voy a matar el tiempo dando una vuelta *meanwhile, I'll go for a walk just to kill time.* 5 *(satisfacer - sed)* to quench; *(- hambre)* to stay, stave off.
▷ *vpr* **matarse** *(involuntariamente)* to die; *(voluntariamente)* to kill os.
matasellos *nm inv* 1 *(marca)* postmark. 2 *(instrumento)* stamp, date stamp.
matasuegras *nm inv* blower, party blower.
mate[1] *adj (sin brillo)* matt.
mate[2] *nm (ajedrez)* mate.
mate[3] *nm (hierba)* maté.
matemática *nf (ciencia)* mathematics: matemática aplicada *applied mathematics.*

See also matemático,-a.

matemáticas *nf pl* mathematics *sing.*
matemático,-a *adj* mathematical.
▷ *nm & nf* mathematician.
materia *nf* 1 *(sustancia)* matter. 2 *(material)* material, substance. 3 *(asignatura)* subject. ■ **en materia de...** on the subject of... ● **materia prima** raw material.
material *adj* 1 *(en general)* material; *(físico)* physical. 2 *(real)* real.
▷ *nm* 1 *(sustancia)* material. 2 *(conjunto de cosas)* material, materials *pl,* equipment.
materialismo *nm* materialism.
materialista *adj* materialistic.
▷ *nm o nf* materialist.
materializar [4] *vt* to put into practice (US practise), carry out.
▷ *vpr* **materializarse** to materialize.
maternal *adj* maternal, motherly.
maternidad *nf* 1 maternity, motherhood. 2 *(hospital)* maternity hospital.
materno,-a *adj (abuelo, etc)* maternal.
matinal *adj* morning.
matiz *nm* 1 *(color)* shade, tint. 2 *(variación)* nuance. 3 *(rasgo)* hint.
▲ *pl* matices.
matizar [4] *vt* 1 ARTE *(colores)* to blend. 2 *(sonido)* to modulate. 3 *(añadir un matiz)* to tinge (de, with).

4 *(añadir)* to add (by way of clarification). 5 *(aclarar)* to qualify, clarify: **esta cuestión habría que matizarla** *let's examine this question more closely.*

matojo *nm* small shrub, bush.

matón,-ona *nm & nf* 1 *fam* bully, thug. 2 *fam (guardaespaldas)* bodyguard.

matorral *nm (maleza)* bushes *pl*, thicket.

matraca *nf* 1 *(instrumento)* wooden rattle. 2 *fam (molestia)* pest, nuisance.

matraz *nm* flask.
▲ *pl* **matraces.**

matriarca *nf* matriarch.

matriarcado *nm* matriarchy.

matriarcal *adj* matriarchal.

matrícula *nf* 1 *(lista)* list, roll. 2 *(registro - de personas)* registration, enrollment; *(de vehículos)* registration: **plazo de matrícula** *registration period.* 3 *(tasa)* registration fee(s), tuition fee(s). 4 AUTO *(número)* registration number, US license number. 5 AUTO *(placa)* number plate, US license plate. ● **matrícula de honor** distinction.

matricular *vt (persona)* to register, enroll; *(vehículo)* to register.
▷ *vpr* **matricularse** to register, enroll: **me he matriculado en Informática** *I've enrolled for computer science.*

matrimonial *adj (derecho)* matrimonial; *(problema)* marital.

matrimonio *nm* 1 *(estado)* marriage, matrimony. 2 *(pareja)* married couple.

matriz *nf* 1 ANAT womb. 2 TÉC mould (US mold). 3 *(original)* original, master copy. 4 *(de talonario)* stub, counterfoil. 5 MAT matrix.
▷ *adj* principal.
▲ *pl* **matrices.**

matrona *nf* 1 *(madre)* matron. 2 *(comadrona)* midwife.

matutino,-a *adj* morning.
▷ *nm* **matutino** *(periódico)* morning paper.

maullar [16] *vi* to mew, miaow, US meow.

Mauritania *nf* Mauritania.

mauritano,-a *adj* Mauritanian.
▷ *nm & nf* Mauritanian.

mausoleo *nm* mausoleum.

maxilar *nm* jaw, jawbone.

máxima *nf* 1 *(frase breve)* maxim, saying. 2 *(regla)* rule, maxim. 3 *(temperatura)* maximum temperature.

máxime *adv fml* especially.

maximizar [4] *vt* to maximize.

máximo,-a *adj (velocidad)* maximum; *(puntuación, condecoración)* highest.
▷ *nm* **máximo** maximum: **tenéis una hora como máximo para acabar** *you must be finished in an hour.*

maya *adj* Mayan.
▷ *nm o nf (persona)* Mayan.
▷ *nm* **maya** *(idioma)* Mayan.

mayestático,-a *adj* majestic.

mayo *nm* 1 May. 2 *(palo)* maypole.

For examples of use, see **marzo.**

mayólica *nf* majolica.

mayonesa *nf* mayonnaise.

mayor *adj* 1 *(comparativo)* bigger, greater, larger; *(persona)* older; *(hermanos, hijos)* elder, older. 2 *(superlativo)* biggest, greatest, largest; *(persona)* oldest; *(hermanos, hijos)* eldest, oldest. 3 *(de edad)* mature, elderly: **la gente mayor** *elderly people.* 4 *(adulto)* grown-up. 5 *(principal)* main. 6 MÚS major.
▷ *nm* 1 MIL major. 2 **mayor que** MAT *(signo)* more than.
▷ *nm pl* **los mayores** *(adultos)* grown-ups, adults; *(antepasados)* ancestors.
▷ *nm & nf* **el/la mayor** *(entre varios)* the oldest; *(entre hermanos, hijos)* the eldest, the oldest.

mayoral *nm* 1 *(pastor)* head shepherd. 2 *(cochero)* coachman. 3 *(capataz)* foreman.

mayordomo *nm* butler.

mayoría *nf* majority: **la mayoría de los hombres...** *most men...* ■ **alcanzar la mayoría de edad** to come of age.

mayorista *nm o nf* wholesaler.

mayoritario,-a *adj* 1 *(de la mayoría)* majority. 2 FIN principal.

mayúscula *nf* capital, capital letter.

mayúsculo,-a *adj* 1 *(enorme)* enormous, gigantic; *(terrible)* terrible. 2 *(letra)* capital.

maza *nf* 1 HIST *(arma)* mace. 2 *(utensilio)* sledgehammer. 3 MÚS drumstick.

mazapán *nm* marzipan.

mazmorra *nf* dungeon.

mazo *nm* 1 *(martillo)* mallet. 2 *(del mortero)* pestle. 3 *(de naipes)* pack, deck; *(de billetes, papeles)* wad.

mazorca *nf* cob. ● **mazorca de maíz** corncob.

me *pron* 1 me: **no me lo dijo** *she didn't tell me;* **dámelo** *give it to me.* 2 *(reflexivo)* myself: **me veo en el espejo** *I can see myself in the mirror.*

meandro *nm* meander.

mear *vi fam* to have a piss, have a wee, have a pee, piss.

MEC *abrev* **(Ministerio de Educación y Ciencia)** ≈ Department of Education and Science; *(abreviatura)* DES.

meca *nf* 1 mecca, Mecca. 2 **la Meca** *(ciudad)* Mecca.

mecachis *interj fam* damn!, US darn!

mecánica *nf* 1 *(ciencia)* mechanics. 2 *(mecanismo)* mechanism. ● **mecánica cuántica** quantum mechanics.

mecánico,-a *adj* mechanical.
▷ *nm & nf* mechanic.

mecanismo *nm* 1 mechanism. 2 *fig (funcionamiento)* working, mechanism.

mecanización *nf* mechanization.

mecanizado,-a *adj* mechanized.

mecanizar [4] *vt* to mechanize.

mecano [Registered trademark.] *nm* Meccano.

mecanografía *nf* typing.

mecanografiar [13] *vt* to type.

mecedora *nf* rocking chair.

mecenas *nm o nf* patron.

mecer [2] *vt* to rock.
▷ *vpr* **mecerse** *(en una silla)* to rock; *(en un columpio)* to swing.

mecha *nf* 1 *(de vela)* wick. 2 MIL fuse.
▷ *nf pl* **mechas** *(de pelo)* highlights.

mechado,-a *adj* larded.

mechar *vt (carne)* to lard.

mechero *nm* (cigarette) lighter.

mechón *nm* 1 *(de pelo)* lock, strand. 2 *(de lana)* tuft.

medalla *nf* medal.

medallero *nm* DEP medals table.
medallista *nm o nf* DEP medallist (US medalist), medal winner.
medallón *nm* **1** *(joya - medalla)* medallion; *(- cajita colgante)* locket. **2** *(de carne, pescado)* médaillon, medallion, slice.
media *nf* **1** *(media calza)* stocking; *(calcetín)* sock. **2** *(promedio)* average. **3** MAT mean. **4 la media** *(hora)* half past, half past the hour. ● **media aritmética** arithmetic mean.
▷ *nf pl* **medias** *(enteras)* tights, pantihose; *(no enteras)* stockings.
mediación *nf* mediation. ■ **por mediación de** through.
mediado,-a *adj (recipiente)* half-full, half-empty; *(sesión, representación)* halfway through. ■ **a mediados de** halfway through.
mediador,-ra *adj* mediating.
▷ *nm & nf* mediator.
mediana *nf* **1** MAT median. **2** *(de la carretera)* central reservation.
medianero,-a *adj* dividing.
mediano,-a *adj* **1** *(de calidad)* average; *(de tamaño)* medium, medium-sized. **2** *(mediocre)* ordinary, mediocre.
medianoche *nf* **1** midnight. **2** CULIN sweet bun.
mediante *adj* by means of.
mediar [12] *vi* **1** *(interceder)* to intercede (**en favor de**, on behalf of). **2** *(interponerse)* to mediate (**en**, in), intervene (**en**, in). **3** *(estar en medio)* to be. **4** *(llegar a la mitad)*.
medicación *nf* medication, medicines *pl*.
medicamento *nm* medicine, drug.
medicar *vt (administrar medicamentos)* to medicate; *(recetar)* to prescribe.
▷ *vpr* **medicarse** to take medicine.
medicina *nf* medicine.
medicinal *adj* medicinal.
medición *nf* **1** *(acción)* measuring. **2** *(número)* measurement.
médico,-a *adj* medical.
▷ *nm & nf* doctor, physician. ● **médico,-a de cabecera** general practitioner, GP. ǀ **médico,-a de familia** family doctor.
medida *nf* **1** *(acción)* measuring; *(dato, número)* measurement. **2** *(disposición)* measure. **3** *(grado)* extent: **en cierta medida** *to a certain extent.* **4** *(prudencia)* moderation. **5** LIT measure, metre. ■ **a (la) medida** *(traje)* made-to-measure. ǀ **a medida que** as. ǀ **en la medida de lo posible** as far as possible.
medidor,-ra *nm* **medidor** AM *(contador)* meter.
medieval *adj* medieval, mediaeval.
medievalista *nm o nf* medievalist, mediaevalist.
medievo *nm* Middle Ages *pl*.
medio,-a *adj* **1** *(mitad)* half: **las dos y media** *half past two;* **un año y medio** *a year and a half.* **2** *(intermedio)* middle: **a media tarde** *in the middle of the afternoon.* **3** *(de promedio)* average.
▷ *adv* half: **medio terminado,-a** *half-finished.*
▷ *nm* **medio 1** *(mitad)* half. **2** *(centro)* middle. **3** *(contexto - físico)* environment. **4** *(social)* circle. ● **medio ambiente** environment.
▷ *nm pl* **medios** *(recursos)* means.
medioambiental *adj* environmental.
mediocampista *nm o nf* midfield player.
mediocre *adj* mediocre.
mediocridad *nf* mediocrity.
mediodía *nm* **1** *(las doce)* noon, midday. **2** *(hora del almuerzo)* lunchtime.
mediopensionista *nm o nf* day student.
medir [34] *vt* **1** *(dimensiones)* to measure. **2** *(riesgos)* to gauge, weigh up. **3** *(palabras)* to weigh, choose carefully. **4** *(versos)* to scan.
▷ *vpr* **medirse** to measure OS.
meditación *nf* meditation.
meditar *vt* to meditate, think.
▷ *vi* to meditate (**sobre**, over), ponder.
mediterráneo,-a *adj* Mediterranean.
▷ *nm & nf* Mediterranean. ● **el (mar) Mediterráneo** the Mediterranean (Sea).
médium *nm o nf* medium.
medo,-a *adj* Median.
▷ *nm & nf (persona)* Mede.
▷ *nm* **medo** *(idioma)* Median.
medrar *vi* **1** *(planta, animal)* to thrive, grow. **2** *(mejorar socialmente)* to get rich, prosper.
médula *nf* **1** ANAT marrow. **2** BOT pith. **3** *fig (esencia)* core, heart. ● **médula espinal** spinal cord.
medular *adj* **1** ANAT marrow. **2** *fig* essential, fundamental.
medusa *nf* jellyfish.
megabyte *nm* megabyte.
megafonía *nf* **1** *(técnica)* sound amplification. **2** *(aparato)* PA system, public-address system.
megáfono *nm* megaphone.
megahercio *nm* megahertz.
megalítico,-a *adj* megalithic.
megalito *nm* megalith.
megalómano,-a *adj* megalomaniac.
▷ *nm & nf* megalomaniac.
megatón *nm* megaton.
megavatio *nm* megawatt.
megavoltio *nm* megavolt.
mejicano,-a *adj* Mexican.
▷ *nm & nf* Mexican.
Méjico *nm* Mexico.
mejilla *nf* cheek.
mejillón *nm* mussel.
mejor *adj* **1** *(comparativo)* better: **este libro es mejor que aquél** *this book is better than that one.* **2** *(superlativo)* best: **mi mejor amigo,-a** *my best friend.* ■ **a lo mejor** perhaps, maybe. ǀ **mejor dicho** or rather.
▷ *adv* **1** *(comparativo)* better: **cada vez mejor** *better and better every day.* **2** *(superlativo)* best.
▷ *nm & nf* **el/la mejor** the best (one).
mejora *nf (progreso)* improvement.
mejorable *adj* which could be improved.
mejorar *vt* to improve.
▷ *vi* to improve, get better.
▷ *vpr* **mejorarse** to get better: **¡que te mejores!** *I hope you get better.*
mejoría *nf* improvement.
melancolía *nf* melancholy, sadness.
melancólico,-a *adj* melancholic, melancholy.
melanina *nf* melanin.

melaza *nf* molasses.
melé *nm* scrum.
melena *nf* 1 *(de persona)* long hair. 2 *(de león, caballo)* mane.
melisa *nf* lemon balm.
mella *nf* 1 *(hendedura)* nick, notch. 2 *(hueco)* hollow, gap; *(en los dientes)* gap.
mellar *vt* 1 *(objeto)* to chip, nick. 2 *fig* to dent, damage.
mellizo,-a *adj* twin.
▷ *nm & nf* twin.
melocotón *nm* peach.
melocotonero *nm* peach tree.
melodía *nf* melody.
melódico,-a *adj* melodic.
melodrama *nm* melodrama.
melodramático,-a *adj* melodramatic.
melómano,-a *adj* music lover.
melón *nm (fruto)* melon.
meloso,-a *adj (dulce)* sweet, honeyed; *(empalagoso)* sickly.
membrana *nf* membrane.
membrillo *nm* 1 *(árbol)* quince tree. 2 *(fruta)* quince. 3 *(dulce)* quince jelly.
memo,-a *adj fam* stupid, dim.
memorable *adj* memorable.
memorándum *nm* 1 *(cuaderno)* notebook. 2 *(informe diplomático)* memorandum.
▲ *pl* **memorándums.**
memoria *nf* 1 *(gen)* memory. 2 *(informe)* report. 3 *(inventario)* inventory. ■ **de memoria** (off) by heart, by memory. ■ **hacer memoria** to try to remember. ● **memoria RAM** RAM memory.
▷ *nf pl* **memorias** *(biografía)* memoirs.
memorial *nm* 1 *(acto)* memorial, conmemoration. 2 *(escrito)* request.
memorizar *vt* to memorize.
mena *nf* ore.
menaje *nm* household goods. ● **menaje de cocina** kitchen equipment.
mención *nf* mention.
mencionar *vt* to mention, cite.
mendelismo *nm* Mendelism, Mendelianism.
mendicante *adj* mendicant.
mendicidad *nf* begging.
mendigar *vi* to beg.
mendigo,-a *nm & nf* beggar.
mendrugo *nm* hard crust (of bread).
menear *vt (cabeza)* to shake; *(cola)* to wag; *(cuerpo, caderas)* to wiggle.
▷ *vpr* **menearse** 1 *(moverse)* to move. 2 *(darse prisa)* to hurry (up), get a move on.
menestra *nf* vegetable stew.
mengua *nf (disminución)* decrease, decline.
menguado,-a *adj* diminished.
menguante *adj (luna)* waning.
menguar [22] *vi* 1 *(número, cantidad)* to diminish, decrease; *(temperatura, nivel)* to fall, drop. 2 *(salud)* decline. 3 *(luna)* to wane. 4 *(labor)* to decrease.
menhir *nm* menhir.
meninge *nm* meninx.
meningitis *nm inv* meningitis.
menisco *nm* meniscus.
menopausia *nf* menopause.
menopáusico,-a *adj* menopausal.
menor *adj* 1 *(comparativo - en tamaño)* smaller; *(- en calidad, importancia)* lesser; *(- en edad)* younger. 2 *(superlativo - en tamaño)* smallest; *(- en calidad, importancia)* least; *(- en edad)* youngest. 3 *(inferior)* minor. 4 MÚS minor.
▷ *nm o nf* JUR minor. ● **menor de edad** minor.
menos *adj* 1 *(comparativo - en cantidad)* less; *(- en número)* fewer: **yo tengo menos años que tú** *I'm younger than you.* 2 *(superlativo - de cantidad)* least; *(- de número)* fewest: **yo soy la que menos culpa tiene** *I'm the least guilty.*
▷ *adv* 1 *(comparativo - de cantidad)* less; *(- de número)* fewer: **voy al gimnasio menos que antes** *I go to the gym less than before.* 2 *(superlativo)* least: **es el menos guapo** *he's the least good-looking.* 3 *(con horas)* to: **las tres menos cuarto** *a quarter to three.* 4 MAT minus. ■ **a menos que** unless. ■ **al menos** at least. ■ **por lo menos** at least.
▷ *prep* but, except: **todo menos eso** *anything but that.*
▷ *pron (cantidad)* less; *(número)* fewer: **me pagó menos** *he paid me less.*
▷ *nm* MAT minus sign.
menospreciar [12] *vt* 1 *(despreciar)* to despise, scorn. 2 *(no valorar)* to undervalue, underrate.
menosprecio *nm* 1 *(desprecio)* scorn, contempt. 2 *(poco aprecio)* underestimation, lack of appreciation.
mensaje *nm* 1 *(en general)* message. 2 *(envío electrónico)* posting.
mensajería *nf* courier service.
mensajero,-a *nm & nf (profesional)* courier; *(que trae un mensaje)* messenger.
menstruación *nf* menstruation.
menstrual *adj* menstrual.
menstruar [11] *vi* to menstruate.
mensual *adj* monthly.
mensualidad *nf (que se cobra)* monthly salary; *(que se paga)* monthly instalment.
mensurable *adj* measurable.
menta *nf* 1 *(hierba)* mint. 2 *(infusión)* mint tea.
mental *adj* mental.
mentalidad *nf* mentality.
mentalizar [4] *vt* to make aware, make realize.
▷ *vpr* **mentalizarse** 1 *(tomar conciencia)* to become aware. 2 *(hacerse a la idea)* to get used to the idea, come to terms with the idea.
mente *nf* 1 *(pensamiento)* mind. 2 *(facultades)* mind, intelligence, intellect.
mentir [35] *vi* to lie.
mentira *nf* lie.
mentiroso,-a *adj* lying.
▷ *nm & nf* liar.
mentón *nm* chin.
mentor *nm* mentor.
menú *nm* 1 CULIN menu. 2 INFORMÁ menu. ● **menú del día** set menu.
▲ *pl* **menús.**
menudo,-a *adj* 1 *(pequeño)* small, tiny. 2 *(enfático)* fine, some, what a...: **¡menudo lío!** *what a mess!* ■ **a menudo** often, frequently.
meñique *adj* little. ● **(dedo) meñique** little finger.

ieollo *nm (lo esencial)* core, heart, crux.
iercader *nm arc* merchant.
iercadería *nf* merchandise.
iercadillo *nm* flea market, bazaar.
iercado *nm* market. ● **mercado bursátil** stock market. ‖ **Mercado Común** Common Market. ‖ **mercado de abastos** wholesale food market.
iercancía *nf (gen)* goods.
iercante *adj* merchant.
iercantil *adj* mercantile, commercial.
iercantilismo *nm* mercantilism.
iercenario,-a *adj* mercenary.
nm & nf mercenary.
iercería *nf* 1 *(artículos)* haberdashery, US notions store. 2 *(tienda)* haberdasher's shop, US notions store.
iercurio *nm* QUÍM mercury, quicksilver.
ierecedor,-ra *adj* worthy. ■ **ser merecedor,-ra de** to be worthy of.
ierecer [43] *vt* 1 to deserve, be worth: **merece la pena verlo** *it's worth a visit.* 2 *(tener necesidad)* to need to be + *pp*, need + *ger*: **la información merece ser comprobada** *the information needs checking.* 3 *(valer)* to earn, get.
ierecido,-a *nm* **merecido** (just) deserts *pl*, come-uppance. ■ **llevar su merecido** to get one's come-uppance.
nerendar [27] *vi* to have an afternoon snack, have tea.
vt to have something for tea.
nerendero *nm* 1 *(instalación)* open-air snack bar. 2 *(en el campo)* picnic spot; *(en la playa)* beachfront snack bar.
nerengue *nm* 1 CULIN meringue. 2 *fam (persona)* weakling, weed. 3 MÚS merengue.
neridiano,-a *adj* 1 *(de mediodía)* midday. 2 *fig (claro)* obvious.
nm meridian.
neridional *adj* southern.
nm o nf southerner.
nerienda *nf* 1 *(a media tarde)* afternoon snack, tea. 2 *(en el campo)* picnic.
nerina *nf* merino sheep.
nérito *nm* 1 *(de alguien)* merit. 2 *(de algo)* merit, worth: **tiene mucho mérito lo que has hecho** *what you have done is quite an achievement.*
nerluza *nf* hake.
nermar *vt* to reduce.
vi to decrease, diminish.
nermelada *nf* jam; *(de cítricos)* marmalade.
nero *nm (pez)* grouper.
nerodear *vi* 1 *(curiosear)* to prowl about. 2 MIL to maraud.
nes *nm* 1 month. 2 *(mensualidad - que cobrar)* monthly salary; *(- que pagar)* monthly instalment (US installment).
nesa *nf* 1 *(gen)* table; *(de oficina)* desk. 2 *(comida)* food. 3 *(personas)* board, committee. ■ **poner la mesa** to set the table, lay the table. ‖ **quitar/recoger la mesa** to clear the table. ● **mesa redonda** *(coloquio)* round table.
neseta *nf* GEOG plateau, tableland, plain.
nesianismo *nm* Messianism.
nesías *nm inv* Messiah.
nesilla *nf* small table. ● **mesilla de noche** bedside table.

mesocarpio *nm* mesocarp.
mesolítico,-a *adj* Mesolithic.
▷ *nm* **el mesolítico** the Mesolithic.
mesón *nm* 1 *(antiguamente)* inn, tavern. 2 *(actualmente)* old-style restaurant.
Mesopotamia *nf* HIST Mesopotamia.
mesopotamio,-a *adj* HIST Mesopotamian.
▷ *nm & nf* HIST Mesopotamian.
mestizaje *nm* crossbreeding.
mestizo,-a *adj* 1 of mixed race, mestizo. 2 *pey* half-breed.
▷ *nm & nf* 1 person of mixed race, mestizo. 2 *pey* half-breed.
mesura *nf* restraint, moderation.
meta *nf* 1 *(en atletismo, motociclismo)* finishing line; *(en carreras de caballos)* winning post. 2 *(portería)* goal. 3 *fig* goal, aim, purpose.
metabolismo *nm* metabolism.
metabolizar *vt* to metabolize.
metacrilato® *nm* 1 QUÍM methacrylate. 2 *(material)* Perspex®.
metadona *nf* methadone.
metafísica *nf* metaphysics.
metáfora *nf* metaphor.
metafórico,-a *adj* metaphorical, metaphoric.
metal *nm* 1 metal. 2 MÚS brass. ● **metal precioso** precious metal.
metalenguaje *nm* metalanguage.
metálico,-a *adj* metallic.
▷ *nm* **metálico** cash.
metalingüística *nf* metalinguistics.
metalista *nm o nf* metal worker.
metalistería *nf* metal work.
metalizado,-a *adj* metallic.
metalizar *vt* to metallize (US metalize).
metalurgia *nf* metallurgy.
metalúrgico,-a *adj* metallurgical.
▷ *nm & nf* metallurgist.
metamórfico,-a *adj* metamorphic.
metamorfosis *nf inv* metamorphosis.
metano *nm* methane.
metanol *nm* methanol.
metástasis *nf inv* metastasis.
metatarso *nm* metatarsus.
meteórico,-a *adj* meteoric.
meteorito *nm* meteorite.
meteoro *nm* meteor.
meteorología *nf* meteorology.
meteorológico,-a *adj* meteorological, weather.
meteorólogo,-a *nm & nf* meteorologist.
metepatas *nm o nf fam* bigmouth.
meter *vt* 1 *(introducir)* to put. 2 *(implicar)* to put into (**en**, -), get into (**en**, -), involve in (**en**, -). 3 *fam (dar)* to give: **menudo susto que nos metió** *he gave us a real fright.* 4 *(hacer)* to make: **no metáis tanto ruido** *don't be so noisy.* 5 *(ropa - acortar)* to take up; *(- estrechar)* to take in.
▷ *vpr* **meterse** 1 *(introducirse en)* to get in: **se metió en la cama** *he got into bed.* 2 *(tomar parte - negocio)* to go into (**en**, -); *(involucrarse en)* to get involved (**en**, in/with), get mixed up (**en**, in/with). 3 *(introducirse)* to get involved (**en**, in): **me metí totalmente en el papel**

I got completely into in the role. 4 *(ir)* to go: **¿dónde se habrá metido?** *where can he have got to?* 5 *(dedicarse)* to go (**en**, into): **quiere meterse en política** *he wants to go into politics.*

meticuloso,-a *adj* 1 *(cuidadoso)* meticulous. 2 *pey (escrupuloso)* fussy, finicky.

metido,-a *adj (envuelto, implicado)* involved (**en**, in).

metileno *nm* methylene.

metílico,-a *adj* methylic.

metódico,-a *adj* methodical.

método *nm* 1 method. 2 *(en pedagogía)* course.

metodología *nf* methodology.

metodológico,-a *adj* methodological.

metonimia *nf* metonymy.

metraje *nm (longitud)* length; *(película rodada)* footage. ● **corto metraje** short (film). ▪ **largo metraje** (full-length) feature film.

metralla *nf* shrapnel.

metralleta *nf* sub-machine-gun.

métrica *nf* metrics *pl*.

métrico,-a *adj* 1 *(sistema, unidad)* metric. 2 *(del verso)* metrical, metric. ● **sistema métrico** metric system.

metro *nm* 1 metre (US meter). 2 *(cinta)* tape measure. 3 *(transporte)* underground, tube, US subway. ● **metro cuadrado** square metre.

metrónomo *nm* metronome.

metrópoli *nf* metropolis.

metropolitano,-a *adj* metropolitan.
▷ *nm* **metropolitano** *fml* underground, tube, US subway.

mexicano,-a *adj* Mexican.
▷ *nm & nf* Mexican.

México *nm* Mexico.

mezcla *nf* 1 *(acción)* mixing, blending. 2 *(producto)* mixture, blend.

mezclar *vt* 1 *(incorporar, unir)* to mix, blend. 2 *(desordenar)* to mix up. 3 *(persona)* to involve (**en**, in).
▷ *vpr* **mezclarse** 1 *(personas)* to mix (**con**, with). 2 *(cosas)* to get mixed up. 3 *(entremeterse)* to interfere (**en**, in).

mezquindad *nf* 1 meanness, stinginess. 2 *(acción)* mean thing.

mezquino,-a *adj* 1 *(avaro)* stingy, niggardly. 2 *(bajo)* low, base. 3 *(pobre)* miserable, poor.

mezquita *nf* mosque.

mg *sím* (**miligramo**) milligramme (US milligram); *(símbolo)* mg.

mi *nm* MÚS E.

mí *pron* me: **éste es para mí** *this one is for me.*

miau *nm* miaow, meow, mew.

mica *nf* GEOL mica.

micénico,-a *adj* Mycenaean.

michelín *nm fam* spare tyre.

mico *nm* 1 *(animal)* (long-tailed) monkey. 2 *fam fig (niño)* little monkey.

micología *nf* mycology.

micosis *nf inv* mycosis.

micra *nf* micron.

micro *nm fam* mike, microphone.

microbio *nm* 1 microbe. 2 *fam (enano)* little squirt.

microbiología *nf* microbiology.

microchip *nm* microchip.

microclima *nm* microclimate.

microcomputador *nm* microcomputer.

microcosmos *nm inv* microcosm.

microeconomía *nf* microeconomics.

microelectrónica *nf* microelectronics.

microfilme *nm* microfilm.

micrófono *nm* microphone.

microondas *nm* microwave. ● **horno microonda[s]** microwave oven.

microordenador *nm* microcomputer.

microprocesador *nm* microprocessor.

microscópico,-a *adj* microscopic.

microscopio *nm* microscope.

miedo *nm* fear. ▪ **tener miedo** to be scared, be frigh[t]ened, be afraid: **tiene miedo a la oscuridad** *he's afra[id] of the dark.*

miedoso,-a *adj* 1 easily frightened. 2 *(cobarde)* cow[]ardly.

miel *nf* honey.

miembro *nm* 1 *(extremidad)* limb. 2 *(socio)* membe[r]. 3 MAT member.

mientras *adv* in the meantime, meanwhile.
▷ *conj* 1 *(temporal)* while, whilst: **mientras estés de vac[a]ciones no pienses en el trabajo** *while you're on holida[y] (US vacation), don't think about work.* 2 *(adversativ[o])* whereas: **yo al menos he estudiado, mientras que t[ú] no** *at least I have studied, whereas you haven't.* 3 *(has[ta] que)* until: **no sabremos quién lo hizo mientras no ten[]gamos las pruebas necesarias** *we won't know who did [it] until we have the necessary evidence.* 4 *(condicional)* a[s] long as: **te lo explico mientras no se lo digas a nadi[e] más** *I'll tell you as long as you don't tell anyone else.*

miércoles *nm* Wednesday.

See also **jueves.**

mierda *nf* 1 *tabú (excremento)* shit: **he pisado una mier[]da de perro** *I've stepped in some dog shit.* 2 *tabú f[ig]* crap: **esta película es una mierda** *this film is crap.*
▷ *interj tabú* shit!

mies *nf* 1 corn, grain. 2 *(cosecha)* harvest time.
▷ *nf pl* **mieses** cornfields.

miga *nf* 1 *(parte blanda del pan)* crumb, soft part; *(pa[n] desmenuzado)* breadcrumbs. 2 *(trocito)* bit, smal[l] piece.
▷ *nf pl* **migas** CULIN fried breadcrumbs. ▪ **hacer buena[s]/malas migas con** to get along well/badly with.

migración *nf* migration.

migraña *nf* migraine.

migrar *vi* to migrate.

migratorio,-a *adj* migratory.

mijo *nm* millet.

mil *adj* 1 thousand. 2 *(milésimo)* thousandth.
▷ *nm* a thousand, one thousand.

See also **seis** and **sexto,-a.**

milagro *nm* miracle.

milagroso,-a *adj* 1 miraculous. 2 *(asombroso)* mar[]vellous.

milanesa ▪ **a la milanesa** done in breadcrumbs.

milano *nm* kite.

milenario,-a *adj* millennial.
▷ *nm* **milenario** millennium.

milenio *nm* millennium.

milésimo,-a *adj* thousandth.
▷ *nm & nf* thousandth.

See also **sexto,-a.**

ıilhojas *nm inv* CULIN millefeuille, puff pastry.
ıili *nf fam* military service. ■ **hacer la mili** *fam* to do one's military service.
ıilicia *nf* **1** *(disciplina)* art of warfare. **2** *(militares)* military. **3** *(gente armada)* militia.
ıiliciano,-a *adj* of the militia.
nm & nf (hombre) militiaman; *(mujer)* militiawoman.
ıiligramo *nm* milligram, milligramme.
ıililitro *nm* millilitre (US milliliter).
ıilimétrico,-a *adj* pinpoint.
ıilímetro *nm* millimetre (US millimeter).
ıilitante *adj* militant.
ıilitar *adj* military.
▷ *nm* military man, soldier.
▷ *vi* **1** MIL to serve. **2** POL *(ser miembro)* to be an active member; *(ser activista)* to be a militant, be an activist.
ıilla *nf* mile. ● **milla náutica** nautical mile.
ıillar *nm* thousand.
ıillón *nm* million.
▷ *nm pl* **millones** a fortune.
ıillonario,-a *nm & nf (hombre)* millionaire; *(mujer)* millionairess.
ıimar *vt (consentir)* to spoil; *(mimar con exceso)* to pamper, mollycoddle.
ıimbre *nm* wicker.
ıimetismo *nm* mimicry.
ıímico,-a *adj* mimic.
ıimo *nm* **1** *(actor)* mime artist. **2** *(cariño)* pampering. **3** *(cuidado)* care: **trátame el cachorro con mucho mimo** *treat the puppy with tender loving care.* ■ **hacerle mimos a ALGN** to pamper SB.
ıimosa *nf* BOT mimosa.
ıimoso,-a *adj* **1** *(mimado)* spoilt. **2** *(cariñoso)* affectionate, loving.
ıina *nf* **1** mine. **2** *fig (cosa)* gold mine: **este negocio es una mina** *this business is a gold mine.* **3** *(explosivo)* mine. **4** *(de lápiz)* lead; *(de bolígrafo)* refill. ● **mina de carbón** coal mine.
ıinar *vt* **1** *(terreno)* to mine. **2** *fig (salud, resistencia)* to undermine, weaken.
minarete *nm* minaret.
ıineral *adj* mineral.
▷ *nm* mineral. ● **agua mineral** mineral water. | **mineral de hierro** iron ore.
minería *nf* **1** *(técnica)* mining. **2** *(mineros)* miners *pl.* **3** *(industria)* mining industry.
minero,-a *adj* mining.
▷ *nm & nf* miner.
miniatura *nf* **1** miniature.
minifalda *nf* mini skirt.
minifundio *nm* smallholding.
minigolf *nm* crazy golf.
mínima *nf (temperatura)* minimum temperature.
minimizar *vt* to minimize.
mínimo,-a *adj* minimum, lowest.
▷ *nm* **mínimo** minimum: **pon el gas en el mínimo** *turn the gas right down.* ■ **como mínimo** at least. ● **mínimo común múltiplo** lowest common multiple.
minino *nm fam* pussy, kitty.
minio *nm* red lead, minium.
minipimer® *nm o nf* hand blender.
ministerio *nm* **1** POL ministry, US department. **2** REL ministry. ● **Ministerio de Asuntos Exteriores** Ministry of Foreign Affairs, GB ≈ Foreign Office, US ≈ State Department. | **Ministerio de Economía y Hacienda** Ministry of Finance, GB ≈ Exchequer, Treasury, US Treasury Department. | **Ministerio de Obras Públicas** Ministry of Public Works, US Department of Public Works.
ministro,-a *nm & nf* **1** POL minister, US secretary. **2** REL minister. ● **primer,-ra ministro,-a** prime minister.
minoico,-a *adj* Minoan.
minoría *nf* minority.
minorista *adj* retail.
▷ *nm o nf* retailer.
minoritario,-a *adj* minority: **un grupo minoritario** *a minority group.*
minucia *nf* trifle.
minucioso,-a *adj* meticulous, thorough, painstaking.
minuendo *nm* minuend.
minúscula *nf (letra)* small letter; *(en imprenta)* lower-case letter.
minúsculo,-a *adj (letra)* small; *(persona, objeto)* minute, minuscule; *(detalle)* insignificant.
minusvalía *nf (de una persona)* handicap, disability.
minusválido,-a *adj* disabled, handicapped.
▷ *nm & nf* disabled person.
minuta *nf* **1** *(factura)* bill; *(de un abogado)* solicitor's fees *pl.* **2** CULIN menu.
minutero *nm* minute hand.
minuto *nm* minute. ■ **al minuto** at once.
mío,-a *adj* my, of mine: **es muy amiga mía** *she's a good friend of mine.*
▷ *pron* mine: **este abrigo es mío** *this coat is mine.* ■ **los míos** *fam* my family *sing,* my folks.
miocardio *nm* myocardium.
miope *adj* short-sighted, myopic.
▷ *nm o nf* short-sighted person.
miopía *nf* short-sightedness.
mira *nf* **1** *(dispositivo)* sight. **2** *fig* intention. ■ **con miras a** with a view to.
mirada *nf (gen)* look; *(vistazo)* glance. ■ **echar una mirada a ALGO/ALGN** to take a look at STH/SB. | **fulminar a ALGN con la mirada** to look daggers at SB. | **levantar la mirada** to look up.
mirador *nm* **1** *(balcón)* glassed-in balcony. **2** *(lugar)* viewing point.
miramiento *nm* consideration. ■ **andarse con miramientos** to be extremely polite.
mirar *vt* **1** *(observar)* to look at; *(con atención)* to watch. **2** *(buscar)* to look; *(registrar)* to search: **me miraron todo al pasar por la aduana** *they went through everything at customs.* **3** *(tener cuidado con)* to watch: **mira bien lo que haces** *watch what you do.* **4** *(averiguar)* to see, find out: **mira (a ver) si lo han vendido ya** *see whether they have sold it yet.*
▷ *vi* **1** *(gen)* to look; *(con atención)* to stare. **2** *(buscar)* to look: **mira debajo de la cama** *look under the bed.* **3** *(tener cuidado)* to mind, watch, be careful: **mira que no te engañen** *mind they don't cheat you.* ■ **¡mira! 1** *(gen)* look! **2** *(con asombro)* well I never!, fancy that! **3** *(como aviso)* look here!
miríada *nf* myriad.

mirilla *nf* peephole, spyhole.
miriópodo *nm* myriapod.
mirlo *nm* blackbird.
mirón,-ona *nm & nf* 1 *fam pey (curioso)* nosy parker. 2 *(espectador)* onlooker. 3 *pey (voyeur)* voyeur, Peeping Tom.
mirra *nf* myrrh.
mirto *nm* myrtle.
misa *nf* mass. ■ **ir a misa** *(asistir)* to go to mass.
misal *nm* missal.
misántropo,-a *nm & nf* misanthrope, misanthropist.
miscelánea *nf* miscellany.
miserable *adj* 1 *(desdichado)* miserable. 2 *(insignificante)* miserly; *(tacaño)* mean. 3 *(malvado)* wretched.
▷ *nm o nf* 1 *(malvado)* wretch. 2 *(tacaño)* miser.
miseria *nf* 1 *(pobreza)* extreme poverty. 2 *(desgracia)* misery, wretchedness. 3 *(tacañería)* meanness. 4 *fam (poco dinero)* pittance.
misericordia *nf* mercy.
mísero,-a *adj* miserable.
misil *nm* missile. ● **misil de crucero** cruise missile.
misión *nf* 1 *(tarea)* mission, task. 2 REL mission.
misionero,-a *adj* mission.
▷ *nm & nf* missionary.
mismo,-a *adj* 1 *(idéntico)* same: **el mismo color** *the same colour.* 2 *(enfático)* very: **en esta misma casa nací yo** *I was born in this very house.*
▷ *pron* same: **es el mismo del año pasado** *it's the same one as last year.*
▷ *adv* **mismo** same: **piensa lo mismo que tu** *he thinks the same as you.* ■ **yo** *(ti, etc)* **mismo,-a** myself *(yourself, etc).* ‖ **es lo mismo** 1 *(la misma cosa)* it amounts to the same thing. 2 *(no importa)* it doesn't matter. ‖ **lo mismo da** it doen't matter.
misógino,-a *adj* misogynous.
míster *nm (en fútbol)* manager, coach.
misterio *nm* mystery.
misterioso,-a *adj* mysterious.
mística *nf* 1 *(misticismo)* mysticism. 2 *(teología)* mystic theology.
misticismo *nm* mysticism.
místico,-a *adj* mystic, mystical.
▷ *nm & nf (persona)* mystic.
mitad *nf* 1 half: **me llevo la mitad** *I'll take half.* 2 *(medio)* middle: **en mitad de la plaza** *in the middle of the square.*
mítico,-a *adj* mythical.
mitificar *vt* 1 *(convertir en mito)* to make a myth of, mythicize. 2 *(adorar)* to hero-worship.
mitin *nm* meeting, rally.
▲ *pl* **mítines.**
mito *nm* myth.
mitología *nf* mythology.
mitológico,-a *adj* mythological.
mitosis *nf inv* mitosis.
mixto,-a *adj* mixed.
ml *sím* **(mililitro)** millilitre (US milliliter); *(símbolo)* ml.
mm *sím* **(milímetro)** millimetre (US millimeter); *(símbolo)* mm.
Mm *sím* **(miriámetro)** myriametre (US myriameter); *(símbolo)* Mm.

mobiliario *nm* furniture.
moca *nf (café)* mocha.
mocasín *nm* moccasin.
mochila *nf* rucksack, backpack.
mochuelo *nm* ZOOL little owl.
moción *nf* motion.
moco *nm* 1 *(mucosidad)* mucus; *(familiarmente)* sno[…] 2 *(de vela)* drips *pl.* 3 *(de pavo)* wattle. ■ **limpiarse lo[…] mocos** *fam* to blow one's nose.
mocoso,-a *nm & nf fam* brat.
moda *nf* 1 fashion: **me gusta ir a la moda** *I like to kee[…] up with fashion.* 2 *(locura)* craze. ■ **estar de moda** to b[…] in fashion.
modales *nm pl* manners.
modalidad *nf* 1 form, method, means, way. 2 *(de[…]porte)* sport; *(en atletismo, esquí)* event; *(en vela)* class[…]
modelado *nm* modelling (US modeling).
modelar *vt* to model, shape.
modélico,-a *adj* model.
modelismo *nm (de arcilla, etc)* modelling; *(de pieza[…])* model-making.
modelo *adj* model.
▷ *nm o nf (persona)* (fashion) model.
▷ *nm* 1 *(patrón)* model: **esto te puede servir de model[…]** *you can use this as a model.* 2 *(diseño)* model. 3 *(traje[…])* number.
módem *nm* modem.
▲ *pl* **módems.**
moderación *nf* moderation.
moderado,-a *adj* moderate.
▷ *nm & nf* moderate.
moderador,-ra *nm & nf (de reunión)* chairperson[…] *(- hombre)* chairman; *(- mujer)* chairwoman; *(de deba[…]te)* moderator.
moderar *vt (gen)* to moderate; *(velocidad)* to reduce.
▷ *vpr* **moderarse** to control OS.
modernismo *nm* 1 *(arte, literatura)* Modernism. 2 *(es[…]tilo español)* Spanish Art Nouveau, Modernismo.
modernista *adj* 1 Modernist. 2 ARTE *(en España[…])* Spanish Art Nouveau, Modernista.
▷ *nm o nf* 1 Modernist. 2 ARTE *(en España)* Modernista
modernizar [4] *vt* to modernize.
▷ *vpr* **modernizarse** to be modernized.
moderno,-a *adj* modern.
modestia *nf* modesty.
modesto,-a *adj* modest.
modificar [1] *vt* to alter, modify.
modista *nm o nf* 1 *(diseñador)* fashion designer. 2 *(de[…] ropa para mujer)* dressmaker; *(de ropa para hombre[…])* tailor.
modisto *nm* 1 *(diseñador)* fashion designer. 2 *(sastre[…])* tailor.
modo *nm* 1 way, manner. 2 LING mood: **el modo subjuntivo** *the subjunctive mood.* ■ **de modo que** so: **de modo que ya lo sabes** *so now you know.* ‖ **en cierto modo** in a way.
▷ *nm pl* **modos** manners. ■ **de todos modos** anyhow, at any rate.
modorra *nf fam* drowsiness, sleepiness.
modular *vt* to modulate.
▷ *adj* modular.
módulo *nm* 1 *(gen)* module. 2 *(mueble)* unit.

mofa *nf* mockery, derision.

mofarse *vpr* to scoff, mock.

mofeta *nf* skunk.

moflete *nm fam* chubby cheek.

mogollón *nm* 1 *fam* heaps *pl*, stacks *pl*, loads *pl*. 2 *fam (alboroto)* racket.
▷ *adv fam* a lot: nos gustó mogollón *it was dead brilliant*.

mohair *nm* mohair.

moho *nm* 1 mould, (US mold). 2 *(de metales - hierro)* rust; *(- cobre)* verdigris.

mohoso,-a *adj* 1 mouldy (US moldy). 2 *(oxidado)* rusty.

mojado,-a *adj (húmedo)* wet, moist; *(empapado)* drenched, soaked, wet through.

mojama *nf* dried salted tuna.

mojar *vt* 1 *(gen)* to wet. 2 *(humedecer)* to dampen. 3 *(alimento)* to dip, dunk. 4 *(cama)* to wet.
▷ *vpr* **mojarse** 1 to get wet. 2 *fam (comprometerse)* to commit OS, get involved.

mojigato,-a *adj (gazmoño)* prudish; *(falso)* sanctimonious.

mojón *nm (poste - de distancia)* milepost; *(piedra)* milestone; *(- de camino)* landmark.

molar *adj* molar.
▷ *nm (diente)* molar.

Moldavia *nf* Moldavia.

moldavo,-a *adj* Moldavian.
▷ *nm & nf* Moldavian.

molde *nm* mould (US mold).

moldeable *adj* mouldable (US moldable).

moldeado,-a *adj* moulded (US molded).
▷ *nm* **moldeado** 1 ARTE moulding (US molding). 2 *(de pelo)* soft perm.

moldear *vt* 1 ARTE *(dar forma)* to mould (US mold); *(- en un molde)* to cast. 2 *(pelo)* to give a soft perm.

moldura *nf* moulding (US molding).

mole *nf* mass, bulk, hulk.

molécula *nf* molecule.

molecular *adj* molecular.

moler [32] *vt* 1 *(gen)* to grind, mill; *(machacar)* to pound. 2 *(cansar)* to wear out.

molestar *vt* 1 *(interrumpir)* to disturb. 2 *(perturbar)* to bother, annoy, upset: me molestan los ruidos *noise bothers me*. 3 *(importunar)* to pester: ¡deja de molestarme ya! *stop pestering me!* 4 *(hacer daño - apretar)* to hurt, be too tight; *(- picar)* to irritate: estos zapatos me molestan *these shoes hurt my feet*. 5 *(ofender)* to upset.
▷ *vpr* **molestarse** 1 *(tomarse la molestia)* to bother: perdone que le moleste *I'm sorry to bother you*. 2 *(ofenderse)* to take offence.

molestia *nf* 1 *(incomodidad)* bother, trouble; *(fastidio)* nuisance. 2 MED trouble, slight pain.

molesto,-a *adj* 1 annoying, troublesome. 2 *(enfadado)* annoyed. 3 *(incómodo)* uncomfortable.

molido,-a *adj* 1 *(café)* ground; *(trigo)* milled. 2 *fam (cansado)* worn-out. ■ **estar molido,-a** *fam* to be worn-out.

molienda *nf (de café)* grinding; *(de trigo)* milling.

moliente ■ **corriente y moliente** run of the mill, common or garden.

molinero,-a *nm & nf* miller.

molinillo *nm* grinder, mill.

molino *nm* mill. ● **molino de viento** windmill.

molla *nf (pulpa)* flesh.

molleja *nf* 1 *(de ave)* gizzard. 2 *(de res)* sweetbread.

mollera *nf fam (inteligencia)* brains *pl*, sense; *(cabeza)* loaf, bonce.

molón,-na *adj argot* cool, brill, fab.

molusco *nm* mollusc (US mollusk).

momentáneo,-a *adj (que dura poco tiempo)* momentary; *(provisional)* temporary.

momento *nm* 1 moment. 2 *(período)* time. 3 *(oportunidad)* time, moment.

momia *nf* mummy.

momificación *nf* mummification.

momificar *vt* to mummify.

monacal *adj* monastic.

monacato *nm* 1 *(profesión)* monkhood. 2 *(institución)* monastic community.

Mónaco *nm* Monaco.

monada *nf* 1 *(cosa bonita)* beauty, lovely thing; *(persona)* gorgeous person, sweet thing, delight. 2 *(gracia)* funny little ways *pl*; *(jugada)* trick: deja ya de hacer monadas *stop fooling around*.

monaguillo *nm* altar boy.

monarca *nm* monarch.

monarquía *nf* monarchy.

monárquico,-a *adj* monarchic, monarchical.

monasterio *nm* monastery.

monástico,-a *adj* monastic.

monda *nf* 1 *(piel)* peel, skin. 2 *(acción)* peeling.

mondadientes *nm inv* toothpick.

mondadura *nf* 1 *(piel - de fruta)* peel; *(- de patata)* peelings *pl*. 2 *(acción)* peeling.

mondar *vt* 1 *(pelar)* to peel. 2 *(podar)* to prune.

mondo,-a *adj (limpio)* bare; *(sencillo)* plain.

mondongo *nm* innards *pl*.

moneda *nf* 1 *(pieza)* coin. 2 *(divisa)* currency.

monedero *nm* purse.

monegasco,-a *adj* Monegasque.
▷ *nm & nf* Monegasque.

monetario,-a *adj* monetary.

monetarismo *nm* monetarism.

monetarista *adj* monetarist.
▷ *nm o nf* monetarist.

mongol,-la *adj* Mongolian, Mongol.
▷ *nm o nf (habitante)* Mongolian, Mongol.
▷ *nm* **mongol** *(idioma)* Mongolian.

Mongolia *nf* Mongolia. ● **Mongolia Interior/Exterior** Inner/Outer Mongolia.

mongólico,-a *adj* 1 affected by Down's syndrome. 2 Mongolian.
▷ *nm & nf* 1 person affected by Down's syndrome. 2 Mongolian.

mongolismo *nm* Down's syndrome, mongolism.

monicaco *nm fam (hombre)* dodgy geezer.

monigote *nm* 1 *(figura)* rag doll, paper doll. 2 *pey (persona)* stooge, puppet. 3 *(dibujo)* matchstick man, doodle.

monismo *nm* monism.

monista *adj* monistic.
▷ *nm o nf* monist.

monitor,-ra *nm & nf (profesor)* instructor.
▷ *nm* **monitor** *(pantalla)* monitor, screen.

monja *nf* nun.
monje *nm* monk.
mono,-a *adj (bonito)* nice, lovely, cute.
▷ *nm & nf* **1** ZOOL monkey. **2** *fam pey (joven)* little brat.
▷ *nm* **mono** *(prenda - de trabajo)* overalls *pl*; *(- de calle)* jump suit, dungarees *pl*; *(- de niños)* rompers *pl*.
monocarril *nm* monorail.
monocolor *adj* monochrome.
monocorde *adj* **1** *(canto)* single-stringed. **2** *fig (monótono)* dull, monotonous.
monocotiledónea *nf* monocotyledon.
monocotiledóneo,-a *adj* monocotyledonous.
monocromático,-a *adj* monochromatic.
monocromía *nf* monochrome.
monocromo,-a *adj* monochrome.
monocular *adj* monocular.
monóculo *nm* monocle.
monocultivo *nm* monoculture.
monódico,-a *adj* monodic.
monofásico,-a *adj* single-phase.
monofonía *nm* mono.
monofónico,-a *adj* mono.
monogamia *nf* monogamy.
monógamo,-a *adj* monogamous.
▷ *nm & nf* monogamist.
monografía *nf* monograph.
monográfico,-a *adj* monographic, single-theme.
monograma *nm* monogram.
monolingüe *adj* monolingual.
monolítico,-a *adj* monolithic.
monolito *nm* monolith.
monologar *vi* to soliloquize.
monólogo *nm (reflexión)* monologue; *(en teatro)* soliloquy.
monomanía *nf* **1** MED monomania. **2** *fam* obsession, fixation.
monomaníaco,-a *adj* MED monomaniac.
monomio *n* MAT monomial.
monoparental *adj* one-parent, single-parent.
monopatín *nm* skateboard.
monoplano *nm* monoplane.
monoplaza *adj* single-seat.
▷ *nm* single-seater.
monopolio *nm* monopoly.
monopolista *adj* monopolistic.
▷ *nm o nf* monopolist.
monopolización *nf* monopolization.
monopolizador,-ra *adj* monopolizing.
▷ *nm & nf* monopolizer.
monopolizar [4] *vt* to monopolize.
monorraíl *nm* monorail.
monosilábico,-a *adj* monosyllabic.
monosílabo,-a *adj* monosyllabic.
▷ *nm* **monosílabo** monosyllable.
monoteísmo *nm* monotheism.
monoteísta *adj* monotheistic.
▷ *nm o nf* monotheist.
monotonía *nf* monotony.
monótono,-a *adj* monotonous.
monovolumen *nm* people carrier.
monóxido *nm* monoxide. ● **monóxido de carbono** carbon monoxide.
monseñor *nm* Monsignor.
monserga *nf fam (lección)* nagging, preaching; *(despropósito)* tall story, drivel, rubbish.
monstruo *adj fam (extraordinario)* fantastic, terrific.
▷ *nm* **1** monster. **2** *fam (genio)* genius, prodigy.
monstruosidad *nf (cosa)* monstrosity; *(fealdad)* hideousness.
monstruoso,-a *adj* **1** *(por tamaño, crueldad)* monstrous. **2** *(por fealdad)* hideous.
monta *nf* **1** *(importancia)* value, account, importance. **2** *(de un caballo)* riding.
montacargas *nm* goods lift, service lift, US freight elevator.
montador,-ra *nm & nf* **1** *(operario)* fitter. **2** *(de joyas)* setter. **3** *(de cine)* film editor.
montadora *nf* splicer, splicing machine.
See also **montador,-ra.**
montaje *nm* **1** *(de piezas)* assembly. **2** *(de una película)* editing. **3** *(de un espectáculo)* staging. **4** *(en foto)* montage. **5** *fam (farsa)* setup.
montante *nm* **1** *(total)* total, total amount. **2** *(pieza vertical)* upright. **3** *(ventana)* skylight.
montaña *nf* mountain.
montañero,-a *nm & nf* mountaineer.
montañés,-esa *nm & nf (de la montaña)* highlander, mountain person.
montañismo *nm* mountaineering, mountain climbing.
montañoso,-a *adj* mountainous.
montaplatos *nm inv* dumb waiter.
montar *vi* **1** *(subir - caballo, bicicleta)* to mount, get on; *(- coche)* to get in; *(- avión)* to get on, board. **2** *(viajar)* to travel; *(cabalgar, ir en bicicleta)* to ride: **¿sabes montar en bicicleta?** *can you ride bicycle?*
▷ *vt* **1** *(subir - caballo)* to mount, get on. **2** *(subir - persona)* to put on: **monté al niño en la bicicleta** *I lifted the kid onto his bike.* **3** *(ensamblar)* to assemble, put together; *(tienda de campaña)* to put up. **4** *(fusil)* to cock. **5** *(sobreponer)* to overlap. **6** *(nata)* to whip; *(claras)* to whisk. **7** TEAT to stage.
▷ *vpr* **montarse** **1** *(subirse)* to get on; *(- en un coche)* to get in; *(- en un caballo)* to mount, get on. **2** *fam (armarse)* to break out: **se montó un buen jaleo** *there was a real to-do.*
montaraz *adj* **1** *(de montaña)* mountain. **2** *(tosco)* rough, coarse.
monte *nm* **1** mountain, mount. **2** *(bosque)* wild, woodland.
montenegrino,-a *adj* Montenegrin.
▷ *nm & nf* Montenegrin.
Montenegro *nm* Montenegro.
montepío *nm* friendly society, benefit society.
montera *nf* bullfighter's hat.
montería *nf (caza)* hunt; *(arte de cazar)* hunting.
montero,-a *nm & nf* hunter.
montés *adj* wild.
montículo *nm* mound, hillock.
monto *nm* total, total amount.
montón *nm* **1** heap, pile. **2** *fam (gran cantidad)* stacks *pl*, loads *pl*, heaps *pl*: **vino un montón de gente** *loads of people came.* ■ **ser del montón** be one of the crowd.

montura *nf* 1 *(cabalgadura)* mount. 2 *(silla)* saddle; *(arreos)* harness. 3 *(armazón - de gafas)* frame; *(- de joyas)* setting.
monumental *adj* monumental.
monumento *nm* ARTE monument.
monzón *nm* monsoon.
monzónico,-a *adj* monsoon.
moña *nf fam (borrachera)* bender. ■ **coger una moña** *fam* to get plastered.
moño *nm* bun. ■ **estar hasta el moño** *fam* to be fed up to the back teeth.
moquear *vi* to have a runny nose.
moqueta *nf* 1 fitted carpet. 2 *(material)* moquette.
moquillo *nm (de perro)* distemper; *(de ave)* pip.
mora *nf* 1 *(de moral)* mulberry. 2 *(zarzamora)* blackberry.
morada *nf* adobe, dwelling.
morado,-a *adj (color)* purple; *(ojo)* black.
▷ *nm* **morado** *(color)* purple.
morador,-ra *nm & nf* dweller, inhabitant.
moral[1] *adj* moral.
▷ *nf* 1 *(reglas)* morals *pl*. 2 *(ánimo)* morale, spirits *pl*.
moral[2] *nm* BOT mulberry tree.
moraleja *nf* moral.
moralidad *nf* morality.
moralina *nf* false morals *pl*.
moralista *adj* moralistic.
moralizador,-ra *adj* moralizing.
moralizar [4] *vi* to moralize.
▷ *vt* to moralize.
morar *vi* to reside, dwell.
moratón *nm fam* bruise.
moratoria *nf* moratorium.
morbidez *nf* softness, tenderness.
morbo *nm* 1 *(enfermedad)* sickness. 2 *fam (excitación)* thrill; *(interés)* morbid curiosity.
morbosidad *nf* 1 *(enfermedad)* morbidity. 2 *(excitación)* morbid pleasure; *(interés)* morbid curiosity.
morboso,-a *adj* 1 MED *(enfermo)* morbid. 2 *fam (obsesión, placer)* morbid; *(persona)* kinky.
morcilla *nf* 1 black pudding. 2 TEAT ad lib.
mordaz *adj* mordant, sarcastic.
mordaza *nf* gag.
mordedura *nf* bite.
morder [32] *vt* to bite: **le ha mordido mi perro** *my dog's bitten him.*
▷ *vi* to bite: **ten cuidado que muerde** *be careful, it bites.*
▷ *vpr* **morderse** to bite. ■ **morderse la lengua** *(callarse)* to hold one's tongue.
mordida *nf fam (soborno)* bribe.
mordiente *nm* mordant.
mordisco *nm* bite.
mordisquear *vt* to nibble.
morena *nf (pez)* moray eel.
moreno,-a *adj* 1 *(pelo)* dark, dark-haired. 2 *(piel)* dark, dark-skinned. 3 *(de raza negra)* black. 4 *(pan, azúcar)* brown.
▷ *nm & nf* 1 *(de pelo)* dark-haired person. 2 *(de piel)* dark-skinned person. 3 *(de raza negra)* black person.
▷ *nm* **moreno** suntan.
morera *nf* white mulberry.
moretón *nm* bruise.
morfema *nm* morpheme.
morfina *nf* morphine.
morfinómano,-a *nm & nf* morphine addict.
morfología *nf* morphology.
morfológico,-a *adj* morphological.
morganático,-a *adj* morganatic.
morgue *nf* morgue.
moribundo,-a *adj* moribund.
morir [33] *vi* 1 *(ser vivo)* to die. 2 *(día)* to finish, come to an end. 3 *(sendero, río)* to end.
▷ *vpr* **morirse** to die. ■ **morirse de vergüenza** to die of embarrassment.
mormón,-ona *adj* Mormon.
▷ *nm & nf* Mormon.
mormónico,-a *adj* Mormon.
moro,-a *adj* 1 Moorish. 2 *fam (árabe)* Arab.
▷ *nm & nf* 1 Moor. 2 *(árabe)* Arab.
morosidad *nf* 1 *(tardanza)* delay; *(- en un pago)* arrears *pl*. 2 *(lentitud)* sluggishness.
moroso,-a *adj* FIN *(cliente)* defaulting, slow in paying, in arrears.
▷ *nm & nf* defaulter.
morral *nm* 1 hunter's bag. 2 MIL knapsack, haversack.
morralla *nf* 1 *(pescado)* small fish. 2 *pey (gente)* riffraff.
morrazo ■ **pegarse un morrazo** *fam* to give OS a bash.
morrena *nf* moraine.
morriña *nf* homesickness.
morrión *nm* helmet.
morro *nm* 1 *fam (de persona - boca)* lips *pl*, mouth; *(cara)* face. 2 *fam (cara dura)* cheek. 3 *(de animal)* snout, nose. 4 *(de coche)* nose.
morrocotudo,-a *adj fam* terrific, fantastic, brilliant.
morrón *adj* **pimiento morrón** sweet red pepper.
morrudo,-a *adj fam* thick-lipped.
morsa *nf* walrus.
Morse *nm* Morse code.
mortadela *nf* mortadella.
mortaja *nf* shroud.
mortal *adj* 1 *(criatura, ser)* mortal. 2 *(peligro, herida)* mortal. 3 *(aburrimiento, susto)* deadly.
▷ *nm o nf* mortal.
mortalidad *nf* mortality.
mortandad *nf* death toll.
mortecino,-a *adj* 1 *(luz)* faint, dull. 2 *(color)* lifeless, dull.
mortero *nm* mortar.
mortífero,-a *adj* deadly, lethal.
mortificación *nf* mortification.
mortificante *adj* mortifying.
mortificar [1] *vt* to mortify.
mortuorio,-a *adj* mortuary.
moruno,-a *adj* Moorish.
mosaico *nm* mosaic.
mosca *nf* 1 fly. 2 *(barba)* tuft. 3 *fam (dinero)* dough.
moscada ● **nuez moscada** nutmeg.
moscardón *nm* 1 blowfly. 2 *(persona)* pest.
moscatel *nm* muscatel.
mosconear *vt fam* to pester.
▷ *vi fam* to be a pest, be a pain.

mosquear *vt fam* to annoy.
▷ *vpr* **mosquearse 1** *fam (enfadarse)* to get cross. **2** *fam (sospechar)* to smell a rat.
mosquete *nm* musket.
mosquetero *nm* musketeer.
mosquetón *nm* **1** *(arma)* short carbine. **2** *(cierre)* snap link.
mosquitera *nf* mosquito net.
mosquitero *nm* mosquito net.
mosquito *nm* mosquito.
mostacera *nf* mustard pot.
mostacho *nm* moustache.
mostaza *nf* mustard.
mosto *nm* **1** *(del vino)* must. **2** *(zumo)* grape juice.
mostrador *nm (de tienda)* counter; *(de bar)* bar.
mostrar *vt* to show.
▷ *vpr* **mostrarse 1** to appear. **2** *(ser)* be; *(resultar ser)* to prove to be, turn out to be: **se mostró un buen padre** *he proved to be a good father.*
mostrenco,-a *adj (grande)* mammoth.
mota *nf* **1** *(partícula)* speck. **2** *(mancha)* spot.
mote *nm* nickname.
moteado,-a *adj* dotted, speckled.
motear *vt* to fleck, speck.
motejar *vt* to nickname.
motel *nm* motel.
motilidad *nf* motility.
motín *nm* **1** *(levantamiento)* riot, uprising. **2** *(de tropas)* mutiny.
motivación *nf* motivation, motive.
motivar *vt* **1** *(causar)* to cause, give rise to. **2** *(estimular)* to motivate.
motivo *nm* **1** motive, reason, cause, grounds *pl.* **2** *(de dibujo, música)* motif, leitmotif.
moto *nf fam (motocicleta)* motorbike.
motocarro *nm* three-wheeled van.
motocicleta *nf* motorcycle, motorbike.
motociclismo *nm* motorcycling.
motociclista *nm o nf* motorcyclist.
motocross *nm* motocross.
motocultivo *nm* mechanised agriculture.
motonáutica *nf* speedboat racing, powerboat racing.
motonáutico,-a *adj* speedboat, powerboat.
motor,-ra *adj* **1** motive. **2** BIOL motor: **función motora** *motor function.*
▷ *nm* **motor** TÉC engine.
motora *nf* small motorboat.
motorismo *nm* motorcycling.
motorista *nm o nf* motorcyclist.
motorizado,-a *adj* motorized.
motorizar [4] *vt* to motorize.
▷ *vpr* **motorizarse** to get wheels, be mobile.
motosierra *nf* power saw.
motriz *adj* [Used only with feminine nouns.] motive.
mousse *nf* CULIN mousse.
mouton *nm* **1** *(piel)* sheepskin. **2** *(abrigo)* sheepskin coat.
movedizo,-a *adj* **1** *(fácil de mover)* easy to move. **2** *(inestable)* unstable.
mover [32] *vt* **1** *(gen)* to move; *(de un sitio a otro)* to move, shift. **2** *(hacer funcionar)* to drive, make work. **3** *(suscitar)* to incite, cause, provoke: **actuó movido por los celos** *he was driven by jealousy.*
▷ *vpr* **moverse 1** *(gen)* to move. **2** *fam (darse prisa)* to get a move on. **3** *fam (espabilarse)* to get a move on.
movible *adj* movable.
movida *nf* **1** *fam (animación)* action. **2** *fam (agitación)* to-do, stir, commotion.
movido,-a *adj* **1** *(día, temporada)* busy, hectic. **2** *(fiesta, concurso)* lively. **3** *(foto)* blurred.
móvil *adj* movable, mobile.
▷ *nm* **1** FÍS moving body. **2** *(motivo)* motive. **3** *(decoración, juguete)* mobile. **4** *(teléfono)* mobile (phone), cell phone.
movilidad *nf* mobility.
movilización *nf* mobilization.
movilizar [4] *vt* to mobilize.
movimiento *nm* **1** *(gen)* movement; *(técnicamente)* motion. **2** *(de gente, ideas)* activity; *(de vehículos)* traffic. **3** *(artístico, político)* movement. **4** *(financiero)* operations *pl.* **5** MÚS *(parte de la composición)* movement; *(velocidad de una composición)* tempo.
moviola® *nf (máquina)* editing projector, Moviola®.
moza *nf* **1** *(chica)* lass. **2** *arc* maid.
Mozambique *nm* Mozambique.
mozambiqueño,-a *adj* Mozambiquean.
▷ *nm & nf* Mozambiquean.
mozárabe *adj* Mozarab.
▷ *nm o nf* Mozarab.
mozo,-a *adj* **1** young. **2** *(soltero)* unmarried, single.
▷ *nm* **mozo 1** *(joven)* young man, lad. **2** *(camarero)* waiter. **3** *(de hotel)* bellboy. **4** *(de estación)* porter. **5** MIL conscript.
MP3 *abrev* (Moving Pictures Experts Group Audio Layer 3) MP3. ● **reproductor MP3** MP3 player.
mu *interj (mugido)* moo.
muaré *nm* moiré.
muchacho,-a *nm & nf (chico)* boy; *(chica)* girl.
▷ *nf (sirvienta)* maid, girl.
muchedumbre *nf* **1** *(de personas)* crowd. **2** *(de cosas)* pile.
mucho,-a *adj* **1** *(singular - en afirmativas)* a lot of; *(- en negativas, interrogativas)* a lot of, much: **hicieron mucho ruido** *they made a lot of noise;* **no tiene mucho dinero** *he hasn't got a lot of/much money.* **2** *(plural - en afirmativas)* a lot of, lots of; *(- en negativas, interrogativas)* a lot of, many: **¿tienes muchos libros?** *have you got a lot of/many books?* **3** *(demasiado - singular)* too much; *(- plural)* too many.
▷ *pron (singular)* a lot, much; *(plural)* a lot, many: **no me queda mucho por hacer** *I haven't got much left to do.*
▷ *adv* **1** *(de cantidad)* a lot, much: **mucho mejor/peor** *much better/worse.* **2** *(de tiempo)*: **mucho antes/después** *much earlier/later;* **3** *(de frecuencia)* often: **no vienen mucho por aquí** *they don't come here often.* ■ **como mucho** at the most: **te pagarán como mucho treinta euros** *they'll pay you thirty euros at the most.*
mucosa *nf* mucous membrane.
mucosidad *nf* mucus.
mucoso,-a *adj* mucous.
muda *nf (de ropa)* change of clothes, *particularly underwear.*
mudable *adj* **1** changeable. **2** *(carácter)* fickle.

mudanza *nf* 1 *(de residencia)* moving. 2 *(cambio)* change.
mudar *vt* 1 to change, alter. 2 *(plumas)* to moult (US molt). 3 *(voz)* to break: **le está mudando la voz** *his voice is breaking.* 4 *(piel)* to shed.
▷ *vpr* **mudarse** 1 to change. 2 *(de residencia)* to move.
mudez *nf* dumbness, muteness.
mudo,-a *adj* 1 *(por defecto)* dumb; *(por voluntad)* silent, quiet. 2 CINE silent. 3 *(vocal, consonante)* mute.
mueble *nm* piece of furniture.
▷ *adj* movable.
▷ *nm pl* **muebles** furniture *sing.*
mueca *nf* 1 *(de burla)* mocking gesture, face. 2 *(de dolor)* grimace.
muela *nf (diente)* tooth, molar.
muelle *nm* 1*(elástico)* spring. 2 MAR dock, wharf; *(malecón)* pier, jetty.
muérdago *nm* mistletoe.
muerdo *nm fam* bite.
muermo *nm fam* drag, pain, bore.
muerte *nf* 1 death. 2 *(asesinato)* murder.
muerto,-a *adj* 1 *(sin vida)* dead; *(sin actividad)* lifeless. 2 *fam (cansado)* tired, worn out.
▷ *nm & nf* 1 dead person; *(cadáver)* corpse. 2 *(víctima)* victim.
▷ *nm* **muerto** *fam* drag, bore.
muesca *nf* 1 *(corte)* nick, notch. 2 *(concavidad)* mortise, mortice.
muesli *nm* muesli.
muestra *nf* 1*(ejemplar)* sample. 2 *(modelo)* pattern. 3 *(señal)* proof, sign: **a mitad de la carrera ya daba muestras de cansancio** *he was showing signs of tiredness halfway through the race.* 4 *(exposición)* show, display.
muestrario *nm* collection of samples.
muestreo *nm (gen)* sampling.
mugido *nm* 1 *(de vaca - uno)* moo; *(- varios)* mooing. 2 *(de toro - uno)* bellow; *(- varios)* bellowing.
mugir [6] *vi* 1 *(vaca)* to moo. 2 *(toro)* to bellow.
mugre *nf* grime, filth.
mugriento,-a *adj* grimy, filthy.
muguete *nm* lily of the valley.
mujer *nf* 1 woman. 2 *(esposa)* wife.
mujeriego,-a *adj pey* fond of the ladies.
mujerona *nf fam* big woman.
mújol *nm* grey mullet.
muladar *nm* dump.
mulato,-a *adj* mulatto.
▷ *nm & nf* mulatto.
mulero *nm* muleteer.
muleta *nf* 1 *(para andar)* crutch. 2 *fig (apoyo)* prop, support. 3 *(en toros)* muleta *red cape.*
muletilla *nf* 1 *(bastón)* cross-handled cane. 2 *(frase repetida)* pet phrase; *(- de persona famosa)* catch phrase; *(palabra)* pet word.
muletón *nm* flannelette.
mulillas *nf pl* team *sing* of mules *(which drag the dead bull from the ring).*
mullido,-a *adj* soft, springy
mullir [41] *vt* 1 *(lana)* to soften; *(almohada, colchón)* to fluff up. 2 *(tierra)* to break up.
mulo,-a *nm & nf (macho)* mule; *(hembra)* she-mule. ■ **estar hecho,-a un/una mulo,-a** to be as strong as an ox. ■ **ser más terco,-a que una mula** to be as stubborn as a mule.
multa *nf (gen)* fine; *(de tráfico)* ticket: **me pusieron una multa por aparcar en la acera** *I got a ticket for parking on the pavement (US sidewalk).* ■ **poner una multa a ALGN** to fine SB, give SB a fine.
multar *vt* to fine: **¿cuánto te multaron?** *how much did they fine you?*
multiacceso *nm* multiaccess.
multicines *nm pl* multiplex *sing,* multi-screen cinema *sing.*1
multicolor *adj* multicoloured, US multicolored.
multicopiar *vt* to duplicate.
multicopista *nf* duplicator.
multicultural *adj* multicultural.
multidimensional *adj* multidimensional.
multidireccional *adj* multidirectional.
multidisciplinar *adj* multidisciplinary.
multifacético,-a *adj* multifaceted.
multiforme *adj* multiform.
multigrado *adj* multigrade.
multilateral *adj* multilateral.
multimedia *adj* multimedia.
▷ *nf* multimedia.
multimillonario,-a *adj (de libras)* multimillion-pound; *(de dólares)* multimillion-dollar: **un contrato multimillonario** *a multimillion-dollar contract.*
▷ *nm & nf* multimillionaire.
multinacional *adj* multinational.
▷ *nf* multinational.
multípara *nf* multiparous.
múltiple *adj* 1 multiple: **un efecto múltiple** *a multiple effect;* **sistema múltiple** *multiple system.* 2 *(muchos)* many, a number of, numerous: **opiniones múltiples** *a number of opinions.*
multiplicable *adj* multipliable.
multiplicación *nf* multiplication.
multiplicador,-ra *adj* multiplying.
▷ *nm* **multiplicador** multiplier.
multiplicar [1] *vt* to multiply (**por**, by).
▷ *vpr* **multiplicarse** 1 *(reproducirse)* to multiply. 2 *fig (atender a todo)* to be everywhere at the same time.
multiplicidad *nf* multiplicity.
múltiplo *adj* multiple.
▷ *nm* multiple.
multipropiedad *nf* time-share.
multirracial *adj* multiracial.
multirriesgo *adj* fully comprehensive.
multitud *nf* 1 *(de personas)* crowd. 2 *(de cosas, ideas)* multitude. ● **baño de multitud** walkabout.
multitudinario,-a *adj* multitudinous.
multiuso *adj* multipurpose.
mundanal *adj* of the world, mundane. ■ **huir del mundanal ruido** to get away from it all.
mundano,-a *adj* of the world, mundane.
mundial *adj* worldwide, world.
▷ *nm* world championship. ■ **de fama mundial** world-famous. ● **mundial de fútbol** World Cup.
mundialmente *adv* worldwide, all over the world. ■ **mundialmente conocido,-a** world-famous.
mundillo *nm* world, circles *pl*: **el mundillo teatral** *theatrical circles.*

mundo *nm* 1 world: ha dado la vuelta al mundo dos veces *he's been around the world twice;* vive aislado en su propio mundo *he's isolated himself in his own little world;* el mundo del cine *the cinema, the world of cinema.* 2 *fig (abismo)* vast difference: entre su forma de vivir y la mía hay un mundo *our ways of life are worlds apart.* 3 *(baúl)* trunk. ■ **caérsele a ALGN el mundo encima** to see one's world turned upside down. | **desde que el mundo es mundo** since the beginning of time. | **el mundo es un pañuelo** it's a small world. | **hacer un mundo de ALGO** to make a big fuss over STH. | **por nada del mundo** not for all the world. | **ser una mujer/un hombre de mundo** to be a woman/man of the world. | **tener mundo** to know the ways of the world. | **venir al mundo** to come into the world. | **el fin del mundo** the end of the world. ● **el Nuevo Mundo** the New World. | **el Tercer Mundo** the Third World.

mundología *nf fam* worldliness. ■ **tener mundología** 1 *(tener experiencia)* to know the ways of the world. 2 *(haber viajado)* to have travelled (US traveled) the world, be a seasoned traveller (US traveler).

munición *nf* ammunition, munitions *pl.*

municipal *adj (gobierno)* town, municipal; *(instalaciones)* council.
▷ *nm o nf (hombre)* policeman; *(mujer)* policewoman.
▷ *nf pl* **las municipales** local elections.

municipio *nm* 1 municipality. 2 *(ayuntamiento)* town council.

muñeca *nf* 1 ANAT wrist. 2 *(juguete)* doll. ● **muñeca de trapo** rag doll.

muñeco *nm* 1 *(juguete)* doll. 2 *fig (títere)* puppet: un muñeco en manos del destino *a puppet in the hands of fate.* ● **muñeco de nieve** snowman. | **muñeco de trapo** rag doll.

muñequera *nf* wristband.

muñir *vt (amañar)* to fix.

muñón *nm* ANAT stump.

mural *adj* mural.
▷ *nm* mural.

muralla *nf* city wall.

murciélago *nm* bat.

murga *nf fam* nuisance. ■ **dar la murga** *fam* to be a pain in the neck.

murmullante *adj* babbling.

murmullo *nm (susurro)* whisper, whispering; *(voz baja)* murmur, murmuring; *(de arroyo)* babbling, burbling; *(de hojas)* rustle, rustling; *(del viento)* sighing, murmur.

murmuración *nf* gossip, backbiting.

murmurador,-ra *adj* gossipy.
▷ *nm & nf* gossip.

murmurar *vt (susurrar)* to murmur, whisper.
▷ *vi* 1 *(criticar)* to gossip. 2 *(persona - susurrar)* to whisper; *(- decir en voz baja)* to murmur; *(agua)* to murmur, babble; *(hojas)* to rustle; *(viento)* to sigh, murmur.

muro *nm* wall.

murria *nf* sadness, melancholy.

mus *nm card game in which players use signs to communicate.*

musa *nf* muse.
▷ *nf pl* **las musas** the Arts.

musaraña *nf* ZOOL shrew. ■ **estar pensando en las musarañas** to daydream.

musculación *nf* body-building.

muscular *adj* muscular.

musculatura *nf* muscles *pl*, musculature.

músculo *nm* muscle.

musculoso,-a *adj* muscular.

muselina *nf* muslin.

museo *nm* museum. ● **museo de arte** art museum | **museo de cera** wax museum.

musgo *nm* moss. ■ **cubierto,-a de musgo** mossy, moss-covered.

musgoso,-a *adj* mossy.

música *nf* music. ■ **irse con la música a otra parte** *fam* to clear off. ● **música ambiental** Muzak. | **música de fondo** background music. | **música clásica** classical music. | **música de cámara** chamber music.

musical *adj* musical.
▷ *nm* musical.

musicalidad *nf* musicality.

musicar *vt* to write the music for, set to music.

músico,-a *adj* musical: composición música *musical composition.*
▷ *nm & nf* musician. ● **instrumento músico** musical instrument.

musicología *nf* musicology.

musicólogo,-a *nm & nf* musicologist.

musiquilla *nf fam pey* tacky music.

musitar *vi (susurrar)* to whisper; *(hablar entre dientes)* to mumble, mutter.

muslo *nm* 1 thigh. 2 CULIN *(de ave)* drumstick.

mustiarse *vi* to wilt, wither.

mustio,-a *adj* 1 *(plantas)* withered, faded. 2 *(persona)* down, downcast, sad.

musulmán,-ana *adj* Muslim, Moslem.
▷ *nm & nf* Muslim, Moslem.

mutabilidad *nf* mutability, changeability.

mutable *adj* mutable.

mutación *nf* 1 change. 2 BIOL mutation.

mutante *adj* mutant.
▷ *nm o nf* mutant.

mutilación *nf* mutilation.

mutilado,-a *adj (persona)* crippled, disabled; *(objeto)* mutilated.
▷ *nm & nf* cripple. ● **mutilado de guerra** war cripple.

mutilar *vt (persona)* to cripple; *(objeto)* to mutilate.

mutis *nm* TEAT exit. ■ **hacer mutis** 1 *(salir)* to make OS scarce. 2 *(callar)* to say nothing. 3 *(en teatro)* to exit.

mutismo *nm* silence.

mutua *nf* mutual benefit society.

mutualidad *nf* 1 *(asociación)* mutual benefit society. 2 *(reciprocidad)* mutuality.

mutualista *adj* of a mutual benefit society.
▷ *nm o nf* member of a mutual benefit society.

mutuamente *adv* mutually: se quieren mutuamente *they love each other, they love one another.*

mutuo,-a *adj* mutual, reciprocal: por mutuo acuerdo *by mutual agreement.*

muy *adv* very: es muy difícil *it's very difficult;* se levantó muy temprano *he got up very early;* lo has hecho muy bien *you've done it very well.* ■ **muy de mañana** very early in the morning. | **por muy ...** no matter how ..., however ...: por muy astuto que sea no nos podrá engañar *now matter how crafty he is he won't be able to con us.*

N

N, n *nf (la letra)* N, n.
N *sím* (norte) north; *(símbolo)* N.
nabo *nm* 1 *(planta)* turnip. 2 *(raíz)* root vegetable. 3 *tabú* prick, cock.
nácar *nm* mother-of-pearl.
nacarado,-a *adj* mother-of-pearl, nacred.
nacer [42] *vi* 1 *(persona)* to be born; *(ave)* to hatch out; *(semilla, planta)* to sprout. 2 *(río)* to rise; *(agua)* to spring; *(camino)* to start, begin. 3 *(sol)* to rise. 4 *(pelo)* to start to grow: ya le ha nacido la barba *his beard has started to grow.* 5 *(idea, sentimiento)* to originate (de, from), spring (de, from), stem (de, from): el miedo nace de la ignorancia *fear stems from ignorance.* ■ al nacer at birth. ▮ nacer con suerte to be born under a lucky star.
nacido,-a *adj* born. ■ bien nacido,-a 1 *(de buena cuna)* of noble birth. 2 *(de buen corazón)* kind-hearted. ▮ mal nacido,-a despicable.
naciente *adj* 1 *(nuevo)* new. 2 *(creciente)* growing.
▷ *nm (este)* East.
nacimiento *nm* 1 birth. 2 *(de río)* source: vamos a visitar el nacimiento del río Segura *we're going to see the source of the river Segura.* 3 *fig* origin, beginning. 4 *(pesebre)* crib, Nativity scene. ■ de nacimiento from birth.
nación *nf* nation. ● Naciones Unidas United Nations.
nacional *adj* 1 national. 2 *(producto, mercado)* domestic. 3 *(vuelo)* domestic; *(noticias)* national.
nacionalidad *nf* nationality.
nacionalismo *nm* nationalism.
nacionalista *adj* nationalist.
▷ *nm o nf* nationalist.
nacionalización *nf* 1 *(de una persona)* naturalization. 2 *(de una empresa)* nationalization.
nacionalizar [4] *vt* 1 *(persona)* to naturalize. 2 *(empresa)* to nationalize.
▷ *vpr* nacionalizarse *(persona)* to become naturalized: nacionalizarse español/británico/etc *to take up Spanish/British/etc citizenship.*
nada *pron* nothing: no quiero nada *I don't want anything.*
▷ *adv* (not) at all: no me gusta nada *I don't like it at all.*
▷ *nf* nothingness. ■ de nada 1 *(no hay de qué)* don't mention it, think nothing of it, (US you're welcome). 2 *(insignificante)* insignificant: gracias, –de nada *thanks, –don't mention it;* es una tontería de nada *it's nothing much.* ▮ dentro de nada in a moment. ▮ nada más ... as soon as..., no sooner...
nadador,-ra *nm & nf* swimmer.
nadar *vi* to swim.
nadería *nf* trifle.
nadie *pron* nobody, not ... anybody: aquí no hay nadie *there's nobody here.*
nado ■ a nado swimming: cruzaron el río a nado *they swam across the river.*
nafta *nf* naphtha.
naftalina *nf* naphthalene. ● bola de naftalina mothball.
naif *adj* naïf, naive.
▷ *nm* naïf art.
nailon [Registered trademark.] *nm* nylon.
naipe *nm* playing card.
nalga *nf* buttock.
Namibia *nf* Namibia.
namibio,-a *adj* Namibian.
▷ *nm & nf* Namibian.
nana *nf* lullaby.
nanay *interj fam* no way!
napa *nf* nappa.
naranja *nf (fruto)* orange.
▷ *adj (color)* orange.
naranjada *nf* orangeade, orange drink.
naranjal *nm* orange grove.
naranjo *nm* orange tree.
narcisismo *nm* narcissism.
narcisista *adj* narcissistic.
▷ *nm o nf* narcissist.
narciso *nm* 1 *(flor)* daffodil, narcissus. 2 *(hombre)* narcissist.
narcótico,-a *adj* narcotic.
▷ *nm* narcótico *(medicamento)* narcotic; *(droga)* drug.
narcotraficante *adj* drug trafficking.
▷ *nm o nf* drug trafficker.
narcotráfico *nm* drug trafficking.
nardo *nm* nard, spikenard.
narigón,-ona *adj fam* big-nosed.
▷ *nm* narigón *fam* huge conk, big nose.
nariz *nf* 1 ANAT nose. 2 *fig (sentido)* sense of smell.
▷ *interj* ¡narices! *fam* not on your life!
▲ *pl* narices. ■ asomar las narices to nose about, nose around. ▮ estar hasta las narices de *fam* to be fed up (to the back teeth) with. ▮ meter las narices en ALGO to poke one's nose into STH.
narración *nf* 1 *(exposición)* narration, account. 2 *(historia)* story.
narrador,-ra *nm & nf* storyteller, narrator.
narrar *vt (gen)* to tell, relate, narrate; *(partido)* to commentate.
narrativa *nf (género)* fiction.
narval *nm* narwhal.
nasa *nf (aparejo)* keepnet; *(cesta)* creel.
nasal *adj* nasal.
▷ *nf (letra)* nasal.

nata *nf* 1 cream. 2 *(de leche hervida)* skin. • **nata montada** whipped cream.
natación *nf* swimming. • **natación sincronizada** synchronized swimming.
natal *adj* native. • **ciudad natal** home town. | **país natal** native country.
natalicio,-a *nm* **natalicio** birthday.
natalidad *nf* birth rate.
natillas *nf pl* custard *sing*.
natividad *nf* nativity.
nativo,-a *adj* native.
nato,-a *adj* born.
natural *adj* 1 *(no artificial)* natural. 2 *(fruta, flor)* fresh. 3 *(sin elaboración)* plain; *(sin alteración)* additive-free: **yogur natural** *plain yoghurt*. 4 *(espontáneo)* unaffected, natural: **en esta foto has quedado más natural** *you look more natural in this photo*. 5 *(lógico)* natural, to be expected.
▷ *nm* 1 *(temperamento)* nature, disposition: **es de natural irritable** *he is irritable by nature*. 2 *(nativo)* native, inhabitant. ■ **al natural** 1 *(en la realidad)* in real life. 2 CULIN in its own juice. | **ser natural de** to be a native of, come from.
naturaleza *nf* 1 nature. 2 *(temperamento)* nature, character. 3 *(complexión)* physical constitution. 4 *(clase, tipo)* nature, kind. ■ **por naturaleza** by nature.
naturalidad *nf* 1 *(sencillez)* naturalness. 2 *(espontaneidad)* ease, spontaneity.
naturalismo *nm* naturalism.
naturalista *adj* naturalist.
▷ *nm o nf* naturalist.
naturalizar [4] *vt* to naturalize.
▷ *vpr* **naturalizarse** to become naturalized: **se ha naturalizado español** *he has taken up Spanish citizenship*.
naturista *adj* naturist.
▷ *nm o nf* naturist.
naturopatía *nf* naturopathy.
naufragar [7] *vi* 1 *(barco)* to sink, be wrecked; *(persona)* to be shipwrecked. 2 *fig* to fail.
naufragio *nm* 1 shipwreck. 2 *fig* failure.
náufrago,-a *adj* wrecked, shipwrecked.
▷ *nm & nf* shipwrecked person, castaway.
Nauru *nm* Nauru.
nauruano,-a *adj* Nauruan.
▷ *nm & nf* Nauruan.
náusea [Often used in plural with the same meaning.] *nf* 1 nausea, sickness. 2 *fig (repugnancia)* repulsion.
nauseabundo,-a *adj* nauseating, sickening.
náutica *nf* navigation, seamanship.
náutico,-a *adj* nautical. • **deportes náuticos** water sports.
navaja *nf* 1 *(cuchillo)* penknife, pocketknife. 2 *(molusco)* razor-shell.
naval *adj* naval.
nave *nf* 1 *(náutica)* ship, vessel. 2 *(espacial)* spaceship, spacecraft. 3 ARQUIT *(central)* nave; *(lateral)* aisle. 4 *(almacén)* industrial warehouse; *(fábrica)* plant. ■ **quemar las naves** to burn one's boats, burn one's bridges. • **nave espacial** spaceship.
navegable *adj* 1 *(río)* navigable. 2 *(barco)* seaworthy.
navegación *nf* 1 *(arte)* navigation. 2 *(tráfico)* shipping. 3 *(viaje por mar)* sea journey, voyage.
navegador *nm (de internet)* browser.
navegante *nm o nf* navigator, seafarer.
navegar [7] *vi* 1 *(persona)* to sail, navigate. 2 *(barco)* to sail. 3 *(avión)* to fly.
Navidad *nf* Christmas. ■ **felicitar las Navidades a** ALGN to wish SB a merry Christmas.
navideño,-a *adj* Christmas.
naviera *nf (empresa)* shipping company.
navío *nm* vessel, ship.
nazi *adj* Nazi.
▷ *nm o nf* Nazi.
nazismo *nm* Nazism.
NE *sím* **(nordeste)** northeast; *(símbolo)* NE.
Neanderthal *adj* Neanderthal.
neblina *nf* mist.
neblinoso,-a *adj* misty.
nebulizador *nm* nebulizer.
nebulosa *nf* nebula.
nebulosidad *nf* nebulosity.
nebuloso,-a *adj* 1 cloudy, hazy. 2 *fig* vague, nebulous.
necedad *nf* 1 *(ignorancia)* stupidity, foolishness. 2 *(acción)* stupid thing to do; *(comentario)* stupid thing to say.
necesario,-a *adj* necessary. ■ **si fuera necesario** if need be, if necessary.
neceser *nm* 1 *(bolsa de aseo)* toilet bag. 2 *(de maquillaje)* make-up bag, make-up kit. 3 *(de viaje)* vanity case. 4 *(de costura)* sewing kit.
necesidad *nf* 1 necessity, need. 2 *(hambre)* hunger. 3 *(pobreza)* poverty, want. ■ **hacer sus necesidades** *fam* to relieve OS. | **pasar necesidades** to be in need, suffer hardship.
necesitado,-a *adj* needy, poor.
necesitar *vt* to need. ■ **«Se necesita piso»** «Flat (US Apartment) wanted».
necio,-a *adj* stupid.
nécora *nf* fiddler crab.
necrología *nf* 1 *(biografía)* obituary. 2 *(lista)* obituaries *pl*.
necrológico,-a *adj* obituary, necrological.
▷ *nf pl* **necrológicas** *(sección prensa)* obituaries *pl*.
necrópolis *nf inv* necropolis.
necrosis *nf inv* necrosis.
néctar *nm* nectar.
nectarina *nf* nectarine.
neerlandés,-esa *adj* Dutch.
▷ *nm & nf* 1 *(persona - hombre)* Dutchman; *(- mujer)* Dutch woman. 2 *(idioma)* Dutch.
nefasto,-a *adj* 1 *(desgraciado)* unlucky, ill-fated, bad. 2 *(perjudicial)* harmful, fatal.
nefrítico,-a *adj* nephritic. • **cólico nefrítico** nephrocolic.
negación *nf* 1 *(de un ideal, derecho)* negation. 2 *(de una acusación)* denial. 3 *(negativa)* refusal. 4 *(en gramática)* negative.
negado,-a *adj (inepto)* hopeless, useless.
negar [48] *vt* 1 *(rechazar)* to deny. 2 *(no conceder)* to refuse.
▷ *vpr* **negarse** to refuse (**a**, to): **se negó a devolverme el dinero** *he refused to give me my money back*.

negativa *nf (negación)* negative answer; *(de una acusación)* denial; *(rechazo)* refusal.
negativo,-a *adj* negative: **su respuesta ha sido negativa** *his answer was no.*
▷ *nm* **negativo** *(en fotografía)* negative.
negligencia *nf* negligence, carelessness.
negligente *adj* negligent.
▷ *nm o nf* negligent person.
negociable *adj* negotiable.
negociación *nf* negotiation. ● **negociación colectiva** collective bargaining.
negociado *nm (sección)* department.
negociador,-ra *adj* negotiating.
▷ *nm & nf* negotiator.
negociante *nm o nf* 1 dealer, merchant. 2 *fam* money-grubber.
negociar [12] *vi (comerciar)* to do business, deal (**con**, in): **negocian con trigo** *they deal in wheat.*
▷ *vt* POL to negotiate.
negocio *nm* 1 *(actividad)* business. 2 *(gestión)* deal, transaction. 3 *(asunto)* affair. 4 *(local)* shop, US store. ■ **hacer negocio** to make a profit.
negra *nf* MÚS crotchet, US quarter note.
negrita *nf* bold, bold type.
negro,-a *adj* 1 *(gen)* black. 2 *(oscuro)* dark. 3 *(poco favorable)* awful, terrible: **llevamos una semana negra** *we've had a terrible week.* 4 *(cine, novela)* detective
▷ *nm & nf (hombre)* black (man); *(mujer)* black (woman).
▷ *nm* **negro** 1 *(color)* black. 2 *(escritor)* ghostwriter. ■ **estar negro,-a** 1 *fam (enfadado)* to be cross. 2 *(bronceado)* to be really brown, be really tanned.
negrura *nf* blackness.
negruzco,-a *adj* blackish.
nene,-a *nm & nf* 1 *(niño)* baby boy; *(niña)* baby girl. 2 *(apelativo)* baby.
nenúfar *nm* water lily.
neoclasicismo *nm* neoclassicism.
neoclásico,-a *adj* neoclassical.
▷ *nm & nf* neoclassicist.
neocolonialismo *nm* neocolonialism.
neófito,-a *nm & nf* neophyte.
neolítico,-a *adj* neolithic.
▷ *nm* **neolítico** Neolithic.
neologismo *nm* neologism.
neón *nm* neon.
neonatal *adj* neonatal.
neonazi *adj* neonazi.
▷ *nm o nf* neonazi.
neorrealismo *nm* neorealism.
neozelandés,-esa *adj* of New Zealand, from New Zealand.
▷ *nm & nf* New Zealander.
Nepal *nm* Nepal.
nepalés,-esa *adj* Nepalese, Nepali.
▷ *nm & nf (persona)* Nepalese, Nepali.
▷ *nm* **nepalés** *(idioma)* Nepalese, Nepali.
nepotismo *nm* nepotism.
nereida *nf* nereid.
nervadura *nf* 1 ARQUIT ribs *pl.* 2 BOT nervures *pl.*
nervio *nm* 1 ANAT nerve. 2 BOT nervure, vein. 3 *(tendón de la carne)* sinew. 4 ARQUIT rib. 5 *(de un libro)* rib. 6 *(vigor)* energy, vitality.
▷ *nm pl* **nervios** nerves. ■ **ponerle los nervios de punta a** ALGN to get on SB's nerves. ■ **tener los nervios de punta** to be on edge.
nerviosismo *nm* 1 *(excitación)* nervousness. 2 *(inquietud)* disquiet.
nervioso,-a *adj* 1 *(gen)* nervous. 2 *(excitable)* excitable. 3 *(intranquilo)* nervous, uptight, edgy. ■ **ponerse nervioso,-a** 1 *(intranquilizarse)* to get nervous. 2 *(impacientarse)* to get all excited.
neto,-a *adj* 1 *(peso, cantidad)* net. 2 *(claro)* neat, clear.
neumático,-a *nm* **neumático** tyre (US tire).
neumonía *nf* pneumonia.
neura *nf fam* obsession.
▷ *adj fam* neurotic.
▷ *nm o nf* neurotic.
neurálgico,-a *adj* 1 MED neuralgic. 2 *fig (fundamental)* key, main.
neurocirujano,-a *nm & nf* neurosurgeon.
neurología *nf* neurology.
neurólogo,-a *nm & nf* neurologist.
neurona *nf* neuron, neurone.
neurosis *nf inv* neurosis.
neurótico,-a *adj* neurotic.
▷ *nm & nf* neurotic.
neutral *adj* neutral.
neutralidad *nf* neutrality.
neutralizar *vt* to neutralize.
neutro,-a *adj* 1 neutral. 2 LING neuter.
▷ *nm* **neutro** neuter.
neutrón *nm* neutron.
nevada *nf* snowfall.
nevado,-a *adj (gen)* covered with snow; *(montaña)* snow-capped.
nevar [27] *vi* [used only in the 3rd person; it does not take a subject.] to snow.
nevera *nf* 1 *(eléctrica)* fridge, refrigerator. 2 *(para excursiones)* cool box. 3 *fam fig* freezing cold place: **esta casa es una nevera** *this house is freezing.*
nevero *nm* ice field.
newton *nm* newton.
▲ *pl* **newtons.**
nexo *nm* 1 *(unión)* connection, link. 2 LING connective.
ni *conj* 1 neither, nor. 2 *(ni siquiera)* not even: **no lo quiero ni regalado** *I wouldn't want it even if they were giving it away.* ■ **¡ni hablar!** no way!
Nicaragua *nf* Nicaragua.
nicaragüense *adj* Nicaraguan.
▷ *nm o nf* Nicaraguan.
nicho *nm* niche.
nicotina *nf* nicotine.
nidada *nf (huevos)* clutch; *(polluelos)* brood.
nidificar *vi* to nest.
nido *nm* nest.
niebla *nf* 1 *(nubes)* fog. 2 *fig* mist.
nieto,-a *nm & nf* grandchild; *(niño)* grandson; *(niña)* granddaughter.
nieve *nf* snow.
NIF *abrev* (**Número de Identificación Fiscal**) *tax identification number.*
Nigeria *nf* Nigeria.
nigeriano,-a *adj* Nigerian.
▷ *nm & nf* Nigerian.

nigromancia *nf* necromancy.
nihilismo *nm* nihilism.
nihilista *adj* nihilistic.
▷ *nm o nf* nihilist.
nilón® *nm* nylon®.
nimbo *nm* nimbus.
nimiedad *nf* **1** *(cualidad)* smallness, triviality. **2** *(cosa nimia)* trifle.
nimio,-a *adj* insignificant, trivial.
ninfa *nf* nymph.
ningún *adj* [Used before a masculine singular noun.] ⟶ **ninguno,-a.** ■ **de ningún modo** in no way.
ninguno,-a *adj* no, not any: **aquí no veo ningún bolígrafo azul** *I can't see any blue ballpoint pen here.*
▷ *pron* **1** *(persona)* nobody, no one: **ninguno lo vio** *no one saw it.* **2** *(objeto)* not any, none: **ninguno me gusta** *I don't like any of them.* ■ **en ninguna parte** nowhere. ‖ **ninguna cosa** nothing. ‖ **ninguno,-a de nosotros** *(ellos etc)* none of us *(them etc)*.

See also **ningún**.

niñato,-a *nm & nf fam* brat.
niñera *nf* nanny.
niñería *nf* **1** *(chiquillada)* childishness, childish behaviour (US behavior). **2** *(nimiedad)* trifle.
niñez *nf (de una persona)* childhood; *(de una idea, proyecto)* infancy.
niño,-a *nm & nf* **1** *(gen)* child; *(chico)* boy, little boy; *(chica)* girl, little girl. **2** *(bebé)* baby. **3** *pey (en comportamiento)* baby; *(en experiencia)* child: **no seas niño y acábate la cena** *don't be such a baby, eat up your dinner!*
▷ *nm pl* **niños** children, kids. ■ **de niño,-a** as a child. ● **niño,-a probeta** test-tube baby.
nipón,-ona *adj* Nipponese.
▷ *nm & nf* Nipponese.
níquel *nm* nickel.
niquelado,-a *adj* nickel-plated.
niquelar *vt* to nickel.
niqui *nm* T-shirt.
nirvana *nm* nirvana.
níscalo *nm* milk cap.
níspero *nm* **1** *(fruto)* medlar. **2** *(árbol)* medlar tree.
nitidez *nf* **1** *(transparencia)* clearness, transparency. **2** *(claridad)* accuracy, precision. **3** *(de imagen)* sharpness.
nítido,-a *adj* **1** *(transparente)* clear, transparent. **2** *(claro)* accurate, precise. **3** *(imagen)* sharp.
nitrato *nm* nitrate.
nítrico,-a *adj* nitric.
nitrito *nm* nitrite.
nitrógeno *nm* nitrogen.
nitroglicerina *nf* nitroglycerine.
nitroso,-a *adj* nitrous.
nivel *nm* **1** *(altura)* level, height. **2** *(categoría)* level, standard, degree: **mis alumnos tienen muy buen nivel de inglés** *my students' English is very good.* **3** *(instrumento)* level. ● **nivel del mar** sea level.
nivelación *nf* **1** *(de un terreno)* levelling (US leveling). **2** *(de diferencias, posturas)* reconciliation.
nivelado,-a *adj* level.
nivelar *vt* **1** *(gen)* to level out, level off. **2** *(diferencias, etc)* to reconcile.
níveo,-a *adj lit* snow-white.
NNE *sím* **(nordnoreste)** north-northeast; *(abreviatura)* NNE.
NNO *sím* **(nordnoroeste)** north-northwest; *(abreviatura)* NNW.
no *adv* **1** no, not. **2** *(en frases negativas)* not: **no lo compres** *don't buy it.* **3** *(en frases interrogativas)*: **¿a que no me pillas?** *I bet you can't catch me.* **4** *(en comparativas)*: **mejor gastarse el dinero ahora que no guardarlo para después** *it's better to spend the money now than to save it for later.* **5** *(prefijo)* non-: **la no violencia** *nonviolence.*
▷ *nm* no: **un no rotundo** *a definite no.*
NO *sím* **(nordoeste)** northwest; *(símbolo)* NW.
nobel *nm* Nobel prize.
nobiliario,-a *adj* noble.
noble *adj (gen)* noble; *(madera)* fine.
▷ *nm o nf (hombre)* nobleman; *(mujer)* noblewoman.
▷ *nm pl* **los nobles** the nobility *sing.*
nobleza *nf* **1** *(cualidad)* nobility, honesty, uprightness. **2** *(los nobles)* nobility.
noche *nf (gen)* night; *(al atardecer)* evening. ■ **ayer (por la) noche** last night. ‖ **buenas noches 1** *(saludo)* good evening. **2** *(despedida)* good night. ‖ **hacer noche en** to spend the night in. ‖ **hacer turno de noche** to work nights. ‖ **por la noche** at night, after dark. ● **media noche** midnight.
Nochebuena *nf* Christmas Eve.
Nochevieja *nf* New Year's Eve.
noción *nf* notion, idea.
▷ *nf pl* **nociones** smattering *sing*, basic knowledge *sing.*
nocividad *nf* noxiousness.
nocivo,-a *adj* noxious, harmful.
noctámbulo,-a *adj* nocturnal.
▷ *nm & nf fam (trasnochador)* night owl, US night hawk.
nocturno,-a *adj* **1** *(gen)* nocturnal; *(vida)* night; *(clase)* evening. **2** ZOOL nocturnal.
nodo *nm* node.
nodriza *nf* **1** *(mujer)* wet nurse. **2** *(vehículo)* supply.
nodular *adj* nodular, nodulated.
nódulo *nm* nodule.
nogal *nm* walnut tree.
nogalina *nf* walnut dye.
nómada *adj* nomadic.
▷ *nm o nf* nomad.
nomadismo *nm* nomadism.
nombrado,-a *adj* well-known.
nombramiento *nm* appointment.
nombrar *vt* **1** *(dar nombre, mencionar)* to name. **2** *(llamar)* to call. **3** *(designar)* to name, appoint.
nombre *nm* **1** name. **2** LING noun. **3** *(fama)* reputation: **es un cirujano de nombre** *he is a well-known surgeon.* ■ **en nombre de** on behalf of. ● **nombre de pila** first name. ‖ **nombre y apellidos** full name *sing.*
nomenclatura *nf* nomenclature.
nomeolvides *nm inv* **1** *(flor)* forget-me-not. **2** *(pulsera)* identity bracelet.
nómina *nf* **1** *(plantilla)* payroll. **2** *(sueldo)* pay cheque (US check); *(papel)* pay slip.
nominación *nf* nomination.
nominal *adj* nominal.
nominalismo *nm* nominalism.
nominalista *adj* nominalist, nominalistic.
▷ *nm o nf* nominalist.

nominalizar *vt* to substantivize.
nominalmente *adv* nominally.
nominar *vt* to nominate.
nominativo,-a *adj* **1** *(cheque)* personal. **2** LING nominative.
▷ *nm* **nominativo** nominative.
non *nm* odd number. ■ **pares y nones** odds and evens.
nonagenario,-a *adj* nonagenarian.
▷ *nm & nf* nonagenarian.
nonagésimo,-a *nm & nf* ninetieth. *adj* ninetieth.
nones *interj* no way!: **me ha dicho que nones** *the answer is no.*
noquear *vt* to knock out.
norcoreano,-a *adj* North Korean.
▷ *nm & nf* North Korean.
nordeste *nm* **1** northeast. **2** *(viento)* northeasterly.
nórdico,-a *adj* **1** *(del norte)* northern. **2** *(de los países del norte)* Nordic.
▷ *nm & nf (persona)* Scandinavian.
▷ *nm* **nórdico** *(idioma)* Norse.
noreste *nm* → **nordeste**.
noria *nf* **1** *(para agua)* water wheel. **2** *(de feria)* big wheel.
norirlandés,-esa *adj* Northern Irish.
▷ *nm & nf (hombre)* Northern Irishman; *(mujer)* Northern Irishwoman
norma *nf* norm, rule.
normal *adj (corriente, habitual)* normal, usual, average; *(lógico)* normal, natural.
▷ *nf* **1** *(escuela)* teacher training college. **2** *(gasolina)* two-star petrol, US regular gasoline. **3** *(en geometría)* perpendicular, normal.
normalidad *nf* normality. ■ **con normalidad** normally, as normal.
normalización *nf* normalization.
normalizar [4] *vt* to normalize, restore to normal.
normativa *nf* rules *pl*, regulations *pl*.
normativo,-a *adj* normative.
noroeste *nm* **1** northwest. **2** *(viento)* northwesterly.
norte *nm* **1** north: **la estrella polar señala el norte** *the Pole Star shows where north is* **2** *(viento)* northerly wind. **3** *fig (dirección, sentido)* direction; *(objetivo)* aim. ● **norte magnético** magnetic North.
Norteamérica *nf (América del Norte)* North America; *(Estados Unidos)* America.
norteamericano,-a *adj (de América del Norte)* North American; *(de Estados Unidos)* American.
▷ *nm & nf (de América del Norte)* North American; *(de Estados Unidos)* American.
Noruega *nf* Norway.
noruego,-a *adj* Norwegian.
▷ *nm & nf (persona)* Norwegian.
▷ *nm* **noruego** *(idioma)* Norwegian.
nos *pron* **1** *(complemento)* us: **nos dijo que no nos moviéramos** *he told us not to move.* **2** *(uso reflexivo)* ourselves: **nos lavamos** *we wash ourselves.* **3** *(uso recíproco)* each other: **nos vemos mucho** *we see each other often.*
nosotros,-as *pron* **1** *(sujeto)* we: **nosotros no fuimos** *we didn't go.* **2** *(complemento)* us: **con nosotros,-as** *with us.*
nostalgia *nf* **1** nostalgia. **2** *(añoranza)* homesickness.
nostálgico,-a *adj* nostalgic.
nota *nf* **1** *(anotación)* note. **2** *(calificación)* mark, grade; *(calificación alta)* high mark: **si quieres nota tendrás que presentarte al oral** *if you want a higher mark you'll have to go for an oral exam.* **3** *(cuenta)* bill: **¿nos trae la nota por favor?** *could you bring us the bill please?* **4** MÚS note.
▷ *nm argot (tipo)* bloke. ■ **dar la nota** *fam* to draw attention to OS. ■ **sacar buenas notas** to get good marks.
notable *adj (apreciable)* noticeable; *(considerable, marcado)* considerable, remarkable.
▷ *nm* **1** *(persona)* dignitary, notable. **2** *(calificación) mark equivalent to between 70% and 80% in the Spanish marking system.*
notación *nf* notation.
notar *vt* **1** *(percibir)* to notice. **2** *(sentir)* to feel: **noto un poco de calor** *I feel a bit hot.*
▷ *vpr* **notarse 1** *(percibirse)* to be noticeable, be evident, show: **apenas se le nota la cicatriz** *you can hardly see his scar* **2** *(sentirse)* to feel. ■ **se nota que ...** one can see that ...
notario,-a *nm & nf* notary, notary public.
noticia *nf* **1** *(información)* news *pl*: **una noticia** *a piece of news.* **2** *(conocimiento)* idea: **no tenía noticia de que hubieran quebrado** *I had no idea they had gone bankrupt.*
▷ *nf pl* **las noticias** the news.
noticiario *nm* news.
notición *nm fam* bombshell.
notificación *nf* notification. ● **notificación judicial** summons *sing*.
notificar [1] *vt* to notify, inform.
notoriedad *nf* **1** *(fama)* fame, prestige. **2** *(evidencia)* obviousness.
notorio,-a *adj* well-known.
novatada *nf (broma)* practical joke *(played on a new student, recruit, etc)*.
novato,-a *adj (persona)* inexperienced, green.
▷ *nm & nf* **1** *(principiante)* novice, beginner. **2** *(universidad)* fresher (US freshman).
novecientos,-as *adj* nine hundred; *(ordinal)* ninehundredth.
▷ *nm pl* **novecientos** nine hundred.

See also **seis**.

novedad *nf* **1** *(cualidad)* newness. **2** *(cosa nueva)* novelty. **3** *(cambio)* change, innovation. ■ **sin novedad** without incident.
novedoso,-a *adj* novel.
novel *adj (escritor, escultor)* novice.
novela *nf* **1** novel. **2** *(en TV, radio)* serial. ● **novela policíaca** detective story.
novelar *vt* to novelize, convert into a novel.
▷ *vi* to write novels.
novelesco,-a *adj* **1** *(de la novela)* fictional, novelistic. **2** *(de novela)* fiction-like.
novelista *nm o nf* novelist.
novena *nf* REL novena.
noveno,-a *adj* ninth.
▷ *nm & nf* ninth.

See also **sexto**.

noventa *adj* ninety.
▷ *nm* ninety.

See also **sesenta**.

novia *nf* 1 *(amiga)* girlfriend. 2 *(prometida)* fiancée; *(en boda)* bride.
noviazgo *nm* engagement.
novicio,-a *nm & nf* 1 *(principiante)* beginner. 2 REL novice.
noviembre *nm* November.
For examples of use, see **marzo**.
novilla *nf* heifer.
novillada *nf* 1 *(corrida)* bullfight with young bulls. 2 *(novillos)* herd of young bulls.
novillero,-a *nm & nf* 1 *(torero)* novice bullfighter. 2 *(estudiante)* truant.
novillo *nm* young bull. ■ **hacer novillos** *fam* to play truant, skip school, US play hooky.
novio *nm* 1 *(amigo)* boyfriend. 2 *(prometido)* fiancé; *(en boda)* bridegroom. ■ **ser novios** 1 *(salir juntos)* to be going out. 2 *(estar prometidos)* to be engaged.
nto. *abrev* (**neto**) net; *(abreviatura)* n.
nubarrón *nm* 1 *(nube)* storm cloud. 2 *fam fig* cloud on the horizon.
nube *nf* 1 cloud. 2 *fig (multitud - de personas)* swarm, crowd; *(- de insectos)* cloud. ■ **estar por las nubes** *(precio)* to be sky-high. | **estar en las nubes** to have one's head in the clouds.
núbil *adj* nubile.
nublado,-a *adj* cloudy, overcast.
▷ *nm* **nublado** storm cloud.
nubosidad *nf* cloudiness.
nuboso,-a *adj* cloudy.
nuca *nf* nape (of the neck).
nuclear *adj* nuclear.
núcleo *nm* 1 nucleus. 2 *(parte central)* core. 3 *(grupo de gente)* circle, group. ● **núcleo urbano** city centre (US center).
nudillo *nm* knuckle.
nudismo *nm* nudism.
nudo *nm* 1 knot. 2 *fig (vínculo)* link, tie. 3 *(de un argumento)* climax. 4 *(en madera)* knot. 5 *(unidad de velocidad)* knot.
nudoso,-a *adj (madera)* knotty, knobbly; *(manos, vara)* gnarled.
nuera *nf* daughter-in-law.
nuestro,-a *adj* our, of ours: **éste es nuestro colegio** *this is our school.*
▷ *pron* ours: **este libro es nuestro** *this book is ours.* ■ **la nuestra** *fam* our chance. | **lo nuestro** 1 *(relación)* our relationship, us. 2 *(asunto)* our business. 3 *(actividad)* our thing. | **los nuestros** *fam* our side *sing*, our people.
nueva *nf* tidings *pl*, news *sing*.
nueve *adj* nine; *(noveno)* ninth.
▷ *nm* nine.
See also **seis**.
nuevo,-a *adj* 1 new. 2 *(adicional)* further.
▷ *nm & nf* newcomer; *(principiante)* beginner; *(universidad)* fresher (US freshman). ■ **de nuevo** again.
nuez *nf* BOT walnut.
▲ *pl* **nueces**.
nulidad *nf* 1 *(ineptitud)* incompetence. 2 *(persona)* hopeless person. 3 JUR nullity.
nulo,-a *adj* 1 *(persona)* useless, totally inept. 2 *(sin valor)* null and void, invalid.
núm. *abrev* (**número**) number; *(abreviatura)* n.
numeración *nf* 1 *(proceso)* numbering. 2 *(conjunto)* numbers *pl*. 3 *(sistema)* numbers *pl*, numerals *pl*. ● **numeración arábiga** Arabic numerals *pl*. | **numeración decimal** decimal system. | **numeración romana** Roman numerals *pl*.
numerador *nm* numerator.
numeral *adj* numeral.
▷ *nm* numeral.
numerar *vt* to number.
▷ *vpr* **numerarse** MIL to number off. ■ **sin numerar** unnumbered.
numérico,-a *adj* numerical.
número *nm* 1 *(gen)* number. 2 *(de una publicación)* number, issue. 3 *(de zapatos)* size: **¿qué número calzas?** *what's your shoe size?, what size shoe do you take?* 4 *(de un espectáculo)* act. 5 *(de lotería)* lottery ticket number. 6 LING number. 7 *fam* scene. ■ **hacer números** to do the figures. | **montar un número** *fam* to make a scene. | **pedir número** to take a numbered ticket. | **ser el número uno** to be the number one. | **sin número** 1 *(edificio)* unnumbered. 2 *(en abundancia)* countless. ● **número arábigo** Arabic numeral. | **número de matrícula** registration number, US license number. | **número de serie** serial number. | **número entero** whole number. | **número fraccionario** fraction. | **número impar** odd number. | **número ordinal** ordinal number. | **número par** even number. | **número primo** prime number. | **número quebrado** fraction. | **número romano** Roman numeral.
numeroso,-a *adj* numerous: **son familia numerosa** *they're a large family.*
numismática *nf* numismatics.
numismático,-a *adj* numismatic.
nunca *adv* 1 never. 2 *(en interrogativa)* ever. ■ **más que nunca** more than ever. | **nunca jamás** never ever. | **nunca más** never again. |
nunciatura *nf* nunciature.
nuncio *nm* nuncio.
nupcial *adj (marcha, tarta)* wedding; *(misa)* nuptial; *(lecho)* marriage.
nupcias *nf pl fml* wedding *sing*, nuptials. ■ **casarse en segundas nupcias** to remarry, marry for the second time.
nurse *nf* nanny.
nutria *nf* otter.
nutrición *nf* nutrition.
nutrido,-a *adj* 1 *(alimentado)* nourished. 2 *fig (abundante)* large: **nutridos aplausos** *enthusiastic applause.*
nutriente *adj* nutrient.
▷ *nm* nutrient.
nutrir *vt* 1 *(alimentar)* to feed, nourish. 2 *fig* to encourage. 3 *(abastecer)* to supply (**de**, with).
▷ *vpr* **nutrirse** 1 *(alimentarse)* to receive nourishment (**de**, from). 2 *fig (abastecerse)* to draw (**de**, on).
nutritivo,-a *adj* nutritious, nourishing. ● **sustancia nutritiva** nutrient. | **valor nutritivo** nutritional value.

Ñ

Ñ, ñ *nf the fifteenth letter of the Spanish alphabet.*
ñandú *nm* AM rhea.
ñoñería *nf (tontería)* inanity, nonsense.
ñoño ,-a *adj* **1** *(soso)* insipid, dull. **2** *(tímido)* shy. **3** *(remilgado)* fussy. **4** *(poco seguro)* wet, drippy, wimpish: **no seas ñoño, no es más que un rasguño** *don't be such a wimp, it's no more than a scratch.* **5** AM old.
ñoqui *nm* gnocchi *pl.*
ñora *nf type of* red pepper.
ñu *nm* gnu.

O

O, o *nf (la letra)* O, o.

o *conj* **1** or: **¿té o café?** *tea or coffee?* **2** *(concesiva)* whether... or: **estudie o no, tiene que aprobar** *whether he studies or not, he has to pass.* ■ **o... o...** either... or...: **o vamos hoy o mañana** *we'll either go today or tomorrow.* ‖ **o sea que** so: **o sea que no vienes** *so you're not coming then.*

Often written «**ó**» between numbers.

O *sím* **(oeste)** west; *(símbolo)* W.

OAA *abrev* **(Organización para la Agricultura y la Alimentación)** Food and Agriculture Organization; *(abreviatura)* FAO.

oasis *nm inv* oasis.

obcecado,-a *adj* blind.

obcecar [1] *vt* to blind.

▷ *vpr* **obcecarse** to be obstinate.

obedecer [43] *vt (autoridad, regla, ley)* to obey: **este niño no obedece** *this child is disobedient.*

▷ *vi* **1** *(persona)* to obey. **2** *(responder)* to respond (**a**, to). **3** *(tener por causa)* to be due (**a**, to): **¿a qué obedece su visita?** *what is the reason for your visit?*

obediencia *nf* obedience.

obediente *adj* obedient.

obertura *nf* MÚS overture.

obesidad *nf* obesity.

obeso,-a *adj* obese.

obispo *nm* bishop.

objeción *nf* objection.

objetar *vt* to object: **no tengo nada que objetar** *I have no objections.*

objetividad *nf* objectivity.

objetivo,-a *adj* objective.

▷ *nm* **objetivo 1** *(fin)* aim, objective. **2** MIL target. **3** *(lente)* lens.

objeto *nm* **1** *(cosa)* object. **2** *(fin)* aim, purpose, object. **3** *(tema)* subject: **el objeto de esta charla es la acupuntura** *the subject of this talk is acupuncture.* ■ **con objeto de** in order to.

objetor,-ra *adj* objecting, dissenting.

▷ *nm & nf* objector. ● **objetor de conciencia** conscientious objector.

oblea *nf* wafer.

oblicuo,-a *adj* oblique.

obligación *nf* **1** *(deber)* duty, obligation. **2** FIN bond.

obligado,-a *adj (forzoso)* required; *(normal)* customary: **la Acrópolis es visita obligada** *visiting the Acropolis is a must.* ■ **estar obligado,-a a hacer ALGO** to be obliged to do STH.

obligar [7] *vt* to force, oblige, make. ■ **obligar a ALGN a hacer ALGO** to force SB to do STH, make SB do STH.

▷ *vpr* **obligarse** to undertake, promise.

obligatorio,-a *adj* compulsory, obligatory.

obnubilar *vt* **1** to cloud, blind. **2** *(fascinar)* to fascinate.

▷ *vpr* **obnubilarse 1** to become confused. **2** *(quedarse fascinado)* to be fascinated, be amazed.

oboe *nm* oboe.

obra *nf* **1** *(trabajo)* work. **2** LIT *(obras completas)* work; *(libro)* book. **3** *(construcción)* building site.

▷ *nf pl* **obras** *(en casa)* alterations, repairs; *(en carretera)* road works. ● **obra de arte** work of art. ‖ **obra de teatro** play.

obrar *vi* **1** *(proceder)* to act, behave: **obró de buena fe** *he acted in good faith.* **2** *(encontrarse)* to be: **la carta obra en mi poder** *the letter is in my hands.*

obrero,-a *adj* working.

▷ *nm & nf* worker, labourer.

obscenidad *nf* obscenity.

obsceno,-a *adj* obscene.

obscurantismo *nm* obscurantism.

obscurantista *adj* obscurantist.

▷ *nm o nf* obscurantist.

obscurecer [43] *vt* **1** *(ensombrecer)* to darken. **2** *fig (ofuscar)* to cloud, obscure.

▷ *vpr* **obscurecerse** *(día, tiempo)* to get cloudy.

obscuridad *nf* **1** darkness. **2** *fig* obscurity.

obscuro,-a *adj* **1** *(cielo, color)* dark. **2** *(idea, razonamiento)* obscure. **3** *(futuro, porvenir)* uncertain, gloomy. **4** *(intención)* dubious, unclear. ■ **a obscuras** in the dark.

obsequiar [12] *vt (regalar)* to give, offer.

obsequio *nm* gift, present.

observación *nf* **1** *(acción)* observation. **2** *(comentario)* observation, comment, remark.

observador,-ra *adj* observant.

▷ *nm & nf* observer.

observar *vt* **1** *(mirar)* to observe, watch. **2** *(notar)* to notice. **3** *(mostrar)* to display, show: **observa buen comportamiento** *he is well behaved.* **4** *(cumplir)* to observe, obey.

observatorio *nm* observatory. ● **observatorio meteorológico** weather station.

obsesión *nf* obsession.

obsesionar *vt* to obsess.

▷ *vpr* **obsesionarse** to get obsessed.

obseso,-a *nm & nf* maniac.

▷ *adj* obsessed.

obsidiana *nf* obsidian.

obsoleto,-a *adj* obsolete.

obstáculo *nm* **1** *(barrera)* obstacle. **2** *(inconveniente)* objection: **no vamos a avanzar si sigues poniendo obstáculos** *we won't get anywhere if you keep raising objections.* **3** *(valla)* fence, jump.

obstante *adv* **no obstante** nevertheless, however.

obstetricia *nf* obstetrics.

obstinado,-a *adj* obstinate, stubborn.

obstinarse *vpr* to persist (**en**, in), insist (**en**, on).

obstrucción *nf* obstruction.
obstruir [62] *vt* to obstruct, block.
▷ *vpr* **obstruirse** to get blocked up.
obtener [87] *vt (beca, resultados)* to get, obtain; *(premio)* to win; *(ganancias)* to make.
obturador *nm* **1** stopper. **2** *(de cámara fotográfica)* shutter.
obtuso,-a *adj* obtuse.
obviar *vt fml* to obviate, remove.
obvio,-a *adj* obvious.
oca *nf* goose. ● **el juego de la oca** ≈ snakes and ladders.
ocasión *nf* **1** *(momento)* occasion. **2** *(oportunidad)* opportunity, chance. **3** COM bargain. **4** *(motivo)* reason: **no me ha dado ocasión para enfadarme con él** *I have never had reason to get annoyed with him.*
ocasional *adj* **1** *(gen)* occasional. **2** *(trabajo)* temporary, casual. **3** *(encuentro)* chance. **4** *(ingreso)* irregular.
ocasionar *vt (causar)* to cause, bring about.
ocaso *nm* **1** *(anochecer)* sunset. **2** *fig (declive)* fall, decline. **3** *(occidente)* west.
occidental *adj* western, occidental.
occidente *nm* the West.
Oceanía *nf* Oceania.
océano [In poetry also written **oceano**.] *nm* ocean.
oceanografía *nf* oceanography.
ochenta *adj* eighty; *(octagésimo)* eightieth.
▷ *nm* eighty.

See also **sesenta**.

ocho *adj* eight; *(octavo)* eighth.
▷ *nm* eight.

See also **seis**.

ochocientos,-as *adj* eight hundred; *(ordinal)* eight hundredth.
▷ *nm & nf* eight hundred.
ocio *nm* **1** *(tiempo libre)* leisure. **2** *(desocupación)* idleness.
ocioso,-a *adj* **1** *(desocupado)* idle. **2** *(innecesario)* pointless.
ocre *adj* ochre.
▷ *nm* ochre.
octagonal *adj* octagonal.
octágono,-a *adj* octagonal.
▷ *nm* **octágono** octagon.
octano *nm* octane.
octava *nf (en música)* octave.
octavilla *nf* **1** *(impreso)* pamphlet. **2** *arc (pliego)* octavo.
octavo,-a *adj* eighth: **llegó en octavo lugar** *he came eighth.*
▷ *nm & nf* eighth: **era la octava en la lista** *she was the eighth on the list.*
▷ *nm* **octavo** *(parte)* eighth.

See also **sexto**.

octeto *nm* octet.
octogésimo,-a *adj* eightieth.
octogonal *adj* octagonal.
octógono *nm* octagon.
octosílabo,-a *adj* octosyllabic.
▷ *nm* **octosílabo** octosyllable.
octubre *nm* October.

For examples of use, see **marzo**.

ocular *adj* eye, ocular.
oculista *nm o nf* eye specialist, ophthalmologist.
ocultar *vt (gen)* to hide, conceal.
oculto,-a *adj (escondido)* hidden: **quedaba oculto tras las ramas** *it was hidden behind the branches.*
ocupación *nf* **1** *(llenado)* occupation. **2** *(empleo)* occupation, employment, job.
ocupado,-a *adj* **1** *(persona)* busy. **2** *(asiento)* taken; *(teléfono)* engaged, US busy; **¿está ocupado el baño?** *is there anyone in the bathroom?*
ocupante *nm o nf* **1** occupant. **2** *(de una vivienda)* occupier, occupant; *(ilegal)* squatter.
ocupar *vt* **1** to occupy, take. **2** *(llenar)* to take up: **la mesa ocupa casi toda la habitación** *the table takes up most of the room.* **3** *(habitar)* to live in, occupy. **4** *(estar - en un cargo)* to hold, fill; *(- en posición)* to occupy, be in. **5** *(dar trabajo)* to employ.
▷ *vpr* **ocuparse de** *(encargarse de)* to take care of.
ocurrencia *nf* **1** *(idea)* idea; *(disparatada)* absurd idea. **2** *(agudeza)* witty remark.
ocurrir *vi* to happen: **¿qué fue lo que ocurrió?** *what happened?* ■ **lo que ocurre es que…** the thing is that…
▷ *vpr* **ocurrirse** to occur to: **no se me ocurre nada** *nothing occurs to me, I can't think of anything.*
oda *nf* ode.
odiar [12] *vt* to hate, loathe. ■ **odio tener que…** I hate having to…
odio *nm* hatred, loathing. ■ **tenerle odio a** ALGN to hate SB.
odioso,-a *adj* hateful, despicable, odious.
odontólogo,-a *nm & nf* dental surgeon, odontologist.
odorífico,-a *adj* odoriferous.
odre *nm* wineskin.
oeste *nm* west.
▷ *adj (ala, viento)* west; *(rumbo)* westerly. ■ **en dirección oeste** westward. ● **películas del oeste** westerns.
ofender *vt* **1** *(herir)* to offend: **no quisiera ofenderte, pero…** *no offence, but…* **2** *(disgustar)* to hurt: **esta decoración ofende a la vista** *this decoration is an eyesore.*
▷ *vpr* **ofenderse** to get offended.
ofendido,-a *adj* offended.
ofensa *nf* offence.
ofensivo,-a *adj* offensive.
oferta *nf* **1** offer. **2** COM bid, tender. **3** *(suministro)* supply. ■ **estar de oferta** to be on (special) offer. ■ **la ley de la oferta y la demanda** the law of supply and demand.
ofertar *vt (ofrecer)* to offer.
off *adj* **1** *(apagado)* off. **2** TEAT offstage. **3** CINE offscreen. ● **voz en off** voice offstage.
office *nm* pantry.
oficial *adj* official.
▷ *nm o nf* **1** *(en oficina)* office worker, clerk; *(en oficio)* assistant. **2** MIL officer. **3** *(en la Administración)* official, officer.
oficiala *nf (operaria)* assistant.
oficialmente *adv* officially.
oficiante *nm o nf* officiant.
oficiar *vt (misa)* to say.
▷ *vi* **1** *(sacerdote)* to officiate. **2** *(ejercer)* to act (**de**, as).
oficina *nf* office. ● **oficina de empleo** job centre, US job office. ■ **oficina de turismo** tourist information office.
oficinista *nm o nf* office worker, clerk.
oficio *nm* **1** *(ocupación)* job, occupation; *(especializado)* trade: **aprender un oficio** *to learn a trade.* **2** *(función)* role, function. **3** REL service.
oficioso,-a *adj (noticia, fuente)* unofficial.
ofidio *nm* snake.

ofimática *nf* office automation, office IT.
ofrecer [43] *vt* **1** *(dar - premio, amistad)* to offer; *(- banquete, fiesta)* to hold; *(- regalo)* to give. **2** *(presentar)* to present: **ofrecer resistencia** *to offer resistance.*
▷ *vpr* **ofrecerse 1** *(prestarse)* to offer, volunteer. **2** *(disponer)* to want. **¿qué se le ofrece?** *what can I do for you?*
ofrecimiento *nm* offer, offering.
ofrenda *nf* offering.
ofrendar *vt* to make an offering of.
oftalmología *nf* ophthalmology.
oftalmólogo,-a *nm & nf* eye specialist, ophthalmologist.
ofuscar [1] *vt* **1** *(confundir)* to muddle, befuddle. **2** *(deslumbrar)* to dazzle.
▷ *vpr* **ofuscarse** to get muddled.
ogro *nm* ogre.
oh *interj* oh!
ohm *nm* ohm.
▲ *pl* **ohms.**
ohmio *nm* ohm.
oídas ■ **de oídas** by hearsay: **yo solo lo sé de oídas** *it's just hearsay.*
oído *nm* **1** *(sentido)* hearing. **2** *(órgano)* ear.
oiga *interj (para llamar la atención)* excuse me!; *(en bar, etc)* waiter!; *(por teléfono)* hello?; *(con enfado)* listen!, look here!
oír [75] *vt* **1** *(percibir sonidos)* to hear: **no se oye ni una mosca** *you could hear a pin drop.* **2** *(atender)* to answer: **¡Dios te oiga!** *if only!*
OIT *abrev* **(Organización Internacional del Trabajo)** International Labour Organization; *(abreviatura)* ILO.
ojal *nm* buttonhole.
ojalá *interj* I hope so: **¡ojalá sea verdad!** *I hope it's true!*
ojeada *nf* glance, quick look. ■ **echar una ojeada 1** *(mirar)* to take a quick look (**a**, at). **2** *(vigilar)* to keep an eye (**a**, on).
ojear *vt (mirar)* to have a quick look at.
ojeras *nf pl* dark rings under the eyes.
ojeriza *nf fam* dislike. ■ **tenerle ojeriza a** ALGN to have it in for SB.
ojeroso,-a *adj* haggard.
ojival *adj (arte)* ogival. ● **arco ojival** lancet arch.
ojo *nm* **1** eye. **2** *(agujero)* hole; *(de aguja)* eye. **3** *(cuidado, precaución)* care: **¡ojo!** *careful!, watch out!* **4** *(perspicacia)* insight, eye: **tiene mucho ojo para los negocios** *she's got a head for business.* ● **cuatro ojos** *fam* four-eyes. ❙ **ojo de la cerradura** keyhole. ❙ **ojos saltones** bulging eyes.
okupa *nm o nf argot* squatter.
ola *nf* wave. ● **ola de frío** cold spell.
oleáceo,-a *adj* oleaceous.
oleada *nf* **1** big wave. **2** *fig* wave.
oleaginoso,-a *adj* oleaginous.
oleaje *nm* swell.
oleicultura *nf* **1** *(cultivo)* olive-growing. **2** *(fabricación)* olive oil industry.
óleo *nm (material)* oil; *(obra)* oil painting. ● **pintura al óleo** oil painting.
oleoducto *nm* pipeline.
oleoso,-a *adj* oily.
oler [60] *vt* to smell.
▷ *vi* to smell: **huele a gas** *it smells of gas in here.*
▷ *vpr* **olerse** to feel, sense: **se ha olido que nos vamos** *she has sensed that we are leaving.*
olfatear *vt* **1** *(oler)* to sniff, smell. **2** *fig (indagar)* to nose into, pry into. **3** *(sospechar)* to suspect.
olfateo *nm* **1** sniffing. **2** *fig* snooping.
olfativo,-a *adj* olfactory.
olfato *nm* **1** sense of smell.. **2** *fig (intuición)* good nose; *(cualidades)* flair.
olfatorio,-a *adj* olfactory.
oligarca *nm o nf* oligarch.
oligarquía *nf* oligarchy.
oligárquico,-a *adj* oligarchic, oligarchical.
oligoelemento *nm* trace element.
oligofrenia *nf* **1** *(enfermedad)* mental handicap. **2** *pey* mental deficiency.
oligofrénico,-a *adj* **1** mentally retarded. **2** *fam pey* moronic.
▷ *nm & nf* **1** mentally retarded person. **2** *fam pey* moron.
olimpiada [Also written **olimpíada.**] *nf* HIST Olympiad. ● **las Olimpiadas** the Olympic Games.
olisquear *vt (olfatear)* to sniff.
▷ *vi fig (curiosear)* to nose around.
oliva *nf* olive.
olivar *nm* olive grove.
olivarero,-a *adj (industria)* olive; *(región)* olive-growing.
▷ *nm & nf* olive grower.
olivo *nm* olive tree.
olla *nf* **1** *(utensilio)* pan. **2** *(comida)* *type of* stew. ● **olla a presión** pressure cooker. ❙ **olla podrida** *type of* meat stew.
olmo *nm* elm tree.
olor *nm* smell.
oloroso,-a *adj* fragrant, sweet-smelling.
▷ *nm (vino)* full-bodied sherry.
olvidadizo,-a *adj* forgetful.
olvidar *vt* to forget.
▷ *vpr* **olvidarse** to forget (**de**, -): **se me ha olvidado tu número de teléfono** *I've forgotten your telephone number.*
olvido *nm* **1** *(desmemoria)* oblivion. **2** *(descuido)* forgetfulness, absent-mindedness. **3** *(lapsus)* oversight, lapse (of memory).
Omán *nm* Oman.
omaní *adj* Omani.
▷ *nm o nf* Omani.
ombligo *nm* navel.
omega *nf (letra)* omega.
omisión *nf* omission.
omitir *vt (no decir)* to omit, leave out.
ómnibus *nm inv* bus.
omnipotente *adj* omnipotent, almighty.
omnipresente *adj* omnipresent.
omnívoro,-a *adj* omnivorous.
omoplato [Also written **omóplato.**] *nm* shoulder blade.
omóplato [Also written **omoplato.**] *nm* shoulder blade.
OMS *abrev* **(Organización Mundial de la Salud)** World Health Organization; *(abreviatura)* WHO.
once *adj* eleven; *(undécimo)* eleventh.
▷ *nm* eleven.
See also **seis.**
onceavo,-a *adj (parte)* eleventh: **la onceava parte de...** *an eleventh of...*
▷ *nm* eleventh: **tres onceavos** *three elevenths.*
See also **sexto.**

oncología *nf* oncology.
oncólogo,-a *nm & nf* oncologist.
onda *nf* wave. ● **onda expansiva** shock wave. ‖ **onda larga** long wave. ‖ **onda media** medium wave.
ondear *vi* 1 *(bandera)* to fly, flutter. 2 *(agua)* to ripple.
ondina *nf* water nymph, undine.
ondulación *nf* 1 undulation, wave. 2 *(agua)* ripple.
ondulado,-a *adj (pelo)* wavy.
ondulante *adj (paisaje, terreno)* undulating, rolling; *(serpiente)* sinuous; *(movimiento, melodía)* rolling.
ondular *vt (pelo)* to wave.
▷ *vi lit (agua)* to undulate.
ondulatorio,-a *adj* undulatory. ● **mecánica ondulatoria** wave mechanics.
oneroso,-a *adj* onerous.
ONG *abrev* (Organización no Gubernamental) nongovernmental organization; *(abreviatura)* NGO.
ónice *nm* onyx.
onírico,-a *adj* dream, of dreams.
ónix *nm* onyx.
ONO *sím* (oesnoroeste) west-northwest; *(símbolo)* WNW.
onomástica *nf* saint's day.
onomástico,-a *adj* onomastic: fiesta onomástica *saint's day.*
onomatopeya *nf* onomatopoeia.
onomatopéyico,-a *adj* onomatopoeic.
ontología *nf* ontology.
ontológico,-a *adj* ontological.
ONU *abrev* (Organización de las Naciones Unidas) United Nations Organization; *(abreviatura)* UNO.
onza *nf (peso)* ounce.
OPA *abrev* (Oferta Pública de Adquisición) takeover bid.
opacidad *nf* opaqueness, opacity.
opaco,-a *adj* opaque.
opalino,-a *adj (de ópalo)* opal; *(opalescente)* opal-like.
ópalo *nm* opal.
opción *nf* 1 *(en general)* option: esta opción es la mejor *this is the best option.* 2 *(alternativa)* option, choice: no tienes otra opción *you have no choice.* 3 *(derecho)* right: esto te da opción a participar otra vez *this gives you the right to take part again.*
opcional *adj* optional.
open *nm inv* DEP open.
OPEP *abrev* (Organización de los Países Exportadores de Petróleo) Organization of Petroleum Exporting Countries; *(abreviatura)* OPEC.
ópera *nf* opera.
operación *nf* 1 *(gen)* operation. 2 FIN transaction, deal.
operador,-ra *nm & nf* 1 *(telefónico)* operator. 2 CINE *(de cámara - hombre)* cameraman; *(- mujer)* camerawoman; *(- de proyector)* projectionist. 3 TÉC operator. 4 FIN trader.
▷ *nm* **operador** MAT *(signo)* operator. ■ **operador turístico** tour operator.
operando *nm* operand.
operante *adj* operative.
operar *vt* 1 MED to operate (a, on): ¿quién te operó? *who operated on you?* 2 *(producir)* to bring about.
▷ *vi* 1 *(actuar)* to operate. 2 *(negociar)* to deal (con, with).
▷ *vpr* **operarse** 1 MED to have an operation: se ha operado del corazón *he has had a heart operation.* 2 *(producirse)* to come about: se han operado grandes cambios en el país *the country has undergone many changes.*
operario,-a *nm & nf* operator, worker.
operativo,-a *adj* operative.
opereta *nf* operetta.
operístico,-a *adj* operatic.
opiáceo,-a *adj* opiate.
opinable *adj* debatable.
opinar *vi* to think (de, about).
opinión *nf (juicio)* opinion, view: en mi opinión *in my opinion, in my view.* ■ **cambiar de opinión** to change one's mind. ● **la opinión pública** public opinion.
opio *nm* opium.
opíparo,-a *adj fml* lavish: una cena opípara *a feast.*
oponente *adj* opposing.
▷ *nm o nf* opponent.
oponer [78] *vt* to reply with, counter with: no tienen nada que oponer a nuestras razones *they cannot reply to our arguments.* ■ **oponer resistencia** to offer resistance.
▷ *vpr* **oponerse** 1 *(estar en contra)* to oppose (a, -), be against (a, -). 2 *(ser contrario)* to be in opposition (a, to), contradict (a, -).
oporto *nm* port.
oportunidad *nf* opportunity, chance.
oportunismo *nm* opportunism.
oportunista *nm o nf* opportunist.
oportuno,-a *adj* 1 *(a tiempo)* opportune, timely: la oferta llegó en el momento oportuno *the offer came at the right time.* 2 *(conveniente)* appropriate: habrá que tomar las medidas oportunas *the appropriate measures will have to be taken.*
oposición *nf* 1 *(antagonismo)* opposition. 2 *(examen)* competitive examination. ■ **preparar las oposiciones** to study for a competitive exam.
opositar *vi (presentarse a examen)* to sit for a competitive exam.
opositor,-ra *nm & nf candidate preparing for an official exam.*
opresión *nf* oppression.
opresivo,-a *adj* oppressive.
opresor,-ra *nm & nf* oppressor.
oprimido,-a *nm & nf* oppressed person.
oprimir *vt* 1 *(botón)* to press: oprima el botón verde *press the green button.* 2 *fig* to oppress.
oprobio *nm* opprobrium.
optar *vi (elegir)* to choose (entre, from): opté por no decir nada *I decided not to say anything.*
optativa *nf* EDUC *(asignatura)* optional subject.
optativo,-a *adj* 1 optional. 2 LING *(oración, modo)* optative.
óptica *nf* 1 *(tienda)* optician's. 2 FÍS optics. 3 *(enfoque)* viewpoint.
óptico,-a *adj (nervio, ángulo)* optic; *(ilusión, instrumento, efecto)* optical.
▷ *nm & nf* optician.
optimismo *nm* optimism.
optimista *adj* optimistic.
▷ *nm o nf* optimist.
optimizar *vt* to optimize.
óptimo,-a *adj* very best, optimum.
opuesto,-a *adj* 1 *(contrario)* contrary, opposed. 2 *(de enfrente)* opposite.

opulencia *nf* opulence.
opulento,-a *adj* opulent.
opus *nm* MÚS opus.
oquedad *nf* 1 *(hueco)* cavity. 2 *fig* vacuity, emptiness.
ora *conj arc* now. ■ **ora... ora...** be it... or...
oración *nf* 1 REL *(plegaria)* prayer; *(acción)* praying. 2 LING clause, sentence. ● **oración principal** main clause. ‖ **oración subordinada** subordinate clause.
oráculo *nm* oracle.
orador,-ra *nm & nf* speaker, orator.
oral *adj* oral.
▷ *nm* EDUC *(examen)* oral, oral exam.
orangután *nm* ZOOL orang-utan, orang-outang.
orar *vi* to pray.
oratoria *nf* oratory.
oratorio,-a *adj (estilo, arte)* oratorical.
▷ *nm* **oratorio** 1 MÚS oratorio. 2 REL oratory.
orbe *nm (esfera)* orb; *(mundo)* world.
órbita *nf* 1 *(de un astro)* orbit. 2 *(del ojo)* socket.
orbital *adj* orbital.
orca *nf* killer whale, orc.
orden *nm* 1 *(ordenación)* order: **clasificados por orden alfabético** *classified in alphabetical order.* 2 BIOL order. 3 ARQUIT order: **el orden jónico** *the Ionic order.*
▷ *nf* 1 *(mandato)* order: **¡es una orden!** *that's an order!* 2 REL order: **la orden franciscana** *the Franciscan order.* ■ **por orden de** by order of. ● **el orden del día** the agenda.
ordenación *nf* 1 *(disposición)* arrangement, organizing. 2 REL ordination.
ordenada *nf* MAT ordinate.
ordenado,-a *adj (habitación)* tidy, in order; *(persona)* tidy, well-organized.
ordenador,-ra *nm* **ordenador** INFORMÁ computer. ● **ordenador personal** personal computer.
ordenamiento *nm* 1 JUR ordinance. 2 *(ordenación)* ordering, arranging.
ordenanza *nm (empleado)* office boy.
▷ *nf (norma)* ordinance. ● **ordenanza municipal** bylaw.
ordenar *vt* 1 *(arreglar)* to put in order; *(habitación)* to tidy up: **los libros estaban ordenados por materias** *the books were classified by subject matter.* 2 *(mandar)* to order 3 REL to ordain.
ordeñar *vt* to milk.
ordinal *adj* ordinal.
▷ *nm* ordinal.
ordinariez *nf* 1 *(defecto)* vulgarity. 2 *(expresión)* vulgar remark.
▲ *pl* **ordinarieces.**
ordinario,-a *adj* 1 *(corriente)* ordinary, common. 2 *(grosero)* vulgar, common. ■ **de ordinario** usually.
orégano *nm* oregano.
oreja *nf* ear.
orejera *nf* earflap.
orejero *nm (sillón)* wing chair.
orfanato *nm* orphanage.
orfandad *nf* orphanage.
orfebre *nm* goldsmith, silversmith.
orfebrería *nf (en oro)* gold work; *(en plata)* silver work.
orfeón *nm* choral society.
órfico,-a *adj lit* orphic.
organdí *nm* organdie.
orgánico,-a *adj* organic.
organigrama *nm (de empresa)* organization chart; *(de informática)* flow chart.
organillero,-a *nm & nf* organ-grinder.
organillo *nm* barrel organ.
organismo *nm* 1 *(humano)* organism. 2 *(institucional)* organization, body.
organista *nm o nf* organist.
organización *nf* organization.
organizar [4] *vt* to organize.
organizativo,-a *adj* organizational.
órgano *nm* organ.
orgasmo *nm* orgasm.
orgía *nf* orgy.
orgullo *nm* 1 *(propia estima)* pride. 2 *(arrogancia)* arrogance, haughtiness.
orgulloso,-a *adj* proud.
orientación *nf* 1 *(capacidad)* sense of direction. 2 *(de un edificio)* aspect. 3 *(dirección)* orientation, tendency.
oriental *adj* eastern, oriental.
▷ *nm o nf* Oriental.
orientalismo *nm* Orientalism.
orientalista *adj* Orientalistic.
▷ *nm o nf* Orientalist.
orientar *vt* 1 *(casa)* to face; *(antena, barco)* to point; *(velas)* to trim. 2 *(esfuerzos, investigaciones)* to direct. 3 *(guiar)* to guide; *(aconsejar)* to advise.
▷ *vpr* **orientarse** to find one's bearings.
oriente *nm* East. ● **el Extremo Oriente** the Far East.
orificio *nm (agujero)* hole; *(abertura)* opening.
origen *nm* 1 *(causa)* cause, origin. 2 *(procedencia - gen)* origin; *(- de persona)* extraction.
▲ *pl* **orígenes.**
original *adj (gen)* original.
▷ *nm* original.
originalidad *nf* originality.
originar *vt* to cause, give rise to.
▷ *vpr* **originarse** to originate.
originario,-a *adj* original. ■ **ser originario,-a de** 1 *(persona)* to come from. 2 *(costumbre)* to originate in.
orilla *nf* 1 *(borde)* edge. 2 *(del río)* bank; *(del mar)* shore.
orillar *vt* 1 *(resolver)* to solve. 2 *(sortear)* to get round.
orina *nf* urine.
orinal *nm* chamber pot; *(para niños)* potty.
orinar *vi* to urinate.
▷ *vt (sangre)* to pass.
▷ *vpr* **orinarse** *fam* to wet OS.
oriundo,-a *adj* native of.
orla *nf* 1 *(adorno)* edging. 2 *(foto)* class graduation photo.
ornamentación *nf* ornamentation.
ornamental *adj* ornamental.
ornamentar *vt* to adorn, decorate.
ornamento *nm* ornament.
ornitología *nf* ornithology.
ornitológico,-a *adj* ornithological.
ornitólogo,-a *nm & nf* ornithologist.
ornitorrinco *nm* platypus.
oro *nm* gold: **un reloj de oro** *a gold watch.*
▷ *nm pl* **oros** *(baraja española)* ≈ diamonds. ■ **hacerse de oro** to make a fortune. ● **oro negro** oil.
orografía *nf* orography.
orográfico,-a *adj* orographic.
orondo,-a *adj* hearty, plump.

orquesta *nf* 1 *(clásica)* orchestra; *(popular)* dance band. 2 *(lugar)* orchestra pit.
orquestal *adj* orchestral.
orquestar *vt* to orchestrate.
orquídea *nf* orchid.
ortiga *nf* nettle.
ortodoncia *nf* orthodontics, dental orthopaedics.
ortodoxia *nf* orthodoxy.
ortodoxo,-a *adj* orthodox.
▷ *nm & nf* orthodox.
ortografía *nf* spelling; *(uso formal)* orthography. ● **falta de ortografía** spelling mistake.
ortográfico,-a *adj* spelling; *(uso formal)* orthographic. ■ **signo ortográfico** 1 punctuation mark. 2 *(tilde)* written accent.
ortopedia *nf* orthopaedics.
ortopédico,-a *adj* orthopaedic.
▷ *nm & nf* orthopaedist.
ortopedista *nm o nf* orthopaedist.
oruga *nf* caterpillar.
orzuelo *nm* sty.
os *pron* 1 *(complemento directo)* you: **os escucho** *I am listening to you.* 2 *(complemento indirecto)* you: **os traje un libro** *I brought you a book.* 3 *(reflexivo)* yourselves: **¿ya os estáis vistiendo?** *are you getting dressed already?* 4 *(recíproco)* each other: **os parecéis mucho** *you look very much alike.*
osadía *nf* 1 *(audacia)* audacity, daring. 2 *(desvergüenza)* effrontery, nerve.
osado,-a *adj* 1 *(audaz)* audacious, daring. 2 *(desvergonzado)* shameless.
osamenta *nf (esqueleto)* skeleton; *(huesos)* bones *pl.*
osar *vi lit* to dare, have the audacity to.
oscilación *nf* 1 *(de precios)* fluctuation. 2 FÍS oscillation.
oscilar *vi* 1 *(variar)* to vary, fluctuate. 2 FÍS to oscillate.
oscilatorio,-a *adj* oscillating.
ósculo *nm lit* kiss.
oscurantismo *nm* obscurantism.
oscuras ■ **a oscuras** in the dark.
óseo,-a *adj (tejido, estructura)* bone.
osera *nf* bear's den.
osezno *nm* bear cub.
osificación *nf* ossification.
osificar *vt* to ossify.
osmio *nm* osmium.
ósmosis *nf inv* osmosis.
oso *nm* bear.
OSO *sím* **(oesudoeste)** west-southwest; *(símbolo)* WSW.
ostentación *nf* ostentation.
ostentar *vt* 1 *(jactarse de)* to show off, flaunt. 2 *(poseer)* to hold.
ostentoso,-a *adj* ostentatious.
osteópata *nm o nf* osteopath.
osteopatía *nf* osteopathy.
osteopático,-a *adj* osteopathic.
ostra *nf* oyster.
ostracismo *nm* ostracism.
ostrero,-a *adj* oyster.
▷ *nm* **ostrero** *(ave)* oystercatcher.
ostrícola *adj* oyster.
OTAN *abrev* **(Organización del Tratado del Atlántico Norte)** North Atlantic Treaty Organization; *(abreviatura)* NATO.
otear *vt (horizonte)* to scan.
otero *nm* hillock.
otitis *nf inv* ear infection, otitis.
otomán *nm (tela)* ottoman.
otomana *nf (cama turca)* ottoman.
otomano,-a *adj* Ottoman.
▷ *nm & nf (persona)* Ottoman.
otoñal *adj* autumnal, autumn, US fall.
otoño *nm* autumn, US fall.
otorgante *adj (de un premio)* awarding.
otorgar [7] *vt* 1 *(conceder)* to grant, give (**a**, to); *(premio)* to award (**a**, to). 2 JUR to execute, draw up.
otorrinolaringólogo,-a *nm & nf* ear, nose and throat specialist, ENT specialist.
otorrinolaringología *nf* ear, nose and throat, ENT.
otro,-a *adj* other, another.
▷ *pron* other, another: **otros** *others.*
OUA *abrev* **(Organización de la Unidad Africana)** Organization of African Unity; *(abreviatura)* OAU.
ovación *nf* ovation, cheering, applause.
ovacionar *vt* to give an ovation (**a**, to), applaud (**a**, -).
oval *adj* oval.
ovalado,-a *adj* oval.
óvalo *nm* oval.
ovario *nm* ovary.
oveja *nf* sheep, ewe. ● **la oveja negra de la familia** the black sheep of the family.
overtura *nf* MÚS overture.
ovillar *vt* to roll into a ball.
ovillo *nm* ball of wool.
ovino,-a *adj* ovine, sheep.
ovíparo,-a *adj* oviparous.
OVNI *abrev* **(Objeto Volador no Identificado)** Unidentified Flying Object; *(abreviatura)* UFO.
ovulación *nf* ovulation.
ovular *adj* ovular.
▷ *vi* to ovulate.
óvulo *nm* ovule.
oxiacetilénico,-a *adj* oxyacetylene.
oxiacetileno *nm* oxyacetylene.
oxidable *adj* oxidizable.
oxidación *nf* 1 QUÍM oxidation. 2 *(proceso)* rusting; *(capa)* rust.
oxidado,-a *adj* 1 rusty. 2 QUÍM oxidized.
oxidante *adj* oxidizing.
▷ *nm* oxidizer.
oxidar *vt* 1 QUÍM to oxidize. 2 *(enmohecer)* to rust.
▷ *vpr* **oxidarse** 1 QUÍM to oxidize. 2 *(enmohecerse)* to rust, go rusty.
óxido *nm* 1 *(herrumbre)* rust. 2 QUÍM oxide.
oxigenación *nf* 1 *fig* airing. 2 QUÍM oxygenation.
oxigenado,-a *adj* 1 QUÍM oxygenated. 2 *(pelo)* bleached.
oxigenar *vt* 1 QUÍM to oxygenate. 2 *(blanquear)* to bleach. 3 *(pulmones)* to get some fresh air in.
▷ *vpr* **oxigenarse** *(persona)* to get some fresh air.
oxígeno *nm* oxygen.
oye *interj fam (para llamar la atención)* hey!; *(con enfado)* listen!, look here!.
oyente *nm o nf* 1 RAD listener. 2 *(alumno)* unregistered student.
ozono *nm* ozone. ● **capa de ozono** ozone layer.

P

P, p *nf (la letra)* P, p.
pabellón *nm* 1 ARQUIT pavilion. 2 *(en una feria)* stand. 3 *(bandera)* flag. 4 ANAT (external) ear.
pabilo *nm* wick.
pábulo *nm* fuel.
pacana *nf* pecan nut.
pacato ,-a *adj fam* prudish.
pacer [42] *vi* to graze.
pachanga *nf (bullicio)* party atmosphere; *(música)* party music.
pachón,-ona *adj* 1 *(perro)* pointer. 2 *fam (persona)* laid-back.
pachorra *nf fam* phlegm.
pachucho ,-a *adj* 1 *fam (persona)* poorly. 2 *fam (fruta)* overripe.
paciencia *nf* patience. ■ **tener paciencia** to be patient.
paciente *adj* patient.
▷ *nm o nf* patient.
pacificación *nf* pacification.
pacíficamente *adv* peacefully.
pacificar [1] *vt* 1 to pacify. 2 *(calmar)* to appease.
pacífico ,-a *adj* peaceful.
pacifismo *nm* pacifism.
pacifista *adj* pacifist.
▷ *nm o nf* pacifist.
pactar *vt* to agree (to).
▷ *vi* to come to an agreement.
pacto *nm* pact, agreement.
padecer [43] *vt* to suffer.
▷ *vi (sufrir)* to suffer (**de**, from).
padecimiento *nm* suffering.
padrastro *nm* 1 *(padre)* stepfather. 2 *(en las uñas)* hangnail.
padrazo *nm fam* loving father.
padre *nm* 1 father. 2 REL *(sacerdote)* father. 3 **Padre** REL Father.
▷ *nm pl* **padres** parents.
padrenuestro *nm* Lord's Prayer.
padrino *nm* 1 *(de bautizo)* godfather. 2 *(de boda)* bride's father *who acts as best man*. 3 *(patrocinador)* sponsor.
▷ *nm pl* **padrinos** godparents.
padrón *nm (censo)* census; *(para votar)* electoral roll.
paella *nf (comida)* paella.
paellera *nf* paella pan.
paga *nf* 1 *(sueldo)* pay. 2 *(de los niños)* pocket money. ● **paga extra** bonus.
pagadero ,-a *adj* payable.
pagador ,-ra *adj* paying.
▷ *nm & nf* 1 *(gen)* payer. 2 *(en banco)* cashier.
paganismo *nm* paganism.
pagano ,-a *adj* REL pagan.
▷ *nm & nf* REL pagan.
pagar [7] *vt* to pay: **ya he pagado lo que debía** *I've already paid what I owed.*
▷ *vi* to pay: **en esta empresa pagan muy bien** *this company pays very well.*
pagaré *nm* promissory note. ● **pagaré del Tesoro** government bond.
página *nf* page. ● **páginas amarillas** yellow pages.
paginación *nf* pagination.
pago *nm* 1 payment. 2 *(recompensa)* reward. ● **pago a cuenta** payment on account.
paguro *nm* 1 *(ermitaño)* hermit crab. 2 *(centolla)* spider crab.
paipái *nm* fan.
país *nm* country.
paisaje *nm* landscape.
paisajista *nm o nf (pintor)* landscape artist.
paisajístico ,-a *adj* landscape.
paisano ,-a *nm & nf* 1 *(compatriota - hombre)* fellow countryman; *(- mujer)* fellow countrywoman. 2 *(campesino - hombre)* countryman; *(- mujer)* countrywoman. ■ **de paisano** 1 *(policía)* in plain clothes. 2 *(soldado)* in civilian clothes.
paja *nf* 1 straw. 2 *fig (relleno)* waffle.
pajar *nm* 1 *(lugar)* hayloft. 2 *(almiar)* haystack.
pajarera *nf* aviary.
pajarería *nf (tienda)* caged-bird shop.
pajarero ,-a *adj* of birds.
pajarita *nf* 1 *(de cuello)* bow tie. 2 *(de papel)* paper bird.
pájaro *nm (animal)* bird. ● **pájaro bobo** penguin. ▮ **pájaro carpintero** woodpecker.
paje *nm* page.
pajita *nf (para beber)* straw.
pajizo ,-a *adj* straw-coloured (US straw-colored).
Pakistán *nm* Pakistan.
pakistaní *adj* Pakistani.
▷ *nm o nf* Pakistani.
▲ *pl* **pakistaníes.**
pala *nf* 1 *(herramienta)* shovel; *(de jardinería)* spade. 2 DEP *(de ping-pong)* bat; *(de remo)* blade; *(de frontón)* bat.
palabra *nf* word. ■ **tener la palabra** to have the floor. ▮ **tener palabra** to keep one's word. ● **palabra de honor** word of honour.
palabrota *nf* swearword. ■ **decir palabrotas** to swear.
palacete *nm* mansion.
palaciego ,-a *adj* palatial.
palacio *nm* palace. ● **palacio de congresos** conference hall.
palada *nf (gen)* shovelful.

paladar *nm* 1 palate. 2 *fig* taste.
paladear *vt* to savour, relish.
paladín *nm* 1 HIST paladin. 2 *fig* champion.
palafito *nm* house on stilts.
palanca *nf (gen)* lever. ■ **hacer palanca** to lever. ● **palanca de cambio** gearstick.
palangana *nf* bowl, washbasin (US washbowl).
palangre *nm (arte de pesca)* boulter *(a long stout line with many hooks)*.
palatal *adj* palatal.
▷ *nf* palatal.
palco *nm (en el teatro)* box.
paleografía *nf* palaeography (US paleography).
paleógrafo ,-a *nm & nf* palaeographer (US paleographer).
paleolítico ,-a *adj* Palaeolithic (US Paleolithic).
▷ *nm* **el paleolítico,-a** the Palaeolithic (US Paleolithic).
paleontología *nf* palaeontology (US paleontology).
paleontólogo ,-a *nm & nf* palaeontologist (US paleontologist).
Palestina *nf* Palestine.
palestino ,-a *adj* Palestinian.
▷ *nm & nf* Palestinian.
palestra *nf* arena, forum.
paleta *nf* 1 *(de pintor)* palette. 2 *(de albañil)* trowel. 3 *(de cocina)* slice. 4 *(pala)* small shovel.
paletada *nf* 1 *(de albañil)* going over with a trowel. 2 *fam* oafish thing to do or say.
paletilla *nf* 1 ANAT shoulder blade. 2 CULIN shoulder.
paleto,-a *nm & nf fam pey* oaf, country bumpkin, yokel.
▷ *adj fam pey* oafish.
paliar [12] *vt* to palliate, alleviate.
paliativo,-a *adj* palliative.
▷ *nm* **paliativo** palliative.
palidecer [43] *vi* 1 to turn pale. 2 *fig* to fade.
palidez *nf* paleness, pallor.
pálido ,-a *adj* pale.
palillero *nm* toothpick holder.
palillo *nm* 1 *(mondadientes)* toothpick. 2 MÚS drumstick.
palíndromo *nm* palindrome.
palio *nm* canopy.
palique *nm fam* chat, small talk.
palisandro *nm* rosewood.
paliza *nf* 1 beating, thrashing. 2 *fam (derrota)* thrashing. 3 *fam (pesadez)* pain.
palma *nf* 1 BOT palm (tree). 2 *(de la mano)* palm.
▷ *nf pl* **palmas** *(aplausos)* clapping *sing*, applause *sing*.
palmada *nf* 1 *(aplauso)* clapping. 2 *(golpe)* slap, pat.
palmadita *nf* slap, pat.
palmar[1] *nm* palm grove.
palmar[2] *loc* **palmarla** *fam* kick the bucket.
palmarés *nm* 1 *(lista)* list of winners. 2 *(historial)* list of achievements; *(de deportista)* record, track record.
palmatoria *nf* candlestick.
palmeado ,-a *adj* 1 BOT palmate. 2 ZOOL *(dedos)* webbed.
palmear *vi* to clap.
palmera *nf* BOT palm tree, palm.
palmeral *nm* palm grove.
palmetazo *nm* stroke of the cane.
palmípedo ,-a *adj* web-footed.
▷ *nf pl* **palmípedas** ZOOL *(género)* web-footed birds.
palmito *nm* 1 CULIN palm heart. 2 BOT palmetto.
palmo *nm (medida)* span.
palmotear *vi* to clap.
palmoteo *nm* clapping.
palo *nm* 1 *(estaca)* stick; *(de valla)* post; *(de telégrafos)* pole. 2 *(golpe)* blow. 3 *(madera)* wood. 4 *(de baraja)* suit. 5 MAR mast. 6 DEP *(de una portería)* goal post. 7 *(de golf)* club. ■ **a palo seco** 1 *(comida)* on its own. 2 *(bebida)* neat.
paloma *nf (gen)* pigeon; *(blanca)* dove.
palomar *nm* dovecote.
palometa *nf* 1 Ray's bream. 2 *(tuerca)* wing nut.
palomilla *nf* 1 *(insecto)* moth. 2 *(tuerca)* wing nut. 3 *(armazón)* bracket.
palomino *nm* young pigeon.
palomita *nf* aniseed and water. ● **palomitas de maíz** popcorn *sing*.
palomo *nm* cock pigeon.
palote *nm* 1 *(palo)* stick. 2 *(dibujo)* stroke.
palpable *adj* 1 palpable. 2 *fig (evidente)* obvious, evident.
palpar *vt* 1 MED to palpate. 2 *fig (percibir)* to sense, feel: **se palpa cierto descontento en el ambiente** *there's discontent in the air.*
palpitación *nf* palpitation.
palpitante *adj* 1 MED palpitating, throbbing. 2 *(tema, cuestión)* burning. 3 *(luz, reflejo)* flashing.
palpitar *vi* to palpitate, throb.
pálpito *nm* hunch, feeling.
paludismo *nm* malaria.
palurdo ,-a *nm & nf* country bumpkin.
palustre *adj (de las lagunas)* lake; *(de los pantanos)* marshy.
pamela *nf* wide-brimmed straw hat.
pampa *nf* pampas *pl*.
pámpano *nm* vine shoot.
pamplina *nf (tontería)* daft thing.
pamplinero,-a *adj* sweet-talking.
pan *nm* 1 *(masa)* bread; *(hogaza)* loaf of bread. 2 *(alimento)* food, bread. ■ **ganarse el pan** to earn one's living. ● **barra de pan** loaf of bread. ‖ **pan de molde** packet sliced bread. ‖ **pan integral** wholemeal bread.
pana *nf* corduroy.
panacea *nf* panacea.
panadería *nf* bakery, baker's.
panadero,-a *nm & nf* baker.
panal *nm* honeycomb.
Panamá *nm* Panama. ● **sombrero panamá** Panama hat.
panameño,-a *adj* Panamanian.
▷ *nm & nf* Panamanian.
panamericano,-a *adj* Pan-American.
panavisión *nf* Panavision.
pancarta *nf* 1 placard. 2 INFORMÁ banner.
panceta *nf* bacon.
panchito *nm* roasted peanut.
pancho ,-a *adj fam* calm, laid-back. ■ **quedarse tan pancho,-a** to behave as if nothing had happened.
páncreas *nm inv* pancreas.
pancreático ,-a *adj* pancreatic.

panda *nm* ZOOL panda.
pandemónium *nm* pandemonium.
pandeo *nm* 1 *(hacia fuera)* bulge; *(hacia abajo)* sag. 2 *(torcedura)* warp.
pandereta *nf* small tambourine.
pandero *nm* tambourine.
pandilla *nf* group of friends.
panecillo *nm* bread roll.
panel *nm* 1 *(gen)* panel. 2 *(tablero)* noticeboard; *(en la carretera)* hoarding, US billboard.
panera *nf* breadbasket.
pánfilo ,-a *adj* 1 *(tonto)* moronic. 2 *(lento)* slow.
panfletario ,-a *adj (estilo)* propagandist.
panfletista *nm o nf* pamphleteer.
panfleto *nm* 1 political pamphlet. 2 *fig* propaganda.
pánico *nm* panic.
panificadora *nf* industrial bakery.
panocha *nf (de maíz)* corncob; *(de trigo)* ear.
panorama *nm* 1 *(paisaje)* panorama, view. 2 *(aspecto)* situation, outlook.
panorámica *nf* panorama.
panorámico ,-a *adj* panoramic. ● **vista panorámica** scenic view, panoramic view.
pantalla *nf* 1 screen. 2 *(de lámpara)* lampshade. ● **la pequeña pantalla** television.
pantalón [Often used in plural with the same meaning.] *nm* trousers *pl*, US pants. ● **pantalón vaquero** jeans *pl*.
pantano *nm* 1 *(artificial)* reservoir. 2 *(cenagoso)* marsh.
pantanoso ,-a *adj* marshy.
panteísmo *nm* pantheism.
panteísta *adj* pantheist.
panteón *nm* pantheon. ● **panteón familiar** family vault.
pantera *nf* panther.
panties *nm pl* tights.
pantomima *nf* 1 *(representación)* pantomime, mime. 2 *fig* farce, pretence.
pantorrilla *nf* calf.
pantufla *nf* slipper.
panty [Often used in plural with the same meaning.] *nm* tights *pl*.
▲ *pl* **pantys.**
panza *nf* belly.
panzada *nf* 1 *fam (atracón de comer)* binge, blowout. 2 *(en el agua)* belly flop.
pañal *nm* nappy, US diaper. ■ **estar en pañales** 1 *(estar verde - persona)* to be very green. 2 *(- proyecto)* to be in its infancy.
pañería *nf* draper's, draper's shop.
paño *nm* 1 *(gen)* cloth; *(de lana)* woollen cloth: **un abrigo de paño** *a woollen coat*. 2 *(para polvo)* duster; *(de cocina)* dishcloth. 3 *(lienzo)* panel, stretch. ■ **en paños menores** 1 *(con la ropa interior)* in one's underwear. 2 *(desnudo)* stark naked.
pañoleta *nf* shawl.
pañuelo *nm* 1 handkerchief. 2 *(chal)* shawl.
papa[1] *nm* 1 *fam* dad. 2 **el Papa** the Pope.
papa[2] *nf (patata)* potato. ● **papas fritas** 1 *(calientes)* chips, US French fries. 2 *(de bolsa)* crisps, US chips.
papá *nm fam* dad, daddy. ● **Papá Noel** Father Christmas, Santa Claus.
papada *nf* double chin.
papado *nm* papacy.
papagayo *nm* 1 parrot. 2 *fig* chatterbox.
papaya *nf* papaya.
papayo *nm* papaya tree.
papel *nm* 1 *(gen)* paper; *(hoja)* piece of paper. 2 *(en obra, película)* role, part. 3 *(función)* role. **¿qué papel desempeñas en la empresa?** *what's your role in the company?* ■ **hacer buen papel** to do well. ‖ **aprenderse el papel** to learn one's lines. ● **papel de aluminio** aluminium foil. ‖ **papel de lija** sandpaper. ‖ **papel higiénico** toilet paper. ‖ **papel pintado** wallpaper.
▷ *nm pl* **papeles** *fam (documentación)* papers: **¿tienes los papeles en regla?** *are your papers in order?*
papeleo *nm fam* red tape, paperwork.
papelera *nf* 1 wastepaper basket. 2 *(en la calle)* litter bin. ● **papelera de reciclaje** trash can.
papelería *nf* stationer's.
papelero ,-a *adj (del papel)* paper: **la industria papelera** *the paper industry*.
papeleta *nf* 1 *(de empeño)* ticket. 2 *(de voto)* ballot paper. 3 *(de examen)* results slip.
paperas *nf pl* mumps.
papi *nm fam* dad, daddy.
papila *nf* papilla.
papilla *nf* 1 *(infantil)* baby food. 2 *(masa espesa)* pap, mush.
papiro *nm* papyrus.
papiroflexia *nf* origami.
papo *nm* 1 *(de ave)* crop; *(de animal)* dewlap. 2 *fam (de persona)* double chin.
papú *adj* Papuan.
▷ *nm o nf* Papuan.
▲ *pl* **papúes.**
Papúa *nf* Papua. ● **Papúa Nueva Guinea** Papua New Guinea.
paquete *nm* 1 *(cajita)* packet, pack; *(bulto)* package; *(postal)* parcel. 2 *(conjunto)* set, packet: **un paquete de medidas** *a package, a package of measures*. ● **paquete postal** parcel.
paquidermo *nm* pachyderm.
Paquistán *nm* Pakistan.
paquistaní *adj* Pakistani.
▷ *nm o nf* Pakistani.
par *adj* 1 equal. 2 MAT even.
▷ *nm* 1 *(dos)* couple; *(pareja)* pair: **un par de naranjas** *a couple of oranges;* **un par de pantalones** *a pair of trousers*. 2 *(título)* peer. ■ **a la par** 1 *(al mismo tiempo)* at the same time. 2 *(juntos)* together. ‖ **de par en par** wide open. ‖ **sin par** matchless.
para *prep* 1 *(finalidad)* for: **es para su cumpleaños** *it's for her birthday*. 2 *(uso, utilidad)* for: **¿tienes algo para el dolor de cabeza?** *have you got anything for a headache?* 3 *(destino, dirección)* for, to: **¿para dónde vas?** *where are you going?* 4 *(tiempo, fechas límites)* by, before: **lo necesito para el viernes** *I need it by Friday*. 5 *(comparación)* for: **pesa poquísimo para lo grande que es** *it's very light for its size*.
▷ *conj* 1 *(finalidad)* to, in order to: **lo hice para ahorrar tiempo** *I did it to save time*. 2 *(suficiente)* enough: **tal como nos han tratado es para no volver nunca más** *the way they treated us is enough to make you never go*

back there again. ■ **para entonces** by then. ■ **para con** towards, to.
parábola *nf* 1 REL parable. 2 MAT parabola.
parabólica *nf* satellite dish.
parabólico ,-a *adj* parabolic. ● **antena parabólica** satellite dish.
parabrisas *nm inv* windscreen.
paracaídas *nm inv* parachute.
paracaidismo *nm* parachuting.
paracaidista *nm o nf* 1 DEP parachutist. 2 MIL paratrooper.
parachoques *nm inv* 1 AUTO bumper, US fender. 2 *(de tren)* buffer.
parada *nf* 1 *(gen)* stop, halt. 2 *(de autobús, etc)* stop. 3 *(pausa)* pause. 4 DEP save, catch. ● **parada de autobus** bus stop.
paradero *nm* whereabouts *pl*.
paradigmático ,-a *adj* paradigmatic.
paradisíaco ,-a *adj* heavenly.
parado ,-a *adj* 1 *(quieto)* still, motionless. 2 *fig (lento)* slow, awkward. 3 *(sin trabajo)* unemployed.
▷ *nm & nf* unemployed person: **los parados** *the unemployed.*
paradójico ,-a *adj* paradoxical.
parador *nm* 1 *(hotel)* state-run hotel. 2 *arc (posada)* inn.
parafina *nf* paraffin.
paraguas *nm inv* umbrella.
Paraguay *nm* Paraguay.
paraguaya *nf type of* peach.
paraguayo ,-a *adj* Paraguayan.
▷ *nm & nf* Paraguayan.
paragüero *nm* umbrella stand.
paraíso *nm* paradise.
paraje *nm* spot.
paralela *nf (línea)* parallel, parallel line.
▷ *nf pl* **paralelas** DEP parallel bars.
paralelo ,-a *adj* parallel.
▷ *nm* **paralelo** parallel.
paralelogramo *nm* parallelogram.
parálisis *nf inv* paralysis.
paralítico ,-a *adj* paralytic.
▷ *nm & nf* paralytic.
paralización *nf* 1 paralysis. 2 COM stagnation.
paralizar [4] *vt* 1 MED to paralyse. 2 *(circulación)* to bring to a standstill; *(obras, actividad)* to bring to a halt.
parámetro *nm* parameter.
páramo *nm* moor.
paranoia *nf* paranoia.
paranoico ,-a *adj* paranoic, paranoiac.
▷ *nm & nf* paranoic, paranoiac.
parapente *nm* paragliding.
parapeto *nm* parapet.
parapléjico ,-a *adj* paraplegic.
▷ *nm & nf* paraplegic.
parapsicología *nf* parapsychology.
parapsicológico ,-a *adj* parapsychological.
parar *vt* 1 to stop. 2 DEP to save, catch: **ha parado tres pelotas** *he's made three saves.*
▷ *vi* 1 to stop: **aquí no para el tren** *the train doesn't stop here.* 2 *(alojarse)* to stay: **¿dónde estás parando?** *where are you staying?* 3 *(hallarse)* to be: **no para en casa** *she's never at home.* 4 *(llegar)* to lead; *(acabar)* to end up: **no se sabe en qué parará esta aventura** *who knows how this adventure will end.*
▷ *vpr* **pararse** to stop.
pararrayos *nm inv* lightning conductor.
parasitario ,-a *adj* parasitic.
parásito ,-a *adj* parasitic.
▷ *nm* **parásito** 1 BIOL parasite. 2 *pey (persona)* parasite, hanger-on.
▷ *nm pl* **parásitos** RAD interference *sing*.
parasol *nm* parasol, sunshade.
parca *nf* **la parca** *fig* death.
parcela *nf* 1 *(de tierra)* plot (of land). 2 *fig* share, portion.
parcelar *vt (finca)* to divide into plots.
parche *nm* 1 patch. 2 *fig (chapuza)* botch job.
parchís *nm inv* ludo.
parcial *adj* 1 *(gen)* partial; *(examen) covering part of the course.* 2 *(tendencioso)* partial, biased.
▷ *nm (examen) examination covering part of the course and counting towards the final mark.*
parcialidad *nf (injusticia)* bias, partiality.
parco ,-a *adj* 1 *(escaso)* frugal, sparing. 2 *(moderado)* moderate, sober.
pardo ,-a *adj* 1 *(color tierra)* brown. 2 *(sin luz)* dark, dim.
pareado ,-a *adj* 1 *(poesía)* rhyming. 2 *(casa)* semidetached.
parecer [43] *nm (opinión)* opinion, mind: **¿has cambiado de parecer?** *have you changed your mind?*
▷ *vi* 1 to seem, look (like): **parece un oso** *it looks like a bear.* 2 *(opinar)* to think: **¿qué te parece?** *what do you think?* 3 [Used only in the 3rd pers, it does not take a subject.] *(aparentar)* to look as if: **parece que va a llover** *it looks as if it's going to rain.*
▷ *vpr* **parecerse** to be alike, look like: **se parecen mucho** *they're very much alike.*
parecido ,-a *adj* similar.
▷ *nm* **parecido** resemblance, likeness.
pared *nf* 1 wall. 2 *(de una montaña)* side.
paredón *nm* 1 *(como defensa)* wall. 2 *(de fusilamiento)* execution wall.
pareja *nf* 1 *(gen)* pair: **he perdido la pareja de este gemelo** *I've lost the other cufflink.* 2 *(de personas)* couple; *(de baile)* partner. 3 *(de cartas)* pair.
parejo,-a *adj (sin diferencia)* the same; *(por igual)* even.
parentela *nf* relatives *pl*, relations *pl*.
parentesco *nm* kinship, relationship: **¿qué parentesco tenéis?** *how are you related?*
paréntesis *nm inv* 1 *(gen)* parenthesis; *(signo)* brackets *pl*. 2 *fig (interrupción)* break, interruption. ■ **entre paréntesis** in brackets, in parentheses.
paria *nm o nf* pariah.
paridad *nf* 1 *(gen)* parity, equality. 2 FIN parity of exchange.
pariente ,-a *nm & nf* relative.
▷ *nf* **la parienta** *fam (esposa)* the missus.
parir *vt fam* to give birth to.
▷ *vi* to give birth.
parking *nm* car park, US parking lot.
párkinson *nm* Parkinson's disease.
parlamentario ,-a *adj* parliamentary.
▷ *nm & nf* member of parliament.
parlamento *nm* 1 parliament. 2 *(discurso)* speech.

parlanchín ,-ina *adj* talkative.
▷ *nm & nf fam* chatterbox.
parlante *adj* talking.
parlotear *vi fam* to chatter, prattle on.
parmesano ,-a *adj* Parmesan.
▷ *nm* **parmesano** *(queso)* Parmesan cheese.
paro *nm* **1** stop. **2** *(desempleo)* unemployment; *(subsidio)* unemployment benefit, US unemployment compensation. **3** *(interrupción)* stoppage, strike. ● **paro cardiaco** cardiac arrest. ‖ **paro indefinido** indefinite strike.
parodia *nf* parody.
parodiar [12] *vt* to parody.
paroxismo *nm* paroxysm.
parpadear *vi* **1** *(ojos)* to blink, wink. **2** *(luz)* to flicker, twinkle.
párpado *nm* eyelid.
parque *nm* **1** *(jardines)* park. **2** *(coches - de un país)* total number; *(- de un propietario)* fleet: **el parque automovilístico español** *the total number of cars in Spain.* **3** *(de niños)* playpen. ● **parque de atracciones** amusement park, funfair. ‖ **parque de bomberos** fire station.
parqué *nm* parquet.
parquímetro *nm* parking meter.
parra *nf* grapevine.
parrafada *nf* **1** *fam (conversación)* chat. **2** *fam (discurso)* spiel, speech.
párrafo *nm* paragraph.
parranda *nf fam* spree. ■ **ir(se) de parranda** to go out on the town.
parrilla *nf* grill, US broiler, barbecue. ■ **a la parrilla** CULIN grilled.
parrillada *nf* mixed grill *(of meat or fish)*.
párroco *nm* parish priest.
parroquia *nf* **1** *(área)* parish. **2** *(iglesia)* parish church. **3** *(feligreses)* parishioners *pl*, congregation.
parsimonia *nf* **1** *(lentitud)* slowness. **2** *(calma)* calmness. **3** *(moderación)* parsimony.
parsimonioso ,-a *adj (tranquilo)* slow, unhurried.
parte *nf* **1** *(gen)* part; *(en una partición)* portion: **divide el pastel en tres partes** *cut the cake into three (slices).* **2** *(en negocio)* share. **3** *(lugar)* place: **no lo venden en ninguna parte** *they don't sell it anywhere.* **4** *(en un conflicto)* side: **las dos partes quieren llevar la razón** *both sides believe they are right.* **5** JUR party.
▷ *nm (comunicado)* official report: **han dicho en el parte que iba a llover** *the weather report said it was going to rain.*
▷ *nf pl* **partes** *fam* privates, private parts. ■ **dar parte** to report. ‖ **de parte de** on behalf of, from. ‖ **en parte** partly: **en parte tienes razón** *you have a point there.* ‖ **por una parte,... por otra...** on the one hand..., on the other hand... ● **parte médico** medical report.
partera *nf* midwife.
parterre *nm* flowerbed.
partición *nf (de una herencia)* partition, division.
participación *nf* **1** *(intervención)* participation, involvement. **2** *(comunicado)* announcement: **¿te han mandado la participación de boda?** *have they notified you of their wedding?* **3** FIN *(acción)* share. **4** *(en lotería)* (part of a) lottery ticket.
participante *nm o nf* participant.
participar *vi (tomar parte - en una conversación)* to participate, take part; *(- en un proyecto)* to take part; *(- en un torneo)* to enter, take part.
▷ *vt (notificar)* to notify, inform.
partícipe *adj* participating.
▷ *nm o nf* participant. ■ **hacer partícipe a** ALGN **de** ALGO **1** *(notificar)* to inform SB about STH. **2** *(compartir)* to share STH with SB.
participio *nm* participle.
partícula *nf* particle.
particular *adj* **1** *(concreto)* particular. **2** *(privado)* private: **en mi domicilio particular** *at my home address.* **3** *(privativo)* peculiar, particular, special.
▷ *nm* **1** *(individuo)* private individual: **compré el coche a un particular** *I bought the car from a private owner.* **2** *(asunto)* matter, subject.
particularidad *nf* **1** *(gen)* peculiarity. **2** *(singularidad)* singularity, peculiarity. **3** *(detalle)* detail.
particularizar *vt* **1** *(distinguir)* to distinguish, make different, differentiate. **2** *(detallar)* to detail.
partida *nf* **1** *(remesa)* consignment, lot. **2** *(documento)* certificate. **3** FIN entry, item. **4** *(juego)* game. ■ **jugar una partida** to play a game. ● **partida de nacimiento** birth certificate.
partidario,-a *adj* supporting.
▷ *nm & nf* supporter. ■ **mostrarse partidario,-a de** ALGO to be in favour of STH.
partidista *adj* biased, partisan.
partido ,-a *adj* **1** *(dividido)* divided. **2** *(roto)* broken, split.
▷ *nm* **partido 1** *(grupo político)* party, group. **2** *(provecho)* profit, advantage. **3** DEP *(equipo)* team; *(juego)* game, match. ■ **sacar partido de** to profit from. ‖ **tomar partido** to take sides. ● **partido amistoso** friendly game.
partir *vt* **1** *(dividir)* to divide, split: **voy a partir pan** *I'll cut some bread.* **2** *(romper)* to break; *(nueces, almendras)* to crack.
▷ *vi* **1** *(irse)* to leave, set out, set off. **2** *(proceder)* to originate from: **¿de quién partió la idea?** *whose idea was it?*
▷ *vpr* **partirse** to break: **se ha partido la pierna** *he's broken his leg.* ■ **a partir de hoy** from now on.
partitivo ,-a *adj* partitive.
▷ *nm* **partitivo** partitive.
partitura *nf* score.
parto *nm (proceso)* delivery, labour (US labor); *(efecto)* childbirth: **fue un parto difícil** *it was a difficult birth.* ■ **estar de parto** to be in labour (US labor).
parvulario *nm* nursery school.
párvulo ,-a *nm & nf* infant.
pasa *nf* raisin.
pasable *adj* passable.
pasadizo *nm* passage.
pasado ,-a *adj* **1** past, gone by. **2** *(año, semana, etc)* last. **3** *(después)* after: **pasadas las once** *after eleven.* **4** *(estropeado)* bad.
▷ *nm* **pasado 1** *(tiempo)* past. **2** LING past, past tense. ● **pasado mañana** the day after tomorrow.
pasador *nm* **1** *(de pelo)* hair slide, slide. **2** *(de puerta, etc)* bolt, fastener.
pasaje *nf* **1** *(tarifa)* fare, ticket. **2** *(pasajeros)* passengers *pl.* **3** *(fragmento)* passage.
pasajero ,-a *adj* passing.
▷ *nm & nf* passenger.

pasamanos *nm inv* handrail.
pasamontañas *nm inv* balaclava.
pasaporte *nm* passport.
pasapurés *nm inv* vegetable mill.
pasar *vi* **1** *(ir)* to pass, pass by, go: **pasa de un idioma a otro sin darse cuenta** *he goes from one language to another without realizing.* **2** *(tiempo)* to pass, go by: **¡cómo pasa el tiempo!** *doesn't time fly!* **3** *(entrar)* to come in, go in: **pasa, está abierto** *come in, it's not locked.* **4** *(cesar)* to pass, cease: **en cuanto pase la tormenta salimos** *we'll go out when the storm has passed.* **5** *(límite)* to exceed (**de**, -). **6** *(ocurrir)* to happen. **7** *(sufrir)* to suffer.
▷ *vt* **1** *(trasladar)* to move, transfer: **pasa este documento al otro CD** *move this file to the other CD.* **2** *(comunicar, dar)* to give: **pásale el informe al jefe** *give this report to the boss.* **3** *(cruzar)* to cross: **pasamos la frontera ayer** *we crossed the border yesterday.* **4** *(alcanzar)* to pass, reach: **pásame la sal, por favor** *pass me the salt, please.* **5** *(aventajar)* to surpass, be better than: **tu hermano ya te pasa en matemáticas** *your brother is better than you at maths.* **6** *(adelantar)* to overtake: **me pasó un deportivo rojo en una curva** *a red sports car overtook me on a bend.* **7** *(deslizar)* to run: **pasó el dedo por el estante** *he ran his finger along the shelf.* **8** *(tolerar)* to overlook: **esta vez te la paso, pero que no se repita** *I'll overlook it this time, but don't let it happen again.* **9** *(aprobar)* to pass: **pasé el examen a la primera** *I passed my test first time.* **10** *(proyectar)* to show: **pasaron unas diapositivas** *they showed some slides.* **11** *(tiempo - estar)* to spend; *(- disfrutar, padecer)* to have: **pasamos unas vacaciones estupendas** *we had a wonderful holiday* (US *vacation).*
▷ *vpr* **pasarse 1** *(desertar)* to pass over (**a**, to): **se ha pasado al otro bando** *she's gone over to the other side.* **2** *(pudrirse)* to go off. **3** *(olvidarse)* to forget: **se me pasó la fecha de entrega** *I forgot about the deadline.* **4** *(ir)* to go by (**por**, -), call in (**por**, at): **pásate por casa cuando quieras** *pop in any time.* **5** *fam (excederse)* to overdo it; *(ir demasiado lejos)* to go too far (**de**, -): **te has pasado de sincero** *you were too honest.*
pasarela *nf* **1** *(puente)* footbridge; *(de un barco)* gangway. **2** *(de modelos)* catwalk.
pasatiempo *nm* pastime, hobby.
▷ *nm pl* **pasatiempos** puzzles.
pascua *nf (cristiana)* Easter; *(judía)* Passover.
▷ *nf pl* **pascuas** Christmas *sing.*
pase *nm* **1** *(permiso)* pass. **2** *(cambio)* move. **3** *(desfile)* show. **4** CINE showing. **5** DEP pass.
pasear *vi* to stroll, go for a walk.
▷ *vt* **1** to take for a walk. **2** *fig (exhibir)* to show off.
paseo *nm* **1** *(a pie)* walk, stroll; *(a caballo)* ride. **2** *(en coche)* drive; *(en bicicleta, moto)* ride. **3** *(calle)* avenue, promenade. ■ **dar un paseo** to go for a walk.
pasillo *nm* corridor.
pasión *nf* passion.
pasional *adj (gen)* passionate.
pasividad *nf* passiveness, passivity.
pasma *nf* **la pasma** *argot* the cops *pl*, the (old) bill.
pasmado ,-a *adj* flabbergasted, open-mouthed.
pasmar *vt* to astonish, amaze.
▷ *vpr* **pasmarse** *fam (asombrarse)* to be astonished, be amazed.
pasmo *nm* **1** *(asombro)* amazement, astonishment: **2** *(resfriado)* chill.
pasmoso ,-a *adj* astonishing, amazing.
paso *nm* **1** *(movimiento)* step, footstep. **2** *(distancia)* pace. **3** *(camino)* passage, way. **4** *(avance)* progress, advance. **5** *(trámite)* step, move. **6** *(de montaña)* mountain pass; *(de mar)* strait. **7** REL float *(used in Holy Week processions).* ■ **abrirse paso** to force one's way through. ‖ **estar de paso** to be passing through. ‖ **«Prohibido el paso»** «No entry». ● **ceda el paso** *(señal)* give way sign, US yield sign. ‖ **paso de cebra** zebra crossing. ‖ **paso de peatones** pedestrian crossing.
pasota *nm o nf* **1** *fam (joven apático)* dropout. **2** *fam (persona despreocupada)* laid-back person: **es un pasota** *he doesn't care about anything.*
pasta *nf* **1** *(masa)* paste. **2** CULIN *(italiana)* pasta; *(de bizcocho, crepes)* mixture; *(para pasteles)* pastry. **3** *(croissant, ensaimada, etc)* pastry; *(de té)* petit four, biscuit, US cookie. **4** *fam (dinero)* dosh, dough, money. **5** *(de encuadernación)* boards *pl.*
pastar *vt* to pasture, graze.
▷ *vi* to pasture, graze.
pastel *adj (color)* pastel.
▷ *nm* **1** CULIN *(tipo bizcocho)* cake; *(tipo empanada)* pie. **2** ARTE *(material, obra)* pastel; *(técnica)* pastel drawing.
pastelería *nf* **1** *(tienda)* cake shop, baker's, confectioner's. **2** *(pasteles)* cakes and pastries.
pastelero ,-a *adj (industria)* baking.
▷ *nm & nf (cocinero)* pastrycook; *(vendedor)* cake seller.
pasteurizado ,-a *adj* pasteurized.
pasteurizar *vt* to pasteurize.
pastilla *nf* **1** *(medicina)* tablet, pill. **2** *(de chocolate, jabón)* bar.
pasto *nm* **1** *(pastizal)* pasture. **2** *(acción)* grazing. ■ **ser pasto de las llamas** to go up in flames.
pastor,-ra *nm & nf (del campo - hombre)* shepherd; *(- mujer)* shepherdess.
▷ *nm* **pastor** REL pastor.
pastoso ,-a *adj* **1** *(sustancia)* pasty, doughy. **2** *(lengua)* furry. **3** *(voz)* mellow.
pata *nf* **1** *(gen)* leg. **2** *(garra)* paw. **3** *(pezuña)* hoof. ■ **a cuatro patas** on all fours. ‖ **meter la pata** *fam* to put one's foot in it. ‖ **patas arriba** upside down. ‖ **tener mala pata** *fam* to have bad luck. ● **patas de gallo** *(arrugas)* crow's feet.
patada *nf* kick. ■ **dar una patada** to kick. ‖ **tratar a patadas** *fam* to treat like dirt.
patalear *vi* **1** *(con enfado)* to stamp one's feet. **2** *(protestar)* to kick up a fuss.
pataleo *nm* **1** *(con los pies)* stamping. **2** *(protesta)* complaining. ● **derecho al pataleo** *fam* the right to complain.
pataleta *nf fam* tantrum.
patán *nm* boor.
patata *nf* potato. ● **patatas fritas 1** *(de bolsa)* crisps, US chips. **2** *(de sartén)* chips, US French fries.
paté *nm* pâté.
patear *vt* **1** to kick. **2** *(andar)* to walk.
▷ *vi (con enfado)* to stamp one's feet.
patentado ,-a *adj* patented.
patentar *vt* to patent.
patente *adj (evidente)* obvious, patent.
▷ *nf* patent.

patera *nf* boat.
paternal *adj* paternal.
paternalista *adj* 1 paternalistic. 2 *pey* patronizing.
paternidad *nf* 1 paternity. 2 *(autoría)* authorship.
paterno ,-a *adj* paternal.
patético ,-a *adj* pathetic.
patíbulo *nm* gallows *sing*.
patilla *nf* 1 *(pata)* leg. 2 *(de las gafas)* arm.
▷ *nf pl* sideboards, US sideburns.
patín *nm* 1 *(de ruedas)* roller skate, skate; *(de hielo)* ice skate. 2 *(tabla)* skateboard. 3 *(patinete)* scooter. 4 *(en el mar)* pedalo.
pátina *nf* patina.
patinador ,-ra *nm & nf* skater.
patinaje *nm* skating. ● **patinaje artístico** figure skating. ‖ **patinaje sobre hielo** ice-skating. ‖ **patinaje sobre ruedas** roller skating.
patinar *vi* 1 *(como diversión)* to skate. 2 *(por accidente)* to slip. 3 *(vehículo)* to skid. 4 *(meter la pata)* to put one's foot in it; *(equivocarse)* to boob, make a boob.
patinazo *nm* 1 skid. 2 *fam (error)* boob, blunder.
patinete *nm* scooter.
patio *nm* 1 *(de una casa)* courtyard; *(de un colegio)* playground. 2 TEAT pit.
patitieso ,-a *adj fam (sorprendido)* flabbergasted; *(inmóvil por el frío)* frozen-stiff.
pato ,-a *nm & nf (ave - en general)* duck; *(- macho)* drake; *(- hembra)* duck.
▷ *nm* **pato** *fam (persona)* clumsy person. ■ **pagar el pato** *fam* to carry the can.
patológico ,-a *adj* pathological.
patoso ,-a *adj* clumsy.
patria *nf* homeland.
patriarca *nm* patriarch.
patriarcado *nm* patriarchy.
patrimonio *nm* 1 *(gen)* patrimony; *(riqueza)* wealth. 2 *(histórico, cultural)* heritage.
patrio ,-a *adj* of one's homeland. ● **patria potestad** custody.
patriota *nm o nf* patriot.
patriótico ,-a *adj* patriotic.
patriotismo *nm* patriotism.
patrocinador ,-ra *adj* sponsoring.
▷ *nm & nf* sponsor.
patrocinar *vt* to sponsor.
patrocinio *nm* sponsorship.
patrón,-ona *nm & nf* 1 *(dueño de una casa)* landlord; *(dueña)* landlady. 2 *(jefe)* employer, boss; *(hombre)* master; *(mujer)* mistress. 3 REL patron saint.
▷ *nm* **patrón** 1 *(en costura)* pattern. 2 *(de barco)* skipper. 3 *(modelo)* standard.
patronal *adj* 1 *(fiesta)* of one's patron saint. 2 *(organización, oferta)* management.
▷ *nf (institución)* employers' association; *(de una empresa)* management.
patronato *nm* 1 *(consejo)* board, council; *(benéfico)* trust. 2 *(patronal)* employers' association.
patrulla *nf* 1 *(de vigilancia)* patrol. 2 *(de rescate)* party.
patrullar *vt* to patrol.
▷ *vi* to be out on patrol.
patuco *nm (de niños)* bootee; *(de adultos)* bedsock.
paulatino ,-a *adj* gradual.
pausa *nf* 1 pause. 2 MÚS rest. ■ **con pausa** slowly.
pausado ,-a *adj* unhurried, slow.
pauta *nf* 1 *(norma)* rule, guideline; *(modelo)* model, pattern. 2 *(en el papel)* lines *pl*. 3 MÚS staff.
pava *nf (hervidora)* kettle.
pavimentar *vt (con losas)* to pave; *(con asfalto)* to surface.
pavimento *nm (de losas)* pavement; *(de asfalto)* road surface.
pavo ,-a *nm & nf* 1 *(ave - macho)* turkey; *(- hembra)* turkey hen. 2 *fam (persona)* drip.
▷ *nm* **pavo** 1 *fam (timidez)* shyness. 2 *fam (antiguamente)* five-peseta coin. ● **pavo real** peacock.
pavonearse *vpr* to brag, swagger.
pavoneo *nm* strutting.
pavor *nm* terror.
pavoroso ,-a *adj* frightful.
payasada *nf* 1 buffoonery, clowning. 2 *fam* silly thing, stupid thing.
payaso ,-a *nm & nf* 1 *(artista de circo)* clown. 2 *fam* joker.
payo ,-a *nm & nf* non-Gypsy *(in Gypsy jargon)*.
paz *nf* peace. ■ **dejar en paz** to leave alone. ‖ **estar en paz** to be even, be quits. ‖ **firmar la paz** to sign a peace treaty. ‖ **hacer las paces** to make up.
▲ *pl* **paces**.
pazo *nm* Galician country house.
PC *abrev* **(ordenador personal)** personal computer; *(abreviatura)* PC.
PDF *abrev* **(portable document format)** portable document format; *(abreviatura)* PDF.
PE *abrev* **(Parlamento Europeo)** European Parliament; *(abreviatura)* EP.
peaje *nm* 1 *(dinero)* toll. 2 *(lugar)* tollbooth.
peana *nf* pedestal, stand.
peatón *nm* pedestrian.
peatonal *adj (calle, zona)* pedestrian.
peca *nf* freckle.
pecado *nm* sin.
pecador ,-ra *nm & nf* sinner.
pecaminoso ,-a *adj* sinful, wicked.
pecar [1] *vi* to sin. ■ **pecar de...** to be too..., be over-...: **pequé de meticulosa** *I was too meticulous.*
pecera *nf (redonda)* fishbowl; *(rectangular)* fish tank.
pechera *nf* 1 *(de camisa)* shirt front; *(de delantal)* bib. 2 *fam (pecho)* bosom.
pechina *nf* scallop.
pecho *nm* 1 *(gen)* chest. 2 *(seno)* breast. ■ **a lo hecho pecho** what's done is done. ‖ **dar el pecho** to breast-feed.
pechuga *nf* 1 *(de un ave)* breast. 2 *fam (de mujer)* bust.
pecíolo *nm* petiole.
pecoso ,-a *adj (persona)* freckly; *(cara)* freckled.
pectina *nf* pectin.
pectoral *nm* 1 *(músculo)* pectoral muscle. 2 *(jarabe)* cough mixture. 3 *(de obispo)* pectoral cross.
pecuario ,-a *adj* cattle.
peculiar *adj* 1 *(raro)* peculiar. 2 *(característico)* particular, personal.
peculiaridad *nf* peculiarity.
pecuniario ,-a *adj* pecuniary.

pedagogía *nf* pedagogy.
pedagógico ,-a *adj* pedagogic(al).
pedagogo ,-a *nm & nf* educator, pedagogue.
pedal *nm* 1 pedal. 2 *fam* bender.
pedalear *vi* to pedal.
pedaleo *nm* pedalling.
pedanía *nf* hamlet.
pedante *adj* pedantic, pompous.
pedantería *nf* pedantry, pomposity.
pedazo *nm* 1 piece, bit. 2 *fam (con insultos)*: **¡pedazo de animal!** *stupid idiot!* ■ **hacer pedazos** to smash to pieces: **me ha hecho pedazos el cenicero** *he's smashed my ashtray.*
pedernal *nm* 1 *(sílex)* flint. 2 *fig* rock.
pedestal *nm* pedestal.
pedestre *adj (a pie)* on foot.
pediatra *nm o nf* paediatrician (US pediatrician).
pediatría *nf* paediatrics (US pediatrics).
pedicuro ,-a *nm & nf* chiropodist.
pedido *nm* 1 *(de mercancías)* order. 2 *(petición)* request, petition. ■ **hacer un pedido** to place an order.
pedigrí *nm* pedigree.
pedigüeño ,-a *nm & nf* pest.
pedir [34] *vt* 1 *(gen)* to ask for: **me pidió que la acompañara** *she asked me to go with her.* 2 *(mercancías, en restaurante)* to order: **¿qué has pedido de postre?** *what did you order for dessert?* 3 *(necesitar)* to need, cry out for.
▷ *vi (por la calle)* to beg.
pedo *nm fam* fart. ■ **tirarse un pedo** *fam* to fart, drop one.
pedorreta *nf fam* raspberry.
pedrada *nf* blow with a stone.
pedregal *nm* rocky ground.
pedregoso ,-a *adj* stony, rocky.
pedrera *nf* stone quarry.
pedrería *nf* precious stones *pl.*
pedrisco *nm (granizo)* hail; *(tormenta)* hailstorm.
pedrusco *nm* rough stone.
pedúnculo *nm* 1 *(de crustáceo)* stalk. 2 *(de planta)* stem.
pega *nf fam (dificultad)* snag: **me pusieron muchas pegas** *they made it difficult for me.*
pegadizo ,-a *adj* 1 *(canción, música)* catchy. 2 *(sustancia)* sticky, adhesive.
pegajoso ,-a *adj* 1 *(mano, dedo)* sticky: **hace un calor pegajoso** *it's really hot and sticky.* 2 *pey (persona)* clingy.
pegamento *nm* glue.
pegar[1] *vt* 1 *(gen)* to stick; *(con pegamento)* to glue, stick with glue; *(con cola)* to paste, stick with paste. 2 *(contagiar)* to give: **me has pegado la gripe** *you've given me your flu.* 3 *(acercar)* to move close to: **pega la estantería a la pared** *move the bookcase against the wall.* 4 INFORMÁ to paste.
▷ *vi (combinar)* to match: **esta blusa no pega con la falda** *this blouse doesn't go with the skirt.*
▷ *vpr* **pegarse** 1 *(quemarse)* to stick: **se me ha vuelto a pegar el arroz** *the rice has stuck again.* 2 *(persona)* to latch onto.
pegar[2] *vt* 1 *(golpear)* to hit: **mamá, Pablo me ha pegado** *mum, Pablo hit me.* 2 *(dar)* to give: **¡vaya susto me has pegado!** *you didn't half scare me!*
▷ *vi (tener fuerza)* to beat down: **¡cómo pega el sol hoy!** *it's a real scorcher today!*
▷ *vpr (tropezar)* to bump (**con**, into).
pegatina *nf* sticker.
pego ■ **dar el pego** *fam* to look like the real thing.
pegote *nm* 1 *fam (masa)* sticky dollop, blob. 2 *fam (chapuza)* botch-up, botched job.
peinado *nm (tocado)* hairdo; *(acción)* combing.
peinado ,-a *adj* combed. ■ **ir bien peinado,-a** to be well groomed.
peinar *vt* 1 *(gen)* to comb; *(con cepillo)* to brush. 2 *(registrar)* to comb, search.
peine *nm* comb.
peineta *nf* ornamental comb.
pela *nf fam (antiguamente)* peseta.
▷ *nf pl* **pelas** *fam (dinero)* dough, money.
peladilla *nf* sugared almond.
pelado ,-a *adj* 1 bald, bare. 2 *(cabeza)* hairless, bald. 3 *(terreno)* barren, treeless. 4 *fam (sin dinero)* broke.
▷ *nm* **pelado** *fam short* haircut.
peladuras *nf pl* peelings.
pelagatos *nm o nf inv fam* nobody.
pelaje *nm* 1 *(de animal)* coat, fur. 2 *fam* looks *pl.*
pelambrera *nf fam* hair.
pelapatatas *nm inv* potato peeler.
pelar *vt* 1 *(persona)* to cut SB's hair. 2 *(animal - quitar las plumas)* to pluck; *(- quitar la piel)* to skin. 3 *(fruta, patata, etc)* to peel.
▷ *vpr* **pelarse** 1 *(cortarse el pelo)* to get one's hair cut. 2 *(piel)* to be peeling.
peldaño *nm* step.
pelea *nf* 1 *(física)* fight; *(verbal)* quarrel, row. 2 *(esfuerzo)* struggle.
peleador ,-ra *adj* argumentative.
▷ *nm & nf* brawler.
pelear *vi* 1 *(físicamente)* to fight; *(verbalmente)* to quarrel, argue. 2 *(hacer un esfuerzo)* to work hard, struggle.
▷ *vpr* **pelearse** *(físicamente)* to fight; *(verbalmente)* to quarrel, argue.
peleón ,-ona *nm & nf (persona)* quarrelsome.
peletería *nf* 1 *(establecimiento)* fur shop, furrier's. 2 *(industria)* fur industry.
peletero ,-a *adj (industria)* fur.
▷ *nm & nf* furrier.
peliagudo ,-a *adj* tricky.
pelícano *nm* pelican.
película *nf* film. ● **película de suspense** thriller. ‖ **película muda** silent movie.
peliculón *nm fam* blockbuster.
peligrar *vi* to be in danger.
peligro *nm* 1 danger. 2 *fam (persona)* menace. ■ **correr peligro de** to be in danger of. ‖ **estar fuera de peligro** to be out of danger.
peligroso ,-a *adj* dangerous.
pelín *nm fam* teeny bit.
pelirrojo ,-a *adj* red-haired.
▷ *nm & nf* redhead.
pellejo *nm (piel)* skin.
pelliza *nf (adornada con piel)* fur-trimmed coat; *(forrada de piel)* fur-lined coat.
pellizcar [1] *vt* to pinch, nip.
pellizco *nm* pinch, nip.

pelma *nm o nf fam* bore.
pelmazo ,-a *nm & nf fam* → **pelma.**
pelo *nm* 1 hair. 2 *(de animal)* coat, fur. 3 *fam* bit: **perdí el tren por un pelo** *I missed the train by seconds.* ■ **con pelos y señales** in great detail, down to the last detail. ‖ **no tener pelos en la lengua** to speak one's mind, not mince words. ‖ **no tener un pelo de tonto,-a** *fam* to be nobody's fool. ‖ **poner los pelos de punta** to make one's hair stand on end. ‖ **tomar el pelo a** ALGN to pull SB's leg.
pelón ,-ona *adj* bald.
▷ *nm & nf* bald person.
pelota *nf* ball. ● **pelota de fútbol** football.
▷ *nm o nf fam* creep.
pelotazo *nm* blow with a ball: **le rompieron las gafas de un pelotazo** *they broke his glasses with a ball.*
peloteo *nm* 1 *(fútbol)* kickabout; *(tenis)* knock-up. 2 *fam* → **pelotilleo.**
pelotera *nf fam* row.
pelotilla *nf* small ball. ■ **hacer la pelotilla a** ALGN *fam* to butter SB up.
pelotillero ,-a *adj* crawling.
▷ *nm & nf fam* creep, crawler.
pelotón *nm* 1 MIL squad. 2 *fig (grupo)* bunch. 3 *(de ciclistas)* pack, peloton.
peltre *nm* pewter.
peluca *nf* wig.
peluche *nm* 1 *(tejido)* plush. 2 *(muñeco)* teddy bear, cuddly toy.
peludo ,-a *adj* hairy.
peluquería *nf* hairdresser's.
peluquero ,-a *nm & nf* hairdresser.
peluquín *nm* hairpiece.
pelusa *nf* 1 *(pelo)* fluff. 2 *fam (celos)* jealousy.
pélvico ,-a *adj* pelvic.
pelvis *nf inv* pelvis.
pena *nf* 1 *(castigo)* sentence, punishment. 2 *(tristeza)* grief, sorrow. 3 *(lástima)* pity: **¡qué pena que no podáis venir!** *it's a shame you can't make it!* 4 *(dificultad)* hardship, trouble. ■ **merecer la pena** to be worth while, be worth it.
penado ,-a *nm & nf* convict.
penal *adj (código)* penal; *(derecho, antecedentes)* criminal.
▷ *nm (prisión)* prison, US penitentiary.
penalidad *nf* trouble, hardship.
penalización *nf* 1 *(acción)* penalization; *(castigo)* pen alty, punishment. 2 DEP penalty.
penalizar [4] *vt* to penalize.
penalti *nm* penalty.
penar *vt (castigar)* to punish, penalize.
▷ *vi (padecer)* to suffer, grieve.
pender *vi* to hang (**de**, from).
pendiente *adj* 1 hanging. 2 *(asunto)* pending, outstanding.
▷ *nf (cuesta)* slope; *(inclinación)* gradient.
▷ *nm (joya)* earring. ■ **estar pendiente de** ALGO 1 *(a la espera)* to be waiting for STH. 2 *(atento)* to follow STH closely.
pendular *adj* pendular.
péndulo *nm* pendulum.
pene *nm* penis.
penetración *nf* 1 penetration. 2 *(perspicacia)* insight.
penetrante *adj* penetrating.
penetrar *vi* 1 *(introducirse - en un territorio)* to penetrate (**en**, -); *(- en una casa, propiedad)* to enter: **no nos atrevimos a penetrar en la selva** *we didn't dare go into the jungle.* 2 *(atravesar)* to penetrate, seep through: **la humedad ha penetrado por el suelo** *damp has seeped through the floor.* 3 *fig (entender)* to comprehend (**en**, -); *(analizar)* to look (**en**, into).
▷ *vt* 1 *(atravesar)* to penetrate; *(ruido)* to pierce. 2 *(descifrar - misterio)* to get to the bottom of; *(- secreto)* to fathom (out).
penicilina *nf* penicillin.
península *nf* 1 peninsula. 2 *(ibérica)* mainland Spain. ● **la Península Ibérica** the Iberian Peninsula.
penique *nm* penny.
penitencia *nf* REL *(virtud)* penitence; *(castigo, sacramento)* penance.
penitenciaría *nf* penitentiary.
penitenciario ,-a *adj (institución, sistema)* prison.
penoso ,-a *adj* 1 *(doloroso)* painful; *(triste)* sad. 2 *(trabajoso)* laborious, hard. 3 *(desastroso)* terrible, awful, dreadful.
pensador ,-ra *nm & nf* thinker.
pensamiento *nm* 1 *(idea)* thought. 2 *(mente)* mind. 3 BOT pansy.
pensante *adj* thinking.
pensar [27] *vi* 1 *(gen)* to think (**en**, of/about): **estuvo pensando en sus amigos** *he was thinking about his friends.* 2 *(considerar)* to consider, think (**en**, about). 3 *(creer)* to think, think about. 4 *(opinar)* to think (**de**, about). 5 *(decidir)* to decide. 6 *(tener la intención)* to intend to, plan, think of.
▷ *vpr* **pensarse** to think about.
pensativo ,-a *adj* pensive.
pensión *nf* 1 *(para jubilados)* pension; *(para ex cónjuge)* maintenance. 2 *(casa de huéspedes)* hostel, boarding house, guesthouse, lodgings *pl.* 3 *(cantidad que se paga)* board and lodging, bed and board. ● **pensión completa** full board.
pensionista *nm o nf (jubilado)* pensioner.
pentagonal *adj* pentagonal.
pentágono *nm* pentagon.
pentagrama *nm* MÚS stave, staff.
pentatlón *nm* pentathlon.
Pentecostés *nm (cristiano)* Pentecost, Whit Sunday; *(judío)* Pentecost.
penúltimo ,-a *adj* penultimate.
▷ *nm & nf* last but one, next to last.
penumbra *nf (gen)* semidarkness; *(de un eclipse)* penumbra.
penuria *nf* 1 *(escasez)* shortage. 2 *(pobreza)* extreme poverty, penury.
peña[1] *nf (piedra)* rock; *(monte)* crag.
peña[2] *nf (grupo)* group of friends; *(asociación)* club.
peñasco *nm* crag.
peñón *nm* craggy rock. ■ **el Peñón de Gibraltar** the Rock of Gibraltar.
peón *nm* 1 *(trabajador)* unskilled labourer (US laborer). 2 *(en el ajedrez)* pawn.
peonía *nf* BOT peony.
peonza *nf* top, spinning top.

peor *adj* 1 *(comparativo)* worse: **tu coche es peor que el mío** *your car is worse than mine.* 2 *(superlativo)* worst.
pepinillo *nm* gherkin.
pepino *nm* cucumber. ■ **me importa un pepino** *fam* I don't give a damn.
pepita *nf* 1 *(de fruta)* ⟶ **seed, pip.** 2 *(de oro)* nugget.
peque *nm* kid.
pequeñez *nf*
▲ *pl* **pequeñeces.** 1 *(de tamaño)* smallness. 2 *(insignificancia)* trifle.
pequeñito ,-a *adj fam* teeny, wee, tiddly.
pequeño ,-a *adj* 1 *(de tamaño)* little, small: **este jersey me está pequeño** *this jumper is too small for me.* 2 *(de edad)* young. 3 *(en tiempo)* short: **nos hemos tomado unas pequenas vacaciones** *we've taken a short holiday (US vacation).*
▷ *nm & nf (niño)* little one: **a esta hora los pequeños tienen que estar en la cama** *kids should be in bed by now.* ■ **de pequeño,-a** as a child.
pequinés ,-esa *adj* Pekinese.
▷ *nm* **pekinés** *(perro)* Pekinese.
pera *nf (fruta)* pear. ■ **pedir peras al olmo** *fam* to ask the impossible.
peral *nm* pear tree.
perca *nf* perch.
percance *nm* mishap.
percatarse *vpr* to notice (**de**, -), realize (**de**, -).
percebe *nm* goose barnacle.
percepción *nf* perception.
perceptible *adj* perceptible, noticeable.
perceptivo ,-a *adj* perceptive.
percha *nf* 1 *(de ropa)* hanger. 2 *(perchero de pie)* coat stand; *(perchero de pared)* rack; *(gancho)* hook.
perchero *nm (de pared)* clothes rack; *(de pie)* coat stand.
percherón ,-ona *adj (caballo)* Percheron.
percibir *vt* 1 *(notar)* to perceive, notice. 2 *(dinero)* to receive.
percusión *nf* percussion.
percusionista *nm o nf* percussionist.
percutir *vt* 1 *(golpear)* to strike. 2 MED to percuss.
perdedor ,-ra *nm & nf* loser.
perder [28] *vt* 1 *(gen)* to lose. 2 *(malgastar, desperdiciar)* to waste: **se pasa el día perdiendo el tiempo** *he's always wasting time.* 3 *(tren, etc)* to miss.
▷ *vi* 1 *(gen)* to lose; *(salir perdiendo)* to lose out. 2 *(empeorar)* to get worse.
▷ *vpr* **perderse** 1 *(extraviarse - persona)* to get lost; *(- animal)* to go missing: **se me ha perdido un pendiente** *I've lost an earring.* 2 *(confundirse)* to get confused, get mixed up: **en cuanto hablan de política me pierdo** *when they talk about politics I get lost.* 3 *(desaparecer)* to disappear, take off: **en cuanto ve problemas, se pierde** *as soon as there's a problem, he disappears.* 4 *(dejar escapar)* to miss: **¡no te lo pierdas!** *don't miss it!*
perdición *nf (moral)* undoing, ruin.
pérdida *nf* 1 *(daño)* loss: **las tormentas han originado muchas pérdidas materiales** *the storms have caused serious damage.* 2 *(desperdicio)* waste. 3 *(acción de perder)* loss: **la pérdida del billete fue un desastre** *losing the ticket was a disaster.* 4 *(escape)* leak.
perdido ,-a *adj* 1 *(extraviado)* lost. 2 *(desperdiciado)* wasted. 3 *(bala)* stray. 4 *(aislado)* isolated, cut-off.
perdigón *nm* 1 pellet. 2 ZOOL young partridge.
perdiguero *nm* gun dog.
perdiz *nf* partridge.
perdón *nm* pardon, forgiveness. ■ **pedir perdón** to apologize, say sorry. ‖ **¡perdón!** 1 *(para excusarse)* sorry! 2 *(para preguntar, hacerse paso)* excuse me.
perdonable *adj* excusable, forgivable, pardonable.
perdonar *vt* 1 *(gen)* to forgive; *(acusado)* to pardon. 2 *(excusar)* to excuse: **perdona que te interrumpa** *excuse me for interrupting, sorry to bother you.* 3 *(deuda)* to write off.
perdurar *vi* to last, continue to exist, live on.
perecedero ,-a *adj* perishable.
perecer [43] *vi* to perish, die.
peregrinación *nf* pilgrimage.
peregrinar *vi* 1 to go on a pilgrimage. 2 *fig* to traipse, trail.
peregrino ,-a *adj* 1 *(en peregrinaje)* travelling. 2 *(ave)* migratory.
▷ *nm & nf* REL pilgrim.
perejil *nm* parsley.
perenne *adj* perennial.
pereza *nf* laziness. ■ **tener pereza** to feel lazy.
perezoso ,-a *adj* lazy.
▷ *nm* **perezoso** ZOOL sloth.
perfección *nf* perfection. ■ **a la perfección** perfectly: **habla inglés a la perfección** *he speaks perfect English.*
perfeccionar *vt* 1 *(mejorar)* to improve. 2 *(hacer perfecto)* to perfect.
perfeccionista *adj* perfectionist.
▷ *nm o nf* perfectionist.
perfecto ,-a *adj* perfect.
perfidia *nf* perfidy.
pérfido ,-a *adj* perfidious.
▷ *nm & nf* traitor.
perfil *nm* 1 *(gen)* profile. 2 *(silueta)* outline. 3 *(para un trabajo)* outline. ■ **de perfil** in profile: **ponte de perfil** *show me your profile.*
perfilar *vt* 1 *(dar forma)* to outline. 2 *(perfeccionar)* to perfect.
▷ *vpr* **perfilarse** to take shape: **se perfila como ganador** *is beginning to look like the winner.*
perforación *nf* 1 *(gen)* perforation. 2 *(en una mina)* drilling, boring. 3 *(de papel)* punching.
perforadora *nf* 1 *(en una mina)* drill. 2 *(de papeles)* punch.
perforar *vt* 1 *(gen)* to perforate. 2 *(terreno)* to drill, bore. 3 *(papel)* to punch.
perfumar *vt* to perfume, scent.
perfume *nm* perfume.
perfumería *nf* 1 *(tienda)* perfumery. 2 *(industria)* perfume industry.
pergamino *nm* parchment.
pérgola *nf* pergola.
pericardio *nm* pericardium.
pericarpio *nm* pericarp.
pericia *nf* skill.
periferia *nf* 1 *(gen)* periphery. 2 *(de una ciudad)* outskirts *pl.*
periférico ,-a *adj* 1 *(gen)* peripheral. 2 *(barrio, zona)* outlying.
▷ *nm* **periférico** INFORMÁ peripheral unit.

perifollo *nm* BOT common chervil.
▷ *nm pl* **perifollos** *fam (adornos)* frills.
perífrasis *nf* periphrasis.
perifrástico ,-a *adj* periphrastic.
perilla *nf* goatee. ■ **venir de perilla** *fam* to come in really handy.
perímetro *nm* perimeter.
periodicidad *nf* periodicity.
periódico ,-a *adj* periodical.
▷ *nm* **periódico** newspaper.
periodismo *nm* journalism.
periodista *nm o nf* journalist.
período *nm* period.
peripecia *nf* incident.
peripuesto ,-a *adj fam* all dressed up.
periquete *nm fam* jiffy. ■ **en un periquete** in a jiffy, in two shakes, in a sec.
periquito ,-a *nm o nf* **periquito** *(gen)* parakeet; *(australiano)* budgerigar.
periscopio *nm* periscope.
peristilo *nm* peristyle.
peritaje *nm* **1** *(informe)* expert's report; *(para el seguro)* loss adjuster's report. **2** *(investigación)* inspection, survey.
perito ,-a *nm & nf* **1** *(experto)* expert; *(en seguros)* loss adjuster. **2** *(en ingeniería)* technician. ● **perito,-a agrónomo,-a** agricultural technician.
perjudicado ,-a *nm & nf* person who loses out, person affected: **los más perjudicados han sido los campesinos** *farmers have been worst affected.*
perjudicar [1] *vt* to adversely affect, be bad for, be detrimental to: **esta sequía perjudica a la agricultura** *the drought is hitting the farmers.*
perjudicial *adj* harmful.
perjuicio *nm (material)* damage; *(económico)* loss.
perjurio *nm* perjury.
perla *nf* **1** pearl. **2** *fig* gem. ■ **de perlas** *fam* perfect: **la fiesta salió de perlas** *the party was a real success.*
permanecer [43] *vi* to stay, remain.
permanencia *nf* **1** *(estancia)* stay. **2** *(continuidad)* continuance.
permanente *adj* permanent, lasting.
▷ *nf (del pelo)* permanent wave: **se ha hecho la permanente** *she's had her hair permed.*
permanganato *nm* permanganate.
permeabilidad *nf* permeability.
permeable *adj* permeable.
permisividad *nf* permissiveness.
permisivo ,-a *adj* permissive.
permiso *nm* **1** permission. **2** *(documento)* permit. **3** MIL leave. ■ **con permiso** excuse me. ‖ **estar de permiso** to be on leave. ● **permiso de conducir** driving licence, US driver's licence.
permitir *vt* to allow, let: **permitió que sus hijas fueran al concierto** *he let his daughters go to the concert.*
▷ *vpr* **permitirse** to allow OS, afford. ■ **¿me permite?** may I?
permuta *nf* exchange.
permutación *nf* permutation.
permutar *vt* **1** to exchange. **2** MAT to permute.
pernicioso ,-a *adj* pernicious, harmful.
pernoctar *vi* to spend the night, stay overnight.
pero *conj* but.
▷ *nm* objection, fault.
perol *nm* cooking pot.
peroné *nm* fibula.
perorata *nf* spiel.
peróxido *nm* peroxide. ● **peróxido de hidrógeno** hydrogen peroxide.
perpendicular *adj* perpendicular.
perpetrar *vt* to perpetrate, commit.
perpetuación *nf* perpetuation.
perpetuar [11] *vt* to perpetuate.
▷ *vpr* **perpetuarse** to be perpetuated.
perpetuidad *nf* perpetuity. ■ **a perpetuidad** for ever and ever.
perpetuo ,-a *adj (gen)* perpetual; *(cargo)* permanent. ● **nieves perpetuas** perpetual snows.
perplejidad *nf* perplexity.
perplejo ,-a *adj* perplexed.
perrera *nf (lugar)* dog pound.
perro ,-a *adj* rotten.
▷ *nm* **perro** ZOOL dog. ■ **ser perro viejo** *fam* to be long in the tooth. ● **perro caliente** hot dog. ‖ **perro callejero** stray dog.
persecución *nf* **1** pursuit. **2** *(represión)* persecution.
perseguidor ,-ora *nm & nf* **1** pursuer. **2** *(represor)* persecutor.
perseguir [56] *vt* **1** to pursue, chase. **2** *fig (seguir)* to follow: **este perro me persigue** *this dog follows me everywhere.* **3** *(reprimir)* to persecute.
perseverante *adj* persevering.
perseverar *vi* to persevere.
persiana *nf* blind.
persignarse *vpr* to cross OS.
persistente *adj* persistent.
persistir *vi* **1** *(mantenerse firme)* to persist, persevere. **2** *(durar)* to continue, persist.
persona *nf* person. ■ **en persona** in person.
personaje *nm* **1** *(famoso)* celebrity. **2** *(en obra, película)* character.
personal *adj* personal.
▷ *nm* **1** *(de una empresa)* personnel, staff. **2** *fam (gente)* everyone, everybody.
▷ *nf* DEP *(falta)* personal foul.
personalidad *nf* **1** *(carácter)* personality. **2** *(personaje)* celebrity.
personalizar *vt* to personalize.
▷ *vi* to get personal.
personarse *vpr* to appear in person, present OS.
personificación *nf* personification.
personificar [1] *vt* to personify.
perspectiva *nf* **1** ARTE perspective. **2** *(posibilidad)* prospect: **este negocio presenta muy buenas perspectivas** *this business has good prospects.* **3** *(vista)* view, perspective. **4** *(punto de vista)* point of view.
perspicacia *nf* sharpness, perspicacity.
perspicaz *adj* sharp, perspicacious.
▲ *pl* **perspicaces.**
persuadir *vt* to persuade, convince.
▷ *vpr* **persuadirse** to be convinced.
persuasión *nf* persuasion.
persuasivo ,-a *adj* persuasive.
pertenecer [43] *vi* to belong (**a**, to).

perteneciente *adj* belonging (**a**, to).
pertenencia *nf* 1 *(propiedad)* property: **esto es de mi pertenencia** *this belongs to me.* 2 *(afiliación)* membership.
▷ *nf pl* **pertenencias** *(bienes)* belongings.
pértiga *nf* pole. ● **salto de pértiga** pole vault.
pertinaz *adj* 1 *(sequía, frío)* prolonged, persistent. 2 *(persona)* obstinate.
▲ *pl* **pertinaces.**
pertinente *adj* 1 *(oportuno)* appropriate. 2 *(relevante)* pertinent, relevant.
pertrechar *vt* to supply (**de**, with).
▷ *vpr* **pertrecharse** to equip OS.
pertrechos *nm pl* 1 equipment *sing.* 2 MIL military equipment *sing.*
perturbación *nf* 1 disruption, disturbance. 2 *(mental)* disorder.
perturbado ,-a *adj* 1 *(trastornado)* mentally disturbed. 2 *(intranquilo)* perturbed.
perturbar *vt* 1 *(alterar)* to disturb, perturb. 2 *(inquietar)* to perturb. ■ **perturbar el orden** to disturb the peace.
Perú *nm* Peru.
peruano ,-a *adj* Peruvian.
▷ *nm & nf* Peruvian.
perversidad *nf (maldad)* wickedness.
perversión *nf* 1 *(maldad)* wickedness. 2 *(sexual)* perversion.
perverso ,-a *adj (malvado)* evil, wicked.
▷ *nm & nf* evil person.
pervertido ,-a *nm & nf* pervert.
pervertir [35] *vt (gen)* to corrupt; *(sexualmente)* to pervert.
pervivencia *nf* survival.
pervivir *vi* to live on, persist, survive.
pesa *nf* weight.
pesadez *nf* 1 *(lentitud)* sluggishness. 2 *(molestia)* bore. 3 *(de un objeto)* heaviness.
pesadilla *nf* nightmare.
pesado ,-a *adj* 1 *(gen)* heavy. 2 *(molesto)* tiresome; *(aburrido)* boring. 3 *(trabajoso)* tough, hard. 4 *(sueño)* deep.
▷ *nm & nf (persona)* bore, pain. ■ **ponerse pesado,-a** to get boring, be a pain.
pesadumbre *nf* sorrow, grief.
pésame *nm* condolences *pl.* ■ **darle el pésame a** ALGN to offer SB one's condolences.
pesar *vi* 1 to weigh: **¿cuánto pesas?** *how much do you weigh?* 2 *(tener mucho peso)* to be heavy. 3 *(sentir)* to be sorry, regret: **me pesa mucho no haberle invitado** *I really regret not having invited him.* 4 *(influir)* to carry weight: **su opinión pesa más que la nuestra** *her opinion carries more weight than ours.*
▷ *vt* to weigh.
▷ *nm* 1 *(pena)* sorrow, grief. 2 *(arrepentimiento)* regret. ■ **a pesar de** despite, in spite of.
pesca *nf* 1 *(actividad)* fishing. 2 *(peces)* fish.
pescadería *nf* fishmonger's, fish shop
pescadero ,-a *nm & nf* fishmonger.
pescadilla *nf* young hake.
pescado *nm* fish. ● **pescado azul** blue fish. ‖ **pescado blanco** white fish.
pescador ,-ra *nm & nf (hombre)* fisherman; *(mujer)* fisherwoman.
pescar [1] *vi (ir a pescar)* to fish, go fishing.
▷ *vt* 1 *(sacar del agua)* to get, catch. 2 *fam (agarrar)* catch: **he pescado un resfriado de aquí te espero** *I've caught a really nasty cold.* 3 *(conseguir)* to get, catch. 4 *fam (comprender)* to understand, get. ■ **ir a pescar** to go fishing.
pescuezo *nm* neck.
pesebre *nm* 1 *(de Navidad)* crib. 2 *(para animales)* manger, stall.
pesimismo *nm* pessimism.
pesimista *adj* pessimistic.
▷ *nm o nf* pessimist.
pésimo ,-a *adj* dreadful, awful.
peso *nm* 1 *(gen)* weight. 2 *(balanza)* scales *pl.* 3 *(carga)* load, burden. ■ **de peso** 1 *(pesado)* heavy. 2 *(importante)* important. 3 *(convincente)* strong, powerful. ● **peso bruto** gross weight.
pespunte *nm* backstitch.
pesquero ,-a *nm* **pesquero** fishing boat.
pesquisa *nf* inquiry.
pestaña *nf* 1 *(del ojo)* eyelash. 2 TÉC flange.
pestañear *vi* to blink.
peste *nf* 1 *(epidemia)* plague. 2 *(mal olor)* stink, stench: **¡qué peste a tabaco hay aquí!** *it stinks of tobacco smoke in here!* 3 *(cosa molesta)* pest. ■ **decir/echar pestes de** ALGN to slag SB off. ● **peste bubónica** bubonic plague.
pesticida *nm* pesticide.
pestilente *adj (apestoso)* stinking.
pestillo *nm* 1 *(de puerta)* bolt; *(de ventana)* catch. 2 *(de una cerradura)* bolt. ■ **cerrar con pestillo** to bolt.
pétalo *nm* petal.
petanca *nf* petanque, boules.
petardo *nm (de verbena)* firecracker, banger.
petate *nm (de soldado, marinero)* kit bag.
petición *nf* 1 *(gen)* request. 2 plea, petition. ■ **a petición de** at the request of.
petirrojo *nm* robin.
petisú *nm* éclair.
peto *nm (pantalón)* pair of dungarees; *(pieza del pantalón)* bib.
pétreo ,-a *adj* stony.
petrificar [1] *vt (fosilizar)* to petrify.
petrodólar *nm* petrodollar.
petróleo *nm* oil.
petrolero ,-a *adj* oil.
▷ *nm* **petrolero** oil tanker.
petrolífero ,-a *adj* oil-bearing.
petroquímica *nf* petrochemistry.
petroquímico ,-a *adj* petrochemical.
petulancia *nf* vanity.
petulante *adj* vain.
petunia *nf* petunia.
peúco *nm* → **patuco.**
peyorativo ,-a *adj* pejorative.
pez *nm* fish. ● **pez espada** swordfish. ‖ **pez gordo** *fig* big shot.
▲ *pl* **peces.**
pezón *nm* nipple.
pezuña *nf* hoof.

piadoso ,-a *adj* 1 pious, devout. 2 *(clemente)* merciful, compassionate.
pianista *nm o nf* pianist.
piano *nm* piano.
pianola [Registered trademark.] *nf* Pianola.
piar [13] *vi* to chirp, tweet.
piara *nf* herd of pigs.
PIB *abrev* **(producto interior bruto)** gross domestic product; *(abreviatura)* GDP.
pibe ,-a *nm & nf* kid.
pica *nf* 1 *(lanza)* pike. 2 *(de picador)* goad. 3 *(de la baraja)* spade. ■ **poner una pica en Flandes** to bring off a coup.
picada *nf* 1 *(picadura - de avispa)* sting; *(- de mosquito)* bite. 2 *(de pez)* bite.
picadero *nm (escuela)* riding school.
picadillo *nm (de carne)* minced meat, mince; *(de verduras)* chopped vegetables.
picado ,-a *adj* 1 CULIN *(cortado - verdura)* finely chopped; *(- carne)* minced. 2 *(vino)* vinegary, sour, off. 3 *(metal)* pitted. 4 *(piel, cara)* pockmarked. 5 *(tabaco)* cut. 6 *(mar)* choppy. 7 *(diente)* decayed. 8 *fam (ofendido)* offended.
picador *nm* 1 *(tauromaquia)* picador. 2 *(minero)* face worker.
picadora *nf* mincer.
picadura *nf* 1 *(de insecto, serpiente)* bite; *(de abeja, avispa)* sting. 2 *(tabaco)* cut tobacco.
picante *adj* 1 *(comida)* hot. 2 *fig (chiste, película)* spicy.
picapedrero *nm* stonecutter.
picaporte *nm* 1 *(para llamar)* door knocker. 2 *(para abrir)* door handle.
picar [1] *vt* 1 *(morder - insecto)* to bite; *(- abeja, avispa)* to sting. 2 *(corroer)* to eat away, rot: **tengo las muelas picadas de comer tantos caramelos** *my teeth are bad from eating so many sweets* (US *so much candy)*. 3 *(perforar - papel, tarjeta)* to punch. 4 *(dar con un pico)* to jab, goad. 5 CULIN *(cortar)* to chop finely; *(carne)* to mince. 6 *(comida)* to nibble: **vamos a salir a picar algo** *we're going to get a bite to eat*. 7 *(incitar)* to arouse: **me picó la curiosidad** *it aroused my curiosity*. 8 *(herir)* to wound: **le ha picado el orgullo** *it has wounded his pride*.
▷ *vi* 1 *(sentir escozor)* to itch: **me pica todo el cuerpo** *I'm itching all over*. 2 *(calentar)* to be hot, be strong: **hoy pica el sol** *the sun's really strong today*. 3 *(estar picante)* to be hot. 4 *(pez)* to bite; *(persona)* to fall for it. 5 *(caer en la cuenta)* to cotton on, twig. 6 *(comer)* to have a nibble.
▷ *vpr* **picarse** 1 *(muela)* to decay, go bad. 2 *(fruta)* to begin to rot. 3 *(tela)* to be moth-eaten. 4 *(mar)* to get choppy. 5 *(vino)* to go vinegary, go sour, go off. 6 *(metal)* to pit. 7 *(ofenderse)* to take offence. 8 *fam (picar el orgullo)* to get annoyed.
picardía *nf* 1 *(astucia)* craftiness. 2 *(atrevimiento)* naughtiness. 3 *(dicho atrevido)* risqué comment.
picaresco ,-a *adj lit* picaresque.
▷ *nf* picaresque genre.
pícaro ,-a *adj* 1 *(astuto)* crafty, sly. 2 *(atrevido)* wicked.
▷ *nm & nf (persona astuta)* slyboots, crafty devil.
picatoste *nm small* crouton.
picazón *nf (picor)* itch.
pichi *nm* pinafore dress, US jumper.
pichichi *nm (goleador)* top goal scorer.
pichón ,-ona *nm & nf* 1 pigeon. 2 *(apelativo)* darling.
picnic *nm* picnic.
pico *nm* 1 *(de ave)* beak. 2 *(herramienta)* pickaxe, pick. 3 *(de montaña)* peak. 4 *(punta)* corner. 5 *fam (boca)* mouth, gob, trap.
▷ *loc* **y pico** *(cantidad)*: **llegaremos sobre las seis y pico** *we'll be there just after six*.
picor *nm* 1 *(gen)* itch. 2 *(de comida)* burning sensation.
picotazo *nm* 1 *(de ave)* peck. 2 *(de insecto, reptil)* bite; *(de abeja, avispa)* sting.
picotear *vt* to peck, peck at.
picoteo *nm* 1 *(de ave)* pecking. 2 *(acción de comer)* nibbling, snacking.
picto ,-a *nm & nf* Pict.
▷ *nm* **picto** Pictish.
pictórico ,-a *adj* pictorial.
picudo ,-a *adj* pointed.
pie *nm* 1 ANAT foot. 2 *(base - de una lámpara)* base; *(- de una escultura)* plinth. 3 *(de un verso)* foot. 4 *(medida de longitud)* foot. 5 *(de un documento)* foot; *(de una fotografía, dibujo)* caption. ■ **a pie** on foot. ‖ **al pie de la letra** word for word. ‖ **dar pie a** to give occasion for. ‖ **no tener ni pies ni cabeza** to be ludicrous, be absurd. ‖ **pararle los pies a** ALGN to put SB in their place. ‖ **ponerse de/en pie** to get to one's feet, stand up.
piedad *nf* 1 *(misericordia)* pity, mercy. 2 *(devoción religiosa)* piety. ■ **tener piedad de** ALGN to have mercy on SB.
piedra *nf* 1 stone. 2 *(granizo)* hailstone. 3 *(en el riñón)* stone. 4 *(de un encendedor)* flint. 5 *(de afilar)* grindstone. ● **piedra pómez** pumice stone. ‖ **piedra preciosa** gem, precious stone.
piel *nf* 1 *(de persona)* skin. 2 *(de animal - sin curtir)* hide; *(- curtida)* leather; *(- con pelo)* fur. 3 *(de la fruta, patatas)* peel. ■ **dejarse la piel** *fam* to give all one's got, sweat blood. ● **piel roja** redskin.
pienso *nm* fodder.
pierna *nf* leg.
pieza *nf* 1 *(gen)* piece; *(de un aparato)* part. 2 MÚS piece, piece of music. 3 TEAT play. 4 *(de un juego de tablero)* piece. 5 *(habitación)* room. ■ **quedarse de una pieza** to be dumbfounded. ● **pieza de recambio** spare part.
pigmentación *nf* pigmentation.
pigmento *nm* pigment.
pigmeo ,-a *adj* 1 *(raza)* Pygmy. 2 *fig* pygmy.
▷ *nm & nf* 1 *(raza)* Pygmy. 2 *fig* pygmy.
pijama *nm* pyjamas (US pajamas) *pl*.
pila *nf* 1 ELEC battery. 2 *(de fregar)* sink. 3 *fam (montón)* pile, heap: **tengo una pila de cosas que hacer** *I've got piles of work to do*. ■ **ponerse las pilas** *fam* to get one's act together.
pilar *nm* pillar.
pilastra *nf* pilaster.
píldora *nf* 1 pill, tablet. 2 **la píldora** *(anticonceptivo)* the pill.
pileta *nf* AM swimming pool.
pillaje *nm* looting.
pillar *vt* 1 *(coger)* to catch. 2 *fam (robar)* to nick. 3 *fam (atropellar)* to run over. 4 *fam (entender)* to catch, get, grasp.

▷ *vi fam (encontrarse)* to be: **me pilla muy cerca de casa** *it's very near home.*
pillo ,-a *nm & nf* 1 *(niño)* little monkey, little devil. 2 *(adulto)* rogue, rascal.
pilón *nm* 1 *(de una fuente)* basin. 2 *(abrevadero)* trough; *(lavadero)* sink.
pilonga *adj* shrivelled. ● **castaña pilonga** dried chestnut.
píloro *nm* pylorus.
pilotar *vt (avión)* to pilot, fly; *(coche)* to drive; *(barco)* to sail.
pilote *nm* pile.
piloto *nm* 1 *(conductor - de avión)* pilot; *(- de coche)* driver; *(- de barco)* pilot; *(- de moto)* rider. 2 *(luz - de un aparato)* pilot light; *(- de un vehículo)* rear light.
▷ *adj (proyecto, programa)* pilot, test.
pimentero *nm* 1 *(recipiente)* pepper pot. 2 *(planta)* pepper plant.
pimentón *nm* paprika. ● **pimentón picante** cayenne pepper.
pimienta *nf (especia)* pepper.
pimiento *nm (gen)* pepper; *(rojo)* red pepper; *(verde)* green pepper. ● **pimiento morrón** sweet pepper.
pinacoteca *nf* art gallery.
pináculo *nm* pinnacle.
pinar *nm* pine grove.
pincel *nm* paintbrush.
pincelada *nf* brush stroke.
pinchadiscos *nm o nf fam* disc jockey, DJ.
pinchar *vt* 1 *(punzar)* to prick. 2 MED *(poner inyección)* to give a injection, give a jab, US give a shot. 3 *(sujetar)* to spear, jab. 4 *(enfadar)* to needle. 5 *(estimular)* to push: **en casa me pinchan para que me apunte al gimnasio** *the family are trying to persuade me to go to the gym.* 6 *fam (intervenir)* to tap. 7 *fam (poner disco)* to play.
▷ *vpr* **pincharse** *fam (droga)* to shoot up.
pinchazo *nm* 1 *(de neumático)* puncture. 2 *(con aguja, etc)* prick. 3 *(inyección)* injection, jab, US shot.
pinche *nm & nf (de cocina)* kitchen assistant.
pincho *nm* 1 *(de una planta)* thorn. 2 *(de un erizo)* spine, prickle. 3 *(de aperitivo)* snack. 4 *(brocheta)* skewer. ● **pincho moruno** shish kebab.
pineal *adj* pineal.
pineda *nf* pine grove.
pingo *nm fam (de ropa)* rag. ■ **ir hecho,-a un pingo** *fam* to look a right mess.
ping-pong *nm* table tennis, ping-pong.
pingüe *adj* substantial.
pingüino *nm* penguin.
pino *nm (árbol)* pine tree; *(madera)* pine.
pinta *nf* 1 *(mancha)* dot. 2 *(medida)* pint. 3 *fam (aspecto)* look: **esta película tiene pinta de estar bien** *this film looks as if it could be good.*
▷ *nm fam pey (persona)* dodgy character.
pintada *nf* graffiti.
pintado ,-a *adj* 1 *(parecido)* identical. 2 *(maquillado)* made-up.
pintalabios *nm inv* lipstick.
pintar *vt* 1 *(gen)* to paint; *(dibujar)* to draw. 2 *(maquillar)* to make up. 3 *fig (describir)* to paint a picture.
▷ *vi* 1 *(gen)* to paint. 2 *(marcar)* to write. 3 *fam (tener que ver)* to do, have to do: **él, ¿qué pintaba allí?** *what was he doing there?;* 4 *(en la baraja)* to be trumps.
▷ *vpr* **pintarse** *(maquillarse)* to put one's make up on.
pintarrajear *vt fam* to daub.
▷ *vpr* **pintarrajearse** to doll OS up.
pintarrajo *nm fam* daub.
pintaúñas *nm inv* nail varnish, nail polish.
pinto ,-a *adj* spotted.
pintor ,-ra *nm & nf (de cuadros)* artist, painter; *(de paredes)* painter and decorator.
pintoresco ,-a *adj* 1 *(lugar)* picturesque. 2 *(persona)* bizarre, colourful (US colorful).
pintura *nf* 1 *(arte)* painting. 2 *(cuadro)* picture. 3 *(producto)* paint: **un bote de pintura** *a tin (US can) of paint.*
pinza *nf* 1 *(de cangrejo)* pincer. 2 *(de la ropa)* clothes peg. 3 *(en pantalón, falda)* pleat.
▷ *nf pl* **pinzas** 1 *(herramienta)* pincers. 2 *(de depilar)* tweezers. 3 *(de servir hielo)* tongs.
pinzamiento *nm* trapped nerve.
pinzón *nm* finch.
piña *nf* 1 *(fruta)* pineapple. 2 *(del pino)* pine cone. 3 *fam (de personas)* clique.
piñata *nf hollow figure filled with sweets (which children try to break open at parties).*
piñón *nm* 1 *(del pino - semilla)* pine seed; *(- comestible)* pine nut kernel. 2 TÉC pinion.
pío *nm* chirp. ■ **no decir ni pío** *fam* not to say a word, not open one's mouth.
pío ,-a *adj* pious.
piojo *nm* louse.
piojoso ,-a *adj* 1 *(lleno de piojos)* lousy, louse-infested. 2 *fam (sucio)* lousy, filthy.
piolet *nm* ice axe (US ax).
pionero ,-a *nm & nf* pioneer.
pipa¹ *nf (de tabaco)* pipe.
pipa² *nf (de girasol)* sunflower seed. ■ **pasarlo pipa** *fam* to have a brilliant time, have a ball.
pipermín *nm (licor)* crème de menthe.
pipeta *nf* pipette.
pipí *nm fam* pee, wee-wee. ■ **hacer pipí** to go for a pee.
pique *nm* 1 *(resentimiento)* pique, grudge. 2 *(rivalidad)* rivalry, needle. ■ **irse a pique** 1 *(barco)* to sink. 2 *(plan, proyecto)* to go under, fall through.
piqueta *nf* pickaxe.
piquete *nm* 1 *(de huelga)* picket. 2 *(de soldados)* squad.
pira *nf* pyre.
pirado ,-a *adj fam (loco)* loony, wacky.
piragua *nf* canoe.
piragüismo *nm* canoeing.
piragüista *nm o nf* canoeist.
piramidal *adj* pyramidal.
pirámide *nf* pyramid.
piraña *nf* piranha.
pirarse *vpr fam* to split, sling one's hook, make OS scarce.
pirata *adj* pirate.
▷ *nm o nf (de la informática)* hacker.
piratear *vt* 1 *(gen)* to pirate. 2 *(informática)* to hack.
piratería *nf (gen)* piracy.

pírex® *nm* pyrex®.
pirindolo *nm fam* thingummy.
pirita *nf* pyrite.
pirómano ,-a *adj* pyromaniacal.
▷ *nm & nf* pyromaniac.
piropear *vt* to make flirtatious comments to.
piropo *nm* compliment, flirtatious comment.
pirotecnia *nf* fireworks *pl*, pyrotechnics.
pirotécnico ,-a *adj* pyrotechnic.
▷ *nm & nf* fireworks expert.
pirueta *nf* pirouette.
piruleta *nf* lollipop.
pirulí *nm fam (de caramelo)* lollipop.
pis *nm fam* wee, pee.
pisada *nf* **1** footstep. **2** *(huella)* footprint.
pisapapeles *nm inv* paperweight.
pisar *vt* **1** *(gen)* to tread on, step on. **2** *(acelerador, embrague)* to put one's foot on. **3** *fig (entrar)* to set foot in. **4** *fam (idea, proyecto)* to steal; *(noticia)* to scoop. **5** *fig (rebajar)* to walk all over: **no se deja pisar por nadie** *nobody walks all over him.*
▷ *vi* to tread, walk, step: **no pises muy fuerte que nos oyen los vecinos** *tread more quietly, the neighbours will hear us.*
piscifactoría *nf* fish farm.
piscina *nf* swimming pool.
Piscis *nm (constelación)* Pisces.
▷ *nm & nf (persona)* Pisces.
piscolabis *nm inv* snack.
piso *nm* **1** *(para vivir)* flat. **2** *(planta)* floor. **3** *(suelo)* floor.
pisotear *vt* **1** *(pisar)* to trample. **2** *fig (persona)* to walk all over.
pisotón *nm* stamp.
pista *nf* **1** *(rastro)* trail, track. **2** *(indicio)* clue. **3** *(de baile)* dance floor. **4** *(camino)* track. **5** *(de tenis)* court. **6** *(de circo)* ring. **7** *(de aterrizaje)* runway. ● **pista de esquí** ski slope. ‖ **pista de tenis** tennis court.
pistachero *nm* pistachio tree.
pistacho *nm* pistachio (nut).
pistilo *nm* pistil.
pisto *nm* type of ratatouille.
pistola *nf* **1** gun. **2** *(para pintar)* spray gun. **3** *(de pan)* loaf of bread.
pistolera *nf* holster.
pistolero *nm* gunman.
pistoletazo *nm* gunshot. ● **pistoletazo de salida** starting signal.
pistón *nm* **1** *(de un motor)* piston. **2** *(de un arma)* cap. **3** MÚS *(corneta)* cornet; *(llave)* key.
pita *nf* BOT pita.
pitada *nf* **1** *(bocinazo)* hoot, honk. **2** *(pitido)* whistle. **3** *(del público)* booing.
pitar *vi* **1** *(silbar)* to blow a whistle. **2** *(tocar la bocina)* to hoot, honk. **3** *(abuchear)* to boo and hiss. ■ **ir/irse pitando** *fam* to rush out, dash off.
▷ *vt* DEP *(falta)* to whistle.
pitido *nm* **1** *(silbido)* whistle. **2** *(bocinazo)* hoot, honk.
pitillera *nf* cigarette case.
pitillo *nm* cigarette. ■ **de pitillo** *(pantalón)* drainpipe.
pito *nm* **1** *(silbato)* whistle. **2** *(de coche)* horn.
pitón[1] *nf* ZOOL python.
pitón[2] *nm* **1** *(del toro)* horn. **2** *(de un botijo)* spout.
pitonisa *nf* fortune teller.
pitorrearse *vpr fam* to make fun (**de**, of).
pitorreo *nm fam (burla)* mocking; *(broma)* joking.
pitorro *nm* spout.
pitufo ,-a *nm & nf fam* little one.
pituitaria *nf* pituitary (gland).
pívot *nm o nf* centre.
pivotar *vi* to pivot.
pivote *nm* pivot.
pizarra *nf* **1** *(mineral)* slate. **2** *(para escribir)* blackboard.
pizca *nf fam (gen)* bit; *(de sal)* pinch.
pizza *nf* pizza.
pizzería *nf* pizzeria, pizza parlour.
placa *nf* **1** *(de metal)* sheet. **2** GEOL plate. **3** *(con el nombre - conmemorativa)* plaque; *(- insignia)* badge; *(- letrero)* sign. **4** *(de matrícula)* number plate, US license plate. **5** *(de cocina)* ring. **6** *(de hielo)* sheet. **7** *(radiografía)* plate. **8** *(dental)* plaque.
placaje *nm* tackle.
placar [1 sacar] *vt (en rugby)* to tackle.
placebo *nm* placebo.
placenta *nf* placenta.
placentero ,-a *adj* pleasant.
placer *nm* pleasure.
▷ *vi* to please: **haz lo que te plazca** *do as you please.*
placidez *nf* placidity.
plácido ,-a *adj* placid, calm.
plafón *nm (lámpara - de techo)* ceiling light; *(- de pared)* wall light.
plaga *nf* **1** *(epidemia)* plague. **2** *(de insectos)* plague, pest. **3** *fig* invasion.
plagar [7] *vt* to plague, infest.
plagiar [12] *vt* to plagiarize.
plagio *nm* plagiarism.
plaguicida *nm* pesticide.
plan *nm* **1** *(intención)* plan. **2** *(programa)* project. **3** *(régimen)* diet. **4** *fam (aventura amorosa)* fling; *(amante)* bit on the side. **5** *fam (para salir)* plans *pl*: **¿tienes plan para el fin de semana?** *are you doing anything this weekend?*
plana *nf (página)* page: **la noticia viene en primera plana** *the news is on the front page.*
plancha *nf* **1** *(de metal)* plate, sheet. **2** *(electrodoméstico)* iron. **3** *(placa de cocina)* griddle, hotplate. ■ **a la plancha** grilled.
planchado ,-a *nm* **planchado** *(acción)* ironing; *(acto)* iron, press.
▷ *adj fam (sorprendido)* lost for words.
planchar *vt* to iron, press.
planchista *nm o nf* panel beater.
plancton *nm* plankton.
planeador *nm* glider.
planear *vt (futuro, idea)* to plan.
▷ *vi (en el aire)* to glide.
planeo *nm* gliding, glide.
planeta *nm* planet.
planetario ,-a *adj* planetary.
▷ *nm* **planetario** planetarium.
planicie *nf* plain.
planificación *nf* planning.
planificador ,-ra *adj* planning.
▷ *nm & nf* planner.

planificar *vt* to plan.
plano ,-a *adj (superficie)* flat.
▷ *nm* **plano 1** *(de una ciudad)* street plan, map. **2** *(de una casa)* plan. **3** *(nivel)* level. **4** CINE shot. **5** MAT plane. **6** *fig (perspectiva)* point of view.
planta *nf* **1** BOT plant. **2** *(del pie)* sole. **3** *(de un edificio - piso)* floor; *(- sección horizontal)* plan. **4** *(industrial)* plant. ● **planta baja** ground floor, US first floor.
plantación *nf* **1** *(terreno)* plantation. **2** *(acción)* planting.
plantar *vt* **1** AGR to plant. **2** *(colocar - gen)* to put, place; *(- tienda de campaña)* to pitch, put up. **3** *fam (persona)* to leave, dump. **4** *(dar)* to give: **le plantó un beso** *she gave him a kiss.*
▷ *vpr* **plantarse 1** *fam (colocarse)* to place OS, position OS: **se plantó en la esquina** *she positioned herself on the corner.* **2** *fam (resistirse)* to dig one's heels in: **se ha plantado en tres millones y no se mueve** *he's holding out for three million and he won't budge.* **3** *(en la baraja)* to stick: **¡me planto!** *I stick.* **4** *fam (llegar)* to get there, be there, arrive.
plante *nm (laboral)* stand, protest action.
planteamiento *nm* **1** MAT *(formulación - de un problema)* formulation; *(- de una teoría)* exposition. **2** *(enfoque)* approach.
plantear *vt* **1** *(pregunta)* to pose, raise; *(cuestión)* to raise; *(acuerdo)* to suggest. **2** *(problema, dificultad)* to cause, give rise to. **3** *(trazar un plan)* to plan, outline. **4** MAT *(problema)* to formulate.
▷ *vpr* **plantearse** to consider.
plantel *nm* cadre.
plantilla *nf* **1** *(patrón)* model, pattern. **2** *(de zapato)* insole. **3** *(personal)* staff.
plantón ■ **darle plantón a ALGN 1** *fam (no presentarse)* to stand SB up. **2** *(llegar con retraso)* to keep SB waiting.
plañidero ,-a *adj* plaintive, mournful.
plañir [40] *vi* to mourn.
plaqueta *nf* **1** *(de sangre)* platelet. **2** *(de gres)* small tile.
plasma *nm* plasma.
plasmar *vt fig* to give expression to, give shape to, capture.
plasta *nf fam (sustancia)* mess.
▷ *nm o nf fam (persona)* pain in the neck, nuisance.
plastelina *nf* Plasticine.
plástica *nf* plastic arts *pl.*
plasticidad *nf* plasticity.
plástico ,-a *adj* **1** plastic. **2** *(lenguaje)* colourful (US colorful), vivid.
▷ *nm* **plástico 1** *(material)* plastic. **2** *argot* record.
plastificado ,-a *adj* laminated.
plastificar *vt* to laminate.
plastilina *nf* Plasticine.
plata *nf* **1** silver. **2** AM money. ● **plata de ley** sterling silver.
plataforma *nf* **1** platform. **2** *fig (trampolín)* springboard. **3** *(conjunto de personas)* group, grouping. ● **plataforma petrolífera** oil rig.
platanal *nm* banana plantation.
platanero ,-a *adj* banana.
▷ *nm* **platanero** banana tree.
plátano *nm* **1** banana. **2** *(árbol)* plane tree.
platea *nf* stalls *pl.*
plateado ,-a *adj (color)* silvery.
platear *vt* to silver-plate.
plateresco ,-a *adj* plateresque.
platería *nf (taller)* silversmith's.
platero ,-a *nm & nf* silversmith.
plática *nf* talk.
platicar [1] *vi* to chat, talk.
platillo *nm* **1** *(de postre)* dessert plate; *(de café)* saucer. **2** *(de balanza)* pan. ● **platillo volante** flying saucer.
platina *nf* **1** *(de microscopio)* slide. **2** MÚS → **pletina.**
platino *nm* platinum.
▷ *nm pl* **platinos** *(de un motor)* contact points.
plato *nm* **1** *(recipiente)* plate, dish. **2** CULIN dish: **hace unos platos buenísimos** *he's a wonderful cook.* **3** *(en comida)* course: **de primer plato hay sopa** *we've got soup for starters.* **4** *(de una balanza)* pan. **5** *(de un tocadiscos)* turntable.
plató *nm (de cine)* set, film set; *(de televisión)* floor.
platónico ,-a *adj* platonic.
plausible *adj* **1** *(admirable)* commendable. **2** *(recomendable)* advisable. **3** *(probable)* plausible.
playa *nf* **1** *(superficie de arena)* beach. **2** *(costa)* seaside.
playeras *nf pl* canvas shoes.
plaza *nf* **1** *(de una población)* square. **2** *(mercado)* marketplace. **3** *(en un vehículo)* seat. **4** *(puesto de trabajo)* position, vacancy. ● **plaza de parking** parking space.
plazo *nm* **1** *(periodo de tiempo)* time. **2** *(de compra)* instalment, US installment. ■ **comprar ALGO a plazos** to buy STH on hire purchase, US buy STH on an installment plan.
plazoleta *nf* small square.
pleamar *nf* high tide.
plebe *nf* **1** *(gen)* common people. **2** HIST masses *pl.*
plebeyo ,-a *adj* plebeian.
▷ *nm & nf* plebeian.
plebiscito *nm* plebiscite.
plegable *adj* folding, collapsible.
plegamiento *nm* folding.
plegar [48] *vt* to fold.
▷ *vpr* **plegarse** to yield, give in.
plegaria *nf* prayer.
pleitear *vi* to sue.
pleito *nm* litigation, lawsuit.
plenamente *adv* fully.
plenario ,-a *adj* plenary.
plenilunio *nm* full moon.
plenitud *nf* **1** *(cúspide)* peak: **está en la plenitud de la vida** *she's in the prime of life.* **2** *(sensación física)* fullness.
pleno ,-a *adj (gen)* full, complete: **en pleno centro de la ciudad** *right in the centre of the city* (US *right downtown).*
▷ *nm* **pleno** *(reunión)* plenary meeting.
pleonasmo *nm* pleonasm.
pletina *nf* deck, cassette deck.
pletórico ,-a *adj* full. ■ **pletórico de alegría** jubilant, euphoric.
pleura *nf* pleura.
plexiglás® *nm* Perspex®.
plexo *nm* plexus.
pliego *nm* **1** *(papel)* sheet of paper. **2** *(documento)* document.
pliegue *nm* **1** fold. **2** *(en la ropa)* pleat.

plinto *nm* 1 ARQUIT plinth. 2 *(en gimnasia)* vaulting horse, box.
plisado ,-a *adj* pleated.
plomada *nf* 1 *(de albañil)* plumb line. 2 *(sonda)* lead. 3 *(para pescar)* weights *pl*.
plomazo *nm o nf fam* bore.
plomizo ,-a *adj (color)* lead-coloured.
plomo *nm* 1 lead. 2 *(pesa)* lead weight. 3 ELEC fuse. 4 *fam fig* bore: **¡vaya un plomo de profe!** *this teacher is such a pain!* ■ **sin plomo** *(gasolina)* unleaded, lead-free.
pluma *nf* 1 *(de ave)* feather. 2 *(de relleno)* feather, down. 3 *(de escribir - estilográfica)* fountain pen.
plumaje *nm (de ave)* plumage.
plumcake *nm* fruitcake.
plumero *nm* 1 *(para el polvo)* feather duster. 2 *(de adorno)* plume. ■ **vérsele el plumero a** ALGN *fam* to see through SB, have SB's number.
plumier *nm* pencil case, pencil box.
plumilla *nf* nib.
plumón *nm* 1 *(de un ave)* down. 2 *(anorak)* down-filled anorak.
plural *adj* plural.
▷ *nm* plural.
pluralidad *nf (gen)* multiplicity; *(diversidad)* diversity.
pluralismo *nm* pluralism.
pluralista *adj* pluralist.
pluralizar *vt* LING to pluralize.
▷ *vi (generalizar)* to generalize.
pluriempleo *nm having more than one job.*
plurilingüe *adj* multilingual.
plus *nm* bonus.
pluscuamperfecto *nm* pluperfect.
plusmarca *nf* record.
plusmarquista *nm o nf* record holder.
plusvalía *nf* 1 *(aumento)* appreciation. 2 *(impuesto)* capital gains tax.
plutocracia *nf* plutocracy.
Plutón *nm* Pluto.
plutonio *nm* plutonium.
pluvial *adj* rain, pluvial.
pluviómetro *nm* rain gauge.
pluviosidad *nf* rainfall.
p.m. *abrev* **(post meridiem** *(después del mediodía))* post meridiem; *(abreviatura)* p.m..
PNB *abrev* **(Producto Nacional Bruto)** gross national product; *(abreviatura)* GNP.
población *nf* 1 *(número de habitantes)* population. 2 *(lugar - ciudad)* town; *(- pueblo)* village. ● **población activa** working population.
poblado ,-a *adj* 1 *(zona)* populated. 2 *(barba, cejas)* bushy.
▷ *nm* **poblado** *(zona habitada)* settlement.
poblamiento *nm* settlement.
poblar *vt* 1 *(ocupar territorio)* to settle. 2 *(habitar)* to inhabit. 3 *(llenar)* to fill: **han poblado de árboles el campo** *they've planted the field with trees.*
pobre *adj* 1 *(gen)* poor. 2 *(infeliz)* poor.
▷ *nm o nf* 1 *(con poco dinero)* poor person; *(mendigo)* beggar. 2 *(infeliz)* poor thing: **la pobre se cree que le van a devolver el dinero** *the poor thing thinks she is going to get her money back.*
pobreza *nf* 1 *(escasez de dinero)* poverty. 2 *(falta)* lack scarcity.
pocho ,-a *adj* 1 *fam (planta)* faded. 2 *fam (alimento* bad. 3 *fam (persona)* off-colour (US off-color), poor ly: **estoy pocha** *I feel poorly.*
pocilga *nf* pigsty.
pócima *nf* 1 *(preparado)* potion. 2 *fam (brebaje)* concoction.
poción *nf* potion.
poco ,-a *adj* little; *(plural)* few, not many: **hago muy poco ejercicio últimamente** *I do very little exercise these days.*
▷ *pron* **poco** little; *(en plural)* not many: **lo poco que aprendí se me ha olvidado** *what little I learned I've forgotten.*
▷ *adv* little, not much: **voy poco por allí** *I rarely go there.*
▷ *nm* **un poco** a little, a bit: **¿me das un poco?** *could you give me a little?*; **espera un poco** *wait a bit.* ■ **dentro de poco** soon, presently. ‖ **hace poco** not long ago. ‖ **poco a poco** slowly, gradually, bit by bit. ‖ **poco antes** shortly before. ‖ **poco después** shortly afterwards. ‖ **por poco** nearly.
poda *nf* pruning.
podadera *nf* pruning shears *pl*.
podar *vt* to prune.
podenco *nm* hound.
poder [77] *vt* 1 *(de facultad)* can, be able to: **¿puedes echarme una mano?** *can you lend me a hand?*; **no pude abrirlo** *I couldn't open it, I was unable to open it.* 2 *(de permiso)* may, can: **pueden pagar en efectivo o con tarjeta** *you can pay in cash or by credit card;* **puede retirarse** *you may leave.* 3 *(conjetura)* may, might: **podría haberlo dejado sobre la mesa** *I may have left it on the table.* 4 *(juicio)* can: **¡podrías habérmelo dicho!** *you could have told me!* 5 *(sugerencias)* can: **podríamos ir a esquiar** *we could go skiing.* ■ **en el poder** *(partido)* in power, in office. ‖ **no poder más** 1 *(comer)* not to be able to manage any more. 2 *(continuar)* not to be able to go on any more. ‖ **no poder ser** to be impossible: **eso no puede ser** *that's impossible, it can't be.* ‖ **puede que** maybe, perhaps: **puede que venga más tarde** *she may come later.*
▷ *vi (superar)* to be stronger than: **tú puedes a todos** *you can beat all of them.*
▷ *nm* 1 *(gen)* power. 2 *(posesión)* possession, hands *pl*: **el documento está ahora en mi poder** *the document is now in my hands.*
poderío *nm* 1 *(autoridad)* power. 2 *(fuerza)* strength.
poderoso ,-a *adj* powerful.
podio *nm* podium.
podólogo ,-a *nm & nf* chiropodist.
podredumbre *nf* 1 *(de un cuerpo)* rottenness. 2 *(lo podrido)* rot. 3 *fig (moral)* corruption.
podrido ,-a *adj* 1 rotten. 2 *fig* corrupt.
poema *nm* poem.
poesía *nf* 1 poetry. 2 *(poema)* poem.
poeta *nm o nf* poet.
poético ,-a *adj* poetic.
poetisa *nf* poetess.
pointer *nm* pointer.
polaco ,-a *adj* Polish.
▷ *nm & nf* 1 *(persona)* Pole. 2 *fam pey (catalán)* Catalan.
▷ *nm* **polaco** *(idioma)* Polish.

polar *adj* polar. ● **estrella polar** Pole Star, Polaris.
polaridad *nf* polarity.
polarizar *vt* 1 FÍS to polarize. 2 *(atención)* to focus.
▷ *vpr* **polarizarse** to become polarized.
polaroid [Registered trademark.] *nf* Polaroid.
polea *nf* pulley.
polémica *nf* controversy.
polémico ,-a *adj* controversial.
polemizar *vi* to debate.
polen *nm* pollen.
poleo *nm* 1 *(planta)* pennyroyal. 2 *(infusión)* mint tea.
poli *nm o nf fam (individuo)* cop.
▷ *nf* **la poli** *fam (cuerpo)* the (old) bill, the cops *pl*.
policía *nf* police, police force.
▷ *nm o nf (gen)* police officer; *(hombre)* policeman; *(mujer)* policewoman.
policíaco ,-a *adj* detective.
policial *adj* police.
policromía *nf* polychromy.
policromo ,-a *adj* polychrome.
polideportivo *nm* sports centre.
poliedro *nm* polyhedron.
poliéster *nm*
▲ *pl* **poliésteres.** polyester.
poliestireno *nm* polystyrene.
polietileno *nm* polythene.
polifacético ,-a *adj* versatile.
polifónico ,-a *adj* polyphonic.
poligamia *nf* polygamy.
polígamo ,-a *adj* polygamous.
▷ *nm & nf* polygamist.
polígloto ,-a *adj* polyglot.
▷ *nm & nf* polyglot.
poligonal *adj* polygonal.
polígono *nm* 1 *(figura)* polygon. 2 *(gen)* area; *(de viviendas)* development, housing estate. ● **polígono industrial** industrial estate.
polígrafo ,-a *nm & nf* polygraph.
poliinsaturado ,-a *adj* polyunsaturated.
polilla *nf* moth.
polímero *nm* polymer.
polimorfo ,-a *adj* polymorphic.
polinización *nf* pollination.
polinizar *vt* to pollinate.
polinomio *nm* polynomial.
poliomielitis *nf inv* poliomyelitis.
polisemia *nf* polysemy.
polisémico ,-a *adj* polysemous.
polisílabo ,-a *adj* polysyllabic.
▷ *nm* **polisílabo** polysyllable.
politécnico ,-a *adj (gen)* polytechnic.
▷ *nm* **politécnico** *(instituto)* technical college.
politeísmo *nm* polytheism.
politeísta *adj* polytheistic.
▷ *nm o nf* polytheist.
política *nf* 1 politics. 2 *(dirección)* policy.
político ,-a *adj* 1 political. 2 *(cortés)* tactful. 3 *(por matrimonio)* -in-law: **madre política** *mother-in-law;* **padre político** *father-in-law.*
▷ *nm & nf* politician.
politizar *vt* to politicize.
poliuretano *nm* polyurethane.
polivalente *adj* 1 *(en química)* polyvalent. 2 *fig (versátil)* versatile, multipurpose.
polivinilo *nm* polyvinyl.
póliza *nf* 1 *(de seguros)* policy. 2 *(sello)* official tax stamp.
polizón *nm* stowaway.
polla *nf* 1 ZOOL young hen. 2 *tabú (órgano sexual)* prick, cock.
pollera *nf* AM skirt.
pollería *nf (tienda)* poultry shop; *(sección de supermercado)* poultry section.
pollino ,-a *nm & nf* 1 ZOOL donkey. 2 *fam* ignoramus.
pollo *nm* chicken.
polluelo *nm* chick.
polo *nm* 1 TÉC pole. 2 *(caramelo)* ice lolly. 3 DEP polo. ● **Polo Norte** North Pole. ‖ **Polo Sur** South Pole.
Polonia *nf* Poland.
poltrona *nf* easy chair.
poltrón ,-ona *adj* lazy.
polución *nf (atmosférica)* pollution.
polucionar *vt* to pollute.
polvareda *nf (de polvo)* cloud of dust.
polvera *nf* (powder) compact.
polvo *nm* 1 *(suciedad)* dust. 2 *(medicamento, etc)* powder. ■ **en polvo** 1 *(leche, cacao)* powdered. 2 *(nieve)* powdery.
▷ *nm pl* **polvos** *(para maquillar)* face powder. ● **polvos de talco** talcum powder *sing.*
pólvora *nf* gunpowder.
polvoriento ,-a *adj* dusty.
pomada *nf* cream.
pomelo *nm (fruto)* grapefruit; *(árbol)* grapefruit tree.
pómez [Also **piedra pómez**.] *nf* pumice stone.
pomo *nm (de puerta)* knob.
pompa *nf* 1 *(de jabón, chicle)* bubble. 2 *(ostentación)* pomp. ● **pompas de jabón** soap bubbles.
pompis *nm inv fam* behind, backside.
pompón *nm* pompom.
pomposo ,-a *adj* pompous.
pómulo *nm* 1 *(hueso)* cheekbone. 2 *(mejilla)* cheek.
ponche *nm* punch.
poncho *nm* poncho.
ponderado ,-a *adj (prudente)* measured.
ponderar *vt* 1 *(sopesar)* to ponder, consider, think over, weigh up. 2 *(alabar)* to praise highly.
ponedero *nm* nest box.
ponedora *adj (gallina)* laying.
ponencia *nf (académica)* paper; *(parlamentaria)* address, speech.
ponente *nm o nf* speaker.
poner [78] *vt* 1 *(gen)* to place, put, set. 2 *(prenda)* to put on: **me pondré el pantalón negro** *I'll put my black trousers on, I'll wear my black trousers.* 3 *(encender)* to turn on, put on: **puso la radio** *she put the radio on.* 4 *(programar)* to set: **he puesto el despertador a las siete** *I've set the alarm clock for seven.* 5 *(instalar)* to install, put in: **¿habéis puesto calefacción?** *have you had central heating put in?* 6 *(establecer)* to open: **han puesto un bar en la esquina** *they've opened a bar on the corner.* 7 *(escribir)* to put, write: **pon tu nombre aquí** *put your name here.* 8 *(decir)* to say: **¿qué pone ese letrero?**

what does that sign say? **9** *(en cine, televisión)* to show: **lo ponen mañana a las tres** *it's on tomorrow at three o'clock.* **10** *(dar nombre)* to name, call: **le pusieron Laura** *they called her Laura.* **11** *(huevos)* to lay. **12** *(dinero)* to put in: **pusimos veinte euros cada uno** *we put in twenty euros each.* **13** *(telegrama, fax)* to send; *(nota)* to leave. **14** *(deber, multa)* to give: **nos han puesto deberes para las vacaciones** *they've given us homework for the holidays* (US *vacation).* **15 poner** + *adj* to make, turn: **la has puesto triste** *you've made her sad.*
▷ *vpr* **ponerse 1** *(sol)* to set. **2** *(volverse)* to become, get, turn: **se puso muy contenta con la noticia** *the news made her very happy.* **3** *(contestar al teléfono)* to answer the phone; *(hablar por teléfono)* to come to the phone: **en este momento no se puede poner** *he can't come to the phone right now.* **4 ponerse a** + *inf* to start + *to* + *inf/* + *-ing*: **se puso a cantar** *he started to sing, he started singing.*
póney *nm* pony.
poniente *nm* **1** *(dirección)* west. **2** *(viento)* west wind, westerly wind.
pontificar *vi* to pontificate.
pontífice *nm* pope, pontiff.
pontón *nm* pontoon.
ponzoña *nf* venom.
ponzoñoso ,-a *adj* venomous.
popa *nf* stern.
pope *nm* pope.
populacho *nm* mob, masses *pl*.
popular *adj* **1** *(del pueblo)* traditional. **2** *(muy conocido)* popular.
popularizar [4] *vt* to popularize.
populista *adj* populist.
populoso ,-a *adj* populous.
popurrí *nm* potpourri.(US *vacation)*
póquer *nm* poker.
por *prep* **1** *(gen)* for: **lo hice por ti** *I did it for you.* **2** *(a través de)* through, by: **iremos por la autopista** *we'll go on the motorway* (US *expressway).* **3** *(calle, carretera)* along, down, up: **íbamos por la calle cuando...** *we were walking along the street when...* **4** *(lugar aproximado)* in, near, round: **está por aquí** *it's somewhere round here.* **5** *(causa)* because of: **suspendieron el concierto por la lluvia** *they cancelled the concert because of the rain.* **6** *(tiempo)* at, for: **nos veremos por vacaciones** *I'll see you during the holidays* (US *vacation).* **7** *(medio)* by: **llegó por correo** *it arrived by post* (US *mail).* **8** *(autoría)* by: **fue escrito por Azorín** *it was written by Azorín.* **9** *(distribución)* per: **cinco por ciento** *five per cent.* **10** *(tras)* by: **les interrogó uno por uno** *he interrogated each one in turn.* **11** *(con pasiva)* by: **fue comprado por la reina** *it was bought by the queen.* **12** *(a favor de)* for, in favour of, US in favor of: **estoy por una amnistía general** *I'm in favour of a general amnesty.* **13** *(en calidad de)* as: **la tomó por esposa** *he took her as his wife.* **14** *(en lugar de)* instead of, in the place of: **ve tú por mi** *you go in my place.* **15** *(multiplicado por)* times, multiplied by: **tres por cuatro, doce** *three fours are twelve, three times four is twelve.* **16 por** *adj* **que** no matter how *adj*: **por caro que sea, lo voy a comprar** *no matter how expensive it is I'm going to buy it.* ■ **estar por** + *inf (a punto de)* to be on the point of + *-ing*. ‖ **por más que** + *subj* however much, no matter how much. ‖ **por mucho que** + *subj* however much, no matter how much.
porcelana *nf* china, porcelain: **una porcelana** *a piece of china.*
porcentaje *nm* percentage.
porcentual *adj* percentage.
porche *nm* veranda(h), US porch.
porcino ,-a *adj* porcine. ● **ganado porcino** pigs *pl*, US hogs *pl*.
porción *nf* **1** *(gen)* portion, part. **2** *(cuota)* share.
pordiosero ,-a *nm & nf* beggar.
porfiar [13] *vi* **1** *(insistir)* to insist (**en**, on). **2** *(discutir)* to squabble.
pormenor *nm* detail. ■ **al pormenor** retail.
pormenorizar [4] *vt* to detail.
porno *adj fam* porno.
▷ *nm* porn.
pornografía *nf* pornography.
pornográfico ,-a *adj* pornographic.
poro *nm* pore.
poroso ,-a *adj* porous.
porque *conj* **1** *(de causa)* because: **no voy porque no quiero** *I'm not going because I don't want to.* **2** *(de finalidad)* in order that, so that.
porqué *nm* cause, reason: **nunca sabremos el porqué** *we'll never know why.*
porquería *nf* **1** *(suciedad)* dirt, filth. **2** *(mala calidad)* rubbish.
porqueriza *nf* pigsty.
porra *nf* **1** *(palo)* club; *(de policía)* truncheon. **2** CULIN *kind of* fritter. **3** *(juego)* sweepstake. ■ **mandar a la porra a** ALGN *fam* to tell SB to get lost, send SB packing.
porrazo *nm (con bastón)* blow; *(al caer)* bump, knock.
porro *nm fam* joint, spliff.
porrón *nm typical glass drinking vessel with a thin spout used for pouring wine into the mouth.*
portaaviones *nm inv* aircraft carrier.
portada *nf* **1** *(de revista, periódico)* front page; *(de libro)* title page. **2** *(tapa de libro)* cover.
portador ,-ra *adj* carrying.
▷ *nm & nf (de un virus)* carrier; *(de un cheque)* bearer.
portaequipajes *nm inv* **1** *(de un coche - maletero)* boot, US trunk; *(- en el techo)* roof rack. **2** *(de un tren)* luggage rack.
portafolios *nm inv* **1** *(carpeta - de piel)* portfolio; *(- de cartón)* folder. **2** *(maletín)* briefcase.
portal *nm (entrada de edificio)* hallway.
portalámparas *nm* bulbholder.
portaminas *nm inv* propelling pencil.
portamonedas *nm inv* purse, US change purse.
portar *vt* to carry.
▷ *vpr* **portarse** to behave. ■ **portarse bien** to be good, behave OS. ‖ **portarse mal** to be naughty.
portátil *adj* portable.
portavoz *nm o nf (gen)* spokesperson; *(hombre)* spokesman; *(mujer)* spokeswoman.
portazo *nm* bang, slam *(of a door)*: **la puerta se cerró de un portazo** *the door slammed shut.*
porte *nm* **1** *(aspecto - de una persona)* bearing; *(- de un edificio, etc)* appearance. **2** *(transporte)* carriage, freight. ● **portes debidos** carriage due. ‖ **portes pagados** carriage paid.

porteador ,-ra *nm & nf* porter.
portentoso ,-a *adj* prodigious.
portería *nf* 1 *(de un edificio)* porter's lodge. 2 DEP goal.
portero ,-a *nm & nf* 1 *(de un edificio)* porter. 2 DEP goalkeeper. ● **portero automático** entryphone.
pórtico *nm* portico.
portillo *nm* breach.
portón *nm* large door.
Portugal *nm* Portugal.
portugués ,-esa *adj* Portuguese.
▷ *nm & nf (persona)* Portuguese.
▷ *nm* **portugués** *(idioma)* Portuguese.
porvenir *nm* future.
pos ■ **en pos de** after, in pursuit of.
posada *nf* inn.
posar *vi (para foto, etc)* to pose.
▷ *vt (colocar)* to rest.
▷ *vpr* **posarse** 1 *(pájaro)* to alight, perch, sit. 2 *(sedimento)* to settle.
posavasos *nm inv* coaster.
posdata *nf* postscript.
pose *nf* 1 *(postura)* pose. 2 *pey (actitud)* pose, air.
poseedor ,-ra *nm & nf* owner.
poseer [61] *vt* 1 *(propiedad)* to own, possess. 2 *(conocimientos, talento, etc)* to have.
posesión *nf* possession. ■ **tomar posesión** 1 *(de un cargo)* to take up. 2 *(de un territorio)* to occupy.
posesivo ,-a *adj* possessive.
poseso ,-a *nm & nf* possessed person: **actuó como un poseso** *he acted like a man possessed.*
posguerra *nf* postwar period.
posibilidad *nf* possibility.
posible *adj* possible. ■ **hacer todo lo posible** to do one's best.
posición *nf* 1 *(postura, situación)* position. 2 *(condición - económica)* situation; *(- social)* status.
positivo ,-a *adj* positive.
▷ *nm* **positivo** positive.
poso *nm* 1 *(del café)* dregs *pl*. 2 *fig* trace.
posología *nf* dosage.
posparto *nm* postpartum.
posponer [78] *vt (en el tiempo)* to postpone, delay, put off; *(en el espacio)* to put back, put in the background.
posta *nf* 1 *(de caballos)* change of horses. 2 *(lugar)* staging post. ■ **a posta** on purpose.
postal *adj* postal.
▷ *nf* postcard.
poste *nm* post.
póster *nm* poster.
▲ *pl* **pósters**.
postergar [7] *vt* 1 *(retrasar)* to postpone, delay. 2 *(perjudicar)* to relegate, put back.
posteridad *nf* posterity.
posterior *adj* 1 *(en el espacio)* back, rear: **en la parte posterior del edificio** *at the back of the building.* 2 *(en el tiempo)* later: **su ascenso fue posterior** *his promotion came later.*
posteriori ■ **a posteriori** a posteriori
postgrado *nm* postgraduate course.
postgraduado ,-a *nm & nf* postgraduate student.
postigo *nm (de ventana)* shutter; *(de puerta)* wicket gate.
postilla *nf* scab.
postizo ,-a *adj* false.
▷ *nm* **postizo** hairpiece.
postor ,-ra *nm & nf* bidder.
postrar *vt* to prostrate.
▷ *vpr* **postrarse** to prostrate OS.
postre *nm* dessert. ■ **a la postre** finally.
postular *vt (defender)* to postulate.
▷ *vi (pedir)* to collect (**para**, for).
póstumo ,-a *adj* posthumous.
postura *nf* 1 *(de un cuerpo)* posture, position. 2 *(actitud)* attitude. 3 *(en una subasta)* bid.
potable *adj* 1 drinkable. 2 *(aceptable)* acceptable.
potaje *nm* 1 CULIN hotpot. 2 *fam (mezcla)* hotchpotch.
potasio *nm* potassium.
pote *nm (vasija)* pot.
potencia *nf* 1 *(capacidad)* power: **este coche tiene mucha potencia** *this car is very powerful.* 2 *(país)* power: **una reunión de las primeras potencias mundiales** *a meeting of the world superpowers.* 3 *(en matemática)* power: **elevamos seis a la tercera potencia** *we raise six to the power of three.* ■ **en potencia** potential, budding.
potencial *adj* potential.
▷ *nm* 1 potential: 2 LING conditional tense.
potenciar *vt* to strengthen.
potentado ,-a *nm* tycoon, potentate.
potente *adj* powerful.
potestad *nf* power.
potestativo ,-a *adj* optional.
potingue *nm* 1 *fam (crema)* face cream. 2 *fam (comida)* concoction.
potrero *nm (lugar)* paddock.
potro ,-a *nm & nf* ZOOL *(macho)* colt; *(hembra)* filly.
▷ *nm* **potro** *(en gimnasia)* horse.
poza *nf* 1 *(charco)* large puddle. 2 *(en un río)* pool. 3 *(foso séptico)* cesspit.
pozo *nm* 1 *(de agua, petróleo)* well. 2 *(de una mina)* shaft.
práctica *nf* 1 practice. 2 *(habilidad)* skill.
▷ *nf pl* **prácticas** practical *sing*. ■ **en la práctica** in practice.
practicable *adj* 1 *(realizable)* feasible. 2 *(transitable)* passable.
practicante *adj* REL practising (US practicing).
▷ *nm o nf (persona)* nurse.
practicar [1] *vt* 1 *(gen)* to practise (US practice). 2 *(hacer)* to make; *(deporte)* to play: **se le practicará la intervención el mes entrante** *he'll be operated on next month.*
▷ *vi* to practise (US practice).
práctico ,-a *adj* 1 *(gen)* practical. 2 *(hábil)* skilful (US skillful). 3 *(pragmático)* practical.
pradera *nf* prairie, grassland.
prado *nf* meadow.
pragmático ,-a *adj* pragmatic.
pragmatismo *nm* pragmatism.
praliné *nm* praline.
preámbulo *nm* preamble.

preaviso *nm* notice.
precalentamiento *nm* DEP warming up.
precalentar *vt* to pre-heat.
precariedad *nf* precariousness.
precario ,-a *adj* precarious.
precaución *nf* precaution. ■ **tomar precauciones** to take precautions.
precavido ,-a *adj* cautious.
precedente *adj* preceding.
▷ *nm* precedent.
preceder *vt* to precede.
preceptiva *nf* precepts *pl*.
preceptivo ,-a *adj* compulsory.
precepto *nm* precept.
preceptor ,-ra *nm & nf* EDUC tutor.
preciado ,-a *adj* precious.
preciarse [12] *vpr* to be proud (**de**, of).
precintar *vt* to seal.
precinto *nm* seal.
precio *nm* **1** *(coste)* price. **2** *fig (valor)* value. ■ **a cualquier precio** at any cost. | **a precio de coste** at cost price.
preciosidad *nf* **1** *(belleza)* loveliness. **2** *(cosa bella)* beautiful thing.
precioso ,-a *adj* **1** *(bello)* beautiful. **2** *(valioso)* precious.
precipicio *nm* cliff, precipice.
precipitación *nf* **1** *(prisa)* rush, haste, hurry. **2** METEOR precipitation, rainfall.
precipitado ,-a *adj (apresurado)* hasty, rash.
precipitar *vt* **1** *(apresurar)* to rush; *(adelantar)* to bring forward. **2** QUÍM to precipitate. **3** *(lanzar)* to push, throw.
▷ *vpr* **precipitarse 1** *(apresurarse)* to rush, be hasty. **2** *(caer)* to fall; *(arrojarse)* to throw os.
precisar *vt* **1** to say exactly: **no sabría precisar cuántos entraron** *I couldn't say exactly how many came in.* **2** *(necesitar)* to need: **«Se precisa cocinero»** *«Cook wanted».*
precisión *nf* precision, accuracy.
preciso ,-a *adj* **1** precise, exact, accurate. **2** *(necesario)* necessary. ■ **ser preciso** to be necessary, be essential: **es preciso que acabes ya** *you must finish now.*
precocinado ,-a *adj* precooked.
preconcebido ,-a *adj* preconceived.
preconizar *vt* to advocate.
precoz *adj* **1** *(persona)* precocious. **2** *(cosecha)* early. **3** *(diagnóstico)* early.
precursor ,-ra *nm & nf* precursor.
predador ,-ra *adj* predatory.
predecesor ,-ra *nm & nf* predecessor.
predecir [79] *vt* to predict.
predestinado ,-a *adj* predestined.
predestinar *vt* to predestine.
predeterminar *vt* to predetermine.
prédica *nf* sermon.
predicación *nf* preaching.
predicado *nm* predicate.
predicador ,-ra *nm & nf* preacher.
predicar [1] *vt* to preach.
predicativo ,-a *adj* predicative.
predicción *nf* prediction.
predilección *nf* predilection. ■ **sentir predilección por** to prefer.
predilecto ,-a *adj* favourite.
predisponer [78] *vt* to predispose.
predisposición *nf* predisposition.
predominante *adj* predominant.
predominar *vt* to predominate.
predominio *nm* predominance.
preeminente *adj* pre-eminent.
preescolar *adj (enseñanza, edad, etapa)* preschool, nursery-school.
preestablecer *vt* to pre-establish.
preestablecido ,-a *adj* pre-established.
preestreno *nm* preview.
prefabricado ,-a *adj* prefabricated.
prefacio *nm* preface.
preferencia *nf* preference. ■ **tener preferencia** AUTO *(de paso)* to have right of way.
preferente *adj* preferential.
preferible *adj* preferable.
preferido ,-a *adj* favourite (US favorite).
preferir [35] *vt* to prefer.
prefijo *nm* **1** LING prefix. **2** *(telefónico)* dialling code, US area code.
pregón *nm* **1** *(anuncio)* public announcement. **2** *(discurso)* speech; *(de fiestas)* opening address, opening speech.
pregonar *vt* **1** *(noticia)* to announce, make public; *(secreto)* to tell everybody, broadcast. **2** *(mercancía)* to cry. **3** *(bando municipal)* to proclaim.
pregonero *nm* town crier.
pregunta *nf* question. ■ **hacer una pregunta a** ALGN to ask SB a question.
preguntar *vt* to ask.
▷ *vpr* **preguntarse** to wonder: **me pregunto si vendrá** *I wonder if he'll come.*
preguntón ,-ona *adj fam* inquisitive, nosy.
prehistoria *nf* prehistory.
prehistórico ,-a *adj* prehistoric.
prejuicio *nm* prejudice.
prejuzgar *vt* to prejudge.
preliminar *adj* preliminary.
▷ *nm* preliminary.
preludio *nm* prelude.
prematrimonial *adj* premarital.
prematuro ,-a *adj* premature.
premeditación *nf* premeditation.
premeditado ,-a *adj* premeditated.
premeditar *vt* to premeditate.
premiado ,-a *adj* prizewinning.
▷ *nm & nf* prizewinner.
premiar [12] *vt* **1** *(otorgar premio)* to award a prize to. **2** *(recompensar)* to reward.
premio *nm* **1** prize. **2** *(recompensa)* reward.
premisa *nf* premise.
premonición *nf* premonition.
premonitorio ,-a *adj* premonitory.
premura *nf* **1** *(prisa)* urgency. **2** *(escasez - de tiempo)* pressure; *(- de espacio)* shortage.
prenatal *adj* antenatal.
prenda *nf* **1** *(de vestir)* garment. **2** *(prueba)* token, pledge: **te dejo este collar en prenda** *I'll leave you this necklace as a pledge.* **3** *(cualidad)* talent. **4** *(en juego)* forfeit. ■ **no soltar prenda** not to say a word.

prendarse *vpr* to fall in love (**de**, with).
prendedor *nm (broche)* brooch; *(alfiler)* pin.
prender *vt* 1 *(agarrar)* to catch; *(arrestar)* to arrest. 2 *(sujetar)* to attach; *(con agujas)* to pin. 3 *(encender - fuego)* to light; *(- luz)* to turn on.
▷ *vi* 1 *(arraigar - planta, costumbre)* to take root. 2 *(fuego, madera, etc)* to catch light, catch fire.
▷ *vpr* **prenderse** to catch fire.
prensa *nf* 1 *(máquina)* press; *(de imprimir)* printing press. 2 *(periodistas)* press; *(periódicos)* papers *pl*. ● **libertad de prensa** freedom of the press.
prensar *vt* to press.
preñado ,-a *adj* pregnant.
preñar *vt (mujer)* to make pregnant; *(animal)* to impregnate.
preocupación *nf* worry.
preocupado ,-a *adj* worried.
preocupar *vt* to worry.
▷ *vpr* **preocuparse** 1 *(sentir preocupación)* to worry (**por**, about), get worried (**por**, about). 2 *(ocuparse)* to mind (**de**, -): **tú preocúpate de lo tuyo** *mind your own business.*
preparación *nf* 1 *(gen)* preparation. 2 *(física, deportiva)* training. 3 *(conocimientos)* knowledge.
preparado ,-a *adj* ready, prepared.
preparador ,-ra *nm & nf* 1 EDUC private tutor *who coaches students for competitive exams*. 2 DEP coach.
preparar *vt* 1 to prepare, get ready: **voy a preparar el desayuno** *I'll get breakfast ready.* 2 *(enseñar)* to teach. 3 DEP *(entrenar)* to train, coach: **se está preparando para el maratón** *she's training for the marathon.* 4 *(estudiar)* to revise for, work for: **¿has preparado el examen de inglés?** *have you studied for the English exam?*
preparativos *nm pl* arrangements, preparations.
preposición *nf* preposition.
prepotencia *nf* 1 *(poder)* dominance. 2 *(arrogancia)* arrogance.
prepotente *adj* arrogant, domineering.
prerrogativa *nf* prerogative.
presa *nf* 1 *(cosa prendida)* prey. 2 *(embalse)* dam. 3 *(acción)* capture. ● **ave de presa** bird of prey.
presagiar [12] *vt* to be a warning of, foretell.
presagio *nm* 1 *(señal)* omen. 2 *(adivinación)* premonition.
presbiteriano ,-a *adj* Presbyterian.
▷ *nm & nf* Presbyterian.
presbítero *nm* priest.
~~**prescindir** *vi*~~ **prescindir de** *(pasar sin)* to do without; *(no contar con)* to leave out.
prescribir *vt* 1 *(recetar)* to prescribe. 2 JUR *(ordenar)* to prescribe, state.
▷ *vi* JUR *(extinguirse)* to expire, lapse.
prescripción *nf* prescription.
presencia *nf* 1 *(gen)* presence. 2 *(aspecto)* appearance. ● **presencia de ánimo** presence of mind.
presenciar [12] *vt (acontecimiento)* to be present at; *(accidente, atraco)* to witness.
presentación *nf* 1 *(de un objeto, documento, etc)* presentation, showing: **la presentación del carné es imprescindible para entrar** *passes must be shown to allow access.* 2 *(de personas)* introduction.
presentador ,-ra *nm & nf* presenter.
presentar *vt* 1 *(gen)* to present; *(mostrar)* to show. 2 *(entregar)* to hand in. 3 *(sacar al mercado)* to launch. 4 *(personas)* to introduce: **¿te han presentado ya?** *have you been introduced yet?* 5 TV to present. 6 *(ofrecer)* to offer, show: **esta cicatriz no presenta buen aspecto** *that scar doesn't look good.*
▷ *vpr* **presentarse** 1 *(comparecer)* to turn up: **nos presentamos en su casa sin previo aviso** *we turned up at her house without prior warning.* 2 *(para elección)* to stand; *(en un concurso)* to enter.
presente *adj* present.
▷ *nm* 1 *(tiempo)* present. 2 LING present tense. 3 *(obsequio)* gift.
▷ *nm pl* **presentes** those present: **los aquí presentes damos por válido el presupuesto** *those of us present approve the budget.*
presentimiento *nm* premonition, presentiment.
presentir [35] *vt* to have a feeling (**que**, that).
preservar *vt* to preserve.
preservativo *nm* condom.
presidencia *nf* 1 POL presidency. 2 *(de una empresa)* chairmanship, US presidency.
presidente ,-ta *nm & nf* 1 POL president. 2 *(de una empresa - hombre)* chairman, US president; *(- mujer)* chairwoman, US president.
presidiario,-a *nm & nf* convict, prisoner.
presidio *nm* prison, penitentiary.
presidir *vt* 1 *(reunión)* to chair, preside over. 2 *(país)* to be president of. 3 *(predominar)* to prevail.
presilla *nf* fastener.
presión *nf* pressure.
presionar *vt* 1 *(objeto)* to press. 2 *(persona)* to pressure, put pressure on.
preso ,-a *nm & nf* prisoner.
prestación *nf* 1 *(servicio)* service. 2 *(de la Seguridad Social)* benefit, allowance. ● **prestación por desempleo** unemployment benefit.
prestado ,-a *adj* lent, on loan. ■ **pedir prestado,-a** to borrow.
prestamista *nm o nf* moneylender.
préstamo *nm* 1 *(crédito)* loan. 2 *(acción de prestar)* lending; *(acción de pedir prestado)* borrowing. 3 LING loanword. ■ **pedir un préstamo** to ask for a loan.
prestar *vt* 1 *(dejar prestado)* to lend, loan. 2 *(pedir prestado)* to borrow. 3 *(servicio)* to do, render. 4 *(ayuda)* to give.
▷ *vpr* **prestarse** 1 *(ofrecerse)* to lend OS: **se prestó para ayudar en la operación de rescate** *he offered to help in the rescue operation.* 2 *(ser motivo)* to lend itself: **estas indicaciones se prestan a malas interpretaciones** *these instructions are open misinterpretation.* 3 *(acceder)* to agree, give in.
prestidigitador ,-ra *nm & nf* conjuror, magician.
prestigio *nm* prestige.
prestigioso ,-a *adj* prestigious.
presto ,-a *adj* 1 *(preparado)* ready. 2 *(rápido)* quick.
presumible *adj* probable, likely.
presumido ,-a *adj (arrogante)* conceited; *(en el vestir)* vain.
presumir *vi* 1 *(vanagloriarse)* to boast (**de**, about), show off (**de**, about). 2 *(ser presumido)* to be vain: **le gusta mucho presumir** *he's really vain.*
▷ *vt (suponer)* to suppose, assume.

presunto ,-a *adj* presumed, alleged.
presuntuoso ,-a *adj (presumido)* conceited, vain; *(arrogante)* presumptuous.
presuponer [78] *vt* to presuppose.
presupuestar *vt (proyecto)* to budget for; *(construcción, obra, etc)* to estimate.
presupuesto ,-a *nm* **presupuesto** 1 *(en finanzas, política)* budget; *(de una obra, reparación, etc)* estimate. 2 *(supuesto)* assumption.
● **los presupuestos generales del Estado** the national budget *sing.*
pretencioso ,-a *adj* pretentious.
▷ *nm & nf* pretentious person.
pretender *vt* 1 *(querer)* to want to: **pretende ganar el concurso** *he wants to win the contest.* 2 *(intentar)* to try to: **no sé qué pretende hacer** *I don't know what he's trying to do.* 3 *(cortejar)* to court.
pretendido ,-a *adj* supposed.
pretendiente *nm (enamorado)* suitor.
▷ *nm o nf* 1 *(a un puesto)* applicant. 2 *(al trono)* pretender.
pretensión *nf* 1 *(intención)* aim; *(ambición)* ambition: **no tengo pretensiones de escritor** *I don't aspire to being a writer.* 2 *(derecho)* claim.
pretérito ,-a *adj* past: **en tiempos pretéritos** *in the past.*
▷ *nm* **pretérito** simple past, preterite.
pretexto *nm* pretext.
prevalecer [43] *vi* to prevail.
prevaricar *vi* JUR to fail deliberately to do one's duty.
prevención *nf* 1 *(precaución)* prevention. 2 *(medida)* measure, preventive measure. 3 *(prejuicio)* prejudice: **al principio le tenía cierta prevención** *at first she was somewhat prejudiced against him.*
prevenido ,-a *adj* forewarned.
prevenir [90] *vt* 1 *(evitar)* to avoid, prevent. 2 *(advertir)* to warn: **me previnieron contra su mal humor** *they warned me about his bad mood.*
preventivo ,-a *adj (medicina, medida, etc)* preventive, preventative.
prever [91] *vt* 1 *(anticipar)* to foresee, forecast. 2 *(preparar)* to plan.
previo ,-a *adj* previous.
previsible *adj* foreseeable.
previsión *nf* 1 *(anticipación)* forecast. 2 *(precaución)* precaution. ● **previsión meteorológica** weather forecast.
previsor ,-ra *adj* farsighted.
prieto ,-a *adj* tight.
prima *nf* 1 *(gratificación)* bonus. 2 *(del seguro)* insurance premium.
primacía *nf* primacy.
primar *vi (predominar)* to be important; *(sobresalir)* to stand out.
primaria *nf* primary education.
primario ,-a *adj* primary.
primate *nm* primate.
primavera *nf* 1 spring. 2 *lit (año)* year.
primaveral *adj* spring, spring-like.
primera *nf* 1 AUTO first gear. 2 *(en transportes)* first class: **viajan siempre en primera** *they always travel first-class.*
primerizo ,-a *nm & nf* beginner: **una madre primeriza** *a first-time mother.*
primero ,-a *adj* first: **el primer día del año** *the first day of the year.*
▷ *nm & nf* first: **es la primera de la clase** *she's top of the class.*
▷ *adv* **primero** *(en primer lugar)* first: **primero vamos a mirarlo en el diccionario** *let's look it up in the dictionary first.* ■ **a primeros de mes/año** at the beginning of the month/year.

Before singular masculine nouns the form **primer** is used.

primicia *nf* 1 BOT first fruit. 2 *(noticia)* scoop.
primigenio ,-a *adj* original.
primitiva *nf (lotería)* ≈ National Lottery.
primitivo ,-a *adj* 1 HIST primitive. 2 *(original)* original. 3 *(rudimentario)* basic.
primo ,-a *nm & nf (familiar)* cousin.
▷ *nm* **primo** *fam* mug, sucker. ■ **hacer el primo** *fam* to be taken for a ride.
primogénito ,-a *adj* first-born, eldest.
▷ *nm & nf* first-born, eldest.
primor *nm* 1 *(delicadeza)* delicateness, delicacy. 2 *(hermosura)* beauty.
primordial *adj* essential.
primoroso ,-a *adj* delicate.
princesa *nf* princess.
principado *nm* principality.
principal *adj* main, chief: **lo principal es que duerma bien** *the main thing is that he sleeps well.*
▷ *nm (piso)* first floor, US second floor.
príncipe *nm* prince.
principiante ,-a *nm & nf* beginner.
principio *nm* 1 *(inicio)* beginning, start: **me voy de vacaciones a principios de mes** *I'm going on holiday (US vacation) at the beginning of the month.* 2 *(base)* principle. 3 *(moral)* principle: **no tiene principios** *he has no principles.*
▷ *nm pl* **principios** rudiments.
pringado ,-a *pp* → **pringar.**
▷ *nm & nf fam pey* mug.
pringar [7] *vt* 1 *(ensuciar)* to make greasy: **me he puesto las manos pringando de grasa** *I've got my hands covered in grease.* 2 *(untar)* to soak in oil.
pringoso ,-a *adj* greasy.
prior ,-ra *nm & nf (hombre)* prior; *(mujer)* prioress.
prioridad *nf* priority.
prioritario ,-a *adj* priority.
prisa *nf* hurry: **¡date prisa que no llegamos!** *hurry up or we'll never make it!* ■ **correr prisa** to be urgent. ■ **tener prisa** to be in a hurry.
prisión *nf* prison.
prisionero ,-a *nm & nf* prisoner.
prisma *nm* 1 prism. 2 *fig (perspectiva)* angle.
prismático ,-a *adj* prismatic.
▷ *nm pl* **prismáticos** binoculars.
privacidad *nf* privacy.
privación *nf* deprivation, privation. ■ **pasar privaciones** to suffer hardship.
privado ,-a *adj* private.
privar *vt (despojar)* to deprive (**de**, of).
privativo ,-a *adj (propio, exclusivo)* exclusive.
privatizar *vt* to privatize.

privilegiado ,-a *adj* privileged.
privilegiar *vt* to privilege.
privilegio *nm* privilege.
pro *nm* advantage.
▷ *prep* pro-, in favour of: **una campaña pro amnistía** *a pro-amnesty campaign.* ● **los pros y los contras** the pros and cons.
proa *nf* bow, prow.
probabilidad *nf* probability.
probable *adj* 1 *(posible)* probable, likely. 2 *(demostrable)* provable.
probado ,-a *adj* proven.
probador *nm* changing room, fitting room.
probar [31] *vt* 1 *(demostrar)* to prove: **esto prueba la veracidad de su testimonio** *this proves the truth of his testimony.* 2 *(comprobar)* to test, check: **prueba el coche a ver cómo responde** *check the car to see how it performs.* 3 *(vino, comida, etc)* to taste, try. 4 *(prenda, zapato)* to try on.
▷ *vi* to try: **prueba a cambiarle la pila** *try changing the battery.*
probeta *nf* test tube.
problema *nm* problem. ■ **tener problemas con** to have trouble with.
problemático ,-a *adj (cuestión)* problematic; *(joven)* difficult.
procedencia *nf* 1 *(de lugar, persona, etc)* origin: **¿conoce la procedencia de este dinero?** *do you know where this money came from?* 2 *(de barco, tren, etc)* origin.
procedente *adj* 1 coming (**de**, from): **el tren procedente de Sevilla** *the train arriving from Seville.* 2 *(adecuado)* appropriate, correct.
proceder *vi* 1 *(pasar a ejecutar)* to proceed: **ahora procedemos a la entrega de premios** *we now move on to the presentation of prizes.* 2 *(actuar)* to act: **en estas situaciones uno no sabe cómo proceder** *one doesn't know what to do in these situations.* 3 *(ser adecuado)* to be appropriate: **se les avisará cuando proceda** *you will be informed in due course.* 4 JUR to start proceedings (**contra**, against).
▷ *nm* conduct, behaviour (US behavior): **su extraño proceder confundió a todos** *his strange behaviour confused everybody.*
procedimiento *nm* 1 *(método)* procedure. 2 JUR proceedings *pl.*
procesado ,-a *adj* 1 INFORMÁ processed. 2 JUR tried.
▷ *nm & nf* **el/la procesado,-a** the accused.
procesador *nm* processor. ● **procesador de textos** INFORMÁ word processor.
procesar *vt* 1 *(gen)* to process. 2 JUR to try.
procesión *nf* procession.
proceso *nm* 1 *(gen)* process. 2 *(en el tiempo)* time. 3 JUR trial. ● **proceso de datos** data processing.
proclamar *vt* 1 *(declarar públicamente)* to proclaim. 2 *(revelar)* to broadcast.
▷ *vpr* **proclamarse** to proclaim OS.
proclive *adj* prone.
procreación *nf* procreation.
procrear *vi* to procreate.
procurador ,-ra *nm & nf* JUR procurator.
procurar *vt* 1 to try. 2 *(proporcionar)* to get: **nos han procurado billetes para el partido** *they've managed to get us some tickets for the match.*
prodigar [7] *vt* to be lavish with.
▷ *vpr* **prodigarse** *(dejarse ver)* to overexpose OS.
prodigio *nm* prodigy, miracle.
prodigioso ,-a *adj* prodigious.
pródigo ,-a *adj* 1 *(generoso - persona)* lavish; *(- naturaleza)* bountiful. 2 *(derrochador)* wasteful.
producción *nf* production.
producir [46] *vt* 1 *(gen)* to produce. 2 *(causar)* to cause. 3 *(cosecha, fruto, etc)* to yield.
▷ *vpr* **producirse** to happen.
productividad *nf* productivity.
productivo ,-a *adj (reunión, tierra)* productive; *(inversión)* profitable.
producto *nm* 1 *(gen)* product: **una amplia gama de productos** *a wide range of products.* 2 MAT product. 3 *(resultado)* result, product. 4 *(provecho)* fruit: **lo compró con el producto de su trabajo** *he bought it with the fruit of his labours.*
productor ,-ra *adj* producing.
▷ *nm & nf* producer.
productora *nf* CINE production company.
proeza *nf* feat, heroic deed.
profanar *vt* to desecrate, profane.
profano ,-a *adj* 1 *(no sagrado)* profane, secular. 2 *(no experto)* lay.
▷ *nm & nf (hombre)* layman; *(mujer)* laywoman.
profecía *nf* prophecy.
proferir [35] *vt (palabra, sonido, etc)* to utter; *(insulto)* to hurl.
profesión *nf* 1 profession. 2 REL taking of vows.
profesional *adj (gen)* professional: **es futbolista profesional** *he's a professional footballer.*
▷ *nm o nf* professional: **trabaja el cuero de maravilla, es todo un profesional** *he does wonders with leather, he's a real professional.*
profesionalidad *nf* professionalism.
profesor ,-ra *nm & nf (de enseñanza media)* teacher; *(de universidad)* lecturer. ● **profesor,-ra particular** private tutor.
profesorado *nm* 1 *(conjunto de profesores)* teaching staff. 2 *(cargo)* teaching post; *(actividad)* teaching profession.
profeta *nm* prophet.
profético ,-a *adj* prophetic.
profetizar [4] *vt* to prophesy.
prófugo ,-a *adj* on the run, fugitive.
▷ *nm & nf* fugitive.
profundidad *nf* 1 depth: **tiene cuatro metros de profundidad** *it's four metres deep.* 2 *(de persona, pensamiento, etc)* depth, profundity.
profundizar [4] *vt* 1 *(agujero, hoyo)* to deepen. 2 **profundizar en** *(tema, cuestión)* to look deeply into, analyse (US analyze) in depth.
profundo ,-a *adj* 1 *(gen)* deep. 2 *(tristeza, dolor, etc)* intense. 3 *(pensamiento, persona, etc)* profound, deep.
profuso ,-a *adj* profuse.
progenitor ,-ra *nm & nf (padre)* father; *(madre)* mother.
▷ *nm pl* **progenitores** parents.

programa *nm* 1 *(gen)* programme (US program). 2 INFORMÁ program. 3 EDUC *(de un curso)* syllabus.
programación *nf* 1 *(de televisión, radi, etco)* programming (US programing). 2 *(de teatro)* billing. 3 *(de vídeo)* programming. 4 INFORMÁ programming.
programador ,-ra *nm & nf* INFORMÁ programmer.
programar *vt* 1 *(gen)* to programme (US program). 2 INFORMÁ to program. 3 *(organizar, planear, etc)* to plan.
progresar *vi* to progress, make progress.
progresión *nf* progression. ● **progresión aritmética** arithmetic progression. | **progresión geométrica** geometric progression.
progresista *adj* progressive.
▷ *nm o nf* progressive.
progresivo ,-a *adj* progressive.
progreso *nm* progress.
prohibición *nf* prohibition, ban.
prohibido ,-a *adj* forbidden.
prohibir [21] *vt* to forbid.
prohibitivo ,-a *adj* prohibitive.
prójimo *nm* fellow man, neighbour (US neighbor).
prole *nf* offspring.
proletariado *nm* proletariat.
proletario ,-a *nm & nf* proletarian.
proliferar *vi* to proliferate.
prolijo ,-a *adj* 1 *(largo en exceso)* long-winded, verbose. 2 *(meticuloso)* meticulous.
prólogo *nm* prologue, US prolog.
prolongación *nf (gen)* prolongation.
prolongado ,-a *adj (largo)* prolonged, lengthy.
prolongar [7] *vt* 1 *(en el tiempo, etc)* to prolong. 2 *(en el espacio)* to extend.
▷ *vpr* **prolongarse** to go on.
promedio *nm* average.
promesa *nf* 1 promise. 2 *(persona)* budding talent.
prometedor ,-ra *adj* promising.
prometer *vt* to promise: **¿lo prometes?** *promise?*
▷ *vi* to be promising: **esta chica es una pintora que promete** *this girl is a promising artist.*
▷ *vpr* **prometerse** *(pareja)* to get engaged.
prometido ,-a *nm & nf (hombre)* fiancé; *(mujer)* fiancée.
prominente *adj* prominent.
promiscuo ,-a *adj* promiscuous.
promoción *nf* 1 *(gen)* promotion. 2 EDUC year, US class.
promocionar *vt* 1 *(gen)* to promote. 2 *(ideas, relaciones, etc)* to foster.
promontorio *nm* promontory, headland.
promotor ,-ra *nm & nf* 1 *(inmobiliario)* developer. 2 *(de una idea, plan, etc)* promoter.
promover [32] *vt* to promote.
promulgar [7] *vt* to enact, promulgate.
pronombre *nm* pronoun.
pronosticar [1] *vt* to predict.
pronóstico *nm* 1 *(del tiempo)* forecast. 2 MED prognosis. ● **pronóstico meteorológico** weather forecast.
pronto ,-a *adj* quick, fast: **la pronta reacción del conductor evitó un desastre** *the driver's quick reaction prevented a disaster.*
▷ *nm* **pronto** *fam (gen)* sudden urge, sudden impulse; *(de ira)* fit: **le dio un pronto de los suyos y se puso a pintar el piso** *he was overcome by a sudden urge and started to paint the flat* (US *apartment).*
▷ *adv* 1 *(rápido)* soon: **no llores que pronto vendrá tu mamá** *don't cry, your mummy will be here soon.* 2 *(temprano)* early: **has llegado demasiado pronto** *you've arrived too early.* ■ **de pronto** suddenly.
pronunciación *nf* 1 pronunciation. 2 pronouncement.
pronunciado ,-a *adj (marcado)* marked, pronounced.
pronunciar [12] *vt* 1 *(gen)* to pronounce. 2 *(discurso)* to make.
▷ *vpr* **pronunciarse** 1 *(expresarse)* to declare OS. 2 *(intensificarse)* to become more pronounced.
propagación *nf* propagation, spreading.
propaganda *nf* 1 *(publicidad)* advertising. 2 *(electoral)* propaganda.
propagar *vt* to propagate, spread.
propano *nm* propane.
propasarse *vpr* to go too far.
propensión *nf* inclination, tendency.
propenso ,-a *adj* inclined. ■ **ser propenso,-a a** ALGO to be prone to STH.
propiciar [12] *vt (favorecer)* to pave the way for, contribute to; *(causar)* to cause, lead to, bring about.
propiciatorio ,-a *adj* propitiatory.
propicio ,-a *adj (gen)* suitable; *(uso formal)* propitious.
propiedad *nf* 1 *(derecho)* ownership. 2 *(bien inmueble)* property. 3 *(corrección)* propriety: **hay que aprender a hablar con propiedad** *one must learn to speak correctly.* ● **propiedad privada** private property.
propietario ,-a *nm & nf* owner.
propina *nf* tip (US *gratuity).*
propinar *vt* to give.
propio ,-a *adj* 1 *(de nuestra propiedad)* own. 2 *(indicado)* proper, appropriate: **lo propio sería mandar una carta de agradecimiento** *the proper thing to do would be to send a thank-you letter.* 3 *(mismo - él)* himself; *(- ella)* herself; *(- cosa, animal)* itself; *(- en plural)* themselves: **el propio profesor no sabía la respuesta** *the teacher himself didn't know the answer.*
proponer [78] *vt (persona, plan, etc)* to propose.
▷ *vpr* **proponerse** to intend.
proporción *nf* proportion.
proporcionado ,-a *adj* in proportion.
proporcional *adj* proportionate, proportional.
proporcionar *vt* 1 *(ayuda, dinero, etc)* to supply; *(consejo)* to give. 2 *(dibujo)* to proportion.
proposición *nf* 1 *(idea)* proposal, proposition; *(sugerencia)* suggestion. 2 LING clause.
propósito *nm* 1 *(intención)* intention. 2 *(objetivo)* aim. ■ **a propósito** 1 *(por cierto)* by the way. 2 *(adrede)* on purpose.
propuesta *nf* proposal.
propugnar *vt* to advocate.
propulsar *vt* 1 *(medida, idea, etc)* to promote. 2 *(cohete, nave, etc)* to propel.
propulsión *nf* propulsion. ● **propulsión a chorro** jet propulsion.
propulsor ,-ra *nm (motor)* motor, engine; *(hélice)* screw, propeller. ● **propulsor de chorro** jet engine.
prórroga *nf* 1 *(de un plazo)* extension. 2 DEP extra time, US overtime.
prorrogable *adj* renewable.

prorrogar [7] *vt* 1 *(aplazar)* to postpone; *(alargar)* to extend. 2 DEP *(partido)* to postpone.
prosa *nf* prose.
prosaico ,-a *adj* prosaic.
proscribir *vt* 1 *(prohibir)* to proscribe, ban. 2 *(exiliar)* to exile.
proscrito ,-a *nm & nf (exiliado)* exile; *(criminal)* outlaw.
proseguir [56] *vt* to continue, carry on.
proselitismo *nm* proselytism.
proselitista *adj* proselytic.
▷ *nm o nf* proselytizer.
prosodia *nf* prosody.
prosopopeya *nf* 1 *(figura retórica)* prosopopoeia. 2 *(solemnidad)* pomposity.
prospección *nf* 1 *(del suelo)* surveying; *(para minerales)* prospecting. 2 *(investigación)* research.
prospecto *nm* leaflet, prospectus.
prosperar *vi* to prosper, thrive.
prosperidad *nf* prosperity.
próspero ,-a *adj* prosperous.
próstata *nf* prostate, prostate gland.
prostitución *nf* prostitution.
prostituir [62] *vt* to prostitute.
▷ *vpr* **prostituirse** to prostitute OS.
prostituta *nf* prostitute.
prostituto *nm* male prostitute.
protagonismo *nm* leading role.
protagonista *adj* main, leading.
▷ *nm o nf* 1 *(de película - actor)* leading man; *(- actriz)* leading lady. 2 *(de novela, obra de teatro, etc)* main character, protagonist. 3 *(de un hecho)* main protagonist.
protagonizar [4] *vt* 1 *(película, etc)* to star in. 2 *(suceso, acontecimiento)* to play a leading part in.
protección *nf* protection.
proteccionismo *nm* protectionism.
proteccionista *adj* protectionist.
▷ *nm o nf* protectionist.
protector ,-ra *adj* protective.
▷ *nm & nf (persona)* protector.
proteger [5] *vt* to protect.
protegido ,-a *nm & nf (hombre)* protégé; *(mujer)* protégée.
proteína *nf* protein.
proteínico ,-a *adj* proteinic.
prótesis *nf* MED *(uso formal)* prosthesis. ● **prótesis dental** denture.
protesta *nf* 1 protest. 2 JUR objection.
protestante *adj* Protestant.
▷ *nm o nf* Protestant.
protestantismo *nm* Protestantism.
protestar *vi* 1 *(mostrar disconformidad)* to protest (**contra**, against). 2 *(refunfuñar)* to moan: **te pasas la vida protestando** *you're always moaning.*
protocolo *nm* 1 *(gen)* protocol. 2 *fig (formalismo)* etiquette, formality.
protón *nm* proton.
protoplasma *nm* protoplasm.
prototipo *nm* prototype.
protozoo *nm* protozoan
protuberancia *nf* protuberance.
provecho *nm* 1 *(beneficio)* benefit: **le ha sacado el máximo provecho a la herencia** *he has made the most of his inheritance.* 2 *(aprovechamiento)* use: **ha estudiado con provecho** *he has benefitted from his studies.* ■ **¡buen provecho!** enjoy your meal!
provechoso ,-a *adj* 1 *(beneficioso)* beneficial; *(lucrativo)* profitable. 2 *(de utilidad)* useful, worthwhile.
proveedor ,-ra *nm & nf* supplier, purveyor.
proveer [61] *vt* 1 *(suministrar)* to provide (**de**, with). 2 *(cubrir)* to fill.
provenir [90] *vi* to come (**de**, from).
proverbial *adj* proverbial.
proverbio *nm* proverb, saying.
providencia *nf* 1 REL providence. 2 JUR ruling.
providencial *adj* providential.
provincia *nf* province. ■ **de provincias** provincial.
provinciano ,-a *adj pey* provincial.
▷ *nm & nf* provincial.
provisión *nf* 1 *(suministro)* provision, supply. 2 *(de un empleo)* filling.
provisional *adj* provisional, temporary.
provisto ,-a *adj* provided (**de**, with), equipped (**de**, with).
provocación *nf* 1 *(gen)* provocation. 2 *(del parto)* induction.
provocar [1] *vt* to incite, to provoke.
provocativo ,-a *adj* provocative.
próximamente *adv* shortly, soon.
proximidad *nf* proximity.
▷ *nf pl* **proximidades** *(vecindad)* vicinity *sing.*
próximo ,-a *adj* 1 *(cerca)* near. 2 *(siguiente)* next: **el mes próximo** *next month.*
proyección *nf* 1 *(gen)* projection. 2 CINE screening, showing. 3 *(alcance)* scope; *(fama)* renown; *(implicaciones)* implications *pl.*
proyectar *vt* 1 *(viaje, escapada)* to plan. 2 *(luz)* to project. 3 *(película)* to show. 4 *(sentimientos)* to project. 5 ARQUIT to design.
proyectil *nm* projectile, missile.
proyecto *nm* 1 *(propósito)* plan. 2 *(plan)* project: **el proyecto del ayuntamiento no satisface al vecindario** *the council's project doesn't satisfy the residents.* 3 ARQUIT designs *pl.* ● **proyecto de ley** JUR bill.
proyector *nm (de cine)* film projector; *(de diapositivas)* slide projector.
prudencia *nf* 1 *(cuidado)* care, caution; *(moderación)* moderation. 2 *(sensatez)* prudence.
prudente *adj* sensible, prudent.
prueba *nf* 1 *(demostración)* proof. 2 *(experimento)* experiment, trial: **haz la prueba** *try it.* 3 *(examen)* test. 4 TÉC trial. 5 MED test. 6 DEP event. 7 JUR evidence. 8 *(en imprenta)* proof: **necesitamos un corrector de pruebas** *we need a proofreader.* 9 *(en costura)* fitting. ■ **poner a prueba** to put to the test. ● **prueba de acceso** entrance examination.
psicoanálisis *nm inv* psychoanalysis.
psicoanalista *nm o nf* psychoanalyst.
psicoanalítico ,-a *adj* psychoanalytic, psychoanalytical.
psicoanalizar *vt* to psychoanalyse (US psychoanalyze).
psicodélico ,-a *adj* psychedelic.
psicología *nf* psychology.
psicológico ,-a *adj* psychological.

psicólogo,-a *nm & nf* psychologist.
psicópata *nm o nf* psychopath.
psicopatía *nf* psychopathy.
psicosis *nf inv* psychosis.
psicosomático,-a *adj* psychosomatic.
psicoterapeuta *nm o nf* psychotherapist.
psicoterapia *nf* psychotherapy.
psique *nf* psyche.
psiquiatra *nm o nf* psychiatrist.
psiquiatría *nf* psychiatry.
psiquiátrico,-a *adj* psychiatric.
psíquico,-a *adj* psychic, psychical.
psoriasis *nf inv* psoriasis.
pterodáctilo *nm* pterodactyl.
púa *nf* 1 *(de peine, cepillo)* tooth. 2 *(de erizo)* quill. 3 MÚS plectrum. 4 *(de alambre)* barb.
pub *nm* pub.
▲ *pl* **pubs o pubes.**
pubertad *nf* puberty.
púbico,-a *adj* pubic.
pubis *nm inv* 1 pubes *pl*. 2 *(hueso)* pubis.
publicable *adj* publishable.
publicación *nf* publication.
publicar [1] *vt* 1 *(libro, noticia, etc)* to publish. 2 *(secreto)* to broadcast, spread.
publicidad *nf* 1 *(comercial)* advertising. 2 *(divulgación)* publicity.
publicista *nm o nf* advertising executive.
publicitario,-a *adj* advertising.
público,-a *adj* public.
▷ *nm* **público** *(de un espectáculo)* audience; *(de televisión)* audience, viewers *pl*: **el público aplaudió entusiasmado** *the audience applauded warmly.* ■ **en público** in public. ● **opinión pública** public opinion.
publirreportaje *nm (documentary style)* television advertisement.
puchero *nm* 1 *(olla)* cooking pot. 2 CULIN meat and vegetable stew. 3 *(gesto)* pout.
púdico,-a *adj* chaste, decent.
pudiente *adj* wealthy, rich.
pudor *nm* 1 *(decencia)* decency. 2 *(modestia)* modesty.
pudoroso,-a *adj* decent, chaste.
pudrir *vt* to rot.
▷ *vpr* **pudrirse** to rot.
pueblerino,-a *adj* 1 *(de pueblo)* village. 2 *pey* countrified.
pueblo *nm* 1 *(población)* village. 2 *(gente)* people.
puente *nm* 1 *(sobre un río, etc)* bridge. 2 *(fiesta) day taken off between a public holiday and the weekend or another holiday*. ● **puente aéreo** shuttle service.
puerco,-a *adj* 1 *fam (sucio)* filthy. 2 *(canalla)* rotten.
▷ *nm & nf (animal - macho)* pig; *(- hembra)* sow. ● **puerco espín** porcupine.
puericultor,-ora *nm & nf* child care specialist.
puericultura *nf* child care.
pueril *adj* 1 *(infantil)* puerile, childish. 2 *(iluso)* naive.
puerro *nm* leek.
puerta *nf* 1 door. 2 *(verja)* gate. 3 DEP *(portería)* goal. ● **puerta de embarque** gate. ❙ **puerta de la calle** main door, front door.
puerto *nm* 1 MAR port, harbour. 2 *(de montaña)* (mountain) pass. ● **puerto deportivo** marina.

Puerto Rico *nm* Puerto Rico.
puertorriqueño,-a *adj* Puerto Rican.
▷ *nm & nf* Puerto Rican.
pues *conj* 1 *(ya que)* since, as. 2 *(por lo tanto)* therefore so. 3 *(repetitivo)* then. 4 *(enfático)* well: **pues bien** *well then;* **¡pues claro!** *of course!;* **pues no** *well no.*
puesta *nf* 1 *(colocación)* setting. 2 *(de huevos)* laying ● **puesta de sol** sunset. ❙ **puesta en escena** staging.
puesto,-a *nm* **puesto** 1 *(sitio)* place: **ya han llegado al primer puesto** *they've made it to the top*. 2 *(de mercado)* stall; *(de feria, etc)* stand. 3 *(empleo)* position, post. 4 MIL post. ■ **estar muy puesto,-a en** ALGO to be well up in STH. ❙ **puesto que** since, as.
puf *nm* pouf, pouffe.
▲ *pl* **pufs.**
púgil *nm* boxer.
pugnar *vi* to fight, struggle.
puja *nf* 1 *(acción)* bidding. 2 *(cantidad)* bid.
pujante *adj* thriving.
pujar *vt (en subasta)* to bid higher.
pulcritud *nf* neatness.
pulcro,-a *adj* neat.
pulga *nf* flea.
pulgada *nf* inch.
pulgar *nm* thumb.
pulgón *nm* aphid.
pulgoso,-a *adj (perro)* flea-ridden.
pulimentar *vt* to polish.
pulir *vt (superficie)* to polish.
▷ *vpr* **pulirse** *fam (dilapidar)* to polish off.
pullover *nm* pullover.
▲ *pl* **pullovers.**
pulmón *nm* lung.
pulmonar *adj* lung, pulmonary.
pulmonía *nf* pneumonia.
pulpa *nf* pulp.
púlpito *nm* pulpit.
pulpo *nm* ZOOL octopus.
pulsación *nf* 1 pulsation. 2 *(de corazón)* beat. 3 *(en mecanografía)* stroke.
pulsador *nm (gen)* push button, button; *(de la luz)* switch.
pulsar *vt* 1 *(botón, timbre, etc)* to press. 2 *(tecla - de máquina de escribir)* to tap; *(- de piano)* to play.
pulsera *nf* 1 bracelet. 2 *(de reloj)* watch strap.
pulso *nm* 1 *(presión sanguínea)* pulse: **déjame que te tome el pulso** *let me take your pulse*. 2 *(firmeza en la mano)* steady hand: **para dibujar hay que tener buen pulso** *to be able to draw you need a steady hand.*
pulular *vi* to swarm.
pulverizador *nm* spray, atomizer.
pulverizar [4] *vt* 1 *(líquido)* to atomize, spray. 2 *(sólido)* to pulverize. 3 *(enemigo)* to crush, wipe out.
puma *nm* puma, mountain lion, cougar.
punción *nf* puncture.
punitivo,-a *adj* punitive.
punk *adj* punk.
▷ *nm* punk.
punta *nf* 1 *(extremo)* tip; *(extremo afilado)* point. 2 CULIN *(pizca)* pinch. ■ **en hora punta** at peak time. ❙ **sacar punta a** 1 *(lápiz)* to sharpen. 2 *(palabras)* to read too much into.

puntada *nf* stitch.
puntal *nm* 1 prop. 2 *fig* support.
puntapié *nm* kick.
puntear *vt* 1 *(dibujar)* to dot. 2 MÚS to pluck.
punteo *nm* MÚS plucking, US picking.
puntera *nf (de zapato, calcetín, etc)* toe; *(protector)* toecap.
puntería *nf* aim: ¡qué buena puntería! *what a good shot!*
puntero ,-a *adj* leading.
▷ *nm* **puntero** *(para señalar)* pointer.
puntiagudo ,-a *adj* pointed.
puntilla *nf* 1 COST lace. 2 *(puñal)* dagger. ■ **de puntillas** on tiptoe.
puntilloso ,-a *adj* 1 *(susceptible)* touchy. 2 *(exigente)* punctilious.
punto *nm* 1 *(gen)* point. 2 *(marca)* dot. 3 *(tanto)* point: nos llevan cinco puntos de ventaja *they're five points ahead of us.* 4 *(detrás de abreviatura)* dot; *(al final de la oración)* full stop, US period. 5 *(lugar)* spot: ¿en qué punto de la carretera se encuentran? *exactly where on the road are they?* 6 *(tema)* point. 7 *(tejido)* knitwear: me he comprado una falda de punto *I bought a knitted skirt.* 8 *(en costura, sutura, etc)* stitch: me caí y me dieron tres puntos en la barbilla *I fell and needed three stitches on my chin.* 9 *(de libro)* bookmark. ■ **en punto** sharp, on the dot: son las tres en punto *it's exactly three o'clock.* ‖ **hasta cierto punto** up to a certain point. ● **dos puntos** colon. ‖ **punto cardinal** cardinal point. ‖ **punto de partida** starting point. ‖ **punto de venta** sales outlet. ‖ **punto de vista** point of view. ‖ **punto débil** weak point. ‖ **punto y coma** semicolon. ‖ **punto y seguido** full stop, new sentence, US period, new sentence.
puntuable *adj* valid.
puntuación *nf* 1 *(en ortografía)* punctuation. 2 *(acción de puntuar)* scoring; *(total de puntos)* score. 3 EDUC *(acción)* marking; *(nota)* mark: obtuvo una puntuación muy alta *she got a very high mark.*
puntual *adj* 1 *(que llega a su hora)* punctual: han llegado muy puntuales *they've arrived right on time.* 2 *(detallado)* detailed. 3 *(aislado)* specific.
puntualidad *nf* punctuality.
puntualización *nf* remark.
puntualizar [4] *vt* 1 *(detallar)* to give full details of. 2 *(especificar)* to point out.
puntuar [11] *vt* 1 LING to punctuate. 2 EDUC to mark.
▷ *vi* DEP to score.
punzada *nf* sharp pain, stab of pain.
punzante *adj* stabbing.
punzar [4] *vt* 1 to prick. 2 *fig* to torment.
punzón *nm* punch.
puñado *nm* handful.
puñal *nm* dagger.
puñalada *nf (acción)* stab; *(herida)* stab wound.
puñetazo *nm* punch.
puño *nm* 1 *(mano)* fist. 2 *(de arma)* handle. 3 *(de camisa, abrigo, etc)* cuff.
pupila *nf* pupil.
pupilaje *nm (de persona)* board and lodging; *(de coche)* garaging: «Se admiten coches a pupilaje» *«Garaging facilities available».*
pupilo ,-a *nm & nf (de un tutor)* pupil.
pupitre *nm* school desk.
purasangre *adj* thoroughbred.
▷ *nm (caballo)* thoroughbred.
puré *nm (espeso)* purée; *(sopa) thick* soup: hoy tenemos puré de zanahoria *today we've got thick carrot soup.* ● **puré de patatas** mashed potatoes.
pureza *nf* 1 *(gen)* purity. 2 *(castidad)* chastity.
purga *nf* purge.
purgación *nf (acción)* purging.
▷ *nf pl* **purgaciones** *fam* blennorrhoea (US blennorrhea).
purgante *adj* purgative.
▷ *nm* purgative, laxative.
purgar [7] *vt* to purge (**de**, of).
purgatorio *nm* purgatory.
purificación *nf* purification.
purificador ,-ra *adj* purifying.
▷ *nm* **purificador** purifier.
purificante *adj* purifying.
purificar *vt* to purify.
purismo *nm* purism.
purista *adj* purist.
▷ *nm o nf* purist.
puritano ,-a *adj* puritan, puritanic.
▷ *nm & nf* puritan.
puro ,-a *adj* 1 *(sin mezcla)* pure: me voy al campo a respirar aire puro *I'm going to the country to breathe some clean air ;* tiene un perro de pura raza *he has a pure-bred dog.* 2 *(mero)* sheer, mere, pure: me enteré por pura casualidad *I found out by pure chance.* 3 *(casto)* chaste, pure.
▷ *nm* **puro** cigar.
púrpura *adj* purple.
▷ *nm* purple.
purpúreo ,-a *adj* purple.
purpurina *nf* glitter.
purulento ,-a *adj* purulent.
pus *nm* pus.
pusilánime *adj* faint-hearted, pusillanimous.
pusilanimidad *nf* faint-heartedness, pusillanimity.
pústula *nf* pustule.
puta *nf tabú* prostitute, whore.
putativo ,-a *adj* putative.
puto ,-a *adj tabú (miserable)* bloody, fucking: no tengo ni un puto duro *I haven't got any fucking money.*
▷ *nm* **puto** 1 *tabú (prostituto)* male prostitute, rent boy. 2 *tabú (sinvergüenza)* bastard, fucker.
putrefacción *nf* putrefaction, rotting.
putrefacto ,-a *adj* putrefied, rotten.
pútrido ,-a *adj* putrefied, rotten.
puya *nf* 1 *(punta de lanza)* tip, point. 2 *(comentario)* gibe.
puyazo *nm* 1 jab with a lance. 2 *(comentario)* gibe.
puzzle *nm* puzzle.

Q

Q, q *nf (la letra)* Q, q.
Qatar *nm* Qatar.
Qm *sím* **(quintal métrico)** quintal.
quásar *nm* quasar.
que[1] *pron* **1** *(sujeto, persona)* who, that; *(cosa)* that, which: **la chica que vino ayer está enferma** *the girl who came yesterday is ill* (US *sick*); **el árbol que se quemó está en el jardín** *the tree that got burnt is in the garden* (US *yard*). **2** *(complemento, persona)* whom, who; *(cosa)* that, which: **el coche que me prestaste está ahí** *the car (that) you lent me is there;* **el niño que viste ayer es mi hijo** *the boy you saw yesterday is my son.* **3** *prep* + **que** *(complemento circunstancial)* which; *(lugar)* where; *(tiempo)* when: **la casa en que vivía estaba lejos** *the house where he lived was far away.* **4** *def art* + **que** the one which, the one that: **ese libro es el que me gusta** *that's the book I like.*
que[2] *conj* **1** that: **dice que no vendrá** *he says (that) he won't come.* **2** *(en comparaciones)* than: **es más alto que su padre** *he is taller than his father.* **3** *(deseo, mandato)*: **¡que te diviertas!** *enjoy yourself!* **4** *(duda, extrañeza)*: **¿que no te hicieron pagar nada?** *(you say) they didn't make you pay anything?* **5** *(causal, consecutiva)*: **¡arriba, que ya son las ocho!** *get up, it's eight o'clock!* **6** *(tanto si... como si...)* whether... or not...: **que llueva que no llueva, iremos de excursión** *whether it rains or not, we're going on a trip.* **7** *(reiterativo)* and: **charla que charla se nos pasó la hora** *we were so busy talking that the hour just flew by.* **8** *(final)* so that: **ven aquí que te vea bien** *come here so that I can see you properly.* **9** *fam (condicional)* if: **que te gusta, te lo quedas; que no te gusta, lo cambias** *if you like it, keep it; if you don't, you can change it.* **10 que no** *(adversativa)* not: **justicia pido, que no gracia** *I want justice, not mercy.* ■ **¿a que no? / ¿a que sí?** right?, isn't that right? ▮ **¿a que no...?** I bet you can't...!: **a que no sabes la respuesta** *I bet you don't know the answer.* ▮ **que yo sepa** as far as I know. ▮ **yo que tú...** if I were you...
qué *pron* what: **no sé qué hacer** *I don't know what to do;* **¿qué querías?** *what did you want?*
▷ *adj* **1** *(cuál)* which: **no sé qué libro quiere** *I don't know which book he wants.* **2** *(en frases interrogativas)* how, what: **¿qué años tienes?** *how old are you?;* **¿qué has dicho?** *what did you say?* **3** *(en frases exclamativas)* how, what: **¡qué bonito!** *how nice!;* **¡qué flor más bonita!** *what a lovely flower!* **4** *(cantidad)* what: **¡qué de gente!** *what a crowd!* ■ **no hay de qué** don't mention it. ▮ **¿qué tal?** *fam* how are things?
quebrada *nf* GEOL *(depresión)* depression; *(paso)* gorge.
quebradizo ,-a *adj* **1** *(frágil)* fragile, brittle; *(pastel)* short. **2** *fig (débil moralmente)* weak, frail.
quebrado ,-a *adj* **1** *(terreno)* rugged, rough, uneven; *(camino)* tortuous. **2** *(número)* fractional.
▷ *nm* **quebrado** MAT fraction.
quebradura *nf* **1** *(grieta)* fissure, crack. **2** GEOL *(depresión)* depression; *(paso)* gorge, ravine.
quebrantado ,-a *adj (debilitado)* feeble, weak.
quebrantahuesos *nm inv* **1** *(ave)* lammergeier. **2** *fig (persona pesada)* bore, pest.
quebrantamiento *nm* **1** *(rotura)* breaking. **2** *(debilitamiento)* weakening. **3** *(de una ley)* violation, infringement.
quebrantar *vt* **1** *(cascar)* to crack. **2** *(romper)* to break, shatter; *(machacar)* to grind. **3** *(debilitar)* to weaken. **4** *fig (salud, posición, fortuna)* to undermine, shatter. **5** *fig (incumplir)* to break, violate. **6** *fig (suavizar)* to take the edge off, temper; *(ablandar)* to soften: **el sol ha quebrantado el frío** *the sun has taken the edge off the cold.* **7** *fig (causar lástima)* to wound, shatter.
▷ *vpr* **quebrantarse 1** *(cascarse)* to crack. **2** *(romperse)* to break. **3** *(la salud)* to be shattered.
quebranto *nm* **1** *fig (desaliento)* discouragement. **2** *fig (lástima)* pity. **3** *fig (pérdida)* severe loss; *(daño)* damage, harm. **4** *fig (aflicción)* grief, pain, sorrow.
quebrar [27] *vt (romper, incumplir)* to break.
▷ *vi* **1** FIN to go bankrupt. **2** *fig (flaquear)* to weaken.
▷ *vpr* **quebrarse 1** *(romperse)* to break. **2** *(herniarse)* to rupture OS. **3** *(interrumpirse)* to be broken, open up: **la cordillera se quiebra a pocos kilómetros** *there is a break in the mountain range in a few kilometres.* **4** *fig (ánimo)* to break, crack.
queda *nf en desuso* curfew.
quedar *vi* **1** *(permanecer)* to remain, stay: **quedó quieto** *he remained still;* **la carta quedó abierta** *the letter was left open.* **2** *fig (terminar)* to end: **la discusión quedó aquí** *the discussion ended here.* **3** *(cita)* to arrange to meet: **quedamos en el aeropuerto a las diez** *we arranged to meet at the airport at ten o'clock.* **4** *(resultado de algo)* to be: **te ha quedado muy bien la tarta** *your cake has turned out really well.* **5** *(favorecer)* to look, fit: **allí quedaría bien un cuadro** *a picture would look nice there.* **6** *(estar situado)* to be: **¿por dónde queda?** *whereabouts is it?* **7** *(restar)* to be left, remain: **quedan tres bombones** *there are three chocolates left.* **8** *(faltar)* to be, be still: **queda mucho que hacer** *there's a lot to be done.* **9 quedar en** *(convenir)* to agree to: **quedamos en volver más tarde** *we agreed to come back later.* **10 quedar por** + *inf* not to have been + *pp*: **la cama quedó por hacer** *the bed had not been made, the bed was left unmade.* **11 quedar** + *gerundio* to be, remain: **cuando me fui el niño quedaba durmiendo** *when I left the child was sleeping.* ■ **¿en qué quedamos?** so what's it to be? ▮ **quedar en nada** to come to nothing.
▷ *vpr* **quedarse 1** *(permanecer)* to remain, stay, be: **se quedaron una semana** *they stayed for a week.* **2** *(resultado de algo)* to be, remain: **quedó entusiasmado** *he was delighted.* **3** *euf (morirse)* to die. **4** *(mar, viento)* to be-

come calm; *(viento)* to drop. **5 quedarse con** *(retener algo)* to keep: **quédese con el cambio** *keep the change.*
quedo ,-a *adj* **1** quiet, still. **2** *(voz)* low.
▷ *adv* **quedo** *(calladamente)* quietly; *(suavemente)* softly.
quehacer *nm* task, chore, job.
queja *nf* **1** *(descontento)* complaint. **2** *(de dolor)* moan, groan.
quejarse *vpr* **1** *(de descontento)* to complain (**de**, about): **¡no te quejes!** *stop complaining!* **2** *(de dolor)* to moan, groan.
quejido *nm* groan, moan.
quejigo *nm* gall oak.
quejumbroso ,-a *adj* **1** *(persona)* whining, plaintive. **2** *(tono)* querulous: **lo dijo con tono quejumbroso** *he said it in a querulous tone.*
quelonio *adj* chelonian.
quema *nf* **1** *(acción, efecto)* burning. **2** *(fuego)* fire. ■ **huir de la quema** to beat it, flee.
quemado ,-a *adj* **1** burnt; *(por el sol)* sunburnt. **2** *fig (resentido)* embittered. **3** *fam (acabado)* spent, burnt-out: **este humorista está muy quemado** *this comedian is burnt-out.*
quemador ,-ra *nm* burner.
quemadura *nf* **1** *(acción)* burning. **2** *(herida)* burn; *(de sol)* sunburn; *(escaldadura)* scald.
quemar *vt* **1** *(gen)* to burn; *(plantas)* to scorch: **quemó un leño** *she burnt a log.* **2** *(incendiar)* to set on fire. **3** *fam (acabar)* to burn out: **dar clase quema mucho** *teaching burns you out.*
▷ *vi (estar muy caliente)* to be burning hot: **esta sopa quema** *this soup is burning hot.*
▷ *vpr* **quemarse** *(persona)* to burn OS; *(cosa)* to be burnt: **se ha quemado la carne** *the meat got burnt.*
quemarropa ■ **a quemarropa** at close range, at point-blank range.
quemazón *nf* **1** *(calor)* intense heat. **2** *fig (ardor)* burning sensation; *(picor)* itch. **3** *fig (dicho picante)* cutting remark.
queratina *nf* keratin.
querella *nf* **1** JUR action, lawsuit. **2** *(queja)* complaint. **3** *(enfrentamiento)* dispute, quarrel.
querellarse *vpr* JUR to take legal action (**contra**, against).
querencia *nf* **1** *(acción)* love. **2** *(inclinación del animal)* homing instinct; *(inclinación del hombre)* homesickness.
querer [80] *vt* **1** *(amar)* to love: **Juan y Elena se quieren** *Juan and Elena love each other.* **2** *(desear)* to want: **quiero que vengas** *I want you to come.* **3** *(buscar)* to be asking for, be looking for: **este chico quiere pelea** *this boy is asking for trouble.* **4** *(petición)* would: **¿quieres venir?** *would you like to come?* **5** *(verificarse)* may, might: **parece que quiere llover** *it looks as if it might rain.*
▷ *nm* love, affection.
querido ,-a *adj (amado)* dear, beloved; *(en carta)* dear.
▷ *nm & nf* **1** *(amante)* lover; *(mujer)* mistress. **2** *fam (apelativo)* darling.
quermes *nm inv* kermes.
quermés *nf* kermis.
queroseno *nm* kerosene.
querubín *nm* cherub.
quesera *nf* **1** *(fábrica)* cheese factory. **2** *(para servirlo)* cheese dish.
quesito *nm* cheese portion.
queso *nm* cheese.
quiasma *nm* chiasma.
quiche *nf* quiche.
quicio *nm* pivot hole. ■ **sacar a ALGN de quicio** *fam* to get on SB's nerves.
quico *nm roasted salted corn.*
quid *nm* crux: **éste es el quid de la cuestión** *this is the crux of the matter.*
quiebra *nf* **1** *(rotura)* break, crack. **2** *(bancarrota)* failure, bankruptcy; *(crack)* crash, collapse: **el último director llevó la empresa a la quiebra** *the last manager led the company into bankruptcy.* **3** *(pérdida)* loss. **4** GEOG gorge. **5** *fig (fracaso)* failure.
quiebro *nm* **1** *(en tauromaquia)* dodge. **2** MÚS trill.
quien *pron* **1** *(sujeto)* who: **me encontré a Toni, quien me dijo que estabas enfermo** *I met Toni, who told me you were ill.* **2** *(complemento)* who, whom: **las personas a quienes me encontré ayer están aquí** *the people (whom) I met yesterday are here.* **3** *(indefinido)* whoever, anyone who: **quien sepa la respuesta que me lo diga** *anyone who knows the answer tell me.* ■ **como quien** as if: **hace como quien no ve** *she acts as if she can't see.* ■ **quien más quien menos** *fig* everybody.
▲ *pl* **quienes.**
quién *pron* **1** *(sujeto)* who: **¿quién te lo dijo?** *who told you?* **2** *(complemento)* who, whom: **¿con quién hablas?** *who are you talking to?*; **¿para quién es?** *who is it for?* **3 de quién** *(posesivo)* whose: **¿de quién es esto?** *whose is this?.*
▲ *pl* **quiénes.**
quienquiera *pron* whoever: **entre, quienquiera que sea** *come in, whoever you may be.*
▲ *pl* **quienesquiera.**
quietismo *nm* **1** *(inercia)* inertia, stagnation. **2** REL quietism.
quieto ,-a *adj* **1** *(sin movimiento)* still, motionless: **¡estáte quieta!** *keep still!, don't move!* **2** *fig (sosegado)* quiet, calm: **el mar estaba quieto** *the sea was calm.*
quietud *nf* **1** *(sin movimiento)* stillness. **2** *fig (sosiego)* calmness, calm.
quijada *nf* jaw, jawbone.
quijotada *nf* quixotic act.
quijote *adj fig* quixotic.
quijotesco ,-a *adj* quixotic.
quijotismo *nm* quixotism.
quilate *nm* **1** *(unidad de peso)* carat. **2** *(unidad del oro)* carat (US karat).
quilla *nf* keel.
quilo[1] *nm (líquido)* chyle.
quilo[2] *nm* → **kilo.**
quilogramo *nm* → **kilogramo.**
quilométrico ,-a *adj* → **kilométrico,-a.**
quilómetro *adj* → **kilómetro.**
quimera *nf* **1** *(mitología)* chimera. **2** *fig (ilusión)* wild fancy, fantasy, pipe dream. **3** *fig (preocupación)* worry; *(sospecha infundada)* unfounded suspicion.
quimérico ,-a *adj* unrealistic, fantastic.
química *nf* chemistry.
químicamente *adv* chemically.
químico ,-a *adj* chemical.
▷ *nm & nf* chemist.
quimioterapia *nf* chemotherapy.

quimo *nm* chyme.
quimono *nm* kimono.
quina *nf* 1 *(corteza)* cinchona bark. 2 *(líquido)* quinine.
quincalla *nf (objetos de metal)* cheap metalware; *(baratija)* trinket.
quincallería *nf* hardware shop.
quincallero ,-a *nm & nf (de objetos de metal)* seller of cheap metalware; *(de baratijas)* trinket seller.
quince *adj (cardinal)* fifteen; *(ordinal)* fifteenth.
▷ *nm* fifteen.
See also seis.
quinceañero ,-a *adj* 1 *(de quince años)* fifteen-year-old. 2 *(adolescente)* teenage.
▷ *nm & nf* 1 *(de quince años)* fifteen-year-old. 2 *(adolescente)* teenager; *(aficionado a música pop)* teenybopper.
quinceavo ,-a *adj* fifth.
▷ *nm & nf* fifth.
See also sexto,-a.
quincena *nf* 1 *(tiempo)* fortnight. 2 *(paga)* fortnightly pay.
quincenal *adj* fortnightly, every two weeks.
quincuagenario ,-a *adj* quinquagenarian.
▷ *nm & nf* quinquagenarian, person in his/her fifties.
quincuagésimo ,-a *adj* fiftieth.
▷ *nm & nf* fiftieth.
See also sexto,-a.
quingentésimo ,-a *adj* five hundredth.
▷ *nm & nf* five hundredth.
See also sexto,-a.
quingombó *nm* okra, ladies' fingers.
quiniela *nf* football pools *pl*.
quinielista *nm o nf* person who does the pools.
quinielístico ,-a *adj to do with football pools*.
quinientista *adj* fifteenth-century.
quinientos ,-as *adj (cardinal)* five hundred; *(ordinal)* five-hundredth.
▷ *nm* quinientos *(número)* five hundred.
See also seis.
quinina *nf* quinine.
quino *nm* cinchona.
quinqué *nm* oil lamp.
▲ *pl* quinqués.
quinquenal *adj* quinquennial, five-year.
quinquenio *nm* quinquennium, five-year period.
quinqui *nm o nf fam* delinquent, petty criminal.
quinta *nf* 1 *(casa)* country house. 2 *(reemplazo militar)* call-up, conscript, US draft. 3 MÚS fifth.
quintaesencia *nf* quintessence.
quintal *nm* quintal *(46 kilograms)*. ● **quintal métrico** quintal *(100 kg)*.
quintar *vt* 1 *(sacar por sorteo)* to take one in five of. 2 *(para el servicio militar)* to conscript, US draft.
quinteto *nm* quintet.
quintilla *nf* five-line stanza.
quintillizo ,-a *nm & nf* quintuplet, quin.
quinto ,-a *adj* fifth.
▷ *nm & nf* fifth.
▷ *nm* quinto 1 MIL conscript, recruit. 2 *fam (de cerveza)* small bottle of beer *(= 20 cl)*.
See also sexto,-a.
quintuplicación *nf* quintupling.
quintuplicar [1] *vt* to quintuple.
quíntuplo ,-a *adj* quintuple.
▷ *nm* quíntuplo quintuple.
quinzavo ,-a *adj-nm & nf* → quinceavo,-a.
quiñón *nm* piece of land.
quiosco *nm* kiosk; *(de periódicos)* newsstand, newspaper stand; *(de música)* bandstand.
quiosquero ,-a *nm & nf* newsagent: su tío es quiosquero *her uncle has a newsstand.*
quiquiriquí *nm* 1 cock-a-doodle-doo. 2 *fig (gallito)* cock of the walk. 3 *(tupé)* quiff.
▲ *pl* quiquiriquíes.
quirófano *nm* operating theatre (US theater).
quiromancia *nf* palmistry, chiromancy.
quiromancía *nf* → quiromancia.
quiromántico ,-a *nm & nf* palmist, chiromancer.
quiromasaje *nm* chiropractic.
quiromasajista *nm & nf* chiropractor.
quirúrgico ,-a *adj* surgical.
quisque *pron* todo quisque everybody, everyone.
quisquilla *nf* 1 *(camarón)* (common) prawn. 2 *(insignificancia)* triviality, trifle.
quisquilloso ,-a *adj* finicky, fussy, touchy.
▷ *nm & nf* fusspot.
quiste *nm* cyst.
quístico ,-a *adj* cystic.
quita *nf* partial acquittance.
quitaesmaltes *nm inv* nail varnish remover.
quitamanchas *nm inv* stain remover.
quitamiedos *nm inv* handrail.
quitanieves *nm inv* snowplough (US snowplow).
quitapinturas *nm inv* paint stripper.
quitar *vt* 1 *(separar)* to remove, take off: quita la tapa *remove the lid.* 2 *(sacar)* to take off, take out; *(prendas)* to take off; *(tiempo)* to take up: quítate los zapatos *take your shoes off.* 3 *(apartar)* to take away, take off: quita eso de ahí *clear that away.* 4 *(hacer desaparecer)* to remove; *(dolor)* to relieve; *(sed)* to quench: eso te quitará el hambre *that'll stop you feeling hungry.* 5 *(despojar)* to take; *(robar)* to steal: me han quitado la cartera *my wallet's been stolen.* 6 *(restar)* to subtract; *(descontar)* to take off. 7 *(prohibir)* to forbid, rule out. 8 *(impedir)* to prevent: eso no quita para que se lo diga *that's no reason not to tell him.* 9 *(disminuir)* to take away: eso no le quita mérito a la obra *that doesn't take anything away from the work.* 10 *fam (radio, agua, etc)* to turn off. ■ **quitar importancia a** ALGO to play STH down. ‖ **quitar la mesa** to clear the table.
▷ *vpr* quitarse 1 *(desaparecer)* to go away, come out: esa mancha no se quita *that stain won't come out.* 2 quitarse de *(del juego, bebida, etc)* to give up: se quitó de fumar *she gave up smoking.*
quitasol *nm* parasol, sunshade.
quite *nm* 1 *(acción de quitar)* removal. 2 *(en esgrima)* parry. 3 *(en tauromaquia) distraction of the bull to allow the escape of another bullfighter.*
quitina *nf* chitin.
quitinoso ,-a *adj* chitinous.
quito ,-a *adj* free, exempt (de, from).
quivi *nm* kiwi fruit.
quizá *adv* → quizás.
quizás *adv* perhaps, maybe.
quórum *nm inv* quorum.

R

R, r *nf (la letra)* R, r.
rabadilla *nf* 1 ANAT coccyx. 2 *(de animal)* rump.
rabanillo *nm* wild radish.
rábano *nm* radish. ■ **¡me importa un rábano!** I don't give a toss!, I couldn't care less!
rabí *nm* rabbi.
▲ *pl* rabíes.
rabia *nf* 1 MED rabies. 2 *fig (enfado)* rage, fury, anger. ■ **dar rabia** to make furious. ‖ **tener rabia a ALGN** not to be able to stand the sight of SB.
rabiar [12] *vi* 1 MED to have rabies. 2 *(enfadarse)* to rage, be furious: **Elena está que rabia** *Elena is furious.* 3 *fig (padecer)* to suffer (**de**, from): **rabiar de dolor** *to writhe in pain.* ■ **hacer rabiar a ALGN** to make SB see red.
rabieta *nf fam* tantrum. ■ **coger una rabieta** *fam* to throw a tantrum.
rabillo *nm* 1 *(pecíolo)* stalk, stem. 2 *(cizaña)* darnel. 3 COST tab, strap. ■ **mirar por el rabillo del ojo** to look out of the corner of one's eye.
rabino *nm* rabbi.
rabioso,-a *adj* 1 MED rabid. 2 *fig (airado)* furious, angry. 3 *fig (excesivo)* terrible, intense. 4 *fam (color)* shocking, gaudy, garish; *(sabor)* very hot. ■ **ponerse rabioso,-a** to fly into a rage.
rabo *nm* 1 *(gen)* tail. 2 *tabú* cock, prick, dick.
racanear *vi* 1 *fam (ser tacaño)* to be mean, be stingy. 2 *fam (ser vago)* to idle, slack.
racanería *nf* 1 *fam (tacañería)* meanness, stinginess. 2 *fam (holgazanería)* idleness, laziness.
rácano,-a *adj* 1 *fam (tacaño)* mean, stingy. 2 *fam (holgazán)* idle, lazy.
racha *nf* 1 *(ráfaga)* gust, squall. 2 *fig (período)* spell, patch. 3 *fig (serie)* string, run, series *sing*: **hubo una racha de incendios** *there was a series of fires.* ■ **a rachas** in fits and starts, on and off. ‖ **tener una buena racha** to have a run of good luck.
racheado,-a *adj* gusty.
racial *adj* racial, race.
racimo *nm* bunch, cluster.
raciocinio *nm* 1 *(razón)* reason. 2 *(argumento)* reasoning.
ración *nf* 1 *(parte)* ration, portion, share. 2 *(de comida)* portion, serving, helping: **«Cuatro raciones»** *«Serves four».*
racional *adj* rational.
racionalista *adj* rationalist.
▷ *nm o nf* rationalist.
racionalización *nf* rationalization.
racionalizar [4] *vt* to rationalize.
racionamiento *nm* rationing.
racionar *vt (limitar)* to ration.
racismo *nm* racism, racialism.
racista *adj* racist, racialist.
▷ *nm o nf* racist, racialist.
rada *nf* bay, inlet.
radar *nm* radar.
▲ *pl* radares.
radiación *nf* radiation.
radiactividad *nf* radioactivity.
radiactivo,-a *adj* radioactive.
radiador *nm* radiator.
radial *adj* radial.
radián *nm* radian.
radiante *adj fig* radiant: **radiante de alegría** *radiant with joy.*
radiar [12] *vi (irradiar)* to radiate, irradiate.
▷ *vt* 1 *(irradiar)* to radiate, irradiate. 2 *(retransmitir)* to broadcast, transmit, radio. 3 MED to X-ray.
radical *adj* radical.
▷ *nm (en gramática, matemática)* root, radical.
radicalismo *nm* radicalism.
radicalizar [4] *vt* 1 to radicalize. 2 *(postura)* to harden.
▷ *vpr* **radicalizarse** 1 *(conflicto)* to intensify. 2 *(postura)* to harden.
radicar [1] *vi* 1 *(encontrarse)* to be (**en**, in), be situated (**en**, in). 2 *fig (consistir)* to lie (**en**, in), stem (**en**, from): **el problema radica en la falta de solidaridad** *the problem lies in the lack of solidarity.* 3 *(arraigar)* to take root.
▷ *vpr* **radicarse** 1 *(arraigarse)* to take root. 2 *(establecerse)* to settle (down).
radio[1] *nm* 1 *(de círculo)* radius: **en un radio de 10 metros** *within a radius of 10 metres.* 2 *(de rueda)* spoke. 3 *(campo)* scope. ● **radio de acción** *fig* field of action, scope.
radio[2] *nf* 1 *(radiodifusión)* radio: **lo oí por la radio** *I heard it on the radio.* 2 *(aparato)* radio, wireless.
▷ *nm o nf fam (persona)* radio operator. ● **radio pirata** pirate radio station.
radio[3] *nm* QUÍM radium.
radioactividad *nf* radioactivity.
radioactivo,-a *adj* radioactive.
radioaficionado,-a *nm & nf* radio ham.
radiocasete *nm* radio cassette, radio cassette player.
radiocomunicación *nf* radio communication.
radiocontrol *nm* radio control.
radiodespertador *nm* radio alarm clock.
radiodifusión *nf* broadcasting.
radioescucha *nm o nf* listener, US auditor.
radiofonía *nf* radio, radiotelephony.
radiofónico,-a *adj* radio: **concurso radiofónico** *radio quiz programme (US program).*
radiofrecuencia *nf* radio frequency.

radiografía *nf* 1 *(técnica)* radiography. 2 *(imagen)* X-ray, radiograph. ■ **hacerse una radiografía** to have an X-ray taken.
radiografiar [13] *vt* to X-ray.
radiología *nf* radiology.
radiólogo,-a *nm & nf* radiologist.
radiometría *nf* radiometry.
radionovela *nf* serial.
radiorreceptor *nm* radio, radio set, radio receiver, wireless, wireless set.
radioscopia *nf* radioscopy.
radiotaxi *nm* radio taxi, radio cab.
radiotelefonía *nf* radiotelephony.
radioteléfono *nm* radiotelephone.
radiotelegrafía *nf* radiotelegraphy.
radiotelegráfico,-a *adj* radiotelegraphic.
radiotelescopio *nm* radio telescope.
radiotelevisión *nf* radio and television.
radioterapia *nf* radiotherapy, radium therapy.
radiotransmisión *nf* radio transmission, broadcasting.
radiotransmisor *nm* radio transmitter.
radiotransmitir *vt* to broadcast.
radioyente *nm o nf* listener.
radón *nm* radon.
RAE *abrev* (**Real Academia Española**) Spanish Royal Academy.
raer [81] *vt* to scrape (off).
ráfaga *nf* 1 *(de viento)* gust, squall. 2 *(de disparos)* burst. 3 *(de luz)* flash.
rafia *nf* raffia.
raglán *adj inv* raglan: **mangas raglán** *raglan sleeves.*
raid *nm (incursión)* raid. ● **raid aéreo** air raid.
▲ *pl* **raids.**
raído,-a *adj (deteriorado)* threadbare, worn.
raigambre *nf* 1 *(raíces)* roots *pl*, root system. 2 *fig* tradition, history.
raíl *nm* rail.
raíz *nf* root. ■ **de raíz** entirely. | **echar raíces** 1 *(planta)* to take root. 2 *(persona)* to settle, put down roots. ● **raíz cuadrada** square root. | **raíz cúbica** cube root.
▲ *pl* **raíces.**
raja *nf* 1 *(corte)* cut, slit. 2 *(hendidura)* crack, split. 3 *(tajada)* slice.
rajá *nm* rajah.
▲ *pl* **rajaes.**
rajar *vt* 1 *(hender)* to split, crack. 2 *(hacer tajadas)* to slice. 3 *argot (acuchillar)* to cut up.
▷ *vi* 1 *fam fig (jactarse)* to show off, boast. 2 *fam fig (hablar mucho)* to chatter, babble on.
▷ *vpr* **rajarse** 1 *(partirse)* to split, crack. 2 *fam (desistir)* to back out, quit.
rajatabla ■ **a rajatabla** to the letter, strictly.
ralea *nf pey* type, sort, kind.
ralentí *nm* CINE slow motion. ■ **al ralentí** *(motor)* ticking over.
ralentizar *vt* to slow down.
rallado,-a *adj (queso, etc)* grated.
rallador *nm* grater.
ralladura *nf* grated rind: **ralladura de limón** *grated lemon rind.*
rallar *vt* to grate.
rally *nm* rally.
▲ *pl* **rallys.**
ralo,-a *adj* 1 *(pelo)* sparse, thin. 2 *(dientes)* with gaps between them.
rama *nf* branch. ■ **andarse por las ramas / irse por las ramas** *fam* to beat about the bush. | **en rama** raw: **canela en rama** *cinnamon stick.*
ramadán *nm* Ramadan.
ramaje *nm* foliage, branches *pl.*
ramal *nm* 1 *(de cuerda)* strand. 2 *(de camino, etc)* branch.
ramalazo *nm fam (ataque)* fit.
rambla *nf* 1 *(lecho de agua)* watercourse, channel. 2 *(paseo)* boulevard, avenue.
ramificación *nf* ramification.
ramificarse [1] *vpr* to ramify, branch (out).
ramillete *nm* 1 posy. 2 *fig (conjunto)* bunch, group, collection.
ramo *nm* 1 *(de flores)* bunch, bouquet. 2 *(de árbol)* branch. 3 *fig (sector)* field: **el ramo de la alimentación** *the food sector, the food industry.*
rampa *nf (pendiente)* ramp. ● **rampa de lanzamiento** launching pad.
rampante *adj* rampant, blatant.
ramplón,-ona *adj fig* coarse, vulgar.
ramplonería *nf* coarseness, vulgarity.
rana *nf* frog. ■ **salir rana** *fam* to be a letdown, be a disappointment.
ranchera *nf* 1 AM *Mexican folk song.* 2 *(coche)* station wagon.
rancho *nm* 1 MIL mess. 2 AM *(granja)* ranch, farm.
rancio,-a *adj* 1 *(comestibles)* stale; *(mantequilla)* rancid. 2 *fig (antiguo)* old, ancient: **de rancio abolengo** *of ancient lineage.* ● **vino rancio** old wine, mellow wine.
rand *nm* rand.
rango *nm* rank. ■ **de alto rango** high-ranking.
ranking *nm* ranking.
▲ *pl* **rankings.**
ranura *nf* 1 *(canal)* groove. 2 *(para monedas, fichas)* slot.
rapacidad *nf* rapacity, rapaciousness.
rapapolvo *nm fam* dressing-down, ticking off.
rapar *vt* 1 *(afeitar)* to shave. 2 *(pelo)* to crop.
rapaz[1] *adj* 1 ZOOL predatory, of prey: **ave rapaz** *bird of prey.* 2 *fig (persona)* rapacious, grasping.
▲ *pl* **rapaces.**
rapaz,-za[2] *nm & nf* youngster; *(muchacho)* lad; *(muchacha)* lass.
▲ *pl* **rapaces.**
rape[1] *nm (pez)* angler fish.
rape[2] *nm fam (rasura)* quick shave. ■ **al rape** close-cropped, short.
rapé *nm* snuff.
rapero,-a *nm & nf* rapper.
rapidez *nf* speed, rapidity: **con rapidez** *quickly.*
rápido,-a *adj* quick, fast.
▷ *adv* quickly: **¡rápido!** *hurry up!, make it snappy!*
▷ *nm* **rápido** *(tren)* fast train, express train.
▷ *nm pl* **rápidos** *(del río)* rapids.
rapiña *nf fam* robbery, theft.
rapiñar *vt fam* to pinch, steal.
raposo,-a *nm & nf* 1 *(macho)* fox; *(hembra)* female fox, vixen. 2 *fig (persona)* sly fox.

rappel *nm* abseiling. ■ **hacer rappel** to abseil.
rapsodia *nf* rhapsody.
raptar *vt* to kidnap, abduct.
rapto *nm* **1** *(secuestro)* kidnapping, abduction. **2** *fig (impulso)* outburst, fit.
raqueta *nf* **1** *(de tenis)* racket; *(de ping-pong)* bat, US paddle. **2** *(para nieve)* snowshoe. **3** *(en casinos)* rake.
raquídeo,-a *adj* → **bulbo raquídeo.**
raquítico,-a *adj* **1** MED rachitic. **2** *fig (exiguo)* meagre (US meager), small. **3** *fig (débil)* weak.
▷ *nm & nf* rachitic person.
raquitismo *nm* rachitis, rickets *pl*.
rareza *nf* **1** *(poco común)* rarity, rareness. **2** *(extravagancia)* eccentricity.
raro,-a *adj* **1** *(poco común)* rare. **2** *(escaso)* scarce, rare: **son raras las personas que saben apreciarlo** *very few people can appreciate it.* **3** *(peculiar)* odd, strange, weird: **últimamente la encuentro rara** *I think she's been acting a little strange recently.* **4** *(excelente)* excellent: **escribió un libro raro, una verdadera obra de arte** *she wrote a very good book, a real work of art.* ■ **¡qué raro!** how odd!, that's strange!
ras ■ **a ras de** (on a) level with. ▮ **a ras de tierra** at ground level. ▮ **al ras** to the brim.
rasante *adj (vuelo)* low, skimming.
▷ *nf (inclinación)* slope. ● **cambio de rasante** brow of a hill.
rascacielos *nm inv* skyscraper.
rascador *nm (para rascar)* scraper.
rascar [1] *vt* **1** *(la piel)* to scratch. **2** *(con rascador)* to scrape, rasp. **3** *(un instrumento)* to strum.
rasero *nm* strickle. ■ **por el mismo rasero** *fig* equally.
rasgado,-a *adj (roto)* torn, ripped.
rasgar [7] *vt* to tear, rip. ■ **rasgarse las vestiduras** *fig* to pull one's hair out.
rasgo *nm* **1** *(línea)* stroke; *(adorno)* flourish. **2** *(facción del rostro)* feature. **3** *(peculiaridad)* characteristic, feature, trait. ■ **explicar a grandes rasgos** to outline, give a general outline of.
rasguear *vt (instrumento)* to strum.
▷ *vi (al escribir)* to write with a flourish.
rasguñar *vt* to scratch, scrape.
rasguño *nm* **1** *(arañazo)* scratch, scrape.
rasilla *nf* **1** *(tela)* serge. **2** *(ladrillo)* tile.
raso,-a *adj* **1** *(plano)* flat, level; *(liso)* smooth: **una cucharada rasa** *a level spoonful.* **2** *(a poca altura)* low. **3** *(atmósfera)* clear, cloudless.
▷ *nm* **raso** *(tejido)* satin. ■ **al raso** in the open, in the open air.
raspa *nf (de pescado)* bone, backbone.
raspado,-a *nm* scraping, scrape.
raspadura *nf* **1** *(ralladura)* scraping, scrapings *pl*. **2** *(señal)* scratch, mark.
raspar *vt* **1** *(rascar)* to scrape (off); *(dañar)* to scratch, graze. **2** *(con lija)* to sand, sand down. **3** *(rasar)* to graze, skim.
rasposo,-a *adj* rough, sharp.
rasqueta *nf* scraper.
rastra *nf* **1** *(rastro)* trail, track. **3** *(sarta)* string. **4** *(para pescar)* trawl, trawl net. ■ **a rastras 1** *(arrastrando)* dragging. **2** *(sin querer)* unwillingly, grudgingly: **llevar a rastras** *to drag along.*
rastrear *vt (seguir el rastro)* to trail, track, trace.
rastrero,-a *adj* **1** BOT creeping. **2** *fig (bajo)* vile, base.
rastrillar *vt (hojas, etc)* to rake.
rastrillo *nm* **1** *(rastro)* rake. **2** *fam (mercadillo)* flea market.
rastro *nm* **1** *(señal)* trace, track, sign; *(olor)* scent: **ni rastro de sangre** *not a trace of blood.* **2** *(vestigio)* vestige. **3** *(mercado)* flea market. ■ **seguir el rastro de** ALGN to follow SB's trail.
rastrojo *nm* **1** *(paja)* stubble. **2** *(campo)* stubble field.
rasurar *vt* to shave.
rata *nf* ZOOL rat.
ratero,-a *nm & nf* pickpocket.
raticida *nm* rat poison.
ratificación *nf* ratification.
ratificar [1] *vt* to ratify.
▷ *vpr* **ratificarse** to be confirmed, be ratified.
rato *nm* **1** *(tiempo)* time, while, moment: **charlamos un rato** *we chatted for a while.* **2** *(espacio)* way: **hay un buen rato hasta Vigo** *it's a long way to Vigo.* **3** *fam (mucho)* very, a lot: **sabe un rato de deportes** *she's a mine of information about sports.* ■ **a ratos** at times. ▮ **pasar un buen rato** to have a good time. ● **ratos libres** free time *sing*.
ratón *nm* mouse.
ratonera *nf* **1** *(trampa)* mousetrap. **2** *fam fig* trap.
raudal *nm* **1** *(agua)* torrent, flood. **2** *fig (abundancia)* flood, wave. ■ **a raudales** in torrents.
raudo,-a *adj lit* swift, rapid.
raviolis *nm pl* ravioli.
raya[1] *nf* **1** *(línea)* line. **2** *(de color)* stripe: **pantalón a rayas** *striped trousers.* **3** *(del pantalón)* crease. **4** *(del pelo)* parting, US part. **5** *(límite)* limit.
raya[2] *nf (pez)* skate.
rayado,-a *adj* **1** *(tejido)* striped. **2** *(papel)* ruled. **3** *(arma)* rifled
▷ *nm* **rayado** stripes *pl*.
rayar *vt* **1** *(líneas)* to draw lines on, line, rule. **2** *(superficie)* to scratch.
▷ *vi* **1** *(limitar)* to border (**con**, on): **su terreno raya con el nuestro** *his plot borders on ours.* **2** *fig (acercarse)* to border (**en**, on): **raya en los cincuenta** *he's nearly fifty.* **3** *(día, alba, luz)* to break.
rayo *nm* **1** ray, beam: **rayo de sol** *sunbeam;* **rayo de luz** *ray of light.* **2** *(relámpago)* lightning, flash of lightning. **3** *fig (persona)* live wire. ● **rayo de luna** moonbeam. ▮ **rayos ultravioletas/UVA** ultraviolet rays. ▮ **rayos X** X-rays.
rayón *nm* rayon.
rayuela *nf* hopscotch.
raza *nf* **1** race. **2** *(animal)* breed. ■ **de raza 1** *(perro)* pedigree. **2** *(caballo)* thoroughbred. ● **raza humana** human race.
razón *nf* **1** *(facultad)* reason. **2** *(motivo)* reason, cause. **3** *(mensaje)* message. **4** *(justicia)* justice. **5** MAT ratio, rate. ■ **dar la razón a** ALGN to agree with SB, say that SB is right. ▮ **perder la razón** to lose one's reason. ▮ **tener razón** to be right.
razonable *adj* reasonable.
razonamiento *nm* reasoning.
razonar *vi* **1** *(discurrir)* to reason. **2** *(hablar)* to talk.
▷ *vt (explicar)* to reason out.
re *nm* re, ray, D.
reabrir *vt* to reopen.

reacción *nf* reaction. ■ **reacción en cadena** chain reaction.
reaccionar *vi* to react.
reaccionario,-a *adj* reactionary.
▷ *nm & nf* reactionary.
reacio,-a *adj* reluctant, unwilling.
reactivación *nf* reactivation.
reactivar *vt* to reactivate.
reactivo,-a *adj* reactive.
▷ *nm* **reactivo** reagent.
reactor *nm* 1 reactor. 2 AV jet, jet plane.
readaptar *vt* to readapt, readjust.
▷ *vpr* **readaptarse** to readapt, readjust.
readmitir *vt (gen)* to readmit; *(un trabajador)* to reinstate.
reafirmar *vt* to reaffirm, reassert.
reagrupar *vt* to regroup.
▷ *vpr* **reagruparse** to regroup.
reajustar *vt* to readjust.
reajuste *nm* readjustment. ● **reajuste ministerial** cabinet reshuffle.
real[1] *adj (verdadero)* real: **en la vida real** *in real life.*
real[2] *adj (regio)* royal.
realce *nm* 1 *(adorno)* relief. 2 *fig (lustre)* prestige, distinction.
realeza *nf* royalty.
realidad *nf* reality. ■ **en realidad** actually, in fact.
realista *adj (de la realidad)* realistic.
▷ *nm o nf (de la realidad)* realist.
realización *nf* 1 *(de un deseo)* fulfilment (US fulfillment). 2 *(ejecución)* execution, carrying out.
realizador,-ra *nm & nf* producer.
realizar [4] *vt* 1 *(ambición)* to realize, fulfil (US fulfill), achieve; *(deseo, esperanza)* to fulfil (US fulfill). 2 *(llevar a cabo)* to accomplish, carry out, do, fulfil (US fulfill). 3 *(un viaje)* to make.
▷ *vpr* **realizarse** 1 *(ambición, deseo)* to be fulfilled, be achieved; *(sueño)* to come true. 2 *(llevarse a cabo)* to be executed, be carried out.
realmente *adv* 1 *(de verdad)* really, truly. 2 *(en realidad)* actually, in fact: **realmente no hacía tanto frío** *in fact it wasn't too cold.*
realquilar *vt* to sublet, sublease.
realzar [4] *vt* 1 *(elevar)* to raise, lift. 2 *fig (engrandecer)* to enhance, heighten. 3 *(pintura)* to highlight.
reanimar *vt* 1 *(persona)* to revive. 2 *(fiesta, conversación)* to liven up.
▷ *vpr* **reanimarse** 1 *(persona)* to revive; *(volver en sí)* to come round. 2 *(fiesta, conversación)* to liven up.
reanudar *vt (gen)* to renew, resume, re-establish.
reaparecer [43] *vi* 1 *(gen)* to reappear. 2 *(un artista, etc)* to make a comeback. 3 *(un fenómeno)* to recur.
reapertura *nf* reopening.
rearme *nm* rearmament, rearming.
reavivar *vt* 1 *(fuego)* to stoke, stoke up. 2 *(dolor)* to intensify; *(interés)* to revive.
rebaba *nf* rough edge.
rebaja *nf* 1 *(reducción)* reduction, lowering. 2 *(descuento)* discount, reduction.
▷ *nf pl* **rebajas** sales.
rebajado,-a *adj* 1 *(de nivel)* lowered; *(arco)* depressed. 2 *(precio)* reduced. 3 *(humillado)* humbled.
rebajar *vt* 1 *(nivel)* to lower. 2 *(precio)* to cut, reduce. 3 *(color)* to soften; *(intensidad)* to diminish. 4 *fig (humillar)* to humiliate.
▷ *vpr* **rebajarse** *fig (humillarse)* to humble OS. ■ **rebajarse a hacer** ALGO to stoop to do STH, lower OS to do STH.
rebanada *nf* slice.
rebañar *vt* 1 *(recoger)* to clean out. 2 *(comida)* to finish off.
rebaño *nm (gen)* herd; *(de ovejas)* flock.
rebasar *vt* 1 *(gen)* to exceed, go beyond, surpass. 2 *(límite, marca)* to overstep. 3 *(náutica)* to pass. 4 AUTO to overtake.
rebatir *vt* to refute.
rebeca *nf* cardigan.
rebeco *nm* chamois.
rebelarse *vpr* to rebel, revolt.
rebelde *adj* 1 rebellious. 2 *fig (tos, etc)* persistent.
▷ *nm o nf* rebel.
rebeldía *nf* 1 rebelliousness. 2 JUR default.
rebelión *nf* rebellion, revolt.
reblandecer [43] *vt* to soften.
▷ *vpr* **reblandecerse** to soften, become soft.
rebobinar *vt* to rewind.
reborde *nm (de mesa)* edge; *(de taza, de tela)* edging.
rebosante *adj* overflowing, brimming: **rebosante de salud** *bursting with health.*
rebosar *vi* 1 *(derramarse)* to overflow, brim over. 2 *fig* to brim (**de**, with), burst (**de**, with): **rebosar de alegría** *to be brimming with joy.*
▷ *vt fig (sentimiento)* to brim with; *(salud)* to exude.
rebotar *vi (pelota)* to bounce, rebound; *(bala)* to ricochet.
rebote *nm* 1 *(de balón)* bounce, rebound. 2 *(de bala)* ricochet. ■ **de rebote** *fig* on the rebound.
rebozado,-a *adj* coated in breadcrumbs, coated in batter.
rebozar [4] *vt* CULIN to coat in breadcrumbs.
rebrotar *vi* to shoot, sprout.
rebullir [41] *vi* to stir, begin to move.
▷ *vpr* **rebullirse** to stir, begin to move.
rebuscado,-a *adj* affected, recherché; *(estilo)* elaborate, contrived.
rebuscar [1] *vt* to search carefully for.
rebuznar *vi* to bray.
rebuzno *nm* bray, braying.
recabar *vt* 1 *(solicitar)* to ask for, entreat. 2 *(obtener)* to attain, obtain, manage to get.
recadero,-a *nm & nf (gen)* messenger.
recado *nm* 1 *(mensaje)* message. 2 *(encargo)* errand: **me hizo un recado** *she ran the errand for me.*
▷ *nm pl* **recados** *(compras)* shopping *sing.*
recaer [67] *vi* 1 *(volver a caer)* to fall again. 2 *(enfermedad)* to relapse, have a relapse. 3 *(vicios, etc)* to relapse, backslide.
recaída *nf* 1 *(enfermedad)* relapse. 2 *(vicios, etc)* relapse, backslide. ■ **sufrir una recaída** to have a relapse.
recalcar [1] *vt fig* to emphasize, stress, underline.
recalentar [27] *vt* 1 *(volver a calentar)* to reheat, warm up. 2 *(calentar demasiado)* to overheat.
recámara *nf* 1 *(cuarto)* dressing room. 2 *(de arma)* chamber.
recambiar [12] *vt* to change (over).

recambio *nm* spare, spare part; *(de pluma, bolígrafo)* refill.

recapacitar *vi* to think (**sobre**, over).

▷ *vt* to think over.

recapitular *vt* to recapitulate, sum up.

recargable *adj (pluma, mechero)* refillable; *(pila)* rechargeable.

recargado,-a *adj fig (exagerado)* overelaborate, exaggerated, contrived.

recargar [7] *vt* 1 *(volver a cargar)* to reload; *(pilas)* to recharge; *(mechero)* to refill. 2 *(sobrecargar)* to overload. 3 *fig (exagerar)* to overelaborate, exaggerate. 4 FIN to increase.

recargo *nm* extra charge, surcharge.

recatado,-a *adj* 1 *(prudente)* cautious, prudent. 2 *(modesto)* modest. 3 *(decente)* decent.

recato *nm* 1 *(cautela)* caution. 2 *(pudor)* modesty.

recauchutado *nm* retreading.

recauchutar *vt* to retread, remould (US remold).

recaudación *nf* 1 *(cobro)* collection. 2 *(cantidad recaudada)* takings *pl.*

recaudador,-ra *nm & nf* tax collector.

recaudar *vt* to collect.

recaudo *nm* 1 *(recaudación)* collection. 2 *(precaución)* precaution.

recelar *vt* 1 *(sospechar)* to suspect, distrust. 2 *(temer)* to fear.

▷ *vi (desconfiar)* to be suspicious (**de**, of): **recela de todos** *he is suspicious of everybody.*

recelo *nm* suspicion.

receloso,-a *adj* suspicious.

recepción *nf* 1 *(gen)* reception. 2 *(de documento, carta, etc)* receipt. 3 *(oficina, etc)* reception, reception desk.

recepcionista *nm o nf* receptionist.

receptáculo *nm* receptacle.

receptividad *nf* receptiveness, receptivity.

receptivo,-a *adj* receptive (**a**, to).

receptor,-ra *nm & nf* receiver, recipient.

▷ *nm* **receptor** *(de radio, etc)* receiver.

recesión *nf* recession.

recesivo,-a *adj* recessive.

receso *nm* recess.

receta *nf* 1 MED prescription. 2 CULIN recipe.

recetar *vt* to prescribe.

recetario *nm* 1 MED prescription pad. 2 CULIN cookery book, US cookbook.

rechazar [4] *vt* 1 *(gen)* to reject, turn down, refuse. 2 *(ataque)* to repel, repulse, drive back. 3 MED to reject.

rechazo *nm* 1 rejection, refusal. 2 MED rejection. 3 *(negativa)* denial, rejection.

rechinante *adj* creaky, squeaky.

rechinar *vi (madera)* to creak; *(metal)* to squeak, screech; *(dientes)* to grind, grate.

rechistar *vi* to say, reply.

rechoncho,-a *adj fam* chubby, tubby.

rechupete ■ **de rechupete** *fam (muy bien)* super, brill, marvellous (US marvelous), fantastic. *(comida)* delicious, scrumptious.

recibidor *nm (de casa)* entrance hall.

recibimiento *nm* reception, welcome.

recibir *vt* 1 *(gen)* to receive. 2 *(invitados)* to entertain. 3 *(salir al encuentro)* to meet: **nos recibió en la puerta** *he met us at the door.*

recibo *nm* 1 *(resguardo)* receipt. 2 *(factura)* invoice, bill. 3 *(recepción)* reception, receiving.

reciclable *adj* recyclable.

reciclado,-a *adj* recycled.

reciclaje *nm (de materias)* recycling.

reciclar *vt (materiales)* to recycle.

recién *adv* [Used only before a past participle.] recently, newly; *(café, pan)* freshly: **un pastel recién hecho** *a freshly baked cake.* ■ **«Recién pintado»** «Wet paint».

reciente *adj* recent.

recinto *nm* grounds *pl*, precincts *pl*, area.

recio,-a *adj* 1 *(fuerte)* strong, robust, sturdy. 2 *(grueso)* thick. 3 *(duro)* hard. 4 *(voz)* loud; *(clima)* harsh, severe.

recipiente *nm* container, receptacle.

reciprocidad *nf* reciprocity.

recíproco,-a *adj* reciprocal, mutual: **un sentimiento recíproco** *a mutual feeling.*

recital *nm* 1 MÚS recital, concert. 2 LIT reading: **recital de poesía** *poetry reading.*

recitar *vt* to recite.

recitativo *nm* recitative.

reclamación *nf* 1 *(demanda)* claim, demand. 2 *(queja)* complaint, protest, objection. ■ **presentar una reclamación** to lodge a complaint.

reclamar *vt* 1 *(pedir)* to demand, claim. 2 *(exigir)* to require, demand.

▷ *vi (protestar)* to protest (**contra**, against): **reclamaron contra aquella medida** *they protested against the measure.*

reclamo *nm* 1 *(para cazar)* decoy bird, lure. 2 *(silbato)* bird call. 3 *(llamada)* call. 4 *(anuncio)* advertisement; *(eslogan)* advertising slogan.

reclinable *adj* reclining.

reclinar *vt* to lean.

▷ *vpr* **reclinarse** to lean back, recline: **se reclinó sobre la almohada** *he lent back on the pillow.*

recluir [62] *vt* 1 *(encerrar)* to shut in. 2 *(en cárcel)* to imprison, intern. 3 *(en manicomio)* to confine.

reclusión *nf* 1 *(encierro)* seclusion. 2 *(encarcelamiento)* imprisonment, internment. 3 *(lugar)* retreat.

recluso,-a *nm & nf* prisoner.

recluta *nm o nf* 1 *(voluntario)* recruit. 2 *(obligado)* conscript.

reclutar *vt* 1 *(voluntarios)* to recruit. 2 *(obligatorio)* to conscript.

recobrar *vt* 1 *(gen)* to recover. 2 *(conocimiento, fuerzas, esperanzas)* to regain; *(aliento)* to get back. 3 *(tiempo)* to make up.

▷ *vpr* **recobrarse** *(recuperarse)* to recover (**de**, from).

recodo *nm* 1 *(de río)* turn, twist; *(de camino)* bend. 2 *(recoveco)* nook.

recogedor *nm* dustpan.

recoger [5] *vt* 1 *(volver a coger)* to take again, take back. 2 *(coger)* to pick up, take back. 3 *(ir a buscar)* to pick up, collect: **me recogerá a las cuatro** *he'll pick me up at four o'clock.* 4 *(cosecha)* to harvest, gather; *(fruta)* to pick. 5 *(juntar)* to gather, collect. 6 *(velas)* to take in; *(cortinas)* to draw. 7 *(dar asilo)* to take in, shelter: **lo recogieron sus abuelos** *he was taken in by his grand-*

parents. 8 *(ordenar)* to clear up, tidy up. 9 *(limpiar)* to clean; *(el polvo)* to wipe off; *(líquido)* to wipe up.
▷ *vpr* **recogerse** 1 *(irse a casa)* to go home. 2 *(irse a dormir)* to go to bed.
recogida *nf* 1 *(gen)* collection. 2 *(cosecha)* harvest, harvesting. ● **recogida de datos** data capture.
recogido,-a *adj* 1 *(apartado)* secluded, withdrawn. 2 *(pelo)* pinned back, tied back. 3 *(pequeño)* small.
recolección *nf* 1 *(recopilación)* collection, gathering. 2 *(cosecha)* harvest, harvesting.
recolectar *vt* 1 *(reunir)* to gather, collect. 2 *(cosechar)* to harvest.
recomendable *adj* recommendable, advisable.
recomendación *nf (consejo)* recommendation, advice; *(para empleo)* reference.
recomendado,-a *adj* recommended.
▷ *nm & nf (hombre)* protégé; *(mujer)* protégée.
recomendar [27] *vt* to recommend, advise: **te recomiendo que estudies más** *I recommend that you study harder.*
recomenzar [47] *vt* to recommence, begin again, start again.
recompensa *nf* reward, recompense. ■ **en recompensa** as a reward, in return.
recompensar *vt* 1 *(compensar)* to compensate. 2 *(remunerar)* to reward, recompense.
recomponer [78] *vt* 1 to repair, mend. 2 *fam (acicalar)* to dress up.
recompuesto,-a *adj (acicalado)* dressed up.
reconcentrar *vt* 1 *(concentrar)* to concentrate (**en**, to). 2 *(reunir)* to bring together.
▷ *vpr* **reconcentrarse** *(ensimismarse)* to become absorbed in thought, concentrate.
reconciliación *nf* reconciliation.
reconciliar [12] *vt* to reconcile.
▷ *vpr* **reconciliarse** *(uso recíproco)* to be reconciled.
recóndito,-a *adj* hidden, secret.
reconfortante *adj* comforting.
reconfortar *vt* 1 *(confortar)* to comfort. 2 *(animar)* to cheer up.
reconocer [44] *vt* 1 *(gen)* to recognize. 2 *(admitir)* to recognize, admit: **reconoció su error** *she admitted her mistake.* 3 *(afrontar)* to face: **reconozcámoslo** *let's face it.* 4 MIL *(terreno)* to reconnoitre (US reconnoiter). 5 MED *(paciente)* to examine.
▷ *vpr* **reconocerse** 1 to recognize each other. 2 *(admitirse)* to admit: **se reconoció culpable** *he admitted his guilt.*
reconocible *adj* recognizable.
reconocido,-a *adj (agradecido)* grateful.
reconocimiento *nm* 1 *(gen)* recognition. 2 *(admisión)* admission. 3 MIL reconnaissance. 4 MED examination, checkup.
reconquista *nf* 1 reconquest. 2 **la Reconquista** the Reconquest *(of Spain, from the Moors).*
reconquistar *vt* to reconquer, recapture, regain.
reconsiderar *vt* to reconsider.
reconstituir [62] *vt* to reconstitute.
reconstituyente *nm* tonic.
reconstrucción *nf* reconstruction.
reconstruir [62] *vt* to reconstruct.
reconvertir [35] *vt* 1 to restructure. 2 *(industria)* to restructure, reorganize.
recopilación *nf (colección)* compilation, collection; *(de leyes)* code.
recopilar *vt* to compile, collect.
récord *adj* record: **en un tiempo récord** *in record time.*
▷ *nm* record.
▲ *pl* **récords.**
recordar [31] *vt* 1 *(rememorar)* to remember: **¿recuerdas?** *do you remember?* 2 *(traer a la memoria)* to remind (**a**, of): **me recuerda a mi hermano** *he reminds me of my brother.*
recordatorio *nm (aviso)* reminder.
recordman *nm* record holder.
recordwoman *nf* record holder.
recorrer *vt* 1 *(distancia)* to cover, travel. 2 *(país)* to tour, travel over, travel round. 3 *(ciudad)* to visit, walk round. 4 *(un escrito)* to look over, go over, look through.
recorrido *nm* 1 *(trayecto)* journey, trip. 2 *(distancia)* distance travelled: **un tren de largo recorrido** *a long-distance train.* 3 *(itinerario)* itinerary, route.
recortado,-a *adj* 1 *(cortado)* cut out. 2 *(borde)* jagged. 3 *(irregular)* uneven, irregular.
recortar *vt* 1 *(muñecos, telas, etc)* to cut out. 2 *(lo que sobra)* to cut off. 3 *(el pelo)* to trim. 4 *fig* to cut, restrict: **han recortado las subvenciones** *subsidies have been cut.*
▷ *vpr* **recortarse** *(sobresalir)* to stand out.
recorte *nm* 1 *(acción)* cutting. 2 *(trozo)* cutting, clipping. 3 *(de periódico)* press clipping, newspaper cutting. 4 *(de pelo)* trim, cut, reduction. 5 *fig (reducción)* cut, reduction: **recorte del presupuesto** *budget cut.*
recostar [31] *vt* to lean.
▷ *vpr* **recostarse** 1 *(apoyarse)* to lean. 2 *(tumbarse)* to lie down.
recoveco *nm* 1 *(vuelta)* turn, bend. 2 *(rincón)* nook, corner.
recreación *nf* recreation.
recrear *vt (divertir)* to amuse, entertain.
▷ *vpr* **recrearse** to amuse OS, enjoy OS.
recreativo,-a *adj* recreational.
recreo *nm* 1 *(diversión)* recreation, amusement, entertainment. 2 *(en la escuela)* playtime, break.
recriminar *vt* 1 *(reprender)* to recriminate. 2 *(reprochar)* to reproach.
recriminatorio,-a *adj* recriminatory.
recrudecer [43] *vi (empeorar)* to worsen, aggravate.
▷ *vpr* **recrudecerse** 1 *(empeorar)* to worsen, aggravate. 2 *(aumentar)* to be increasing.
recrudecimiento *nm* 1 *(empeoramiento)* worsening. 2 *(aumento)* rise (**de**, in), deepening, upsurge.
recta *nf* 1 *(línea)* straight line. 2 *(en carretera)* straight.
rectangular *adj* rectangular.
rectángulo,-a *adj* rectangular: **triángulo rectángulo** *right-angled triangle,* US *right triangle.*
▷ *nm* **rectángulo** rectangle.
rectificación *nf* 1 rectification. 2 *(corrección)* correction, remedy.
rectificar [1] *vt* 1 to rectify. 2 *(corregir)* to correct.
rectilíneo,-a *adj* rectilinear.
rectitud *nf* 1 straightness. 2 *fig* rectitude.
recto,-a *adj* 1 *(derecho)* straight. 2 *fig (honesto)* honest, upright. 3 *(ángulo)* right.
▷ *nm* **recto** ANAT rectum.
▷ *adv* straight, straight on: **vaya todo recto** *go straight on.*

rector,-ra *nm & nf* 1 EDUC vice chancellor, US president. 2 REL rector.
rectorado *nm* 1 EDUC *(cargo)* vice chancellorship, US presidency. 2 REL *(cargo)* rectorship; *(oficina)* rector's office.
recua *nf* 1 *(de animales)* train. 2 *fig* string, drove, line.
recuadro *nm* 1 *(cuadro)* frame. 2 *(en prensa)* box.
recubrir *vt* to cover (**con/de**, with); *(con pintura)* to coat (**con/de**, with).
recuento *nm* recount, count.
recuerdo *nm* 1 *(imagen)* memory, recollection. 2 *(regalo)* souvenir, keepsake.
▷ *nm pl* **recuerdos** *(saludos)* regards, greetings; *(en carta)* best wishes: **me dio recuerdos para ti** *he sends you his regards.* ■ **en recuerdo de** in memory of.
recular *vi (retroceder)* to go back.
recuperación *nf* recovery, recuperation, retrieval.
recuperar *vt* 1 *(gen)* to recover, recuperate, retrieve. 2 *(afecto)* to win back; *(conocimiento)* to regain; *(tiempo, clases)* to make up.
▷ *vpr* **recuperarse** 1 *(disgusto, emoción)* to get over (**de**, -), recover (**de**, from). 2 *(enfermedad)* to recover (**de**, from), recuperate (**de**, from).
recurrir *vi* 1 JUR to appeal. 2 *(acogerse - a algo)* to resort (**a**, to); *(- a ALGN)* to turn (**a**, to): **recurrió a sus padres** *she turned to her parents.*
recurso *nm* 1 *(medio)* resort. 2 JUR appeal.
▷ *nm pl* **recursos** resources, means.
recusar *vt* 1 to reject, refuse. 2 JUR to challenge.
red *nf* 1 *(gen)* net. 2 *(redecilla)* hairnet. 3 *(sistema)* network, system. 4 ELEC mains *pl.* 5 INFORMÁ network. 6 *(estadística)* graph. 7 *fig (trampa)* trap. ● **red de carreteras** road network.
redacción *nf* 1 *(escritura)* writing. 2 *(escrito)* composition, essay. 3 *(estilo)* wording. 4 *(prensa)* editing. 5 *(oficina)* editorial office. 6 *(redactores)* editorial staff.
redactar *vt* 1 *(escribir)* to write, compose. 2 *(tratado, discurso, etc)* to draft, draw up. 3 *(prensa)* to edit.
redactor,-ra *nm & nf* editor. ● **redactor jefe** editor in chief.
redada *nf fig (en un sitio)* raid; *(en varios sitios a la vez)* round-up.
redecilla *nf* 1 *(tejido)* net, netting. 2 *(de pelo)* hairnet.
redención *nf* redemption.
redescubrir *vt* to rediscover.
redicho,-a *adj fam* affected, pretentious.
redil *nm* fold, sheepfold.
redimir *vt* to redeem.
▷ *vpr* **redimirse** to redeem OS.
rediseñar *vt* to redesign.
redistribución *nf* redistribution.
redistribuir [62] *vt* to redistribute.
rédito *nm* interest, yield.
redoblar *vt (aumentar)* to redouble, intensify: **redoblar esfuerzos** *to redouble one's efforts.*
▷ *vi (tambores)* to roll.
redoble *nm* roll.
redoma *nf* flask.
redonda *nf* MÚS semibreve, US whole note. ■ **a la redonda** around.
redondeado,-a *adj* rounded.
redondear *vt* 1 *(poner redondo)* to round, make round. 2 *(cantidad)* to round off, round up, make up to a round figure.
redondel *nm (círculo)* circle, ring.
redondo,-a *adj* 1 *(circular)* round. 2 *fig (perfecto)* perfect, excellent: **un beneficio redondo** *an excellent profit.* 3 *fig (cantidad)* round: **en números redondos** *in round figures.*
reducción *nf* reduction.
reducido,-a *adj* 1 *(limitado)* limited; *(pequeño)* small. 2 *(precio)* low.
reducir [46] *vt* 1 *(gen)* to reduce: **reducir a cenizas** *to reduce to ashes.* 2 *(disminuir)* to reduce, cut, cut down on: **reducir gastos** *to cut down on expenses.* 3 *(vencer)* to subdue.
▷ *vpr* **reducirse** 1 *(gen)* to be reduced. 2 *(resultar)* to come down (**a**, to): **todo se redujo a una equivocación** *it all came down to a mistake.*
redundancia *nf* redundancy.
redundante *adj* redundant.
redundar *vi* 1 *(abundar)* to abound. 2 *(resultar)* to redound (**en**, to): **redundó en nuestro beneficio** *it was to our advantage.*
reedición *nf (de libro)* reprint, reissue; *(de disco)* rerelease.
reedificar [1] *vt* to rebuild.
reeditar *vt (libro)* to reprint, reissue; *(disco)* to rerelease.
reeducar [1] *vt* to re-educate.
reelección *nf* re-election.
reelegir [55] *vt* to re-elect.
reembolsar *vt* 1 *(pagar)* to reimburse; *(cantidad)* to repay. 2 *(devolver)* to refund.
reembolso *nm* 1 *(pago)* reimbursement; *(cantidad)* payment. 2 *(devolución)* refund. ● **contra reembolso** cash on delivery.
reemplazar [4] *vt* to replace.
reemplazo *nm* 1 replacement. 2 MIL call-up.
reemprender *vt* to start again.
reencarnación *nf* reincarnation.
reencontrarse [31] *vpr* to find OS again.
reencuentro *nm* reunion.
reestreno *nm (teatro)* revival; *(cine)* rerelease, rerun.
reestructuración *nf* restructuring, reorganization.
reestructurar *vt* to restructure, reorganize.
reexaminar *vt* to reexamine.
reexpedir [34] *vt* to return, send back.
reexportar *vt* to re-export.
refajo *nm* petticoat, underskirt.
referencia *nf (relación)* reference. ■ **hacer referencia a ALGO** to refer to STH.
▷ *nf pl* **referencias** *(informes)* references.
referéndum *nm inv* referendum.
referente *adj* concerning (**a**, -), regarding (**a**, -).
referir [35] *vt* 1 *(expresar)* to tell, relate. 2 *(remitir)* to refer.
▷ *vpr* **referirse** to refer (**a**, to).
refilón ■ **mirar ALGO de refilón** to look at STH out of the corner of one's eye.
refinado,-a *adj* 1 *(gen)* refined. 2 *fig (astuto)* sly.
refinamiento *nm* 1 *(esmero)* refinement. 2 *(ensañamiento)* cruelty.
refinar *vt (azúcar, etc)* to refine.
refinería *nf* refinery.
reflación *nf* reflation.

reflectante *adj* reflective.
reflector,-ra *adj* reflecting.
▷ *nm* **reflector 1** *(cuerpo)* reflector. **2** ELEC searchlight, spotlight.
reflejar *vt* **1** *(gen)* to reflect. **2** *(mostrar)* to show: **su rostro refleja sus sentimientos** *her face shows her feelings.*
▷ *vpr* **reflejarse** to be reflected.
reflejo,-a *adj* **1** GRAM reflexive. **2** *(movimiento)* reflex.
▷ *nm* **reflejo 1** *(imagen)* reflection. **2** *(destello)* gleam, glint. **3** *(movimiento)* reflex.
▷ *nm pl* **reflejos** *(mechas)* streaks, highlights.
réflex *nm inv* **1** *(sistema)* reflex. **2** *(cámara)* reflex camera.
reflexión *nf* reflection.
reflexionar *vi* to reflect (**sobre**, on), think (**sobre**, about): **reflexionamos sobre el tema** *we reflected on the subject.*
reflexivo,-a *adj* **1** reflective, thoughtful. **2** GRAM reflexive.
reflexoterapia *nf* reflexology.
reflotar *vt* to refloat.
reflujo *nm* ebb tide, ebb.
reforestación *nf* reforestation, reafforestation.
reforestar *vt* to reforest, reafforest.
reforma *nf* **1** *(gen)* reform. **2** *(mejora)* improvement. **3 la Reforma** REL the Reformation.
▷ *nf pl* **reformas** *(en construcción)* alterations, repairs, improvements. • **reforma agraria** agrarian reform.
reformar *vt* **1** *(gen)* to reform. **2** ARQUIT to renovate, do up. **3** *(una prenda)* to alter.
▷ *vpr* **reformarse** *(corregirse)* to reform OS.
reformatear *vt* INFORMÁ to reformat.
reformatorio *nm* reformatory, reform school. • **reformatorio de menores** remand home.
reformista *adj* reformist.
▷ *nm o nf* reformist.
reforzado,-a *adj* reinforced, strengthened.
reforzar [50] *vt* to reinforce, strengthen.
refracción *nf* refraction. • **ángulo de refracción** angle of refraction.
refractario,-a *adj* **1** *(al fuego)* heat-resistant. **2** *(persona - que rehúsa)* reluctant, unwilling; *(- opuesta)* opposed: **es refractario al progreso** *he's opposed to progress.*
refrán *nm* proverb, saying.
refranero *nm* collection of proverbs, collection of sayings.
refregar [48] *vt* **1** to rub hard. **2** *fam fig* to rub in: **me refregó mi error** *he kept on about my mistake.*
refrenar *vt* **1** *(contener)* to restrain, curb, control. **2** *(al caballo)* to rein in.
refrendar *vt (aprobar)* to ratify, approve.
refrescante *adj* refreshing.
refrescar [1] *vt* **1** *(poner fresco)* to cool, refresh. **2** *fig (la memoria)* to refresh; *(idiomas)* to brush up on.
▷ *vi* **1** *(el tiempo)* to get cooler, cool down, turn cooler. **2** *(comida, bebida)* to be refreshing.
▷ *vpr* **refrescarse 1** *(gen)* to cool down, cool off; *(lavarse)* to freshen up; *(tomar el fresco)* to get a breath of fresh air. **2** *(beber)* to have a cold drink.
refresco *nm (bebida)* soft drink.
refriega *nf* **1** *(lucha)* scuffle, brawl. **2** *(escaramuza)* skirmish.
refrigeración *nf* **1** refrigeration. **2** *(aire acondicionado)* air conditioning. **3** *(sistema)* cooling system.
refrigerado,-a *adj* **1** *(enfriado)* refrigerated, cooled. **2** *(con aire acondicionado)* air-conditioned.
refrigerador *nm* fridge, refrigerator.
refrigerar *vt* **1** *(enfriar)* to refrigerate. **2** *(con aire acondicionado)* to air-condition.
refrigerio *nm* refreshments *pl*, snack.
refrito,-a *nm* **refrito** *fam fig* rehash.
refuerzo *nm (fortalecimiento)* reinforcement, strengthening.
refugiado,-a *nm & nf* refugee. • **refugiado político** political refugee.
refugiar [12] *vt* to shelter, give refuge to.
▷ *vpr* **refugiarse** *(gen)* to take refuge; *(de la lluvia)* to shelter.
refugio *nm* **1** *(gen)* shelter, refuge. **2** *fig* refuge.
refulgente *adj* radiant, brilliant.
refulgir [6] *vi (brillar)* to shine; *(resplandecer)* to glitter, sparkle.
refundir *vt* **1** *(metales)* to recast. **2** *fig (comedia, etc)* to adapt.
refunfuñar *vi fam* to grumble, moan, complain.
refunfuñón,-ona *nm & nf fam* grumbler, moaner.
refutable *adj* refutable, disprovable.
refutar *vt* to refute, disprove.
regadera *nf* watering can.
regadío,-a *adj* irrigable.
▷ *nm* **regadío 1** *(acción)* irrigation, watering. **2** *(tierras)* irrigated land. • **cultivo de regadío** irrigation farming.
regalado,-a *adj* **1** *(de regalo)* given as a present. **2** *(muy barato)* dirt cheap. **3** *(gratis)* free. **4** *(agradable)* comfortable, pleasant: **llevar una vida regalada** *to lead an easy life, lead a pleasant life.*
regalar *vt* **1** *(dar un regalo)* to give as a present: **le podemos regalar un libro para su cumpleaños** *we can get him a book for his birthday.* **2** *(halagar)* to flatter.
regaliz *nm* liquorice (US licorice).
regalo *nm* **1** *(obsequio)* gift, present. **2** *(complacencia)* pleasure, joy. **3** *(ganga)* bargain, steal.
regañadientes ■ **a regañadientes** reluctantly, grudgingly, unwillingly.
regañar *vt* to scold, tell off.
▷ *vi (reñir)* to argue, quarrel, fall out: **no hacen más que regañar** *they're always quarrelling.*
regañina *nf (reprensión)* scolding, telling-off.
regañón,-ona *adj fam* grumpy, irritable.
regar [48] *vt* **1** *(plantas, tierra, río)* to water. **2** *(calle)* to wash down, hose down.
regata[1] *nf* MAR regatta, boat race.
regata[2] *nf (surco)* irrigation channel.
regatear *vt* **1** *(un precio)* to haggle over, barter for. **2** *(escatimar)* to be sparing with. ■ **no regatear esfuerzos** to spare no effort.
▷ *vi* **1** *(comerciar)* to haggle, bargain. **2** DEP to dribble. **3** MAR to race.
regateo *nm* **1** *(precios)* haggling, bargaining. **2** DEP dribbling.
regatista *nm o nf (hombre)* yachtsman; *(mujer)* yachtswoman.

regazo *nm* lap.
regencia *nf* regency.
regeneración *nf* regeneration.
regenerador,-ra *adj* regenerative.
regenerar *vt* to regenerate.
regentar *vt* 1 POL to govern, rule. 2 *(cargo)* to hold. 3 *(dirigir)* to manage, direct.
regente,-a *adj* ruling, governing.
▷ *nm o nf* 1 POL regent. 2 JUR magistrate. 3 *(director)* manager.
reggae *nm* reggae.
regidor,-ra *adj* ruling, governing.
▷ *nm & nf* 1 *(concejal)* town councillor. 2 TEAT stage manager.
régimen *nm* 1 POL regime. 2 MED diet. 3 *(condiciones)* system, regime, rules *pl*; *(forma de producirse)* pattern. 4 LING government. ■ **estar a régimen** to be on a diet.
▲ *pl* **regímenes.**
regimiento *nm* regiment.
regio,-a *adj (real)* royal, regal.
región *nf* region.
regional *adj* regional.
regionalista *adj* regionalist.
▷ *nm o nf* regionalist.
regir [55] *vt* 1 *(gobernar)* to govern, rule. 2 *(dirigir)* to manage, direct, run. 3 LING to govern.
▷ *vi (ley, etc)* to be in force, apply: **esta ley aún rige** *this law is still in force.*
▷ *vpr* **regirse** *(guiarse)* to follow, abide (**por**, by), go (**por**, by): **se rige por la opinión de su padre** *he goes by his father's opinion.*
registrado,-a *adj* registered, recorded, noted, listed.
registrador,-ra *adj* registering, recording: **caja registradora** *cash register.*
▷ *nm & nf* registrar.
registrar *vt* 1 *(inspeccionar)* to search, inspect, look through. 2 *(cachear)* to frisk. 3 *(inscribir)* to register, record, note. 4 *(grabar)* to record.
▷ *vpr* **registrarse** 1 *(matricularse)* to register, enrol (US enroll). 2 *(detectarse)* to be recorded. 3 *(ocurrir)* to happen: **se ha registrado un terremoto** *there has been an earthquake.*
registro *nm* 1 *(inspección)* search, inspection. 2 *(inscripción)* registration, recording; *(matriculación)* enrolment (US enrollment), registration. 3 JUR *(oficina)* registry; *(libro)* register. 4 MÚS register. 5 INFORMÁ register. 6 TÉC inspection hole. ● **registro civil** *(oficina)* registry office.
regla *nf* 1 *(norma)* rule, regulation, norm. 2 *(pauta)* pattern, rule. 3 *(instrumento)* ruler. 4 MAT rule. 5 *(menstruación)* period. ■ **en regla** in order.
reglado,-a *adj* 1 *(moderado)* moderate. 2 *(regulado)* regulated. 3 *(papel)* ruled, lined.
reglamentación *nf* 1 *(reglamento)* regulations *pl*, rules *pl*. 2 *(acción)* regulation.
reglamentar *vt* to regulate.
reglamentario,-a *adj* statutory, prescribed, required; *(arma)* regulation.
reglamento *nm* regulations *pl*, rules *pl*.
reglar *vt (regular)* to regulate.
regleta *nf* space.
regocijar *vpr* **regocijarse** 1 *(alegrarse)* to be delighted (**con**, by). 2 *(regodearse)* to delight (**de**, in), take pleasure (**de**, in).
regocijo *nm (placer)* delight, joy, happiness.
regodearse *vpr fam* to delight (**en/con**, in), take pleasure (**en/con**, in).
regodeo *nm fam* delight, pleasure.
regordete,-a *adj fam* chubby, tubby.
regresar *vi* to return, come back, go back.
regresión *nf* 1 *(retroceso)* regression. 2 *(disminución)* drop, decrease.
regresivo,-a *adj* regressive.
regreso *nm* return. ■ **estar de regreso** to be back.
reguero *nm* 1 *(corriente)* trickle of water. 2 *(señal)* trail, trickle. 3 *(reguera)* irrigation channel.
regulable *adj* adjustable.
regulación *nf* 1 *(control)* regulation, control. 2 *(ajuste)* adjustment.
regulador,-ra *adj* regulating.
regular *adj* 1 *(gen)* regular. 2 *fam (pasable)* so-so, average, not bad.
▷ *vt* 1 *(gen)* to regulate. 2 *(ajustar)* to adjust.
regularidad *nf* regularity. ■ **con regularidad** regularly.
regularización *nf* regularization.
regularizar [4] *vt* to regularize; *(normalizar)* to standardize; *(arreglar)* to sort out.
regurgitar *vt* to regurgitate.
rehabilitación *nf* 1 rehabilitation. 2 *(en rango)* rehabilitation, reinstatement.
rehabilitar *vt* to rehabilitate.
▷ *nf (en rango)* to rehabilitate, reinstate.
rehacer [73] *vt (volver a hacer)* to do again, redo.
▷ *vpr* **rehacerse** *(recuperarse)* to recover, recuperate.
rehén *nm o nf* hostage.
rehogar [7] *vt* to fry lightly.
rehuir [62] *vt* to avoid, shun.
rehusar [18] *vt* to refuse, decline, turn down: **rehusé la invitación** *I declined the invitation.*
reimplantar *vt* to implant again.
reimpresión *nf* 1 *(acción)* reprinting. 2 *(ejemplar)* reprint.
reimprimir *vt* to reprint.
reina *nf (gen)* queen.
reinado *nm* reign.
reinante *adj* 1 *(que reina)* reigning. 2 *(existente)* prevailing, reigning: **el silencio reinante** *the reigning silence.*
reinar *vi* 1 to reign. 2 *fig (prevalecer)* to reign, prevail: **reina el desconcierto** *disorder reigns.*
reincidente *adj* 1 relapsing. 2 JUR reoffending, recidivist.
▷ *nm o nf* JUR reoffender, recidivist.
reincidir *vi* 1 to relapse (**en**, into), fall back (**en**, into). 2 JUR to reoffend.
reincorporar *vt* to reincorporate; *(a un trabajo)* to reinstate.
▷ *vpr* **reincorporarse** to rejoin (**a**, -): **se reincorporará al trabajo el lunes** *she will go back to work on Monday.*
reindustrialización *nf* reindustrialization.
reingresar *vt* to readmit.
▷ *vi* to return.
reingreso *nm* return.

reinicializar [4] *vt (gen)* to reset; *(ordenador)* to reboot.
reiniciar *vt* to restart.
reino *nm* kingdom, reign.
reinserción *nf* reintegration, rehabilitation: **la reinserción social** *social rehabilitation.*
reinsertar *vt* to reintegrate.
▷ *vpr* **reinsertarse** to reintegrate.
reinstalar *vt* to reinstall, reinstal.
reintegrar *vt* **1** *(reincorporar)* to reinstate, restore. **2** *(pagar)* to refund, reimburse; *(banco)* to credit.
▷ *vpr* **reintegrarse** *(volver a ejercer)* to return (**a**, to): **se reintegró a su puesto** *he returned to his job.*
reintegro *nm* **1** *(reincorporación)* reinstatement. **2** FIN reimbursement, repayment, refund; *(bancario)* credit. **3** *(de lotería)* refund of the price of the ticket.
reinterpretar *vt* to reinterpret.
reintroducir [46] *vt* to reintroduce.
reinvertir *vt* to reinvest.
reír [37] *vt* to laugh at: **reír las gracias** *to laugh at jokes.*
▷ *vi* to laugh.
▷ *vpr* **reírse** to laugh (**de**, at): **¿de qué te ríes?** *what are you laughing at?*
reiteración *nf* reiteration.
reiterar *vt* to reiterate, repeat.
reiterativo,-a *adj* repetitive, repetitious, reiterative.
reivindicación *nf* claim, demand.
reivindicar [1] *vt* to claim, demand.
reivindicativo,-a *adj* protest.
reja *nf (de ventana)* grill, grille, bar.
rejilla *nf* **1** *(celosía)* grill, grille. **2** *(de chimenea)* grate. **3** *(de silla)* wickerwork. **4** *(de horno)* grid iron. **5** *(de ventilador)* grill. **6** *(para equipaje)* luggage rack.
rejón *nm* lance.
rejoneador,-ra *nm & nf* bullfighter on horseback.
rejonear *vt* to fight on horseback.
rejoneo *nm* bullfighting on horseback.
rejuvenecer [43] *vt* to rejuvenate.
▷ *vpr* **rejuvenecerse** to become rejuvenated.
rejuvenecimiento *nm* rejuvenation.
relación *nf* **1** *(correspondencia)* relation, relationship. **2** *(conexión)* link, connection. **3** *(lista)* list, record. **4** *(relato)* account, telling. **5** *(en matemática)* ratio.
▷ *nf pl* **relaciones** *(conocidos)* acquaintances; *(contactos)* contacts, connections. ■ **con relación a / en relación a** with regard to, regarding.
relacionar *vt* **1** *(poner en relación)* to relate, connect, associate. **2** *(relatar)* to tell, list.
▷ *vpr* **relacionarse** **1** *(estar conectado)* to be related (**con**, to), be connected (**con**, with). **2** *(alternar)* to get acquainted (**con**, with), mix (**con**, with), meet (**con**, -).
relajación *nf (gen)* relaxation.
relajante *adj* relaxing.
relajar *vt (gen)* to relax.
▷ *vpr* **relajarse** *(descansar)* to relax.
relajo *nm* **1** *(descanso)* relaxation, rest; *(tranquilidad)* peace. **2** *(falta de orden)* relaxed attitude.
relamer *vt* to lick.
▷ *vpr* **relamerse** to lick one's lips repeatedly.
relamido,-a *adj (pulcro)* prim and proper.
relámpago *nm* flash of lightning.
relampaguear *vi* [Used only in the 3rd pers; it does not take a subject.] to flash.
relanzar *vt* to relaunch.
relatar *vt* **1** *(una historia)* to narrate, tell. **2** *(un suceso)* to report, tell.
relatividad *nf* relativity.
relativizar [4] *vt* to lessen the importance of, play down.
relativo,-a *adj* relative.
▷ *nm* **relativo** LING relative.
relato *nm* **1** *(narración)* story, tale. **2** *(informe)* report, account.
relax *nm inv* relaxation.
releer [61] *vt* to reread, read again.
relegar [7] *vt* to relegate (**a**, to), consign (**a**, to).
relente *nm* dew.
relevancia *nf* **1** *(significación)* relevance. **2** *(importancia)* importance.
relevante *adj* **1** *(significativo)* relevant. **2** *(importante)* excellent, outstanding.
relevar *vt* **1** *(sustituir)* to relieve, take over from. **2** *(eximir)* to exempt (**de**, from). **3** *(destituir)* to dismiss, remove, relieve. **4** *fig (engrandecer)* to exaggerate.
▷ *vpr* **relevarse** to take turns.
relevo *nm* **1** MIL relief, change of the guard. **2** DEP relay.
relieve *nm* **1** relief. **2** *fig (renombre)* renown, fame. ■ **en relieve** in relief. ■ **poner de relieve** *fig* to emphasize, highlight, underline.
religión *nf* religion.
religioso,-a *adj* religious.
▷ *nm & nf (hombre)* monk; *(mujer)* nun.
relinchar *vi* to neigh, whinny.
reliquia *nf* relic.
rellamada *nf* redial.
rellano *nm* landing.
rellenar *vt* **1** *(volver a llenar)* to refill, fill again. **2** *(llenar del todo)* to cram, pack, stuff. **3** *(cuestionario)* to fill in, fill out. **4** CULIN *(ave)* to stuff; *(pastel)* to fill. **5** COST to pad.
relleno,-a *adj* **1** *(totalmente lleno)* stuffed, crammed, packed. **2** *(cara)* full. **3** CULIN stuffed; *(pasteles)* filled.
▷ *nm* **relleno** CULIN *(aves)* stuffing; *(pasteles)* filling.
reloj *nm* clock; *(de pulsera)* watch. ■ **contra reloj** against the clock. ● **reloj de arena** hourglass. ● **reloj de pulsera** wristwatch.
relojería *nf* **1** *(arte)* watchmaking, clockmaking. **2** *(tienda)* watchmaker's, jeweller's.
relojero,-a *nm & nf* watchmaker, clockmaker.
reluciente *adj* bright, shining, gleaming, glittering.
relucir [45] *vi* **1** *(brillar)* to shine, gleam, glitter. **2** *fig (destacar)* to excel, stand out, shine. ■ **sacar a relucir** ALGO to bring up STH.
relumbrar *vi* to shine, dazzle, gleam.
remachadora *nf* riveting machine.
remachar *vt (clavo, etc)* to clinch; *(metal)* to rivet.
remache *nm* rivet.
remanente *adj* **1** *(que queda)* remaining, residual. **2** *(extra)* surplus.
▷ *nm* **1** *(restos)* remainder, remains *pl.* **2** *(extra)* surplus.
remangar *vt (mangas, pantalones)* to roll up; *(faldas, vestidos)* to pull up, hitch up.

▷ *vpr* **remangarse** *fig* to decide quickly, make a snap decision.
remanso *nm* 1 *(estanque)* pool. 2 *(lugar tranquilo)* quiet place.
remar *vi* to row.
remarcar [1] *vt* to stress, underline.
rematado,-a *adj* 1 absolute, utter, out-and-out. 2 convicted.
rematar *vt* 1 *(acabar)* to finish off, round off, put the finishing touches to. 2 *(precios)* to knock down. 3 *(matar)* to kill, finish off. 4 DEP to shoot.
▷ *vi* DEP to take a shot at goal, shoot.
remate *nm* 1 *(final)* end, finish. 2 DEP shot. ■ **de remate** *fam* utter, out-and-out, total.
remedar *vt* 1 *(imitar)* to imitate, copy. 2 *(con burla)* to ape.
remediar [12] *vt* 1 *(poner remedio)* to remedy. 2 *(reparar)* to repair, make good. 3 *(resolver)* to solve. 4 *(evitar)* to avoid, prevent.
remedio *nm* 1 *(cura)* remedy, cure. 2 *fig (solución)* solution. 3 remedy, recourse. ■ **como último remedio** as a last resort. ‖ **no tener más remedio que** to have no choice but to, have no option but to.
rememoración *nf* remembrance, recollection.
rememorar *vt* to remember, recall.
remendar [27] *vt* COST to mend; *(ropas)* to patch; *(calcetines)* to darn.
remera *nf (pluma)* remex, quill feather.
See also **remero,-a.**
remero,-a *nm & nf* DEP rower; *(hombre)* oarsman; *(mujer)* oarswoman.
remesa *nf* 1 *(de dinero)* remittance. 2 *(de mercancías)* consignment, shipment.
remeter *vt (meter adentro)* to tuck in.
remiendo *nm* mend, darn.
remilgado,-a *adj* 1 *(afectado)* affected. 2 *(con la comida)* fussy, finicky.
remilgo *nm* affectation.
reminiscencia *nf* reminiscence.
remisión *nf* 1 *(referencia)* reference. 2 *(envío)* sending.
remiso,-a *adj (reacio)* reluctant, unwilling.
remite *nm* sender's name and address.
remitente *nm o nf* sender.
remitido *nm* advertisement, announcement.
remitir *vt* 1 *(enviar)* to remit, send. 2 *(referir)* to refer.
▷ *vi (ceder)* to subside: **la fiebre ha remitido** *the fever has subsided.*
▷ *vpr* **remitirse** *(atenerse)* to refer (**a**, to): **se remitió a su propio acuerdo** *he referred to his own agreement.*
remo *nm* 1 *(pala)* oar, paddle. 2 DEP rowing.
remodelación *nf* 1 *(modificación)* reshaping. 2 *(reorganización)* reorganization.
remodelar *vt* 1 *(modificar)* to reshape. 2 *(reorganizar)* to reorganize. 3 *(ministerio)* to reshuffle.
remojar *vt (empapar)* to soak (**en**, in).
remojo *nm* soaking. ■ **poner en remojo** to soak, leave to soak.
remolacha *nf* beetroot. ● **remolacha azucarera** sugar beet.
remolcador *nm* 1 MAR tug, tugboat. 2 AUTO breakdown truck, US tow truck.
remolcar [1] *vt* to tow.
remolino *nm* 1 *(de polvo)* whirl, cloud; *(de agua)* whirlpool, eddy; *(de aire)* whirlwind. 2 *(de pelo)* tuft, US cowlick. 3 *(de gente)* throng, crowd, mass.
remolón,-ona *adj* lazy, slack.
remolonear *vi* to shirk, slack.
remolque *nm* 1 *(acción)* towing. 2 *(vehículo)* trailer.
remontar *vt* 1 *(elevar)* to raise. 2 *(subir)* to go up. 3 *(río)* to sail up; *(vuelo)* to soar.
▷ *vpr* **remontarse** 1 *(al volar)* to soar. 2 *(datar)* to go back (**a**, to).
rémora *nf* 1 *(pez)* remora. 2 *fig (obstáculo)* hindrance.
remorder [32] *vt fig (desasosegar)* to trouble, worry.
remordimiento *nm* remorse.
remoto,-a *adj* remote, far-off.
remover [32] *vt* 1 *(trasladar)* to move. 2 *(tierra)* to turn over, dig up. 3 *(líquido)* to stir. 4 *(comida)* to stir; *(ensalada)* to toss. 5 *fig (agitar)* to get moving, stir up. 6 *fig (recuerdo)* to stir up; *(tema)* to bring up.
▷ *vpr* **removerse** to stir, shift.
remozar *vt* 1 *(fachada)* to renovate, modernize; *(decorar)* to redecorate; *(limpiar)* to brighten up. 2 *(ropa)* to brighten up.
remplazar *vt* → **reemplazar.**
remuneración *nf* remuneration, pay.
remunerado,-a *adj* paid.
remunerar *vt* to remunerate, reward, pay.
renacimiento *nm* 1 *(vuelta a nacer)* rebirth. 2 *fig* revival, renaissance. 3 **el Renacimiento** HIST the Renaissance.
renacuajo *nm* 1 ZOOL tadpole. 2 *fam (niño)* shrimp.
renal *adj* renal, kidney.
rencilla *nf* quarrel.
rencor *nm* 1 *(odio)* rancour (US rancor). 2 *(resentimiento)* resentment.
rencoroso,-a *adj* 1 *(hostil)* rancorous. 2 *(resentido)* resentful.
rendición *nf* surrender.
rendido,-a *adj* 1 *(sumiso)* humble, submissive. 2 *(muy cansado)* worn out, exhausted.
rendija *nf* crack, split.
rendimiento *nm* 1 *(producción - de terreno)* yield; *(- de máquina)* output; *(- de persona)* progress, performance; *(- de inversión)* yield, return. 2 *(trabajo - de motor, máquina)* efficiency, performance.
rendir [34] *vt* 1 *(vencer)* to defeat, conquer. 2 *(cansar)* to exhaust, wear out. 3 *(restituir)* to render, give back. 4 *(producir)* to yield, produce; *(progresar)* to progress.
▷ *vi (dar fruto)* to pay.
▷ *vpr* **rendirse** 1 *(entregarse al enemigo)* to surrender, give in. 2 *(darse por vencido)* to give up: **¡me rindo!** *I give up!*
renegado,-a *adj* renegade.
▷ *nm & nf* renegade.
renegar [48] *vt (negar)* to deny vigorously.
▷ *vi* 1 *(gen)* to renounce (**de**, -); *(familia)* to disown (**de**, -). 2 *(protestar)* to grumble, complain.
renegociar [12] *vt* to renegotiate.
renglón *nm (línea)* line.
reno *nm* reindeer.
renombrado,-a *adj* renowned, famous.
renombrar *vt* to rename.
renombre *nm* renown, fame.
renovable *adj* renewable.

renovación *nf* 1 *(de contrato, etc)* renewal. 2 *(de casa)* renovation.
renovador,-ra *adj (gen)* revitalizing, refreshing; *(en política)* progressive.
renovar [31] *vt* 1 *(gen)* to renew. 2 *(casa)* to renovate; *(de decoración)* to redecorate. 3 *(de personal)* to reorganize.
renquear *vi* 1 *(de la pierna)* to limp; *(del pie)* to hobble. 2 *fig (vacilar)* to dither.
renta *nf* 1 *(ingresos)* income. 2 *(declaración de renta)* tax return. 3 *(beneficio)* interest, return. 4 *(alquiler)* rent. ● **renta per cápita** per capita income.
rentabilidad *nf* profitability.
rentabilizar [4] *vt* to make profitable.
rentable *adj* profitable.
rentar *vt* to produce, yield.
renuente *adj* reluctant, unwilling.
renuevo *nm* 1 BOT shoot, sprout. 2 *(renovación)* renewal.
renuncia *nf* 1 renunciation. 2 *(dimisión)* resignation.
renunciar [12] *vi* 1 *(abandonar)* to give up (**a**, -), abandon (**a**, -). 2 *(dimitir)* to resign. 3 to renounce (**a**, -), relinquish (**a**, -).
renuncio *nm fig* lie, contradiction.
reñido,-a *adj* 1 *(enemistado)* on bad terms, at odds. 2 *(de rivalidad)* bitter, tough, hard-fought. 3 *(incompatible)* incompatible.
reñir [36] *vi* 1 *(discutir)* to quarrel, argue. 2 *(pelear)* to fight. 3 *(desavenirse)* to fall out.
▷ *vt (reprender)* to scold, tell off.
reo *nm o nf* 1 JUR *(acusado)* defendant, accused. 2 JUR *(culpable)* culprit.
reojo ■ **de reojo** out of the corner of one's eye.
reordenar *vt* to rearrange.
reorganización *nf* reorganization.
reorganizar [4] *vt* to reorganize.
reorientación *nf* reorientation.
reorientar *vt fig* to redirect.
repantigarse [7] *vpr fam* to lounge, loll.
reparable *adj* repairable.
reparación *nf* 1 *(arreglo)* repair, repairing. 2 *fig (desagravio)* reparation, redress *pl*.
reparador,-ra *adj* restorative, refreshing.
reparar *vt* 1 *(arreglar)* to repair, mend, fix. 2 *(remediar - daño)* to make good; *(- perjuicio, insulto)* to make up for. 3 *(vengarse)* to avenge. 4 *(restablecer)* to restore, renew.
▷ *vi (advertir)* to notice, see: **repare usted en esto** *look at this.*
reparo *nm* objection. ■ **no tener reparos en** not to hesitate to.
repartición *nf* distribution, sharing out.
repartidor,-ra *nm & nf (hombre)* delivery man; *(mujer)* delivery woman; *(chico)* delivery boy; *(chica)* delivery girl.
repartir *vt* 1 *(dividir)* to distribute, divide, share out. 2 *(entregar)* to give out, hand out; *(correo, leche)* to deliver; *(premios)* to give out. 3 *(comida)* to hand out. 4 *(distribuir)* to spread out.
reparto *nm* 1 *(división)* sharing out, division; *(distribución)* distribution. 2 *(de un terreno)* parcelling out; *(de un país)* partition. 3 *(entrega)* handing out; *(de mercancías)* delivery. 4 *(naipes - acción)* dealing; *(- turno)* deal. 5 *(de obra, película)* cast.
repasar *vt* 1 *(volver a examinar)* to revise (US to review), go over. 2 *(máquina, etc)* to check, overhaul.
repaso *nm* 1 revision, check; *(lección)* review. 2 COST mending. ● **curso de repaso** refresher course.
repatriación *nf* repatriation.
repatriar [14] *vt* to repatriate.
repecho *nm* short steep slope.
repeinado,-a *adj fig* dolled up.
repelencia *nf* repulse.
repelente *adj* repellent, repulsive.
repeler *vt* 1 *(rechazar)* to repel, repulse. 2 *(repugnar)* to disgust, repel.
repelús *nm fam* shiver.
repensar [27] *vt* to think over.
repente *nm* 1 *fam (movimiento)* sudden movement, start. 2 *fam (ataque)* fit, outburst. ■ **de repente** suddenly, all of a sudden.
repentino,-a *adj* sudden.
repentizar [4] *vi* MÚS to sight read.
repercusión *nf* repercussion.
repercutir *vi fig (trascender)* to have repercussions (**en**, on), affect.
repertorio *nm* 1 *(resumen)* list, index. 2 TEAT repertoire, repertory.
repesca *nf fam* second chance; *(examen)* resit. ■ **hacer un examen de repesca** to resit an exam.
repetición *nf* 1 *(gen)* repetition. 2 *(de programa)* repeat.
repetido,-a *adj* repeated.
repetidor,-ra *nm & nf* EDUC repeat student.
▷ *nm* **repetidor** TÉC relay, booster station.
repetir [34] *vt* 1 *(gen)* to repeat: **se lo repetí dos veces** *I told him twice.* 2 *(volver a hacer)* to do again, do over again.
▷ *vi* 1 *(volver a servirse)* to have a second helping: 2 *(venir a la boca)* to repeat (on one), come up: **el ajo repite** *garlic repeats.* 3 EDUC to repeat a year.
▷ *vpr* **repetirse** 1 *(persona)* to repeat OS. 2 *(hecho)* to recur.
repetitivo,-a *adj* repetitive.
repicar [1] *vt* 1 *(campanas)* to peal, ring out. 2 *(picar)* to chop, mince.
repintar *vt* to repaint.
repipi *adj fam* la-di-da, affected.
repique *nm* peal, ringing.
repisa *nf* ledge, shelf.
replanteamiento *nm* rethink.
replantar *vt* 1 *(volver a plantar)* to replant. 2 *(trasplantar)* to transplant.
replantear *vt* 1 ARQUIT to redesign. 2 *(asunto, problema)* to re-examine, reconsider, rethink.
replegable *adj* retracable.
replegarse [48] *vpr* to withdraw, fall back, retreat.
repleto,-a *adj* full up, full (**de**, of), jam-packed (**de**, with).
réplica *nf* 1 *(respuesta)* answer, reply; *(objeción)* retort. 2 ARTE *(copia)* replica.
replicar [1] *vt* 1 *(contestar)* to answer, reply. 2 *(poner objeciones)* to argue, answer back. 3 JUR to answer.
▷ *vi* to argue, answer back.
repliegue *nm* 1 *(pliegue)* fold, crease. 2 MIL withdrawal, retreat.

repoblación *nf* repopulation. ● **repoblación forestal** reafforestation, reforestation.
repoblar [31] *vt* to repopulate; *(bosque)* to reafforest, reforest.
repollo *nm* cabbage.
reponer [78] *vt* 1 *(reemplazar)* to replace. 2 *(en el teatro)* to put on again, restage; *(en el cine)* to rerun.
▷ *vpr* **reponerse** *(salud, susto)* to recover.
reportaje *nm* 1 *(prensa, radio)* report. 2 *(noticias)* article, news item. 3 *(documental)* documentary.
reportar *vt* 1 *(proporcionar)* to bring.
reporte *nm* report.
reportero,-a *nm & nf* reporter.
reposacabezas *nm inv* headrest.
reposado,-a *adj* calm, quiet, peaceful.
reposapiés *nm inv* footrest.
reposar *vi* 1 *(descansar)* to rest, take a rest. 2 *(yacer)* to rest, lie, be buried. 3 *(un líquido)* to settle. ■ **dejar reposar** CULIN to leave to stand.
reposición *nf* 1 *(restitución)* restoration. 2 *(en el teatro)* revival; *(en el cine)* rerun.
reposo *nm* 1 *(descanso)* rest. 2 *(tranquilidad)* peace.
repostar *vt* 1 *(provisiones)* to stock up with. 2 *(avión)* to refuel; *(coche)* to fill up.
repostería *nf (pastas)* cakes *pl*; *(chocolate, bombones)* confectionery.
repostero,-a *nm & nf (de pasteles)* pastrycook; *(de chocolate, bombones)* confectioner.
reprender *vt* to reprimand, scold.
reprensión *nf* reprimand, scolding.
represa *nf* dam.
represalia *nf* reprisal, retaliation.
represaliado,-a *adj* sanctioned.
represaliar *vt* to sanction.
representación *nf* 1 *(gen)* representation. 2 TEAT performance. ■ **en representación de** as a representative of, representing.
representante *adj* representative.
▷ *nm o nf* 1 representative. 2 *(actor)* actor; *(actriz)* actress.
representar *vt* 1 *(gen)* to represent. 2 *(símbolo)* to represent, stand for: **una paloma representa la paz** *a dove stands for peace.* 3 TEAT *(obra)* to perform; *(papel)* to play (the part of). 4 *(aparentar)* to appear to be, look: **representa veinte años** *she looks twenty.*
representativo,-a *adj* representative.
represión *nf* repression.
represivo,-a *adj* repressive.
reprimenda *nf* reprimand.
reprimido,-a *adj* repressed.
▷ *nm & nf* repressed person.
reprimir *vt (gen)* to repress, suppress.
▷ *vpr* **reprimirse** to control OS.
reprivatización *nf* return to private ownership.
reprivatizar *vt* to return to private ownership.
reprobable *adj* reproachable, reprehensible.
reprobación *nf* reprobation, reproof.
reprobar [31] *vt* to condemn, to censure.
reprobatorio,-a *adj* reproving.
reprochable *adj* reproachable.
reprochar *vt* to reproach, censure.
reproche *nm* reproach, criticism.
reproducción *nf* reproduction.
reproducir [46] *vt* to reproduce, repeat.
▷ *vpr* **reproducirse** 1 *(gen)* to reproduce. 2 *(volver a ocurrir)* to happen again, recur.
reproductor,-ra *adj* 1 *(gen)* reproducing. 2 ANAT reproductive. 3 *(animal)* breeding.
▷ *nm & nf (animal)* breeder.
reprografía *nf* reprography.
reprogramar *vt* to reprogramme (US reprogram).
reptar *vi (arrastrarse)* to crawl, slither.
reptil *nm* reptile.
república *nf* republic.
republicanismo *nm* republicanism.
republicano,-a *adj* republican.
▷ *nm & nf* republican.
repudiar [12] *vt* to repudiate.
repudio *nm* repudiation.
repuesto,-a *adj (recuperado)* recovered.
▷ *nm* **repuesto** 1 *(prevención)* store, supply, stock. 2 *(recambio)* spare, spare part. ■ **de repuesto** spare, in reserve.
repugnancia *nf* repugnance, disgust.
repugnante *adj* repugnant, disgusting.
repugnar *vt* 1 *(negar)* to deny. 2 *(contradecir)* to contradict.
repujado,-a *adj* embossed, repoussé.
repujar *vt* to emboss.
repulsa *nf* 1 *(rechazo)* rebuff. 2 *(condena)* condemnation.
repulsión *nf* repulsion, repugnance.
repulsivo,-a *adj* repulsive, revolting.
repuntar *vi* 1 *(la marea)* to turn. 2 *(economía)* to recover, pick up.
reputación *nf* reputation.
reputado,-a *adj* reputed, reputable.
reputar *vt* to consider, deem.
requemado,-a *adj* scorched, burnt.
requemar *vt (gen)* to scorch, burn.
requerimiento *nm* 1 *(súplica)* request. 2 JUR *(aviso)* summons *pl*; *(intimación)* injunction.
requerir [35] *vt* 1 *(necesitar)* to require, need: **esto requiere gran paciencia** *this requires a lot of patience.* 2 *(decir con autoridad)* to demand, call for. 3 *(solicitar)* to request.
requesón *nm* cottage cheese.
requiebro *nm* compliment, flirtatious remark.
réquiem *nm* requiem.
requisa *nf* 1 *(inspección)* inspection. 2 *(embargo)* requisition.
requisar *vt* 1 MIL to requisition. 2 *fam (apropiarse)* to grab, swipe.
requisito *nm* requisite, requirement.
requisitoria *nf* requisition, demand.
res *nf (gen)* beast, animal; *(cabeza de ganado)* head.
resabiar [12] *vt* make fall into bad habits.
resabio *nm* 1 *(mal sabor)* bad aftertaste. 2 *(vicio)* bad habit.
resaca *nf* 1 *(de las olas)* undertow, undercurrent. 2 *(de borrachera)* hangover.
resalado,-a *adj fam (gracioso)* charming.
resaltar *vi fig (distinguirse)* to stand out (**de**, from).
▷ *vt* to highlight, stress, emphasize.
resalte *nm* ledge.
resarcir [3] *vt* to compensate, indemnify.
▷ *vpr* **resarcirse** to make up for.
resbaladizo,-a *adj* slippery.

resbalar *vi* 1 *(deslizarse)* to slide. 2 *(sin querer - persona)* to slip.
resbalón *nm* slip.
resbaloso,-a *adj* slippery.
rescatar *vt* 1 *(rehén, náufrago, persona atrapada, etc)* to rescue; *(cadáver)* to recover; *(ciudad)* to recapture. 2 *(recuperar)* to recover.
rescate *nm* 1 *(salvamento)* rescue; *(de ciudad)* recapture. 2 *(dinero)* ransom. 3 *(recuperación)* recovery, recapture.
rescindir *vt* to rescind, cancel, terminate.
rescisión *nf* cancellation, termination.
rescoldo *nm* 1 *(brasa)* embers *pl*. 2 *fig (recelo)* lingering doubt.
resecar [1] *vt* to dry up.
▷ *vpr* **resecarse** to dry up.
reseco,-a *adj (seco)* very dry, parched.
resentido,-a *adj* resentful. ■ **estar resentido,-a con** ALGN to bear resentment towards SB.
resentimiento *nm* resentment.
resentirse [35] *vpr* 1 *(sentirse)* to suffer (**de**, from), feel the effects (**de**, of). 2 *(flaquear)* to be weakened. 3 *fig (enojarse)* to become resentful, feel resentment.
reseña *nf* 1 *(crítica)* review; *(en prensa)* write-up. 2 *(descripción)* description.
reseñar *vt* 1 *(crítica)* to review. 2 *(describir)* to describe.
reserva *nf* 1 *(de plazas, entradas)* booking, reservation. 2 *(provisión)* reserve; *(existencias)* stock. 3 *(cautela)* reservation. 4 *(discreción)* discretion, reserve. 5 *(vino)* vintage. 6 *(de animales)* reserve; *(de personas)* reservation. 7 MIL reserve, reserves *pl*.
▷ *nf pl* **reservas** COM reserves, stock *sing*.
reservado,-a *adj* 1 *(persona)* reserved. 2 *(asunto)* confidential.
▷ *nm* **reservado** *(en local)* private room; *(en tren)* reserved compartment.
reservar *vt* 1 *(plazas, etc)* to book, reserve. 2 *(guardar)* to keep, save. 3 *(ocultar)* to withhold, keep to OS.
▷ *vpr* **reservarse** 1 *(conservarse)* to save OS (**para**, for). 2 to withhold, keep to OS: **se reservó su opinión** *she kept her opinion to herself*.
reservista *nm o nf* reservist.
resfriado,-a *adj* with a cold.
▷ *nm* **resfriado** cold.
resfriar [13] *vt (enfriar)* to cool.
▷ *vpr* **resfriarse** MED to catch a cold.
resfrío *nm* cold.
resguardar *vt* 1 *(proteger)* to protect (**de**, from), shelter (**de**, from). 2 *(salvaguardar)* to safeguard (**de**, against).
▷ *vpr* **resguardarse** *(protegerse)* to protect OS.
resguardo *nm* 1 *(protección)* protection, shelter. 2 *(garantía)* safeguard, guarantee. 3 *(recibo)* receipt, ticket.
residencia *nf (gen)* residence. ● **residencia de ancianos** old people's home.
residencial *adj* residential.
residente *adj* resident, residing.
▷ *nm o nf* resident.
residir *vi* 1 to reside (**en**, in), live (**en**, in). 2 *fig* to lie (**en**, in).
residual *adj* residual.
residuo *nm* residue.
▷ *nm pl* **residuos** waste *sing*, refuse *sing*.

resignación *nf* resignation.
resignado,-a *adj* resigned.
resignar *vt* to resign, relinquish.
▷ *vpr* **resignarse** to resign OS (**a**, to).
resina *nf* resin.
resinoso,-a *adj* resinous.
resistencia *nf* 1 *(gen)* resistance. 2 *(aguante)* endurance, stamina. 3 *(oposición)* resistance, opposition 4 ELEC resistance. 5 *(de materiales)* strength.
resistente *adj* 1 *(que resiste)* resistant (**a**, to). 2 *(fuerte)* tough, strong.
resistir *vi* 1 *(aguantar - algo)* to hold (out); *(- alguien)* to hold out, take (it), have endurance. 2 *(durar)* to endure, last. 3 *(ejército)* to hold out, resist.
▷ *vt* 1 *(soportar)* to stand, tolerate. 2 *(peso, etc)* to bear, withstand, take. 3 *(tentación, etc)* to resist.
▷ *vpr* **resistirse** 1 *(rechazar)* to resist. 2 *fam (costar)* to be difficult, be hard: **la física se le resiste** *he's struggling with physics*. 3 *(negarse)* to refuse: **me resisto a creerlo** *I find it hard to believe*.
resma *nf* ream, ream of paper.
resolución *nf* 1 *(decisión)* resolution, decision; *(determinación)* determination, resolve. 2 *(solución)* solution; *(de un conflicto)* settlement; *(en técnica)* resolution.
resolutivo,-a *adj* resolvent.
resolver [32] *vt* 1 *(solucionar - gen)* to resolve, solve; *(- asunto, conflicto)* to resolve, settle; *(- dificultad)* to overcome. 2 *(decidir)* to resolve, decide (-, to): 3 *(deshacer)* to resolve. 4 QUÍM to dissolve.
▷ *vpr* **resolverse** 1 *(solucionarse)* to be solved; *(resultar)* to work out. 2 *(reducirse)* to end up (**en**, in), turn out.
resonancia *nf* 1 resonance. 2 *(eco)* echo. 3 *fig (importancia)* importance; *(consecuencias)* repercussions *pl*.
resonante *adj* 1 resounding. 2 *fig* important.
resonar [31] *vi* 1 *(gen)* to resound. 2 *(cristal, metales)* to ring. 3 *(tener eco)* to echo.
resoplar *vi* 1 to breathe heavily. 2 *(de cansancio)* to puff and pant.
resoplido *nm* 1 *(resuello)* heavy breathing; *(silbido)* wheezing; *(por cansancio)* panting. 2 *(de enfado)* snort.
resorte *nm* 1 spring. 2 *fig* means *pl*.
respaldar *vt* to support, back (up).
▷ *vpr* **respaldarse** 1 to lean back (**en**, on). 2 *(apoyarse)* to lean (**en**, on).
respaldo *nm* 1 back. 2 *fig* support, backing.
respectivamente *adv* respectively.
respectivo,-a *adj* respective. ■ **en lo respectivo a** with regard to, regarding.
respecto *nm* regard, respect. ■ **con respecto a** with regard to, regarding.
respetabilidad *nf* respectability.
respetable *adj* respectable.
respetar *vt* to respect.
respeto *nm* 1 *(gen)* respect. 2 *fam (miedo)* fear.
▷ *nm pl* **respetos** respects. ● **falta de respeto** lack of respect.
respetuosamente *adv* respectfully.
respetuoso,-a *adj* respectful.
respingo *nm* 1 *(sacudida)* start, jump. 2 *fig (ademán)* gesture of unwillingness.

respingón,-ona *adj* snub, upturned: **nariz respingona** *snub nose.*

respiración *nf* 1 *(acción)* breathing, respiration. 2 *(aliento)* breath more easily, breathe.

respiradero *nm* 1 TÉC air vent. 2 *fig* rest.

respirar *vi* 1 to breathe. 2 *(estar vivo)* to be breathing. 3 *fig (relajarse)* to breathe more easily, breathe a sigh of relief: **al oír al doctor, respiramos** *when we heard what the doctor had to say we breathed a sigh of relief.* ■ **sin respirar** 1 *(sin descanso)* nonstop. 2 *(con atención)* attentively.
▷ *vt (absorber)* to breathe, breathe in, inhale.

respiratorio,-a *adj* respiratory.

respiro *nm* 1 *(resuello)* breathing. 2 *fig (descanso)* breather, break. 3 *fig (alivio)* relief, respite.

resplandecer [43] *vi* 1 *(sol)* to shine; *(metal)* to gleam, glint; *(fuego)* to glow. 2 *fig* to glow (**de**, with), shine (**de**, with).

resplandeciente *adj* 1 *(brillante)* shining; *(metales)* gleaming, glittering; *(fuego)* glowing; *(ojos)* sparkling. 2 *fig (radiante)* resplendent, radiant.

resplandor *nm (de luz)* brightness, brilliance; *(de metales, cristales)* gleam, glitter; *(del fuego)* glow, blaze.

responder *vt (contestar)* to answer.
▷ *vi* 1 *(contestar)* to answer, reply. 2 *(replicar)* to answer back. 3 *(corresponder)* to answer, respond to: **tengo que responder a su amabilidad** *I have to respond to his kindness.* 4 *(tener el efecto deseado)* to respond: **el motor respondió bien** *the engine responded well.* 5 *(ser responsable)* to answer (**de**, for), accept responsibility (**de**, for).

responsabilidad *nf* responsibility.

responsabilizar [4] *vt* hold responsible (**de**, for).
▷ *vpr* **responsabilizarse** to take responsibility (**de**, for), claim responsibility (**de**, for).

responsable *adj* responsible.
▷ *nm o nf* 1 *(encargado)* person in charge. 2 *(de un crimen)* perpetrator, culprit, person responsible. ■ **hacerse responsable de** ALGO to assume responsibility for STH.

responso *nm* 1 REL *prayer for the dead.* 2 *fam (reprimenda)* ticking-off.

respuesta *nf* 1 *(gen)* answer, reply. 2 *(reacción)* response. ■ **en respuesta a** in response to.

resquebrajar *vt* to crack.
▷ *vpr* **resquebrajarse** to crack.

resquemor *nm* resentment, ill feeling.

resquicio *nm* 1 *(abertura)* crack, chink. 2 *fig* glimmer; *(oportunidad)* chance; *(posibilidad)* possibility, chance: **un resquicio de esperanza** *a glimmer of hope;*

resta *nf* subtraction.

restablecer [43] *vt (gen)* to reestablish; *(orden, monarquía)* to restore.
▷ *vpr* **restablecerse** 1 *(gen)* to be reestablished; *(orden, etc)* to be restored. 2 MED to recover, get better.

restablecimiento *nm* 1 *(gen)* reestablishment; *(orden, etc)* restoration. 2 MED recovery.

restallar *vi* 1 *(látigo)* to crack. 2 *(hacer ruido)* to crackle.

restallido *nm* crack.

restante *adj* remaining.
▷ *nm* **lo restante** the rest, the remainder, what is left over.

restañar *vt* to staunch.

restar *vt* 1 MAT to subtract, take (away). 2 *fig (quitar)* to reduce, deduct. 3 DEP to return.
▷ *vi (quedar)* to be left, remain. ■ **restar importancia a** ALGO to play STH down, play down the importance of STH.

restauración *nf (restablecimiento)* restoration.

restaurante *nm* restaurant.

restaurar *vt (obra, etc)* to restore.

restitución *nf* restitution.

restituir [62] *vt* 1 *(restablecer)* to restore. 2 *(devolver)* to return, give back.

resto *nm* 1 remainder, rest. 2 MAT remainder.
▷ *nm pl* **restos** 1 *(gen)* remains; *(ruinas)* ruins. 2 *(de comida)* leftovers.

restregar [48] *vt* 1 *(frotar)* to rub hard. 2 *(fregar)* to scrub.

restricción *nf* restriction.

restrictivo,-a *adj* restrictive.

restringir [6] *vt* 1 *(limitar)* to restrict, limit. 2 *(astringir)* to contract.

resucitar *vt* 1 to resuscitate. 2 *fig* to revive.
▷ *vi* to resuscitate.

resuello *nm* 1 *(acción)* breathing. 2 *(aliento)* breath, gasp.

resuelto,-a *adj (decidido)* resolute, determined.

resulta *nf* consequence. ■ **de resultas de** as a result of.

resultado *nm* result.

resultante *adj* resultant.

resultar *vi* 1 *(gen)* to result, be the result of. 2 *(ser)* to be: **resultó vencedor** *he won.* 3 *(acabar siendo)* to turn out to be: **resultó ser muy agradable** *he turned out to be very nice.* 4 *(salir)* to come out, turn out, work out: **todo resultó como esperábamos** *it all worked out as we expected.* 5 *(ocurrir)* to turn out: **resulta que está enfermo y no puede venir** *it turns out that he's ill and can't come.* 6 *(ser conveniente)* to be advisable. 7 *(tener éxito)* to be a success, come off: **el negocio resultó** *the business was a success.* ■ **resulta que** it turns out that.

resumen *nm* summary.

resumir *vt* 1 *(reducir)* to summarize. 2 *(concluir)* to sum up: **resumiendo, es una novela excelente** *in short, it's an excellent novel.*
▷ *vpr* **resumirse** 1 to be summarized, be summed up. 2 *(venir a ser)* to be reduced (**en**, to), boil down (**en**, to).

resurgir [6] *vi* 1 *(volver a aparecer)* to reappear. 2 *(revivir)* to revive.

resurrección *nf* resurrection.

retablo *nm* altarpiece, reredos.

retaco *nm fam fig (persona)* shorty, dumpling.

retador,-ra *adj* challenging.

retaguarda *nf* rearguard. ■ **ir a la retaguarda** to bring up the rear.

retahíla *nf* string, series: **una retahíla de chistes** *a series of jokes.*

retal *nm (de tela)* offcut, remnant.

retama *nf* broom.

retapizar [4] *vt* to reupholster.

retar *vt* 1 *(desafiar)* to challenge. 2 *fam (reprender)* to scold.

retardado,-a *adj* delayed, retarded: **de efecto retardado** *delayed-action.*

retardar *vt* 1 *(detener)* to slow down; *(retrasar)* to delay. 2 *(posponer)* to postpone.

retazo *nm* remnant, fragment.

retén *nm* MIL reserves *pl,* reinforcements *pl.*

retención *nf* 1 *(gen)* retention. 2 FIN withholding, deduction. 3 *(de tráfico)* traffic jam, (traffic) hold-up.
retener [87] *vt* 1 *(contener)* to restrain, hold back. 2 *(no dejar marchar)* to keep, keep back: **no quiero retenerte** *I don't want to keep you.* 3 *(no devolver)* to keep. 4 *(en la memoria)* to retain, remember. 5 *(detener)* to detain; *(arrestar)* to arrest. 6 FIN to deduct, withhold. 7 *(absorber)* to retain, hold: **el algodón retiene el agua** *cotton holds water.*
▷ *vpr* **retenerse** to restrain OS, hold OS back.
retentiva *nf* retentiveness, memory.
reticencia *nf* 1 *(reserva)* reticence, reserve. 2 *(insinuación)* insinuation, innuendo.
reticente *adj* insinuating.
retícula *nf* reticle.
reticular *adj* reticular.
retina *nf* retina.
retintín *nm fig* innuendo, sarcastic tone.
retirada *nf* MIL retreat, withdrawal.
retirado,-a *adj* 1 *(apartado)* remote. 2 *(tranquilo)* secluded, quiet. 3 *(jubilado)* retired.
▷ *nm & nf* retired person, US retiree.
retirar *vt* 1 *(apartar - gen)* to take away, remove; *(- un mueble)* to move away. 2 *(un carnet)* to take away. 3 *(algo dicho)* to take back. 4 *(dinero, ley, moneda)* to withdraw. 5 *(jubilar)* to retire.
▷ *vpr* **retirarse** 1 MIL to retreat, withdraw. 2 *(apartarse del mundo)* to go into seclusion. 3 *(apartarse)* to withdraw, draw back, move back: **retírate, no veo** *move back, I can't see.* 4 *(alejarse)* to move away: **retírate de la ventana** *move away from the window.* 5 *(irse a descansar)* to retire: **se retiró a su habitación** *she retired to her bedroom.* 6 *(jubilarse)* to retire. ■ **no se retire** *(al teléfono)* hold on, don't hang up.
retiro *nm* 1 *(jubilación)* retirement. 2 *(pensión)* pension.
reto *nm* challenge.
retocar [1] *vt (dibujo, fotografía)* to touch up, retouch.
retomar *vt* 1 *(territorio)* to retake. 2 *(tema)* to return to.
retoñar *vi (rebrotar)* to shoot, sprout.
retoño *nm* 1 BOT sprout, shoot. 2 *fig* kid.
retoque *nm* finishing touch.
retorcer [54] *vt* 1 *(gen)* to twist. 2 *(ropa)* to wring (out).
▷ *vpr* **retorcerse** 1 *(gen)* to become twisted, twist. 2 *(doblarse)* to bend. ■ **retorcerse de risa** *fig* to double up with laughter.
retorcido,-a *adj fig* twisted.
retórica *nf* rhetoric.
retórico,-a *adj* rhetorical.
retornable *adj* returnable. ■ **«Envase no retornable»** «Non-returnable».
retornar *vt (restituir)* to return, give back.
retorno *nm* 1 return. 2 *(recompensa)* reward.
retortijón *nm (de tripas)* stomach cramp.
retozar [4] *vi* to frolic, gambol.
retozo *nm* frolic.
retozón,-ona *adj* frolicsome, playful.
retractar *vt* to retract, revoke, withdraw.
▷ *vpr* **retractarse** to retract, take back.
retráctil *adj* 1 *(uña, etc)* retractile. 2 *(tren de aterrizaje)* retractable.
retraer [88] *vt (reprochar)* to reproach: **le retrajo sus faltas** *she reproached him for his faults.*
▷ *vpr* **retraerse** 1 *(apartarse)* to be dissuaded. 2 *(refugiarse)* to take refuge.
retraído,-a *adj* 1 *(tímido)* shy, reserved. 2 *(poco comunicativo)* unsociable, withdrawn.
retraimiento *nm (timidez)* shyness, retiring nature.
retransmisión *nf* broadcast, transmission.
retransmisor *nm* transmitter.
retransmitir *vt* RAD TV to broadcast. ■ **retransmitir ALGO en directo** to broadcast STH live.
retrasado,-a *adj* 1 *(en conocimientos, trabajo)* behind. 2 *(pagos)* late. 3 *(reloj)* slow. 4 *(tren, avión, etc)* delayed. 5 *(país)* backward, underdeveloped.
▷ *nm & nf* mentally retarded person.
retrasar *vt* 1 *(atrasar)* to delay, put off, postpone. 2 *(reloj)* to put back. 3 DEP to pass back.
▷ *vpr* **retrasarse** 1 *(atrasarse)* to be late, arrive late, be delayed. 2 *(reloj)* to be slow. 3 *(trabajo, conocimientos, pagos)* to fall behind.
retraso *nm* 1 *(demora)* delay. 2 *(subdesarrollo)* backwardness, underdevelopment.
retratar *vt* 1 *(pintura)* to portray, paint a portrait of. 2 *(foto)* to photograph, take a photograph of. 3 *fig* to describe, portray, depict.
▷ *vpr* **retratarse** *(darse a conocer)* to be described.
retratista *nm o nf* 1 *(pintor)* portrait painter, portrait artist. 2 *(fotógrafo)* photographer.
retrato *nm* 1 *(pintura)* portrait. 2 *(foto)* photograph. 3 *fig (descripción)* description, depiction, portrayal. ■ **ser el vivo retrato de ALGN** to be the spitting image of SB.
retrete *nm* toilet, lavatory.
retribución *nf* 1 *(pago)* pay, payment. 2 *(recompensa)* recompense, reward.
retribuir [62] *vt* 1 *(pagar)* to pay. 2 *(recompensar)* to remunerate, reward.
retributivo,-a *adj* retributive.
retro *adj inv* 1 *fam (reaccionario)* reactionary. 2 *fam (del pasado)* old-fashioned.
retroactivo,-a *adj* retroactive: **ley con efecto retroactivo** *retroactive law.*
retroalimentación *nf* feedback.
retroceder *vi* 1 *(recular)* to go back, move back. 2 *(bajar de nivel)* to go down.
retroceso *nm* 1 *(movimiento)* backward movement. 2 *(económico)* recession.
retrógrado,-a *adj* 1 *(que retrocede)* retrograde. 2 *fig (reaccionario)* reactionary.
▷ *nm & nf (reaccionario)* reactionary.
retroproyector *nm* overhead projector.
retrospección *nf* retrospection.
retrospectivo,-a *adj* retrospective.
retrotraer [88] *vt* to predate.
retumbante *adj* 1 resounding. 2 *fig* ostentatious, pretentious.
retumbar *vi* 1 *(resonar)* to resound, echo. 2 *(tronar)* to thunder, boom.
retumbo *nm (sordo)* rumble; *(estruendoso)* boom.
reuma *nm* rheumatism.
reúma *nm* rheumatism.
reumático,-a *adj* rheumatic.
▷ *nm & nf* rheumatic.
reumatismo *nm* rheumatism.
reumatología *nf* rheumatology.

reumatólogo,-a *nm & nf* rheumatologist.
reunificación *nf* reunification.
reunificar [1] *vt* to reunify.
reunión *nf (gen)* meeting, gathering.
reunir [19] *vt* **1** *(congregar)* get together. **2** *(juntar algo)* to put together: **reunimos todos nuestros libros** *we put all our books together.* **3** *(recoger)* to gather (together); *(dinero)* to raise. **4** *(coleccionar)* to collect. **5** *(tener)* to have, possess. **6** *(requisitos)* to satisfy, meet, fulfil (US fulfill).
▷ *vpr* **reunirse** to meet (**con**, -), get together, have a meeting with.
reurbanizar [4] *vt* to redevelop.
reutilizable *adj* reusable.
reutilizar [4] *vt* to reuse.
reválida *nf* final examination.
revalidar *vt* to confirm, ratify, validate.
revalorización *nf (de moneda)* revaluation; *(de precio)* appreciation, increase in value.
revalorizar [4] *vt (moneda)* to revalue; *(precio)* to increase the value of.
▷ *vpr* **revalorizarse** *(moneda)* to revalue; *(precio)* to appreciate, go up in value.
revaluar *vt* to revalue.
revancha *nf* **1** revenge. **2** *(en naipes)* return game. **3** DEP return match.
revanchismo *nm* revanchism.
revanchista *adj* revanchist.
▷ *nm o nf* revanchist.
revelación *nf* revelation.
revelado *nm* developing.
revelador,-ra *adj* revealing.
▷ *nm* **revelador** developer.
revelar *vt* **1** to reveal, disclose. **2** *(fotos)* to develop.
revendedor,-ra *nm & nf (de entradas)* ticket tout, US scalper.
revender *vt* **1** *(gen)* to resell. **2** *(al por menor)* to retail. **3** *(entradas)* to tout.
reventa *nf* **1** *(gen)* resale. **2** *(al por menor)* retail. **3** *(de entradas)* touting.
reventar [27] *vt* **1** *(gen)* to burst. **2** *(neumático)* to puncture, burst. **3** *(romper)* to break, smash. **4** *(estropear)* to ruin, spoil. **5** *fig (agotar)* to exhaust, tire out.
▷ *vi* **1** *fam (fastidiar)* to annoy: **me revientan sus preguntas** *her questions get on my nerves.* **2** *(estallar)* to burst: **la cañería reventó** *the pipe burst.*
▷ *vpr* **reventarse 1** *(estallar)* to burst. **2** *fam (cansarse)* to tire OS out.
reventón,-ona *nm* **1** *(de cañería)* burst. **2** *(de neumático)* blowout.
reverberación *nf* reverberation, reflection.
reverberar *vi* to reverberate, reflect.
reverdecer [43] *vi* **1** to grow green again. **2** *fig* to revive.
reverencia *nf* **1** *(respeto)* reverence. **2** *(gesto)* bow.
reverenciar [12] *vt* to revere, venerate.
reverendo,-a *adj* **1** reverend. **2** *fam (enorme)* enormous, great.
▷ *nm & nf* reverend.
reverente *adj* reverent.
reversible *adj* reversible.
reverso *nm* reverse, back.
revertir [35] *vi* **1** *(volver)* to revert, return, go back. **2** *(resultar)* to result (**en**, in).
revés *nm* **1** *(reverso)* back, reverse, wrong side; *(de tela)* wrong side. **2** *(bofetada)* slap; *(golpe)* backhander. **3** *(en tenis)* backhand (stroke). **4** *fig (contrariedad)* misfortune, setback, reverse. ■ **al revés** *(al contrario)* the other way round.
revestimiento *nm* covering, coating.
revestir [34] *vt* **1** *(recubrir)* to cover (**de**, with), coat (**de**, with), line (**de**, with). **2** *fig (presentar)* to take on.
▷ *vpr* **revestirse** to arm OS: **revestirse de paciencia** *to arm OS with patience.*
revisar *vt* **1** *(gen)* to revise, go through, check. **2** *(examen, etc)* to check, look over. **3** *(cuentas)* to check, audit.
revisión *nf* **1** *(gen)* revision, checking. **2** *(de billetes)* inspection. **3** *(de coche)* service, overhaul. ● **revisión médica** checkup.
revisionismo *nm* revisionism.
revisionista *adj* revisionist.
▷ *nm o nf* revisionist.
revisor,-ra *nm & nf* ticket inspector.
revista *nf* **1** *(publicación)* magazine, review, journal. **2** *(inspección)* inspection. **3** MIL review. **4** TEAT revue.
revistero *nm* magazine rack.
revitalización *nf* revitalization.
revitalizar [4] *vt* to revitalize.
revivificar [1] *vt* to revivify, revive.
revivir *vi* **1** to revive.
▷ *vt* to revive, bring back to life.
revocable *adj* revocable.
revocar [1] *vt (ley)* to revoke; *(orden)* to cancel, rescind.
revolcar [49] *vt (derribar al suelo)* to knock down, knock over.
▷ *vpr* **revolcarse** *(echarse)* to roll about.
revolotear *vi* to fly about, flutter about, hover.
revoloteo *nm* fluttering, hovering.
revoltijo *nm (mezcla)* mess, clutter, jumble.
revoltillo *nm* → **revoltijo.**
revoltoso,-a *adj* **1** *(rebelde)* rebellious.
▷ *nm & nf* rebel, troublemaker.
revolución *nf* revolution.
revolucionar *vt* to revolutionize.
revolucionario,-a *adj* revolutionary.
▷ *nm & nf* revolutionary.
revolver [32] *vt* **1** *(agitar)* to stir. **2** *(mezclar)* to mix. **3** *(ensalada)* to toss. **4** *(habitación, casa, etc)* to turn upside down. **5** *(papeles)* to rummage through; *(bolso, bolsillo, etc)* to rummage in. **6** *(producir náuseas)* to upset, turn: **le revolvió el estómago** *it turned his stomach.*
▷ *vpr* **revolverse 1** *(moverse)* to fidget. **2** *(volverse con rapidez)* to turn around, spin round. **3** *(tiempo)* to turn stormy; *(mar)* to become rough.
revólver *nm* revolver.
revoque *nm (enlucido)* plastering.
revuelo *nm* **1** *(revoloteo)* fluttering. **2** *fig* commotion, stir.
revuelta *nf (revolución)* revolt, riot.
revuelto,-a *adj* **1** *(desordenado)* confused, mixed up, in a mess. **2** *(gente)* agitated, restless, up in arms. **3** *(tiempo)* stormy, unsettled; *(mar)* rough. **4** *(época)* turbulent: **tiempos revueltos** *turbulent times.*
revulsivo,-a *adj* revulsive.
rey *nm* king.
reyerta *nf* quarrel, row, fight.
rezagado,-a *nm & nf* straggler, latecomer.

rezagar [7] *vt (atrasar)* to delay, put off, postpone.
▷ *vpr* **rezagarse** to fall behind, lag behind.
rezar [4] *vi* 1 *(orar)* to pray. 2 *(decir)* to say, read.
rezo *nm* 1 *(acción)* praying. 2 *(oración)* prayer.
rezongar [7] *vi fam fig* to grumble, moan.
rezongón,-ona *nm & nf fam* grumbler, griper.
rezumar *vt* 1 *(transpirar)* to ooze. 2 *fig* to exude, ooze: **rezumar alegría** *to ooze happiness.*
ría *nf (gen)* estuary, river mouth; *(técnicamente)* ria.
riachuelo *nm* brook, stream.
riada *nf* 1 flood, flooding. 2 *fig* flood.
ribazo *nm* embankment, bank.
ribera *nf* 1 *(de río)* bank. 2 *(del mar)* shore, seashore. 3 *(tierra cercana a un río)* riverside, waterfront.
ribereño,-a *adj* riverside, waterfront.
▷ *nm & nf* riverside dweller, waterfront dweller.
ribete *nm (cinta)* border, trimming, edging.
ribeteado,-a *adj* edged, bordered.
ribetear *vt* to edge, border.
ribonucleico,-a *adj* ribonucleic.
ricachón,-ona *nm & nf fam* moneybags.
ricamente *adv* 1 *(con riquezas)* richly. 2 *fam (estupendamente)* very well.
ricino *nm* castor-oil plant.
rico,-a *adj* 1 *(acaudalado)* rich, wealthy. 2 *(abundante)* rich: **rico en potasio** *rich in potassium.* 3 *(sabroso)* tasty, delicious. 4 *(tierra)* rich, fertile. 5 *(excelente)* rich, excellent. 6 *fam (bonito)* lovely, adorable: **tiene un niño muy rico** *she's got a lovely boy.*
▷ *nm & nf* rich person.
ridiculez *nf* 1 *(cualidad)* ridiculousness. 2 *(cosa, hecho)* ridiculous thing, ridiculous action.
ridiculizar [4] *vt* to ridicule, deride.
ridículo,-a *adj* ridiculous, absurd.
▷ *nm* **ridículo** ridicule. ■ **hacer el ridículo** to make a fool of OS.
riego *nm* irrigation, watering. ● **riego sanguíneo** blood circulation.
riel *nm* rail.
rielar *vi lit* to shimmer, gleam.
rienda *nf* 1 rein. 2 *fig (control)* restraint. ■ **llevar las riendas** *fig* to hold the reins, be in control.
riesgo *nm* risk, danger. ■ **a todo riesgo** *(seguro)* fully-comprehensive.
rifa *nf* raffle.
rifar *vt* to raffle (off).
▷ *vpr* **rifarse** 1 MAR to split. 2 *(solicitar, desear)* to fight over.
rifle *nm* rifle.
rigidez *nf* 1 *(dureza)* stiffness, rigidity. 2 *fig (rectitud)* strictness, firmness, inflexibility.
▲ *pl* **rigideces.**
rígido,-a *adj* 1 *(duro)* rigid, stiff. 2 *fig (severo)* strict, firm, inflexible.
rigor *nm* 1 *(severidad)* rigour (US rigor), strictness, severity. 2 *(dureza)* rigour (US rigor), harshness. 3 *(exactitud)* precision, exactness.
rigurosamente *adv* 1 *(con severidad)* rigorously, severely, strictly. 2 *(con exactitud)* accurately. 3 *(minuciosamente)* meticulously. 4 *(totalmente)* absolutely.
rigurosidad *nf* rigorousness, strictness.
riguroso,-a *adj* 1 *(severo)* rigorous, severe, strict. 2 *(clima)* rigorous, severe, harsh. 3 *(exacto)* exact. 4 *(minucioso)* meticulous.
rima *nf* rhyme.
▷ *nf pl* **rimas** poem *sing.*
rimar *vt* to rhyme.
▷ *vi* to rhyme.
rimbombante *adj (lenguaje)* pretentious, pompous.
rímel® *nm* mascara.
rincón *nm* corner.
rinconera *nf* corner unit.
ring *nm* ring.
▲ *pl* **rings.**
rinitis *nf inv* rhinitis.
rinoceronte *nm* rhinoceros.
riña *nf* 1 *(pelea)* fight. 2 *(discusión)* quarrel.
riñón *nm* kidney.
riñonera *nf* 1 *(faja)* back support. 2 *(bolsa)* bum bag.
río *nm* 1 river. 2 *fig* stream, river: **un río de sangre** *a river of blood.*
riostra *nf* brace, strut.
ripio *nm (palabrería)* padding, verbiage, waffle.
riqueza *nf (cualidad)* richness, wealthiness.
risa *nf* 1 laugh. 2 *(risas)* laughter. ■ **darle risa a ALGN** to make SB laugh. ■ **entrar la risa** to begin to laugh. ● **ataque de risa** fit of laughter.
risco *nm* crag, cliff.
risilla *nf* giggle, titter; *(falsa)* false laugh.
risotada *nf* guffaw.
ristra *nf* string.
ristre ■ **en ristre** at the ready.
risueño,-a *adj* 1 *(sonriente)* smiling. 2 *(animado)* cheerful.
rítmico,-a *adj* rhythmic, rhythmical.
ritmo *nm* 1 rhythm. 2 *fig* pace, speed.
rito *nm* 1 REL rite. 2 *fig (costumbre)* ritual.
ritual *adj* ritual.
▷ *nm* ritual.
rival *adj* rival.
▷ *nm o nf* rival.
rivalidad *nf* rivalry.
rivalizar [4] *vi* to rival.
rivera *nf* brook, stream.
rizado,-a *adj* 1 *(pelo)* curly. 2 MAR choppy.
▷ *nm* **rizado** *(de pelo)* curling.
rizador *nm* curling tongs *pl*, curling iron.
rizar [4] *vt (pelo)* to curl.
▷ *vpr* **rizarse** 1 *(pelo)* to curl, go curly. 2 *(el mar)* to ripple.
rizo *nm* 1 *(de pelo)* curl. 2 *(en el agua)* ripple. 3 *(tejido)* towelling (US toweling), terry towelling. 4 AV loop.
rizoma *nm* rhizome.
rizópodo *nm* rhizopod.
rizoso,-a *adj* naturally curly.
robalo *nm* bass.
róbalo *nm* bass.
robar *vt* 1 *(banco, persona)* to rob; *(objeto)* to steal; *(casa)* to break into, burgle. 2 *(raptar)* to kidnap. 3 *(en naipes)* to draw. 4 *fig (cobrar muy caro)* to rip off. 5 *fig (corazón, alma)* to steal.
robinia *nf* robinia, false acacia.
roble *nm* oak, oak tree.
robledal *nm* oak grove, oak wood.
robledo *nm* oak grove, oak wood.

robo *nm* 1 *(gen)* theft, robbery; *(en casa)* burglary; *(en banco)* robbery. 2 *(en naipes)* draw. 3 *fig (estafa)* robbery.
robot *nm* robot.
robótica *nf* robotics.
robótico,-a *adj* robotic, robot-like.
robotizar *vt* to automate.
robustecer [43] *vt* to strengthen.
▷ *vpr* **robustecerse** to grow stronger, gain strength.
robustez *nf* robustness, strength, sturdiness.
robusto,-a *adj* robust, strong, sturdy.
roca *nf* rock.
rocalla *nf* pebbles *pl*, stone chippings *pl*.
rocambolesco,-a *adj fam* incredible.
roce *nm* 1 *(fricción)* rubbing; *(en piel)* chafing. 2 *(señal - en zapatos)* scuff mark; *(- en piel)* graze; *(- en coche, etc)* mark. 3 *(contacto físico)* light touch, brush. 4 *fam (trato)* contact. 5 *fam (disensión)* friction, brush.
rociada *nf* 1 *(acción)* spraying, sprinkling. 2 *(rocío)* dew.
rociador *nm (para la ropa)* spray; *(para el jardín, incendios)* sprinkler.
rociar [13] *vt* 1 *(salpicar)* to spray, sprinkle. 2 *fig (esparcir)* to scatter, strew.
rocín *nm (caballo)* nag, hack.
rocinante *nm fig* nag, hack.
rocío *nm* dew.
rock *nm* rock.
rockero,-a *nm & nf (músico)* rock musician; *(fan)* rock fan.
rococó *adj* rococo.
rocoso,-a *adj* rocky, stony.
roda *nf* stem.
rodaballo *nm* turbot.
rodada *nf* tyre mark, (US tyre mark).
rodado,-a *adj* 1 AUTO *(que tiene ruedas)* wheeled, on wheels; *(que ha pasado el rodaje)* run-in. 2 *(piedra)* rounded, smooth. 3 *fig (persona)* experienced.
rodaja *nf* slice. ■ **en rodajas** sliced.
rodaje *nm* 1 CINE filming, shooting. 2 AUTO running-in.
rodamiento *nm* bearing.
rodante *adj* rolling.
rodapié *nm* skirting board, US baseboard.
rodar [31] *vi* 1 *(dar vueltas)* to roll; *(rueda)* to turn. 2 *(caer rodando)* to roll down. 3 *fig (ir de un lado a otro)* to roam. 4 *(vehículos)* to run; *(velocidad)* to do.
▷ *vt* 1 *(hacer que de vueltas)* to roll. 2 CINE to film, shoot. 3 AUTO to run in. 4 *(recorrer)* to travel.
rodear *vt (cercar)* to surround, encircle.
▷ *vpr* **rodearse** to surround OS (**de**, with).
rodela *nf* round shield.
rodeno,-a *adj* red.
rodeo *nm* 1 *(desviación)* detour. 2 *fig (elusión)* evasiveness.
rodera *nf* tyre (US tire) mark, track.
rodete *nm* 1 *(de pelo)* bun, chignon. 2 *(para llevar peso en la cabeza)* (ring-shaped) pad.
rodilla *nf* 1 ANAT knee. 2 *(paño)* cloth, floorcloth.
rodillazo *nm* blow with the knee, blow to the knee.
rodillera *nf* 1 DEP knee pad. 2 COST knee patch.
rodillo *nm* 1 roller. 2 CULIN rolling pin.
rodio *nm* rhodium.
rododendro *nm* rhododendron.
rodomiel *nm* rose honey.
rodrigón *nm* stake, stick.
roedor,-ra *adj* rodent.
▷ *nm* **roedor** rodent.
roedura *nf (señal)* gnaw mark.
roela *nf* blank.
roer [82] *vt* 1 *(hueso)* to gnaw. 2 *fig (desgastar)* to wear away.
rogar [52] *vt (pedir)* to request, ask; *(implorar)* to beg, implore, plead.
rogativa *nf* rogation.
roído,-a *adj* gnawed, eaten away.
rojear *vi* to redden, turn red.
rojez *nf* redness.
rojiblanco,-a *adj* red-and-white.
rojizo,-a *adj* reddish.
rojo,-a *adj (color)* red.
▷ *nm & nf* POL *(gen)* red, Communist.
▷ *nm* **rojo** red.
rol *nm (papel)* role.
▲ *pl* **roles**.
rollista *nm o nf fam (cuentista)* over-dramatic person.
rollizo,-a *adj* plump, chubby.
rollo *nm* 1 *(gen)* roll. 2 *fam (aburrimiento)* drag, bore, pain: **esta peli es un rollo** *this film is a drag.* 3 *fam (discurso, explicación, etc)* long drawn-out speech, boring lecture. 4 *fam (amorío)* affair. 5 *fam (asunto)* business.
romance *adj* LING Romance.
▷ *nm* 1 LING *(gen)* Romance language; *(castellano)* Spanish. 2 *(amorío)* romance.
romancero *nm* collection of romances.
romaní *nm o nf* gipsy, gypsy.
románico,-a *adj* 1 *(arquitectura, arte - gen)* Romanesque. 2 *(lengua)* Romance.
romanismo *nm* Romanism.
romanista *nm & nf* Romanist.
romanizar [4] *vt* to Romanize.
romanticismo *nm* romanticism.
romántico,-a *adj* romantic.
▷ *nm & nf* romantic.
romanza *nf* romance.
rómbico,-a *adj* rhombic.
rombo *nm* 1 rhombus. 2 *(naipes)* diamond.
romboedro *nm* rhombohedron.
romboide *nm* rhomboid.
romeo *nm* Romeo.
romería *nf* pilgrimage.
romero *nm* BOT rosemary.
romo,-a *adj (sin punta)* blunt, dull.
rompecabezas *nm inv* 1 *(juego)* (jigsaw) puzzle. 2 *fig (problema)* riddle, puzzle, conundrum.
rompecocos *nm inv* brain-teaser.
rompecorazones *nm o nf inv fam* heart-throb, heartbreaker.
rompedera *nf* punch.
rompehielos *nm inv* icebreaker.
rompehuelgas *nm o nf inv* strikebreaker.
rompeolas *nm inv* breakwater, jetty.
romper *vt* 1 *(gen)* to break; *(papel, tela)* to tear; 2 *(rajar, reventar)* to split. 3 *(gastar)* to wear out. 4 *fig (relaciones)* to break off. 5 *fig (ley)* to break. 6 *fig (cerca, límite)* to break through, break down.

▷ *vi* 1 *fig (acabar - con algo)* to break; *(- con alguien)* to split up, US break up. 2 *(olas, día)* to break. 3 **romper a** + *inf fig (empezar)* to burst out: **romper a reír** *to burst out laughing.* 4 **romper en** + *sust fig (prorrumpir)* to burst into: **romper en llanto** *to burst into tears.*

▷ *vpr* **romperse** 1 *(gen)* to break: **se me ha roto esta uña** *I've broken this nail.* 2 *(papel, tela)* to tear, rip. 3 *(rajarse, reventarse)* to split. 4 *(desgastarse)* to wear out: **se me han roto los zapatos** *my shoes are worn out.* 5 *(coche)* to break down.

rompetechos *nm o nf inv fam fig* shorty, dumpling.

rompible *adj* breakable.

rompiente *nm* reef, shoal.

rompimiento *nm* 1 *(rotura)* breaking, breakage. 2 *fig (relación)* breaking-off.

ron *nm* rum.

roncamente *adv* roughly, coarsely.

roncar [1] *vi* to snore.

roncha *nf (en la piel)* swelling, lump, spot.

ronco,-a *adj* hoarse.

ronda *nf* 1 *(patrulla)* patrol, watch. 2 *(de policía)* beat. 3 *(vuelta)* round. 4 *(de bebidas, cartas)* round. 5 *(negociaciones)* round. ■ **hacer la ronda** to do one's rounds.

rondalla *nf* MÚS group of strolling minstrels.

rondar *vt* 1 *(vigilar)* to patrol, do the rounds of. 2 *(merodear)* to prowl around, hang about, haunt: **siempre ronda la casa** *he's always prowling around the house.* 3 *fig (años)* to be about: **ronda los cincuenta** *she's about fifty.*

▷ *vi* 1 *(vigilar)* to patrol. 2 *(merodear)* to prowl around, roam around.

rondel *nm* rondel.

ronquear *vi* to be hoarse.

ronquedad *nf* joarseness.

ronquera *nf* hoarseness.

ronquido *nm* snore, snoring.

ronronear *vi* to purr.

ronroneo *nm* purring.

ronzal *nm* halter.

ronzar[1] [4] *vt* to crunch, munch.

ronzar[2] [4] *vt* MAR to lever.

roña *nf (suciedad)* filth, dirt.

roñería *nf fam* meanness, stinginess.

roñica *nm o nf fam* scrooge, miser.

roñoso,-a *adj* 1 *(sucio)* filthy, dirty. 2 *fam (tacaño)* mean, stingy.

▷ *nm & nf fam* scrooge, miser.

ropa *nf* clothing, clothes *pl*: **ropa de invierno** *winter clothes;* **ropa de esquí** *ski wear.* ● **ropa blanca** linen, household linen. **ropa interior** underwear.

ropaje *nm* robes *pl*, apparel.

ropavejero,-a *nm & nf* second-hand clothes dealer.

ropero *nm* wardrobe, US closet.

roque *nm* rook. ■ **estar roque** *fam* to be asleep.

roqueda *nf* rocky place.

roquedal *nm* rocky place.

roquedo *nm* rock.

roquefort *nm (específicamente)* Roquefort; *(en general)* blue cheese.

roqueño,-a *adj* 1 *(lleno de rocas)* rocky. 2 *(duro)* hard.

roquero,-a *adj-nm & nf* → **rockero,-a**.

rorro *nm fam* baby.

rosa *nf (flor)* rose.

▷ *nm (color)* pink.

▷ *adj* 1 *(color)* pink. 2 *fig (novela)* romantic. ■ **fresco,-a como una rosa** *fig* as fresh as a daisy.

rosáceo,-a *adj* rose-coloured (US rose-colored), rosy.

rosado,-a *adj* 1 *(color)* rosy, pink. 2 *(vino)* rosé.

▷ *nm* **rosado** *(vino)* rosé.

rosal *nm* rosebush.

rosaleda *nf* rose garden.

rosario *nm* 1 REL rosary, beads *pl.* 2 *fig* string, series: **rosario de mentiras** *string of lies.* ■ **rezar el rosario** to say the rosary.

rosbif *nm* roast beef.

rosca *nf* 1 *(de tornillo)* thread. 2 CULIN doughnut. 3 *(carnosidad)* roll of fat. 4 *(anilla)* ring.

rosco *nm* ring-shaped bread roll.

roscón *nm* ring-shaped pastry; *(de Pascua)* Easter ring.

rosetón *nm* rose window.

rosquilla *nf* doughnut, ring-shaped pastry.

rostro *nm fml (cara)* face.

rotación *nf* rotation.

rotativa *nf* rotary press.

rotativo,-a *adj* rotary, revolving.

▷ *nm* **rotativo** newspaper.

rotatorio,-a *adj* rotary, rotating, revolving.

roto,-a *adj* 1 *(gen)* broken. 2 *(tela, papel)* torn. 3 *(gastado)* worn out. 4 *(cansado)* tired.

▷ *nm* **roto** *(agujero)* hole, tear.

rotonda *nf* 2 *(plaza)* roundabout, US traffic circle.

rotor *nm* rotor.

rótula *nf* ANAT kneecap.

rotulación *nf* lettering, labelling.

rotulador *nm* felt-tip pen.

rotular *vt* to label.

rotulista *nm o nf* signwriter.

rótulo *nm* 1 *(letrero)* sign; *(luminoso)* neon sign. 2 *(titular)* heading, title.

rotundamente *adv* 1 *(negar)* flatly, categorically. 2 *(afirmar)* emphatically.

rotundidad *nf* firmness.

rotundo,-a *adj* 1 *(redondo)* round. 2 *fig (éxito)* resounding. 3 *(negativa)* flat, categorical; *(afirmación)* categorical, emphatic: **un no rotundo** *a flat refusal.*

rotura *nf* 1 *(gen)* break, breaking, crack. 2 *(en tela, papel)* tear, rip. 3 MED fracture.

roturación *nf* ploughing (US plowing).

roturadora *nf* plough (US plow).

roturar *vt* to plough (US plow).

roulotte *nf* caravan.

rozadura *nf* scratch, abrasion.

rozagante *adj* 1 *(vestido)* showy. 2 *fig* splendid.

rozamiento *nm (roce)* rubbing, friction.

rozar [4] *vt* 1 *(tocar ligeramente)* to touch lightly, brush. 2 *(raspar)* to rub against, brush against; *(herir)* to graze: **el zapato me roza el pie** *my shoe's rubbing my foot.*

▷ *vi* 1 *(raspar)* to rub. 2 *fig (tener relación)* to border (**con**, on), verge (**con**, on).

▷ *vpr* **rozarse** 1 *(rasparse)* to rub (**con**, against), brush (**con**, against). 2 *(desgastarse)* to wear (out). 3 *fig (tratarse)* to come into contact (**con**, with), rub shoulders (**con**, with).

r.p.m. *abrev* **(revoluciones por minuto)** revolutions per minute; *(abreviatura)* rpm.
rúa *nf* street.
Ruanda *nf* Rwanda.
ruandés,-esa *adj* Rwandan.
▷ *nm & nf* Rwandan.
rubeola *nf* German measles, rubella.
rubéola *nf* German measles, rubella.
rubí *nm* ruby.
▲ *pl* **rubíes.**
rubia *nf* blonde.
rubiales *nm o nf inv fam* blondie.
rubicán,-ana *adj* roan.
rubicundo,-a *adj* rosy, rubicund, reddish.
rubidio *nm* rubidium.
rubio,-a *adj* **1** *(cabello)* fair; *(persona)* fair-haired; *(hombre)* blond; *(mujer)* blonde. **2** *(tabaco)* Virginia.
▷ *nm & nf (hombre)* blond; *(mujer)* blonde.
rublo *nm* rouble.
rubor *nm* blush, flush.
ruborizarse [4] *vpr* to blush, go red, redden.
rúbrica *nf* **1** *(de firma)* flourish (in signature). **2** *(título)* title, heading.
rubricar [1] *vt* **1** *(firmar)* to sign with a flourish. **2** *(respaldar)* to endorse, ratify.
rubro,-a *adj fml* red.
rucio,-a *adj (pardo)* grey.
▷ *nm & nf (asno)* donkey.
ruda *nf* rue.
rudeza *nf* roughness, coarseness.
rudimentario,-a *adj* rudimentary.
rudimento *nm* rudiment.
rudo,-a *adj* rough, coarse.
rueca *nf* distaff.
rueda *nf* **1** *(gen)* wheel: **de cuatro ruedas** *four-wheeled.* **2** *(círculo)* circle, ring. ● **rueda de la fortuna** wheel of fortune. ▮ **rueda de molino** millstone. ▮ **rueda de prensa** press conference. ▮ **rueda de recambio** spare wheel. ▮ **rueda delantera** front wheel.
ruedo *nm (en las plazas de toros)* bullring, arena.
ruego *nm* request, petition. ● **ruegos y preguntas** any other business.
rufián *nm (canalla)* scoundrel, villain, ruffian.
rufianesco,-a *adj* villainous.
rugby *nm* rugby.
rugido *nm* roar, bellow.
rugiente *adj* howling, roaring.
ruginoso,-a *adj* rusty.
rugir [6] *vi* to roar, bellow; *(viento)* to howl; *(tripas)* to rumble.
rugosidad *nf* rugosity.
rugoso,-a *adj* rough, wrinkled.
ruibarbo *nm* rhubarb.
ruido *nm* **1** *(gen)* noise. **2** *(sonido)* sound. **3** *(jaleo)* din, row. **4** *fig* stir, commotion. ■ **hacer ruido 1** to make a noise. **2** *fig* to cause a stir..
ruidosamente *adv* noisily, loudly.
ruidoso,-a *adj* **1** noisy, loud. **2** *fig* sensational.
ruin *adj* **1** *pey (vil)* mean, base, despicable, vile. **2** *(pequeño)* petty, insignificant. **3** *(tacaño)* stingy, mean.
ruina *nf* **1** ruin, collapse. **2** *fig* fall, end, downfall.
▷ *nf pl* **ruinas** ruins. ■ **estar hecho,-a una ruina** *fig* to be a wreck.
ruindad *nf* **1** *(maldad)* meanness, vileness. **2** *(acto)* mean act, low trick.
ruinoso,-a *adj* **1** ruinous, disastrous. **2** *fig* tumbledown, dilapidated.
ruiseñor *nm* nightingale.
rular *vt (funcionar)* to work.
ruleta *nf* roulette.
rulo *nm* **1** *(para pelo)* curler, roller. **2** *(rizo)* curl, ringlet. **3** CULIN rolling pin.
rulot *nf* caravan.
Rumanía *nf* Romania.
rumano,-a *adj* Romanian, Rumanian.
▷ *nm & nf (persona)* Romanian, Rumanian.
▷ *nm* **rumano** *(idioma)* Romanian, Rumanian.
rumba *nf* rumba, rhumba.
rumbo *nm* **1** *(dirección)* course, direction. **2** *fam fig (pompa)* pomp, show. **3** *fam fig (generosidad)* lavishness, generosity. ■ **perder el rumbo 1** to go off course. **2** *fig* to lose one's bearings.
rumboso,-a *adj fam* lavish, sumptuous.
rumia *nf* rumination.
rumiante *adj* ruminant.
▷ *nm* ruminant.
rumiar [12] *vi (animal)* to ruminate, chew the cud.
▷ *vt* **1** *(mascar)* to chew. **2** *fig (pensar)* to ruminate, chew over, reflect on.
rumor *nm* **1** *(murmullo)* murmur. **2** *(noticia, voz)* rumour (US rumor).
rumorearse *vpr* [Used only in the 3rd pers; it does not take a subject.] to be rumoured (US rumored).
rumoroso,-a *adj* murmuring.
runrún *nm* **1** *(ruido)* buzz, noise, murmur. **2** *fam (rumor)* rumour (US rumor).
runrunearse *vpr* [Used only in the 3rd pers; it does not take a subject.] *fam* to be rumoured (US rumored).
runruneo *nm* buzz, noise, murmur.
rupestre *adj* rock. ● **pintura rupestre** cave painting.
rupia *nf* rupee.
ruptura *nf* **1** *(rotura)* breaking, breakage, break. **2** *fig* breaking-off, break-up.
rural *adj* rural, country: **médico rural** *country doctor.*
Rusia *nf* Russia.
ruso,-a *adj* Russian.
▷ *nm & nf (persona)* Russian.
▷ *nm* **ruso** *(idioma)* Russian.
rústico,-a *adj* rustic, rural.
▷ *nm* **rústico** peasant. ■ **en rústica** in paperback.
ruta *nf* route, way, road. ● **ruta aérea** air route, airway.
rutenio *nm* ruthenium.
rutilante *adj lit* shining, sparkling, gleaming.
rutilar *vi lit* to shine, sparkle, gleam.
rutina *nf* routine: **la rutina diaria** *the daily routine.*
rutinario,-a *adj* **1** *(gen)* routine. **2** *(persona)* unimaginative, dull.

S

S, s *nf (la letra)* S, s.
S *sím* **(sur)** south; *(símbolo)* S.
S. *abrev* **(san, santo,-a)** Saint; *(abreviatura)* St.
S.A. *abrev* **(Sociedad Anónima)** Public Limited Company; *(abreviatura)* PLC.
sábado *nm* Saturday.
See also **jueves.**
sabana *nf* savanna, savannah.
sábana *nf* sheet.
sabandija *nf* ZOOL bug.
sabañón *nm* chilblain.
sabático,-a *adj* sabbatical.
sabelotodo *nm o nf inv pey* know-all, know-it-all.
saber [83] *nm* knowledge.
▷ *vt* **1** *(gen)* to know: **no sé lo que pasó allí** *I don't know what happened there.* **2** *(tener habilidad)* to be able to, know how to: **sabe coser** *she knows how to sew.* **3** *(enterarse)* to learn, find out: **lo acabamos de saber** *we've just found out.*
▷ *vi (tener sabor)* to taste (**a**, of).
▷ *vpr* **saberse** to know: **se sabe la tabla de memoria** *she knows the table off by heart.*
sabido,-a *adj* known.
sabiduría *nf* **1** *(conocimientos)* knowledge. **2** *(prudencia)* wisdom.
sabiendas ■ **a sabiendas** knowingly: **lo hizo a sabiendas de que se equivocaba** *he did it knowing full well that he was wrong.*
sabihondo,-a *nm & nf fam pey* pedant, know-all, smart aleck.
sabio,-a *adj* **1** *(con conocimientos)* learned, knowledgeable. **2** *(con prudencia)* wise, sensible.
▷ *nm & nf* **1** *(instruido)* learned person. **2** *(prudente)* sage, wise person.
sablazo *nm fam (de dinero)* scrounging. ■ **dar un sablazo a** ALGN *fam* to scrounge some money off SB.
sable *nm* sabre (US saber).
sablear *vt fam* to touch for money, scrounge money from, scrounge money off.
sabor *nm* **1** taste, flavour (US flavor). **2** *fig* feeling.
saborear *vt* **1** to taste. **2** *fig* to savour (US savor), relish.
saboreo *nm* savouring (US savoring).
sabotaje *nm* sabotage.
saboteador,-ra *nm & nf* saboteur.
sabotear *vt* to sabotage.
sabroso,-a *adj* **1** *(con mucho sabor)* tasty, delicious. **2** *(agradable)* pleasant, delightful.
sabueso *nm* **1** *(perro)* bloodhound. **2** *fig (persona)* sleuth.
saca *nf* large sack.
sacacorchos *nm inv* corkscrew.
sacamuelas *nm o nf inv fam* dentist.
sacapuntas *nm inv* pencil sharpener.
sacar [1] *vt* **1** *(poner en el exterior)* to take out, pull out, get out. **2** *(obtener - gen)* to get; *(- premio)* to win; *(- dinero)* to get, make, earn; *(- billete)* to get, buy. **3** *(dinero del banco)* to draw, withdraw, take out. **4** *(resolver)* to work out, solve. **5** *(encontrar)* to get, find. **6** *(enseñar)* to show. **7** *(quitar)* to remove. **8** *(extraer de algo)* to extract, obtain: **sacar caucho de un árbol** *to extract rubber from a tree.* **9** *(agua)* to draw. **10** *(llevar fuera)* to take out: **luego sacó el perro** *then he took the dog out for a walk.* **11** *(fotografía)* to take; *(fotocopia, copia)* to make. **12** *(producir)* to produce. **13** *(moda)* to introduce, set; *(nuevo producto)* to bring out. **14** *(publicar)* to publish, bring out. **15** *fam (ir por delante)* to be ahead: **nos saca media hora** *she's half an hour ahead of us.* **16** *fam (ser más alto)* to be taller: **te saca un palmo** *he's six inches taller than you.* **17** DEP *(tenis)* to serve; *(fútbol)* to kick off. **18** MAT *(restar)* to subtract; *(raíz)* to extract, find out. **19** *(mineral)* to extract. **20** QUÍM to extract.
▷ *vpr* **sacarse 1** *(desvestirse)* to take off. **2** *(fotografía)* to have taken.
sacarina *nf* saccharin.
sacarosa *nf* sucrose, saccharose.
sacerdocio *nm* priesthood.
sacerdotal *adj* priestly.
sacerdote *nm* priest.
sacerdotisa *nf* priestess.
saciable *adj* satiable.
saciar [12] *vt* **1** *(hambre)* to satiate; *(sed)* to quench. **2** *fig (deseos)* to satisfy; *(ambiciones)* to fulfil (US fulfill).
▷ *vpr* **saciarse** to satiate OS, be satiated.
saciedad *nf* satiety, satiation.
saco *nm* **1** *(bolsa)* sack, bag. **2** AM *(americana)* jacket.
sacralizar [4] *vt* to consecrate.
sacramental *adj* sacramental. ● **auto sacramental** LIT mystery play.
sacramento *nm* sacrament.
sacrificado,-a *adj (persona)* self-sacrificing.
sacrificar [1] *vt* **1** *(gen)* to sacrifice. **2** *fig (reses)* to slaughter; *(animal doméstico)* to destroy, put down.
▷ *vpr* **sacrificarse** to sacrifice OS (**por**, for).
sacrificio *nm* sacrifice.
sacrilegio *nm* sacrilege.
sacrílego,-a *adj* sacrilegious.
sacristán,-ana *nm & nf* verger, sexton.
sacristía *nf* vestry, sacristy.
sacro,-a *adj* **1** *(sagrado)* sacred. **2** ANAT sacrum.
▷ *nm* **sacro** *(hueso)* sacrum.
sacudida *nf* **1** *(gen)* shake. **2** *(movimiento violento)* jolt, jerk. **3** *(terremoto)* earthquake.
sacudir *vt* **1** *(gen)* to shake. **2** *(alfombra, etc)* to shake out; *(polvo, arena)* to shake off. **3** *(golpear algo)* to

beat. **4** *(cabeza)* to shake. **5** *(dar una paliza)* to beat up. **6** *fig (emocionar, alterar)* to shake.

sádico,-a *adj* sadistic.
▷ *nm & nf* sadist.

sadismo *nm* sadism.

saeta *nf* **1** *(arma)* arrow, dart. **2** *(copla) religious flamenco song sung in Holy Week celebrations.*

saetera *nf* loophole, embrasure.

safari *nm* **1** *(expedición)* safari. **2** *(lugar)* safari park.

saga *nf* saga.

sagacidad *nf* **1** sagacity. **2** *(astucia)* shrewdness.

sagaz *adj* **1** clever, sagacious. **2** *(astuto)* shrewd, astute.

Sagitario *nm* Sagittarius.
▷ *pl* Sagitario.

sagrado,-a *adj* sacred, holy. ● **Sagrada Biblia** Holy Bible.

sah *nm* shah.

Sáhara *nm* Sahara.

saharaui *adj* Saharan.
▷ *nm o nf* Saharan.

sahariana *nf* safari shirt, safari jacket.

sahariano,-a *adj* Saharan.

sainete *nm* TEAT comic sketch, one-act farce.

sainetista *nm o nf* writer of *sainetes*.

sajadura *nf* incision.

sajar *vt* to make an incision in.

sake *nm* sake.

sal *nf* salt. ● **sal fina** table salt.
▷ *nf pl* **sales** smelling salts.

sala *nf* **1** *(aposento)* room; *(grande)* hall. **2** *(sala de estar)* lounge, living room. **3** *(de hospital)* ward; *(de cine)* cinema; *(de teatro)* theatre. **4** JUR *(tribunal)* court.

salacot *nm* pith helmet, topee, topi.

saladero *nm* saltery.

salado,-a *adj* **1** *(con sal)* salted; *(con demasiada sal)* salty: **agua salada** *salt water.* **2** *fam fig (agudo)* witty; *(gracioso)* funny; *(encantador)* charming, attractive.

salamandra *nf* salamander.

salamanquesa *nf* ZOOL gecko.

salame *nm* salami.

salami *nm* salami.

salar *vt* **1** *(curar)* to salt. **2** *(sazonar)* to salt, add salt to.

salarial *adj* salary, wage.

salario *nm* salary, wages *pl*, wage.

salazón *nf* **1** *(acción)* salting. **2** *(carne)* salted meat; *(pescado)* salted fish.

salchicha *nf* sausage.

salchichería *nf* pork butcher's (shop).

salchichón *nm* salami-type sausage.

salcochar *vt* to boil in salt water.

saldar *vt* **1** *(cuenta)* to settle; *(deuda)* to pay off. **2** *(rebajar)* to sell off. **3** *fig (diferencias)* to settle, resolve.

saldo *nm* **1** *(de una cuenta)* balance. **2** *(pago)* liquidation, settlement. **3** *(resto de mercancía)* remnant, leftover, remainder. **4** *(venta a bajo precio)* sale.

saledizo,-a *nm* **saledizo** projection, ledge.

salero *nm* **1** *(recipiente)* saltcellar, US salt shaker. **2** *fig (gracia)* charm, wit.

saleroso,-a *adj fig* charming, witty.

sálico,-a *adj* Salic. ● **ley Sálica** Salic law.

salida *nf* **1** *(partida)* departure: **la salida del tren es a las dos** *the train leaves at two.* **2** *(puerta, etc)* exit, way out. **3** *(momento de salir)*: **nos encontramos a la salida del cine** *we met coming out of the cinema.* **4** *(viaje corto)* trip. **5** *(de un astro)* rising. **6** DEP start. **7** COM outlet, market: **estas prendas no tienen salida** *there's no market for these clothes.* **8** FIN outlay, expenditure. **9** *fig (ocurrencia)* witty remark, witticism. **10** *fig (escapatoria)* solution, way out. **11** *fig (perspectiva)* opening. **12** TÉC outlet. **13** INFORMÁ output.

salido,-a *adj* **1** *(que sobresale)* projecting, prominent. **2** *(ojos)* bulging. **3** *(animal en celo)* on heat, in heat.

saliente *adj* **1** *(que sobresale)* projecting. **2** *(cesante)* outgoing.
▷ *nm* projection, overhang, ledge.

salina *nf* **1** *(mina)* salt mine. **2** *(establecimiento)* salt works.

salinidad *nf* salinity.

salino,-a *adj* saline.

salir [84] *vi* **1** *(ir hacia afuera)* to go out (**de**, of): **salir de casa** *to go out of the house.* **2** *(venir de dentro)* to come out: **ven, sal al jardín** *come out here into the garden* (US *yard).* **3** *(partir)* to leave: **el autobús sale a las tres** *the bus leaves at three.* **4** *(no estar)* to be out: **lo siento, ha salido** *I'm sorry, she's out.* **5** *(amigos, novios)* to go out. **6** *(aparecer)* to appear, be: **salió en los periódicos** *he appeared in the newspapers.* **7** *(revista, novela, etc)* to come out; *(moda)* to come in. **8** *(proceder)* to come (**de**, from): **de la aceituna sale el aceite** *olive oil comes from olives.* **9** *(resultar)* to turn out, turn out to be: **salió demasiado salado** *it turned out too salty.* **10** *(examen, prueba)* to go, turn out: **¿cómo te salió?** *how did it go?, how did you do?* **11** *(venir a costar)* to come to, cost, work out. **12** *(sobresalir)* to project, stick out. **13** *(sol, etc)* to rise, come out; *(vegetales)* to come up; *(flores)* to come out. **14** *(granos)* to get, break out in, come out in; *(pelo)* to grow; *(diente)* to cut: **le salieron granos** *he broke out in spots.* **15** *(mancha)* to come out, come off. **16** *(parecerse)* to take after (**a**, -): **ha salido a su padre** *she takes after her father.* **17** *(al azar)* to be drawn. **18** *(nombre, palabra)* to be able to think of: **no me sale un sinónimo** *I can't think of a synonym.* **19** *(solucionar)* to work out: **no me sale** *I can't work it out.* **20** *(librarse)* to get out (**de**, of). **21** *(trabajo, oportunidad)* to come up. **22** *(dar a)* to open (**a**, onto), come out (**a**, at): **esta calle sale a la avenida** *this street comes out at the avenue.*
▷ *vpr* **salirse 1** *(líquido, gas)* to leak, leak out; *(río)* to overflow. **2** *(al hervir)* to boil over. **3** *(tornillo, etc)* to come off, come out. **4** *(de la carretera)* to go off (**de**, -).

salitre *nm* saltpetre (US saltpeter).

saliva *nf* saliva.

salivación *nf* salivation.

salival *adj* salivary.

salivar *vi* to salivate.

salmo *nm* psalm.

salmodia *nf* **1** REL psalmody. **2** *fam fig (canturreo)* drone.

salmodiar *vi (salmear)* to sing psalms.
▷ *vt fam fig (canturrear)* to drone.

salmón *nm (pez)* salmon.
▷ *adj (color)* salmon, salmon pink.

salmonado,-a *adj (asalmonado)* salmon, salmon-like: **trucha salmonada** *salmon trout.*

salmonelosis *nf inv* salmonellosis, food poisoning.

salmonero,-a *adj* salmon.

salmonete *nm* red mullet.

salmuera *nf* brine.

salobre *adj* 1 *(agua)* brackish, slightly salty. 2 *(salado)* salty; *(muy salado)* briny.
salobridad *nf* brackishness.
Salomón *nm* Solomon. ● **Islas Salomón** Solomon Islands.
salomónico,-a *adj* Solomonic, Solomonian.
salón *nm* 1 *(en casa)* sitting room, drawing room, lounge. 2 *(en edificio público)* hall. 3 *(exposición)* show, exhibition.
salpicadero *nm* dashboard.
salpicadura *nf* 1 *(acción)* splashing. 2 *(gotas)* splash.
salpicar [1] *vt* 1 *(rociar)* to sprinkle. 2 *(caer gotas)* to splash.
salpicón *nm* 1 *(salpicadura)* splash. 2 CULIN cocktail.
salpimentar [27] *vt* 1 to season. 2 *fig* to season, spice.
salpullido *nm* rash.
salsa *nf* 1 sauce. 2 *fam fig (gracia)* zest. 3 MÚS salsa.
salsera *nf* gravy boat.
saltador,-ra *adj* jumping, leaping.
▷ *nm & nf* jumper.
▷ *nm* **saltador** *(cuerda)* skipping rope.
saltamontes *nm inv* grasshopper.
saltar *vi* 1 *(gen)* to jump, leap: **saltó de la cama** *she jumped out of bed.* 2 *(en paracaídas)* to parachute. 3 *(romperse)* to break; *(estallar)* to burst. 4 *(desprenderse)* to come off. 5 *(tapón, corcho)* to pop out, pop off. 6 *fig (enfadarse)* to blow up, explode: **salta por todo** *he flies off the handle at the slightest thing.* 7 *fig (de una cosa a otra)* to jump, skip. 8 *fig (decir)* to come out (**con**, with); *(contestar)* to answer (**con**, with).
▷ *vt* 1 *fig (salvar de un salto)* to jump (over), leap (over). 2 *(arrancar)* to pull off. 3 *(ajedrez, etc)* to jump. 4 *fig (omitir)* to skip, miss out.
▷ *vpr* **saltarse** 1 *(ley, etc)* to ignore. 2 *(omitir)* to skip, miss out. 3 *(desprenderse)* to come off; *(- lentilla)* to fall out.
saltarín,-ina *nm & nf (que salta)* energetic person.
salteado,-a *adj* 1 *(espaciado)* spaced out. 2 CULIN sauté, sautéed.
salteador,-ra *nm & nf (hombre)* highwayman; *(mujer)* female highwayman.
saltear *vt* CULIN to sauté.
salterio *nm* 1 *(libro)* Psalter. 2 *(instrumento)* psaltery.
saltimbanqui *nm o nf* acrobat, tumbler.
salto *nm* 1 *(gen)* jump, leap. 2 DEP jump; *(natación)* dive. 3 *(de agua)* waterfall. 4 *(despeñadero)* precipice. 5 *fig (omisión)* gap.
salubre *adj* salubrious, healthy.
salubridad *nf (estado de salud)* healthiness; *(de lugar, clima)* salubriousness, salubrity.
salud *nf* health.
saludable *adj* 1 *(sano)* healthy. 2 *fig (beneficioso)* good.
saludar *vt* 1 *(demostrar cortesía)* to greet. 2 *(decir hola)* to say hello to. 3 MIL to salute.
saludo *nm* 1 greeting. 2 MIL salute.
salva *nf (con arma)* salvo, volley. ● **salva de aplausos** *fig* round of applause.
salvable *adj (gen)* savable; *(de un desastre)* salvageable.
salvación *nf* 1 *(gen)* salvation, rescue. 2 REL salvation.
salvado *nm* bran.
salvador,-ra *nm & nf* saviour (US savior), rescuer.
Salvador *nm* **El Salvador** 1 El Salvador. 2 REL the Saviour (US Savior).
salvadoreño,-a *adj* Salvadorian, Salvadoran.
▷ *nm & nf* Salvadorian, Salvadoran.
salvaguardar *vt* to safeguard (**de**, from).
salvaguardia *nf* 1 *(papel)* safe-conduct. 2 *fig (protección)* safeguard, protection.
salvaje *adj* 1 *(planta)* wild. 2 *(animal)* wild. 3 *(pueblo, tribu)* savage, uncivilized. 4 *fam fig (violento)* savage, wild. 5 *(bruto)* uncouth, boorish.
▷ *nm o nf* 1 *(no civilizado)* savage. 2 *(bruto)* brute, boor.
salvajismo *nm* savagery.
salvamanteles *nm inv* table mat.
salvamento *nm* rescue.
salvamiento *nm* rescue.
salvar *vt* 1 *(librar de peligro)* to save, rescue. 2 *(barco)* to salvage. 3 *(honor, ruina)* to save. 4 *(obstáculo)* to clear. 5 *(dificultad)* to overcome, get round. 6 *(distancia)* to cover.
▷ *vpr* **salvarse** 1 *(sobrevivir)* to survive. 2 *(escaparse)* to escape (**de**, from). 3 REL to be saved, save one's soul.
salvapantallas *nm inv* INFORMÁ screensaver.
salvavidas *nm inv* life belt.
salvedad *nf (excepción)* exception.
salvia *nf* sage.
salvo,-a *adj (ileso)* unharmed, safe.
▷ *adv* **salvo** except, except for.
salvoconducto *nm* safe-conduct.
samaritano,-a *adj* Samaritan.
samba *nf* samba.
sambenito *nm* 1 HIST *(escapulario)* sanbenito. 2 *fig (deshonra)* disgrace; *(descrédito)* stigma. ■ **colgarle un sambenito a** ALGN *fig* to give SB a bad name.
Samoa *nf* Samoa.
samoano,-a *adj* Samoan.
▷ *nm & nf (persona)* Samoan.
▷ *nm* **samoano** *(idioma)* Samoan.
samovar *nm* samovar.
samurái *nm*
▲ *pl* **samuráis.** samurái.
samuray *nm* samurai.
▲ *pl* **samurais.**
san *adj* saint: **San Carlos** *Saint Charles.*

Used before names of male saints except for **Tomás, Tomé, Toribio** and **Domingo**. See also **santo,-a**.

sanador,-ra *adj* curative.
▷ *nm & nf* curer.
sanar *vt* to heal, cure.
▷ *vi* 1 *(enfermo)* to recover, get better. 2 *(herida)* to heal.
sanatorio *nm* clinic, nursing home; *(hospital)* hospital.
sanción *nf* 1 *(aprobación)* sanction, approval. 2 *(pena)* sanction, penalty.
sancionable *adj* punishable.
sancionar *vt* 1 *(aprobar)* to sanction. 2 *(penar)* to penalize.
sancochar *vt* to parboil.
sancocho *nm* parboiled food.
sandalia *nf* sandal.
sándalo *nm* sandalwood.
sandez *nf* piece of nonsense.
sandía *nf* watermelon.
sándwich *nm* sandwich.
sandwichera *nf* sandwich toaster.
sandwichería *nf* sandwich bar.
saneado,-a *adj* sound, healthy.

saneamiento *nm* 1 *(de terreno)* drainage. 2 *(de edificio)* cleaning, disinfection. 3 *(de moneda)* stabilization.
sanear *vt* 1 *(limpiar)* to clean; *(desinfectar)* to disinfect. 2 *(económicamente)* to make financially viable.
sangrado *nm* indention, indentation, indent.
sangrante *adj* 1 bleeding. 2 *fig* flagrant, blatant.
sangrar *vt* 1 *(abrir una vena)* to bleed. 2 *(dar salida a un líquido)* to drain. 3 *fam fig (dejar sin dinero)* to bleed dry. 4 *(en impresión)* to indent.
sangre *nf* blood. ● **sangre fría** *fig* sang froid.
sangría *nf* 1 *(bebida)* sangria. 2 MED bleeding, blood-letting. 3 *fig (de dinero, etc)* drain.
sangriento,-a *adj* 1 *(que echa sangre)* bleeding. 2 *(con sangre)* bloody.
sanguijuela *nf* leech, bloodsucker.
sanguina *nf (lápiz)* red chalk.
sanguinaria *nf (piedra)* bloodstone.
sanguinario,-a *adj* bloodthirsty.
sanguíneo,-a *adj* blood.
sanguino,-a *adj* blood.
sanguinolento,-a *adj* 1 *(que echa sangre)* bleeding. 2 *(con sangre)* bloody, bloodstained; *(ojos)* bloodshot.
sanidad *nf* 1 *(calidad de sano)* health, healthiness. 2 *(servicios)* health: **sanidad pública** *public health.*
sanitario,-a *adj* sanitary, health.
▷ *nm & nf* health officer.
▷ *nm pl* **sanitarios** bathroom fittings.
sano,-a *adj* 1 *(con salud)* healthy, fit. 2 *(saludable)* healthy, wholesome. 3 *fig (sin corrupción)* sound.
sanseacabó ■ **y sanseacabó** *fam* and that's that!
sansón *nm fam* he-man.
santería *nf* sanctimoniousness.
santero,-a *adj* sanctimonious.
santidad *nf* saintliness, holiness.
santificación *nf* sanctification.
santificar [1] *vt* 1 *(hacer santo)* to sanctify, make holy. 2 *(fiestas, etc)* to keep, observe.
santiguar [22] *vt* to bless, make the sign of the cross over.
▷ *vpr* **santiguarse** *(uso reflexivo)* to cross OS, make the sign of the cross.
santísimo,-a *adj* most holy.
▷ *nm* **el Santísimo** the Holy Sacrament.
santo,-a *adj* 1 *(gen)* holy, sacred. 2 *(persona)* holy, saintly. 3 *fam (para enfatizar)* hell of a, real, right. 4 *(como título)* saint: **Santa Elena** *Saint Helen.*
▷ *nm & nf* saint.
▷ *nm* **santo** 1 *(imagen)* image of a saint. 2 *fam (dibujo)* picture. 3 *(onomástica)* saint's day.

See also **san**.

santón *nm* REL holy man.
santoral *nm* 1 *(libro)* hagiography. 2 *(lista de santos)* calendar of saints' feast days.
santuario *nm* sanctuary, shrine.
santurrón,-ona *nm & nf* sanctimonious person.
santurronería *nf* sanctimoniousness.
saña *nf* 1 *(enojo)* rage, fury. 2 *(crueldad)* cruelty.
sapiencia *nf* 1 *fml (sabiduría)* wisdom. 2 *(conocimiento)* knowledge.
sapo *nm* toad.
saponificar [1] *vt* to saponify.
saque *nm* 1 *(tenis)* service. 2 *(fútbol)* kick-off. ● **saque de banda** *(fútbol)* throw-in.
saqueador,-ra *nm & nf (de ciudades)* plunderer, pillager; *(de casas, comercios)* looter.
saquear *vt (casas)* to plunder, pillage; *(casas, comercios)* to loot.
saqueo *nm (de ciudades)* sacking, plundering; *(de casa, comercio)* looting.
sarampión *nm* measles *pl.*
sarao *nm* 1 *(reunión)* soirée. 2 *fam (jaleo)* knees-up.
sarcasmo *nm* sarcasm.
sarcástico,-a *adj* sarcastic.
sarcófago *nm* sarcophagus.
sarcoma *nm* sarcoma.
sardina *nf* sardine.
sardónico,-a *adj* sardonic.
sarga *nf* serge, twill.
sargazo *nm* sargasso.
sargento *nm* 1 MIL sergeant. 2 *fig* tyrant.
sari *nm* sari.
sarmentoso,-a *adj fig (dedos, etc)* bony, scrawny.
sarmiento *nm* vine shoot.
sarna *nf* MED *(en personas)* scabies; *(en animales)* mange.
sarnoso,-a *adj (piel)* itchy, scabby; *(animal)* mangy.
sarpullido *nm* rash.
sarraceno,-a *adj* Saracen.
▷ *nm & nf* Saracen.
sarro *nm* 1 *(en los dientes)* tartar. 2 *(sedimento)* deposit.
sarta *nf* string. ● **sarta de mentiras** *fam* pack of lies.
sartén *nf* frying pan, US fry pan.
sartenada *nf* panful.
sastra *nf (en teatro, cine)* wardrobe mistress.
sastre,-a *nm & nf* tailor.
sastrería *nf* 1 *(tienda)* tailor's (shop). 2 *(oficio)* tailoring.
satánico,-a *adj* satanic.
▷ *nm & nf* Satanist.
satanismo *nm* Satanism.
satélite *nm* satellite.
satén *nm* satin.
satinado,-a *adj (gen)* satiny, shiny; *(pintura)* satin.
sátira *nf* satire.
satírico,-a *adj* 1 *(de la sátira)* satiric. 2 *(del sátiro)* satyric.
satirizar [4] *vt* to satirize.
sátiro *nm* satyr.
satisfacción *nf (gen)* satisfaction.
satisfacer [85] *vt* 1 *(gen)* to satisfy. 2 *(deuda)* to pay. 3 *(requisitos, exigencias)* to meet, fulfil satisfy. 4 *(agravio, ofensa)* to make amends for.
satisfactorio,-a *adj* satisfactory.
satisfecho,-a *adj* 1 *(contento)* satisfied, pleased. 2 *(pagado de sí mismo)* self-satisfied.
sátrapa *nm* 1 HIST satrap. 2 *fig* despot, satrap.
saturación *nf* saturation.
saturado,-a *adj* 1 saturated. 2 *fig* sick, tired.
saturar *vt* to saturate.
saturnismo *nm* lead poisoning.
Saturno *nm* Saturn.
sauce *nm* willow
saúco *nm* elder.
saudade *nf* nostalgia, homesickness.
saudí *adj* Saudi.
▷ *nm o nf* Saudi.

saudita *adj-nm o nf* → **saudí.**
sauna *nf* sauna.
saurio,-a *adj* saurian.
▷ *nm & nf* saurian.
savia *nf* 1 BOT sap. 2 *fig* sap, vitality.
saxo *nm fam* → **saxofón.**
saxofón *nm (instrumento)* saxophone, sax.
▷ *nm o nf (músico)* saxophonist, sax player.
saxofonista *nm o nf* saxophonist.
saya *nf* 1 *(falda)* skirt. 2 *(enagua)* petticoat.
sayal *nm* sackcloth.
sayo *nm* cassock, smock.
sazón *nf* 1 *(madurez)* ripeness. 2 *(sabor)* taste, flavour (US flavor). 3 *(aderezo)* seasoning.
sazonado,-a *adj fig* witty.
sazonar *vt* 1 *(madurar)* to ripen, mature. 2 *(comida)* to season, flavour (US flavor).
se[1] *pron* 1 *(reflexivo - él)* himself; *(- ella)* herself; *(- usted, ustedes)* yourself, yourselves; *(- ellos, ellas)* themselves; *(- esto)* itself. 2 *(recíproco)* each other, one another: **se quieren** *they love each other.* 3 *(pasiva)*: **se han abierto las puertas** *the doors have been opened.* 4 *(impersonal)*: **se ve que no** *apparently not.*
se[2] *pron (objeto indirecto - a él)* him, to him; *(- a ella)* her, to her; *(- a ellos, ellas)* them, to them; *(- a esto)* it, to it; *(- a usted, ustedes)* you, to you: **se lo dije** *I told her.*

Used before the pronouns **la, las, lo** and **los** instead of **le** or **les.**

sé[1] *pres indic* → **saber.**
sé[2] *imperat* → **ser.**
SE *sím* **(sureste)** southeast; *(símbolo)* SE.
sebáceo,-a *adj* sebaceous.
sebo *nm* 1 *(grasa)* fat. 2 CULIN suet. 3 *(para velas)* tallow.
seborrea *nf* seborrhoea (US seborrhea).
seboso,-a *adj* greasy.
seca *nf (sequía)* drought.
secadero *nm* drying room.
secado *nm* drying.
secador *nm* 1 dryer, drier. 2 *(de pelo)* hairdryer.
secadora *nf* tumble dryer, dryer.
secano *nm* dry land.
secante[1] *adj* 1 *(que seca)* drying. 2 *(papel)* blotting.
▷ *nm* 1 *(papel)* blotting paper. 2 DEP marker.
secante[2] *adj (geometría)* secant.
▷ *nf* secant.
secar [1] *vt* 1 *(gen)* to dry. 2 *(lágrimas, vajilla)* to wipe; *(líquido)* to wipe up, mop up. 3 *(planta)* to wither, dry up; *(río, fuente, etc)* to dry up.
▷ *vpr* **secarse** 1 *(gen)* to dry. 2 *(líquido, río, etc)* to dry up; *(planta)* to wither, dry up.
sección *nf* 1 *(corte)* section, cut. 2 *(geometría)* section. 3 *(departamento)* section, department. 4 *(en periódico, revista)* page, section.
seccionar *vt* to section, cut.
secesión *nf* secession.
secesionismo *nm* secessionism.
secesionista *adj* secessionist.
▷ *nm o nf* secessionist.
seco,-a *adj* 1 *(gen)* dry. 2 *(frutos, flores)* dried. 3 *(marchito)* withered, dried up. 4 *fig (carácter)* dry; *(tono, respuesta)* curt, sharp. 5 *fig (golpe, ruido)* sharp.
secreción *nf* secretion.
secreta *nf fam* secret police.
secretar *vt* to secrete.
secretaría *nf* 1 *(cargo)* secretaryship. 2 *(oficina)* secretary's office; *(en la administración)* secretariat.
secretariado *nm* 1 *(cargo)* secretaryship. 2 *(oficina)* secretariat. 3 *(estudios)* secretarial course.
secretario,-a *nm & nf* secretary.
secreteo *nm* whispering.
secreter *nm* writing desk, bureau.
secreto,-a *adj* secret.
▷ *nm* **secreto** 1 *(lo reservado)* secret. 2 *(reserva)* secrecy.
secretor,-ra *adj* secretory.
secretorio,-a *adj* secretory.
secta *nf* sect.
sectario,-a *adj* sectarian.
sectarismo *nm* sectarianism.
sector *nm* 1 *(gen)* sector. 2 *fig (zona)* area. 3 *fig (parte)* section.
sectorial *adj* sectorial.
secuaz *nm o nf* follower; *(uso peyorativo)* underling.
secuela *nf* consequence, result.
secuencia *nf* sequence.
secuencial *adj* sequential.
secuenciar [12] *vt* to arrange in sequence.
secuestrador,-ra *nm & nf* kidnapper.
secuestrar *vt* 1 *(personas)* to kidnap; *(avión)* to hijack. 2 JUR to sequester, seize, confiscate.
secuestro *nm* 1 *(personas)* kidnapping; *(de avión)* hijacking. 2 JUR sequestration, seizure, confiscation.
secular *adj* 1 *(seglar)* secular, lay. 2 *fig (antiquísimo)* ancient, age-old.
secularidad *nf* secularity.
secularización *nf* secularization.
secularizar [4] *vt* to secularize.
secundar *vt* to support, second.
secundaria *nf* EDUC secondary education.
secundario,-a *adj* secondary.
▷ *nm* **secundario** GEOL secondary.
secuoya *nf* sequoia, redwood.
sed *nf* thirst.
seda *nf* silk. ■ **como una seda** *fig* smoothly.
sedación *nf* sedation.
sedal *nm* fishing line.
sedante *adj* 1 MED sedative. 2 *fig* soothing.
sedar *vt* to sedate.
sede *nf* 1 *(oficina central)* headquarters, central office. 2 *(del gobierno)* seat.
sedentario,-a *adj* sedentary.
sedente *adj* seated, sitting.
sedería *nf* 1 *(industria)* silk trade. 2 *(tienda)* silk shop.
sedición *nf* sedition.
sedicioso,-a *adj* seditious.
▷ *nm & nf* rebel.
sediento,-a *adj* 1 thirsty. 2 *fig (poder, etc)* hungry (**de**, for).
sedimentación *nf* sedimentation.
sedimentar *vt* to settle, deposit.
▷ *vpr* **sedimentarse** to settle.
sedimentario,-a *adj* sedimentary.
sedimento *nm* sediment, deposit.
sedoso,-a *adj* silky, silken.
seducción *nf* seduction.

seducir [46] *vt* 1 *(gen)* to seduce. 2 *(persuadir)* to tempt, seduce. 3 *(cautivar)* to captivate.
seductor,-ra *adj* 1 seductive. 2 *(atractivo)* captivating. 3 *(persuasivo)* tempting.
▷ *nm & nf* seducer.
sefardí *adj* Sephardic.
▷ *nm o nf* Sephardi.
▲ *pl* sefardíes.
sefardita *adj-nm o nf* → sefardí.
segador,-ra *nm & nf* harvester, reaper.
segadora *nf* harvester, reaper; *(de césped)* lawnmower.
segar [48] *vt* 1 *(gen)* to reap, cut; *(césped)* to mow. 2 *fig (matar)* to mow down. 3 *fig (truncar)* to cut off.
seglar *nm o nf* lay person.
segmentación *nf* segmentation.
segmentar *vt* to segment.
segmento *nm* 1 *(gen)* segment. 2 INFORMÁ overlay.
segregación *nf* 1 *(separación)* segregation. 2 *(secreción)* secretion.
segregacionista *adj* segregationist.
▷ *nm o nf* segregationist.
segregar [7] *vt* 1 *(separar)* to segregate. 2 *(secretar)* to secrete.
segueta *nf* fret saw.
seguido,-a *adj* 1 *(continuo)* continuous. 2 *(consecutivo)* consecutive. 3 *(en línea recta)* straight, direct.
▷ *adv* seguido straight: todo seguido *straight on.*
seguidor,-ra *nm & nf* 1 follower. 2 DEP supporter, fan.
seguimiento *nm* 1 *(perseguimiento)* pursuit. 2 *(continuación)* continuation. 3 *fig (de un cliente, etc)* follow-up.
seguir [56] *vt* 1 *(gen)* to follow: ¡sígame! *follow me!* 2 *(perseguir)* to pursue, chase. 3 *(continuar)* to continue, carry on. 4 *(un camino)* to continue on. 5 *(curso, etc)* to do; *(explicaciones)* to follow.
▷ *vi* 1 *(proseguir)* to go on, carry on: siga todo recto *go straight on.* 2 *(continuar)* to follow on, continue: siguió leyendo *she kept on reading.* 3 *(permanecer, mantenerse)* to continue to be, be still: sigue ocupado *he's still busy.*
▷ *vpr* seguirse 1 *(inferirse)* to deduce. 2 *(suceder a continuación)* to follow.
según *prep* 1 *(conforme)* according to: según su opinión *in his opinion.* 2 *(dependiendo)* depending on: según el tiempo *depending on the weather.* 3 *(como)* just as: todo quedó según estaba *everything stayed just as it was.* 4 *(a medida que)* as: según la miraba me di cuenta de que ya nos habíamos visto *as I looked at her I realized we had met before.* 5 *(tal vez)* it depends.
segunda *nf* 1 *(tren, etc)* second class. 2 *(marcha del auto)* second, second gear. 3 *fig (intención)* ulterior motive.
segundero *nm* second hand.
segundo,-a *adj* second.
▷ *nm & nf* second.
▷ *nm* segundo *(tiempo)* second.
See also sexto,-a.
segundón *nm* second son.
seguridad *nf* 1 *(gen)* security. 2 *(física)* safety. 3 *(certeza)* certainty, sureness. 4 *(confianza)* confidence. ● seguridad social ≈ National Health Service.
seguro,-a *adj* 1 *(asegurado)* secure. 2 *(a salvo)* safe. 3 *(firme)* firm, steady. 4 *(cierto)* certain, sure: estoy segura de que fue allí *I'm sure she went there.* 5 *(de fiar)* reliable. 6 *(confiado)* confident: está muy seguro de sí mismo *he's very self-confident.*
▷ *nm* seguro 1 *(contrato, póliza)* insurance. 2 *(mecanismo)* safety device, safety catch.
▷ *adv* for sure, definitely: seguro que no *definitely not.*
seis *adj* 1 six: son las seis en punto *it's exactly six o'clock;* el seis de junio *the sixth of June;* somos seis *there are six of us.* 2 *(sexto)* sixth: soy el seis de la lista *I'm sixth on the list.*
▷ *nm* six: el seis *number six;* mide seis por seis *it measures six by six.*
seisavo,-a *adj-nm & nf* → sexto,-a.
seiscientos,-as *adj (cardinal)* six hundred; *(ordinal)* six hundredth.
▷ *nm* seiscientos *(número)* six hundred.
See also seis.
seísmo *nm (terremoto)* earthquake.
selección *nf* 1 *(gen)* selection. 2 DEP *(gen)* team; *(fútbol)* squad.
seleccionador,-ra *nm & nf* selector.
seleccionar *vt* to select.
selectividad *nf* EDUC university entrance examination.
selectivo,-a *adj* selective.
selecto,-a *adj* 1 select. 2 *(escogido)* exclusive.
selector *nm* selector button.
selenio *nm* selenium.
self-service *nm inv* self-service cafeteria.
sellador,-ra *adj* sealing.
▷ *nm* sellador sealant.
sellar *vt* 1 *(timbrar)* to stamp; *(oficial)* to seal. 2 *(monedas, etc)* to hallmark, stamp. 3 *fig (habitación, etc)* to close (up), seal up. 4 *fig (dejar señal)* to stamp, brand. 5 *fig (concluir)* to seal, settle, conclude.
▷ *vi* to sign on.
sello *nm* 1 *(de correos)* stamp. 2 *(de estampar, precinto)* seal.
selva *nf* 1 *(bosque)* forest. 2 *(jungla)* jungle.
selvático,-a *adj* 1 forest, jungle. 2 *fig* uncouth.
selvicultura *nf* forestry.
semáforo *nm* traffic lights *pl.*
semana *nf* 1 *(tiempo)* week. 2 *fig (salario)* weekly wage.
semanada *nf* weekly wage.
semanal *adj* weekly.
semanario,-a *adj* weekly.
▷ *nm* weekly magazine.
semántica *nf* semantics.
semántico,-a *adj* semantic.
semblante *nm* 1 *(cara)* face. 2 *(expresión)* countenance. 3 *fig (apariencia)* look.
semblanza *nf* portrait.
sembrado,-a *adj fig (cubierto)* covered (de, with), full (de, of): la página está sembrada de correcciones *the page is covered with corrections.*
▷ *nm* sembrado sown field.
sembrador,-ra *nm & nf* sower.
sembradora *nf* seed drill.
sembrar [27] *vt* 1 AGR to sow. 2 *fig (esparcir)* to scatter.
semejante *adj* 1 *(parecido)* similar. 2 *pey (tal)* such, like that: no voy a permitir semejante insolencia *I won't allow such insolence.* 3 *(geometría)* similar.
▷ *nm* fellow being.
semejanza *nf* similarity, likeness.
semejar *vi* to resemble, be alike.
▷ *vpr* semejarse to be similar, be alike.

semen *nm* semen.
semental *nm* stud.
sementera *nf* 1 *(acción)* sowing, seeding. 2 *(tierra)* sown field.
semestral *adj* half-yearly, semestral.
semestre *nm* 1 six-month period. 2 EDUC semester.
semicircular *adj* semicircular.
semicírculo *nm* semicircle.
semicircunferencia *nf* semicircumference.
semiconductor *nm* semiconductor.
semiconsciente *adj* half-conscious.
semicorchea *nf* semiquaver, sixteenth note.
semidiós,-osa *nm & nf* demigod.
semidirecto,-a *adj* 1 semidirect. 2 *(tren)* express.
▷ *nm* **semidirecto** *(tren)* express train.
semiesférico,-a *adj* hemispheroidal.
semifinal *nf* semifinal.
semifinalista *nm o nf* semifinalist.
semifusa *nf* hemidemisemiquaver, sixty-fourth note.
semilla *nf* 1 seed. 2 *fig* seed, seeds.
semillero *nm* 1 seedbed. 2 *fig* hotbed.
seminal *adj* seminal.
seminario *nm* 1 EDUC seminar. 2 REL seminary.
seminarista *nm* seminarian.
seminuevo,-a *adj* nearly new.
semioficial *adj* semiofficial.
semiología *nf* semiology.
semiótica *nf* semiotics.
semiprecioso,-a *adj* semiprecious.
semiseco,-a *adj* medium dry.
semi-seco,-a *adj* medium-dry.
semita *adj* Semitic.
▷ *nm o nf* Semite.
semítico,-a *adj* Semitic.
semitono *nm* semitone, half-step.
semivocal *adj* semivocal.
▷ *nf* semivowel.
sémola *nf* semolina.
sempiterno,-a *adj* 1 everlasting. 2 *lit* sempiternal.
senado *nm* 1 senate. 2 *fig (reunión)* assembly.
senador,-ra *nm & nf* senator.
senatorial *adj* senatorial.
sencillez *nf* 1 *(gen)* simplicity. 2 *(naturalidad)* simplicity, lack of affectation. 3 *(ingenuidad)* naivety.
sencillo,-a *adj* 1 *(sin adornos)* simple, plain. 2 *(fácil)* simple, easy. 3 *(no compuesto)* single. 4 *fig (persona - natural)* natural, unaffected; *(- ingenua)* naive, gullible.
senda *nf* path.
senderismo *nm* trekking.
sendero *nm* path.
sendos,-as *adj* each, either.
senectud *nf* old age.
Senegal *nm* Senegal.
senegalés,-esa *adj* Senegalese.
▷ *nm & nf* Senegalese.
senil *adj* senile.
senilidad *nf* senility.
sénior *adj* senior: **Juan Sánchez sénior** *Juan Sánchez Senior.*
▲ *pl* **séniores.**
seno *nm* 1 *(pecho)* breast, bosom. 2 *(hueco entre el pecho y la ropa)* bosom. 3 *(matriz)* womb. 4 *(cavidad)* cavity, hollow, hole. 5 MAT sine. 6 ANAT sinus.
sensación *nf* 1 *(impresión)* sensation, feeling: **sensación de calor** *feeling of warmth.* 2 *(emoción)* sensation.
sensacional *adj* sensational.
sensacionalismo *nm* sensationalism.
sensacionalista *adj* sensational, sensationalistic.
sensatez *nf* good sense.
sensato,-a *adj* sensible.
sensibilidad *nf* 1 *(percepción, sentido artístico)* sensitivity, feeling. 2 *(emotividad)* sensibility. 3 *(precisión)* sensitivity.
sensibilización *nf* raising of awareness.
sensibilizar [4] *vt* 1 *(gen)* to sensitize. 2 *fig (concienciar)* to sensitize, make aware.
sensible *adj* 1 *(capaz de sentir)* sentient. 2 *(impresionable)* sensitive. 3 *(piel, oído)* sensitive. 4 *(perceptible)* perceptible, appreciable, noticeable. 5 *(considerable)* significant, considerable, sizeable. 6 *(que causa pena)* terrible, sad. 7 TÉC *(preciso)* sensitive.
sensiblería *nf* mawkishness, sentimentality.
sensiblero,-a *adj* mawkish, sentimental.
sensitivo,-a *adj* 1 *(sensible)* sensitive. 2 *(que siente)* sentient. 3 *(de los sentidos)* sense: **órganos sensitivos** *sense organs.*
sensor *nm* sensor.
sensorial *adj* sensory.
sensual *adj* sensual.
sensualidad *nf* sensuality.
sentada *nf* 1 *(acción)* sitting: **lo hicimos de una sentada** *we did it in one sitting.* 2 *(protesta)* sit-in.
sentado,-a *adj* 1 seated, sitting. 2 *(establecido)* established, settled.
sentar [27] *vt* 1 *(en silla, etc)* to sit, seat. 2 *fig (establecer)* to establish.
▷ *vi* 1 *(color, ropa, etc)* to suit: **esta corbata no te sienta** *this tie doesn't suit you.* 2 *(comida, etc)* to do; *(comentario, etc)* to take.
▷ *vpr* **sentarse** 1 *(en silla, etc)* to sit, sit down. 2 *(líquido)* to settle. 3 *(tiempo)* to settle, settle down.
sentencia *nf* 1 JUR *(decisión)* judgement; *(condena)* sentence. 2 *(aforismo)* proverb, maxim, saying, motto.
sentenciar [12] *vt* to sentence (**a**, to).
sentencioso,-a *adj* sententious.
sentido,-a *adj* 1 *(muerte, etc)* deeply felt: **nuestro más sentido pésame** *our deepest sympathy.* 2 *(sensible)* touchy, sensitive.
▷ *nm* **sentido** 1 *(gen)* sense. 2 *(significado)* sense, meaning. 3 *(conocimiento)* consciousness. 4 *(dirección)* direction.
sentimental *adj* sentimental.
▷ *nm o nf* sentimental person.
sentimentalismo *nm* sentimentality.
sentimiento *nm* 1 *(gen)* feeling: **no tiene sentimientos** *he's got no feelings.* 2 *(pena)* sorrow, grief.
sentina *nf* 1 *(de nave)* bilge. 2 *fig (albañal)* sewer.
sentir [35] *nm* 1 *(sentimiento)* feeling. 2 *(opinión)* opinion, view.
▷ *vt* 1 *(gen)* to feel: **sentir amor** *to feel love.* 2 *(lamentar)* to regret, be sorry about, feel sorry: **lo siento mucho** *I'm very sorry.* 3 *(oír)* to hear: **¿sientes algo?** *can you hear anything?* 4 *(presentir)* to feel, think, have a feeling

that: **siento que todo acabará bien** *I think everything will turn out all right.*

▷ *vpr* **sentirse** to feel.

seña *nf* 1 *(indicio, gesto)* sign. 2 *(señal)* mark.

▷ *nf pl* **señas** address *sing.* ■ **hacer señas a** ALGN to signal to SB.

señal *nf* 1 *(signo)* sign, indication. 2 *(marca)* mark; *(en libro)* bookmark. 3 *(aviso, comunicación)* signal. 4 *(placa, letrero)* sign. 5 *(vestigio)* trace. 6 *(cicatriz)* scar. 7 *(de teléfono)* tone. 8 *(de pago)* deposit.

señalado,-a *adj* 1 *(famoso)* distinguished, famous. 2 *(fijado)* appointed, fixed: **llegamos a la hora señalada** *we arrived at the the appointed time.* 3 *(significativo)* noticeable. 4 *(marcado)* marked, scarred: **tiene la espalda señalada** *his back is scarred.*

señalar *vt* 1 *(marcar)* to mark. 2 *(hacer notar)* to point out: **señaló algunas contradicciones** *she pointed out some contradictions.* 3 *(apuntar hacia)* to point to, show: **la manecilla pequeña señala las dos** *the little hand is pointing to two.* 4 *(con el dedo)* to point at. 5 *(fijar - cita)* to arrange, make; *(fecha, lugar, precio)* to set, fix.

señalización *nf* 1 *(señales)* road signs *pl*; *(de aeropuerto, estación)* signposting, signs *pl.* 2 *(colocación)* signposting.

señalizar [4] *vt* to signpost.

señero,-a *adj* 1 *(solo)* alone. 2 *(único)* unique. 3 *(destacado)* outstanding.

señor,-ra *adj* 1 *(noble)* distinguished, noble. 2 *fam* fine: **es un señor coche** *it's quite a car.*

▷ *nm & nf* 1 *(hombre)* man, gentleman; *(mujer)* woman, lady. 2 *(amo - hombre)* master; *(- mujer)* mistress. 3 *(tratamiento - hombre)* sir; *(- mujer)* madam, US ma'am: **buenos días, señora** *good morning, madam.* 4 *(ante apellido - hombre)* Mr; *(- mujer)* Mrs: **el Sr. Rodríguez** *Mr Rodríguez.*

señora *nf (esposa)* wife.

señoría *nf fml (para hombre)* lordship; *(para mujer)* ladyship.

señorial *adj* stately, majestic.

señorío *nm* 1 *(mando)* dominion, rule. 2 *(territorio)* estate, domain.

señorita *nf* 1 *(mujer joven)* young woman; *(con más formalidad)* young lady. 2 *(tratamiento)* Miss: **Señorita Rodríguez** *Miss Rodríguez.* 3 *fam (puro)* small cigar. 4 **la señorita** EDUC the teacher, Miss.

señorito *nm* 1 *(tratamiento)* master (of the house). 2 *fam pey (joven rico)* daddy's boy, rich kid.

señuelo *nm* 1 decoy. 2 *fig* bait.

sépalo *nm* sepal.

separación *nf* 1 separation. 2 *(espacio)* space, gap.

separado,-a *adj* 1 separate. 2 *(divorciado)* separated. ■ **por separado** separately, individually.

separador,-ra *adj* separative.

▷ *nm* **separador** separator, divider.

separar *vt* 1 *(gen)* to separate. 2 *(hacer grupos)* to separate, sort out. 3 *(guardar aparte)* to set aside, put aside: **te he separado un trozo de pastel** *I've put aside a piece of cake for you.* 4 *(apartar)* to move away (**de**, from). 5 *(de empleo, cargo)* to remove (**de**, from), dismiss (**de**, from). 6 *fig (mantener alejado)* to keep away (**de**, from).

▷ *vpr* **separarse** 1 *(tomar diferente camino)* to separate, part company. 2 *(matrimonio)* to separate. 3 *(apartarse)* to move away (**de**, from). 4 *(desprenderse)* to separate (**de**, from), come off (**de**, -). 5 *(de amigo, etc)* to part company (**de**, with). 6 **separarse de** *(dejar algo)* to part with.

separata *nf* offprint.

separatismo *nm* separatism.

separatista *adj* separatist.

▷ *nm o nf* separatist.

sepelio *nm* burial, interment.

sepia *nf (pez)* cuttlefish.

sepsia *nf* sepsis.

septenario,-a *adj* septenary.

▷ *nm* **septenario** septenary.

septenio *nm* septennium.

septentrional *adj* northern.

septeto *nm* septet.

septicemia *nf* septicaemia (US septicemia).

séptico,-a *adj* septic.

septiembre *nm* September.

For examples of use, see **marzo**.

séptimo,-a *adj* seventh.

See also **sexto,-a.**

septuagenario,-a *nm & nf* septuagenarian.

septuagésimo,-a *adj* seventieth.

See also **sexto,-a.**

sepulcral *adj* sepulchral.

sepulcro *nm* tomb.

sepultar *vt* to bury.

sepultura *nf* 1 *(lugar)* grave. 2 *(acto)* burial.

sepulturero,-a *nm & nf* gravedigger.

sequedad *nf* dryness.

sequía *nf* drought.

séquito *nm* 1 *(personas)* entourage, retinue. 2 POL group of followers.

ser [86] *vi* 1 *(gen)* to be: **Sócrates era filósofo** *Socrates was a philosopher.* 2 *(pertenecer)* to be, belong (**de**, to): **estas sillas son nuestras** *these chairs are ours.* 3 *(ser propio)* to be like (**de**, -): **es muy de Pilar** *it's just like Pilar.* 4 *(costar)* to be, cost: **¿cuánto es?** *how much is it?* 5 *(causar)* to cause, be. 6 *(consistir en)* to lie in, consist of. 7 *(suceder)* to happen (**de**, to): **¿qué fue de Iván?** *what happened to Iván?* 8 *(ocurrir, tener lugar)* to take place, be held: **la reunión será en el salón de actos** *the meeting will be held in the assembly hall.* 9 **ser de** *(proceder)* to be from, come from: **Santi es de Cáceres** *Santi is from Cáceres.* 10 *(indica material)* to be made of: **la puerta es de madera** *the door is made of wood.* 11 *(devenir)* to become of: **¡qué sería de nosotros sin ti!** *what would become of us without you!* 12 *(estar escrito)* to be by, be written by: **es de García Márquez** *it's by García Márquez.* 13 **ser de** + *inf (ser digno)* to be worth: **es de ver** *it's worth seeing;* **es de admirar** *she's to be admired.*

▷ *aux (pasiva)* to be: **fue encontrado por Raúl** *it was found by Raúl.*

▷ *nm* 1 *(ente)* being. 2 *(esencia)* essence, substance. 3 *(valor)* core, heart. 4 *(vida)* life, existence. ● **ser humano** human being.

serafín *nm* seraph.

serbal *nm* service tree.

serbio,-a *adj* Serb, Serbian.

▷ *nm & nf* Serb, Serbian.

▷ *nm* **serbio** *(idioma)* Serbian.

serena *nf* serenade.
serenar *vt* 1 *(gen)* to calm. 2 *fig (a alguien)* to calm down.
▷ *vpr* **serenarse** 1 METEOR to clear up. 2 *(mar)* to grow calm. 3 *fig (persona)* to calm down.
serenata *nf* serenade.
serenidad *nf* serenity, calm. ■ **conservar la serenidad** to keep calm, remain calm.
sereno,-a *adj* 1 METEOR *(cielo)* clear; *(tiempo)* fine, good. 2 *fig (persona - tranquila)* calm. 3 *fig (ambiente, etc)* calm, peaceful, quiet.
▷ *nm* **sereno** 1 *(vigilante)* night watchman. 2 *(ambiente de la noche)* night air, night dew. ■ **dormir al sereno** to sleep out in the open.
serial *nm* serial.
seriar [12] *vt* to serialize.
serie *nf* 1 *(gen)* series. 2 *(conjunto)* series, string, succession: **una serie de accidentes** *a series of accidents.*
seriedad *nf* 1 *(gravedad)* seriousness, gravity. 2 *(formalidad)* reliability, dependability. ■ **con seriedad** seriously.
serigrafía *nf* serigraphy, silk-screen printing.
serio,-a *adj* 1 *(importante)* serious, grave. 2 *(severo)* serious. 3 *(formal)* reliable, responsible, dependable. 4 *(color)* sober; *(traje, etc)* formal. ■ **tomar en serio** to take seriously.
sermón *nm* 1 REL sermon. 2 *fam* sermon, ticking-off.
sermonear *vi* 1 REL to preach. 2 *fam (reprender)* to lecture.
seropositivo,-a *adj* 1 seropositive. 2 *(con el VIH)* HIV positive.
seroso,-a *adj* serous.
serpentear *vi* 1 *(gen)* to crawl, wriggle. 2 *(camino)* to wind, twist; *(río)* to wind, meander.
serpentín *nm* coil.
serpentina *nf (de papel)* streamer.
serpiente *nf* snake.
serpol *nm* wild thyme.
serraduras *nf pl* sawdust *sing.*
serrallo *nm* harem.
serranía *nf* mountain range, mountains *pl.*
serrano,-a *adj* mountain, highland.
▷ *nm & nf* highlander.
serrar [27] *vt* to saw.
serrería *nf* sawmill.
serrín *nm* sawdust.
serrucho *nm* handsaw.
servible *adj* usable, serviceable.
servicial *adj* obliging, helpful, accommodating.
servicio *nm* 1 *(gen)* service. 2 *(criados)* servants *pl*; *(asistente)* domestic help. 3 *(juego, conjunto)* set: **servicio de té** *tea set.* 4 *(favor)* service, favour (US favor). 5 DEP service, serve. 6 [Also **servicios**.] *(retrete)* toilet, US rest room. ● **servicio a domicilio** home delivery service. ‖ **servicio de urgencias** emergency service.
servidor,-ra *nm & nf* 1 servant. 2 *euf* myself.
▷ *nm* **servidor** 1 MIL gunner. 2 INFORMÁ server.
servidumbre *nf* 1 *(condición)* servitude. 2 *(criados)* servants *pl*, staff of servants. 3 *(obligación)* obligation. 4 JUR servitude.
servil *adj* 1 *(humilde)* servile. 2 *(obediente)* subservient. 3 *(rastrero)* base.
servilismo *nm* 1 *(humildad)* servility. 2 *(obediencia)* subservience.
servilleta *nf* napkin, serviette.
servilletero *nm* napkin ring, serviette ring.
servio,-a *adj* Serb, Serbian.
▷ *nm & nf* Serb, Serbian.
▷ *nm* **servio** *(idioma)* Serbian.
servir [34] *vt* 1 *(gen)* to serve. 2 *(comida, bebida)* to serve, wait on. 3 *(ayudar)* to help: **¿en qué puedo servirle?** *how may I help you?* 4 COM *(suministrar)* to serve, supply with; *(entregar)* to deliver.
▷ *vi* 1 *(gen)* to serve. 2 *(ser útil)* to be useful, be helpful, be a help. 3 *(objeto)* to be no good: **esto no sirve** *this is no good.* 4 *(estar al servicio de otro)* to be a servant, be in service. 5 *(asistir a la mesa)* to serve (**en**, at), wait (**en**, at): **servir en la mesa** *to wait at table.* ■ **servir para** to be used for, be for: **también sirve para abrir latas** *it's also used for opening tins (US cans).*
▷ *vpr* **servirse** 1 *(comida, etc)* to serve OS, help OS. 2 *(usar)* to use (**de**, -), make use of (**de**, -).
servofreno *nm* servo brake.
servomotor *nm* servomotor.
sésamo *nm* sesame.
sesear *vi* to pronounce Spanish **c** before **e** or **i**, and **z**, as **s**.
sesenta *adj (cardinal)* sixty; *(ordinal)* sixtieth.
▷ *nm (número)* sixty.
See also **seis.**
sesentavo,-a *adj* sixtieth.
See also **sexto,-a.**
sesentón,-ona *nm & nf fam* sixty-year old.
seseo *nm* pronunciation of Spanish **c**, before **e** or **i**, and **z**, as **s**.
sesera *nf fam* brain, brains *pl.*
sesgar [7] *vt* 1 *(cortar)* to cut on the bias, cut on a slant. 2 *(torcer)* to slant.
sesgo *nm* 1 *(torcimiento)* slant. 2 *fig (curso)* slant, turn. ■ **tomar un sesgo favorable** *fig* to take a turn for the better.
sesión *nf* 1 *(reunión)* session, meeting. 2 CINE showing. ● **sesión continua** continuous session. ‖ **sesión plenaria** plenary session.
seso *nm* 1 brain. 2 *fam fig* brains *pl*, grey matter, sense. ■ **devanarse los sesos** *fam* to rack one's brains.
▷ *nm pl* **sesos** CULIN brains.
sestear *vi* to have a nap.
sestercio *nm* sesterce.
sesudo,-a *adj* 1 *(sensato)* sensible; *(prudente)* wise. 2 *(inteligente)* intelligent, brainy.
set *nm* set.
▲ *pl* **sets.**
seta *nf (comestible)* mushroom; *(no comestible)* toadstool.
setecientos,-as *adj (cardinal)* seven hundred; *(ordinal)* seven-hundredth.
▷ *nm* **setecientos** *(número)* seven hundred.
See also **seis.**
setenta *adj (cardinal)* seventy; *(ordinal)* seventieth.
▷ *nm (número)* seventy.
See also **seis.**
setentavo,-a *adj* seventieth.
▷ *nm & nf* seventieth.
See also **sexto,-a.**

setiembre *nm* September.

For examples of use, see **marzo**.

seto *nm* hedge.

seudónimo *nm (gen)* pseudonym.

severidad *nf* **1** *(gravedad)* severity, harshness. **2** *(rigurosidad)* strictness.

severo,-a *adj* **1** *(grave)* severe, harsh. **2** *(riguroso)* strict.

sevicia *nf* cruelty.

sexagenario,-a *adj* sexagenarian.
▷ *nm & nf* sexagenarian.

sexagesimal *adj* sexagesimal.

sexagésimo,-a *adj* sixtieth.
▷ *nm & nf* sixtieth.

See also **sexto,-a.**

sexenio *nm* six-year period.

sexi *adj* sexy.
▷ *nm* sex appeal.

sexismo *nm* sexism.

sexista *adj* **1** sexist. **2** *(machista)* chauvinistic.
▷ *nm* **1** sexist. **2** *(machista)* male chauvinist.

sexo *nm* **1** sex. **2** *(órganos)* sexual organs *pl*, genitals *pl*.

sextante *nm* sextant.

sexteto *nm* sextet.

sextillizo,-a *nm & nf* sextuplet.

sexto,-a *adj* sixth: **una sexta parte** *a sixth;* **viven en el sexto piso** *they live on the sixth floor;* **Alfonso sexto** *Alfonso the Sixth.*
▷ *nm & nf* sixth: **le correspondió un sexto de la herencia** *he got a sixth of the inheritance.*

sextuplicar [1] *vt* to multiply by six, sextuplicate.

séxtuplo,-a *adj* sextuple.
▷ *nm* **séxtuplo** six times as much, six times as many.

sexuado,-a *adj* sexed.

sexual *adj (gen)* sex; *(relaciones)* sexual: **vida sexual** *sex life.*

sexualidad *nf* sexuality.

sexy *adj* sexy.
▷ *nm* sex appeal.

Seychelles *nm pl* **las (islas) Seychelles** the Seychelles.

sha *nm* shah.

shah *nm* shah.

shérif *nm* sheriff.

shetland *nm* Shetland wool.

short *nm* shorts *pl*.

show *nm* **1** *(espectáculo)* show. **2** *fam (numerito)* show, display.

si[1] *conj* **1** *(condicional)* if: **si quieres puedes venir con nosotros** *you can come with us if you want to.* **2** *(disyuntiva, duda)* if, whether: **no sé si decírselo (o no)** *I don't know whether to tell her (or not).* **3** *(énfasis)* but: **¡pero si es facilísimo!** *¡but it's really easy!* ■ **como si** as if. ■ **por si acaso** just in case: **llévatelo por si acaso** *take it with you just in case.*

si[2] *nm* MÚS ti, si, B.
▲ *pl* **sis.**

sí[1] *pron* **1** *(él)* himself; *(ella)* herself; *(cosa)* itself; *(ellos, ellas)* themselves; *(usted)* yourself; *(ustedes)* yourselves: **lo hizo por sí misma** *she did it by herself;* **hablaban para sí** *they were talking to themselves.* **2** *(uno mismo)* oneself. **3** *(recíproco)* each other: **hablaban entre sí** *they were talking to each other.*

sí[2] *adv* **1** yes: **dijo que sí** *she said yes.* **2** *(enfático)* of course: **sí que me gusta** *of course I like it.*
▷ *nm* [*pl* **síes.**] yes. ■ **creo que sí** I think so. ■ **porque sí 1** *(sin razón)* just because I *(you, etc)* say so. **2** *(por naturaleza)* that's the way it is: **no puedes marcharte porque sí** *you can't leave just because you feel like it.*

sial *nm* sial.

sibarita *adj* sybarite, sybaritic.
▷ *nm o nf* sybarite, bon vivant.

sibarítico,-a *adj* sybaritic.

sibaritismo *nm* sybaritism.

siberiano,-a *adj* Siberian.
▷ *nm & nf* Siberian.

sibilino,-a *adj* **1** sibylline. **2** *fig* cryptic, enigmatic.

sicario *nm* **1** hired gunman. **2** *(matón)* heavy, thug.

sicoanálisis *nm inv* psychoanalysis.

sicoanalista *nm o nf* psychoanalyst.

sicoanalítico,-a *adj* psychoanalytical.

sicoanalizar *vt* psychoanalyse (US psychoanalyze).

sicodélico,-a *adj* psychedelic.

sicodrama *nm* psychodrama.

sicofármaco *nm* psychoactive drug.

sicología *nf* psychology.

sicológico,-a *adj* psychological.

sicólogo,-a *nm & nf* psychologist.

sicópata *nm o nf* psychopath.

sicopatía *nf* psychopathy.

sicopatología *nf* psychopathology.

sicosis *nf inv* psychosis.

sicosomático,-a *adj* psychosomatic.

sicoterapeuta *nm o nf* psychotherapist.

sicoterapia *nf* psychotherapy.

sicótico,-a *adj* psychotic.

sida *nm* AIDS.

SIDA *abrev* MED **(síndrome de inmunodeficiencia adquirida)** acquired immune deficiency syndrome; *(abreviatura)* AIDS.

sidecar *nm* sidecar.

sideral *adj* sidereal, astral.

siderurgia *nf* iron and steel industry.

siderúrgico,-a *adj* iron and steel.

sidra *nf* cider, US hard cider.

siega *nf* **1** *(acción)* harvesting, reaping. **2** *(época)* harvest, harvest time. **3** *(mieses)* harvest.

siembra *nf* **1** *(acción)* sowing. **2** *(época)* sowing time. **3** *(sembrado)* sown field.

siempre *adv* always.

siempreviva *nf* everlasting flower, immortelle.

sien *nf* temple.

siena *adj* sienna, dark yellow.

sierra *nf* **1** TÉC saw. **2** GEOG mountain range.

Sierra Leona *nf* Sierra Leone.

sierraleonés,-esa *adj* Sierra Leonean.
▷ *nm & nf* Sierra Leonean.

siervo,-a *nm & nf* **1** *(esclavo)* slave. **2** HIST serf.

siesta *nf* siesta, afternoon nap.

siete *adj (cardinal)* seven; *(séptimo)* seventh.
▷ *nm* **1** *(número)* seven. **2** *fam (rasgón)* tear.

See also **seis.**

sietemesino,-a *adj* seven-month.
▷ *nm & nf* baby born two months premature.

sífilis *nf inv* syphilis.

sifilítico,-a *adj* syphilitic.
▷ *nm & nf* syphilitic.
sifón *nm* 1 *(tubo encorvado)* siphon. 2 *(tubo acodado)* U-bend, trap. 3 *(bebida)* soda, soda water. 4 *(botella)* soda siphon.
sigilo *nm* 1 *(secreto)* secrecy. 2 *(discreción)* discretion.
sigilografía *nf* sigillography.
sigiloso,-a *adj* 1 *(discreto)* secretive. 2 *(silencioso)* quiet.
sigla *nf* acronym, abbreviation.
siglo *nm* 1 century. 2 *fig (vida mundana)* world. ● **el Siglo de Oro** the Golden Age.
sigma *nf* sigma.
signatura *nf* 1 *(en biblioteca)* catalogue (US catalog) number. 2 *(firma)* signature.
significación *nf* 1 *(sentido)* meaning. 2 *(trascendencia)* significance.
significado,-a *adj* well-known, important.
▷ *nm* **significado** 1 meaning. 2 LING signifier.
significante *nm* significant.
significar [1] *vt* 1 to mean: **no sé lo que significa** *I don't know what it means.* 2 *(hacer saber)* to make known, express.
significativo,-a *adj* 1 *(que da a entender)* meaningful. 2 *(importante)* significant.
signo *nm* 1 *(gen)* sign. 2 GRAM mark. 3 *(destino)* fate, destiny. 4 *(tendencia)* tendency.
siguiente *adj* following, next: **vamos a leer el capítulo siguiente** *we're going to read the next chapter.* ■ **¡el siguiente!** next, please!
sij *adj* Sikh.
▷ *nm o nf* Sikh.
▲ *pl* **sijs.**
sílaba *nf* syllable.
silabario *nm* spelling book.
silabear *vi* to divide words into syllables.
silábico,-a *adj* syllabic.
silba *nf* hissing.
silbar *vi* 1 to whistle. 2 *(abuchear)* to hiss, boo.
silbato *nm* whistle.
silbido *nm* 1 *(acción)* whistle, whistling. 2 *(abucheo)* hissing.
silbo *nm* whistle, whistling.
silenciador *nm* 1 *(de arma)* silencer. 2 AUTO silencer, US muffler.
silenciar [12] *vt* 1 *(ocultar)* to hush up. 2 *(pasar por alto)* not to mention.
silencio *nm* silence. ■ **guardar silencio** to keep quiet.
silencioso,-a *adj (persona)* quiet; *(objeto)* silent.
silepsis *nf inv* syllepsis.
sílex *nm inv* flint.
sílfide *nf* sylph.
silicato *nm* silicate.
sílice *nf* silica.
silíceo,-a *adj* flinty.
silícico,-a *adj* silicic.
silicio *nm* silicon.
silicona *nf* silicone.
silla *nf* 1 chair. 2 *(de montar)* saddle.
sillar *nm (piedra)* ashlar.
sillería *nf* 1 *(sillas)* chairs *pl*, set of chairs *pl*. 2 *(del coro)* choir stalls *pl*. 3 ARQUIT ashlar.
sillín *nm* saddle.
sillita ● **sillita de niño** pushchair.
sillón *nm* armchair.
silo *nm* silo.
silogismo *nm* syllogism.
silueta *nf* 1 *(contorno)* silhouette. 2 *(figura)* figure, shape.
siluetear *vt* to silhouette.
silva *nf* 1 *(colección)* miscellany. 2 *(poema)* type of poem.
silvestre *adj* wild: **una fresa silvestre** *a wild strawberry.*
silvicultor,-ra *nm & nf* forestry expert.
silvicultura *nf* forestry.
sima *nf* abyss, chasm.
simbiosis *nf inv* symbiosis.
simbiótico,-a *adj* symbiotic.
simbólico,-a *adj* symbolic, symbolical.
simbolismo *nm* symbolism.
simbolista *adj* symbolist.
▷ *nm o nf* symbolist.
simbolizar [4] *vt* to symbolize.
símbolo *nm* symbol.
simetría *nf* symmetry.
simétrico,-a *adj* symmetric, symmetrical.
simiente *nf* seed.
simiesco,-a *adj* simian, apelike.
símil *nm* 1 *(comparación)* comparison. 2 *(semejanza)* resemblance, similarity. 3 LIT simile.
similar *adj* similar.
similitud *nf* similarity, resemblance.
simio *nm* simian, monkey.
simpatía *nf* 1 *(cordialidad)* affection (**por**, for), liking (**por**, for). 2 *(amabilidad)* warmth, pleasantness. 3 *(afinidad)* affinity (**por**, with). 4 *(solidaridad)* sympathy (**por**, towards), solidarity (**con**, with). 5 MED sympathy.
simpático,-a *adj* 1 *(amable)* nice, likeable; *(agradable)* kind, friendly; *(encantador)* charming: **Pepe me cae simpático** *I think Pepe's a nice guy.* 2 MED sympathetic.
simpatizante *nm o nf* supporter.
simpatizar [4] *vi* 1 *(con persona)* to get on (**con**, with): **simpatizamos enseguida** *we hit it off at once.* 2 *(con idea, etc)* to sympathize (**con**, with).
simple *adj* 1 *(gen)* simple. 2 *(único)* single, just one: **con una simple llamada lo hubiera arreglado** *he could have settled it with just one phone call.* 3 *(mero)* mere. 4 *(persona)* simple, simple-minded.
simpleza *nf* 1 *(idiotez)* simple-mindedness. 2 *(tontería)* nonsense.
simplicidad *nf* 1 simplicity. 2 *(ingenuidad)* naivety, ingenuousness.
simplificación *nf* simplification.
simplificar [1] *vt* to simplify.
simplista *adj* simplistic, oversimple.
simplón,-ona *adj* simple, naive.
▷ *nm & nf* simpleton.
simposio *nm* symposium.
simulación *nf* simulation.
simulacro *nm* sham, pretence (US pretense): **simulacro de incendio** *fire drill.*
simulado,-a *adj* simulated.
simulador,-ra *adj* simulative.
▷ *nm & nf* pretender.
▷ *nm* **simulador** TÉC simulator.
simular *vt* 1 to simulate. 2 *(fingir)* to pretend.

simultanear *vt* 1 *(hacer dos cosas)* to do simultaneously, do at the same time. 2 *(combinar)* to combine.
simultaneidad *nf* simultaneity.
simultáneo,-a *adj* simultaneous.
simún *nm* simoom.
sin *prep* 1 *(carencia)* without. 2 *(además de)* not counting. ■ **estar sin** + *inf* not to have been + *pp*: **está sin planchar** *it hasn't been ironed.* ■ **sin querer** accidentally, by mistake: **lo hizo sin querer** *he didn't mean to do it.*
sinagoga *nf* synagogue.
sinalefa *nf* synalepha, synaloepha, elision.
sincerarse *vpr (abrirse)* to open one's heart (**con**, to).
sinceridad *nf* sincerity.
sincero,-a *adj* sincere.
sinclinal *nm* syncline.
síncopa *nf* 1 MÚS syncopation. 2 LING syncope.
sincopado,-a *adj* MÚS syncopated.
sincopar *vt* 1 *(notas, palabras)* to syncopate. 2 *fig (abreviar)* to abridge.
síncope *nm* syncope.
sincretismo *nm* syncretism.
sincronía *nf* synchrony.
sincrónico,-a *adj* synchronic.
sincronismo *nm* synchronism.
sincronización *nf* synchronization.
sincronizar [4] *vt* to synchronize.
sindicado,-a *adj* who belongs to a trade union.
sindical *adj* trade union, union.
sindicalismo *nm* trade unionism, unionism.
sindicalista *nm o nf* trade unionist, unionist.
sindicar [1] *vt* to unionize.
▷ *vpr* **sindicarse** *(unirse a un sindicato)* to join a trade union.
sindicato *nm* trade union, union.
síndico *nm* 1 POL elected representative. 2 *(depositario)* trustee.
síndrome *nm* syndrome.
sinécdoque *nf* synecdoche.
sinéresis *nf inv* syneresis, synaeresis.
sinergia *nf* synergy.
sinfín *nm* endless number: **tuvieron un sinfín de problemas** *they had no end of problems.*
sinfonía *nf* symphony.
sinfónico,-a *adj* symphonic.
Singapur *nm* Singapore.
singladura *nf* 1 MAR day's run. 2 *fig* path, course.
singular *adj* 1 *(único)* singular, single. 2 *(excepcional)* extraordinary, exceptional.
▷ *nm* GRAM singular. ■ **en singular** GRAM in the singular.
singularidad *nf* 1 *(unicidad)* singularity. 2 *(excepcionalidad)* strangeness, uniqueness.
singularizar [4] *vt* 1 *(distinguir)* to distinguish, single out. 2 GRAM to use in the singular.
▷ *vpr* **singularizarse** to distinguish OS (**por**, by/with), stand out ((por, for).
siniestra *nf (izquierda)* left hand.
siniestrado,-a *adj lit* damaged.
siniestro,-a *adj* 1 *lit (izquierdo)* left, left-hand. 2 *(malo)* sinister, ominous.
▷ *nm* **siniestro** disaster, catastrophe; *(accidente)* accident; *(incendio)* fire.
sinnúmero *nm* endless number.
sino[1] *conj* 1 *(contraposición)* but: **no es blanco sino negro** *it isn't white but black.* 2 *(excepción)* but, except for: **nadie lo sabe sino Antonio** *nobody knows except for Antonio.*
sino[2] *nm (destino)* fate, destiny.
sínodo *nm* synod.
sinología *nf* sinology.
sinonimia *nf* synonymy.
sinónimo,-a *adj* synonymous.
▷ *nm* **sinónimo** synonym.
sinopsis *nf inv* synopsis.
sinóptico,-a *adj* synoptic, synoptical.
sinovial *adj* synovial.
sinrazón *nf* wrong, injustice.
sinsabor *nm fig* worry, trouble, heartache.
sintáctico,-a *adj* syntactic, syntactical.
sintagma *nm* phrase. ● **sintagma nominal** noun phrase.
sintaxis *nf inv* syntax.
síntesis *nf inv* synthesis.
sintético,-a *adj* synthetic.
sintetizador *nm* synthesizer.
sintetizar [4] *vt* 1 to synthesize. 2 *(resumir)* to summarize: **sintetizando diría que...** *to sum up, I'd like to say that...*
sintoísmo *nm* Shinto, Shintoism.
sintoísta *nm o nf* Shintoist.
síntoma *nm* symptom.
sintomático,-a *adj* 1 symptomatic. 2 *fig* significant.
sintomatología *nf* symptomatology.
sintonía *nf* 1 *(de radio)* tuning. 2 *(música)* signature tune. 3 *fig (armonía)* harmony. ■ **estar en sintonía con** ALGN *fig* to be in tune with SB, be on SB's wavelength.
sintonizador *nm* 1 *(botón)* tuning knob. 2 *(de cadena de sonido)* tuner.
sintonizar [4] *vt (radio)* to tune in to: **sintonizó una emisora local** *he tuned in to a local radio station.*
▷ *vi fig (llevarse bien)* to get on well, be on the same wavelength.
sinuosidad *nf* 1 *(cualidad)* sinuosity. 2 *(curva)* bend, curve. 3 *fig (de argumento, etc)* tortuousness; *(de persona)* deviousness.
sinuoso,-a *adj* 1 *(camino)* winding. 2 *fig (argumento)* tortuous; *(persona)* devious.
sinusitis *nf inv* sinusitis.
sinvergüenza *nm o nf* 1 *(pícaro)* rotter, swine, louse. 2 *(descarado)* cheeky devil.
sique *nf* psyche.
siquiatra *nm o nf* psychiatrist.
siquiatría *nf* psychiatry.
siquiátrico,-a *adj-nm* → **psiquiátrico,-a.**
síquico,-a *adj* → **psiquico,-a.**
siquiera *conj* 1 *(adversativa)* even though, even if: **quisiera hablar contigo, siquiera fuera un momento** *I would like to speak to you, even if it's only for a moment.* 2 *(distributiva)* whether.
▷ *adv (por lo menos)* at least: **dame siquiera la mitad** *give me at least half of it.*
sir *nm* sir.
▲ *pl* **sires.**
sirena *nf* 1 *(ninfa)* siren, mermaid. 2 *(alarma)* siren.
Siria *nf* Syria.

sirio,-a *adj* Syrian.
▷ *nm & nf* Syrian.
siroco *nm* sirocco (wind).
sirope *nm* syrup.
sirviente,-a *nm & nf* servant.
sisa *nf* 1 COST armhole. 2 *(hurto)* petty theft, pilfering.
sisal *nm* sisal.
sisar *vt* 1 COST to dart, take in. 2 *(hurtar)* to pilfer, pinch, nick; *(estafar)* to cheat.
sisear *vi* to hiss.
▷ *vt* to hiss.
siseo *nm* hiss, hissing.
sísmico,-a *adj* seismic.
sismo *nm* earthquake, tremor.
sismógrafo *nm* seismograph.
sismología *nf* seismology.
sismológico,-a *adj* seismological.
sismólogo,-a *nm & nf* seismologist.
sistema *nm* system. ● **sistema de ecuaciones** simultaneous equations *pl*. ‖ **sistema métrico decimal** decimal metric system. ‖ **sistema nervioso** nervous system. ‖ **sistema operativo** operative system.
sistemático,-a *adj* systematic.
sistematizar [4] *vt* to systematize.
sístole *nf* systole.
sistólico,-a *adj* systolic.
sitar *nm* sitar.
sitiado,-a *adj* besieged.
▷ *nm & nf* besieged.
sitial *nm* seat of honour (US honor).
sitiar [12] *vt* to besiege, lay siege to.
sitio *nm* 1 *(lugar)* place. 2 *(espacio)* space, room: **hay mucho sitio** *there's plenty of room.* 3 *(asiento)* seat. 4 MIL siege. ● **sitio web** website.
sito,-a *adj fml* located, situated.
situación *nf* 1 *(circunstancia)* situation: **la situación política** *the political situation.* 2 *(posición)* position: **su situación social** *his social position.* 3 *(emplazamiento)* situation, location.
situado,-a *adj* situated, located.
situar [11] *vt* to place, locate, situate, put: **no puedo situarlo en el mapa** *I can't locate it on the map.*
▷ *vpr* **situarse** 1 *(colocarse)* to be placed, be located, be situated. 2 *(lograr una posición)* to get on, do well, be successful.
siux *nm o nf* Sioux, Siouan.
skay [Registered trademark.] *nm* leatherette.
S.L. *abrev* **(Sociedad Limitada)** Limited Company; *(abreviatura)* Ltd, Co.
slalom *nm* slalom.
slip *nm* ⟶ **eslip.**
slogan *nm* ⟶ **eslogan.**
SME *abrev* **(Sistema Monetario Europeo)** European Monetary System; *(abreviatura)* EMS.
smoking *nm* ⟶ **esmoquin.**
SMS *abrev* **(short message service [servicio de mensajes cortos])** short message service; *(abreviatura)* SMS.
snob *adj-nm o nf* ⟶ **esnob.**
snobismo *nm* ⟶ **esnobismo.**
so[1] *prep fml* under. ■ **so pena de** under penalty of, on pain of.
so[2] *interj fam*: **¡so tonto!** *you damned fool!*
so[3] *interj (para caballerías)* whoa!
SO *sím* **(suroeste)** southwest; *(símbolo)* SW.
soasar *vt* to roast lightly.
sobaco *nm* armpit.
sobado,-a *adj* 1 *(desgastado)* worn, shabby. 2 *(manoseado)* well-thumbed, dog-eared. 3 *fig (manido)* well-worn.
sobar *vt* 1 *(ablandar)* to knead. 2 *fig (manosear - objeto)* to finger; *(- persona)* to grope, paw, touch up.
soberanía *nf* sovereignty.
soberano,-a *adj* 1 sovereign. 2 *fig* extreme, supreme. 3 *fam* huge, great.
▷ *nm & nf* sovereign.
soberbia *nf* 1 *(orgullo)* pride; *(arrogancia)* arrogance, haughtiness. 2 *(cólera)* rage, anger.
soberbio,-a *adj* 1 *(orgulloso)* proud; *(arrogante)* arrogant, haughty. 2 *(suntuoso)* sumptuous, magnificent. 3 *(magnífico)* superb, splendid, magnificent.
sobón,-ona *nm & nf* groper: **es un sobón** *he can't keep his hands to himself.*
sobornable *adj* bribable, venal.
sobornar *vt* to bribe, suborn.
soborno *nm* 1 *(acción)* bribery. 2 *(regalo, etc)* bribe.
sobra *nf (exceso)* excess, surplus. ■ **saber ALGO de sobra** to know STH only too well.
▷ *nf pl* **sobras** *(desperdicios)* leftovers.
sobrado,-a *adj (que sobra)* ample, more than enough, plenty of.
sobrante *adj* leftover, remaining, spare.
sobrar *vi* 1 *(haber más de lo necesario)* to be more than enough, be too much: **sobra arroz** *there's too much rice.* 2 *(estar de más)* to be superfluous, be unnecessary: **ese comentario sobra** *that remark is unnecessary.* 3 *(quedar)* to have left over, be left over: **nos sobraron quince euros** *we had fifteen euros left over.*
sobre *prep* 1 *(encima)* on, upon, on top of: **sobre de la mesa** *on the table.* 2 *(por encima)* over, above: **volamos sobre la ciudad** *we're flying over the town.* 3 *(acerca de)* about, on: **el primer capítulo trata sobre los derechos humanos** *chapter one is about human rights.* 4 *(alrededor de)* about, around: **vendré sobre las dos** *I'll come about two.*
▷ *nm* 1 *(de correo)* envelope. 2 *(de sopa, etc)* packet. ■ **sobre todo** above all, especially.
sobre- *pref* super-, over-.
sobreabundancia *nf* superabundance, overabundance.
sobrealimentar *vt* to overfeed.
sobreático *nm* penthouse.
sobrecarga *nf* 1 overload. 2 *fig* additional burden, further worry.
sobrecargar [7] *vt* 1 to overload. 2 *fig* to overburden.
sobrecogedor,-ra *adj* 1 *(conmovedor)* dramatic, awesome. 2 *(que da miedo)* frightening.
sobrecoger [5] *vt* 1 *(coger de repente)* to startle, take by surprise. 2 *(asustar)* to frighten, scare.
sobrecubierta *nf* jacket, dust cover.
sobredosis *nf inv* overdose.
sobreentender [28] *vt* 1 *(comprender)* to understand. 2 *(deducir)* to deduce.

▷ *vpr* **sobreentenderse** to be implied, be inferred: **se sobreentiende que su respuesta será afirmativa** *one assumes that she will say yes.*
sobreexcitación *nf* overexcitement.
sobreexcitar *vt* to overexcite.
▷ *vpr* **sobreexcitarse** to get overexcited.
sobreexponer [78] *vt* to overexpose.
sobreexposición *nf* overexposure.
sobrehilar *vt* COST to whipstitch.
sobrehumano,-a *adj* superhuman.
sobreimpresión *nf* overprint.
sobrellevar *vt* to bear, endure.
sobremanera *adv* exceedingly.
sobremesa *nf* 1 *(período)* afternoon: **la programación de la sobremesa** *the afternoon's television programmes.* 2 *(charla)* table talk.
sobrenadar *vi* to float.
sobrenatural *adj* supernatural.
sobrenombre *nm* nickname.
sobrentender [28] *vt-vpr* → **sobreentender.**
sobrepaga *nf* bonus.
sobrepasar *vt* 1 to exceed, surpass, be in excess of. 2 *(competición)* to beat.
sobrepeso *nm* 1 overload, excess weight. 2 *(de persona)* excess weight.
sobreponer [78] *vt* to put on top (**en**, of), superimpose (**en**, on).
▷ *vpr* **sobreponerse** 1 *fig (al dolor, etc)* to overcome (**a**, -). 2 *fig (animarse)* to pull OS together.
sobreproducción *nf* excess production, overproduction.
sobresaliente *adj* 1 sticking out, protruding. 2 *fig* outstanding, excellent.
▷ *nm (calificación - colegio)* A; *(- universidad)* first, US A.
sobresalir [84] *vi* 1 to stick out, protrude. 2 *fig* to stand out, excel.
sobresaltar *vt* to startle.
▷ *vpr* **sobresaltarse** to be startled.
sobresalto *nm* start; *(de temor)* fright, shock.
sobresdrújulo,-a *adj* accented on the antepenultimate syllable.
sobreseído,-a *pp* → **sobreseer.**
sobreseimiento *nm* dismissal.
sobrestimar *vt* to overestimate.
sobresueldo *nm* extra pay, bonus.
sobretasa *nf* surcharge.
sobretodo *nm* *(abrigo)* overcoat.
sobrevalorar *vt* to overestimate.
sobrevenir [90] *vi* to happen to, befall: **no sabremos nunca lo que le sobrevino** *we'll never know what happened to her.*
sobreviviente *nm o nf* survivor.
sobrevivir *vi* 1 *(gen)* to survive. 2 *(a alguien)* to outlive.
sobrevolar [31] *vt* to fly over.
sobrexcitación *nf* overexcitement.
sobrexcitar *vt-vpr* → **sobreexcitar.**
sobrexponer [78] *vt* → **sobreexponer.**
sobriedad *nf* sobriety, moderation, restraint.
sobrino,-a *nm & nf (hombre)* nephew; *(mujer)* niece.
sobrio,-a *adj* 1 *(estilo, color, etc)* sober, plain. 2 *(persona)* sober, moderate, restrained.

socaire *nm* lee. ■ **al socaire** MAR leeward. | **al socaire de** *fig* under the protection of.
socarrón,-ona *adj* 1 *(astuto)* sly, cunning. 2 *(burlón)* sarcastic, ironic, wry.
socarronería *nf* 1 *(astucia)* slyness. 2 *(ironía)* sarcasm, wryness.
socavar *vt* 1 *(excavar)* to dig under. 2 *fig* to undermine.
socavón *nm* 1 *(cueva excavada)* excavation. 2 *(bache)* hollow, hole. 3 *(de una mina)* gallery, tunnel.
sochantre *nm* succentor.
sociabilidad *nf* sociability.
sociable *adj* sociable, friendly.
social *adj* social.
socialdemocracia *nf* social democracy.
socialdemócrata *adj* social democratic.
▷ *nm o nf* social democrat.
socialismo *nm* socialism.
socialista *adj* socialist.
▷ *nm o nf* socialist.
socialización *nf* 1 *(gen)* socialization. 2 *(nacionalización)* nationalization.
socializar [4] *vt* 1 *(gen)* to socialize. 2 *(nacionalizar)* to nationalize.
sociedad *nf* 1 *(gen)* society. 2 COM company. 3 *(asociación)* society, association.
socio,-a *nm & nf* 1 *(miembro)* member. 2 COM partner, associate. 3 *(accionista)* shareholder, member.
socioeconómico,-a *adj* socioeconomic.
sociología *nf* sociology.
sociológico,-a *adj* sociological.
sociólogo,-a *nm & nf* sociologist.
socorrer *vt* to help, assist, come to the aid of, go to the aid of.
socorrido,-a *adj* 1 *(útil)* useful, handy. 2 *(abastecido)* well-stocked. 3 *(trillado, manido)* hackneyed, well-worn.
socorrismo *nm* life-saving.
socorrista *nm o nf* life-saver, lifeguard.
socorro *nm* 1 *(ayuda)* help, aid, assistance. 2 *(provisiones)* supplies *pl*, provisions *pl*.
▷ *interj* help!
socrático,-a *adj* Socratic.
▷ *nm & nf* Socratic.
soda *nf* 1 *(bebida)* soda water. 2 QUÍM soda.
sódico,-a *adj* sodium.
sodio *nm* sodium.
sodomía *nf* sodomy.
sodomita *adj* sodomitic.
▷ *nm o nf* sodomite, bugger.
sodomizar [4] *vt* to sodomize, bugger.
soez *adj* vulgar, crude, rude.
sofá *nm* sofa, settee.
sofá-cama *nm* sofa bed, studio couch.
sofisma *nm* sophism.
sofista *adj* sophistic.
▷ *nm o nf* sophist.
sofisticación *nf* sophistication.
sofisticado,-a *adj* sophisticated.
sofisticar [1] *vt* to sophisticate.
soflama *nf* 1 *(llama)* flicker, glow. 2 *(rubor)* blush. 3 *(arenga)* harangue.
sofocante *adj* suffocating, stifling.

sofocar [1] *vt* 1 *(ahogar)* to suffocate, stifle, smother. 2 *fig (incendio)* to put out, extinguish; *(rebelión)* to suppress, put down.
▷ *vpr* **sofocarse** 1 *(de calor, etc)* to suffocate. 2 *fig (ruborizarse)* to blush.

sofoco *nm* 1 *(ahogo)* suffocation, stifling sensation. 2 *fig (vergüenza)* embarrassment; *(rubor)* blushing. 3 *fam (disgusto)* shock.

sofocón *nm fam* shock. ■ **llevarse un sofocón** *fam* to get into a state.

sofreír [37] *vt* to fry lightly, brown.

sofrito,-a *nm* **sofrito** fried tomato and onion sauce.

software *nm* software.

soga *nf* rope, cord.

soja *nf* soya bean, US soybean. ● **salsa de soja** soy sauce.

sojuzgar [7] *vt* to subjugate.

sol[1] *nm* 1 *(estrella)* sun. 2 *(luz)* sun, sunlight, sunshine. 3 *fam (persona)* darling. 4 *(moneda de Perú)* sol, standard monetary unit of Peru. ■ **hace sol** it's sunny, the sun's shining. ‖ **tomar el sol** 1 *(tendido)* to sunbathe. 2 *(al caminar)* to get some sun.

sol[2] *nm* MÚS sol, G.

solana *nf* 1 *(lugar donde da el sol)* sunny spot, suntrap. 2 *(de una casa - interior)* sun lounge; *(- exterior)* sun terrace.

solanera *nf* 1 *(insolación)* sunstroke. 2 *(lugar al sol)* sunny place, suntrap. 3 *(de una casa)* sun lounge, US sunporch.

solano *nm* 1 *(viento)* easterly wind. 2 BOT nightshade.

solapa *nf* 1 *(de prenda)* lapel. 2 *(de sobre, libro)* flap.

solapado,-a *adj fig* sly, evasive.

solapar *vt* 1 COST to put lapels on. 2 *fig (ocultar)* to conceal, cover up.
▷ *vi (cubrir)* to overlap.

solar[1] *adj (del sol)* solar.

solar[2] *nm* 1 *(terreno)* plot, lot; *(en obras)* building site. 2 *(casa solariega)* ancestral home.

solar[3] [31] *vt (suelo)* to floor.

solario *nm* solarium.

solárium *nm* solarium.

solaz *nm* 1 *(esparcimiento)* recreation, entertainment. 2 *(descanso)* rest, relaxation.

solazar [4] *vt* 1 *(entretener)* to amuse, entertain. 2 *(descansar)* to rest, relax.
▷ *vpr* **solazarse** 1 *(divertirse)* to enjoy OS. 2 *(relajarse)* to relax.

soldado *nm* soldier. ● **soldado raso** private.

soldador,-ra *nm & nf* welder.
▷ *nm* **soldador** soldering iron.

soldadura *nf* 1 *(acción)* welding, soldering. 2 *(unión)* weld, soldered joint.

soldar [31] *vt* 1 *(metal)* to weld, solder. 2 *fig (enmendar)* to mend.
▷ *vpr* **soldarse** *(huesos)* to knit.

soleado,-a *adj* sunny.

solear *vt* to expose to the sun, put in the sun.

soledad *nf* 1 *(estado)* solitude. 2 *(sentimiento)* loneliness. 3 *(lugar)* lonely place.

solemne *adj* 1 solemn, majestic. 2 *pey* downright: **es una solemne tontería** *it's downright stupidity.*

solemnidad *nf* 1 *(pompa)* solemnity, pomp, formality. 2 *(acto, ceremonia)* solemn ceremony, ceremonial occasion.

solemnizar [4] *vt (celebrar)* to solemnize, celebrate; *(conmemorar)* to commemorate.

soler [32] *vi (acostumbrar - presente)* to be in the habit of + -*ing*; *(- pasado)* used to: **solía venir cada martes** *she used to come every Tuesday.*

Used only in present and past tenses.

solera *nf* 1 *(soporte)* support, prop. 2 *(de molino)* lower millstone. 3 *(de horno)* floor. 4 *(del vino)* lees *pl.* 5 *fig (tradición)* tradition. ■ **de solera / de mucha solera** 1 *(familia, etc)* old-established. 2 *(vino)* vintage.

solfa *nf* MÚS sol-fa, musical notation.

solfear *vt* MÚS to sol-fa.

solfeo *nm* MÚS sol-fa, solfeggio.

solicitante *nm o nf* applicant.

solicitar *vt* 1 *(pedir)* to request. 2 *(trabajo)* to apply for; *(permiso, etc)* to ask for; *(votos)* to canvass for. 3 *(persona)* to chase after. 4 *(cortejar)* to woo, court.

solícito,-a *adj* obliging, attentive.

solicitud *nf* 1 *(petición)* request; *(de trabajo)* application; *(- impreso)* application form. 2 *(instancia)* petition. 3 *(diligencia)* solicitude, care. ● **solicitud de empleo** job application.

solidaridad *nf* solidarity.

solidario,-a *adj* 1 *(ligado)* united. 2 *(responsabilidad, causa)* common.

solidarizarse [4] *vpr* 1 *(gen)* to show one's solidarity (**con**, with). 2 *(apoyar)* to support (**con**, -).

solidez *nf (resistencia)* solidity, strength; *(firmeza)* firmness.

solidificación *nf* solidification.

solidificar [1] *vt* 1 *(líquido)* to solidify. 2 *(pasta)* to harden, set.
▷ *vpr* **solidificarse** 1 *(líquido)* to solidify. 2 *(pasta)* to harden, set.

sólido,-a *adj* 1 *(fuerte)* solid, strong; *(firme)* firm. 2 *fig (color)* fast. 3 *fig (principios, etc)* sound.
▷ *nm* **sólido** solid.

soliloquio *nm* soliloquy.

solista *nm o nf* soloist.

solitaria *nf* MED tapeworm.

solitario,-a *adj* 1 *(que está solo)* solitary, lone. 2 *(que se siente solo)* lonely. 3 *(lugar)* deserted, lonely.
▷ *nm & nf (persona)* solitary person.
▷ *nm* **solitario** *(diamante, naipes)* solitaire.

sólito,-a *adj* usual, customary.

soliviantar *vt* 1 *(inducir)* to rouse, stir up. 2 *(irritar)* to irritate.

sollozar [4] *vi* to sob.

sollozo *nm* sob.

sólo *adv* → **solo**[1].

solo[1] *adv* [**Sólo** is used if confusion with the adjective or the noun is possible.] only, just: **solo quiero café** *I just want a coffee.*

solo,-a[2] *adj* 1 *(sin compañía)* alone, on one's own, by OS; *(sin ayuda)* (by) OS, (for) OS. 2 *(solitario)* lonely: **me siento sola** *I feel lonely.* 3 *(único)* only, sole, single: **ni una sola vez** *not even once.* 4 *(café)* black.
▷ *nm* **solo** 1 *(naipes)* solitaire. 2 *fam (café)* black coffee. 3 MÚS solo. ■ **a solas** alone, by OS.

solomillo *nm* sirloin.
solsticio *nm* solstice.
soltar [31] *vt* **1** *(desasir)* to let go of, release, drop: **me soltó la mano** *he let go of my hand.* **2** *(desatar)* to untie, unfasten, undo; *(aflojar)* to loosen. **3** *(preso)* to release, free, set free. **4** *(animal)* to let out; *(perro)* to unleash. **5** *(humo, olor)* to give off. **6** *(puntos)* to drop. **7** *(de vientre)* to loosen. **8** *fam (arrear)* to give, deal: **le soltó una torta** *he gave him a slap.* **9** *fam (decir)* to come out with, blurt out: **nos soltó un rollo** *he gave us a boring lecture.*
▷ *vpr* **soltarse 1** *(desatarse)* to come untied, come unfastened. **2** *(desprenderse)* to come off. **3** *(tornillo, etc)* to come loose. **4** *(animal)* to get loose, break loose. **5** *(puntos)* to come undone. **6** *(vientre)* to loosen. **7** *fig (adquirir habilidad)* to become proficient, get the knack: **ya se suelta en inglés** *he's getting fluent in English.* **8** *fig (desenvolverse)* to become self-confident, loosen up.
soltería *nf (gen)* single state; *(de hombre)* bachelorhood.
soltero,-a *adj* single, unmarried.
▷ *nm & nf (hombre)* bachelor, single man; *(mujer)* single woman.
solterón,-ona *nm & nf pey (hombre)* old unmarried man, confirmed bachelor; *(mujer)* old maid, spinster.
soltura *nf* **1** *(agilidad)* agility. **2** *fig (seguridad)* confidence, assurance. **3** *fig (al hablar)* fluency, ease.
solubilidad *nf* solubility.
soluble *adj* soluble.
solución *nf* solution.
solucionar *vt* **1** *(problema)* to solve. **2** *(huelga, asunto)* to settle.
solvencia *nf* **1** FIN solvency. **2** *(pago)* settlement. **3** *(fiabilidad)* reliability; *(reputación)* good reputation.
solventar *vt* **1** *(dificultad, problema)* to solve, resolve. **2** *(deuda, asunto)* to settle.
solvente *adj* **1** FIN solvent. **2** *(fiable)* reliable.
▷ *nm* QUÍM solvent.
somalí *adj* Somali.
▷ *nm o nf* Somali.
Somalia *nf* Somalia.
somanta *nf fam* beating, thrashing.
somatén *nm* **1** civilian militia. **2** *fig* uproar.
somático,-a *adj* somatic.
somatología *nf* somatology.
sombra *nf* **1** *(falta de sol)* shade. **2** *(silueta)* shadow. **3** *(espectro)* ghost, shade. **4** *fig (persona que sigue a otra)* shadow. **5** *fam fig (gracia)* wit. **6** *fig (parte pequeña)* trace, shadow, bit. **7** *fig (clandestinidad)* secrecy.
sombreado *nm* shading.
sombrear *vt* **1** *(dar sombra)* to cast a shadow upon, shade. **2** *(en dibujo)* to shade, shade in.
sombrerera *nf* hatbox.
sombrerería *nf (gen)* hat shop; *(de señoras)* milliner's; *(de señores)* hatter's.
sombrerero,-a *nm & nf (gen)* hat maker; *(para señoras)* milliner; *(para señores)* hatter.
sombrero *nm* **1** *(prenda)* hat. **2** *(de hongo)* cap.
sombrilla *nf* parasol, sunshade.
sombrío,-a *adj* **1** *(lugar)* dark. **2** *fig (tenebroso)* gloomy, sombre (US somber). **3** *fig (persona)* gloomy, sullen.
somero,-a *adj fig (superficial)* superficial, shallow; *(breve)* brief.
someter *vt* **1** *(rebeldes)* to subdue, put down; *(rebelión)* to quell. **2** *(hacer recibir)* to subject (**a**, to). **3** *(pasiones)* to subdue. **4** *(proponer, presentar)* to submit, present.
▷ *vpr* **someterse 1** *(rendirse)* to surrender (**a**, to). **2** *(tratamiento, etc)* to undergo (**a**, -). ■ **someter a prueba** to test, put to the test. ▮ **someter** ALGO **a votación** to put STH to the vote, vote on STH.
sometimiento *nm* **1** *(dominación)* subjection, subjugation. **2** *(presentación, propuesta)* submission, presentation.
somier *nm* sprung bed base.
▲ *pl* **somieres.**
somnífero,-a *nm* **somnífero** sleeping pill.
somnolencia *nf* sleepiness, drowsiness, somnolence.
somnoliento,-a *adj* sleepy, drowsy.
somorgujo *nm* grebe.
somormujo *nm* grebe.
son *nm* **1** *(sonido)* sound. **2** *fig (modo)* manner, way: **a mi son** *my way.* ■ **en son de paz** in peace.
sonado,-a *adj* **1** *(conocido)* famous. **2** *(escándalo, etc)* much talked-about. **3** *fam fig (loco)* mad, crazy.
sonajero *nm* baby's rattle.
sonambulismo *nm* sleepwalking, somnambulism.
sonámbulo,-a *nm & nf* sleepwalker, somnambulist.
sonar[1] [31] *vi* **1** *(hacer ruido)* to sound. **2** *(timbre, teléfono, etc)* to ring. **3** *(alarma, reloj)* to go off. **4** *(instrumento)* to play. **5** *(letra)* to be pronounced: **esa letra no suena** *that letter is not pronounced.*
▷ *vt* **1** *(conocer vagamente)* to sound familiar, ring a bell: **no me suena esa calle** *that street doesn't ring a bell.* **2** *(timbre, etc)* to ring; *(bocina)* to blow, sound; *(instrumento)* to play.
▷ *vpr* **sonarse** *(nariz)* to blow.
sonar[2] *nm* MAR sonar.
sonata *nf* sonata.
sonda *nf* **1** MED *(para intervenciones quirúrgicas)* probe; *(para evacuar líquidos)* catheter. **2** MAR sounding line. **3** *(barreno)* drill, bore. **4** *(atmosférica)* sonde; *(espacio)* probe.
sondar *vt* → **sondear.**
sondear *vt* **1** MED to sound, probe. **2** MAR to sound. **3** *(subsuelo)* to drill, bore. **4** *fig (encuestar)* to sound out, test.
sondeo *nm* **1** MED sounding, probing. **2** MAR sounding. **3** *(del subsuelo)* drilling, boring. **4** *fig (encuesta)* poll.
soneto *nm* sonnet.
sónico,-a *adj* sonic.
sonido *nm* sound.
sonoridad *nf* sonority.
sonorización *nf* **1** *(de película)* recording of the soundtrack. **2** *(amplificación)* amplification. **3** LING voicing.
sonorizar [4] *vt* **1** *(película)* to record the soundtrack. **2** *(amplificar)* to install amplifying equipment in. **3** LING to voice.
sonoro,-a *adj* **1** *(resonante)* loud, resounding. **2** LING sound.
sonreír [37] *vi* to smile.
▷ *vt* **1** to smile at: **le sonrió** *she smiled at him.* **2** *fig (favorecer)* to smile on, smile upon: **la fortuna no le sonríe** *fortune doesn't smile upon him.*
▷ *vpr* **sonreírse** to smile.

sonriente *adj* smiling.
sonrisa *nf* smile.
sonrojar *vt* to make blush.
▷ *vpr* **sonrojarse** to blush.
sonrojo *nm* **1** *(rubor)* blush, blushing. **2** *(vergüenza)* shame, embarrassment.
sonrosado,-a *adj* rosy, pink.
sonsacar [1] *vt* **1** *(gen)* to wheedle. **2** *fig (secreto)* to get out of, worm out.
soñador,-ra *nm & nf* dreamer.
soñar [31] *vt* **1** *(al dormir)* to dream. **2** *fig (fantasear)* to daydream, dream.
▷ *vi* **1** *(al dormir)* to dream (**con**, about/of): **soñé contigo** *I dreamt about you.* **2** *fig (fantasear)* to daydream (**con**, about), dream (**con**, about/of). ■ **soñar despierto** to daydream.
soñolencia *nf* sleepiness, drowsiness.
soñoliento,-a *adj* drowsy, sleepy.
sopa *nf (plato)* soup.
sopapo *nm fam* slap.
sopera *nf* soup tureen.
sopero,-a *adj* soup.
▷ *nm* **sopero** *(plato)* soup dish.
sopesar *vt* **1** to try the weight of. **2** *fig* to weigh up.
sopetón *nm (trozo de pan)* toast soaked in oil. ■ **de sopetón** all of a sudden.
soplado,-a *adj* **1** *fam fig (demasiado compuesto)* overdressed. **2** *fam fig (estirado)* conceited.
▷ *nm* **soplado** TÉC glass-blowing.
soplador,-ra *nm* glass-blower.
soplar *vi* **1** *(viento, etc)* to blow. **2** *fam (denunciar)* to squeal. **3** *fam (beber)* to booze.
▷ *vt* **1** *(polvo, etc)* to blow away, blow off; *(vela)* to blow out; *(sopa)* to blow on; *(globo)* to blow up. **2** *(vidrio)* to blow. **3** *fam fig (delatar)* to split on, grass on. **4** *fam fig (en un examen, etc)* to whisper the answer, tell the answer.
soplete *nm* blowtorch, blowlamp.
soplido *nm* blow, puff.
soplo *nm* **1** *(con la boca)* blow, puff. **2** *(de viento)* puff. **3** *fig (momento)* moment, minute. **4** MED murmur. **5** *fam (de secreto, etc)* tip-off.
soplón,-ona *nm & nf fam (niño)* telltale, sneak; *(adulto)* informer, grass.
sopor *nm* drowsiness, sleepiness.
soporífero,-a *adj* **1** soporific, sleep-inducing. **2** *fig* dull, boring.
soporífico,-a *adj* ⟶ **soporífero,-a.**
soportable *adj* bearable.
soportal *nm* porch.
▷ *nm pl* **soportales** arcade *sing.*
soportar *vt* **1** *(aguantar)* to support, bear. **2** *fig (sufrir)* to stand, bear, endure. **3** *fig (lluvia, tormenta, etc)* to weather.
soporte *nm* support. ● **soporte de datos** INFORMÁ data carrier.
soprano *nm o nf* soprano.
sor *nf* sister.
sorber *vt* **1** *(líquido)* to sip. **2** *fig (absorber)* to absorb, soak up.
sorbete *nm* sorbet, US sherbet.
sorbo *nm* **1** *(acción)* sip. **2** *(trago)* gulp.
sordera *nf* deafness.
sordidez *nf* **1** *(suciedad)* squalor. **2** *(mezquindad)* meanness.
sórdido,-a *adj* **1** *(sucio)* squalid, sordid. **2** *(mezquino)* mean.
sordina *nf (de instrumentos de viento)* mute, sordino; *(de piano)* damper.
sordo,-a *adj* **1** *(persona)* deaf. **2** *(sonido, dolor, golpe)* dull. **3** LING voiceless, unvoiced.
▷ *nm & nf (persona)* deaf person.
sordomudez *nf* deaf-mutism.
sordomudo,-a *adj* deaf and dumb, deaf mute.
▷ *nm & nf* deaf and dumb person, deaf mute.
sorgo *nm* sorghum.
soriasis *nf inv* psoriasis.
sorna *nf fig (mofa)* mocking tone; *(ironía)* sarcasm.
sorprendente *adj* surprising, amazing, astonishing.
sorprender *vt* **1** *(coger desprevenido)* to catch unawares, take by surprise. **2** *fig (descubrir)* to discover; *(conversación)* to overhear. **3** *fig (maravillar)* to surprise, astonish, amaze.
▷ *vpr* **sorprenderse** *fig* to be surprised.
sorpresa *nf* surprise.
sortear *vt* **1** *(echar a suertes)* to draw lots for, cast lots for. **2** *(rifar)* to raffle. **3** MIL to draft. **4** *fig (obstáculos, dificultad)* to get round, overcome; *(preguntas)* to dodge, evade, get round.
sorteo *nm* draw; *(rifa)* raffle.
sortija *nf (anillo)* ring.
sortilegio *nm* **1** *(hechicería)* sorcery, witchcraft. **2** *(hechizo)* spell.
sosa *nf* **1** QUÍM soda. **2** BOT saltwort.
sosegado,-a *adj* calm, quiet.
sosegar [48] *vt (aplacar)* to calm, quieten.
▷ *vpr* **sosegarse** *(calmarse)* to calm down.
soseras *nm o nf vin fam* dull person, bore.
sosería *nf* insipidity, dullness.
sosia *nm* double, lookalike.
sosiego *nm* calmness, peace, tranquillity.
soslayar *vt* **1** *(ladear)* to slant, put on a slant. **2** *fig (evitar)* to avoid, dodge.
soslayo ■ **de soslayo** sideways: **me miró de soslayo** *he looked at me sideways.*
soso,-a *adj* **1** *(insípido)* tasteless; *(sin sal)* unsalted. **2** *fig* dull, insipid.
sospecha *nf* suspicion.
sospechar *vt (imaginar)* to suspect, think, suppose.
▷ *vi (desconfiar)* to suspect (**de**, -).
sospechoso,-a *adj* suspicious.
▷ *nm & nf* suspect.
sostén *nm* **1** *(apoyo)* support. **2** *(sustento)* sustenance. **3** [Also used in plural with the same meaning.] *(prenda)* bra, brassiere.
sostener [87] *vt* **1** *(mantener firme)* to support, hold up. **2** *(sujetar)* to hold. **3** *fig (apoyar)* to support, back. **4** *fig (afirmar)* to maintain, affirm. **5** *fig (alimentar)* to support, keep. **6** *fig (velocidad, correspondencia, relación, etc)* to keep up, maintain.
▷ *vpr* **sostenerse** **1** *(mantenerse)* to support OS; *(de pie)* to stand up. **2** *(permanecer)* to stay, remain.
sostenibilidad *nf* sustainability.
sostenible *adj (gen)* sustainable; *(argumento)* tenable.

sostenido,-a *adj* 1 *(continuado)* sustained; *(constante)* steady. 2 MÚS sharp: fa sostenido *F sharp*.
▷ *nm* sostenido MÚS sharp.
sota *nf (cartas)* jack, knave.
sotana *nf* cassock, soutane.
sótano *nm (gen)* basement; *(de casa)* cellar, basement.
sotavento *nm* lee, leeward.
sotechado *nm* shed.
soterrado,-a *adj* 1 buried. 2 *fig* hidden, concealed.
soterrar [27] *vt* 1 to bury. 2 *fig* to hide, conceal.
soto *nm* 1 *(arboleda)* grove, copse. 2 *(matorrales)* thicket.
soufflé *nm* soufflé.
souvenir *nm* souvenir.
sponsor *nm* sponsor.
sport • ropa de sport casual clothes *pl*, casual wear, sportswear, leisure wear.
spot *nm* commercial, advert, ad.
spray *nm* spray.
sprint *nm* sprint.
sprínter *nm o nf* sprinter.
squash *nm* squash.
Sr. *abrev* (señor) mister; *(abreviatura)* Mr.
Sra. *abrev* (señora) Mrs.
Sri Lanka *nf* Sri Lanka.
SSE *sím* (sudsudeste) south-southeast; *(símbolo)* SSE.
SSO *sím* (sudsudoeste) south-southwest; *(símbolo)* SSW.
Sta. *abrev* (santa) Saint; *(abreviatura)* St.
stand *nm* stand.
standard *adj inv* standard.
▷ *nm* standard.
standing *nm* standing.
stárter *nm* choke.
status *nm inv* status.
Sto. *abrev* (Santo) Saint; *(abreviatura)* St.
stock *nm* stock.
stop *nm* 1 *(señal)* stop sign. 2 *(parada)* stop.
su *adj (de él)* his; *(de ella)* her; *(de usted, de ustedes)* your; *(de ellos, de ellas)* their; *(de animales, cosas)* its; *(de uno)* one's: es su coche (de ella) *it's her car;* me dieron sus libros *they gave me their books;* abra su maleta, por favor *open your suitcase, please.*
suave *adj* 1 *(agradable al tacto)* soft, smooth. 2 *(liso, llano)* smooth, even. 3 *fig (apacible)* gentle, mild. 4 *fig (tranquilo)* easy. 5 *fig (música, palabras, voz, luz, movimiento, viento)* soft, gentle. 6 *fig (clima)* mild, clement.
suavidad *nf* 1 *(dulzura)* softness. 2 *(lisura)* smoothness, evenness. 3 *fig (tranquilidad)* ease. 4 *fig (de música, palabras, viento, etc)* softness, gentleness. 5 *fig (del clima, tabaco, sabor)* mildness.
suavizante *nm* 1 *(de pelo)* hair conditioner, conditioner. 2 *(de ropa)* fabric softener, fabric conditioner.
suavizar [4] *vt* 1 *(hacer agradable)* to soften. 2 *(alisar)* to smooth (out). 3 *fig* to soften.
subacuático,-a *adj* underwater, subaquatic.
subafluente *nm* tributary.
subalimentación *nf* undernourishment.
subalimentar *vt* to undernourish, underfeed.
subalterno,-a *nm & nf* subordinate, subaltern.
subarrendar [27] *vt* to sublet, sublease.
subarriendo *nm* sublease.
subasta *nf* 1 *(venta)* auction. 2 *(adjudicación de obra)* invitation to tender.
subastador,-ra *nm & nf* auctioneer.
subastar *vt* to auction (off), sell at auction.
subatómico,-a *adj* subatomic.
subcampeón,-ona *nm & nf (en competición)* runner-up; *(en ránking)* number two.
subclase *nf* subclass.
subcomisión *nf* subcommittee.
subcomité *nm* subcommittee.
subconjunto *nm* subset.
subconsciente *adj* subconscious.
▷ *nm* subconscious.
subcontinente *nm* subcontinent.
subcontratar *vt* to subcontract.
subcontrato *nm* subcontract.
subcultura *nf* subculture.
subcutáneo,-a *adj* subcutaneous.
subdelegación *nf* subdelegation.
subdelegado,-a *nm & nf* subdelegate.
subdesarrollado,-a *adj* underdeveloped.
subdesarrollo *nm* underdevelopment.
subdirector,-ra *nm & nf* assistant director, assistant manager.
súbdito,-a *nm & nf* 1 *(de un rey)* subject. 2 *(ciudadano)* citizen.
subdividir *vt* to subdivide.
subdivisión *nf* subdivision.
subempleado,-a *adj* underemployed.
subempleo *nm* underemployment.
suberoso,-a *adj* suberose.
subespecie *nf* subspecies.
subestación *nf* substation.
subestimar *vt* to underestimate.
subexponer [78] *vt* to underexpose.
subexposición *nf* underexposure.
subfusil *nm* sub-machine-gun.
subgénero *nm* subgenus.
subgrupo *nm* subgroup.
subida *nf* 1 *(ascenso)* ascent, climb. 2 *(pendiente)* slope, hill. 3 *fig (aumento - gen)* increase; *(- de temperatura)* rise; *(- de precios, salario)* rise, increase.
subido,-a *adj* 1 *(gen)* high. 2 *(color, olor)* strong.
subíndice *nm* subscript, subindex.
subir *vi* 1 *(ir hacia arriba - gen)* to go up, come up; *(- avión)* to climb. 2 *(en un vehículo - coche)* to get in; *(autobús, avión, barco, tren)* to get on, get onto. 3 *(montar - bicicleta)* to get on; *(- caballo)* to get on, mount. 4 *(a un árbol)* to climb up. 5 *fig (elevarse, aumentar)* to rise. 6 *fig (categoría, puesto)* to be promoted.
▷ *vt* 1 *(escaleras, calle)* to go up, climb; *(montaña)* to climb. 2 *(mover arriba)* to carry up, take up, bring up; *(poner arriba)* to put upstairs. 3 *(cabeza, etc)* to lift, raise. 4 *(pared)* to raise. 5 *fig (precio, salario, etc)* to raise, put up. 6 *fig (subir el volumen - voz)* to raise; *(- aparato)* to turn up. 7 *fig (color)* to strengthen.
▷ *vpr* subirse 1 *(piso, escalera)* to go up. 2 *(árbol, muro, etc)* to climb up (a, -). 3 *(en un vehículo - coche)* to get in (a, -); *(autobús)* to get on (a, -); *(avión, barco, tren)* to get on (a, -), get onto (a,-). ¡súbete, súbete al coche! *get in, get into the car!* 4 *(en animales, bicicleta)* to get on (a, -), mount. 5 *(ropa, calcetines)* to pull up; *(cremallera)* to do up, zip up; *(mangas)* to roll up.
súbito,-a *adj* sudden.

subjefe,-a *nm o nf* second in command.
subjetividad *nf* subjectivity, subjectiveness.
subjetivo,-a *adj* subjective.
subjuntivo,-a *adj* subjunctive.
▷ *nm* **subjuntivo** subjunctive.
sublevación *nf* uprising, revolt, rebellion.
sublevar *vt* **1** to incite to rebellion. **2** *fig (indignar)* to infuriate.
▷ *vpr* **sublevarse** to rebel, revolt.
sublimación *nf* sublimation.
sublimar *vt* **1** *(gen)* to sublimate. **2** *(ensalzar)* to praise, exalt.
sublime *adj* sublime.
subliminal *adj* subliminal.
submarinismo *nm* skin diving.
submarinista *nm o nf* skin-diver.
submarino,-a *adj* underwater, submarine.
▷ *nm* **submarino** submarine.
submúltiplo,-a *adj* submultiple.
▷ *nm* **submúltiplo** submultiple.
subnormal *adj* MED mentally handicapped, subnormal.
▷ *nm o nf* **1** MED subnormal. **2** *fam* blockhead.
suboficial *nm* **1** MIL noncommissioned officer. **2** MAR petty officer.
subordinación *nf* subordination.
subordinado,-a *adj* subordinate.
▷ *nm & nf* subordinate.
subordinar *vt* to subordinate.
▷ *vpr* **subordinarse** to subordinate OS.
subproducto *nm* by-product.
subrayar *vt* **1** to underline. **2** *fig* to emphasize, underline, stress.
subreino *nm* subkingdom.
subrepticio,-a *adj* surreptitious.
subrogar [7] *vt* to subrogate, substitute.
subsanar *vt* **1** *(remediar)* to rectify, correct. **2** *(dificultad, etc)* to overcome.
subscribir *vt-vpr* → **suscribir.**
subscriptor,-ra *nm & nf* subscriber.
subscrito,-a *adj-nm & nf* → **suscrito,-a.**
subsecretaría *nf* **1** *(cargo)* under-secretaryship. **2** *(oficina)* under-secretary's office.
subsecretario,-a *nm & nf* under-secretary.
subsidiario,-a *adj* subsidiary.
subsidio *nm* allowance, benefit.
subsistencia *nf* **1** *(hecho)* subsistence. **2** *(lo necesario para vivir)* sustenance.
▷ *nf pl* **subsistencias** *(provisiones)* food *sing*, provisions, supplies.
subsistir *vi* **1** *(conservarse)* to subsist, remain, last. **2** *(vivir)* to subsist, live on, survive.
substancia *nf* → **sustancia.**
substancial *adj* → **sustancial.**
substanciar [12] *vt* to condense, abridge.
substancioso,-a *adj* → **sustancioso,-a.**
substantivar *vt* to use as a noun.
substantivo,-a *adj-nm* → **sustantivo.**
substitución *nf* substitution, replacement.
substituible *adj* replaceable, expendable.
substituir [62] *vt* → **sustituir.**
substituto,-a *nm & nf* → **sustituto,-a.**
substracción *nf* → **sustracción.**
substraendo *nm* subtrahend.
substraer [88] *vt-vpr* → **sustraer.**
substrato *nm* substratum.
subsuelo *nm* subsoil.
subteniente *nm* second lieutenant.
subterfugio *nm (escapatoria)* subterfuge; *(pretexto)* pretext.
subterráneo,-a *adj* subterranean, underground.
▷ *nm* **subterráneo** underground passage, tunnel, subway.
subtipo *nm* subtype.
subtitular *vt* CINE to subtitle.
subtítulo *nm* **1** subtitle. **2** LIT subhead, subheading.
subtotal *nm* subtotal.
subtropical *adj* subtropical.
suburbano,-a *adj* suburban.
▷ *nm* **suburbano** suburban train.
suburbial *adj* suburban.
suburbio *nm (periferia)* suburb.
subvención *nf* subsidy, grant.
subvencionar *vt* to subsidize.
subversión *nf* subversion.
subversivo,-a *adj* subversive.
subyacente *adj* underlying.
subyacer [92] *vi* to underlie (**en**, -).
subyugar [7] *vt* **1** to subjugate. **2** *fig* to captivate.
succionar *vt* to suck up.
sucedáneo,-a *adj* substitute.
▷ *nm* **sucedáneo** substitute: **sucedáneo de café** *coffee substitute.*
suceder *vi* **1** [Used only in the 3rd person; it does not take a subject.] *(acontecer)* to happen, occur: **¿qué sucede?** *what's the matter?* **2** *(seguir)* to follow (**a**, -), succeed (**a**, -): **sucedió a su padre en el puesto** *he succeeded his father in the job.* **3** *(heredar)* to succeed.
▷ *vpr* **sucederse** to follow one another.
sucesión *nf* **1** *(herencia)* succession, inheritance. **2** *(descendencia)* issue, heirs *pl.* **3** *(al trono)* succession. **4** *(serie)* series, succession.
sucesivo,-a *adj* **1** *(siguiente)* following, successive. **2** *(consecutivo)* consecutive, running.
suceso *nm* **1** *(hecho)* event, happening, occurrence. **2** *(incidente)* incident. **3** *(delito)* crime.
sucesor,-ra *nm & nf* successor.
suciedad *nf* **1** *(inmundicia)* dirt, filth. **2** *(calidad)* dirtiness, filthiness.
sucinto,-a *adj* concise, succinct.
sucio,-a *adj* **1** *(con manchas)* dirty, filthy. **2** *(que se ensucia fácilmente)* which dirties easily, which shows the dirt. **3** *fig (deshonesto)* shady, underhand. **4** DEP *fig* foul, dirty, unfair. **5** *fig (trabajo, lenguaje)* dirty, filthy.
▷ *adv* **sucio** *fig* in an underhand way, dirty: **jugar sucio** *to play dirty.* ■ **en sucio** in rough.
suculencia *nf* succulence, juiciness.
suculento,-a *adj* juicy, succulent.
sucumbir *vi* **1** *(rendirse)* to succumb (**a**, to), yield (**a**, to). **2** *(morir)* to perish. **3** *fig (tentación, etc)* to give in (**a**, to), yield (**a**, to).
sucursal *nf* **1** *(oficina)* branch, branch office. **2** *(delegación)* subsidiary.
sudación *nf* sweating.

sudadera *nf* 1 *(prenda)* sweatshirt. 2 *fam (acción)* sweat.
Sudáfrica *nf* South Africa.
sudafricano,-a *adj* South African.
Sudamérica *nf* South America.
sudamericano,-a *adj* South American.
Sudán *nm* Sudan.
sudanés,-esa *adj* Sudanese.
▷ *nm & nf* Sudanese.
sudar *vi (transpirar)* to sweat, perspire.
sudario *nm* shroud.
sudeste *adj* 1 *(del sudeste)* southeast, southeastern; *(hacia el sudeste)* southeasterly. 2 *(viento)* southeast.
▷ *nm* 1 *(punto cardinal)* southeast. 2 *(viento)* southeast wind.
sudista *adj* Southern.
▷ *nm o nf* Southerner.
sudoeste *adj* 1 *(del sudoeste)* southwest, southwestern; *(hacia el sudoeste)* southwesterly. 2 *(viento)* southwest.
▷ *nm* 1 *(punto cardinal)* southwest. 2 *(viento)* southwest wind.
sudor *nm* 1 sweat, perspiration. 2 *fig* effort, hard work.
sudoríparo,-a *adj* sudoriferous, sweat. ● **glándulas sudoríparas** sweat glands.
sudoroso,-a *adj* sweaty.
Suecia *nf* Sweden.
sueco,-a *adj* Swedish.
▷ *nm & nf (persona)* Swede.
▷ *nm* **sueco** *(idioma)* Swedish.
suegro,-a *nm & nf (hombre)* father-in-law; *(mujer)* mother-in-law.
suela *nf (del calzado)* sole.
sueldo *nm* salary, pay, wages *pl*. ■ **estar a sueldo** to be on a salary.
suelo *nm* 1 *(superficie)* ground; *(de interior)* floor. 2 *fig (tierra)* soil, land; *(mundo)* earth. 3 *(territorio)* soil, land. 4 *(terreno)* land. 5 *(pavimento)* surface. 6 *fig (de vasija, etc)* bottom.
suelto,-a *adj* 1 *(no sujeto)* loose: **tornillo suelto** *loose screw*. 2 *(desatado)* undone, untied. 3 *(no envasado o empaquetado)* loose. 4 *(desaparejado)* odd: **un guante suelto** *an odd glove*. 5 *(dinero)* in change: **no llevo nada suelto** *I haven't got any change*. 6 *(en libertad)* free; *(huido)* at large. 7 *(disgregado)* scattered. 8 *(con diarrea)* loose. 9 *(prenda)* loose, loose-fitting. 10 *fig (ligero)* agile, nimble; *(veloz)* swift.
▷ *nm* **suelto** *(cambio)* change, small change, loose change.
sueño *nm* 1 *(acto)* sleep. 2 *(ganas de dormir)* sleepiness. 3 *(lo soñado)* dream. 4 *fig (ilusión)* dream, illusion.
suero *nm* 1 MED serum. 2 *(de la leche)* whey.
suerte *nf* 1 *(fortuna)* luck, fortune. 2 *(azar)* chance. 3 *(destino)* destiny, fate. 4 *(estado, condición)* lot, situation. 5 *fml (tipo)* sort, kind, type: **toda suerte de libros** *all kinds of books*. ■ **¡buena suerte!** good luck!
suéter *nm* sweater.
suficiente *adj* 1 *(bastante)* sufficient, enough. 2 *(apto)* suitable. 3 *fig (engreído)* smug, complacent.
sufijo,-a *adj* suffixal.
▷ *nm* **sufijo** suffix.
sufragar [7] *vt (costear - gastos)* to defray, pay; *(- empresa)* to finance.
sufragio *nm* 1 suffrage. 2 *(voto)* vote.
sufragista *nm & nf (hombre)* suffragist; *(mujer)* suffragette.
sufrido,-a *adj* 1 *(persona)* patient, long-suffering. 2 *(color)* practical, that does not show the dirt; *(tejido)* hardwearing.
sufridor,-ra *nm & nf* sufferer.
sufrimiento *nm* suffering.
sufrir *vt* 1 *(padecer)* to suffer. 2 *(accidente, ataque)* to have; *(operación)* to undergo. 3 *(dificultades, cambios)* to experience; *(derrota, consecuencias)* to suffer. 4 *(aguantar)* to bear, stand, put up with: **no la puedo sufrir** *I can't stand her*.
▷ *vi (padecer)* to suffer.
sugerencia *nf* suggestion.
sugerente *adj* suggestive.
sugerir [35] *vt* 1 to suggest. 2 *(insinuar)* to hint, hint at. 3 *(suscitar)* to suggest, make think: **sus cuadros no me sugieren nada** *his paintings don't do anything for me*.
sugestión *nf* suggestion.
sugestionar *vt* to influence, persuade.
sugestivo,-a *adj (que atrae)* fascinating, attractive.
suicida *adj* suicidal.
▷ *nm o nf* 1 suicide. 2 *fig* madcap.
suicidarse *vpr* to commit suicide.
suicidio *nm* suicide.
suite *nf* suite.
Suiza *nf* Switzerland.
suizo,-a *adj* Swiss.
▷ *nm & nf* Swiss.
sujeción *nf (acción)* subjection.
sujetador,-ra *adj* fastening.
▷ *nm* **sujetador** bra, brassiere.
sujetar *vt* 1 *(fijar)* to fix, secure, hold. 2 *(agarrar, sostener)* to hold, hold on to. 3 *(papeles)* to fasten; *(pelo)* to hold in place. 4 *fig (dominar, someter)* to control, restrain.
▷ *vpr* **sujetarse** 1 *(agarrarse)* to hold on, hold tight. 2 *fig (someterse)* to subject OS (**a**, to).
sujeto,-a *adj* 1 *(sometido)* subject (**a**, to), liable (**a**, to). 2 *(agarrado, atado)* fastened, secure.
▷ *nm* **sujeto** 1 LING subject. 2 *(individuo)* fellow, individual, character.
sulfato *nm* sulphate (US sulfate).
sulfhídrico,-a *adj* sulphuretted (US sulfureted).
sulfito *nm* sulphite (US sulfite).
sulfurar *vt* 1 QUÍM to sulphurate (US sulfurate). 2 *fam fig (irritar)* to infuriate.
▷ *vpr* **sulfurarse** *fam fig* to blow one's top, lose one's rag.
sulfúrico,-a *adj* sulphuric (US sulfuric).
sulfuro *nm* sulphide (US sulfide).
sulfuroso,-a *adj* sulphurous (US sulfurous).
sultán,-ana *nm & nf (hombre)* sultan; *(mujer)* sultana.
sultanato *nm* sultanate.
suma *nf* 1 *(cantidad)* sum, amount. 2 MAT sum, addition. 3 *(resumen)* summary.
sumando *nm* addend.
sumar *vt* 1 MAT to add, add up. 2 *(componer una cantidad)* to total, amount to, come to. 3 *(compendiar)* to summarize, sum up.
▷ *vpr* **sumarse** *(unirse)* to join (**a**, in).
sumario,-a *adj* 1 summary, brief. 2 JUR summary.
▷ *nm* **sumario** 1 *(resumen)* summary. 2 JUR legal proceedings *pl*, indictment.

sumergible *adj* submergible, submersible.
▷ *nm* submarine.
sumergir [6] *vt* 1 *(meter bajo líquido)* to submerge, submerse, immerse. 2 *fig (hundir)* to plunge, sink.
▷ *vpr* **sumergirse** 1 *(meterse bajo líquido)* to submerge (**en**, in), go underwater. 2 *fig* to become immersed (**en**, in).
sumidero *nm* drain, sewer.
sumiller *nm* chamberlain.
suministrador,-ra *nm & nf* supplier.
suministrar *vt* to provide, supply.
suministro *nm* supply, supplying.
sumir *vt fig* to plunge.
▷ *vpr* **sumirse** 1 *(hundirse)* to sink. 2 *fig* to immerse OS (**en**, in), lose OS (**en**, in).
sumisión *nf* 1 *(acto)* submission. 2 *(carácter)* submissiveness.
sumiso,-a *adj* submissive, obedient.
sumo,-a *adj* 1 *(supremo)* supreme, highest. 2 *fig (muy grande)* greatest.
suntuario,-a *adj* sumptuary.
suntuoso,-a *adj* sumptuous, magnificent.
supeditar *vt* 1 *(subordinar)* to subordinate (**a**, to). 2 *(condicionar)* to subject (**a**, to).
▷ *vpr* **supeditarse** *(someterse)* to subject OS (**a**, to.
súper *nm fam (supermercado)* supermarket.
▷ *nf fam (gasolina)* four-star.
superable *adj* surmountable.
superabundante *adj* superabundant.
superación *nf* 1 *(problemas, etc)* overcoming. 2 *(de uno mismo)* self-improvement.
superar *vt* 1 *(exceder)* to surpass, exceed, excel. 2 *(obstáculo, etc)* to overcome, surmount.
▷ *vpr* **superarse** 1 *(sobrepasarse)* to excel OS. 2 *(mejorarse)* to improve OS, better OS.
superávit *nm inv* surplus.
superconductividad *nf* superconductivity.
superconductor *nm* superconductor.
superdotado,-a *nm & nf* genius.
superestrato *nm* superstratum.
superestructura *nf* superstructure.
superficial *adj* superficial.
superficialidad *nf* superficiality.
superficie *nf* 1 *(parte externa)* surface. 2 *(área)* area.
superfluo,-a *adj* superfluous.
superhombre *nm* superman.
superíndice *nm* superscript.
superintendente *nm o nf* superintendent.
superior *adj* 1 *(encima de)* upper, top: **labio superior** *upper lip*. 2 *(por encima de)* greater (**a**, than), higher (**a**, than), above (**a**, -): **es superior a cuatro** *it's greater than four*. 3 *fig (persona - que supera)* superior; *(- mejor)* better. 4 *fig (calidad, etc)* superior, high, excellent. 5 EDUC higher.
▷ *nm* 1 *(jefe)* superior. 2 REL superior.
superiora *nf* REL mother superior.
superioridad *nf (persona)* superiority.
superlativo,-a *adj* superlative.
▷ *nm* **superlativo** superlative.
supermercado *nm* supermarket.
supernova *nf* supernova.
superpoblación *nf* overpopulation, overcrowding.
superpoblado,-a *adj* overpopulated, overcrowded.
superponer [78] *vt* 1 to superimpose, lay on top. 2 *fig* to put before.
superposición *nf* superimposition.
superpotencia *nf* superpower.
superpuesto,-a *pp* → **superponer.**
supersónico,-a *adj* supersonic.
superstición *nf* superstition.
supersticioso,-a *adj* superstitious.
supervisar *vt* to supervise.
supervisión *nf* supervision, control.
supervisor,-ra *nm & nf* supervisor.
supervivencia *nf* survival.
superviviente *adj* surviving.
▷ *nm o nf* survivor.
suplantación *nf* 1 *(falsificación)* forgery. 2 *(de una persona)* supplantation, replacement.
suplantar *vt* 1 *(una persona)* to supplant, take the place of. 2 *(falsificar)* to forge.
suplementario,-a *adj* 1 supplementary, extra, additional. 2 *(geometría)* supplementary.
suplemento *nm* 1 *(de revista, etc)* supplement. 2 *(de dinero)* extra charge. 3 *(geometría)* supplement.
suplencia *nf* substitution.
suplente *nm o nf* 1 *(gen)* substitute. 2 DEP reserve player. 3 TEAT understudy.
supletorio,-a *adj* supplementary, additional, extra: **cama supletoria** *extra bed*.
▷ *nm* **supletorio** *(teléfono)* extension.
súplica *nf* 1 request, entreaty, plea. 2 JUR petition.
suplicar [1] *vt* 1 to beseech, beg, implore. 2 JUR to appeal to.
suplicio *nm (castigo)* torture.
suplir *vt* 1 *(reemplazar)* to replace, substitute. 2 *(compensar)* to make up for.
suponer [78] *vt* 1 *(gen)* to suppose, assume. 2 *(significar)* to mean. 3 *(conllevar)* to mean, entail, require. 4 *(adivinar)* to guess; *(imaginar)* to imagine, think. 5 *(creer)* to think.
▷ *nm fam* supposition.
suposición *nf* supposition, assumption.
supositorio *nm* suppository.
supranacional *adj* supranational.
suprarrenal *adj* suprarenal.
supremacía *nf* supremacy.
supremo,-a *adj* 1 *(gen)* supreme. 2 *(decisivo)* decisive. 3 *(último)* last, final.
supresión *nf* 1 *(de libertad, etc)* suppression; *(de ley, impuesto)* abolition; *(de dificultades)* elimination; *(de restricciones)* lifting. 2 *(de palabra)* deletion. 3 *(omisión)* omission.
suprimir *vt* 1 *(libertad, etc)* to suppress; *(ley, impuestos)* to abolish; *(dificultades)* to eliminate, remove; *(restricciones)* to lift. 2 *(tabaco, alcohol)* to cut out. 3 *(palabra)* to delete, take out, leave out. 4 *(omitir)* to omit.
supuesto,-a *adj* 1 *(que se supone)* supposed, assumed. 2 *(pretendido)* so-called, self-styled.
▷ *nm* **supuesto** 1 *(suposición)* supposition, assumption. 2 *(hipótesis)* hypothesis.
supurar *vi* to suppurate.
sur *nm* 1 south. 2 *(viento)* south wind.
Suramérica *nf* South America.
suramericano,-a *adj-nm & nf* → **sudamericano,-a.**

surcar [1] *vt* 1 AGR to plough (US plow). 2 *(agua)* to cut through, cross; *(aire)* to fly through.
surco *nm* 1 *(en tierra)* furrow. 2 *(arruga)* wrinkle. 3 *(de disco)* groove.
surcoreano,-a *adj* South Korean.
▷ *nm & nf* South Korean.
sureño,-a *adj* southern.
▷ *nm & nf* southerner.
sureste *adj-nm* → **sudeste.**
surf *nm* surf.
surfista *nm o nf* surfer.
surgir [6] *vi* 1 *(agua)* to spring forth, spurt up. 2 *fig (aparecer - gen)* to appear, emerge; *(- dificultades)* to crop up, arise, come up. 3 MAR to anchor.
Surinam *nm* Surinam.
suroeste *adj-nm* → **sudoeste.**
surrealismo *nm* surrealism.
surrealista *adj* surrealist, surrealistic.
▷ *nm o nf* surrealist.
surtido,-a *adj* 1 *(variado)* assorted. 2 *(bien provisto)* well stocked.
▷ *nm* **surtido** assortment, selection.
surtidor *nm* 1 *(fuente)* fountain. 2 *(chorro)* jet, spout.
surtir *vt (proveer)* to supply (**de**, with), provide (**de**, with).
▷ *vi (brotar)* to spout, spurt.
▷ *vpr* **surtirse** to supply OS, provide OS.
susceptibilidad *nf* 1 *(gen)* susceptibility. 2 *(sensibilidad)* sensitivity.
susceptible *adj* 1 *(gen)* susceptible. 2 *(sensible)* oversensitive.
suscitar *vt* 1 *(gen)* to cause, provoke. 2 *(rebelión)* to stir up, arouse; *(discusión)* to start; *(problemas)* to cause, raise; *(interés)* to arouse.
suscribir *vt* 1 FIN to subscribe. 2 *fig (convenir con alguien)* to subscribe to, endorse. 3 *(a una revista, etc)* to take out a subscription for. 4 *fml (firmar)* to subscribe.
▷ *vpr* **suscribirse** *(abonarse)* to subscribe.
suscripción *nf* subscription.
suscriptor,-ra *nm & nf* subscriber.
suscrito,-a *adj* 1 *(abonado)* subscribed. 2 *(firmado)* undersigned.
▷ *nm & nf* undersigned.
susodicho,-a *adj fml* above-mentioned, aforesaid.
suspender *vt* 1 *(levantar)* to hang, hang up, suspend. 2 *(aplazar - gen)* to postpone, put off, delay; *(- reunión)* to adjourn. 3 EDUC *fig* to fail. 4 *fig (pagos)* to suspend; *(servicio)* to discontinue.
suspense *nm* suspense.
suspensión *nf* 1 *(acto de levantar)* hanging, hanging up, suspension. 2 AUTO suspension. 3 *(aplazamiento - gen)* delay, postponement; *(- de reunión)* adjournment. 4 *(supresión)* suspension, discontinuation.
suspenso,-a *adj* 1 *(colgado)* hanging, suspended. 2 REL *fig (alumno)* failed. 3 *fig (asombrado)* bewildered.
▷ *nm* **suspenso** EDUC fail.
suspicacia *nf (sospecha)* suspicion.
suspicaz *adj* 1 *(desconfiado)* mistrustful, distrustful. 2 *(que sospecha)* suspicious.
suspirar *vi* to sigh.
suspiro *nm* sigh.
sustancia *nf* 1 *(gen)* substance. 2 *(esencia)* substance, essence.
sustancial *adj* 1 *(gen)* substantial. 2 *(fundamental)* essential, fundamental. 3 *(importante)* important.
sustanciar [12] *vt* to condense, abridge.
sustancioso,-a *adj* 1 *(nutritivo)* wholesome. 2 *fig (libro, etc)* meaty.
sustantivar *vt* to use as a noun.
sustantivo,-a *nm* noun, substantive.
sustentable *adj* tenable.
sustentación *nf* 1 *(soporte)* support. 2 *(mantenimiento)* sustenance, maintenance.
sustentar *vt* 1 *(familia, etc)* to maintain, support, sustain. 2 *(sostener)* to hold up, support. 3 *(teoría, opinión)* to support, defend.
sustento *nm* 1 *(alimento)* sustenance, food. 2 *(apoyo)* support.
sustitución *nf* substitution, replacement.
sustituible *adj* replaceable, expendable.
sustituir [62] *vt (reemplazar)* to substitute (**por**, with), replace (**por**, with).
sustitutivo,-a *adj* substitutive.
▷ *nm* **sustitutivo** substitute.
sustituto,-a *nm & nf* substitute, stand-in.
susto *nm* fright, scare, shock.
sustracción *nf* 1 *(robo)* theft. 2 MAT subtraction.
sustraendo *nm* subtrahend.
sustraer [88] *vt* 1 *(robar)* to steal. 2 MAT to subtract.
▷ *vpr* **sustraerse** *(faltar al cumplimiento)* to evade (**a**, -), elude (**a**, -); *(tentaciones)* to resist (**a**, -).
sustrato *nm* substratum.
susurrar *vi* to whisper.
susurro *nm* 1 whisper. 2 *fig (agua)* murmur; *(hojas)* rustle.
sutil *adj* 1 *(delgado)* thin, fine. 2 *(aroma)* delicate; *(color)* soft. 3 *(brisa)* gentle. 4 *fig* subtle.
sutileza *nf* 1 thinness, fineness. 2 *fig* subtlety.
sutura *nf* suture.
suturar *vt* to stitch.
suyo,-a *adj (de él)* his, of his; *(de ella)* her, of hers; *(de animales, cosas)* its; *(de usted, de ustedes)* yours, of yours; *(de ellos, de ellas)* theirs, of theirs: **este libro es suyo** *this book is hers;* **aquel amigo suyo** *that friend of yours.*
▷ *pron (de él)* his; *(de ella)* hers; *(de usted, de ustedes)* yours; *(de ellos, de ellas)* theirs: **éstos son los míos, los suyos están sobre la mesa** *there are mine, hers are on the table.*
▷ *nf* **la suya** *(ocasión, oportunidad)* one's chance, one's opportunity.
▷ *nm* **lo suyo** 1 *(lo que toca)* what one deserves. 2 *(habilidad)* forte, one's thing: **lo suyo es el tenis** *tennis is his thing.* 3 *fam (mucho)* a lot: **comió lo suyo** *he ate a lot.*
▷ *nm pl* **los suyos** *(familiares)* his *(her, your, etc)* family *sing;* *(amigos)* his *(her, your, etc)* friends, his *(her, your, etc)* people.
Swazilandia *nf* Swaziland.
swing *nm* swing.

T

T, t *nf (la letra)* T, t.
T. *abrev* **(tara)** tare.
tabaco *nm* **1** *(gen)* tobacco. **2** *(cigarrillos)* cigarettes *pl*; *(cigarro)* cigar. **3** *(enfermedad)* black rot. ● **tabaco rubio** Virginia tobacco.
tábano *nm* horsefly.
tabaquera *nf (caja - para tabaco)* tobacco tin; *(- para rapé)* snuffbox.
tabaquismo *nm* nicotine poisoning, nicotinism.
tabardo *nm* tabard.
tabarra *nf fam* pain in the neck, bore. ■ **dar la tabarra** *fam* to be a pain in the neck.
tabasco [Registered trademark.] *nm* Tabasco sauce.
taberna *nf* pub, bar.
tabernáculo *nm* tabernacle.
tabicar [1] *vt* **1** *(ventana, puerta)* to wall up. **2** *(habitación)* to partition off, divide.
tabique *nm* partition, partition wall.
tabla *nf* **1** *(de madera)* board, plank. **2** *(de piedra)* slab; *(de metal)* sheet. **3** *(estante)* shelf. **4** ARTE panel. **5** COST pleat. **6** *(índice)* index. **7** *(lista)* list; *(catálogo)* catalogue (US catalog). **8** MAT table. ● **tabla de multiplicar** multiplication table.
▷ *nf pl* **tablas** **1** TEAT stage *sing*, boards. **2** *(ajedrez)* stalemate *sing*, draw *sing*.
tablado *nm* **1** *(suelo)* wooden floor. **2** *(entarimado)* wooden platform. **3** *(del escenario)* stage.
tablero *nm* **1** *(tablón)* panel, board. **2** *(en juegos)* board. **3** *(encerado)* blackboard. **4** AUTO dashboard. **5** INFORMÁ display board. ● **tablero de ajedrez** chessboard.
tableta *nf* **1** *(pastilla)* tablet. **2** *(de chocolate)* bar.
tablilla *nf* **1** small board. **2** MED splint.
tablón *nm* **1** plank. **2** *(en construcción)* board. ● **tablón de anuncios** notice board, US bulletin board.
tabú *adj inv* taboo.
▲ *pl* **tabúes o tabús.**
tabulación *nf* tabulation.
tabulador *nm* tabulator.
tabular *adj* tabular.
▷ *vt* to tabulate.
taburete *nm* stool.
tacañería *nf* stinginess, meanness.
tacaño,-a *adj* mean, stingy.
tacatá *nm* baby-walker.
tacataca *nm* baby-walker.
tacha[1] *nf* **1** *(defecto)* flaw, blemish, defect. **2** *(descrédito)* blemish.
tacha[2] *nf (tachuela)* tack.
tachadura *nf* crossing out.
tachar *vt* **1** *(borrar)* to cross out. **2** *(culpar)* to accuse **(de,** of): **lo tachan de fascista** *they accuse him of being a fascist.*
tachón *nm (tachadura)* crossing out.
tachonar *vt* **1** *(con tachones)* to stud, cover with studs. **2** *fig (salpicar)* to stud, dot.
tachuela *nf* tack, stud.
tacita *nf* little cup.
tácito,-a *adj* tacit.
taciturno,-a *adj* **1** *(callado)* taciturn, silent. **2** *(triste)* sad, melancholy.
taco *nm* **1** *(tarugo)* plug, stopper. **2** *(para pared)* plug, Rawlplug. **3** *(bloc de notas)* notepad, writing pad; *(calendario)* tear-off calendar. **4** *(de entradas)* book; *(de billetes)* wad. **5** *(de billar)* cue. **6** CULIN *(de queso, etc)* cube, piece; *(en Méjico)* taco, rolled-up tortilla. **7** *fam (palabrota)* swearword.
tacógrafo *nm* tachograph.
tacómetro *nm* tachometer.
tacón *nm* heel.
taconear *vi (pisar)* to tap one's heels, click one's heels; *(golpear)* to stamp one's heels.
taconeo *nm (pisada)* heel-tapping, clicking of the heels; *(golpe)* stamping with the heels.
táctica *nf* tactic, tactics *pl*, strategy.
táctico,-a *adj* tactical.
▷ *nm & nf* tactician.
táctil *adj* tactile.
tacto *nm* **1** *(sentido)* touch. **2** *(acción)* touch, touching. **3** *fig (delicadeza)* tact. ■ **tener tacto** to be tactful.
Tadjikistán *nm* Tadzhikistan.
tadjiko,-a *adj* Tadzhiki.
▷ *nm o nf (persona)* Tadzhik.
▷ *nm* **tadjiko** *(idioma)* Tadzhiki.
taekwondo *nm* tae kwon do.
tafetán *nm* taffeta.
tafilete *nm* Morocco leather.
tagalo,-a *adj* Tagalog.
▷ *nm & nf* Tagalog.
▷ *nm* **tagalo** *(idioma)* Tagalog.
Tahití *nm* Tahiti.
tahitiano,-a *adj* Tahitian.
▷ *nm & nf (persona)* Tahitian.
▷ *nm* **tahitiano** *(idioma)* Tahitian.
tahona *nf* **1** *(molino)* flour-mill. **2** *(panadería)* bakery.
tahúr,-ura *nm & nf* cardsharper, cardsharp.
taifa *nf* **1** *(facción)* faction. **2** *fam fig* gang of villains. ● **reinos de taifa** *small Spanish kingdoms after the disintegration of the Caliphate of Córdoba in 1031.*
taiga *nf* taiga.
tailandés,-esa *adj* Thai.
▷ *nm & nf (persona)* Thai.
▷ *nm* **tailandés** *(idioma)* Thai.
Tailandia *nf* Thailand.
taimado,-a *adj* sly, crafty.
Taiwán *nm* Taiwan.

taiwanés,-esa *adj* Taiwanese.
> *nm & nf* Taiwanese.
tajada *nf* **1** *(rodaja)* slice. **2** *(corte)* cut; *(cuchillada)* stab.
tajante *adj fig* emphatic, categorical.
tajar *vt* to cut, chop, slice (off).
tajo *nm* **1** *(corte)* cut, slash. **2** *(filo)* cutting edge. **3** *(escarpa)* steep cliff.
tal *adj* **1** *(semejante)* such: **en tales condiciones** *in such conditions.* **2** *(tan grande)* such, so: **tal es su ignorancia que...** *he is so ignorant that...* **3** *(cosa sin especificar)* such and such: **tal día** *such and such a day.* **4** *(persona sin especificar)* someone called, a certain: **vino un tal Alberto** *someone called Alberto came.*
▷ *pron (alguno - cosa)* such a thing, something; *(- persona)* someone, somebody: **yo no dije tal cosa** *I didn't say such a thing.*
▷ *adv (así)* in such a way, so: **tal me contestó que no supe cómo reaccionar** *he answered in such a way that I didn't know how to react.* ■ **tal como 1** *(ejemplos)* such as. **2** *(de la misma manera)* just as. ‖ **tal cual** just as it is. ‖ **tal y como** just as, as.
tala *nf* tree felling.
taladrador,-ra *nm & nf* driller, borer.
taladradora *nf (herramienta)* drill.
taladrar *vt* **1** *(gen)* to drill; *(pared)* to bore through. **2** *fig (los oídos)* to pierce.
taladro *nm* **1** *(herramienta)* drill, bore. **2** *(agujero)* hole.
tálamo *nm (lecho conyugal)* nuptial bed.
talante *nm* **1** *(disposición)* disposition, mood. **2** *(voluntad)* willingness.
talar *vt* **1** *(cortar)* to fell. **2** *(destruir)* to devastate.
talasoterapia *nf* thalassotherapy.
talco *nm* talc.
talega *nf (bolsa)* bag, sack.
talego *nm* **1** *(bolsa)* long bag, long sack. **2** *(contenido)* bagful, sackful. **3** *argot fig (cárcel)* clink, hole. **4** *argot fig (antiguamente)* one-thousand peseta note.
talento *nm* **1** *(entendimiento)* talent, intelligence. **2** *(aptitud)* gift, talent.
talentoso,-a *adj* talented, gifted.
talio *nm* thallium.
talión *nm* talion. ■ **la ley del talión** an eye for an eye, a tooth for a tooth.
talismán *nm* talisman, lucky charm.
talla *nf* **1** *(estatura)* height. **2** *fig (moral, intelectual)* stature. **3** *(de prenda)* size: **¿qué talla usa?** *what size is he?* **4** *(escultura)* carving, sculpture. **5** *(tallado - piedras)* cutting; *(- metal)* engraving.
tallado,-a *adj (piedra)* cut; *(madera)* carved.
tallador,-ra *nm & nf (grabador)* engraver.
tallar *vt* **1** *(madera, piedra)* to carve, shape; *(piedras preciosas)* to cut; *(metales)* to engrave. **2** *(medir)* to measure the height of.
tallarín *nm* noodle, tagliatelle *sing.*
talle *nm* **1** *(cintura)* waist. **2** *(figura - de hombre)* build, physique; *(- de mujer)* figure, shape.
taller *nm* **1** *(obrador)* workshop. **2** *(de artista)* studio. **3** *(en fábrica)* shop, workshop. **4** AUTO garage, repair shop.
tallista *nm o nf* woodcarver, carver.
tallo *nm* BOT stem, stalk; *(renuevo)* sprout, shoot.
talludo,-a *adj* **1** *(planta)* leggy, tall. **2** *fig (crecido)* grown, grown-up.
talmud *nm* Talmud.
talo *nm* thallus.
talón *nm* **1** *(de pie, zapato, etc)* heel. **2** *(cheque)* cheque (US check). ● **talón bancario** counter cheque (US check). ‖ **talón de Aquiles** Achilles' heel.
talonario *nm (de cheques)* cheque book (US check book); *(de recibos)* stub book.
talonera *nf (pantalones)* binding; *(medias, etc)* heel-piece; *(de fijación)* heel-grip.
talud *nm* slope.
tamaño,-a *adj (semejante)* such a, so big a: **no pude aguantar tamaña impertinencia** *I couldn't tolerate such an impertinent remark.*
▷ *nm* **tamaño** *(medida)* size.
tamarindo *nm* tamarind.
tamarisco *nm* tamarisk.
tambalearse *vpr* **1** *(persona)* to stagger, totter; *(mueble)* to wobble. **2** *fig* to be shaky.
tambaleo *nm* **1** *(de persona)* staggering, reeling. **2** *(de mueble)* wobble, wobbling.
también *adv* **1** *(igualmente)* also, too, as well, so: **Pedro también estaba** *Pedro was also there, Pedro was there too, Pedro was there as well.* **2** *(además)* besides, in addition.
tambor *nm* **1** *(instrumento)* drum. **2** *(maquinaria)* drum. **3** *(de arma)* cylinder, barrel. **4** *(de lavadora)* drum. **5** *(de freno)* brake drum.
tamboril *nm* small drum.
tamborilear *vi* **1** *(golpear el tambor)* to play the drum. **2** *(repiquetear)* to drum.
tamborileo *nm* drumming.
tamborilero,-a *nm & nf* drummer.
tamiz *nm* sieve.
tamizar [4] *vt* **1** *(harina, tierra)* to sieve. **2** *(luz)* to filter. **3** *fig (seleccionar)* to screen.
tampoco *adv* neither, nor, not... either: **no quiere estudiar y tampoco quiere ir al cine** *he doesn't want to study and he doesn't want to go to the cinema either.*
tampón *nm* **1** *(de entintar)* inkpad. **2** MED tampon.
tam-tam *nm* tom-tom.
tan *adv* **1** *(tanto)* such, such a, so: **no seas tan cruel** *don't be so cruel.* **2** *(comparativo - como)* as... as, so... (that); *(- que)* so..., so... (that): **está tan gordo como tú** *he's as fat as you (are).* ■ **tan solo** only, just: **tan solo quiero uno** *I only want one.*
tanatorio *nm* chapel of rest.
tanda *nf* **1** *(conjunto)* batch, lot; *(serie)* series, course. **2** *(turno)* shift. **3** *(en billar)* game.
tándem *nm* **1** *(bicicleta)* tandem. **2** *fig (de dos personas)* team of two, tandem.
▲ *pl* **tándemes.**
tanga *nm* G-string, tanga.
tangencial *adj* tangential.
tangente *adj* tangent.
▷ *nf* tangent.
tangible *adj* tangible.
tango *nm* tango.
tanino *nm* tannin.
tanque *nm* **1** *(depósito)* tank, reservoir. **2** MIL tank. **3** *(vehículo cisterna)* tanker.
tantear *vt* **1** *(calcular)* to estimate, guess. **2** *(probar medidas)* to size up. **3** *fig (ensayar)* to try out, put to the test. **4** *fig (persona)* to sound out. **5** *(dibujo)* to sketch.

▷ *vi* **1** DEP to score, keep score. **2** *(andar a tientas)* to feel one's way.

tanteo *nm* **1** *(cálculo aproximado)* estimate, guess. **2** *(prueba)* reckoning, rough estimate; *(de medidas)* sizing up. **3** *(sondeo)* trial, test. **4** *(de persona)* sounding out. **5** DEP score.

tanto,-a *adj* **1** *(incontables)* so much; *(contables)* so many: **no comas tantos caramelos** *don't eat so many sweets (US so much candy)*. **2** *(comparación - incontable)* as much; *(- contables)* as many: **tengo tantos libros como tú** *I've got as many books as you.*

▷ *pron (incontable)* so much; *(contable)* so many: **no había tantos** *there weren't so many.*

▷ *adv* **1** *(cantidad)* so much: **¡te quiero tanto!** *I love you so much!* **2** *(tiempo)* so long: **esperamos tanto** *we waited for so long.* **3** *(frecuencia)* so often: **no los telefonees tanto** *don't phone them so often.*

▷ *nm* **tanto 1** *(punto)* point; *(fútbol)* goal. **2** *(cantidad imprecisa)* so much, a certain amount: **percibes un tanto al mes** *you get so much a month.* **3** *(poco)* bit: **es un tanto estrecho** *it's a bit narrow.* ■ **a las tantas** *fam* very late, at an unearthly hour. ‖ **por lo tanto** therefore.

Tanzania *nf* Tanzania.

tanzano,-a *adj* Tanzanian.

▷ *nm & nf* Tanzanian.

tañedor,-ra *nm & nf* player: **un tañedor de laúd** *a lute player, a lutanist.*

tañer [38] *vt* **1** *(instrumento)* to play. **2** *(campanas)* to ring, toll.

tañido *nm* **1** *(de instrumento)* sound. **2** *(de campanas)* ringing, toll, peal.

taoísmo *nm* Taoism.

taoísta *adj* Taoist.

tapa *nf* **1** *(cubierta)* lid, top; *(de botella)* cap, top, stopper. **2** *(de libro)* cover. **3** *(de zapato)* heel-plate. **4** CULIN *(comida)* appetizer, savoury (US savory), tapa.

tapacubos *nm inv* hubcap.

tapadera *nf* **1** cover, lid. **2** *fig* cover, front.

tapajuntas *nm inv* beading, fillet.

tapar *vt* **1** *(cubrir)* to cover; *(con tapa)* to put the lid on, put the top on. **2** *(con ropas, etc)* to wrap up. **3** *(obstruir)* to obstruct; *(tubería)* to block. **4** *(ocultar)* to hide; *(a la vista)* to block. **5** *fig (encubrir)* to cover up.

▷ *vpr* **taparse 1** *(abrigarse)* to wrap up. **2** *(la nariz)* to be blocked up.

tapete *nm* **1** *(alfombra)* rug. **2** *(paño)* runner.

tapia *nf (cerca)* garden wall; *(de adobe)* mud wall.

tapiado,-a *adj* walled.

tapiar [12] *vt* **1** *(área)* to wall in, wall off. **2** *fig (puerta, ventana)* to wall up, close up.

tapicería *nf* **1** ARTE tapestry making. **2** *(tapices)* tapestries *pl*. **3** *(de muebles, etc)* upholstery. **4** *(tienda)* upholsterer's, upholsterer's workshop.

tapicero,-a *nm & nf* **1** *(de muebles, coche)* upholsterer. **2** ARTE tapestry maker.

tapioca *nf* tapioca.

tapir *nm* tapir.

tapiz *nm* **1** *(de pared)* tapestry. **2** *(alfombra)* rug, carpet.

tapizado *nm* **1** *(acción)* upholstering. **2** *(material)* upholstery material.

tapizar [4] *vt (muebles)* to upholster.

tapón *nm* **1** stopper, plug; *(de botella)* cap, cork. **2** *(de oído)* wax in the ear. **3** *(baloncesto)* block. **4** *(embotellamiento)* traffic jam.

taponamiento *nm* plugging, obturation.

taponar *vt* **1** *(orificio, etc)* to plug, stop. **2** *(atascar)* to block. **3** *(poner el tapón)* to put the plug in. **4** MED to tampon, plug.

tapujo *nm* **1** *(embozo)* muffler. **2** *fig (disimulo)* deceit, secrecy.

taquicardia *nf* tachycardia.

taquigrafía *nf* tachygraphy, shorthand.

taquigráfico,-a *adj* written in shorthand.

taquígrafo,-a *nm & nf* tachygrapher, stenographer.

taquilla *nf* **1** *(de tren, etc)* ticket office, booking office; *(de cine, teatro)* box office. **2** *(recaudación)* takings *pl*, returns *pl*. **3** *(casillero)* pigeonholes *pl*. **4** *(armario)* locker.

taquillero,-a *nm & nf* booking clerk, ticket clerk.

▷ *adj fig* popular, big at the box office: **una película taquillera** *a film which is a box-office hit.*

taquimecanografía *nf* shorthand and typing.

taquimecanógrafo,-a *nm & nf* shorthand typist.

taquímetro *nm* tacheometer, tachymeter.

tara *nf* **1** *(peso)* tare. **2** *(defecto)* defect, blemish, fault.

taracea *nf* marquetry.

taraceado,-a *adj* inlaid.

taracear *vt* to inlay.

tarado,-a *adj* **1** *(defectuoso)* defective, damaged. **2** *(persona)* handicapped.

▷ *nm & nf fam fig* idiot, nitwit.

tarántula *nf* tarantula.

tarar *vt* to tare.

tararear *vt* to hum.

tarareo *nm* humming.

tardanza *nf* delay.

tardar *vt (emplear tiempo)* to take.

▷ *vi (demorar)* to take a long time: **se tarda más a pie** *it takes longer on foot.*

tarde *nf* **1** *(hasta las cinco aprox.)* afternoon. **2** *(después de las cinco aprox.)* evening.

▷ *adv* **1** *(hora avanzada)* late: **se está haciendo tarde** *it's getting late.* **2** *(demasiado tarde)* too late.

tardío,-a *adj* late, belated.

tardón,-ona *adj fam* very slow.

▷ *nm & nf fam* slowcoach.

tarea *nf* task, job.

tarifa *nf* **1** *(precio)* tariff, rate; *(de transporte)* fare. **2** *(lista de precios)* price list.

tarifar *vt (fijar tarifa)* to put a price to, price.

tarima *nf* platform, dais.

tarjeta *nf* card. ● **tarjeta de crédito** credit card. ‖ **tarjeta de memoria** memory card, chip card. ‖ **tarjeta de presentación** business card. ‖ **tarjeta postal** postcard.

tarjetero *nm* wallet for visiting-cards.

tarlatana *nf* tarlatan.

tarot *nm* tarot.

tarrina *nf* tub.

tarro *nm* **1** *(vasija)* jar, pot, tub. **2** *fam (cabeza)* bonce.

tarso *nm* tarsus.

tarta *nf* flan, tart, pie: **tarta de manzana** *apple pie.*

tartaleta *nf* small pastry case.

tartamudeante *adj* stammering.

tartamudear *vi* to stammer, stutter.

tartamudeo *nm* 1 *(acción)* stammering, stuttering. 2 *(defecto)* stammer, stutter.
tartamudez *nf* stammering, stuttering.
tartamudo,-a *nm & nf* stutterer, stammerer.
tartán [Registered trademark.] *nm (tela)* tartan.
tartana *nf* 1 *(embarcación)* tartan. 2 *(carruaje)* trap. 3 *fam fig (coche)* banger, heap.
tártaro[1] *nm (depósito)* tartar.
tártaro,-a[2] *adj* Tartar.
▷ *nm & nf* Tartar.
tartera *nf (fiambrera)* lunchbox.
tarugo *nm* 1 *(de madera)* lump of wood. 2 *fam fig (persona)* blockhead.
tarumba *adj fam* mad, crazy, bonkers.
tas *nm* anvil.
tasa *nf* 1 *(valoración)* valuation, appraisal. 2 *(precio)* fee, charge. 3 *(impuesto)* tax, levy. 4 *(límite)* limit; *(medida)* measure. 5 *(índice)* rate. ● **tasa de natalidad** birth rate.
tasación *nf* valuation, appraisal.
tasador,-ra *nm & nf* valuer.
tasar *vt* 1 *(valorar)* to value, appraise. 2 *(poner precio)* to set the price of, fix the price of.
Tasmania *nf* Tasmania.
tasmano,-a *adj* Tasmanian.
▷ *nm & nf* Tasmanian.
tata *nf fam* nanny.
tatami *nm* judo mat.
tatarabuelo,-a *nm & nf (hombre)* great-great-grandfather; *(mujer)* great-great-grandmother.
tataranieto,-a *nm & nf (hombre)* great-great-grandson; *(mujer)* great-great-granddaughter.
tatuaje *nm* 1 *(dibujo)* tattoo. 2 *(técnica)* tattooing.
tatuar [11] *vt* to tattoo.
tau *nf* tau.
taumaturgia *nf* thaumaturgy.
taumaturgo,-a *nm & nf* thaumaturge.
taurino,-a *adj (del toro)* taurine; *(de la fiesta)* bullfighting.
Tauro *nm* Taurus.
tauromaquia *nf* bullfighting, tauromachy.
tautología *nf* tautology.
taxativo,-a *adj* precise, restricted, specific.
taxi *nm* taxi, cab.
taxidermia *nf* taxidermy.
taxidermista *nm o nf* taxidermist.
taxímetro *nm* taximeter, clock.
taxista *nm o nf* taxi driver.
taxonomía *nf* taxonomy.
taza *nf* 1 *(recipiente)* cup. 2 *(contenido)* cupful. 3 *(de retrete)* bowl.
tazón *nm* bowl.
te[1] *nf* 1 *name of the letter* t. 2 *(regla)* T-square.
te[2] *pron* 1 you, to you, for you: **te mandaré una carta** *I'll send you a letter.* 2 *(uso reflexivo)* yourself: **ponte el abrigo** *put your coat on.* 3 *(uso pronominal) no se traduce*: **vete a casa** *go home.*
té *nm* tea. ● **la hora del té** teatime.
teatral *adj* 1 *(del teatro)* theatrical, dramatic. 2 *fig (exagerado)* stagy, stagey, theatrical.
teatralidad *nf* theatricality, staginess.
teatralizar *vt* 1 to stage. 2 *fig* to dramatize.
teatro *nm* 1 theatre (US theater). 2 ARTE theatre (US theater), stage. 3 *fig (exageración)* show, play-acting.
tebeo *nm* children's comic.
teca *nf (árbol, madera)* teak.
techado *nm* roof, covering.
techar *vt* to roof.
techo *nm* 1 *(interior)* ceiling; *(de coche, tejado)* roof. 2 *fig (límite superior)* ceiling.
techumbre *nf (techo)* roof; *(materiales)* covering.
tecla *nf* key.
teclado *nm* keyboard.
teclear *vi (piano)* to press the keys; *(máquina de escribir, ordenador)* to type, tap the keys.
tecleo *nm* 1 MÚS fingering. 2 *(ruido)* rattle, clatter.
teclista *nm o nf* MÚS keyboard player.
técnica *nf* 1 *(tecnología)* technique, technology. 2 *(habilidad)* technique. 3 *(ingeniería)* engineering.
tecnicismo *nm* technical term, technical expression.
técnico,-a *adj* technical.
▷ *nm & nf* technician, technical expert.
tecnicolor® *nm* Technicolor®.
tecnocracia *nf* technocracy.
tecnócrata *nm o nf* technocrat.
tecnocrático,-a *adj* technocratic.
tecnología *nf* technology.
tecnológico,-a *adj* technological.
tectónica *nf* tectonics.
tectónico,-a *adj* tectonic.
tedio *nm* tedium, boredom.
tedioso,-a *adj* tedious, boring.
tegumento *nm* integument, tegument.
teína *nf* theine.
teísmo *nm* theism.
teja *nf (de barro)* tile.
tejado *nm* roof.
tejano,-a *adj* Texan.
▷ *nm & nf* Texan.
▷ *nm pl* **tejanos** *(pantalón)* jeans.
tejar *vt* to tile.
tejedor,-ra *nm & nf* weaver.
tejemaneje *nm fam (enredos)* intrigue, scheming.
tejer *vt* 1 *(en telar)* to weave. 2 *(hacer punto)* to knit. 3 *(araña)* to spin. 4 *fig (plan)* to weave, plot, scheme.
tejido *nm* 1 *(tela)* fabric, textile. 2 ANAT tissue.
tejo[1] *nm* 1 *(juego del chito)* quoits *pl.* 2 *(juego del caracol)* hopscotch.
tejo[2] *nm (árbol)* yew tree.
tejón *nm* badger.
tela *nf* 1 *(textil)* material, fabric, cloth. 2 *(de araña)* cobweb. 3 ARTE *(lienzo)* canvas; *(cuadro)* painting. 4 *fam (dinero)* dough. 5 *fam (asunto, tema)* subject, matter
telar *nm* 1 *(para tejer)* loom. 2 *(para encuadernar)* sewing press.
telaraña *nf* cobweb, spider's web.
tele *nf fam* telly, TV.
teleadicto,-a *nm & nf* telly addict.
telearrastre *nm* ski lift, drag lift.
telecabina *nf* cable car.
teleclub *nm* television club.
telecomedia *nf* situation comedy.
telecomunicación *nf* telecommunication.
telediario *nm* television news bulletin, TV news.
teledifusión *nf* television broadcast.

teledirigido,-a *adj* remote-controlled.
teledirigir [6] *vt* to operate by remote control.
teleférico *nm* cable car, cable railway.
telefilm *nm* TV film (US TV movie).
telefonear *vi* to phone.
telefonía *nf* telephony, telephone system.
telefonista *nm o nf* telephonist.
teléfono *nm* telephone, phone. ● **teléfono móvil** mobile phone, cellular phone.
telegrafía *nf* telegraphy.
telegrafiar [13] *vt* to telegraph, wire.
telegráfico,-a *adj* telegraphic.
telegrafista *nm o nf* telegraphist, telegrapher.
telégrafo *nm* telegraph.
telegrama *nm* telegram, cable.
telemando *nm* remote control.
telemanía *nf* telly addiction.
telemaratón *nm* telethon.
telemática *nf* telematics.
telemático,-a *adj* telematic.
telemetría *nf* telemetry.
telémetro *nm* telemeter, rangefinder.
telenovela *nf* soap opera.
teleobjetivo *nm* telephoto lens.
telepatía *nf* telepathy.
telepático,-a *adj* telepathic.
teleprocesar *vt* to teleprocess.
teleproceso *nm* teleprocessing.
telequinesia *nf* telekinesis.
telescópico,-a *adj* telescopic.
telescopio *nm* telescope.
telesilla *nm* chair lift.
telespectador,-ra *nm & nf* TV viewer.
telesquí *nm* ski lift, drag lift.
teletexto *nm* teletext.
teletipo® *nm* 1 *(aparato)* Teletype, teleprinter. 2 *(noticia)* piece of news *(from an agency)*.
televidente *nm o nf* TV viewer.
televisar *vt* to televise.
televisión *nf* 1 *(sistema)* television. 2 *fam (aparato)* television set.
televisivo,-a *adj* television.
televisor *nm* television set.
télex® *nm* telex.
telón *nm* curtain. ● **telón de acero** POL iron curtain. ‖ **telón de fondo** TEAT backdrop.
telonero,-a *adj* first on stage, support.
telúrico,-a *adj* telluric.
tema *nm* 1 *(de discurso, escrito, etc)* topic, subject, theme. 2 MÚS theme.
temario *nm (de examen)* programme (US program).
temática *nf* subject matter.
temático,-a *adj* 1 thematic. 2 LING stem.
temblar [27] *vi* 1 *(de frío)* to shiver (**de**, with); *(de miedo)* to tremble (**de**, with). 2 *(voz)* to quiver.
temblón,-ona *adj fam* trembling, shaky.
temblor *nm* 1 *(gen)* tremor, shudder; *(de frío)* shivering, shivers *pl*. 2 *fig* shiver.
tembloroso,-a *adj (de frío)* shivering; *(de miedo)* trembling; *(con sacudidas)* shaking, shaky.
temer *vt* to fear, be afraid of..
▷ *vi* 1 *(tener miedo)* to be afraid. 2 *(preocuparse)* to worry.
▷ *vpr* **temerse** to be afraid: **me temo que sí** *I'm afraid so.*
temerario,-a *adj* reckless, rash.
temeridad *nf* 1 *(actitud)* temerity, rashness. 2 *(acto temerario)* reckless act.
temeroso,-a *adj* fearful.
temible *adj* dreadful, fearful, fearsome.
temor *nm* fear.
témpano *nm* ice floe.
temperamental *adj* temperamental.
temperamento *nm* temperament, nature.
temperar *vt* to temper, mitigate.
temperatura *nf* temperature.
tempestad *nf* 1 storm. 2 *fig* turmoil, uproar.
tempestuoso,-a *adj* stormy.
templado,-a *adj* 1 *(agua)* warm; *(clima, temperatura)* temperate. 2 *(moderado)* moderate; *(sereno)* composed. 3 *(valiente)* brave. 4 MÚS tuned. 5 *(metal)* tempered.
templanza *nf* moderation, restraint.
templar *vt* 1 *(moderar)* to moderate, temper. 2 *(algo frío)* to warm up; *(algo caliente)* to cool down. 3 *fig (cólera)* to appease; *(apaciguar)* to calm down. 4 *(cuerda, tornillo)* to tighten (up). 5 MÚS to tune. 6 TÉC to temper. 7 *(colores)* to match.
▷ *vpr* **templarse** *(contenerse)* to restrain OS, control OS.
templete *nm* pavilion, kiosk.
templo *nm* temple.
temporada *nf* 1 *(en artes, deportes, moda)* season. 2 *(período)* period, time. ● **temporada alta** high season. ‖ **temporada baja** low season.
temporal[1] *adj* 1 *(transitorio)* temporary, provisional.
▷ *nm* METEOR storm.
temporal[2] *adj* ANAT temporal.
▷ *nm* ANAT temporal bone.
temporalidad *nf* temporality.
temporero,-a *adj* seasonal, temporary.
▷ *nm & nf* seasonal worker.
temporizador *nm* timer.
tempranero,-a *adj* 1 *(persona)* early-riser: **es tempranero** *he's an early-riser.* 2 *(cosecha)* early.
temprano,-a *adj* early.
▷ *adv* early.
tenacidad *nf* tenacity, perseverance.
tenacillas *nf pl* 1 *(para rizar el pelo)* curling tongs. 2 *(para el azúcar)* sugar tongs.
tenaz *adj* 1 *(persona)* tenacious.
tenaza *nf* [Often used in plural with the same meaning.] *(herramienta)* pliers *pl*, pincers *pl*; *(para el fuego)* tongs *pl*.
tendal *nm* 1 *(toldo)* awning. 2 *(tendedero)* drying place.
tendedero *nm* clothesline.
tendencia *nf (inclinación)* tendency, inclination, predisposition, leaning; *(movimiento)* trend.
tendenciosidad *nf* tendentiousness, partiality.
tendencioso,-a *adj* tendentious, biased.
tendente *adj* directed (**a**, at), aimed (**a**, at).
tender [28] *vt* 1 *(extender - mantel, etc)* to spread; *(- red)* to cast. 2 *(puente)* to throw; *(vía, cable)* to lay; *(cuerda)* to stretch. 3 *(ropa, colada)* to hang out. 4 *(mano)* to stretch out, hold out. 5 *(emboscada, trampa)* to lay, set.
▷ *vi (tener tendencia)* to tend (**a**, to), have a tendency (**a**, to): **tiende al aburrimiento** *it tends to be boring.*
▷ *vpr* **tenderse** *(tumbarse)* to lie down, stretch out.

tenderete *nm (puesto)* stall.
tendero,-a *nm & nf* shopkeeper.
tendido,-a *adj* 1 *(extendido)* spread out, laid out. 2 *(ropa, colada)* hung out.
▷ *nm* **tendido** 1 *(de cable, vía)* laying; *(de puente)* construction. 2 *(colada)* wash, washing. 3 *(en los toros)* front tiers of seats, US bleachers *pl.*
tendón *nm* tendon, sinew.
tenebrismo *nm* tenebrism.
tenebrista *adj* tenebrist.
tenebroso,-a *adj* 1 *(sombrío)* dark, gloomy. 2 *fig (siniestro)* sinister, shady.
tenedor,-ra *nm (utensilio)* fork.
teneduría *nf* bookkeeping.
tenencia *nf* tenancy, possession.
tener [87] *vt* 1 *(gen)* to have, have got: **tuvimos un día estupendo** *we had a wonderful day.* 2 *(poseer)* to own, possess. 3 *(sostener)* to hold: **¿qué tienes en la mano?** *what are you holding?* 4 *(coger)* to take: **ten tu copa** *take your glass.* 5 *(sensación, sentimiento)* to be, feel: **tengo hambre** *I'm hungry.* 6 *(mantener)* to keep: **la lluvia me ha tenido despierta toda la noche** *the rain has kept me up all night.* 7 *(medir)* to measure. 8 *(contener)* to hold, contain. 9 *(edad)* to be. 10 *(un hijo)* to have. 11 *(celebrar)* to hold: **tener una reunión** *to hold a meeting.* 12 *(considerar)* to consider, think: **lo tienen por muy listo** *they think he's very smart.* ■ **¡ahí tienes!** so, there you are! ‖ **tener cariño a** to be fond of. ‖ **tener compasión** to take pity (**de**, on). ‖ **tener ilusión** to be enthusiastic.
▷ *aux* **tener que** *(obligación)* to have to, have got to, must: **tengo que quedarme** *I must stay.*
▷ *vpr* **tenerse** *(sostenerse)* to stand up. ■ **tenerse por** to consider OS, think OS: **se tiene por guapo** *he thinks he's handsome.*
tenería *nf* tannery.
tenia *nf* tapeworm.
teniente *nm* lieutenant.
tenis *nm (deporte)* tenis. ● **tennis de mesa** table tennis, ping-pong.
tenista *nm o nf* tennis player.
tenor *nm* 1 MÚS tenor. 2 *(conforme)* tenor, purport.
tensado,-a *adj* 1 *(cuerda, cable)* taut, tautened, tense. 2 *(arco)* drawn.
tensar *vt* 1 *(cable, cuerda)* to tauten. 2 *(arco)* to draw.
tensión *nf* 1 ELEC tension, voltage. 2 *(de materiales)* stress; *(de gases)* pressure. 3 MED pressure. 4 *fig (de una situación)* tension, tenseness; *(de una persona)* stress, strain. ● **alta tensión** ELEC high tension. ‖ **tensión arterial** blood pressure.
tenso,-a *adj* 1 *(cable, cuerda)* tense, taut. 2 *fig (relaciones)* strained. 3 *fig (persona)* tense.
tensor,-ra *adj* tensile, tightening.
▷ *nm* **tensor** 1 *(músculo)* tensor. 2 *(para musculación)* chest expander. 3 *(mecanismo)* turnbuckle.
tentación *nf* temptation.
tentáculo *nm* tentacle.
tentador,-ra *adj* tempting, enticing.
tentar [27] *vt* 1 *(palpar)* to feel, touch. 2 *(incitar)* to tempt.
tentativa *nf* attempt, try.
tentempié *nm fam (refrigerio)* snack, bite.
tenue *adj* 1 *(delgado)* thin, light, tenuous. 2 *(tela)* flimsy, thin. 3 *(luz, sonido)* subdued, faint.
teñido,-a *adj* 1 dyed; *(pelo)* tinted, dyed. 2 *fig* tinged.
teñir [36] *vt* 1 *(dar un color)* to dye. 2 *(rebajar un color)* to tone down.
▷ *vpr* **teñirse** *(el pelo)* to dye one's hair.
teocracia *nf* theocracy.
teodolito *nm* theodolite.
teologal *adj* theological.
teología *nf* theology.
teológico,-a *adj* theological.
teólogo,-a *nm & nf* theologian, theologist.
teorema *nm* theorem.
teoría *nf* theory. ■ **en teoría** theoretically.
teórica *nf* theory, theoretics.
teórico,-a *adj* theoretic, theoretical.
▷ *nm & nf* theoretician, theorist.
teorizar [4] *vi* to theorize (**sobre**, on).
teosofía *nf* theosophy.
tequila *nf* tequila.
terapeuta *nm o nf* therapist.
terapéutica *nf* therapeutics, therapy.
terapéutico,-a *adj* therapeutic.
terapia *nf* therapy.
tercer *adj* [Used before singular masculine nouns.] third: **el tercer mundo** *the third world.*
See also **tercero,-a.**
tercera *nf* 1 *(clase)* third class. 2 *(marcha de auto)* third gear, third. 3 MÚS third.
tercermundista *adj* third-world.
tercero,-a *adj (ordinal)* third.
▷ *nm & nf (parte)* third.
▷ *nm* **tercero** 1 *(mediador)* mediator. 2 *(persona ajena)* outsider. 3 JUR third party.
See also **sexto,-a.**
terceto *nm* 1 *(poesía)* tercet. 2 MÚS trio.
terciado,-a *adj (intermedio)* medium-size.
terciana *nf* tertian fever.
terciar [12] *vi* 1 *(mediar)* to mediate, arbitrate. 2 *(participar)* to take part, participate: **terciaron en el debate** *they took part in the debate.*
▷ *vt (poner en diagonal)* to place diagonally.
▷ *vpr* **terciarse** *(venir bien, darse)* to arise.
terciario,-a *adj* tertiary.
tercio,-a *adj* third.
▷ *nm* **tercio** 1 *(parte)* third. 2 *(en tauromaquia)* stage.
terciopelo *nm* velvet.
terco,-a *adj* obstinate, stubborn.
tergal® *nm type of synthetic textile fibre.*
tergiversar *vt* to twist, distort.
termal *adj* thermal.
termas *nf pl (baños)* spa *sing,* hot baths, hot springs.
termia *nf* therm.
térmico,-a *adj* thermal.
terminación *nf* 1 *(acción)* ending, termination. 2 *(conclusión)* completion. 3 *(parte final)* end. 4 GRAM ending.
terminado,-a *adj* finished, completed.
terminal *adj (último)* final, terminal.
▷ *nf* 1 *(estación)* terminus. 2 *(en aeropuerto)* terminal.
▷ *nm (de ordenador)* terminal.
terminante *adj* 1 *(categórico)* categorical, final. 2 *(dato, resultado)* conclusive, definitive, definite.
terminar *vt* 1 *(acabar)* to finish. 2 *(dar fin)* to end.

▷ *vi* 1 *(acabar)* to finish, end: **terminó a las cuatro** *it finished at four.* 2 *(acabar de)* to have just (**de**, -): **termina de marchar** *he has just left.* 3 *(final de una acción, de un estado)* to end up: **terminó por marcharse** *he ended up leaving.* 4 *(eliminar)* to put an end (**con**, **to**). 5 *(estropear)* to damage (**con**, -), ruin (**con**, -): **la lluvia terminó con la cosecha** *the rain damaged the crops.* 6 *(reñir)* to break up (**con**, with). 7 *(enfermedad)* to come to the final stage.
▷ *vpr* **terminarse** 1 *(acabarse)* to finish, end, be over. 2 *(agotarse)* to run out: **se ha terminado el azúcar** *the sugar has run out.*
término *nm* 1 *(fin)* end, finish. 2 *(estación)* terminus, terminal. 3 *(límite)* limit, boundary; *(hito)* boundary marker. 4 *(plazo)* term, time, period. 5 *(palabra)* term, word: **término técnico** *technical term.* 6 *(estado)* condition, state. 7 *(lugar, posición)* place. 8 *(en matemáticas, gramática)* term. ■ **dar término a** ALGO to conclude STH.
▷ *nm pl* **términos** *(condiciones)* conditions, terms.
terminología *nf* terminology.
terminológico,-a *adj* terminological.
termita *nf* termite.
termitero *nm* termite's nest.
termo *nm (recipiente)* flask, thermos flask.
termoaislante *adj* insulating.
termodinámica *nf* thermodynamics.
termodinámico,-a *adj* thermodynamic.
termometría *nf* thermometry.
termométrico,-a *adj* thermometrical.
termómetro *nm* thermometer.
termonuclear *adj* thermonuclear.
termostato *nm* thermostat.
terna *nf* list of three candidates.
ternario,-a *adj* ternary.
ternera *nf* CULIN veal, beef.
ternero,-a *nm & nf (animal)* calf.
ternilla *nf* cartilage.
terno *nm* 1 *(tres cosas)* set of three, group of three. 2 *(traje)* three-piece suit. 3 *fam (juramento)* swearword.
ternura *nf* tenderness, gentleness.
terquedad *nf (obstinación)* obstinacy, stubbornness.
terracota *nf* terracotta.
terrado *nm* flat roof, terrace.
terraplén *nm* embankment.
terráqueo,-a *adj* earth.
terrateniente *nm o nf* landowner.
terraza *nf* 1 *(balcón)* terrace, balcony. 2 *(azotea)* roof terrace, terrace. 3 *(de un café)* terrace.
terrazo *nm* terrazzo.
terremoto *nm* earthquake.
terrenal *adj* earthly, worldly.
terreno,-a *adj* worldly, earthly.
▷ *nm* **terreno** 1 *(tierra)* land, piece of land, ground; *(solar)* plot, site. 2 GEOG terrain. 3 AGR *(de cultivo)* soil; *(campo)* field. 4 DEP field, ground.
terrestre *adj* 1 *(de la tierra)* terrestrial, earthly. 2 *(por tierra)* by land.
terrible *adj* terrible, awful.
terrícola *nm o nf* earth dweller.
territorial *adj* territorial.
territorialidad *nf* territoriality.
territorio *nm* territory.
terrón *nm* 1 *(de tierra)* clod. 2 *(de azúcar, etc)* lump.
terror *nm* 1 *(gen)* terror. 2 CINE horror.
terrorífico,-a *adj* terrifying, frightening.
terrorismo *nm* terrorism.
terrorista *adj* terrorist.
▷ *nm o nf* terrorist.
terroso,-a *adj* 1 *(de la tierra)* earthy. 2 *(color)* earth-coloured (US earth-colored).
terruño *nm* 1 *(masa de tierra)* clod. 2 *(tierra natal)* homeland, native land. 3 *(tierra que se trabaja)* land.
terso,-a *adj* 1 *(liso)* smooth. 2 *(brillante)* shiny, glossy. 3 *fig (estilo)* polished, fluent.
tersura *nf* 1 *(lisura)* smoothness. 2 *(brillo)* shine.
tertulia *nf* 1 *(reunión)* get-together. 2 *(lugar en cafés)* back room. ● **tertulia literaria** literary gathering.
tertuliano,-a *nm & nf* person who participates in a gathering.
tesina *nf* degree dissertation.
tesis *nf inv* 1 thesis. 2 *(opinión)* view, theory. ● **tesis doctoral** doctoral thesis.
tesitura *nf fig (estado de ánimo)* mood, frame of mind.
tesón *nm* tenacity, firmness.
tesorería *nf (oficina)* treasurer's office; *(cargo)* treasurer.
tesorero,-a *nm & nf* treasurer.
tesoro *nm* 1 *(gen)* treasure. 2 *fig* treasure, gem. ● **Tesoro Público** Treasury.
test *nm* test.
▲ *pl* tests o test.
testa *nf* head.
testado,-a *adj* testate.
testador,-ra *nm & nf (hombre)* testator; *(mujer)* testatrix.
testaferro *nm* front man.
testamentario,-a *adj* testamentary.
▷ *nm & nf (hombre)* executor; *(mujer)* executrix.
testamento *nm* 1 JUR will, testament. 2 REL Testament. ■ **hacer testamento** to make one's will, draw up one's will. ● **Antiguo Testamento / Nuevo Testamento** Old Testament / New Testament.
testar *vi* to make one's will.
testarudez *nf* stubbornness, obstinacy.
testarudo,-a *adj* obstinate, stubborn, pig-headed.
testículo *nm* testicle.
testifical *adj* attesting, witnessing.
testificar [1] *vt* to testify.
testigo *nm o nf* witness.
▷ *nm* 1 *(prueba)* proof, evidence, witness. 2 DEP baton.
testimonial *adj* testimonial.
testimoniar [12] *vt* 1 JUR to bear witness to, testify to, attest to. 2 *fig* to show, prove, bear witness to.
testimonio *nm* 1 JUR testimony. 2 *(prueba)* evidence.
testosterona *nf* testosterone.
testuz *nm & nf* 1 *(frente)* forehead. 2 *(nuca)* nape.
teta *nf* 1 breast; *(más familiarmente)* tit, boob. 2 *(de animal)* udder.
tetánico,-a *adj* tetanic.
tétano *nm* tetanus.
tétanos *nm inv* tetanus.
tetera *nf* teapot.
tetilla *nf* 1 ANAT man's nipple. 2 *(tetina)* teat, rubber teat.
tetina *nf* teat, rubber teat.
tetrabrik® *nm* carton.
tetraedro *nm* tetrahedron.
tetragonal *adj* tetragonal.

tetralogía *nf* tetralogy.
tetrarquía *nf* tetrarchy.
tetrasílabo,-a *adj* tetrasyllabic.
▷ *nm* **tetrasílabo** tetrasyllable.
tétrico,-a *adj* gloomy, dull, dismal.
textil *adj* textile.
▷ *nm* textile.
texto *nm* text.
textual *adj* 1 textual. 2 *(exacto)* literal, precise, exact.
textura *nf* 1 *(textil)* texture. 2 *(minerales)* structure.
tez *nf* complexion.
ti *pron* [Used only after a preposition.] you: **te lo doy a ti** *I'll give it to you.*
tía *nf* 1 *(pariente)* aunt. 2 *fam (persona)* girl, woman.
tibia *nf* tibia, shinbone.
tibieza *nf* 1 tepidity, tepidness. 2 *fig* lack of enthusiasm, coolness, tepidity.
tibio,-a *adj* 1 tepid, lukewarm. 2 *fig* tepid, unenthusiastic, cool.
tiburón *nm* shark.
tic *nm* 1 tic, twitch. 2 *fig (manía)* habit.
ticket *nm* → **tique.**
tictac *nm* tick-tock, ticking.
tic-tac *nm* tick-tock.
tiempo *nm* 1 *(gen)* time. 2 *(época)* time, period, age, days *pl*: **en tiempo de los romanos** *in Roman times.* 3 METEOR weather: **¿qué tiempo hace?** *what's the weather like?* 4 *(edad)* age: **¿qué tiempo tiene el niño?** *how old is your baby?* 5 *(temporada)* season, time: **fruta del tiempo** *fruit in season.* 6 *(momento)* moment, time: **no es tiempo de preguntarle eso** *it's not the time to ask him that.* 7 MÚS tempo, movement. 8 DEP *(parte)* half. 9 GRAM tense. 10 TÉC stroke. ■ **a tiempo** 1 *(en el momento oportuno)* in time. 2 *(a la hora)* on time. ‖ **hacer buen tiempo** the weather is good. ● **tiempo libre** free time.
tienda *nf* 1 *(establecimiento)* shop, US store. 2 *(de campaña)* tent. 3 *(de carro)* cover. ■ **ir de tiendas** to go shopping. ● **tienda de campaña** tent.
tienta *nf (sagacidad)* sagacity, cleverness. ■ **a tientas** by touch.
tiento *nm* 1 *(tacto)* tact, feel. 2 *(prudencia)* caution. ■ **con tiento** tactfully.
tierno,-a *adj* 1 *(blando)* tender, soft. 2 *fig (reciente)* fresh: **pan tierno** *fresh bread.* 3 *fig (cariñoso)* affectionate.
tierra *nf* 1 *(planeta)* earth. 2 *(superficie sólida)* land. 3 *(terreno cultivado)* soil, land. 4 *(país)* country, land. 5 *(suelo)* ground. 6 ELEC earth, US ground.
▷ *nf pl* **tierras** land *sing.* ■ **tierra adentro** inland. ● **tierra de nadie** no-man's-land. ‖ **tierra firme** terra firma, dry land.
tieso,-a *adj* 1 *(rígido)* stiff, rigid. 2 *(erguido)* upright, erect. 3 *(tenso)* taut, tight.
tiesto *nm* flowerpot.
tifoideo,-a *adj* typhoid. ● **fiebre tifoidea** typhoid fever.
tifón *nm* typhoon.
tifus *nm inv* typhus, typhus fever.
tigre *nm* tiger.
tigresa *nf fig* femme fatale.
tijera *nf* [Generally used in plural.] *(instrumento)* scissors *pl*, pair of scissors.
tijereta *nf (insecto)* earwig.
tijeretazo *nm* snip.
tila *nf* 1 *(tilo)* lime. 2 *(flor)* lime blossom. 3 *(infusión)* lime-blossom tea.
tildar *vt* 1 *(poner tilde)* to put a written accent on; *(de la ñ)* to put a tilde on. 2 *(a una persona)* to call, brand: **lo tildaron de mentiroso** *they branded him a liar.*
tilde *nf* 1 *(gen)* written accent; *(de la ñ)* tilde. 2 *fig (tacha)* fault, flaw.
tilo *nm* lime tree.
timador,-ra *nm & nf* swindler, cheat.
timar *vt* to swindle, cheat, trick.
timba *nf fam (partida)* game, hand.
timbal *nm* MÚS kettledrum.
timbrado,-a *adj* stamped.
timbrar *vt* to stamp, mark.
timbrazo *nm* loud ring, long ring.
timbre *nm* 1 *(de la puerta)* bell. 2 *(sello)* stamp, seal. 3 MÚS timbre.
timidez *nf* shyness, timidity.
tímido,-a *adj* shy, timid.
timo[1] *nm (estafa)* swindle.
timo[2] *nm (glándula)* thymus.
timón *nm* 1 *(barco, avión)* rudder. 2 *(del arado)* beam. 3 *fig (negocio, etc)* helm.
timonel *nm* steersman, helmsman.
timonera *nf* rectrix.
Timor Oriental *nm* East Timor.
timorato,-a *adj (tímido)* shy, timid.
tímpano *nm (del oído)* eardrum.
tina *nf* 1 *(recipiente)* vat, tub. 2 *(tinaja)* large earthenware vat. 3 *(bañera)* bath, bathtub.
tinaja *nf* large earthenware jar.
tinglado *nm* 1 *(cobertizo)* shed. 2 *(tablado)* platform, raised floor. 3 *fig (embrollo)* mess.
tiniebla *nf* [Also used in plural with the same meaning.] *(oscuridad)* darkness.
▷ *nf pl* **tinieblas** *fig (ignorancia)* ignorance *sing*, confusion *sing*.
tino *nm* 1 *(puntería)* good aim, aim. 2 *fig (juicio)* good judgement, sense. 3 *fig (moderación)* moderation.
tinta *nf* 1 *(gen)* ink. 2 *(tinte)* dyeing.
▷ *nf pl* **tintas** colours (US colors), hues. ■ **cargar las tintas** *fig* to exaggerate. ‖ **saber ALGO de buena tinta** *fig* to get STH straight from the horse's mouth. ‖ **sudar tinta** *fig* to sweat blood. ● **tinta china** Indian ink.
tintar *vt* to dye.
tinte *nm* 1 *(colorante)* dye. 2 *(proceso)* dyeing. 3 *(tintorería)* dry-cleaner's. 4 *fig (aspecto)* shade, colouring (US coloring), overtones *pl*.
tintero *nm* inkwell.
tintinear *vi* → **tintinar.**
tintineo *nm* 1 *(de vidrio)* clink, clinking, chink. 2 *(de campanillas)* jingling, ting-a-ling.
tinto,-a *adj* 1 *(teñido)* dyed, stained. 2 *(vino)* red.
▷ *nm* **tinto** *(vino)* red wine.
tintorería *nf* dry-cleaner's.
tintorero,-a *nm & nf* dry-cleaner.
tintura *nf* 1 *(colorante)* dye. 2 *(proceso)* dyeing. 3 *(disolución)* tincture.
tiña *nf* 1 *(larva)* honeycomb moth. 2 MED tinea.
tiñoso,-a *adj* MED scabby, mangy.
tío *nm* 1 *(pariente)* uncle. 2 *fam (hombre)* bloke, guy.
▷ *nm pl* **tíos** aunt and uncle.

tiovivo *nm* merry-go-round, US carrousel.
tipi *nm* tepee, wigwam.
típico,-a *adj* 1 *(característico)* typical, characteristic. 2 *(pintoresco)* picturesque; *(tradicional)* traditional.
tipificación *nf* 1 *(normalización)* standardization. 2 *(caracterización)* typification.
tipificar [1] *vt* 1 *(normalizar)* to standardize. 2 *(caracterizar)* to typify.
tiple *nm o nf (cantante)* soprano, soprano singer.
tipo *nm* 1 *(clase)* type, kind. 2 FIN rate. 3 ANAT *(de hombre)* build, physique; *(de mujer)* figure. 4 *fam (persona)* guy, fellow, bloke. 5 *(en impresión)* type. ■ **aguantar el tipo** *fig* to keep cool, keep calm. ● **tipo de interés** FIN rate of interest.
tipografía *nf* typography.
tipográfico,-a *adj* typographic, typographical. ● **error tipográfico** printing error.
tipógrafo,-a *nm & nf* typographer.
tipología *nf* typology.
tíquet *nm* → **tique**.
▲ *pl* **tíquets**.
tiquismiquis *nm pl* 1 *(escrúpulos)* fussing *sing*. 2 *(riñas)* bickering *sing*.
▷ *nm o nf inv fam (persona)* fusspot.
tira *nf* 1 *(cinta, banda)* strip. 2 *(de dibujos)* comic strip.
▷ *loc* **la tira** *(cantidad)* a lot, loads; *(mucho tiempo)* for yonks.
tirabuzón *nm (rizo)* ringlet.
tirachinas *nm inv* catapult, US slingshot.
tirada *nf* 1 *(acción)* throw: **en la segunda tirada le salieron dos seises** *he got two sixes on the second throw*. 2 *(impresión)* print run: **una tirada de cinco mil ejemplares** *a print run of five thousand*. 3 *(distancia)* stretch: **hay una buena tirada hasta allí** *it's a good few miles away*. 4 *(serie)* series, long series. ■ **de una tirada** in one go.
tirado,-a *adj* 1 *fam (precio)* dirt cheap. 2 *fam (problema, asunto)* dead easy. 3 *fam (abandonado)* let down.
tirador,-ra *nm & nf (persona)* shooter, marksman.
▷ *nm (de puerta, cajón)* knob, handle.
tiraje *nm* 1 *(impresión)* printing. 2 *(distribución)* circulation.
tiralíneas *nm inv* drawing pen.
tiranía *nf* tyranny.
tiránico,-a *adj* tyrannic, tyrannical.
tiranizar [4] *vt* to tyrannize.
tirano,-a *nm & nf* tyrant.
tirante *adj* 1 taut, tight. 2 *fig (relación, situación)* tense.
▷ *nm* 1 *(de tela)* strap. 2 TÉC brace. 3 ARQUIT beam.
▷ *nm pl* **tirantes** *(de pantalón)* braces, US suspenders.
tirantez *nf* 1 *(tensión)* tautness, tightness. 2 *fig (de relación, etc)* tension, strain.
tirar *vt* 1 *(echar)* to throw, fling. 2 *(dejar caer)* to drop. 3 *(desechar)* to throw away. 4 *(derribar)* to knock down; *(casa, árbol)* to pull down. 5 *(derramar)* to spill. 6 *(vaso, botella)* to knock over. 7 *(estirar)* to pull. 8 *(imprimir)* to print. 9 *(un tiro)* to fire; *(una bomba)* to drop; *(cohete)* to launch. 10 DEP to take. 11 *fig (malgastar)* to waste.
▷ *vi* 1 *(cuerda, puerta)* to pull (**de**, -). 2 *(estufa, etc)* to draw. 3 *(en juegos)* to be a player's move, be a player's turn: **tira él** *it's his turn*. 4 *fam (funcionar)* to work, run: **esto ya no tira** *this doesn't work any more*. 5 *fam (durar)* to last: **con esta reparación tirará un par de meses** *after these repairs it'll last for a couple of months*. 6 *fam fig (atraer)* to attract, appeal: **no le tira la mecánica** *mechanics doesn't appeal to him*. 7 *fig (inclinarse)* to be attracted (**a/hacia**, to), be drawn (**a/hacia**, to): **esta chica tira hacia las artes** *this girl is drawn to the arts*. 8 *fig (mantenerse)* to get by, get along: **ella tira con poco dinero** *she gets by with little money*. 9 *(disparar)* to shoot, fire. 10 DEP *(fútbol)* to shoot; *(ciclismo)* to set the pace.
▷ *vpr* **tirarse** 1 *(lanzarse)* to throw OS, hurl OS. 2 *(abalanzarse)* to rush (**sobre**, at), jump (**sobre**, on). 3 *(tumbarse)* to lie down. 4 *fam (tiempo)* to spend: **se tiró una hora en la ducha** *he spent an hour in the shower*.
tirita® *nf* sticking plaster, plaster, Elastoplast, Band-aid.
tiritar *vi (gen)* to shiver, shake, tremble.
tiritera *nf (gen)* shivering, shivers *pl*.
tiritona *nf* → **tiritera**.
tiro *nm* 1 *(lanzamiento)* throw. 2 *(disparo, ruido)* shot. 3 *(galería de tiro)* shooting gallery. 4 DEP shooting. 5 *(caballerías)* team. 6 COST *(vestido)* shoulder width; *(de pantalón)* distance between waist and crotch. 7 *(de chimenea)* draught (US draft). 8 *(fútbol, etc)* shot. ● **tiro al blanco** target shooting.
tiroideo,-a *adj* thyroid.
tiroides *nm* thyroid, thyroid gland.
tirón *nm* pull, tug. ■ **de un tirón** *fam* in one go.
tirotear *vt* to shoot, snipe.
tiroteo *nm* shooting, exchange of shots.
tirria *nf fam* dislike. ■ **tener tirria a** *fam* to dislike.
tisana *nf* infusion, tisane.
tísico,-a *nm & nf* consumptive.
tisis *nf inv* consumption, tuberculosis, phthisis.
tisú *nm (de oro)* gold lamé; *(de plata)* silver lamé.
titán *nm* titan.
titánico,-a *adj* titanic.
titanio *nm* titanium.
títere *nm* 1 *(marioneta)* puppet, marionette. 2 *fig (persona)* puppet, dupe.
▷ *nm pl* **títeres** puppet show *sing*. ■ **no dejar títere con cabeza** *fam (destruir)* to break everything in sight.
titi *nm argot (hombre)* young guy; *(mujer)* young girl.
tití *nm* titi.
titilante *adj (temblor)* quivering.
titilar *vi* 1 *(temblar)* to quiver. 2 *(luz)* to flicker; *(de estrella)* to twinkle.
titileo *nm* 1 *(temblor)* quiver. 2 *(de luz)* flicker; *(de estrella)* twinkle.
titiritero,-a *nm & nf* 1 *(de títeres)* puppeteer. 2 *(saltimbanqui)* travelling acrobat.
tito,-a *nm & nf fam (tío)* uncle; *(tía)* aunt.
titubeante *adj* 1 *(tambaleante)* staggering, shaky. 2 *(al hablar)* stammering. 3 *fig (indeciso)* hesitant.
titubear *vi* 1 *(tambalearse)* to stagger, totter, shake. 2 *(tartamudear)* to stammer. 3 *fig (vacilar)* to hesitate.
titubeo *nm* 1 *(temblor)* stagger, staggering, tottering. 2 *(tartamudeo)* stammering. 3 *fig (duda)* hesitation.
titulación *nf* qualifications *pl*.
titulado,-a *adj* 1 *(llamado)* called. 2 EDUC *(diplomado)* qualified; *(licenciado)* graduate.
titular *vt* to entitle, title, call.
▷ *adj* regular.
▷ *nm o nf* 1 *(poseedor)* holder. 2 *(de un puesto)* office holder; *(de cátedra)* professor.
▷ *nm (prensa)* headline.
▷ *vpr* **titularse** 1 *(llamarse)* to be called, be titled. 2 EDUC to graduate (**en**, in).

titularidad *nf* entitlement.
título *nm* 1 *(de obra)* title. 2 *(de texto legal)* heading. 3 *(dignidad)* title. 4 *(persona noble)* noble (person). 5 EDUC *(licenciatura)* degree; *(diploma)* certificate, diploma. 6 *(documento)* title. 7 *(titular de prensa)* headline.
▷ *nm pl* **títulos** *(titulación)* qualifications; *(méritos)* qualities. ● **título de propiedad** deeds *pl.*
tiza *nf* chalk.
tiznado,-a *adj* sooty, blackened.
tiznar *vt* 1 to blacken, soil with soot.
tizne *nm* soot.
tiznón *nm* smudge.
tizón *nm* 1 half-burnt stick, brand. 2 *fig* stain.
Tm *sím* metric ton.
TNT *abrev* **(trinitrotolueno)** trinitrotoluene; *(abreviatura)* TNT.
toalla *nf* towel. ● **toalla de baño** bath towel.
toallero *nm* towel rail, towel rack.
toallita *nf* flannel, face flannel.
toba *nf* 1 *(piedra)* tufa. 2 *(sarro)* tartar. 3 *fig (capa)* layer.
tobera *nf (gen)* nozzle.
tobillera *nf* ankle sock, ankle support.
tobillo *nm* ankle.
tobogán *nm* 1 *(rampa)* slide. 2 *(trineo)* toboggan.
toca *nf (sombrero)* headdress; *(de monja)* wimple.
tocadiscos *nm inv* record-player.
tocado[1] *nm* 1 *(peinado)* coiffure. 2 *(prenda)* hat.
tocado,-a[2] *adj* 1 *(fruta)* bad, rotten. 2 *fam (perturbado)* crazy, touched. 3 DEP injured.
tocador *nm* 1 *(mueble)* dressing-table. 2 *(habitación)* dressing-room, boudoir.
tocar [1] *vt* 1 *(gen)* to touch: **no tocar la mercancía** *do not handle the goods.* 2 *(sentir por el tacto)* to feel: **tócalo, está frío** *feel it, it's cold.* 3 *(revolver)* to rummage amongst, root around: **no toques mis papeles** *leave my papers alone.* 4 *(hacer sonar - instrumento, canción)* to play; *(timbre)* to ring; *(bocina)* to blow, honk; *(campanas)* to strike. 5 *(la hora)* to strike. 6 DEP *(diana)* to hit; *(esgrima)* to touch. 7 *fig (mencionar)* to touch on. 8 *fig (impresionar)* to touch, reach: **me tocó el corazón** *he touched my heart.*
▷ *vi* 1 *(ser el turno)* to be one's turn: **le toca a él** *it's his turn.* 2 *(corresponder)* to be up to: **le toca a él explicarse** *it's up to him to explain himself.* 3 *(ganar)* to win. 4 *(en un reparto, etc)* to fall. 5 *(un destino)* to be posted: **le tocó en Cartagena** *he was posted to Cartagena.* 6 *(tener que)* to have to: **nos tocó llevarla** *we had to take her.* 7 *(afectar)* to concern, affect: **le toca directamente** *it directly concerns you.* 8 *(entrar en contacto)* to touch.
▷ *vpr* **tocarse** *(uso reflexivo)* to touch OS; *(uso recíproco)* to touch each other.
tocayo,-a *nm & nf* namesake.
tocho *nm* 1 *(lingote)* iron ingot. 2 *fam (libro grande)* tome; *(libro aburrido)* boring book.
tocinería *nf* pork butcher's.
tocino *nm* 1 *(carne)* bacon. 2 *(grasa)* fat, lard.
tocología *nf* tocology, obstetrics.
tocólogo,-a *nm & nf* tocologist, obstetrician.
tocón *nm (de tronco)* stump.
todavía *adv* 1 *(a pesar de ello)* still. 2 *(tiempo)* still, yet: **todavía están allí** *they're still there.* 3 *(para reforzar)* even: **esto todavía está mejor** *this is even better.*
todo,-a *adj* 1 *(sin excluir nada)* all: **todos los vecinos lo vieron** *all the neighbours saw it.* 2 *(verdadero)* real: **era todo un reto** *it was a real challenge.* 3 *(cada)* every: **todos los días** *every day.*
▷ *pron* 1 *(sin excluir nada)* all, everything: **llamaron todos** *they all phoned.* 2 *(cualquiera)* anybody: **todo el que yo diga** *anybody I say.*
▷ *nm* **todo** *(totalidad)* whole.
▷ *adv* completely, totally, all: **está todo mojado** *it's all wet.*
todopoderoso,-a *adj* almighty.
todoterreno *adj* four-wheel-drive.
▷ *nm* four-wheel-drive vehicle.
tofe *nm* toffee.
tofu *nm* tofu.
toga *nf* 1 *(de romanos)* toga. 2 *(de magistrado, etc)* gown.
togado,-a *adj (magistrado, etc)* robed.
▷ *nm & nf (juez)* judge; *(abogado)* lawyer.
Togo *nm* Togo.
togolés,-esa *adj* Togolese.
▷ *nm & nf* Togolese.
toldo *nm* 1 *(cubierta)* awning. 2 *(de playa)* sunshade.
tolerable *adj* tolerable.
tolerado,-a *adj (película, etc)* suitable for children.
tolerancia *nf* tolerance.
tolerante *adj* tolerant, lenient.
tolerar *vt* 1 *(permitir, soportar)* to tolerate, put up with: **no te toleraré esa actitud** *I won't put up with that attitude.* 2 *(inconvenientes)* to stand.
tolueno *nm* toluene.
tolva *nf* hopper.
toma *nf* 1 *(acción)* taking. 2 MED dose. 3 MIL capture. 4 *(de aire)* intake, inlet; *(de agua)* outlet, tap; *(de electricidad)* plug, socket. 5 *(grabación)* recording. 6 CINE take, shot. ● **toma de conciencia** awareness. ▮ **toma de posesión** takeover.
tomador,-ra *nm o nf (de letra de cambio)* drawee; *(de seguro)* policy holder.
tomar *vt* 1 *(gen)* to take: **lo tomó en broma** *she took it as a joke.* 2 *(baño, ducha)* to have, take; *(foto)* to take. 3 *(comer, beber)* to have; *(beber)* to drink; *(comer)* to eat: **tómate la leche** *drink your milk.* 4 *(el autobús, el tren)* to catch. 5 *(aceptar)* to accept, take. 6 *(comprar)* to buy, get, have. 7 *(adquirir)* to acquire, get into: **tomar una costumbre** *to acquire a habit.* 8 MIL to capture, take.
▷ *vi (encaminarse)* to go, turn.
▷ *vpr* **tomarse** 1 *(gen)* to take: **me tomé una aspirina** *I took an aspirin.* 2 *(beber)* to drink; *(comer)* to eat. ■ **tomarse las cosas con calma** to take it easy.
tomate *nm (fruto)* tomato.
tomatera *nf (planta)* tomato plant.
tomatero,-a *nm & nf* tomato seller.
tomavistas *nm* cine camera, US movie camera.
tómbola *nf* tombola.
tomillo *nm* thyme.
tomismo *nm* Thomism.
tomo *nm (volumen)* volume.
ton ■ **sin ton ni son** without rhyme or reason.
tonada *nf* tune, song.
tonadilla *nf* ditty, little tune.
tonadillero,-a *nm & nf (cantante)* singer of ditties.
tonal *adj* tonal.
tonalidad *nf* tonality, tone.

tonel *nm* barrel, cask.
tonelada *nf* ton. ● **tonelada métrica** metric ton, tonne.
tonelaje *nm* tonnage.
tonelería *nf* 1 *(fabricación)* cooperage, barrel-making. 2 *(tienda)* barrel shop.
tonelero,-a *nm & nf* cooper, barrel-maker.
Tonga *nf* Tonga.
tongada *nf* pile, heap.
tongano,-a *adj* Tongan.
▷ *nm & nf (persona)* Tongan.
▷ *nm* **tongano** *(idioma)* Tongan.
tongo *nm* fix: **en la carrera hubo tongo** *the race was fixed, the race was rigged.*
tónica *nf* 1 *(tendencia)* tendency. 2 *(bebida)* tonic.
tónico,-a *adj* 1 *(sílaba)* tonic, stressed. 2 *(nota musical)* tonic.
▷ *nm* **tónico** MED tonic.
tonificante *adj* invigorating.
tonificar [1] *vt* to tone up, invigorate.
tonillo *nm* 1 *(sonsonete)* drone, monotone. 2 *(acento)* accent, lilt. 3 *(retintín)* sarcastic tone.
tono *nm* 1 *(gen)* tone: **el tono de su discurso** *the tone of her speech.* 2 *(energía)* energy. ■ **fuera de tono** *fig* inappropriate, out of place.
tontear *vi (decir tonterías)* to act the clown.
tontería *nf* 1 *(calidad de tonto)* stupidity, silliness. 2 *(dicho, hecho)* silly thing, stupid thing. 3 *(insignificancia)* trifle. ■ **hacer tonterías** to mess about.
tonto,-a *adj* silly, stupid, US dumb: **¡qué idea más tonta!** *what a stupid idea!*
▷ *nm & nf* fool, idiot. ■ **hacerse el tonto** to play dumb.
topacio *nm* topaz.
topar *vi* 1 *(chocar)* to bump into: **el coche topó contra un poste** *the car bumped into a pole.* 2 *(encontrar - algo)* to come across, find; *(- alguien)* to bump into, run into. 3 *fig (dificultades, etc)* to come up against, run into.
tope *nm* 1 *(límite)* limit, end. 2 TÉC stop, check. 3 *(de ferrocarril)* buffer, bumping post, bumper. 4 MAR masthead.
▷ *adj fig* top, maximum.
▷ *adv argot* really, absolutely: **la fiesta fue tope divertida** *the party was absolutely brilliant.* ■ **a tope** 1 *argot (al límite)* flat out. 2 *(lleno)* jam-packed, chock-a-block.
topetazo *nm* butt, bump.
topetón *nm* → **topetazo.**
tópico,-a *adj* MED external: **uso tópico** *external use.*
▷ *nm* **tópico** commonplace, cliché.
topless *nm* topless. ■ **en topless** topless.
topo *nm* mole.
topografía *nf* topography.
topográfico,-a *adj* topographic.
topógrafo,-a *nm & nf* topographer.
topología *nf* topology.
toponimia *nf* 1 *(ciencia)* toponymy. 2 *(nombres)* place names *pl.*
toponímico,-a *adj* toponymic, toponymical.
topónimo *nm* place name, toponym.
toque *nm* 1 *(acto)* touch. 2 *(de campana)* ringing, peal, pealing; *(de trompeta)* blare, sounding; *(de claxon)* honk; *(de sirena)* hoot; *(de tambor)* beat, beating. 3 *(pincelada)* touch. 4 *fig (advertencia)* warning. ■ **dar un toque a** ALGN 1 *(llamar)* to take SB to task. 2 *(llamar la atención)* to call SB's attention.
toquilla *nf* shawl, knitted shawl.
torácico,-a *adj* thoracic. ● **caja torácica** chest cavity.
tórax *nm inv* thorax.
torbellino *nm* 1 *(de viento)* whirlwind; *(de agua)* whirlpool; *(de polvo)* whirl, cloud.
torcedura *nf* 1 *(acción)* twist, twisting. 2 MED sprain.
torcer [54] *vt* 1 *(gen)* to twist. 2 *(doblar)* to bend.
▷ *vi (girar)* to turn: **torció a la derecha** *he turned right.*
▷ *vpr* **torcerse** 1 *(gen)* to twist. 2 *(doblarse)* to bend; *(madera)* to warp. 3 *(ladearse)* to become slanted. 4 MED to sprain, twist. 5 *fig (plan)* to fall through.
torcido,-a *adj* 1 *(que no es recto)* twisted. 2 *(madera)* warped; *(metal)* bent. 3 *(ladeado)* slanted, crooked, lopsided: **el cuadro está torcido** *the painting is crooked.*
tordo,-a *nm* **tordo** *(pájaro)* thrush.
torear *vt* 1 *(lidiar)* to fight. 2 *fig (entretener)* to put off. 3 *fig (burlar)* to tease, confuse. 4 *fig (asunto, etc)* to tackle skilfully, handle well. 5 *fig (evitar)* to avoid.
▷ *vi (lidiar)* to fight.
toreo *nm* bullfighting.
torera *nf* bolero jacket, bolero.
torero,-a *nm & nf* bullfighter, matador.
toril *nm* bullpen.
tormenta *nf* storm.
tormento *nm* 1 *(tortura)* torture. 2 *(dolor)* torment.
tormentoso,-a *adj* stormy.
torna *nf* return.
tornado *nm* tornado.
tornar *vt* 1 *(devolver)* to give back (**a**, to), return (**a**, to). 2 *(mudar)* to transform (**en**, into), turn (**en**, into).
▷ *vi* 1 *(regresar)* to go back (**a**, to), return (**a**, to). 2 *(volver a)* to start again: **tornó a beber** *he started drinking again.*
▷ *vpr* **tornarse** to become, turn.
tornasol *nm* 1 BOT sunflower. 2 *(luz)* iridescense.
tornasolado,-a *adj* iridescent.
torneado,-a *adj* TÉC lathed, turned on the lathe.
▷ *nm* **torneado** TÉC turning.
tornear *vt* to turn.
torneo *nm* 1 *(justa)* tourney, joust. 2 DEP tournament.
tornero,-a *nm & nf* turner, lathe operator.
tornillo *nm* screw, bolt.
torniquete *nm* MED tourniquet.
torno *nm* 1 TÉC lathe. 2 *(elevador)* winch, windlass. ■ **en torno a** 1 *(alrededor de)* around. 2 *(acerca de)* about, concerning. ● **torno de alfarero** potter's wheel.
toro *nm (animal)* bull.
▷ *nm pl* **los toros** *(corrida)* bullfight *sing; (arte)* bullfighting *sing.*
toronja *nf* grapefruit.
torpe *adj* 1 *(poco hábil)* clumsy. 2 *(de movimiento)* slow, awkward. 3 *(poco inteligente)* dim, thick.
torpedear *vt* to torpedo.
torpedero,-a *nm* **torpedero** torpedo boat.
torpedo *nm* MIL torpedo.
torpeza *nf* 1 *(falta de habilidad)* clumsiness, awkwardness. 2 *(mental)* dimness, stupidity. 3 *(de movimiento)* slowness, heaviness. 4 *(error)* blunder.
torre *nf* 1 *(gen)* tower. 2 *(campanario)* bell tower. 3 *(chalé)* country house, house, villa. 4 *(ajedrez)* rook, castle. ● **torre de comunicaciones** communications tower.

torrefacto,-a *adj* high roast.
torrencial *adj* torrential.
torrente *nm* 1 *(de agua)* mountain stream, torrent. 2 *fig (abundancia)* flood, stream.
torrentera *nf* gully.
torreón *nm* fortified tower.
torreta *nf* turret, small tower.
torrezno *nm* rasher of fried bacon.
tórrido,-a *adj* torrid.
torrija *nf type of* French toast.
torsión *nf* 1 *(torcedura)* twist, twisting. 2 TÉC torsion.
torso *nm* 1 ANAT torso. 2 *(estatua)* bust.
torta *nf* 1 CULIN cake. 2 *fam (golpe)* blow, crack; *(bofetada)* slap, wallop. ■ **ni torta** *fam* not a thing: **no ve ni torta** *he can't see a thing.*
tortazo *nm* 1 *fam (golpe)* whack, thump. 2 *fam (bofetada)* slap, punch.
tortícolis *nf inv* stiff neck, crick in the neck.
tortilla *nf* 1 omelette (US omelet). 2 AM tortilla, pancake. ● **tortilla a la francesa** omelette, plain omelette. ‖ **tortilla de patatas** potato omelette, Spanish omelette.
tortita *nf* pancake.
tórtola *nf* → **tórtolo,-a.**
tortolito,-a *adj* inexperienced, green.
tórtolo,-a *nm & nf (macho)* male turtledove; *(hembra)* turtledove.
tortuga *nf* 1 *(de tierra)* tortoise. 2 *(marina)* turtle.
tortuoso,-a *adj* tortuous, winding.
tortura *nf (tormento)* torture.
torturador,-ra *nm & nf* torturer.
torturar *vt* to torture.
torvo,-a *adj* grim, fierce.
torzal *nm* 1 *(de seda)* silk twist. 2 *fig (de varias cosas)* twist, twine.
tos *nf* cough, coughing. ■ **tener tos** to have a cough.
tosca *nf* 1 *(piedra)* tufa. 2 *(sarro)* tartar.
tosco,-a *adj* 1 *(basto)* rough, rustic. 2 *(persona)* uncouth.
toser *vi* to cough.
tosquedad *nf* roughness, crudeness.
tostada *nf* toast, slice of toast.
tostadero *nm* roaster.
tostado,-a *adj* 1 *(pan)* toasted; *(café)* roasted. 2 *fig (moreno)* tanned, brown.
tostador,-ra *nm & nf (de pan)* toaster; *(de café)* roaster.
tostar [31] *vt* 1 *(pan)* to toast; *(café)* to roast; *(carnes)* to brown. 2 *fig (piel)* to tan.
▷ *vpr* **tostarse** *fig (la piel)* to get brown, turn brown, tan.
tostón *nm fam fig* bore, drag: **la peli fue un tostón** *the film was a drag.*
total *adj* total, complete, overall: **anestesia total** *general anaesthetic.*
▷ *nm* 1 *(totalidad)* whole: **el total de la población** *the whole population.* 2 *(suma)* total, sum.
▷ *adv* 1 *(en conclusión)* in short, so: **total, que se fueron porque quisieron** *they left because they wanted to.* 2 *(al fin y al cabo)* after all.
totalidad *nf* whole, totality. ■ **en su totalidad** as a whole.
totalitario,-a *adj* totalitarian.
totalitarismo *nm* totalitarianism, dictatorship.
totalitarista *adj* totalitarian.
tótem *nm* totem; *(efigie)* totem pole.
totovía *nf* wood lark.
tournée *nf (gira)* tour; *(viaje)* touring holiday.
touroperador *nm* travel firm.
toxicidad *nf* toxicity.
tóxico,-a *adj* toxic, poisonous.
▷ *nm* **tóxico** toxicant, poison.
toxicología *nf* toxicology.
toxicológico,-a *adj* toxicologic, toxicological.
toxicólogo,-a *nm & nf* toxicologist.
toxicomanía *nf* drug addiction.
toxicómano,-a *nm & nf* drug addict.
toxina *nf* toxin.
tozudez *nf* stubbornness, obstinacy.
tozudo,-a *adj* stubborn, obstinate.
traba *nf fig (impedimento)* hindrance, obstacle.
trabado,-a *adj* 1 *(sujeto)* fastened; *(atascado)* jammed. 2 *fig (robusto)* robust. 3 *fig (coherente)* coherent.
trabajado,-a *adj* elaborate, carefully worked.
trabajador,-ra *adj* 1 *(que trabaja)* working. 2 *(laborioso)* hard-working, industrious.
▷ *nm & nf* worker, labourer (US laborer).
trabajar *vi* 1 *(gen)* to work: **trabaja mucho** *she works hard.* 2 *(en obra, película)* to act, perform: **¿quién trabaja en la obra?** *who's in the play?* 3 *fig (soportar)* to be under stress: **esta cuerda trabaja mucho** *this rope is under stress.*
▷ *vt* 1 *(materiales)* to work (on). 2 *(idea, idioma, etc)* to work on. 3 *(la tierra)* to till. 4 CULIN *(pasta)* to knead.
trabajo *nm* 1 *(ocupación)* work. 2 *(tarea)* task, job. 3 *(empleo)* job, employment. 4 *(esfuerzo)* effort. 5 EDUC report, paper.
▷ *nm pl* **trabajos** *fig (penalidades)* hardships. ● **trabajos manuales** arts and crafts, handicrafts.
trabajoso,-a *adj* 1 hard, laborious. 2 *(difícil)* difficult.
trabalenguas *nm inv* tongue twister.
trabar *vt* 1 *(unir)* to join, link. 2 *(sujetar)* to lock, fasten. 3 *(mecanismo)* to jam. 4 *(prender a alguien)* to shackle. 5 *(caballería)* to hobble. 6 *fig (empezar)* to start. 7 *fig (conversación, amistad)* to strike up. 8 *fig (impedir)* to impede, hinder, shackle.
▷ *vpr* **trabarse** *(enredarse)* to get tangled up. ■ **trabársele la lengua a** ALGN to get tongue-tied.
trabilla *nf (de pantalón)* stirrup; *(de chaqueta)* half-belt.
trabuco *nm* blunderbuss.
traca *nf* string of firecrackers.
tracción *nf* traction. ● **tracción delantera** front-wheel drive.
tracto *nm* tract.
tractor,-ra *nm* **tractor** tractor.
tractorista *nm o nf* tractor driver.
tradición *nf* tradition.
tradicional *adj* traditional.
tradicionalismo *nm* 1 traditionalism. 2 POL radical conservatism.
tradicionalista *nm o nf* 1 traditionalist. 2 POL radical conservative.
traducción *nf* translation.
traducir [46] *vt* 1 *(gen)* to translate. 2 *(expresar)* to express, show.
▷ *vpr* **traducirse** *(resulta)* to result in, give.
traductor,-ra *adj* translating.
▷ *nm & nf* translator.

traer [88] *vt* 1 *(gen)* to bring. 2 *(llevar consigo)* to carry: traía un bolso *she was carrying a bag.* 3 *(vestir)* to wear. 4 *(causar)* to cause, bring: esto le trajo muchos problemas *it caused him a lot of problems.* 5 *(llevar noticias)* to carry, contain: la revista traía varias fotos *the magazine contained several pictures.* 6 *(contener)* to contain: el paquete trae un regalo *the package contains a gift.*
▷ *vpr* traerse *(llevar consigo)* to bring along: tráete al bebé *bring your baby along.*
traficante *nm o nf* 1 trader, dealer. 2 *(ilegal)* trafficker.
traficar [1] *vi* 1 to deal. 2 *(de forma ilegal)* to traffic (en, in), deal (en, in): trafica en/con drogas *he traffics in drugs.*
tráfico *nm* 1 AUTO traffic. 2 COM traffic, trade.
tragaderas *nf pl* 1 *fam (faringe)* throat *sing.* 2 *fam fig (credulidad)* gullibility.
tragaluz *nm* skylight.
tragaperras ● máquina tragaperras slot machine.
tragar [7] *vt* 1 *(ingerir)* to swallow. 2 *(absorber)* to soak up. 3 *fig (hacer desaparecer)* to swallow up. 4 *fig (gastar, consumir)* to eat up, guzzle: este coche traga mucha gasolina *this car guzzles petrol (US gas).* 5 *fig (creer)* to swallow, believe. 6 *fig (aguantar)* to put up with; *(disimular)* to hide: tuvo que tragar sus exigencias *she had to put up with his demands.* 7 *fig (soportar a alguien)* to stand, stomach: no trago a Pedro *I can't stand Pedro.*
▷ *vi* to swallow, swallow up.
▷ *vpr* tragarse *(ingerir)* to swallow: se tragó un botón *he swallowed a button.*
tragedia *nf* tragedy.
trágico,-a *adj* tragic.
tragicomedia *nf* tragicomedy.
tragicómico,-a *adj* tragicomic.
trago *nm* 1 *(sorbo)* swig, drop. 2 *fam (bebida)* drink. 3 *fam fig (adversidad)* rough time.
tragón,-ona *nm & nf fam* glutton, big eater.
traguito *nm* swallow dram.
traición *nf* treason. ■ a traición treacherously.
traicionar *vt* 1 *(gen)* to betray. 2 *fig (delatar)* to give away, betray.
traicionero,-a *adj* treacherous.
traidor,-ra *adj* treacherous.
▷ *nm & nf* traitor.
tráiler *nm* 1 CINE trailer, US preview. 2 AUTO articulated lorry, US trailer truck.
traílla *nf* 1 *(cuerda)* leash. 2 *(para allanar)* strickle.
traína *nf* trawl, trawl net.
trainera *nf* trawler.
traje *nm* 1 *(de hombre)* suit. 2 *(de mujer)* dress. ● traje de chaqueta tailored suit. | traje de noche evening dress.
trajín *nm fam fig* comings and goings *pl.*
trajinar *vi (moverse)* to bustle about, run about.
tralla *nf* 1 *(cuerda)* rope. 2 *(látigo)* whip.
trama *nf* 1 *(textil)* weft, woof. 2 *(argumento)* plot.
tramar *vt* 1 *(tejidos)* to weave. 2 *fig (maquinar)* to plot.
tramitación *nf* JUR procedure, steps *pl.*
tramitar *vt* 1 *(gestionar)* to deal with, process: tramitaremos su pasaporte *we'll get your passport sorted out.* 2 *(solicitar, negociar)* to arrange, negotiate: tramitar un préstamo *to negotiate a loan.*
trámite *nm* 1 *(paso)* step. 2 *(formalidad)* formality.
tramo *nm* 1 *(camino, etc)* stretch, section. 2 *(de escalera)* flight. 3 *(de terreno)* lot, plot.
tramoya *nf (máquina)* stage machinery.
tramoyista *nm o nf* TEAT sceneshifter, stagehand.
trampa *nf* 1 *(abertura)* trapdoor, hatch. 2 *(para cazar)* trap, snare. 3 *fig (engaño)* fiddle; *(truco)* trick. 4 *fig (deuda)* debt. ■ tender una trampa to set a trap, lay a trap.
trampear *vi (estafar)* to be on the fiddle; *(vivir de su ingenio)* to live by one's wits.
trampero,-a *nm & nf* trapper.
trampilla *nf* trapdoor, hatch.
trampolín *nm* 1 *(de piscina)* springboard, divingboard. 2 *(de esquí)* ski jump.
tramposo,-a *adj* deceitful, tricky.
▷ *nm & nf* trickster, cheat; *(en las cartas)* cardsharp.
tranca *nf* 1 *(palo)* club, cudgel. 2 *(para puertas, etc)* bar.
trancazo *nm* 1 *(golpe)* blow with a cudgel. 2 *fam fig (resfriado)* cold; *(gripe)* flu.
trance *nm* 1 *(momento crítico)* critical moment. 2 *(dificultad)* fix, tight spot. 3 *(éxtasis)* trance. ■ pasar por un trance to hit a bad patch.
tranco *nm* stride.
tranquilidad *nf (quietud)* calmness, tranquillity (US tranquility); *(sosiego)* peace and quiet. ● paz y tranquilidad peace and quiet.
tranquilizante *nm* tranquillizer (US tranquilizer).
tranquilizar [4] *vt* 1 *(calmar)* to calm down, tranquillize (US tranquilize). 2 *(dar confianza)* to reassure, set one's mind at rest.
▷ *vpr* tranquilizarse 1 *(calmarse)* to calm down. 2 to set one's mind at rest, be reassured.
tranquilo,-a *adj* 1 *(sin inquietud)* calm, relaxed, tranquil. 2 *(sin preocupación)* reassured. 3 *(sin movimiento)* calm, still, quiet. 4 *(sin ruidos)* quiet, still, peaceful. 5 *(persona)* calm, easy-going, placid. 6 *(agua)* still; *(conciencia)* clear.
transacción *nf* transaction, deal.
transatlántico,-a *adj* transatlantic.
▷ *nm* transatlántico liner, ocean liner.
transbordar *vt* to transfer.
▷ *vi* change *(de tren, etc).*
transbordador *nm* ferry, car ferry. ● transbordador espacial space shuttle.
transbordo *nm* 1 *(de vehículo)* change, US transfer. 2 *(de barco)* transshipment.
transcribir *vt* to transcribe.
transcripción *nf* transcription.
transcurrir *vi* 1 *(tiempo)* to pass, elapse. 2 *(acontecer)* to take place, go off.
transcurso *nm* 1 *(paso)* course, passing. 2 *(duración)* space, period. ■ en el transcurso de los años over the course of the years.
transeúnte *nm o nf (peatón)* pedestrian.
transexual *adj* transsexual.
▷ *nm o nf* transsexual.
transexualismo *nm* transsexualism.
transferencia *nf* FIN transfer.
transferible *adj* transferable.
transferir [35] *vt* FIN to transfer, convey.
transfigurar *vt* to transfigure.
▷ *vpr* transfigurarse to become transfigured.
transformación *nf* transformation.
transformador,-ra *adj* transforming.
▷ *nm* transformador transformer.
transformar *vt* to transform, change.

▷ *vpr* **transformarse** to change, be transformed: **se transformó completamente** *he was completely transformed.* ■ **transformarse en 1** *(persona)* to become. **2** *(objeto)* to convert into.
tránsfuga *nm o nf* **1** MIL deserter. **2** POL turncoat.
transfuguismo *nm* POL tendency to change political colours (US colors).
transfusión *nf* transfusion. ● **transfusión de sangre** blood transfusion.
transgénico,-a *adj* genetically modified, GM.
transgredir *vt* to transgress, break.
Used only in forms which include the letter i in their endings: **transgredía, transgrediré, transgrediendo.**
transgresión *nf* transgression.
transgresor,-ra *nm & nf* transgressor, law-breaker.
transición *nf* transition.
transicional *adj* transitional.
transido,-a *adj fig (angustiado)* distressed.
transigencia *nf* **1** *(actitud)* tolerance, lenience. **2** *(concesión)* compromise.
transigente *adj* accommodating, tolerant, lenient.
transigir [6] *vi* **1** *(ceder)* to compromise, give in, yield. **2** *(tolerar)* to tolerate, bear.
transistor *nm* transistor.
transitable *adj* passable.
transitado,-a *adj* busy.
transitar *vi* **1** *(viajar)* to travel, travel about. **2** *(pasar)* to pass, go, walk.
transitivo,-a *adj* transitive.
tránsito *nm* **1** *(acción)* passage, movement. **2** AUTO traffic. **3** *euf (muerte)* death, passing. **4** *(lugar de parada)* stopping place.
transitoriedad *nf* transience, transiency.
transitorio,-a *adj (pasajero)* transitory; *(de transición)* transitional, interim.
transmediterráneo,-a *adj* trans-Mediterranean.
transmisible *adj* transmissible.
transmisión *nf* **1** *(propagación)* transmission. **2** JUR transfer, transference. **3** RAD TV broadcast. **4** TÉC drive.
▷ *nf pl* **transmisiones** MIL signals. ● **transmisión en directo** RAD TV live broadcast.
transmisor,-ra *adj* transmitting.
▷ *nm & nf* transmitter.
transmitir *vt* **1** *(gen)* to transmit. **2** RAD TV to broadcast. **3** *(enfermedad)* to transmit, pass on. **4** JUR to transfer, hand down.
transmutación *nf* transmutation.
transmutar *vt* to transmute.
▷ *vpr* **transmutarse** to change, transform.
transoceánico,-a *adj* transoceanic.
transparencia *nf* **1** transparency, transparence. **2** *(diapositiva)* transparency, slide.
transparentar *vt fig (emociones, etc)* to reveal.
▷ *vpr* **transparentarse 1** *(ser transparente)* to be transparent, show through. **2** *fig (emociones, etc)* to show.
transparente *adj* **1** *(gen)* transparent. **2** *(tela, vestido)* transparent, see-through. **3** *fig* straight, plain.
transpiración *nf* perspiration, transpiration.
transpirar *vi* to perspire, transpire.
transplantar *vt* **1** *(gen)* to transplant. **2** *(trasladar)* to transfer.
transplante *nm* transplant.
transponer [78] *vt* **1** *(cambiar de sitio)* to move. **2** *(atravesar)* to cross over. **3** *(trasplantar)* to transplant. **4** *(desaparecer)* to disappear.
▷ *vpr* **transponerse 1** *(astro)* to set, go down. **2** *(quedarse dormido)* to doze off.
transportable *adj* transportable.
transportar *vt* **1** *(gen)* to transport. **2** *(pasajeros)* to carry; *(mercancías en barco)* to ship. **3** MAT to transfer. **4** MÚS to transpose. **5** *fig (hacer perder la razón)* to carry away, send into raptures.
▷ *vpr* **transportarse** *fig* to be transported, be enraptured, be carried away.
transporte *nm* **1** *(medio)* transport. **2** *(acción)* transport, US transportation. **3** COM freight, freightage. **4** MÚS transposition. **5** *fig* transport, ecstasy, bliss. ● **transporte público** public transport.
transportista *nm o nf* carrier.
transposición *nf* transposition.
transvasar *vt* **1** *(líquidos)* to decant. **2** *(entre ríos)* to transfer.
transvase *nm* **1** *(de líquidos)* decanting. **2** *(de ríos)* transfer.
transversal *adj* transversal, transverse, crosswise.
transverso,-a *adj* transverse, crosswise.
tranvía *nm* **1** *(sistema)* tramway. **2** *(vehículo)* tram, tramcar, US streetcar.
trapacería *nf* trick, fiddle.
trapecio *nm* **1** DEP trapeze. **2** *(geometría)* trapezium, US trapezoid. **3** ANAT *(hueso)* trapezium; *(músculo)* trapezius.
trapecista *nm o nf* trapeze artist.
trapería *nf* secondhand clothes shop.
trapero,-a *nm & nf (hombre)* rag-and-bone man, US junkman; *(mujer)* rag-and-bone woman.
trapezoide *nm* trapezoid, US trapezium.
trapo *nm* **1** *(tela vieja)* rag. **2** *(paño, bayeta)* cloth. **3** MAR sails *pl*. **4** *(telón)* curtain. **5** *(del torero)* red cape.
▷ *nm pl* **trapos** clothes, rags. ■ **poner a** ALGN **como un trapo (sucio)** *fam* to tear SB apart. ● **trapo del polvo** duster.
tráquea *nf* trachea, windpipe.
traqueal *adj* tracheal.
traqueotomía *nf* tracheotomy.
traquetear *vi (hacer ruido)* to clatter, rattle.
▷ *vt (agitar)* to shake, bang about.
traqueteo *nm* **1** *(ruido)* rattle, clatter. **2** *(movimiento)* jolting, bumping.
tras *prep* **1** *(después de)* after: **tras la salida del avión** *after the departure of the plane.* **2** *(detrás)* behind: **tras el muro** *behind the wall.* **3** *(en pos de)* after, in pursuit of: **iba siempre tras el éxito** *he was always in pursuit of success.* ■ **día tras día** day after day.
trasbordador *nm* ferry, car ferry.
trasbordar *vt-vi* → **transbordar.**
trasbordo *nm* → **transbordo.**
trascendencia *nf* **1** *(importancia)* significance, importance. **2** *(filosofía)* transcendence, transcendency.
trascendental *adj* **1** *(importante)* significant, very important, consequential; *(de gran alcance)* far-reaching. **2** *(filosofía)* transcendent, transcendental.
trascendente *adj* → **trascendental.**
trascender [28] *vi* **1** *(olor - despedir)* to smell; *(- llegar hasta)* to reach. **2** *(darse a conocer)* to become known,

leak out: **el resultado trascendió** *the result leaked out.* **3** *(extenderse)* to spread, have a wide effect.
trascribir *vt* to transcribe.
trascripción *nf* transcription.
trasegar [48] *vt* **1** *(mudar)* to move about, shuffle. **2** *(líquidos)* to decant.
trasero,-a *adj* back, rear.
▷ *nm* **trasero** *fam euf* bottom, bum.
trasferencia *nf* ⟶ **transferencia.**
trasferible *adj* transferable.
trasferir [35] *vt* ⟶ **transferir.**
trasfiguración *nf* transfiguration.
trasfigurar *vt-vpr* ⟶ **transfigurar.**
trasfondo *nm* **1** background. **2** *fig* undertone.
trasformación *nf* transformation.
trasformador,-ra *adj-nm* ⟶ **transformador,-ra.**
trasformar *vt-vpr* ⟶ **transformar.**
trásfuga *nm o nf* ⟶ **tránsfuga.**
trasfuguismo *nm* ⟶ **transfuguismo.**
trasfusión *nf* ⟶ **transfusión.**
trasgo *nm* goblin, imp.
trasgredir *vt* ⟶ **transgredir.**
trasgresión *nf* transgression.
trasgresor,-ra *nm & nf* transgressor, law-breaker.
trashumancia *nf* transhumance.
trashumante *adj* transhumant.
trasiego *nm* comings and goings *pl*, hustle and bustle.
traslación *nf* **1** *(de la Tierra)* passage, movement. **2** *(en matemáticas)* translation.
trasladar *vt* **1** *(cambiar de sitio)* to move. **2** *(de cargo, etc)* to transfer. **3** *(aplazar)* to postpone, put off.
▷ *vpr* **trasladarse 1** *(ir)* to go. **2** *(cambiar de residencia)* to move.
traslado *nm* **1** *(cambio de lugar)* move, moving; *(de residencia)* removal. **2** *(de cargo, etc)* transfer. **3** *(copia)* copy. **4** JUR notification.
traslúcido,-a *adj* translucent, semitransparent.
traslucir [45] *vt fig* to show, reveal, betray.
▷ *vpr* **traslucirse 1** *(material)* to be translucent. **2** *fig (dejar ver)* to show, show through.
trasluz *nm* diffused light, reflected light. ■ **mirar** ALGO **al trasluz** to look at STH against the light.
trasmano *nm o nf* second hand.
trasmigración *nf* transmigration.
trasmisión *nf* ⟶ **transmisión.**
trasmisor *adj-nm* ⟶ **transmisor,-ra.**
trasmitir *vt* ⟶ **transmitir.**
trasmutación *nf* transmutation.
trasnochado,-a *adj* **1** *fig (viejo)* old, hackneyed. **2** *fig (desmejorado)* haggard, bleary-eyed.
trasnochador,-ra *nm & nf* night bird, nighthawk.
trasnochar *vi* to stay up late.
traspapelado,-a *adj* mislaid, misplaced.
traspapelar *vt* to mislay, misplace.
▷ *vpr* **traspapelarse** to get mislaid, get misplaced.
traspasar *vt* **1** *(atravesar)* to go through, cross. **2** *(cambiar de lugar)* to move. **3** *(perforar)* to go through, pierce. **4** *(dar, pasar)* to transfer; *(vender)* to sell. **5** *fig (exceder)* to exceed, go beyond.
traspaso *nm* **1** *(de negocio, etc)* transfer, sale. **2** *(precio)* transfer fee.
traspié *nm* **1** *(tropezón)* stumble, trip. **2** *fig (equivocación)* blunder.
▲ *pl* **traspiés.**
trasponer [78] *vt-vpr* ⟶ **transponer.**
trasportista *nm o nf* carrier.
trasposición *nf* transposition.
traspuesto,-a ■ **quedarse traspuesto,-a** to nod off.
traspunte *nm* callboy.
trasquilado,-a *adj* **1** *(oveja)* sheared; *(pelo)* hacked, unevenly cut. **2** *fam fig* curtailed, cut down.
trasquilador,-ra *nm & nf* shearer.
trasquilar *vt* **1** *(animales)* to shear. **2** *(pelo)* to hack, cut unevenly. **3** *fig* to curtail.
trasquilón *nm* **1** *fam (de pelo)* hacked cut, chop. **2** *fam fig (de dinero)* loot, catch.
trastabillar *vi* **1** *(dar traspiés)* to stumble, trip. **2** *(tambalearse)* to stagger, totter.
trastada *nf fam (mala pasada)* dirty trick.
trastazo *nm fam* whack, wallop, thump. ■ **darse un trastazo** *fam* to come a cropper.
traste *nm* MÚS fret. ■ **irse al traste** *fig* to fall through.
trastear *vt* **1** MÚS to play. **2** *(revolver)* to rummage in. **3** *fig (manejar)* to twist around one's little finger.
▷ *vi (revolver)* to rummage.
trastero,-a *nm* junk room.
trastienda *nf* **1** *(de tienda)* back room. **2** *fig (astucia)* cunning.
trasto *nm* **1** *(algo inútil)* piece of junk. **2** *fam (niño)* little devil. **3** *fam (persona)* useless person, good-for-nothing, dead loss.
▷ *nm pl* **trastos 1** *(utensilios)* tackle *sing*, gear *sing*. **2** *fam (pertenencias)* belongings, things. ■ **tirarse los trastos a la cabeza** *fig* to have a blazing row.
trastocar [1] *vt (cambiar)* to change.
▷ *vpr* **trastocarse** *(trastornarse)* to go mad.
trastornado,-a *adj* **1** *(preocupado)* upset. **2** *(loco)* mad. **3** *(mente)* unbalanced.
trastornar *vt* **1** *(revolver)* to turn round. **2** *(alterar - planes)* to disrupt; *(- paz, orden)* to disturb. **3** *(estómago)* to upset. **4** *fig (enloquecer)* to drive crazy.
▷ *vpr* **trastornarse** *(perturbarse)* to go mad.
trastorno *nm* **1** *(desorden)* confusion. **2** *(molestia)* trouble, inconvenience. **3** *(perturbación)* disruption, upheaval, upset. **4** MED upset.
trastrocar [49] *vt* **1** *(gen)* to switch around, change around. **2** *(orden)* to invert, reverse.
trasunto *nm* **1** *(copia)* copy. **2** *(representación)* representation.
trata *nf* slave trade.
tratable *adj* friendly, congenial.
tratadista *nm o nf* treatise writer.
tratado *nm* **1** *(pacto)* treaty. **2** *(estudio)* treatise.
tratamiento *nm* **1** *(gen)* treatment. **2** *(de datos, materiales)* processing. **3** *(título)* title, form of address. ● **tratamiento de textos** word processing.
tratante *nm o nf* dealer.
tratar *vt* **1** *(gen - objeto)* to treat, handle; *(- persona)* to treat: **nos trató bien** *he treated us well.* **2** *(asunto, tema)* to discuss, deal with. **3** *(gestionar)* to handle, run. **4** *(dar tratamiento)* to address as. **5** *(calificar, considerar)* to consider, call: **lo trató de idiota** *she called him an idiot.* **6** MED to treat. **7** *(datos, texto)* to process. **8** QUÍM to treat.

▷ *vi* 1 *(relacionarse)* to be acquainted (**con**, with), know (**con**, -). 2 *(tener tratos)* to deal (**con**, with). 3 *(negociar)* to negotiate (**con**, with). 4 *(intentar)* to try (**de**, to): **trata de hacerlo** *try to do it*. 5 *(versar)* to be about: **trata de/sobre espías** *it's about spies*.
▷ *vpr* **tratarse** 1 *(relacionarse)* to talk to each other, be on speaking terms: **no se tratan** *they're not on speaking terms*. 2 *(llamarse)* to address each other as, call each other. 3 *(referirse)* to be about: **se trataba de un atraco** *it was about a robbery*.
trato *nm* 1 *(acción)* treatment. 2 *(modales)* manner. 3 *(contacto)* contact. 4 *(acuerdo)* agreement. 5 COM deal. 6 *(tratamiento)* title. ■ **cerrar un trato** to close a deal. ‖ **¡trato hecho!** it's a deal!
trauma *nm* trauma.
traumático,-a *adj* traumatic.
traumatismo *nm* traumatism.
traumatizar [4] *vt* 1 MED to traumatize. 2 *fam* to shock.
traumatología *nf* traumatology.
travelín *nm* travelling (US traveling) shot.
través *nm* 1 *(inclinación)* slant. 2 *(pieza de madera)* crosspiece, crossbeam. 3 MAR beam. 4 *fig (desgracia)* misfortune. ■ **a través de** 1 *(de un lado a otro)* across, over. 2 *(por dentro)* through. 3 *(mediante)* through, from.
travesaño *nm* 1 ARQUIT crosspiece. 2 DEP crossbar.
travesía *nf* 1 *(viaje)* crossing; *(por mar)* voyage, crossing. 2 *(calle)* cross-street, passage. 3 *(distancia)* distance.
travesti *nm o nf* transvestite.
travestí *nm o nf* transvestite.
travestido,-a *nm & nf* transvestite.
travesura *nf* piece of mischief, childish prank. ■ **hacer travesuras** to get into mischief.
traviesa *nf* 1 *(de ferrocarril)* sleeper, US tie. 2 *(en construcción)* trimmer.
travieso,-a *adj* mischievous, naughty.
trayecto *nm* 1 *(distancia)* distance, way. 2 *(recorrido)* route, itinerary.
trayectoria *nf* 1 trajectory. 2 *fig* line, course, path.
traza *nf fig (apariencia)* looks *pl*, appearance.
trazado *nm* 1 *(plano)* layout, plan. 2 *(dibujo)* drawing, sketch. 3 *(de carretera, ferrocarril)* route, course.
trazar [4] *vt* 1 *(línea, plano, dibujo)* to draw, draw up. 2 *(parque)* to lay out; *(edificio)* to design. 3 *(itinerario)* to trace. 4 *fig (plan, etc)* to outline, draft.
trazo *nm* 1 *(línea)* line. 2 *(de una letra)* stroke. 3 *fig (rasgo facial)* feature.
trébol *nm* 1 *(planta)* clover, trefoil. 2 *(naipes)* club.
trece *adj (cardinal)* thirteen; *(ordinal)* thirteenth.
▷ *nm (número)* thirteen; *(fecha)* thirteenth.
See also **seis**.
treceavo,-a *adj* thirteenth.
▷ *nm & nf* thirteenth.
See also **sexto,-a**.
trecho *nm* 1 *(espacio)* distance, way; *(tiempo)* while, time. 2 *(de camino, ruta)* stretch. 3 AGR plot, patch. 4 *fam (parte)* piece, bit.
tregua *nf* 1 truce. 2 *fig* respite, rest.
treinta *adj (cardinal)* thirty; *(ordinal)* thirtieth.
▷ *nm (número)* thirty; *(fecha)* thirtieth.
See also **seis**.
treintañero,-a *adj* thirty-year-old.
▷ *nm & nf* thirty-year-old person.
treintavo,-a *adj* thirtieth.
▷ *nm & nf* thirtieth.
See also **sexto,-a**.
treintena *nf (exacto)* thirty; *(aproximado)* about thirty.
tremebundo,-a *adj* terrible, dreadful.
tremendista *adj* sensationalist.
tremendo,-a *adj* 1 *(terrible)* terrible, dreadful, frightful. 2 *(muy grande)* huge, enormous, tremendous. 3 *(travieso)* terrible. ■ **tomarse** ALGO **por la tremenda** *fig* to make a great fuss about STH.
trementina *nf* turpentine.
tremolar *vt* to wave.
▷ *vi* to wave, flutter.
tremolina *nf fam fig* uproar, fuss, shindy.
trémulo,-a *adj* 1 *(tembloroso)* tremulous, quivering. 2 *(luz, llama)* flickering.
tren *nm* 1 *(ferrocarril)* train. 2 *(conjunto de máquinas)* convoy, line. 3 *fig (ritmo, modo)* speed, pace. ■ **coger el tren** to catch a train. ● **tren de alta velocidad** high-speed train.
trenca *nf (abrigo)* duffel coat, duffle coat.
trenza *nf* 1 *(peluquería)* plait, US braid. 2 COST braid.
trenzado *nm* 1 *(trenza - de pelo)* plait, US braid; *(- de costura)* braid. 2 *(en danza)* entrechat. 3 *(de caballo)* crossover step.
trenzar [4] *vt* 1 to plait. 2 *(peluquería)* to plait, US braid.
trepador,-ra *adj (planta)* climbing.
▷ *nm & nf fam pey* go-getter, social climber.
trepanación *nf* trepanation, trephination.
trepanar *vi* to trepan, trephine.
trépano *nm* 1 MED trephine. 2 TÉC bit.
trepar[1] *vt (escalar)* to climb.
▷ *vi (escalar)* to climb.
trepar[2] *vt* 1 *(taladrar)* to drill. 2 *(un bordado)* to trim.
trepidante *adj* 1 vibrating, shaking. 2 *fig (vida, etc)* hectic, frantic.
trepidar *vi* to vibrate, shake.
tres *adj (cardinal)* three; *(ordinal)* third.
▷ *nm* [*pl* **treses**.] *(número)* three; *(fecha)* third. ● **tres en raya** noughts and crosses, US tick-tack-toe.
See also **seis**.
trescientos,-as *adj (cardinal)* three hundred; *(ordinal)* three hundredth.
▷ *nm (número)* three hundred.
See also **seis**.
tresillo *nm (mueble)* suite, three-piece suite.
treta *nf* trick, ruse.
tríada *nf* triad.
trial *nm* trial.
triangular *adj* triangular.
triángulo,-a *adj* triangular.
▷ *nm* **triángulo** triangle. ● **triángulo equilátero** equilateral triangle. ‖ **triángulo isósceles** isosceles triangle. ‖ **triángulo rectángulo** right-angled triangle.
triatlón *nm* triathlon.
tribal *adj* tribal, tribe.
tribu *nf* tribe.
tribuna *nf* 1 *(plataforma)* rostrum, dais. 2 DEP grandstand.
tribunal *nm* 1 JUR court. 2 *(de examen)* board of examiners. ■ **llevar a los tribunales** to take to court. ● **Tribunal Supremo** High Court, US Supreme Court.
tributación *nf* taxation, levy.

tributar *vt* to pay.
tributario,-a *adj* tributary, tax.
▷ *nm & nf* taxpayer.
tributo *nm* 1 *(impuesto)* tax. 2 *(a cambio de algo)* tribute. 3 *fig (carga)* price. 4 *fig (de sentimiento)* token.
tricéfalo,-a *adj* tricephalous.
tríceps *nm inv* triceps.
triciclo *nm* tricycle.
tricornio *nm (sombrero)* three-cornered hat.
tricotar *vt* to knit.
tridente *nm* trident.
tridimensional *adj* three-dimensional.
triedro *nm* trihedron.
trienal *adj* triennial.
trienio *nm* triennium.
trifásico,-a *adj* ELEC three-phase.
trigal *nm* wheat field.
trigémino,-a *adj* trigeminal.
▷ *nm* **trigémino** trigeminal nerve.
trigésimo,-a *adj* thirtieth.
▷ *nm & nf* thirtieth.
See also **sexto,-a**.
triglifo *nm* triglyph.
trigo *nm (cereal)* wheat.
trigonometría *nf* trigonometry.
trigonométrico,-a *adj* trigonometric.
trigueño,-a *adj* 1 *(pelo)* corn-coloured (US corn-colored), dark blonde. 2 *(piel)* dark, swarthy. 3 *(persona)* olive-skinned.
triguero,-a *adj* wheat.
trilateral *adj* three-sided, trilateral.
trilingüe *adj* trilingual.
trilita *nf* TNT, trinitrotoluene.
trilla *nf* threshing.
trillado,-a *adj* 1 *(camino)* beaten, well-trodden. 2 *fig (expresión, etc)* overworked, well-worn.
trilladora *nf* threshing machine.
trillar *vt* 1 to thresh. 2 *fig* to wear out.
trillizo,-a *nm & nf* triplet.
trilogía *nf* trilogy.
trimestral *adj* quarterly, three-monthly, trimestral.
trimestre *nm* 1 quarter, trimester. 2 EDUC term.
trimotor *nm* three-engined aircraft.
trinar *vi* 1 *(ave)* to warble. 2 MÚS to trill. 3 *fam (enfadarse)* to rage, fume: **Pedro está que trina** *Pedro is fuming.*
trinchar *vt* to carve, slice (up).
trinchera *nf* trench.
trineo *nm* sleigh, sled, sledge.
trinidad *nf* trinity.
Trinidad *nf* Trinidad. ● **Trinidad y Tobago** Trinidad and Tobago.
trinitrotolueno *nm* trinitrotoluene.
trino *nm* 1 *(ave)* warble, trill. 2 MÚS trill.
trino,-a *adj* trine.
trinomio *nm* trinomial.
trinquete[1] *nm (lengüeta)* pawl; *(mecanismo)* ratchet.
trinquete[2] *nm* 1 *(frontón)* pelota court. 2 MAR *(palo)* foremast; *(vela)* foresail.
trío *nm* trio.
tripa *nf* 1 *(intestino)* gut, intestine. 2 *(barriga)* gut, stomach. 3 *(de vasija)* belly. 4 *fam (embarazo)* belly.
▷ *nf pl* **tripas** *fam (interior)* innards.
tripartito,-a *adj* tripartite.
triple *adj* 1 triple. 2 *(tres veces)* three times: **pagamos el triple del precio real** *we paid three times the real price.*
▷ *nm* triple. ● **triple salto** triple jump.
triplicado *nm* triplicate.
triplicar [1] *vt* to triple, treble.
trípode *nm* tripod.
tríptico *nm* triptych.
triptongo *nm* triphthong.
tripulación *nf* crew.
tripulante *nm* crew member.
tripular *vt* to man.
triquinosis *nf inv* trichinosis.
triquiñuela *nf fam* trick, dodge.
tris *nm fam fig* bit; *(sonido)* crack. ■ **en un tris** *fam* in a jiffy: **lo hizo en un tris** *he did it in a jiffy.*
trisílabo,-a *adj* trisyllabic.
▷ *nm* **trisílabo** trisyllable.
triste *adj* 1 *(infeliz)* sad, unhappy; *(futuro)* bleak. 2 *(oscuro, sombrío)* gloomy, dismal. 3 *(único)* single, only: **ni un triste libro** *not a single book.* 4 *(insignificante)* poor, humble. ■ **es triste que…** it's a pity…: **es triste que no los podamos ayudar** *it's a pity we can't help them.*
tristeza *nf* sadness.
▷ *nf pl* **tristezas** problems, sufferings.
tristón,-ona *adj fam* gloomy, sad, melancholy.
tritón *nm* 1 *(anfibio)* newt. 2 **Tritón** *(mitología)* Triton.
triturado,-a *adj* 1 ground, crushed. 2 *fig* crumpled up.
triturador,-ra *adj* grinding, crushing, triturating.
▷ *nm* **triturador** waste disposal unit, US garbage disposal unit.
trituradora *nf* grinder, crushing machine. ● **trituradora de papel** paper shredder.
triturar *vt* 1 to grind (up), crush; *(papel)* to shred. 2 *fig (físicamente)* to beat (up); *(moralmente)* to tear apart.
triunfador,-ra *adj* winning.
▷ *nm & nf* winner.
triunfal *adj* triumphant.
triunfalismo *nm* 1 triumphalism. 2 POL jingoism.
triunfalista *adj* 1 triumphalist. 2 POL jingoistic.
▷ *nm o nf* 1 triumphalist. 2 POL jingoist.
triunfar *vi* to triumph. ■ **triunfar en la vida** to succeed in life.
triunfo *nm* 1 *(victoria)* triumph, victory. 2 DEP win. 3 *(éxito)* success. 4 *(naipes)* trump.
trivial *adj* trivial, petty.
trivialidad *nf* triviality, pettiness.
trivializar *vt* to trivialize, minimize.
triza *nf* bit, fragment. ■ **estar hecho,-a trizas** *fam* to feel washed out.
trocar [49] *vt* 1 *(permutar)* to exchange, swap. 2 *(transformar)* to turn (**en**, into), convert (**en**, into).
trocear *vt* to cut up.
trofeo *nm* trophy.
trófico,-a *adj* food.
troglodita *nm o nf* troglodyte.
trola *nf fam* lie, fib.
trolebús *nm* trolley bus.
tromba *nf* waterspout. ● **tromba de agua** downpour.
trombo *nm* thrombus.
trombón *nm* MÚS trombone.

▷ *nm o nf* trombonist. ● **trombón de varas** slide trombone.
trombosis *nf inv* thrombosis.
trompa *nf* **1** MÚS horn. **2** *(de elefante)* trunk. **3** *(de insecto)* proboscis. **4** ANAT tube. **5** *fam fig (nariz)* hooter, snout. ■ **estar trompa** *fam* to be plastered. ● **trompa de Eustaquio** Eustachian tube. | **trompa de Falopio** Fallopian tube.
▷ *nm o nf* MÚS horn player.
trompazo *nm* bump. ■ **darse un trompazo** to have a bump, have a crash.
trompeta *nf* MÚS trumpet.
▷ *nm o nf* trumpet player.
trompetista *nm o nf* trumpet player, trumpeter.
trompicón *nm* **1** *(tropezón)* trip, stumble. **2** *(golpe)* blow, hit. ■ **a trompicones** in fits and starts.
trompo *nm* top, spinning top.
tronar [31] *vi* **1** [Used only in the 3rd person; it does not take a subject.] *(trueno)* to thunder. **2** *(cañón, etc)* to thunder.
tronchar *vt* **1** *(árboles)* to cut down, fell. **2** *fig* to destroy. ■ **troncharse de risa** *fam* to split one's sides with laughter.
troncho *adj* stem, stalk.
tronco *nm* **1** ANAT trunk, torso. **2** BOT *(tallo de árbol)* trunk; *(leño)* log. **3** *fig (linaje)* family stock. **4** *fig (persona inútil)* blockhead. **5** *(geometría)* frustum. **6** *argot (compañero)* mate, pal, chum. ■ **dormir como un tronco** *fam* to sleep like a log. ● **tronco de cono** truncated cone.
tronera *nf* **1** *(de fortificación)* loophole, embrasure. **2** *(de barco)* porthole. **3** *(de billar)* pocket.
tronido *nm* **1** thunderclap. **2** *fig (ruina)* fall, downfall.
trono *nm* throne.
tropa *nf* **1** MIL troops *pl*, soldiers *pl*. **2** *(muchedumbre)* crowd.
▷ *nf pl* **tropas** MIL troops, fighting soldiers.
tropel *nm* throng, mob. ■ **en tropel** in a mad rush.
tropelía *nf* **1** *(atropello)* outrage. **2** *(tropel)* throng, mob. **3** *(delito)* crime.
tropezar [47] *vi* **1** *(trompicar)* to trip, stumble: **tropezó con mi pie** *he tripped over my foot.* **2** *fig (encontrar a alguien)* to come (**con**, across), bump (**con**, into). **3** *fig (encontrar dificultades, etc)* to come up (**con**, against), run (**con**, into).
tropezón *nm* **1** *(traspié)* trip, stumble. **2** *fig (error)* slip-up, faux pas. **3** *fam (de comida)* chunk of food. ■ **dar un tropezón** to trip.
tropical *adj* tropical.
trópico *nm* tropic.
▷ *nm pl* **trópicos** tropics.
tropiezo *nm* **1** *(obstáculo)* trip. **2** *fig (error)* blunder, faux pas; *(revés)* setback, mishap. **3** *(riña)* quarrel.
tropismo *nm* tropism.
tropo *nm* trope.
troposfera *nf* troposphere.
troquel *nm* die.
troqueladora *nf* stamping machine.
troquelar *vt (gen)* to stamp; *(monedas)* to strike; *(cuero)* to emboss.
trotamundos *nm o nf inv* globe-trotter.
trotar *vi* **1** to trot. **2** *fig (andar)* to bustle, run.
trote *nm* **1** *(de caballo)* trot. **2** *fam fig (actividad)* chasing about, hustle and bustle, bustle. ■ **al trote** at a trot.
troupe *nf* troupe.
trova *nf* poem.
trovador,-ra *nm & nf* troubadour, minstrel.
trozo *nm* piece, chunk.
trucaje *nm* trick photography.
trucar [1] *vt* **1** *(foto, etc)* to doctor, alter, tamper with. **2** AUTO to soup up.
trucha *nf* trout.
truco *nm* **1** *(ardid)* trick. **2** *(fotográfico)* trick effect, trick camera shot. **3** *(tranquillo)* knack. ■ **coger el truco a ALGO** *fam* to get the knack of STH, get the hang of STH.
truculencia *nf* **1** cruelty. **2** *fig* sensationalism.
truculento,-a *adj* **1** *(cruel)* cruel. **2** *fig (excesivo)* sensationalistic.
trueno *nm* **1** thunder. **2** *fam (joven)* hare brain.
trueque *nm* exchange, swap.
trufa *nf* **1** *(hongo)* truffle. **2** *(de chocolate)* chocolate truffle.
trufar *vt* to stuff with truffles.
▷ *vi fig* to tell lies.*f*
truhan,-ana *nm & nf* rogue, crook.
trullo *nm argot* clink.
truncado,-a *adj (geometría)* truncated.
truncar [1] *vt* **1** *(cortar)* to truncate. **2** *fig (ilusiones, esperanzas)* to shatter, cut short. **3** *fig (escrito)* to leave unfinished; *(sentido)* to upset.
▷ *vpr* **truncarse** *fig (ilusiones, etc)* to cut short.
trust *nm* trust, cartel.
▲ *pl* **trusts.**
tu *adj* your: **tu coche** *your car;* **tus coches** *your cars.*
tú *pron* **1** you. **2** REL Thou. ■ **tratar de tú** to address as *tú.*
tuareg *adj* Tuareg.
▷ *nm* Tuareg.
tuba *nf* tuba.
tubérculo *nm* **1** BOT tuber. **2** MED tubercle.
tuberculosis *nf inv* tuberculosis.
tuberculoso,-a *adj* **1** BOT tuberous. **2** MED tubercular, tuberculous.
tubería *nf* **1** *(de agua)* piping, pipes *pl*, plumbing. **2** *(de gas, petróleo)* pipeline.
tuberoso,-a *adj* tuberous.
tubo *nm* **1** *(de ensayo, etc)* tube. **2** *(tubería)* pipe. **3** ANAT tube. ● **tubo de ensayo** test tube. | **tubo de escape** exhaust pipe, exhaust. | **tubo digestivo** alimentary canal.
tubular *adj* tubular.
▷ *nm* bicycle tyre.
tucán *nm* toucan.
tuerca *nf* nut.
tuerto,-a *adj* one-eyed, blind in one eye.
▷ *nm & nf* one-eyed person.
tuétano *nm* **1** marrow. **2** *fig* essence, core.
tufo *nm* **1** *(mal olor)* pong, foul smell, stink. **2** *(emanación)* fume, vapour (US vapor).
tugurio *nm* **1** *(choza)* shepherd's hut. **2** *(casucha)* hovel, shack. **3** *fig* hole, dive.
tul *nm* tulle.
tulipa *nf* **1** *(bot)* small tulip. **2** *(lámpara)* tulip-shaped lampshade.
tulipán *nm* tulip.
tullido,-a *adj* crippled, disabled.
▷ *nm & nf* cripple.

tumbado,-a *adj (estirado)* lying, stretched out: **tumbado al sol** *lying in the sun.*
tumbar *vt* 1 *(derribar)* to knock out, knock over. 2 EDUC *fam* to fail.
▷ *vpr* **tumbarse** *(acostarse)* to lie down, stretch out.
tumbo *nm* jolt, bump. ■ **dar tumbos** to jolt, bump along.
tumbona *nf* 1 *(hamaca)* deck-chair. 2 *(silla extensible)* lounger.
tumefacto,-a *adj* swollen.
tumor *nm* tumour (US tumor).
túmulo *nm* 1 *(montecillo)* tumulus, burial mound, barrow. 2 *(catafalco)* catafalque.
tumulto *nm* tumult, commotion.
tumultuoso,-a *adj* tumultuous, riotous.
tuna *nf* student minstrel group.
tunda *nf* 1 *fam* thrashing, beating. 2 *fig (trabajo agotador)* exhausting job, drag.
tundra *nf* tundra.
tunecino,-a *adj* Tunisian.
▷ *nm & nf* Tunisian.
túnel *nm* tunnel.
Túnez *nm* 1 *(ciudad)* Tunis. 2 *(país)* Tunisia.
tungsteno *nm* tungsten.
túnica *nf* tunic.
tuno[1] *nm* BOT prickly pear.
tuno,-a[2] *nm & nf* rogue, crook.
▷ *nm* **tuno** *(de la tuna)* member of a *tuna.*
tupé *nm* 1 *(copete)* tuft of hair, quiff. 2 *fam fig (atrevimiento)* nerve, cheek.
tupí *adj* Tupi.
▷ *nm & nf* Tupi.
▷ *nm (idioma)* Tupi.
tupido,-a *adj* 1 dense, thick. 2 *fig (torpe)* clumsy.
tupir *vi (apretar)* to pack tight, press down.
▷ *vpr* **tupirse** 1 *(comiendo)* to stuff OS. 2 *(ofuscarse)* to get muddled up, get in a muddle.
turba[1] *nf* 1 *(combustible)* peat, turf. 2 *(abono)* peat.
turba[2] *nf (muchedumbre)* mob, crowd.
turbación *nf* 1 *(alteración)* disturbance. 2 *(preocupación)* anxiety, worry. 3 *(desconcierto)* confusion, uneasiness.
turbado,-a *adj* 1 *(alterado)* disturbed, unsettled. 2 *(preocupado)* worried, upset. 3 *(desconcertado)* confused.
turbador,-ra *adj* 1 *(que altera)* disturbing, unsettling. 2 *(preocupante)* worrying, upsetting. 3 *(desconcertante)* confusing, disconcerting.
turbante *nm* turban.
turbar *vt* 1 *(alterar)* to unsettle, disturb. 2 *(enturbiar)* to stir up. 3 *(preocupar)* to upset, worry. 4 *(desconcertar)* to baffle, put off.
▷ *vpr* **turbarse** 1 *(preocuparse)* to be upset, become upset. 2 *(desconcertarse)* to be confused, be baffled.
turbera *nf* peat bog.
turbina *nf* turbine.
turbio,-a *adj* 1 *(oscurecido)* cloudy, muddy, turbid. 2 *fig (dudoso)* shady, dubious. 3 *fig (turbulento)* turbulent. 4 *fig (confuso)* confused. 5 *fig (vista)* blurred.
turbo *nm* turbo.
turbogenerador *nm* turbogenerator.
turbohélice *nm* turboprop.
turborreactor *nm* turbojet, turbojet engine.
turbulencia *nf* turbulence.
turbulento,-a *adj* turbulent, troubled.
turco,-a *adj* Turkish.
▷ *nm & nf (persona)* Turk.
▷ *nm* **turco** *(idioma)* Turkish.
turgencia *nf* turgidity, turgidness.
turgente *adj* turgid.
turismo *nm* 1 *(gen)* tourism. 2 *(industria)* tourist trade, tourist industry. 3 AUTO private car, saloon. ■ **hacer turismo** 1 *(país)* to go touring. 2 *(ciudad, pueblo)* to go sightseeing.
turista *nm o nf* tourist.
turístico,-a *adj* tourist. ■ **de interés turístico** of interest to tourists.
Turkmenistán *nm* Turkmenistan.
turmalina *nf* tourmaline.
túrmix [Registered trademark.] *nm inv* liquidizer, blender.
turnar *vi* to alternate.
▷ *vpr* **turnarse** to take turns.
turnedó *nm* tournedos.
turno *nm* 1 *(tanda)* turn, go: **es mi turno** *it's my turn;* **¿a quién le toca el turno?** *who's next?* 2 *(período de trabajo)* shift. ■ **estar de turno** to be on duty. ● **turno de día / turno de noche** day shift / night shift.
turquesa *adj* turquoise.
▷ *nf (piedra)* turquoise.
▷ *nm (color)* turquoise.
Turquía *nf* Turkey.
turrón *nm type of* nougat.
turronería *nf* shop selling nougat.
turulato,-a *adj fam* flabbergasted, flummoxed.
tute *nm* 1 *(naipes)* card game. 2 *fig (esfuerzo)* beating.
tutear *vt* 1 to address as *tú.* 2 *fig* to be on familiar terms with.
▷ *vpr* **tutearse** *(uso recíproco)* to address each other as *tú.*
tutela *nf* 1 JUR guardianship, tutelage. 2 *fig* protection, guidance. ■ **bajo la tutela de** under the protection of.
tutelar *adj* tutelary.
tuteo *nm* use of the *tú* form of address.
tutor,-ra *nm & nf* 1 JUR guardian. 2 *fig* protector, guide. 3 EDUC tutor.
▷ *nm* **tutor** AGR stake, prop.
tutoría *nf* 1 JUR guardianship. 2 EDUC post of tutor.
tutti frutti *adj* tutti-frutti.
tutú *nm* tutu.
Tuvalu *nm* Tuvalu.
tuyo,-a *adj* of yours, one of your: **¿es primo tuyo?** *is he a cousin of yours?, is he your cousin?*
▷ *pron* yours, your own: **el tuyo está allí** *yours is there.*
▷ *nm* **lo tuyo** *(lo que es tuyo)* what is yours; *(lo que te concierne)* your business, your own business.
▷ *nm pl* **los tuyos** *(familiares)* your family *sing; (amigos)* your friends.
TV *abrev* **(televisión)** television; *(abreviatura)* TV.
twist *nm* twist.

U

U, u *nf*
▲ *pl* úes. *(la letra)* U, u.
u [Used before words beginning with o or ho.] *conj* or: diez u once *ten or eleven.*
See also o.
ubicación *nf* location, position.
ubicar [1] *vi* to be, be situated.
▷ *vt* AM *(situar)* to locate, situate, place.
ubicuidad *nf* ubiquity.
ubicuo,-a *adj* ubiquitous, omnipresent.
ubre *nf* udder.
UCI *abrev* MED (Unidad de Cuidados Intensivos) intensive care unit; *(abreviatura)* ICU.
ucraniano,-a *adj* Ukrainian.
▷ *nm & nf (persona)* Ukrainian.
Ud. *abrev* (usted) you.
Uds. *abrev* (ustedes) you.
UE *abrev* (Unión Europea) European Union; *(abreviatura)* EU.
UEFA *abrev* (Unión de Asociaciones Europeas de Fútbol) Union of European Football Associations; *(abreviatura)* UEFA.
ufanarse *vpr* to boast (con/de, of).
ufano,-a *adj* **1** *(engreído)* conceited, arrogant. **2** *(satisfecho)* satisfied, happy. **3** *(desenvuelto)* confident.
ufología *nf* ufology.
Uganda *nf* Uganda.
ugandés,-esa *adj* Ugandan.
▷ *nm & nf* Ugandan.
ujier *nm* usher.
ukelele *nm* ukulele, ukelele.
úlcera *nf* ulcer. ● úlcera de estómago stomach ulcer.
ulceración *nf* ulceration.
ulcerar *vt* to ulcerate.
▷ *vpr* ulcerarse to ulcerate.
ulceroso,-a *adj* ulcerous.
ulterior *adj* **1** *(más allá)* further. **2** *(siguiente)* subsequent; *(posterior)* later, further.
ultimación *nf* completion, conclusion.
ultimar *vt* to finish, complete, conclude.
ultimátum *nm inv* **1** ultimatum. **2** *fam* final word.
último,-a *adj* **1** last. **2** *(más reciente)* latest; *(de dos)* latter. **3** *(más alejado)* furthest; *(más abajo)* bottom, lowest; *(más arriba)* top; *(más atrás)* back. **4** *(definitivo)* final
ultra *adj fam* extreme right-wing.
▷ *nm o nf fam* extreme right-winger.
ultra- *pref* ultra.
ultracongelado *adj* deep-frozen.
ultracongelar *vt* to deep-freeze.
ultraconservador,-ra *adj* ultraconservative.
▷ *nm & nf* ultraconservative.
ultraderecha *nf* extreme right (wing).
ultraderechista *adj* extreme right-wing.
▷ *nm o nf* extreme right-winger.
ultraísmo *nm* ultraism.
ultrajante *adj* outrageous, insulting, offensive.
ultrajar *vt* to outrage, insult, offend.
ultraje *nm* outrage, insult, offence (US offense).
ultraligero *adj* ultralight.
▷ *nm* ultraligero *(avión)* microlight.
ultramar *nm* overseas.
ultramarino,-a *adj* overseas.
▷ *nm* ultramarino *(tienda)* grocer's (shop), US grocery (store).
▷ *nm pl* ultramarinos *(comestibles)* groceries.
ultramoderno,-a *adj* ultramodern.
ultranza ■ a ultranza **1** *(a muerte)* to the death. **2** *(a todo trance)* at all costs, at any price. **3** *(acérrimo)* out-and-out.
ultrapasar *vt* to surpass, go beyond.
ultrasónico,-a *adj* ultrasonic.
ultrasonido *nm* ultrasound.
ultratumba *adv* beyond the grave.
▷ *nf* afterlife.
ultravioleta *adj inv* ultraviolet.
ulular *vi (animal)* to howl; *(búho)* to hoot.
ululato *nm (de animal)* howl; *(de búho)* hoot.
umbilical *adj* umbilical.
umbral *nm* **1** threshold. **2** *fig* threshold, outset.
umbrela *nf* umbrella.
umbría *nf* shady place.
umbrío,-a *adj* shady.
umbroso,-a *adj* shady.
un,-na *art indef* a, an: un libro *a book;* un ojo *an eye.*
▷ *adj* **1** *(numeral)* one: tiene un año *he's one year old.* **2** *(indef)* some: un día volverá *he'll come some day.*
See also uno,-a.
unánime *adj* unanimous.
unanimidad *nf* unanimity.
unción *nf* **1** unction. **2** *fig (devoción)* devotion, fervour.
uncir [3] *vt* to yoke.
undécimo,-a *adj* eleventh.
▷ *nm & nf (ordinal, partitivo)* eleventh.
See also sexto,-a.
undulación *nf* undulation; *(agua)* ripple.
ungir [6] *vt* to anoint.
ungüento *nm* ointment.
ungulado,-a *adj* ungulate, hoofed.
▷ *nm* ungulado ungulate, hoofed animal.
unicameral *adj* unicameral, single-chamber.
unicelular *adj* unicellular, single-cell.
unicidad *nf* uniqueness.
único,-a *adj* **1** *(solo)* only, sole: la única persona *the only person.* **2** *(extraordinario)* unique.
unicolor *adj* of one colour, single-coloured.
unicornio *nm* unicorn.
unidad *nf* **1** unit. **2** *(barco)* vessel; *(avión)* aircraft; *(de tren)* carriage, coach. **3** *(cohesión)* unity.

unidimensional *adj* one-dimensional.
unidireccional *adj* unidirectional.
unido,-a *adj* 1 *(junto)* united. 2 *(avenido)* attached: **estar muy unidos** *to be very close.*
unifamiliar • **vivienda unifamiliar** detached house.
unificación *nf* unification.
unificador,-ra *adj* unifying.
▷ *nm & nf* unifier.
unificar [1] *vt* to unify.
uniformado,-a *adj* in uniform, uniformed.
uniformar *vt* 1 *(igualar)* to make uniform, standardize. 2 *(poner un uniforme)* to put into uniform, give a uniform.
uniforme *adj* 1 uniform. 2 *(superficie)* even.
▷ *nm (prenda)* uniform.
uniformidad *nf* 1 *(igualdad)* uniformity. 2 *(de superficie)* evenness.
uniformizar [4] *vt* to standardize.
unigénito,-a *adj* only-begotten.
▷ *nm* **el Unigénito** the Son of God, Jesus Christ.
unilateral *adj* unilateral.
unión *nf* 1 union. 2 TÉC *(acoplamiento)* joining; *(junta)* joint.
unionismo *nm* unionism.
unionista *adj* unionist.
unipersonal *adj* 1 single, individual. 2 GRAM unipersonal.
unir *vt* 1 *(juntar)* to unite, join, join together. 2 *(combinar)* to combine (**a**, with). 3 *(enlazar)* to link (**a**, to).
unisex *adj inv* unisex.
unísono,-a *adj* unisonous, in harmony.
unitario,-a *adj* unitary.
univalvo,-a *adj* univalve.
universal *adj* universal.
▷ *nm pl* **universales** *(filosofía, lingüística, etc)* universals.
universalidad *nf* universality.
universalizar *vt* to universalize.
universidad *nf* university.
universitario,-a *adj* university.
▷ *nm & nf (que está estudiando)* university student; *(licenciado)* university graduate.
universo *nm* universe.
unívoco,-a *adj* univocal.
uno,-a *adj (numeral)* one: **el número uno** *number one.*
▷ *pron* 1 one: **uno (de ellos)** *one of them.* 2 *(impersonal)* one, you: **uno tiene que velar por sus intereses** *one has to look after one's own interests.* 3 *fam (persona)* someone, somebody: **estaba hablando con una** *he was talking to some woman.*
▷ *nm* **uno** *(número)* one.
▷ *nf* **la una** *(hora)* one o'clock.
▷ *adj vpr* **unos,-as** *(indefinido)* some; *(aproximado)* about, around: **unas cajas** *some boxes;* **habrá unos treinta** *there must be around thirty.* ■ **a (la) una** together. | **de uno,-a en uno,-a** one by one.
untar *vt* 1 to grease, smear: **untar pan con mantequilla** *to spread butter on bread.* 2 *fam (sobornar)* to bribe.
unto *nm* grease, ointment.
untuosidad *nf* greasiness, oiliness.
untuoso,-a *adj* unctuous, greasy, oily.
uña *nf* 1 nail; *(del dedo)* fingernail; *(del dedo del pie)* toenail. 2 *(garra)* claw; *(pezuña)* hoof.
uñero *nm* 1 *(inflamación)* whitlow. 2 *(uña clavada)* ingrowing nail.
uperización *nf* UHT treatment.
uperizar [4] *vt* to treat at an ultrahigh temperature. • **leche uperizada** UHT milk.
uralita [Registered trademark.] *nf* uralite.
uranio *nm* uranium.
Urano *nm* Uranus.
urbanidad *nf* urbanity, politeness.
urbanismo *nm* town planning.
urbanista *nm o nf* town planner.
urbanístico,-a *adj* town-planning, urban.
urbanización *nf* 1 *(proceso)* urbanization. 2 *(conjunto residencial)* housing development, housing estate.
urbanizar [4] *vt* to urbanize, develop.
urbano,-a *adj* urban, city.
urbe *nf* large city, metropolis.
urdimbre *nf* 1 *(textil)* warp. 2 *fig (trama)* intrigue.
urdir *vt* 1 *(textil)* to warp. 2 *fig (tramar)* to plot, scheme.
urea *nf* urea.
uremia *nf* uraemia, US uremia.
uréter *nm* ureter.
uretra *nf* urethra.
urgencia *nf* 1 urgency. 2 *(necesidad)* urgent need, pressing need. 3 *(emergencia)* emergency.
▷ *nf pl* **urgencias** *(servicio)* casualty department *sing*, casualty *sing*, US emergency room. ■ **en (un) caso de urgencia** in an emergency.
urgente *adj* 1 urgent. 2 *(correo)* express (post, US mail), first-class (post, US mail).
urgir [6] *vi* to be urgent, be pressing.
úrico,-a *adj* uric.
urinario,-a *adj* urinary.
▷ *nm* **urinario** *(retrete)* urinal.
urna *nf* 1 POL ballot box. 2 *(vasija)* urn. 3 *(caja)* glass case.
urogallo *nm* capercaillie.
urogenital *adj* urogenital.
urología *nf* urology.
urólogo,-a *nm & nf* urologist.
urraca *nf* 1 magpie. 2 *fig (cotorra)* chatterbox.
urticante *adj* stinging.
urticaria *nf* hives *pl*, urticaria.
Uruguay *nm* Uruguay.
uruguayo,-a *adj* Uruguayan.
▷ *nm & nf* Uruguayan.
usado,-a *adj* 1 *(gastado)* worn out, old. 2 *(de segunda mano)* second-hand, used.
usar *vt* 1 to use. 2 *(prenda)* to wear.
▷ *vi* to use (**de**, -).
▷ *vpr* **usarse** *(estar de moda)* to be used, be in fashion.
usía *pron fml (hombre)* Your Lordship; *(mujer)* Your Ladyship.
uso *nm* 1 use. 2 *(ejercicio)* exercise. 3 *(de prenda)* wearing. 4 *(costumbre)* usage, custom. 5 GRAM usage.
usted *pron fml* you.
▲ *pl* **ustedes**.
usual *adj* usual, common.
usuario,-a *nm & nf* user.
usufructo *nm* usufruct, use.

usufructuar [11] *vt* to have the usufruct of, usufruct.
usufructuario,-a *adj* usufructuary.
▷ *nm & nf* usufructuary.
usura *nf* usury.
usurero,-a *nm & nf* usurer.
usurpación *nf* usurpation.
usurpador,-ra *adj* usurping.
▷ *nm & nf* usurper.
usurpar *vt* to usurp.
utensilio *nm* **1** *(herramienta)* tool, utensil. **2** *(aparato)* device, implement.
uterino,-a *adj* uterine.
útero *nm* uterus, womb.
útil[1] *adj* useful.
útil[2] *nm (herramienta)* tool, instrument.
utilería *nf* (stage) props *pl*.
utilidad *nf* **1** utility, usefulness. **2** *(beneficio)* profit.
utilitario,-a *adj* utilitarian.
▷ *nm* **utilitario** *(coche)* utility vehicle.
utilitarista *adj* utilitarian.
▷ *nm o nf* utilitarian.
utilizable *adj* usable, fit for use.
utilización *nf* use.
utilizar [4] *vt* to use, make use of.
utillaje *nm* tools *pl*, equipment.
utopía *nf* Utopia.
utópico,-a *adj* Utopian.
utopista *adj* Utopian.
uva *nf* grape.
uve *nf name of the letter* **v**.
UVI *abrev* MED **(unidad de vigilancia intensiva)** intensive care unit; *(abreviatura)* ICU.
úvula *nf* uvula.
uvular *adj* uvular.
uzbeco,-a *adj* Uzbek.
▷ *nm & nf (persona)* Uzbek.
▷ *nm* **uzbeco** *(idioma)* Uzbek.
Uzbekistán *nm* Uzbekistan.

V

V, v *nf (la letra)* V, v.
V *sím* **(voltio)** volt; *(símbolo)* V.
vaca *nf* **1** cow. **2** *(carne)* beef. **3** *(cuero)* cowhide.
vacaciones *nf pl* holiday, holidays *pl*, US vacation: **se fueron de vacaciones a Mallorca** *they went to Majorca for their holidays (US vacation).* ■ **estar de vacaciones** to be on holiday (US vacation).
vacante *adj* vacant.
▷ *nf* vacancy.
vaciado *nm* **1** *(fabricación en molde)* casting, moulding (US molding). **2** *(de un documento)* extraction of information. **3** *(dejar vacío)* emptying; *(dejar hueco)* hollowing out. **4** INFORMÁ dumping.
vaciar [13] *vt* **1** *(recipiente)* to empty; *(local)* to empty, clear. **2** *(contenido)* to pour away. **3** *(dejar hueco)* to hollow out. **4** *(moldear)* to cast, mould (US mold).
vaciedad *nf* stupid remark.
vacilación *nf* **1** *(duda)* hesitation, wavering. **2** *(oscilación)* swaying, vacillation.
vacilante *adj* **1** *(dubitativo)* hesitating. **2** *(voz)* hesitant; *(luz)* flickering; *(paso, mesa, etc)* unsteady, shaky.
vacilar *vi* **1** *(oscilar)* to sway, vacillate. **2** *(estar poco firme)* to wobble. **3** *(al andar)* to sway, stagger, wobble; *(al hablar)* to falter. **4** *(luz)* to flicker. **5** *fig (dudar)* to hesitate, waver. **6** *fam (tomar el pelo)* to joke, tease: **¡no me vaciles!** *don't tease me!* **7** *fam (presumir)* to show off.
vacilón,-ona *nm & nf fam* teaser, joker.
vacío,-a *adj* **1** *(gen)* empty: **el cine está vacío** *the cinema is empty.* **2** *(no ocupado)* vacant, unoccupied; *(sin muebles)* unfurnished. **3** *(hueco)* hollow.
▷ *nm* **vacío 1** *(gen)* emptiness. **2** *(hueco)* gap; *(espacio)* space; *(espacio en blanco)* blank space. **3** *(vacante)* vacancy. **4** FÍS vacuum. **5** *fig (falta)* emptiness, void.
vacuidad *nf* vacuity, emptiness.
vacuna *nf* MED vaccine.
vacunación *nf* MED vaccination.
vacunar *vt* MED to vaccinate (**contra**, against).
▷ *vpr* **vacunarse** to be vaccinated.
vacuno,-a *adj* bovine.
vacuo,-a *adj* vacuous, empty.
vacuola *nf* vacuole.
vadear *vt* **1** *(río)* to ford. **2** *fig (dificultad)* to overcome.
vademécum *nm inv* handbook, vade mecum.
vado *nm* **1** *(de río)* ford. **2** *(de acera)* dropped kerb.
vagabundear *vi (vagar)* to wander, roam.
vagabundeo *nm (merodeo)* wandering, roaming.
vagabundo,-a *adj* **1** wandering. **2** *pey* vagrant.
▷ *nm & nf* **1** *(trotamundos)* wanderer, rover. **2** *pey* vagrant, tramp, US hobo. **3** *(sin casa)* tramp, US hobo.
vagancia *nf* **1** *(estar ocioso,-a)* idleness. **2** JUR vagrancy.
vagar[1] [7] *vi (estar ocioso)* to idle about, loaf around.
vagar[2] [7] *vi (errar)* to wander (**por**, about), roam (**por**, about).
vagina *nf* vagina.
vaginal *adj* vaginal.
vago,-a[1] *adj* **1** *(vacío)* empty. **2** *(holgazán)* lazy, idle.
vago,-a[2] *adj (impreciso)* vague: **idea vaga** *vague idea.*
vagón *nm* **1** *(para pasajeros)* carriage, coach, US car. **2** *(para mercancías)* wagon, truck, US boxcar, freight car.
vagoneta *nf* small open wagon.
vaguada *nf* lowest part of a valley, stream bed.
vaguear *vi* → **vagar 1 and vagar 2.**
vaguedad *nf* **1** *(imprecisión)* vagueness: **la vaguedad de sus pensamientos** *the vagueness of his thoughts.* **2** *(expresión imprecisa)* vague remark.
vaharada *nf* puff, breath.
vahído *nm* dizzy spell, fainting spell.
vaho *nm* **1** *(vapor)* vapour (US vapor), steam. **2** *(aliento)* breath.
vaina *nf* **1** *(de espada, etc)* sheath, scabbard. **2** *(de instrumento, etc)* case. **3** BOT pod, husk.
vainica *nf* hemstitch.
vainilla *nf* vanilla.
vaivén *nm* **1** *(oscilación)* swaying; *(balanceo)* rocking. **2** *(ir y venir)* coming and going, bustle. **3** *fig (cambio)* fluctuation, change. **4** *fig (intercambio)* exchange.
vajilla *nf* tableware, dishes *pl*, crockery. ● **una vajilla** a dinner service.
vale *nm* **1** *(comprobante)* voucher; *(recibo)* receipt. **2** *(pagaré)* IOU, promissory note.
▷ *interj fam* OK!
valedero,-a *adj* valid.
valedor,-ra *nm & nf* protector, patron.
valencia *nf* valency.
valentía *nf (valor)* bravery, courage.
valer [89] *vt* **1** *(tener un valor de)* to be worth: **no vale nada** *it is worthless.* **2** *(costar)* to cost, be: **vale siete euros el kilo** *it costs seven euros a kilo* **3** *(hacer merecedor)* to win, earn, get: **el suspenso le valió un rapapolvo** *failing the exam earned him a strong repremand.* **4** *(ocasionar)* to cause: **me ha valido muchos problemas** *he's caused me a lot of problems.* **5** MAT to equal.
▷ *vi* **1** *(tener un valor de)* to be worth. **2** *(ser útil, adecuado)* to be useful, be of use, be good for: **¿te vale este libro?** *is this book any use (to you)?* **3** *(costar)* to cost, be worth. **4** *(ser válido, contar)* to count. **5** *(tener validez)* to be valid; *(monedas)* to be legal tender: **ese billete aún vale** *that ticket is still valid.* **6** *(ser suficiente, bastar)* to do, be enough: **con esto ya me vale** *this will be enough for me.* **7** *(estar permitido)* to be allowed, be permitted.
▷ *nm (valía)* value.
▷ *vpr* **valerse 1** *(utilizar)* to use (**de**, of), make use (**de**, of): **se valió de un bastón** *he used a stick.* **2** *(espabilarse)* to manage, cope.
valeriana *nf* BOT valerian.

valeroso,-a *adj* courageous, brave.
valía *nf* 1 *(objeto)* value, worth. 2 *(persona)* worth, merit.
validación *nf (de documento)* validation.
validar *vt (documento)* to validate, make valid.
validez *nf* validity.
valido *nm* favourite (US favorite).
válido,-a *adj* valid.
valiente *adj* 1 *(valeroso)* brave, courageous, bold. 2 *(fuerte)* strong, vigorous.
valija *nf* 1 *(maleta)* suitcase, case. 2 *(de correos)* mailbag. ● **valija diplomática** diplomatic bag.
valioso,-a *adj* valuable, precious.
valla *nf* 1 *(cerca)* fence; *(construcción)* wall. 2 MIL stockade, fortification. 3 DEP hurdle. 4 *(para publicidad)* hoarding, US billboard. 5 *fig* obstacle, hindrance.
vallado *nm* 1 *(cerca)* fence. 2 MIL stockade.
vallar *vt* to fence (in), build a fence around.
valle *nm* valley.
valor *nm* 1 *(valía)* value, worth, merit: **una persona de gran valor** *a person of great merit.* 2 *(precio)* price. 3 *(validez)* value: **estas monedas dejarán de tener valor muy pronto** *these coins will soon be of no value.* 4 *(importancia)* importance. 5 *(coraje)* courage, valour (US valor). 6 MAT value.
▷ *nm pl* **valores** 1 FIN securities. 2 *(principios)* values.
valoración *nf* 1 *(tasación)* valuation, valuing. 2 *(revalorización)* appreciation.
valorar *vt* 1 *(tasar)* to value, calculate the value of. 2 *(aumentar el valor)* to raise the value of.
valorización *nf* 1 *(tasación)* valuation, valuing. 2 *(revalorización)* appreciation.
valorizar [4] *vt* 1 *(tasar)* to value. 2 *(revalorizar)* to raise the value of.
valquiria *nf* Valkyrie.
vals *nm* waltz.
valuar [11] *vt* to value.
valva *nf* valve.
válvula *nf* valve. ● **válvula de seguridad** safety valve.
valvular *adj* valvular.
vampiresa *nf fam* vamp, femme fatale.
vampirismo *nm* vampirism.
vampiro *nm* 1 *(espectro)* vampire. 2 *(mamífero)* vampire bat. 3 *fig* leech, parasite.
vanadio *nm* vanadium.
vanagloriarse [12] *vpr* to boast (**de**, of).
vandalismo *nm* vandalism.
vándalo,-a *adj* Vandal.
▷ *nm & nf* 1 Vandal. 2 *fig* vandal.
vanguardia *nf* 1 *(corriente)* avant-garde, vanguard. 2 *(parte de ejército)* vanguard, van.
vanguardismo *nm* avant-garde movement.
vanguardista *adj* avant-garde.
▷ *nm o nf* avant-gardist.
vanidad *nf* vanity, conceit.
vanidoso,-a *adj* vain, conceited.
vano,-a *adj* 1 *(inútil)* vain, useless. 2 *(ilusorio)* illusory, futile. 3 *(frívolo)* frivolous. ■ **en vano** in vain.
Vanuatu *nm* Vanuatu.
vapor *nm* 1 *(gas)* vapour (US vapor), steam. 2 *(barco)* steamship, steamer. ■ **al vapor** CULIN steamed. ● **vapor de agua** water vapour (US vapor).
vaporización *nf* vaporization.
vaporizador *nm* vaporizer, spray, atomizer.
vaporizar [4] *vt* to vaporize.
vaporoso,-a *adj* 1 vaporous. 2 *fig (tejido)* sheer.
vapulear *vt* 1 *(azotar)* to beat, thrash. 2 *fig (criticar)* to criticize, slate.
vapuleo *nm* 1 *(zurra)* beating, thrashing. 2 *fig (crítica)* slating, hammering.
vaquería *nf* 1 *(establo)* cowshed. 2 *(lechería)* dairy.
vaqueriza *nf* cowshed.
vaquerizo,-a *adj* cattle.
▷ *nm & nf* cowherd.
vaquero,-a *adj* cow, cattle.
▷ *nm & nf (pastor)* cowherd, US cowboy.
▷ *nm pl* **vaqueros** *(pantalones)* jeans, pair of jeans.
vaqueta *nf* cowhide.
vaquilla *nf* heifer.
vara *nf* 1 *(palo)* staff, rod, pole. 2 *(de mando)* staff, mace. 3 *(medida de longitud)* unit of length equal to approximately 33 inches. 4 *(tauromaquia)* lance, pike.
varapalo *nm* 1 *(palo)* long pole. 2 *(golpe)* blow with a pole. 3 *fam fig (daño)* blow, setback.
varar *vi* 1 MAR *(encallar)* to run aground. 2 *fig (un negocio)* to come to a standstill.
varear *vt* 1 *(golpear)* to beat with a pole. 2 *(fruta)* to knock down (with a pole).
vareo *nm* knocking down (fruit from trees).
variabilidad *nf* variability.
variable *adj* variable, changeable.
▷ *nf* MAT variable.
variación *nf* variation, change.
variado,-a *adj* 1 varied. 2 *(galletas, helados)* assorted.
variante *adj* variable.
▷ *nf* 1 *(versión)* variant. 2 *(diferencia)* difference.
variar [13] *vt* 1 *(cambiar)* to change. 2 *(dar variedad)* to vary, give some variety to.
▷ *vi* 1 *(cambiar)* to change: **han variado de planes** *they have changed their plans.* 2 *(diferir)* to be different (**de**, to), differ (**de**, from): **lo que dices varía de tus primeras declaraciones** *what you're saying differs from your first statement.* 3 MAT to vary. ■ **para variar** *irón* as usual, just for a change.
varicela *nf* MED chickenpox, varicella.
varicoso,-a *adj* varicose.
variedad *nf* 1 *(diversidad)* variety, diversity: **una gran variedad de productos** *a wide variety of products.* 2 *(clase, tipo)* variety.
▷ *nf pl* **variedades** *(espectáculo)* variety show *sing.*
varilla *nf* 1 *(vara)* stick, rod. 2 *(de paraguas, abanico)* rib; *(de corsé)* stay.
vario,-a *adj* 1 *(diverso)* different, diverse. 2 *(variado)* varied, assorted. 3 *(mudable)* changeable, variable.
▷ *nm pl* **varios** *(algunos)* some, several, a number of.
variopinto,-a *adj (diverso)* diverse, assorted.
varita *nf* small stick. ● **varita mágica** magic wand.
variz *nf* varicose vein.
▲ *pl* **varices.**
varón *nm* 1 *(hombre)* man; *(chico)* boy. 2 *(sexo)* male.
varonil *adj* manly, virile, male.
vasallaje *nm* 1 HIST vassalage. 2 *fig* servitude.
vasallo,-a *nm & nf* 1 HIST vassal. 2 *(súbdito)* subject.
vasar *nm* kitchen shelf.
vasco,-a *adj* Basque.
▷ *nm & nf (persona)* Basque.
▷ *nm* **vasco** *(idioma)* Basque. ● **País Vasco** Basque Country.

vascular *adj* vascular.
vascularización *nf* vascularization.
vasectomía *nf* vasectomy.
vaselina® *nf* 1 *(sustancia)* Vaseline, petroleum jelly. 2 *(en fútbol)* chip.
vasija *nf* vessel, pot, jar.
vaso *nm* 1 *(para beber)* glass. 2 *(para flores)* vase. 3 ANAT vessel. ● **vaso capilar** capillary..
vasoconstricción *nf* vasoconstriction.
vasodilatación *nf* vasodilation.
vástago *nm* 1 BOT shoot, bud. 2 *fig (descendencia)* offspring. 3 TÉC rod, stem.
vastedad *nf* vastness, immensity.
vasto,-a *adj* vast, immense, huge.
váter *nm fam* toilet.
vaticinador,-ra *adj* prophesying, predicting.
▷ *nm & nf* prophet, seer.
vaticinar *vt* to predict, foretell, prophesy.
vaticinio *nm* prophecy, prediction.
vatio *nm* watt.
vaya *interj* what a: **¡vaya idea!** *what an idea!*
Vd. *abrev* **(usted)** you.
vecinal *adj* local.
vecindad *nf* 1 *(lugar)* neighbourhood (US neighborhood), vicinity. 2 *(vecinos)* neighbours *pl* (US neighbors *pl*), residents *pl*, community.
vecindario *nm* 1 *(lugar)* neighbourhood (US neighborhood). 2 *(vecinos)* neighbours *pl* (US neighbors *pl*), community, residents *pl*.
vecino,-a *adj* nearby, neighbouring (US neighboring).
▷ *nm & nf* 1 *(del barrio)* neighbour (US neighbor). 2 *(residente)* resident. 3 *(habitante)* inhabitant.
vector *nm* vector.
vectorial *adj* vectorial.
veda *nf* 1 *(prohibición)* prohibition. 2 *(de caza)* close season, US closed season.
vedado,-a *adj* forbidden, prohibited.
▷ *nm* **vedado** game preserve.
vedar *vt (prohibir)* to prohibit, forbid, ban.
vedette *nf* TEAT *(variedades)* star.
vega *nf* fertile lowland, fertile plain.
vegetación *nf* vegetation.
▷ *nf pl* **vegetaciones** MED adenoids.
vegetal *adj* vegetable.
▷ *nm* 1 vegetable, plant. 2 *(persona)* vegetable.
vegetar *vi* 1 *(plantas)* to vegetate, grow. 2 *fig (persona)* to vegetate.
vegetarianismo *nm* vegetarianism.
vegetariano,-a *adj* vegetarian.
▷ *nm & nf* vegetarian.
vegetativo,-a *adj* vegetative.
vehemencia *nf* vehemence.
vehemente *adj* vehement.
vehículo *nm* 1 *(gen)* vehicle. 2 *(coche)* car. 3 *fig* vehicle. 4 *fig (enfermedades)* transmitter, carrier.
veinte *adj (cardinal)* twenty; *(vigésimo)* twentieth.
▷ *nm (número)* twenty; *(fecha)* twentieth. ● **los años veinte** the twenties.
See also **seis.**
veinteavo,-a *adj* twentieth.
▷ *nm & nf* twentieth.
See also **sexto,-a.**
veintena *nf (exacto)* twenty; *(aproximado)* about twenty.
veinticinco *adj (cardinal)* twenty-five; *(ordinal)* twenty-fifth.
▷ *nm (número)* twenty-five; *(fecha)* twenty-fifth.
veinticuatro *adj (cardinal)* twenty-four; *(ordinal)* twenty-fourth.
▷ *nm (número)* twenty-four; *(fecha)* twenty-fourth.
veintidós *adj (cardinal)* twenty-two; *(ordinal)* twenty-second.
▷ *nm (número)* twenty-two; *(fecha)* twenty-second.
veintinueve *adj (cardinal)* twenty-nine; *(ordinal)* twenty-ninth.
▷ *nm (número)* twenty-nine; *(fecha)* twenty-ninth.
veintiocho *adj (cardinal)* twenty-eight; *(ordinal)* twenty-eighth.
▷ *nm (número)* twenty-eight; *(fecha)* twenty-eighth.
veintiséis *adj (cardinal)* twenty-six; *(ordinal)* twenty-sixth.
▷ *nm (número)* twenty-six; *(fecha)* twenty-sixth.
veintisiete *adj (cardinal)* twenty-seven; *(ordinal)* twenty-seventh.
▷ *nm (número)* twenty-seven; *(fecha)* twenty-seventh.
veintitrés *adj (cardinal)* twenty-three; *(ordinal)* twenty-third.
▷ *nm (número)* twenty-three; *(fecha)* twenty-third.
veintiún *adj* [Used only before masculine nouns.] twenty-one.
See also **veintiuno,-a.**
veintiuna *nf* pontoon, blackjack.
See also **veintiuno,-a.**
veintiuno,-a *adj (cardinal)* twenty-one; *(ordinal)* twenty-first.
▷ *nm (número)* twenty-one; *(fecha)* twenty-first.
vejación *nf* 1 *(maltrato)* vexation. 2 *(humillación)* humiliation.
vejar *vt* 1 *(molestar)* to vex. 2 *(humillar)* to humiliate.
vejatorio,-a *adj* 1 *(molesto)* vexatious, annoying. 2 *(humillante)* humiliating.
vejez *nf* old age.
vejiga *nf* bladder.
vela[1] *nf* 1 *(vigilia)* watch, vigil; *(de muerto)* wake. 2 *(desvelo)* wakefulness. 3 *(candela)* candle. ■ **pasar la noche en vela** to have a sleepless night.
vela[2] *nf* 1 *(de barco)* sail. 2 DEP sailing. 3 *fig (barco de vela)* sailing ship.
velada *nf* evening, soirée.
velado,-a *adj* 1 *(oculto)* hidden. 2 *(fotografía)* blurred.
velador,-ra *nm* 1 *(vigilante)* watchman, guard. 2 *(candelero)* candlestick. 3 *(mesita)* pedestal table.
veladura *nf* 1 *(en pintura)* glaze. 2 *(en fotografía)* fog.
velaje *nm* sails *pl*.
velamen *nm* sails *pl*.
velar[1] *vi* 1 *(no dormir)* to stay awake; *(no acostarse)* to stay up. 2 *fig (cuidar)* to watch (**por**, over), look (**por**, after): **velaron por él** *they looked after him.*
▷ *vt (enfermo)* to sit up with; *(muerto)* to keep vigil over.
velar[2] *adj* LING velar.
▷ *vt* 1 *fig (cubrir)* to hide, cover, veil. 2 *(fotografía)* to fog, expose. 3 *(pintura)* to glaze.
▷ *vpr* **velarse** *(fotografía)* to become fogged.
velatorio *nm* wake, vigil.
velcro® *nm* velcro.

veleidad *nf* 1 *(capricho)* caprice, whim. 2 *(inconstancia)* inconstancy, fickleness.
veleidoso,-a *adj* inconstant, fickle.
velero,-a *nm & nf (fabricante de velas)* sailmaker.
▷ *nm* **velero** sailing ship, sailing boat.
veleta *nf (para el viento)* weathercock, weather vane.
▷ *nm o nf fam fig (persona)* fickle person.
velita *nf* nightlight.
vello *nm* 1 *(de persona - pelusa)* down; *(- en las piernas, etc)* hair. 2 *(de fruta, planta)* down, bloom.
vellón *nm* fleece.
vellosidad *nf* 1 *(vello)* down. 2 *(abundancia - de pelusa)* downiness; *(en las piernas, etc)* hairiness.
velloso,-a *adj* downy, hairy, fluffy.
velludo,-a *adj* downy, hairy, fluffy.
velo *nm* 1 *(gen)* veil. 2 ANAT velum.
velocidad *nf* 1 *(rapidez)* speed, velocity. 2 AUTO *(marcha)* gear. ■ **a toda velocidad** at full speed. ● **velocidad de transmisión** INFORMÁ bit rate.
velocímetro *nm* speedometer.
velocípedo *nm* velocipede.
velocista *nm o nf* DEP sprinter.
velódromo *nm* cycle track, US velodrome.
velomotor *nm* moped.
velón *nm* oil lamp.
velorio[1] *nm (velatorio)* wake.
velorio[2] *nm* REL taking of the veil.
veloz *adj* fast, quick, swift, rapid.
vena *nf* 1 ANAT vein. 2 *(yacimiento)* vein. 3 BOT vein. 4 *(en mármol, etc)* vein, streak. 5 *fig (disposición)* mood.
venablo *nm* javelin, dart.
venado *nm* 1 ZOOL stag, deer. 2 CULIN venison.
venal *adj* 1 *(vendible)* venal, saleable. 2 *fig (sobornable)* venal, corrupt.
venalidad *nf* venality.
vencedor,-ra *adj* winning, victorious.
▷ *nm & nf* 1 *(equipo, etc)* winner, victor.
vencejo[1] *nm (ave)* swift.
vencejo[2] *nf (atadura)* bond.
vencer [2] *vt* 1 DEP to beat. 2 *(exceder)* to outdo, surpass: **la vence en belleza** *she surpasses her in beauty.* 3 *(problema, etc)* to overcome. 4 *(ser dominado)* to overcome: **la venció el cansancio** *she was overcome by tiredness.*
▷ *vi* 1 *(ganar)* to win. 2 *(deuda, etc)* to fall due, be payable. 3 *(plazo)* to expire.
▷ *vpr* **vencerse** 1 *(romperse)* to break; *(doblarse)* to bend, incline. 2 *fig (reprimir)* to control OS.
vencido,-a *adj* 1 *(derrotado)* defeated, beaten. 2 *(deuda)* due, payable. 3 *(plazo)* expired. ■ **darse por vencido,-a** *fig* to give up, accept defeat.
vencimiento *nm* 1 *(pago, etc)* maturity. 2 *(plazo)* expiry.
venda *nf* bandage.
vendaje *nm* dressing.
vendar *vt* to bandage.
vendaval *nm* strong wind, gale.
vendedor,-ra *adj* selling.
▷ *nm & nf* 1 *(gen)* seller; *(hombre)* salesman; *(mujer)* saleswoman. 2 *(dependiente)* shop assistant.
vender *vt* 1 *(gen)* to sell. 2 *fig (traicionar)* to betray.
▷ *vpr* **venderse** 1 *(uso impersonal)* to be on sale, be sold: **se vende en farmacias** *on sale at your chemist's.* 2 *(dejarse sobornar)* to sell OS. ■ **«Se vende»** «For sale».
vendible *adj* saleable, marketable.
vendido,-a *adj* sold.
vendimia *nf (cosecha)* grape harvest.
vendimiador,-ra *nm & nf* grape picker.
vendimiar [12] *vt* to harvest.
veneno *nm (química, vegetal)* poison; *(animal)* venom.
venenoso *adj* 1 poisonous. 2 *fig* spiteful, venomous.
venerable *adj* venerable.
veneración *nf* veneration, worship.
venerar *vt* to venerate, worship, revere.
venéreo,-a *adj* venereal.
venezolano,-a *adj* Venezuelan.
▷ *nm & nf* Venezuelan.
Venezuela *nf* Venezuela.
vengador,-ra *nm & nf* avenger.
venganza *nf* revenge, vengeance.
vengar [7] *vt* to avenge.
▷ *vpr* **vengarse** to take revenge (**de**, on).
vengativo,-a *adj* vengeful, vindictive.
venia *nf* 1 *fml (licencia)* permission. 2 *fml (perdón)* pardon.
venial *adj* venial.
venialidad *nf* veniality.
venida *nf* coming, arrival.
venidero,-a *adj* future, coming.
venir [90] *vi* 1 *(gen)* to come: **el mes que viene** *next month.* 2 *(llegar)* to arrive: **vino tarde** *he arrived late.* 3 *(proceder)* to come (**de**, from): **viene de París** *it comes from Paris.* 4 *(estar, aparecer)* to be, come: **las explicaciones vienen en español** *the instructions are in Spanish.* 5 *(ser)* to be: **eso te viene grande** *that's too big for you.*
▷ *aux* 1 **venir a** + *inf (aproximación)* to be about; *(alcanzar, llegar a)* to arrive at; *(terminar por)* to end up. 2 **venir** + *ger (acción durativa)*: **lo venía avisando desde hace tiempo** *he has been warning us about it for a long time.* 3 **venir** + *pp (ser, estar)* to be: **eso viene motivado por la inflación** *it's caused by inflation.*
▷ *vpr* **venirse** to come back, go back.
venoso,-a *adj* 1 *(sangre)* venous. 2 *(manos, etc)* veined.
venta *nf* 1 *(acción)* sale, selling. 2 *(hostal)* country inn.
ventaja *nf* 1 *(gen)* advantage. 2 *(provecho)* profit; *(beneficio)* benefit.
ventajoso,-a *adj* advantageous, profitable.
ventana *nf* 1 ARQUIT window. 2 *(de la nariz)* nostril.
ventanal *nm* large window.
ventanilla *nf* 1 *(banco, coche, sobre, etc)* window. 2 *(barco)* porthole. 3 *(de taquilla)* window. 4 *(de la nariz)* nostril.
ventanuco *nm* small window.
ventarrón *nm* strong wind, gale.
ventear *vt* 1 *(husmear)* to sniff. 2 *(airear)* to air, air out. 3 *fig (indagar)* to snoop.
ventero,-a *nm & nf* innkeeper.
ventilación *nf* ventilation.
ventilador *nm* ventilator, fan.
ventilar *vt* 1 *(lugar)* to air, ventilate. 2 *(agitar al viento)* to air. 3 *fig (dar a conocer)* to air. 4 *fig (discutir)* to discuss.
▷ *vpr* **ventilarse** 1 *(lugar)* to be ventilated. 2 *(objeto)* to be aired. 3 *fam (terminar)* to finish off.
ventisca *nf* snowstorm, blizzard.
ventolera *nf* 1 *(golpe)* gust of wind. 2 *fig* caprice.
ventosa *nf* 1 *(pieza cóncava)* suction cup. 2 *(de animal)* sucker.
ventosidad *nf* wind, flatulence.

ventoso,-a *adj* windy.
ventrículo *nm* ventricle.
ventrílocuo,-a *adj* ventriloquistic.
▷ *nm & nf* ventriloquist.
ventriloquia *nf* ventriloquy, ventriloquism.
ventura *nf* **1** *(felicidad)* happiness. **2** *(casualidad)* fortune, chance; *(suerte)* luck. **3** *(azar)* hazard, risk.
venturoso,-a *adj* lucky, fortunate.
ver [91] *vt* **1** *(gen)* to see: **no te veo** *I can't see you.* **2** *(mirar)* to look (at). **3** *(televisión)* to watch. **4** *fig (entender)* to see, understand: **no veo por qué lo hizo** *I can't understand why she did it.* **5** *(visitar)* to visit, see: **ven a verme** *come and see me.* **6** JUR to try, hear. **7** *(parecer)* to look: **te veo triste** *you look sad.* ■ **a ver** let me see.
▷ *nm* **1** *(vista)* sight. **2** *(apariencia)* looks *pl*, appearance.
▷ *vpr* **verse 1** *(ser visto)* to be seen: **aquí dentro no se ve nada** *you can't see a thing in here.* **2** *(con* ALGN*)* to meet, see each other. **3** *(en una situación, etc)* to find OS, be: **se vio en un apuro** *he was in a fix.* **4** *(imaginarse)* to imagine OS.
vera *nf* edge, side. ■ **a la vera de** beside, next to.
veracidad *nf* veracity, truthfulness.
veranda *nf* veranda.
veraneante *nm o nf* holiday-maker, US vacationist.
veranear *vi* to spend the summer (holiday) (**en**, in/at).
veraneo *nm* summer holiday.
veraniego,-a *adj* summer, summery.
verano *nm* summer.
veras ■ **de veras** really, seriously.
veraz *adj* truthful, veracious.
verbal *adj* verbal, oral.
verbalizar *vt* to verbalize.
verbena *nf* **1** BOT verbena. **2** *(fiesta)* night party.
verbigracia *adv fml* for example, for instance.
verbo *nm* verb.
verborrea *nf fam* verbosity.
verdad *nf* truth, truthfulness: **es verdad** *it's true.*
verdadero,-a *adj* true, real.
verde *adj* **1** *(color)* green. **2** *(fruta)* unripe, green. **3** *fig (persona)* green, immature. **4** *fam (chiste)* blue, dirty.
▷ *nm* **1** *(color)* green. **2** *(hierba)* grass. **3** POL green: **los verdes** *the Greens.*
verderón *nm* greenfinch.
verdín *nm* **1** *(de plantas)* verdure. **2** *(capa - de algas)* green slime; *(- de paredes, frutas)* green mould (US mold).
verdor *nm (color)* verdure, greenness.
verdoso,-a *adj* greenish.
verdugo *nm* **1** *(persona)* executioner. **2** *(prenda)* balaclava.
verdugón *nm* weal.
verdulera *nf fig* coarse woman.
See also **verdulero,-a.**
verdulería *nf* greengrocer's (shop).
verdulero,-a *nm & nf* greengrocer.
verdura *nf* **1** *(hortaliza)* vegetables *pl* **2** *(color)* greenness.
vereda *nf* footpath, path.
veredicto *nm* verdict.
vergel *nm* orchard.
verglás *nm* black ice, ice.
vergonzante *adj* shamefaced.
vergonzoso,-a *adj* **1** *(acto)* shameful. **2** *(persona)* shy.
vergüenza *nf* **1** *(deshonor, etc)* shame. **2** *(timidez)* shyness: **me da vergüenza bailar** *I'm too shy to dance.* **3** *(escándalo)* disgrace, shame: **lo que han hecho es una vergüenza** *what they did is a disgrace.*
vericueto *nm* rough path, dirt track.
verídico,-a *adj* truthful, true.
verificación *nf* **1** *(comprobación)* verification, checking. **2** *(cumplimiento)* carrying out, conducting.
verificar [1] *vt* **1** *(comprobar)* to verify, check. **2** *(probar)* to prove. **3** *(efectuar)* to carry out, perform.
▷ *vpr* **verificarse 1** *(comprobarse)* to come true. **2** *(efectuarse)* to take place.
verja *nf* **1** *(reja)* grating, grille. **2** *(cerca)* railing, railings *pl.* **3** *(puerta)* iron gate.
vermú *nm* **1** *(bebida)* vermouth. **2** *(aperitivo)* aperitive.
▲ *pl* **vermuts.**
vermut *nm* → **vermú.**
vernáculo,-a *adj* vernacular. ● **lengua vernácula** vernacular.
verosímil *adj (probable)* likely; *(creíble)* credible.
verosimilitud *nf (probabilidad)* probability, likeliness; *(credibilidad)* credibility, verisimilitude.
verraco *nm* boar, hog.
verruga *nf* wart.
versado,-a *adj* versed (**en**, in), proficient (**en**, in).
versal *adj* capital.
▷ *nf* capital, capital letter.
versalita *adj* small capital.
▷ *nf* small capital letter, small capital.
versar *vi* **1** *(tratar)* to deal (**sobre**, with), be (**sobre**, about/on): **la conferencia versó sobre la lingüística** *the lecture was on linguistics.* **2** *(dar vueltas)* to revolve, turn.
versátil *adj* **1** *(gen)* versatile. **2** *fig (voluble)* fickle.
versatilidad *nf* **1** *(gen)* versatility. **2** *fig* fickleness.
versículo *nm* verse, versicle.
versificación *nf* versification.
versificar [1] *vt* to put into verse, versify.
▷ *vi* to versify, write in verse.
versión *nf* **1** *(gen)* version, account. **2** *(traducción)* translation. **3** *(adaptación)* adaptation.
versionar *vt* to cover, do a version of.
verso *nm* **1** LIT verse. **2** *fam (poema)* poem.
vértebra *nf* vertebra.
vertebrado,-a *adj* vertebrate.
▷ *nm pl* **los vertebrados** the vertebrates.
vertebral *adj* vertebral, spinal.
vertebrar *vt fig* to be the backbone of, structure.
vertedero *nm* rubbish dump, rubbish tip.
verter [28] *vt* **1** *(líquido - voluntariamente)* to pour. **2** *(derramar)* to spill. **3** *(vaciar)* to empty, empty out. **4** *(basura)* to dump. **5** *fig (conceptos, ideas, etc)* to express.
vertical *adj* vertical: **lo puso vertical** *she put it upright.*
▷ *nf* vertical, vertical line.
▷ *nm* vertical.
vértice *nm* vertex.
vertido,-a *nm (consciente)* dumping; *(fortuito)* spillage.
vertiente *nf* **1** *(gen)* slope. **2** *fig (aspecto)* angle.
vertiginoso,-a *adj* dizzy, giddy.
vértigo *nm* **1** MED vertigo. **2** *(mareo)* dizziness. **3** *fig* frenzy.
vesícula *nf* vesicle. ● **vesícula biliar** gall bladder.
vesicular *adj* vesicular.
vespertino,-a *adj* evening.
▷ *nm* **vespertino** evening newspaper.
vespino® *nm* moped.

vestal *adj* vestal.
vestíbulo *nm* 1 *(de casa)* hall, entrance. 2 *(de hotel, etc)* hall, lobby, vestibule, foyer.
vestido,-a *adj* dressed: **vestida de blanco** *dressed in white.*
▷ *nm* **vestido** 1 *(indumentaria)* clothes *pl*, dress, costume. 2 *(de mujer)* dress; *(de hombre)* suit.
vestidor *nm* dressing room.
vestidura [Generally used in plural.] *nf* 1 *(gen)* clothing, clothes *pl*. 2 REL vestments *pl*.
vestigio *nm* vestige, trace, remains *pl*.
vestimenta *nf* clothes *pl*, garments *pl*.
vestir [34] *vt* 1 *(llevar)* to wear, be dressed in: **vestía un vestido rojo** *she was wearing a red dress.* 2 *(ayudar a vestirse)* to dress; *(hacer vestidos)* to make clothes for. 3 *(cubrir)* to cover (**de**, with).
▷ *vi* 1 to dress: **vestir de negro** *to dress in black.* 2 *(ser elegante, lucir)* to be classy, look smart.
▷ *vpr* **vestirse** 1 *(uso reflexivo)* to dress OS, get dressed. 2 *(comprarse la ropa)* to buy one's clothes: **se viste en Milán** *she buys her clothes in Milan.*
vestuario *nm* 1 *(ropas)* wardrobe, clothes *pl*. 2 TEAT *(ropa)* wardrobe, costumes *pl*; *(camerino)* dressing room. 3 DEP changing room (US locker room).
veta *nf* 1 *(de mármol, roca)* seam, vein; *(de madera)* streak. 2 *fig* streak.
vetar *vt* to veto, put a veto on.
veteado,-a *adj (mármol, etc)* veined; *(madera)* grained.
vetear *vt* to grain, streak.
veteranía *nf* 1 seniority. 2 MIL long service.
veterano,-a *adj* veteran.
▷ *nm & nf* veteran.
veterinaria *nf* veterinary medicine.
veterinario,-a *adj* veterinary.
▷ *nm & nf* veterinary surgeon, vet, US veterinarian.
veto *nm* veto. ■ **poner el veto a** to put a veto on, veto.
vetustez *nf fml (antigüedad)* antiquity; *(vejez)* great age.
vetusto,-a *adj fml (antiguo)* ancient; *(viejo)* very old.
vez *nf* 1 time: **fue la única vez que la vi** *it was the only time I saw her;* **una vez** *once;* **dos veces** *twice;* **cuatro veces** *four times.* 2 *(turno)* turn; *(ocasión)* occasion.
▲ *pl* **veces.**
vía *nf* 1 *(camino)* road, way; *(calle)* street; *(carril)* lane. 2 *(de tren)* track, line; *(en la estación)* platform: **el tren de la vía uno** *the train at platform one.* 3 ANAT passage, canal, track. 4 *fig (modo)* way, manner, means. 5 JUR procedure. 6 *(rumbo, dirección)* via, through: **Barcelona-Singapur vía Frankfurt** *Barcelona-Singapore via Frankfurt.*
viabilidad *nf* viability.
viable *adj* viable.
viaducto *nm* viaduct.
viajante *nm* commercial traveller (US traveler), travelling (US traveling) salesman.
viajar *vi* to travel: **ha viajado por el mundo entero** *she's travelled all over the world.*
viaje *nm* 1 *(gen)* journey, trip. 2 *(en coche)* drive, journey. 3 *(travesía por mar)* voyage. 4 [Usually used in plural.] *(concepto de viajar)* travel. 5 *(carga)* load. ● **viaje de ida y vuelta** return trip, US round trip.
viajero,-a *adj* travelling (US traveling).
▷ *nm & nf* 1 traveller (US traveler). 2 *(en transporte público)* passenger.
vial *adj* road.
vianda *nf* food, victuals *pl*.
viandante *nm o nf* pedestrian, passer-by.
viario,-a *adj* road, highway.
viático *nm* REL viaticum.
víbora *nf* viper.
vibración *nf* 1 vibration. 2 LING rolling, trilling.
vibráfono *nm* vibraphone.
vibrante *adj* 1 *(enérgico)* vibrant, vigorous; *(emocionante)* exciting, stirring: **un partido vibrante** *an exciting match.* 2 LING rolled, trilled.
vibrar *vi* 1 *(gen)* to vibrate; *(pulsar)* to throb, pulsate: **toda la ciudad vibraba de actividad** *the whole city throbbed with activity.* 2 *fig (conmoverse)* to be moved, be overcome with emotion: **el cantante hizo vibrar al público** *the singer thrilled the audience.* 3 LING to roll, trill.
vibratorio,-a *adj* vibratory.
vicaría *nf* 1 *(dignidad)* vicarship. 2 *(lugar)* vicarage.
vicario,-a *nm & nf* vicar.
vicepresidente,-a *nm & nf* 1 *(gen)* vice-chairperson. 2 POL vice president.
vicetiple *nf* chorus girl.
viceversa *adv* vice versa.
viciado,-a *adj (aire - mal olor)* foul, foul-smelling; *(- cargado)* stuffy; *(- contaminado)* polluted.
viciar [12] *vt* 1 *(corromper)* to corrupt, lead astray. 2 *(aire)* to pollute.
▷ *vpr* **viciarse** 1 *(enviciarse)* to take to vice, become corrupted. 2 *(objeto)* to go out of shape.
vicio *nm* 1 *(corrupción)* vice, corruption. 2 *(mala costumbre)* bad habit; *(inmoralidad)* vice. 3 *(del lenguaje)* incorrect usage. 4 *(defecto)* defect.
vicioso,-a *adj* 1 *(cosa)* faulty. 2 *(persona)* depraved.
▷ *nm & nf* depraved person.
vicisitud *nf* vicissitude.
víctima *nf* victim, casualty.
victimizar *vt* to victimize.
victoria *nf* victory, triumph.
victorioso,-a *adj* victorious, triumphant.
vicuña *nf* ZOOL vicuna, vicuña.
vid *nf* grapevine, vine.
vida *nf* 1 *(gen)* life. 2 *(viveza)* liveliness. 3 *(tiempo)* lifetime, life. 4 *(modo de vivir)* life, way of life. 5 *(medios)* living, livelihood. ■ **ganarse la vida** to earn one's living. ● **vida familiar** family life.
vidente *nm o nf (persona que adivina)* clairvoyant.
vídeo *nm (aparato)* video; *(cinta)* video, video tape.
videocámara *nf* video camera.
videocasete *nf* video cassette.
videoconferencia *nf* videoconference.
videoconsola *nf* games console.
videoclip *nm* video, pop video.
videoclub *nm* video club.
videófono *nm* videophone.
videojuego *nm* video game.
videoteca *nf* video library.
videoteléfono *nm* videophone.
videotexto *nm* videotext, teletext.
vidriado,-a *adj* glazed.
▷ *nm* **vidriado** 1 *(cerámica)* glazed earthenware. 2 *(barniz)* glaze. 3 *(acción)* glazing.
vidriar [14] *vt (cerámica)* to glaze.

vidriera *nf* 1 *(ventana)* picture window. 2 *(puerta)* glass door. 3 *(de balcón, galería)* French window. 4 *(vitral)* stained-glass window. 5 *(escaparate)* shop window.
vidriero,-a *nm & nf* 1 *(fabricante)* glass-maker. 2 *(colocador)* glazier.
vidrio *nm (material)* glass.
vidrioso,-a *adj* 1 *(gen)* glassy; *(quebradizo)* brittle, glass-like. 2 *(ojos)* glazed. 3 *fig (asunto, etc)* touchy.
vieira *nf* scallop.
viejo,-a *adj* 1 *(gen)* old: **un coche viejo** *an old car.* 2 *(desgastado)* old, worn-out. 3 *(antiguo)* old, ancient.
▷ *nm & nf (hombre)* old man; *(mujer)* old woman. ■ **hacerse viejo,-a** to grow old.
viento *nm* 1 *(gen)* wind. 2 *(rumbo)* direction. 3 *(de caza)* scent. 4 *(cuerda)* rope, guy. 5 *fam (flatulencia)* wind, flatulence. ■ **hacer viento** to be windy.
vientre *nm* 1 ANAT belly, abdomen. 2 *(vísceras)* bowels *pl.* 3 *(de embarazada)* womb.
viernes *nm inv* Friday. ● **Viernes Santo** Good Friday.
See also **jueves.**
Vietnam *nm* Vietnam.
vietnamita *adj* Vietnamese.
▷ *nm & nf (persona)* Vietnamese.
▷ *nm* **vietnamita** *(idioma)* Vietnamese.
viga *nf* 1 *(de madera)* beam. 2 *(de acero, etc)* girder.
vigencia *nf* validity.
vigente *adj* in force, valid.
vigésimo,-a *adj* twentieth: **vigésimo primero** *twenty-first.*
▷ *nm & nf* twentieth.
See also **sexto,-a.**
vigía *nm o nf* lookout.
vigilancia *nf* 1 *(acción)* surveillance. 2 *(cuidado)* vigilance, watchfulness.
vigilante *adj* 1 *(que vigila)* vigilant. 2 *(alerta)* alert.
▷ *nm o nf (hombre)* guard, watchman; *(mujer)* guard.
vigilar *vt* 1 *(cuidar)* to watch (over), look after: **vigila al niño** *look after the baby.* 2 *(con armas, etc)* to guard. 3 *(supervisar)* to oversee. 4 *(estar atento)* to keep an eye on, take care of.
▷ *vi (gen)* to keep watch.
vigilia *nf (estado de no dormir)* wakefulness, sleeplessness.
vigor *nm* 1 *(fuerza)* vigour (US vigor), strength. 2 *(validez)* force, effect. ■ **en vigor** in force.
vigorizante *adj* invigorating.
vigorizar [4] *vt* to invigorate, fortify.
vigoroso,-a *adj* vigorous, strong.
vigueta *nf (de madera)* small beam; *(de metal)* small girder.
VIH *abrev* MED **(virus de inmunodeficiencia humana)** Human Immune Deficiency Virus; *(abreviatura)* HIV.
vihuela *nf* vihuela, *type of* guitar.
vikingo,-a *adj* Viking.
▷ *nm & nf* Viking.
vil *adj* vile, base, despicable.
vileza *nf* 1 *(cualidad)* vileness. 2 *(acto)* vile act.
vilipendiar [12] *vt* 1 *(ofender)* to revile, insult. 2 *(despreciar)* to despise.
vilipendio *nm* 1 *(ofensa)* offence (US offense); *(humillación)* humiliation. 2 *(desprecio)* scorn, contempt.
villa *nf* 1 *(casa)* villa. 2 *(pueblo)* small town; *(ciudad)* town.
villancico *nm* carol, Christmas carol.
villanía *nf* 1 *(bajeza)* vileness, baseness. 2 *fig (acción)* vile deed, despicable act.
villano,-a *nm & nf* 1 HIST serf. 2 *fig (persona ruin)* villain.
villorrio *nm pey* one-horse town.
vilo ■ **en vilo** 1 *(suspendido)* in the air, suspended. 2 *fig (indeciso)* in suspense, on tenterhooks.
vinagre *nm* 1 vinegar. 2 *fig* sourpuss.
vinagrera *nf* vinegar bottle.
▷ *nf pl* **vinagreras** cruet *sing*, cruet set *sing.*
vinagreta *nf* vinaigrette sauce.
vinajera *nf* altar cruet.
vinatería *nf* 1 *(comercio)* wine trade. 2 *(tienda)* wine shop.
vinatero,-a *nm & nf* wine merchant.
vinculación *nf* 1 *(acción)* linking. 2 *(vínculo)* link, bond.
vincular *vt* 1 *(unir)* to link (**a**, to), bind (**a**, to). 2 *(relacionar)* to relate (**con**, to), connect (**con**, with), link (**con**, with). 3 JUR to entail.
▷ *vpr* **vincularse** to link OS (**a**, to).
vínculo *nm* 1 tie, bond, link. 2 *fig* link.
vindicación *nf (defensa)* vindication.
vindicar [1] *vt (defender)* to vindicate.
vindicativo,-a *adj* 1 *(que defiende)* vindicatory. 2 *(vengativo)* vindictive. 3 JUR punitive.
vinícola *adj* wine-producing.
vinicultor,-ra *nm & nf* wine producer.
vinicultura *nf* wine production, wine growing.
vinificación *nf* wine-making process.
vinílico,-a *adj* vinyl.
vinilo *nm* vinyl.
vino *nm* wine. ● **vino tinto** red wine.
viña *nf* vineyard.
viñedo *nm* vineyard.
viñeta *nf* 1 *(en impresión)* vignette. 2 *(dibujo humorístico)* cartoon.
viola *nf* viola.
violáceo,-a *adj* violaceous, violet.
violación *nf* 1 *(transgresión)* violation, infringement. 2 *(de persona)* rape.
violador,-ra *nm & nf* 1 *(de leyes, etc)* violator. 2 rapist.
violar *vt* 1 *(transgredir)* to violate. 2 *(persona)* to rape.
violencia *nf* 1 *(fuerza)* violence. 2 *(embarazo)* embarrassment. 3 *(situación embarazosa)* embarrassing situation. 4 *(violación)* rape.
violentar *vt* 1 *(forzar algo)* to force, break open. 2 *(obligar a alguien)* to force, use force on. 3 *fig (entrar)* to break into, enter by force.
▷ *vpr* **violentarse** 1 *fig (molestarse)* to get annoyed. 2 *fig (avergonzarse)* to feel ashamed.
violento,-a *adj* 1 *(gen)* violent. 2 *(molesto)* embarrassed, awkward, ill at ease.
violeta *adj (color)* violet.
▷ *nm (color)* violet.
▷ *nf* BOT violet.
violín *nm* violin.
violinista *nm o nf* violinist.
violón *nm* double bass.
violoncelista *nm o nf* cellist, violoncello.
violoncelo *nm* cello.
violonchelista *nm o nf* cellist, violoncello.
violonchelo *nm* cello.
viperino,-a *adj* 1 viperine, viperous. 2 *fig* venomous.

viraje *nm* 1 *(curva)* turn, bend. 2 *(en coche)* turn. 3 MAR tack. 4 *(fotografía)* toning.
viral *adj* viral.
virar *vi* 1 MAR to tack, put about. 2 AUTO to turn round.
virgen *adj* 1 *(persona)* virgin. 2 *(puro)* virgin, pure.
▷ *nm o nf* virgin. ● **la Santísima Virgen** the Blessed Virgin.
virginal *adj* 1 virginal. 2 REL of the Virgin.
virginidad *nf* virginity.
virgo *nm* 1 *(virginidad)* virginity. 2 *(himen)* hymen. 3 *(astrología)* Virgo.
vírico,-a *adj* viral.
viril *adj* virile, manly.
virilidad *nf* virility.
virología *nf* virology.
virólogo,-a *nm & nf* virologist.
virreina *nf (que gobierna)* vicereine, female viceroy.
virreinato *nm* viceroyalty.
virrey *nm* viceroy.
virtual *adj* virtual.
virtud *nf* 1 *(cualidad)* virtue. 2 *(propiedad, eficacia)* property, quality.
virtuosismo *nm* virtuosity.
virtuoso,-a *adj* virtuous.
▷ *nm & nf* virtuous person.
viruela *nf* 1 MED smallpox. 2 *(marca)* pockmark.
virulencia *nf* virulence.
virulento,-a *adj* virulent.
virus *nm inv* virus.
viruta *nf* shaving.
vis ● **vis cómica** comic sense, humour (US humor).
visado,-a *adj* endorsed with a visa.
▷ *nm* **visado** visa.
visar *vt* 1 *(pasaporte)* to endorse with a visa. 2 *(documento)* to endorse, approve.
víscera *nf* internal organ.
▷ *nf pl* **vísceras** viscera, entrails.
visceral *adj* 1 visceral. 2 *fig* profound, deep-rooted.
viscosa *nf* viscose.
viscosidad *nf* viscosity.
viscoso,-a *adj* viscous.
visera *nf* 1 *(de gorra)* peak; *(de casco)* visor. 2 *(suelta)* eyeshade. 3 AUTO sun visor.
visibilidad *nf* visibility.
visigodo,-a *nm & nf* Visigoth.
visigótico,-a *adj* Visigothic.
visillo *nm* small lace curtain.
visión *nf* 1 *(acción)* vision. 2 *(vista)* sight. 3 *(ilusión)* vision. 4 *fig (persona fea)* fright, sight. ■ **ver visiones** to dream.
visionar *vt* to view.
visionario,-a *adj* visionary.
▷ *nm & nf* visionary.
visir *nm* vizier.
visita *nf* 1 *(acción)* visit. 2 *(invitado)* visitor, guest; *(invitados)* visitors *pl*, guests *pl*. ■ **estar de visita en** to be visiting. ● **horas de visita** MED surgery hours.
visitante *nm o nf* visitor.
visitar *vt* 1 *(ir a ver a alguien)* to visit, pay a visit to, call on, go and see: **vamos a ver a la abuela** *let's go and visit grandma.* 2 *(lugar)* to visit, see. 3 *(inspeccionar)* to inspect.
vislumbrar *vt* 1 *(ver)* to glimpse. 2 *fig (conjeturar)* to begin to see: **vislumbraron una solución al problema** *they began to see a solution to the problem.*
viso *nm* 1 *(reflejo)* sheen, shimmer. 2 *(ropa interior)* underskirt. 3 *fig (apariencia)* appearance. ■ **tener visos de** to seem, appear.
visón *nm* mink.
visor *nm* 1 *(de arma)* sight. 2 *(de máquina fotográfica)* viewfinder.
víspera *nf* 1 *(día anterior)* day before. 2 *(de fiesta)* eve.
▷ *nf pl* **vísperas** REL vespers.
vista *nf* 1 *(visión)* sight, vision. 2 *(ojo)* eye, eyes *pl*. 3 *(panorama)* view. 4 *(aspecto)* appearance, aspect, look. 5 *(dibujo, cuadro, foto)* view. 6 *(intención)* intention. 7 *(propósito)* outlook, prospect. 8 JUR trial, hearing.
▷ *nf pl* **vistas** view *sing*: **la habitación tiene vistas al mar** *the room has a view of the sea.* ■ **a simple vista** at first sight: **a primera vista parecía más complicado** *at first sight it looked more complicated.* ■ **ser corto,-a de vista** to be short-sighted. ■ **tener vista de lince** *fig* to be eagle-eyed, have eyes like a hawk.
vistazo *nm* glance. ■ **echar un vistazo a** ALGO 1 *(mirar)* to have a look at STH. 2 *(vigilar)* to keep an eye on.
visto,-a *adj* 1 *(anticuado)* old-fashioned. 2 *(dado)* in view of, considering. 3 *(corriente)* common. 4 *(ladrillo, viga, obra)* exposed.
▷ *nm* **visto** approval. ■ **dar el visto bueno a** ALGO to approve STH, O.K. STH.
vistosidad *nf* showiness.
vistoso,-a *adj* 1 *(llamativo)* showy, flashy. 2 *(colorido)* bright, colourful (US colorful).
visual *adj* visual.
▷ *nf (línea)* line of vision, line of sight.
visualización *nf* display.
visualizar [4] *vt* 1 to visualize. 2 INFORMÁ to display.
vital *adj* 1 *(de la vida)* vital. 2 *fig (esencial)* essential, vital.
vitalicio,-a *adj* life, for life: **un cargo vitalicio** *a post held for life.*
vitalidad *nf* vitality.
vitalizar [4] *vt* to vitalize.
vitamina *nf* vitamin.
vitaminado,-a *adj* vitamin-enriched.
vitamínico,-a *adj* vitamin.
vitelo *nm* vitellus.
vitícola *adj* wine-growing, wine-producing.
viticultor,-ra *nm & nf* wine grower, viticulturist.
viticultura *nf* wine-growing, viticulture.
vitola *nf* 1 *(de cigarro)* cigar band. 2 *fig (facha)* appearance.
vitorear *vt (aclamar)* to cheer, acclaim.
vitral *nm* stained-glass window.
vítreo,-a *adj* vitreous.
vitrina *nf* 1 *(armario)* glass cabinet. 2 *(de exposición)* glass case, showcase. 3 *(escaparate)* shop window.
vitriólico,-a *adj* vitriolic.
vitriolo *nm* vitriol.
vitro *loc* **in vitro** in vitro. ● **fecundación in vitro** in vitro fertilization.
vitrocerámica ● **encimera vitrocerámica** ceramic hob.
vitualla *nf* [Generally used in plural.] provisions *pl*, food.
vituperar *vt* to vituperate, censure, condemn.
vituperio *nm* vituperation, censure, condemnation.
viudedad *nf* 1 *(estado)* widowhood. 2 *(pensión - hombre)* widower's pension; *(- mujer)* widow's pension.

viudez *nf* widowhood.
viudo,-a *adj* widowed.
▷ *nm & nf (hombre)* widower; *(mujer)* widow.
viva *nm* cheer, shout.
vivac *nm* bivouac.
▲ *pl* **vivaques.**
vivacidad *nf* vivacity, liveliness.
vivaque *nm* bivouac.
vivaz *adj* **1** *(vivo)* vivacious, lively. **2** *(perspicaz)* sharp, quick-witted.
vivencia *nf* personal experience.
víveres *nm pl* food *sing*, provisions, supplies.
vivero *nm* **1** *(de plantas)* nursery. **2** *(de peces)* fish farm, fish hatchery; *(de moluscos)* bed.
viveza *nf* **1** *(persona)* liveliness, vivacity. **2** *(color, relato)* vividness. **3** *(al hablar)* vehemence. **4** *(agudeza)* sharpness, quick-wittedness.
vívido,-a *adj* vivid.
vividor,-ra *nm & nf* **1** *(persona que sabe vivir)* person who makes the most of life. **2** *pey (aprovechado)* sponger, scrounger.
vivienda *nf* **1** *(gen)* housing, accommodation. **2** *(morada)* dwelling. **3** *(casa)* house. **4** *(piso)* flat.
vivificar [1] *vt* to vivify, give life to, enliven.
vivíparo,-a *adj* viviparous.
vivir *vi* **1** *(tener vida)* to live; *(estar vivo)* to be alive: **vivió hasta los ochenta años** *he lived to the age of eighty.* **2** *(habitar)* to live: **vive en Barcelona** *she lives in Barcelona.* **3** *(mantenerse)* to live, live on, make a living: **ese trabajo no le da para vivir** *he can't live on what that job pays.* **4** *fig (durar)* to last, live on.
▷ *vt (pasar por, experimentar)* to live through, go through, experience: **mi abuelo vivió la guerra** *my grandfather lived through the war.*
vivisección *nf* vivisection.
vivo,-a *adj* **1** *(que tiene vida)* living; *(que está)* alive: **materia viva** *living matter;* **Pepe está vivo** *Pepe is alive.* **2** *(fuego, llama)* live, burning. **3** *(lengua)* living. **4** *fig (color, etc)* bright, vivid. **5** *fig (animado)* lively, vivacious. **6** *fig (dolor, emoción, etc)* acute, deep, intense. **7** *fig (descripción, etc)* lively, graphic. **8** *fig (carácter)* quick, irritable. **9** *fig (listo)* quick-witted. **10** *fig (astuto)* shrewd, sly. **11** *fig (llaga, herida)* open. ■ **en vivo** TV live.
▷ *nm & nf* **1** living person: **los vivos** *the living.* **2** *fam fig (astuto)* quick-witted person.
VO *abrev* CINE **(Versión Original)** original language version.
vocablo *nm* word, term.
vocabulario *nm* vocabulary.
vocación *nf* vocation, calling.
vocacional *adj* vocational.
vocal *adj* vocal.
▷ *nf* vowel.
▷ *nm o nf (de junta, etc)* member.
vocálico,-a *adj* vocalic.
vocalista *nm o nf* vocalist, singer.
vocalización *nf* vocalization.
vocalizar [4] *vi* to vocalize.
▷ *vt* to vocalize.
vocativo *nm* vocative.
vocear *vi (dar voces)* to shout, cry out.
▷ *vt* **1** *(divulgar)* to publish. **2** *(gritar)* to shout, cry out. **3** *(divulgar)* to publish, proclaim. **4** *(aclamar)* to cheer, acclaim.
vocerío *nm* shouting, uproar.
vocero,-a *nm & nf (gen)* spokesperson; *(hombre)* spokesman; *(mujer)* spokeswoman.
vociferar *vi* to vociferate, shout.
▷ *vt* to vociferate, shout.
vodevil *nm* vaudeville, music hall.
vodka *nm* vodka.
voladizo,-a *adj* projecting, jutting out.
▷ *nm* **voladizo** projection.
volado,-a *adj* **1** *(en impresión)* superior. **2** ARQUIT projecting.
volador,-ra *adj* flying.
volandero,-a *adj* **1** *(que cuelga)* hanging; *(que está suelto)* loose. **2** *fig (imprevisto)* unexpected, unforeseen. **3** *fig (que vagabundea)* wandering, restless.
volante *adj (que vuela)* flying.
▷ *nm* **1** COST flounce; *(adorno)* frill, ruffle. **2** AUTO steering wheel. **3** TÉC flywheel.
volar [31] *vi* **1** *(ir por el aire)* to fly. **2** *fig (papeles, etc)* to be blown away. **3** *fig (ir deprisa)* to fly: **el tiempo vuela** *time flies.* **4** *fam fig (desaparecer)* to disappear, vanish. **5** *fig (sobresalir de un edificio)* to jut out, project. **6** *fig (noticia, etc)* to spread rapidly.
▷ *vt* **1** *fig (hacer explotar - edificio)* to blow up, demolish; *(- caja fuerte)* to blow open; *(- en minería)* to blast. **2** *fig (en impresión)* to raise. **3** *(en caza)* to flush.
▷ *vpr* **volarse** *(papeles, etc)* to be blown away. ■ **echarse a volar** to fly away, fly off.
volátil *adj* volatile.
volatilizar [4] *vt* to volatilize.
▷ *vpr* **volatilizarse** **1** to volatilize. **2** *fig* to vanish into thin air.
volcado,-a ● **volcado de memoria** dump.
volcán *nm* volcano.
volcánico,-a *adj* volcanic.
volcanismo *nm* volcanism, vulcanism.
volcar [49] *vi* **1** *(coche, etc)* to turn over, overturn. **2** MAR to capsize.
▷ *vt* **1** *(gen)* to turn over, knock over, upset. **2** *(vaciar)* to empty out, pour out. **3** *fig (hacer cambiar de parecer)* to make change one's mind.
▷ *vpr* **volcarse** *fig (entregarse)* to do one's utmost.
volea *nf* DEP volley.
volear *vt* to volley.
voleibol *nm* volleyball.
voleo *nm* DEP volley. ■ **a voleo / al voleo** *fig* at random, haphazardly.
volframio *nm* wolfram.
volición *nf* volition.
volitivo,-a *adj* volitive.
volován *nm* vol-au-vent.
volquete *nm* dumper-truck.
voltaje *nm* voltage.
voltear *vt* **1** *(dar vueltas)* to whirl, twirl. **2** *(poner al revés)* to turn over, toss. **3** *(campanas)* to peal, ring out. **4** *(a una persona)* to toss up in the air.
voltereta *nf* somersault. ■ **dar volteretas** to do somersaults.
voltímetro *nm* voltmeter.

voltio *nm* volt.
volubilidad *nf* changeability, fickleness.
voluble *adj* changeable, fickle.
volumen *nm* **1** *(gen)* volume. **2** *(tamaño)* size. ● **volumen de negocios** turnover.
volumetría *nf* volumetry.
voluminoso,-a *adj* **1** voluminous. **2** *(enorme)* bulky.
voluntad *nf* **1** *(cualidad)* will. **2** *(fuerza de voluntad)* willpower: **tiene mucha voluntad** *she's very strong-willed.* **3** *(deseo)* wish. **4** *(propósito)* intention, purpose: **tiene buena voluntad** *her intentions are good.* **5** *(afecto)* affection. ■ **a voluntad** at will. | **buena voluntad** goodwill. ● **voluntad de hierro / voluntad férrea** will of iron, iron will.
voluntariado *nm* **1** MIL voluntary enlistment. **2** *(civil)* group of volunteers.
voluntario,-a *adj* voluntary.
▷ *nm & nf* volunteer.
voluntarioso,-a *adj (con voluntad)* willing.
voluptuosidad *nf* voluptuousness.
voluptuoso,-a *adj* voluptuous.
voluta *nf* **1** ARQUIT volute, scroll. **2** *(espiral)* spiral, column. **3** *(de humo)* ring.
volver [32] *vt* **1** *(dar vuelta a)* to turn, turn over; *(hacia abajo)* to turn upside down; *(de dentro afuera)* to turn inside out; *(lo de atrás hacia delante)* to turn back to front: **volver la tortilla** *to turn the omelette.* **2** *(convertir)* to turn, make, change: **el dinero ha vuelto tonto a Paco** *money has made Paco foolish.* **3** *(devolver)* to give back; *(a su lugar)* to put back.
▷ *vi* **1** *(regresar)* to return; *(ir)* to go back; *(venir)* to come back: **vuelve cuando quieras** *come back whenever you want.* **2** *(a un tema, etc)* to return, revert. **3 volver a** *(hacer otra vez)* to do again: **volver a leer** *to read again.* ■ **volver a las andadas** to fall back into one's old habits. | **volver del revés** to turn inside out. | **volver en sí** to regain consciousness, come round. |
▷ *vpr* **volverse 1** *(regresar - ir)* to go back; *(- venir)* to come back. **2** *(darse la vuelta)* to turn. **3** *(convertirse)* to turn, become.
vomitar *vt* **1** to vomit. **2** *fig* to belch, spew out.
▷ *vi* to be sick, vomit: **tengo ganas de vomitar** *I feel sick.*
vomitivo,-a *adj* emetic.
▷ *nm* **vomitivo** emetic.
vómito *nm* **1** *(resultado)* vomit. **2** *(acción)* vomiting.
vomitona *nf* vomit.
voracidad *nf* voracity, voraciousness.
vorágine *nf* vortex, whirlpool.
voraz *adj* **1** voracious. **2** *fig* fierce, raging.
▲ *pl* **voraces.**
vórtice *nf* **1** vortex, whirlpool. **2** *(de ciclón)* centre (US center) of a cyclone.
vos *pron* **1** *arc (usted)* thou, you. **2** AM *(tú)* you.
vosear *vt* to address as *vos.*
voseo *nm* use of *vos.*
vosotros,-as *pron (sujeto)* you; *(objeto)* you, yourselves: **con vosotros** *with you;* **entre vosotras** *among yourselves;* **¿cómo lo sabéis vosotros?** *how do you know?*
votación *nf* **1** *(voto)* vote, ballot. **2** *(acto)* vote, voting.
votante *nm o nf* voter.
votar *vi (dar el voto)* to vote.
▷ *vt (proponer para aprobar)* to pass.
voto *nm* **1** *(gen)* vote: **tres votos a favor** *three votes for.* **2** REL vow. **3** *(deseo)* wish. **4** *(blasfemia)* curse, oath. ● **derecho al voto** the right to vote.
voz *nf* **1** *(sonido)* voice. **2** *(grito)* shout. **3** *(vocablo, palabra)* word. **4** GRAM voice: **voz activa** *active voice.* **5** MÚS *(de instrumento)* tone; *(cantante)* voice: **canción a tres voces** *three-part song.* **6** *fig (rumor)* rumour (US rumor). **7** *fig (en asamblea - facultad de hablar)* voice, say; *(- voto)* vote.
vudú *nm* voodoo.
vuelco *nm* **1** *(gen)* tumble, upset. **2** *(barco)* capsizing. **3** *fig* change.
vuelo *nm* **1** *(acto, etc)* flight. **2** *(acción)* flying. **3** ARQUIT *(voladizo)* projection. ● **vuelo chárter** charter flight.
vuelta *nf* **1** *(giro)* turn. **2** *(en un circuito)* lap, circuit. **3** *(paseo)* walk, stroll: **vamos a dar una vuelta** *let's go for a walk.* **4** *(regreso, retorno)* return; *(viaje de regreso)* return journey, journey back: **a la vuelta de las vacaciones** *after the holidays (US vacation).* **5** *(dinero de cambio)* change: **quédese con la vuelta** *keep the change.* **6** *(curva)* bend, curve. **7** *(reverso)* back, reverse. **8** *(de torneo, etc)* round. **9** *(cambio)* change, alteration. **10** COST *(de pantalón)* turn-up; *(forro)* lining. **11** *(al hacer punto)* row.
vuelto,-a *adj (cuello)* roll: **jersey de cuello vuelto** *rollneck sweater.*
vuestro,-a *adj* your, of yours: **vuestra casa** *your house;* **un amigo vuestro** *a friend of yours.*
▷ *pron* yours: **éstas son las vuestras** *these are yours.*
▷ *nm* **lo vuestro** what is yours, what belongs to you.
vulcanismo *nm* vulcanism, volcanism.
vulcanizar *vt* to vulcanize.
vulcanología *nf* volcanology, vulcanology.
vulcanólogo,-a *nm & nf* volcanologist.
vulgar *adj* **1** *(grosero)* vulgar, coarse, common: **lenguaje vulgar** *coarse language.* **2** *(general)* common, general. **3** *(banal)* banal, ordinary; *(idea)* commonplace. **4** *(no técnico)* lay: **término vulgar** *lay term.*
vulgaridad *nf* **1** *(grosería)* vulgarity. **2** *(banalidad)* banality.
vulgarismo *nm* vulgarism.
vulgarización *nf* vulgarization, popularization.
vulgarizar [4] *vt* **1** *(popularizar)* to popularize, vulgarize. **2** *(hacer vulgar)* to make common.
▷ *vpr* **vulgarizarse** *(popular)* to become popular; *(grosero)* to become vulgar, become common.
vulgo *nm pey* common people *pl*, masses *pl*.
vulnerabilidad *nf* vulnerability.
vulnerable *adj* vulnerable.
vulneración *nf* **1** *(gen)* violation. **2** *fig (reputación)* damaging, harming.
vulnerar *vt* **1** *(ley, etc)* to violate. **2** *fig (honor, etc)* to damage, harm.
vulva *nf* vulva.

W

W, w *nf (la letra)* W, w.
W *sím* (vatio) watt; *(símbolo)* W.
walkie-talkie *nm* walkie-talkie.
walkman® *nm* Walkman.
▲ *pl* walkmans.
WAP *abrev* (wireless application protocol [protocolo de aplicaciones inalámbricas]) wireless application protocol; *(abreviatura)* WAP.
wáter *nm*
▲ *pl* wáteres. *fam* toilet.
waterpolo *nm* water polo.
watt *nm* watt.
▲ *pl* watts.
See also vatio.
W.C. *abrev* (retrete) water closet; *(abreviatura)* WC.
web *nf* website.
wélter *nm* welterweight.
whiskería *nf* whisky bar.
whisky *nm* whisky; *(irlandés)* whiskey. ■ **whisky escocés** Scotch, Scotch whisky.
whist *nm* whist.
windsurf *nm* windsurfing.
windsurfing *nm* windsurfing.
windsurfista *nm o nf* windsurfer.
wok *nm* wok.
wolfram *nm* wolfram.
wolframio *nm* wolfram.
wombat *nm* wombat.
WWF/Adena *abrev* (World Wildlife Fund/ Asociación para la Defensa de la Naturaleza) World Wildlife Fund; *(abreviatura)* WWF.

X

X, x *nf (la letra)* X, x.
xenofilia *nf* xenophilia.
xenófilo,-a *adj* xenophilous.
▷ *nm & nf* xenophile.
xenofobia *nf* xenophobia.
xenófobo,-a *adj* xenophobic.
▷ *nm & nf* xenophobe.
xenón *nm* xenon.
xerocopia *nf* Xerox, photocopy.
xerocopiar *vt* to Xerox, photocopy.
xerografía *nf* xerography.
xileno *nm* xylene.
xilofonista *nm o nf* xylophonist.
xilófono *nm* xylophone.
xilografía *nf* **1** *(arte)* xylography. **2** *(impresión)* xylograph.
xilográfico,-a *adj* xylographic.
xilógrafo,-a *nm & nf* xylographer.
Xunta *nm & nf* *autonomous government of Galicia.*

Y

Y, y *nf (la letra)* Y, y.

y *conj* **1** and: **Alberto y María** *Alberto and María.* **2** *(hora)* past: **son las tres y cuarto** *it's a quarter past three.* **3** *(en pregunta)* what about. **4** *(repetición)* after.

See also **e**.

ya *adv* **1** already: **esa película ya la he visto** *I've already seen that film.* **2** *(más tarde)* later: **ya lo haré** *I'll do it later.* **3** *(ahora mismo)* at once, right now, straightaway: **¡ya voy!** *I'm coming!* **4** *(ahora)* now: **ya viven en el piso nuevo** *they're living in the new flat (US apartment) now.* **5** *(uso enfático)*: **ya lo sé** *I know that.* **6** *(para afirmar)* I know, yes.
▷ *interj irón* oh yes!

yac *nm* yak.

yacente *adj* lying. ■ **estatua yacente** recumbent statue.

yacer [92] *vi* **1** *(estar enterrado)* to lie. **2** *fml (hallarse)* to lie. **3** *lit (dormir)* to be lying; *(acostarse)* to lie (**con**, with)

yacimiento *nm* bed, deposit.

yaguar *nm* jaguar.

yak *nm* ZOOL yak.

Yakarta *nm* Djakarta, Jakarta.

yanqui *nm o nf* **1** HIST Yankee. **2** *pey* Yank.
▷ *adj* **1** HIST Yankee. **2** *pey* Yankee.

yantar *nm arc* fare, viands *pl.*
▷ *vi arc* to eat.

yarda *nf* yard.

yate *nm* yacht.

yayo,-a *nm & nf fam (abuelo)* granddad; *(abuela)* grandma.

yaz *nm* ⟶ **jazz.**

yazgo *pres indic* ⟶ **yacer.**

yedra *nf* ivy.

yegua *nf* mare.

yeguada *nf* herd of horses.

yeísmo *nm* pronunciation of **ll** as **y**.

yelmo *nm arc* helmet.

yema *nf* **1** *(de huevo)* yolk. **2** BOT bud. **3** *(del dedo)* fingertip. **4** CULIN *sweet made from sugar and egg yolk.*

Yemen *nm* Yemen.

yemení *adj* Yemeni.
▷ *nm o nf* Yemeni.

yen *nm* yen.

yermo,-a *adj* **1** *(estéril)* barren. **2** *(despoblado)* deserted.
▷ *nm (terreno inculto)* wasteland.

yerno *nm* son-in-law.

yernocracia *nf fam* nepotism.

yerro *nm en desuso* error.
▷ *pres indic* ⟶ **errar.**

yerto,-a *adj* rigid, stiff: **yerto de frío** *rigid with cold.*

yesal *nm* gypsum quarry.

yesca *nf* tinder. ■ **mechero de yesca** wick lighter.

yesería *nf* **1** plasterwork. **2** *(fábrica)* gypsum kiln.
▷ *nf pl* **yeserías** ARTE plasterwork.

yesero,-a *nm & nf* plasterer.

yeso *nm* **1** *(mineral)* gypsum. **2** *(para la construcción)* plaster. **3** *(tiza)* chalk. **4** *(escultura)* plaster cast.

yeti *nm* **1** yeti. **2 el Yeti** the Abominable Snowman.

yeyuno *nm* jejunum.

yiddish *adj* Yiddish.
▷ *nm (idioma)* Yiddish.1

yihad *nf* jihad.

yiu-yitsu *nm* jiujitsu.

yo *pron* I: **el jefe soy yo** *I'm the boss;* **soy yo** *it's me;* **fui yo quien se lo dijo** *it was me who told him;* **entre tú y yo** *between you and me;* **yo en tu lugar...** *if I were you...;* **yo que tú...** *if I were you....*
▷ *nm* **el yo** the ego, the self.

yodado,-a *pp* ⟶ **yodar.**
▷ *adj* iodized.

yodar *vt* to iodize.

yodo *nm* iodine.

yoduro *nm* iodide.

yoga *nm* yoga.

yogui *nm o nf* yogi.

yogur *nm* yoghurt.
▲ *pl* **yogures.**

yogurt *nm*
▲ *pl* **yogurts.** yoghurt.

yogurtera *nf* yoghurt maker.

yola *nf* yawl.

yonqui *nm o nf argot* junkie.

yóquey *nm* jockey.

yoqui *nm* jockey.

yoyó® *nm* yo-yo.

yuca *nf* **1** *(planta)* yucca. **2** *(harina)* cassava, manioc.

yudo *nm* judo.

yudoka *nm o nf* judoka.

yugo *nm* yoke. ● **bajo el yugo de** under the yoke of.

Yugoslavia *nf* Yugoslavia.

yugoslavo,-a *adj* Yugoslav, Yugosalvian.
▷ *nm & nf* Yugoslav, Yugosalvian.

yugular *adj* jugular.
▷ *nf* jugular vein.

yuju *interj fam*⟶ **yupi.**

yunque *nm* anvil.

yunta *nf* team of oxen, yoke.

yupi *interj fam* whoopee!, yippee!

yuppie *adj* yuppie.
▷ *nm o nf* yuppie.

yute *nm* jute.

yuxtaponer [78] *vt* to juxtapose.
▲ *pp* **yuxtapuesto,-a.**

yuxtaposición *nf* juxtaposition.

yuxtapuesto,-a *pp* ⟶ **yuxtaponer.**

Z

Z, z *nf (la letra)* Z, z.
zafarse *vpr* to get away (**de**, from), free OS (**de**, from), escape (**de**, from): **logró zafarse de la policía** *he managed to get away from the police.*
zafiedad *nf* uncouthness.
zafio,-a *adj* **1** uncouth. **2** *fig* gauche.
zafiro *nm* sapphire.
zaga *nf* **1** rear. **2** *(en deporte)* defence (US defense).
zagal,-la *nm \ nf* **1** *(muchacho)* lad; *(muchacha)* lass. **2** *(pastor)* shepherd; *(pastora)* shepherdess.
zaguán *nm* hall, hallway.
zaherir [35] *vt* **1** to wound, hurt. **2** *(sentimientos)* to hurt.
zahorí *nm o nf* **1** *(adivino)* seer, clairvoyant; *(buscador de agua)* water diviner. **2** *fig* mindreader.
▲ *pl* **zahoríes.**
zaino,-a *adj* **1** *(traidor)* treacherous. **2** *(caballo)* chestnut; *(res vacuna)* black.
Zaire *nm* Zaire.
zaireño,-a *adj* Zairean.
▷ *nm \ nf* Zairean.
zalamería *nf* winning ways *pl.*
zalamero,-a *adj* charming, winning.
▷ *nm \ nf* charmer. ● **ponerse zalamero,-a** to turn on the charm.
zamarra *nf* sheepskin jacket.
Zambesi *nm* **el Zambesi** the Zambesi.
Zambia *nf* Zambia.
zambiano,-a *adj* Zambian.
▷*nm \ nf* Zambian.
zambo,-a *adj* knock-kneed.
▷ *nm (mono)* spider monkey.
zambomba *nf* rumbling pot.
▷ *interj fam* gosh!
zambullir *vt* to plunge.
zambullirse *vpr* **1** *(en el agua)* to plunge in, dive in: **se zambulló en el agua** *he plunged into the water.* **2** *(en una actividad)* to throw OS (**en**, into).
zampar *vi fam* to stuff oneself.
zampón,-ona *nm \ nf* guzzler, gannet.
zampoña *nf* panpipes.
zampullín *nm* grebe.
zanahoria *nf* carrot.
zancada *nf* stride. ● **en dos zancadas** in two shakes.
zancadilla *nf* **1** trip. **2** *fam (engaño)* ruse, trick.
zanco *nm* stilt.
zancudas *nf pl* waders, wading birds.
zancudo,-a *adj* **1** long-legged. **2** *(ave)* wading.
▷ *nm* **zancudo** AM mosquito. ■ **aves zancudas** waders, wading birds.
zanganear *vi* to loaf around.
zángano,-a *nm \ nf fam (persona)* loafer.
▷ *nm (insecto)* drone.
zangolotino ■ **niño zangolotino** *en desuso* big baby.
zanja *nf* trench. ● **abrir una zanja** to dig a trench.
zanjar *vt fig (asunto)* to settle.
zapata *nf* **1** *(arandela)* washer. **2** TÉC shoe. **3** *(de cámara fotográfica)* hot shoe. ■ **zapata de freno** brake shoe.
zapatería *nf* **1** *(tienda)* shoe shop. **2** *(taller de reparación)* shoe repairer's, cobbler's; *(taller de fabricación)* shoemaker's. **3** *(oficio)* shoemaking.
zapatero,-a *nm \ nf* **1** *(que arregla)* shoe repairer, cobbler. **2** *(que fabrica)* shoemaker. **3** *(que vende)* shoe seller. ● **¡zapatero a tus zapatos!** the cobbler should stick to his last. ■ **zapatero remendón** cobbler.
zapatilla *nf* **1** *(de estar en casa)* slipper. **2** *(de loneta)* plimsoll. ■ **zapatilla de ballet** ballet shoe. | **zapatilla de deporte** trainer, running shoe. | **zapatilla de puntas** toe shoe.
zapato *nm* shoe. ■ **zapatos de tacón** high-heeled shoes.
zapatón *nm fam* clodhopper.
zape *interj fam (asombro)* gosh!; *(al gato)* shoo!
zapoteca *adj* Zapotec, Zapotecan.
▷ *nm o nf (persona)* Zapotec, Zapotecan.
▷ *nm (idioma)* Zapotec.
zapping *nm* channel-zapping, channel-hopping: **se pasa la vida haciendo zapping** *he spends all day channel-hopping.*
zar *nm* tsar, czar.
zarabanda *nf* **1** MÚS saraband. **2** *fam (jaleo)* bustle, confusion.
zaragata *nf* rumpus.
Zaragoza *nf* Saragossa.
zaragüelles *nm pl* **1** *(calzones)* breeches. **2** *(pantalones)* baggy trousers.
zaranda *nf* sieve.
zarandajas *nf pl fam* trifles.
zarandear *vt* **1** *(sacudir)* to shake; *(empujar)* to jostle, knock about. **2** *(cribar)* to sieve.
zarandearse *vpr* **1** *(ajetrearse)* to bustle about, rush about. **2** *(contonearse)* to swagger, strut.
zarandeo *nm* **1** *(sacudida)* shaking; *(empujones)* jostling about. **2** *(criba)* sieving. **3** *(contoneo)* swaggering, strutting.
zarapito *nm (ave)* curlew.
zarcero *nm (ave)* melodious warbler.
zarcillo *nm* **1** *(pendiente)* earring. **2** BOT tendril.
zarco,-a *adj* blue.
zarigüeya *nf* opossum.
zarina *nf* tsarina, czarina.
zarismo *nm* tsarism, czarism.
zarista *adj* tsarist, czarist.
▷ *nm o nf* tsarist, czarist.
zarpa *nf* claw, paw. ● **echarle la zarpa a** ALGO **1** *(animal)* to pounce on STH. **2** *(persona)* to grab STH.
zarpar *vi* to weigh anchor, set sail.

zarpazo *nm (marca)* claw mark. ● **dar un zarpazo, pegar un zarpazo** to claw.
zarrapastroso,-a *adj fam* scruffy.
▷ *nm \ nf* scruff.
zarza *nf* bramble, blackberry bush.
zarzal *nm* bramble patch.
zarzamora *nf (zarza)* blackberry bush; *(fruto)* blackberry.
zarzaparrilla *nf* sarsaparilla.
zarzuela *nf* 1 MÚS zarzuela, *Spanish operetta*. 2 CULIN fish stew.
zarzuelero,-a *adj* in the style of an operetta.
zarzuelístico,-a *adj* MÚS *to do with* zarzuela.
zas *interj (ruido)* bang!, crash!, smack!; *(al caer al agua)* splash!; *(de repente)* suddenly, all of a sudden.
zascandil *nm* 1 *(alocado)* madcap, featherbrain. 2 *(entrometido)* busybody, meddler.
zascandilear *vi* to meddle.
zeda *nf* → **zeta.**
zéjel *nm* LIT *Hispano-Arabic stanza.*
zenit *nm* zenith.
zepelín *nm* zeppelin.
zeta *nf (letra)* zed, US zee.
▷ *nm argot* police car.
zigzag *nm*
▲ *pl* **zigzags o zigzagues.** zigzag.
zigzagueante *adj* zigzag.
zigzaguear *vi* to zigzag.
zimbabuo,-a *adj-nm \ nf* → **zimbabwense.**
Zimbabwe *nm* Zimbabwe.
zimbabwense *adj* Zimbabwean.
▷ *nm o nf* Zimbabwean.
zinc *nm* zinc.
zíngaro,-a *nm \ nf* Tzigane, Hungarian gypsy.
▷ *adj* Tzigane.
zipizape *nm fam* rumpus: **se armó un zipizape tremendo** *there was a hell of a rumpus.*
zócalo *nm* 1 *(de habitación)* skirting board; *(de edificio)* plinth course, plinth. 2 *(pedestal)* plinth, socle.
zoco *nm* souk, suq, *open-air marketplace in some Arab countries* .
zodiacal *adj* zodiacal.
zodiaco *nm* zodiac.
zodíaco *nm* zodiac.
zombi *nm o nf* zombie. ● **estar zombi 1** *fam (atontado)* to be groggy. 2 *(loco)* to be loopy.
zombie *nm o nf* → **zombi.**
zona *nf* 1 area. 2 *(fronteriza, militar)* zone.
▷ *nm* MED *(herpes)* shingles. ■ **zona azul** parking meter zone. ■ **zona edificada** built-up area. ‖ **zona fronteriza** border zone. ‖ **zona glacial** frigid zone. ‖ **zona templada** temperate zone. ‖ **zona tórrida** torrid zone. ‖ **zona verde** green zone.
zonal *adj* zonal.
zonzo,-a *adj* AM silly.
zoo *nm* zoo.
zoología *nf* zoology.
zoológico,-a *adj* zoological.
▷ *nm* zoo.
zoólogo,-a *nm \ nf* zoologist.
zoom *nm* zoom, zoom lens.
zopenco,-a *nm \ nf fam* oaf.
▷ *adj fam* oafish.
zoquete *nm fam* nincompoop, numskull.
zorcico *nm* MÚS *Basque dance and song.*
zorra *nf* 1 *(animal)* vixen. 2 *tabú (mujer)* bitch. ● **ni zorra** *fam* sod all. ‖ **no tener ni zorra idea** *fam* not to have a clue.
zorrera *nf* 1 *(madriguera)* foxhole. 2 *fam* smoke-filled room.
zorrería *nf fam* dirty trick: **¡qué zorrería!** *what a rotten thing to do!*
zorrillo *nm* ZOOL zorilla.
zorro,-a *adj (astuto)* cunning, sly.
▷ *nm* **zorro** 1 *(animal)* fox; *(macho)* dog fox, fox. 2 *(piel)* fox-fur, fox-skin. 3 *(persona)* old fox.
▷ *nm pl* **zorros** *(para el polvo)* duster *sing*. ● **estar hecho,-a unos zorros** *fam* to be bushed. ■ **zorro azul** blue fox. ‖ **zorro viejo** sly old fox.
zorrupia *nf fam* trollop.
zorzal *nm (ave)* thrush. ■ **zorzal alirrojo** redwing. ‖ **zorzal charlo** mistle thrush. ‖ **zorzal real** fieldfare.
zote *adj* dim-witted.
▷ *nm o nf* dimwit.
zozobra *nf* 1 *(de un barco)* sinking, capsizing. 2 *fig (congoja)* anguish, anxiety.
zozobrar *vi* 1 *(barco)* to sink, capsize. 2 *(persona)* to worry, be anxious. 3 *(proyecto)* to fail, be ruined.
zueco *nm* clog.
zulo *nm* hide-out.
zumba *nf* 1 *(burla)* teasing. 2 *(paliza)* thrashing.
zumbado,-a *adj fam* crazy, loony.
zumbador,-ra *adj* buzzing.
▷ *nm* **zumbador** buzzer.
zumbar *vi (abejorro, oídos)* to buzz: **me zumban los oídos** *my ears are buzzing.*
▷ *vt fam (pegar)* to thrash. ● **salir zumbando** *fam* to zoom off. ‖ **zumbarse de** ALGN *(burlarse)* to make fun of SB, tease SB.
zumbido *nm* buzzing.
zumbón,-ona *adj* teasing, joking.
▷ *nm \ nf* joker.
zumo *nm* juice: **zumo de naranja** *orange juice.*
zurcido *nm* 1 darn, mend. 2 *(acción)* darning.
zurcir [3] *vt* to darn, mend. ● **¡que te zurzan!** get lost!
zurdo,-a *adj (persona)* left-handed; *(mano)* left.
▷ *nm \ nf* left-hander, left-handed person.
▷ *nf (mano)* left hand: **un golpe con la zurda** *a left-handed blow.*
zurear *vi (palomas)* to coo.
zureo *nm* billing and cooing.
zurra *nf fam* thrashing.
zurrapa *nf* 1 *(de posos)* dregs *pl*. 2 *tabú (de excrementos)* skid mark.
zurrar *vt* 1 *fam* to thrash. 2 *fam (cuero)* to tan. ● **zurrarle la badana a** ALGN to tan SB's hide.
zurriagazo *nm* 1 *(latigazo)* lash, stroke. 2 *fam (desgracia)* blow, stroke of bad luck.
zurriago *nm* whip.
zurriburri *nm* 1 *fam (mezcla de gente)* hotchpotch, mishmash. 2 *(grupo ruidoso)* rowdy bunch, noisy crowd.
zurrón *nm* shepherd's pouch, shepherd's bag.

Appendices
Apéndices

False friends / Falsos amigos

Some of the following Spanish words appear to be cognates of English words, but they are *not*: e.g., **sopa** in Spanish does *not* mean 'soap' in English, and **parientes** does not mean 'parents' in English. Other words sometimes suggest an English equivalent, but can also have a very different meaning: e.g., **real** in Spanish can be interpreted at times to mean 'real' in English but more often should be translated as 'royal', and **equipo** in Spanish can mean 'equipment' in English but is more often translated as 'team'.

In the Spanish to English column, certain English words are in brackets to indicate that *only sometimes* the Spanish word has the meaning of the bracketed English word. In the English to Spanish column the abbreviations —*(adj)* = adjective, *(n)* = noun, and *(v)* = verb— are used in a few cases for clarity.

Spanish-English

acre: sharp, sour, rude, harsh, [acre]
actual: current, present *(time)*
admirar: to astonish, surprise, [admire]
apuntar: to point, aim; write down, make a note of
asignación: allowance, assignment, [assignation]
asistir: to attend, be present, to help, [to assist]
atender: to pay attention, take care of, [attend to]

carpeta: portfolio; file folder
carta: letter *(mail)*, charter, [playing card]

cigarro: cigarette
colegio: school *(private or high school)*
conferencia: lecture, interview, meeting, [conference]
constipado: suffering from a cold
contar: to tell, relate, [count]
contento: happy, glad, satisfied, [contented]
costumbre: custom

decepción: disillusionment, disappointment, [deception]
desgracia: misfortune, mishap, disfavour
desgraciado: unfortunate, wretched, unlucky
deshonesto: immodest, indecent
dirección: address *(mail)*, [direction]
disgusto: quarrel, annoyance, sorrow, [disgust]
distinto: different; clear; several; [distinct]

embarazada: pregnant
equipo: team; fittings; squad; [equipment]
equivocación: error, mistake
éxito: success
expedir: to issue *(a decree)*; send, ship; dispatch, [expedite]
explanar: to level, grade (ground); [explain]

fábrica: factory, mill, structure, [fabric]
falta: shortage, lack; blemish; defect, [fault]

Inglés-Español

acre: acre, unidad de medida
actual: verdadero, real
admire: considerar con placer, admirar
appoint: nombrar, señalar
assignation: asignación, destinación
assist: ayudar, asistir
attend: asistir a, cuidar, atender

carpet: alfombra
cart: carro, carreta
card: tarjeta, naipe, carta
cigar: puro
college: universidad
conference: junta, sesión, entrevista, conferencia
constipated: estreñido
count: *(v)* contar
contented: satisfecho, tranquilo, contento
costume: vestuario, traje

deception: engaño, fraude, decepción
disgrace: *(n)* deshonra, vergüenza, ignominia
disgraced: deshonrado, avergonzado
dishonest: engañoso, falso, poco honrado
direction: dirección
disgust: hastío, asco, repugnancia, disgusto
distinct: claro, visible; inequívoco; diferente, distinto

embarrassed: turbado, desconcertado
equipment: aparatos, equipo
equivocation: equívoco; subterfugio, engaño
exit: salida
expedite: acelerar, facilitar; apresurar, despachar
explain: explicar, aclarar

fabric: tela, textura; fábrica; construcción
fault: *(n)* culpa; defecto, falta

formal: reliable, trustworthy; grave; definite [formal]
frase: sentence, [phrase]
fray: priest, friar

golpe: blow
gracioso: amusing, witty; graceful, charming
grande: large, big, great, [grand]

honesto: decent, pore, virtuous; reasonable [honest]

idioma: language, [idiom]
ignorar: to be unaware or ignorant of

largo: long
lectura: reading
leer: to read
liar: to fie, bind, roll up

media: stocking

ordinario: coarse, vulgar; usual, [ordinary]

parientes: relatives
probar: to test, taste, try out

quitar: to take away, deprive of, subtract

real: royal, [real]
realizar: to fulfil, achieve, carry out; [realize]
recordar: to remember, recall, remind, awaken
regular: ordinary; so so, fairly well; systematic, [regular]
renta: interest, revenue, [rent]
repente: start, sudden movement
replicar: to reply, answer, retort, [replicate]
ropa: clothes, clothing
ruin: vile, mean; petty, stingy; little

salvo: sate; easily; omitted
sano: healthy; sound; whole; [sane]
sauce: willow
sensible: sentient; sensitive; perceptible; [sensible]
simpático: agreeable, pleasant, congenial
sopa: soup
suceder: to happen, come about, [succeed]
suceso: event, incident

taller: workshop; laboratory; studio
tuna: prickly pear; idle and vagrant life
tutor: guardian, [tutor]

vagón: railway car or coach
vale: note, sales slip, coupon

formal: convencional, ceremonioso, formal
phrase: expresión, frase
fray: *(v)* raerse, deshilacharse; *(n)* alboroto, riña

gulp: *(n)* trago
gracious: afable, cortés; atractivo; bondadoso
grand: magnífico; grandioso, majestuoso; grande

honest: honrado, integro, recto; sincero

idiom: modismo; lenguaje
ignore: no hacer caso de; desconocer

large: grande
lecture: *(n)* conferencia; lección; plática
leer: *(v)* mirar de soslayo; *(n)* mirada de soslayo
liar: *(n)* mentiroso, embustero

media: (*pl* of **medium**) medias; medios de comunicación (radio, televisión, etc.)

ordinary: corriente, común, ordinario, mediocre

parents: padres
probe: *(v)* tentar; examinar a fondo; sondear

quit: abandonar, cesar, parar, dejar (de hacer algo)

real: *(adj)* verdadero, real
realize: darse cuenta de; comprender; efectuar, llevar a cabo; realizar
record: *(v)* registrar, apuntar, asentar, inscribir; grabar en disco
regular: metódico, ordenado, regular
rent: *(n)* alquilar; *(n)* arrendamiento, rente; rasgadura
repent: arrepentirse
replicate: *(v)* duplicar, repetir, replicar
rope: *(n)* soga, cuerda
ruin: *(v)* arruinar, estropear; *(n)* ruina, destrucción

salvo: salva; pretexto
sane: cuerdo; razonable; sano
sauce: salsa, condimento
sensible: sensato, razonable, juicioso
sympathetic: compasivo; simpatizante
soap: jabón
succeed: lograr(se); medrar, salir bien; suceder
success: éxito

taller: más alto
tuna: atún
tutor: *(n)* maestro particular, tutor

wagon: carro, carreta, carretón
vale: valle, cañada

Examples of letters

Formal salutations
Dear Mr/Mrs/Ms…
Dear Sirs
Dear Sir or Madam
To whom it may concern

Informal salutations
Hi/ hello/dearest

Formal complimentary closes
Yours sincerely
Yours faithfully

Informal complimentary closes
Love/ With all my love
Yours / Yours affectionately
Kind/warm/best regards

Job application

B TRANSLATORS
98, Lyneham Road
LUTON, Beds
LU2 9ys

July 16, 2007

Dear Sirs

I am writing to apply for the position of Translator/Interpreter at your London headquarters, advertised in yesterday's "Daily News".

You will find an account of my career and qualifications on my enclosed résumé, and I have added the names of two referees and copies of two recent testimonials.

My mother is English and my father Spanish, so I am bilingual in those two languages, and I also speak French and German fairly fluently. I have considerable experience as an interpreter, and have translated a great deal of technical material, but it has always been my ambition to find a permanent position in a firm of international standing.

If you feel that my qualifications meet with your requirements, I shall be pleased to come for an interview.

Yours Sincerely,
William Smith

Formal letter of business introduction

J. Cockburn & Co
52 Park Road
MANCHESTER,
MCR 2RD

10th February 2007

Me. J.J. Sen,
Managing Director
Calcutta Papers Ltd.
Chowringhee Road
Calcutta,
W. Bengal.

Dear Mr Sen,

We have recently appointed a new Overseas Sales Manager, Mr D. Thompson, who will be visiting India, especially Bengal, at the end of next month. We are writing this to introduce him to you and we should be much obliged if you would extend to him the courtesy and help which you invariably gave to his predecessor, Mr T. Nelson.

Mr Thompson is thoroughly familiar with the Indian market and would like to discuss various projects which he feels might be to our mutual advantage.

Yours sincerely,

Donald Cross
Director

Booking a hotel room by email

Nuevo mensaje
Enviar Chat Adjuntar Agenda Tipo de letra Colores Borrador
Para: myroom@nights.com
Cc:
Asunto: booking
Cuenta:

Dear Sir,
I would like to book room for the week of April 2 (six nights). I should like to know of accommodation will be available for this period. We would require one double room with private bathroom. Please send your rates, giving inclusive terms for bed and breakfast.
As we will be coming by car, it is important that the hotel should provide garage space.
I look forward to receiving your reply.
Yours faithfully,

Peter Brown

Ejemplos de cartas

Saludos formales
Estimado,-a(-as)/a Sr./Sra./Srta./Sres./Sras.
Apreciado,-a Sr./Sra.
A quien pueda interesar

Saludos informales
¡Hola!
Querido,-a

Despedidas formales
Atentamente/Le saluda atentamente
Un saludo
Con mis mejores deseos

Despedidas informales
Con cariño/Con todo mi amor/Afectuosamente
Un fuerte abrazo/Besos

Demanda de empleo

Editorial Corondel
c/ del Medio, 8
34001 Palencia

26 de julio de 2007

Estimados Sres.

Me dirijo a ustedes por la oferta de empleo para un editor de libros de texto que su empresa ha publicado ayer en la prensa local.

Cuento con una experiencia de más de diez años en la edición de libros de texto para enseñanza media y enseñanza primaria, período en el que he desempeñado tareas de coordinación editorial, como free lance, para diferentes empresas del sector.

Les adjunto mi curriculum vitae, en el que se detallan mis datos personales, mi titulación y formación académica complementaria, así como los principales trabajos efectuados y las empresas para la que éstos fueron realizados.

Espero que mi formación y experiencia profesional se adapten al perfil que ustedes demandan.

Sin otro particular, quedo a la espera de sus noticias.

Un saludo cordial,
Elisa López

Carta de gestión comercial

SOFIMAX S.L.
Polígono industrial Las Heras s/n
47014 Valladolid

Sr. Enrique González
Director comercial
CEFITEX S.L.
c/ Mayor, 73
Pamplona

15 de mayo de 2007

Estimado Sr. González,

La empresa que represento, a la vista de su catálogo, está interesada en la adquisición de algunos de los componentes electrónicos que ustedes producen. Por este motivo, consideramos que sería interesante visitar su empresa para conocer en detalle estos productos y concretar los precios y los posibles plazos de entrega de los futuros pedidos.

Si le parece oportuno, visitaríamos su empresa a principios de la semana próxima. Les ruego que concreten la fecha que les resulte más conveniente y nos lo comuniquen.

Atentamente,

Javier Hernández
Director comercial

Hacer una reserva de hotel por e-mail

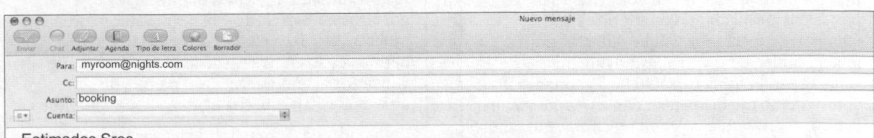

Nuevo mensaje

Enviar Chat Adjuntar Agenda Tipo de letra Colores Borrador

Para: myroom@nights.com
Cc:
Asunto: booking
Cuenta:

Estimados Sres.

Quisiera reservar una habitación en su hotel para la semana del 12 al 17 de mayo (seis noches). Les ruego que me confirmen a la mayor brevedad posible si tendrán habitaciones disponibles en esas fechas y, en caso afirmativo, que me remitan las tarifas de una habitación doble con baño, en régimen de alojamiento y desayuno.

Atentamente,

Pepe Pérez

Examples of letters / Ejemplos de cartas

Informal letters

Carrer del Sol, 54
08173 Sant Cugat del Vallés
Barcelona
21st May 2003

Dear John,

How are you these days? I haven't heard from you for ages. I'm writing to you now because I need your help. I'm thinking of coming to England next year to improve my English. I'd like to stay for a year. Naturally, I can't afford a year's holiday and I'm wondering if you know of any job I could apply for.

I'm really sorry to bother you with this but I have no idea where to make enquiries myself. It would be a great help if you could put me in touch with a firm or agency that I could write to. When are you thinking of coming to Spain? You know you will be very welcome to stay with us.

I'm looking forward to hearing from you soon.

Kind regards,

Beth

[...]
Dear John,

Your name and address was given to me by my English teacher, who told me that you might like to correspond with a boy of your age in Spain. I'm sixteen years old and I was born in Madrid, although I live in Sant Cugat, a little town near Barcelona. My father is a doctor, and besides him and myself, there are three people in my family: my mother and my two younger sisters.

My main interests are cycling on my mountain bike, chatting on the Internet and downloading music on to my MP3 player, which I take with me everywhere I go. When you write to me, please tell me all about your hobbies and interests. I expect they will be different from mine. I understand you are studying my language and I think it would be a good idea if you wrote to me in Spanish while I wrote you in English. This would be good practice for us, and if I make any bad mistakes I hope you will correct them for me.

I'm looking forward very much to hearing from you.

Yours sincerely,

Cartas informales

256 Back Street
08173 Sant Cugat del Vallés
Barcelona
21st May 2003

Querido Francisco,

¿Cómo estás? ¿Qué tal está tu familia? Te escribo porque necesito tu ayuda. Estoy pensando ir a España durante un año para perfeccionar mi español. He pedido excedencia en el trabajo desde el próximo mes de enero, por lo que en esas fechas estaría en condiciones de trasladarme a Madrid. Para llevar a cabo este proyecto debo encontrar allí un trabajo y un lugar donde alojarme (sería suficiente con una habitación en un piso compartido).

Yo ya he iniciado gestiones desde aquí a través de Internet, e incluso he enviado varios currículums a escuelas de idiomas para ofrecerme como profesor de inglés. Lamento molestarte, pero creo que es importante que estés al corriente de mis planes por si puedes echarme una mano. Te adjunto mi CV por si lo necesitas.

¿Piensas volver este verano a Inglaterra? Si así fuera, ya sabes que puedes alojarte en casa.

Te llamaré dentro de unos días para comentar todo esto de viva voz.

Muchas gracias por adelantado por tu apoyo.

Recibe un fuerte abrazo.

¡Hasta pronto!

Peter

Queridos Isabel y Ernesto,

Ya estamos de nuevo en casa y hemos retomado nuestras rutinas: los dos hemos vuelto al trabajo y los niños han empezado las clases.

Hemos pasado unos días maravillosos con vosotros en Barcelona y os recordamos con mucho cariño. La ciudad nos pareció muy hermosa y los niños no dejan de pedirnos que volvamos al año que viene al parque de atracciones tan espectacular en el que estuvimos.

Os agradecemos mucho todas vuestras atenciones y os esperamos pronto aquí: aunque no hace tan buen tiempo como en Barcelona, ¡Londres también tiene sus encantos!

Un gran abrazo a todos y hasta pronto.

Anne y Paul

Numbers / Numerales

Cardinal numbers		Números cardinales
zero	0	cero
one	1	uno
two	2	dos
three	3	tres
four	4	cuatro
five	5	cinco
six	6	seis
seven	7	siete
eight	8	ocho
nine	9	nueve
ten	10	diez
eleven	11	once
twelve	12	doce
thirteen	13	trece
fourteen	14	catorce
fifteen	15	quince
sixteen	16	deiciséis
seventeen	17	diecisiete
eighteen	18	dieciocho
nineteen	19	diecinueve

Cardinal numbers		Números cardinales
twenty	20	veinte
twenty-one	21	veintiuno
twenty-two	22	veintidós
twenty-three	23	veintitrés
twenty-four	24	veinticuatro
twenty-five	25	veinticinco
twenty-six	26	veintiséis
twenty seven	27	veintisiete
twenty-eight	28	veintiocho
twenty-nine	29	veintinueve
thirty	30	treinta
forty	40	cuarenta
fifty	50	cincuenta
sixty	60	sesenta
seventy	70	setenta
eighty	80	ochenta
ninety	90	noventa
one hundred	100	cien
five hundred	500	quinientos
one thousand	1000	mil

Números ordinales

1st	first
2nd	second
3rd	third
4th	fourth
5th	fifth
6th	sixth
7th	seventh
8th	eighth
9th	ninth
10th	tenth
11th	eleventh
12th	twelfth
13th	thirteenth
14th	fourteenth
15th	fifteenth
16th	sixteenth
17th	seventeenth
18th	eighteenth
19th	nineteenth
20th	twentieth
21st	twenty first
22nd	twenty second
30th	thirtieth
40th	fortieth
50th	fiftieth
60th	sixtieth
70th	seventieth
80th	eightieth
90th	ninetieth
100th	hundredth

Números ordinales

1.º, 1.ª	primero, -a
2.º, 2.ª	segundo, -a
3.º, 3.ª	tercero, -a
4.º, 4.ª	cuarto, -a
5.º, 5.ª	quinto, -a
6.º, 6.ª	sexto, -a
7.º, 7.ª	séptimo, -a
8.º, 8.ª	octavo, -a
9.º, 9.ª	noveno, -a
10.º, 10.ª	décimo, -a
11.º, 11.ª	undécimo, -a
12.º, 12.ª	duodécimo, -a
13.º, 13.ª	decimotercero, -a / decimotercio, -a
14.º, 14.ª	decimocuarto, -a
1.5º, 15.ª	decimoquinto -a
16.º, 16.ª	decimosexto, -a
17.º, 17.ª	decimoséptimo, -a
18.º, 18.ª	decimoctavo, -a
19.º, 19.ª	decimonoveno, -a / decimonono, -a
20.º, 20.ª	vigésimo, -a
21.º, 21.ª	vigésimo, -a primero, -a
22.º, 22.ª	vigésimo, -a segundo, -a
30.º, 30.ª	trigésimo, -a
40.º, 40.ª	cuadragésimo, -a
50.º, 50.ª	quincuagésimo, -a
60.º, 60.ª	sexagésimo, -a
70.º, 70.ª	septuagésimo, -a
80.º, 80.ª	octogésimo, -a
90.º, 90.ª	nonagésimo, -a
100.º, 100.ª	centésimo, -a

Weights and measures

Metric System

Unit	Abbreviation	Approximate US Equivalent	
LENGTH			
1 millimeter	mm	0.04	inch
1 centimeter	cm	0.39	inch
1 meter	m	39.37	inches
		1.094	yards
1 kilometer	km	3,281.5	feet
		0.62	mile
AREA			
1 square centimeter	sq cm (cm^2)	0.155	square inch
1 square meter	m^2	10.764	square feet
		1.196	square yards
1 hectare	ha	2.471	acres
1 square kilometer	sq km (km^2)	247.105	acres
		0.386	square mile
VOLUME			
1 cubic centimeter	cu cm (cm^3)	0.061	cubic inch
1 stere	s	1.308	cubic yards
1 cubic meter	m^3	1.308	cubic yards
CAPACITY (Liquid Measure)			
1 decilitre	dl	0.21	pint
1 litre	1	1.057	quarts
1 decalitre	dal	2.6	gallons
CAPACITY (Dry Measure)			
1 decilitre	dl	0.18	pint
1 litre	l	0.908	quart
1 decalitre	dal	1.14	pecks
1 hectolitre	hl	2.84	bushels
CAPACITY (Cubic Measure)			
1 decilitre	dl	6.1	cubic inches
1 litre	l	61.02	cubic inches
1 decalitre	dal	0.35	cubic foot
1 hectolitre	hl	3.53	cubic feet
1 kilolitre	kl	1.31	cubic yards
MASS AND WEIGHT			
1 gram	g, gm	0.035	ounce
1 decagram	dag	0.353	ounce
1 hectogram	hg	3.527	ounces
1 kilogram	kg	2.2046	pounds
1 quintal	q	220.46	pounds
1 metric ton	MT, t	1.1	tons

Pesos y medidas

Sistema métrico

Unidad	Abreviatura	Equivalente aproximado del sistemas americano	
LONGITUD			
1 milímetro	mm	0,04	pulgada
1 centímetro	cm	0,39	pulgada
1 metro	m	39,37	pulgadas
		1,094	yardas
1 kilómetro	km	3.281,5	pies
		0,62	milla
ÁREA			
1 centímetro cuadrado	cm^2	0,155	pulgada cuadrada
1 metro cuadrado	m^2	10,764	pies cuadrados
		1,196	yardas cuadradas
1 hectárea	ha	2,471	acres
1 kilómetro cuadrado	km^2	247,105	acres
		0,386	milla cuadrada
VOLUMEN			
1 centímetro cúbico	cm^3	0,061	pulgada cúbica
1 metro cúbico	m^3	1,308	yardas cúbicas
CAPACIDAD (Medida líquida)			
1 decilitro	dl	0,21	pinta
1 litro	l	1,057	quarts
1 decalitro	Dl	2,64	galones
CAPACIDAD (Medida árida)			
1 decilitro	dl	0,18	pinta
1 litro	l	0,908	quart
1 decalitro	Dl	1,14	pecks
1 hectolitro	Hl	2,84	bushels
CAPACIDAD (Medida cúbica)			
1 decilitro	dl	6,1	pulgadas cúbicas
1 litro	l	61,02	pulgadas cúbicas
1 decalitro	Dl	0,35	pie cúbico
1 hectolitro	Hl	3,53	pies cúbicos
1 kilolitro	Kl	1,31	yardas cúbicas
MASA Y PESO			
1 gramo	g	0,035	onza
1 decagramo	Dg	0,353	onza
1 hectogramo	Hg	3,527	onzas
1 kilogramo	Kg	2,2046	libra
1 quintal métrico	q	220,46	libra
1 tonelada métrica	t	1,1	toneladas

US Customary Weights and Measures / Unidades de pesos y medidas estadounidenses

Linear measure / Medida de longitud

1 foot / pie	=	12 inches / pulgadas
1 yard / yarda	=	36 inches / pulgadas
		3 feet / pies
1 rod	=	$5^1/_2$ yards / yardas
1 mile / milla	=	5,280 feet / 5.280 pies
		1,760 yards / 1.760 yardas

Liquid measure / Medida líquida

1 pint / pinta	=	4 gills
1 quart / quart líquido	=	2 pints / pintas
1 gallon / galón	=	4 quarts / quarts líquidos

Area measure / Medida de superficie

1 square foot / pie cuadrado	=	144 square inches / pulgadas cuadradas
1 square yard / yarda cuadrada	=	9 square feet / pies cuadrados
1 square rod/ rod cuadrado	=	$30^1/_4$ square yards / yardas cuadradas
1 square mile / milla cuadrada	=	160 square rods / rods cuadrados
		640 acres

Dry measure / Medida árida

1 quart	=	2 pints / pintas áridas
1 peck	=	8 quarts
1 bushel	=	4 pecks

Some useful measures / Unas medidas útiles

Quantity / Cantidad

1 dozen / docena	=	12 units / unidades
1 gross / gruesa	=	12 dozen / docenas

Quantity of paper / Cantidad de papel

1 quire / mano	=	24 or 25 sheets / hojas
1 ream / resma	=	500 sheets / hojas
		20 quires / manos

Electricity / Electricidad

charge / carga	=	coulomb / culombio
power / potencia	=	watt / vatio
		kilowatt / kilovatio
resistance / resistencia	=	ohm / ohmio
strength / fuerza	=	ampere / amperio
voltage / voltaje	=	volt / voltio

Idioms and Expressions / Modismos y expresiones

A

Above all
Ante todo, por encima de todo, sobre todo

According to the rules
Como Dios manda

Act a fool
Hacer el ridículo, hacerse el tonto

Act without restraint
Soltar la rienda

Add fuel to the fire
Echar leña al fuego

After all
A fin de cuentas, después de todo, en resumidas cuentas

Against all odds
Contra viento y marea

Against the grain
A contrapelo

A litte more
Y pico

All along
Desde el principio

All at once
De un golpe, de un tirón, de una tirada

All by oneself (himself)
Por su cuenta

All day
Todo el día

All joking aside
Bromas a un lado, fuera de broma

All of a sudden
De buenas a primeras, de repente

All the time
A cada rato, todo el tiempo

All together
En conjunto, en junto

And so on
Y así sucesivamente

Anything at all
Cualquier cosa

Any way you look at it
A todas luces

Around the corner
A la vuelta de, a la vuelta de la esquina

As a general rule
Por regla general, por lo general

As a last resort
Como último recurso

As a matter of fact
En realidad

As a result (of)
A consecuencia de, de resultas

As a rule
Por lo regular

As far as I'm concerned
Por mi parte

As for
En cuanto a

As if by magic
Como por ensalmo

As long as
Siempre que

As much as
Tanto como

As soon as possible
Cuanto antes, lo más pronto posible

As the saying goes
Como dijo el otro

As usual
Como de costumbre, como siempre, sin novedad

As well as
Así como

As you like
A la voluntad

At all costs
A toda costa, a todo trance

At all times
A toda hora

At any cost
Cueste lo que cueste

At any rate
Como quiera que sea, de cualquier modo, de todas maneras, de todos modos

At any time
A toda hora

At arm's length
A una brazada

At first
Al principio

At full speed (or greatest speed)
A escape, a toda prisa, a toda vela, a todo correr

At home
En casa

At last
A la postre, al fin, al fin y al cabo, por fin, último

At (the) least
Al menos, a lo menos, como mínimo, menos mal, por lo menos

At most
A lo más, a lo sumo

At once
Ahora mismo, al instante, al punto, de pronto, de una vez, desde luego, en el acto, en seguida

At one stroke
De una vez

At one time
A un tiempo, de una vez

At random
A la buena de Dios, a la ventura, al azar

At that time
A la sazón, en aquel tiempo

At the same time
A la vez, al mismo tiempo, de paso, entre tanto

At times
A ratos, a veces

At will
A la voluntad, a voluntad

At worst
A lo más

Average person
El común de las gentes

B

Back and forth
De aquí para allá

Backward(s)
Al revés, hacia atrás

Be about to
Estar a punto de, estar para

Be a fan of
Ser aficionado a

Be afraid
Tener miedo

Be against
Estar en pugna con, ponerse en contra de

Be alert
Estar a la mira de, ponerse chango

Be all right, OK
Estar bien

Be a load off one's mind
Quitarse uno un peso de encima

Be anxious to
No ver la hora de

Be a part of
Formar parte de

Bear in mind
Tener presente (de lo que)

Be ashamed
Tener vergüenza

Beat around the bush
Andarse con rodeos, andarse por las ramas

Be at the end of one's rope or resources
Estar en las últimas

Be broke
Estar bruja

Be disappointed
Llevarse un chasco

Be dull
No tener sal en la mollera

Be eager to
Tener deseos de

Be equal to (a task)
Estar a la altura de

Be exhausted
No poder más

Be fed up with
Estar harto de

Be fond of
Estar afecto a

Before one's (very) eyes
A ojos vistas

Begin to understand
Ir entendiendo

Be good for nothing
No servir para nada

Behind one's back
A espaldas de

Be in a bad mood
Estar mal templado, estar de mal humor, mal genio

Be in a good mood
Estar de buen humor, buen genio

Be in a hurry
Estar (or andar) de prisa, tener prisa

Be in big trouble
Estar con el agua al cuello

Be in charge of
Estar a cargo de, estar encargado de

Be indebted to
Estar en deuda con

Be in favour (us favor) of
Estar por

Be in good health
Estar bien de salud, sin novedad

Be in need of
Hacer falta

Be in the mood (for)
Estar de (o en) vena (para)

Be in the same boat
Estar en las mismas

Be in the way
Estar de sobra

Be irritable (or a grouchy person)
Ser un erizo

Be left alone
Estar de non, quedar de non

Be long (in doing)
Tardar en

Be lucky
Tener suerte, tocarle a uno la suerte

Be mistaken
Estar en un error

Be oliged to
Verse obligado a

Be obvious
Saltar a la vista

Be on duty
Estar de turno

Be on good terms with
Acordar con

Be on one's last legs
Estar en las últimas

Be on the lookout for
Estar a la mira de

Be on vacation
Estar de vacaciones

Be out of a job
Medir las calles

Be out of luck
Andar de malas, estar de malas, tener la de malas

Be out of the house
Estar fuera de la casa

Be pleased with
Quedar contento con

Be a question of
Tratarse de

Be responsible for
Hacerse cargo de

Be right
Andar bien; tener razón

Be satisfied
Estar uno hasta la coronilla

Be short of money
Estar (or andar) escaso de dinero

Be sorry for someone
Pesarle a uno

Be successful
Salir bien, tener éxito

Be terribly sorry
Sentir en el alma

Be thirsty
Tener sed

Be to blame
Tener la culpa

Better late than never
Más vale tarde que nunca

Between the devil and the deep blue sea
Entre la espada y la pared

Be unlucky
Estar salado

Be up to date
Estar al cabo de, estar al corriente de, estar en corriente

Be used as
Servir de

Be used for
Servir para

Be used (or accustomed) to ...
Tener la costumbre de...

Be very difficult
Costar trabajo

Be well-informed
Estar al cabo de, estar al corriente de, estar en corriente

Be well off
Estar desahogado

Be worse off
Estar peor que antes

Be worth
Valer por

Be worthless
No ser ni chicha ni limonada

Be worthwhile
Merecer la pena, valer la pena

Be wrong
Estar en un error, no tener razón

Be ... years old
Tener ... años

Break one's word
Faltar a su palabra, pintarle un violín

Break the news
Dar la noticia

Bump into each other
Darse un encontrón

Burn the midnight oil
Quemarse las pestañas (or las cejas)

By all means
A toda costa, a todas luces, de todos modos, sin falta

By chance
Al azar, por casualidad

By ear
Al oído, de oído

By heart
De memoria

By means of
Por medio de

By mistake
Por equivocación, por descuido

By oneself
Por sí solo, por su mano

By sight
A ojo

By the way
A propósito, de paso, entre paréntesis

By word of mouth
De palabra, de viva voz

C

Call on the phone (telephone)
Llamar por teléfono

Catch cold
Coger catarro, coger un resfriado

Cause pain or worry
Hacer mella

Certainly
A buen seguro

Certainly not
Claro que no

Change one's mind
Cambiar de idea (...opinión, ... pensamiento)

Change the subject
Cambiar de tema

Cock and bull story
Cuento chino

Come hell or high water
Contra viento y marea

Come out poorly
Salir mal

Come out well
Quedar bien, salir bien, surtir efecto

Come to a boil
Soltar (or alzar) el hervor

Come to an agreement
Ponerse de acuerdo

Come to blows
Venir a las manos

Come to know
Llegar a saber

Come what may
Contra viento y marea, suceda lo que suceda

Considering that
Visto que

Cost an arm and a leg
Costar un ojo de la cara

Cut class
Faltar a (la) clase, hacer pinta

D

Daily grind
La rutina diaria

Dating from
Desde hace

Day after day
Día tras día

Decide upon
Optar por

Don't worry
¡No se ocupe!, ¡no se preocupe usted!

Do one's best
Hacer lo posible, poner todo de su parte

Do over
Hacer de nuevo, hacer otra vez, volver a hacer

Do without
Pasarse sin, prescindir de

Drive someone crazy
Volver loco a uno

Drop out (of)
Darse de baja, dejar de asistir, retirarse (de)

During the week
A mediados de la semana, entre semana

E

Each one
Cada cual, cada uno

Each other
El uno al otro, unos a otros

Each time
A cada rato, cada vez

Earn a living
Ganar para comer, ganarse la vida

End up as
Venir a parar

End up by (doing something)
Acabar por

Enjoy your meal!
¡Buen provecho!

Et cetera
Y así sucesivamente

Even so
Así y todo

Even though
Aun cuando, ni siquiera

Ever since
Desde entonces

Every other day
Cada dos días, un día sí y otro no, un día y un día no

Everything else
Todo lo demás

Every time
Todas las veces (que)

Exactly the opposite
Todo lo contrario

Except for
Si no fuera por, si no fuera porque

F

Face to face
Cara a cara

Farther away
Más allá de

Farther on
Más adelante

Fast asleep
Profundamente dormido

Feel like
Tener gana(s) de

Feel OK
Estar regular

Feel sorry for
Tener lástima de

Few, a
Unas cuantas, unos cuantos

Few words, a
Cuatro palabras

Find fault with
Poner defectos, poner faltas

First of all
Ante todo

Fit of anger
Arranque de cólera, ímpetu de ira

Follow in the footsteps (of)
Seguir las pisadas

Fond of
Amante de, amigo de

Foot the bill
Pagar los gastos

For a change
Para variar

For and against
En pro y en contra

For example
Por ejemplo

For now
Por ahora

For some reason
Por algo

For some time now
De algún tiempo para acá

For sure
De seguro

For that reason
Por esa razón, por eso

For the first time
Por primera vez

For the last time
Por última vez

For the time being
De momento, por ahora, por el momento, por lo pronto

From a distance
De lejos, desde lejos

From bad to worse
De mal en peor

From beginning to end
De cabo a rabo

From now on
De ahora en adelante, de aquí en adelante, de hoy en adelante, desde ahora, en adelante

From one side to the other
De parte a parte

From that time on
De aquel tiempo en adelante, de aquel entonces

From the beginning
Desde el principio

From time to time
A ratos, de tarde en tarde

From top to bottom
De arriba abajo

G

Get along well with
Llevarse bien con, quedar bien con

Get going
Poner en marcha

Get lost!
¡Vete a bañar!

Get out of a difficulty
Salir del paso

Get out of here!
¡Largo de aquí!, ¡quítese de aquí!

Get the point
Caer en la cuenta

Get to one's feet
Ponerse de pie

Get to sleep
Conciliar el sueño

Get well
Ponerse bien

Get worse
Subir de punto

Give a party
Dar una fiesta

Give good results
Surtir efecto

Give regards
Dar los recuerdos

Give thanks
Dar las gracias

Give up (or get rid of) something
Quitarse de una cosa

Go arm in arm
Ir del brazo

Go back on one's word
Echarse para atrás, volverse atrás

Go jump in the lake!
¡Vete a bañar!

Good-looking
Bien parecido, de buen ver

Good luck
Que le vaya bien

Go on foot
Ir a pie

Go on holiday (us vacation)
Ir de vacaciones

Go out to meet
Salir al encuentro de

Go over carefully
Pasar revista a

Go shopping
Ir de compras

Grown up
Hecho y derecho

H

Half done
A medio hacer

Happy-go-lucky
Chueco o derecho

Hard cash
Dinero contante y sonante

Hard time
Un rato desagradable

Have a bad time
Sudar la gota gorda

Have a big mouth
Tener la lengua larga

Have a birthday
Cumplir años

Have a good day
Que lo pase bien

Have a good time
Pasar un buen rato

Have a screw loose
Faltarle a uno un tornillo

Have in mind
Tener en la mente

Have nothing to do with
No tener nada que ver con

Have no way out
No tener alternativa (or elección)

Have one's own way
Salirse con la suya

Have on the tip of one's tongue
Tener en la punta de la lengua

Have the misfortune to
Tener la pena de

Have time off
Tener tiempo libre

Heads or tails
Águila o pico, águila o sello, cara o cruz

Help yourself
Sírvase usted

Hit a nerve
Tocar en lo vivo

Hit or miss
Al tanteo, chueco o derecho

Hit the ceiling
Poner el grito en el cielo

Hit the nail on the head
Dar en el clavo, dar en (or con) el chiste, dar uno en la tecla

How awful!
¡Qué horror!

How do you like ...?
¿Qué le parece ...?

How do you say ...?
¿Cómo se dice ...?

How far?
¿Hasta dónde?

How goes it? (or how is it going?)
¿Qué hubo?

How often?
¿Cada cuánto tiempo?

How should I know?
¿Qué sé yo?

How unfortunate!
¡Qué desgracia!

I

If not
De lo contrario, donde no

If so
En caso afirmativo

In accordance with
Conforme a, de acuerdo con

In addition to
Además de, a más de, sobre que

In advance
Con anticipación, con tiempo, de antemano, por adelantado

In a jiffy
Como por ensalmo, en un credo, en un chiflido, en un soplo

In a little while
Dentro de poco

In all
En junto, en conjunto

In a minute
En un credo

In any case
Al fin de cuentas, de todos modos

In brief
En resolución, en resumen

In broad daylight
En pleno día

In case
Por si acaso

In cold blood
En sangre fría

In compliance with
En conformidad con, estar de conformidad con

In conclusion
En fin

In days gone by
En días pasados

In detail
Por extenso, por menudo

In due course or time
A su (debido) tiempo

In either case
En ambos casos

In fact
De hecho, en efecto, en rigor

In front of
Al frente de, delante de, frente a

In good taste
De buen tono, de buen gusto

In many respects
En muchos puntos

In my opinion
A mi entender, a mi modo de ver

In order
En regla

In order that
A fin de que, para que

In other words
En otros términos, es decir

In particular
En especial

In passing
De paso

In poor taste
De mal gusto

In the presence of
A vista de

In short
Al fin y al cabo, en fin, en resumidas cuentas

In some way or other
De un modo u otro

In spite of
A despecho de, a pesar de

In spite of everything
A pesar de todo

In spite of the fact that
A pesar de que

In such a way
De suerte que

Intend to
Pensar en, tener la intención de

In that way
De esa manera, de ese modo

In the act
En fragante

In the background
En lontananza

In the direction of
Con rumbo a

In the event of
En caso de

In the final analysis
A fin de cuentas

In the future
De ahora en adelante, en adelante, en lo futuro, en lo sucesivo

In the hands of
En poder de

In the long run
A la larga

In the morning (afternoon, etc.)
Por la mañana (la tarde, etc.)

In the nick of time
En el momento preciso

In the open air
Al aire libre, al raso

In the opposite way
Al revés

In the same way
Del mismo modo

In the style of
A (la) manera de

In this way
De esta manera, de este modo

In writing
Por escrito

I should say not!
¡De ninguna manera!

I should say so!
¡Ya lo creo!

Is that so?
¿De veras?, ¿de verdad?, ¡no diga!

It can't be helped
No hay remedio, no tiene remedio

It doesn't matter
No le hace, no tiene importancia

It is good (bad) weather
Hace buen (mal) clima

It is no wonder that
No es mucho que

It is time for
Es (la) hora de

It is time to go
Es (la) hora de partir

It makes no difference
Darle lo mismo, es lo de menos, lo mismo da, no le hace

It must be true
Ha de ser verdad

It's a deal!
¡Trato hecho!

It's almost time
Falta poco

It seems to me that
Me parece que

It serves me right
Bien me lo merezco

It's none of your (my) business
No es asunto suyo (mío)

It's not important
No tiene importancia

It's time to ...
Ya es hora de ...

It's too late now
Ya es tarde

J

Jump to conclusions
Hacer deducciones precipitadas

Just in case
Por lo que pueda tronar, por si acaso

Just right
Al centavo, al pelo

K

Keep one's word
Cumplir (con) su palabra

Keep track of
Llevar la cuenta, llevar cuenta de

Keep up to date, informed, posted
Tener al corriente

Kick out
Dar de baja

Kill two birds with one stone
Matar dos pájaros de un tiro

Know absolutely nothing (about that)
No saber ni papa (de eso)

Know how to (sew, dance, etc.)
Saber (coser, bailar, etc.)

L

Last month
El mes pasado

Last straw
La gota que derrama el vaso

Last week
La semana pasada

Learn by heart
Aprender de memoria

Leave alone
Dejar en paz, dejar tranquilo

Leave (someone) in the lurch
Dejar (a uno) plantado, dejar en las astas del toro

Less than
Menos de, menos que

Like always
Como siempre

Little by little
Poco a poco

Live together
Hacer vida

Long ago
Hace mucho tiempo

Look for a needle in a haystack
Buscar una aguja en un pajar

Look well
Tener buena cara

Lose one's head
Saltar las trancas

Lose sight of
Perder de vista

Lots of
La mar de

M

Majority of people, the
El común de las gentes

Make a deal
Hacer un trato

Make a fool of
Poner en ridículo

Make a mistake
No dar pie con bola

Make an appointment
Dar una cita

Make friends with
Hacerse amigo de

Make fun of
Burlarse de, hacer cuco a, hacer burla de

Make hay while the sun shines
Hacer su agosto

Make no difference
Dar lo mismo, no irle ni venirle a uno

Make oneself understood
Hacerse entender

Make up for
Resarcirse de

Make use of
Valerse de

Make way for
Abrir paso para

Meet face to face
Enfrentarse con

Mind your own business!
¿Quién te mete, Juan Copete?

More than
Más de, más que

More than anyone
Más que nadie

More than enough
De sobra

More than ever
Más que nunca

More than once
Más de una vez, una y otra vez

Most of
La mayoría de, la mayor parte de

N

Neither fish nor fowl
No ser ni chicha ni limonada

Never mind
¡No importa!, ¡no se ocupe!

Next to
Al lado de, junto a

No ... (smoking, eating, etc.)
Se prohibe ... (fumar, comer, etc.)

Nobody else
Ningún otro

No comment
Sin comentarios

No kidding!
¡Palabrita de honor!

No longer
Ya no

No matter how much
Por mucho que

No matter what
Por ningún motivo, suceda lo que suceda

No sooner said than done
Dicho y hecho

Not by a long shot
Ni con mucho

Not by any means
Ni mucho menos

Nothing at all
Nada en absoluto

Nothing unusual
Nada de particular

Not much
Poca cosa

Not only ... but also
No sólo ... sino también

No trespassinig
Prohibida la entrada, prohibido el paso, se prohibe entrar (pasar)

Not to be a laughing matter
No ser cosa de juego

Not to feel well
Sentirse destemplado

Not to know anything
No saber una (or ni) jota

Not to my knowledge
No que yo sepa

Not to say a word
No despegar los labios

Not to sleep a wink
Pasar la noche en claro (or en blanco)

Not to worry
Perder cuidado

Not yet
Aún no, todavía no

Now and then
De tarde en tarde, de vez en cuando

No wonder!
¡Con razón!

O

Of course
Claro que sí, ¿cómo no?, desde luego, por supuesto, seguro que sí, ya se ve

Of course not
Claro que no

Of little value or importance
De poca monta, lo de menos

On a large scale
En grande

On all sides
Para todos lados

On approval
A vistas

Once and for all
De una vez, de una vez por todas

Once in a blue moon
Allá a las quinientas, como visita de obispo, de tarde en tarde

Once upon a time
Había una vez, érase que se era, érase una vez, y va de cuento

One at a time
De uno en uno, uno a la vez

One by one
Uno por uno

One of these (fine) days
Un día de estos

One or the other
El uno o el otro, uno u otro

On one's back
De espaldas

On one's knees
De rodillas

On purpose
A propósito, de propósito

On the contrary
Al contrario, por el contrario

On the fence
Entre azul y buenas noches

On the following day
Al día siguiente, al otro día

On the other hand
En cambio, por otra parte, por otro lado

On the road to
Camino de

On the run
A la carrera

On the spur of the moment
De buenas a primeras

On the way
De camino, de tránsito, (estar) en camino

On time
A buena hora, a tiempo

Out of breath
Con la lengua de corbata, con la lengua de pechera

Out of date
Pasado de moda

Out of style
Pasado de moda

Out of the country
En el extranjero

Out of the ordinary
Fuera de lo corriente

Over and over again
Repetidas veces, una y otra vez

Over here
Por acá, por aquí

Over there
Por ahí, por allá

P

Pay attention (to)
Dar atención, fijarse en, hacer caso (a or de), prestar atención

Pay a visit
Hacer una visita

Pay by cash
Pagar al contado

Per day
Al día

Pick a fight or quarrel with
Meterse con

Place hope in someone
Esperar en alguien

Place one's hope in
Cifrar la esperanza en

Plain and simple truth
La verdad clara y desnuda

Play a trick
Pegar un chasco

Play hooky
Hacer pinta, pintar venado

Play second fiddle
Ser plato de sugunda mesa

Point blank
A quema ropa, a quemarropa

Pretend not to hear
Hacerse el sordo

Pretend not to notice
Hacerse el desentendido

Prick up one's ears
Aguzar las orejas (or los oídos)

Provided that
Con tal (de) que, dado el caso que, siempre que

Pull one's leg
Tomarle el pelo

Put into practice
Poner por obra

Put in writing
Hacer por escrito

Put one's foot in one's mouth
Meter la pata

Put the cart before the horse
Tomar el rábano por las hojas

Q

Quarrel with
Meterse con

Quickly
Al trote, de prisa, de un salto, en un salto

R

Rack one's brain
Devanarse los sesos, quebrarse una lo cabeza, romperse los cascos

Rain or shine
Que llueva o no

Rather than
Antes que, más bien que

Regardless of
Sin hacer caso de

Regards to
Recuerdos a

Repeat mechanically
Repetir de carretilla

Rest of them, the
Los (las) demás

Right away
En el acto

Right here
Aquí mismo

Right now
Ahora mismo, en seguida, más ahorita

S

Safe and sound
Sano y salvo

Same as, the
El (or lo) mismo que, igual que

Save time
Ganar tiempo

Say goodbye to
Despedirse de

Say to oneself
Decir para sí

See to it that
Ver de, ver que

Set in motion
Poner en juego

Set out (on a trip, etc.)
Ponerse en camino

Set the table
Poner la mesa

Shake hands (with)
Dar la mano, darse la mano, estrechar la mano (a)

Shortly thereafter
Poco después de

Shut tight
A piedra y lodo

Since then
Desde entonces

Sky high
Por las nubes

Slam the door
Dar un portazo

Sleep it off
Dormir la mona

Sleep on it
Consultar con la almohada

Sleep soundly
Dormir a pierna suelta

Something is wrong
Hay moros en la costa

So much the better
Tanto mejor

So much the worse
Tanto peor

Sooner or later
A la corta o a la larga, tarde o temprano

Sooner the better, the
Antes hoy que mañana

So-so
Así así, tal cual

So what?
¡A mí qué!, ¿de modo qué?, ¿pues qué?, ¿y qué?

Spare no expense
Echar la casa por la ventana

Speak frankly
Hablar al alma, no tener pelillos en la lengua

Speak loudly
Hablar alto, hablar en voz alta

Split hairs
Pararse en pelillos

Stand a chance
Tener probabilidad

Stark raving mad
Loco de remate

Start a conversation
Entablar una conversación

Stay in bed
Guardar (la) cama

Stop (smoking, etc.)
Dejar de (fumar, etc.)

Stop beating around the bush
Dejarse de cuentos, dejarse de rodeos

Stop short (or suddenly)
Parar en seco

Straw that broke the camel's back, the
La gota que derrama el vaso

Study hard
Quemarse las pestañas (or las cejas)

Such as
Tal como, tales como, tal cual

Suit perfectly
Venir a (or al) pelo

Sure enough
Dicho y hecho

Swarm of people
Un hervidero de gente, un remolino de gente

Sweat blood
Sudar la gota gorda

T

Take a chance
Correr riesgo

Take advantage of the situation
Aprovechar la ocasión

Take a long time (in doing something)
Tardar en (hacer algo)

Take a long weekend
Hacer puente

Take a nap
Descabezar el sueño, echar un sueño, echar una siesta

Take a stand against
Salir al encuentro de

Take a walk, take a ride
Dar un paseo

Take care of someone
Mirar por alguien

Take for granted
Dar por descontado, dar por hecho, dar por sabido (or sentado or supuesto), tomar por cierto

Take into account
Hacer caso a (or de), tener en cuenta, tomar en cuenta

Take lightly
Tomar a risa

Take pity on
Tener lástima de

Take seriously
Tomar a pecho(s)

Take time off
Tomar tiempo libre

Take to heart
Tomar a (or en) pecho(s), tomar en serio

Talk too much
Hablar por los codos

Talk to oneself
Hablar para sus adentros

Tear to pieces
Hacer garras, hacer trizas

That can't be helped
Eso no tiene quite

That is a horse of a different color
Eso es harina de otro costal

That is the limit!
¡Eso es el colmo!

That is why
Por algo, por esa razón
That's not the point (or the question)
No se trata de eso
That's right
Eso es
That's the last straw!
¡No faltaba más!
The fact is
El caso es
The more ... the less
Mientras más ... mientras menos
There are no two ways about it
No hay que darle vueltas, no tiene vuelta de hoja
There is more than meets the eye
Hay gato encerrado
There is no doubt (that)
No cabe duda (que)
There is no way around it
No hay que darle vueltas
There is the heart of the matter!
¡Allí está el toque!
There's nothing to do except ...
No hay más remedio que ...
This will do
Así está bien
Thousand thanks, a
Mil gracias
Through thick and thin
Por toda suerte de penalidades
Throw a party
Dar una fiesta
To and fro
De aquí para allá
Tomorrow afternoon
Mañana por la tarde
Tomorrow is another day
Mañana Dios dirá
Tomorrow morning
Mañana por la mañana, mañana temprano
Tomorrow night
Mañana por la noche
Too bad!
¡Qué lástima!
To oneself
Consigo mismo
To one's heart's content
A pedir de boca
To the limit
Hasta más no poder
Towards the end of (a period of time)
A fines de
Turn a deaf ear
Hacerse el sordo
Turn one's back (on)
Dar las espaldas (a), voltear la espalda
Turn out to be
Venir a parar, venir a ser
Turn the corner
Doblar a la esquina
Turn the page
Darle vuelta a la hoja
Two by two
De dos en dos
Two of a kind
Tal para cual
Two-way
De dos sentidos

U

Ups and downs
Subidas y bajadas
Up to a point
Hasta cierto punto
Up to date
A la moda, hasta la fecha
Up to the top
Hasta el tope

V

Various times
Repetidas veces
Very much
Con (or en or por) extremo, de lo lindo
Very often
Con mucha frecuencia, muy a menudo
Very thought of, the
La mera idea de

W

Wait in line
Hacer cola
Wash one's hands of
Lavarse las manos de
Watch out (for)
Tener cuidado (con)
Wear oneself out
Hacerse uno rajas
Well done!
¡Así se hace!
Well-done (well-cooked)
Bien asado, bien cocido
Well then
Pues bien
Well worth it
Digno de
What a mess!
¡Qué batingue!
What a pleasure!
¡Qué gusto!
What does it mean?
¿Qué quiere decir?, ¿qué significa?
What do you think of it?
¿Qué le parece?
What happened?
¿Qué pasó?
What if ...?
¿Y si ...?
What is it?
¿Qué haces?
What is more
Más aún
What is the point of that?
¿A qué viene eso?
What nonsense!
¡Qué barbaridad!
What's going on?
¿Qué pasa?
What's new?
¿Qué hay de nuevo?
What's the difference?
¡Qué más da!
What's the matter with you?
¿Qué le (or te) pasa?
What's up?
¿Qué hubo?, ¿qué pasa?
What's wrong with that?
¿Qué hay de malo con eso?
What time is it?
¿Qué hora es?, ¿qué horas son?
When all is said and done
A la postre
Whether one likes it or not
Por las buenas o por las malas
Whole truth, the
La verdad clara y desnuda
With great difficulty
A duras penas
Within a week
Dentro de una semana
Within view
A vista de
Without fail
Sin falta
Without help
Sin remedio
Without interruption
De seguida
Without question
Sin disputa
Without realizing
Sin sentir
Without risk
Sobre seguro
Without stopping
De corrida, de hilo
Without warning
A quema ropa, a quemarropa
With pleasure
De (buena) voluntad
With regard to
Acerca de, con respecto a, en cuanto a, respecto a
With the aim of
Con el propósito de

With your permission
Con permiso

Word of honor!
¡Palabrita de honor!

Work hard
Dar batería, sudar la gota gorda

Work well
Andar bien

Worry about
Preocuparse por

Worry about nothing
Ahogarse en poca agua

Worse than
Peor que

Worth seeing
Ser de ver, ser para ver

Y

Year before last
Año antepasado

Yesterday afternoon
Ayer por la tarde

You don't say!
¡No diga!

You're welcome
De nada, no hay de qué

Modismos y expresiones / Idioms and Expressions

A

A buen santo te encomiendas
To bark up the wrong tree

A buen seguro
Certainly, very probably

A cada paso
At every turn (or step)

A cada rato
Each time, all the time

A contrapelo
Against the grain

A deshora(s)
At all hours, unexpectedly; at an untimely moment

A duras penas
With great difficulty, hardly, scarcely

A escondidas
On the sly, undercover

A fin de cuentas
After all, in the final analysis

A las claras
Clearly, openly, frankly, publicly

A las mil maravillas
Beautifully, wonderfully well

A los cuatro vientos
In all directions

A más ver (or hasta más ver)
Goodbye

A mi entender
In my opinion, as I understand it

A mi modo de ver
In my opinion

¡A mí qué!
What's that to me?, so what?

A ojo
By sight, by guess

A ojos cerrados
Blindly

A ojos vistas
Visibly, clearly; before one's eyes

A pesar de (todo)
In spite of (everything)

A pie(s) juntillas
With both feet together; believe strongly

A propósito
By the way, apropos; on purpose

A puerta cerrada
Secretly, behind closed doors

¿A qué viene eso?
What is the point of that?

A quema ropa (or a quemarropa)
Very close, point blank, without warning

A rienda suelta
Free rein, violently, swiftly

A sangre fría
In cold blood

A toda costa
By all means, at whatever costs

A toda vela
Under full sail, at full speed

A todas luces
By all means, any way you look at it

A vuelo de pájaro
As the crow flies

Acabar de
To have just (done something)

Acabar por
To end up by (doing something)

Acordar con
To be on good terms with

Acostarse con las gallinas
To go to bed early

Agachar las orejas
To hang one's head

Aguantar el chubasco
To weather the storm

Aguzar las orejas (los oídos)
To prick up one's ears

¡Ahí está el detalle!
That's the point!

Ahora es cuando
Now is the time; now is your chance

Al contado
Cash

Al habla
Within speaking distance; speaking! (in answering a telephone)

Al pan, pan y al vino, vino
Call a spade a spade

Al pie de la letra
Literally, to the letter

Al revés
Backward(s), wrong side out, in the opposite way

Allá a las quinientas
Once in a blue moon

¡Allí está el toque!
There is the heart of the matter!

Andar agitado
To be out of sorts

Andar de malas
Be out of luck

Andarse con rodeos
To beat around the bush

Andarse el tiempo
Meanwhile, as time goes on

Andarse por las ramas
To beat around the bush

Antes hoy que mañana
The sooner the better

Aprendiz de todo y oficial de nada
Jack of all trades

Aprovechar la ocasión
To take advantage of the situation

Así está bien
This will do (be OK)

¡Así se hace!
Well done!, bully for you!

Aun cuando
Even if, even though

Ayer por la tarde
Yesterday afternoon

B

Bien arreglado
Neatly dressed

Bien asado
Well-done (well-cooked)

Bien cocido
Well-done (well-cooked)

Bien me lo merezco
It serves me right

Bien parecido
Good-looking

Boca abajo
Face down, prone

Boca arriba
Face up, supine

Bromas aparte
All joking aside

Buen tipo
Good fellow

Buscarle tres (cuartro) pies al gato
To look for trouble

Buscar una aguja en un pajar
To look for a needle in a haystack

C

¿Cada cuánto tiempo?
How often?

Cada dos días
Every other day

Cada uno
Apiece

¡Cállate la trompa!
Shut up!

Callejón sin salida
Blind alley, dead end

Caminar con pies de plomo
To go cautiously

Camino trillado
Beaten path

Cara o cruz
Heads or tails

Cargar con el muerto
To get the blame unjustly

Carne de gallina
Goosebumps

Castañetear con los dedos
To snap one's fingers

Chueco o derecho
Hit or miss, happy-go-lucky

Claro que no
Of course not, certainly not

Claro que sí
Of course, naturally

Como dijo el otro
As someone said, as the saying goes

Como Dios manda
According to the rules

¡Cómo no!
Of course, why not!

Como por ensalmo
As if by magic, in a jiffy

Como quiera que sea
At any rate

Como siempre
As usual, like always

Como último recurso
As a last resort

Como visita de obispo
Once in a blue moon

Con la lengua de corbata (or con la lengua de pechera)
Out of breath, with tongue hanging out

Con motivo de
With the idea of, because of, on the occasion of, on account of

¿Con qué cara?
How can I (one) have the nerve?

¡Con razón!
No wonder!

Con todo (or con todos) los obstáculos
In spite of that

Consultar con la almohada
To sleep on it

Contra viento y marea
Against all odds, come hell or high water, come what may

Cortar el hilo
To break the thread of a story, to interrupt

Costar trabajo
To be very difficult

Costar un ojo de la cara
To cost an arm and a leg, be very expensive

Cualquier cosa
Anything at all

Cualquiera (or cualesquiera) de los dos
Either of the two

Cuanto antes
As soon as possible

Cuento chino
Cock and bull story

Cueste lo que cueste
At any cost

D

Dar al traste con
To ruin, destroy

Dar al través con
To ruin, destroy

Dar ánimo
To cheer up

Dar atención
To pay attention

Dar batería
To raise a rumpus, to work hard

Dar cima
To complete, carry out

Dar coba
To flatter, play up to, softsoap

Dar disgustos a
To cause distress or grief to

Dar el visto bueno
To approve, OK

Dar en el clavo
To hit the nail on the head

Dar en (or dar con) el chiste
To guess right, hit the nail on the head

Dar esquinazo
To ditch, avoid meeting someone

Dar gato por liebre
To cheat or swindle

Dar guerra
To make trouble

Dar la mano
To help, shake hands

Dar la noticia
To break the news

Dar la razón
To agree, to be of same opinion

Dar largas
To postpone or delay, or give someone the run around

Dar las espaldas a
To turn one's back on

Dar las gracias
To give thanks, to thank

Dar lo mismo
To make no difference

Dar los recuerdos
To give regards

Dar parte
To inform

Dar por descontado
To take for granted

Dar por hecho
To take for granted, to consider as done

Dar propina
To tip (give a gratuity)

Dar que hacer
To cause extra work

Dar un paseo
To take a walk or ride

Dar un portazo
To slam the door

Dar un vistazo a
To glance over, peruse

Dar una cita
To make an appointment

Dar una fiesta
To give (throw) a party

Dar una satisfacción
To apologize

Dar uno en la tecla
To hit the nail on the head,
find the right way to do something

Darle a uno mala espina
To arouse one's suspicions

Darse cuenta de (que)
To realize (that), to notice

Darse de baja
To drop out

Darse farol
To show off, put on airs

Darse un tropezón
To trip, stumble

Darse un encontrón
To collide with, bump into each other

De ahí que
Hence

De algún tiempo para acá
From some time now

De arriba abajo
From top to bottom

De aquí en adelante
From now on

De aquí para allá
To and fro, back and forth

De broma
Jokingly, in jest

De buen ver
Good-looking

De buenas a primeras
All of a sudden, unexpectedly, on the spur of the moment

De cabo a rabo
From beginning to end

De copete
High rank, important, proud

De cualquier modo
At any rate

¡De dónde!
Nonsense!

De dos sentidos
Two-way

De ese modo (or de esa manera)
In that way

De este modo (or de esta manera)
In this way

De etiqueta
Formal

De golpe
Suddenly

De gorra
At another's expense

De hecho
In fact

De hilo
Without stopping

De improviso
Unexpectedly

De lado
Tilted, oblique, sideways

De lo lindo
Wonderfully, very much, to the utmost

De mal en peor
From bad to worse

De mala gana
Unwillingly

De memoria
By heart

De momento
For the time being

De nada
Don't mention it; you're welcome

¡De ninguna manera!
By no means!, I should say not!

De ocasión
Reduced price, a bargain

De oídos
Hearsay

De paso
In passing, at the same time, by the way, in transit

De poca monta
Of little value or importance

De punto
By the minute

De pura casualidad
By pure chance

De rebote
On the rebound, indirectly

De repente
Suddenly, all of a sudden

De repuesto
Spare, extra

De resultas
As a result, consequently

De rigor
A must, it must

De seguida
Continuously, without interruption

De sobra
More than enough, unnecessarily

De sol a sol
Sunrise to sunset

De su (propia) cosecha
Of one's own making or invention

De tarde en tarde
From time to time, now and then, once in a blue moon

De tejas abajo
Here below, in this world

De todos modos
At any rate, in any case, anyhow, by all means

De un salto
Quickly

De una vez
At once, at one time, at one stroke, once and for all

De una vez por todas
Once and for all

De uso
Secondhand

De veras (¿De veras?)
Really, in truth, in earnest (really?, is that so?)

De viva voz
By word of mouth

De (buena) voluntad
Willingly, with pleasure

De vuelta
Again

Dejar a uno plantado
To stand someone up, leave someone in the lurch

Dejar en las astas del toro
To leave in the lurch

Dejar saber
To let on, pretend

Dejarse de cuentos
Come to the point, stop beating around the bush

Dejarse de rodeos
Stop the excuses, stop beating around the bush

Desayunarse con la noticia
To hear a piece of news early or for the first time

Desde luego
Actually, of course, at once

Despedirse de
To say goodbye to

Devanarse los sesos
To rack one's brain

Día hábil
Weekday, workday

Días de semana
Weekdays

Dicho y hecho
Sure enough, no sooner said than done

Digno de
Well worth it

Digno de confianza
Reliable, trustworthy

Dinero contante y sonante
Ready (or hard) cash

Dinero menudo
Change (re money)

Donde no
Otherwise, if not

Dondequiera que (or por dondequiera que)
Wherever

E

Echar al olvido
To forget on purpose

Echar de menos
To miss

Echar de ver
To notice, observe

Echar espumarajos
To froth at the mouth, to be very angry

Echar flores
To throw bouquets, to flatter, to compliment

Echar la casa por la ventana
To spare no expense, squander everything

Echar leña al fuego
To add fuel to the fire

Echar papas
To fib

Echar un piropo
To compliment, flatter

Echar una cana al aire
To go out for a good time

Echarle la bendición a una cosa
To give something up for lost

Echarse para atrás
To back out, go back on one's word

El caso es
The fact is

El común de las gentes
The majority of the people, the average person

El gusto es mío
The pleasure is mine

El mismísimo hombre
The very man

El pro y el contro
Pro and con

El uno o el otro (or uno u otro)
Either, one or the other

En aquel tiempo (en aquel entonces)
At that time, in those days

En cambio
On the other hand

En caso de
In the event of

En conformidad con
In compliance with

En el quinto infierno (or los quintos infiernos)
Very far away

En el sigilo (or silencio) de la noche
In the dead of the night

En fragante
In the act

En grande
On a large scale

En lo más crudo del invierno
In the dead of winter

En lontananza
In the distance, in the background

En muchos puntos
In many respects

En otros términos
In other words

En pleno día
In broad daylight

En realidad
As a matter of fact

En resumen
Summing up, in brief

En resumidas cuentas
In short, after all

En todas partes
Everywhere

En todo caso
In any event

En un credo
In a jiffy, in a minute

En un chiflido
In a jiffy, in a second

En un santiamén
Instantly, in the twinkling of an eye

Entre azul y buenas noches
Undecided, on the fence

Entre la espada y la pared
Between the devil and the deep blue sea

Entre tanto
Meanwhile, all the while, at the same time

Es decir
That is to say, in other words

Es (la) hora de (partir)
It is time for, it is time to (go)

Es lo de menos
It makes no difference, that's the least of the troubles

Eso corre prisa
That is urgent

¡Eso el el colmo!
That is the limit!

Eso es harina de otro costal
That's a horse of a different color

Esperar todo el santo día
To wait the whole blessed day

Estamos a mano
We are even, quits

Estar a buen recaudo
To be safe

Estar a cargo de
To be in charge of

Estar a gusto
To be contented or comfortable

Estar a punto de
To be about to

Estar al cabo de
To be well-informed, up-to-date

Estar al corriente de
To be informed, to be up-to-date

Estar afecto a
To be fond of

Estar con el agua al cuello
To be in big trouble

Estar de malas
To be out of luck

Estar de mal humor (or de mal genio)
To be in a bad mood

Estar (or quedar) de non
To be left alone, without a partner or companion

Estar de vacaciones
To be on vacation

Estar de viaje
To be on the road

Estar desahogado
To be well off

Estar en las mismas
To be in the same boat

Estar en las últimas
To be on one's last legs, to be at the end of one's rope, out of resources

Estar en pañales
To be in infancy, to possess scant knowledge

Estar en un aprieto
To be in a jam, to be in trouble

Estar entre la espada y la pared
To be between the devil and the deep blue sea

Estar fuera de la casa
To be out of the house, away from home

Estar harto de
To be fed up with

Estar mal templado
To be in a bad mood

Estar peor que antes
To be worse off

Estar salado
To be unlucky; to be witty, salty

Estar torcido con
To be on unfriendly terms with

Estar uno en sus cabales
To be in one's right mind

Estar uno hasta el copete
To be stuffed, fed up

Estrechar la mano (a)
To shake hands, grasp (or squeeze) a hand

Explicar una cátedra
To teach a course

F

Faltar a clase
To cut class

Faltar a su palabra
To break one's word

Faltarle a uno un tornillo
To have little sense, to have a screw loose

Fruncir las cejas
To frown, knit the eyebrows

Fuera de propósito
Irrelevant

G

Ganar para comer
To earn a living

Ganarse la vida
To make one's living

Guardar rencor
To bear or hold a grudge

Guardar silencio
To keep silent

H

Había una vez
Once upon a time

Hablar al caso
To speak to the point, or in plain language

Hablar por los codos
To talk too much, chatter constantly

Hace buen (mal) tiempo
It is good (bad) weather

Hacer cocos
To make eyes at, flirt

Hacer cola
To form a line, wait in line

Hacer cuco a
To fool, make fun of

Hacer deducciones precipitadas
To jump to conclusions

Hacer destacar
To emphasize

Hacer el (or hacer un) papel
To play a role

Hacer favoritismos en prejudicio de
To discriminate against

Hacer gracia
To amuse, to make laugh

Hacer la corte
To court, woo

Hacer las maletas
To pack, get ready to leave

Hacer las paces
To make up after a quarrel

Hacer mal papel
To make a poor showing

Hacer mella
To make a dent or impression,
to cause pain or worry

Hacer pinta
To play hooky, cut class

Hacer por escrito
To put in writing

Hacer puente
To take a long weekend

Hacer su agosto
To make hay while the sun shines

Hacer teatro
To show off

Hacer un trato
To make a deal

Hacer una plancha
To make a ridiculous blunder

Hacer una vista
To pay a visit

Hacerse amigo
To make friends with

Hacerse cargo
To take charge, to be responsible for

Hacerse el desentendido
To pretend not to notice

Hacerse el sordo
To pretend not to hear,
turn a deaf ear

Hacerse entender
To make oneself understood

Hacerse un lío
To get tangled up, become confused

Hasta cierto punto
In a way, up to a point

Hasta más no poder
To the limit, utmost

Hasta la fecha
Up to date, up to now

Hay gato encerrado
There is more than meets the eye

I

Ida y vuela
Round trip, return trip

Idas y venidas
Comings and goings

Inaplicable al caso
Irrelevant

Incurrir en el odio de
To incur the hatred of

Ir a medias (or ir a la mitad)
To go halves (50-50)

Ir de compras
To go shopping

Ir de jarana
To go on a spree

Ir de vacaciones
To go on vacation

Ir del brazo
To go arm in arm

Ir entendiendo
To begin to understand

J

Juego limpio
Fair play

Juego sucio
Foul play

Junto a
Near to, or next to

Junto con
With, along with

L

La comidilla de la vecindad
The talk of the town

La cosa no cuajó
The thing did not work well

La cuestión palpitante
The burning question

La gota que derrama el vaso
The last straw, the straw that broke
the camel's back

La rutina diaria
The daily grind

La verdad clara y desnuda
The whole truth, the plain
and simple truth

Lavarse las manos de
To wash one's hands of

Levantar la mesa
To clear the table

Limpio de polvo y paja
Net, entirely free, clear profit

Llamar al pan pan, y al vino vino
To call a spade a spade

Llamar por teléfono
To call on the telephone

Llevar a cabo
To carry through, to accomplish

Llevar la cuenta (or llevar cuenta de)
To keep track of

Llevar ventaja
To have the lead, to be ahead

Llevarse adelante
To carry out

Llevarse un chasco
To be disappointed

Llover a cántaros
To rain cats and dogs (pitchforks)

Lo de menos
Of little importance, the least of it

Lo más pronto posible
As soon as possible

Lo mismo da
It makes no difference

Loco de remate
Stark raving mad

M

Más ahorita
Right now

Más de una vez
More than once

Más pesado que una mosca
Pesky as a fly

Más que nadie
More than anyone

Más que nunca
More than ever

Más vale tarde que nunca
Better late than never

Matar dos pájaros de un tiro
To kill two birds with one stone

Matar el gusano
To satisfy a need or desire (hunger, etc.)

Me lloran los ojos
My eyes water

Media cuchara
A mediocre person

Medir las calles
To walk the streets, be out of a job

Meterse de por medio
To intervene, meddle in a dispute

Meterse en un lío
To get oneself in a mess

Mirar con el rabo del ojo
To look out of the corner
of one's eye

Mirar por encima del hombro
To look down on; despise

Muchas subidas y bajadas
Many ups and downs,
much going up and down

Muy trabajador
Hard-working

N

Nada de eso
Nothing like that

Nada en absoluto
Nothing at all

Ni con mucho
Not by far, not by a long shot, far from

Ni mucho menos
Not by any means, not anything like it

No da abasto a
To be unable to cope with

No dar pie con bola
To make a mistake, not to get things right

No darse cuenta
Not to realize

To despegar los labios
Not to say a word, not to open one's mouth

¡No diga!
Is that so? you don't say!

No es asunto mío (suyo, etc.)
It's none of my (your, etc.) business

No es mucho que
It is no wonder that

¡No faltaba más!
That's the last straw! why, the very idea!

No hay de qué
You're welcome; don't mention it

No hay más remedio que
There's no other way but to; there's nothing to do except

No hay prisa
There's no hurry

No hay que darle vueltas
There's no way around it; there are no two ways about it

¡No importa!
Never mind!

No le hace
It doesn't matter, it makes no difference

No nos debemos nada
We are even (quits)

No poder con
Not to be able to stand, endure, control, carry

No poder menos de
Not to be able to help; Ex.: **No puede menos de hacerlo** *he can't help doing it*

No saber ni papa (de eso)
To know absolutely nothing (about that)

¡No se ocupe!
Never mind!, don't worry!

No se trata de eso
That's not the point; that's not the question

No ser cosa de juego
Not to be a laughing matter

No ser ni chicha ni limonada
To be worthless, neither fish nor fowl

No tener alternativa (or elección)
To have no alternative, no way out

No tener sal en la mollera
To be dull, stupid

No tiene vuelta de hoja
There's no two ways about it

No vale una cuartilla
Not worth a penny

No viene al cuento (or no viene al caso)
It is not opportune, or to the point

O

O sea que
That is to say

Oír decir que
To hear that

Oír hablar de
To hear about

¡Otra, otra!
Encore

Otra vez
Again

P

Pagado de sí mismo
To be pleased with oneself

Pagar el pato
To be the scapegoat, get the blame

¡Palabrita de honor!
Word of honor, honestly; no kidding

¿Para qué?
What for?, for what use?

Para unos fines u otros
For one purpose or another

Para variar
For a change

Pararse en pelillos
To split hairs

Pasado de moda
Out of style, out of date

Pasado mañana
Day after tomorrow

Pasar de la raya
To overstep bounds, take undue liberties

Pasar por alto
To omit, overlook

Pasar un buen rato
To have a good time

Pasear a pie
To take a walk

Pasear en coche
To go for a drive (by auto)

Patas arriba
Upside down

Pecar de oscuro
To be very unclear, too complicated

Pegar un chasco
To play a trick, surprise, disappoint

Peor que peor
That is even worse

Perder prestigo
To lose face

Perderse de vista
To vanish, to be lost from view, to drop out of sight

Pintar venado
To play hooky

Pintarle un violín
To break one's word

Poner al corriente
To inform, to bring up to date

Poner defectos
To find fault with

Poner el grito en el cielo
To complain loudly, to hit the ceiling

Poner en limpio
To make a clean copy, to recopy

Poner en marcha
To get going

Poner en razón
To pacify

Poner la mira
To fix one's eyes on, aim at

Poner por las nubes
To praise to the skies

Poner por obra
To undertake, put into practice

Poner todo de su parte
To do one's best

Ponerse bien
To get well

Ponerse colorado
To blush

Ponerse de acuerdo
To come to an agreement

Ponerse en contra de
To oppose, be against

Por accidente
By accident

Por ahora
For the time being, for now

Por algo
For some reason; that's why

Por aquí cerca
Around here, in this vicinity

Por casualidad
By chance, by accident

Por consiguiente
Consequently, therefore

Por de (or por lo) pronto
For the present

Por desgracia
Unfortunately

Por el estilo
Such as that, of that kind

Por encima de todo
Above all

Por fuera
From the outside, on the outside

Por las buenas o por las malas
Whether one likes it or not

Por lo demás
Moreover, as for the rest (of us), aside from this

Por lo general
Usually, generally

Por lo menos
At least

Por lo pronto
For the time being

Por lo regular
Usually, as a rule

Por lo visto
Apparently, by the looks of, evidently

Por menudo
In detail, retail

Por mi parte
As far as I'm concerned

Por mucho que
No matter how much

Por ningún motivo
Under no circumstances, no matter what

Por regla general
As a general rule, usually

Por si acaso
In case, just in case

Por su mano
By oneself

Por término medio
On an average

Por toda suerte de penalidades
Through thick and thin

Por todo el mundo
All over the world

Por todo lo alto
Not sparing expense

Por última vez
For the last time, finally

Presencia de ánimo
Presence of mind, serenity

Prestar atención
To pay attention

Puede ser que
It may be that

Pues bien
Now then, well then, all right then

Pues mire
Well, look

Q

¡Qué barbaridad!
What nonsense!, what an atrocity!

¡Qué batingue!
What a mess!

¡Qué de!
What a lot!, how much!

¡Qué desgracia!
How unfortunate!

¡Qué gusto!
What a pleasure! I am delighted!

¿Qué haces?
What's the matter?, what is it?

¿Qué hay de malo con eso?
What's wrong with that? So, what's so bad about that?

¿Qué hora es? (or ¿qué horas son?)
What time is it?

¡Qué horror!
How awful!

¿Qué hubo?
How goes it?, what's up?

¡Qué lástima!
Too bad!, what a pity!

Qué le vaya bien
Good luck

¿Qué mosca te ha picado?
What's eating you?

¿Qué pasa?
What's up?, what's going on?

¡Qué quiere decir?
What does it mean?

¡Qué se divierta!
Have a good time!

¿Qué tal?
Hello! How are you?

Quebrarse uno la cabeza
To rack one's brain

Quedar contento con
To be pleased with

Quedar entendido que
To be understood, agreed to

Quemarse las pestañas (or las cejas)
To burn the midnight oil, study hard

¿Quién te mete, Juan Copete?
Mind your own business. What's it to you?

Quiere llover
It is trying (is about) to rain

Quitarse uno un peso de encima
To be relieved of, to be a load off one's

R

Ratos perdidos
Leisure hours

Recuerdos a
Regards to ...

Reírse para sus adentros
To laugh up one's sleeve

Repetidas veces
Over and over again, various times

Repetir de carretilla
To rattle off, repeat mechanically

Reunión de confianza
Informal gathering or party

Romperse los cascos
To rack one's brains

Rosario de desdichas
Chain of misfortune

S

Saber de memoria
To know by heart

Sacar el cuerpo
To dodge

Salida de pie de banco
Silly remark, nonsense

Salir al encuentro de
To go out to meet, to oppose, take a stand against

Salir bien
To be successful, to come out well

Salir del paso
To get out of a difficulty

Salirse con la suya
To have one's own way

Saltar las trancas
To lose patience, lose one's head

Sano y salvo
Safe and sound

Santo y bueno
Well and good

Se dice
It is said, they say

Se prohibe (fumar)
It is forbidden (to smoke); no (smoking)

Seguir la pisadas
To follow in the footsteps (of), emulate

Según y conforme (or según y como)
Exactly as, just as, that depends

Sentar bien a
To fit well

Sentir en el alma
To be terribly sorry, to regret very much

Ser aficionado a
To be a fan, a buff

Ser de carne y hueso
To be only human

Ser de rigor
To be indispensable, to be required by custom

Ser de (or ser para) ver
Worth seeing

Ser plato de segunda mesa
To play second fiddle

Ser un cero a la izquierda
To be of no account

Ser un erizo
To be irritable; a grouchy person

Sin falta
By all means, without fail, without fault

Sin fin
An infinite quantity

Sin novedad
As usual (to be well, in good health)

Sin qué ni para qué
Without rhyme or reason

Sin rebozo
Openly, frankly

Sin reserva
Unreserved, frankly

Sin sentir
Without realizing, inadvertently, unnoticed

Sin ton ni son
Without rhyme or reason

Sobradas veces
Repeatedly, many times

Sobre manera
Excessively

Sobre todo
Especially, above all

Soltar el hervor
To come to a boil

Soltar la rienda
To let loose, act without restraint

Su punto flaco
His weakness, her weak side

Subidas y bajadas
Ups and downs

Subir de punto
To increase, get worse

Suceda lo que suceda
Come what may, no matter what

Sudar la gota gorda
To sweat profusely, work hard, sweat blood, have a bad time

T

Tal cual
Such as, so-so, fair

Tal para cual
Two of a kind

Tal vez sea que
It may be that

Tanto mejor
So much the better

Tanto peor
So much the worse

Tarde o temprano
Sooner or later

Tener al corriente
To keep up-to-date (informed, posted)

Tener ... años
To be ... years old

Tener deseos de
To want to, to be eager to

Tener en cuenta
To consider, to take into account

Tener en la punta de la lengua
To have on the tip of one's tongue

Tener gana(s) de
To feel like

Tener gusto en
To be glad to

Tener la costumbre de
To be used (accustomed) to ...

Tener la lengua larga
To have a big mouth

Tener la pena de
To have the misfortune to

Tener murria
To be sulky, to have the blues

Tener presente (de or que)
To bear in mind

Tener probabilidad
To stand a chance

Tener roce con
To have contact with a person

Tener tiempo libre
To have time off

Tenerle tirria a una persona
To have a dislike for (or grudge against) a person

Tirarse una plancha
To put oneself in a ridiculous situation

Tocar de oído
To play by ear

Tocar en lo vivo
To hurt to the quick, hit a nerve, touch a sore spot

Tocarle a uno
To be one's turn

Toda clase de
All kinds of

Todas las veces (que)
Every time, whenever

Todavía no
Not yet

Todo el año
All year round

Todo el día
All day

Todo el mundo
Everybody

Todo el tiempo
All the time

Todo hombre
Everyone

Todo lo contrario
Exactly the opposite

Todo lo demás
Everything else

Todo sigue bien
All goes well

Tomar a broma
To take as a joke

Tomar a pecho(s)
To take to heart, to take seriously

Tomar el rábano por las hojas
To put the cart before the horse, to misinterpret or misconstrue

Tomar el sol
To sunbathe

Tomar en cuenta
To consider, take into account

Tomar en serio
To take to heart

Tomar tiempo libre
To take time off

Tomarlo con calma
To take it easy

Tratarse de
To be a question of

¡Trato hecho!
It's a deal!

U

Un día sí y otro no
Every other day

Un día sí y un día no
Every other day

Un no sé qué
Something indefinable

Un nudo en la garganta
A lump in the throat

Una infinidad de
A large number of

Una que otra vez
Once in a while

Una y otra vez
More than once, over and over again

Uno a la vez
One at a time

Uno por uno
One by one

Unos a otros
Each other

V

Valer la pena
To be worthwhile.
Ex.: **No vale la pena** *it's not worth the trouble*

Valerse de
To make use of

Varias veces
Several times

Venir a (or al) pelo
To come at the right moment, to suit perfectly, to be opportune

Verse obligado a
To be obliged to or forced to

Volver a
To do ... again

Volver a las andadas
To fall back into old habits

Y

Y así sucesivamente
And so on, et cetera

Y pico
(A) little more

Ya es hora de
It's time to

Ya es tarde
It's too late now

Ya mero
Very soon, just about to ...

¡Ya lo creo!
I should say so! Yes, of course

Ya no sopla
To be no good, of no use as ...

Ya se ve
Of course; it is clear

Ya voy
I am coming

North America / América del Norte

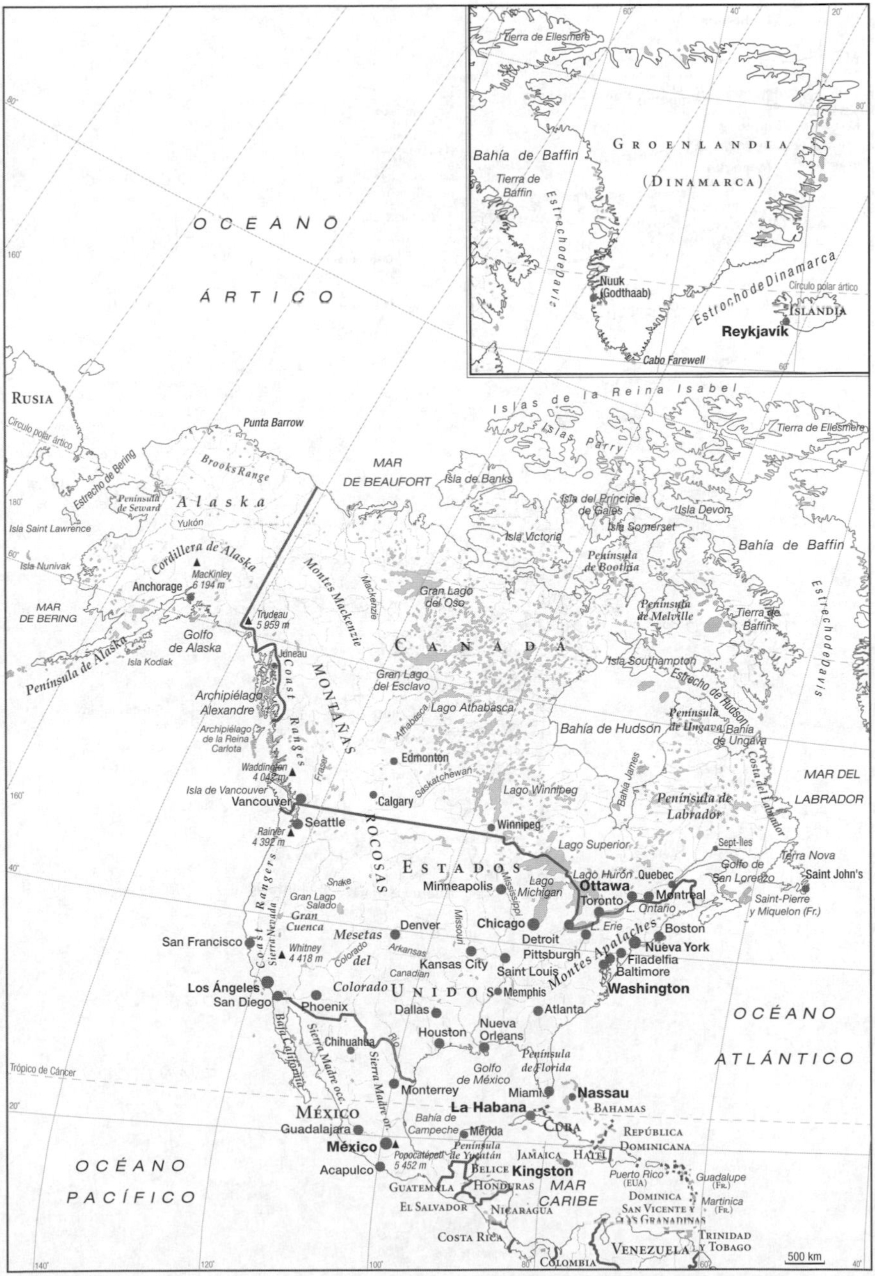

South and Central America / América Central y del Sur

Spain / España

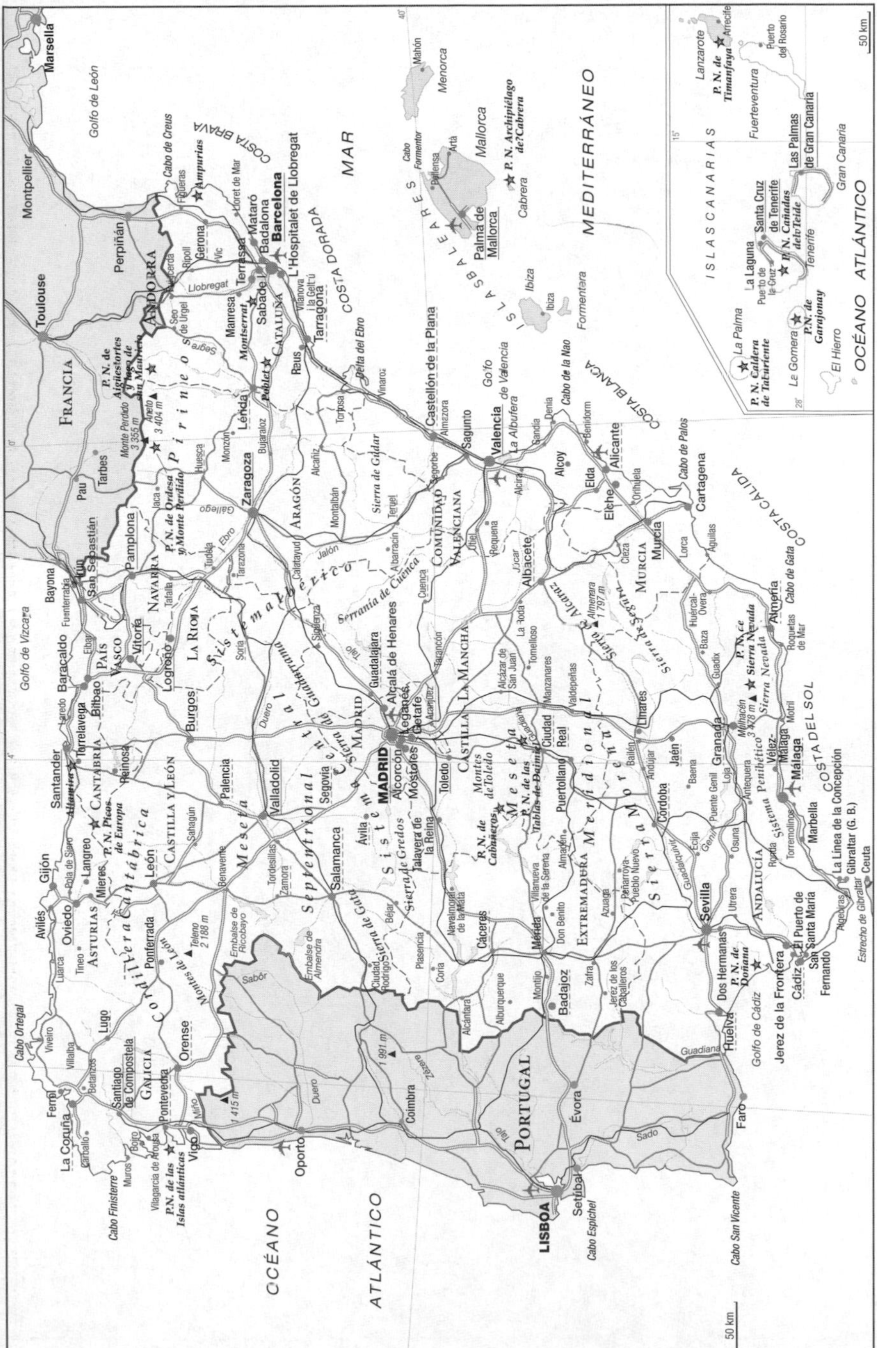